*Paul B. Harris*

To Zachary

From an UNCLE you will probably never meet....
From what I hear you'll get a lot of use from these Books.

Proverbs 3:5,6

# VOLUME 1
# A ~ K

## The Outline Bible Five Translation

# PRACTICAL WORD STUDIES IN THE NEW TESTAMENT

## Five Translations

- King James Version
- New King James Version
- New International Version
- New American Standard
- New Living Translation

VOLUME 1

A - K

The Outline Bible Five Translation

# PRACTICAL WORD STUDIES IN THE NEW TESTAMENT

Five Translations

- King James Version
- New King James Version
- New International Version
- New American Standard
- New Living Translation

# Volume 1
## A ~ K

### The Outline Bible Five Translation

# PRACTICAL WORD STUDIES IN THE NEW TESTAMENT

Leadership Ministries Worldwide
PO Box 21310
Chattanooga, TN 37424-0310

PRACTICAL WORD STUDIES IN THE NEW TESTAMENT
COPYRIGHT © 1998
By Alpha-Omega Ministries, Inc.

All rights reserved. No part of
The Outline Bible Five Translation,
Practical Word Studies In The New Testament
may be reproduced in any
manner without written permission.

Scripture quotations marked (NIV) are taken from THE HOLY BIBLE, NEW INTERNATIONAL VERSION®.
NIV®. Copyright © 1973, 1978, 1984 by International Bible Society
Used by permission of Zondervan Publishing House. All rights reserved.

Scripture quotations marked (NASB) are taken from the NEW AMERICAN STANDARD BIBLE®, © Copyright
The Lockman Foundation 1960, 1962, 1963, 1968, 1971, 1972, 1973, 1975, 1977
Used by permission. All rights reserved. http://www.lockman.org

Scripture quotations marked (NKJV) are taken from the NEW KING JAMES VERSION,
Copyright © 1982, Thomas Nelson, Inc. Used by permission. All rights reserved.

Scripture quotations marked (NLT) are taken from the *HOLY BIBLE*, NEW LIVING TRANSLATION,
Copyright © 1996. Used by permission of Tyndale House Publishers, Inc., Wheaton, Illinois 60189. All rights reserved.

Scripture taken from THE GREEK NEW TESTAMENT, Fourth Revised Edition. Edited by BARBARA ALAND, KURT ALAND,
JOHANNES KARAVIDOPOULOS, CARLO M. MARTINI and BRUCE M. METZGER, Copyright © 1993, 1994, 1998
Deutsche Bibelgesellschaft German Bible Society, Stuttgart, GERMANY. Used by permission

Scripture taken from the F.H.A. SCRIVENER 1881 - THEODORE BEZA 1598 TEXTUS RECEPTUS GREEK
NEW TESTAMENT (GNS), Copyright ©1992 by Dr. Kirk D. DiVietro, Grace Baptist Church. Used by permission

BWHEBB, BWHEBL [Hebrew]; BWGRKL, BWGRKN, and BWGRKI [Greek] Postscript® Type 1 and TrueType fonts
Copyright © 1994-1999 BibleWorks, L.L.C. All rights reserved. These Biblical Greek and Hebrew fonts are used
with permission and are from BibleWorks for Windows, the premier exegetical and research Bible software system.

The Outline Bible Five Translation, Practical Word Studies In The New Testament is written for God's people to use in their preparation for preaching and teaching. Leadership Ministries Worldwide wants God's people to use The Outline Bible Five Translation, Practical Word Studies In The New Testament. The purpose of the copyright is to prevent the reproduction, misuse, and abuse of the material.

May our Lord bless us all as we preach, teach, and write for Him, fulfilling His great commission to make disciples of all nations.

Please address all requests for information or permission to:
Leadership Ministries Worldwide
PO Box 21310
Chattanooga, TN 37424-0310
Ph.# (800) 987-8790   FAX (423) 855-8616 E-Mail outlinebible@compuserve.com
http://www.outlinebible.org

Library of Congress Catalog Card Number: 98-75730
International Standard Book Number: 1-57407-107-6

Printed in the United States of America

Publisher & Distributor

# DEDICATED:

To all the men and women of the world
who preach and teach the Gospel of our
Lord Jesus Christ
and
To the Mercy and Grace of God.

————  ————

- Demonstrated to us in Christ Jesus our Lord.

  "In whom we have redemption through His blood, the forgiveness of sins, according to the riches of His grace." (Eph. 1:7)

- Out of the mercy and grace of God His Word has flowed. Let every person know that God will have mercy upon him, forgiving and using him to fulfill His glorious plan of salvation.

  "For God so loved the world, that he gave his only begotten Son, that whosoever believeth in him should not perish, but have everlasting life. For God sent not his Son into the world to condemn the world; but that the world through him might be saved." (Jn 3:16-17)

  "For this is good and acceptable in the sight of God our Saviour; who will have all men to be saved, and to come unto the knowledge of the truth." (I Tim. 2:3-4)

————  ————

**The Preacher's Outline and Study Bible®**
is written for God's people to use
in their study and teaching of God's Holy Word.

## OUR VISION, PASSION & PURPOSE:

- To share the Word of God with the world.
- To help the believer, both minister and layman alike, in his understanding, preaching, and teaching of God's Word.
- To do everything we possibly can to lead men, women, boys, and girls to give their hearts and lives to Jesus Christ and to secure the eternal life which He offers.
- To do all we can to minister to the needy of the world.
- To give Jesus Christ His proper place, the place which the Word gives Him. Therefore — No work of Leadership Ministries Worldwide will ever be personalized.

# TABLE OF CONTENTS

| | Page |
|---|---|
| HOW TO USE THE PRACTICAL WORD STUDY | i |
| SPECIAL FEATURES OF THE PRACTICAL WORD STUDY | ii |
| A BRIEF HISTORICAL OVERVIEW OF THE TRANSLATIONS | iii - v |
| A BRIEF HISTORICAL OVERVIEW OF THE GREEK NEW TESTAMENT | vi - vii |
| ABBREVIATIONS | viii - ix |
| PRACTICAL WORD STUDY, Volume 1, A - K | 1 - 1208 |
| PRACTICAL WORD STUDY, Volume 1, L -Z | 1209-2380 |
| A SIMPLIFIED GREEK PRIMER FOR BEGINNERS | 2381 - 2384 |
| GREEK INDEX | 2385 - 2428 |
| BIBLIOGRAPHY | 2429 - 2432 |

# TABLE OF CONTENTS

| | Page |
|---|---|
| HOW TO USE THE PRACTICAL WORD STUDY | i |
| SPECIAL FEATURES OF THE PRACTICAL WORD STUDY | ii |
| A BRIEF HISTORICAL OVERVIEW OF THE TRANSLATIONS | iii - v |
| A BRIEF HISTORICAL OVERVIEW OF THE GREEK NEW TESTAMENT | vi - vii |
| ABBREVIATIONS | viii - ix |
| PRACTICAL WORD STUDY, Volume I: A - K | 1 - 1298 |
| PRACTICAL WORD STUDY, Volume II: L - Z | 1299 - 2380 |
| A SIMPLIFIED GREEK TRACER FOR BEGINNERS | 2381 - 2388 |
| GREEK INDEX | 2389 - 2428 |
| BIBLIOGRAPHY | 2429 - 2432 |

# HOW TO USE...
## THE PRACTICAL WORD STUDY

**W**hen you look up an English word, this simple, easy-to-use word study chart will give you the following information:

(#1) The English Word

(#2) How Five Different Translations Use the Same Word

(#3) The Preacher's Outline & Sermon Bible® Reference where you can secure additional information

(#4) The Greek Word, English Transliteration, Pronunciation, and Grammatical Parsing

(#5) The Reference Number for the Root Word from the Three Major Concordances

(#6) The Verse Written Out for Five Major Translations with the Key Word(s) in Bold Type

(#7) The Actual Greek Text (Textus Receptus [GNS] and UBS4-NA27 [GNT]) with the Key Word(s) in Bold)

(#8) The Greek Meaning of the Word Defined with Simple, Easy-to-Understand Terms

(#9) The Practical Application For Study, Preaching, And Teaching

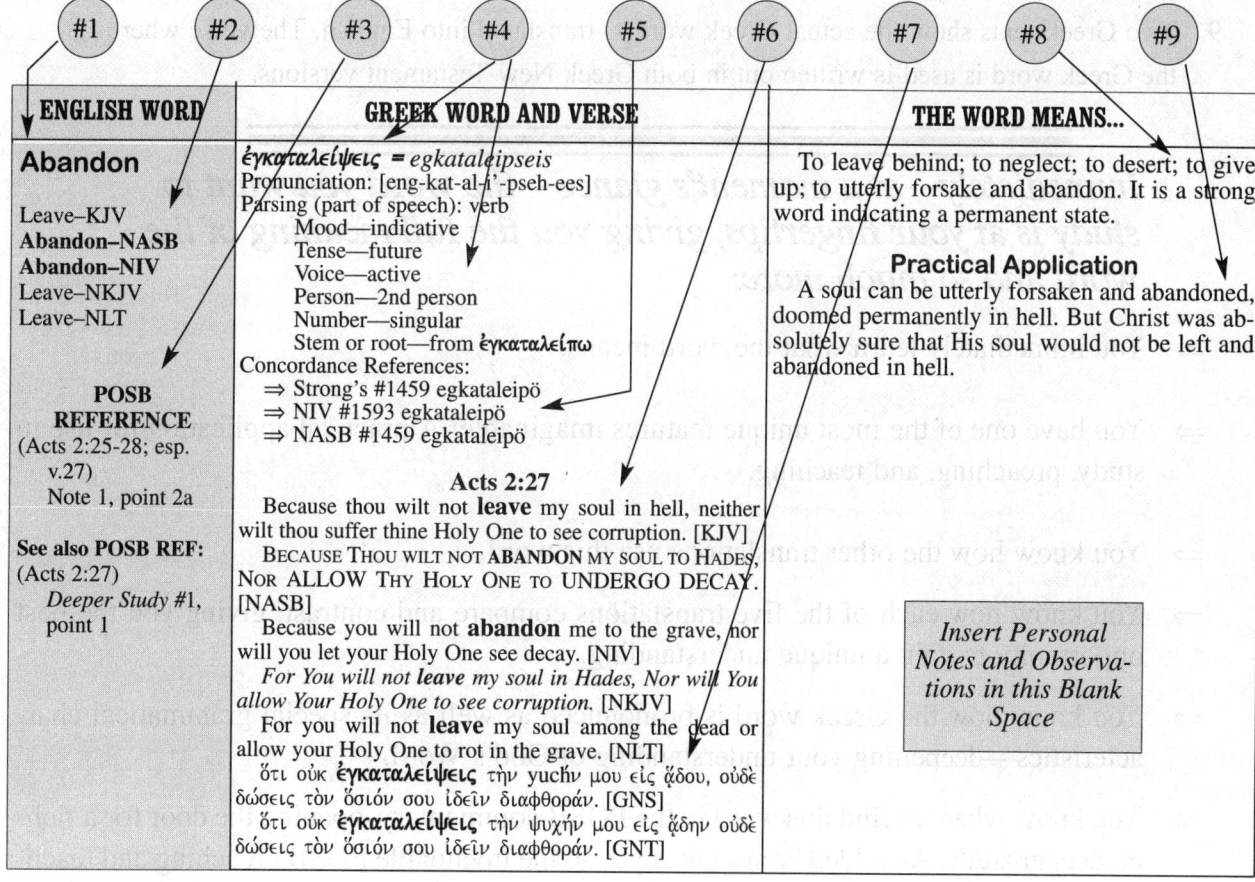

*Read on for more ...*
## ...SPECIAL FEATURES →

i

# SPECIAL FEATURES OF...
# THE PRACTICAL WORD STUDY

1. The Full Meaning of Each Word is given.
2. Five Major Translations are given to show just how the English word is used.
3. Practical Application is given for each word.
4. The Greek Word is given and phonetically pronounced. No more embarrassing stumbles from the pulpit or lectern trying to pronounce the Greek word.
5. Full and easy-to-understand parsing is given using simple, meaningful terms.
6. Concordance numbers from all three of the major concordances are given for each word: the concordance numbers from Strong's, the NIV, and the NASB. This allows for a quick, more exhaustive search for a particular word.
7. Each Scripture verse is written out in full, providing clear understanding with the key word in bold type.
8. **The Preacher's Outline & Sermon Bible** Reference is given for quick and easy access to more commentary and outlines.
9. Two Greek texts show the actual Greek word(s) translated into English. The verse where the Greek word is used is written out in both Greek New Testament versions.

---

*Immediately—at a moment's glance—the word you want to study is at your fingertips, giving you the full meaning of the word and so much more:*

⇒ You immediately learn what the word means.

⇒ You have one of the most unique features imaginable: A practical application for use in study, preaching, and teaching.

⇒ You know how the other translations use this word.

⇒ You know how each of the five translations compare and contrast, giving you the best opportunity to gain a unique understanding.

⇒ You know how the Greek word is pronounced as well as its special grammatical characteristics—deepening your understanding of God's Word.

⇒ You know where to find this word in the POSB commentary, opening the door for a richer, deeper study. An added bonus takes you to the invaluable POSB preaching and teaching outlines, giving you additional preparation for your message or lesson.

⇒ You know where to find the word from your favorite concordance.

# A BRIEF HISTORICAL OVERVIEW OF THE TRANSLATIONS

One of the great benefits of the *Practical Word Studies In The New Testament (PWS)* is the use of five popular English translations. The reader will quickly discover the value of being able to compare the translations with one another. Below is a quick overview of the five translations. (Note: they are listed in chronological order.)

1. **KING JAMES VERSION—KJV (or the AUTHORIZED VERSION—AV)**

    ⇒ **DATE**: The KJV (both Old and New Testaments) was published in 1611.

    ⇒ **PURPOSE**: "That a translation be made of the whole Bible, as constant as can be to the original Hebrew and Greek; and this to be set out and printed, without any marginal notes, and only to be used in all Churches of England in time of divine service"—from *History of the English Bible* by F. F. Bruce; New York: Oxford University Press, 1978, third edition, p.96.

    ⇒ **HISTORY**: The idea for a new translation came out of the Hamton Court Conference in January 1604. At the forefront was Dr. John Reynolds (or Rainolds), the President of Corpus Christi College in Oxford England. The momentum for a translation that would replace the Geneva Bible was halting at first. However, with the blessing and strong leadership of King James I of England, the translation by 47 translators soon began. The KJV was translated from the earliest known Greek and Hebrew texts.

    Note carefully King James' very own words on why he desired a new Bible translation:

    *"I profess...I could never yet see a Bible well translated in English; but I think that, of all, that of Geneva is the worst. I wish some special pains were taken for a uniform translation, which should be done by the best-learned men in both Universities, then reviewed by the Bishops, presented to the Privy Council, lastly ratified by Royal authority, to be read in the whole Church, and none other."* —Bruce, p.96-97.

    ⇒ **FEATURES OF THE KJV**: Since its inception in 1611, it remains the best-selling Bible in the world. The KJV is noted for its poetic beauty, for its majestic literary splendor using "The King's English."

2. **NEW AMERICAN STANDARD BIBLE—NASB**

    ⇒ **DATE**: The NASB (both Old and New Testaments) was published in 1971.

    ⇒ **PURPOSE**: "The Editorial Board had a twofold purpose in making this translation: to adhere as closely as possible to the original languages of the Holy Scriptures, and to make the translation in a fluent and readable style according to current English usage."

    The fourfold aim of the Lockman Foundation as printed in each copy of the NASB is as follows:
    1. These publications shall be true to the original Hebrew and Greek.
    2. They shall be grammatically correct.
    3. They shall be understandable to the masses.
    4. They shall give the Lord Jesus Christ His proper place, the place which the Word gives Him; therefore, no work will ever be personalized.

    ⇒ **HISTORY**: "The King James Version, a landmark in the history of English Bible translation, is a revision of the Bishops' Bible of 1568. The KJV became the basis for the English Revised Version appearing in 1881 (New Testament) and 1885 (Old Testament). The American counterpart of this last work was published in 1901 as the American Standard Version. The ASV, a product of both British and American scholarship, has been highly regarded for its scholarship, and accuracy.

    Recognizing the values of the American Standard Version, The Lockman Foundation felt an urgency to preserve these and other lasting values of the ASV, by incorporating recent discoveries of Hebrew and Greek textual sources and by rendering it into more current English. Therefore, in 1959 a new translation project was launched, based on the time-honored principles of translation of the ASV and KJV. **The result is the *New American Standard Bible*®**. Under the sponsorship of The Lockman Foundation of La Habra, California, a dedicated team of scholars worked for more than ten years to produce the *New American Standard Bible*."—from The Lockman Foundation web site.

    ⇒ **FEATURES OF THE NEW AMERICAN STANDARD BIBLE**: This translation is noted as the most accurate, word for word, translation available. The NASB translation attempts to bridge the beauty of the King's English with a language that can be understood by the contemporary reader. "The *NASB*® is excellent for Bible study because it aims at a precise translation of the original Hebrew, Aramaic, and Greek. As such, it renders, where practical, the original order of words and phrases. In passages where this literalness produces unacceptable English, the translators used modern English idioms and indicated the literal renderings in marginal notes. In New Testament Greek, questions are worded in a way that shows whether the expected answer is yes or no. The *NASB®* translation is faithful to this treatment. In places where the English language would describe past action with a past-tense verb, the Greek uses the present tense for special vividness. The *NASB®* indicates such cases with an asterisk (or star) before the past-tense verb. Among the other distinctives are the *NASB*'s clear indicating of all phrases that quote or allude to the Old Testament; it includes quotation marks for dialogue and quoted material and capitalizes personal pronouns and words referring to Deity; and supplied words are in italic type."—from The Lockman Foundation web site.

3. **NEW INTERNATIONAL VERSION—NIV**

   ⇒ **DATE**: The NIV New Testament was published in 1973. The NIV Old Testament was published in 1979.
   ⇒ **PURPOSE**: "From the beginning of the project, the Committee on Bible Translation held to certain goals for the New International Version: that it would be an accurate translation and one that would have clarity and literary quality and so prove suitable for public and private reading, teaching, preaching, memorizing and liturgical use. The Committee also sought to preserve some measure of continuity with the long tradition of translating the Scriptures into English."—from the Preface of the NIV Study Bible, Zondervan, 1985.
   ⇒ **HISTORY**: "The New International Version is a completely new translation of the Holy Bible made by over a hundred scholars working directly from the best available Hebrew, Aramaic and Greek texts. It had its beginning in 1965 when, after several years of exploratory study by committees from the Christian Reformed Church and the National Association of Evangelicals, a group of scholars met at Palos Heights, Illinois, and concurred in the need for a new translation of the Bible in contemporary English. This group, though not made up of official church representatives, was transdenominational. Its conclusion was endorsed by a large number of leaders from many denominations who met in Chicago in 1966.

   "Responsibility for the new version was delegated by the Palos Heights group to a self-governing body of fifteen, the Committee on Bible Translation, composed for the most part of biblical scholars from colleges, universities and seminaries. In 1967 the New York Bible Society (now the International Bible Society) generously undertook the financial sponsorship of the project—a sponsorship that made it possible to enlist the help of many distinguished scholars. The fact that participants from the United States, Great Britain, Canada, Australia and New Zealand worked together give the project its international scope. That they were from many denominations—including Anglican, Assemblies of God, Baptist, Brethren, Christian Reformed, Church of Christ, Evangelical Free, Lutheran, Mennonite, Methodist, Nazarene, Presbyterian, Wesleyan and other churches—helped to safeguard the translation from sectarian bias."—from the Preface of the NIV Study Bible, Zondervan, 1985.
   ⇒ **FEATURES OF THE NEW INTERNATIONAL VERSION**: This translation is a popular modern-language Bible. It attempts to find the balance between two translation methods: the literal method and the dynamic translation method. Many Bible scholars credit the NIV for both its accuracy and its readability.

4. **NEW KING JAMES VERSION—NKJV**

   ⇒ **DATE**: The New King James Version NT was published in 1979. The New King James Version OT was published in 1982.
   ⇒ **PURPOSE**: "In the Preface to the 1611 edition, the translators of the Authorized Version, known popularly as the King James Bible, state that it was not their purpose 'to make a new translation...but to make a good one better.' Indebted to the earlier work of William Tyndale and others, they saw their best contribution to consist in revising and enhancing the excellence of the English versions which had sprung from the Reformation of the sixteenth century. In harmony with the purpose of the King James scholars, the translators and editors of the present work [NKJV] have not pursued a goal of innovation. They have perceived the Holy Bible, New King James Version, as a continuation of the labors of the earlier translators, thus unlocking for today's readers the spiritual treasures found especially in the Authorized Version of the Holy Scriptures." —from the preface, The New Open Bible Study Edition, Thomas Nelson, 1990, p.12.
   ⇒ **HISTORY**: "The versions of 1881, 1901, and 1952 had used a New Testament Greek text that differed considerably from the traditional text and from the great majority of biblical manuscripts. There was growing concern among large segments of the Christian community that there was insufficient reason for many of these differences.

   "In 1975 Thomas Nelson Publishers, successor to the British firm that had first published the English Revised Version (1885), the American Standard Version (1901), and the Revised Standard Version (1952), determined to evaluate interest in a possible new revision. Such a revision would retain the traditional text while taking into account of variant readings in footnotes.

iv

"Because any revision of the Scriptures must meet the needs of public worship, Christian education and personal reading and study, leading clergymen and lay Christians were invited to meetings in Chicago, Illinois, and Nashville, Tennessee, in 1975, and in London, England, in 1976 to discuss the need for revision. Almost one hundred church leaders from a broad spectrum of Christian churches gave strong endorsement to a new revision.

"Biblical scholars representing a broad cross section of evangelical Christendom were selected to work on this major project. They came from Canada, England, Scotland, New Zealand, Australia, the Netherlands, and Taiwan, as well as from the United States, so that the New King James Version would reflect internationally accepted English use.

"Each translator worked privately and recommended changes in the King James text. In the translator's work he used the *Biblia Hebraica Stuttgartensia* (for the Old Testament) or the Scrivener Greek Text (for the New Testament) and a copy of the 1611 King James Version as revised in 1769 (the edition in general use today). His work was then submitted to the executive editor for the Old or New Testament. An elaborate concordance and word studies of the English, Greek, and Hebrew were prepared especially for this revision by the executive editors and their associates. In addition, using the original texts, the King James Bible, and other guidelines, the executive editor for the Old or New Testament carefully reviewed each scholar's work. Where necessary, they made recommendations for further changes or, in some cases, for restoration of the King James reading….Throughout the entire editing process, the work was regularly reviewed by the clergy and lay advisors who served on the British and North American Overview Committees. The final exhaustive review process was carried out by a separate Executive Review Committee for each Testament over a period of four years…The review process was completed in July 1981, at St. Andrews University in northeast Scotland, not far from King James' residence, historic Stirling Castle."—from the forward, The New Open Bible Study Edition, Thomas Nelson, 1990, p.10-11.

⇒ **FEATURES OF THE NEW KING JAMES VERSION**: The NKJV is noted as the translation that retains the elegant style of the KJV while "modernizing" the language. The NKJV is a word for word translation, replacing archaic words with contemporary ones.

5. **NEW LIVING TRANSLATION—NLT**

⇒ **DATE**: The New Living Translation was published in 1996.
⇒ **PURPOSE**: "The goal of any Bible translation is to convey the meaning of the ancient Hebrew and Greek texts as accurately as possible to the modern reader. The New Living Translation is based on the most recent scholarship in the theory of translation. The challenge for the translators was to create a text that would make the same impact in the life of modern readers that the original text had for the original readers. In the New Living translation, this is accomplished by translating entire thoughts (rather than just words) into natural, everyday English. The end result is a translation that is easy to read and understand and that accurately communicates the meaning of the original text."—from A Note To Readers, The New Living Translation, Tyndale, 1996.
⇒ **HISTORY**: "With 40 million copies in print, *The Living Bible* has been meeting a great need in people's hearts for more than thirty years. But even good things can be improved, so ninety evangelical scholars from various theological backgrounds and denominations were commissioned in 1989 to begin revising *The Living Bible*. The end result of this seven year process in the *Holy Bible*, New Living Translation—a general-purpose translation that is accurate, easy to read, and excellent for study."—from A Note To Readers, The New Living Translation, Tyndale, 1996.
⇒ **FEATURES OF THE NEW LIVING TRANSLATION**: The NLT is a meaning-for-meaning translation. "The goal of any Bible translation is to convey the **meaning** of the ancient Hebrew and Greek texts as accurately as possible to the modern reader. The New Living Translation is based on the most recent scholarship in the theory of translation. The challenge for the translators was to create a text that would make the same **impact** in the life of modern readers that the original text had for the original readers. In the New Living Translation, this is accomplished by translating **entire thoughts** (rather than just words) into natural, everyday English. The end result is a translation that is easy to read and understand and that accurately communicates the meaning of the original text."—from Tyndale's web site.

# A BRIEF HISTORICAL OVERVIEW OF THE GREEK NEW TESTAMENT

Throughout history, God has preserved the integrity of the Bible as it has been passed down from generation to generation. Because of God's love for man and His wisdom and power, we can trust the authority of the Bible. It is important to know how we got the Bible and why we can trust its authority for our lives. There are three principle sources for the New Testament text that give us our English Bibles:

1. There are the Greek manuscripts (some 4,000 to 5,000 in number).
   a. The earliest form of these Greek manuscripts is called "papyri." This paper scroll was made from the Egyptian papyrus plant that grew on the banks of the Nile River.
   b. From the fourth to tenth century, the manuscripts were written on parchment from animal skins. Of the many manuscripts, four stand out for their authority:
      1) *The Sinaitic Codex* was written in the fourth century and contains the entire New Testament. Discovered in a monastery on Mt. Sinai by Constantin Tischendorf, it was brought to Russia in 1859. In 1933 it was purchased by the British government from the Soviets. This important manuscript is on display at the British Museum in London England.
      2) *The Vatican Codex* was also written in the fourth century. It contains the complete New Testament except for the Pastoral epistles, a portion of Hebrews, and the book of Revelation. It is on display in the Library of the Vatican in Rome Italy.
      3) The *Alexandrian Codex* was written in the fifth century. It contains the complete New Testament except for most of the Gospel of Matthew and portions of John and 2 Corinthians. This manuscript contains almost all of the Greek Old Testament. A gift to King James I, it is on display at the British Museum.
      4) The *Ephraem Codex* was written in the fifth century. It contains the New Testament but in fragmentary form. This manuscript is on display in the National Library of Paris France.
2. There are different versions that had a significant impact on the New Testament text, the most important being Jerome's Latin Vulgate (382 A.D.)
3. There are the quotations of the New Testament from the writings of the early church fathers; men like Ambrose, Athanasius, Augustine, Clement of Alexandria, Irenaeus, Jerome, and Origen. The majority of their writings are in Greek and Latin.

## IMPORTANT DATES AND EVENTS IN THE HISTORY OF THE NEW TESTAMENT

| NAME OF MANUSCRIPT OR TRANSLATION | DATE | AUTHOR/EDITOR | HISTORICAL FACTS/REMARKS |
| --- | --- | --- | --- |
| *The Original Autographs* | Most of the New Testament books were written before the destruction of the Temple in Jerusalem by Rome in A.D. 70 | The New Testament writers | The original autographs are perfect, without error. The whole Bible is God's inerrant, infallible revelation to man, and is to be the only supreme authority in all matters of faith and conduct. |
| *The Earliest Greek Manuscripts* | Written in the second and third centuries | Early Church fathers | ⇒ The earliest Greek manuscripts were written on papyrus. |
| *The Codex Manuscripts* | Dated as early as the fourth century | Scribes, monks | ⇒ The Codex Manuscripts are the basis for most modern editions of the Greek New Testament. |
| *The Majority Text (from the Byzantine family of Greek Manuscripts)* | Dated in the 15th century | Scribes, monks | ⇒ The Majority Text became the basis of all English translations of the New Testament until the nineteenth century. |
| *The Gutenberg Bible* | Dated in the fifteenth century (1456) | Johann Gutenberg | ⇒ The Latin Vulgate edition of the Bible was the first Bible to be printed from a printing press. 47 known copies still exist. |
| *The Complutensian Polygot* | Dated in the sixteenth century (1522) | Cardinal Ximenes of Spain | ⇒ The Complutensian Polygot was the first printed Greek New Testament from a printing press. |

| NAME OF MANUSCRIPT OR TRANSLATION | DATE | AUTHOR/EDITOR | HISTORICAL FACTS/REMARKS |
|---|---|---|---|
| *The Textus Receptus* | Dated in the sixteenth century (1516) | Desiderius Erasmus | ⇒ The Textus Receptus (TR) is based primarily on the manuscripts from the Byzantine text family.<br>⇒ The TR influenced biblical studies and theology for centuries.<br>⇒ The TR was the first published Greek New Testament made available for sale. |
| *The Revision of the Textus Receptus* | Dated in the sixteenth century (1550-1551) | Robert (Estienne) or Stephanus | ⇒ This popular edition of the TR became the standard until the late nineteenth century.<br>⇒ It was Stephanus who inserted verse divisions. |
| *The Revision of the Textus Receptus* | Dated in the sixteenth century (1565-1604) | Theodore Beza | ⇒ Beza published nine editions of the TR.<br>⇒ Beza popularized the form of Erasmus and Stephanus. |
| *The King James Version* | Dated in the seventeenth century (1611) | 47 translators | ⇒ The KJV is based upon the Textus Receptus. |
| *Bengel's Greek New Testament* | Dated in the eighteenth century (1734) | Johann Bengel | ⇒ Bengel followed the Textus Receptus, but also offered comments and corrections in the text in the margin. |
| *Westcott and Hort's Greek New Testament* | Dated in the nineteenth century (1881-1882) | Brooke Foss Westcott and Fenton John Anthony Hort | ⇒ Westcott and Hort's Greek text became known as a "critical text." They departed from the Textus Receptus and worked from other Greek manuscripts.<br>⇒ Their work become the forerunner for modern Greek New Testament translations; i.e. The Greek New Testament UBS4, the fourth edition of the United Bible Society's standard New Testament text in the original Greek language. |
| *The Greek New Testament (GNT UBS4 - NA27)* | First copyright was in 1966. Later revisions were completed in 1968 and 1975 | Edited by Kurt Aland, Matthew Black, Carlo M. Martini, Bruce M. Metzger, and Allen Wikgren, in cooperation with the Institute for New Testament Textual Research, Munster/Westphalia, Fourth Edition (with exactly the same text as the Nestle - Aland 27th Edition of the Greek New Testament) | ⇒ Most modern translations are based upon this Greek text. |

# ABBREVIATIONS

## BIBLE ABBREVIATIONS

| | | |
|---|---|---|
| KJV | = | King James Version |
| NASB | = | New American Standard Bible |
| NIV | = | New International Version |
| NKJV | = | New King James Version |
| NLT | = | New Living Translation |
| GNS | = | The F. H. A. Scrivener 1881 - Theodore Beza 1598 Textus Receptus Greek New Testament, ASCII edition |
| GNT | = | The Greek New Testament (UBS4 - NA27) |
| RV | = | Revised Version |

## BIBLE RESOURCES ABBREVIATIONS

| | | |
|---|---|---|
| POSB | = | The Preacher's Outline & Sermon Bible® |
| PWS | = | Practical Word Studies in the New Testament |

## NEW TESTAMENT ABBREVIATIONS

| | | |
|---|---|---|
| Mt. | = | Matthew |
| Mk. | = | Mark |
| Lk. | = | Luke |
| Jn. | = | John |
| Acts | = | Acts |
| Ro. | = | Romans |
| 1 Cor. | = | 1 Corinthians |
| 2 Cor. | = | 2 Corinthians |
| Gal. | = | Galatians |
| Eph. | = | Ephesians |
| Ph. | = | Philippians |
| Col. | = | Colossians |
| 1 Th. | = | 1 Thessalonians |
| 2 Th. | = | 2 Thessalonians |
| 1 Tim. | = | 1 Timothy |
| 2 Tim. | = | 2 Timothy |
| Tit. | = | Titus |
| Phile. | = | Philemon |
| Heb. | = | Hebrews |
| Jas. | = | James |
| 1 Pt. | = | 1 Peter |
| 2 Pt. | = | 2 Peter |
| 1 Jn. | = | 1 John |
| 2 Jn. | = | 2 John |
| 3 Jn. | = | 3 John |
| Jude | = | Jude |
| Rev. | = | Revelation |

## MISCELLANEOUS ABBREVIATIONS

| | | |
|---|---|---|
| & | = | And |
| Arg. | = | Argument |
| Bckgrd. | = | Background |
| Bc. | = | Because |
| Circ. | = | Circumstance |
| Concl. | = | Conclusion |
| Cp. | = | Compare |
| Ct. | = | Contrast |
| Dif. | = | Different |
| e.g. | = | For example |
| Et. | = | Eternal |
| f. | = | Following |
| Govt. | = | Government |
| Id. | = | Identity or Identification |
| Illust. | = | Illustration |
| K. | = | Kingdom, K. of God, K. of Heaven, etc. |
| No. | = | Number |
| N.T. | = | New Testament |
| O.T. | = | Old Testament |
| Pt. | = | Point |
| Quest. | = | Question |
| Rel. | = | Religion |
| Resp. | = | Responsibility |
| Rev. | = | Revelation |
| Rgt. | = | Righteousness |
| Thru | = | Through |
| V. | = | Verse |
| Vs. | = | Verses |
| Vs. | = | Versus |

# PRACTICAL WORD STUDIES
## in the NEW TESTAMENT

| ENGLISH WORD | GREEK WORD AND VERSE | THE WORD MEANS... |
|---|---|---|
| **#1**<br>**Abaddon**<br><br>Abaddon–KJV<br>**Abaddon–NASB**<br>**Abaddon–NIV**<br>Abaddon–NKJV<br>Abaddon–NLT<br><br>**POSB REFERENCE**<br>(Rev.9:11)<br>Note 6, point 4 | Ἀβαδδών = *Abaddōn*<br>Pronunciation: [ab-ad-dohn']<br>Parsing (part of speech): noun<br>    Case—nominative<br>    Gender—masculine<br>    Number—singular<br>    Stem or root—from Ἀβαδδών<br>Concordance References:<br>  ⇒ Strong's #3 Abaddōn<br>  ⇒ NIV #3 Abaddōn<br>  ⇒ NASB #3 Abaddōn<br><br>**Rev. 9:11**<br>And they had a king over them, *which is* the angel of the bottomless pit, whose name in the Hebrew tongue *is* **Abaddon**, but in the Greek tongue hath *his* name Apollyon. [KJV]<br>They have as king over them, the angel of the abyss; his name in Hebrew is **Abaddon**, and in the Greek he has the name Apollyon. [NASB]<br>They had as king over them the angel of the Abyss, whose name in Hebrew is **Abaddon**, and in Greek, Apollyon. [NIV]<br>And they had as king over them the angel of the bottomless pit, whose name in Hebrew is **Abaddon**, but in Greek he has the name Apollyon. [NKJV]<br>Their king is the angel from the bottomless pit; his name in Hebrew is *Abaddon*, and in Greek, *Apollyon*—the Destroyer. [NLT]<br>καὶ ἔχουσιν ἐπ' αὐτῶν βασιλέα τὸν ἄγγελον τῆς ἀβύσσου· ὄνομα αὐτῷ Ἑβραϊστὶ **Ἀβαδδών**, καὶ ἐν τῇ Ἑλληνικῇ ὄνομα ἔχει Ἀπολλύων. [GNS]<br>ἔχουσιν ἐπ' αὐτῶν βασιλέα τὸν ἄγγελον τῆς ἀβύσσου, ὄνομα αὐτῷ Ἑβραϊστὶ **Ἀβαδδών**, καὶ ἐν τῇ Ἑλληνικῇ ὄνομα ἔχει Ἀπολλύων. [GNT] | The angel of the Abyss (bottomless pit). This angel has both a Greek and an Hebrew name. His Hebrew name is Abaddon which means *destruction*, and his Greek name is Apollyon which means *destroyer*.<br><br>**Practical Application**<br>What better name could there be to describe this ruler of the demonic locusts? No creature nor force leaves behind any more destruction than that of the ferocious locust. Who is this fallen angel? It has to be either Satan himself or one of his commanding angels. |
| **#2**<br>**Abandon**<br><br>Leave–KJV<br>**Abandon–NASB**<br>**Abandon–NIV**<br>Leave–NKJV<br>Leave–NLT<br><br>**POSB REFERENCE**<br>(Acts 2:25-28; esp. v.27)<br>Note 1, point 2a<br><br>See also POSB REF:<br>(Acts 2:27)<br>*Deeper Study #1,* point 1 | ἐγκαταλείψεις = *egkataleipseis*<br>Pronunciation: [eng-kat-al-i'-pseh-ees]<br>Parsing (part of speech): verb<br>    Mood—indicative<br>    Tense—future<br>    Voice—active<br>    Person—2nd person<br>    Number—singular<br>    Stem or root—from ἐγκαταλείπω<br>Concordance References:<br>  ⇒ Strong's #1459 egkataleipō<br>  ⇒ NIV #1593 egkataleipō<br>  ⇒ NASB #1459 egkataleipō<br><br>**Acts 2:27**<br>Because thou wilt not **leave** my soul in hell, neither wilt thou suffer thine Holy One to see corruption. [KJV]<br>BECAUSE THOU WILT NOT **ABANDON** MY SOUL TO HADES, NOR ALLOW THY HOLY ONE TO UNDERGO DECAY. [NASB]<br>Because you will not **abandon** me to the grave, nor will you let your Holy One see decay. [NIV]<br>*For You will not* **leave** *my soul in Hades, Nor will You allow Your Holy One to see corruption.* [NKJV]<br>For you will not **leave** my soul among the dead or allow your Holy One to rot in the grave. [NLT]<br>ὅτι οὐκ **ἐγκαταλείψεις** τὴν ψυχήν μου εἰς ᾅδου, οὐδὲ δώσεις τὸν ὅσιόν σου ἰδεῖν διαφθοράν. [GNS]<br>ὅτι οὐκ **ἐγκαταλείψεις** τὴν ψυχήν μου εἰς ᾅδην οὐδὲ δώσεις τὸν ὅσιόν σου ἰδεῖν διαφθοράν. [GNT] | To leave behind; to neglect; to desert; to give up; to utterly forsake and abandon. It is a strong word indicating a permanent state.<br><br>**Practical Application**<br>A soul can be utterly forsaken and abandoned, doomed permanently in hell. But Christ was absolutely sure that His soul would not be left and abandoned in hell. |
| **#3**<br>**Abandoned–Abandons** | ἐγκαταλειπόμενοι = *egkataleipomenoi*<br>Pronunciation: [eng-kat-al-i'-po-mehn-oy]<br>Parsing (part of speech): verb<br>    Mood—participle<br>    Tense—present<br>    Voice—passive | To leave behind; to neglect; to desert; to give up; to utterly forsake and abandon. It is a strong word indicating a permanent state.<br><br>**Practical Application**<br>God never forsakes, abandons, or deserts his |

# PRACTICAL WORD STUDIES
## in the New Testament

| ENGLISH WORD | GREEK WORD AND VERSE | THE WORD MEANS... |
|---|---|---|
| Forsaken–KJV<br>Forsaken–NASB<br>**Abandoned–NIV**<br>Forsaken–NKJV<br>**Abandons–NLT**<br><br>**POSB<br>REFERENCE**<br>(2 Cor.4:7-9; esp. v.9)<br>Note 2, point 3 | Case—nominative<br>Gender—masculine<br>Person—1st person<br>Number—plural<br>Stem or root—from ἐγκαταλείπω<br>Concordance References:<br>⇒ Strong's #1459 egkataleipō<br>⇒ NIV #1593 egkataleipō<br>⇒ NASB #1459 egkataleipō<br><br>**2 Cor. 4:9**<br>Persecuted, but not **forsaken**; cast down, but not destroyed; [KJV]<br>Persecuted, but not **forsaken**; struck down, but not destroyed; [NASB]<br>Persecuted, but not **abandoned**; struck down, but not destroyed. [NIV]<br>Persecuted, but not **forsaken**; struck down, but not destroyed— [NKJV]<br>We are hunted down, but God never **abandons** us. We get knocked down, but we get up again and keep going. [NLT]<br>διωκόμενοι, ἀλλ' οὐκ **ἐγκαταλειπόμενοι**, καταβαλλόμενοι ἀλλ' οὐκ ἀπολλύμενοι· [GNS]<br>διωκόμενοι ἀλλ' οὐκ **ἐγκαταλειπόμενοι**, καταβαλλόμενοι ἀλλ' οὐκ ἀπολλύμενοι, [GNT] | dear servant. God never leaves him alone. The companionship of God, His presence and power, is always with His dear servant. |
| **#4<br>Abba**<br><br>Abba–KJV<br>Abba–NASB<br>Abba–NIV<br>Abba–NKJV<br>Abba–NLT<br><br>**POSB<br>REFERENCE**<br>(Mk.14:36)<br>Note 3, point 3 | Ἀββα = Abba<br>Pronunciation: [ab-bah']<br>Parsing (part of speech): noun<br>Case—vocative<br>Gender—masculine<br>Person—singular<br>Stem or root—from ἀββά<br>Concordance References:<br>⇒ Strong's #5 Abba<br>⇒ NIV #5 Abba<br>⇒ NASB #5 Abba<br><br>**Mark 14:36**<br>And he said, **Abba**, Father, all things *are* possible unto thee; take away this cup from me: nevertheless not what I will, but what thou wilt. [KJV]<br>And He was saying, "**Abba**! Father! All things are possible for Thee; remove this cup from Me; yet not what I will, but what Thou wilt." [NASB]<br>"**Abba**, Father," he said, "everything is possible for you. Take this cup from me. Yet not what I will, but what you will." [NIV]<br>And He said, "**Abba**, Father, all things *are* possible for You. Take this cup away from Me; nevertheless, not what I will, but what You *will*." [NKJV]<br>"**Abba**, Father," he said, "everything is possible for you. Please take this cup of suffering away from me. Yet I want your will, not mine." [NLT]<br>καὶ ἔλεγεν, **Ἀββα**, ὁ πατήρ, πάντα δυνατά σοι· παρένεγκε τὸ ποτήριον ἀπ' ἐμοῦ τοῦτο· ἀλλ' οὐ τί ἐγὼ θέλω, ἀλλὰ τί σύ. [GNS]<br>καὶ ἔλεγεν, **Ἀββα** ὁ πατήρ, πάντα δυνατά σοι· παρένεγκε τὸ ποτήριον τοῦτο ἀπ' ἐμοῦ· ἀλλ' οὐ τί ἐγὼ θέλω ἀλλὰ τί σύ. [GNT] | Father, my father. The word "Abba" is from the Aramaic word meaning Father. When used in the New Testament, Abba is used as an intimate term for God.<br><br>**Practical Application**<br>Note in this Scripture: Jesus addressed God as "Father." This was what a small child called his father from day to day. It was the address of a child's love and dependency. The child knew that His father would hear and turn to him when he called "Father." Just like a child, Jesus Christ cried out to His Father in childlike brokenness and dependency, knowing that His Father would hear and turn to help Him. |
| **#5<br>Abhor**<br><br>Abhor–KJV<br>Abhor–NASB<br>Hate–NIV<br>Abhor–NKJV<br>Hate–NLT | ἀποστυγοῦντες = apostugountes<br>Pronunciation: [ap-os-toog-oon-tehs]<br>Parsing (part of speech): verb<br>Mood—participle (imperative sense)<br>Tense—present<br>Voice—active<br>Case—nominative<br>Gender—masculine<br>Person—2nd person<br>Number—plural<br>Stem or root—from ἀποστυγέω | To hate; to abhor. It means to hate with intense feeling; to loathe; to look upon with horror.<br><br>**Practical Application**<br>The believer is to love by hating evil. Love desires the very best for people; therefore, love hates evil for evil destroys human life. The believer stands against evil, doing all he can to fight... |

# PRACTICAL WORD STUDIES
## in the NEW TESTAMENT

| ENGLISH WORD | GREEK WORD AND VERSE | THE WORD MEANS... |
|---|---|---|
| **POSB REFERENCE** (Romans. 12:9-10, esp. v.9) Note 1, point 1 | Concordance References:<br>⇒ Strong's #655 apostugeö<br>⇒ NIV #696 apostugeö<br>⇒ NASB #655 apostugeö<br><br>**Romans 12:9**<br>*Let love be without dissimulation.* **Abhor** *that which is evil; cleave to that which is good.* [KJV]<br>Let love be without hypocrisy. **Abhor** what is evil; cling to what is good. [NASB]<br>Love must be sincere. **Hate** what is evil; cling to what is good. [NIV]<br>*Let love be without hypocrisy.* **Abhor** *what is evil. Cling to what is good.* [NKJV]<br>Don't just pretend that you love others. Really love them. **Hate** what is wrong. Stand on the side of the good. [NLT]<br>Ἡ ἀγάπη ἀνυπόκριτος. **ἀποστυγοῦντες** τὸ πονηρόν, κολλώμενοι τῷ ἀγαθῷ. [GNS]<br>Ἡ ἀγάπη ἀνυπόκριτος. **ἀποστυγοῦντες** τὸ πονηρόν, κολλώμενοι τῷ ἀγαθῷ, [GNT] | • hunger and poverty<br>• hurt and pain<br>• drunkenness and drugs<br>• cursing and bitterness<br>• suggestive and enticing dress<br>• unjust and improper behavior<br>• hoarding and stealing<br>• disease and suffering<br>• ignorance and godless education<br>• family divisiveness and divorce<br>• off-colored and dirty talk<br>• immorality and destructive sex<br>• selfishness and greed<br>• corruption and death<br><br>The list could go on and on. The point is that the believer must love, and he shows his love by hating and fighting against that which is evil. |
| **#6 Abide**<br><br>Abide–KJV<br>Abide–NASB<br>Remain–NIV<br>Abide–NKJV<br>Remain–NLT<br><br>**POSB REFERENCE** (Jn.15:4) Deeper Study #2<br><br>See also POSB REF: (1 Jn.2:24) Note 1 | μείνατε = *meinate*<br>Pronunciation: [meh-een'-ah-teh]<br>Parsing (part of speech): verb<br>    Mood—imperative<br>    Tense—aorist<br>    Voice—active<br>    Person—2nd person<br>    Number—plural<br>    Stem or root—from μένω<br>Concordance References:<br>⇒ Strong's #3306 meno<br>⇒ NIV #3531 meno<br>⇒ NASB #3306 meno<br><br>**John 15:4**<br>**Abide** *in me, and I in you. As the branch cannot bear fruit of itself, except it abide in the vine; no more can ye, except ye abide in me.* [KJV]<br>"**Abide** in Me, and I in you. As the branch cannot bear fruit of itself, unless it abides in the vine, so neither *can* you, unless you abide in Me. [NASB]<br>**Remain** in me, and I will remain in you. No branch can bear fruit by itself; it must remain in the vine. Neither can you bear fruit unless you remain in me [NIV]<br>**Abide** in Me, and I in you. As the branch cannot bear fruit of itself, unless it abides in the vine, neither can you, unless you abide in Me. [NKJV]<br>**Remain** in me, and I will remain in you. For a branch cannot produce fruit if it is severed from the vine, and you cannot be fruitful apart from me. [NLT]<br>**μείνατε** ἐν ἐμοί, κἀγὼ ἐν ὑμῖν. καθὼς τὸ κλῆμα οὐ δύναται καρπὸν φέρειν ἀφ' ἑαυτοῦ, ἐὰν μὴ μείνῃ ἐν τῇ ἀμπέλῳ, οὕτως οὐδὲ ὑμεῖς, ἐὰν μὴ ἐν ἐμοὶ μένητε. [GNS]<br>**μείνατε** ἐν ἐμοί, κἀγὼ ἐν ὑμῖν. καθὼς τὸ κλῆμα οὐ δύναται καρπὸν φέρειν ἀφ' ἑαυτοῦ ἐὰν μὴ μένῃ ἐν τῇ ἀμπέλῳ, οὕτως οὐδὲ ὑμεῖς ἐὰν μὴ ἐν ἐμοὶ μένητε. [GNT] | To hold; to continue; to abide; to remain; to keep on obeying. It means to dwell, continue, stay, sojourn, rest in or upon; to live; to rest; to nest.<br><br>**Practical Application**<br>It is being set and fixed and remaining there. It is continuing on and on in a fixed state, condition, or being. (See POSB *Deeper Study* #1, Abide—John 15:1-8; POSB note—John 6:56.) The more a branch abides in the vine, that is, the closer the branch abides to the heart of the vine, the more nourishment a branch draws from the vine and the more fruit it bears. |
| **#7 Abide**<br><br>Rest–KJV<br>Abide–NASB<br>Live–NIV<br>Rest–NKJV<br>Rests–NLT<br><br>**POSB REFERENCE** (Acts 2:25-28; esp. v.26) Note 1, point 1c | κατασκηνώσει = *kataskēnōsei*<br>Pronunciation: [ka-tah-skay-no-seh-ee]<br>Parsing (part of speech): verb<br>    Mood—indicative<br>    Tense—future<br>    Voice—active<br>    Person—3rd person<br>    Number—singular<br>    Stem or root—from κατασκηνόω<br>Concordance References:<br>⇒ Strong's #2681 kataskēnoö<br>⇒ NIV #2942 kataskēnoö<br>⇒ NASB #2681 kataskēnoö | To hold; to continue; to abide; to remain; to keep on obeying. It means to dwell, continue, stay, sojourn, rest in or upon; to live; to rest; to nest.<br><br>**Practical Application**<br>The word "abide" means to tabernacle or pitch a tent. Jesus' flesh rested, tabernacled, pitched its tent, encamped and made its abode upon hope—the hope of conquering death, of being resurrected. Hope of living forever was the basis and foundation of Jesus' life upon earth, that for which He came to earth. He focused His whole life upon the hope of the cross and of the |

3

# PRACTICAL WORD STUDIES
## in the NEW TESTAMENT

| ENGLISH WORD | GREEK WORD AND VERSE | THE WORD MEANS... |
|---|---|---|
| | **Acts 2:26**<br>Therefore did my heart rejoice, and my tongue was glad; moreover also my flesh shall **rest** in hope: [KJV]<br>'THEREFORE MY HEART WAS GLAD AND MY TONGUE EXULTED; MOREOVER MY FLESH ALSO WILL **ABIDE** IN HOPE; [NASB]<br>Therefore my heart is glad and my tongue rejoices; my body also will **live** in hope, [NIV]<br>*Therefore my heart rejoiced, and my tongue was glad; Moreover my flesh also will **rest** in hope.* [NKJV]<br>No wonder my heart is filled with joy, and my mouth shouts his praises! My body **rests** in hope. [NLT]<br>Διὰ τοῦτο εὐφράνθη ἡ καρδία μου, καὶ ἠγαλλιάσατο ἡ γλῶσσά μου· ἔτι δὲ καὶ ἡ σάρξ μου **κατασκηνώσει** ἐπ' ἐλπίδι· [GNS]<br>διὰ τοῦτο ηὐφράνθη ἡ καρδία μου καὶ ἠγαλλιάσατο ἡ γλῶσσά μου, ἔτι δὲ καὶ ἡ σάρξ μου **κατασκηνώσει** ἐπ' ἐλπίδι, [GNT] | glorious resurrection from the dead (cp. Paul's testimony—Phil. 3:7-16, esp. Phil. 3:11). |
| **#8**<br>**Abide**<br><br>Continue–KJV<br>**Abide–NASB**<br>Hold–NIV<br>**Abide–NKJV**<br>Keep obeying–NLT<br><br>**POSB REFERENCE**<br>(Jn.8:31)<br>Note 1, point 2 | μείνητε = meinēte<br>Pronunciation: [meen'-ay-teh]<br>Parsing (part of speech): verb<br>  Mood—subjunctive<br>  Tense—aorist<br>  Voice—active<br>  Person—2nd person<br>  Number—plural<br>  Stem or root—from μένω<br>Concordance References:<br>⇒ Strong's #3306 meno<br>⇒ NIV #3531 menö<br>⇒ NASB #3306 meno<br><br>**John 8:31**<br>Then said Jesus to those Jews which believed on him, If ye **continue** in my word, *then* are ye my disciples indeed; [KJV]<br>Jesus therefore was saying to those Jews who had believed Him, "If you **abide** in My word, *then* you are truly disciples of Mine; [NASB]<br>To the Jews who had believed him, Jesus said, "If you **hold** to my teaching, you are really my disciples. [NIV]<br>Then Jesus said to those Jews who believed Him, "If you **abide** in My word, you are My disciples indeed. [NKJV]<br>Jesus said to the people who believed in him, "You are truly my disciples if you **keep obeying** my teachings. [NLT]<br>Ἔλεγεν οὖν ὁ Ἰησοῦς πρὸς τοὺς πεπιστευκότας αὐτῷ Ἰουδαίους, Ἐὰν ὑμεῖς **μείνητε** ἐν τῷ λόγῳ τῷ ἐμῷ, ἀληθῶς μαθηταί μού ἐστε· [GNS]<br>Ἔλεγεν οὖν ὁ Ἰησοῦς πρὸς τοὺς πεπιστευκότας αὐτῷ Ἰουδαίους, Ἐὰν ὑμεῖς **μείνητε** ἐν τῷ λόγῳ τῷ ἐμῷ, ἀληθῶς μαθηταί μού ἐστε [GNT] | To hold; to continue; to abide; to remain; to keep on obeying. It means to dwell, continue, stay, sojourn, rest in or upon; to live; to rest; to nest.<br><br>**Practical Application**<br>The idea is that of dwelling, just as a person dwells at home. The Word of the Lord is the believer's dwelling place. He continues and abides in God's Word. Very simply, what Jesus was saying is this:<br>⇒ A person who really begins to believe will "continue in" or "hold on to" the Lord's Word. He will continue both to study and to do the Word (2 Tim. 2:15).<br>⇒ A person who does not really believe will not "hold on" to the Lord's Word.<br>⇒ The proof that a person "really believes" is that he does "continue" in the Lord's Word.<br>⇒ The proof that a person has made only a false or a superficial profession is that he does not "continue in" the Lord's Word. He just does not obey the Word of God. |
| **#9**<br>**Abides**<br><br>Dwelleth–KJV<br>**Abides–NASB**<br>Remains–NIV<br>**Abides–NKJV**<br>Remain–NLT<br><br>**POSB REFERENCE**<br>(Jn.6:56)<br>Note 4 | μένει = menei<br>Pronunciation: [mehn'-ee]<br>Parsing (part of speech): verb<br>  Mood—indicative<br>  Tense—present<br>  Voice—active<br>  Person—3rd person<br>  Number—singular<br>  Stem or root—from μένω<br>Concordance References:<br>⇒ Strong's #3306 meno<br>⇒ NIV #3531 menö<br>⇒ NASB #3306 meno<br><br>**John 6:56**<br>He that eateth my flesh, and drinketh my blood, **dwelleth** in me, and I in him. [KJV]<br>"He who eats My flesh and drinks My blood **abides** in Me, and I in him. [NASB] | To hold; to continue; to abide; to remain; to keep on obeying. It means to dwell, stay, sojourn, rest in or upon; to live; to rest; to nest.<br><br>**Practical Application**<br>It is being fixed and set and remaining there, continuing on and on. Such is the state and condition and being of the person who receives Christ. The person receives Christ into his being, and Christ enters the person's life and abides within him. The person is also taken and placed into Christ, that is, placed with all other believers into the spiritual body of Christ. |

# PRACTICAL WORD STUDIES
## in the NEW TESTAMENT

| ENGLISH WORD | GREEK WORD AND VERSE | THE WORD MEANS... |
|---|---|---|
| | Whoever eats my flesh and drinks my blood **remains** in me, and I in him. [NIV]<br>He who eats My flesh and drinks My blood **abides** in Me, and I in him. [NKJV]<br>All who eat my flesh and drink my blood **remain** in me, and I in them. [NLT]<br>ὁ τρώγων μου τὴν σάρκα, καὶ πίνων μου τὸ αἷμα, ἐν ἐμοὶ **μένει**, κἀγὼ ἐν αὐτῷ. [GNS]<br>ὁ τρώγων μου τὴν σάρκα καὶ πίνων μου τὸ αἷμα ἐν ἐμοὶ **μένει** κἀγὼ ἐν αὐτῷ. [GNT] | |
| **#10**<br>**Ability**<br><br>Gifts–KJV<br>Gifts–NASB<br>Gifts–NIV<br>Gifts–NKJV<br>Ability–NLT<br><br>**POSB REFERENCE**<br>(Rom.12:6-8; esp. v.6)<br>Note 2 | χαρίσματα = charismata<br>Pronunciation: [khar'-is-mah-tah]<br>Parsing (part of speech): noun<br>  Case—accusative<br>  Gender—neuter<br>  Number—plural<br>  Stem or root—from χάρισμα, τος<br>Concordance References:<br>⇒ Strong's #5486 charisma<br>⇒ NIV #5922 charisma<br>⇒ NASB #5486 charisma<br><br>**Romans 12:6**<br>Having then **gifts** differing according to the grace that is given to us, whether prophecy, *let us prophesy* according to the proportion of faith; [KJV]<br>And since we have **gifts** that differ according to the grace given to us, *let each exercise them accordingly:* if prophecy, according to the proportion of his faith; [NASB]<br>We have different **gifts**, according to the grace given us. If a man's gift is prophesying, let him use it in proportion to his faith. [NIV]<br>Having then **gifts** differing according to the grace that is given to us, *let us use them:* if prophecy, *let us prophesy* in proportion to our faith; [NKJV]<br>God has given each of us the **ability** to do certain things well. So if God has given you the ability to prophesy, speak out when you have faith that God is speaking through you. [NLT]<br>ἔχοντες δὲ **χαρίσματα** κατὰ τὴν χάριν τὴν δοθεῖσαν ἡμῖν διάφορα, εἴτε προφητείαν κατὰ τὴν ἀναλογίαν τῆς πίστεως· [GNS]<br>ἔχοντες δὲ **χαρίσματα** κατὰ τὴν χάριν τὴν δοθεῖσαν ἡμῖν διάφορα, εἴτε προφητείαν κατὰ τὴν ἀναλογίαν τῆς πίστεως, [GNT] | Gifts, ability. It means the very special ability given to the believer by God.<br><br>**Practical Application**<br>Note that the ability is from God; it is not a natural talent. The believer could not have attained nor secured the ability himself. It is a spiritual ability; that is, it is given by the Spirit of God for spiritual purposes. It is given to the believer so that he can fulfill his task on earth.<br>Note also that the abilities are said to be given in order "to do certain things well." This means that the abilities are given after we come to know the grace of God. This is part of our heritage in Christ, the glorious privilege...<br>• of being given a very special task upon earth.<br>• of being given purpose and meaning and significance in life.<br>• of being given a very special gift or gifts to fulfill our task on earth. |
| **#11**<br>**Ability To Give Wise Advice**<br><br>Word of wisdom–KJV<br>Word of wisdom–NASB<br>Message of wisdom–NIV<br>Word of wisdom–NKJV<br>Ability to give wise advice–NLT<br><br>**POSB REFERENCE**<br>(1 Cor.12:8-10; esp. v.8)<br>Note 3, point 1 | σοφίας λόγος = sophias logos<br>Pronunciation: [sof-ee'-ahs log'-os]<br>Parsing *sophias* (part of speech): noun<br>  Case—genitive<br>  Gender—feminine<br>  Number—singular<br>  Stem or root—from σοφία, ας<br>Concordance References:<br>⇒ Strong's #3056 logos + 4678 sophia<br>⇒ NIV #3364 logos [message of] + 5053 sophia [wisdom]<br>⇒ NASB #3056 logos + 4678 sophia<br><br>**1 Cor. 12:8**<br>For to one is given by the Spirit the **word of wisdom**; to another the word of knowledge by the same Spirit; [KJV]<br>For to one is given the **word of wisdom** through the Spirit, and to another the word of knowledge according to the same Spirit; [NASB]<br>To one there is given through the Spirit the **message of wisdom**, to another the message of knowledge by means of the same Spirit, [NIV]<br>For to one is given the **word of wisdom** through the Spirit, to another the word of knowledge through the same | Message or word of wisdom; the ability to give wise advice; insight, intelligence, knowledge, the wisdom of God.<br><br>**Practical Application**<br>The wisdom of God is the truth which God has now revealed to man; it is the whole system of truth revealed by God—the truth about God and man and the world. Therefore, the ability to give wise advice is the gift to share the wisdom and truth of God with men—to share the truth in simple and understandable language. |

# PRACTICAL WORD STUDIES
## in the NEW TESTAMENT

| ENGLISH WORD | GREEK WORD AND VERSE | THE WORD MEANS... |
|---|---|---|
| | Spirit, [NKJV]<br>To one person the Spirit gives the **ability to give wise advice**; to another he gives the gift of special knowledge. [NLT]<br>ᾧ μὲν γὰρ διὰ τοῦ Πνεύματος δίδοται λόγος **σοφίας**, ἄλλῳ δὲ **λόγος** γνώσεως, κατὰ τὸ αὐτὸ Πνεῦμα· [GNS]<br>ᾧ μὲν γὰρ διὰ τοῦ πνεύματος δίδοται λόγος **σοφίας**, ἄλλῳ δὲ **λόγος** γνώσεως κατὰ τὸ αὐτὸ πνεῦμα, [GNT] | |
| **#12**<br>**Abode**<br><br>Abode–KJV<br>Gathering together–NASB<br>Came together–NIV<br>Staying–NKJV<br>Returned–NLT<br><br>**POSB REFERENCE**<br>(Mt.17:22)<br>Note 1, point 1 | Συστρεφομένων = Sustrephomenōn<br>Pronunciation: [sus-tref'-o-me'-known]<br>Parsing (part of speech): verb<br>    Mood—participle<br>    Tense—present<br>    Voice—passive<br>    Case—genative<br>    Gender—masculine<br>    Person—plural<br>    Stem or root—from συστρέφω<br>Concordance References:<br>⇒ Strong's #390 anastrepho<br>⇒ NIV #5370 sustrephō<br>⇒ NASB #4962 sustrephō<br><br>**Matthew 17:22**<br>And while they **abode** in Galilee, Jesus said unto them, The Son of man shall be betrayed into the hands of men: [KJV]<br>And while they were **gathering together** in Galilee, Jesus said to them, "The Son of Man is going to be delivered into the hands of men; [NASB]<br>When they **came together** in Galilee, he said to them, "The Son of Man is going to be betrayed into the hands of men. [NIV]<br>Now while they were **staying** in Galilee, Jesus said to them, "The Son of Man is about to be betrayed into the hands of men, [NKJV]<br>One day after they had **returned** to Galilee, Jesus told them, "The Son of Man is going to be betrayed. [NLT]<br>Ἀνατρεφομένων δὲ αὐτῶν ἐν τῇ Γαλιλαίᾳ εἶπεν αὐτοῖς ὁ Ἰησοῦς, Μέλλει ὁ υἱὸς τοῦ ἀνθρώπου παραδίδοσθαι εἰς χεῖρας ἀνθρώπων, [GNS]<br>Συστρεφομένων δὲ αὐτῶν ἐν τῇ Γαλιλαίᾳ εἶπεν αὐτοῖς ὁ Ἰησοῦς, Μέλλει ὁ υἱὸς τοῦ ἀνθρώπου παραδίδοσθαι εἰς χεῖρας ἀνθρώπων, [GNT] | To have gathered; to come together; to abide; to return; to go to and fro; a picture of having gathered military troops for a review.<br><br>**Practical Application**<br>    The force of this word takes on a fresh meaning when the context of this Scripture is understood.<br>    Jesus Christ is preparing the "troops"—His disciples—for the time when He would no longer be with them. He was drilling into them the fact that He was to be killed and raised from the dead. Jesus had to continue talking about His death and resurrection because it was so hard to understand. There were three primary reasons why the disciples had difficulty in grasping the fact.<br>1. The Messiah's death and resurrection were new experiences, new happenings. History was to be made. The talk of a literal death and resurrection was bound to be understood in symbolic and spiritual language (see POSB note—Matthew 18:1-2). (How like so many to spiritualize the two events—even though the events really took place and are so strongly proclaimed by the disciples.) (Cp. 1 Cor. 15:3-8. See POSB note—Mark 9:32; POSB note—Mark 9:34.)<br>2. The Messiah's death and resurrection were thought to be impossible. How could God die? Most men proclaim that God cannot die. Of course, the disciples had not yet seen what death really is—basically separation from God (see POSB *Deeper Study* #1—Hebrews 9:27). They had to learn that God was dealing with spiritual and eternal life (and death), not just with physical and temporal life (and death) on this earth.<br>3. The Messiah's death and resurrection were contrary to all their hopes and expectations. It was just different from all the disciples had ever heard or been taught. The Messiah was thought to be a Messiah of power and sovereign rule not a Messiah who had to suffer and die in order to save man. (See POSB note—Matthew 1:1; POSB *Deeper Study* #2—Matthew 1:18; POSB *Deeper Study* #2—Matthew 3:11; POSB note—Matthew 11:1-6; POSB note—Matthew 11:2-3; POSB *Deeper Study* #1—Matthew 11:5; POSB *Deeper Study* #2—Matthew 11:6; POSB *Deeper Study* #1—Matthew 12:16; POSB note—Matthew 22:42; POSB note—Luke 7:21-23.) |
| **#13**<br>**Abomination That Causes Desolation– Abomination Of Desolation** | βδέλυγμα ἐρημώσεως = bdelugma erēmōseōs<br>Pronunciation: [bdel'-oog-mah er-ay'-mo-say'-os]<br>Parsing *bdelugma* (part of speech): noun<br>    Case—accusative<br>    Gender—neuter<br>    Number—singular<br>    Stem or root—from βδέλυγμα, τος | To detest or detestable.<br><br>**Practical Application**<br>    It is a picture of becoming sick with nausea. The abomination that causes desolation is translated three other times as "abomination" or |

# PRACTICAL WORD STUDIES
## in the NEW TESTAMENT

| ENGLISH WORD | GREEK WORD AND VERSE | THE WORD MEANS... |
|---|---|---|
| **Abomination of desolation–KJV**<br>**ABOMINATION OF DESOLATION–NASB**<br>**Abomination that causes desolation–NIV**<br>**Abomination of desolation–NKJV**<br>Sacrilegious object that causes desecration–NLT<br><br>**POSB REFERENCE**<br>(Mt.24:15)<br>*Deeper Study #1*<br><br>See also POSB REF:<br>(Mk.13:14)<br>*Deeper Study #1* | Parsing *erëmöseös* (part of speech): noun<br>   Case—genitive<br>   Gender—feminine<br>   Number—singular<br>   Stem or root—from ἐρήμωσις, εως<br>Concordance References:<br>⇒ Strong's #946 bdelugma + 2050 erëmösis<br>⇒ NIV #1007 bdelugma [abomination] + 3836 ho + 2247 erëmösis [desolation]<br>⇒ NASB #946 bdelugma + 2050 erëmösis<br><br>**Matthew 24:15**<br>When ye therefore shall see the **abomination of desolation**, spoken of by Daniel the prophet, stand in the holy place, (whoso readeth, let him understand:) [KJV]<br>"Therefore when you see the ABOMINATION OF DESOLATION which was spoken of through Daniel the prophet, standing in the holy place (let the reader understand), [NASB]<br>"So when you see standing in the holy place 'the **abomination that causes desolation**,' spoken of through the prophet Daniel—let the reader understand— [NIV]<br>"Therefore when you see the *'abomination of desolation,'* spoken of by Daniel the prophet, standing in the holy place" (whoever reads, let him understand), [NKJV]<br>"The time will come when you will see what Daniel the prophet spoke about: the **sacrilegious object that causes desecration** standing in the holy place"—reader, pay attention! [NLT]<br>Ὅταν οὖν ἴδητε τὸ **βδέλυγμα** τῆς **ἐρημώσεως** τὸ ῥηθὲν διὰ Δανιὴλ τοῦ προφήτου ἑστὸς ἐν τόπῳ ἁγίῳ, -- ὁ ἀναγινώσκων νοείτω, [GNS]<br>Ὅταν οὖν ἴδητε τὸ **βδέλυγμα** τῆς **ἐρημώσεως** τὸ ῥηθὲν διὰ Δανιὴλ τοῦ προφήτου ἑστὸς ἐν τόπῳ ἁγίῳ, ὁ ἀναγινώσκων νοείτω, [GNT] | "abominable" in the New Testament (See Mark 13:14 and Rev.17:4-5).<br>The word "desolation" comes from the Greek word *erëmösis* and means a wilderness or a desert and, in this context, a wasted, desolate place.<br><br>**Practical Application**<br>Without the presence of God, a place and person are like a wilderness, deserted and left all alone. They are left to waste away. |
| **#14**<br>**Abound**<br><br>**Abound–KJV**<br>Increased–NASB<br>Increase–NIV<br>**Abound–NKJV**<br>Rampant–NLT<br><br>**POSB REFERENCE**<br>(Mt.24:12)<br>*Deeper Study #7*<br><br>See also POSB REF:<br>(2 Pt.1:8-11; esp. v.8)<br>Note 2 | πληθυνθῆναι = *plëthunthënai*<br>Pronunciation: [play-thoon'-thay-nai]<br>Parsing (part of speech): verb<br>   Mood—infinitive<br>   Tense—aorist<br>   Voice—passive<br>   Case—accusative<br>   Stem or root—from πληθύνω<br>Concordance References:<br>⇒ Strong's #4129 plethuno<br>⇒ NIV #4437 plëthunö<br>⇒ NASB #4129 plethuno<br><br>**Matthew 24:12**<br>And because iniquity shall **abound**, the love of many shall wax cold. [KJV]<br>"And because lawlessness is **increased**, most people's love will grow cold. [NASB]<br>Because of the **increase** of wickedness, the love of most will grow cold, [NIV]<br>And because lawlessness will **abound**, the love of many will grow cold. [NKJV]<br>Sin will be **rampant** everywhere, and the love of many will grow cold. [NLT]<br>καὶ διὰ τὸ **πληθυνθῆναι** τὴν ἀνομίαν ψυγήσεται ἡ ἀγάπη τῶν πολλῶν· [GNS]<br>καὶ διὰ τὸ **πληθυνθῆναι** τὴν ἀνομίαν ψυγήσεται ἡ ἀγάπη τῶν πολλῶν. [GNT] | To increase; to overflow; to multiply; to abound; to be rampant; to grow in numbers; to greatly increase.<br><br>**Practical Application**<br>What are the consequences that will come to the world when wickedness becomes rampant? Scripture declares emphatically that these events are going to happen.<br>⇨ The Lord is returning to gather His people together in the most spectacular and joyful occasion of human history.<br>⇨ The great and terrible day of the Lord is going to fall upon the earth. Unbelievers—all those who have cursed, rebelled, denied, ignored, neglected, and rejected Christ—are going to bear the justice of God.<br>⇨ The great apostasy is going to be witnessed by the earth: millions are going to turn away from Christ.<br>⇨ <u>The antichrist is going to arise upon the world scene and bring a material utopia to the earth and some form of state worship—all in utter rebellion and denial of God Himself.</u><br>The point is this: the end times are coming upon the world. Therefore, people must be taught so that some can be saved and escape the things coming upon the earth. (See POSB outline—Matthew 24:1-51 and POSB notes—Matthew 24:1-51 for more of a picture as to what makes the tribulation of the last days worse than what men usually suffer upon earth.) |

# PRACTICAL WORD STUDIES
## in the NEW TESTAMENT

| ENGLISH WORD | GREEK WORD AND VERSE | THE WORD MEANS... |
|---|---|---|
| **#15**<br>**Abound**<br><br>Abound–KJV<br>Abound–NASB<br>Overflow–NIV<br>Abound–NKJV<br>Overflow–NLT<br><br>**POSB REFERENCE**<br>(1 Th.3:12)<br>Note 2 | περισσεύσαι = *perisseusai*<br>Pronunciation: [per-is-syoo'-sah-ee]<br>Parsing (part of speech): verb<br>    Mood—optative<br>    Tense—aorist<br>    Voice—active<br>    Person—3rd person<br>    Number—singular<br>    Stem or root—from περισσεύω<br>Concordance References:<br>  ⇒ Strong's #4052 perisseuō<br>  ⇒ NIV #4355 perisseuō<br>  ⇒ NASB #4052 perisseuō<br><br>**1 Thes. 3:12**<br>And the Lord make you to increase and **abound** in love one toward another, and toward all *men*, even as we *do* toward you: [KJV]<br>And may the Lord cause you to increase and **abound** in love for one another, and for all men, just as we also *do* for you; [NASB]<br>May the Lord make your love increase and **overflow** for each other and for everyone else, just as ours does for you. [NIV]<br>And may the Lord make you increase and **abound** in love to one another and to all, just as we *do* to you, [NKJV]<br>And may the Lord make your love grow and **overflow** to each other and to everyone else, just as our love overflows toward you. [NLT]<br>ὑμᾶς δὲ ὁ Κύριος πλεονάσαι καὶ **περισσεύσαι** τῇ ἀγάπῃ εἰς ἀλλήλους καὶ εἰς πάντας, καθάπερ καὶ ἡμεῖς εἰς ὑμᾶς, [GNS]<br>ὑμᾶς δὲ ὁ κύριος πλεονάσαι καὶ **περισσεύσαι** τῇ ἀγάπῃ εἰς ἀλλήλους καὶ εἰς πάντας καθάπερ καὶ ἡμεῖς εἰς ὑμᾶς, [GNT] | To increase; to overflow; to multiply; to abound; to be rampant. The word "abound" (*perisseusai*) means to excel and overflow (Amplified New Testament).<br><br>**Practical Application**<br>    The great need is to grow in love—to overflow—to excel and overflow in love. But note the crucial point: the love being spoken about is not what the world means by love. This is seen in two significant points.<br>1. The love that we must grow in is the love that makes us love *all men*, not just one another.<br>2. The source of love is the Lord. There is no other source, not for the kind of love that can love *all men*. This is the reason Paul went before the Lord and requested such a love. Paul knew that it was impossible for him or the Thessalonians to work up the kind of love that could reach out and overflow toward all men. |
| **#16**<br>**About, Not To Worry**<br><br>Nothing doubting–KJV<br>Without misgivings–NASB<br>No hesitation–NIV<br>Doubting nothing–NKJV<br>**Not to worry about–NLT**<br><br>**POSB REFERENCE**<br>(Acts 11:4-15; esp. v.12)<br>Note 2, point 3 | μηδὲν διακρίναντα = *mēden diakrinanta*<br>Pronunciation: [may-dehn' dee-ak-ree'-nahn-tah]<br>Parsing *diakrinanta* (part of speech): verb<br>    Mood—participle<br>    Tense—aorist<br>    Voice—active<br>    Case—accusative<br>    Gender—masculine<br>    Person—1st person<br>    Number—singular<br>    Stem or root—from διακρίνω<br>Concordance References:<br>  ⇒ Strong's #3367 mēdeis + 1252 diakrinō<br>  ⇒ NIV #3594 mēdeis [no] + 1359 diakrinō [hesitation]<br>  ⇒ NASB #3367 mēdeis + 1252 diakrinō<br><br>**Acts 11:12**<br>And the spirit bade me go with them, **nothing doubting**. Moreover these six brethren accompanied me, and we entered into the man's house: [KJV]<br>"And the Spirit told me to go with them **without misgivings**. And these six brethren also went with me, and we entered the man's house. [NASB]<br>The Spirit told me to have **no hesitation** about going with them. These six brothers also went with me, and we entered the man's house. [NIV]<br>Then the Spirit told me to go with them, **doubting nothing.** Moreover these six brethren accompanied me, and we entered into the man's house. [NKJV]<br>The Holy Spirit told me to go with them and **not to worry about** their being Gentiles. These six brothers here accompanied me, and we soon arrived at the home of the man who had sent for us. [NLT]<br>εἶπε δὲ μοι τὸ Πνεῦμά συνελθεῖν αὐτοῖς, **μηδὲν** | No hesitation; to be without misgivings; not to worry about; not to doubt.<br><br>**Practical Application**<br>    It means that they were to make no distinction. God tells Peter in no uncertain terms, "Go with them [the Gentiles] making no distinctions."<br>    The same command is given to all believers of all generations. Believers are not to make distinctions, not to discriminate in proclaiming the gospel. What an indictment against so many! How many *withdraw* from the poor? How many do not reach out to people of other races and social classes? |

# PRACTICAL WORD STUDIES
## in the New Testament

| ENGLISH WORD | GREEK WORD AND VERSE | THE WORD MEANS... |
|---|---|---|
| | διακρινόμενον. ἦλθον δὲ σὺν ἐμοὶ καὶ οἱ ἓξ ἀδελφοὶ οὗτοι, καὶ εἰσήλθομεν εἰς τὸν οἶκον τοῦ ἀνδρός. [GNS]<br>εἶπεν δὲ τὸ πνεῦμά μοι συνελθεῖν αὐτοῖς **μηδὲν διακρίναντα**. ἦλθον δὲ σὺν ἐμοὶ καὶ οἱ ἓξ ἀδελφοὶ οὗτοι καὶ εἰσήλθομεν εἰς τὸν οἶκον τοῦ ἀνδρός. [GNT] | |
| **#17**<br>**Above**<br><br>Preferring–KJV<br>Give preference–NASB<br>**Above–NIV**<br>Giving preference–NKJV<br>Take delight–NLT<br><br>**POSB REFERENCE**<br>(Rom.12:9-10; esp. v.10)<br>Note 1, point 4 | προηγούμενοι = *proëgoumenoi*<br>Pronunciation: [pro-ay-goo'-mehn-oy]<br>Parsing (part of speech): verb<br>  Mood—participle (imperative sense)<br>  Tense—present<br>  Voice—middle or passive deponent<br>  Case—nominative<br>  Gender—masculine<br>  Person—2nd person<br>  Number—plural<br>  Stem or root—from προηγέομαι<br>Concordance References:<br>⇒ Strong's #4285 proëgeomai<br>⇒ NIV #4605 proëgeomai<br>⇒ NASB #4285 proëgeomai<br><br>**Romans 12:10**<br>*Be* kindly affectioned one to another with brotherly love; in honour **preferring** one another; [KJV]<br>Be devoted to one another in brotherly love; **give preference** to one another in honor; [NASB]<br>Be devoted to one another in brotherly love. Honor one another **above** yourselves. [NIV]<br>*Be* kindly affectionate to one another with brotherly love, in honor **giving preference** to one another; NKJV]<br>Love each other with genuine affection, and **take delight** in honoring each other. [NLT]<br>τῇ φιλαδελφίᾳ εἰς ἀλλήλους φιλόστοργοι· τῇ τιμῇ ἀλλήλους **προηγούμενοι** [GNS]<br>τῇ φιλαδελφίᾳ εἰς ἀλλήλους φιλόστοργοι, τῇ τιμῇ ἀλλήλους **προηγούμενοι**, [GNT] | Above; preferring; to give preference; to take delight. It means to go before; to lead; to set an example.<br><br>**Practical Application**<br>The charge is clear: the believer is to take the lead in esteeming and expressing respect for others. Imagine a church full of believers with each taking the lead in esteeming and honoring the other. What a picture of true love and care, of real warmth and tenderness, of great strength and manliness. |
| **#18**<br>**Above Reproach**<br><br>Blameless–KJV<br>**Above reproach–NASB**<br>**Above reproach–NIV**<br>Blameless–NKJV<br>Life cannot be spoken against–NLT<br><br>**POSB REFERENCE**<br>(1 Tim.3:2-3; esp. v.2)<br>Note 2, point 1 | ἀνεπίλημπτον = *anepilëmpton*<br>Pronunciation: [an-ep-il'-amp-ton]<br>Parsing (part of speech): adjective<br>  Case—accusative<br>  Gender—masculine<br>  Number—singular<br>  Stem or root—from ἀνεπίλημπτος, ον<br>Concordance References:<br>⇒ Strong's #423 anepilëmptos<br>⇒ NIV #455 anepilëmptos<br>⇒ NASB #423 anepilëmptos<br><br>**1 Tim. 3:2**<br>A bishop then must be **blameless**, the husband of one wife, vigilant, sober, of good behaviour, given to hospitality, apt to teach; [KJV]<br>An overseer, then, must be **above reproach**, the husband of one wife, temperate, prudent, respectable, hospitable, able to teach, [NASB]<br>Now the overseer must be **above reproach**, the husband of but one wife, temperate, self-controlled, respectable, hospitable, able to teach, [NIV]<br>A bishop then must be **blameless**, the husband of one wife, temperate, sober-minded, of good behavior, hospitable, able to teach; [NKJV]<br>For an elder must be a man whose **life cannot be spoken against**. He must be faithful to his wife. He must exhibit self-control, live wisely, and have a good reputation. He must enjoy having guests in his home and must be able to teach. [NLT]<br>δεῖ οὖν τὸν ἐπίσκοπον **ἀνεπίλημπτον** εἶναι, μιᾶς γυναικὸς ἄνδρα, νηφάλιον, σώφρονα, κόσμιον, φιλόξενον, διδακτικόν· [GNS]<br>δεῖ οὖν τὸν ἐπίσκοπον **ἀνεπίλημπτον** εἶναι, μιᾶς γυναικὸς ἄνδρα, νηφάλιον σώφρονα κόσμιον φιλόξενον διδακτικόν, [GNT] | To be without fault; to be without rebuke; to be above reproach; to live an innocent life; to have a life that cannot be spoken against; to be without blemish, spot, or defect.<br><br>**Practical Application**<br>The minister or overseer of God must be qualified; he must meet some personal qualifications; he must be a person of great Christian character. The minister or overseer must be "above reproach" (*anepilëmpton*): blameless; not open to attack; not able to be criticized by the enemy at all (*The Pulpit Commentary*, Vol.21, Edited by H.D.M. Spence & Joseph S. Exell. Grand Rapids, MI: Eerdmans Publishing Co., 1950, p.50). He must be completely above reproach. |

# PRACTICAL WORD STUDIES
## in the NEW TESTAMENT

| ENGLISH WORD | GREEK WORD AND VERSE | THE WORD MEANS... |
|---|---|---|
| **#19**<br>**Above Reproach**<br><br>Without rebuke–KJV<br>**Above reproach–NASB**<br>Without fault–NIV<br>Without fault–NKJV<br>Innocent lives–NLT<br><br>**POSB REFERENCE**<br>(Philip.2:15)<br>Note 4, point 3 | ἄμωμα = amöma<br>Pronunciation: [am-o'-mah]<br>Parsing (part of speech): adjective<br>    Case—nominative<br>    Gender—neuter<br>    Number—plural<br>    Stem or root—from ἄμωμος, ον<br>Concordance References:<br>⇒ Strong's #298 amömetos<br>⇒ NIV #320 amömos<br>⇒ NASB #299b amömos<br><br>**Philip. 2:15**<br>That ye may be blameless and harmless, the sons of God, **without rebuke**, in the midst of a crooked and perverse nation, among whom ye shine as lights in the world; [KJV]<br>That you may prove yourselves to be blameless and innocent, children of God **above reproach** in the midst of a crooked and perverse generation, among whom you appear as lights in the world, [NASB]<br>So that you may become blameless and pure, children of God **without fault** in a crooked and depraved generation, in which you shine like stars in the universe [NIV]<br>That you may become blameless and harmless, children of God **without fault** in the midst of a crooked and perverse generation, among whom you shine as lights in the world, [NKJV]<br>So that no one can speak a word of blame against you. You are to live clean, **innocent lives** as children of God in a dark world full of crooked and perverse people. Let your lives shine brightly before them. [NLT]<br>ἵνα γένησθε ἄμεμπτοι καὶ ἀκέραιοι, τέκνα Θεοῦ **ἀμώμητα** ἐν μέσῳ γενεᾶς σκολιᾶς καὶ διεστραμμένης, ἐν οἷς φαίνεσθε ὡς φωστῆρες ἐν κόσμῳ, [GNS]<br>ἵνα γένησθε ἄμεμπτοι καὶ ἀκέραιοι, τέκνα θεοῦ **ἄμωμα** μέσον γενεᾶς σκολιᾶς καὶ διεστραμμένης, ἐν οἷς φαίνεσθε ὡς φωστῆρες ἐν κόσμῳ, [GNT] | To be without fault; to be without rebuke; to be above reproach; to live innocent lives; to be without blemish, spot, or defect.<br><br>**Practical Application**<br>This is a word that is taken from the Old Testament sacrifices made to God. The idea is that the believer is to live upon earth under the eyes and scrutiny of God. He is to walk without any blemish, spot, or defect.<br>    However, note a fact: the believer lives in a crooked and perverse generation. The world is wicked and evil, twisted and perverted; therefore, the believer has a difficult path to walk. But walk he must, for he is to be the light of the world. He is to shine as a light in the world. He is to reflect the purity, holiness and quietness of God Himself. |
| **#20**<br>**Above Reproach**<br><br>Unreproveable–KJV<br>Beyond reproach–NASB<br>Free from accusation–NIV<br>**Above reproach–NKJV**<br>Without a single fault–NLT<br><br>**POSB REFERENCE**<br>(Col.1:22)<br>Note 3, point 3 | ἀνεγκλήτους = anegklëtous<br>Pronunciation: [an-eng'-klay-toos]<br>Parsing (part of speech): adjective<br>    Case—accusative<br>    Gender—masculine<br>    Number—plural<br>    Stem or root—from ἀνέγκλητος, ον<br>Concordance References:<br>⇒ Strong's #410 anegklëtos<br>⇒ NIV #441 anegklëtos<br>⇒ NASB #410 anegklëtos<br><br>**Col. 1:22**<br>In the body of his flesh through death, to present you holy and unblameable and **unreproveable** in his sight: [KJV]<br>Yet He has now reconciled you in His fleshly body through death, in order to present you before Him holy and blameless and **beyond reproach**—[NASB]<br>But now he has reconciled you by Christ's physical body through death to present you holy in his sight, without blemish and **free from accusation**—[NIV]<br>In the body of His flesh through death, to present you holy, and blameless, and **above reproach** in His sight—[NKJV]<br>Yet now he has brought you back as his friends. He has done this through his death on the cross in his own human body. As a result, he has brought you into the very presence of God, and you are holy and blameless as you stand before him **without a single fault**. [NLT]<br>νυνὶ δὲ ἀποκατήλλαξεν ἐν τῷ σώματι τῆς σαρκὸς αὐτοῦ διὰ τοῦ θανάτου, παραστῆσαι ὑμᾶς ἁγίους καὶ ἀμώμους καὶ **ἀνεγκλήτους** κατενώπιον αὐτοῦ·[GNS]<br>νυνὶ δὲ ἀποκατήλλαξεν ἐν τῷ σώματι τῆς σαρκὸς αὐτοῦ διὰ τοῦ θανάτου παραστῆσαι ὑμᾶς ἁγίους καὶ ἀμώμους καὶ **ἀνεγκλήτους** κατενώπιον αὐτοῦ, [GNT] | To be free from accusation; to be beyond reproach; to have nothing against them; to be without a single fault, unreproveable, blameless, unchargeable.<br><br>**Practical Application**<br>Imagine standing before God holy, unblameable, and beyond reproach. Imagine how pleased God would be! How He would joy and rejoice in us—that we had honored Christ, His only Son, by trusting Him so much! As we are presented to God, what would He say? What would His first words be to us? We would be speechless, no doubt. But what a day of coronation, of glory, of greatness—standing face to face with our Father, the God of all glory, the Sovereign Majesty of the whole universe.<br>    This is God's one great purpose in reconciliation: to present us perfect before Him. |

# PRACTICAL WORD STUDIES
## in the NEW TESTAMENT

| ENGLISH WORD | GREEK WORD AND VERSE | THE WORD MEANS... |
|---|---|---|
| **#21**<br>**Abusers**<br><br>Revilers–KJV<br>Revilers–NASB<br>Slanderers–NIV<br>Revilers–NKJV<br>**Abusers–NLT**<br><br>**POSB REFERENCE**<br>(1 Cor.6:10)<br>Note 3, point 4 | λοίδοροι = loidoroi<br>Pronunciation: [loy'-dor-oy-ee]<br>Parsing (part of speech): noun<br>    Case—nominative<br>    Gender—masculine<br>    Number—plural<br>    Stem or root—from λοίδορος, ου<br>Concordance References:<br>  ⇒ Strong's #3060 loidoros<br>  ⇒ NIV #3368 loidoros<br>  ⇒ NASB #3060 loidoros<br><br>**1 Cor. 6:10**<br>Nor thieves, nor covetous, nor drunkards, nor **revilers**, nor extortioners, shall inherit the kingdom of God. [KJV]<br><br>Nor thieves, nor the covetous, nor drunkards, nor **revilers**, nor swindlers, shall inherit the kingdom of God. [NASB]<br><br>Nor thieves nor the greedy nor drunkards nor **slanderers** nor swindlers will inherit the kingdom of God. [NIV]<br><br>Nor thieves, nor covetous, nor drunkards, nor **revilers**, nor extortioners will inherit the kingdom of God. [NKJV]<br><br>Thieves, greedy people, drunkards, **abusers**, and swindlers—none of these will have a share in the Kingdom of God. [NLT]<br><br>οὔτε κλέπται, οὔτε πλεονέκται, οὐ μέθυσοι, οὐ **λοίδοροι**, οὐχ ἅρπαγες, βασιλείαν Θεοῦ οὐ κληρονομήσουσι. [GNS]<br><br>οὔτε κλέπται οὔτε πλεονέκται οὐ μέθυσοι οὐ **λοίδοροι**, οὐχ ἅρπαγες βασιλείαν θεοῦ κληρονομήσουσιν. [GNT] | Slanderers, revilers, abusers.<br><br>**Practical Application**<br>Abusers (*anepilëmpton*) are people who mistreat others through scolding, ranting and raving, insolent and abusive language, cursing and slanderous language. |
| **#22**<br>**Abusers Of Themselves With Mankind**<br><br>Abusers of themselves with mankind–KJV<br>Homosexuals–NASB<br>Homosexual offenders–NIV<br>Sodomites–NKJV<br>Homosexuals–NLT<br><br>**POSB REFERENCE**<br>(1 Cor.6:9)<br>Note 2, point 4 | ἀρσενοκοῖται = arsenokoitai<br>Pronunciation: [ar-sen-ok-oy'-tah-ee]<br>Parsing (part of speech): noun<br>    Case—nominative<br>    Gender—masculine<br>    Number—plural<br>    Stem or root—from ἀρσενοκοίτης, ου<br>Concordance References:<br>  ⇒ Strong's #733 arsenokoitës<br>  ⇒ NIV #780 arsenokoitës<br>  ⇒ NASB #733 arsenokoitës<br><br>**1 Cor. 6:9**<br>Know ye not that the unrighteous shall not inherit the kingdom of God? Be not deceived: neither fornicators, nor idolaters, nor adulterers, nor effeminate, nor **abusers of themselves with mankind**, [KJV]<br><br>Or do you not know that the unrighteous shall not inherit the kingdom of God? Do not be deceived; neither fornicators, nor idolaters, nor adulterers, nor effeminate, nor **homosexuals**, [NASB]<br><br>Do you not know that the wicked will not inherit the kingdom of God? Do not be deceived: Neither the sexually immoral nor idolaters nor adulterers nor male prostitutes nor **homosexual offenders** [NIV]<br><br>Do you not know that the unrighteous will not inherit the kingdom of God? Do not be deceived. Neither fornicators, nor idolaters, nor adulterers, nor homosexuals, nor **sodomites**, [NKJV]<br><br>Don't you know that those who do wrong will have no share in the Kingdom of God? Don't fool yourselves. Those who indulge in sexual sin, who are idol worshipers, adulterers, male prostitutes, **homosexuals**, [NLT]<br><br>ἢ οὐκ οἴδατε ὅτι ἄδικοι βασιλείαν Θεοῦ οὐ κληρονομήσουσι; μὴ πλανᾶσθε· οὔτε πόρνοι, οὔτε εἰδωλολάτραι, οὔτε μοιχοί, οὔτε μαλακοί, οὔτε **ἀρσενοκοῖται**, [GNS] | Homosexual offenders; sodomites, perverts; the abusers of themselves with mankind.<br><br>**Practical Application**<br>The warning is clear and sobering: the practicing homosexual, those who are "abusers of themselves with mankind" (*arsenokoitai*), will not inherit the kingdom of God. |

# PRACTICAL WORD STUDIES
## in the NEW TESTAMENT

| ENGLISH WORD | GREEK WORD AND VERSE | THE WORD MEANS... |
|---|---|---|
| | ἢ οὐκ οἴδατε ὅτι ἄδικοι θεοῦ βασιλείαν οὐ κληρονομήσουσιν; μὴ πλανᾶσθε· οὔτε πόρνοι οὔτε εἰδωλολάτραι οὔτε μοιχοὶ οὔτε μαλακοὶ οὔτε **ἀρσενοκοῖται** [GNT] | |
| **#23**<br>**Abusive**<br><br>Blasphemers–KJV<br>Revilers–NASB<br>**Abusive–NIV**<br>Blasphemers–NKJV<br>Scoffing at God–NLT<br><br>**POSB REFERENCE**<br>(2 Tim.3:2-4; esp. v.2)<br>Note 2, point 5 | **βλάσφημοι** = *blasphēmoi*<br>Pronunciation: [blas'-fay-moy]<br>Parsing (part of speech): adjective<br>  Case—nominative<br>  Gender—masculine<br>  Number—plural<br>  Stem or root—from βλάσφημος, ον<br>Concordance References:<br>⇒ Strong's #989 blasphēmos<br>⇒ NIV #1061 blasphēmos<br>⇒ NASB #989 blasphēmos<br><br>**2 Tim. 3:2**<br>For men shall be lovers of their own selves, covetous, boasters, proud, **blasphemers**, disobedient to parents, unthankful, unholy, [KJV]<br><br>For men will be lovers of self, lovers of money, boastful, arrogant, **revilers**, disobedient to parents, ungrateful, unholy, [NASB]<br><br>People will be lovers of themselves, lovers of money, boastful, proud, **abusive**, disobedient to their parents, ungrateful, unholy, [NIV]<br><br>For men will be lovers of themselves, lovers of money, boasters, proud, **blasphemers**, disobedient to parents, unthankful, unholy, [NKJV]<br><br>For people will love only themselves and their money. They will be boastful and proud, **scoffing at God**, disobedient to their parents, and ungrateful. They will consider nothing sacred. [NLT]<br><br>ἔσονται γὰρ οἱ ἄνθρωποι φίλαυτοι, φιλάργυροι, ἀλαζόνες, ὑπερήφανοι, **βλάσφημοι**, γονεῦσιν ἀπειθεῖς, ἀχάριστοι, ἀνόσιοι, [GNS]<br><br>ἔσονται γὰρ οἱ ἄνθρωποι φίλαυτοι φιλάργυροι ἀλαζόνες ὑπερήφανοι **βλάσφημοι**, γονεῦσιν ἀπειθεῖς, ἀχάριστοι ἀνόσιοι [GNT] | To be verbally abusive; to blaspheme; to revile; to openly scoff at God; to slander, to insult, rail, reproach, curse.<br><br>**Practical Application**<br>The word "abusive" or "blasphemy" (*blasphēmoi*) is usually thought to be against God, and it is. But it is also a sin against men. Men can blaspheme men. Think of the cursing and insults that are thrown against God and men today. Practically everyone is cursing and reviling others: mothers, fathers, children, teachers, professionals, actors, comedians, politicians, even some professing religionists feel the need to occasionally curse in order to be acceptable.<br>Why is there so much cursing and profanity today? Because there is a loss of respect for both self and others, for both position and authority. People rail, revile, insult, reproach, and curse when they are disturbed within—when they sense dissatisfaction, disapproval, unacceptance, bitterness, emptiness, loneliness, and reaction within their heart. A disturbed and dissatisfied heart causes people to blaspheme God and man, including themselves (blaming and cursing themselves when they fail and come ever so short). |
| **#24**<br>**Abusive**<br><br>Railer–KJV<br>Reviler–NASB<br>Slanderer–NIV<br>Reviler–NKJV<br>**Abusive–NLT**<br><br>**POSB REFERENCE**<br>(1 Cor.5:11)<br>Note 5 | **λοίδορος** = *loidoros*<br>Pronunciation: [loy'-dor-os]<br>Parsing (part of speech): noun<br>  Case—nominative<br>  Gender—masculine<br>  Number—singular<br>  Stem or root—from λοίδορος, ου<br>Concordance References:<br>⇒ Strong's #3060 loidoros<br>⇒ NIV #3368 loidoros<br>⇒ NASB #3060 loidoros<br><br>**1 Cor. 5:11**<br>But now I have written unto you not to keep company, if any man that is called a brother be a fornicator, or covetous, or an idolater, or a **railer**, or a drunkard, or an extortioner; with such an one no not to eat. [KJV]<br><br>But actually, I wrote to you not to associate with any so-called brother if he should be an immoral person, or covetous, or an idolater, or a **reviler**, or a drunkard, or a swindler—not even to eat with such a one. [NASB]<br><br>But now I am writing you that you must not associate with anyone who calls himself a brother but is sexually immoral or greedy, an idolater or a **slanderer**, a drunkard or a swindler. With such a man do not even eat. [NIV]<br><br>But now I have written to you not to keep company with anyone named a brother, who is sexually immoral, or covetous, or an idolater, or a **reviler**, or a drunkard, or an extortioner—not even to eat with such a person. [NKJV]<br><br>What I meant was that you are not to associate with anyone who claims to be a Christian yet indulges in sexual sin, or is greedy, or worships idols, or is **abusive**, or a | Someone who is a slanderer; railer; reviler; an abusive person.<br><br>**Practical Application**<br>The abuser (*loidoros*) is a person who rants and scolds; reviles and abuses; uses insolent, abusive, and slanderous language. |

# PRACTICAL WORD STUDIES
## in the NEW TESTAMENT

| ENGLISH WORD | GREEK WORD AND VERSE | THE WORD MEANS... |
|---|---|---|
| | drunkard, or a swindler. Don't even eat with such people. [NLT]<br><br>νυνὶ δὲ ἔγραψα ὑμῖν μὴ συναναμίγνυσθαι, ἐάν τις ἀδελφὸς ὀνομαζόμενος ᾖ πόρνος, ἢ πλεονέκτης, ἢ εἰδωλολάτρης, ἢ **λοίδορος**, ἢ μέθυσος ἢ ἅρπαξ· τῷ τοιούτῳ μηδὲ Συνεσθίειν. [GNS]<br><br>νυνὶ δὲ ἔγραψα ὑμῖν μὴ συναναμίγνυσθαι ἐάν τις ἀδελφὸς ὀνομαζόμενος ᾖ πόρνος ἢ πλεονέκτης ἢ εἰδωλολάτρης ἢ **λοίδορος** ἢ μέθυσος ἢ ἅρπαξ, τῷ τοιούτῳ μηδὲ συνεσθίειν. [GNT] | |
| **#25**<br>**Abusive Speech**<br><br>Filthy communication–KJV<br>**Abusive speech– NASB**<br>Filthy language–NIV<br>Filthy language–NKJV<br>Dirty language–NLT<br><br>**POSB REFERENCE**<br>(Col.3:8-11; esp. v.8)<br>Note 2, point 1e | αἰσχρολογίαν = aischrologian<br>Pronunciation: [ahee-skhrol-og-ee'-ahn]<br>Parsing (part of speech): noun<br>   Case—accusative<br>   Gender—feminine<br>   Number—singular<br>   Stem or root—from αἰσχρολογία, ας<br>Concordance References:<br>⇒ Strong's #148 aischrologia<br>⇒ NIV #155 aischrologia<br>⇒ NASB #148 aischrologia<br><br>**Col. 3:8**<br>But now ye also put off all these; anger, wrath, malice, blasphemy, **filthy communication** out of your mouth. [KJV]<br>But now you also, put them all aside: anger, wrath, malice, slander, *and* **abusive speech** from your mouth. [NASB]<br>But now you must rid yourselves of all such things as these: anger, rage, malice, slander, and **filthy language** from your lips. [NIV]<br>But now you yourselves are to put off all these: anger, wrath, malice, blasphemy, **filthy language** out of your mouth. [NKJV]<br>But now is the time to get rid of anger, rage, malicious behavior, slander, and **dirty language**. [NLT]<br>νυνὶ δὲ ἀπόθεσθε καὶ ὑμεῖς τὰ πάντα, ὀργήν, θυμόν, κακίαν, βλασφημίαν, **αἰσχρολογίαν** ἐκ τοῦ στόματος ὑμῶν· [GNS]<br>νυνὶ δὲ ἀπόθεσθε καὶ ὑμεῖς τὰ πάντα, ὀργήν, θυμόν, κακίαν, βλασφημίαν, **αἰσχρολογίαν** ἐκ τοῦ στόματος ὑμῶν· [GNT] | Filthy language, filthy communication, abusive speech, dirty language, obscene speech.<br><br>**Practical Application**<br>If a believer is to follow and imitate God, he has to be pure in speech and conversation; he has to keep his mouth or tongue clean. He cannot let his mouth become foul and polluted, filthy and vile.<br>He is never, not once, to be engaged in "abusive speech" (*aischrologian*): using the mouth in obscene, shameful, foul, polluted, base, immoral conduct and conversation. What an indictment of our day—a day of sodomy and perversion. And note: the word refers to both conduct and speech. How polluted and foul-mouthed so many have become—so much so that society could easily be known as a second Sodom and Gomorrah. |
| **#26**<br>**Accept**<br><br>Receive–KJV<br>**Accept–NASB**<br>**Accept–NIV**<br>Receive–NKJV<br>**Accept–NLT**<br><br>**POSB REFERENCE**<br>(Rom.14:1-2; esp. v.1)<br>Note 1<br><br>See also POSB REF:<br>(Rom.15:7-12; esp. v.7)<br>Note 4 | προσλαμβάνεσθε = proslambanesthe<br>Pronunciation: [pros-lam-ban'-ehs-theh]<br>Parsing (part of speech): verb<br>   Mood—imperative<br>   Tense—present<br>   Voice—middle<br>   Person— 2nd person<br>   Number—plural<br>   Stem or root—from προσλαμβάνομαι<br>Concordance References:<br>⇒ Strong's #4355 proslambanō<br>⇒ NIV #4689 proslambanō<br>⇒ NASB #4355 proslambanō<br><br>**Romans 14:1**<br>Him that is weak in the faith **receive** ye, *but* not to doubtful disputations. [KJV]<br>Now **accept** the one who is weak in faith, *but* not for *the purpose of* passing judgment on his opinions. [NASB]<br>**Accept** him whose faith is weak, without passing judgment on disputable matters. [NIV]<br>**Receive** one who is weak in the faith, *but* not to disputes over doubtful things. [NKJV]<br>**Accept** Christians who are weak in faith, and don't argue with them about what they think is right or wrong. [NLT]<br>Τὸν δὲ ἀσθενοῦντα τῇ πίστει **προσλαμβάνεσθε**, μὴ εἰς διακρίσεις διαλογισμῶν. [GNS]<br>Τὸν δὲ ἀσθενοῦντα τῇ πίστει **προσλαμβάνεσθε**, μὴ εἰς διακρίσεις διαλογισμῶν. [GNT] | To accept; to receive; to welcome; to take to oneself.<br><br>**Practical Application**<br>It means...<br>• to accept a weak person just as God graciously accepts people.<br>• to take a weak person to oneself just as God graciously takes people to Himself.<br>The believer is to "accept" the weak brother just as God accepts him. The exhortation is both forceful and tender, demanding and hopeful. It is forceful and demanding in that it gives the believer the opportunity to act as God acts, and it gives the weak believer great hope in being cared for and looked after. |

## Practical Word Studies in the New Testament

| ENGLISH WORD | GREEK WORD AND VERSE | THE WORD MEANS... |
|---|---|---|
| **#27**<br>**Accept–**<br>**Acceptable**<br><br>Acceptable–KJV<br>Acceptable–NASB<br>Pleasing–NIV<br>Acceptable–NKJV<br>Accept–NLT<br><br>**POSB**<br>**REFERENCE**<br>(Romans 12:1)<br>Note 4, point 2 | εὐάρεστον = euareston<br>Pronunciation: [yoo-ar'-es-ton]<br>Parsing (part of speech): adjective<br>    Case—accusative<br>    Gender—feminine<br>    Number—singular<br>    Stem or root—from εὐάρεστος, ον<br>Concordance References:<br>⇒ Strong's #2101 euarestos<br>⇒ NIV #2298 euarestos<br>⇒ NASB #2101 euarestos<br><br>**Romans 12:1**<br>I beseech you therefore, brethren, by the mercies of God, that ye present your bodies a living sacrifice, holy, **acceptable** unto God, *which is* your reasonable service. [KJV]<br><br>I urge you therefore, brethren, by the mercies of God, to present your bodies a living and holy sacrifice, **acceptable** to God, *which is* your spiritual service of worship. [NASB]<br><br>Therefore, I urge you, brothers, in view of God's mercy, to offer your bodies as living sacrifices, holy and **pleasing** to God—this is your spiritual act of worship. [NIV]<br><br>I beseech you therefore, brethren, by the mercies of God, that you present your bodies a living sacrifice, holy, **acceptable** to God, *which is* your reasonable service. [NKJV]<br><br>And so, dear brothers and sisters, I plead with you to give your bodies to God. Let them be a living and holy sacrifice—the kind he will **accept**. When you think of what he has done for you, is this too much to ask? [NLT]<br><br>Παρακαλῶ οὖν ὑμᾶς, ἀδελφοί, διὰ τῶν οἰκτιρμῶν τοῦ Θεοῦ, παραστῆσαι τὰ σώματα ὑμῶν θυσίαν ζῶσαν, ἁγίαν εὐάρεστον τῷ Θεῷ, τὴν λογικὴν λατρείαν ὑμῶν. [GNS]<br><br>Παρακαλῶ οὖν ὑμᾶς, ἀδελφοί, διὰ τῶν οἰκτιρμῶν τοῦ θεοῦ παραστῆσαι τὰ σώματα ὑμῶν θυσίαν ζῶσαν ἁγίαν εὐάρεστον τῷ θεῷ, τὴν λογικὴν λατρείαν ὑμῶν· [GNT] | Pleasing, acceptable. The word means well-pleasing, approving and extremely satisfying to God.<br><br>**Practical Application**<br>The dedication of the body to God is acceptable (*euareston*). God accepts and joys and rejoices over a body that is dedicated and living for Him.<br>This is the very thing for which believers should seek: to be acceptable and well-pleasing to God. We should seek to cause Him to joy and to rejoice in our bodies. Our bodies should be so dedicated—so pure and holy and clean, and so committed and involved in helping people—that God's heart is just flooded with joy and rejoicing. |
| **#28**<br>**Accept The**<br>**Authority**<br><br>Subjection–KJV<br>Submissive–NASB<br>Submissive–NIV<br>Submissive–NKJV<br>Accept the authority–NLT<br><br>**POSB**<br>**REFERENCE**<br>(1 Pt.3:1)<br>Note 1<br><br>See also POSB REF:<br>(Col.3:18)<br>Note 1, point 1<br>(1 Pt.5:5)<br>Note 1 | ὑποτασσόμεναι = hupotassomenai<br>Pronunciation: [hoop-ot-as'-so-mehn-ah-ee]<br>Parsing (part of speech): verb<br>    Mood—participle (imperative sense)<br>    Tense—present<br>    Voice—passive<br>    Case—nominative<br>    Gender—feminine<br>    Person—2nd person<br>    Number—plural<br>    Stem or root—from ὑποτάσσω<br>Concordance References:<br>⇒ Strong's #5293 hupotassomenai<br>⇒ NIV #5718 hupotassomenai<br>⇒ NASB #5293 hupotassomenai<br><br>**1 Peter 3:1**<br>Likewise, ye wives, *be* in **subjection** to your own husbands; that, if any obey not the word, they also may without the word be won by the conversation of the wives; [KJV]<br><br>In the same way, you wives, be **submissive** to your own husbands so that even if any *of them* are disobedient to the word, they may be won without a word by the behavior of their wives, [NASB]<br><br>Wives, in the same way be **submissive** to your husbands so that, if any of them do not believe the word, they may be won over without words by the behavior of their wives, [NIV]<br><br>Wives, likewise, *be* **submissive** to your own husbands, that even if some do not obey the word, they, with- | To be submissive; to accept the authority; to submit to; to be under the authority of.<br><br>**Practical Application**<br>The wife's duty is to subject herself to her own husband even if he does not obey God's Word. Scripture is clear and pointed about this. The phrase "accept the authority" (*hupotassomenai*) mean just what it says—to be in subjection; to submit oneself. The Greek scholar Marvin Vincent says that it is used of the *submission of servants* (*Word Studies in the New Testament*, Vol.1. Grand Rapids, MI: Eerdmans, 1946, p.65). (Cp. 1 Peter 2:18.) The word means that a Christian wife is to place herself under the authority and control of her husband; that she is to subject and submit herself to her own husband's authority, control, and leadership. There is no question but that this is what the word means.<br>⇒ Vine says that it is primarily a military term meaning to *rank under* (*Expository Dictionary of New Testament Words*. Old Tappan, NJ: Fleming H. Revell, 1966).<br>⇒ Robertson says that the word has a military air and that the word is the same kind of obedience that a citizen is to give to the government. (See his comments on Col. 3:18, *Word Pictures in the New Testament*, Vol.6.) |

# Practical Word Studies
## in the New Testament

| ENGLISH WORD | GREEK WORD AND VERSE | THE WORD MEANS... |
|---|---|---|
| | out a word, may be won by the conduct of their wives, [NKJV]<br><br>In the same way, you wives must **accept the authority** of your husbands, even those who refuse to accept the Good News. Your godly lives will speak to them better than any words. They will be won over [NLT]<br><br>Ὁμοίως, αἱ γυναῖκες **ὑποτασσόμεναι** τοῖς ἰδίοις ἀνδράσιν, ἵνα καὶ εἴ τινες ἀπειθοῦσι τῷ λόγῳ, διὰ τῆς τῶν γυναικῶν ἀναστροφῆς ἄνευ λόγου κερδηθήσωνται [GNS]<br><br>Ὁμοίως [αἱ] γυναῖκες, **ὑποτασσόμεναι** τοῖς ἰδίοις ἀνδράσιν, ἵνα καὶ εἴ τινες ἀπειθοῦσιν τῷ λόγῳ, διὰ τῆς τῶν γυναικῶν ἀναστροφῆς ἄνευ λόγου κερδηθήσονται, [GNT] | In modern society this is strong; in fact, it is too strong for many. Many reject the idea of woman's submission as archaic, outdated, and old-fashioned. Some even react in anger and hostility against the Word of God and those who preach the duty of wives.<br><br>Are they right? Has Scripture gone too far in declaring that wives should accept the authority of their husbands? Has God made a mistake within the order of the family? To the Christian, the answer is "no". The problem is not in what God has said, but in our *understanding of what He has said* or in our rebellion against what He wills. Any wife who reacts to God's command is reacting either because she does not understand what God is saying or is just *unwilling to give her life to God and follow Him as He says*. What does God mean by subjection? God does not mean *dictatorial subjection*...<br>• that a wife is to subject herself to a tyrant.<br>• that a wife is to submit herself to the demands of a husband who acts like a beast.<br>• that a wife is to be a slave or footstool for the husband.<br>• that a wife is to serve her husband without restraint.<br>• that a wife is to be treated as inferior to her husband.<br><br>What God means by submission is order, cooperation, relationship, and partnership—that a husband and wife are to walk *together*, *hand in hand*, throughout life. Every body of people—even when the body is only two persons—must have a leader who takes the lead in plowing through the wilderness of the world and its trials and temptations and difficulties. Between the two, wife and husband, one of them has to be the primary leader. God's order for the two is that the husband take the lead. The Christian wife, in obedience to her Lord, accept the authority of her husband's leadership, authority, and control.<br><br>Note one other factor that points out just how seriously God takes the wife's subjection to her husband. Even if the husband does not obey God's Word, the wife is to subject herself to him. Imagine what is being said to the wife, how strong this exhortation is:<br>⇒ Some husbands are unbelievers; they just refuse to heed God's Word.<br>⇒ Some husbands not only fail to believe in God, they rebel against and curse God. And they make life difficult for their wives because their wives do trust God.<br>⇒ Some husbands disobey God's Word by living unholy and sinful lives, and they neglect and ignore their wives.<br>⇒ Some husbands are believers in Christ, but they do not obey God's Word. They, too, mistreat their wives.<br><br>What does God expect of the wife? This passage of Scripture is clear: the wife is to accept the authority of her own husband. But note why: that the husband may be won to Christ by the godly behavior of the wife. By living a life of purity and reverence and by demonstrating a quiet and meek spirit, the wife stands a good chance of winning her husband to the Lord. |

# PRACTICAL WORD STUDIES
## in the NEW TESTAMENT

| ENGLISH WORD | GREEK WORD AND VERSE | THE WORD MEANS... |
|---|---|---|
| **#29**<br>**Accept, Not**<br><br>Receiveth not–KJV<br>Not accept–NASB<br>Not accept–NIV<br>Not receive–NKJV<br>Can't understand–NLT<br><br>**POSB REFERENCE**<br>(1 Cor.2:14)<br>Note 1, point 1 | οὐ δέχεται = ou dechetai<br>Pronunciation: [oo dekh'-eh-tah-ee]<br>Parsing *dechetai* (part of speech): verb<br>    Mood—indicative<br>    Tense—present<br>    Voice—middle or passive deponent<br>    Person—3rd person<br>    Number—singular<br>    Stem or root—from δέχομαι<br>Concordance References:<br>  ⇒ Strong's #3756 ou + 1209 dechomai<br>  ⇒ NIV #4024 ou [not] + 1312 dechomai [accept]<br>  ⇒ NASB #3756 ou + 1209 dechomai<br><br>**1 Cor. 2:14**<br>But the natural man **receiveth not** the things of the Spirit of God: for they are foolishness unto him: neither can he know *them*, because they are spiritually discerned. [KJV]<br>But a natural man does **not accept** the things of the Spirit of God; for they are foolishness to him, and he cannot understand them, because they are spiritually appraised. [NASB]<br>The man without the Spirit does **not accept** the things that come from the Spirit of God, for they are foolishness to him, and he cannot understand them, because they are spiritually discerned. [NIV]<br>But the natural man does **not receive** the things of the Spirit of God, for they are foolishness to him; nor can he know *them*, because they are spiritually discerned. [NKJV]<br>But people who aren't Christians **can't understand** these truths from God's Spirit. It all sounds foolish to them because only those who have the Spirit can understand what the Spirit means. [NLT]<br>ψυχικὸς δὲ ἄνθρωπος **οὐ δέχεται** τὰ τοῦ Πνεύματος τοῦ Θεοῦ· μωρία γὰρ αὐτῷ ἐστι, καὶ οὐ δύναται γνῶναι, ὅτι πνευματικῶς ἀνακρίνεται·[GNS]<br>ψυχικὸς δὲ ἄνθρωπος **οὐ δέχεται** τὰ τοῦ πνεύματος τοῦ θεοῦ, μωρία γὰρ αὐτῷ ἐστιν, καὶ οὐ δύναται γνῶναι, ὅτι πνευματικῶς ἀνακρίνεται·[GNT] | Not receive; not accept; not take; not welcome; not bear with; to refuse and regret; not obtain.<br><br>**Practical Application**<br>The man without the Spirit is the natural man. He does not accept the things that come from the Spirit of God. The phrase "not accept" (*ou dechetai*) means that spiritual things are not welcomed as a guest, are not accepted. It means to refuse and reject. Spiritual things are of little if any concern to the natural man. His mind is primarily upon this world, upon...<br>• bigger and better things<br>• acquiring more and more<br>• desires and feelings<br>• wants and cravings<br>• position and wealth<br>• attention and recognition<br>• ambition and promotion<br>• socials and parties<br>• play and recreation<br>• comfort and ease<br>• drinking and eating<br>• dress and appearance<br><br>The natural man's life and mind are spent focusing upon the natural, upon this world and not upon the spiritual; therefore, in God's eyes he is classified as the natural man. His heart welcomes only the world; it is closed to God. As stated, God is not welcomed into his life. Therefore, he does not accept the things that come from the Spirit of God. |
| **#30**<br>**Accepted**<br><br>Accepted–KJV<br>Pleasing–NASB<br>Please–NIV<br>Pleasing–NKJV<br>Please–NLT<br><br>**POSB REFERENCE**<br>(2 Cor.5:9-10; esp. v.9)<br>Note 4 | εὐάρεστοι εἶναι = euarestoi einai<br>Pronunciation: [yoo-ar'-es-toy ee-nah-ee]<br>Parsing *euarestoi* (part of speech): adjective<br>    Case—nominative<br>    Gender—masculine<br>    Number—plural<br>    Stem or root—from εὐάρεστος, ον<br>Parsing *einai* (part of speech): verb<br>    Mood—infinitive<br>    Tense—present<br>    Voice—active<br>    Stem or root—from εἰμί<br>Concordance References:<br>  ⇒ Strong's #1510+2101 eimi euarestos<br>  ⇒ NIV #1639+2298 eimi euarestos<br>  ⇒ NASB #1510+2101 eimi euarestos<br><br>**2 Cor. 5:9**<br>Wherefore we labour, that, whether present or absent, we may be **accepted** of him. [KJV]<br>Therefore also we have as our ambition, whether at home or absent, to be **pleasing** to Him. [NASB]<br>So we make it our goal to **please** him, whether we are at home in the body or away from it. [NIV]<br>Therefore we make it our aim, whether present or absent, to be well **pleasing** to Him. [NKJV]<br>So our aim is to **please** him always, whether we are here in this body or away from this body. [NLT]<br>διὸ καὶ φιλοτιμούμεθα, εἴτε ἐνδημοῦντες, εἴτε ἐκδημοῦντες, **εὐάρεστοι** αὐτῷ **εἶναι**. [GNS]<br>διὸ καὶ φιλοτιμούμεθα, εἴτε ἐνδημοῦντες εἴτε ἐκδημοῦντες, **εὐάρεστοι** αὐτῷ **εἶναι**. [GNT] | To please; to be accepted. The word means well pleasing in the sense of being accepted.<br><br>**Practical Application**<br>Paul says that he is to be judged; therefore, he works his fingers to the bone. Why? That he may be accepted (*euarestoi*) by God. |

# PRACTICAL WORD STUDIES
## in the NEW TESTAMENT

| ENGLISH WORD | GREEK WORD AND VERSE | THE WORD MEANS... |
|---|---|---|
| **#31**<br>**Access**<br><br>Access–KJV<br>Obtained our introduction–NASB<br>Access–NIV<br>Access–NKJV<br>Brought us into this place–NLT<br><br>**POSB REFERENCE**<br>(Romans 5:2)<br>Note 3, point 2 | προσαγωγὴν = *prosagōgēn*<br>Pronunciation: [pros-ag-ogue-ayn']<br>Parsing (part of speech): noun<br>    Case—accusative<br>    Gender—feminine<br>    Number—singular<br>    Stem or root—from προσαγωγή, ῆς<br>Concordance References:<br>⇒ Strong's #4318 prosagōgē<br>⇒ NIV #4643 prosagōgē<br>⇒ NASB #4318 prosagōgē<br><br>**Romans 5:2**<br>By whom also we have **access** by faith into this grace wherein we stand, and rejoice in hope of the glory of God. [KJV]<br><br>Through whom also we have **obtained our introduction** by faith into this grace in which we stand; and we exult in hope of the glory of God. [NASB]<br><br>Through whom also we have gained **access** by faith into this grace in which we now stand. And we rejoice in the hope of the glory of God. [NIV]<br><br>Through whom also we have **access** by faith into this grace in which we stand, and rejoice in hope of the glory of God. [NKJV]<br><br>Because of our faith, Christ has **brought us into this place** of highest privilege where we now stand, and we confidently and joyfully look forward to sharing God's glory. [NLT]<br><br>δι' οὗ καὶ τὴν **προσαγωγὴν** ἐσχήκαμεν τῇ πίστει εἰς τὴν χάριν ταύτην ἐν ᾗ ἑστήκαμεν, καὶ καυχώμεθα ἐπ' ἐλπίδι τῆς δόξης τοῦ Θεοῦ. [GNS]<br><br>δι' οὗ καὶ τὴν **προσαγωγὴν** ἐσχήκαμεν [τῇ πίστει] εἰς τὴν χάριν ταύτην ἐν ᾗ ἑστήκαμεν καὶ καυχώμεθα ἐπ' ἐλπίδι τῆς δόξης τοῦ Θεοῦ. [GNT] | Access; to bring to; to move to; to introduce; to present. It is the freedom or right to enter.<br><br>**Practical Application**<br>Note it is through Christ that we have access into this grace. The thought is that of being in a royal court and being presented and introduced to the King of kings. Jesus Christ is the One who throws open the door into God's presence. He is the One who presents us to God, the Sovereign Majesty of the universe. |
| **#32**<br>**Access**<br><br>Access–KJV<br>Access–NASB<br>Access–NIV<br>Access–NKJV<br>May come to–NLT<br><br>**POSB REFERENCE**<br>(Eph.2:18)<br>Note 5<br><br>See also POSB REF:<br>(Romans 5:2)<br>Note 3, point 2 | προσαγωγὴν = *prosagōgēn*<br>Pronunciation: [pros-ag-ogue-ayn']<br>Parsing (part of speech): noun<br>    Case—accusative<br>    Gender—feminine<br>    Number—singular<br>    Stem or root—from προσαγωγή, ῆς<br>Concordance References:<br>⇒ Strong's #4318 prosagōgē<br>⇒ NIV #4643 prosagōgē<br>⇒ NASB #4318 prosagōgē<br><br>**Ephes. 2:18**<br>For through him we both have **access** by one Spirit unto the Father. [KJV]<br><br>For through Him we both have our **access** in one Spirit to the Father. [NASB]<br><br>For through him we both have **access** to the Father by one Spirit. [NIV]<br><br>For through Him we both have **access** by one Spirit to the Father. [NKJV]<br><br>Now all of us, both Jews and Gentiles, **may come to** the Father through the same Holy Spirit because of what Christ has done for us. [NLT]<br><br>ὅτι δι' αὐτοῦ ἔχομεν τὴν **προσαγωγὴν** οἱ ἀμφότεροι ἐν ἑνὶ Πνεύματι πρὸς τὸν πατέρα. [GNS]<br><br>ὅτι δι' αὐτοῦ ἔχομεν τὴν **προσαγωγὴν** οἱ ἀμφότεροι ἐν ἑνὶ πνεύματι πρὸς τὸν πατέρα. [GNT] | Access; to bring to; to move to; to introduce; to present.<br><br>**Practical Application**<br>The thought is that of being in a royal court and being presented and introduced to the King of kings. Jesus Christ is the One who throws open the door into God's presence. He is the One who presents us to God, the Sovereign Majesty of the universe.<br><br>Note that it is the Holy Spirit who escorts us into God's presence. The idea is that of daily access—hour by hour, moment by moment. The Holy Spirit keeps us in the presence of God.<br>⇒ The Holy Spirit is the Divine Nature of God within us that gives us permanent access into God's presence. (John 3:5; Romans 8:11; 2 Peter 1:4).<br>⇒ The Holy Spirit is the One who works in us to stir us to move more and more into God's presence (Romans 8:14; Galatians 4:6-7).<br>⇒ The Holy Spirit is the constant companion with us, teaching us to live in God's presence (John 14:26; 1 Cor. 2:12-13).<br>⇒ The Holy Spirit is the One within us who bears witness that we are the children of God and should approach God continually (Romans 8:15-16; Galatians 4:4-6). |
| **#33**<br>**Accomplish Purpose** | τελειοῦμαι = *teleioumai*<br>Pronunciation: [tel-i-oo'-mah-ee]<br>Parsing (part of speech): verb<br>    Mood—indicative<br>    Tense—present | To reach a goal; to complete an assignment; to accomplish a specific purpose; to finish a task. |

## PRACTICAL WORD STUDIES
### in the NEW TESTAMENT

| ENGLISH WORD | GREEK WORD AND VERSE | THE WORD MEANS... |
|---|---|---|
| Perfected–KJV<br>Reach goal–NASB<br>Reach goal–NIV<br>Perfected–NKJV<br>**Accomplish purpose–NLT**<br><br>**POSB REFERENCE**<br>(Lk.13:31-33; esp. v.32)<br>Note 2, point 1 | Voice—passive<br>Person—1st person<br>Number—singular<br>Stem or root—from τελειόω<br>Concordance References:<br>⇒ Strong's #5048 teleioo<br>⇒ NIV #5457 teleioö<br>⇒ NASB #5048 teleioo<br><br>**Luke 13:32**<br>And he said unto them, Go ye, and tell that fox, Behold, I cast out devils, and I do cures to day and to morrow, and the third *day* I shall be **perfected**. [KJV]<br>And He said to them, "Go and tell that fox, 'Behold, I cast out demons and perform cures today and tomorrow, and the third *day* I **reach** My goal.' [NASB]<br>He replied, "Go tell that fox, 'I will drive out demons and heal people today and tomorrow, and on the third day I will **reach** my goal.' [NIV]<br>And He said to them, "Go, tell that fox, 'Behold, I cast out demons and perform cures today and tomorrow, and the third *day* I shall be **perfected**.' [NKJV]<br>Jesus replied, "Go tell that fox that I will keep on casting out demons and doing miracles of healing today and tomorrow; and the third day I will **accomplish** my **purpose**. [NLT]<br>καὶ εἶπεν αὐτοῖς, Πορευθέντες εἴπατε τῇ ἀλώπεκι ταύτῃ, Ἰδοὺ ἐκβάλλω δαιμόνια, καὶ ἰάσεις ἐπιτελῶ σήμερον καὶ αὔριον, καὶ τῇ τρίτῃ **τελειοῦμαι**. [GNS]<br>καὶ εἶπεν αὐτοῖς, Πορευθέντες εἴπατε τῇ ἀλώπεκι ταύτῃ, Ἰδοὺ ἐκβάλλω δαιμόνια καὶ ἰάσεις ἀποτελῶ σήμερον καὶ αὔριον καὶ τῇ τρίτῃ **τελειοῦμαι**. [GNT] | **Practical Application**<br>His ministry of delivering men spiritually and physically (casting out evil spirits and healing) will not be stopped by any man, even rulers such as Herod.<br>The words "the third day I will accomplish my purpose" mean that His witness and delivering power will be completed and finished. There is a definite time for it, then His witness will stop. It will be no more. But until that day, nothing can stop His ministry and witness. This is, of course, a reference to Jesus' death and His resurrection on the third day. Note that His resurrection is the perfection of His ministry. It is by arising from the dead that He conquered death and completed man's salvation. |
| **#34**<br>**Accomplished**<br><br>Most surely believed–KJV<br>**Accomplished–NASB**<br>Fulfilled–NIV<br>Fulfilled–NKJV<br>Took place–NLT<br><br>**POSB REFERENCE**<br>(Lk.1:1)<br>Note 1, point 2<br><br>**See also POSB REF:**<br>(Lk.21:24)<br>Note 5, point 1 | πεπληροφορημένων* peplērophorēmenōn<br>Pronunciation: [pe-play-rof-or-ee-men-own]<br>Parsing (part of speech): verb<br>Mood—participle<br>Tense—perfect<br>Voice—passive<br>Case—genitive<br>Gender—neuter<br>Number—plural<br>Stem or root—from πληροφορέω<br>Concordance References:<br>⇒ Strong's #4135 plerophoreo<br>⇒ NIV #4442 plērophoreö<br>⇒ NASB #4135 plerophoreo<br><br>**Luke 1:1**<br>Forasmuch as many have taken in hand to set forth in order a declaration of those things which are **most surely believed** among us, [KJV]<br>Inasmuch as many have undertaken to compile an account of the things **accomplished** among us, [NASB]<br>Many have undertaken to draw up an account of the things that have been **fulfilled** among us, [NIV]<br>Inasmuch as many have taken in hand to set in order a narrative of those things which have been **fulfilled** among us, [NKJV]<br>Most honorable Theophilus:Many people have written accounts about the events that **took place** among us. [NLT]<br>Ἐπειδήπερ πολλοὶ ἐπεχείρησαν ἀνατάξασθαι διήγησιν περὶ τῶν **πεπληροφορημένων** ἐν ἡμῖν πραγμάτων, [GNS]<br>Ἐπειδήπερ πολλοὶ ἐπεχείρησαν ἀνατάξασθαι διήγησιν περὶ τῶν **πεπληροφορημένων** ἐν ἡμῖν πραγμάτων, [GNT] | To fill; to fill up; to make full; to come to an end; to bring to completion; to finish. It means things that were fulfilled, that were accomplished, that were actually performed, or that had run their full course (cp. 2 Tim. 4:5).<br><br>**Practical Application**<br>Luke is saying that the *things of Christ* were not only believed, but they were also accomplished or fulfilled among the believers of that day. The *things* (events, matters) of Christ actually took place; they were purposeful; they were destined to be accomplished and fulfilled.<br>The point is this: the things of Christ are a record of historical events, things that actually happened and that actually fulfilled the purpose of God. Therefore, the things are "most surely believed among us [believers]." What are the *things* accomplished and believed? Both the things of the New Testament and of the Old Testament. The whole Bible is a record of "those things". |
| **#35**<br>**Accomplished The Whole Purpose** | τέλος = telos<br>Pronunciation: [tel'-os]<br>Parsing (part of speech): noun<br>Case—nominative | The purposed end; the determined goal; the destined climax; the sought after consummation; the fulfillment; the result; the outcome; the last; |

# PRACTICAL WORD STUDIES
in the NEW TESTAMENT

| ENGLISH WORD | GREEK WORD AND VERSE | THE WORD MEANS... |
|---|---|---|
| End–KJV<br>End–NASB<br>End–NIV<br>End–NKJV<br>**Accomplished the whole purpose–NLT**<br><br>**POSB REFERENCE**<br>(Romans 10:4)<br>Note 2 | Gender—neuter<br>Number—singular<br>Stem or root—from τέλος, ους<br>Concordance References:<br>⇒ Strong's #5056 telos<br>⇒ NIV #5465 telos<br>⇒ NASB #5056 telos<br><br>**Romans 10:4**<br>For Christ *is* the **end** of the law for righteousness to every one that believeth. [KJV]<br>For Christ is the **end** of the law for righteousness to everyone who believes. [NASB]<br>Christ is the **end** of the law so that there may be righteousness for everyone who believes. [NIV]<br>For Christ *is* the **end** of the law for righteousness to everyone who believes. [NKJV]<br>For Christ has **accomplished the whole purpose** of the law. All who believe in him are made right with God. [NLT]<br>τέλος γὰρ νόμου Χριστὸς εἰς δικαιοσύνην παντὶ τῷ πιστεύοντι. [GNS]<br>τέλος γὰρ νόμου Χριστὸς εἰς δικαιοσύνην παντὶ τῷ πιστεύοντι. [GNT] | the full extent of the termination; accomplished the whole purpose.<br><br>**Practical Application**<br>Jesus Christ is the One who accomplished the whole purpose (*telos*) of the law. Through Jesus Christ, man no longer has to seek righteousness through the law. Man no longer has to work and work to be acceptable to God, to work and work knowing full well that he is coming ever so short of God's glory and demand. Man no longer has to live under the enslaving power of sin, under its guilt and shame and punishment. Man no longer has to live under the weight and pressure of failing and of being ever so unworthy and hopeless, lonely and alienated. Man can now be set free, knowing full well that he is acceptable to God. Man can now have a heart that swells with assurance and confidence, the perfect knowledge that he is God's and God is his. Man can know that he is accepted as righteous before God. How? Through the righteousness of Jesus Christ. |
| **#36**<br>**Account A Wrong Suffered, Does Not Take Into**<br><br>Thinketh no evil–KJV<br>**Does not take into account a wrong suffered–NASB**<br>Record of wrongs–NIV<br>Thinks no evil–NKJV<br>No record of when it has been wronged–NLT<br><br>**POSB REFERENCE**<br>(1 Cor.13:4-7; esp. v.5)<br>Note 2, point 9 | οὐ λογίζεται τὸ κακόν =oo logizetai to kakon<br>Pronunciation: [oo log-id'-eh-tah-ee to kak-on']<br>Parsing *logizetai* (part of speech): verb<br>   Mood—indicative<br>   Tense—present<br>   Voice—middle or passive deponent<br>   Person—3rd person<br>   Number—singular<br>   Stem or root—from λογίζομαι<br>Parsing *kakon* (part of speech): pronominal adjective<br>   Case—accusative<br>   Gender—neuter<br>   Number—singular<br>   Stem or root—from κακός, ή, όν<br>Concordance References:<br>⇒ Strong's #3756 ou + 3049 logizomai + 2556 kakos<br>⇒ NIV #4024 ou [no] 3357 logizomai [record of] + 2805 kakos [wrongs]<br>⇒ NASB #3756 ou + 3049 logizomai + 2556 kakos<br><br>**1 Cor. 13:5**<br>Doth not behave itself unseemly, seeketh not her own, is not easily provoked, **thinketh no evil**; [KJV]<br>Does not act unbecomingly; it does not seek its own, is not provoked, **does not take into account a wrong suffered**, [NASB]<br>It is not rude, it is not self-seeking, it is not easily angered, it keeps no **record of wrongs**. [NIV]<br>Does not behave rudely, does not seek its own, is not provoked, **thinks no evil**; [NKJV]<br>Or rude. Love does not demand its own way. Love is not irritable, and it keeps **no record of when it has been wronged**. [NLT]<br>οὐκ ἀσχημονεῖ, οὐ ζητεῖ τὰ ἑαυτῆς, οὐ παροξύνεται, **οὐ λογίζεται τὸ κακόν**, [GNS]<br>οὐκ ἀσχημονεῖ, οὐ ζητεῖ τὰ ἑαυτῆς, οὐ παροξύνεται, **οὐ λογίζεται τὸ κακόν**, [GNT] | To count, to reckon; not to claim a record of wrongs; not to think evil; not to keep an account of wrongs suffered.<br><br>**Practical Application**<br>Love does not consider the wrong suffered; is not resentful; does not hold the evil done to oneself. Love suffers the evil done to it and forgets it. |
| **#37**<br>**Accounted**<br><br>Reckoned–KJV<br>Reckoned–NASB<br>Credited–NIV<br>**Accounted–NKJV**<br>Declared–NLT | Ἐλογίσθη *elogisthë*<br>Pronunciation: [eh-log-ees'-thay]<br>Parsing (part of speech): verb<br>   Mood—indicative<br>   Tense—aorist<br>   Voice—passive<br>   Person—3rd person<br>   Number—singular<br>   Stem or root—from λογίζομαι | Credited, reckoned, declared; to count; to deposit; to put to one's account; to impute; to consider; to evaluate; to calculate.<br><br>**Practical Application**<br>Abraham's faith was counted for righteousness or credited as righteousness (see POSB note, Justification—Romans 4:1-3; POSB note—Romans 4:6-8; POSB *Deeper Study* #1— |

# PRACTICAL WORD STUDIES
## in the New Testament

| ENGLISH WORD | GREEK WORD AND VERSE | THE WORD MEANS... |
|---|---|---|
| **POSB REFERENCE** (Romans 4:9) Note 2 | Concordance References:<br>⇒ Strong's #3049 logizomai<br>⇒ NIV #3357 logizomai<br>⇒ NASB #3049 logizomai<br><br>**Romans 4:9**<br>Cometh this blessedness then upon the circumcision only, or upon the uncircumcision also? for we say that faith was **reckoned** to Abraham for righteousness. [KJV]<br>Is this blessing then only on the circumcised, or upon the uncircumcised also? For we say, "Faith was **reckoned** to Abraham as righteousness." [NASB]<br>Is this blessedness only for the circumcised, or also for the uncircumcised? We have been saying that Abraham's faith was **credited** to him as righteousness. [NIV]<br>Does this blessedness then come upon the circumcised only, or upon the uncircumcised also? For we say that faith was **accounted** to Abraham for righteousness. [NKJV]<br>Now then, is this blessing only for the Jews, or is it for Gentiles, too? Well, what about Abraham? We have been saying he was **declared** righteous by God because of his faith. [NLT]<br>ὁ μακαρισμὸς οὖν οὗτος ἐπὶ τὴν περιτομὴν ἢ καὶ ἐπὶ τὴν ἀκροβυστίαν; λέγομεν γὰρ ὅτι **Ἐλογίσθη** τῷ Ἀβραὰμ ἡ πίστις εἰς δικαιοσύνην. [GNS]<br>ὁ μακαρισμὸς οὖν οὗτος ἐπὶ τὴν περιτομὴν ἢ καὶ ἐπὶ τὴν ἀκροβυστίαν; λέγομεν γάρ, **Ἐλογίσθη** τῷ Ἀβραὰμ ἡ πίστις εἰς δικαιοσύνην. [GNT] | Romans 4:22; POSB *Deeper Study #2*—Romans 4:22; POSB note—Romans 5:1 for more discussion).<br>Note that Abraham was justified or counted righteous by faith; he was not justified...<br>• by being religious.<br>• by performing good deeds.<br>• by doing some good work.<br>• by being good and virtuous.<br>• by submitting to a ritual.<br>• by joining some body of believers. |
| **#38**<br>**Accounted**<br><br>Imputed–KJV<br>Reckoned–NASB<br>Credited–NIV<br>**Accounted–NKJV**<br>Declared–NLT<br><br>**POSB REFERENCE** (Romans 4:22) *Deeper Study #1* | ἐλογίσθη = elogisthē<br>Pronunciation: [eh-log-ees'-thay]<br>Parsing (part of speech): verb<br>    Mood—indicative<br>    Tense—aorist<br>    Voice—passive<br>    Person—3rd person<br>    Number—singular<br>    Stem or root—from λογίζομαι<br>Concordance References:<br>⇒ Strong's #3049 logizomai<br>⇒ NIV #3357 logizomai<br>⇒ NASB #3049 logizomai<br><br>**Romans 4:22**<br>And therefore it was **imputed** to him for righteousness. [KJV]<br>Therefore also it was **reckoned** to him as righteousness. [NASB]<br>This is why "it was **credited** to him as righteousness." [NIV]<br>And therefore "it was **accounted** to him for righteousness." [NKJV]<br>And because of Abraham's faith, God **declared** him to be righteous. [NLT]<br>διὸ καὶ **ἐλογίσθη** αὐτῷ εἰς δικαιοσύνην. [GNS]<br>διὸ [καὶ] **ἐλογίσθη** αὐτῷ εἰς δικαιοσύνην. [GNT] | To credit; to impute; to reckon; to declare; to count; to compute; to ascribe; to deposit; to put to one's account.<br><br>**Practical Application**<br>Abraham's faith was counted for righteousness. (See POSB *Deeper Study #1*, Reckon—Romans 6:11 for a fuller discussion.) Abraham deposited his faith with God, and God credited Abraham's faith as righteousness. |
| **#39**<br>**Accredited**<br><br>Approved–KJV<br>Attested–NASB<br>**Accredited–NIV**<br>Attested–NKJV<br>Endorsed–NLT<br><br>**POSB REFERENCE** (Acts 2:22-24; esp. v.22) Note 3, point 1 | ἀποδεδειγμένον = apodedeigmenon<br>Pronunciation: [ap-od-eh-deeng-meh'-non]<br>Parsing (part of speech): verb<br>    Mood—participle<br>    Tense—perfect<br>    Voice—passive<br>    Case—accusative<br>    Gender—masculine<br>    Number—singular<br>    Stem or root—from ἀποδείκνυμι<br>Concordance References:<br>⇒ Strong's #584 apodeiknumi<br>⇒ NIV #617 apodeiknumi<br>⇒ NASB #584 apodeiknumi | To accredit; to approve; to endorse; to point out; to display; to show; to attest; to sanction; to certify.<br><br>**Practical Application**<br>God put His stamp of approval upon Jesus. He demonstrated and showed all men that Jesus is perfectly acceptable to Him. Jesus of Nazareth had God's approval, His perfect acceptance. |

# PRACTICAL WORD STUDIES
## in the NEW TESTAMENT

| ENGLISH WORD | GREEK WORD AND VERSE | THE WORD MEANS... |
|---|---|---|
| | **Acts 2:22**<br>Ye men of Israel, hear these words; Jesus of Nazareth, a man **approved** of God among you by miracles and wonders and signs, which God did by him in the midst of you, as ye yourselves also know: [KJV]<br>"Men of Israel, listen to these words: Jesus the Nazarene, a man **attested** to you by God with miracles and wonders and signs which God performed through Him in your midst, just as you yourselves know— [NASB]<br>"Men of Israel, listen to this: Jesus of Nazareth was a man **accredited** by God to you by miracles, wonders and signs, which God did among you through him, as you yourselves know. [NIV]<br>"Men of Israel, hear these words: Jesus of Nazareth, a Man **attested** by God to you by miracles, wonders, and signs which God did through Him in your midst, as you yourselves also know— [NKJV]<br>"People of Israel, listen! God publicly **endorsed** Jesus of Nazareth by doing wonderful miracles, wonders, and signs through him, as you well know. [NLT]<br>ἄνδρες Ἰσραηλῖται, ἀκούσατε τοὺς λόγους τούτους· Ἰησοῦν τὸν Ναζωραῖον, ἄνδρα ἀπὸ τοῦ Θεοῦ **ἀποδεδειγμένον** εἰς ὑμᾶς δυνάμεσι καὶ τέρασι καὶ σημείοις, οἷς ἐποίησε δι' αὐτοῦ ὁ Θεὸς ἐν μέσῳ ὑμῶν, καθὼς καὶ αὐτοὶ οἴδατε, [GNS]<br>Ἄνδρες Ἰσραηλῖται, ἀκούσατε τοὺς λόγους τούτους· Ἰησοῦν τὸν Ναζωραῖον, ἄνδρα **ἀποδεδειγμένον** ἀπὸ τοῦ θεοῦ εἰς ὑμᾶς δυνάμεσι καὶ τέρασι καὶ σημείοις οἷς ἐποίησεν δι' αὐτοῦ ὁ θεὸς ἐν μέσῳ ὑμῶν καθὼς αὐτοὶ οἴδατε, [GNT] | |
| **#40**<br>**Accurately–Accuracy**<br><br>Diligently–KJV<br>**Accurately–NASB**<br>**Accurately–NIV**<br>**Accurately–NKJV**<br>**Accuracy–NLT**<br><br>POSB<br>REFERENCE<br>(Acts 18:25)<br>Note 5 | ἀκριβῶς = *akribōs*<br>Pronunciation: [ak-ree-boce']<br>Parsing (part of speech): adjective adverb<br>   Stem or root—from ἀκριβῶς<br>Concordance References:<br>   ⇒ Strong's #199 akribōs<br>   ⇒ NIV #209 akribōs<br>   ⇒ NASB #199 akribōs<br><br>**Acts 18:25**<br>This man was instructed in the way of the Lord; and being fervent in the spirit, he spake and taught **diligently** the things of the Lord, knowing only the baptism of John. [KJV]<br>This man had been instructed in the way of the Lord; and being fervent in spirit, he was speaking and teaching **accurately** the things concerning Jesus, being acquainted only with the baptism of John; [NASB]<br>He had been instructed in the way of the Lord, and he spoke with great fervor and taught about Jesus **accurately**, though he knew only the baptism of John. [NIV]<br>This man had been instructed in the way of the Lord; and being fervent in spirit, he spoke and taught **accurately** the things of the Lord, though he knew only the baptism of John. [NKJV]<br>He had been taught the way of the Lord and talked to others with great enthusiasm and **accuracy** about Jesus. However, he knew only about John's baptism. [NLT]<br>οὗτος ἦν κατηχημένος τὴν ὁδὸν τοῦ Κυρίου, καὶ ζέων τῷ πνεύματι ἐλάλει καὶ ἐδίδασκεν **ἀκριβῶς** τὰ περὶ τοῦ Κύριον, ἐπιστάμενος μόνον τὸ βάπτισμα Ἰωάννου· [GNS]<br>οὗτος ἦν κατηχημένος τὴν ὁδὸν τοῦ κυρίου καὶ ζέων τῷ πνεύματι ἐλάλει καὶ ἐδίδασκεν **ἀκριβῶς** τὰ περὶ τοῦ Ἰησοῦ, ἐπιστάμενος μόνον τὸ βάπτισμα Ἰωάννου [GNT] | Accurately, diligently, with care.<br><br>**Practical Application**<br>The stress is that Apollos taught accurately (*akribōs*), that is, carefully and diligently.<br>⇒ He was true to the Scriptures, weighing carefully what they said.<br>⇒ He proclaimed what the Scriptures taught and all that they taught. He did not neglect subjects his listeners might not like to hear.<br>⇒ He did not twist the Scriptures, adding to or taking away from them. |
| **#41**<br>**Accursed**<br><br>Anathema–KJV<br>**Accursed–NASB** | ἀνάθεμα = *anathema*<br>Pronunciation: [an-ath'-em-ah]<br>Parsing (part of speech): noun<br>   Case—nominative<br>   Gender—neuter<br>   Number—singular | Curse, accursed, under the ban, cast away. It is something doomed to utter destruction.<br><br>**Practical Application**<br>There was the terrifying importance of love for Christ. Paul uses the word four times |

## PRACTICAL WORD STUDIES
### in the NEW TESTAMENT

| ENGLISH WORD | GREEK WORD AND VERSE | THE WORD MEANS... |
|---|---|---|
| Curse–NIV<br>**Accursed–NKJV**<br>Cursed–NLT<br><br>**POSB REFERENCE**<br>(1 Cor.16:19-24; esp. v.22)<br>Note 6, point 2 | Stem or root—from ἀνάθεμα, τος<br>Concordance References:<br>⇒ Strong's #331 anathema<br>⇒ NIV #353 anathema<br>⇒ NASB #331 anathema<br><br>**1 Cor. 16:22**<br>If any man love not the Lord Jesus Christ, let him be **Anathema** Maranatha. [KJV]<br>If anyone does not love the Lord, let him be **accursed**. Maranatha. [NASB]<br>If anyone does not love the Lord—a **curse** be on him. Come, O Lord! [NIV]<br>If anyone does not love the Lord Jesus Christ, let him be **accursed**. O Lord, come! [NKJV]<br>If anyone does not love the Lord, that person is **cursed**. Our Lord, come! [NLT]<br>εἴ τις οὐ φιλεῖ τὸν Κύριον Ἰησοῦν Χριστόν, ἤτω **ἀνάθεμα**. Μαρὰν ἀθα. [GNS]<br>εἴ τις οὐ φιλεῖ τὸν κύριον, ἤτω **ἀνάθεμα**. Μαρανα θα. [GNT] | (Romans 9:3; 1 Cor. 12:3; 1 Cor. 16:22; Galatians 1:8; cp. Acts 23:14). The word "maranatha" means the Lord comes! The idea is that any man who does not love the Lord Jesus Christ will be accursed. And the Lord is coming: they will be accursed. |
| **#42**<br>**Accursed**<br><br>Accursed–KJV<br>Accursed–NASB<br>Cursed–NIV<br>Accursed–NKJV<br>Cursed–NLT<br><br>**POSB REFERENCE**<br>(Rom.9:1-3; esp. v.3)<br>Note 1, point 3 | ἀνάθεμα = anathema<br>Pronunciation: [an-ath'-em-ah]<br>Parsing (part of speech): noun<br>   Case—nominative<br>   Gender—neuter<br>   Number—singular<br>Stem or root—from ἀνάθεμα, τος<br>Concordance References:<br>⇒ Strong's #331 anathema<br>⇒ NIV #353 anathema<br>⇒ NASB #331 anathema<br><br>**Romans 9:3**<br>For I could wish that myself were **accursed** from Christ for my brethren, my kinsmen according to the flesh: [KJV]<br>For I could wish that I myself were **accursed**, *separated* from Christ for the sake of my brethren, my kinsmen according to the flesh, [NASB]<br>For I could wish that I myself were **cursed** and cut off from Christ for the sake of my brothers, those of my own race, [NIV]<br>For I could wish that I myself were **accursed** from Christ for my brethren, my countrymen according to the flesh, [NKJV]<br>For my people, my Jewish brothers and sisters. I would be willing to be forever **cursed**—cut off from Christ!—if that would save them. [NLT]<br>ηὐχόμην γὰρ αὐτὸς ἐγὼ **ἀνάθεμα** εἶναι ἀπὸ τοῦ Χριστοῦ ὑπὲρ τῶν ἀδελφῶν μου, τῶν συγγενῶν μου κατὰ σάρκα· [GNS]<br>ηὐχόμην γὰρ **ἀνάθεμα** εἶναι αὐτὸς ἐγὼ ἀπὸ τοῦ Χριστοῦ ὑπὲρ τῶν ἀδελφῶν μου τῶν συγγενῶν μου κατὰ σάρκα, [GNT] | Curse, accursed, under the ban, cast away. It is something doomed to utter destruction.<br><br>**Practical Application**<br>The picture is that of a man who had an unbelievable willingness to be sacrificed for his people. Paul could wish to be accursed (*anathema*), that is, separated from Christ if it would save his people. He could be willing to swap his salvation for their doom if it would lead to their salvation. Paul felt the deepest love and concern for his people. |
| **#43**<br>**Act Of Worship**<br><br>Service–KJV<br>Service of worship–NASB<br>**Act of worship–NIV**<br>Service–NKJV<br>Not translated–NLT<br><br>**POSB REFERENCE**<br>(Rom.12:1)<br>Note 2, point 2b | λατρείαν = latreian<br>Pronunciation: [lat-ri'-ahn]<br>Parsing (part of speech): noun<br>   Case—accusative<br>   Gender—feminine<br>   Number—singular<br>Stem or root—from λατρεία, ας<br>Concordance References:<br>⇒ Strong's #2999 latreia<br>⇒ NIV #3301 latreia<br>⇒ NASB #2999 latreia<br><br>**Romans 12:1**<br>I beseech you therefore, brethren, by the mercies of God, that ye present your bodies a living sacrifice, holy, acceptable unto God, *which is* your reasonable **service**. [KJV] | An act of worship; a service of worship; a ministry; a service.<br><br>**Practical Application**<br>The believer is to use his mind in dedicating his body as an act of worship. He is to study the Scriptures and intelligently think about how to best serve God as he walks through life day by day. |

## PRACTICAL WORD STUDIES
### in the NEW TESTAMENT

| ENGLISH WORD | GREEK WORD AND VERSE | THE WORD MEANS... |
|---|---|---|
| | I urge you therefore, brethren, by the mercies of God, to present your bodies a living and holy sacrifice, acceptable to God, *which is* your spiritual **service of worship**. [NASB]<br><br>Therefore, I urge you, brothers, in view of God's mercy, to offer your bodies as living sacrifices, holy and pleasing to God—this is your spiritual **act of worship**. [NIV]<br><br>I beseech you therefore, brethren, by the mercies of God, that you present your bodies a living sacrifice, holy, acceptable to God, *which is* your reasonable **service**. [NKJV]<br><br>And so, dear brothers and sisters, I plead with you to give your bodies to God. Let them be a living and holy sacrifice—the kind he will accept. When you think of what he has done for you, is this too much to ask? [NLT]—NOT TRANSLATED<br><br>Παρακαλῶ οὖν ὑμᾶς, ἀδελφοί, διὰ τῶν οἰκτιρμῶν τοῦ Θεοῦ, παραστῆσαι τὰ σώματα ὑμῶν θυσίαν ζῶσαν, ἁγίαν εὐάρεστον τῷ Θεῷ, τὴν λογικὴν **λατρείαν** ὑμῶν. [GNS]<br><br>Παρακαλῶ οὖν ὑμᾶς, ἀδελφοί, διὰ τῶν οἰκτιρμῶν τοῦ θεοῦ παραστῆσαι τὰ σώματα ὑμῶν θυσίαν ζῶσαν ἁγίαν εὐάρεστον τῷ θεῷ, τὴν λογικὴν **λατρείαν** ὑμῶν· [GNT] | |
| **#44**<br>**Act Unbecomingly**<br><br>Behave itself unseemly–KJV<br>**Act unbecomingly–NASB**<br>Rude–NIV<br>Behave rudely–NKJV<br>Rude–NLT<br><br>**POSB REFERENCE**<br>(1 Cor.13:4-7; esp. v.5)<br>Note 2, point 6 | ἀσχημονεῖ = *aschēmonei*<br>Pronunciation: [as-kay-mon-ee']<br>Parsing (part of speech): verb<br>    Mood—indicative<br>    Tense—present<br>    Voice—active<br>    Person—3rd person<br>    Number—singular<br>    Stem or root—from ἀσχημονέω<br>Concordance References:<br>  ⇒ Strong's #807 aschēmoneō<br>  ⇒ NIV #858 aschēmoneō<br>  ⇒ NASB #807 aschēmoneō<br><br>**1 Cor. 13:5**<br>Doth not **behave itself unseemly**, seeketh not her own, is not easily provoked, thinketh no evil; [KJV]<br><br>Does not **act unbecomingly**; it does not seek its own, is not provoked, does not take into account a wrong *suffered*, [NASB]<br><br>It is not **rude**, it is not self-seeking, it is not easily angered, it keeps no record of wrongs. [NIV]<br><br>Does not **behave rudely**, does not seek its own, is not provoked, thinks no evil; [NKJV]<br><br>Or **rude**. Love does not demand its own way. Love is not irritable, and it keeps no record of when it has been wronged. [NLT]<br><br>οὐκ **ἀσχημονεῖ**, οὐ ζητεῖ τὰ ἑαυτῆς, οὐ παροξύνεται, οὐ λογίζεται τὸ Κακόν, [GNS]<br><br>οὐκ **ἀσχημονεῖ**, οὐ ζητεῖ τὰ ἑαυτῆς, οὐ παροξύνεται, οὐ λογίζεται τὸ κακόν, [GNT] | Unbecomingly, rudely, indecently, unmannerly, disgracefully.<br><br>**Practical Application**<br>Love does nothing to shame oneself. Love is orderly and controlled; and it behaves and treats all persons with respect, honoring and respecting who they are. |
| **#45**<br>**Active**<br><br>Powerful–KJV<br>**Active–NASB**<br>**Active–NIV**<br>Powerful–NKJV<br>Power–NLT<br><br>**POSB REFERENCE**<br>(Heb.4:11-13; esp. v.12)<br>Note 5, point 2a | ἐνεργής = *energēs*<br>Pronunciation: [en-er-gace']<br>Parsing (part of speech): adjective<br>    Case—nominative<br>    Gender—masculine<br>    Number—singular<br>    Stem or root—from ἐνεργής, ές<br>Concordance References:<br>  ⇒ Strong's #1756 energēs<br>  ⇒ NIV #1921 energēs<br>  ⇒ NASB #1756 energēs<br><br>**Hebrews 4:12**<br>For the word of God *is* quick, and **powerful**, and sharper than any twoedged sword, piercing even to the dividing asunder of soul and spirit, and of the joints and | Active, powerful, effective.<br><br>**Practical Application**<br>God's word of promise, His rest of salvation, is active and powerful. It is not dormant and inactive. It is actually active and working, energizing the heart of the believer. |

# PRACTICAL WORD STUDIES
## in the NEW TESTAMENT

| ENGLISH WORD | GREEK WORD AND VERSE | THE WORD MEANS... |
|---|---|---|
| | marrow, and *is* a discerner of the thoughts and intents of the heart. [KJV]<br><br>For the word of God is living and **active** and sharper than any two-edged sword, and piercing as far as the division of soul and spirit, of both joints and marrow, and able to judge the thoughts and intentions of the heart. [NASB]<br><br>For the word of God is living and **active**. Sharper than any double-edged sword, it penetrates even to dividing soul and spirit, joints and marrow; it judges the thoughts and attitudes of the heart. [NIV]<br><br>For the word of God *is* living and **powerful**, and sharper than any two-edged sword, piercing even to the division of soul and spirit, and of joints and marrow, and is a discerner of the thoughts and intents of the heart. [NKJV]<br><br>For the word of God is full of living **power**. It is sharper than the sharpest knife, cutting deep into our innermost thoughts and desires. It exposes us for what we really are. [NLT]<br><br>ζῶν γὰρ ὁ λόγος τοῦ Θεοῦ, καὶ **ἐνεργὴς**, καὶ τομώτερος ὑπὲρ πᾶσαν μάχαιραν δίστομον, καὶ διϊκνούμενος· ἄχρι μερισμοῦ ψυχῆς τε καὶ πνεύματος, ἁρμῶν τε καὶ μυελῶν, καὶ κριτικὸς ἐνθυμήσεων καὶ ἐννοιῶν καρδίας. [GNS]<br><br>Ζῶν γὰρ ὁ λόγος τοῦ θεοῦ καὶ **ἐνεργὴς** καὶ τομώτερος ὑπὲρ πᾶσαν μάχαιραν δίστομον καὶ διϊκνούμενος ἄχρι μερισμοῦ ψυχῆς καὶ πνεύματος, ἁρμῶν τε καὶ μυελῶν, καὶ κριτικὸς ἐνθυμήσεων καὶ ἐννοιῶν καρδίας·. [GNT] | |
| **#46**<br>**Add**<br><br>**Add**–KJV<br>Applying–NASB<br>**Add**–NIV<br>**Add**–NKJV<br>Apply–NLT<br><br>**POSB REFERENCE**<br>(2 Pt.1:5-7; esp. v.5)<br>Note 1 | ἐπιχορηγήσατε = *epichorēgēsate*<br>Pronunciation: [ep-ee-khor-ayg-eh'-sah-teh]<br>Parsing (part of speech): verb<br>    Mood—imperative<br>    Tense—aorist<br>    Voice—active<br>    Person—2nd person<br>    Number—plural<br>    Stem or root—from ἐπιχορηγέω<br>Concordance References:<br>  ⇒ Strong's #2023 epichorēgeō<br>  ⇒ NIV #2220 epichorēgeō<br>  ⇒ NASB #2023 epichorēgeō<br><br>**2 Peter 1:5**<br>And beside this, giving all diligence, **add** to your faith virtue; and to virtue knowledge; [KJV]<br><br>Now for this very reason also, **applying** all diligence, in your faith supply moral excellence, and in *your* moral excellence, knowledge; [NASB]<br><br>For this very reason, make every effort to **add** to your faith goodness; and to goodness, knowledge; [NIV]<br><br>But also for this very reason, giving all diligence, **add** to your faith virtue, to virtue knowledge, [NKJV]<br><br>So make every effort to **apply** the benefits of these promises to your life. Then your faith will produce a life of moral excellence. A life of moral excellence leads to knowing God better. [NLT]<br><br>καὶ αὐτὸ τοῦτο δὲ σπουδὴν πᾶσαν παρεισενέγκαντες, **ἐπιχορηγήσατε** ἐν τῇ πίστει ὑμῶν τὴν ἀρετήν, ἐν δὲ τῇ ἀρετῇ τὴν γνῶσιν, [GNS]<br><br>καὶ αὐτὸ τοῦτο δὲ σπουδὴν πᾶσαν παρεισενέγκαντες **ἐπιχορηγήσατε** ἐν τῇ πίστει ὑμῶν τὴν ἀρετήν, ἐν δὲ τῇ ἀρετῇ τὴν γνῶσιν, [GNT] | To add; to apply.<br><br>**Practical Application**<br>The word "add" (*epichorēgēsate*) means in addition to God's great salvation—right along side of what God has done—add *these qualities*. *Make every effort* to add them. Hasten, jump, act now to add them; don't wait. Be energetic and earnest, strenuously work to add *these qualities* to your faith and salvation. |
| **#47**<br>**Addicted**<br><br>Addicted–KJV<br>Devoted–NASB<br>Devoted–NIV<br>Devoted–NKJV<br>Spending their lives–NLT | ἔταξαν = *etaxan*<br>Pronunciation: [eh-taxs'-ahn]<br>Parsing (part of speech): verb<br>    Mood—indicative<br>    Tense—aorist<br>    Voice—active<br>    Person—3rd person<br>    Number—plural<br>    Stem or root—from τάσσω | Devoted, addicted, loyal, faithful, devout, dutiful, established; spending their lives.<br><br>**Practical Application**<br>It means they [Stephanas and his household] devoted themselves, appointed themselves, diligently gave themselves to meeting the day-to-day needs of the believers. They not only minis- |

**PRACTICAL WORD STUDIES**
in the NEW TESTAMENT

| ENGLISH WORD | GREEK WORD AND VERSE | THE WORD MEANS... |
|---|---|---|
| **POSB REFERENCE** (1 Cor.16:15-18; esp. v.15) Note 5 | Concordance References:<br>⇒ Strong's #5021 tassö<br>⇒ NIV #5435 tassö<br>⇒ NASB #5021 tassö<br><br>**1 Cor. 16:15**<br>I beseech you, brethren, (ye know the house of Stephanas, that it is the firstfruits of Achaia, and *that* they have **addicted** themselves to the ministry of the saints,) [KJV]<br>Now I urge you, brethren (you know the household of Stephanas, that they were the first fruits of Achaia, and that they have **devoted** themselves for ministry to the saints), [NASB]<br>You know that the household of Stephanas were the first converts in Achaia, and they have **devoted** themselves to the service of the saints. I urge you, brothers, [NIV]<br>I urge you, brethren—you know the household of Stephanas, that it is the firstfruits of Achaia, and *that* they have **devoted** themselves to the ministry of the saints— [NKJV]<br>You know that Stephanas and his household were the first to become Christians in Greece, and they are **spending their lives** in service to other Christians. I urge you, dear brothers and sisters, [NLT]<br>Παρακαλῶ δὲ ὑμᾶς, ἀδελφοί· -- οἴδατε τὴν οἰκίαν Στεφανᾶ, ὅτι ἐστὶν ἀπαρχὴ τῆς Ἀχαΐας, καὶ εἰς διακονίαν τοῖς ἁγίοις **ἔταξαν** ἑαυτούς -- [GNS]<br>Παρακαλῶ δὲ ὑμᾶς, ἀδελφοί· οἴδατε τὴν οἰκίαν Στεφανᾶ, ὅτι ἐστὶν ἀπαρχὴ τῆς Ἀχαΐας καὶ εἰς διακονίαν τοῖς ἁγίοις **ἔταξαν** ἑαυτούς· [GNT] | tered to others; they were addicted to meeting the needs of believers. |
| **#48**<br>**Adequate**<br><br>Perfect–KJV<br>**Adequate–NASB**<br>Thoroughly–NIV<br>Complete–NKJV<br>Preparing us in every way–NLT<br><br>**POSB REFERENCE** (2 Tim. 3:17) Note 5 | ἄρτιος = *artios*<br>Pronunciation: [ar'-tee-os]<br>Parsing (part of speech): adjective<br>  Case—nominative<br>  Gender—masculine<br>  Number—singular<br>  Stem or root—from ἄρτιος, α, ον<br>Concordance References:<br>⇒ Strong's #739 artios<br>⇒ NIV #787 artios<br>⇒ NASB #739 artios<br><br>**2 Tim. 3:17**<br>That the man of God may be **perfect**, throughly furnished unto all good works. [KJV]<br>That the man of God may be **adequate**, equipped for every good work. [NASB]<br>So that the man of God may be **thoroughly** equipped for every good work. [NIV]<br>That the man of God may be **complete**, thoroughly equipped for every good work. [NKJV]<br>It is God's way of **preparing us in every way**, fully equipped for every good thing God wants us to do. [NLT]<br>ἵνα **ἄρτιος** ᾖ ὁ τοῦ Θεοῦ ἄνθρωπος, πρὸς πᾶν ἔργον ἀγαθὸν ἐξηρτισμένος. [GNS]<br>ἵνα **ἄρτιος** ᾖ ὁ τοῦ θεοῦ ἄνθρωπος, πρὸς πᾶν ἔργον ἀγαθὸν ἐξηρτισμένος. [GNT] | To be thorough; to be perfect; to be adequate; to be prepared in every way. It means complete, matured, filled.<br><br>**Practical Application**<br>Scripture perfects a man and equips him for every good work. By "adequate" (*artios*) is meant complete, matured, perfect, filled. No person is complete or mature apart from Scripture. Man was made for God and he is to live by the Word of God. If he tries to live without God and His Word, man fails in life. He lives an incomplete, immature, and misfitted life. This is particularly true of the *man of God*, the person who claims to be a minister or teacher of God's Word. |
| **#49**<br>**Administering**<br><br>Serve–KJV<br>Serve–NASB<br>Wait on–NIV<br>Serve–NKJV<br>**Administering–NLT** | διακονεῖν = *diakonein*<br>Pronunciation: [dee-ak-on-een']<br>Parsing (part of speech): verb<br>  Mood—infinitive<br>  Tense—present<br>  Voice—active<br>  Stem or root—from διακονέω<br>Concordance References:<br>⇒ Strong's #1247 diakoneo<br>⇒ NIV #1354 diakoneö<br>⇒ NASB #1247 diakoneo | To wait on; to serve; to administer; to minister; to care for; to see after; to provide for.<br><br>**Practical Application**<br>The word "administering" (*diakonein*) is used of ministers throughout the New Testament, both preachers of the Word and deacons who serve as ministers in meeting the day-to-day needs of the flock (cp. Acts 6:4; Acts 12:25; Acts 21:19; Romans 11:13). The deacons were being chosen to minister as much as the apostles, but in a dif- |

# PRACTICAL WORD STUDIES
## in the NEW TESTAMENT

| ENGLISH WORD | GREEK WORD AND VERSE | THE WORD MEANS... |
|---|---|---|
| **POSB REFERENCE** (Acts 6:2) *Deeper Study #1* | **Acts 6:2**<br>Then the twelve called the multitude of the disciples *unto them,* and said, It is not reason that we should leave the word of God, and **serve** tables. [KJV]<br>And the twelve summoned the congregation of the disciples and said, "It is not desirable for us to neglect the word of God in order to **serve** tables. [NASB]<br>So the Twelve gathered all the disciples together and said, "It would not be right for us to neglect the ministry of the word of God in order to **wait on** tables. [NIV]<br>Then the twelve summoned the multitude of the disciples and said, "It is not desirable that we should leave the word of God and **serve** tables. [NKJV]<br>So the Twelve called a meeting of all the believers. "We apostles should spend our time preaching and teaching the word of God, not **administering** a food program," they said. [NLT]<br>προσκαλεσάμενοι δὲ οἱ δώδεκα τὸ πλῆθος τῶν μαθητῶν, εἶπον, Οὐκ ἀρεστόν ἐστιν ἡμᾶς, καταλείψαντας τὸν λόγον τοῦ Θεοῦ, **διακονεῖν** τραπέζαις. [GNS]<br>προσκαλεσάμενοι δὲ οἱ δώδεκα τὸ πλῆθος τῶν μαθητῶν εἶπαν, Οὐκ ἀρεστόν ἐστιν ἡμᾶς καταλείψαντας τὸν λόγον τοῦ θεοῦ **διακονεῖν** τραπέζαις. [GNT] | ferent area of concentration.<br>This does not mean the apostles never met day-to-day needs of the flock nor that the deacons never shared the Word. Both apostles and deacons served in both areas, but each concentrated upon his primary call and mission. (See POSB *Deeper Study* #1, Deacon—1 Tim. 3:8-13 for more discussion.) |
| **#50 Administration**<br><br>Dispensation–KJV<br>**Administration–NASB**<br>Put into effect–NIV<br>Dispensation–NKJV<br>This is his plan–NLT<br><br>**POSB REFERENCE** (Eph.1:9-10; esp. v.10) Note 6, point 3 | οἰκονομίαν = oikonomian<br>Pronunciation: [oy-kon-om-ee'-ahn]<br>Parsing (part of speech): noun<br>    Case—accusative<br>    Gender—feminine<br>    Number—singular<br>    Stem or root—from οἰκονομία, ας<br>Concordance References:<br>  ⇒ Strong's #3622 oikonomia<br>  ⇒ NIV #3873 oikonomia<br>  ⇒ NASB #3622 oikonomia<br><br>**Ephes. 1:10**<br>That in the **dispensation** of the fulness of times he might gather together in one all things in Christ, both which are in heaven, and which are on earth; even in him: [KJV]<br>With a view to an **administration** suitable to the fulness of the times, that is, the summing up of all things in Christ, things in the heavens and things upon the earth. In Him [NASB]<br>To be **put into effect** when the times will have reached their fulfillment—to bring all things in heaven and on earth together under one head, even Christ. [NIV]<br>That in the **dispensation** of the fulness of the times He might gather together in one all things in Christ, both which are in heaven and which are on earth—in Him. [NKJV]<br>And **this is his plan**: At the right time he will bring everything together under the authority of Christ—everything in heaven and on earth. [NLT]<br>εἰς **οἰκονομίαν** τοῦ πληρώματος τῶν καιρῶν, ἀνακεφαλαιώσασθαι τὰ πάντα ἐν τῷ Χριστῷ, τά τε ἐν τοῖς οὐρανοῖς καὶ τὰ ἐπὶ τῆς γῆς· ἐν αὐτῷ, [GNS]<br>εἰς **οἰκονομίαν** τοῦ πληρώματος τῶν καιρῶν, ἀνακεφαλαιώσασθαι τὰ πάντα ἐν τῷ Χριστῷ, τὰ ἐπὶ τοῖς οὐρανοῖς καὶ τὰ ἐπὶ τῆς γῆς ἐν αὐτῷ. [GNT] | To put into effect; administration; to have a plan. The word Paul uses literally means "household arrangement."<br><br>**Practical Application**<br>The idea is that the universe is a house under the management of God. God is handling, planning, arranging, and administering all things toward a climactic consummation for Christ and His followers. In that climactic day all disharmony and division and evil will be subjected and harmonized (*anakephalaioo*) under Christ. A new and perfect and eternal creation will be established for the Lord and His followers throughout the universe. |
| **#51 Administration**<br><br>Dispensation–KJV<br>Stewardship–NASB<br>**Administration–NIV**<br>Dispensation–NKJV<br>Special ministry–NLT | οἰκονομίαν = oikonomian<br>Pronunciation: [oy-kon-om-ee'-ahn]<br>Parsing (part of speech): noun<br>    Case—accusative<br>    Gender—feminine<br>    Number—singular<br>    Stem or root—from οἰκονομία, ας<br>Concordance References:<br>  ⇒ Strong's #3622 oikonomia<br>  ⇒ NIV #3873 oikonomia<br>  ⇒ NASB #3622 oikonomia | Administration, stewardship, management, ownership; to have a special ministry.<br><br>**Practical Application**<br>Paul existed to be a steward of God. Paul was given the duty to oversee and administer the grace of God to the world. |

## PRACTICAL WORD STUDIES
### in the NEW TESTAMENT

| ENGLISH WORD | GREEK WORD AND VERSE | THE WORD MEANS... |
|---|---|---|
| **POSB REFERENCE** (Eph.3:2) Note 1, point 2 | **Ephes. 3:2**<br>If ye have heard of the **dispensation** of the grace of God which is given me to youward: [KJV]<br>If indeed you have heard of the **stewardship** of God's grace which was given to me for you; [NASB]<br>Surely you have heard about the **administration** of God's grace that was given to me for you, [NIV]<br>If indeed you have heard of the **dispensation** of the grace of God which was given to me for you, [NKJV]<br>As you already know, God has given me this **special ministry** of announcing his favor to you Gentiles. [NLT]<br>- εἴγε ἠκούσατε τὴν **οἰκονομίαν** τῆς χάριτος τοῦ Θεοῦ τῆς δοθείσης μοι εἰς ὑμᾶς, [GNS]<br>εἴ γε ἠκούσατε τὴν **οἰκονομίαν** τῆς χάριτος τοῦ θεοῦ τῆς δοθείσης μοι εἰς ὑμᾶς, [GNT] | |
| **#52 Administrations**<br><br>Governments–KJV<br>**Administrations–NASB**<br>Those with gifts of administration–NIV<br>**Administrations–NKJV**<br>Those who can get others to work together–NLT<br><br>**POSB REFERENCE** (1 Cor.12:27-30; esp. v.28) Note 5, point 1g | κυβερνήσεις = *kubernēseis*<br>Pronunciation: [koo-ber'-nay-sees]<br>Parsing (part of speech): noun<br>    Case—accusative<br>    Gender—feminine<br>    Number—plural<br>    Stem or root—from κυβέρνησις, εως<br>Concordance References:<br>  ⇒ Strong's #2941 kubernēsis<br>  ⇒ NIV #3236 kubernēsis<br>  ⇒ NASB #2941 kubernēsis<br><br>**1 Cor. 12:28**<br>And God hath set some in the church, first apostles, secondarily prophets, thirdly teachers, after that miracles, then gifts of healings, helps, **governments**, diversities of tongues. [KJV]<br>And God has appointed in the church, first apostles, second prophets, third teachers, then miracles, then gifts of healings, helps, **administrations**, *various* kinds of tongues. [NASB]<br>And in the church God has appointed first of all apostles, second prophets, third teachers, then workers of miracles, also those having gifts of healing, those able to help others, **those with gifts of administration**, and those speaking in different kinds of tongues. [NIV]<br>And God has appointed these in the church: first apostles, second prophets, third teachers, after that miracles, then gifts of healings, helps, **administrations**, varieties of tongues. [NKJV]<br>Here is a list of some of the members that God has placed in the body of Christ: first are apostles, second are prophets, third are teachers, then those who do miracles, those who have the gift of healing, those who can help others, **those who can get others to work together**, those who speak in unknown languages. [NLT]<br>καὶ οὓς μὲν ἔθετο ὁ Θεὸς ἐν τῇ ἐκκλησίᾳ πρῶτον ἀποστόλους, δεύτερον προφήτας, τρίτον διδασκάλους, ἔπειτα δυνάμεις, εἶτα χαρίσματα ἰαμάτων, ἀντιλήψεις, **κυβερνήσεις**, γένη γλωσσῶν. [GNS]<br>καὶ οὓς μὲν ἔθετο ὁ θεὸς ἐν τῇ ἐκκλησίᾳ πρῶτον ἀποστόλους, δεύτερον προφήτας, τρίτον διδασκάλους, ἔπειτα δυνάμεις, ἔπειτα χαρίσματα ἰαμάτων, ἀντιλήμψεις, **κυβερνήσεις**, γένη γλωσσῶν. [GNT] | Those with gifts of administration; those who can get others to work together; a God-given ability to lead.<br><br>**Practical Application**<br>The Greek word is descriptive (*kubernēseis*). It refers to the pilot of a ship, the person who steers the ship through the dangerous channels of the oceans. The church, of course, needs such persons who can give it direction as it moves along on its journey to reach the destination God has appointed for it. |
| **#53 Admirable**<br><br>Good report–KJV<br>Good repute–NASB<br>**Admirable–NIV**<br>Good report–NKJV<br>**Admirable–NLT** | εὔφημα = *euphēma*<br>Pronunciation: [yoo'-fay-mah]<br>Parsing (part of speech): adjective<br>    Case—nominative<br>    Gender—neuter<br>    Number—plural<br>    Stem or root—from εὔφημος, ον<br>Concordance References:<br>  ⇒ Strong's #2163 euphēmos<br>  ⇒ NIV #2368 euphēmos<br>  ⇒ NASB #2163 euphēmos | Admirable; of good repute; of good report. It means worthy of praise, reputable, high-toned, things of the highest quality.<br><br>**Practical Application**<br>The believer is to think only upon worthy things. He is not to listen to *bad reports*, no matter how juicy they may seem. Neither is he to fill his mind with junk, whether through rumor, radio, television, music, off-colored jokes, or by whatever source. His thoughts are to be focused |

# PRACTICAL WORD STUDIES
## in the NEW TESTAMENT

| ENGLISH WORD | GREEK WORD AND VERSE | THE WORD MEANS... |
|---|---|---|
| **POSB REFERENCE** (Philip.4:8-9; esp. v.8) Note 2, point 1f | **Philip. 4:8**<br>Finally, brethren, whatsoever things are true, whatsoever things *are* honest, whatsoever things *are* just, whatsoever things *are* pure, whatsoever things *are* lovely, whatsoever things *are* of **good report**; if *there be* any virtue, and if *there be* any praise, think on these things. [KJV]<br>Finally, brethren, whatever is true, whatever is honorable, whatever is right, whatever is pure, whatever is lovely, whatever is of **good repute**, if there is any excellence and if anything worthy of praise, let your mind dwell on these things. [NASB]<br>Finally, brothers, whatever is true, whatever is noble, whatever is right, whatever is pure, whatever is lovely, whatever is **admirable**—if anything is excellent or praiseworthy—think about such things. [NIV]<br>Finally, brethren, whatever things are true, whatever things *are* noble, whatever things *are* just, whatever things *are* pure, whatever things *are* lovely, whatever things *are* of **good report**, if *there is* any virtue and if *there is* anything praiseworthy—meditate on these things. [NKJV]<br>And now, dear brothers and sisters, let me say one more thing as I close this letter. Fix your thoughts on what is true and honorable and right. Think about things that are pure and lovely and **admirable**. Think about things that are excellent and worthy of praise. [NLT]<br>Τὸ λοιπόν, ἀδελφοί, ὅσα ἐστὶν ἀληθῆ, ὅσα σεμνά, ὅσα δίκαια, ὅσα ἀγνά, ὅσα προσφιλῆ, ὅσα **εὔφημα**, εἴ τις ἀρετὴ καὶ εἴ τις ἔπαινος, ταῦτα λογίζεσθε· [GNS]<br>Τὸ λοιπόν, ἀδελφοί, ὅσα ἐστὶν ἀληθῆ, ὅσα σεμνά, ὅσα δίκαια, ὅσα ἀγνά, ὅσα προσφιλῆ, ὅσα **εὔφημα**, εἴ τις ἀρετὴ καὶ εἴ τις ἔπαινος, ταῦτα λογίζεσθε· [GNT] | only upon worthy things—only upon that which is admirable. |
| **#54 Admonish**<br><br>Warn–KJV<br>**Admonish**–NASB<br>Warning–NIV<br>Warn–NKJV<br>Watch and care–NLT<br><br>**POSB REFERENCE** (Acts 20:28-31; esp. v.31) Note 2, point 4a<br><br>See also POSB REF: (Rom.15:14) Note 1, point 2c | **νουθετῶν** = *noutheton*<br>Pronunciation: [noo-thet-own']<br>Parsing (part of speech): verb<br>    Mood—participle<br>    Tense—present<br>    Voice—active<br>    Case—nominative<br>    Gender—masculine<br>    Person—1st person<br>    Number—singular<br>    Stem or root—from **νουθετέω**<br>Concordance References:<br>⇒ Strong's #3560 noutheteö<br>⇒ NIV #3805 noutheteö<br>⇒ NASB #3560 noutheteö<br><br>**Acts 20:31**<br>Therefore watch, and remember, that by the space of three years I ceased not to **warn** every one night and day with tears. [KJV]<br>"Therefore be on the alert, remembering that night and day for a period of three years I did not cease to **admonish** each one with tears. [NASB]<br>So be on your guard! Remember that for three years I never stopped **warning** each of you night and day with tears. [NIV]<br>Therefore watch, and remember that for three years I did not cease to **warn** everyone night and day with tears. [NKJV]<br>Watch out! Remember the three years I was with you—my constant **watch and care** over you night and day, and my many tears for you. [NLT]<br>διὸ γρηγορεῖτε, μνημονεύοντες ὅτι τριετίαν νύκτα καὶ ἡμέραν οὐκ ἐπαυσάμην μετὰ δακρύων **νουθετῶν** ἕνα ἕκαστον. [GNS]<br>διὸ γρηγορεῖτε μνημονεύοντες ὅτι τριετίαν νύκτα καὶ ἡμέραν οὐκ ἐπαυσάμην μετὰ δακρύων **νουθετῶν** ἕνα ἕκαστον. [GNT] | To warn; to admonish; to watch and care; to instruct; to teach.<br><br>**Practical Application**<br>The word means both to give advice and to warn. It is a picture of urgency; of a desperate need to share the truth. The message is so important that the messenger is overcome with tears—both night and day. |

# PRACTICAL WORD STUDIES
## in the NEW TESTAMENT

| ENGLISH WORD | GREEK WORD AND VERSE | THE WORD MEANS... |
|---|---|---|
| **#55**<br>**Admonition**<br><br>Admonition–KJV<br>Instruction–NASB<br>Instruction–NIV<br>Admonition–NKJV<br>Instruction–NLT<br><br>**POSB REFERENCE**<br>(Eph.6:4)<br>Note 2, point 2 | νουθεσία = *nouthesia*<br>Pronunciation: [noo-thes-ee'-ah]<br>Parsing (part of speech): noun<br>    Case—dative<br>    Gender—feminine<br>    Number—singular<br>    Stem or root—from νουθεσία, ας<br>Concordance References:<br>⇒ Strong's #3559 nouthesia<br>⇒ NIV #3804 nouthesia<br>⇒ NASB #3559 nouthesia<br><br>**Ephes. 6:4**<br>And, ye fathers, provoke not your children to wrath: but bring them up in the nurture and **admonition** of the Lord. [KJV]<br><br>And, fathers, do not provoke your children to anger; but bring them up in the discipline and **instruction** of the Lord. [NASB]<br><br>Fathers, do not exasperate your children; instead, bring them up in the training and **instruction** of the Lord. [NIV]<br><br>And you, fathers, do not provoke your children to wrath, but bring them up in the training and **admonition** of the Lord. [NKJV]<br><br>And now a word to you fathers. Don't make your children angry by the way you treat them. Rather, bring them up with the discipline and **instruction** approved by the Lord. [NLT]<br><br>καὶ οἱ πατέρες, μὴ παροργίζετε τὰ τέκνα ὑμῶν, ἀλλ᾽ ἐκτρέφετε αὐτὰ ἐν παιδείᾳ καὶ **νουθεσίᾳ** Κυρίου. [GNS]<br><br>Καὶ οἱ πατέρες, μὴ παροργίζετε τὰ τέκνα ὑμῶν ἀλλὰ ἐκτρέφετε αὐτὰ ἐν παιδείᾳ καὶ **νουθεσίᾳ** κυρίου. [GNT] | Instruction, admonition, warning. It means counsel, exhortation, correction.<br><br>**Practical Application**<br>Note that the parent is not to rear the child after his own ideas and notions of what is best for the child, but after the nurture and admonition *of the Lord*. The Lord's Word is to be the guide for Christian parents in rearing their child. The benefits in bringing up a child in the Lord are innumerable. Just a few are as follows:<br>1. A child who is brought to Christ grows up learning love: that he is loved by God and by all who trust God. He grows no matter how evil some may act, knowing that he is to love even those who do wrong.<br>2. A child who is brought to Christ grows up learning power and triumph: that God will help His followers through all; that there is a supernatural power available to help, a power to help when mother and dad and loved ones have done all they can.<br>3. A child who is brought to Christ grows up learning hope and faith: that no matter what happens, no matter how great a trial, we can still trust God and hope in Him. He has provided a very special strength to carry us through the trials of this life (no matter how painful); that He has provided a very special place called heaven where He will carry us and our loved ones when we face death.<br>4. A child who is brought to Christ grows up learning the truth of life and endurance (service): that God has given us the privilege of life and of living in a beautiful earth and universe; that the evil and bad which exists in the world is caused by evil and bad people; that despite such evil, we are to serve in appreciation for life and the beautiful earth upon which God has placed us. We are to work and work diligently, making the greatest contribution we can.<br>5. A child who is brought to Christ grows up learning trust and endurance: that life is full of temptations and pitfalls which can easily rob us of joy and destroy our lives and the fulfillment of our purposes; that the way to escape the temptations and pitfalls is to follow Christ and endure in our work and purpose.<br>6. A child who is brought to Christ grows up learning peace: that there is an inner peace despite the turbulent waters of this world; that peace is knowing and trusting Christ. |
| **#56**<br>**Adopt Us As His Very Own Children**<br><br>Adoption of sons–KJV<br>Adoption as sons–NASB<br>Full rights of sons–NIV<br>Adoption as sons–NKJV | υἱοθεσίαν = *huiothesian*<br>Pronunciation: [hwee-oth-es-ee'-ahn]<br>Parsing (part of speech): noun<br>    Case—accusative<br>    Gender—feminine<br>    Number—singular<br>    Stem or root—from υἱοθεσία, ας<br>Concordance References:<br>⇒ Strong's #5206 huiothesia<br>⇒ NIV #5625 huiothesia<br>⇒ NASB #5206 huiothesia<br><br>**Galatians 4:5**<br>To redeem them that were under the law, that we might receive the **adoption of sons**. [KJV] | To have the full rights of sons; to be placed as a son; to be adopted as sons; to be adopted as God's very own children; to be given and to possess full sonship.<br><br>**Practical Application**<br>The picture of adoption is a beautiful picture of what God does for the Christian. In the ancient world the family was based on a Roman law called "patria potestas," the father's power. The law gave the father absolute authority over his children so long as the father lived. He could |

# PRACTICAL WORD STUDIES
## in the NEW TESTAMENT

| ENGLISH WORD | GREEK WORD AND VERSE | THE WORD MEANS... |
|---|---|---|
| **Adopt us as his very own children–NLT**<br><br>**POSB REFERENCE**<br>(Gal. 4:5-6; esp. v.5)<br>*Deeper Study #2* | In order that He might redeem those who were under the Law, that we might receive the **adoption as sons**. [NASB]<br>To redeem those under law, that we might receive the **full rights of sons**. [NIV]<br>To redeem those who were under the law, that we might receive the **adoption as sons**. [NKJV]<br>God sent him to buy freedom for us who were slaves to the law, so that he could **adopt us as his very own children**. [NLT]<br>ἵνα τοὺς ὑπὸ νόμον ἐξαγοράσῃ, ἵνα τὴν **υἱοθεσίαν** ἀπολάβωμεν. [GNS]<br>ἵνα τοὺς ὑπὸ νόμον ἐξαγοράσῃ, ἵνα τὴν **υἱοθεσίαν** ἀπολάβωμεν. [GNT] | work, enslave, sell and, if he wished, he could pronounce the death penalty. Regardless of the child's adult age, the father held all power over personal and property rights.<br>Therefore, adoption was a serious matter. Yet, it was a common practice to ensure that a family would not become extinct by having no male children. And when a child was adopted, three legal steps were taken.<br>1. The adopted son was adopted permanently. He could not be adopted today and disinherited tomorrow. He became a son of the father—forever. He was eternally secure as a son.<br>2. The adopted son immediately had all the rights of a legitimate son in the new family.<br>3. The adopted son completely lost all rights in his old family. The adopted son was looked upon as a new person—so new that old debts and obligations connected with his former family were cancelled and abolished as if they never existed.<br><br>The Bible says several things about the believer's adoption as a son of God.<br>1. The believer's adoption establishes a new relationship with God—forever. He is eternally secure as a child of God. But the new relationship is established only when a person comes to Christ through faith (Galatians 3:26; Galatians 4:4-5).<br>2. The believer's adoption establishes a new relationship with God as father. The believer has all the rights and privileges of a genuine son of God (Romans 8:16-17; 1 John 3:1-2).<br>3. The believer's adoption establishes a new dynamic experience with God as father, a moment-by-moment access into His very presence (Romans 8:14, 16; Galatians 4:6).<br>4. The believer's adoption gives him a very special relationship with other children of God—a family relationship that binds him with others in an unparalleled spiritual union (see POSB note—Ephes. 2:11-18; POSB note—Ephes. 2:19-22; POSB note—Ephes. 3:6; POSB note—Ephes. 4:4-6; and POSB note—Ephes. 4:17-19. Cp. Acts 2:42. See POSB outline—Matthew 12:46-50 and POSB notes—Matthew 12:46-50.)<br>5. The believer's adoption makes him a new person. The believer has been taken out from under the authority and power of the world and its sin. The believer is placed as a son into the family and authority of God. The old life with all of its debts and obligations are cancelled and wiped out (2 Cor. 5:17; Galatians 3:23-27; 2 Peter 1:4. See POSB *Deeper Study #1*—Ephes. 4:22; POSB *Deeper Study #3*—Ephes. 4:24.)<br>6. The believer's adoption is to be fully realized in the future at the return of Jesus Christ (Romans 8:19; Ephes. 1:14; 1 Thes. 4:14-17; 1 John 3:2).<br>7. The believer's adoption and its joy will be shared by all creation on a cosmic scale (Romans 8:21). There is to be a new heavens and earth (2 Peter 3:12-14; Rev. 21:1-7). |

# PRACTICAL WORD STUDIES
## in the NEW TESTAMENT

| ENGLISH WORD | GREEK WORD AND VERSE | THE WORD MEANS... |
|---|---|---|
| **#57**<br>**Adoption As Sons, Of Sons**<br><br>**Adoption of sons–KJV**<br>**Adoption as sons–NASB**<br>**Full rights of sons–NIV**<br>**Adoption as sons–NKJV**<br>Adopt us as his very own children–NLT<br><br>**POSB REFERENCE**<br>(Gal.4:5-6; esp. v.5)<br>*Deeper Study #2* | υἱοθεσίαν = huiothesian<br>Pronunciation: [hwee-oth-es-ee'-ahn]<br>Parsing (part of speech): noun<br>    Case—accusative<br>    Gender—feminine<br>    Number—singular<br>    Stem or root—from υἱοθεσία, ας<br>Concordance References:<br>⇒ Strong's #5206 huiothesia<br>⇒ NIV #5625 huiothesia<br>⇒ NASB #5206 huiothesia<br><br>**Galatians 4:5**<br>To redeem them that were under the law, that we might receive the **adoption of sons**. [KJV]<br>In order that He might redeem those who were under the Law, that we might receive the **adoption as sons**. [NASB]<br>To redeem those under law, that we might receive the **full rights of sons**. [NIV]<br>To redeem those who were under the law, that we might receive the **adoption as sons**. [NKJV]<br>God sent him to buy freedom for us who were slaves to the law, so that he could **adopt us as his very own children**. [NLT]<br>ἵνα τοὺς ὑπὸ νόμον ἐξαγοράσῃ, ἵνα τὴν **υἱοθεσίαν** ἀπολάβωμεν. [GNS]<br>ἵνα τοὺς ὑπὸ νόμον ἐξαγοράσῃ, ἵνα τὴν **υἱοθεσίαν** ἀπολάβωμεν. [GNT] | To have the full rights of sons; to be placed as a son; to be adopted as sons; to be adopted as God's very own children; to be given and to possess full sonship.<br><br>**Practical Application**<br>The picture of adoption is a beautiful picture of what God does for the Christian. In the ancient world the family was based on a Roman law called "patria potestas," the father's power. The law gave the father absolute authority over his children so long as the father lived. He could work, enslave, sell and, if he wished, he could pronounce the death penalty. Regardless of the child's adult age, the father held all power over personal and property rights.<br>(See **Adopt Us As His Very Own Children,** for more discussion). |
| **#58**<br>**Adorn**<br><br>**Adorn–KJV**<br>**Adorn–NASB**<br>Dress–NIV<br>**Adorn–NKJV**<br>Wear–NLT<br><br>**POSB REFERENCE**<br>(1 Tim.2:9-10; esp. v.9)<br>Note 1 | κοσμεῖν = kosmein<br>Pronunciation: [kos-meh'-in]<br>Parsing (part of speech): verb<br>    Mood—infinitive<br>    Tense—present<br>    Voice—active<br>    Stem or root—from κοσμέω<br>Concordance References:<br>⇒ Strong's #2885 kosmeō<br>⇒ NIV #3175 kosmeō<br>⇒ NASB #2885 kosmeō<br><br>**1 Tim. 2:9**<br>In like manner also, that women **adorn** themselves in modest apparel, with shamefacedness and sobriety; not with broided hair, or gold, or pearls, or costly array; [KJV]<br>Likewise, *I want* women to **adorn** themselves with proper clothing, modestly and discreetly, not with braided hair and gold or pearls or costly garments; [NASB]<br>I also want women to **dress** modestly, with decency and propriety, not with braided hair or gold or pearls or expensive clothes, [NIV]<br>In like manner also, that the women **adorn** themselves in modest apparel, with propriety and moderation, not with braided hair or gold or pearls or costly clothing, [NKJV]<br>And I want women to be modest in their appearance. They should **wear** decent and appropriate clothing and not draw attention to themselves by the way they fix their hair or by wearing gold or pearls or expensive clothes. [NLT]<br>ὡσαύτως καὶ τὰς γυναῖκας ἐν καταστολῇ κοσμίῳ, μετὰ αἰδοῦς καὶ σωφροσύνης, **κοσμεῖν** ἑαυτάς, μὴ ἐν πλέγμασιν, ἢ χρυσῷ, ἢ μαργαρίταις, ἢ ἱματισμῷ πολυτελεῖ, [GNS]<br>ὡσαύτως [καὶ] γυναῖκας ἐν καταστολῇ κοσμίῳ μετὰ αἰδοῦς καὶ σωφροσύνης **κοσμεῖν** ἑαυτάς, μὴ ἐν πλέγμασιν καὶ χρυσίῳ ἢ μαργαρίταις ἢ ἱματισμῷ πολυτελεῖ, [GNT] | To dress; to adorn; to wear.<br><br>**Practical Application**<br>The word "adorn" (*kosmein*) is really a better translation of what Scripture means. The word means the dress, ornaments, and arrangement of clothing upon the body. But the word *adorn* also refers to behavior and demeanor, that is, the way a woman carries herself, walks, moves, and behaves in public. Remember: this passage is being written to genuine Christian women—women who truly believe in the Lord and wish to honor the Lord in order to have a strong testimony for Him. The Christian woman wants to guard her clothing and to dress modestly; she wants to watch the way she dresses, walks, moves, and behaves in public. She wants to bring honor to the Lord and to build a strong testimony—a testimony that she loves the Lord and has committed her life...<br>• to help people, not to seduce them.<br>• to serve people, not to destroy them.<br>• to point people to Christ, not to attract them to herself.<br>• to teach people righteous behavior, not fleshly and worldly behavior. |
| **#59**<br>**Adorning–Adornment** | κόσμος = kosmos<br>Pronunciation: [kos'-mos]<br>Parsing (part of speech): noun<br>    Case—nominative | Adornment, beauty.<br><br>**Practical Application**<br>The point is that the wife does not dress, |

# PRACTICAL WORD STUDIES
## in the NEW TESTAMENT

| ENGLISH WORD | GREEK WORD AND VERSE | THE WORD MEANS... |
|---|---|---|
| **Adorning–KJV**<br>**Adornment–NASB**<br>**Adornment–NIV**<br>**Adornment–NKJV**<br>Beauty–NLT<br><br>**POSB REFERENCE**<br>(1 Pt.3:3)<br>Note 4 | Gender—masculine<br>Number—singular<br>Stem or root—from κόσμος<br>Concordance References:<br>⇒ Strong's #2889 kosmos<br>⇒ NIV #3180 kosmos<br>⇒ NASB #2889 kosmos<br><br>**1 Peter 3:3**<br>Whose **adorning** let it not be that outward *adorning* of plaiting the hair, and of wearing of gold, or of putting on of apparel; [KJV]<br>And let not your **adornment** be *merely* external—braiding the hair, and wearing gold jewelry, or putting on dresses; [NASB]<br>Your beauty should not come from outward **adornment**, such as braided hair and the wearing of gold jewelry and fine clothes. [NIV]<br>Do not let your **adornment** be *merely* outward—arranging the hair, wearing gold, or putting on *fine* apparel— [NKJV]<br>Don't be concerned about the outward **beauty** that depends on fancy hairstyles, expensive jewelry, or beautiful clothes. [NLT]<br>ὧν ἔστω οὐχ ὁ ἔξωθεν ἐμπλοκῆς τριχῶν, καὶ περιθέσεως χρυσίων, ἢ ἐνδύσεως ἱματίων **κόσμος**· [GNS]<br>ὧν ἔστω οὐχ ὁ ἔξωθεν ἐμπλοκῆς τριχῶν καὶ περιθέσεως χρυσίων ἢ ἐνδύσεως ἱματίων **κόσμος** [GNT] | walk, move, speak, or behave to attract attention to her body. She is not to adorn herself...<br>• with elaborate hairstyles: hairstyles that are so different that they break away from acceptable custom and attract attention to herself.<br>• with gold or expensive clothing: elaborate jewelry and clothing that is extravagant, ostentatious, flamboyant, attracting attention to herself.<br>How a woman dresses shows whether she lives in the fear and reverence of God or has desires for the world and the gaping and lustful attention of men. The Christian woman is not to adorn herself in a sensual or excessive manner.<br>⇒ She is not to adorn herself with unusual hairstyles.<br>⇒ She is not to adorn herself with extremely expensive clothes and jewelry.<br>⇒ She is not to adorn herself in any manner that will be immodest or impure and unclean.<br>⇒ She must not dress or behave *in any manner that would not be modest enough to appear before and to be seen by God*—in any manner that does not show fear and reverence for God.<br>⇒ She must not adorn herself in any manner that would cause her to be proud or puffed up.<br>⇒ She must not adorn herself with any dress or behavior that would attract and cause sensual or tempting thoughts to a man. (This shows anything but fear and reverence for God.) |
| **#60**<br>**Adulterating**<br><br>Deceitfully–KJV<br>**Adulterating–NASB**<br>Distort–NIV<br>Deceitfully–NKJV<br>Distort–NLT<br><br>**POSB REFERENCE**<br>(2 Cor.4:2)<br>Note 2 | δολοῦντες = dolountes<br>Pronunciation: [dol-oon'-tehs]<br>Parsing (part of speech): verb<br>Mood—participle<br>Tense—present<br>Voice—active<br>Case—nominative<br>Number—masculine<br>Person—1st person<br>Number—plural<br>Stem or root—from δολόω<br>Concordance References:<br>⇒ Strong's #1389 doloö<br>⇒ NIV #1516 doloö<br>⇒ NASB #1389 doloö<br><br>**2 Cor. 4:2**<br>But have renounced the hidden things of dishonesty, not walking in craftiness, nor handling the word of God **deceitfully**; but by manifestation of the truth commending ourselves to every man's conscience in the sight of God. [KJV]<br>But we have renounced the things hidden because of shame, not walking in craftiness or **adulterating** the word of God, but by the manifestation of truth commending ourselves to every man's conscience in the sight of God. [NASB]<br>Rather, we have renounced secret and shameful ways; we do not use deception, nor do we **distort** the word of God. On the contrary, by setting forth the truth plainly we commend ourselves to every man's conscience in the sight of God. [NIV]<br>But we have renounced the hidden things of shame, not walking in craftiness nor handling the word of God | To distort; to falsify; to adulterate; to corrupt; to deceive; to ensnare.<br><br>**Practical Application**<br>The minister is not to adulterate (*dolountes*) the "word of God." It is "the Word *of God*"; that is, it has come from God, not man. The Author of the Word of God is God. God is the *Authority* of the Word of God. The minister is only the *spokesman* for God; therefore, he is...<br>• not to falsify the Word of God.<br>• not to adulterate the Word of God.<br>• not to corrupt the Word of God.<br>• not to deceive or ensnare people by mishandling the Word of God.<br><br>The minister is not *to add* the ideas, traditions, philosophies, or speculations of men to the Word of God. Neither is he to take away portions of Scripture, denying that they are the Word of God; nor is he to neglect, ignore, or keep silent about some part of God's Word. The minister of God is not to distort the Word of God in any form or fashion. |

# PRACTICAL WORD STUDIES
## in the NEW TESTAMENT

| ENGLISH WORD | GREEK WORD AND VERSE | THE WORD MEANS... |
|---|---|---|
| | **deceitfully**, but by manifestation of the truth commending ourselves to every man's conscience in the sight of God. [NKJV]<br><br>We reject all shameful and underhanded methods. We do not try to trick anyone, and we do not **distort** the word of God. We tell the truth before God, and all who are honest know that. [NLT]<br><br>ἀλλ ἀπειπάμεθα τὰ κρυπτὰ τῆς αἰσχύνης, μὴ περιπατοῦντες ἐν πανουργίᾳ μηδὲ **δολοῦντες** τὸν λόγον τοῦ Θεοῦ, ἀλλὰ τῇ φανερώσει τῆς ἀληθείας συνιστῶντες ἑαυτοὺς πρὸς πᾶσαν συνείδησιν ἀνθρώπων ἐνώπιον τοῦ Θεοῦ. [GNS]<br><br>ἀλλὰ ἀπειπάμεθα τὰ κρυπτὰ τῆς αἰσχύνης, μὴ περιπατοῦντες ἐν πανουργίᾳ μηδὲ **δολοῦντες** τὸν λόγον τοῦ θεοῦ ἀλλὰ τῇ φανερώσει τῆς ἀληθείας συνιστάνοντες ἑαυτοὺς πρὸς πᾶσαν συνείδησιν ἀνθρώπων ἐνώπιον τοῦ θεοῦ. [GNT] | |
| **#61**<br>**Adulterers**<br><br>**Adulterers–KJV**<br>**Adulterers–NASB**<br>**Adulterers–NIV**<br>**Adulterers–NKJV**<br>**Adulterers–NLT**<br><br>**POSB REFERENCE**<br>(1 Cor.6:9)<br>Note 2, point 3 | μοιχοὶ = *moichoi*<br>Pronunciation: [moy-khoy']<br>Parsing (part of speech): noun<br>    Case—nominative<br>    Gender—masculine<br>    Number—plural<br>    Stem or root—from μοιχός, οῦ<br>Concordance References:<br>  ⇒ Strong's #3432 moichos<br>  ⇒ NIV #3659 moichos<br>  ⇒ NASB #3432 moichos<br><br>**1 Cor. 6:9**<br>Know ye not that the unrighteous shall not inherit the kingdom of God? Be not deceived: neither fornicators, nor idolaters, nor **adulterers**, nor effeminate, nor abusers of themselves with mankind, [KJV]<br><br>Or do you not know that the unrighteous shall not inherit the kingdom of God? Do not be deceived; neither fornicators, nor idolaters, nor **adulterers**, nor effeminate, nor homosexuals, [NASB]<br><br>Do you not know that the wicked will not inherit the kingdom of God? Do not be deceived: Neither the sexually immoral nor idolaters nor **adulterers** nor male prostitutes nor homosexual offenders [NIV]<br><br>Do you not know that the unrighteous will not inherit the kingdom of God? Do not be deceived. Neither fornicators, nor idolaters, nor **adulterers**, nor homosexuals, nor sodomites, [NKJV]<br><br>Don't you know that those who do wrong will have no share in the Kingdom of God? Don't fool yourselves. Those who indulge in sexual sin, who are idol worshipers, **adulterers**, male prostitutes, homosexuals, [NLT]<br><br>ἢ οὐκ οἴδατε ὅτι ἄδικοι βασιλείαν Θεοῦ οὐ κληρονομήσουσι; μὴ πλανᾶσθε· οὔτε πόρνοι, οὔτε εἰδωλολάτραι, οὔτε **μοιχοί**, οὔτε μαλακοὶ, οὔτε ἀρσενοκοῖται, [GNS]<br><br>ἢ οὐκ οἴδατε ὅτι ἄδικοι θεοῦ βασιλείαν οὐ κληρονομήσουσιν; μὴ πλανᾶσθε· οὔτε πόρνοι οὔτε εἰδωλολάτραι οὔτε **μοιχοί** οὔτε μαλακοὶ οὔτε ἀρσενοκοῖται [GNT] | Adulterers.<br><br>**Practical Application**<br>Adulterers (*moichoi*) are those...<br>• who are sexually unfaithful to their wife or husband.<br>• who look on a woman or a man to lust after her or him. Looking at and lusting after the opposite sex in person, in magazines, in books, on beaches or wherever is adultery. Imagining and lusting within the heart is the very same as committing the act. |
| **#62**<br>**Adulteries**<br><br>Fornication–KJV<br>Immorality–NASB<br>**Adulteries–NIV**<br>Fornication–NKJV<br>Immorality–NLT | πορνείας = *porneias*<br>Pronunciation: [por-ni'-ahs]<br>Parsing (part of speech): noun<br>    Case—genitive<br>    Gender—feminine<br>    Number—singular<br>    Stem or root—from πορνεία, ας<br>Concordance References:<br>  ⇒ Strong's #4202 porneia<br>  ⇒ NIV #4518 porneia<br>  ⇒ NASB #4202 porneia | Adulteries, spiritual fornication, immorality; sexual sin. It means the rejection of God and the turning to other gods.<br><br>**Practical Application**<br>The world of the end time will be days of secularism, humanism, and materialism. Man will worship himself and his secular society. He will focus his life around...<br>• technology<br>• pleasures<br>• science |

## PRACTICAL WORD STUDIES
### in the NEW TESTAMENT

| ENGLISH WORD | GREEK WORD AND VERSE | THE WORD MEANS... |
|---|---|---|
| **POSB REFERENCE** (Rev.18:2-7; esp. v.3) Note 2 | **Rev. 18:3** <br> For all nations have drunk of the wine of the wrath of her **fornication**, and the kings of the earth have committed fornication with her, and the merchants of the earth are waxed rich through the abundance of her delicacies. [KJV] <br> "For all the nations have drunk of the wine of the passion of her **immorality**, and the kings of the earth have committed *acts of* immorality with her, and the merchants of the earth have become rich by the wealth of her sensuality." [NASB] <br> For all the nations have drunk the maddening wine of her **adulteries**. The kings of the earth committed adultery with her, and the merchants of the earth grew rich from her excessive luxuries." [NIV] <br> For all the nations have drunk of the wine of the wrath of her **fornication**, the kings of the earth have committed fornication with her, and the merchants of the earth have become rich through the abundance of her luxury." [NKJV] <br> For all the nations have drunk the wine of her passionate **immorality**. The rulers of the world have committed adultery with her, and merchants throughout the world have grown rich as a result of her luxurious living." [NLT] <br> ὅτι ἐκ τοῦ οἴνου τοῦ θυμοῦ τῆς **πορνείας** αὐτῆς πέπωκε πάντα τὰ ἔθνη, καὶ οἱ βασιλεῖς τῆς γῆς μετ' αὐτῆς ἐπόρνευσαν, καὶ οἱ ἔμποροι τῆς γῆς ἐκ τῆς δυνάμεως τοῦ στρήνους αὐτῆς ἐπλούτησαν. [GNS] <br> ὅτι ἐκ τοῦ οἴνου τοῦ θυμοῦ τῆς **πορνείας** αὐτῆς πέπωκαν πάντα τὰ ἔθνη καὶ οἱ βασιλεῖς τῆς γῆς μετ' αὐτῆς ἐπόρνευσαν, καὶ οἱ ἔμποροι τῆς γῆς ἐκ τῆς δυνάμεως τοῦ στρήνους αὐτῆς ἐπλούτησαν. [GNT] | - recreation <br> - education <br> - comforts <br><br> Babylon, the capital of the world, will take the lead in the secular society. The city will have economic wealth that will literally intoxicate the world. The businessmen and merchants of the world will grow rich because of Babylon's wealth. Its wealth will be so vast that it will be able to control nations and leaders and businessmen all over the world. <br><br> The point is this: the capital city will use its influence for evil, for secularism and power. The city will manipulate the nations and leaders of the world to follow its own evil purposes. Those evil purposes will be a secular society, a worship of the state and its leader as the answer to the utopian society, that is, to meeting the needs of the people. The city will lead the nations to exterminate the Jews, Christian believers, and the faithful of all other religions who refuse to give their first loyalty to the state. Babylon will be able to seduce the nations and leaders to follow in this evil plot because of its wealth. (See POSB pt.6—Rev. 13:4-8 for more discussion.) |
| **#63 Adultery** <br><br> **Adultery–KJV** <br> Not translated–NASB <br> Not translated–NIV <br> **Adultery–NKJV** <br> Not translated–NLT <br><br> **POSB REFERENCE** (Gal.5:19-21; esp. v.19) Note 2 | μοιχεία = moicheia <br> Pronunciation: [moy-khi'-ah] <br> Parsing (part of speech): noun <br>     Case—genitive <br>     Gender—feminine <br>     Stem or root—from μοιχεύω <br> Concordance References: <br> ⇒ Strong's #3430 moicheia <br> ⇒ NIV #Not translated <br> ⇒ NASB #Not translated <br><br> **Galatians 5:19** <br> Now the works of the flesh are manifest, which are *these*; **Adultery**, fornication, uncleanness, lasciviousness, [KJV] <br> Now the deeds of the flesh are evident, which are: immorality, impurity, sensuality, [NASB]—NOT TRANSLATED <br> The acts of the sinful nature are obvious: sexual immorality, impurity and debauchery; [NIV]—NOT TRANSLATED <br> Now the works of the flesh are evident, which are: **adultery**, fornication, uncleanness, lewdness, [NKJV] <br> When you follow the desires of your sinful nature, your lives will produce these evil results: sexual immorality, impure thoughts, eagerness for lustful pleasure, [NLT]—NOT TRANSLATED <br> φανερὰ δέ ἐστι τὰ ἔργα τῆς σαρκός, ἅτινά ἐστι **μοιχεία**, πορνεία, ἀκαθαρσία, ἀσέλγεια, [GNS] <br> φανερὰ δέ ἐστιν τὰ ἔργα τῆς σαρκός, ἅτινά ἐστιν πορνεία, ἀκαθαρσία, ἀσέλγεια, [GNT] | Sexual immorality; sexual promiscuity; sexual impurity; adultery, lewdness, fornication (pre-marital sex). <br><br> **Practical Application** <br> Adultery is also looking on a woman or a man to lust after her or him. Looking at and lusting after the opposite sex whether in person, magazines, books, on beaches or anywhere else is adultery. Imagining and lusting within the heart is the very same as committing the act. |
| **#64 Adultery** <br><br> **Adultery–KJV** <br> **Adultery–NASB** <br> **Adultery–NIV** <br> **Adultery–NKJV** <br> **Adultery–NLT** | ἐμοίχευσεν = emoicheusen <br> Pronunciation: [eh-moy-khyoo'-sen] <br> Parsing (part of speech): verb <br>     Mood—indicative <br>     Tense—aorist <br>     Voice—active <br>     Person—3rd person <br>     Number—singular <br>     Stem or root—from μοιχεύω | Sexual immorality; sexual promiscuity; sexual impurity; adultery, lewdness, fornication (pre-marital sex). <br><br> **Practical Application** <br> Adultery is often said to be sexual unfaithfulness by a married person. This is true, but it is much more. Man's idea of adultery is shattered |

# PRACTICAL WORD STUDIES
## in the NEW TESTAMENT

| ENGLISH WORD | GREEK WORD AND VERSE | THE WORD MEANS... |
|---|---|---|
| **POSB REFERENCE** (Mt.5:28) Note 2 | Concordance References:<br>⇒ Strong's #3431 moicheuo<br>⇒ NIV #3658 moicheuo<br>⇒ NASB #3431 moicheuo<br><br>**Matthew 5:28**<br>But I say unto you, That whosoever looketh on a woman to lust after her hath committed **adultery** with her already in his heart. [KJV]<br>But I say to you, that everyone who looks on a woman to lust for her has committed **adultery** with her already in his heart. [NASB]<br>But I tell you that anyone who looks at a woman lustfully has already committed **adultery** with her in his heart. [NIV]<br>But I say to you that whoever looks at a woman to lust for her has already committed **adultery** with her in his heart. [NKJV]<br>But I say, anyone who even looks at a woman with lust in his eye has already committed **adultery** with her in his heart. [NLT]<br>ἐγὼ δὲ λέγω ὑμῖν, ὅτι πᾶς ὁ βλέπων γυναῖκα πρὸς τὸ ἐπιθυμῆσαι αὐτῆς ἤδη **ἐμοίχευσεν** αὐτὴν ἐν τῇ καρδίᾳ αὐτοῦ. [GNS]<br>ἐγὼ δὲ λέγω ὑμῖν ὅτι πᾶς ὁ βλέπων γυναῖκα πρὸς τὸ ἐπιθυμῆσαι αὐτὴν ἤδη **ἐμοίχευσεν** αὐτὴν ἐν τῇ καρδίᾳ αὐτοῦ. [GNT] | by Christ (see POSB *Deeper Study* #5—Matthew 19:9). Christ says adultery is not only the actual act, but adultery is committed by any one of five acts:<br>⇒ A deliberate look.<br>⇒ Passion within the heart: desiring and lusting.<br>⇒ The actual act of sex with someone other than one's own spouse.<br>⇒ Divorce relationships (Matthew 5:32; Matthew 19:9-11; Mark 10:11-12; Luke 16:18).<br>⇒ Spiritual unfaithfulness toward God or apostasy from God (Matthew 12:39; Matthew 16:4; Mark 8:38; James 4:4; cp. Ezekiel 16:15f; Ezekiel 23:43f). |
| **#65 Adultery**<br><br>Chambering–KJV<br>Sexual promiscuity–NASB<br>Sexual immorality–NIV<br>Lewdness–NKJV<br>**Adultery–NLT**<br><br>**POSB REFERENCE** (Rom.13:13) Note 4, point 3 | κοίταις = *koitais*<br>Pronunciation: [koy'-tays]<br>Parsing (part of speech): noun<br>  Case—dative<br>  Gender—feminine<br>  Number—plural<br>  Stem or root—from κοίτη, ης<br>Concordance References:<br>⇒ Strong's #2845 koitē<br>⇒ NIV #3130 koitē<br>⇒ NASB #2845 koitē<br><br>**Romans 13:13**<br>Let us walk honestly, as in the day; not in rioting and drunkenness, not in **chambering** and wantonness, not in strife and envying. [KJV]<br>Let us behave properly as in the day, not in carousing and drunkenness, not in **sexual promiscuity** and sensuality, not in strife and jealousy. [NASB]<br>Let us behave decently, as in the daytime, not in orgies and drunkenness, not in **sexual immorality** and debauchery, not in dissension and jealousy. [NIV]<br>Let us walk properly, as in the day, not in revelry and drunkenness, not in **lewdness** and lust, not in strife and envy. [NKJV]<br>We should be decent and true in everything we do, so that everyone can approve of our behavior. Don't participate in wild parties and getting drunk, or in **adultery** and immoral living, or in fighting and jealousy. [NLT]<br>ὡς ἐν ἡμέρᾳ, εὐσχημόνως περιπατήσωμεν, μὴ κώμοις καὶ μέθαις, μὴ **κοίταις** καὶ ἀσελγείαις, μὴ ἔριδι καὶ ζήλῳ. [GNS]<br>ὡς ἐν ἡμέρᾳ εὐσχημόνως περιπατήσωμεν, μὴ κώμοις καὶ μέθαις, μὴ **κοίταις** καὶ ἀσελγείαις, μὴ ἔριδι καὶ ζήλῳ. [GNT] | Sexual immorality; sexual promiscuity; sexual impurity; adultery, lewdness, fornication (pre-marital sex).<br><br>**Practical Application**<br>The charge is straightforward. The believer is not to participate...<br>• in wild parties<br>• in getting drunk<br>• in adultery<br>• in immoral living<br>• in jealousy |
| **#66 Adultery– Adulteries**<br><br>Adulteries–KJV<br>Adulteries–NASB<br>Adultery–NIV<br>Adulteries–NKJV<br>Adultery–NLT | μοιχεῖαι = *moicheiai*<br>Pronunciation: [moy-khi'-ah-ee]<br>Parsing (part of speech): noun<br>  Case—nominative<br>  Gender—feminine<br>  Number—plural<br>  Stem or root—from μοιχεία, ας<br>Concordance References:<br>⇒ Strong's #3430 moicheia | Adultery; sexual unfaithfulness to husband or wife. It is also looking on a woman or a man to lust after her or him.<br><br>**Practical Application**<br>Looking at and lusting after the opposite sex, whether in person, in magazines, in books, on beaches, or anywhere else, is adultery. |

# PRACTICAL WORD STUDIES
## in the NEW TESTAMENT

| ENGLISH WORD | GREEK WORD AND VERSE | THE WORD MEANS... |
|---|---|---|
| **POSB REFERENCE** (Mk.7:21) *Deeper Study #4* | ⇒ NIV #3657 moicheia<br>⇒ NASB #3430 moicheia<br><br>**Mark 7:21**<br>(Note: in the NLT & GNT greek, *moicheiai* is in verse 22)<br><br>For from within, out of the heart of men, proceed evil thoughts, **adulteries**, fornications, murders, [KJV]<br>"For from within, out of the heart of men, proceed the evil thoughts, fornications, thefts, murders, **adulteries**, [NASB]<br>For from within, out of men's hearts, come evil thoughts, sexual immorality, theft, murder, **adultery**, [NIV]<br>For from within, out of the heart of men, proceed evil thoughts, **adulteries**, fornications, murders, [NKJV]<br>For from within, out of a person's heart, come evil thoughts, sexual immorality, theft, murder, [NLT]—**Mark 7:21**<br>**Adultery**, greed, wickedness, deceit, eagerness for lustful pleasure, envy, slander, pride, and foolishness. [NLT]—**Mark 7:22**<br>ἔσωθεν γὰρ ἐκ τῆς καρδίας τῶν ἀνθρώπων οἱ διαλογισμοὶ οἱ κακοὶ ἐκπορεύονται, **μοιχεῖαι**, πορνεῖαι, φόνοι, κλοπαί, **Mark 7:21** [GNS]<br>ἔσωθεν γὰρ ἐκ τῆς καρδίας τῶν ἀνθρώπων οἱ διαλογισμοὶ οἱ κακοὶ ἐκπορεύονται, πορνεῖαι, κλοπαί, φόνοι, **Mark 7:21** [GNT]<br>πλεονεξίαι, πονηρίαι, δόλος, ἀσέλγεια, ὀφθαλμὸς πονηρός, βλασφημία, ὑπερηφανία, ἀφροσύνη· **Mark 7:22** [GNS]<br>**μοιχεῖαι**, πλεονεξίαι, πονηρίαι, δόλος, ἀσέλγεια, ὀφθαλμὸς πονηρός, βλασφημία, ὑπερηφανία, ἀφροσύνη· **Mark 7:22** [GNT] | Imagining and lusting within the heart is the very same as committing the act. (See POSB note—Matthew 5:28; POSB *Deeper Study #5*—Matthew 19:9 for discussion.) Adultery is a sin against the seventh commandment. |
| **#67<br>Adversary**<br><br>Adversary–KJV<br>Adversary–NASB<br>Enemy–NIV<br>Adversary–NKJV<br>Enemy–NLT<br><br>**POSB REFERENCE**<br>(1 Pt.5:8)<br>Note 2 | ἀντίδικος = *antidikos*<br>Pronunciation: [an-tid'-ee-kos]<br>Parsing (part of speech): noun<br>    Case—nominative<br>    Gender—masculine<br>    Number—singular<br>    Stem or root—from ἀντίδικος, ου<br>Concordance References:<br>⇒ Strong's #476 antidikos<br>⇒ NIV #508 antidikos<br>⇒ NASB #476 antidikos<br><br>**1 Peter 5:8**<br>Be sober, be vigilant; because your **adversary** the devil, as a roaring lion, walketh about, seeking whom he may devour: [KJV]<br>Be of sober *spirit*, be on the alert. Your **adversary**, the devil, prowls about like a roaring lion, seeking someone to devour. [NASB]<br>Be self-controlled and alert. Your **enemy** the devil prowls around like a roaring lion looking for someone to devour. [NIV]<br>Be sober, be vigilant; because your **adversary** the devil walks about like a roaring lion, seeking whom he may devour. [NKJV]<br>Be careful! Watch out for attacks from the Devil, your great **enemy**. He prowls around like a roaring lion, looking for some victim to devour. [NLT]<br>νήψατε, γρηγορήσατε, ὅτι ὁ **ἀντίδικος** ὑμῶν διάβολος, ὡς λέων ὠρυόμενος περιπατεῖ ζητῶν τινα καταπίῃ· [GNS]<br>Νήψατε, γρηγορήσατε. ὁ **ἀντίδικος** ὑμῶν διάβολος ὡς λέων ὠρυόμενος περιπατεῖ ζητῶν [τινα] καταπιεῖν· [GNT] | Enemy, adversary, opponent; an adversary who is seeking to take one to court.<br><br>**Practical Application**<br>The Greek word means a legal opponent such as an opponent in a lawsuit. It also means a common day-to-day opponent like a neighbor who opposes and stands as an enemy against us. The picture is that of the devil opposing us in every conceivable way.<br>⇒ It is the picture of Satan standing in a law court, standing as an adversary in the court of God and accusing us before God.<br>⇒ It is the picture of Satan standing here on earth, standing against us and doing all he can to trip us up and to defeat and destroy us. |

## PRACTICAL WORD STUDIES
### in the NEW TESTAMENT

| ENGLISH WORD | GREEK WORD AND VERSE | THE WORD MEANS... |
|---|---|---|
| **#68**<br>**Advocate**<br><br>**Advocate–KJV**<br>**Advocate–NASB**<br>Speaks...in...defense–NIV<br>**Advocate–NKJV**<br>Someone to plead for you–NLT<br><br>**POSB REFERENCE**<br>(1 Jn.2:1-2; esp. v.1)<br>Note 3, point 1 | παράκλητον = *paraklēton*<br>Pronunciation: [par-ak'-lay-ton]<br>Parsing (part of speech): noun<br>    Case—accusative<br>    Gender—masculine<br>    Number—singular<br>    Stem or root—from παράκλητος, ου<br>Concordance References:<br>  ⇒ Strong's #3875 paraklētos<br>  ⇒ NIV #4156 paraklētos<br>  ⇒ NASB #3875 paraklētos<br><br>**1 John 2:1**<br>My little children, these things write I unto you, that ye sin not. And if any man sin, we have an **advocate** with the Father, Jesus Christ the righteous: [KJV]<br><br>My little children, I am writing these things to you that you may not sin. And if anyone sins, we have an **Advocate** with the Father, Jesus Christ the righteous; [NASB]<br><br>My dear children, I write this to you so that you will not sin. But if anybody does sin, we have one who **speaks** to the Father **in** our **defense**—Jesus Christ, the Righteous One. [NIV]<br><br>My little children, these things I write to you, so that you may not sin. And if anyone sins, we have an **Advocate** with the Father, Jesus Christ the righteous. [NKJV]<br><br>My dear children, I am writing this to you so that you will not sin. But if you do sin, there is **someone to plead for you** before the Father. He is Jesus Christ, the one who pleases God completely. [NLT]<br><br>Τεκνία μου, ταῦτα γράφω ὑμῖν, ἵνα μὴ ἁμάρτητε. καὶ ἐάν τις ἁμάρτῃ, **παράκλητον** ἔχομεν πρὸς τὸν πατέρα, Ἰησοῦν Χριστὸν δίκαιον· [GNS]<br><br>Τεκνία μου, ταῦτα γράφω ὑμῖν ἵνα μὴ ἁμάρτητε. καὶ ἐάν τις ἁμάρτῃ, **παράκλητον** ἔχομεν πρὸς τὸν πατέρα Ἰησοῦν Χριστὸν δίκαιον·[GNT] | One who speaks in defense; an advocate; someone who pleads for another person; a Helper; an Intercessor. This word is associated with Christ and the Holy Spirit.<br><br>**Practical Application**<br>Jesus Christ is our "Advocate" (*paraklēton*). The word means someone who is called in to stand by the side of another. The purpose is to help in any way possible. This is the word [*parakletos*] used of the Holy Spirit. (See POSB *Deeper Study* #1—John 14:16 for discussion.)<br>⇒ There is the picture of a friend called in to help a person who is troubled or distressed or confused.<br>⇒ There is the picture of a commander called in to help a discouraged and dispirited army.<br>⇒ There is the picture of a lawyer, an advocate called in to help a defendant who needs his case pleaded.<br><br>There is no one word that can adequately translate *paracletos*. The word that probably comes closest is simply *helper*. Sin causes the believer to be distressed and confused, discouraged and dispirited. Sin separates the believer from God, making him guilty of transgression and worthy of condemnation and punishment. But Jesus Christ is the believer's Helper—His *Advocate*. Jesus Christ stands before God to plead the case of the believer. |
| **#69**<br>**Advocates A Different Doctrine**<br><br>Teach otherwise–KJV<br>**Advocates a different doctrine–NASB**<br>Teaches false doctrines–NIV<br>Teaches otherwise–NKJV<br>Deny these things–NLT<br><br>**POSB REFERENCE**<br>(1 Tim.6:3)<br>Note 1 | ἑτεροδιδασκαλεῖ = *heterodidaskalei*<br>Pronunciation: [het-er-od-id-as-kal-eh'-ee]<br>Parsing (part of speech): verb<br>    Mood—indicative<br>    Tense—present<br>    Voice—active<br>    Person—3rd person<br>    Number—singular<br>    Stem or root—from ἑτεροδιδασκαλέω<br>Concordance References:<br>  ⇒ Strong's #2085 heterodidaskaleō<br>  ⇒ NIV #2281 heterodidaskaleō<br>  ⇒ NASB #2085 heterodidaskaleō<br><br>**1 Tim. 6:3**<br>If any man **teach otherwise**, and consent not to wholesome words, *even* the words of our Lord Jesus Christ, and to the doctrine which is according to godliness; [KJV]<br><br>If anyone **advocates a different doctrine**, and does not agree with sound words, those of our Lord Jesus Christ, and with the doctrine conforming to godliness, [NASB]<br><br>If anyone **teaches false doctrines** and does not agree to the sound instruction of our Lord Jesus Christ and to godly teaching, [NIV]<br><br>If anyone **teaches otherwise** and does not consent to wholesome words, *even* the words of our Lord Jesus Christ, and to the doctrine which accords with godliness, [NKJV]<br><br>Some false teachers may **deny these things**, but these are the sound, wholesome teachings of the Lord Jesus Christ, and they are the foundation for a godly life. [NLT] | Teaches false doctrines; to advocate a different doctrine.<br><br>**Practical Application**<br>The false teacher advocates a different doctrine. He does not teach the words of the Lord Jesus Christ. This is a terrible indictment. Imagine being in the pulpit of a Christian church and claiming to be a teacher of the Lord Jesus Christ, yet not teaching His words. How many of us are guilty of this indictment? How many of us are guilty of advocating a different doctrine? |

## PRACTICAL WORD STUDIES
## in the NEW TESTAMENT

| ENGLISH WORD | GREEK WORD AND VERSE | THE WORD MEANS... |
|---|---|---|
| | Εἴ τις ἑτεροδιδασκαλεῖ, καὶ μὴ προσέρχεται ὑγιαίνουσι λόγοις, τοῖς τοῦ Κυρίου ἡμῶν Ἰησοῦ Χριστοῦ, καὶ τῇ κατ᾽ εὐσέβειαν διδασκαλίᾳ, [GNS]<br>εἴ τις ἑτεροδιδασκαλεῖ καὶ μὴ προσέρχεται ὑγιαίνουσιν λόγοις τοῖς τοῦ κυρίου ἡμῶν Ἰησοῦ Χριστοῦ καὶ τῇ κατ᾽ εὐσέβειαν διδασκαλίᾳ, [GNT] | |
| #70<br>**Affection On, Set**<br><br>Set...affection on–KJV<br>Set...mind on–NASB<br>Set...minds on–NIV<br>Set...mind on–NKJV<br>Thoughts–NLT<br><br>**POSB REFERENCE**<br>(Col.3:1-4; esp. v.2)<br>Note 2 | φρονεῖτε = phroneite<br>Pronunciation: [fron-eh'-ee-teh]<br>Parsing (part of speech): verb<br>   Mood—imperative<br>   Tense—present<br>   Voice—active<br>   Person—2nd person<br>   Number—plural<br>   Stem or root—from φρονέω<br>Concordance References:<br>  ⇒ Strong's #5426 phroneō<br>  ⇒ NIV #5858 phroneō<br>  ⇒ NASB #5426 phroneō<br><br>**Col. 3:2**<br>**Set** your **affection on** things above, not on things on the earth. [KJV]<br>**Set** your **mind on** the things above, not on the things that are on earth. [NASB]<br>**Set** your **minds on** things above, not on earthly things. [NIV]<br>**Set** your **mind on** things above, not on things on the earth. [NKJV]<br>Let heaven fill your **thoughts**. Do not think only about things down here on earth. [NLT]<br>τὰ ἄνω φρονεῖτε, μὴ τὰ ἐπὶ τῆς γῆς. [GNS]<br>τὰ ἄνω φρονεῖτε, μὴ τὰ ἐπὶ τῆς γῆς. [GNT] | To set one's mind on; to set one's thoughts on; to have one's mind controlled. It means to set and focus one's mind constantly upon heavenly things, not upon earthly things.<br><br>**Practical Application**<br>Very simply, the things of Christ and of heaven are to consume the believer's life and mind. But for the believer to keep his affection on the things of Christ he must know what those things are. Therefore, the question naturally arises: What are the things of Christ and the things of heaven which are to consume our thoughts?<br>The resurrection of Christ tells us what the things of Christ and of heaven are. It is His resurrection that allows us to be "*risen with Christ.*" Remember: we actually take part and participate in the resurrection of Christ. This is a *positional relationship* to God. When we accept Christ, God places us in Christ positionally. He begins to see us *in* Christ, *already seated in the heavenlies and perfected forever* (cp. Ephes. 2:4-7). Because of this glorious position which God has given we should seek the things of Christ and of heaven. |
| #71<br>**Afflicted**<br><br>Troubled–KJV<br>**Afflicted–NASB**<br>Hard pressed–NIV<br>Hard pressed–NKJV<br>Pressed–NLT<br><br>**POSB REFERENCE**<br>(2 Cor.4:7-9; esp. v.8)<br>Note 2 | θλιβόμενοι = thlibomenoi<br>Pronunciation: [thlee'-bo-mehn-oy]<br>Parsing (part of speech): verb<br>   Mood—participle<br>   Tense—present<br>   Voice—passive<br>   Case—nominative<br>   Gender—masculine<br>   Person—1st person<br>   Number—plural<br>   Stem or root—from θλίβω<br>Concordance References:<br>  ⇒ Strong's #2346 thlibō<br>  ⇒ NIV #2567 thlibō<br>  ⇒ NASB #2346 thlibō<br><br>**2 Cor. 4:8**<br>*We are* **troubled** *on every side, yet not distressed; we are* perplexed, but not in despair; [KJV]<br>*We are* **afflicted** in every way, but not crushed; perplexed, but not despairing; [NASB]<br>*We are* **hard pressed** on every side, but not crushed; perplexed, but not in despair; [NIV]<br>*We are* **hard pressed** on every side, yet not crushed; *we are* perplexed, but not in despair; [NKJV]<br>We are **pressed** on every side by troubles, but we are not crushed and broken. We are perplexed, but we don't give up and quit. [NLT]<br>ἐν παντὶ θλιβόμενοι, ἀλλ᾽ οὐ στενοχωρούμενοι· ἀπορούμενοι ἀλλ᾽ οὐκ ἐξαπορούμενοι· [GNS]<br>ἐν παντὶ θλιβόμενοι ἀλλ᾽ οὐ στενοχωρούμενοι, ἀπορούμενοι ἀλλ᾽ οὐκ ἐξαπορούμενοι, [GNT] | To be hard pressed, troubled, afflicted, squeezed, oppressed, hedged in; to have difficulty; to be pressed.<br><br>**Practical Application**<br>The power of God sustains the minister. The minister (and believers) of God faces all kinds of trouble and difficult situations in life. However, he has one great resource: the presence and power of God within him. God never forsakes him; God saves and delivers him through every situation and trial, no matter how difficult. The minister (or believer) may be afflicted in every way, but God's power saves him from distress. |
| #72<br>**Affliction** | θλίψει = thlipsei<br>Pronunciation: [thlip'-seh-ee]<br>Parsing (part of speech): noun<br>   Case—dative<br>   Gender—feminine | To have trouble, tribulation, affliction, distress; to suffer from hard circumstances; to be weighed down exceedingly; to be pressed and crushed. It means persecution, affliction, crushing troubles, hard circumstances, terrible suffering. |

# PRACTICAL WORD STUDIES
## in the NEW TESTAMENT

| ENGLISH WORD | GREEK WORD AND VERSE | THE WORD MEANS... |
|---|---|---|
| Tribulation–KJV<br>**Affliction–NASB**<br>Troubles–NIV<br>Tribulation–NKJV<br>Troubles–NLT<br><br>**POSB<br>REFERENCE**<br>(2 Cor.1:4)<br>Note 2<br><br>See also POSB REF:<br>(1 Thes.3:7-10; esp. v.7)<br>Note 4, point 1 | Number—singular<br>Stem or root—from θλίψις, εως<br>Concordance References:<br>⇒ Strong's #2347 thlipsis<br>⇒ NIV #2568 thlipsis<br>⇒ NASB #2347 thlipsis<br><br>**2 Cor. 1:4**<br>Who comforteth us in all our **tribulation**, that we may be able to comfort them which are in any trouble, by the comfort wherewith we ourselves are comforted of God. [KJV]<br>Who comforts us in all our **affliction** so that we may be able to comfort those who are in any affliction with the comfort with which we ourselves are comforted by God. [NASB]<br>Who comforts us in all our **troubles**, so that we can comfort those in any trouble with the comfort we ourselves have received from God. [NIV]<br>Who comforts us in all our **tribulation**, that we may be able to comfort those who are in any trouble, with the comfort with which we ourselves are comforted by God. [NKJV]<br>He comforts us in all our **troubles** so that we can comfort others. When others are troubled, we will be able to give them the same comfort God has given us. [NLT]<br>ὁ παρακαλῶν ἡμᾶς ἐπὶ πάσῃ τῇ **θλίψει** ἡμῶν, εἰς τὸ δύνασθαι ἡμᾶς παρακαλεῖν τοὺς ἐν πάσῃ θλίψει, διὰ τῆς παρακλήσεως ἧς παρακαλούμεθα αὐτοὶ ὑπὸ τοῦ Θεοῦ· [GNS]<br>ὁ παρακαλῶν ἡμᾶς ἐπὶ πάσῃ τῇ **θλίψει** ἡμῶν, εἰς τὸ δύνασθαι ἡμᾶς παρακαλεῖν τοὺς ἐν πάσῃ θλίψει διὰ τῆς παρακλήσεως ἧς παρακαλούμεθα αὐτοὶ ὑπὸ τοῦ θεοῦ· [GNT] | **Practical Application**<br>It is the picture of a beast of burden being crushed beneath a load that is just too heavy. It is the picture of a person having a heavy weight placed on his breast and being pressed and crushed to the point that he feels he is going to die. Note the word is used four times in 2 Cor. 1:3-7. |
| #73<br>**Afflictions**<br><br>Tribulation–KJV<br>Tribulation–NASB<br>**Afflictions–NIV**<br>Tribulation–NKJV<br>Suffering–NLT<br><br>**POSB<br>REFERENCE**<br>(Rev.2:9)<br>Note 3, point 1 | θλῖψιν = thlipsin<br>Pronunciation: [thlip'-sin]<br>Parsing (part of speech): noun<br>  Case—accusative<br>  Gender—feminine<br>  Number—singular<br>Stem or root—from θλίψις, εως<br>Concordance References:<br>⇒ Strong's #2347 thlipsis<br>⇒ NIV #2568 thlipsis<br>⇒ NASB #2347 thlipsis<br><br>**Rev. 2:9**<br>I know thy works, and **tribulation**, and poverty, (but thou art rich) and *I know* the blasphemy of them which say they are Jews, and are not, but *are* the synagogue of Satan. [KJV]<br>'I know your **tribulation** and your poverty (but you are rich), and the blasphemy by those who say they are Jews and are not, but are a synagogue of Satan. [NASB]<br>I know your **afflictions** and your poverty—yet you are rich! I know the slander of those who say they are Jews and are not, but are a synagogue of Satan. [NIV]<br>I know your works, **tribulation**, and poverty (but you are rich); and *I know* the blasphemy of those who say they are Jews and are not, but *are* a synagogue of Satan. [NKJV]<br>"I know about your **suffering** and your poverty—but you are rich! I know the slander of those opposing you. They say they are Jews, but they really aren't because theirs is a synagogue of Satan. [NLT]<br>Οἶδά σου τὰ ἔργα καὶ τὴν **θλῖψιν** καὶ τὴν πτωχείαν, -- πλούσιος δὲ εἶ -- , καὶ τὴν βλασφημίαν τῶν λεγόντων Ἰουδαίους εἶναι ἑαυτούς, καὶ οὐκ εἰσίν, ἀλλὰ συναγωγὴ τοῦ Σατανᾶ. [GNS]<br>Οἶδά σου τὴν **θλῖψιν** καὶ τὴν πτωχείαν, ἀλλὰ πλούσιος εἶ, καὶ τὴν βλασφημίαν ἐκ τῶν λεγόντων Ἰουδαίους εἶναι ἑαυτούς, καὶ οὐκ εἰσὶν ἀλλὰ συναγωγὴ τοῦ Σατανᾶ. [GNT] | Afflictions, trials, tribulation, persecution, suffering, trouble. It means the pressure of crushing affliction. It means troubles, hard circumstances, distress, pressure, strain, tension that comes both from within and without.<br><br>**Practical Application**<br>This word indicates that the trials and persecution were most severe. But the believers were holding up under the attacks and refusing to deny Christ. They were faithful to Christ despite all the ridicule, mockery, abuse, cursing, loss of property, possible imprisonment and martyrdom. |

# PRACTICAL WORD STUDIES
## in the NEW TESTAMENT

| ENGLISH WORD | GREEK WORD AND VERSE | THE WORD MEANS... |
|---|---|---|
| **#74**<br>**Afflictions**<br><br>**Afflictions–KJV**<br>**Afflictions–NASB**<br>Troubles–NIV<br>Tribulations–NKJV<br>Troubles–NLT<br><br>**POSB REFERENCE**<br>(2 Cor.6:4-5; esp. v.4)<br>Note 3<br><br>See also POSB REF:<br>(2 Thes.1:4-5; esp. v.4)<br>Note 6 | θλίψεσιν = *thlipsesin*<br>Pronunciation: [thlips'-seh-sin]<br>Parsing (part of speech): noun<br>    Case—dative<br>    Gender—feminine<br>    Number—plural<br>    Stem or root—from θλῖψις, εως<br>Concordance References:<br>  ⇒ Strong's #2347 thlipsis<br>  ⇒ NIV #2568 thlipsis<br>  ⇒ NASB #2347 thlipsis<br><br>**2 Cor. 6:4**<br>But in all *things* approving ourselves as the ministers of God, in much patience, in **afflictions**, in necessities, in distresses, [KJV]<br>But in everything commending ourselves as servants of God, in much endurance, in **afflictions**, in hardships, in distresses, [NASB]<br>Rather, as servants of God we commend ourselves in every way: in great endurance; in **troubles**, hardships and distresses; [NIV]<br>But in all *things* we commend ourselves as ministers of God: in much patience, in **tribulations**, in needs, in distresses, [NKJV]<br>In everything we do we try to show that we are true ministers of God. We patiently endure **troubles** and hardships and calamities of every kind. [NLT]<br>ἀλλ' ἐν παντὶ συνίσταντες ἑαυτοὺς ὡς Θεοῦ διάκονοι, ἐν ὑπομονῇ πολλῇ, ἐν **θλίψεσιν**, ἐν ἀνάγκαις, ἐν στενοχωρίαις, [GNS]<br>ἀλλ' ἐν παντὶ συνίσταντες ἑαυτοὺς ὡς θεοῦ διάκονοι, ἐν ὑπομονῇ πολλῇ, ἐν **θλίψεσιν**, ἐν ἀνάγκαις, ἐν στενοχωρίαις, [GNT] | To have trouble, tribulation, affliction, distress; to suffer from hard circumstances; to be weighed down exceedingly; to be pressed and crushed. It means persecution, affliction, crushing troubles, hard circumstances, terrible suffering.<br><br>**Practical Application**<br>Things often press in upon a man, weigh upon and burden down his heart. Sometimes the pressure is so heavy and tight that a man feels like he is going to explode or be crushed. The pressure may come from some lustful temptation or from some strong trial, but no matter, he is to steadfastly endure all pressing troubles. |
| **#75**<br>**Afraid of**<br><br>Fear–KJV<br>Fear–NASB<br>**Afraid–NIV**<br>Fear–NKJV<br>Fear–NLT<br><br>**POSB REFERENCE**<br>(Mt.10:29)<br>*Deeper Study* #2<br>[Note: the word afraid is used in Mt.10:26, 28, 31] | φοβεῖσθε = *phobeisthe*<br>Pronunciation: [fob-ees-the]<br>Parsing (part of speech): verb<br>    Mood—imperative<br>    Tense—present<br>    Voice—middle or passive deponent<br>    Person—2nd person<br>    Number—plural<br>    Stem or root—from φοβέομαι<br>Concordance References:<br>  ⇒ Strong's #5399 phobeo<br>  ⇒ NIV #5828 phobeo<br>  ⇒ NASB #5399 phobeo<br><br>**Matthew 10:28**<br>And fear not them which kill the body, but are not able to kill the soul: but rather **fear** him which is able to destroy both soul and body in hell. [KJV]<br>"And do not fear those who kill the body, but are unable to kill the soul; but rather **fear** Him who is able to destroy both soul and body in hell. [NASB]<br>Do not be afraid of those who kill the body but cannot kill the soul. Rather, be **afraid of** the One who can destroy both soul and body in hell. [NIV]<br>And do not fear those who kill the body but cannot kill the soul. But rather **fear** Him who is able to destroy both soul and body in hell. [NKJV]<br>"Don't be afraid of those who want to kill you. They can only kill your body; they cannot touch your soul. **Fear** only God, who can destroy both soul and body in hell. [NLT]<br>καὶ μὴ φοβηθῆτε ἀπὸ τῶν ἀποκτεινόντων τὸ σῶμα, τὴν δὲ ψυχὴν μὴ δυναμένων ἀποκτεῖναι. **φοβηθήτε** δὲ μᾶλλον τὸν δυνάμενον καὶ ψυχὴν καὶ σῶμα ἀπολέσαι ἐν γεέννῃ. [GNS]<br>καὶ μὴ φοβεῖσθε ἀπὸ τῶν ἀποκτεννόντων τὸ σῶμα, τὴν δὲ ψυχὴν μὴ δυναμένων ἀποκτεῖναι· **φοβεῖσθε** δὲ μᾶλλον τὸν δυνάμενον καὶ ψυχὴν καὶ σῶμα ἀπολέσαι ἐν γεέννῃ. [GNT] | Fear, fright, alarm, dread, terror.<br><br>**Practical Application**<br>In relation to God it means to fear; to show reverence, to sense a reverential fear; to stand in awe because of a holy fear. It means we fear God because He is God: holy, righteous, pure, and just. It means that we fear and stand in awe and reverence of God who will reveal His holiness when He executes His justice in some future day of judgment. |

## PRACTICAL WORD STUDIES
### in the NEW TESTAMENT

| ENGLISH WORD | GREEK WORD AND VERSE | THE WORD MEANS... |
|---|---|---|
| **#76**<br>**Afraid, Don't Be**<br><br>Fear not–KJV<br>Do not fear–NASB<br>**Don't be afraid– NIV**<br>Do not be afraid–NKJV<br>**Don't be afraid–NLT**<br><br>**POSB REFERENCE**<br>(Lk.5:10)<br>Note 7, point 1<br><br>**See also POSB REF:**<br>(Lk.8:49-56; esp. v.50)<br>Note 4, point 2 | Μὴ φοβοῦ = mē phobou<br>Pronunciation: [may fob-oo']<br>Parsing (part of speech): verb<br>    Mood—imperative<br>    Tense—present<br>    Voice—middle or passive deponent<br>    Person—2nd person<br>    Number—singular<br>    Stem or root—from φοβέομαι<br>Concordance References:<br>⇒ Strong's #3361 me + 5399 phobeomai<br>⇒ NIV #3590 mē + 5828 phobeomai<br>⇒ NASB #3361 me + 5399 phobeomai<br><br>**Luke 5:10**<br>And so *was* also James, and John, the sons of Zebedee, which were partners with Simon. And Jesus said unto Simon, **Fear not**; from henceforth thou shalt catch men. [KJV]<br>And so also James and John, sons of Zebedee, who were partners with Simon. And Jesus said to Simon, "**Do not fear**, from now on you will be catching men." [NASB]<br>And so were James and John, the sons of Zebedee, Simon's partners. Then Jesus said to Simon, "**Don't be afraid**; from now on you will catch men." [NIV]<br>And so also *were* James and John, the sons of Zebedee, who were partners with Simon. And Jesus said to Simon, "**Do not be afraid**. From now on you will catch men." [NKJV]<br>His partners, James and John, the sons of Zebedee, were also amazed. Jesus replied to Simon, "**Don't be afraid**! From now on you'll be fishing for people!" [NLT]<br>ὁμοίως δὲ καὶ Ἰάκωβον καὶ Ἰωάννην, υἱοὺς Ζεβεδαίου, οἳ ἦσαν κοινωνοὶ τῷ Σίμωνι. καὶ εἶπε πρὸς τὸν Σίμωνα ὁ Ἰησοῦς, **Μὴ φοβοῦ**· ἀπὸ τοῦ νῦν ἀνθρώπους ἔσῃ ζωγρῶν. [GNS]<br>ὁμοίως δὲ καὶ Ἰάκωβον καὶ Ἰωάννην υἱοὺς Ζεβεδαίου, οἳ ἦσαν κοινωνοὶ τῷ Σίμωνι. καὶ εἶπεν πρὸς τὸν Σίμωνα ὁ Ἰησοῦς, **Μὴ φοβοῦ**· ἀπὸ τοῦ νῦν ἀνθρώπους ἔσῃ ζωγρῶν. [GNT] | Do not have fear, dread, terror; do not be afraid.<br><br>**Practical Application**<br>The words "Don't be afraid" indicate that Peter was actually scared and frightened. Jesus was calming him, telling him to trust and stop fearing. |
| **#77**<br>**After A While**<br><br>Many days–KJV<br>Many days–NASB<br>Many days–NIV<br>Many days–NKJV<br>**After a while–NLT**<br><br>**POSB REFERENCE**<br>(Acts 9:23)<br>*Deeper Study* #1 | ἡμέραι ἱκαναί = hēmerai hikanai<br>Pronunciation: [hay-mer'-ah-ee hik-an-ah-ee']<br>Parsing *hēmerai* (part of speech): noun<br>    Case—nominative<br>    Gender—feminine<br>    Number—plural<br>    Stem or root—from ἡμέρα<br>Parsing *hikanai* (part of speech): adjective<br>    Case—nominative<br>    Gender—feminine<br>    Number—plural<br>    Stem or root—from ἱκανός<br>Concordance References:<br>⇒ Strong's #2425 hikanos + 2250 hēmera<br>⇒ NIV #2653 hikanos [many] + 2465 hēmera [days]<br>⇒ NASB #2425 hikanos + 2250 hēmera<br><br>**Acts 9:23**<br>And after that **many days** were fulfilled, the Jews took counsel to kill him: [KJV]<br>And when **many days** had elapsed, the Jews plotted together to do away with him, [NASB]<br>After **many days** had gone by, the Jews conspired to kill him, [NIV]<br>Now after **many days** were past, the Jews plotted to kill him. [NKJV]<br>**After a while** the Jewish leaders decided to kill him. [NLT] | Many days; after a while.<br><br>**Practical Application**<br>This is a term indicating a short time (Acts 9:19). |

41

# PRACTICAL WORD STUDIES
## in the NEW TESTAMENT

| ENGLISH WORD | GREEK WORD AND VERSE | THE WORD MEANS... |
|---|---|---|
| | Ὡς δὲ ἐπληροῦντο **ἡμέραι ἱκαναί**, συνεβουλεύσαντο οἱ Ἰουδαῖοι ἀνελεῖν αὐτόν· [GNS]<br>Ὡς δὲ ἐπληροῦντο **ἡμέραι ἱκαναί**, συνεβουλεύσαντο οἱ Ἰουδαῖοι ἀνελεῖν αὐτόν· [GNT] | |
| **#78**<br>**After This**<br><br>Afterward–KJV<br>Soon afterwards–NASB<br>**After this–NIV**<br>Afterward–NKJV<br>Not long afterward–NLT<br><br>**POSB REFERENCE**<br>(Lk.8:1)<br>Note 1 | ἐν τῷ καθεξῆς = *en tö kathexës*<br>Pronunciation: [en tow kath-ex-ace']<br>Parsing (part of speech): adjective adverb<br>    Stem or root—from καθεξῆς<br>Concordance References:<br>⇒ Strong's #1722 en + 2517 kathexes + 3588 ho<br>⇒ NIV #1877 en + 2759 kathexës [after this] + 3836 ho<br>⇒ NASB #1722 en + 2517 kathexes + 3588 ho<br><br>**Luke 8:1**<br>And it came to pass **afterward**, that he went throughout every city and village, preaching and showing the glad tidings of the kingdom of God: and the twelve *were* with him, [KJV]<br>And it came about **soon afterwards**, that He *began* going about from one city and village to another, proclaiming and preaching the kingdom of God; and the twelve were with Him, [NASB]<br>**After this**, Jesus traveled about from one town and village to another, proclaiming the good news of the kingdom of God. The Twelve were with him, [NIV]<br>Now it came to pass, **afterward**, that He went through every city and village, preaching and bringing the glad tidings of the kingdom of God. And the twelve *were* with Him, [NKJV]<br>**Not long afterward** Jesus began a tour of the nearby cities and villages to announce the Good News concerning the Kingdom of God. He took his twelve disciples with him, [NLT]<br>Καὶ ἐγένετο **ἐν τῷ καθεξῆς**, καὶ αὐτὸς διώδευε κατὰ πόλιν καὶ κώμην, κηρύσσων καὶ εὐαγγελιζόμενος τὴν βασιλείαν τοῦ Θεοῦ· καὶ οἱ δώδεκα σὺν αὐτῷ, [GNS]<br>Καὶ ἐγένετο **ἐν τῷ καθεξῆς** καὶ αὐτὸς διώδευεν κατὰ πόλιν καὶ κώμην κηρύσσων καὶ εὐαγγελιζόμενος τὴν βασιλείαν τοῦ θεοῦ καὶ οἱ δώδεκα σὺν αὐτῷ, [GNT] | After this; one after the other; in sequence; an orderly, successive step.<br><br>**Practical Application**<br>Right after the banquet at Simon's home, Jesus got up and went about His primary task, that of preaching and proclaiming the gospel. He did not linger in fellowship nor in any other pursuits, no matter their legitimacy or enjoyment. He was faithful and consistent in preaching and proclaiming the gospel. |
| **#79**<br>**Afterward–Afterwards**<br><br>Afterward–KJV<br>Soon afterwards–NASB<br>After this–NIV<br>**Afterward–NKJV**<br>Not long afterward–NLT<br><br>**POSB REFERENCE**<br>(Lk.8:1)<br>Note 1 | ἐν τῷ καθεξῆς = *en tö kathexës*<br>Pronunciation: [en tow kath-ex-ace']<br>Parsing (part of speech): adjective adverb<br>    Stem or root—from καθεξῆς<br>Concordance References:<br>⇒ Strong's #1722 en + 2517 kathexes + 3588 ho<br>⇒ NIV #1877 en + 2759 kathexës [after this] + 3836 ho<br>⇒ NASB #1722 en + 2517 kathexes + 3588 ho<br><br>**Luke 8:1**<br>And it came to pass **afterward**, that he went throughout every city and village, preaching and showing the glad tidings of the kingdom of God: and the twelve *were* with him, [KJV]<br>And it came about **soon afterwards**, that He *began* going about from one city and village to another, proclaiming and preaching the kingdom of God; and the twelve were with Him, [NASB]<br>**After this**, Jesus traveled about from one town and village to another, proclaiming the good news of the kingdom of God. The Twelve were with him, [NIV]<br>Now it came to pass, **afterward**, that He went through every city and village, preaching and bringing the glad tidings of the kingdom of God. And the twelve *were* with Him, [NKJV]<br>**Not long afterward** Jesus began a tour of the nearby cities and villages to announce the Good News concerning the Kingdom of God. He took his twelve disciples with him, [NLT] | After this; one after the other; in sequence; an orderly, successive step.<br><br>**Practical Application**<br>Right after the banquet at Simon's home, Jesus got up and went about His primary task, that of preaching and proclaiming the gospel. He did not linger in fellowship nor in any other pursuits, no matter their legitimacy or enjoyment. He was faithful and consistent in preaching and proclaiming the gospel. |

## PRACTICAL WORD STUDIES
### in the NEW TESTAMENT

| ENGLISH WORD | GREEK WORD AND VERSE | THE WORD MEANS... |
|---|---|---|
| | Καὶ ἐγένετο ἐν τῷ καθεξῆς, καὶ αὐτὸς διώδευε κατὰ πόλιν καὶ κώμην, κηρύσσων καὶ εὐαγγελιζόμενος τὴν βασιλείαν τοῦ Θεοῦ· καὶ οἱ δώδεκα σὺν αὐτῷ, [GNS]<br><br>Καὶ ἐγένετο ἐν τῷ καθεξῆς καὶ αὐτὸς διώδευεν κατὰ πόλιν καὶ κώμην κηρύσσων καὶ εὐαγγελιζόμενος τὴν βασιλείαν τοῦ θεοῦ καὶ οἱ δώδεκα σὺν αὐτῷ, [GNT] | |
| **#80**<br>**Again**<br><br>Again–KJV<br>Again–NASB<br>Again–NIV<br>Again–NKJV<br>Again–NLT<br><br>**POSB REFERENCE**<br>(Jn.3:3)<br>Note 2, point 1 | ἄνωθεν = anōthen<br>Pronunciation: [an'-o-then]<br>Parsing (part of speech): adjective adverb<br>Stem or root—from ἄνωθεν<br>Concordance References:<br>⇒ Strong's #509 anothen<br>⇒ NIV #540 anōthen<br>⇒ NASB #509 anothen<br><br>**John 3:3**<br>Jesus answered and said unto him, Verily, verily, I say unto thee, Except a man be born **again**, he cannot see the kingdom of God. [KJV]<br>Jesus answered and said to him, "Truly, truly, I say to you, unless one is born **again**, he cannot see the kingdom of God." [NASB]<br>In reply Jesus declared, "I tell you the truth, no one can see the kingdom of God unless he is born **again**." [NIV]<br>Jesus answered and said to him, "Most assuredly, I say to you, unless one is born **again**, he cannot see the kingdom of God." [NKJV]<br>Jesus replied, "I assure you, unless you are born **again**, you can never see the Kingdom of God." [NLT]<br>Ἀπεκρίθη ὁ Ἰησοῦς καὶ εἶπεν αὐτῷ, Ἀμὴν ἀμὴν λέγω σοι, ἐὰν μή τις γεννηθῇ **ἄνωθεν**, οὐ δύναται ἰδεῖν τὴν βασιλείαν τοῦ Θεοῦ. [GNS]<br>ἀπεκρίθη Ἰησοῦς καὶ εἶπεν αὐτῷ, Ἀμὴν ἀμὴν λέγω σοι, ἐὰν μή τις γεννηθῇ **ἄνωθεν**, οὐ δύναται ἰδεῖν τὴν βασιλείαν τοῦ θεοῦ. [GNT] | Literally to be born from above.<br><br>**Practical Application**<br>Note: the word "again" has three different meanings in Greek. It means...<br>⇒ From the first: from the beginning or completely and fully (cp. Luke 1:3).<br>⇒ Again: a second time, a repeated act (John 3:4) (cp. Galatians 4:9).<br>⇒ From above: from the top, which means from God (cp. John 19:11).<br><br>The point is this. A person must be "born again." A person must be...<br>⇒ born completely and fully, a complete and full change.<br>⇒ born all over again, in the sense of a second time.<br>⇒ born from above, from God. |
| **#81**<br>**Again**<br><br>Flourished again–KJV<br>Revived–NASB<br>Renewed–NIV<br>Flourished again–NKJV<br>Again–NLT<br><br>**POSB REFERENCE**<br>(Philip.4:10)<br>Note 1 | ἀνεθάλετε = anethalete<br>Pronunciation: [an-ath-al'-eh-teh]<br>Parsing (part of speech): verb<br>  Mood—indicative<br>  Tense—aorist<br>  Voice—active<br>  Person—2nd person<br>  Number—plural<br>  Stem or root—from ἀναθάλλω<br>Concordance References:<br>⇒ Strong's #330 anathallō<br>⇒ NIV #352 anathallō<br>⇒ NASB #330 anathallō<br><br>**Philip. 4:10**<br>But I rejoiced in the Lord greatly, that now at the last your care of me hath **flourished again**; wherein ye were also careful, but ye lacked opportunity. [KJV]<br>But I rejoiced in the Lord greatly, that now at last you have **revived** your concern for me; indeed, you were concerned *before,* but you lacked opportunity. [NASB]<br>I rejoice greatly in the Lord that at last you have **renewed** your concern for me. Indeed, you have been concerned, but you had no opportunity to show it. [NIV]<br>But I rejoiced in the Lord greatly that now at last your care for me has **flourished again**; though you surely did care, but you lacked opportunity. [NKJV]<br>How grateful I am, and how I praise the Lord that you are concerned about me **again**. I know you have always been concerned for me, but for a while you didn't have the chance to help me. [NLT]<br>Ἐχάρην δὲ ἐν Κυρίῳ μεγάλως, ὅτι ἤδη ποτὲ **ἀνεθάλετε** τὸ ὑπὲρ ἐμοῦ φρονεῖν,, ἐφ' ᾧ καὶ ἐφρονεῖτε, ἠκαιρεῖσθε δέ. [GNS]<br>Ἐχάρην δὲ ἐν κυρίῳ μεγάλως ὅτι ἤδη ποτὲ **ἀνεθάλετε** τὸ ὑπὲρ ἐμοῦ φρονεῖν, ἐφ' ᾧ καὶ ἐφρονεῖτε, ἠκαιρεῖσθε δέ. [GNT] | To renew; to flourish again; to revive again.<br><br>**Practical Application**<br>It is the picture of plants and flowers sprouting, shooting up, and blossoming *again.* The key word is *again.* When the church had been founded, the believers had supported Paul and his mission work on a regular basis. But for some reason they had dropped their mission support. That had probably been over ten to twelve years before (Lehman Strauss. *Devotional Studies in Philippians.* Neptune, NJ: Loizeaux Brothers, 1959). Why they had stopped sending support to Paul is not known. However, the point to see is the glorious revival of mission support that took place in the church. They picked up the support of Paul once again, and their giving flourished and blossomed anew. The joy and rejoicing of Paul's heart can just be imagined. He says, "I rejoiced greatly in the Lord." |

# PRACTICAL WORD STUDIES
## in the NEW TESTAMENT

| ENGLISH WORD | GREEK WORD AND VERSE | THE WORD MEANS... |
|---|---|---|
| **#82**<br>**Against**<br><br>Contrary–KJV<br>Contrary–NASB<br>**Against–NIV**<br>Contrary–NKJV<br>Headwinds–NLT<br><br>**POSB REFERENCE**<br>(Acts 27:4-12; esp. v.4)<br>Note 2, point 1a | ἐναντίους = enantious<br>Pronunciation: [en-an-tee'-oos]<br>Parsing (part of speech): adjective<br>    Case—accusative<br>    Gender—masculine<br>    Number—plural<br>    Stem or root—from ἐναντίος<br>Concordance References:<br>⇒ Strong's #1727 enantios<br>⇒ NIV #1885 enantios<br>⇒ NASB #1727 enantios<br><br>**Acts 27:4**<br>And when we had launched from thence, we sailed under Cyprus, because the winds were **contrary**. [KJV]<br>And from there we put out to sea and sailed under the shelter of Cyprus because the winds were **contrary**. [NASB]<br>From there we put out to sea again and passed to the lee of Cyprus because the winds were **against** us. [NIV]<br>When we had put to sea from there, we sailed under *the shelter of* Cyprus, because the winds were **contrary**. [NKJV]<br>Putting out to sea from there, we encountered **headwinds** that made it difficult to keep the ship on course, so we sailed north of Cyprus between the island and the mainland. [NLT]<br>κἀκεῖθεν ἀναχθέντες ὑπεπλεύσαμεν τὴν Κύπρον, διὰ τὸ τοὺς ἀνέμους εἶναι **ἐναντίους**, [GNS]<br>κἀκεῖθεν ἀναχθέντες ὑπεπλεύσαμεν τὴν Κύπρον διὰ τὸ τοὺς ἀνέμους εἶναι **ἐναντίους**, [GNT] | Against, contrary, opposed, hostile headwinds.<br><br>**Practical Application**<br>The winds were "against": strong and forceful; a northwest headwind faced them. Therefore, they could not strike a straight course through the open sea. |
| **#83**<br>**Age**<br><br>World–KJV<br>**Age–NASB**<br>**Age–NIV**<br>**Age–NKJV**<br>World–NLT<br><br>**POSB REFERENCE**<br>(1 Cor.2:6)<br>Note 2, point 2 | αἰῶνος = aiönos<br>Pronunciation: [ahee-ohn'-os]<br>Parsing (part of speech): noun<br>    Case—genitive<br>    Gender—masculine<br>    Number—singular<br>    Stem or root—from αἰών, ῶνος<br>Concordance References:<br>⇒ Strong's #165 aiön<br>⇒ NIV #172 aiön<br>⇒ NASB #165 aiön<br><br>**1 Cor. 2:6**<br>Howbeit we speak wisdom among them that are perfect: yet not the wisdom of this **world**, nor of the princes of this **world**, that come to nought: [KJV]<br>Yet we do speak wisdom among those who are mature; a wisdom, however, not of this **age**, nor of the rulers of this **age**, who are passing away; [NASB]<br>We do, however, speak a message of wisdom among the mature, but not the wisdom of this **age** or of the rulers of this **age**, who are coming to nothing. [NIV]<br>However, we speak wisdom among those who are mature, yet not the wisdom of this **age**, nor of the rulers of this **age**, who are coming to nothing. [NKJV]<br>Yet when I am among mature Christians, I do speak with words of wisdom, but not the kind of wisdom that belongs to this **world**, and not the kind that appeals to the rulers of this **world**, who are being brought to nothing. [NLT]<br>Σοφίαν δὲ λαλοῦμεν ἐν τοῖς τελείοις· σοφίαν δὲ οὐ τοῦ **αἰῶνος** τούτου, οὐδὲ τῶν ἀρχόντων τοῦ **αἰῶνος** τούτου, τῶν καταργουμένων· [GNS]<br>Σοφίαν δὲ λαλοῦμεν ἐν τοῖς τελείοις, σοφίαν δὲ οὐ τοῦ **αἰῶνος** τούτου οὐδὲ τῶν ἀρχόντων τοῦ **αἰῶνος** τούτου τῶν καταργουμένων·[GNT] | This age, this world that is passing on as fast as the flower of the field which is here today and gone tomorrow.<br><br>**Practical Application**<br>The wisdom of this age and of its leaders is here today and gone tomorrow. Man's ideas about God and truth fade and pass away almost as quickly as man himself does. |
| **#84**<br>**Ages** | αἰῶσιν = aiösin<br>Pronunciation: [ah-ee-o-sin]<br>Parsing (part of speech): noun<br>    Case—dative | Ages, world order, life, time.<br><br>**Practical Application**<br>God has done so much for us through Christ |

## PRACTICAL WORD STUDIES
## in the NEW TESTAMENT

| ENGLISH WORD | GREEK WORD AND VERSE | THE WORD MEANS... |
|---|---|---|
| **Ages**–KJV<br>**Ages**–NASB<br>**Ages**–NIV<br>**Ages**–NKJV<br>Not translated–NLT<br><br>**POSB<br>REFERENCE**<br>(Eph.2:7)<br>Note 4 | Gender—masculine<br>Number—plural<br>Stem or root—from αἰών, ῶνος<br>Concordance References:<br>⇒ Strong's #165 aiön<br>⇒ NIV #172 aiön<br>⇒ NASB #165 aiön<br><br>**Ephes. 2:7**<br>That in the **ages** to come he might show the exceeding riches of his grace in *his* kindness toward us through Christ Jesus. [KJV]<br>In order that in the **ages** to come He might show the surpassing riches of His grace in kindness toward us in Christ Jesus. [NASB]<br>In order that in the coming **ages** he might show the incomparable riches of his grace, expressed in his kindness to us in Christ Jesus. [NIV]<br>That in the **ages** to come He might show the exceeding riches of His grace in *His* kindness toward us in Christ Jesus. [NKJV]<br>And so God can always point to us as examples of the incredible wealth of his favor and kindness toward us, as shown in all he has done for us through Christ Jesus. [NLT]—NOT TRANSLATED<br>ἵνα ἐνδείξηται ἐν τοῖς **αἰῶσι** τοῖς ἐπερχομένοις τὸν ὑπερβάλλοντα πλοῦτον τῆς χάριτος αὐτοῦ ἐν χρηστότητι ἐφ᾽ ἡμᾶς ἐν Χριστῷ Ἰησοῦ· [GNS]<br>ἵνα ἐνδείξηται ἐν τοῖς **αἰῶσιν** τοῖς ἐπερχομένοις τὸ ὑπερβάλλον πλοῦτος τῆς χάριτος αὐτοῦ ἐν χρηστότητι ἐφ᾽ ἡμᾶς ἐν Χριστῷ Ἰησοῦ. [GNT] | Jesus our Lord, so much that it will take an eternity to show it all off. "Ages" (*aiösin*) literally means the ages that just come in one upon another; that just roll in one upon another. It means an eternity of ages. Grasping the verse is helped by breaking it up like this...<br>• the exceeding riches<br>• of His grace in His kindness<br>• toward us<br>• through Christ Jesus<br>God is going to be eternally glorified for His grace and kindness toward us. All creatures will live in stark amazement at God's wondrous mercy shown toward men—all through Christ Jesus (cp. Ephes. 3:10). |
| **#85<br>Agitating**<br><br>Stirred up–KJV<br>Stirring up–NASB<br>**Agitating**–NIV<br>Stirred up–NKJV<br>Stirred up–NLT<br><br>**POSB<br>REFERENCE**<br>(Acts 17:13-15; esp. v.13)<br>Note 7 | σαλεύοντες = *saleuontes*<br>Pronunciation: [sal-yoo'-on-tehs]<br>Parsing (part of speech): verb<br>  Mood—participle<br>  Tense—present<br>  Voice—active<br>  Case—nominative<br>  Gender—masculine<br>  Number—plural<br>  Stem or root—from σαλεύω<br>Concordance References:<br>⇒ Strong's #4531 saleuö<br>⇒ NIV #4888 saleuö<br>⇒ NASB #4531 saleuö<br><br>**Acts 17:13**<br>But when the Jews of Thessalonica had knowledge that the word of God was preached of Paul at Berea, they came thither also, and **stirred up** the people. [KJV]<br>But when the Jews of Thessalonica found out that the word of God had been proclaimed by Paul in Berea also, they came there likewise, agitating and **stirring up** the crowds. [NASB]<br>When the Jews in Thessalonica learned that Paul was preaching the word of God at Berea, they went there too, **agitating** the crowds and stirring them up. [NIV]<br>But when the Jews from Thessalonica learned that the word of God was preached by Paul at Berea, they came there also and **stirred up** the crowds. [NKJV]<br>But when some Jews in Thessalonica learned that Paul was preaching the word of God in Berea, they went there and **stirred up** trouble. [NLT]<br>ὡς δὲ ἔγνωσαν οἱ ἀπὸ τῆς Θεσσαλονίκης Ἰουδαῖοι ὅτι καὶ ἐν τῇ Βεροίᾳ κατηγγέλη ὑπὸ τοῦ Παύλου ὁ λόγος τοῦ Θεοῦ, ἦλθον κἀκεῖ **σαλεύοντες** τοὺς ὄχλους. [GNS]<br>Ὡς δὲ ἔγνωσαν οἱ ἀπὸ τῆς Θεσσαλονίκης Ἰουδαῖοι ὅτι καὶ ἐν τῇ Βεροίᾳ κατηγγέλη ὑπὸ τοῦ Παύλου ὁ λόγος τοῦ θεοῦ, ἦλθον κἀκεῖ **σαλεύοντες** καὶ ταράσσοντες τοὺς ὄχλους. [GNT] | To agitate; to stir up; to shake; to sway; to be unsettled.<br><br>**Practical Application**<br>The idea is a volcanic stirring or shaking of the people. The stirring was of earthquake proportions. (Cp. the Galatian Jews who also pursued Paul to keep him from preaching, Acts 14:19.) |

# PRACTICAL WORD STUDIES
## in the NEW TESTAMENT

| ENGLISH WORD | GREEK WORD AND VERSE | THE WORD MEANS... |
|---|---|---|
| **#86**<br>**Agonized**<br><br>Conflict–KJV<br>Struggle–NASB<br>Struggling–NIV<br>Conflict–NKJV<br>**Agonized–NLT**<br><br>**POSB REFERENCE**<br>(Col.2:1)<br>Note 1 | ἀγῶνα = agōna<br>Pronunciation: [ag-on'-ah]<br>Parsing (part of speech): noun<br>    Case—accusative<br>    Gender—masculine<br>    Number—singular<br>    Stem or root—from ἀγών, ῶνος<br>Concordance References:<br>⇒ Strong's #73 agōn<br>⇒ NIV #74 agōn<br>⇒ NASB #73 agōn<br><br>**Col. 2:1**<br>For I would that ye knew what great **conflict** I have for you, and *for* them at Laodicea, and *for* as many as have not seen my face in the flesh; [KJV]<br><br>For I want you to know how great a **struggle** I have on your behalf, and for those who are at Laodicea, and for all those who have not personally seen my face, [NASB]<br><br>I want you to know how much I am **struggling** for you and for those at Laodicea, and for all who have not met me personally. [NIV]<br><br>For I want you to know what a great **conflict** I have for you and those in Laodicea, and *for* as many as have not seen my face in the flesh, [NKJV]<br><br>I want you to know how much I have **agonized** for you and for the church at Laodicea, and for many other friends who have never known me personally. [NLT]<br><br>Θέλω γὰρ ὑμᾶς εἰδέναι ἡλίκον **ἀγῶνα** ἔχω ὑπὲρ περὶ ὑμῶν καὶ τῶν ἐν Λαοδικείᾳ, καὶ ὅσοι οὐχ ἑώρακασι τὸ πρόσωπόν μου ἐν σαρκί, [GNS]<br><br>Θέλω γὰρ ὑμᾶς εἰδέναι ἡλίκον **ἀγῶνα** ἔχω ὑπὲρ ὑμῶν καὶ τῶν ἐν Λαοδικείᾳ καὶ ὅσοι οὐκ ἑόρακαν τὸ πρόσωπόν μου ἐν σαρκί, [GNT] | To struggle; to agonize; to fight. It means to strive, agonize, struggle, and wrestle in prayer for the believers of the churches.<br><br>**Practical Application**<br>It is the picture of an athlete exerting every ounce of energy he has in the struggle of the contest. The idea is that Paul labored hard, toiled, strove, agonized, struggled, and wrestled in prayer. |
| **#87**<br>**Agony**<br><br>Pains–KJV<br>**Agony–NASB**<br>**Agony–NIV**<br>Pains–NKJV<br>Horrors–NLT<br><br>**POSB REFERENCE**<br>(Acts 2:24)<br>*Deeper Study* #4,<br>point 2 | ὠδῖνας = ōdinas<br>Pronunciation: [o-deen'-ahs]<br>Parsing (part of speech): noun<br>    Case—accusative<br>    Gender—feminine<br>    Number—plural<br>    Stem or root—from ὠδίν<br>Concordance References:<br>⇒ Strong's #5604 ōdin<br>⇒ NIV #6047 ōdin<br>⇒ NASB #5604 ōdin<br><br>**Acts 2:24**<br>Whom God hath raised up, having loosed the **pains** of death: because it was not possible that he should be holden of it. [KJV]<br><br>"And God raised Him up again, putting an end to the **agony** of death, since it was impossible for Him to be held in its power. [NASB]<br><br>But God raised him from the dead, freeing him from the **agony** of death, because it was impossible for death to keep its hold on him. [NIV]<br><br>Whom God raised up, having loosed the **pains** of death, because it was not possible that He should be held by it. [NKJV]<br><br>However, God released him from the **horrors** of death and raised him back to life again, for death could not keep him in its grip. [NLT]<br><br>ὃν ὁ Θεὸς ἀνέστησε, λύσας τὰς **ὠδῖνας** τοῦ θανάτου, καθότι οὐκ ἦν δυνατὸν κρατεῖσθαι αὐτὸν ὑπ' αὐτοῦ· [GNS]<br><br>ὃν ὁ θεὸς ἀνέστησεν λύσας τὰς **ὠδῖνας** τοῦ θανάτου, καθότι οὐκ ἦν δυνατὸν κρατεῖσθαι αὐτὸν ὑπ' αὐτοῦ· [GNT] | Agony, pains, horrors, suffering; birth pangs.<br><br>**Practical Application**<br>For the unbeliever, there is great pain in death, pain such as that experienced by a woman in giving birth. But man no longer has to suffer the agony of death nor does he have to fear suffering through death. Christ has conquered and abolished death, made it completely harmless. Death is actually the most glorious and joyful experience for the believer, an experience that simply explodes human imagination. (Cp. John 5:24; Hebrews 2:14-15.)<br><br>How can this be said? Because the believer actually never experiences death. Quicker than the eye can blink, God transfers the believer into His presence—to live with Him eternally. |

# PRACTICAL WORD STUDIES
## in the NEW TESTAMENT

| ENGLISH WORD | GREEK WORD AND VERSE | THE WORD MEANS... |
|---|---|---|
| **#88**<br>**Agony**<br><br>**Being in an agony–**<br>KJV<br>**Being in agony–**<br>NASB<br>**Being in anguish–**NIV<br>**Being in agony–**<br>NKJV<br>**In such agony–**NLT<br><br>**POSB**<br>**REFERENCE**<br>(Lk.22:43-44; esp.<br>v.44)<br>Note 4, point 2 | γενόμενος ἐν ἀγωνίᾳ = genomenos en agönia<br>Pronunciation: [ghin'-om-en-os en ag-o-nee'-ah]<br>Parsing *genomenos* (part of speech): verb<br>    Mood—participle<br>    Tense—aorist<br>    Voice—middle deponent<br>    Case—nominative<br>    Gender—masculine<br>    Number—singular<br>    Stem or root—from γίνομαι<br>Parsing *agönia* (part of speech): noun<br>    Case—dative<br>    Gender—feminine<br>    Number—singular<br>    Stem or root—from ἀγωνία, ας<br>Concordance References:<br>⇒ Strong's #1096 ginomai + 1722 en + 74 agonia<br>⇒ NIV #1181 ginomai [being] + 1877 en [in] + 75 agönia [anguish]<br>⇒ NASB #1096 ginomai + 1722 en + 74 agonia<br><br>**Luke 22:44**<br>And **being in an agony** he prayed more earnestly: and his sweat was as it were great drops of blood falling down to the ground. [KJV]<br>And **being in agony** He was praying very fervently; and His sweat became like drops of blood, falling down upon the ground. [NASB]<br>And **being in anguish**, he prayed more earnestly, and his sweat was like drops of blood falling to the ground. [NIV]<br>And **being in agony**, He prayed more earnestly. Then His sweat became like great drops of blood falling down to the ground. [NKJV]<br>He prayed more fervently, and he was **in such agony** of spirit that his sweat fell to the ground like great drops of blood. [NLT]<br>καὶ **γενόμενος ἐν ἀγωνίᾳ**, ἐκτενέστερον προσηύχετο. ἐγένετο δὲ ὁ ἱδρὼς αὐτοῦ ὡσεὶ θρόμβοι αἵματος καταβαίνοντος ἐπὶ τὴν γῆν. [GNS]<br>καὶ **γενόμενος ἐν ἀγωνίᾳ** ἐκτενέστερον προσηύχετο· καὶ ἐγένετο ὁ ἱδρὼς αὐτοῦ ὡσεὶ θρόμβοι αἵματος καταβαίνοντος ἐπὶ τὴν γῆν. [GNT] | To be in agony, anguish, a very real pain. It means to be distressed, grieved, pained with great anguish.<br><br>**Practical Application**<br>The Greek *genomenos* (aorist participle) means Jesus experienced a growing agony. The weight upon Him was not only intense, it grew more and more intense. The pressure and sense of suffering became heavier and heavier. The picture is that of His becoming engrossed and embodied in agony. Thus, He prayed more and more earnestly. His prayer grew and increased in intensity even as His agony intensified. |
| **#89**<br>**Agree**<br><br>Agree–KJV<br>Agree–NASB<br>Agree–NIV<br>Agree–NKJV<br>Agree–NLT<br><br>**POSB**<br>**REFERENCE**<br>(Mt.18:19-20; esp.<br>v.19)<br>*Deeper Study #3* | συμφωνήσωσιν = sumphönësösin<br>Pronunciation: [soom-fo-neh'-so-sin]<br>Parsing (part of speech): verb<br>    Mood—subjunctive<br>    Tense—aorist<br>    Voice—active<br>    Person—3rd person<br>    Number—plural<br>    Stem or root—from συμφωνέω<br>Concordance References:<br>⇒ Strong's #4856 sumphoneo<br>⇒ NIV #5244 sumphöneö<br>⇒ NASB #4856 sumphoneo<br><br>**Matthew 18:19**<br>Again I say unto you, That if two of you shall **agree** on earth as touching any thing that they shall ask, it shall be done for them of my Father which is in heaven. [KJV]<br>"Again I say to you, that if two of you **agree** on earth about anything that they may ask, it shall be done for them by My Father who is in heaven. [NASB]<br>"Again, I tell you that if two of you on earth **agree** about anything you ask for, it will be done for you by my Father in heaven. [NIV]<br>Again I say to you that if two of you **agree** on earth concerning anything that they ask, it will be done for them by My Father in heaven. [NKJV]<br>"I also tell you this: If two of you **agree** down here on | To be in complete accord; to harmonize together like that of a symphony; to sound together; to act together in each other's nature; to consent.<br><br>**Practical Application**<br>It is the very opposite of wandering thoughts, half-hearted commitment, disconnected purpose, disjointed and misplaced understanding, unsynchronized spirits, and incomplete and piece-meal knowledge. |

## Practical Word Studies in the New Testament

| ENGLISH WORD | GREEK WORD AND VERSE | THE WORD MEANS... |
|---|---|---|
| | earth concerning anything you ask, my Father in heaven will do it for you. [NLT]<br>Πάλιν ἀμὴν λέγω ὑμῖν, ὅτι ἐὰν δύο ὑμῶν **συμφωνήσωσιν** ἐπὶ τῆς γῆς περὶ παντὸς πράγματος οὗ ἐὰν αἰτήσωνται, γενήσεται αὐτοῖς παρὰ τοῦ πατρός μου τοῦ ἐν οὐρανοῖς. [GNS]<br>Πάλιν [ἀμὴν] λέγω ὑμῖν ὅτι ἐὰν δύο **συμφωνήσωσιν** ἐξ ὑμῶν ἐπὶ τῆς γῆς περὶ παντὸς πράγματος οὗ ἐὰν αἰτήσωνται, γενήσεται αὐτοῖς παρὰ τοῦ πατρός μου τοῦ ἐν οὐρανοῖς. [GNT] | |
| **#90**<br>**Agree**<br><br>Consent–KJV<br>**Agree–NASB**<br>**Agree–NIV**<br>**Agree–NKJV**<br>**Agree–NLT**<br><br>**POSB REFERENCE**<br>(Rom.7:14-17; esp. v.16)<br>Note 2, point 2 | σύμφημι = *sumphēmi*<br>Pronunciation: [soom'-fay-mee]<br>Parsing (part of speech): verb<br>    Mood—indicative<br>    Tense—present<br>    Voice—active<br>    Person—1st person<br>    Number—singular<br>    Stem or root—from σύμφημι<br>Concordance References:<br>  ⇒ Strong's #4852 sumphēmi<br>  ⇒ NIV #5238 sumphēmi<br>  ⇒ NASB #4852 sumphēmi<br><br>**Romans 7:16**<br>If then I do that which I would not, I **consent** unto the law that *it is* good. [KJV]<br>But if I do the very thing I do not wish *to do*, I **agree** with the Law, *confessing* that it is good. [NASB]<br>And if I do what I do not want to do, I **agree** that the law is good. [NIV]<br>If, then, I do what I will not to do, I **agree** with the law that *it is* good. [NKJV]<br>I know perfectly well that what I am doing is wrong, and my bad conscience shows that I **agree** that the law is good. [NLT]<br>εἰ δὲ ὃ οὐ θέλω, τοῦτο ποιῶ, **σύμφημι** τῷ νόμῳ ὅτι καλός. [GNS]<br>εἰ δὲ ὃ οὐ θέλω τοῦτο ποιῶ, **σύμφημι** τῷ νόμῳ ὅτι καλός. [GNT] | To agree; to consent; to be in complete accord; to harmonize together like that of a symphony; to sound together; to act together in each other's nature.<br><br>**Practical Application**<br>The word "agree" (*sumphēmi*) means to agree, to say the same thing, to speak right along with the law, to prove and demonstrate that the law is right. The law proves and demonstrates that a man cannot live a perfectly righteous life. A carnal man proves the very same thing. He sins, finding himself doing exactly what the law says not to do and what he himself prefers not to do.<br>The point is this: when a carnal man sins, the law points out his sin. The law tells the carnal man the truth: he is a sinner doomed to die. Knowing this, the carnal man is able to seek the Lord and His forgiveness. Therefore, the carnal man agrees with the law; the law is very good, for it tells him that he must seek the Savior and His forgiveness. He may not actually follow through and seek the Lord, but the law has at least fulfilled its function and shown the carnal man what he needs to do. |
| **#91**<br>**Agree To, With**<br><br>Consent–KJV<br>**Agree with–NASB**<br>**Agree to–NIV**<br>Consent–NKJV<br>Deny–NLT<br><br>**POSB REFERENCE**<br>(1 Tim.6:3)<br>Note 1, point 1, 2 | προσέρχεται = *proserchetai*<br>Pronunciation: [pros-er'-kheh-tah-ee]<br>Parsing (part of speech): verb<br>    Mood—indicative<br>    Tense—present<br>    Voice—middle or passive deponent<br>    Person—3rd person<br>    Number—singular<br>    Stem or root—from προσέρχομαι<br>Concordance References:<br>  ⇒ Strong's #4334 proserchomai<br>  ⇒ NIV #4665 proserchomai<br>  ⇒ NASB #4334 proserchomai<br><br>**1 Tim. 6:3**<br>If any man teach otherwise, and **consent** not to wholesome words, *even* the words of our Lord Jesus Christ, and to the doctrine which is according to godliness; [KJV]<br>If anyone advocates a different doctrine, and does not **agree with** sound words, those of our Lord Jesus Christ, and with the doctrine conforming to godliness, [NASB]<br>If anyone teaches false doctrines and does not **agree to** the sound instruction of our Lord Jesus Christ and to godly teaching, [NIV]<br>If anyone teaches otherwise and does not **consent** to wholesome words, *even* the words of our Lord Jesus Christ, and to the doctrine which accords with godliness, [NKJV]<br>Some false teachers may **deny** these things, but these are the sound, wholesome practicings of the Lord Jesus | To agree to; to agree with; to consent.<br><br>**Practical Application**<br>The words "agree to" or "agree with" (*proserchetai*) have the sense of "attaching oneself to" Christ (Daniel Guthrie. *The Pastoral Epistles.* "Tyndale New Testament Commentaries," p.110f). The false teacher is just not willing to attach himself to the *Lord Jesus Christ*. He is...<br>• not willing to confess that Jesus is the *Lord God* from heaven, the very Son of God Himself.<br>• not willing to confess that Jesus is the *Christ*, the Messiah and Savior of the world.<br>The false teacher does not consent to the teachings of godliness. He is...<br>• not willing to accept the righteousness of God revealed in Jesus Christ.<br>• not willing to separate himself from the world nor to set his life wholly apart unto God.<br>One or both of these reasons are why the false teacher does not teach the wholesome words of Christ but rather chooses to teach a different doctrine and way of life. He has committed his life to the *profession* of the ministry...<br>• as a way to serve mankind.<br>• as a way to earn a livelihood. |

# PRACTICAL WORD STUDIES
## in the NEW TESTAMENT

| ENGLISH WORD | GREEK WORD AND VERSE | THE WORD MEANS... |
|---|---|---|
| | Christ, and they are the foundation for a godly life. [NLT]<br>Εἴ τις ἑτεροδιδασκαλεῖ, καὶ μὴ **προσέρχεται** ὑγιαίνουσι λόγοις, τοῖς τοῦ Κυρίου ἡμῶν Ἰησοῦ Χριστοῦ, καὶ τῇ κατ' εὐσέβειαν διδασκαλίᾳ, [GNS]<br>εἴ τις ἑτεροδιδασκαλεῖ καὶ μὴ **προσέρχεται** ὑγιαίνουσιν λόγοις τοῖς τοῦ κυρίου ἡμῶν Ἰησοῦ Χριστοῦ καὶ τῇ κατ' εὐσέβειαν διδασκαλίᾳ, [GNT] | But he is not committed to represent Christ and His Word. As a result, the person is called a false teacher by both the Holy Scriptures and Christ. |
| **#92**<br>**Agreement**<br><br>**Agreement–KJV**<br>**Agreement–NASB**<br>**Agreement–NIV**<br>**Agreement–NKJV**<br>Union–NLT<br><br>**POSB**<br>**REFERENCE**<br>(2 Cor.6:14-16; esp. v.16)<br>Note 2 | συγκατάθεσις = *sugkatathesis*<br>Pronunciation: [soong-kat-ath'-es-is]<br>Parsing (part of speech): noun<br>    Case—nominative<br>    Gender—feminine<br>    Number—singular<br>    Stem or root—from συγκατάθεσις, εως<br>Concordance References:<br>  ⇒ Strong's #4783 sugkatathesis<br>  ⇒ NIV #5161 sugkatathesis<br>  ⇒ NASB #4783 sugkatathesis<br><br>**2 Cor. 6:16**<br>And what **agreement** hath the temple of God with idols? for ye are the temple of the living God; as God hath said, I will dwell in them, and walk in *them;* and I will be their God, and they shall be my people. [KJV]<br>Or what **agreement** has the temple of God with idols? For we are the temple of the living God; just as God said, "I WILL DWELL IN THEM AND WALK AMONG THEM; AND I WILL BE THEIR GOD, AND THEY SHALL BE MY PEOPLE. [NASB]<br>What **agreement** is there between the temple of God and idols? For we are the temple of the living God. As God has said: "I will live with them and walk among them, and I will be their God, and they will be my people." [NIV]<br>And what **agreement** has the temple of God with idols? For you are the temple of the living God. As God has said: *"I will dwell in them And walk among them. I will be their God, And they shall be My people."* [NKJV]<br>And what **union** can there be between God's temple and idols? For we are the temple of the living God. As God said: "I will live in them and walk among them. I will be their God, and they will be my people. [NLT]<br>τίς δὲ **συγκατάθεσις** ναῷ Θεοῦ μετὰ εἰδώλων; ἡμεῖς γὰρ ναὸς Θεοῦ ἐστε ζῶντος, καθὼς εἶπεν ὁ Θεὸς ὅτι Ἐνοικήσω ἐν αὐτοῖς, καὶ ἐμπεριπατήσω· καὶ ἔσομαι αὐτῶν Θεός, καὶ αὐτοὶ ἔσονταί μοι λαός. [GNS]<br>τίς δὲ **συγκατάθεσις** ναῷ θεοῦ μετὰ εἰδώλων; ἡμεῖς γὰρ ναὸς θεοῦ ἐσμεν ζῶντος, καθὼς εἶπεν ὁ θεὸς ὅτι Ἐνοικήσω ἐν αὐτοῖς καὶ ἐμπεριπατήσω καὶ ἔσομαι αὐτῶν θεὸς καὶ αὐτοὶ ἔσονταί μου λαός. [GNT] | Agreement; close agreement; a close union and bond of mind and spirit.<br><br>**Practical Application**<br>There can be no agreement, no union, and no bond whatsoever between the temple of God and idols. Above all else, idolatry is despised by God, for an idol is the substitute god of a man. An idol replaces God in a man's life. A man's worship or idol may be ranging from self or personal ideas over to graven images or possessions. A man may worship and make an idol out of anything. An idol can be anything to which a man gives his primary allegiance—his time, energy, money. Wherever a man puts his primary time, energy, money, and allegiance is where his heart and worship are. |
| **#93**<br>**Aid**<br><br>He took–KJV<br>Help–NASB<br>Helps–NIV<br>**Aid–NKJV**<br>Help–NLT<br><br>**POSB**<br>**REFERENCE**<br>(Heb.2:14-16; esp. v.16)<br>Note 1, point 5 | ἐπιλαμβάνεται = *epilambanetai*<br>Pronunciation: [ep-ee-lam-ban'-eh-tah-ee]<br>Parsing (part of speech): verb<br>    Mood—indicative<br>    Tense—present<br>    Voice—middle or passive deponent<br>    Person—3rd person<br>    Number—singular<br>    Stem or root—from ἐπιλαμβάνομαι<br>Concordance References:<br>  ⇒ Strong's #1949 epilambanomai<br>  ⇒ NIV #2138 epilambanomai<br>  ⇒ NASB #1949 epilambanomai<br><br>**Hebrews 2:16**<br>For verily **he took** not on him the nature of angels; but he took on him the seed of Abraham. [KJV]<br>For assuredly He does not give **help** to angels, but He gives help to the descendant of Abraham. [NASB]<br>For surely it is not angels he **helps**, but Abraham's descendants. [NIV] | To help; to take; to lay hold of; to catch; to seize; to take by the hand.<br><br>**Practical Application**<br>Jesus Christ has delivered us from the bondage of the flesh. This tells us a most wonderful truth: Jesus Christ did not only take hold of man's nature, He took hold of man's hand. He took us by the hand and delivered us. The picture is that of love and tender care, of His delivering us out of the bondages of the flesh and of human nature. Note: it is not angels that He took by the hand, but the seed of Abraham, that is, the spiritual seed of Abrahm, those who believe and trust in the Lord Jesus Christ as their Savior. |

## PRACTICAL WORD STUDIES
### in the NEW TESTAMENT

| ENGLISH WORD | GREEK WORD AND VERSE | THE WORD MEANS... |
|---|---|---|
| | For indeed He does not give **aid** to angels, but He does give aid to the seed of Abraham. [NKJV]<br>We all know that Jesus came to **help** the descendants of Abraham, not to help the angels. [NLT]<br>οὐ γὰρ δήπου ἀγγέλων **ἐπιλαμβάνεται**, ἀλλὰ σπέρματος Ἀβραὰμ ἐπιλαμβάνεται, [GNS]<br>οὐ γὰρ δήπου ἀγγέλων **ἐπιλαμβάνεται** ἀλλὰ σπέρματος Ἀβραὰμ ἐπιλαμβάνεται. [GNT] | |
| #94<br>**Aid**<br><br>Succour–KJV<br>Come to the aid–<br>  NASB<br>Help–NIV<br>**Aid–NKJV**<br>Help–NLT<br><br>**POSB<br>REFERENCE**<br>(Heb 2:17-18, esp. v.18)<br>Note 2, point 4 | βοηθῆσαι = *boëthësai*<br>Pronunciation: [bo-ay-thay'-sah-ee]<br>Parsing (part of speech): verb<br>    Mood—infinitive<br>    Tense—aorist<br>    Voice—active<br>    Stem or root—from βοηθέω<br>Concordance References:<br>  ⇒ Strong's #997 boëtheö<br>  ⇒ NIV #1070 boëtheö<br>  ⇒ NASB #997 boëtheö<br><br>**Hebrews 2:18**<br>For in that he himself hath suffered being tempted, he is able to **succour** them that are tempted. [KJV]<br>For since He Himself was tempted in that which He has suffered, He is able to **come to the aid** of those who are tempted. [NASB]<br>Because he himself suffered when he was tempted, he is able to **help** those who are being tempted. [NIV]<br>For in that He Himself has suffered, being tempted, He is able to **aid** those who are tempted. [NKJV]<br>Since he himself has gone through suffering and temptation, he is able to **help** us when we are being tempted. [NLT]<br>ἐν ᾧ γὰρ πέπονθεν αὐτὸς πειρασθείς, δύναται τοῖς πειραζομένοις **βοηθῆσαι**. [GNS]<br>ἐν ᾧ γὰρ πέπονθεν αὐτὸς πειρασθείς, δύναται τοῖς πειραζομένοις **βοηθῆσαι**. [GNT] | To help; to succour; to come to the aid. It means to relieve, assist; to be so eager to help that one runs to the cry of a person.<br><br>**Practical Application**<br>Jesus Christ became the High Priest so that He could help man when he faces the trials and temptations of life.<br>What a picture of Jesus Christ! He has heard our cry in all of our suffering and pain, trial and temptation; and He has run to help and deliver us. Just think! He has been made like us in order to feel with us and deliver us. He has become the perfect High Priest. He needed to do this in order to experience every situation, condition, and trial of man. He experienced the most humiliating experiences imaginable. He experienced...<br>• being born to an unwed mother (Matthew 1:18-19).<br>• being born in a stable, the worst of conditions (Luke 2:7).<br>• being born to poor parents (Luke 2:24).<br>• having his life threatened as a baby (Matthew 2:13f).<br>• being the cause of unimaginable sorrow (Matthew 2:16f).<br>• having to be moved and shifted about as a baby (Matthew 2:13f).<br>• being reared in a despicable place, Nazareth (Luke 2:39).<br>• having His father die during His youth (see POSB note, pt. 3—Matthew 13:53-58).<br>• having to support His mother and brothers and sisters (see POSB note, pt. 3—Matthew 13:53-58).<br>• having no home, not even a place to lay His head (Matthew 8:20; Luke 9:58).<br>• being hated and opposed by religionists (Mark 14:1-2).<br>• being charged with insanity (Mark 3:21).<br>• being charged with demon possession (Mark 3:22).<br>• being opposed by His own family (Mark 3:31-32).<br>• being rejected, hated, and opposed by listeners (Matthew 13:53-58; Luke 4:28-29).<br>• being betrayed by a close friend (Mark 14:10-11, 18).<br>• being left alone, rejected, and forsaken by all His friends (Mark 14:50).<br>• being tried before the high court of the land on the charge of treason (John 18:33).<br>• being executed by crucifixion, the worst possible death (John 19:16f).<br>And Jesus Christ suffered so much more, but the point to note is this: in each of these experiences His suffering reached the depth of humiliation. Christ stooped to the lowest point of human experience in every condition in order to |

# PRACTICAL WORD STUDIES
## in the NEW TESTAMENT

| ENGLISH WORD | GREEK WORD AND VERSE | THE WORD MEANS... |
|---|---|---|
| | | become the *Perfect Sympathizer* (Savior). This is the reason He can now identify with and feel for any person's circumstances. No person ever comes close to the depth of suffering and humiliation He bore. Jesus Christ can succor—help, feel for, care for, and look after—every person no matter his condition, trial, or temptation. |
| **#95**<br>**Aides**<br><br>Servants–KJV<br>Servants–NASB<br>Attendants–NIV<br>Servants–NKJV<br>**Aides–NLT**<br><br>**POSB REFERENCE**<br>(Mt.22:11-14; esp. v.13)<br>Note 4, point 2 | διακόνοις = diakonois<br>Pronunciation: [di'ak-o'-nois]<br>Parsing (part of speech): noun<br>   Case—dative<br>   Gender—masculine<br>   Number—plural<br>   Stem or root—from διάκονος, ου<br>Concordance References:<br>  ⇒ Strong's #1401 doulos<br>  ⇒ NIV #1356 diakonos<br>  ⇒ NASB #1249 diakonos<br><br>**Matthew 22:13**<br>Then said the king to the **servants**, Bind him hand and foot, and take him away, and cast *him* into outer darkness; there shall be weeping and gnashing of teeth. [KJV]<br>"Then the king said to the **servants**, 'Bind him hand and foot, and cast him into the outer darkness; in that place there shall be weeping and gnashing of teeth.' [NASB]<br>"Then the king told the **attendants**, 'Tie him hand and foot, and throw him outside, into the darkness, where there will be weeping and gnashing of teeth.' [NIV]<br>Then the king said to the **servants**, 'Bind him hand and foot, take him away, and cast *him* into outer darkness; there will be weeping and gnashing of teeth.' [NKJV]<br>Then the king said to his **aides**, 'Bind him hand and foot and throw him out into the outer darkness, where there is weeping and gnashing of teeth.' [NLT]<br>τότε εἶπεν ὁ βασιλεὺς τοῖς **διακόνοις**, Δήσαντες αὐτοῦ πόδας καὶ χεῖρας, ἄρατε αὐτὸν καὶ ἐκβάλετε εἰς τὸ σκότος τὸ ἐξώτερον· ἐκεῖ ἔσται ὁ κλαυθμὸς καὶ ὁ βρυγμὸς τῶν ὀδόντων. [GNS]<br>τότε ὁ βασιλεὺς εἶπεν τοῖς **διακόνοις**, Δήσαντες αὐτοῦ πόδας καὶ χεῖρας ἐκβάλετε αὐτὸν εἰς τὸ σκότος τὸ ἐξώτερον· ἐκεῖ ἔσται ὁ κλαυθμὸς καὶ ὁ βρυγμὸς τῶν ὀδόντων. [GNT] | To serve or to be a servant or helper; a deacon or minister.<br><br>**Practical Application**<br>*Diakonos* means acts of service or ministry. Diakonos includes but does not limit itself to the church office of the deacon. In this Scripture, the word refers to God's angels. The aides (*diakonois*) were not the same servants who delivered the invitations. They were not the disciples (Matthew 22:3,4) and preachers (Matthew 22:8,10) of the Lord. They were the angelic guardians of heaven who minister to the Godhead (cp. Matthew 13:41-43, 49-50). Three things were done.<br>1. The man was bound hand and foot. The hand and foot are usually the bodily parts used by man to sin. The hands are bound so there is no resistance. The feet are bound so there is no escape. Whatever the King says is done in the Great Day of the Feast. No man can resist or flee.<br>2. The man was taken away, out of the King's presence and out of the presence of His Son and of the other guests. He was not allowed to share in the joy and bounty of the occasion.<br>3. The man was cast into outer darkness, far, far away from everyone else. He was not only cut off from the sharing of the occasion but from ever seeing the occasion. Whatever light and splendor there was in the Great Wedding Feast, he was cast into the *outer* regions of darkness, never to glimpse the light. |
| **#96**<br>**Aim For Perfection**<br><br>Be perfect–KJV<br>Be made complete–NASB<br>**Aim for perfection–NIV**<br>Become complete–NKJV<br>Change your ways–NLT<br><br>**POSB REFERENCE**<br>(2 Cor.13:11-13; esp. v.11)<br>Note 3 | καταρτίζεσθε = katartizesthe<br>Pronunciation: [kat-ar-tid'-zehs-the]<br>Parsing (part of speech):verb<br>   Mood—imperative<br>   Tense—present<br>   Voice—passive<br>   Person—2nd person<br>   Number—plural<br>   Stem or root—from καταρτίζω<br>Concordance References:<br>  ⇒ Strong's #2675 katartizō<br>  ⇒ NIV #2936 katartizō<br>  ⇒ NASB #2675 katartizō<br><br>**2 Cor. 13:11**<br>Finally, brethren, farewell. **Be perfect**, be of good comfort, be of one mind, live in peace; and the God of love and peace shall be with you. [KJV]<br>Finally, brethren, rejoice, **be made complete**, be comforted, be like-minded, live in peace; and the God of love and peace shall be with you. [NASB]<br>Finally, brothers, good-by. **Aim for perfection**, listen to my appeal, be of one mind, live in peace. And the God of love and peace will be with you. [NIV]<br>Finally, brethren, farewell. **Become complete**. Be of good comfort, be of one mind, live in peace; and the God of love and peace will be with you. [NKJV] | To aim and strive for perfection; to be made complete; to prepare; to change one's ways; to restore, reform, correct, and mend oneself and one's ways.<br><br>**Practical Application**<br>Paul's challenge to his Corinthian brothers is blunt and to the point: Stop your sinning and aim for perfection. |

## PRACTICAL WORD STUDIES
### in the NEW TESTAMENT

| ENGLISH WORD | GREEK WORD AND VERSE | THE WORD MEANS... |
|---|---|---|
| | Dear brothers and sisters, I close my letter with these last words: Rejoice. **Change your ways**. Encourage each other. Live in harmony and peace. Then the God of love and peace will be with you. [NLT]<br>Λοιπόν, ἀδελφοί, χαίρετε· **καταρτίζεσθε**, παρακαλεῖσθε, τὸ αὐτὸ φρονεῖτε, εἰρηνεύετε· καὶ ὁ Θεὸς τῆς ἀγάπης καὶ εἰρήνης ἔσται μεθ' ὑμῶν. [GNS]<br>Λοιπόν, ἀδελφοί, χαίρετε, **καταρτίζεσθε**, παρακαλεῖσθε, τὸ αὐτὸ φρονεῖτε, εἰρηνεύετε, καὶ ὁ Θεὸς τῆς ἀγάπης καὶ εἰρήνης ἔσται μεθ' ὑμῶν. [GNT] | |
| **#97**<br>**Aim Is**<br><br>Labour–KJV<br>Ambition–NASB<br>Make it...goal–NIV<br>Make it...aim–NKJV<br>**Aim is–NLT**<br><br>**POSB REFERENCE**<br>(2 Cor.5:9-10; esp. v.9)<br>Note 4 | φιλοτιμούμεθα = *philotimoumetha*<br>Pronunciation: [fil-ot-im-oo'-meh-tha]<br>Parsing (part of speech): verb<br>    Mood—indicative<br>    Tense—present<br>    Voice—middle or passive deponent<br>    Person—1st person<br>    Number—plural<br>    Stem or root—from φιλοτιμέομαι<br>Concordance References:<br>  ⇒ Strong's #5389 philotimeomai<br>  ⇒ NIV #5818 philotimeomai<br>  ⇒ NASB #5389 philotimeomai<br><br>**2 Cor. 5:9**<br>Wherefore we **labour**, that, whether present or absent, we may be accepted of him. [KJV]<br>Therefore also we have as our **ambition**, whether at home or absent, to be pleasing to Him. [NASB]<br>So we **make it** our **goal** to please him, whether we are at home in the body or away from it. [NIV]<br>Therefore we **make it** our **aim**, whether present or absent, to be well pleasing to Him. [NKJV]<br>So our **aim is** to please him always, whether we are here in this body or away from this body. [NLT]<br>διὸ καὶ **φιλοτιμούμεθα**, εἴτε ἐνδημοῦντες, εἴτε ἐκδημοῦντες, εὐάρεστοι αὐτῷ εἶναι. [GNS]<br>διὸ καὶ **φιλοτιμούμεθα**, εἴτε ἐνδημοῦντες εἴτε ἐκδημοῦντες, εὐάρεστοι αὐτῷ εἶναι. [GNT] | To make a goal; to constantly aim; to be constantly ambitious; to strive earnestly.<br><br>**Practical Application**<br>Judgment stirs in us the longing to please God and to receive our heavenly home. Judgment stirs us to adopt one great "aim" (*philotimoumetha*) in life: to please God. Paul says that he is to be judged; therefore, he works his fingers to the bone. Why? That he may please (*euarestoi*) God. |
| **#98**<br>**Alarmed, Not**<br><br>Not troubled–KJV<br>Not frightened–NASB<br>**Not alarmed–NIV**<br>Not troubled–NKJV<br>Don't panic–NLT<br><br>**POSB REFERENCE**<br>(Mt.24:6-7; esp. v.6)<br>Note 3, point 2<br><br>**See also POSB REF:**<br>(Mk.13:7-8; esp. v.7)<br>Note 3, point 2 | μὴ θροεῖσθε = *mē throeisthe*<br>Pronunciation: [meh-thro-eis'-the]<br>Parsing *throeisthe* (part of speech): verb<br>    Mood—imperfect<br>    Tense—present<br>    Voice—passive<br>    Person—2nd person<br>    Number—plural<br>    Stem or root—from θροέομαι<br>Concordance References:<br>  ⇒ Strong's #2360 throeo<br>  ⇒ NIV # 3590 mē + 2583 throeö<br>  ⇒ NASB #2360 throeo<br><br>**Matthew 24:6**<br>And ye shall hear of wars and rumours of wars: see that ye be **not troubled**: for all *these things* must come to pass, but the end is not yet. [KJV]<br>"And you will be hearing of wars and rumors of wars; see that you are **not frightened**, for *those things* must take place, but *that* is not yet the end. [NASB]<br>You will hear of wars and rumors of wars, but see to it that you are **not alarmed**. Such things must happen, but the end is still to come. [NIV]<br>And you will hear of wars and rumors of wars. See that you are **not troubled**; for all *these things* must come to pass, but the end is not yet. [NKJV]<br>And wars will break out near and far, but **don't panic**. Yes, these things must come, but the end won't follow immediately. [NLT]<br>ὁρᾶτε, **μὴ θροεῖσθε** δεῖ γὰρ γενέσθαι· ἀλλ' οὔπω ἐστὶ τὸ τέλος. [GNS] | Not to be disturbed, startled, frightened, alarmed, panicked, troubled, or confused.<br><br>**Practical Application**<br>World violence can disturb and frighten. It can lead us into confusion and commotion; to cry out within our inner being. But Christ says this is not to be the case with His disciples. Our hearts are to be fixed upon God, trusting His presence, care, and security (Matthew 10:28; Luke 12:4).<br>Three things can happen to the believer in looking at world-wide trouble.<br>1. The believer can become overly affected by the news of world affairs and turmoil. Such news can become so interesting and captivating that it can dominate the believer's life. He begins to live and thrive on the news.<br>2. The believer can become overly apprehensive about the personal safety of himself and his family. He can begin to fear so much that he forgets that his security is in God, not in this world. Fear over world affairs tends to emphasize the importance of the earth over the importance of God; it tends to emphasize the worldly over the spiritual. The world, of course, is important; but what needs to be stressed is the spiritual. And it is the believer's responsibility to stress the spiritual, the security and peace of heart that is found in |

# PRACTICAL WORD STUDIES
## in the NEW TESTAMENT

| ENGLISH WORD | GREEK WORD AND VERSE | THE WORD MEANS... |
|---|---|---|
| | μελλήσετε δὲ ἀκούειν πολέμους καὶ ἀκοὰς πολέμων· ὁρᾶτε **μὴ θροεῖσθε**· δεῖ γὰρ γενέσθαι, ἀλλ' οὔπω ἐστὶν τὸ τέλος. [GNT] | Christ.<br>3. The believer can become so alarmed over world affairs that he neglects his spiritual duties. The believer is naturally concerned over the world, as all men should be. But he is not to allow world affairs to interfere with his witnessing for Christ. He is to be at peace and to be secure with God, and he is to demonstrate the peace and security of God, going about his daily duties as much as possible within a turbulent world. The point is, the believer is to be witnessing for Christ no matter the turbulence of the world. |
| **#99**<br>**Alert**<br><br>Vigilant–KJV<br>Be on the alert–NASB<br>**Alert–NIV**<br>Vigilant–NKJV<br>Watch out–NLT<br><br>**POSB REFERENCE**<br>(1 Pt.5:8)<br>Note 1, point 2 | γρηγορήσατε = grēgorēsate<br>Pronunciation: [gray-gor-ay'-sah-teh]<br>Parsing (part of speech): verb<br>    Mood—imperative<br>    Tense—aorist<br>    Voice—active<br>    Person—2nd person<br>    Number—plural<br>    Stem or root—from γρηγορέω<br>Concordance References:<br>  ⇒ Strong's #1127 grēgoreō<br>  ⇒ NIV #1213 grēgoreō<br>  ⇒ NASB #1127 grēgoreō<br><br>**1 Peter 5:8**<br>Be sober, be **vigilant**; because your adversary the devil, as a roaring lion, walketh about, seeking whom he may devour: [KJV]<br>Be of sober *spirit*, **be on the alert**. Your adversary, the devil, prowls about like a roaring lion, seeking someone to devour. [NASB]<br>Be self-controlled and **alert**. Your enemy the devil prowls around like a roaring lion looking for someone to devour. [NIV]<br>Be sober, be **vigilant**; because your adversary the devil walks about like a roaring lion, seeking whom he may devour. [NKJV]<br>Be careful! **Watch out** for attacks from the Devil, your great enemy. He prowls around like a roaring lion, looking for some victim to devour. [NLT]<br>νήψατε, **γρηγορήσατε**, ὅτι ὁ ἀντίδικος ὑμῶν διάβολος, ὡς λέων ὠρυόμενος περιπατεῖ ζητῶν τινα καταπίῃ. [GNS]<br>Νήψατε, **γρηγορήσατε**. ὁ ἀντίδικος ὑμῶν διάβολος ὡς λέων ὠρυόμενος περιπατεῖ ζητῶν [τινα] καταπιεῖν· [GNT] | To be alert; to be vigilant; to watch out. The word means to be watchful and awake.<br><br>**Practical Application**<br>It has the idea of being constantly aroused and on the lookout; to always be aroused, awake, and watching for the devil and his attacks. If a person's mind and body are dull, flabby, and weak from drink, drugs, overeating, slothfulness, and indulgence in sleep, recreation, pleasure, or in anything else—that person cannot be watching and waiting; he cannot be constantly aroused to look for the devil's temptations and attacks.<br>The believer must be sober and serious about the devil; he must be alert and vigilant in looking for the devil's temptations and attacks. It is the only conceivable way the believer can conquer and overcome in this life; it is the only way he can keep his life and testimony from being destroyed by the devil. |
| **#100**<br>**Alert**<br><br>Watch–KJV<br>Keeping alert–NASB<br>Watchful–NIV<br>Vigilant–NKJV<br>**Alert–NLT**<br><br>**POSB REFERENCE**<br>(Col.4:2-4; esp. v.2)<br>Note 1, point 2 | γρηγοροῦντες = grēgorountes<br>Pronunciation: [gray-gor-yoon'-tehs]<br>Parsing (part of speech): verb<br>    Mood—participle (imperative sense)<br>    Tense—present<br>    Voice—active<br>    Case—nominative<br>    Gender—masculine<br>    Person—2nd person<br>    Number—plural<br>    Stem or root—from γρηγορέω<br>Concordance References:<br>  ⇒ Strong's #1127 grēgoreō<br>  ⇒ NIV #1213 grēgoreō<br>  ⇒ NASB #1127 grēgoreō<br><br>**Col. 4:2**<br>Continue in prayer, and **watch** in the same with thanksgiving; [KJV]<br>Devote yourselves to prayer, **keeping alert** in it with *an attitude of* thanksgiving; [NASB]<br>Devote yourselves to prayer, being **watchful** and | To be watchful; to keep alert; to be alive; to stay awake, sleepless, active; to concentrate.<br><br>**Practical Application**<br>It means to fight against distractions, drowsiness, sluggishness, wandering thoughts, and useless daydreaming. It means to discipline our minds and control our thoughts in prayer. Being very honest, this is a problem that afflicts every believer sometime. Overwork, tiredness, pressure, strain—an innumerable list of things can make it very difficult to concentrate in prayer. This is the very reason Paul stresses the need to watch in prayer. But note: vigilance in prayer is the duty of the believer. Again, it is not something that God does for us. We are responsible for watching and concentrating. We are the ones who are to discipline our minds and control our thoughts. For this reason, we must never give up in prayer. We must... |

## PRACTICAL WORD STUDIES in the NEW TESTAMENT

| ENGLISH WORD | GREEK WORD AND VERSE | THE WORD MEANS... |
|---|---|---|
| | thankful. [NIV]<br>Continue earnestly in prayer, being **vigilant** in it with thanksgiving; [NKJV]<br>Devote yourselves to prayer with an **alert** mind and a thankful heart. [NLT]<br>Τῇ προσευχῇ προσκαρτερεῖτε, **γρηγοροῦντες** ἐν αὐτῇ ἐν εὐχαριστίᾳ· [GNS]<br>Τῇ προσευχῇ προσκαρτερεῖτε, **γρηγοροῦντες** ἐν αὐτῇ ἐν εὐχαριστίᾳ, [GNT] | • always struggle against drowsiness and wandering thoughts.<br>• learn to concentrate—to discipline our minds and control our thoughts.<br>• teach ourselves to be watchful in prayer. |
| #101<br>**Alert, Be On The**<br><br>Watch–KJV<br>**Be on the alert**– NASB<br>Keep watch–NIV<br>Watch–NKJV<br>Be prepared–NLT<br><br>**POSB REFERENCE**<br>(Mt.24:42)<br>Note 1<br><br>See also POSB REF:<br>(Mk.13:37)<br>*Deeper Study* #1<br>(1 Pt.5:8)<br>Note 1, point 2 | γρηγορεῖτε = *grēgoreite*<br>Pronunciation: [gray-gor-ee'-teh]<br>Parsing (part of speech): verb<br>    Mood—imperfect<br>    Tense—present<br>    Voice—active<br>    Person—2nd person<br>    Number—plural<br>    Stem or root—from γρηγορέω<br>Concordance References:<br>  ⇒ Strong's #1127 gregoreuo<br>  ⇒ NIV #1213 grēgoreō<br>  ⇒ NASB #1127 gregoreuo<br><br>**Matthew 24:42**<br>**Watch** therefore: for ye know not what hour your Lord doth come. [KJV]<br>"Therefore **be on the alert**, for you do not know which day your Lord is coming. [NASB]<br>"Therefore **keep watch**, because you do not know on what day your Lord will come. [NIV]<br>**Watch** therefore, for you do not know what hour your Lord is coming. [NKJV]<br>So **be prepared**, because you don't know what day your Lord is coming. [NLT]<br>**γρηγορεῖτε** οὖν, ὅτι οὐκ οἴδατε ποίᾳ ὥρᾳ ὁ Κύριος ὑμῶν ἔρχεται· [GNS]<br>**γρηγορεῖτε** οὖν, ὅτι οὐκ οἴδατε ποίᾳ ἡμέρᾳ ὁ κύριος ὑμῶν ἔρχεται. [GNT] | To watch; to stay alert; to be ready; to pay strict attention; to keep awake; to be watchful and sleepless; to be vigilant; to be prepared.<br><br>**Practical Application**<br>It also includes the idea of being motivated, of keeping one's attention (mind) upon a thing. Being on the alert also has the idea of being alert at the right time. It is at night that a person really needs to stay awake and watch for the thief (cp. 1 Thes. 5:4-9). |
| #102<br>**Alert, On The**<br><br>Watch–KJV<br>**On the alert**–NASB<br>On the watch–NIV<br>Watch–NKJV<br>Constant watch–NLT<br><br>**POSB REFERENCE**<br>(Lk.21:36)<br>Note 2 | ἀγρυπνεῖτε = *agrupneite*<br>Pronunciation: [ag-roop-neeh'-te]<br>Parsing (part of speech): verb<br>    Mood—imperfect<br>    Tense—present<br>    Voice—active<br>    Person—2nd person<br>    Number—plural<br>    Stem or root—from ἀγρυπνέω<br>Concordance References:<br>  ⇒ Strong's #69 agrupneo<br>  ⇒ NIV #70 agrupneō<br>  ⇒ NASB #69 agrupneo<br><br>**Luke 21:36**<br>**Watch** ye therefore, and pray always, that ye may be accounted worthy to escape all these things that shall come to pass, and to stand before the Son of man. [KJV]<br>"But keep **on the alert** at all times, praying in order that you may have strength to escape all these things that are about to take place, and to stand before the Son of Man." [NASB]<br>Be always **on the watch**, and pray that you may be able to escape all that is about to happen, and that you may be able to stand before the Son of Man." [NIV]<br>**Watch** therefore, and pray always that you may be counted worthy to escape all these things that will come to pass, and to stand before the Son of Man." [NKJV]<br>Keep a **constant watch**. And pray that, if possible, you may escape these horrors and stand before the Son of Man." [NLT]<br>**Ἀγρυπνεῖτε** οὖν ἐν παντὶ καιρῷ δεόμενοι ἵνα καταξιωθῆτε ἐκφυγεῖν ταῦτα πάντα τὰ μέλλοντα γίνεσθαι, καὶ σταθῆναι ἔμπροσθεν τοῦ υἱοῦ τοῦ | To be sleepless, awake, on guard; to be on a constant watch.<br><br>**Practical Application**<br>It means a spirit of being wakeful; of being restless; of guarding. In this Scripture, to watch is to pray. What does it mean to watch and pray? Praying always means the believer is to live in a spirit of prayer...<br>• praying all day, as he walks throughout the day.<br>• praying on all occasions and about everything.<br>• praying at appointed times, times set aside for nothing but prayer and devotions or quiet times. |

# PRACTICAL WORD STUDIES
## in the NEW TESTAMENT

| ENGLISH WORD | GREEK WORD AND VERSE | THE WORD MEANS... |
|---|---|---|
| | ἀνθρώπου. [GNS]<br>ἀγρυπνεῖτε δὲ ἐν παντὶ καιρῷ δεόμενοι ἵνα κατισχύσητε ἐκφυγεῖν ταῦτα πάντα τὰ μέλλοντα γίνεσθαι καὶ σταθῆναι ἔμπροσθεν τοῦ υἱοῦ τοῦ ἀνθρώπου. [GNT] | |
| **#103**<br>**Alienated From–**<br>**Alienated**<br><br>**Alienated**–KJV<br>**Alienated**–NASB<br>**Alienated from**–NIV<br>**Alienated**–NKJV<br>**So far away**–NLT<br><br>**POSB**<br>**REFERENCE**<br>(Col.1:21-22; esp. v.21)<br>Note 2<br><br>See also POSB REF:<br>(Eph.4:17-19; esp. v.18)<br>Note 1, point 3 | ἀπηλλοτριωμένους = apēllotriōmenous<br>Pronunciation: [ap-ayl-lot-ree-o'-mehn-oos]<br>Parsing (part of speech): verb<br>    Mood—participle<br>    Tense—perfect<br>    Voice—passive<br>    Case—accusative<br>    Gender—masculine<br>    Person—2nd person<br>    Number—plural<br>    Stem or root—from ἀπαλλοτριόω<br>Concordance References:<br>  ⇒ Strong's #526 apallotrioō<br>  ⇒ NIV #558 apallotrioō<br>  ⇒ NASB #526 apallotrioō<br><br>**Col. 1:21**<br>And you, that were sometime **alienated** and enemies in *your* mind by wicked works, yet now hath he reconciled [KJV]<br>And although you were formerly **alienated** and hostile in mind, *engaged* in evil deeds, [NASB]<br>Once you were **alienated from** God and were enemies in your minds because of your evil behavior. [NIV]<br>And you, who once were **alienated** and enemies in your mind by wicked works, yet now He has reconciled [NKJV]<br>This includes you who were once **so far away** from God. You were his enemies, separated from him by your evil thoughts and actions, [NLT]<br>καὶ ὑμᾶς ποτε ὄντας **ἀπηλλοτριωμένους** καὶ ἐχθροὺς τῇ διανοίᾳ ἐν τοῖς ἔργοις τοῖς πονηροῖς,. [GNS]<br>Καὶ ὑμᾶς ποτε ὄντας **ἀπηλλοτριωμένους** καὶ ἐχθροὺς τῇ διανοίᾳ ἐν τοῖς ἔργοις τοῖς πονηροῖς, [GNT] | To be alienated from; to be far away. The word means estranged, excluded, alienated, and separated because of dislike; it means to be unattached because of indifferent and unfriendly feelings.<br><br>**Practical Application**<br>Man is alienated from God...<br>• because he dislikes who God is and is unwilling to submit to the sovereignty of God and to the Lordship of Christ.<br>• because he dislikes what God says, and he refuses to give up all he is and has to obey God fully.<br>• because he feels God will overlook his sin. Man just feels that God would never condemn him, not in the final analysis.<br>• because he thinks God is far away, mostly removed from the world and the affairs of daily life. Man thinks that God is unconcerned and that He has little interest in day-to-day living. |
| **#104**<br>**Aliens**<br><br>Foreigners–KJV<br>**Aliens**–NASB<br>**Aliens**–NIV<br>Foreigners–NKJV<br>Foreigners–NLT<br><br>**POSB**<br>**REFERENCE**<br>(Eph.2:19)<br>Note 1<br><br>See also POSB REF:<br>(1 Pt.2:11)<br>Note 1 | πάροικοι = paroikoi<br>Pronunciation: [par'-oy-koy]<br>Parsing (part of speech): adjective<br>    Case—nominative<br>    Gender—masculine<br>    Number—plural<br>    Stem or root—from πάροικος, ου<br>Concordance References:<br>  ⇒ Strong's #3941 paroikos<br>  ⇒ NIV #4230 paroikos<br>  ⇒ NASB #3941 paroikos<br><br>**Ephes. 2:19**<br>Now therefore ye are no more strangers and **foreigners**, but fellowcitizens with the saints, and of the household of God; [KJV]<br>So then you are no longer strangers and **aliens**, but you are fellow citizens with the saints, and are of God's household, [NASB]<br>Consequently, you are no longer foreigners and **aliens**, but fellow citizens with God's people and members of God's household, [NIV]<br>Now, therefore, you are no longer strangers and **foreigners**, but fellow citizens with the saints and members of the household of God, [NKJV]<br>So now you Gentiles are no longer strangers and **foreigners**. You are citizens along with all of God's holy people. You are members of God's family. [NLT]<br>ἄρα οὖν οὐκέτι ἐστὲ ξένοι καὶ **πάροικοι**, ἀλλὰ συμπολῖται τῶν ἁγίων καὶ οἰκεῖοι τοῦ Θεοῦ,. [GNS]<br>ἄρα οὖν οὐκέτι ἐστὲ ξένοι καὶ **πάροικοι** ἀλλὰ ἐστὲ συμπολῖται τῶν ἁγίων καὶ οἰκεῖοι τοῦ θεοῦ, [GNT] | An alien; a sojourner; a migrant; a stranger; a foreigner; an exile.<br><br>**Practical Application**<br>It is the picture of an alien or foreigner who is in a country for a while, long enough to rent or lease a house, but he is not a permanent resident. He has no legal rights or status. He is a stranger, an exile or a foreigner who dwells in a strange land (B.C. Coffin. *First Peter*. "The Pulpit Commentary," Vol.22, p.72). There was a time when we...<br>• were outside God and His kingdom.<br>• were unknown to God and His kingdom.<br>• did not belong to God and His kingdom.<br>• were sojourners, living outside God and outside His kingdom.<br>• were alien to God and to His kingdom.<br>• were migrants, not belonging to God nor to His kingdom.<br>• were exiles to God and to His kingdom.<br>There was a time when we were as a stranger and an alien or a foreigner to God, when we were not citizens of God's kingdom. We had no relationship and no fellowship with God and no home and no rights to citizenship in His kingdom.<br><br>But note the glorious news: we are no longer strangers and aliens or foreigners to God. Jesus Christ has brought us to God (see POSB outline and notes—Ephes. 2:13-18). We are now *fellow citizens* with all of God's people. We now have a home and all the rights of citizenship in God's kingdom. |

# PRACTICAL WORD STUDIES
## in the NEW TESTAMENT

| ENGLISH WORD | GREEK WORD AND VERSE | THE WORD MEANS... |
|---|---|---|
| **#105**<br>**Aliens**<br><br>Strangers—KJV<br>**Aliens**—NASB<br>Strangers—NIV<br>Pilgrims—NKJV<br>Foreigners—NLT<br><br>**POSB<br>REFERENCE**<br>(1 Pt.1:1)<br>Note 1<br><br>See also POSB REF:<br>(1 Pt.2:11)<br>Note 1, point 2 | παρεπιδήμοις = *parepidēmois*<br>Pronunciation: [par-ep-id'-ay-moys]<br>Parsing (part of speech): pronominal adjective<br>    Case—dative<br>    Gender—masculine<br>    Number—plural<br>    Stem or root—from παρεπίδημος, ου<br>Concordance References:<br>  ⇒ Strong's #3927 parepidēmos<br>  ⇒ NIV #4215 parepidēmos<br>  ⇒ NASB #3927 parepidēmos<br><br>**1 Peter 1:1**<br>Peter, an apostle of Jesus Christ, to the **strangers** scattered throughout Pontus, Galatia, Cappadocia, Asia, and Bithynia, [KJV]<br>Peter, an apostle of Jesus Christ, to those who reside as **aliens**, scattered throughout Pontus, Galatia, Cappadocia, Asia, and Bithynia, who are chosen [NASB]<br>Peter, an apostle of Jesus Christ, To God's elect, **strangers** in the world, scattered throughout Pontus, Galatia, Cappadocia, Asia and Bithynia, [NIV]<br>Peter, an apostle of Jesus Christ, To the **pilgrims** of the Dispersion in Pontus, Galatia, Cappadocia, Asia, and Bithynia, [NKJV]<br>This letter is from Peter, an apostle of Jesus Christ. I am writing to God's chosen people who are living as **foreigners** in the lands of Pontus, Galatia, Cappadocia, the province of Asia, and Bithynia. [NLT]<br>Πέτρος, ἀπόστολος Ἰησοῦ Χριστοῦ ἐκλεκτοῖς **παρεπιδήμοις** διασπορᾶς Πόντου, Γαλατίας, Καππαδοκίας, Ἀσίας, καὶ Βιθυνίας, [GNS]<br>Πέτρος ἀπόστολος Ἰησοῦ Χριστοῦ ἐκλεκτοῖς **παρεπιδήμοις** διασπορᾶς Πόντου, Γαλατίας, Καππαδοκίας, Ἀσίας καὶ Βιθυνίας, [GNT] | Strangers, aliens, pilgrims, foreigners. The word means pilgrim, sojourner, refugee, visitor, or exile.<br><br>**Practical Application**<br>The chosen are believers, believers who are only strangers scattered over the earth. This is the descriptive picture being painted in 1 Peter 1:1. Believers are only aliens (*parepidēmois*) on earth. The idea is that of a person visiting a place for a while, but he is not a permanent resident. Believers are citizens of heaven; their home is in heaven *with God*, not on earth with the rulers of this world. The rulers and people of this earth may persecute believers, but believers are here on earth only temporarily—only as strangers, pilgrims, sojourners, aliens and exiles. |
| **#106**<br>**All**<br><br>All–KJV<br>All–NASB<br>All–NIV<br>All–NKJV<br>All–NLT<br><br>**POSB<br>REFERENCE**<br>(Lk.9:1)<br>Note 1, point 4a | πάντα = *panta*<br>Pronunciation: [pan-ta]<br>Parsing (part of speech): adjective<br>    Case—accusative<br>    Gender—neuter<br>    Number—plural<br>    Stem or root—from πᾶς, πᾶσα, πᾶν<br>Concordance References:<br>  ⇒ Strong's #3956 pas<br>  ⇒ NIV #4246 pas<br>  ⇒ NASB #3956 pas<br><br>**Luke 9:1**<br>Then he called his twelve disciples together, and gave them power and authority over **all** devils, and to cure diseases. [KJV]<br>And He called the twelve together, and gave them power and authority over **all** the demons, and to heal diseases. [NASB]<br>When Jesus had called the Twelve together, he gave them power and authority to drive out **all** demons and to cure diseases, [NIV]<br>Then He called His twelve disciples together and gave them power and authority over **all** demons, and to cure diseases. [NKJV]<br>One day Jesus called together his twelve apostles and gave them power and authority to cast out demons and to heal **all** diseases. [NLT]<br>Συγκαλεσάμενος δὲ τοὺς δώδεκα μαθητὰς αὐτοῦ, ἔδωκεν αὐτοῖς δύναμιν καὶ ἐξουσίαν ἐπὶ **πάντα** τὰ δαιμόνια, καὶ νόσους θεραπεύειν. [GNS]<br>Συγκαλεσάμενος δὲ τοὺς δώδεκα ἔδωκεν αὐτοῖς δύναμιν καὶ ἐξουσίαν ἐπὶ **πάντα** τὰ δαιμόνια καὶ νόσους θεραπεύειν [GNT] | All, any, entire, total, every, the whole.<br><br>**Practical Application**<br>The word "all" (*panta*) means that the disciple was to have power over all kinds of evil, no matter how evil and enslaving, strong and fierce, subtle and undetected. It also points to the glorious purpose of Jesus. He had come to defeat and conquer the evil forces of this world, to rout and triumph over "all" of them. |

# PRACTICAL WORD STUDIES
## in the NEW TESTAMENT

| ENGLISH WORD | GREEK WORD AND VERSE | THE WORD MEANS... |
|---|---|---|
| **#107**<br>**All Deceit**<br><br>All subtilty–KJV<br>All deceit–NASB<br>All...deceit–NIV<br>All deceit–NKJV<br>Villainy–NLT<br><br>**POSB REFERENCE**<br>(Acts 13:8-11; esp. v.10)<br>Note 4, point 3 | παντὸς δόλου = pantos dolou<br>Pronunciation: [pahn-tos dol'-oo]<br>Parsing *pantos* (part of speech): adjective<br>    Case—genative<br>    Gender—masculine<br>    Person—singular<br>    Stem or root—from πᾶς<br>Parsing *dolou* (part of speech): noun<br>    Case—genative<br>    Gender—masculine<br>    Number—singular<br>    Stem or root—from δόλος<br>Concordance References:<br>  ⇒ Strong's #3956 pas + 1388 dolos<br>  ⇒ NIV #4246 pas [all] + 1515 dolos [deceit]<br>  ⇒ NASB #3956 pas + 1388 dolos<br><br>**Acts 13:10**<br>And said, O full of **all subtilty** and all mischief, *thou* child of the devil, *thou* enemy of all righteousness, wilt thou not cease to pervert the right ways of the Lord? [KJV]<br>And said, "You who are full of **all deceit** and fraud, you son of the devil, you enemy of all righteousness, will you not cease to make crooked the straight ways of the Lord? [NASB]<br>"You are a child of the devil and an enemy of everything that is right! You are full of **all kinds of deceit** and trickery. Will you never stop perverting the right ways of the Lord? [NIV]<br>and said, "O full of **all deceit** and all fraud, *you* son of the devil, *you* enemy of all righteousness, will you not cease perverting the straight ways of the Lord? [NKJV]<br>"You son of the Devil, full of every sort of trickery and **villainy**, enemy of all that is good, will you never stop perverting the true ways of the Lord? [NLT]<br>εἶπεν, Ὦ πλήρης **παντὸς δόλου** καὶ πάσης ῥᾳδιουργίας, υἱὲ διαβόλου, ἐχθρὲ πάσης δικαιοσύνης, οὐ παύσῃ διαστρέφων τὰς ὁδοὺς Κυρίου τὰς εὐθείας; [GNS]<br>εἶπεν, Ὦ πλήρης **παντὸς δόλου** καὶ πάσης ῥᾳδιουργίας, υἱὲ διαβόλου, ἐχθρὲ πάσης δικαιοσύνης, οὐ παύσῃ διαστρέφων τὰς ὁδοὺς [τοῦ] κυρίου τὰς εὐθείας; [GNT] | All deceit, subtilty, villainy, treachery.<br><br>**Practical Application**<br>It means to be full of all craftiness, guile, trickery, deceit, treachery, seeking to bait and catch, to enslave in error and untruth. |
| **#108**<br>**All Gone Out Of The Way**<br><br>All gone out of the way–KJV<br>All have turned aside–NASB<br>All have turned away–NIV<br>Have all turned aside–NKJV<br>All have turned away from God–NLT<br><br>**POSB REFERENCE**<br>(Romans 3:10-12; esp. v.12)<br>Note 2, point 4 | πάντες ἐξέκλιναν = pantes exeklinan<br>Pronunciation: [pahn-tehs ek-ehk-lee'-nahn]<br>Parsing *exeklinan* (part of speech): verb<br>    Mood—indicative<br>    Tense—aorist<br>    Voice—active<br>    Person—3rd person<br>    Number—plural<br>    Stem or root—from ἐκκλίνω<br>Concordance References:<br>  ⇒ Strong's #3956 pas + 1578 ekklinō<br>  ⇒ NIV #4246 pas [all] + 1712 ekklinō [turned away]<br>  ⇒ NASB #3956 pas + 1578 ekklinō<br><br>**Romans 3:12**<br>They are **all gone out of the way**, they are together become unprofitable; there is none that doeth good, no, not one. [KJV]<br>**ALL HAVE TURNED ASIDE**, TOGETHER THEY HAVE BECOME USELESS; THERE IS NONE WHO DOES GOOD, THERE IS NOT EVEN ONE." [NASB]<br>**All have turned away**, they have together become worthless; there is no one who does good, not even one." [NIV]<br>They **have all turned aside**; They have together become unprofitable; There is none who does good, no, not one." [NKJV]<br>**All have turned away from God**; all have gone | To turn away; to turn aside; to go out of the way.<br><br>**Practical Application**<br>The Greek means that men lean out, turn away, and turn aside...<br>• from God.<br>• from the way that leads to God.<br>• to another way.<br>Men are crooked; they are not straight with God. They do not follow God nor pursue the right way to God. They take another path, another road, another way. |

## PRACTICAL WORD STUDIES
### in the NEW TESTAMENT

| ENGLISH WORD | GREEK WORD AND VERSE | THE WORD MEANS... |
|---|---|---|
| | wrong. No one does good, not even one." [NLT]<br>πάντες ἐξέκλιναν, ἅμα ἠχρειώθησαν· οὐκ ἔστι ὁ ποιῶν χρηστότητα, οὐκ ἔστιν ἕως ἑνός. [GNS]<br>πάντες ἐξέκλιναν ἅμα ἠχρεώθησαν· οὐκ ἔστιν ὁ ποιῶν χρηστότητα, [οὐκ ἔστιν] ἕως ἑνός. [GNT] | |
| **#109**<br>**All It Contains**<br><br>Fashion–KJV<br>Form–NASB<br>Present form–NIV<br>Form–NKJV<br>**All it contains–NLT**<br><br>**POSB<br>REFERENCE**<br>(1 Cor.7:29-31; esp. v.31)<br>Note 3 | σχῆμα = schëma<br>Pronunciation: [skhay'-mah]<br>Parsing (part of speech): noun<br>    Case—nominative<br>    Gender—neuter<br>    Number—singular<br>    Stem or root—from σχῆμα, τος<br>Concordance References:<br>⇒ Strong's #4976 schëma<br>⇒ NIV #5386 schëma [present form]<br>⇒ NASB #4976 schëma<br><br>**1 Cor. 7:31**<br>And they that use this world, as not abusing *it:* for the **fashion** of this world passeth away. [KJV]<br>And those who use the world, as though they did not make full use of it; for the **form** of this world is passing away. [NASB]<br>Those who use the things of the world, as if not engrossed in them. For this world in its **present form** is passing away. [NIV]<br>And those who use this world as not misusing *it.* For the **form** of this world is passing away. [NKJV]<br>Those in frequent contact with the things of the world should make good use of them without becoming attached to them, for this world and **all it contains** will pass away. [NLT]<br>καὶ οἱ χρώμενοι τῷ κόσμῳ τοπύτῳ, ὡς μὴ καταχρώμενοι· παράγει γὰρ τὸ **σχῆμα** τοῦ κόσμου τούτου. [GNS]<br>καὶ οἱ χρώμενοι τὸν κόσμον ὡς μὴ καταχρώμενοι· παράγει γὰρ τὸ **σχῆμα** τοῦ κόσμου τούτου. [GNT] | Present form, fashion, likeness, nature, all it [the world] contains.<br><br>**Practical Application**<br>It is a word taken from the theater. The world is nothing more than the passing scenes of a film that will soon end. The world is destined to end in its present form or fashion. The present state of things will cease just as the scenes of a film cease. The believer must keep this in mind; he must not live for the passing form of this world and all it contains. He must live for eternity, keeping before his mind that time is short, ever so short. |
| **#110**<br>**All Longsuffering**<br><br>All longsuffering–KJV<br>Great patience–NASB<br>Great patience–NIV<br>All longsuffering–NKJV<br>Patiently–NLT<br><br>**POSB<br>REFERENCE**<br>(2 Tim. 4:2)<br>Note 2, point 5a | πάσῃ μακροθυμίᾳ = pasë makrothumia<br>Pronunciation: [pah'-say mak-roth-oo-mee'-ah]<br>Parsing *pasë* (part of speech): adjective<br>    Case—dative<br>    Gender—feminine<br>    Number—singular<br>    Stem or root—from πᾶς, πᾶσα, πᾶν<br>Parsing *makrothumia* (part of speech): noun<br>    Case—dative<br>    Gender—feminine<br>    Number—singular<br>    Stem or root—from μακροθυμία, ας<br>Concordance References:<br>⇒ Strong's #3115+3956 makrothumia pas<br>⇒ NIV #3429+4246 makrothumia pas [great patience]<br>⇒ NASB #3115+3956 makrothumia pas<br><br>**2 Tim. 4:2**<br>Preach the word; be instant in season, out of season; reprove, rebuke, exhort with **all longsuffering** and doctrine. [KJV]<br>Preach the word; be ready in season *and* out of season; reprove, rebuke, exhort, with **great patience** and instruction. [NASB]<br>Preach the Word; be prepared in season and out of season; correct, rebuke and encourage—with **great patience** and careful instruction. [NIV]<br>Preach the word! Be ready in season *and* out of season. Convince, rebuke, exhort, with **all longsuffering** and teaching. [NKJV]<br>Preach the word of God. Be persistent, whether the time is favorable or not. **Patiently** correct, rebuke, and encourage your people with good teaching. [NLT] | Great patience, all longsuffering, patiently.<br><br>**Practical Application**<br>The minister must "exhort with all longsuffering" (*pasë makrothumia*). The idea is that the minister patiently endures in exhorting people—no matter the circumstances. He exhorts and exhorts, encourages and encourages. He suffers a long, long time with people...<br>• enduring whatever weaknesses and failings they have.<br>• enduring whatever evil and injury is done.<br>The minister suffers a long, long time without resentment or anger; and he never gives up, for he knows the power of Christ to change lives. |

**PRACTICAL WORD STUDIES**
**in the NEW TESTAMENT**

| ENGLISH WORD | GREEK WORD AND VERSE | THE WORD MEANS... |
|---|---|---|
| | κήρυξον τὸν λόγον, ἐπίστηθι εὐκαίρως, ἀκαίρως, ἔλεγξον, ἐπιτίμησον, παρακάλεσον, ἐν **πάσῃ μακροθυμίᾳ** καὶ διδαχῇ [GNS]<br>κήρυξον τὸν λόγον, ἐπίστηθι εὐκαίρως ἀκαίρως, ἔλεγξον, ἐπιτίμησον, παρακάλεσον, ἐν **πάσῃ μακροθυμίᾳ** καὶ διδαχῇ. [GNT] | |
| #111<br>**All Right**<br><br>Whole–KJV<br>Well–NASB<br>Healed–NIV<br>Well–NKJV<br>**All right**–NLT<br><br>**POSB**<br>**REFERENCE**<br>(Lk.8:49-56; esp. v.50)<br>Note 4, point 2<br><br>See also POSB REF:<br>(Acts 4:9-10; esp. v.9)<br>Deeper Study #4 | σωθήσεται = sōthēsetai<br>Pronunciation: [so-they'-se-tah-ee]<br>Parsing (part of speech): verb<br>   Mood—indicative<br>   Tense—future<br>   Voice—passive<br>   Person—3rd person<br>   Number—singular<br>   Stem or root—from σῴζω<br>Concordance References:<br>  ⇒ Strong's #4982 sozo<br>  ⇒ NIV #5392 sözö<br>  ⇒ NASB #4982 sozo<br><br>**Luke 8:50**<br>But when Jesus heard *it*, he answered him, saying, Fear not: believe only, and she shall be made **whole**. [KJV]<br>But when Jesus heard *this*, He answered him, "Do not be afraid *any longer*; only believe, and she shall be made **well**." [NASB]<br>Hearing this, Jesus said to Jairus, "Don't be afraid; just believe, and she will be **healed**." [NIV]<br>But when Jesus heard *it*, He answered him, saying, "Do not be afraid; only believe, and she will be made **well**." [NKJV]<br>But when Jesus heard what had happened, he said to Jairus, "Don't be afraid. Just trust me, and she will be **all right**." [NLT]<br>ὁ δὲ Ἰησοῦς ἀκούσας ἀπεκρίθη αὐτῷ, λέγων, Μὴ φοβοῦ. μόνον πίστευε, καὶ **σωθήσεται**. [GNS]<br>ὁ δὲ Ἰησοῦς ἀκούσας ἀπεκρίθη αὐτῷ, μόνον πίστευσον, καὶ **σωθήσεται**. [GNT] | Restored, made alive, saved; to make well; to preserve; to make all right.<br><br>**Practical Application**<br>Imagine the strong faith required to believe simply because of Jesus' Word, because of what He said. Jesus demonstrated His great love and amazing power. He raised Jairus' daughter. He showed that He cared for the man and the family who approached Him in belief and trust. |
| #112<br>**All Subtilty**<br><br>All subtilty–KJV<br>All deceit–NASB<br>All...deceit–NIV<br>All deceit–NKJV<br>Villainy–NLT<br><br>**POSB**<br>**REFERENCE**<br>(Acts 13:8-11; esp. v.10)<br>Note 4, point 3 | παντὸς δόλου = pantos dolou<br>Pronunciation: [pahn-tos dol'-oo]<br>Parsing *pantos* (part of speech): adjective<br>   Case—genative<br>   Gender—masculine<br>   Number—singular<br>   Stem or root—from πᾶς<br>Parsing *dolou* (part of speech): noun<br>   Case—genative<br>   Gender—masculine<br>   Number—singular<br>   Stem or root—from δόλος<br>Concordance References:<br>  ⇒ Strong's #3956 pas + 1388 dolos<br>  ⇒ NIV #4246 pas + 1515 dolos<br>  ⇒ NASB #3956 pas + 1388 dolos<br><br>**Acts 13:10**<br>And said, O full of **all subtilty** and all mischief, *thou* child of the devil, *thou* enemy of all righteousness, wilt thou not cease to pervert the right ways of the Lord? [KJV]<br>And said, "You who are full of **all deceit** and fraud, you son of the devil, you enemy of all righteousness, will you not cease to make crooked the straight ways of the Lord? [NASB]<br>"You are a child of the devil and an enemy of everything that is right! You are full of **all kinds of deceit** and trickery. Will you never stop perverting the right ways of the Lord? [NIV]<br>And said, "O full of **all deceit** and all fraud, *you* son of the devil, *you* enemy of all righteousness, will you not cease perverting the straight ways of the Lord? [NKJV] | All deceit, subtilty, villainy, treachery.<br><br>**Practical Application**<br>It means to be full of all craftiness, guile, trickery, deceit, treachery, seeking to bait and catch, to enslave in error and untruth. |

## PRACTICAL WORD STUDIES
### in the NEW TESTAMENT

| ENGLISH WORD | GREEK WORD AND VERSE | THE WORD MEANS... |
|---|---|---|
| | "You son of the Devil, full of every sort of trickery and **villainy**, enemy of all that is good, will you never stop perverting the true ways of the Lord? [NLT]<br>εἶπεν, Ὦ πλήρης **παντὸς δόλου** καὶ πάσης ῥᾳδιουργίας, υἱὲ διαβόλου, ἐχθρὲ πάσης δικαιοσύνης, οὐ παύσῃ διαστρέφων τὰς ὁδοὺς Κυρίου τὰς εὐθείας; [GNS]<br>εἶπεν, Ὦ πλήρης **παντὸς δόλου** καὶ πάσης ῥᾳδιουργίας, υἱὲ διαβόλου, ἐχθρὲ πάσης δικαιοσύνης, οὐ παύσῃ διαστρέφων τὰς ὁδοὺς [τοῦ] κυρίου τὰς εὐθείας; [GNT] | |
| **#113**<br>**All Things**<br><br>All things–KJV<br>All things–NASB<br>All things–NIV<br>All things–NKJV<br>Everything there is–NLT<br><br>**POSB REFERENCE**<br>(Jn.1:3)<br>Note 2, point 1<br><br>See also POSB REF:<br>(Col.1:16)<br>Note 1, point 2 | πάντα = panta<br>Pronunciation: [pahn-tah]<br>Parsing (part of speech): pronominal adjective<br>    Case—nominative<br>    Gender—neuter<br>    Number—plural<br>    Stem or root—from πᾶς, πᾶσα, πᾶν<br>Concordance References:<br> ⇒ Strong's #3956 pas<br> ⇒ NIV #4246 pas<br> ⇒ NASB #3956 pas<br><br>**John 1:3**<br>**All things** were made by him; and without him was not any thing made that was made. [KJV]<br>**All things** came into being by Him, and apart from Him nothing came into being that has come into being. [NASB]<br>Through him **all things** were made; without him nothing was made that has been made. [NIV]<br>**All things** were made through Him, and without Him nothing was made that was made. [NKJV]<br>He created **everything there is**. Nothing exists that he didn't make. [NLT]<br>**πάντα** δι' αὐτοῦ ἐγένετο, καὶ χωρὶς αὐτοῦ ἐγένετο οὐδὲ ἕν, ὃ γέγονεν. [GNS]<br>**πάντα** δι' αὐτοῦ ἐγένετο, καὶ χωρὶς αὐτοῦ ἐγένετο οὐδὲ ἕν. ὃ γέγονεν [GNT] | All things; everything there is; every detail of creation—not creation as a whole, but every single detail.<br><br>**Practical Application**<br>Each element and thing, each being and person—whether material or spiritual, angelic or human—has come into being by Christ. The words "all things" (*panta*) are very significant. They mean...<br>• "all things" collectively, that is, all the things within the universe were created by Christ.<br>• "all things" individually, that is, every single detail of creation, was created by Christ. Each particle and thing, each being and element has come into being by Christ and by Him alone.<br>The point is that nothing exists that was not created by Christ. All things were made by Him, even the very details of every single thing. |
| **#114**<br>**All You Need**<br><br>Sufficient–KJV<br>Sufficient–NASB<br>Sufficient–NIV<br>Sufficient–NKJV<br>All you need–NLT<br><br>**POSB REFERENCE**<br>(2 Cor.12:7-10; esp. v.9)<br>Note 3 | Ἀρκεῖ = Arkei<br>Pronunciation: [ar-keh'-ee]<br>Parsing (part of speech): verb<br>    Mood—indicative<br>    Tense—present<br>    Voice—active<br>    Person—3rd person<br>    Number—singular<br>    Stem or root—from ἀρκέω<br>Concordance References:<br> ⇒ Strong's #714 arkeö<br> ⇒ NIV #758 arkeö<br> ⇒ NASB #714 arkeö<br><br>**2 Cor. 12:9**<br>And he said unto me, My grace is **sufficient** for thee: for my strength is made perfect in weakness. Most gladly therefore will I rather glory in my infirmities, that the power of Christ may rest upon me. [KJV]<br>And He has said to me, "My grace is **sufficient** for you, for power is perfected in weakness." Most gladly, therefore, I will rather boast about my weaknesses, that the power of Christ may dwell in me. [NASB]<br>But he said to me, "My grace is **sufficient** for you, for my power is made perfect in weakness." Therefore I will boast all the more gladly about my weaknesses, so that Christ's power may rest on me. [NIV]<br>And He said to me, "My grace is **sufficient** for you, for My strength is made perfect in weakness." Therefore most gladly I will rather boast in my infirmities, that the power of Christ may rest upon me. [NKJV]<br>Each time he said, "My gracious favor is **all you need**. My power works best in your weakness." So now I | Sufficient, all you need; to be enough; the power or strength to withstand any danger.<br><br>**Practical Application**<br>The presence, love, favor, and blessings of God are sufficient to help the believer walk through any suffering. God's grace within the believer can carry the believer through anything. In Paul's case, it was physical suffering. In our case it may be either physical or spiritual attacks; but no matter: God's grace is sufficient to see us through whatever the thorn is. |

## Practical Word Studies
### in the New Testament

| ENGLISH WORD | GREEK WORD AND VERSE | THE WORD MEANS... |
|---|---|---|
| | am glad to boast about my weaknesses, so that the power of Christ may work through me. [NLT]<br><br>καὶ εἴρηκέ μοι, Ἀρκεῖ σοι ἡ χάρις μου· ἡ γὰρ δύναμις μου ἐν ἀσθενείᾳ τελειοῦται. ἥδιστα οὖν μᾶλλον καυχήσομαι ἐν ταῖς ἀσθενείαις μου, ἵνα ἐπισκηνώσῃ ἐπ' ἐμὲ ἡ δύναμις τοῦ Χριστοῦ [GNS]<br><br>καὶ εἴρηκέν μοι· Ἀρκεῖ σοι ἡ χάρις μου, ἡ γὰρ δύναμις ἐν ἀσθενείᾳ τελεῖται. ἥδιστα οὖν μᾶλλον καυχήσομαι ἐν ταῖς ἀσθενείαις μου, ἵνα ἐπισκηνώσῃ ἐπ' ἐμὲ ἡ δύναμις τοῦ Χριστοῦ. [GNT] | |
| **#115**<br>**All, One Died For**<br><br>One died for all–KJV<br>One died for all–NASB<br>One died for all–NIV<br>One died for all–NKJV<br>Christ died for everyone–NLT<br><br>**POSB REFERENCE**<br>(2 Cor.5:14-16; esp. v.14)<br>Note 4, point 1 | εἷς ὑπὲρ πάντων ἀπέθανεν = heis huper pantōn apethanen<br>Pronunciation: [ice who-pare pawn-town ap-eh-tha-nehn]<br>Parsing *pantōn* (part of speech): pronominal adjective<br>    Case—genitive<br>    Gender—masculine<br>    Number—plural<br>    Stem or root—from πᾶς, πᾶσα, πᾶν<br>Concordance References:<br>⇒ Strong's #1520 heis + 599 apothnēskō + 5228 huper + 3956 pas<br>⇒ NIV #1651 heis [one] + 633 apothnēskō [died] +5642 huper [for] + 4246 pas [all]<br>⇒ NASB #1520 heis + 599 apothnēskō + 5228 huper + 3956 pas<br><br>**2 Cor. 5:14**<br>For the love of Christ constraineth us; because we thus judge, that if **one died for all**, then were all dead: [KJV]<br>For the love of Christ controls us, having concluded this, that **one died for all**, therefore all died; [NASB]<br>For Christ's love compels us, because we are convinced that **one died for all**, and therefore all died. [NIV]<br>For the love of Christ compels us, because we judge thus: that if **One died for all**, then all died; [NKJV]<br>Whatever we do, it is because Christ's love controls us. Since we believe that **Christ died for everyone**, we also believe that we have all died to the old life we used to live. [NLT]<br>ἡ γὰρ ἀγάπη τοῦ Χριστοῦ συνέχει ἡμᾶς, κρίναντας τοῦτο, ὅτι εἰ **εἷς ὑπὲρ πάντων ἀπέθανεν**, ἄρα οἱ πάντες ἀπέθανον [GNS]<br>ἡ γὰρ ἀγάπη τοῦ Χριστοῦ συνέχει ἡμᾶς, κρίναντας τοῦτο, ὅτι **εἷς ὑπὲρ πάντων ἀπέθανεν**, ἄρα οἱ πάντες ἀπέθανον· [GNT] | One died for *all*; Christ died for *everyone*.<br><br>**Practical Application**<br>Christ died that all persons might die *in Him*. In the Greek this verse says:<br>⇒ "One died for all" (*heis huper pantōn apethanen*).<br>⇒ "Therefore, all died" (*ara hoi pantes apethanon*).<br>Note the exact words: "One died for all; therefore, all died." Paul is saying...<br>• that Jesus Christ died for all men; therefore all men died when He died.<br>• that since Christ died for all, then it follows that all men died in Him.<br>• that all men were represented in Christ when He died.<br>• that all men are counted as having died when Christ died.<br>• that Jesus Christ died the ideal death, the death that stands for all men.<br>Of course, this is simply saying the same thing in different ways so that we can more easily grasp exactly what Paul is saying. But note: the word "all" is not teaching universal salvation, that is, that every human being is saved by the death of Christ. This passage has to be kept in context with the rest of Scripture; therefore, "all" means all who are redeemed by faith in the death of Christ. |
| **#116**<br>**Allotted To**<br><br>Heritage–KJV<br>Allotted to–NASB<br>Entrusted to–NIV<br>Entrusted to–NKJV<br>Assigned to–NLT<br><br>**POSB REFERENCE**<br>(1 Pt.5:2-3; esp. v.3)<br>Note 2, point 3 | κλήρων = klērōn<br>Pronunciation: [klay'-rown]<br>Parsing (part of speech): noun<br>    Case—genitive<br>    Gender—masculine<br>    Number—plural<br>    Stem or root—from κλῆρος, ου<br>Concordance References:<br>⇒ Strong's #2819 klēros<br>⇒ NIV #3102 klēros<br>⇒ NASB #2819 klēros<br><br>**1 Peter 5:3**<br>Neither as being lords over *God's* **heritage**, but being ensamples to the flock. [KJV]<br>Nor yet as lording it over those **allotted to** your charge, but proving to be examples to the flock. [NASB]<br>Not lording it over those **entrusted to** you, but being examples to the flock. [NIV]<br>Nor as being lords over those **entrusted to** you, but being examples to the flock; [NKJV]<br>Don't lord it over the people **assigned to** your care, but lead them by your good example. [NLT]<br>μηδ' ὡς κατακυριεύοντες τῶν **κλήρων**, ἀλλὰ τύποι | Entrusted to; allotted to; assigned to.<br><br>**Practical Application**<br>This is the word that was used of Israel in the Old Testament. It means that the Jews were the people who were set apart and allotted and assigned to God. They were His very special allotment and assignment—His treasures—the people charged to His care and oversight. This is the picture painted of the elder or minister and the flock of God. God has given the minister a very special heritage or allotment and assignment: the minister has been assigned to feed the heritage of God, the very flock that belongs to God Himself.<br>Now note how the minister is to lead God's flock. He is not to lord it over them, but he is to lead by example. The minister...<br>• is not to be a dictator but an example.<br>• is not to preach one thing and do something else.<br>The minister is to lead people by living for |

# PRACTICAL WORD STUDIES
## in the NEW TESTAMENT

| ENGLISH WORD | GREEK WORD AND VERSE | THE WORD MEANS... |
|---|---|---|
| | γινόμενοι τοῦ ποιμνίου. [GNS]<br>μηδ' ὡς κατακυριεύοντες τῶν **κλήρων** ἀλλὰ τύποι γινόμενοι τοῦ ποιμνίου· [GNT] | Christ. He is to preach and teach Christ, but he is to first of all live a pure and righteous life just like Christ lived. The minister is to live exactly what he preaches. He is to be a pattern and model for Christ, a pattern and model of just what God wants His people to be. |
| **#117**<br>**Allow**<br>**Loose**<br>Loose–KJV<br>Loose–NASB<br>Loose–NIV<br>Loose–NKJV<br>Allow–NLT<br><br>**POSB REFERENCE**<br>(Mt.18:17-18; esp. v.18)<br>Note 2, point 2 | λύσητε = lusëte<br>Pronunciation: [loo'-say-teh]<br>Parsing (part of speech): verb<br>    Mood—subjunctive<br>    Tense—aorist<br>    Voice—active<br>    Person—2nd person<br>    Number—plural<br>    Stem or root—from λύω<br>Concordance References:<br>⇒ Strong's #3089 luo<br>⇒ NIV #3395 luö<br>⇒ NASB #3089 luo<br><br>**Matthew 18:18**<br>Verily I say unto you, Whatsoever ye shall bind on earth shall be bound in heaven: and whatsoever ye shall **loose** on earth shall be loosed in heaven. [KJV]<br>"Truly I say to you, whatever you shall bind on earth shall be bound in heaven; and whatever you **loose** on earth shall be loosed in heaven. [NASB]<br>"I tell you the truth, whatever you bind on earth will be bound in heaven, and whatever you **loose** on earth will be loosed in heaven. [NIV]<br>Assuredly, I say to you, whatever you bind on earth will be bound in heaven, and whatever you **loose** on earth will be loosed in heaven. [NKJV]<br>I tell you this: Whatever you prohibit on earth is prohibited in heaven, and whatever you **allow** on earth is allowed in heaven. [NLT]<br>Ἀμὴν λέγω ὑμῖν, ὅσα ἐὰν δήσητε ἐπὶ τῆς γῆς, ἔσται δεδεμένα ἐν τῷ οὐρανῷ· καὶ ὅσα ἐὰν **λύσητε** ἐπὶ τῆς γῆς, ἔσται λελυμένα ἐν τῷ οὐρανῷ. [GNS]<br>Ἀμὴν λέγω ὑμῖν· ὅσα ἐὰν δήσητε ἐπὶ τῆς γῆς ἔσται δεδεμένα ἐν οὐρανῷ, καὶ ὅσα ἐὰν **λύσητε** ἐπὶ τῆς γῆς ἔσται λελυμένα ἐν τῷ οὐρανῷ. [GNT] | To unbind; to release; to set free; to loosen what has been bound or tied. To loose a person means to set him free from spiritual bondage.<br><br>**Practical Application**<br>Why is it so important to free offending believers from the clutches of sin? There are several passages of Scripture that issue a severe warning and speak of the sinful behavior of believers...<br>• sinful behavior that causes loss of all reward by fire—a loss so great one is stripped as much as a burned-out building. It is the loss of all except the bare salvation of oneself (1 Cor. 3:11-15, esp. 1 Cor. 3:15).<br>• sinful behavior that destroys the flesh so that the Spirit may be saved (1 Cor. 5:5).<br>• sinful behavior that can cause a person to become a castaway (1 Cor. 9:27).<br>• sinful behavior that causes death for a believer (1 Cor. 11:29-30, esp. 1 John 5:30; 1 John 5:16).<br>• sinful behavior that merits no escape (Hebrews 2:1-3; Hebrews 12:25f).<br>• sinful behavior that prohibits a person from ever repenting again (Hebrews 6:4f).<br>• sinful behavior that causes a person to miss God's rest (Hebrews 4:1f).<br>• sinful behavior that prohibits any future sacrifice for sins and merits terrible punishment (Hebrews 10:26f).<br>• sinful behavior that entangles a person in the pollutions of the world after he has come to the knowledge of the Lord Jesus Christ (2 Peter 2:20).<br>• sinful behavior that leads to death (1 John 5:16). |
| **#118**<br>**Almighty–**<br>**Almighty One**<br><br>Almighty–KJV<br>Almighty–NASB<br>Almighty–NIV<br>Almighty–NKJV<br>Almighty One–NLT<br><br>**POSB REFERENCE**<br>(Rev.1:8)<br>Note 4, point 3 | παντοκράτωρ = pantokratör<br>Pronunciation: [pan-tok-rat'-ore]<br>Parsing (part of speech): noun<br>    Case—nominative<br>    Gender—masculine<br>    Number—singular<br>    Stem or root—from παντοκράτωρ, ορος<br>Concordance References:<br>⇒ Strong's #3841 pantokratör<br>⇒ NIV #4120 pantokratör<br>⇒ NASB #3841 pantokratör<br><br>**Rev. 1:8**<br>I am Alpha and Omega, the beginning and the ending, saith the Lord, which is, and which was, and which is to come, the **Almighty**. [KJV]<br>"I am the Alpha and the Omega," says the Lord God, "who is and who was and who is to come, the **Almighty**." [NASB]<br>"I am the Alpha and the Omega," says the Lord God, "who is, and who was, and who is to come, the **Almighty**." [NIV]<br>"I am the Alpha and the Omega, *the* Beginning and *the* End," says the Lord, "who is and who was and who is to | The Almighty; the Almighty One; the Controller of all; the Ruler over all.<br><br>**Practical Application**<br>Jesus Christ is the Almighty (*pantokratör*). He is the One who controls all things and rules over all things in the whole universe. This means that Jesus Christ possesses all power: He is omnipotent, able to do anything. He controls everything: the universe and every being within the universe. He controls the atoms, protons, neutrons, and electrons of space and matter. He even controls every circumstance, event, and happening throughout the universe. |

## PRACTICAL WORD STUDIES
### in the NEW TESTAMENT

| ENGLISH WORD | GREEK WORD AND VERSE | THE WORD MEANS... |
|---|---|---|
| | come, the **Almighty**." [NKJV]<br><br>"I am the Alpha and the Omega—the beginning and the end," says the Lord God. "I am the one who is, who always was, and who is still to come, the **Almighty One**." [NLT]<br><br>Ἐγώ εἰμι τὸ Α καὶ τὸ Ω, ἀρχὴ καὶ τέλος, λέγει οἱ Κύριος, ὁ ὢν καὶ ὁ ἦν καὶ ὁ ἐρχόμενος, ὁ **παντοκράτωρ**. [GNS]<br><br>Ἐγώ εἰμι τὸ Ἄλφα καὶ τὸ Ὦ, λέγει κύριος ὁ θεός, ὁ ὢν καὶ ὁ ἦν καὶ ὁ ἐρχόμενος, ὁ **παντοκράτωρ**. [GNT] | |
| **#119**<br>**Almsdeeds... Did**<br><br>Almsdeeds...did–KJV<br>Charity...continually Did–NASB<br>Helping the poor–NIV<br>Charitable deeds...did–NKJV<br>Helping the poor–NLT<br><br>**POSB REFERENCE**<br>(Acts 9:36-39; esp. v.36)<br>Note 2, point 1c | ἐλεημοσυνῶν ἐποίει = eleëmosunön epoiei<br>Pronunciation: [el-eh-ay-mos-oon'-own eh-poy-eh'-ee]<br>Parsing *eleëmosunön* (part of speech): noun<br>    Case—genitive<br>    Gender—feminine<br>    Number—plural<br>    Stem or root—from ἐλεημοσύνη, ης<br>Parsing *epoiei* (part of speech): verb<br>    Mood—indicative<br>    Tense—imperfect<br>    Voice—active<br>    Person—3rd person<br>    Number—singular<br>    Stem or root—from ποιέω<br>Concordance References:<br>  ⇒ Strong's #1654 + 4160 eleëmosunē poieō<br>  ⇒ NIV #1797+4472 eleëmosunē poieō [helping the poor]<br>  ⇒ NASB #1654 + 4160 eleëmosunē poieō<br><br>**Acts 9:36**<br>Now there was at Joppa a certain disciple named Tabitha, which by interpretation is called Dorcas: this woman was full of good works and **almsdeeds** which she **did**. [KJV]<br><br>Now in Joppa there was a certain disciple named Tabitha (which translated *in Greek* is called Dorcas); this woman was abounding with deeds of kindness and **charity**, which she **continually did**. [NASB]<br><br>In Joppa there was a disciple named Tabitha (which, when translated, is Dorcas), who was always doing good and **helping the poor**. [NIV]<br><br>At Joppa there was a certain disciple named Tabitha, which is translated Dorcas. This woman was full of good works and **charitable deeds** which she **did**. [NKJV]<br><br>There was a believer in Joppa named Tabitha (which in Greek is Dorcas). She was always doing kind things for others and **helping the poor**. [NLT]<br><br>Ἐν Ἰόππῃ δέ τις ἦν μαθήτρια ὀνόματι Ταβιθά, ἣ διερμηνευομένη λέγεται Δορκάς· αὕτη ἦν πλήρης ἀγαθῶν ἔργων καὶ **ἐλεημοσυνῶν** ὧν **ἐποίει**. [GNS]<br><br>Ἐν Ἰόππῃ δέ τις ἦν μαθήτρια ὀνόματι Ταβιθά, ἣ διερμηνευομένη λέγεται Δορκάς· αὕτη ἦν πλήρης ἔργων ἀγαθῶν καὶ **ἐλεημοσυνῶν** ὧν **ἐποίει**. [GNT] | To help the poor; to do almsdeeds; to show charity; to give to needy people; to do charitable deeds.<br><br>**Practical Application**<br>The emphasis is that Tabitha (or Dorcas) gave things, gifts which she herself made. |
| **#120**<br>**Altars**<br><br>Devotions–KJV<br>Objects of...worship–NASB<br>Objects of worship–NIV<br>Objects of...worship–NKJV<br>Altars–NLT<br><br>**POSB REFERENCE**<br>(Acts 17:23)<br>Note 3, point 1 | τὰ σεβάσματα* = ta sebasmata<br>Pronunciation: [tah seb'-as-mah-tah]<br>Parsing *sebasmata* (part of speech): noun<br>    Case—accusative<br>    Gender—neuter<br>    Number—plural<br>    Stem or root—from σέβασμα, τος<br>Concordance References:<br>  ⇒ Strong's #3588 ho + 4574 sebasma<br>  ⇒ NIV #3836 ho + 4934 sebasma<br>  ⇒ NASB #3588 ho + 4574 sebasma<br><br>**Acts 17:23**<br>For as I passed by, and beheld your **devotions**, I found an altar with this inscription, TO THE UNKNOWN GOD. Whom therefore ye ignorantly worship, him declare I unto you. [KJV] | Objects of worship; altars; places of devotion and worship.<br><br>**Practical Application**<br>It means the objects of worship such as idols, altars, images. |

## PRACTICAL WORD STUDIES
### in the NEW TESTAMENT

| ENGLISH WORD | GREEK WORD AND VERSE | THE WORD MEANS... |
|---|---|---|
| | "For while I was passing through and examining the **objects of** your **worship**, I also found an altar with this inscription, 'TO AN UNKNOWN GOD.' What therefore you worship in ignorance, this I proclaim to you. [NASB]<br><br>For as I walked around and looked carefully at your **objects of worship**, I even found an altar with this inscription: TO AN UNKNOWN GOD. Now what you worship as something unknown I am going to proclaim to you. [NIV]<br><br>For as I was passing through and considering the **objects of** your **worship,** I even found an altar with this inscription: TO THE UNKNOWN GOD. Therefore, the One whom you worship without knowing, Him I proclaim to you: [NKJV]<br><br>For as I was walking along I saw your many **altars**. And one of them had this inscription on it—'To an Unknown God.' You have been worshiping him without knowing who he is, and now I wish to tell you about him. [NLT]<br><br>διερχόμενος γὰρ καὶ ἀναθεωρῶν **τὰ σεβάσματα** ὑμῶν, εὗρον καὶ βωμὸν ἐν ᾧ ἐπεγέγραπτο, Ἀγνώστῳ Θεῷ. ὃν οὖν ἀγνοοῦντες εὐσεβεῖτε, τοῦτον ἐγὼ καταγγέλλω ὑμῖν. [GNS]<br><br>διερχόμενος γὰρ καὶ ἀναθεωρῶν **τὰ σεβάσματα** ὑμῶν εὗρον καὶ βωμὸν ἐν ᾧ ἐπεγέγραπτο, Ἀγνώστῳ θεῷ. ὃ οὖν ἀγνοοῦντες εὐσεβεῖτε, τοῦτο ἐγὼ καταγγέλλω ὑμῖν. [GNT] | |
| **#121**<br>**Always**<br><br>Continuing instant–KJV<br>Devoted–NASB<br>Faithful–NIV<br>Continuing steadfastly–NKJV<br>**Always–NLT**<br><br>**POSB REFERENCE**<br>(Romans 12:12)<br>Note 3, point 3 | **προσκαρτεροῦντες** = *proskarterountes*<br>Pronunciation: [pros-kar-ter-oon'-tehs]<br>Parsing (part of speech): verb<br>    Mood—participle (imperative sense)<br>    Tense—present<br>    Voice—active<br>    Case—nominative<br>    Gender—masculine<br>    Person—2nd person<br>    Number—plural<br>    Stem or root—from **προσκαρτερέω**<br>Concordance References:<br>  ⇒ Strong's #4342 proskartereō<br>  ⇒ NIV #4674 proskartereō<br>  ⇒ NASB #4342 proskartereō<br><br>**Romans 12:12**<br>Rejoicing in hope; patient in tribulation; **continuing instant** in prayer; [KJV]<br>Rejoicing in hope, persevering in tribulation, **devoted** to prayer, [NASB]<br>Be joyful in hope, patient in affliction, **faithful** in prayer. [NIV]<br>rejoicing in hope, patient in tribulation, **continuing steadfastly** in prayer; [NKJV]<br>Be glad for all God is planning for you. Be patient in trouble, and **always** be prayerful. [NLT]<br>τῇ ἐλπίδι χαίροντες· τῇ θλίψει ὑπομένοντες· τῇ προσευχῇ **προσκαρτεροῦντες·** [GNS]<br>τῇ ἐλπίδι χαίροντες, τῇ θλίψει ὑπομένοντες, τῇ προσευχῇ **προσκαρτεροῦντες,** [GNT] | To be faithful; to be devoted and attentive to; to give constant attention to; to give unceasing care to; to wait steadfastly upon; to persevere.<br><br>**Practical Application**<br>Very simply, the believer overcomes trials by giving constant attention to God and waiting upon His delivering power. The believer stays in constant communion with his Lord, depending upon Him to supply the strength to walk through the trials of daily living. |
| **#122**<br>**Always Honor**<br><br>Worthy–KJV<br>Worthy–NASB<br>Worthy–NIV<br>Worthy–NKJV<br>**Always honor–NLT**<br><br>**POSB REFERENCE**<br>(Col.1:10)<br>Note 2 | **ἀξίως** = *axiōs*<br>Pronunciation: [ax-ee'-oce]<br>Parsing (part of speech): adjective<br>    Type—adverb<br>    Stem or root—from **ἀξίως**<br>Concordance References:<br>  ⇒ Strong's #516 axiōs<br>  ⇒ NIV #547 axiōs<br>  ⇒ NASB #516 axiōs<br><br>**Col. 1:10**<br>That ye might walk **worthy** of the Lord unto all pleasing, being fruitful in every good work, and increasing in | Worthy; in a manner worthy of; to always honor.<br><br>**Practical Application**<br>Knowing the will of God is of no value until we have committed our lives to do it. The words "worthy" [always honor] (*axios*) means to have the weight of something else or to weigh as much as something else (Wuest, *Ephesians and Colossians,* Vol.1, p.176).<br>This means an amazing thing: our walk is to weigh as much as the walk of Christ. Our con- |

# PRACTICAL WORD STUDIES
## in the NEW TESTAMENT

| ENGLISH WORD | GREEK WORD AND VERSE | THE WORD MEANS... |
|---|---|---|
| | the knowledge of God; [KJV]<br>So that you may walk in a manner **worthy** of the Lord, to please *Him* in all respects, bearing fruit in every good work and increasing in the knowledge of God; [NASB]<br>And we pray this in order that you may live a life **worthy** of the Lord and may please him in every way: bearing fruit in every good work, growing in the knowledge of God, [NIV]<br>That you may walk **worthy** of the Lord, fully pleasing *Him,* being fruitful in every good work and increasing in the knowledge of God; [NKJV]<br>Then the way you live will **always honor** and please the Lord, and you will continually do good, kind things for others. All the while, you will learn to know God better and better. [NLT]<br>περιπατῆσαι ὑμᾶς **ἀξίως** τοῦ Κυρίου εἰς πᾶσαν ἀρεσκείαν, ἐν παντὶ ἔργῳ ἀγαθῷ καρποφοροῦντες καὶ αὐξανόμενοι εἰς τὴν ἐπιγνώσιν τοῦ Θεοῦ· [GNS]<br>περιπατῆσαι **ἀξίως** τοῦ κυρίου εἰς πᾶσαν ἀρεσκείαν, ἐν παντὶ ἔργῳ ἀγαθῷ καρποφοροῦντες καὶ αὐξανόμενοι τῇ ἐπιγνώσει τοῦ θεοῦ, [GNT] | duct is to conform to the will of God as much as the conduct of Christ. We are to live a life just as worthy as the life of Christ. The will of God is to control our behavior as much as it did the behavior of Christ. |
| **#123**<br>**Always Keep Yourselves**<br><br>Endeavouring–KJV<br>Being diligent–NASB<br>Make every effort–NIV<br>Endeavoring–NKJV<br>**Always keep yourselves–NLT**<br><br>**POSB REFERENCE**<br>(Eph.4:3)<br>Note 2 | σπουδάζοντες = *spoudazontes*<br>Pronunciation: [spoo-dad'-zon-tes]<br>Parsing (part of speech): verb<br>  Mood—participle (imperative sense)<br>  Tense—present<br>  Voice—active<br>  Case—nominative<br>  Gender—masculine<br>  Person—2nd person<br>  Number—plural<br>  Stem or root—from σπουδάζω<br>Concordance References:<br>  ⇒ Strong's #4704 spoudazō<br>  ⇒ NIV #5079 spoudazō<br>  ⇒ NASB #4704 spoudazō<br><br>**Ephes. 4:3**<br>**Endeavouring** to keep the unity of the Spirit in the bond of peace. [KJV]<br>**Being diligent** to preserve the unity of the Spirit in the bond of peace. [NASB]<br>**Make every effort** to keep the unity of the Spirit through the bond of peace. [NIV]<br>**Endeavoring** to keep the unity of the Spirit in the bond of peace. [NKJV]<br>**Always keep yourselves** united in the Holy Spirit, and bind yourselves together with peace. [NLT]<br>**σπουδάζοντες** τηρεῖν τὴν ἑνότητα τοῦ Πνεύματος ἐν τῷ συνδέσμῳ τῆς εἰρήνης. [GNS]<br>**σπουδάζοντες** τηρεῖν τὴν ἑνότητα τοῦ πνεύματος ἐν τῷ συνδέσμῳ τῆς εἰρήνης· [GNT] | To make every effort; to work hard; to be eager; to do one's best, being diligent, working to take care and to do one's very best, and to make haste to do it.<br><br>**Practical Application**<br>The only way to walk worthy of God's great calling is to work at keeping the peace and unity which God has given us. Nothing cuts the heart of God like divisiveness between His people, divisiveness which tears apart His church. The very thing God is doing is creating a new body of people to live together in the love and unity of His Son. He is going to create a new heavens and earth in which there will be no other spirit. Therefore, He expects us to live in the love and unity of His Spirit now. |
| **#124**<br>**Amazed**<br><br>Astonished–KJV<br>**Amazed–NASB**<br>**Amazed–NIV**<br>Astonished–NKJV<br>**Amazed–NLT**<br><br>**POSB REFERENCE**<br>(Lk.2:46-47; esp. v.47)<br>Note 3, point 2c | ἐξίσταντο δὲ = *existanto de*<br>Pronunciation: [ex-is'-tahn-tow de]<br>Parsing (part of speech): verb<br>  Mood—indicative<br>  Tense—imperfect<br>  Voice—middle<br>  Person—3rd person<br>  Number—plural<br>  Stem or root—from ἐξίστημι and ἐξιστάνω<br>Concordance References:<br>  ⇒ Strong's #1839 existēmi<br>  ⇒ NIV #2014 existēmi<br>  ⇒ NASB #1839 existēmi<br><br>**Luke 2:47**<br>And all that heard him were **astonished** at his understanding and answers. [KJV]<br>And all who heard Him were **amazed** at His under- | To be amazed or astonished; to be shocked or confounded; to be overwhelmed; to be in awe; to wonder; to admire; to marvel; to be surprised; to be perplexed, bewildered, dazed, confused, disconcerted.<br><br>**Practical Application**<br>In this Scripture, the word means that all were astonished, overwhelmed, bewildered, and wondered at His understanding. This is a striking lesson for both children and adults.<br>1. Every opportunity to learn the truth should be grasped.<br>2. We should thirst for knowledge and understanding. |

# PRACTICAL WORD STUDIES in the NEW TESTAMENT

| ENGLISH WORD | GREEK WORD AND VERSE | THE WORD MEANS... |
|---|---|---|
| | standing and His answers. [NASB]<br>Everyone who heard him was **amazed** at his understanding and his answers. [NIV]<br>And all who heard Him were **astonished** at His understanding and answers. [NKJV]<br>And all who heard him were **amazed** at his understanding and his answers. [NLT]<br>ἐξίσταντο δὲ πάντες οἱ ἀκούοντες αὐτοῦ ἐπὶ τῇ συνέσει καὶ ταῖς ἀποκρίσεσιν αὐτοῦ. [GNS]<br>ἐξίσταντο δὲ πάντες οἱ ἀκούοντες αὐτοῦ ἐπὶ τῇ συνέσει καὶ ταῖς ἀποκρίσεσιν αὐτοῦ. [GNT] | |
| **#125**<br>**Amazed**<br><br>Amazed–KJV<br>Amazed–NASB<br>Amazed–NIV<br>Amazed–NKJV<br>Awe–NLT<br><br>**POSB REFERENCE**<br>(Lk.9:42-43; esp. v.43)<br>Note 3, point 2<br><br>See also POSB REF:<br>(Mk.1:22)<br>Note 3 | ἐξεπλήσσοντο = *explēssonto*<br>Pronunciation: [ek-e-place'-son-tow]<br>Parsing (part of speech): verb<br>    Mood—indicative<br>    Tense—imperfect<br>    Voice—passive<br>    Person—3rd person<br>    Number—plural<br>    Stem or root—from ἐκπλήσσω<br>Concordance References:<br>  ⇒ Strong's #1605 ekplēssō<br>  ⇒ NIV #1742 ekplēssō<br>  ⇒ NASB #1605 ekplēssō<br><br>**Luke 9:43**<br>And they were all **amazed** at the mighty power of God. But while they wondered every one at all things which Jesus did, he said unto his disciples, [KJV]<br>And they were all **amazed** at the greatness of God. But while everyone was marveling at all that He was doing, He said to His disciples, [NASB]<br>And they were all **amazed** at the greatness of God. While everyone was marveling at all that Jesus did, he said to his disciples, [NIV]<br>And they were all **amazed** at the majesty of God. But while everyone marveled at all the things which Jesus did, He said to His disciples, [NKJV]<br>**Awe** gripped the people as they saw this display of God's power. While everyone was marveling over all the wonderful things he was doing, Jesus said to his disciples, [NLT]<br>ἐξεπλήσσοντο δὲ πάντες ἐπὶ τῇ μεγαλειότητι τοῦ Θεοῦ. Πάντων δὲ θαυμαζόντων ἐπὶ πᾶσιν οἷς ἐποίει ὁ Ἰησοῦς, εἶπε πρὸς τοὺς μαθητὰς αὐτοῦ, [GNS]<br>ἐξεπλήσσοντο δὲ πάντες ἐπὶ τῇ μεγαλειότητι τοῦ θεοῦ. Πάντων δὲ θαυμαζόντων ἐπὶ πᾶσιν οἷς ἐποίει εἶπεν πρὸς τοὺς μαθητὰς αὐτοῦ, [GNT] | To be amazed; to be overwhelmed; to be in awe.<br><br>**Practical Application**<br>Note the dramatic account found in this Scripture: The people who observed Jesus' delivering the boy from the unclean spirit marvelled at what they had seen. They were all *amazed* at "the greatness of God." |
| **#126**<br>**Amazed**<br><br>Wondered–KJV<br>Wondering–NASB<br>Amazed–NIV<br>Marveled–NKJV<br>Amazed–NLT<br><br>**POSB REFERENCE**<br>(Lk.4:22-23; esp. v.22)<br>Note 4, point 1 | ἐθαύμαζον = *ethaumazon*<br>Pronunciation: [eh-thou-mad'-zon]<br>Parsing (part of speech): verb<br>    Mood—indicative<br>    Tense—imperfect<br>    Voice—active<br>    Person—3rd person<br>    Number—plural<br>    Stem or root—from θαυμάζω<br>Concordance References:<br>  ⇒ Strong's #2296 thaumazō<br>  ⇒ NIV #2513 thaumazō<br>  ⇒ NASB #2296 thaumazō<br><br>**Luke 4:22**<br>And all bare him witness, and **wondered** at the gracious words which proceeded out of his mouth. And they said, Is not this Joseph's son? [KJV]<br>And all were speaking well of Him, and **wondering** at the gracious words which were falling from His lips; and they were saying, "Is this not Joseph's son?" [NASB]<br>All spoke well of him and were **amazed** at the gracious words that came from his lips. "Isn't this Joseph's | To wonder; to be amazed; to marvel.<br><br>**Practical Application**<br>The people of Jesus' home town began to marvel and to be amazed at the gracious words flowing from His mouth. They were taking pride in one of the sons of their neighbors, a son who was so capable. |

## PRACTICAL WORD STUDIES in the NEW TESTAMENT

| ENGLISH WORD | GREEK WORD AND VERSE | THE WORD MEANS... |
|---|---|---|
| | son?" they asked. [NIV]<br>So all bore witness to Him, and **marveled** at the gracious words which proceeded out of His mouth. And they said, "Is this not Joseph's son?" [NKJV]<br>All who were there spoke well of him and were **amazed** by the gracious words that fell from his lips. "How can this be?" they asked. "Isn't this Joseph's son?" [NLT]<br>καὶ πάντες ἐμαρτύρουν αὐτῷ, καὶ **ἐθαύμαζον** ἐπὶ τοῖς λόγοις τῆς χάριτος, τοῖς ἐκπορευομένοις ἐκ τοῦ στόματος αὐτοῦ, καὶ ἔλεγον, Οὐχ οὗτος ἐστιν οἱ υἱός Ἰωσὴφ; [GNS]<br>Καὶ πάντες ἐμαρτύρουν αὐτῷ καὶ **ἐθαύμαζον** ἐπὶ τοῖς λόγοις τῆς χάριτος τοῖς ἐκπορευομένοις ἐκ τοῦ στόματος αὐτοῦ καὶ ἔλεγον, Οὐχὶ υἱός ἐστιν Ἰωσὴφ οὗτος; [GNT] | |
| **#127**<br>**Amazed**<br><br>**Amazed**–KJV<br>**Amazed**–NASB<br>Astonished–NIV<br>**Amazed**–NKJV<br>**Amazed**–NLT<br><br>**POSB REFERENCE**<br>(Acts 9:21)<br>Note 4<br><br>See also POSB REF:<br>(Acts 10:44-45; esp. v.45)<br>Note 1, point 4 | ἐξίσταντο = existanto<br>Pronunciation: [ex-is'-tahn-tow]<br>Parsing (part of speech): verb<br>    Mood—indicative<br>    Tense—imperfect<br>    Voice—middle<br>    Person—3rd person<br>    Number—plural<br>    Stem or root—from ἐξίστημι and ἐξιστάνω<br>Concordance References:<br>⇒ Strong's #1839 existēmi<br>⇒ NIV #2014 existēmi<br>⇒ NASB #1839 existēmi<br><br>**Acts 9:21**<br>But all that heard *him* were **amazed**, and said; Is not this he that destroyed them which called on this name in Jerusalem, and came hither for that intent, that he might bring them bound unto the chief priests? [KJV]<br>And all those hearing him continued to be **amazed**, and were saying, "Is this not he who in Jerusalem destroyed those who called on this name, and *who* had come here for the purpose of bringing them bound before the chief priests?" [NASB]<br>All those who heard him were **astonished** and asked, "Isn't he the man who raised havoc in Jerusalem among those who call on this name? And hasn't he come here to take them as prisoners to the chief priests?" [NIV]<br>Then all who heard were **amazed**, and said, "Is this not he who destroyed those who called on this name in Jerusalem, and has come here for that purpose, so that he might bring them bound to the chief priests?" [NKJV]<br>All who heard him were **amazed**. "Isn't this the same man who persecuted Jesus' followers with such devastation in Jerusalem?" they asked. "And we understand that he came here to arrest them and take them in chains to the leading priests." [NLT]<br>**ἐξίσταντο** δὲ πάντες οἱ ἀκούοντες, καὶ ἔλεγον, Οὐχ οὗτός ἐστιν ὁ πορθήσας εἰς Ἰερουσαλὴμ τοὺς ἐπικαλουμένους τὸ ὄνομα τοῦτο, καὶ ὧδε εἰς τοῦτο ἐληλύθει ἵνα δεδεμένους αὐτοὺς ἀγάγῃ ἐπὶ τοὺς ἀρχιερεῖς; [GNS]<br>**ἐξίσταντο** δὲ πάντες οἱ ἀκούοντες καὶ ἔλεγον, Οὐχ οὗτός ἐστιν ὁ πορθήσας εἰς Ἰερουσαλὴμ τοὺς ἐπικαλουμένους τὸ ὄνομα τοῦτο, καὶ ὧδε εἰς τοῦτο ἐληλύθει ἵνα δεδεμένους αὐτοὺς ἀγάγῃ ἐπὶ τοὺς ἀρχιερεῖς; [GNT] | To be astonished; to be amazed; to be shocked or confounded, overwhelmed, bewildered.<br><br>**Practical Application**<br>It means that they were amazed, astounded, shocked at what they were seeing. Paul stood as a testimony to the community. The public and leaders of the synagogue were amazed (*existanto*), astonished, astounded, shocked at what they were seeing.<br>1. They were expecting an inflamed antagonist storming the homes and meeting places of those who "called on the name of Jesus." They knew he had been sent to arrest and chain not only the men but the women followers of Jesus and to drag them back to Jerusalem for treason and death.<br>2. Instead, they were witnessing a man radically changed, a man...<br>• associating and identifying himself with those whom he had come to destroy.<br>• preaching like a flaming evangel, proclaiming Jesus to be the Messiah and the Son of God. |
| **#128**<br>**Amazed**<br><br>Greatly amazed–KJV<br>**Amazed**–NASB<br>Overwhelmed with wonder–NIV<br>**Amazed**–NKJV<br>In awe–NLT | ἐξεθαμβήθησαν = exethambēthēsan<br>Pronunciation: [ek-eh-tham-bayth'-ay-sahn]<br>Parsing (part of speech): verb<br>    Mood—indicative<br>    Tense—aorist<br>    Voice—passive<br>    Person—3rd person<br>    Number—plural<br>    Stem or root—from ἐκθαμβέομαι | To be filled with wonder; to be overwhelmed with wonder and awe; to be amazed—greatly amazed.<br><br>**Practical Application**<br>What amazed the people when they "saw" Jesus?<br>1. Perhaps Jesus retained some of the glory of |

## PRACTICAL WORD STUDIES
### in the New Testament

| ENGLISH WORD | GREEK WORD AND VERSE | THE WORD MEANS... |
|---|---|---|
| **POSB REFERENCE** (Mk.9:15) *Deeper Study #1* | Concordance References:<br>⇒ Strong's #1568 ekthambeo<br>⇒ NIV #1701 ekthambeō<br>⇒ NASB #1568 ekthambeo<br><br>**Mark 9:15**<br>And straightway all the people, when they beheld him, were **greatly amazed**, and running to *him* saluted him. [KJV]<br>And immediately, when the entire crowd saw Him, they were **amazed**, and *began* running up to greet Him. [NASB]<br>As soon as all the people saw Jesus, they were **overwhelmed with wonder** and ran to greet him. [NIV]<br>Immediately, when they saw Him, all the people were greatly **amazed**, and running to *Him*, greeted Him. [NKJV]<br>The crowd watched Jesus **in awe** as he came toward them, and then they ran to greet him. [NLT]<br>καὶ εὐθέως πᾶς ὁ ὄχλος ἰδὼν αὐτὸν **ἐξεθαμβήθη**, καὶ προστρέχοντες ἠσπάζοντο αὐτόν. [GNS]<br>καὶ εὐθὺς πᾶς ὁ ὄχλος ἰδόντες αὐτὸν **ἐξεθαμβήθησαν** καὶ προστρέχοντες ἠσπάζοντο αὐτόν. [GNT] | the transfiguration (cp. Exodus 34:29 when Moses came down from the mountain after having been with God). The people may have seen a glow, a majestic countenance about Jesus.<br>2. Perhaps Jesus came at such an opportune time that the people were amazed to see Him, as though His timing was destined. He arrived just when His disciples needed help.<br>3. Perhaps Jesus walked with a renewed air, a more authoritative and decisive countenance than before. Just coming from the transfiguration was bound to instill a renewed confidence and authority within Him. |
| **#129**<br>**Amazed–Amazement**<br><br>Amazed–KJV<br>Amazed–NASB<br>Amazed–NIV<br>Amazed–NKJV<br>Amazement–NLT<br><br>**POSB REFERENCE** (Mk.1:27-28; esp. v.27) Note 3, point 1 | ἐθαμβήθησαν = ethambethesan<br>Pronunciation: [eh-tham-bay'-thay-sahn]<br>Parsing (part of speech): verb<br>   Mood—indicative<br>   Tense—aorist<br>   Voice—passive<br>   Person—3rd person<br>   Number—plural<br>   Stem or root—from θαμβέομαι<br>Concordance References:<br>⇒ Strong's #2284 thambeo<br>⇒ NIV #2501 thambeō<br>⇒ NASB #2284 thambeo<br><br>**Mark 1:27**<br>And they were all **amazed**, insomuch that they questioned among themselves, saying, What thing is this? what new doctrine *is* this? for with authority commandeth he even the unclean spirits, and they do obey him. [KJV]<br>And they were all **amazed**, so that they debated among themselves, saying, "What is this? A new teaching with authority! He commands even the unclean spirits, and they obey Him." [NASB]<br>The people were all so **amazed** that they asked each other, "What is this? A new teaching—and with authority! He even gives orders to evil spirits and they obey him." [NIV]<br>Then they were all **amazed**, so that they questioned among themselves, saying, "What is this? What new doctrine *is* this? For with authority He commands even the unclean spirits, and they obey Him." [NKJV]<br>**Amazement** gripped the audience, and they began to discuss what had happened. "What sort of new teaching is this?" they asked excitedly. "It has such authority! Even evil spirits obey his orders!" [NLT]<br>καὶ **ἐθαμβήθησαν** πάντες, ὥστε συζητεῖν πρὸς αὐτοὺς, λέγοντας, Τί ἐστι τοῦτο; τις ἡ διδαχὴ ἡ καινὴ αὕτη, ὅτι κατ' ἐξουσίαν καὶ τοῖς πνεύμασι τοῖς ἀκαθάρτοις ἐπιτάσσει, καὶ ὑπακούουσιν αὐτῷ. [GNS]<br>καὶ **ἐθαμβήθησαν** ἅπαντες ὥστε συζητεῖν πρὸς ἑαυτοὺς λέγοντας, Τί ἐστιν τοῦτο; διδαχὴ καινὴ κατ' ἐξουσίαν· καὶ τοῖς πνεύμασι τοῖς ἀκαθάρτοις ἐπιτάσσει, καὶ ὑπακούουσιν αὐτῷ. [GNT] | To be filled with wonder, to be overwhelmed with wonder and awe, to be amazed—greatly amazed.<br><br>**Practical Application**<br>In this Scripture, the word literally means to be knocked silly, to be struck with amazement. The people were amazed at Jesus' teaching and His ability to subject evil spirits to His authority. |
| **#130**<br>**Amazed–Amazement** | ἐξίσταντο = existanto<br>Pronunciation: [ex-is'-tawn-tow]<br>Parsing (part of speech): verb<br>   Mood—indicative | To be astonished; to be amazed; to be shocked or confounded, overwhelmed, bewildered, and left wondering. |

# PRACTICAL WORD STUDIES
## in the NEW TESTAMENT

| ENGLISH WORD | GREEK WORD AND VERSE | THE WORD MEANS... |
|---|---|---|
| Amazed–KJV<br>Amazement–NASB<br>Amazed–NIV<br>Amazed–NKJV<br>Amazed–NLT<br><br>**POSB REFERENCE**<br>(Acts 2:12-13; esp. v.12)<br>Note 6 | Tense—imperfect<br>Voice—middle<br>Person—3rd person<br>Number—plural<br>Stem or root—from ἐξίστημι<br>Concordance References:<br>⇒ Strong's #1839 existëmi<br>⇒ NIV #2014 existëmi<br>⇒ NASB #1839 existëmi<br><br>**Acts 2:12**<br>And they were all **amazed**, and were in doubt, saying one to another, What meaneth this? [KJV]<br>And they all continued in **amazement** and great perplexity, saying to one another, "What does this mean?" [NASB]<br>**Amazed** and perplexed, they asked one another, "What does this mean?" [NIV]<br>So they were all **amazed** and perplexed, saying to one another, "Whatever could this mean?" [NKJV]<br>They stood there **amazed** and perplexed. "What can this mean?" they asked each other. [NLT]<br>Ἐξίσταντο δὲ πάντες καὶ διηπόρουν, ἄλλος πρὸς ἄλλον λέγοντες, Τί ἂν θέλει τοῦτο εἶναι; [GNS]<br>ἐξίσταντο δὲ πάντες καὶ διηπόρουν, ἄλλος πρὸς ἄλλον λέγοντες, Τί θέλει τοῦτο εἶναι; [GNT] | **Practical Application**<br>All were amazed (*existanto*) and astonished, marveling at what was happening. There was a twofold reaction.<br>1. Some were attracted, perplexed and wondering, at a loss as to what was happening. But they were attracted enough to seek meaning in it all.<br>2. Others simply mocked, accusing the disciples of being drunk. (Just imagine the ecstatic joy flooding their hearts for them to behave in a way to cause such a charge! Where is the infilling of such joy today?) |
| **#131**<br>**Ambassadors**<br><br>Ambassadors–KJV<br>Ambassadors–NASB<br>Ambassadors–NIV<br>Ambassadors–NKJV<br>Ambassadors–NLT<br><br>**POSB REFERENCE**<br>(2 Cor.5:20)<br>Note 3, point 1 | πρεσβεύομεν = *presbeuomen*<br>Pronunciation: [pres-byoo'-o-mehn]<br>Parsing (part of speech): verb<br>  Mood—indicative<br>  Tense—present<br>  Voice—active<br>  Person—1st person<br>  Number—plural<br>  Stem or root—from πρεσβεύω<br>Concordance References:<br>⇒ Strong's #4243 presbeuö<br>⇒ NIV #4563 presbeuö<br>⇒ NASB #4243 presbeuö<br><br>**2 Cor. 5:20**<br>Now then we are **ambassadors** for Christ, as though God did beseech *you* by us: we pray *you* in Christ's stead, be ye reconciled to God. [KJV]<br>Therefore, we are **ambassadors** for Christ, as though God were entreating through us; we beg you on behalf of Christ, be reconciled to God. [NASB]<br>We are therefore Christ's **ambassadors**, as though God were making his appeal through us. We implore you on Christ's behalf: Be reconciled to God. [NIV]<br>Now then, we are **ambassadors** for Christ, as though God were pleading through us: we implore *you* on Christ's behalf, be reconciled to God. [NKJV]<br>We are Christ's **ambassadors**, and God is using us to speak to you. We urge you, as though Christ himself were here pleading with you, "Be reconciled to God!" [NLT]<br>ὑπὲρ Χριστοῦ οὖν **πρεσβεύομεν**, ὡς τοῦ θεοῦ παρακαλοῦντος δι' ἡμῶν· δεόμεθα ὑπὲρ Χριστοῦ, καταλλάγητε τῷ θεῷ. [GNS]<br>ὑπὲρ Χριστοῦ οὖν **πρεσβεύομεν** ὡς τοῦ θεοῦ παρακαλοῦντος δι' ἡμῶν· δεόμεθα ὑπὲρ Χριστοῦ, καταλλάγητε τῷ θεῷ. [GNT] | Ambassadors, representatives, envoys, messengers.<br><br>**Practical Application**<br>Ministers and other believers are given the highest of titles: they are "Christ's ambassadors." The "ambassadors" (*presbeuomen*) are persons who are sent forth as official envoys to represent the Sender and to announce the message of the Sender. Four things are always true about the ambassador.<br>⇒ The ambassador belongs to the One who sent him out.<br>⇒ The ambassador is commissioned to be sent out. He exists only for the purpose for which he was sent.<br>⇒ The ambassador possesses all the authority and power of the One who sent him out.<br>⇒ The ambassador is sent forth with the message of the Sender. |
| **#132**<br>**Ambition**<br><br>Labour–KJV<br>**Ambition**–NASB<br>Make it...goal–NIV<br>Make it...aim–NKJV<br>Aim is–NLT | φιλοτιμούμεθα = *philotimoumetha*<br>Pronunciation: [fil-ot-im-oo'-meh-tha]<br>Parsing (part of speech): verb<br>  Mood—indicative<br>  Tense—present<br>  Voice—middle or passive deponent<br>  Person—1st person<br>  Number—plural<br>  Stem or root—from φιλοτιμέομαι | To make a goal; to constantly aim; to be constantly ambitious; to strive earnestly.<br><br>**Practical Application**<br>Judgment stirs in us the longing to please God and to receive our heavenly home. Judgment stirs "ambition" (*philotimoumetha*) in order to please God. Paul says that he is to be judged; |

PRACTICAL WORD STUDIES
in the NEW TESTAMENT

| ENGLISH WORD | GREEK WORD AND VERSE | THE WORD MEANS... |
|---|---|---|
| **POSB REFERENCE** (2 Cor.5:9-10; esp. v.9) Note 4 | Concordance References:<br>⇒ Strong's #5389 philotimeomai<br>⇒ NIV #5818 philotimeomai<br>⇒ NASB #5389 philotimeomai<br><br>**2 Cor. 5:9**<br>Wherefore we **labour**, that, whether present or absent, we may be accepted of him. [KJV]<br>Therefore also we have as our **ambition**, whether at home or absent, to be pleasing to Him. [NASB]<br>So we **make it** our **goal** to please him, whether we are at home in the body or away from it. [NIV]<br>Therefore we **make it** our **aim**, whether present or absent, to be well pleasing to Him. [NKJV]<br>So our **aim is** to please him always, whether we are here in this body or away from this body. [NLT]<br>διὸ καὶ **φιλοτιμούμεθα**, εἴτε ἐνδημοῦντες, εἴτε ἐκδημοῦντες, εὐάρεστοι αὐτῷ εἶναι. [GNS]<br>διὸ καὶ **φιλοτιμούμεθα**, εἴτε ἐνδημοῦντες εἴτε ἐκδημοῦντες, εὐάρεστοι αὐτῷ εἶναι. [GNT] | therefore, he works his fingers to the bone. Why? That he may please (*euarestoi*) God. |
| **#133**<br>**Ambition, Make It**<br><br>Study–KJV<br>**Make it...ambition**–NASB<br>**Make it...ambition**–NIV<br>Aspire–NKJV<br>**Ambition**–NLT<br><br>**POSB REFERENCE** (1 Thes.4:11) Note 2 | φιλοτιμεῖσθαι = *philotimeisthai*<br>Pronunciation: [fil-ot-im-ees'-tha-ee]<br>Parsing (part of speech): verb<br>   Mood—infinitive<br>   Tense—present<br>   Voice—middle or passive deponent<br>   Stem or root—from φιλοτιμέομαι<br>Concordance References:<br>⇒ Strong's #5389 philotimeomai<br>⇒ NIV #5818 philotimeomai<br>⇒ NASB #5389 philotimeomai<br><br>**1 Thes. 4:11**<br>And that ye **study** to be quiet, and to do your own business, and to work with your own hands, as we commanded you; [KJV]<br>And to **make it** your **ambition** to lead a quiet life and attend to your own business and work with your hands, just as we commanded you; [NASB]<br>**Make it** your **ambition** to lead a quiet life, to mind your own business and to work with your hands, just as we told you, [NIV]<br>That you also **aspire** to lead a quiet life, to mind your own business, and to work with your own hands, as we commanded you, [NKJV]<br>This should be your **ambition**: to live a quiet life, minding your own business and working with your hands, just as we commanded you before. [NLT]<br>καὶ **φιλοτιμεῖσθαι** ἡσυχάζειν καὶ πράσσειν τὰ ἴδια, καὶ ἐργάζεσθαι ταῖς ἰδίαις χερσὶν ὑμῶν, καθὼς ὑμῖν παρηγγείλαμεν· [GNS]<br>καὶ **φιλοτιμεῖσθαι** ἡσυχάζειν καὶ πράσσειν τὰ ἴδια καὶ ἐργάζεσθαι ταῖς [ἰδίαις] χερσὶν ὑμῶν, καθὼς ὑμῖν παρηγγείλαμεν, [GNT] | To make it one's ambition or goal; to study; to aspire; to endeavor; to be ambitious; to strive eagerly; to seek with all one's energy.<br><br>**Practical Application**<br>The very meaning of the word *ambition* shows the supreme importance of quietness. We must seek to be quiet and learn to be quiet. |
| **#134**<br>**Among You**<br><br>Within you–KJV<br>In your midst–NASB<br>Within you–NIV<br>Within you–NKJV<br>**Among you**–NLT<br><br>**POSB REFERENCE** (Lk.17:20-21; esp. v.21) Note 1, point 2 | ἐντὸς ὑμῶν = *entos humōn*<br>Pronunciation: [en-tos' hu-mown]<br>Parsing *entos* (part of speech): preposition<br>   Case—genitive<br>   Stem or root—from ἐντός<br>Parsing *humōn* (part of speech): noun pronoun<br>   Case—genitive<br>   Person—2nd person<br>   Number—plural<br>   Stem or root—from σύ<br>Concordance References:<br>⇒ Strong's #1787 entos + 5216 humon<br>⇒ NIV #1955 entos [within] + 5148 su [you]<br>⇒ NASB #1787 entos + 5216 humon<br><br>**Luke 17:21**<br>Neither shall they say, Lo here! or, lo there! for, behold, the kingdom of God is **within you**. [KJV] | Within you, among you, inside of you, or in your midst.<br><br>**Practical Application**<br>Some say this should be translated "among you." If so, then Christ is saying that He is the embodiment of the Kingdom of God. He is setting up the Kingdom of God among them, right there and then. God is already beginning to rule and reign in the lives He is touching.<br>Others say the words mean "within you." If so, then the kingdom is to be looked for within the hearts and lives of people. The Kingdom of God is spiritual; it is the changing of hearts, the rule and reign of God within men's lives. It is the power of God to take a sinful, immoral, and |

# PRACTICAL WORD STUDIES
## in the NEW TESTAMENT

| ENGLISH WORD | GREEK WORD AND VERSE | THE WORD MEANS... |
|---|---|---|
| | nor will they say, 'Look, here *it is!*' or, 'There *it is!*' For behold, the kingdom of God is **in your midst**." [NASB]<br>Nor will people say, 'Here it is,' or 'There it is,' because the kingdom of God is **within you**." [NIV]<br>Nor will they say, 'See here!' or 'See there!' For indeed, the kingdom of God is **within you**." [NKJV]<br>You won't be able to say, 'Here it is!' or 'It's over there!' For the Kingdom of God is **among you**." [NLT]<br>οὐδὲ ἐροῦσιν, Ἰδοὺ ὧδε, ἤ, Ἰδοὺ ἐκεῖ. ἰδοὺ γὰρ, ἡ βασιλεία τοῦ Θεοῦ **ἐντὸς ὑμῶν** ἐστιν. [GNS]<br>οὐδὲ ἐροῦσιν, Ἰδοὺ ὧδε ἤ, Ἐκεῖ, ἰδοὺ γὰρ ἡ βασιλεία τοῦ θεοῦ **ἐντὸς ὑμῶν** ἐστιν. [GNT] | unjust man and change him into a servant of God. |
| **#135**<br>**Anathema**<br><br>Anathema–KJV<br>Accursed–NASB<br>Curse–NIV<br>Accursed–NKJV<br>Cursed–NLT<br><br>**POSB REFERENCE**<br>(1 Cor.16:19-24; esp. v.22)<br>Note 6, point 2 | ἀνάθεμα = *anathema*<br>Pronunciation: [an-ath'-em-ah]<br>Parsing (part of speech): noun<br>    Case—nominative<br>    Gender—neuter<br>    Number—singular<br>    Stem or root—from ἀνάθεμα, τος<br>Concordance References:<br>  ⇒ Strong's #331 anathema<br>  ⇒ NIV #353 anathema<br>  ⇒ NASB #331 anathema<br><br>**1 Cor. 16:22**<br>If any man love not the Lord Jesus Christ, let him be **Anathema** Maranatha. [KJV]<br>If anyone does not love the Lord, let him be **accursed**. Maranatha. [NASB]<br>If anyone does not love the Lord—a **curse** be on him. Come, O Lord! [NIV]<br>If anyone does not love the Lord Jesus Christ, let him be **accursed**. O Lord, come! [NKJV]<br>If anyone does not love the Lord, that person is **cursed**. Our Lord, come! [NLT]<br>εἴ τις οὐ φιλεῖ τὸν Κύριον Ἰησοῦν Χριστόν, ἤτω **ἀνάθεμα**. Μαρὰν ἀθα. [GNS]<br>εἴ τις οὐ φιλεῖ τὸν κύριον, ἤτω **ἀνάθεμα**. Μαρανα θα. [GNT] | Cursed, accursed, under the ban, cast away. It is something doomed to utter destruction.<br><br>**Practical Application**<br>There was the terrifying importance of love for Christ. Paul uses the word (*anathema*) four times (Romans 9:3; 1 Cor. 12:3; 1 Cor. 16:22; Galatians 1:8; cp. Acts 23:14). The word "maranatha" means the Lord comes! The idea is that any man (singular) who does not love the Lord Jesus Christ will be accursed. And the Lord is coming; therefore this person will be accursed (*anathema*). |
| **#136**<br>**Anchor**<br><br>Anchor–KJV<br>Anchor–NASB<br>Anchor–NIV<br>Anchor–NKJV<br>Anchor–NLT<br><br>**POSB REFERENCE**<br>(Heb.6:18-20; esp. v.19)<br>Note 6, point 2 | ἄγκυραν = *agkuran*<br>Pronunciation: [ang'-koo-rahn]<br>Parsing (part of speech): noun<br>    Case—accusative<br>    Gender—feminine<br>    Number—singular<br>    Stem or root—from ἄγκυρα, ας<br>Concordance References:<br>  ⇒ Strong's #45 agkura<br>  ⇒ NIV #46 agkura<br>  ⇒ NASB #45 agkura<br><br>**Hebrews 6:19**<br>Which *hope* we have as an **anchor** of the soul, both sure and stedfast, and which entereth into that within the veil; [KJV]<br>This hope we have as an **anchor** of the soul, a *hope* both sure and steadfast and one which enters within the veil, [NASB]<br>We have this hope as an **anchor** for the soul, firm and secure. It enters the inner sanctuary behind the curtain, [NIV]<br>This *hope* we have as an **anchor** of the soul, both sure and steadfast, and which enters the Presence *behind* the veil, [NKJV]<br>This confidence is like a strong and trustworthy **anchor** for our souls. It leads us through the curtain of heaven into God's inner sanctuary. [NLT]<br>ἣν ὡς **ἄγκυραν** ἔχομεν τῆς ψυχῆς ἀσφαλῆ τε καὶ βεβαίαν, καὶ εἰσερχομένην εἰς τὸ ἐσώτερον τοῦ καταπετάσματος [GNS]<br>ἣν ὡς **ἄγκυραν** ἔχομεν τῆς ψυχῆς ἀσφαλῆ τε καὶ βεβαίαν καὶ εἰσερχομένην εἰς τὸ ἐσώτερον τοῦ καταπετάσματος, [GNT] | Anchor, base, support, tie-down.<br><br>**Practical Application**<br>Our hope in God is an anchor for the believer's soul. The word "anchor" (*agkuran*) refers to the anchor used by ships to hold the ship in a certain place. The anchor keeps it from floating aimlessly about and being damaged or sunk by floating upon the rocks of forbidden shores. God's promise of an eternal land (heaven) is what anchors the believer's soul and...<br>• keeps it from floating aimlessly about.<br>• keeps it from floating upon the rocks of forbidden shores.<br>Note: the anchor of hope is both sure and steadfast. It cannot slip and it cannot break; it will hold the believer no matter what storms or violence are launched against it. |

## PRACTICAL WORD STUDIES
### in the NEW TESTAMENT

| ENGLISH WORD | GREEK WORD AND VERSE | THE WORD MEANS... |
|---|---|---|
| **#137**<br>**And**<br><br>And–KJV<br>And–NASB<br>And–NIV<br>And–NKJV<br>And–NLT<br><br>**POSB REFERENCE**<br>(Jn.3:5)<br>*Deeper Study #2* | καί = *kai*<br>Pronunciation: [kah-ee]<br>Parsing (part of speech): conjunction<br>    Type—coordinating<br>    Stem or root—from καί<br>Concordance References:<br>  ⇒ Strong's #2532 kai<br>  ⇒ NIV #2779 kai<br>  ⇒ NASB #2532 kai<br><br>**John 3:5**<br>Jesus answered, Verily, verily, I say unto thee, Except a man be born of water **and** *of* the Spirit, he cannot enter into the kingdom of God. [KJV]<br>Jesus answered, "Truly, truly, I say to you, unless one is born of water **and** the Spirit, he cannot enter into the kingdom of God. [NASB]<br>Jesus answered, "I tell you the truth, no one can enter the kingdom of God unless he is born of water **and** the Spirit. [NIV]<br>Jesus answered, "Most assuredly, I say to you, unless one is born of water **and** the Spirit, he cannot enter the kingdom of God. [NKJV]<br>Jesus replied, "The truth is, no one can enter the Kingdom of God without being born of water **and** the Spirit. [NLT]<br>ἀπεκρίθη ὁ Ἰησοῦς, Ἀμὴν ἀμὴν λέγω σοι, ἐὰν μή τις γεννηθῇ ἐξ ὕδατος **καὶ** Πνεύματος, οὐ δύναται εἰσελθεῖν εἰς τὴν βασιλείαν τοῦ Θεοῦ. [GNS]<br>ἀπεκρίθη Ἰησοῦς, Ἀμὴν ἀμὴν λέγω σοι, ἐὰν μή τις γεννηθῇ ἐξ ὕδατος **καὶ** πνεύματος, οὐ δύναται εἰσελθεῖν εἰς τὴν βασιλείαν τοῦ θεοῦ. [GNT] | In addition to, also, plus, including, together with. The word "and" can also be translated "even."<br><br>**Practical Application**<br>The word "and" (*kai*) translated here is left up to the translator. In light of the rest of Scripture, it probably should be translated "even." This would mean that water with all of its cleansing power is a symbol of the Holy Spirit: "No one can enter the kingdom of God unless he is born of water even the Spirit." A strong argument for this is in the very next verse where the new birth is said to be spiritual, apart from any natural phenomenon. It has nothing to do with any physical substance, including water. It is not of the flesh, not of any material thing. It is of the Spirit (cp. Romans 8:11; Ephes. 2:1). |
| **#138**<br>**And You–**<br>**And Thou**<br><br>And thou–KJV<br>And you–NASB<br>And you–NIV<br>And you–NKJV<br>And you–NLT<br><br>**POSB REFERENCE**<br>(Rom.11:17)<br>Note 1, point 2 | σὺ δέ = *su de*<br>Pronunciation: [soo deh]<br>Parsing (part of speech): noun pronoun<br>    Case—nominative<br>    Person—2nd person<br>    Number—singular<br>    Stem or root—from σύ<br>Concordance References:<br>  ⇒ Strong's #1161 de + 4771 su<br>  ⇒ NIV #1254 de [and]+ 5148 su [you]<br>  ⇒ NASB #1161 de + 4771 su<br><br>**Romans 11:17**<br>And if some of the branches be broken off, **and thou**, being a wild olive tree, wert graffed in among them, and with them partakest of the root and fatness of the olive tree; [KJV]<br>But if some of the branches were broken off, **and you**, being a wild olive, were grafted in among them and became partaker with them of the rich root of the olive tree, [NASB]<br>If some of the branches have been broken off, **and you**, though a wild olive shoot, have been grafted in among the others and now share in the nourishing sap from the olive root, [NIV]<br>And if some of the branches were broken off, **and you,** being a wild olive tree, were grafted in among them, and with them became a partaker of the root and fatness of the olive tree, [NKJV]<br>But some of these branches from Abraham's tree, some of the Jews, have been broken off. **And you** Gentiles, who were branches from a wild olive tree, were grafted in. So now you also receive the blessing God has promised Abraham and his children, sharing in God's rich nourishment of his special olive tree. [NLT]<br>εἰ δέ τινες τῶν κλάδων ἐξεκλάσθησαν, **σὺ δὲ** ἀγριέλαιος ὢν ἐνεκεντρίσθης ἐν αὐτοῖς, καὶ συγκοινωνὸς τῆς ῥίζης καὶ τῆς πιότητος τῆς ἐλαίας ἐγένου, [GNS]<br>Εἰ δέ τινες τῶν κλάδων ἐξεκλάσθησαν, **σὺ δὲ** ἀγριέλαιος ὢν ἐνεκεντρίσθης ἐν αὐτοῖς καὶ συγκοινωνὸς τῆς ῥίζης τῆς πιότητος τῆς ἐλαίας ἐγένου, [GNT] | And you.<br><br>**Practical Application**<br>Some wild olive branches were grafted into the shoot. Note that the words "and thou" or "you" (*kai su*) is singular. Paul is not speaking to Gentiles as a whole, but to the individual Gentile. Note two things:<br>a. The Gentile believer is said to have been a *wild olive branch*. The word "wild" means that the Gentile was not part of the olive shoot (God); he was outside and estranged and alienated from the olive shoot (God). Therefore, he was...<br>  • part of the desert wilderness and uncultivated world.<br>  • growing loose and uncontrolled.<br>  • useless and worthless.<br>  • uncared for and unprotected.<br>  • insect-infested and sour and inferior.<br><br>b. The Gentile believer is now said to have been grafted into the olive shoot. He is now attached to God, that is, in a right relationship with God: Therefore, he now partakes of the root and fatness of the olive shoot. Very simply, this means that the believer is fed and nourished by God. |

# PRACTICAL WORD STUDIES
## in the NEW TESTAMENT

| ENGLISH WORD | GREEK WORD AND VERSE | THE WORD MEANS... |
|---|---|---|
| **#139**<br>**Angels**<br><br>**Angels–KJV**<br>**Angels–NASB**<br>**Angels–NIV**<br>**Angels–NKJV**<br>**Angels–NLT**<br><br>**POSB**<br>**REFERENCE**<br>(Heb.1:4-14; esp. v.4)<br>*Deeper Study* #1<br><br>See also POSB REF:<br>(Rev.2:8)<br>Note 1<br>(Rev.20:1-2; esp. v.1)<br>Note 1<br>(Rev.1:20)<br>Note 7 | ἀγγέλων = aggelōn<br>Pronunciation: [ang'-el-on]<br>Parsing (part of speech): noun<br>    Case—genitive<br>    Gender—masculine<br>    Number—plural<br>    Stem or root—from ἄγγελος, ου<br>Concordance References:<br>   ⇒ Strong's #32 aggelos<br>   ⇒ NIV #34 aggelos<br>   ⇒ NASB #32 aggelos<br><br>**Hebrews 1:4**<br>Being made so much better than the **angels**, as he hath by inheritance obtained a more excellent name than they. [KJV]<br>Having become as much better than the **angels**, as He has inherited a more excellent name than they. [NASB]<br>So he became as much superior to the **angels** as the name he has inherited is superior to theirs. [NIV]<br>Having become so much better than the **angels**, as He has by inheritance obtained a more excellent name than they. [NKJV]<br>This shows that God's Son is far greater than the **angels**, just as the name God gave him is far greater than their names. [NLT]<br>τοσούτῳ κρείττων γενόμενος τῶν **ἀγγέλων**, ὅσῳ διαφορώτερον παρ' αὐτοὺς κεκληρονόμηκεν ὄνομα. [GNS]<br>τοσούτῳ κρείττων γενόμενος τῶν **ἀγγέλων** ὅσῳ διαφορώτερον παρ' αὐτοὺς κεκληρονόμηκεν ὄνομα. [GNT] | Angel, messenger, one who is sent.<br><br>**Practical Application**<br>The word is used at least five different ways in Scripture.<br>⇒ It is used of men (Luke 7:24; James 2:25; Rev. 1:20; Rev. 2:1, 8, 12, 18; Rev. 3:1, 7, 14).<br>⇒ It is used of Christ (Rev. 8:3-5).<br>⇒ It is used of the "angel of the Lord" or the "angel of God," meaning the presence of deity in angelic form (Genesis 16:1-13; Genesis 21:17-19; Genesis 22:11-16; Genesis 31:11-13; Exodus 3:2-4; Judges 2:1; Judges 6:12-16; Judges 13:3-22).<br>⇒ It is used of prophets (Haggai 1:13).<br>⇒ It is used of spiritual beings who serve God (Psalm 104:4; Hebrews 1:14; Hebrews 2:2, 5).<br><br>1. The important facts about angels seem to be as follows:<br>  a. Angels are created beings, superior to men (Psalm 104:4; cp. Hebrews 1:14; Col. 1:16).<br>  b. Angels are numerous (Psalm 68:17; Matthew 26:53; Hebrews 12:22; Rev. 5:11).<br>  c. Angels are extremely superior to men in intelligence and knowledge (2 Samuel 14:20; Psalm 103:20; Psalm 104:4).<br>  d. Angels have great power (2 Kings 19:35; Matthew 28:3; 2 Peter 2:11; Rev. 20:1-2).<br>  e. Angels observe men (Eccles. 5:6; 1 Cor. 4:9; Ephes. 3:10).<br>  f. Some angels have fallen with Satan from their original state (2 Peter 2:4; Jude 6; Rev. 20:10. See POSB Master Subject Index—Satan and POSB Master Subject Index—Evil Spirits.)<br><br>2. Apparently, angels were created in various ranks and for specific functions to be performed *before God Himself.*<br>  a. There is the archangel Michael who stands above all the other angels. He is the prime administrator of God (Daniel 10:21; Daniel 12:1, 7-12; 1 Thes. 4:16; Jude 9). Some believe Satan was an archangel, before his fall, superior even to Michael, (see POSB note—Rev. 12:7).<br>  b. There is the angel Gabriel who is God's very special messenger of mercy (Daniel 8:15-16; Daniel 9:21; Luke 1:19-33). He is never called an archangel.<br>  c. The Scripture gives the titles of other angelic orders.<br>    ⇒ There are the seraphim, whose function seems to be to praise God (Isaiah 6:1-6, the only reference to them).<br>    ⇒ There are the cherubim, whose function seems to be to proclaim the glory of God (Genesis 3:24; Exodus 25:18; Psalm 80:1; Psalm 99:2).<br>  d. Other angels are said to have various functions... |

## PRACTICAL WORD STUDIES
### in the NEW TESTAMENT

| ENGLISH WORD | GREEK WORD AND VERSE | THE WORD MEANS... |
|---|---|---|
| | | • to worship God (Neh. 9:6; Luke 2:13-14).<br>• to rejoice in the repentance of a single sinner (Luke 15:10).<br>• to accompany Christ at His second coming (Matthew 24:31; Matthew 25:31; Mark 8:38; 1 Thes. 4:16).<br>• to execute the judgments of God (Genesis 3:24; Genesis 19:1; Judges 5:23; 2 Samuel 24:16; 1 Chron. 2:15; 2 Chron. 32:32; Acts 12:23; 2 Peter 2:4; Jude 6; Rev. 12:9).<br><br>3. Angels have a very important function in God's dealings with believers. Note what Scripture says: "They [are] ministering spirits sent to serve those who will inherit salvation" (Hebrews 1:14—NIV).<br>   a. They protect and deliver believers either through or from trials (Psalm 34:7; Psalm 91:11; Isaiah 63:9; Daniel 3:28; Daniel 6:22; Acts 12:7-11).<br>   b. They guide and lead believers in their ministry (1 Kings 19:5; Matthew 2:13, 19-20; Acts 5:19; Acts 8:26).<br>   c. They escort believers into heaven (Luke 16:22).<br>   d. They encourage believers (Acts 27:23-25). Note: this assistance seems to begin at childhood and to continue on throughout life (Hebrews 1:14; cp. Matthew 18:10; Psalm 91:11). |
| **#140**<br>**Angels, Like Angels, Equal Unto The**<br><br>Equal unto the angels–KJV<br>Like angels–NASB<br>Like angels–NIV<br>Equal to the angels–NKJV<br>Like angels–NLT<br><br>**POSB REFERENCE**<br>(Lk.20:36)<br>Note 5, point 1 | ἰσάγγελοι = *isaggeloi*<br>Pronunciation: [ee-sang'-el-o-ee]<br>Parsing (part of speech): adjective<br>    Case—nominative<br>    Gender—masculine<br>    Number—plural<br>    Stem or root—from ἰσάγγελος, ον<br>Concordance References:<br>  ⇒ Strong's #2465 isaggelos<br>  ⇒ NIV #2694 isaggelos<br>  ⇒ NASB #2465 isaggelos<br><br>**Luke 20:36**<br>Neither can they die any more: for they are **equal unto the angels**; and are the children of God, being the children of the resurrection. [KJV]<br>For neither can they die anymore, for they are **like angels**, and are sons of God, being sons of the resurrection. [NASB]<br>And they can no longer die; for they are **like** the **angels**. They are God's children, since they are children of the resurrection. [NIV]<br>Nor can they die anymore, for they are **equal to the angels** and are sons of God, being sons of the resurrection. [NKJV]<br>And they will never die again. In these respects they are **like angels**. They are children of God raised up to new life. [NLT]<br>οὔτε γὰρ ἀποθανεῖν ἔτι δύνανται, **ἰσάγγελοι** γάρ εἰσι, καὶ υἱοί εἰσι τοῦ θεοῦ, τῆς ἀναστάσεως υἱοὶ ὄντες. [GNS]<br>οὐδὲ γὰρ ἀποθανεῖν ἔτι δύνανται, **ἰσάγγελοι** γάρ εἰσιν καὶ υἱοί εἰσιν θεοῦ τῆς ἀναστάσεως υἱοὶ ὄντες. [GNT] | Like or equal to an angel.<br><br>**Practical Application**<br>This word means that believers will have a nature like the angels: be glorified, be their peers, live in the joy of working and serving God just as the angels do. It means believers will have all the glorious being and privileges and responsibilities that angels have. |
| **#141**<br>**Anger** | θυμός = *thumos*<br>Pronunciation: [thoo-mos']<br>Parsing (part of speech): noun<br>    Case—nominative | Anger, wrath, fury, indignation, rage. It means God's wrath against sin. |

# PRACTICAL WORD STUDIES
## in the New Testament

| ENGLISH WORD | GREEK WORD AND VERSE | THE WORD MEANS... |
|---|---|---|
| Wrath–KJV<br>Indignation–NASB<br>**Anger–NIV**<br>Wrath–NKJV<br>**Anger–NLT**<br><br>**POSB REFERENCE**<br>(Romans 2:8)<br>*Deeper Study #7* | Gender—masculine<br>Number—singular<br>Stem or root—from θυμός, ου<br>Concordance References:<br>⇒ Strong's #2372 thumos<br>⇒ NIV #2596 thumos<br>⇒ NASB #2372 thumos<br><br>**Romans 2:8**<br>But unto them that are contentious, and do not obey the truth, but obey unrighteousness, indignation and **wrath**, [KJV]<br>But to those who are selfishly ambitious and do not obey the truth, but obey unrighteousness, wrath and **indignation**. [NASB]<br>But for those who are self-seeking and who reject the truth and follow evil, there will be wrath and **anger**. [NIV]<br>But to those who are self-seeking and do not obey the truth, but obey unrighteousness—indignation and **wrath**, [NKJV]<br>But he will pour out his **anger** and wrath on those who live for themselves, who refuse to obey the truth and practice evil deeds. [NLT]<br>τοῖς δὲ ἐξ ἐριθείας, καὶ ἀπειθοῦσι μὲν τῇ ἀληθείᾳ πειθομένοις δὲ τῇ ἀδικίᾳ, **θυμός** καὶ ὀργή, [GNS]<br>τοῖς δὲ ἐξ ἐριθείας καὶ ἀπειθοῦσι τῇ ἀληθείᾳ πειθομένοις δὲ τῇ ἀδικίᾳ ὀργὴ καὶ **θυμός**. [GNT] | **Practical Application**<br>*Thumos* is an anger that is felt more deeply than the *orge* anger of God; therefore, it arises more quickly. *Thumos* anger is the anger that arises out of deep hurt; therefore, it bursts forth with terrifying judgment. (See POSB *Deeper Study #1*, God's Wrath—Romans 1:18 for verses.) |
| #142<br>**Anger–Angry**<br><br>Angry–KJV<br>Angry–NASB<br>Anger–NIV<br>Angry–NKJV<br>Anger–NLT<br><br>**POSB REFERENCE**<br>(Eph.4:26-27; esp. v.26)<br>Note 2<br><br>See also POSB REF:<br>(Eph.4:31)<br>Note 6, point 3<br>(Col.3:8-11; esp. v.8)<br>Note 2<br>(Romans 1:18)<br>*Deeper Study #1* | ὀργίζεσθε = *orgizesthe*<br>Pronunciation: [or-gid'-zehs-theh]<br>Parsing (part of speech): verb<br>  Mood—imperative<br>  Tense—present<br>  Voice—middle or passive deponent<br>  Person—2nd person<br>  Number—plural<br>Concordance References:<br>⇒ Strong's #3710 orgizō<br>⇒ NIV #3974 orgizō<br>⇒ NASB #3710 orgizō<br><br>**Ephes. 4:26**<br>Be ye **angry**, and sin not: let not the sun go down upon your wrath: [KJV]<br>BE ANGRY, AND *yet* DO NOT SIN; do not let the sun go down on your anger, [NASB]<br>"In your **anger** do not sin": Do not let the sun go down while you are still angry, [NIV]<br>"Be **angry**, and do not sin": do not let the sun go down on your wrath, [NKJV]<br>And "don't sin by letting **anger** gain control over you." Don't let the sun go down while you are still angry, [NLT]<br>**ὀργίζεσθε** καὶ μὴ ἁμαρτάνετε· ὁ ἥλιος μὴ ἐπιδυέτω ἐπὶ τῷ παροργισμῷ ὑμῶν, [GNS]<br>**ὀργίζεσθε** καὶ μὴ ἁμαρτάνετε· ὁ ἥλιος μὴ ἐπιδυέτω ἐπὶ [τῷ] παροργισμῷ ὑμῶν, [GNT] | To be angry, enraged, furious.<br><br>**Practical Application**<br>The believer is to strip away the garment of anger. Men do become angry: note that Scripture recognizes this. There are times when anger is called for, but we are to guard against sinning when we become angry. Anger causes us to either react, lash out and hurt others, or else it motivates us to right wrongs and correct injustices.<br>1. There is wrong anger or what may be called unjustified or selfish anger.<br>  a. There is the anger that broods, that is selfish. It harbors malice; it will not forget; it lingers; it broods; it wills revenge and sometimes seeks revenge.<br>  b. There is the anger that holds contempt (*raca*). It despises; it ridicules; it arrogantly exalts self and calls another person empty and useless. This is an anger that is full of malice. It despises and scorns (*raca*). It arises from pride—a proud wrath (Proverbs 21:24). Such feelings or anger walk over and trample a person. It says that whatever ill comes upon a person is deserved.<br>  c. There is the anger that curses. It seeks to destroy a man and his reputation morally, intellectually, and spiritually.<br>2. There is right anger or what may be called justified anger (*orgizesthe*). The believer must be an angry person—angry with those who sin and do wrong and who are unjust and selfish in their behavior. However, a justified anger is always disciplined and controlled; it is always limited to those who do wrong either against God or against others. The distinguishing mark between justified and unjustified anger is that a justified anger is never selfish; it is never shown |

# PRACTICAL WORD STUDIES
## in the NEW TESTAMENT

| ENGLISH WORD | GREEK WORD AND VERSE | THE WORD MEANS... |
|---|---|---|
| | | because of what has happened to oneself. It is an anger that is purposeful. The believer knows that he is angry for a legitimate reason, and he seeks to correct the situation in the most peaceful way possible (see POSB note—Romans 12:18; POSB note—John 2:12-16). |
| **#143**<br>**Angry Tempers**<br><br>Wraths–KJV<br>**Angry tempers–**<br>**NASB**<br>Outbursts of anger–NIV<br>Outbursts of wrath–NKJV<br>Outbursts of anger–NLT<br><br>**POSB**<br>**REFERENCE**<br>(2 Cor.12:19-21; esp. v.20)<br>Note 3, point 2 | θυμοί = thumoi<br>Pronunciation: [thoo-moy']<br>Parsing (part of speech): noun<br>    Case—nominative<br>    Gender—masculine<br>    Number—plural<br>    Stem or root—from θυμός, ου<br>Concordance References:<br>  ⇒ Strong's #2372 thumos<br>  ⇒ NIV #2596 thumos<br>  ⇒ NASB #2372 thumos<br><br>**2 Cor. 12:20**<br>For I fear, lest, when I come, I shall not find you such as I would, and *that* I shall be found unto you such as ye would not: lest *there be* debates, envyings, **wraths**, strifes, backbitings, whisperings, swellings, tumults: [KJV]<br>For I am afraid that perhaps when I come I may find you to be not what I wish and may be found by you to be not what you wish; that perhaps *there may be* strife, jealousy, **angry tempers**, disputes, slanders, gossip, arrogance, disturbances; [NASB]<br>For I am afraid that when I come I may not find you as I want you to be, and you may not find me as you want me to be. I fear that there may be quarreling, jealousy, **outbursts of anger**, factions, slander, gossip, arrogance and disorder. [NIV]<br>For I fear lest, when I come, I shall not find you such as I wish, and *that* I shall be found by you such as you do not wish; lest *there be* contentions, jealousies, **outbursts of wrath**, selfish ambitions, backbitings, whisperings, conceits, tumults; [NKJV]<br>For I am afraid that when I come to visit you I won't like what I find, and then you won't like my response. I am afraid that I will find quarreling, jealousy, **outbursts of anger**, selfishness, backstabbing, gossip, conceit, and disorderly behavior. [NLT]<br>φοβοῦμαι γὰρ μή πως ἐλθὼν οὐχ οἵους θέλω εὕρω ὑμᾶς, κἀγὼ εὑρεθῶ ὑμῖν οἷον οὐ θέλετε· μή πως ἔρις, ζῆλοι, **θυμοί**, ἐριθεῖαι, καταλαλιαί, ψιθυρισμοί, φυσιώσεις, ἀκαταστασίαι [GNS]<br>φοβοῦμαι γὰρ μή πως ἐλθὼν οὐχ οἵους θέλω εὕρω ὑμᾶς κἀγὼ εὑρεθῶ ὑμῖν οἷον οὐ θέλετε· μή πως ἔρις, ζῆλος, **θυμοί**, ἐριθεῖαι, καταλαλιαί, ψιθυρισμοί, φυσιώσεις, ἀκαταστασίαι [GNT] | Outbursts of anger; angry tempers; fiery anger; intense fits of anger.<br><br>**Practical Application**<br>Paul was stricken with fear, fear lest the church fail to be what it should be and reject him and his ministry. Paul feared that the church would fail to deal with the carnal critics and continue putting up with their evil attacks against him. He lists eight evils, including angry tempers (*thumoi*) that were and still are characteristic of divisive critics in the church. |
| **#144**<br>**Angry, Had**<br>**Been Very**<br><br>Was...displeased–KJV<br>Was very angry–NASB<br>Had been quarreling–NIV<br>**Had been very**<br>**angry–NKJV**<br>Was very angry–NLT<br><br>**POSB**<br>**REFERENCE**<br>(Acts 12:18-23; esp. v.20)<br>Note 3, point 1 | Ἦν θυμομαχῶν = Ēn thumomachōn<br>Pronunciation: [ayne thoo-mom-ach-on]<br>Parsing *thumomachōn* (part of speech): verb<br>    Mood—participle<br>    Tense—present<br>    Voice—active<br>    Case—nominative<br>    Gender—masculine<br>    Number—singular<br>    Stem or root—from θυμομαχέω<br>Concordance References:<br>  ⇒ Strong's #1510 eimi + 2371 thumomacheō<br>  ⇒ NIV #1639 eimi [been] + 2595 thumomacheō [quarreling]<br>  ⇒ NASB #1510 eimi + 2371 thumomacheō<br><br>**Acts 12:20**<br>And Herod **was** highly **displeased** with them of Tyre and Sidon: but they came with one accord to him, and, | To be very angry; to be displeased; to quarrel in an irate way.<br><br>**Practical Application**<br>Herod's nature is seen in the phrase "had been very angry" (*Ēn thumomachōn*). It means to be inflamed; to be filled with violent hostility. It is very hot anger, an emotion that should never characterize the leader of a nation. |

# PRACTICAL WORD STUDIES
## in the NEW TESTAMENT

| ENGLISH WORD | GREEK WORD AND VERSE | THE WORD MEANS... |
|---|---|---|
| | having made Blastus the king's chamberlain their friend, desired peace; because their country was nourished by the king's *country*. [KJV]<br><br>Now he **was very angry** with the people of Tyre and Sidon; and with one accord they came to him, and having won over Blastus the king's chamberlain, they were asking for peace, because their country was fed by the king's country. [NASB]<br><br>He **had been quarreling** with the people of Tyre and Sidon; they now joined together and sought an audience with him. Having secured the support of Blastus, a trusted personal servant of the king, they asked for peace, because they depended on the king's country for their food supply. [NIV]<br><br>Now Herod **had been very angry** with the people of Tyre and Sidon; but they came to him with one accord, and having made Blastus the king's personal aide their friend, they asked for peace, because their country was supplied with food by the king's *country*. [NKJV]<br><br>Now Herod **was very angry** with the people of Tyre and Sidon. So they sent a delegation to make peace with him because their cities were dependent upon Herod's country for their food. They made friends with Blastus, Herod's personal assistant, [NLT]<br><br>Ἦν δὲ ὁ Ἡρώδης **θυμομαχῶν** Τυρίοις καὶ Σιδωνίοις· τὴν ὁμοθυμαδὸν δὲ παρῆσαν πρὸς αὐτόν, καὶ πείσαντες Βλάστον τὸν ἐπὶ τοῦ κοιτῶνος τοῦ βασιλέως, ᾐτοῦντο εἰρήνην, διὰ τὸ τρέφεσθαι αὐτῶν τὴν χώραν ἀπὸ τῆς βασιλικῆς. [GNS]<br><br>Ἦν δὲ **θυμομαχῶν** Τυρίοις καὶ Σιδωνίοις· ὁμοθυμαδὸν δὲ παρῆσαν πρὸς αὐτόν καὶ πείσαντες Βλάστον, τὸν ἐπὶ τοῦ κοιτῶνος τοῦ βασιλέως, ᾐτοῦντο εἰρήνην διὰ τὸ τρέφεσθαι αὐτῶν τὴν χώραν ἀπὸ τῆς βασιλικῆς. [GNT] | |
| **#145**<br>**Angry, Was Very**<br><br>Was...displeased–KJV<br>**Was very angry–NASB**<br>Had been quarreling–NIV<br>Had been very angry–NKJV<br>**Was very angry–NLT**<br><br>**POSB REFERENCE**<br>(Acts 12:18-23; esp. v.20)<br>Note 3, point 1 | Ἦν θυμομαχῶν = Ēn thumomachōn<br>Pronunciation: [ayne thoo-mom-ach-on]<br>Parsing *thumomachōn* (part of speech): verb<br>    Mood—participle<br>    Tense—present<br>    Voice—active<br>    Case—nominative<br>    Gender—masculine<br>    Number—singular<br>    Stem or root—from θυμομαχέω<br>Concordance References:<br>⇒ Strong's #1510 eimi + 2371 thumomacheō<br>⇒ NIV #1639 eimi [been] + 2595 thumomacheō [quarreling]<br>⇒ NASB #1510 eimi + 2371 thumomacheō<br><br>**Acts 12:20**<br>And Herod **was** highly **displeased** with them of Tyre and Sidon: but they came with one accord to him, and, having made Blastus the king's chamberlain their friend, desired peace; because their country was nourished by the king's *country*. [KJV]<br><br>Now he **was very angry** with the people of Tyre and Sidon; and with one accord they came to him, and having won over Blastus the king's chamberlain, they were asking for peace, because their country was fed by the king's country. [NASB]<br><br>He **had been quarreling** with the people of Tyre and Sidon; they now joined together and sought an audience with him. Having secured the support of Blastus, a trusted personal servant of the king, they asked for peace, because they depended on the king's country for their food supply. [NIV]<br><br>Now Herod **had been very angry** with the people of Tyre and Sidon; but they came to him with one accord, and having made Blastus the king's personal aide their friend, they asked for peace, because their country was supplied with food by the king's *country*. [NKJV]<br><br>Now Herod **was very angry** with the people of Tyre | To be very angry; to be displeased; to quarrel in an irate way.<br><br>**Practical Application**<br>Herod's nature is seen in the phrase "was very angry" (*Ēn thumomachōn*). The phase means to be inflamed; to be filled with violent hostility. It is very hot anger, an emotion that should never characterize the leader of a nation. |

# PRACTICAL WORD STUDIES
## in the NEW TESTAMENT

| ENGLISH WORD | GREEK WORD AND VERSE | THE WORD MEANS... |
|---|---|---|
| | and Sidon. So they sent a delegation to make peace with him because their cities were dependent upon Herod's country for their food. They made friends with Blastus, Herod's personal assistant. [NLT]<br><br>Ἦν δὲ ὁ Ἡρῴδης **θυμομαχῶν** Τυρίοις καὶ Σιδωνίοις· τὴν ὁμοθυμαδὸν δὲ παρῆσαν πρὸς αὐτόν, καὶ πείσαντες Βλάστον τὸν ἐπὶ τοῦ κοιτῶνος τοῦ βασιλέως, ᾐτοῦντο εἰρήνην, διὰ τὸ τρέφεσθαι αὐτῶν τὴν χώραν ἀπὸ τῆς βασιλικῆς. [GNS]<br><br>Ἦν δὲ **θυμομαχῶν** Τυρίοις καὶ Σιδωνίοις· ὁμοθυμαδὸν δὲ παρῆσαν πρὸς αὐτόν καὶ πείσαντες Βλάστον, τὸν ἐπὶ τοῦ κοιτῶνος τοῦ βασιλέως, ᾐτοῦντο εἰρήνην διὰ τὸ τρέφεσθαι αὐτῶν τὴν χώραν ἀπὸ τῆς βασιλικῆς. [GNT] | |
| **#146**<br>**Anguish**<br><br>Being in an agony– KJV<br>Being in agony–NASB<br>**Being in anguish– NIV**<br>Being in agony–NKJV<br>In such agony–NLT<br><br>**POSB REFERENCE**<br>(Lk.22:43-44; esp. v.44)<br>Note 4, point 2 | γενόμενος ἐν ἀγωνίᾳ = *genomenos en agōnia*<br>Pronunciation: [ghin'-om-en-os en ag-o-nee'-ah]<br>Parsing *genomenos* (part of speech): verb<br>   Mood—participle<br>   Tense—aorist<br>   Voice—middle deponent<br>   Case—nominative<br>   Gender—masculine<br>   Number—singular<br>   Stem or root—from γίνομαι<br>Parsing *agōnia* (part of speech): noun<br>   Case—dative<br>   Gender—feminine<br>   Number—singular<br>   Stem or root—from ἀγωνία, ας<br>Concordance References:<br>⇒ Strong's #1096 ginomai + 1722 en + 74 agonia<br>⇒ NIV #1181 ginomai [being] + 1877 en [in] + 75 agōnia [anguish]<br>⇒ NASB #1096 ginomai + 1722 en + 74 agonia<br><br>**Luke 22:44**<br>And **being in an agony** he prayed more earnestly: and his sweat was as it were great drops of blood falling down to the ground. [KJV]<br>And **being in agony** He was praying very fervently; and His sweat became like drops of blood, falling down upon the ground. [NASB]<br>And **being in anguish**, he prayed more earnestly, and his sweat was like drops of blood falling to the ground. [NIV]<br>And **being in agony**, He prayed more earnestly. Then His sweat became like great drops of blood falling down to the ground. [NKJV]<br>He prayed more fervently, and he was **in such agony** of spirit that his sweat fell to the ground like great drops of blood. [NLT]<br>καὶ **γενόμενος ἐν ἀγωνίᾳ**, ἐκτενέστερον προσηύχετο. ἐγένετο δὲ ὁ ἱδρὼς αὐτοῦ ὡσεὶ θρόμβοι αἵματος καταβαίνοντος ἐπὶ τὴν γῆν. [GNS]<br>καὶ **γενόμενος ἐν ἀγωνίᾳ** ἐκτενέστερον προσηύχετο· καὶ ἐγένετο ὁ ἱδρὼς αὐτοῦ ὡσεὶ θρόμβοι αἵματος καταβαίνοντος ἐπὶ τὴν γῆν. [GNT] | To be in agony, anguish, a very real pain. It means to be distressed, grieved, pained with great anguish.<br><br>**Practical Application**<br>The Greek *genomenos* (aorist participle) means Jesus experienced a growing anguish. The weight upon Him was not only intense, it grew more and more intense. The pressure and sense of suffering became heavier and heavier. The picture is that of His becoming engrossed and embodied in anguish. Thus, He prayed more and more earnestly. His prayer grew and increased in intensity even as His anguish intensified. |
| **#147**<br>**Anguish**<br><br>Sorrowful–KJV<br>Grieved–NASB<br>Sorrowful–NIV<br>Sorrowful–NKJV<br>**Anguish–NLT**<br><br>**POSB REFERENCE**<br>(Mt.26:37)<br>*Deeper Study* #3 | λυπεῖσθαι = *lupeisthai*<br>Pronunciation: [loo-pehs'-thigh]<br>Parsing (part of speech): verb<br>   Mood—infinitive<br>   Tense—present<br>   Voice—passive<br>   Stem or root—from λυπέω<br>Concordance References:<br>⇒ Strong's #3076 lupeö<br>⇒ NIV #3382 lupeö<br>⇒ NASB #3076 lupeö<br><br>**Matthew 26:37**<br>And he took with him Peter and the two sons of | To be distressed; to be grieved; to be saddened; to be hurt; to be pained with great anguish. It means to be *consumed* with intense sorrow of heart.<br><br>**Practical Application**<br>What was the source behind this great anguish that Christ experienced? Apparently all that Christ had been through and was about to go through was opened up to His mind. His whole being was now focusing in upon the suffering He had to experience as the sin-bearer for the world. The mental vision literally compressed |

## PRACTICAL WORD STUDIES
### in the NEW TESTAMENT

| ENGLISH WORD | GREEK WORD AND VERSE | THE WORD MEANS... |
|---|---|---|
| | Zebedee, and began to be **sorrowful** and very heavy. [KJV]<br>And He took with Him Peter and the two sons of Zebedee, and began to be **grieved** and distressed. [NASB]<br>He took Peter and the two sons of Zebedee along with him, and he began to be **sorrowful** and troubled. [NIV]<br>And He took with Him Peter and the two sons of Zebedee, and He began to be **sorrowful** and deeply distressed. [NKJV]<br>He took Peter and Zebedee's two sons, James and John, and he began to be filled with **anguish** and deep distress. [NLT]<br>καὶ παραλαβὼν τὸν Πέτρον καὶ τοὺς δύο υἱοὺς Ζεβεδαίου, ἤρξατο **λυπεῖσθαι** καὶ ἀδημονεῖν. [GNS]<br>καὶ παραλαβὼν τὸν Πέτρον καὶ τοὺς δύο υἱοὺς Ζεβεδαίου ἤρξατο **λυπεῖσθαι** καὶ ἀδημονεῖν. [GNT] | His physical body, almost to the point of crushing Him. (See POSB *Deeper Study #2*—Matthew 26:37-38.) |
| **#148**<br>**Anguish**<br><br>**Anguish–KJV**<br>Distress–NASB<br>Distress–NIV<br>**Anguish–NKJV**<br>Calamity–NLT<br><br>**POSB REFERENCE**<br>(Rom.2:9)<br>*Deeper Study #9* | στενοχωρία = stenochōria<br>Pronunciation: [sten-okh-o-ree'-ah]<br>Parsing (part of speech): noun<br>    Case—nominative<br>    Gender—feminine<br>    Number—singular<br>    Stem or root—from στενοχωρία, ας<br>Concordance References:<br>⇒ Strong's #4730 stenochōria<br>⇒ NIV #5103 stenochōria<br>⇒ NASB #4730 stenochōria<br><br>**Romans 2:9**<br>Tribulation and **anguish**, upon every soul of man that doeth evil, of the Jew first, and also of the Gentile; [KJV]<br>*There will be* tribulation and **distress** for every soul of man who does evil, of the Jew first and also of the Greek, [NASB]<br>There will be trouble and **distress** for every human being who does evil: first for the Jew, then for the Gentile; [NIV]<br>Tribulation and **anguish**, on every soul of man who does evil, of the Jew first and also of the Greek; [NKJV]<br>There will be trouble and **calamity** for everyone who keeps on sinning—for the Jew first and also for the Gentile. [NLT]<br>θλῖψις καὶ **στενοχωρία** ἐπὶ πᾶσαν ψυχὴν ἀνθρώπου τοῦ κατεργαζομένου τὸ κακόν, Ἰουδαίου τε πρῶτον καὶ Ἕλληνος [GNS]<br>θλῖψις καὶ **στενοχωρία** ἐπὶ πᾶσαν ψυχὴν ἀνθρώπου τοῦ κατεργαζομένου τὸ κακόν, Ἰουδαίου τε πρῶτον καὶ Ἕλληνος· [GNT] | Distress, anguish, calamity, trouble, hardship, difficulty. It means to be put into a narrow place; to be compressed together; to experience extreme pain, sorrow, and affliction.<br><br>**Practical Application**<br>Every evil-doer is to be judged, both Jew and Gentile. No evil-doer will escape. Every soul of man that does evil will suffer, and the judgment will be severe and terrible. His judgment will involve indignation and wrath, tribulation and anguish (see POSB *Deeper Study #6*—Romans 2:8; POSB *Deeper Study #7*—Romans 2:8; POSB *Deeper Study #8*—Romans 2:9; and POSB *Deeper Study #9*—Romans 2:9 for discussion). |
| **#149**<br>**Anguish**<br><br>Sorrow–KJV<br>Grief–NASB<br>**Anguish–NIV**<br>Grief–NKJV<br>Grief–NLT<br><br>**POSB REFERENCE**<br>(Rom.9:1-3; esp. v.2),<br>Note 1, point 2 | ὀδύνη = odunē<br>Pronunciation: [od-oo'-nay]<br>Parsing (part of speech): noun<br>    Case—nominative<br>    Gender—feminine<br>    Number—singular<br>    Stem or root—from ὀδύνη, ης<br>Concordance References:<br>⇒ Strong's #3601 odunē<br>⇒ NIV #3850 odunē<br>⇒ NASB #3601 odunē<br><br>**Romans 9:2**<br>That I have great heaviness and continual **sorrow** in my heart. [KJV]<br>That I have great sorrow and unceasing **grief** in my heart. [NASB]<br>I have great sorrow and unceasing **anguish** in my heart. [NIV]<br>That I have great sorrow and continual **grief** in my heart. [NKJV]<br>My heart is filled with bitter sorrow and unending **grief** [NLT]<br>ὅτι λύπη μοί ἐστι μεγάλη, καὶ ἀδιάλειπτος **ὀδύνη** τῇ καρδίᾳ μου. [GNS]<br>ὅτι λύπη μοί ἐστιν μεγάλη καὶ ἀδιάλειπτος **ὀδύνη** τῇ καρδίᾳ μου. [GNT] | Intense anguish, sorrow, grief, pain, torment.<br><br>**Practical Application**<br>Note this is continuous and unceasing anguish. Paul was always bearing pain for the salvation of his kinsmen. The depth of Paul's love and concern is graphically seen in what he said. |

# PRACTICAL WORD STUDIES
## in the NEW TESTAMENT

| ENGLISH WORD | GREEK WORD AND VERSE | THE WORD MEANS... |
|---|---|---|
| **#150**<br>**Announce**<br><br>Preaching–KJV<br>Proclaiming–NASB<br>Proclaiming the good news–NIV<br>Preaching–NKJV<br>**Announce–NLT**<br><br>**POSB REFERENCE**<br>(Lk.8:1)<br>*Deeper Study #1* | κηρύσσων = *kërussön*<br>Pronunciation: [kay-roos'-sown]<br>Parsing (part of speech): verb<br>    Mood—participle<br>    Tense—present<br>    Voice—active<br>    Case—nominative<br>    Gender—masculine<br>    Number—singular<br>    Stem or root—from κηρύσσω<br>Concordance References:<br>  ⇒ Strong's #2784 kerusso<br>  ⇒ NIV #3062 kërussö NOTE: Repeated Greek word. The NIV translates with NIV #2294 euaggelizö as "proclaiming the good news." See below, Lk.8:1 for translation comparison.<br>  ⇒ NASB #2784 kerusso<br><br>**Luke 8:1**<br>And it came to pass afterward, that he went throughout every city and village, **preaching** and showing the glad tidings of the kingdom of God: and the twelve *were* with him, [KJV]<br><br>And it came about soon afterwards, that He *began* going about from one city and village to another, **proclaiming** and preaching the kingdom of God; and the twelve were with Him, [NASB]<br><br>After this, Jesus traveled about from one town and village to another, **proclaiming the good news** of the kingdom of God. The Twelve were with him, [NIV]<br><br>Now it came to pass, afterward, that He went through every city and village, **preaching** and bringing the glad tidings of the kingdom of God. And the twelve *were* with Him, [NKJV]<br><br>Not long afterward Jesus began a tour of the nearby cities and villages to **announce** the Good News concerning the Kingdom of God. He took his twelve disciples with him, [NLT]<br><br>Καὶ ἐγένετο ἐν τῷ καθεξῆς, καὶ αὐτὸς διώδευε κατὰ πόλιν καὶ κώμην, **κηρύσσων** καὶ εὐαγγελιζόμενος τὴν βασιλείαν τοῦ Θεοῦ· καὶ οἱ δώδεκα σὺν αὐτῷ, [GNS]<br><br>Καὶ ἐγένετο ἐν τῷ καθεξῆς καὶ αὐτὸς διώδευεν κατὰ πόλιν καὶ κώμην **κηρύσσων** καὶ εὐαγγελιζόμενος τὴν βασιλείαν τοῦ θεοῦ καὶ οἱ δώδεκα σὺν αὐτῷ, [GNT] | To proclaim; to publish; to be a herald; to preach the gospel as a herald; to preach; to declare; to announce; to make known.<br><br>**Practical Application**<br>In this Scripture, Jesus began a tour of nearby cities and villages "to announce the Good News." He had an ache, a compassion for all and was not willing that any should perish. He sought everyone within His reach. Note that He did not seek the limelight of the cities. He went out into the villages of the countryside as well. He had been sent to preach, and He preached anywhere and everywhere He could reach. The whole thrust of His being was to reach people for God, to reach everyone He could. |
| **#151**<br>**Announce The Good News**<br><br>Showing the glad tidings–KJV<br>Preaching–NASB<br>Proclaiming the good news–NIV<br>Bringing the glad tidings–NKJV<br>**Announce the good news–NLT**<br><br>**POSB REFERENCE**<br>(Lk.8:1)<br>*Deeper Study #2* | εὐαγγελιζόμενος = *euaggelizomenos*<br>Pronunciation: [yoo-ang-ghel-id'-zo-men-os]<br>Parsing (part of speech): verb<br>    Mood—participle<br>    Tense—present<br>    Voice—middle<br>    Case—nominative<br>    Gender—masculine<br>    Number—plural<br>    Stem or root—from εὐαγγελίζω<br>Concordance References:<br>  ⇒ Strong's #2097 euaggelizö<br>  ⇒ NIV #2294 euaggelizö<br>  ⇒ NASB #2097 euaggelizö<br><br>**Luke 8:1**<br>And it came to pass afterward, that he went throughout every city and village, preaching and **showing the glad tidings** of the kingdom of God: and the twelve *were* with him, [KJV]<br><br>And it came about soon afterwards, that He *began* going about from one city and village to another, proclaiming and **preaching** the kingdom of God; and the twelve were with Him, [NASB]<br><br>After this, Jesus traveled about from one town and village to another, **proclaiming the good news** of the kingdom of God. The Twelve were with him, [NIV]<br><br>Now it came to pass, afterward, that He went through | To preach glad tidings; to announce glad tidings; to declare good news; to bring the glad tidings; to proclaim the gospel of Jesus Christ.<br><br>**Practical Application**<br>Note the Greek word, how it resembles the word *evangelism*. The English word *evangelism* comes from it. By the very nature of his work, the preacher is an evangelist. He is a herald who comes in the name of the King, representing the King (cp. 2 Cor. 5:20). He announces *only* the message of the King; he has no message of his own. If and when he begins to announce his own message, he is no longer the representative or the spokesman of the King. |

# PRACTICAL WORD STUDIES
## in the NEW TESTAMENT

| ENGLISH WORD | GREEK WORD AND VERSE | THE WORD MEANS... |
|---|---|---|
| | every city and village, preaching and **bringing the glad tidings** of the kingdom of God. And the twelve were with Him, [NKJV]<br><br>Not long afterward Jesus began a tour of the nearby cities and villages to **announce the Good News** concerning the Kingdom of God. He took his twelve disciples with him, [NLT]<br><br>Καὶ ἐγένετο ἐν τῷ καθεξῆς, καὶ αὐτὸς διώδευε κατὰ πόλιν καὶ κώμην, κηρύσσων καὶ **εὐαγγελιζόμενος** τὴν βασιλείαν τοῦ Θεοῦ· καὶ οἱ δώδεκα σὺν αὐτῷ, [GNS]<br><br>Καὶ ἐγένετο ἐν τῷ καθεξῆς καὶ αὐτὸς διώδευεν κατὰ πόλιν καὶ κώμην κηρύσσων καὶ **εὐαγγελιζόμενος** τὴν βασιλείαν τοῦ θεοῦ καὶ οἱ δώδεκα σὺν αὐτῷ, [GNT] | |
| **#152**<br>**Announcing**<br><br>Preaching–KJV<br>Proclaiming–NASB<br>Preaching–NIV<br>Preaching–NKJV<br>Announcing–NLT<br><br>**POSB REFERENCE**<br>(Mt.9:35)<br>*Deeper Study #1* | κηρύσσων = *kērussōn*<br>Pronunciation: [kay-roos'-sown]<br>Parsing (part of speech): verb<br>  Mood—participle<br>  Tense—present<br>  Voice—active<br>  Case—nominative<br>  Gender—masculine<br>  Number—singular<br>  Stem or root— from κηρύσσω<br>Concordance References:<br>  ⇒ Strong's #2784 kērussō<br>  ⇒ NIV #3062 kērussō<br>  ⇒ NASB #2784 kērussō<br><br>**Matthew 9:35**<br>And Jesus went about all the cities and villages, teaching in their synagogues, and **preaching** the gospel of the kingdom, and healing every sickness and every disease among the people. [KJV]<br>And Jesus was going about all the cities and the villages, teaching in their synagogues, and **proclaiming** the gospel of the kingdom, and healing every kind of disease and every kind of sickness. [NASB]<br>Jesus went through all the towns and villages, teaching in their synagogues, **preaching** the good news of the kingdom and healing every disease and sickness. [NIV]<br>Then Jesus went about all the cities and villages, teaching in their synagogues, **preaching** the gospel of the kingdom, and healing every sickness and every disease among the people. [NKJV]<br>Jesus traveled through all the cities and villages of that area, teaching in the synagogues and **announcing** the Good News about the Kingdom. And wherever he went, he healed people of every sort of disease and illness. [NLT]<br>Καὶ περιῆγεν ὁ Ἰησοῦς τὰς πόλεις πάσας καὶ τὰς κώμας, διδάσκων ἐν ταῖς συναγωγαῖς αὐτῶν, καὶ **κηρύσσων** τὸ εὐαγγέλιον τῆς βασιλείας, καὶ θεραπεύων πᾶσαν νόσον καὶ πᾶσαν μαλακίαν ἐν τῷ λαῷ. [GNS]<br>Καὶ περιῆγεν ὁ Ἰησοῦς τὰς πόλεις πάσας καὶ τὰς κώμας διδάσκων ἐν ταῖς συναγωγαῖς αὐτῶν καὶ **κηρύσσων** τὸ εὐαγγέλιον τῆς βασιλείας καὶ θεραπεύων πᾶσαν νόσον καὶ πᾶσαν μαλακίαν. [GNT] | To proclaim, preach, announce, herald, publish.<br><br>**Practical Application**<br>The preacher is a herald who comes in the name of the King and who represents the King (cp. 2 Cor. 5:20). He comes to announce or proclaim the message of the King and *only* the message of the King. He has no message of his own. If and when he begins to announce or proclaim his own message, he is no longer the herald or the spokesman of the King. |
| **#153**<br>**Announcing**<br><br>Show–KJV<br>Proclaim–NASB<br>Proclaim–NIV<br>Proclaim–NKJV<br>Announcing–NLT | καταγγέλλετε = *kataggellete*<br>Pronunciation: [kat-ang-gel'-leh-teh]<br>Parsing (part of speech): verb<br>  Mood—indicative<br>  Tense—present<br>  Voice—active<br>  Person—2nd person<br>  Number—plural<br>  Stem or root—from καταγγέλλω<br>Concordance References:<br>  ⇒ Strong's #2605 kataggellō<br>  ⇒ NIV #2859 kataggellō<br>  ⇒ NASB #2605 kataggellō | To proclaim; to preach; to declare; to announce; to report; to make known.<br><br>**Practical Application**<br>The Lord's Supper is both a picture and sermon which announces...<br>• the Lord's death.<br>• the Lord's return.<br>The point is this: Christ died for us that we might live eternally with Him. Therefore, His death pictures both what He has done for us and what He is going to do for us when He returns. |

# PRACTICAL WORD STUDIES
## in the New Testament

| ENGLISH WORD | GREEK WORD AND VERSE | THE WORD MEANS... |
|---|---|---|
| **POSB REFERENCE**<br>(1 Cor.11:23-26; esp. v.26)<br>Note 3, point 3 | **1 Cor. 11:26**<br>For as often as ye eat this bread, and drink *this* cup, ye do **show** the Lord's death till he come. [KJV]<br>For as often as you eat this bread and drink the cup, you **proclaim** the Lord's death until He comes. [NASB]<br>For whenever you eat this bread and drink this cup, you **proclaim** the Lord's death until he comes. [NIV]<br>For as often as you eat this bread and drink this cup, you **proclaim** the Lord's death till He comes. [NKJV]<br>For every time you eat this bread and drink this cup, you are **announcing** the Lord's death until he comes again. [NLT]<br>ὁσάκις γὰρ ἂν ἐσθίητε τὸν ἄρτον τοῦτον, καὶ τὸ ποτήριον τοῦτο πίνητε, τὸν θάνατον τοῦ Κυρίου **καταγγέλλετε** ἄχρις οὗ ἂν ἔλθῃ. [GNS]<br>ὁσάκις γὰρ ἐὰν ἐσθίητε τὸν ἄρτον τοῦτον καὶ τὸ ποτήριον πίνητε, τὸν θάνατον τοῦ κυρίου **καταγγέλλετε** ἄχρις οὗ ἔλθῃ. [GNT] | His death is a picture of both our past and present redemption. But it is also a picture of our future redemption when we will be conformed to His image of perfection. |
| **#154**<br>**Annoyed**<br><br>Grieved–KJV<br>**Annoyed**–NASB<br>Troubled–NIV<br>**Annoyed**–NKJV<br>Exasperated–NLT<br><br>**POSB REFERENCE**<br>(Acts 16:18)<br>Note 2, point 2 | διαπονηθείς = *diaponētheis*<br>Pronunciation: [dee-ap-on-ay'-theh-ees]<br>Parsing (part of speech): verb<br>    Mood—participle<br>    Tense—aorist<br>    Voice—passive deponent<br>    Case—nominative<br>    Gender—masculine<br>    Number—singular<br>    Stem or root—from διαπονέομαι<br>Concordance References:<br>⇒ Strong's #1278 diaponeomai<br>⇒ NIV #1387 diaponeomai<br>⇒ NASB #1278 diaponeomai<br><br>**Acts 16:18**<br>And this did she many days. But Paul, being **grieved**, turned and said to the spirit, I command thee in the name of Jesus Christ to come out of her. And he came out the same hour. [KJV]<br>And she continued doing this for many days. But Paul was greatly **annoyed**, and turned and said to the spirit, "I command you in the name of Jesus Christ to come out of her!" And it came out at that very moment. [NASB]<br>She kept this up for many days. Finally Paul became so **troubled** that he turned around and said to the spirit, "In the name of Jesus Christ I command you to come out of her!" At that moment the spirit left her. [NIV]<br>And this she did for many days. But Paul, greatly **annoyed**, turned and said to the spirit, "I command you in the name of Jesus Christ to come out of her." And he came out that very hour. [NKJV]<br>This went on day after day until Paul got so **exasperated** that he turned and spoke to the demon within her. "I command you in the name of Jesus Christ to come out of her," he said. And instantly it left her. [NLT]<br>τοῦτο δὲ ἐποίει ἐπὶ πολλὰς ἡμέρας. **διαπονηθείς** δὲ ὁ Παῦλος, καὶ ἐπιστρέψας, τῷ πνεύματι εἶπε, Παραγγέλλω σοι ἐν τῷ ὀνόματι Ἰησοῦ Χριστοῦ, ἐξελθεῖν ἀπ' αὐτῆς. Καὶ ἐξῆλθεν αὐτῇ τῇ ὥρᾳ. [GNS]<br>τοῦτο δὲ ἐποίει ἐπὶ πολλὰς ἡμέρας. **διαπονηθείς** δὲ Παῦλος καὶ ἐπιστρέψας τῷ πνεύματι εἶπεν, Παραγγέλλω σοι ἐν ὀνόματι Ἰησοῦ Χριστοῦ ἐξελθεῖν ἀπ' αὐτῆς· καὶ ἐξῆλθεν αὐτῇ τῇ ὥρᾳ. [GNT] | Troubled, grieved, annoyed, exasperated. The word means pained, deeply troubled, worked up, annoyed, and angry (a righteous anger).<br><br>**Practical Application**<br>Paul was troubled and hurting...<br>• over the girl's being enslaved by sin.<br>• over the girl's being so used by greedy and lustful men.<br>• over the false witness to the Lord's name.<br>• over the mockery and ridicule of his ministry as the servant of Christ. |
| **#155**<br>**Anointed**<br><br>Anointed–KJV<br>Anointed–NASB<br>Anointed–NIV<br>Anointed–NKJV<br>Commissioned–NLT | χρίσας = *chrisas*<br>Pronunciation: [khre'-sahs]<br>Parsing (part of speech): verb<br>    Mood—participle<br>    Tense—aorist<br>    Voice—active<br>    Case—nominative<br>    Gender—masculine | To anoint; to commission; to be consecrated and qualified for service.<br><br>**Practical Application**<br>Note who it is that anoints us: God Himself. What is the anointing, the unction that He gives? The Holy Spirit. |

# PRACTICAL WORD STUDIES
## in the NEW TESTAMENT

| ENGLISH WORD | GREEK WORD AND VERSE | THE WORD MEANS... |
|---|---|---|
| **POSB REFERENCE** (2 Cor.1:21-22; esp. v.21) Note 5 <br><br> See also POSB REF: (1 Jn.2:20-21) Note 3, point 1 | Number—singular <br> Stem or root—from χρίω <br> Concordance References: <br> ⇒ Strong's #5548 chriō <br> ⇒ NIV #5987 chriō <br> ⇒ NASB #5548 chriō <br><br> **2 Cor. 1:21** <br> Now he which stablisheth us with you in Christ, and hath **anointed** us, *is* God; [KJV] <br> Now He who establishes us with you in Christ and **anointed** us is God, [NASB] <br> Now it is God who makes both us and you stand firm in Christ. He **anointed** us, [NIV] <br> Now He who establishes us with you in Christ and has **anointed** us *is* God, [NKJV] <br> It is God who gives us, along with you, the ability to stand firm for Christ. He has **commissioned** us, [NLT] <br> ὁ δὲ βεβαιῶν ἡμᾶς σὺν ὑμῖν εἰς Χριστὸν, καὶ **χρίσας** ἡμᾶς, Θεός, [GNS] <br> ὁ δὲ βεβαιῶν ἡμᾶς σὺν ὑμῖν εἰς Χριστὸν καὶ **χρίσας** ἡμᾶς θεός, [GNT] | |
| **#156** <br> **Another** <br><br> Another–KJV <br> Another–NASB <br> Another–NIV <br> Another–NKJV <br> Someone else–NLT <br><br> **POSB REFERENCE** (Jn.5:32) Note 2 | ἄλλος = allos <br> Pronunciation: [al'-los] <br> Parsing (part of speech): adjective <br>   Case—nominative <br>   Gender—masculine <br>   Number—singular <br>   Stem or root— from ἄλλος, η <br> Concordance References: <br> ⇒ Strong's #243 allos <br> ⇒ NIV #257 allos <br> ⇒ NASB #243 allos <br><br> **John 5:32** <br> There is **another** that beareth witness of me; and I know that the witness which he witnesseth of me is true. [KJV] <br> "There is **another** who bears witness of Me, and I know that the testimony which He bears of Me is true. [NASB] <br> There is **another** who testifies in my favor, and I know that his testimony about me is valid. [NIV] <br> There is **another** who bears witness of Me, and I know that the witness which He witnesses of Me is true. [NKJV] <br> But **someone else** is also testifying about me, and I can assure you that everything he says about me is true. [NLT] <br> ἄλλος ἐστὶν ὁ μαρτυρῶν περὶ ἐμοῦ, καὶ οἶδα ὅτι ἀληθής ἐστιν ἡ μαρτυρία ἣν μαρτυρεῖ περὶ ἐμοῦ. [GNS] <br> ἄλλος ἐστὶν ὁ μαρτυρῶν περὶ ἐμοῦ, καὶ οἶδα ὅτι ἀληθής ἐστιν ἡ μαρτυρία ἣν μαρτυρεῖ περὶ ἐμοῦ. [GNT] | Another, someone else, some other, different one. <br><br> **Practical Application** <br> Christ did not identify who He meant by "another" (*allos*). (Cp. John 14:16.) Most commentators believe He was referring to God Himself. However, there are three reasons why the Holy Spirit is thought to be the One to whom Christ was referring. <br> 1. The Holy Spirit had already been given to Christ "without measure" (see POSB note—John 3:34). He was, of course, very conscious of the witness of the Spirit both within and without Him. The Spirit was empowering Him and doing the works of God through Him. <br> 2. The Holy Spirit is One of the witnesses that bears witness to Christ (cp. 1 John 5:6-12). When John the apostle discusses the witness to Christ in his epistle, he mentions the Spirit. If the present verse is not referring to the Spirit, then the Spirit is not listed as one of the witnesses in the present passage. This would be most unlikely, especially since the witness of the Father is covered in John 5:37-38, and the ministry and witness of the Spirit is covered so thoroughly in this Gospel. (See POSB outline and notes—John 14:15-26; POSB notes—John 16:7-15.) <br> 3. Note how the verse reads. Christ seems to be talking about an inner witness, the witness of a Presence which He senses within His innermost Being, a Power that works in and through Him. This of course could be God; but again, it could also be the Spirit which would seem to fit more naturally in the context. <br><br> Note the Lord's words, "I know that his testimony about me is valid."[NIV] The Lord meant at least two things. <br> 1. He knew the truth of the witness within His own heart and life. He had the consciousness, the sense, the awareness, the personal knowledge of the Spirit's witness within His own inner Being. The Spirit bore witness with |

# Practical Word Studies in the New Testament

| ENGLISH WORD | GREEK WORD AND VERSE | THE WORD MEANS... |
|---|---|---|
| | | Jesus' own Spirit that He was the Son of God Himself.<br>2. He knew that the witness and the work of the Holy Spirit, in and through Him, was true. The Spirit was convicting men, working in their hearts and lives, convincing them of the claims of Christ. (See POSB outline and notes—John 16:7-15 for the Lord's discussion of the Spirit's work.) |
| #157<br>**Another**<br><br>**Another**–KJV<br>Different–NASB<br>Different–NIV<br>Different–NKJV<br>Different–NLT<br><br>**POSB REFERENCE**<br>(Gal.1:6-7; esp. v.6)<br>Note 2 | ἕτερον = *heteron*<br>Pronunciation: [et'-er-on]<br>Parsing (part of speech): adjective<br>   Case—accusative<br>   Gender—neuter<br>   Number—singular<br>   Stem or root—from ἕτερος, α, ον<br>Concordance References:<br>  ⇒ Strong's #2087 heteros<br>  ⇒ NIV #2283 heteros<br>  ⇒ NASB #2087 heteros<br><br>**Galatians 1:6**<br>I marvel that ye are so soon removed from him that called you into the grace of Christ unto **another** gospel: [KJV]<br>I am amazed that you are so quickly deserting Him who called you by the grace of Christ, for a **different** gospel; [NASB]<br>I am astonished that you are so quickly deserting the one who called you by the grace of Christ and are turning to a **different** gospel—[NIV]<br>I marvel that you are turning away so soon from Him who called you in the grace of Christ, to a **different** gospel, [NKJV]<br>I am shocked that you are turning away so soon from God, who in his love and mercy called you to share the eternal life he gives through Christ. You are already following a **different** way [NLT]<br>Θαυμάζω ὅτι οὕτω ταχέως μετατίθεσθε ἀπὸ τοῦ καλέσαντος ὑμᾶς ἐν χάριτι Χριστοῦ εἰς **ἕτερον** εὐαγγέλιον· [GNS]<br>Θαυμάζω ὅτι οὕτως ταχέως μετατίθεσθε ἀπὸ τοῦ καλέσαντος ὑμᾶς ἐν χάριτι [Χριστοῦ] εἰς **ἕτερον** εὐαγγέλιον, [GNT] | Different, unnatural, changed or altered in a strange way.<br><br>**Practical Application**<br>It means a different kind of gospel, not just a difference in emphasis or spirit (A.T. Robertson. *Word Pictures in the New Testament*, Vol.4. Nashville: Broadman Press, 1931, p.276). It means another kind of gospel that presents...<br>• another Jesus<br>• another grace<br>• another way to be saved<br>• another God<br>• another picture of God's love<br><br>But note what Scripture declares: the gospel to which the Galatians were turning was *not a different or another gospel*. There is no other gospel; there is only one true gospel by which men can become acceptable to God, and that is the gospel of God Himself revealed in the death of His Son, even "the grace of Christ." |
| #158<br>**Answer**<br><br>**Answer**–KJV<br>Defense–NASB<br>**Answer**–NIV<br>Defense–NKJV<br>Explain–NLT<br><br>**POSB REFERENCE**<br>(1 Pt.3:15)<br>Note 3 | ἀπολογίαν = *apologian*<br>Pronunciation: [ap-ol-og-ee'-ahn]<br>Parsing (part of speech): noun<br>   Case—accusative<br>   Gender—feminine<br>   Number—singular<br>   Stem or root—from ἀπολογία, ας<br>Concordance References:<br>  ⇒ Strong's #627 apologia<br>  ⇒ NIV #665 apologia<br>  ⇒ NASB #627 apologia<br><br>**1 Peter 3:15**<br>But sanctify the Lord God in your hearts: and *be* ready always to *give* an **answer** to every man that asketh you a reason of the hope that is in you with meekness and fear: [KJV]<br>But sanctify Christ as Lord in your hearts, always *being* ready to make a **defense** to everyone who asks you to give an account for the hope that is in you, yet with gentleness and reverence; [NASB]<br>But in your hearts set apart Christ as Lord. Always be prepared to give an **answer** to everyone who asks you to give the reason for the hope that you have. But do this with gentleness and respect, [NIV]<br>But sanctify the Lord God in your hearts, and always *be* ready to *give* a **defense** to everyone who asks you a | To answer; to reply; to defend; to explain. It means a decision, response, discovery, solution.<br><br>**Practical Application**<br>One answer to persecution is to readily defend the hope of salvation to every man and to do so with gentleness and respect. The word "answer" or "defend" (*apologian*) means just that, to answer back or to give a defense of the believer's hope (A.T. Robertson. *Word Pictures in the New Testament*, Vol.6, p.114). |

# PRACTICAL WORD STUDIES
## in the NEW TESTAMENT

| ENGLISH WORD | GREEK WORD AND VERSE | THE WORD MEANS... |
|---|---|---|
| | reason for the hope that is in you, with meekness and fear; [NKJV]<br><br>Instead, you must worship Christ as Lord of your life. And if you are asked about your Christian hope, always be ready to **explain** it. [NLT]<br><br>Κύριον δὲ τὸν Θεὸν ἁγιάσατε ἐν ταῖς καρδίαις ὑμῶν· ἕτοιμοι δὲ ἀεὶ πρὸς **ἀπολογίαν** παντὶ τῷ αἰτοῦντι ὑμᾶς λόγον περὶ τῆς ἐν ὑμῖν ἐλπίδος, [GNS]<br><br>ύριον δὲ τὸν Χριστὸν ἁγιάσατε ἐν ταῖς καρδίαις ὑμῶν, ἕτοιμοι ἀεὶ πρὸς **ἀπολογίαν** παντὶ τῷ αἰτοῦντι ὑμᾶς λόγον περὶ τῆς ἐν ὑμῖν ἐλπίδος, [GNT] | |
| **#159**<br>**Answers**<br><br>Answers–KJV<br>Answers–NASB<br>Answers–NIV<br>Answers–NKJV<br>Answers–NLT<br><br>**POSB REFERENCE**<br>(Lk.2:46-47; esp. v.47)<br>Note 3, point 2c | **ἀποκρίσεσιν** = *apokrisesin*<br>Pronunciation: [ap-ok'-ree-seh-sin]<br>Parsing (part of speech): noun<br>    Case—dative<br>    Gender—feminine<br>    Number—plural<br>    Stem or root—from **ἀπόκρισις**, εως<br>Concordance References:<br>  ⇒ Strong's #612 apokrisis<br>  ⇒ NIV #647 apokrisis<br>  ⇒ NASB #612 apokrisis<br><br>**Luke 2:47**<br>And all that heard him were astonished at his understanding and **answers**. [KJV]<br><br>And all who heard Him were amazed at His understanding and His **answers**. [NASB]<br><br>Everyone who heard him was amazed at his understanding and his **answers**. [NIV]<br><br>And all who heard Him were astonished at His understanding and **answers**. [NKJV]<br><br>And all who heard him were amazed at his understanding and his **answers**. [NLT]<br><br>ἐξίσταντο δὲ πάντες οἱ ἀκούοντες αὐτοῦ ἐπὶ τῇ συνέσει καὶ ταῖς **ἀποκρίσεσιν** αὐτοῦ. [GNS]<br>ἐξίσταντο δὲ πάντες οἱ ἀκούοντες αὐτοῦ ἐπὶ τῇ συνέσει καὶ ταῖς **ἀποκρίσεσιν** αὐτοῦ. [GNT] | Answers, explanations, discoveries, resolutions, solutions.<br><br>**Practical Application**<br>In the context of this Scripture, note what Jesus did:<br>  ⇒ He wanted answers, more understanding.<br>  ⇒ He thirsted for truth and sought it.<br><br>Note that His questions and answers revealed phenomenal knowledge and understanding. Everyone was astonished, even the doctors. |
| **#160**<br>**Antitype**<br><br>Figure–KJV<br>Corresponding–NASB<br>Symbolizes–NIV<br>Antitype–NKJV<br>Picture–NLT<br><br>**POSB REFERENCE**<br>(1 Pt.3:21)<br>Note 1, point 3a | **ἀντίτυπον** = *antitupon*<br>Pronunciation: [an-teet'-oo-pon]<br>Parsing (part of speech): adjective adverb OR adjective<br>    Case—nominative<br>    Gender—neuter<br>    Number—singular<br>    Stem or root—from **ἀντίτυπος**, ον<br>Concordance References:<br>  ⇒ Strong's #499 antitupos<br>  ⇒ NIV #531 antitupos<br>  ⇒ NASB #499 antitupos<br><br>**1 Peter 3:21**<br>The like **figure** whereunto even baptism doth also now save us (not the putting away of the filth of the flesh, but the answer of a good conscience toward God,) by the resurrection of Jesus Christ: [KJV]<br><br>And **corresponding** to that, baptism now saves you—not the removal of dirt from the flesh, but an appeal to God for a good conscience—through the resurrection of Jesus Christ, [NASB]<br><br>And this water **symbolizes** baptism that now saves you also—not the removal of dirt from the body but the pledge of a good conscience toward God. It saves you by the resurrection of Jesus Christ, [NIV]<br><br>There is also an **antitype** which now saves us—baptism (not the removal of the filth of the flesh, but the answer of a good conscience toward God), through the resurrection of Jesus Christ, [NKJV]<br><br>And this is a **picture** of baptism, which now saves you by the power of Jesus Christ's resurrection. Baptism is not a removal of dirt from your body; it is an appeal to God from a clean conscience. [NLT] | Symbolize, figure, copy, antitype.<br><br>**Practical Application**<br>Jesus Christ saves the believer through baptism: not the baptism by water, but the baptism of a good conscience wrought by the power of the resurrection of Jesus Christ (1 Peter 3:21).<br>The water which saved Noah and his family is a type of the cleansing that saves us. The water...<br>• bore up the ark and saved them through the judgment of God.<br>• delivered them from the ridicule and mockery of evil men.<br>• delivered them from the corruption of the world and led them to a new life.<br>• put to death the old world and gave them the hope of a new world.<br>• put to death their old life and gave them a new beginning.<br>• saved the race of man and created a new people of God.<br>• delivered them from the old world right into the new world.<br><br>What is Peter saying? Note the word "antitype" (*antitupon*). The figure or picture of baptism is just like the water that saved Noah and his family.<br>⇒ The *flooding waters* of Noah's day picture the judgment of God upon sin. The flooding waters picture how man was saved |

## PRACTICAL WORD STUDIES
### in the NEW TESTAMENT

| ENGLISH WORD | GREEK WORD AND VERSE | THE WORD MEANS... |
|---|---|---|
| | ᾧ καὶ ἡμᾶς **ἀντίτυπον** νῦν σῴζει βάπτισμα, οὐ σαρκὸς ἀπόθεσις ῥύπου, ἀλλὰ συνειδήσεως ἀγαθῆς ἐπερώτημα εἰς Θεόν, δι' ἀναστάσεως Ἰησοῦ Χριστοῦ, [GNS]<br>ὃ καὶ ὑμᾶς **ἀντίτυπον** νῦν σῴζει βάπτισμα, οὐ σαρκὸς ἀπόθεσις ῥύπου ἀλλὰ συνειδήσεως ἀγαθῆς ἐπερώτημα εἰς θεόν, δι' ἀναστάσεως Ἰησοῦ Χριστοῦ, [GNT] | from a corruptible world and carried into a new world.<br>⇒ The *baptismal water* pictures the judgment of God upon Christ, a judgment of death that was due sinners. It pictures how man is saved from a corruptible life and world and carried into a new life and world by the resurrection of Christ. |
| **#161**<br>**Anxiety**<br><br>Care–KJV<br>**Anxiety–NASB**<br>**Anxiety–NIV**<br>Care–NKJV<br>Worries and cares–NLT<br><br>**POSB**<br>**REFERENCE**<br>(1 Pt.5:6-7; esp. v.7)<br>Note 3, point 3 | **μέριμναν** = *merimnan*<br>Pronunciation: [mer'-im-nahn]<br>Parsing (part of speech): noun<br>    Case—accusative<br>    Gender—feminine<br>    Number—singular<br>    Stem or root—from μέριμνα, ης<br>Concordance References:<br>⇒ Strong's #3308 *merimna*<br>⇒ NIV #3533 *merimna*<br>⇒ NASB #3308 *merimna*<br><br>**1 Peter 5:7**<br>Casting all your **care** upon him; for he careth for you. [KJV]<br>Casting all your **anxiety** upon Him, because He cares for you. [NASB]<br>Cast all your **anxiety** on him because he cares for you. [NIV]<br>Casting all your **care** upon Him, for He cares for you. [NKJV]<br>Give all your **worries and cares** to God, for he cares about what happens to you. [NLT]<br>πᾶσαν τὴν **μέριμναν** ὑμῶν ἐπιρρίψαντες ἐπ' αὐτόν, ὅτι αὐτῷ μέλει περὶ ὑμῶν. [GNS]<br>πᾶσαν τὴν **μέριμναν** ὑμῶν ἐπιρίψαντες ἐπ' αὐτόν, ὅτι αὐτῷ μέλει περὶ ὑμῶν. [GNT] | Anxiety, care, worries, concern.<br><br>**Practical Application**<br>God cares for us; He cares about all our anxiety. Remember: the believers of Peter's day were suffering terrible persecution. They had been forced to flee for their lives, leaving everything behind: homes, jobs, and possessions. They had only what they could carry by hand, and they fled to whatever places they felt were safe. They were, so to speak, an underground people. They had to live, work, and worship in secret and to find housing and food wherever they could. They never knew when they would be discovered and forced to flee again.<br>The point is this: imagine the anxiety, the pressure, tension, and stress being experienced by the believers. Yet there was great help: God was available to help them. Note that the exhortation is not only clearly stated; it is a command: "cast all your anxiety (*merimna*) upon Him, because He cares for you." God's mighty hand will...<br>• save and deliver you<br>• look after and care for you<br>• strengthen and secure you<br>• provide and protect you<br>• give you assurance and confidence |
| **#162**<br>**Anxious**<br><br>Take no thought–KJV<br>**Anxious–NASB**<br>Worry about–NIV<br>Worry about–NKJV<br>Worry about–NLT<br><br>**POSB**<br>**REFERENCE**<br>(Lk.12:22-34; esp. v.22)<br>Outline<br>Introduction<br><br>**See also POSB REF:**<br>(Mt.6:25)<br>Note 1 | **μεριμνᾶτε** = *merimnate*<br>Pronunciation: [mer-im-nah'-teh]<br>Parsing (part of speech): verb<br>    Mood—imperfect<br>    Tense—present<br>    Voice—active<br>    Person—2nd person<br>    Number—plural<br>    Stem or root—from μεριμνάω<br>Concordance References:<br>⇒ Strong's #3309 *merimnao*<br>⇒ NIV #3534 *merimnaö*<br>⇒ NASB #3309 *merimnao*<br><br>**Luke 12:22**<br>And he said unto his disciples, Therefore I say unto you, **Take no thought** for your life, what ye shall eat; neither for the body, what ye shall put on. [KJV]<br>And He said to His disciples, "For this reason I say to you, do not be **anxious** for *your* life, *as to* what you shall eat; nor for your body, *as to* what you shall put on. [NASB]<br>Then Jesus said to his disciples: "Therefore I tell you, do not **worry about** your life, what you will eat; or about your body, what you will wear. [NIV]<br>Then He said to His disciples, "Therefore I say to you, do not **worry about** your life, what you will eat; nor about the body, what you will put on. [NKJV]<br>Then turning to his disciples, Jesus said, "So I tell you, don't **worry about** everyday life—whether you have enough food to eat or clothes to wear. [NLT]<br>Εἶπε δὲ πρὸς τοὺς μαθητὰς αὐτοῦ, Διὰ τοῦτο ὑμῖν λέγω, μὴ **μεριμνᾶτε** τῇ ψυχῇ ὑμῶν, τί φάγητε· μηδὲ τῷ σώματι, τί ἐνδύσησθε. [GNS]<br>Εἶπεν δὲ πρὸς τοὺς μαθητὰς [αὐτοῦ], Διὰ τοῦτο λέγω ὑμῖν· μὴ **μεριμνᾶτε** τῇ ψυχῇ τί φάγητε, μηδὲ τῷ σώματι τί ἐνδύσησθε. [GNT] | Do not worry; do not be anxious; do not overly concerned and caring (cp. Phil. 4:6).<br><br>**Practical Application**<br>"Do not be anxious." Being worried and overly concerned is a constant problem among men. It is not to be so among God's people. (See POSB outline—Matthew 6:25-34 and POSB notes—Matthew 6:25-34 for more discussion and application.) |

# PRACTICAL WORD STUDIES
## in the NEW TESTAMENT

| ENGLISH WORD | GREEK WORD AND VERSE | THE WORD MEANS... |
|---|---|---|
| **#163**<br>**Anxious About, For**<br><br>Careful for–KJV<br>**Anxious for–NASB**<br>**Anxious about–NIV**<br>**Anxious for–NKJV**<br>Worry about–NLT<br><br>**POSB REFERENCE**<br>(Philip.4:6-7; esp. v.6)<br>Note 1 | μεριμνᾶτε = *merimnate*<br>Pronunciation: [mer-im-nah'-teh]<br>Parsing (part of speech): verb<br>  Mood—imperative<br>  Tense—present<br>  Voice—active<br>  Person—2nd person<br>  Number—plural<br>  Stem or root—from μεριμνάω<br>Concordance References:<br>  ⇒ Strong's #3309 merimnaö<br>  ⇒ NIV #3534 merimnaö<br>  ⇒ NASB #3309 merimnaö<br><br>**Philip. 4:6**<br>Be **careful for** nothing; but in every thing by prayer and supplication with thanksgiving let your requests be made known unto God. [KJV]<br>Be **anxious for** nothing, but in everything by prayer and supplication with thanksgiving let your requests be made known to God. [NASB]<br>Do not be **anxious about** anything, but in everything, by prayer and petition, with thanksgiving, present your requests to God. [NIV]<br>Be **anxious for** nothing, but in everything by prayer and supplication, with thanksgiving, let your requests be made known to God; [NKJV]<br>Don't **worry about** anything; instead, pray about everything. Tell God what you need, and thank him for all he has done. [NLT]<br>μηδὲν **μεριμνᾶτε**, ἀλλ' ἐν παντὶ τῇ προσευχῇ καὶ τῇ δεήσει μετὰ εὐχαριστίας τὰ αἰτήματα ὑμῶν γνωριζέσθω πρὸς τὸν Θεόν, [GNS]<br>μηδὲν **μεριμνᾶτε**, ἀλλ' ἐν παντὶ τῇ προσευχῇ καὶ τῇ δεήσει μετὰ εὐχαριστίας τὰ αἰτήματα ὑμῶν γνωριζέσθω πρὸς τὸν θεόν. [GNT] | To be anxious about; to be anxious for; to be careful for; to worry about; to be concerned about.<br><br>**Practical Application**<br>The idea is that the believer is not to worry or fret about a single thing. The word "anything" or "nothing" (*meden*) means not even one thing. Humanly speaking, the Philippians had every reason to worry and be anxious.<br>⇒ They were suffering severe persecution (Phil. 1:18-19).<br>⇒ They were facing a disturbance in the church, some disunity and quarreling (Phil. 1:27, 42).<br>⇒ They had some carnal members within their fellowship, some members who were prideful, super-spiritual, and self-centered (Phil. 2:3-4; Phil. 3:12).<br>⇒ They were facing some false teachers who had joined their fellowship, and the teachers were fierce in attacking the cross of Christ (Phil. 3:2-3, 18-19).<br>⇒ Some of the believers were having to struggle for the necessities of life: food, clothing, and shelter (Phil. 4:19).<br>There was little else that could confront these dear believers. They were facing about every trial and temptation imaginable, the kind of trouble that arouses anxiety and worry. Humanly, a person is going to fret, worry and suffer anxiety...<br>• when he is either about to lose or lacks food, clothing, or shelter.<br>• when he is persecuted, ridiculed, abused, or threatened.<br>• when he is surrounded by quarrels, disturbance, carnality, or false teaching.<br>In the midst of such circumstances, the only way a person can keep from worrying is to receive an injection of supernatural power.<br>This is the very point of Scripture. There is an answer to worry and anxiety, a supernatural answer: the peace of God. God will *enable* the believer to conquer worry and anxiety. God will overcome the trials of life for the believer, no matter how terrible and pressuring they may be. God will infuse the believer with peace—with the very peace of God Himself—a peace so great and so wonderful that it carries the believer right through the trial. Of course, this does not mean the believer is not to be concerned about the problems of life. He is, but there is a difference between concern and anxiety or worry. Concern drives us to arise and tackle the problems of life with an indomitable courage and diligence. Concern drives us to tackle and conquer all that we can handle. Anxiety and worry cause all kinds of problems. |
| **#164**<br>**Anxious Longing Of**<br><br>Earnest expectation of–KJV<br>**Anxious longing of–NASB**<br>Eager expectation for–NIV | ἀποκαραδοκία* *apokaradokia*<br>Pronunciation: [ap-ok-ar-ad-ok-ee'-ah]<br>Parsing (part of speech): noun<br>  Case—nominative<br>  Gender—feminine<br>  Number—singular<br>  Stem or root—from ἀποκαραδοκία, ας<br>Concordance References:<br>  ⇒ Strong's #603 apokaradokia<br>  ⇒ NIV #638 apokaradokia | Eager longing; deep desire; eager expectation for; earnest expectation.<br><br>**Practical Application**<br>The creation suffers and struggles for deliverance from corruption. The word "creation" refers to everything under man: animal, plant, and mineral. All creation is pictured as living and waiting expectantly for the day when the sons of God will be glorified. The words "anx- |

# PRACTICAL WORD STUDIES
## in the NEW TESTAMENT

| ENGLISH WORD | GREEK WORD AND VERSE | THE WORD MEANS... |
|---|---|---|
| Earnest expectation of– NKJV<br>Waiting eagerly for– NLT<br><br>**POSB REFERENCE**<br>(Romans 8:19-22; esp. v.19)<br>Note 2 | ⇒ NASB #603 apokaradokia<br><br>**Romans 8:19**<br>For the **earnest expectation of** the creature waiteth for the manifestation of the sons of God. [KJV]<br>For the **anxious longing of** the creation waits eagerly for the revealing of the sons of God. [NASB]<br>The creation waits in **eager expectation for** the sons of God to be revealed. [NIV]<br>For the **earnest expectation of** the creation eagerly waits for the revealing of the sons of God. [NKJV]<br>For all creation is **waiting eagerly for** that future day when God will reveal who his children really are. [NLT]<br>ἡ γὰρ **ἀποκαραδοκία** τῆς κτίσεως τὴν ἀποκάλυψιν τῶν υἱῶν τοῦ Θεοῦ ἀπεκδέχεται· [GNS]<br>ἡ γὰρ **ἀποκαραδοκία** τῆς κτίσεως τὴν ἀποκάλυψιν τῶν υἱῶν τοῦ θεοῦ ἀπεκδέχεται. [GNT] | ious longing of" (*apokaradokia*) mean to watch with the neck outstretched and the head erect. It is a persistent, unswerving expectation, an expectation that does not give up but keeps looking until the event happens. |
| **#165**<br>**Anyone Who Runs Ahead, Who Goes Too Far**<br><br>Whosoever transgresseth–KJV<br>Anyone who goes too far–NASB<br>Anyone who runs ahead–NIV<br>Whoever transgresses–NKJV<br>Wander beyond–NLT<br><br>**POSB REFERENCE**<br>(2 Jn.1:9)<br>Note 3 | πᾶς ὁ προάγων = pas ho proagōn<br>Pronunciation: [pas ho pro-ag'-own]<br>Parsing *proagōn* (part of speech): verb<br>  Mood—participle<br>  Tense—present<br>  Voice—active<br>  Case—nominative<br>  Gender—masculine<br>  Number—singular<br>  Stem or root—from προάγω<br>Concordance References:<br>⇒ Strong's #3956 pas + 3588 ho + 3845 parabaino<br>⇒ NIV #4246 pas [Anyone] + 3836 ho [who] + 4575 proagō [runs ahead]<br>⇒ NASB #3956 pas + 3588 ho + 4254 proagō<br><br>**2 John 1:9**<br>**Whosoever transgresseth**, and abideth not in the doctrine of Christ, hath not God. He that abideth in the doctrine of Christ, he hath both the Father and the Son. [KJV]<br>**Anyone who goes too far** and does not abide in the teaching of Christ, does not have God; the one who abides in the teaching, he has both the Father and the Son. [NASB]<br>**Anyone who runs ahead** and does not continue in the teaching of Christ does not have God; whoever continues in the teaching has both the Father and the Son. [NIV]<br>**Whoever transgresses** and does not abide in the doctrine of Christ does not have God. He who abides in the doctrine of Christ has both the Father and the Son. [NKJV]<br>For if you **wander beyond** the teaching of Christ, you will not have fellowship with God. But if you continue in the teaching of Christ, you will have fellowship with both the Father and the Son. [NLT]<br>πᾶς ὁ **παραβαίνω** καὶ μὴ μένων ἐν τῇ διδαχῇ τοῦ Χριστοῦ, Θεὸν οὐκ ἔχει· ὁ μένων ἐν τῇ διδαχῇ τοῦ Χριστοῦ, οὗτος καὶ τὸν πατέρα καὶ τὸν υἱὸν ἔχει. [GNS]<br>πᾶς ὁ **προάγων** καὶ μὴ μένων ἐν τῇ διδαχῇ τοῦ Χριστοῦ θεὸν οὐκ ἔχει· ὁ μένων ἐν τῇ διδαχῇ, οὗτος καὶ τὸν πατέρα καὶ τὸν υἱὸν ἔχει. [GNT] | To transgress against God by going too far, by trying to move out ahead of Christ; to wander beyond.<br><br>**Practical Application**<br>The person who does not continue in the teachings of Christ does not have or possess God. There are many teachers—ministers and laymen alike—who would like to be progressive and creative to come up with a novel idea, to make some advancement in thought. They want people to recognize and approve them; therefore, they try to impress people. In so doing, they go beyond Christ and what He taught. They twist or branch off from the teachings of Christ. John warns against this: if a person does not stay in the teachings of Christ, then he does not have God. He is not saved; he is not truly born of God. The only person who is born of God is the person who stays in the teachings of Christ. This does not mean that believers are not to be creative and thoughtful. It means that we must not move out beyond Christ and what He taught. |
| **#166**<br>**Anything, Not**<br><br>Nothing–KJV<br>Nothing–NASB<br>**Not...anything–NIV**<br>Nothing–NKJV<br>**Anything–NLT** | μηδέν = mēden<br>Pronunciation: [may-dehn]<br>Parsing (part of speech): pronominal adjective<br>  Type—cardinal<br>  Case—accusative<br>  Gender—neuter<br>  Number—singular<br>  Stem or root—from μηδείς, μηδεμία, μηδέν<br>Concordance References:<br>⇒ Strong's #3367 mēdeis | Not anything, nothing, not even one thing; not anyone.<br><br>**Practical Application**<br>Humanly, a person is going to fret, worry and suffer anxiety...<br>• when he is either about to lose or lacks food, clothing, or shelter.<br>• when he is persecuted, ridiculed, abused, |

# PRACTICAL WORD STUDIES
## in the NEW TESTAMENT

| ENGLISH WORD | GREEK WORD AND VERSE | THE WORD MEANS... |
|---|---|---|
| **POSB REFERENCE** (Philip.4:6-7; esp. v.6) Note 1 | ⇒ NIV #3594 mēdeis<br>⇒ NASB #3367 mēdeis<br><br>**Philip. 4:6**<br>Be careful for **nothing**; but in every thing by prayer and supplication with thanksgiving let your requests be made known unto God. [KJV]<br>Be anxious for **nothing**, but in everything by prayer and supplication with thanksgiving let your requests be made known to God. [NASB]<br>Do **not** be anxious about **anything**, but in everything, by prayer and petition, with thanksgiving, present your requests to God. [NIV]<br>Be anxious for **nothing**, but in everything by prayer and supplication, with thanksgiving, let your requests be made known to God; [NKJV]<br>Don't worry about **anything**; instead, pray about everything. Tell God what you need, and thank him for all he has done. [NLT]<br>**μηδὲν** μεριμνᾶτε, ἀλλ' ἐν παντὶ τῇ προσευχῇ καὶ τῇ δεήσει μετὰ εὐχαριστίας τὰ αἰτήματα ὑμῶν γνωριζέσθω πρὸς τὸν Θεόν, [GNS]<br>**μηδὲν** μεριμνᾶτε, ἀλλ' ἐν παντὶ τῇ προσευχῇ καὶ τῇ δεήσει μετὰ εὐχαριστίας τὰ αἰτήματα ὑμῶν γνωριζέσθω πρὸς τὸν θεόν. [GNT] | or threatened.<br>• when he is surrounded by quarrels, disturbance, carnality, or false teaching.<br>In the midst of such circumstances, the only way a person can keep from worrying is to receive an injection of supernatural power: the peace of God (Ph.4:7). |
| **#167**<br>**Apart From The Law**<br><br>Without law–KJV<br>Without the law–NASB<br>Apart from the law–NIV<br>Without law–NKJV<br>Never had God's written law–NLT<br><br>**POSB REFERENCE** (Romans 2:11-15; esp. v.12) Note 4, point 1a | *ἀνόμως* = *anomōs*<br>Pronunciation: [an-om'-oce]<br>Parsing (part of speech): adverb adjective<br>    Stem or root—from ἀνόμως<br>Concordance References:<br>  ⇒ Strong's #460 anomōs<br>  ⇒ NIV #492 anomōs<br>  ⇒ NASB #460 anomōs<br><br>**Romans 2:12**<br>For as many as have sinned **without law** shall also perish without law: and as many as have sinned in the law shall be judged by the law; [KJV]<br>For all who have sinned **without the Law** will also perish without the Law; and all who have sinned under the Law will be judged by the Law; [NASB]<br>All who sin **apart from the law** will also perish apart from the law, and all who sin under the law will be judged by the law. [NIV]<br>For as many as have sinned **without law** will also perish without law, and as many as have sinned in the law will be judged by the law [NKJV]<br>God will punish the Gentiles when they sin, even though they **never had God's written law**. And he will punish the Jews when they sin, for they do have the law. [NLT]<br>ὅσοι γὰρ **ἀνόμως** ἥμαρτον, ἀνόμως καὶ ἀπολοῦνται· καὶ ὅσοι ἐν νόμῳ ἥμαρτον, διὰ νόμου κριθήσονται·[GNS]<br>ὅσοι γὰρ **ἀνόμως** ἥμαρτον, ἀνόμως καὶ ἀπολοῦνται, καὶ ὅσοι ἐν νόμῳ ἥμαρτον, διὰ νόμου κριθήσονται [GNT] | Apart from the law; to be without the law; to never have God's written law.<br><br>**Practical Application**<br>The man who sins "apart from the law" (*anomōs*) will also perish apart from the law. The word for "law" is a general word. It refers to the law of God in both the Scriptures and nature. Therefore, the man who does not have the law of Scripture does have the law of nature to guide him. If he sins against the law of nature, he will still be judged and perish. He had the opportunity to know through nature itself. |
| **#168**<br>**Apollyon**<br><br>Apollyon–KJV<br>Apollyon–NASB<br>Apollyon–NIV<br>Apollyon–NKJV<br>Apollyon–the Destroyer–NLT | *Ἀπολλύων* = *Apolluōn*<br>Pronunciation: [ap-ol-loo'-ohn]<br>Parsing (part of speech): noun<br>    Case—nominative<br>    Gender—masculine<br>    Number—singular<br>    Stem or root—from Ἀπολλύων, ονος<br>Concordance References:<br>  ⇒ Strong's #623 Apolluōn<br>  ⇒ NIV #661 Apolluōn<br>  ⇒ NASB #623 Apolluōn<br><br>**Rev. 9:11**<br>And they had a king over them, *which is* the angel of the bottomless pit, whose name in the Hebrew tongue *is* | Apollyon, the destroyer. It is his Greek name.<br><br>**Practical Application**<br>What better name could there be to describe this ruler of the demonic locusts? No creature nor force leaves behind any more destruction than that of the ferocious locust. Who is this fallen angel? It has to be either Satan himself or one of his commanding angels. |

# PRACTICAL WORD STUDIES
## in the NEW TESTAMENT

| ENGLISH WORD | GREEK WORD AND VERSE | THE WORD MEANS... |
|---|---|---|
| **POSB REFERENCE**<br>(Rev.9:11)<br>Note 6 | Abaddon, but in the Greek tongue hath *his* name **Apollyon**. [KJV]<br>They have as king over them, the angel of the abyss; his name in Hebrew is Abaddon, and in the Greek he has the name **Apollyon**. [NASB]<br>They had as king over them the angel of the Abyss, whose name in Hebrew is Abaddon, and in Greek, **Apollyon**. [NIV]<br>And they had as king over them the angel of the bottomless pit, whose name in Hebrew *is* Abaddon, but in Greek he has the name **Apollyon**. [NKJV]<br>Their king is the angel from the bottomless pit; his name in Hebrew is *Abaddon,* and in Greek, ***Apollyon—the Destroyer***. [NLT]<br>καὶ ἔχουσιν ἐπ' αὐτῶν βασιλέα τὸν ἄγγελον τῆς ἀβύσσου· ὄνομα αὐτῷ Ἑβραϊστὶ Ἀβαδδών, καὶ ἐν τῇ Ἑλληνικῇ ὄνομα ἔχει **Ἀπολλύων**. [GNS]<br>ἔχουσιν ἐπ' αὐτῶν βασιλέα τὸν ἄγγελον τῆς ἀβύσσου, ὄνομα αὐτῷ Ἑβραϊστὶ Ἀβαδδών, καὶ ἐν τῇ Ἑλληνικῇ ὄνομα ἔχει **Ἀπολλύων**. [GNT] | |
| **#169**<br>**Apostles**<br><br>Apostles–KJV<br>Apostles–NASB<br>Apostles–NIV<br>Apostles–NKJV<br>Apostles–NLT<br><br>**POSB REFERENCE**<br>(Mt.10:2)<br>*Deeper Study #5*<br><br>See also POSB REF:<br>(Lk.6:13)<br>Note 3, point 1<br>(Rom.1:1)<br>Note 2<br>(1 Cor.12:28)<br>*Deeper Study #1*<br>(Gal.1:1)<br>Note 1<br>(Eph.1:1)<br>Note 1, point 2<br>(Eph.4:11)<br>Note 3, point 1<br>(Col.1:1)<br>Note 1, point 2<br>(1 Tim.1:1)<br>Note 1<br>(1 Tim.2:3-7; esp. v.7)<br>Note 3, point 5b<br>(2 Tim.1:1)<br>Note 1<br>(Tit.1:1)<br>Note 1, point 2<br>(2 Pt.1:1)<br>Note 1, point 2 | ἀποστόλων = *apostolōn*<br>Pronunciation: [ap-os'-tol-own]<br>Parsing (part of speech): noun<br>    Case—genitive<br>    Gender—masculine<br>    Number—plural<br>    Stem or root—from ἀπόστολος, ου<br>Concordance References:<br>  ⇒ Strong's #652 apostolos<br>  ⇒ NIV #693 apostolos<br>  ⇒ NASB #652 apostolos<br><br>**Matthew 10:2**<br>Now the names of the twelve **apostles** are these; The first, Simon, who is called Peter, and Andrew his brother; James *the son* of Zebedee, and John his brother; [KJV]<br>Now the names of the twelve **apostles** are these: The first, Simon, who is called Peter, and Andrew his brother; and James the *son* of Zebedee, and John his brother; [NASB]<br>These are the names of the twelve **apostles**: first, Simon (who is called Peter) and his brother Andrew; James son of Zebedee, and his brother John; [NIV]<br>Now the names of the twelve **apostles** are these: first, Simon, who is called Peter, and Andrew his brother; James the *son* of Zebedee, and John his brother; [NKJV]<br>Here are the names of the twelve **apostles**: first Simon (also called Peter), then Andrew (Peter's brother), James (son of Zebedee), John (James's brother); [NLT]<br>Τῶν δὲ δώδεκα **ἀποστόλων** τὰ ὀνόματά ἐστι ταῦτα· πρῶτος Σίμων ὁ λεγόμενος Πέτρος, καὶ Ἀνδρέας ὁ ἀδελφὸς αὐτοῦ· Ἰάκωβος ὁ τοῦ Ζεβεδαίου, καὶ Ἰωάννης ὁ ἀδελφὸς αὐτοῦ·[GNS]<br>Τῶν δὲ δώδεκα **ἀποστόλων** τὰ ὀνόματά ἐστιν ταῦτα· πρῶτος Σίμων ὁ λεγόμενος Πέτρος καὶ Ἀνδρέας ὁ ἀδελφὸς αὐτοῦ, καὶ Ἰάκωβος ὁ τοῦ Ζεβεδαίου καὶ Ἰωάννης ὁ ἀδελφὸς αὐτοῦ, [GNT] | To send out. An apostle is a representative, a messenger, an ambassador, a person who is sent out into one country to represent another country. The word "apostle" has both a narrow and a broad usage in the New Testament. Three things are true of the apostle:<br>⇒ He belongs to the One who has sent him out.<br>⇒ He is commissioned to be sent out.<br>⇒ He possesses all the authority and power of the One who sends him out.<br><br>**Practical Application**<br>The apostle...<br>• is like an *ambassador* who is sent forth to represent the Person who called and appointed him.<br>• is like a very special *messenger* who is called and sent forth to proclaim the message of the Sender.<br>• is like a very special *minister* who is called and sent forth to serve as the Leader wills.<br>• is like a very special *servant* who is called and sent forth to do the bidding of the Master.<br>Now, note three additional points:<br>1. An apostle is a man chosen directly by the Lord Himself or by the Holy Spirit (cp. Matthew 10:1-2; Mark 3:13-14; Luke 6:13; Acts 9:6, 15; Acts 13:2; Acts 22:10, 14-15; Romans 1:1). He was a man who had either seen or been a companion of the Lord Jesus.<br>2. Jesus called Himself an apostle (*apesteilos*, John 17:3), and He is called the Apostle and High Priest of our profession (Hebrews 3:1).<br>3. Others were also called apostles (Acts 14:4, 14, 17; 1 Thes. 2:6; 2 Cor. 8:23; Phil. 2:25; Galatians 1:19; Romans 16:7). However, there is a distinct difference between all these and the twelve whom Christ chose. The first twelve were...<br>• chosen by the Lord Himself while on earth.<br>• chosen to be with Him during His earthly ministry (Mark 3:14).<br>• chosen to be trained by Him alone, personally. |

# PRACTICAL WORD STUDIES
## in the NEW TESTAMENT

| ENGLISH WORD | GREEK WORD AND VERSE | THE WORD MEANS... |
|---|---|---|
| | | • chosen to be the eyewitnesses of His resurrection (Acts 1:22).<br>• chosen to be the ones who were to carry forth His message which had come from His very own mouth.<br>There is a sense in which the gift of apostleship is still given and used in the ministry today. The Lord's servants of all generations must *see* the Lord and know Him intimately. Similarly, we must personally *see and experience* the power of the resurrection. Certainly there are some in every generation who have *so seen* the Lord Jesus and who *so know* and *so experience* the power of the Lord's resurrection. Perhaps the Lord Jesus endues some with the very special gift of an apostle to be used in a very special way throughout His most precious domain—the church. |
| #170<br>**Appeal**<br><br>Beseech–KJV<br>Exhort–NASB<br>**Appeal–NIV**<br>Plead–NKJV<br>**Appeal–NLT**<br><br>**POSB<br>REFERENCE**<br>(1 Cor.1:10)<br>Note 1<br><br>See also POSB REF:<br>(1 Tim.5:1-2; esp. v.1)<br>Introduction | Παρακαλῶ = *Parakalō*<br>Pronunciation: [par-ak-al-o']<br>Parsing (part of speech): verb<br>   Mood—indicative<br>   Tense—present<br>   Voice—active<br>   Person—1st person<br>   Number—singular<br>   Stem or root—from παρακαλέω<br>Concordance References:<br>⇒ Strong's #3870 parakaleō<br>⇒ NIV #4151 parakaleō<br>⇒ NASB #3870 parakaleō<br><br>**1 Cor. 1:10**<br>Now I **beseech** you, brethren, by the name of our Lord Jesus Christ, that ye all speak the same thing, and *that* there be no divisions among you; but *that* ye be perfectly joined together in the same mind and in the same judgment. [KJV]<br>Now I **exhort** you, brethren, by the name of our Lord Jesus Christ, that you all agree, and there be no divisions among you, but you be made complete in the same mind and in the same judgment. [NASB]<br>I **appeal** to you, brothers, in the name of our Lord Jesus Christ, that all of you agree with one another so that there may be no divisions among you and that you may be perfectly united in mind and thought. [NIV]<br>Now I **plead** with you, brethren, by the name of our Lord Jesus Christ, that you all speak the same thing, and *that* there be no divisions among you, but *that* you be perfectly joined together in the same mind and in the same judgment. [NKJV]<br>Now, dear brothers and sisters, I **appeal** to you by the authority of the Lord Jesus Christ to stop arguing among yourselves. Let there be real harmony so there won't be divisions in the church. I plead with you to be of one mind, united in thought and purpose. [NLT]<br>Παρακαλῶ δὲ ὑμᾶς, ἀδελφοί, διὰ τοῦ ὀνόματος τοῦ Κυρίου ἡμῶν Ἰησοῦ Χριστοῦ, ἵνα τὸ αὐτὸ λέγητε πάντες, καὶ μὴ ᾖ ἐν ὑμῖν σχίσματα, ἦτε δὲ κατηρτισμένοι ἐν τῷ αὐτῷ νοῒ καὶ ἐν τῇ αὐτῇ γνώμῃ. [GNS]<br>Παρακαλῶ δὲ ὑμᾶς, ἀδελφοί, διὰ τοῦ ὀνόματος τοῦ κυρίου ἡμῶν Ἰησοῦ Χριστοῦ, ἵνα τὸ αὐτὸ λέγητε πάντες καὶ μὴ ᾖ ἐν ὑμῖν σχίσματα, ἦτε δὲ κατηρτισμένοι ἐν τῷ αὐτῷ νοῒ καὶ ἐν τῇ αὐτῇ γνώμῃ. [GNT] | To appeal; to ask; to exhort; to encourage; to beseech; to beg; to urge; to request; to summon; to call to one's side.<br><br>**Practical Application**<br>Paul says, "I call you to my side; come, let's share together, talk the matter over. I ask, plead, beg—hear what I have to say." |
| #171<br>**Appear, To** | ἐμφανῆ γενέσθαι = *emphanē genesthai*<br>Pronunciation: [em-fan-ay' ghin'-es-tha-ee]<br>Parsing *emphanē* (part of speech): adjective<br>   Case—accusative<br>   Gender—masculine | To be seen; to become visible; to appear; to reveal; to show openly. |

# PRACTICAL WORD STUDIES
## in the NEW TESTAMENT

| ENGLISH WORD | GREEK WORD AND VERSE | THE WORD MEANS... |
|---|---|---|
| Showed...openly–KJV<br>Become visible–NASB<br>Be seen–NIV<br>Showed openly–NKJV<br>**To appear–NLT**<br><br>**POSB REFERENCE**<br>(Acts 10:40-41; esp. v.40)<br>Note 6, point 1 | Number—singular<br>Stem or root—from ἐμφανής<br>Parsing *genesthai* (part of speech): verb<br>  Mood—infinitive<br>  Tense—aorist<br>  Voice—middle deponent<br>  Stem or root—from γίνομαι<br>Concordance References:<br>⇒ Strong's #1717 emphanës + 1096 ginomai<br>⇒ NIV #1871 [seen] emphanës + 1181 ginomai [be]<br>⇒ NASB #1717 emphanës + 1096 ginomai<br><br>**Acts 10:40**<br>Him God raised up the third day, and **showed** him **openly**; [KJV]<br>"God raised Him up on the third day, and granted that He should **become visible**, [NASB]<br>But God raised him from the dead on the third day and caused him to **be seen**. [NIV]<br>Him God raised up on the third day, and **showed** Him **openly**, [NKJV]<br>But God raised him to life three days later. Then God allowed him **to appear**, [NLT]<br>Τοῦτον ὁ Θεὸς ἤγειρε τῇ τρίτῃ ἡμέρᾳ, καὶ ἔδωκεν αὐτὸν **ἐμφανῆ γενέσθαι**, [GNS]<br>τοῦτον ὁ θεὸς ἤγειρεν [ἐν] τῇ τρίτῃ ἡμέρᾳ καὶ ἔδωκεν αὐτὸν **ἐμφανῆ γενέσθαι**, [GNT] | **Practical Application**<br>God showed Jesus openly—He allowed Him to appear—which means that God set Jesus before people, so that He could be visibly, openly, and publicly seen. God manifested, showed, and set Him forth as the Risen Lord. (See POSB note—Acts 1:3 and POSB *Deeper Study* #1, Jesus, Resurrection—Acts 1:3 for more discussion.) |
| **#172**<br>**Appearance**<br><br>Brightness–KJV<br>**Appearance–NASB**<br>Splendor–NIV<br>Brightness–NKJV<br>Splendor–NLT<br><br>**POSB REFERENCE**<br>(2 Thes.2:8)<br>Note 4, point 2 | ἐπιφανείᾳ = *epiphaneia*<br>Pronunciation: [ep-if-an'-ee-ah]<br>Parsing (part of speech): noun<br>  Case—dative<br>  Gender—feminine<br>  Number—singular<br>  Stem or root—from ἐπιφάνεια, ας<br>Concordance References:<br>⇒ Strong's #2015 epiphaneia<br>⇒ NIV #2211 epiphaneia<br>⇒ NASB #2015 epiphaneia<br><br>**2 Thes. 2:8**<br>And then shall that Wicked be revealed, whom the Lord shall consume with the spirit of his mouth, and shall destroy with the **brightness** of his coming: [KJV]<br>And then that lawless one will be revealed whom the Lord will slay with the breath of His mouth and bring to an end by the **appearance** of His coming; [NASB]<br>And then the lawless one will be revealed, whom the Lord Jesus will overthrow with the breath of his mouth and destroy by the **splendor** of his coming. [NIV]<br>And then the lawless one will be revealed, whom the Lord will consume with the breath of His mouth and destroy with the **brightness** of His coming. [NKJV]<br>Then the man of lawlessness will be revealed, whom the Lord Jesus will consume with the breath of his mouth and destroy by the **splendor** of his coming. [NLT]<br>καὶ τότε ἀποκαλυφθήσεται ὁ ἄνομος, ὃν ὁ Κύριος ἀναλώσει τῷ πνεύματι τοῦ στόματος αὐτοῦ, καὶ καταργήσει τῇ **ἐπιφανείᾳ** τῆς παρουσίας αὐτοῦ [GNS]<br>καὶ τότε ἀποκαλυφθήσεται ὁ ἄνομος, ὃν ὁ κύριος [Ἰησοῦς] ἀνελεῖ τῷ πνεύματι τοῦ στόματος αὐτοῦ καὶ καταργήσει τῇ **ἐπιφανείᾳ** τῆς παρουσίας αὐτοῦ, [GNT] | Splendor, brightness, appearance.<br><br>**Practical Application**<br>The Lord of glory will destroy the antichrist with the brightness of His coming. The word "appearance" (*epiphaneia*) is a very special word. It is a word chosen by the New Testament to refer only to the coming (*parousia*) of the Lord. It is used only five times in all the New Testament, and in every instance it refers to the Lord's coming into the world. It refers once to His first coming (2 Tim. 1:10) and four times to His second coming (1 Tim. 6:14; 2 Tim. 4:1, 8; Titus 2:13). The whole idea of *appearance* or *splendor* is brightness, radiance, glory, and light. Someone has pointed out that when Jesus Christ returns to earth, there will be such a spectacular display of glory and splendor that the explosion of every star in the universe could not match the sight of the Lord (source unknown). When Christ first appears, there will apparently be the energizing of a laser beam of glory zeroed in on the antichrist, and he will be immediately destroyed by the radiance of the Lord's glory and light—quicker than the eye can blink. Simply by showing Himself, the Lord will destroy the antichrist. Note: the word "destroy" does not mean to annihilate, but to make inoperative; to make powerless; to end; to put a stop to his evil work. |
| **#173**<br>**Appearance Changed**<br><br>Transfigured–KJV<br>Transfigured–NASB<br>Transfigured–NIV<br>Transfigured–NKJV | μετεμορφώθη = *metemorphōthē*<br>Pronunciation: [met-am-or-fo'-thay]<br>Parsing (part of speech): verb<br>  Mood—indicative<br>  Tense—aorist<br>  Voice—passive<br>  Person—3rd person<br>  Number—singular<br>  Stem or root—from μεταμορφόομαι | A change into another form; a transformation; a change of countenance; a complete change.<br><br>**Practical Application**<br>Luke said, "the appearance of his face changed" (Luke 9:29). Note how the gospel writers described what happened. |

## PRACTICAL WORD STUDIES
### in the NEW TESTAMENT

| ENGLISH WORD | GREEK WORD AND VERSE | THE WORD MEANS... |
|---|---|---|
| **Appearance changed–NLT**<br><br>**POSB REFERENCE**<br>(Mt.17:2)<br>Note 2<br><br>See also POSB REF:<br>(Mk.9:2-3; esp. v.2)<br>*Deeper Study #2* | Concordance References:<br>⇒ Strong's #3339 metamorphoö<br>⇒ NIV #3565 metamorphoö<br>⇒ NASB #3339 metamorphoö<br><br>**Matthew 17:2**<br>And was **transfigured** before them: and his face did shine as the sun, and his raiment was white as the light. [KJV]<br>And He was **transfigured** before them; and His face shone like the sun, and His garments became as white as light. [NASB]<br>There he was **transfigured** before them. His face shone like the sun, and his clothes became as white as the light. [NIV]<br>and He was **transfigured** before them. His face shone like the sun, and His clothes became as white as the light. [NKJV]<br>As the men watched, Jesus' **appearance changed** so that his face shone like the sun, and his clothing became dazzling white. [NLT]<br>καὶ **μετεμορφώθη** ἔμπροσθεν αὐτῶν, καὶ ἔλαμψε τὸ πρόσωπον αὐτοῦ ὡς ὁ ἥλιος, τὰ δὲ ἱμάτια αὐτοῦ ἐγένετο λευκὰ ὡς τὸ φῶς. [GNS]<br>καὶ **μετεμορφώθη** ἔμπροσθεν αὐτῶν, καὶ ἔλαμψεν τὸ πρόσωπον αὐτοῦ ὡς ὁ ἥλιος, τὰ δὲ ἱμάτια αὐτοῦ ἐγένετο λευκὰ ὡς τὸ φῶς. [GNT] | *As the men watched, Jesus' appearance changed so that his face shone like the sun, and his clothing became dazzling white. (Matthew 17:2) [NLT]*<br>*And his clothing became dazzling white, far whiter than any earthly process could ever make it. (Mark 9:3) [NLT]*<br>*And as he was praying, the appearance of his face changed, and his clothing became dazzling white. (Luke 9:29) [NLT]* |
| **#174**<br>**Appeared**<br><br>Made–KJV<br>Made–NASB<br>Made–NIV<br>Coming–NKJV<br>**Appeared–NLT**<br><br>**POSB REFERENCE**<br>(Philip.2:7)<br>Note 3, point 2 | γενόμενος = genomenos<br>Pronunciation: [ghin'-om-eh-nos]<br>Parsing (part of speech): verb<br>  Mood—participle<br>  Tense—aorist<br>  Voice—middle deponent<br>  Case—nominative<br>  Gender—masculine<br>  Number—singular<br>  Stem or root—from γίνομαι<br>Concordance References:<br>⇒ Strong's #1096 ginomai<br>⇒ NIV #1181 ginomai<br>⇒ NASB #1096 ginomai<br><br>**Philip. 2:7**<br>But made himself of no reputation, and took upon him the form of a servant, and was **made** in the likeness of men: [KJV]<br>But emptied Himself, taking the form of a bond-servant, *and* being **made** in the likeness of men. [NASB]<br>But made himself nothing, taking the very nature of a servant, being **made** in human likeness. [NIV]<br>But made Himself of no reputation, taking the form of a bondservant, *and* **coming** in the likeness of men. [NKJV]<br>He made himself nothing; he took the humble position of a slave and **appeared** in human form. [NLT]<br>ἀλλ᾽ ἑαυτὸν ἐκένωσε, μορφὴν δούλου λαβών, ἐν ὁμοιώματι ἀνθρώπων **γενόμενος**· καὶ σχήματι εὑρεθεὶς ὡς ἄνθρωπος, [GNS]<br>ἀλλὰ ἑαυτὸν ἐκένωσεν μορφὴν δούλου λαβών, ἐν ὁμοιώματι ἀνθρώπων **γενόμενος**· καὶ σχήματι εὑρεθεὶς ὡς ἄνθρωπος [GNT] | To be made; to become; to arrive; to appear. It means a definite entrance into time.<br><br>**Practical Application**<br>It is not a permanent state. Jesus became a man, but it was not to be a permanent state. It was only for a time, a particular period. In the fullness of time, He made a definite entrance into the world as a man.<br>Note that Jesus Christ did not come to earth as a prince or some great leader upon earth. He did not come to receive the homage and service of men. He came as the humblest of men, as a servant to serve men. "He was brought up meanly, probably working with his supposed father at his trade. His whole life was a life of humiliation, meanness, poverty, and disgrace; he had nowhere to lay his head, lived upon alms, was a man of sorrows and acquainted with grief, did not appear with external pomp or any marks of distinction from other men. This was the humiliation of his life" (Matthew Henry. *Matthew Henry's Commentary*, Vol.6. Old Tappan, NJ: Fleming H. Revell Co., p.732f). |
| **#175**<br>**Appeared**<br><br>Showed–KJV<br>Presented–NASB<br>Showed–NIV<br>Presented–NKJV<br>**Appeared–NLT** | παρέστησεν = parestēsen<br>Pronunciation: [par-is'-tay-sen]<br>Parsing (part of speech): verb<br>  Mood—indicative<br>  Tense—aorist<br>  Voice—active<br>  Person—3rd person<br>  Number—singular<br>  Stem or root—from παρίστημι | To show; to present; to offer; to appear; to bring near; to hand over.<br><br>**Practical Application**<br>Jesus showed, presented Himself alive. Note the exciting facts in this Scripture during the forty days after His crucifixion:<br>⇒ He personally appeared to the apostles.<br>⇒ He proved to them in many ways that He |

# PRACTICAL WORD STUDIES
## in the NEW TESTAMENT

| ENGLISH WORD | GREEK WORD AND VERSE | THE WORD MEANS... |
|---|---|---|
| **POSB REFERENCE**<br>(Acts 1:3)<br>Note 3, point 1 | Concordance References:<br>⇒ Strong's #3936 paristēmi<br>⇒ NIV #4225 paristēmi<br>⇒ NASB ##3936 paristēmi<br><br>**Acts 1:3**<br>To whom also he **showed** himself alive after his passion by many infallible proofs, being seen of them forty days, and speaking of the things pertaining to the kingdom of God. [KJV]<br>To these He also **presented** Himself alive, after His suffering, by many convincing proofs, appearing to them over *a period of* forty days, and speaking of the things concerning the kingdom of God. [NASB]<br>After his suffering, he **showed** himself to these men and gave many convincing proofs that he was alive. He appeared to them over a period of forty days and spoke about the kingdom of God. [NIV]<br>To whom He also **presented** Himself alive after His suffering by many infallible proofs, being seen by them during forty days and speaking of the things pertaining to the kingdom of God. [NKJV]<br>During the forty days after his crucifixion, he **appeared** to the apostles from time to time and proved to them in many ways that he was actually alive. On these occasions he talked to them about the Kingdom of God. [NLT]<br>οἷς καὶ **παρέστησεν** ἑαυτὸν ζῶντα μετὰ τὸ παθεῖν αὐτὸν ἐν πολλοῖς τεκμηρίοις, δι' ἡμερῶν τεσσεράκοντα ὀπτανόμενος αὐτοῖς, καὶ λέγων τὰ περὶ τῆς βασιλείας τοῦ Θεοῦ. [GNS]<br>οἷς καὶ **παρέστησεν** ἑαυτὸν ζῶντα μετὰ τὸ παθεῖν αὐτὸν ἐν πολλοῖς τεκμηρίοις, δι' ἡμερῶν τεσσεράκοντα ὀπτανόμενος αὐτοῖς καὶ λέγων τὰ περὶ τῆς βασιλείας τοῦ θεοῦ· [GNT] | was actually alive.<br>⇒ He talked to them about the Kingdom of God. |
| **#176**<br>**Appearing–Appears**<br><br>Appearing–KJV<br>Appearing–NASB<br>Appearing–NIV<br>Appearing–NKJV<br>Appears–NLT<br><br>**POSB REFERENCE**<br>(2 Tim.4:1)<br>Note 1, point 2 | ἐπιφάνειαν = epiphaneian<br>Pronunciation: [ep-if-an'-ee-ahn]<br>Parsing (part of speech): noun<br>    Case—accusative<br>    Gender—feminine<br>    Number—singular<br>    Stem or root—from ἐπιφάνεια, ας<br>Concordance References:<br>⇒ Strong's #2015 epiphaneia<br>⇒ NIV #2211 epiphaneia<br>⇒ NASB #2015 epiphaneia<br><br>**2 Tim. 4:1**<br>I charge *thee* therefore before God, and the Lord Jesus Christ, who shall judge the quick and the dead at his **appearing** and his kingdom; [KJV]<br>I solemnly charge *you* in the presence of God and of Christ Jesus, who is to judge the living and the dead, and by His **appearing** and His kingdom: [NASB]<br>In the presence of God and of Christ Jesus, who will judge the living and the dead, and in view of his **appearing** and his kingdom, I give you this charge: [NIV]<br>I charge *you* therefore before God and the Lord Jesus Christ, who will judge the living and the dead at His **appearing** and His kingdom: [NKJV]<br>And so I solemnly urge you before God and before Christ Jesus—who will someday judge the living and the dead when he **appears** to set up his Kingdom: [NLT]<br>Διαμαρτύρομαι οὖν ἐγὼ ἐνώπιον τοῦ Θεοῦ, καὶ τοῦ κυρίου Ἰησοῦ Χριστοῦ, τοῦ μέλλοντος κρίνειν ζῶντας καὶ νεκρούς, κατὰ τὴν **ἐπιφάνειαν** αὐτοῦ καὶ τὴν βασιλείαν αὐτοῦ, [GNS]<br>Διαμαρτύρομαι ἐνώπιον τοῦ θεοῦ καὶ Χριστοῦ Ἰησοῦ τοῦ μέλλοντος κρίνειν ζῶντας καὶ νεκρούς, καὶ τὴν **ἐπιφάνειαν** αὐτοῦ καὶ τὴν βασιλείαν αὐτοῦ· [GNT] | Appearing. It means the glorious and visible appearance of the Lord Jesus (Kenneth Wuest. *Word Studies in the Greek New Testament*, Vol.2. Grand Rapids, MI: Eerdmans Publishing Co., 1966, p.153).<br><br>**Practical Application**<br>The history of the word is found in the appearance of the great Roman Emperor, especially when he was scheduled to visit a city. Thorough preparations were made: buildings and streets were scrubbed and cleaned; people worked hard to prepare themselves and their city for their coming king. They were excited about his coming and focused their attention and energy upon his coming. This is exactly what the minister must do: he must preach the Word, keeping his mind upon the return of the Lord Jesus Christ. He must be prepared for His return, and the minister of the Lord prepares by preaching the Word. The conquering Lord is returning; if we fail to preach the Word, we will stand before Him unprepared—embarrassed and ashamed. If we fail to be subjected to Him now—fail to preach His Word—we will be subjected and judged by Him. |

## PRACTICAL WORD STUDIES
### in the NEW TESTAMENT

| ENGLISH WORD | GREEK WORD AND VERSE | THE WORD MEANS... |
|---|---|---|
| **#177**<br>**Appears**<br><br>Revealed–KJV<br>Revealed–NASB<br>Revealed–NIV<br>Revealed–NKJV<br>**Appears–NLT**<br><br>**POSB<br>REFERENCE**<br>(2 Thes.1:7-8; esp. v.7)<br>Note 2, point 1 | ἀποκαλύψει = *apokalupsei*<br>Pronunciation: [ap-ok-al'-oop-seh-ee]<br>Parsing (part of speech): noun<br>    Case—dative<br>    Gender—feminine<br>    Number—singular<br>    Stem or root—from ἀποκάλυψις, εως<br>Concordance References:<br>  ⇒ Strong's #602 apokalupsis<br>  ⇒ NIV #637 apokalupsis<br>  ⇒ NASB #602 apokalupsis<br><br>**2 Thes. 1:7**<br>And to you who are troubled rest with us, when the Lord Jesus shall be **revealed** from heaven with his mighty angels, [KJV]<br>And *to give* relief to you who are afflicted and to us as well when the Lord Jesus shall be **revealed** from heaven with His mighty angels in flaming fire, [NASB]<br>And give relief to you who are troubled, and to us as well. This will happen when the Lord Jesus is **revealed** from heaven in blazing fire with his powerful angels. [NIV]<br>And to *give* you who are troubled rest with us when the Lord Jesus is **revealed** from heaven with His mighty angels, [NKJV]<br>And God will provide rest for you who are being persecuted and also for us when the Lord Jesus **appears** from heaven. He will come with his mighty angels, [NLT]<br>καὶ ὑμῖν τοῖς θλιβομένοις ἄνεσιν μεθ' ἡμῶν, ἐν τῇ **ἀποκαλύψει** τοῦ Κυρίου Ἰησοῦ ἀπ' οὐρανοῦ μετ' ἀγγέλων δυνάμεως αὐτοῦ, [GNS]<br>καὶ ὑμῖν τοῖς θλιβομένοις ἄνεσιν μεθ' ἡμῶν, ἐν τῇ **ἀποκαλύψει** τοῦ κυρίου Ἰησοῦ ἀπ' οὐρανοῦ μετ' ἀγγέλων δυνάμεως αὐτοῦ [GNT] | To reveal, to appear; to be unveiled and uncovered; a revelation<br><br>**Practical Application**<br>Jesus' return in judgment shall be a spectacular appearance from heaven. The day is coming when Jesus Christ shall rent the heavens and return to earth in judgment. As Matthew Henry says, "He will come in all the pomp and power of the upper world" (*Matthew Henry's Commentary*, Vol.6, p.794). He will be revealed as the Supreme Majesty and Judge of the world. |
| **#178**<br>**Appetite**<br><br>Belly–KJV<br>**Appetite–NASB**<br>Stomach–NIV<br>Belly–NKJV<br>**Appetite–NLT**<br><br>**POSB<br>REFERENCE**<br>(Philip.3:18-19; esp. v.19)<br>Note 2, point 2 | κοιλία = *koilia*<br>Pronunciation: [koy-lee'-ah]<br>Parsing (part of speech): noun<br>    Case—nominative<br>    Gender—feminine<br>    Number—singular<br>    Stem or root—from κοιλία, ας<br>Concordance References:<br>  ⇒ Strong's #2836 koilia<br>  ⇒ NIV #3120 koilia<br>  ⇒ NASB #2836 koilia<br><br>**Philip. 3:19**<br>Whose end *is* destruction, whose God *is their* **belly**, and *whose* glory *is* in their shame, who mind earthly things.) [KJV]<br>Whose end is destruction, whose god is *their* **appetite**, and *whose* glory is in their shame, who set their minds on earthly things. [NASB]<br>Their destiny is destruction, their god is their **stomach**, and their glory is in their shame. Their mind is on earthly things. [NIV]<br>Whose end *is* destruction, whose god *is their* **belly**, and *whose* glory *is* in their shame—who set their mind on earthly things. [NKJV]<br>Their future is eternal destruction. Their god is their **appetite**, they brag about shameful things, and all they think about is this life here on earth. [NLT]<br>ὧν τὸ τέλος ἀπώλεια, ὧν ὁ θεὸς ἡ **κοιλία**, καὶ ἡ δόξα ἐν τῇ αἰσχύνῃ αὐτῶν, οἱ τὰ ἐπίγεια φρονοῦντες. [GNS]<br>ὧν τὸ τέλος ἀπώλεια, ὧν ὁ θεὸς ἡ **κοιλία** καὶ ἡ δόξα ἐν τῇ αἰσχύνῃ αὐτῶν, οἱ τὰ ἐπίγεια φρονοῦντες. [GNT] | Stomach, belly, appetite.<br><br>**Practical Application**<br>Their god is their appetite (*koilia*), that is, their stomach, their sensuality, their desire for the physical pleasures of this world. Physical and material gratification is their god. They center their lives around...<br>• possessions and property<br>• houses and furnishings<br>• food and appetite<br>• comfort and plenty<br>• position and success<br>• pleasure and sex<br>• acceptance and social standing<br>• money and wealth<br>• honor and fame<br>Just take a moment to think about any of the above, how some persons center and focus their lives upon such things. Some persons spend more time in front of a mirror or eating or thinking about acceptance or success or possessions or some business deal than they do in prayer. |
| **#179**<br>**Appetites** | κοιλία = *koilia*<br>Pronunciation: [koy-lee'-ah]<br>Parsing (part of speech): noun<br>    Case—dative | Appetites, personal interests. It means the stomach and its physical appetites. |

## PRACTICAL WORD STUDIES
### in the NEW TESTAMENT

| ENGLISH WORD | GREEK WORD AND VERSE | THE WORD MEANS... |
|---|---|---|
| Belly–KJV<br>**Appetites–NASB**<br>**Appetites–NIV**<br>Belly–NKJV<br>Personal interests–NLT<br><br>**POSB REFERENCE**<br>(Rom.16:17-18; esp. v.18)<br>Note 1, point 2 | Gender—feminine<br>Number—singular<br>Stem or root—from κοιλία, ας<br>Concordance References:<br>⇒ Strong's #2836 koilia<br>⇒ NIV #3120 koilia<br>⇒ NASB #2836 koilia<br><br>**Romans 16:18**<br>For they that are such serve not our Lord Jesus Christ, but their own **belly**; and by good words and fair speeches deceive the hearts of the simple. [KJV]<br>For such men are slaves, not of our Lord Christ but of their own **appetites**; and by their smooth and flattering speech they deceive the hearts of the unsuspecting. [NASB]<br>For such people are not serving our Lord Christ, but their own **appetites**. By smooth talk and flattery they deceive the minds of naive people. [NIV]<br>For those who are such do not serve our Lord Jesus Christ, but their own **belly**, and by smooth words and flattering speech deceive the hearts of the simple. [NKJV]<br>Such people are not serving Christ our Lord; they are serving their own **personal interests**. By smooth talk and glowing words they deceive innocent people. [NLT]<br>οἱ γὰρ τοιοῦτοι τῷ Κυρίῳ ἡμῶν Ἰησοῦ Χριστῷ οὐ δουλεύουσιν, ἀλλὰ τῇ ἑαυτῶν **κοιλίᾳ**· καὶ διὰ τῆς χρηστολογίας καὶ εὐλογίας ἐξαπατῶσι τὰς καρδίας τῶν ἀκάκων. [GNS]<br>οἱ γὰρ τοιοῦτοι τῷ κυρίῳ ἡμῶν Χριστῷ οὐ δουλεύουσιν ἀλλὰ τῇ ἑαυτῶν **κοιλίᾳ**, καὶ διὰ τῆς χρηστολογίας καὶ εὐλογίας ἐξαπατῶσιν τὰς καρδίας τῶν ἀκάκων. [GNT] | **Practical Application**<br>A divisive person does not serve Christ, but his own desires. A divisive person is gripped by...<br>• selfish desires<br>• base ambition<br>• personal urges<br>• physical appetites<br>• wanting his own way<br>• getting what he wants<br><br>Note: Scripture clearly says that divisive persons do not serve Christ. They call themselves Christians, but their Lord is not Christ. They are not committed to His honor and glory and mission, but to themselves—to getting and doing what they want. The divisive person is still given over to the things of this carnal, sensual, and secular world. |
| #180<br>**Apply–<br>Applying**<br><br>Add–KJV<br>**Applying–NASB**<br>Add–NIV<br>Add–NKJV<br>**Apply–NLT**<br><br>**POSB REFERENCE**<br>(2 Pt.1:5-7; esp. v.5)<br>Note 1 | ἐπιχορηγήσατε = *epichorëgësate*<br>Pronunciation: [ep-ee-khor-ayg-eh'-sah-teh]<br>Parsing (part of speech): verb<br>   Mood—imperative<br>   Tense—aorist<br>   Voice—active<br>   Person—2nd person<br>   Number—plural<br>   Stem or root—from ἐπιχορηγέω<br>Concordance References:<br>⇒ Strong's #2023 epichorëgeö<br>⇒ NIV #2220 epichorëgeö<br>⇒ NASB #2023 epichorëgeö<br><br>**2 Peter 1:5**<br>And beside this, giving all diligence, **add** to your faith virtue; and to virtue knowledge; [KJV]<br>Now for this very reason also, **applying** all diligence, in your faith supply moral excellence, and in *your* moral excellence, knowledge; [NASB]<br>For this very reason, make every effort to **add** to your faith goodness; and to goodness, knowledge; [NIV]<br>But also for this very reason, giving all diligence, **add** to your faith virtue, to virtue knowledge, [NKJV]<br>So make every effort to **apply** the benefits of these promises to your life. Then your faith will produce a life of moral excellence. A life of moral excellence leads to knowing God better. [NLT]<br>καὶ αὐτὸ τοῦτο δὲ σπουδὴν πᾶσαν παρεισενέγκαντες, **ἐπιχορηγήσατε** ἐν τῇ πίστει ὑμῶν τὴν ἀρετήν, ἐν δὲ τῇ ἀρετῇ τὴν γνῶσιν, [GNS]<br>καὶ αὐτὸ τοῦτο δὲ σπουδὴν πᾶσαν παρεισενέγκαντες **ἐπιχορηγήσατε** ἐν τῇ πίστει ὑμῶν τὴν ἀρετήν, ἐν δὲ τῇ ἀρετῇ τὴν γνῶσιν, [GNT] | To add; to apply.<br><br>**Practical Application**<br>The word "apply" or "applying" (*epichorëgësate*) means in addition to God's great salvation apply them—right along side of what God has done—add *these qualities*. *Make every effort* to add them. Hasten, jump, act now to add them; don't wait. Be energetic and earnest, strenuously work to add *these qualities* to your faith and salvation. |
| #181<br>**Appointed** | ἐποίησεν = *epoiesen*<br>Pronunciation: [eh-poy-eh'-sen]<br>Parsing (part of speech): verb<br>   Mood—indicative<br>   Tense—aorist | To be ordained, chosen, designated, commissioned, picked, elected, selected, or appointed.<br><br>**Practical Application**<br>The word is taken from the Greek root word |

## PRACTICAL WORD STUDIES
### in the NEW TESTAMENT

| ENGLISH WORD | GREEK WORD AND VERSE | THE WORD MEANS... |
|---|---|---|
| Ordained–KJV<br>**Appointed–NASB**<br>**Appointed–NIV**<br>**Appointed–NKJV**<br>Selected–NLT<br><br>**POSB**<br>**REFERENCE**<br>(Mk.3:14)<br>*Deeper Study #1* | Voice—active<br>Person—3rd person<br>Number—singular<br>Stem or root—from ποιέω<br>Concordance References:<br>⇒ Strong's #4160 poieö<br>⇒ NIV #4472 poieö<br>⇒ NASB #4160 poieö<br><br>**Mark 3:14**<br>And he **ordained** twelve, that they should be with him, and that he might send them forth to preach, [KJV]<br>And He **appointed** twelve, that they might be with Him, and that He might send them out to preach, [NASB]<br>He **appointed** twelve—designating them apostles—that they might be with him and that he might send them out to preach [NIV]<br>Then He **appointed** twelve, that they might be with Him and that He might send them out to preach, [NKJV]<br>Then he **selected** twelve of them to be his regular companions, calling them apostles. He sent them out to preach, [NLT]<br>καὶ **ἐποίησε** δώδεκα, ἵνα ὦσι μετ' αὐτοῦ, καὶ ἵνα ἀποστέλλῃ αὐτοὺς κηρύσσειν, [GNS]<br>καὶ **ἐποίησεν** δώδεκα [οὓς καὶ ἀποστόλους ὠνόμασεν] ἵνα ὦσιν μετ' αὐτοῦ καὶ ἵνα ἀποστέλλῃ αὐτοὺς κηρύσσειν [GNT] | *poieö* which means to do, to make, to appoint with credentials. The word is often used to refer to a person's being appointed to some high position or office. The picture is that of Jesus Christ, the future King of the universe, taking twelve men and appointing them to be His. He appointed (ordained) them to the *office* of being His ministers and representatives on earth. |
| **#182**<br>**Appointed**<br><br>Ordained–KJV<br>**Appointed–NASB**<br>**Appointed–NIV**<br>**Appointed–NKJV**<br>**Appointed–NLT**<br><br>**POSB**<br>**REFERENCE**<br>(Acts 14:23)<br>*Deeper Study #3* | χειροτονήσαντες = *cheirotonēsantes*<br>Pronunciation: [khi-rot-on-ay-sahn-tehs]<br>Parsing (part of speech): verb<br>  Mood—participle<br>  Tense—aorist<br>  Voice—active<br>  Case—nominative<br>  Gender—masculine<br>  Number—plural<br>  Stem or root—from χειροτονέω<br>Concordance References:<br>⇒ Strong's #5500 cheirotoneö<br>⇒ NIV #5936 cheirotoneö<br>⇒ NASB #5500 cheirotoneö<br><br>**Acts 14:23**<br>And when they had **ordained** them elders in every church, and had prayed with fasting, they commended them to the Lord, on whom they believed. [KJV]<br>And when they had **appointed** elders for them in every church, having prayed with fasting, they commended them to the Lord in whom they had believed. [NASB]<br>Paul and Barnabas **appointed** elders for them in each church and, with prayer and fasting, committed them to the Lord, in whom they had put their trust. [NIV]<br>So when they had **appointed** elders in every church, and prayed with fasting, they commended them to the Lord in whom they had believed. [NKJV]<br>Paul and Barnabas also **appointed** elders in every church and prayed for them with fasting, turning them over to the care of the Lord, in whom they had come to trust. [NLT]<br>χειροτονήσαντες δὲ αὐτοῖς πρεσβυτέρους κατ' ἐκκλησίαν προσευξάμενοι μετὰ νηστειῶν, παρέθεντο αὐτοὺς τῷ Κυρίῳ εἰς ὃν πεπιστεύκεισαν. [GNS]<br>χειροτονήσαντες δὲ αὐτοῖς κατ' ἐκκλησίαν πρεσβυτέρους, προσευξάμενοι μετὰ νηστειῶν παρέθεντο αὐτοὺς τῷ κυρίῳ εἰς ὃν πεπιστεύκεισαν. [GNT] | To appoint; to ordain; to elect; to choose by stretching out the hand.<br><br>**Practical Application**<br>The word is used to refer to both God and men choosing others. Note the striking facts in this Scripture:<br>⇒ Paul and Barnabas appointed the leaders.<br>⇒ Paul and Barnabas appointed elders in *every* church.<br>⇒ Paul and Barnabas appointed the elders with prayer and fasting.<br>⇒ Paul and Barnabas appointed the elders, commending them to the Lord.<br>⇒ Paul and Barnabas did all of this, trusting in the Lord. |
| **#183**<br>**Appointed**<br><br>Raised...up–KJV<br>Raised...up–NASB | ἐξήγειρά = *exēgeira*<br>Pronunciation: [ex-eg-i'-rah]<br>Parsing (part of speech): verb<br>  Mood—indicative<br>  Tense—aorist<br>  Voice—active | To be raised up; to be appointed.<br><br>**Practical Application**<br>God shows justice as He wills. Scripture says that God "appointed" (*exēgeira*) Pharaoh. This means that God allowed Pharaoh to appear, |

# PRACTICAL WORD STUDIES
## in the NEW TESTAMENT

| ENGLISH WORD | GREEK WORD AND VERSE | THE WORD MEANS... |
|---|---|---|
| Raised...up–NIV<br>Raised...up–NKJV<br>Appointed–NLT<br><br>**POSB REFERENCE**<br>(Rom.9:15-18; esp. v.17)<br>Note 2, point 2a | Person—1st person<br>Number—singular<br>Stem or root—from ἐξεγείρω<br>Concordance References:<br>⇒ Strong's #1825 exegeirō<br>⇒ NIV #1995 exegeirō<br>⇒ NASB #1825 exegeirō<br><br>**Romans 9:17**<br>For the scripture saith unto Pharaoh, Even for this same purpose have I **raised** thee **up**, that I might show my power in thee, and that my name might be declared throughout all the earth. [KJV]<br><br>For the Scripture says to Pharaoh, "FOR THIS VERY PURPOSE I **RAISED** YOU **UP**, TO DEMONSTRATE MY POWER IN YOU, AND THAT MY NAME MIGHT BE PROCLAIMED THROUGHOUT THE WHOLE EARTH." [NASB]<br><br>For the Scripture says to Pharaoh: "I **raised** you **up** for this very purpose, that I might display my power in you and that my name might be proclaimed in all the earth." [NIV]<br><br>For the Scripture says to Pharaoh, *"For this very purpose I have **raised** you **up**, that I may show My power in you, and that My name may be declared in all the earth."* [NKJV]<br><br>For the Scriptures say that God told Pharaoh, "I have **appointed** you for the very purpose of displaying my power in you, and so that my fame might spread throughout the earth." [NLT]<br><br>λέγει γὰρ ἡ γραφὴ τῷ Φαραὼ ὅτι Εἰς αὐτὸ τοῦτο **ἐξήγειρά** σε, ὅπως ἐνδείξωμαι ἐν σοὶ τὴν δύναμίν μου, καὶ ὅπως διαγγελῇ τὸ ὄνομά μου ἐν πάσῃ τῇ γῇ. [GNS]<br><br>λέγει γὰρ ἡ γραφὴ τῷ Φαραὼ ὅτι Εἰς αὐτὸ τοῦτο **ἐξήγειρά** σε ὅπως ἐνδείξωμαι ἐν σοὶ τὴν δύναμίν μου καὶ ὅπως διαγγελῇ τὸ ὄνομά μου ἐν πάσῃ τῇ γῇ. [GNT] | brought him forth upon the scene of world history. We must always remember the teaching of Scripture:<br><br>*"Obey the government, for God is the one who put it there. All governments have been placed in power by God." (Romans 13:1)* [NLT] |
| **#184**<br>**Appointed Time**<br><br>Time–KJV<br>Time–NASB<br>Appointed time–NIV<br>Time–NKJV<br>Time–NLT<br><br>**POSB REFERENCE**<br>(Mt.26:17-19; esp. v.18)<br>Note 1, point 2<br><br>**See also POSB REF:**<br>(John 7:6-9; esp. v.6)<br>Note 3, point 1b | καιρός = kairos<br>Pronunciation: [kahee-ros']<br>Parsing (part of speech): noun<br>Case—masculine<br>Gender—masculine<br>Number—singular<br>Stem or root—from καιρός, οῦ<br>Concordance References:<br>⇒ Strong's #2540 kairos<br>⇒ NIV #2789 kairos<br>⇒ NASB #2540 kairos<br><br>**Matthew 26:18**<br>And he said, Go into the city to such a man, and say unto him, The Master saith, My **time** is at hand; I will keep the passover at thy house with my disciples. [KJV]<br><br>And He said, "Go into the city to a certain man, and say to him, 'The Teacher says, "My **time** is at hand; I *am to* keep the Passover at your house with My disciples."'" [NASB]<br><br>He replied, "Go into the city to a certain man and tell him, 'The Teacher says: My **appointed time** is near. I am going to celebrate the Passover with my disciples at your house.'" [NIV]<br><br>And He said, "Go into the city to a certain man, and say to him, 'The Teacher says, "My **time** is at hand; I will keep the Passover at your house with My disciples."'" [NKJV]<br><br>"As you go into the city," he told them, "you will see a certain man. Tell him, 'The Teacher says, My **time** has come, and I will eat the Passover meal with my disciples at your house.'" [NLT]<br><br>ὁ δὲ εἶπεν, Ὑπάγετε εἰς τὴν πόλιν πρὸς τὸν δεῖνα καὶ εἴπατε αὐτῷ, Ὁ διδάσκαλος λέγει, Ὁ **καιρός** μου ἐγγύς ἐστι· πρὸς σὲ ποιῶ τὸ πάσχα μετὰ τῶν μαθητῶν μου. [GNS]<br><br>ὁ δὲ εἶπεν, Ὑπάγετε εἰς τὴν πόλιν πρὸς τὸν δεῖνα καὶ εἴπατε αὐτῷ, Ὁ διδάσκαλος λέγει, Ὁ **καιρός** μου ἐγγύς ἐστιν, πρὸς σὲ ποιῶ τὸ πάσχα μετὰ τῶν μαθητῶν μου. [GNT] | The right time; the best time; the appointed time; the right season; the right opportunity; the significant window of opportunity; a definite moment in history.<br><br>**Practical Application**<br>Jesus knew His purpose for coming to earth. It was...<br>• not to live for Himself.<br>• not to overthrow human governments.<br>• not to place a band-aid on the spiritual cancer of sin.<br><br>Jesus was declaring that now was the appointed time for Him to go to the cross and to die for the sins of the world. |

# PRACTICAL WORD STUDIES
## in the NEW TESTAMENT

| ENGLISH WORD | GREEK WORD AND VERSE | THE WORD MEANS... |
|---|---|---|
| **#185**<br>**Appointed To Death**<br><br>**Appointed to death–KJV**<br>Condemned to death–NASB<br>Condemned to die–NIV<br>Condemned to death–NKJV<br>Condemned to die–NLT<br><br>**POSB REFERENCE**<br>(1 Cor.4:9-10; esp. v.9)<br>Note 4, point 1 | ἐπιθανατίους = *epithanatious*<br>Pronunciation: [ep-ee-than-at'-ee-oos]<br>Parsing (part of speech): adjective<br>    Case—accusative<br>    Gender—masculine<br>    Number—plural<br>    Stem or root—from ἐπιθανάτιος, ον<br>Concordance References:<br>⇒ Strong's #1935 epithanatios<br>⇒ NIV #2119 epithanatios<br>⇒ NASB #1935 epithanatios<br><br>**1 Cor. 4:9**<br>For I think that God hath set forth us the apostles last, as it were **appointed to death**: for we are made a spectacle unto the world, and to angels, and to men. [KJV]<br>For, I think, God has exhibited us apostles last of all, as men **condemned to death**; because we have become a spectacle to the world, both to angels and to men. [NASB]<br>For it seems to me that God has put us apostles on display at the end of the procession, like men **condemned to die** in the arena. We have been made a spectacle to the whole universe, to angels as well as to men. [NIV]<br>For I think that God has displayed us, the apostles, last, as men **condemned to death**; for we have been made a spectacle to the world, both to angels and to men. [NKJV]<br>But sometimes I think God has put us apostles on display, like prisoners of war at the end of a victor's parade, **condemned to die**. We have become a spectacle to the entire world—to people and angels alike. [NLT]<br>δοκῶ γάρ, ὅτι ὁ Θεὸς ἡμᾶς τοὺς ἀποστόλους ἐσχάτους ἀπέδειξεν ὡς **ἐπιθανατίους**· ὅτι θέατρον ἐγενήθημεν τῷ κόσμῳ, καὶ ἀγγέλοις καὶ ἀνθρώποις. [GNS]<br>δοκῶ γάρ, ὁ θεὸς ἡμᾶς τοὺς ἀποστόλους ἐσχάτους ἀπέδειξεν ὡς **ἐπιθανατίους**, ὅτι θέατρον ἐγενήθημεν τῷ κόσμῳ καὶ ἀγγέλοις καὶ ἀνθρώποις. [GNT] | Condemned to die; appointed to death; sentenced to death.<br><br>**Practical Application**<br>This is the picture of a doomed gladiator. He is marched through the city streets and before the screaming mobs of the arena. He is made a spectacle before the world, and he has to endure it, for he has no choice.<br>Paul sees ministers as being spectacles. They are being marched across the scene of world history to carry on their combat as ordained by the Emperor and King. They are mere spectacles to the world and to angels and men, with few ever understanding and fully accepting them. And from among the few who do accept them, some eventually withdraw and turn against them. |
| **#186**<br>**Appraised**<br><br>Discerned–KJV<br>**Appraised–NASB**<br>Discerned–NIV<br>Discerned–NKJV<br>Means–NLT<br><br>**POSB REFERENCE**<br>(1 Cor.2:14)<br>Note 1, point 3 | ἀνακρίνεται = *anakrinetai*<br>Pronunciation: [an-ak-ree'-neh-tah-ee]<br>Parsing (part of speech): verb<br>    Mood—indicative<br>    Tense—present<br>    Voice—passive<br>    Person—3rd person<br>    Number—singular<br>    Stem or root—from ἀνακρίνω<br>Concordance References:<br>⇒ Strong's #350 anakrinō<br>⇒ NIV #373 anakrinō<br>⇒ NASB #350 anakrinō<br><br>**1 Cor. 2:14**<br>But the natural man receiveth not the things of the Spirit of God: for they are foolishness unto him: neither can he know *them*, because they are spiritually **discerned**. [KJV]<br>But a natural man does not accept the things of the Spirit of God; for they are foolishness to him, and he cannot understand them, because they are spiritually **appraised**. [NASB]<br>The man without the Spirit does not accept the things that come from the Spirit of God, for they are foolishness to him, and he cannot understand them, because they are spiritually **discerned**. [NIV]<br>But the natural man does not receive the things of the Spirit of God, for they are foolishness to him; nor can he know *them*, because they are spiritually **discerned**. [NKJV]<br>But people who aren't Christians can't understand these truths from God's Spirit. It all sounds foolish to them because only those who have the Spirit can under- | Discerned, investigated, judged, scrutinized, examined, appraised, estimated.<br><br>**Practical Application**<br>Spiritual things have to be appraised by a living spirit, not by a natural man—a man without the Spirit—not by a man who is primarily living by his animal nature. Spiritual things can be appraised only by a spirit that is living. Spiritual things can be...<br>• investigated only by a living spirit.<br>• judged only by a living spirit.<br>• examined only by a living spirit.<br>• estimated and valued only by a living spirit. |

# PRACTICAL WORD STUDIES
## in the NEW TESTAMENT

| ENGLISH WORD | GREEK WORD AND VERSE | THE WORD MEANS... |
|---|---|---|
| | stand what the Spirit **means**. [NLT]<br>ψυχικὸς δὲ ἄνθρωπος οὐ δέχεται τὰ τοῦ Πνεύματος τοῦ Θεοῦ· μωρία γὰρ αὐτῷ ἐστι, καὶ οὐ δύναται γνῶναι, ὅτι πνευματικῶς **ἀνακρίνεται** [GNS]<br>ψυχικὸς δὲ ἄνθρωπος οὐ δέχεται τὰ τοῦ πνεύματος τοῦ θεοῦ, μωρία γὰρ αὐτῷ ἐστιν, καὶ οὐ δύναται γνῶναι, ὅτι πνευματικῶς **ἀνακρίνεται** [GNT] | |
| **#187**<br>**Appreciate**<br><br>Know–KJV<br>**Appreciate–NASB**<br>Respect–NIV<br>Recognize–NKJV<br>Honor–NLT<br><br>**POSB**<br>**REFERENCE**<br>(1 Thes.5:12-13;<br>esp.v.12)<br>Note 1, point 1 | εἰδέναι = eidenai<br>Pronunciation: [i'-dehn-ah-ee]<br>Parsing (part of speech): verb<br>    Mood—infinitive<br>    Tense—perfect<br>    Voice—active<br>    Stem or root—from οἶδα<br>Concordance References:<br>  ⇒ Strong's #1492 eido<br>  ⇒ NIV #3857 oida<br>  ⇒ NASB #3609a oida<br><br>**1 Thes. 5:12**<br>And we beseech you, brethren, to **know** them which labour among you, and are over you in the Lord, and admonish you; [KJV]<br>But we request of you, brethren, that you **appreciate** those who diligently labor among you, and have charge over you in the Lord and give you instruction, [NASB]<br>Now we ask you, brothers, to **respect** those who work hard among you, who are over you in the Lord and who admonish you. [NIV]<br>And we urge you, brethren, to **recognize** those who labor among you, and are over you in the Lord and admonish you, [NKJV]<br>Dear brothers and sisters, **honor** those who are your leaders in the Lord's work. They work hard among you and warn you against all that is wrong. [NLT]<br>Ἐρωτῶμεν δὲ ὑμᾶς, ἀδελφοί, **εἰδέναι** τοὺς κοπιῶντας ἐν ὑμῖν, καὶ προϊσταμένους ὑμῶν ἐν Κυρίῳ, καὶ νουθετοῦντας ὑμᾶς, [GNS]<br>Ἐρωτῶμεν δὲ ὑμᾶς, ἀδελφοί, **εἰδέναι** τοὺς κοπιῶντας ἐν ὑμῖν καὶ προϊσταμένους ὑμῶν ἐν κυρίῳ καὶ νουθετοῦντας ὑμᾶς [GNT] | To respect; to know; to appreciate; to recognize; to honor; to be acquainted with; to acknowledge; to know the value of.<br><br>**Practical Application**<br>Believers are to appreciate the leaders of their church. Few people labor as much as a committed church leader. |
| **#188**<br>**Appropriate**<br><br>Holiness–KJV<br>Reverent–NASB<br>Reverent–NIV<br>Reverent–NKJV<br>**Appropriate–NLT**<br><br>**POSB**<br>**REFERENCE**<br>(Tit.2:3)<br>Note 3, point 1 | ἱεροπρεπεῖς = hieroprepeis<br>Pronunciation: [hee-er-op-rep-ice']<br>Parsing (part of speech): adjective<br>    Case—accusative<br>    Gender—feminine<br>    Number—plural<br>    Stem or root—from ἱεροπρεπής, ές<br>Concordance References:<br>  ⇒ Strong's #2412 hieroprepēs<br>  ⇒ NIV #2640 hieroprepēs<br>  ⇒ NASB #2412 hieroprepēs<br><br>**Titus 2:3**<br>The aged women likewise, that *they be* in behaviour as becometh **holiness**, not false accusers, not given to much wine, teachers of good things; [KJV]<br>Older women likewise are to be **reverent** in their behavior, not malicious gossips, nor enslaved to much wine, teaching what is good, [NASB]<br>Likewise, teach the older women to be **reverent** in the way they live, not to be slanderers or addicted to much wine, but to teach what is good. [NIV]<br>The older women likewise, that they be **reverent** in behavior, not slanderers, not given to much wine, teachers of good things—[NKJV]<br>Similarly, teach the older women to live in a way that is **appropriate** for someone serving the Lord. They must not go around speaking evil of others and must not be heavy drinkers. Instead, they should teach others what is | Reverent, devout, holy, different and set apart in purity of behavior and thought.<br><br>**Practical Application**<br>Elderly women are to live and move about in an appropriate spirit and be focused upon sacred things. Matthew Henry says that elderly women are to keep "a pious [holy] decency and decorum in clothing and gesture, in looks and speech, and in all their deportment [behavior]" (*Matthew Henry's Commentary*, Vol.6, p.862). |

# PRACTICAL WORD STUDIES
## in the NEW TESTAMENT

| ENGLISH WORD | GREEK WORD AND VERSE | THE WORD MEANS... |
|---|---|---|
| | good. [NLT]<br>Πρεσβύτιδας ὡσαύτως ἐν καταστήματι **ἱεροπρεπεῖς**, μὴ διαβόλους, μὴ οἴνῳ πολλῷ δεδουλωμένας, καλοδιδασκάλους [GNS]<br>πρεσβύτιδας ὡσαύτως ἐν καταστήματι **ἱεροπρεπεῖς**, μὴ διαβόλους μηδὲ οἴνῳ πολλῷ δεδουλωμένας, καλοδιδασκάλους, [GNT] | |
| **#189**<br>**Approved**<br><br>**Approved–KJV**<br>Attested–NASB<br>Accredited–NIV<br>Attested–NKJV<br>Endorsed–NLT<br><br>**POSB REFERENCE**<br>(Acts 2:22-24; esp. v.22)<br>Note 3, point 1 | **ἀποδεδειγμένον** = *apodedeigmenon*<br>Pronunciation: [ap-od-eh-deeng-meh'-non]<br>Parsing (part of speech): verb<br>    Mood—participle<br>    Tense—perfect<br>    Voice—passive<br>    Case—accusative<br>    Gender—masculine<br>    Number—singular<br>    Stem or root—from ἀποδείκνυμι<br>Concordance References:<br>  ⇒ Strong's #584 apodeiknumi<br>  ⇒ NIV #617 apodeiknumi<br>  ⇒ NASB #584 apodeiknumi<br><br>**Acts 2:22**<br>Ye men of Israel, hear these words; Jesus of Nazareth, a man **approved** of God among you by miracles and wonders and signs, which God did by him in the midst of you, as ye yourselves also know: [KJV]<br>"Men of Israel, listen to these words: Jesus the Nazarene, a man **attested** to you by God with miracles and wonders and signs which God performed through Him in your midst, just as you yourselves know— [NASB]<br>"Men of Israel, listen to this: Jesus of Nazareth was a man **accredited** by God to you by miracles, wonders and signs, which God did among you through him, as you yourselves know. [NIV]<br>"Men of Israel, hear these words: Jesus of Nazareth, a Man **attested** by God to you by miracles, wonders, and signs which God did through Him in your midst, as you yourselves also know—[NKJV]<br>"People of Israel, listen! God publicly **endorsed** Jesus of Nazareth by doing wonderful miracles, wonders, and signs through him, as you well know. [NLT]<br>ἄνδρες Ἰσραηλῖται, ἀκούσατε τοὺς λόγους τούτους· Ἰησοῦν τὸν Ναζωραῖον, ἄνδρα ἀπὸ τοῦ Θεοῦ **ἀποδεδειγμένον** εἰς ὑμᾶς δυνάμεσι καὶ τέρασι καὶ σημείοις, οἷς ἐποίησε δι' αὐτοῦ ὁ Θεὸς ἐν μέσῳ ὑμῶν, καθὼς καὶ αὐτοὶ οἴδατε, [GNS]<br>Ἄνδρες Ἰσραηλῖται, ἀκούσατε τοὺς λόγους τούτους· Ἰησοῦν τὸν Ναζωραῖον, ἄνδρα **ἀποδεδειγμένον** ἀπὸ τοῦ θεοῦ εἰς ὑμᾶς δυνάμεσι καὶ τέρασι καὶ σημείοις οἷς ἐποίησεν δι' αὐτοῦ ὁ θεὸς ἐν μέσῳ ὑμῶν καθὼς αὐτοὶ οἴδατε, [GNT] | To accredit; to approve; to endorse; to point out; to display; to show; to attest; to sanction; to certify.<br><br>**Practical Application**<br>God put His stamp of approval upon Jesus. He demonstrated and showed all men that Jesus is perfectly acceptable to Him. Jesus of Nazareth had God's approval, His perfect acceptance. |
| **#190**<br>**Argue**<br><br>Strife–KJV<br>Dispute–NASB<br>Dispute–NIV<br>Dispute–NKJV<br>**Argue–NLT**<br><br>**POSB REFERENCE**<br>(Lk.22:24)<br>Note 1, point 1 | **φιλονεικία** = *philoneikia*<br>Pronunciation: [fil-on-i-kee'-ah]<br>Parsing (part of speech): noun<br>    Case—nominative<br>    Gender—feminine<br>    Number—singular<br>    Stem or root—from φιλονεικία, ας<br>Concordance References:<br>  ⇒ Strong's #5379 philoneikia<br>  ⇒ NIV #5808 philoneikia<br>  ⇒ NASB #5379 philoneikia<br><br>**Luke 22:24**<br>And there was also a **strife** among them, which of them should be accounted the greatest. [KJV]<br>And there arose also a **dispute** among them *as to* which one of them was regarded to be greatest. [NASB]<br>Also a **dispute** arose among them as to which of them | Being eager and ready to argue, debate and contend; being alert to strive for one's position.<br><br>**Practical Application**<br>It conveys the idea of giving no ground, of standing up no matter what, of being stubborn, of resisting regardless of circumstances. |

# PRACTICAL WORD STUDIES
## in the NEW TESTAMENT

| ENGLISH WORD | GREEK WORD AND VERSE | THE WORD MEANS... |
|---|---|---|
| | was considered to be greatest. [NIV]<br>Now there was also a **dispute** among them, as to which of them should be considered the greatest. [NKJV]<br>And they began to **argue** among themselves as to who would be the greatest in the coming Kingdom. [NLT]<br>Ἐγένετο δὲ καὶ **φιλονεικία** ἐν αὐτοῖς τὸ, τίς αὐτῶν δοκεῖ εἶναι μείζων. [GNS]<br>Ἐγένετο δὲ καὶ **φιλονεικία** ἐν αὐτοῖς, τὸ τίς αὐτῶν δοκεῖ εἶναι μείζων. [GNT] | |
| **#191**<br>**Argue Sharply–**<br>**Argue–**<br>**Arguing**<br><br>Strove–KJV<br>**Argue–NASB**<br>**Argue sharply–NIV**<br>Quarreled–NKJV<br>**Arguing–NLT**<br><br>**POSB**<br>**REFERENCE**<br>(Jn.6:52-53; esp. v.52)<br>Note 1 | Ἐμάχοντο = *Emachonto*<br>Pronunciation: [eh-mach'-on-tow]<br>Parsing (part of speech): verb<br>   Mood—indicative<br>   Tense—imperfect<br>   Voice—middle or passive deponent<br>   Person—3rd person<br>   Number—plural<br>   Stem or root—from μάχομαι<br>Concordance References:<br>  ⇒ Strong's #3164 machomai<br>  ⇒ NIV #3481 machomai<br>  ⇒ NASB #3164 machomai<br><br>**John 6:52**<br>The Jews therefore **strove** among themselves, saying, How can this man give us *his* flesh to eat? [KJV]<br>The Jews therefore *began* to **argue** with one another, saying, "How can this man give us *His* flesh to eat?" [NASB]<br>Then the Jews began to **argue sharply** among themselves, "How can this man give us his flesh to eat?" [NIV]<br>The Jews therefore **quarreled** among themselves, saying, "How can this *Man* give us *His* flesh to eat?" [NKJV]<br>Then the people began **arguing** with each other about what he meant. "How can this man give us his flesh to eat?" they asked. [NLT]<br>Ἐμάχοντο οὖν πρὸς ἀλλήλους οἱ Ἰουδαῖοι, λέγοντες, Πῶς δύναται οὗτος ἡμῖν δοῦναι τὴν σάρκα αὐτοῦ φαγεῖν; [GNS]<br>Ἐμάχοντο οὖν πρὸς ἀλλήλους οἱ Ἰουδαῖοι λέγοντες, Πῶς δύναται οὗτος ἡμῖν δοῦναι τὴν σάρκα [αὐτοῦ] φαγεῖν; [GNT] | To argue sharply; to strive with words; to fuss; to debate; to strongly differ; to hotly dispute. In a most literal sense it means to fight as a soldier would fight in war; to fight by using words.<br><br>**Practical Application**<br>In this Scripture, the religionists were debating what Jesus meant. The Jews (religionists) began to argue over the meaning of the words. "How can this man give us His flesh to eat?"<br>⇒ Some interpreted His words as a parable, in a figurative and symbolic way. They knew He often spoke in parables.<br>⇒ Others had no idea what He meant, but they did see that He was claiming to be the most important person in the world, the very Savior of men. This, of course, bothered them beyond reason. How could any man claim to be so important to the world? As materialists and humanists they asked, "How can this be? He is but a man. How can He give His flesh for the world and the world receive eternal life?"<br>⇒ A few disciples, genuine followers of the Lord, perhaps understood.<br>The point is that the religionists were disturbed. The message had been going on for a long time and Jesus had made claim after claim—all most unusual. Moreover, what He was saying was not clear and some of it was offensive. Therefore, they were angry and perplexed and began to argue among themselves about what He meant and how they should respond to Him. |
| **#192**<br>**Arguing**<br><br>Disputings–KJV<br>Disputing–NASB<br>**Arguing–NIV**<br>Disputing–NKJV<br>**Arguing–NLT**<br><br>**POSB**<br>**REFERENCE**<br>(Philip.2:14)<br>Note 3<br><br>See also POSB REF:<br>(Lk.9:46)<br>Note 1, point 1 | διαλογισμῶν = *dialogismōn*<br>Pronunciation: [dee-al-og-is-mon']<br>Parsing (part of speech): noun<br>   Case—genitive<br>   Gender—masculine<br>   Number—plural<br>   Stem or root—from διαλογισμός, οῦ<br>Concordance References:<br>  ⇒ Strong's #1261 dialogismos<br>  ⇒ NIV #1369 dialogismos<br>  ⇒ NASB #1261 dialogismos<br><br>**Philip. 2:14**<br>Do all things without murmurings and **disputings**: [KJV]<br>Do all things without grumbling or **disputing**; [NASB]<br>Do everything without complaining or **arguing**, [NIV]<br>Do all things without complaining and **disputing**, [NKJV]<br>In everything you do, stay away from complaining and **arguing**, [NLT] | Arguing, disputes. It means outward and vocal questionings, and expressions of doubt.<br><br>**Practical Application**<br>Simply stated, it is just as Scripture says: disputes or arguments that have broken out into the open. Note several significant facts.<br>1. Complaining and arguing are not to be allowed in the church. As the verse says: Do everything without complaining or "arguing." If complaining begins among a clique or even between two people, the spiritual leaders of the church are to deal with it just as Christ laid out (see POSB outline and notes—Matthew 18:15-20). It is not to be allowed to fester. Complaints, unless they are stopped, will lead to disputes, turmoil, and divisiveness.<br>2. Complaining and arguing are *never of God—never*! This is the very point of this charge. *Everything*—nothing is left out—is to be done without complaining or arguing. |

# PRACTICAL WORD STUDIES
## in the New Testament

| ENGLISH WORD | GREEK WORD AND VERSE | THE WORD MEANS... |
|---|---|---|
| | πάντα ποιεῖτε χωρὶς γογγυσμῶν καὶ **διαλογισμῶν**, [GNS]<br>πάντα ποιεῖτε χωρὶς γογγυσμῶν καὶ **διαλογισμῶν**, [GNT] | 3. Complaining and arguing were the very sins that brought judgment upon so many Jews in the wilderness wanderings of Israel.<br>4. The person who complains and argues is not working at his salvation or deliverance. He is doing the very opposite: working to bring judgment upon himself. |
| **#193**<br>**Arguing**<br><br>Disputing–KJV<br>Reasoning–NASB<br>**Arguing–NIV**<br>Reasoning–NKJV<br>**Arguing–NLT**<br><br>**POSB REFERENCE**<br>(Acts 19:2-9; esp. v.8)<br>Note 2, point 2a | διαλεγόμενος = *dialegomenos*<br>Pronunciation: [dee-al-eg'-om-ehn-os]<br>Parsing (part of speech): verb<br>    Mood—participle<br>    Tense—present<br>    Voice—middle or passive deponent<br>    Case—nominative<br>    Gender—masculine<br>    Number—singular<br>    Stem or root—from διαλέγομαι<br>Concordance References:<br>⇒ Strong's #1256 dialegomai<br>⇒ NIV #1363 dialegomai<br>⇒ NASB #1256 dialegomai<br><br>**Acts 19:8**<br>And he went into the synagogue, and spake boldly for the space of three months, **disputing** and persuading the things concerning the kingdom of God. [KJV]<br>And he entered the synagogue and continued speaking out boldly for three months, **reasoning** and persuading *them* about the kingdom of God. [NASB]<br>Paul entered the synagogue and spoke boldly there for three months, **arguing** persuasively about the kingdom of God. [NIV]<br>And he went into the synagogue and spoke boldly for three months, **reasoning** and persuading concerning the things of the kingdom of God. [NKJV]<br>Then Paul went to the synagogue and preached boldly for the next three months, **arguing** persuasively about the Kingdom of God. [NLT]<br>Εἰσελθὼν δὲ εἰς τὴν συναγωγήν, ἐπαρρησιάζετο, ἐπὶ μῆνας τρεῖς **διαλεγόμενος**, καὶ πείθων τὰ περὶ τῆς βασιλείας τοῦ Θεοῦ. [GNS]<br>Εἰσελθὼν δὲ εἰς τὴν συναγωγὴν ἐπαρρησιάζετο ἐπὶ μῆνας τρεῖς **διαλεγόμενος** καὶ πείθων [τὰ] περὶ τῆς βασιλείας τοῦ θεοῦ. [GNT] | To argue; to dispute; to reason; to discuss; to convince; to debate; to answer questions.<br><br>**Practical Application**<br>Paul preached boldly in the synagogue of the Jews. He discussed the gospel, asking and answering questions, convincing all who were willing to be convinced. |
| **#194**<br>**Arguing About**<br><br>Disputed–KJV<br>Discussing–NASB<br>**Arguing about–NIV**<br>Disputed–NKJV<br>Discussing–NLT<br><br>**POSB REFERENCE**<br>(Mk.9:33)<br>Note 1 | διελογίζεσθε = *dielogizesthe*<br>Pronunciation: [dee-el-og-id'-zehs-theh]<br>Parsing (part of speech): verb<br>    Mood—indicative<br>    Tense—imperfect<br>    Voice—middle or passive deponent<br>    Person—2nd person<br>    Number—plural<br>    Stem or root—from διαλογίζομαι<br>Concordance References:<br>⇒ Strong's #1260 dialogizomai<br>⇒ NIV #1368 dialogizomai<br>⇒ NASB #1260 dialogizomai<br><br>**Mark 9:33**<br>And he came to Capernaum: and being in the house he asked them, What was it that ye **disputed** among yourselves by the way? [KJV]<br>And they came to Capernaum; and when He was in the house, He *began* to question them, "What were you **discussing** on the way?" [NASB]<br>They came to Capernaum. When he was in the house, he asked them, "What were you **arguing about** on the road?" [NIV]<br>Then He came to Capernaum. And when He was in the house He asked them, "What was it you **disputed** among yourselves on the road?" [NKJV] | To dispute; to discuss. It is arguing, complaining, questioning, contesting, hairsplitting, nit-picking, and bickering as well as reasoning.<br><br>**Practical Application**<br>In this Scripture, the word pictures an intense debate between the disciples of Christ. They argued over which of them would be the greatest in the kingdom of Christ. |

**PRACTICAL WORD STUDIES
in the NEW TESTAMENT**

| ENGLISH WORD | GREEK WORD AND VERSE | THE WORD MEANS... |
|---|---|---|
| | After they arrived at Capernaum, Jesus and his disciples settled in the house where they would be staying. Jesus asked them, "What were you **discussing** out on the road?" [NLT]<br><br>Καὶ ἦλθεν εἰς Καπερναούμ· καὶ ἐν τῇ οἰκίᾳ γενόμενος, ἐπηρώτα αὐτούς, Τί ἐν τῇ ὁδῷ πρὸς ἑαυτοὺς **διελογίζεσθε**; [GNS]<br><br>Καὶ ἦλθον εἰς Καφαρναούμ. καὶ ἐν τῇ οἰκίᾳ γενόμενος ἐπηρώτα αὐτούς, Τί ἐν τῇ ὁδῷ **διελογίζεσθε**; [GNT] | |
| **#195**<br>**Arguments**<br><br>Contentions–KJV<br>Quarrels–NASB<br>Quarrels–NIV<br>Contentions–NKJV<br>**Arguments–NLT**<br><br>**POSB<br>REFERENCE**<br>(1 Cor.1:11)<br>Note 2 | ἔριδες = *erides*<br>Pronunciation: [er'-i-des]<br>Parsing (part of speech): noun<br>    Case—nominative<br>    Gender—feminine<br>    Number—plural<br>    Stem or root—from ἔρις, ιδος<br>Concordance References:<br>  ⇒ Strong's #2054 eris<br>  ⇒ NIV #2251 eris<br>  ⇒ NASB #2054 eris<br><br>**1 Cor. 1:11**<br>For it hath been declared unto me of you, my brethren, by them *which are of the house* of Chloe, that there are **contentions** among you. [KJV]<br>For I have been informed concerning you, my brethren, by Chloe's *people,* that there are **quarrels** among you. [NASB]<br>My brothers, some from Chloe's household have informed me that there are **quarrels** among you. [NIV]<br>For it has been declared to me concerning you, my brethren, by those of Chloe's *household,* that there are **contentions** among you. [NKJV]<br>For some members of Chloe's household have told me about your **arguments**, dear brothers and sisters. [NLT]<br>ἐδηλώθη γάρ μοι περὶ ὑμῶν, ἀδελφοί μου, ὑπὸ τῶν Χλόης ὅτι **ἔριδες** ἐν ὑμῖν εἰσι. [GNS]<br>ἐδηλώθη γάρ μοι περὶ ὑμῶν, ἀδελφοί μου, ὑπὸ τῶν Χλόης ὅτι **ἔριδες** ἐν ὑμῖν εἰσιν. [GNT] | Wranglings, strifes, quarrels, fightings, factions.<br><br>**Practical Application**<br>Note: the nature of division is more clearly defined by the word. The church was arguing and splitting into groups, contending and quarreling over something. There was a severe strife between factions and cliques in the church. |
| **#196**<br>**Arguments**<br><br>Imaginations–KJV<br>Speculations–NASB<br>**Arguments–NIV**<br>**Arguments–NKJV**<br>Every proud argument–NLT<br><br>**POSB<br>REFERENCE**<br>(2 Cor.10:3-5; esp. v.5)<br>Note 2 | λογισμοὺς = *logismous*<br>Pronunciation: [log-is-moos']<br>Parsing (part of speech): noun<br>    Case—accusative<br>    Gender—masculine<br>    Number—plural<br>    Stem or root—from λογισμός, οῦ<br>**Note: this comes from verse 4 in the greek, but is translated in the English Bible in verse 5**<br>Concordance References:<br>  ⇒ Strong's #3053 logismos<br>  ⇒ NIV #3361 logismos<br>  ⇒ NASB #3053 logismos<br><br>**2 Cor. 10:5**<br>Casting down **imaginations**, and every high thing that exalteth itself against the knowledge of God, and bringing into captivity every thought to the obedience of Christ; [KJV]<br>*We are* destroying **speculations** and every lofty thing raised up against the knowledge of God, and *we are* taking every thought captive to the obedience of Christ, [NASB]<br>We demolish **arguments** and every pretension that sets itself up against the knowledge of God, and we take captive every thought to make it obedient to Christ. [NIV]<br>Casting down **arguments** and every high thing that exalts itself against the knowledge of God, bringing every thought into captivity to the obedience of Christ, [NKJV]<br>With these weapons we break down **every proud argument** that keeps people from knowing God. With | Arguments, speculations, false reasoning.<br><br>**Practical Application**<br>The believer is to *demolish or cast down arguments*: thoughts and imaginations that are uncontrolled, wild, evil, lustful, immoral, unjust, wrong, untrue, devilish, and set against God. |

| ENGLISH WORD | GREEK WORD AND VERSE | THE WORD MEANS... |
|---|---|---|
| | these weapons we conquer their rebellious ideas, and we teach them to obey Christ. [NLT]<br><br>τὰ γὰρ ὅπλα τῆς στρατείας ἡμῶν οὐ σαρκικὰ, ἀλλὰ δυνατὰ τῷ Θεῷ πρὸς καθαίρεσιν ὀχυρωμάτων -- , **λογισμοὺς** καθαιροῦντες **2 Cor. 10:4** [GNS]<br><br>καὶ πᾶν ὕψωμα ἐπαιρόμενον κατὰ τῆς γνώσεως τοῦ Θεοῦ, καὶ αἰχμαλωτίζοντες πᾶν νόημα εἰς τὴν ὑπακοὴν τοῦ Χριστοῦ, **2 Cor. 10:5** [GNS]<br><br>τὰ γὰρ ὅπλα τῆς στρατείας ἡμῶν οὐ σαρκικὰ ἀλλὰ δυνατὰ τῷ θεῷ πρὸς καθαίρεσιν ὀχυρωμάτων, **λογισμοὺς** καθαιροῦντες **2 Cor. 10:4** [GNT]<br><br>καὶ πᾶν ὕψωμα ἐπαιρόμενον κατὰ τῆς γνώσεως τοῦ θεοῦ, καὶ αἰχμαλωτίζοντες πᾶν νόημα eivj τὴν ὑπακοὴν τοῦ Χριστοῦ, **2 Cor. 10:5** [GNT] | |
| **#197**<br>**Arguments**<br><br>Convinced–KJV<br>Refuted–NASB<br>Refuted–NKJV<br>Refuted–NIV<br>**Arguments–NLT**<br><br>**POSB**<br>**REFERENCE**<br>(Acts 18:27-28; esp. v.28)<br>Note 8, point 2b | **διακατηλέγχετο** = *diakatëlegcheto*<br>Pronunciation: [dee-ak-at-el-eng'-cheh-tow]<br>Parsing (part of speech): verb<br>    Mood—indicative<br>    Tense—imperfect<br>    Voice—middle or passive deponent<br>    Person—3rd person<br>    Number—singular<br>    Stem or root—from **διακατελέγχομαι**<br>Concordance References:<br>  ⇒ Strong's #1246 diakatelegchomai<br>  ⇒ NIV #1352 diakatelegchomai<br>  ⇒ NASB #1246 diakatelegchomai<br><br>**Acts 18:28**<br>For he mightily **convinced** the Jews, *and that* publickly, showing by the scriptures that Jesus was Christ. [KJV]<br><br>For he powerfully **refuted** the Jews in public, demonstrating by the Scriptures that Jesus was the Christ. [NASB]<br><br>For he vigorously **refuted** the Jews in public debate, proving from the Scriptures that Jesus was the Christ. [NIV]<br><br>For he vigorously **refuted** the Jews publicly, showing from the Scriptures that Jesus is the Christ. [NKJV]<br><br>He refuted all the Jews with powerful **arguments** in public debate. Using the Scriptures, he explained to them, "The Messiah you are looking for is Jesus." [NLT]<br><br>εὐτόνως γὰρ τοῖς Ἰουδαίοις **διακατηλέγχετο** δημοσίᾳ ἐπιδεικνὺς διὰ τῶν γραφῶν εἶναι τὸν Χριστὸν, Ἰησοῦν. [GNS]<br><br>εὐτόνως γὰρ τοῖς Ἰουδαίοις **διακατηλέγχετο** δημοσίᾳ ἐπιδεικνὺς διὰ τῶν γραφῶν εἶναι τὸν Χριστὸν Ἰησοῦν. [GNT] | Refuted to the very last point, confronted, defeated in argument; to be argued down.<br><br>**Practical Application**<br>Apollos did it publicly. But note: he was not using human reason to argue; he was using the Scripture. And his purpose was to prove that Jesus is the Messiah. (See POSB *Deeper Study* #2—Matthew 1:18 for discussion.) |
| **#198**<br>**Arose**<br><br>Arose–KJV<br>Rose up–NASB<br>Opposition arose–NIV<br>**Arose–NKJV**<br>Started–NLT<br><br>**POSB**<br>**REFERENCE**<br>(Acts 6:9-10; esp. v.9)<br>Note 2, point 2 | **ἀνέστησαν** = *anestësan*<br>Pronunciation: [an-is'-tay-san]<br>Parsing (part of speech): verb<br>    Mood—indicative<br>    Tense—aorist<br>    Voice—active<br>    Person—3rd person<br>    Number—plural<br>    Stem or root—from **ἀνίστημι**<br>Concordance References:<br>  ⇒ Strong's #450 anistemi<br>  ⇒ NIV #482 anistēmi<br>  ⇒ NASB #450 anistemi<br><br>**Acts 6:9**<br>Then there **arose** certain of *the synagogue*, which is called the synagogue of the Libertines, and Cyrenians, and Alexandrians, and of them of Cilicia and of Asia, disputing with Stephen. [KJV]<br><br>But some men from what was called the Synagogue of the Freedmen, *including* both Cyrenians and Alexandrians, and some from Cilicia and Asia, **rose up** | Opposition arose; stood up.<br><br>**Practical Application**<br>Five synagogues in particular stood up against Stephen. They opposed what he was preaching. There was a strong reason for the opposition of the Grecian Jews. They and their forefathers had been forcibly deported out of their homeland and scattered across the world by the Romans. While living in the foreign lands of the world, they had remained faithful to their Jewish religion. The message of Jesus Christ was a threat to them and their religion. |

# PRACTICAL WORD STUDIES
## in the NEW TESTAMENT

| ENGLISH WORD | GREEK WORD AND VERSE | THE WORD MEANS... |
|---|---|---|
| | and argued with Stephen. [NASB]<br>**Opposition arose**, however, from members of the Synagogue of the Freedmen (as it was called)—Jews of Cyrene and Alexandria as well as the provinces of Cilicia and Asia. These men began to argue with Stephen, [NIV]<br>Then there **arose** some from what is called the Synagogue of the Freedmen (Cyrenians, Alexandrians, and those from Cilicia and Asia), disputing with Stephen. [NKJV]<br>But one day some men from the Synagogue of Freed Slaves, as it was called, **started** to debate with him. They were Jews from Cyrene, Alexandria, Cilicia, and the province of Asia. [NLT]<br>ἀνέστησαν δέ τινες τῶν ἐκ τῆς συναγωγῆς τῆς λεγομένης Λιβερτίνων, καὶ Κυρηναίων, καὶ Ἀλεξανδρέων, καὶ τῶν ἀπὸ Κιλικίας καὶ Ἀσίας, συζητοῦντες τῷ Στεφάνῳ. [GNS]<br>ἀνέστησαν δέ τινες τῶν ἐκ τῆς συναγωγῆς τῆς λεγομένης Λιβερτίνων καὶ Κυρηναίων καὶ Ἀλεξανδρέων καὶ τῶν ἀπὸ Κιλικίας καὶ Ἀσίας συζητοῦντες τῷ Στεφάνῳ, [GNT] | |
| **#199**<br>**Arrogance**<br><br>Pride–KJV<br>Pride–NASB<br>**Arrogance–NIV**<br>Pride–NKJV<br>Pride–NLT<br><br>**POSB REFERENCE**<br>(Mk.7:22)<br>*Deeper Study* #14<br><br>See also POSB REF:<br>(Jas.4:16)<br>Note 4 | ὑπερηφανία = *huperephania*<br>Pronunciation: [hoop-er-ay-fan-ee´-ah]<br>Parsing (part of speech): noun<br>    Case—nominative<br>    Gender—feminine<br>    Number—singular<br>    Stem or root—from ὑπερηφανία, ας<br>Concordance References:<br>  ⇒ Strong's #5243 huperephania<br>  ⇒ NIV #5661 huperēphania<br>  ⇒ NASB #5243 huperephania<br><br>**Mark 7:22**<br>Thefts, covetousness, wickedness, deceit, lasciviousness, an evil eye, blasphemy, **pride**, foolishness: [KJV]<br>Deeds of coveting *and* wickedness, *as well as* deceit, sensuality, envy, slander, **pride** *and* foolishness. [NASB]<br>Greed, malice, deceit, lewdness, envy, slander, **arrogance** and folly. [NIV]<br>Thefts, covetousness, wickedness, deceit, lewdness, an evil eye, blasphemy, **pride**, foolishness. [NKJV]<br>Adultery, greed, wickedness, deceit, eagerness for lustful pleasure, envy, slander, **pride**, and foolishness. [NLT]<br>πλεονεξίαι, πονηρίαι, δόλος, ἀσέλγεια, ὀφθαλμὸς πονηρός, βλασφημία, **ὑπερηφανία**, ἀφροσύνη· [GNS]<br>μοιχεῖαι, πλεονεξίαι, πονηρίαι, δόλος, ἀσέλγεια, ὀφθαλμὸς πονηρός, βλασφημία, **ὑπερηφανία**, ἀφροσύνη· [GNT] | Self-exaltation, conceit, pride, puffed up, arrogance, haughtiness, insolence, putting oneself above others, looking down upon others, scorn, contempt.<br><br>**Practical Application**<br>It means to lift one's head above another, to hold contempt for another, to compare oneself with others. Arrogance can be hidden in the heart as well as openly displayed. God opposes the proud (James 4:6; 1 Peter 5:5; Proverbs 3:24). |
| **#200**<br>**Arrogance**<br><br>Swellings–KJV<br>**Arrogance–NASB**<br>**Arrogance–NIV**<br>Conceits–NKJV<br>Conceit–NLT<br><br>**POSB REFERENCE**<br>(2 Cor.12:19-21; esp. v.20)<br>Note 3, point 2 | φυσιώσεις = *phusiōseis*<br>Pronunciation: [foo-see´-o-seh-ees]<br>Parsing (part of speech): noun<br>    Case—nominative<br>    Gender—feminine<br>    Number—plural<br>    Stem or root—from φυσίωσις, εως<br>Concordance References:<br>  ⇒ Strong's #5450 phusiōsis<br>  ⇒ NIV #5883 phusiōsis<br>  ⇒ NASB #5450 phusiōsis<br><br>**2 Cor. 12:20**<br>For I fear, lest, when I come, I shall not find you such as I would, and *that* I shall be found unto you such as ye would not: lest *there be* debates, envyings, wraths, strifes, backbitings, whisperings, **swellings**, tumults: [KJV]<br>For I am afraid that perhaps when I come I may find you to be not what I wish and may be found by you to be not what you wish; that perhaps *there may be* strife, jealousy, angry tempers, disputes, slanders, gossip, arro- | Conceit, pride, swellings, puffed up, arrogance, haughtiness, insolence, putting oneself above others, looking down upon others, scorn, contempt.<br><br>**Practical Application**<br>The arrogant, the conceited, the proud person feels that he is better than others. Note that this is a feeling within the heart. The proud person may appear quiet and humble; but within his heart, he secretly feels better than others. God opposes the proud. |

# PRACTICAL WORD STUDIES
## in the NEW TESTAMENT

| ENGLISH WORD | GREEK WORD AND VERSE | THE WORD MEANS... |
|---|---|---|
| | gance, disturbances; [NASB]<br>For I am afraid that when I come I may not find you as I want you to be, and you may not find me as you want me to be. I fear that there may be quarreling, jealousy, outbursts of anger, factions, slander, gossip, **arrogance** and disorder. [NIV]<br>For I fear lest, when I come, I shall not find you such as I wish, and *that* I shall be found by you such as you do not wish; lest *there be* contentions, jealousies, outbursts of wrath, selfish ambitions, backbitings, whisperings, **conceits**, tumults; [NKJV]<br>For I am afraid that when I come to visit you I won't like what I find, and then you won't like my response. I am afraid that I will find quarreling, jealousy, outbursts of anger, selfishness, backstabbing, gossip, **conceit**, and disorderly behavior. [NLT]<br>φοβοῦμαι γὰρ μή πως ἐλθὼν οὐχ οἵους θέλω εὕρω ὑμᾶς, κἀγὼ εὑρεθῶ ὑμῖν οἷον οὐ θέλετε· μή πως ἔρις, ζῆλοι, θυμοί, ἐριθεῖαι, καταλαλιαί, ψιθυρισμοί, **φυσιώσεις**, ἀκαταστασίαι·[GNS]<br>φοβοῦμαι γὰρ μή πως ἐλθὼν οὐχ οἵους θέλω εὕρω ὑμᾶς, κἀγὼ εὑρεθῶ ὑμῖν οἷον οὐ θέλετε· μή πως ἔρις, ζῆλος, θυμοί, ἐριθεῖαι, καταλαλιαί, ψιθυρισμοί, **φυσιώσεις**, ἀκαταστασίαι·[GNT] | |
| **#201**<br>**Arrogance**<br><br>Boastings–KJV<br>**Arrogance–NASB**<br>Brag–NIV<br>**Arrogance–NKJV**<br>Your own plans–NLT<br><br>**POSB REFERENCE**<br>(Jas.4:16)<br>Note 4 | ἐν ταῖς ἀλαζονείαις = en tais alazoneiais<br>Pronunciation: [en tace al-ad-zon-i'-ah-is]<br>Parsing *alazoneiais* (part of speech): noun<br>    Case—dative<br>    Gender—feminine<br>    Number—plural<br>    Stem or root—from ἀλαζονεία, ας<br>Concordance References:<br>⇒ Strong's #212+1722+3588 alazoneia en ho<br>⇒ NIV #224+1877+3836 alazoneia en ho [brag]<br>⇒ NASB #212+1722+3588 alazoneia en ho<br><br>**James 4:16**<br>But now ye rejoice in your **boastings**: all such rejoicing is evil. [KJV]<br>But as it is, you boast in your **arrogance**; all such boasting is evil. [NASB]<br>As it is, you boast and **brag**. All such boasting is evil. [NIV]<br>But now you boast in your **arrogance**. All such boasting is evil. [NKJV]<br>Otherwise you will be boasting about **your own plans**, and all such boasting is evil. [NLT]<br>νῦν δὲ καυχᾶσθε **ἐν ταῖς ἀλαζονείαις** ὑμῶν· πᾶσα καύχησις τοιαύτη πονηρά ἐστιν. [GNS]<br>νῦν δὲ καυχᾶσθε **ἐν ταῖς ἀλαζονείαις** ὑμῶν· πᾶσα καύχησις τοιαύτη πονηρά ἐστιν. [GNT] | To brag; to boast; to be proud of; to be arrogant.<br><br>**Practical Application**<br>The word "arrogance" (*alazoniais*) means an empty boaster (A.T. Robertson. *Word Pictures in the New Testament*, Vol. 6, p.56). That is, it is a person who boasts about something he thinks he has, but he does not really have it. He lives in an unreal world. Any person who goes through life without God is just like this. He lives and plans, thinking that he controls his life and the future. His life is one big boast of self-sufficiency, and it is wrong, totally wrong. A thousand things can happen to change his plans—to injure him or to radically change his life and work, or to snatch his life right out of this world.<br>Most people—laymen and ministers alike—boast of their work, what they have done, their abilities and possessions. But note a fact seldom thought about: most boasting is not done by word of mouth. It is done by the way we live. We boast by flaunting our abilities and successes through our possessions and activities such as expensive houses, clothes and cars, exclusive clubs, friendships, and recreation.<br>We have an urge, a tendency to boast and to be seen and recognized as better and more successful than others. And note what Scripture says: we rejoice in our boastings—that we are more successful in our work than some others. But such boastings—such pride and arrogance—are evil. Why? Because a man's ability and life are due to God and rest in the hands of God. And in addition to this: the future—tomorrow and even one hour from now—is in the hands of God. It may be a heart attack—it may be a thief—it may be an accident—it is all in the hands of God. What a person needs to do is trust God and commit all his ways into the hands of God, acknowledging Him in all things and at every turn of every day. |

## PRACTICAL WORD STUDIES
### in the NEW TESTAMENT

| ENGLISH WORD | GREEK WORD AND VERSE | THE WORD MEANS... |
|---|---|---|
| **#202**<br>**Arrogant**<br><br>Puffed up–KJV<br>**Arrogant–NASB**<br>Proud–NIV<br>Puffed up–NKJV<br>Proud–NLT<br><br>**POSB REFERENCE**<br>(1 Cor.13:4-7; esp. v.4)<br>Note 2, point 5 | φυσιοῦται = *phusioutai*<br>Pronunciation: [foo-see-oo'-tah-ee]<br>Parsing (part of speech): verb<br>    Mood—indicative<br>    Tense—present<br>    Voice—passive<br>    Person—3rd person<br>    Number—singular<br>    Stem or root—from φυσιόω<br>Concordance References:<br>⇒ Strong's #5448 phusioö<br>⇒ NIV #5881 phusioö<br>⇒ NASB #5448 phusioö<br><br>**1 Cor. 13:4**<br>Charity suffereth long, *and* is kind; charity envieth not; charity vaunteth not itself, is not **puffed up**, [KJV]<br>Love is patient, love is kind, *and* is not jealous; love does not brag *and* is not **arrogant**, [NASB]<br>Love is patient, love is kind. It does not envy, it does not boast, it is not **proud**. [NIV]<br>Love suffers long *and* is kind; love does not envy; love does not parade itself, is not **puffed up**; [NKJV]<br>Love is patient and kind. Love is not jealous or boastful or **proud** [NLT]<br>ἡ ἀγάπη μακροθυμεῖ, χρηστεύεται· ἡ ἀγάπη, οὐ ζηλοῖ· ἡ ἀγάπη οὐ περπερεύεται, οὐ **φυσιοῦται**, [GNS]<br>Ἡ ἀγάπη μακροθυμεῖ, χρηστεύεται ἡ ἀγάπη, οὐ ζηλοῖ, [ἡ ἀγάπη] οὐ περπερεύεται, οὐ **φυσιοῦται**, [GNT] | Proud, puffed up, arrogant, conceited.<br><br>**Practical Application**<br>Love is not arrogant (*phusioutai*): prideful, conceited, puffed up; does not think nor act as though oneself is better or above others. Love is modest and humble and recognizes and honors others. |
| **#203**<br>**Arrogant**<br><br>Proud–KJV<br>**Arrogant–NASB**<br>**Arrogant–NIV**<br>Proud–NKJV<br>Proud–NLT<br><br>**POSB REFERENCE**<br>(Romans 1:30)<br>*Deeper Study* #15<br><br>See also POSB REF:<br>(2 Tim.3:2-4; esp. v.2)<br>Note 2, point 4 | ὑπερηφάνους = *huperëphanous*<br>Pronunciation: [hoop-er-ay'-fan-oos]<br>Parsing (part of speech): pronominal adjective<br>    Case—accusative<br>    Gender—masculine<br>    Number—plural<br>    Stem or root—from ὑπερήφανος, ον<br>Concordance References:<br>⇒ Strong's #5244 huperëphanos<br>⇒ NIV #5662 huperëphanos<br>⇒ NASB #5244 huperëphanos<br><br>**Romans 1:30**<br>Backbiters, haters of God, despiteful, **proud**, boasters, inventors of evil things, disobedient to parents, [KJV]<br>Slanderers, haters of God, insolent, **arrogant**, boastful, inventors of evil, disobedient to parents, [NASB]<br>Slanderers, God-haters, insolent, **arrogant** and boastful; they invent ways of doing evil; they disobey their parents; [NIV]<br>Backbiters, haters of God, violent, **proud**, boasters, inventors of evil things, disobedient to parents, [NKJV]<br>They are backstabbers, haters of God, insolent, **proud**, and boastful. They are forever inventing new ways of sinning and are disobedient to their parents. [NLT]<br>ψιθυριστάς, καταλάλους, θεοστυγεῖς, ὑβριστάς, **ὑπερηφάνους**, ἀλαζόνας, ἐφευρετὰς κακῶν, γονεῦσιν ἀπειθεῖς, [GNS]<br>καταλάλους θεοστυγεῖς ὑβριστὰς **ὑπερηφάνους** ἀλαζόνας, ἐφευρετὰς κακῶν, γονεῦσιν ἀπειθεῖς, [GNT] | Pride, arrogance, conceit, swellings, puffed up, arrogance, haughtiness, insolence, putting oneself above others, looking down upon others, scorn, contempt.<br><br>**Practical Application**<br>It means to show oneself, to lift one's head above another, to hold contempt for another, to compare oneself with others. Arrogance can be hidden in the heart as well as openly displayed. God opposes the proud (James 4:6; 1 Peter 5:5; Proverbs 3:24). |
| **#204**<br>**Arrogant**<br><br>Selfwilled–KJV<br>Self-willed–NASB<br>Overbearing–NIV<br>Self-willed–NKJV<br>**Arrogant–NLT** | αὐθάδη = *authadë*<br>Pronunciation: [ow-thad'-ay]<br>Parsing (part of speech): adjective<br>    Case—accusative<br>    Gender—masculine<br>    Number—singular<br>    Stem or root—from αὐθάδης, ες<br>Concordance References:<br>⇒ Strong's #829 authadës<br>⇒ NIV #881 authadës<br>⇒ NASB #829 authadës | Overbearing, self-willed, self-pleasing, arrogant, haughty, and self-centered.<br><br>**Practical Application**<br>It is a person who thinks too highly of himself, who looks at his own things and ignores or neglects the things of others. It is a person who is harsh to others; who criticizes, grumbles, and condemns others; who downs others and elevates himself in his own mind. |

# PRACTICAL WORD STUDIES
## in the NEW TESTAMENT

| ENGLISH WORD | GREEK WORD AND VERSE | THE WORD MEANS... |
|---|---|---|
| **POSB REFERENCE** (Tit.1:7-8; esp. v.7) Note 3, point 1a | **Titus 1:7**<br>For a bishop must be blameless, as the steward of God; not **selfwilled**, not soon angry, not given to wine, no striker, not given to filthy lucre; [KJV]<br>For the overseer must be above reproach as God's steward, not **self-willed**, not quick-tempered, not addicted to wine, not pugnacious, not fond of sordid gain, [NASB]<br>Since an overseer is entrusted with God's work, he must be blameless—not **overbearing**, not quick-tempered, not given to drunkenness, not violent, not pursuing dishonest gain. [NIV]<br>For a bishop must be blameless, as a steward of God, not **self-willed**, not quick-tempered, not given to wine, not violent, not greedy for money, [NKJV]<br>An elder must live a blameless life because he is God's minister. He must not be **arrogant** or quick-tempered; he must not be a heavy drinker, violent, or greedy for money. [NLT]<br>δεῖ γὰρ τὸν ἐπίσκοπον ἀνέγκλητον εἶναι, ὡς Θεοῦ οἰκονόμον· μὴ **αὐθάδη**, μὴ ὀργίλον, μὴ πάροινον, μὴ πλήκτην, μὴ αἰσχροκερδῆ, [GNS]<br>δεῖ γὰρ τὸν ἐπίσκοπον ἀνέγκλητον εἶναι ὡς θεοῦ οἰκονόμον, μὴ **αὐθάδη**, μὴ ὀργίλον, μὴ πάροινον, μὴ πλήκτην, μὴ αἰσχροκερδῆ, [GNT] | |
| **#205**<br>**As Precious As**<br><br>Like precious–KJV<br>Same kind–NASB<br>**As precious as–NIV**<br>Like precious–NKJV<br>Same precious–NLT<br><br>**POSB REFERENCE** (2 Pt.1:1) Note 2 | ἰσότιμον = isotimon<br>Pronunciation: [ee-sot'-ee-mon]<br>Parsing (part of speech): adjective<br>  Case—accusative<br>  Gender—feminine<br>  Number—singular<br>  Stem or root—from ἰσότιμος, ον<br>Concordance References:<br>⇒ Strong's #2472 isotimos<br>⇒ NIV #2700 isotimos<br>⇒ NASB #2472 isotimos<br><br>**2 Peter 1:1**<br>Simon Peter, a servant and an apostle of Jesus Christ, to them that have obtained **like precious** faith with us through the righteousness of God and our Saviour Jesus Christ: [KJV]<br>Simon Peter, a bond-servant and apostle of Jesus Christ, to those who have received a faith of the **same kind** as ours, by the righteousness of our God and Savior, Jesus Christ: [NASB]<br>Simon Peter, a servant and apostle of Jesus Christ, To those who through the righteousness of our God and Savior Jesus Christ have received a faith **as precious as** ours: [NIV]<br>Simon Peter, a bondservant and apostle of Jesus Christ, To those who have obtained **like precious** faith with us by the righteousness of our God and Savior Jesus Christ: [NKJV]<br>This letter is from Simon Peter, a slave and apostle of Jesus Christ. I am writing to all of you who share the **same precious** faith we have, faith given to us by Jesus Christ, our God and Savior, who makes us right with God. [NLT]<br>Σίμων Πέτρος, δοῦλος καὶ ἀπόστολος Ἰησοῦ Χριστοῦ, τοῖς **ἰσότιμον** ἡμῖν λαχοῦσι πίστιν ἐν δικαιοσύνῃ τοῦ Θεοῦ ἡμῶν καὶ σωτῆρος ἡμῶν Ἰησοῦ Χριστοῦ· [GNS]<br>Συμεὼν Πέτρος δοῦλος καὶ ἀπόστολος Ἰησοῦ Χριστοῦ τοῖς **ἰσότιμον** ἡμῖν λαχοῦσιν πίστιν ἐν δικαιοσύνῃ τοῦ θεοῦ ἡμῶν καὶ σωτῆρος Ἰησοῦ Χριστοῦ, [GNT] | As precious as; equally valuable; of the same kind.<br><br>**Practical Application**<br>Note this: the faith of Jesus Christ is the *same precious faith* that is given to all believers. The Greek word that Peter uses for "precious" (*isotimon*) is an unusual word. This is the only time it is used in the New Testament. It is really a double word. The *isos* means *equal*, and *time* means *honor* (A.T. Robertson. *Word Pictures in the New Testament*, Vol.6, p.147). Therefore, *faith as precious as* is meant *like faith*, a faith that is like everyone else's faith. This is a most wonderful thing. It means that we are all given the very same faith; we are all equal in value and honor and privilege before God. God does not discriminate; He does not have favorites. God loves us all equally, and He values and honors us all as much as He did Peter, James, John and Paul. |
| **#206**<br>**As The Prophets Foretold** | διὰ γραφῶν προφητικῶν = dia graphōn prophētikōn<br>Pronunciation: [di-ah graf-own' prof-ay-tik-own']<br>Parsing *dia* (part of speech): preposition<br>  Case—genitive<br>  Stem or root—from διά<br>Parsing *graphōn* (part of speech): noun | Through the prophetic writings, by the Scriptures of the prophets, as the prophets foretold.<br><br>**Practical Application**<br>God wants the world to know the gospel; therefore, He has commanded that it be revealed |

# PRACTICAL WORD STUDIES
## in the NEW TESTAMENT

| ENGLISH WORD | GREEK WORD AND VERSE | THE WORD MEANS... |
|---|---|---|
| By the scriptures of the prophets–KJV<br>By the Scriptures of the prophets–NASB<br>Through the prophetic writings–NIV<br>By the prophetic Scriptures–NKJV<br>**As the prophets foretold–NLT**<br><br>**POSB REFERENCE**<br>(Romans 16:25-26, esp. v.26)<br>Note 3, point 2 | Case—genitive<br>Gender—feminine<br>Number—plural<br>Stem or root—from γραφή, ῆς<br>Parsing *prophētikōn* (part of speech): adjective<br>Case—genitive<br>Gender—feminine<br>Number—plural<br>Stem or root—from προφητικός, ή, όν<br>Concordance References:<br>⇒ Strong's #1223 dia + 1124 graphē + 4397 prophētikos<br>⇒ NIV #1328 dia [through] + 1210 graphē [writings] + 4738 prophētikos [prophetic]<br>⇒ NASB #1223 dia + 1124 graphē + 4397 prophētikos<br><br>**Romans 16:26**<br>But now is made manifest, and **by the scriptures of the prophets**, according to the commandment of the everlasting God, made known to all nations for the obedience of faith: [KJV]<br>But now is manifested, and **by the Scriptures of the prophets**, according to the commandment of the eternal God, has been made known to all the nations, *leading* to obedience of faith; [NASB]<br>But now revealed and made known **through the prophetic writings** by the command of the eternal God, so that all nations might believe and obey him—[NIV]<br>But now has been made manifest, and **by the prophetic Scriptures** has been made known to all nations, according to the commandment of the everlasting God, for obedience to the faith— [NKJV]<br>But now **as the prophets foretold** and as the eternal God has commanded, this message is made known to all Gentiles everywhere, so that they might believe and obey Christ. [NLT]<br>φανερωθέντος δὲ νῦν **διά** τε **γραφῶν προφητικῶν**, κατ' ἐπιταγὴν τοῦ αἰωνίου Θεοῦ, εἰς ὑπακοὴν πίστεως εἰς πάντα τὰ ἔθνη γνωρισθέντος, [GNS]<br>φανερωθέντος δὲ νῦν **διά** τε **γραφῶν προφητικῶν** κατ' ἐπιταγὴν τοῦ αἰωνίου θεοῦ εἰς ὑπακοὴν πίστεως εἰς πάντα τὰ ἔθνη γνωρισθέντος, [GNT] | and proclaimed to the world. But note the crucial point: it is revealed as the prophets foretold, by the prophetic Scriptures *(dia graphōn prophētikōn)*. This is extremely important, for it tells us exactly where we are to find out about God and His message to the world. We do not discover God by natural reasoning: God reveals Himself to us.<br>There are two questions that desperately need to be studied by everyone.<br>1. Since God has revealed how men are to become acceptable to Him, why do men continue to create their own ideas about how to reach God? Why do men continue to think they will be acceptable to God if they can just do enough good to pacify God? Why do most men continue to think that God will never reject them, that they are not evil enough to be unacceptable to God?<br>2. Since God has revealed the gospel in the prophetic Scriptures, why do men not rush to the Scriptures to find the truth? Why do men not search the Scriptures daily to find out what God has revealed? (cp. Acts 17:11). |
| **#207**<br>**Ascension**<br><br>Received up–KJV<br>**Ascension–NASB**<br>Taken up–NIV<br>Received up–NKJV<br>Return–NLT<br><br>**POSB REFERENCE**<br>(Lk.9:51)<br>*Deeper Study #1* | ἀναλήμψεως = *analēmpseōs*<br>Pronunciation: [an-al'-aimp-se-os]<br>Parsing (part of speech): noun<br>Case—genitive<br>Gender—feminine<br>Number—singular<br>Stem or root—from ἀνάλημψις, εως<br>Concordance References:<br>⇒ Strong's #354 analepsis<br>⇒ NIV #378 analēmpsis<br>⇒ NASB #354 analēmpsis<br><br>**Luke 9:51**<br>And it came to pass, when the time was come that he should be **received up**, he stedfastly set his face to go to Jerusalem, [KJV]<br>And it came about, when the days were approaching for His **ascension**, that He resolutely set His face to go to Jerusalem; [NASB]<br>As the time approached for him to be **taken up** to heaven, Jesus resolutely set out for Jerusalem. [NIV]<br>Now it came to pass, when the time had come for Him to be **received up**, that He steadfastly set His face to go to Jerusalem, [NKJV]<br>As the time drew near for his **return** to heaven, Jesus resolutely set out for Jerusalem. [NLT]<br>Ἐγένετο δὲ ἐν τῷ συμπληροῦσθαι τὰς ἡμέρας τῆς **ἀναλήψεως** αὐτοῦ, καὶ αὐτὸς τὸ πρόσωπον αὐτοῦ | Taken up, ascensed, received up, returned.<br><br>**Practical Application**<br>This word refers to the ascension of Christ (cp. *analambano*, Acts 1:2, 11, 22; 1 Tim. 3:16). Salvation was to be secured by the ascension of Christ. How? The Ascended Lord means at least four things.<br>1. It means the Risen Lord. The ascension means that Christ arose from the dead. If He had remained in the grave, He would still be there in the form of dust. He could not have ascended. If He were to be "received up," He had to be raised up—quickened—made alive—taken up. No one can be taken up without first being raised up. Therefore, to speak of the ascension is to mean that Christ is risen. Death is conquered; man can now be saved from death.<br>2. It means the Advocate or Representative Lord. On earth Christ lived a perfect life; He was without sin (2 Cor. 5:21; Hebrews 4:15; 1 Peter 1:19; 1 Peter 2:22; John 8:46). He was "obedient unto death, even the death of the cross. Wherefore God also hath highly exalted Him" (Phil. 2:8-9). He is "sitting on the right hand of God (Col. 3:1). He is "Jesus |

# PRACTICAL WORD STUDIES
## in the NEW TESTAMENT

| ENGLISH WORD | GREEK WORD AND VERSE | THE WORD MEANS... |
|---|---|---|
| | ἐστήριξε τοῦ πορεύεσθαι εἰς Ἰερουσαλήμ, [GNS]<br>Ἐγένετο δὲ ἐν τῷ συμπληροῦσθαι τὰς ἡμέρας τῆς **ἀναλήμψεως** αὐτοῦ καὶ αὐτὸς τὸ πρόσωπον ἐστήρισεν τοῦ πορεύεσθαι εἰς Ἰερουσαλήμ. [GNT] | Christ the righteous"; therefore, He is our "advocate with the Father" (1 John 2:1). He is able to represent us before God because He has lived upon earth and secured a perfect righteousness. He is the Ideal Man (see note—Matthew 5:17-18), our advocate, the One who is qualified to plead our case before God and see to it that we are saved.<br>3. It means the Priestly or Intercessory Lord. Every man suffers while on earth: suffers pain, trial, need, want, temptation, loss, illness, and eventually death. We are incapable of even knowing how to pray as we ought in order to secure the help we need. But Christ knows and understands. He has been to earth and suffered just as we suffer. Therefore, He knows how to intercede for us and how to deliver us.<br>4. It means the exalted Lord. Christ has ascended to be exalted, to rule and reign over the universe for God. There is a great day of judgment coming upon the world, a day when all men will bow the knee and acknowledge that Jesus is Lord, the Son of the living God. |
| **#208**<br>**Ashamed**<br><br>**Ashamed–KJV**<br>Disappoint–NASB<br>Disappoint–NIV<br>Disappoint–NKJV<br>Disappoint–NLT<br><br>**POSB REFERENCE**<br>(Rom.5:3-5; esp. v.5)<br>Note 5, point 4 | καταισχύνει = *kataischunei*<br>Pronunciation: [kat-ahee-skhoo'-neh-ee]<br>Parsing (part of speech): verb<br>    Mood—indicative<br>    Tense—present<br>    Voice—active<br>    Person—3rd person<br>    Number—singular<br>    Stem or root—from καταισχύνω<br>Concordance References:<br>⇒ Strong's #2617 *kataischunō*<br>⇒ NIV #2875 *kataischunō*<br>⇒ NASB #2617 *kataischunō*<br><br>**Romans 5:5**<br>And hope maketh not **ashamed**; because the love of God is shed abroad in our hearts by the Holy Ghost which is given unto us. [KJV]<br>And hope does not **disappoint**, because the love of God has been poured out within our hearts through the Holy Spirit who was given to us. [NASB]<br>And hope does not **disappoint** us, because God has poured out his love into our hearts by the Holy Spirit, whom he has given us. [NIV]<br>Now hope does not **disappoint**, because the love of God has been poured out in our hearts by the Holy Spirit who was given to us. [NKJV]<br>And this expectation will not **disappoint** us. For we know how dearly God loves us, because he has given us the Holy Spirit to fill our hearts with his love. [NLT]<br>ἡ δὲ ἐλπὶς οὐ **καταισχύνει**, ὅτι ἡ ἀγάπη τοῦ Θεοῦ ἐκκέχυται ἐν ταῖς καρδίαις ἡμῶν διὰ Πνεύματος Ἁγίου τοῦ δοθέντος ἡμῖν, [GNS]<br>ἡ δὲ ἐλπὶς οὐ **καταισχύνει**, ὅτι ἡ ἀγάπη τοῦ θεοῦ ἐκκέχυται ἐν ταῖς καρδίαις ἡμῶν διὰ πνεύματος ἁγίου τοῦ δοθέντος ἡμῖν. [GNT] | To disappoint; to embarrass; to make ashamed; to humiliate; to disgrace.<br><br>**Practical Application**<br>Hope never disappoints: never shames, deludes, deceives, confounds, confuses. The believer, the person who is truly justified, will never be disappointed or shamed. He will see his hope fulfilled. He will live forever in the presence of God inheriting the promises God has given in His Word. |
| **#209**<br>**Ashamed**<br><br>**Ashamed–KJV**<br>Shame–NASB<br>Unashamed–NIV<br>**Ashamed–NKJV**<br>Shame–NLT | μὴ αἰσχυνθῶμεν = *mē aischunthōmen*<br>Pronunciation: [may ahee-skhoo'-tho-mehn]<br>Parsing (part of speech): verb<br>    Mood—subjunctive<br>    Tense—aorist<br>    Voice—passive deponent<br>    Person—1st person<br>    Number—plural<br>    Stem or root—from αἰσχύνομαι | To be ashamed, shamed. It means not to shrink back; to sense guilt and disgrace; to feel embarrassment.<br><br>**Practical Application**<br>If we do not abide in Christ, we will be ashamed when Jesus Christ returns to earth. Note a fact that is so often ignored by believers, a fact that is seldom if ever thought about. There |

# PRACTICAL WORD STUDIES
## in the NEW TESTAMENT

| ENGLISH WORD | GREEK WORD AND VERSE | THE WORD MEANS... |
|---|---|---|
| **POSB REFERENCE** (1 Jn.2:28) Note 2 | Concordance References:<br>⇒ Strong's #153+3361 aischunomai mē<br>⇒ NIV #159+3590 aischunomai mē [unashamed]<br>⇒ NASB #153+3361 aischunomai mē<br><br>**1 John 2:28**<br>And now, little children, abide in him; that, when he shall appear, we may have confidence, and not be **ashamed** before him at his coming. [KJV]<br>And now, little children, abide in Him, so that when He appears, we may have confidence and not shrink away from Him in **shame** at His coming. [NASB]<br>And now, dear children, continue in him, so that when he appears we may be confident and **unashamed** before him at his coming. [NIV]<br>And now, little children, abide in Him, that when He appears, we may have confidence and not be **ashamed** before Him at His coming. [NKJV]<br>And now, dear children, continue to live in fellowship with Christ so that when he returns, you will be full of courage and not shrink back from him in **shame**. [NLT]<br>καὶ νῦν, τεκνία, μένετε ἐν αὐτῷ· ἵνα ὅταν φανερωθῇ ἔχωμεν παρρησίαν, καὶ μὴ **αἰσχυνθῶμεν** ἀπ' αὐτοῦ, ἐν τῇ παρουσίᾳ αὐτοῦ. [GNS]<br>Καὶ νῦν, τεκνία, μένετε ἐν αὐτῷ, ἵνα ἐὰν φανερωθῇ σχῶμεν παρρησίαν καὶ μὴ **αἰσχυνθῶμεν** ἀπ' αὐτοῦ ἐν τῇ παρουσίᾳ αὐτοῦ. [GNT] | will be shame, disgrace, and embarrassment when Christ returns. Some believers will shrink back from Christ. The picture of nothing but joy and rejoicing when Christ returns is not a true picture. There is going to be judgment: the judgment of every man's works no matter what the works are, and there will be the judgment of sinners no matter who they are, all unbelievers.<br>There will be joy and rejoicing for some believers, for those who have been abiding in Christ. But there will be shame, guilt, disgrace, and embarrassment—a shrinking back—for those who have been walking unfaithfully. |
| **#210 Ask**<br><br>Beseech–KJV<br>Request–NASB<br>**Ask–NIV**<br>Urge–NKJV<br>Not translated–NLT<br><br>**POSB REFERENCE** (1 Thes.4:1-2) Note 1, point 1 | **ἐρωτῶμεν** = erōtōmen<br>Pronunciation: [er-o-to'-mehn]<br>Parsing (part of speech): verb<br>  Mood—indicative<br>  Tense—present<br>  Voice—active<br>  Person—1st person<br>  Number—plural<br>  Stem or root—from ἐρωτάω<br>Concordance References:<br>⇒ Strong's #2065 erōtaō<br>⇒ NIV #2263 erōtaō<br>⇒ NASB #2065 erōtaō<br><br>**1 Thes. 4:1**<br>Furthermore then we **beseech** you, brethren, and exhort *you* by the Lord Jesus, that as ye have received of us how ye ought to walk and to please God, *so* ye would abound more and more. [KJV]<br>Finally then, brethren, we **request** and exhort you in the Lord Jesus, that, as you received from us *instruction* as to how you ought to walk and please God (just as you actually do walk), that you may excel still more. [NASB]<br>Finally, brothers, we instructed you how to live in order to please God, as in fact you are living. Now we **ask** you and urge you in the Lord Jesus to do this more and more. [NIV]<br>Finally then, brethren, we **urge** and exhort in the Lord Jesus that you should abound more and more, just as you received from us how you ought to walk and to please God; [NKJV]<br>Finally, dear brothers and sisters, we urge you in the name of the Lord Jesus to live in a way that pleases God, as we have taught you. You are doing this already, and we encourage you to do so more and more. [NLT]—NOT TRANSLATED<br>Τὸ λοιπὸν οὖν, ἀδελφοί, **ἐρωτῶμεν** ὑμᾶς καὶ παρακαλοῦμεν ἐν Κυρίῳ Ἰησοῦ, καθὼς παρελάβετε παρ' ἡμῶν τὸ πῶς δεῖ ὑμᾶς περιπατεῖν καὶ ἀρέσκειν Θεῷ, ἵνα περισσεύητε μᾶλλον. [GNS]<br>Λοιπὸν οὖν, ἀδελφοί, **ἐρωτῶμεν** ὑμᾶς καὶ παρακαλοῦμεν ἐν κυρίῳ Ἰησοῦ, ἵνα καθὼς παρελάβετε παρ' ἡμῶν τὸ πῶς δεῖ ὑμᾶς περιπατεῖν καὶ ἀρέσκειν θεῷ, καθὼς καὶ περιπατεῖτε, ἵνα περισσεύητε μᾶλλον. [GNT] | To ask; to beseech; to invite; to request; to beg; to urge.<br><br>**Practical Application**<br>This word always has a sense of urgency about it. Paul was tenderly requesting his dear brothers to continue to please God in their daily walk, but it was an urgent request. Their walking to please God was an absolute necessity, a necessity that carried with it great blessings for obedience and terrible judgment for disobedience (the displeasure of God). |

## PRACTICAL WORD STUDIES
in the NEW TESTAMENT

| ENGLISH WORD | GREEK WORD AND VERSE | THE WORD MEANS... |
|---|---|---|
| **#211**<br>**Asked**<br><br>Desired–KJV<br>Demanded permission–NASB<br>**Asked–NIV**<br>**Asked–NKJV**<br>**Asked–NLT**<br><br>**POSB REFERENCE**<br>(Lk.22:31)<br>Note 1, point 2 | ἐξητήσατο = *exētēsato*<br>Pronunciation: [ex-ahee-teh'-saw-tow]<br>Parsing (part of speech): verb<br>    Mood—indicative<br>    Tense—aorist<br>    Voice—middle<br>    Person—3rd person<br>    Number—singular<br>    Stem or root—from ἐξαιτέομαι<br>Concordance References:<br>  ⇒ Strong's #1809 exaiteomai<br>  ⇒ NIV #1977 exaiteō<br>  ⇒ NASB #1809 exaiteō<br><br>**Luke 22:31**<br>And the Lord said, Simon, Simon, behold, Satan hath **desired** *to have* you, that he may sift *you* as wheat: [KJV]<br>"Simon, Simon, behold, Satan has **demanded permission** to sift you like wheat; [NASB]<br>"Simon, Simon, Satan has **asked** to sift you as wheat. [NIV]<br>And the Lord said, "Simon, Simon! Indeed, Satan has **asked** for you, that he may sift *you* as wheat. [NKJV]<br>"Simon, Simon, Satan has **asked** to have all of you, to sift you like wheat. [NLT]<br>εἶπε δὲ ὁ Κύριος, Σίμων Σίμων, ἰδοὺ ὁ Σατανᾶς **ἐξητήσατο** ὑμᾶς, τοῦ σινιάσαι ὡς τὸν σῖτον· [GNS]<br>Σίμων Σίμων, ἰδοὺ ὁ Σατανᾶς **ἐξητήσατο** ὑμᾶς τοῦ σινιάσαι ὡς τὸν σῖτον· [GNT] | To beg for something; to desire; to make an appeal; to demand; to obtain by asking.<br><br>**Practical Application**<br>Jesus pictured Satan as begging permission of God to trip the disciples. It is the same picture that is found in Job (Job 1:6f). The Bible is clear in its teaching: God is sovereign; anything that goes on in the universe goes on because God allows it, even temptation. The truth to see is that...<br>• Jesus did give a glimpse into the spiritual world.<br>• Satan begged God to let him test and try the disciples.<br>• Satan is subject to God and has no right or power to tempt believers unless God allows it.<br>• The Lord's prayer does include the words, "Deliver us from the evil one" (*a po tou poneron*) (see POSB *Deeper Study #9*—Matthew 6:13. |
| **#212**<br>**Asked**<br><br>Besought–KJV<br>Begging–NASB<br>Invited–NIV<br>Begged–NKJV<br>**Asked–NLT**<br><br>**POSB REFERENCE**<br>(Acts 13:42-45; esp. v.42)<br>Note 1, point 1 | παρεκάλουν = *parekaloun*<br>Pronunciation: [par-ek-al-oon]<br>Parsing (part of speech): verb<br>    Mood—indicative<br>    Tense—imperfect<br>    Voice—active<br>    Person—3rd person<br>    Number—plural<br>    Stem or root—from παρακαλέω<br>Concordance References:<br>  ⇒ Strong's #3870 parakaleō<br>  ⇒ NIV #4151 parakaleō<br>  ⇒ NASB #3870 parakaleō<br><br>**Acts 13:42**<br>And when the Jews were gone out of the synagogue, the Gentiles **besought** that these words might be preached to them the next sabbath. [KJV]<br>And as Paul and Barnabas were going out, the people kept **begging** that these things might be spoken to them the next Sabbath. [NASB]<br>As Paul and Barnabas were leaving the synagogue, the people **invited** them to speak further about these things on the next Sabbath. [NIV]<br>So when the Jews went out of the synagogue, the Gentiles **begged** that these words might be preached to them the next Sabbath. [NKJV]<br>As Paul and Barnabas left the synagogue that day, the people **asked** them to return again and speak about these things the next week. [NLT]<br>Ἐξιόντων ἐκ τῆς συναγωγῆς τῶν Ἰουδαίων, δὲ αὐτῶν **παρεκάλουν** τὰ ἔθνη εἰς τὸ μεταξὺ σάββατον λαληθῆναι αὐτοῖς τὰ ῥήματα ταῦτα. [GNS]<br>Ἐξιόντων δὲ αὐτῶν **παρεκάλουν** εἰς τὸ μεταξὺ σάββατον λαληθῆναι αὐτοῖς τὰ ῥήματα ταῦτα. [GNT] | Invited, urged, besought, begged, asked; requested urgently; appealed to; pleaded with.<br><br>**Practical Application**<br>It is continuous action: the heathen continued to beseech. The picture is that they asked and asked Paul to share more about the forgiveness of sins which is in Jesus. |
| **#213**<br>**Asking Questions**<br><br>Asking questions–KJV | ἐπερωτῶντα = *eperōtōnta*<br>Pronunciation: [ep-er-o-town'-tah]<br>Parsing (part of speech): verb<br>    Mood—participle<br>    Tense—passive<br>    Voice—active<br>    Case—accusative | To ask questions; to interrogate; to inquire.<br><br>**Practical Application**<br>In this Scripture, Christ was "asking them questions." He wanted answers, more understanding. He thirsted for truth and sought it. |

## Practical Word Studies
### in the New Testament

| ENGLISH WORD | GREEK WORD AND VERSE | THE WORD MEANS... |
|---|---|---|
| Asking questions–NASB<br>Asking questions–NIV<br>Asking questions–NKJV<br>Discussing deep questions–NLT<br><br>**POSB REFERENCE**<br>(Lk.2:46-47; esp. v.46)<br>Note 3, point 2b<br><br>See also POSB REF:<br>(Mk.8:29)<br>Note 3, point 1 | Gender—masculine<br>Number—singular<br>Stem or root—from ἐπερωτάω<br>Concordance References:<br>⇒ Strong's #1905 eperötaö<br>⇒ NIV #2089 eperötaö<br>⇒ NASB #1905 eperötaö<br><br>**Luke 2:46**<br>And it came to pass, that after three days they found him in the temple, sitting in the midst of the doctors, both hearing them, and **asking** them **questions**. [KJV]<br>And it came about that after three days they found Him in the temple, sitting in the midst of the teachers, both listening to them, and **asking** them **questions**. [NASB]<br>After three days they found him in the temple courts, sitting among the teachers, listening to them and **asking** them **questions**. [NIV]<br>Now so it was *that* after three days they found Him in the temple, sitting in the midst of the teachers, both listening to them and **asking** them **questions**. [NKJV]<br>Three days later they finally discovered him. He was in the Temple, sitting among the religious teachers, **discussing deep questions** with them. [NLT]<br>καὶ ἐγένετο, μεθ' ἡμέρας τρεῖς εὗρον αὐτὸν ἐν τῷ ἱερῷ, καθεζόμενον ἐν μέσῳ τῶν διδασκάλων, καὶ ἀκούοντα αὐτῶν, καὶ **ἐπερωτῶντα** αὐτούς. [GNS]<br>καὶ ἐγένετο μετὰ ἡμέρας τρεῖς εὗρον αὐτὸν ἐν τῷ ἱερῷ καθεζόμενον ἐν μέσῳ τῶν διδασκάλων καὶ ἀκούοντα αὐτῶν καὶ **ἐπερωτῶντα** αὐτούς· [GNT] | |
| **#214**<br>**Asleep, Fell**<br><br>Slept–KJV<br>Sleep–NASB<br>**Fell asleep–NIV**<br>Slept–NKJV<br>Slept–NLT<br><br>**POSB REFERENCE**<br>(Mt.25:5)<br>*Deeper Study #4* | ἐκάθευδον = ekatheudön<br>Pronunciation: [eh-kath-yoo'-don]<br>Parsing (part of speech): verb<br>  Mood—indicative<br>  Tense—imperfect<br>  Voice—active<br>  Person—3rd person<br>  Number—plural<br>  Stem or root—from καθεύδω<br>Concordance References:<br>⇒ Strong's #2518 katheudö<br>⇒ NIV #2761 katheudö<br>⇒ NASB #2518 katheudö<br><br>**Matthew 25:5**<br>While the bridegroom tarried, they all slumbered and **slept**. [KJV]<br>"Now while the bridegroom was delaying, they all got drowsy and *began* to **sleep**. [NASB]<br>The bridegroom was a long time in coming, and they all became drowsy and **fell asleep**. [NIV]<br>But while the bridegroom was delayed, they all slumbered and **slept**. [NKJV]<br>When the bridegroom was delayed, they all lay down and **slept**. [NLT]<br>χρονίζοντος δὲ τοῦ νυμφίου ἐνύσταξαν πᾶσαι καὶ **ἐκάθευδον**. [GNS]<br>χρονίζοντος δὲ τοῦ νυμφίου ἐνύσταξαν πᾶσαι καὶ **ἐκάθευδον**. [GNT] | To fall asleep; to go to sleep. This is the natural sleep of a person at night.<br><br>**Practical Application**<br>Even the wise and strong grow weary and find it difficult to stay awake and alert, to stay at peak performance all the time. No believer, whoever he is, walks anywhere as close to God as he should. The world is too dark and the darkness too heavy for the believer to see enough light that he can always be victorious over the pull of heavy eyelids.<br>⇒ His body is too weak to be *always laboring*.<br>⇒ His mind is too undeveloped to be *always concentrating*.<br>⇒ His energy is too limited to be *always driving*.<br>⇒ His spirit is too young to be *always sacrificing*.<br>⇒ His motives are too self-centered to be *always walking unselfishly*. |
| **#215**<br>**Aspire**<br><br>Study–KJV<br>Make it... ambition–NASB<br>Make it... ambition–NIV<br>**Aspire–NKJV**<br>Ambition–NLT | φιλοτιμεῖσθαι = philotimeisthai<br>Pronunciation: [fil-ot-im-ees'-tha-ee]<br>Parsing (part of speech): verb<br>  Mood—infinitive<br>  Tense—present<br>  Voice—middle or passive deponent<br>  Stem or root—from φιλοτιμέομαι<br>Concordance References:<br>⇒ Strong's #5389 philotimeomai<br>⇒ NIV #5818 philotimeomai<br>⇒ NASB #5389 philotimeomai | To make it one's ambition or goal; to study; to aspire; to endeavor; to be ambitious; to strive eagerly; to seek with all one's energy.<br><br>**Practical Application**<br>The very meaning of the word *aspire* shows the supreme importance of quietness. We must seek to be quiet and learn to be quiet. |

# PRACTICAL WORD STUDIES
## in the NEW TESTAMENT

| ENGLISH WORD | GREEK WORD AND VERSE | THE WORD MEANS... |
|---|---|---|
| **POSB REFERENCE** (1 Thes.4:11) Note 2 | **1 Thes. 4:11** And that ye **study** to be quiet, and to do your own business, and to work with your own hands, as we commanded you; [KJV] And to **make it** your **ambition** to lead a quiet life and attend to your own business and work with your hands, just as we commanded you; [NASB] **Make it** your **ambition** to lead a quiet life, to mind your own business and to work with your hands, just as we told you, [NIV] That you also **aspire** to lead a quiet life, to mind your own business, and to work with your hands, as we commanded you, [NKJV] This should be your **ambition**: to live a quiet life, minding your own business and working with your hands, just as we commanded you before. [NLT] καὶ **φιλοτιμεῖσθαι** ἡσυχάζειν καὶ πράσσειν τὰ ἴδια, καὶ ἐργάζεσθαι ταῖς ἰδίαις χερσὶν ὑμῶν, καθὼς ὑμῖν παρηγγείλαμεν· [GNS] καὶ **φιλοτιμεῖσθαι** ἡσυχάζειν καὶ πράσσειν τὰ ἴδια καὶ ἐργάζεσθαι ταῖς [ἰδίαις] χερσὶν ὑμῶν, καθὼς ὑμῖν παρηγγείλαμεν, [GNT] | |
| **#216** **Assayed** Assayed–KJV Trying–NASB Tried–NIV Tried–NKJV Tried–NLT **POSB REFERENCE** (Acts 9:26-28; esp. v.26) Note 2, point 1 | ἐπείραζεν = epeirazen Pronunciation: [eh-peh-i'-rahd-zen] Parsing (part of speech): verb   Mood—indicative   Tense—imperfect   Voice—active   Person—3rd person   Number—singular   Stem or root—from πειράζω Concordance References:   ⇒ Strong's #3985 peirazö   ⇒ NIV #4279 peirazö   ⇒ NASB #3985 peirazö **Acts 9:26** And when Saul was come to Jerusalem, he **assayed** to join himself to the disciples: but they were all afraid of him, and believed not that he was a disciple. [KJV] And when he had come to Jerusalem, he was **trying** to associate with the disciples; and they were all afraid of him, not believing that he was a disciple. [NASB] When he came to Jerusalem, he **tried** to join the disciples, but they were all afraid of him, not believing that he really was a disciple. [NIV] And when Saul had come to Jerusalem, he **tried** to join the disciples; but they were all afraid of him, and did not believe that he was a disciple. [NKJV] When Saul arrived in Jerusalem, he **tried** to meet with the believers, but they were all afraid of him. They thought he was only pretending to be a believer! [NLT] Παραγενόμενος δὲ ὁ Σαῦλος εἰς Ἰερουσαλήμ, **ἐπείρατο** κολλᾶσθαι τοῖς μαθηταῖς· καὶ πάντες ἐφοβοῦντο αὐτόν, μὴ πιστεύοντες ὅτι ἐστὶ μαθητής. [GNS] Παραγενόμενος δὲ εἰς Ἰερουσαλὴμ **ἐπείραζεν** κολλᾶσθαι τοῖς μαθηταῖς, καὶ πάντες ἐφοβοῦντο αὐτόν μὴ πιστεύοντες ὅτι ἐστὶν μαθητής. [GNT] | To try; to try repeatedly; to put to the test; to attempt. **Practical Application** Paul was faithful in seeking fellowship with believers, but they rejected him. Paul fled to Jerusalem. Note these facts. 1. Paul tried and tried to join the disciples at Jerusalem. 2. Paul was persecuted by his past as the arch-persecutor of believers; the believers would not accept him. They did not believe his testimony. They were suspicious, thinking he was an imposter trying to work his way into the circle of believers...   • to spy upon them.   • to identify all the disciples so he could arrest them. 3. Paul was befriended by Barnabas. Somehow Barnabas began to sense Paul may be telling the truth. Apparently, he sat down with Paul and had Paul relate his experiences with Christ. Barnabas became thoroughly convinced that Paul was truthful and took Paul to the apostles. (By apostles is meant Peter and James, the half-brother of Jesus who was to become, if he were not already, the pastor of the church at Jerusalem [Galatians 1:18-19]. The other apostles were probably out of town on some mission.) Note that Barnabas, after introducing Paul to Peter and James, shared three things about Paul: ⇒ that Paul's conversion was real—that he had actually seen the Lord on the road to Damascus. ⇒ that the Lord had actually spoken to Paul. ⇒ that Paul had been preaching boldly in Damascus. 4. Paul was finally accepted. Peter was convinced and invited Paul to stay with him. Paul did, and he stayed fifteen glorious days, fellowshipping with the man whom the Lord Himself had chosen to be the first leader of His dear people (cp. Galatians 1:18. Note: Paul said his primary purpose for coming to Jerusalem was to see Peter.) This was important for it meant he had not gone for the pur- |

# PRACTICAL WORD STUDIES
## in the NEW TESTAMENT

| ENGLISH WORD | GREEK WORD AND VERSE | THE WORD MEANS... |
|---|---|---|
| | | pose of ministering, but to learn about Jesus from the leader of the apostolic band. Note also that while there, Paul was not sitting around revelling in the fellowship of Peter and James. He still ministered, still bore witness of the saving grace of God. He went out to preach Jesus.<br><br>Note the great struggle Paul went through just to be able to worship and fellowship with other believers. There was no thought whatsoever about forsaking the assembly of believers, no thoughts about worshipping alone out in nature or wherever. He fought to fellowship with other believers, fought until they accepted him. |
| **#217**<br>**Assembled**<br><br>**Assembled–KJV**<br>Gathered together–NASB<br>Came together–NIV<br>**Assembled–NKJV**<br>Gathered–NLT<br><br>**POSB**<br>**REFERENCE**<br>(Mk.14:53)<br>Note 1 | συνέρχονται = sunerchontai<br>Pronunciation: [soon-er'-khon-tah-ee]<br>Parsing (part of speech): verb<br>    Mood—indicative<br>    Tense—present<br>    Voice—middle or passive deponent<br>    Person—3rd person<br>    Number—plural<br>    Stem or root—from συνέρχομαι<br>Concordance References:<br>  ⇒ Strong's #4905 sunerchomai<br>  ⇒ NIV #5302 sunerchomai<br>  ⇒ NASB #4905 sunerchomai<br><br>**Mark 14:53**<br>And they led Jesus away to the high priest: and with him were **assembled** all the chief priests and the elders and the scribes. [KJV]<br>And they led Jesus away to the high priest; and all the chief priests and the elders and the scribes **gathered together**. [NASB]<br>They took Jesus to the high priest, and all the chief priests, elders and teachers of the law **came together**. [NIV]<br>And they led Jesus away to the high priest; and with him were **assembled** all the chief priests, the elders, and the scribes. [NKJV]<br>Jesus was led to the high priest's home where the leading priests, other leaders, and teachers of religious law had **gathered**. [NLT]<br>Καὶ ἀπήγαγον τὸν Ἰησοῦν πρὸς τὸν ἀρχιερέα· καὶ **συνέρχονται** αὐτῷ πάντες οἱ ἀρχιερεῖς καὶ οἱ πρεσβύτεροι καὶ οἱ γραμματεῖς. [GNS]<br>Καὶ ἀπήγαγον τὸν Ἰησοῦν πρὸς τὸν ἀρχιερέα, καὶ **συνέρχονται** πάντες οἱ ἀρχιερεῖς καὶ οἱ πρεσβύτεροι καὶ οἱ γραμματεῖς. [GNT] | To assemble; to gather; to draw together; to come together; to flock together; to resort; to meet with.<br><br>**Practical Application**<br>The word also has the idea of accompanying one another. The picture is that of the Jewish leaders flocking or herding together around Jesus, of being called to accompany one another to their respective seats, ready to pounce on Jesus. |
| **#218**<br>**Assembly**<br><br>Church–KJV<br>Congregation–NASB<br>**Assembly–NIV**<br>Congregation–NKJV<br>**Assembly–NLT**<br><br>**POSB**<br>**REFERENCE**<br>(Acts 7:38)<br>*Deeper Study #4* | ἐκκλησία = ekklēsia<br>Pronunciation: [ek-klay-see'-ah]<br>Parsing (part of speech): noun<br>    Case—dative<br>    Gender—feminine<br>    Number—singular<br>    Stem or root— from ἐκκλησία<br>Concordance References:<br>  ⇒ Strong's #1577 ekklēsia<br>  ⇒ NIV #1711 ekklēsia<br>  ⇒ NASB #1577 ekklēsia<br><br>**Acts 7:38**<br>This is he, that was in the **church** in the wilderness with the angel which spake to him in the mount Sina, and *with* our fathers: who received the lively oracles to give unto us: [KJV]<br>"This is the one who was in the **congregation** in the wilderness together with the angel who was speaking to | Assembly, church, congregation, gathering.<br><br>**Practical Application**<br>Israel was God's church, God's assembly, God's congregation in the wilderness. Israel was a type of the church in the world. |

# PRACTICAL WORD STUDIES
## in the NEW TESTAMENT

| ENGLISH WORD | GREEK WORD AND VERSE | THE WORD MEANS... |
|---|---|---|
| | him on Mount Sinai, and *who was* with our fathers; and he received living oracles to pass on to you. [NASB]<br><br>He was in the **assembly** in the desert, with the angel who spoke to him on Mount Sinai, and with our fathers; and he received living words to pass on to us. [NIV]<br><br>This is he who was in the **congregation** in the wilderness with the Angel who spoke to him on Mount Sinai, and *with* our fathers, the one who received the living oracles to give to us, [NKJV]<br><br>Moses was with the **assembly** of God's people in the wilderness. He was the mediator between the people of Israel and the angel who gave him life-giving words on Mount Sinai to pass on to us. [NLT]<br><br>οὗτός ἐστιν ὁ γενόμενος ἐν τῇ **ἐκκλησίᾳ** ἐν τῇ ἐρήμῳ, μετὰ τοῦ ἀγγέλου τοῦ λαλοῦντος αὐτῷ ἐν τῷ ὄρει Σινᾶ καὶ τῶν πατέρων ἡμῶν· ὃς ἐδέξατο λόγια ζῶντα δοῦναι ἡμῖν· [GNS]<br><br>οὗτός ἐστιν ὁ γενόμενος ἐν τῇ **ἐκκλησίᾳ** ἐν τῇ ἐρήμῳ μετὰ τοῦ ἀγγέλου τοῦ λαλοῦντος αὐτῷ ἐν τῷ ὄρει Σινᾶ καὶ τῶν πατέρων ἡμῶν, ὃς ἐδέξατο λόγια ζῶντα δοῦναι ἡμῖν, [GNT] | |
| **#219**<br>**Assigned To**<br><br>Heritage–KJV<br>Allotted to–NASB<br>Entrusted to–NIV<br>Entrusted to–NKJV<br>**Assigned to–NLT**<br><br>**POSB REFERENCE**<br>(1 Pt.5:2-3; esp. v.3)<br>Note 2, point 3 | κλήρων = klērōn<br>Pronunciation: [klay'-rown]<br>Parsing (part of speech): noun<br>    Case—genitive<br>    Gender—masculine<br>    Number—plural<br>    Stem or root—from κλῆρος, ου<br>Concordance References:<br>  ⇒ Strong's #2819 klēros<br>  ⇒ NIV #3102 klēros<br>  ⇒ NASB #2819 klēros<br><br>**1 Peter 5:3**<br>Neither as being lords over *God's* **heritage**, but being ensamples to the flock. [KJV]<br><br>Nor yet as lording it over those **allotted to** your charge, but proving to be examples to the flock. [NASB]<br><br>Not lording it over those **entrusted to** you, but being examples to the flock. [NIV]<br><br>Nor as being lords over those **entrusted to** you, but being examples to the flock; [NKJV]<br><br>Don't lord it over the people **assigned to** your care, but lead them by your good example. [NLT]<br><br>μηδ' ὡς κατακυριεύοντες τῶν **κλήρων**, ἀλλὰ τύποι γινόμενοι τοῦ ποιμνίου. [GNS]<br><br>μηδ' ὡς κατακυριεύοντες τῶν **κλήρων** ἀλλὰ τύποι γινόμενοι τοῦ ποιμνίου· [GNT] | Entrusted to; allotted to; assigned to.<br><br>**Practical Application**<br>This is the word that was used of Israel in the Old Testament. It means that the Jews were the people who were set apart and allotted and assigned to God. They were His very special allotment and assignment—His treasure—the people charged to His care and oversight. This is the picture painted of the elder or minister and the flock of God. God has given the minister a very special heritage or allotment and assignment: the minister has been assigned to feed the heritage of God, the very flock that belongs to God Himself.<br><br>Now note how the minister is to lead God's flock. He is not to lord it over them, but he is to lead by example. The minister...<br>- is not to be a dictator but an example.<br>- is not to preach one thing and do something else. |
| **#220**<br>**Assistant**<br><br>Minister–KJV<br>Helper–NASB<br>Helper–NIV<br>**Assistant–NKJV**<br>**Assistant–NLT**<br><br>**POSB REFERENCE**<br>(Acts 13:5-6; esp. v.5)<br>Note 2, point 2 | ὑπηρέτην = hupēretēn<br>Pronunciation: [hoop-ay-ret'-ayn]<br>Parsing (part of speech): noun<br>    Case—accusative<br>    Gender—masculine<br>    Number—singular<br>    Stem or root—from ὑπηρέτης, ου<br>Concordance References:<br>  ⇒ Strong's #5257 hupēretēs<br>  ⇒ NIV #5677 hupēretēs<br>  ⇒ NASB #5257 hupēretēs<br><br>**Acts 13:5**<br>And when they were at Salamis, they preached the word of God in the synagogues of the Jews: and they had also John to *their* **minister**. [KJV]<br><br>And when they reached Salamis, they *began* to proclaim the word of God in the synagogues of the Jews; and they also had John as their **helper**. [NASB]<br><br>When they arrived at Salamis, they proclaimed the word of God in the Jewish synagogues. John was with them as their **helper**. [NIV]<br><br>And when they arrived in Salamis, they preached the | The minister is to lead people by living for Christ. He is to preach and teach Christ, but he is to first of all live a pure and righteous life just like Christ lived. The minister is to live exactly what he preaches. He is to be a pattern and model for Christ, a pattern and model of just what God wants His people to be.<br><br>Helper, minister, assistant, attendant, servant.<br><br>**Practical Application**<br>Mark was assisting under Barnabas and Paul, being discipled by them—helping, serving, ministering right with them, learning all he could. Apparently he was somewhat younger. |

# PRACTICAL WORD STUDIES
## in the NEW TESTAMENT

| ENGLISH WORD | GREEK WORD AND VERSE | THE WORD MEANS... |
|---|---|---|
| | word of God in the synagogues of the Jews. They also had John as *their* **assistant**. [NKJV]<br>There, in the town of Salamis, they went to the Jewish synagogues and preached the word of God. (John Mark went with them as their **assistant**.) [NLT]<br>καὶ γενόμενοι ἐν Σαλαμῖνι, κατήγγελλον τὸν λόγον τοῦ Θεοῦ ἐν ταῖς συναγωγαῖς τῶν Ἰουδαίων· εἶχον δὲ καὶ Ἰωάννην **ὑπηρέτην**. [GNS]<br>καὶ γενόμενοι ἐν Σαλαμῖνι κατήγγελλον τὸν λόγον τοῦ θεοῦ ἐν ταῖς συναγωγαῖς τῶν Ἰουδαίων. εἶχον δὲ καὶ Ἰωάννην **ὑπηρέτην**. [GNT] | |
| **#221**<br>**Associate With**<br><br>Company with–KJV<br>**Associate with–NASB**<br>**Associate with–NIV**<br>Keep company with–NKJV<br>**Associate with–NLT**<br><br>**POSB REFERENCE**<br>(1 Cor.5:9-10; esp. v.9)<br>Note 4 | συναναμίγνυσθαι = *sunanamignusthai*<br>Pronunciation: [soon-an-am-ig'-noos-thah-ee]<br>Parsing (part of speech): verb<br>    Mood—infinitive<br>    Tense—present<br>    Voice—middle or passive<br>    Stem or root—from συναναμίγνυμι<br>Concordance References:<br>  ⇒ Strong's #4874 sunanameignumi<br>  ⇒ NIV #5264 sunanameignumi<br>  ⇒ NASB #4874 sunanameignumi<br><br>**1 Cor. 5:9**<br>I wrote unto you in an epistle not to **company with** fornicators: [KJV]<br>I wrote you in my letter not to **associate with** immoral people; [NASB]<br>I have written you in my letter not to **associate with** sexually immoral people—[NIV]<br>I wrote to you in my epistle not to **keep company with** sexually immoral people. [NKJV]<br>When I wrote to you before, I told you not to **associate with** people who indulge in sexual sin. [NLT]<br>Ἔγραψα ὑμῖν ἐν τῇ ἐπιστολῇ μὴ **συναναμίγνυσθαι** πόρνοις· [GNS]<br>Ἔγραψα ὑμῖν ἐν τῇ ἐπιστολῇ μὴ **συναναμίγνυσθαι** πόρνοις, [GNT] | Associate with, company with; have dealings with; mix up.<br><br>**Practical Application**<br>The church and its believers cannot go out of the world; therefore, some contact with the unbelievers of the world is necessary. This is understandable to any thinking and honest person. However, it is also understandable that the church must not become *mixed up* with the shameful sinners of the world. The church and its believers must be separate in their behavior and fellowship. The church and the believers are to be holy and pure and righteous before God and to hold up the banner of holiness and purity and righteousness before the people of the world. Believers are *in the world*, but they must not be *of the world*. |
| **#222**<br>**Assurance**<br><br>Substance–KJV<br>**Assurance–NASB**<br>Sure–NIV<br>Substance–NKJV<br>Confident assurance–NLT<br><br>**POSB REFERENCE**<br>(Heb.11:1)<br>Note 1 | ὑπόστασις = *hupostasis*<br>Pronunciation: [hoop-os'-tas-is]<br>Parsing (part of speech): noun<br>    Case—nominative<br>    Gender—feminine<br>    Number—singular<br>    Stem or root—from ὑπόστασις, εως<br>Concordance References:<br>  ⇒ Strong's #5287 hupostasis<br>  ⇒ NIV #5712 hupostasis<br>  ⇒ NASB #5287 hupostasis<br><br>**Hebrews 11:1**<br>Now faith is the **substance** of things hoped for, the evidence of things not seen. [KJV]<br>Now faith is the **assurance** of *things* hoped for, the conviction of things not seen. [NASB]<br>Now faith is being **sure** of what we hope for and certain of what we do not see. [NIV]<br>Now faith is the **substance** of things hoped for, the evidence of things not seen. [NKJV]<br>What is faith? It is the **confident assurance** that what we hope for is going to happen. It is the evidence of things we cannot yet see. [NLT]<br>Ἔστι δὲ πίστις ἐλπιζομένων **ὑπόστασις**, πραγμάτων ἔλεγχος οὐ βλεπομένων. [GNS]<br>Ἔστιν δὲ πίστις ἐλπιζομένων **ὑπόστασις**, πραγμάτων ἔλεγχος οὐ βλεπομένων. [GNT] | The foundation, assurance, title-deed, and guarantee of things hoped for.<br><br>**Practical Application**<br>Look closely at what is being said and note that faith is being described as an act, an act of the mind and heart. That is, our hearts and minds believe something, and we have assurance and conviction that it is true. This is certainly true; faith is an act of the mind and heart. But many of the earlier interpreters understood "assurance" (*hupostasis*) to mean *real being, substantial nature, the real nature of a thing*. Vincent points this out and even says that it suggests the real sense, but he backs off of the meaning and concludes that faith is basically an act of what he calls "moral intelligence directed at an object" Marvin Vincent. *Word Studies in the New Testament*, Vol. 4. Grand Rapids, MI: Eerdmans Publishing Co., 1969, p.510).<br>Now, what does all this discussion mean? It means this: faith is the *assurance, the actual possession*, of things hoped for, the *evidence and reality* of things not seen. It is *both an act and a possession* of the thing believed. It is believing and trusting in that which actually exists—in that which we can possess. We may not be able to see it, but it is real and existing; and we can possess it by believing and having faith in it. We can possess it now—we cannot see it, but we can actually possess the very substance of it by believing and entrusting our lives to it. |

## PRACTICAL WORD STUDIES
## in the NEW TESTAMENT

| ENGLISH WORD | GREEK WORD AND VERSE | THE WORD MEANS... |
|---|---|---|
| | | ⇒ Faith is *trusting and possessing* all that God is and says.<br>⇒ Faith is *believing and possessing* all that God is and says.<br>⇒ Faith is *having confidence in and possessing* all that God is and says.<br>⇒ Faith is *hoping for something and possessing it* because God is (exists) and has promised it.<br>Note what Biblical faith is not. It is not...<br>• "I think so; I hope so."<br>• "It may be so; it may not be so."<br>• "It might be true; it might not be true."<br>Biblical faith does not deal with what is unreal, imaginary, fanciful, visionary, superficial, or deceptive. Biblical faith is the knowledge, experience, and *possession* of things hoped for. True Biblical faith deals only with truth and reality. It is...<br>• knowing what is real.<br>• experiencing what is real.<br>• possessing what is real. |
| #223<br>**Assured–**<br>**Assuredly**<br><br>**Assuredly–KJV**<br>Certain–NASB<br>**Assured–NIV**<br>**Assuredly–NKJV**<br>Clearly known–NLT<br><br>**POSB**<br>**REFERENCE**<br>(Acts 2:33-36; esp. v.36)<br>Note 4, point 3 | ἀσφαλῶς γινωσκέτω = *asphalōs ginōsketō*<br>Pronunciation: [as-fal-oce' ghin-oce'-keh-tow]<br>Parsing *asphalōs* (part of speech): adverb adjective<br>    Stem or root—from ἀσφαλῶς<br>Parsing *ginōsketō* (part of speech): verb<br>    Mood—imperative<br>    Tense—present<br>    Voice—active<br>    Person—3rd person<br>    Number—singular<br>    Stem or root—from γινώσκω<br>Concordance References:<br>⇒ Strong's #806+1097 asphalōs ginōskō<br>⇒ NIV #857+1182 asphalōs ginōskō [assured]<br>⇒ NASB #806+1097 asphalōs ginōskō<br><br>            **Acts 2:36**<br>Therefore let all the house of Israel know **assuredly**, that God hath made that same Jesus, whom ye have crucified, both Lord and Christ. [KJV]<br>"Therefore let all the house of Israel know for **certain** that God has made Him both Lord and Christ— this Jesus whom you crucified." [NASB]<br>"Therefore let all Israel be **assured** of this: God has made this Jesus, whom you crucified, both Lord and Christ." [NIV]<br>"Therefore let all the house of Israel know **assuredly** that God has made this Jesus, whom you crucified, both Lord and Christ." [NKJV]<br>So let it be **clearly known** by everyone in Israel that God has made this Jesus whom you crucified to be both Lord and Messiah!" [NLT]<br>ἀσφαλῶς οὖν γινωσκέτω πᾶς οἶκος Ἰσραὴλ, ὅτι καὶ Κύριον καὶ Χριστὸν αὐτὸν ὁ Θεός ἐποίησε, τοῦτον τὸν Ἰησοῦν ὃν ὑμεῖς ἐσταυρώσατε. [GNS]<br>ἀσφαλῶς οὖν γινωσκέτω πᾶς οἶκος Ἰσραηλ ὅτι καὶ κύριον αὐτὸν καὶ Χριστὸν ἐποίησεν ὁ θεός, τοῦτον τὸν Ἰησοῦν ὃν ὑμεῖς ἐσταυρώσατε. [GNT] | To be assured; to be aware of; to know about; to be sure; to be certain; to know beyond a doubt.<br><br>**Practical Application**<br>The word is emphatic. It means without any doubt whatsoever, with perfect assurance and certainty. |
| #224<br>**Assuredly**<br>**Gathering**<br><br>**Assuredly gathering–**<br>KJV<br>Concluding–NASB<br>Concluding–NIV | συμβιβάζοντες = *sumbibazontes*<br>Pronunciation: [soom-bib-ad'-zon-tehs]<br>Parsing (part of speech): verb<br>    Mood—participle<br>    Tense—present<br>    Voice—active<br>    Case—nominative<br>    Gender—masculine<br>    Person—1st person<br>    Number—plural<br>    Stem or root—from συμβιβάζω | To conclude or concluding; to prove, put together, set side by side; to bring together.<br><br>**Practical Application**<br>The picture is that of the three men's discussing and reasoning, considering all that had happened to them. They were logically setting the facts together, side by side and coming to their conclusion. |

## PRACTICAL WORD STUDIES
### in the New Testament

| ENGLISH WORD | GREEK WORD AND VERSE | THE WORD MEANS... |
|---|---|---|
| Concluding–NKJV<br>Conclude–NLT<br><br>**POSB<br>REFERENCE**<br>(Acts 16:10)<br>Note 3 | Concordance References:<br>⇒ Strong's #4822 sumbibazō<br>⇒ NIV #5204 sumbibazō<br>⇒ NASB #4822 sumbibazō<br><br>**Acts 16:10**<br>And after he had seen the vision, immediately we endeavoured to go into Macedonia, **assuredly gathering** that the Lord had called us for to preach the gospel unto them. [KJV]<br>And when he had seen the vision, immediately we sought to go into Macedonia, **concluding** that God had called us to preach the gospel to them. [NASB]<br>After Paul had seen the vision, we got ready at once to leave for Macedonia, **concluding** that God had called us to preach the gospel to them. [NIV]<br>Now after he had seen the vision, immediately we sought to go to Macedonia, **concluding** that the Lord had called us to preach the gospel to them. [NKJV]<br>So we decided to leave for Macedonia at once, for we could only **conclude** that God was calling us to preach the Good News there. [NLT]<br>ὡς δὲ τὸ ὅραμα εἶδεν, εὐθέως ἐζητήσαμεν ἐξελθεῖν εἰς τὴν Μακεδονίαν, **συμβιβάζοντες** ὅτι προσκέκληται ἡμᾶς ὁ Κύριος εὐαγγελίσασθαι αὐτούς. [GNS]<br>ὡς δὲ τὸ ὅραμα εἶδεν, εὐθέως ἐζητήσαμεν ἐξελθεῖν εἰς Μακεδονίαν **συμβιβάζοντες** ὅτι προσκέκληται ἡμᾶς ὁ θεὸς εὐαγγελίσασθαι αὐτούς. [GNT] | |
| #225<br>**Astonished**<br><br>Amazed–KJV<br>Amazed–NASB<br>**Astonished–NIV**<br>Amazed–NKJV<br>Amazed–NLT<br><br>**POSB<br>REFERENCE**<br>(Acts 9:21)<br>Note 4<br><br>**See also POSB REF:**<br>(Acts 10:44-45; esp. v.45)<br>Note 1, point 4 | ἐξίσταντο = existanto<br>Pronunciation: [ex-is'-tahn-tow]<br>Parsing (part of speech): verb<br>   Mood—indicative<br>   Tense—imperfect<br>   Voice—middle<br>   Person—3rd person<br>   Number—plural<br>   Stem or root—from ἐξίστημι and ἐξιστάνω<br>Concordance References:<br>⇒ Strong's #1839 existēmi<br>⇒ NIV #2014 existēmi<br>⇒ NASB #1839 existēmi<br><br>**Acts 9:21**<br>But all that heard *him* were **amazed**, and said; Is not this he that destroyed them which called on this name in Jerusalem, and came hither for that intent, that he might bring them bound unto the chief priests? [KJV]<br>And all those hearing him continued to be **amazed**, and were saying, "Is this not he who in Jerusalem destroyed those who called on this name, and *who* had come here for the purpose of bringing them bound before the chief priests?" [NASB]<br>All those who heard him were **astonished** and asked, "Isn't he the man who raised havoc in Jerusalem among those who call on this name? And hasn't he come here to take them as prisoners to the chief priests?" [NIV]<br>Then all who heard were **amazed**, and said, "Is this not he who destroyed those who called on this name in Jerusalem, and has come here for that purpose, so that he might bring them bound to the chief priests?" [NKJV]<br>All who heard him were **amazed**. "Isn't this the same man who persecuted Jesus' followers with such devastation in Jerusalem?" they asked. "And we understand that he came here to arrest them and take them in chains to the leading priests." [NLT]<br>ἐξίσταντο δὲ πάντες οἱ ἀκούοντες, καὶ ἔλεγον, Οὐχ οὗτός ἐστιν ὁ πορθήσας εἰς Ἰερουσαλὴμ τοὺς ἐπικαλουμένους τὸ ὄνομα τοῦτο, καὶ ὧδε εἰς τοῦτο ἐληλύθει ἵνα δεδεμένους αὐτοὺς ἀγάγῃ ἐπὶ τοὺς ἀρχιερεῖς; [GNS] | To be astonished; to be amazed; to be shocked or confounded, overwhelmed, bewildered.<br><br>**Practical Application**<br>Paul stood as a testimony to the community. The public and leaders of the synagogue were amazed (*existanto*), astonished, astounded, shocked at what they were seeing.<br>1. They were expecting an inflamed antagonist storming the homes and meeting places of those who "called on the name of Jesus." They knew he had been sent to arrest and chain not only the men but the women followers of Jesus and to drag them back to Jerusalem for treason and death.<br>2. Instead, they were witnessing a man radically changed, a man...<br>• associating and identifying himself with those whom he had come to destroy.<br>• preaching like a flaming evangel, proclaiming Jesus to be the Messiah and the Son of God. |

## PRACTICAL WORD STUDIES
## in the NEW TESTAMENT

| ENGLISH WORD | GREEK WORD AND VERSE | THE WORD MEANS... |
|---|---|---|
| | ἐξίσταντο δὲ πάντες οἱ ἀκούοντες καὶ ἔλεγον, Οὐχ οὗτός ἐστιν ὁ πορθήσας εἰς Ἰερουσαλὴμ τοὺς ἐπικαλουμένους τὸ ὄνομα τοῦτο, καὶ ὧδε εἰς τοῦτο ἐληλύθει ἵνα δεδεμένους αὐτοὺς ἀγάγῃ ἐπὶ τοὺς ἀρχιερεῖς; [GNT] | |
| **#226**<br>**Astonished**<br><br>**Astonished–KJV**<br>Amazed–NASB<br>Amazed–NIV<br>**Astonished–NKJV**<br>Amazed–NLT<br><br>**POSB REFERENCE**<br>(Lk.2:46-47; esp. v.47)<br>Note 3, point 2c | ἐξίσταντο δὲ = existanto de<br>Pronunciation: [ex-is'-tahn-tow de]<br>Parsing (part of speech): verb<br>    Mood—indicative<br>    Tense—imperfect<br>    Voice—middle<br>    Person—3rd person<br>    Number—plural<br>    Stem or root—from ἐξίστημι and ἐξιστάνω<br>Concordance References:<br>  ⇒ Strong's #1839 existēmi<br>  ⇒ NIV #2014 existēmi<br>  ⇒ NASB #1839 existēmi<br><br>**Luke 2:47**<br>And all that heard him were **astonished** at his understanding and answers. [KJV]<br>And all who heard Him were **amazed** at His understanding and His answers. [NASB]<br>Everyone who heard him was **amazed** at his understanding and his answers. [NIV]<br>And all who heard Him were **astonished** at His understanding and answers. [NKJV]<br>And all who heard Him were **amazed** at his understanding and his answers. [NLT]<br>ἐξίσταντο δὲ πάντες οἱ ἀκούοντες αὐτοῦ ἐπὶ τῇ συνέσει καὶ ταῖς ἀποκρίσεσιν αὐτοῦ. [GNS]<br>ἐξίσταντο δὲ πάντες οἱ ἀκούοντες αὐτοῦ ἐπὶ τῇ συνέσει καὶ ταῖς ἀποκρίσεσιν αὐτοῦ. [GNT] | To be amazed or astonished; to be shocked or confounded; to be overwhelmed; to be in awe; to wonder; to admire; to marvel; to be surprised; to be perplexed, bewildered, dazed, confused, disconcerted.<br><br>**Practical Application**<br>In this Scripture, the word means that all were astonished, overwhelmed, bewildered, and wondered at His understanding. This is a striking lesson for both children and adults.<br>1. Every opportunity to learn the truth should be grasped.<br>2. We should thirst for knowledge and understanding. |
| **#227**<br>**Astonished**<br><br>Marvelled–KJV<br>Marveled–NASB<br>Surprised–NIV<br>Marveled–NKJV<br>**Astonished–NLT**<br><br>**POSB REFERENCE**<br>(Jn.4:27)<br>Note 3 | ἐθαύμαζον = ethaumazon<br>Pronunciation: [eh-thou-mah'-sahn]<br>Parsing (part of speech): verb<br>    Mood—indicative<br>    Tense—imperfect<br>    Voice—active<br>    Person—3rd person<br>    Number—plural<br>    Stem or root—from θαυμάζω<br>Concordance References:<br>  ⇒ Strong's #2296 thaumazo<br>  ⇒ NIV #2513 thaumazō<br>  ⇒ NASB #2296 thaumazo<br><br>**John 4:27**<br>And upon this came his disciples, and **marvelled** that he talked with the woman: yet no man said, What seekest thou? or, Why talkest thou with her? [KJV]<br>And at this point His disciples came, and they **marveled** that He had been speaking with a woman; yet no one said, "What do You seek?" or, "Why do You speak with her?" [NASB]<br>Just then his disciples returned and were **surprised** to find him talking with a woman. But no one asked, "What do you want?" or "Why are you talking with her?" [NIV]<br>And at this point His disciples came, and they **marveled** that He talked with a woman; yet no one said, "What do You seek?" or, "Why are You talking with her?" [NKJV]<br>Just then his disciples arrived. They were **astonished** to find him talking to a woman, but none of them asked him why he was doing it or what they had been discussing. [NLT]<br>Καὶ ἐπὶ τούτῳ ἦλθον οἱ μαθηταὶ αὐτοῦ, καὶ ἐθαύμαζον ὅτι μετὰ γυναικὸς ἐλάλει· οὐδεὶς μέντοι εἶπε, Τί ζητεῖς; ἤ, Τί λαλεῖς μετ' αὐτῆς; [GNS]<br>Καὶ ἐπὶ τούτῳ ἦλθαν οἱ μαθηταὶ αὐτοῦ καὶ ἐθαύμαζον ὅτι μετὰ γυναικὸς ἐλάλει· οὐδεὶς μέντοι εἶπεν, Τί ζητεῖς ἢ Τί λαλεῖς μετ' αὐτῆς; [GNT] | To be astonished, amazed, bewildered; to be surprised; to marvel.<br><br>**Practical Application**<br>Just as Jesus made His phenomenal claims (See John 4:13-26), the disciples arrived. They were surprised because He was talking with the woman. There were two reasons for their reaction.<br>1. She was a woman. The Rabbis of that day would not be *alone* or *talk* with women in public. They feared what people might think and say. Very honestly, there is some merit to this idea. A person, especially a leader, must guard himself and his thoughts around the opposite sex. Of course, one can carry the practice too far. Wisdom and self-control are both needed.<br>2. She was a Samaritan, a person considered despicable, below their social standing, unfit to be seen with in public. Note how Christ tore down the barriers of both problems and how the disciples controlled their tongue from questioning and gossiping. |

## Practical Word Studies
## in the New Testament

| ENGLISH WORD | GREEK WORD AND VERSE | THE WORD MEANS... |
|---|---|---|
| **#228**<br>**Astray**<br><br>Spoil–KJV<br>Captive–NASB<br>Captive–NIV<br>Cheat–NKJV<br>**Astray–NLT**<br><br>**POSB**<br>**REFERENCE**<br>(Col.2:8)<br>Note 1 | ἔσται συλαγωγῶν = estai sulagōgōn<br>Pronunciation: [es-tah-ee soo-lag-og-o'-gon']<br>Parsing *sulagōgōn* (part of speech): verb<br>    Mood—participle<br>    Tense—present<br>    Voice—active<br>    Case—nominative<br>    Gender—masculine<br>    Number—singular<br>    Stem or root—from συλαγωγέω<br>Concordance References:<br>  ⇒ Strong's #1510 eimi + 4812 sulagōgeō<br>  ⇒ NIV #1639+5194 eimi sulagōgeō [takes captive]<br>  ⇒ NASB #1510 eimi + 4812 sulagōgeō<br><br>**Col. 2:8**<br>    Beware lest any man **spoil** you through philosophy and vain deceit, after the tradition of men, after the rudiments of the world, and not after Christ. [KJV]<br>    See to it that no one takes you **captive** through philosophy and empty deception, according to the tradition of men, according to the elementary principles of the world, rather than according to Christ. [NASB]<br>    See to it that no one takes you **captive** through hollow and deceptive philosophy, which depends on human tradition and the basic principles of this world rather than on Christ. [NIV]<br>    Beware lest anyone **cheat** you through philosophy and empty deceit, according to the tradition of men, according to the basic principles of the world, and not according to Christ. [NKJV]<br>    Don't let anyone lead you **astray** with empty philosophy and high-sounding nonsense that come from human thinking and from the evil powers of this world, and not from Christ. [NLT]<br>    βλέπετε μή τις ὑμᾶς ἔσται ὁ συλαγωγῶν διὰ τῆς φιλοσοφίας καὶ κενῆς ἀπάτης, κατὰ τὴν παράδοσιν τῶν ἀνθρώπων, κατὰ τὰ στοιχεῖα τοῦ κόσμου, καὶ οὐ κατὰ Χριστόν· [GNS]<br>    βλέπετε μή τις ὑμᾶς ἔσται ὁ συλαγωγῶν διὰ τῆς φιλοσοφίας καὶ κενῆς ἀπάτης κατὰ τὴν παράδοσιν τῶν ἀνθρώπων, κατὰ τὰ στοιχεῖα τοῦ κόσμου καὶ οὐ κατὰ Χριστόν· [GNT] | To take captive; to lead astray; to lead into captivity or slavery; to cheat.<br><br>**Practical Application**<br>    Some men are in a genuine search for truth and reality. They seek to learn the truth and reality of the universe and the problems that face them, but they limit themselves to the universe.<br>    Other persons have novel ideas or philosophies about truth and reality, but they become more interested in their positions than the truth. They need others to accept their positions or else their ideas die. Therefore, they have to present and persuade people of their ideas and philosophies whether they are sound or not.<br>    Believers must, therefore, beware and guard against worldly philosophies and ideas lest they become ensnared and enslaved. |
| **#229**<br>**Astray**<br><br>Untoward–KJV<br>Perverse–NASB<br>Corrupt–NIV<br>Perverse–NKJV<br>**Astray–NLT**<br><br>**POSB**<br>**REFERENCE**<br>(Acts 2:40)<br>Note 5, point 2 | σκολιᾶς = skolias<br>Pronunciation: [skol-ee-ahs']<br>Parsing (part of speech): adjective<br>    Case—genitive<br>    Gender—feminine<br>    Number—singular<br>    Stem or root—from σκολιός, ά, όν<br>Concordance References:<br>  ⇒ Strong's #4646 skolios<br>  ⇒ NIV #5021 skolios<br>  ⇒ NASB #4646 skolios<br><br>**Acts 2:40**<br>    And with many other words did he testify and exhort, saying, Save yourselves from this **untoward** generation. [KJV]<br>    And with many other words he solemnly testified and kept on exhorting them, saying, "Be saved from this **perverse** generation!" [NASB]<br>    With many other words he warned them; and he pleaded with them, "Save yourselves from this **corrupt** generation." [NIV]<br>    And with many other words he testified and exhorted them, saying, "Be saved from this **perverse** generation." [NKJV]<br>    Then Peter continued preaching for a long time, strongly urging all his listeners, "Save yourselves from this generation that has gone **astray**!" [NLT] | To be corrupt; to be harsh; to be perverse; to go astray; to be crooked or bent out of shape.<br><br>**Practical Application**<br>    People are far from being straight and far from being in the shape intended by God. They are crooked and bent, unrighteous and ungodly, sinful and corrupt. |

# PRACTICAL WORD STUDIES
## in the NEW TESTAMENT

| ENGLISH WORD | GREEK WORD AND VERSE | THE WORD MEANS... |
|---|---|---|
| | ἑτέροις τε λόγοις πλείοσι διεμαρτύρετο καὶ παρεκάλει, λέγων, Σώθητε ἀπὸ τῆς γενεᾶς τῆς **σκολιᾶς** ταύτης. [GNS]<br>ἑτέροις τε λόγοις πλείοσιν διεμαρτύρατο καὶ παρεκάλει αὐτοὺς λέγων, Σώθητε ἀπὸ τῆς γενεᾶς τῆς **σκολιᾶς** ταύτης. [GNT] | |
| **#230**<br>**At Many Times–**<br>**At Sundry**<br>**Times**<br><br>At sundry times–KJV<br>In many portions–NASB<br>At many times–NIV<br>At various times–NKJV<br>Many times–NLT<br><br>**POSB**<br>**REFERENCE**<br>(Heb.1:1-2; esp. v.1)<br>Note 1, point 1 | Πολυμερῶς = Polumerös<br>Pronunciation: [pol-oo-mer'-oce]<br>Parsing (part of speech): adverb adjective<br>Stem or root—from πολυμερῶς<br>Concordance References:<br>⇒ Strong's #4181 polumerös<br>⇒ NIV #4495 polumerös<br>⇒ NASB #4181 polumerös<br><br>**Hebrews 1:1**<br>God, who **at sundry times** and in divers manners spake in time past unto the fathers by the prophets, [KJV]<br>God, after He spoke long ago to the fathers in the prophets **in many portions** and in many ways, [NASB]<br>In the past God spoke to our forefathers through the prophets **at many times** and in various ways, [NIV]<br>God, who **at various times** and in various ways spoke in time past to the fathers by the prophets, [NKJV]<br>Long ago God spoke **many times** and in many ways to our ancestors through the prophets. [NLT]<br>Πολυμερῶς καὶ πολυτρόπως πάλαι ὁ Θεὸς λαλήσας τοῖς πατράσιν ἐν τοῖς προφήταις, [GNS]<br>Πολυμερῶς καὶ πολυτρόπως πάλαι ὁ θεὸς λαλήσας τοῖς πατράσιν ἐν τοῖς προφήταις [GNT] | At many times; that is, in many portions; in many parts; in many separate revelations; at many different times; little by little.<br><br>**Practical Application**<br>God's Word is found in the prophets. In ancient times God spoke to man by His prophets, that is, by persons whom He had chosen to proclaim His Word to the world. Who are these persons? They are the men and women of the Old Testament Scriptures. But note a significant fact: God spoke through the prophets...<br>• "at many times, at sundry times"<br>• in various ways, in diverse manners<br>What does this mean? No man could possibly receive and understand or explain the whole revelation of God. God and the truth of God is too big for any one man. Therefore, God had to make many revelations to many different people, and He had to use many different ways to speak to men. No man could ever contain or share the whole revelation of God. |
| **#231**<br>**At Once**<br><br>Not delay–KJV<br>Do not delay–NASB<br>**At once**–NIV<br>Not to delay–NKJV<br>Come as soon as possible–NLT<br><br>**POSB**<br>**REFERENCE**<br>(Acts 9:36-39; esp. v.38)<br>Note 2, point 3c | Μὴ ὀκνήσῃς = Më oknësës<br>Pronunciation: [may hok-nay'-says]<br>Parsing *oknēsēs* (part of speech): verb<br>   Mood—subjunctive or imperative<br>   Tense—aorist<br>   Voice—active<br>   Person—2nd person<br>   Number—singular<br>   Stem or root—from ὀκνέω<br>Concordance References:<br>⇒ Strong's #3361 + 3635 më okneö<br>⇒ NIV #3590 + 3890 më okneö [at once]<br>⇒ NASB #3361 + 3635 më okneö<br><br>**Acts 9:38**<br>And forasmuch as Lydda was nigh to Joppa, and the disciples had heard that Peter was there, they sent unto him two men, desiring *him* that he would **not delay** to come to them. [KJV]<br>And since Lydda was near Joppa, the disciples, having heard that Peter was there, sent two men to him, entreating him, "**Do not delay** to come to us." [NASB]<br>Lydda was near Joppa; so when the disciples heard that Peter was in Lydda, they sent two men to him and urged him, "Please come **at once**!" [NIV]<br>And since Lydda was near Joppa, and the disciples had heard that Peter was there, they sent two men to him, imploring *him* **not to delay** in coming to them. [NKJV]<br>But they had heard that Peter was nearby at Lydda, so they sent two men to beg him, "Please **come as soon as possible**!" [NLT]<br>ἐγγὺς δὲ οὔσης Λύδδης τῇ Ἰόππῃ, οἱ μαθηταὶ ἀκούσαντες ὅτι Πέτρος ἐστὶν ἐν αὐτῇ, ἀπέστειλαν δύο ἄνδρας πρὸς αὐτὸν παρακαλοῦντες **μὴ ὀκνῆσαι** διελθεῖν ἕως αὐτῶν. [GNS]<br>ἐγγὺς δὲ οὔσης Λύδδας τῇ Ἰόππῃ οἱ μαθηταὶ ἀκούσαντες ὅτι Πέτρος ἐστὶν ἐν αὐτῇ ἀπέστειλαν δύο ἄνδρας πρὸς αὐτὸν παρακαλοῦντες, **Μὴ ὀκνήσῃς** διελθεῖν ἕως ἡμῶν. [GNT] | At once; without delay; to come as soon as possible.<br><br>**Practical Application**<br>It means not to hesitate, not to be reluctant, but to act and act now, quickly, without questioning. |

## PRACTICAL WORD STUDIES
### in the NEW TESTAMENT

| ENGLISH WORD | GREEK WORD AND VERSE | THE WORD MEANS... |
|---|---|---|
| **#232**<br>**At Various Times**<br><br>At sundry times–KJV<br>In many portions–NASB<br>At many times–NIV<br>**At various times–NKJV**<br>Many times–NLT<br><br>**POSB REFERENCE**<br>(Heb.1:1-2; esp. v.1)<br>Note 1, point 1 | Πολυμερῶς = Polumerōs<br>Pronunciation: [pol-oo-mer'-oce]<br>Parsing (part of speech): adverb adjective<br>    Stem or root—from πολυμερῶς<br>Concordance References:<br>  ⇒ Strong's #4181 polumerōs<br>  ⇒ NIV #4495 polumerōs<br>  ⇒ NASB #4181 polumerōs<br><br>**Hebrews 1:1**<br>God, who **at sundry times** and in divers manners spake in time past unto the fathers by the prophets, [KJV]<br>God, after He spoke long ago to the fathers in the prophets **in many portions** and in many ways, [NASB]<br>In the past God spoke to our forefathers through the prophets **at many times** and in various ways, [NIV]<br>God, who **at various times** and in various ways spoke in time past to the fathers by the prophets, [NKJV]<br>Long ago God spoke **many times** and in many ways to our ancestors through the prophets. [NLT]<br>Πολυμερῶς καὶ πολυτρόπως πάλαι ὁ Θεὸς λαλήσας τοῖς πατράσιν ἐν τοῖς προφήταις, [GNS]<br>Πολυμερῶς καὶ πολυτρόπως πάλαι ὁ θεὸς λαλήσας τοῖς πατράσιν ἐν τοῖς προφήταις [GNT] | At many times; that is, in many portions; in many parts; in many separate revelations; at many different times; little by little.<br><br>**Practical Application**<br>God's Word is found in the prophets. In ancient times God spoke to man by His prophets, that is, by persons whom He had chosen to proclaim His Word to the world. Who are these persons? They are the men and women of the Old Testament Scriptures. But note a significant fact: God spoke through the prophets...<br>  • "at various times"<br>  • in various ways<br>What does this mean? No man could possibly receive and understand or explain the whole revelation of God. God and the truth of God is too big for any one man. Therefore, God had to make many revelations to many different people, and He had to use many different ways to speak to men. No man could ever contain or share the whole revelation of God. |
| **#233**<br>**At Work In–**<br>**At Work Within**<br><br>Did work in–KJV<br>**At work in–NASB**<br>**At work in–NIV**<br>**At work in–NKJV**<br>At work within–NLT<br><br>**POSB REFERENCE**<br>(Rom.7:5)<br>Note 1, point 1 | ἐνηργεῖτο ἐν = enērgeito en<br>Pronunciation: [en-ayrg-ee'-tow hen]<br>Parsing enērgeito (part of speech): verb<br>    Mood—indicative<br>    Tense—imperfect<br>    Voice—middle<br>    Person—3rd person<br>    Number—singular<br>    Stem or root—from ἐνεργέω<br>Concordance References:<br>  ⇒ Strong's #1722 + 1754 en energeō<br>  ⇒ NIV #1877 + 1919 en energeō [at work in]<br>  ⇒ NASB #1722 + 1754 en energeō<br><br>**Romans 7:5**<br>For when we were in the flesh, the motions of sins, which were by the law, **did work in** our members to bring forth fruit unto death. [KJV]<br>For while we were in the flesh, the sinful passions, which were *aroused* by the Law, were **at work in** the members of our body to bear fruit for death. [NASB]<br>For when we were controlled by the sinful nature, the sinful passions aroused by the law were **at work in** our bodies, so that we bore fruit for death. [NIV]<br>For when we were in the flesh, the sinful passions which were aroused by the law were **at work in** our members to bear fruit to death. [NKJV]<br>When we were controlled by our old nature, sinful desires were **at work within** us, and the law aroused these evil desires that produced sinful deeds, resulting in death. [NLT]<br>ὅτε γὰρ ἦμεν ἐν τῇ σαρκί, τὰ παθήματα τῶν ἁμαρτιῶν τὰ διὰ τοῦ νόμου ἐνηργεῖτο ἐν τοῖς μέλεσιν ἡμῶν εἰς τὸ καρποφορῆσαι τῷ θανάτῳ, [GNS]<br>ὅτε γὰρ ἦμεν ἐν τῇ σαρκί, τὰ παθήματα τῶν ἁμαρτιῶν τὰ διὰ τοῦ νόμου ἐνηργεῖτο ἐν τοῖς μέλεσιν ἡμῶν, εἰς τὸ καρποφορῆσαι τῷ θανάτῳ [GNT] | To be at work in or within; to do work in or within.<br><br>**Practical Application**<br>Sinful feelings are actually "at work" (*energeito*) in our members—at work by the statement or restriction of the law. When the law prohibits and forbids something, it actually creates within us...<br>• an interest<br>• an attraction<br>• an excitement<br>• an appeal<br>• a tug or pull<br>• a fascination<br>• a seduction<br>• an arousal<br><br>There is within man something that makes him want to do what he is forbidden to do. When he is restricted or fenced in, he wants to break through the restriction or fence. He wants to go beyond where he is allowed, to take control of his own life as he wishes and wills. (See POSB note—Romans 7:8 for more discussion.) |
| **#234**<br>**Athletes**<br>**Practice**<br><br>Striveth–KJV<br>Competes in the games–NASB<br>Competes in the games–NIV | ἀγωνιζόμενος = agōnizomenos<br>Pronunciation: [ag-o-nid'-zom-eh-nos]<br>Parsing (part of speech): verb<br>    Mood—participle<br>    Tense—present<br>    Voice—middle or passive deponent<br>    Case—nominative<br>    Gender—masculine<br>    Number—singular<br>    Stem or root—from ἀγωνίζομαι | To compete in games; to compete as a highly disciplined athlete; to struggle in competition; to struggle; to make every effort.<br><br>**Practical Application**<br>Every runner and boxer is highly disciplined in body, mind, thought, spirit, exercise, workouts, and contests. He is disciplined...<br>• in body: what he eats and how much he |

# PRACTICAL WORD STUDIES
## in the NEW TESTAMENT

| ENGLISH WORD | GREEK WORD AND VERSE | THE WORD MEANS... |
|---|---|---|
| Competes–NKJV<br>**Athletes practice**–NLT<br><br>**POSB REFERENCE**<br>(1 Cor.9:25)<br>Note 2 | Concordance References:<br>⇒ Strong's #75 agōnizomai<br>⇒ NIV #76 agōnizomai<br>⇒ NASB #75 agōnizomai<br><br>**1 Cor. 9:25**<br>And every man that **striveth** for the mastery is temperate in all things. Now they *do it* to obtain a corruptible crown; but we an incorruptible. [KJV]<br>And everyone who **competes in the games** exercises self-control in all things. They then *do it* to receive a perishable wreath, but we an imperishable. [NASB]<br>Everyone who **competes in the games** goes into strict training. They do it to get a crown that will not last; but we do it to get a crown that will last forever. [NIV]<br>And everyone who **competes** *for the prize* is temperate in all things. Now they *do it* to obtain a perishable crown, but we *for* an imperishable *crown*. [NKJV]<br>All **athletes practice** strict self-control. They do it to win a prize that will fade away, but we do it for an eternal prize. [NLT]<br>πᾶς δὲ ὁ **ἀγωνιζόμενος** πάντα ἐγκρατεύεται, ἐκεῖνοι μὲν οὖν ἵνα φθαρτὸν στέφανον λάβωσιν, ἡμεῖς δὲ ἄφθαρτον. [GNS]<br>πᾶς δὲ ὁ **ἀγωνιζόμενος** πάντα ἐγκρατεύεται, ἐκεῖνοι μὲν οὖν ἵνα φθαρτὸν στέφανον λάβωσιν, ἡμεῖς δὲ ἄφθαρτον. [GNT] | eats.<br>• in mind and thought: his concentration on the goal and how to best gear his body, spirit, and mind to that end.<br>• In spirit: keeping his spirit strong and motivated for the strain necessary to work out day by day and to reach his goal.<br>The minister or believer is to do no less. He must be just as disciplined as the athlete. He disciplines himself to the point of pain. And note: the discipline "goes into strict training." It covers his body, mind, and spirit, the place where God's presence actually dwells. Therefore, he does not allow anything to *touch or enter* his body not anything, that is corrupt, impure, polluted, or that will cause a more rapid deterioration of the temple. |
| **#235**<br>**Atoning Sacrifice**<br><br>Propitiation–KJV<br>Propitiation–NASB<br>Atoning sacrifice–NIV<br>Propitiation–NKJV<br>Sacrifice–NLT<br><br>**POSB REFERENCE**<br>(1 Jn.2:1-2; esp. v.2)<br>Note 3, point 2<br><br>See also POSB REF:<br>(1 Jn.2:2)<br>*Deeper Study* #1 | ἱλασμός = *hilasmos*<br>Pronunciation: [hil-as-mos']<br>Parsing (part of speech): noun<br>  Case—nominative<br>  Gender—masculine<br>  Number—singular<br>  Stem or root—from ἱλασμός, οῦ<br>Concordance References:<br>⇒ Strong's #2434 hilasmos<br>⇒ NIV #2662 hilasmos<br>⇒ NASB #2434 hilasmos<br><br>**1 John 2:2**<br>And he is the **propitiation** for our sins: and not for ours only, but also for *the sins of* the whole world. [KJV]<br>And He Himself is the **propitiation** for our sins; and not for ours only, but also for *those of* the whole world. [NASB]<br>He is the **atoning sacrifice** for our sins, and not only for ours but also for the sins of the whole world. [NIV]<br>And He Himself is the **propitiation** for our sins, and not for ours only but also for the whole world. [NKJV]<br>He is the **sacrifice** for our sins. He takes away not only our sins but the sins of all the world. [NLT]<br>καὶ αὐτὸς **ἱλασμός** ἐστι περὶ τῶν ἁμαρτιῶν ἡμῶν· οὐ περὶ τῶν ἡμετέρων δὲ μόνον, ἀλλὰ καὶ περὶ ὅλου τοῦ κόσμου. [GNS]<br>καὶ αὐτὸς **ἱλασμός** ἐστιν περὶ τῶν ἁμαρτιῶν ἡμῶν, οὐ περὶ τῶν ἡμετέρων δὲ μόνον ἀλλὰ καὶ περὶ ὅλου τοῦ κόσμου. [GNT] | Atoning sacrifice, propitiation. It means to be a sacrifice, a covering, a satisfaction, a payment, an appeasement for sin. It means to turn away anger or to make reconciliation between God and man.<br><br>**Practical Application**<br>Jesus Christ is *the atoning sacrifice, the propitiation for our sins.* Remember: God is holy and just. He is perfect love, but He is also perfect holiness and justice. Therefore, He must execute justice against the sinner. He must judge and condemn sin. His justice must be perfectly satisfied. Now there is only one way God's justice can be perfectly satisfied: His justice has to be cast against the *perfect sacrifice.* If there were a Perfect and Ideal Man, that Man could accept the guilt and punishment for sin. The Perfect Man could step forward to bear the punishment for sin and satisfy the justice of God.<br>This is the glorious gospel, the wonderful love and provision of God. Jesus Christ is the Ideal and Perfect Man. Therefore, He sacrificed His life for man and His sacrifice covered all men. As the Ideal Man, Jesus Christ accepted the guilt and punishment of sin for all men. He died for all men. When He died, He died as the perfect sacrifice for sins. Therefore, God accepts His death...<br>• as the *sacrifice* for our sins.<br>• as the *covering* for our sins.<br>• as the *satisfaction* for our sins.<br>• as the *payment* for the penalty of our sins.<br>• as the *appeasement* of His wrath against sin.<br>When Jesus Christ carries a man's case before God, He pleads His own righteousness and death, and God accepts His righteousness and death for man. It is by this, by His sacrifice and death for our sins, that we become acceptable to God.<br>Note one other point: Jesus Christ is the propitiation for the sins of the *whole world.* He is |

# PRACTICAL WORD STUDIES
## in the NEW TESTAMENT

| ENGLISH WORD | GREEK WORD AND VERSE | THE WORD MEANS... |
|---|---|---|
| | | the eternal Son of God, the Ideal and Perfect Man. Therefore, all that He ever did covers eternity. His sacrifice for sin covers the first man ever born and spans all of time over to the last man, and then it continues right on throughout all of eternity. Jesus Christ paid the penalty of sin for all sinners of all generations. He died for the sins of all people, no matter who they are or what they have done.<br><br>But note a critical fact: a person has to come to Jesus Christ, trusting Him to be his advocate before God. Jesus Christ is the only Person who has the right to stand as an advocate in the court of God's perfect justice. He is the only Person who can present man's case before God and have man declared righteous. Therefore, a person is not covered by the advocacy of Christ unless he comes to Christ and has Christ represent him before God. |
| **#236**<br>**Attendants**<br><br>Servants—KJV<br>Servants—NASB<br>**Attendants—NIV**<br>Servants—NKJV<br>Aides—NLT<br><br>**POSB REFERENCE**<br>(Mt.22:11-14; esp. v.13)<br>Note 4, point 2 | διακόνοις = *diakonois*<br>Pronunciation: [di'ak-o'-nois]<br>Parsing (part of speech): noun<br>    Case—dative<br>    Gender—masculine<br>    Number—plural<br>    Stem or root—from διάκονος, ου<br>Concordance References:<br>  ⇒ Strong's #1401 doulos<br>  ⇒ NIV #1356 diakonos<br>  ⇒ NASB #1249 diakonos<br><br>**Matthew 22:13**<br>Then said the king to the **servants**, Bind him hand and foot, and take him away, and cast *him* into outer darkness; there shall be weeping and gnashing of teeth. [KJV]<br>"Then the king said to the **servants**, 'Bind him hand and foot, and cast him into the outer darkness; in that place there shall be weeping and gnashing of teeth.' [NASB]<br>"Then the king told the **attendants**, 'Tie him hand and foot, and throw him outside, into the darkness, where there will be weeping and gnashing of teeth.' [NIV]<br>Then the king said to the **servants**, 'Bind him hand and foot, take him away, and cast *him* into outer darkness; there will be weeping and gnashing of teeth.' [NKJV]<br>Then the king said to his **aides**, 'Bind him hand and foot and throw him out into the outer darkness, where there is weeping and gnashing of teeth.' [NLT]<br>τότε εἶπεν ὁ βασιλεὺς τοῖς **διακόνοις**, Δήσαντες αὐτοῦ πόδας καὶ χεῖρας, ἄρατε αὐτὸν καὶ ἐκβάλετε εἰς τὸ σκότος τὸ ἐξώτερον· ἐκεῖ ἔσται ὁ κλαυθμὸς καὶ ὁ βρυγμὸς τῶν ὀδόντων. [GNS]<br>τότε ὁ βασιλεὺς εἶπεν τοῖς **διακόνοις**, Δήσαντες αὐτοῦ πόδας καὶ χεῖρας ἐκβάλετε αὐτὸν εἰς τὸ σκότος τὸ ἐξώτερον· ἐκεῖ ἔσται ὁ κλαυθμὸς καὶ ὁ βρυγμὸς τῶν ὀδόντων. [GNT] | To serve or to be a servant or helper; a deacon or minister.<br><br>**Practical Application**<br>Diakonos means acts of service or ministry. Diakonos includes but does not limit itself to the church office of the deacon. In this Scripture, the word refers to God's angels. The attendants (*diakonois*) were not the same servants who delivered the invitations. They were not the disciples (Matthew 22:3,4) and preachers (Matthew 22:8,10) of the Lord. They were the angelic guardians of heaven who minister to the Godhead (cp. Matthew 13:41-43, 49-50). Three things were done.<br>1. The man was bound hand and foot. The hand and foot are usually the bodily parts used by man to sin. The hands are bound so there is no resistance. The feet are bound so there is no escape. Whatever the King says is done in the Great Day of the Feast. No man can resist or flee.<br>2. The man was taken away, out of the King's presence and out of the presence of His Son and of the other guests. He was not allowed to share in the joy and bounty of the occasion.<br>3. The man was cast into outer darkness, far, far away from everyone else. He was not only cut off from the sharing of the occasion but from ever seeing the occasion. Whatever light and splendor there was in the Great Wedding Feast, he was cast into the *outer* regions of darkness, never to glimpse the light. |
| **#237**<br>**Attentive**<br><br>**Attentive—KJV**<br>Hanging upon—NASB<br>Hung on—NIV<br>**Attentive—NKJV**<br>Hung on—NLT<br><br>**POSB REFERENCE**<br>(Lk.19:47-48; esp. v.48)<br>Note 3, point 2 | ἐξεκρέματο = *exekremato*<br>Pronunciation: [ex-e-krem'-ah-tow]<br>Parsing (part of speech): verb<br>    Mood—indicative<br>    Tense—aorist<br>    Voice—middle<br>    Person—3rd person<br>    Number—singular<br>    Stem or root—from ἐκκρέμαμαι<br>Concordance References:<br>  ⇒ Strong's #1582 ekkremannumi<br>  ⇒ NIV #1717 ekkremannumi<br>  ⇒ NASB #1582 ekkremannumi | To be attentive; to pay close attention; to hang on the words of someone speaking.<br><br>**Practical Application**<br>The word means that they hung upon Jesus, gave Him rapt attention, were struck by Him. |

# PRACTICAL WORD STUDIES
## in the NEW TESTAMENT

| ENGLISH WORD | GREEK WORD AND VERSE | THE WORD MEANS... |
|---|---|---|
| | **Luke 19:48**<br>And could not find what they might do: for all the people were very **attentive** to hear him. [KJV]<br>And they could not find anything that they might do, for all the people were **hanging upon** His words. [NASB]<br>Yet they could not find any way to do it, because all the people **hung on** his words. [NIV]<br>And were unable to do anything; for all the people were very **attentive** to hear Him. [NKJV]<br>But they could think of nothing, because all the people **hung on** every word he said. [NLT]<br>καὶ οὐχ εὕρισκον τὸ τί ποιήσωσιν· ὁ λαὸς γὰρ ἅπας **ἐξεκρέματο** αὐτοῦ ἀκούων. [GNS]<br>καὶ οὐχ εὕρισκον τὸ τί ποιήσωσιν, ὁ λαὸς γὰρ ἅπας **ἐξεκρέματο** αὐτοῦ ἀκούων. [GNT] | |
| **#238**<br>**Attested**<br><br>Approved–KJV<br>**Attested–NASB**<br>Accredited–NIV<br>**Attested–NKJV**<br>Endorsed–NLT<br><br>**POSB REFERENCE**<br>(Acts 2:22-24; esp. v.22)<br>Note 3, point 1 | **ἀποδεδειγμένον** = *apodedeigmenon*<br>Pronunciation: [ap-od-eh-deeng-meh'-non]<br>Parsing (part of speech): verb<br>  Mood—participle<br>  Tense—perfect<br>  Voice—passive<br>  Case—accusative<br>  Gender—masculine<br>  Number—singular<br>  Stem or root—from **ἀποδείκνυμι**<br>Concordance References:<br>  ⇒ Strong's #584 apodeiknumi<br>  ⇒ NIV #617 apodeiknumi<br>  ⇒ NASB #584 apodeiknumi<br><br>**Acts 2:22**<br>Ye men of Israel, hear these words; Jesus of Nazareth, a man **approved** of God among you by miracles and wonders and signs, which God did by him in the midst of you, as ye yourselves also know: [KJV]<br>"Men of Israel, listen to these words: Jesus the Nazarene, a man **attested** to you by God with miracles and wonders and signs which God performed through Him in your midst, just as you yourselves know— [NASB]<br>"Men of Israel, listen to this: Jesus of Nazareth was a man **accredited** by God to you by miracles, wonders and signs, which God did among you through him, as you yourselves know. [NIV]<br>"Men of Israel, hear these words: Jesus of Nazareth, a Man **attested** by God to you by miracles, wonders, and signs which God did through Him in your midst, as you yourselves also know— [NKJV]<br>"People of Israel, listen! God publicly **endorsed** Jesus of Nazareth by doing wonderful miracles, wonders, and signs through him, as you well know. [NLT]<br>ἄνδρες Ἰσραηλῖται, ἀκούσατε τοὺς λόγους τούτους· Ἰησοῦν τὸν Ναζωραῖον, ἄνδρα ἀπὸ τοῦ Θεοῦ **ἀποδεδειγμένον** εἰς ὑμᾶς δυνάμεσι καὶ τέρασι καὶ σημείοις, οἷς ἐποίησε δι' αὐτοῦ ὁ Θεὸς ἐν μέσῳ ὑμῶν, καθὼς καὶ αὐτοὶ οἴδατε, [GNS]<br>Ἄνδρες Ἰσραηλῖται, ἀκούσατε τοὺς λόγους τούτους· Ἰησοῦν τὸν Ναζωραῖον, ἄνδρα **ἀποδεδειγμένον** ἀπὸ τοῦ θεοῦ εἰς ὑμᾶς δυνάμεσι καὶ τέρασι καὶ σημείοις οἷς ἐποίησεν δι' αὐτοῦ ὁ θεὸς ἐν μέσῳ ὑμῶν καθὼς αὐτοὶ οἴδατε, [GNT] | To accredit; to approve; to endorse; to point out; to display; to show; to attest; to sanction; to certify.<br><br>**Practical Application**<br>God put His stamp of approval upon Jesus. He demonstrated and showed all men that Jesus is perfectly acceptable to Him. Jesus of Nazareth had God's approval, His perfect acceptance. |
| **#239**<br>**Attracted**<br><br>Carried about–KJV<br>Carried away–NASB<br>Carried away–NIV<br>Carried about–NKJV<br>**Attracted–NLT** | **παραφέρεσθε** = *parapheresthe*<br>Pronunciation: [par-a-fer'-ehs-the]<br>Parsing (part of speech): verb<br>  Mood—imperative<br>  Tense—present<br>  Voice—passive<br>  Person—2nd person<br>  Number—plural<br>  Stem or root—from **παραφέρω** | To be carried away; to be blown along; to be attracted to the wrong thing; to lead away; to be carried away or astray.<br><br>**Practical Application**<br>To be attracted or carried away from the grace of God is the most dangerous thing that can happen to a person, for it is the grace of God that |

# PRACTICAL WORD STUDIES
## in the NEW TESTAMENT

| ENGLISH WORD | GREEK WORD AND VERSE | THE WORD MEANS... |
|---|---|---|
| **POSB REFERENCE** (Heb.13:9-11; esp. v.9) Note 1 | Concordance References:<br>⇒ Strong's #3911 paraphero<br>⇒ NIV #4195 paraphero<br>⇒ NASB #3911 paraphero<br><br>**Hebrews 13:9**<br>Be not **carried about** with divers and strange doctrines. For *it is* a good thing that the heart be established with grace; not with meats, which have not profited them that have been occupied therein. [KJV]<br>Do not be **carried away** by varied and strange teachings; for it is good for the heart to be strengthened by grace, not by foods, through which those who were thus occupied were not benefited. [NASB]<br>Do not be **carried away** by all kinds of strange teachings. It is good for our hearts to be strengthened by grace, not by ceremonial foods, which are of no value to those who eat them. [NIV]<br>Do not be **carried about** with various and strange doctrines. For *it is* good that the heart be established by grace, not with foods which have not profited those who have been occupied with them. [NKJV]<br>So do not be **attracted** by strange, new ideas. Your spiritual strength comes from God's special favor, not from ceremonial rules about food, which don't help those who follow them. [NLT]<br>διδαχαῖς ποικίλαις καὶ ξέναις μὴ **περιφέρεσθε**· καλὸν γὰρ χάριτι βεβαιοῦσθαι τὴν καρδίαν, οὐ βρώμασιν, ἐν οἷς οὐκ ὠφελήθησαν οἱ περιπατήσαντες. [GNS]<br>διδαχαῖς ποικίλαις καὶ ξέναις μὴ **παραφέρεσθε**· καλὸν γὰρ χάριτι βεβαιοῦσθαι τὴν καρδίαν, οὐ βρώμασιν, ἐν οἷς οὐκ ὠφελήθησαν οἱ περιπατοῦντες. [GNT] | saves a person. A person can become acceptable to God only if he approaches God through God's grace demonstrated in the Lord Jesus Christ. |
| **#240 Austere**<br><br>Austere–KJV<br>Exacting–NASB<br>Hard–NIV<br>Austere–NKJV<br>Tough–NLT<br><br>**POSB REFERENCE** (Lk.19:15-23; esp. v.22) Note 5, point 6b | αὐστηρός = *austēros*<br>Pronunciation: [ow-stay-ros']<br>Parsing (part of speech): adjective<br>  Case—nominative<br>  Gender—masculine<br>  Number—singular<br>  Stem or root—from αὐστηρός, ά, όν<br>Concordance References:<br>⇒ Strong's #840 austēros<br>⇒ NIV #893 austēros<br>⇒ NASB #840 austēros<br><br>**Luke 19:22**<br>And he saith unto him, Out of thine own mouth will I judge thee, *thou* wicked servant. Thou knewest that I was an **austere** man, taking up that I laid not down, and reaping that I did not sow: [KJV]<br>"He said to him, 'By your own words I will judge you, you worthless slave. Did you know that I am an **exacting** man, taking up what I did not lay down, and reaping what I did not sow? [NASB]<br>"His master replied, 'I will judge you by your own words, you wicked servant! You knew, did you, that I am a **hard** man, taking out what I did not put in, and reaping what I did not sow? [NIV]<br>And he said to him, 'Out of your own mouth I will judge you, *you* wicked servant. You knew that I was an **austere** man, collecting what I did not deposit and reaping what I did not sow. [NKJV]<br>"'You wicked servant!' the king roared. 'Hard, am I? If you knew so much about me and how **tough** I am, [NLT]<br>λέγει δὲ αὐτῷ, Ἐκ τοῦ στόματός σου κρίνω σε, πονηρὲ δοῦλε. ᾔδεις ὅτι ἐγὼ ἄνθρωπος **αὐστηρός** εἰμι, αἴρων ὃ οὐκ ἔθηκα, καὶ θερίζων ὃ οὐκ ἔσπειρα· [GNS]<br>λέγει αὐτῷ, Ἐκ τοῦ στόματός σου κρινῶ σε, πονηρὲ δοῦλε. ᾔδεις ὅτι ἐγὼ ἄνθρωπος **αὐστηρός** εἰμι, αἴρων ὃ οὐκ ἔθηκα καὶ θερίζων ὃ οὐκ ἔσπειρα; [GNT] | Sharp, hard, exacting, tough, austere, stringent.<br><br>**Practical Application**<br>In this Scripture, the unfaithful servant accused the Lord of being too hard. He felt that the Lord was too demanding and strict; and if he committed himself to the Lord's affairs, he would lose out on too much of the pleasures and comforts of life. But note: this was merely an excuse for his failure. He had chosen to live a life of selfishness and comfort and worldliness in the kingdom of the Lord without paying the price of helping to build it. He had been complacent and idle, doing very little. He had to cover up his failure or else face judgment, but his excuse was unacceptable. Perfect justice was executed: "Out of your own mouth I will judge you." [NKJV] The very excuse, as well as the life, of the unfaithful servant determined his judgment. |

# Practical Word Studies
## in the New Testament

| ENGLISH WORD | GREEK WORD AND VERSE | THE WORD MEANS... |
|---|---|---|
| **#241**<br>**Author**<br><br>Captain–KJV<br>**Author**–NASB<br>**Author**–NIV<br>Captain–NKJV<br>Perfect leader–NLT<br><br>**POSB<br>REFERENCE**<br>(Heb.2:9-13; esp. v.10)<br>Note 3, point 2b | ἀρχηγὸν = *archēgon*<br>Pronunciation: [ar-khay-gon']<br>Parsing (part of speech): noun<br>    Case—accusative<br>    Gender—masculine<br>    Number—singular<br>    Stem or root—from ἀρχηγός, οῦ<br>Concordance References:<br>  ⇒ Strong's #747 *archēgos*<br>  ⇒ NIV #795 *archēgos*<br>  ⇒ NASB #747 *archēgos*<br><br>**Hebrews 2:10**<br>For it became him, for whom *are* all things, and by whom *are* all things, in bringing many sons unto glory, to make the **captain** of their salvation perfect through sufferings. [KJV]<br><br>For it was fitting for Him, for whom are all things, and through whom are all things, in bringing many sons to glory, to perfect the **author** of their salvation through sufferings. [NASB]<br><br>In bringing many sons to glory, it was fitting that God, for whom and through whom everything exists, should make the **author** of their salvation perfect through suffering. [NIV]<br><br>For it was fitting for Him, for whom *are* all things and by whom *are* all things, in bringing many sons to glory, to make the **captain** of their salvation perfect through sufferings. [NKJV]<br><br>And it was only right that God—who made everything and for whom everything was made—should bring his many children into glory. Through the suffering of Jesus, God made him a **perfect leader**, one fit to bring them into their salvation. [NLT]<br><br>ἔπρεπε γὰρ αὐτῷ, δι' ὃν τὰ πάντα καὶ δι' οὗ τὰ πάντα, πολλοὺς υἱοὺς εἰς δόξαν ἀγαγόντα, τὸν **ἀρχηγὸν** τῆς σωτηρίας αὐτῶν διὰ παθημάτων τελειῶσαι [GNS]<br><br>Ἔπρεπεν γὰρ αὐτῷ, δι' ὃν τὰ πάντα καὶ δι' οὗ τὰ πάντα, πολλοὺς υἱοὺς εἰς δόξαν ἀγαγόντα τὸν **ἀρχηγὸν** τῆς σωτηρίας αὐτῶν διὰ παθημάτων τελειῶσαι. [GNT] | Author, leader, pioneer, pathfinder, founder, originator, perfect leader. It means the one who blazes forth, cutting through something so that others may follow.<br><br>**Practical Application**<br>Jesus Christ opened up the way or trail to God. This He did by suffering all the experiences of man—perfectly. He remained perfect through all His sufferings. He never sinned; He never failed, not even once. He learned obedience by the things which He suffered—perfectly. And by such, He secured a perfect, eternal righteousness for man. He is the perfect pioneer who has cut the perfect path to God. He is the Ideal and Perfect Man who stands for and covers all persons...<br>• all who believe and trust Him to cover them.<br>• all who believe and trust Him to make them presentable to God. |
| **#242**<br>**Author**<br><br>**Author**–KJV<br>**Author**–NASB<br>**Author**–NIV<br>**Author**–NKJV<br>Start–NLT<br><br>**POSB<br>REFERENCE**<br>(Heb.12:2)<br>Note 3, point 1 | τὸν ἀρχηγὸν = *ton archēgon*<br>Pronunciation: [ton ar-khay-gon']<br>Parsing (part of speech): noun<br>    Case—accusative<br>    Gender—masculine<br>    Number—singular<br>    Stem or root—from ἀρχηγός, οῦ<br>Concordance References:<br>  ⇒ Strong's #3588 ho + 747 *archēgos*<br>  ⇒ NIV #3836 ho + 795 *archēgos* [author]<br>  ⇒ NASB #3588 ho + 747 *archēgos*<br><br>**Hebrews 12:2**<br>Looking unto Jesus the **author** and finisher of *our* faith; who for the joy that was set before him endured the cross, despising the shame, and is set down at the right hand of the throne of God. [KJV]<br><br>Fixing our eyes on Jesus, the **author** and perfecter of faith, who for the joy set before Him endured the cross, despising the shame, and has sat down at the right hand of the throne of God. [NASB]<br><br>Let us fix our eyes on Jesus, the **author** and perfecter of our faith, who for the joy set before him endured the cross, scorning its shame, and sat down at the right hand of the throne of God. [NIV]<br><br>Looking unto Jesus, the **author** and finisher of *our* faith, who for the joy that was set before Him endured the cross, despising the shame, and has sat down at the right hand of the throne of God. [NKJV] | Author, leader, pioneer, pathfinder, founder, originator, perfect leader. It means the one who blazes forth and cuts through something so that others may follow.<br><br>**Practical Application**<br>Jesus Christ participated in the race Himself; He actually ran the race of faith. In fact, He is the very Author and Finisher of faith. The Author (*ton archēgon*) means that He authored, began, originated, created, and gave birth to the Christian race. |

# PRACTICAL WORD STUDIES
## in the NEW TESTAMENT

| ENGLISH WORD | GREEK WORD AND VERSE | THE WORD MEANS... |
|---|---|---|
| | We do this by keeping our eyes on Jesus, on whom our faith depends from **start** to finish. He was willing to die a shameful death on the cross because of the joy he knew would be his afterward. Now he is seated in the place of highest honor beside God's throne in heaven. [NLT]<br><br>ἀφορῶντες εἰς τὸν τῆς πίστεως ἀρχηγὸν καὶ τελειωτὴν Ἰησοῦν, ὃς ἀντὶ τῆς προκειμένης αὐτῷ χαρᾶς, ὑπέμεινε σταυρὸν αἰσχύνης καταφρονήσας, ἐν δεξιᾷ τε τοῦ θρόνου τοῦ Θεοῦ ἐκάθισεν. [GNS]<br><br>ἀφορῶντες εἰς τὸν τῆς πίστεως ἀρχηγὸν καὶ τελειωτὴν Ἰησοῦν, ὃς ἀντὶ τῆς προκειμένης αὐτῷ χαρᾶς ὑπέμεινεν σταυρὸν αἰσχύνης καταφρονήσας ἐν δεξιᾷ τε τοῦ θρόνου τοῦ Θεοῦ κεκάθικεν. [GNT] | |
| **#243**<br>**Authorities**<br><br>Powers–KJV<br>Powers–NASB<br>**Authorities–NIV**<br>Powers–NKJV<br>**Authorities–NLT**<br><br>**POSB REFERENCE**<br>(Eph.6:12)<br>Note 3, point 5 | ἐξουσίας = *exousias*<br>Pronunciation: [ex-oo-see'-ahs]<br>Parsing (part of speech): noun<br>   Case—accusative<br>   Gender—feminine<br>   Number—plural<br>   Stem or root—from ἐξουσία, ας<br>Concordance References:<br>  ⇒ Strong's #1849 exousia<br>  ⇒ NIV #2026 exousia<br>  ⇒ NASB #1849 exousia<br><br>**Ephes. 6:12**<br>For we wrestle not against flesh and blood, but against principalities, against **powers**, against the rulers of the darkness of this world, against spiritual wickedness in high *places*. [KJV]<br>For our struggle is not against flesh and blood, but against the rulers, against the **powers**, against the world forces of this darkness, against the spiritual *forces* of wickedness in the heavenly *places*. [NASB]<br>For our struggle is not against flesh and blood, but against the rulers, against the **authorities**, against the powers of this dark world and against the spiritual forces of evil in the heavenly realms. [NIV]<br>For we do not wrestle against flesh and blood, but against principalities, against **powers**, against the rulers of the darkness of this age, against spiritual *hosts* of wickedness in the heavenly *places*. [NKJV]<br>For we are not fighting against people made of flesh and blood, but against the evil rulers and **authorities** of the unseen world, against those mighty powers of darkness who rule this world, and against wicked spirits in the heavenly realms. [NLT]<br><br>ὅτι οὐκ ἔστιν ἡμῖν ἡ πάλη πρὸς αἷμα καὶ σάρκα, ἀλλὰ πρὸς τὰς ἀρχάς, πρὸς τὰς **ἐξουσίας**, πρὸς τοὺς κοσμοκράτορας τοῦ σκότους τοῦ αἰῶνος τούτου, πρὸς τὰ πνευματικὰ τῆς πονηρίας ἐν τοῖς ἐπουρανίοις. [GNS]<br><br>ὅτι οὐκ ἔστιν ἡμῖν ἡ πάλη πρὸς αἷμα καὶ σάρκα, ἀλλὰ πρὸς τὰς ἀρχάς, πρὸς τὰς **ἐξουσίας**, πρὸς τοὺς κοσμοκράτορας τοῦ σκότους τούτου, πρὸς τὰ πνευματικὰ τῆς πονηρίας ἐν τοῖς ἐπουρανίοις. [GNT] | Authorities, powers, supernatural power, ruling power; the demons of Satan in the lower atmosphere who constitute his kingdom in the air.<br><br>**Practical Application**<br>Some persons have always scoffed at the idea of a personal devil or demons who actually exist in a so-called spiritual world. They feel they are too educated and intelligent to believe such nonsense. They proclaim that such ideas are outdated and belong to the dark ages of man's ignorance and superstitions. But note a significant fact: man is ever so conscious of what he terms...<br>• *sub-conscious horrors* that affect both his mind and body.<br>• *unseen and uncontrollable forces* that greatly affect his behavior.<br>• *unregulated behavior* that he cannot control even when he knows better and wills to do differently.<br>• *cosmic forces* that affect and determine his behavior.<br>• *blind fate* that controls his life like a puppet. |
| **#244**<br>**Authority**<br><br>Power–KJV<br>**Authority–NASB**<br>**Authority–NIV**<br>Power–NKJV<br>**Authority–NLT**<br><br>**POSB REFERENCE**<br>(Mt.10:1)<br>*Deeper Study #2* | ἐξουσίαν = *exousia*<br>Pronunciation: [ex-oo-see'-ah]<br>Parsing (part of speech): noun<br>   Case—accusative<br>   Gender—feminine<br>   Number—singular<br>   Stem or root—from ἐξουσία, ας<br>Concordance References:<br>  ⇒ Strong's #1849 exousia<br>  ⇒ NIV #2026 exousia<br>  ⇒ NASB #1849 exousia<br><br>**Matthew 10:1**<br>And when he had called unto *him* his twelve disciples, he gave them **power** *against* unclean spirits, to cast them out, and to heal all manner of sickness and all manner of | Authority, authorization, power, sanction.<br><br>**Practical Application**<br>In this Scripture, Christ was giving *His own authority* to His messengers. They were being sent forth by Him on a very special mission; therefore, they were given His authority and power to minister.<br>Notice that the authority to save or convert the lost is not given. Why? Only God can save and penetrate the spiritual world or dimension. Man's authority is limited to the physical world and dimension. |

# PRACTICAL WORD STUDIES
## in the NEW TESTAMENT

| ENGLISH WORD | GREEK WORD AND VERSE | THE WORD MEANS... |
|---|---|---|
| | disease. [KJV]<br>And having summoned His twelve disciples, He gave them **authority** over unclean spirits, to cast them out, and to heal every kind of disease and every kind of sickness. [NASB]<br>He called his twelve disciples to him and gave them **authority** to drive out evil spirits and to heal every disease and sickness. [NIV]<br>And when He had called His twelve disciples to *Him*, He gave them **power** over unclean spirits, to cast them out, and to heal all kinds of sickness and all kinds of disease. [NKJV]<br>Jesus called his twelve disciples to him and gave them **authority** to cast out evil spirits and to heal every kind of disease and illness. [NLT]<br>καὶ προσκαλεσάμενος τοὺς δώδεκα μαθητὰς αὐτοῦ, ἔδωκεν αὐτοῖς **ἐξουσίαν** πνευμάτων ἀκαθάρτων, ὥστε ἐκβάλλειν αὐτὰ, καὶ θεραπεύειν πᾶσαν νόσον καὶ πᾶσαν μαλακίαν. [GNS]<br>Καὶ προσκαλεσάμενος τοὺς δώδεκα μαθητὰς αὐτοῦ ἔδωκεν αὐτοῖς **ἐξουσίαν** πνευμάτων ἀκαθάρτων ὥστε ἐκβάλλειν αὐτὰ καὶ θεραπεύειν πᾶσαν νόσον καὶ πᾶσαν μαλακίαν. [GNT] | |
| **#245**<br>**Authority,<br>All–Complete**<br><br>All power–KJV<br>All authority–NASB<br>All authority–NIV<br>All authority–NKJV<br>Complete authority–NLT<br><br>**POSB<br>REFERENCE**<br>(Mt.28:18)<br>Note 2 | πᾶσα ἐξουσία = *pasa exousia*<br>Pronunciation: [pas-ah ex-oo-see'-ah]<br>Parsing *pasa* (part of speech): adjective<br>    Case—nominative<br>    Gender—feminine<br>    Number—singular<br>    Stem or root—from πᾶς, πᾶσα, πᾶν<br>Parsing *exousia* (part of speech): noun<br>    Case—nominative<br>    Gender—feminine<br>    Number—singular<br>    Stem or root—from ἐξουσία, ας<br>Concordance References:<br>  ⇒ Strong's #3956 pas + 1849 exousia<br>  ⇒ NIV #4246 pas [all] + #2026 exousia [authority]<br>  ⇒ NASB #3956 pas + 1849 exousia<br><br>**Matthew 28:18**<br>And Jesus came and spake unto them, saying, **All power** is given unto me in heaven and in earth. [KJV]<br>And Jesus came up and spoke to them, saying, "**All authority** has been given to Me in heaven and on earth. [NASB]<br>Then Jesus came to them and said, "**All authority** in heaven and on earth has been given to me. [NIV]<br>And Jesus came and spoke to them, saying, "**All authority** has been given to Me in heaven and on earth. [NKJV]<br>Jesus came and told his disciples, "I have been given **complete authority** in heaven and on earth. [NLT]<br>καὶ προσελθὼν ὁ Ἰησοῦς ἐλάλησεν αὐτοῖς λέγων, Ἐδόθη μοι **πᾶσα ἐξουσία** ἐν οὐρανῷ καὶ ἐπὶ τῆς γῆς. [GNS]<br>καὶ προσελθὼν ὁ Ἰησοῦς ἐλάλησεν αὐτοῖς λέγων, Ἐδόθη μοι **πᾶσα ἐξουσία** ἐν οὐρανῷ καὶ ἐπὶ [τῆς] γῆς. [GNT] | The ability, the power, the authority, the right to do something.<br><br>**Practical Application**<br>God the Father entrusted Jesus Christ with this kind of authority. Christ has been given complete freedom over *all*. This means...<br>• all freedom to impose His authority in heaven.<br>• all freedom to impose His authority on earth.<br>• all freedom to impose His authority over every disciple.<br>• all freedom to impose His authority over every person and every nation.<br>On the basis of His authority, believers are to go, and as we go we are to follow His instructions completely. |
| **#246**<br>**Avoid**<br><br>Avoid–KJV<br>Away–NASB<br>Away–NIV<br>Avoid–NKJV<br>Away–NLT | ἐκκλίνετε = *ekklinete*<br>Pronunciation: [ek-klee'-nah-teh]<br>Parsing (part of speech): verb<br>    Mood—imperative<br>    Tense—present<br>    Voice—active<br>    Person—2nd person<br>    Number—plural<br>    Stem or root—from ἐκκλίνω<br>Concordance References:<br>  ⇒ Strong's #1578 ekklinō<br>  ⇒ NIV #1712 ekklinō<br>  ⇒ NASB #1578 ekklinō | To avoid; to shun; to turn away from; to keep away from; to remove oneself from.<br><br>**Practical Application**<br>Get away from divisive persons and have absolutely nothing to do with them. Avoid them because of the terrible devastation that a divisive person can do to the strength of a church. |

# PRACTICAL WORD STUDIES
## in the NEW TESTAMENT

| ENGLISH WORD | GREEK WORD AND VERSE | THE WORD MEANS... |
|---|---|---|
| **POSB REFERENCE** (Rom.16:17-18; esp. v.17) Note 1, point 1b | **Romans 16:17** Now I beseech you, brethren, mark them which cause divisions and offences contrary to the doctrine which ye have learned; and **avoid** them. [KJV]<br><br>Now I urge you, brethren, keep your eye on those who cause dissensions and hindrances contrary to the teaching which you learned, and turn **away** from them. [NASB]<br><br>I urge you, brothers, to watch out for those who cause divisions and put obstacles in your way that are contrary to the teaching you have learned. Keep **away** from them. [NIV]<br><br>Now I urge you, brethren, note those who cause divisions and offenses, contrary to the doctrine which you learned, and **avoid** them. [NKJV]<br><br>And now I make one more appeal, my dear brothers and sisters. Watch out for people who cause divisions and upset people's faith by teaching things that are contrary to what you have been taught. Stay **away** from them. [NLT]<br><br>Παρακαλῶ δὲ ὑμᾶς, ἀδελφοί, σκοπεῖν τοὺς τὰς διχοστασίας καὶ τὰ σκάνδαλα, παρὰ τὴν διδαχὴν ἣν ὑμεῖς ἐμάθετε, ποιοῦντας· καὶ **ἐκκλίνατε** ἀπ' αὐτῶν. [GNS]<br><br>Παρακαλῶ δὲ ὑμᾶς, ἀδελφοί, σκοπεῖν τοὺς τὰς διχοστασίας καὶ τὰ σκάνδαλα παρὰ τὴν διδαχὴν ἣν ὑμεῖς ἐμάθετε ποιοῦντας, καὶ **ἐκκλίνετε** ἀπ' αὐτῶν· [GNT] | |
| **#247 Awake**<br><br>Awake–KJV<br>Become sober minded–NASB<br>Come back to your senses–NIV<br>Awake–NKJV<br>Come to your senses–NLT<br><br>**POSB REFERENCE** (1 Cor.15:34) Note 4 | ἐκνήψατε = eknēpsate<br>Pronunciation: [ek-nay'-fah-teh]<br>Parsing (part of speech): verb<br>  Mood—imperative<br>  Tense—aorist<br>  Voice—active<br>  Person—2nd person<br>  Number—plural<br>  Stem or root—from ἐκνήφω<br>Concordance References:<br>  ⇒ Strong's #1594 eknēphō<br>  ⇒ NIV #1729 eknēphō<br>  ⇒ NASB #1594 eknēphō<br><br>**1 Cor. 15:34**<br>**Awake** to righteousness, and sin not; for some have not the knowledge of God: I speak *this* to your shame. [KJV]<br><br>**Become sober-minded** as you ought, and stop sinning; for some have no knowledge of God. I speak *this* to your shame. [NASB]<br><br>**Come back to your senses** as you ought, and stop sinning; for there are some who are ignorant of God—I say this to your shame. [NIV]<br><br>**Awake** to righteousness, and do not sin; for some do not have the knowledge of God. I speak *this* to your shame. [NKJV]<br><br>**Come to your senses** and stop sinning. For to your shame I say that some of you don't even know God. [NLT]<br><br>**ἐκνήψατε** δικαίως καὶ μὴ ἁμαρτάνετε· ἀγνωσίαν γὰρ Θεοῦ τινες ἔχουσι· πρὸς ἐντροπὴν ὑμῖν λέγω. [GNS]<br><br>**ἐκνήψατε** δικαίως καὶ μὴ ἁμαρτάνετε, ἀγνωσίαν γὰρ θεοῦ τινες ἔχουσιν, πρὸς ἐντροπὴν ὑμῖν λαλῶ. [GNT] | Come back to your senses; become sober; arouse yourself out of a drunken, sleepy state.<br><br>**Practical Application**<br>Some in the Corinthian church were following the false teachers as though they were drunken and senseless, in a stupor, in a stupid state. They desperately needed to awaken to righteousness—to stop sinning. The denial of a resurrection is totally wrong; it is sin. There is to be a resurrection of the dead. To deny this fact is to put oneself in a drunken, senseless, unthinking state of mind. |
| **#248 Awake–Awaken**<br><br>Awake–KJV<br>Awaken–NASB<br>Wake up–NIV<br>Awake–NKJV<br>Wake up–NLT | ἐγερθῆναι = egerthēnai<br>Pronunciation: [eg-er'-thay-nah-ee]<br>Parsing (part of speech): verb<br>  Mood—infinitive<br>  Tense—aorist<br>  Voice—passive<br>  Stem or root—from ἐγείρω<br>Concordance References:<br>  ⇒ Strong's #1453 egeirō<br>  ⇒ NIV #1586 egeirō<br>  ⇒ NASB #1453 egeirō | To wake up; to awake, awaken.<br><br>**Practical Application**<br>Too many believers are slumbering and paying no attention to what is going on in the world; too many are not watching; too many are not observing the signs of the time. Too many are complacent and slothful, lazily passing through life with little commitment to serving Christ. Too few are meeting the needs of the suffering |

# PRACTICAL WORD STUDIES
## in the NEW TESTAMENT

| ENGLISH WORD | GREEK WORD AND VERSE | THE WORD MEANS... |
|---|---|---|
| **POSB REFERENCE** (Rom.13:11-12; esp. v.11) Note 2 | **Romans 13:11**<br>And that, knowing the time, that now *it is* high time to **awake** out of sleep: for now *is* our salvation nearer than when we believed. [KJV]<br>And this *do*, knowing the time, that it is already the hour for you to **awaken** from sleep; for now salvation is nearer to us than when we believed. [NASB]<br>And do this, understanding the present time. The hour has come for you to **wake up** from your slumber, because our salvation is nearer now than when we first believed. [NIV]<br>And *do* this, knowing the time, that now *it is* high time to **awake** out of sleep; for now our salvation *is* nearer than when we *first* believed. [NKJV]<br>Another reason for right living is that you know how late it is; time is running out. **Wake up**, for the coming of our salvation is nearer now than when we first believed. [NLT]<br>Καὶ τοῦτο, εἰδότες τὸν καιρόν, ὅτι ὥρα ὑμᾶς ἤδη ἐξ ὕπνου **ἐγερθῆναι**· νῦν γὰρ ἐγγύτερον ἡμῶν ἡ σωτηρία ἢ ὅτε ἐπιστεύσαμεν. [GNS]<br>Καὶ τοῦτο εἰδότες τὸν καιρόν, ὅτι ὥρα ἤδη ὑμᾶς ἐξ ὕπνου **ἐγερθῆναι**, νῦν γὰρ ἐγγύτερον ἡμῶν ἡ σωτηρία ἢ ὅτε ἐπιστεύσαμεν. [GNT] | and dying massses of the world. It is time "to awake" *(egerthēnai)* out of sleep: time to wake up, to be aroused and stirred. It is time to get up and move and act—now—before it is too late. |
| **#249 Away**<br>Avoid–KJV<br>**Away**–NASB<br>**Away**–NIV<br>Avoid–NKJV<br>**Away**–NLT<br>**POSB REFERENCE** (Rom.16:17-18; esp. v.17) Note 1, point 1b | ἐκκλίνετε = *ekklinete*<br>Pronunciation: [ek-klee'-nah-teh]<br>Parsing (part of speech): verb<br>   Mood—imperative<br>   Tense—present<br>   Voice—active<br>   Person—2nd person<br>   Number—plural<br>   Stem or root—from ἐκκλίνω<br>Concordance References:<br>  ⇒ Strong's #1578 ekklinō<br>  ⇒ NIV #1712 ekklinō<br>  ⇒ NASB #1578 ekklinō<br><br>**Romans 16:17**<br>Now I beseech you, brethren, mark them which cause divisions and offences contrary to the doctrine which ye have learned; and **avoid** them. [KJV]<br>Now I urge you, brethren, keep your eye on those who cause dissensions and hindrances contrary to the teaching which you learned, and turn **away** from them. [NASB]<br>I urge you, brothers, to watch out for those who cause divisions and put obstacles in your way that are contrary to the teaching you have learned. Keep **away** from them. [NIV]<br>Now I urge you, brethren, note those who cause divisions and offenses, contrary to the doctrine which you learned, and **avoid** them. [NKJV]<br>And now I make one more appeal, my dear brothers and sisters. Watch out for people who cause divisions and upset people's faith by teaching things that are contrary to what you have been taught. Stay **away** from them. [NLT]<br>Παρακαλῶ δὲ ὑμᾶς, ἀδελφοί, σκοπεῖν τοὺς τὰς διχοστασίας καὶ τὰ σκάνδαλα, παρὰ τὴν διδαχὴν ἣν ἐμάθετε, ποιοῦντας· καὶ **ἐκκλίνατε** ἀπ' αὐτῶν. [GNS]<br>Παρακαλῶ δὲ ὑμᾶς, ἀδελφοί, σκοπεῖν τοὺς τὰς διχοστασίας καὶ τὰ σκάνδαλα παρὰ τὴν διδαχὴν ἣν ὑμεῖς ἐμάθετε ποιοῦντας, καὶ **ἐκκλίνετε** ἀπ' αὐτῶν· [GNT] | To avoid; to shun; to turn away from; to keep away from; to remove oneself from.<br><br>**Practical Application**<br>Get away from divisive persons and have absolutely nothing to do with them. Avoid them because of the terrible devastation that a divisive person can do to the strength of a church. |
| **#250 Away– Away From**<br>Depart–KJV<br>Depart–NASB | ἀποχωρεῖτε ἀπ' = *apochōreite ap'*<br>Pronunciation: [ap-okh-o-reh'-i-teh ap]<br>Parsing (part of speech): verb<br>   Mood—imperative<br>   Tense—present<br>   Voice—active<br>   Person—2nd person<br>   Number—plural<br>   Stem or root—from ἀποχωρέω | To depart from; to go away; to be cut off from; to leave a place.<br><br>**Practical Application**<br>In this Scripture, the idea is the enormous distance, the great gulf, placed between the person making a false profession and the Lord's pres- |

# PRACTICAL WORD STUDIES
## in the NEW TESTAMENT

| ENGLISH WORD | GREEK WORD AND VERSE | THE WORD MEANS... |
|---|---|---|
| **Away from–NIV**<br>Depart–NKJV<br>**Away–NLT**<br><br>**POSB REFERENCE**<br>(Mt.7:23)<br>*Deeper Study #1* | Concordance References:<br>⇒ Strong's #672 apochōreō + 575 apo<br>⇒ NIV #608+713 apochōreō apo<br>⇒ NASB #672 apochōreō + 575 apo<br><br>**Matthew 7:23**<br>And then will I profess unto them, I never knew you: **depart** from me, ye that work iniquity. [KJV]<br>"And then I will declare to them, 'I never knew you; DEPART FROM ME, YOU WHO PRACTICE LAWLESSNESS.' [NASB]<br>Then I will tell them plainly, 'I never knew you. **Away from** me, you evildoers!' [NIV]<br>And then I will declare to them, 'I never knew you; **depart** from Me, you who practice lawlessness!' [NKJV]<br>But I will reply, 'I never knew you. Go **away**; the things you did were unauthorized.' [NLT]<br>καὶ τότε ὁμολογήσω αὐτοῖς, ὅτι οὐδέποτε ἔγνων ὑμᾶς· **ἀποχωρεῖτε ἀπ'** ἐμοῦ οἱ ἐργαζόμενοι τὴν ἀνομίαν. [GNS]<br>καὶ τότε ὁμολογήσω αὐτοῖς ὅτι Οὐδέποτε ἔγνων ὑμᾶς· **ἀποχωρεῖτε ἀπ'** ἐμοῦ οἱ ἐργαζόμενοι τὴν ἀνομίαν. [GNT] | ence. There will never be a sadder moment in a person's life than to hear Christ's command to "go away from Me, depart from Me...I never knew you!" |
| **#251**<br>**Awe**<br><br>Amazed–KJV<br>Amazed–NASB<br>Amazed–NIV<br>Amazed–NKJV<br>**Awe–NLT**<br><br>**POSB REFERENCE**<br>(Lk.9:42-43; esp. v.43)<br>Note 3, point 2 | ἐξεπλήσσοντο = *exeplēssonto*<br>Pronunciation: [ek-e-place'-son-tow]<br>Parsing (part of speech): verb<br>  Mood—indicative<br>  Tense—imperfect<br>  Voice—passive<br>  Person—3rd person<br>  Number—plural<br>  Stem or root—from ἐκπλήσσω<br>Concordance References:<br>⇒ Strong's #1605 eklpesso<br>⇒ NIV #1742 ekplēssō<br>⇒ NASB #1605 eklpesso<br><br>**Luke 9:43**<br>And they were all **amazed** at the mighty power of God. But while they wondered every one at all things which Jesus did, he said unto his disciples, [KJV]<br>And they were all **amazed** at the greatness of God. But while everyone was marveling at all that He was doing, He said to His disciples, [NASB]<br>And they were all **amazed** at the greatness of God. While everyone was marveling at all that Jesus did, he said to his disciples, [NIV]<br>And they were all **amazed** at the majesty of God. But while everyone marveled at all the things which Jesus did, He said to His disciples, [NKJV]<br>**Awe** gripped the people as they saw this display of God's power. While everyone was marveling over all the wonderful things he was doing, Jesus said to his disciples, [NLT]<br>**ἐξεπλήσσοντο** δὲ πάντες ἐπὶ τῇ μεγαλειότητι τοῦ Θεοῦ. Πάντων δὲ θαυμαζόντων ἐπὶ πᾶσιν οἷς ἐποίει ὁ Ἰησοῦς, εἶπε πρὸς τοὺς μαθητὰς αὐτοῦ, [GNS]<br>**ἐξεπλήσσοντο** δὲ πάντες ἐπὶ τῇ μεγαλειότητι τοῦ Θεοῦ. Πάντων δὲ θαυμαζόντων ἐπὶ πᾶσιν οἷς ἐποίει εἶπεν πρὸς τοὺς μαθητὰς αὐτοῦ, [GNT] | To be amazed; to be overwhelmed; to be in awe.<br><br>**Practical Application**<br>Note the dramatic account found in this Scripture: The people who observed Jesus' delivering the boy from the unclean spirit marveled at what they had seen. They were all *marvelling over the wonderful things Jesus was doing.* |
| **#252**<br>**Awe**<br><br>Fear–KJV<br>Fear–NASB<br>**Awe–NIV**<br>Fear–NKJV<br>Wonder–NLT | φόβος = *phobos*<br>Pronunciation: [fob'-os]<br>Parsing (part of speech): noun<br>  Case—nominative<br>  Gender—masculine<br>  Number—singular<br>  Stem or root—from φόβος, ου | Awe, fear, wonder.<br><br>**Practical Application**<br>It does not mean to fear God's presence, to shrink and withdraw from Him. To the contrary, it means that a person reverences and stands in awe of Him, wanting to approach and know Him because He is the majestic and sovereign Being |

## PRACTICAL WORD STUDIES
## in the NEW TESTAMENT

| ENGLISH WORD | GREEK WORD AND VERSE | THE WORD MEANS... |
|---|---|---|
| **POSB REFERENCE** (Lk.1:64-66; esp. v.65) Note 3, point 2  See also POSB REF: (Acts 2:43) Note 3 (Acts 9:31) *Deeper Study #1* | Concordance References:<br>⇒ Strong's #5401 phobos<br>⇒ NIV #5832 phobos<br>⇒ NASB #5401 phobos<br><br>**Luke 1:65**<br>And **fear** came on all that dwelt round about them: and all these sayings were noised abroad throughout all the hill country of Judaea. [KJV]<br>And **fear** came on all those living around them; and all these matters were being talked about in all the hill country of Judea. [NASB]<br>The neighbors were all filled with **awe**, and throughout the hill country of Judea people were talking about all these things. [NIV]<br>Then **fear** came on all who dwelt around them; and all these sayings were discussed throughout all the hill country of Judea. [NKJV]<br>**Wonder** fell upon the whole neighborhood, and the news of what had happened spread throughout the Judean hills. [NLT]<br>καὶ ἐγένετο ἐπὶ πάντας **φόβος** τοὺς περιοικοῦντας αὐτούς· καὶ ἐν ὅλῃ τῇ ὀρεινῇ τῆς Ἰουδαίας διελαλεῖτο πάντα τὰ ῥήματα ταῦτα, [GNS]<br>καὶ ἐγένετο ἐπὶ πάντας **φόβος** τοὺς περιοικοῦντας αὐτούς, καὶ ἐν ὅλῃ τῇ ὀρεινῇ τῆς Ἰουδαίας διελαλεῖτο πάντα τὰ ῥήματα ταῦτα, [GNT] | of the universe. It means that a person does not fear...<br>• to trust and believe Him.<br>• to approach and worship Him.<br>• to do His will.<br>• to serve Him.<br><br>Fear does not mean terror or fright. It means...<br>• a godly fear, a fear of God, of His displeasure and judgment.<br>• a holy sense of God's presence.<br>• a consciousness that God is working.<br>• a reverence for God and for what is happening.<br>• a sense of awe and wonder. |
| **#253**<br>**Awe**<br><br>Godly fear–KJV<br>**Awe**–NASB<br>**Awe**–NIV<br>Godly fear–NKJV<br>**Awe**–NLT<br><br>**POSB REFERENCE**<br>(Heb.12:28-29; esp. v.28) Note 3, point 2 | δέους = *deous*<br>Pronunciation: [dee'-oos]<br>Parsing (part of speech): noun<br>  Case—genitive<br>  Gender—neuter<br>  Number—singular<br>  Stem or root—from δέος, ους<br>Concordance References:<br>⇒ Strong's #127 aidos<br>⇒ NIV #1290 deos<br>⇒ NASB #1190a deos<br><br>**Hebrews 12:28**<br>Wherefore we receiving a kingdom which cannot be moved, let us have grace, whereby we may serve God acceptably with reverence and **godly fear**: [KJV]<br>Therefore, since we receive a kingdom which cannot be shaken, let us show gratitude, by which we may offer to God an acceptable service with reverence and **awe**; [NASB]<br>Therefore, since we are receiving a kingdom that cannot be shaken, let us be thankful, and so worship God acceptably with reverence and **awe**, [NIV]<br>Therefore, since we are receiving a kingdom which cannot be shaken, let us have grace, by which we may serve God acceptably with reverence and **godly fear**. [NKJV]<br>Since we are receiving a kingdom that cannot be destroyed, let us be thankful and please God by worshiping him with holy fear and **awe**. [NLT]<br>διὸ βασιλείαν ἀσάλευτον παραλαμβάνοντες, ἔχωμεν χάριν δι' ἧς λατρεύωμεν εὐαρέστως τῷ Θεῷ μετὰ **αἰδοῦς** καὶ εὐλαβείας· [GNS]<br>Διὸ βασιλείαν ἀσάλευτον παραλαμβάνοντες ἔχωμεν χάριν, δι' ἧς λατρεύωμεν εὐαρέστως τῷ θεῷ μετὰ εὐλαβείας καὶ **δέους**· [GNT] | Awe, reverence, godly fear. It means being apprehensive because some danger can lurk over the horizon.<br><br>**Practical Application**<br>A person must do exactly what this verse says: *serve God acceptably* with reverence and godly fear. God must be feared, for He is Lord. A person must serve God and serve Him in an acceptable way. |
| **#254**<br>**Awe, In**<br><br>Greatly amazed–KJV<br>Amazed–NASB<br>Overwhelmed with wonder–NIV<br>Greatly amazed–NKJV<br>**In awe**–NLT | ἐξεθαμβήθησαν = *exethambēthēsan*<br>Pronunciation: [ek-eh-tham-bayth'-ay-sahn]<br>Parsing (part of speech): verb<br>  Mood—indicative<br>  Tense—aorist<br>  Voice—passive<br>  Person—3rd person<br>  Number—plural<br>  Stem or root—from ἐκθαμβέομαι<br>Concordance References:<br>⇒ Strong's #1568 ekthambeo<br>⇒ NIV #1701 ekthambeō<br>⇒ NASB #1568 ekthambeo | To be filled with wonder; to be overwhelmed with wonder and awe; to be amazed—greatly amazed.<br><br>**Practical Application**<br>What amazed the people when they "saw" Jesus?<br>1. Perhaps Jesus retained some of the glory of the transfiguration. The people may have seen a glow, a majestic countenance about Jesus. (cp. Exodus 34:29 when Moses came |

# PRACTICAL WORD STUDIES
## in the NEW TESTAMENT

| ENGLISH WORD | GREEK WORD AND VERSE | THE WORD MEANS... |
|---|---|---|
| **POSB REFERENCE** (Mk.9:15) *Deeper Study #1* | **Mark 9:15**<br>And straightway all the people, when they beheld him, were **greatly amazed**, and running to *him* saluted him. [KJV]<br>And immediately, when the entire crowd saw Him, they were **amazed**, and *began* running up to greet Him. [NASB]<br>As soon as all the people saw Jesus, they were **overwhelmed with wonder** and ran to greet him. [NIV]<br>Immediately, when they saw Him, all the people were **greatly amazed**, and running to *Him*, greeted Him. [NKJV]<br>The crowd watched Jesus **in awe** as he came toward them, and then they ran to greet him. [NLT]<br>καὶ εὐθέως πᾶς ὁ ὄχλος ἰδὼν αὐτὸν **ἐξεθαμβήθη**, καὶ προστρέχοντες ἠσπάζοντο αὐτόν. [GNS]<br>καὶ εὐθὺς πᾶς ὁ ὄχλος ἰδόντες αὐτὸν **ἐξεθαμβήθησαν** καὶ προστρέχοντες ἠσπάζοντο αὐτόν. [GNT] | down from the mountain after having been with God).<br>2. Perhaps Jesus came at such an opportune time that the people were amazed to see Him, as though His timing was destined. He arrived just when His disciples needed help.<br>3. Perhaps Jesus walked with a renewed air, a more authoritative and decisive countenance than before. Just coming from the transfiguration was bound to instill a renewed confidence and authority within Him. |

## PRACTICAL WORD STUDIES
### in the NEW TESTAMENT

| ENGLISH WORD | GREEK WORD AND VERSE | THE WORD MEANS... |
|---|---|---|
| **#255**<br>**Babble–**<br>**Babbling**<br><br>Vain repetitions–KJV<br>Meaningless repetitions–NASB<br>**Babbling–NIV**<br>Vain repetitions–NKJV<br>**Babble–NLT**<br><br>**POSB**<br>**REFERENCE**<br>(Mt.6:7)<br>*Deeper Study #1* | βατταλογήσητε = *battologesete*<br>Pronunciation: [bat-tol-og-ay say-teh]<br>Parsing (part of speech): verb<br>    Mood—subjunctive or imperative<br>    Tense—aorist<br>    Voice—active<br>    Person—2nd person<br>    Number—plural<br>    Stem or root—from βατταλογέω<br>Concordance References:<br>  ⇒ Strong's #945 battalogeö<br>  ⇒ NIV #1006 battalogeö<br>  ⇒ NASB #945 battalogeö<br><br>**Matthew 6:7**<br>But when ye pray, use not **vain repetitions**, as the heathen do: for they think that they shall be heard for their much speaking. [KJV]<br>"And when you are praying, do not use **meaningless repetition**, as the Gentiles do, for they suppose that they will be heard for their many words. [NASB]<br>And when you pray, do not keep on **babbling** like pagans, for they think they will be heard because of their many words. [NIV]<br>And when you pray, do not use **vain repetitions** as the heathen do. For they think that they will be heard for their many words. [NKJV]<br>"When you pray, don't **babble** on and on as people of other religions do. They think their prayers are answered only by repeating their words again and again. [NLT]<br>Προσευχόμενοι δὲ μὴ **βατταλογήσητε**, ὥσπερ οἱ ἐθνικοί· δοκοῦσι γὰρ ὅτι ἐν τῇ πολυλογίᾳ αὐτῶν εἰσακουσθήσονται. [GNS]<br>Προσευχόμενοι δὲ μὴ **βατταλογήσητε** ὥσπερ οἱ ἐθνικοί, δοκοῦσιν γὰρ ὅτι ἐν τῇ πολυλογίᾳ αὐτῶν εἰσακουσθήσονται. [GNT] | To babble; to use many phrases; to speak idle or vain words; to speak meaningless words.<br><br>**Practical Application**<br>Babbling means at least two things.<br>1. It means saying the same words over and over again without putting one's heart and thought into what is being said.<br>2. It means using certain religious words or phrases (sometimes over and over again) and thinking God hears because one is using such religious talk. |
| **#256**<br>**Babes**<br><br>**Babes–KJV**<br>Immature–NASB<br>Infants–NIV<br>**Babes–NKJV**<br>Children–NLT<br><br>**POSB**<br>**REFERENCE**<br>(Romans 2:17-20; esp. v.20)<br>Note 1, point 9 | νηπίων = *nëpiön*<br>Pronunciation: [nay'-pee-own]<br>Parsing (part of speech): pronominal adjective<br>    Case—genitive<br>    Gender—masculine<br>    Number—plural<br>    Stem or root—from νήπιος, α, ον<br>Concordance References:<br>  ⇒ Strong's #3516 nëpios<br>  ⇒ NIV #3758 nëpios<br>  ⇒ NASB #3516 nëpios<br><br>**Romans 2:20**<br>An instructor of the foolish, a teacher of **babes**, which hast the form of knowledge and of the truth in the law. [KJV]<br>A corrector of the foolish, a teacher of the **immature**, having in the Law the embodiment of knowledge and of the truth, [NASB]<br>An instructor of the foolish, a teacher of **infants**, because you have in the law the embodiment of knowledge and truth—[NIV]<br>An instructor of the foolish, a teacher of **babes**, having the form of knowledge and truth in the law. [NKJV]<br>You think you can instruct the ignorant and teach **children** the ways of God. For you are certain that in God's law you have complete knowledge and truth. [NLT]<br>παιδευτὴν ἀφρόνων, διδάσκαλον **νηπίων**, ἔχοντα τὴν μόρφωσιν τῆς γνώσεως καὶ τῆς ἀληθείας ἐν τῷ νόμῳ·[GNS]<br>παιδευτὴν ἀφρόνων, διδάσκαλον **νηπίων**, ἔχοντα τὴν μόρφωσιν τῆς γνώσεως καὶ τῆς ἀληθείας ἐν τῷ νόμῳ· [GNT] | The infant; the immature; the novice; the children; the proselyte; the innocent; the baby; the new church member.<br><br>**Practical Application**<br>A person is not mature in God just because he...<br>• has been baptized and has been a church member for a long time.<br>• thinks he is mature.<br>• serves as a teacher.<br>What makes a person mature and capable of teaching the immature of the world is experience with Christ, having walked and served with Christ for a long time. |

# PRACTICAL WORD STUDIES
## in the NEW TESTAMENT

| ENGLISH WORD | GREEK WORD AND VERSE | THE WORD MEANS... |
|---|---|---|
| **#257**<br>**Backbiters**<br><br>**Backbiters**–KJV<br>Slanderers–NASB<br>Slanderers–NIV<br>**Backbiters**–NKJV<br>Backstabbers–NLT<br><br>**POSB REFERENCE**<br>(Romans 1:30)<br>*Deeper Study* #12 | καταλάλους = katalalous<br>Pronunciation: [kat-al'-al-oos]<br>Parsing (part of speech): pronominal adjective<br>    Case—accusative<br>    Gender—masculine<br>    Number—plural<br>    Stem or root—from κατάλαλος, ου<br>Concordance References:<br>⇒ Strong's #2637 katalalos<br>⇒ NIV #2897 katalalos<br>⇒ NASB #2637 katalalos<br><br>**Romans 1:30**<br>**Backbiters**, haters of God, despiteful, proud, boasters, inventors of evil things, disobedient to parents, [KJV]<br>**Slanderers**, haters of God, insolent, arrogant, boastful, inventors of evil, disobedient to parents, [NASB]<br>**Slanderers**, God-haters, insolent, arrogant and boastful; they invent ways of doing evil; they disobey their parents; [NIV]<br>**Backbiters**, haters of God, violent, proud, boasters, inventors of evil things, disobedient to parents, [NKJV]<br>They are **backstabbers**, haters of God, insolent, proud, and boastful. They are forever inventing new ways of sinning and are disobedient to their parents. [NLT]<br>ψιθυριστάς, **καταλάλους**, θεοστυγεῖς, ὑβριστάς, ὑπερηφάνους, ἀλαζόνας, ἐφευρετάς κακῶν, γονεῦσιν ἀπειθεῖς, [GNS]<br>**καταλάλους** θεοστυγεῖς ὑβριστάς ὑπερηφάνους ἀλαζόνας, ἐφευρετάς κακῶν, γονεῦσιν ἀπειθεῖς, [GNT] | Slanderers, backbiters, backstabbers; one who speaks evil of another.<br><br>**Practical Application**<br>The word differs from the quiet, secret backbiter. It is a loud, open backbiter, a person who broadcasts the tale. The tale may be true or not: it does not matter. The backbiting slanderer burns within to tell the gossip to everyone. |
| **#258**<br>**Backbitings**<br><br>**Backbitings**–KJV<br>Slanders–NASB<br>Slander–NIV<br>**Backbitings**–NKJV<br>Backstabbing–NLT<br><br>**POSB REFERENCE**<br>(2 Cor.12:19-21; esp. v.20)<br>Note 3, point 2<br><br>See also POSB REF:<br>(1 Pt.2:1)<br>Note 1, point 5 | καταλαλιαι = katalaliai<br>Pronunciation: [kat-al-al-ee'-ah-ee]<br>Parsing (part of speech): noun<br>    Case—nominative<br>    Gender—feminine<br>    Number—plural<br>    Stem or root—from καταλαλιά, ᾶς<br>Concordance References:<br>⇒ Strong's #2636 katalalia<br>⇒ NIV #2896 katalalia<br>⇒ NASB #2636 katalalia<br><br>**2 Cor. 12:20**<br>For I fear, lest, when I come, I shall not find you such as I would, and that I shall be found unto you such as ye would not: lest there be debates, envyings, wraths, strifes, **backbitings**, whisperings, swellings, tumults: [KJV]<br>For I am afraid that perhaps when I come I may find you to be not what I wish and may be found by you to be not what you wish; that perhaps there may be strife, jealousy, angry tempers, disputes, **slanders**, gossip, arrogance, disturbances; [NASB]<br>For I am afraid that when I come I may not find you as I want you to be, and you may not find me as you want me to be. I fear that there may be quarreling, jealousy, outbursts of anger, factions, **slander**, gossip, arrogance and disorder. [NIV]<br>For I fear lest, when I come, I shall not find you such as I wish, and that I shall be found by you such as you do not wish; lest there be contentions, jealousies, outbursts of wrath, selfish ambitions, **backbitings**, whisperings, conceits, tumults; [NKJV]<br>For I am afraid that when I come to visit you I won't like what I find, and then you won't like my response. I am afraid that I will find quarreling, jealousy, outbursts of anger, selfishness, **backstabbing**, gossip, conceit, and disorderly behavior. [NLT]<br>φοβοῦμαι γὰρ μή πως ἐλθών οὐχ οἵους θέλω εὕρω ὑμᾶς, κἀγὼ εὑρεθῶ ὑμῖν οἷον οὐ θέλετε· μή πως ἔρις, ζῆλοι, θυμοί, ἐριθεῖαι, **καταλαλιαί**, ψιθυρισμοί, φυσιώσεις, ἀκαταστασίαι·[GNS] | Slander, backbiting, insult, vilification, verbal attack.<br><br>**Practical Application**<br>This means to criticize, judge, backbite, gossip, censor, condemn, and grumble against another person. It means to talk about and tear down another person, to spread tales about another person that cut and hurt him and that lower his image and reputation in the eyes of others.<br>When we criticize a brother or sister in Christ, we are slandering one of God's own children. Just think: we are actually slandering a son or daughter of God. This alone should keep us from backbiting another believer. |

# PRACTICAL WORD STUDIES
## in the NEW TESTAMENT

| ENGLISH WORD | GREEK WORD AND VERSE | THE WORD MEANS... |
|---|---|---|
| | φοβοῦμαι γὰρ μή πως ἐλθὼν οὐχ οἵους θέλω εὕρω ὑμᾶς κἀγὼ εὑρεθῶ ὑμῖν οἷον οὐ θέλετε· μή πως ἔρις, ζῆλος, θυμοί, ἐριθεῖαι, **καταλαλιαί**, ψιθυρισμοί, φυσιώσεις, ἀκαταστασίαι· [GNT] | |
| **#259**<br>**Backstabbers**<br><br>Backbiters–KJV<br>Slanderers–NASB<br>Slanderers–NIV<br>Backbiters–NKJV<br>**Backstabbers–NLT**<br><br>**POSB REFERENCE**<br>(Rom.1:30)<br>*Deeper Study* #12 | καταλάλους = katalalous<br>Pronunciation: [kat-al'-al-oos]<br>Parsing (part of speech): pronominal adjective<br>    Case—accusative<br>    Gender—masculine<br>    Number—plural<br>    Stem or root—from κατάλαλος, ου<br>Concordance References:<br>  ⇒ Strong's #2637 katalalos<br>  ⇒ NIV #2897 katalalos<br>  ⇒ NASB #2637 katalalos<br><br>**Romans 1:30**<br>**Backbiters**, haters of God, despiteful, proud, boasters, inventors of evil things, disobedient to parents, [KJV]<br>**Slanderers**, haters of God, insolent, arrogant, boastful, inventors of evil, disobedient to parents, [NASB]<br>**Slanderers**, God-haters, insolent, arrogant and boastful; they invent ways of doing evil; they disobey their parents; [NIV]<br>**Backbiters**, haters of God, violent, proud, boasters, inventors of evil things, disobedient to parents, [NKJV]<br>They are **backstabbers**, haters of God, insolent, proud, and boastful. They are forever inventing new ways of sinning and are disobedient to their parents. [NLT]<br>ψιθυριστάς, **καταλάλους**, θεοστυγεῖς, ὑβριστάς, ὑπερηφάνους, ἀλαζόνας, ἐφευρετὰς κακῶν, γονεῦσιν ἀπειθεῖς, [GNS]<br>**καταλάλους** θεοστυγεῖς ὑβριστάς ὑπερηφάνους ἀλαζόνας, ἐφευρετὰς κακῶν, γονεῦσιν ἀπειθεῖς, [GNT] | Slanderers, backbiters, backstabbers; one who speaks evil of another.<br><br>**Practical Application**<br>The word differs from the quiet, secret backstabber. It is a loud, open backstabber, a person who broadcasts the tale. The tale may be true or not: it does not matter. The backbiting slanderer burns within to tell the gossip to everyone. |
| **#260**<br>**Backstabbing**<br><br>Backbitings–KJV<br>Slanders–NASB<br>Slander–NIV<br>Backbitings–NKJV<br>**Backstabbing–NLT**<br><br>**POSB REFERENCE**<br>(2 Cor.12:19-21; esp. v.20)<br>Note 3, point 2<br><br>See also POSB REF:<br>(1 Pet.2:1)<br>Note 1, point 5 | καταλαλιαί = katalaliai<br>Pronunciation: [kat-al-al-ee'-ah-ee]<br>Parsing (part of speech): noun<br>    Case—nominative<br>    Gender—feminine<br>    Number—plural<br>    Stem or root—from καταλαλιά, ᾶς<br>Concordance References:<br>  ⇒ Strong's #2636 katalalia<br>  ⇒ NIV #2896 katalalia<br>  ⇒ NASB #2636 katalalia<br><br>**2 Cor. 12:20**<br>For I fear, lest, when I come, I shall not find you such as I would, and that I shall be found unto you such as ye would not: lest there be debates, envyings, wraths, strifes, **backbitings**, whisperings, swellings, tumults: [KJV]<br>For I am afraid that perhaps when I come I may find you to be not what I wish and may be found by you to be not what you wish; that perhaps there may be strife, jealousy, angry tempers, disputes, **slanders**, gossip, arrogance, disturbances; [NASB]<br>For I am afraid that when I come I may not find you as I want you to be, and you may not find me as you want me to be. I fear that there may be quarreling, jealousy, outbursts of anger, factions, **slander**, gossip, arrogance and disorder. [NIV]<br>For I fear lest, when I come, I shall not find you such as I wish, and that I shall be found by you such as you do not wish; lest there be contentions, jealousies, outbursts of wrath, selfish ambitions, **backbitings**, whisperings, conceits, tumults; [NKJV]<br>For I am afraid that when I come to visit you I won't like what I find, and then you won't like my response. I am afraid that I will find quarreling, jealousy, outbursts of anger, selfishness, **backstabbing**, gossip, conceit, and disorderly behavior. [NLT] | Slander, backbiting, insult, vilification, verbal attack.<br><br>**Practical Application**<br>This means to criticize, judge, backbite, gossip, censor, condemn, and grumble against another person. It means to talk about and tear down another person, to spread tales about another person that cut and hurt him and that lower his image and reputation in the eyes of others.<br>When we criticize a brother or sister in Christ, we are slandering one of God's own children. Just think: we are actually slandering a son or daughter of God. This alone should keep us from backbiting another believer. |

# Practical Word Studies
## in the New Testament

| ENGLISH WORD | GREEK WORD AND VERSE | THE WORD MEANS... |
|---|---|---|
| | φοβοῦμαι γὰρ μή πως ἐλθὼν οὐχ οἵους θέλω εὕρω ὑμᾶς, κἀγὼ εὑρεθῶ ὑμῖν οἷον οὐ θέλετε· μή πως ἔρις, ζῆλοι, θυμοί, ἐριθεῖαι, **καταλαλιαί**, ψιθυρισμοί, φυσιώσεις, ἀκαταστασίαι· [GNS]<br><br>φοβοῦμαι γὰρ μή πως ἐλθὼν οὐχ οἵους θέλω εὕρω ὑμᾶς κἀγὼ εὑρεθῶ ὑμῖν οἷον οὐ θέλετε· μή πως ἔρις, ζῆλος, θυμοί, ἐριθεῖαι, **καταλαλιαί**, ψιθυρισμοί, φυσιώσεις, ἀκαταστασίαι· [GNT] | |
| **#261**<br>**Bag**<br><br>Scrip–KJV<br>**Bag–NASB**<br>**Bag–NIV**<br>Knapsack–NKJV<br>Traveler's bag–NLT<br><br>**POSB REFERENCE**<br>(Lk.10:4)<br>Note 4, point 1 | **πήραν** = përan<br>Pronunciation: [pay'-rahn]<br>Parsing (part of speech): noun<br>    Case—accusative<br>    Gender—feminine<br>    Number—singular<br>    Stem or root—from πήρα, ας<br>Concordance References:<br>⇒ Strong's #4082 pēra<br>⇒ NIV #4385 pēra<br>⇒ NASB #4082 pēra<br><br>**Luke 10:4**<br>Carry neither purse, nor **scrip**, nor shoes: and salute no man by the way. [KJV]<br>"Carry no purse, no **bag**, no shoes; and greet no one on the way. [NASB]<br>Do not take a purse or **bag** or sandals; and do not greet anyone on the road. [NIV]<br>Carry neither money bag, **knapsack**, nor sandals; and greet no one along the road. [NKJV]<br>Don't take along any money, or a **traveler's bag**, or even an extra pair of sandals. And don't stop to greet anyone on the road. [NLT]<br>μὴ βαστάζετε βαλάντιον, μὴ **πήραν**, μὴ ὑποδήματα· καὶ μηδένα κατὰ τὴν ὁδὸν ἀσπάσησθε. [GNS]<br>μὴ βαστάζετε βαλλάντιον, μὴ **πήραν**, μὴ ὑποδήματα, καὶ μηδένα κατὰ τὴν ὁδὸν ἀσπάσησθε. [GNT] | A traveler's bag, wallet, or sack usually made of animal skin (leather). This bag was used to carry the possessions that a traveler would need for his journey.<br><br>**Practical Application**<br>Note Jesus' clear instructions: they were not to carry a money-bag (purse, *ballantion*) or a traveler's bag (*përan*) or two pair of sandals. They were to trust God for provisions, not worrying about money for food, housing, or clothing (Matthew 6:24-34). Worrying about such things would be cumbersome, taking away precious time that should be spent in ministering. Also, they were preaching a message of faith and trust in God. They needed to live what they were preaching and become a living picture of the dependency that God wants from every man. |
| **#262**<br>**Band**<br><br>**Band–KJV**<br>Cohort–NASB<br>Detachment of soldiers– NIV<br>Detachment of troops–NKJV<br>Battalion of Roman soldiers–NLT<br><br>**POSB REFERENCE**<br>(Jn.18:3)<br>Deeper Study #1 | **σπεῖραν** = speiran<br>Pronunciation: [spi'-rahn]<br>Parsing (part of speech): noun<br>    Case—accusative<br>    Gender—feminine<br>    Number—singular<br>    Stem or root—from σπεῖρα, ης<br>Concordance References:<br>⇒ Strong's #4686 speira<br>⇒ NIV #5061 speira<br>⇒ NASB #4686 speira<br><br>**John 18:3**<br>Judas then, having received a **band** of men and officers from the chief priests and Pharisees, cometh thither with lanterns and torches and weapons. [KJV]<br>Judas then, having received the Roman **cohort**, and officers from the chief priests and the Pharisees, came there with lanterns and torches and weapons. [NASB]<br>So Judas came to the grove, guiding a **detachment of soldiers** and some officials from the chief priests and Pharisees. They were carrying torches, lanterns and weapons. [NIV]<br>Then Judas, having received a **detachment of troops**, and officers from the chief priests and Pharisees, came there with lanterns, torches, and weapons. [NKJV]<br>The leading priests and Pharisees had given Judas a **battalion of Roman soldiers** and Temple guards to accompany him. Now with blazing torches, lanterns, and weapons, they arrived at the olive grove. [NLT]<br>ὁ οὖν Ἰούδας, λαβὼν τὴν **σπεῖραν**, καὶ ἐκ τῶν ἀρχιερέων καὶ Φαρισαίων ὑπηρέτας ἔρχεται ἐκεῖ μετὰ φανῶν καὶ λαμπάδων καὶ ὅπλων. [GNS]<br>ὁ οὖν Ἰούδας λαβὼν τὴν **σπεῖραν** καὶ ἐκ τῶν ἀρχιερέων καὶ ἐκ τῶν Φαρισαίων ὑπηρέτας ἔρχεται ἐκεῖ μετὰ φανῶν καὶ λαμπάδων καὶ ὅπλων. [GNT] | A detachment; a company; a battalion; a band; a cohort of Roman soldiers; a regiment.<br><br>**Practical Application**<br>This usually meant a cohort or battalion which was made up of six hundred soldiers. However, "band" (*speiran*) sometimes meant maniple. Every detachment of soldiers consisted of three maniples, about two hundred soldiers. Which is meant here is not known. Most believe the number of soldiers was large, certainly close to the two hundred serving in a maniple. |

## PRACTICAL WORD STUDIES
### in the New Testament

| ENGLISH WORD | GREEK WORD AND VERSE | THE WORD MEANS... |
|---|---|---|
| **#263**<br>**Band Of Soldiers**<br><br>Band of soldiers–KJV<br>Cohort–NASB<br>Company of soldiers–NIV<br>Garrison–NKJV<br>Battalion–NLT<br><br>**POSB REFERENCE**<br>(Mt.27:26-38; esp. v.27)<br>Note 2, point 2 | σπεῖραν = *speiran*<br>Pronunciation: [spi'-rahn]<br>Parsing (part of speech): noun<br>  Case—accusative<br>  Gender—feminine<br>  Number—singular<br>  Stem or root—from σπεῖρα, ης<br>Concordance References:<br>  ⇒ Strong's #4686 speira<br>  ⇒ NIV #5061 speira<br>  ⇒ NASB #4686 speira<br><br>**Matthew 27:27**<br>Then the soldiers of the governor took Jesus into the common hall, and gathered unto him the whole **band of soldiers**. [KJV]<br>Then the soldiers of the governor took Jesus into the Praetorium and gathered the whole Roman **cohort** around Him. [NASB]<br>Then the governor's soldiers took Jesus into the Praetorium and gathered the whole **company of soldiers** around him. [NIV]<br>Then the soldiers of the governor took Jesus into the Praetorium and gathered the whole **garrison** around Him. [NKJV]<br>Some of the governor's soldiers took Jesus into their headquarters and called out the entire **battalion**. [NLT]<br>Τότε οἱ στρατιῶται τοῦ ἡγεμόνος παραλαβόντες τὸν Ἰησοῦν εἰς τὸ πραιτώριον συνήγαγον ἐπ' αὐτὸν ὅλην τὴν σπεῖραν· [GNS]<br>Τότε οἱ στρατιῶται τοῦ ἡγεμόνος παραλαβόντες τὸν Ἰησοῦν εἰς τὸ πραιτώριον συνήγαγον ἐπ' αὐτὸν ὅλην τὴν σπεῖραν. [GNT] | A company, battalion, detachment, garrison or band of soldiers; a regiment.<br><br>**Practical Application**<br>This usually meant a cohort or battalion which was made up of six hundred soldiers. However, "band of soldiers" (*speiran*) sometimes meant maniple. Every cohort consisted of three maniples, about two hundred soldiers. Which is meant here is not known. Most believe the number of soldiers was large, certainly close to the two hundred serving in a maniple. |
| **#264**<br>**Banquetings**<br><br>Banquetings–KJV<br>Drinking parties–NASB<br>Carousing–NIV<br>Drinking parties–NKJV<br>Wild parties–NLT<br><br>**POSB REFERENCE**<br>(1 Pt.4:3)<br>Note 3, point 5 | πότοις = *potois*<br>Pronunciation: [pot'-oys]<br>Parsing (part of speech): noun<br>  Case—dative<br>  Gender—masculine<br>  Number—plural<br>  Stem or root—from πότος, ου<br>Concordance References:<br>  ⇒ Strong's #4224 potos<br>  ⇒ NIV #4542 potos<br>  ⇒ NASB #4224 potos<br><br>**1 Peter 4:3**<br>For the time past of our life may suffice us to have wrought the will of the Gentiles, when we walked in lasciviousness, lusts, excess of wine, revellings, **banquetings**, and abominable idolatries: [KJV]<br>For the time already past is sufficient for you to have carried out the desire of the Gentiles, having pursued a course of sensuality, lusts, drunkenness, carousals, **drinking parties** and abominable idolatries. [NASB]<br>For you have spent enough time in the past doing what pagans choose to do—living in debauchery, lust, drunkenness, orgies, **carousing** and detestable idolatry. [NIV]<br>For we have spent enough of our past lifetime in doing the will of the Gentiles—when we walked in lewdness, lusts, drunkenness, revelries, **drinking parties**, and abominable idolatries. [NKJV]<br>You have had enough in the past of the evil things that godless people enjoy—their immorality and lust, their feasting and drunkenness and **wild parties**, and their terrible worship of idols. [NLT]<br>ἀρκετὸς γὰρ ἡμῖν ὁ παρεληλυθὼς χρόνος τὸ βίου τὸ θέλημα τῶν ἐθνῶν κατεργάσασθαι, πεπορευμένους ἐν ἀσελγείαις, ἐπιθυμίαις, οἰνοφλυγίαις, κώμοις, **πότοις**, καὶ ἀθεμίτοις εἰδωλολατρείαις·[GNS] | Carousing, banquetings, drunkenness; drinking parties; wild parties; partying and getting drunk; a drunken orgy.<br><br>**Practical Application**<br>The believer's life is divided into two parts: *his old life* and *his new life*. Note the force of this verse: in his *old life*, he sinned enough. He has already followed the desires and lusts of the ungodly (Gentiles) enough. He has already worked the will of the ungodly. He has walked after them, walked just as they walk, and enough is enough. The believer is no longer to fulfill the desires of the flesh. |

# PRACTICAL WORD STUDIES
## in the NEW TESTAMENT

| ENGLISH WORD | GREEK WORD AND VERSE | THE WORD MEANS... |
|---|---|---|
| | ἀρκετὸς γὰρ ὁ παρεληλυθὼς χρόνος τὸ βούλημα τῶν ἐθνῶν κατειργάσθαι πεπορευμένους ἐν ἀσελγείαις, ἐπιθυμίαις, οἰνοφλυγίαις, κώμοις, **πότοις** καὶ ἀθεμίτοις εἰδωλολατρίαις. [GNT] | |
| **#265**<br>**Banquets, Enjoying**<br><br>Eating–KJV<br>Eating–NASB<br>Eating–NIV<br>Eating–NKJV<br>Enjoying banquets–NLT<br><br>**POSB REFERENCE**<br>(Mt.24:38)<br>*Deeper Study #3* | τρώγοντες = *trōgontes*<br>Pronunciation: [tro'-gon-tes]<br>Parsing (part of speech): verb<br>   Mood—participle<br>   Tense—present<br>   Voice—active<br>   Case—nominative<br>   Gender—masculine<br>   Number—plural<br>   Stem or root—from τρώγω<br>Concordance References:<br>⇒ Strong's #5176 trōgō<br>⇒ NIV #5592 trōgō<br>⇒ NASB #5176 trōgō<br><br>**Matthew 24:38**<br>For as in the days that were before the flood they were **eating** and drinking, marrying and giving in marriage, until the day that Noe entered into the ark, [KJV]<br>"For as in those days which were before the flood they were **eating** and drinking, they were marrying and giving in marriage, until the day that Noah entered the ark, [NASB]<br>For in the days before the flood, people were **eating** and drinking, marrying and giving in marriage, up to the day Noah entered the ark; [NIV]<br>For as in the days before the flood, they were **eating** and drinking, marrying and giving in marriage, until the day that Noah entered the ark, [NKJV]<br>In those days before the Flood, the people were **enjoying banquets** and parties and weddings right up to the time Noah entered his boat. [NLT]<br>ὥσπερ γὰρ ἦσαν ἐν ταῖς ἡμέραις ταῖς πρὸ τοῦ κατακλυσμοῦ **τρώγοντες** καὶ πίνοντες, γαμοῦντες καὶ ἐκγαμίζοντες, ἄχρι ἧς ἡμέρας εἰσῆλθε Νῶε εἰς τὴν κιβωτόν, [GNS]<br>ὡς γὰρ ἦσαν ἐν ταῖς ἡμέραις [ἐκείναις] ταῖς πρὸ τοῦ κατακλυσμοῦ **τρώγοντες** καὶ πίνοντες, γαμοῦντες καὶ γαμίζοντες, ἄχρι ἧς ἡμέρας εἰσῆλθεν Νῶε εἰς τὴν κιβωτόν, [GNT] | To eat; to gnaw; to chew; to feed on. It has the idea of grabbing and gnawing greedily like a hungry dog.<br><br>**Practical Application**<br>Here it means the habitual practice of eating with a gluttonous appetite, eating excessively.<br>The gluttonous, the well-fed are those who are filled with all that the world has to offer; in essence, they are full of themselves, their own desires, urges, and cravings. They have no hunger for righteousness at all. Scripture identifies the full as those...<br>• who fill their bellies with the pods of the world (Luke 15:16).<br>• who serve their own personal interests and not the Lord Jesus Christ (Romans 16:18).<br>• who indulge in the foods (things, sins) of the world (1 Cor. 6:13; cp. 1 Cor. 6:9-13).<br>• who make their god their appetite (Phil. 3:19).<br>• who "became full of every kind of wickedness, sin, greed, hate, envy, murder, fighting, deception, malicious behavior, and gossip. They are backstabbers, haters of God, insolent, proud, and boastful. They are forever inventing new ways of sinning and are disobedient to their parents. They refuse to understand, break their promises, and are heartless and unforgiving. They are fully aware of God's death penalty for those who do these things, yet they go right ahead and do them anyway. And, worse yet, they encourage others to do them, too" (Romans 1:29-32).<br>The judgment of the full will be hunger. This means they...<br>• will leave all that filled them behind when they die (Luke 12:20; Luke 16:25).<br>• will have no desires filled after this life.<br>• will have no delights fulfilled throughout eternity.<br>• will hunger for good things (righteous things) throughout eternity. |
| **#266**<br>**Baptize**<br><br>**Baptize–KJV**<br>**Baptize–NASB**<br>**Baptize–NIV**<br>**Baptize–NKJV**<br>**Baptize–NLT**<br><br>**POSB REFERENCE**<br>(Mt.3:11)<br>*Deeper Study #2*<br><br>**See also POSB REF:**<br>(Lk.3:16)<br>*Deeper Study #1* | βαπτίσει = *baptisei*<br>Pronunciation: [bap-tis'-see]<br>Parsing (part of speech): verb<br>   Mood—indicative<br>   Tense—future<br>   Voice—active<br>   Person—3rd person<br>   Number—singular<br>   Stem or root—from βαπτίζω<br>Concordance References:<br>⇒ Strong's #907 baptizō<br>⇒ NIV #966 baptizō<br>⇒ NASB #907 baptizō<br><br>**Matthew 3:11**<br>I indeed baptize you with water unto repentance: but he that cometh after me is mightier than I, whose shoes I am not worthy to bear: he shall **baptize** you with the Holy Ghost, and with fire: [KJV]<br>"As for me, I baptize you with water for repentance, but He who is coming after me is mightier than I, and I am not fit to remove His sandals; He will **baptize** you with | To baptize; to dip; to immerse; to wash; to submerge; to place into.<br><br>**Practical Application**<br>In this Scripture, two kinds of baptism are noted:<br>⇒ There is the baptism with water for repentance; the baptism that was given by John.<br>⇒ There is the baptism with the Holy Spirit and with fire, the baptism that is given by Christ.<br>Note the distinctions between the two baptisms:<br>1. John's baptism was both a preparation and a symbol of the spiritual baptism that Jesus was to bring. John's water baptism meant two things.<br>  a. It symbolized cleansing from all sin. A person was being prepared for the cleansing that Christ would provide.<br>  b. It symbolized separation or dedication. A |

# PRACTICAL WORD STUDIES
## in the NEW TESTAMENT

| ENGLISH WORD | GREEK WORD AND VERSE | THE WORD MEANS... |
|---|---|---|
| | the Holy Spirit and fire. [NASB]<br>"I baptize you with water for repentance. But after me will come one who is more powerful than I, whose sandals I am not fit to carry. He will **baptize** you with the Holy Spirit and with fire. [NIV]<br>I indeed baptize you with water unto repentance, but He who is coming after me is mightier than I, whose sandals I am not worthy to carry. He will **baptize** you with the Holy Spirit and fire. [NKJV]<br>"I baptize with water those who turn from their sins and turn to God. But someone is coming soon who is far greater than I am—so much greater that I am not even worthy to be his slave. He will **baptize** you with the Holy Spirit and with fire. [NLT]<br>ἐγὼ μὲν βαπτίζω ὑμᾶς ἐν ὕδατι εἰς μετάνοιαν· ὁ δὲ ὀπίσω μου ἐρχόμενος ἰσχυρότερός μού ἐστιν, οὗ οὐκ εἰμὶ ἱκανὸς τὰ ὑποδήματα βαστάσαι· αὐτὸς ὑμᾶς **βαπτίσει** ἐν Πνεύματι Ἁγίῳ καὶ πυρί· [GNS]<br>ἐγὼ μὲν ὑμᾶς βαπτίζω ἐν ὕδατι εἰς μετάνοιαν, ὁ δὲ ὀπίσω μου ἐρχόμενος ἰσχυρότερός μού ἐστιν, οὗ οὐκ εἰμὶ ἱκανὸς τὰ ὑποδήματα βαστάσαι· αὐτὸς ὑμᾶς **βαπτίσει** ἐν πνεύματι ἁγίῳ καὶ πυρί· [GNT] | person was setting his life apart to God in a renewed spirit of dedication. He was committing himself to the Christ about whom John was preaching.<br>Note: John's baptism is called "the baptism of repentance"; that is, the person who repented was baptized. There could be no question; it was understood: if a person repented and actually turned to the Lord, he was baptized.<br>2. Jesus' spiritual baptism was a double baptism. (Only one preposition is used in the Greek for "the Spirit and fire," the preposition "in.")<br>a. Jesus baptizes the person in the Spirit. He dips, immerses, and places the person in the Spirit. Whereas the person was carnal and materialistic minded, he now becomes spiritual minded (Romans 8:5-7). The Jews had looked and longed for the day when the Spirit would come. The prophets had predicted His coming time and again. Therefore, the people knew exactly what John was predicting. The Spirit was expected to awaken and excite the people to such a degree that they would mobilize behind the Messiah and follow Him in the overthrow of all oppressors. The Spirit was to lead the people in freeing Israel and establishing it as one of the greatest nations on earth (cp. Ezekiel 36:26-27; Ezekiel 37:14; Ezekiel 39:29; Isaiah 44:3; Joel 2:28).<br>b. Jesus baptizes the person in fire. Fire has several functions that graphically symbolize the work of Christ. It illuminates, warms, melts, burns, and utterly destroys. The difference between baptism with water and fire is the difference between an outward work and an inward work. Water only cleanses the outside; fire purifies within, that is, the heart. Jesus Christ separates a person from his former life and purifies him within by the fire of His Spirit. It should be noted that in John's mind the "baptism of fire" meant that the Messiah was to destroy the enemies of Israel. It was "the messianic fire of judgment" that was to come from the throne of David (see POSB *Deeper Study* #2—Matthew 1:18; POSB notes—Matthew 11:1-6; POSB note—Matthew 11:2-3; POSB *Deeper Study* #1—Matthew 11:5; POSB *Deeper Study* #2—Matthew 11:6; POSB *Deeper Study* #1—Matthew 12:16; POSB *Deeper Study* #1—Matthew 22:42; POSB note—Luke 7:21.) |
| **#267**<br>**Bare**<br><br>Bare–KJV<br>Carried–NASB<br>Carried–NIV<br>Bore–NKJV<br>Removed–NLT | ἐβάστασεν = *ebastasen*<br>Pronunciation: [eh-bas-ta'-sen]<br>Parsing (part of speech): verb<br>   Mood—indicative<br>   Tense—aorist<br>   Voice—active<br>   Person—3rd person<br>   Number—singular<br>   Stem or root—from βαστάζω<br>Concordance References:<br>  ⇒ Strong's #941 bastazō<br>  ⇒ NIV #1002 bastazō | To bear; to bear with; to endure; to take up; to carry; to support; to sustain; to remove; to endure hardship.<br><br>**Practical Application**<br>In this Scripture, Christ did not just heal our sicknesses as any other minister, but He "Himself took (*elaben*) our infirmities, and bare (*ebastasen*) our sicknesses." This means at least two things. |

# PRACTICAL WORD STUDIES
## in the NEW TESTAMENT

| ENGLISH WORD | GREEK WORD AND VERSE | THE WORD MEANS... |
|---|---|---|
| **POSB REFERENCE** (Mt.8:17) Note 3 | ⇒ NASB #941 bastazö<br><br>**Matthew 8:17**<br>That it might be fulfilled which was spoken by Esaias the prophet, saying, Himself took our infirmities, and **bare** our sicknesses. [KJV]<br>In order that what was spoken through Isaiah the prophet might be fulfilled, saying, "He Himself took our infirmities, and **CARRIED** AWAY OUR DISEASES." [NASB]<br>This was to fulfill what was spoken through the prophet Isaiah: "He took up our infirmities and **carried** our diseases." [NIV]<br>That it might be fulfilled which was spoken by Isaiah the prophet, saying: "He Himself took our infirmities And **bore** our sicknesses." [NKJV]<br>This fulfilled the word of the Lord through Isaiah, who said, "He took our sicknesses and **removed** our diseases." [NLT]<br>ὅπως πληρωθῇ τὸ ῥηθὲν διὰ Ἡσαΐου τοῦ προφήτου, λέγοντος, Αὐτὸς τὰς ἀσθενείας ἡμῶν ἔλαβε, καὶ τὰς νόσους **ἐβάστασεν**. [GNS]<br>ὅπως πληρωθῇ τὸ ῥηθὲν διὰ Ἡσαΐου τοῦ προφήτου λέγοντος, Αὐτὸς τὰς ἀσθενείας ἡμῶν ἔλαβεν καὶ τὰς νόσους **ἐβάστασεν**. [GNT] | 1. He carried our infirmities and sicknesses to the ultimate degree when He died on the cross for us. It was there that He bore them (see POSB *Deeper Study #2*—Mt.8:17 for discussion). (Cp. Jn.1:29.)<br>2. He carried each fresh illness in a way that will never be understood.<br>  a. Each need that stood before Him was a reminder that He had to bear the sin of the world. And He knew what this meant and all that it was to include. Seeing the needs of people standing before Him reminded Him of the suffering He was to bear.<br>  b. Each need that He met was a "foretaste of the cross. The thought of what He had to bear was upon His mind day by day and hour by hour as He went about ministering. This was bound to weigh ever so heavily upon Him. |
| **#268**<br>**Bare Witness– Borne Witness**<br><br>Bare witness–KJV<br>Borne witness–NASB<br>Testified–NIV<br>Borne witness–NKJV<br>Preached–NLT<br><br>**POSB REFERENCE** (Jn.5:33-35; esp. v.33) Note 3, point 1 | μεμαρτύρηκεν = memarturëken<br>Pronunciation: [meh-mar-too-ray'-kehn]<br>Parsing (part of speech): verb<br>  Mood—indicative<br>  Tense—perfect<br>  Voice—active<br>  Person—3rd person<br>  Number—singular<br>  Stem or root—from μαρτυρέω<br>Concordance References:<br>⇒ Strong's #3140 martureö<br>⇒ NIV #3455 martureö<br>⇒ NASB #3140 martureö<br><br>**John 5:33**<br>Ye sent unto John, and he **bare witness** unto the truth. [KJV]<br>"You have sent to John, and he has **borne witness** to the truth. [NASB]<br>"You have sent to John and he has **testified** to the truth. [NIV]<br>You have sent to John, and he has **borne witness** to the truth. [NKJV]<br>In fact, you sent messengers to listen to John the Baptist, and he **preached** the truth. [NLT]<br>ὑμεῖς ἀπεστάλκατε πρὸς Ἰωάννην, καὶ **μεμαρτύρηκε** τῇ ἀληθείᾳ. [GNS]<br>ὑμεῖς ἀπεστάλκατε πρὸς Ἰωάννην, καὶ **μεμαρτύρηκεν** τῇ ἀληθείᾳ· [GNT] | A permanent and continuing witness; to testify; to preach; to bear witness; to speak well of; to approve; to affirm; to confirm; to tell about.<br><br>**Practical Application**<br>John's message was not a fly-by-night witness that appeared on the scene and suddenly disappeared. His witness continued and still continues and will always continue. It was a trustworthy message, a witness to the truth. (Cp. John 1:19-27, 29-36.) |
| **#269**<br>**Barren**<br><br>Barren–KJV<br>Useless–NASB<br>Ineffective–NIV<br>Barren–NKJV<br>Productive–NLT<br><br>**POSB REFERENCE** (2 Pt.1:8-11; esp. v.8) Note 2, point 1 | ἀργούς = argous<br>Pronunciation: [ar-goos']<br>Parsing (part of speech): adjective<br>  Case—accusative<br>  Gender—masculine<br>  Number—plural<br>  Stem or root—from ἀργός, ή, όν<br>Concordance References:<br>⇒ Strong's #692 argos<br>⇒ NIV #734 argos<br>⇒ NASB #692 argos<br><br>**2 Peter 1:8**<br>For if these things be in you, and abound, they make you that ye shall neither be **barren** nor unfruitful in the knowledge of our Lord Jesus Christ. [KJV]<br>For if these qualities are yours and are increasing, they | To be ineffective; to be barren; to be lazy; to be careless; to be doing nothing. It means to be idle and slothful, empty and useless.<br><br>**Practical Application**<br>It is the very opposite of being fruitful and productive in life. Therefore if we possess *these things*, if we really work at our salvation, we will not live an ineffective, dry life. We will not be unfruitful nor live a life that is empty and useless, idle and slothful. On the contrary, we will live a life that flows with nourishment and that bears the ripest of fruit: love, joy, and peace (cp. Galatians 5:22-23).<br>But note the source of such a life: the source |

# PRACTICAL WORD STUDIES
## in the NEW TESTAMENT

| ENGLISH WORD | GREEK WORD AND VERSE | THE WORD MEANS... |
|---|---|---|
| | render you neither **useless** nor unfruitful in the true knowledge of our Lord Jesus Christ. [NASB]<br>  For if you possess these qualities in increasing measure, they will keep you from being **ineffective** and unproductive in your knowledge of our Lord Jesus Christ. [NIV]<br>  For if these things are yours and abound, you will be neither **barren** nor unfruitful in the knowledge of our Lord Jesus Christ. [NKJV]<br>  The more you grow like this, the more you will become **productive** and useful in your knowledge of our Lord Jesus Christ. [NLT]<br>  ταῦτα γὰρ ὑμῖν ὑπάρχοντα, καὶ πλεονάζοντα, οὐκ **ἀργοὺς** οὐδὲ ἀκάρπους καθίστησιν εἰς τὴν τοῦ Κυρίου ἡμῶν Ἰησοῦ Χριστοῦ ἐπίγνωσιν· [GNS]<br>  ταῦτα γὰρ ὑμῖν ὑπάρχοντα καὶ πλεονάζοντα οὐκ **ἀργοὺς** οὐδὲ ἀκάρπους καθίστησιν εἰς τὴν τοῦ κυρίου ἡμῶν Ἰησοῦ Χριστοῦ ἐπίγνωσιν· [GNT] | is our Lord Jesus Christ. We must know Him and grow in the knowledge of Him. The knowledge of Him must be our aim and purpose in life. Only as we know Him can we overcome the barrenness and unfruitfulness of life. He and He alone can give us real life. Therefore, we must possess *these things*—really work at our salvation—really seek fellowship and communion with Christ moment by moment and day by day—in order not to be barren or unfruitful in the knowledge of Him. We must learn to pray all day long and to take *set times* for prayer every day, set times for concentrated prayer. We must learn to *keep our minds* on Christ. |
| **#270**<br>**Base**<br><br>Base–KJV<br>Meek–NASB<br>Timid–NIV<br>Lowly–NKJV<br>Timid–NLT<br><br>**POSB REFERENCE**<br>(2 Cor.10:1-2; esp. v.1)<br>Note 1 | ταπεινός = *tapeinos*<br>Pronunciation: [tap-i-nos']<br>Parsing (part of speech): adjective<br>   Case—nominative<br>   Gender—masculine<br>   Number—singular<br>   Stem or root—from ταπεινός, ή, όν<br>Concordance References:<br>  ⇒ Strong's #5011 tapeinos<br>  ⇒ NIV #5424 tapeinos<br>  ⇒ NASB #5011 tapeinos<br><br>**2 Cor. 10:1**<br>Now I Paul myself beseech you by the meekness and gentleness of Christ, who in presence am **base** among you, but being absent am bold toward you: [KJV]<br>  Now I, Paul, myself urge you by the meekness and gentleness of Christ— I who am **meek** when face to face with you, but bold toward you when absent! [NASB]<br>  By the meekness and gentleness of Christ, I appeal to you—I, Paul, who am "**timid**" when face to face with you, but "bold" when away! [NIV]<br>  Now I, Paul, myself am pleading with you by the meekness and gentleness of Christ—who in presence am **lowly** among you, but being absent am bold toward you. [NKJV]<br>  Now I, Paul, plead with you. I plead with the gentleness and kindness that Christ himself would use, even though some of you say I am bold in my letters but **timid** in person. [NLT]<br>  Αὐτὸς δὲ ἐγὼ Παῦλος παρακαλῶ ὑμᾶς διὰ τῆς πραότητος καὶ ἐπιεικείας τοῦ Χριστοῦ, ὃς κατὰ πρόσωπον μὲν **ταπεινὸς** ἐν ὑμῖν, ἀπὼν δὲ θαρρῶ εἰς ὑμᾶς· [GNS]<br>  Αὐτὸς δὲ ἐγὼ Παῦλος παρακαλῶ ὑμᾶς διὰ τῆς πραΰτητος καὶ ἐπιεικείας τοῦ Χριστοῦ, ὃς κατὰ πρόσωπον μὲν **ταπεινὸς** ἐν ὑμῖν, ἀπὼν δὲ θαρρῶ εἰς ὑμᾶς· [GNT] | Timid, meek, base, humble, lowly, gentle.<br><br>**Practical Application**<br>Some were saying that Paul was a coward. This is what is meant by the word "base" (*tapeinos*). They were saying that Paul was bold in his instructions; that is, he rebuked the church when he was writing to them, but he was a coward when it came to speaking face to face with them. |
| **#271**<br>**Basic Principles**<br><br>Rudiments–KJV<br>Elementary principles–NASB<br>**Basic principles–NIV**<br>**Basic principles–NKJV**<br>Evil powers–NLT | στοιχείων = *stoicheiön*<br>Pronunciation: [stoy-khi'-on]<br>Parsing (part of speech): noun<br>   Case—genitive<br>   Gender—neuter<br>   Number—plural<br>   Stem or root—from στοιχεῖα, ων<br>Concordance References:<br>  ⇒ Strong's #4747 stoicheion<br>  ⇒ NIV #5122 stoicheion<br>  ⇒ NASB #4747 stoicheion<br><br>**Col. 2:20**<br>Wherefore if ye be dead with Christ from the **rudiments** of the world, why, as though living in the world, | Basic principles; rudiments; elements; elementary principles; first lessons; evil powers.<br><br>**Practical Application**<br>The term "basic principles" (*stoicheiön*) means two things and Christ saves us from both. (See POSB note, Philosophy—Col. 2:8 for more discussion.)<br>1. *Basic principles* means crude notions of men about the universe—that is, about God, reality, and truth. It is man's ideas and philosophies, their elementary or rudimentary teachings, their ABC understanding of God and the |

# PRACTICAL WORD STUDIES
## in the NEW TESTAMENT

| ENGLISH WORD | GREEK WORD AND VERSE | THE WORD MEANS... |
|---|---|---|
| **POSB REFERENCE** (Col.2:20) Note 1 | are ye subject to ordinances, [KJV]<br>If you have died with Christ to the **elementary principles** of the world, why, as if you were living in the world, do you submit yourself to decrees, such as, [NASB]<br>Since you died with Christ to the **basic principles** of this world, why, as though you still belonged to it, do you submit to its rules: [NIV]<br>Therefore, if you died with Christ from the **basic principles** of the world, why, as though living in the world, do you subject yourselves to regulations— [NKJV]<br>You have died with Christ, and he has set you free from the **evil powers** of this world. So why do you keep on following rules of the world, such as, [NLT]<br>Εἰ οὖν ἀπεθάνετε σὺν τῷ Χριστῷ, ἀπὸ τῶν **στοιχείων** τοῦ κόσμου, τί ὡς ζῶντες ἐν κόσμῳ δογματίζεσθε, [GNS]<br>Εἰ ἀπεθάνετε σὺν Χριστῷ ἀπὸ τῶν **στοιχείων** τοῦ κόσμου, τί ὡς ζῶντες ἐν κόσμῳ δογματίζεσθε; [GNT] | universe, reality, and truth. When men think of God, they come up with all kinds of ways and laws to reach Him and to secure His approval and acceptance. However, there are three basic problems with man's approach to God.<br>a. First, we cannot keep rules and laws—not in a perfect sense. No matter what way we choose to reach God, we cannot walk a straight path to Him.<br>b. Second, once we have broken a rule or law, we stand guilty before God. Therefore, we must be judged, condemned, and punished for having broken the law. A law breaker is guilty and unacceptable and the punishment must be borne. Therefore, rules and laws cannot make us acceptable to God. They can only lead to guilt and condemnation.<br>c. Third, we die; we do not live forever. Moreover, there is no law or force on this earth that can give us the energy and power to live forever. Rules and laws only condemn us when we break them. They have no power to save us from death nor to give us eternal life. Because of this, rules and laws cannot be the way to approach God.<br>　How then can we approach God? If the best thinking of men about the universe and God are not the way to approach God, what is the way? The answer will be discussed in a moment, but first look at the second meaning of the term b*asic principles*.<br>2. *Basic principles* means the basic elements or materials of the universe, the things that men say lie behind the universe or at the very base of reality. Down through the centuries men have posed all kinds of forces, energies, powers, principalities, spirits, angels, and beings as standing behind the universe and life. As a result, men have committed their lives to and worshipped all sorts of creatures and forces or elements and materials. However, there is a critical problem with this approach to God, a problem that dooms all who seek truth and who approach God through the elements of this universe or through the spirits of the spiritual world.<br>a. First, there is the problem of corruption. Everything in the universe is corruptible, aging, dying, deteriorating, and decaying. Therefore, there is nothing in the universe that can save man, for the way of all things—all elements and all materials—is the way of change and death.<br>b. Second, there is a problem with seeking truth and God through the spirits or angels of a spiritual world.<br>⇒ First, man cannot penetrate the spiritual world. He is physical, and the physical just cannot move over into the world of the spiritual no matter what any person claims. If the spiritual world is ever to be known, then the spiritual has to reveal itself to us. |

# PRACTICAL WORD STUDIES
## in the NEW TESTAMENT

| ENGLISH WORD | GREEK WORD AND VERSE | THE WORD MEANS... |
|---|---|---|
| | | ⇒ Second, any person who claims to have been given visions or revelations by the spiritual world still has the same problems that everyone else has: the problems of imperfection (unrighteousness), death, and eternal life. No angel, spirit, or any other intermediary has ever taken care of the problem of sin and death and of eternal life for us. We have already sinned, and we are already imperfect. Therefore, someone, someplace must *bear our sin* or punishment for us or else we have to pay for it ourselves. And, in addition, someone has to go through the experience of death and conquer it to tell us how to do the same or else we are going to die and never reach God.<br>This is the glorious message of the gospel. God is love, eternal and infinite love, so He has done all this for us. He did it through His Son, Jesus Christ. |
| #272<br>**Basic Things**<br><br>First principles–KJV<br>Elementary principles–NASB<br>Elementary truths–NIV<br>First principles–NKJV<br>**Basic things–NLT**<br><br>**POSB REFERENCE**<br>(Heb.5:12)<br>Note 2 | στοιχεῖα τῆς ἀρχῆς = *stoicheia tēs archēs*<br>Pronunciation: [stoy-khi'-ah tace ar-khays']<br>Parsing *stoicheia* (part of speech): noun<br>    Case—accusative<br>    Gender—neuter<br>    Number—plural<br>    Stem or root—from στοιχεῖα, ων<br>Parsing *archēs* (part of speech): noun<br>    Case—genitive<br>    Gender—feminine<br>    Number—singular<br>    Stem or root—from ἀρχή, ῆς<br>Concordance References:<br>  ⇒ Strong's #746+3588+4747 archē ho stoicheion<br>  ⇒ NIV #794+3836+5122 archē ho stoicheion [elementary truths]<br>  ⇒ NASB #746+3588+4747 archē ho stoicheion<br><br>**Hebrews 5:12**<br>For when for the time ye ought to be teachers, ye have need that one teach you again which be the **first principles** of the oracles of God; and are become such as have need of milk, and not of strong meat. [KJV]<br>For though by this time you ought to be teachers, you have need again for someone to teach you the **elementary principles** of the oracles of God, and you have come to need milk and not solid food. [NASB]<br>In fact, though by this time you ought to be teachers, you need someone to teach you the **elementary truths** of God's word all over again. You need milk, not solid food! [NIV]<br>For though by this time you ought to be teachers, you need someone to teach you again the **first principles** of the oracles of God; and you have come to need milk and not solid food. [NKJV]<br>You have been Christians a long time now, and you ought to be teaching others. Instead, you need someone to teach you again the **basic things** a beginner must learn about the Scriptures. You are like babies who drink only milk and cannot eat solid food. [NLT]<br>καὶ γὰρ ὀφείλοντες εἶναι διδάσκαλοι, διὰ τὸν χρόνον, πάλιν χρείαν ἔχετε τοῦ διδάσκειν ὑμᾶς τὰ **στοιχεῖα τῆς ἀρχῆς** τῶν λογίων τοῦ Θεοῦ· καὶ γεγόνατε χρείαν ἔχοντες γάλακτος, καὶ οὐ στερεᾶς τροφῆς. [GNS]<br>καὶ γὰρ ὀφείλοντες εἶναι διδάσκαλοι διὰ τὸν χρόνον, πάλιν χρείαν ἔχετε τοῦ διδάσκειν ὑμᾶς τινὰ τὰ **στοιχεῖα τῆς ἀρχῆς** τῶν λογίων τοῦ θεοῦ καὶ γεγόνατε χρείαν ἔχοντες γάλακτος [καὶ] οὐ στερεᾶς τροφῆς. [GNT] | Elementary truths; elementary principles; first principles; basic things.<br><br>**Practical Application**<br>A person becomes immature because he refuses to grow up spiritually. The Hebrew believers refused to move beyond the first principles of God's Word. "Basic things" (*stoicheia*) means the basic principles of God's Word, the elementary teachings, the ABC's of God's Word. They are the very basic teachings of salvation and of spiritual growth, such teachings as...<br>• a person should be saved<br>• a person should grow spiritually<br>• a person should live righteously<br>• a person should worship<br>• a person should keep the rituals and ceremonies of religion<br><br>Such basic truths as these are the milk of God's Word. They are truths for young believers, for babes in Christ. They are to be learned and learned quickly by the believer, and then he is to move on to maturity. Note that the Christian life is compared to physical growth. A young believer is said to be a babe in Christ, and the first principles of God's Word are said to be the milk upon which he is to feed. A young believer is to feed upon the milk of the Word, the first principles, but he is expected to grow until he is feeding upon the meat of the Word—studying and growing a mature understanding of the Christian life. |

# PRACTICAL WORD STUDIES
## in the NEW TESTAMENT

| ENGLISH WORD | GREEK WORD AND VERSE | THE WORD MEANS... |
|---|---|---|
| **#273**<br>**Basketfuls–**<br>**Baskets–**<br>**Baskets full**<br><br>Baskets full–KJV<br>Baskets full–NASB<br>Basketfuls–NIV<br>Baskets full–NKJV<br>Baskets–NLT<br><br>**POSB**<br>**REFERENCE**<br>(Mt.15:37)<br>*Deeper Study #1* | σπυρίδας πλήρεις:= *spuridas plēreis*<br>Pronunciation: [spur-i-das play'-race]<br>Parsing *spuridas* (part of speech): noun<br>    Case—accusative<br>    Gender—feminine<br>    Number—plural<br>    Stem or root—from σπυρίς, ίδος<br>Parsing *plēreis* (part of speech): adjective<br>    Case—accusative<br>    Gender—feminine<br>    Number—plural<br>    Stem or root—from πλήρης, ες<br>Concordance References:<br>⇒ Strong's #4711 spuris + 4134 pleres<br>⇒ NIV #5083 spuris [baskets] + 4441 pleres [full]<br>⇒ NASB #4711 spuris + 4134 pleres<br><br>**Matthew 15:37**<br>And they did all eat, and were filled: and they took up of the broken meat that was left seven **baskets full**. [KJV]<br>And they all ate, and were satisfied, and they picked up what was left over of the broken pieces, seven large **baskets full**. [NASB]<br>They all ate and were satisfied. Afterward the disciples picked up seven **basketfuls** of broken pieces that were left over. [NIV]<br>So they all ate and were filled, and they took up seven large **baskets full** of the fragments that were left. [NKJV]<br>They all ate until they were full, and when the scraps were picked up, there were seven large **baskets** of food left over! [NLT]<br>καὶ ἔφαγον πάντες καὶ ἐχορτάσθησαν. καὶ ἦραν τὸ περισσεῦον τῶν κλασμάτων, ἑπτὰ **σπυρίδας πλήρεις**. [GNS]<br>καὶ ἔφαγον πάντες καὶ ἐχορτάσθησαν. καὶ τὸ περισσεῦον τῶν κλασμάτων ἦραν ἑπτὰ **σπυρίδας πλήρεις**. [GNT] | Basketfuls, baskets that are completely full; large wicker, hamper-like baskets used by Gentiles, often large enough to carry a man inside.<br><br>**Practical Application**<br>These were small pouch-like baskets usually carried by Jews to hold their food when journeying. |
| **#274**<br>**Battalion**<br><br>Band of soldiers–KJV<br>Cohort–NASB<br>Company of soldiers–NIV<br>Garrison–NKJV<br>**Battalion–NLT**<br><br>**POSB**<br>**REFERENCE**<br>(Mt.27:26-38; esp. v.27)<br>Note 2, point 2 | σπεῖραν = *speiran*<br>Pronunciation: [spi'-rahn]<br>Parsing (part of speech): noun<br>    Case—accusative<br>    Gender—feminine<br>    Number—singular<br>    Stem or root—from σπεῖρα, ης<br>Concordance References:<br>⇒ Strong's #4686 speira<br>⇒ NIV #5061 speira<br>⇒ NASB #4686 speira<br><br>**Matthew 27:27**<br>Then the soldiers of the governor took Jesus into the common hall, and gathered unto him the whole **band of soldiers**. [KJV]<br>Then the soldiers of the governor took Jesus into the Praetorium and gathered the whole Roman **cohort** around Him. [NASB]<br>Then the governor's soldiers took Jesus into the Praetorium and gathered the whole **company of soldiers** around him. [NIV]<br>Then the soldiers of the governor took Jesus into the Praetorium and gathered the whole **garrison** around Him. [NKJV]<br>Some of the governor's soldiers took Jesus into their headquarters and called out the entire **battalion**. [NLT]<br>Τότε οἱ στρατιῶται τοῦ ἡγεμόνος παραλαβόντες τὸν Ἰησοῦν εἰς τὸ πραιτώριον συνήγαγον ἐπ' αὐτὸν ὅλην τὴν **σπεῖραν**· [GNS]<br>Τότε οἱ στρατιῶται τοῦ ἡγεμόνος παραλαβόντες τὸν Ἰησοῦν εἰς τὸ πραιτώριον συνήγαγον ἐπ' αὐτὸν ὅλην τὴν **σπεῖραν**. [GNT] | A company, battalion, detachment, garrison or band of soldiers; a regiment.<br><br>**Practical Application**<br>This usually meant a cohort which was made up of six hundred soldiers. However, "battalion" (*speiran*) sometimes meant maniple. Every cohort consisted of three maniples, about two hundred soldiers. Which is meant here is not known. Most believe the number of soldiers was large, certainly close to the two hundred serving in a maniple. |

## PRACTICAL WORD STUDIES
## in the NEW TESTAMENT

| ENGLISH WORD | GREEK WORD AND VERSE | THE WORD MEANS... |
|---|---|---|
| **#275**<br>**Battalion Of Roman Soldiers**<br><br>Band–KJV<br>Cohort–NASB<br>Detachment of soldiers–NIV<br>Detachment of troops–NKJV<br>**Battalion of Roman soldiers–NLT**<br><br>**POSB REFERENCE**<br>(Jn.18:3)<br>*Deeper Study #1* | σπεῖραν = *speiran*<br>Pronunciation: [spi'-rahn]<br>Parsing (part of speech): noun<br>    Case—accusative<br>    Gender—feminine<br>    Number—singular<br>    Stem or root—from σπεῖρα, ης<br>Concordance References:<br>  ⇒ Strong's #4686 speira<br>  ⇒ NIV #5061 speira<br>  ⇒ NASB #4686 speira<br><br>**John 18:3**<br>Judas then, having received a **band** of men and officers from the chief priests and Pharisees, cometh thither with lanterns and torches and weapons. [KJV]<br>Judas then, having received the Roman **cohort**, and officers from the chief priests and the Pharisees, came there with lanterns and torches and weapons. [NASB]<br>So Judas came to the grove, guiding a **detachment of soldiers** and some officials from the chief priests and Pharisees. They were carrying torches, lanterns and weapons. [NIV]<br>Then Judas, having received a **detachment of troops**, and officers from the chief priests and Pharisees, came there with lanterns, torches, and weapons. [NKJV]<br>The leading priests and Pharisees had given Judas a **battalion of Roman soldiers** and Temple guards to accompany him. Now with blazing torches, lanterns, and weapons, they arrived at the olive grove. [NLT]<br>ὁ οὖν Ἰούδας, λαβὼν τὴν **σπεῖραν**, καὶ ἐκ τῶν ἀρχιερέων καὶ Φαρισαίων ὑπηρέτας ἔρχεται ἐκεῖ μετὰ φανῶν καὶ λαμπάδων καὶ ὅπλων. [GNS]<br>ὁ οὖν Ἰούδας λαβὼν τὴν **σπεῖραν** καὶ ἐκ τῶν ἀρχιερέων καὶ ἐκ τῶν Φαρισαίων ὑπηρέτας ἔρχεται ἐκεῖ μετὰ φανῶν καὶ λαμπάδων καὶ ὅπλων. [GNT] | A detachment; company, garrison, battalion, band or cohort of Roman soldiers; a regiment.<br><br>**Practical Application**<br>This usually meant a cohort which was made up of six hundred soldiers. However, "battalion of Roman soldiers" (*speiran*) sometimes meant maniple. Every detachment of soldiers consisted of three maniples, about two hundred soldiers. Which is meant here is not known. Most believe the number of soldiers was large, certainly close to the two hundred serving in a maniple. |
| **#276**<br>**Battered**<br><br>Tossed–KJV<br>**Battered–NASB**<br>Buffeted–NIV<br>Tossed–NKJV<br>Fighting–NLT<br><br>**POSB REFERENCE**<br>(Mt.14:24-27, esp.v.24)<br>Note 2, point 1 | βασανιζόμενον = *basanizomenon*<br>Pronunciation: [bas-an-id'-zo-me-non]<br>Parsing (part of speech): verb<br>    Mood—participle<br>    Tense—present<br>    Voice—passive<br>    Case—nominative<br>    Gender—neuter<br>    Number—singular<br>    Stem or root—from βασανίζω<br>Concordance References:<br>  ⇒ Strong's #928 basanizō<br>  ⇒ NIV #989 basanizō<br>  ⇒ NASB #928 basanizō<br><br>**Matthew 14:24**<br>But the ship was now in the midst of the sea, **tossed** with waves: for the wind was contrary. [KJV]<br>But the boat was already many stadia away from the land, **battered** by the waves; for the wind was contrary. [NASB]<br>But the boat was already a considerable distance from land, **buffeted** by the waves because the wind was against it. [NIV]<br>But the boat was now in the middle of the sea, **tossed** by the waves, for the wind was contrary. [NKJV]<br>Meanwhile, the disciples were in trouble far away from land, for a strong wind had risen, and they were **fighting** heavy waves. [NLT]<br>τὸ δὲ πλοῖον ἤδη μέσον τῆς θαλάσσης ἦν, **βασανιζόμενον** ὑπὸ τῶν κυμάτων· ἦν γὰρ ἐναντίος ὁ ἄνεμος. [GNS]<br>τὸ δὲ πλοῖον ἤδη σταδίους πολλοὺς ἀπὸ τῆς γῆς ἀπεῖχεν **βασανιζόμενον** ὑπὸ τῶν κυμάτων, ἦν γὰρ ἐναν γίνεσθε οὖν μιμηταὶ τοῦ θεοῦ ὡς τέκνα ἀγαπητά [GNT] | To be buffeted, beaten, battered, or tossed about with great force; to be tormented; to be tortured.<br><br>**Practical Application**<br>In this Scripture, it is a picture of being completely at the mercy of a force greater than any possible human resistance. It is a picture of the awesome power of unleashed nature and mankind's inability to resist its effects. |

# PRACTICAL WORD STUDIES
## in the NEW TESTAMENT

| ENGLISH WORD | GREEK WORD AND VERSE | THE WORD MEANS... |
|---|---|---|
| **#277** <br> **Be** <br><br> Be–KJV <br> Be–NASB <br> Be–NIV <br> Be–NKJV <br> **Follow–NLT** <br><br> **POSB REFERENCE** <br> (Eph.5:1) <br> Note 1 | γίνεσθε = ginesthe <br> Pronunciation: [ghen-ehs-theh] <br> Parsing (part of speech): verb <br>     Mood—imperative <br>     Tense—present <br>     Voice—middle or passive deponent <br>     Person—2nd person <br>     Number—plural <br>     Stem or root—from γίνομαι <br> Concordance References: <br> ⇒ Strong's #1096 ginomai <br> ⇒ NIV #1181 ginomai <br> ⇒ NASB #1096 ginomai <br><br> **Ephes. 5:1** <br> **Be** ye therefore followers of God, as dear children; [KJV] <br> Therefore **be** imitators of God, as beloved children; [NASB] <br> **Be** imitators of God, therefore, as dearly loved children [NIV] <br> Therefore **be** imitators of God as dear children. [NKJV] <br> **Follow** God's example in everything you do, because you are his dear children. [NLT] <br> Γίνεσθε οὖν μιμηταὶ τοῦ Θεοῦ, ὡς τέκνα ἀγαπητά· [GNS] <br> γίνεσθε οὖν μιμηταὶ τοῦ θεοῦ ὡς τέκνα ἀγαπητά [GNT]τίος ὁ ἄνεμος. [GNT] | To be; to follow; to become. <br><br> **Practical Application** <br> It means *to become* a follower of God. The idea is that of commitment, attachment, devotion, allegiance, attention. Before a person can be a follower of God, he must commit and attach himself to God. He must surrender and devote his life to God and then begin to follow after God. |
| **#278** <br> **Be** <br><br> Be–KJV <br> Become–NASB <br> Become–NIV <br> Become–NKJV <br> Become–NLT <br><br> **POSB REFERENCE** <br> (Jn.12:34-36; esp. v.36) <br> Note 5, point 2 <br><br> See also POSB REF: <br> (Jn.1:12-13; esp. v.12) <br> Note 3, point 2 <br> (Eph.5:1) <br> Note 1 | γένησθε = genësthe <br> Pronunciation: [ghen-ace-theh] <br> Parsing (part of speech): verb <br>     Mood—subjunctive <br>     Tense—aorist <br>     Voice—middle deponent <br>     Person—2nd person <br>     Number—plural <br>     Stem or root—from γίνομαι <br> Concordance References: <br> ⇒ Strong's #1096 ginomai <br> ⇒ NIV #1181 ginomai <br> ⇒ NASB #1096 ginomai <br><br> **John 12:36** <br> While ye have light, believe in the light, that ye may **be** the children of light. These things spake Jesus, and departed, and did hide himself from them. [KJV] <br> "While you have the light, believe in the light, in order that you may **become** sons of light." These things Jesus spoke, and He departed and hid Himself from them. [NASB] <br> Put your trust in the light while you have it, so that you may **become** sons of light." When he had finished speaking, Jesus left and hid himself from them. [NIV] <br> While you have the light, believe in the light, that you may **become** sons of light." These things Jesus spoke, and departed, and was hidden from them. [NKJV] <br> Believe in the light while there is still time; then you will **become** children of the light." After saying these things, Jesus went away and was hidden from them. [NLT] <br> ἕως τὸ φῶς ἔχετε, πιστεύετε εἰς τὸ φῶς, ἵνα υἱοὶ φωτὸς **γένησθε**. Ταῦτα ἐλάλησεν ὁ Ἰησοῦς, καὶ ἀπελθὼν ἐκρύβη ἀπ' αὐτῶν. [GNS] <br> ὡς τὸ φῶς ἔχετε, πιστεύετε εἰς τὸ φῶς, ἵνα υἱοὶ φωτὸς **γένησθε**. Ταῦτα ἐλάλησεν Ἰησοῦς, καὶ ἀπελθὼν ἐκρύβη ἀπ' αὐτῶν. [GNT] | To become; to be; to come into existence; to take on a new form; to be made; to change. <br><br> **Practical Application** <br> "Be" is a once-for-all act, a personal experience that happens all at once. A person who truly sees Jesus Christ as the Light of the world believes and continues to believe. And the very moment his heart leaps toward Christ in belief, he becomes a child of the Light, a child of God Himself. The person sees the Light and begins to walk in the Light, living the kind of life he should. |
| **#279** <br> **Be Afflicted** | ταλαιπωρήσατε = talaipörësate <br> Pronunciation: [tal-ahee-po-ray'-sah-teh] <br> Parsing (part of speech): verb <br>     Mood—imperative | To lament; to grieve; to be afflicted; to be miserable; to be distressed; to suffer deep grief; to endure toils (A.T. Robertson. *Word Pictures in the New Testament*, Vol. 6, p.53); to discipline |

# PRACTICAL WORD STUDIES
## in the NEW TESTAMENT

| ENGLISH WORD | GREEK WORD AND VERSE | THE WORD MEANS... |
|---|---|---|
| **Be afflicted**–KJV<br>Be miserable–NASB<br>Grieve–NIV<br>Lament–NKJV<br>Deep grief–NLT<br><br>**POSB REFERENCE**<br>(Jas 4:9)<br>Note 3 | Tense—aorist<br>Voice—active<br>Person—2nd person<br>Number—plural<br>Stem or root—from ταλαιπωρέω<br>Concordance References:<br>⇒ Strong's #5003 talaipōreō<br>⇒ NIV #5415 talaipōreō<br>⇒ NASB #5003 talaipōreō<br><br>**James 4:9**<br>**Be afflicted**, and mourn, and weep: let your laughter be turned to heaviness, and your joy to heaviness. [KJV]<br>**Be miserable** and mourn and weep; let your laughter be turned into mourning, and your joy to gloom. [NASB]<br>**Grieve**, mourn and wail. Change your laughter to mourning and your joy to gloom. [NIV]<br>**Lament** and mourn and weep! Let your laughter be turned to mourning and your joy to gloom. [NKJV]<br>Let there be tears for the wrong things you have done. Let there be sorrow and **deep grief**. Let there be sadness instead of laughter, and gloom instead of joy. [NLT]<br>ταλαιπωρήσατε καὶ πενθήσατε καὶ κλαύσατε· ὁ γέλως ὑμῶν εἰς πένθος μετατραπήτω, καὶ ἡ χαρὰ εἰς κατήφειαν. [GNS]<br>ταλαιπωρήσατε καὶ πενθήσατε καὶ κλαύσατε. ὁ γέλως ὑμῶν εἰς πένθος μετατραπήτω καὶ ἡ χαρὰ εἰς κατήφειαν. [GNT] | and to voluntarily abstain (William Barclay. *The Letters of James and Peter.* "Daily Study Bible Series." Philadelphia, PA: Westminster Press, Began in 1953, p.127).<br><br>**Practical Application**<br>How can we overcome temptation? Endure. Be deeply and mournfully concerned. Note how descriptive this verse is:<br><br>*"Be afflicted, and mourn, and weep: let your laughter be turned to mourning, and your joy to heaviness" (James 4:9). [KJV]*<br><br>The picture is this: when temptation strikes us, it is not time...<br>• to be laughing and joking aroud<br>• to be lighthearted<br>• to be complacent<br>• to be at ease<br>• to be jolly<br>• to be teasing<br>• to be unconcerned<br>• to be uncomfortable<br>• to be lying around<br>Temptation is affliction; therefore, it is time to be disciplined and to control the comforts and joys of life. Temptation is a time for rigorous warfare—for battle and the discipline and endurance of battle. |
| **#280**<br>**Be Careful How You Live**<br><br>Honest–KJV<br>Excellent–NASB<br>Good–NIV<br>Honorable–NKJV<br>**Be careful how you live**–NLT<br><br>**POSB REFERENCE**<br>(1 Pt.2:12)<br>Note 3 | καλήν = kalēn<br>Pronunciation: [kal-ayn']<br>Parsing (part of speech): adjective<br>Case—accusative<br>Gender—feminine<br>Number—singular<br>Stem or root—from καλός, ή, όν<br>Concordance References:<br>⇒ Strong's #2570 kalos<br>⇒ NIV #2819 kalos<br>⇒ NASB #2570 kalos<br><br>**1 Peter 2:12**<br>Having your conversation **honest** among the Gentiles: that, whereas they speak against you as evildoers, they may by your good works, which they shall behold, glorify God in the day of visitation. [KJV]<br>Keep your behavior **excellent** among the Gentiles, so that in the thing in which they slander you as evildoers, they may on account of your good deeds, as they observe them, glorify God in the day of visitation. [NASB]<br>Live such **good** lives among the pagans that, though they accuse you of doing wrong, they may see your good deeds and glorify God on the day he visits us. [NIV]<br>Having your conduct **honorable** among the Gentiles, that when they speak against you as evildoers, they may, by your good works which they observe, glorify God in the day of visitation. [NKJV]<br>**Be careful how you live** among your unbelieving neighbors. Even if they accuse you of doing wrong, they will see your honorable behavior, and they will believe and give honor to God when he comes to judge the world. [NLT]<br>τὴν ἀναστροφὴν ὑμῶν ἐν τοῖς ἔθνεσιν ἔχοντες **καλήν**, ἵνα, ἐν ᾧ καταλαλοῦσιν ὑμῶν ὡς κακοποιῶν, ἐκ τῶν καλῶν ἔργων ἐποπτεύσαντες δοξάσωσι τὸν Θεὸν ἐν ἡμέρᾳ ἐπισκοπῆς. [GNS]<br>τὴν ἀναστροφὴν ὑμῶν ἐν τοῖς ἔθνεσιν ἔχοντες **καλήν**, ἵνα, ἐν ᾧ καταλαλοῦσιν ὑμῶν ὡς κακοποιῶν ἐκ τῶν καλῶν ἔργων ἐποπτεύοντες δοξάσωσιν τὸν θεὸν ἐν ἡμέρᾳ ἐπισκοπῆς. [GNT] | Good, honest, excellent, honorable, proper; to be careful how one lives.<br><br>**Practical Application**<br>The word for "be careful how you live" (*kalēn*) means a good life, a life that is honorable, righteous, pure, lovely, decent, excellent, upright, and noble. It means a life that is without blame, that cannot be justly or accurately blamed with any sin or evil. The world watches a genuine believer to see if he really lives what he professes. Therefore, we must live good lives, honest lives, lives that are just what we profess: holy, righteous, and pure. |

## PRACTICAL WORD STUDIES
### in the NEW TESTAMENT

| ENGLISH WORD | GREEK WORD AND VERSE | THE WORD MEANS... |
|---|---|---|
| **#281**<br>**Be Careful Then**<br><br>Take heed–KJV<br>Take care–NASB<br>See to it–NIV<br>Beware–NKJV<br>**Be careful then–NLT**<br><br>**POSB REFERENCE**<br>(Heb.3:12)<br>Note 2 | Βλέπετε = *Blepete*<br>Pronunciation: [blep'-eh-teh]<br>Parsing (part of speech): verb<br>    Mood—imperative<br>    Tense—present<br>    Voice—active<br>    Person—2nd person<br>    Number—plural<br>    Stem or root—from βλέπω<br>Concordance References:<br>  ⇒ Strong's #991 blepö<br>  ⇒ NIV #1063 blepö<br>  ⇒ NASB #991 blepö<br><br>**Hebrews 3:12**<br>**Take heed**, brethren, lest there be in any of you an evil heart of unbelief, in departing from the living God. [KJV]<br>**Take care**, brethren, lest there should be in any one of you an evil, unbelieving heart, in falling away from the living God. [NASB]<br>**See to it**, brothers, that none of you has a sinful, unbelieving heart that turns away from the living God. [NIV]<br>**Beware**, brethren, lest there be in any of you an evil heart of unbelief in departing from the living God; [NKJV]<br>**Be careful then**, dear brothers and sisters. Make sure that your own hearts are not evil and unbelieving, turning you away from the living God. [NLT]<br>**βλέπετε**, ἀδελφοί, μή ποτε ἔσται ἔν τινι ὑμῶν καρδία πονηρὰ ἀπιστίας, ἐν τῷ ἀποστῆναι ἀπὸ Θεοῦ ζῶντος· [GNS]<br>**Βλέπετε**, ἀδελφοί, μήποτε ἔσται ἔν τινι ὑμῶν καρδία πονηρὰ ἀπιστίας ἐν τῷ ἀποστῆναι ἀπὸ θεοῦ ζῶντος, [GNT] | Be alert and stay alert; be on the lookout and do it constantly; watch and keep on watching.<br><br>**Practical Application**<br>There is great danger that believers might depart from the living God. They might do just what Israel did. Therefore, be careful—take heed (*Blepete*). Keep a watchful eye on your trust and obedience to God. Watch for an evil heart of unbelief. What is an evil heart of unbelief? It is a heart that...<br>• stands off from God<br>• stands aloof from God<br>• renounces God<br>• rebels against God<br>• does not believe in God<br>• does not trust God and His promises<br>• does not follow God as He demands |
| **#282**<br>**Be Clothed**<br><br>**Be clothed–KJV**<br>Clothe...with–NASB<br>Clothe...with–NIV<br>**Be clothed–NKJV**<br>Serve each other–NLT<br><br>**POSB REFERENCE**<br>(1 Pt.5:5)<br>Note 2, point 2 | ἐγκομβώσασθε = *egkombösasthe*<br>Pronunciation: [eng-kom-bo'-sahs-theh]<br>Parsing (part of speech): verb<br>    Mood—imperative<br>    Tense—aorist<br>    Voice—middle deponent<br>    Person—2nd person<br>    Number—plural<br>    Stem or root—from ἐγκομβόομαι<br>Concordance References:<br>  ⇒ Strong's #1463 egkomboomai<br>  ⇒ NIV #1599 egkomboomai<br>  ⇒ NASB #1463 egkomboomai<br><br>**1 Peter 5:5**<br>Likewise, ye younger, submit yourselves unto the elder. Yea, all of you be subject one to another, and **be clothed** with humility: for God resisteth the proud, and giveth grace to the humble. [KJV]<br>You younger men, likewise, be subject to your elders; and all of you, **clothe** yourselves **with** humility toward one another, for God is opposed to the proud, but gives grace to the humble. [NASB]<br>Young men, in the same way be submissive to those who are older. All of you, **clothe** yourselves **with** humility toward one another, because, "God opposes the proud but gives grace to the humble." [NIV]<br>Likewise you younger people, submit yourselves to your elders. Yes, all of you be submissive to one another, and **be clothed** with humility, for "God resists the proud, But gives grace to the humble." [NKJV]<br>You younger men, accept the authority of the elders. And all of you, **serve each other** in humility, for "God sets himself against the proud, but he shows favor to the humble." [NLT]<br>ὁμοίως, νεώτεροι, ὑποτάγητε πρεσβυτέροις· πάντες δὲ | To clothe with; to be clothed; to put on; to serve; to gird oneself with some clothing.<br><br>**Practical Application**<br>It is the picture of what Jesus did in the upper room when He girded Himself with an apron to assume the role of a servant and wash the feet of the disciples. Jesus, the Son of God and Sovereign Majesty of the universe, actually clothed Himself with the apron of humility and served the disciples. |

# PRACTICAL WORD STUDIES
## in the New Testament

| ENGLISH WORD | GREEK WORD AND VERSE | THE WORD MEANS... |
|---|---|---|
| | ἀλλήλοις ὑποτασσόμενοι, τὴν ταπεινοφροσύνην **ἐγκομβώσασθε**· ὅτι ὁ Θεὸς ὑπερηφάνοις ἀντιτάσσεται, ταπεινοῖς δὲ δίδωσι χάρινἈ [GNS]<br><br>Ὁμοίως, νεώτεροι, ὑποτάγητε πρεσβυτέροις· πάντες δὲ ἀλλήλοις τὴν ταπεινοφροσύνην **ἐγκομβώσασθε**, ὅτι Ὁ[O] θεὸς ὑπερηφάνοις ἀντιτάσσεται, ταπεινοῖς δὲ δίδωσιν χάριν. [GNT] | |
| **#283**<br>**Be Diligent**<br><br>Be diligent–KJV<br>Be diligent–NASB<br>Make every effort–NIV<br>Be diligent–NKJV<br>Make every effort–NLT<br><br>**POSB REFERENCE**<br>(2 Pt.3:14)<br>Note 4 | σπουδάσατε = *spoudasate*<br>Pronunciation: [spoo-das-teh]<br>Parsing (part of speech): verb<br>  Mood—imperative<br>  Tense—aorist<br>  Voice—active<br>  Person—2nd person<br>  Number—plural<br>  Stem or root—from σπουδάζω<br>Concordance References:<br>⇒ Strong's #4704 spoudazō<br>⇒ NIV #5079 spoudazō<br>⇒ NASB #4704 spoudazō<br><br>**2 Peter 3:14**<br>Wherefore, beloved, seeing that ye look for such things, **be diligent** that ye may be found of him in peace, without spot, and blameless. [KJV]<br><br>Therefore, beloved, since you look for these things, **be diligent** to be found by Him in peace, spotless and blameless, [NASB]<br><br>So then, dear friends, since you are looking forward to this, **make every effort** to be found spotless, blameless and at peace with him. [NIV]<br><br>Therefore, beloved, looking forward to these things, **be diligent** to be found by Him in peace, without spot and blameless; [NKJV]<br><br>And so, dear friends, while you are waiting for these things to happen, **make every effort** to live a pure and blameless life. And be at peace with God. [NLT]<br><br>Διό, ἀγαπητοί, ταῦτα προσδοκῶντες, **σπουδάσατε** ἄσπιλοι καὶ ἀμώμητοι αὐτῷ εὑρεθῆναι ἐν εἰρήνῃ. [GNS]<br><br>Διό, ἀγαπητοί, ταῦτα προσδοκῶντες **σπουδάσατε** ἄσπιλοι καὶ ἀμώμητοι αὐτῷ εὑρεθῆναι ἐν εἰρήνῃ [GNT] | To make every effort; to be diligent; to do one's very best; to work hard; to be eager; to strive earnestly; to be zealous in seeking after.<br><br>**Practical Application**<br>Believers must be diligent and prepared for the coming of Christ. The believer is to be diligent, that is, eager, earnest and zealous in preparing himself for the return of the Lord. Why? So that the Lord will find him prepared. |
| **#284**<br>**Be Encouraged**<br><br>Good cheer–KJV<br>Take courage–NASB<br>Take courage–NIV<br>Good cheer–NKJV<br>Be encouraged–NLT<br><br>**POSB REFERENCE**<br>(Acts 23:11)<br>Note 5 | Θάρσει = *Tharsei*<br>Pronunciation: [thar-seh'-ee]<br>Parsing (part of speech): verb<br>  Mood—imperfect<br>  Tense—present<br>  Voice—active<br>  Person—2nd person<br>  Number—singular<br>  Stem or root—from θαρσέω<br>Concordance References:<br>⇒ Strong's #2293 tharseō<br>⇒ NIV #2510 tharseō<br>⇒ NASB #2293 tharseō<br><br>**Acts 23:11**<br>And the night following the Lord stood by him, and said, Be of **good cheer**, Paul: for as thou hast testified of me in Jerusalem, so must thou bear witness also at Rome. [KJV]<br><br>But on the night immediately following, the Lord stood at his side and said, "**Take courage**; for as you have solemnly witnessed to My cause at Jerusalem, so you must witness at Rome also." [NASB]<br><br>The following night the Lord stood near Paul and said, "**Take courage**! As you have testified about me in Jerusalem, so you must also testify in Rome." [NIV]<br><br>But the following night the Lord stood by him and said, "Be of **good cheer**, Paul; for as you have testified for Me in Jerusalem, so you must also bear witness at Rome." [NKJV] | To take courage; to be of good cheer; to be encouraged; to cheer up; to take heart.<br><br>**Practical Application**<br>The Lord wishes His servants to always be encouraged (*Tharsei*) and courageous and full of cheer, no matter the trial. The life of His servant is under the care and leadership of the Lord. |

# PRACTICAL WORD STUDIES
## in the NEW TESTAMENT

| ENGLISH WORD | GREEK WORD AND VERSE | THE WORD MEANS... |
|---|---|---|
| | That night the Lord appeared to Paul and said, "**Be encouraged**, Paul. Just as you have told the people about me here in Jerusalem, you must preach the Good News in Rome." [NLT]<br><br>Τῇ δὲ ἐπιούσῃ νυκτὶ ἐπιστὰς αὐτῷ ὁ Κύριος εἶπε, **Θάρσει** Παῦλε· ὡς γὰρ διεμαρτύρω τὰ περὶ ἐμοῦ εἰς Ἰερουσαλὴμ, οὕτω σε δεῖ καὶ εἰς Ῥώμην μαρτυρῆσαι. [GNS]<br><br>Τῇ δὲ ἐπιούσῃ νυκτὶ ἐπιστὰς αὐτῷ ὁ κύριος εἶπεν, **Θάρσει** ὡς γὰρ διεμαρτύρω τὰ περὶ ἐμοῦ εἰς Ἰερουσαλὴμ, οὕτω σε δεῖ καὶ εἰς Ῥώμην μαρτυρῆσαι. [GNT] | |
| **#285**<br>**Be Made Complete**<br><br>Be perfect–KJV<br>**Be made complete–NASB**<br>Aim for perfection–NIV<br>Become complete–NKJV<br>Change your ways–NLT<br><br>**POSB REFERENCE**<br>(2 Cor.13:11-13; esp. v.11)<br>Note 3 | καταρτίζεσθε = katartizesthe<br>Pronunciation: [kat-ar-tid'-zehs-the]<br>Parsing (part of speech):verb<br>    Mood—imperative<br>    Tense—present<br>    Voice—passive<br>    Person—2nd person<br>    Number—plural<br>    Stem or root—from καταρτίζω<br>Concordance References:<br>  ⇒ Strong's #2675 katartizō<br>  ⇒ NIV #2936 katartizō<br>  ⇒ NASB #2675 katartizō<br><br>**2 Cor. 13:11**<br>Finally, brethren, farewell. **Be perfect**, be of good comfort, be of one mind, live in peace; and the God of love and peace shall be with you. [KJV]<br>Finally, brethren, rejoice, **be made complete**, be comforted, be like-minded, live in peace; and the God of love and peace shall be with you. [NASB]<br>Finally, brothers, good-by. **Aim for perfection**, listen to my appeal, be of one mind, live in peace. And the God of love and peace will be with you. [NIV]<br>Finally, brethren, farewell. **Become complete**. Be of good comfort, be of one mind, live in peace; and the God of love and peace will be with you. [NKJV]<br>Dear brothers and sisters, I close my letter with these last words: Rejoice. **Change your ways**. Encourage each other. Live in harmony and peace. Then the God of love and peace will be with you. [NLT]<br>Λοιπόν, ἀδελφοί, χαίρετε· **καταρτίζεσθε**, παρακαλεῖσθε, τὸ αὐτὸ φρονεῖτε, εἰρηνεύετε· καὶ ὁ Θεὸς τῆς ἀγάπης καὶ εἰρήνης ἔσται μεθ' ὑμῶν. [GNS]<br>Λοιπόν, ἀδελφοί, χαίρετε, **καταρτίζεσθε**, παρακαλεῖσθε, τὸ αὐτὸ φρονεῖτε, εἰρηνεύετε, καὶ ὁ θεὸς τῆς ἀγάπης καὶ εἰρήνης ἔσται μεθ' ὑμῶν. [GNT] | To aim and strive for perfection; to be made complete; to prepare; to change one's ways; to restore, reform, correct, and mend oneself and one's ways.<br><br>**Practical Application**<br>Paul's challenge to his Corinthian brothers is blunt and to the point: Stop your sinning and be made complete. |
| **#286**<br>**Be Miserable**<br><br>Be afflicted–KJV<br>**Be miserable–NASB**<br>Grieve–NIV<br>Lament–NKJV<br>Deep grief–NLT<br><br>**POSB REFERENCE**<br>(Jas 4:9)<br>Note 3 | ταλαιπωρήσατε = talaipōrēsate<br>Pronunciation: [tal-ahee-po-ray'-sah-teh]<br>Parsing (part of speech): verb<br>    Mood—imperative<br>    Tense—aorist<br>    Voice—active<br>    Person—2nd person<br>    Number—plural<br>    Stem or root—from ταλαιπωρέω<br>Concordance References:<br>  ⇒ Strong's #5003 talaipōreō<br>  ⇒ NIV #5415 talaipōreō<br>  ⇒ NASB #5003 talaipōreō<br><br>**James 4:9**<br>**Be afflicted**, and mourn, and weep: let your laughter be turned to mourning, and your joy to heaviness. [KJV]<br>**Be miserable** and mourn and weep; let your laughter be turned into mourning, and your joy to gloom. [NASB]<br>**Grieve**, mourn and wail. Change your laughter to mourning and your joy to gloom. [NIV]<br>**Lament** and mourn and weep! Let your laughter be | To lament; to grieve; to be afflicted; to be miserable; to be distressed; to suffer deep grief; to endure toils (A.T. Robertson. *Word Pictures in the New Testament*, Vol. 6, p.53); to discipline and to voluntarily abstain (William Barclay. *The Letters of James and Peter*, p.127).<br><br>**Practical Application**<br>How can we overcome temptation? Endure. Be deeply and mournfully concerned. Note how descriptive this verse is:<br><br>*"Be miserable and mourn and weep; let your laughter be turned into mourning, and your joy to gloom" (James 4:9).* [NASB]<br><br>The picture is this: when temptation strikes us, it is not time...<br>• to be laughing<br>• to be joking around |

# PRACTICAL WORD STUDIES
## in the NEW TESTAMENT

| ENGLISH WORD | GREEK WORD AND VERSE | THE WORD MEANS... |
|---|---|---|
| | turned to mourning and your joy to gloom. [NKJV]<br>Let there be tears for the wrong things you have done. Let there be sorrow and **deep grief**. Let there be sadness instead of laughter, and gloom instead of joy. [NLT]<br>ταλαιπωρήσατε καὶ πενθήσατε καὶ κλαύσατε· ὁ γέλως ὑμῶν εἰς πένθος μετατραπήτω, καὶ ἡ χαρὰ εἰς κατήφειαν. [GNS]<br>ταλαιπωρήσατε καὶ πενθήσατε καὶ κλαύσατε. ὁ γέλως ὑμῶν εἰς πένθος μετατραπήτω καὶ ἡ χαρὰ εἰς κατήφειαν. [GNT] | • to be lighthearted<br>• to be complacent<br>• to be at ease<br>• to be jolly<br>• to be teasing<br>• to be unconcerned<br>• to be uncomfortable<br>• to be lying around<br>Temptation is affliction; therefore, it is time to be disciplined and to control the comforts and joys of life. Temptation is a time for rigorous warfare—for battle and the discipline and endurance of battle. |
| #287<br>**Be On Guard**<br><br>Take heed–KJV<br>**Be on guard–NASB**<br>Keep watch over–NIV<br>Take heed–NKJV<br>Beware–NLT<br><br>**POSB REFERENCE**<br>(Acts 20:28)<br>Note 1, point 1 | προσέχετε = prosechete<br>Pronunciation: [pros-ech'-eh-teh]<br>Parsing (part of speech): verb<br>   Mood—imperfect<br>   Tense—present<br>   Voice—active<br>   Person—2nd person<br>   Number—plural<br>   Stem or root—from προσέχω<br>Concordance References:<br> ⇒ Strong's #4337 prosechō<br> ⇒ NIV #4668 prosechō<br> ⇒ NASB #4337 prosechō<br><br>**Acts 20:28**<br>**Take heed** therefore unto yourselves, and to all the flock, over the which the Holy Ghost hath made you overseers, to feed the church of God, which he hath purchased with his own blood. [KJV]<br>"**Be on guard** for yourselves and for all the flock, among which the Holy Spirit has made you overseers, to shepherd the church of God which He purchased with His own blood. [NASB]<br>**Keep watch over** yourselves and all the flock of which the Holy Spirit has made you overseers. Be shepherds of the church of God, which he bought with his own blood. [NIV]<br>Therefore **take heed** to yourselves and to all the flock, among which the Holy Spirit has made you overseers, to shepherd the church of God which He purchased with His own blood. [NKJV]<br>"And now **beware**! Be sure that you feed and shepherd God's flock—his church, purchased with his blood—over whom the Holy Spirit has appointed you as elders. [NLT]<br>προσέχετε οὖν ἑαυτοῖς καὶ παντὶ τῷ ποιμνίῳ, ἐν ᾧ ὑμᾶς τὸ Πνεῦμα τὸ Ἅγιον ἔθετο ἐπισκόπους, ποιμαίνειν τὴν ἐκκλησίαν τοῦ Θεοῦ, ἣν περιεποιήσατο διὰ τοῦ ἰδίου αἵματος. [GNS]<br>προσέχετε ἑαυτοῖς καὶ παντὶ τῷ ποιμνίῳ, ἐν ᾧ ὑμᾶς τὸ πνεῦμα τὸ ἅγιον ἔθετο ἐπισκόπους ποιμαίνειν τὴν ἐκκλησίαν τοῦ θεοῦ, ἣν περιεποιήσατο διὰ τοῦ αἵματος τοῦ ἰδίου. [GNT] | To keep watch over; to take heed; to be on guard; to beware; to be careful, oh so careful. It means to give attention, concentrate upon, focus upon, attend to, watch after, and guard his life.<br><br>**Practical Application**<br>There are specific areas in which the believer must guard.<br>1. He must guard against false teaching (Luke 12:1).<br>2. He must guard against an unforgiving spirit (Luke 17:3-4).<br>3. He must guard against self-indulgence, drunkenness, and the possessions of this life (Luke 21:34).<br>4. He must guard against the fables, myths, speculations, ideas, and false doctrines of men, and depending upon one's genealogy or heritage for salvation (1 Tim. 1:4).<br>5. He must watch and give himself to reading, exhortation and doctrine (1 Tim. 4:13).<br>6. He must especially give himself to the doctrine (*te didaskalia*), the teaching of Scripture (1 Tim. 4:16). |
| #288<br>**Be On The Alert**<br><br>Vigilant–KJV<br>**Be on the alert–NASB**<br>Alert–NIV<br>Vigilant–NKJV<br>Watch out–NLT | γρηγορήσατε = grēgorēsate<br>Pronunciation: [gray-gor-ay'-sah-teh]<br>Parsing (part of speech): verb<br>   Mood—imperative<br>   Tense—aorist<br>   Voice—active<br>   Person—2nd person<br>   Number—plural<br>   Stem or root—from γρηγορέω<br>Concordance References:<br> ⇒ Strong's #1127 grēgoreō<br> ⇒ NIV #1213 grēgoreō<br> ⇒ NASB #1127 grēgoreō | To be alert; to be vigilant; to watch out; to be on guard. The word means to be watchful and awake.<br><br>**Practical Application**<br>It has the idea of being constantly aroused and on the lookout; to always be aroused, awake, and watching for the devil and his attacks. If a person's mind and body are dull, flabby, and weak from drink, drugs, overeating, slothfulness, and indulgence in sleep, recreation, pleasure, or in anything else—that person cannot be watching and waiting; he cannot be constantly |

# PRACTICAL WORD STUDIES
## in the NEW TESTAMENT

| ENGLISH WORD | GREEK WORD AND VERSE | THE WORD MEANS... |
|---|---|---|
| **POSB REFERENCE** (1 Pt.5:8) Note 1, point 2 | **1 Peter 5:8** Be sober, be **vigilant**; because your adversary the devil, as a roaring lion, walketh about, seeking whom he may devour. [KJV] Be of sober spirit, **be on the alert**. Your adversary, the devil, prowls about like a roaring lion, seeking someone to devour. [NASB] Be self-controlled and **alert**. Your enemy the devil prowls around like a roaring lion looking for someone to devour. [NIV] Be sober, be **vigilant**; because your adversary the devil walks about like a roaring lion, seeking whom he may devour. [NKJV] Be careful! **Watch out** for attacks from the Devil, your great enemy. He prowls around like a roaring lion, looking for some victim to devour. [NLT] νήψατε, **γρηγορήσατε**, ὅτι ὁ ἀντίδικος ὑμῶν διάβολος, ὡς λέων ὠρυόμενος περιπατεῖ ζητῶν τινα καταπίῃ· [GNS] Νήψατε, **γρηγορήσατε**. ὁ ἀντίδικος ὑμῶν διάβολος ὡς λέων ὠρυόμενος περιπατεῖ ζητῶν [τινα] καταπιεῖν· [GNT] | aroused to look for the devil's temptations and attacks. The believer must be sober and serious about the devil; he must be alert and vigilant in looking for the devil's temptations and attacks. It is the only conceivable way the believer can conquer and overcome in life; it is the only way he can keep his life and testimony from being destroyed by the devil. |
| **#289 Be Perfect** Be perfect–KJV Be made complete–NASB Aim for perfection–NIV Become complete–NKJV Change your ways–NLT **POSB REFERENCE** (2 Cor.13:11-13; esp. v.11) Note 3 | **καταρτίζεσθε** = katartizesthe Pronunciation: [kat-ar-tid'-zehs-the] Parsing (part of speech): verb  Mood—imperative  Tense—present  Voice—passive  Person—2nd person  Number—plural  Stem or root—from **καταρτίζω** Concordance References: ⇒ Strong's #2675 katartizō ⇒ NIV #2936 katartizō ⇒ NASB #2675 katartizō **2 Cor. 13:11** Finally, brethren, farewell. **Be perfect**, be of good comfort, be of one mind, live in peace; and the God of love and peace shall be with you. [KJV] Finally, brethren, rejoice, **be made complete**, be comforted, be like-minded, live in peace; and the God of love and peace shall be with you. [NASB] Finally, brothers, good-by. **Aim for perfection**, listen to my appeal, be of one mind, live in peace. And the God of love and peace will be with you. [NIV] Finally, brethren, farewell. **Become complete**. Be of good comfort, be of one mind, live in peace; and the God of love and peace will be with you. [NKJV] Dear brothers and sisters, I close my letter with these last words: Rejoice. **Change your ways**. Encourage each other. Live in harmony and peace. Then the God of love and peace will be with you. [NLT] Λοιπόν, ἀδελφοί, χαίρετε· **καταρτίζεσθε**, παρακαλεῖσθε, τὸ αὐτὸ φρονεῖτε, εἰρηνεύετε· καὶ ὁ Θεὸς τῆς ἀγάπης καὶ εἰρήνης ἔσται μεθ' ὑμῶν. [GNS] Λοιπόν, ἀδελφοί, χαίρετε, **καταρτίζεσθε**, παρακαλεῖσθε, τὸ αὐτὸ φρονεῖτε, εἰρηνεύετε, καὶ ὁ Θεὸς τῆς ἀγάπης καὶ εἰρήνης ἔσται μεθ' ὑμῶν. [GNT] | To aim and strive for perfection; to be made complete; to prepare; to change one's ways; to restore, reform, correct, and mend oneself and one's ways. **Practical Application** Paul's challenge to his Corinthian brothers is blunt and to the point: Stop your sinning (criticism, divisiveness, immorality). |
| **#290 Bear With– Bearing With** Forbearing–KJV **Bearing with–NASB Bear with–NIV Bearing with–NKJV** Make allowance–NLT | **ἀνεχόμενοι** = anechomenoi Pronunciation: [an-ekh'-om-ehn-oy] Parsing (part of speech): verb  Mood—participle (imperative sense)  Tense—present  Voice—middle  Case—nominative  Gender—masculine  Person—2nd person  Number—plural  Stem or root—from **ἀνέχομαι** Concordance References: ⇒ Strong's #430 anechomai | To bear with; to be patient with; to make allowance for; forbearance. It means to hold back; to put up with; to refrain; to endure; to control. **Practical Application** People have to put up with a great deal of things when dealing with us. There is a reason for this: everyone of us is guilty of... • some weakness • some unattractive behavior • some wrong behavior |

# PRACTICAL WORD STUDIES
## in the NEW TESTAMENT

| ENGLISH WORD | GREEK WORD AND VERSE | THE WORD MEANS... |
|---|---|---|
| **POSB REFERENCE** (Col.3:13) Note 7 | ⇒ NIV #462 anechomai<br>⇒ NASB #430 anechomai<br><br>**Col. 3:13**<br>**Forbearing** one another, and forgiving one another, if any man have a quarrel against any: even as Christ forgave you, so also do ye. [KJV]<br>**Bearing with** one another, and forgiving each other, whoever has a complaint against anyone; just as the Lord forgave you, so also should you. [NASB]<br>**Bear with** each other and forgive whatever grievances you may have against one another. Forgive as the Lord forgave you. [NIV]<br>**Bearing with** one another, and forgiving one another, if anyone has a complaint against another; even as Christ forgave you, so you also must do. [NKJV]<br>You must **make allowance** for each other's faults and forgive the person who offends you. Remember, the Lord forgave you, so you must forgive others. [NLT]<br>ἀνεχόμενοι ἀλλήλων, καὶ χαριζόμενοι ἑαυτοῖς ἐάν τις πρός τινα ἔχῃ μομφήν· καθὼς καὶ ὁ Χριστὸς ἐχαρίσατο ὑμῖν, οὕτω καὶ ὑμεῖς· [GNS]<br>ἀνεχόμενοι ἀλλήλων καὶ χαριζόμενοι ἑαυτοῖς ἐάν τις πρός τινα ἔχῃ μομφήν· καθὼς καὶ ὁ κύριος ἐχαρίσατο ὑμῖν, οὕτως καὶ ὑμεῖς· [GNT] | • some mistreatment<br>• some neglect<br>• some failure<br>• some bad habit<br>• some irritating behavior<br><br>There are some things about us that just turn some people off. None of us escapes this fact. In addition, everyone of us does things that irritate some people. Again, there is no escaping the fact. Any person can be looked at and have his flaws and weaknesses picked out.<br>But note: this is not what Scripture says to do. Scripture says that the believer is to put on the clothing of forbearance. The believer is to forbear the flaws of others. He is to put up with and bear with the weaknesses of other believers. |
| **#291**<br>**Beareth–<br>Bears**<br><br>Beareth–KJV<br>Bears–NASB<br>Protects–NIV<br>Bears–NKJV<br>Never gives up–NLT<br><br>**POSB REFERENCE** (1 Cor.13:4-7; esp. v.7) Note 2, point 12 | στέγει = *stegei*<br>Pronunciation: [steg'-ee]<br>Parsing (part of speech): verb<br>   Mood—indicative<br>   Tense—present<br>   Voice—active<br>   Person—3rd person<br>   Number—singular<br>   Stem or root—from στέγω<br>Concordance References:<br>⇒ Strong's #4722 stegō<br>⇒ NIV #5095 stegō<br>⇒ NASB #4722 stegō<br><br>**1 Cor. 13:7**<br>**Beareth** all things, believeth all things, hopeth all things, endureth all things. [KJV]<br>**Bears** all things, believes all things, hopes all things, endures all things. [NASB]<br>It always **protects**, always trusts, always hopes, always perseveres. [NIV]<br>**Bears** all things, believes all things, hopes all things, endures all things. [NKJV]<br>Love **never gives up**, never loses faith, is always hopeful, and endures through every circumstance. [NLT]<br>πάντα **στέγει**, πάντα πιστεύει, πάντα ἐλπίζει, πάντα ὑπομένει. [GNS]<br>πάντα **στέγει**, πάντα πιστεύει, πάντα ἐλπίζει, πάντα ὑπομένει. [GNT] | To protect; to bear; to never give up; to endure; to put up with; to stand.<br><br>**Practical Application**<br>It means both to cover all things and to bear up under all things. Love does both: it stands up under the weight and onslaught of all things, and it covers up the faults of others. It has no pleasure in exposing the wrong and weaknesses of others. Love bears up under any neglect, abuse, ridicule—anything that is thrown against it. |
| **#292**<br>**Beat**<br><br>Smote–KJV<br>Beat–NASB<br>Struck–NIV<br>Struck–NKJV<br>Beat–NLT<br><br>**POSB REFERENCE** (Mt.27:26-38; esp. v.30) Note 2, point 7 | ἔτυπτον = *etupton*<br>Pronunciation: [eh-toop'-ton]<br>Parsing (part of speech): verb<br>   Mood—indicative<br>   Tense—imperfect<br>   Voice—active<br>   Person—3rd person<br>   Number—plural<br>   Stem or root—from τύπτω<br>Concordance References:<br>⇒ Strong's #5180 tuptō<br>⇒ NIV #5597 tuptō<br>⇒ NASB #5180 tuptō<br><br>**Matthew 27:30**<br>And they spit upon him, and took the reed, and **smote** him on the head. [KJV] | Struck, smote, hit, wound, beat; injure. It means to literally strike with the fist, to beat and injure.<br><br>**Practical Application**<br>In the context of this Scripture, they kept on beating Christ. They took the staff, the mock scepter, and used it as a weapon, beating Him on the head continuously. They probably passed the staff from one soldier to another, giving many an opportunity to vent their folly and spite. He was bruised and bleeding, a horrible sight. |

# PRACTICAL WORD STUDIES
## in the NEW TESTAMENT

| ENGLISH WORD | GREEK WORD AND VERSE | THE WORD MEANS... |
|---|---|---|
| | And they spat on Him, and took the reed and *began* to **beat** Him on the head. [NASB]<br>They spit on him, and took the staff and **struck** him on the head again and again. [NIV]<br>Then they spat on Him, and took the reed and **struck** Him on the head. [NKJV]<br>And they spit on him and grabbed the stick and **beat** him on the head with it. [NLT]<br>καὶ ἐμπτύσαντες εἰς αὐτὸν ἔλαβον τὸν κάλαμον καὶ **ἔτυπτον** εἰς τὴν κεφαλὴν αὐτοῦ. [GNS]<br>καὶ ἐμπτύσαντες εἰς αὐτὸν ἔλαβον τὸν κάλαμον καὶ **ἔτυπτον** εἰς τὴν κεφαλὴν αὐτοῦ. [GNT] | |
| **#293**<br>**Beaten–**<br>**Beatings**<br><br>Stripes–KJV<br>**Beatings–NASB**<br>**Beatings–NIV**<br>Stripes–NKJV<br>**Beaten–NLT**<br><br>**POSB**<br>**REFERENCE**<br>(2 Cor. 6:4-5; esp. v.5)<br>Note 3 | πληγαῖς = plēgais<br>Pronunciation: [play-gah-ees]<br>Parsing (part of speech): noun<br>  Case—dative<br>  Gender—feminine<br>  Number—plural<br>  Stem or root—from πληγή, ῆς<br>Concordance References:<br>⇒ Strong's #4127 plēgē<br>⇒ NIV #4435 plēgē<br>⇒ NASB #4127 plēgē<br><br>**2 Cor. 6:5**<br>In **stripes**, in imprisonments, in tumults, in labours, in watchings, in fastings; [KJV]<br>In **beatings**, in imprisonments, in tumults, in labors, in sleeplessness, in hunger, [NASB]<br>In **beatings**, imprisonments and riots; in hard work, sleepless nights and hunger; [NIV]<br>In **stripes**, in imprisonments, in tumults, in labors, in sleeplessness, in fastings; [NKJV]<br>We have been **beaten**, been put in jail, faced angry mobs, worked to exhaustion, endured sleepless nights, and gone without food. [NLT]<br>ἐν **πληγαῖς**, ἐν φυλακαῖς, ἐν ἀκαταστασίαις, ἐν κόποις, ἐν ἀγρυπνίαις, ἐν νηστείαις, [GNS]<br>ἐν **πληγαῖς**, ἐν φυλακαῖς, ἐν ἀκαταστασίαις, ἐν κόποις, ἐν ἀγρυπνίαις, ἐν νηστείαις, [GNT] | Scourgings, beatings, floggings, lashings, whippings; to wound.<br><br>**Practical Application**<br>This was a savage, excruciating punishment. The whip (*phagellow*) was made of leather straps with two small balls attached to the end of each strap. The balls were made of rough lead or sharp bones or spikes, so that they would cut deeply into the flesh. Paul's hands were tied to a post above his head as he was scourged. It was the custom for the prisoner to be lashed until he was judged near death by the presiding centurion (Jewish trials allowed only forty lashes.) The criminal's back was, of course, nothing more than an unrecognizable mass of torn flesh.<br>Paul was scourged at least eight times—just imagine! Eight times—five times by the Jews and three times by the Gentiles (2 Cor. 11:24-25). Tragically, believers all over the world are sometimes whipped and abused because of their testimony for the Lord Jesus. In such times, only one thing can give the believer a consistent life and testimony: steadfast endurance. |
| **#294**<br>**Beauty**<br><br>Adorning–KJV<br>Adornment–NASB<br>Adornment–NIV<br>Adornment–NKJV<br>**Beauty–NLT**<br><br>**POSB**<br>**REFERENCE**<br>(1 Pt.3:3)<br>Note 4 | κόσμος = kosmos<br>Pronunciation: [kos'-mos]<br>Parsing (part of speech): noun<br>  Case—nominative<br>  Gender—masculine<br>  Number—singular<br>  Stem or root—from κόσμος<br>Concordance References:<br>⇒ Strong's #2889 kosmos<br>⇒ NIV #3180 kosmos<br>⇒ NASB #2889 kosmos<br><br>**1 Peter 3:3**<br>Whose **adorning** let it not be that outward *adorning* of plaiting the hair, and of wearing of gold, or of putting on of apparel; [KJV]<br>And let not your **adornment** be *merely* external—braiding the hair, and wearing gold jewelry, or putting on dresses; [NASB]<br>Your beauty should not come from outward **adornment**, such as braided hair and the wearing of gold jewelry and fine clothes. [NIV]<br>Do not let your **adornment** be *merely* outward—arranging the hair, wearing gold, or putting on *fine* apparel— [NKJV]<br>Don't be concerned about the outward **beauty** that depends on fancy hairstyles, expensive jewelry, or beautiful clothes. [NLT]<br>ὧν ἔστω οὐχ ὁ ἔξωθεν ἐμπλοκῆς τριχῶν, καὶ περιθέσεως χρυσίων, ἢ ἐνδύσεως ἱματίων **κόσμος**· [GNS]<br>ὧν ἔστω οὐχ ὁ ἔξωθεν ἐμπλοκῆς τριχῶν καὶ περιθέσεως χρυσίων ἢ ἐνδύσεως ἱματίων **κόσμος** [GNT] | Adornment, beauty, decoration, comeliness.<br><br>**Practical Application**<br>The word "beauty" (*kosmos*) is really an accurate translation of what Scripture means. The word means the dress, ornaments, and arrangement of clothing upon the body. But the word also refers to behavior and demeanor, that is, the way a woman carries herself, walks, moves, and behaves in public. Remember: this passage is being written to genuine Christian women—women who truly believe in the Lord and wish to honor the Lord and to have a strong testimony for Him. The Christian woman wants to guard her clothing in order to dress modestly; she wants to watch the way she dresses, walks, moves, and behaves in public. She wants to bring honor to the Lord and to build a strong testimony—a testimony that she does love the Lord and has committed her life...<br>• to help people, not to seduce them.<br>• to serve people, not to destroy them.<br>• to point people to Jesus, not to attract them to herself.<br>• to teach people righteous behavior, not fleshly and worldly behavior.<br>The point is that the Christian woman does not dress, walk, move, speak, or behave to attract attention to her body. She is not to adorn |

# PRACTICAL WORD STUDIES
## in the NEW TESTAMENT

| ENGLISH WORD | GREEK WORD AND VERSE | THE WORD MEANS... |
|---|---|---|
| | | herself...<br>• with *fancy hairstyles*: elaborate hairstyles; hairstyles that are so different that they break away from acceptable custom and attract attention to herself.<br>• with expensive jewelry or beautiful elaborate jewelry and clothing that is extravagant, ostentatious, flamboyant, attracting attention to herself.<br>How a woman dresses shows whether she lives in the fear and reverence of God or has desires for the world and the gaping and lustful attention of men. The Christian woman is not to adorn herself in a sensual or excessive manner.<br>⇒ She is not to adorn herself with unusual hairstyles.<br>⇒ She is not to adorn herself with extremely expensive clothes and jewelry.<br>⇒ She is not to adorn herself in any manner that will be immodest or impure and unclean.<br>⇒ She must not dress or behave *in any manner that would not be modest enough to appear before and to be seen by God*—in any manner that does not show fear and reverence for God.<br>⇒ She must not adorn herself in any manner that would cause her to be proud or puffed up.<br>⇒ She must not adorn herself with any dress or behavior that would attract and cause sensual or tempting thoughts to a man. (This shows anything but fear and reverence for God.) |
| #295<br>**Became**<br><br>Took part–KJV<br>Partook–NASB<br>Shared in–NIV<br>Shared in–NKJV<br>**Became**–NLT<br><br>**POSB<br>REFERENCE**<br>(Heb. 2:14-16; esp. v.14)<br>Note 1. point 1 | μετέσχεν = meteschen<br>Pronunciation: [met-es-khehn]<br>Parsing (part of speech): verb<br>    Mood—indicative<br>    Tense—aorist<br>    Voice—active<br>    Person—3rd person<br>    Number—singular<br>    Stem or root—from μετέχω<br>Concordance References:<br>⇒ Strong's #3348 metechō<br>⇒ NIV #3576 metechō<br>⇒ NASB #3348 metechō<br><br>**Hebrews 2:14**<br>Forasmuch then as the children are partakers of flesh and blood, he also himself likewise **took part** of the same; that through death he might destroy him that had the power of death, that is, the devil; [KJV]<br>Since then the children share in flesh and blood, He Himself likewise also **partook** of the same, that through death He might render powerless him who had the power of death, that is, the devil; [NASB]<br>Since the children have flesh and blood, he too **shared in** their humanity so that by his death he might destroy him who holds the power of death—that is, the devil—[NIV]<br>Inasmuch then as the children have partaken of flesh and blood, He Himself likewise **shared in** the same, that through death He might destroy him who had the power of death, that is, the devil, [NKJV]<br>Because God's children are human beings—made of flesh and blood—Jesus also **became** flesh and blood by being born in human form. For only as a human being could he die, and only by dying could he break the power | To share in; to take part of; to partake of; to become; to hold with.<br><br>**Practical Application**<br>Christ took part of or "became" (*meteschen*) human nature. The idea is that Christ became human nature and held human nature with man. He added human nature to His divine nature. His human nature was an addition to His divine nature. As God the Son, Jesus Christ had absolutely no part of flesh and blood, but as the Son of Man, He took hold of man's nature. The point is this: Jesus Christ became man, and as Man He became flesh and blood, willingly and voluntarily. Jesus Christ loves us so much that He would pay the ultimate price to deliver us. He would humble Himself to such a degree that He would leave heaven above in order to come to earth and live as a Man. (See POSB notes—Hebrews 2:17-18 for more discussion.) (Kenneth Wuest points this out in an excellent discussion and Marvin Vincent quotes the Biblical scholar B.F. Westcott as making the same point.) |

| ENGLISH WORD | GREEK WORD AND VERSE | THE WORD MEANS... |
|---|---|---|
| | of the Devil, who had the power of death. [NLT]<br>ἐπεὶ οὖν τὰ παιδία κεκοινώνηκε σαρκός καὶ αἵματος, καὶ αὐτὸς παραπλησίως **μετέσχε** τῶν αὐτῶν, ἵνα διὰ τοῦ θανάτου καταργήσῃ τὸν τὸ κράτος ἔχοντα τοῦ θανάτου, τοῦτ' ἔστι τὸν διάβολον, [GNS]<br>ἐπεὶ οὖν τὰ παιδία κεκοινώνηκεν αἵματος καὶ σαρκός, καὶ αὐτὸς παραπλησίως **μετέσχεν** τῶν αὐτῶν, ἵνα διὰ τοῦ θανάτου καταργήσῃ τὸν τὸ κράτος ἔχοντα τοῦ θανάτου, τοῦτ' ἔστιν τὸν διάβολον, [GNT] | |
| #296<br>**Because [You] Cannot**<br><br>No longer–KJV<br>For you can no longer–NASB<br>**Because [you] cannot–NIV**<br>No longer–NKJV<br>You are going to be dismissed –NLT<br><br>**POSB REFERENCE**<br>(Lk.16:1-7; esp. v.2)<br>Note 1, point 2a | οὐ γὰρ δύνῃ = *ou gar dunë*<br>Pronunciation: [oo gar doo-nay]<br>Parsing *dunë* (part of speech): verb<br>  Mood—indicative<br>  Tense—present<br>  Voice—middle or passive deponent<br>  Person—2nd person<br>  Number—singular<br>  Stem or root—from δύναμαι<br>Concordance References:<br>⇒ Strong's #1063 gar + dunamai 1410 + 3756 ou<br>⇒ NIV #1142 gar [because] + 1538 dunamai + 4024 ou [cannot]<br>⇒ NASB #1063 gar + dunamai 1410 + 3756 ou<br><br>**Luke 16:2**<br>And he called him, and said unto him, How is it that I hear this of thee? give an account of thy stewardship; for thou mayest be **no longer** steward. [KJV]<br>"And he called him and said to him, 'What is this I hear about you? Give an account of your stewardship, **for you can no longer** be steward.' [NASB]<br>So he called him in and asked him, 'What is this I hear about you? Give an account of your management, **because you cannot** be manager any longer.' [NIV]<br>So he called him and said to him, 'What is this I hear about you? Give an account of your stewardship, for you can **no longer** be steward.' [NKJV]<br>So his employer called him in and said, 'What's this I hear about your stealing from me? Get your report in order, because **you are going to be dismissed**.' [NLT]<br>καὶ φωνήσας αὐτὸν, εἶπεν αὐτῷ, Τί τοῦτο ἀκούω περὶ σοῦ; ἀπόδος τὸν λόγον τῆς οἰκονομίας σου· **οὐ γὰρ δυνήσῃ** ἔτι οἰκονομεῖν. [GNS]<br>καὶ φωνήσας αὐτὸν εἶπεν αὐτῷ, Τί τοῦτο ἀκούω περὶ σοῦ; ἀπόδος τὸν λόγον τῆς οἰκονομίας σου, **οὐ γὰρ δύνῃ** ἔτι οἰκονομεῖν. [GNT] | Because you cannot; for you can no longer; you are going to be dismissed; not capable of; cannot do; not able to do.<br><br>**Practical Application**<br>In this Scripture, the manager is required to give an account of his actions, to prepare a final accounting. Note two important facts:<br>1. The Lord hears that the manager has been misusing His "possessions" (cp. Lk.16:1). The Lord had only heard about the embezzlement. The full evidence against the manager was not yet fully known. The Lord gave the manager a chance to prove his trust and faithfulness. The accounting did not mean that the manager would be dismissed from the Lord's estate (heaven, Kingdom of God), only that he must prove his trust and faithfulness. Of course, if the manager had not been faithful in looking after the Lord's goods, then he would be dismissed: "because you cannot [*ou gar dunë*] be manager any longer."<br>2. The final accounting is at death (Hebrews 9:27). If the manager is found to have been untrustworthy, he will be dismissed and discharged from the Lord's estate (kingdom, heaven, eternal life. See POSB *Deeper Study* #3—Matthew 19:23-24.) |
| #297<br>**Because Of Him**<br><br>Of him–KJV<br>By His doing–NASB<br>**Because of him–NIV**<br>Of Him–NKJV<br>God alone made it possible–NLT<br><br>**POSB REFERENCE**<br>(1 Cor.1:30-31; esp. v.30)<br>Note 4 | ἐξ αὐτοῦ = *ex autou*<br>Pronunciation: [ex ow-too']<br>Parsing *autou* (part of speech): noun<br>  Type—pronoun<br>  Case—genitive<br>  Gender—masculine<br>  Person—3rd person<br>  Number—singular<br>  Stem or root—from αὐτός, ή, ό<br>Concordance References:<br>⇒ Strong's #1537 ek + 846 autos<br>⇒ NIV #1666 ek [because of] + 899 autos [him]<br>⇒ NASB #1537 ek + 846 autos<br><br>**1 Cor. 1:30**<br>But **of him** are ye in Christ Jesus, who of God is made unto us wisdom, and righteousness, and sanctification, and redemption: [KJV]<br>But **by His doing** you are in Christ Jesus, who became to us wisdom from God, and righteousness and sanctification, and redemption, [NASB]<br>It is **because of him** that you are in Christ Jesus, who has become for us wisdom from God—that is, our righteousness, holiness and redemption, [NIV]<br>But **of Him** you are in Christ Jesus, who became for | Because of God; out of God; out of His nature of love and salvation; by God's doing.<br><br>**Practical Application**<br>God chooses the believer to be in Christ (see POSB *Deeper Study* #1, Position in Christ—Romans 8:1 for discussion). Again, the stress is that it is God who saves a person; the person does not save himself, no matter how capable he is or how much good he may do. How is God able to save men? By Christ. God presented Christ to the world as the wisdom of God. |

# PRACTICAL WORD STUDIES
## in the NEW TESTAMENT

| ENGLISH WORD | GREEK WORD AND VERSE | THE WORD MEANS... |
|---|---|---|
| | us wisdom from God—and righteousness and sanctification and redemption— [NKJV]<br>**God alone made it possible** for you to be in Christ Jesus. For our benefit God made Christ to be wisdom itself. He is the one who made us acceptable to God. He made us pure and holy, and he gave himself to purchase our freedom. [NLT]<br>ἐξ αὐτοῦ δὲ ὑμεῖς ἐστε ἐν Χριστῷ Ἰησοῦ, ὃς ἐγενήθη ἡμῖν σοφία ἀπὸ Θεοῦ, δικαιοσύνη τε καὶ ἁγιασμός, καὶ ἀπολύτρωσις, [GNS]<br>ἐξ αὐτοῦ δὲ ὑμεῖς ἐστε ἐν Χριστῷ Ἰησοῦ, ὃς ἐγενήθη σοφία ἡμῖν ἀπὸ θεοῦ, δικαιοσύνη τε καὶ ἁγιασμὸς καὶ ἀπολύτρωσις, [GNT] | |
| **#298**<br>**Because They Are Mine**<br><br>In my name–KJV<br>In My name–NASB<br>In my name–NIV<br>In My name–NKJV<br>**Because they are mine–NLT**<br><br>**POSB REFERENCE**<br>(Mt.18:19-20; esp. v.20)<br>*Deeper Study* #3 | εἰς τὸ ἐμὸν ὄνομα = *eis to emon onoma*<br>Pronunciation: [ice to e-mon-on'-om-ah]<br>Parsing *onoma* (part of speech): noun<br>  Case—accusative<br>  Gender—neuter<br>  Number—singular<br>  Stem or root—from ὄνομα, τος<br>Concordance References:<br>⇒ Strong's #3686 onoma<br>⇒ NIV #1650 eis [in] + 1847 emos [my] + 3950 onoma [name]<br>⇒ NASB #3686 onoma<br><br>**Matthew 18:20**<br>For where two or three are gathered together **in my name**, there am I in the midst of them. [KJV]<br>"For where two or three have gathered together **in My name**, there I am in their midst." [NASB]<br>For where two or three come together **in my name**, there am I with them." [NIV]<br>For where two or three are gathered together **in My name**, I am there in the midst of them." [NKJV]<br>For where two or three gather together **because they are mine**, I am there among them." [NLT]<br>οὐ γάρ εἰσι δύο ἢ τρεῖς συνηγμένοι εἰς τὸ ἐμὸν ὄνομα, ἐκεῖ εἰμι ἐν μέσῳ αὐτῶν. [GNS]<br>οὗ γάρ εἰσιν δύο ἢ τρεῖς συνηγμένοι εἰς τὸ ἐμὸν ὄνομα, ἐκεῖ εἰμι ἐν μέσῳ αὐτῶν. [GNT] | Literally "into my name."<br><br>**Practical Application**<br>The idea is close and intimate union with Christ. It is a "getting into" the Spirit of Christ; a longing to be in union with Him and to act only for His glory. It is a depth of spiritual union demonstrated by so few. Note: it comes not only from private prayer but from prayer with others. |
| **#299**<br>**Because You Belong To The Lord**<br><br>In the Lord–KJV<br>In the Lord–NASB<br>In the Lord–NIV<br>In the Lord–NKJV<br>**Because you belong to the Lord–NLT**<br><br>**POSB REFERENCE**<br>(Eph.6:1-3; esp. v.1)<br>Note 1, point 1 | ἐν κυρίῳ = *en kuriō*<br>Pronunciation: [en koo'-ree-o]<br>Parsing *kuriō* (part of speech): noun<br>  Case—dative<br>  Gender—masculine<br>  Number—sing from κύριος, ου ular<br>  Stem or root—<br>Concordance References:<br>⇒ Strong's #1722 en + 2962 kurios<br>⇒ NIV #1877 en [in] + 3261 kurios [the Lord]<br>⇒ NASB #1722 en + 2962 kurios<br><br>**Ephes. 6:1**<br>Children, obey your parents **in the Lord**: for this is right. [KJV]<br>Children, obey your parents **in the Lord**, for this is right. [NASB]<br>Children, obey your parents **in the Lord**, for this is right. [NIV]<br>Children, obey your parents **in the Lord**, for this is right. [NKJV]<br>Children, obey your parents **because you belong to the Lord**, for this is the right thing to do. [NLT]<br>Τὰ τέκνα, ὑπακούετε τοῖς γονεῦσιν ὑμῶν ἐν Κυρίῳ· τοῦτο γάρ ἐστι δίκαιον. [GNS]<br>Τὰ τέκνα, ὑπακούετε τοῖς γονεῦσιν ὑμῶν [ἐν κυρίῳ]· τοῦτο γάρ ἐστιν δίκαιον. [GNT] | In the Lord; because you belong to the Lord, Master, Owner.<br><br>**Practical Application**<br>First, to obey means to obey *because you belong to the Lord*. Note the command again: "Children, obey your parents because you belong to the Lord." (*en kuriō*) The phrase "because you belong to the Lord" means at least two things.<br>1. There is a limit to the child's obedience. When a parent is not acting in the Lord, he is not to be obeyed. The Lord has nothing whatsoever to do with the filth of unrighteousness and abuse of precious children. If a child can break away to free himself from such parental corruption, he has every right to be freed from his parent. The Lord came to set men free from the abuse and the filth of sin, not to enslave men to it and especially not to enslave children to it.<br>One of the most severe warnings ever issued in all of history was issued by the Lord Jesus to adults who abuse children:<br><br>*"But if anyone causes one of these little ones who trusts in me to lose faith, it would be better for that person to be thrown into* |

# PRACTICAL WORD STUDIES
## in the NEW TESTAMENT

| ENGLISH WORD | GREEK WORD AND VERSE | THE WORD MEANS... |
|---|---|---|
| | | the sea with a large millstone tied around the neck. If your hand causes you to sin, cut it off. It is better to enter heaven with only one hand than to go into the unquenchable fires of hell with two hands. If your foot causes you to sin, cut it off. It is better to enter heaven with only one foot than to be thrown into hell with two feet. And if your eye causes you to sin, gouge it out. It is better to enter the Kingdom of God half blind than to have two eyes and be thrown into hell, 'where the worm never dies and the fire never goes out.'" (Mark 9:42-48). [NLT] |
| | | 2. The phrase "because you belong to the Lord" also tells why the child is to obey his parents. "Children, obey your parents because you belong to the Lord"—obeying your parents is right; it is of the Lord; it pleases the Lord; therefore, obey them. When they guide and instruct you, follow them (cp. Col. 3:20). |
| **#300**<br>**Become**<br><br>Be–KJV<br>**Become–NASB**<br>**Become–NIV**<br>**Become–NKJV**<br>**Become–NLT**<br><br>**POSB<br>REFERENCE**<br>(Jn.12:34-36; esp. v.36)<br>Note 5, point 2<br><br>See also POSB REF:<br>(Jn.1:12-13; esp. v.12)<br>Note 3, point 2<br>(Eph.5:1)<br>Note 1 | γένησθε = genësthe<br>Pronunciation: [ghen-ace-theh]<br>Parsing (part of speech): verb<br>   Mood—subjunctive<br>   Tense—aorist<br>   Voice—middle deponent<br>   Person—2nd person<br>   Number—plural<br>   Stem or root—from γίνομαι<br>Concordance References:<br> ⇒ Strong's #1096 ginomai<br> ⇒ NIV #1181 ginomai<br> ⇒ NASB #1096 ginomai<br><br>**John 12:36**<br>While ye have light, believe in the light, that ye **be** the children of light. These things spake Jesus, and departed, and did hide himself from them. [KJV]<br>"While you have the light, believe in the light, in order that you may **become** sons of light." These things Jesus spoke, and He departed and hid Himself from them. [NASB]<br>Put your trust in the light while you have it, so that you may **become** sons of light." When he had finished speaking, Jesus left and hid himself from them. [NIV]<br>While you have the light, believe in the light, that you may **become** sons of light." These things Jesus spoke, and departed, and was hidden from them. [NKJV]<br>Believe in the light while there is still time; then you will **become** children of the light." After saying these things, Jesus went away and was hidden from them. [NLT]<br>ἕως τὸ φῶς ἔχετε, πιστεύετε εἰς τὸ φῶς, ἵνα υἱοὶ φωτὸς **γένησθε**. Ταῦτα ἐλάλησεν ὁ Ἰησοῦς, καὶ ἀπελθὼν ἐκρύβη ἀπ' αὐτῶν. [GNS]<br>ὡς τὸ φῶς ἔχετε, πιστεύετε εἰς τὸ φῶς, ἵνα υἱοὶ φωτὸς **γένησθε**. Ταῦτα ἐλάλησεν Ἰησοῦς, καὶ ἀπελθὼν ἐκρύβη ἀπ' αὐτῶν. [GNT] | To become; to be; to come into existence; to take on a new form; to be made; to change.<br><br>**Practical Application**<br>"Become" is a once-for-all act, a personal experience that happens all at once. A person who truly sees Jesus Christ as the Light of the world believes and continues to believe. And the very moment his heart leaps toward Christ in belief, he becomes a child of the Light, a child of God Himself. The person sees the Light and begins to walk in the Light, living the kind of life he should. |
| **#301**<br>**Become [Your]<br>Father**<br><br>Begotten–KJV<br>Begotten–NASB<br>**Become [your]<br>Father–NIV**<br>Begotten–NKJV | γεγέννηκά = gegennëka<br>Pronunciation: [ghe-ghen-nay'-kah]<br>Parsing (part of speech): verb<br>   Mood—indicative<br>   Tense—perfect<br>   Voice—active<br>   Person—1st person<br>   Number—singular<br>   Stem or root—from γεννάω<br>Concordance References:<br> ⇒ Strong's #1080 gennaö | To become a father of; to beget; to give birth to; to conceive; to be born.<br><br>**Practical Application**<br>Jesus Christ is the Son of God; God and God alone is the Father of Christ" (*gegennëka*); that is, He was born or sent into the world by God. God did not send or cause an angel to be born into the world; He sent His only begotten Son, His one and only Son. |

# PRACTICAL WORD STUDIES
## in the NEW TESTAMENT

| ENGLISH WORD | GREEK WORD AND VERSE | THE WORD MEANS... |
|---|---|---|
| **Become [your] Father–NLT**<br><br>**POSB REFERENCE**<br>(Heb.1:4-6; esp. v.5)<br>Note 1, point 1 | ⇒ NIV #1164 gennaö<br>⇒ NASB #1080 gennaö<br><br>**Hebrews 1:5**<br>For unto which of the angels said he at any time, Thou art my Son, this day have I **begotten** thee? And again, I will be to him a Father, and he shall be to me a Son? [KJV]<br><br>For to which of the angels did He ever say, "Thou art My Son, Today I have **begotten** Thee"? And again, "I will be a Father to Him And He shall be a Son to Me"? [NASB]<br><br>For to which of the angels did God ever say, "You are my Son; today I have **become** your **Father**"? Or again, "I will be his Father, and he will be my Son"? [NIV]<br><br>For to which of the angels did He ever say: "You are My Son, Today I have **begotten** You"? And again: "I will be to Him a Father, And He shall be to Me a Son"? [NKJV]<br><br>For God never said to any angel what he said to Jesus: "You are my Son. Today I have **become** your **Father**." And again God said, "I will be his Father, and he will be my Son." [NLT]<br><br>τίνι γὰρ εἶπέ ποτε τῶν ἀγγέλων, Υἱός μου εἶ σύ, ἐγὼ σήμερον **γεγέννηκά** σε; Καὶ πάλιν, Ἐγὼ ἔσομαι αὐτῷ εἰσπατέρα, καὶ αὐτὸς ἔσται μοι εἰς υἱόν; [GNS]<br><br>Τίνι γὰρ εἶπέν ποτε τῶν ἀγγέλων, Υἱός μου εἶ σύ, ἐγὼ σήμερον **γεγέννηκά** σε; καὶ πάλιν, Ἐγὼ ἔσομαι αὐτῷ εἰς πατέρα, καὶ αὐτὸς ἔσται μοι εἰς υἱόν; [GNT] | |
| **#302**<br>**Become Arrogant**<br><br>Puffed up–KJV<br>Become arrogant–NASB<br>Take pride–NIV<br>Puffed up–NKJV<br>Brag–NLT<br><br>**POSB REFERENCE**<br>(1 Cor.4:6)<br>Note 1, point 2 | φυσιοῦσθε = *phusiousthe*<br>Pronunciation: [foo-see-o'-oos-the]<br>Parsing (part of speech): verb<br>  Mood—indicative<br>  Tense—present<br>  Voice—passive<br>  Person—2nd person<br>  Number—plural<br>  Stem or root—from φυσιόω<br>Concordance References:<br>⇒ Strong's #5448 phusioö<br>⇒ NIV #5881 phusioö<br>⇒ NASB #5448 phusioö<br><br>**1 Cor. 4:6**<br>And these things, brethren, I have in a figure transferred to myself and to Apollos for your sakes; that ye might learn in us not to think of men above that which is written, that no one of you be **puffed up** for one against another. [KJV]<br><br>Now these things, brethren, I have figuratively applied to myself and Apollos for your sakes, that in us you might learn not to exceed what is written, in order that no one of you might **become arrogant** in behalf of one against the other. [NASB]<br><br>Now, brothers, I have applied these things to myself and Apollos for your benefit, so that you may learn from us the meaning of the saying, "Do not go beyond what is written." Then you will not **take pride** in one man over against another. [NIV]<br><br>Now these things, brethren, I have figuratively transferred to myself and Apollos for your sakes, that you may learn in us not to think beyond what is written, that none of you may be **puffed up** on behalf of one against the other. [NKJV]<br><br>Dear brothers and sisters, I have used Apollos and myself to illustrate what I've been saying. If you pay attention to the Scriptures, you won't **brag** about one of your leaders at the expense of another. [NLT]<br><br>Ταῦτα δέ, ἀδελφοί, μετεσχημάτισα εἰς ἐμαυτὸν καὶ Ἀπολλῶν δι' ὑμᾶς, ἵνα ἐν ἡμῖν μάθητε τὸ μὴ ὑπὲρ ὃ γέγραπται φρονεῖν, ἵνα μὴ εἰς ὑπὲρ τοῦ ἑνὸς **φυσιοῦσθε** | To take pride; to become arrogant; to brag; to be conceited; to be inflated.<br><br>**Practical Application**<br>It is a picture of puffed up air bags. The point is the judging of ministers and the feelings that one can judge ministers is nothing but hot air in puffed up or inflated balloons. It is meaningless. It means absolutely nothing to God. (Cp. 1 Cor. 4:18-19; 1 Cor. 5:2; 1 Cor. 8:1; 1 Cor. 13:4.) |

# PRACTICAL WORD STUDIES
## in the NEW TESTAMENT

| ENGLISH WORD | GREEK WORD AND VERSE | THE WORD MEANS... |
|---|---|---|
| | κατὰ τοῦ ἑτέρου. [GNS]<br>Ταῦτα δέ, ἀδελφοί, μετεσχημάτισα εἰς ἐμαυτὸν καὶ Ἀπολλῶν δι' ὑμᾶς, ἵνα ἐν ἡμῖν μάθητε τὸ Μὴ ὑπὲρ ἃ γέγραπται, ἵνα μὴ εἰς ὑπὲρ τοῦ ἑνὸς **φυσιοῦσθε** κατὰ τοῦ ἑτέρου. [GNT] | |
| **#303**<br>**Become Complete**<br><br>Be perfect–KJV<br>Be made complete–NASB<br>Aim for perfection–NIV<br>**Become complete–NKJV**<br>Change your ways–NLT<br><br>**POSB REFERENCE**<br>(2 Cor.13:11-13; esp. v.11)<br>Note 3 | **καταρτίζεσθε** = katartizesthe<br>Pronunciation: [kat-ar-tid'-zehs-the]<br>Parsing (part of speech): verb<br>    Mood—imperative<br>    Tense—present<br>    Voice—passive<br>    Person—2nd person<br>    Number—plural<br>    Stem or root—from καταρτίζω<br>Concordance References:<br>  ⇒ Strong's #2675 katartizō<br>  ⇒ NIV #2936 katartizō<br>  ⇒ NASB #2675 katartizō<br><br>**2 Cor. 13:11**<br>Finally, brethren, farewell. **Be perfect**, be of good comfort, be of one mind, live in peace; and the God of love and peace shall be with you. [KJV]<br>Finally, brethren, rejoice, **be made complete**, be comforted, be like-minded, live in peace; and the God of love and peace shall be with you. [NASB]<br>Finally, brothers, good-by. **Aim for perfection**, listen to my appeal, be of one mind, live in peace. And the God of love and peace will be with you. [NIV]<br>Finally, brethren, farewell. **Become complete**. Be of good comfort, be of one mind, live in peace; and the God of love and peace will be with you. [NKJV]<br>Dear brothers and sisters, I close my letter with these last words: Rejoice. **Change your ways**. Encourage each other. Live in harmony and peace. Then the God of love and peace will be with you. [NLT]<br>Λοιπόν, ἀδελφοί, χαίρετε· **καταρτίζεσθε**, παρακαλεῖσθε, τὸ αὐτὸ φρονεῖτε, εἰρηνεύετε· καὶ ὁ Θεὸς τῆς ἀγάπης καὶ εἰρήνης ἔσται μεθ' ὑμῶν. [GNS]<br>Λοιπόν, ἀδελφοί, χαίρετε, **καταρτίζεσθε**, παρακαλεῖσθε, τὸ αὐτὸ φρονεῖτε, εἰρηνεύετε, καὶ ὁ θεὸς τῆς ἀγάπης καὶ εἰρήνης ἔσται μεθ' ὑμῶν. [GNT] | To aim and strive for perfection; to be made complete; to prepare; to change one's ways; to restore, reform, correct, and mend oneself and one's ways.<br><br>**Practical Application**<br>Paul's challenge to his Corinthian brothers is blunt and to the point: Stop your sinning (criticism, divisiveness, immorality). |
| **#304**<br>**Become Sober Minded**<br><br>Awake–KJV<br>**Become sober minded–NASB**<br>Come back to your senses–NIV<br>Awake–NKJV<br>Come to your senses–NLT<br><br>**POSB REFERENCE**<br>(1 Cor.15:34)<br>Note 4 | **ἐκνήψατε** = eknēpsate<br>Pronunciation: [ek-nay'-fah-teh]<br>Parsing (part of speech): verb<br>    Mood—imperative<br>    Tense—aorist<br>    Voice—active<br>    Person—2nd person<br>    Number—plural<br>    Stem or root—from ἐκνήφω<br>Concordance References:<br>  ⇒ Strong's #1594 eknēphō<br>  ⇒ NIV #1729 eknēphō<br>  ⇒ NASB #1594 eknēphō<br><br>**1 Cor. 15:34**<br>**Awake** to righteousness, and sin not; for some have not the knowledge of God: I speak this to your shame. [KJV]<br>**Become sober-minded** as you ought, and stop sinning; for some have no knowledge of God. I speak this to your shame. [NASB]<br>**Come back to your senses** as you ought, and stop sinning; for there are some who are ignorant of God—I say this to your shame. [NIV]<br>**Awake** to righteousness, and do not sin; for some do not have the knowledge of God. I speak this to your shame. [NKJV]<br>**Come to your senses** and stop sinning. For to your shame I say that some of you don't even know God. | Come back to your senses; become sober; arouse yourself out of a drunken, sleepy state.<br><br>**Practical Application**<br>Some in the Corinthian church were following the false teachers as though they were drunken and senseless, in a stupor, in a stupid state. They desperately needed to awaken to righteousness—to stop sinning. The denial of a resurrection is totally wrong; it is sin. There is to be a resurrection of the dead. To deny this fact is to put oneself in a drunken, senseless, unthinking state of mind. |

# PRACTICAL WORD STUDIES
## in the NEW TESTAMENT

| ENGLISH WORD | GREEK WORD AND VERSE | THE WORD MEANS... |
|---|---|---|
| | [NLT]<br>ἐκνήψατε δικαίως καὶ μὴ ἁμαρτάνετε· ἀγνωσίαν γὰρ Θεοῦ τινες ἔχουσι· πρὸς ἐντροπὴν ὑμῖν λέγω. [GNS]<br>ἐκνήψατε δικαίως καὶ μὴ ἁμαρτάνετε, ἀγνωσίαν γὰρ θεοῦ τινες ἔχουσιν, πρὸς ἐντροπὴν ὑμῖν λαλῶ. [GNT] | |
| **#305**<br>**Become Unprofitable**<br><br>Become unprofitable–KJV<br>Become useless–NASB<br>Become worthless–NIV<br>Become unprofitable–NKJV<br>Gone wrong–NLT<br><br>**POSB REFERENCE**<br>(Rom.3:10-12; esp. v.12)<br>Note 2, point 5 | ἠχρεώθησαν = ēchreōthēsan<br>Pronunciation: [aykh-ri-o'-thay-sahn]<br>Parsing (part of speech): verb<br>   Mood—indicative<br>   Tense—aorist<br>   Voice—passive<br>   Person—3rd person<br>   Number—plural<br>   Stem or root—from ἀχρειόομαι<br>Concordance References:<br>  ⇒ Strong's #889 achreioö<br>  ⇒ NIV #946 achreioö<br>  ⇒ NASB #889 achreioö<br><br>**Romans 3:12**<br>They are all gone out of the way, they are together **become unprofitable**; there is none that doeth good, no, not one. [KJV]<br>ALL HAVE TURNED ASIDE, TOGETHER THEY HAVE **BECOME USELESS**; THERE IS NONE WHO DOES GOOD, THERE IS NOT EVEN ONE." [NASB]<br>All have turned away, they have together **become worthless**; there is no one who does good, not even one." [NIV]<br>*They have all turned aside; They have together **become unprofitable**; There is none who does good, no, not one."* [NKJV]<br>All have turned away from God; all have **gone wrong**. No one does good, not even one." [NLT]<br>πάντες ἐξέκλιναν, ἅμα **ἠχρεώθησαν**· οὐκ ἔστι ὁ ποιῶν χρηστότητα, οὐκ ἔστιν ἕως ἑνός. [GNS]<br>πάντες ἐξέκλιναν ἅμα **ἠχρεώθησαν**· οὐκ ἔστιν ὁ ποιῶν χρηστότητα, [οὐκ ἔστιν] ἕως ἑνός. [GNT] | To become worthless; unprofitable, useless, sour, bad, debased. (Cp. sour milk.) It means to go wrong.<br><br>**Practical Application**<br>A sinful nature is unprofitable (Romans 3:12; cp. Psalm 14:3). All men without Christ are worthless, useless, sour, bad. |
| **#306**<br>**Become Useless**<br><br>Become unprofitable–KJV<br>**Become useless–NASB**<br>Become worthless–NIV<br>Become unprofitable–KJV<br>Gone wrong–NLT<br><br>**POSB REFERENCE**<br>(Rom.3:10-12; esp. v.12)<br>Note 2, point 5 | ἠχρεώθησαν = ēchreōthēsan<br>Pronunciation: [aykh-ri-o'-thay-sahn]<br>Parsing (part of speech): verb<br>   Mood—indicative<br>   Tense—aorist<br>   Voice—passive<br>   Person—3rd person<br>   Number—plural<br>   Stem or root—from ἀχρειόομαι<br>Concordance References:<br>  ⇒ Strong's #889 achreioö<br>  ⇒ NIV #946 achreioö<br>  ⇒ NASB #889 achreioö<br><br>**Romans 3:12**<br>They are all gone out of the way, they are together **become unprofitable**; there is none that doeth good, no, not one. [KJV]<br>ALL HAVE TURNED ASIDE, TOGETHER THEY HAVE **BECOME USELESS**; THERE IS NONE WHO DOES GOOD, THERE IS NOT EVEN ONE." [NASB]<br>All have turned away, they have together **become worthless**; there is no one who does good, not even one." [NIV]<br>*They have all turned aside; They have together **become unprofitable**; There is none who does good, no, not one."* [NKJV]<br>All have turned away from God; all have **gone wrong**. No one does good, not even one." [NLT]<br>πάντες ἐξέκλιναν, ἅμα **ἠχρεώθησαν**· οὐκ ἔστι ὁ ποιῶν χρηστότητα, οὐκ ἔστιν ἕως ἑνός. [GNS]<br>πάντες ἐξέκλιναν ἅμα **ἠχρεώθησαν**· οὐκ ἔστιν ὁ ποιῶν χρηστότητα, [οὐκ ἔστιν] ἕως ἑνός. [GNT] | To become worthless; unprofitable, useless, sour, bad, debased. (Cp. sour milk.) It means to go wrong.<br><br>**Practical Application**<br>A sinful nature is useless (Romans 3:12; cp. Psalm 14:3). All men without Christ are worthless, useless, sour, bad. |

# PRACTICAL WORD STUDIES
## in the NEW TESTAMENT

| ENGLISH WORD | GREEK WORD AND VERSE | THE WORD MEANS... |
|---|---|---|
| **#307**<br>**Become Visible**<br><br>Showed openly–KJV<br>**Become visible–NASB**<br>Be seen–NIV<br>Showed openly–NKJV<br>To appear–NLT<br><br>**POSB REFERENCE**<br>(Acts 10:40-41; esp. v.40)<br>Note 6, point 1 | ἐμφανῆ γενέσθαι = emphanē genesthai<br>Pronunciation: [em-fan-ay' ghin'-es-tha-ee]<br>Parsing *emphanē* (part of speech): adjective<br>    Case—accusative<br>    Gender—masculine<br>    Number—singular<br>    Stem or root—from ἐμφανής<br>Parsing *genesthai* (part of speech): verb<br>    Mood—infinitive<br>    Tense—aorist<br>    Voice—middle deponent<br>    Stem or root—from γίνομαι<br>Concordance References:<br>⇒ Strong's #1717 emphanēs + 1096 ginomai<br>⇒ NIV #1871 [seen] emphanēs + 1181 genesthai [be]<br>⇒ NASB #1717 emphanēs + 1096 ginomai<br><br>**Acts 10:40**<br>Him God raised up the third day, and **showed** him **openly**; [KJV]<br>"God raised Him up on the third day, and granted that He should **become visible**, [NASB]<br>But God raised him from the dead on the third day and caused him to **be seen**. [NIV]<br>Him God raised up on the third day, and **showed** Him **openly**, [NKJV]<br>But God raised him to life three days later. Then God allowed him **to appear**, [NLT]<br>Τοῦτον ὁ Θεὸς ἤγειρε τῇ τρίτῃ ἡμέρᾳ, καὶ ἔδωκεν αὐτὸν ἐμφανῆ γενέσθαι, [GNS]<br>τοῦτον ὁ θεὸς ἤγειρεν [ἐν] τῇ τρίτῃ ἡμέρᾳ καὶ ἔδωκεν αὐτὸν ἐμφανῆ γενέσθαι, [GNT] | To be seen; to become visible; to appear; to show openly; to be revealed.<br><br>**Practical Application**<br>God granted that Christ should become visible—He allowed Him to appear—which means that God set Jesus before people so that He could be visibly, openly, and publicly seen. God manifested, showed, and set Him forth as the Risen Lord. (See POSB note—Acts 1:3 and POSB *Deeper Study* #1, Jesus, Resurrection—Acts 1:3 for more discussion.) |
| **#308**<br>**Become Worthless**<br><br>Become unprofitable–KJV<br>Become useless–NASB<br>**Become worthless–NIV**<br>Become unprofitable–NKJV<br>Gone wrong–NLT<br><br>**POSB REFERENCE**<br>(Rom.3:10-12; esp. v.12)<br>Note 2, point 5 | ἠχρεώθησαν = ēchreōthēsan<br>Pronunciation: [aykh-ri-o'-thay-sahn]<br>Parsing (part of speech): verb<br>    Mood—indicative<br>    Tense—aorist<br>    Voice—passive<br>    Person—3rd person<br>    Number—plural<br>    Stem or root—from ἀχρειόομαι<br>Concordance References:<br>⇒ Strong's #889 achreioō<br>⇒ NIV #946 achreioō<br>⇒ NASB #889 achreioō<br><br>**Romans 3:12**<br>They are all gone out of the way, they are together **become unprofitable**; there is none that doeth good, no, not one. [KJV]<br>ALL HAVE TURNED ASIDE, TOGETHER THEY HAVE BECOME USELESS; THERE IS NONE WHO DOES GOOD, THERE IS NOT EVEN ONE." [NASB]<br>All have turned away, they have together **become worthless**; there is no one who does good, not even one." [NIV]<br>They have all turned aside; They have together **become unprofitable**; There is none who does good, no, not one." [NKJV]<br>All have turned away from God; all have **gone wrong**. No one does good, not even one." [NLT]<br>πάντες ἐξέκλιναν, ἅμα **ἠχρεώθησαν**· οὐκ ἔστι ὁ ποιῶν χρηστότητα, οὐκ ἔστιν ἕως ἑνός. [GNS]<br>πάντες ἐξέκλιναν ἅμα **ἠχρεώθησαν**· οὐκ ἔστιν ὁ ποιῶν χρηστότητα, [οὐκ ἔστιν] ἕως ἑνός. [GNT] | To become worthless; unprofitable, useless, sour, bad, debased. (Cp. sour milk.) It means to go wrong.<br><br>**Practical Application**<br>A sinful nature is worthless (Romans 3:12; cp. Psalm 14:3). All men without Christ are worthless, useless, sour, bad. |
| **#309**<br>**Becometh**<br><br>Becometh–KJV<br>In a manner | ἀξίως = axiōs<br>Pronunciation: [ax-ee'-oce]<br>Parsing (part of speech): adjective adverb<br>    Stem or root—from ἀξίως<br>Concordance References: | To fit; to be suitable; to correspond; to be worthy.<br><br>**Practical Application**<br>The believer's behavior is to... |

## PRACTICAL WORD STUDIES
### in the NEW TESTAMENT

| ENGLISH WORD | GREEK WORD AND VERSE | THE WORD MEANS... |
|---|---|---|
| worthy–NASB<br>In a manner worthy–NIV<br>Be worthy–NKJV<br>In a manner worthy–NLT<br><br>**POSB REFERENCE**<br>(Philip.1:27)<br>Note 2 | ⇒ Strong's #516 axiös<br>⇒ NIV #547 axiös<br>⇒ NASB #516 axiös<br><br>**Philip. 1:27**<br>Only let your conversation be as it **becometh** the gospel of Christ: that whether I come and see you, or else be absent, I may hear of your affairs, that ye stand fast in one spirit, with one mind striving together for the faith of the gospel; [KJV]<br>Only conduct yourselves **in a manner worthy** of the gospel of Christ; so that whether I come and see you or remain absent, I may hear of you that you are standing firm in one spirit, with one mind striving together for the faith of the gospel; [NASB]<br>Whatever happens, conduct yourselves **in a manner worthy** of the gospel of Christ. Then, whether I come and see you or only hear about you in my absence, I will know that you stand firm in one spirit, contending as one man for the faith of the gospel [NIV]<br>Only let your conduct **be worthy** of the gospel of Christ, so that whether I come and see you or am absent, I may hear of your affairs, that you stand fast in one spirit, with one mind striving together for the faith of the gospel, [NKJV]<br>But whatever happens to me, you must live **in a manner worthy** of the Good News about Christ, as citizens of heaven. Then, whether I come and see you again or only hear about you, I will know that you are standing side by side, fighting together for the Good News. [NLT]<br>μόνον **ἀξίως** τοῦ εὐαγγελίου τοῦ Χριστοῦ πολιτεύεσθε, ἵνα εἴτε ἐλθὼν καὶ ἰδὼν ὑμᾶς, εἴτε ἀπὼν, ἀκούσω τὰ περὶ ὑμῶν, ὅτι στήκετε ἐν ἑνὶ πνεύματι, μιᾷ ψυχῇ συναθλοῦντες τῇ πίστει τοῦ εὐαγγελίου, [GNS]<br>Μόνον **ἀξίως** τοῦ εὐαγγελίου τοῦ Χριστοῦ πολιτεύεσθε, ἵνα εἴτε ἐλθὼν καὶ ἰδὼν ὑμᾶς εἴτε ἀπὼν ἀκούω τὰ περὶ ὑμῶν, ὅτι στήκετε ἐν ἑνὶ πνεύματι, μιᾷ ψυχῇ συναθλοῦντες τῇ πίστει τοῦ εὐαγγελίου [GNT] | • fit the gospel he professes.<br>• correspond to the gospel he professes.<br>• be suitable to the gospel he professes.<br>• be worthy of the gospel he professes.<br><br>No church and no believer within the church is to bring dishonor to the gospel. If a person professes the gospel, he is to live worthy of the gospel. His conduct and behavior is to fit and correspond to the gospel he professes. |
| **#310**<br>**Been Put In Jail**<br><br>Imprisonments–KJV<br>Imprisonments–NASB<br>Imprisonments–NIV<br>Imprisonments–NKJV<br>**Been put in jail**–NLT<br><br>**POSB REFERENCE**<br>(2 Cor.6:4-5; esp. v.5)<br>Note 3 | φυλακαῖς = phulakais<br>Pronunciation: [foo-lak-ah-ees]<br>Parsing (part of speech): noun<br>    Case—dative<br>    Gender—feminine<br>    Number—plural<br>    Stem or root—from φυλακή, ῆς<br>Concordance References:<br>⇒ Strong's #5438 phulakē<br>⇒ NIV #5871 phulakē<br>⇒ NASB #5438 phulakē<br><br>**2 Cor. 6:5**<br>In stripes, in **imprisonments**, in tumults, in labours, in watchings, in fastings; [KJV]<br>In beatings, in **imprisonments**, in tumults, in labors, in sleeplessness, in hunger, [NASB]<br>In beatings, **imprisonments** and riots; in hard work, sleepless nights and hunger; [NIV]<br>In stripes, in **imprisonments**, in tumults, in labors, in sleeplessness, in fastings; [NKJV]<br>We have been beaten, **been put in jail**, faced angry mobs, worked to exhaustion, endured sleepless nights, and gone without food. [NLT]<br>ἐν πληγαῖς, ἐν **φυλακαῖς**, ἐν ἀκαταστασίαις, ἐν κόποις, ἐν ἀγρυπνίαις, ἐν νηστείαις, [GNS]<br>ἐν πληγαῖς, ἐν **φυλακαῖς**, ἐν ἀκαταστασίαις, ἐν κόποις, ἐν ἀγρυπνίαις, ἐν νηστείαις, [GNT] | Imprisonments; to be put in jail.<br><br>**Practical Application**<br>Paul was arrested and imprisoned several times: in Philippi (Acts 16), Jerusalem, Cesarea, and Rome. The early church Christian Clement of Rome (A.D. 96) says that Paul was imprisoned seven times throughout the whole span of his ministry. When the believer, minister, or layman faces imprisonment for Christ, the call of the hour is for consistency: he must endure despite the threat. He must not weaken lest he become an offense to the name of Christ and to the ministry. |
| **#311**<br>**Before Eyes**<br><br>Beheld–KJV | βλεπόντων = blepontön<br>Pronunciation: [blep'-own-tone]<br>Parsing (part of speech): verb<br>    Mood—participle<br>    Tense—present | To see; to behold; to look upon; to watch.<br><br>**Practical Application**<br>Jesus Christ began to slowly arise from the |

# PRACTICAL WORD STUDIES
## in the NEW TESTAMENT

| ENGLISH WORD | GREEK WORD AND VERSE | THE WORD MEANS... |
|---|---|---|
| Looking on–NASB<br>**Before...eyes–NIV**<br>Watched–NKJV<br>Watching–NLT<br><br>**POSB REFERENCE**<br>(Acts 1:9)<br>Note 4 | Voice—active<br>Case—genitive<br>Gender—masculine<br>Number—plural<br>Stem or root—from βλέπω<br>Concordance References:<br>⇒ Strong's #991 blepō<br>⇒ NIV #1063 blepō<br>⇒ NASB #991 blepō<br><br>**Acts 1:9**<br>And when he had spoken these things, while they **beheld**, he was taken up; and a cloud received him out of their sight. [KJV]<br>And after He had said these things, He was lifted up while they were **looking on**, and a cloud received Him out of their sight. [NASB]<br>After he said this, he was taken up **before** their very **eyes**, and a cloud hid him from their sight. [NIV]<br>Now when He had spoken these things, while they **watched**, He was taken up, and a cloud received Him out of their sight. [NKJV]<br>It was not long after he said this that he was taken up into the sky while they were **watching**, and he disappeared into a cloud. [NLT]<br>καὶ ταῦτα εἰπών, **βλεπόντων** αὐτῶν ἐπήρθη, καὶ νεφέλη ὑπέλαβεν αὐτὸν ἀπὸ τῶν ὀφθαλμῶν αὐτῶν. [GNS]<br>καὶ ταῦτα εἰπὼν **βλεπόντων** αὐτῶν ἐπήρθη, καὶ νεφέλη ὑπέλαβεν αὐτὸν ἀπὸ τῶν ὀφθαλμῶν αὐτῶν. [GNT] | earth, ascending ever upward toward the sky above. The disciples were shocked and spellbound, gazing at the spectacular sight. They were beholding one of the most dramatic and phenomenal events ever experienced:<br>⇒ the Ascension of the Lord Jesus Christ.<br>⇒ the return of God's Son into heaven, into the spiritual world and dimension of being. |
| #312<br>**Beg**<br><br>Pray–KJV<br>**Beg–NASB**<br>Implore–NIV<br>Implore–NKJV<br>Urge–NLT<br><br>**POSB REFERENCE**<br>(2 Cor.5:20)<br>Note 3 | δεόμεθα = deometha<br>Pronunciation: [deh'-om-eh-tha]<br>Parsing (part of speech): verb<br>    Mood—indicative<br>    Tense—present<br>    Voice—middle or passive deponent<br>    Person—1st person<br>    Number—plural<br>    Stem or root—from δέομαι<br>Concordance References:<br>⇒ Strong's #1189 deomai<br>⇒ NIV #1289 deomai<br>⇒ NASB #1189a deomai<br><br>**2 Cor. 5:20**<br>Now then we are ambassadors for Christ, as though God did beseech you by us: we **pray** you in Christ's stead, be ye reconciled to God. [KJV]<br>Therefore, we are ambassadors for Christ, as though God were entreating through us; we **beg** you on behalf of Christ, be reconciled to God. [NASB]<br>We are therefore Christ's ambassadors, as though God were making his appeal through us. We **implore** you on Christ's behalf: Be reconciled to God. [NIV]<br>Now then, we are ambassadors for Christ, as though God were pleading through us: we **implore** you on Christ's behalf, be reconciled to God. [NKJV]<br>We are Christ's ambassadors, and God is using us to speak to you. We **urge** you, as though Christ himself were here pleading with you, "Be reconciled to God!" [NLT]<br>ὑπὲρ Χριστοῦ οὖν πρεσβεύομεν, ὡς τοῦ Θεοῦ παρακαλοῦντος δι' ἡμῶν· **δεόμεθα** ὑπὲρ Χριστοῦ, καταλλάγητε τῷ Θεῷ. [GNS]<br>ὑπὲρ Χριστοῦ οὖν πρεσβεύομεν ὡς τοῦ θεοῦ παρακαλοῦντος δι' ἡμῶν· **δεόμεθα** ὑπὲρ Χριστοῦ, καταλλάγητε τῷ θεῷ. [GNT] | To implore; to pray; to beg; to urge; to intreat; to cry; to ask; and to plead with.<br><br>**Practical Application**<br>Note that it is "for Christ's sake" that we are to plead with men. Christ has paid the ultimate price to make reconciliation available to men: He has taken the sins of men upon Himself and borne the condemnation for them. Because He has done so much, every man owes his life to Christ—every man owes it to Christ to be reconciled to God. For Christ's sake, a man should give himself to God. |
| #313<br>**Begged**<br><br>Besought–KJV | ἠρώτα = erota<br>Pronunciation: [er-o-tah']<br>Parsing (part of speech): verb<br>    Mood—indicative<br>    Tense—imperfect | To ask; to plead, beseech, or implore; to beg and to keep on begging.<br><br>**Practical Application**<br>The woman begged Christ to heal her demon- |

# PRACTICAL WORD STUDIES
## in the NEW TESTAMENT

| ENGLISH WORD | GREEK WORD AND VERSE | THE WORD MEANS... |
|---|---|---|
| Kept asking–NASB<br>**Begged–NIV**<br>Kept asking–NKJV<br>**Begged–NLT**<br><br>**POSB<br>REFERENCE**<br>(Mk.7:26-28; esp.<br>v.26)<br>Note 3 | Voice—active<br>Person—3rd person<br>Number—singular<br>Stem or root—from ἐρωτάω<br>Concordance References:<br>⇒ Strong's #2065 erōtaō<br>⇒ NIV #2263 erōtaō<br>⇒ NASB #2065 erōtaō<br><br>**Mark 7:26**<br>The woman was a Greek, a Syrophenician by nation; and she **besought** him that he would cast forth the devil out of her daughter. [KJV]<br>Now the woman was a Gentile, of the Syrophoenician race. And she **kept asking** Him to cast the demon out of her daughter. [NASB]<br>The woman was a Greek, born in Syrian Phoenicia. She **begged** Jesus to drive the demon out of her daughter. [NIV]<br>The woman was a Greek, a Syro-Phoenician by birth, and she **kept asking** Him to cast the demon out of her daughter. [NKJV]<br>She **begged** him to release her child from the demon's control. Since she was a Gentile, born in Syrian Phoenicia, [NLT]<br>ἐν δὲ ἡ δὲ γυνὴ Ἑλληνίς, Συροφοινίσσα τῷ γένει· καὶ **ἠρώτα** αὐτὸν ἵνα τὸ δαιμόνιον ἐκβάλῃ ἐκ τῆς θυγατρὸς αὐτῆς. [GNS]<br>ἡ δὲ γυνὴ ἦν Ἑλληνίς, Συροφοινίκισσα τῷ γένει· καὶ **ἠρώτα** αὐτὸν ἵνα τὸ δαιμόνιον ἐκβάλῃ ἐκ τῆς θυγατρὸς αὐτῆς. [GNT] | possessed daughter. The word "begged" is in the Greek imperfect tense which means she kept on begging and begging. Note that Jesus kept on listening and listening. |
| **#314<br>Begged**<br><br>Stayed–KJV<br>Keep–NASB<br>Keep–NIV<br>Keep–NKJV<br>**Begged–NLT**<br><br>**POSB<br>REFERENCE**<br>(Lk.4:43-44; esp. v.42)<br>Note 8 | κατεῖχον = kateichon<br>Pronunciation: [kat-ay'-chon]<br>Parsing (part of speech): verb<br>   Mood—indicative<br>   Tense—imperfect<br>   Voice—active<br>   Person—3rd person<br>   Number—plural<br>   Stem or root—from κατέχω<br>Concordance References:<br>⇒ Strong's #2722 katechō<br>⇒ NIV #2988 katechō<br>⇒ NASB #2722 katechō<br><br>**Luke 4:42**<br>And when it was day, he departed and went into a desert place: and the people sought him, and came unto him, and **stayed** him, that he should not depart from them. [KJV]<br>And when day came, He departed and went to a lonely place; and the multitudes were searching for Him, and came to Him, and tried to **keep** Him from going away from them. [NASB]<br>At daybreak Jesus went out to a solitary place. The people were looking for him and when they came to where he was, they tried to **keep** him from leaving them. [NIV]<br>Now when it was day, He departed and went into a deserted place. And the crowd sought Him and came to Him, and tried to **keep** Him from leaving them; [NKJV]<br>Early the next morning Jesus went out into the wilderness. The crowds searched everywhere for him, and when they finally found him, they **begged** him not to leave them. [NLT]<br>ενομένης δὲ ἡμέρας, ἐξελθὼν ἐπορεύθη εἰς ἔρημον τόπον, καὶ οἱ ὄχλοι ἐζήτουν αὐτόν, καὶ ἦλθον ἕως αὐτοῦ, καὶ **κατεῖχον** αὐτὸν τοῦ μὴ πορεύεσθαι ἀπ' αὐτῶν. [GNS]<br>Γενομένης δὲ ἡμέρας ἐξελθὼν ἐπορεύθη εἰς ἔρημον τόπον· καὶ οἱ ὄχλοι ἐπεζήτουν αὐτόν καὶ ἦλθον ἕως αὐτοῦ καὶ **κατεῖχον** αὐτὸν τοῦ μὴ πορεύεσθαι ἀπ' αὐτῶν. [GNT] | Tried to prevent; hinder; stop; hold back; restrain; to physically try to keep someone from leaving.<br><br>**Practical Application**<br>Jesus remained faithful to His mission despite the pressure of some persons to sidetrack Him. Jesus had to preach in other cities as well, so He could not stay with those clamoring after Him. He had to fulfill His mission. He could not be sidetracked. Everyone had to hear the Gospel. He had to give others the opportunity as well. He knew that the more He could reach and disciple, the more others would hear and be reached. So He set His face like a flint and marched on despite all who "begged (*kateichon*) Him not to leave them." |

## PRACTICAL WORD STUDIES
## in the NEW TESTAMENT

| ENGLISH WORD | GREEK WORD AND VERSE | THE WORD MEANS... |
|---|---|---|
| **#315**<br>**Begged**<br><br>Besought–KJV<br>Requesting–NASB<br>**Begged–NIV**<br>Implored–NKJV<br>**Begged–NLT**<br><br>**POSB<br>REFERENCE**<br>(Jn.4:46-47; esp. v.47)<br>Note 1, point 4 | ἠρώτα = ërōta<br>Pronunciation: [ay-ro-tah']<br>Parsing (part of speech): verb<br>   Mood—indicative<br>   Tense—imperfect<br>   Voice—active<br>   Person—3rd person<br>   Number—singular<br>   Stem or root—from ἐρωτάω<br>Concordance References:<br>⇒ Strong's #2065 erōtaō<br>⇒ NIV #2263 erōtaō<br>⇒ NASB #2065 erōtaō<br><br>**John 4:47**<br>When he heard that Jesus was come out of Judaea into Galilee, he went unto him, and **besought** him that he would come down, and heal his son: for he was at the point of death. [KJV]<br>When he heard that Jesus had come out of Judea into Galilee, he went to Him, and was **requesting** Him to come down and heal his son; for he was at the point of death. [NASB]<br>When this man heard that Jesus had arrived in Galilee from Judea, he went to him and **begged** him to come and heal his son, who was close to death. [NIV]<br>When he heard that Jesus had come out of Judea into Galilee, he went to Him and **implored** Him to come down and heal his son, for he was at the point of death. [NKJV]<br>When he heard that Jesus had come from Judea and was traveling in Galilee, he went over to Cana. He found Jesus and **begged** him to come to Capernaum with him to heal his son, who was about to die. [NLT]<br>οὗτος ἀκούσας ὅτι Ἰησοῦς ἥκει ἐκ τῆς Ἰουδαίας εἰς τὴν Γαλιλαίαν, ἀπῆλθε πρὸς αὐτόν, καὶ **ἠρώτα** αὐτὸν ἵνα καταβῇ καὶ ἰάσηται αὐτοῦ τὸν υἱόν· ἤμελλε γὰρ ἀποθνήσκειν. [GNS]<br>οὗτος ἀκούσας ὅτι Ἰησοῦς ἥκει ἐκ τῆς Ἰουδαίας εἰς τὴν Γαλιλαίαν ἀπῆλθεν πρὸς αὐτὸν καὶ **ἠρώτα** ἵνα καταβῇ καὶ ἰάσηται αὐτοῦ τὸν υἱόν, ἤμελλεν γὰρ ἀποθνήσκειν. [GNT] | To ask; to request; to implore; to plead desperately; to urge; to beseech; to appeal; to supplicate; to pray for immediate help.<br><br>**Practical Application**<br>Note an important lesson from this Scripture: The man did not let his high position keep him from Jesus. He did not wrap himself in pride nor did he allow what others might say keep him from Jesus. He swallowed his pride and confessed his need in the face of all who ridiculed, and he went to Jesus. |
| **#316**<br>**Begged–<br>Begging**<br><br>Besought–KJV<br>**Begging–NASB**<br>Invited–NIV<br>**Begged–NKJV**<br>Asked–NLT<br><br>**POSB<br>REFERENCE**<br>(Acts 13:42-45; esp. v.42)<br>Note 1, point 1 | παρεκάλουν = parekaloun<br>Pronunciation: [par-ek-al-oon]<br>Parsing (part of speech): verb<br>   Mood—indicative<br>   Tense—imperfect<br>   Voice—active<br>   Person—3rd person<br>   Number—plural<br>   Stem or root—from παρακαλέω<br>Concordance References:<br>⇒ Strong's #3870 parakaleō<br>⇒ NIV #4151 parakaleō<br>⇒ NASB #3870 parakaleō<br><br>**Acts 13:42**<br>And when the Jews were gone out of the synagogue, the Gentiles **besought** that these words might be preached to them the next sabbath. [KJV]<br>And as Paul and Barnabas were going out, the people kept **begging** that these things might be spoken to them the next Sabbath. [NASB]<br>As Paul and Barnabas were leaving the synagogue, the people **invited** them to speak further about these things on the next Sabbath. [NIV]<br>So when the Jews went out of the synagogue, the Gentiles **begged** that these words might be preached to them the next Sabbath. [NKJV]<br>As Paul and Barnabas left the synagogue that day, the people **asked** them to return again and speak about these | Invited, urged, besought, begged, asked; requested urgently; appealed to; pleaded with.<br><br>**Practical Application**<br>It is continuous action: the heathen continued to beseech. The picture is that they begged and begged Paul to share more about the forgiveness of sins which is in Jesus. |

# PRACTICAL WORD STUDIES
## in the NEW TESTAMENT

| ENGLISH WORD | GREEK WORD AND VERSE | THE WORD MEANS... |
|---|---|---|
| | things the next week. [NLT]<br>Ἐξιόντων ἐκ τῆς συναγωγῆς τῶν Ἰουδαίων, δὲ αὐτῶν **παρεκάλουν** τὰ ἔθνη εἰς τὸ μεταξὺ σάββατον λαληθῆναι αὐτοῖς τὰ ῥήματα ταῦτα. [GNS]<br>Ἐξιόντων δὲ αὐτῶν **παρεκάλουν** εἰς τὸ μεταξὺ σάββατον λαληθῆναι αὐτοῖς τὰ ῥήματα ταῦτα. [GNT] | |
| #317<br>**Beginning**<br><br>Beginning–KJV<br>Beginning–NASB<br>Beginning–NIV<br>Beginning–NKJV<br>First of all–NLT<br><br>**POSB REFERENCE**<br>(Col.1:18)<br>Note 2 | ἀρχή = *archē*<br>Pronunciation: [ar-khay']<br>Parsing (part of speech): noun<br>    Case—nominative<br>    Gender—feminine<br>    Number—singular<br>    Stem or root—from ἀρχή, ῆς<br>Concordance References:<br>   ⇒ Strong's #746 archē<br>   ⇒ NIV #794 archē<br>   ⇒ NASB #746 archē<br><br>**Col. 1:18**<br>And he is the head of the body, the church: who is the **beginning**, the firstborn from the dead; that in all things he might have the preeminence. [KJV]<br>He is also head of the body, the church; and He is the **beginning**, the first-born from the dead; so that He Himself might come to have first place in everything. [NASB]<br>And he is the head of the body, the church; he is the **beginning** and the firstborn from among the dead, so that in everything he might have the supremacy. [NIV]<br>And He is the head of the body, the church, who is the **beginning**, the firstborn from the dead, that in all things He may have the preeminence. [NKJV]<br>Christ is the head of the church, which is his body. He is the **first of all** who will rise from the dead, so he is first in everything. [NLT]<br>καὶ αὐτός ἐστιν ἡ κεφαλὴ τοῦ σώματος, τῆς ἐκκλησίας· ὅς ἐστιν **ἀρχή**, πρωτότοκος ἐκ τῶν νεκρῶν, ἵνα γένηται ἐν πᾶσιν αὐτὸς πρωτεύων· [GNS]<br>καὶ αὐτός ἐστιν ἡ κεφαλὴ τοῦ σώματος τῆς ἐκκλησίας· ὅς ἐστιν **ἀρχή**, πρωτότοκος ἐκ τῶν νεκρῶν, ἵνα γένηται ἐν πᾶσιν αὐτὸς πρωτεύων, [GNT] | Beginning, first of all, origin, the genesis, the dawn, the conception, the start, the commencement.<br><br>**Practical Application**<br>The word "beginning" (*archē*) has a twofold idea.<br>1. "Beginning" means creative power. When something first begins, it is created or brought into being by some person or thing greater than itself. Jesus Christ was the Person who gave birth to the church. He is greater than the church; therefore, He had the power to create the church and bring it into existence.<br>⇒ The church is the idea of His mind: He was the One who dreamed of the church, thought it up, and saw the great purpose it could accomplish upon earth.<br>⇒ The church is the plan of His heart: He saw how the church could be founded and built upon the earth, and His heart wanted it.<br>⇒ The church is the desire of His will: He desired and longed for the church; therefore, He willed to create it.<br>⇒ The church is the activity of His hands and life. Jesus Christ came to earth and gave birth to the church (see POSB outline and note—Matthew 16:18; and POSB *Deeper Study* #1, Church—Matthew 16:18).<br>⇒ The church is the result of His love. He loved the world; therefore, He founded His church and He reaches out to the world through His church.<br>⇒ The church is the subject of His care: He looks after and oversees the welfare of His church, making sure that it fulfills its purpose on earth. Even the very gates of hell cannot prevail against the church because of His love and care (Matthew 16:18).<br>The point is this: Jesus Christ began the church. He is the beginning, the creative power who founded and gave birth to the church.<br>2. "Beginning" means *first in time*. Jesus Christ was the first Person of the church. He began the church; therefore, He was the first member, the great and glorious Founder of the church. All others who come into the church follow Him. |
| #318<br>**Beginning**<br><br>Beginning–KJV<br>Beginning–NASB<br>First–NIV<br>Beginning–NKJV<br>Early–NLT | ἀρχῆς = *archēs*<br>Pronunciation: [ar-khays']<br>Parsing (part of speech): noun<br>    Case—genitive<br>    Gender—feminine<br>    Number—singular<br>    Stem or root—from ἀρχή, ῆς<br>Concordance References:<br>   ⇒ Strong's #746 archē<br>   ⇒ NIV #794 archē<br>   ⇒ NASB #746 archē | The beginning, the first of all, the origin, the genesis, the dawn, the conception, the start, the commencement.<br><br>**Practical Application**<br>In the context of this Scripture, Luke notes that the ministers of the Word were eyewitnesses "from the beginning, from the first." They were eyewitnesses of every event and word of Christ, eyewitnesses of His life day by day. |

# PRACTICAL WORD STUDIES
## in the New Testament

| ENGLISH WORD | GREEK WORD AND VERSE | THE WORD MEANS... |
|---|---|---|
| **POSB REFERENCE** (Lk.1:3, esp. v.2) Note 3, point 2 | **Luke 1:2** Even as they delivered them unto us, which from the **beginning** were eyewitnesses, and ministers of the word; [KJV]<br><br>Just as those who from the **beginning** were eyewitnesses and servants of the word have handed them down to us, [NASB]<br><br>Just as they were handed down to us by those who from the **first** were eyewitnesses and servants of the word. [NIV]<br><br>Just as those who from the **beginning** were eyewitnesses and ministers of the word delivered them to us, [NKJV]<br><br>They used as their source material the reports circulating among us from the **early** disciples and other eyewitnesses of what God has done in fulfillment of his promises. [NLT]<br><br>καθὼς παρέδοσαν ἡμῖν οἱ ἀπ' **ἀρχῆς** αὐτόπται καὶ ὑπηρέται γενόμενοι τοῦ λόγου, [GNS]<br><br>καθὼς παρέδοσαν ἡμῖν οἱ ἀπ' **ἀρχῆς** αὐτόπται καὶ ὑπηρέται γενόμενοι τοῦ λόγου, [GNT] | |
| #319 **Beginning, From The**<br><br>First–KJV<br>Beginning–NASB<br>From the beginning–NIV<br>First–NKJV<br>Beginning–NLT<br><br>**POSB REFERENCE** (Lk.1:3) Note 3, point 2 | **ἄνωθεν** = anōthen<br>Pronunciation: [an'-o-then]<br>Parsing (part of speech): adjective adverb<br>   Stem or root—from ἄνωθεν<br>Concordance References:<br>  ⇒ Strong's #509 anōthen<br>  ⇒ NIV #540 anōthen<br>  ⇒ NASB #509 anōthen<br><br>**Luke 1:3**<br>It seemed good to me also, having had perfect understanding of all things from the very **first**, to write unto thee in order, most excellent Theophilus, [KJV]<br><br>It seemed fitting for me as well, having investigated everything carefully from the **beginning**, to write it out for you in consecutive order, most excellent Theophilus; [NASB]<br><br>Therefore, since I myself have carefully investigated everything **from the beginning**, it seemed good also to me to write an orderly account for you, most excellent Theophilus, [NIV]<br><br>It seemed good to me also, having had perfect understanding of all things from the very **first**, to write to you an orderly account, most excellent Theophilus, [NKJV]<br><br>Having carefully investigated all of these accounts from the **beginning**, I have decided to write a careful summary for you, [NLT]<br><br>ἔδοξε κἀμοὶ παρηκολουθηκότι **ἄνωθεν** πᾶσιν ἀκριβῶς, καθεξῆς σοι γράψαι, κράτιστε Θεόφιλε, [GNS]<br><br>ἔδοξε κἀμοὶ παρηκολουθηκότι **ἄνωθεν** πᾶσιν ἀκριβῶς, καθεξῆς σοι γράψαι, κράτιστε Θεόφιλε, [GNT] | From the beginning, from the first, from above, from a higher place (heaven). The words "beginning or first" can and often do mean from above.<br><br>**Practical Application**<br>Some understand Luke to be saying that he had investigated the things from above. Several things point to this translation.<br>1. If Luke meant from the first or beginning why did he not use the same word (*arches*) which he used in verse 2? It seems to be much more accurate to say he chooses a different word (*anōthen*) because he is saying something different, "from above."<br>2. The prophets are said to have proclaimed things from above. They are said to have searched intently and with the greatest care, trying to find out the time and circumstances to which the Spirit of Christ in them was pointing when he predicted the sufferings of Christ and the glories that would follow. It was revealed to them that they were not serving themselves but you, when they spoke of the things that have now been told you by those who have preached the gospel to you by the Holy Spirit sent from heaven. Even angels long to look into these things. (1 Peter 1:10-12). Scripture also says, "for no prophecy was ever made by an act of human will, but men moved by the Holy Spirit spoke from God." (2 Peter 1:21).<br>3. Luke is certainly recording all things "from above," investigating and searching diligently to write what "the Spirit of Christ in them was pointing when he predicted the sufferings of Christ and the glories that would follow." (1 Peter 1:11). [NIV] He is certainly speaking as a holy man of God "moved by the Holy Spirit" (2 Peter 1:21). He is certainly proclaiming the gospel of the Lord Jesus Christ, the good news of Him who came "from above." |

# PRACTICAL WORD STUDIES
## in the NEW TESTAMENT

| ENGLISH WORD | GREEK WORD AND VERSE | THE WORD MEANS... |
|---|---|---|
| **#320**<br>**Begotten**<br><br>**Begotten–KJV**<br>**Begotten–NASB**<br>Become [your]<br>Father–NIV<br>**Begotten–NKJV**<br>Become [your]<br>Father–NLT<br><br>**POSB REFERENCE**<br>(Heb.1:4-6; esp. v.5)<br>Note 1, point 1 | γεγέννηκά = *gegennēka*<br>Pronunciation: [ghe-ghen-nay'-kah]<br>Parsing (part of speech): verb<br>   Mood—indicative<br>   Tense—perfect<br>   Voice—active<br>   Person—1st person<br>   Number—singular<br>   Stem or root—from γεννάω<br>Concordance References:<br>⇒ Strong's #1080 gennaō<br>⇒ NIV #1164 gennaō<br>⇒ NASB #1080 gennaō<br><br>**Hebrews 1:5**<br>For unto which of the angels said he at any time, Thou art my Son, this day have I **begotten** thee? And again, I will be to him a Father, and he shall be to me a Son? [KJV]<br>For to which of the angels did He ever say, "Thou art My Son, Today I have **begotten** Thee"? And again, "I will be a Father to Him And He shall be a Son to Me"? [NASB]<br>For to which of the angels did God ever say, "You are my Son; today I have **become** your **Father**"? Or again, "I will be his Father, and he will be my Son"? [NIV]<br>For to which of the angels did He ever say: "You are My Son, Today I have **begotten** You"? And again: "I will be to Him a Father, And He shall be to Me a Son"? [NKJV]<br>For God never said to any angel what he said to Jesus: "You are my Son. Today I have **become** your **Father**." And again God said, "I will be his Father, and he will be my Son." [NLT]<br>τίνι γὰρ εἶπέ ποτε τῶν ἀγγέλων, Υἱός μου εἶ σύ, ἐγὼ σήμερον **γεγέννηκά** σε; Καὶ πάλιν, Ἐγὼ ἔσομαι αὐτῷ εἰς πατέρα, καὶ αὐτὸς ἔσται μοι εἰς υἱόν; [GNS]<br>Τίνι γὰρ εἶπέν ποτε τῶν ἀγγέλων, Υἱός μου εἶ σύ, ἐγὼ σήμερον **γεγέννηκά** σε; καὶ πάλιν, Ἐγὼ ἔσομαι αὐτῷ εἰς πατέρα, καὶ αὐτὸς ἔσται μοι εἰς υἱόν; [GNT] | To become a father of; to beget; to give birth to; to conceive; to be born. *As man/God*<br><br>**Practical Application**<br>Jesus Christ is the Son of God; He and He alone has been "begotten" (*gegennēka*); that is, born or sent into the world by God. God did not send or cause an angel to be born into the world; He sent His only begotten Son, His one and only Son. *He exists from eternity Alpha/omega Beginning/ending* |
| **#321**<br>**Beguile**<br><br>**Beguile–KJV**<br>Delude–NASB<br>Deceive–NIV<br>Deceive–NKJV<br>Deceive–NLT<br><br>**POSB REFERENCE**<br>(Col.2:4)<br>Note 3 | παραλογίζηται = *paralogizētai*<br>Pronunciation: [par-al-og-id'-zay-tah-ee]<br>Parsing (part of speech): verb<br>   Mood—subjunctive<br>   Tense—present<br>   Voice—middle or passive deponent<br>   Person—3rd person<br>   Number—singular<br>   Stem or root—from παραλογίζομαι<br>Concordance References:<br>⇒ Strong's #3884 paralogizomai<br>⇒ NIV #4165 paralogizomai<br>⇒ NASB #3884 paralogizomai<br><br>**Col. 2:4**<br>And this I say, lest any man should **beguile** you with enticing words. [KJV]<br>I say this in order that no one may **delude** you with persuasive argument. [NASB]<br>I tell you this so that no one may **deceive** you by fine-sounding arguments. [NIV]<br>Now this I say lest anyone should **deceive** you with persuasive words. [NKJV]<br>I am telling you this so that no one will be able to **deceive** you with persuasive arguments. [NLT]<br>τοῦτο δὲ λέγω, ἵνα μη τις ὑμᾶς **παραλογίζηται** ἐν πιθανολογίᾳ. [GNS]<br>Τοῦτο λέγω ἵνα μηδεὶς ὑμᾶς **παραλογίζηται** ἐν πιθανολογίᾳ. [GNT] | To deceive; to delude; to beguile; to mislead, cheat, seduce, and lead someone astray.<br><br>**Practical Application**<br>Note how the seduction takes place: by "enticing words" (*pithanologiai*), that is, by words that are persuasive, appealing, eloquent, flowery, and attractive. |

# PRACTICAL WORD STUDIES
## in the NEW TESTAMENT

| ENGLISH WORD | GREEK WORD AND VERSE | THE WORD MEANS... |
|---|---|---|
| **#322**<br>**Beguile**<br><br>Beguile–KJV<br>Defrauding–NASB<br>Disqualify...for–NIV<br>Cheat–NKJV<br>Condemn–NLT<br><br>**POSB REFERENCE**<br>(Col.2:18-19; esp. v.18)<br>Note 2 | καταβραβευέτω = katabrabeuetō<br>Pronunciation: [kat-ab-rab-yoo'-eh-tow]<br>Parsing (part of speech): verb<br>   Mood—imperative<br>   Tense—present<br>   Voice—active<br>   Person—3rd person<br>   Number—singular<br>   Stem or root—from καταβραβεύω<br>Concordance References:<br>  ⇒ Strong's #2603 katabrabeuō<br>  ⇒ NIV #2857 katabrabeuō<br>  ⇒ NASB #2603 katabrabeuō<br><br>**Col. 2:18**<br>Let no man **beguile** you of your reward in a voluntary humility and worshipping of angels, intruding into those things which he hath not seen, vainly puffed up by his fleshly mind, [KJV]<br>Let no one keep **defrauding** you of your prize by delighting in self-abasement and the worship of the angels, taking his stand on visions he has seen, inflated without cause by his fleshly mind, [NASB]<br>Do not let anyone who delights in false humility and the worship of angels **disqualify** you **for** the prize. Such a person goes into great detail about what he has seen, and his unspiritual mind puffs him up with idle notions. [NIV]<br>Let no one **cheat** you of your reward, taking delight in false humility and worship of angels, intruding into those things which he has not seen, vainly puffed up by his fleshly mind, [NKJV]<br>Don't let anyone **condemn** you by insisting on self-denial. And don't let anyone say you must worship angels, even though they say they have had visions about this. These people claim to be so humble, but their sinful minds have made them proud. [NLT]<br>μηδεὶς ὑμᾶς **καταβραβευέτω** θέλων ἐν ταπεινοφροσύνῃ καὶ θρησκείᾳ τῶν ἀγγέλων, ἃ μὴ ἑώρακεν ἐμβατεύων, εἰκῇ φυσιούμενος ὑπὸ τοῦ νοὸς τῆς σαρκὸς αὐτοῦ, [GNS]<br>μηδεὶς ὑμᾶς **καταβραβευέτω** θέλων ἐν ταπεινοφροσύνῃ καὶ θρησκείᾳ τῶν ἀγγέλων, ἃ ἑόρακεν ἐμβατεύων, εἰκῇ φυσιούμενος ὑπὸ τοῦ νοὸς τῆς σαρκὸς αὐτοῦ, [GNT] | To disqualify; to beguile; to defraud; to cheat; to condemn. It means to rob; to defraud; to cheat a person out of his reward.<br><br>**Practical Application**<br>It is possible for believers to be cheated out of their reward by false teachers. How? By following those who teach that there is another approach to God other than Christ. Christ is God's appointed way to approach Him, and there is no other way. |
| **#323**<br>**Behave**<br><br>Behave–KJV<br>Conduct–NASB<br>Conduct–NIV<br>Conduct–NKJV<br>Conduct–NLT<br><br>**POSB REFERENCE**<br>(1 Tim.3:14-15; esp. v.15)<br>Note 1 | ἀναστρέφεσθαι = anastrephesthai<br>Pronunciation: [an-as-tref'-ehs-tha-ee]<br>Parsing (part of speech): verb<br>   Mood—infinitive<br>   Tense—present<br>   Voice—passive<br>   Stem or root—from ἀναστρέφω<br>Concordance References:<br>  ⇒ Strong's #390 anastrephō<br>  ⇒ NIV #418 anastrephō<br>  ⇒ NASB #390 anastrephō<br><br>**1 Tim. 3:15**<br>But if I tarry long, that thou mayest know how thou oughtest to **behave** thyself in the house of God, which is the church of the living God, the pillar and ground of the truth. [KJV]<br>But in case I am delayed, I write so that you may know how one ought to **conduct** himself in the household of God, which is the church of the living God, the pillar and support of the truth. [NASB]<br>If I am delayed, you will know how people ought to **conduct** themselves in God's household, which is the church of the living God, the pillar and foundation of the truth. [NIV]<br>But if I am delayed, I write so that you may know how you ought to **conduct** yourself in the house of God, which is the church of the living God, the pillar and ground of the truth. [NKJV] | To conduct; to behave; to live.<br><br>**Practical Application**<br>The word "behave" (*anastrephesthai*) means the conduct, walk, and behavior of a person; but it especially refers to how a person relates to other people. Therefore, the great concern of the Pastoral Epistles is how believers behave in their relationships to God, to each other, and to the unbelievers of the world.<br>Remember: Timothy was in Ephesus and Paul was writing from Macedonia. Paul hoped to visit Ephesus and Timothy soon, but he was not quite sure that he would be able to leave Macedonia. Therefore, he was spelling out in some detail...<br>• how Christian believers are to conduct themselves within the church.<br>• how Christian believers are to behave and witness to a world that is lost and reeling under the weight of corruption and evil. |

# PRACTICAL WORD STUDIES
## in the NEW TESTAMENT

| ENGLISH WORD | GREEK WORD AND VERSE | THE WORD MEANS... |
|---|---|---|
| | So that if I can't come for a while, you will know how people must **conduct** themselves in the household of God. This is the church of the living God, which is the pillar and support of the truth. [NLT]<br><br>ἐὰν δὲ βραδύνω, ἵνα εἰδῇς πῶς δεῖ ἐν οἴκῳ Θεοῦ **ἀναστρέφεσθαι**, ἥτις ἐστὶν ἐκκλησία Θεοῦ ζῶντος, στῦλος καὶ ἑδραίωμα τῆς ἀληθείας. [GNS]<br><br>ἐὰν δὲ βραδύνω, ἵνα εἰδῇς πῶς δεῖ ἐν οἴκῳ θεοῦ **ἀναστρέφεσθαι**, ἥτις ἐστὶν ἐκκλησία θεοῦ ζῶντος, στῦλος καὶ ἑδραίωμα τῆς ἀληθείας. [GNT] | |
| **#324**<br>**Behave Itself Unseemly**<br><br>Behave itself unseemly–KJV<br>Act unbecomingly–NASB<br>Rude–NIV<br>Behave rudely–NKJV<br>Rude–NLT<br><br>**POSB REFERENCE**<br>(1 Cor.13:4-7; esp. v.5)<br>Note 2, point 6 | ἀσχημονεῖ = aschēmonei<br>Pronunciation: [as-kay-mon-ee']<br>Parsing (part of speech): verb<br>    Mood—indicative<br>    Tense—present<br>    Voice—active<br>    Person—3rd person<br>    Number—singular<br>    Stem or root—from ἀσχημονέω<br>Concordance References:<br>⇒ Strong's #807 aschēmoneō<br>⇒ NIV #858 aschēmoneō<br>⇒ NASB #809 aschēmoneō<br><br>**1 Cor. 13:5**<br>Doth not **behave itself unseemly**, seeketh not her own, is not easily provoked, thinketh no evil; [KJV]<br>Does not **act unbecomingly**; it does not seek its own, is not provoked, does not take into account a wrong suffered, [NASB]<br>It is not **rude**, it is not self-seeking, it is not easily angered, it keeps no record of wrongs. [NIV]<br>Does not **behave rudely**, does not seek its own, is not provoked, thinks no evil; [NKJV]<br>Or **rude**. Love does not demand its own way. Love is not irritable, and it keeps no record of when it has been wronged. [NLT]<br>οὐκ **ἀσχημονεῖ**, οὐ ζητεῖ τὰ ἑαυτῆς, οὐ παροξύνεται, οὐ λογίζεται τὸ κακόν, [GNS]<br>οὐκ **ἀσχημονεῖ**, οὐ ζητεῖ τὰ ἑαυτῆς, οὐ παροξύνεται, οὐ λογίζεται τὸ κακόν, [GNT] | Unbecomingly, rudely, indecently, unmannerly, disgracefully; acting improperly.<br><br>**Practical Application**<br>Love does nothing to shame oneself. Love is orderly and controlled; and it behaves and treats all persons with respect, honoring and respecting who they are. |
| **#325**<br>**Behave Rudely**<br><br>Behave itself unseemly–KJV<br>Act unbecomingly–NASB<br>Rude–NIV<br>Behave rudely–NKJV<br>Rude–NLT<br><br>**POSB REFERENCE**<br>(1 Cor.13:4-7; esp. v.5)<br>Note 2, point 6 | ἀσχημονεῖ = aschēmonei<br>Pronunciation: [as-kay-mon-ee']<br>Parsing (part of speech): verb<br>    Mood—indicative<br>    Tense—present<br>    Voice—active<br>    Person—3rd person<br>    Number—singular<br>    Stem or root—from ἀσχημονέω<br>Concordance References:<br>⇒ Strong's #807 aschēmoneō<br>⇒ NIV #858 aschēmoneō<br>⇒ NASB #809 aschēmoneō<br><br>**1 Cor. 13:5**<br>Doth not **behave itself unseemly**, seeketh not her own, is not easily provoked, thinketh no evil; [KJV]<br>Does not **act unbecomingly**; it does not seek its own, is not provoked, does not take into account a wrong suffered, [NASB]<br>It is not **rude**, it is not self-seeking, it is not easily angered, it keeps no record of wrongs. [NIV]<br>Does not **behave rudely**, does not seek its own, is not provoked, thinks no evil; [NKJV]<br>Or **rude**. Love does not demand its own way. Love is not irritable, and it keeps no record of when it has been wronged. [NLT]<br>οὐκ **ἀσχημονεῖ**, οὐ ζητεῖ τὰ ἑαυτῆς, οὐ παροξύνεται, οὐ λογίζεται τὸ κακόν, [GNS]<br>οὐκ **ἀσχημονεῖ**, οὐ ζητεῖ τὰ ἑαυτῆς, οὐ παροξύνεται, οὐ λογίζεται τὸ κακόν, [GNT] | Unbecomingly, rudely, indecently, unmannerly, disgracefully; acting improperly.<br><br>**Practical Application**<br>Love does nothing to shame oneself. Love is orderly and controlled; and it behaves and treats all persons with respect, honoring and respecting who they are. |

# PRACTICAL WORD STUDIES
## in the NEW TESTAMENT

| ENGLISH WORD | GREEK WORD AND VERSE | THE WORD MEANS... |
|---|---|---|
| **#326**<br>**Beheld**<br><br>**Beheld–KJV**<br>Observing–NASB<br>Watched–NIV<br>Saw–NKJV<br>Watched–NLT<br><br>**POSB REFERENCE**<br>(Mk.12:41-42; esp. v.41)<br>Note 1 | ἐθεώρει = etheōrei<br>Pronunciation: [eh-theh-o-reh'-ee]<br>Parsing (part of speech): verb<br>    Mood—indicative<br>    Tense—imperfect<br>    Voice—active<br>    Person—3rd person<br>    Number—singular<br>    Stem or root—from θεωρέω<br>Concordance References:<br>  ⇒ Strong's #2334 theōreō<br>  ⇒ NIV #2555 theōreō<br>  ⇒ NASB #2334 theōreō<br><br>**Mark 12:41**<br>And Jesus sat over against the treasury, and **beheld** how the people cast money into the treasury: and many that were rich cast in much. [KJV]<br>And He sat down opposite the treasury, and began **observing** how the multitude were putting money into the treasury; and many rich people were putting in large sums. [NASB]<br>Jesus sat down opposite the place where the offerings were put and **watched** the crowd putting their money into the temple treasury. Many rich people threw in large amounts. [NIV]<br>Now Jesus sat opposite the treasury and **saw** how the people put money into the treasury. And many who were rich put in much. [NKJV]<br>Jesus went over to the collection box in the Temple and sat and **watched** as the crowds dropped in their money. Many rich people put in large amounts. [NLT]<br>Καὶ καθίσας ὁ Ἰησοῦς κατέναντι τοῦ γαζοφυλακίου, **ἐθεώρει** πῶς ὁ ὄχλος βάλλει χαλκὸν εἰς τὸ γαζοφυλάκιον· καὶ πολλοὶ πλούσιοι ἔβαλλον πολλά. [GNS]<br>Καὶ καθίσας κατέναντι τοῦ γαζοφυλακίου **ἐθεώρει** πῶς ὁ ὄχλος βάλλει χαλκὸν εἰς τὸ γαζοφυλάκιον. καὶ πολλοὶ πλούσιοι ἔβαλλον πολλά. [GNT] | To observe, watch, behold, look at, notice; to see; to carefully observe; to look on; to gaze upon; to perceive.<br><br>**Practical Application**<br>Christ was deliberately observing, discerning the motives of the people as they made their offerings. Christ knows the motives—the sacrifices made or the "tips" offered—behind every gift given to Him.<br>There is a great difference between giving what one can spare and giving sacrificially, actually giving up something in order to give. Sacrificial giving costs something. Sacrificial giving is giving when it hurts, when a person has nothing left, nothing to spare. The difference needs to be stressed, for God expects sacrificial giving. If the world is ever to be reached for Christ and its desperate needs met, then every believer must give sacrificially. |
| **#327**<br>**Beheld**<br><br>**Beheld–KJV**<br>Watching–NASB<br>Saw–NIV<br>Saw–NKJV<br>Saw–NLT<br><br>**POSB REFERENCE**<br>(Lk.10:18)<br>Note 2 | Ἐθεώρουν = etheōroun<br>Pronunciation: [eh-theh-o-reh'-o]<br>Parsing (part of speech): verb<br>    Mood—indicative<br>    Tense—imperfect<br>    Voice—active<br>    Person—1st person<br>    Number—singular<br>    Stem or root—from θεωρέω<br>Concordance References:<br>  ⇒ Strong's #2334 theōreō<br>  ⇒ NIV #2555 theōreō<br>  ⇒ NASB #2334 theōreō<br><br>**Luke 10:18**<br>And he said unto them, I **beheld** Satan as lightning fall from heaven. [KJV]<br>And He said to them, "I was **watching** Satan fall from heaven like lightning. [NASB]<br>He replied, "I **saw** Satan fall like lightning from heaven. [NIV]<br>And He said to them, "I **saw** Satan fall like lightning from heaven. [NKJV]<br>"Yes," he told them, "I **saw** Satan falling from heaven as a flash of lightning! [NLT]<br>εἶπε δὲ αὐτοῖς, **Ἐθεώρουν** τὸν Σατανᾶν ὡς ἀστραπὴν ἐκ τοῦ οὐρανοῦ πεσόντα. [GNS]<br>εἶπεν δὲ αὐτοῖς, **Ἐθεώρουν** τὸν Σατανᾶν ὡς ἀστραπὴν ἐκ τοῦ οὐρανοῦ πεσόντα. [GNT] | To see; to carefully observe; to behold; to watch; to look on; to gaze upon; to perceive; to notice.<br><br>**Practical Application**<br>The word means that Jesus thought upon, gave full attention to, contemplated, envisioned Satan's falling from his summit of power as the god and prince of this world (see POSB *Deeper Study* #1, Satan—Rev. 12:9). |

# PRACTICAL WORD STUDIES
## in the NEW TESTAMENT

| ENGLISH WORD | GREEK WORD AND VERSE | THE WORD MEANS... |
|---|---|---|
| **#328**<br>**Beheld**<br><br>Beheld–KJV<br>Beheld–NASB<br>Seen–NIV<br>Beheld–NKJV<br>Seen–NLT<br><br>**POSB REFERENCE**<br>(Jn.1:14)<br>Note 1 | ἐθεασάμεθα = etheasametha<br>Pronunciation: [eh-theh-ah-sah'-meh-thah]<br>Parsing (part of speech): verb<br>    Mood—indicative<br>    Tense—aorist<br>    Voice—middle deponent<br>    Person—1st person<br>    Number—plural<br>    Stem or root—from θεάομαι<br>Concordance References:<br>  ⇒ Strong's #2300 theaomai<br>  ⇒ NIV #2517 theaomai<br>  ⇒ NASB #2300 theaomai<br><br>**John 1:14**<br>And the Word was made flesh, and dwelt among us, (and we **beheld** his glory, the glory as of the only begotten of the Father,) full of grace and truth. [KJV]<br><br>And the Word became flesh, and dwelt among us, and we **beheld** His glory, glory as of the only begotten from the Father, full of grace and truth. [NASB]<br><br>The Word became flesh and made his dwelling among us. We have **seen** his glory, the glory of the One and Only, who came from the Father, full of grace and truth. [NIV]<br><br>And the Word became flesh and dwelt among us, and we **beheld** His glory, the glory as of the only begotten of the Father, full of grace and truth. [NKJV]<br><br>So the Word became human and lived here on earth among us. He was full of unfailing love and faithfulness. And we have **seen** his glory, the glory of the only Son of the Father. [NLT]<br><br>καὶ ὁ λόγος σὰρξ ἐγένετο, καὶ ἐσκήνωσεν ἐν ἡμῖν, -- καὶ **ἐθεασάμεθα** τὴν δόξαν αὐτοῦ, δόξαν ὡς μονογενοῦς παρὰ πατρός -- , πλήρης χάριτος καὶ ἀληθείας. [GNS]<br><br>Καὶ ὁ λόγος σὰρξ ἐγένετο καὶ ἐσκήνωσεν ἐν ἡμῖν, καὶ **ἐθεασάμεθα** τὴν δόξαν αὐτοῦ, δόξαν ὡς μονογενοῦς παρὰ πατρός, πλήρης χάριτος καὶ ἀληθείας. [GNT] | To be seen, beheld; to notice; to look at; to observe.<br><br>**Practical Application**<br>The word actually means seeing with the human eye. It is used about twenty times in the New Testament. There is no room whatever for saying that God's becoming a man was merely a vision of some man's mind or imagination. John was saying that he and others actually saw the Word made flesh. Jesus Christ was beyond question God Himself who became man, who partook of the very same flesh as all other men. (Cp. 1 John 1:1-4.) (See POSB *Deeper Study* #1, Flesh—John 1:14 for the meaning of "flesh" and why Jesus Christ had to become flesh. Also see POSB *Deeper Study* #1, Flesh—1 Cor. 3:1-4 for more discussion.) |
| **#329**<br>**Beheld**<br><br>Beheld–KJV<br>Looking on–NASB<br>Before...eyes–NIV<br>Watched–NKJV<br>Watching–NLT<br><br>**POSB REFERENCE**<br>(Acts 1:9)<br>Note 4 | βλεπόντων = blepontōn<br>Pronunciation: [blep'-own-tone]<br>Parsing (part of speech): verb<br>    Mood—participle<br>    Tense—present<br>    Voice—active<br>    Case—genitive<br>    Gender—masculine<br>    Number—plural<br>    Stem or root—from βλέπω<br>Concordance References:<br>  ⇒ Strong's #991 blepō<br>  ⇒ NIV #1063 blepō<br>  ⇒ NASB #991 blepō<br><br>**Acts 1:9**<br>And when he had spoken these things, while they **beheld**, he was taken up; and a cloud received him out of their sight. [KJV]<br><br>And after He had said these things, He was lifted up while they were **looking on**, and a cloud received Him out of their sight. [NASB]<br><br>After he said this, he was taken up **before** their very **eyes**, and a cloud hid him from their sight. [NIV]<br><br>Now when He had spoken these things, while they **watched**, He was taken up, and a cloud received Him out of their sight. [NKJV]<br><br>It was not long after he said this that he was taken up into the sky while they were **watching**, and he disappeared into a cloud. [NLT]<br><br>καὶ ταῦτα εἰπών, **βλεπόντων** αὐτῶν ἐπήρθη, καὶ νεφέλη ὑπέλαβεν αὐτὸν ἀπὸ τῶν ὀφθαλμῶν αὐτῶν. [GNS]<br><br>καὶ ταῦτα εἰπὼν **βλεπόντων** αὐτῶν ἐπήρθη, καὶ νεφέλη ὑπέλαβεν αὐτὸν ἀπὸ τῶν ὀφθαλμῶν αὐτῶν. [GNT] | To see; to behold; to look upon; to watch.<br><br>**Practical Application**<br>Jesus Christ began to slowly arise from the earth, ascending ever upward toward the sky above. The disciples were shocked and spellbound, gazing at the spectacular sight. They were beholding one of the most dramatic and phenomenal events ever experienced:<br>  ⇒ the Ascension of the Lord Jesus Christ.<br>  ⇒ the return of God's Son into heaven, into the spiritual world and dimension of being. |

# PRACTICAL WORD STUDIES
## in the NEW TESTAMENT

| ENGLISH WORD | GREEK WORD AND VERSE | THE WORD MEANS... |
|---|---|---|
| **#330**<br>**Beheld**<br><br>Beheld–KJV<br>Looked at–NASB<br>Looked at–NIV<br>Looked at–NKJV<br>Looked intently–NLT<br><br>**POSB REFERENCE**<br>(Jn.1:42)<br>Note 6, point 1 | ἐμβλέψας = emblepsas<br>Pronunciation: [em-blehps'-ahs]<br>Parsing (part of speech): verb<br>    Mood—participle<br>    Tense—aorist<br>    Voice—active<br>    Case—nominative<br>    Gender—masculine<br>    Number—singular<br>    Stem or root—from ἐμβλέπω<br>Concordance References:<br> ⇒ Strong's #1689 emblepō<br> ⇒ NIV #1838 emblepō<br> ⇒ NASB #1689 emblepō<br><br>**John 1:42**<br>And he brought him to Jesus. And when Jesus **beheld** him, he said, Thou art Simon the son of Jona: thou shalt be called Cephas, which is by interpretation, A stone. [KJV]<br><br>He brought him to Jesus. Jesus **looked at** him, and said, "You are Simon the son of John; you shall be called Cephas" (which is translated Peter). [NASB]<br><br>And he brought him to Jesus.Jesus **looked at** him and said, "You are Simon son of John. You will be called Cephas" (which, when translated, is Peter). [NIV]<br><br>And he brought him to Jesus. Now when Jesus **looked at** him, He said, "You are Simon the son of Jonah. You shall be called Cephas" (which is translated, A Stone). [NKJV]<br><br>Then Andrew brought Simon to meet Jesus. **Looking intently** at Simon, Jesus said, "You are Simon, the son of John—but you will be called Cephas" (which means Peter). [NLT]<br><br>καὶ ἤγαγεν αὐτὸν πρὸς τὸν Ἰησοῦν. ἐμβλέψας δὲ αὐτῷ ὁ Ἰησοῦς εἶπε, Σὺ εἶ Σίμων ὁ υἱὸς Ἰωνᾶ· σὺ κληθήσῃ Κηφᾶς, -- ὃ ἑρμηνεύεται Πέτρος. --[GNS]<br><br>ἤγαγεν αὐτὸν πρὸς τὸν Ἰησοῦν. ἐμβλέψας αὐτῷ ὁ Ἰησοῦς εἶπεν, Σὺ εἶ Σίμων ὁ υἱὸς Ἰωάννου, σὺ κληθήσῃ Κηφᾶς ὃ ἑρμηνεύεται Πέτρος. [GNT] | To look upon with an intense, earnest look; to concentrate; to stare and gaze upon.<br><br>**Practical Application**<br>Jesus looked into the innermost being of Peter. Note two significant facts.<br>1. Jesus "beholds" a person: studies and knows him intimately. This is both a comfort and a warning, depending upon a person's response.<br>2. Jesus sees the potential within a person and longs to change that person to make him everything he can become. |
| **#331**<br>**Beheld**<br><br>Looked upon–KJV<br>**Beheld–NASB**<br>Looked at–NIV<br>Looked upon–NKJV<br>Saw–NLT<br><br>**POSB REFERENCE**<br>(1 Jn.1:1)<br>Note 2, point 3 | ἐθεασάμεθα = etheasametha<br>Pronunciation: [eh-theh-ahs'-ah-meh-tha]<br>Parsing (part of speech): verb<br>    Mood—indicative<br>    Tense—aorist<br>    Voice—middle deponent<br>    Person—1st person<br>    Number—plural<br>    Stem or root—from θεάομαι<br>Concordance References:<br> ⇒ Strong's #2300 theaomai<br> ⇒ NIV #2517 theaomai<br> ⇒ NASB #2300 theaomai<br><br>**1 John 1:1**<br>That which was from the beginning, which we have heard, which we have seen with our eyes, which we have **looked upon**, and our hands have handled, of the Word of life; [KJV]<br><br>What was from the beginning, what we have heard, what we have seen with our eyes, what we **beheld** and our hands handled, concerning the Word of Life—[NASB]<br><br>That which was from the beginning, which we have heard, which we have seen with our eyes, which we have **looked at** and our hands have touched—this we proclaim concerning the Word of life. [NIV]<br><br>That which was from the beginning, which we have heard, which we have seen with our eyes, which we have **looked upon,** and our hands have handled, concerning the Word of life—[NKJV]<br><br>The one who existed from the beginning is the one we | To look at; to look upon; to behold; to see; to gaze and look upon for a long time in order to study and understand and grasp. It means to look intensely and earnestly; it means to grasp the meaning and significance of a person.<br><br>**Practical Application**<br>John is testifying that he and the other apostles and believers beheld and gazed upon Jesus Christ in order...<br>• to study and understand Him.<br>• to seek and grasp the meaning and significance of His person.<br><br>A person will never see and understand who Christ is by just glancing at Him. If a person wants to know Christ, he has to look intensely and seriously; he has to seek to understand if Christ really is who John and other believers claim He is. |

# PRACTICAL WORD STUDIES
## in the NEW TESTAMENT

| ENGLISH WORD | GREEK WORD AND VERSE | THE WORD MEANS... |
|---|---|---|
| | have heard and seen. We **saw** him with our own eyes and touched him with our own hands. He is Jesus Christ, the Word of life. [NLT]<br>Ὃ ἦν ἀπ' ἀρχῆς, ὃ ἀκηκόαμεν, ὃ ἑωράκαμεν τοῖς ὀφθαλμοῖς ἡμῶν, ὃ **ἐθεασάμεθα**, καὶ αἱ χεῖρες ἡμῶν ἐψηλάφησαν, περὶ τοῦ λόγου τῆς ζωῆς [GNS]<br>Ὃ ἦν ἀπ' ἀρχῆς, ὃ ἀκηκόαμεν, ὃ ἑωράκαμεν τοῖς ὀφθαλμοῖς ἡμῶν, ὃ **ἐθεασάμεθα** καὶ αἱ χεῖρες ἡμῶν ἐψηλάφησαν περὶ τοῦ λόγου τῆς ζωῆς [GNT] | |
| **#332**<br>**Behold**<br><br>Behold–KJV<br>Take note–NASB<br>Consider–NIV<br>Look on–NKJV<br>Hear–NLT<br><br>**POSB REFERENCE**<br>(Acts 4:29-30; esp. v.29)<br>Note 4, point 1b | ἔπιδε ἐπὶ = *epide epi*<br>Pronunciation: [ep-i'-deh ep-ee]<br>Parsing *epide* (part of speech): verb<br>    Mood—imperative<br>    Tense—aorist<br>    Voice—active<br>    Person—2nd person<br>    Number—singular<br>    Stem or root—from ἐπεῖδον<br>Parsing *epi* (part of speech): preposition<br>    Case—accusative<br>    Stem or root—from ἐπί<br>Concordance References:<br>⇒ Strong's #1896 + 1909 epeidon epi<br>⇒ NIV #2078 + 2093 epeidon epi<br>⇒ NASB #1896 + 1909 epeidon epi<br><br>**Acts 4:29**<br>And now, Lord, **behold** their threatenings: and grant unto thy servants, that with all boldness they may speak thy word, [KJV]<br>"And now, Lord, **take note** of their threats, and grant that Thy bond-servants may speak Thy word with all confidence, [NASB]<br>Now, Lord, **consider** their threats and enable your servants to speak your word with great boldness. [NIV]<br>Now, Lord, **look on** their threats, and grant to Your servants that with all boldness they may speak Your word, [NKJV]<br>And now, O Lord, **hear** their threats, and give your servants great boldness in their preaching. [NLT]<br>καὶ τὰ νῦν, Κύριε, **ἔπιδε ἐπὶ** τὰς ἀπειλὰς αὐτῶν, καὶ δὸς τοῖς δούλοις σου μετὰ παρρησίας πάσης λαλεῖν τὸν λόγον σου, [GNS]<br>καὶ τὰ νῦν, κύριε, **ἔπιδε ἐπὶ** τὰς ἀπειλὰς αὐτῶν καὶ δὸς τοῖς δούλοις σου μετὰ παρρησίας πάσης λαλεῖν τὸν λόγον σου, [GNT] | To consider; to behold; to take note; to hear; to look upon.<br><br>**Practical Application**<br>The church was asking God to concentrate and focus upon the persecution; to deal with it and to overrule the enemy; to give whatever was necessary to endure through it all. |
| **#333**<br>**Behold**<br><br>Behold–KJV<br>Behold–NASB<br>Where–NIV<br>Behold–NKJV<br>There–NLT<br><br>**POSB REFERENCE**<br>(Acts 16:1-3; esp. v.1)<br>Note 1, point 1 | καὶ ἰδού = *kai idou*<br>Pronunciation: [kah-ee id-oo']<br>Parsing *idou* (part of speech): particle sentence<br>    Stem or root—from ἰδού<br>Concordance References:<br>⇒ Strong's #2400 + 2532 idou kai<br>⇒ NIV #2627 + 2779 idou kai<br>⇒ NASB #2400 + 2532 idou kai<br><br>**Acts 16:1**<br>Then came he to Derbe and Lystra: and, **behold**, a certain disciple was there, named Timotheus, the son of a certain woman, which was a Jewess, and believed; but his father was a Greek: [KJV]<br>And he came also to Derbe and to Lystra. And **behold**, a certain disciple was there, named Timothy, the son of a Jewish woman who was a believer, but his father was a Greek, [NASB]<br>He came to Derbe and then to Lystra, **where** a disciple named Timothy lived, whose mother was a Jewess and a believer, but whose father was a Greek. [NIV]<br>Then he came to Derbe and Lystra. And **behold**, a certain disciple was there, named Timothy, the son of a certain Jewish woman who believed, but his father was Greek. [NKJV] | To behold; to look and listen.<br><br>**Practical Application**<br>The word "behold" (*kai idou*) has the idea of looking and gazing at a wonderful discovery, at an unexpected surprise. |

# PRACTICAL WORD STUDIES
## in the NEW TESTAMENT

| ENGLISH WORD | GREEK WORD AND VERSE | THE WORD MEANS... |
|---|---|---|
| | Paul and Silas went first to Derbe and then on to Lystra. **There** they met Timothy, a young disciple whose mother was a Jewish believer, but whose father was a Greek. [NLT]<br><br>Κατήντησε δὲ εἰς Δέρβην καὶ Λύστραν· **καὶ ἰδοὺ**, μαθητής τις ἦν ἐκεῖ, ὀνόματι Τιμόθεος, υἱὸς γυναικὸς τινος Ἰουδαίας πιστῆς, πατρὸς δὲ Ἕλληνος. [GNS]<br><br>Κατήντησεν δὲ [καὶ] εἰς Δέρβην καὶ εἰς Λύστραν. **καὶ ἰδοὺ** μαθητής τις ἦν ἐκεῖ ὀνόματι Τιμόθεος, υἱὸς γυναικὸς Ἰουδαίας πιστῆς, πατρὸς δὲ Ἕλληνος, [GNT] | |
| **#334**<br>**Being**<br><br>Being–KJV<br>Is–NASB<br>Is–NIV<br>Being–NKJV<br>Not translated–NLT<br><br>**POSB REFERENCE**<br>(Heb.1:3)<br>Note 4 | ὤν = ōn<br>Pronunciation: [own]<br>Parsing (part of speech): verb<br>   Mood—participle<br>   Tense—present<br>   Voice—active<br>   Case—nominative<br>   Gender—masculine<br>   Number—singular<br>   Stem or root—from εἰμί<br>Concordance References:<br>  ⇒ Strong's #1510 eimi<br>  ⇒ NIV #1639 eimi<br>  ⇒ NASB #1510 eimi<br><br>**Hebrews 1:3**<br>Who **being** the brightness of his glory, and the express image of his person, and upholding all things by the word of his power, when he had by himself purged our sins, sat down on the right hand of the Majesty on high; [KJV]<br><br>And He **is** the radiance of His glory and the exact representation of His nature, and upholds all things by the word of His power. When He had made purification of sins, He sat down at the right hand of the Majesty on high; [NASB]<br><br>The Son **is** the radiance of God's glory and the exact representation of his being, sustaining all things by his powerful word. After he had provided purification for sins, he sat down at the right hand of the Majesty in heaven. [NIV]<br><br>Who **being** the brightness of His glory and the express image of His person, and upholding all things by the word of His power, when He had by Himself purged our sins, sat down at the right hand of the Majesty on high, [NKJV]<br><br>The Son reflects God's own glory, and everything about him represents God exactly. He sustains the universe by the mighty power of his command. After he died to cleanse us from the stain of sin, he sat down in the place of honor at the right hand of the majestic God of heaven. [NLT]—Not Translated<br><br>ὃς **ὢν** ἀπαύγασμα τῆς δόξης, καὶ χαρακτὴρ τῆς ὑποστάσεως αὐτοῦ, φέρων τε τὰ πάντα τῷ ῥήματι τῆς δυνάμεως αὐτοῦ, δι' ἑαυτοῦ καθαρισμὸν ποιησάμενος τῶν ἁμαρτιῶν ἡμῶν, ἐκάθισεν ἐν δεξιᾷ τῆς μεγαλωσύνης ἐν ὑψηλοῖς, [GNS]<br><br>ὃς **ὢν** ἀπαύγασμα τῆς δόξης καὶ χαρακτὴρ τῆς ὑποστάσεως αὐτοῦ, φέρων τε τὰ πάντα τῷ ῥήματι τῆς δυνάμεως αὐτοῦ, καθαρισμὸν τῶν ἁμαρτιῶν ποιησάμενος ἐκάθισεν ἐν δεξιᾷ τῆς μεγαλωσύνης ἐν ὑψηλοῖς, [GNT] | Is; being; existing. It means "absolute and timeless existence" (A.T. Robertson. *Word Pictures in the New Testament*, Vol. 5, p.335).<br><br>**Practical Application**<br>This means that Jesus Christ Himself possessed the glory of God before He ever came into the world. He has always existed in the glory of God; He is eternal.<br><br>What does glory mean? It means all the brightness of God—all the brilliance, radiance, splendor, and light of God's Being. It means that God's very presence—in all of His light and purity—dwells among us in the person of Jesus Christ. It meant that in Christ "dwelt all the fullness [glory] of God" (Col. 2:9). Men could look at Jesus Christ and see the glory of God in Him—the very light and radiance of God's Being. |
| **#335**<br>**Being**<br><br>Person–KJV<br>Nature–NASB<br>Being–NIV<br>Person–NKJV<br>God–NLT | ὑποστάσεως = hupostaseōs<br>Pronunciation: [hoop-os'-tas-eh-os]<br>Parsing (part of speech): noun<br>   Case—genitive<br>   Gender—feminine<br>   Number—singular<br>   Stem or root—from ὑπόστασις, εως<br>Concordance References:<br>  ⇒ Strong's #5287 hupostasis<br>  ⇒ NIV #5712 hupostasis<br>  ⇒ NASB #5287 hupostasis | Being, person, nature, substance.<br><br>**Practical Application**<br>Jesus Christ is the very substance, the very Being, Person, and embodiment of God. |

# PRACTICAL WORD STUDIES
## in the New Testament

| ENGLISH WORD | GREEK WORD AND VERSE | THE WORD MEANS... |
|---|---|---|
| **POSB REFERENCE** (Heb.1:3) Note 5 | **Hebrews 1:3**<br>Who being the brightness of *his* glory, and the express image of his **person**, and upholding all things by the word of his power, when he had by himself purged our sins, sat down on the right hand of the Majesty on high; [KJV]<br>And He is the radiance of His glory and the exact representation of His **nature**, and upholds all things by the word of His power. When He had made purification of sins, He sat down at the right hand of the Majesty on high; [NASB]<br>The Son is the radiance of God's glory and the exact representation of his **being**, sustaining all things by his powerful word. After he had provided purification for sins, he sat down at the right hand of the Majesty in heaven. [NIV]<br>Who being the brightness of *His* glory and the express image of His **person**, and upholding all things by the word of His power, when He had by Himself purged our sins, sat down at the right hand of the Majesty on high, [NKJV]<br>The Son reflects God's own glory, and everything about him represents **God** exactly. He sustains the universe by the mighty power of his command. After he died to cleanse us from the stain of sin, he sat down in the place of honor at the right hand of the majestic God of heaven. [NLT]<br>ὃς ὢν ἀπαύγασμα τῆς δόξης, καὶ χαρακτὴρ τῆς **ὑποστάσεως** αὐτοῦ, φέρων τε τὰ πάντα τῷ ῥήματι τῆς δυνάμεως αὐτοῦ, δι' εαυτοῦ καθαρισμὸν ποιησάμενος τῶν ἁμαρτιῶν ημῶν, ἐκάθισεν ἐν δεξιᾷ τῆς μεγαλωσύνης ἐν ὑψηλοῖς, [GNS]<br>ὃς ὢν ἀπαύγασμα τῆς δόξης καὶ χαρακτὴρ τῆς **ὑποστάσεως** αὐτοῦ, φέρων τε τὰ πάντα τῷ ῥήματι τῆς δυνάμεως αὐτοῦ, καθαρισμὸν τῶν ἁμαρτιῶν ποιησάμενος ἐκάθισεν ἐν δεξιᾷ τῆς μεγαλωσύνης ἐν ὑψηλοῖς, [GNT] | |
| **#336 Being**<br><br>**Being**–KJV<br>Existed–NASB<br>**Being**–NIV<br>**Being**–NKJV<br>Was–NLT<br><br>**POSB REFERENCE** (Philip.2:6) Note 2, point 1 | ὑπάρχων = *huparchōn*<br>Pronunciation: [hoop-ar'-khown]<br>Parsing (part of speech): verb<br>  Mood—participle<br>  Tense—present<br>  Voice—active<br>  Case—nominative<br>  Gender—masculine<br>  Number—singular<br>  Stem or root—from ὑπάρχω<br>Concordance References:<br>  ⇒ Strong's #5225 huparchō<br>  ⇒ NIV #5639 huparchō<br>  ⇒ NASB #5225 huparchō<br><br>**Philip. 2:6**<br>Who, **being** in the form of God, thought it not robbery to be equal with God: [KJV]<br>Who, although He **existed** in the form of God, did not regard equality with God a thing to be grasped, [NASB]<br>Who, **being** in very nature God, did not consider equality with God something to be grasped, [NIV]<br>Who, **being** in the form of God, did not consider it robbery to be equal with God, [NKJV]<br>Though he **was** God, he did not demand and cling to his rights as God. [NLT]<br>ὃς ἐν μορφῇ Θεοῦ **ὑπάρχων**, οὐχ ἁρπαγμὸν ἡγήσατο τὸ εἶναι ἴσα Θεῷ, [GNS]<br>ὃς ἐν μορφῇ θεοῦ **ὑπάρχων** οὐχ ἁρπαγμὸν ἡγήσατο τὸ εἶναι ἴσα θεῷ, [GNT] | Being, existed, was. The word "being" (*huparchōn*) means existence, what a person is within and without.<br><br>**Practical Application**<br>It is the very essence of a person, what a person is; that part of a person that cannot be changed. It is who a person is and all that he is.<br>This is a most glorious truth because it means that *Jesus Christ is God*; He is the very *being of God*. |
| **#337 Being Built Up**<br><br>Edified–KJV<br>**Being built up**–NASB | οἰκοδομουμένη = *oikodomoumenē*<br>Pronunciation: [oy-kod-om-oo'-mehn-ah-ee]<br>Parsing (part of speech): verb<br>  Mood—participle<br>  Tense—present | To be strengthened; to be edified; to build; to encourage; to restore.<br><br>**Practical Application**<br>The word means to build up; to grow spiritu- |

# PRACTICAL WORD STUDIES
## in the NEW TESTAMENT

| ENGLISH WORD | GREEK WORD AND VERSE | THE WORD MEANS... |
|---|---|---|
| Strengthened–NIV<br>Edified–NKJV<br>Grew in strength–NLT<br><br>**POSB REFERENCE**<br>(Acts 9:31)<br>Note 2 | Voice—passive<br>Case—nominative<br>Gender—feminine<br>Number—singular<br>Stem or root—from οἰκοδομέω<br>Concordance References:<br>⇒ Strong's #3618 oikodomeö<br>⇒ NIV #3868 oikodomeö<br>⇒ NASB #3618 oikodomeö<br><br>**Acts 9:31**<br>Then had the churches rest throughout all Judaea and Galilee and Samaria, and were **edified**; and walking in the fear of the Lord, and in the comfort of the Holy Ghost, were multiplied. [KJV]<br>So the church throughout all Judea and Galilee and Samaria enjoyed peace, **being built up**; and, going on in the fear of the Lord and in the comfort of the Holy Spirit, it continued to increase. [NASB]<br>Then the church throughout Judea, Galilee and Samaria enjoyed a time of peace. It was **strengthened**; and encouraged by the Holy Spirit, it grew in numbers, living in the fear of the Lord. [NIV]<br>Then the churches throughout all Judea, Galilee, and Samaria had peace and were **edified**. And walking in the fear of the Lord and in the comfort of the Holy Spirit, they were multiplied. [NKJV]<br>The church then had peace throughout Judea, Galilee, and Samaria, and it **grew in strength** and numbers. The believers were walking in the fear of the Lord and in the comfort of the Holy Spirit. [NLT]<br>Αἱ μὲν οὖν ἐκκλησίαι καθ' ὅλης τῆς Ἰουδαίας καὶ Γαλιλαίας καὶ Σαμαρείας εἶχον εἰρήνην, **οἰκοδο**μούμεναι καὶ πορευόμεναι τῷ φόβῳ τοῦ Κυρίου, καὶ τῇ παρακλήσει τοῦ Ἁγίου Πνεύματος ἐπληθύνετο. [GNS]<br>Ἡ μὲν οὖν ἐκκλησία καθ' ὅλης τῆς Ἰουδαίας καὶ Γαλιλαίας καὶ Σαμαρείας εἶχεν εἰρήνην **οἰκοδομουμένη** καὶ πορευομένη τῷ φόβῳ τοῦ κυρίου καὶ τῇ παρακλήσει τοῦ ἁγίου πνεύματος ἐπληθύνετο. [GNT] | ally; to promote spiritual growth; to strengthen; to establish; to confirm in the faith. The tense is continuous action. |
| #338<br>**Being Diligent**<br><br>Endeavouring–KJV<br>**Being diligent–NASB**<br>Make every effort–NIV<br>Endeavoring–NKJV<br>Always keep yourselves–NLT<br><br>**POSB REFERENCE**<br>(Eph.4:3)<br>Note 2 | σπουδάζοντες = *spoudazontes*<br>Pronunciation: [spoo-dad'-zon-tes]<br>Parsing (part of speech): verb<br>Mood—participle (imperative sense)<br>Tense—present<br>Voice—active<br>Case—nominative<br>Gender—masculine<br>Person—2nd person<br>Number—plural<br>Stem or root—from σπουδάζω<br>Concordance References:<br>⇒ Strong's #4704 spoudazö<br>⇒ NIV #5079 spoudazö<br>⇒ NASB #4704 spoudazö<br><br>**Ephes. 4:3**<br>**Endeavouring** to keep the unity of the Spirit in the bond of peace. [KJV]<br>**Being diligent** to preserve the unity of the Spirit in the bond of peace. [NASB]<br>**Make every effort** to keep the unity of the Spirit through the bond of peace. [NIV]<br>**Endeavoring** to keep the unity of the Spirit in the bond of peace. [NKJV]<br>**Always keep yourselves** united in the Holy Spirit, and bind yourselves together with peace. [NLT]<br>**σπουδάζοντες** τηρεῖν τὴν ἑνότητα τοῦ Πνεύματος ἐν τῷ συνδέσμῳ τῆς εἰρήνης. [GNS]<br>**σπουδάζοντες** τηρεῖν τὴν ἑνότητα τοῦ πνεύματος ἐν τῷ συνδέσμῳ τῆς εἰρήνης· [GNT] | To make every effort; to work hard; to be eager; to do one's best, being diligent, to work at, taking care and doing one's very best, and to make haste to do it.<br><br>**Practical Application**<br>The only way to walk worthy of God's great calling is to work at keeping the peace and unity which God has given us. Nothing cuts the heart of God like divisiveness between His people, divisiveness which tears apart His church. The very thing God is doing is creating a new body of people to live together in the love and unity of His Son. He is going to create a new heavens and earth in which there will be no other spirit. Therefore, He expects us to live in the love and unity of His Spirit now. |

# PRACTICAL WORD STUDIES
## in the NEW TESTAMENT

| ENGLISH WORD | GREEK WORD AND VERSE | THE WORD MEANS... |
|---|---|---|
| **#339**<br>**Believe**<br><br>Believe–KJV<br>Believe–NASB<br>Put your trust–NIV<br>Believe–NKJV<br>Believe–NLT<br><br>**POSB REFERENCE**<br>(Jn.12:34-36; esp. v.36)<br>Note 5, point 2 | πιστεύετε = *pisteuete*<br>Pronunciation: [pist-yoo'-eh-teh]<br>Parsing (part of speech): verb<br>   Mood—imperative<br>   Tense—present<br>   Voice—active<br>   Person—2nd person<br>   Number—plural<br>   Stem or root—from πιστεύω<br>Concordance References:<br>  ⇒ Strong's #4100 pisteuo<br>  ⇒ NIV #4409 pisteuo<br>  ⇒ NASB #4100 pisteuo<br><br>**John 12:36**<br>While ye have light, **believe** in the light, that ye may be the children of light. These things spake Jesus, and departed, and did hide himself from them. [KJV]<br>"While you have the light, **believe** in the light, in order that you may become sons of light." These things Jesus spoke, and He departed and hid Himself from them. [NASB]<br>**Put your trust** in the light while you have it, so that you may become sons of light." When he had finished speaking, Jesus left and hid himself from them. [NIV]<br>While you have the light, **believe** in the light, that you may become sons of light." These things Jesus spoke, and departed, and was hidden from them. [NKJV]<br>**Believe** in the light while there is still time; then you will become children of the light." After saying these things, Jesus went away and was hidden from them. [NLT]<br>ἕως τὸ φῶς ἔχετε, **πιστεύετε** εἰς τὸ φῶς, ἵνα υἱοὶ φωτὸς γένησθε. Ταῦτα ἐλάλησεν ὁ Ἰησοῦς, καὶ ἀπελθὼν ἐκρύβη ἀπ' αὐτῶν. [GNS]<br>ὡς τὸ φῶς ἔχετε, **πιστεύετε** εἰς τὸ φῶς, ἵνα υἱοὶ φωτὸς γένησθε. Ταῦτα ἐλάλησεν Ἰησοῦς, καὶ ἀπελθὼν ἐκρύβη ἀπ' αὐτῶν. [GNT] | To believe; to put trust in; to be convinced; to have no doubt; to be certain of.<br><br>**Practical Application**<br>Note this important grammatical form of the word "believe" (*pisteuete*): it is continuous action. A person who truly sees Jesus Christ as the Light of the world believes and continues to believe. And the very moment his heart leaps toward Christ in belief, he becomes a child of the Light, a child of God Himself. The person sees the Light and begins to walk in the Light, living the kind of life he should. |
| **#340**<br>**Believe–Believing**<br><br>Believing–KJV<br>Believe–NASB<br>Believe–NIV<br>Believing–NKJV<br>Trust–NLT<br><br>**POSB REFERENCE**<br>(1 Pt.1:8-9; esp. v.8)<br>Note 3, point 2 | πιστεύοντες = *pisteuontes*<br>Pronunciation: [pist-yoo'-on-tehs]<br>Parsing (part of speech): verb<br>   Mood—participle<br>   Tense—present<br>   Voice—active<br>   Case—nominative<br>   Gender—masculine<br>   Person—2nd person<br>   Number—plural<br>   Stem or root—from πιστεύω<br>Concordance References:<br>  ⇒ Strong's #4100 pisteuō<br>  ⇒ NIV #4409 pisteuō<br>  ⇒ NASB #4100 pisteuō<br><br>**1 Peter 1:8**<br>Whom having not seen, ye love; in whom, though now ye see him not, yet **believing**, ye rejoice with joy unspeakable and full of glory: [KJV]<br>And though you have not seen Him, you love Him, and though you do not see Him now, but **believe** in Him, you greatly rejoice with joy inexpressible and full of glory, [NASB]<br>Though you have not seen him, you love him; and even though you do not see him now, you **believe** in him and are filled with an inexpressible and glorious joy, [NIV]<br>Whom having not seen you love. Though now you do not see Him, yet **believing**, you rejoice with joy inexpressible and full of glory, [NKJV]<br>You love him even though you have never seen him. Though you do not see him, you **trust** him; and even now | To believe; to trust; to have faith in God and Christ; to have the utmost confidence in.<br><br>**Practical Application**<br>Trials and temptations are to be conquered by our belief in Jesus Christ. Note the verse: we do not see Jesus, but we do believe in Him. The word "believe" (*pisteuontes*) is in the present continuous tense. That is, it is continuous action, continuous belief—a belief that continues on and on. It is believing and never ceasing to believe and trust Jesus Christ. The point is clear: if we are continuing to believe in Jesus Christ, then we are following Christ. We are doing what He says...<br>• rejecting and turning away from all temptations.<br>• standing firm and relying upon His presence and power to conquer and to carry us through all trials. |

## PRACTICAL WORD STUDIES
### in the NEW TESTAMENT

| ENGLISH WORD | GREEK WORD AND VERSE | THE WORD MEANS... |
|---|---|---|
| | you are happy with a glorious, inexpressible joy. [NLT]<br>ὃν οὐκ εἰδότες ἀγαπᾶτε, εἰς ὃν ἄρτι μὴ ὁρῶντες **πιστεύοντες** δὲ, ἀγαλλιᾶσθε χαρᾷ ἀνεκλαλήτῳ καὶ δεδοξασμένῃ, [GNS]<br>ὃν οὐκ ἰδόντες ἀγαπᾶτε, εἰς ὃν ἄρτι μὴ ὁρῶντες **πιστεύοντες** δὲ ἀγαλλιᾶσθε χαρᾷ ἀνεκλαλήτῳ καὶ δεδοξασμένῃ [GNT] | |
| **#341**<br>**Believe, Did Not**<br><br>Believed not–KJV<br>Disobedient–NASB<br>Refused to believe–NIV<br>**Did not believe–NKJV**<br>Rejected–NLT<br><br>**POSB REFERENCE**<br>(Acts 19:2-9; esp. v.9)<br>Note 2, point 2d | ἠπείθουν = ëpeithoun<br>Pronunciation: [ap-i-thoon']<br>Parsing (part of speech): verb<br>   Mood—indicative<br>   Tense—imperfect<br>   Voice—active<br>   Person—3rd person<br>   Number—plural<br>   Stem or root—from ἀπειθέω<br>Concordance References:<br>⇒ Strong's #544 apeitheō<br>⇒ NIV #578 apeitheō<br>⇒ NASB #544 apeitheō<br><br>**Acts 19:9**<br>But when divers were hardened, and **believed not**, but spake evil of that way before the multitude, he departed from them, and separated the disciples, disputing daily in the school of one Tyrannus. [KJV]<br>But when some were becoming hardened and **disobedient**, speaking evil of the Way before the multitude, he withdrew from them and took away the disciples, reasoning daily in the school of Tyrannus. [NASB]<br>But some of them became obstinate; they **refused to believe** and publicly maligned the Way. So Paul left them. He took the disciples with him and had discussions daily in the lecture hall of Tyrannus. [NIV]<br>But when some were hardened and **did not believe**, but spoke evil of the Way before the multitude, he departed from them and withdrew the disciples, reasoning daily in the school of Tyrannus. [NKJV]<br>But some **rejected** his message and publicly spoke against the Way, so Paul left the synagogue and took the believers with him. Then he began preaching daily at the lecture hall of Tyrannus. [NLT]<br>ὡς δέ τινες ἐσκληρύνοντο καὶ **ἠπείθουν**, κακολογοῦντες τὴν ὁδὸν ἐνώπιον τοῦ πλήθους, ἀποστὰς ἀπ' αὐτῶν ἀφώρισε τοὺς μαθητάς, καθ' ἡμέραν διαλεγόμενος ἐν τῇ σχολῇ τυράννου τινός. [GNS]<br>ὡς δέ τινες ἐσκληρύνοντο καὶ **ἠπείθουν** κακολογοῦντες τὴν ὁδὸν ἐνώπιον τοῦ πλήθους, ἀποστὰς ἀπ' αὐτῶν ἀφώρισεν τοὺς μαθητὰς καθ' ἡμέραν διαλεγόμενος ἐν τῇ σχολῇ Τυράννου. [GNT] | To refuse to believe; to be disobedient; to reject.<br><br>**Practical Application**<br>Take note of this, for rejecting the gospel is not just unbelief. It is much worse: it is disobeying God. God demands that men believe in His Son Jesus Christ. Not believing is an act of outright disobedience, an affront to God, an act of rebellion and hostility against His commandment. |
| **#342**<br>**Believe, Does Not**<br><br>Believeth not–KJV<br>Who does not obey–NASB<br>Whoever rejects–NIV<br>**Does not believe–NKJV**<br>Who don't obey–NLT<br><br>**POSB REFERENCE**<br>(Jn.3:36)<br>Deeper Study #4 | ὁ ἀπειθῶν = ho apeithōn<br>Pronunciation: [ho ap-i-thown']<br>Parsing apeithōn (part of speech): verb<br>   Mood—participle<br>   Tense—present<br>   Voice—active<br>   Case—nominative<br>   Gender—masculine<br>   Number—singular<br>   Stem or root—from ἀπειθέω<br>Concordance References:<br>⇒ Strong's #3588 ho + 544 apeitheō<br>⇒ NIV #3836 ho [whoever] + 578 apeitheō [rejects]<br>⇒ NASB #3588 ho + 544 apeitheō<br><br>**John 3:36**<br>He that believeth on the Son hath everlasting life: and he that **believeth not** the Son shall not see life; but the wrath of God abideth on him. [KJV]<br>"He who believes in the Son has eternal life; but he | To reject; to believe not; to obey not; to disobey; to be an unbeliever.<br><br>**Practical Application**<br>If a person does not obey, he does not really believe. Conversely, if a person really believes, he obeys. (See POSB note—John 2:24 and POSB *Deeper Study* #2—John 2:24; POSB *Deeper Study* #1—Hebrews 5:9.) The man who believes *on* the Son has everlasting life (see POSB *Deeper Study* #2—John 1:4; POSB *Deeper Study* #1—John 10:10; POSB *Deeper Study* #1—John 17:2-3). God will receive and honor anyone who receives and honors His Son whom He loves so much. It does not matter who the person is or what the person has done. If the person believes on God's only Son, God gives everlasting life to him.<br>The person who does not believe the Son |

# PRACTICAL WORD STUDIES
## in the NEW TESTAMENT

| ENGLISH WORD | GREEK WORD AND VERSE | THE WORD MEANS... |
|---|---|---|
| | **who does not obey** the Son shall not see life, but the wrath of God abides on him." [NASB]<br>Whoever believes in the Son has eternal life, but **whoever rejects** the Son will not see life, for God's wrath remains on him." [NIV]<br>He who believes in the Son has everlasting life; and he who **does not believe** the Son shall not see life, but the wrath of God abides on him." [NKJV]<br>And all who believe in God's Son have eternal life. Those **who don't obey** the Son will never experience eternal life, but the wrath of God remains upon them." [NLT]<br>ὁ πιστεύων εἰς τὸν υἱὸν ἔχει ζωὴν αἰώνιον· ὁ δὲ **ἀπειθῶν** τῷ υἱῷ, οὐκ ὄψεται ζωήν, ἀλλ' ἡ ὀργὴ τοῦ Θεοῦ μένει ἐπ' αὐτόν. [GNS]<br>ὁ πιστεύων εἰς τὸν υἱὸν ἔχει ζωὴν αἰώνιον· ὁ δὲ **ἀπειθῶν** τῷ υἱῷ οὐκ ὄψεται ζωήν, ἀλλ' ἡ ὀργὴ τοῦ θεοῦ μένει ἐπ' αὐτόν. [GNT] | faces two things.<br>1. He will not see life. He perishes (see POSB *Deeper Study* #2, Perish—John 3:16).<br>2. The wrath of God abides on him (see POSB *Deeper Study* #5—John 3:36). |
| **#343**<br>**Believe, Not–Believe, Didn't–Believed Them Not**<br><br>**Believed them not–KJV**<br>**Not believe–NASB**<br>**Not believe–NIV**<br>**Not believe–NKJV**<br>**Didn't believe–NLT**<br><br>**POSB REFERENCE**<br>(Lk.24:9-11; esp. v.11)<br>Note 6 | ἠπίστουν = ëpistoun<br>Pronunciation: [ayp-is'-toon]<br>Parsing (part of speech): verb<br>    Mood—indicative<br>    Tense—imperfect<br>    Voice—active<br>    Person—3rd person<br>    Number—plural<br>    Stem or root—from ἀπιστέω<br>Concordance References:<br>⇒ Strong's #569 apisteö<br>⇒ NIV #601 apisteö<br>⇒ NASB #569 apisteö<br><br>**Luke 24:11**<br>And their words seemed to them as idle tales, and they **believed them not**. [KJV]<br>And these words appeared to them as nonsense, and they would **not believe** them. [NASB]<br>But they did **not believe** the women, because their words seemed to them like nonsense. [NIV]<br>And their words seemed to them like idle tales, and they did **not believe** them. [NKJV]<br>But the story sounded like nonsense, so they **didn't believe** it. [NLT]<br>καὶ ἐφάνησαν ἐνώπιον αὐτῶν ὡσεὶ λῆρος τὰ ῥήματα αὐτῶν, καὶ **ἠπίστουν** αὐταῖς. [GNS]<br>καὶ ἐφάνησαν ἐνώπιον αὐτῶν ὡσεὶ λῆρος τὰ ῥήματα ταῦτα, καὶ **ἠπίστουν** αὐταῖς. [GNT] | Not to believe; a habitual lack of confidence; a failure to believe; a refusal to believe; to be unfaithful; to be faithless.<br><br>**Practical Application**<br>The Greek word is disbelieved and is in the imperfect active tense which means the disciples "kept on disbelieving," kept on putting no trust or confidence in what the women were claiming. The disciples were gripped with a skeptical, unbelieving spirit. |
| **#344**<br>**Believed**<br><br>**Believed–KJV**<br>**Believed–NASB**<br>**Believed–NIV**<br>**Believed–NKJV**<br>Convinced–NLT<br><br>**POSB REFERENCE**<br>(Jn.2:23)<br>Note 1, point 1<br><br>See also POSB REF:<br>(Jn.2:23-24; esp. v.23)<br>*Deeper Study* #2 | ἐπίστευσαν = episteusan<br>Pronunciation: [eh-pist-yoo'-sahn]<br>Parsing (part of speech): <u>verb</u><br>    Mood—indicative<br>    Tense—aorist<br>    Voice—<u>active</u><br>    Person—3rd person<br>    Number—plural<br>    Stem or root—from πιστεύω<br>Concordance References:<br>⇒ Strong's #4100 pisteuö<br>⇒ NIV #4409 pisteuö<br>⇒ NASB #4100 pisteuö<br><br>**John 2:23**<br>Now when he was in Jerusalem at the passover, in the feast day, <u>many **believed** in his name</u>, when they saw the miracles which he did. [KJV]<br>Now when He was in Jerusalem at the Passover, during the feast, many **believed** in His name, beholding His signs which He was doing. [NASB]<br>Now while he was in Jerusalem at the Passover Feast, many people saw the miraculous signs he was doing and **believed** in his name. [NIV] | To trust; to have faith in; to be persuaded; to accept; to have no doubt; to be convinced; to believe; to rely on.<br><br>**Practical Application**<br>The word "believed" (*episteusan*) is in the Greek aorist tense, which means they believed *once-for-all*. In this Scripture, their belief was genuine, at least the belief of some. However, the belief of others was not genuine. The fact that Jesus knew "all men" (all those professing belief) and did not commit Himself to them shows the inadequacy of their faith (John 2:24). |

# PRACTICAL WORD STUDIES
## in the NEW TESTAMENT

| ENGLISH WORD | GREEK WORD AND VERSE | THE WORD MEANS... |
|---|---|---|
| | Now when He was in Jerusalem at the Passover, during the feast, many **believed** in His name when they saw the signs which He did. [NKJV]<br><br>Because of the miraculous signs he did in Jerusalem at the Passover celebration, many people were **convinced** that he was indeed the Messiah. [NLT]<br><br>Ὡς δὲ ἦν ἐν Ἱεροσολύμοις ἐν τῷ πάσχα ἐν τῇ ἑορτῇ, πολλοὶ **ἐπίστευσαν** εἰς τὸ ὄνομα αὐτοῦ, θεωροῦντες αὐτοῦ τὰ σημεῖα ἃ ἐποίει. [GNS]<br><br>Ὡς δὲ ἦν ἐν τοῖς Ἱεροσολύμοις ἐν τῷ πάσχα ἐν τῇ ἑορτῇ, πολλοὶ **ἐπίστευσαν** εἰς τὸ ὄνομα αὐτοῦ θεωροῦντες αὐτοῦ τὰ σημεῖα ἃ ἐποίει· [GNT] | |
| **#345**<br>**Believed Not**<br><br>**Believed not–KJV**<br>Disobedient–NASB<br>Refused to believe–NIV<br>Did not believe–NKJV<br>Rejected–NLT<br><br>**POSB REFERENCE**<br>(Acts 19:2-9; esp. v.9)<br>Note 2, point 2d | ἠπείθουν = ëpeithoun<br>Pronunciation: [ayp-i-thoon']<br>Parsing (part of speech): verb<br>  Mood—indicative<br>  Tense—imperfect<br>  Voice—active<br>  Person—3rd person<br>  Number—plural<br>  Stem or root—from ἀπειθέω<br>Concordance References:<br>  ⇒ Strong's #544 apeitheō<br>  ⇒ NIV #578 apeitheō<br>  ⇒ NASB #544 apeitheō<br><br>**Acts 19:9**<br>But when divers were hardened, and **believed not**, but spake evil of that way before the multitude, he departed from them, and separated the disciples, disputing daily in the school of one Tyrannus. [KJV]<br><br>But when some were becoming hardened and **disobedient**, speaking evil of the Way before the multitude, he withdrew from them and took away the disciples, reasoning daily in the school of Tyrannus. [NASB]<br><br>But some of them became obstinate; they **refused to believe** and publicly maligned the Way. So Paul left them. He took the disciples with him and had discussions daily in the lecture hall of Tyrannus. [NIV]<br><br>But when some were hardened and **did not believe**, but spoke evil of the Way before the multitude, he departed from them and withdrew the disciples, reasoning daily in the school of Tyrannus. [NKJV]<br><br>But some **rejected** his message and publicly spoke against the Way, so Paul left the synagogue and took the believers with him. Then he began preaching daily at the lecture hall of Tyrannus. [NLT]<br><br>ὡς δέ τινες ἐσκληρύνοντο καὶ **ἠπείθουν**, κακολογοῦντες τὴν ὁδὸν ἐνώπιον τοῦ πλήθους, ἀποστὰς ἀπ' αὐτῶν ἀφώρισε τοὺς μαθητάς, καθ' ἡμέραν διαλεγόμενος ἐν τῇ σχολῇ τυράννου τινός. [GNS]<br><br>ὡς δέ τινες ἐσκληρύνοντο καὶ **ἠπείθουν** κακολογοῦντες τὴν ὁδὸν ἐνώπιον τοῦ πλήθους, ἀποστὰς ἀπ' αὐτῶν ἀφώρισεν τοὺς μαθητάς καθ' ἡμέραν διαλεγόμενος ἐν τῇ σχολῇ Τυράννου. [GNT] | Refused to believe; to believe not; to be disobedient; to reject.<br><br>**Practical Application**<br>Take note of this, for rejecting the gospel is not just unbelief. It is much worse: it is disobeying God. God demands that men believe in His Son Jesus Christ. Not believing is an act of outright disobedience, an affront to God, an act of rebellion and hostility against His commandment. |
| **#346**<br>**Believed Not**<br><br>**Believed not–KJV**<br>Disobedient–NASB<br>Disobeyed–NIV<br>Did not obey–NKJV<br>Disobeyed–NLT<br><br>**POSB REFERENCE**<br>(Heb.3:13-19; esp. v.18)<br>Note 3, point 7 | ἀπειθήσασιν = apeithēsasin<br>Pronunciation: [ap-i-thay'-sah-sin]<br>Parsing (part of speech): verb<br>  Mood—participle<br>  Tense—aorist<br>  Voice—active<br>  Case—dative<br>  Gender—masculine<br>  Number—plural<br>  Stem or root—from ἀπειθέω<br>Concordance References:<br>  ⇒ Strong's #544 apeitheō<br>  ⇒ NIV #578 apeitheō<br>  ⇒ NASB #544 apeitheō | To disobey; to fail to believe; to be disobedient; to refuse to be persuaded; to refuse to believe; to withhold belief.<br><br>**Practical Application**<br>God judges unbelief. It is a person who just refuses to be persuaded despite the evidence that Jesus Christ is truly the Savior of the world; the kind of person who chooses to continue living for the world and self despite the fact of coming judgment. The unbeliever will not be allowed to enter God's promised land of heaven nor God's eternal rest. |

# PRACTICAL WORD STUDIES
## in the NEW TESTAMENT

| ENGLISH WORD | GREEK WORD AND VERSE | THE WORD MEANS... |
|---|---|---|
| | **Hebrews 3:18**<br>And to whom sware he that they should not enter into his rest, but to them that **believed not**? [KJV]<br>And to whom did He swear that they should not enter His rest, but to those who were **disobedient**? [NASB]<br>And to whom did God swear that they would never enter his rest if not to those who **disobeyed**? [NIV]<br>And to whom did He swear that they would not enter His rest, but to those who **did not obey**? [NKJV]<br>And to whom was God speaking when he vowed that they would never enter his place of rest? He was speaking to those who **disobeyed** him. [NLT]<br>τίσι δὲ ὤμοσε μὴ εἰσελεύσεσθαι εἰς τὴν κατάπαυσιν αὐτοῦ, εἰ μὴ τοῖς **ἀπειθήσασι**; [GNS]<br>τίσιν δὲ ὤμοσεν μὴ εἰσελεύσεσθαι εἰς τὴν κατάπαυσιν αὐτοῦ εἰ μὴ τοῖς **ἀπειθήσασιν**; [GNT] | |
| **#347**<br>**Believeth Not**<br><br>Believeth not–KJV<br>Who does not obey–NASB<br>Whoever rejects–NIV<br>Does not believe–NKJV<br>Who don't obey–NLT<br><br>**POSB REFERENCE**<br>(Jn.3:36)<br>*Deeper Study* #4 | ὁ ἀπειθῶν = *ho apeithōn*<br>Pronunciation: [ho ap-i-thown']<br>Parsing *apeithōn* (part of speech): verb<br>    Mood—participle<br>    Tense—present<br>    Voice—active<br>    Case—nominative<br>    Gender—masculine<br>    Number—singular<br>    Stem or root—from ἀπειθέω<br>Concordance References:<br>⇒ Strong's #3588 ho + 544 apeitheō<br>⇒ NIV #3836 ho [whoever] + 578 apeitheō [rejects]<br>⇒ NASB #3588 ho + 544 apeitheō<br><br>**John 3:36**<br>He that believeth on the Son hath everlasting life: and he that **believeth not** the Son shall not see life; but the wrath of God abideth on him. [KJV]<br>"He who believes in the Son has eternal life; but he **who does not obey** the Son shall not see life, but the wrath of God abides on him." [NASB]<br>Whoever believes in the Son has eternal life, but **whoever rejects** the Son will not see life, for God's wrath remains on him." [NIV]<br>He who believes in the Son has everlasting life; and he who **does not believe** the Son shall not see life, but the wrath of God abides on him." [NKJV]<br>And all who believe in God's Son have eternal life. Those **who don't obey** the Son will never experience eternal life, but the wrath of God remains upon them." [NLT]<br>ὁ πιστεύων εἰς τὸν υἱὸν ἔχει ζωὴν αἰώνιον· ὁ δὲ **ἀπειθῶν** τῷ υἱῷ, οὐκ ὄψεται ζωήν, ἀλλ' ἡ ὀργὴ τοῦ Θεοῦ μένει ἐπ' αὐτόν. [GNS]<br>ὁ πιστεύων εἰς τὸν υἱὸν ἔχει ζωὴν αἰώνιον· ὁ δὲ **ἀπειθῶν** τῷ υἱῷ οὐκ ὄψεται ζωήν, ἀλλ' ἡ ὀργὴ τοῦ θεοῦ μένει ἐπ' αὐτόν. [GNT] | To reject; to believe not; to obey not; to disobey; to be an unbeliever.<br><br>**Practical Application**<br>If a person does not obey, he does not really believe. Conversely, if a person really believes, he obeys. (See POSB note—John 2:24 and POSB *Deeper Study* #2—John 2:24; POSB *Deeper Study* #1—Hebrews 5:9.) The man who believes *on* the Son has everlasting life (see POSB *Deeper Study* #2—John 1:4; POSB *Deeper Study* #1—John 10:10; POSB *Deeper Study* #1—John 17:2-3). God will receive and honor anyone who receives and honors His Son whom He loves so much. It does not matter who the person is or what the person has done. If the person believes on God's only Son, God gives everlasting life to him.<br>The person who does not believe the Son faces two things.<br>1. He will not see life. He perishes (see POSB *Deeper Study* #2, Perish—John 3:16).<br>2. The wrath of God abides on him (see POSB *Deeper Study* #5—John 3:36). |
| **#348**<br>**Belly**<br><br>Belly–KJV<br>Appetites–NASB<br>Appetites–NIV<br>Belly–NKJV<br>Personal interests–NLT<br><br>**POSB REFERENCE**<br>(Rom.16:17-18; esp. v.18)<br>Note 1, point 2 | κοιλία = *koilia*<br>Pronunciation: [koy-lee'-ah]<br>Parsing (part of speech): noun<br>    Case—dative<br>    Gender—feminine<br>    Number—singular<br>    Stem or root—from κοιλία, ας<br>Concordance References:<br>⇒ Strong's #2836 koilia<br>⇒ NIV #3120 koilia<br>⇒ NASB #2836 koilia<br><br>**Romans 16:18**<br>For they that are such serve not our Lord Jesus Christ, but their own **belly**; and by good words and fair speeches deceive the hearts of the simple. [KJV]<br>For such men are slaves, not of our Lord Christ but of their own **appetites**; and by their smooth and flattering | Appetites, personal interests. It means the stomach or belly and its physical appetites.<br><br>**Practical Application**<br>A divisive person does not serve Christ, but his own desires. A divisive person is gripped by...<br>• selfish desires<br>• base ambition<br>• personal urges<br>• physical appetites<br>• wanting his own way<br>• getting what he wants<br><br>Note: Scripture clearly says that divisive persons do not serve Christ. They call themselves |

# PRACTICAL WORD STUDIES
## in the NEW TESTAMENT

| ENGLISH WORD | GREEK WORD AND VERSE | THE WORD MEANS... |
|---|---|---|
| | speech they deceive the hearts of the unsuspecting. [NASB]<br>    For such people are not serving our Lord Christ, but their own **appetites**. By smooth talk and flattery they deceive the minds of naive people. [NIV]<br>    For those who are such do not serve our Lord Jesus Christ, but their own **belly**, and by smooth words and flattering speech deceive the hearts of the simple. [NKJV]<br>    Such people are not serving Christ our Lord; they are serving their own **personal interests**. By smooth talk and glowing words they deceive innocent people. [NLT]<br>    οἱ γὰρ τοιοῦτοι τῷ Κυρίῳ ἡμῶν Ἰησοῦ Χριστῷ οὐ δουλεύουσιν, ἀλλὰ τῇ ἑαυτῶν **κοιλίᾳ**. καὶ διὰ τῆς χρηστολογίας καὶ εὐλογίας ἐξαπατῶσι τὰς καρδίας τῶν ἀκάκων. [GNS]<br>    οἱ γὰρ τοιοῦτοι τῷ κυρίῳ ἡμῶν Χριστῷ οὐ δουλεύουσιν ἀλλὰ τῇ ἑαυτῶν **κοιλίᾳ**, καὶ διὰ τῆς χρηστολογίας καὶ εὐλογίας ἐξαπατῶσιν τὰς καρδίας τῶν ἀκάκων. [GNT] | Christians, but their Lord is not Christ. They are not committed to His honor and glory and mission, but to themselves—to getting and doing what they want. The divisive person is still given over to the things of this carnal, sensual, and secular world. |
| **#349**<br>**Belly**<br><br>Belly–KJV<br>Appetite–NASB<br>Stomach–NIV<br>**Belly–NKJV**<br>Appetite–NLT<br><br>**POSB REFERENCE**<br>(Philip.3:18-19; esp. v.19)<br>Note 2, point 2 | κοιλία = *koilia*<br>Pronunciation: [koy-lee'-ah]<br>Parsing (part of speech): noun<br>    Case—nominative<br>    Gender—feminine<br>    Number—singular<br>    Stem or root—from κοιλία, ας<br>Concordance References:<br>⇒ Strong's #2836 koilia<br>⇒ NIV #3120 koilia<br>⇒ NASB #2836 koilia<br><br>**Philip. 3:19**<br>    Whose end is destruction, whose God is their **belly**, and whose glory is in their shame, who mind earthly things.) [KJV]<br>    Whose end is destruction, whose god is their **appetite**, and whose glory is in their shame, who set their minds on earthly things. [NASB]<br>    Their destiny is destruction, their god is their **stomach**, and their glory is in their shame. Their mind is on earthly things. [NIV]<br>    Whose end is destruction, whose god is their **belly**, and whose glory is in their shame—who set their mind on earthly things. [NKJV]<br>    Their future is eternal destruction. Their god is their **appetite**, they brag about shameful things, and all they think about is this life here on earth. [NLT]<br>    ὧν τὸ τέλος ἀπώλεια, ὧν ὁ θεὸς ἡ **κοιλία**, καὶ ἡ δόξα ἐν τῇ αἰσχύνῃ αὐτῶν, οἱ τὰ ἐπίγεια φρονοῦντες. [GNS]<br>    ὧν τὸ τέλος ἀπώλεια, ὧν ὁ θεὸς ἡ **κοιλία** καὶ ἡ δόξα ἐν τῇ αἰσχύνῃ αὐτῶν, οἱ τὰ ἐπίγεια φρονοῦντες. [GNT] | Stomach, belly, appetite.<br><br>**Practical Application**<br>    Their god is their belly (*koilia*), that is, their stomach, their sensuality, their desire for the physical pleasures of this world. Physical and material gratification is their god. They center their lives around...<br>• possessions and property<br>• houses and furnishings<br>• food and appetite<br>• comfort and plenty<br>• position and success<br>• pleasure and sex<br>• acceptance and social standing<br>• money and wealth<br>• honor and fame<br><br>    Just take a moment to think about any of the above, how some persons center and focus their lives upon such things. Some persons spend more time in front of a mirror or eating or thinking about acceptance or success or possessions or some business deal than they do in prayer. |
| **#350**<br>**Belong To God**<br><br>Holy–KJV<br>Holy–NASB<br>Holy–NIV<br>Holy–NKJV<br>**Belong to God–NLT**<br><br>**POSB REFERENCE**<br>(Heb.3:1)<br>Note 1, point 1 | ἅγιοι = *hagioi*<br>Pronunciation: [hag'-ee-oy]<br>Parsing (part of speech): adjective<br>    Case—vocative<br>    Gender—masculine<br>    Number—plural<br>    Stem or root—from ἅγιος, α, ον<br>Concordance References:<br>⇒ Strong's #40 hagios<br>⇒ NIV #41 hagios<br>⇒ NASB #40 hagios<br><br>**Hebrews 3:1**<br>    Wherefore, **holy** brethren, partakers of the heavenly calling, consider the Apostle and High Priest of our profession, Christ Jesus; [KJV]<br>    Therefore, **holy** brethren, partakers of a heavenly calling, consider Jesus, the Apostle and High Priest of our confession. [NASB]<br>    Therefore, **holy** brothers, who share in the heavenly | Holy; to be set apart or separated to Christ; to belong to God; to be morally pure; saints; devoted; set apart.<br><br>**Practical Application**<br>1. Believers should fix their attention upon Jesus Christ because of who they are.<br>⇒ Believers are holy brothers. The words "belong to God" or "holy" (*hagioi*) mean to be set apart or separated to Christ. It means that we have turned away from the unclean things of the world and from the religions of the world and have turned to Christ. We are holy, set apart to be a brother to Christ. Therefore, we should be following and focusing our attention upon Christ.<br>⇒ Believers are partakers of the heavenly calling. We have been called by Christ to live with God in heaven. We are not to live for this earth; we are to live for heaven. |

# PRACTICAL WORD STUDIES
## in the NEW TESTAMENT

| ENGLISH WORD | GREEK WORD AND VERSE | THE WORD MEANS... |
|---|---|---|
| | calling, fix your thoughts on Jesus, the apostle and high priest whom we confess. [NIV]<br>Therefore, **holy** brethren, partakers of the heavenly calling, consider the Apostle and High Priest of our confession, Christ Jesus, [NKJV]<br>And so, dear brothers and sisters who **belong to God** and are bound for heaven, think about this Jesus whom we declare to be God's Messenger and High Priest. [NLT]<br>Ὅθεν, ἀδελφοὶ **ἅγιοι**, κλήσεως ἐπουρανίου μέτοχοι, κατανοήσατε τὸν ἀπόστολον καὶ ἀρχιερέα τῆς ὁμολογίας ἡμῶν Χριστὸν Ἰησοῦν, [GNS]<br>Ὅθεν, ἀδελφοὶ **ἅγιοι**, κλήσεως ἐπουρανίου μέτοχοι, κατανοήσατε τὸν ἀπόστολον καὶ ἀρχιερέα τῆς ὁμολογίας ἡμῶν Ἰησοῦν,. [GNT] | Therefore, our attention is to be fixed upon heaven, especially upon Christ who is our glorious Savior and who has made it possible for us to live in heaven.<br>2. Believers should fix their attention upon Jesus Christ because of who Christ is.<br>  a. Jesus Christ is the *Apostle* of our confession. The word *apostle* means a person who is sent forth as an ambassador: sent forth by a king or a country on a special mission with a special message. And note: the person is always sent forth with the full authority and power of the king and country which he represents. This is Jesus Christ. Note the word *profession* or *confession*: we confess that Jesus Christ is the Supreme Apostle of our faith and lives. We confess that He is the One whom God sent from heaven to earth...<br>  • as the supreme representative of God, the One who shows us exactly what God is like.<br>  • as the supreme messenger of God, the One who tells us the truth about God and ourselves and the world.<br>  • with all the authority and power of God, the One who has control over all the world and over all the trials and circumstances of our lives.<br>  b. Jesus Christ is the High Priest of our confession (see POSB *Deeper Study* #2, Jesus Christ, High Priest—Hebrews 3:1 for discussion). |
| #351<br>**Belonged To This World**<br><br>Carnal–KJV<br>Men of flesh–NASB<br>Worldly–NIV<br>Carnal–NKJV<br>**Belonged to this world**–NLT<br><br>**POSB REFERENCE**<br>(1 Cor.3:1-4; esp. v.1)<br>*Deeper Study* #1 | σαρκίνοις = *sarkinois*<br>Pronunciation: [sar-kee'-noys]<br>Parsing (part of speech): pronominal adjective<br>  Case—dative<br>  Gender—masculine<br>  Number—plural<br>  Stem or root—from σάρκινος, η, ον<br>Concordance References:<br>  ⇒ Strong's #4560 sarkinos<br>  ⇒ NIV #4921 sarkinos<br>  ⇒ NASB #4560 sarkinos<br><br>**1 Cor. 3:1**<br>And I, brethren, could not speak unto you as unto spiritual, but as unto **carnal**, even as unto babes in Christ. [KJV]<br>And I, brethren, could not speak to you as to spiritual men, but as to **men of flesh**, as to babes in Christ. [NASB]<br>Brothers, I could not address you as spiritual but as **worldly**—mere infants in Christ. [NIV]<br>And I, brethren, could not speak to you as to spiritual people but as to **carnal**, as to babes in Christ. [NKJV]<br>Dear brothers and sisters, when I was with you I couldn't talk to you as I would to mature Christians. I had to talk as though you **belonged to this world** or as though you were infants in the Christian life. [NLT]<br>Καὶ ἐγώ, ἀδελφοί, οὐκ ἠδυνήθην λαλῆσαι ὑμῖν ὡς πνευματικοῖς, ἀλλ' ὡς **σαρκίνοις**, ὡς νηπίοις ἐν Χριστῷ. [GNS]<br>Κἀγώ, ἀδελφοί, οὐκ ἠδυνήθην λαλῆσαι ὑμῖν ὡς πνευματικοῖς ἀλλ' ὡς **σαρκίνοις**, ὡς νηπίοις ἐν Χριστῷ. [GNT] | Worldly, carnal, fleshly, unspiritual, belonging to this world.<br><br>**Practical Application**<br>The ending "inois" [*sarkinois*] means "to be made of." Paul is saying that the Corinthians were human beings, made of flesh. Their problem was that they were living as though they were nothing but flesh. They were still living at the human level of life. They had never gotten beyond the affairs and material things of this life. They acted as though this world was all there was. |

# PRACTICAL WORD STUDIES
## in the NEW TESTAMENT

| ENGLISH WORD | GREEK WORD AND VERSE | THE WORD MEANS... |
|---|---|---|
| **#352**<br>**Benefactors**<br><br>**Benefactors**–KJV<br>**Benefactors**–NASB<br>**Benefactors**–NIV<br>**Benefactors**–NKJV<br>Friends of the people–NLT<br><br>**POSB REFERENCE**<br>(Lk.22:25)<br>Note 2, point 2 | εὐεργέται = *euergetai*<br>Pronunciation: [yoo-erg-et'-ah-ee]<br>Parsing (part of speech): noun<br>    Case—nominative<br>    Gender—masculine<br>    Number—plural<br>    Stem or root—from εὐεργέτης, ου<br>Concordance References:<br>  ⇒ Strong's #2110 euergetēs<br>  ⇒ NIV #2309 euergetēs<br>  ⇒ NASB #2110 euergetēs<br><br>**Luke 22:25**<br>And he said unto them, The kings of the Gentiles exercise lordship over them; and they that exercise authority upon them are called **benefactors**. [KJV]<br>And He said to them, "The kings of the Gentiles lord it over them; and those who have authority over them are called '**Benefactors**.' [NASB]<br>Jesus said to them, "The kings of the Gentiles lord it over them; and those who exercise authority over them call themselves **Benefactors**. [NIV]<br>And He said to them, "The kings of the Gentiles exercise lordship over them, and those who exercise authority over them are called '**benefactors**.' [NKJV]<br>Jesus told them, "In this world the kings and great men order their people around, and yet they are called '**friends of the people**.' [NLT]<br>ὁ δὲ εἶπεν αὐτοῖς, Οἱ βασιλεῖς τῶν ἐθνῶν κυριεύουσιν αὐτῶν, καὶ οἱ ἐξουσιάζοντες αὐτῶν, **εὐεργέται** καλοῦνται. [GNS]<br>ὁ δὲ εἶπεν αὐτοῖς, Οἱ βασιλεῖς τῶν ἐθνῶν κυριεύουσιν αὐτῶν καὶ οἱ ἐξουσιάζοντες αὐτῶν **εὐεργέται** καλοῦνται. [GNT] | Benefactor; a friend of people; a person who gives and helps others.<br><br>**Practical Application**<br>The worldly benefactor wants to be known and called a benefactor, recognized and honored for his help and contribution. He desires to be known as a great person, a friend of the people, a person who is generous, thoughtful, concerned, honorable. |
| **#353**<br>**Beneficial**<br><br>Expedient–KJV<br>Profitable–NASB<br>**Beneficial**–NIV<br>Helpful–NKJV<br>Good for you–NLT<br><br>**POSB REFERENCE**<br>(1 Cor.6:12)<br>Note 1, point 1 | συμφέρει = *sumpherei*<br>Pronunciation: [soom-fer'-eh-ee]<br>Parsing (part of speech): verb<br>    Mood—indicative<br>    Tense—present<br>    Voice—active<br>    Person—3rd person<br>    Number—singular<br>    Stem or root—from συμφέρω<br>Concordance References:<br>  ⇒ Strong's #4851 sumpherö<br>  ⇒ NIV #5237 sumpherö<br>  ⇒ NASB #4851 sumpherö<br><br>**1 Cor. 6:12**<br>All things are lawful unto me, but all things are not **expedient**: all things are lawful for me, but I will not be brought under the power of any. [KJV]<br>All things are lawful for me, but not all things are **profitable**. All things are lawful for me, but I will not be mastered by anything. [NASB]<br>"Everything is permissible for me"—but not everything is **beneficial**. "Everything is permissible for me"—but I will not be mastered by anything. [NIV]<br>All things are lawful for me, but all things are not **helpful**. All things are lawful for me, but I will not be brought under the power of any. [NKJV]<br>You may say, "I am allowed to do anything." But I reply, "Not everything is **good for you**." And even though "I am allowed to do anything," I must not become a slave to anything. [NLT]<br>Πάντα μοι ἔξεστιν, ἀλλ' οὐ πάντα **συμφέρει**· πάντα μοι ἔξεστιν, ἀλλ' οὐκ ἐγὼ ἐξουσιασθήσομαι ὑπό τινος. [GNS]<br>Πάντα μοι ἔξεστιν ἀλλ' οὐ πάντα **συμφέρει**. πάντα μοι ἔξεστιν ἀλλ' οὐκ ἐγὼ ἐξουσιασθήσομαι ὑπό τινος. [GNT] | Beneficial, expedient, useful, helpful, worthwhile, advisable, profitable, good for you.<br><br>**Practical Application**<br>For example, it is beneficial to eat fish; it is unprofitable to eat poisonous berries. It is advisable to keep active for the sake of the body; it is harmful to lie around and become inactive. Note that doing some activities is lawful, but others are not good and profitable. |

# PRACTICAL WORD STUDIES
## in the NEW TESTAMENT

| ENGLISH WORD | GREEK WORD AND VERSE | THE WORD MEANS... |
|---|---|---|
| **#354**<br>**Beseech**<br><br>**Beseech–KJV**<br>Exhort–NASB<br>Appeal–NIV<br>Plead–NKJV<br>Appeal–NLT<br><br>**POSB REFERENCE**<br>(1 Cor.1:10)<br>Note 1<br><br>See also POSB REF:<br>(1 Tim.5:1-2; esp. v.1)<br>Introduction | Παρακαλῶ = *Parakalō*<br>Pronunciation: [par-ak-al-o']<br>Parsing (part of speech): verb<br>   Mood—indicative<br>   Tense—present<br>   Voice—active<br>   Person—1st person<br>   Number—singular<br>   Stem or root—from παρακαλέω<br>Concordance References:<br> ⇒ Strong's #3870 parakaleō<br> ⇒ NIV #4151 parakaleō<br> ⇒ NASB #3870 parakaleō<br><br>**1 Cor. 1:10**<br>Now I **beseech** you, brethren, by the name of our Lord Jesus Christ, that ye all speak the same thing, and that there be no divisions among you; but that ye be perfectly joined together in the same mind and in the same judgment. [KJV]<br>Now I **exhort** you, brethren, by the name of our Lord Jesus Christ, that you all agree, and there be no divisions among you, but you be made complete in the same mind and in the same judgment. [NASB]<br>I **appeal** to you, brothers, in the name of our Lord Jesus Christ, that all of you agree with one another so that there may be no divisions among you and that you may be perfectly united in mind and thought. [NIV]<br>Now I **plead** with you, brethren, by the name of our Lord Jesus Christ, that you all speak the same thing, and that there be no divisions among you, but that you be perfectly joined together in the same mind and in the same judgment. [NKJV]<br>Now, dear brothers and sisters, I **appeal** to you by the authority of the Lord Jesus Christ to stop arguing among yourselves. Let there be real harmony so there won't be divisions in the church. I plead with you to be of one mind, united in thought and purpose. [NLT]<br>Παρακαλῶ δὲ ὑμᾶς, ἀδελφοί, διὰ τοῦ ὀνόματος τοῦ Κυρίου ἡμῶν Ἰησοῦ Χριστοῦ, ἵνα τὸ αὐτὸ λέγητε πάντες, καὶ μὴ ᾖ ἐν ὑμῖν σχίσματα, ἦτε δὲ κατηρτισμένοι ἐν τῷ αὐτῷ νοῒ καὶ ἐν τῇ αὐτῇ γνώμῃ. [GNS]<br>Παρακαλῶ δὲ ὑμᾶς, ἀδελφοί, διὰ τοῦ ὀνόματος τοῦ κυρίου ἡμῶν Ἰησοῦ Χριστοῦ, ἵνα τὸ αὐτὸ λέγητε πάντες καὶ μὴ ᾖ ἐν ὑμῖν σχίσματα, ἦτε δὲ κατηρτισμένοι ἐν τῷ αὐτῷ νοῒ καὶ ἐν τῇ αὐτῇ γνώμῃ. [GNT] | To appeal; to ask; to exhort; to plead; to encourage; to beseech; to beg; to urge; to request; to summon; to call to one's side.<br><br>**Practical Application**<br>Paul says, "I call you to my side; come, let's share together, talk the matter over. I ask, plead, beg—hear what I have to say." |
| **#355**<br>**Beseech**<br><br>**Beseech–KJV**<br>Urge–NASB<br>Urge–NIV<br>**Beseech–NKJV**<br>Plead with–NLT<br><br>**POSB REFERENCE**<br>(Rom.12:1)<br>Note 1 | Παρακαλῶ = *Parakalō*<br>Pronunciation: [par-ak-al-o]<br>Parsing (part of speech): verb<br>   Mood—indicative<br>   Tense—present<br>   Voice—active<br>   Person—1st person<br>   Number—singular<br>   Stem or root—from παρακαλέω<br>Concordance References:<br> ⇒ Strong's #3870 parakaleō<br> ⇒ NIV #4151 parakaleō<br> ⇒ NASB #3870 parakaleō<br><br>**Romans 12:1**<br>I **beseech** you therefore, brethren, by the mercies of God, that ye present your bodies a living sacrifice, holy, acceptable unto God, which is your reasonable service. [KJV]<br>I **urge** you therefore, brethren, by the mercies of God, to present your bodies a living and holy sacrifice, acceptable to God, which is your spiritual service of worship. [NASB]<br>Therefore, I **urge** you, brothers, in view of God's mercy, to offer your bodies as living sacrifices, holy and | To urge; to beseech; to plead with; to beg; to request; to ask.<br><br>**Practical Application**<br>Note a significant point: what is about to be said is not being said to the world, that is, to the lost. It is being directed to brothers in Christ: "I beseech you therefore, brethren." Devotion to God is strongly urged. |

## PRACTICAL WORD STUDIES
### in the NEW TESTAMENT

| ENGLISH WORD | GREEK WORD AND VERSE | THE WORD MEANS... |
|---|---|---|
| | pleasing to God—this is your spiritual act of worship. [NIV]<br><br>I **beseech** you therefore, brethren, by the mercies of God, that you present your bodies a living sacrifice, holy, acceptable to God, which is your reasonable service. [NKJV]<br><br>And so, dear brothers and sisters, I **plead with** you to give your bodies to God. Let them be a living and holy sacrifice—the kind he will accept. When you think of what he has done for you, is this too much to ask? [NLT]<br><br>Παρακαλῶ οὖν ὑμᾶς, ἀδελφοί, διὰ τῶν οἰκτιρμῶν τοῦ Θεοῦ, παραστῆσαι τὰ σώματα ὑμῶν θυσίαν ζῶσαν, ἁγίαν εὐάρεστον τῷ Θεῷ, τὴν λογικὴν λατρείαν ὑμῶν. [GNS]<br><br>Παρακαλῶ οὖν ὑμᾶς, ἀδελφοί, διὰ τῶν οἰκτιρμῶν τοῦ θεοῦ παραστῆσαι τὰ σώματα ὑμῶν θυσίαν ζῶσαν ἁγίαν εὐάρεστον τῷ θεῷ, τὴν λογικὴν λατρείαν ὑμῶν· [GNT] | |
| **#356**<br>**Beseech**<br><br>Beseech–KJV<br>Request–NASB<br>Ask–NIV<br>Urge–NKJV<br>Not translated–NLT<br><br>**POSB REFERENCE**<br>(1 Thes.4:1-2)<br>Note 1, point 1 | ἐρωτῶμεν = erōtōmen<br>Pronunciation: [er-o-to'-mehn]<br>Parsing (part of speech): verb<br>   Mood—indicative<br>   Tense—present<br>   Voice—active<br>   Person—1st person<br>   Number—plural<br>   Stem or root—from ἐρωτάω<br>Concordance References:<br>  ⇒ Strong's #2065 erōtaō<br>  ⇒ NIV #2263 erōtaō<br>  ⇒ NASB #2065 erōtaō<br><br>**1 Thes. 4:1**<br>Furthermore then we **beseech** you, brethren, and exhort you by the Lord Jesus, that as ye have received of us how ye ought to walk and to please God, so ye would abound more and more. [KJV]<br><br>Finally then, brethren, we **request** and exhort you in the Lord Jesus, that, as you received from us instruction as to how you ought to walk and please God (just as you actually do walk), that you may excel still more. [NASB]<br><br>Finally, brothers, we instructed you how to live in order to please God, as in fact you are living. Now we **ask** you and urge you in the Lord Jesus to do this more and more. [NIV]<br><br>Finally then, brethren, we **urge** and exhort in the Lord Jesus that you should abound more and more, just as you received from us how you ought to walk and to please God; [NKJV]<br><br>Finally, dear brothers and sisters, we urge you in the name of the Lord Jesus to live in a way that pleases God, as we have taught you. You are doing this already, and we encourage you to do so more and more. [NLT]—Not Translated<br><br>Τὸ λοιπὸν οὖν, ἀδελφοί, **ἐρωτῶμεν** ὑμᾶς καὶ παρακαλοῦμεν ἐν Κυρίῳ Ἰησοῦ, καθὼς παρελάβετε παρ' ἡμῶν τὸ πῶς δεῖ ὑμᾶς περιπατεῖν καὶ ἀρέσκειν Θεῷ, ἵνα περισσεύητε μᾶλλον. [GNS]<br><br>Λοιπὸν οὖν, ἀδελφοί, **ἐρωτῶμεν** ὑμᾶς καὶ παρακαλοῦμεν ἐν κυρίῳ Ἰησοῦ, ἵνα καθὼς παρελάβετε παρ' ἡμῶν τὸ πῶς δεῖ ὑμᾶς περιπατεῖν καὶ ἀρέσκειν θεῷ, καθὼς καὶ περιπατεῖτε, ἵνα περισσεύητε μᾶλλον. [GNT] | To ask; to beseech; to invite; to request; to beg; to urge.<br><br>**Practical Application**<br>This word always has a sense of urgency about it. Paul was tenderly requesting his dear brothers to continue to please God in their daily walk, but it was an urgent request. Their walking to please God was an absolute necessity, a necessity that carried with it great blessings for obedience and terrible judgment for disobedience (the displeasure of God). |
| **#357**<br>**Beside Ourselves**<br><br>Beside ourselves–KJV<br>Beside ourselves–NASB | ἐξέστημεν = exestēmen<br>Pronunciation: [ex-is'-tay-mehn]<br>Parsing (part of speech): verb<br>   Mood—indicative<br>   Tense—aorist<br>   Voice—active<br>   Person—1st person<br>   Number—plural<br>   Stem or root—from ἐξίστημι and ἐξιστάνω | To be crazy; to be beside oneself; to be out of one's mind; to be insane.<br><br>**Practical Application**<br>One of the charges against Paul was that he was beside himself (*exestemen*), that he was mad, insane. It means to act in the extreme, abnormally, unlike what others act. Paul was |

# PRACTICAL WORD STUDIES
## in the NEW TESTAMENT

| ENGLISH WORD | GREEK WORD AND VERSE | THE WORD MEANS... |
|---|---|---|
| Out of...mind–NIV<br>**Beside ourselves–NKJV**<br>Crazy–NLT<br><br>**POSB REFERENCE**<br>(2 Cor.5:13)<br>Note 3 | Concordance References:<br>⇒ Strong's #1839 existēmi<br>⇒ NIV #2014 existēmi<br>⇒ NASB #1839 existēmi<br><br>**2 Cor. 5:13**<br>For whether we be **beside ourselves**, it is to God: or whether we be sober, it is for your cause. [KJV]<br>For if we are **beside ourselves**, it is for God; if we are of sound mind, it is for you. [NASB]<br>If we are **out of** our **mind**, it is for the sake of God; if we are in our right mind, it is for you. [NIV]<br>For if we are **beside ourselves**, it is for God; or if we are of sound mind, it is for you. [NKJV]<br>If it seems that we are **crazy**, it is to bring glory to God. And if we are in our right minds, it is for your benefit. [NLT]<br>εἴτε γὰρ ἐξέστημεν, Θεῷ· εἴτε σωφρονοῦμεν, ὑμῖν. [GNS]<br>εἴτε γὰρ ἐξέστημεν, Θεῷ· εἴτε σωφρονοῦμεν, ὑμῖν. [GNT] | charged with being a "fool" for Christ. Note that he accepts the charge as true. |
| **#358**<br>**Besought**<br><br>Besought–KJV<br>Kept asking–NASB<br>Begged–NIV<br>Kept asking–NKJV<br>Begged–NLT<br><br>**POSB REFERENCE**<br>(Mk.7:26-28; esp. v.26)<br>Note 3 | ἠρώτα = *erota*<br>Pronunciation: [er-o-tah']<br>Parsing (part of speech): verb<br>  Mood—indicative<br>  Tense—imperfect<br>  Voice—active<br>  Person—3rd person<br>  Number—singular<br>  Stem or root—from ἐρωτάω<br>Concordance References:<br>⇒ Strong's #2065 erōtaō<br>⇒ NIV #2263 erōtaō<br>⇒ NASB #2065 erōtaō<br><br>**Mark 7:26**<br>The woman was a Greek, a Syrophenician by nation; and she **besought** him that he would cast forth the devil out of her daughter. [KJV]<br>Now the woman was a Gentile, of the Syrophoenician race. And she **kept asking** Him to cast the demon out of her daughter. [NASB]<br>The woman was a Greek, born in Syrian Phoenicia. She **begged** Jesus to drive the demon out of her daughter. [NIV]<br>The woman was a Greek, a Syro-Phoenician by birth, and she **kept asking** Him to cast the demon out of her daughter. [NKJV]<br>She **begged** him to release her child from the demon's control. Since she was a Gentile, born in Syrian Phoenicia, [NLT]<br>ἐν δὲ ἡ δὲ γυνὴ Ἑλληνίς, Συροφοινίσσα τῷ γένει· καὶ **ἠρώτα** αὐτὸν ἵνα τὸ δαιμόνιον ἐκβάλῃ ἐκ τῆς θυγατρὸς αὐτῆς. [GNS]<br>ἡ δὲ γυνὴ ἦν Ἑλληνίς, Συροφοινίκισσα τῷ γένει· καὶ **ἠρώτα** αὐτὸν ἵνα τὸ δαιμόνιον ἐκβάλῃ ἐκ τῆς θυγατρὸς αὐτῆς. [GNT] | To ask, to plead, to beseech, or to implore; to beg and to keep on begging.<br><br>**Practical Application**<br>The woman begged or besought Christ to heal her demon-possessed daughter. The word "besought" is in the Greek imperfect tense which means she kept on begging and begging. Note that Jesus kept on listening and listening. |
| **#359**<br>**Besought**<br><br>Besought–KJV<br>Entreated–NASB<br>Pleaded...with–NIV<br>Begged–NKJV<br>Pleading with–NLT<br><br>**POSB REFERENCE**<br>(Mk.5:22-24; esp. v.23)<br>Note 2 point 3 | παρακαλεῖ = *parakalei*<br>Pronunciation: [par-ak-al-eh'-ee]<br>Parsing (part of speech): verb<br>  Mood—indicative<br>  Tense—present<br>  Voice—active<br>  Person—3rd person<br>  Number—singular<br>  Stem or root—from παρακαλέω<br>Concordance References:<br>⇒ Strong's #3870 parakaleō<br>⇒ NIV #4151 parakaleō<br>⇒ NASB #3870 parakaleō | To plead with; to entreat; to beseech; to call to one's side for help; to beg; to urge; to appeal to; to request.<br><br>**Practical Application**<br>In this Scripture, the ruler had a pleading attitude. He pleaded with and begged Jesus to come and heal his daughter. |

# PRACTICAL WORD STUDIES
## in the NEW TESTAMENT

| ENGLISH WORD | GREEK WORD AND VERSE | THE WORD MEANS... |
|---|---|---|
|  | **Mark 5:23**<br>And **besought** him greatly, saying, My little daughter lieth at the point of death: I pray thee, come and lay thy hands on her, that she may be healed; and she shall live. [KJV]<br>And **entreated** Him earnestly, saying, "My little daughter is at the point of death; please come and lay Your hands on her, that she may get well and live." [NASB]<br>And **pleaded** earnestly **with** him, "My little daughter is dying. Please come and put your hands on her so that she will be healed and live." [NIV]<br>And **begged** Him earnestly, saying, "My little daughter lies at the point of death. Come and lay Your hands on her, that she may be healed, and she will live." [NKJV]<br>**Pleading with** him to heal his little daughter. "She is about to die," he said in desperation. "Please come and place your hands on her; heal her so she can live." [NLT]<br>καὶ **παρακαλεῖ** αὐτὸν πολλὰ, λέγων ὅτι Τὸ θυγάτριόν μου ἐσχάτως ἔχει· ἵνα ἐλθὼν ἐπιθῇς αὐτῇ τὰς χεῖρας, ὅπως σωθῇ καὶ ζήσεται. [GNS]<br>καὶ **παρακαλεῖ** αὐτὸν πολλὰ λέγων ὅτι Τὸ θυγάτριόν μου ἐσχάτως ἔχει, ἵνα ἐλθὼν ἐπιθῇς τὰς χεῖρας αὐτῇ ἵνα σωθῇ καὶ ζήσῃ. [GNT] |  |
| **#360**<br>**Besought**<br><br>Besought–KJV<br>Requesting–NASB<br>Begged–NIV<br>Implored–NKJV<br>Begged–NLT<br><br>**POSB REFERENCE**<br>(Jn.4:46-47; esp. v.47)<br>Note 1, point 4 | ἠρώτα = *ërōta*<br>Pronunciation: [ay-ro-tah']<br>Parsing (part of speech): verb<br>    Mood—indicative<br>    Tense—imperfect<br>    Voice—active<br>    Person—3rd person<br>    Number—singular<br>    Stem or root—from ἐρωτάω<br>Concordance References:<br>⇒ Strong's #2065 *erōtaō*<br>⇒ NIV #2263 *erōtaō*<br>⇒ NASB #2065 *erōtaō*<br><br>**John 4:47**<br>When he heard that Jesus was come out of Judaea into Galilee, he went unto him, and **besought** him that he would come down, and heal his son: for he was at the point of death. [KJV]<br>When he heard that Jesus had come out of Judea into Galilee, he went to Him, and was **requesting** Him to come down and heal his son; for he was at the point of death. [NASB]<br>When this man heard that Jesus had arrived in Galilee from Judea, he went to him and **begged** him to come and heal his son, who was close to death. [NIV]<br>When he heard that Jesus had come out of Judea into Galilee, he went to Him and **implored** Him to come down and heal his son, for he was at the point of death. [NKJV]<br>When he heard that Jesus had come from Judea and was traveling in Galilee, he went over to Cana. He found Jesus and **begged** him to come to Capernaum with him to heal his son, who was about to die. [NLT]<br>οὗτος ἀκούσας ὅτι Ἰησοῦς ἥκει ἐκ τῆς Ἰουδαίας εἰς τὴν Γαλιλαίαν, ἀπῆλθε πρὸς αὐτόν, καὶ **ἠρώτα** αὐτὸν ἵνα καταβῇ καὶ ἰάσηται αὐτοῦ τὸν υἱόν· ἤμελλε γὰρ ἀποθνήσκειν. [GNS]<br>οὗτος ἀκούσας ὅτι Ἰησοῦς ἥκει ἐκ τῆς Ἰουδαίας εἰς τὴν Γαλιλαίαν ἀπῆλθεν πρὸς αὐτὸν καὶ **ἠρώτα** ἵνα καταβῇ καὶ ἰάσηται αὐτοῦ τὸν υἱόν, ἤμελλεν γὰρ ἀποθνήσκειν. [GNT] | To ask; to request; to implore; to plead desperately; to urge; to beseech; to appeal; to supplicate; to pray for immediate help.<br><br>**Practical Application**<br>Note an important lesson from this Scripture: The man did not let his high position keep him from Jesus. He did not wrap himself in pride nor did he allow what others might say keep him from Jesus. He swallowed his pride and confessed his need in the face of all who ridiculed, and he went to Jesus. |
| **#361**<br>**Besought**<br><br>Besought–KJV<br>Begging–NASB | παρεκάλουν = *parekaloun*<br>Pronunciation: [par-ek-al-oon]<br>Parsing (part of speech): verb<br>    Mood—indicative<br>    Tense—imperfect<br>    Voice—active | Invited, urged, besought, begged, asked; requested urgently; appealed to; pleaded with.<br><br>**Practical Application**<br>It is continuous action: the heathen continued |

## Practical Word Studies in the New Testament

| ENGLISH WORD | GREEK WORD AND VERSE | THE WORD MEANS... |
|---|---|---|
| Invited–NIV<br>Begged–NKJV<br>Asked–NLT<br><br>**POSB REFERENCE**<br>(Acts 13:42-45; esp. v.42)<br>Note 1, point 1 | Person—3rd person<br>Number—plural<br>Stem or root—from παρακαλέω<br>Concordance References:<br>⇒ Strong's #3870 parakaleö<br>⇒ NIV #4151 parakaleö<br>⇒ NASB #3870 parakaleö<br><br>**Acts 13:42**<br>And when the Jews were gone out of the synagogue, the Gentiles **besought** that these words might be preached to them the next sabbath. [KJV]<br>And as Paul and Barnabas were going out, the people kept **begging** that these things might be spoken to them the next Sabbath. [NASB]<br>As Paul and Barnabas were leaving the synagogue, the people **invited** them to speak further about these things on the next Sabbath. [NIV]<br>So when the Jews went out of the synagogue, the Gentiles **begged** that these words might be preached to them the next Sabbath. [NKJV]<br>As Paul and Barnabas left the synagogue that day, the people **asked** them to return again and speak about these things the next week. [NLT]<br>Ἐξιόντων ἐκ τῆς συναγωγῆς τῶν Ἰουδαίων, δὲ αὐτῶν **παρεκάλουν** τὰ ἔθνη εἰς τὸ μεταξὺ σάββατον λαληθῆναι αὐτοῖς τὰ ῥήματα ταῦτα. [GNS]<br>Ἐξιόντων δὲ αὐτῶν **παρεκάλουν** εἰς τὸ μεταξὺ σάββατον λαληθῆναι αὐτοῖς τὰ ῥήματα ταῦτα. [GNT] | to beseech. The picture is that they begged and begged Paul to share more about the forgiveness of sins which is in Jesus. |
| **#362**<br>**Best**<br><br>Exercise–KJV<br>**Best–NASB**<br>Strive–NIV<br>Strive–NKJV<br>Try–NLT<br><br>**POSB REFERENCE**<br>(Acts 24:14-16; esp. v.16)<br>Note 3, point 4a | ἀσκῶ = askö<br>Pronunciation: [as-ko']<br>Parsing (part of speech): verb<br>   Mood—indicative<br>   Tense—present<br>   Voice—active<br>   Person—1st person<br>   Number—singular<br>   Stem or root—from ἀσκέω<br>Concordance References:<br>⇒ Strong's #778 askeö<br>⇒ NIV #828 askeö<br>⇒ NASB #778 askeö<br><br>**Acts 24:16**<br>And herein do I **exercise** myself, to have always a conscience void of offence toward God, and toward men. [KJV]<br>"In view of this, I also do my **best** to maintain always a blameless conscience both before God and before men. [NASB]<br>So I **strive** always to keep my conscience clear before God and man. [NIV]<br>This being so, I myself always **strive** to have a conscience without offense toward God and men. [NKJV]<br>Because of this, I always **try** to maintain a clear conscience before God and everyone else. [NLT]<br>ἐν τούτῳ δὲ αὐτὸς **ἀσκῶ**, ἀπρόσκοπον συνείδησιν ἔχειν πρὸς τὸν Θεὸν καὶ τοὺς ἀνθρώπους διὰ παντός. [GNS]<br>ἐν τούτῳ καὶ αὐτὸς **ἀσκῶ** ἀπρόσκοπον συνείδησιν ἔχειν πρὸς τὸν θεὸν καὶ τοὺς ἀνθρώπους διὰ παντός. [GNT] | To strive; to exercise; to try; to endeavor; to give one's best.<br><br>**Practical Application**<br>Paul exercised himself—actively trained, disciplined, practiced, labored, strove, struggled, even to the point of pain—to keep a pure conscience. |
| **#363**<br>**Best Places**<br><br>Chief rooms–KJV<br>Places of honor at the table–NASB<br>Places of honor at the table–NIV | τὰς πρωτοκλισίας = tas prötoklisias<br>Pronunciation: [tas pro-tok-lis-ee'-ahs]<br>Parsing prötoklisias (part of speech): noun<br>   Case—accusative<br>   Gender—feminine<br>   Number—plural<br>   Stem or root—from πρωτοκλισία, ας<br>Concordance References:<br>⇒ Strong's #4411 prötoklisia | The places of honor at a table; the head of the table; the chief seats.<br><br>**Practical Application**<br>In this Scripture, it was time for everyone to be seated for the meal, and Jesus noticed how some guests scrambled for the places of honor at the table. Today, we usually place the names of |

## Practical Word Studies in the New Testament

| ENGLISH WORD | GREEK WORD AND VERSE | THE WORD MEANS... |
|---|---|---|
| Best places–NKJV<br>Head of the table–NLT<br><br>**POSB<br>REFERENCE**<br>(Lk.14:7)<br>Note 1 | ⇒ NIV #4752 prōtoklisia<br>⇒ NASB #4411 prōtoklisia<br><br>**Luke 14:7**<br>And he put forth a parable to those which were bidden, when he marked how they chose out the **chief rooms**; saying unto them, [KJV]<br>And He began speaking a parable to the invited guests when He noticed how they had been picking out the **places of honor at the table**; saying to them, [NASB]<br>When he noticed how the guests picked the **places of honor at the table**, he told them this parable: [NIV]<br>So He told a parable to those who were invited, when He noted how they chose the **best places**, saying to them: [NKJV]<br>When Jesus noticed that all who had come to the dinner were trying to sit near the **head of the table**, he gave them this advice: [NLT]<br>Ἔλεγε δὲ πρὸς τοὺς κεκλημένους παραβολήν, ἐπέχων πῶς **τὰς πρωτοκλισίας** ἐξελέγοντο, λέγων πρὸς αὐτούς, [GNS]<br>Ἔλεγεν δὲ πρὸς τοὺς κεκλημένους παραβολήν, ἐπέχων πῶς **τὰς πρωτοκλισίας** ἐξελέγοντο, λέγων πρὸς αὐτούς, [GNT] | the most honored guests at the plates. However, in Jesus' day the highest seat of honor was on the right of the host and the next highest on his left, and so the ranking continued alternating back and forth until the lowest ranked person sat the farthest away from the host. Very simply, the closer one sat to the host, the higher the honor. When Jesus saw how some quickly moved up close to the host, He saw an opportunity to teach the great importance of humility. |
| **#364<br>Bethany**<br><br>Bethany–KJV<br>Bethany–NASB<br>Bethany–NIV<br>Bethany–NKJV<br>Bethany–NLT<br><br>**POSB<br>REFERENCE**<br>(Mt.21:17-18; esp. v.17)<br>Note 1 | Βηθανίαν = Bēthanian<br>Pronunciation: [bay-than-ee'-ahn]<br>Parsing (part of speech): noun<br>    Case—accusative<br>    Gender—feminine<br>    Number—singular<br>    Stem or root—from Βηθανία, ας<br>Concordance References:<br>⇒ Strong's #963 Bēthania<br>⇒ NIV #1029 Bēthania<br>⇒ NASB #963 Bēthania<br><br>**Matthew 21:17**<br>And he left them, and went out of the city into **Bethany**; and he lodged there. [KJV]<br>And He left them and went out of the city to **Bethany**, and lodged there. [NASB]<br>And he left them and went out of the city to **Bethany**, where he spent the night. [NIV]<br>Then He left them and went out of the city to **Bethany**, and He lodged there. [NKJV]<br>Then he returned to **Bethany**, where he stayed overnight. [NLT]<br>καὶ καταλιπὼν αὐτοὺς ἐξῆλθεν ἔξω τῆς πόλεως εἰς **Βηθανίαν**, καὶ ηὐλίσθη ἐκεῖ. [GNS]<br>Καὶ καταλιπὼν αὐτοὺς ἐξῆλθεν ἔξω τῆς πόλεως εἰς **Βηθανίαν** καὶ ηὐλίσθη ἐκεῖ. [GNT] | House of unripe dates or figs.<br><br>**Practical Application**<br>Bethany was a suburb of the great city of Jerusalem [located about two miles to the south east]. This town is significant for several reasons:<br>⇒ It was the home of Mary, Martha, and Lazarus (John 11:8).<br>⇒ It was the place where Jesus raised Lazarus from the grave (John 11:38-44).<br>⇒ It was near the location where Jesus ascended to Heaven (Luke 24:50-51). |
| **#365<br>Bethphage**<br><br>Bethphage–KJV<br>Bethphage–NASB<br>Bethphage–NIV<br>Bethphage–NKJV<br>Bethphage–NLT<br><br>**POSB<br>REFERENCE**<br>(Mt.21:1)<br>*Deeper Study #2*<br><br>See also POSB REF:<br>(Lk.19:29)<br>*Deeper Study #1* | Βηθφαγή = Bēthphagē<br>Pronunciation: [bayth-fag-ay']<br>Parsing (part of speech): noun<br>    Case—accusative<br>    Gender—feminine<br>    Number—singular<br>    Stem or root—from Βηθφαγή<br>Concordance References:<br>⇒ Strong's #967 Bēthphagē<br>⇒ NIV #1036 Bēthphagē<br>⇒ NASB #967 Bēthphagē<br><br>**Matthew 21:1**<br>And when they drew nigh unto Jerusalem, and were come to **Bethphage**, unto the mount of Olives, then sent Jesus two disciples, [KJV]<br>And when they had approached Jerusalem and had come to **Bethphage**, to the Mount of Olives, then Jesus sent two disciples, [NASB]<br>As they approached Jerusalem and came to | Literally "fig-house"; "house or place of unripe, green figs."<br><br>**Practical Application**<br>Bethphage (known as beth paghah in the Hebrew language) was a small village near Jerusalem lying toward the Mount of Olives. The village was located on the road going from Jerusalem to Jericho. Bethphage was the place where the colt was obtained that Jesus rode into Jerusalem (Matthew 21:1-11; Mark 11:1-11; Luke 19:28-40). |

PRACTICAL WORD STUDIES
in the NEW TESTAMENT

| ENGLISH WORD | GREEK WORD AND VERSE | THE WORD MEANS... |
|---|---|---|
| | **Bethphage** on the Mount of Olives, Jesus sent two disciples, [NIV]<br>Now when they drew near Jerusalem, and came to **Bethphage**, at the Mount of Olives, then Jesus sent two disciples, [NKJV]<br>As Jesus and the disciples approached Jerusalem, they came to the town of **Bethphage** on the Mount of Olives. Jesus sent two of them on ahead. [NLT]<br>Καὶ ὅτε ἤγγισαν εἰς Ἱεροσόλυμα καὶ ἦλθον εἰς **Βηθφαγὴ** πρὸς τὸ ὄρος τῶν ἐλαιῶν, τότε Ἰησοῦς ἀπέστειλε δύο μαθητὰς, [GNS]<br>Καὶ ὅτε ἤγγισαν εἰς Ἱεροσόλυμα καὶ ἦλθον εἰς **Βηθφαγὴ** εἰς τὸ Ὄρος τῶν Ἐλαιῶν, τότε Ἰησοῦς ἀπέστειλεν δύο μαθητὰς [GNT] | |
| **#366**<br>**Betray–**<br>**Betrayed**<br><br>Traitors–KJV<br>Treacherous–NASB<br>Treacherous–NIV<br>Traitors–NKJV<br>**Betray–NLT**<br><br>**POSB**<br>**REFERENCE**<br>(2 Tim. 3:2-4; esp. v.4)<br>Note 2, point 15 | προδόται = *prodotai*<br>Pronunciation: [prod-ot'-ah-ee]<br>Parsing (part of speech): noun<br>    Case—nominative<br>    Gender—masculine<br>    Number—plural<br>    Stem or root—from προδότης, ου<br>Concordance References:<br>  ⇒ Strong's #4273 prodotēs<br>  ⇒ NIV #4595 prodotēs<br>  ⇒ NASB #4273 prodotēs<br><br>**2 Tim. 3:4**<br>**Traitors**, heady, highminded, lovers of pleasures more than lovers of God; [KJV]<br>**Treacherous**, reckless, conceited, lovers of pleasure rather than lovers of God; [NASB]<br>**Treacherous**, rash, conceited, lovers of pleasure rather than lovers of God—[NIV]<br>**Traitors**, headstrong, haughty, lovers of pleasure rather than lovers of God, [NKJV]<br>They will **betray** their friends, be reckless, be puffed up with pride, and love pleasure rather than God. [NLT]<br>προδόται, προπετεῖς, τετυφωμένοι, φιλήδονοι μᾶλλον ἢ φιλόθεοι, [GNS]<br>προδόται προπετεῖς τετυφωμένοι, φιλήδονοι μᾶλλον ἢ φιλόθεοι, [GNT] | Treacherous, traitor, to betray.<br><br>**Practical Application**<br>People will be betrayers (*prodotai*): betraying a trust refers to a person who...<br>• betrays his country<br>• betrays his team<br>• betrays his friends<br>• betrays his family<br><br>It refers to a person who betrays any trust or any commitment. The most tragic betrayal of all is the person who betrays Christ and the church—who turns his back upon Christ and returns to the world and its crowd. The last days will see an increase in traitors. |
| **#367**<br>**Betrayed**<br><br>Deliver–KJV<br>Delivered–NASB<br>Hand...over–NIV<br>Deliver–NKJV<br>**Betrayed–NLT**<br><br>**POSB**<br>**REFERENCE**<br>(Mk.10:33)<br>Note 4 | παραδοθήσεται = *paradothesetai*<br>Pronunciation: [par-ad-o-theh-seh-tah-ee]<br>Parsing (part of speech): verb<br>    Mood—indicative<br>    Tense—future<br>    Voice—passive<br>    Person—3rd person<br>    Number—singular<br>    Stem or root—from παραδίδωμι<br>Concordance References:<br>  ⇒ Strong's #3860 paradidōmi<br>  ⇒ NIV #4140 paradidōmi<br>  ⇒ NASB #3860 paradidōmi<br><br>**Mark 10:33**<br>Saying, Behold, we go up to Jerusalem; and the Son of man shall be delivered unto the chief priests, and unto the scribes; and they shall condemn him to death, and shall **deliver** him to the Gentiles: [KJV]<br>Saying, "Behold, we are going up to Jerusalem, and the Son of Man will be **delivered** to the chief priests and the scribes; and they will condemn Him to death, and will deliver Him to the Gentiles. [NASB]<br>"We are going up to Jerusalem," he said, "and the Son of Man will be betrayed to the chief priests and teachers of the law. They will condemn him to death and will **hand** him **over** to the Gentiles, [NIV]<br>"Behold, we are going up to Jerusalem, and the Son of Man will be betrayed to the chief priests and to the scribes; and they will condemn Him to death and **deliver** | To hand over; to turn over; to be betrayed, to be abandoned; to be put in prison; to be delivered over and into death.<br><br>**Practical Application**<br>It means that His death was determined, ordained, set in the plan and counsel of God. Note that Jesus said, "The Son of Man will be betrayed." His death was right before His face, ready to take place. |

# PRACTICAL WORD STUDIES
## in the NEW TESTAMENT

| ENGLISH WORD | GREEK WORD AND VERSE | THE WORD MEANS... |
|---|---|---|
| | Him to the Gentiles; [NKJV]<br>"When we get to Jerusalem," he told them, "the Son of Man will be **betrayed** to the leading priests and the teachers of religious law. They will sentence him to die and hand him over to the Romans. [NLT]<br>ὅτι Ἰδοὺ ἀναβαίνομεν εἰς Ἱεροσόλυμα· καὶ ὁ υἱὸς τοῦ ἀνθρώπου **παραδοθήσεται** τοῖς ἀρχιερεῦσι καὶ τοῖς γραμματεῦσι, καὶ κατακρινοῦσιν αὐτὸν θανάτῳ, καὶ παραδώσουσιν αὐτὸν τοῖς ἔθνεσι, [GNS]<br>ὅτι Ἰδοὺ ἀναβαίνομεν εἰς Ἱεροσόλυμα, καὶ ὁ υἱὸς τοῦ ἀνθρώπου **παραδοθήσεται** τοῖς ἀρχιερεῦσιν καὶ τοῖς γραμματεῦσιν, καὶ κατακρινοῦσιν αὐτὸν θανάτῳ καὶ παραδώσουσιν αὐτὸν τοῖς ἔθνεσιν [GNT] | |
| **#368**<br>**Betrayed, Shall Be, Will Be**<br><br>Shall be betrayed–KJV<br>Will be delivered–NASB<br>Will be betrayed–NIV<br>Will be betrayed–NKJV<br>Will be betrayed–NLT<br><br>**POSB REFERENCE**<br>(Mt.20:18)<br>Note 2, point 1<br><br>See also POSB REF:<br>(Mt.17:22)<br>Note 1, point 2<br>(Mk.9:31)<br>Note 2, point 2<br>(Lk.9:44-45; esp. v.44)<br>Note 4, point 2 | **παραδοθήσεται** = *paradothësetai*<br>Pronunciation: [par-ad-o-the'-say-tai]<br>Parsing (part of speech): verb<br>   Mood—indicative<br>   Tense—future<br>   Voice—passive<br>   Person—3rd person<br>   Number—singular<br>   Stem or root—from **παραδίδωμι**<br>Concordance References:<br>  ⇒ Strong's #3860 paradidömi<br>  ⇒ NIV #4140 paradidömi<br>  ⇒ NASB #3860 paradidömi<br><br>**Matthew 20:18**<br>Behold, we go up to Jerusalem; and the Son of man **shall be betrayed** unto the chief priests and unto the scribes, and they shall condemn him to death, [KJV]<br>"Behold, we are going up to Jerusalem, and the Son of Man **will be delivered** to the chief priests and scribes, and they will condemn Him to death, [NASB]<br>"We are going up to Jerusalem, and the Son of Man **will be betrayed** to the chief priests and the teachers of the law. They will condemn him to death [NIV]<br>"Behold, we are going up to Jerusalem, and the Son of Man **will be betrayed** to the chief priests and to the scribes; and they will condemn Him to death, [NKJV]<br>"When we get to Jerusalem," he said, "the Son of Man **will be betrayed** to the leading priests and the teachers of religious law. They will sentence him to die. [NLT]<br>Ἰδοὺ ἀναβαίνομεν εἰς Ἱεροσόλυμα, καὶ ὁ υἱὸς τοῦ ἀνθρώπου **παραδοθήσεται** τοῖς ἀρχιερεῦσι καὶ γραμματεῦσι καὶ κατακρινοῦσιν αὐτὸν θανάτῳ, [GNS]<br>Ἰδοὺ ἀναβαίνομεν εἰς Ἱεροσόλυμα, καὶ ὁ υἱὸς τοῦ ἀνθρώπου **παραδοθήσεται** τοῖς ἀρχιερεῦσιν καὶ γραμματεῦσιν, καὶ κατακρινοῦσιν αὐτὸν θανάτῳ [GNT] | To be betrayed; to be delivered up into the power of someone else; to hand over; to give over; to be arrested.<br><br>**Practical Application**<br>This betrayal led to the handing over of Jesus Christ to the Gentiles. He was mocked, flogged, and crucified. Was Christ taken aback by this betrayal? Was He caught off guard?<br>God knows every person's heart. Even a person's inner thoughts are known to God, as well as what a person does. No one can hide what He does from God, not even a thought. God knows if a man is betraying His Son. He even knows if a man is thinking about sinning and turning his back on Jesus. The more a man thinks about sinning, the more likely he is to turn back. His betrayal can be predicted.<br>Note: the greatest act of betrayal in all of history was conquered when Jesus Christ rose from the dead. No human betrayal can divert the purpose of God. |
| **#369**<br>**Bewailed**<br><br>Bewailed–KJV<br>Mourning–NASB<br>Mourned–NIV<br>Mourned–NKJV<br>Grief-stricken–NLT<br><br>**POSB REFERENCE**<br>(Lk.23:27)<br>Note 2 | **ἐκόπτοντο** = *ekoptonto*<br>Pronunciation: [eh-kop'-tawn-tow]<br>Parsing (part of speech): verb<br>   Mood—indicative<br>   Tense—imperfect<br>   Voice—middle<br>   Person—3rd person<br>   Number—plural<br>   Stem or root—from **κόπτω**<br>Concordance References:<br>  ⇒ Strong's #2875 koptö<br>  ⇒ NIV #3164 koptö<br>  ⇒ NASB #2875 koptö<br><br>**Luke 23:27**<br>And there followed him a great company of people, and of women, which also **bewailed** and lamented him. [KJV]<br>And there were following Him a great multitude of the people, and of women who were **mourning** and lamenting Him. [NASB]<br>A large number of people followed him, including | To mourn; to be grief-stricken; to lament; to wail; to cut, strike, smite, beat.<br><br>**Practical Application**<br>They were cut to the core of their hearts, actually feeling pain for Jesus. A natural response to the Lord's sufferings is not enough. A person must understand why Christ suffered and must feel a godly sorrow over Christ's having to bear the sins of the world (see POSB *Deeper Study* #1—2 Cor. 7:10). |

# PRACTICAL WORD STUDIES
## in the NEW TESTAMENT

| ENGLISH WORD | GREEK WORD AND VERSE | THE WORD MEANS... |
|---|---|---|
| | women who **mourned** and wailed for him. [NIV]<br>And a great multitude of the people followed Him, and women who also **mourned** and lamented Him. [NKJV]<br>Great crowds trailed along behind, including many **grief-stricken** women. [NLT]<br>Ἠκολούθει δὲ αὐτῷ πολὺ πλῆθος τοῦ λαοῦ, καὶ γυναικῶν αἳ καὶ **ἐκόπτοντο** καὶ ἐθρήνουν αὐτόν. [GNS]<br>Ἠκολούθει δὲ αὐτῷ πολὺ πλῆθος τοῦ λαοῦ καὶ γυναικῶν αἳ **ἐκόπτοντο** καὶ ἐθρήνουν αὐτόν. [GNT] | |
| **#370**<br>**Beware**<br><br>Beware–KJV<br>Beware–NASB<br>Watch out–NIV<br>Beware–NKJV<br>Beware–NLT<br><br>**POSB**<br>**REFERENCE**<br>(Mt.7:15)<br>Note 1 | Προσέχετε = *Prosechete*<br>Pronunciation: [pros-ekh'-eh-teh]<br>Parsing (part of speech): verb<br>    Mood—imperative<br>    Tense—present<br>    Voice—active<br>    Person—2nd person<br>    Number—plural<br>    Stem or root—from προσέχω<br>Concordance References:<br>  ⇒ Strong's #4337 prosechō<br>  ⇒ NIV #4668 prosechō<br>  ⇒ NASB #4337 prosechō<br><br>**Matthew 7:15**<br>**Beware** of false prophets, which come to you in sheep's clothing, but inwardly they are ravening wolves. [KJV]<br>"**Beware** of the false prophets, who come to you in sheep's clothing, but inwardly are ravenous wolves. [NASB]<br>"**Watch out** for false prophets. They come to you in sheep's clothing, but inwardly they are ferocious wolves. [NIV]<br>"**Beware** of the false prophets, who come to you in sheep's clothing, but inwardly they are ravenous wolves. [NKJV]<br>"**Beware** of false prophets who come disguised as harmless sheep, but are really wolves that will tear you apart. [NLT]<br>Προσέχετε δὲ ἀπὸ τῶν ψευδοπροφητῶν, οἵτινες ἔρχονται πρὸς ὑμᾶς ἐν ἐνδύμασι προβάτων, ἔσωθεν δέ εἰσι λύκοι ἅρπαγες. [GNS]<br>Προσέχετε ἀπὸ τῶν ψευδοπροφητῶν, οἵτινες ἔρχονται πρὸς ὑμᾶς ἐν ἐνδύμασιν προβάτων, ἔσωθεν δέ εἰσιν λύκοι ἅρπαγες. [GNT] | To beware; to take heed; to guard; to watch; to keep yourself. It means to pay close attention to; to be careful.<br><br>**Practical Application**<br>The word is emphatic; the warning is clear and strong. The believer has been warned; therefore, he must now beware, guard and stand against the error of false teachers. If he does not stay alert and guard against the teaching of false teachers, he will be led away by their error. The believer will fall and no longer be steadfast. He will lose the exciting hope of the Lord's return and no longer look forward to the glorious union with Christ nor to eternal life with God the Father. |
| **#371**<br>**Beware**<br><br>Beware–KJV<br>Beware–NASB<br>Watch out–NIV<br>Beware–NKJV<br>Beware–NLT<br><br>**POSB**<br>**REFERENCE**<br>(Mk.8:15)<br>*Deeper Study #2* | βλέπετε = *blepete*<br>Pronunciation: [blep'-eh-teh]<br>Parsing (part of speech): verb<br>    Mood—imperative<br>    Tense—present<br>    Voice—active<br>    Person—2nd person<br>    Number—plural<br>    Stem or root—from βλέπω<br>Concordance References:<br>  ⇒ Strong's #991 blepō<br>  ⇒ NIV #1063 blepō<br>  ⇒ NASB #991 blepō<br><br>**Mark 8:15**<br>And he charged them, saying, Take heed, **beware** of the leaven of the Pharisees, and of the leaven of Herod. [KJV]<br>And He was giving orders to them, saying, "Watch out! **Beware** of the leaven of the Pharisees and the leaven of Herod." [NASB]<br>"Be careful," Jesus warned them. "**Watch out** for the yeast of the Pharisees and that of Herod." [NIV]<br>Then He charged them, saying, "Take heed, **beware** of the leaven of the Pharisees and the leaven of Herod." [NKJV] | To watch out; to beware; to see, perceive, grasp, and understand in order to watch out for something; to turn the mind upon an object and consider and keep a watchful eye upon it; to guard and protect against something.<br><br>**Practical Application**<br>Again, the charge is a *present imperative*. The person is to begin immediately to beware and to continue his watch, always looking out for the danger. |

# PRACTICAL WORD STUDIES
## in the NEW TESTAMENT

| ENGLISH WORD | GREEK WORD AND VERSE | THE WORD MEANS... |
|---|---|---|
| | As they were crossing the lake, Jesus warned them, "**Beware** of the yeast of the Pharisees and of Herod." [NLT]<br><br>καὶ διεστέλλετο αὐτοῖς, λέγων, Ὁρᾶτε, **βλέπετε** ἀπὸ τῆς ζύμης τῶν Φαρισαίων, καὶ τῆς ζύμης Ἡρώδου [GNS]<br><br>καὶ διεστέλλετο αὐτοῖς λέγων, Ὁρᾶτε, **βλέπετε** ἀπὸ τῆς ζύμης τῶν Φαρισαίων καὶ τῆς ζύμης Ἡρῴδου. [GNT] | |
| **#372**<br>**Beware**<br><br>Beware–KJV<br>On...guard–NASB<br>On...guard–NIV<br>Beware–NKJV<br>Beware–NLT<br><br>**POSB REFERENCE**<br>(Rom.12:15-19; esp. v.15)<br>Note 2, point 1 | φυλάσσεσθε = *phulassesthe*<br>Pronunciation: [foo-las'-say-the]<br>Parsing (part of speech): verb<br>    Mood—imperative<br>    Tense—present<br>    Voice—middle<br>    Person—2nd person<br>    Number—plural<br>    Stem or root—from φυλάσσω<br>Concordance References:<br>  ⇒ Strong's #5442 phulassō<br>  ⇒ NIV #5875 phulassō<br>  ⇒ NASB #5442 phulassō<br><br>**Luke 12:15**<br>And he said unto them, Take heed, and **beware** of covetousness: for a man's life consisteth not in the abundance of the things which he possesseth. [KJV]<br>And He said to them, "Beware, and be **on your guard** against every form of greed; for not even when one has an abundance does his life consist of his possessions." [NASB]<br>Then he said to them, "Watch out! Be **on your guard** against all kinds of greed; a man's life does not consist in the abundance of his possessions." [NIV]<br>And He said to them, "Take heed and **beware** of covetousness, for one's life does not consist in the abundance of the things he possesses." [NKJV]<br>Then he said, "**Beware**! Don't be greedy for what you don't have. Real life is not measured by how much we own." [NLT]<br>ἶπε δὲ πρὸς αὐτούς, Ὁρᾶτε καὶ **φυλάσσεσθε** ἀπὸ πάσης πλεονεξίας· ὅτι οὐκ ἐν τῷ περισσεύειν τινὶ ἡ ζωὴ αὐτοῦ ἐστιν ἐκ τῶν ὑπαρχόντων αὐτοῦ. [GNS]<br>εἶπεν δὲ πρὸς αὐτούς, Ὁρᾶτε καὶ **φυλάσσεσθε** ἀπὸ πάσης πλεονεξίας, ὅτι οὐκ ἐν τῷ περισσεύειν τινὶ ἡ ζωὴ αὐτοῦ ἐστιν ἐκ τῶν ὑπαρχόντων αὐτῷ. [GNT] | To be on guard; to beware; to guard oneself; to keep safe; to defend; to protect oneself from some dangerous enemy.<br><br>**Practical Application**<br>What is the purpose of such a strong warning? Why should a person seek protection from covetousness and greed? Because it is a craving, a desire for more and more. It is greediness, a dissatisfaction with what is enough. It includes the cravings for both material things and fleshly indulgence. It is desiring what belongs to others; snatching at something that belongs to others; a love of having, a cry of give me, give me (cp. 2 Peter 2:14).<br>⇒ It is a lust so deep within a man that he finds his happiness in things instead of in God.<br>⇒ It is a covetousness so deep that it desires the power that things bring more than the things themselves.<br>⇒ It is an intense appetite for gain; a passion for the pleasure that things can bring. It goes beyond the pleasure of possessing things for their own sakes. |
| **#373**<br>**Beware**<br><br>Take heed–KJV<br>Be on guard–NASB<br>Keep watch over–NIV<br>Take heed–NKJV<br>Beware–NLT<br><br>**POSB REFERENCE**<br>(Acts 20:28)<br>Note 1, point 1 | προσέχετε = *prosechete*<br>Pronunciation: [pros-ech'-eh-teh]<br>Parsing (part of speech): verb<br>    Mood—imperfect<br>    Tense—present<br>    Voice— active<br>    Person—2nd person<br>    Number—plural<br>    Stem or root—from προσέχω<br>Concordance References:<br>  ⇒ Strong's #4337 prosechō<br>  ⇒ NIV #4668 prosechō<br>  ⇒ NASB #4337 prosechō<br><br>**Acts 20:28**<br>**Take heed** therefore unto yourselves, and to all the flock, over the which the Holy Ghost hath made you overseers, to feed the church of God, which he hath purchased with his own blood. [KJV]<br>"**Be on guard** for yourselves and for all the flock, among which the Holy Spirit has made you overseers, to shepherd the church of God which He purchased with His own blood. [NASB]<br>**Keep watch over** yourselves and all the flock of which the Holy Spirit has made you overseers. Be shep- | To keep watch over; to take heed; to be on guard; to beware; to be careful, oh so careful. It means to give attention, concentrate upon, focus upon, attend to, watch after, and guard his life.<br><br>**Practical Application**<br>There are specific areas the believer must guard.<br>1. He must guard against false teaching (Luke 12:1).<br>2. He must guard against an unforgiving spirit (Luke 17:3-4).<br>3. He must guard against self-indulgence, drunkenness, and the possessions of this life (Luke 21:34).<br>4. He must guard against the fables, myths, speculations, ideas, and false doctrines of men, and trusting in genealogies for salvation (1 Tim. 1:4).<br>5. He must watch and give himself to reading, exhortation and doctrine (1 Tim. 4:13).<br>6. He must especially give himself to *the doctrine* (*te didaskalia*), the teaching of Scripture |

# PRACTICAL WORD STUDIES
## in the NEW TESTAMENT

| ENGLISH WORD | GREEK WORD AND VERSE | THE WORD MEANS... |
|---|---|---|
| | herds of the church of God, which he bought with his own blood. [NIV]<br><br>Therefore **take heed** to yourselves and to all the flock, among which the Holy Spirit has made you overseers, to shepherd the church of God which He purchased with His own blood. [NKJV]<br><br>"And now **beware**! Be sure that you feed and shepherd God's flock—his church, purchased with his blood—over whom the Holy Spirit has appointed you as elders. [NLT]<br><br>προσέχετε οὖν ἑαυτοῖς καὶ παντὶ τῷ ποιμνίῳ, ἐν ᾧ ὑμᾶς τὸ Πνεῦμα τὸ Ἅγιον ἔθετο ἐπισκόπους, ποιμαίνειν τὴν ἐκκλησίαν τοῦ Θεοῦ, ἣν περιεποιήσατο διὰ τοῦ ἰδίου αἵματος. [GNS]<br><br>προσέχετε ἑαυτοῖς καὶ παντὶ τῷ ποιμνίῳ, ἐν ᾧ ὑμᾶς τὸ πνεῦμα τὸ ἅγιον ἔθετο ἐπισκόπους ποιμαίνειν τὴν ἐκκλησίαν τοῦ θεοῦ, ἣν περιεποιήσατο διὰ τοῦ αἵματος τοῦ ἰδίου. [GNT] | (1 Tim. 4:16). |
| **#374**<br>**Beware**<br><br>Take heed–KJV<br>Take care–NASB<br>See to it–NIV<br>**Beware–NKJV**<br>Be careful then–NLT<br><br>**POSB REFERENCE**<br>(Heb.3:12)<br>Note 2 | Βλέπετε = Blepete<br>Pronunciation: [blep'-eh-teh]<br>Parsing (part of speech): verb<br>  Mood—imperative<br>  Tense—present<br>  Voice—active<br>  Person—2nd person<br>  Number—plural<br>  Stem or root—from βλέπω<br>Concordance References:<br>  ⇒ Strong's #991 blepō<br>  ⇒ NIV #1063 blepō<br>  ⇒ NASB #991 blepō<br><br>**Hebrews 3:12**<br>**Take heed**, brethren, lest there be in any of you an evil heart of unbelief, in departing from the living God. [KJV]<br><br>**Take care**, brethren, lest there should be in any one of you an evil, unbelieving heart, in falling away from the living God. [NASB]<br><br>**See to it**, brothers, that none of you has a sinful, unbelieving heart that turns away from the living God. [NIV]<br><br>**Beware**, brethren, lest there be in any of you an evil heart of unbelief in departing from the living God; [NKJV]<br><br>**Be careful then**, dear brothers and sisters. Make sure that your own hearts are not evil and unbelieving, turning you away from the living God. [NLT]<br><br>βλέπετε, ἀδελφοί, μή ποτε ἔσται ἔν τινι ὑμῶν καρδία πονηρὰ ἀπιστίας, ἐν τῷ ἀποστῆναι ἀπὸ Θεοῦ ζῶντος· [GNS]<br><br>Βλέπετε, ἀδελφοί, μήποτε ἔσται ἔν τινι ὑμῶν καρδία πονηρὰ ἀπιστίας ἐν τῷ ἀποστῆναι ἀπὸ θεοῦ ζῶντος, [GNT] | Be alert and stay alert; be on the lookout and do it constantly; watch and keep on watching.<br><br>**Practical Application**<br>There is great danger that believers might depart from the living God. They might do just what Israel did. Therefore, be careful—beware (*Blepete*). Keep a watchful eye on your trust and obedience to God. Watch for an evil heart of unbelief. What is an evil heart of unbelief? It is a heart that...<br>• stands off from God<br>• stands aloof from God<br>• renounces God<br>• rebels against God<br>• does not believe in God<br>• does not trust God and His promises<br>• does not follow God as He demands |
| **#375**<br>**Beware**<br><br>Beware–KJV<br>See to it–NASB<br>See to it–NIV<br>**Beware–NKJV**<br>Don't let–NLT<br><br>**POSB REFERENCE**<br>(Col.2:8)<br>Note 1<br><br>See also POSB REF:<br>(Heb.12:25-29; esp. | βλέπετε = blepete<br>Pronunciation: [blep'-eh-teh]<br>Parsing (part of speech): verb<br>  Mood—imperative<br>  Tense—present<br>  Voice—active<br>  Person—2nd person<br>  Number—plural<br>  Stem or root—from βλέπω<br>Concordance References:<br>  ⇒ Strong's #991 blepō<br>  ⇒ NIV #1063 blepō<br>  ⇒ NASB #991 blepō<br><br>**Col. 2:8**<br>**Beware** lest any man spoil you through philosophy and vain deceit, after the tradition of men, after the rudiments of the world, and not after Christ. [KJV] | To see to it, to beware of; to not let; to take heed, look out, guard yourself.<br><br>**Practical Application**<br>Why is this important, "lest anyone cheat you through philosophy and empty deceit?"<br>⇒ Some men are in a genuine search for truth and reality. They seek to learn the truth and reality of the universe and the problems that face them, but they limit themselves to the universe.<br>⇒ Other persons have novel ideas or philosophies about truth and reality, but they become more interested in their position than the truth. They need others to accept their positions or else their ideas die. Therefore, they have to present and per- |

| ENGLISH WORD | GREEK WORD AND VERSE | THE WORD MEANS... |
|---|---|---|
| v.25)<br>Introduction | **See to it** that no one takes you captive through philosophy and empty deception, according to the tradition of men, according to the elementary principles of the world, rather than according to Christ. [NASB]<br>**See to it** that no one takes you captive through hollow and deceptive philosophy, which depends on human tradition and the basic principles of this world rather than on Christ. [NIV]<br>**Beware** lest anyone cheat you through philosophy and empty deceit, according to the tradition of men, according to the basic principles of the world, and not according to Christ. [NKJV]<br>**Don't let** anyone lead you astray with empty philosophy and high-sounding nonsense that come from human thinking and from the evil powers of this world, and not from Christ. [NLT]<br>βλέπετε μή τις ὑμᾶς ἔσται ὁ συλαγωγῶν διὰ τῆς φιλοσοφίας καὶ κενῆς ἀπάτης, κατὰ τὴν παράδοσιν τῶν ἀνθρώπων, κατὰ τὰ στοιχεῖα τοῦ κόσμου, καὶ οὐ κατὰ Χριστόν· [GNS]<br>βλέπετε μή τις ὑμᾶς ἔσται ὁ συλαγωγῶν διὰ τῆς φιλοσοφίας καὶ κενῆς ἀπάτης κατὰ τὴν παράδοσιν τῶν ἀνθρώπων, κατὰ τὰ στοιχεῖα τοῦ κόσμου καὶ οὐ κατὰ Χριστόν· [GNT] | suade people of their ideas and philosophies whether they are sound or not.<br><br>Believers must, therefore, beware and guard against worldly philosophies and ideas lest they become ensnared and enslaved. |
| #376<br>**Bewitched**<br><br>**Bewitched–KJV**<br>**Bewitched–NASB**<br>**Bewitched–NIV**<br>**Bewitched–NKJV**<br>What magician has cast an evil spell– NLT<br><br>**POSB REFERENCE**<br>(Gal.3:1)<br>Note 1 | ἐβάσκανεν = ebaskanen<br>Pronunciation: [eh-bas-kah'-nen]<br>Parsing (part of speech): verb<br>    Mood—indicative<br>    Tense—aorist<br>    Voice—active<br>    Person—3rd person<br>    Number—singular<br>    Stem or root—from βασκαίνω<br>Concordance References:<br>  ⇒ Strong's #940 baskainō<br>  ⇒ NIV #1001 baskainō<br>  ⇒ NASB #940 baskainō<br><br>**Galatians 3:1**<br>O foolish Galatians, who hath **bewitched** you, that ye should not obey the truth, before whose eyes Jesus Christ hath been evidently set forth, crucified among you? [KJV]<br>You foolish Galatians, who has **bewitched** you, before whose eyes Jesus Christ was publicly portrayed as crucified? [NASB]<br>You foolish Galatians! Who has **bewitched** you? Before your very eyes Jesus Christ was clearly portrayed as crucified. [NIV]<br>O foolish Galatians! Who has **bewitched** you that you should not obey the truth, before whose eyes Jesus Christ was clearly portrayed among you as crucified? [NKJV]<br>Oh, foolish Galatians! **What magician has cast an evil spell** on you? For you used to see the meaning of Jesus Christ's death as clearly as though I had shown you a signboard with a picture of Christ dying on the cross. [NLT]<br>Ὦ ἀνόητοι Γαλάται, τίς ὑμᾶς **ἐβάσκανε** τῇ ἀληθείᾳ μὴ πείθεσθαι, οἷς κατ' ὀφθαλμοὺς Ἰησοῦς Χριστὸς προεγράφη ἐν ὑμῖν ἐσταυρωμένος; [GNS]<br>Ὦ ἀνόητοι Γαλάται, τίς ὑμᾶς **ἐβάσκανεν**, οἷς κατ' ὀφθαλμοὺς Ἰησοῦς Χριστὸς προεγράφη ἐσταυρωμένος; [GNT] | To be bewitched; to be placed under an evil spell; to cast a spell upon; to mislead, deceive.<br><br>**Practical Application**<br>The false teachers were charismatic, very capable, fluent, and persuasive speakers. They had dynamic personalities. Their teaching sounded reasonable and logical:<br>⇒ A man must keep the ritual of religion.<br>⇒ A man must do good works to be good.<br>⇒ A man must keep the law in order to be acceptable to God.<br><br>It all sounded reasonable and logical, especially to a person who was not thinking and comparing the teaching to the gospel of Christ. The error was *bewitching*, deceiving the believers. |
| #377<br>**Beyond Reproach**<br><br>Unreproveable–KJV<br>**Beyond reproach– NASB** | ἀνεγκλήτους = anegklētous<br>Pronunciation: [an-eng'-klay-toos]<br>Parsing (part of speech): adjective<br>    Case—accusative<br>    Gender—masculine<br>    Number—plural<br>    Stem or root—from ἀνέγκλητος, ον<br>Concordance References: | To be free from accusation; to be beyond reproach; to have nothing against them; to be without a single fault, unreproveable, blameless, unchargeable.<br><br>**Practical Application**<br>Imagine standing before God holy, unblame- |

# PRACTICAL WORD STUDIES
## in the NEW TESTAMENT

| ENGLISH WORD | GREEK WORD AND VERSE | THE WORD MEANS... |
|---|---|---|
| Free from accusation–NIV<br>Above reproach–NKJV<br>Without a single fault–NLT<br><br>**POSB REFERENCE**<br>(Col.1:22)<br>Note 3, point 3 | ⇒ Strong's #410 anegklētos<br>⇒ NIV #441 anegklētos<br>⇒ NASB #410 anegklētos<br><br>**Col. 1:22**<br>In the body of his flesh through death, to present you holy and unblameable and **unreproveable** in his sight: [KJV]<br>Yet He has now reconciled you in His fleshly body through death, in order to present you before Him holy and blameless and **beyond reproach**—[NASB]<br>But now he has reconciled you by Christ's physical body through death to present you holy in his sight, without blemish and **free from accusation**—[NIV]<br>In the body of His flesh through death, to present you holy, and blameless, and **above reproach** in His sight—[NKJV]<br>Yet now he has brought you back as his friends. He has done this through his death on the cross in his own human body. As a result, he has brought you into the very presence of God, and you are holy and blameless as you stand before him **without a single fault**. [NLT]<br>νυνὶ δὲ ἀποκατήλλαξεν ἐν τῷ σώματι τῆς σαρκὸς αὐτοῦ διὰ τοῦ θανάτου, παραστῆσαι ὑμᾶς ἁγίους καὶ ἀμώμους καὶ **ἀνεγκλήτους** κατενώπιον αὐτοῦ· [GNS]<br>νυνὶ δὲ ἀποκατήλλαξεν ἐν τῷ σώματι τῆς σαρκὸς αὐτοῦ διὰ τοῦ θανάτου παραστῆσαι ὑμᾶς ἁγίους καὶ ἀμώμους καὶ **ἀνεγκλήτους** κατενώπιον αὐτοῦ, [GNT] | able, and beyond reproach. Imagine how pleased God would be! How He would joy and rejoice in us—that we had honored Christ, His only Son, by trusting Him so much! As we are presented to God, what would He say? What would His first words be to us? We would be speechless, no doubt. But what a day of coronation, of glory, of greatness—standing face to face with our Father, the God of all glory, the Sovereign Majesty of the whole universe.<br>This is God's one great purpose in reconciliation: to present us perfect before Him. |
| #378<br>**Beyond The Reach**<br><br>Fadeth not away–KJV<br>Not fade away–NASB<br>Fade–NIV<br>Not fade away–NKJV<br>**Beyond the reach–NLT**<br><br>**POSB REFERENCE**<br>(1 Pt.1:4)<br>Note 2, point 3 | ἀμίαντον = amaranton<br>Pronunciation: [am-ar'-an-ton]<br>Parsing (part of speech): adjective<br>   Case—accusative<br>   Gender—feminine<br>   Number—singular<br>   Stem or root—from ἀμάραντος, ον<br>Concordance References:<br>⇒ Strong's #263 amarantos<br>⇒ NIV #278 amarantos<br>⇒ NASB #263 amarantos<br><br>**1 Peter 1:4**<br>To an inheritance incorruptible, and undefiled, and that **fadeth not away**, reserved in heaven for you, [KJV]<br>To obtain an inheritance which is imperishable and undefiled and will **not fade away**, reserved in heaven for you, [NASB]<br>And into an inheritance that can never perish, spoil or **fade**—kept in heaven for you, [NIV]<br>To an inheritance incorruptible and undefiled and that does **not fade away**, reserved in heaven for you, [NKJV]<br>For God has reserved a priceless inheritance for his children. It is kept in heaven for you, pure and undefiled, **beyond the reach** of change and decay. [NLT]<br>εἰς κληρονομίαν ἄφθαρτον καὶ ἀμίαντον καὶ **ἀμάραντον**, τετηρημένην ἐν οὐρανοῖς εἰς ὑμᾶς [GNS]<br>εἰς κληρονομίαν ἄφθαρτον καὶ **ἀμίαντον** καὶ ἀμάραντον, τετηρημένην ἐν οὐρανοῖς εἰς ὑμᾶς [GNT] | To not fade away; to be unfading; to be permanent.<br><br>**Practical Application**<br>Our priceless inheritance is beyond the reach (*amaranton*) of change and decay. It will last forever and ever. The splendor and beauty of it all—of life and of all the positions and possessions which God will give us—none of the splendor and beauty will fade or diminish whatsoever. Nothing, not even our energy and bodies, shall wear out or waste away. |
| #379<br>**Bind**<br><br>**Bind–KJV**<br>**Bind–NASB**<br>**Bind–NIV**<br>**Bind–NKJV**<br>Prohibit–NLT<br><br>**POSB REFERENCE**<br>(Mt.18:17-18; esp. | δήσητε = dēsēte<br>Pronunciation: [day'-say-teh]<br>Parsing (part of speech): verb<br>   Mood—subjunctive<br>   Tense—aorist<br>   Voice—active<br>   Person—2nd person<br>   Number—plural<br>   Stem or root—from δέω<br>Concordance References:<br>⇒ Strong's #1210 deō<br>⇒ NIV #1313 deō<br>⇒ NASB #1210 deō | To bind or tie as with a rope, chain, or cord; a loss of spiritual freedom.<br><br>**Practical Application**<br>What does it really mean to "bind" someone on earth? One thing is sure—it cannot mean that any man or any church has the power to forgive or not forgive sins. No man or church has the power to doom or save and set free a person.<br>What it probably means is this: when a brother chooses sin and refuses to be reconciled after the church reaches out after him, he is lost to the |

# PRACTICAL WORD STUDIES
## in the NEW TESTAMENT

| ENGLISH WORD | GREEK WORD AND VERSE | THE WORD MEANS... |
|---|---|---|
| v.18)<br>Note 2, point 2 | **Matthew 18:18**<br>Verily I say unto you, Whatsoever ye shall **bind** on earth shall be bound in heaven: and whatsoever ye shall loose on earth shall be loosed in heaven. [KJV]<br>"Truly I say to you, whatever you shall **bind** on earth shall be bound in heaven; and whatever you loose on earth shall be loosed in heaven. [NASB]<br>"I tell you the truth, whatever you **bind** on earth will be bound in heaven, and whatever you loose on earth will be loosed in heaven. [NIV]<br>Assuredly, I say to you, whatever you **bind** on earth will be bound in heaven, and whatever you loose on earth will be loosed in heaven. [NKJV]<br>I tell you this: Whatever you **prohibit** on earth is prohibited in heaven, and whatever you allow on earth is allowed in heaven. [NLT]<br>Ἀμὴν λέγω ὑμῖν, ὅσα ἐὰν **δήσητε** ἐπὶ τῆς γῆς, ἔσται δεδεμένα ἐν τῷ οὐρανῷ· καὶ ὅσα ἐὰν λύσητε ἐπὶ τῆς γῆς, ἔσται λελυμένα ἐν τῷ οὐρανῷ. [GNS]<br>Ἀμὴν λέγω ὑμῖν· ὅσα ἐὰν **δήσητε** ἐπὶ τῆς γῆς ἔσται δεδεμένα ἐν οὐρανῷ, καὶ ὅσα ἐὰν λύσητε ἐπὶ τῆς γῆς ἔσται λελυμένα ἐν οὐρανῷ. [GNT] | church. There is no relationship between him and the church. The church failed to reach him; therefore, he is *bound to the earth* and to being treated as an outsider. Thus heaven—God Himself—will reckon him to be bound by sin as an outsider just as the church binds (counts) him. Similarly, if he is ever reached by the church and "loosed" from the bondage of sin, heaven will reckon him loosed. God will receive him back as a redeemed brother, as an insider. |
| #380<br>**Birth Pains–**<br>**Birth Pangs**<br><br>Sorrows–KJV<br>**Birth pangs**–NASB<br>**Birth pains**–NIV<br>Sorrows–NKJV<br>Horrors to come–NLT<br><br>**POSB**<br>**REFERENCE**<br>(Mt.24:8)<br>*Deeper Study #5*<br><br>See also POSB REF:<br>(Mk.13:8)<br>*Deeper Study #4* | ὠδίνων = ōdinōn<br>Pronunciation: [o-deen'-own]<br>Parsing (part of speech): noun<br>   Case—genitive<br>   Gender—feminine<br>   Number—plural<br>   Stem or root—from ὠδίν, ῖνος<br>Concordance References:<br>⇒ Strong's #5604 ōdin<br>⇒ NIV #6047 ōdin<br>⇒ NASB #5604 ōdin<br><br>**Matthew 24:8**<br>All these are the beginning of **sorrows**. [KJV]<br>"But all these things are merely the beginning of **birth pangs**. [NASB]<br>All these are the beginning of **birth pains**. [NIV]<br>All these are the beginning of **sorrows**. [NKJV]<br>But all this will be only the beginning of the **horrors to come**. [NLT]<br>πάντα δὲ ταῦτα ἀρχὴ **ὠδίνων**. [GNS]<br>πάντα δὲ ταῦτα ἀρχὴ **ὠδίνων**. [GNT] | Birth pains; labor pains; travailings; agony; great sorrow; intolerable anguish; horror; quick, sharp, violent travailing pain.<br><br>**Practical Application**<br>The Bible speaks of a time in human history when the world will reel under the weight of intolerable anguish. There will be three great disasters of nature that will cause these birth pains:<br>1. Famines. There is evidently to be terrible famine in the last days. The black horse of the four horsemen of the Apocalypse indicates terrible famine (see POSB note—Rev. 6:5-6). The unbearable pain and terrible evil that hunger can cause is graphically described by Scripture.<br><br>   *Better are those slain with the sword Than those slain with hunger; For they pine away, being stricken For lack of the fruits of the field. The hands of compassionate women Boiled their own children; They became food for them Because of the destruction of the daughter of my people. Lament. 4:9-10 [NASB]*<br><br>2. Pestilence or disease. Pestilence will also be one of the terrible sufferings at the end time. Part of the suffering caused by the pale horse of the four horsemen of the Apocalypse includes pestilences.<br><br>   *They (Death and Hell) were given power over a fourth of the earth to kill by sword, famine and plague, and by the wild beasts of the earth. Rev. 6:8 [NIV]* (see POSB note—Rev. 6:8).<br><br>3. Earthquakes. Earthquakes will occur in many places during the last days of the earth (Rev. 6:12; Rev. 11:12-13, 19; Rev. 16:17-19). |

# PRACTICAL WORD STUDIES
## in the New Testament

| ENGLISH WORD | GREEK WORD AND VERSE | THE WORD MEANS... |
|---|---|---|
| **#381**<br>**Bishop**<br><br>**Bishop–KJV**<br>Guardian–NASB<br>Overseer–NIV<br>Overseer–NKJV<br>Guardian–NLT<br><br>**POSB REFERENCE**<br>(1 Pt.2:25)<br>Note 3, point 2 | ἐπίσκοπον = *episkopon*<br>Pronunciation: [ep-is'-kop-on]<br>Parsing (part of speech): noun<br>    Case—accusative<br>    Gender—masculine<br>    Number—singular<br>    Stem or root—from ἐπίσκοπος, ου<br>Concordance References:<br>⇒ Strong's #1985 *episkopos*<br>⇒ NIV #2176 *episkopos*<br>⇒ NASB #1985 *episkopos*<br><br>**1 Peter 2:25**<br>For ye were as sheep going astray; but are now returned unto the Shepherd and **Bishop** of your souls. [KJV]<br>For you were continually straying like sheep, but now you have returned to the Shepherd and **Guardian** of your souls. [NASB]<br>For you were like sheep going astray, but now you have returned to the Shepherd and **Overseer** of your souls. [NIV]<br>For you were like sheep going astray, but have now returned to the Shepherd and **Overseer** of your souls. [NKJV]<br>Once you were wandering like lost sheep. But now you have turned to your Shepherd, the **Guardian** of your souls. [NLT]<br>ἦτε γὰρ ὡς πρόβατα πλανώμενα· ἀλλ ἐπεστράφητε νῦν ἐπὶ τὸν ποιμένα καὶ **ἐπίσκοπον** τῶν ψυχῶν ὑμῶν. [GNS]<br>ἦτε γὰρ ὡς πρόβατα πλανώμενοι, ἀλλὰ ἐπεστράφητε νῦν ἐπὶ τὸν ποιμένα καὶ **ἐπίσκοπον** τῶν ψυχῶν ὑμῶν. [GNT] | Overseer and caretaker, guardian, protector, guide, and director (William Barclay. *The Letters of James and Peter*, p.258).<br><br>**Practical Application**<br>It is the picture of Christ's watching over our souls and looking after them with the greatest of care. Jesus Christ is our Overseer, Bishop, Caretaker, Guardian, Protector, Guide, and Director. When we come to Him, He takes complete charge of our lives. |
| **#382**<br>**Bishoprick**<br><br>**Bishoprick–KJV**<br>Office–NASB<br>Place of leadership–NIV<br>Office–NKJV<br>Position–NLT<br><br>**POSB REFERENCE**<br>(Acts 1:16-20; esp. v.20)<br>Note 2, point 6a | ἐπισκοπὴν = *episkopēn*<br>Pronunciation: [ep-is-kop-ayn']<br>Parsing (part of speech): noun<br>    Case—accusative<br>    Gender—feminine<br>    Number—singular<br>    Stem or root—from ἐπισκοπή, ῆς<br>Concordance References:<br>⇒ Strong's #1984 *episkopē*<br>⇒ NIV #2175 *episkopē*<br>⇒ NASB #1984 *episkopē*<br><br>**Acts 1:20**<br>For it is written in the book of Psalms, Let his habitation be desolate, and let no man dwell therein: and his **bishoprick** let another take. [KJV]<br>"For it is written in the book of Psalms, 'Let his homestead be made desolate, And let no man dwell in it'; and, 'His **OFFICE** LET ANOTHER MAN TAKE.' [NASB]<br>"For," said Peter, "it is written in the book of Psalms, " 'May his place be deserted; let there be no one to dwell in it,' and, "'May another take his **place of leadership**.' [NIV]<br>"For it is written in the book of Psalms: 'Let his dwelling place be desolate, And let no one live in it'; and, 'Let another take his **office**.' [NKJV]<br>Peter continued, "This was predicted in the book of Psalms, where it says, 'Let his home become desolate, with no one living in it.' And again, 'Let his **position** be given to someone else.' [NLT]<br>γέγραπται γὰρ ἐν βίβλῳ Ψαλμῶν, Γενηθήτω ἡ ἔπαυλις αὐτοῦ ἔρημος, καὶ μὴ ἔστω ὁ κατοικῶν ἐν αὐτῇ· καί, Τὴν **ἐπισκοπὴν** αὐτοῦ λάβοι ἕτερος. [GNS]<br>Γέγραπται γὰρ ἐν βίβλῳ ψαλμῶν, Γενηθήτω ἡ ἔπαυλις αὐτοῦ ἔρημος καὶ μὴ ἔστω ὁ κατοικῶν ἐν αὐτῇ, καί, Τὴν **ἐπισκοπὴν** αὐτοῦ λαβέτω ἕτερος. [GNT] | Place of leadership; office; position; place of service; overseership.<br><br>**Practical Application**<br>It is the word from which the office of overseer or bishop is taken. The idea is that Judas' office of overseeing the flock of God was to be filled by another person. Judas had lost his ministry completely. |

# PRACTICAL WORD STUDIES
in the NEW TESTAMENT

| ENGLISH WORD | GREEK WORD AND VERSE | THE WORD MEANS... |
|---|---|---|
| **#383**<br>**Bishops**<br><br>**Bishops**–KJV<br>Overseers–NASB<br>Overseers–NIV<br>**Bishops**–NKJV<br>Elders–NLT<br><br>**POSB REFERENCE**<br>(Philip.1:1)<br>Note 4, point 1 | ἐπισκόποις = *episkopois*<br>Pronunciation: [ep-is'-kop-oys]<br>Parsing (part of speech): noun<br>  Case—dative<br>  Gender—masculine<br>  Number—plural<br>  Stem or root—from ἐπίσκοπος, ου<br>Concordance References:<br>⇒ Strong's #1985 *episkopos*<br>⇒ NIV #2176 *episkopos*<br>⇒ NASB #1985 *episkopos*<br><br>**Philip. 1:1**<br>Paul and Timotheus, the servants of Jesus Christ, to all the saints in Christ Jesus which are at Philippi, with the **bishops** and deacons: [KJV]<br>Paul and Timothy, bond-servants of Christ Jesus, to all the saints in Christ Jesus who are in Philippi, including the **overseers** and deacons: [NASB]<br>Paul and Timothy, servants of Christ Jesus,To all the saints in Christ Jesus at Philippi, together with the **overseers** and deacons: [NIV]<br>Paul and Timothy, bondservants of Jesus Christ, To all the saints in Christ Jesus who are in Philippi, with the **bishops** and deacons: [NKJV]<br>This letter is from Paul and Timothy, slaves of Christ Jesus.It is written to all of God's people in Philippi, who believe in Christ Jesus, and to the **elders** and deacons. [NLT]<br>Παῦλος καὶ Τιμόθεος δοῦλοι Ἰησοῦ Χριστοῦ, πᾶσι τοῖς ἁγίοις ἐν Χριστῷ Ἰησοῦ τοῖς οὖσιν ἐν Φιλίπποις, σὺν **ἐπισκόποις** καὶ διακόνοις· [GNS]<br>Παῦλος καὶ Τιμόθεος δοῦλοι Χριστοῦ Ἰησοῦ πᾶσιν τοῖς ἁγίοις ἐν Χριστῷ Ἰησοῦ τοῖς οὖσιν ἐν Φιλίπποις σὺν **ἐπισκόποις** καὶ διακόνοις, [GNT] | To oversee; to look after; to manage; to guard; to be an elder, a bishop.<br><br>**Practical Application**<br>The bishops (*episkopois*) were apparently the same as the elders (*presbuteros*) or ministers of a church. The two words are used interchangeably to refer to the same men (Acts 20:17, 28; Titus 1:5, 7).<br>The instructions in the *Epistle of Titus* say that his duties included primarily exhortation and overseeing the lives of the believers. The overseer was the person whom we call the minister of the church. (See POSB *Deeper Study* #1—Titus 1:5-9 for full discussion.) |
| **#384**<br>**Bitterness**<br><br>**Bitterness**–KJV<br>**Bitterness**–NASB<br>**Bitterness**–NIV<br>**Bitterness**–NKJV<br>**Bitterness**–NLT<br><br>**POSB REFERENCE**<br>(Eph.4:31)<br>Note 1, point 1 | πικρία = *pikria*<br>Pronunciation: [pik-ree'-ah]<br>Parsing (part of speech): noun<br>  Case—nominative<br>  Gender—feminine<br>  Number—singular<br>  Stem or root—from πικρία, ας<br>Concordance References:<br>⇒ Strong's #4088 *pikria*<br>⇒ NIV #4394 *pikria*<br>⇒ NASB #4088 *pikria*<br><br>**Ephes. 4:31**<br>Let all **bitterness**, and wrath, and anger, and clamour, and evil speaking, be put away from you, with all malice: [KJV]<br>Let all **bitterness** and wrath and anger and clamor and slander be put away from you, along with all malice. [NASB]<br>Get rid of all **bitterness**, rage and anger, brawling and slander, along with every form of malice. [NIV]<br>Let all **bitterness**, wrath, anger, clamor, and evil speaking be put away from you, with all malice. [NKJV]<br>Get rid of all **bitterness**, rage, anger, harsh words, and slander, as well as all types of malicious behavior. [NLT]<br>πᾶσα **πικρία** καὶ θυμὸς καὶ ὀργὴ καὶ κραυγὴ καὶ βλασφημία ἀρθήτω ἀφ' ὑμῶν, σὺν πάσῃ κακίᾳ·[GNS]<br>πᾶσα **πικρία** καὶ θυμὸς καὶ ὀργὴ καὶ κραυγὴ καὶ βλασφημία ἀρθήτω ἀφ' ὑμῶν σὺν πάσῃ κακίᾳ. [GNT] | Bitterness, spite, resentment, harshness, bitter feelings.<br><br>**Practical Application**<br>A person who is bitter is often...<br>• sharp<br>• resentful<br>• cynical<br>• intense<br>• relentless<br>• cold<br>• harsh<br>• stressful<br>• distasteful<br>• unpleasant<br><br>Any expression involving any of these is sin to God. God desires a person to be filled with love and joy and peace and to express such. Anything less than the expression of these is sin. |
| **#385**<br>**Blame, Without**<br><br>Without blame–KJV<br>Blameless–NASB | ἀμώμους = *amōmous*<br>Pronunciation: [am'-o-moos]<br>Parsing (part of speech): adjective<br>  Case—accusative<br>  Gender—masculine<br>  Number—plural | To be blameless; to be without blame; to be faultless; to be unblemished.<br><br>**Practical Application**<br>The words "without blame" (*amōmous*) mean |

# PRACTICAL WORD STUDIES
## in the NEW TESTAMENT

| ENGLISH WORD | GREEK WORD AND VERSE | THE WORD MEANS... |
|---|---|---|
| Blameless–NIV<br>**Without blame–NKJV**<br>Without fault–NLT<br><br>**POSB REFERENCE**<br>(Eph.1:4)<br>Note 2, point 2 | Stem or root—from ἄμωμος, ον<br>Concordance References:<br>⇒ Strong's #299 amōmos<br>⇒ NIV #320 amōmos<br>⇒ NASB #299 amōmos<br><br>**Ephes. 1:4**<br>According as he hath chosen us in him before the foundation of the world, that we should be holy and **without blame** before him in love: [KJV]<br>Just as He chose us in Him before the foundation of the world, that we should be holy and **blameless** before Him. In love [NASB]<br>For he chose us in him before the creation of the world to be holy and **blameless** in his sight. In love [NIV]<br>Just as He chose us in Him before the foundation of the world, that we should be holy and **without blame** before Him in love, [NKJV]<br>Long ago, even before he made the world, God loved us and chose us in Christ to be holy and **without fault** in his eyes. [NLT]<br>καθὼς ἐξελέξατο ἡμᾶς ἐν αὐτῷ πρὸ καταβολῆς κόσμου, εἶναι ἡμᾶς ἁγίους, καὶ **ἀμώμους** κατενώπιον αὐτοῦ ἐν ἀγάπῃ, [GNS]<br>καθὼς ἐξελέξατο ἡμᾶς ἐν αὐτῷ πρὸ καταβολῆς κόσμου εἶναι ἡμᾶς ἁγίους καὶ **ἀμώμους** κατενώπιον αὐτοῦ ἐν ἀγάπῃ, [GNT] | to be free from sin, dirt, and filth; to be above reproach and without blemish; to be without fault and defilement. |
| **#386<br>Blameless**<br><br>Blameless–KJV<br>Blameless–NASB<br>Blameless–NIV<br>Blameless–NKJV<br>Free from all blame–NLT<br><br>**POSB REFERENCE**<br>(1 Cor.1:8)<br>Note 3 | ἀνεγκλήτους = anegklētous<br>Pronunciation: [an-eng'-klay-toos]<br>Parsing (part of speech): adjective<br>    Case—accusative<br>    Gender—masculine<br>    Number—plural<br>    Stem or root—from ἀνέγκλητος, ον<br>Concordance References:<br>⇒ Strong's #410 anegklētos<br>⇒ NIV #441 anegklētos<br>⇒ NASB #410 anegklētos<br><br>**1 Cor. 1:8**<br>Who shall also confirm you unto the end, that ye may be **blameless** in the day of our Lord Jesus Christ. [KJV]<br>Who shall also confirm you to the end, **blameless** in the day of our Lord Jesus Christ. [NASB]<br>He will keep you strong to the end, so that you will be **blameless** on the day of our Lord Jesus Christ. [NIV]<br>Who will also confirm you to the end, that you may be **blameless** in the day of our Lord Jesus Christ. [NKJV]<br>He will keep you strong right up to the end, and he will keep you **free from all blame** on the great day when our Lord Jesus Christ returns. [NLT]<br>ὃς καὶ βεβαιώσει ὑμᾶς ἕως τέλους, **ἀνεγκλήτους** ἐν τῇ ἡμέρᾳ τοῦ Κυρίου ἡμῶν Ἰησοῦ Χριστοῦ. [GNS]<br>ὃς καὶ βεβαιώσει ὑμᾶς ἕως τέλους **ἀνεγκλήτους** ἐν τῇ ἡμέρᾳ τοῦ κυρίου ἡμῶν Ἰησοῦ [Χριστοῦ]. [GNT] | Blameless; beyond reproach; unreproveable; without fault; guiltless; free from accusation.<br><br>**Practical Application**<br>It means that no one will be able to accuse or bring any accusation against the believer when he stands before Christ in the day of judgment. The "day of our Lord Jesus Christ" will bring about the judgment seat of Christ. Only those who are preserved by the blood and power of Jesus Christ will be counted blameless (1 Cor. 1:8). |
| **#387<br>Blameless**<br><br>Void of offence–KJV<br>**Blameless–NASB**<br>Clear–NIV<br>Without offense–NKJV<br>Clear–NLT<br><br>**POSB REFERENCE**<br>(Acts 24:14-16; esp. v.16)<br>Note 3, point 4b | ἀπρόσκοπον = aproskopon<br>Pronunciation: [ap-ros'-kop-on]<br>Parsing (part of speech): adjective<br>    Case—accusative<br>    Gender—feminine<br>    Number—singular<br>    Stem or root—from ἀπρόσκοπος<br>Concordance References:<br>⇒ Strong's #677 aproskopos<br>⇒ NIV #718 aproskopos<br>⇒ NASB #677 aproskopos<br><br>**Acts 24:16**<br>And herein do I exercise myself, to have always a conscience **void of offence** toward God, and toward men. [KJV] | To be clear; to be blameless; to be clear in conscience.<br><br>**Practical Application**<br>It means to keep from stumbling, to keep from causing others to stumble, to keep from hurting oneself and from hurting others. |

## PRACTICAL WORD STUDIES in the NEW TESTAMENT

| ENGLISH WORD | GREEK WORD AND VERSE | THE WORD MEANS... |
|---|---|---|
| | "In view of this, I also do my best to maintain always a **blameless** conscience both before God and before men. [NASB]<br>So I strive always to keep my conscience **clear** before God and man. [NIV]<br>This being so, I myself always strive to have a conscience **without offense** toward God and men. [NKJV]<br>Because of this, I always try to maintain a **clear** conscience before God and everyone else. [NLT]<br>ἐν τούτῳ δὲ αὐτὸς ἀσκῶ, **ἀπρόσκοπον** συνείδησιν ἔχειν πρὸς τὸν θεὸν καὶ τοὺς ἀνθρώπους διὰ παντός. [GNS]<br>ἐν τούτῳ καὶ αὐτὸς ἀσκῶ **ἀπρόσκοπον** συνείδησιν ἔχειν πρὸς τὸν θεὸν καὶ τοὺς ἀνθρώπους διὰ παντός. [GNT] | |
| **#388**<br>**Blameless**<br><br>Without blame–KJV<br>**Blameless–NASB**<br>**Blameless–NIV**<br>Without blame–NKJV<br>Without fault–NLT<br><br>**POSB REFERENCE**<br>(Eph.1:4)<br>Note 2, point 2 | ἀμώμους = *amōmous*<br>Pronunciation: [am'-o-moos]<br>Parsing (part of speech): adjective<br>    Case—accusative<br>    Gender—masculine<br>    Number—plural<br>    Stem or root—from ἄμωμος, ον<br>Concordance References:<br>⇒ Strong's #299 amōmos<br>⇒ NIV #320 amōmos<br>⇒ NASB #299 amōmos<br><br>**Ephes. 1:4**<br>According as he hath chosen us in him before the foundation of the world, that we should be holy and **without blame** before him in love: [KJV]<br>Just as He chose us in Him before the foundation of the world, that we should be holy and **blameless** before Him. In love [NASB]<br>For he chose us in him before the creation of the world to be holy and **blameless** in his sight. In love [NIV]<br>Just as He chose us in Him before the foundation of the world, that we should be holy and **without blame** before Him in love, [NKJV]<br>Long ago, even before he made the world, God loved us and chose us in Christ to be holy and **without fault** in his eyes. [NLT]<br>καθὼς ἐξελέξατο ἡμᾶς ἐν αὐτῷ πρὸ καταβολῆς κόσμου, εἶναι ἡμᾶς ἁγίους, καὶ **ἀμώμους** κατενώπιον αὐτοῦ ἐν ἀγάπῃ, [GNS]<br>καθὼς ἐξελέξατο ἡμᾶς ἐν αὐτῷ πρὸ καταβολῆς κόσμου εἶναι ἡμᾶς ἁγίους καὶ **ἀμώμους** κατενώπιον αὐτοῦ ἐν ἀγάπῃ, [GNT] | To be blameless; to be without blame; to be faultless; to be unblemished.<br><br>**Practical Application**<br>The word "blameless" (*amōmous*) means to be free from sin, dirt, and filth; to be above reproach and without blemish; to be without fault and defilement. |
| **#389**<br>**Blameless**<br><br>Unblameable–KJV<br>Unblamable–NASB<br>**Blameless–NIV**<br>**Blameless–NKJV**<br>**Blameless–NLT**<br><br>**POSB REFERENCE**<br>(1 Thes.3:13)<br>Note 3 | ἀμέμπτους = *amemptous*<br>Pronunciation: [am'-ehmp-toos]<br>Parsing (part of speech): adjective<br>    Case—accusative<br>    Gender—feminine<br>    Number—plural<br>    Stem or root—from ἄμεμπτος, ον<br>Concordance References:<br>⇒ Strong's #273 amemptos<br>⇒ NIV #289 amemptos<br>⇒ NASB #273 amemptos<br><br>**1 Thes. 3:13**<br>To the end he may stablish your hearts **unblameable** in holiness before God, even our Father, at the coming of our Lord Jesus Christ with all his saints. [KJV]<br>So that He may establish your hearts **unblamable** in holiness before our God and Father at the coming of our Lord Jesus with all His saints. [NASB]<br>May he strengthen your hearts so that you will be **blameless** and holy in the presence of our God and Father when our Lord Jesus comes with all his holy ones. [NIV] | Blameless, unblameable, faultless.<br><br>**Practical Application**<br>The word "blameless" (*amemptous*) means to be free from fault and blame; to be free from all charges (W.E. Vine. *Expository Dictionary of New Testament Words*). It is the Lord Jesus Christ who can make our hearts *unblameable in holiness* before God. He alone can free us from the faults and charges of sin; He alone can present us blameless and holy before God. Just think about it: Who else has such power? Do you know such a person? The thinking and honest person has to answer no. And to be honest, if Christ does not have the righteousness and power to present us unblameable before God, then we are hopelessly doomed. Why? Because He is the only Person who has ever risen from the dead, the only Person never to die again and to live eternally with God. If He is not our Savior, then we will die and never arise, never |

## PRACTICAL WORD STUDIES in the NEW TESTAMENT

| ENGLISH WORD | GREEK WORD AND VERSE | THE WORD MEANS... |
|---|---|---|
| | So that He may establish your hearts **blameless** in holiness before our God and Father at the coming of our Lord Jesus Christ with all His saints. [NKJV]<br><br>As a result, Christ will make your hearts strong, **blameless**, and holy when you stand before God our Father on that day when our Lord Jesus comes with all those who belong to him. [NLT]<br><br>εἰς τὸ στηρίξαι ὑμῶν τὰς καρδίας **ἀμέμπτους** ἐν ἁγιωσύνῃ, ἔμπροσθεν τοῦ Θεοῦ καὶ πατρὸς ἡμῶν, ἐν τῇ παρουσίᾳ τοῦ Κυρίου ἡμῶν Ἰησοῦ Χριστοῦ μετὰ πάντων τῶν ἁγίων αὐτοῦ. [GNS]<br><br>εἰς τὸ στηρίξαι ὑμῶν τὰς καρδίας **ἀμέμπτους** ἐν ἁγιωσύνῃ ἔμπροσθεν τοῦ Θεοῦ καὶ πατρὸς ἡμῶν ἐν τῇ παρουσίᾳ τοῦ κυρίου ἡμῶν Ἰησοῦ μετὰ πάντων τῶν ἁγίων αὐτοῦ, [ἀμήν]. [GNT] | live with God. Man's only hope is Christ, the hope that He has the righteousness and power to set us blameless before God. |
| **#390**<br>**Blameless**<br><br>**Blameless–KJV**<br>Above reproach–NASB<br>Above reproach–NIV<br>**Blameless–NKJV**<br>Life cannot be spoken against–NLT<br><br>**POSB REFERENCE**<br>(1 Tim.3:2-3; esp. v.2)<br>Note 2, point 1 | **ἀνεπίλημπτον** = anepilēmpton<br>Pronunciation: [an-ep-il'-amp-ton]<br>Parsing (part of speech): adjective<br>    Case—accusative<br>    Gender—masculine<br>    Number—singular<br>    Stem or root—from **ἀνεπίλημπτος**, ον<br>Concordance References:<br>  ⇒ Strong's #423 anepilēmptos<br>  ⇒ NIV #455 anepilēmptos<br>  ⇒ NASB #423 anepilēmptos<br><br>**1 Tim. 3:2**<br>A bishop then must be **blameless**, the husband of one wife, vigilant, sober, of good behaviour, given to hospitality, apt to teach; [KJV]<br><br>An overseer, then, must be **above reproach**, the husband of one wife, temperate, prudent, respectable, hospitable, able to teach, [NASB]<br><br>Now the overseer must be **above reproach**, the husband of but one wife, temperate, self-controlled, respectable, hospitable, able to teach, [NIV]<br><br>A bishop then must be **blameless**, the husband of one wife, temperate, sober-minded, of good behavior, hospitable, able to teach; [NKJV]<br><br>For an elder must be a man whose **life cannot be spoken against**. He must be faithful to his wife. He must exhibit self-control, live wisely, and have a good reputation. He must enjoy having guests in his home and must be able to teach. [NLT]<br><br>δεῖ οὖν τὸν ἐπίσκοπον **ἀνεπίλημπτον** εἶναι, μιᾶς γυναικὸς ἄνδρα, νηφάλιον, σώφρονα, κόσμιον, φιλόξενον, διδακτικόν· [GNS]<br><br>δεῖ οὖν τὸν ἐπίσκοπον **ἀνεπίλημπτον** εἶναι, μιᾶς γυναικὸς ἄνδρα, νηφάλιον σώφρονα κόσμιον φιλόξενον διδακτικόν, [GNT] | To be without fault; to be without rebuke; to be above reproach; to live an innocent life; to have a life that cannot be spoken against; to be without blemish, spot, or defect.<br><br>**Practical Application**<br>The minister or overseer of God must be qualified; he must meet some personal qualifications; he must be a person of great Christian character. The minister or overseer must be "blameless" (*anepilēmpton*): above reproach; not open to attack; not able to be criticized by the enemy at all (*The Pulpit Commentary*, Vol.21, p.50). He must be completely above reproach. |
| **#391**<br>**Blameless**<br><br>Harmless–KJV<br>Innocent–NASB<br>**Blameless–NIV**<br>Harmless–NKJV<br>**Blameless–NLT**<br><br>**POSB REFERENCE**<br>(Heb.7:26)<br>Note 2, point 2 | **ἄκακος** = akakos<br>Pronunciation: [ak'-ak-os]<br>Parsing (part of speech): adjective<br>    Case—nominative<br>    Gender—masculine<br>    Number—singular<br>    Stem or root—from **ἄκακος**, ον<br>Concordance References:<br>  ⇒ Strong's #172 akakos<br>  ⇒ NIV #179 akakos<br>  ⇒ NASB #172 akakos<br><br>**Hebrews 7:26**<br>For such an high priest became us, who is holy, **harmless**, undefiled, separate from sinners, and made higher than the heavens; [KJV]<br><br>For it was fitting that we should have such a high priest, holy, **innocent**, undefiled, separated from sinners and exalted above the heavens; [NASB]<br><br>Such a high priest meets our need—one who is holy, | Blameless, harmless, innocent, unsuspecting, naive; free from all guile, deception, envy, and malice against anyone.<br><br>**Practical Application**<br>William Barclay says that "Jesus *never hurt any man*" (*The Letter to the Hebrews*, p.89). We might say that Jesus Christ was so good that there was nothing but good in Him. There was nothing but the goodness and love of God in Him, and that was all that He ever shared with man. Jesus Christ is absolutely *harmless and blameless*. |

# PRACTICAL WORD STUDIES
## in the NEW TESTAMENT

| ENGLISH WORD | GREEK WORD AND VERSE | THE WORD MEANS... |
|---|---|---|
| | **blameless**, pure, set apart from sinners, exalted above the heavens. [NIV]<br><br>For such a High Priest was fitting for us, who is holy, **harmless**, undefiled, separate from sinners, and has become higher than the heavens; [NKJV]<br><br>He is the kind of high priest we need because he is holy and **blameless**, unstained by sin. He has now been set apart from sinners, and he has been given the highest place of honor in heaven. [NLT]<br><br>Τοιοῦτος γὰρ ἡμῖν ἔπρεπεν ἀρχιερεύς, ὅσιος, **ἄκακος**, ἀμίαντος, κεχωρισμένος ἀπὸ τῶν ἁμαρτωλῶν, καὶ ὑψηλότερος τῶν οὐρανῶν γενόμενος· [GNS]<br><br>Τοιοῦτος γὰρ ἡμῖν καὶ ἔπρεπεν ἀρχιερεύς, ὅσιος **ἄκακος** ἀμίαντος, κεχωρισμένος ἀπὸ τῶν ἁμαρτωλῶν καὶ ὑψηλότερος τῶν οὐρανῶν γενόμενος, [GNT] | |
| **#392**<br>**Blameless**<br><br>Offence–KJV<br>**Blameless**–NASB<br>**Blameless**–NIV<br>Offense–NKJV<br>**Blameless**–NLT<br><br>**POSB REFERENCE**<br>(Philip.1:9-10; esp. v.10)<br>Note 7, point 3 | ἀπρόσκοποι = aproskopoi<br>Pronunciation: [ap-ros'-kop-oy]<br>Parsing (part of speech): adjective<br>    Case—nominative<br>    Gender—masculine<br>    Number—plural<br>    Stem or root—from ἀπρόσκοπος, ον<br>Concordance References:<br>⇒ Strong's #677 aproskopos<br>⇒ NIV #718 aproskopos<br>⇒ NASB #677 aproskopos<br><br>**Philip. 1:10**<br>That ye may approve things that are excellent; that ye may be sincere and without **offence** till the day of Christ; [KJV]<br><br>So that you may approve the things that are excellent, in order to be sincere and **blameless** until the day of Christ; [NASB]<br><br>So that you may be able to discern what is best and may be pure and **blameless** until the day of Christ, [NIV]<br><br>That you may approve the things that are excellent, that you may be sincere and **offense** till the day of Christ, [NKJV]<br><br>For I want you to understand what really matters, so that you may live pure and **blameless** lives until Christ returns. [NLT]<br><br>εἰς τὸ δοκιμάζειν ὑμᾶς τὰ διαφέροντα, ἵνα ἦτε εἰλικρινεῖς καὶ **ἀπρόσκοποι** εἰς ἡμέραν Χριστοῦ, [GNS]<br><br>εἰς τὸ δοκιμάζειν ὑμᾶς τὰ διαφέροντα, ἵνα ἦτε εἰλικρινεῖς καὶ **ἀπρόσκοποι** εἰς ἡμέραν Χριστοῦ, [GNT] | Blameless; without offense; clear; faultless; inoffensive.<br><br>**Practical Application**<br>A growing love is needed to keep us blameless, from causing others to stumble. We must always guard against being blameless (*aproskopoi*) or a stumbling block to others. Note: we must be willing to choose the best and the excellent for the sake of others. We may be able to control, but others may not be able to control...<br>• drinking<br>• television<br>• social functions<br>• the latest fashion and dress<br>• dancing<br>• movies<br>• eating<br>• makeup<br>The list could go on and on with almost everything we do. We must control everything we do, not slipping over into the questionable—sometimes not even doing the acceptable and good. We must choose the best. Discern what is best. Why?<br>⇒ To keep from causing a brother to stumble.<br>⇒ To offer up to the Lord the very best we can. This point should *break our hearts*. Just think how often we have chosen to do less than the best for our Lord. We have offered up to Him behavior, words, thoughts, deeds, works that were second best—and we knew it! How His heart must have been cut—especially when He went to the ultimate limit in loving and giving Himself for us. |
| **#393**<br>**Blameless**<br><br>**Blameless**–KJV<br>**Blameless**–NASB<br>**Blameless**–NIV<br>**Blameless**–NKJV<br>Word of blame–NLT<br><br>**POSB REFERENCE**<br>(Philip.2:15)<br>Note 4 | ἄμεμπτοι = amemptoi<br>Pronunciation: [am'-emp-toy]<br>Parsing (part of speech): adjective<br>    Case—nominative<br>    Gender—masculine<br>    Number—plural<br>    Stem or root—from ἄμεμπτος, ον<br>Concordance References:<br>⇒ Strong's #273 amemptos<br>⇒ NIV #289 amemptos<br>⇒ NASB #273 amemptos<br><br>**Philip. 2:15**<br>That ye may be **blameless** and harmless, the sons of God, without rebuke, in the midst of a crooked and perverse nation, among whom ye shine as lights in the world; [KJV] | To be blameless, faultless, free from fault and censure; to be above reproach and rebuke; to have nothing wrong with.<br><br>**Practical Application**<br>The believer is to live a blameless, faultless and pure life, both in the church and in the world. No person should be able to point to the believer to accuse him with anything. The believer is to be clean, unpolluted, spotless, holy, righteous, and pure before man and God. |

# PRACTICAL WORD STUDIES
## in the NEW TESTAMENT

| ENGLISH WORD | GREEK WORD AND VERSE | THE WORD MEANS... |
|---|---|---|
| | That you may prove yourselves to be **blameless** and innocent, children of God above reproach in the midst of a crooked and perverse generation, among whom you appear as lights in the world, [NASB]<br>So that you may become **blameless** and pure, children of God without fault in a crooked and depraved generation, in which you shine like stars in the universe [NIV]<br>That you may become **blameless** and harmless, children of God without fault in the midst of a crooked and perverse generation, among whom you shine as lights in the world, [NKJV]<br>So that no one can speak a **word of blame** against you. You are to live clean, innocent lives as children of God in a dark world full of crooked and perverse people. Let your lives shine brightly before them. [NLT]<br>ἵνα γένησθε **ἄμεμπτοι** καὶ ἀκέραιοι, τέκνα Θεοῦ ἀμώμητα ἐν μέσῳ γενεᾶς σκολιᾶς καὶ διεστραμμένης, ἐν οἷς φαίνεσθε ὡς φωστῆρες ἐν κόσμῳ, [GNS]<br>ἵνα γένησθε **ἄμεμπτοι** καὶ ἀκέραιοι, τέκνα θεοῦ ἄμωμα μέσον γενεᾶς σκολιᾶς καὶ διεστραμμένης, ἐν οἷς φαίνεσθε ὡς φωστῆρες ἐν κόσμῳ, [GNT] | |
| **#394**<br>**Blameless**<br><br>Unblameable–KJV<br>**Blameless**–NASB<br>Without blemish–NIV<br>**Blameless**–NKJV<br>**Blameless**–NLT<br><br>**POSB REFERENCE**<br>(Col.1:22)<br>Note 3, point 2 | ἀμώμους = *amōmous*<br>Pronunciation: [am'-o-moos]<br>Parsing (part of speech): adjective<br>   Case—accusative<br>   Gender—masculine<br>   Number—plural<br>   Stem or root—from ἄμωμος, ον<br>Concordance References:<br>  ⇒ Strong's #299 amōmos<br>  ⇒ NIV #320 amōmos<br>  ⇒ NASB #299 amōmos<br><br>**Col. 1:22**<br>In the body of his flesh through death, to present you holy and **unblameable** and unreproveable in his sight: [KJV]<br>Yet He has now reconciled you in His fleshly body through death, in order to present you before Him holy and **blameless** and beyond reproach—[NASB]<br>But now he has reconciled you by Christ's physical body through death to present you holy in his sight, **without blemish** and free from accusation—[NIV]<br>In the body of His flesh through death, to present you holy, and **blameless**, and above reproach in His sight [NKJV]<br>Yet now he has brought you back as his friends. He has done this through his death on the cross in his own human body. As a result, he has brought you into the very presence of God, and you are holy and **blameless** as you stand before him without a single fault. [NLT]<br>νυνὶ δὲ ἀποκατήλλαξεν ἐν τῷ σώματι τῆς σαρκὸς αὐτοῦ διὰ τοῦ θανάτου, παραστῆσαι ὑμᾶς ἁγίους καὶ **ἀμώμους** καὶ ἀνεγκλήτους κατενώπιον αὐτοῦ·[GNS]<br>νυνὶ δὲ ἀποκατήλλαξεν ἐν τῷ σώματι τῆς σαρκὸς αὐτοῦ διὰ τοῦ θανάτου παραστῆσαι ὑμᾶς ἁγίους καὶ **ἀμώμους** καὶ ἀνεγκλήτους κατενώπιον αὐτοῦ, [GNT] | Without blemish; without spot; without fault; without any defect whatsoever.<br><br>**Practical Application**<br>We must also be "blameless" (*amomous*). We must be without spot, faultless, without any defect whatsoever. |
| **#395**<br>**Blameless**<br><br>**Blameless**–KJV<br>**Blameless**–NASB<br>**Blameless**–NIV<br>**Blameless**–NKJV<br>**Blameless**–NLT<br><br>**POSB REFERENCE**<br>(2 Pt.3:14)<br>Note 4, point 3 | ἀμώμητοι = *amōmētoi*<br>Pronunciation: [am-o'-may-toy]<br>Parsing (part of speech): adjective<br>   Case—nominative<br>   Gender—masculine<br>   Number—plural<br>   Stem or root—from ἀμώμητος, ον<br>Concordance References:<br>  ⇒ Strong's #298 amōmētos<br>  ⇒ NIV #318 amōmētos<br>  ⇒ NASB #298 amōmētos<br><br>**2 Peter 3:14**<br>Wherefore, beloved, seeing that ye look for such things, be diligent that ye may be found of him in peace, | Blameless; faultless; free from fault and censure; above reproach and rebuke; nothing wrong with.<br><br>**Practical Application**<br>The believer is to live a blameless, faultless, and pure life, both in the church and in the world. No one is to be able to point to the believer and accuse him with anything. The believer is to be clean, unpolluted, spotless, holy, righteous, and pure before man and God. |

PRACTICAL WORD STUDIES
in the NEW TESTAMENT

| ENGLISH WORD | GREEK WORD AND VERSE | THE WORD MEANS... |
|---|---|---|
| | without spot, and **blameless**. [KJV]<br>Therefore, beloved, since you look for these things, be diligent to be found by Him in peace, spotless and **blameless**, [NASB]<br>So then, dear friends, since you are looking forward to this, make every effort to be found spotless, **blameless** and at peace with him. [NIV]<br>Therefore, beloved, looking forward to these things, be diligent to be found by Him in peace, without spot and **blameless**; [NKJV]<br>And so, dear friends, while you are waiting for these things to happen, make every effort to live a pure and **blameless** life. And be at peace with God. [NLT]<br>Διό, ἀγαπητοί, ταῦτα προσδοκῶντες, σπουδάσατε ἄσπιλοι καὶ **ἀμώμητοι** αὐτῷ εὑρεθῆναι ἐν εἰρήνῃ. [GNS]<br>Διό, ἀγαπητοί, ταῦτα προσδοκῶντες σπουδάσατε ἄσπιλοι καὶ **ἀμώμητοι** αὐτῷ εὑρεθῆναι ἐν εἰρήνῃ [GNT] | |
| **#396**<br>**Blameless**<br><br>Faultless–KJV<br>**Blameless–NASB**<br>Without Fault–NIV<br>Faultless–NKJV<br>Innocent of sin–NLT<br><br>**POSB REFERENCE**<br>(Jude 1:24-25; esp. v.24)<br>Note 4, point 2 | ἀμώμους = *amōmous*<br>Pronunciation: [am'-o-moos]<br>Parsing (part of speech): adjective<br>    Case—accusative<br>    Gender—masculine<br>    Number—plural<br>    Stem or root—from ἄμωμος, ον<br>Concordance References:<br>⇒ Strong's #299 amōmos<br>⇒ NIV #320 amōmos<br>⇒ NASB #299 amōmos<br><br>**Jude 1:24**<br>Now unto him that is able to keep you from falling, and to present you **faultless** before the presence of his glory with exceeding joy, [KJV]<br>Now to Him who is able to keep you from stumbling, and to make you stand in the presence of His glory **blameless** with great joy, [NASB]<br>To him who is able to keep you from falling and to present you before his glorious presence **without fault** and with great joy—[NIV]<br>Now to Him who is able to keep you from stumbling, And to present you **faultless** Before the presence of His glory with exceeding joy, [NKJV]<br>And now, all glory to God, who is able to keep you from stumbling, and who will bring you into his glorious presence **innocent of sin** and with great joy. [NLT]<br>Τῷ δὲ δυναμένῳ φυλάξαι ὑμᾶς ἀπταίστους, καὶ στῆσαι κατενώπιον τῆς δόξης αὐτοῦ **ἀμώμους** ἐν ἀγαλλιάσει, [GNS]<br>Τῷ δὲ δυναμένῳ φυλάξαι ὑμᾶς ἀπταίστους καὶ στῆσαι κατενώπιον τῆς δόξης αὐτοῦ **ἀμώμους** ἐν ἀγαλλιάσει, [GNT] | To be without fault, blameless; to be innocent of sin; to be faultless, without blemish; to be spotless and pure, without any defilement whatsoever.<br><br>**Practical Application**<br>God is *able to make us blameless* when we come face to face with Him. The word "blameless" (*amōmous*) means to be spotless and pure, without any defilement whatsoever. God is able to accept us in Jesus Christ, the spotless Lamb of God. If we will continue to approach God in Christ—in the name of Christ and His death—then God will accept us and count our faith as righteousness. He will accept us in the righteousness of His Son, the Lord Jesus Christ. God is able to do this, and He will do it if we will draw near Him *in Christ*. |
| **#397**<br>**Blasphemers**<br><br>**Blasphemers–KJV**<br>Revilers–NASB<br>Abusive–NIV<br>**Blasphemers–NKJV**<br>Scoffing at God–NLT<br><br>**POSB REFERENCE**<br>(2 Tim.3:2-4; esp. v.2)<br>Note 2, point 5 | βλάσφημοι = *blasphēmoi*<br>Pronunciation: [blas'-fay-moy]<br>Parsing (part of speech): adjective<br>    Case—nominative<br>    Gender—masculine<br>    Number—plural<br>    Stem or root—from βλάσφημος, ον<br>Concordance References:<br>⇒ Strong's #989 blasphēmos<br>⇒ NIV #1061 blasphēmos<br>⇒ NASB #989 blasphēmos<br><br>**2 Tim. 3:2**<br>For men shall be lovers of their own selves, covetous, boasters, proud, **blasphemers**, disobedient to parents, unthankful, unholy, [KJV]<br>For men will be lovers of self, lovers of money, boastful, arrogant, **revilers**, disobedient to parents, ungrateful, unholy, [NASB]<br>People will be lovers of themselves, lovers of money, boastful, proud, **abusive**, disobedient to their parents, | To be verbally abusive; to blaspheme; to revile; to openly scoff at God; to slander, insult, rail, reproach, curse.<br><br>**Practical Application**<br>The word "blasphemers" (*blasphēmoi*) is usually thought to be against God, and it is. But it is also a sin against men. Men can blaspheme men. Think of the cursing and insults that will be thrown against God and men today. Practically everyone is cursing and reviling others: mothers, fathers, children, teachers, professionals, actors, comedians, politicians, even some professing religionists feel the need to occasionally curse in order to be acceptable.<br>Why is there so much cursing and profanity today? Because there is a loss of respect for both self and others, for both position and authority. People rail, revile, insult, reproach, and curse |

## Practical Word Studies in the New Testament

| ENGLISH WORD | GREEK WORD AND VERSE | THE WORD MEANS... |
|---|---|---|
| | ungrateful, unholy, [NIV]<br>　For men will be lovers of themselves, lovers of money, boasters, proud, **blasphemers**, disobedient to parents, unthankful, unholy, [NKJV]<br>　For people will love only themselves and their money. They will be boastful and proud, **scoffing at God**, disobedient to their parents, and ungrateful. They will consider nothing sacred. [NLT]<br>　ἔσονται γὰρ οἱ ἄνθρωποι φίλαυτοι, φιλάργυροι, ἀλαζόνες, ὑπερήφανοι, **βλάσφημοι**, γονεῦσιν ἀπειθεῖς, ἀχάριστοι, ἀνόσιοι, [GNS]<br>　ἔσονται γὰρ οἱ ἄνθρωποι φίλαυτοι φιλάργυροι ἀλαζόνες ὑπερήφανοι **βλάσφημοι**, γονεῦσιν ἀπειθεῖς, ἀχάριστοι ἀνόσιοι [GNT] | when they are disturbed within—when they sense dissatisfaction, disapproval, unacceptance, bitterness, emptiness, loneliness, and reaction within their heart. A disturbed and dissatisfied heart causes people to blaspheme God and man, including themselves (blaming and cursing themselves when they fail and come ever so short). |
| **#398**<br>**Blasphemes–**<br>**Blasphemeth–**<br>**Blaspheming–**<br>**Blasphemy**<br><br>Blasphemeth–KJV<br>Blasphemes–NASB<br>Blaspheming–NIV<br>Blasphemes–NKJV<br>Blasphemy–NLT<br><br>**POSB**<br>**REFERENCE**<br>(Mt.9:3)<br>*Deeper Study #4* | βλασφημεῖ = *blasphēmei*<br>Pronunciation: [blas-fay-meh'-ee]<br>Parsing (part of speech): verb<br>　Mood—indicative<br>　Tense—present<br>　Voice—active<br>　Person—3rd person<br>　Number—singular<br>　Stem or root—from βλασφημέω<br>Concordance References:<br>　⇒ Strong's #987 blasphēmeō<br>　⇒ NIV #1059 blasphēmeō<br>　⇒ NASB #987 blasphēmeō<br><br>**Matthew 9:3**<br>　And, behold, certain of the scribes said within themselves, This man **blasphemeth**. [KJV]<br>　And behold, some of the scribes said to themselves, "This fellow **blasphemes**." [NASB]<br>　At this, some of the teachers of the law said to themselves, "This fellow is **blaspheming**!" [NIV]<br>　And at once some of the scribes said within themselves, "This Man **blasphemes**!" [NKJV]<br>　"**Blasphemy**! This man talks like he is God!" some of the teachers of religious law said among themselves. [NLT]<br>　καὶ ἰδού, τινες τῶν γραμματέων εἶπον ἐν ἑαυτοῖς, Οὗτος **βλασφημεῖ**. [GNS]<br>　καὶ ἰδοὺ τινες τῶν γραμματέων εἶπαν ἐν ἑαυτοῖς, Οὗτος **βλασφημεῖ**. [GNT] | To blaspheme; to speak against God; to curse; to slander, insult, rail at, revile, reproach.<br><br>**Practical Application**<br>In this Scripture, Jesus Himself was claiming to do what only God could do—forgive sins. |
| **#399**<br>**Blasphemy**<br><br>Blasphemy–KJV<br>Slander–NASB<br>Slander–NIV<br>Blasphemy–NKJV<br>Slander–NLT<br><br>**POSB**<br>**REFERENCE**<br>(Mk.7:22)<br>*Deeper Study #13*<br><br>See also POSB REF:<br>(Col.3:8-11; esp. v.8)<br>Note 2, point 1 | βλασφημία = *blasphemia*<br>Pronunciation: [blas-fay-me'-ah]<br>Parsing (part of speech): noun<br>　Case—nominative<br>　Gender—feminine<br>　Number—singular<br>　Stem or root—from βλασφημία, ας<br>Concordance References:<br>　⇒ Strong's #988 blasphemia<br>　⇒ NIV #1060 blasphemia<br>　⇒ NASB #988 blasphemia<br><br>**Mark 7:22**<br>　Thefts, covetousness, wickedness, deceit, lasciviousness, an evil eye, **blasphemy**, pride, foolishness: [KJV]<br>　Deeds of coveting and wickedness, as well as deceit, sensuality, envy, **slander**, pride and foolishness. [NASB]<br>　Greed, malice, deceit, lewdness, envy, **slander**, arrogance and folly. [NIV]<br>　Thefts, covetousness, wickedness, deceit, lewdness, an evil eye, **blasphemy**, pride, foolishness. [NKJV]<br>　Adultery, greed, wickedness, deceit, eagerness for lustful pleasure, envy, **slander**, pride, and foolishness. [NLT]<br>　λεονεξίαι, πονηρίαι, δόλος, ἀσέλγεια, ὀφθαλμὸς πονηρός, **βλασφημία**, ὑπερηφανία, ἀφροσύνη· [GNS]<br>　μοιχεῖαι, πλεονεξίαι, πονηρίαι, δόλος, ἀσέλγεια, ὀφθαλμὸς πονηρός, **βλασφημία**, ὑπερηφανία, ἀφροσύνη· [GNT] | To slander, blaspheme, insult, revile, defame, speak evil of God or people; to have malicious talkman.<br><br>**Practical Application**<br>In this Scripture, Jesus was listing the bad things that come out of a person's heart that makes him unclean. |

# PRACTICAL WORD STUDIES
## in the NEW TESTAMENT

| ENGLISH WORD | GREEK WORD AND VERSE | THE WORD MEANS... |
|---|---|---|
| **#400** **Blemishes** Spots–KJV Hidden reefs–NASB **Blemishes–NIV** Spots–NKJV Dangerous reefs–NLT **POSB REFERENCE** (Jude 1:12) Note 14 | σπιλάδες = *spilades* Pronunciation: [spee-la-des'] Parsing (part of speech): noun    Case—nominative    Gender—feminine    Number—plural    Stem or root—from σπιλάς, άδος Concordance References: ⇒ Strong's #4694 spilas ⇒ NIV #5069 spilas ⇒ NASB #4694 spilas **Jude 1:12** These are **spots** in your feasts of charity, when they feast with you, feeding themselves without fear: clouds they are without water, carried about of winds; trees whose fruit withereth, without fruit, twice dead, plucked up by the roots; [KJV] These men are those who are **hidden reefs** in your love feasts when they feast with you without fear, caring for themselves; clouds without water, carried along by winds; autumn trees without fruit, doubly dead, uprooted; [NASB] These men are **blemishes** at your love feasts, eating with you without the slightest qualm—shepherds who feed only themselves. They are clouds without rain, blown along by the wind; autumn trees, without fruit and uprooted—twice dead. [NIV] These are **spots** in your love feasts, while they feast with you without fear, serving only themselves. They are clouds without water, carried about by the winds; late autumn trees without fruit, twice dead, pulled up by the roots; [NKJV] When these people join you in fellowship meals celebrating the love of the Lord, they are like **dangerous reefs** that can shipwreck you. They are shameless in the way they care only about themselves. They are like clouds blowing over dry land without giving rain, promising much but producing nothing. They are like trees without fruit at harvesttime. They are not only dead but doubly dead, for they have been pulled out by the roots. [NLT] οὗτοί εἰσιν ἐν ταῖς ἀγάπαις ὑμῶν **σπιλάδες**, συνευωχούμενοι ὑμῖν, ἀφόβως ἑαυτοὺς ποιμαίνοντες· νεφέλαι ἄνυδροι, ὑπὸ ἀνέμων περιφερόμεναι· δένδρα φθινοπωρινά, ἄκαρπα, δὶς ἀποθανόντα, ἐκριζωθέντα· [GNS] οὗτοί εἰσιν οἱ ἐν ταῖς ἀγάπαις ὑμῶν **σπιλάδες** συνευωχούμενοι ἀφόβως, ἑαυτοὺς ποιμαίνοντες, νεφέλαι ἄνυδροι ὑπὸ ἀνέμων παραφερόμεναι, δένδρα φθινοπωρινὰ ἄκαρπα δὶς ἀποθανόντα ἐκριζωθέντα, [GNT] | Blemishes, spots, hidden reefs, dangerous reefs; anything that which poses a dangerous threat. **Practical Application** False teachers are *spots and blemishes* upon the fellowship of the church. The Greek word for "blemishes" (*spilades*) can mean *submerged rocks or hidden reefs* that can wreck a ship. False teachers are reefs within the church that can wreck the fellowship of the church. Translators differ as to which meaning Jude intended. Perhaps he meant both, for both are certainly true. The *love feasts* referred to were called *love feasts* by the early church. They were fellowship meals that the church celebrated after the services on the Lord's Day. Each family brought what food they could. This, of course, meant that the wealthy brought plenty and the poor brought little or nothing. Remember that many of the believers were slaves in that day, so some of them would not be able to bring any food whatsoever. Some churches had the most joyful fellowship around the love feasts. It provided a time when the believers could share the warmth of their hearts and grow in fellowship together. It was a time when the Holy Spirit could draw the hearts of believers together in love and joy and care and sharing. It was a time that the Holy Spirit could use to bind believers together in feelings for one another and in warmth and tenderness. The point is this: fellowship among believers is a most wonderful time, a unique opportunity to grow and share together. But when false teachers are present, the scene is entirely different. ⇒ False teachers are spots or blemishes upon the fellowship of believers. They dirty and soil the name of Christ and the testimony of the church. They profess to be believers and are even teachers of God's Word, but they are not pure. Their false teaching disturbs genuine believers and causes division within the fellowship of the church. Those who are not rooted in Christ and in God's Word follow and support the false teacher; those who are rooted in Christ and in God's Word reject the false teacher. False teachers always spot and dirty the fellowship of the church because they cause division among the people and destroy the Spirit of Christ among them. ⇒ False teachers are reefs or submerged rocks that wreck the fellowship of the church. Their teaching is often injected into the church quietly and insidiously, completely unknown to the general membership. Therefore, the fellowship is subject to being shipwrecked upon the reefs of false teaching. Note that the false teachers feed themselves—that is, they fellowship with believers—without fear. There is no fear of God nor thought about the damage they are doing to the fellowship of the church. Their interest is to boost themselves forward; to be recognized as an excellent teacher or preacher, a person of unusual gifts, a teacher with new insights, a teacher who is progressive, who is a notch above others. |

# PRACTICAL WORD STUDIES
## in the NEW TESTAMENT

| ENGLISH WORD | GREEK WORD AND VERSE | THE WORD MEANS... |
|---|---|---|
| **#401**<br>**Bless–**<br>**Blessing**<br><br>Bless–KJV<br>Bless–NASB<br>Bless–NIV<br>Bless–NKJV<br>Bless–NLT<br><br>**POSB REFERENCE**<br>(Rom.12:14)<br>Note 1<br><br>See also POSB REF:<br>(1 Pt.3:9)<br>Note 6, point 2 | εὐλογεῖτε = *eulogeite*<br>Pronunciation: [yoo-log-ee'-teh]<br>Parsing (part of speech): verb<br>    Mood—imperative<br>    Tense—present<br>    Voice—active<br>    Person—2nd person<br>    Number—plural<br>    Stem or root—from εὐλογέω<br>Concordance References:<br>  ⇒ Strong's #2127 eulogeö<br>  ⇒ NIV #2328 eulogeö<br>  ⇒ NASB #2127 eulogeö<br><br>**Romans 12:14**<br>**Bless** them which persecute you: **bless**, and curse not. [KJV]<br>**Bless** those who persecute you; **bless** and curse not. [NASB]<br>**Bless** those who persecute you; **bless** and do not curse. [NIV]<br>**Bless** those who persecute you; **bless** and do not curse. [NKJV]<br>If people persecute you because you are a Christian, don't curse them; pray that God will **bless** them. [NLT]<br>εὐλογεῖτε τοὺς διώκοντας ὑμᾶς· εὐλογεῖτε, καὶ μὴ καταρᾶσθε. [GNS]<br>εὐλογεῖτε τοὺς διώκοντας [ὑμᾶς], εὐλογεῖτε καὶ μὴ καταρᾶσθε. [GNT] | To bless; to speak well of; to bestow a blessing upon; to praise.<br><br>**Practical Application**<br>What does it mean to bless and to speak well of?<br>1. It means to speak well to our persecutors. We do not react against them by cursing, speaking harshly, or striking out at them. We do not try to hurt them either verbally or physically. On the contrary, we seek to find something that is commendable about them, and we commend them for it.<br>2. It means to speak well about our persecutors. When speaking to others, we do not down the persecutor, but we mention some commendable trait. We praise some "good thing" about the person; we do not tear him down.<br>3. It means to pray for our persecutors. We must do as Jesus said and did.<br>4. It means to do good to our persecutors. |
| **#402**<br>**Blessed**<br><br>Blessed–KJV<br>Blessed–NASB<br>Blessed–NIV<br>Blessed–NKJV<br>Blessed–NLT<br><br>**POSB REFERENCE**<br>(Mk.14:61)<br>Note 5 | εὐλογητοῦ = *eulogētou*<br>Pronunciation: [yoo-log-ay-too']<br>Parsing (part of speech): pronominal adjective<br>    Case—genitive<br>    Gender—masculine<br>    Number—singular<br>    Stem or root—from εὐλογητός, ή, όν<br>Concordance References:<br>  ⇒ Strong's #2128 eulogētos<br>  ⇒ NIV #2329 eulogētos<br>  ⇒ NASB #2128 eulogētos<br><br>**Mark 14:61**<br>But he held his peace, and answered nothing. Again the high priest asked him, and said unto him, Art thou the Christ, the Son of the **Blessed**? [KJV]<br>But He kept silent, and made no answer. Again the high priest was questioning Him, and saying to Him, "Are You the Christ, the Son of the **Blessed** One?" [NASB]<br>But Jesus remained silent and gave no answer. Again the high priest asked him, "Are you the Christ, the Son of the **Blessed** One?" [NIV]<br>But He kept silent and answered nothing. Again the high priest asked Him, saying to Him, "Are You the Christ, the Son of the **Blessed**?" [NKJV]<br>Jesus made no reply. Then the high priest asked him, "Are you the Messiah, the Son of the **blessed** God?" [NLT]<br>ὁ δὲ ἐσιώπα, καὶ οὐδέν ἀπεκρίνατο. πάλιν ὁ ἀρχιερεὺς ἐπηρώτα αὐτὸν, καὶ λέγει αὐτῷ, Σὺ εἶ ὁ Χριστὸς, ὁ υἱὸς τοῦ εὐλογητοῦ; [GNS]<br>ὁ δὲ ἐσιώπα καὶ οὐκ ἀπεκρίνατο οὐδέν. πάλιν ὁ ἀρχιερεὺς ἐπηρώτα αὐτὸν καὶ λέγει αὐτῷ, Σὺ εἶ ὁ Χριστὸς ὁ υἱὸς τοῦ εὐλογητοῦ; [GNT] | Blessed, the Blessed One; a title for God.<br><br>**Practical Application**<br>The Jews, when mentioning God's name, would usually say, "God, blessed for ever." The word "blessed" came to be a title for God. |
| **#403**<br>**Blessed**<br><br>Blessed–KJV<br>Blessed–NASB<br>Good–NIV<br>Blessed–NKJV<br>Special favor–NLT | μακάριοι = *makarioi*<br>Pronunciation: [mak-ar'-ee-o-ee]<br>Parsing (part of speech): adjective<br>    Case—nominative<br>    Gender—masculine<br>    Number—plural<br>    Stem or root—from μακάριος, α, ον | Good, blessed; to have special favor; to pronounce a person happy, fortunate or blessed.<br><br>**Practical Application**<br>It is a judgment that affirms a person's condition as being "blessed." The idea is that Christ is going to bestow special favor and make the |

215

# PRACTICAL WORD STUDIES
## in the NEW TESTAMENT

| ENGLISH WORD | GREEK WORD AND VERSE | THE WORD MEANS... |
|---|---|---|
| **POSB REFERENCE** (Lk.12:35-40; esp. v.37) Note 1, point 3 | Concordance References:<br>⇒ Strong's #3107 makarios<br>⇒ NIV #3421 makarios<br>⇒ NASB #3107 makarios<br><br>**Luke 12:37**<br>**Blessed** are those servants, whom the lord when he cometh shall find watching: verily I say unto you, that he shall gird himself, and make them to sit down to meat, and will come forth and serve them. [KJV]<br>"**Blessed** are those slaves whom the master shall find on the alert when he comes; truly I say to you, that he will gird himself to serve, and have them recline at the table, and will come up and wait on them. [NASB]<br>It will be **good** for those servants whose master finds them watching when he comes. I tell you the truth, he will dress himself to serve, will have them recline at the table and will come and wait on them. [NIV]<br>**Blessed** are those servants whom the master, when he comes, will find watching. Assuredly, I say to you that he will gird himself and have them sit down to eat, and will come and serve them. [NKJV]<br>There will be **special favor** for those who are ready and waiting for his return. I tell you, he himself will seat them, put on an apron, and serve them as they sit and eat! [NLT]<br>μακάριοι οἱ δοῦλοι ἐκεῖνοι, οὓς ἐλθὼν ὁ κύριος εὑρήσει γρηγοροῦντας· ἀμὴν λέγω ὑμῖν ὅτι περιζώσεται καὶ ἀνακλινεῖ αὐτοὺς, καὶ παρελθὼν διακονήσει αὐτοῖς. [GNS]<br>μακάριοι οἱ δοῦλοι ἐκεῖνοι, οὓς ἐλθὼν ὁ κύριος εὑρήσει γρηγοροῦντας· ἀμὴν λέγω ὑμῖν ὅτι περιζώσεται καὶ ἀνακλινεῖ αὐτοὺς καὶ παρελθὼν διακονήσει αὐτοῖς. [GNT] | believer happy and blessed. Happiness and blessedness will become a state of being, the constant experience of the believer. |
| **#404 Blessed**<br><br>Blessed–KJV<br>Blessed–NASB<br>Blessed–NIV<br>Blessed–NKJV<br>Wonderful–NLT<br><br>**POSB REFERENCE** (Tit.2:13) Note 3 | μακαρίαν = makarian<br>Pronunciation: [mak-ar'-ee-ahn]<br>Parsing (part of speech): adjective<br>    Case—accusative<br>    Gender—feminine<br>    Number—singular<br>    Stem or root—from μακάριος, α, ον<br>Concordance References:<br>⇒ Strong's #3107 makarios<br>⇒ NIV #3421 makarios<br>⇒ NASB #3107 makarios<br><br>**Titus 2:13**<br>Looking for that **blessed** hope, and the glorious appearing of the great God and our Saviour Jesus Christ; [KJV]<br>Looking for the **blessed** hope and the appearing of the glory of our great God and Savior, Christ Jesus; [NASB]<br>While we wait for the **blessed** hope—the glorious appearing of our great God and Savior, Jesus Christ, [NIV]<br>Looking for the **blessed** hope and glorious appearing of our great God and Savior Jesus Christ, [NKJV]<br>While we look forward to that **wonderful** event when the glory of our great God and Savior, Jesus Christ, will be revealed. [NLT]<br>προσδεχόμενοι τὴν **μακαρίαν** ἐλπίδα καὶ ἐπιφάνειαν τῆς δόξης τοῦ μεγάλου Θεοῦ καὶ σωτῆρος ἡμῶν Ἰησοῦ Χριστοῦ, [GNS]<br>προσδεχόμενοι τὴν **μακαρίαν** ἐλπίδα καὶ ἐπιφάνειαν τῆς δόξης τοῦ μεγάλου θεοῦ καὶ σωτῆρος ἡμῶν Ἰησοῦ Χριστοῦ, [GNT] | Blessed, wonderful. It means to be filled with happiness, prosperity, richness, benefits, the highest good—all the great and glorious benefits imaginable.<br><br>**Practical Application**<br>The blessed hope of the Lord's return is to be filled with all that one can imagine and more...<br>• all the *happiness* imaginable and more.<br>• all the *prosperity* imaginable and more.<br>• all the *richness* imaginable and more.<br>• all the *benefits* imaginable and more.<br><br>If one can imagine the highest good and all the richness of life possible, the appearing of the glory of the Lord Jesus Christ will be this and more—much more. |
| **#405 Blessed– Blesses** | Μακάριος = Makarios<br>Pronunciation: [mak-ar'-ee-os]<br>Parsing (part of speech): adjective<br>    Case—nominative<br>    Gender—masculine<br>    Number—singular | Blessed, fortunate, happy.<br><br>**Practical Application**<br>The person who perseveres under trial will be "blessed" (*Makarios*). This refers to this life, to |

# PRACTICAL WORD STUDIES
## in the NEW TESTAMENT

| ENGLISH WORD | GREEK WORD AND VERSE | THE WORD MEANS... |
|---|---|---|
| Blessed–KJV<br>Blessed–NASB<br>Blessed–NIV<br>Blessed–NKJV<br>Blesses–NLT<br><br>**POSB<br>REFERENCE**<br>(Jas.1:12)<br>Note 3, point 1<br><br>See also POSB REF:<br>(Mt.5:3)<br>*Deeper Study* #1<br>(Rev.20:6)<br>Note 3, point 1 | Stem or root—from μακάριος, α, ον<br>Concordance References:<br>⇒ Strong's #3107 makarios<br>⇒ NIV #3421 makarios<br>⇒ NASB #3107 makarios<br><br>**James 1:12**<br>**Blessed** is the man that endureth temptation: for when he is tried, he shall receive the crown of life, which the Lord hath promised to them that love him. [KJV]<br>**Blessed** is a man who perseveres under trial; for once he has been approved, he will receive the crown of life, which the Lord has promised to those who love Him. [NASB]<br>**Blessed** is the man who perseveres under trial, because when he has stood the test, he will receive the crown of life that God has promised to those who love him. [NIV]<br>**Blessed** is the man who endures temptation; for when he has been approved, he will receive the crown of life which the Lord has promised to those who love Him. [NKJV]<br>God **blesses** the people who patiently endure testing. Afterward they will receive the crown of life that God has promised to those who love him. [NLT]<br>Μακάριος ἀνὴρ ὃς ὑπομένει πειρασμόν· ὅτι δόκιμος γενόμενος λήμψεται τὸν στέφανον τῆς ζωῆς, ὃν ἐπηγγείλατο ὁ Κύριος τοῖς ἀγαπῶσιν αὐτόν. [GNS]<br>Μακάριος ἀνὴρ ὃς ὑπομένει πειρασμόν, ὅτι δόκιμος γενόμενος λήμψεται τὸν στέφανον τῆς ζωῆς ὃν ἐπηγγείλατο τοῖς ἀγαπῶσιν αὐτόν. [GNT] | the here and now. The word *blessed* means inward and spiritual joy and satisfaction; an inner assurance and confidence that carries one through all the trials and temptations of life no matter the pain, sorrow, loss, or grief. Simply stated, the person is secure in this life. He knows that God is looking after and caring for him and is going to deliver him from all the corruption and evil of this life including death, and give him life eternal. |
| **#406<br>Blessing**<br><br>Gift–KJV<br>Gift–NASB<br>Gift–NIV<br>Gift–NKJV<br>Blessing–NLT<br><br>**POSB<br>REFERENCE**<br>(Rom.1:10-13; esp. v.11)<br>Note 4, point 1 | χάρισμα = charisma<br>Pronunciation: [khar'-is-mah]<br>Parsing (part of speech): noun<br>    Case—accusative<br>    Gender—neuter<br>    Number—singular<br>Stem or root—from χάρισμα, τος<br>Concordance References:<br>⇒ Strong's #5486 charisma<br>⇒ NIV #5922 charisma<br>⇒ NASB #5486 charisma<br><br>**Romans 1:11**<br>For I long to see you, that I may impart unto you some spiritual **gift**, to the end ye may be established; [KJV]<br>For I long to see you in order that I may impart some spiritual **gift** to you, that you may be established; [NASB]<br>I long to see you so that I may impart to you some spiritual **gift** to make you strong—[NIV]<br>For I long to see you, that I may impart to you some spiritual **gift**, so that you may be established [NKJV]<br>For I long to visit you so I can share a spiritual **blessing** with you that will help you grow strong in the Lord. [NLT]<br>ἐπιποθῶ γὰρ ἰδεῖν ὑμᾶς, ἵνα τι μεταδῶ **χάρισμα** ὑμῖν πνευματικὸν εἰς τὸ στηριχθῆναι ὑμᾶς, [GNS]<br>ἐπιποθῶ γὰρ ἰδεῖν ὑμᾶς, ἵνα τι μεταδῶ **χάρισμα** ὑμῖν πνευματικὸν εἰς τὸ στηριχθῆναι ὑμᾶς, [GNT] | A gift; a divine blessing; a gift of grace.<br><br>**Practical Application**<br>The term often refers to specific gifts given by the Holy Spirit (Romans 12:6-8), but here it means the truths of the grace of God, of His spiritual blessings to man revealed in Christ Jesus our Lord. Very simply, Paul longed to share the truths of the gospel with the believers at Rome. God's spiritual blessings were overflowing in his heart, and he was aching to share the gift of God's blessings. |
| **#407<br>Blind**<br><br>Blind–KJV<br>Blind–NASB<br>Blind–NIV<br>Blind–NKJV<br>Blind–NLT | τυφλός = tuphlos<br>Pronunciation: [toof-los']<br>Parsing (part of speech): pronominal adjective<br>    Case—nominative<br>    Gender—masculine<br>    Number—singular<br>Stem or root—from τυφλός, ή, όν<br>Concordance References:<br>⇒ Strong's #5185 tuphlos<br>⇒ NIV #5603 tuphlos<br>⇒ NASB #5185 tuphlos | To be blind.<br><br>**Practical Application**<br>The church was spiritually "blind" (*tuphlos*). They could see only what was in the world: money and human ability and effort. They did not look beyond to the spiritual need of the human soul nor to the possibility of spiritual and supernatural power working within the church and the lives of people. |

# PRACTICAL WORD STUDIES
## in the NEW TESTAMENT

| ENGLISH WORD | GREEK WORD AND VERSE | THE WORD MEANS... |
|---|---|---|
| **POSB REFERENCE** (Rev.3:16-17; esp. v.17) Note 4 | **Rev. 3:17** Because thou sayest, I am rich, and increased with goods, and have need of nothing; and knowest not that thou art wretched, and miserable, and poor, and **blind**, and naked: [KJV]<br><br>'Because you say, "I am rich, and have become wealthy, and have need of nothing," and you do not know that you are wretched and miserable and poor and **blind** and naked, [NASB]<br><br>You say, 'I am rich; I have acquired wealth and do not need a thing.' But you do not realize that you are wretched, pitiful, poor, **blind** and naked. [NIV]<br><br>Because you say, 'I am rich, have become wealthy, and have need of nothing'—and do not know that you are wretched, miserable, poor, **blind**, and naked [NKJV]<br><br>You say, 'I am rich. I have everything I want. I don't need a thing!' And you don't realize that you are wretched and miserable and poor and **blind** and naked. [NLT]<br><br>ὅτι λέγεις, ὅτι Πλούσιός εἰμι, καὶ πεπλούτηκα καὶ οὐδενὸς χρείαν ἔχω, καὶ οὐκ οἶδας ὅτι σὺ εἶ ὁ ταλαίπωρος καὶ ἐλεεινὸς καὶ πτωχὸς καὶ **τυφλὸς** καὶ γυμνός· [GNS]<br><br>ὅτι λέγεις ὅτι Πλούσιός εἰμι καὶ πεπλούτηκα καὶ οὐδὲν χρείαν ἔχω, καὶ οὐκ οἶδας ὅτι σὺ εἶ ὁ ταλαίπωρος καὶ ἐλεεινὸς καὶ πτωχὸς καὶ **τυφλὸς** καὶ γυμνός, [GNT] | |
| **#408 Blindness**<br><br>**Blindness–KJV**<br>Hardness–NASB<br>Hardening–NIV<br>**Blindness–NKJV**<br>Shut their minds and hardened–NLT<br><br>**POSB REFERENCE** (Eph.4:17-19; esp. v.18) Note 1, point 3 | πώρωσιν = *pörösin*<br>Pronunciation: [po'-ro-sin]<br>Parsing (part of speech): noun<br>    Case—accusative<br>    Gender—feminine<br>    Number—singular<br>    Stem or root—from πώρωσις, εως<br>Concordance References:<br>  ⇒ Strong's #4457 pörösis<br>  ⇒ NIV #4801 pörösis<br>  ⇒ NASB #4457 pörösis<br><br>**Ephes. 4:18**<br>Having the understanding darkened, being alienated from the life of God through the ignorance that is in them, because of the **blindness** of their heart: [KJV]<br><br>Being darkened in their understanding, excluded from the life of God, because of the ignorance that is in them, because of the **hardness** of their heart; [NASB]<br><br>They are darkened in their understanding and separated from the life of God because of the ignorance that is in them due to the **hardening** of their hearts. [NIV]<br><br>Having their understanding darkened, being alienated from the life of God, because of the ignorance that is in them, because of the **blindness** of their heart; [NKJV]<br><br>Their closed minds are full of darkness; they are far away from the life of God because they have **shut their minds and hardened** their hearts against him. [NLT]<br><br>ἐσκοτισμένοι τῇ διανοίᾳ ὄντες ἀπηλλοτριωμένοι τῆς ζωῆς τοῦ Θεοῦ διὰ τὴν ἄγνοιαν τὴν οὖσαν ἐν αὐτοῖς, διὰ τὴν **πώρωσιν** τῆς καρδίας αὐτῶν· [GNS]<br><br>ἐσκοτωμένοι τῇ διανοίᾳ ὄντες, ἀπηλλοτριωμένοι τῆς ζωῆς τοῦ θεοῦ διὰ τὴν ἄγνοιαν τὴν οὖσαν ἐν αὐτοῖς, διὰ τὴν **πώρωσιν** τῆς καρδίας αὐτῶν, [GNT] | Hardening, hardness. It is a stubbornness, a numbing, a lack of feeling.<br><br>**Practical Application**<br>Unbelievers are alienated from God because of their own willful ignorance and hardness of heart. Note the words "in them." The cause is "in them":<br>⇒ They choose to be ignorant within their minds—choose to be ignorant of God.<br>⇒ They choose to harden their own hearts.<br><br>Unbelievers are responsible for their own death. God has provided the fountain of youth for man, the way for man to live forever. God had given His life, that is, eternal life, to man. The only way man can ever miss God's gift of eternal life is to reject God and His gift. |
| **#409 Blotted Out**<br><br>**Blotted out–KJV**<br>Wiped away–NASB<br>Wiped out–NIV<br>**Blotted out–NKJV**<br>Cleansed–NLT | ἐξαλειφθῆναι = *exaleiphthēnai*<br>Pronunciation: [ex-al-eef'-thay-nah-ee]<br>Parsing (part of speech): verb<br>    Mood—infinitive<br>    Tense—aorist<br>    Voice—passive<br>    Case—accusative<br>    Stem or root—from ἐξαλείφω<br>Concordance References:<br>  ⇒ Strong's #1813 exaleiphō<br>  ⇒ NIV #1981 exaleiphō<br>  ⇒ NASB #1813 exaleiphō | Wiped out; wiped away; blotted out; cleansed; destroyed; removed; canceled.<br><br>**Practical Application**<br>It means erased, smeared out, rubbed off, wiped out, obliterated—just like handwriting is erased and wiped off a wall. |

# PRACTICAL WORD STUDIES
## in the New Testament

| ENGLISH WORD | GREEK WORD AND VERSE | THE WORD MEANS... |
|---|---|---|
| **POSB REFERENCE** (Acts 3:19) Note 7, point 1 | **Acts 3:19**<br>Repent ye therefore, and be converted, that your sins may be **blotted out**, when the times of refreshing shall come from the presence of the Lord; [KJV]<br>"Repent therefore and return, that your sins may be **wiped away**, in order that times of refreshing may come from the presence of the Lord; [NASB]<br>Repent, then, and turn to God, so that your sins may be **wiped out**, that times of refreshing may come from the Lord, [NIV]<br>Repent therefore and be converted, that your sins may be **blotted out**, so that times of refreshing may come from the presence of the Lord, [NKJV]<br>Now turn from your sins and turn to God, so you can be **cleansed** of your sins. [NLT]<br>μετανοήσατε οὖν καὶ ἐπιστρέψατε, εἰς τὸ **ἐξαλειφθῆναι** ὑμῶν τὰς ἁμαρτίας, [GNS]<br>μετανοήσατε οὖν καὶ ἐπιστρέψατε εἰς τὸ **ἐξαλειφθῆναι** ὑμῶν τὰς ἁμαρτίας, [GNT] | |
| **#410**<br>**Boast**<br>Boast–KJV<br>Boast–NASB<br>Brag about–NIV<br>Boast–NKJV<br>Boast–NLT<br><br>**POSB REFERENCE** (Rom.2:17-20; esp. v.17) Note 1, point 2 | καυχᾶσαι = *kauchasai*<br>Pronunciation: [kow-khah'-sahee]<br>Parsing (part of speech): verb<br>   Mood—indicative<br>   Tense—present<br>   Voice—middle or passive deponent<br>   Person—2nd person<br>   Number—singular<br>   Stem or root—from καυχάομαι<br>Concordance References:<br>   ⇒ Strong's #2744 kauchaomai<br>   ⇒ NIV #3016 kauchaomai<br>   ⇒ NASB #2744 kauchaomai<br><br>**Romans 2:17**<br>Behold, thou art called a Jew, and restest in the law, and makest thy **boast** of God, [KJV]<br>But if you bear the name "Jew," and rely upon the Law, and **boast** in God, [NASB]<br>Now you, if you call yourself a Jew; if you rely on the law and **brag about** your relationship to God; [NIV]<br>Indeed you are called a Jew, and rest on the law, and make your **boast** in God, [NKJV]<br>If you are a Jew, you are relying on God's law for your special relationship with him. You **boast** that all is well between yourself and God. [NLT]<br>Ἴδε σὺ Ἰουδαῖος ἐπονομάζῃ καὶ ἐπαναπαύῃ τῷ νόμῳ, καὶ **καυχᾶσαι** ἐν Θεῷ, [GNS]<br>Εἰ δὲ σὺ Ἰουδαῖος ἐπονομάζῃ καὶ ἐπαναπαύῃ νόμῳ καὶ **καυχᾶσαι** ἐν θεῷ [GNT] | To brag about; to boast; to glory; to take pride in; to feel proud about one's profession of God and religion.<br><br>**Practical Application**<br>The idea is that one openly professes that he believes in God. He is not ashamed of his belief and religious affiliation. He believes in God, and he feels safe and secure in his belief. He confesses God, and he feels that God accepts him because of his profession.<br>However, this is the mistake of the religionist. God is not interested in a man's profession but in a man's life. God wants a man's living for Him, not just professing and talking about Him. |
| **#411**<br>**Boast–Boastful**<br>Vaunteth–KJV<br>Brag–NASB<br>Boast–NIV<br>Parade–NKJV<br>Boastful–NLT<br><br>**POSB REFERENCE** (1 Cor.13:4-7; esp. v.4) Note 2, point 4 | περπερεύεται = *perpereuetai*<br>Pronunciation: [per-per-yoo'-eh-tah-ee]<br>Parsing (part of speech): verb<br>   Mood—indicative<br>   Tense—present<br>   Voice—middle or passive deponent<br>   Person—3rd person<br>   Number—singular<br>   Stem or root—from περπερεύομαι<br>Concordance References:<br>   ⇒ Strong's #4068 perpereuomai<br>   ⇒ NIV #4371 perpereuomai<br>   ⇒ NASB #4068 perpereuomai<br><br>**1 Cor. 13:4**<br>Charity suffereth long, and is kind; charity envieth not; charity **vaunteth** not itself, is not puffed up, [KJV]<br>Love is patient, love is kind, and is not jealous; love does not **brag** and is not arrogant, [NASB]<br>Love is patient, love is kind. It does not envy, it does not **boast**, it is not proud. [NIV] | To boast; to brag; to be boastful; to be conceited.<br><br>**Practical Application**<br>Love does not boast (*perpereuetai*): is not boastful; does not brag nor seek recognition, honor, or applause from others. On the contrary, love seeks to give: to recognize, to honor, to applaud the other person. |

# PRACTICAL WORD STUDIES
## in the NEW TESTAMENT

| ENGLISH WORD | GREEK WORD AND VERSE | THE WORD MEANS... |
|---|---|---|
| | Love suffers long and is kind; love does not envy; love does not **parade** itself, is not puffed up; [NKJV]<br>Love is patient and kind. Love is not jealous or **boastful** or proud [NLT]<br>ἡ ἀγάπη μακροθυμεῖ, χρηστεύεται· ἡ ἀγάπη, οὐ ζηλοῖ· ἡ ἀγάπη οὐ **περπερεύεται**, οὐ φυσιοῦται, [GNS]<br>Ἡ ἀγάπη μακροθυμεῖ, χρηστεύεται ἡ ἀγάπη, οὐ ζηλοῖ, [ἡ ἀγάπη] οὐ **περπερεύεται**, οὐ φυσιοῦται, [GNT] | |
| **#412**<br>**Boast–**<br>**Boasting**<br><br>Glorying–KJV<br>**Boasting–NASB**<br>**Boasting–NIV**<br>Glorying–NKJV<br>**Boast–NLT**<br><br>**POSB**<br>**REFERENCE**<br>(1 Cor.5:6)<br>Note 1 | καύχημα = kauchēma<br>Pronunciation: [kow'-khay-mah]<br>Parsing (part of speech): noun<br>   Case—nominative<br>   Gender—neuter<br>   Number—singular<br>   Stem or root—from καύχημα, τος<br>Concordance References:<br>  ⇒ Strong's #2745 kauchēma<br>  ⇒ NIV #3017 kauchēma<br>  ⇒ NASB #2745 kauchēma<br><br>**1 Cor. 5:6**<br>Your **glorying** is not good. Know ye not that a little leaveneth the whole lump? [KJV]<br>Your **boasting** is not good. Do you not know that a little leaven leavens the whole lump of dough? [NASB]<br>Your **boasting** is not good. Don't you know that a little yeast works through the whole batch of dough? [NIV]<br>Your **glorying** is not good. Do you not know that a little leaven leavens the whole lump? [NKJV]<br>How terrible that you should **boast** about your spirituality, and yet you let this sort of thing go on. Don't you realize that if even one person is allowed to go on sinning, soon all will be affected? [NLT]<br>Οὐ καλὸν τὸ **καύχημα** ὑμῶν. οὐκ οἴδατε ὅτι μικρὰ ζύμη ὅλον τὸ φύραμα ζυμοῖ; [GNS]<br>Οὐ καλὸν τὸ **καύχημα** ὑμῶν. οὐκ οἴδατε ὅτι μικρὰ ζύμη ὅλον τὸ φύραμα ζυμοῖ; [GNT] | Boasting, glorying, taking pride in.<br><br>**Practical Application**<br>It means that some believers in the Corinthian Church were boasting, glorying, and taking pride in the man despite the known fact of his sin. Perhaps he was a man of outstanding leadership in the community or the city of Corinth. Perhaps he had become a leader of one of the factions in the church. Whatever the case, the church overlooked his sin and took great pride in the fact that a man of his stature would join and become a part of their fellowship. |
| **#413**<br>**Boasters–**<br>**Boastful**<br><br>Boasters–KJV<br>**Boastful–NASB**<br>**Boastful–NIV**<br>Boasters–NKJV<br>**Boastful–NLT**<br><br>**POSB**<br>**REFERENCE**<br>(Rom.1:30)<br>*Deeper Study* #16<br><br>See also POSB REF:<br>(2 Tim.3:2-4; esp. v.2)<br>Note 2, point 3 | ἀλαζόνας = alazonas<br>Pronunciation: [al-ad-zone'-ahs]<br>Parsing (part of speech): noun<br>   Case—accusative<br>   Gender—masculine<br>   Number—plural<br>   Stem or root—from ἀλαζών, ονος<br>Concordance References:<br>  ⇒ Strong's #213 alazōn<br>  ⇒ NIV #225 alazōn<br>  ⇒ NASB #213 alazōn<br><br>**Romans 1:30**<br>Backbiters, haters of God, despiteful, proud, **boasters**, inventors of evil things, disobedient to parents, [KJV]<br>Slanderers, haters of God, insolent, arrogant, **boastful**, inventors of evil, disobedient to parents, [NASB]<br>Slanderers, God-haters, insolent, arrogant and **boastful**; they invent ways of doing evil; they disobey their parents; [NIV]<br>Backbiters, haters of God, violent, proud, **boasters**, inventors of evil things, disobedient to parents, [NKJV]<br>They are backstabbers, haters of God, insolent, proud, and **boastful**. They are forever inventing new ways of sinning and are disobedient to their parents. [NLT]<br>ψιθυριστάς, καταλάλους, θεοστυγεῖς, ὑβριστάς, ὑπερηφάνους, **ἀλαζόνας**, ἐφευρετὰς κακῶν, γονεῦσιν ἀπειθεῖς, [GNS]<br>καταλάλους θεοστυγεῖς ὑβριστὰς ὑπερηφάνους **ἀλαζόνας**, ἐφευρετὰς κακῶν, γονεῦσιν ἀπειθεῖς, [GNT] | Boastful, boasters, braggarts, pretenders, vaunters, swaggerts; to be arrogant.<br><br>**Practical Application**<br>It is a person who...<br>• boasts in what he has.<br>• boasts in what he can do.<br>• pretends to have what he does not have or pretends to have done what he has not done.<br><br>Bragging may involve a job, a deal, a possession, an achievement—anything that may impress others. It is a person who feels the need to push himself above others even if it involves *pretension, deception, make believe,* or *lies*.<br>⇒ The world is full of boasters and braggarts: teachers who pretend to be wise.<br>⇒ politicians who pretend to know the way to the utopian state.<br>⇒ business people who pretend to have the product that brings health, beauty, and happiness.<br>⇒ religionists who pretend to have the revelation and gifts and to be more spiritual than others. |

# Practical Word Studies
## in the New Testament

| ENGLISH WORD | GREEK WORD AND VERSE | THE WORD MEANS... |
|---|---|---|
| **#414**<br>**Boastings**<br><br>Boastings–KJV<br>Arrogance–NASB<br>Brag–NIV<br>Arrogance–NKJV<br>Your own plans–NLT<br><br>**POSB REFERENCE**<br>(Jas.4:16)<br>Note 4 | ἐν ταῖς ἀλαζονείαις = *en tais alazoneiais*<br>Pronunciation: [en tace al-ad-zon-i'-ah-is]<br>Parsing *alazoneiais* (part of speech): noun<br>    Case—dative<br>    Gender—feminine<br>    Number—plural<br>    Stem or root—from ἀλαζονεία, ας<br>Concordance References:<br>⇒ Strong's #212+1722+3588 alazoneia en ho<br>⇒ NIV #224+1877+3836 alazoneia en ho [brag]<br>⇒ NASB #212+1722+3588 alazoneia en ho<br><br>**James 4:16**<br>But now ye rejoice in your **boastings**: all such rejoicing is evil. [KJV]<br>But as it is, you boast in your **arrogance**; all such boasting is evil. [NASB]<br>As it is, you boast and **brag**. All such boasting is evil. [NIV]<br>But now you boast in your **arrogance**. All such boasting is evil. [NKJV]<br>Otherwise you will be boasting about **your own plans**, and all such boasting is evil. [NLT]<br>νῦν δὲ καυχᾶσθε ἐν ταῖς ἀλαζονείαις ὑμῶν· πᾶσα καύχησις τοιαύτη πονηρά ἐστιν. [GNS]<br>νῦν δὲ καυχᾶσθε ἐν ταῖς ἀλαζονείαις ὑμῶν· πᾶσα καύχησις τοιαύτη πονηρά ἐστιν. [GNT] | To brag; to boast; to be proud of; to be arrogant.<br><br>**Practical Application**<br>The word "boastings" (*alazoniais*) means an empty boaster (A.T. Robertson. *Word Pictures in the New Testament*, Vol. 6, p.56). That is, it is a person who boasts about something he thinks he has, but he does not really have it. He lives in an unreal world. Any person who goes through life without God is just like this. He lives and plans, thinking that he controls his life and the future. His life is one big boast of self-sufficiency, and it is wrong, totally wrong. A thousand things can happen to change his plans—to injure him or to radically change his life and work, or to snatch his life right out of this world.<br>Most people—laymen and ministers alike—boast of their work, what they have done, their abilities and possessions. But note a fact seldom thought about: most boasting is not done by word of mouth. It is done by the way we live. We boast by flaunting our abilities and successes through our possessions and activities such as expensive houses, clothes and cars, exclusive clubs, friendships, and recreation.<br>We have an urge, a tendency to boast and to be seen and recognized as better and more successful than others. And note what Scripture says: we rejoice in our boastings—that we are more successful in our work than some others. But such boastings—such pride and arrogance—are evil. Why? Because a man's ability and life are due to God and rest in the hands of God. And in addition to this: the future—tomorrow and even one hour from now—is in the hands of God. It may be a heart attack—it may be a thief—it may be an accident—it is all in the hands of God. What a person needs to do is trust God and commit all his ways into the hands of God, acknowledging Him in all things and at every turn of every day. |
| **#415**<br>**Body**<br><br>Vessel–KJV<br>Vessel–NASB<br>**Body–NIV**<br>Vessel–NKJV<br>**Body–NLT**<br><br>**POSB REFERENCE**<br>(1 Thes.4:3-5; esp. v.4)<br>Note 2, point 2 | σκεῦος = *skeuos*<br>Pronunciation: [skyoo'-os]<br>Parsing (part of speech): noun<br>    Case—accusative<br>    Gender—neuter<br>    Number—singular<br>    Stem or root—<br>Concordance References:<br>⇒ Strong's #4632 skeuos<br>⇒ NIV #5007 skeuos<br>⇒ NASB #4632 skeuos<br><br>**1 Thes. 4:4**<br>That every one of you should know how to possess his **vessel** in sanctification and honour; [KJV]<br>That each of you know how to possess his own **vessel** in sanctification and honor, [NASB]<br>That each of you should learn to control his own **body** in a way that is holy and honorable, [NIV]<br>That each of you should know how to possess his own **vessel** in sanctification and honor, [NKJV]<br>Then each of you will control your **body** and live in holiness and honor—[NLT]<br>εἰδέναι ἕκαστον ὑμῶν τὸ ἑαυτοῦ **σκεῦος** κτᾶσθαι ἐν ἁγιασμῷ καὶ τιμῇ [GNS]<br>εἰδέναι ἕκαστον ὑμῶν τὸ ἑαυτοῦ **σκεῦος** κτᾶσθαι ἐν ἁγιασμῷ καὶ τιμῇ, [GNT] | Body, vessel.<br><br>**Practical Application**<br>Sanctification means that a person knows how to control his body and his spouse. Leon Morris points out that the word body or "vessel" (*skeuos*) can refer either to a person's own body or to a person's spouse (*The Epistles of Paul to the Thessalonians*. "Tyndale New Testament Commentaries," ed. by RVG Tasker. Grand Rapids, MI: Eerdmans, 1956, p.75). Both hold great meaning for the Christian believer. A believer is to know how to control his own body and how to control his spouse. A person can neglect, ignore, and abuse his body and a person can neglect, ignore, and abuse his or her spouse. In discussing a person's spouse, it is important to note 1 Cor. 7:4-5. Neglecting, ignoring, or abusing one's spouse can bring about temptation and can contribute significantly to the spouse's becoming unfaithful and impure.<br>Note that the believer is to *learn how to control*, to possess his or her body and spouse in a way that is holy and honorable. There is no excuse for ignorance in this matter nor for disobedience. The believer is to learn that it is his |

## PRACTICAL WORD STUDIES
### in the New Testament

| ENGLISH WORD | GREEK WORD AND VERSE | THE WORD MEANS... |
|---|---|---|
| | | duty to keep his body and spouse pure, learn this...<br>• beyond a shadow of a doubt<br>• without equivocation<br>• without question<br><br>The point is strong: it is unthinkable that a believer would engage in sexual immorality, that he would bring dishonor to his Lord and to his spouse, family, and himself. The believing husband and wife are to know that they must keep themselves and each other in sanctification and honor. They must not give themselves to dishonorable and immoral neighbors nor to harlots. |
| **#416**<br>**Bold–**<br>**Boldness**<br><br>**Bold**–KJV<br>**Boldness**–NASB<br>Dared–NIV<br>**Bold**–NKJV<br>Courage–NLT<br><br>**POSB**<br>**REFERENCE**<br>(1 Thes.2:2)<br>Note 2 | ἐπαρρησιασάμεθα = *eparrēsiasametha*<br>Pronunciation: [ep-ar-hray-see-ahs-ah-meh-tha]<br>Parsing (part of speech): verb<br>    Mood—indicative<br>    Tense—aorist<br>    Voice—middle deponent<br>    Person—1st person<br>    Number—plural<br>    Stem or root—from παρρησιάζομαι<br>Concordance References:<br>  ⇒ Strong's #3955 parrēsiazomai<br>  ⇒ NIV #4245 parrēsiazomai<br>  ⇒ NASB #3955 parrēsiazomai<br><br>**1 Thes. 2:2**<br>But even after that we had suffered before, and were shamefully entreated, as ye know, at Philippi, we were **bold** in our God to speak unto you the gospel of God with much contention. [KJV]<br>But after we had already suffered and been mistreated in Philippi, as you know, we had the **boldness** in our God to speak to you the gospel of God amid much opposition. [NASB]<br>We had previously suffered and been insulted in Philippi, as you know, but with the help of our God we **dared** to tell you his gospel in spite of strong opposition. [NIV]<br>But even after we had suffered before and were spitefully treated at Philippi, as you know, we were **bold** in our God to speak to you the gospel of God in much conflict. [NKJV]<br>You know how badly we had been treated at Philippi just before we came to you and how much we suffered there. Yet our God gave us the **courage** to declare his Good News to you boldly, even though we were surrounded by many who opposed us. [NLT]<br>ἀλλὰ καὶ προπαθόντες καὶ ὑβρισθέντες, καθὼς οἴδατε, ἐν Φιλίπποις, **ἐπαρρησιασάμεθα** ἐν τῷ Θεῷ ἡμῶν λαλῆσαι πρὸς ὑμᾶς τὸ εὐαγγέλιον τοῦ Θεοῦ ἐν πολλῷ ἀγῶνι. [GNS]<br>ἀλλὰ προπαθόντες καὶ ὑβρισθέντες, καθὼς οἴδατε, ἐν Φιλίπποις **ἐπαρρησιασάμεθα** ἐν τῷ θεῷ ἡμῶν λαλῆσαι πρὸς ὑμᾶς τὸ εὐαγγέλιον, τοῦ θεοῦ ἐν πολλῷ ἀγῶνι. [GNT] | Boldness, courage, daring. It means to speak boldly and freely; to speak out and to speak publicly without fear.<br><br>**Practical Application**<br>Too many fail to witness for Christ because they fear ridicule, embarrassment, mockery, and persecution. They are secret believers of Christ instead of bold witnesses for Christ. |
| **#417**<br>**Boldness–**<br>**Boldly**<br><br>**Boldness**–KJV<br>Confidence–NASB<br>Confidence–NIV<br>**Boldness**–NKJV<br>**Boldly**–NLT | παρρησίαν = *parrēsian*<br>Pronunciation: [par-rhay-see'-ahn]<br>Parsing (part of speech): noun<br>    Case—accusative<br>    Gender—feminine<br>    Number—singular<br>    Stem or root—from παρρησία, ας<br>Concordance References:<br>  ⇒ Strong's #3954 parrēsia<br>  ⇒ NIV #4244 parrēsia<br>  ⇒ NASB #3954 parrēsia | Confidence, boldness, unshakable assurance.<br><br>**Practical Application**<br>The word "boldness" (*parrēsian*) means to enter God's presence freely and openly, with confidence and assurance. Just imagine...<br>• being able to enter the presence of God freely and openly.<br>• knowing God personally and intimately.<br>• fellowshipping and communing with God.<br>• having God guide and direct, look after and care for, provide and protect, strengthen |

# PRACTICAL WORD STUDIES
## in the NEW TESTAMENT

| ENGLISH WORD | GREEK WORD AND VERSE | THE WORD MEANS... |
|---|---|---|
| **POSB REFERENCE** (Heb.10:19-20; esp. v.19) Note 1 | **Hebrews 10:19**<br>Having therefore, brethren, **boldness** to enter into the holiest by the blood of Jesus, [KJV]<br>Since therefore, brethren, we have **confidence** to enter the holy place by the blood of Jesus, [NASB]<br>Therefore, brothers, since we have **confidence** to enter the Most Holy Place by the blood of Jesus, [NIV]<br>Therefore, brethren, having **boldness** to enter the Holiest by the blood of Jesus, [NKJV]<br>And so, dear brothers and sisters, we can **boldly** enter heaven's Most Holy Place because of the blood of Jesus. [NLT]<br>Ἔχοντες οὖν, ἀδελφοί, **παρρησίαν** εἰς τὴν εἴσοδον τῶν ἁγίων ἐν τῷ αἵματι Ἰησοῦ, [GNS]<br>Ἔχοντες οὖν, ἀδελφοί, **παρρησίαν** εἰς τὴν εἴσοδον τῶν ἁγίων ἐν τῷ αἵματι Ἰησοῦ, [GNT] | and deliver us with joy, rejoicing, assurance, confidence, and victory over all the trials and temptations in life.<br>Imagine having God take care of one's life like that. This is what the new and living faith is: it is *boldness* to enter God's presence, to know God intimately and personally, experiencing His fellowship, presence, and power all the time. It is living and moving and having our being in God.<br>How is this possible? How can a person know God so personally and intimately? By the blood of Jesus Christ. The death of Jesus Christ opened up a new and living way for us to approach God. It opened up a way that brings us right into the holiest place of all, into the very presence of God. |
| **#418**<br>**Bond Servant–Bondservant**<br><br>Servant–KJV<br>**Bond-servant–NASB**<br>Servant–NIV<br>**Bondservant–NKJV**<br>Slave–NLT<br><br>**POSB REFERENCE**<br>(Jas 1:1)<br>Note 1, point 1<br><br>**See also POSB REF:**<br>(Romans 1:1)<br>Note 1<br>(2 Cor.4:5)<br>Note 4<br>(Gal.1:10)<br>Note 1<br>(Philip.1:1)<br>Note 2<br>(2 Pt.1:1)<br>Note 1, point 1 | δοῦλος = *doulos*<br>Pronunciation: [doo'-los]<br>Parsing (part of speech): noun<br>  Case—nominative<br>  Gender—masculine<br>  Number—singular<br>Stem or root—from δοῦλος, η, ον<br>Concordance References:<br>⇒ Strong's #1401 doulos<br>⇒ NIV #1528 doulos1<br>⇒ NASB #1401 doulos<br><br>**James 1:1**<br>James, a **servant** of God and of the Lord Jesus Christ, to the twelve tribes which are scattered abroad, greeting. [KJV]<br>James, a **bond-servant** of God and of the Lord Jesus Christ, to the twelve tribes who are dispersed abroad, greetings. [NASB]<br>James, a **servant** of God and of the Lord Jesus Christ, To the twelve tribes scattered among the nations: Greetings. [NIV]<br>James, a **bondservant** of God and of the Lord Jesus Christ,To the twlve tribes which are scattered abroad:Greetings. [NKJV]<br>This letter is from James, a **slave** of God and of the Lord Jesus Christ.It is written to Jewish Christians scattered among the nations.Greetings! [NLT]<br>Ἰάκωβος, Θεοῦ καὶ Κυρίου Ἰησοῦ Χριστοῦ **δοῦλος**, ταῖς δώδεκα φυλαῖς ταῖς ἐν τῇ διασπορᾷ, χαίρειν. [GNS]<br>Ἰάκωβος θεοῦ καὶ κυρίου Ἰησοῦ Χριστοῦ **δοῦλος** ταῖς δώδεκα φυλαῖς ταῖς ἐν τῇ διασπορᾷ χαίρειν. [GNT] | To be a servant; to be a bond-servant; to be as a slave.<br><br>**Practical Application**<br>The word "bond-servant" (*doulos*) in the Greek means far more than just a servant. It means a slave totally possessed by the master. It means a *bond-servant* bound by law to a master. A look at the slave market of James's day shows more clearly what James meant when he said he was a "slave of Jesus Christ."<br>1. The slave was owned by his master; he was totally possessed by his master. This is what James meant. James was purchased and possessed by Christ, the Son of the living God. Christ had looked upon him and had seen his rebellious and needful condition. And when Christ looked, the most wonderful thing happened: Christ loved him and bought him; therefore, he was now the possession of Christ.<br>2. The slave existed for his master, and he had no other reason for existence. He had no personal rights whatsoever. The same was true with James: he existed only for Christ. His rights were the rights of Christ only.<br>3. The slave served his master, and he existed only for the purpose of service. He was at the master's disposal any hour of the day. So it was with James: he lived only to serve Christ—hour by hour and day by day.<br>4. The slave's will belonged to his master. He was allowed no will and no ambition other than the will and ambition of the master. He was completely subservient to the master, owing total obedience to the will of the master. James belonged to Christ. In fact, he fought and struggled to bring "every thought into captivity to the obedience of Christ" (2 Cor. 10:3-5, esp. 2 Cor. 10:5).<br>5. There is a fifth and most precious thing that James meant by "a slave of Jesus Christ." He meant that he had the highest and most honored and kingly profession in all the world. Men of God, the greatest men of history, have always been called "the servants of God." It was the highest title of honor. The believer's slavery to Jesus Christ is no cringing, cowardly, shameful subjection. It is the position of honor—the honor that bestows upon a man the privileges and responsibilities of serving the King of kings and Lord of lords. |

# PRACTICAL WORD STUDIES
## in the NEW TESTAMENT

| ENGLISH WORD | GREEK WORD AND VERSE | THE WORD MEANS... |
|---|---|---|
| **#419**<br>**Bond-Servants**<br><br>Servants–KJV<br>**Bond-servants–NASB**<br>Servants–NIV<br>Servants–NKJV<br>Servants–NLT<br><br>**POSB REFERENCE**<br>(Acts 4:29-30; esp. v.29)<br>Note 4, point 1c | δούλοις = *doulois*<br>Pronunciation: [doo'-lo-ees]<br>Parsing (part of speech): noun<br>    Case—dative<br>    Gender—masculine<br>    Number—plural<br>    Stem or root—from δοῦλος, η, ον<br>Concordance References:<br>  ⇒ Strong's #1401 *doulos*<br>  ⇒ NIV #1528 *doulos*1<br>  ⇒ NASB #1401 *doulos*<br><br>**Acts 4:29**<br>And now, Lord, behold their threatenings: and grant unto thy **servants**, that with all boldness they may speak thy word, [KJV]<br>"And now, Lord, take note of their threats, and grant that Thy **bond-servants** may speak Thy word with all confidence, [NASB]<br>Now, Lord, consider their threats and enable your **servants** to speak your word with great boldness. [NIV]<br>Now, Lord, look on their threats, and grant to Your **servants** that with all boldness they may speak Your word, [NKJV]<br>And now, O Lord, hear their threats, and give your **servants** great boldness in their preaching. [NLT]<br>καὶ τὰ νῦν, Κύριε, ἔπιδε ἐπὶ τὰς ἀπειλὰς αὐτῶν, καὶ δὸς τοῖς **δούλοις** σου μετὰ παρρησίας πάσης λαλεῖν τὸν λόγον σου, [GNS]<br>καὶ τὰ νῦν, κύριε, ἔπιδε ἐπὶ τὰς ἀπειλὰς αὐτῶν καὶ δὸς τοῖς **δούλοις** σου μετὰ παρρησίας πάσης λαλεῖν τὸν λόγον σου, [GNT] | To be a servant; to be a bond-servant; to be as a slave.<br><br>**Practical Application**<br>The word "bond-servants" (*doulois*) is the word for bond-slaves. The church was saying that they were the bond-servants of the Lord, to do His will, to share and speak God's Word despite persecution. |
| **#420**<br>**Bondslave**<br><br>Handmaid–KJV<br>**Bondslave–NASB**<br>Servant–NIV<br>Maidservant–NKJV<br>Servant–NLT<br><br>**POSB REFERENCE**<br>(Lk.1:38)<br>Note 8 | δούλη = *doulë*<br>Pronunciation: [doo'-lay]<br>Parsing (part of speech): noun<br>    Case—nominative<br>    Gender—feminine<br>    Number—singular<br>    Stem or root—from δούλη, ης<br>Concordance References:<br>  ⇒ Strong's #1399 *doulë*<br>  ⇒ NIV #1527 *doulë*<br>  ⇒ NASB #1399 *doulë*<br><br>**Luke 1:38**<br>And Mary said, Behold the **handmaid** of the Lord; be it unto me according to thy word. And the angel departed from her. [KJV]<br>And Mary said, "Behold, the **bondslave** of the Lord; be it done to me according to your word." And the angel departed from her. [NASB]<br>"I am the Lord's **servant**," Mary answered. "May it be to me as you have said." Then the angel left her. [NIV]<br>Then Mary said, "Behold the **maidservant** of the Lord! Let it be to me according to your word." And the angel departed from her. [NKJV]<br>Mary responded, "I am the Lord's **servant**, and I am willing to accept whatever he wants. May everything you have said come true." And then the angel left. [NLT]<br>εἶπε δὲ Μαριάμ, Ἰδοὺ ἡ **δούλη** Κυρίου· γένοιτό μοι κατὰ τὸ ῥῆμά σου. καὶ ἀπῆλθεν ἀπ' αὐτῆς ὁ ἄγγελος. [GNS]<br>εἶπεν δὲ Μαριάμ, Ἰδοὺ ἡ **δούλη** κυρίου· γένοιτό μοι κατὰ τὸ ῥῆμά σου. καὶ ἀπῆλθεν ἀπ' αὐτῆς ὁ ἄγγελος. [GNT] | Slave girl; a handmaid; a maidservant; a female servant; a bondslave.<br><br>**Practical Application**<br>Mary was saying that she was a bondslave, willing to sell herself out completely to God. She would possess herself no longer but would give herself completely to God. |
| **#421**<br>**Bore**<br><br>Bare–KJV<br>Carried–NASB | ἐβάστασεν = *ebastasen*<br>Pronunciation: [e-bas-ta'-sen]<br>Parsing (part of speech): verb<br>    Mood—indicative<br>    Tense—aorist<br>    Voice—active | To bear; to endure; to take up; to carry; to support; to sustain; to remove; to tolerate.<br><br>**Practical Application**<br>In this Scripture, Christ did not just heal our |

# PRACTICAL WORD STUDIES
## in the NEW TESTAMENT

| ENGLISH WORD | GREEK WORD AND VERSE | THE WORD MEANS... |
|---|---|---|
| Carried–NIV<br>**Bore–NKJV**<br>Removed–NLT<br><br>**POSB REFERENCE**<br>(Mt.8:17)<br>Note 3 | Person—3rd person<br>Number—singular<br>Stem or root—from βαστάζω<br>Concordance References:<br>⇒ Strong's #941 bastazō<br>⇒ NIV #1002 bastazō<br>⇒ NASB #941 bastazō<br><br>**Matthew 8:17**<br>That it might be fulfilled which was spoken by Esaias the prophet, saying, Himself took our infirmities, and **bare** our sicknesses. [KJV]<br>In order that what was spoken through Isaiah the prophet might be fulfilled, saying, "He Himself took our infirmities, and **CARRIED** AWAY OUR DISEASES." [NASB]<br>This was to fulfill what was spoken through the prophet Isaiah: "He took up our infirmities and **carried** our diseases." [NIV]<br>That it might be fulfilled which was spoken by Isaiah the prophet, saying: "He Himself took our infirmities And **bore** our sicknesses." [NKJV]<br>This fulfilled the word of the Lord through Isaiah, who said, "He took our sicknesses and **removed** our diseases." [NLT]<br>ὅπως πληρωθῇ τὸ ῥηθὲν διὰ Ἡσαΐου τοῦ προφήτου, λέγοντος, Αὐτὸς τὰς ἀσθενείας ἡμῶν ἔλαβε, καὶ τὰς νόσους **ἐβάστασεν**. [GNS]<br>ὅπως πληρωθῇ τὸ ῥηθὲν διὰ Ἡσαΐου τοῦ προφήτου λέγοντος, Αὐτὸς τὰς ἀσθενείας ἡμῶν ἔλαβεν καὶ τὰς νόσους **ἐβάστασεν**. [GNT] | sicknesses as any other minister, but He "Himself took [*elaben*] our infirmities, and bore [*ebastasen*] our sicknesses." This means at least two things.<br>1. He carried our infirmities and sicknesses to the ultimate degree when He died on the cross for us. It was there that He bore them (see POSB *Deeper Study* #2—Mt.8:17 for discussion). (Cp. Jn.1:29.)<br>2. He carried each fresh illness in a way that will never be understood.<br>  a. Each need that stood before Him was a reminder that He had to bear the sin of the world. And He knew what this meant and all that it was to include. Seeing the needs of men standing before Him reminded Him of the suffering He was to bear.<br>  b. Each need that He met was a foretaste of the cross. The thought of what He had to bear was upon His mind day by day and hour by hour as He went about ministering. This was bound to weigh ever so heavily upon Him. |
| #422<br>**Born Of A Woman**<br><br>Made of a woman–KJV<br><br>**Born of a woman–NASB**<br><br>**Born of a woman–NIV**<br><br>**Born of a woman–NKJV**<br><br>**Born of a woman–NLT**<br><br>**POSB REFERENCE**<br>(Gal.4:4-7; esp. v.4)<br>Note 2 | γενόμενον ἐκ γυναικός = genomenon ek gunaikos<br>Pronunciation: [ghin'-om-eh-non ek goo-nee-kos]<br>Parsing *genomenon* (part of speech): verb<br>  Mood—participle<br>  Tense—aorist<br>  Voice—middle deponent<br>  Case—accusative<br>  Gender—masculine<br>  Number—singular<br>  Stem or root—from γίνομαι<br>Parsing *ek* (part of speech): preposition<br>  Case—genitive<br>  Stem or root—from ἐκ<br>Parsing *gunaikos* (part of speech): noun<br>  Case—genitive<br>  Gender—feminine<br>  Number—singular<br>  Stem or root—from γυνή, αικός<br>Concordance References:<br>⇒ Strong's #1096 ginomai + 1537 ek + 1135 gunē<br>⇒ NIV #1181 ginomai [born] + 1666 ek [of] + 1222 gunē [woman]<br>⇒ NASB #1096 ginomai + 1537 ek + 1135 gunē<br><br>**Galatians 4:4**<br>But when the fulness of the time was come, God sent forth his Son, **made of a woman**, made under the law, [KJV]<br>But when the fulness of the time came, God sent forth His Son, **born of a woman**, born under the Law, [NASB]<br>But when the time had fully come, God sent his Son, **born of a woman**, born under law, [NIV]<br>But when the fullness of the time had come, God sent forth His Son, **born of a woman**, born under the law, [NKJV]<br>But when the right time came, God sent his Son, **born of a woman**, subject to the law. [NLT]<br>ὅτε δὲ ἦλθε τὸ πλήρωμα τοῦ χρόνου, ἐξαπέστειλεν ὁ Θεὸς τὸν υἱὸν αὐτοῦ, **γενόμενον ἐκ γυναικός**, γενόμενον ὑπὸ νόμον, [GNS]<br>ὅτε δὲ ἦλθεν τὸ πλήρωμα τοῦ χρόνου, ἐξαπέστειλεν ὁ θεὸς τὸν υἱὸν αὐτοῦ, **γενόμενον ἐκ γυναικός**, γενόμενον ὑπὸ νόμον, [GNT] | Born of a woman; made of a woman.<br><br>**Practical Application**<br>Christ came into the world just as all men do, through a woman. But note the most glorious truth: He was "sent" by God. Jesus Christ was "His Son," the Son of God. God spoke the Word and the woman conceived miraculously. The Virgin Birth did take place: God's very own Son has been sent into the world *as a man* to save people. (See POSB *Deeper Study* #3, Jesus Christ, Birth—Matthew 1:16; POSB *Deeper Study* #8—Matthew 1:23; POSB note—Luke 1:27 and POSB *Deeper Study* #1—Luke 1:27; POSB note—Luke 1:34-35. Especially see Luke 1:27.) |

# PRACTICAL WORD STUDIES
## in the NEW TESTAMENT

| ENGLISH WORD | GREEK WORD AND VERSE | THE WORD MEANS... |
|---|---|---|
| **#423**<br>**Bothered**<br><br>Troubled–KJV<br>**Bothered–NASB**<br>Upset–NIV<br>Troubled–NKJV<br>Upset–NLT<br><br>**POSB REFERENCE**<br>(Lk.10:41-42; esp. v.41)<br>Note 4, point 2 | θορυβάζῃ = thorubazë<br>Pronunciation: [tho-ru-bad'-zay]<br>Parsing (part of speech): verb<br>    Mood—indicative<br>    Tense—present<br>    Voice—passive<br>    Person—2nd person<br>    Number—singular<br>    Stem or root—from θορυβάζω<br>Concordance References:<br>  ⇒ Strong's #5182 thorubazö<br>  ⇒ NIV #2571 thorubazö<br>  ⇒ NASB #2350a thorubazö<br><br>**Luke 10:41**<br>And Jesus answered and said unto her, Martha, Martha, thou art careful and **troubled** about many things: [KJV]<br>But the Lord answered and said to her, "Martha, Martha, you are worried and **bothered** about so many things; [NASB]<br>"Martha, Martha," the Lord answered, "you are worried and **upset** about many things, [NIV]<br>And Jesus answered and said to her, "Martha, Martha, you are worried and **troubled** about many things. [NKJV]<br>But the Lord said to her, "My dear Martha, you are so **upset** over all these details! [NLT]<br>ἀποκριθεὶς δὲ εἶπεν αὐτῇ ὁ Ἰησοῦς, Μάρθα Μάρθα, μεριμνᾷς καὶ **τυρβάζῃ** περὶ πολλά· [GNS]<br>ἀποκριθεὶς δὲ εἶπεν αὐτῇ ὁ κύριος, Μάρθα Μάρθα, μεριμνᾷς καὶ **θορυβάζῃ** περὶ πολλά, [GNT] | To be upset; to be bothered; to be troubled; to be disturbed, agitated, in turmoil, stirred up, ruffled.<br><br>**Practical Application**<br>In this Scripture, Martha sought to please Jesus with her service and ministering, but two things were wrong.<br>⇒ She was looking after "many things," too many. She was trying to do too much for so many.<br>⇒ She had become anxious and troubled. |
| **#424**<br>**Bought**<br><br>Bought–KJV<br>Bought–NASB<br>Bought–NIV<br>Bought–NKJV<br>Bought–NLT<br><br>**POSB REFERENCE**<br>(1 Cor.6:20)<br>Deeper Study #2 | ἠγοράσθητε = ëgorasthëte<br>Pronunciation: [ayg-or-ahs'-thay-teh]<br>Parsing (part of speech): verb<br>    Mood—indicative<br>    Tense—aorist<br>    Voice—passive<br>    Person—2nd person<br>    Number—plural<br>    Stem or root—from ἀγοράζω<br>Concordance References:<br>  ⇒ Strong's #59 agorazö<br>  ⇒ NIV #60 agorazö<br>  ⇒ NASB #59 agorazö<br><br>**1 Cor. 6:20**<br>For ye are **bought** with a price: therefore glorify God in your body, and in your spirit, which are God's. [KJV]<br>For you have been **bought** with a price: therefore glorify God in your body. [NASB]<br>You were **bought** at a price. Therefore honor God with your body. [NIV]<br>For you were **bought** at a price; therefore glorify God in your body and in your spirit, which are God's. [NKJV]<br>For God **bought** you with a high price. So you must honor God with your body. [NLT]<br>ἠγοράσθητε γὰρ τιμῆς· δοξάσατε δὴ τὸν Θεὸν ἐν τῷ σώματι ὑμῶν, καὶ ἐν τῷ πνεύματι ὑμῶν, ἅτινά ἐστι τοῦ Θεοῦ. [GNS]<br>**ἠγοράσθητε** γὰρ τιμῆς· δοξάσατε δὴ τὸν θεὸν ἐν τῷ σώματι ὑμῶν. [GNT] | To buy; to purchase; to redeem; to ransom; to buy in the marketplace of slavery.<br><br>**Practical Application**<br>The idea is that Jesus Christ has paid our ransom and bought us...<br>• out of our enslavement to sin.<br>• out of our enslavement to death.<br>• out of our enslavement to hell.<br>His death met all the demands of God's perfect justice. God's justice was completely satisfied with Jesus Christ's...<br>• taking our sin upon Himself.<br>• dying for us.<br>• suffering hell or separation from God for us.<br>Therefore we are freed, liberated from sin, death, and hell. We are now free to live righteously and eternally in God's presence—all because Jesus Christ paid our ransom. He is our redemption. (See POSB note—2 Cor. 5:21; POSB note—Ephes. 1:7.) |
| **#425**<br>**Bought**<br><br>Purchased–KJV<br>Purchased–NASB<br>**Bought–NIV**<br>Purchased–NKJV<br>Purchased–NLT | περιεποιήσατο = periepoiësato<br>Pronunciation: [per-ee-poy-eh'-sah-tow]<br>Parsing (part of speech): verb<br>    Mood—indicative<br>    Tense—aorist<br>    Voice—middle<br>    Person—3rd person<br>    Number—singular<br>    Stem or root—from περιποιέομαι | Bought, purchased, obtained, acquired.<br><br>**Practical Application**<br>Jesus "bought" the church. He died as our substitute; He died for us; and because He died for us, we never have to die. This is what Scripture means when it says that Jesus Christ gave Himself for us. This is how God demonstrated His grace to the world: He gave His Son |

# PRACTICAL WORD STUDIES
## in the NEW TESTAMENT

| ENGLISH WORD | GREEK WORD AND VERSE | THE WORD MEANS... |
|---|---|---|
| **POSB REFERENCE** (Acts 20:28-31; esp. v.28) Note 2, point 1b | Concordance References:<br>⇒ Strong's #4046 peripoieō<br>⇒ NIV #4347 peripoieō<br>⇒ NASB #4046 peripoieō<br><br>**Acts 20:28**<br>Take heed therefore unto yourselves, and to all the flock, over the which the Holy Ghost hath made you overseers, to feed the church of God, which he hath **purchased** with his own blood. [KJV]<br>"Be on guard for yourselves and for all the flock, among which the Holy Spirit has made you overseers, to shepherd the church of God which He **purchased** with His own blood. [NASB]<br>Keep watch over yourselves and all the flock of which the Holy Spirit has made you overseers. Be shepherds of the church of God, which he **bought** with his own blood. [NIV]<br>Therefore take heed to yourselves and to all the flock, among which the Holy Spirit has made you overseers, to shepherd the church of God which He **purchased** with His own blood. [NKJV]<br>"And now beware! Be sure that you feed and shepherd God's flock—his church, **purchased** with his blood—over whom the Holy Spirit has appointed you as elders. [NLT]<br>προσέχετε οὖν ἑαυτοῖς καὶ παντὶ τῷ ποιμνίῳ, ἐν ᾧ ὑμᾶς τὸ Πνεῦμα τὸ Ἅγιον ἔθετο ἐπισκόπους, ποιμαίνειν τὴν ἐκκλησίαν τοῦ Θεοῦ, ἣν **περιεποιήσατο** διὰ τοῦ ἰδίου αἵματος. [GNS]<br>προσέχετε ἑαυτοῖς καὶ παντὶ τῷ ποιμνίῳ, ἐν ᾧ ὑμᾶς τὸ πνεῦμα τὸ ἅγιον ἔθετο ἐπισκόπους ποιμαίνειν τὴν ἐκκλησίαν τοῦ θεοῦ, ἣν **περιεποιήσατο** διὰ τοῦ αἵματος τοῦ ἰδίου. [GNT] | to die for the sins of men. |
| **#426 Bound**<br><br>Bound–KJV<br>Ought–NASB<br>Ought–NIV<br>Bound–NKJV<br>Not translated–NLT<br><br>**POSB REFERENCE** (2 Thes.1:3) Note 4 | ὀφείλομεν = *opheilomen*<br>Pronunciation: [of-i'-lo-mehn]<br>Parsing (part of speech): verb<br>    Mood—indicative<br>    Tense—present<br>    Voice—active<br>    Person—1st person<br>    Number—plural<br>    Stem or root—from ὀφείλω<br>Concordance References:<br>⇒ Strong's #3784 opheilō<br>⇒ NIV #4053 opheilō<br>⇒ NASB #3784 opheilō<br><br>**2 Thes. 1:3**<br>We are **bound** to thank God always for you, brethren, as it is meet, because that your faith groweth exceedingly, and the charity of every one of you all toward each other aboundeth; [KJV]<br>We **ought** always to give thanks to God for you, brethren, as is only fitting, because your faith is greatly enlarged, and the love of each one of you toward one another grows ever greater; [NASB]<br>We **ought** always to thank God for you, brothers, and rightly so, because your faith is growing more and more, and the love every one of you has for each other is increasing. [NIV]<br>We are **bound** to thank God always for you, brethren, as it is fitting, because your faith grows exceedingly, and the love of every one of you all abounds toward each other, [NKJV]<br>Dear brothers and sisters, we always thank God for you, as is right, for we are thankful that your faith is flourishing and you are all growing in love for each other. [NLT]—NOT TRANSLATED<br>Εὐχαριστεῖν **ὀφείλομεν** τῷ Θεῷ πάντοτε περὶ ὑμῶν, ἀδελφοί, καθὼς ἄξιόν ἐστιν, ὅτι ὑπεραυξάνει ἡ πίστις ὑμῶν, καὶ πλεονάζει ἡ ἀγάπη ἑνὸς ἑκάστου πάντων ὑμῶν | Ought, bound, compulsion and obligation.<br><br>**Practical Application**<br>The church's growing faith compelled Paul to thank God for the church—for their faith. Imagine how a minister's heart would joy and rejoice over his people's growing like the Thessalonian believers did. |

# PRACTICAL WORD STUDIES
## in the NEW TESTAMENT

| ENGLISH WORD | GREEK WORD AND VERSE | THE WORD MEANS... |
|---|---|---|
| | εἰς ἀλλήλους· [GNS]<br>Εὐχαριστεῖν **ὀφείλομεν** τῷ θεῷ πάντοτε περὶ ὑμῶν, ἀδελφοί, καθὼς ἄξιόν ἐστιν, ὅτι ὑπεραυξάνει ἡ πίστις ὑμῶν καὶ πλεονάζει ἡ ἀγάπη ἑνὸς ἑκάστου πάντων ὑμῶν εἰς ἀλλήλους, [GNT] | |
| **#427**<br>**Bound Over**<br><br>Concluded–KJV<br>Shut up–NASB<br>**Bound over–NIV**<br>Committed–NKJV<br>Imprisoned–NLT<br><br>**POSB REFERENCE**<br>(Rom.11:32)<br>Note 5 | συνέκλεισεν = *sunekleisen*<br>Pronunciation: [soon-he-kli'-sehn]<br>Parsing (part of speech): verb<br>  Mood—indicative<br>  Tense—aorist<br>  Voice—active<br>  Person—3rd person<br>  Number—singular<br>  Stem or root—from συγκλείω<br>Concordance References:<br>  ⇒ Strong's #4788 sugkleiō<br>  ⇒ NIV #5168 sugkleiō<br>  ⇒ NASB #4788 sugkleiō<br><br>**Romans 11:32**<br>For God hath **concluded** them all in unbelief, that he might have mercy upon all. [KJV]<br>For God has **shut up** all in disobedience that He might show mercy to all. [NASB]<br>For God has **bound** all men **over** to disobedience so that he may have mercy on them all. [NIV]<br>For God has **committed** them all to disobedience, that He might have mercy on all. [NKJV]<br>For God has **imprisoned** all people in their own disobedience so he could have mercy on everyone. [NLT]<br>συνέκλεισε γὰρ ὁ Θεὸς τοὺς πάντας εἰς ἀπείθειαν ἵνα τοὺς πάντας ἐλεήσῃ. [GNS]<br>συνέκλεισεν γὰρ ὁ Θεὸς τοὺς πάντας εἰς ἀπείθειαν, ἵνα τοὺς πάντας ἐλεήσῃ. [GNT] | To be bound over; to imprison; to shut up in a place; to close up; to lock up; to be committed to disobedience.<br><br>**Practical Application**<br>This is an unusual idea: God has taken men, both Jews and Gentiles, and shut them up to unbelief (*apeitheian*) or disobedience. This is the judicial judgment of God (see POSB *Deeper Study* #2—Romans 11:7-10; POSB note—Romans 1:24; POSB *Deeper Study* #1—John 12:39-41). It is the picture of God's using sin and events for good. God takes sin and works it out for the good of the world. Man has chosen sin, choosing to go his own way in life, so God allows man to do his own thing. God locks man up in his own world of selfishness, allowing man to roam around in his world of sin. Why? So that man's true nature of sinfulness will be clearly seen, and thereby cause the honest and thinking man to seek God. God wishes to have mercy upon all, both Jew and Gentile; but before men can come to God, they must confess two things:<br>  ⇒ that they are sinful and dying creatures in desperate need of God.<br>  ⇒ that God exists and that He will have mercy upon the person who diligently seeks Him (Heb.11:6). |
| **#428**<br>**Bound Together**<br><br>Unequally yoked together–KJV<br>**Bound together–NASB**<br>Yoked together–NIV<br>Unequally yoked together–NKJV<br>Team up–NLT<br><br>**POSB REFERENCE**<br>(2 Cor.6:14-16; esp. v.14)<br>Note 2 | ἑτεροζυγοῦντες = *heterozugountes*<br>Pronunciation: [het-er-od-zoog-oon-tehs]<br>Parsing (part of speech): verb<br>  Mood—participle<br>  Tense—present<br>  Voice—active<br>  Case—nominative<br>  Gender—masculine<br>  Person—2nd person<br>  Number—plural<br>  Stem or root—from ἑτεροζυγέω<br>Concordance References:<br>  ⇒ Strong's #2086 heterozugeō<br>  ⇒ NIV #2282 heterozugeō<br>  ⇒ NASB #2086 heterozugeō<br><br>**2 Cor. 6:14**<br>Be ye not **unequally yoked together** with unbelievers: for what fellowship hath righteousness with unrighteousness? and what communion hath light with darkness? [KJV]<br>Do not be **bound together** with unbelievers; for what partnership have righteousness and lawlessness, or what fellowship has light with darkness? [NASB]<br>Do not be **yoked together** with unbelievers. For what do righteousness and wickedness have in common? Or what fellowship can light have with darkness? [NIV]<br>Do not be **unequally yoked together** with unbelievers. For what fellowship has righteousness with lawlessness? And what communion has light with darkness? [NKJV]<br>Don't **team up** with those who are unbelievers. How can goodness be a partner with wickedness? How can light live with darkness? [NLT]<br>Μὴ γίνεσθε **ἑτεροζυγοῦντες** ἀπίστοις· τίς γὰρ μετοχὴ δικαιοσύνῃ καὶ ἀνομίᾳ; τίς δὲ κοινωνία φωτὶ | To be yoked together; to be bound together; to team up; to be unequally yoked; to be mismated.<br><br>**Practical Application**<br>It refers back to the Old Testament where God forbade the plowing of an ox with an ass (Deut. 22:10) or the union of different kinds of animals (Leviticus 19:19). The point is...<br>• that the union of a genuine believer with an unbeliever would be as different as the union between two kinds of animals.<br>• that the plowing through life of a believer with an unbeliever would be as difficult as the plowing of a field with an ox and an ass yoked together.<br><br>Genuine believers are radically different from unbelievers. |

## Practical Word Studies
### in the New Testament

| ENGLISH WORD | GREEK WORD AND VERSE | THE WORD MEANS... |
|---|---|---|
| | πρὸς σκότος; [GNS]<br>Μὴ γίνεσθε **ἑτεροζυγοῦντες** ἀπίστοις· τίς γὰρ μετοχὴ δικαιοσύνῃ καὶ ἀνομίᾳ, ἢ τίς κοινωνία φωτὶ πρὸς σκότος; [GNT] | |
| **#429**<br>**Bowed Down**<br><br>Worshipped–KJV<br>**Bowed down–NASB**<br>Knelt–NIV<br>Worshiped–NKJV<br>Worshiping–NLT<br><br>**POSB REFERENCE**<br>(Mt.8:2)<br>Note 2, point 2 | προσεκύνει = *prosekunei*<br>Pronunciation: [pros-koo-neh'-ee]<br>Parsing (part of speech): verb<br>   Mood—indicative<br>   Tense—imperfect<br>   Voice—active<br>   Person—3rd person<br>   Number—singular<br>   Stem or root—from προσκυνέω<br>Concordance References:<br>⇒ Strong's #4352 proskuneō<br>⇒ NIV #4686 proskuneō<br>⇒ NASB #4352 proskuneō<br><br>**Matthew 8:2**<br>And, behold, there came a leper and **worshipped** him, saying, Lord, if thou wilt, thou canst make me clean. [KJV]<br>And behold, a leper came to Him, and **bowed down** to Him, saying, "Lord, if You are willing, You can make me clean." [NASB]<br>A man with leprosy came and **knelt** before him and said, "Lord, if you are willing, you can make me clean." [NIV]<br>And behold, a leper came and **worshiped** Him, saying, "Lord, if You are willing, You can make me clean." [NKJV]<br>Suddenly, a man with leprosy approached Jesus. He knelt before him, **worshiping**. "Lord," the man said, "if you want to, you can make me well again." [NLT]<br>καὶ ἰδοὺ, λεπρὸς ἐλθὼν **προσεκύνει** αὐτῷ λέγων, Κύριε, ἐὰν θέλῃς δύνασαί με καθαρίσαι. [GNS]<br>καὶ ἰδοὺ λεπρὸς προσελθὼν **προσεκύνει** αὐτῷ λέγων, Κύριε, ἐὰν θέλῃς δύνασαί με καθαρίσαι. [GNT] | To worship; to bow down; to reverence; to pay homage.<br><br>**Practical Application**<br>In this Scripture, it is a bowing down, a genuine worship that is directed to the Lord. The leper demonstrated two significant things by rushing up and worshipping Jesus.<br>⇒ His desire and willingness to break away from the world and its restrictions.<br>⇒ His acknowledgment that Jesus was worthy of worship. |
| **#430**<br>**Brag**<br><br>Puffed up–KJV<br>Become arrogant–NASB<br>Take pride–NIV<br>Puffed up–NKJV<br>**Brag–NLT**<br><br>**POSB REFERENCE**<br>(1 Cor.4:6)<br>Note 1, point 2 | φυσιοῦσθε = *phusiousthe*<br>Pronunciation: [foo-see-o'-oos-the]<br>Parsing (part of speech): verb<br>   Mood—indicative<br>   Tense—present<br>   Voice—passive<br>   Person—2nd person<br>   Number—plural<br>   Stem or root—from φυσιόω<br>Concordance References:<br>⇒ Strong's #5448 phusioō<br>⇒ NIV #5881 phusioō<br>⇒ NASB #5448 phusioō<br><br>**1 Cor. 4:6**<br>And these things, brethren, I have in a figure transferred to myself and to Apollos for your sakes; that ye might learn in us not to think of men above that which is written, that no one of you be **puffed up** for one against another. [KJV]<br>Now these things, brethren, I have figuratively applied to myself and Apollos for your sakes, that in us you might learn not to exceed what is written, in order that no one of you might **become arrogant** in behalf of one against the other. [NASB]<br>Now, brothers, I have applied these things to myself and Apollos for your benefit, so that you may learn from us the meaning of the saying, "Do not go beyond what is written." Then you will not **take pride** in one man over against another. [NIV]<br>Now these things, brethren, I have figuratively transferred to myself and Apollos for your sakes, that you may learn in us not to think beyond what is written, that none | To take pride; to become arrogant; to brag; to be conceited; to be inflated; to be puffed up.<br><br>**Practical Application**<br>It is a picture of puffed up air bags. The point is the judging of ministers and the feelings that one can judge ministers is nothing but hot air in *puffed up* or inflated balloons. It is meaningless. It means absolutely nothing to God. (Cp. 1 Cor. 4:18-19; 1 Cor. 5:2; 1 Cor. 8:1; 1 Cor. 13:4.) |

## PRACTICAL WORD STUDIES
### in the NEW TESTAMENT

| ENGLISH WORD | GREEK WORD AND VERSE | THE WORD MEANS... |
|---|---|---|
| | of you may be **puffed up** on behalf of one against the other. [NKJV]<br><br>Dear brothers and sisters, I have used Apollos and myself to illustrate what I've been saying. If you pay attention to the Scriptures, you won't **brag** about one of your leaders at the expense of another. [NLT]<br><br>Ταῦτα δέ, ἀδελφοί, μετεσχημάτισα εἰς ἐμαυτὸν καὶ Ἀπολλῶν δι' ὑμᾶς, ἵνα ἐν ἡμῖν μάθητε τὸ μὴ ὑπὲρ ὃ γέγραπται φρονεῖν, ἵνα μὴ εἷς ὑπὲρ τοῦ ἑνὸς **φυσιοῦσθε** κατὰ τοῦ ἑτέρου. [GNS]<br><br>Ταῦτα δέ, ἀδελφοί, μετεσχημάτισα εἰς ἐμαυτὸν καὶ Ἀπολλῶν δι' ὑμᾶς, ἵνα ἐν ἡμῖν μάθητε τὸ Μὴ ὑπὲρ ἃ γέγραπται, ἵνα μὴ εἷς ὑπὲρ τοῦ ἑνὸς **φυσιοῦσθε** κατὰ τοῦ ἑτέρου. [GNT] | |
| **#431**<br>**Brag**<br><br>Vaunteth–KJV<br>**Brag**–NASB<br>Boast–NIV<br>Parade–NKJV<br>Boastful–NLT<br><br>**POSB REFERENCE**<br>(1 Cor.13:4-7; esp. v.4)<br>Note 2, point 4 | **περπερεύεται** = *perpereuetai*<br>Pronunciation: [per-per-yoo'-eh-tah-ee]<br>Parsing (part of speech): verb<br>   Mood—indicative<br>   Tense—present<br>   Voice—middle or passive deponent<br>   Person—3rd person<br>   Number—singular<br>   Stem or root—from περπερεύομαι<br>Concordance References:<br> ⇒ Strong's #4068 perpereuomai<br> ⇒ NIV #4371 perpereuomai<br> ⇒ NASB #4068 perpereuomai<br><br>**1 Cor. 13:4**<br>Charity suffereth long, and is kind; charity envieth not; charity **vaunteth** not itself, is not puffed up, [KJV]<br><br>Love is patient, love is kind, and is not jealous; love does not **brag** and is not arrogant, [NASB]<br><br>Love is patient, love is kind. It does not envy, it does not **boast**, it is not proud. [NIV]<br><br>Love suffers long and is kind; love does not envy; love does not **parade** itself, is not puffed up; [NKJV]<br><br>Love is patient and kind. Love is not jealous or **boastful** or proud [NLT]<br><br>ἡ ἀγάπη μακροθυμεῖ, χρηστεύεται· ἡ ἀγάπη, οὐ ζηλοῖ· ἡ ἀγάπη οὐ **περπερεύεται**, οὐ φυσιοῦται, [GNS]<br><br>Ἡ ἀγάπη μακροθυμεῖ, χρηστεύεται ἡ ἀγάπη, οὐ ζηλοῖ, [ἡ ἀγάπη] οὐ **περπερεύεται**, οὐ φυσιοῦται, [GNT] | To boast; to brag; to be boastful; to be conceited; to parade.<br><br>**Practical Application**<br>Love does not brag (*perpereuetai*): is not boastful; does not brag nor seek recognition, honor, or applause from others. On the contrary, love seeks to give: to recognize, to honor, to applaud the other person. |
| **#432**<br>**Brag**<br><br>Boastings–KJV<br>Arrogance–NASB<br>**Brag**–NIV<br>Arrogance–NKJV<br>Your own plans–NLT<br><br>**POSB REFERENCE**<br>(Jas.4:16)<br>Note 4 | **ἐν ταῖς ἀλαζονείαις** = *en tais alazoneiais*<br>Pronunciation: [en tace al-ad-zon-i'-ah-is]<br>Parsing *alazoneiais* (part of speech): noun<br>   Case—dative<br>   Gender—feminine<br>   Number—plural<br>   Stem or root—from ἀλαζονεία, ας<br>Concordance References:<br> ⇒ Strong's #212+1722+3588 alazoneia en ho<br> ⇒ NIV #224+1877+3836 alazoneia en ho [brag]<br> ⇒ NASB #212+1722+3588 alazoneia en ho<br><br>**James 4:16**<br>But now ye rejoice in your **boastings**: all such rejoicing is evil. [KJV]<br><br>But as it is, you boast in your **arrogance**; all such boasting is evil. [NASB]<br><br>As it is, you boast and **brag**. All such boasting is evil. [NIV]<br><br>But now you boast in your **arrogance**. All such boasting is evil. [NKJV]<br><br>Otherwise you will be boasting about **your own plans**, and all such boasting is evil. [NLT]<br><br>νῦν δὲ καυχᾶσθε **ἐν ταῖς ἀλαζονείαις** ὑμῶν· πᾶσα καύχησις τοιαύτη πονηρά ἐστιν. [GNS]<br><br>νῦν δὲ καυχᾶσθε **ἐν ταῖς ἀλαζονείαις** ὑμῶν· πᾶσα καύχησις τοιαύτη πονηρά ἐστιν. [GNT] | To brag; to boast; to be proud of; to be arrogant.<br><br>**Practical Application**<br>The word "brag" (*alazoniais*) means an empty boaster (A.T. Robertson. *Word Pictures in the New Testament*, Vol. 6, p.56). That is, it is a person who boasts about something he thinks he has, but he does not really have it. He lives in an unreal world. Any person who goes through life without God is just like this. He lives and plans, thinking that he controls his life and the future. His life is one big boast of self-sufficiency, and it is wrong, totally wrong. A thousand things can happen to change his plans—to injure him or to radically change his life and work, or to snatch his life right out of this world.<br><br>Most people—laymen and ministers alike—boast of their work, what they have done, their abilities and possessions. But note a fact seldom thought about: most boasting is not done by word of mouth. It is done by the way we live. We boast by flaunting our abilities and successes through our possessions and activities such as expensive houses, clothes and cars, exclusive clubs, friendships, and recreation. |

# Practical Word Studies in the New Testament

| ENGLISH WORD | GREEK WORD AND VERSE | THE WORD MEANS... |
|---|---|---|
| | | We have an urge, a tendency to boast and to be seen and recognized as better and more successful than others. And note what Scripture says: we rejoice in our boastings—that we are more successful in our work than some others. But such boastings—such pride and arrogance—are evil. Why? Because a man's ability and life are due to God and rest in the hands of God. And in addition to this: the future—tomorrow and even one hour from now—is in the hands of God. It may be a heart attack—it may be a thief—it may be an accident—it is all in the hands of God. What a person needs to do is trust God and commit all his ways into the hands of God, acknowledging Him in all things and at every turn of every day. |
| **#433**<br>**Brag About**<br><br>Boast–KJV<br>Boast–NASB<br>**Brag about–NIV**<br>Boast–NKJV<br>Boast–NLT<br><br>**POSB REFERENCE**<br>(Rom.2:17-20; esp. v.17)<br>Note 1, point 2 | καυχᾶσαι = *kauchasai*<br>Pronunciation: [kow-khah'-sahee]<br>Parsing (part of speech): verb<br>  Mood—indicative<br>  Tense—present<br>  Voice—middle or passive deponent<br>  Person—2nd person<br>  Number—singular<br>  Stem or root—from καυχάομαι<br>Concordance References:<br>  ⇒ Strong's #2744 kauchaomai<br>  ⇒ NIV #3016 kauchaomai<br>  ⇒ NASB #2744 kauchaomai<br><br>**Romans 2:17**<br>Behold, thou art called a Jew, and restest in the law, and makest thy **boast** of God, [KJV]<br>But if you bear the name "Jew," and rely upon the Law, and **boast** in God, [NASB]<br>Now you, if you call yourself a Jew; if you rely on the law and **brag about** your relationship to God; [NIV]<br>Indeed you are called a Jew, and rest on the law, and make your **boast** in God, [NKJV]<br>If you are a Jew, you are relying on God's law for your special relationship with him. You **boast** that all is well between yourself and God. [NLT]<br>Ἴδε σὺ Ἰουδαῖος ἐπονομάζῃ καὶ ἐπαναπαύῃ τῷ νόμῳ, καὶ **καυχᾶσαι** ἐν Θεῷ, [GNS]<br>Εἰ δὲ σὺ Ἰουδαῖος ἐπονομάζῃ καὶ ἐπαναπαύῃ νόμῳ καὶ **καυχᾶσαι** ἐν θεῷ [GNT] | To brag about; to boast; to glory; to take pride in; to feel proud about one's profession of God and religion.<br><br>**Practical Application**<br>The idea is that one openly professes that he believes in God. He is not ashamed of his belief and religious affiliation. He believes in God, and he feels safe and secure in his belief. He confesses God, and he feels that God accepts him because of his profession.<br>However, this is the mistake of the religionist. God is not interested in a man's profession but in a man's life. God wants a man's living for Him, not just professing and talking about Him. |
| **#434**<br>**Brag, Don't**<br><br>Meekness–KJV<br>Gentleness–NASB<br>Humility–NIV<br>Meekness–NKJV<br>**Don't brag–NLT**<br><br>**POSB REFERENCE**<br>(Jas 3:13)<br>Note 1, point 2 | πραΰτητι = *prautëti*<br>Pronunciation: [prah-oo'-tay-tee]<br>Parsing (part of speech): noun<br>  Case—dative<br>  Gender—feminine<br>  Number—singular<br>  Stem or root—from πραΰτης, ητος<br>Concordance References:<br>  ⇒ Strong's #4240 prautës<br>  ⇒ NIV #4559 prautës<br>  ⇒ NASB #4240 prautës<br><br>**James 3:13**<br>Who is a wise man and endued with knowledge among you? let him show out of a good conversation his works with **meekness** of wisdom. [KJV]<br>Who among you is wise and understanding? Let him show by his good behavior his deeds in the **gentleness** of wisdom. [NASB]<br>Who is wise and understanding among you? Let him show it by his good life, by deeds done in the **humility** that comes from wisdom. [NIV]<br>Who is wise and understanding among you? Let him show by good conduct that his works are done in the | Humility, meekness, gentleness; to be gentle, tender, humble, mild, considerate, but strongly so.<br><br>**Practical Application**<br>Humility, a refusal to brag, has the strength to control and discipline; and it does so at the right time.<br>1. Humility has *a humble state of mind*. But this does not mean the teacher is weak, cowardly, and bowing. The meek teacher simply loves people and loves peace; therefore, he walks humbly among men regardless of their status and circumstance in life. Associating with the poor and lowly of this earth does not bother the meek teacher. He desires to be a friend to all and to help all as much as possible.<br>2. Humility has *a strong state of mind*. It looks at situations and wants justice and right to be done. It is not a weak mind that ignores and neglects evil and wrongdoing, abuse and suffering. |

# PRACTICAL WORD STUDIES
## in the NEW TESTAMENT

| ENGLISH WORD | GREEK WORD AND VERSE | THE WORD MEANS... |
|---|---|---|
| | **meekness** of wisdom. [NKJV]<br>If you are wise and understand God's ways, live a life of steady goodness so that only good deeds will pour forth. And if you **don't brag** about the good you do, then you will be truly wise! [NLT]<br>Τίς σοφὸς καὶ ἐπιστήμων ἐν ὑμῖν; δειξάτω ἐκ τῆς καλῆς ἀναστροφῆς τὰ ἔργα αὐτοῦ ἐν **πραΰτητι** σοφίας. [GNS]<br>Τίς σοφὸς καὶ ἐπιστήμων ἐν ὑμῖν; δειξάτω ἐκ τῆς καλῆς ἀναστροφῆς τὰ ἔργα αὐτοῦ ἐν **πραΰτητι** σοφίας. [GNT] | ⇒ If someone is suffering, humility steps in to do what it can to help.<br>⇒ If evil is being done, humility does what it can to stop and correct it.<br>⇒ If evil is running rampant and indulging itself, humility actually strikes out in anger. However, note a crucial point: the anger is always at the right time and against the right thing.<br>3. Humility has *strong self-control*. The humble teacher controls his spirit and mind. He controls the lusts of his flesh. He does not give way to ill-temper, retaliation, passion, indulgence, or license. The meek teacher dies to himself, to what his flesh would like to do, and he does the right thing—exactly what God wants done.<br>In summary, the humble man walks in a humble, tender, but strong state of mind; denies himself, giving utmost consideration to others. He shows a control and righteous anger against injustice and evil. A humble man forgets and lives for others because of what Christ has done for him. |
| **#435**<br>**Brawler, Not A**<br><br>**Not a brawler**–KJV<br>Uncontentious–NASB<br>Not quarrelsome–NIV<br>Not quarrelsome–NKJV<br>Peace loving–NLT<br><br>**POSB REFERENCE**<br>(1 Tim.3-2-3; esp. v.3)<br>Note 2, point 12 | ἄμαχον = *amachon*<br>Pronunciation: [am'-akh-on]<br>Parsing (part of speech): adjective<br>    Case—accusative<br>    Gender—masculine<br>    Number—singular<br>    Stem or root—from ἄμαχος, ον<br>Concordance References:<br>⇒ Strong's #269 amachos<br>⇒ NIV #285 amachos<br>⇒ NASB #269 amachos<br><br>**1 Tim. 3:3**<br>Not given to wine, no striker, not greedy of filthy lucre; but patient, **not a brawler**, not covetous; [KJV]<br>Not addicted to wine or pugnacious, but gentle, **uncontentious**, free from the love of money. [NASB]<br>Not given to drunkenness, not violent but gentle, **not quarrelsome**, not a lover of money. [NIV]<br>Not given to wine, not violent, not greedy for money, but gentle, **not quarrelsome**, not covetous; [NKJV]<br>He must not be a heavy drinker or be violent. He must be gentle, **peace loving**, and not one who loves money. [NLT]<br>μὴ πάροινον, μὴ πλήκτην, μὴ αἰσχροκερδῆ, ἀλλ᾽ ἐπιεικῆ, **ἄμαχον**, ἀφιλάργυρον· [GNS]<br>μὴ πάροινον μὴ πλήκτην, ἀλλὰ ἐπιεικῆ **ἄμαχον** ἀφιλάργυρον, [GNT] | Not quarrelsome; not a brawler; not contentious; not a fighter; to be peace loving, peaceable, peaceful.<br><br>**Practical Application**<br>The minister or bishop must not be quarrelsome (*amachon*): He must be a man of peace, a mild-mannered person, always under control. Again, this refers to the tongue as well as to the hands. He must be a man who is deeply touched when there is unrest, controversy, or disturbance in the church or among believers. He must be a person who is so touched that he will work and seek for peace. |
| **#436**<br>**Brawlers**<br><br>**Brawlers**–KJV<br>Uncontentious–NASB<br>Peaceable–NIV<br>Peaceable–NKJV<br>Quarreling–NLT<br><br>**POSB REFERENCE**<br>(Tit.3:2)<br>Note 4 | ἀμάχους = *amachous*<br>Pronunciation: [am'-akh-oos]<br>Parsing (part of speech): adjective<br>    Case—accusative<br>    Gender—masculine<br>    Number—plural<br>    Stem or root—from ἄμαχος, ον<br>Concordance References:<br>⇒ Strong's #269 amachos<br>⇒ NIV #285 amachos<br>⇒ NASB #269 amachos<br><br>**Titus 3:2**<br>To speak evil of no man, to be no **brawlers**, but gentle, showing all meekness unto all men. [KJV]<br>To malign no one, to be **uncontentious**, gentle, showing every consideration for all men. [NASB]<br>To slander no one, to be **peaceable** and considerate, | To be peaceable; uncontentious; not to be quarreling or brawling.<br><br>**Practical Application**<br>The Christian is not to be a fighting, contentious person; not to be a person who is always walking around looking for an argument or fight; not to be a person who walks around with a chip on his shoulder looking for some controversy or argument; not to be so opinionated and stubborn that everyone else is always wrong; not to be a person who is always criticizing or talking about others, stirring up trouble and disturbing feelings and causing division. The Christian citizen is to be the very opposite: meek and peaceful. This, of course, does not mean that the |

# PRACTICAL WORD STUDIES
## in the NEW TESTAMENT

| ENGLISH WORD | GREEK WORD AND VERSE | THE WORD MEANS... |
|---|---|---|
| | and to show true humility toward all men. [NIV]<br>To speak evil of no one, to be **peaceable**, gentle, showing all humility to all men. [NKJV]<br>They must not speak evil of anyone, and they must avoid **quarreling**. Instead, they should be gentle and show true humility to everyone. [NLT]<br>μηδένα βλασφημεῖν, **ἀμάχους** εἶναι, ἐπιεικεῖς, πᾶσαν ἐνδεικνυμένους πραότητα πρὸς πάντας ἀνθρώπους. [GNS]<br>μηδένα βλασφημεῖν, **ἀμάχους** εἶναι, ἐπιεικεῖς, πᾶσαν ἐνδεικνυμένους πραΰτητα πρὸς πάντας ἀνθρώπους. [GNT] | Christian citizen does not speak up for what is right; he does. And he is strong in his stand, refusing to give in to the license and indulgence of evil. But he seeks peace where it is possible, and he seeks to lead others to be peaceable. |
| **#437**<br>**Brawling**<br><br>Clamour–KJV<br>Clamor–NASB<br>**Brawling–NIV**<br>Clamor–NKJV<br>Harsh words–NLT<br><br>**POSB REFERENCE**<br>(Eph.4:31)<br>Note 6, point 4 | κραυγή = *kraugē*<br>Pronunciation: [krow-gay']<br>Parsing (part of speech): noun<br>    Case—nominative<br>    Gender—feminine<br>    Number—singular<br>    Stem or root—from κραυγή, ῆς<br>Concordance References:<br>⇒ Strong's #2906 kraugē<br>⇒ NIV #3199 kraugē<br>⇒ NASB #2906 kraugē<br><br>**Ephes. 4:31**<br>Let all bitterness, and wrath, and anger, and **clamour**, and evil speaking, be put away from you, with all malice: [KJV]<br>Let all bitterness and wrath and anger and **clamor** and slander be put away from you, along with all malice. [NASB]<br>Get rid of all bitterness, rage and anger, **brawling** and slander, along with every form of malice. [NIV]<br>Let all bitterness, wrath, anger, **clamor**, and evil speaking be put away from you, with all malice. [NKJV]<br>Get rid of all bitterness, rage, anger, **harsh words**, and slander, as well as all types of malicious behavior. [NLT]<br>πᾶσα πικρία καὶ θυμὸς καὶ ὀργὴ καὶ **κραυγὴ** καὶ βλασφημία ἀρθήτω ἀφ' ὑμῶν, σὺν πάσῃ κακίᾳ· [GNS]<br>πᾶσα πικρία καὶ θυμὸς καὶ ὀργὴ καὶ **κραυγὴ** καὶ βλασφημία ἀρθήτω ἀφ' ὑμῶν σὺν πάσῃ κακίᾳ. [GNT] | Brawling, clamor, harsh words, angry words. It means insulting, boisterous behavior, and loud talking.<br><br>**Practical Application**<br>What must be the believer's relationship with brawling?<br>⇒ He is to get rid of it.<br>⇒ He is to put brawling behind him.<br>⇒ He is to never give brawling a place in his life. |
| **#438**<br>**Bread, The**<br><br>The Bread–KJV<br>The Bread–NASB<br>The Bread–NIV<br>The Bread–NKJV<br>The Bread–NLT<br><br>**POSB REFERENCE**<br>(Jn.6:33)<br>Note 3, point 1d | ὁ ἄρτος = *ho artos*<br>Pronunciation: [ho ar'-tos]<br>Parsing *artos* (part of speech): noun<br>    Case—nominative<br>    Gender—masculine<br>    Number—singular<br>    Stem or root—from ἄρτος, ου<br>Concordance References:<br>⇒ Strong's #740 artos<br>⇒ NIV #788 artos<br>⇒ NASB #740 artos<br><br>**John 6:33**<br>For the **bread** of God is he which cometh down from heaven, and giveth life unto the world. [KJV]<br>"For the **bread** of God is that which comes down out of heaven, and gives life to the world." [NASB]<br>For the **bread** of God is he who comes down from heaven and gives life to the world." [NIV]<br>For the **bread** of God is He who comes down from heaven and gives life to the world." [NKJV]<br>The true **bread** of God is the one who comes down from heaven and gives life to the world." [NLT]<br>ὁ γὰρ **ἄρτος** τοῦ θεοῦ ἐστιν ὁ καταβαίνων ἐκ τοῦ οὐρανοῦ, καὶ ζωὴν διδοὺς τῷ κόσμῳ. [GNS]<br>ὁ γὰρ **ἄρτος** τοῦ θεοῦ ἐστιν ὁ καταβαίνων ἐκ τοῦ οὐρανοῦ καὶ ζωὴν διδοὺς τῷ κόσμῳ. [GNT] | The Bread; the bread that is spiritual and divine; a loaf; food.<br><br>**Practical Application**<br>The Bread of God was a person. Note the personal pronoun "He," and the word "bread" which is masculine. Note that "He," the Bread of God who feeds and nourishes man, came down or "out of" heaven. He was not born of the earth. He came from the very presence of God Himself.<br>The Bread of God gives *life* to the world. The purpose of bread is to give life. (See POSB *Deeper Study* #2—John 1:4; POSB *Deeper Study* #1—John 10:10; POSB *Deeper Study* #1—John 17:2-3.) Bread gives life by...<br>• nourishing and sustaining<br>• satisfying<br>• energizing<br>• being partaken on a regular basis<br>• creating desire (the need) for more (See POSB note—Luke 4:3-4. Cp. Neh. 9:15) |
| **#439**<br>**Break** | ἀκυροῦντες = *akurountes*<br>Pronunciation: [ak-oo-roon'-tehs]<br>Parsing (part of speech): verb<br>    Mood—participle | To nullify; to be of no effect; to make void, ineffective; to annul; to cancel; to disregard; to deprive of authority and power; to invalidate. |

# PRACTICAL WORD STUDIES
## in the NEW TESTAMENT

| ENGLISH WORD | GREEK WORD AND VERSE | THE WORD MEANS... |
|---|---|---|
| Of none effect–KJV<br>Invalidating–NASB<br>Nullify–NIV<br>Of no effect–NKJV<br>**Break–NLT**<br><br>**POSB REFERENCE**<br>(Mk.7:13)<br>*Deeper Study* #2 | Tense—present<br>Voice—active<br>Case—nominative<br>Gender—masculine<br>Person—2nd person<br>Number—plural<br>Stem or root—from ἀκυρόω<br>Concordance References:<br>⇒ Strong's #208 akuroö<br>⇒ NIV #218 akuroö<br>⇒ NASB #208 akuroö<br><br>**Mark 7:13**<br>Making the word of God **of none effect** through your tradition, which ye have delivered: and many such like things do ye. [KJV]<br>Thus **invalidating** the word of God by your tradition which you have handed down; and you do many things such as that." [NASB]<br>Thus you **nullify** the word of God by your tradition that you have handed down. And you do many things like that." [NIV]<br>Making the word of God **of no effect** through your tradition which you have handed down. And many such things you do." [NKJV]<br>As such, you **break** the law of God in order to protect your own tradition. And this is only one example. There are many, many others." [NLT]<br>ἀκυροῦντες τὸν λόγον τοῦ Θεοῦ τῇ παραδόσει ὑμῶν ᾗ παρεδώκατε· καὶ παρόμοια τοιαῦτα πολλὰ ποιεῖτε. [GNS]<br>ἀκυροῦντες τὸν λόγον τοῦ Θεοῦ τῇ παραδόσει ὑμῶν ᾗ παρεδώκατε· καὶ παρόμοια τοιαῦτα πολλὰ ποιεῖτε. [GNT] | **Practical Application**<br>In this Scripture, Christ is rebuking anyone who places human traditions on an equal or higher authority than the Word of God. Jesus charged the religionists with setting aside God's Word for tradition. Religious traditions may be described as institutional or personal.<br>1. Institutional traditions are such things as rituals, rules, regulations, schedules, forms, services, procedures, organizations—anything that gives order and security to the persons involved.<br>2. Personal traditions are such things as church attendance, prayers, habits, ceremonies, objects which a person uses (somewhat superstitiously) to keep himself religiously secure.<br>Jesus was attacking the fact that so many religionists put their traditions first while neglecting and ignoring God's Word. (See POSB notes—Matthew 12:1-8; POSB note—Matthew 12:10 and POSB *Deeper Study* #1—Matthew 12:10). |
| #440<br>**Break**<br><br>Destroy–KJV<br>Render powerless–NASB<br>Destroy–NIV<br>Destroy–NKJV<br>**Break–NLT**<br><br>**POSB REFERENCE**<br>(Heb.2:14-16; esp. v.14)<br>Note 1, point 3 | καταργήσῃ = katargēsē<br>Pronunciation: [kat-arg-ay'-say]<br>Parsing (part of speech): verb<br>Mood—subjunctive<br>Tense—aorist<br>Voice—active<br>Person—3rd person<br>Number—singular<br>Stem or root—from καταργέω<br>Concordance References:<br>⇒ Strong's #2673 katargeō<br>⇒ NIV #2934 katargeō<br>⇒ NASB #2673 katargeō<br><br>**Hebrews 2:14**<br>Forasmuch then as the children are partakers of flesh and blood, he also himself likewise took part of the same; that through death he might **destroy** him that had the power of death, that is, the devil; [KJV]<br>Since then the children share in flesh and blood, He Himself likewise also partook of the same, that through death He might **render powerless** him who had the power of death, that is, the devil; [NASB]<br>Since the children have flesh and blood, he too shared in their humanity so that by his death he might **destroy** him who holds the power of death—that is, the devil—[NIV]<br>Inasmuch then as the children have partaken of flesh and blood, He Himself likewise shared in the same, that through death He might **destroy** him who had the power of death, that is, the devil, [NKJV]<br>Because God's children are human beings—made of flesh and blood—Jesus also became flesh and blood by being born in human form. For only as a human being could he die, and only by dying could he **break** the power of the Devil, who had the power of death. [NLT]<br>ἐπεὶ οὖν τὰ παιδία κεκοινώνηκε σαρκὸς καὶ αἵματος, καὶ αὐτὸς παραπλησίως μετέσχε τῶν αὐτῶν, ἵνα διὰ τοῦ θανάτου **καταργήσῃ** τὸν τὸ κράτος ἔχοντα τοῦ θανάτου, | To destroy; to render powerless; to break; to abolish; to render ineffective; to cancel; to nullify; to bring to nothing; to do away; to make inoperative.<br><br>**Practical Application**<br>Jesus Christ alone has broken and destroyed the power of Satan over sin and death. Satan's power over sin and death functions and operates within man, and what a power it is—the awesome power to separate men from God for eternity. But Jesus Christ has broken that power. He has made the power of Satan ineffective and inoperative. Man no longer has to be enslaved by sin and its guilt nor by death. He is delivered from death because Jesus Christ has broken Satan's power over death. |

## PRACTICAL WORD STUDIES
in the NEW TESTAMENT

| ENGLISH WORD | GREEK WORD AND VERSE | THE WORD MEANS... |
|---|---|---|
| | τοῦτ᾽ ἔστι τὸν διάβολον, [GNS]<br>ἐπεὶ οὖν τὰ παιδία κεκοινώνηκεν αἵματος καὶ σαρκός, καὶ αὐτὸς παραπλησίως μετέσχεν τῶν αὐτῶν, ἵνα διὰ τοῦ θανάτου **καταργήσῃ** τὸν τὸ κράτος ἔχοντα τοῦ θανάτου, τοῦτ᾽ ἔστιν τὸν διάβολον, [GNT] | |
| **#441**<br>**Break Their Promises**<br><br>Covenantbreakers–KJV<br>Untrustworthy–NASB<br>Faithless–NIV<br>Untrustworthy–NKJV<br>**Break their promises–NLT**<br><br>**POSB REFERENCE**<br>(Rom.1:31)<br>*Deeper Study* #20 | ἀσυνθέτους = asunthetous<br>Pronunciation: [as-oon´-thet-oos]<br>Parsing (part of speech): adjective<br>    Case—accusative<br>    Gender—masculine<br>    Number—plural<br>    Stem or root—from ἀσύνθετος, ον<br>Concordance References:<br>  ⇒ Strong's #802 asunthetos<br>  ⇒ NIV #853 asunthetos<br>  ⇒ NASB #802 asunthetos<br><br>**Romans 1:31**<br>Without understanding, **covenantbreakers**, without natural affection, implacable, unmerciful: [KJV]<br>Without understanding, **untrustworthy**, unloving, unmerciful; [NASB]<br>They are senseless, **faithless**, heartless, ruthless. [NIV]<br>Undiscerning, **untrustworthy**, unloving, unforgiving, unmerciful; [NKJV]<br>They refuse to understand, **break their promises**, and are heartless and unforgiving. [NLT]<br>ἀσυνέτους, **ἀσυνθέτους**, ἀστόργους, ἀσπόνδους, ἀνελεήμονας· [GNS]<br>ἀσυνέτους **ἀσυνθέτους** ἀστόργους ἀνελεήμονας [GNT] | Faithless, untrustworthy, disloyal, covenant breakers, breakers of promises or agreements.<br><br>**Practical Application**<br>It is a person who tragically does not keep his word or promise. He is simply untrustworthy, not dependable. |
| **#442**<br>**Breath**<br><br>Spirit–KJV<br>**Breath–NASB**<br>**Breath–NIV**<br>**Breath–NKJV**<br>**Breath–NLT**<br><br>**POSB REFERENCE**<br>(2 Thes.2:8)<br>Note 4, point 1 | πνεύματι = pneumati<br>Pronunciation: [pnyoo´-mah-tee]<br>Parsing (part of speech): noun<br>    Case—dative<br>    Gender—neuter<br>    Number—singular<br>    Stem or root—from πνεῦμα, τος<br>Concordance References:<br>  ⇒ Strong's #4151 pneuma<br>  ⇒ NIV #4460 pneuma<br>  ⇒ NASB #4151 pneuma<br><br>**2 Thes. 2:8**<br>And then shall that Wicked be revealed, whom the Lord shall consume with the **spirit** of his mouth, and shall destroy with the brightness of his coming: [KJV]<br>And then that lawless one will be revealed whom the Lord will slay with the **breath** of His mouth and bring to an end by the appearance of His coming; [NASB]<br>And then the lawless one will be revealed, whom the Lord Jesus will overthrow with the **breath** of his mouth and destroy by the splendor of his coming. [NIV]<br>And then the lawless one will be revealed, whom the Lord will consume with the **breath** of His mouth and destroy with the brightness of His coming. [NKJV]<br>Then the man of lawlessness will be revealed, whom the Lord Jesus will consume with the **breath** of His mouth and destroy by the splendor of his coming. [NLT]<br>καὶ τότε ἀποκαλυφθήσεται ὁ ἄνομος, ὃν ὁ Κύριος ἀναλώσει τῷ **πνεύματι** τοῦ στόματος αὐτοῦ, καὶ καταργήσει τῇ ἐπιφανείᾳ τῆς παρουσίας αὐτοῦ· [GNS]<br>καὶ τότε ἀποκαλυφθήσεται ὁ ἄνομος, ὃν ὁ κύριος [Ἰησοῦς] ἀνελεῖ τῷ **πνεύματι** τοῦ στόματος αὐτοῦ καὶ καταργήσει τῇ ἐπιφανείᾳ τῆς παρουσίας αὐτοῦ, [GNT] | Breath, the Spirit of God, wind.<br><br>**Practical Application**<br>The Lord Jesus will slay the antichrist with the breath of His mouth. What is *the breath of Jesus' mouth*? It is the spirit of truth, holiness, and unlimited power. When Jesus speaks, what He says is of God and unstoppable. When He rents the sky to slay the antichrist, there will be no battle, for all the forces of heaven and earth combined would be as nonexistent against the Lord God of the universe. Christ will speak the Word, and the antichrist will be slain. It will be like the blowing of a little breath and the dust particle is removed never to return. |
| **#443**<br>**Brightness**<br><br>**Brightness–KJV**<br>Appearance–NASB | ἐπιφανείᾳ = epiphaneia<br>Pronunciation: [ep-if-an´-ee-ah]<br>Parsing (part of speech): noun<br>    Case—dative<br>    Gender—feminine<br>    Number—singular | Splendor, brightness, appearance.<br><br>**Practical Application**<br>The Lord of glory will destroy the antichrist with the brightness of His coming. The word |

# PRACTICAL WORD STUDIES
## in the NEW TESTAMENT

| ENGLISH WORD | GREEK WORD AND VERSE | THE WORD MEANS... |
|---|---|---|
| Splendor–NIV<br>**Brightness–NKJV**<br>Splendor–NLT<br><br>**POSB REFERENCE**<br>(2 Thes.2:8)<br>Note 4, point 2 | Stem or root—from ἐπιφάνεια, ας<br>Concordance References:<br>⇒ Strong's #2015 epiphaneia<br>⇒ NIV #2211 epiphaneia<br>⇒ NASB #2015 epiphaneia<br><br>**2 Thes. 2:8**<br>And then shall that Wicked be revealed, whom the Lord shall consume with the spirit of his mouth, and shall destroy with the **brightness** of his coming: [KJV]<br>And then that lawless one will be revealed whom the Lord will slay with the breath of His mouth and bring to an end by the **appearance** of His coming; [NASB]<br>And then the lawless one will be revealed, whom the Lord Jesus will overthrow with the breath of his mouth and destroy by the **splendor** of his coming. [NIV]<br>And then the lawless one will be revealed, whom the Lord will consume with the breath of His mouth and destroy with the **brightness** of His coming. [NKJV]<br>Then the man of lawlessness will be revealed, whom the Lord Jesus will consume with the breath of his mouth and destroy by the **splendor** of his coming. [NLT]<br>καὶ τότε ἀποκαλυφθήσεται ὁ ἄνομος, ὃν ὁ Κύριος ἀναλώσει τῷ πνεύματι τοῦ στόματος αὐτοῦ, καὶ καταργήσει τῇ **ἐπιφανείᾳ** τῆς παρουσίας αὐτοῦ· [GNS]<br>καὶ τότε ἀποκαλυφθήσεται ὁ ἄνομος, ὃν ὁ κύριος [Ἰησοῦς] ἀνελεῖ τῷ πνεύματι τοῦ στόματος αὐτοῦ καὶ καταργήσει τῇ **ἐπιφανείᾳ** τῆς παρουσίας αὐτοῦ, [GNT] | "brightness" (*epiphaneia*) is a very special word. It is a word chosen by the New Testament to refer only to the coming (*parousia*) of the Lord. It is used only five times in all the New Testament, and in every instance it refers to the Lord's coming into the world. It refers once to His first coming (2 Tim. 1:10) and four times to His second coming (1 Tim. 6:14; 2 Tim. 4:1, 8; Titus 2:13). The whole idea of *splendor* is brightness, radiance, glory, and light. Someone has pointed out that when Jesus Christ returns to earth, there will be such a spectacular display of glory and splendor that the explosion of every star in the universe could not match the sight of the Lord (source unknown). When Christ first appears, there will apparently be the energizing of a laser beam of glory zeroed in on the antichrist, and he will be immediately destroyed by the radiance of the Lord's glory and light—quicker than we could blink an eye. Simply by showing Himself, the Lord will destroy the antichrist. Note: the word "destroy" does not mean to annihilate but to make inoperative; to make powerless; to end; to put a stop to his evil work. |
| #444<br>**Bring**<br><br>Direct–KJV<br>Direct–NASB<br>Direct–NIV<br>Direct–NKJV<br>**Bring–NLT**<br><br>**POSB REFERENCE**<br>(2 Thes.3:3-5; esp. v.5)<br>Note 2, point 3 | κατευθῦναι = *kateuthunai*<br>Pronunciation: [kat-yoo-thoo'-nah-ee]<br>Parsing (part of speech): verb<br>  Mood—optative<br>  Tense—aorist<br>  Voice—active<br>  Person—3rd person<br>  Number—singular<br>  Stem or root—from κατευθύνω<br>Concordance References:<br>⇒ Strong's #2720 kateuthunō<br>⇒ NIV #2985 kateuthunō<br>⇒ NASB #2720 kateuthunō<br><br>**2 Thes. 3:5**<br>And the Lord **direct** your hearts into the love of God, and into the patient waiting for Christ. [KJV]<br>And may the Lord **direct** your hearts into the love of God and into the steadfastness of Christ. [NASB]<br>May the Lord **direct** your hearts into God's love and Christ's perseverance. [NIV]<br>Now may the Lord **direct** your hearts into the love of God and into the patience of Christ. [NKJV]<br>May the Lord **bring** you into an ever deeper understanding of the love of God and the endurance that comes from Christ. [NLT]<br>ὁ δὲ Κύριος **κατευθύναι** ὑμῶν τὰς καρδίας εἰς τὴν ἀγάπην τοῦ Θεοῦ, καὶ εἰς τὴν ὑπομονὴν τοῦ Χριστοῦ. [GNS]<br>Ὁ δὲ κύριος **κατευθύναι** ὑμῶν τὰς καρδίας εἰς τὴν ἀγάπην τοῦ θεοῦ καὶ εἰς τὴν ὑπομονὴν τοῦ Χριστοῦ. [GNT] | To direct; to bring; to guide; to make straight or to be straight. It means to remove obstacles out of the way or to open up.<br><br>**Practical Application**<br>The Lord Jesus Christ takes the genuine believer and opens up his heart; He straightens, directs, and focuses the believer's heart upon the love of God. The result is that the believer learns to love God more and more. His attention and focus become more and more set upon God's love. Therefore, when trials, trouble, temptation, and evil attack the believer, he is able to stand in the love of God and overcome the attack. |
| #445<br>**Bring Everything Together**<br><br>Gather together in one all things–KJV<br>Summing up of all things–NASB | ἀνακεφαλαιώσασθαι = *anakephalaiōsasthai*<br>Pronunciation: [an-ak-ef-al-ah'ee-o-sahs-tha-ee]<br>Parsing (part of speech): verb<br>  Mood—infinitive<br>  Tense—aorist<br>  Voice—middle deponent<br>  Stem or root—from ἀνακεφαλαιόω<br>Concordance References:<br>⇒ Strong's #346 anakephalaioō<br>⇒ NIV #368 anakephalaioō<br>⇒ NASB #346 anakephalaioō | To bring together under one head; to gather together in one all things; to sum up all things; to bring everything together; to unite.<br><br>**Practical Application**<br>There is to be a consummation, a climax of history—a *fullness of time*, a new order—in which all things will be unified and harmonized and brought to a peaceful state under the authority of Jesus Christ. History is in the hands of |

# PRACTICAL WORD STUDIES
## in the NEW TESTAMENT

| ENGLISH WORD | GREEK WORD AND VERSE | THE WORD MEANS... |
|---|---|---|
| Bring...together under one head–NIV<br>Gather together in one all things–NKJV<br>**Bring everything together–NLT**<br><br>**POSB REFERENCE**<br>(Eph.1:9-10; esp. v.10)<br>Note 6, point 3 | **Ephes. 1:10**<br>That in the dispensation of the fulness of times he might **gather together in one all things** in Christ, both which are in heaven, and which are on earth; even in him: [KJV]<br>With a view to an administration suitable to the fulness of the times, that is, the **summing up of all things** in Christ, things in the heavens and things upon the earth. In Him [NASB]<br>To be put into effect when the times will have reached their fulfillment—to **bring** all things in heaven and on earth **together under one head**, even Christ. [NIV]<br>That in the dispensation of the fullness of the times He might **gather together in one all things** in Christ, both which are in heaven and which are on earth—in Him. [NKJV]<br>And this is his plan: At the right time he will **bring everything together** under the authority of Christ—everything in heaven and on earth. [NLT]<br>εἰς οἰκονομίαν τοῦ πληρώματος τῶν καιρῶν, **ἀνακεφαλαιώσασθαι** τὰ πάντα ἐν τῷ Χριστῷ, τὰ τε ἐν τοῖς οὐρανοῖς καὶ τὰ ἐπὶ τῆς γῆς· ἐν αὐτῷ, [GNS]<br>εἰς οἰκονομίαν τοῦ πληρώματος τῶν καιρῶν, **ἀνακεφαλαιώσασθαι** τὰ πάντα ἐν τῷ Χριστῷ, τὰ ἐπὶ τοῖς οὐρανοῖς καὶ τὰ ἐπὶ τῆς γῆς ἐν αὐτῷ. [GNT] | God.<br>God is handling, planning, arranging, and administering all things toward a climactic consummation for Christ and His followers. In that climactic day all disharmony and division and evil will be subjected and harmonized (*anakephalaiösasthai*) under Christ. A new and perfect and eternal creation will be established for the Lord and His followers throughout the universe. |
| **#446**<br>**Bring Sorrow**<br><br>Grieve–KJV<br>Grieve–NASB<br>Grieve–NIV<br>Grieve–NKJV<br>**Bring sorrow–NLT**<br><br>**POSB REFERENCE**<br>(Eph.4:30)<br>Note 5 | λυπεῖτε = *lupeite*<br>Pronunciation: [loo-peh'-ee-teh]<br>Parsing (part of speech): verb<br>    Mood—imperative<br>    Tense—present<br>    Voice—active<br>    Person—2nd person<br>    Number—plural<br>    Stem or root—from λυπέω<br>Concordance References:<br>⇒ Strong's #3076 lupeö<br>⇒ NIV #3382 lupeö<br>⇒ NASB #3076 lupeö<br><br>**Ephes. 4:30**<br>And **grieve** not the holy Spirit of God, whereby ye are sealed unto the day of redemption. [KJV]<br>And do not **grieve** the Holy Spirit of God, by whom you were sealed for the day of redemption. [NASB]<br>And do not **grieve** the Holy Spirit of God, with whom you were sealed for the day of redemption. [NIV]<br>And do not **grieve** the Holy Spirit of God, by whom you were sealed for the day of redemption. [NKJV]<br>And do not **bring sorrow** to God's Holy Spirit by the way you live. Remember, he is the one who has identified you as his own, guaranteeing that you will be saved on the day of redemption. [NLT]<br>καὶ μὴ **λυπεῖτε** τὸ Πνεῦμα τὸ Ἅγιον τοῦ Θεοῦ, ἐν ᾧ ἐσφραγίσθητε εἰς ἡμέραν ἀπολυτρώσεως. [GNS]<br>καὶ μὴ **λυπεῖτε** τὸ πνεῦμα τὸ ἅγιον τοῦ θεοῦ, ἐν ᾧ ἐσφραγίσθητε εἰς ἡμέραν ἀπολυτρώσεως. [GNT] | To grieve; to distress; to bring sorrow; to hurt; to pain; to offend; to vex; to injure; to sadden the Holy Spirit.<br><br>**Practical Application**<br>When a child acts contrary to the counsel of his parents, he hurts and brings sorrow to them. So when a person acts contrary to the counsel of the Holy Spirit, he hurts and brings sorrow to Him. Note three points.<br>1. The command is forceful, very forceful. This is seen in the name of the Holy Spirit. He is not only called the Holy Spirit here, He is called both the Holy Spirit and "the Spirit of God"—a double reference.<br>2. There are at least four ways the Holy Spirit can be grieved.<br>  a. He is *grieved* when believers allow impure things to penetrate their lives or thoughts.<br>  b. He is *grieved* when believers behave immorally.<br>  c. He is *grieved* when believers act unjustly.<br>  d. He is *grieved* when believers participate in anything contrary to the nature of the Holy Spirit. Note the context of this passage: the command to "grieve not the Spirit" is surrounded by a series of negative commands.<br>3. The reason we should not grieve the Spirit of God is because of His great ministry to us: He has sealed us until the day of redemption (see POSB note, Holy Spirit, Seal—Ephes. 1:13-14 for discussion). |
| **#447**<br>**Bring Together Under One Head**<br><br>Gather together in one all things–KJV<br>Summing up of all things–NASB | ἀνακεφαλαιώσασθαι = *anakephalaiösasthai*<br>Pronunciation: [an-ak-ef-al-ah'ee-o-sahs-tha-ee]<br>Parsing (part of speech): verb<br>    Mood—infinitive<br>    Tense—aorist<br>    Voice—middle deponent<br>    Stem or root—from ἀνακεφαλαιόω<br>Concordance References:<br>⇒ Strong's #346 anakephalaioö<br>⇒ NIV #368 anakephalaioö | To bring together under one head; to gather together in one all things; to sum up all things; to bring everything together; to unite.<br><br>**Practical Application**<br>There is to be a consummation, a climax of history—a *fullness of time*, a new order—in which all things will be unified and harmonized and brought to a peaceful state under the author- |

## PRACTICAL WORD STUDIES
### in the New Testament

| ENGLISH WORD | GREEK WORD AND VERSE | THE WORD MEANS... |
|---|---|---|
| **Bring...together under one head–NIV**<br>Gather together in one all things–NKJV<br>Bring everything together–NLT<br><br>**POSB REFERENCE**<br>(Eph.1:9-10; esp. v.10)<br>Note 6, point 3 | ⇒ NASB #346 anakephalaioö<br><br>**Ephes. 1:10**<br>That in the dispensation of the fulness of times he might **gather together in one all things** in Christ, both which are in heaven, and which are on earth; even in him: [KJV]<br>With a view to an administration suitable to the fulness of the times, that is, the **summing up of all things** in Christ, things in the heavens and things upon the earth. In Him [NASB]<br>To be put into effect when the times will have reached their fulfillment—to **bring** all things in heaven and on earth **together under one head**, even Christ. [NIV]<br>That in the dispensation of the fullness of the times He might **gather together in one all things** in Christ, both which are in heaven and which are on earth—in Him. [NKJV]<br>And this is his plan: At the right time he will **bring everything together** under the authority of Christ—everything in heaven and on earth. [NLT]<br>εἰς οἰκονομίαν τοῦ πληρώματος τῶν καιρῶν, **ἀνακεφαλαιώσασθαι** τὰ πάντα ἐν τῷ Χριστῷ, τὰ τε ἐν τοῖς οὐρανοῖς καὶ τὰ ἐπὶ τῆς γῆς· ἐν αὐτῷ, [GNS]<br>εἰς οἰκονομίαν τοῦ πληρώματος τῶν καιρῶν, **ἀνακεφαλαιώσασθαι** τὰ πάντα ἐν τῷ Χριστῷ, τὰ ἐπὶ τοῖς οὐρανοῖς καὶ τὰ ἐπὶ τῆς γῆς ἐν αὐτῷ. [GNT] | ity of Jesus Christ. History is in the hands of God.<br>God is handling, planning, arranging, and administering all things toward a climactic consummation for Christ and His followers. In that climactic day all disharmony and division and evil will be subjected and harmonized (*anakephalaiösasthai*) under Christ. A new and perfect and eternal creation will be established for the Lord and His followers throughout the universe. |
| **#448**<br>**Bringing**<br><br>Brought–KJV<br>**Bringing–NASB**<br>**Bringing–NIV**<br>Brought–NKJV<br>Brought–NLT<br><br>**POSB REFERENCE**<br>(Mk.10:13)<br>*Deeper Study #1* | προσέφερον = *prospheron*<br>Pronunciation: [pros-fer'-on]<br>Parsing (part of speech): verb<br>  Mood—indicative<br>  Tense—imperfect<br>  Voice—active<br>  Person—3rd person<br>  Number—plural<br>  Stem or root—from προσφέρω<br>Concordance References:<br>⇒ Strong's #4374 prospherō<br>⇒ NIV #4712 prospherō<br>⇒ NASB #4374 prospherō<br><br>**Mark 10:13**<br>And they **brought** young children to him, that he should touch them: and his disciples rebuked those that brought them. [KJV]<br>And they were **bringing** children to Him so that He might touch them; and the disciples rebuked them. [NASB]<br>People were **bringing** little children to Jesus to have him touch them, but the disciples rebuked them. [NIV]<br>Then they **brought** little children to Him, that He might touch them; but the disciples rebuked those who brought them. [NKJV]<br>One day some parents **brought** their children to Jesus so he could touch them and bless them, but the disciples told them not to bother him. [NLT]<br>Καὶ **προσέφερον** αὐτῷ παιδία, ἵνα ἄψηται αὐτῶν· οἱ δὲ μαθηταὶ ἐπετίμων τοῖς προσφέρρουσιν. [GNS]<br>Καὶ **προσέφερον** αὐτῷ παιδία ἵνα αὐτῶν ἄψηται· οἱ δὲ μαθηταὶ ἐπετίμησαν αὐτοῖς. [GNT] | To bring to; to bring unto; to fetch; to offer; to present.<br><br>**Practical Application**<br>It is the word used in connection with offerings. The idea is that whatever is brought is being brought as an offering. It is a dedication to God (cp. Matthew 5:23-24). |
| **#449**<br>**Bringing The Glad Tidings**<br><br>Showing the glad tidings–KJV<br>Preaching–NASB<br>Proclaiming the good news–NIV<br>**Bringing the glad tidings–NKJV** | εὐαγγελιζόμενος = *euaggelizomenos*<br>Pronunciation: [yoo-ang-ghel-id'-zo-men-os]<br>Parsing (part of speech): verb<br>  Mood—participle<br>  Tense—present<br>  Voice—middle<br>  Case—nominative<br>  Gender—masculine<br>  Number—plural<br>  Stem or root—from εὐαγγελίζω<br>Concordance References:<br>⇒ Strong's #2097 euaggelizo | To preach glad tidings; to announce glad tidings; to declare good news; to bring the glad tidings; to proclaim the gospel of Jesus Christ.<br><br>**Practical Application**<br>Note the Greek word, how it resembles the word *evangelism*. The English word *evangelism* comes from it. By the very nature of his work, the preacher is an evangelist. He is a herald who comes in the name of the King, representing the King (cp. 2 Cor. 5:20). He proclaims *only* the |

# PRACTICAL WORD STUDIES
## in the NEW TESTAMENT

| ENGLISH WORD | GREEK WORD AND VERSE | THE WORD MEANS... |
|---|---|---|
| Announce the Good News–NLT<br><br>**POSB REFERENCE**<br>(Lk.8:1)<br>*Deeper Study #2* | ⇒ NIV #2294 euaggelizō<br>⇒ NASB #2097 euaggelizo<br><br>**Luke 8:1**<br>And it came to pass afterward, that he went throughout every city and village, preaching and **showing the glad tidings** of the kingdom of God: and the twelve were with him, [KJV]<br>And it came about soon afterwards, that He began going about from one city and village to another, proclaiming and **preaching** the kingdom of God; and the twelve were with Him, [NASB]<br>After this, Jesus traveled about from one town and village to another, **proclaiming the good news** of the kingdom of God. The Twelve were with him, [NIV]<br>Now it came to pass, afterward, that He went through every city and village, preaching and **bringing the glad tidings** of the kingdom of God. And the twelve were with Him, [NKJV]<br>Not long afterward Jesus began a tour of the nearby cities and villages to **announce the Good News** concerning the Kingdom of God. He took his twelve disciples with him, [NLT]<br>Καὶ ἐγένετο ἐν τῷ καθεξῆς, καὶ αὐτὸς διώδευε κατὰ πόλιν καὶ κώμην, κηρύσσων καὶ **εὐαγγελιζόμενος** τὴν βασιλείαν τοῦ Θεοῦ· καὶ οἱ δώδεκα σὺν αὐτῷ, [GNS]<br>Καὶ ἐγένετο ἐν τῷ καθεξῆς καὶ αὐτὸς διώδευεν κατὰ πόλιν καὶ κώμην κηρύσσων καὶ **εὐαγγελιζόμενος** τὴν βασιλείαν τοῦ θεοῦ καὶ οἱ δώδεκα σὺν αὐτῷ, [GNT] | message of the King; he has no message of his own. If and when he begins to proclaim his own message, he is no longer the representative or the spokesman of the King. |
| **#450**<br>**Broke Down**<br><br>Thought thereon–KJV<br>Not translated–NASB<br>**Broke down**–NIV<br>Thought about it–NKJV<br>**Broke down**–NLT<br><br>**POSB REFERENCE**<br>(Mk.14:72)<br>Note 5 | ἐπιβαλών = epibalon<br>Pronunciation: [ep-ee-bal'-lon]<br>Parsing (part of speech): verb<br>  Mood—participle<br>  Tense—aorist<br>  Voice—active<br>  Case—nominative<br>  Gender—masculine<br>  Number—singular<br>  Stem or root—from ἐπιβάλλω<br>Concordance References:<br>⇒ Strong's #1911 epiballō<br>⇒ NIV #2095 epiballō<br>⇒ NASB #1911 epiballō<br><br>**Mark 14:72**<br>And the second time the cock crew. And Peter called to mind the word that Jesus said unto him, Before the cock crow twice, thou shalt deny me thrice. And when he **thought thereon**, he wept. [KJV]<br>And immediately a cock crowed a second time. And Peter remembered how Jesus had made the remark to him, "Before a cock crows twice, you will deny Me three times." And he began to weep. [NASB]—NOT TRANSLATED<br>Immediately the rooster crowed the second time. Then Peter remembered the word Jesus had spoken to him: "Before the rooster crows twice you will disown me three times." And he **broke down** and wept. [NIV]<br>A second time the rooster crowed. Then Peter called to mind the word that Jesus had said to him, "Before the rooster crows twice, you will deny Me three times." And when he **thought about it**, he wept. [NKJV]<br>And immediately the rooster crowed the second time. Suddenly, Jesus' words flashed through Peter's mind: "Before the rooster crows twice, you will deny me three times." And he **broke down** and cried. [NLT]<br>καὶ ἐκ δευτέρου ἀλέκτωρ ἐφώνησε. καὶ ἀνεμνήσθη ὁ Πέτρος τοῦ ῥήματος οὗ εἶπεν αὐτῷ ὁ Ἰησοῦς. ὅτι Πρὶν ἀλέκτορα φωνῆσαι δὶς, ἀπαρνήσῃ με τρίς. καὶ **ἐπιβαλών** ἔκλαιε. [GNS]<br>καὶ εὐθὺς ἐκ δευτέρου ἀλέκτωρ ἐφώνησεν. καὶ ἀνεμνήσθη ὁ Πέτρος τὸ ῥῆμα ὡς εἶπεν αὐτῷ ὁ Ἰησοῦς ὅτι Πρὶν ἀλέκτορα φωνῆσαι δὶς τρίς με ἀπαρνήσῃ· καὶ **ἐπιβαλών** ἔκλαιεν. [GNT] | To break down; to throw upon; to set the mind upon a specific thing.<br><br>**Practical Application**<br>Peter "broke down and wept." He remembered what Jesus had said: that he, Peter, would deny Jesus three times. Peter's mind was fastened upon what Jesus had told him. His mind would not let Jesus' words go. |

# PRACTICAL WORD STUDIES
## in the NEW TESTAMENT

| ENGLISH WORD | GREEK WORD AND VERSE | THE WORD MEANS... |
|---|---|---|
| **#451**<br>**Brotherly**<br><br>Love as brethren–KJV<br>**Brotherly**–NASB<br>Love as brothers–NIV<br>Love as brothers–NKJV<br>Loving one another–NLT<br><br>**POSB REFERENCE**<br>(1 Pt.3:8)<br>Note 3 | φιλάδελφοι = *philadelphoi*<br>Pronunciation: [fil-ad'-el-foy]<br>Parsing (part of speech): adjective<br>    Case—nominative<br>    Gender—masculine<br>    Number—plural<br>    Stem or root—from φιλάδελφος, ον<br>Concordance References:<br>  ⇒ Strong's #5361 *philadelphos*<br>  ⇒ NIV #5790 *philadelphos*<br>  ⇒ NASB #5361 *philadelphos*<br><br>**1 Peter 3:8**<br>Finally, be ye all of one mind, having compassion one of another, **love as brethren**, be pitiful, be courteous: [KJV]<br>To sum up, let all be harmonious, sympathetic, **brotherly**, kindhearted, and humble in spirit; [NASB]<br>Finally, all of you, live in harmony with one another; be sympathetic, **love as brothers**, be compassionate and humble. [NIV]<br>Finally, all of you be of one mind, having compassion for one another; **love as brothers**, be tenderhearted, be courteous; [NKJV]<br>Finally, all of you should be of one mind, full of sympathy toward each other, **loving one another** with tender hearts and humble minds. [NLT]<br>Τὸ δὲ τέλος, πάντες ὁμόφρονες, συμπαθεῖς, **φιλάδελφοι**, εὔσπλαγχνοι, φιλόφρονες· [GNS]<br>Τὸ δὲ τέλος πάντες ὁμόφρονες, συμπαθεῖς, **φιλάδελφοι**, εὔσπλαγχνοι, ταπεινόφρονες, [GNT] | To love as brothers; to be brotherly; to love one another; to love another believer.<br><br>**Practical Application**<br>  There is no greater force than love. If two people truly love each other, they will do anything for the other. There is no greater bond on earth than true love. This is especially true of the love between believers. Why? Is there a difference between the love that believers have for one another and the love that neighbors have for one another? Scripture says yes, emphatically yes. Believers are to have a different kind of love than neighbors have for one another. The love that believers are to have for one another is what the Greek calls *philadelphia* love, a very special kind of love. |
| **#452**<br>**Brotherly Kindness**<br><br>**Brotherly kindness**–KJV<br>**Brotherly kindness**–NASB<br>**Brotherly kindness**–NIV<br>**Brotherly kindness**–NKJV<br>Love for other Christians–NLT<br><br>**POSB REFERENCE**<br>(2 Pt.1:5-7; esp. v.7)<br>Note 1, point 6 | φιλαδελφίαν = *philadelphian*<br>Pronunciation: [fil-ad-el-fee'-ahn]<br>Parsing (part of speech): noun<br>    Case—accusative<br>    Gender—feminine<br>    Number—singular<br>    Stem or root—from φιλαδελφία, ας<br>Concordance References:<br>  ⇒ Strong's #5360 *philadelphia*<br>  ⇒ NIV #5789 *philadelphia*<br>  ⇒ NASB #5360 *philadelphia*<br><br>**2 Peter 1:7**<br>And to godliness **brotherly kindness**; and to brotherly kindness charity. [KJV]<br>And in your godliness, **brotherly kindness**, and in your brotherly kindness, love. [NASB]<br>And to godliness, **brotherly kindness**; and to brotherly kindness, love. [NIV]<br>To godliness **brotherly kindness**, and to brotherly kindness love. [NKJV]<br>Godliness leads to **love for other Christians**, and finally you will grow to have genuine love for everyone. [NLT]<br>ἐν δὲ τῇ εὐσεβείᾳ τὴν **φιλαδελφίαν**, ἐν δὲ τῇ φιλαδελφίᾳ τὴν ἀγάπην. [GNS]<br>ἐν δὲ τῇ εὐσεβείᾳ τὴν **φιλαδελφίαν**, ἐν δὲ τῇ φιλαδελφίᾳ τὴν ἀγάπην. [GNT] | Brotherly kindness; love for other Christians; loving each other as brothers; the very special love that exists between brothers and sisters within a loving family; brothers and sisters who truly cherish one another.<br><br>**Practical Application**<br>It is the kind of love...<br>• that binds one another together as a family, as a brotherly clan.<br>• that binds one another in an unbreakable union.<br>• that holds one another ever so dearly within the heart.<br>• that knows deep affection for one another.<br>• that nourishes and nurtures one another.<br>• that shows concern for and looks after the welfare of one another.<br>• that joins hands with one another in a common purpose *under one father* (Leon Morris. *The Epistles of Paul to the Thessalonians.* "Tyndale New Testament Commentary," p.80).<br><br>  How can people possibly love one another like this when they are not true blood brothers and sisters? Here is how. The Greek word "brother" (*adelphos*) means *from the same womb*. The word used for love is "phileo" which means deep-seated affection and care, deep and warm feelings within the heart. It is the kind of love that holds a person near and dear to one's heart. Now note: the two Greek words are combined together by the writer to convey what he means by *brotherly love*.<br>⇒ People who have *brotherly love* have come from the same womb, that is, from the same source. They have been *born* |

## PRACTICAL WORD STUDIES
### in the NEW TESTAMENT

| ENGLISH WORD | GREEK WORD AND VERSE | THE WORD MEANS... |
|---|---|---|
| | | *again* by the Spirit of God through faith in the Lord Jesus Christ. When they receive this new birth, God gives them a new spirit—a spirit that melts and binds their hearts and lives in love for all the family of God.<br><br>Believers may not even know one another. They may even be from different parts of the world, but there is a *brotherly love* between them because they have been given a new birth and a new spirit of love by God. They are brothers and sisters in the family of God—the family of those who truly believe in God's Son, the Lord Jesus Christ—the family who has received a new spirit that binds them together in brotherly love. This new spirit, of course, comes from the Holy Spirit of God Himself. (See POSB *Deeper Study* #3, Fellowship—Acts 2:42 for more discussion.) |
| **#453**<br>**Brotherly Love**<br><br>**Brotherly love–KJV**<br>Love of the brethren–NASB<br>**Brotherly love–NIV**<br>**Brotherly love–NKJV**<br>Shown among God's people–NLT<br><br>**POSB REFERENCE**<br>(1 Thes.4:9-10; esp. v.9)<br>Note 1 | φιλαδελφίας = *philadelphias*<br>Pronunciation: [fil-ad-el-fee'-ahs]<br>Parsing (part of speech): noun<br>    Case—genitive<br>    Gender—feminine<br>    Number—singular<br>    Stem or root—from φιλαδελφία, ας<br>Concordance References:<br>  ⇒ Strong's #5360 *philadelphia*<br>  ⇒ NIV #5789 *philadelphia*<br>  ⇒ NASB #5360 *philadelphia*<br><br>**1 Thes. 4:9**<br>But as touching **brotherly love** ye need not that I write unto you: for ye yourselves are taught of God to love one another. [KJV]<br>Now as to the **love of the brethren**, you have no need for anyone to write to you, for you yourselves are taught by God to love one another; [NASB]<br>Now about **brotherly love** we do not need to write to you, for you yourselves have been taught by God to love each other. [NIV]<br>But concerning **brotherly love** you have no need that I should write to you, for you yourselves are taught by God to love one another; [NKJV]<br>But I don't need to write to you about the Christian **love** that should be **shown among God's people**. For God himself has taught you to love one another. [NLT]<br>Περὶ δὲ τῆς **φιλαδελφίας** οὐ χρείαν ἔχετε γράφειν ὑμῖν· αὐτοὶ γὰρ ὑμεῖς θεοδίδακτοί ἐστε εἰς τὸ ἀγαπᾶν ἀλλήλους· [GNS]<br>Περὶ δὲ τῆς **φιλαδελφίας** οὐ χρείαν ἔχετε γράφειν ὑμῖν, αὐτοὶ γὰρ ὑμεῖς θεοδίδακτοί ἐστε εἰς τὸ ἀγαπᾶν ἀλλήλους, [GNT] | Brotherly love; love of the brothers shown among God's people; loving one another as brothers.<br><br>**Practical Application**<br>In the Greek the word "love" is not the word that is usually used for love. The word that is usually used for Christian love is *agape*, but the word used here is *philadelphia*, a very special kind of love. The word means *brotherly love*, the very special love that exists between brothers and sisters within a loving family, brothers and sisters who truly cherish each other. It is the kind of love...<br>• that binds one another together as a family, as a brotherly clan.<br>• that binds each in an unbreakable union.<br>• that holds one another ever so deeply within the heart.<br>• that knows deep affection for one another.<br>• that nourishes and nurtures one another.<br>• that shows concern and looks after the welfare of one another.<br>• that joins hands with one another in a common purpose *under one father* (Leon Morris, *The Epistles of Paul to the Thessalonians*. "Tyndale New Testament Commentaries," p.80). |
| **#454**<br>**Brotherly Love**<br><br>**Brotherly Love–KJV**<br>Love of the brethren–NASB<br>Loving each other as brothers–NIV<br>**Brotherly love–NKJV**<br>Love each other with true Christian love–NLT | φιλαδελφία = *philadelphia*<br>Pronunciation: [fil-ad-el-fee'-ahs]<br>Parsing (part of speech): noun<br>    Case—genitive<br>    Gender—feminine<br>    Number—singular<br>    Stem or root—from φιλαδελφία, ας<br>Concordance References:<br>  ⇒ Strong's #5360 *philadelphia*<br>  ⇒ NIV #5789 *philadelphia*<br>  ⇒ NASB #5360 *philadelphia*<br><br>**Hebrews 13:1**<br>Let **brotherly love** continue. [KJV]<br>Let **love of the brethren** continue. [NASB]<br>Keep on **loving each other as brothers**. [NIV]<br>Let **brotherly love** continue. [NKJV] | Brotherly love; love of the brothers shown among God's people; loving one another as brothers.<br><br>**Practical Application**<br>Note that the love existing among believers is a special kind of love. It is a "brotherly love" (*philadelphia*), the very special love that exists between brothers and sisters within a loving family, brothers and sisters who truly cherish one another. It is the kind of love...<br>• that binds each other together as a family, as a brotherly clan.<br>• that binds each other in an unbreakable union. |

## PRACTICAL WORD STUDIES
### in the NEW TESTAMENT

| ENGLISH WORD | GREEK WORD AND VERSE | THE WORD MEANS... |
|---|---|---|
| **POSB REFERENCE** (Heb.13:1) Note 1, point 1 | Continue to **love each other with true Christian love**. [NLT] <br> Ἡ **φιλαδελφία** μενέτω. [GNS] <br> Ἡ **φιλαδελφία** μενέτω. [GNT] | • that holds each other ever so deeply within the heart. <br> • that knows deep affection for each other. <br> • that nourishes and nurtures each other. <br> • that shows concern and looks after the welfare of each other. <br> • that joins hands with each other in a common purpose *under one father* (Leon Morris. *The Epistles of Paul to the Thessalonians*. "Tyndale New Testament Commentary," p.80). |
| **#455 Brought** <br><br> **Brought**–KJV <br> Bringing–NASB <br> Bringing–NIV <br> **Brought**–NKJV <br> **Brought**–NLT <br><br> **POSB REFERENCE** (Mk.10:13) *Deeper Study #1* | προσέφερον = prospheron <br> Pronunciation: [pros-fer'-on] <br> Parsing (part of speech): verb <br>     Mood—indicative <br>     Tense—imperfect <br>     Voice—active <br>     Person—3rd person <br>     Number—plural <br>     Stem or root—from προσφέρω <br> Concordance References: <br>   ⇒ Strong's #4374 prospheröˉ <br>   ⇒ NIV #4712 prospheröˉ <br>   ⇒ NASB #4374 prospheröˉ <br><br> **Mark 10:13** <br> And they **brought** young children to him, that he should touch them: and his disciples rebuked those that brought them. [KJV] <br> And they were **bringing** children to Him so that He might touch them; and the disciples rebuked them. [NASB] <br> People were **bringing** little children to Jesus to have him touch them, but the disciples rebuked them. [NIV] <br> Then they **brought** little children to Him, that He might touch them; but the disciples rebuked those who brought them. [NKJV] <br> One day some parents **brought** their children to Jesus so he could touch them and bless them, but the disciples told them not to bother him. [NLT] <br> Καὶ **προσέφερον** αὐτῷ παιδία, ἵνα ἅψηται αὐτῶν· οἱ δὲ μαθηταὶ ἐπετίμων τοῖς προσφέρουσιν. [GNS] <br> Καὶ **προσέφερον** αὐτῷ παιδία ἵνα αὐτῶν ἅψηται· οἱ δὲ μαθηταὶ ἐπετίμησαν αὐτοῖς. [GNT] | To bring to; to fetch; to get; to lift; to offer; to present. <br><br> **Practical Application** <br> It is the word used in connection with offerings. The idea is that whatever is brought is being brought as an offering. It is a dedication to God (cp. Matthew 5:23-24). |
| **#456 Brought** <br><br> Caught–KJV <br> Dragged..away–NASB <br> Seized–NIV <br> Seized–NKJV <br> **Brought**–NLT <br><br> **POSB REFERENCE** (Acts 6:11-14; esp. v.12) Note 3, point 3 | συνήρπασαν = sunërpasan <br> Pronunciation: [soon-ayr-pa'-sahn] <br> Parsing (part of speech): verb <br>     Mood—indicative <br>     Tense—aorist <br>     Voice—active <br>     Person—3rd person <br>     Number—plural <br>     Stem or root—from συναρπάζω <br> Concordance References: <br>   ⇒ Strong's #4884 sunarpazöˉ <br>   ⇒ NIV #5275 sunarpazöˉ <br>   ⇒ NASB #4884 sunarpazöˉ <br><br> **Acts 6:12** <br> And they stirred up the people, and the elders, and the scribes, and came upon him, and **caught** him, and brought him to the council, [KJV] <br> And they stirred up the people, the elders and the scribes, and they came upon him and **dragged** him **away**, and brought him before the Council. [NASB] <br> So they stirred up the people and the elders and the teachers of the law. They **seized** Stephen and brought him before the Sanhedrin. [NIV] <br> And they stirred up the people, the elders, and the scribes; and they came upon him, **seized** him, and | To seize; to catch; to drag away; to bring. <br><br> **Practical Application** <br> The word "brought" (*sunërpasan*) means to seize with violence. The picture is that they seized and literally dragged him to court (cp. Luke 8:29; Acts 19:29; Acts 27:15). |

## PRACTICAL WORD STUDIES
## in the NEW TESTAMENT

| ENGLISH WORD | GREEK WORD AND VERSE | THE WORD MEANS... |
|---|---|---|
| | brought him to the council. [NKJV]<br>Naturally, this roused the crowds, the elders, and the teachers of religious law. So they arrested Stephen and **brought** him before the high council. [NLT]<br>συνεκίνησάν τε τὸν λαὸν καὶ τοὺς πρεσβυτέρους καὶ τοὺς γραμματεῖς, καὶ ἐπιστάντες **συνήρπασαν** αὐτὸν, καὶ ἤγαγον εἰς τὸ συνέδριον, [GNS]<br>συνεκίνησάν τε τὸν λαὸν καὶ τοὺς πρεσβυτέρους καὶ τοὺς γραμματεῖς, καὶ ἐπιστάντες **συνήρπασαν** αὐτὸν καὶ ἤγαγον εἰς τὸ συνέδριον, [GNT] | |
| **#457**<br>**Brought Us Into This Place**<br>Access–KJV<br>Obtained our introduction–NASB<br>Access–NIV<br>Access–NKJV<br>**Brought us into this place**–NLT<br><br>**POSB REFERENCE**<br>(Rom.5:2)<br>Note 3, point 2 | **προσαγωγὴν** = *prosagōgēn*<br>Pronunciation: [pros-ag-ogue-ayn']<br>Parsing (part of speech): noun<br>    Case—accusative<br>    Gender—feminine<br>    Number—singular<br>    Stem or root—from προσαγωγή, ῆς<br>Concordance References:<br>  ⇒ Strong's #4318 prosagōgē<br>  ⇒ NIV #4643 prosagōgē<br>  ⇒ NASB #4318 prosagōgē<br><br>**Romans 5:2**<br>By whom also we have **access** by faith into this grace wherein we stand, and rejoice in hope of the glory of God. [KJV]<br>Through whom also we have **obtained our introduction** by faith into this grace in which we stand; and we exult in hope of the glory of God. [NASB]<br>Through whom we have gained **access** by faith into this grace in which we now stand. And we rejoice in the hope of the glory of God. [NIV]<br>Through whom also we have **access** by faith into this grace in which we stand, and rejoice in hope of the glory of God. [NKJV]<br>Because of our faith, Christ has **brought us into this place** of highest privilege where we now stand, and we confidently and joyfully look forward to sharing God's glory. [NLT]<br>δι' οὗ καὶ τὴν **προσαγωγὴν** ἐσχήκαμεν τῇ πίστει εἰς τὴν χάριν ταύτην ἐν ᾗ ἑστήκαμεν, καὶ καυχώμεθα ἐπ' ἐλπίδι τῆς δόξης τοῦ Θεοῦ. [GNS]<br>δι' οὗ καὶ τὴν **προσαγωγὴν** ἐσχήκαμεν [τῇ πίστει] εἰς τὴν χάριν ταύτην ἐν ᾗ ἑστήκαμεν καὶ καυχώμεθα ἐπ' ἐλπίδι τῆς δόξης τοῦ θεοῦ. [GNT] | Access; to bring to; to move to; to introduce; to present. It is the freedom or right to enter.<br><br>**Practical Application**<br>Note it is through Christ that we have access into this grace. The thought is that of being in a royal court and being presented and introduced to the King of kings. Jesus Christ is the One who throws open the door into God's presence. He is the One who presents us to God, the Sovereign Majesty of the universe. |
| **#458**<br>**Brutal**<br>Fierce–KJV<br>**Brutal**–NASB<br>**Brutal**–NIV<br>**Brutal**–NKJV<br>Cruel–NLT<br><br>**POSB REFERENCE**<br>(2 Tim. 3:2-4; esp. v.3)<br>Note 2, point 13 | **ἀνήμεροι** = *anēmeroi*<br>Pronunciation: [an-ay'-mer-oy]<br>Parsing (part of speech): adjective<br>    Case—nominative<br>    Gender—masculine<br>    Number—plural<br>    Stem or root—from ἀνήμερος, ον<br>Concordance References:<br>  ⇒ Strong's #434 anēmeros<br>  ⇒ NIV #466 anēmeros<br>  ⇒ NASB #434 anēmeros<br><br>**2 Tim. 3:3**<br>Without natural affection, trucebreakers, false accusers, incontinent, **fierce**, despisers of those that are good, [KJV]<br>Unloving, irreconcilable, malicious gossips, without self-control, **brutal**, haters of good, [NASB]<br>Without love, unforgiving, slanderous, without self-control, **brutal**, not lovers of the good, [NIV]<br>Unloving, unforgiving, slanderers, without self-control, **brutal**, despisers of good, [NKJV]<br>They will be unloving and unforgiving; they will slander others and have no self-control; they will be **cruel** and have no interest in what is good. [NLT]<br>ἄστοργοι, ἄσπονδοι, διάβολοι, ἀκρατεῖς, **ἀνήμεροι**, ἀφιλάγαθοι, [GNS]<br>ἄστοργοι ἄσπονδοι διάβολοι ἀκρατεῖς **ἀνήμεροι** ἀφιλάγαθοι [GNT] | Brutal, fierce, cruel, savage, and untamed.<br><br>**Practical Application**<br>It is the word that describes the savage beast of the wild that is unrestrained in its fierceness. It is a word that should never be true of people, yet tragically it is. Never in the history of the world have men become as fierce and savage as they are today.<br>1. People no longer just murder...<br>  • they mutilate<br>  • they torture<br>  • they kill at random<br>  • they kill by twos and threes and by thousands and millions (for example, Hitler, Stalin)<br>And they take pleasure in their torture and savagery.<br>2. People no longer just correct and rebuke children, spouse, friend, neighbor, employee, or stranger...<br>  • they curse<br>  • they abuse<br>  • they attack<br>  • they maim<br>  • they act violently<br>The last days will see an increase in brutal, fierce and savage behavior. |

## Practical Word Studies
### in the New Testament

| ENGLISH WORD | GREEK WORD AND VERSE | THE WORD MEANS... |
|---|---|---|
| **#459**<br>**Buffeted**<br><br>Tossed–KJV<br>Battered–NASB<br>**Buffeted–NIV**<br>Tossed–NKJV<br>Fighting–NLT<br><br>**POSB REFERENCE**<br>(Mt.14:24-27, esp.v.24)<br>Note 2, point 1 | βασανιζόμενον = basanizomenon<br>Pronunciation: [bas-an-id'-zo-me-non]<br>Parsing (part of speech): verb<br>    Mood—participle<br>    Tense—present<br>    Voice—passive<br>    Case—nominative<br>    Gender—neuter<br>    Number—singular<br>    Stem or root—from βασανίζω<br>Concordance References:<br>  ⇒  Strong's #928 basanizō<br>  ⇒  NIV #989 basanizō<br>  ⇒  NASB #928 basanizō<br><br>**Matthew 14:24**<br>But the ship was now in the midst of the sea, **tossed** with waves: for the wind was contrary. [KJV]<br>But the boat was already many stadia away from the land, **battered** by the waves; for the wind was contrary. [NASB]<br>But the boat was already a considerable distance from land, **buffeted** by the waves because the wind was against it. [NIV]<br>But the boat was now in the middle of the sea, **tossed** by the waves, for the wind was contrary. [NKJV]<br>Meanwhile, the disciples were in trouble far away from land, for a strong wind had risen, and they were **fighting** heavy waves. [NLT]<br>τὸ δὲ πλοῖον ἤδη μέσον τῆς θαλάσσης ἦν, **βασανιζόμενον** ὑπὸ τῶν κυμάτων· ἦν γὰρ ἐναντίος ὁ ἄνεμος. [GNS]<br>τὸ δὲ πλοῖον ἤδη σταδίους πολλοὺς ἀπὸ τῆς γῆς ἀπεῖχεν **βασανιζόμενον** ὑπὸ τῶν κυμάτων, ἦν γὰρ ἐναντίος ὁ ἄνεμος. [GNT] | To be buffeted, beaten, battered, or tossed about with great force; to be tormented.<br><br>**Practical Application**<br>In this Scripture, it is a picture of being completely at the mercy of a force greater than any possible human resistance. It is a picture of the awesome power of unleashed nature and mankind's inability to resist its effects. |
| **#460**<br>**Build Up**<br><br>Edify–KJV<br>**Build up–NASB**<br>**Build...up–NIV**<br>Edify–NKJV<br>**Build...up–NLT**<br><br>**POSB REFERENCE**<br>(1 Thes.5:11)<br>Note 4 | οἰκοδομεῖτε = oikodomeite<br>Pronunciation: [oy-kod-om-eh'-ee-teh]<br>Parsing (part of speech): verb<br>    Mood—imperative<br>    Tense—present<br>    Voice—active<br>    Person—2nd person<br>    Number—plural<br>    Stem or root—from οἰκοδομέω<br>Concordance References:<br>  ⇒  Strong's #3618 oikodomeō<br>  ⇒  NIV #3868 oikodomeō<br>  ⇒  NASB #3618 oikodomeō<br><br>**1 Thes. 5:11**<br>Wherefore comfort yourselves together, and **edify** one another, even as also ye do. [KJV]<br>Therefore encourage one another, and **build up** one another, just as you also are doing. [NASB]<br>Therefore encourage one another and **build** each other **up**, just as in fact you are doing. [NIV]<br>Therefore comfort each other and **edify** one another, just as you also are doing. [NKJV]<br>So encourage each other and **build** each other **up**, just as you are already doing. [NLT]<br>διὸ παρακαλεῖτε ἀλλήλους, καὶ **οἰκοδομεῖτε** εἰς τὸν ἕνα, καθὼς καὶ ποιεῖτε. [GNS]<br>Διὸ παρακαλεῖτε ἀλλήλους καὶ **οἰκοδομεῖτε** εἰς τὸν ἕνα, καθὼς καὶ ποιεῖτε. [GNT] | To build up; to edify; to strengthen; to encourage; to restore; to erect; to rebuild.<br><br>**Practical Application**<br>We are to "*build up*" (*oikodomeite*) one another: strengthen and build one another up. The believer is to speak only that which is good and which will edify or build up people. Speech is for the purpose...<br>• of sharing good things.<br>• of building up and strengthening people.<br>• of ministering grace (favor, blessings) and helping one another as we plow through life. |
| **#461**<br>**Burned**<br><br>**Burned–KJV**<br>**Burned–NASB**<br>**Burned–NIV** | καίεται = kaietai<br>Pronunciation: [kah'ee-eh-tah-ee]<br>Parsing (part of speech): verb<br>    Mood—indicative<br>    Tense—present<br>    Voice—passive<br>    Person—3rd person | To burn; to be consumed with fire; to incinerate; to char; to kindle; to ignite; to be on fire.<br><br>**Practical Application**<br>Note the tragic fate of the person who does not remain or abide in Christ. The unattached branch is doomed. It is thrown away to wither |

# PRACTICAL WORD STUDIES
## in the NEW TESTAMENT

| ENGLISH WORD | GREEK WORD AND VERSE | THE WORD MEANS... |
|---|---|---|
| **Burned–NKJV**<br>**Burned–NLT**<br><br>**POSB<br>REFERENCE**<br>(Jn.15:4-6; esp. v.6)<br>Note 4, point 4d | Number—singular<br>Stem or root—from καίω<br>Concordance References:<br>⇒ Strong's #2545 kaio<br>⇒ NIV #2794 kaio<br>⇒ NASB #2545 kaio<br><br>**John 15:6**<br>If a man abide not in me, he is cast forth as a branch, and is withered; and men gather them, and cast them into the fire, and they are **burned**. [KJV]<br>"If anyone does not abide in Me, he is thrown away as a branch, and dries up; and they gather them, and cast them into the fire, and they are **burned**. [NASB]<br>If anyone does not remain in me, he is like a branch that is thrown away and withers; such branches are picked up, thrown into the fire and **burned**. [NIV]<br>If anyone does not abide in Me, he is cast out as a branch and is withered; and they gather them and throw them into the fire, and they are **burned**. [NKJV]<br>Anyone who parts from me is thrown away like a useless branch and withers. Such branches are gathered into a pile to be **burned**. [NLT]<br>ἐὰν μή τις μείνῃ ἐν ἐμοί, ἐβλήθη ἔξω ὡς τὸ κλῆμα, καὶ ἐξηράνθη, καὶ συνάγουσιν αὐτά, καὶ εἰς πῦρ βάλλουσι, καὶ **καίεται**. [GNS]<br>ἐὰν μή τις μένῃ ἐν ἐμοί, ἐβλήθη ἔξω ὡς τὸ κλῆμα καὶ ἐξηράνθη καὶ συνάγουσιν αὐτὰ καὶ εἰς τὸ πῦρ βάλλουσιν καὶ **καίεται**. [GNT] | and to be picked up and thrown into the fire and burned.<br>1. The branch is *thrown away* (*eblethe exo*): to be plucked off and cast out, thrown away, discarded, disposed of. The unattached branch wants and chooses to be unattached, so God lets it. It is given over and given up to be unattached. God abandons it. It is thrown away and out of the way and left to itself, to do as it chooses. (See POSB outline and notes—Romans 1:24-32.)<br>2. The branch *withers* (*exeranthe*): to be dried up, wrinkled, peeled; to become sapless and bare; to lose energy and strength. The unattached branch experiences everything withering away—its...<br>• gifts and abilities<br>• life and body<br>• family and friends<br>• fate and destiny<br>• hopes and dreams<br>• confidence and assurance<br>• purpose and meaning<br>3. The branch is *picked up* (*sunagousin*): the day of judgment arrives. In the Greek text, who it is that picks up is not given. The Greek simply says, "they picked up or gathered." This is probably God's having His angels gather up all the unattached branches, "everything that causes sin and all who do evil" (cp. Matthew 13:41).<br>4. The branch is thrown into the fire and "*burned*" (*kaietai*). (See POSB *Deeper Study* #2—Matthew 5:22; POSB note—Matthew 8:12; POSB *Deeper Study* #4—Luke 16:24. Cp. Matthew 13:42, 50; Rev. 20:15; Rev. 21:8.) |
| **#462<br>Business**<br><br>**Business–KJV**<br>Diligence–NASB<br>Zeal–NIV<br>Diligence–NKJV<br>Work–NLT<br><br>**POSB<br>REFERENCE**<br>(Rom.12:11)<br>Note 2, point 1 | σπουδῇ = *spoudē*<br>Pronunciation: [spoo-day']<br>Parsing (part of speech): noun<br>    Case—dative<br>    Gender—feminine<br>    Number—singular<br>    Stem or root—from σπουδή, ῆς<br>Concordance References:<br>⇒ Strong's #4710 spoudē<br>⇒ NIV #5082 spoudē<br>⇒ NASB #4710 spoudē<br><br>**Romans 12:11**<br>Not slothful in **business**; fervent in spirit; serving the Lord; [KJV]<br>Not lagging behind in **diligence**, fervent in spirit, serving the Lord; [NASB]<br>Never be lacking in **zeal**, but keep your spiritual fervor, serving the Lord. [NIV]<br>Not lagging in **diligence**, fervent in spirit, serving the Lord; [NKJV]<br>Never be lazy in your **work**, but serve the Lord enthusiastically. [NLT]<br>τῇ **σπουδῇ** μὴ ὀκνηροί· τῷ πνεύματι ζέοντες· τῷ Κυρίῳ δουλεύοντες· [GNS]<br>τῇ **σπουδῇ** μὴ ὀκνηροί, τῷ πνεύματι ζέοντες, τῷ κυρίῳ δουλεύοντες, [GNT] | Zeal, diligence, work, earnestness, effort.<br><br>**Practical Application**<br>The exhortation is clear: the believer must...<br>• not be lazy or slow-moving in zeal.<br>• not be sluggish or lethargic in diligence.<br>• not be hesitating or delaying in earnestness.<br>The believer just cannot approach life in a lackadaisical, easy going, slow-moving fashion. The world is reeling in pain, with millions starving and suffering due to man's selfishness and sin, hoarding, disease, war, death—and the list could go on and on. The believer must not give in to sluggishness and complacency. He must serve the Lord with all diligence and zeal and earnestness. He must be enthusiastic in his service. |
| **#463<br>Busy At Home** | οἰκουργούς = *oikourgous*<br>Pronunciation: [oy-koor-goos']<br>Parsing (part of speech): pronominal adjective OR adjective<br>    Case—accusative | To be busy at home; to be keepers at home; to be workers at home; to take care of business [at home]; to be homemakers, devoted to duties at home. |

# PRACTICAL WORD STUDIES
## in the New Testament

| ENGLISH WORD | GREEK WORD AND VERSE | THE WORD MEANS... |
|---|---|---|
| Chaste, keepers at home–KJV<br>Workers at home–NASB<br>**Busy at home–NIV**<br>Chaste, homemakers–NKJV<br>Pure, take care of their homes–NLT<br><br>**POSB REFERENCE**<br>(Tit.2:4-5; esp. v.5)<br>Note 4, point 6 | Gender—feminine<br>Number—plural<br>Stem or root—from **οἰκουργός**, όν<br>Concordance References:<br>⇒ Strong's #3626 oikourgos<br>⇒ NIV #3877 oikourgos<br>⇒ NASB #3626 oikourgos<br><br>**Titus 2:5**<br>To be discreet, **chaste, keepers at home**, good, obedient to their own husbands, that the word of God be not blasphemed. [KJV]<br>To be sensible, pure, **workers at home**, kind, being subject to their own husbands, that the word of God may not be dishonored. [NASB]<br>To be self-controlled and pure, to be **busy at home**, to be kind, and to be subject to their husbands, so that no one will malign the word of God. [NIV]<br>To be discreet, **chaste, homemakers**, good, obedient to their own husbands, that the word of God may not be blasphemed. [NKJV]<br>To live wisely and be **pure**, to **take care of their homes**, to do good, and to be submissive to their husbands. Then they will not bring shame on the word of God. [NLT]<br>σώφρονας, ἁγνάς, **οἰκουργούς** ἀγαθάς, ὑποτασσομένας τοῖς ἰδίοις ἀνδράσιν, ἵνα μὴ ὁ λόγος τοῦ Θεοῦ βλασφημῆται. [GNS]<br>σώφρονας ἁγνάς **οἰκουργούς** ἀγαθάς, ὑποτασσομένας τοῖς ἰδίοις ἀνδράσιν, ἵνα μὴ ὁ λόγος τοῦ θεοῦ βλασφημῆται. [GNT] | **Practical Application**<br>Young women are to be *busy at home*: homemakers. No better exposition of this command could be given than that written by Oliver Greene:<br><br>*"This does not mean that the wife is never to go out of the home, never to take part in any outside interests; but she is not to neglect the duties of the home in order to participate in things outside the home. In other words, she is not to be better known outside the home than in the home, by her own husband and family. She is to be diligent at home—not lazy or slothful, not unconcerned about the home and the things pertaining thereto—but to give her best to the home, seeing that things are in order and that the home is kept as becomes a Christian....The duty of a Christian mother is first to her home, and these other interests must be secondary"* (*The Epistles of Paul the Apostle to Timothy and Titus*. Greenville, SC: The Gospel Hour, Inc., 1964, p.444f). |
| **#464**<br>**By Christ Jesus**<br><br>In Christ Jesus–KJV<br>In Christ Jesus–NASB<br>**By Christ Jesus–NIV**<br>In Christ Jesus–NKJV<br>Through Christ Jesus–NLT<br><br>**POSB REFERENCE**<br>(Romans 3:24)<br>Note 3, point 2 | ἐν Χριστῷ Ἰησοῦ· = *en Christō Iēsou*<br>Pronunciation: [en khris-tow' ee-ay-soo']<br>Parsing *en* (part of speech): preposition<br>Case—dative<br>Stem or root—from ἐν<br>Concordance References:<br>⇒ Strong's #1722 en + 5547 Christos + 2424 Iēsous<br>⇒ NIV #1877 en [by] + 5986 Christos [Christ] + 2652 Iēsous [Jesus]<br>⇒ NASB #1722 en + 5547 Christos + 2424 Iēsous<br><br>**Romans 3:24**<br>Being justified freely by his grace through the redemption that is **in Christ Jesus**: [KJV]<br>Being justified as a gift by His grace through the redemption which is **in Christ Jesus**; [NASB]<br>And are justified freely by his grace through the redemption that came **by Christ Jesus**. [NIV]<br>Being justified freely by His grace through the redemption that is **in Christ Jesus**, [NKJV]<br>Yet now God in his gracious kindness declares us not guilty. He has done this **through Christ Jesus**, who has freed us by taking away our sins. [NLT]<br>δικαιούμενοι δωρεὰν τῇ αὐτοῦ χάριτι διὰ τῆς ἀπολυτρώσεως τῆς **ἐν Χριστῷ Ἰησοῦ**· [GNS]<br>δικαιούμενοι δωρεὰν τῇ αὐτοῦ χάριτι διὰ τῆς ἀπολυτρώσεως τῆς **ἐν Χριστῷ Ἰησοῦ**· [GNT] | *By* Christ Jesus, *in* Christ Jesus, *through* Christ Jesus.<br><br>**Practical Application**<br>Redemption is "by Christ Jesus," wrought through His death and sufferings. Of this there can be no doubt; the fact is critical to a person's destiny. Redemption is not brought about...<br>• by the life of Christ.<br>• by the power of Christ.<br>• by the example of Christ.<br>Scripture is abundantly clear about this. His cross and His sacrifice in death are what brought about redemption. Redemption is because of the shed blood of Jesus Christ, God's very own Son. Through Christ and Christ alone, redemption is...<br>• accomplished<br>• a reality<br>• wrought<br>• a truth<br>• a fact<br>• fulfilled |
| **#465**<br>**By Him**<br><br>By him–KJV<br>**By Him–NASB**<br>**By him–NIV**<br>**By Him–NKJV**<br>Christ is the one through–NLT | ἐν αὐτῷ = *en autō*<br>Pronunciation: [en ow-tow']<br>Parsing *autō* (part of speech): pronoun<br>Case—dative<br>Gender—masculine<br>Person—3rd person<br>Number—singular<br>Stem or root—from αὐτός, ή, ό<br>Concordance References:<br>⇒ Strong's #1722 en + 846 autos<br>⇒ NIV #1877 en [by] + 899 autos [him]<br>⇒ NASB #1722 en + 846 autos | By Him; Christ is the One through. The words "by Him" (*en autō*) mean *in Him*; that is, creation took place *in* Christ, *within* His very being.<br><br>**Practical Application**<br>⇒ The heart of Christ desired the world.<br>⇒ The mind of Christ planned the world.<br>⇒ The will of Christ destined the world.<br>⇒ The Word of Christ created the world.<br>⇒ The creation of the world took place with- |

# PRACTICAL WORD STUDIES
## in the NEW TESTAMENT

| ENGLISH WORD | GREEK WORD AND VERSE | THE WORD MEANS... |
|---|---|---|
| **POSB REFERENCE** (Col.1:16) Note 1, point 1 | **Col. 1:16**<br>For **by him** were all things created, that are in heaven, and that are in earth, visible and invisible, whether they be thrones, or dominions, or principalities, or powers: all things were created by him, and for him: [KJV]<br>For **by Him** all things were created, both in the heavens and on earth, visible and invisible, whether thrones or dominions or rulers or authorities—all things have been created by Him and for Him. [NASB]<br>For **by him** all things were created: things in heaven and on earth, visible and invisible, whether thrones or powers or rulers or authorities; all things were created by him and for him. [NIV]<br>For **by Him** all things were created that are in heaven and that are on earth, visible and invisible, whether thrones or dominions or principalities or powers. All things were created through Him and for Him. [NKJV]<br>**Christ is the one through** whom God created everything in heaven and earth. He made the things we can see and the things we can't see—kings, kingdoms, rulers, and authorities. Everything has been created through him and for him. [NLT]<br>ὅτι **ἐν αὐτῷ** ἐκτίσθη τὰ πάντα, τὰ ἐν τοῖς οὐρανοῖς καὶ τὰ ἐπὶ τῆς γῆς, τὰ ὁρατὰ καὶ τὰ ἀόρατα, εἴτε θρόνοι, εἴτε κυριότητες, εἴτε ἀρχαί, εἴτε ἐξουσίαι· τὰ πάντα δι᾽ αὐτοῦ καὶ εἰς αὐτὸν ἔκτισται· [GNS]<br>ὅτι **ἐν αὐτῷ** ἐκτίσθη τὰ πάντα ἐν τοῖς οὐρανοῖς καὶ ἐπὶ τῆς γῆς, τὰ ὁρατὰ καὶ τὰ ἀόρατα, εἴτε θρόνοι εἴτε κυριότητες εἴτε ἀρχαὶ εἴτε ἐξουσίαι· τὰ πάντα δι᾽ αὐτοῦ καὶ εἰς αὐτὸν ἔκτισται· [GNT] | in Christ, within His personality and being. The world was born within Him.<br>⇒ It was the *love of Christ* that moved His heart to create the world.<br>⇒ It was the *knowledge of Christ* that aroused His mind to plan the world.<br>⇒ It was the *riches of His grace* that stirred Him to will the world.<br>⇒ It was the *power of His Word* that energized or brought the world into existence.<br><br>The universe exists because of Christ and because of Him alone. The idea for the universe was born in Him, and the actual creation of the universe took place by His own energy and effort. Jesus Christ Himself brought the universe into existence. |
| **#466**<br>**By His Doing**<br><br>Of him–KJV<br>**By His doing–NASB**<br>Because of him–NIV<br>Of Him–NKJV<br>God alone made it possible–NLT<br><br>**POSB REFERENCE**<br>(1 Cor.1:30-31; esp. v.30)<br>Note 4 | ἐξ αὐτοῦ = *ex autou*<br>Pronunciation: [ex ow-too']<br>Parsing *autou* (part of speech): noun<br>    Type—pronoun<br>    Case—genitive<br>    Gender—masculine<br>    Person—3rd person<br>    Number—singular<br>    Stem or root—from αὐτός, ή, ό<br>Concordance References:<br>  ⇒ Strong's #1537 ek + 846 autos<br>  ⇒ NIV #1666 ek [because of] + 899 autos [him]<br>  ⇒ NASB #1537 ek + 846 autos<br><br>**1 Cor. 1:30**<br>But **of him** are ye in Christ Jesus, who of God is made unto us wisdom, and righteousness, and sanctification, and redemption: [KJV]<br>But **by His doing** you are in Christ Jesus, who became to us wisdom from God, and righteousness and sanctification, and redemption, [NASB]<br>It is **because of him** that you are in Christ Jesus, who has become for us wisdom from God—that is, our righteousness, holiness and redemption. [NIV]<br>But **of Him** you are in Christ Jesus, who became for us wisdom from God—and righteousness and sanctification and redemption— [NKJV]<br>**God alone made it possible** for you to be in Christ Jesus. For our benefit God made Christ to be wisdom itself. He is the one who made us acceptable to God. He made us pure and holy, and he gave himself to purchase our freedom. [NLT]<br>ἐξ αὐτοῦ δὲ ὑμεῖς ἐστε ἐν Χριστῷ Ἰησοῦ, ὃς ἐγενήθη ἡμῖν σοφία ἀπὸ Θεοῦ, δικαιοσύνη τε καὶ ἁγιασμός, καὶ ἀπολύτρωσις, [GNS]<br>ἐξ αὐτοῦ δὲ ὑμεῖς ἐστε ἐν Χριστῷ Ἰησοῦ, ὃς ἐγενήθη σοφία ἡμῖν ἀπὸ θεοῦ, δικαιοσύνη τε καὶ ἁγιασμὸς καὶ ἀπολύτρωσις, [GNT] | Because of (God); out of God; out of His nature (of love and salvation); by God's doing.<br><br>**Practical Application**<br>God chooses the believer to be in Christ (see POSB *Deeper Study* #1, Position in Christ—Romans 8:1 for discussion). Again, the stress is that it is God who saves a person; the person does not save himself, no matter how capable he is or how much good he may do. How is God able to save people? By Christ. God took Christ and presented Him to the world as the wisdom of God. |

# PRACTICAL WORD STUDIES
## in the NEW TESTAMENT

| ENGLISH WORD | GREEK WORD AND VERSE | THE WORD MEANS... |
|---|---|---|
| **#467**<br>**By The Prophetic Scriptures**<br><br>By the scriptures of the prophets–KJV<br>By the Scriptures of the prophets–NASB<br>Through the prophetic writings–NIV<br>**By the prophetic Scriptures–NKJV**<br>As the prophets foretold–NLT<br><br>**POSB REFERENCE**<br>(Rom.16:25-26, esp. v.26)<br>Note 3, point 2 | διά γραφῶν προφητικῶν = dia graphōn prophētikōn<br>Pronunciation: [di-ah graf-own' prof-ay-tik-own']<br>Parsing *dia* (part of speech): preposition<br>  Case—genitive<br>  Stem or root—from διά<br>Parsing *graphōn* (part of speech): noun<br>  Case—genitive<br>  Gender—feminine<br>  Number—plural<br>  Stem or root—from γραφή, ῆς<br>Parsing *prophētikōn* (part of speech): adjective<br>  Case—genitive<br>  Gender—feminine<br>  Number—plural<br>  Stem or root—from προφητικός, ή, όν<br>Concordance References:<br>⇒ Strong's #1223 dia + 1124 graphē + 4397 prophētikos<br>⇒ NIV #1328 dia [through] + 1210 graphē [writings] + 4738 prophētikos [prophetic]<br>⇒ NASB #1223 dia + 1124 graphē + 4397 prophētikos<br><br>**Romans 16:26**<br>But now is made manifest, and **by the scriptures of the prophets**, according to the commandment of the everlasting God, made known to all nations for the obedience of faith: [KJV]<br>But now is manifested, and **by the Scriptures of the prophets**, according to the commandment of the eternal God, has been made known to all the nations, leading to obedience of faith; [NASB]<br>But now revealed and made known **through the prophetic writings** by the command of the eternal God, so that all nations might believe and obey him—[NIV]<br>But now has been made manifest, and **by the prophetic Scriptures** has been made known to all nations, according to the commandment of the everlasting God, for obedience to the faith— [NKJV]<br>But now **as the prophets foretold** and as the eternal God has commanded, this message is made known to all Gentiles everywhere, so that they might believe and obey Christ. [NLT]<br>φανερωθέντος δὲ νῦν **διά τε γραφῶν προφητικῶν**, κατ' ἐπιταγὴν τοῦ αἰωνίου Θεοῦ, εἰς ὑπακοὴν πίστεως εἰς πάντα τὰ ἔθνη γνωρισθέντος, [GNS]<br>φανερωθέντος δὲ νῦν **διά τε γραφῶν προφητικῶν** κατ' ἐπιταγὴν τοῦ αἰωνίου θεοῦ εἰς ὑπακοὴν πίστεως εἰς πάντα τὰ ἔθνη γνωρισθέντος, [GNT] | Through the prophetic writings; by the Scriptures of the prophets; as the prophets foretold.<br><br>**Practical Application**<br>God wants the world to know the gospel; therefore, He has commanded that it be revealed and proclaimed to the world. But note the crucial point: it is revealed by the prophetic Scriptures (*dia graphōn prophētikōn*). This is extremely important, for it tells us exactly where we are to find out about God and His message to the world. We do not discover God by natural reasoning: God reveals Himself to us.<br>    There are two questions that desperately need to be studied by everyone.<br>1. Since God has revealed how men are to become acceptable to Him, why do men continue to create their own ideas about how to reach God? Why do men continue to think they will be acceptable to God if they can just do enough good to pacify God? Why do most men continue to think that God will never reject them, that they are not evil enough to be unacceptable to God?<br>2. Since God has revealed the gospel in the prophetic Scriptures, why do men not rush to the Scriptures to find the truth? Why do men not search the Scriptures daily to find out what God has revealed? (Acts 17:11). |
| **#468**<br>**By The Scriptures Of The Prophets**<br><br>**By the scriptures of the prophets–KJV**<br>**By the Scriptures of the prophets–NASB**<br>Through the prophetic writings–NIV<br>By the prophetic Scriptures–NKJV<br>As the prophets foretold–NLT | διά γραφῶν προφητικῶν = dia graphōn prophētikōn<br>Pronunciation: [di-ah graf-own' prof-ay-tik-own']<br>Parsing *dia* (part of speech): preposition<br>  Case—genitive<br>  Stem or root—from διά<br>Parsing *graphōn* (part of speech): noun<br>  Case—genitive<br>  Gender—feminine<br>  Number—plural<br>  Stem or root—from γραφή, ῆς<br>Parsing *prophētikōn* (part of speech): adjective<br>  Case—genitive<br>  Gender—feminine<br>  Number—plural<br>  Stem or root—from προφητικός, ή, όν<br>Concordance References:<br>⇒ Strong's #1223 dia + 1124 graphē + 4397 prophētikos<br>⇒ NIV #1328 dia [through] + 1210 graphē [writings] + 4738 prophētikos [prophetic]<br>⇒ NASB #1223 dia + 1124 graphē + 4397 prophētikos | Through the prophetic writings; by the Scriptures of the prophets; as the prophets foretold.<br><br>**Practical Application**<br>God wants the world to know the gospel; therefore, He has commanded that it be revealed and proclaimed to the world. But note the crucial point: it is revealed by the prophetic Scriptures (*dia graphōn prophētikōn*). This is extremely important, for it tells us exactly where we are to find out about God and His message to the world. We do not discover God by natural reasoning: God reveals Himself to us.<br>    There are two questions that desperately need to be studied by everyone.<br>1. Since God has revealed how men are to become acceptable to Him, why do men continue to create their own ideas about how to reach God? Why do men continue to think |

| ENGLISH WORD | GREEK WORD AND VERSE | THE WORD MEANS |
|---|---|---|
| **POSB REFERENCE** (Rom.16:25-26, esp. v.26) Note 3, point 2 | **Romans 16:26**<br>But now is made manifest, and **by the scriptures of the prophets**, according to the commandment of the everlasting God, made known to all nations for the obedience of faith: [KJV]<br>But now is manifested, and **by the Scriptures of the prophets**, according to the commandment of the eternal God, has been made known to all the nations, leading to obedience of faith; [NASB]<br>But now has been made manifest, and **by the prophetic Scriptures** has been made known to all nations, according to the commandment of the everlasting God, for obedience to the faith—[NKJV]<br>But now **as the prophets foretold** and as the eternal God has commanded, this message is made known to all Gentiles everywhere, so that they might believe and obey Christ. [NLT]<br>φανερωθέντος δὲ νῦν **διά τε γραφῶν προφητικῶν**, κατ' ἐπιταγὴν τοῦ αἰωνίου Θεοῦ, εἰς ὑπακοὴν πίστεως εἰς πάντα τὰ ἔθνη γνωρισθέντος, [GNS]<br>φανερωθέντος δὲ νῦν **διά τε γραφῶν προφητικῶν** κατ' ἐπιταγὴν τοῦ αἰωνίου θεοῦ εἰς ὑπακοὴν πίστεως εἰς πάντα τὰ ἔθνη γνωρισθέντος, [GNT] | they will be acceptable to God if they can just do enough good to pacify God? Why do most men continue to think that God will never reject them, that they are not evil enough to be unacceptable to God?<br>2. Since God has revealed the gospel in the prophetic Scriptures, why do men not rush to the Scriptures to find the truth? Why do men not search the Scriptures daily to find out what God has revealed? (cp. Acts 17:11). |

# PRACTICAL WORD STUDIES
## in the NEW TESTAMENT

| ENGLISH WORD | GREEK WORD AND VERSE | THE WORD MEANS... |
|---|---|---|
| **#469**<br>**Calamities**<br><br>Distresses–KJV<br>Distresses–NASB<br>Distresses–NIV<br>Distresses–NKJV<br>**Calamities–NLT**<br><br>**POSB<br>REFERENCE**<br>(2 Cor.6:4-5; esp. v.4)<br>Note 3 | στενοχωρίαις = stenochōriais<br>Pronunciation: [sten-okh-o-ree'-ah-ees]<br>Parsing (part of speech): noun<br>    Case—dative<br>    Gender—feminine<br>    Number—plural<br>    Stem or root—from στενοχωρία, ας<br>Concordance References:<br>  ⇒ Strong's #4730 stenochōria<br>  ⇒ NIV #5103 stenochōria<br>  ⇒ NASB #4730 stenochōria<br><br>**2 Cor. 6:4**<br>But in all things approving ourselves as the ministers of God, in much patience, in afflictions, in necessities, in **distresses**, [KJV]<br>But in everything commending ourselves as servants of God, in much endurance, in afflictions, in hardships, in **distresses**, [NASB]<br>Rather, as servants of God we commend ourselves in every way: in great endurance; in troubles, hardships and **distresses**; [NIV]<br>But in all things we commend ourselves as ministers of God: in much patience, in tribulations, in needs, in **distresses**, [NKJV]<br>In everything we do we try to show that we are true ministers of God. We patiently endure troubles and hardships and **calamities** of every kind. [NLT]<br>ἀλλ' ἐν παντὶ συνίσταντες ἑαυτοὺς ὡς Θεοῦ διάκονοι, ἐν ὑπομονῇ πολλῇ, ἐν θλίψεσιν, ἐν ἀνάγκαις, ἐν **στενοχωρίαις**, [GNS]<br>ἀλλ' ἐν παντὶ συνίσταντες ἑαυτοὺς ὡς θεοῦ διάκονοι, ἐν ὑπομονῇ πολλῇ, ἐν θλίψεσιν, ἐν ἀνάγκαις, ἐν **στενοχωρίαις**, [GNT] | Distresses, difficulties, troubles, straits, calamities; hard places; tight places; inescapable situations.<br><br>**Practical Application**<br>It is the picture of being cornered and being unable to escape; a picture of having no room or place to turn, of being forced to confront the situation or else being utterly devastated and defeated. When the minister or servant is cornered by temptation or trial—when there seems to be no escape—his only resource is endurance. He must steadfastly endure lest he offend the gospel and become a stumbling block to others. |
| **#470**<br>**Calamity**<br><br>Anguish–KJV<br>Distress–NASB<br>Distress–NIV<br>Anguish–NKJV<br>**Calamity–NLT**<br><br>**POSB<br>REFERENCE**<br>(Rom.2:9)<br>*Deeper Study #9* | στενοχωρία = stenochōria<br>Pronunciation: [sten-okh-o-ree'-ah]<br>Parsing (part of speech): noun<br>    Case—nominative<br>    Gender—feminine<br>    Number—singular<br>    Stem or root—from στενοχωρία, ας<br>Concordance References:<br>  ⇒ Strong's #4730 stenochōria<br>  ⇒ NIV #5103 stenochōria<br>  ⇒ NASB #4730 stenochōria<br><br>**Romans 2:9**<br>Tribulation and **anguish**, upon every soul of man that doeth evil, of the Jew first, and also of the Gentile; [KJV]<br>There will be tribulation and **distress** for every soul of man who does evil, of the Jew first and also of the Greek, [NASB]<br>There will be trouble and **distress** for every human being who does evil: first for the Jew, then for the Gentile; [NIV]<br>Tribulation and **anguish**, on every soul of man who does evil, of the Jew first and also of the Greek; [NKJV]<br>There will be trouble and **calamity** for everyone who keeps on sinning—for the Jew first and also for the Gentile. [NLT]<br>θλῖψις καὶ **στενοχωρία** ἐπὶ πᾶσαν ψυχὴν ἀνθρώπου τοῦ κατεργαζομένου τὸ κακόν, Ἰουδαίου τε πρῶτον καὶ Ἕλληνος· [GNS]<br>θλῖψις καὶ **στενοχωρία** ἐπὶ πᾶσαν ψυχὴν ἀνθρώπου τοῦ κατεργαζομένου τὸ κακόν, Ἰουδαίου τε πρῶτον καὶ Ἕλληνος· [GNT] | Distress, anguish, calamity, trouble, hardship, difficulty. It means to be put into a narrow place; to be compressed together; to experience extreme pain, sorrow, and affliction.<br><br>**Practical Application**<br>Every evil-doer is to be judged, both Jew and Gentile. No evil-doer will escape. Every soul of man that does evil will suffer, and the judgment will be severe and terrible. His judgment will involve indignation and wrath, tribulation and anguish (see POSB *Deeper Study #6*—Romans 2:8; POSB *Deeper Study #7*—Romans 2:8; POSB *Deeper Study #8*—Romans 2:9; and POSB *Deeper Study #9*—Romans 2:9 for discussion). |
| **#471**<br>**Call–Called** | ὅσους ἂν προσκαλέσηται = hosous an proskalesētai<br>Pronunciation: [ha-soos an pros-kal-eh'-say-tah-ee]<br>Parsing *proskalesētai* (part of speech): verb<br>    Mood—subjunctive<br>    Tense—aorist | To call; to be called; to summon; to invite; to gather together. |

# PRACTICAL WORD STUDIES
## in the NEW TESTAMENT

| ENGLISH WORD | GREEK WORD AND VERSE | THE WORD MEANS... |
|---|---|---|
| Many..shall call–KJV<br>Many..shall call–NASB<br>All whom..call–NIV<br>Will call–NKJV<br>All who have been called–NLT<br><br>**POSB REFERENCE**<br>(Acts 2:39)<br>*Deeper Study #3* | Voice—middle deponent<br>Person—3rd person<br>Number—singular<br>Stem or root—from προσκαλέομαι<br>Concordance References:<br>⇒ Strong's #302+ 3745 an hosos + 4341 proskaleō<br>⇒ NIV #323+ 4012 an hosos + 4673 proskaleō<br>⇒ NASB #302+ 3745 an hosos + 4341 proskaleō<br><br>**Acts 2:39**<br>For the promise is unto you, and to your children, and to all that are afar off, even as **many** as the Lord our God **shall call**. [KJV]<br>"For the promise is for you and your children, and for all who are far off, as **many** as the Lord our God **shall call** to Himself." [NASB]<br>The promise is for you and your children and for all who are far off—for **all whom** the Lord our God will **call**." [NIV]<br>For the promise is to you and to your children, and to all who are afar off, as many as the Lord our God **will call**." [NKJV]<br>This promise is to you and to your children, and even to the Gentiles—**all who have been called** by the Lord our God." [NLT]<br>ὑμῖν γάρ ἐστιν ἡ ἐπαγγελία καὶ τοῖς τέκνοις ὑμῶν, καὶ πᾶσι τοῖς εἰς μακράν, **ὅσους ἂν προσκαλέσηται** Κύριος ὁ Θεὸς ἡμῶν. [GNS]<br>ὑμῖν γάρ ἐστιν ἡ ἐπαγγελία καὶ τοῖς τέκνοις ὑμῶν καὶ πᾶσιν τοῖς εἰς μακρὰν **ὅσους ἂν προσκαλέσηται** κύριος ὁ θεὸς ἡμῶν. [GNT] | **Practical Application**<br>God has to call a person to Himself because man is dead to God and resists the gospel. Man's deadness and resistance are seen in the very word call. The word call has both the idea of initiative and deadness and of constraint and resistance. For example, the calling of a person to simply come involves both actions...<br>• of pulling him to come.<br>• of being dead (unaware and not knowing or resisting the fact that one was to come).<br>Man, self-centered and rebellious toward God, likes to feel independent. Consequently, man is dead to God and resistant to the pulling call and quickening power of God. |
| **#472**<br>**Call Out– Called Out**<br><br>Cried–KJV<br>Call out–NASB<br>Called out–NIV<br>Cried–NKJV<br>Called out–NLT<br><br>**POSB REFERENCE**<br>(Lk.8:5-8; esp. v.8)<br>Note 2, point 4 | ἐφώνει = *ephōnei*<br>Pronunciation: [eh-fo-neh'-ee]<br>Parsing (part of speech): verb<br>  Mood—indicative<br>  Tense—imperfect<br>  Voice—active<br>  Person—3rd person<br>  Number—singular<br>  Stem or root—from φωνέω<br>Concordance References:<br>⇒ Strong's #5455 phōneō<br>⇒ NIV #5888 phōneō<br>⇒ NASB #5455 phōneō<br><br>**Luke 8:8**<br>And other fell on good ground, and sprang up, and bare fruit an hundredfold. And when he had said these things, he **cried**, He that hath ears to hear, let him hear. [KJV]<br>"And other seed fell into the good soil, and grew up, and produced a crop a hundred times as great." As He said these things, He would **call out**, "He who has ears to hear, let him hear." [NASB]<br>Still other seed fell on good soil. It came up and yielded a crop, a hundred times more than was sown."When he said this, he **called out**, "He who has ears to hear, let him hear." [NIV]<br>But others fell on good ground, sprang up, and yielded a crop a hundredfold." When He had said these things He **cried**, "He who has ears to hear, let him hear!" [NKJV]<br>Still other seed fell on fertile soil. This seed grew and produced a crop one hundred times as much as had been planted." When he had said this, he **called out**, "Anyone who is willing to hear should listen and understand!" [NLT]<br>καὶ ἕτερον ἔπεσεν ἐπὶ τὴν γῆν τὴν ἀγαθήν, καὶ φυὲν ἐποίησε καρπὸν ἑκατονταπλασίονα. Ταῦτα λέγων, **ἐφώνει**, Ὁ ἔχων ὦτα ἀκούειν ἀκουέτω. [GNS]<br>καὶ ἕτερον ἔπεσεν εἰς τὴν γῆν τὴν ἀγαθήν καὶ φυὲν ἐποίησεν καρπὸν ἑκατονταπλασίονα. ταῦτα λέγων **ἐφώνει**, Ὁ ἔχων ὦτα ἀκούειν ἀκουέτω. [GNT] | To call out; to cry; to summon; to call out with a loud voice.<br><br>**Practical Application**<br>In this Scripture, note what Jesus did. Immediately upon finishing the parable, He called out (*ephōnei*) with a loud shout: "He who has ears to hear, let him hear." He warned: "Hear!" He issued a strong warning. |

# Practical Word Studies
## in the New Testament

| ENGLISH WORD | GREEK WORD AND VERSE | THE WORD MEANS... |
|---|---|---|
| **#473**<br>**Called**<br><br>Called–KJV<br>Called–NASB<br>Called–NIV<br>Called–NKJV<br>Called–NLT<br><br>**POSB REFERENCE**<br>(Jude 1:1-2; esp. v.1)<br>Note 2, point 3 | κλητοῖς = klētois<br>Pronunciation: [klay-toys]<br>Parsing (part of speech): pronominal adjective<br>    Case—dative<br>    Gender—masculine<br>    Number—plural<br>    Stem or root—from κλητός, ή, όν<br>Concordance References:<br>  ⇒ Strong's #2822 klētos<br>  ⇒ NIV #3105 klētos<br>  ⇒ NASB #2822 klētos<br><br>**Jude 1:1**<br>Jude, the servant of Jesus Christ, and brother of James, to them that are sanctified by God the Father, and preserved in Jesus Christ, and **called**: [KJV]<br>Jude, a bond-servant of Jesus Christ, and brother of James, to those who are the **called**, beloved in God the Father, and kept for Jesus Christ: [NASB]<br>Jude, a servant of Jesus Christ and a brother of James, To those who have been **called**, who are loved by God the Father and kept by Jesus Christ: [NIV]<br>Jude, a bondservant of Jesus Christ, and brother of James, To those who are **called**, sanctified by God the Fater, and preserved in Jesus Christ: [NKJV]<br>This letter is from Jude, a slave of Jesus Christ and a brother of James. I am writing to all who are **called** to live in the love of God the Father and the care of Jesus Christ. [NLT]<br><br>Ἰούδας Ἰησοῦ Χριστοῦ δοῦλος, ἀδελφὸς δὲ Ἰακώβου, τοῖς ἐν Θεῷ πατρὶ ἡγιασμένοις, καὶ Ἰησοῦ Χριστῷ τετηρημένοις, **κλητοῖς**· [GNS]<br>Ἰούδας Ἰησοῦ Χριστοῦ δοῦλος, ἀδελφὸς δὲ Ἰακώβου, τοῖς ἐν θεῷ πατρὶ ἠγαπημένοις καὶ Ἰησοῦ Χριστῷ τετηρημένοις **κλητοῖς**· [GNT] | Called, invited, named.<br><br>**Practical Application**<br>Believers are "called" (klētois). This means several things.<br>1. It means that believers are the persons who have responded to the call of the gospel. God calls man to accept the gospel. He tugs and pulls at the heart strings, convicts and convinces man to accept Jesus Christ as His Son, but man has to respond to the call of God. God cannot make the decision for man. The believer is a person who has genuinely accepted the call of God. God summoned him, called him, and the believer responded. He became a believer, a person who truly believed in Jesus Christ.<br>2. It means that a believer has been called to be a *saint*, that is, to live a life of holiness. The word "saint" (*hagios*) means holy one or holiness. The believer is called to be holy and pure and righteous just as God is.<br>3. It means that the believer is called to have a heavenly hope. He is called to an eternal hope, the hope of living forever with God. He is called to be perfected and conformed to the image of the Lord Jesus Christ forever.<br>4. It means that the believer is appointed to a very special task and duty while on earth. He is called to serve Jesus Christ. |
| **#474**<br>**Called Out**<br><br>Cried–KJV<br>Cried out–NASB<br>Cried out–NIV<br>Cried out–NKJV<br>**Called out–NLT**<br><br>**POSB REFERENCE**<br>(Jn.7:25-31; esp. v.28)<br>Note 2 | ἔκραξεν = ekraxen<br>Pronunciation: [eh-krahd'-zehn]<br>Parsing (part of speech): verb<br>    Mood—indicative<br>    Tense—aorist<br>    Voice—active<br>    Person—3rd person<br>    Number—singular<br>    Stem or root—from κράζω<br>Concordance References:<br>  ⇒ Strong's #2896 krazo<br>  ⇒ NIV #3189 krazo<br>  ⇒ NASB #2896 krazo<br><br>**John 7:28**<br>Then **cried** Jesus in the temple as he taught, saying, Ye both know me, and ye know whence I am: and I am not come of myself, but he that sent me is true, whom ye know not. [KJV]<br>Jesus therefore **cried out** in the temple, teaching and saying, "You both know Me and know where I am from; and I have not come of Myself, but He who sent Me is true, whom you do not know. [NASB]<br>Then Jesus, still teaching in the temple courts, **cried out**, "Yes, you know me, and you know where I am from. I am not here on my own, but he who sent me is true. You do not know him, [NIV]<br>Then Jesus **cried out**, as He taught in the temple, saying, "You both know Me, and you know where I am from; and I have not come of Myself, but He who sent Me is true, whom you do not know. [NKJV]<br>While Jesus was teaching in the Temple, he **called out**, "Yes, you know me, and you know where I come from. But I represent one you don't know, and he is true. [NLT]<br><br>ἔκραξεν οὖν ἐν τῷ ἱερῷ διδάσκων ὁ Ἰησοῦς καὶ | To call out with a loud voice; to cry out with great emotion; to shout; to scream; to exclaim.<br><br>**Practical Application**<br>In this Scripture, we discover what Christ called out in the temple courts:<br>1. He *is* a man, and men do know where He came from. He was born of Mary and did come from Nazareth, but that is not all. There is much, much more.<br>2. He has come *from God*. God sent Him. Note exactly what Jesus claimed.<br>  a. "I am not here on my own": His mission and message were not His own. He did not dream up nor plan them. He was not out for self glory or to build a movement and a following. What He did was not of Himself.<br>  b. "He who sent me is true." A real Person sent Jesus, and note: the Person is not only real, He is true. He is a Person who is the very embodiment of truth. (See POSB *Deeper Study* #1—John 1:9; POSB *Deeper Study* #2—John 14:6.) What Jesus was claiming and doing was exactly what He had been sent and commissioned to claim and to do.<br>  c. "You do not know Him." They did not know that Person who is truth. Jesus was saying, of course, that they did not know God. If they knew God, really knew Him, they would recognize and know that Jesus' mission and works were of God. They would know that only God's perfect love |

# PRACTICAL WORD STUDIES
## in the NEW TESTAMENT

| ENGLISH WORD | GREEK WORD AND VERSE | THE WORD MEANS... |
|---|---|---|
| | λέγων, Κἀμὲ οἴδατε, καὶ οἴδατε πόθεν εἰμί, καὶ ἀπ' ἐμαυτοῦ οὐκ ἐλήλυθα, ἀλλ' ἔστιν ἀληθινὸς ὁ πέμψας με, ὃν ὑμεῖς οὐκ οἴδατε· [GNS]<br>ἔκραξεν οὖν ἐν τῷ ἱερῷ διδάσκων ὁ Ἰησοῦς καὶ λέγων, Κἀμὲ οἴδατε καὶ οἴδατε πόθεν εἰμί· καὶ ἀπ' ἐμαυτοῦ οὐκ ἐλήλυθα, ἀλλ' ἔστιν ἀληθινὸς ὁ πέμψας με, ὃν ὑμεῖς οὐκ οἴδατε· [GNT] | and power could speak and do as Jesus did.<br>3. "I know Him [God]." Jesus told how He knew God.<br>a. He knew God because He was from God (see POSB *Deeper Study* #1—John 3:31 for verses of Scripture). He actually came from God's presence, from being face to face with Him.<br>b. He knew God because He was sent by God (see POSB Deeper *Study* #3—John 3:34). While face to face with God, God commissioned Him to go forth to *proclaim* and *live* the truth before men. (See POSB *Deeper Study* #2—John 14:6.) |
| **#475**<br>**Called Out**<br><br>Loud voice–KJV<br>Loud voice–NASB<br>**Called out–NIV**<br>Loud voice–NKJV<br>Called to him in a loud voice–NLT<br><br>**POSB REFERENCE**<br>(Acts 14:8-13; esp. v.10)<br>Note 2, point 1e | εἶπεν μεγάλῃ φωνῇ = eipen megalë phönë<br>Pronunciation: [ep'-ee meg'-ah-lay fo-nay']<br>Parsing *eipen* (part of speech): verb<br>   Mood—indicative<br>   Tense—aorist<br>   Voice—active<br>   Person—3rd person<br>   Number—singular<br>   Stem or root—from εἶπον aor. of λέγω<br>Parsing *megalë* (part of speech): adjective<br>   Case—dative<br>   Gender—feminine<br>   Number—singular<br>   Stem or root—from μέγας<br>Parsing *phönë* (part of speech): noun<br>   Case—dative<br>   Gender—feminine<br>   Number—singular<br>   Stem or root—from φωνη<br>Concordance References:<br>⇒ Strong's #44832036 + 3173 + 5456 legö megas phönë<br>⇒ NIV #3306 + 3489 + 5889 legö megas phönë [called out]<br>⇒ NASB #44832036 + 3173 + 5456 legö megas phönë<br><br>**Acts 14:10**<br>Said with a **loud voice**, Stand upright on thy feet. And he leaped and walked. [KJV]<br>Said with a **loud voice**, "Stand upright on your feet." And he leaped up and began to walk. [NASB]<br>And **called out**, "Stand up on your feet!" At that, the man jumped up and began to walk. [NIV]<br>Said with a **loud voice**, "Stand up straight on your feet!" And he leaped and walked. [NKJV]<br>So Paul **called to him in a loud voice**, "Stand up!" And the man jumped to his feet and started walking. [NLT]<br>εἶπε μεγάλῃ τῇ φωνῇ, Ἀνάστηθι ἐπὶ τοὺς πόδας σου ὀρθός. καὶ ἥλλετο καὶ περιεπάτει. [GNS]<br>εἶπεν μεγάλῃ φωνῇ, Ἀνάστηθι ἐπὶ τοὺς πόδας σου ὀρθός. καὶ ἥλατο καὶ περιεπάτει. [GNT] | To call out; to call out with a loud voice, a loud cry, at the top of voice; to give a shout.<br><br>**Practical Application**<br>Paul did not reach out for the man; he did not touch the man at all. He simply spoke to the man. The power was of Christ and the faith was within the man. The man had to exercise his faith, believe in and really trust in the Lord Jesus to be healed just as he did to be saved. |
| **#476**<br>**Called Together**<br><br>Called...together–KJV<br>Called...together–NASB<br>Called...together–NIV<br>Called...together–NKJV<br>Called together–NLT | Συγκαλεσάμενος = sugkalesamenos<br>Pronunciation: [soong-kal-eh'-sah-men-os]<br>Parsing (part of speech): verb<br>   Mood—participle<br>   Tense—aorist<br>   Voice—middle<br>   Case—nominative<br>   Gender—masculine<br>   Number—singular<br>   Stem or root—from συγκαλέω<br>Concordance References:<br>⇒ Strong's #4779 sugkaleö<br>⇒ NIV #5157 sugkaleö<br>⇒ NASB #4779 sugkaleö | To call together; to contact; to summon; to send for; to collect; to assemble.<br><br>**Practical Application**<br>The meaning of this word reveals several things to us.<br>1. The disciples had families and responsibilities. We tend to glamorize the disciples and Jesus, forgetting the disciples were ordinary men with day to day duties. They were not with the Lord at this time. They had to spend some time at home taking care of their families and whatever other duties they had. No |

# PRACTICAL WORD STUDIES
## in the NEW TESTAMENT

| ENGLISH WORD | GREEK WORD AND VERSE | THE WORD MEANS... |
|---|---|---|
| **POSB REFERENCE** (Lk.9:1) Note 1 | **Luke 9:1** Then he **called** his twelve disciples **together**, and gave them power and authority over all devils, and to cure diseases. [KJV] And He **called** the twelve **together**, and gave them power and authority over all the demons, and to heal diseases. [NASB] When Jesus had **called** the Twelve **together**, he gave them power and authority to drive out all demons and to cure diseases, [NIV] Then He **called** His twelve disciples **together** and gave them power and authority over all demons, and to cure diseases. [NKJV] One day Jesus **called together** his twelve apostles and gave them power and authority to cast out demons and to heal all diseases. [NLT] συγκαλεσάμενος δὲ τοὺς δώδεκα μαθητὰς αὐτοῦ, ἔδωκεν αὐτοῖς δύναμιν καὶ ἐξουσίαν ἐπὶ πάντα τὰ δαιμόνια, καὶ νόσους θεραπεύειν. [GNS] Συγκαλεσάμενος δὲ τοὺς δώδεκα ἔδωκεν αὐτοῖς δύναμιν καὶ ἐξουσίαν ἐπὶ πάντα τὰ δαιμόνια καὶ νόσους θεραπεύειν [GNT] | doubt they did spend most of their time with Jesus as traveling evangelists; but at certain times, they returned home in order to tend to family affairs. 2. The basic ingredient for ministry is *togetherness*. Note the words, "called... together." The very thrust of the words points to the importance of coming together. 3. The purpose for coming together is to minister. Jesus was completing His Galilean ministry. He was now ready to set His face toward Jerusalem (Luke 9:51). His ministry had been successful. Multitudes knew of His coming to earth, many had been helped and some did believe and trust. Now, before He left the area, He wanted to reach out one more time to those who were close to believing and to more deeply root and ground those who already believed. 4. The call of Jesus was for the disciples to have power over "all devils, and to cure diseases." a. "Power...over all demons." The word "all" means that the disciple was to have power over all kinds of evil, no matter how evil and enslaving, strong and fierce, subtle and undetected. It also points to the glorious purpose of Jesus. He had come to defeat and conquer the evil forces of this world, to rout and triumph over "all" of them. b. "Power...to cure diseases." This would demonstrate the great compassion of the Lord and draw people to Him (John 12:32). It would also help tremendously in confirming the faith of some. |
| **#477 Came** Was made–KJV Was born–NASB Was–NIV Was born–NKJV **Came–NLT** **POSB REFERENCE** (Romans 1:1-4; esp. v.3) Note 3, point. 2a | γενομένου = genomenou Pronunciation: [ghin'-om-hen-oo] Parsing (part of speech): verb     Mood—participle     Tense—aorist     Voice—middle deponent     Case—genitive     Gender—masculine     Number—singular     Stem or root—from γίνομαι Concordance References:   ⇒ Strong's #1096 ginomai   ⇒ NIV #1181 ginomai   ⇒ NASB #1096 ginomai **Romans 1:3** Concerning his Son Jesus Christ our Lord, which **was made** of the seed of David according to the flesh; [KJV] Concerning His Son, who **was born** of a descendant of David according to the flesh, [NASB] Regarding his Son, who as to his human nature **was** a descendant of David, [NIV] Concerning His Son Jesus Christ our Lord, who **was born** of the seed of David according to the flesh, [NKJV] It is the Good News about his Son, Jesus, who **came** as a man, born into King David's royal family line. [NLT] περὶ τοῦ υἱοῦ αὐτοῦ τοῦ γενομένου ἐκ σπέρματος Δαβὶδ κατὰ σάρκα, [GNS] περὶ τοῦ υἱοῦ αὐτοῦ τοῦ γενομένου ἐκ σπέρματος Δαυὶδ κατὰ σάρκα, [GNT] | Was; was made; was born; came; became; happened; came into being. **Practical Application** The point is this: God sent His Son into the world in human flesh. God's Son became a man—flesh and blood—just like all other men. He had a human nature, and because He had a human nature... • He suffered all the trials of life which we suffer. • He is able to help us through all the trials of life. |
| **#478 Came Down** | καταβάς = katabas Pronunciation: [kat-ab-ah's] Parsing (part of speech): verb     Mood—participle     Tense—aorist | To come down; to descend; to come from a higher place to a lower place. **Practical Application** The phrase "came down" is again in the aorist |

# PRACTICAL WORD STUDIES
## in the NEW TESTAMENT

| ENGLISH WORD | GREEK WORD AND VERSE | THE WORD MEANS... |
|---|---|---|
| Came down–KJV<br>Came down–NASB<br>Came down–NIV<br>Came down–NKJV<br>Came down–NLT<br><br>**POSB REFERENCE**<br>(Jn.6:47-51; esp. v.51)<br>Note 3, point 3b | Voice—active<br>Case—nominative<br>Gender—masculine<br>Person—1st person<br>Number—singular<br>Stem or root—from καταβαίνω<br>Concordance References:<br>⇒ Strong's #2597 katabainō<br>⇒ NIV #2849 katabainō<br>⇒ NASB #2597 katabainō<br><br>**John 6:51**<br>I am the living bread which **came down** from heaven: if any man eat of this bread, he shall live for ever: and the bread that I will give is my flesh, which I will give for the life of the world. [KJV]<br>"I am the living bread that **came down** out of heaven; if anyone eats of this bread, he shall live forever; and the bread also which I shall give for the life of the world is My flesh." [NASB]<br>I am the living bread that **came down** from heaven. If anyone eats of this bread, he will live forever. This bread is my flesh, which I will give for the life of the world." [NIV]<br>I am the living bread which **came down** from heaven. If anyone eats of this bread, he will live forever; and the bread that I shall give is My flesh, which I shall give for the life of the world." [NKJV]<br>I am the living bread that **came down** out of heaven. Anyone who eats this bread will live forever; this bread is my flesh, offered so the world may live." [NLT]<br>ἐγώ εἰμι ὁ ἄρτος ὁ ζῶν, ὁ ἐκ τοῦ οὐρανοῦ **καταβάς**· ἐάν τις φάγῃ ἐκ τούτου τοῦ ἄρτου, ζήσεται εἰς τὸν αἰῶνα. καὶ ὁ ἄρτος δὲ ὃν ἐγὼ δώσω, ἡ σάρξ μου ἐστίν, ἣν ἐγὼ δώσω ὑπὲρ τῆς τοῦ κόσμου ζωῆς. [GNS]<br>ἐγώ εἰμι ὁ ἄρτος ὁ ζῶν ὁ ἐκ τοῦ οὐρανοῦ **καταβάς**· ἐάν τις φάγῃ ἐκ τούτου τοῦ ἄρτου ζήσει εἰς τὸν αἰῶνα, καὶ ὁ ἄρτος δὲ ὃν ἐγὼ δώσω ἡ σάρξ μού ἐστιν ὑπὲρ τῆς τοῦ κόσμου ζωῆς. [GNT] | tense which means Christ came once. The incarnation had never taken place before, nor will it ever take place again. The miraculous entrance of the living Bread into the world is a one-time-only event. |
| **#479**<br>**Came Into Being**<br><br>Were made–KJV<br>**Came into being–NASB**<br>Were made–NIV<br>Were made–NKJV<br>Created–NLT<br><br>**POSB REFERENCE**<br>(Jn.1:3)<br>Note 2, point 2 | ἐγένετο = egeneto<br>Pronunciation: [eh-ghin'-eh-tow]<br>Parsing (part of speech): verb<br>  Mood—indicative<br>  Tense—aorist<br>  Voice—middle deponent<br>  Person—3rd person<br>  Number—singular<br>  Stem or root—from γίνομαι<br>Concordance References:<br>⇒ Strong's #1096 ginomai<br>⇒ NIV #1181 ginomai<br>⇒ NASB #1096 ginomai<br><br>**John 1:3**<br>All things **were made** by him; and without him was not any thing made that was made. [KJV]<br>All things **came into being** by Him, and apart from Him nothing came into being that has come into being. [NASB]<br>Through him all things **were made**; without him nothing was made that has been made. [NIV]<br>All things **were made** through Him, and without Him nothing was made that was made. [NKJV]<br>He **created** everything there is. Nothing exists that he didn't make. [NLT]<br>πάντα δι' αὐτοῦ **ἐγένετο**, καὶ χωρὶς αὐτοῦ **ἐγένετο** οὐδὲ ἕν, ὃ γέγονεν. [GNS]<br>πάντα δι' αὐτοῦ **ἐγένετο**, καὶ χωρὶς αὐτοῦ **ἐγένετο** οὐδὲ ἕν. ὃ γέγονεν [GNT] | Were made; came into being or became; created; to take place; to happen.<br><br>**Practical Application**<br>Note what this is saying. Nothing was existing—no substance, no matter whatsoever. Matter is not eternal. God did not take something outside of Himself, something less than perfect (evil) to create the world. Christ, the Word, took nothing but His will and power; and He spoke the Word and created every single thing out of nothing (*ex nihilo*). |

# PRACTICAL WORD STUDIES
in the NEW TESTAMENT

| ENGLISH WORD | GREEK WORD AND VERSE | THE WORD MEANS... |
|---|---|---|
| **#480**<br>**Came No More**<br><br>**Came not as yet**–KJV<br>**Came no more**–NASB<br>**Not return**–NIV<br>**Came no more**–NKJV<br>**Didn't return**–NLT<br><br>**POSB REFERENCE**<br>(2 Cor.1:23-2:4; esp. v.23)<br>Note 1, 2<br><br>(Special note: see also 2 Cor.2:1, Note 2 for more discussion) | οὐκέτι ἦλθον = ouketi ëlthon<br>Pronunciation: [oo-keh-tee ale'-thon]<br>Parsing ëlthon (part of speech): verb<br>    Mood—indicative<br>    Tense—aorist<br>    Voice—active<br>    Person—1st person<br>    Number—singular<br>    Stem or root—from ἔρχομαι<br>Concordance References:<br>  ⇒ Strong's #3765 ouketi + 2064 erchomai<br>  ⇒ NIV #4033 ouketi [not] + 2262 erchomai [return]<br>  ⇒ NASB #3765 ouketi + 2064 erchomai<br><br>**2 Cor. 1:23**<br>Moreover I call God for a record upon my soul, that to spare you I **came not as yet** unto Corinth. [KJV]<br>But I call God as witness to my soul, that to spare you I **came no more** to Corinth. [NASB]<br>I call God as my witness that it was in order to spare you that I did **not return** to Corinth. [NIV]<br>Moreover I call God as witness against my soul, that to spare you I **came no more** to Corinth. [NKJV]<br>Now I call upon God as my witness that I am telling the truth. The reason I **didn't return** to Corinth was to spare you from a severe rebuke. [NLT]<br>Ἐγὼ δὲ μάρτυρα τὸν Θεὸν ἐπικαλοῦμαι ἐπὶ τὴν ἐμὴν ψυχήν, ὅτι φειδόμενος ὑμῶν **οὐκέτι ἦλθον** εἰς Κόρινθον. [GNS]<br>Ἐγὼ δὲ μάρτυρα τὸν θεὸν ἐπικαλοῦμαι ἐπὶ τὴν ἐμὴν ψυχήν, ὅτι φειδόμενος ὑμῶν **οὐκέτι ἦλθον** εἰς Κόρινθον. [GNT] | Did not return; did not make his way back; did not go back.<br><br>**Practical Application**<br>The statement "I came no more to Corinth" points toward Paul's having made a quick visit to Corinth after writing his first letter, a visit that resulted in the people's rejecting him and breaking his heart (see POSB Introduction, Special Features, pt. 3—1 Corinthians for more discussion). |
| **#481**<br>**Came Not As Yet**<br><br>**Came not as yet**–KJV<br>**Came no more**–NASB<br>**Not return**–NIV<br>**Came no more**–NKJV<br>**Didn't return**–NLT<br><br>**POSB REFERENCE**<br>(2 Cor.1:23-2:4; esp. v.23)<br>Note 1, 2<br><br>(Special note: see also 2 Cor.2:1, Note 2 for more discussion) | οὐκέτι ἦλθον = ouketi ëlthon<br>Pronunciation: [oo-keh-tee ale'-thon]<br>Parsing ëlthon (part of speech): verb<br>    Mood—indicative<br>    Tense—aorist<br>    Voice—active<br>    Person—1st person<br>    Number—singular<br>    Stem or root—from ἔρχομαι<br>Concordance References:<br>  ⇒ Strong's #3765 ouketi + 2064 erchomai<br>  ⇒ NIV #4033 ouketi [not] + 2262 erchomai [return]<br>  ⇒ NASB #3765 ouketi + 2064 erchomai<br><br>**2 Cor. 1:23**<br>Moreover I call God for a record upon my soul, that to spare you I **came not as yet** unto Corinth. [KJV]<br>But I call God as witness to my soul, that to spare you I **came no more** to Corinth. [NASB]<br>I call God as my witness that it was in order to spare you that I did **not return** to Corinth. [NIV]<br>Moreover I call God as witness against my soul, that to spare you I **came no more** to Corinth. [NKJV]<br>Now I call upon God as my witness that I am telling the truth. The reason I **didn't return** to Corinth was to spare you from a severe rebuke. [NLT]<br>Ἐγὼ δὲ μάρτυρα τὸν Θεὸν ἐπικαλοῦμαι ἐπὶ τὴν ἐμὴν ψυχήν, ὅτι φειδόμενος ὑμῶν **οὐκέτι ἦλθον** εἰς Κόρινθον. [GNS]<br>Ἐγὼ δὲ μάρτυρα τὸν θεὸν ἐπικαλοῦμαι ἐπὶ τὴν ἐμὴν ψυχήν, ὅτι φειδόμενος ὑμῶν **οὐκέτι ἦλθον** εἰς Κόρινθον. [GNT] | Did not return; did not make his way back; did not go back.<br><br>**Practical Application**<br>The statement "I came not as yet" can be equally translated, "I came no more to Corinth." This, too, points toward Paul's having made a quick visit to Corinth after writing his first letter, a visit that resulted in the people's rejecting him and breaking his heart (see POSB Introduction, Special Features, pt. 3—1 Corinthians for more discussion). |
| **#482**<br>**Came On** | ἐπέπεσεν ἐπὶ = epepesen epi<br>Pronunciation: [eh-pehp-ehs-en ehp-ee]<br>Parsing epepesen (part of speech): verb<br>    Mood—indicative<br>    Tense—aorist | Came upon; fell upon; fell on.<br><br>**Practical Application**<br>Peter was still preaching; he had not finished his message when the Holy Spirit fell. God and |

# PRACTICAL WORD STUDIES
## in the NEW TESTAMENT

| ENGLISH WORD | GREEK WORD AND VERSE | THE WORD MEANS... |
|---|---|---|
| Fell on–KJV<br>Fell upon–NASB<br>**Came on–NIV**<br>Fell upon–NKJV<br>Fell upon–NLT<br><br>**POSB REFERENCE**<br>(Acts 10:44-45; esp. v.44)<br>Note 1, point 3 | Voice—active<br>Person—3rd person<br>Number—singular<br>Stem or root—from ἐπιπίπτω<br>Parsing *epi* (part of speech): preposition<br>Case—accusative<br>Stem or root—from ἐπί<br>Concordance References:<br>⇒ Strong's #1909 + 1968 epi epipiptö<br>⇒ NIV #2093 + 2158 epi epipiptö<br>⇒ NASB #1909 + 1968 epi epipiptö<br><br>### Acts 10:44<br>While Peter yet spake these words, the Holy Ghost **fell on** all them which heard the word. [KJV]<br>While Peter was still speaking these words, the Holy Spirit **fell upon** all those who were listening to the message. [NASB]<br>While Peter was still speaking these words, the Holy Spirit **came on** all who heard the message. [NIV]<br>While Peter was still speaking these words, the Holy Spirit **fell upon** all those who heard the word. [NKJV]<br>Even as Peter was saying these things, the Holy Spirit **fell upon** all who had heard the message. [NLT]<br>Ἔτι λαλοῦντος τοῦ Πέτρου τὰ ῥήματα ταῦτα, **ἐπέπεσε** τὸ Πνεῦμα τὸ Ἅγιον **ἐπὶ** πάντας τοὺς ἀκούοντας τὸν λόγον. [GNS]<br>Ἔτι λαλοῦντος τοῦ Πέτρου τὰ ῥήματα ταῦτα **ἐπέπεσεν** τὸ πνεῦμα τὸ ἅγιον **ἐπὶ** πάντας τοὺς ἀκούοντας τὸν λόγον. [GNT] | God alone caused the Holy Spirit to fall upon the Gentile believers, not the hands of Peter...<br>• anointing them<br>• being laid upon them<br>• baptizing them<br><br>No man had anything to do with God's pouring His Spirit upon these believers. The gift of the Spirit was the act of God and God's alone. |
| #483<br>**Came Together**<br><br>Abode–KJV<br>Gathering together–NASB<br>**Came together–NIV**<br>Staying–NKJV<br>Returned–NLT<br><br>**POSB REFERENCE**<br>(Mt.17:22)<br>Note 1, point 1 | Συστρεφομένων = *Sustrephomenön*<br>Pronunciation: [sus-tref'-o-me'-known]<br>Parsing (part of speech): verb<br>Mood—participle<br>Tense—present<br>Voice—passive<br>Case—genitive<br>Gender—masculine<br>Person—plural<br>Stem or root—from συστρέφω<br>Concordance References:<br>⇒ Strong's #390 anastrepho<br>⇒ NIV #5370 sustrephö<br>⇒ NASB #390 anastrepho<br><br>### Matthew 17:22<br>And while they **abode** in Galilee, Jesus said unto them, The Son of man shall be betrayed into the hands of men: [KJV]<br>And while they were **gathering together** in Galilee, Jesus said to them, "The Son of Man is going to be delivered into the hands of men; [NASB]<br>When they **came together** in Galilee, he said to them, "The Son of Man is going to be betrayed into the hands of men. [NIV]<br>Now while they were **staying** in Galilee, Jesus said to them, "The Son of Man is about to be betrayed into the hands of men, [NKJV]<br>One day after they had **returned** to Galilee, Jesus told them, "The Son of Man is going to be betrayed. [NLT]<br>Ἀνατρεφομένων δὲ αὐτῶν ἐν τῇ Γαλιλαίᾳ εἶπεν αὐτοῖς ὁ Ἰησοῦς, Μέλλει ὁ υἱὸς τοῦ ἀνθρώπου παραδίδοσθαι εἰς χεῖρας ἀνθρώπων, [GNS]<br>**Συστρεφομένων** δὲ αὐτῶν ἐν τῇ Γαλιλαίᾳ εἶπεν αὐτοῖς ὁ Ἰησοῦς, Μέλλει ὁ υἱὸς τοῦ ἀνθρώπου παραδίδοσθαι εἰς χεῖρας ἀνθρώπων, [GNT] | To have gathered; to come together; to abiode; to return; to go to and fro; a picture of having gathered military troops for a review.<br><br>### Practical Application<br>The force of this word takes on a fresh meaning when the context of this Scripture is understood.<br>Jesus Christ was preparing the "troops"—His disciples—for the time when He would no longer be with them. He was drilling into them the fact that He was to be killed and raised from the dead. Jesus had to continue talking about His death and resurrection because it was so hard to understand. There were three primary reasons why the disciples had difficulty in grasping the fact.<br>1. The Messiah's death and resurrection were new experiences, new happenings. History was to be made. The talk of a literal death and resurrection was bound to be understood in symbolic and spiritual language (see POSB note—Matthew 18:1-2). (How like so many to spiritualize the two events—even though the events really took place and are so strongly proclaimed by the disciples.) (Cp. 1 Cor. 15:3-8. See POSB note—Mark 9:32; POSB note—Mark 9:34.)<br>2. The Messiah's death and resurrection were thought to be impossible. How could God die? Most men proclaim that God cannot die. Of course, the disciples had not yet seen what death really is—basically separation from God (see POSB *Deeper Study* #1—Hebrews 9:27). They had to learn that God was dealing with spiritual and eternal life (and death), not just with physical and temporal life (and death) on this earth. |

## PRACTICAL WORD STUDIES
## in the NEW TESTAMENT

| ENGLISH WORD | GREEK WORD AND VERSE | THE WORD MEANS... |
|---|---|---|
| | | 3. The Messiah's death and resurrection were contrary to all their hopes and expectations. It was just different from all the disciples had ever heard or been taught. The Messiah was thought to be a Messiah of power and sovereign rule not a Messiah who had to suffer and die in order to save man. (See POSB note—Matthew 1:1; POSB *Deeper Study* #2—Matthew 1:18; POSB *Deeper Study* #2—Matthew 3:11; POSB note—Matthew 11:1-6; POSB note—Matthew 11:2-3; POSB *Deeper Study* #1—Matthew 11:5; POSB *Deeper Study* #2—Matthew 11:6; POSB *Deeper Study* #1—Matthew 12:16; POSB note—Matthew 22:42; POSB note—Luke 7:21-23.) |
| #484<br>**Came Together**<br><br>Assembled–KJV<br>**Gathered together–NASB**<br>**Came together–NIV**<br>Assembled–NKJV<br>**Gathered–NLT**<br><br>**POSB REFERENCE**<br>(Mk.14:53)<br>Note 1 | συνέρχονται = sunerchontai<br>Pronunciation: [soon-er'-khon-tah-ee]<br>Parsing (part of speech): verb<br>   Mood—indicative<br>   Tense—present<br>   Voice—middle or passive deponent<br>   Person—3rd person<br>   Number—plural<br>   Stem or root—from συνέρχομαι<br>Concordance References:<br>  ⇒ Strong's #4905 sunerchomai<br>  ⇒ NIV #5302 sunerchomai<br>  ⇒ NASB #4905 sunerchomai<br><br>**Mark 14:53**<br>And they led Jesus away to the high priest: and with him were **assembled** all the chief priests and the elders and the scribes. [KJV]<br>And they led Jesus away to the high priest; and all the chief priests and the elders and the scribes **gathered together**. [NASB]<br>They took Jesus to the high priest, and all the chief priests, elders and teachers of the law **came together**. [NIV]<br>And they led Jesus away to the high priest; and with him were **assembled** all the chief priests, the elders, and the scribes. [NKJV]<br>Jesus was led to the high priest's home where the leading priests, other leaders, and teachers of religious law had **gathered**. [NLT]<br>Καὶ ἀπήγαγον τὸν Ἰησοῦν πρὸς τὸν ἀρχιερέα· καὶ **συνέρχονται** αὐτῷ πάντες οἱ ἀρχιερεῖς καὶ οἱ πρεσβύτεροι καὶ οἱ γραμματεῖς. [GNS]<br>Καὶ ἀπήγαγον τὸν Ἰησοῦν πρὸς τὸν ἀρχιερέα, καὶ **συνέρχονται** πάντες οἱ ἀρχιερεῖς καὶ οἱ πρεσβύτεροι καὶ οἱ γραμματεῖς. [GNT] | To assemble; to gather; to draw together; to come together; to flock together; to resort; to meet with.<br><br>**Practical Application**<br>The word also has the idea of accompanying one another. The picture is that of the Jewish leaders flocking or herding together around Jesus, of being called to accompany one another to their respective seats, ready to pounce on Jesus. |
| #485<br>**Came Upon Him**<br><br>Came upon him–KJV<br>Came upon him–NASB<br>Not translated–NIV<br>Came upon him–NKJV<br>Not translated–NLT<br><br>**POSB REFERENCE**<br>(Acts 6:11-14; esp. v.12)<br>Note 3, point 2 | ἐπιστάντες = epistantes<br>Pronunciation: [ep-is'-tan-tes]<br>Parsing (part of speech): verb<br>   Mood—participle<br>   Tense—aorist<br>   Voice—active<br>   Case—nominative<br>   Gender—masculine<br>   Person—plural<br>   Stem or root—from ἐφίστημι<br>Concordance References:<br>  ⇒ Strong's #2186 ephistēmi<br>  ⇒ NIV #2392 ephistēmi<br>  ⇒ NASB #2186 ephistēmi<br><br>**Acts 6:12**<br>And they stirred up the people, and the elders, and the scribes, and **came upon him**, and caught him, and brought him to the council, [KJV] | Came upon Him; to stand near; to appear; stood beside.<br><br>**Practical Application**<br>The words "came upon him" mean they rushed at him in fury, anger, and violence. |

## PRACTICAL WORD STUDIES
### in the NEW TESTAMENT

| ENGLISH WORD | GREEK WORD AND VERSE | THE WORD MEANS... |
|---|---|---|
| | And they stirred up the people, the elders and the scribes, and they **came upon him** and dragged him away, and brought him before the Council. [NASB]<br>So they stirred up the people and the elders and the teachers of the law. They seized Stephen and brought him before the Sanhedrin. [NIV] —Not Translated<br>And they stirred up the people, the elders, and the scribes; and they **came upon him**, seized him, and brought him to the council. [NKJV]<br>Naturally, this roused the crowds, the elders, and the teachers of religious law. So they arrested Stephen and brought him before the high council. [NLT]—Not Translated<br>συνεκίνησάν τε τὸν λαὸν καὶ τοὺς πρεσβυτέρους καὶ τοὺς γραμματεῖς, καὶ **ἐπιστάντες** συνήρπασαν αὐτόν, καὶ ἤγαγον εἰς τὸ συνέδριον, [GNS]<br>συνεκίνησάν τε τὸν λαὸν καὶ τοὺς πρεσβυτέρους καὶ τοὺς γραμματεῖς, καὶ **ἐπιστάντες** συνήρπασαν αὐτὸν καὶ ἤγαγον εἰς τὸ συνέδριον, [GNT] | |
| **#486**<br>**Can't Understand**<br><br>Receiveth not–KJV<br>Not accept–NASB<br>Not accept–NIV<br>Not receive–NKJV<br>Can't understand–NLT<br><br>**POSB REFERENCE**<br>(1 Cor.2:14)<br>Note 1, point 1 | οὐ δέχεται = ou dechetai<br>Pronunciation: [oo dekh'-eh-tah-ee]<br>Parsing *dechetai* (part of speech): verb<br>  Mood—indicative<br>  Tense—present<br>  Voice—middle or passive deponent<br>  Person—3rd person<br>  Number—singular<br>  Stem or root—from δέχομαι<br>Concordance References:<br> ⇒ Strong's #3756 ou + 1209 dechomai<br> ⇒ NIV #4024 ou [not] + 1312 dechomai [accept]<br> ⇒ NASB #3756 ou + 1209 dechomai<br><br>**1 Cor. 2:14**<br>But the natural man **receiveth not** the things of the Spirit of God: for they are foolishness unto him: neither can he know them, because they are spiritually discerned. [KJV]<br>But a natural man does **not accept** the things of the Spirit of God; for they are foolishness to him, and he cannot understand them, because they are spiritually appraised. [NASB]<br>The man without the Spirit does **not accept** the things that come from the Spirit of God, for they are foolishness to him, and he cannot understand them, because they are spiritually discerned. [NIV]<br>But the natural man does **not receive** the things of the Spirit of God, for they are foolishness to him; nor can he know them, because they are spiritually discerned. [NKJV]<br>But people who aren't Christians **can't understand** these truths from God's Spirit. It all sounds foolish to them because only those who have the Spirit can understand what the Spirit means. [NLT]<br>ψυχικὸς δὲ ἄνθρωπος **οὐ δέχεται** τὰ τοῦ Πνεύματος τοῦ Θεοῦ· μωρία γὰρ αὐτῷ ἐστι, καὶ οὐ δύναται γνῶναι, ὅτι πνευματικῶς ἀνακρίνεται· [GNS]<br>ψυχικὸς δὲ ἄνθρωπος **οὐ δέχεται** τὰ τοῦ πνεύματος τοῦ θεοῦ, μωρία γὰρ αὐτῷ ἐστιν, καὶ οὐ δύναται γνῶναι, ὅτι πνευματικῶς ἀνακρίνεται· [GNT] | Not receive; not accept; not take; not welcome; not bear with; to refuse and regret; not obtain.<br><br>**Practical Application**<br>The man without the Spirit is the natural man. He does not accept the things that come from the Spirit of God. The phrase "can't understand" (*dechetai*) means that spiritual things are not welcomed as a guest, are not accepted. It means to refuse and reject. Spiritual things are of little, if any, concern to the natural man. His mind is primarily upon this world, upon...<br>• bigger and better things<br>• acquiring more and more<br>• desires and feelings<br>• wants and cravings<br>• position and wealth<br>• attention and recognition<br>• ambition and promotion<br>• socials and parties<br>• play and recreation<br>• comfort and ease<br>• drinking and eating<br>• dress and appearance<br><br>The natural man's life and mind are spent focusing upon the natural, upon this world and not upon the spiritual; therefore, in God's eyes he is classified as the natural man. His heart welcomes only the world; it is closed to God. As stated, God is not welcomed into his life. Therefore, he does not accept the things that come from the Spirit of God. |
| **#487**<br>**Captain**<br><br>Captain–KJV<br>Author–NASB<br>Author–NIV<br>Captain–NKJV<br>Perfect leader–NLT | ἀρχηγὸν = archēgon<br>Pronunciation: [ar-khay-gon']<br>Parsing (part of speech): noun<br>  Case—accusative<br>  Gender—masculine<br>  Number—singular<br>  Stem or root—from ἀρχηγός, οῦ<br>Concordance References:<br> ⇒ Strong's #747 archēgos<br> ⇒ NIV #795 archēgos<br> ⇒ NASB #747 archēgos | Author, leader, pioneer, pathfinder, founder, originator, perfect leader. It means the one who blazes forth, cutting through something so that others may follow.<br><br>**Practical Application**<br>Jesus Christ opened up the way or trail to God. This He did by suffering all the experiences of men—perfectly. He remained perfect through all His sufferings. He never sinned; He |

# PRACTICAL WORD STUDIES
## in the NEW TESTAMENT

| ENGLISH WORD | GREEK WORD AND VERSE | THE WORD MEANS... |
|---|---|---|
| **POSB REFERENCE**<br>(Heb.2:9-13; esp. v.10)<br>Note 3, point 2b | **Hebrews 2:10**<br>For it became him, for whom are all things, and by whom are all things, in bringing many sons unto glory, to make the **captain** of their salvation perfect through sufferings. [KJV]<br>For it was fitting for Him, for whom are all things, and through whom are all things, in bringing many sons to glory, to perfect the **author** of their salvation through sufferings. [NASB]<br>In bringing many sons to glory, it was fitting that God, for whom and through whom everything exists, should make the **author** of their salvation perfect through suffering. [NIV]<br>For it was fitting for Him, for whom are all things and by whom are all things, in bringing many sons to glory, to make the **captain** of their salvation perfect through sufferings. [NKJV]<br>And it was only right that God—who made everything and for whom everything was made—should bring his many children into glory. Through the suffering of Jesus, God made him a **perfect leader**, one fit to bring them into their salvation. [NLT]<br>ἔπρεπε γὰρ αὐτῷ, δι' ὃν τὰ πάντα καὶ δι' οὗ τὰ πάντα, πολλοὺς υἱοὺς εἰς δόξαν ἀγαγόντα, τὸν **ἀρχηγὸν** τῆς σωτηρίας αὐτῶν διὰ παθημάτων τελειῶσαι· [GNS]<br>Ἔπρεπεν γὰρ αὐτῷ, δι' ὃν τὰ πάντα καὶ δι' οὗ τὰ πάντα, πολλοὺς υἱοὺς εἰς δόξαν ἀγαγόντα τὸν **ἀρχηγὸν** τῆς σωτηρίας αὐτῶν διὰ παθημάτων τελειῶσαι. [GNT] | never failed, not even once. He learned obedience by the things which He suffered—perfectly. And by such, He secured a perfect and an eternal righteousness for man. He is the perfect pioneer who has cut the perfect path to God. He is the Ideal and Perfect Man who stands for and covers all persons...<br>• all who believe and trust Him to cover them.<br>• all who believe and trust Him to make them presentable to God. |
| **#488**<br>**Captive**<br>Spoil–KJV<br>**Captive–NASB**<br>**Captive–NIV**<br>Cheat–NKJV<br>Astray–NLT<br>**POSB REFERENCE**<br>(Col.2:8)<br>Note 1 | ἔσται συλαγωγῶν = estai sulagōgōn<br>Pronunciation: [es-tah-ee soo-lag-og-o'-gon']<br>Parsing *sulagōgōn* (part of speech): verb<br>  Mood—participle<br>  Tense—present<br>  Voice—active<br>  Case—nominative<br>  Gender—masculine<br>  Number—singular<br>  Stem or root—from συλαγωγέω<br>Concordance References:<br>⇒ Strong's #1510 eimi + 4812 sulagōgeō<br>⇒ NIV #1639+5194 eimi sulagōgeō [takes captive]<br>⇒ NASB #1510 eimi + 4812 sulagōgeō<br><br>**Col. 2:8**<br>Beware lest any man **spoil** you through philosophy and vain deceit, after the tradition of men, after the rudiments of the world, and not after Christ. [KJV]<br>See to it that no one takes you **captive** through philosophy and empty deception, according to the tradition of men, according to the elementary principles of the world, rather than according to Christ. [NASB]<br>See to it that no one takes you **captive** through hollow and deceptive philosophy, which depends on human tradition and the basic principles of this world rather than on Christ. [NIV]<br>Beware lest anyone **cheat** you through philosophy and empty deceit, according to the tradition of men, according to the basic principles of the world, and not according to Christ. [NKJV]<br>Don't let anyone lead you **astray** with empty philosophy and high-sounding nonsense that come from human thinking and from the evil powers of this world, and not from Christ. [NLT]<br>βλέπετε μή τις ὑμᾶς **ἔσται** ὁ **συλαγωγῶν** διὰ τῆς φιλοσοφίας καὶ κενῆς ἀπάτης, κατὰ τὴν παράδοσιν τῶν ἀνθρώπων, κατὰ τὰ στοιχεῖα τοῦ κόσμου, καὶ οὐ κατὰ Χριστόν· [GNS]<br>βλέπετε μή τις ὑμᾶς **ἔσται** ὁ **συλαγωγῶν** διὰ τῆς φιλοσοφίας καὶ κενῆς ἀπάτης κατὰ τὴν παράδοσιν τῶν ἀνθρώπων, κατὰ τὰ στοιχεῖα τοῦ κόσμου καὶ οὐ κατὰ Χριστόν. [GNT] | To take captive; to lead astray; to lead into captivity or slavery.<br><br>**Practical Application**<br>Some men are in a genuine search for truth and reality. They seek to learn the truth and reality of the universe and the problems that face them, but they limit themselves to the universe.<br>Other persons have novel ideas or philosophies about truth and reality, but they become more interested in their positions than the truth. They need others to accept their positions or else their ideas die. Therefore, they have to present and persuade people of their ideas and philosophies whether they are sound or not.<br>Believers must, therefore, beware and guard against worldly philosophies and ideas lest they become ensnared and enslaved. |

## PRACTICAL WORD STUDIES
### in the NEW TESTAMENT

| ENGLISH WORD | GREEK WORD AND VERSE | THE WORD MEANS... |
|---|---|---|
| **#489**<br>**Care**<br><br>**Care**–KJV<br>Anxiety–NASB<br>Anxiety–NIV<br>**Care**–NKJV<br>Worries and cares–NLT<br><br>**POSB REFERENCE**<br>(1 Pt.5:6-7; esp. v.7)<br>Note 3, point 3 | μέριμναν = *merimnan*<br>Pronunciation: [mer'-im-nahn]<br>Parsing (part of speech): noun<br>   Case—accusative<br>   Gender—feminine<br>   Number—singular<br>   Stem or root—from μέριμνα, ης<br>Concordance References:<br>  ⇒ Strong's #3308 merimna<br>  ⇒ NIV #3533 merimna<br>  ⇒ NASB #3308 merimna<br><br>**1 Peter 5:7**<br>Casting all your **care** upon him; for he careth for you. [KJV]<br>Casting all your **anxiety** upon Him, because He cares for you. [NASB]<br>Cast all your **anxiety** on him because he cares for you. [NIV]<br>Casting all your **care** upon Him, for He cares for you. [NKJV]<br>Give all your **worries and cares** to God, for he cares about what happens to you. [NLT]<br>πᾶσαν τὴν **μέριμναν** ὑμῶν ἐπιρρίψαντες ἐπ' αὐτόν, ὅτι αὐτῷ μέλει περὶ ὑμῶν." [GNS]<br>πᾶσαν τὴν **μέριμναν** ὑμῶν ἐπιρίψαντες ἐπ' αὐτόν, ὅτι αὐτῷ μέλει περὶ ὑμῶν· μέλει περὶ ὑμῶν. [GNT] | Anxiety, care, worries, concern, distress, pressure.<br><br>**Practical Application**<br>God cares for us; He cares about all our needs. Remember: the believers of Peter's day were suffering terrible persecution. They had been forced to flee for their lives, leaving everything behind: homes, jobs, and possessions. They had only what they could carry by hand, and they fled to whatever places they felt were safe. They were, so to speak, an underground people. They had to live, work, and worship in secret and to find housing and food wherever they could. They never knew when they would be discovered and forced to flee again.<br>  The point is this: imagine the anxiety, the pressure, tension, and stress being experienced by the believers. Yet there was great help: God was available to help them. Note that the exhortation is not only clearly stated; it is a command: "casting all your care (*merimna*) upon Him, for He cares for you." God's mighty hand will...<br>• save and deliver you<br>• look after and care for you<br>• strengthen and secure you<br>• provide and protect you<br>• give you assurance and confidence |
| **#490**<br>**Care**<br><br>Preserved–KJV<br>Kept–NASB<br>Kept–NIV<br>Preserved–NKJV<br>**Care**–NLT<br><br>**POSB REFERENCE**<br>(Jude 1:1-2; esp. v.1)<br>Note 2, point 2 | τετηρημένοις = *tetēremenois*<br>Pronunciation: [teh-tay-ray'-men-oys]<br>Parsing (part of speech): verb<br>   Mood—participle<br>   Tense—perfect<br>   Voice—passive<br>   Case—dative<br>   Gender—masculine<br>   Number—plural<br>   Stem or root—from τηρέω<br>Concordance References:<br>  ⇒ Strong's #5083 tereō<br>  ⇒ NIV #5498 tereō<br>  ⇒ NASB #5083 tereō<br><br>**Jude 1:1**<br>Jude, the servant of Jesus Christ, and brother of James, to them that are sanctified by God the Father, and **preserved** in Jesus Christ, and called: [KJV]<br>Jude, a bond-servant of Jesus Christ, and brother of James, to those who are the called, beloved in God the Father, and **kept** for Jesus Christ: [NASB]<br>Jude, a servant of Jesus Christ and a brother of James,To those who have been called, who are loved by God the Father and **kept** by Jesus Christ: [NIV]<br>Jude, a bondservant of Jesus Christ, and brother of James, To those who are called, sanctified by God the Father, and **preserved** in Jesus Christ: [NKJV]<br>This letter is from Jude, a slave of Jesus Christ and a brother of James. I am writing to all who are called to live in the love of God the Father and the **care** of Jesus Christ. [NLT]<br>Ἰούδας Ἰησοῦ Χριστοῦ δοῦλος, ἀδελφὸς δὲ Ἰακώβου, τοῖς ἐν Θεῷ πατρὶ ἡγιασμένοις, καὶ Ἰησοῦ Χριστῷ **τετηρημένοις**, κλητοῖς· [GNS]<br>Ἰούδας Ἰησοῦ Χριστοῦ δοῦλος, ἀδελφὸς δὲ Ἰακώβου, τοῖς ἐν θεῷ πατρὶ ἠγαπημένοις καὶ Ἰησοῦ Χριστῷ **τετηρημένοις** κλητοῖς· [GNT] | To be kept; to be guarded and watched after; to reserve; to protect.<br><br>**Practical Application**<br>Believers are "in the care of Jesus Christ." The word "care" (*tetēremenois*) means to be kept; to be guarded and watched after. God keeps the believer, guards and watches over him. The believer is a person...<br>• who is watched over by God.<br>• who is guided and directed by God day by day.<br>• who is strengthened by God to walk through all the trials and temptations of life.<br>• who is protected from all the enemies of life, even death.<br>• who is to be escorted into heaven quicker than the blink of an eye when the time comes for him to leave this world.<br>• who is given life, both abundant and eternal.<br>• who is given assurance of God's presence and love through all of life.<br><br>The true believer is a person who is preserved and kept by God. He is a person who is looked after and cared for by God. But note: it is *in Jesus Christ* that God keeps a person. The believer is a person who has placed his life into Jesus Christ; he is a person who is *trusting* Jesus Christ to save him. It is the true believer in Jesus Christ whom God preserves. |

# PRACTICAL WORD STUDIES
## in the NEW TESTAMENT

| ENGLISH WORD | GREEK WORD AND VERSE | THE WORD MEANS... |
|---|---|---|
| **#491**<br>**Care For The Flock Of God**<br><br>Feed the flock of God–KJV<br>Shepherd the flock of God–NASB<br>Be shepherds of–NIV<br>Shepherd the flock of God–NKJV<br>**Care for the flock of God–NLT**<br><br>**POSB REFERENCE**<br>(1 Pt.5:2-3)<br>Note 2<br><br>See also POSB REF:<br>(Acts 20:28-31; esp. v.28)<br>Note 2 | ποιμάνατε = poimanate<br>Pronunciation: [poy-mah'nah-teh]<br>Parsing (part of speech): verb<br>    Mood—imperative<br>    Tense—aorist<br>    Voice—active<br>    Person—2nd person<br>    Number—plural<br>    Stem or root—from ποιμαίνω<br>Concordance References:<br>⇒ Strong's #4165 poimainō<br>⇒ NIV #4477 poimainō<br>⇒ NASB #4165 poimainō<br><br>**1 Peter 5:2**<br>**Feed the flock of God** which is among you, taking the oversight thereof, not by constraint, but willingly; not for filthy lucre, but of a ready mind; [KJV]<br>**Shepherd the flock of God** among you, exercising oversight not under compulsion, but voluntarily, according to the will of God; and not for sordid gain, but with eagerness; [NASB]<br>**Be shepherds of** God's flock that is under your care, serving as overseers—not because you must, but because you are willing, as God wants you to be; not greedy for money, but eager to serve; [NIV]<br>**Shepherd the flock of God** which is among you, serving as overseers, not by compulsion but willingly, not for dishonest gain but eagerly; [NKJV]<br>**Care for the flock of God** entrusted to you. Watch over it willingly, not grudgingly—not for what you will get out of it, but because you are eager to serve God. [NLT]<br>ποιμάνατε τὸ ἐν ὑμῖν ποίμνιον τοῦ Θεοῦ, ἐπισκοποῦντες μὴ ἀναγκαστῶς, ἀλλ' ἑκουσίως· μηδὲ αἰσχροκερδῶς, ἀλλὰ προθύμως, [GNS]<br>ποιμάνατε τὸ ἐν ὑμῖν ποίμνιον τοῦ θεοῦ [ἐπισκοποῦντες] μὴ ἀναγκαστῶς ἀλλὰ ἑκουσίως κατὰ θεόν, μηδὲ αἰσχροκερδῶς ἀλλὰ προθύμως, [GNT] | To feed the flock of God; to shepherd the flock of God; to care for the flock of God; to be shepherds of.<br><br>**Practical Application**<br>The exhortation to ministers is direct and forceful, but as clear as it can be. "Care for the flock of God." The phrase "care for the flock of God" (*poimanate*) is an all-inclusive phrase that covers all the duties of the minister. It means not only to preach and teach the Word of God but to tend and shepherd the flock. It means to act like a shepherd, to carry out the duties of a shepherd. The duties of the shepherd are several fold (see *Deeper Study #2—1 Peter 2:25* for more discussion):<br>⇒ to feed the sheep even if he has to gather them in his arms to carry them to the pasture.<br>⇒ to guide the sheep to the pasture and away from the rough places and precipices.<br>⇒ to seek and save the sheep who get lost.<br>⇒ to protect the sheep. He is even willing to sacrifice his life for the sheep.<br>⇒ to restore the sheep who go astray and return.<br>⇒ to reward the sheep for obedience and faithfulness.<br>⇒ to keep the sheep separate from the goats.<br>But note this: in all the duties of tending and looking after the flock of God, we must never forget what the great Greek scholar W.E. Vine stresses:<br>*In the spiritual care of God's children, the feeding of the flock from the Word of God is the constant and regular necessity; it is to have the foremost place. The tending (which includes this) consists of other acts, of discipline, authority, restoration, material assistance of individuals, but they are incidental in comparison with the feeding (Expository Dictionary of New Testament Words. Old Tappan, NJ: Fleming H. Revell, 1966).* |
| **#492**<br>**Careful**<br><br>Take heed–KJV<br>On guard–NASB<br>**Careful–NIV**<br>Take heed–NKJV<br>Watch out–NLT<br><br>**POSB REFERENCE**<br>(Lk.21:34-35; esp. v.34)<br>Note 1 | Προσέχετε = prosechete<br>Pronunciation: [pros-ekh'-eh-teh]<br>Parsing (part of speech): verb<br>    Mood—imperative<br>    Tense—present<br>    Voice—active<br>    Person—2nd person<br>    Number—plural<br>    Stem or root—from προσέχω<br>Concordance References:<br>⇒ Strong's #4337 prosechō<br>⇒ NIV #4668 prosechō<br>⇒ NASB #4337 prosechō<br><br>**Luke 21:34**<br>And **take heed** to yourselves, lest at any time your hearts be overcharged with surfeiting, and drunkenness, and cares of this life, and so that day come upon you unawares. [KJV]<br>"Be **on guard**, that your hearts may not be weighted down with dissipation and drunkenness and the worries of life, and that day come on you suddenly like a trap; [NASB]<br>"Be **careful**, or your hearts will be weighed down with dissipation, drunkenness and the anxieties of life, and that day will close on you unexpectedly like a trap. [NIV] | To give attention; to focus one's mind; to watch out; to guard; to beware; to take care; to be on guard; to pay close attention to; to carefully consider.<br><br>**Practical Application**<br>The end time and the day of the Lord's return demands taking care. Note this important fact: the believer is to be careful (*prosechete*); that is, to guard his life. How? By not engaging in worldliness. His heart is not to be weighed down (*barethosin*): heavy, weighed down, burdened, overloaded, filled up, indulged. |

# PRACTICAL WORD STUDIES
## in the NEW TESTAMENT

| ENGLISH WORD | GREEK WORD AND VERSE | THE WORD MEANS... |
|---|---|---|
| | "But **take heed** to yourselves, lest your hearts be weighed down with carousing, drunkenness, and cares of this life, and that Day come on you unexpectedly. [NKJV]<br>"**Watch out!** Don't let me find you living in careless ease and drunkenness, and filled with the worries of this life. Don't let that day catch you unaware, [NLT]<br>Προσέχετε δὲ ἑαυτοῖς, μήποτε βαρυνθῶσιν ὑμῶν αἱ καρδίαι ἐν κραιπάλῃ καὶ μέθῃ καὶ μερίμναις βιωτικαῖς, καὶ αἰφνίδιος ἐφ' ὑμᾶς ἐπιστῇ ἡ ἡμέρα ἐκείνη· [GNS]<br>Προσέχετε δὲ ἑαυτοῖς μήποτε βαρηθῶσιν ὑμῶν αἱ καρδίαι ἐν κραιπάλῃ καὶ μέθῃ καὶ μερίμναις βιωτικαῖς καὶ ἐπιστῇ ἐφ' ὑμᾶς αἰφνίδιος ἡ ἡμέρα ἐκείνη [GNT] | |
| **#493**<br>**Careful**<br><br>Careful–KJV<br>Worried–NASB<br>Worried–NIV<br>Worried–NKJV<br>Upset–NLT<br><br>**POSB REFERENCE**<br>(Lk.10:41-42; esp. v.41)<br>Note 4, point 2 | μεριμνᾷς = merimnas<br>Pronunciation: [mer-im-nahs']<br>Parsing (part of speech): verb<br>   Mood—indicative<br>   Tense—present<br>   Voice—active<br>   Person—2nd person<br>   Number—singular<br>   Stem or root—from μεριμνάω<br>Concordance References:<br>  ⇒ Strong's #3309 merimnaō<br>  ⇒ NIV #3534 merimnaō<br>  ⇒ NASB #3309 merimnaō<br><br>**Luke 10:41**<br>And Jesus answered and said unto her, Martha, Martha, thou art **careful** and troubled about many things: [KJV]<br>But the Lord answered and said to her, "Martha, Martha, you are **worried** and bothered about so many things; [NASB]<br>"Martha, Martha," the Lord answered, "you are **worried** and upset about many things, [NIV]<br>And Jesus answered and said to her, "Martha, Martha, you are **worried** and troubled about many things. [NKJV]<br>But the Lord said to her, "My dear Martha, you are so **upset** over all these details! [NLT]<br>ἀποκριθεὶς δὲ εἶπεν αὐτῇ ὁ Ἰησοῦς, Μάρθα Μάρθα, μεριμνᾷς καὶ τυρβάζῃ περὶ πολλά· [GNS]<br>ἀποκριθεὶς δὲ εἶπεν αὐτῇ ὁ κύριος, Μάρθα Μάρθα, μεριμνᾷς καὶ θορυβάζῃ περὶ πολλά, [GNT] | To worry; to be anxious; to be cautious; to be mindful; to be upset; to be overly concerned and caring (cp. Phil. 4:6).<br><br>**Practical Application**<br>It has the idea of being inwardly torn and divided in two, of being distracted from what one's mind and heart and life should be focused upon. |
| **#494**<br>**Careful**<br><br>Provide–KJV<br>Respect–NASB<br>**Careful–NIV**<br>Have regard–NKJV<br>Do things in such a way–NLT<br><br>**POSB REFERENCE**<br>(Rom.12:17)<br>Note 4, point 2 | προνοούμενοι = pronooumenoi<br>Pronunciation: [pro-no-oo-meh'-noy]<br>Parsing (part of speech): verb<br>   Mood—participle (imperative sense)<br>   Tense—present<br>   Voice—middle<br>   Case—nominative<br>   Gender—masculine<br>   Person—2nd person<br>   Number—plural<br>   Stem or root—from προνοέω<br>Concordance References:<br>  ⇒ Strong's #4306 pronoeō<br>  ⇒ NIV #4629 pronoeō<br>  ⇒ NASB #4306 pronoeō<br><br>**Romans 12:17**<br>Recompense to no man evil for evil. **Provide** things honest in the sight of all men. [KJV]<br>Never pay back evil for evil to anyone. **Respect** what is right in the sight of all men. [NASB]<br>Do not repay anyone evil for evil. Be **careful** to do what is right in the eyes of everybody. [NIV]<br>Repay no one evil for evil. **Have regard** for good things in the sight of all men. [NKJV]<br>Never pay back evil for evil to anyone. **Do things in such a way** that everyone can see you are honorable. [NLT] | To be careful; to provide; to respect; to do things in such a way; to take care of; to think before acting; to take pains.<br>The believer is to demonstrate good behavior in the sight of all men. The word "careful" (*pronooumenoi*) means to think before acting.<br><br>**Practical Application**<br>The idea is this: when someone does evil against the believer, the believer is to think before he acts. He is to think and pray through his behavior. Why? So that he can respond in the right and proper way. The believer needs to do what is right and noble, and the only way to do it is to think through the situation. |

# PRACTICAL WORD STUDIES
## in the NEW TESTAMENT

| ENGLISH WORD | GREEK WORD AND VERSE | THE WORD MEANS... |
|---|---|---|
| | μηδενὶ κακὸν ἀντὶ κακοῦ ἀποδιδόντες. **προνοούμενοι** καλὰ ἐνώπιον πάντων ἀνθρώπων. [GNS]<br>μηδενὶ κακὸν ἀντὶ κακοῦ ἀποδιδόντες, **προνοούμενοι** καλὰ ἐνώπιον πάντων ἀνθρώπων· [GNT] | |
| **#495**<br>**Careful**<br><br>Sober–KJV<br>Sober spirit–NASB<br>Self-controlled–NIV<br>Sober–NKJV<br>Careful–NLT<br><br>**POSB<br>REFERENCE**<br>(1 Pt.5:8)<br>Note 1 | Νήψατε = Nēpsate<br>Pronunciation: [nay'-psah-teh]<br>Parsing (part of speech): verb<br>   Mood—imperative<br>   Tense—aorist<br>   Voice—active<br>   Person—2nd person<br>   Number—plural<br>   Stem or root—from νήφω<br>Concordance References:<br>  ⇒ Strong's #3525 nēphō<br>  ⇒ NIV #3768 nēphō<br>  ⇒ NASB #3525 nēphō<br><br>**1 Peter 5:8**<br>Be **sober**, be vigilant; because your adversary the devil, as a roaring lion, walketh about, seeking whom he may devour: [KJV]<br>Be of **sober** *spirit*, be on the alert. Your adversary, the devil, prowls about like a roaring lion, seeking someone to devour. [NASB]<br>Be **self-controlled** and alert. Your enemy the devil prowls around like a roaring lion looking for someone to devour. [NIV]<br>Be **sober**, be vigilant; because your adversary the devil walks about like a roaring lion, seeking whom he may devour. [NKJV]<br>Be **careful**! Watch out for attacks from the Devil, your great enemy. He prowls around like a roaring lion, looking for some victim to devour. [NLT]<br>**νήψατε**, γρηγορήσατε, ὅτι ὁ ἀντίδικος ὑμῶν διάβολος, ὡς λέων ὠρυόμενος περιπατεῖ ζητῶν τινα καταπίῃ· [GNS]<br>**Νήψατε**, γρηγορήσατε. ὁ ἀντίδικος ὑμῶν διάβολος ὡς λέων ὠρυόμενος περιπατεῖ ζητῶν [τινα] καταπιεῖν· [GNT] | To be self-controlled; to be sober in mind and behavior; to live a strong life; to keep one's head.<br><br>**Practical Application**<br>How can we stand against the attacks and temptations of the devil? There is only one way: we must be careful, be vigilant. The word means...<br>• not to become intoxicated with drugs or alcohol of any kind.<br>• to be sober in mind and behavior; to be controlled in all things; not given over to indulgence, license, or extravagance. It is the opposite of indulgence in anything such as eating, drinking, and recreation. It means to live a sober, solid, controlled, and strong life.<br>The believer has to be careful as he watches for the attacks of the devil. If he is not sober, he will not be alert enough to conquer the attacks and the temptations of the devil. The believer will be overcome and led into sin and destruction. And no believer can be alert enough to stand up against the devil if he indulges and gratifies his flesh in...<br>• sex<br>• food<br>• sleep<br>• relaxation<br>• alcohol and drugs<br>• recognition<br>• pornography<br>• position<br>• clothing<br>• possessions<br>• power<br>The believer is to live a careful and controlled life. He is to stay alert to the devil and his temptations at all times. He must be alert enough to see the temptations and attacks coming and have a mind and spirit strong enough to stand against the temptations and attacks. |
| **#496**<br>**Careful**<br><br>Careful–KJV<br>Careful–NASB<br>Careful–NIV<br>Careful–NKJV<br>Careful–NLT<br><br>**POSB<br>REFERENCE**<br>(Tit.3:8)<br>Note 1 | φροντίζωσιν = phrontizōsin<br>Pronunciation: [fron-tid'-zo-sin]<br>Parsing (part of speech): verb<br>   Mood—subjunctive<br>   Tense—present<br>   Voice—active<br>   Person—3rd person<br>   Number—plural<br>   Stem or root—from φροντίζω<br>Concordance References:<br>  ⇒ Strong's #5431 phrontizō<br>  ⇒ NIV #5863 phrontizō<br>  ⇒ NASB #5431 phrontizō<br><br>**Titus 3:8**<br>*This is* a faithful saying, and these things I will that thou affirm constantly, that they which have believed in God might be **careful** to maintain good works. These things are good and profitable unto men. [KJV]<br>This is a trustworthy statement; and concerning these | To be careful; to be concerned about.<br><br>**Practical Application**<br>The word means...<br>• to think upon doing what is good (or doing good works).<br>• to consider good works.<br>• to give careful attention to good works.<br>• to focus upon good works.<br>The idea is that the very thoughts of a person's mind are to be centered and focused upon doing good works. Good works are to be the very concentration and primary purpose of a person's life. But note: this is not all. The necessity of doing good works is brought out by another factor. The minister is instructed to affirm constantly—to insist that believers persevere in doing good works. The idea is that the minister |

# PRACTICAL WORD STUDIES
## in the NEW TESTAMENT

| ENGLISH WORD | GREEK WORD AND VERSE | THE WORD MEANS... |
|---|---|---|
| | things I want you to speak confidently, so that those who have believed God may be **careful** to engage in good deeds. These things are good and profitable for men. [NASB]<br>This is a trustworthy saying. And I want you to stress these things, so that those who have trusted in God may be **careful** to devote themselves to doing what is good. These things are excellent and profitable for everyone. [NIV]<br>This is a faithful saying, and these things I want you to affirm constantly, that those who have believed in God should be **careful** to maintain good works. These things are good and profitable to men. [NKJV]<br>These things I have told you are all true. I want you to insist on them so that everyone who trusts in God will be **careful** to do good deeds all the time. These things are good and beneficial for everyone. [NLT]<br>πιστὸ ὁ λόγος, καὶ περὶ τούτων βούλομαί σε διαβεβαιοῦσθαι, ἵνα **φροντίζωσι** καλῶν ἔργων προΐστασθαι οἱ πεπιστευκότες τῷ Θεῷ. ταῦτά ἐστι τὰ καλὰ καὶ ὠφέλιμα τοῖς ἀνθρώποις· [GNS]<br>Πιστὸς ὁ λόγος· καὶ περὶ τούτων βούλομαί σε διαβεβαιοῦσθαι, ἵνα **φροντίζωσιν** καλῶν ἔργων προΐστασθαι οἱ πεπιστευκότες θεῷ· ταῦτά ἐστιν καλὰ καὶ ὠφέλιμα τοῖς ἀνθρώποις. [GNT] | must...<br>• earnestly insist<br>• constantly insist<br>• steadfastly insist<br>The minister of God must press believers to maintain good works. Why so much emphasis on good works? Matthew Henry says, "Because a bare, inactive faith will not save a person; only a working active faith will save a person. Saving faith is a faith that bears righteousness and purity; it actively works at being righteous and pure and at leading others to live righteous and pure lives."<br>Note one other point: good works are good and profitable to men. Good works alone will build the kind of society and world for which the human heart longs: a world of love, joy, and peace. But remember what Scripture says: we are not saved *by our works of righteousness*; we are saved by the mercy and grace of God through faith in Christ Jesus. |
| **#497**<br>**Careful–**<br>**Careful, Very**<br><br>Circumspectly–KJV<br>**Careful–NASB**<br>**Very careful–NIV**<br>Circumspectly–NKJV<br>**Careful–NLT**<br><br>**POSB**<br>**REFERENCE**<br>(Eph.5:15)<br>Note 1 | ἀκριβῶς = akribōs<br>Pronunciation: [ak-ree-boce']<br>Parsing (part of speech): adjective adverb<br>    Stem or root—from ἀκριβῶς<br>Concordance References:<br>⇒ Strong's #199 akribōs<br>⇒ NIV #209 akribōs<br>⇒ NASB #199 akribōs<br><br>**Ephes. 5:15**<br>See then that ye walk **circumspectly**, not as fools, but as wise, [KJV]<br>Therefore be **careful** how you walk, not as unwise men, but as wise, [NASB]<br>Be **very careful**, then, how you live—not as unwise but as wise, [NIV]<br>See then that you walk **circumspectly**, not as fools but as wise, [NKJV]<br>So be **careful** how you live, not as fools but as those who are wise. [NLT]<br>Βλέπετε οὖν **ἀκριβῶς** περιπατεῖτε, μὴ ὡς ἄσοφοι, ἀλλ' ὡς σοφοί, [GNS]<br>Βλέπετε οὖν **ἀκριβῶς** πῶς περιπατεῖτε μὴ ὡς ἄσοφοι ἀλλ' ὡς σοφοί, [GNT] | To be very careful; circumspectly, accurately; to be more adequate.<br><br>**Practical Application**<br>Life is a walk, a path that we trod every day. When we arise in the morning, we begin to walk about. God expects us to walk very carefully, that is, circumspectly and accurately—exactly as we should. |
| **#498**<br>**Careful For**<br><br>Careful for–KJV<br>Anxious for–NASB<br>Anxious about–NIV<br>Anxious for–NKJV<br>Worry about–NLT<br><br>**POSB**<br>**REFERENCE**<br>(Philip.4:6-7; esp. v.6)<br>Note 1 | μεριμνᾶτε = merimnate<br>Pronunciation: [mer-im-nah'-teh]<br>Parsing (part of speech): verb<br>    Mood—imperative<br>    Tense—present<br>    Voice—active<br>    Person—2nd person<br>    Number—plural<br>    Stem or root—from μεριμνάω<br>Concordance References:<br>⇒ Strong's #3309 merimnaō<br>⇒ NIV #3534 merimnaō<br>⇒ NASB #3309 merimnaō<br><br>**Philip. 4:6**<br>Be **careful for** nothing; but in every thing by prayer and supplication with thanksgiving let your requests be made known unto God. [KJV]<br>Be **anxious for** nothing, but in everything by prayer and supplication with thanksgiving let your requests be made known to God. [NASB]<br>Do not be **anxious about** anything, but in every- | To be anxious about; to be anxious for; to be careful for; to worry about; to be concerned about.<br><br>**Practical Application**<br>The idea is that the believer is not to worry or fret about a single thing. The word "nothing" (*meden*) means not even one thing. Humanly speaking, the Philippians had every reason to worry and be anxious.<br>⇒ They were suffering severe persecution (Phil. 1:18-19).<br>⇒ They were facing a disturbance in the church, some disunity and quarreling (Phil. 1:27, 42).<br>⇒ They had some carnal members within their fellowship, some members who were prideful, super-spiritual, and self-centered (Phil. 2:3-4; Phil. 3:12).<br>⇒ They were facing some false teachers who |

# Practical Word Studies
## in the New Testament

| ENGLISH WORD | GREEK WORD AND VERSE | THE WORD MEANS... |
|---|---|---|
| | thing, by prayer and petition, with thanksgiving, present your requests to God. [NIV]<br>Be **anxious for** nothing, but in everything by prayer and supplication, with thanksgiving, let your requests be made known to God; [NKJV]<br>Don't **worry about** anything; instead, pray about everything. Tell God what you need, and thank him for all he has done. [NLT]<br>πᾶσαν τὴν **μέριμναν** ὑμῶν ἐπιρρίψαντες ἐπ' αὐτόν, ὅτι αὐτῷ μέλει περὶ ὑμῶν. [GNS]<br>μηδὲν **μεριμνᾶτε**, ἀλλ' ἐν παντὶ τῇ προσευχῇ καὶ τῇ δεήσει μετὰ εὐχαριστίας τὰ αἰτήματα ὑμῶν γνωριζέσθω πρὸς τὸν θεόν. [GNT] | had joined their fellowship, and the teachers were fierce in attacking the cross of Christ (Phil. 3:2-3, 18-19).<br>⇒ Some of the believers were having to struggle for the necessities of life: food, clothing, and shelter (Phil. 4:19).<br>There was little else that could confront these dear believers. They were facing about every trial and temptation imaginable, the kind of trouble that arouses anxiety and worry. Humanly, a person is going to fret, worry and suffer anxiety...<br>• when he is either about to lose or lacks food, clothing, or shelter.<br>• when he is persecuted, ridiculed, abused, or threatened.<br>• when he is surrounded by quarrels, disturbance, carnality, or false teaching.<br>In the midst of such circumstances, the only way a person can keep from worrying is to receive an injection of supernatural power.<br>This is the very point of Scripture. There is an answer to worry and anxiety, a supernatural answer: the peace of God. God will *enable* the believer to conquer worry and anxiety. God will overcome the trials of life for the believer, no matter how terrible and pressuring they may be. God will infuse the believer with peace—with the very peace of God Himself—a peace so great and so wonderful that it carries the believer right through the trial. Of course, this does not mean the believer is not to be concerned about the problems of life. He is, but there is a difference between concern and anxiety or worry. Concern drives us to arise and tackle the problems of life with an indomitable courage and diligence. Concern drives us to tackle and conquer all that we can handle. Anxiety and worry cause all kinds of problems. |
| #499<br>**Careful Summary**<br><br>In order–KJV<br>Consecutive order–NASB<br>Orderly–NIV<br>Orderly–NKJV<br>**Careful summary–NLT**<br><br>**POSB REFERENCE**<br>(Lk.1:3)<br>Note 3, point 3 | καθεξῆς = kathexës<br>Pronunciation: [kath-ex-ace']<br>Parsing (part of speech): adjective adverb<br>   Stem or root—from **καθεξῆς**<br>Concordance References:<br>   ⇒ Strong's #2517 kathexës<br>   ⇒ NIV #2759 kathexës<br>   ⇒ NASB #2517 kathexës<br><br>**Luke 1:3**<br>It seemed good to me also, having had perfect understanding of all things from the very first, to write unto thee **in order**, most excellent Theophilus, [KJV]<br>It seemed fitting for me as well, having investigated everything carefully from the beginning, to write *it* out for you in **consecutive order**, most excellent Theophilus; [NASB]<br>Therefore, since I myself have carefully investigated everything from the beginning, it seemed good also to me to write an **orderly** account for you, most excellent Theophilus, [NIV]<br>It seemed good to me also, having had perfect understanding of all things from the very first, to write to you an **orderly** account, most excellent Theophilus, [NKJV]<br>Having carefully investigated all of these accounts from the beginning, I have decided to write a **careful summary** for you, [NLT]<br>ἔδοξε κἀμοὶ παρηκολουθηκότι ἄνωθεν πᾶσιν ἀκριβῶς, **καθεξῆς** σοι γράψαι, κράτιστε Θεόφιλε, [GNS]<br>ἔδοξε κἀμοὶ παρηκολουθηκότι ἄνωθεν πᾶσιν ἀκριβῶς **καθεξῆς** σοι γράψαι, κράτιστε Θεόφιλε, [GNT] | Orderly; in order; in consecutive order; in a careful summary; methodical; precise; correct.<br><br>**Practical Application**<br>Luke is the only writer in the New Testament to use this word. He uses it in the gospel only once and in Acts twice (Acts 11:4; Acts 18:23). The question is, what does Luke mean by orderly? Consecutive or chronological arrangement? Logical arrangement? Subject arrangement? Inspired or Spirit-led arrangement? The meaning is not clear. Perhaps he is saying that he is writing a full account of the life of Christ and that his account is a better arrangement; that is, it has more order and is better arranged than those in existence. |

# PRACTICAL WORD STUDIES
## in the New Testament

| ENGLISH WORD | GREEK WORD AND VERSE | THE WORD MEANS... |
|---|---|---|
| **#500**<br>**Careful, Be**<br><br>Take heed–KJV<br>Watch out–NASB<br>**Be careful–NIV**<br>Take heed–NKJV<br>Warned–NLT<br><br>**POSB REFERENCE**<br>(Mk.8:15)<br>*Deeper Study* #1 | Ὁρᾶτε = Horate<br>Pronunciation: [hor-ah'-teh]<br>Parsing (part of speech): verb<br>    Mood—imperative<br>    Tense—present<br>    Voice—active<br>    Person—2nd person<br>    Number—plural<br>    Stem or root—from ὁράω<br>Concordance References:<br>⇒ Strong's #3708 horaö<br>⇒ NIV #3972 horaö<br>⇒ NASB #3708 horaö<br><br>**Mark 8:15**<br>And he charged them, saying, **Take heed**, beware of the leaven of the Pharisees, and *of* the leaven of Herod. [KJV]<br>And He was giving orders to them, saying, "**Watch out**! Beware of the leaven of the Pharisees and the leaven of Herod." [NASB]<br>"**Be careful**," Jesus warned them. "Watch out for the yeast of the Pharisees and that of Herod." [NIV]<br>Then He charged them, saying, "**Take heed**, beware of the leaven of the Pharisees and the leaven of Herod." [NKJV]<br>As they were crossing the lake, Jesus **warned** them, "Beware of the yeast of the Pharisees and of Herod." [NLT]<br>καὶ διεστέλλετο αὐτοῖς, λέγων, Ὁρᾶτε, βλέπετε ἀπὸ τῆς ζύμης τῶν Φαρισαίων, καὶ τῆς ζύμης Ἡρώδου. [GNS]<br>καὶ διεστέλλετο αὐτοῖς λέγων, Ὁρᾶτε, βλέπετε ἀπὸ τῆς ζύμης τῶν Φαρισαίων καὶ τῆς ζύμης Ἡρώδου. [GNT] | To see, behold, discern, and acquaint oneself by closely observing and experiencing. It means to take heed; to watch out; to be warned; to be careful; to make sure.<br><br>**Practical Application**<br>Two things are needed for a person to "be careful": active thought and a discerning mind. The thing to be heeded must be actively observed, thought through, and discerned.<br>In the present passage, the charge is a *present imperative*. Beginning right now, the disciple is to "be careful" of yeast (leaven) and he is to continue being careful, always observing and discerning. |
| **#501**<br>**Careful, Be**<br><br>Considering–KJV<br>Looking–NASB<br>Watch–NIV<br>Considering–NKJV<br>**Be careful–NLT**<br><br>**POSB REFERENCE**<br>(Gal.6:1)<br>Note 3 | σκοπῶν = skopön<br>Pronunciation: [skop-own]<br>Parsing (part of speech): verb<br>    Mood—participle (imperative sense)<br>    Tense—present<br>    Voice—active<br>    Case—nominative<br>    Gender—masculine<br>    Person—2nd person<br>    Number—singular<br>    Stem or root—from σκοπέω<br>Concordance References:<br>⇒ Strong's #4648 skopeö<br>⇒ NIV #5023 skopeö<br>⇒ NASB #4648 skopeö<br><br>**Galatians 6:1**<br>Brethren, if a man be overtaken in a fault, ye which are spiritual, restore such an one in the spirit of meekness; **considering** thyself, lest thou also be tempted. [KJV]<br>Brethren, even if a man is caught in any trespass, you who are spiritual, restore such a one in a spirit of gentleness; *each one* **looking** to yourself, lest you too be tempted. [NASB]<br>Brothers, if someone is caught in a sin, you who are spiritual should restore him gently. But **watch** yourself, or you also may be tempted. [NIV]<br>Brethren, if a man is overtaken in any trespass, you who *are* spiritual restore such a one in a spirit of gentleness, **considering** yourself lest you also be tempted. [NKJV]<br>Dear brothers and sisters, if another Christian is overcome by some sin, you who are godly should gently and humbly help that person back onto the right path. And **be careful** not to fall into the same temptation yourself. [NLT] | To watch; to carefully consider; to look to oneself; to keep one's attention on; to fix eyes on; to take note of; to think about oneself and to give attention to oneself. It means to keep an attentive eye on oneself.<br><br>**Practical Application**<br>If we really watch and consider the matter, then we will reach out in love and gentleness to help our fallen brothers. We have to help them, for we are all ever so subject to being caught in a sin. |

## PRACTICAL WORD STUDIES
in the NEW TESTAMENT

| ENGLISH WORD | GREEK WORD AND VERSE | THE WORD MEANS... |
|---|---|---|
| | Ἀδελφοί, ἐὰν καὶ προληφθῇ ἄνθρωπος ἔν τινι παραπτώματι, ὑμεῖς οἱ πνευματικοὶ καταρτίζετε τὸν τοιοῦτον ἐν πνεύματι πραότητος, **σκοπῶν** σεαυτόν, μὴ καὶ σὺ πειρασθῇς. [GNS]<br><br>Ἀδελφοί, ἐὰν καὶ προλημφθῇ ἄνθρωπος ἔν τινι παραπτώματι, ὑμεῖς οἱ πνευματικοὶ καταρτίζετε τὸν τοιοῦτον ἐν πνεύματι πραΰτητος, **σκοπῶν** σεαυτόν μὴ καὶ σὺ πειρασθῇς. [GNT] | |
| **#502**<br>**Careless**<br><br>Idle–KJV<br>**Careless**–NASB<br>**Careless**–NIV<br>Idle–NKJV<br>Idle–NLT<br><br>**POSB REFERENCE**<br>(Mt.12:36)<br>*Deeper Study #1* | ἀργὸν = argon<br>Pronunciation: [ar-gon]<br>Parsing (part of speech): adjective<br>    Case—accusative<br>    Gender—neuter<br>    Number—singular<br>    Stem or root—from ἀργός, ή, όν<br>Concordance References:<br>  ⇒ Strong's #692 argos<br>  ⇒ NIV #734 argos<br>  ⇒ NASB #692 argos<br><br>**Matthew 12:36**<br>But I say unto you, That every **idle** word that men shall speak, they shall give account thereof in the day of judgment. [KJV]<br>"And I say to you, that every **careless** word that men shall speak, they shall render account for it in the day of judgment. [NASB]<br>But I tell you that men will have to give account on the day of judgment for every **careless** word they have spoken. [NIV]<br>But I say to you that for every **idle** word men may speak, they will give account of it in the day of judgment. [NKJV]<br>And I tell you this, that you must give an account on judgment day of every **idle** word you speak. [NLT]<br>λέγω δὲ ὑμῖν, ὅτι πᾶν ῥῆμα **ἀργὸν** ὃ ἐὰν λαλήσωσιν οἱ ἄνθρωποι, ἀποδώσουσι περὶ αὐτοῦ λόγον ἐν ἡμέρᾳ κρίσεως. [GNS]<br>λέγω δὲ ὑμῖν ὅτι πᾶν ῥῆμα **ἀργὸν** ὃ λαλήσουσιν οἱ ἄνθρωποι ἀποδώσουσιν περὶ αὐτοῦ λόγον ἐν ἡμέρᾳ κρίσεως· [GNT] | Careless, idle, negative, irresponsible, worthless, useless, unfruitful, barren, ineffective, idle word.<br><br>**Practical Application**<br>In this Scripture, the term "careless or idle words" conveys very well what Christ means. Note several lessons:<br>1. God hears and records every careless, idle word that we speak. (Psalm 139:4)<br>2. Unprofitable words make us, and show us to be, unprofitable servants.<br>3. Our idle words must be confessed to God and His mercy must be requested, for we are guilty of this unprofitable and wasteful sin.<br>4. Scripture flows with charge after charge governing the tongue. (cp. Romans 14:19; 1 Cor. 14:26; Ephes. 5:3-4; 1 Thes. 5:11; Job 15:3) |
| **#503**<br>**Careless Ease**<br><br>Surfeiting–KJV<br>Dissipation–NASB<br>Dissipation–NIV<br>Carousing–NKJV<br>**Careless ease**–NLT<br><br>**POSB REFERENCE**<br>(Lk.21:34-35; esp. v.34)<br>Note 1, point 1 | κραιπάλη = kraipalë<br>Pronunciation: [krahee-pal'-ay]<br>Parsing (part of speech): noun<br>    Case—dative<br>    Gender—feminine<br>    Number—singular<br>    Stem or root—from κραιπάλη, ης<br>Concordance References:<br>  ⇒ Strong's #2897 kraipalë<br>  ⇒ NIV #3190 kraipalë<br>  ⇒ NASB #2897 kraipalë<br><br>**Luke 21:34**<br>And take heed to yourselves, lest at any time your hearts be overcharged with **surfeiting**, and drunkenness, and cares of this life, and so that day come upon you unawares. [KJV]<br>"Be on guard, that your hearts may not be weighted down with **dissipation** and drunkenness and the worries of life, and that day come on you suddenly like a trap; [NASB]<br>"Be careful, or your hearts will be weighed down with **dissipation**, drunkenness and the anxieties of life, and that day will close on you unexpectedly like a trap. [NIV]<br>"But take heed to yourselves, lest your hearts be weighed down with **carousing**, drunkenness, and cares of this life, and that Day come on you unexpectedly. [NKJV]<br>"Watch out! Don't let me find you living in **careless ease** and drunkenness, and filled with the worries of this | Dissipation, surfeiting, careless ease; to be light hearted, silly, frivolous, giddy.<br><br>**Practical Application**<br>Medically, it referred to drunken nausea or headaches. It is the kind of light heartedness, silliness, frivolity, and giddiness that comes from partying and drinking. It is the loose, giddy, suggestive movements and talk that take place...<br>• at parties<br>• at social gatherings<br>• on dates<br>• behind closed doors<br>• at luncheons & dinner engagements<br>• at dances<br>• at clubs<br>• on business trips<br>• in the dark |

## PRACTICAL WORD STUDIES
### in the NEW TESTAMENT

| ENGLISH WORD | GREEK WORD AND VERSE | THE WORD MEANS... |
|---|---|---|
| | life. Don't let that day catch you unaware, [NLT]<br>Προσέχετε δὲ ἑαυτοῖς, μήποτε βαρυνθῶσιν ὑμῶν αἱ καρδίαι ἐν **κραιπάλῃ** καὶ μέθῃ καὶ μερίμναις βιωτικαῖς, καὶ αἰφνίδιος ἐφ' ὑμᾶς ἐπιστῇ ἡ ἡμέρα ἐκείνη· [GNS]<br>Προσέχετε δὲ ἑαυτοῖς μήποτε βαρηθῶσιν ὑμῶν αἱ καρδίαι ἐν **κραιπάλῃ** καὶ μέθῃ καὶ μερίμναις βιωτικαῖς καὶ ἐπιστῇ ἐφ' ὑμᾶς αἰφνίδιος ἡ ἡμέρα ἐκείνη [GNT] | |
| **#504**<br>**Cares**<br><br>Nourisheth–KJV<br>Nourishes–NASB<br>Feeds–NIV<br>Nourishes–NKJV<br>**Cares–NLT**<br><br>**POSB REFERENCE**<br>(Eph.5:25-33; esp. v.29)<br>Note 2, point 2 | ἐκτρέφει = *ektrephei*<br>Pronunciation: [ek-tref'-eh-ee]<br>Parsing (part of speech): verb<br>    Mood—indicative<br>    Tense—present<br>    Voice—active<br>    Person—3rd person<br>    Number—singular<br>    Stem or root—from ἐκτρέφω<br>Concordance References:<br>  ⇒ Strong's #1625 ektrephō<br>  ⇒ NIV #1763 ektrephō<br>  ⇒ NASB #1625 ektrephō<br><br>**Ephes. 5:29**<br>For no man ever yet hated his own flesh; but **nourisheth** and cherisheth it, even as the Lord the church: [KJV]<br>For no one ever hated his own flesh, but **nourishes** and cherishes it, just as Christ also *does* the church, [NASB]<br>After all, no one ever hated his own body, but he **feeds** and cares for it, just as Christ does the church—[NIV]<br>For no one ever hated his own flesh, but **nourishes** and cherishes it, just as the Lord *does* the church. [NKJV]<br>No one hates his own body but lovingly **cares** for it, just as Christ cares for his body, which is the church. [NLT]<br>οὐδεὶς γάρ ποτε τὴν ἑαυτοῦ σάρκα ἐμίσησεν, ἀλλ **ἐκτρέφει** καὶ θάλπει αὐτήν, καθὼς καὶ ὁ Κύριος τὴν ἐκκλησίαν· [GNS]<br>οὐδεὶς γάρ ποτε τὴν ἑαυτοῦ σάρκα ἐμίσησεν ἀλλὰ **ἐκτρέφει** καὶ θάλπει αὐτήν, καθὼς καὶ ὁ Χριστὸς τὴν ἐκκλησίαν, [GNT] | To feed; to clothe; to nurture; to look after until she is mature in the marriage and then to continue nourishing her as long as she lives.<br><br>**Practical Application**<br>The love which the husband is to have for his wife is the very same love he has for his own body. This is a startling statement. Note again what it says: the husband is to love his wife just as much as he loves *his own body*. This means that he is to care for his wife as he does his own body.<br>What a difference would exist in marriage if the husband just *cares for* his wife as he does his own body. Think through the meaning of the two words for just a moment and imagine the difference that could exist. |
| **#505**<br>**Cares For**<br><br>Cherisheth–KJV<br>Cherishes–NASB<br>**Cares for–NIV**<br>Cherishes–NKJV<br>Lovingly–NLT<br><br>**POSB REFERENCE**<br>(Eph.5:25-33; esp. v.29)<br>Note 2, point 2a | θάλπει = *thalpei*<br>Pronunciation: [thal'-peh-ee]<br>Parsing (part of speech): verb<br>    Mood—indicative<br>    Tense—present<br>    Voice—active<br>    Person—3rd person<br>    Number—singular<br>    Stem or root—from θάλπω<br>Concordance References:<br>  ⇒ Strong's #2282 thalpō<br>  ⇒ NIV #2499 thalpō<br>  ⇒ NASB #2282 thalpō<br><br>**Ephes. 5:29**<br>For no man ever yet hated his own flesh; but nourisheth and **cherisheth** it, even as the Lord the church: [KJV]<br>For no one ever hated his own flesh, but nourishes and **cherishes** it, just as Christ also *does* the church, [NASB]<br>After all, no one ever hated his own body, but he feeds and **cares for** it, just as Christ does the church—[NIV]<br>For no one ever hated his own flesh, but nourishes and **cherishes** it, just as the Lord *does* the church. [NKJV]<br>No one hates his own body but **lovingly** cares for it, just as Christ cares for his body, which is the church. [NLT]<br>οὐδεὶς γάρ ποτε τὴν ἑαυτοῦ σάρκα ἐμίσησεν, ἀλλ ἐκτρέφει καὶ **θάλπει** αὐτήν, καθὼς καὶ ὁ Κύριος τὴν ἐκκλησίαν· [GNS]<br>οὐδεὶς γάρ ποτε τὴν ἑαυτοῦ σάρκα ἐμίσησεν ἀλλὰ ἐκτρέφει καὶ **θάλπει** αὐτήν, καθὼς καὶ ὁ Χριστὸς τὴν ἐκκλησίαν, [GNT] | To care for; to cherish; to lovingly care for; to take care of.<br><br>**Practical Application**<br>The word "cares for" (*thalpei*) means to hold ever so dear within the heart; to treat with warmth, tenderness, care, affection, and appreciation. |

# PRACTICAL WORD STUDIES
## in the NEW TESTAMENT

| ENGLISH WORD | GREEK WORD AND VERSE | THE WORD MEANS... |
|---|---|---|
| **#506** **Carnal** Carnal–KJV Men of flesh–NASB Worldly–NIV Carnal–NKJV Belonged to this world–NLT **POSB REFERENCE** (1 Cor.3:1-4; esp. v.1) *Deeper Study #1* | σαρκίνοις = sarkinois Pronunciation: [sar-kee'-noys] Parsing (part of speech): pronominal adjective     Case—dative     Gender—masculine     Number—plural     Stem or root—from σάρκινος, η, ον Concordance References: ⇒ Strong's #4560 sarkinos ⇒ NIV #4921 sarkinos ⇒ NASB #4560 sarkinos **1 Cor. 3:1** And I, brethren, could not speak unto you as unto spiritual, but as unto **carnal**, *even* as unto babes in Christ. [KJV] And I, brethren, could not speak to you as to spiritual men, but as to **men of flesh**, as to babes in Christ. [NASB] Brothers, I could not address you as spiritual but as **worldly**—mere infants in Christ. [NIV] And I, brethren, could not speak to you as to spiritual *people* but as to **carnal**, as to babes in Christ. [NKJV] Dear brothers and sisters, when I was with you I couldn't talk to you as I would to mature Christians. I had to talk as though you **belonged to this world** or as though you were infants in the Christian life. [NLT] Καὶ ἐγώ, ἀδελφοί, οὐκ ἠδυνήθην λαλῆσαι ὑμῖν ὡς πνευματικοῖς, ἀλλ' ὡς **σαρκίνοις**, ὡς νηπίοις ἐν Χριστῷ. [GNS] Κἀγώ, ἀδελφοί, οὐκ ἠδυνήθην λαλῆσαι ὑμῖν ὡς πνευματικοῖς ἀλλ' ὡς **σαρκίνοις**, ὡς νηπίοις ἐν Χριστῷ. [GNT] | Worldly, carnal, fleshly, controlled by your own sinful desires, unspiritual, belonging to this world. **Practical Application** The ending "inois" [sark*inois*] means "to be made of." Paul is saying that the Corinthians were human beings, made of flesh. Their problem was that they were living as though they were nothing but flesh. They were still living at the human level of life. They had never gotten beyond the affairs and material things of this life. They acted as though this world was all there was. |
| **#507** **Carnal** Carnal–KJV Fleshly–NASB Worldly–NIV Carnal–NKJV Controlled by your own sinful desires–NLT **POSB REFERENCE** (1 Cor.3:1-4; esp. v.3) *Deeper Study #1* | σαρκικοί = sarkikoi Pronunciation: [sar-kee-koy'] Parsing (part of speech): adjective     Case—nominative     Gender—masculine     Number—plural     Stem or root—from σαρκικός, ή, όν Concordance References: ⇒ Strong's #4559 sarkikos ⇒ NIV #4920 sarkikos ⇒ NASB #4559 sarkikos **1 Cor. 3:3** For ye are yet **carnal**: for whereas *there is* among you envying, and strife, and divisions, are ye not carnal, and walk as men? [KJV] For you are still **fleshly**. For since there is jealousy and strife among you, are you not fleshly, and are you not walking like mere men? [NASB] You are still **worldly**. For since there is jealousy and quarreling among you, are you not worldly? Are you not acting like mere men? [NIV] For you are still **carnal**. For where *there are* envy, strife, and divisions among you, are you not carnal and behaving like *mere* men? [NKJV] For you are still **controlled by your own sinful desires**. You are jealous of one another and quarrel with each other. Doesn't that prove you are controlled by your own desires? You are acting like people who don't belong to the Lord. [NLT] ἔτι γὰρ **σαρκικοί** ἐστε· ὅπου γὰρ ἐν ὑμῖν ζῆλος καὶ ἔρις καὶ διχοστασίαι, οὐχὶ σαρκικοί ἐστε, καὶ κατὰ ἄνθρωπον περιπατεῖτε; [GNS] ἔτι γὰρ **σαρκικοί** ἐστε. ὅπου γὰρ ἐν ὑμῖν ζῆλος καὶ ἔρις, οὐχὶ σαρκικοί ἐστε καὶ κατὰ ἄνθρωπον περιπατεῖτε; [GNT] | Worldly, carnal, fleshly, sinful; controlled by your own sinful desires. **Practical Application** The ending "ikoi" means to be "characterized by." Paul is saying that the Corinthians were not only "made of flesh" but characterized and "dominated by the flesh." They were allowing the flesh and its passions to captivate and control their behavior. They were living on the level of the flesh, dominated by it. |

# PRACTICAL WORD STUDIES
## in the NEW TESTAMENT

| ENGLISH WORD | GREEK WORD AND VERSE | THE WORD MEANS... |
|---|---|---|
| **#508** <br> **Carnal** <br><br> **Carnal**–KJV <br> Flesh–NASB <br> Unspiritual–NIV <br> **Carnal**–NKJV <br> With me–NLT <br><br> **POSB REFERENCE** <br> (Rom.7:14-17; esp. v.14) <br> Note 2 | σάρκινός = sarkinos <br> Pronunciation: [sahr-kee-nos'] <br> Parsing (part of speech): adjective <br>　　Case—nominative <br>　　Gender—masculine <br>　　Number—singular <br>　　Stem or root—from σάρκινος, η, ον <br> Concordance References: <br> ⇒ Strong's #4559 sarkikos <br> ⇒ NIV #4921 sarkinos <br> ⇒ NASB #4560 sarkinos <br><br> **Romans 7:14** <br> For we know that the law is spiritual: but I am **carnal**, sold under sin. [KJV] <br> For we know that the Law is spiritual; but I am of **flesh**, sold into bondage to sin. [NASB] <br> We know that the law is spiritual; but I am **unspiritual**, sold as a slave to sin. [NIV] <br> For we know that the law is spiritual, but I am **carnal**, sold under sin. [NKJV] <br> The law is good, then. The trouble is not with the law but **with me**, because I am sold into slavery, with sin as my master. [NLT] <br> οἴδαμεν γὰρ ὅτι ὁ νόμος πνευματικός ἐστιν· ἐγὼ δὲ **σάρκικός** εἰμι, πεπραμένος ὑπὸ τὴν ἁμαρτίαν. [GNS] <br> οἴδαμεν γὰρ ὅτι ὁ νόμος πνευματικός ἐστιν, ἐγὼ δὲ **σάρκινός** εἰμι πεπραμένος ὑπὸ τὴν ἁμαρτίαν. [GNT] | Unspiritual, carnal, fleshly, human, worldly; by sinful nature; to belong to this world; to be made of flesh; to consist of flesh; to have a body of flesh and blood. It means the flesh with which a man is born, the fleshly nature one inherits from his parents when he is born. <br><br> **Practical Application** <br> The word carnal also means to be given up to the flesh, that is, to live a fleshly, sensual life; to be given over to animal appetites; to be controlled by one's sinful nature. (See POSB *Deeper Study* #1, Carnal—1 Cor. 3:1-4 for more discussion.) |
| **#509** <br> **Carnally Minded, To Be** <br><br> To be carnally minded–KJV <br> Mind set on the flesh–NASB <br> Mind of sinful man–NIV <br> To be carnally minded–NKJV <br> Sinful nature controls your mind–NLT <br><br> **POSB REFERENCE** <br> (Rom.8:5-8; esp. v.6) <br> Note 3, point 1 | τὸ φρόνημα τῆς σαρκός = to phronēma tēs sarkos <br> Pronunciation: [to fron'-ay-mah tace sar-kos] <br> Parsing *phronēma* (part of speech): noun <br>　　Case—nominative <br>　　Gender—neuter <br>　　Number—singular <br>　　Stem or root—from φρόνημα, τος <br> Parsing *sarkos* (part of speech): noun <br>　　Case—genitive <br>　　Gender—feminine <br>　　Number—singular <br>　　Stem or root—from σάρξ <br> Concordance References: <br> ⇒ Strong's #3588 ho + 5427 phronēma + 3588 ho + 4561 sarx <br> ⇒ NIV #3836 ho [The] + 5859 phronēma [mind] + 3836 ho [Not in English] + 4922 sarx [sinful man] <br> ⇒ NASB #3588 ho + 5427 phronēma + 3588 ho + 4561 sarx <br><br> **Romans 8:6** <br> For **to be carnally minded** *is* death; but to be spiritually minded *is* life and peace. [KJV] <br> For **the mind set on the flesh** is death, but the mind set on the Spirit is life and peace, [NASB] <br> **The mind of sinful man** is death, but the mind controlled by the Spirit is life and peace; [NIV] <br> For **to be carnally minded** *is* death, but to be spiritually minded *is* life and peace. [NKJV] <br> If your **sinful nature controls your mind**, there is death. But if the Holy Spirit controls your mind, there is life and peace. [NLT] <br> τὸ γὰρ φρόνημα τῆς σαρκὸς θάνατος· τὸ δὲ φρόνημα τοῦ πνεύματος ζωὴ καὶ εἰρήνη· [GNS] <br> τὸ γὰρ φρόνημα τῆς σαρκὸς θάνατος, τὸ δὲ φρόνημα τοῦ πνεύματος ζωὴ καὶ εἰρήνη· [GNT] | To have a worldly, carnal, fleshly, mind and thoughts; to be controlled by your own sinful desires; to be unspiritual. <br><br> **Practical Application** <br> This is one of the most important passages in all of Scripture, for it discusses the human mind: <br><br> *"For as he [a man] thinks in his heart, so is he." (Proverbs 23:7).* <br><br> Where a man keeps his mind and what he thinks about determine who he is and what he does. If a man keeps his mind and thoughts in the gutter, he becomes part of the filth in the gutter. If he keeps his mind upon the *good*, he becomes good. If he focuses upon achievement and success, he achieves and succeeds. If his mind is filled with religious thoughts, he becomes religious. If his thoughts are focused upon God and righteousness, he becomes godly and righteous. A man becomes and does what he thinks. It is the law of the mind. |
| **#510** <br> **Carousals** <br><br> Revellings–KJV <br> **Carousals**–NASB <br> Orgies–NIV | κώμοις = kōmois <br> Pronunciation: [ko'-moys] <br> Parsing (part of speech): noun <br>　　Case—dative <br>　　Gender—masculine <br>　　Number—plural <br>　　Stem or root—from κῶμος, ου | Orgies, revelings, carousals; feasting, uncontrolled license, indulgence, and pleasure; taking part in wild parties or in drinking parties or in orgies; lying around indulging in feeding the lusts of the flesh, the desires of the sinful nature. |

# PRACTICAL WORD STUDIES
## in the NEW TESTAMENT

| ENGLISH WORD | GREEK WORD AND VERSE | THE WORD MEANS... |
|---|---|---|
| Revelries–NKJV<br>Feasting–NLT<br><br>**POSB REFERENCE**<br>(1 Pt.4:3)<br>Note 3, point 4 | Concordance References:<br>⇒ Strong's #2970 kōmos<br>⇒ NIV #3269 kōmos<br>⇒ NASB #2970 kōmos<br><br>**1 Peter 4:3**<br>For the time past of *our* life may suffice us to have wrought the will of the Gentiles, when we walked in lasciviousness, lusts, excess of wine, **revellings**, banquetings, and abominable idolatries: [KJV]<br>For the time already past is sufficient *for you* to have carried out the desire of the Gentiles, having pursued a course of sensuality, lusts, drunkenness, **carousals**, drinking parties and abominable idolatries. [NASB]<br>For you have spent enough time in the past doing what pagans choose to do—living in debauchery, lust, drunkenness, **orgies**, carousing and detestable idolatry. [NIV]<br>For we *have spent* enough of our past lifetime in doing the will of the Gentiles—when we walked in lewdness, lusts, drunkenness, **revelries**, drinking parties, and abominable idolatries. [NKJV]<br>You have had enough in the past of the evil things that godless people enjoy—their immorality and lust, their **feasting** and drunkenness and wild parties, and their terrible worship of idols. [NLT]<br>ἀρκετὸς γὰρ ἡμῖν ὁ παρεληλυθὼς χρόνος τὸ βίου τὸ θέλημα τῶν ἐθνῶν κατεργάσασθαι, πεπορευμένους ἐν ἀσελγείαις, ἐπιθυμίαις, οἰνοφλυγίαις, **κώμοις**, πότοις, καὶ ἀθεμίτοις εἰδωλολατρείαις· [GNS]<br>ἀρκετὸς γὰρ ὁ παρεληλυθὼς χρόνος τὸ βούλημα τῶν ἐθνῶν κατειργάσθαι πεπορευμένους ἐν ἀσελγείαις, ἐπιθυμίαις, οἰνοφλυγίαις, **κώμοις**, πότοις καὶ ἀθεμίτοις εἰδωλολατρίαις. [GNT] | **Practical Application**<br>It is a graphic picture of a life that is out of control, a life that has cast off reason and pursued a course of carousals. |
| **#511**<br>**Carousing**<br><br>Revellings–KJV<br>Carousing–NASB<br>Orgies–NIV<br>Revelries–NKJV<br>Wild parties–NLT<br><br>**POSB REFERENCE**<br>(Gal.5:19-21; esp. v.21)<br>Note 2<br><br>**See also POSB REF:**<br>(Rom.13:13)<br>Note 4, point 1 | κῶμοι = kōmoi<br>Pronunciation: [ko'-moy]<br>Parsing (part of speech): noun<br>  Case—nominative<br>  Gender—masculine<br>  Number—plural<br>  Stem or root—from κῶμος, ου<br>Concordance References:<br>⇒ Strong's #2970 kōmos<br>⇒ NIV #3269 kōmos<br>⇒ NASB #2970 kōmos<br><br>**Galatians 5:21**<br>Envyings, murders, drunkenness, **revellings**, and such like: of the which I tell you before, as I have also told *you* in time past, that they which do such things shall not inherit the kingdom of God. [KJV]<br>Envying, drunkenness, **carousing**, and things like these, of which I forewarn you just as I have forewarned you that those who practice such things shall not inherit the kingdom of God. [NASB]<br>And envy; drunkenness, **orgies**, and the like. I warn you, as I did before, that those who live like this will not inherit the kingdom of God. [NIV]<br>Envy, murders, drunkenness, **revelries**, and the like; of which I tell you beforehand, just as I also told *you* in time past, that those who practice such things will not inherit the kingdom of God. [NKJV]<br>Envy, drunkenness, **wild parties**, and other kinds of sin. Let me tell you again, as I have before, that anyone living that sort of life will not inherit the Kingdom of God. [NLT]<br>φθόνοι, φόνοι, μέθαι, **κῶμοι**, καὶ τὰ ὅμοια τούτοις· ἃ προλέγω ὑμῖν, καθὼς καὶ προεῖπον, ὅτι οἱ τὰ τοιαῦτα πράσσοντες βασιλείαν Θεοῦ οὐ κληρονομήσουσιν. [GNS]<br>φθόνοι, μέθαι, **κῶμοι** καὶ τὰ ὅμοια τούτοις, ἃ προλέγω ὑμῖν καθὼς προεῖπον ὅτι οἱ τὰ τοιαῦτα πράσσοντες βασιλείαν θεοῦ οὐ κληρονομήσουσιν. [GNT] | Orgies, rioting, carousing, wild parties. It means reveling, carousing, partying, feasting, intemperance, debauchery, unrestrained revelry and indulgence, giving license to basic urges.<br><br>**Practical Application**<br>This word graphically describes a life of uncontrolled license, indulgence, and pleasure; taking part in wild parties or in drinking parties; lying around indulging in feeding the lusts of the flesh. |

# PRACTICAL WORD STUDIES
## in the NEW TESTAMENT

| ENGLISH WORD | GREEK WORD AND VERSE | THE WORD MEANS... |
|---|---|---|
| **#512**<br>**Carousing**<br><br>Banquetings–KJV<br>Drinking parties–NASB<br>**Carousing–NIV**<br>Drinking parties–NKJV<br>Wild parties–NLT<br><br>**POSB REFERENCE**<br>(1 Pt.4:3)<br>Note 3, point 5 | πότοις = *potois*<br>Pronunciation: [pot'-oys]<br>Parsing (part of speech): noun<br>    Case—dative<br>    Gender—masculine<br>    Number—plural<br>    Stem or root—from πότος, ου<br>Concordance References:<br>  ⇒ Strong's #4224 *potos*<br>  ⇒ NIV #4542 *potos*<br>  ⇒ NASB #4224 *potos*<br><br>**1 Peter 4:3**<br>For the time past of our life may suffice us to have wrought the will of the Gentiles, when we walked in lasciviousness, lusts, excess of wine, revellings, **banquetings**, and abominable idolatries: [KJV]<br>For the time already past is sufficient for you to have carried out the desire of the Gentiles, having pursued a course of sensuality, lusts, drunkenness, carousals, **drinking parties** and abominable idolatries. [NASB]<br>For you have spent enough time in the past doing what pagans choose to do—living in debauchery, lust, drunkenness, orgies, **carousing** and detestable idolatry. [NIV]<br>For we have spent enough of our past lifetime in doing the will of the Gentiles—when we walked in lewdness, lusts, drunkenness, revelries, **drinking parties**, and abominable idolatries. [NKJV]<br>You have had enough in the past of the evil things that godless people enjoy—their immorality and lust, their feasting and drunkenness and **wild parties**, and their terrible worship of idols. [NLT]<br>ἀρκετὸς γὰρ ἡμῖν ὁ παρεληλυθὼς χρόνος τὸ βίου τὸ θέλημα τῶν ἐθνῶν κατεργάσασθαι, πεπορευμένους ἐν ἀσελγείαις, ἐπιθυμίαις, οἰνοφλυγίαις, κώμοις, **πότοις**, καὶ ἀθεμίτοις εἰδωλολατρείαις· [GNS]<br>ἀρκετὸς γὰρ ὁ παρεληλυθὼς χρόνος τὸ βούλημα τῶν ἐθνῶν κατειργάσθαι πεπορευμένους ἐν ἀσελγείαις, ἐπιθυμίαις, οἰνοφλυγίαις, κώμοις, **πότοις** καὶ ἀθεμίτοις εἰδωλολατρίαις. [GNT] | Carousing, banquetings, drunkenness; drinking parties; wild parties; partying and getting drunk; a drunken orgy.<br><br>**Practical Application**<br>The believer's life is divided into two parts: *his old life and his new life*. Note the force of this verse: in his *old life*, he sinned enough. He has already followed the desires and lusts of the ungodly (Gentiles) enough. He has already worked the will of the ungodly. He has walked after them, walked just as they walk, and enough is enough. The believer is no longer to fulfill the desires of the flesh. |
| **#513**<br>**Carousing**<br><br>Surfeiting–KJV<br>Dissipation–NASB<br>Dissipation–NIV<br>**Carousing–NKJV**<br>Careless ease–NLT<br><br>**POSB REFERENCE**<br>(Lk.21:34-35; esp. v.34)<br>Note 1, point 1 | κραιπάλῃ = *kraipalē*<br>Pronunciation: [krahee-pal'-ay]<br>Parsing (part of speech): noun<br>    Case—dative<br>    Gender—feminine<br>    Number—singular<br>    Stem or root—from κραιπάλη, ης<br>Concordance References:<br>  ⇒ Strong's #2897 *kraipalē*<br>  ⇒ NIV #3190 *kraipalē*<br>  ⇒ NASB #2897 *kraipalē*<br><br>**Luke 21:34**<br>And take heed to yourselves, lest at any time your hearts be overcharged with **surfeiting**, and drunkenness, and cares of this life, and so that day come upon you unawares. [KJV]<br>"Be on guard, that your hearts may not be weighted down with **dissipation** and drunkenness and the worries of life, and that day come on you suddenly like a trap; [NASB]<br>"Be careful, or your hearts will be weighed down with **dissipation**, drunkenness and the anxieties of life, and that day will close on you unexpectedly like a trap. [NIV]<br>"But take heed to yourselves, lest your hearts be weighed down with **carousing**, drunkenness, and cares of this life, and that Day come on you unexpectedly. [NKJV]<br>"Watch out! Don't let me find you living in **careless ease** and drunkenness, and filled with the worries of this life. Don't let that day catch you unaware, [NLT] | Dissipation, surfeiting, carousing; careless ease; to be light-hearted, silly, frivolous, giddy.<br><br>**Practical Application**<br>Medically, it referred to drunken nausea or headaches. It is the kind of light heartedness, silliness, frivolity, and giddiness that comes from partying and drinking. It is the loose, giddy, suggestive movements and talk that take place...<br>• at parties<br>• at social gatherings<br>• on dates<br>• behind closed doors<br>• at luncheons & dinner engagements<br>• at dances<br>• at clubs<br>• on business trips<br>• in the dark |

## Practical Word Studies
### in the New Testament

| ENGLISH WORD | GREEK WORD AND VERSE | THE WORD MEANS... |
|---|---|---|
| | Προσέχετε δὲ ἑαυτοῖς, μήποτε βαρυνθῶσιν ὑμῶν αἱ καρδίαι ἐν **κραιπάλῃ** καὶ μέθῃ καὶ μερίμναις βιωτικαῖς, καὶ αἰφνίδιος ἐφ' ὑμᾶς ἐπιστῇ ἡ ἡμέρα ἐκείνη· [GNS] <br><br> Προσέχετε δὲ ἑαυτοῖς μήποτε βαρηθῶσιν ὑμῶν αἱ καρδίαι ἐν **κραιπάλῃ** καὶ μέθῃ καὶ μερίμναις βιωτικαῖς καὶ ἐπιστῇ ἐφ' ὑμᾶς αἰφνίδιος ἡ ἡμέρα ἐκείνη [GNT] | |
| **#514** <br> **Carried** <br><br> Bare–KJV <br> **Carried–NASB** <br> **Carried–NIV** <br> Bore–NKJV <br> Removed–NLT <br><br> **POSB REFERENCE** <br> (Mt.8:17) <br> Note 3 | ἐβάστασεν = ebastasen <br> Pronunciation: [e-bas-ta'-sen] <br> Parsing (part of speech): verb <br>    Mood—indicative <br>    Tense—aorist <br>    Voice—active <br>    Person—3rd person <br>    Number—singular <br>    Stem or root—from βαστάζω <br> Concordance References: <br>  ⇒ Strong's #941 bastazō <br>  ⇒ NIV #1002 bastazō <br>  ⇒ NASB #941 bastazō <br><br> **Matthew 8:17** <br> That it might be fulfilled which was spoken by Esaias the prophet, saying, Himself took our infirmities, and **bare** our sicknesses. [KJV] <br><br> In order that what was spoken through Isaiah the prophet might be fulfilled, saying, "HE HIMSELF TOOK OUR INFIRMITIES, AND **CARRIED** AWAY OUR DISEASES." [NASB] <br><br> This was to fulfill what was spoken through the prophet Isaiah: "He took up our infirmities and **carried** our diseases." [NIV] <br><br> That it might be fulfilled which was spoken by Isaiah the prophet, saying: *"He Himself took our infirmities And **bore** our sicknesses."* [NKJV] <br><br> This fulfilled the word of the Lord through Isaiah, who said, "He took our sicknesses and **removed** our diseases." [NLT] <br><br> ὅπως πληρωθῇ τὸ ῥηθὲν διὰ Ἡσαΐου τοῦ προφήτου, λέγοντος, Αὐτὸς τὰς ἀσθενείας ἡμῶν ἔλαβε, καὶ τὰς νόσους **ἐβάστασεν**. [GNS] <br><br> ὅπως πληρωθῇ τὸ ῥηθὲν διὰ Ἡσαΐου τοῦ προφήτου λέγοντος, Αὐτὸς τὰς ἀσθενείας ἡμῶν ἔλαβεν καὶ τὰς νόσους **ἐβάστασεν**. [GNT] | To bear; to bear with; to endure; to take up; to carry; to support; to sustain; to remove; to endure hardship. <br><br> **Practical Application** <br> In this Scripture, Christ did not just heal our sicknesses as any other minister, but He "took up [*elaben*] our infirmities and carried away [*ebastasen*] our diseases." This means at least two things. <br> 1. He carried our infirmities and diseases to the ultimate degree when He died on the cross for us. It was there that He bore them (see POSB *Deeper Study* #2—Mt.8:17 for discussion). (Cp. Jn.1:29.) <br> 2. He carried each fresh illness in a way that will never be understood. <br>   a. Each need that stood before Him was a reminder that He had to bear the sin of the world. And He knew what this meant and all that it was to include. Seeing the needs of people standing before Him reminded Him of the suffering He was to bear. <br>   b. Each need that He met was a foretaste of the cross. The thought of what He had to bear was upon His mind day by day and hour by hour as He went about ministering. This was bound to weigh ever so heavily upon Him. |
| **#515** <br> **Carried About– Carried Away** <br><br> **Carried about–KJV** <br> **Carried away–NASB** <br> **Carried away–NIV** <br> **Carried about–NKJV** <br> Attracted–NLT <br><br> **POSB REFERENCE** <br> (Heb.13:9-11; esp. v.9) <br> Note 1 | παραφέρεσθε = *parapheresthe* <br> Pronunciation: [par-a-fer'-ehs-the] <br> Parsing (part of speech): verb <br>    Mood—imperative <br>    Tense—present <br>    Voice—passive <br>    Person—2nd person <br>    Number—plural <br>    Stem or root—from παραφέρω <br> Concordance References: <br>  ⇒ Strong's #3911 *parapherō* <br>  ⇒ NIV #4195 *parapherō* <br>  ⇒ NASB #3911 *parapherō* <br><br> **Hebrews 13:9** <br> Be not **carried about** with divers and strange doctrines. For *it is* a good thing that the heart be established with grace; not with meats, which have not profited them that have been occupied therein. [KJV] <br><br> Do not be **carried away** by varied and strange teachings; for it is good for the heart to be strengthened by grace, not by foods, through which those who were thus occupied were not benefited. [NASB] <br><br> Do not be **carried away** by all kinds of strange teachings. It is good for our hearts to be strengthened by grace, not by ceremonial foods, which are of no value to those who eat them. [NIV] <br><br> Do not be **carried about** with various and strange doctrines. For *it is* good that the heart be established by | To be carried away; to be blown along; to be attracted to the wrong thing; to lead away; to be carried away or astray. <br><br> **Practical Application** <br> To be carried away from the grace of God is the most dangerous thing that can happen to a person, for it is the grace of God that saves a person. A person can become acceptable to God only if he approaches God through God's grace demonstrated in the Lord Jesus Christ. |

# PRACTICAL WORD STUDIES
## in the NEW TESTAMENT

| ENGLISH WORD | GREEK WORD AND VERSE | THE WORD MEANS... |
|---|---|---|
| | grace, not with foods which have not profited those who have been occupied with them. [NKJV]<br><br>So do not be **attracted** by strange, new ideas. Your spiritual strength comes from God's special favor, not from ceremonial rules about food, which don't help those who follow them. [NLT]<br><br>διδαχαῖς ποικίλαις καὶ ξέναις μὴ **περιφέρεσθε**· καλὸν γὰρ χάριτι βεβαιοῦσθαι τὴν καρδίαν, οὐ βρώμασιν, ἐν οἷς οὐκ ὠφελήθησαν οἱ περιπατήσαντες. [GNS]<br><br>διδαχαῖς ποικίλαις καὶ ξέναις μὴ **παραφέρεσθε**· καλὸν γὰρ χάριτι βεβαιοῦσθαι τὴν καρδίαν, οὐ βρώμασιν, ἐν οἷς οὐκ ὠφελήθησαν οἱ περιπατοῦντες. [GNT] | |
| **#516**<br>**Cast**<br><br>Cast–KJV<br>Threw–NASB<br>Flung–NIV<br>Threw–NKJV<br>Threw–NLT<br><br>**POSB REFERENCE**<br>(Rev.12:3-4; esp.v.4)<br>Note 2 | ἔβαλεν = *ebalen*<br>Pronunciation: [eh-bal'-lehn]<br>Parsing (part of speech): verb<br>    Mood—indicative<br>    Tense—aorist<br>    Voice—active<br>    Person—3rd person<br>    Number—singular<br>    Stem or root—from βάλλω<br>Concordance References:<br>  ⇒ Strong's #906 *ballō*<br>  ⇒ NIV #965 *ballō*<br>  ⇒ NASB #906 *ballō*<br><br>**Rev. 12:4**<br>And his tail drew the third part of the stars of heaven, and did **cast** them to the earth: and the dragon stood before the woman which was ready to be delivered, for to devour her child as soon as it was born. [KJV]<br><br>And his tail swept away a third of the stars of heaven, and **threw** them to the earth. And the dragon stood before the woman who was about to give birth, so that when she gave birth he might devour her child. [NASB]<br><br>His tail swept a third of the stars out of the sky and **flung** them to the earth. The dragon stood in front of the woman who was about to give birth, so that he might devour her child the moment it was born. [NIV]<br><br>His tail drew a third of the stars of heaven and **threw** them to the earth. And the dragon stood before the woman who was ready to give birth, to devour her Child as soon as it was born. [NKJV]<br><br>His tail dragged down one-third of the stars, which he **threw** to the earth. He stood before the woman as she was about to give birth to her child, ready to devour the baby as soon as it was born. [NLT]<br><br>καὶ ἡ οὐρὰ αὐτοῦ σύρει τὸ τρίτον τῶν ἀστέρων τοῦ οὐρανοῦ, καὶ **ἔβαλεν** αὐτοὺς εἰς τὴν γῆν· καὶ ὁ δράκων ἔστηκεν ἐνώπιον τῆς γυναικὸς τῆς μελλούσης τεκεῖν, ἵνα, ὅταν τέκῃ τὸ τέκνον αὐτῆς, καταφάγῃ. [GNS]<br><br>καὶ ἡ οὐρὰ αὐτοῦ σύρει τὸ τρίτον τῶν ἀστέρων τοῦ οὐρανοῦ καὶ **ἔβαλεν** αὐτοὺς εἰς τὴν γῆν· καὶ ὁ δράκων ἔστηκεν ἐνώπιον τῆς γυναικὸς τῆς μελλούσης τεκεῖν, ἵνα ὅταν τέκῃ τὸ τέκνον αὐτῆς καταφάγῃ. [GNT] | To fling; to throw; to hurl; to chuck; to toss.<br><br>**Practical Application**<br>He "cast" (*ebalen*) them down or threw them down. This is aorist tense which means a once-for-all act; that is, it tells us what Satan did long ago.<br><br>The point is this: today, in the present moment, Satan has authority over one third of the stars or angels of heaven. How? Because in the past, he cast them down with himself. |
| **#517**<br>**Cast Away**<br><br>Cast away–KJV<br>Forfeits–NASB<br>Forfeit–NIV<br>Lost–NKJV<br>Forfeit–NLT<br><br>**POSB REFERENCE**<br>(Lk.9:25)<br>*Deeper Study #2* | ζημιωθείς = *zēmiōtheis*<br>Pronunciation: [dzay-mee-o'-thace]<br>Parsing (part of speech): verb<br>    Mood—participle<br>    Tense—aorist<br>    Voice—passive<br>    Case—nominative<br>    Gender—masculine<br>    Number—singular<br>    Stem or root—from ζημιόω<br>Concordance References:<br>  ⇒ Strong's #2210 *zēmioō*<br>  ⇒ NIV #2423 *zēmioō*<br>  ⇒ NASB #2210 *zēmioō* | To forfeit; to cast away; to harm; to suffer the loss of; to lose what is of greatest value; to be punished by forfeiting and losing.<br><br>**Practical Application**<br>Note that this is a stated fact, an inevitable and sure result. The person who seeks to please himself is doomed to "be cast away." He tried to find himself here on earth, but he never did. He lost himself. He lost the greatest things in all the world: certainty, assurance, confidence, and satisfaction of knowing that he is eternally secure and destined to live and serve God forever. |

## PRACTICAL WORD STUDIES
### in the NEW TESTAMENT

| ENGLISH WORD | GREEK WORD AND VERSE | THE WORD MEANS... |
|---|---|---|
|  | **Luke 9:25**<br>For what is a man advantaged, if he gain the whole world, and lose himself, or be **cast away**? [KJV]<br>"For what is a man profited if he gains the whole world, and loses or **forfeits** himself? [NASB]<br>What good is it for a man to gain the whole world, and yet lose or **forfeit** his very self? [NIV]<br>For what profit is it to a man if he gains the whole world, and is himself destroyed or **lost**? [NKJV]<br>And how do you benefit if you gain the whole world but lose or **forfeit** your own soul in the process? [NLT]<br>τί γὰρ ὠφελεῖται ἄνθρωπος, κερδήσας τὸν κόσμον ὅλον, ἑαυτὸν δὲ ἀπολέσας, ἢ **ζημιωθείς**; [GNS]<br>τί γὰρ ὠφελεῖται ἄνθρωπος κερδήσας τὸν κόσμον ὅλον ἑαυτὸν δὲ ἀπολέσας ἢ **ζημιωθείς**; [GNT] |  |
| **#518**<br>**Cast Away**<br><br>**Cast away**–KJV<br>Rejected–NASB<br>Reject–NIV<br>**Cast away**–NKJV<br>Rejected–NLT<br><br>**POSB REFERENCE**<br>(Romans 11:1)<br>Note 1 | ἀπώσατο = *apōsato*<br>Pronunciation: [ap-o-sah-tow]<br>Parsing (part of speech): verb<br>    Mood—indicative<br>    Tense—aorist<br>    Voice—middle deponent<br>    Person—3rd person<br>    Number—singular<br>    Stem or root—from ἀπωθέομαι<br>Concordance References:<br> ⇒ Strong's #683 apōtheōmai<br> ⇒ NIV #723 apōtheō<br> ⇒ NASB #683 apōtheōmai<br><br>**Romans 11:1**<br>I say then, Hath God **cast away** his people? God forbid. For I also am an Israelite, of the seed of Abraham, of the tribe of Benjamin. [KJV]<br>I say then, God has not **rejected** His people, has He? May it never be! For I too am an Israelite, a descendant of Abraham, of the tribe of Benjamin. [NASB]<br>I ask then: Did God **reject** his people? By no means! I am an Israelite myself, a descendant of Abraham, from the tribe of Benjamin. [NIV]<br>I say then, has God **cast away** His people? Certainly not! For I also am an Israelite, of the seed of Abraham, *of* the tribe of Benjamin. [NKJV]<br>I ask, then, has God **rejected** his people, the Jews? Of course not! Remember that I myself am a Jew, a descendant of Abraham and a member of the tribe of Benjamin. [NLT]<br>Λέγω οὖν, Μὴ **ἀπώσατο** ὁ Θεὸς τὸν λαὸν αὐτοῦ; μὴ γένοιτο. καὶ γὰρ ἐγὼ Ἰσραηλίτης εἰμί, ἐκ σπέρματος Ἀβραάμ, φυλῆς Βενϊαμίν. [GNS]<br>Λέγω οὖν, μὴ **ἀπώσατο** ὁ θεὸς τὸν λαὸν αὐτοῦ; μὴ γένοιτο· καὶ γὰρ ἐγὼ Ἰσραηλίτης εἰμί, ἐκ σπέρματος Ἀβραάμ, φυλῆς Βενϊαμίν. [GNT] | To cast away; to push away, to thrust away; to repel; to repudiate; to push aside; to reject; to fail to listen to (one's conscience)<br><br>**Practical Application**<br>The idea is to utterly and totally and finally reject. Has God utterly rejected Jews? Paul shouts: "May it never be!" (*me genoito*). It is impossible! It must never be! It can never be! God has not broken and violated His Word to Israel. God's promises to Israel did not mean that all Jews were locked in to salvation no matter how sinful and disobedient they were. It did not mean that an unbelieving and disobedient Jew was acceptable to God simply because he had been born a Jew. God's promises were intended for those who believed and obeyed Him. The people who believed and obeyed Him have always been "His people." |
| **#519**<br>**Cast Down**<br><br>**Cast down**–KJV<br>Struck down–NASB<br>Struck down–NIV<br>Struck down–NKJV<br>Knocked down–NLT<br><br>**POSB REFERENCE**<br>(2 Cor.4:7-9; esp. v.9)<br>Note 2, point 4 | καταβαλλόμενοι = *kataballomenoi*<br>Pronunciation: [kat-ab-al-lo'-mehn-oy]<br>Parsing (part of speech): verb<br>    Mood—participle<br>    Tense—present<br>    Voice—passive<br>    Case—nominative<br>    Gender—masculine<br>    Person—1st person<br>    Number—plural<br>    Stem or root—from καταβάλλω<br>Concordance References:<br> ⇒ Strong's #2598 kataballō<br> ⇒ NIV #2850 kataballō<br> ⇒ NASB #2598 kataballō<br><br>**2 Cor. 4:9**<br>Persecuted, but not forsaken; **cast down**, but not | To be struck down; to be cast down; to be smitten down; to be knocked down; to be laying down.<br><br>**Practical Application**<br>The minister (or believer) may be "cast down," (*kataballomenoi*) but he is never destroyed. The minister (or believer) may be struck down, but he is never allowed to strike out; he may be knocked down, but he is never knocked out. |

# PRACTICAL WORD STUDIES
## in the NEW TESTAMENT

| ENGLISH WORD | GREEK WORD AND VERSE | THE WORD MEANS... |
|---|---|---|
| | destroyed; [KJV]<br>Persecuted, but not forsaken; **struck down**, but not destroyed; [NASB]<br>Persecuted, but not abandoned; **struck down**, but not destroyed. [NIV]<br>Persecuted, but not forsaken; **struck down**, but not destroyed— [NKJV]<br>We are hunted down, but God never abandons us. We get **knocked down**, but we get up again and keep going. [NLT]<br>διωκόμενοι, ἀλλ' οὐκ ἐγκαταλειπόμενοι, **καταβαλλόμενοι** ἀλλ' οὐκ ἀπολλύμενοι· [GNS]<br>διωκόμενοι, ἀλλ' οὐκ ἐγκαταλειπόμενοι, **καταβαλλόμενοι** ἀλλ' οὐκ ἀπολλύμενοι, [GNT] | |
| **#520**<br>**Cast Forth–**<br>**Cast Out**<br><br>**Cast forth**–KJV<br>Thrown away–NASB<br>Thrown away–NIV<br>**Cast out**–NKJV<br>Thrown away–NLT<br><br>**POSB**<br>**REFERENCE**<br>(Jn.15:4-6; esp. v.6)<br>Note 4, point 4a | ἐβλήθη ἔξω = eblēthē exō<br>Pronunciation: [eh-blay-thay ex'-o]<br>Parsing eblēthē (part of speech): verb<br>    Mood—indicative<br>    Tense—aorist<br>    Voice—passive<br>    Person—3rd person<br>    Number—singular<br>    Stem or root—from βάλλω<br>Parsing exō (part of speech): adjective adverb<br>    Stem or root—from ἔξω<br>Concordance References:<br>⇒ Strong's #906 ballo + 1854 exō<br>⇒ NIV #965 ballo [thrown] + 2032 exō [away]<br>⇒ NASB #906 ballo + 1854 exō<br><br>**John 15:6**<br>If a man abide not in me, he is **cast forth** as a branch, and is withered; and men gather them, and cast *them* into the fire, and they are burned. [KJV]<br>"If anyone does not abide in Me, he is **thrown away** as a branch, and dries up; and they gather them, and cast them into the fire, and they are burned. [NASB]<br>If anyone does not remain in me, he is like a branch that is **thrown away** and withers; such branches are picked up, thrown into the fire and burned. [NIV]<br>If anyone does not abide in Me, he is **cast out** as a branch and is withered; and they gather them and throw *them* into the fire, and they are burned. [NKJV]<br>Anyone who parts from me is **thrown away** like a useless branch and withers. Such branches are gathered into a pile to be burned. [NLT]<br>ἐὰν μή τις μείνῃ ἐν ἐμοί, **ἐβλήθη ἔξω** ὡς τὸ κλῆμα, καὶ ἐξηράνθη, καὶ συνάγουσιν αὐτὰ, καὶ εἰς πῦρ βάλλουσι, καὶ καίεται. [GNS]<br>ἐὰν μή τις μένῃ ἐν ἐμοί, **ἐβλήθη ἔξω** ὡς τὸ κλῆμα καὶ ἐξηράνθη καὶ συνάγουσιν αὐτὰ καὶ εἰς τὸ πῦρ βάλλουσιν καὶ καίεται. [GNT] | To be plucked off and cast out, thrown away, discarded, disposed of; to be hurled; to be flung.<br><br>**Practical Application**<br>The unattached branch wants and chooses to be unattached, so God lets it. It is given over and given up to be unattached. God abandons it. It is thrown off—cast off and out of the way and left to itself, to do as it chooses. (See POSB outline—Romans 1:24-32 and POSB notes—Romans 1:24-32.) |
| **#521**<br>**Cast Out**<br><br>**Cast out**–KJV<br>**Cast out**–NASB<br>Driven out–NIV<br>**Cast out**–NKJV<br>**Cast out**–NLT<br><br>**POSB**<br>**REFERENCE**<br>(Jn.12:31)<br>*Deeper Study* #3,<br>point 3 | ἐκβληθήσεται ἔξω = ekblēthēsetai exō<br>Pronunciation: [ek-blay-thay-seh-tah-ee ex-o]<br>Parsing ekblēthēsetai (part of speech): verb<br>    Mood—indicative<br>    Tense—future<br>    Voice—passive<br>    Person—3rd person<br>    Number—singular<br>    Stem or root—from ἐκβάλλω<br>Parsing exō (part of speech): adjective adverb<br>    Stem or root— from ἔξω<br>Concordance References:<br>⇒ Strong's #1544 ekballo + 1854 exō<br>⇒ NIV #1675 ekballo [driven] + 2032 exō [out]<br>⇒ NASB #1544 ekballo + 1854 exō<br><br>**John 12:31**<br>Now is the judgment of this world: now shall the prince of this world be **cast out**. [KJV] | To drive out; to cast out; to cast from or forth; to reject; to expel; to exclude; to cast clean out (exo) of a place; to throw out; to pluck out; to put outside.<br><br>**Practical Application**<br>Note the words "cast out" (*ekblēthēsetai exō*, future passive of ekballo which means a sure fact lying in the future). The words mean Satan in all his power, rule, and reign is driven out by the death of Christ. His power, rule, and reign over lives is now broken. |

## PRACTICAL WORD STUDIES
### in the NEW TESTAMENT

| ENGLISH WORD | GREEK WORD AND VERSE | THE WORD MEANS... |
|---|---|---|
| | "Now judgment is upon this world; now the ruler of this world shall be **cast out**. [NASB]<br>Now is the time for judgment on this world; now the prince of this world will be **driven out**. [NIV]<br>Now is the judgment of this world; now the ruler of this world will be **cast out**. [NKJV]<br>The time of judgment for the world has come, when the prince of this world will be **cast out**. [NLT]<br>νῦν κρίσις ἐστὶ τοῦ κόσμου τούτου· νῦν ὁ ἄρχων τοῦ κόσμου τούτου **ἐκβληθήσεται ἔξω**. [GNS]<br>νῦν κρίσις ἐστὶν τοῦ κόσμου τούτου, νῦν ὁ ἄρχων τοῦ κόσμου τούτου **ἐκβληθήσεται ἔξω**· [GNT] | |
| **#522**<br>**Cast Vote Against**<br><br>Voice against–KJV<br>Cast...vote against–NASB<br>Cast...vote against–NIV<br>Cast...vote against–NKJV<br>Cast...vote against–NLT<br><br>**POSB REFERENCE**<br>(Acts 26:9-11; esp. v.10)<br>Note 4 | κατήνεγκα ψῆφον = katēnegka psēphon<br>Pronunciation: [kat-ay-nehg'-kah psay'-fon]<br>Parsing *katēnegka* (part of speech): verb<br>   Mood—indicative<br>   Tense—aorist<br>   Voice—active<br>   Person—1st person<br>   Number—singular<br>   Stem or root—from καταφέρω<br>Parsing *psēphon* (part of speech): noun<br>   Case—accusative<br>   Gender—feminine<br>   Number—singular<br>   Stem or root—from ψῆφος<br>Concordance References:<br>⇒ Strong's #2702 katapherö + 5586 psëphos<br>⇒ NIV #2965 katapherö [cast against] + 6029 psëphos [vote]<br>⇒ NASB #2702 katapherö + 5586 psëphos<br><br>**Acts 26:10**<br>Which thing I also did in Jerusalem: and many of the saints did I shut up in prison, having received authority from the chief priests; and when they were put to death, I gave my **voice against** them. [KJV]<br>"And this is just what I did in Jerusalem; not only did I lock up many of the saints in prisons, having received authority from the chief priests, but also when they were being put to death I **cast** my **vote against** them. [NASB]<br>And that is just what I did in Jerusalem. On the authority of the chief priests I put many of the saints in prison, and when they were put to death, I **cast** my **vote against** them. [NIV]<br>This I also did in Jerusalem, and many of the saints I shut up in prison, having received authority from the chief priests; and when they were put to death, I **cast** my **vote against** them. [NKJV]<br>Authorized by the leading priests, I caused many of the believers in Jerusalem to be sent to prison. And I **cast** my **vote against** them when they were condemned to death. [NLT]<br>ὃ καὶ ἐποίησα ἐν Ἱεροσολύμοις, καὶ πολλοὺς τῶν ἁγίων ἐγὼ φυλακαῖς κατέκλεισα, τὴν παρὰ τῶν ἀρχιερέων ἐξουσίαν λαβών, ἀναιρουμένων τε αὐτῶν **κατήνεγκα ψῆφον**. [GNS]<br>ὃ καὶ ἐποίησα ἐν Ἱεροσολύμοις, καὶ πολλούς τε τῶν ἁγίων ἐγὼ ἐν φυλακαῖς κατέκλεισα τὴν παρὰ τῶν ἀρχιερέων ἐξουσίαν λαβών ἀναιρουμένων τε αὐτῶν **κατήνεγκα ψῆφον**. [GNT] | To cast a vote against; to vote against.<br><br>**Practical Application**<br>The word actually means a little stone or pebble used by the Sanhedrin that was thrown into an urn indicating how a person was voting. A black pebble meant condemnation. The point to note is this: Paul was saying that he was a member of the Sanhedrin, actually casting a vote against the Christian believers. |
| **#523**<br>**Castaway**<br><br>Castaway–KJV<br>Disqualified–NASB<br>Disqualified–NIV<br>Disqualified–NKJV<br>Disqualified–NLT | ἀδόκιμος = adokimos<br>Pronunciation: [ad-ok'-ee-mos]<br>Parsing (part of speech): adjective<br>   Case—nominative<br>   Gender—masculine<br>   Number—singular<br>   Stem or root—from ἀδόκιμος, ον<br>Concordance References:<br>⇒ Strong's #96 adokimos<br>⇒ NIV #99 adokimos<br>⇒ NASB #96 adokimos | Disqualified, reprobate, worthless, rejected, disapproved, depraved, unfit; failing to stand the test.<br><br>**Practical Application**<br>What does Paul mean? Most writers think that Paul is referring to salvation, that when he comes to the end of the race, he sees the possibility of being rejected—if he has not *lived* what he has preached to others. |

# PRACTICAL WORD STUDIES
## in the NEW TESTAMENT

| ENGLISH WORD | GREEK WORD AND VERSE | THE WORD MEANS... |
|---|---|---|
| **POSB REFERENCE** (1 Cor.9:27) Note 6, point 2 | **1 Cor. 9:27**<br>But I keep under my body, and bring *it* into subjection: lest that by any means, when I have preached to others, I myself should be a **castaway**. [KJV]<br>But I buffet my body and make it my slave, lest possibly, after I have preached to others, I myself should be **disqualified**. [NASB]<br>No, I beat my body and make it my slave so that after I have preached to others, I myself will not be **disqualified** for the prize. [NIV]<br>But I discipline my body and bring *it* into subjection, lest, when I have preached to others, I myself should become **disqualified**. [NKJV]<br>I discipline my body like an athlete, training it to do what it should. Otherwise, I fear that after preaching to others I myself might be **disqualified**. [NLT]<br>ἀλλὰ ὑπωπιάζω μου τὸ σῶμα καὶ δουλαγωγῶ, μήπως, ἄλλοις κηρύξας αὐτὸς **ἀδόκιμος** γένωμαι. [GNS]<br>ἀλλὰ ὑπωπιάζω μου τὸ σῶμα καὶ δουλαγωγῶ, μή πως ἄλλοις κηρύξας αὐτὸς **ἀδόκιμος** γένωμαι. [GNT] | The very fact that most writers understand Paul to be dealing with salvation clearly speaks to all ministers of the gospel: we must heed the Scripture.<br>Now, what does Paul mean? Five things are sure about Paul's teaching in Scripture.<br>**First**, Paul definitely pictured himself in a life-long struggle for salvation. The great Greek scholar A.T. Robertson says that Paul alone uses the Greek word *adokimos* in a moral sense in the New Testament, and Paul definitely says that he subjects his body and keeps it under control lest he be a *castaway*. Look at Paul's use of the word. It stands as a beneficial warning to us all—to live what we preach, and profess and live it with the utmost diligence and effort. (*Word Pictures in the New Testament*, Vol. 4. Nashville, TN: Broadman Press, 1931, p.150.)<br>**Second**, Paul definitely pictured himself as having to struggle against sin throughout life, and he struggled against sin for two reasons:<br>⇒ to attain to the resurrection of the dead (Philip.3:11).<br>⇒ to conquer the flesh, the sinful nature.<br>**Third**, Paul was perfectly assured of his salvation; he was perfectly assured that he would run the race and run it well. He was persuaded of two things:<br>⇒ that nothing in heaven or earth, in fact, nothing present and nothing to come, could ever separate him from the love of God (Ro.8:35-39).<br>⇒ that the Lord was able to *keep him* until the day of redemption.<br>**Fourth**, Paul was convinced that only those who walked in the Spirit and were committed to a deadly struggle against sin were saved and given the absolute assurance of their salvation (see POSB outline—Romans 8:1-17 and POSB notes—Romans 8:1-17).<br>**Fifth**, Paul was not perfect, and he confessed the fact, confessing that he was far from perfect. Therefore, until he was made perfect, he was going to struggle, follow, press, and strive for perfection; that is, to be conformed to the image of Christ (Ro.8:29; Philip.3:10-11). |
| **#524**<br>**Catch**<br><br>Catch–KJV<br>Catching–NASB<br>Catch–NIV<br>Catch–NKJV<br>Fishing–NLT<br><br>**POSB REFERENCE** (Lk.5:10) Note 7, point 2 | ἔσῃ ζωγρῶν = *esē zōgrōn*<br>Pronunciation: [es-ee dzogue-rohn']<br>Parsing *esē* (part of speech): verb<br>  Mood—indicative<br>  Tense—future<br>  Voice—middle deponent<br>  Person—2nd person<br>  Number—singular<br>  Stem or root—from εἰμί<br>Parsing *zōgrōn* (part of speech): verb<br>  Mood—participle<br>  Tense—present<br>  Voice—active<br>  Case—nominative<br>  Gender—masculine<br>  Person—2nd person<br>  Number—singular<br>  Stem or root—from ζωγρέω<br>Concordance References:<br>  ⇒ Strong's #1488 eimi +2221 zōgreō<br>  ⇒ NIV #1639 eimi +2436 zōgreō<br>  ⇒ NASB #1488 eimi +2221 zōgreō | To catch alive or to catch for life; to capture; to nab; to fish; to seize; to snare; to grab; to take.<br><br>**Practical Application**<br>The idea is that Peter was no longer to catch (fish) for death, but he was to catch (men) for life. |

# PRACTICAL WORD STUDIES
## in the NEW TESTAMENT

| ENGLISH WORD | GREEK WORD AND VERSE | THE WORD MEANS... |
|---|---|---|
| | **Luke 5:10**<br>And so *was* also James, and John, the sons of Zebedee, which were partners with Simon. And Jesus said unto Simon, Fear not; from henceforth thou shalt **catch** men. [KJV]<br>And so also James and John, sons of Zebedee, who were partners with Simon. And Jesus said to Simon, "Do not fear, from now on you will be **catching** men." [NASB]<br>And so were James and John, the sons of Zebedee, Simon's partners. Then Jesus said to Simon, "Don't be afraid; from now on you will **catch** men." [NIV]<br>And so also *were* James and John, the sons of Zebedee, who were partners with Simon. And Jesus said to Simon, "Do not be afraid. From now on you will **catch** men." [NKJV]<br>His partners, James and John, the sons of Zebedee, were also amazed. Jesus replied to Simon, "Don't be afraid! From now on you'll be **fishing** for people!" [NLT]<br>ὁμοίως δὲ καὶ Ἰάκωβον καὶ Ἰωάννην, υἱοὺς Ζεβεδαίου, οἳ ἦσαν κοινωνοὶ τῷ Σίμωνι. καὶ εἶπε πρὸς τὸν Σίμωνα ὁ Ἰησοῦς, Μὴ φοβοῦ· ἀπὸ τοῦ νῦν ἀνθρώπους **ἔσῃ ζωγρῶν**. [GNS]<br>ὁμοίως δὲ καὶ Ἰάκωβον καὶ Ἰωάννην υἱοὺς Ζεβεδαίου, οἳ ἦσαν κοινωνοὶ τῷ Σίμωνι. καὶ εἶπεν πρὸς τὸν Σίμωνα ὁ Ἰησοῦς, Μὴ φοβοῦ· ἀπὸ τοῦ νῦν ἀνθρώπους **ἔσῃ ζωγρῶν**. [GNT] | |
| **#525**<br>**Caught**<br><br>Caught–KJV<br>Dragged..away–NASB<br>Seized–NIV<br>Seized–NKJV<br>Brought–NLT<br><br>**POSB REFERENCE**<br>(Acts 6:11-14; esp. v.12)<br>Note 3, point 3 | συνήρπασαν = sunërpasan<br>Pronunciation: [soon-ayr-pa'-sahn]<br>Parsing (part of speech): verb<br>  Mood—indicative<br>  Tense—aorist<br>  Voice—active<br>  Person—3rd person<br>  Number—plural<br>  Stem or root—from συναρπάζω<br>Concordance References:<br>⇒ Strong's #4884 sunarpazo<br>⇒ NIV #5275 sunarpazö<br>⇒ NASB #4884 sunarpazo<br><br>**Acts 6:12**<br>And they stirred up the people, and the elders, and the scribes, and came upon *him,* and **caught** him, and brought *him* to the council, [KJV]<br>And they stirred up the people, the elders and the scribes, and they came upon him and **dragged** him **away**, and brought him before the Council. [NASB]<br>So they stirred up the people and the elders and the teachers of the law. They **seized** Stephen and brought him before the Sanhedrin. [NIV]<br>And they stirred up the people, the elders, and the scribes; and they came upon *him,* **seized** him, and brought *him* to the council. [NKJV]<br>Naturally, this roused the crowds, the elders, and the teachers of religious law. So they arrested Stephen and **brought** him before the high council. [NLT]<br>συνεκίνησάν τε τὸν λαὸν καὶ τοὺς πρεσβυτέρους καὶ τοὺς γραμματεῖς, καὶ ἐπιστάντες **συνήρπασαν** αὐτόν, καὶ ἤγαγον εἰς τὸ συνέδριον, [GNS]<br>συνεκίνησάν τε τὸν λαὸν καὶ τοὺς πρεσβυτέρους καὶ τοὺς γραμματεῖς, καὶ ἐπιστάντες **συνήρπασαν** αὐτὸν καὶ ἤγαγον εἰς τὸ συνέδριον, [GNT] | To seize; to catch; to drag away; to bring; to lay hold of; to carry off.<br><br>**Practical Application**<br>The word "caught" (*sunërpasan*) means to seize with violence. The picture is that they caught and literally dragged him to court (cp. Luke 8:29; Acts 19:29; Acts 27:15). |
| **#526**<br>**Caught Away**<br><br>Caught away–KJV<br>Snatched...away–NASB | ἥρπασεν = hërpasen<br>Pronunciation: [heyr-pah'-sehn]<br>Parsing (part of speech): verb<br>  Mood—indicative<br>  Tense—aorist<br>  Voice—active<br>  Person—3rd person<br>  Number—singular | To be suddenly taken away; to be caught away; to be snatched away; to be taken by force.<br><br>**Practical Application**<br>The word for "caught...away" (*hërpasen*) is strong. It means to be snatched away quickly, immediately, miraculously. It is the same word |

# PRACTICAL WORD STUDIES
## in the NEW TESTAMENT

| ENGLISH WORD | GREEK WORD AND VERSE | THE WORD MEANS... |
|---|---|---|
| Suddenly took...away–NIV<br>Caught...away–NKJV<br>Caught...away–NLT<br><br>**POSB REFERENCE**<br>(Acts 8:39-40; esp. v.39)<br>Note 7, point 1 | Stem or root—from ἁρπάζω<br>Concordance References:<br>⇒ Strong's #726 harpazö<br>⇒ NIV #773 harpazö<br>⇒ NASB #726 harpazö<br><br>**Acts 8:39**<br>And when they were come up out of the water, the Spirit of the Lord **caught away** Philip, that the eunuch saw him no more: and he went on his way rejoicing. [KJV]<br>And when they came up out of the water, the Spirit of the Lord **snatched** Philip **away**; and the eunuch saw him no more, but went on his way rejoicing. [NASB]<br>When they came up out of the water, the Spirit of the Lord **suddenly took** Philip **away**, and the eunuch did not see him again, but went on his way rejoicing. [NIV]<br>Now when they came up out of the water, the Spirit of the Lord **caught** Philip **away**, so that the eunuch saw him no more; and he went on his way rejoicing. [NKJV]<br>When they came up out of the water, the Spirit of the Lord **caught** Philip **away**. The eunuch never saw him again but went on his way rejoicing. [NLT]<br>ὅτε δὲ ἀνέβησαν ἐκ τοῦ ὕδατος, Πνεῦμα Κυρίου **ἥρπασε** τὸν Φίλιππον· καὶ οὐκ εἶδεν αὐτὸν οὐκέτι ὁ εὐνοῦχος, ἐπορεύετο γὰρ τὴν ὁδὸν αὐτοῦ χαίρων. [GNS]<br>ὅτε δὲ ἀνέβησαν ἐκ τοῦ ὕδατος, πνεῦμα κυρίου **ἥρπασεν** τὸν Φίλιππον καὶ οὐκ εἶδεν αὐτὸν οὐκέτι ὁ εὐνοῦχος, ἐπορεύετο γὰρ τὴν ὁδὸν αὐτοῦ χαίρων. [GNT] | used for the rapture of the church. It means to catch up into heaven during the rapture. |
| **#527**<br>**Cause To Stumble**<br><br>Stumblingblock–KJV<br>Stumbling block–NASB<br>Stumbling block–NIV<br>Stumbling block–NKJV<br>Cause...to stumble–NLT<br><br>**POSB REFERENCE**<br>(1 Cor.8:9-11; esp. v.9)<br>Note 3<br><br>See also POSB REF:<br>(Rom.14:13-15; esp. v.13)<br>Note 6 | πρόσκομμα = proskomma<br>Pronunciation: [pros'-kom-mah]<br>Parsing (part of speech): noun<br>   Case—nominative<br>   Gender—neuter<br>   Number—singular<br>   Stem or root—from πρόσκομμα, τος<br>Concordance References:<br>⇒ Strong's #4348 proskomma<br>⇒ NIV #4682 proskomma<br>⇒ NASB #4348 proskomma<br><br>**1 Cor. 8:9**<br>But take heed lest by any means this liberty of yours become a **stumblingblock** to them that are weak. [KJV]<br>But take care lest this liberty of yours somehow become a **stumbling block** to the weak. [NASB]<br>Be careful, however, that the exercise of your freedom does not become a **stumbling block** to the weak. [NIV]<br>But beware lest somehow this liberty of yours become a **stumbling block** to those who are weak. [NKJV]<br>But you must be careful with this freedom of yours. Do not **cause** a brother or sister with a weaker conscience **to stumble**. [NLT]<br>βλέπετε δὲ μήπως ἡ ἐξουσία ὑμῶν αὕτη **πρόσκομμα** γένηται τοῖς ἀσθενέσιν. [GNS]<br>βλέπετε δὲ μή πως ἡ ἐξουσία ὑμῶν αὕτη **πρόσκομμα** γένηται τοῖς ἀσθενέσιν. [GNT] | A stone, an obstacle, a stumbling block; an occasion, an offense or something that causes a person to stumble and fall into sin.<br><br>**Practical Application**<br>A believer's liberty can cause a weak believer to fall into sin. In the case of the Corinthians, some believers were participating in the social functions where meat had been offered to idols. Some were even attending the functions in the idol's temple (1 Cor. 8:10). Apparently, this was causing some of the weaker believers to do the same. But they were not able to handle the situation. |
| **#528**<br>**Causes Lust**<br><br>Offend–KJV<br>Makes you stumble–NASB<br>Causes...sin–NIV<br>Causes...sin–NKJV<br>**Causes...lust–NLT** | σκανδαλίζει = skandalizei<br>Pronunciation: [skan-dal-idz-eh-ee]<br>Parsing (part of speech): verb<br>   Mood—indicative<br>   Tense—present<br>   Voice—active<br>   Person—3rd person<br>   Number—singular<br>   Stem or root—from σκανδαλίζω<br>Concordance References:<br>⇒ Strong's #4624 skandalizö<br>⇒ NIV #4997 skandalizö<br>⇒ NASB #4624 skandalizö | To stumble; to fall away; to sin; to succumb to lust; to offend; to be baited; to be lured; to be tripped up; to cause someone to sin or fall into sin.<br><br>**Practical Application**<br>In this particular Scripture, the eyes and hands are said to be stumbling blocks. |

# PRACTICAL WORD STUDIES
## in the New Testament

| ENGLISH WORD | GREEK WORD AND VERSE | THE WORD MEANS... |
|---|---|---|
| **POSB REFERENCE** (Mt.5:29) Note 4 | **Matthew 5:29** And if thy right eye **offend** thee, pluck it out, and cast *it* from thee: for it is profitable for thee that one of thy members should perish, and not *that* thy whole body should be cast into hell. [KJV]<br><br>"And if your right eye **makes you stumble**, tear it out, and throw it from you; for it is better for you that one of the parts of your body perish, than for your whole body to be thrown into hell. [NASB]<br><br>If your right eye **causes** you to **sin**, gouge it out and throw it away. It is better for you to lose one part of your body than for your whole body to be thrown into hell. [NIV]<br><br>If your right eye **causes** you to **sin**, pluck it out and cast *it* from you; for it is more profitable for you that one of your members perish, than for your whole body to be cast into hell. [NKJV]<br><br>So if your eye—even if it is your good eye—**causes** you to **lust**, gouge it out and throw it away. It is better for you to lose one part of your body than for your whole body to be thrown into hell. [NLT]<br><br>εἰ δὲ ὁ ὀφθαλμός σου ὁ δεξιὸς **σκανδαλίζει** σε, ἔξελε αὐτὸν καὶ βάλε ἀπὸ σοῦ· συμφέρει γάρ σοι ἵνα ἀπόληται ἓν τῶν μελῶν σου, καὶ μὴ ὅλον τὸ σῶμά σου βληθῇ εἰς γέενναν. [GNS]<br><br>εἰ δὲ ὁ ὀφθαλμός σου ὁ δεξιὸς **σκανδαλίζει** σε, ἔξελε αὐτὸν καὶ βάλε ἀπὸ σοῦ· συμφέρει γάρ σοι ἵνα ἀπόληται ἓν τῶν μελῶν σου καὶ μὴ ὅλον τὸ σῶμά σου βληθῇ εἰς γέενναν. [GNT] | |
| **#529**<br>**Causes Sin**<br><br>Offend–KJV<br>Makes you stumble–NASB<br>**Causes...sin**–NIV<br>**Causes...sin**–NKJV<br>Causes...lust–NLT<br><br>**POSB REFERENCE** (Mt.5:29) Note 4 | σκανδαλίζει = *skandalizei*<br>Pronunciation: [skan-dal-idz-eh-ee]<br>Parsing (part of speech): verb<br>    Mood—indicative<br>    Tense—present<br>    Voice—active<br>    Person—3rd person<br>    Number—singular<br>    Stem or root—from σκανδαλίζω<br>Concordance References:<br>  ⇒ Strong's #4624 skandalizō<br>  ⇒ NIV #4997 skandalizō<br>  ⇒ NASB #4624 skandalizō<br><br>**Matthew 5:29**<br>And if thy right eye **offend** thee, pluck it out, and cast *it* from thee: for it is profitable for thee that one of thy members should perish, and not *that* thy whole body should be cast into hell. [KJV]<br><br>"And if your right eye **makes you stumble**, tear it out, and throw it from you; for it is better for you that one of the parts of your body perish, than for your whole body to be thrown into hell. [NASB]<br><br>If your right eye **causes** you to **sin**, gouge it out and throw it away. It is better for you to lose one part of your body than for your whole body to be thrown into hell. [NIV]<br><br>If your right eye **causes** you to **sin**, pluck it out and cast *it* from you; for it is more profitable for you that one of your members perish, than for your whole body to be cast into hell. [NKJV]<br><br>So if your eye—even if it is your good eye—**causes** you to **lust**, gouge it out and throw it away. It is better for you to lose one part of your body than for your whole body to be thrown into hell. [NLT]<br><br>εἰ δὲ ὁ ὀφθαλμός σου ὁ δεξιὸς **σκανδαλίζει** σε, ἔξελε αὐτὸν καὶ βάλε ἀπὸ σοῦ· συμφέρει γάρ σοι ἵνα ἀπόληται ἓν τῶν μελῶν σου, καὶ μὴ ὅλον τὸ σῶμά σου βληθῇ εἰς γέενναν. [GNS]<br><br>εἰ δὲ ὁ ὀφθαλμός σου ὁ δεξιὸς **σκανδαλίζει** σε, ἔξελε αὐτὸν καὶ βάλε ἀπὸ σοῦ· συμφέρει γάρ σοι ἵνα ἀπόληται ἓν τῶν μελῶν σου καὶ μὴ ὅλον τὸ σῶμά σου βληθῇ εἰς γέενναν. [GNT] | To stumble; to fall away; to sin; to succumb to lust; to offend; to be baited; to be lured; to be tripped up; to cause someone to sin or fall into sin.<br><br>**Practical Application**<br>In this particular Scripture, the eyes and hands are said to be stumbling blocks. |

# Practical Word Studies
## in the New Testament

| ENGLISH WORD | GREEK WORD AND VERSE | THE WORD MEANS... |
|---|---|---|
| **#530**<br>**Causes To Lose Faith**<br><br>Offend–KJV<br>Causes...to stumble–NASB<br>Causes...to sin–NIV<br>Causes...to stumble–NKJV<br>**Causes...to lose faith–NLT**<br><br>**POSB REFERENCE**<br>(Mk.9:42)<br>Note 1 | σκανδαλίσῃ = skandalisë<br>Pronunciation: [skan-dal-i'-see]<br>Parsing (part of speech): verb<br>    Mood—subjunctive<br>    Tense—aorist<br>    Voice—active<br>    Person—3rd person<br>    Number—singular<br>    Stem or root—from σκανδαλίζω<br>Concordance References:<br>  ⇒ Strong's #4624 skandalizö<br>  ⇒ NIV #4997 skandalizö<br>  ⇒ NASB #4624 skandalizö<br><br>**Mark 9:42**<br>And whosoever shall **offend** one of *these* little ones that believe in me, it is better for him that a millstone were hanged about his neck, and he were cast into the sea. [KJV]<br><br>"And whoever **causes** one of these little ones who believe **to stumble**, it would be better for him if, with a heavy millstone hung around his neck, he had been cast into the sea. [NASB]<br><br>"And if anyone **causes** one of these little ones who believe in me **to sin**, it would be better for him to be thrown into the sea with a large millstone tied around his neck. [NIV]<br><br>"But whoever **causes** one of these little ones who believe in Me **to stumble**, it would be better for him if a millstone were hung around his neck, and he were thrown into the sea. [NKJV]<br><br>"But if anyone **causes** one of these little ones who trusts in me **to lose faith**, it would be better for that person to be thrown into the sea with a large millstone tied around the neck. [NLT]<br><br>καὶ ὃς ἂν **σκανδαλίσῃ** ἕνα τῶν μικρῶν τούτων τῶν πιστευόντων εἰς ἐμέ, καλόν ἐστι αὐτῷ μᾶλλον, εἰ περίκειται λίθος μυλικὸς περὶ τὸν τράχηλον αὐτοῦ, καὶ βέβληται εἰς τὴν θάλασσαν. [GNS]<br><br>Καὶ ὃς ἂν **σκανδαλίσῃ** ἕνα τῶν μικρῶν τούτων τῶν πιστευόντων [εἰς ἐμέ], καλόν ἐστιν αὐτῷ μᾶλλον εἰ περίκειται μύλος ὀνικὸς περὶ τὸν τράχηλον αὐτοῦ καὶ βέβληται εἰς τὴν θάλασσαν. [GNT] | To cause a person to sin or stumble; to offend or cause a person to lose faith.<br><br>**Practical Application**<br>Christ seemed to be saying, "The most terrible sin of all is leading another person to sin. There is no sin any worse than leading another person astray. It is the worst conceivable sin." There are several ways we cause others to sin.<br>1. By leading them into sin and teaching them to sin. "Oh, come on, no one will know. It's not going to hurt you."<br>2. By example, things that we do. Example is not a direct vocal suggestion. We are not necessarily aware that "the child" sees or is observing us; nevertheless, he sees and learns from what we do. He thinks to himself: "If it's all right for him, then it is bound to be all right for me."<br>3. By overlooking or passing over wrong; by giving soft names to it; by considering some sins to be merely minor sins. "Oh, that's all right. There's not that much to it. It isn't going to hurt anyone. Don't pay any attention to it. Just forget it."<br>4. By ridiculing or poking fun at, or by joking and sneering at a person's attempt to do right. "Oh, don't be a fuddy-duddy, a square; you're acting like a fanatic. You and your religion."<br>5. By looking at, touching, and tasting some things that are socially acceptable; but that are sinful to God. They are harmful, habit forming, and physically stimulating when they should not be. "Wow, look at that." "Taste that." "What a turn on!"<br>6. By persecuting and threatening "a child" or a believer. The threat can range all the way from loss of promotion, job, friendship, or acceptance to imprisonment and death. |
| **#531**<br>**Causes To Sin**<br><br>Offend–KJV<br>Causes...to stumble–NASB<br>**Causes...to sin–NIV**<br>Causes...to stumble–NKJV<br>Causes...to lose faith–NLT<br><br>**POSB REFERENCE**<br>(Mk.9:42)<br>Note 1 | σκανδαλίσῃ = skandalisë<br>Pronunciation: [skan-dal-i'-see]<br>Parsing (part of speech): verb<br>    Mood—subjunctive<br>    Tense—aorist<br>    Voice—active<br>    Person—3rd person<br>    Number—singular<br>    Stem or root—from σκανδαλίζω<br>Concordance References:<br>  ⇒ Strong's #4624 skandalizö<br>  ⇒ NIV #4997 skandalizö<br>  ⇒ NASB #4624 skandalizö<br><br>**Mark 9:42**<br>And whosoever shall **offend** one of *these* little ones that believe in me, it is better for him that a millstone were hanged about his neck, and he were cast into the sea. [KJV]<br><br>"And whoever **causes** one of these little ones who believe **to stumble**, it would be better for him if, with a heavy millstone hung around his neck, he had been cast into the sea. [NASB]<br><br>"And if anyone **causes** one of these little ones who believe in me **to sin**, it would be better for him to be thrown into the sea with a large millstone tied around his neck. [NIV]<br><br>"But whoever **causes** one of these little ones who | To cause a person to sin or stumble; to offend or cause a person to lose faith.<br><br>**Practical Application**<br>Christ seemed to be saying, "The most terrible sin of all is leading another person to sin. There is no sin any worse than leading another person astray. It is the worst conceivable sin." (See **Causes To Lose Faith** for more application). |

## PRACTICAL WORD STUDIES
### in the NEW TESTAMENT

| ENGLISH WORD | GREEK WORD AND VERSE | THE WORD MEANS... |
|---|---|---|
| | believe in Me **to stumble**, it would be better for him if a millstone were hung around his neck, and he were thrown into the sea. [NKJV]<br><br>"But if anyone **causes** one of these little ones who trusts in me **to lose faith**, it would be better for that person to be thrown into the sea with a large millstone tied around the neck. [NLT]<br><br>καὶ ὃς ἂν **σκανδαλίσῃ** ἕνα τῶν μικρῶν τούτων τῶν πιστευόντων εἰς ἐμέ, καλόν ἐστι αὐτῷ μᾶλλον, εἰ περίκειται λίθος μυλικὸς περὶ τὸν τράχηλον αὐτοῦ, καὶ βέβληται εἰς τὴν θάλασσαν. [GNS]<br><br>Καὶ ὃς ἂν **σκανδαλίσῃ** ἕνα τῶν μικρῶν τούτων τῶν πιστευόντων [εἰς ἐμέ], καλόν ἐστιν αὐτῷ μᾶλλον εἰ περίκειται μύλος ὀνικὸ [GNT] | |
| **#532**<br>**Causes To Stumble**<br><br>Offend–KJV<br>**Causes...to stumble–NASB**<br>Causes...to sin–NIV<br>**Causes...to stumble–NKJV**<br>Causes...to lose faith–NLT<br><br>**POSB REFERENCE**<br>(Mk.9:42)<br>Note 1 | σκανδαλίσῃ = *skandalisë*<br>Pronunciation: [skan-dal-i'-see]<br>Parsing (part of speech): verb<br>   Mood—subjunctive<br>   Tense—aorist<br>   Voice—active<br>   Person—3rd person<br>   Number—singular<br>   Stem or root—from σκανδαλίζω<br>Concordance References:<br>  ⇒ Strong's #4624 skandalizō<br>  ⇒ NIV #4997 skandalizō<br>  ⇒ NASB #4624 skandalizō<br><br>**Mark 9:42**<br>And whosoever shall **offend** one of *these* little ones that believe in me, it is better for him that a millstone were hanged about his neck, and he were cast into the sea. [KJV]<br><br>"And whoever **causes** one of these little ones who believe **to stumble**, it would be better for him if, with a heavy millstone hung around his neck, he had been cast into the sea. [NASB]<br><br>"And if anyone **causes** one of these little ones who believe in me **to sin**, it would be better for him to be thrown into the sea with a large millstone tied around his neck. [NIV]<br><br>"But whoever **causes** one of these little ones who believe in Me **to stumble**, it would be better for him if a millstone were hung around his neck, and he were thrown into the sea. [NKJV]<br><br>"But if anyone **causes** one of these little ones who trusts in me **to lose faith**, it would be better for that person to be thrown into the sea with a large millstone tied around the neck. [NLT]<br><br>καὶ ὃς ἂν **σκανδαλίσῃ** ἕνα τῶν μικρῶν τούτων τῶν πιστευόντων εἰς ἐμέ, καλόν ἐστι αὐτῷ μᾶλλον, εἰ περίκειται λίθος μυλικὸς περὶ τὸν τράχηλον αὐτοῦ, καὶ βέβληται εἰς τὴν θάλασσαν. [GNS]<br><br>Καὶ ὃς ἂν **σκανδαλίσῃ** ἕνα τῶν μικρῶν τούτων τῶν πιστευόντων [εἰς ἐμέ], καλόν ἐστιν αὐτῷ μᾶλλον εἰ περίκειται μύλος ὀνικὸ [GNT] | To cause a person to sin or stumble; to offend or cause a person to lose faith.<br><br>**Practical Application**<br>Christ seemed to be saying, "The most terrible sin of all is leading another person to sin. There is no sin any worse than leading another person astray. It is the worst conceivable sin." (See **Causes To Lose Faith** for more application). |
| **#533**<br>**Certain**<br><br>Assuredly–KJV<br>**Certain–NASB**<br>Assured–NIV<br>Assuredly–NKJV<br>Clearly known–NLT<br><br>**POSB REFERENCE**<br>(Acts 2:33-36; esp. v.36)<br>Note 4, point 3 | ἀσφαλῶς γινωσκέτω = *asphalōs ginōsketō*<br>Pronunciation: [as-fal-oce' ghin-oce'-keh-tow]<br>Parsing *asphalōs* (part of speech): adjective adverb<br>   Type—adverb<br>   Stem or root—from ἀσφαλῶς<br>Parsing *ginōsketō* (part of speech): verb<br>   Mood—imperative<br>   Tense—present<br>   Voice—active<br>   Person—3rd person<br>   Number—singular<br>   Stem or root—from γινώσκω<br>Concordance References:<br>  ⇒ Strong's #806+1097 asphalōs ginōskō<br>  ⇒ NIV #857+1182 asphalōs ginōskō [assured]<br>  ⇒ NASB #806+1097 asphalōs ginōskō | To be assured; to be aware of; to know about; to be sure; to be certain; to know beyond a doubt.<br><br>**Practical Application**<br>The word is emphatic. It means without any doubt whatsoever, with perfect assurance and certainty. |

# PRACTICAL WORD STUDIES
## in the NEW TESTAMENT

| ENGLISH WORD | GREEK WORD AND VERSE | THE WORD MEANS... |
|---|---|---|
| | **Acts 2:36**<br>Therefore let all the house of Israel know **assuredly**, that God hath made that same Jesus, whom ye have crucified, both Lord and Christ. [KJV]<br>"Therefore let all the house of Israel know for **certain** that God has made Him both Lord and Christ— this Jesus whom you crucified." [NASB]<br>"Therefore let all Israel be **assured** of this: God has made this Jesus, whom you crucified, both Lord and Christ." [NIV]<br>"Therefore let all the house of Israel know **assuredly** that God has made this Jesus, whom you crucified, both Lord and Christ." [NKJV]<br>So let it be **clearly known** by everyone in Israel that God has made this Jesus whom you crucified to be both Lord and Messiah!" [NLT]<br>ἀσφαλῶς οὖν **γινωσκέτω** πᾶς οἶκος Ἰσραήλ, ὅτι καὶ Κύριον καὶ Χριστὸν αὐτὸν ὁ Θεός ἐποίησε, τοῦτον τὸν Ἰησοῦν ὃν ὑμεῖς ἐσταυρώσατε. [GNS]<br>ἀσφαλῶς οὖν **γινωσκέτω** πᾶς οἶκος Ἰσραὴλ ὅτι καὶ κύριον αὐτὸν καὶ Χριστὸν ἐποίησεν ὁ θεός, τοῦτον τὸν Ἰησοῦν ὃν ὑμεῖς ἐσταυρώσατε. [GNT] | |
| **#534**<br>**Certain Days**<br><br>**Certain days**–KJV<br>Several days–NASB<br>Several days–NIV<br>Some days–NKJV<br>Few days–NLT<br><br>**POSB REFERENCE**<br>(Acts 9:19)<br>Note 2 | ἡμέρας τινάς = hēmeras tinas<br>Pronunciation: [hay-mer'-ahs ti'-nahs]<br>Parsing *hēmeras* (part of speech): noun<br>    Case—accusative<br>    Gender—feminine<br>    Number—plural<br>    Stem or root—from ἡμέρα, ας<br>Parsing *tinas* (part of speech): adjective<br>    Type—indefinite<br>    Case—accusative<br>    Gender—feminine<br>    Number—plural<br>    Stem or root—from τὶς, τὶ<br>Concordance References:<br>⇒ Strong's #2250 hēmera + 5100 tis<br>⇒ NIV #2465 hēmera [days] + 5516 tis [several]<br>⇒ NASB #2250 hēmera + 5100 tis<br><br>**Acts 9:19**<br>And when he had received meat, he was strengthened. Then was Saul **certain days** with the disciples which were at Damascus. [KJV]<br>And he took food and was strengthened. Now for **several days** he was with the disciples who were at Damascus, [NASB]<br>And after taking some food, he regained his strength. Saul spent **several days** with the disciples in Damascus. [NIV]<br>So when he had received food, he was strengthened. Then Saul spent **some days** with the disciples at Damascus. [NKJV]<br>Afterward he ate some food and was strengthened. Saul stayed with the believers in Damascus for a **few days**. [NLT]<br>καὶ λαβὼν τροφὴν ἐνίσχυσεν. Ἐγένετο δὲ ὁ Σαῦλος μετὰ τῶν ἐν Δαμασκῷ μαθητῶν **ἡμέρας τινάς**. [GNS]<br>καὶ λαβὼν τροφὴν ἐνίσχυσεν. Ἐγένετο δὲ μετὰ τῶν ἐν Δαμασκῷ μαθητῶν **ἡμέρας τινάς** [GNT] | Several days; a few days; certain days. It is a term indicating a short time.<br><br>**Practical Application**<br>Paul joined and became associated and identified with other believers. What happened is important to note, for it holds a much needed lesson for every generation. Paul joined the other believers at Damascus because he was a *true* believer. His old nature, the old man, had truly died; and he now had the new nature of believers. He was *bound* to join those who had the same nature as he. It was their presence he desired. He wanted to share in...<br>• their companionship and fellowship (see POSB *Deeper Study #3*—Acts 2:42 for more discussion).<br>• their love, concern, and care.<br>• their beliefs and principles.<br>• their study of the Word.<br>• their growth in Christ.<br>• their edifying and building up of each other.<br>• their witness and service.<br><br>Saul (or Paul) associated and became identified with the church so that the world might know that he was a believer. He wanted to openly and publicly declare that he was now...<br>• a new creature in Christ Jesus.<br>• a follower of "the Way" which he had opposed and persecuted.<br>• a true disciple of the Lord Jesus. |
| **#535**<br>**Certainly Not**<br><br>God forbid–KJV<br>May it never be–NASB<br>Not at all–NIV<br>**Certainly not**–NKJV<br>Of course not–NLT | μὴ γένοιτο = mē genoito<br>Pronunciation: [may ghin'-oy-tow]<br>Parsing *genoito* (part of speech): verb<br>    Mood—optative<br>    Tense—aorist<br>    Voice—middle dep<br>    Person—3rd person<br>    Number—singular<br>    Stem or root—from γίνομαι<br>Concordance References:<br>⇒ Strong's #1096 + 3361 ginomai mē | God forbid; not at all; may it never be; certainly not; of course not.<br><br>**Practical Application**<br>The question is, "If you say some Jews do not believe and are condemned, doesn't that void God's promises and make God a liar?" Or to say it another way, "What if some disbelieve and reject God's Word, will their unbelief cause God to void His Word and promises? God promised |

# PRACTICAL WORD STUDIES
## in the NEW TESTAMENT

| ENGLISH WORD | GREEK WORD AND VERSE | THE WORD MEANS... |
|---|---|---|
| **POSB REFERENCE** (Romans 3:5-8; esp. v.4) Note 3, point 1<br><br>See also POSB REF: (Rom.11:1) Note 1 | ⇒ NIV #1181 + 3590 ginomai mē [Not at all]<br>⇒ NASB #1096+ 3361 ginomai mē<br><br>**Romans 3:4**<br>**God forbid**: yea, let God be true, but every man a liar; as it is written, That thou mightest be justified in thy sayings, and mightest overcome when thou art judged. [KJV]<br>**May it never be**! Rather, let God be found true, though every man be found a liar, as it is written, "That Thou mightest be justified in Thy words, And mightest prevail when Thou ART JUDGED." [NASB]<br>**Not at all**! Let God be true, and every man a liar. As it is written: "So that you may be proved right when you speak and prevail when you judge." [NIV]<br>**Certainly not**! Indeed, let God be true but every man a liar. As it is written: *"That You may be justified in Your words, And may overcome when You are judged."* [NKJV]<br>**Of course not**! Though everyone else in the world is a liar, God is true. As the Scriptures say, "He will be proved right in what he says, and he will win his case in court." [NLT]<br>μὴ γένοιτο· γινέσθω δὲ ὁ Θεὸς ἀληθής, πᾶς δὲ ἄνθρωπος ψεύστης, καθὼς γέγραπται, "Ὅπως ἂν δικαιωθῇς ἐν τοῖς λόγοις σου, καὶ νικήσεις ἐν τῷ κρίνεσθαί σε. [GNS]<br>μὴ γένοιτο· γινέσθω δὲ ὁ Θεὸς ἀληθής, πᾶς δὲ ἄνθρωπος ψεύστης, καθὼς γέγραπται, "Ὅπως ἂν δικαιωθῇς ἐν τοῖς λόγοις σου καὶ νικήσεις ἐν τῷ κρίνεσθαί σε. [GNT] | the Jews a special place and special privileges through Abraham and his seed (see POSB Deeper Study #1—John 4:22). If some Jews do not believe God's promises and God condemns them, isn't He breaking His promise to Abraham and his seed? Isn't He voiding His Word and Covenant and making Himself a liar? God's Word could not be based on heart religion and on moral character alone. There has to be something else, something outward—a rite (circumcision, baptism, church membership)—that shows we are religious (Jews). If we go through the rite or ritual, then God is bound to accept us. He has promised to so accept us. He is not going to break His Word."<br>The application of this question concerns every religionist. The thinking religionist poses the same objection and question: "If you say some religionists do not believe and are condemned, doesn't that void God's Word and make God a liar? God's Word promises the religious person special privileges and the hope of eternal life. His Word tells us to believe Christ and to possess His Word, to be baptized and join the fellowship of the church. If we do that and God still condemns us, is He not voiding His Word and becoming a liar?"<br>⇒ Certainly not.<br>⇒ God will be faithful. His Word and promise of salvation will stand even if *every* man lies about believing and lies about giving his heart to serve Jesus.<br>⇒ God will prove His Word: He will be justified and proven faithful in what He has said. He will still save *any person* who obediently gives his heart to Jesus.<br>⇒ In fact, God will overcome; He will prove His Word another way. He will judge all who make a false profession and who judge Him and His Word, who accuse Him of being unfaithful and voiding His Word. David himself said that God would judge the unfaithful or disobedient man (Psalm 51:4). David had sinned greatly, not keeping the commandments of God, so God judged David and charged him with sin. David did the right thing: he confessed his sin and repented and began to live righteously. But David did something else: he declared that God's charge and judgment against him were *just*, that God was perfectly justified. And God was, for God is always just, and He is always justified in what He says and does. |
| **#536**<br>**Certificate Of Debt**<br><br>Handwriting–KJV<br>**Certificate of debt– NASB**<br>Written code–NIV<br>Handwriting–NKJV<br>Record–NLT<br><br>**POSB REFERENCE** | χειρόγραφον = *cheirographon*<br>Pronunciation: [khi-rog'-raf-on]<br>Parsing (part of speech): noun<br>    Case—accusative<br>    Gender—neuter<br>    Number—singular<br>    Stem or root—from χειρόγραφον, ου<br>Concordance References:<br>⇒ Strong's #5498 cheirographon<br>⇒ NIV #5934 cheirographon<br>⇒ NASB #5498 cheirographon<br><br>**Col. 2:14**<br>Blotting out the **handwriting** of ordinances that was against us, which was contrary to us, and took it out of the | Written code, handwriting, certificate of debt, record of one's debts. It actually means a legal note or debt, what Barclay calls *a charge list* or a list of charges against man (*The Letters to the Philippians, Colossians, and Thessalonians*, p.170).<br><br>**Practical Application**<br>Man's concept of the law is twofold.<br>1. Some men see the law as a list of rules that God has led great religious men to write down in either the Bible or other religious books. |

# PRACTICAL WORD STUDIES
## in the NEW TESTAMENT

| ENGLISH WORD | GREEK WORD AND VERSE | THE WORD MEANS... |
|---|---|---|
| (Col.2:14)<br>Note 2, point 1 | way, nailing it to his cross; [KJV]<br>Having canceled out the **certificate of debt** consisting of decrees against us and which was hostile to us; and He has taken it out of the way, having nailed it to the cross. [NASB]<br>Having canceled the **written code**, with its regulations, that was against us and that stood opposed to us; He took it away, nailing it to the cross. [NIV]<br>Having wiped out the **handwriting** of requirements that was against us, which was contrary to us. And He has taken it out of the way, having nailed it to the cross. [NKJV]<br>He canceled the **record** that contained the charges against us. He took it and destroyed it by nailing it to Christ's cross. [NLT]<br>ἐξαλείψας τὸ καθ' ἡμῶν **χειρόγραφον** τοῖς δόγμασιν, ὃ ἦν ὑπεναντίον ἡμῖν· καὶ αὐτὸ ἦρκεν ἐκ τοῦ μέσου, προσηλώσας αὐτὸ τῷ σταυρῷ· [GNS]<br>ἐξαλείψας τὸ καθ' ἡμῶν **χειρόγραφον** τοῖς δόγμασιν ὃ ἦν ὑπεναντίον ἡμῖν, καὶ αὐτὸ ἦρκεν ἐκ τοῦ μέσου προσηλώσας αὐτὸ τῷ σταυρῷ· [GNT] | 2. Other men see the laws of God as unwritten laws that are rooted in the nature of man and the world. Man just instinctively senses what is right and wrong, and he is to live as his instinct tells him (cp. Romans 2:14-15).<br>Man just senses the handwriting of laws against him—laws that condemn him when he goes contrary to what they say or what he senses. The point is this: man senses the list of charges against him. And he should sense the wrong he has done, for it is his violation of God's law that condemns him to eternal death. Only as he senses and acknowledges his transgressions will he ever turn to God to save him. |
| #537<br>**Certify**<br><br>Certify–KJV<br>Know–NASB<br>Know–NIV<br>Make known–NKJV<br>Solemnly assure–NLT<br><br>**POSB<br>REFERENCE**<br>(Gal.1:11-12; esp. v.11)<br>Note 2 | Γνωρίζω = Gnōrizō<br>Pronunciation: [gno-rid'-zo]<br>Parsing (part of speech): verb<br>  Mood—indicative<br>  Tense—present<br>  Voice—active<br>  Person—1st person<br>  Number—singular<br>  Stem or root—from γνωρίζω<br>Concordance References:<br>  ⇒ Strong's #1107 gnōrizō<br>  ⇒ NIV #1192 gnōrizō<br>  ⇒ NASB #1107 gnōrizō<br><br>**Galatians 1:11**<br>But I **certify** you, brethren, that the gospel which was preached of me is not after man. [KJV]<br>For I would have you **know**, brethren, that the gospel which was preached by me is not according to man. [NASB]<br>I want you to **know**, brothers, that the gospel I preached is not something that man made up. [NIV]<br>But I **make known** to you, brethren, that the gospel which was preached by me is not according to man. [NKJV]<br>Dear brothers and sisters, I **solemnly assure** you that the Good News of salvation which I preach is not based on mere human reasoning or logic. [NLT]<br>Γνωρίζω δὲ ὑμῖν, ἀδελφοί, τὸ εὐαγγέλιον τὸ εὐαγγελισθὲν ὑπ' ἐμοῦ, ὅτι οὐκ ἔστι κατὰ ἄνθρωπον. [GNS]<br>Γνωρίζω γὰρ ὑμῖν, ἀδελφοί, τὸ εὐαγγέλιον τὸ εὐαγγελισθὲν ὑπ' ἐμοῦ ὅτι οὐκ ἔστιν κατὰ ἄνθρωπον· [GNT] | To certify; to make known; to solemnly assure.<br><br>**Practical Application**<br>The minister proclaimed the gospel. Some critics of Paul were saying that he was not a true apostle of the Lord Jesus because he had not been a follower of the Lord when the Lord was upon the earth. Therefore, what he was teaching was a man-made gospel taught by mistaken and misguided men.<br>Note that the word "certify" (*Gnōrizō*) is a solemn word, a strong declaration that what follows is of crucial importance and needs to be heard. |
| #538<br>**Chambering**<br><br>Chambering–KJV<br>Sexual promiscuity–NASB<br>Sexual immorality–NIV<br>Lewdness–NKJV<br>Adultery–NLT<br><br>**POSB<br>REFERENCE**<br>(Rom.13:13)<br>Note 4, point 3 | κοίταις = koitais<br>Pronunciation: [koy'-tays]<br>Parsing (part of speech): noun<br>  Case—dative<br>  Gender—feminine<br>  Number—plural<br>  Stem or root—from κοίτη, ης<br>Concordance References:<br>  ⇒ Strong's #2845 koitē<br>  ⇒ NIV #3130 koitē<br>  ⇒ NASB #2845 koitē<br><br>**Romans 13:13**<br>Let us walk honestly, as in the day; not in rioting and drunkenness, not in **chambering** and wantonness, not in strife and envying. [KJV]<br>Let us behave properly as in the day, not in carousing | Sexual immorality; sexual promiscuity; sexual impurity; adultery, lewdness, fornication (pre-marital sex).<br><br>**Practical Application**<br>The charge is straightforward. The believer is not to participate...<br>• in wild parties<br>• in getting drunk<br>• in adultery<br>• in immoral living<br>• in jealousy |

## PRACTICAL WORD STUDIES
### in the NEW TESTAMENT

| ENGLISH WORD | GREEK WORD AND VERSE | THE WORD MEANS... |
|---|---|---|
| | and drunkenness, not in **sexual promiscuity** and sensuality, not in strife and jealousy. [NASB]<br>　Let us behave decently, as in the daytime, not in orgies and drunkenness, not in **sexual immorality** and debauchery, not in dissension and jealousy. [NIV]<br>　Let us walk properly, as in the day, not in revelry and drunkenness, not in **lewdness** and lust, not in strife and envy. [NKJV]<br>　We should be decent and true in everything we do, so that everyone can approve of our behavior. Don't participate in wild parties and getting drunk, or in **adultery** and immoral living, or in fighting and jealousy. [NLT]<br>　ὡς ἐν ἡμέρᾳ, εὐσχημόνως περιπατήσωμεν, μὴ κώμοις καὶ μέθαις, μὴ **κοίταις** καὶ ἀσελγείαις, μὴ ἔριδι καὶ ζήλῳ. [GNS]<br>　ὡς ἐν ἡμέρᾳ εὐσχημόνως περιπατήσωμεν, μὴ κώμοις καὶ μέθαις, μὴ **κοίταις** καὶ ἀσελγείαις, μὴ ἔριδι καὶ ζήλῳ, [GNT] | |
| **#539**<br>**Change**<br><br>Converted–KJV<br>Converted–NASB<br>**Change–NIV**<br>Converted–NKJV<br>Turn–NLT<br><br>**POSB REFERENCE**<br>(Mt.18:3)<br>Note 2 | στραφῆτε = *straphēte*<br>Pronunciation: [stref'-ee-teh]<br>Parsing (part of speech): verb<br>　Mood—subjunctive<br>　Tense—aorist<br>　Voice—passive<br>　Person—2nd person<br>　Number—plural<br>　Stem or root—from στρέφω<br>Concordance References:<br>⇒ Strong's #4762 strephō<br>⇒ NIV #5138 strephō<br>⇒ NASB #4762 strephō<br><br>**Matthew 18:3**<br>　And said, Verily I say unto you, Except ye be **converted**, and become as little children, ye shall not enter into the kingdom of heaven. [KJV]<br>　And said, "Truly I say to you, unless you are **converted** and become like children, you shall not enter the kingdom of heaven. [NASB]<br>　And he said: "I tell you the truth, unless you **change** and become like little children, you will never enter the kingdom of heaven. [NIV]<br>　And said, "Assuredly, I say to you, unless you are **converted** and become as little children, you will by no means enter the kingdom of heaven. [NKJV]<br>　Then he said, "I assure you, unless you **turn** from your sins and become as little children, you will never get into the Kingdom of Heaven. [NLT]<br>　καὶ εἶπεν, Ἀμὴν λέγω ὑμῖν, ἐὰν μὴ **στραφῆτε** καὶ γένησθε ὡς τὰ παιδία, οὐ μὴ εἰσέλθητε εἰς τὴν βασιλείαν τῶν οὐρανῶν. [GNS]<br>　καὶ εἶπεν, Ἀμὴν λέγω ὑμῖν, ἐὰν μὴ **στραφῆτε** καὶ γένησθε ὡς τὰ παιδία, οὐ μὴ εἰσέλθητε εἰς τὴν βασιλείαν τῶν οὐρανῶν. [GNT] | To change; to turn around; to be converted; to turn from one thing to something else.<br><br>**Practical Application**<br>　How is a person changed or converted? By turning and becoming as a little child. What does it mean "to become as a little child"? When Christ *called* the child to Him, the child demonstrated exactly what Christ meant.<br>1. The child *trusted* Christ. The child responded to the call of Christ. He sensed the openness, warmth, tenderness, care, and love of Christ; so he felt free to respond and to trust Christ's call.<br>2. The child *surrendered* himself to Christ. He was willing to give up what he was doing to go to Christ, willing to surrender whatever it was that was occupying his thoughts and behavior.<br>3. The child *obeyed* Christ. He was obedient, doing exactly what Christ requested, and it was probably difficult to do so. There were at least thirteen adult men standing or sitting there, and the child was being asked to walk into the midst of these men. Note that he obeyed despite the difficulty and obeyed simply because Christ asked him.<br>4. The child *humbled* himself before Christ. All the above traits show humility. However, there is something often overlooked and abused by the adult world. Little children do not push themselves forward. They are not interested in prominence, fame, power, wealth, or position. They do not want to be placed in the midst of a group of adults, for they prefer to be in the background, away from staring, gawking eyes. Such embarrasses them and makes them feel self-conscious. Therefore, they prefer to be left in their obscure world. They are by nature humble, knowing little if anything of the competitive world that surrounds them; that is, they know little of it until they are brought into it by adults. |
| **#540**<br>**Change Your Ways**<br><br>Be perfect–KJV<br>Be made complete–NASB | καταρτίζεσθε = *katartizesthe*<br>Pronunciation: [kat-ar-tid'-zehs-the]<br>Parsing (part of speech): verb<br>　Mood—imperative<br>　Tense—present<br>　Voice—passive<br>　Person—2nd person | To aim and strive for perfection; to be made complete; to prepare; to change one's ways; to restore, reform, correct, and mend oneself and one's ways. |

# PRACTICAL WORD STUDIES
## in the NEW TESTAMENT

| ENGLISH WORD | GREEK WORD AND VERSE | THE WORD MEANS... |
|---|---|---|
| Aim for perfection–NIV<br>Become complete–NKJV<br>**Change your ways–NLT**<br><br>**POSB REFERENCE**<br>(2 Cor.13:11-13; esp. v.11)<br>Note 3 | Number—plural<br>Stem or root—from καταρτίζω<br>Concordance References:<br>⇒ Strong's #2675 katartizō<br>⇒ NIV #2936 katartizō<br>⇒ NASB #2675 katartizō<br><br>**2 Cor. 13:11**<br>Finally, brethren, farewell. **Be perfect**, be of good comfort, be of one mind, live in peace; and the God of love and peace shall be with you. [KJV]<br>Finally, brethren, rejoice, **be made complete**, be comforted, be like-minded, live in peace; and the God of love and peace shall be with you. [NASB]<br>Finally, brothers, good-by. **Aim for perfection**, listen to my appeal, be of one mind, live in peace. And the God of love and peace will be with you. [NIV]<br>Finally, brethren, farewell. **Become complete**. Be of good comfort, be of one mind, live in peace; and the God of love and peace will be with you. [NKJV]<br>Dear brothers and sisters, I close my letter with these last words: Rejoice. **Change your ways**. Encourage each other. Live in harmony and peace. Then the God of love and peace will be with you. [NLT]<br>Λοιπόν, ἀδελφοί, χαίρετε· **καταρτίζεσθε**, παρακαλεῖσθε, τὸ αὐτὸ φρονεῖτε, εἰρηνεύετε· καὶ ὁ Θεὸς τῆς ἀγάπης καὶ εἰρήνης ἔσται μεθ' ὑμῶν. [GNS]<br>Λοιπόν, ἀδελφοί, χαίρετε, **καταρτίζεσθε**, παρακαλεῖσθε, τὸ αὐτὸ φρονεῖτε, εἰρηνεύετε, καὶ ὁ θεὸς τῆς ἀγάπης καὶ εἰρήνης ἔσται μεθ' ὑμῶν. [GNT] | **Practical Application**<br>Paul's challenge to his Corinthian brothers is blunt and to the point: Stop your sinning (criticism, divisiveness, immorality). |
| **#541**<br>**Changing**<br><br>Renewing–KJV<br>Renewing–NASB<br>Renewing–NIV<br>Renewing–NKJV<br>**Changing–NLT**<br><br>**POSB REFERENCE**<br>(Rom.12:2)<br>Note 4, point 1 | ἀνακαινώσει = anakainōsei<br>Pronunciation: [an-ak-ah'ee-no-seh-ee]<br>Parsing (part of speech): noun<br>    Case—dative<br>    Gender—feminine<br>    Number—singular<br>    Stem or root—from ἀνακαίνωσις<br>Concordance References:<br>⇒ Strong's #342 anakainōsis<br>⇒ NIV #364 anakainōsis<br>⇒ NASB #342 anakainōsis<br><br>**Romans 12:2**<br>And be not conformed to this world: but be ye transformed by the **renewing** of your mind, that ye may prove what is that good, and acceptable, and perfect, will of God. [KJV]<br>And do not be conformed to this world, but be transformed by the **renewing** of your mind, that you may prove what the will of God is, that which is good and acceptable and perfect. [NASB]<br>Do not conform any longer to the pattern of this world, but be transformed by the **renewing** of your mind. Then you will be able to test and approve what God's will is—his good, pleasing and perfect will. [NIV]<br>And do not be conformed to this world, but be transformed by the **renewing** of your mind, that you may prove what *is* that good and acceptable and perfect will of God. [NKJV]<br>Don't copy the behavior and customs of this world, but let God transform you into a new person by **changing** the way you think. Then you will know what God wants you to do, and you will know how good and pleasing and perfect his will really is. [NLT]<br>καὶ μὴ συσχηματίζεσθε τῷ αἰῶνι τούτῳ, ἀλλὰ μεταμορφοῦσθε τῇ **ἀνακαινώσει** τοῦ νοός ὑμῶν, εἰς τὸ δοκιμάζειν ὑμᾶς τί τὸ θέλημα τοῦ Θεοῦ, τὸ ἀγαθὸν καὶ εὐάρεστον καὶ τέλειον. [GNS]<br>αἱ μὴ συσχηματίζεσθε τῷ αἰῶνι τούτῳ, ἀλλὰ μεταμορφοῦσθε τῇ **ἀνακαινώσει** τοῦ νοός εἰς τὸ δοκιμάζειν ὑμᾶς τί τὸ θέλημα τοῦ θεοῦ, τὸ ἀγαθὸν καὶ εὐάρεστον καὶ τέλειον. [GNT] | Renewing, changing; to be renewed; to be made new, readjusted, changed, turned around, regenerated.<br><br>**Practical Application**<br>How is a man transformed within his inner person? The Bible declares as simply as can be stated, "by changing the way you think." The believer's mind is to be changed (*anakainōsei*), which means to be made new, readjusted, changed, turned around, regenerated.<br>The mind of man has been affected by sin. It desperately needs to be renewed. The mind is far from perfect. It is basically worldly, that is...<br>• selfish<br>• self-centered<br>• self-seeking<br>• centered on this world<br>• centered on the flesh<br>• centered on this life<br>Scripture is clear about the corruption of man's mind. The human mind has been tragically corrupted by man's selfishness and sin. |

## PRACTICAL WORD STUDIES
### in the NEW TESTAMENT

| ENGLISH WORD | GREEK WORD AND VERSE | THE WORD MEANS... |
|---|---|---|
| **#542**<br>**Character**<br><br>Conversation–KJV<br>**Character–NASB**<br>Lives–NIV<br>Conduct–NKJV<br>Not translated–NLT<br><br>**POSB REFERENCE**<br>(Heb.13:5-6; esp. v.5)<br>Note 5 | τρόπος = tropos<br>Pronunciation: [trop'-os]<br>Parsing (part of speech): noun<br>    Case—nominative<br>    Gender—masculine<br>    Number—singular<br>    Stem or root—from τρόπος, ου<br>Concordance References:<br>  ⇒ Strong's #5158 tropos<br>  ⇒ NIV #5573 tropos<br>  ⇒ NASB #5158 tropos<br><br>**Hebrews 13:5**<br>Let your **conversation** be without covetousness; and be content with such things as ye have: for he hath said, I will never leave thee, nor forsake thee. [KJV]<br>Let your **character** be free from the love of money, being content with what you have; for He Himself has said, "I WILL NEVER DESERT YOU, NOR WILL I EVER FORSAKE YOU," [NASB]<br>Keep your **lives** free from the love of money and be content with what you have, because God has said, "Never will I leave you; never will I forsake you." [NIV]<br>Let your **conduct** be without covetousness; be content with such things as you have. For He Himself has said, "I will never leave you nor forsake you." [NKJV]<br>Stay away from the love of money; be satisfied with what you have. For God has said, "I will never fail you. I will never forsake you." [NLT]—NOT TRANSLATED<br>ἀφιλάργυρος ὁ **τρόπος**, ἀρκούμενοι τοῖς παροῦσιν· αὐτὸς γὰρ εἴρηκεν, Οὐ μή σε ἀνῶ, οὐδ' οὐ μήσε ἐγκαταλίπω. [GNS]<br>Ἀφιλάργυρος ὁ **τρόπος**, ἀρκούμενοι τοῖς παροῦσιν. αὐτὸς γὰρ εἴρηκεν, Οὐ μή σε ἀνῶ οὐδ' οὐ μή σε ἐγκαταλίπω, [GNT] | Character, conversation, lives, ways, conduct. Thomas Hewitt points out that the Greek word for "conversation" [character] (*tropos*) means *manner of life*, or *the way of thought and life* (*The Epistle to the Hebrews*. "Tyndale New Testament Commentaries," p.206).<br><br>**Practical Application**<br>The believer's very thoughts are to be free from covetousness. His thoughts are to be focused upon Christ and the glorious hope of eternity, not upon this passing world and its possessions. The believer is to have no secret lust for the things of this world. |
| **#543**<br>**Character, Proven, Strength Of**<br><br>Experience–KJV<br>**Proven character–NASB**<br>Character–NIV<br>Character–NKJV<br>Strength of character–NLT<br><br>**POSB REFERENCE**<br>(Rom.5:3-5; esp. v.4)<br>Note 5, point 2 | δοκιμήν = dokimēn<br>Pronunciation: [dok-ee-mayn']<br>Parsing (part of speech): noun<br>    Case—accusative<br>    Gender—feminine<br>    Number—singular<br>    Stem or root—from δοκιμή, ῆς<br>Concordance References:<br>  ⇒ Strong's #1382 dokimē<br>  ⇒ NIV #1509 dokimē<br>  ⇒ NASB #1382 dokimē<br><br>**Romans 5:4**<br>And patience, **experience**; and experience, hope: [KJV]<br>And perseverance, **proven character**; and proven character, hope; [NASB]<br>Perseverance, **character**; and character, hope. [NIV]<br>And perseverance, **character**; and character, hope. [NKJV]<br>And endurance develops **strength of character** in us, and character strengthens our confident expectation of salvation. [NLT]<br>ἡ δὲ ὑπομονὴ **δοκιμήν**, ἡ δὲ δοκιμὴ ἐλπίδα· [GNS]<br>ἡ δὲ ὑπομονὴ **δοκιμήν**, ἡ δὲ δοκιμὴ ἐλπίδα. [GNT] | Character, experience; proven character; strength of character; integrity; strength. The idea is that of proven experience, of gaining strength through the trials of life; therefore, the word is more accurately translated "character."<br><br>**Practical Application**<br>When a justified man endures trials, he comes out of it stronger than ever before. He is a man of much stronger character and integrity. He knows much more about the presence and strength of God. |
| **#544**<br>**Charge**<br><br>Charge–KJV<br>Instruct–NASB<br>Command–NIV<br>**Charge–NKJV**<br>Stop–NLT | παραγγείλῃς = paraggeilēs<br>Pronunciation: [par-ang-geh-i-lays]<br>Parsing (part of speech): verb<br>    Mood—subjunctive<br>    Tense—aorist<br>    Voice—active<br>    Person—2nd person<br>    Number—singular<br>    Stem or root—from παραγγέλλω<br>Concordance References:<br>  ⇒ Strong's #3853 paraggellō | To command; to charge; to instruct; to give strict orders to stop.<br><br>**Practical Application**<br>Timothy was in Ephesus and Paul was in Macedonia, a great distance apart. Ephesus was in Asia and Macedonia was in Europe, north of Greece. Note that Paul had to urge Timothy to stay at Ephesus. The church was in trouble because false teaching had seeped in, and the |

# PRACTICAL WORD STUDIES
## in the NEW TESTAMENT

| ENGLISH WORD | GREEK WORD AND VERSE | THE WORD MEANS... |
|---|---|---|
| **POSB REFERENCE** (1 Tim.1:3) Note 1 | ⇒ NIV #4133 paraggellö<br>⇒ NASB #3853 paraggellö<br><br>**1 Tim. 1:3**<br>As I besought thee to abide still at Ephesus, when I went into Macedonia, that thou mightest **charge** some that they teach no other doctrine, [KJV]<br>As I urged you upon my departure for Macedonia, remain on at Ephesus, in order that you may **instruct** certain men not to teach strange doctrines, [NASB]<br>As I urged you when I went into Macedonia, stay there in Ephesus so that you may **command** certain men not to teach false doctrines any longer [NIV]<br>As I urged you when I went into Macedonia—remain in Ephesus that you may **charge** some that they teach no other doctrine, [NKJV]<br>When I left for Macedonia, I urged you to stay there in Ephesus and **stop** those who are teaching wrong doctrine. [NLT]<br>Καθὼς παρεκάλεσά σε προσμεῖναι ἐν Ἐφέσῳ, πορευόμενος εἰς Μακεδονίαν, ἵνα **παραγγείλῃς** τισὶ μὴ ἑτεροδιδασκαλεῖν, [GNS]<br>Καθὼς παρεκάλεσά σε προσμεῖναι ἐν Ἐφέσῳ, πορευόμενος εἰς Μακεδονίαν, ἵνα **παραγγείλῃς** τισὶν μὴ ἑτεροδιδασκαλεῖν [GNT] | church needed Timothy. Apparently, Timothy felt incapable and wanted to join Paul until Paul could return to Ephesus and handle the situation himself. However, false teaching is so serious a matter that it has to be handled immediately when it raises its ugly head. Therefore, Timothy had to remain in Ephesus so that he could *command* the church to stop the false teaching. The word "charge" (*paraggeilës*) is a strong word. It is a military word that means to pass commands down through the ranks. Timothy was to *give orders and charge* the false teachers to stop teaching false doctrine, and if this did not work, he was to order and charge the church to handle the false teachers. |
| **#545**<br>**Charge**<br><br>**Charge**–KJV<br>Command–NASB<br>Instruction–NIV<br>**Charge**–NKJV<br>Instructions–NLT<br><br>**POSB REFERENCE** (1 Tim.1:18) Note 1 | παραγγελίαν = *paraggelian*<br>Pronunciation: [par-ang-gel-ee'-ahn]<br>Parsing (part of speech): noun<br>    Case—accusative<br>    Gender—feminine<br>    Number—singular<br>    Stem or root—from παραγγελία, ας<br>Concordance References:<br>⇒ Strong's #3852 paraggelia<br>⇒ NIV #4132 paraggelia<br>⇒ NASB #3852 paraggelia<br><br>**1 Tim. 1:18**<br>This **charge** I commit unto thee, son Timothy, according to the prophecies which went before on thee, that thou by them mightest war a good warfare; [KJV]<br>This **command** I entrust to you, Timothy, my son, in accordance with the prophecies previously made concerning you, that by them you may fight the good fight, [NASB]<br>Timothy, my son, I give you this **instruction** in keeping with the prophecies once made about you, so that by following them you may fight the good fight, [NIV]<br>This **charge** I commit to you, son Timothy, according to the prophecies previously made concerning you, that by them you may wage the good warfare, [NKJV]<br>Timothy, my son, here are my **instructions** for you, based on the prophetic words spoken about you earlier. May they give you the confidence to fight well in the Lord's battles. [NLT]<br>Ταύτην τὴν **παραγγελίαν** παρατίθεμαί σοι, τέκνον Τιμόθεε, κατὰ τὰς προαγούσας ἐπὶ σὲ προφητείας, ἵνα στρατεύῃ ἐν αὐταῖς τὴν καλὴν στρατείαν, [GNS]<br>Ταύτην τὴν **παραγγελίαν** παρατίθεμαί σοι, τέκνον Τιμόθεε, κατὰ τὰς προαγούσας ἐπὶ σὲ προφητείας, ἵνα στρατεύῃ ἐν αὐταῖς τὴν καλὴν στρατείαν, [GNT] | A command; an urgent command; a military command; a mandate; a decree; strict orders or instructions.<br><br>**Practical Application**<br>The charge to the young minister is forceful—fight a good warfare! Paul is giving a "charge" (*paraggelian*) to Timothy. It is a command that lays upon a person the most urgent and critical obligation. Donald Guthrie says, "The ministry is not a matter to be trifled with, but an order from the commander-in-chief" (*The Pastoral Epistles*. "Tyndale New Testament Commentaries," p.67). W.E. Vine points out that the "charge" is always a command from a superior that is to be transmitted to others; that is, this charge—the charge to fight a good warfare—is to be given to the young minister and he, in turn, is to pass the charge on to others (*Expository Dictionary of New Testament Words*). |
| **#546**<br>**Charge**<br><br>**Charge**–KJV<br>Instruct–NASB<br>Command–NIV<br>Command–NKJV<br>Tell–NLT | παράγγελλε = *paraggelle*<br>Pronunciation: [par-ang-gel'-leh]<br>Parsing (part of speech): verb<br>    Mood—imperative<br>    Tense—present<br>    Voice—active<br>    Person—2nd person<br>    Number—singular<br>    Stem or root—from παραγγέλλω<br>Concordance References: | To command; to charge; to instruct; to tell; to order; to rule.<br><br>**Practical Application**<br>The word "charge" (*paraggelle*) is a strong word. It has the force of a military command, yet it has the tenderness of an appeal to it. It means to beg and beseech a person—strongly so—to the point that the person is commanded to act. In |

## PRACTICAL WORD STUDIES
## in the NEW TESTAMENT

| ENGLISH WORD | GREEK WORD AND VERSE | THE WORD MEANS... |
|---|---|---|
| POSB REFERENCE (1 Tim.6:17-19; esp. v.17) Note 1 | Strong's #3853 paraggellö<br>NIV #4133 paraggellö<br>NASB #3853 paraggellö<br><br>**1 Tim. 6:17**<br>**Charge** them that are rich in this world, that they be not highminded, nor trust in uncertain riches, but in the living God, who giveth us richly all things to enjoy; [KJV]<br>**Instruct** those who are rich in this present world not to be conceited or to fix their hope on the uncertainty of riches, but on God, who richly supplies us with all things to enjoy. [NASB]<br>**Command** those who are rich in this present world not to be arrogant nor to put their hope in wealth, which is so uncertain, but to put their hope in God, who richly provides us with everything for our enjoyment. [NIV]<br>**Command** those who are rich in this present age not to be haughty, nor to trust in uncertain riches but in the living God, who gives us richly all things to enjoy. [NKJV]<br>**Tell** those who are rich in this world not to be proud and not to trust in their money, which will soon be gone. But their trust should be in the living God, who richly gives us all we need for our enjoyment. [NLT]<br>Τοῖς πλουσίοις ἐν τῷ νῦν αἰῶνι **παράγγελλε** μὴ ὑψηλοφρονεῖν, μηδὲ ἠλπικέναι ἐπὶ πλούτου ἀδηλότητι, ἀλλ' ἐν Θεῷ τῷ ζῶντι, τῷ παρέχοντι ἡμῖν πλουσίως πάντα εἰς ἀπόλαυσιν· [GNS]<br>Τοῖς πλουσίοις ἐν τῷ νῦν αἰῶνι **παράγγελλε** μὴ ὑψηλοφρονεῖν μηδὲ ἠλπικέναι ἐπὶ πλούτου ἀδηλότητι ἀλλ' ἐπὶ Θεῷ τῷ παρέχοντι ἡμῖν πάντα πλουσίως εἰς ἀπόλαυσιν, [GNT] | this charge, God is appealing and begging the rich person, but He is doing it so strongly that it is a command. The rich person is approached in love and tenderness and an appeal is made to him, but he is expected to do exactly what God says. |
| **#547 Charged**<br><br>Charged–KJV<br>Gave [them] orders–NASB<br>Commanded–NIV<br>Commanded–NKJV<br>Told–NLT<br><br>POSB REFERENCE (Mk.7:36) Note 5 | διεστείλατο = diesteilato<br>Pronunciation: [dee-es-teel'-ah-tow]<br>Parsing (part of speech): verb<br>    Mood—indicative<br>    Tense—aorist<br>    Voice—middle<br>    Person—3rd person<br>    Number—singular<br>    Stem or root—from διαστέλλω<br>Concordance References:<br>  ⇒ Strong's #1291 diastellomai<br>  ⇒ NIV #1403 diastellö<br>  ⇒ NASB #1291 diastellö<br><br>**Mark 7:36**<br>And he **charged** them that they should tell no man: but the more he charged them, so much the more a great deal they published *it*; [KJV]<br>And He **gave them orders** not to tell anyone; but the more He ordered them, the more widely they continued to proclaim it. [NASB]<br>Jesus **commanded** them not to tell anyone. But the more he did so, the more they kept talking about it. [NIV]<br>Then He **commanded** them that they should tell no one; but the more He commanded them, the more widely they proclaimed *it*. [NKJV]<br>Jesus **told** the crowd not to tell anyone, but the more he told them not to, the more they spread the news, [NLT]<br>καὶ **διεστείλατο** αὐτοῖς ἵνα μηδενὶ εἴπωσιν· ὅσον δὲ αὐτὸς αὐτοῖς διεστέλλετο μᾶλλον περισσότερον ἐκήρυσσον· [GNS]<br>καὶ **διεστείλατο** αὐτοῖς ἵνα μηδενὶ λέγωσιν· ὅσον δὲ αὐτοῖς διεστέλλετο, αὐτοὶ μᾶλλον περισσότερον ἐκήρυσσον. [GNT] | To charge; to give a command; to give orders; to tell someone what to do or what not to do; to warn.<br><br>**Practical Application**<br>The word for "charged" (*diesteilato*) is strong. The order was clearly given. There is a lesson on humility in the command. Jesus was not after the applause or praise of people. The miracles were not done for that reason. All that He was and all that He had done was to help people by pointing them to God. People were lost, and He had come to seek and save the lost, not to win their applause (cp. Luke 19:10). |
| **#548 Charitable Deeds** | ἐλεημοσυνῶν ἐποίει = eleëmosunön epoiei<br>Pronunciation: [el-eh-ay-mos-oon'-own eh-poy-eh'-ee]<br>Parsing *eleëmosunön* (part of speech): noun<br>    Case—genitive<br>    Gender—feminine | To help the poor; to do almsdeeds; to show charity; to give to needy people; to do charitable deeds. |

# PRACTICAL WORD STUDIES
## in the NEW TESTAMENT

| ENGLISH WORD | GREEK WORD AND VERSE | THE WORD MEANS... |
|---|---|---|
| Almsdeeds...did–KJV<br>Charity..continually did–NASB<br>Helping the poor–NIV<br>**Charitable deeds... did–NKJV**<br>Helping the poor–NLT<br><br>**POSB REFERENCE**<br>(Acts 9:36-39; esp. v.36)<br>Note 2, point 1c | Number—plural<br>Stem or root—from ἐλεημοσύνη, ης<br>Parsing *epoiei* (part of speech): verb<br>  Mood—indicative<br>  Tense—imperfect<br>  Voice—active<br>  Person—3rd person<br>  Number—singular<br>  Stem or root—from ποιέω<br>Concordance References:<br>⇒ Strong's #1654 + 4160 eleëmosunë poieö<br>⇒ NIV #1797 + 4472 eleëmosunë poieö [helping the poor]<br>⇒ NASB #1654 + 4160 eleëmosunë poieö<br><br>**Acts 9:36**<br>Now there was at Joppa a certain disciple named Tabitha, which by interpretation is called Dorcas: this woman was full of good works and **almsdeeds** which she **did**. [KJV]<br>Now in Joppa there was a certain disciple named Tabitha (which translated *in Greek* is called Dorcas); this woman was abounding with deeds of kindness and **charity**, which she **continually did**. [NASB]<br>In Joppa there was a disciple named Tabitha (which, when translated, is Dorcas), who was always doing good and **helping the poor**. [NIV]<br>At Joppa there was a certain disciple named Tabitha, which is translated Dorcas. This woman was full of good works and **charitable deeds** which she **did**. [NKJV]<br>There was a believer in Joppa named Tabitha (which in Greek is Dorcas). She was always doing kind things for others and **helping the poor**. [NLT]<br>Ἐν Ἰόππῃ δέ τις ἦν μαθήτρια ὀνόματι Ταβιθά, ἣ διερμηνευομένη λέγεται Δορκάς· αὕτη ἦν πλήρης ἀγαθῶν ἔργων καὶ **ἐλεημοσυνῶν** ὧν **ἐποίει**. [GNS]<br>Ἐν Ἰόππῃ δέ τις ἦν μαθήτρια ὀνόματι Ταβιθά, ἣ διερμηνευομένη λέγεται Δορκάς· αὕτη ἦν πλήρης ἔργων ἀγαθῶν καὶ **ἐλεημοσυνῶν** ὧν **ἐποίει**. [GNT] | **Practical Application**<br>The emphasis is that she gave things, gifts which she herself made. |
| **#549**<br>**Charity**<br><br>Charity–KJV<br>Love–NASB<br>Love–NIV<br>Love–NKJV<br>Love–NLT<br><br>**POSB REFERENCE**<br>(1 Cor.13:1-13; esp. v.1)<br>*Deeper Study* #1<br><br>See also POSB REF:<br>(Rom.5:6-11; esp. v.8)<br>Introduction<br>(Col.3:14)<br>Note 9<br>(I Tim.1:5-6; esp. v.5)<br>Note 3<br>(2 Pet.1:5-7; esp.v.7)<br>Note 1, point 7<br>(2 Jn.1:5)<br>*Deeper Study* #1 | ἀγάπην = *agapën*<br>Pronunciation: [ag-ah'-payn]<br>Parsing (part of speech): noun<br>  Case—accusative<br>  Gender—feminine<br>  Number—singular<br>  Stem or root—from ἀγάπη, ης<br>Concordance References:<br>⇒ Strong's #26 agapë<br>⇒ NIV #27 agapë<br>⇒ NASB #26 agapë<br><br>**1 Cor. 13:1**<br>Though I speak with the tongues of men and of angels, and have not **charity**, I am become *as* sounding brass, or a tinkling cymbal. [KJV]<br>If I speak with the tongues of men and of angels, but do not have **love**, I have become a noisy gong or a clanging cymbal. [NASB]<br>If I speak in the tongues of men and of angels, but have not **love**, I am only a resounding gong or a clanging cymbal. [NIV]<br>Though I speak with the tongues of men and of angels, but have not **love**, I have become sounding brass or a clanging cymbal. [NKJV]<br>If I could speak in any language in heaven or on earth but didn't **love** others, I would only be making meaningless noise like a loud gong or a clanging cymbal. [NLT]<br>Ἐὰν ταῖς γλώσσαις τῶν ἀνθρώπων λαλῶ καὶ τῶν ἀγγέλων, **ἀγάπην** δὲ μὴ ἔχω, γέγονα χαλκὸς ἠχῶν ἢ κύμβαλον ἀλαλάζον. [GNS]<br>Ἐὰν ταῖς γλώσσαις τῶν ἀνθρώπων λαλῶ καὶ τῶν ἀγγέλων, **ἀγάπην** δὲ μὴ ἔχω, γέγονα χαλκὸς ἠχῶν ἢ κύμβαλον ἀλαλάζον. [GNT] | Love, the "God-kind of love;" Christian love; the highest level of concern and interest.<br><br>**Practical Application**<br>The meaning of *agape love* is more clearly seen by contrasting it with the various kinds of love. There are essentially four kinds of love. Whereas the English language has only the word *love* to describe all the affectionate experiences of men, the Greek language had a different word to describe each kind of love.<br>1. There is *passionate love* or *eros love*. This is the physical love between sexes; the patriotic love of a person for his nation; the ambition of a person for power, wealth, or fame. Briefly stated, *eros love* is the base love of a man that arises from his own inner passion. Sometimes *eros love* is focused upon good and other times it is focused upon bad. It should be noted that *eros love* is never used in the New Testament.<br>2. There is *affectionate love* or *storge love*. This is the kind of love that exists between parent and child and between loyal citizens and a trustworthy ruler. *Storge love* is also not used in the New Testament.<br>3. There is an *endearing love*, the love that cherishes. This is *phileo love*, the love of a husband and wife for each other, of a brother for a brother, of a friend for the dearest of friends. |

# PRACTICAL WORD STUDIES
## in the NEW TESTAMENT

| ENGLISH WORD | GREEK WORD AND VERSE | THE WORD MEANS... |
|---|---|---|
| | | It is the love that cherishes, that holds someone or something ever so dear to one's heart.<br>4. There is *selfless and sacrificial love* or *agape love*. Agape love is the love of the mind, of the reason, of the will. It is the love that goes so far...<br>• that it loves a person even if he does not deserve to be loved.<br>• that it actually loves the person who is utterly unworthy of being loved.<br>(Note: For more discussion concerning love, see POSB note, pt. 4, Love—John 21:15-17 and POSB *Deeper Study* #1, pt.4, Love—1 Cor.13:1-13.) |
| **#550**<br>**Charity...Continually Did**<br><br>Almsdeed...did–KJV<br>**Charity..continually did–NASB**<br>Helping the poor–NIV<br>Charitable deeds...did–NKJV<br>Helping the poor–NLT<br><br>**POSB REFERENCE**<br>(Acts 9:36-39; esp. v.36)<br>Note 2, point 1c | ἐλεημοσυνῶν ἐποίει = eleëmosunön epoiei<br>Pronunciation: [el-eh-ay-mos-oon'-own he-poy-eh'-ee]<br>Parsing *eleëmosunön* (part of speech): noun<br>    Case—genitive<br>    Gender—feminine<br>    Number—plural<br>    Stem or root—from ἐλεημοσύνη, ης<br>Parsing *epoiei* (part of speech): verb<br>    Mood—indicative<br>    Tense—imperfect<br>    Voice—active<br>    Person—3rd person<br>    Number—singular<br>    Stem or root—from ποιέω<br>Concordance References:<br>⇒ Strong's #1654 + 4160 eleëmosunë poieö<br>⇒ NIV #1797 + 4472 eleëmosunë poieö [helping the poor]<br>⇒ NASB #1654 + 4160 eleëmosunë poieö<br><br>**Acts 9:36**<br>Now there was at Joppa a certain disciple named Tabitha, which by interpretation is called Dorcas: this woman was full of good works and **almsdeeds** which she **did**. [KJV]<br>Now in Joppa there was a certain disciple named Tabitha (which translated *in Greek* is called Dorcas); this woman was abounding with deeds of kindness and **charity**, which she **continually did**. [NASB]<br>In Joppa there was a disciple named Tabitha (which, when translated, is Dorcas), who was always doing good and **helping the poor**. [NIV]<br>At Joppa there was a certain disciple named Tabitha, which is translated Dorcas. This woman was full of good works and **charitable deeds** which she **did**. [NKJV]<br>There was a believer in Joppa named Tabitha (which in Greek is Dorcas). She was always doing kind things for others and **helping the poor**. [NLT]<br>Ἐν Ἰόππῃ δέ τις ἦν μαθήτρια ὀνόματι Ταβιθά, ἣ διερμηνευομένη λέγεται Δορκάς· αὕτη ἦν πλήρης ἀγαθῶν ἔργων καὶ **ἐλεημοσυνῶν** ὧν **ἐποίει**. [GNS]<br>Ἐν Ἰόππῃ δέ τις ἦν μαθήτρια ὀνόματι Ταβιθά, ἣ διερμηνευομένη λέγεται Δορκάς· αὕτη ἦν πλήρης ἔργων ἀγαθῶν καὶ **ἐλεημοσυνῶν** ὧν **ἐποίει**. [GNT] | To help the poor; to do almsdeeds; to show charity; to give to needy people; to do charitable deeds.<br><br>**Practical Application**<br>The emphasis is that she gave things, gifts which she herself made. |
| **#551**<br>**Chaste**<br><br>**Chaste–KJV**<br>**Chaste–NASB**<br>Purity–NIV<br>**Chaste–NKJV**<br>Pure–NLT<br><br>**POSB REFERENCE**<br>(1 Pt.3:2)<br>Note 2 | ἁγνήν = hagnën<br>Pronunciation: [hag-nayn']<br>Parsing (part of speech): adjective<br>    Case—accusative<br>    Gender—feminine<br>    Number—singular<br>    Stem or root—from ἁγνός, ή, όν<br>Concordance References:<br>⇒ Strong's #53 hagnos<br>⇒ NIV #54 hagnos<br>⇒ NASB #53 hagnos | Pure, chaste. The word "chaste" (*hagnën*) means to be pure from all fault; to be clean and holy and free from all defilement; to act and behave in the most pure and modest way possible.<br><br>**Practical Application**<br>When a woman marries a man, she sets herself apart for him and him alone. She keeps herself clean and pure for him and for him alone. Note that the verse says, "Likewise, ye wives, *be* in subjection to your own husbands" (3:1). She |

# PRACTICAL WORD STUDIES
## in the NEW TESTAMENT

| ENGLISH WORD | GREEK WORD AND VERSE | THE WORD MEANS... |
|---|---|---|
| | **1 Peter 3:2**<br>While they behold your **chaste** conversation *coupled* with fear. [KJV]<br>as they observe your **chaste** and respectful behavior. [NASB]<br>When they see the **purity** and reverence of your lives. [NIV]<br>When they observe your **chaste** conduct *accompanied* by fear. [NKJV]<br>By watching your **pure**, godly behavior. [NLT]<br>ἐποπτεύσαντες τὴν ἐν φόβῳ **ἁγνὴν** ἀναστροφὴν ὑμῶν. [GNS]<br>ἐποπτεύσαντες τὴν ἐν φόβῳ **ἁγνὴν** ἀναστροφὴν ὑμῶν. [GNT] | does not subject or give herself to some other husband or man. She is her husband's and his alone.<br>A dirty wife or husband is never to be named among Christian believers. Nothing destroys the testimony of believers any more than sexual impurity. And nothing affects the love and the trust that couples can put in one another any more than sexual impurity. For this reason, the Christian wife is to subject herself to her own husband by living a pure life. |
| **#552**<br>**Chaste,**<br>**Keepers At**<br>**Home**<br><br>Chaste, keepers at home–KJV<br>Workers at home–NASB<br>Busy at home–NIV<br>Homemakers–NKJV<br>Pure, take care of their homes–NLT<br><br>**POSB**<br>**REFERENCE**<br>(Tit.2:4-5; esp. v.5)<br>Note 4, point 6<br>Introduction | οἰκουργούς = *oikourgous*<br>Pronunciation: [oy-koor-goos']<br>Parsing (part of speech): pronominal adjective OR adjective<br>   Case—accusative<br>   Gender—feminine<br>   Number—plural<br>   Stem or root—from οἰκουργός, όν<br>Concordance References:<br>  ⇒ Strong's #3626 oikourgos<br>  ⇒ NIV #3877 oikourgos<br>  ⇒ NASB #3626 oikourgos<br><br>**Titus 2:5**<br>*To be* discreet, **chaste, keepers at home**, good, obedient to their own husbands, that the word of God be not blasphemed. [KJV]<br>*To be* sensible, pure, **workers at home**, kind, being subject to their own husbands, that the word of God may not be dishonored. [NASB]<br>To be self-controlled and pure, to be **busy at home**, to be kind, and to be subject to their husbands, so that no one will malign the word of God. [NIV]<br>To be discreet, chaste, **homemakers**, good, obedient to their own husbands, that the word of God may not be blasphemed. [NKJV]<br>To live wisely and be **pure**, to **take care of their homes**, to do good, and to be submissive to their husbands. Then they will not bring shame on the word of God. [NLT]<br>σώφρονας, ἁγνάς, **οἰκουργούς** ἀγαθάς, ὑποτασσομένας τοῖς ἰδίοις ἀνδράσιν, ἵνα μὴ ὁ λόγος τοῦ Θεοῦ βλασφημῆται· [GNS]<br>σώφρονας ἁγνάς **οἰκουργούς** ἀγαθάς, ὑποτασσομένας τοῖς ἰδίοις ἀνδράσιν, ἵνα μὴ ὁ λόγος τοῦ θεοῦ βλασφημῆ [GNT] | To be busy at home; to be keepers at home; to be workers at home; to take care of business [at home]; to be homemakers, devoted to duties at home.<br><br>**Practical Application**<br>Young women are to be *keepers or workers at home*: homemakers. No better exposition of this command could be given than that written by Oliver Greene:<br><br>*"This does not mean that the wife is never to go out of the home, never to take part in any outside interests; but she is not to neglect the duties of the home in order to participate in things outside the home. In other words, she is not to be better known outside the home than in the home, by her own husband and family. She is to be diligent at home—not lazy or slothful, not unconcerned about the home and the things pertaining thereto—but to give her best to the home, seeing that things are in order and that the home is kept as becomes a Christian....The duty of a Christian mother is first to her home, and these other interests must be secondary"* (The Epistles of Paul the Apostle to Timothy and Titus. Greenville, SC: The Gospel Hour, Inc., 1964, p.444f). |
| **#553**<br>**Chasteneth–**<br>**Chastens**<br><br>Chasteneth–KJV<br>Disciplines–NASB<br>Disciplines–NIV<br>**Chastens–NKJV**<br>Disciplines–NLT<br><br>**POSB**<br>**REFERENCE**<br>(Heb.12:5-13; esp. v.6)<br>Introduction | παιδεύει = *paideuei*<br>Pronunciation: [pahee-dyoo'-eh-ee]<br>Parsing (part of speech): verb<br>   Mood—indicative<br>   Tense—present<br>   Voice—active<br>   Person—3rd person<br>   Number—singular<br>   Stem or root—from παιδεύω<br>Concordance References:<br>  ⇒ Strong's #3811 paideuō<br>  ⇒ NIV #4084 paideuō<br>  ⇒ NASB #3811 paideuō<br><br>**Hebrews 12:6**<br>For whom the Lord loveth he **chasteneth**, and scourgeth every son whom he receiveth. [KJV]<br>For those whom the Lord loves He **disciplines**, And He scourges every son whom He receives." [NASB]<br>Because the Lord **disciplines** those he loves, and he punishes everyone he accepts as a son." [NIV] | Disciplines, chastens; to correct; to train; to instruct; to teach; to beat; to whip; to punish.<br><br>**Practical Application**<br>God does not cause bad and evil in life. God loves man and loves this world. Therefore, God's concern is not to cause problems and pain for us; His concern is to deliver us through all the trouble and pain on earth and to save us for heaven and eternity. How does God do this? By disciplining us. What does chastening (*paideuei*) mean? When we think of discipline, we usually think of chastisement and correction and it does mean this. But it also means to train and teach and instruct a person. Both meanings are included in the Biblical word *discipline and chastisement* (cp. A.T. Robertson. *Word Pictures in the New Testament*, Vol. 5, p.435). God does two things with us:<br>1. First, when we face some trial and sin in life, |

| ENGLISH WORD | GREEK WORD AND VERSE | THE WORD MEANS... |
|---|---|---|
| | *For whom the LORD loves He **chastens**, And scourges every son whom e receives."* [NKJV]<br><br>For the Lord **disciplines** those he loves, and he punishes those he accepts as his children." [NLT]<br><br>ὃν γὰρ ἀγαπᾷ Κύριος **παιδεύει**· μαστιγοῖ δὲ πάντα υἱὸν ὃν παραδέχεται. [GNS]<br><br>ὃν γὰρ ἀγαπᾷ κύριος **παιδεύει**, μαστιγοῖ δὲ πάντα υἱὸν ὃν παραδέχεται. [GNT] | God stirs us to stand fast and to conquer the trial or to turn away from the sin. He guides, directs, teaches, trains, and instructs us all along the way, making us stronger and stronger in life and drawing us closer and closer to Him. God does not want the trials and sins of life to defeat and engulf us; He wants them to strengthen us. He wants to use them to discipline and teach us more and more endurance, and He wants to teach us to trust and depend upon Him more and more. But note this: we have to let God work in our hearts to use the trials to strengthen us. We cannot wallow around in self-pity or react against the trials and problems that attack us. We must turn to God—truly turn to God—and ask Him for help and strength and let Him help us.<br><br>An illustration is this. A small innocent baby who is crippled in an automobile accident by a drunkard is not being chastised or corrected by God. The child has done nothing for which to be chastised. The child is crippled because of a sinful man who followed the path of Satan, crippled because he lives in a corruptible world. God loves the child, and God will look after the child as the child grows if the child will look to God for help. God will use the child's sufferings...<br><br>• God will teach and discipline the *growing child* to endure more and more, making him stronger and stronger.<br>• God will teach and discipline the *growing child* to trust and depend upon Christ more and more and to fellowship and commune with Christ more and more.<br>• God will use the endurance and faith of the *growing child* as a testimony to the love and care of God—as a testimony to the living reality and delivering power of God that can conquer all the trials and sorrows of life, even that of death.<br><br>2. Second, when we fail and cave in to the trial and sin, God lets us reap what we have sown. We bear the results of our sin, but even during sin and failure, God loves us. He loves and works with us, convicting us by His Spirit to repent. He then uses the suffering of the sin to stir us to think of Him and our failure. God takes the sufferings that are caused by trials and sins and uses them to correct and discipline us. This is the key statement, and it is what we must always remember when dealing with all the bad and evil things upon earth. God does not cause them; we cause them, and the corruptible world in which we live causes them, and the archenemy Satan causes them. God loves us and has nothing in mind for us except love and the very best of everything. Therefore, God takes all the bad and evil—all the suffering of bad and evil—and He uses it all to make us think about Him and our failure. He uses the suffering caused by sin and trials to correct and discipline us, to stir us to draw near Him in trust, dependence, and love, and to live like we should. |

# Practical Word Studies
## in the New Testament

| ENGLISH WORD | GREEK WORD AND VERSE | THE WORD MEANS... |
|---|---|---|
| **#554**<br>**Chatter**<br><br>Vain babblings–KJV<br>Empty chatter–NASB<br>**Chatter–NIV**<br>Idle babblings–NKJV<br>Foolish discussions–NLT<br><br>**POSB REFERENCE**<br>(1 Tim.6:20)<br>Note 2, point 2a | κενοφωνίας = kenophōnias<br>Pronunciation: [ken-of-o-nee'-ahs]<br>Parsing (part of speech): noun<br>    Case—accusative<br>    Gender—feminine<br>    Number—plural<br>    Stem or root—from κενοφωνία, ας<br>Concordance References:<br>  ⇒ Strong's #2757 kenophōnia<br>  ⇒ NIV #3032 kenophōnia<br>  ⇒ NASB #2757 kenophōnia<br><br>**1 Tim. 6:20**<br>O Timothy, keep that which is committed to thy trust, avoiding profane *and* **vain babblings**, and oppositions of science falsely so called: [KJV]<br>O Timothy, guard what has been entrusted to you, avoiding worldly *and* **empty chatter** *and* the opposing arguments of what is falsely called "knowledge"— [NASB]<br>Timothy, guard what has been entrusted to your care. Turn away from godless **chatter** and the opposing ideas of what is falsely called knowledge, [NIV]<br>O Timothy! Guard what was committed to your trust, avoiding the profane *and* **idle babblings** and contradictions of what is falsely called knowledge— [NKJV]<br>Timothy, guard what God has entrusted to you. Avoid godless, **foolish discussions** with those who oppose you with their so-called knowledge. [NLT]<br>Ὦ Τιμόθεε, τὴν παρακαταθήκην φύλαξον, ἐκτρεπόμενος τὰς βεβήλους **κενοφωνίας** καὶ ἀντιθέσεις τῆς ψευδωνύμου γνώσεως· [GNS]<br>Ὦ Τιμόθεε, τὴν παραθήκην φύλαξον ἐκτρεπόμενος τὰς βεβήλους **κενοφωνίας** καὶ ἀντιθέσεις τῆς ψευδωνύμου γνώσεως, [GNT] | Chatter; vain babblings; idle babblings; empty chatter; foolish discussions; foolish talk.<br><br>**Practical Application**<br>The charge is to take all *empty talk* and turn away from it. Have absolutely nothing to do with common, irreverent, godless *empty voices*—no matter who is sounding forth the words. This would, of course, include...<br>• false claims to truth<br>• worldly philosophy<br>• cursing<br>• criticism<br>• suggestive talk<br>• all forms of false teaching<br>• novel ideas of religion<br>• gossip<br>• off-colored jokes |
| **#555**<br>**Cheat**<br><br>Spoil–KJV<br>Captive–NASB<br>Captive–NIV<br>**Cheat–NKJV**<br>Astray–NLT<br><br>**POSB REFERENCE**<br>(Col.2:8)<br>Note 1 | ἔσται συλαγωγῶν = estai sulagōgōn<br>Pronunciation: [es-tah-ee soo-lag-og-o'-gon']<br>Parsing *sulagōgōn* (part of speech): verb<br>    Mood—participle<br>    Tense—present<br>    Voice—active<br>    Case—nominative<br>    Gender—masculine<br>    Number—singular<br>    Stem or root—from συλαγωγέω<br>Concordance References:<br>  ⇒ Strong's #1510 eimi + 4812 sulagōgeō<br>  ⇒ NIV #1639+5194 eimi sulagōgeō [takes captive]<br>  ⇒ NASB #1510 eimi + 4812 sulagōgeō<br><br>**Col. 2:8**<br>Beware lest any man **spoil** you through philosophy and vain deceit, after the tradition of men, after the rudiments of the world, and not after Christ. [KJV]<br>See to it that no one takes you **captive** through philosophy and empty deception, according to the tradition of men, according to the elementary principles of the world, rather than according to Christ. [NASB]<br>See to it that no one takes you **captive** through hollow and deceptive philosophy, which depends on human tradition and the basic principles of this world rather than on Christ. [NIV]<br>Beware lest anyone **cheat** you through philosophy and empty deceit, according to the tradition of men, according to the basic principles of the world, and not according to Christ. [NKJV]<br>Don't let anyone lead you **astray** with empty philosophy and high-sounding nonsense that come from human thinking and from the evil powers of this world, and not from Christ. [NLT]<br>βλέπετε μή τις ὑμᾶς **ἔσται ὁ συλαγωγῶν** διὰ τῆς | To take captive; to lead astray; to lead into captivity or slavery; to cheat.<br><br>**Practical Application**<br>Some men are in a genuine search for truth and reality. They seek to learn the truth and reality of the universe and the problems that face them, but they limit themselves to the universe.<br>Other persons have novel ideas or philosophies about truth and reality, but they become more interested in their positions than the truth. They need others to accept their positions or else their ideas die. Therefore, they have to present and persuade people of their ideas and philosophies whether they are sound or not.<br>Believers must, therefore, beware and guard against worldly philosophies and ideas lest they become ensnared and enslaved. |

# PRACTICAL WORD STUDIES
## in the NEW TESTAMENT

| ENGLISH WORD | GREEK WORD AND VERSE | THE WORD MEANS... |
|---|---|---|
| | φιλοσοφίας καὶ κενῆς ἀπάτης, κατὰ τὴν παράδοσιν τῶν ἀνθρώπων, κατὰ τὰ στοιχεῖα τοῦ κόσμου, καὶ οὐ κατὰ Χριστόν· [GNS]<br><br>βλέπετε μή τις ὑμᾶς **ἔσται ὁ συλαγωγῶν** διὰ τῆς φιλοσοφίας καὶ κενῆς ἀπάτης κατὰ τὴν παράδοσιν τῶν ἀνθρώπων, κατὰ τὰ στοιχεῖα τοῦ κόσμου καὶ οὐ κατὰ Χριστόν· [GNT] | |
| **#556**<br>**Cheat**<br><br>Beguile–KJV<br>Defrauding–NASB<br>Disqualify...for–NIV<br>**Cheat–NKJV**<br>Condemn–NLT<br><br>**POSB REFERENCE**<br>(Col.2:18-19; esp. v.18)<br>Note 2 | καταβραβευέτω = *katabrabeuetō*<br>Pronunciation: [kat-ab-rab-yoo'-eh-tow]<br>Parsing (part of speech): verb<br>  Mood—imperative<br>  Tense—present<br>  Voice—active<br>  Person—3rd person<br>  Number—singular<br>  Stem or root—from καταβραβεύω<br>Concordance References:<br>⇒ Strong's #2603 katabrabeuō<br>⇒ NIV #2857 katabrabeuō<br>⇒ NASB #2603 katabrabeuō<br><br>**Col. 2:18**<br>Let no man **beguile** you of your reward in a voluntary humility and worshipping of angels, intruding into those things which he hath not seen, vainly puffed up by his fleshly mind, [KJV]<br>Let no one keep **defrauding** you of your prize by delighting in self-abasement and the worship of the angels, taking his stand on visions he has seen, inflated without cause by his fleshly mind, [NASB]<br>Do not let anyone who delights in false humility and the worship of angels **disqualify** you **for** the prize. Such a person goes into great detail about what he has seen, and his unspiritual mind puffs him up with idle notions. [NIV]<br>Let no one **cheat** you of your reward, taking delight in *false* humility and worship of angels, intruding into those things which he has not seen, vainly puffed up by his fleshly mind, [NKJV]<br>Don't let anyone **condemn** you by insisting on self-denial. And don't let anyone say you must worship angels, even though they say they have had visions about this. These people claim to be so humble, but their sinful minds have made them proud. [NLT]<br>μηδεὶς ὑμᾶς **καταβραβευέτω** θέλων ἐν ταπεινοφροσύνῃ καὶ θρησκείᾳ τῶν ἀγγέλων, ἃ μὴ ἑώρακεν ἐμβατεύων, εἰκῇ φυσιούμενος ὑπὸ τοῦ νοὸς τῆς σαρκὸς αὐτοῦ, [GNS]<br>μηδεὶς ὑμᾶς **καταβραβευέτω** θέλων ἐν ταπεινοφροσύνῃ καὶ θρησκείᾳ τῶν ἀγγέλων, ἃ ἑόρακεν ἐμβατεύων, εἰκῇ φυσιούμενος ὑπὸ τοῦ νοὸς τῆς σαρκὸς αὐτοῦ, [GNT] | To disqualify; to beguile; to defraud; to cheat; to condemn. It means to rob; to defraud; to cheat a person out of his reward.<br><br>**Practical Application**<br>It is possible for believers to be disqualified for their reward by false teachers. How? By following those who teach that there is another approach to God other than Christ. Christ is God's appointed way to approach Him, and there is no other way. |
| **#557**<br>**Cheek**<br><br>**Cheek–KJV**<br>**Cheek–NASB**<br>**Cheek–NIV**<br>**Cheek–NKJV**<br>**Cheek–NLT**<br><br>**POSB REFERENCE**<br>(Lk.6:27-31; esp. v.29)<br>Note 1, point 1e | σιαγόνα = *siagona*<br>Pronunciation: [see-ag-own'-ah]<br>Parsing (part of speech): noun<br>  Case—accusative<br>  Gender—feminine<br>  Number—singular<br>  Stem or root—from σιαγών, όνος<br>Concordance References:<br>⇒ Strong's #4600 siagōn<br>⇒ NIV #4965 siagōn<br>⇒ NASB #4600 siagōn<br><br>**Luke 6:29**<br>And unto him that smiteth thee on the *one* **cheek** offer also the other; and him that taketh away thy cloke forbid not *to take thy* coat also. [KJV]<br>"Whoever hits you on the **cheek**, offer him the other also; and whoever takes away your coat, do not withhold your shirt from him either. [NASB]<br>If someone strikes you on one **cheek**, turn to him the other also. If someone takes your cloak, do not stop him | Cheek, the jaw or jawbone.<br><br>**Practical Application**<br>It is a strong blow, a punch and not just a slap of contempt. Of course, there is contempt and bitterness, but there is also physical injury. Christ is saying that the believer is not to strike back, not to retaliate against...<br>• bitter insults or contempt.<br>• bodily threats or injury.<br><br>When suffering for the gospel's sake, for his personal testimony for Christ, the believer is to respond to physical abuse just as his Lord did. He is to demonstrate moral strength through a quiet and meek spirit, trusting God to touch the heart of his persecutors. (See POSB notes—Matthew 5:38-39 for more discussion.) |

# Practical Word Studies in the New Testament

| ENGLISH WORD | GREEK WORD AND VERSE | THE WORD MEANS... |
|---|---|---|
| | from taking your tunic. [NIV]<br>To him who strikes you on the *one* **cheek**, offer the other also. And from him who takes away your cloak, do not withhold *your* tunic either. [NKJV]<br>If someone slaps you on one **cheek**, turn the other **cheek**. If someone demands your coat, offer your shirt also. [NLT]<br>τῷ τύπτοντί σε ἐπὶ τὴν **σιαγόνα**, πάρεχε καὶ τὴν ἄλλην· καὶ ἀπὸ τοῦ αἴροντός σου τὸ ἱμάτιον, καὶ τὸν χιτῶνα μὴ κωλύσῃς. [GNS]<br>τῷ τύπτοντί σε ἐπὶ τὴν **σιαγόνα** πάρεχε καὶ τὴν ἄλλην, καὶ ἀπὸ τοῦ αἴροντός σου τὸ ἱμάτιον καὶ τὸν χιτῶνα μὴ κωλύσῃς. [GNT] | |
| **#558**<br>**Cheer**<br><br>Comfort–KJV<br>Not translated–NASB<br>Not translated–NIV<br>**Cheer**–NKJV<br>Not translated–NLT<br><br>**POSB REFERENCE**<br>(Lk.8:43-48; esp. v.48)<br>Note 3, point 5b | Θάρσει = *tharsei*<br>Pronunciation: [thar-seh'-ee]<br>Parsing (part of speech): verb<br>    Mood—imperative<br>    Tense—present<br>    Person—2nd person<br>    Number—singular<br>    Stem or root—from Θάρσέω<br>Note: the correct parsing for this word is debatable. In referring to different Greek sources, the above is selected from Moulton's Analytical Greek Lexicon Revised 1978 Edition, p.191.<br>Concordance References:<br>⇒ Strong's #2293 tharseo<br>⇒ NIV #—NOT TRANSLATED<br>⇒ NASB #—NOT TRANSLATED<br><br>**Luke 8:48**<br>And he said unto her, Daughter, be of good **comfort**: thy faith hath made thee whole; go in peace. [KJV]<br>And He said to her, "Daughter, your faith has made you well; go in peace." [NASB]—NOT TRANSLATED<br>Then he said to her, "Daughter, your faith has healed you. Go in peace." [NIV]—NOT TRANSLATED<br>And He said to her, "Daughter, be of good **cheer**; your faith has made you well. Go in peace." [NKJV]<br>"Daughter," he said to her, "your faith has made you well. Go in peace." [NLT]—NOT TRANSLATED<br>ὁ δὲ εἶπεν αὐτῇ, **Θάρσει**, θυγάτηρ, ἡ πίστις σου σέσωκέ σε· πορεύου εἰς εἰρήνην. [GNS]<br>ὁ δὲ εἶπεν αὐτῇ, Θυγάτηρ, ἡ πίστις σου σέσωκέν σε· πορεύου εἰς εἰρήνην. [GNT] | Comfort, or more accurately, cheer, courage, confidence, and boldness in her faith and healing.<br><br>**Practical Application**<br>The woman was to rest assured and be comforted; her faith was rewarded, wonderfully so. Her faith caused Jesus to meet her face to face; her faith did some wonderful things for her.<br>1. She was called, "Daughter." This was the only time Jesus ever called a woman, "Daughter." What a distinct privilege! It meant she had become a child of God's.<br>2. She was given comfort. [KJV only]<br>3. She was assured that she was well permanently. Her deliverance would last.<br>4. She was given peace (see POSB note—John 14:27). |
| **#559**<br>**Cheerful– Cheerfully**<br><br>Cheerful–KJV<br>Cheerful–NASB<br>Cheerful–NIV<br>Cheerful–NKJV<br>Cheerfully–NLT<br><br>**POSB REFERENCE**<br>(2 Cor.9:7)<br>Note 4 | ἱλαρὸν = *hilaron*<br>Pronunciation: [hil-ar-on']<br>Parsing (part of speech): adjective<br>    Case—accusative<br>    Gender—masculine<br>    Number—singular<br>    Stem or root—from ἱλαρός, ά, όν<br>Concordance References:<br>⇒ Strong's #2431 hilaros<br>⇒ NIV #2659 hilaros<br>⇒ NASB #2431 hilaros<br><br>**2 Cor. 9:7**<br>Every man according as he purposeth in his heart, *so let him give*; not grudgingly, or of necessity: for God loveth a **cheerful** giver. [KJV]<br>Let each one *do* just as he has purposed in his heart; not grudgingly or under compulsion; for God loves a **cheerful** giver. [NASB]<br>Each man should give what he has decided in his heart to give, not reluctantly or under compulsion, for God loves a **cheerful** giver. [NIV]<br>*So let* each one *give* as he purposes in his heart, not grudgingly or of necessity; for God loves a **cheerful** giver. [NKJV]<br>You must each make up your own mind as to how much you should give. Don't give reluctantly or in | Cheerful, cheerfully, joyful.<br><br>**Practical Application**<br>The giver must give cheerfully if he wishes God to accept his gift. The giver is pleased and delighted to give to meet the needs of God's people and of the world. Note that God *loves* the cheerful giver, for the cheerful giver is just like His Son, Jesus Christ. Jesus Christ willingly and cheerfully gave all He was and had to meet the needs of the world. |

# PRACTICAL WORD STUDIES
## in the NEW TESTAMENT

| ENGLISH WORD | GREEK WORD AND VERSE | THE WORD MEANS... |
|---|---|---|
| | response to pressure. For God loves the person who gives **cheerfully**. [NLT]<br><br>ἕκαστος καθὼς προαιρεῖται τῇ καρδίᾳ· μὴ ἐκ λύπης ἢ ἐξ ἀνάγκης· **ἱλαρὸν** γὰρ δότην ἀγαπᾷ ὁ Θεός. [GNS]<br><br>ἕκαστος καθὼς προῄρηται τῇ καρδίᾳ, μὴ ἐκ λύπης ἢ ἐξ ἀνάγκης· **ἱλαρὸν** γὰρ δότην ἀγαπᾷ ὁ θεός. [GNT] | |
| **#560**<br>**Cheerfully–**<br>**Cheerfulness**<br><br>Cheerfulness–KJV<br>Cheerfulness–NASB<br>Cheerfully–NIV<br>Cheerfulness–NKJV<br>Gladly–NLT<br><br>**POSB**<br>**REFERENCE**<br>(Rom.12:6-8; esp. v.8)<br>Note 2, point 7 | ἐν ἱλαρότητι = *en hilarotëti*<br>Pronunciation: [en hil-ar-ot'-ay-tee]<br>Parsing *hilarotëti* (part of speech): noun<br>   Case—dative<br>   Gender—feminine<br>   Number—singular<br>   Stem or root—from ἱλαρότης, ητος<br>Concordance References:<br>⇒ Strong's #1722 + 2432 en hilarotēs<br>⇒ NIV #1877 + 2660 en hilarotēs [cheerfully]<br>⇒ NASB #1722 + 2432 en hilarotēs<br><br>**Romans 12:8**<br>Or he that exhorteth, on exhortation: he that giveth, *let him do it* with simplicity; he that ruleth, with diligence; he that sheweth mercy, with **cheerfulness**. [KJV]<br>Or he who exhorts, in his exhortation; he who gives, with liberality; he who leads, with diligence; he who shows mercy, with **cheerfulness**. [NASB]<br>If it is encouraging, let him encourage; if it is contributing to the needs of others, let him give generously; if it is leadership, let him govern diligently; if it is showing mercy, let him do it **cheerfully**. [NIV]<br>He who exhorts, in exhortation; he who gives, with liberality; he who leads, with diligence; he who shows mercy, with **cheerfulness**. [NKJV]<br>If your gift is to encourage others, do it! If you have money, share it generously. If God has given you leadership ability, take the responsibility seriously. And if you have a gift for showing kindness to others, do it **gladly**. [NLT]<br><br>εἴτε ὁ παρακαλῶν, ἐν τῇ παρακλήσει· ὁ μεταδιδοὺς ἐν ἁπλότητι, ὁ προϊστάμενος, ἐν σπουδῇ· ὁ ἐλεῶν **ἐν ἱλαρότητι**. [GNS]<br><br>εἴτε ὁ παρακαλῶν ἐν τῇ παρακλήσει· ὁ μεταδιδοὺς ἐν ἁπλότητι, ὁ προϊστάμενος ἐν σπουδῇ, ὁ ἐλεῶν **ἐν ἱλαρότητι**. [GNT] | To be cheerful; to be joyful; to be happy; to be glad; to be merry.<br><br>**Practical Application**<br>There is the gift of mercy (*eleon*). This is a person who is full of forgiveness and compassion, pity and mercy toward others. Note that the merciful person is to show mercy with a cheerful (*hilarotëti*) heart. The person with the gift of mercy...<br>• is not to forgive grudgingly.<br>• is not to hesitate in forgiving others.<br>• is not to show mercy in an annoyed spirit.<br>• is not to show mercy in a spirit of criticism and rebuke toward the person who needs help. (This often happens when the person is down and out because of unemployment, lack of education, or some other unfortunate circumstance.)<br><br>The believer who has the spirit of mercy is to show mercy with a cheerful and joyful heart, doing all he can to lift up the person needing kindness. |
| **#561**<br>**Cherishes–**<br>**Cherisheth**<br><br>Cherisheth–KJV<br>Cherishes–NASB<br>Cares for–NIV<br>Cherishes–NKJV<br>Lovingly–NLT<br><br>**POSB**<br>**REFERENCE**<br>(Eph.5:25-33; esp. v.29)<br>Note 2, point 2a | θάλπει = *thalpei*<br>Pronunciation: [thal'-peh-ee]<br>Parsing (part of speech): verb<br>   Mood—indicative<br>   Tense—present<br>   Voice—active<br>   Person—3rd person<br>   Number—singular<br>   Stem or root—from θάλπω<br>Concordance References:<br>⇒ Strong's #2282 thalpō<br>⇒ NIV #2499 thalpō<br>⇒ NASB #2282 thalpō<br><br>**Ephes. 5:29**<br>For no man ever yet hated his own flesh; but nourisheth and **cherisheth** it, even as the Lord the church: [KJV]<br>For no one ever hated his own flesh, but nourishes and **cherishes** it, just as Christ also *does* the church, [NASB]<br>After all, no one ever hated his own body, but he feeds and **cares for** it, just as Christ does the church—[NIV]<br>For no one ever hated his own flesh, but nourishes and **cherishes** it, just as the Lord *does* the church. [NKJV]<br>No one hates his own body but **lovingly** cares for it, just as Christ cares for his body, which is the church. [NLT]<br><br>οὐδεὶς γάρ ποτε τὴν ἑαυτοῦ σάρκα ἐμίσησεν, ἀλλ | To care for; to cherish; to lovingly care for; to take care of.<br><br>**Practical Application**<br>The word "cherishes" or "cherisheth" (*thalpei*) means to hold ever so dear within the heart; to treat with warmth, tenderness, care, affection, and appreciation. |

## Practical Word Studies
### in the New Testament

| ENGLISH WORD | GREEK WORD AND VERSE | THE WORD MEANS... |
|---|---|---|
| | ἐκτρέφει καὶ **θάλπει** αὐτήν, καθὼς καὶ ὁ Κύριος τὴν ἐκκλησίαν· [GNS]<br>οὐδεὶς γάρ ποτε τὴν ἑαυτοῦ σάρκα ἐμίσησεν ἀλλὰ ἐκτρέφει καὶ **θάλπει** αὐτήν, καθὼς καὶ ὁ Χριστὸς τὴν ἐκκλησίαν, [GNT] | |
| **#562**<br>**Chief**<br><br>Chief–KJV<br>First–NASB<br>First–NIV<br>First–NKJV<br>First–NLT<br><br>**POSB REFERENCE**<br>(Mt.20:23-28; esp. v.27)<br>Note 3, point 3 | πρῶτος = *prōtos*<br>Pronunciation: [pro'-tos]<br>Parsing (part of speech): adjective<br>    Type—ordinal<br>    Case—nominative<br>    Gender—masculine<br>    Number—singular<br>    Stem or root—from πρῶτος, η, ον<br>Concordance References:<br>  ⇒ Strong's #4413 prōtos<br>  ⇒ NIV #4755 prōtos<br>  ⇒ NASB #4413 prōtos<br><br>**Matthew 20:27**<br>And whosoever will be **chief** among you, let him be your servant: [KJV]<br>And whoever wishes to be **first** among you shall be your slave; [NASB]<br>And whoever wants to be **first** must be your slave— [NIV]<br>And whoever desires to be **first** among you, let him be your slave— [NKJV]<br>And whoever wants to be **first** must become your slave. [NLT]<br>καὶ ὃς ἐὰν θέλῃ ἐν ὑμῖν εἶναι **πρῶτος** ἔστω ὑμῶν δοῦλος· [GNS]<br>καὶ ὃς ἂν θέλῃ ἐν ὑμῖν εἶναι **πρῶτος** ἔσται ὑμῶν δοῦλος· [GNT] | To be first in importance; chief; foremost; prominent; to be "in charge."<br><br>**Practical Application**<br>If a person wants to be chief, what essential thing must be done? This person must learn to become a great servant. The word servant (*doulos*) means far more than just a servant. It means a slave totally possessed by the master. It is a *bondservant* bound by law to a master.<br>A look at the slave market of the New Testament day shows clearly what it meant to be a "slave or servant of Jesus Christ."<br>1. The slave was owned by his master; he was totally possessed by his master. The New Testament believer was purchased and possessed by Christ.<br>2. The slave existed for his master, and he had no other reason for existence. He had no personal rights whatsoever. The same was true of the New Testament believer: he existed only for Christ. His rights were the rights of Christ only.<br>3. The slave served his master, and he existed only for the purpose of service. He was at the master's disposal any hour of the day. So it was with the New Testament believer: he lived only to serve Christ—hour by hour and day by day.<br>4. The slave's will belonged to his master. He was allowed no will and no ambition other than the will and ambition of the master. He was completely subservient to the Master and owed total obedience to the will of the master. The New Testament believer belonged to Christ.<br>5. There is a fifth and most precious thing that the New Testament believer meant by "a slave of Jesus Christ." He meant that he had the highest and most honored and kingly profession in all the world. Men of God, the greatest men of history, have always been called *the servants of God*. It was the highest title of honor. The believer's slavery to Jesus Christ is no cringing, cowardly, shameful subjection. It is the position of honor—the honor that bestows upon a man the privileges and responsibilities of serving the King of kings and Lord of lords. |
| **#563**<br>**Chief Rooms**<br><br>Chief rooms–KJV<br>Places of honor at the table–NASB<br>Places of honor at the table–NIV<br>Best places–NKJV<br>Head of the table–NLT<br><br>**POSB REFERENCE**<br>(Lk.14:7)<br>Note 1 | τὰς πρωτοκλισίας = *tas prōtoklisias*<br>Pronunciation: [tas pro-tok-lis-ee'-ahs]<br>Parsing *prōtoklisias* (part of speech): noun<br>    Case—accusative<br>    Gender—feminine<br>    Number—plural<br>    Stem or root—from πρωτοκλισία, ας<br>Concordance References:<br>  ⇒ Strong's #4411 prōtoklisia<br>  ⇒ NIV #4752 prōtoklisia<br>  ⇒ NASB #4411 prōtoklisia<br><br>**Luke 14:7**<br>And he put forth a parable to those which were bidden, when he marked how they chose out the **chief rooms**; saying unto them, [KJV] | The places of honor at a table; the head of the table; the chief seats.<br><br>**Practical Application**<br>In this Scripture, it was time for everyone to be seated for the meal, and Jesus noticed how some guests scrambled for the places of honor at the table. Today, we usually place the names of the most honored guests at the plates. However, in Jesus' day the highest seat of honor was on the right of the host and the next highest on his left, and so the ranking continued alternating back and forth until the lowest ranked person sat the farthest away from the host. Very simply, the |

# PRACTICAL WORD STUDIES
## in the NEW TESTAMENT

| ENGLISH WORD | GREEK WORD AND VERSE | THE WORD MEANS... |
|---|---|---|
|  | And He *began* speaking a parable to the invited guests when He noticed how they had been picking out the **places of honor at the table**; saying to them, [NASB]<br><br>When he noticed how the guests picked the **places of honor at the table**, he told them this parable: [NIV]<br><br>So He told a parable to those who were invited, when He noted how they chose the **best places**, saying to them: [NKJV]<br><br>When Jesus noticed that all who had come to the dinner were trying to sit near the **head of the table**, he gave them this advice: [NLT]<br><br>Ἔλεγε δὲ πρὸς τοὺς κεκλημένους παραβολήν, ἐπέχων πῶς **τὰς πρωτοκλισίας** ἐξελέγοντο, λέγων πρὸς αὐτούς, [GNS]<br><br>Ἔλεγεν δὲ πρὸς τοὺς κεκλημένους παραβολήν, ἐπέχων πῶς **τὰς πρωτοκλισίας** ἐξελέγοντο, λέγων πρὸς αὐτούς, [GNT] | closer one sat to the host, the higher the honor. When Jesus saw how some quickly moved up close to the host, He saw an opportunity to teach the great importance of humility. |
| **#564**<br>**Children**<br><br>**Children–KJV**<br>Sons–NASB<br>Sons–NIV<br>Sons–NKJV<br>Children–NLT<br><br>**POSB REFERENCE**<br>(Jn.12:34-36; esp. v.36)<br>Note 5, point 2 | υἱοί = *huioi*<br>Pronunciation: [hwee-o-ee']<br>Parsing (part of speech): noun<br>    Case—nominative<br>    Gender—masculine<br>    Number—plural<br>    Stem or root—from υἱός, οῦ<br>Concordance References:<br>  ⇒ Strong's #5207 *huios*<br>  ⇒ NIV #5626 *huios*<br>  ⇒ NASB #5207 *huios*<br><br>**John 12:36**<br>While ye have light, believe in the light, that ye may be the **children** of light. These things spake Jesus, and departed, and did hide himself from them. [KJV]<br><br>"While you have the light, believe in the light, in order that you may become **sons** of light." These things Jesus spoke, and He departed and hid Himself from them. [NASB]<br><br>Put your trust in the light while you have it, so that you may become **sons** of light." When he had finished speaking, Jesus left and hid himself from them. [NIV]<br><br>While you have the light, believe in the light, that you may become **sons** of light." These things Jesus spoke, and departed, and was hidden from them. [NKJV]<br><br>Believe in the light while there is still time; then you will become **children** of the light." After saying these things, Jesus went away and was hidden from them. [NLT]<br><br>ἕως τὸ φῶς ἔχετε, πιστεύετε εἰς τὸ φῶς, ἵνα **υἱοὶ** φωτὸς γένησθε. Ταῦτα ἐλάλησεν ὁ Ἰησοῦς, καὶ ἀπελθὼν ἐκρύβη ἀπ' αὐτῶν. [GNS]<br><br>ὡς τὸ φῶς ἔχετε, πιστεύετε εἰς τὸ φῶς, ἵνα **υἱοὶ** φωτὸς γένησθε. Ταῦτα ἐλάλησεν Ἰησοῦς, καὶ ἀπελθὼν ἐκρύβη ἀπ' αὐτῶν. [GNT] | Sons, children, descendants, offsprings, heirs, followers.<br><br>**Practical Application**<br>A person must believe in the Light. If people believe, something significant will happen. They will become children (*huioi*, sons) of the Light.<br>  ⇒ "Believe" (*pisteuete*) is continuous action.<br>  ⇒ "Become" (*genesthe*) is a once-for-all act, a personal experience that happens all at once.<br><br>A person who truly sees Jesus Christ as the Light of the world believes and continues to believe. And the very moment his heart leaps toward Christ in belief, he becomes a child of the Light, a child of God Himself. The person sees the Light and begins to walk in the Light, living the kind of life he should. |
| **#565**<br>**Children**<br><br>Babes–KJV<br>Immature–NASB<br>Infants–NIV<br>Babes–NKJV<br>**Children–NLT**<br><br>**POSB REFERENCE**<br>(Romans 2:17-20; esp. v.20)<br>Note 1, point 9 | νηπίων = *nēpiōn*<br>Pronunciation: [nay'-pee-own]<br>Parsing (part of speech): pronominal adjective<br>    Case—genitive<br>    Gender—masculine<br>    Number—plural<br>    Stem or root—from νήπιος, α, ον<br>Concordance References:<br>  ⇒ Strong's #3516 *nēpios*<br>  ⇒ NIV #3758 *nēpios*<br>  ⇒ NASB #3516 *nēpios*<br><br>**Romans 2:20**<br>An instructor of the foolish, a teacher of **babes**, which hast the form of knowledge and of the truth in the law. [KJV]<br><br>A corrector of the foolish, a teacher of the **immature**, having in the Law the embodiment of knowledge and of | The infant; the immature; the novice; the children; the proselyte; the innocent; the baby; the new church member.<br><br>**Practical Application**<br>A person is not mature in God just because he...<br>• has been baptized and has been a church member for a long time.<br>• thinks he is mature.<br>• serves as a teacher.<br><br>What makes a person mature and capable of teaching the immature of the world is experience with Christ, having walked and served with Christ for a long time. |

# PRACTICAL WORD STUDIES
## in the NEW TESTAMENT

| ENGLISH WORD | GREEK WORD AND VERSE | THE WORD MEANS... |
|---|---|---|
| | the truth, [NASB]<br>An instructor of the foolish, a teacher of **infants**, because you have in the law the embodiment of knowledge and truth—[NIV]<br>An instructor of the foolish, a teacher of **babes**, having the form of knowledge and truth in the law. [NKJV]<br>You think you can instruct the ignorant and teach **children** the ways of God. For you are certain that in God's law you have complete knowledge and truth. [NLT]<br>παιδευτὴν ἀφρόνων, διδάσκαλον **νηπίων**, ἔχοντα τὴν μόρφωσιν τῆς γνώσεως καὶ τῆς ἀληθείας ἐν τῷ νόμῳ· [GNS]<br>παιδευτὴν ἀφρόνων, διδάσκαλον **νηπίων**, ἔχοντα τὴν μόρφωσιν τῆς γνώσεως καὶ τῆς ἀληθείας ἐν τῷ νόμῳ· [GNT] | |
| **#566**<br>**Children Of God**<br><br>Sons of God–KJV<br>Children of God–NASB<br>Children of God–NIV<br>Children of God–NKJV<br>Children of God–NLT<br><br>**POSB REFERENCE**<br>(Jn.1:12-13; esp. v.12)<br>Note 3, point 2 | τέκνα θεοῦ = *tekna theou*<br>Pronunciation: [tek'-nah theh'-oo]<br>Parsing *tekna* (part of speech): noun<br>    Case—accusative<br>    Gender—neuter<br>    Number—plural<br>    Stem or root—from τέκνον, ου<br>Concordance References:<br>⇒ Strong's #5043 teknon + 2316 theos<br>⇒ NIV #5451 teknon [children] + 2536 theos [God]<br>⇒ NASB #5043 teknon + 2316 theos<br><br>**John 1:12**<br>But as many as received him, to them gave he power to become the **sons of God**, *even* to them that believe on his name: [KJV]<br>But as many as received Him, to them He gave the right to become **children of God**, *even* to those who believe in His name, [NASB]<br>Yet to all who received Him, to those who believed in his name, he gave the right to become **children of God**—[NIV]<br>But as many as received Him, to them He gave the right to become **children of God**, to those who believe in His name: [NKJV]<br>But to all who believed him and accepted him, he gave the right to become **children of God**. [NLT]<br>ὅσοι δὲ ἔλαβον αὐτόν, ἔδωκεν αὐτοῖς ἐξουσίαν **τέκνα θεοῦ** γενέσθαι, τοῖς πιστεύουσιν εἰς τὸ ὄνομα αὐτοῦ· [GNS]<br>ὅσοι δὲ ἔλαβον αὐτόν, ἔδωκεν αὐτοῖς ἐξουσίαν **τέκνα θεοῦ** γενέσθαι, τοῖς πιστεύουσιν εἰς τὸ ὄνομα αὐτοῦ, [GNT] | Children, people, descendants—male or female—of God; sons of God.<br><br>**Practical Application**<br>It is important to understand how a person becomes a child of God. There is only one way—the way of adoption. The picture of adoption is a beautiful picture of what God does for the Christian believer. In the ancient world the family was based on a Roman law called "patria potestas," the father's power. The law gave the father absolute authority over his children so long as the father lived. He could work, enslave, sell, and if he wished, he could pronounce the death penalty. Regardless of the child's adult age, the father held all power over personal and property rights.<br>Therefore, adoption was a serious matter. Yet, it was a common practice to ensure that a family would not become extinct by having no male children. And when a child was adopted, three legal steps were taken.<br>1. The adopted son was adopted permanently. He could not be adopted today and disinherited tomorrow. He became a son of the father—forever. He was eternally secure as a son.<br>2. The adopted son immediately had all the rights of a legitimate son in the new family.<br>3. The adopted son completely lost all rights in his old family. The adopted son was looked upon as a new person—so new that old debts and obligations connected with his former family were canceled out and abolished as if they never existed. |
| **#567**<br>**Chose– Chosen**<br><br>Chosen–KJV<br>Chosen–NASB<br>Chose–NIV<br>Chosen–NKJV<br>Chose–NLT<br><br>**POSB REFERENCE**<br>(1 Cor.1:27-28)<br>Note 2 | ἐξελέξατο = *exelexato*<br>Pronunciation: [ek-eh-lek'-ah-to]<br>Parsing (part of speech): verb<br>    Mood—indicative<br>    Tense—aorist<br>    Voice—middle<br>    Person—3rd person<br>    Number—singular<br>    Stem or root—from ἐκλέγομαι<br>Concordance References:<br>⇒ Strong's #1586 eklegomai<br>⇒ NIV #1721 eklegomai<br>⇒ NASB #1586 eklegomai<br><br>**1 Cor. 1:27-28**<br>But God hath **chosen** the foolish things of the world to confound the wise; and God hath **chosen** the weak things of the world to confound the things which are mighty; And base things of the world, and things which | To be chosen, selected; to make a choice.<br><br>**Practical Application**<br>The fact that men do not save themselves, but God saves them, is stressed three times in the words "calling" and "chosen" (1 Cor. 1:26-28). God is the One who takes the initiative in saving men. It is God...<br>• who does not call many outstanding people.<br>• who does call the simple and humble people.<br>The point to see is this: God's choice is not arbitrary, not without reason. He knows why He chooses the simple and humble over the outstanding. |

# PRACTICAL WORD STUDIES
## in the NEW TESTAMENT

| ENGLISH WORD | GREEK WORD AND VERSE | THE WORD MEANS... |
|---|---|---|
| | are despised, hath God **chosen**, yea, and things which are not, to bring to nought things that are: [KJV]<br><br>But God has **chosen** the foolish things of the world to shame the wise, and God has **chosen** the weak things of the world to shame the things which are strong, and the base things of the world and the despised, God has **chosen**, the things that are not, that He might nullify the things that are, [NASB]<br><br>But God **chose** the foolish things of the world to shame the wise; God **chose** the weak things of the world to shame the strong. He **chose** the lowly things of this world and the despised things—and the things that are not—to nullify the things that are, [NIV]<br><br>But God has **chosen** the foolish things of the world to put to shame the wise, and God has **chosen** the weak things of the world to put to shame the things which are mighty; and the base things of the world and the things which are despised God has **chosen**, and the things which are not, to bring to nothing the things that are, [NKJV]<br><br>Instead, God deliberately **chose** things the world considers foolish in order to shame those who think they are wise. And he **chose** those who are powerless to shame those who are powerful. God **chose** things despised by the world, things counted as nothing at all, and used them to bring to nothing what the world considers important, [NLT]<br><br>ἀλλὰ τὰ μωρὰ τοῦ κόσμου **ἐξελέξατο** ὁ Θεὸς, ἵνα τοὺς σοφοὺς καταισχύνῃ· καὶ τὰ ἀσθενῆ τοῦ κόσμου **ἐξελέξατο** ὁ Θεὸς, ἵνα καταισχύνῃ τὰ ἰσχυρά· καὶ τὰ ἀγενῆ τοῦ κόσμου καὶ τὰ ἐξουθενημένα **ἐξελέξατο** ὁ Θεὸς, καὶ τὰ μὴ ὄντα, ἵνα τὰ ὄντα καταργήσῃ. [GNS]<br><br>ἀλλὰ τὰ μωρὰ τοῦ κόσμου **ἐξελέξατο** ὁ θεός, ἵνα καταισχύνῃ τοὺς σοφούς, καὶ τὰ ἀσθενῆ τοῦ κόσμου **ἐξελέξατο** ὁ θεός, ἵνα καταισχύνῃ τὰ ἰσχυρά, καὶ τὰ ἀγενῆ τοῦ κόσμου καὶ τὰ ἐξουθενημένα **ἐξελέξατο** ὁ θεός, τὰ μὴ ὄντα, ἵνα τὰ ὄντα καταργήσῃ, [GNT] | |
| **#568**<br>**Chose Him For This Pupose Long Before**<br><br>Foreordained–KJV<br>Foreknown–NASB<br>Chosen before–NIV<br>Foreordained–NKJV<br>**Chose him for this pupose long before–NLT**<br><br>**POSB REFERENCE**<br>(1 Pt.1:18-20; esp. v.20)<br>Note 4, point 3b | προεγνωσμένου πρό = *proegnösmenou pro*<br>Pronunciation: [pro-ehg-noce'-men-oo pro]<br>Parsing *proegnösmenou* (part of speech): verb<br>    Mood—participle<br>    Tense—perfect<br>    Voice—passive<br>    Case—genitive<br>    Gender—masculine<br>    Number—singular<br>    Stem or root—from προγινώσκω<br>Concordance References:<br>⇒ Strong's #4253+4267 pro proginöskö<br>⇒ NIV #4574+4589 pro proginöskö [chosen before]<br>⇒ NASB #4253+4267 pro proginöskö<br><br>**1 Peter 1:20**<br>Who verily was **foreordained** before the foundation of the world, but was manifest in these last times for you, [KJV]<br><br>For He was **foreknown** before the foundation of the world, but has appeared in these last times for the sake of you [NASB]<br><br>He was **chosen before** the creation of the world, but was revealed in these last times for your sake. [NIV]<br><br>He indeed was **foreordained** before the foundation of the world, but was manifest in these last times for you [NKJV]<br><br>God **chose him for this purpose long before** the world began, but now in these final days, he was sent to the earth for all to see. And he did this for you. [NLT]<br><br>προεγνωσμένου μὲν πρὸ καταβολῆς κόσμου, φανερωθέντος δὲ ἐπ' ἐσχάτων τῶν χρόνων δι' ὑμᾶς, [GNS]<br><br>προεγνωσμένου μὲν πρὸ καταβολῆς κόσμου φανερωθέντος δὲ ἐπ' ἐσχάτου τῶν χρόνων δι' ὑμᾶς [GNT] | Chosen before, foreordained, foreknown; already known.<br><br>**Practical Application**<br>God foreordained that Christ—chosen before the foundation of the world—redeem us by His blood. God foreordained this even before the foundation of the world. The word (*proegnösmenou*) is used three different ways in Scripture:<br>⇒ to know something beforehand, ahead of time.<br>⇒ to know something immediately by loving and accepting and approving it.<br>⇒ to elect, foreordain, and predetermine something.<br><br>Note that all three meanings are at work in this passage. Before the world was ever created, God knew, approved, and predestined Christ to redeem man by coming to earth and dying for man. (See POSB *Deeper Study* #1, Foreknowledge—1 Peter 1:2 for more discussion.) |

# PRACTICAL WORD STUDIES
## in the NEW TESTAMENT

| ENGLISH WORD | GREEK WORD AND VERSE | THE WORD MEANS... |
|---|---|---|
| **#569**<br>**Chose Them**<br><br>Predestinate–KJV<br>Predestined–NASB<br>Predestined–NIV<br>Predestined–NKJV<br>Chose them–NLT<br><br>**POSB REFERENCE**<br>(Rom.8:29)<br>Note 2, point 3 | προώρισεν = proörisen<br>Pronunciation: [pro-or-i'-sehn]<br>Parsing (part of speech): verb<br>  Mood—indicative<br>  Tense—aorist<br>  Voice—active<br>  Person—3rd person<br>  Stem or root—from προορίζω<br>Concordance References:<br>  ⇒ Strong's #4309 proorizō<br>  ⇒ NIV #4633 proorizō<br>  ⇒ NASB #4309 proorizō<br><br>**Romans 8:29**<br>For whom he did foreknow, he also did **predestinate** *to be* conformed to the image of his Son, that he might be the firstborn among many brethren. [KJV]<br><br>For whom He foreknew, He also **predestined** *to become* conformed to the image of His Son, that He might be the first-born among many brethren; [NASB]<br><br>For those God foreknew he also **predestined** to be conformed to the likeness of his Son, that he might be the firstborn among many brothers. [NIV]<br><br>For whom He foreknew, He also **predestined** *to be* conformed to the image of His Son, that He might be the firstborn among many brethren. [NKJV]<br><br>For God knew his people in advance, and he **chose them** to become like his Son, so that his Son would be the firstborn, with many brothers and sisters. [NLT]<br><br>ὅτι οὓς προέγνω, καὶ **προώρισε** συμμόρφους τῆς εἰκόνος τοῦ υἱοῦ αὐτοῦ, εἰς τὸ εἶναι αὐτὸν πρωτότοκον ἐν πολλοῖς ἀδελφοῖς· [GNS]<br><br>ὅτι οὓς προέγνω, καὶ **προώρισεν** συμμόρφους τῆς εἰκόνος τοῦ υἱοῦ αὐτοῦ, εἰς τὸ εἶναι αὐτὸν πρωτότοκον ἐν πολλοῖς ἀδελφοῖς· [GNT] | Decide from the beginning or beforehand, predestine; set apart from the beginning or beforehand. The predestination of God; to destine or appoint before; to foreordain; to predetermine. The basic Greek word (*proorizö*) means to mark off or to set off the boundaries of something.<br><br>**Practical Application**<br>The idea is a glorious picture of what God is doing for the believer. The boundary is marked and set off for the believer: the boundary of being conformed to the image of God's dear Son. The believer will be made just like Christ, conformed to His very likeness and image. Nothing can stop God's purpose for the believer. It is predestinated, set, and marked off. The believer may struggle and suffer through the sin and shame of this world; he may even stumble and fall or become discouraged and downhearted. But if he is a genuine child of God, he will not be defeated, not totally. He will soon arise from his fall and begin to follow Christ again. He is predestinated to be a brother of Christ, to worship and serve Christ throughout all eternity. And Christ will not be disappointed. God loves His Son too much to allow Him to be disappointed by losing a single brother. Jesus Christ will have His joy fulfilled; He will see every brother of His face to face, conformed perfectly to His image. He will have the worship and service of every brother chosen to be His by God the Father. The believer's eternal destiny, that of being an adopted brother to the Lord Jesus Christ, is determined. The believer can rest assured of this glorious truth. God has predestinated him to be delivered from the suffering and struggling of this sinful world. (See POSB note, Predestination—John 6:37; POSB note, Predestination—John 6:39; POSB note, Predestination—John 6:44-46 for God's part and man's part in salvation. See POSB *Deeper Study* #3—Acts 2:23; POSB *Deeper Study* #1—Romans 9:10-13; POSB note—Romans 9:14-33 for more discussion.) |
| **#570**<br>**Chose You Long Ago**<br><br>Foreknowledge–KJV<br>Foreknowledge–NASB<br>Foreknowledge–NIV<br>Foreknowledge–NKJV<br>Chose you long ago–NLT<br><br>**POSB REFERENCE**<br>(1 Pt.1:2)<br>*Deeper Study* #1<br><br>See also POSB REF:<br>(Acts 2:23)<br>*Deeper Study* #3 | πρόγνωσιν = prognösin<br>Pronunciation: [prog'-no-sin]<br>Parsing (part of speech): noun<br>  Case—accusative<br>  Gender—feminine<br>  Number—singular<br>  Stem or root—from πρόγνωσις, εως<br>Concordance References:<br>  ⇒ Strong's #4268 prognōsis<br>  ⇒ NIV #4590 prognōsis<br>  ⇒ NASB #4268 prognōsis<br><br>**1 Peter 1:2**<br>Elect according to the **foreknowledge** of God the Father, through sanctification of the Spirit, unto obedience and sprinkling of the blood of Jesus Christ: Grace unto you, and peace, be multiplied. [KJV]<br><br>According to the **foreknowledge** of God the Father, by the sanctifying work of the Spirit, that you may obey Jesus Christ and be sprinkled with His blood: May grace and peace be yours in fullest measure. [NASB]<br><br>Who have been chosen according to the **foreknowledge** of God the Father, through the sanctifying work of | To see before; to know beforehand; to see and know the future; to foreordain.<br><br>**Practical Application**<br>God is God; therefore He sees the future. No matter how far a person looks into the future, God sees it. God knows...<br>• exactly what *will* happen, every single event and its consequences.<br>• exactly what *could* happen (but will not), every single possibility and its consequences.<br>Therefore God knows...<br>• exactly what man *will* do, every single act and its consequences.<br>• exactly what man *could* do (but will not), every single possibility and its consequences.<br>God is God. He is eternal and omniscient (knowing all). He knows the past, the present, and the future. And note: He knows it all eternally, forever. God knew... |

# PRACTICAL WORD STUDIES
## in the NEW TESTAMENT

| ENGLISH WORD | GREEK WORD AND VERSE | THE WORD MEANS... |
|---|---|---|
| | the Spirit, for obedience to Jesus Christ and sprinkling by his blood: Grace and peace be yours in abundance. [NIV]<br><br>Elect according to the **foreknowledge** of God the Father, in sanctification of the Spirit, for obedience and sprinkling of the blood of Jesus Christ:Grace to you and peace be multiplied. [NKJV]<br><br>God the Father **chose you long ago**, and the Spirit has made you holy. As a result, you have obeyed Jesus Christ and are cleansed by his blood. May you have more and more of God's special favor and wonderful peace. [NLT]<br><br>κατὰ **πρόγνωσιν** Θεοῦ πατρός, ἐν ἁγιασμῷ Πνεύματος, εἰς ὑπακοὴν καὶ ῥαντισμὸν αἵματος Ἰησοῦ Χριστοῦ· χάρις ὑμῖν καὶ εἰρήνη πληθυνθείη. [GNS]<br><br>κατὰ **πρόγνωσιν** θεοῦ πατρός ἐν ἁγιασμῷ πνεύματος εἰς ὑπακοὴν καὶ ῥαντισμὸν αἵματος Ἰησοῦ Χριστοῦ, χάρις ὑμῖν καὶ εἰρήνη πληθυνθείη. [GNT] | • every event of world history before the *foundation of the world*.<br>• every event of a person's life before the *foundation of the world* (cp. Ephes. 1:4). |
| **#571**<br>**Chosen**<br><br>Elect–KJV<br>Elect–NASB<br>**Chosen–NIV**<br>Elect–NKJV<br>**Chosen–NLT**<br><br>**POSB REFERENCE**<br>(Lk.18:7)<br>*Deeper Study* #1 | ἐκλεκτῶν = eklektōn<br>Pronunciation: [ek-lek-ton]<br>Parsing (part of speech): pronominal adjective<br>    Case—genitive<br>    Gender—masculine<br>    Number—plural<br>    Stem or root—from ἐκλεκτός, ή, όν<br>Concordance References:<br> ⇒ Strong's #1588 eklektos<br> ⇒ NIV #1723 eklektos<br> ⇒ NASB #1588 eklektos<br><br>**Luke 18:7**<br>And shall not God avenge his own **elect**, which cry day and night unto him, though he bear long with them? [KJV]<br><br>now shall not God bring about justice for His **elect**, who cry to Him day and night, and will He delay long over them? [NASB]<br><br>And will not God bring about justice for his **chosen** ones, who cry out to him day and night? Will he keep putting them off? [NIV]<br><br>And shall God not avenge His own **elect** who cry out day and night to Him, though He bears long with them? [NKJV]<br><br>Even he rendered a just decision in the end, so don't you think God will surely give justice to his **chosen** people who plead with him day and night? Will he keep putting them off? [NLT]<br><br>ὁ δὲ Θεὸς οὐ μὴ ποιήσει τὴν ἐκδίκησιν τῶν **ἐκλεκτῶν** αὐτοῦ τῶν βοώντων πρὸς αὐτῷ ἡμέρας καὶ νυκτός, καὶ μακροθυμῶν ἐπ' αὐτοῖς; [GNS]<br><br>ὁ δὲ θεὸς οὐ μὴ ποιήσῃ τὴν ἐκδίκησιν τῶν **ἐκλεκτῶν** αὐτοῦ τῶν βοώντων αὐτῷ ἡμέρας καὶ νυκτός, καὶ μακροθυμεῖ ἐπ' αὐτοῖς; [GNT] | The chosen; the elect; the selected; the favored; the choice; the person picked out.<br><br>**Practical Application**<br>The chosen or elect are the believers, the disciples of Christ, the people who genuinely belong to God (Matthew 24:22, 24, 31; Mark 13:20, 22, 27; Romans 8:33; Col. 3:12; 2 Tim. 2:10; Titus 1:1; 1 Peter 1:1; 1 Peter 2:9. Also cp. where the word is translated "chosen," Matthew 20:16; Matthew 22:14; Romans 16:13 [NIV only]; 2 John 1:1, 13; Rev. 17:14.)<br><br>The focus of the word is upon God's choice. There is no doubt about this, for the word itself means that God does the choosing and the picking out. But note: the choosing is for service, not for salvation or position (John 15:16). The believer is chosen to bear fruit (see POSB *Deeper Study* #1—John 15:1-8). |
| **#572**<br>**Chosen**<br><br>Inheritance–KJV<br>Inheritance–NASB<br>**Chosen–NIV**<br>Inheritance–NKJV<br>Inheritance–NLT<br><br>**POSB REFERENCE**<br>(Eph.1:11-13; esp. v.11)<br>Note 7, point 2 | ἐκληρώθημεν = eklērōthēmen<br>Pronunciation: [eh-klay-ro'-thay-mehn]<br>Parsing (part of speech): verb<br>    Mood—indicative<br>    Tense—aorist<br>    Voice—passive<br>    Person—1st person<br>    Number—plural<br>    Stem or root—from κληρόω<br>Concordance References:<br> ⇒ Strong's #2820 klēroō<br> ⇒ NIV #3103 klēroō<br> ⇒ NASB #2820 klēroō<br><br>**Ephes. 1:11**<br>In whom also we have obtained an **inheritance**, being predestinated according to the purpose of him who worketh all things after the counsel of his own will: [KJV]<br><br>Also we have obtained an **inheritance**, having been predestined according to His purpose who works all | Chosen, inheritance, heritage.<br><br>**Practical Application**<br>God takes the believer and makes him His own heritage and possession. The believer himself is made the inheritance of God. He is given the glorious privilege of *being*, of living and existing forever as God's most *cherished possession and heritage*. He becomes the most precious gem and treasure of God. This is the believer's inheritance, his heritage. |

# PRACTICAL WORD STUDIES
## in the NEW TESTAMENT

| ENGLISH WORD | GREEK WORD AND VERSE | THE WORD MEANS... |
|---|---|---|
| | things after the counsel of His will, [NASB]<br>　In him we were also **chosen**, having been predestined according to the plan of him who works out everything in conformity with the purpose of his will, [NIV]<br>　In Him also we have obtained an **inheritance**, being predestined according to the purpose of Him who works all things according to the counsel of His will, [NKJV]<br>　Furthermore, because of Christ, we have received an **inheritance** from God, for he chose us from the beginning, and all things happen just as he decided long ago. [NLT]<br>　ἐν ᾧ καὶ **ἐκληρώθημεν**, προορισθέντες κατὰ πρόθεσιν τοῦ τὰ πάντα ἐνεργοῦντος κατὰ τὴν βουλὴν τοῦ θελήματος αὐτοῦ, [GNS]<br>　ἐν ᾧ καὶ **ἐκληρώθημεν** προορισθέντες κατὰ πρόθεσιν τοῦ τὰ πάντα ἐνεργοῦντος κατὰ τὴν βουλὴν τοῦ θελήματος αὐτοῦ [GNT] | |
| **#573**<br>**Chosen**<br><br>Elect–KJV<br>**Chosen–NASB**<br>**Chosen–NIV**<br>Elect–NKJV<br>**Chosen–NLT**<br><br>**POSB REFERENCE**<br>(2 Jn.1:1)<br>Note 1 | ἐκλεκτῇ = eklektë<br>Pronunciation: [ek-lek-tay']<br>Parsing (part of speech): adjective<br>　Case—dative<br>　Gender—feminine<br>　Number—singular<br>　Stem or root—from ἐκλεκτός, ή, όν<br>Concordance References:<br>　⇒ Strong's #1588 eklektos<br>　⇒ NIV #1723 eklektos<br>　⇒ NASB #1588 eklektos<br><br>**2 John 1:1**<br>　The elder unto the **elect** lady and her children, whom I love in the truth; and not I only, but also all they that have known the truth; [KJV]<br>　The elder to the **chosen** lady and her children, whom I love in truth; and not only I, but also all who know the truth, [NASB]<br>　The elder, To the **chosen** lady and her children, whom I love in the truth—and not only I, but also all who know the truth—[NIV]<br>　The Elder, To the **elect** lady and her children, whom I love in truth, and not only I, but also all those who have known he truth, [NKJV]<br>　This letter is from John the Elder. It is written to the **chosen** lady and to her children, whom I love in the truth, as does everyone else who knows God's truth—[NLT]<br>　Ὁ πρεσβύτερος **ἐκλεκτῇ** κυρίᾳ, καὶ τοῖς τέκνοις αὐτῆς, οὓς ἐγὼ ἀγαπῶ ἐν ἀληθείᾳ, καὶ οὐκ ἐγὼ μόνος ἀλλὰ καὶ πάντες οἱ ἐγνωκότες τὴν ἀλήθειαν, [GNS]<br>　Ὁ πρεσβύτερος **ἐκλεκτῇ** κυρίᾳ καὶ τοῖς τέκνοις αὐτῆς, οὓς ἐγὼ ἀγαπῶ ἐν ἀληθείᾳ, καὶ οὐκ ἐγὼ μόνος ἀλλὰ καὶ πάντες οἱ ἐγνωκότες τὴν ἀλήθειαν, [GNT] | Chosen, elected, selected. It means to be chosen by God.<br><br>**Practical Application**<br>　It means to be one of God's *holy and beloved* followers. This dear mother was elected or chosen by God to be one of His chosen, one of His *holy and beloved* followers. |
| **#574**<br>**Chosen**<br><br>Elect–KJV<br>**Chosen–NASB**<br>Elect–NIV<br>Elect–NKJV<br>**Chosen–NLT**<br><br>**POSB REFERENCE**<br>(Tit.1:1)<br>Note 2 | ἐκλεκτῶν = eklektön<br>Pronunciation: [ek-lek-ton']<br>Parsing (part of speech): pronominal adjective<br>　Case—genitive<br>　Gender—masculine<br>　Number—plural<br>　Stem or root—from ἐκλεκτός, ή, όν<br>Concordance References:<br>　⇒ Strong's #1588 eklektos<br>　⇒ NIV #1723 eklektos<br>　⇒ NASB #1588 eklektos<br><br>**Titus 1:1**<br>　Paul, a servant of God, and an apostle of Jesus Christ, according to the faith of God's **elect**, and the acknowledging of the truth which is after godliness; [KJV]<br>　Paul, a bond-servant of God, and an apostle of Jesus Christ, for the faith of those **chosen** of God and the knowledge of the truth which is according to godliness, [NASB] | The chosen, the elect, the selected, the person picked out. It means to be chosen by God; separated or set apart.<br><br>**Practical Application**<br>　The purpose of God's servant is to stir believers. Note that believers are called "those chosen of God." (*eklektön*) They are the persons whom God has chosen to be His "holy and beloved" people.<br>　God called believers out of the world and away from the old life it offered, the old life of sin and death. He called believers to be separated and set apart unto Himself and the new life He offers, the new life of righteousness and eternity. |

## PRACTICAL WORD STUDIES in the NEW TESTAMENT

| ENGLISH WORD | GREEK WORD AND VERSE | THE WORD MEANS... |
|---|---|---|
| | Paul, a servant of God and an apostle of Jesus Christ for the faith of God's **elect** and the knowledge of the truth that leads to godliness—[NIV]<br><br>Paul, a bondservant of God and an apostle of Jesus Christ, according to the faith of God's **elect** and the acknowledgment of the truth which accords with godliness, [NKJV]<br><br>This letter is from Paul, a slave of God and an apostle of Jesus Christ. I have been sent to bring faith to those God has **chosen** and to teach them to know the truth that shows them how to live godly lives. [NLT]<br><br>Παῦλος, δοῦλος Θεοῦ, ἀπόστολος δὲ Ἰησοῦ Χριστοῦ, κατὰ πίστιν **ἐκλεκτῶν** Θεοῦ καὶ ἐπίγνωσιν ἀληθείας τῆς κατ' εὐσέβειαν, [GNS]<br><br>Παῦλος, δοῦλος θεοῦ, ἀπόστολος δὲ Ἰησοῦ Χριστοῦ κατὰ πίστιν **ἐκλεκτῶν** θεοῦ καὶ ἐπίγνωσιν ἀληθείας τῆς κατ' εὐσέβειαν [GNT] | |
| **#575**<br>**Chosen Before**<br><br>Foreordained–KJV<br>Foreknown–NASB<br>**Chosen before–NIV**<br>Foreordained–NKJV<br>Chose him for this purpose long before–NLT<br><br>**POSB REFERENCE**<br>(1 Pt.1:18-20; esp. v.20)<br>Note 4, point 3b | προεγνωσμένου πρό = *proegnösmenou pro*<br>Pronunciation: [pro-ehg-noce'-men-oo pro]<br>Parsing *proegnösmenou* (part of speech): verb<br>    Mood—participle<br>    Tense—perfect<br>    Voice—passive<br>    Case—genitive<br>    Gender—masculine<br>    Number—singular<br>    Stem or root—from προγινώσκω<br>Concordance References:<br>  ⇒ Strong's #4253+4267 pro proginöskö<br>  ⇒ NIV #4574+4589 pro proginöskö [chosen before]<br>  ⇒ NASB #4253+4267 pro proginöskö<br><br>**1 Peter 1:20**<br>Who verily was **foreordained** before the foundation of the world, but was manifest in these last times for you, [KJV]<br>For He was **foreknown** before the foundation of the world, but has appeared in these last times for the sake of you [NASB]<br>He was **chosen before** the creation of the world, but was revealed in these last times for your sake. [NIV]<br>He indeed was **foreordained** before the foundation of the world, but was manifest in these last times for you [NKJV]<br>God **chose him for this purpose long before** the world began, but now in these final days, he was sent to the earth for all to see. And he did this for you. [NLT]<br>προεγνωσμένου μὲν **πρὸ** καταβολῆς κόσμου, φανερωθέντος δὲ ἐπ' ἐσχάτων τῶν χρόνων δι' ὑμᾶς, [GNS]<br>προεγνωσμένου μὲν **πρὸ** καταβολῆς κόσμου φανερωθέντος δὲ ἐπ' ἐσχάτου τῶν χρόνων δι' ὑμᾶς [GNT] | Chosen before, foreordained, foreknown; already known.<br><br>**Practical Application**<br>God foreordained that Christ—chosen before the foundation of the world—redeem us by His blood. God foreordained this even before the foundation of the world. The word (*proegnösmenou*) is used three different ways in Scripture:<br>⇒ to know something beforehand, ahead of time.<br>⇒ to know something immediately by loving and accepting and approving it.<br>⇒ to elect, foreordain, and predetermine something.<br><br>Note that all three meanings are at work in this passage. Before the world was ever created, God knew, approved, and predestined Christ to redeem man by coming to earth and dying for man. (See POSB *Deeper Study* #1, Foreknowledge—1 Peter 1:2 for more discussion.) |
| **#576**<br>**Chosen Generation**<br><br>Chosen generation–KJV<br>Chosen race–NASB<br>Chosen people–NIV<br>**Chosen generation–NKJV**<br>Chosen people–NLT<br><br>**POSB REFERENCE**<br>(1 Pt.2:9)<br>Note 1, point 1 | γένος ἐκλεκτόν = *genos eklekton*<br>Pronunciation: [ghen'-os ek-lek-ton']<br>Parsing *genos* (part of speech): noun<br>    Case—nominative<br>    Gender—neuter<br>    Number—singular<br>    Stem or root—from γένος, ους<br>Parsing *eklekton* (part of speech): adjective<br>    Case—nominative<br>    Gender—neuter<br>    Number—singular<br>    Stem or root—from ἐκλεκτός, ή, όν<br>Concordance References:<br>  ⇒ Strong's #1085 genos + 1588 eklektos<br>  ⇒ NIV #1169 genos [people] + 1723 eklektos [chosen]<br>  ⇒ NASB #1085 genos + 1588 eklektos<br><br>**1 Peter 2:9**<br>But ye *are* a **chosen generation**, a royal priesthood, | Chosen people; chosen generation; chosen race; chosen family; chosen nation; chosen descendants.<br><br>**Practical Application**<br>The Greek words actually mean a *chosen or elect race*. Peter takes the term from the Old Testament where God stated the same thing about Israel. It means those who are the recipients of the eternal, saving, atoning, grace of God.<br><br>*My people, My chosen. This people I have formed for Myself (Isaiah 43:20-21)—*[NKJV]<br><br>The idea is that of a new race of people, a new species that differs entirely from the other races upon earth. This is a shocking statement to some |

# PRACTICAL WORD STUDIES
## in the NEW TESTAMENT

| ENGLISH WORD | GREEK WORD AND VERSE | THE WORD MEANS... |
|---|---|---|
| | an holy nation, a peculiar people; that ye should shew forth the praises of him who hath called you out of darkness into his marvellous light: [KJV]<br><br>But you are A **CHOSEN RACE**, A royal PRIESTHOOD, A HOLY NATION, A PEOPLE FOR *God's* OWN POSSESSION, that you may proclaim the excellencies of Him who has called you out of darkness into His marvelous light; [NASB]<br><br>But you are a **chosen people**, a royal priesthood, a holy nation, a people belonging to God, that you may declare the praises of him who called you out of darkness into his wonderful light. [NIV]<br><br>But you *are* a **chosen generation**, a royal priesthood, a holy nation, His own special people, that you may proclaim the praises of Him who called you out of darkness into His marvelous light; [NKJV]<br><br>But you are not like that, for you are a **chosen people**. You are a kingdom of priests, God's holy nation, his very own possession. This is so you can show others the goodness of God, for he called you out of the darkness into his wonderful light. [NLT]<br><br>ὑμεῖς δὲ **γένος ἐκλεκτόν**, βασίλειον ἱεράτευμα, ἔθνος ἅγιον, λαὸς εἰς περιποίησιν, ὅπως τὰς ἀρετὰς ἐξαγγείλητε τοῦ ἐκ σκότους ὑμᾶς καλέσαντος εἰς τὸ θαυμαστὸν αὐτοῦ φῶς· [GNS]<br><br>Ὑμεῖς δὲ **γένος ἐκλεκτόν**, βασίλειον ἱεράτευμα, ἔθνος ἅγιον, λαὸς εἰς περιποίησιν, ὅπως τὰς ἀρετὰς ἐξαγγείλητε τοῦ ἐκ σκότους ὑμᾶς καλέσαντος εἰς τὸ θαυμαστὸν αὐτοῦ φῶς· [GNT] | people; nevertheless, it is exactly what the Word of God claims. God is actually creating a new race of people upon earth. How? How can it be that believers from China, Russia, Asia, Africa, India, Europe, the Americas, the Islands, Canada, and all the other nations of the world form a new race of people? By the Spirit of God. The Spirit of God is changing people inwardly, not outwardly. He is not changing facial and skin features. These mean little; they are only superficial differences that change, age, perish, die, and decay ever so rapidly. God is changing people within their hearts and minds and lives, changing them where it really matters. God is implanting His divine nature within believers. When a person believes in Jesus Christ, God's divine nature is immediately implanted into his heart and life. |
| **#577**<br>**Chosen Ones**<br><br>Elect–KJV<br>Elect–NASB<br>Elect–NIV<br>Elect–NKJV<br>**Chosen ones–NLT**<br><br>**POSB REFERENCE**<br>(Mt.24:31)<br>Note 6 | ἐκλεκτούς = *eklektous*<br>Pronunciation: [ek-lek-toos']<br>Parsing (part of speech): pronominal adjective<br>    Case—accusative<br>    Gender—masculine<br>    Number—plural<br>    Stem or root—from ἐκλεκτός, ή, όν<br>Concordance References:<br>  ⇒ Strong's #1588 eklektos<br>  ⇒ NIV #1723 eklektos<br>  ⇒ NASB #1588 eklektos<br><br>**Matthew 24:31**<br>And he shall send his angels with a great sound of a trumpet, and they shall gather together his **elect** from the four winds, from one end of heaven to the other. [KJV]<br>"And He will send forth His angels with A GREAT TRUMPET and THEY WILL GATHER TOGETHER His **elect** from the four winds, from one end of the sky to the other. [NASB]<br>And he will send his angels with a loud trumpet call, and they will gather his **elect** from the four winds, from one end of the heavens to the other. [NIV]<br>And He will send His angels with a great sound of a trumpet, and they will gather together His **elect** from the four winds, from one end of heaven to the other. [NKJV]<br>And he will send forth his angels with the sound of a mighty trumpet blast, and they will gather together his **chosen ones** from the farthest ends of the earth and heaven. [NLT]<br>καὶ ἀποστελεῖ τοὺς ἀγγέλους αὐτοῦ μετὰ σάλπιγγος φωνῆς μεγάλης, καὶ ἐπισυνάξουσι τοὺς **ἐκλεκτοὺς** αὐτοῦ ἐκ τῶν τεσσάρων ἀνέμων ἀπ' ἄκρων οὐρανῶν ἕως ἄκρων αὐτῶν. [GNS]<br>καὶ ἀποστελεῖ τοὺς ἀγγέλους αὐτοῦ μετὰ σάλπιγγος μεγάλης, καὶ ἐπισυνάξουσιν τοὺς **ἐκλεκτοὺς** αὐτοῦ ἐκ τῶν τεσσάρων ἀνέμων ἀπ' ἄκρων οὐρανῶν ἕως [τῶν] ἄκρων αὐτῶν. [GNT] | To be chosen; to be elected; the chosen ones; to be selected; those who are the recipients of the eternal, saving, atoning grace of God.<br><br>**Practical Application**<br>Who are the chosen ones?<br>⇒ They are the people who cry—pray, converse, share with God—day and night (Luke 18:7).<br>⇒ They are the people who are justified by God (Romans 8:33).<br>⇒ They are the people who are "holy and loved," who "clothe [them]selves with tenderhearted mercy, kindness, humility, gentleness, and patience." (Col.3:12)—[NLT] |
| **#578**<br>**Chosen People** | γένος ἐκλεκτόν = *genos eklekton*<br>Pronunciation: [ghen'-os ek-lek-ton']<br>Parsing *genos* (part of speech): noun<br>    Case—nominative | Chosen people; chosen generation; chosen race; chosen family; chosen nation; chosen descendants. |

# PRACTICAL WORD STUDIES
## in the NEW TESTAMENT

| ENGLISH WORD | GREEK WORD AND VERSE | THE WORD MEANS... |
|---|---|---|
| Chosen generation–KJV<br>Chosen race–NASB<br>**Chosen people–NIV**<br>Chosen generation–NKJV<br>**Chosen people–NLT**<br><br>**POSB REFERENCE**<br>(1 Pt.2:9)<br>Note 1, point 1 | Gender—neuter<br>Number—singular<br>Stem or root—from γένος, ους<br>Parsing *eklekton* (part of speech): adjective<br>Case—nominative<br>Gender—neuter<br>Number—singular<br>Stem or root—from ἐκλεκτός, ή, όν<br>Concordance References:<br>⇒ Strong's #1085 genos + 1588 eklektos<br>⇒ NIV #1169 genos [people] + 1723 eklektos [chosen]<br>⇒ NASB #1085 genos + 1588 eklektos<br><br>**1 Peter 2:9**<br>But ye *are* a **chosen generation**, a royal priesthood, an holy nation, a peculiar people; that ye should shew forth the praises of him who hath called you out of darkness into his marvellous light: [KJV]<br><br>But you are A **CHOSEN RACE**, A royal PRIESTHOOD, A HOLY NATION, A PEOPLE FOR *God's* OWN POSSESSION, that you may proclaim the excellencies of Him who has called you out of darkness into His marvelous light; [NASB]<br><br>But you are a **chosen people**, a royal priesthood, a holy nation, a people belonging to God, that you may declare the praises of him who called you out of darkness into his wonderful light. [NIV]<br><br>But you *are* a **chosen generation**, a royal priesthood, a holy nation, His own special people, that you may proclaim the praises of Him who called you out of darkness into His marvelous light; [NKJV]<br><br>But you are not like that, for you are a **chosen people**. You are a kingdom of priests, God's holy nation, his very own possession. This is so you can show others the goodness of God, for he called you out of the darkness into his wonderful light. [NLT]<br><br>ὑμεῖς δὲ **γένος ἐκλεκτόν**, βασίλειον ἱεράτευμα, ἔθνος ἅγιον, λαὸς εἰς περιποίησιν, ὅπως τὰς ἀρετὰς ἐξαγγείλητε τοῦ ἐκ σκότους ὑμᾶς καλέσαντος εἰς τὸ θαυμαστὸν αὐτοῦ φῶς· [GNS]<br><br>Ὑμεῖς δὲ **γένος ἐκλεκτόν**, βασίλειον ἱεράτευμα, ἔθνος ἅγιον, λαὸς εἰς περιποίησιν, ὅπως τὰς ἀρετὰς ἐξαγγείλητε τοῦ ἐκ σκότους ὑμᾶς καλέσαντος εἰς τὸ θαυμαστὸν αὐτοῦ φῶς· [GNT] | **Practical Application**<br>The Greek words actually mean a *chosen or elect race*. Peter takes the term from the Old Testament where God stated the same thing about Israel. It means those who are the recipients of the eternal, saving, atoning, grace of God.<br><br>*"My people, my chosen. This people have I formed for myself"* (Isaiah 43:20-21)—[NIV]<br><br>The idea is that of a new race of people, a new species that differs entirely from the other races upon earth. This is a shocking statement to some people; nevertheless, it is exactly what the Word of God claims. God is actually creating a new race of people upon earth. How? How can it be that believers from China, Russia, Asia, Africa, India, Europe, the Americas, the Islands, Canada, and all the other nations of the world form a new race of people? By the Spirit of God. The Spirit of God is changing people inwardly, not outwardly. He is not changing facial and skin features. These mean little; they are only superficial differences that change, age, perish, die, and decay ever so rapidly. God is changing people within their hearts and minds and lives, changing them where it really matters. God is implanting His divine nature within believers. When a person believes in Jesus Christ, God's divine nature is immediately implanted into his heart and life. |
| **#579**<br>**Chosen Race**<br><br>Chosen generation–KJV<br>**Chosen race–NASB**<br>Chosen people–NIV<br>Chosen generation–NKJV<br>Chosen people–NLT<br><br>**POSB REFERENCE**<br>(1 Pt.2:9)<br>Note 1, point 1 | **γένος ἐκλεκτόν** = genos eklekton<br>Pronunciation: [ghen'-os ek-lek-ton']<br>Parsing *genos* (part of speech): noun<br>Case—nominative<br>Gender—neuter<br>Number—singular<br>Stem or root—from γένος, ους<br>Parsing *eklekton* (part of speech): adjective<br>Case—nominative<br>Gender—neuter<br>Number—singular<br>Stem or root—from ἐκλεκτός, ή, όν<br>Concordance References:<br>⇒ Strong's #1085 genos + 1588 eklektos<br>⇒ NIV #1169 genos [people] + 1723 eklektos [chosen]<br>⇒ NASB #1085 genos + 1588 eklektos<br><br>**1 Peter 2:9**<br>But ye *are* a **chosen generation**, a royal priesthood, an holy nation, a peculiar people; that ye should shew forth the praises of him who hath called you out of darkness into his marvellous light: [KJV]<br><br>But you are A **CHOSEN RACE**, A royal PRIESTHOOD, A HOLY NATION, A PEOPLE FOR *God's* OWN POSSESSION, that you may proclaim the excellencies of Him who has called you out of darkness into His marvelous light; [NASB] | Chosen people; chosen generation; chosen race; chosen family; chosen nation; chosen descendants.<br><br>**Practical Application**<br>The Greek words actually mean a *chosen or elect race*. Peter takes the term from the Old Testament where God stated the same thing about Israel. It means those who are the recipients of the eternal, saving, atoning, grace of God.<br><br>*My chosen people. "The people whom I formed for Myself,"* (Isaiah 43:20-21)—[NASB]<br><br>The idea is that of a new race of people, a new species that differs entirely from the other races upon earth. (See above for more application). |

# PRACTICAL WORD STUDIES
## in the NEW TESTAMENT

| ENGLISH WORD | GREEK WORD AND VERSE | THE WORD MEANS... |
|---|---|---|
| | But you are a **chosen people**, a royal priesthood, a holy nation, a people belonging to God, that you may declare the praises of him who called you out of darkness into his wonderful light. [NIV]<br><br>But you *are* a **chosen generation**, a royal priesthood, a holy nation, His own special people, that you may proclaim the praises of Him who called you out of darkness into His marvelous light; [NKJV]<br><br>But you are not like that, for you are a **chosen people**. You are a kingdom of priests, God's holy nation, his very own possession. This is so you can show others the goodness of God, for he called you out of the darkness into his wonderful light. [NLT]<br><br>ὑμεῖς δὲ **γένος ἐκλεκτόν**, βασίλειον ἱεράτευμα, ἔθνος ἅγιον, λαὸς εἰς περιποίησιν, ὅπως τὰς ἀρετὰς ἐξαγγείλητε τοῦ ἐκ σκότους ὑμᾶς καλέσαντος εἰς τὸ θαυμαστὸν αὐτοῦ φῶς· [GNS]<br><br>Ὑμεῖς δὲ **γένος ἐκλεκτόν**, βασίλειον ἱεράτευμα, ἔθνος ἅγιον, λαὸς εἰς περιποίησιν, ὅπως τὰς ἀρετὰς ἐξαγγείλητε τοῦ ἐκ σκότους ὑμᾶς καλέσαντος εἰς τὸ θαυμαστὸν αὐτοῦ φῶς· [GNT] | |
| **#580**<br>**Chosen, Already, Before, Beforehand**<br><br>Chosen before–KJV<br>Chosen beforehand–NASB<br>Already chosen–NIV<br>Chosen before–NKJV<br>Chosen beforehand–NLT<br><br>**POSB REFERENCE**<br>(Acts 10:40-41; esp. v.41)<br>Note 6, point 2 | προκεχειροτονημένοις = *prokecheirotonëmenois*<br>Pronunciation: [pro-kech-ee-rot-on-eh'-men-ois]<br>Parsing (part of speech): verb<br>    Mood—participle<br>    Tense—perfect<br>    Voice—passive<br>    Case—dative<br>    Gender—masculine<br>    Number—plural<br>    Stem or root—from προχειροτονέω<br>Concordance References:<br>  ⇒ Strong's #4401 procheirotoneō<br>  ⇒ NIV #4742 procheirotoneō<br>  ⇒ NASB #4401 procheirotoneō<br><br>**Acts 10:41**<br>Not to all the people, but unto witnesses **chosen before** of God, *even* to us, who did eat and drink with him after he rose from the dead. [KJV]<br><br>not to all the people, but to witnesses who were **chosen beforehand** by God, *that is*, to us, who ate and drank with Him after He arose from the dead. [NASB]<br><br>He was not seen by all the people, but by witnesses whom God had **already chosen**—by us who ate and drank with him after he rose from the dead. [NIV]<br><br>Not to all the people, but to witnesses **chosen before** by God, *even* to us who ate and drank with Him after He arose from the dead. [NKJV]<br><br>not to the general public, but to us whom God had **chosen beforehand** to be his witnesses. We were those who ate and drank with him after he rose from the dead. [NLT]<br><br>οὐ παντὶ τῷ λαῷ, ἀλλὰ μάρτυσι τοῖς **προκεχειροτονημένοις** ὑπὸ τοῦ θεοῦ, ἡμῖν, οἵτινες συνεφάγομεν καὶ συνεπίομεν αὐτῷ μετὰ τὸ ἀναστῆναι αὐτὸν ἐκ νεκρῶν. [GNS]<br><br>οὐ παντὶ τῷ λαῷ ἀλλὰ μάρτυσιν τοῖς **προκεχειροτονημένοις** ὑπὸ τοῦ θεοῦ, ἡμῖν, οἵτινες συνεφάγομεν καὶ συνεπίομεν αὐτῷ μετὰ τὸ ἀναστῆναι αὐτὸν ἐκ νεκρῶν· [GNT] | To choose in advance; already chosen; chosen beforehand; chosen before. It means to be pointed out, to be designated, to be appointed (cp. John 17:6).<br><br>**Practical Application**<br>Before Christ ever arose, God chose some people to be witnesses of His Son's resurrection. They were chosen for the very purpose of proclaiming the resurrection to a world of dying men. |
| **#581**<br>**Christ**<br><br>Christ–KJV<br>Christ–NASB<br>Christ–NIV<br>Christ–NKJV<br>Messiah–NLT | Χριστοῦ = *Christou*<br>Pronunciation: [khris-too']<br>Parsing (part of speech): noun<br>    Case—genitive<br>    Gender—masculine<br>    Number—singular<br>    Stem or root—from Χριστός, οῦ<br>Concordance References:<br>  ⇒ Strong's #5547 Christos<br>  ⇒ NIV #5986 Christos<br>  ⇒ NASB #5547 Christos | The Christ; the Messiah; the Anointed One.<br><br>**Practical Application**<br>The words "Christ" (*Christou*) and "Messiah" are the same word. *Messiah* is the Hebrew word and *Christ* is the Greek word. Both words refer to the same person and mean the same thing: the *Anointed One*. The Messiah is the *Anointed One of God*. Matthew says Jesus "is called Christ" (Matthew 1:16); that is, He is |

# PRACTICAL WORD STUDIES
## in the NEW TESTAMENT

| ENGLISH WORD | GREEK WORD AND VERSE | THE WORD MEANS... |
|---|---|---|
| **POSB REFERENCE**<br>(Mk.1:1)<br>*Deeper Study #2*<br><br>See also POSB REF:<br>(Jn.1:20)<br>*Deeper Study #2*<br>(Mt.22:41-42; esp. v.42)<br>Note 2, point 1<br>(Mk.12:35)<br>Note 2, point 1 | **Mark 1:1**<br>The beginning of the gospel of Jesus **Christ**, the Son of God; [KJV]<br>The beginning of the gospel of Jesus **Christ**, the Son of God. [NASB]<br>The beginning of the gospel about Jesus **Christ**, the Son of God. [NIV]<br>The beginning of the gospel of Jesus **Christ**, the Son of God. [NKJV]<br>Here begins the Good News about Jesus the **Messiah**, the Son of God. [NLT]<br>Ἀρχη τοῦ εὐαγγελίου Ἰησοῦ **Χριστοῦ** υἱοῦ Θεοῦ. [GNS]<br>Ἀρχὴ τοῦ εὐαγγελίου Ἰησοῦ **Χριστοῦ** [υἱοῦ θεοῦ]. [GNT] | recognized as the *Anointed One of God*, the Messiah Himself.<br>In the day of Jesus Christ, people feverishly panted for the coming of the long promised Messiah. The weight of life was harsh, hard, and impoverished. Under the Romans the people felt that God could not wait much longer to fulfill His promise. Such longings for deliverance left the people gullible. Many arose who claimed to be the Messiah and led the gullible followers into rebellion against the Roman State. The insurrectionist Barabbas, who was set free in the place of Jesus at Jesus' trial, is an example (Mark 15:6f). (See POSB notes—Matthew 1:1; POSB *Deeper Study #2*—Matthew 3:11; POSB notes—Matthew 11:1-6; POSB note—Matthew 11:2-3; POSB *Deeper Study #1*—Matthew 11:5; POSB *Deeper Study #2*—Matthew 11:6; POSB note—Luke 7:21-23.)<br>The Messiah was thought to be several things. (See POSB note, Davidic Prophecies—Luke 3:24-31.)<br>1. Nationally, He was to be the leader from David's line who would free the Jewish state as an independent nation and lead it to be the greatest nation the world had ever known.<br>2. Militarily, He was to be a great military leader who would lead Jewish armies victoriously over all the world.<br>3. Religiously, He was to be a supernatural figure straight from God who would bring righteousness over all the earth.<br>4. Personally, He was to be the One who would bring peace to the whole world.<br>Jesus Christ accepted the title of Messiah on three different occasions (Matthew 16:17; Mark 14:61; John 4:26). The name "Jesus" shows Him to be man. The name "Christ" shows Him to be God's Anointed One, God's very own Son. *Christ* is Jesus' official title. It identifies Him officially as *Prophet* (Deut. 18:15-19), *Priest* (Psalm 110:4), and *King* (2 Samuel 7:12-13). These three officials were always anointed with oil, a symbol of the Holy Spirit who was to perfectly anoint the Christ, the Messiah (Matthew 3:16; Mark 1:10-11; Luke 3:21-22; John 1:32-33). (See POSB note—Luke 3:32-38 for more discussion, verses and fulfillment.) |
| **#582**<br>**Christ**<br><br>Christ–KJV<br>Christ–NASB<br>Christ–NIV<br>Christ–NKJV<br>Christ–NLT<br><br>**POSB REFERENCE**<br>(Jas 1:1)<br>Note 1 | Χριστοῦ = *Christou*<br>Pronunciation: [khris-too']<br>Parsing (part of speech): noun<br>    Case—genitive<br>    Gender—masculine<br>    Number—singular<br>    Stem or root—from Χριστός, οῦ<br>Concordance References:<br>  ⇒ Strong's #5547 Christos<br>  ⇒ NIV #5986 Christos<br>  ⇒ NASB #5547 Christos<br><br>**James 1:1**<br>James, a servant of God and of the Lord Jesus **Christ**, to the twelve tribes which are scattered abroad, greeting. [KJV]<br>James, a bond-servant of God and of the Lord Jesus **Christ**, to the twelve tribes who are dispersed abroad, greetings. [NASB]<br>James, a servant of God and of the Lord Jesus **Christ**, | Christ; the Anointed One; the Messiah.<br><br>**Practical Application**<br>By Christ (*Christou*), James meant the Messiah, the Savior whom God had promised down through the centuries.<br>This is striking and touching, for James had lived as a brother to Jesus for years. Day in and day out, hour by hour, month by month, and year by year James had played, eaten, worked, slept, and gone to school with Jesus. He had roamed the surrounding hills with Jesus as a boy and seen Him play with other children and relate to the neighbors and adults of their neighborhood. James had seen how his brother received and responded to adult instruction, teaching, and supervision. He had also probably seen Jesus take over the head of the household when their father, Joseph, had died. |

# PRACTICAL WORD STUDIES
## in the NEW TESTAMENT

| ENGLISH WORD | GREEK WORD AND VERSE | THE WORD MEANS... |
|---|---|---|
| | To the twelve tribes scattered among the nations: Greetings. [NIV]<br>James, a bondservant of God and of the Lord Jesus **Christ**, To the twelve tribes which are scattered abroad: Greetings. [NKJV]<br>This letter is from James, a slave of God and of the Lord Jesus **Christ**. It is written to Jewish Christians scattered among the nations. Greetings! [NLT]<br>Ἰάκωβος, Θεοῦ καὶ Κυρίου Ἰησοῦ **Χριστοῦ** δοῦλος, ταῖς δώδεκα φυλαῖς ταῖς ἐν τῇ διασπορᾷ, χαίρειν. [GNS]<br>Ἰάκωβος θεοῦ καὶ κυρίου Ἰησοῦ **Χριστοῦ** δοῦλος ταῖς δώδεκα φυλαῖς ταῖς ἐν τῇ διασπορᾷ χαίρειν. [GNT] | Just imagine the daily, monthly, and yearly contact James had with Jesus, and still James calls Him...<br>• the Lord Jesus Christ, the Lord and Christ of the Old Testament Scriptures.<br>• the Lord of glory (James 2:1).<br>• the Lord who is coming again (James 5:7).<br>• the Lord whose coming draws near (James 5:8).<br>The point is this: James is saying that the Lord Jesus Christ is God, the very Son of God who is equal to God the Father. He is saying that his brother, Jesus the carpenter from Nazareth, is of the very nature and character of God, of the very being and essence of God. |
| #583<br>**Christ Is The One Through**<br><br>By him–KJV<br>By Him–NASB<br>By him–NIV<br>By Him–NKJV<br>**Christ is the one through–NLT**<br><br>**POSB REFERENCE**<br>(Col.1:16)<br>Note 1, point 1 | ἐν αὐτῷ = en autō<br>Pronunciation: [en ow'-tow']<br>Parsing autō (part of speech): pronoun<br>  Case—dative<br>  Gender—masculine<br>  Person—3rd person<br>  Number—singular<br>  Stem or root—from αὐτός, ή, ό<br>Concordance References:<br>⇒ Strong's #1722 en + 846 autos<br>⇒ NIV #1877 en [by] + 899 autos [him]<br>⇒ NASB #1722 en + 846 autos<br><br>**Col. 1:16**<br>For **by him** were all things created, that are in heaven, and that are in earth, visible and invisible, whether they be thrones, or dominions, or principalities, or powers: all things were created by him, and for him: [KJV]<br>For **by Him** all things were created, both in the heavens and on earth, visible and invisible, whether thrones or dominions or rulers or authorities—all things have been created by Him and for Him. [NASB]<br>For **by him** all things were created: things in heaven and on earth, visible and invisible, whether thrones or powers or rulers or authorities; all things were created by him and for him. [NIV]<br>For **by Him** all things were created that are in heaven and that are on earth, visible and invisible, whether thrones or dominions or principalities or powers. All things were created through Him and for Him. [NKJV]<br>**Christ is the one through** whom God created everything in heaven and earth. He made the things we can see and the things we can't see—kings, kingdoms, rulers, and authorities. Everything has been created through him and for him. [NLT]<br>ὅτι **ἐν αὐτῷ** ἐκτίσθη τὰ πάντα, τὰ ἐν τοῖς οὐρανοῖς καὶ τὰ ἐπὶ τῆς γῆς, τὰ ὁρατὰ καὶ τὰ ἀόρατα, εἴτε θρόνοι, εἴτε κυριότητες, εἴτε ἀρχαί, εἴτε ἐξουσίαι· τὰ πάντα δι' αὐτοῦ καὶ εἰς αὐτὸν ἔκτισται· [GNS]<br>ὅτι **ἐν αὐτῷ** ἐκτίσθη τὰ πάντα ἐν τοῖς οὐρανοῖς καὶ ἐπὶ τῆς γῆς, τὰ ὁρατὰ καὶ τὰ ἀόρατα, εἴτε θρόνοι εἴτε κυριότητες εἴτε ἀρχαί εἴτε ἐξουσίαι· τὰ πάντα δι' αὐτοῦ καὶ εἰς αὐτὸν ἔκτισται· [GNT] | By Him; Christ is the One through. The words "Christ is the one through" (*en autō*) mean *in Him*; that is, creation took place *in* Christ, *within* His very being.<br><br>**Practical Application**<br>⇒ The heart of Christ desired the world.<br>⇒ The mind of Christ planned the world.<br>⇒ The will of Christ destined the world.<br>⇒ The Word of Christ created the world.<br>⇒ The creation of the world took place within Christ, within His personality and being. The world was born within Him.<br>⇒ It was the *love of Christ* that moved His heart to create the world.<br>⇒ It was the *knowledge of Christ* that aroused His mind to plan the world.<br>⇒ It was the *riches of His grace* that stirred Him to will the world.<br>⇒ It was the *power of His Word* that energized or brought the world into existence.<br>The universe exists because of Christ and because of Him alone. The idea for the universe was born in Him, and the actual creation of the universe took place by His own energy and effort. Jesus Christ Himself brought the universe into existence. |
| #584<br>**Christian Teaching**<br><br>Ordinances–KJV<br>Traditions–NASB<br>Teachings–NIV<br>Traditions–NKJV<br>**Christian teaching– NLT** | παραδόσεις = paradoseis<br>Pronunciation: [par-ad'-os-ees]<br>Parsing (part of speech): noun<br>  Case—accusative<br>  Gender—feminine<br>  Number—plural<br>  Stem or root—from παράδοσις, εως<br>Concordance References:<br>⇒ Strong's #3862 paradosis<br>⇒ NIV #4142 paradosis<br>⇒ NASB #3862 paradosis | Teachings, traditions or instructions that are passed down by word of mouth from generation to generation.<br><br>**Practical Application**<br>This is important to see, for this passage is dealing...<br>• with traditions.<br>• with unwritten laws of behavior.<br>• with customs.<br>• with local practice. |

# PRACTICAL WORD STUDIES
## in the NEW TESTAMENT

| ENGLISH WORD | GREEK WORD AND VERSE | THE WORD MEANS... |
|---|---|---|
| **POSB REFERENCE**<br>(1 Cor.11:2)<br>Note 1<br><br>See also POSB REF:<br>(2 Thes.2:15)<br>Note 4 | **1 Cor. 11:2**<br>Now I praise you, brethren, that ye remember me in all things, and keep the **ordinances**, as I delivered *them* to you. [KJV]<br>Now I praise you because you remember me in everything, and hold firmly to the **traditions**, just as I delivered them to you. [NASB]<br>I praise you for remembering me in everything and for holding to the **teachings**, just as I passed them on to you. [NIV]<br>Now I praise you, brethren, that you remember me in all things and keep the **traditions** just as I delivered *them* to you. [NKJV]<br>I am so glad, dear friends, that you always keep me in your thoughts and you are following the **Christian teaching** I passed on to you. [NLT]<br>Ἐπαινῶ δὲ ὑμᾶς, ἀδελφοί, ὅτι πάντα μου μέμνησθε καὶ καθὼς παρέδωκα ὑμῖν τὰς **παραδόσεις** κατέχετε. [GNS]<br>Ἐπαινῶ δὲ ὑμᾶς ὅτι πάντα μου μέμνησθε καί, καθὼς παρέδωκα ὑμῖν, τὰς **παραδόσεις** κατέχετε. [GNT] | • with preferences of a particular people or body.<br>• with long-established patterns of a people or group.<br><br>Leon Morris quotes J.B. Lightfoot: "The prominent idea of *paradoseis* [tradition]...is that of an authority external to the teacher himself." Leon Morris himself says:<br><br>*This is another way of putting the truth...that the gospel is not of human origin, and the preacher is not at liberty to substitute his own thoughts for that which he has received* (The Epistles of Paul to the Thessalonians. "Tyndale New Testament Commentaries," p.138). |
| **#585**<br>**Christians In Jerusalem**<br><br>Saints–KJV<br>Saints–NASB<br>Saints–NIV<br>Saints–NKJV<br>Christians in Jerusalem–NLT<br><br>**POSB REFERENCE**<br>(2 Cor.9:1-2; esp. v.1)<br>Note 1 | ἁγίους = *hagious*<br>Pronunciation: [hag'-ee-oos]<br>Parsing (part of speech): pronominal adjective<br>    Case—accusative<br>    Gender—masculine<br>    Number—plural<br>    Stem or root—from ἅγιος, α, ον<br>Concordance References:<br>⇒ Strong's #40 hagios<br>⇒ NIV #41 hagios<br>⇒ NASB #40 hagios<br><br>**2 Cor. 9:1**<br>For as touching the ministering to the **saints**, it is superfluous for me to write to you: [KJV]<br>For it is superfluous for me to write to you about this ministry to the **saints**; [NASB]<br>There is no need for me to write to you about this service to the **saints**. [NIV]<br>Now concerning the ministering to the **saints**, it is superfluous for me to write to you; [NKJV]<br>I really don't need to write to you about this gift for the **Christians in Jerusalem**. [NLT]<br>Περὶ μὲν γὰρ τῆς διακονίας τῆς εἰς τοὺς **ἁγίους** περισσόν μοί ἐστι τὸ γράφειν ὑμῖν· [GNS]<br>Περὶ μὲν γὰρ τῆς διακονίας τῆς εἰς τοὺς **ἁγίους** περισσόν μοί ἐστιν τὸ γράφειν ὑμῖν· [GNT] | Saints, consecrated, pure, holy, sacred, upright; those who are set apart and devoted to God. It is a term referring to genuine believers.<br><br>**Practical Application**<br>The point is striking. Some fellow believers were in desperate need. The churches in Judea were poor and desperately needed help; therefore the Corinthians were expected to help them. In fact, the expectation was so strong there was little need to even say anything about it. |
| **#586**<br>**Church**<br><br>Church–KJV<br>Church–NASB<br>Church–NIV<br>Church–NKJV<br>Church–NLT<br><br>**POSB REFERENCE**<br>(Mt.16:18)<br>*Deeper Study* #1<br><br>See also POSB REF:<br>(1 Tim.3:15)<br>Note 2, point 2 | ἐκκλησίαν = *ekklēsian*<br>Pronunciation: [ek-klay-see'-ahn]<br>Parsing (part of speech): noun<br>    Case—accusative<br>    Gender—feminine<br>    Number—singular<br>    Stem or root—from ἐκκλησία, ας<br>Concordance References:<br>⇒ Strong's #1577 ekklēsia<br>⇒ NIV #1711 ekklēsia<br>⇒ NASB #1577 ekklēsia<br><br>**Matthew 16:18**<br>And I say also unto thee, That thou art Peter, and upon this rock I will build my **church**; and the gates of hell shall not prevail against it. [KJV]<br>"And I also say to you that you are Peter, and upon this rock I will build My **church**; and the gates of Hades shall not overpower it. [NASB]<br>And I tell you that you are Peter, and on this rock I will build my **church**, and the gates of Hades will not overcome it. [NIV]<br>And I also say to you that you are Peter, and on this rock I will build My **church**, and the gates of Hades shall | Church; to call out a gathering; an assembly; a congregation.<br><br>**Practical Application**<br>In the Greek there is no spiritual significance ascribed to the word itself, but in the New Testament *ekklēsian* usually refers to the members of a local church or to the church, world wide. What is the difference then between such secular gatherings and the church of God?<br>1. It is God who calls together and gathers His church. His church is the body of people "called out" from the world by Him. They are His body of people, a people sanctified or *set apart* by Him to form the church of the living God.<br>2. God dwells within the very presence of believers when they gather together (see POSB note—1 Cor. 3:16-17).<br>3. The gathering of God meets together for two purposes—worship and mission. God is the object of worship, and His mission becomes |

# PRACTICAL WORD STUDIES
## in the NEW TESTAMENT

| ENGLISH WORD | GREEK WORD AND VERSE | THE WORD MEANS... |
|---|---|---|
| | not prevail against it. [NKJV]<br>Now I say to you that you are Peter, and upon this rock I will build my **church**, and all the powers of hell will not conquer it. [NLT]<br>κἀγὼ δέ σοι λέγω, ὅτι σὺ εἶ πέτρος, καὶ ἐπὶ ταύτῃ τῇ πέτρᾳ οἰκοδομήσω μου τὴν **ἐκκλησίαν**, καὶ πύλαι ᾅδου οὐ κατισχύσουσιν αὐτῆς. [GNS]<br>κἀγὼ δέ σοι λέγω ὅτι σὺ εἶ Πέτρος, καὶ ἐπὶ ταύτῃ τῇ πέτρᾳ οἰκοδομήσω μου τὴν **ἐκκλησίαν** καὶ πύλαι ᾅδου οὐ κατισχύσουσιν αὐτῆς. [GNT] | the objective of the church. Therefore, God's church, the local assembly, gathers together to worship and to pool its resources in order to carry out the mission of God Himself. It should be noted that this is the first mention of the church in the New Testament. (See POSB notes—Matthew 16:18; POSB note—Ephes. 2:20; POSB note—Ephes. 4:4-6 for more discussion.) |
| **#587**<br>**Church**<br><br>Church–KJV<br>Congregation–NASB<br>Assembly–NIV<br>Congregation–NKJV<br>Assembly–NLT<br><br>**POSB REFERENCE**<br>(Acts 7:38)<br>*Deeper Study #4* | ἐκκλησίᾳ = ekklēsia<br>Pronunciation: [ek-klay-see'-ah]<br>Parsing (part of speech): noun<br>    Case—dative<br>    Gender—feminine<br>    Number—singular<br>    Stem or root—from ἐκκλησία<br>Concordance References:<br>  ⇒ Strong's #1577 ekklēsia<br>  ⇒ NIV #1711 ekklēsia<br>  ⇒ NASB #1577 ekklēsia<br><br>**Acts 7:38**<br>This is he, that was in the **church** in the wilderness with the angel which spake to him in the mount Sina, and *with* our fathers: who received the lively oracles to give unto us: [KJV]<br>"This is the one who was in the **congregation** in the wilderness together with the angel who was speaking to him on Mount Sinai, and *who was* with our fathers; and he received living oracles to pass on to you. NASB]<br>He was in the **assembly** in the desert, with the angel who spoke to him on Mount Sinai, and with our fathers; and he received living words to pass on to us. [NIV]<br>This is he who was in the **congregation** in the wilderness with the Angel who spoke to him on Mount Sinai, and *with* our fathers, the one who received the living oracles to give to us, [NKJV]<br>Moses was with the **assembly** of God's people in the wilderness. He was the mediator between the people of Israel and the angel who gave him life-giving words on Mount Sinai to pass on to us. [NLT]<br>οὗτός ἐστιν ὁ γενόμενος ἐν τῇ **ἐκκλησίᾳ** ἐν τῇ ἐρήμῳ, μετὰ τοῦ ἀγγέλου τοῦ λαλοῦντος αὐτῷ ἐν τῷ ὄρει Σινᾶ καὶ τῶν πατέρων ἡμῶν· ὃς ἐδέξατο λόγια ζῶντα δοῦναι ἡμῖν· [GNS]<br>οὗτός ἐστιν ὁ γενόμενος ἐν τῇ **ἐκκλησίᾳ** ἐν τῇ ἐρήμῳ μετὰ τοῦ ἀγγέλου τοῦ λαλοῦντος αὐτῷ ἐν τῷ ὄρει Σινᾶ καὶ τῶν πατέρων ἡμῶν, ὃς ἐδέξατο λόγια ζῶντα δοῦναι ἡμῖν, [GNT] | Assembly, church, congregation, gathering.<br><br>**Practical Application**<br>Israel was God's church, God's assembly, God's congregation in the wilderness. Israel was a type of the church in the world. |
| **#588**<br>**Church, The**<br><br>The church–KJV<br>The church–NASB<br>The church–NIV<br>The church–NKJV<br>The church–NLT<br><br>**POSB REFERENCE**<br>(Rom.16:1-2; esp. v.1)<br>Note 1 | τῆς ἐκκλησίας = tēs ekklēsias<br>Pronunciation: [tays ek-klay-see'-ahs]<br>Parsing *ekklēsias* (part of speech): noun<br>    Case—genitive<br>    Gender—feminine<br>    Number—singular<br>    Stem or root—from ἐκκλησία, ας<br>Concordance References:<br>  ⇒ Strong's #3588 ho + 1577 ekklēsia<br>  ⇒ NIV #3836 ho [the] + 1711 ekklēsia [church]<br>  ⇒ NASB #3588 ho + 1577 ekklēsia<br><br>**Romans 16:1**<br>I commend unto you Phebe our sister, which is a servant of **the church** which is at Cenchrea: [KJV]<br>I commend to you our sister Phoebe, who is a servant of **the church** which is at Cenchrea; [NASB]<br>I commend to you our sister Phoebe, a servant of **the church** in Cenchrea. [NIV]<br>I commend to you Phoebe our sister, who is a servant of **the church** in Cenchrea, [NKJV] | The church, congregation, gathering, assembly.<br><br>**Practical Application**<br>The words "of the church" (*tēs ekklēsias*) modify servant or deaconess. Phoebe was a servant or a deaconess of the church which is at Cenchrea. Paul is not saying she is a servant of the Lord to all of God's people in general. She was, of course, just as all believers are. But this is not what Paul is saying. He is very clear about the matter: she is an official "servant [deaconess] of the church which is at Cenchrea."<br>The separation of the sexes in that day would almost necessitate some official office of women to minister to the women of the church. This would be especially true in the area of ministry where women would be alone, for example, in visiting and caring for the sick and in distribut- |

# PRACTICAL WORD STUDIES
## in the NEW TESTAMENT

| ENGLISH WORD | GREEK WORD AND VERSE | THE WORD MEANS... |
|---|---|---|
| | Our sister Phoebe, a deacon in **the church** in Cenchrea, will be coming to see you soon. [NLT]<br>Συνίστημι δὲ ὑμῖν Φοίβην τὴν ἀδελφὴν ἡμῶν, οὖσαν διάκονον **τῆς ἐκκλησίας** τῆς ἐν Κεγχρεαῖς· [GNS]<br>Συνίστημι δὲ ὑμῖν Φοίβην τὴν ἀδελφὴν ἡμῶν, οὖσαν [καὶ] διάκονον **τῆς ἐκκλησίας** τῆς ἐν Κεγχρεαῖς, [GNT] | ing food and clothing among the needful. |
| **#589**<br>**Circumspectly**<br><br>**Circumspectly**–KJV<br>Careful–NASB<br>Very careful–NIV<br>**Circumspectly**–NKJV<br>Careful–NLT<br><br>**POSB REFERENCE**<br>(Eph.5:15)<br>Note 1 | **ἀκριβῶς** = *akribōs*<br>Pronunciation: [ak-ree-boce']<br>Parsing (part of speech): adjective adverb<br>Stem or root—from ἀκριβῶς<br>Concordance References:<br>⇒ Strong's #199 akribōs<br>⇒ NIV #209 akribōs<br>⇒ NASB #199 akribōs<br><br>**Ephes. 5:15**<br>See then that ye walk **circumspectly**, not as fools, but as wise, [KJV]<br>Therefore be **careful** how you walk, not as unwise men, but as wise, [NASB]<br>Be **very careful**, then, how you live—not as unwise but as wise, [NIV]<br>See then that you walk **circumspectly**, not as fools but as wise, [NKJV]<br>So be **careful** how you live, not as fools but as those who are wise. [NLT]<br>Βλέπετε οὖν **ἀκριβῶς** περιπατεῖτε, μὴ ὡς ἄσοφοι, ἀλλ' ὡς σοφοί, [GNS]<br>Βλέπετε οὖν **ἀκριβῶς** πῶς περιπατεῖτε μὴ ὡς ἄσοφοι ἀλλ' ὡς σοφοί, [GNT] | To be very careful; circumspectly; accurately.<br><br>**Practical Application**<br>Life is a walk, a path that we trod every day. When we arise in the morning, we begin to walk about. God expects us to walk circumspectly, that is, carefully and accurately—exactly as we should. |
| **#590**<br>**Citizens– Citizenship**<br><br>Conversation–KJV<br>**Citizenship**–NASB<br>**Citizenship**–NIV<br>**Citizenship**–NKJV<br>**Citizens**–NLT<br><br>**POSB REFERENCE**<br>(Philip.3:20-21; esp. v.20)<br>Note 1, point 1 | **πολίτευμα** = *politeuma*<br>Pronunciation: [pol-it'-yoo-mah]<br>Parsing (part of speech): noun<br>  Case—nominative<br>  Gender—neuter<br>  Number—singular<br>Stem or root—from πολίτευμα, τος<br>Concordance References:<br>⇒ Strong's #4175 politeuma<br>⇒ NIV #4487 politeuma<br>⇒ NASB #4175 politeuma<br><br>**Philip. 3:20**<br>For our **conversation** is in heaven; from whence also we look for the Saviour, the Lord Jesus Christ: [KJV]<br>For our **citizenship** is in heaven, from which also we eagerly wait for a Savior, the Lord Jesus Christ; [NASB]<br>But our **citizenship** is in heaven. And we eagerly await a Savior from there, the Lord Jesus Christ, [NIV]<br>For our **citizenship** is in heaven, from which we also eagerly wait for the Savior, the Lord Jesus Christ, [NKJV]<br>But we are **citizens** of heaven, where the Lord Jesus Christ lives. And we are eagerly waiting for him to return as our Savior. [NLT]<br>ἡμῶν γὰρ τὸ **πολίτευμα** ἐν οὐρανοῖς ὑπάρχει, ἐξ οὗ καὶ Σωτῆρα ἀπεκδεχόμεθα, Κύριον Ἰησοῦν Χριστόν· [GNS]<br>ἡμῶν γὰρ τὸ **πολίτευμα** ἐν οὐρανοῖς ὑπάρχει, ἐξ οὗ καὶ σωτῆρα ἀπεκδεχόμεθα κύριον Ἰησοῦν Χριστόν, [GNT] | Citizenship; to be a citizen of; to be in the place of citizenship.<br><br>**Practical Application**<br>The believer's life is to be heaven-centered, for his citizenship is in heaven. Remember that Philippi was a Roman colony and its citizens, although in Macedonia, were citizens of Rome. The citizens of Roman colonies lived as Romans: they dressed as Romans, spoke the Roman language, lived by the laws of Rome, engaged in Roman pleasures and social affairs, and worshiped the Roman gods. Despite the fact that they lived in Macedonia, their citizenship was in Rome. (See POSB note, Citizenship, Heavenly—Phil. 1:27 for more discussion; cp. Ephes. 2:6.)<br>The point to see is this: the Philippian believers knew exactly what it meant to live in one place and to be a citizen of another place. They knew exactly what it would mean to live upon the earth and...<br>• to dress as a citizen of heaven and not of the earth.<br>• to speak as a citizen of heaven and not of the earth.<br>• to engage in the pleasures of a citizen of heaven and not of the earth.<br>• to live by the laws of heaven as well as the laws of earth.<br>• to worship the God of heaven and not the religions and gods of this earth. |
| **#591**<br>**Clamor– Clamour**<br><br>**Clamour**–KJV | **κραυγή** = *kraugē*<br>Pronunciation: [krow-gay']<br>Parsing (part of speech): noun<br>  Case—nominative<br>  Gender—feminine<br>  Number—singular<br>Stem or root—from κραυγή, ῆς | Brawling; clamor; harsh words; uproar; angry words. It means insulting, boisterous behavior, and loud talking.<br><br>**Practical Application**<br>What must be the believer's relationship with |

# PRACTICAL WORD STUDIES
## in the NEW TESTAMENT

| ENGLISH WORD | GREEK WORD AND VERSE | THE WORD MEANS... |
|---|---|---|
| **Clamor–NASB**<br>Brawling–NIV<br>**Clamor–NKJV**<br>Harsh words–NLT<br><br>**POSB REFERENCE**<br>(Eph.4:31)<br>Note 6, point 4 | Concordance References:<br>⇒ Strong's #2906 kraugë<br>⇒ NIV #3199 kraugë<br>⇒ NASB #2906 kraugë<br><br>**Ephes. 4:31**<br>Let all bitterness, and wrath, and anger, and **clamour**, and evil speaking, be put away from you, with all malice: [KJV]<br>Let all bitterness and wrath and anger and **clamor** and slander be put away from you, along with all malice. [NASB]<br>Get rid of all bitterness, rage and anger, **brawling** and slander, along with every form of malice. [NIV]<br>Let all bitterness, wrath, anger, **clamor**, and evil speaking be put away from you, with all malice. [NKJV]<br>Get rid of all bitterness, rage, anger, **harsh words**, and slander, as well as all types of malicious behavior. [NLT]<br>πᾶσα πικρία καὶ θυμὸς καὶ ὀργὴ καὶ **κραυγὴ** καὶ βλασφημία ἀρθήτω ἀφ' ὑμῶν, σὺν πάσῃ κακίᾳ· [GNS]<br>πᾶσα πικρία καὶ θυμὸς καὶ ὀργὴ καὶ **κραυγὴ** καὶ βλασφημία ἀρθήτω ἀφ' ὑμῶν σὺν πάσῃ κακίᾳ. [GNT] | clamoring?<br>⇒ He is to get rid of it.<br>⇒ He is to put clamoring behind him.<br>⇒ He is to never give clamoring a place in his life. |
| **#592**<br>**Clean**<br><br>Harmless–KJV<br>Innocent–NASB<br>Pure–NIV<br>Harmless–NKJV<br>Clean–NLT<br><br>**POSB REFERENCE**<br>(Philip.2:15)<br>Note 4, point 2 | ἀκέραιοι = akeraioi<br>Pronunciation: [ak-er'-ah-ee-oy]<br>Parsing (part of speech): adjective<br>    Case—nominative<br>    Gender—masculine<br>    Number—plural<br>    Stem or root—from ἀκέραιος, ον<br>Concordance References:<br>⇒ Strong's #185 akeraios<br>⇒ NIV #193 akeraios<br>⇒ NASB #185 akeraios<br><br>**Philip. 2:15**<br>That ye may be blameless and **harmless**, the sons of God, without rebuke, in the midst of a crooked and perverse nation, among whom ye shine as lights in the world; [KJV]<br>That you may prove yourselves to be blameless and **innocent**, children of God above reproach in the midst of a crooked and perverse generation, among whom you appear as lights in the world, [NASB]<br>So that you may become blameless and **pure**, children of God without fault in a crooked and depraved generation, in which you shine like stars in the universe [NIV]<br>That you may become blameless and **harmless**, children of God without fault in the midst of a crooked and perverse generation, among whom you shine as lights in the world, [NKJV]<br>So that no one can speak a word of blame against you. You are to live **clean**, innocent lives as children of God in a dark world full of crooked and perverse people. Let your lives shine brightly before them. [NLT]<br>ἵνα γένησθε ἄμεμπτοι καὶ **ἀκέραιοι**, τέκνα Θεοῦ ἀμώμητα ἐν μέσῳ γενεᾶς σκολιᾶς καὶ διεστραμμένης, ἐν οἷς φαίνεσθε ὡς φωστῆρες ἐν κόσμῳ, [GNS]<br>ἵνα γένησθε ἄμεμπτοι καὶ **ἀκέραιοι**, τέκνα θεοῦ ἄμωμα μέσον γενεᾶς σκολιᾶς καὶ διεστραμμένης, ἐν οἷς φαίνεσθε ὡς φωστῆρες ἐν κόσμῳ, [GNT] | Pure, harmless, innocent, clean, without guile, unmixed and unadulterated.<br><br>**Practical Application**<br>Believers are to work at being clean (*akeraioi*). It is the idea of flour or grain passing through a sieve to separate the pure from the impure. It means that our thoughts and lives...<br>• are not to be polluted by watching, reading, and listening to worldly and sexual attractions.<br>• are not to be given over to worldly and sexual attractions.<br><br>Our thoughts and lives are to be pure, clean, uncontaminated, and unpolluted. |
| **#593**<br>**Clean–**<br>**Cleansed**<br><br>Clean–KJV<br>Cleansed–NASB<br>Clean–NIV<br>Cleansed–NKJV<br>Healed–NLT | καθαρίσθητι = katharisthëti<br>Pronunciation: [kath-ar-is-thay-tee]<br>Parsing (part of speech): verb<br>    Mood—imperative<br>    Tense—aorist<br>    Voice—passive<br>    Person—2nd person<br>    Number—singular<br>    Stem or root—from καθαρίζω<br>Concordance References: | To be clean and pure physically, to be healed from the effects of leprosy; to be purified; to be washed; to be cleaned.<br><br>**Practical Application**<br>In this Scripture, the word also includes the idea of being made morally clean and pure, of being spiritually cleansed and healed. |

# PRACTICAL WORD STUDIES in the NEW TESTAMENT

| ENGLISH WORD | GREEK WORD AND VERSE | THE WORD MEANS... |
|---|---|---|
| **POSB REFERENCE** (Mt.8:3) Note 3 | ⇒ Strong's #2511 katharizō<br>⇒ NIV #2751 katharizō<br>⇒ NASB #2511 katharizō<br><br>**Matthew 8:3**<br>And Jesus put forth *his* hand, and touched him, saying, I will; be thou **clean**. And immediately his leprosy was cleansed. [KJV]<br>And He stretched out His hand and touched him, saying, "I am willing; be **cleansed**." And immediately his leprosy was cleansed. [NASB]<br>Jesus reached out his hand and touched the man. "I am willing," he said. "Be **clean**!" Immediately he was cured of his leprosy. [NIV]<br>Then Jesus put out His hand and touched him, saying, "I am willing; be **cleansed**." Immediately his leprosy was cleansed. [NKJV]<br>Jesus touched him. "I want to," he said. "Be **healed**!" And instantly the leprosy disappeared. [NLT]<br>καὶ ἐκτείνας τὴν χεῖρα, ἥψατο αὐτοῦ ὁ Ἰησοῦς λέγων, Θέλω, **καθαρίσθητι**. καὶ εὐθέως ἐκαθαρίσθη αὐτοῦ ἡ λέπρα. [GNS]<br>καὶ ἐκτείνας τὴν χεῖρα ἥψατο αὐτοῦ λέγων, Θέλω, **καθαρίσθητι**· καὶ εὐθέως ἐκαθαρίσθη αὐτοῦ ἡ λέπρα. [GNT] | |
| **#594**<br>**Cleansed**<br><br>Blotted out–KJV<br>Wiped away–NASB<br>Wiped out–NIV<br>Blotted out–NKJV<br>Cleansed–NLT<br><br>**POSB REFERENCE** (Acts 3:19) Note 7, point 1 | ἐξαλειφθῆναι = *exaleiphthēnai*<br>Pronunciation: [ex-al-eef'-thay-nah-ee]<br>Parsing (part of speech): verb<br>    Mood—infinitive<br>    Tense—aorist<br>    Voice—passive<br>    Case—accusative<br>    Stem or root—from ἐξαλείφω<br>Concordance References:<br>⇒ Strong's #1813 exaleiphō<br>⇒ NIV #1981 exaleiphō<br>⇒ NASB #1813 exaleiphō<br><br>**Acts 3:19**<br>Repent ye therefore, and be converted, that your sins may be **blotted out**, when the times of refreshing shall come from the presence of the Lord; [KJV]<br>"Repent therefore and return, that your sins may be **wiped away**, in order that times of refreshing may come from the presence of the Lord; [NASB]<br>Repent, then, and turn to God, so that your sins may be **wiped out**, that times of refreshing may come from the Lord, [NIV]<br>Repent therefore and be converted, that your sins may be **blotted out**, so that times of refreshing may come from the presence of the Lord, [NKJV]<br>Now turn from your sins and turn to God, so you can be **cleansed** of your sins. [NLT]<br>μετανοήσατε οὖν καὶ ἐπιστρέψατε, εἰς τὸ **ἐξαλειφθῆναι** ὑμῶν τὰς ἁμαρτίας, [GNS]<br>μετανοήσατε οὖν καὶ ἐπιστρέψατε εἰς τὸ **ἐξαλειφθῆναι** ὑμῶν τὰς ἁμαρτίας, [GNT] | Wiped out; wiped away; blotted out; cleansed; destroyed; removed; canceled.<br><br>**Practical Application**<br>It means erased, smeared out, rubbed off, wiped out, obliterated—just like handwriting is erased and wiped off a wall. |
| **#595**<br>**Clear**<br><br>Void of offence–KJV<br>Blameless–NASB<br>Clear–NIV<br>Without offense–NKJV<br>Clear–NLT | ἀπρόσκοπον = *aproskopon*<br>Pronunciation: [ap-ros'-kop-on]<br>Parsing (part of speech): adjective<br>    Case—accusative<br>    Gender—feminine<br>    Number—singular<br>    Stem or root—from ἀπρόσκοπος<br>Concordance References:<br>⇒ Strong's #677 aproskopos<br>⇒ NIV #718 aproskopos<br>⇒ NASB #677 aproskopos<br><br>**Acts 24:16**<br>And herein do I exercise myself, to have always a con- | To be clear; to be blameless; to be clear in conscience.<br><br>**Practical Application**<br>It means to keep from stumbling, to keep from causing others to stumble, to keep from hurting oneself and from hurting others. |

# PRACTICAL WORD STUDIES
## in the NEW TESTAMENT

| ENGLISH WORD | GREEK WORD AND VERSE | THE WORD MEANS... |
|---|---|---|
| **POSB REFERENCE** (Acts 24:14-16; esp. v.16) Note 3, point 4b | science **void of offence** toward God, and *toward* men. [KJV]<br>"In view of this, I also do my best to maintain always a **blameless** conscience *both* before God and before men. [NASB]<br>So I strive always to keep my conscience **clear** before God and man. [NIV]<br>This *being* so, I myself always strive to have a conscience **without offense** toward God and men. [NKJV]<br>Because of this, I always try to maintain a **clear** conscience before God and everyone else. [NLT]<br>ἐν τούτῳ δὲ αὐτὸς ἀσκῶ, **ἀπρόσκοπον** συνείδησιν ἔχειν πρὸς τὸν Θεὸν καὶ τοὺς ἀνθρώπους διὰ παντός. [GNS]<br>ἐν τούτῳ καὶ αὐτὸς ἀσκῶ **ἀπρόσκοπον** συνείδησιν ἔχειν πρὸς τὸν θεὸν καὶ τοὺς ἀνθρώπους διὰ παντός. [GNT] | |
| **#596**<br>**Clear Minded**<br><br>Sober–KJV<br>Sound judgment–NASB<br>**Clear minded–NIV**<br>Serious–NKJV<br>Earnest–NLT<br><br>**POSB REFERENCE** (1 Pt.4:7) Note 1 | σωφρονήσατε = *söphronësate*<br>Pronunciation: [so-fron-ay'-sah-teh]<br>Parsing (part of speech): verb<br>    Mood—imperative<br>    Tense—aorist<br>    Voice—active<br>    Person—2nd person<br>    Number—plural<br>    Stem or root—from σωφρονέω<br>Concordance References:<br>  ⇒ Strong's #4993 söphroneö<br>  ⇒ NIV #5404 söphroneö<br>  ⇒ NASB #4993 söphroneö<br><br>**1 Peter 4:7**<br>But the end of all things is at hand: be ye therefore **sober**, and watch unto prayer. [KJV]<br>The end of all things is at hand; therefore, be of **sound judgment** and sober *spirit* for the purpose of prayer. [NASB]<br>The end of all things is near. Therefore be **clear minded** and self-controlled so that you can pray. [NIV]<br>But the end of all things is at hand; therefore be **serious** and watchful in your prayers. [NKJV]<br>The end of the world is coming soon. Therefore, be **earnest** and disciplined in your prayers. [NLT]<br>Πάντων δὲ τὸ τέλος ἤγγικε· **σωφρονήσατε** οὖν καὶ νήψατε εἰς τὰς προσευχάς. [GNS]<br>Πάντων δὲ τὸ τέλος ἤγγικεν. **σωφρονήσατε** οὖν καὶ νήψατε εἰς προσευχάς. [GNT] | To be clear minded; to be sober; to exhibit sound judgment; to be earnest. This means to be serious and to have a sound mind; to be in control of oneself and to be self-restrained; to be calm and sensible.<br><br>**Practical Application**<br>The believer lives under the climax of history; he keeps his mind upon the return of Christ by doing three things.<br>1. He keeps a serious and sound mind about everything. He is not a jolly, back slapping, frivolous type of person. He takes life seriously, knowing that man has a purpose for being on earth, that life is the most meaningful and significant possession that man has. Therefore, he measures the importance of things. He measures all things in light of eternity as well as time. He considers the future as well as the present. He knows that his life could be snatched from him overnight by some accident or by the news of some disease. The believer who keeps his mind upon the climax of history, upon the return of the Lord Jesus Christ, is a sober person; he is a serious-and sound-minded person.<br>2. He controls and restrains his desires and lusts and appetites. He never gives in to excess—to the lust for more and more. He controls sex and uses it for marriage. He controls desire for food and uses it for health. He controls the desire for material possessions and uses it to meet the needs of his family and the desperate needs of the world.<br>3. He is calm and sensible about all things. He is not overly shaken by trouble, problems, or circumstances that arise within his family, employment, society, or world. Family problems and world events just do not shake him. He is concerned but not shaken. He does not get overly excited with recreation, sports, or any other happening of life. He enjoys the happenings and experiences of life, but he keeps a sensible perspective of all things and gives each thing its proper place. |
| **#597**<br>**Clearly**<br><br>Expressly–KJV<br>Explicitly–NASB<br>**Clearly–NIV** | ῥητῶς = *hrëtös*<br>Pronunciation: [hray-toce']<br>Parsing (part of speech): adjective adverb<br>    Stem or root—from ῥητῶς<br>Concordance References:<br>  ⇒ Strong's #4490 hrëtös | Clearly, expressly, explicitly, specifically.<br><br>**Practical Application**<br>The Spirit has spoken "clearly" (*hrëtös*), that is, in specific terms, in plain words, distinctly, so that there can be no question about what is being said. False teachers will arise in the latter times. |

320

# PRACTICAL WORD STUDIES
## in the NEW TESTAMENT

| ENGLISH WORD | GREEK WORD AND VERSE | THE WORD MEANS... |
|---|---|---|
| Expressly–NKJV<br>Clearly–NLT<br><br>**POSB<br>REFERENCE**<br>(1 Tim.4:1)<br>Note 1 | ⇒ NIV #4843 hrētös<br>⇒ NASB #4490 hrētös<br><br>**1 Tim. 4:1**<br>Now the Spirit speaketh **expressly**, that in the latter times some shall depart from the faith, giving heed to seducing spirits, and doctrines of devils; [KJV]<br>But the Spirit **explicitly** says that in later times some will fall away from the faith, paying attention to deceitful spirits and doctrines of demons, [NASB]<br>The Spirit **clearly** says that in later times some will abandon the faith and follow deceiving spirits and things taught by demons. [NIV]<br>Now the Spirit **expressly** says that in latter times some will depart from the faith, giving heed to deceiving spirits and doctrines of demons, [NKJV]<br>Now the Holy Spirit tells us **clearly** that in the last times some will turn away from what we believe; they will follow lying spirits and teachings that come from demons. [NLT]<br>Τὸ δὲ Πνεῦμα **ῥητῶς** λέγει, ὅτι ἐν ὑστέροις καιροῖς ἀποστήσονταί τινες τῆς πίστεως, προσέχοντες πνεύμασι πλάνοις καὶ διδασκαλίαις δαιμονίων, [GNS]<br>Τὸ δὲ πνεῦμα **ῥητῶς** λέγει ὅτι ἐν ὑστέροις καιροῖς ἀποστήσονταί τινες τῆς πίστεως προσέχοντες πνεύμασιν πλάνοις καὶ διδασκαλίαις δαιμονίων, [GNT] | |
| **#598<br>Clearly Known**<br><br>Assuredly–KJV<br>Certain–NASB<br>Assured–NIV<br>Assuredly–NKJV<br>Clearly known–NLT<br><br>**POSB<br>REFERENCE**<br>(Acts 2:33-36; esp. v.36)<br>Note 4, point 3 | ἀσφαλῶς γινωσκέτω = *asphalös ginösketö*<br>Pronunciation: [as-fal-oce' ghin-oce'-keh-tow]<br>Parsing *asphalös* (part of speech): adjective adverb<br>    Stem or root—from ἀσφαλῶς<br>Parsing *ginösketö* (part of speech): verb<br>    Mood—imperative<br>    Tense—present<br>    Voice—active<br>    Person—3rd person<br>    Number—singular<br>    Stem or root—from γινώσκω<br>Concordance References:<br>⇒ Strong's #806+1097 asphalös ginöskö<br>⇒ NIV #857+1182 asphalös ginöskö [assured]<br>⇒ NASB #806+1097 asphalös ginöskö<br><br>**Acts 2:36**<br>Therefore let all the house of Israel know **assuredly**, that God hath made that same Jesus, whom ye have crucified, both Lord and Christ. [KJV]<br>"Therefore let all the house of Israel know for **certain** that God has made Him both Lord and Christ— this Jesus whom you crucified." [NASB]<br>"Therefore let all the house of Israel know **assuredly** that God has made this Jesus, whom you crucified, both Lord and Christ." [NKJV]<br>"Therefore let all Israel be **assured** of this: God has made this Jesus, whom you crucified, both Lord and Christ." [NIV]<br>"Therefore let all the house of Israel know **assuredly** that God has made this Jesus, whom you crucified, both Lord and Christ." [NKJV]<br>So let it be **clearly known** by everyone in Israel that God has made this Jesus whom you crucified to be both Lord and Messiah!" [NLT]<br>**ἀσφαλῶς** οὖν **γινωσκέτω** πᾶς οἶκος Ἰσραήλ, ὅτι καὶ Κύριον καὶ Χριστὸν αὐτὸν ὁ Θεὸς ἐποίησε, τοῦτον τὸν Ἰησοῦν ὃν ὑμεῖς ἐσταυρώσατε. [GNS]<br>**ἀσφαλῶς** οὖν **γινωσκέτω** πᾶς οἶκος Ἰσραὴλ ὅτι καὶ κύριον αὐτὸν καὶ Χριστὸν ἐποίησεν ὁ θεός, τοῦτον τὸν Ἰησοῦν ὃν ὑμεῖς ἐσταυρώσατε. [GNT] | To be assured; to be aware of; to know about; to be sure; to be certain; to know beyond a doubt.<br><br>**Practical Application**<br>The word is emphatic. It means without any doubt whatsoever, with perfect assurance and certainty. |
| **#599<br>Clearly Predicted** | οὐχὶ ἔδει = *ouchi edei*<br>Pronunciation: [oo-chee eh-dee]<br>Parsing *edei* (part of speech): verb<br>    Mood—indicative<br>    Tense—imperfect | Not have to; ought not; not necessary; clearly predicted. |

# PRACTICAL WORD STUDIES
## in the NEW TESTAMENT

| ENGLISH WORD | GREEK WORD AND VERSE | THE WORD MEANS... |
|---|---|---|
| Ought not–KJV<br>Not necessary–NASB<br>Not...have to–NIV<br>Ought not–NKJV<br>Clearly predicted–NLT<br><br>**POSB REFERENCE**<br>(Lk.24:15-27; esp. v.26)<br>Note 2, point 3b | Voice—active<br>Person—3rd person<br>Number—singular<br>Stem or root—from δεῖ<br>Concordance References:<br>⇒ Strong's #3780 ouchi + 1163 dei<br>⇒ NIV #4049 ouchi [not] + 1256 dei [have to]<br>⇒ NASB #3780 ouchi + 1163 dei<br><br>**Luke 24:26**<br>**Ought not** Christ to have suffered these things, and to enter into his glory? [KJV]<br>"Was it **not necessary** for the Christ to suffer these things and to enter into His glory?" [NASB]<br>Did **not** the Christ **have to** suffer these things and then enter his glory?" [NIV]<br>**Ought not** the Christ to have suffered these things and to enter into His glory?" [NKJV]<br>Wasn't it **clearly predicted** by the prophets that the Messiah would have to suffer all these things before entering his time of glory?" [NLT]<br>οὐχὶ ταῦτα ἔδει παθεῖν τὸν Χριστὸν καὶ εἰσελθεῖν εἰς τὴν δόξαν αὐτοῦ; [GNS]<br>οὐχὶ ταῦτα ἔδει παθεῖν τὸν Χριστὸν καὶ εἰσελθεῖν εἰς τὴν δόξαν αὐτοῦ; [GNT] | **Practical Application**<br>It means that the death of Christ was an absolute necessity. The words "clearly predicted" are strong. They mean there was a constraint, an imperative, a necessity laid upon the Messiah to die and arise. He had no choice. His death and resurrection had been planned and willed by God through all eternity. |
| #600<br>**Cleave to**<br><br>Cleave to–KJV<br>Cling to–NASB<br>Cling to–NIV<br>Cling to–NKJV<br>Stand on the side of–NLT<br><br>**POSB REFERENCE**<br>(Rom.12:9-10; esp. v.9)<br>Note 1, point 2 | κολλώμενοι = kollōmenoi<br>Pronunciation: [kol-lo'-mehn-oy]<br>Parsing (part of speech): verb<br>  Mood—participle (imperative sense)<br>  Tense—present<br>  Voice—passive<br>  Case—nominative<br>  Gender—masculine<br>  Person—2nd person<br>  Number—plural<br>  Stem or root—from κολλάομαι<br>Concordance References:<br>⇒ Strong's #2853 kollaō<br>⇒ NIV #3140 kollaō<br>⇒ NASB #2853 kollaō<br><br>**Romans 12:9**<br>*Let* love be without dissimulation. Abhor that which is evil; **cleave to** that which is good. [KJV]<br>Let love be without hypocrisy. Abhor what is evil; **cling to** what is good. [NASB]<br>Love must be sincere. Hate what is evil; **cling to** what is good. [NIV]<br>*Let* love *be* without hypocrisy. Abhor what is evil. **Cling to** what is good. [NKJV]<br>Don't just pretend that you love others. Really love them. Hate what is wrong. **Stand on the side of** the good. [NLT]<br>Ἡ ἀγάπη ἀνυπόκριτος. ἀποστυγοῦντες τὸ πονηρόν, κολλώμενοι τῷ ἀγαθῷ. [GNS]<br>Ἡ ἀγάπη ἀνυπόκριτος, ἀποστυγοῦντες τὸ πονηρόν, κολλώμενοι τῷ ἀγαθῷ, [GNT] | To cling; to cleave; to stand on the side of; to join or fasten together, to attach or glue together.<br><br>**Practical Application**<br>The believer is to love by cleaving to that which is good. The believer is to desire only the very best—all the good possible—for people. He is to cleave to the good and to work for everyone to know and experience the good. The believer shows that he truly loves people by holding fast and working for the good. |
| #601<br>**Cleave To**<br><br>Cleave to–KJV<br>Cleave to–NASB<br>United to–NIV<br>Joined to–NKJV<br>Joined to–NLT<br><br>**POSB REFERENCE**<br>(Mt.19:5)<br>*Deeper Study* #2 | κολληθήσεται = kollēthēsetai<br>Pronunciation: [kol-lay-thay-seh-tah-ee]<br>Parsing (part of speech): verb<br>  Mood—indicative<br>  Tense—future<br>  Voice—passive<br>  Person—3rd person<br>  Number—singular<br>  Stem or root—from κολλάομαι<br>Concordance References:<br>⇒ Strong's #2853 kollaō<br>⇒ NIV #3140 kollaō<br>⇒ NASB #2853 kollaō<br><br>**Matthew 19:5** | To unite to; to cleave; to join fast together; to glue together; to cement together; to be joined in the closest union possible; to be bound together; to be so totally united together that two become one.<br><br>**Practical Application**<br>To be united means a spiritual union. It is a union higher and stronger than the union of parent and child. It is a union that means more than living together, more than having sex and bearing offspring. Animals do this. It is a union that can be wrought by God alone (Matthew 19:11). |

# PRACTICAL WORD STUDIES
## in the NEW TESTAMENT

| ENGLISH WORD | GREEK WORD AND VERSE | THE WORD MEANS... |
|---|---|---|
|  | And said, For this cause shall a man leave father and mother, and shall **cleave to** his wife: and they twain shall be one flesh. [KJV]<br><br>And said, 'FOR THIS CAUSE A MAN SHALL LEAVE HIS FATHER AND MOTHER, AND SHALL **CLEAVE TO** HIS WIFE; AND THE TWO SHALL BECOME ONE FLESH'? [NASB]<br><br>And said, 'For this reason a man will leave his father and mother and be **united to** his wife, and the two will become one flesh'? [NIV]<br><br>And said, '*For this reason a man shall leave his father and mother and be **joined to** his wife, and the two shall become one flesh*'? [NKJV]<br><br>And he said, 'This explains why a man leaves his father and mother and is **joined to** his wife, and the two are united into one.' [NLT]<br><br>καὶ εἶπεν, Ἔνεκα τούτου καταλείψει ἄνθρωπος τὸν πατέρα καὶ τὴν μητέρα, καὶ **προσκολληθήσεται** τῇ γυναικὶ αὐτοῦ, καὶ ἔσονται οἱ δύο εἰς σάρκα μίαν. [GNS]<br><br>καὶ εἶπεν, Ἔνεκα τούτου καταλείψει ἄνθρωπος τὸν πατέρα καὶ τὴν μητέρα καὶ **κολληθήσεται** τῇ γυναικὶ αὐτοῦ, καὶ ἔσονται οἱ δύο εἰς σάρκα μίαν. [GNT] | It is a spiritual union that places man above the physical plane of animals. It is a spiritual fullness, a spiritual sharing of life together: a dedication, a consecration, a completeness, a satisfaction that makes a person the exclusive possession of God and of the spouse. As said, such a cleaving or spiritual union is wrought by God alone. Both husband and wife must be willing and submissive for God to bring about such a union in their lives. |
| **#602**<br>**Cleave To**<br><br>Joined unto–KJV<br>**Cleave to–NASB**<br>United to–NIV<br>Joined to–NKJV<br>Joined to–NLT<br><br>**POSB REFERENCE**<br>(Eph.5:31)<br>*Deeper Study #1* | προσκολληθήσεται πρός = *proskollēthēsetai pros*<br>Pronunciation: [pros-kol-lay'-thay-seh-tah-ee pros]<br>Parsing *proskollēthēsetai* (part of speech): verb<br>    Mood—indicative<br>    Tense—future<br>    Voice—passive<br>    Person—3rd person<br>    Number—singular<br>    Stem or root—from προσκολλάομαι<br>Concordance References:<br>⇒ Strong's #4314+4347 pros proskollaō<br>⇒ NIV #4639+4681 pros proskollaō [united to]<br>⇒ NASB #4314+4347 pros proskollaō<br><br>**Ephes. 5:31**<br>For this cause shall a man leave his father and mother, and shall **joined unto** his wife, and they two shall be one flesh. [KJV]<br>FOR THIS CAUSE A MAN SHALL LEAVE HIS FATHER AND MOTHER, AND SHALL **CLEAVE TO** HIS WIFE; AND THE TWO SHALL BECOME ONE FLESH. [NASB]<br>"For this reason a man will leave his father and mother and be **united to** his wife, and the two will become one flesh." [NIV]<br>"*For this reason a man shall leave his father and mother and **be joined to** his wife, and the two shall become one flesh.*" [NKJV]<br>As the Scriptures say, "A man leaves his father and mother and is **joined to** his wife, and the two are united into one." [NLT]<br>ἐκ τῆς σαρκὸς αὐτοῦ καὶ ἐκ τῶν ὀστέων αὐτοῦ. Ἀντὶ τούτου καταλείψει ἄνθρωπος τὸν πατέρα αὐτοῦ καὶ τὴν μητέρα, καὶ **προσκολληθήσεται πρός** τὴν γυναῖκα αὐτοῦ, καὶ ἔσονται οἱ δύο εἰς σάρκα μίαν. [GNS]<br>ἀντὶ τούτου καταλείψει ἄνθρωπος [τὸν] πατέρα καὶ [τὴν] μητέρα καὶ **προσκολληθήσεται πρός** τὴν γυναῖκα αὐτοῦ, καὶ ἔσονται οἱ δύο εἰς σάρκα μίαν. [GNT] | To cleave to; to join fast together; to glue together; to cement together; to be joined in the closest union possible; to be bound together; to be so totally united that two become one.<br><br>**Practical Application**<br>To cleave means a spiritual union. It is a union higher and stronger than the union of parent and child. It is a union that means more than living together, more than having sex and bearing offspring. Animals do this. It is a union that can be wrought by God alone (Ephes. 5:31). It is a spiritual union that places man above the physical plane of animals. It is a spiritual fullness, a spiritual sharing of life together: a dedication, a consecration, a completeness, a satisfaction that makes a person the exclusive possession of God and of the spouse. As said, such a cleaving or spiritual union is wrought by God alone. Both husband and wife must be willing and submissive for God to bring about such a cleaving in their lives. "Submitting yourselves one to another in the fear [trust] of God" (Ephes. 5:21; see POSB outlines—Ephes. 5:22-33 and POSB notes—Ephes. 5:22-33).<br>There are three unions within a true marriage, that is, a marriage that *really cleaves* and is really *joined together* by God (Mat. 19:6).<br>1. There is the physical union: the sharing of each other's body (1 Cor. 7:2-5).<br>2. There is the mental union: the sharing of each other's life and dreams and hopes, and the working together to realize those dreams and hopes. It is important to note that this union still deals only with the physical and material world.<br>3. There is the spiritual union: the sharing and melting and molding of each other's spirit (see Ephes. 5:25-33). This can be wrought only by God. Therefore, there has to be a sharing together with God for there to be a *nourishing* and *nurturing* of the spirit. (For a detailed commentary, see POSB *Deeper Study #1*—Eph.5:31) |

# PRACTICAL WORD STUDIES
## in the NEW TESTAMENT

| ENGLISH WORD | GREEK WORD AND VERSE | THE WORD MEANS... |
|---|---|---|
| **#603**<br>**Cling**<br><br>Cleave–KJV<br>**Cling**–NASB<br>**Cling**–NIV<br>**Cling**–NKJV<br>Stand on the side of–NLT<br><br>**POSB REFERENCE**<br>(Rom.12:9-10; esp. v.9)<br>Note 1, point 2 | κολλώμενοι = *kollōmenoi*<br>Pronunciation: [kol-lo'-mehn-oy]<br>Parsing (part of speech): verb<br>    Mood—participle (imperative sense)<br>    Tense—present<br>    Voice—passive<br>    Case—nominative<br>    Gender—masculine<br>    Person—2nd person<br>    Number—plural<br>    Stem or root—from κολλάομαι<br>Concordance References:<br>  ⇒ Strong's #2853 kollaō<br>  ⇒ NIV #3140 kollaō<br>  ⇒ NASB #2853 kollaō<br><br>**Romans 12:9**<br>*Let* love be without dissimulation. Abhor that which is evil; **cleave** to that which is good. [KJV]<br>Let love be without hypocrisy. Abhor what is evil; **cling** to what is good. [NASB]<br>Love must be sincere. Hate what is evil; **cling** to what is good. [NIV]<br>*Let* love *be* without hypocrisy. Abhor what is evil. **Cling** to what is good. [NKJV]<br>Don't just pretend that you love others. Really love them. Hate what is wrong. **Stand on the side of** the good. [NLT]<br>Ἡ ἀγάπη ἀνυπόκριτος. ἀποστυγοῦντες τὸ πονηρόν, **κολλώμενοι** τῷ ἀγαθῷ. [GNS]<br>Ἡ ἀγάπη ἀνυπόκριτος. ἀποστυγοῦντες τὸ πονηρόν, **κολλώμενοι** τῷ ἀγαθῷ. [GNT] | To cling; to cleave; to stand on the side of; to join or fasten together, to attach or glue together.<br><br>**Practical Application**<br>The believer is to love by clinging to that which is good. The believer is to desire only the very best—all the good possible—for people. He is to cleave to the good and to work for everyone to know and experience the good. The believer shows that he truly loves people by holding fast and working for the good. |
| **#604**<br>**Cloth**<br><br>Napkin–KJV<br>**Cloth**–NASB<br>**Cloth**–NIV<br>**Cloth**–NKJV<br>Headcloth–NLT<br><br>**POSB REFERENCE**<br>(Jn.11:44)<br>*Deeper Study #2* | σουδαρίῳ = *soudariō*<br>Pronunciation: [soo-dar'-ee-o]<br>Parsing (part of speech): noun<br>    Case—dative<br>    Gender—neuter<br>    Number—singular<br>    Stem or root—from σουδάριον, ου<br>Concordance References:<br>  ⇒ Strong's #4676 soudarion<br>  ⇒ NIV #5051 soudarion<br>  ⇒ NASB #4676 soudarion<br><br>**John 11:44**<br>And he that was dead came forth, bound hand and foot with graveclothes: and his face was bound about with a **napkin**. Jesus saith unto them, Loose him, and let him go. [KJV]<br>He who had died came forth, bound hand and foot with wrappings; and his face was wrapped around with a **cloth**. Jesus said to them, "Unbind him, and let him go." [NASB]<br>The dead man came out, his hands and feet wrapped with strips of linen, and a **cloth** around his face. Jesus said to them, "Take off the grave clothes and let him go." [NIV]<br>And he who had died came out bound hand and foot with graveclothes, and his face was wrapped with a **cloth**. Jesus said to them, "Loose him, and let him go." [NKJV]<br>And Lazarus came out, bound in graveclothes, his face wrapped in a **headcloth**. Jesus told them, "Unwrap him and let him go!" [NLT]<br>καὶ ἐξῆλθεν ὁ τεθνηκὼς δεδεμένος τοὺς πόδας καὶ τὰς χεῖρας κειρίαις, καὶ ἡ ὄψις αὐτοῦ **σουδαρίῳ** περιεδέδετο. λέγει αὐτοῖς ὁ Ἰησοῦς, Λύσατε αὐτὸν, καὶ ἄφετε ὑπάγειν. [GNS]<br>ἐξῆλθεν ὁ τεθνηκὼς δεδεμένος τοὺς πόδας καὶ τὰς χεῖρας κειρίαις, καὶ ἡ ὄψις αὐτοῦ **σουδαρίῳ** περιεδέδετο. λέγει αὐτοῖς ὁ Ἰησοῦς, Λύσατε αὐτὸν καὶ ἄφετε αὐτὸν ὑπάγειν. [GNT] | A cloth, napkin, headcloth, graveclothes, or handkerchief; a piece of cloth.<br><br>**Practical Application**<br>In this Scripture, there was a cloth wrapped around the face of Lazarus. This is important to note for two reasons.<br>1. Jesus had a cloth wrapped around His face when He was buried. After His resurrection it was folded either by Him or an angel and laid to the side. The folded cloth was the immediate thing that convinced John of the Lord's resurrection. (See POSB note—John 20:7-10.)<br>2. The cloth showed that the grave clothes of Jesus' day included at least two pieces of clothing. There was a separate cloth or napkin wrapped around the face. It is mentioned two times in the New Testament (John 11:44; John 20:7. Cp. Luke 19:20; Acts 19:12 for two other uses of the same Greek word, *soudarioi*.) |

# PRACTICAL WORD STUDIES
## in the NEW TESTAMENT

| ENGLISH WORD | GREEK WORD AND VERSE | THE WORD MEANS... |
|---|---|---|
| **#605**<br>**Clothe With**<br><br>Put on–KJV<br>Put on–NASB<br>**Clothe with–NIV**<br>Put on–NKJV<br>Take control–NLT<br><br>**POSB REFERENCE**<br>(Rom.13:14)<br>*Deeper Study #2*<br><br>See also POSB REF:<br>(Col.3:12-14; esp. v.12)<br>Note 1 | ἐνδύσασθε = endusasthe<br>Pronunciation: [en-doo'-sahs-theh]<br>Parsing (part of speech): verb<br>   Mood—imperative<br>   Tense—aorist<br>   Voice—middle<br>   Person—2nd person<br>   Number—plural<br>   Stem or root—from ἐνδύω<br>Concordance References:<br>  ⇒ Strong's #1746 enduō<br>  ⇒ NIV #1907 enduō<br>  ⇒ NASB #1746 enduō<br><br>**Romans 13:14**<br>But **put** ye **on** the Lord Jesus Christ, and make not provision for the flesh, to *fulfil* the lusts *thereof.* [KJV]<br>But **put on** the Lord Jesus Christ, and make no provision for the flesh in regard to *its* lusts. [NASB]<br>Rather, **clothe** yourselves **with** the Lord Jesus Christ, and do not think about how to gratify the desires of the sinful nature. [NIV]<br>But **put on** the Lord Jesus Christ, and make no provision for the flesh, to *fulfill its* lusts. [NKJV]<br>But let the Lord Jesus Christ **take control** of you, and don't think of ways to indulge your evil desires. [NLT]<br>ἀλλ **ἐνδύσασθε** τὸν Κύριον Ἰησοῦν Χριστόν, καὶ τῆς σαρκὸς πρόνοιαν μὴ ποιεῖσθε, εἰς ἐπιθυμίας. [GNS]<br>ἀλλὰ **ἐνδύσασθε** τὸν κύριον Ἰησοῦν Χριστόν καὶ τῆς σαρκὸς πρόνοιαν μὴ ποιεῖσθε εἰς ἐπιθυμίας. [GNT] | To clothe with; to put on; to wear; to dress; to take control.<br><br>**Practical Application**<br>Scripture lists seven things that the believer is to put on or with which he is to clothe himself.<br>1. The believer is to put on and be "endued or clothed" (*endusesthe*) with the Holy Spirit (Luke 24:49).<br>2. The believer is to put on and be clothed with the Lord Jesus Christ (Romans 13:14; Galatians 3:27).<br>3. The believer is to put on and be clothed with immortality (1 Cor. 15:53-54; 2 Cor. 5:3).<br>4. The believer is to put on and be clothed with the new man (Ephes. 4:24; Col. 3:10).<br>5. The believer is to put on and be clothed with the nature of God (Col. 3:12).<br>6. The believer is to put on and be clothed with the armor of light and of God (Romans 13:14; Ephes. 6:11f).<br>7. The believer is to put on and be clothed with love (Col. 3:14). |
| **#606**<br>**Clothe With**<br><br>Be clothed–KJV<br>**Clothe...with–NASB**<br>**Clothe...with–NIV**<br>**Clothed with–NKJV**<br>Serve each other–NLT<br><br>**POSB REFERENCE**<br>(1 Pt.5:5)<br>Note 2, point 2 | ἐγκομβώσασθε = egkombōsasthe<br>Pronunciation: [eng-kom-bo'-sahs-theh]<br>Parsing (part of speech): verb<br>   Mood—imperative<br>   Tense—aorist<br>   Voice—middle deponent<br>   Person—2nd person<br>   Number—plural<br>   Stem or root—from ἐγκομβόομαι<br>Concordance References:<br>  ⇒ Strong's #1463 egkomboomai<br>  ⇒ NIV #1599 egkomboomai<br>  ⇒ NASB #1463 egkomboomai<br><br>**1 Peter 5:5**<br>Likewise, ye younger, submit yourselves unto the elder. Yea, all *of you* be subject one to another, and **be clothed** with humility: for God resisteth the proud, and giveth grace to the humble. [KJV]<br>You younger men, likewise, be subject to your elders; and all of you, **clothe** yourselves **with** humility toward one another, for GOD IS OPPOSED TO THE PROUD, BUT GIVES GRACE TO THE HUMBLE. [NASB]<br>Young men, in the same way be submissive to those who are older. All of you, **clothe** yourselves **with** humility toward one another, because, "God opposes the proud but gives grace to the humble." [NIV]<br>Likewise you younger people, submit yourselves to *your* elders. Yes, all *of you* be submissive to one another, and be **clothed with** humility, for *"God resists the roud, But gives grace to the humble."* [NKJV]<br>You younger men, accept the authority of the elders. And all of you, **serve each other** in humility, for "God sets himself against the proud, but he shows favor to the humble." [NLT]<br>ὁμοίως, νεώτεροι, ὑποτάγητε πρεσβυτέροις· πάντες δὲ ἀλλήλοις ὑποτασσόμενοι, τὴν ταπεινοφροσύνην **ἐγκομβώσασθε**· ὅτι ὁ Θεὸς ὑπερηφάνοις ἀντιτάσσεται, ταπεινοῖς δὲ δίδωσι χάριν. [GNS]<br>Ὁμοίως, νεώτεροι, ὑποτάγητε πρεσβυτέροις· πάντες δὲ ἀλλήλοις τὴν ταπεινοφροσύνην **ἐγκομβώσασθε**, ὅτι [Ὁ] θεὸς ὑπερηφάνοις ἀντιτάσσεται, ταπεινοῖς δὲ δίδωσιν χάριν. [GNT] | To clothe with; to be clothed; to put on; to serve; to gird oneself with an apron.<br><br>**Practical Application**<br>It is the picture of what Jesus did in the upper room when He girded Himself with an apron to assume the role of a servant and wash the feet of the disciples. Jesus, the Son of God and Sovereign Majesty of the universe, actually clothed Himself with the apron of humility to serve the disciples. |

# PRACTICAL WORD STUDIES
## in the NEW TESTAMENT

| ENGLISH WORD | GREEK WORD AND VERSE | THE WORD MEANS... |
|---|---|---|
| **#607**<br>**Clothed With**<br><br>Endued with–KJV<br>Clothed with–NASB<br>Clothed with–NIV<br>Endued with–NKJV<br>Comes and fills–NLT<br><br>**POSB REFERENCE**<br>(Lk.24:44-49; esp. v.49)<br>Note 2, point 4c | ἐνδύσησθε = endusësthe<br>Pronunciation: [en-doo'-sees-thay]<br>Parsing (part of speech): verb<br>    Mood—subjunctive<br>    Tense—aorist<br>    Voice—middle<br>    Person—2nd person<br>    Number—plural<br>    Stem or root—from ἐνδύω<br>Concordance References:<br>  ⇒ Strong's #1746 enduö<br>  ⇒ NIV #1907 enduö<br>  ⇒ NASB #1746 enduö<br><br>**Luke 24:49**<br>And, behold, I send the promise of my Father upon you: but tarry ye in the city of Jerusalem, until ye be **endued with** power from on high. [KJV]<br>"And behold, I am sending forth the promise of My Father upon you; but you are to stay in the city until you are **clothed with** power from on high." [NASB]<br>I am going to send you what my Father has promised; but stay in the city until you have been **clothed with** power from on high." [NIV]<br>Behold, I send the Promise of My Father upon you; but tarry in the city of Jerusalem until you are **endued with** power from on high." [NKJV]<br>"And now I will send the Holy Spirit, just as my Father promised. But stay here in the city until the Holy Spirit **comes and fills** you with power from heaven." [NLT]<br>καὶ ἰδοὺ ἐγὼ ἀποστέλλω τὴν ἐπαγγελίαν τοῦ πατρός μου ἐφ' ὑμᾶς· ὑμεῖς δὲ καθίσατε ἐν τῇ πόλει Ἰερουσαλήμ, ἕως οὗ **ἐνδύσησθε** δύναμιν ἐξ ὕψους. [GNS]<br>καὶ [ἰδοὺ] ἐγὼ ἀποστέλλω τὴν ἐπαγγελίαν τοῦ πατρός μου ἐφ' ὑμᾶς· ὑμεῖς δὲ καθίσατε ἐν τῇ πόλει ἕως οὗ **ἐνδύσησθε** ἐξ ὕψους δύναμιν. [GNT] | To put on a garment; to be clothed with; to wear; to dress.<br><br>**Practical Application**<br>In this Scripture, we find that the source of the Spirit and power was God.<br>  ⇒ Christ was to send the promise.<br>  ⇒ The promise was from the Father. God gave the promise.<br>  ⇒ Believers had to stay; to tarry; that is, to wait upon the Lord and pray for the promise.<br>  ⇒ The promise was to come from "on high." God Himself was the Source of power for all evangelism. |
| **#608**<br>**Clothed, Be**<br><br>Be clothed–KJV<br>Clothe...with–NASB<br>Clothe...with–NIV<br>Be clothed–NKJV<br>Serve each other–NLT<br><br>**POSB REFERENCE**<br>(1 Pt.5:5)<br>Note 2, point 2 | ἐγκομβώσασθε = egkombösasthe<br>Pronunciation: [eng-kom-bo'-sahs-theh]<br>Parsing (part of speech): verb<br>    Mood—imperative<br>    Tense—aorist<br>    Voice—middle deponent<br>    Person—2nd person<br>    Number—plural<br>    Stem or root—from ἐγκομβόομαι<br>Concordance References:<br>  ⇒ Strong's #1463 egkomboomai<br>  ⇒ NIV #1599 egkomboomai<br>  ⇒ NASB #1463 egkomboomai<br><br>**1 Peter 5:5**<br>Likewise, ye younger, submit yourselves unto the elder. Yea, all *of you* be subject one to another, and **be clothed** with humility: for God resisteth the proud, and giveth grace to the humble. [KJV]<br>You younger men, likewise, be subject to your elders; and all of you, **clothe** yourselves **with** humility toward one another, for GOD IS OPPOSED TO THE PROUD, BUT GIVES GRACE TO THE HUMBLE. [NASB]<br>Young men, in the same way be submissive to those who are older. All of you, **clothe** yourselves **with** humility toward one another, because, "God opposes the proud but gives grace to the humble." [NIV]<br>Likewise you younger people, submit yourselves to *your* elders. Yes, all of *you* be submissive to one another, and **be clothed** with humility, for "God resists the proud, But gives grace to the humble." [NKJV]<br>You younger men, accept the authority of the elders. And all of you, **serve each other** in humility, for "God sets himself against the proud, but he shows favor to the humble." [NLT] | To clothe with; to be clothed; to put on; to serve; to gird oneself with some clothing.<br><br>**Practical Application**<br>It is the picture of what Jesus did in the upper room when He girded Himself with an apron and assumed the role of a servant and washed the feet of the disciples. Jesus, the Son of God and Sovereign Majesty of the universe, actually clothed Himself with the apron of humility to serve the disciples. |

# PRACTICAL WORD STUDIES
## in the NEW TESTAMENT

| ENGLISH WORD | GREEK WORD AND VERSE | THE WORD MEANS... |
|---|---|---|
| | ὁμοίως, νεώτεροι, ὑποτάγητε πρεσβυτέροις· πάντες δὲ ἀλλήλοις ὑποτασσόμενοι, τὴν ταπεινοφροσύνην **ἐγκομβώσασθε**· ὅτι ὁ Θεὸς ὑπερηφάνοις ἀντιτάσσεται, ταπεινοῖς δὲ δίδωσι χάριν. [GNS]<br><br>Ὁμοίως, νεώτεροι, ὑποτάγητε πρεσβυτέροις· πάντες δὲ ἀλλήλοις τὴν ταπεινοφροσύνην **ἐγκομβώσασθε**, ὅτι [Ὁ] Θεὸς ὑπερηφάνοις ἀντιτάσσεται, ταπεινοῖς δὲ δίδωσιν χάριν. [GNT] | |
| **#609**<br>**Cloven**<br><br>**Cloven–KJV**<br>Distributing–NASB<br>Separated–NIV<br>Divided–NKJV<br>Not translated–NLT<br><br>**POSB REFERENCE**<br>(Acts 2:2-4; esp. v.3)<br>Note 4, point 2 | διαμεριζόμεναι = *diamerizomenai*<br>Pronunciation: [dee-am-er-id'-zo-men-ah-ee]<br>Parsing (part of speech): verb<br>   Mood—participle<br>   Tense—present<br>   Voice—middle or passive<br>   Case—nominative<br>   Gender—feminine<br>   Number—plural<br>   Stem or root—from διαμερίζω<br>Concordance References:<br>⇒ Strong's #1266 diamerizō<br>⇒ NIV #1374 diamerizō<br>⇒ NASB #1266 diamerizō<br><br>**Acts 2:3**<br>And there appeared unto them **cloven** tongues like as of fire, and it sat upon each of them. [KJV]<br>And there appeared to them tongues as of fire **distributing** themselves, and they rested on each one of them. [NASB]<br>They saw what seemed to be tongues of fire that **separated** and came to rest on each of them. [NIV]<br>Then there appeared to them **divided** tongues, as of fire, and *one* sat upon each of them. [NKJV]<br>Then, what looked like flames or tongues of fire appeared and settled on each of them. [NLT]—Not Translated<br>καὶ ὤφθησαν αὐτοῖς **διαμεριζόμεναι** γλῶσσαι ὡσεὶ πυρός, καὶ ἐκάθισε τε ἐφ' ἕνα ἕκαστο αὐτῶν. [GNS]<br>καὶ ὤφθησαν αὐτοῖς **διαμεριζόμεναι** γλῶσσαι ὡσεὶ πυρός καὶ ἐκάθισεν ἐφ' ἕνα ἕκαστον αὐτῶν, [GNT] | Separated, distributed; divided.<br><br>**Practical Application**<br>The Greek means a tongue that was cloven, that is, parted asunder. The idea is that a single tongue appeared and then began to split and divide itself, resting upon each of the disciples. |
| **#610**<br>**Coarse Jesting**<br><br>Jesting–KJV<br>**Coarse jesting–NASB**<br>Coarse joking–NIV<br>**Coarse jesting–NKJV**<br>Coarse jokes–NLT<br><br>**POSB REFERENCE**<br>(Eph.5:4)<br>Note 4, point 3 | εὐτραπελία = *eutrapelia*<br>Pronunciation: [yoo-trap-el-ee'-ah]<br>Parsing (part of speech): noun<br>   Case—nominative<br>   Gender—feminine<br>   Number—singular<br>   Stem or root—from εὐτραπελία, ας<br>Concordance References:<br>⇒ Strong's #2160 eutrapelia<br>⇒ NIV #2365 eutrapelia<br>⇒ NASB #2160 eutrapelia<br><br>**Ephes. 5:4**<br>Neither filthiness, nor foolish talking, nor **jesting**, which are not convenient: but rather giving of thanks. [KJV]<br>And *there must be no* filthiness and silly talk, or **coarse jesting**, which are not fitting, but rather giving of thanks. [NASB]<br>Nor should there be obscenity, foolish talk or **coarse joking**, which are out of place, but rather thanksgiving. [NIV]<br>Neither filthiness, nor foolish talking, nor **coarse jesting**, which are not fitting, but rather giving of thanks. [NKJV]<br>Obscene stories, foolish talk, and **coarse jokes**—these are not for you. Instead, let there be thankfulness to God. [NLT]<br>καὶ αἰσχρότης, καὶ μωρολογία, ἡ **εὐτραπελία**, τὰ οὐκ ἀνήκοντα· ἀλλὰ μᾶλλον εὐχαριστία. [GNS]<br>καὶ αἰσχρότης καὶ μωρολογία ἡ **εὐτραπελία**, ἃ οὐκ ἀνῆκεν, ἀλλὰ μᾶλλον εὐχαριστία. [GNT] | Coarse joking; jesting; vulgar or dirty talk. It means to joke, talk foolishly, poke fun, act or speak without thought; to be suggestive in conversation; to make wisecracks.<br><br>**Practical Application**<br>It also has the idea of being cunning and clever, of being polished in suggestive and off-colored joking and using it to attract attention and win favors (Kenneth Wuest. *Ephesians and Colossians*, Vol.1, p.121). Coarse jesting is often used in off-colored jokes or conversation at parties or work breaks in order to be suggestive. |

# PRACTICAL WORD STUDIES
## in the NEW TESTAMENT

| ENGLISH WORD | GREEK WORD AND VERSE | THE WORD MEANS... |
|---|---|---|
| **#611**<br>**Coarse Joking, Jokes**<br><br>Jesting–KJV<br>Coarse jesting–NASB<br>**Coarse joking–NIV**<br>Coarse jesting–NKJV<br>**Coarse jokes–NLT**<br><br>**POSB REFERENCE**<br>(Eph.5:4)<br>Note 4, point 3 | εὐτραπελία = eutrapelia<br>Pronunciation: [yoo-trap-el-ee'-ah]<br>Parsing (part of speech): noun<br>    Case—nominative<br>    Gender—feminine<br>    Number—singular<br>    Stem or root—from εὐτραπελία, ας<br>Concordance References:<br>⇒ Strong's #2160 eutrapelia<br>⇒ NIV #2365 eutrapelia<br>⇒ NASB #2160 eutrapelia<br><br>**Ephes. 5:4**<br>Nor should there be obscenity, foolish talk or **coarse joking**, which are out of place, but rather thanksgiving. [NIV]<br>Neither filthiness, nor foolish talking, nor **jesting**, which are not convenient: but rather giving of thanks. [KJV]<br>And *there must be no* filthiness and silly talk, or **coarse jesting**, which are not fitting, but rather giving of thanks. [NASB]<br>Neither filthiness, nor foolish talking, nor **coarse jesting**, which are not fitting, but rather giving of thanks. [NKJV]<br>Obscene stories, foolish talk, and **coarse jokes**—these are not for you. Instead, let there be thankfulness to God. [NLT]<br>Obscene stories, foolish talk, and **coarse jokes**—these are not for you. Instead, let there be thankfulness to God. [NLT]<br>καὶ αἰσχρότης, καὶ μωρολογία, ἢ **εὐτραπελία**, τὰ οὐκ ἀνήκοντα· ἀλλὰ μᾶλλον εὐχαριστία. [GNS]<br>καὶ αἰσχρότης καὶ μωρολογία ἢ **εὐτραπελία**, ἃ οὐκ ἀνῆκεν, ἀλλὰ μᾶλλον εὐχαριστία. [GNT] | Coarse joking; jesting; vulgar or dirty talk. It means to joke, talk foolishly, poke fun, act or speak without thought; to be suggestive in conversation; to make wisecracks.<br><br>**Practical Application**<br>It also has the idea of being cunning and clever, of being polished in suggestive and off-colored joking and using it to attract attention and win favors (Kenneth Wuest. *Ephesians and Colossians*, Vol.1, p.121). Coarse joking is often used in off-colored jokes or conversation at parties or work breaks in order to be suggestive. |
| **#612**<br>**Cohort**<br><br>Band of soldiers–KJV<br>**Cohort–NASB**<br>Company of soldiers–NIV<br>Garrison–NKJV<br>Battalion–NLT<br><br>**POSB REFERENCE**<br>(Mt.27:26-38; esp. v.27)<br>Note 2, point 2 | σπεῖραν = speiran<br>Pronunciation: [spi'-rahn]<br>Parsing (part of speech): noun<br>    Case—accusative<br>    Gender—feminine<br>    Number—singular<br>    Stem or root—from σπεῖρα, ης<br>Concordance References:<br>⇒ Strong's #4686 speira<br>⇒ NIV #5061 speira<br>⇒ NASB #4686 speira<br><br>**Matthew 27:27**<br>Then the soldiers of the governor took Jesus into the common hall, and gathered unto him the whole **band of soldiers**. [KJV]<br>Then the soldiers of the governor took Jesus into the Praetorium and gathered the whole *Roman* **cohort** around Him. [NASB]<br>Then the soldiers of the governor took Jesus into the Praetorium and gathered the whole **garrison** around Him. [NKJV]<br>Some of the governor's soldiers took Jesus into their headquarters and called out the entire **battalion**. [NLT]<br>Τότε οἱ στρατιῶται τοῦ ἡγεμόνος παραλαβόντες τὸν Ἰησοῦν εἰς τὸ πραιτώριον συνήγαγον ἐπ' αὐτὸν ὅλην τὴν **σπεῖραν**· [GNS]<br>Τότε οἱ στρατιῶται τοῦ ἡγεμόνος παραλαβόντες τὸν Ἰησοῦν εἰς τὸ πραιτώριον συνήγαγον ἐπ' αὐτὸν ὅλην τὴν **σπεῖραν**. [GNT] | A company, battalion, detachment, cohort, garrison or band of soldiers; a regiment.<br><br>**Practical Application**<br>This usually meant a cohort or battalion which was made up of six hundred soldiers. However, "cohort" (*speiran*) sometimes meant maniple. Every cohort consisted of three maniples, about two hundred soldiers. Which is meant here is not known. Most believe the number of soldiers was large, certainly close to the two hundred serving in a maniple. |
| **#613**<br>**Cohort**<br><br>Band–KJV<br>**Cohort–NASB** | σπεῖραν = speiran<br>Pronunciation: [spi'-rahn]<br>Parsing (part of speech): noun<br>    Case—accusative<br>    Gender—feminine<br>    Number—singular | A detachment; a company; a battalion; a band; a cohort of Roman soldiers; a regiment.<br><br>**Practical Application**<br>This usually meant a cohort or battalion |

# PRACTICAL WORD STUDIES
## in the NEW TESTAMENT

| ENGLISH WORD | GREEK WORD AND VERSE | THE WORD MEANS... |
|---|---|---|
| Detachment of soldiers–NIV<br>Detachment of troops–NKJV<br>Battalion of Roman soldiers–NLT<br><br>**POSB REFERENCE**<br>(Jn.18:3)<br>*Deeper Study #1* | Stem or root—from σπεῖρα, ης<br>Concordance References:<br>⇒ Strong's #4686 speira<br>⇒ NIV #5061 speira<br>⇒ NASB #4686 speira<br><br>**John 18:3**<br>Judas then, having received a **band** *of men* and officers from the chief priests and Pharisees, cometh thither with lanterns and torches and weapons. [KJV]<br>Judas then, having received the *Roman* **cohort**, and officers from the chief priests and the Pharisees, came there with lanterns and torches and weapons. [NASB]<br>So Judas came to the grove, guiding a **detachment of soldiers** and some officials from the chief priests and Pharisees. They were carrying torches, lanterns and weapons. [NIV]<br>Then Judas, having received a **detachment *of troops***, and officers from the chief priests and Pharisees, came there with lanterns, torches, and weapons. [NKJV]<br>The leading priests and Pharisees had given Judas a **battalion of Roman soldiers** and Temple guards to accompany him. Now with blazing torches, lanterns, and weapons, they arrived at the olive grove. [NLT]<br>ὁ οὖν Ἰούδας, λαβὼν τὴν **σπεῖραν**, καὶ ἐκ τῶν ἀρχιερέων καὶ Φαρισαίων ὑπηρέτας ἔρχεται ἐκεῖ μετὰ φανῶν καὶ λαμπάδων καὶ ὅπλων. [GNS]<br>ὁ οὖν Ἰούδας λαβὼν τὴν **σπεῖραν** καὶ ἐκ τῶν ἀρχιερέων καὶ ἐκ τῶν Φαρισαίων ὑπηρέτας ἔρχεται ἐκεῖ μετὰ φανῶν καὶ λαμπάδων καὶ ὅπλων. [GNT] | which was made up of six hundred soldiers. However, "cohort" (*speiran*) sometimes meant maniple. Every detachment of soldiers consisted of three maniples, about two hundred soldiers. Which is meant here is not known. Most believe the number of soldiers was large, certainly close to the two hundred serving in a maniple. |
| **#614**<br>**Collection Box**<br><br>Treasury–KJV<br>Treasury–NASB<br>Temple treasury–NIV<br>Treasury–NKJV<br>**Collection box–NLT**<br><br>**POSB REFERENCE**<br>(Lk.21:1)<br>*Deeper Study #1* | γαζοφυλάκιον = gazophulakion<br>Pronunciation: [gad-zof-oo-lak'-ee-on]<br>Parsing (part of speech): noun<br>    Case—accusative<br>    Gender—neuter<br>    Number—singular<br>Stem or root—from γαζοφυλάκιον, ου<br>Concordance References:<br>⇒ Strong's #1049 gazophulakion<br>⇒ NIV #1126 gazophulakion<br>⇒ NASB #1049 gazophulakion<br><br>**Luke 21:1**<br>And he looked up, and saw the rich men casting their gifts into the **treasury**. [KJV]<br>And He looked up and saw the rich putting their gifts into the **treasury**. [NASB]<br>As he looked up, Jesus saw the rich putting their gifts into the **temple treasury**. [NIV]<br>And He looked up and saw the rich putting their gifts into the **treasury**, [NKJV]<br>While Jesus was in the Temple, he watched the rich people putting their gifts into the **collection box**. [NLT]<br>Ἀναβλέψας δὲ εἶδε τοὺς βάλλοντας τὰ δῶρα αὐτῶν εἰς τὸ **γαζοφυλάκιον** αὐτῶν πλουσίους· [GNS]<br>Ἀναβλέψας δὲ εἶδεν τοὺς βάλλοντας εἰς τὸ **γαζοφυλάκιον** τὰ δῶρα αὐτῶν πλουσίους. [GNT] | The temple treasury; a collection box; an offering box; the place where the offerings were put.<br><br>**Practical Application**<br>The collection box was in the court of the women. A section of the court had thirteen trumpet shaped collection boxes. Each box had written on it the purpose for which the offerings were to be used. People simply dropped their offerings into the box of the ministry they wished to support. |
| **#615**<br>**Combined**<br><br>Tempered–KJV<br>Comosed–NASB<br>**Combined–NIV**<br>Composed–NKJV<br>Put...together–NLT<br><br>**POSB REFERENCE**<br>(1 Cor.12:24-26; esp. v.24)<br>Note 4 | συνεκέρασεν = sunekerasen<br>Pronunciation: [soon-eh-ker'-ahn-sehn]<br>Parsing (part of speech): verb<br>    Mood—indicative<br>    Tense—aorist<br>    Voice—active<br>    Person—3rd person<br>    Number—singular<br>Stem or root—from συγκεράννυμι<br>Concordance References:<br>⇒ Strong's #4786 sugkerannumi<br>⇒ NIV #5166 sugkerannumi<br>⇒ NASB #4786 sugkerannumi | To mix; to combine; to unite; to put together; to arrange and blend together.<br><br>**Practical Application**<br>God has arranged the church as it is: the gifted and less gifted mix, combine, and blend together. And He has done it in such a manner that more honor really belongs to those who are not as gifted. The prayer warrior is much more essential than the soloist who is out before the people. The lay witness for Christ is more necessary than the preacher who stands in the pulpit. The person who ministers to the sick or eld- |

# PRACTICAL WORD STUDIES
## in the NEW TESTAMENT

| ENGLISH WORD | GREEK WORD AND VERSE | THE WORD MEANS... |
|---|---|---|
| | **1 Cor. 12:24**<br>For our comely *parts* have no need: but God hath **tempered** the body together, having given more abundant honour to that *part* which lacked: [KJV]<br>Whereas our seemly *members* have no need *of it*. But God has *so* **composed** the body, giving more abundant honor to that *member* which lacked, [NASB]<br>While our presentable parts need no special treatment. But God has **combined** the members of the body and has given greater honor to the parts that lacked it, [NIV]<br>But our presentable *parts* have no need. But God **composed** the body, having given greater honor to that *part* which lacks it, [NKJV]<br>While other parts do not require this special care. So God has **put** the body **together** in such a way that extra honor and care are given to those parts that have less dignity. [NLT]<br>τὰ δὲ εὐσχήμονα ἡμῶν οὐ χρείαν ἔχει· ἀλλ ὁ Θεὸς **συνεκέρασε** τὸ σῶμα, τῷ ὑστερουντι περισσοτέραν δοὺς τιμήν, [GNS]<br>τὰ δὲ εὐσχήμονα ἡμῶν οὐ χρείαν ἔχει. ἀλλὰ ὁ Θεὸς **συνεκέρασεν** τὸ σῶμα τῷ ὑστερουμένῳ περισσοτέραν δοὺς τιμήν, [GNT] | erly is more honorable than the committee chairman who leads the whole congregation in administrative matters. |
| **#616**<br>**Come**<br><br>Follow–KJV<br>Follow–NASB<br>Follow–NIV<br>Follow–NKJV<br>Come–NLT<br><br>**POSB REFERENCE**<br>(Jn.1:43)<br>*Deeper Study #1* | Ἀκολούθει = akolouthei<br>Pronunciation: [ak-ol-oo-theh'-ee]<br>Parsing (part of speech): verb<br>   Mood—imperative<br>   Tense—present<br>   Voice—active<br>   Person—2nd person<br>   Number—singular<br>   Stem or root—from ἀκολουθέω<br>Concordance References:<br>  ⇒ Strong's #190 akoloutheō<br>  ⇒ NIV #199 akoloutheō<br>  ⇒ NASB #190 akoloutheō<br><br>**John 1:43**<br>The day following Jesus would go forth into Galilee, and findeth Philip, and saith unto him, **Follow** me. [KJV]<br>The next day He purposed to go forth into Galilee, and He found Philip. And Jesus said to him, "**Follow** Me." [NASB]<br>The next day Jesus decided to leave for Galilee. Finding Philip, he said to him, "**Follow** me." [NIV]<br>The following day Jesus wanted to go to Galilee, and He found Philip and said to him, "**Follow** Me." [NKJV]<br>he next day Jesus decided to go to Galilee. He found Philip and said to him, "**Come**, be my disciple." [NLT]<br>Τῇ ἐπαύριον ἠθέλησεν ὁ Ἰησοῦς ἐξελθεῖν εἰς τὴν Γαλιλαίαν, καὶ εὑρίσκει Φίλιππον, καὶ λέγει αὐτῷ, **Ἀκολούθει** μοι. [GNS]<br>Τῇ ἐπαύριον ἠθέλησεν ἐξελθεῖν εἰς τὴν Γαλιλαίαν καὶ εὑρίσκει Φίλιππον. καὶ λέγει αὐτῷ ὁ Ἰησοῦς, **Ἀκολούθει** μοι. [GNT] | To follow; to come; to accompany; to become a close companion, a close follower, a disciple.<br><br>**Practical Application**<br>Two significant ideas are in the word: union and likeness, or cleaving and conformity. To come to Christ means...<br>• to cleave, to be united to Him, to be in close union with Him.<br>• to become like Him, to be conformed to Him. |
| **#617**<br>**Come–**<br>**Cometh–**<br><br>Cometh–KJV<br>Coming–NASB<br>Coming–NIV<br>Coming–NKJV<br>Come–NLT<br><br>**POSB REFERENCE**<br>(Jn.4:25)<br>Note 1, point 1 | ἔρχεται = erchetai<br>Pronunciation: [er'-cheh-tah-ee]<br>Parsing (part of speech): verb<br>   Mood—indicative<br>   Tense—present<br>   Voice—middle or passive deponent<br>   Person—3rd person<br>   Number—singular<br>   Stem or root—from ἔρχομαι<br>Concordance References:<br>  ⇒ Strong's #2064 erchomai<br>  ⇒ NIV #2262 erchomai<br>  ⇒ NASB #2064 erchomai<br><br>**John 4:25**<br>The woman saith unto him, I know that Messias **cometh**, which is called Christ: when he is come, he will | To come; to arrive; to enter; to be bound to come; to be present.<br><br>**Practical Application**<br>The idea in this Scripture is that the Messiah was coming soon. His coming was at hand, imminent. The woman's belief was based upon such Scriptures as Genesis 3:15; Genesis 49:10; Numbers 24:17; Deut. 18:15. For example, note what happened in the prophetic blessing of Jacob (Genesis 49:10c-12). These points have a double reference, referring to both Judah and the Lord Jesus Christ.<br>⇒ The people would gather to offer their obedience to Judah, but even more, they would |

## PRACTICAL WORD STUDIES in the NEW TESTAMENT

| ENGLISH WORD | GREEK WORD AND VERSE | THE WORD MEANS... |
|---|---|---|
| | tell us all things. [KJV]<br>The woman said to Him, "I know that Messiah is **coming** (He who is called Christ); when that One comes, He will declare all things to us." [NASB]<br>The woman said to Him, "I know that Messiah is **coming**" (who is called Christ). "When He comes, He will tell us all things." [NKJV]<br>The woman said, "I know the Messiah will **come**—the one who is called Christ. When he comes, he will explain everything to us." [NLT]<br>λέγει αὐτῷ ἡ γυνή, Οἶδα ὅτι Μεσσίας **ἔρχεται** -- ὁ λεγόμενος Χριστός· -- ὅταν ἔλθῃ ἐκεῖνος, ἀναγγελεῖ ἡμῖν πάντα. [GNS]<br>λέγει αὐτῷ ἡ γυνή, Οἶδα ὅτι Μεσσίας **ἔρχεται** ὁ λεγόμενος Χριστός· ὅταν ἔλθῃ ἐκεῖνος, ἀναγγελεῖ ἡμῖν ἅπαντα. [GNT] | eternally gather to offer their obedience to Shiloh, the Messiah (Genesis 49:10c).<br>⇒ Judah would bring great prosperity and abundance to Israel, but even more, Shiloh, the Messiah, would bring prosperity and abundance to the people of the earth. Note the figurative language used to describe this fact: the vineyards would be producing so much fruit that Judah would tie his donkey to a vine, and the loss of the vine destroyed by the tied strap would not be felt. There would be such an abundance of fruit that he could wash his clothes in the juice of the grapes.<br>⇒ Judah would bring health to the people, but even more, Shiloh, the Messiah, would bring health (Genesis 49:12). Again, the language is figurative. His eyes would be darker or duller than wine and his teeth whiter than milk. The thought is that of a healthy color, of good nourishment and health. |
| **#618**<br>**Come–**<br>**Come, Full–**<br>**Come, Fully**<br><br>Full come–KJV<br>Fully come–NASB<br>Come–NIV<br>Fully come–NKJV<br>Come–NLT<br><br>**POSB REFERENCE**<br>(Jn.7:6-9; esp. v.8)<br>Note 3, point 3 | πεπλήρωται = *peplērōtai*<br>Pronunciation: [peh-play-ro'-tah-ee]<br>Parsing (part of speech): verb<br>   Mood—indicative<br>   Tense—perfect<br>   Voice—passive<br>   Person—3rd person<br>   Number—singular<br>   Stem or root— from πληρόω<br>Concordance References:<br>  ⇒ Strong's #4137 pleroo<br>  ⇒ NIV #4444 pleroo<br>  ⇒ NASB #4137 pleroo<br><br>**John 7:8**<br>Go ye up unto this feast: I go not up yet unto this feast; for my time is not yet **full come**. [KJV]<br>"Go up to the feast yourselves; I do not go up to this feast because My time has not yet **fully come**." [NASB]<br>You go to the Feast. I am not yet going up to this Feast, because for me the right time has not yet **come**." [NIV]<br>You go up to this feast. I am not yet going up to this feast, for My time has not yet **fully come**." [NKJV]<br>You go on. I am not yet ready to go to this festival, because my time has not yet **come**." [NLT]<br>ὑμεῖς ἀνάβητε εἰς τὴν ἑορτὴν ταύτην· ἐγὼ οὔπω ἀναβαίνω εἰς τὴν ἑορτὴν ταύτην, ὅτι ὁ καιρὸς ὁ ἐμὸς οὔπω **πεπλήρωται**. [GNS]<br>ὑμεῖς ἀνάβητε εἰς τὴν ἑορτήν· ἐγὼ οὐκ ἀναβαίνω εἰς τὴν ἑορτὴν ταύτην, ὅτι ὁ ἐμὸς καιρὸς οὔπω **πεπλήρωται**. [GNT] | To come; to fully come; to fill; to fulfill; to fill up completely and entirely; to bring to completion; to make complete.<br><br>**Practical Application**<br>In this Scripture, it is not time for Jesus' full revelation. His predestined hour to die for the world was not to be, not yet. It was to come, but in God's time. And when it came, His claims and works would be validated and proven beyond question. Many would proclaim Him to be both Lord and Savior, the Bread of Life who alone can fill and satisfy the desperate and starving needs of men. |
| **#619**<br>**Come (Back)**<br>**To Your**<br>**Senses**<br><br>Awake–KJV<br>Become sober minded–NASB<br>Come back to your senses–NIV<br>Awake–NKJV<br>Come to your senses–NLT<br><br>**POSB REFERENCE**<br>(1 Cor.15:34)<br>Note 4 | ἐκνήψατε = *eknēpsate*<br>Pronunciation: [ek-nay'-fah-teh]<br>Parsing (part of speech): verb<br>   Mood—imperative<br>   Tense—aorist<br>   Voice—active<br>   Person—2nd person<br>   Number—plural<br>   Stem or root—from ἐκνήφω<br>Concordance References:<br>  ⇒ Strong's #1594 eknēphō<br>  ⇒ NIV #1729 eknēphō<br>  ⇒ NASB #1594 eknēphō<br><br>**1 Cor. 15:34**<br>**Awake** to righteousness, and sin not; for some have not the knowledge of God: I speak *this* to your shame. [KJV]<br>**Become sober-minded** as you ought, and stop sinning; for some have no knowledge of God. I speak *this* to | Come back to your senses; become sober; arouse yourself out of a drunken, sleepy state.<br><br>**Practical Application**<br>Some in the Corinthian church were following the false teachers as though they were drunken and senseless, in a stupor, in a stupid state. They desperately needed to awaken to righteousness—to stop sinning. The denial of a resurrection is totally wrong; it is sin. There is to be a resurrection of the dead. To deny this fact is to put oneself in a drunken, senseless, unthinking state of mind. |

# PRACTICAL WORD STUDIES
## in the NEW TESTAMENT

| ENGLISH WORD | GREEK WORD AND VERSE | THE WORD MEANS... |
|---|---|---|
| | your shame. [NASB]<br>**Come back to your senses** as you ought, and stop sinning; for there are some who are ignorant of God—I say this to your shame. [NIV]<br>**Awake** to righteousness, and do not sin; for some do not have the knowledge of God. I speak *this* to your shame. [NKJV]<br>**Come to your senses** and stop sinning. For to your shame I say that some of you don't even know God. [NLT]<br>ἐκνήψατε δικαίως καὶ μὴ ἁμαρτάνετε· ἀγνωσίαν γὰρ Θεοῦ τινες ἔχουσι· πρὸς ἐντροπὴν ὑμῖν λέγω. [GNS]<br>ἐκνήψατε δικαίως καὶ μὴ ἁμαρτάνετε, ἀγνωσίαν γὰρ θεοῦ τινες ἔχουσιν, πρὸς ἐντροπὴν ὑμῖν λαλῶ. [GNT] | |
| **#620**<br>**Come As Soon As Possible**<br><br>Not delay–KJV<br>Do not delay–NASB<br>At once–NIV<br>Not to delay–NKJV<br>**Come as soon as possible–NLT**<br><br>**POSB REFERENCE**<br>(Acts 9:36-39; esp. v.38)<br>Note 2, point 3c | Μὴ ὀκνήσῃς = Mē oknēsēs<br>Pronunciation: [may ok-nay'-says]<br>Parsing *oknēsēs* (part of speech): verb<br>   Mood—subjunctive or imperative<br>   Tense—aorist<br>   Voice—active<br>   Person—2nd person<br>   Number—singular<br>   Stem or root—from ὀκνέω<br>Concordance References:<br>  ⇒ Strong's #3361 + 3635 mē okneō<br>  ⇒ NIV #3590 + 3890 mē okneō [at once]<br>  ⇒ NASB #3361 + 3635 mē okneō<br><br>**Acts 9:38**<br>And forasmuch as Lydda was nigh to Joppa, and the disciples had heard that Peter was there, they sent unto him two men, desiring *him* that he would **not delay** to come to them. [KJV]<br>And since Lydda was near Joppa, the disciples, having heard that Peter was there, sent two men to him, entreating him, "**Do not delay** to come to us." [NASB]<br>Lydda was near Joppa; so when the disciples heard that Peter was in Lydda, they sent two men to him and urged him, "Please come **at once**!" [NIV]<br>And since Lydda was near Joppa, and the disciples had heard that Peter was there, they sent two men to him, imploring *him* **not to delay** in coming to them. [NKJV]<br>But they had heard that Peter was nearby at Lydda, so they sent two men to beg him, "Please **come as soon as possible**!" [NLT]<br>ἐγγὺς δὲ οὔσης Λύδδης τῇ Ἰόππῃ, οἱ μαθηταὶ ἀκούσαντες ὅτι Πέτρος ἐστιν ἐν αὐτῇ, ἀπέστειλαν δύο ἄνδρας πρὸς αὐτὸν παρακαλοῦντες **μὴ ὀκνῆσαι** διελθεῖν ἕως αὐτῶν. [GNS]<br>ἐγγὺς δὲ οὔσης Λύδδας τῇ Ἰόππῃ οἱ μαθηταὶ ἀκούσαντες ὅτι Πέτρος ἐστὶν ἐν αὐτῇ ἀπέστειλαν δύο ἄνδρας πρὸς αὐτὸν παρακαλοῦντες, **Μὴ ὀκνήσῃς** διελθεῖν ἕως ἡμῶν. [GNT] | At once; without delay; to come as soon as possible.<br><br>**Practical Application**<br>It means not to hesitate, not to be reluctant, but to act and act now, quickly, without questioning. |
| **#621**<br>**Come To Know**<br><br>Knowledge–KJV<br>Knowledge–NASB<br>Knowledge–NIV<br>Knowledge–NKJV<br>**Come to know–NLT**<br><br>**POSB REFERENCE**<br>(2 Pt.1:2)<br>Note 3, point 3 | ἐπιγνώσει = epignōsei<br>Pronunciation: [ep-ig'-no-seh-ee]<br>Parsing (part of speech): noun<br>   Case—dative<br>   Gender—feminine<br>   Number—singular<br>   Stem or root—from ἐπίγνωσις, εως<br>Concordance References:<br>  ⇒ Strong's #1922 epignōsis<br>  ⇒ NIV #2106 epignōsis<br>  ⇒ NASB #1922 epignōsis<br><br>**2 Peter 1:2**<br>Grace and peace be multiplied unto you through the **knowledge** of God, and of Jesus our Lord, [KJV]<br>Grace and peace be multiplied to you in the **knowledge** of God and of Jesus our Lord; [NASB]<br>Grace and peace be yours in abundance through the **knowledge** of God and of Jesus our Lord. [NIV]<br>Grace and peace be multiplied to you in the **knowledge** of God and of Jesus our Lord, [NKJV] | Full, personal, precise, and correct; to know and possess full understanding; to know in a personal, conscious way.<br><br>**Practical Application**<br>Note that Jesus Christ multiplies grace and peace. He gives an abundance of grace and peace; He causes grace and peace to overflow in the life of the genuine believer. There is never to be a lack of grace and peace in the life of any true believer. Every believer is to always be overflowing with joy, with the favor and blessings of God and with peace within his own spirit and with God and others.<br>How can a person always be overflowing with the grace and peace of God? Through the knowledge of God and of Jesus our Lord. We have to know God in order to receive the grace and peace of God. What does it mean to know |

# PRACTICAL WORD STUDIES
## in the NEW TESTAMENT

| ENGLISH WORD | GREEK WORD AND VERSE | THE WORD MEANS... |
|---|---|---|
| | May God bless you with his special favor and wonderful peace as you **come to know** Jesus, our God and Lord, better and better. [NLT]<br>χάρις ὑμῖν καὶ εἰρήνη πληθυνθείη ἐν **ἐπιγνώσει** τοῦ Θεοῦ καὶ Ἰησοῦ τοῦ Κυρίου ἡμῶν· [GNS]<br>χάρις ὑμῖν καὶ εἰρήνη πληθυνθείη ἐν **ἐπιγνώσει** τοῦ θεοῦ καὶ Ἰησοῦ τοῦ κυρίου ἡμῶν. [GNT] | God? The words "come to know" (*epignōsei*) mean "full, personal, precise, and correct" knowledge (The Amplified New Testament).<br>⇒ It means to know Christ personally; to know Him by experience. It means to know Christ just like we know any person: by walking and talking with Him.<br>⇒ It means to know Christ fully; to know Him in all of His person, exactly who He is. It means to be precise and correct in what we know about Him.<br>The point is this: if a person knows Christ fully and personally, precisely and correctly, then he knows Christ as Savior and Lord. He knows Christ as the Son of God who was sent to earth by the Father to save the world. The person does not look upon Christ as a mere man, as a great religious leader who founded the religion of Christianity. The person looks upon Jesus Christ as the Savior and Lord of men, and he knows Christ personally. He experiences Christ: he comes to Christ and asks Christ to save him and to be the Lord of his life. He gives all that he is and has to Christ, surrendering totally to Christ as his Lord. It is the person who so surrenders to Christ that comes to know Christ, and day by day, the person experiences the overflow of the Lord's grace and peace. |
| **#622**<br>**Come To The Aid**<br><br>Succour–KJV<br>Come to the aid–NASB<br>Help–NIV<br>Aid–NKJV<br>Help–NLT<br><br>**POSB REFERENCE**<br>(Heb 2:17-18, esp. v.18)<br>Note 2 | βοηθῆσαι = *boëthësai*<br>Pronunciation: [bo-ay-thay'-sah-ee]<br>Parsing (part of speech): verb<br>    Mood—infinitive<br>    Tense—aorist<br>    Voice—active<br>    Stem or root—from βοηθέω<br>Concordance References:<br>  ⇒ Strong's #997 boëtheō<br>  ⇒ NIV #1070 boëtheō<br>  ⇒ NASB #997 boëtheō<br><br>**Hebrews 2:18**<br>For in that he himself hath suffered being tempted, he is able to **succour** them that are tempted. [KJV]<br>For since He Himself was tempted in that which He has suffered, He is able to **come to the aid** of those who are tempted. [NASB]<br>Because he himself suffered when he was tempted, he is able to **help** those who are being tempted. [NIV]<br>For in that He Himself has suffered, being tempted, He is able to **aid** those who are tempted. [NKJV]<br>Since he himself has gone through suffering and temptation, he is able to **help** us when we are being tempted. [NLT]<br>ἐν ᾧ γὰρ πέπονθεν αὐτὸς πειρασθείς, δύναται τοῖς πειραζομένοις **βοηθῆσαι**. [GNS]<br>ἐν ᾧ γὰρ πέπονθεν αὐτὸς πειρασθείς, δύναται τοῖς πειραζομένοις **βοηθῆσαι**. [GNT] | To help; to aid; to relieve, to assist; to come to the aid.<br><br>**Practical Application**<br>Jesus Christ became the High Priest so that He could come to the aid of man when he faces the trials and temptations of life. The words "come to the aid" (*boëthësai*) mean to help, relieve, assist; to be so eager to help that one runs to the cry of a person. What a picture of Jesus Christ! He has heard our cry in all of our suffering and pain, trial and temptation; and He has run to help and deliver us. Just think! He has been made like us in order to feel with us and deliver us. He has become the perfect High Priest. He needed to do this in order to experience every situation, condition, and trial of man. He experienced the most humiliating experiences imaginable. He experienced...<br>• being born to an unwed mother (Matthew 1:18-19).<br>• being born in a stable, the worst of conditions (Luke 2:7).<br>• being born to poor parents (Luke 2:24).<br>• having his life threatened as a baby (Matthew 2:13f).<br>• being the cause of unimaginable sorrow (Matthew 2:16f).<br>• having to be moved and shifted about as a baby (Matthew 2:13f).<br>• being reared in a despicable place, Nazareth (Luke 2:39).<br>• having His father die during His youth (see POSB note, pt. 3—Matthew 13:53-58).<br>• having to support His mother and brothers and sisters (see POSB note, pt. 3—Matthew 13:53-58).<br>• having no home, not even a place to lay |

# PRACTICAL WORD STUDIES
## in the NEW TESTAMENT

| ENGLISH WORD | GREEK WORD AND VERSE | THE WORD MEANS... |
|---|---|---|
| | | His head (Matthew 8:20; Luke 9:58).<br>• being hated and opposed by religionists (Mark 14:1-2).<br>• being charged with insanity (Mark 3:21).<br>• being charged with demon possession (Mark 3:22).<br>• being opposed by His own family (Mark 3:31-32).<br>• being rejected, hated, and opposed by listeners (Matthew 13:53-58; Luke 4:28-29).<br>• being betrayed by a close friend (Mark 14:10-11, 18).<br>• being left alone, rejected, and forsaken by all of His friends (Mark 14:50).<br>• being tried before the high court of the land on the charge of treason (John 18:33).<br>• being executed by crucifixion, the worst possible death (John 19:16f).<br>And Jesus Christ suffered so much more, but the point to note is this: in each of these experiences His suffering reached the depth of humiliation. Christ stooped to the lowest point of human experience in every condition in order to become the *Perfect Sympathizer* (Savior). This is the reason He can now identify with and feel for any person's circumstances. No person ever comes close to the depth of suffering and humiliation He bore. Jesus Christ can succor—help, feel for, care for, and look after—every person no matter his condition, trial, or temptation. |
| #623<br>**Come, O Lord!–<br>Come, Our Lord,**<br><br>Maranatha–KJV<br>Maranatha–NASB<br>**Come, O Lord!–NIV**<br>**O Lord, come–NKJV**<br>**Our Lord, come!–NLT**<br><br>**POSB REFERENCE**<br>(1 Cor.16:19-24; esp. v.22)<br>Note 6, point 2 | Μαρανα θα = *Marana tha*<br>Pronunciation: [mar'-an-ah thah']<br>Parsing *Marana* (part of speech): noun<br>    Case—vocative<br>    Gender—masculine<br>    Number—singular<br>    Stem or root—from μαράνα θα<br>Parsing *tha* (part of speech): verb<br>    Mood—imperative<br>    Tense—aorist<br>    Voice—active<br>    Person—2nd person<br>    Number—singular<br>    Stem or root—from μαράνα θα<br>Concordance References:<br>⇒ Strong's #3134 marana tha<br>⇒ NIV #3448 marana tha<br>⇒ NASB #3134 marana tha<br><br>**1 Cor. 16:22**<br>If any man love not the Lord Jesus Christ, let him be Anathema **Maranatha**. [KJV]<br>If anyone does not love the Lord, let him be accursed. **Maranatha**. [NASB]<br>If anyone does not love the Lord—a curse be on him. **Come, O Lord!** [NIV]<br>If anyone does not love the Lord Jesus Christ, let him be accursed. **O Lord, come**! [NKJV]<br>If anyone does not love the Lord, that person is cursed. **Our Lord, come!** [NLT]<br>εἴ τις οὐ φιλεῖ τὸν Κύριον Ἰησοῦν Χριστόν, ἤτω ἀνάθεμα. **Μαρὰν ἀθα.** [GNS]<br>εἴ τις οὐ φιλεῖ τὸν κύριον, ἤτω ἀνάθεμα. **Μαρανα θα.** [GNT] | Come, O Lord!; Our Lord, come! (in Aramaic).<br><br>**Practical Application**<br>How do we know that Christ is going to return to earth and take believers to live with God forever? Because God raised up Christ from the dead. By resurrecting Christ, God...<br>• proved that He is the God of all power.<br>• proved that He has the power to raise the dead.<br>• proved that He is going to do just as Christ taught: raise all men, some to eternal life and some to eternal death, that is, to be eternally separated from God. |
| #624<br>**Comes And Fills** | ἐνδύσησθε = *endusësthe*<br>Pronunciation: [en-doo'-sees-thay]<br>Parsing (part of speech): verb<br>    Mood—subjunctive<br>    Tense—aorist<br>    Voice—middle | To put on a garment; to be clothed with; to wear; to dress.<br><br>**Practical Application**<br>In this Scripture, we find that the source of the Spirit and power was God. |

# PRACTICAL WORD STUDIES
## in the New Testament

| ENGLISH WORD | GREEK WORD AND VERSE | THE WORD MEANS... |
|---|---|---|
| Enued with–KJV<br>Clothed with–NASB<br>Clothed with–NIV<br>Endued with–NKJV<br>**Comes and fills–NLT**<br><br>**POSB REFERENCE**<br>(Lk.24:44-49; esp. v.49)<br>Note 2, point 4c | Person—2nd person<br>Number—plural<br>Stem or root—from ἐνδύω<br>Concordance References:<br>⇒ Strong's #1746 enduō<br>⇒ NIV #1907 enduō<br>⇒ NASB #1746 enduō<br><br>**Luke 24:49**<br>And, behold, I send the promise of my Father upon you: but tarry ye in the city of Jerusalem, until ye be **endued with** power from on high. [KJV]<br>"And behold, I am sending forth the promise of My Father upon you; but you are to stay in the city until you are **clothed with** power from on high." [NASB]<br>I am going to send you what my Father has promised; but stay in the city until you have been **clothed with** power from on high." [NIV]<br>Behold, I send the Promise of My Father upon you; but tarry in the city of Jerusalem until you are **endued with** power from on high." [NKJV]<br>"And now I will send the Holy Spirit, just as my Father promised. But stay here in the city until the Holy Spirit **comes and fills** you with power from heaven." [NLT]<br>καὶ ἰδοὺ ἐγὼ ἀποστέλλω τὴν ἐπαγγελίαν τοῦ πατρός μου ἐφ' ὑμᾶς· ὑμεῖς δὲ καθίσατε ἐν τῇ πόλει Ἰερουσαλήμ, ἕως οὗ **ἐνδύσησθε** δύναμιν ἐξ ὕψους. [GNS]<br>καὶ [ἰδοὺ] ἐγὼ ἀποστέλλω τὴν ἐπαγγελίαν τοῦ πατρός μου ἐφ' ὑμᾶς· ὑμεῖς δὲ καθίσατε ἐν τῇ πόλει ἕως οὗ **ἐνδύσησθε** ἐξ ὕψους δύναμιν. [GNT] | ⇒ Christ was to send the promise.<br>⇒ The promise was from the Father. God gave the promise.<br>⇒ Believers had to stay; to tarry; that is, to wait upon the Lord and pray for the promise.<br>⇒ The promise was to come "from heaven." God Himself was the Source of power for all evangelism. |
| #625<br>**Comes To An End**<br><br>Fulfilled–KJV<br>Fulfilled–NASB<br>Fulfilled–NIV<br>Fulfilled–NKJV<br>**Comes to an end–NLT**<br><br>**POSB REFERENCE**<br>(Lk.21:24)<br>Note 5, point 1 | πληρωθῶσιν = plērōthōsin<br>Pronunciation: [play-ro'-tho-sin]<br>Parsing (part of speech): verb<br>  Mood—subjunctive<br>  Tense—aorist<br>  Voice—passive<br>  Person—3rd person<br>  Number—plural<br>  Stem or root—from πληρόω<br>Concordance References:<br>⇒ Strong's #4137 plēroō<br>⇒ NIV #4444 plēroō<br>⇒ NASB #4137 plēroō<br><br>**Luke 21:24**<br>And they shall fall by the edge of the sword, and shall be led away captive into all nations: and Jerusalem shall be trodden down of the Gentiles, until the times of the Gentiles be **fulfilled**. [KJV]<br>And they will fall by the edge of the sword, and will be led captive into all the nations; and Jerusalem will be trampled under foot by the Gentiles until the times of the Gentiles be **fulfilled**. [NASB]<br>They will fall by the sword and will be taken as prisoners to all the nations. Jerusalem will be trampled on by the Gentiles until the times of the Gentiles are **fulfilled**. [NIV]<br>And they will fall by the edge of the sword, and be led away captive into all nations. And Jerusalem will be trampled by Gentiles until the times of the Gentiles are **fulfilled**. [NKJV]<br>They will be brutally killed by the sword or sent away as captives to all the nations of the world. And Jerusalem will be conquered and trampled down by the Gentiles until the age of the Gentiles **comes to an end**. [NLT]<br>αἱ πεσοῦνται στόματι μαχαίρης, καὶ αἰχμαλωτισθήσονται εἰς πάντα τὰ ἔθνη· καὶ Ἰερουσαλὴμ ἔσται πατουμένη ὑπὸ ἐθνῶν, ἄχρι **πληρωθῶσι** καιροὶ ἐθνῶν. [GNS]<br>καὶ πεσοῦνται στόματι μαχαίρης καὶ αἰχμαλωτισθήσονται εἰς τὰ ἔθνη πάντα, καὶ Ἰερουσαλὴμ ἔσται πατουμένη ὑπὸ ἐθνῶν, ἄχρι οὗ **πληρωθῶσιν** καιροὶ ἐθνῶν. [GNT] | To fill; to fill up; to make full; to come to an end; to bring to completion; to finish.<br><br>**Practical Application**<br>It means that God is in control of the ages. There is a purpose to "the age of the Gentiles" and to what has happened and is yet to happen. God is in control of history. |

**PRACTICAL WORD STUDIES**
**in the NEW TESTAMENT**

| ENGLISH WORD | GREEK WORD AND VERSE | THE WORD MEANS... |
|---|---|---|
| **#626**<br>**Comfort**<br><br>**Comfort**–KJV<br>Not translated–NASB<br>Not translated–NIV<br>Cheer–NKJV<br>Not translated–NLT<br><br>**POSB**<br>**REFERENCE**<br>(Lk.8:43-48; esp. v.48)<br>Note 3, point 5b | Θάρσει = *tharsei*<br>Pronunciation: [thar-seh'-ee]<br>Parsing (part of speech): verb<br>    Mood—imperative<br>    Tense—present<br>    Person—2nd person<br>    Number—singular<br>    Stem or root—from Θαρσέω<br>Note: the correct parsing for this word is debatable. In referring to different Greek sources, the above is selected from Moulton's Analytical Greek Lexicon Revised 1978 Edition, p.191.<br>Concordance References:<br>  ⇒ Strong's #2293 tharseo<br>  ⇒ NIV #—Not Translated<br>  ⇒ NASB #—Not Translated<br><br>**Luke 8:48**<br>And he said unto her, Daughter, be of good **comfort**: thy faith hath made thee whole; go in peace. [KJV]<br>And He said to her, "Daughter, your faith has made you well; go in peace." [NASB]—Not Translated<br>Then he said to her, "Daughter, your faith has healed you. Go in peace." [NIV]—Not Translated<br>And He said to her, "Daughter, be of good **cheer**; your faith has made you well. Go in peace." [NKJV]<br>"Daughter," he said to her, "your faith has made you well. Go in peace." [NLT]—Not Translated<br>ὁ δὲ εἶπεν αὐτῇ, **Θάρσει**, θυγάτηρ, ἡ πίστις σου σέσωκέ σε· πορεύου εἰς εἰρήνην. [GNS]<br>ὁ δὲ εἶπεν αὐτῇ, Θυγάτηρ, ἡ πίστις σου σέσωκέν σε· πορεύου εἰς εἰρήνην. [GNT] | Comfort, or more accurately, cheer, courage, confidence, and boldness in her faith and healing.<br><br>**Practical Application**<br>The woman was to rest assured and be comforted; her faith was rewarded, wonderfully so. Her faith caused Jesus to meet her face to face; her faith did some wonderful things for her.<br>1. She was called, "Daughter." This was the only time Jesus ever called a woman, "Daughter." What a distinct privilege! It meant she had become a child of God's.<br>2. She was given comfort. [KJV only]<br>3. She was assured that she was well permanently. Her deliverance would last.<br>4. She was given peace (see POSB note—John 14:27). |
| **#627**<br>**Comfort**<br><br>Consolation–KJV<br>**Comfort**–NASB<br>**Comfort**–NIV<br>Consolation–NKJV<br>Happiness–NLT<br><br>**POSB**<br>**REFERENCE**<br>(Lk.6:24-26; esp. v.24)<br>Note 2, point 1d<br><br>**See also POSB REF:**<br>(Acts 15:30-35; esp. v.31)<br>Note 5, point 1 | παράκλησιν = *paraklēsin*<br>Pronunciation: [par-ak'-lay-sin]<br>Parsing (part of speech): noun<br>    Case—accusative<br>    Gender—feminine<br>    Number—singular<br>    Stem or root—from παράκλησις, εως<br>Concordance References:<br>  ⇒ Strong's #3874 paraklesis<br>  ⇒ NIV #4155 paraklēsis<br>  ⇒ NASB #3874 paraklesis<br><br>**Luke 6:24**<br>But woe unto you that are rich! for ye have received your **consolation**. [KJV]<br>"But woe to you who are rich, for you are receiving your **comfort** in full. [NASB]<br>"But woe to you who are rich, for you have already received your **comfort**. [NIV]<br>But woe to you who are rich, For you have received your **consolation**. [NKJV]<br>"What sorrows await you who are rich, for you have your only **happiness** now. [NLT]<br>πλὴν οὐαὶ ὑμῖν τοῖς πλουσίοις, ὅτι ἀπέχετε τὴν **παράκλησιν** ὑμῶν. [GNS]<br>Πλὴν οὐαὶ ὑμῖν τοῖς πλουσίοις, ὅτι ἀπέχετε τὴν **παράκλησιν** ὑμῶν. [GNT] | Comfort, help, aid, happiness, consolation, encouragement.<br><br>**Practical Application**<br>Their (the rich) only "comfort" is to be on this earth—the wealth they have. There will be no comfort after this life—no help, no aid, no encouragement, no cheer. They are paid in full. |
| **#628**<br>**Comfort**<br><br>**Comfort**–KJV<br>**Comfort**–NASB<br>Encouraged–NIV<br>**Comfort**–NKJV<br>**Comfort**–NLT | παρακλήσει = *paraklēsei*<br>Pronunciation: [par-ak'-lay-seh-ee]<br>Parsing (part of speech): noun<br>    Case—dative<br>    Gender—feminine<br>    Number—singular<br>    Stem or root—from παράκλησις, εως<br>Concordance References:<br>  ⇒ Strong's #3874 paraklēsis<br>  ⇒ NIV #4155 paraklēsis<br>  ⇒ NASB #3874 paraklēsis | Encouragement, comfort, help.<br><br>**Practical Application**<br>The word "comfort" (*paraklēsei*) means paraclete, the very title by which Christ called the Holy Spirit. It means comforter, advisor, helper, encourager, exhorter. The picture is that of One who is called to stand by the believer's side (just as Jesus did). |

# PRACTICAL WORD STUDIES
## in the NEW TESTAMENT

| ENGLISH WORD | GREEK WORD AND VERSE | THE WORD MEANS... |
|---|---|---|
| **POSB REFERENCE** (Acts 9:31) Note 3, point 2  See also POSB REF: (Rom.15:4) Note 2, point 2b | **Acts 9:31** Then had the churches rest throughout all Judaea and Galilee and Samaria, and were edified; and walking in the fear of the Lord, and in the **comfort** of the Holy Ghost, were multiplied. [KJV]  So the church throughout all Judea and Galilee and Samaria enjoyed peace, being built up; and, going on in the fear of the Lord and in the **comfort** of the Holy Spirit, it continued to increase. [NASB]  Then the church throughout Judea, Galilee and Samaria enjoyed a time of peace. It was strengthened; and **encouraged** by the Holy Spirit, it grew in numbers, living in the fear of the Lord. [NIV]  Then the churches throughout all Judea, Galilee, and Samaria had peace and were edified. And walking in the fear of the Lord and in the **comfort** of the Holy Spirit, they were multiplied. [NKJV]  The church then had peace throughout Judea, Galilee, and Samaria, and it grew in strength and numbers. The believers were walking in the fear of the Lord and in the **comfort** of the Holy Spirit. [NLT]  Αἱ μὲν οὖν ἐκκλησίαι καθ' ὅλης τῆς Ἰουδαίας καὶ Γαλιλαίας καὶ Σαμαρείας εἶχον εἰρήνην, οἰκοδομουμέναι καὶ πορευομέναι τῷ φόβῳ τοῦ Κυρίου, καὶ τῇ **παρακλήσει** τοῦ Ἁγίου Πνεύματος ἐπληθύνετο. [GNS]  Ἡ μὲν οὖν ἐκκλησία καθ' ὅλης τῆς Ἰουδαίας καὶ Γαλιλαίας καὶ Σαμαρείας εἶχεν εἰρήνην οἰκοδομουμένη καὶ πορευομένη τῷ φόβῳ τοῦ κυρίου καὶ τῇ **παρακλήσει** τοῦ ἁγίου πνεύματος ἐπληθύνετο. [GNT] | |
| **#629 Comfort**  Comfort–KJV Consolation–NASB Comfort–NIV Comfort–NKJV Comfort–NLT  **POSB REFERENCE** (Philip.2:1) Note 2 | παραμύθιον = *paramuthion* Pronunciation: [par-am-oo'-thee-on] Parsing (part of speech): noun  Case—nominative  Gender—feminine  Number—singular  Stem or root—from παράκλησις, εως Concordance References: ⇒ Strong's #3890 paramuthion ⇒ NIV #4172 paramuthion ⇒ NASB #3890 paramuthion  **Philip. 2:1** If *there be* therefore any consolation in Christ, if any **comfort** of love, if any fellowship of the Spirit, if any bowels and mercies, [KJV]  If therefore there is any encouragement in Christ, if there is any **consolation** of love, if there is any fellowship of the Spirit, if any affection and compassion, [NASB]  If you have any encouragement from being united with Christ, if any **comfort** from his love, if any fellowship with the Spirit, if any tenderness and compassion, [NIV]  Therefore if *there is* any consolation in Christ, if any **comfort** of love, if any fellowship of the Spirit, if any affection and mercy, [NKJV]  Is there any encouragement from belonging to Christ? Any **comfort** from his love? Any fellowship together in the Spirit? Are your hearts tender and sympathetic? [NLT]  Εἴ τις οὖν παράκλησις ἐν Χριστῷ, εἴ τι **παραμύθιον** ἀγάπης, εἴ τις κοινωνία Πνεύματος, εἴ τινα σπλάγχνα καὶ οἰκτιρμοί, [GNS]  Εἴ τις οὖν παράκλησις ἐν Χριστῷ, εἴ τι **παραμύθιον** ἀγάπης, εἴ τις κοινωνία πνεύματος, εἴ τις σπλάγχνα καὶ οἰκτιρμοί, [GNT] | Comfort, consolation, encouragement, help.  **Practical Application**  There is a comfort (*paramuthion*) of love that is in Christ. The love of Christ stirs a person to keep the unity with other believers. The word "love" is *agape* love, the love that is selfless and sacrificial. *Agape love* is the love of the mind, of the reason, and of the will. It is the love that goes so far...  • that it loves a person even if he does not deserve to be loved.  • that actually loves the person who is utterly unworthy of being loved.  Agape love is the love of Christ, the love which He showed when He gave and sacrificed Himself for us. We did not deserve it and were utterly unworthy of such love, yet Christ loved us despite all.  Imagine the spirit of unity that would exist within a church if every member would let the love of Christ flow through him. There would be no bitterness, anger, or strife—no action that would hurt another person whatsoever. If the person were wrong and deserved punishment, the church's members would sacrifice and give themselves for him. |
| **#630 Comfort**  Comfort–KJV Comfort–NASB Encourage–NIV | παρακαλέσαι = *parakalesai* Pronunciation: [par-ak-al-eh'-sah-ee] Parsing (part of speech): verb  Mood—optative  Tense—aorist  Voice—active  Person—3rd person | The word means exhortation, encouragement, admonition, comfort.  **Practical Application**  The person who is saved receives comfort (*parakalesai*). Note that God and Christ are the Ones who can comfort, exhort, and encourage |

# PRACTICAL WORD STUDIES
## in the NEW TESTAMENT

| ENGLISH WORD | GREEK WORD AND VERSE | THE WORD MEANS... |
|---|---|---|
| **Comfort–NKJV**<br>**Comfort–NLT**<br><br>**POSB<br>REFERENCE**<br>(2 Thes.2:16-17; esp. v.17)<br>Note 5, point 4 | Number—singular<br>Stem or root—from παρακαλέω<br>Concordance References:<br>⇒ Strong's #3870 parakaleō<br>⇒ NIV #4151 parakaleō<br>⇒ NASB #3870 parakaleō<br><br>**2 Thes. 2:17**<br>**Comfort** your hearts, and stablish you in every good word and work. [KJV]<br>**Comfort** and strengthen your hearts in every good work and word. [NASB]<br>**Encourage** your hearts and strengthen you in every good deed and word. [NIV]<br>**Comfort** your hearts and establish you in every good word and work. [NKJV]<br>**Comfort** your hearts and give you strength in every good thing you do and say. [NLT]<br>**παρακαλέσαι** ὑμῶν τὰς καρδίας, καὶ στηρίξαι ὑμᾶς ἐν παντὶ λόγῳ καὶ ἔργῳ ἀγαθῷ. [GNS]<br>**παρακαλέσαι** ὑμῶν τὰς καρδίας καὶ στηρίξαι ἐν παντὶ ἔργῳ καὶ λόγῳ ἀγαθῷ. [GNT] | the believer to live like they should. When the believer comes to Christ for strength, Christ will comfort and encourage him. |
| **#631<br>Comfort–<br>Comforting**<br><br>**Comfort–KJV**<br>Consolation–NASB<br>**Comfort–NIV**<br>**Comfort–NKJV**<br>**Comforting–NLT**<br><br>**POSB<br>REFERENCE**<br>(1 Cor.14:3)<br>*Deeper Study #1,*<br>point 3 | *παραμυθίαν* = *paramuthian*<br>Pronunciation: [par-am-oo-thee'-ahn]<br>Parsing (part of speech): noun<br>    Case—accusative<br>    Gender—feminine<br>    Number—singular<br>Stem or root—from παραμυθία, ας<br>Concordance References:<br>⇒ Strong's #3889 paramuthia<br>⇒ NIV #4171 paramuthia<br>⇒ NASB #3889 paramuthia<br><br>**1 Cor. 14:3**<br>But he that prophesieth speaketh unto men *to* edification, and exhortation, and **comfort**. [KJV]<br>But one who prophesies speaks to men for edification and exhortation and **consolation**. [NASB]<br>But everyone who prophesies speaks to men for their strengthening, encouragement and **comfort**. [NIV]<br>But he who prophesies speaks edification and exhortation and **comfort** to men. [NKJV]<br>But one who prophesies is helping others grow in the Lord, encouraging and **comforting** them. [NLT]<br>ὁ δὲ προφητεύων ἀνθρώποις λαλεῖ οἰκοδομὴν καὶ παράκλησιν καὶ **παραμυθίαν**. [GNS]<br>ὁ δὲ προφητεύων ἀνθρώποις λαλεῖ οἰκοδομὴν καὶ παράκλησιν καὶ **παραμυθίαν**. [GNT] | Comfort, consolation; to give strength and hope to; to ease the grief or trouble of someone.<br><br>**Practical Application**<br>Comfort (*paramuthian*) has the idea of comforting through the most severe experiences of life, for example, through death (cp. John 11:19, 31). |
| **#632<br>Comfort–<br>Comforts**<br><br>**Comfort–KJV**<br>**Comfort–NASB**<br>**Comfort–NIV**<br>**Comfort–NKJV**<br>**Comforts–NLT**<br><br>**POSB<br>REFERENCE**<br>(2 Cor.1:3)<br>Note 1 | *παρακλήσεως* = *paraklēseōs*<br>Pronunciation: [par-ak'-lay-seh-os]<br>Parsing (part of speech): noun<br>    Case—genitive<br>    Gender—feminine<br>    Number—singular<br>Stem or root—from παράκλησις, εως<br>Concordance References:<br>⇒ Strong's #3874 paraklēsis<br>⇒ NIV #4155 paraklēsis<br>⇒ NASB #3874 paraklēsis<br><br>**2 Cor. 1:3**<br>Blessed *be* God, even the Father of our Lord Jesus Christ, the Father of mercies, and the God of all **comfort**; [KJV]<br>Blessed *be* the God and Father of our Lord Jesus Christ, the Father of mercies and God of all **comfort**; [NASB]<br>Praise be to the God and Father of our Lord Jesus Christ, the Father of compassion and the God of all **comfort**, [NIV] | To comfort; to be by the side of another; to relieve and support; to give solace, consolation, and encouragement.<br><br>**Practical Application**<br>There is the idea of strength, an enablement, a confidence. It consoles and relieves a person, but it strengthens him at the same time. It charges a person to go out and face the world. Note the word is used ten times in 2 Cor. 1:3-7. |

# PRACTICAL WORD STUDIES
## in the NEW TESTAMENT

| ENGLISH WORD | GREEK WORD AND VERSE | THE WORD MEANS... |
|---|---|---|
| | Blessed *be* the God and Father of our Lord Jesus Christ, the Father of mercies and God of all **comfort**, [NKJV]<br>All praise to the God and Father of our Lord Jesus Christ. He is the source of every mercy and the God who **comforts** us. [NLT]<br>Εὐλογητὸς ὁ Θεὸς καὶ πατὴρ τοῦ Κυρίου ἡμῶν Ἰησοῦ Χριστοῦ, ὁ πατὴρ τῶν οἰκτιρμῶν καὶ Θεὸς πάσης **παρακλήσεως**, [GNS]<br>Εὐλογητὸς ὁ θεὸς καὶ πατὴρ τοῦ κυρίου ἡμῶν Ἰησοῦ Χριστοῦ, ὁ πατὴρ τῶν οἰκτιρμῶν καὶ θεὸς πάσης **παρακλήσεως**, [GNT] | |
| **#633**<br>**Comfort, Be Of Good**<br><br>Be of good comfort–KJV<br>Be comforted–NASB<br>Listen to...appeal–NIV<br>Be of good comfort–NKJV<br>Encourage each other–NLT<br><br>**POSB REFERENCE**<br>(2 Cor.13:11-13; esp. v.11)<br>Note 3 | **παρακαλεῖσθε** = *parakaleisthe*<br>Pronunciation: [par-ak-al-eehs'-the]<br>Parsing (part of speech): verb<br>    Mood—imperative<br>    Tense—present<br>    Voice—passive<br>    Person—2nd person<br>    Number—plural<br>    Stem or root—from παρακαλέω<br>Concordance References:<br>  ⇒ Strong's #3870 parakaleō<br>  ⇒ NIV #4151 parakaleō<br>  ⇒ NASB #3870 parakaleō<br><br>**2 Cor. 13:11**<br>Finally, brethren, farewell. Be perfect, **be of good comfort**, be of one mind, live in peace; and the God of love and peace shall be with you. [KJV]<br>Finally, brethren, rejoice, be made complete, **be comforted**, be like-minded, live in peace; and the God of love and peace shall be with you. [NASB]<br>Finally, brothers, good-by. Aim for perfection, **listen to** my **appeal**, be of one mind, live in peace. And the God of love and peace will be with you. [NIV]<br>Finally, brethren, farewell. Become complete. **Be of good comfort**, be of one mind, live in peace; and the God of love and peace will be with you. [NKJV]<br>Dear brothers and sisters, I close my letter with these last words: Rejoice. Change your ways. **Encourage each other**. Live in harmony and peace. Then the God of love and peace will be with you. [NLT]<br>Λοιπόν, ἀδελφοί, χαίρετε· καταρτίζεσθε, **παρακαλεῖσθε**, τὸ αὐτὸ φρονεῖτε, εἰρηνεύετε· καὶ ὁ Θεὸς τῆς ἀγάπης καὶ εἰρήνης ἔσται μεθ' ὑμῶν. [GNS]<br>Λοιπόν, ἀδελφοί, χαίρετε, καταρτίζεσθε, **παρακαλεῖσθε**, τὸ αὐτὸ φρονεῖτε, εἰρηνεύετε, καὶ ὁ θεὸς τῆς ἀγάπης καὶ εἰρήνης ἔσται μεθ' ὑμῶν. [GNT] | To be comforted; to encourage each other; to cheer up; to be assured, consoled. The word could also mean "be exhorted"; that is, listen and heed what I have said.<br><br>**Practical Application**<br>If the believers of the church would do these four things...<br>• be perfect, that is, complete<br>• be of good comfort<br>• be of one mind<br>• live in peace<br><br>...then the God of love and peace would be with them. Note that God is the Author, the Giver of love and peace. Therefore, if a man wishes to know true love and true peace, he must accept the challenge to live accordingly. |
| **#634**<br>**Comforted**<br><br>Comforted–KJV<br>Encouraged–NASB<br>Encouraged–NIV<br>Encouraged–NKJV<br>Encouraged–NLT<br><br>**POSB REFERENCE**<br>(Col.2:2-3; esp. v.2)<br>Note 2 | **παρακληθῶσιν** = *paraklēthōsin*<br>Pronunciation: [par-ak-lay-tho'-sin]<br>Parsing (part of speech): verb<br>    Mood—subjunctive<br>    Tense—aorist<br>    Voice—passive<br>    Person—3rd person<br>    Number—plural<br>    Stem or root—from παρακαλέω<br>Concordance References:<br>  ⇒ Strong's #3870 parakaleō<br>  ⇒ NIV #4151 parakaleō<br>  ⇒ NASB #3870 parakaleō<br><br>**Col. 2:2**<br>That their hearts might be **comforted**, being knit together in love, and unto all riches of the full assurance of understanding, to the acknowledgement of the mystery of God, and of the Father, and of Christ; [KJV]<br>That their hearts may be **encouraged**, having been knit together in love, and attaining to all the wealth that comes from the full assurance of understanding, resulting in a true knowledge of God's mystery, that is, Christ Himself, [NASB] | To be encouraged; to be comforted; to be consoled; to be appeased; to urge; to plead with. The word "comforted" (*paraklēthōsin*) means to be strong, strengthened, established and braced (Vincent. *Word Studies in the New Testament*, Vol.3, p.482).<br><br>**Practical Application**<br>It is the kind of strength...<br>• that stirs confidence and assurance.<br>• that braces a person to withstand the onslaught of false teaching, trials, and temptations.<br>• that comforts and builds assurance and confidence in life, both now and eternally.<br><br>The human heart aches for such strength, for this kind of confidence, assurance, and comfort. |

## PRACTICAL WORD STUDIES
### in the NEW TESTAMENT

| ENGLISH WORD | GREEK WORD AND VERSE | THE WORD MEANS... |
|---|---|---|
| | My purpose is that they may be **encouraged** in heart and united in love, so that they may have the full riches of complete understanding, in order that they may know the mystery of God, namely, Christ, [NIV]<br><br>That their hearts may be **encouraged**, being knit together in love, and *attaining* to all riches of the full assurance of understanding, to the knowledge of the mystery of God, both of the Father and of Christ, [NKJV]<br><br>My goal is that they will be **encouraged** and knit together by strong ties of love. I want them to have full confidence because they have complete understanding of God's secret plan, which is Christ himself. [NLT]<br><br>ἵνα **παρακληθῶσιν** αἱ καρδίαι αὐτῶν, συμβιβασθέντων ἐν ἀγάπῃ, καὶ εἰς πᾶν πλοῦτον τῆς πληροφορίας τῆς συνέσεως, εἰς ἐπίγνωσιν τοῦ μυστηρίου τοῦ Θεοῦ καὶ πατρὸς καὶ τοῦ Χριστοῦ, [GNS]<br><br>ἵνα **παρακληθῶσιν** αἱ καρδίαι αὐτῶν, συμβιβασθέντες ἐν ἀγάπῃ καὶ εἰς πᾶν πλοῦτος τῆς πληροφορίας τῆς συνέσεως, εἰς ἐπίγνωσιν τοῦ μυστηρίου τοῦ θεοῦ, Χριστοῦ, [GNT] | |
| **#635**<br>**Comforted Together**<br><br>Comforted together– KJV<br>Encouraged together– NASB<br>Mutually encouraged– NIV<br>Encouraged together– NKJV<br>Encouraged by yours– NLT<br><br>**POSB REFERENCE**<br>(Rom.1:10-13; esp. v.12)<br>Note 4, point 2 | συμπαρακληθῆναι = sumparaklēthēnai<br>Pronunciation: [soom-par-ak-leh'-thay-nah-ee]<br>Parsing (part of speech): verb<br>    Mood—infinitive<br>    Tense—aorist<br>    Voice—passive<br>    Case—accusative<br>    Stem or root—from συμπαρακαλέομαι<br>Concordance References:<br>  ⇒ Strong's #4837 sumparakaleō<br>  ⇒ NIV #5220 sumparakaleō<br>  ⇒ NASB #4837 sumparakaleō<br><br>**Romans 1:12**<br>That is, that I may be **comforted together** with you by the mutual faith both of you and me. [KJV]<br><br>That is, that I may be **encouraged together** with you *while* among you, each of us by the other's faith, both yours and mine. [NASB]<br><br>That is, that you and I may be **mutually encouraged** by each other's faith. [NIV]<br><br>That is, that I may be **encouraged together** with you by the mutual faith both of you and me. [NKJV]<br><br>I'm eager to encourage you in your faith, but I also want to be **encouraged by yours**. In this way, each of us will be a blessing to the other. [NLT]<br><br>τοῦτο δέ ἐστι, **συμπαρακληθῆναι** ἐν ὑμῖν διὰ τῆς ἐν ἀλλήλοις πίστεως ὑμῶν τε καὶ ἐμοῦ. [GNS]<br><br>τοῦτο δέ ἐστιν **συμπαρακληθῆναι** ἐν ὑμῖν διὰ τῆς ἐν ἀλλήλοις πίστεως ὑμῶν τε καὶ ἐμοῦ. [GNT] | To be encouraged together; to be mutually encouraged; to be strengthened and consoled together.<br><br>**Practical Application**<br>Paul wished to be comforted together with other believers. Paul expected to be taught and strengthened by the believers as well as to teach and to strengthen them. There was to be a mutual sharing among all. Paul expected all believers to be actively sharing the gospel. He even expected them to share with him so that he might grow and be more firmly rooted in the faith. |
| **#636**<br>**Comforted, Be**<br><br>Be of good comfort– KJV<br>**Be comforted–NASB**<br>Listen to appeal–NIV<br>Be of good comfort– NKJV<br>Encourage each other– NLT<br><br>**POSB REFERENCE**<br>(2 Cor.13:11-13; esp. v.11)<br>Note 3 | παρακαλεῖσθε = parakaleisthe<br>Pronunciation: [par-ak-al-eehs'-the]<br>Parsing (part of speech): verb<br>    Mood—imperative<br>    Tense—present<br>    Voice—passive<br>    Person—2nd person<br>    Number—plural<br>    Stem or root—from παρακαλέω<br>Concordance References:<br>  ⇒ Strong's #3870 parakaleō<br>  ⇒ NIV #4151 parakaleō<br>  ⇒ NASB #3870 parakaleō<br><br>**2 Cor. 13:11**<br>Finally, brethren, farewell. Be perfect, **be of good comfort**, be of one mind, live in peace; and the God of love and peace shall be with you. [KJV]<br><br>Finally, brethren, rejoice, be made complete, **be comforted**, be like-minded, live in peace; and the God of love and peace shall be with you. [NASB]<br><br>Finally, brothers, good-by. Aim for perfection, **listen** | To listen to an appeal; to be comforted; to encourage each other; to cheer up; to be assured, consoled. The word could also mean "be exhorted"; that is, listen to and heed what I have said.<br><br>**Practical Application**<br>If the believers of the church would do these four things...<br>• be made complete<br>• be comforted<br>• be like-minded<br>• live in peace<br><br>...then the God of love and peace would be with them. Note that God is the Author, the Giver of love and peace. Therefore, if a man wishes to know true love and true peace, he must accept the challenge and live accordingly. |

# PRACTICAL WORD STUDIES
## in the NEW TESTAMENT

| ENGLISH WORD | GREEK WORD AND VERSE | THE WORD MEANS... |
|---|---|---|
| | to my **appeal**, be of one mind, live in peace. And the God of love and peace will be with you. [NIV]<br><br>Finally, brethren, farewell. Become complete. **Be of good comfort**, be of one mind, live in peace; and the God of love and peace will be with you. [NKJV]<br><br>Dear brothers and sisters, I close my letter with these last words: Rejoice. Change your ways. **Encourage each other**. Live in harmony and peace. Then the God of love and peace will be with you. [NLT]<br><br>Λοιπόν, ἀδελφοί, χαίρετε· καταρτίζεσθε, **παρακαλεῖσθε**, τὸ αὐτὸ φρονεῖτε, εἰρηνεύετε· καὶ ὁ Θεὸς τῆς ἀγάπης καὶ εἰρήνης ἔσται μεθ' ὑμῶν. [GNS]<br><br>Λοιπόν, ἀδελφοί, χαίρετε, καταρτίζεσθε, **παρακαλεῖσθε**, τὸ αὐτὸ φρονεῖτε, εἰρηνεύετε, καὶ ὁ Θεὸς τῆς ἀγάπης καὶ εἰρήνης ἔσται μεθ' ὑμῶν. [GNT] | |
| **#637**<br>**Comforter**<br><br>Comforter–KJV<br>Helper–NASB<br>Counselor–NIV<br>Helper–NKJV<br>Counselor–NLT<br><br>**POSB REFERENCE**<br>(Jn.14:16)<br>*Deeper Study #1* | παράκλητον = *paraklēton*<br>Pronunciation: [par-ak'-lay-ton]<br>Parsing (part of speech): noun<br>   Case—accusative<br>   Gender—masculine<br>   Number—singular<br>   Stem or root—from παράκλητος, ου<br>Concordance References:<br>  ⇒ Strong's #3875 parakletos<br>  ⇒ NIV #4156 parakletos<br>  ⇒ NASB #3875 parakletos<br><br>**John 14:16**<br>And I will pray the Father, and he shall give you another **Comforter**, that he may abide with you for ever; [KJV]<br><br>"And I will ask the Father, and He will give you another **Helper**, that He may be with you forever; [NASB]<br><br>And I will ask the Father, and he will give you another **Counselor** to be with you forever—[NIV]<br><br>And I will pray the Father, and He will give you another **Helper**, that He may abide with you forever—[NKJV]<br><br>And I will ask the Father, and he will give you another **Counselor**, who will never leave you. [NLT]<br><br>καὶ ἐγὼ ἐρωτήσω τὸν πατέρα καὶ ἄλλον **παράκλητον** δώσει ὑμῖν, μένῃ ἵνα μεθ' ὑμῶν εἰς τὸν αἰῶνα, [GNS]<br><br>κἀγὼ ἐρωτήσω τὸν πατέρα καὶ ἄλλον **παράκλητον** δώσει ὑμῖν, ἵνα μεθ' ὑμῶν εἰς τὸν αἰῶνα ᾖ, [GNT] | Counselor, Comforter, Helper, Intercessor; One called in; One called to the side of another.<br><br>**Practical Application**<br>The purpose is to help in any way possible.<br>1. There is the picture of a friend called in to help a person who is troubled or distressed or confused.<br>2. There is the picture of a commander called in to help a discouraged and dispirited army.<br>3. There is the picture of a lawyer, an advocate called in to help a defendant who needs his case pleaded. There is no one word that can adequately translate *paracletos*. The word that probably comes closest is simply *Helper*. |
| **#638**<br>**Comfortless**<br><br>Comfortless–KJV<br>Orphans–NASB<br>Orphans–NIV<br>Orphans–NKJV<br>Orphans–NLT<br><br>**POSB REFERENCE**<br>(Jn.14:18-20; esp. v.18)<br>Note 4, point 1 | ὀρφανούς = *orphanous*<br>Pronunciation: [or-fan-oos']<br>Parsing (part of speech): pronominal adjective<br>   Case—accusative<br>   Gender—masculine<br>   Number—plural<br>   Stem or root—from ὀρφανός, ή, όν<br>Concordance References:<br>  ⇒ Strong's #3737 orphanos<br>  ⇒ NIV #4003 orphanos<br>  ⇒ NASB #3737 orphanos<br><br>**John 14:18**<br>I will not leave you **comfortless**: I will come to you. [KJV]<br><br>"I will not leave you as **orphans**; I will come to you. [NASB]<br><br>I will not leave you as **orphans**; I will come to you. [NIV]<br><br>I will not leave you **orphans**; I will come to you. [NKJV]<br><br>No, I will not abandon you as **orphans**—I will come to you. [NLT]<br><br>οὐκ ἀφήσω ὑμᾶς **ὀρφανούς**· ἔρχομαι πρὸς ὑμᾶς. [GNS]<br><br>Οὐκ ἀφήσω ὑμᾶς **ὀρφανούς**, ἔρχομαι πρὸς ὑμᾶς. [GNT] | Orphans; comfortless; to be without care of parents; to be alone; to be helpless; to be friendless.<br><br>**Practical Application**<br>Jesus would not leave them to struggle through the trials of life alone. Jesus' presence with His followers began with His resurrection and with the coming of the Holy Spirit. Jesus was saying that He would come to the believer in the person of the Holy Spirit. |

# PRACTICAL WORD STUDIES
## in the NEW TESTAMENT

| ENGLISH WORD | GREEK WORD AND VERSE | THE WORD MEANS... |
|---|---|---|
| **#639**<br>**Coming**<br><br>Cometh–KJV<br>**Coming–NASB**<br>**Coming–NIV**<br>**Coming–NKJV**<br>Come–NLT<br><br>**POSB REFERENCE**<br>(Jn.4:25)<br>Note 1, point 1 | ἔρχεται = *erchetai*<br>Pronunciation: [er'-cheh-tah-ee]<br>Parsing (part of speech): verb<br>    Mood—indicative<br>    Tense—present<br>    Voice—middle or passive deponent<br>    Person—3rd person<br>    Number—singular<br>    Stem or root—from ἔρχομαι<br>Concordance References:<br>    Strong's #2064 *erchomai*<br>    NIV #2262 *erchomai*<br>    NASB #2064 *erchomai*<br><br>**John 4:25**<br>The woman saith unto him, I know that Messias **cometh**, which is called Christ: when he is come, he will tell us all things. [KJV]<br>The woman said to Him, "I know that Messiah is **coming** (He who is called Christ); when that One comes, He will declare all things to us." [NASB]<br>The woman said to Him, "I know that Messiah is **coming**" (who is called Christ). "When He comes, He will tell us all things." [NKJV]<br>The woman said, "I know the Messiah will **come**—the one who is called Christ. When he comes, he will explain everything to us." [NLT]<br>λέγει αὐτῷ ἡ γυνή, Οἶδα ὅτι Μεσσίας **ἔρχεται** -- ὁ λεγόμενος Χριστός· ὅταν ἔλθῃ ἐκεῖνος, ἀναγγελεῖ ἡμῖν πάντα. [GNS]<br>λέγει αὐτῷ ἡ γυνή, Οἶδα ὅτι Μεσσίας **ἔρχεται** ὁ λεγόμενος Χριστός· ὅταν ἔλθῃ ἐκεῖνος, ἀναγγελεῖ ἡμῖν ἅπαντα. [GNT] | To come; to arrive; to enter; to be bound to come; to be present.<br><br>**Practical Application**<br>The idea in this Scripture is that the Messiah was coming soon. His coming was at hand, imminent. The woman's belief was based upon such Scriptures as Genesis 3:15; Genesis 49:10; Numbers 24:17; Deut. 18:15. For example, note what happened in the prophetic blessing of Jacob (Genesis 49:10c-12). These points have a double reference, referring to both Judah and the Lord Jesus Christ.<br>⇒ The people would gather to offer their obedience to Judah, but even more, they would eternally gather to offer their obedience to *Shiloh*, the Messiah (Genesis 49:10c).<br>⇒ Judah would bring great prosperity and abundance to Israel, but even more, *Shiloh*, the Messiah, would bring prosperity and abundance to the people of the earth. Note the figurative language used to describe this fact: the vineyards would be producing so much fruit that Judah would tie his donkey to a vine, and the loss of the vine destroyed by the tied strap would not be felt. There would be such an abundance of fruit that he could wash his clothes in the juice of the grapes.<br>⇒ Judah would bring health to the people, but even more, *Shiloh*, the Messiah, would bring health (Genesis 49:12). Again, the language is figurative. His eyes would be darker or duller than wine and his teeth whiter than milk. The thought is that of a healthy color, of good nourishment and health. |
| **#640**<br>**Coming**<br><br>**Coming–KJV**<br>**Coming–NASB**<br>**Coming–NIV**<br>**Coming–NKJV**<br>**Coming–NLT**<br><br>**POSB REFERENCE**<br>(2 Thes.2:8)<br>Note 4, point 2 | παρουσίας = *parousias*<br>Pronunciation: [par-oo-see'-ahs]<br>Parsing (part of speech): noun<br>    Case—genitive<br>    Gender—feminine<br>    Number—singular<br>    Stem or root—from παρουσία, ας<br>Concordance References:<br>    ⇒ Strong's #3952 *parousia*<br>    ⇒ NIV #4242 *parousia*<br>    ⇒ NASB #3952 *parousia*<br><br>**2 Thes. 2:8**<br>And then shall that Wicked be revealed, whom the Lord shall consume with the spirit of his mouth, and shall destroy with the brightness of his **coming**:[KJV]<br>And then that lawless one will be revealed whom the Lord will slay with the breath of His mouth and bring to an end by the appearance of His **coming**; [NASB]<br>And then the lawless one will be revealed, whom the Lord Jesus will overthrow with the breath of his mouth and destroy by the splendor of his **coming**. [NIV]<br>And then the lawless one will be revealed, whom the Lord will consume with the breath of His mouth and destroy with the brightness of His **coming**. [NKJV]<br>Then the man of lawlessness will be revealed, whom the Lord Jesus will consume with the breath of his mouth and destroy by the splendor of his **coming**. [NLT]<br>καὶ τότε ἀποκαλυφθήσεται ὁ ἄνομος, ὃν ὁ Κύριος ἀναλώσει τῷ πνεύματι τοῦ στόματος αὐτοῦ, καὶ καταργήσει τῇ ἐπιφανείᾳ τῆς **παρουσίας** αὐτοῦ· [GNS]<br>καὶ τότε ἀποκαλυφθήσεται ὁ ἄνομος, ὃν ὁ κύριος [Ἰησοῦς] ἀνελεῖ τῷ πνεύματι τοῦ στόματος αὐτοῦ καὶ καταργήσει τῇ ἐπιφανείᾳ τῆς **παρουσίας** αὐτοῦ, [GNT] | Coming, arrival, presence.<br><br>**Practical Application**<br>The Lord of glory will destroy the antichrist with the brightness of His coming. The word "brightness, appearance or splendor" (*epiphaneia*) is a very special word. It is a word chosen by the New Testament to refer only to the coming (*parousias*) of the Lord. It is used only five times in all the New Testament, and in every instance it refers to the Lord's coming into the world. It refers once to His first coming (2 Tim. 1:10) and four times to His second coming (1 Tim. 6:14; 2 Tim. 4:1, 8; Titus 2:13). The whole idea of *brightness* is splendor, radiance, glory, and light. Someone has pointed out that when Jesus Christ returns to earth, there will be such a spectacular display of glory and splendor that the explosion of every star in the universe could not match the sight of the Lord (source unknown). When Christ first appears, there will apparently be the energizing of a laser beam of glory zeroed in on the antichrist, and he shall be immediately destroyed by the radiance of the Lord's glory and light—quicker than we could blink an eye. Simply by showing Himself, the Lord will destroy the antichrist. Note: the word "destroy" does not mean to annihilate, but to make inoperative; to make powerless; to end; to put a stop to his evil work. |

# PRACTICAL WORD STUDIES
## in the NEW TESTAMENT

| ENGLISH WORD | GREEK WORD AND VERSE | THE WORD MEANS... |
|---|---|---|
| **#641**<br>**Coming**<br><br>Made–KJV<br>Made–NASB<br>Made–NIV<br>**Coming–NKJV**<br>Appeared–NLT<br><br>**POSB REFERENCE**<br>(Philip.2:7)<br>Note 3, point 2 | γενόμενος = *genomenos*<br>Pronunciation: [ghin'-om-eh-nos]<br>Parsing (part of speech): verb<br>   Mood—participle<br>   Tense—aorist<br>   Voice—middle deponent<br>   Case—nominative<br>   Gender—masculine<br>   Number—singular<br>   Stem or root—from γίνομαι<br>Concordance References:<br>⇒ Strong's #1096 ginomai<br>⇒ NIV #1181 ginomai<br>⇒ NASB #1096 ginomai<br><br>**Philip. 2:7**<br>But made himself of no reputation, and took upon him the form of a servant, and was **made** in the likeness of men: [KJV]<br>But emptied Himself, taking the form of a bond-servant, *and* being **made** in the likeness of men. [NASB]<br>But made himself nothing, taking the very nature of a servant, being **made** in human likeness. [NIV]<br>But made Himself of no reputation, taking the form of a bondservant, *and* **coming** in the likeness of men. [NKJV]<br>He made himself nothing; he took the humble position of a slave and **appeared** in human form. [NLT]<br>ἀλλ᾽ ἑαυτὸν ἐκένωσε, μορφὴν δούλου λαβών, ἐν ὁμοιώματι ἀνθρώπων **γενόμενος**· καὶ σχήματι εὑρεθεὶς ὡς ἄνθρωπος, [GNS]<br>ἀλλὰ ἑαυτὸν ἐκένωσεν μορφὴν δούλου λαβών, ἐν ὁμοιώματι ἀνθρώπων **γενόμενος**· καὶ σχήματι εὑρεθεὶς ὡς ἄνθρωπος [GNT] | To be made; to become; to appear. It means a definite entrance into time.<br><br>**Practical Application**<br>It is not a permanent state. Jesus became a man, but it was not to be a permanent state. It was only for a time, a particular period. In the fullness of time, He made a definite entrance into the world as a man.<br>Note that Jesus Christ did not come to earth as a prince or some great leader upon earth. He did not come to receive the homage and service of men. He came as the humblest of men, as a servant to serve men. "He was brought up meanly, probably working with his supposed father at his trade. His whole life was a life of humiliation, meanness, poverty, and disgrace; he had nowhere to lay his head, lived upon alms, was a man of sorrows and acquainted with grief, did not appear with external pomp or any marks of distinction from other men. This was the humiliation of his life" (Matthew Henry. *Matthew Henry's Commentary*, Vol.6, p.732f). |
| **#642**<br>**Command**<br><br>Commandment–KJV<br>Commandment–NASB<br>**Command–NIV**<br>Commandment–NKJV<br>**Command–NLT**<br><br>**POSB REFERENCE**<br>(1 Tim.1:1)<br>Note 1, point 1 | ἐπιταγὴν = *epitagēn*<br>Pronunciation: [ep-ee-tag-ayn']<br>Parsing (part of speech): noun<br>   Case—accusative<br>   Gender—feminine<br>   Number—singular<br>   Stem or root—from ἐπιταγή, ῆς<br>Concordance References:<br>⇒ Strong's #2003 epitagē<br>⇒ NIV #2198 epitagē<br>⇒ NASB #2003 epitagē<br><br>**1 Tim. 1:1**<br>Paul, an apostle of Jesus Christ by the **commandment** of God our Saviour, and Lord Jesus Christ, *which is* our hope; [KJV]<br>Paul, an apostle of Christ Jesus according to the **commandment** of God our Savior, and of Christ Jesus, *who is* our hope; [NASB]<br>Paul, an apostle of Christ Jesus by the **command** of God our Savior and of Christ Jesus our hope, [NIV]<br>Paul, an apostle of Jesus Christ, by the **commandment** of God our Svior and the Lord Jesus Christ, our hope, [NKJV]<br>This letter is from Paul, an apostle of Christ Jesus, appointed by the **command** of God our Savior and by Christ Jesus our hope. [NLT]<br>Παῦλος ἀπόστολος Ἰησοῦ Χριστοῦ κατ᾽ **ἐπιταγὴν** Θεοῦ σωτῆρος ἡμῶν, καὶ Κυρίου Ἰησοῦ Χριστοῦ τῆς ἐλπίδος ἡμῶν, [GNS]<br>Παῦλος ἀπόστολος Χριστοῦ Ἰησοῦ κατ᾽ **ἐπιταγὴν** Θεοῦ σωτῆρος ἡμῶν καὶ Χριστοῦ Ἰησοῦ τῆς ἐλπίδος ἡμῶν [GNT] | Command, commandment, authority, order, mandate, rule.<br><br>**Practical Application**<br>The word command (*epitagen*) means to be under orders; to be placed under obligation. It is the instructions given by some high official that must be carried out, for example, the word of a king. The word *command* has the sense of compulsion, force, and necessity.<br>Paul—the minister of God—was a man sent forth by the command and order of the King of kings, God Himself. The compulsion, force, and necessity of God's command drove him to be a minister of Christ Jesus. |
| **#643**<br>**Command** | παραγγείλῃς = *paraggeilēs*<br>Pronunciation: [par-ang-geh-i-lays]<br>Parsing (part of speech): verb<br>   Mood—subjunctive | To command; to charge; to instruct; to give strict orders to stop. |

# PRACTICAL WORD STUDIES
## in the NEW TESTAMENT

| ENGLISH WORD | GREEK WORD AND VERSE | THE WORD MEANS... |
|---|---|---|
| Charge–KJV<br>Instruct–NASB<br>**Command–NIV**<br>Charge–NKJV<br>Stop–NLT<br><br>**POSB REFERENCE**<br>(1 Tim.1:3)<br>Note 1 | Tense—aorist<br>Voice—active<br>Person—2nd person<br>Number—singular<br>Stem or root—from παραγγέλλω<br>Concordance References:<br>  Strong's #3853 paraggellö<br>  NIV #4133 paraggellö<br>  NASB #3853 paraggellö<br><br>**1 Tim. 1:3**<br>As I besought thee to abide still at Ephesus, when I went into Macedonia, that thou mightest **charge** some that they teach no other doctrine, [KJV]<br>As I urged you upon my departure for Macedonia, remain on at Ephesus, in order that you may **instruct** certain men not to teach strange doctrines, [NASB]<br>As I urged you when I went into Macedonia, stay there in Ephesus so that you may **command** certain men not to teach false doctrines any longer [NIV]<br>As I urged you when I went into Macedonia—remain in Ephesus that you may **charge** some that they teach no other doctrine, [NKJV]<br>When I left for Macedonia, I urged you to stay there in Ephesus and **stop** those who are teaching wrong doctrine. [NLT]<br>Καθὼς παρεκάλεσά σε προσμεῖναι ἐν Ἐφέσῳ, πορευόμενος εἰς Μακεδονίαν, ἵνα **παραγγείλῃς** τισὶ μὴ ἑτεροδιδασκαλεῖν, [GNS]<br>Καθὼς παρεκάλεσά σε προσμεῖναι ἐν Ἐφέσῳ πορευόμενος εἰς Μακεδονίαν, ἵνα **παραγγείλῃς** τισὶν μὴ ἑτεροδιδασκαλεῖν [GNT] | **Practical Application**<br>Timothy was in Ephesus and Paul was in Macedonia, a great distance apart. Ephesus was in Asia and Macedonia was in Europe, north of Greece. Note that Paul had to urge Timothy to stay at Ephesus. The church was in trouble because false teaching had seeped in, and the church needed Timothy. Apparently, Timothy felt incapable and wanted to join Paul until Paul could return to Ephesus and handle the situation himself. However, false teaching is so serious a matter that it has to be handled immediately when it raises its ugly head. Therefore, Timothy had to remain in Ephesus so that he could *command* the church to stop the false teaching. The word "command" (*paraggeilës*) is a strong word. It is a military word that means to pass commands down through the ranks. Timothy was to *give orders and charge* the false teachers to stop teaching false doctrine, and if this did not work, he was to order and charge the church to handle the false teachers. |
| #644<br>**Command**<br><br>Charge–KJV<br>**Command–NASB**<br>Instruction–NIV<br>Charge–NKJV<br>Instructions–NLT<br><br>**POSB REFERENCE**<br>(1 Tim.1:18)<br>Note 1 | παραγγελίαν = *paraggelian*<br>Pronunciation: [par-ang-gel-ee'-ahn]<br>Parsing (part of speech): noun<br>  Case—accusative<br>  Gender—feminine<br>  Number—singular<br>  Stem or root—from παραγγελία, ας<br>Concordance References:<br>⇒ Strong's #3852 paraggelia<br>⇒ NIV #4132 paraggelia<br>⇒ NASB #3852 paraggelia<br><br>**1 Tim. 1:18**<br>This **charge** I commit unto thee, son Timothy, according to the prophecies which went before on thee, that thou by them mightest war a good warfare; [KJV]<br>This **command** I entrust to you, Timothy, my son, in accordance with the prophecies previously made concerning you, that by them you may fight the good fight, [NASB]<br>Timothy, my son, I give you this **instruction** in keeping with the prophecies once made about you, so that by following them you may fight the good fight, [NIV]<br>This **charge** I commit to you, son Timothy, according to the prophecies previously made concerning you, that by them you may wage the good warfare, [NKJV]<br>Timothy, my son, here are my **instructions** for you, based on the prophetic words spoken about you earlier. May they give you the confidence to fight well in the Lord's battles. [NLT]<br>Ταύτην τὴν **παραγγελίαν** παρατίθεμαί σοι, τέκνον Τιμόθεε, κατὰ τὰς προαγούσας ἐπὶ σὲ προφητείας, ἵνα στρατεύῃ ἐν αὐταῖς τὴν καλὴν στρατείαν [GNS]<br>Ταύτην τὴν **παραγγελίαν** παρατίθεμαί σοι, τέκνον Τιμόθεε, κατὰ τὰς προαγούσας ἐπὶ σὲ προφητείας, ἵνα στρατεύῃ ἐν αὐταῖς τὴν καλὴν στρατείαν [GNT] | A command; an urgent command; a military command; a mandate; a decree; strict orders or instructions.<br><br>**Practical Application**<br>The command to the young minister is forceful—fight a good warfare! Paul is giving a "command" (*paraggelian*) to Timothy. It is a command that lays upon a person the most urgent and critical obligation. Donald Guthrie says, "The ministry is not a matter to be trifled with, but an order from the commander-in-chief" (*The Pastoral Epistles.* "Tyndale New Testament Commentaries," p.67). W.E. Vine points out that the "charge" is always a command from a superior that is to be transmitted to others; that is, this charge—the charge to fight a good warfare—is to be given to the young minister and he, in turn, is to pass the charge on to others (*Expository Dictionary of New Testament Words*). |

# PRACTICAL WORD STUDIES
## in the NEW TESTAMENT

| ENGLISH WORD | GREEK WORD AND VERSE | THE WORD MEANS... |
|---|---|---|
| **#645**<br>**Command**<br><br>Charge–KJV<br>Instruct–NASB<br>**Command–NIV**<br>**Command–NKJV**<br>Tell–NLT<br><br>**POSB REFERENCE**<br>(1 Tim.6:17-19; esp. v.17)<br>Note 1 | παράγγελλε = *paraggelle*<br>Pronunciation: [par-ang-gel'-leh]<br>Parsing (part of speech): verb<br>   Mood—imperative<br>   Tense—present<br>   Voice—active<br>   Person—2nd person<br>   Number—singular<br>   Stem or root—from παραγγέλλω<br>Concordance References:<br>  ⇒ Strong's #3853 *paraggellö*<br>  ⇒ NIV #4133 *paraggellö*<br>  ⇒ NASB #3853 *paraggellö*<br><br>**1 Tim. 6:17**<br>**Charge** them that are rich in this world, that they be not highminded, nor trust in uncertain riches, but in the living God, who giveth us richly all things to enjoy; [KJV]<br>**Instruct** those who are rich in this present world not to be conceited or to fix their hope on the uncertainty of riches, but on God, who richly supplies us with all things to enjoy. [NASB]<br>**Command** those who are rich in this present world not to be arrogant nor to put their hope in wealth, which is so uncertain, but to put their hope in God, who richly provides us with everything for our enjoyment. [NIV]<br>**Command** those who are rich in this present age not to be haughty, nor to trust in uncertain riches but in the living God, who gives us richly all things to enjoy. [NKJV]<br>**Tell** those who are rich in this world not to be proud and not to trust in their money, which will soon be gone. But their trust should be in the living God, who richly gives us all we need for our enjoyment. [NLT]<br>Τοῖς πλουσίοις ἐν τῷ νῦν αἰῶνι **παράγγελλε** μὴ ὑψηλοφρονεῖν, μηδὲ ἠλπικέναι ἐπὶ πλούτου ἀδηλότητι, ἀλλ' ἐν Θεῷ τῷ ζῶντι, τῷ παρέχοντι ἡμῖν πλουσίως πάντα εἰς ἀπόλαυσιν· [GNS]<br>Τοῖς πλουσίοις ἐν τῷ νῦν αἰῶνι **παράγγελλε** μὴ ὑψηλοφρονεῖν μηδὲ ἠλπικέναι ἐπὶ πλούτου ἀδηλότητι ἀλλ' ἐπὶ θεῷ τῷ παρέχοντι ἡμῖν πάντα πλουσίως εἰς ἀπόλαυσιν, [GNT] | To command; to charge; to instruct; to tell; to order; to rule.<br><br>**Practical Application**<br>The word "command" (*paraggelle*) is a strong word. It has the force of a military command, yet it has the tenderness of an appeal to it. It means to beg and beseech a person—strongly so—to the point that the person is commanded to act. In this charge, God is appealing and begging the rich person, but He is doing it so strongly that it is a command. The rich person is approached in love and tenderness and an appeal is made to him, but he is expected to do exactly what God says. |
| **#646**<br>**Commandment**<br><br>**Commandment–KJV**<br>**Commandment–NASB**<br>Command–NIV<br>**Commandment–NKJV**<br>Command–NLT<br><br>**POSB REFERENCE**<br>(1 Tim.1:1)<br>Note 1, point 1 | ἐπιταγήν = *epitagën*<br>Pronunciation: [ep-ee-tah-gayn']<br>Parsing (part of speech): noun<br>   Case—accusative<br>   Gender—feminine<br>   Number—singular<br>   Stem or root—from ἐπιταγή, ῆς<br>Concordance References:<br>  ⇒ Strong's #2003 *epitagë*<br>  ⇒ NIV #2198 *epitagë*<br>  ⇒ NASB #2003 *epitagë*<br><br>**1 Tim. 1:1**<br>Paul, an apostle of Jesus Christ by the **commandment** of God our Saviour, and Lord Jesus Christ, which is our hope; [KJV]<br>Paul, an apostle of Christ Jesus according to the **commandment** of God our Savior, and of Christ Jesus, who is our hope; [NASB]<br>Paul, an apostle of Christ Jesus by the **command** of God our Savior and of Christ Jesus our hope, [NIV]<br>Paul, an apostle of Jesus Christ, by the **commandment** of God our Svior and the Lord Jesus Christ, our hope, [NKJV]<br>This letter is from Paul, an apostle of Christ Jesus, appointed by the **command** of God our Savior and by Christ Jesus our hope. [NLT]<br>Παῦλος ἀπόστολος Ἰησοῦ Χριστοῦ κατ' **ἐπιταγὴν** Θεοῦ σωτῆρος ἡμῶν, καὶ Κυρίου Ἰησοῦ Χριστοῦ τῆς | Command, commandment, authority, order, mandate, rule.<br><br>**Practical Application**<br>The word "commandment" (*epitagën*) means to be under orders; to be placed under obligation. It is the instructions given by some high official that must be carried out, for example, the word of a king. The word *commandment* has the sense of compulsion, force, and necessity. Paul—the minister of God—was a man sent forth by the command and order of the King of kings, God Himself. The compulsion, force, and necessity of God's command drove him to be a minister of Christ Jesus. |

# PRACTICAL WORD STUDIES
## in the New Testament

| ENGLISH WORD | GREEK WORD AND VERSE | THE WORD MEANS... |
|---|---|---|
| | ἐλπίδος ἡμῶν, [GNS]<br>Παῦλος ἀπόστολος Χριστοῦ Ἰησοῦ κατ' **ἐπιταγὴν** θεοῦ σωτῆρος ἡμῶν καὶ Χριστοῦ Ἰησοῦ τῆς ἐλπίδος ἡμῶν [GNT] | |
| **#647**<br>**Commanded**<br><br>Charged–KJV<br>Gave [them] orders–NASB<br>**Commanded–NIV**<br>**Commanded–NKJV**<br>Told–NLT<br><br>**POSB REFERENCE**<br>(Mk.7:36)<br>Note 5 | διεστείλατο = *diesteilato*<br>Pronunciation: [dee-es-teel'-ah-tow]<br>Parsing (part of speech): verb<br>    Mood—indicative<br>    Tense—aorist<br>    Voice—middle<br>    Person—3rd person<br>    Number—singular<br>    Stem or root—from διαστέλλω<br>Concordance References:<br>  ⇒ Strong's #1291 diastellomai<br>  ⇒ NIV #1403 diastellō<br>  ⇒ NASB #1291 diastellō<br><br>**Mark 7:36**<br>And he **charged** them that they should tell no man: but the more he charged them, so much the more a great deal they published it; [KJV]<br><br>And He **gave them orders** not to tell anyone; but the more He ordered them, the more widely they continued to proclaim it. [NASB]<br><br>Jesus **commanded** them not to tell anyone. But the more he did so, the more they kept talking about it. [NIV]<br><br>Then He **commanded** them that they should tell no one; but the more He commanded them, the more widely they proclaimed it. [NKJV]<br><br>Jesus **told** the crowd not to tell anyone, but the more he told them not to, the more they spread the news, [NLT]<br><br>καὶ **διεστείλατο** αὐτοῖς ἵνα μηδενὶ εἴπωσιν· ὅσον δὲ αὐτὸς αὐτοῖς διεστέλλετο μᾶλλον περισσότερον ἐκήρυσσον· [GNS]<br><br>καὶ **διεστείλατο** αὐτοῖς ἵνα μηδενὶ λέγωσιν· ὅσον δὲ αὐτοῖς διεστέλλετο, αὐτοὶ μᾶλλον περισσότερον ἐκήρυσσον. [GNT] | To charge; to give a command; to give orders; to tell someone what to do or what not to do.<br><br>**Practical Application**<br>The word for "commanded" (*diesteilato*) is strong. The order was clearly given. There is a lesson on humility in the command. Jesus was not after the applause or praise of people. The miracles were not done for that reason. All that He was and all that He had done was to help people by pointing them to God. People were lost, and He had come to seek and save the lost, not to win their applause (cp. Luke 19:10). |
| **#648**<br>**Commanded**<br><br>Commanded–KJV<br>Ordered–NASB<br>Ordered–NIV<br>**Commanded–NKJV**<br>Gave orders–NLT<br><br>**POSB REFERENCE**<br>(Acts 10:48)<br>Note 4 | προσέταξεν = *prosetaxen*<br>Pronunciation: [pros-eh'-tahxs-ehn]<br>Parsing (part of speech): verb<br>    Mood—indicative<br>    Tense—aorist<br>    Voice—active<br>    Person—3rd person<br>    Number—singular<br>    Stem or root—from προστάσσω<br>Concordance References:<br>  ⇒ Strong's #4367 prostassō<br>  ⇒ NIV #4705 prostassō<br>  ⇒ NASB #4367 prostassō<br><br>**Acts 10:48**<br>And he **commanded** them to be baptized in the name of the Lord. Then prayed they him to tarry certain days. [KJV]<br><br>And he **ordered** them to be baptized in the name of Jesus Christ. Then they asked him to stay on for a few days. [NASB]<br><br>So he **ordered** that they be baptized in the name of Jesus Christ. Then they asked Peter to stay with them for a few days. [NIV]<br><br>And he **commanded** them to be baptized in the name of the Lord. Then they asked him to stay a few days. [NKJV]<br><br>So he **gave orders** for them to be baptized in the name of Jesus Christ. Afterward Cornelius asked him to stay with them for several days. [NLT]<br><br>**προσέταξε** τε αὐτοὺς βαπτισθῆναι ἐν τῷ ὀνόματι τοῦ Κυρίου. τότε ἠρώτησαν αὐτὸν ἐπιμεῖναι ἡμέρας τινάς. [GNS]<br><br>**προσέταξεν** δὲ αὐτοὺς ἐν τῷ ὀνόματι Ἰησοῦ Χριστοῦ βαπτισθῆναι. τότε ἠρώτησαν αὐτὸν ἐπιμεῖναι ἡμέρας τινάς. [GNT] | To order; to give a command; to give orders.<br><br>**Practical Application**<br>Peter commanded (*prosetaxen*) the Gentile believers to be baptized. Evidently, he commanded the six Jewish brothers to baptize them. Note: the Gentiles...<br>• had "heard the Word" (Acts 10:44).<br>• "believed on the Lord Jesus Christ" (Acts 11:17).<br>• experienced "the Holy Spirit" falling (Acts 10:44), and being "poured" upon them (Acts 10:45). They had "received the Holy Spirit" (Acts 10:47).<br>• were "baptized in the name of the Lord" (Acts 10:48). |

# PRACTICAL WORD STUDIES
## in the NEW TESTAMENT

| ENGLISH WORD | GREEK WORD AND VERSE | THE WORD MEANS... |
|---|---|---|
| **#649**<br>**Commend**<br><br>**Commend–KJV**<br>**Commend–NASB**<br>Commit–NIV<br>**Commend–NKJV**<br>Entrust–NLT<br><br>**POSB REFERENCE**<br>(Acts 20:32)<br>Note 3 | παρατίθεμαι = *paratithemai*<br>Pronunciation: [par-at-ith'-eh-mah-ee]<br>Parsing (part of speech): verb<br>   Mood—indicative<br>   Tense—present<br>   Voice—middle<br>   Person—1st person<br>   Number—singular<br>   Stem or root—from παρατίθημι<br>Concordance References:<br>  ⇒ Strong's #3908 paratithēmi<br>  ⇒ NIV #4192 paratithēmi<br>  ⇒ NASB #3908 paratithēmi<br><br>**Acts 20:32**<br>And now, brethren, I **commend** you to God, and to the word of his grace, which is able to build you up, and to give you an inheritance among all them which are sanctified. [KJV]<br>"And now I **commend** you to God and to the word of His grace, which is able to build you up and to give you the inheritance among all those who are sanctified. [NASB]<br>"Now I **commit** you to God and to the word of his grace, which can build you up and give you an inheritance among all those who are sanctified. [NIV]<br>So now, brethren, I **commend** you to God and to the word of His grace, which is able to build you up and give you an inheritance among all those who are sanctified. [NKJV]<br>"And now I **entrust** you to God and the word of his grace—his message that is able to build you up and give you an inheritance with all those he has set apart for himself. [NLT]<br>καὶ τὰ νῦν **παρατίθεμαι** ὑμᾶς, ἀδελφοί, τῷ Θεῷ καὶ τῷ λόγῳ τῆς χάριτος αὐτοῦ τῷ δυναμένῳ ἐποικοδομῆσαι, καὶ δοῦναι ὑμῖν κληρονομίαν ἐν τοῖς ἡγιασμένοις πᾶσιν. [GNS]<br>καὶ τὰ νῦν **παρατίθεμαι** ὑμᾶς τῷ θεῷ καὶ τῷ λόγῳ τῆς χάριτος αὐτοῦ, τῷ δυναμένῳ οἰκοδομῆσαι καὶ δοῦναι τὴν κληρονομίαν ἐν τοῖς ἡγιασμένοις πᾶσιν. [GNT] | To commit; to commend; to entrust.<br><br>**Practical Application**<br>The believer is to be committed to God's Word; that is, he is to place, commit, entrust, fix, lay, and deposit his life with God and His Word. Very simply, the church leader is to totally entrust his life to God and His Word, laying himself completely upon both. |
| **#650**<br>**Commendeth**<br><br>**Commendeth–KJV**<br>Demonstrates–NASB<br>Demonstrates–NIV<br>Demonstrates–NKJV<br>Showed–NLT<br><br>**POSB REFERENCE**<br>(Rom.5:8-9; esp. v.8)<br>Note 2 | συνίστησιν = *sunistēsin*<br>Pronunciation: [soon-is-tay'-sin]<br>Parsing (part of speech): verb<br>   Mood—indicative<br>   Tense—present<br>   Voice—active<br>   Person—3rd person<br>   Number—singular<br>   Stem or root—from συνίστημι and συνιστάνω<br>Concordance References:<br>  ⇒ Strong's #4921 sunistēmi<br>  ⇒ NIV #5319 sunistēmi<br>  ⇒ NASB #4921 sunistēmi<br><br>**Romans 5:8**<br>But God **commendeth** his love toward us, in that, while we were yet sinners, Christ died for us. [KJV]<br>But God **demonstrates** His own love toward us, in that while we were yet sinners, Christ died for us. [NASB]<br>But God **demonstrates** his own love for us in this: While we were still sinners, Christ died for us. [NIV]<br>But God **demonstrates** His own love toward us, in that while we were still sinners, Christ died for us. [NKJV]<br>But God **showed** his great love for us by sending Christ to die for us while we were still sinners. [NLT]<br>**συνίστησι** δὲ τὴν ἑαυτοῦ ἀγάπην εἰς ἡμᾶς ὁ Θεὸς ὅτι ἔτι ἁμαρτωλῶν ὄντων ἡμῶν Χριστὸς ὑπὲρ ἡμῶν ἀπέθανε. [GNS]<br>**συνίστησιν** δὲ τὴν ἑαυτοῦ ἀγάπην εἰς ἡμᾶς ὁ θεός, ὅτι ἔτι ἁμαρτωλῶν ὄντων ἡμῶν Χριστὸς ὑπὲρ ἡμῶν ἀπέθανεν. [GNT] | Recommends; commends; gives approval to; shows, proves, demonstrates; to stand with or beside.<br><br>**Practical Application**<br>We were sinners, yet God proved His love to us. The word "commendeth" (*sunistēsin*) means to show, prove, exhibit. It is the present tense: God is always showing and proving His love to us. |

**PRACTICAL WORD STUDIES**
in the NEW TESTAMENT

| ENGLISH WORD | GREEK WORD AND VERSE | THE WORD MEANS... |
|---|---|---|
| **#651**<br>**Commission**<br><br>Dispensation–KJV<br>Stewardship–NASB<br>**Commission–NIV**<br>Stewardship–NKJV<br>Responsibility–NLT<br><br>**POSB**<br>**REFERENCE**<br>(Col.1:25)<br>Note 2 | οἰκονομίαν = oikonomian<br>Pronunciation: [oy-kon-om-ee'-ahn]<br>Parsing (part of speech): noun<br>    Case—accusative<br>    Gender—feminine<br>    Number—singular<br>    Stem or root—from οἰκονομία, ας<br>Concordance References:<br>  ⇒ Strong's #3622 oikonomia<br>  ⇒ NIV #3873 oikonomia<br>  ⇒ NASB #3622 oikonomia<br><br>**Col. 1:25**<br>Whereof I am made a minister, according to the **dispensation** of God which is given to me for you, to fulfil the word of God; [KJV]<br>Of this church I was made a minister according to the **stewardship** from God bestowed on me for your benefit, that I might fully carry out the preaching of the word of God, [NASB]<br>I have become its servant by the **commission** God gave me to present to you the word of God in its fullness—[NIV]<br>Of which I became a minister according to the **stewardship** from God which was given to me for you, to fulfill the word of God, [NKJV]<br>God has given me the **responsibility** of serving his church by proclaiming his message in all its fullness to you Gentiles. [NLT]<br>ἧς ἐγενόμην ἐγὼ διάκονος, κατὰ τὴν **οἰκονομίαν** τοῦ Θεοῦ τὴν δοθεῖσάν μοι εἰς ὑμᾶς, πληρῶσαι τὸν λόγον τοῦ Θεοῦ, [GNS]<br>ἧς ἐγενόμην ἐγὼ διάκονος κατὰ τὴν **οἰκονομίαν** τοῦ θεοῦ τὴν δοθεῖσάν μοι εἰς ὑμᾶς πληρῶσαι τὸν λόγον τοῦ θεοῦ, [GNT] | Commission, dispensation, stewardship, responsibility; management of; responsibility of, duty of.<br><br>**Practical Application**<br>The word "commission" (*oikonomian*) refers to the steward who oversees the household and property of the owner. The minister is the steward of God, the person chosen to oversee the house or church of God. This fact is almost unbelievable, but it is true: God has actually chosen some persons to oversee His affairs for Him. The minister has actually been chosen by God to be the steward of His world and church and people. God has literally taken His church and people and placed them into the hands of His ministers, into...<br>• their stewardship<br>• their supervision<br>• their administration<br>• their ministry<br>• their responsibility<br>• their management<br>• their care<br>• their lives<br>• their love<br>What an enormous call and responsibility, yet it comes from God; therefore, it must be fulfilled. |
| **#652**<br>**Commissioned**<br><br>Anointed–KJV<br>Anointed–NASB<br>Anointed–NIV<br>Anointed–NKJV<br>**Commissioned–NLT**<br><br>**POSB**<br>**REFERENCE**<br>(2 Cor.1:21-22; esp. v.21)<br>Note 5 | χρίσας = chrisas<br>Pronunciation: [khre'-sahs]<br>Parsing (part of speech): verb<br>    Mood—participle<br>    Tense—aorist<br>    Voice—active<br>    Case—nominative<br>    Gender—masculine<br>    Number—singular<br>    Stem or root—from χρίω<br>Concordance References:<br>  ⇒ Strong's #5548 chriö<br>  ⇒ NIV #5987 chriö<br>  ⇒ NASB #5548 chriö<br><br>**2 Cor. 1:21**<br>Now he which stablisheth us with you in Christ, and hath **anointed** us, is God; [KJV]<br>Now He who establishes us with you in Christ and **anointed** us is God, [NASB]<br>Now it is God who makes both us and you stand firm in Christ. He **anointed** us, [NIV]<br>Now He who establishes us with you in Christ and has **anointed** us is God, [NKJV]<br>It is God who gives us, along with you, the ability to stand firm for Christ. He has **commissioned** us, [NLT]<br>ὁ δὲ βεβαιῶν ἡμᾶς σὺν ὑμῖν εἰς Χριστόν, καὶ **χρίσας** ἡμᾶς, Θεός, [GNS]<br>ὁ δὲ βεβαιῶν ἡμᾶς σὺν ὑμῖν εἰς Χριστὸν καὶ **χρίσας** ἡμᾶς θεός, [GNT] | To anoint; to commission; to be consecrated and qualified for service.<br><br>**Practical Application**<br>Note who it is that commissions or anoints us: God Himself. What is the commissioning or anointing, the unction that He gives? The Holy Spirit. |
| **#653**<br>**Commit**<br><br>**Commit–KJV**<br>Entrusting–NASB<br>Entrust–NIV | ἐπίστευεν = episteuen<br>Pronunciation: [eh-pist-yoo'-ehn]<br>Parsing (part of speech): verb<br>    Mood—indicative<br>    Tense—imperfect<br>    Voice—active<br>    Person—3rd person | To entrust; to commit; to trust; to believe; to have faith in; to confide in; to have confidence in.<br><br>**Practical Application**<br>The Greek word "commit" is the very same word "believe" (cp. John 2:23). This gives an |

# PRACTICAL WORD STUDIES
## in the NEW TESTAMENT

| ENGLISH WORD | GREEK WORD AND VERSE | THE WORD MEANS... |
|---|---|---|
| **Commit–NKJV**<br>Trust–NLT<br><br>**POSB REFERENCE**<br>(Jn.2:24)<br>*Deeper Study #2* | Number—singular<br>Stem or root—from πιστεύω<br>Concordance References:<br>⇒ Strong's #4100 pisteuo<br>⇒ NIV #4409 pisteuō<br>⇒ NASB #4100 pisteuo<br><br>**John 2:24**<br>But Jesus did not **commit** himself unto them, because he knew all men, [KJV]<br>But Jesus, on His part, was not **entrusting** Himself to them, for He knew all men, [NASB]<br>But Jesus would not **entrust** himself to them, for he knew all men. [NIV]<br>But Jesus did not **commit** Himself to them, because He knew all *men*, [NKJV]<br>But Jesus didn't **trust** them, because he knew what people were really like. [NLT]<br>αὐτὸς δὲ ὁ Ἰησοῦς οὐκ **ἐπίστευεν** ἑαυτὸν αὐτοῖς, διὰ τὸ αὐτὸν γινώσκειν πάντας, [GNS]<br>αὐτὸς δὲ Ἰησοῦς οὐκ **ἐπίστευεν** αὐτὸν αὐτοῖς διὰ τὸ αὐτὸν γινώσκειν πάντας [GNT] | excellent picture of saving faith, of what genuine faith is—of the kind of faith that really saves a person. Note the circumstances behind this Scripture.<br>Jesus did not trust nor believe in the people; He did not commit Himself into their lives or hands. The verb is continuous action: Jesus kept on refusing to trust men, kept on refusing to commit Himself into their lives. Two reasons are given for this continuing attitude of Jesus.<br>1. Jesus knew all men. The idea is that He knew every single man personally. Not a person escaped His knowledge.<br>2. Jesus knew what was in man. No one needed to tell Him about man. He knew man's nature: his depravity, evil, deception, and fickleness. He knew the men He could trust and could not trust. He knew every man who professed to believe, yet would...<br>• betray Him.<br>• deny his faith under pressure.<br>• forsake Him, turning back to the world.<br>• slip and fall back into sin.<br>• be weak and easily influenced, tossed to and fro.<br>• prove untrustworthy.<br>• lack zeal and genuine commitment.<br>• lack courage to stand.<br>Jesus knew all this about every man. Nothing was hid from Him. Therefore, He was not able to commit Himself and His blessings to some men despite the fact that they professed to believe. |
| **#654**<br>**Commit**<br><br>Commend–KJV<br>Commend–NASB<br>**Commit–NIV**<br>Commend–NKJV<br>Entrust–NLT<br><br>**POSB REFERENCE**<br>(Acts 20:32)<br>Note 3 | παρατίθεμαι = *paratithemai*<br>Pronunciation: [par-at-ith'-eh-mah-ee]<br>Parsing (part of speech): verb<br>  Mood—indicative<br>  Tense—present<br>  Voice—middle<br>  Person—1st person<br>  Number—singular<br>  Stem or root—from παρατίθημι<br>Concordance References:<br>⇒ Strong's #3908 paratithēmi<br>⇒ NIV #4192 paratithēmi<br>⇒ NASB #3908 paratithēmi<br><br>**Acts 20:32**<br>And now, brethren, I **commend** you to God, and to the word of his grace, which is able to build you up, and to give you an inheritance among all them which are sanctified. [KJV]<br>"And now I **commend** you to God and to the word of His grace, which is able to build you up and to give you the inheritance among all those who are sanctified. [NASB]<br>"Now I **commit** you to God and to the word of his grace, which can build you up and give you an inheritance among all those who are sanctified. [NIV]<br>So now, brethren, I **commend** you to God and to the word of His grace, which is able to build you up and give you an inheritance among all those who are sanctified. [NKJV]<br>"And now I **entrust** you to God and the word of his grace—his message that is able to build you up and give you an inheritance with all those he has set apart for himself. [NLT]<br>καὶ τὰ νῦν **παρατίθεμαι** ὑμᾶς, ἀδελφοί, τῷ Θεῷ καὶ τῷ λόγῳ τῆς χάριτος αὐτοῦ τῷ δυναμένῳ ἐποικοδομῆσαι, | To commit; to commend; to entrust.<br><br>**Practical Application**<br>The believer is to be committed to God's Word; that is, he is to place, commit, entrust, fix, lay, and deposit his life with God and His Word. Very simply, the church leader is to totally entrust his life to God and His Word, laying himself completely upon both. |

# PRACTICAL WORD STUDIES
## in the NEW TESTAMENT

| ENGLISH WORD | GREEK WORD AND VERSE | THE WORD MEANS... |
|---|---|---|
| | καὶ δοῦναι ὑμῖν κληρονομίαν ἐν τοῖς ἡγιασμένοις πᾶσιν. [GNS]<br>καὶ τὰ νῦν **παρατίθεμαι** ὑμᾶς τῷ θεῷ καὶ τῷ λόγῳ τῆς χάριτος αὐτοῦ, τῷ δυναμένῳ οἰκοδομῆσαι καὶ δοῦναι τὴν κληρονομίαν ἐν τοῖς ἡγιασμένοις πᾶσιν. [GNT] | |
| **#655**<br>**Commit**<br><br>**Commit**–KJV<br>Entrust–NASB<br>**Commit**–NIV<br>**Commit**–NKJV<br>Trust–NLT<br><br>**POSB REFERENCE**<br>(1 Pt.4:19)<br>Note 7 | **παρατιθέσθωσαν** = *paratithesthōsan*<br>Pronunciation: [par-at-ith'-ehs-tho'-sahn]<br>Parsing (part of speech): verb<br>    Mood—imperative<br>    Tense—present<br>    Voice—middle<br>    Person—3rd person<br>    Number—plural<br>    Stem or root—from παρατίθημι<br>Concordance References:<br>  ⇒ Strong's #3908 paratithēmi<br>  ⇒ NIV #4192 paratithēmi<br>  ⇒ NASB #3908 paratithēmi<br><br>**1 Peter 4:19**<br>Wherefore let them that suffer according to the will of God **commit** the keeping of their souls to him in well doing, as unto a faithful Creator. [KJV]<br>Therefore, let those also who suffer according to the will of God **entrust** their souls to a faithful Creator in doing what is right. [NASB]<br>So then, those who suffer according to God's will should **commit** themselves to their faithful Creator and continue to do good. [NIV]<br>Therefore let those who suffer according to the will of God **commit** their souls *to Him* in doing good, as to a faithful Creator. [NKJV]<br>So if you are suffering according to God's will, keep on doing what is right, and **trust** yourself to the God who made you, for he will never fail you. [NLT]<br>ὥστε καὶ οἱ πάσχοντες κατὰ τὸ θέλημα τοῦ Θεοῦ, ὡς πιστῷ κτίστῃ **παρατιθέσθωσαν** τὰς ψυχὰς ἑαυτῶν ἐν ἀγαθοποιΐᾳ. [GNS]<br>ὥστε καὶ οἱ πάσχοντες κατὰ τὸ θέλημα τοῦ θεοῦ πιστῷ κτίστῃ **παρατιθέσθωσαν** τὰς ψυχὰς αὐτῶν ἐν ἀγαθοποιΐᾳ. [GNT] | To commit; to entrust; to trust; to deposit; to entrust into the hands of a trusted banker or friend.<br><br>**Practical Application**<br>God can be trusted; He will not fail the believer. He will either deliver the believer through the suffering or else take him home to be with Christ forever. God will save the believer's soul. The believer can trust God, trust Him far more than any friend on earth, for God never fails. God is a faithful Creator. He has created us to be with Him eternally, and His plan will not be defeated. If we commit our souls to Him, no matter what men may do to us, God will save us. He will fulfill His plan and purpose in our lives. |
| **#656**<br>**Commit Sacrilege**<br><br>**Commit sacrilege**–KJV<br>Rob temples–NASB<br>Rob temples–NIV<br>Rob temples–NKJV<br>Steal from pagan temples–NLT<br><br>**POSB REFERENCE**<br>(Romans 2:21-24; esp. v.22)<br>Note 2, point 4 | **ἱεροσυλεῖς** = *hierosuleis*<br>Pronunciation: [hee-er-os-ool-ice]<br>Parsing (part of speech): verb<br>    Mood—indicative<br>    Tense—present<br>    Voice—active<br>    Person—2nd person<br>    Number—singular<br>    Stem or root—from ἱεροσυλέω<br>Concordance References:<br>  ⇒ Strong's #2416 hierosuleō<br>  ⇒ NIV #2644 hierosuleō<br>  ⇒ NASB #2416 hierosuleō<br><br>**Romans 2:22**<br>Thou that sayest a man should not commit adultery, dost thou commit adultery? thou that abhorrest idols, dost thou **commit sacrilege**? [KJV]<br>You who say that one should not commit adultery, do you commit adultery? You who abhor idols, do you **rob temples**? [NASB]<br>You who say that people should not commit adultery, do you commit adultery? You who abhor idols, do you **rob temples**? [NIV]<br>You who say, "Do not commit adultery," do you commit adultery? You who abhor idols, do you **rob temples**? [NKJV]<br>You say it is wrong to commit adultery, but do you do it? You condemn idolatry, but do you **steal from pagan temples**? [NLT] | Commit sacrilege; rob temples; to violate one's commitment to God and to rob from God.<br><br>**Practical Application**<br>It means to consider something more important than God, something so important that it requires...<br>• the commitment that you owe God.<br>• the tithes and offerings that you owe God.<br><br>You say that you worship God and abhor idols; yet you take what belongs to God–your commitment, your time, your energy, your tithes–and you give it to something else. You make something else more important than God; you make it an idol. This is one of the major sins of the religionists. |

350

# PRACTICAL WORD STUDIES
## in the NEW TESTAMENT

| ENGLISH WORD | GREEK WORD AND VERSE | THE WORD MEANS... |
|---|---|---|
| | ὁ λέγων μὴ μοιχεύειν μοιχεύεις; ὁ βδελυσσόμενος τὰ εἴδωλα, ἱεροσυλεῖς; [GNS]<br>ὁ λέγων μὴ μοιχεύειν μοιχεύεις; ὁ βδελυσσόμενος τὰ εἴδωλα ἱεροσυλεῖς; [GNT] | |
| **#657**<br>**Committed**<br><br>Concluded–KJV<br>Shut up–NASB<br>Bound over–NIV<br>**Committed–NKJV**<br>Imprisoned–NLT<br><br>**POSB REFERENCE**<br>(Rom.11:32)<br>Note 5 | συνέκλεισεν = *sunekleisen*<br>Pronunciation: [soon-he-kli'-sehn]<br>Parsing (part of speech): verb<br>  Mood—indicative<br>  Tense—aorist<br>  Voice—active<br>  Person—3rd person<br>  Number—singular<br>  Stem or root—from συγκλείω<br>Concordance References:<br>⇒ Strong's #4788 sugkleiō<br>⇒ NIV #5168 sugkleiō<br>⇒ NASB #4788 sugkleiō<br><br>**Romans 11:32**<br>For God hath **concluded** them all in unbelief, that he might have mercy upon all. [KJV]<br>For God has **shut up** all in disobedience that He might show mercy to all. [NASB]<br>For God has **bound** all men **over** to disobedience so that he may have mercy on them all. [NIV]<br>For God has **committed** them all to disobedience, that He might have mercy on all. [NKJV]<br>For God has **imprisoned** all people in their own disobedience so he could have mercy on everyone. [NLT]<br>συνέκλεισε γὰρ ὁ Θεὸς τοὺς πάντας εἰς ἀπείθειαν ἵνα τοὺς πάντας ἐλεήσῃ. [GNS]<br>συνέκλεισεν γὰρ ὁ θεὸς τοὺς πάντας εἰς ἀπείθειαν, ἵνα τοὺς πάντας ἐλεήσῃ. [GNT] | To be bound over; to imprison; to shut up in a place; to close up; to lock up; to be committed to disobedience.<br><br>**Practical Application**<br>This is an unusual idea: God has taken men, both Jews and Gentiles, and shut them up to unbelief (*apeitheian*) or disobedience. This is the judicial judgment of God (see POSB *Deeper Study* #2—Romans 11:7-10; POSB note—Romans 1:24; POSB *Deeper Study* #1—John 12:39-41). It is the picture of God's using sin and events for good. God takes sin and works it out for the good of the world. Man has chosen sin, choosing to go his own way in life, so God allows man to do his own thing. God locks man up in his own world of selfishness, allowing man to roam around in his world of sin. Why? So that man's true nature of sinfulness will be clearly seen and thereby cause the honest and thinking man to seek God. God wishes to have mercy upon all, both Jew and Gentile; but before men can come to God, they must confess two things:<br>⇒ that they are sinful and dying creatures in desperate need of God.<br>⇒ that God exists and that He will have mercy upon the person who diligently seeks Him (Heb.11:6). |
| **#658**<br>**Committed To–<br>Committed Unto**<br><br>Committed unto–KJV<br>Entrusted to–NASB<br>Entrusted to–NIV<br>**Committed to–NKJV**<br>Entrusted to–NLT<br><br>**POSB REFERENCE**<br>(2 Tim. 1:11-12 esp. v.12)<br>Note 5, point 2b | παραθήκην = *parathēkēn*<br>Pronunciation: [par-ath-ay'-kayn]<br>Parsing (part of speech): noun<br>  Case—accusative<br>  Gender—feminine<br>  Number—singular<br>  Stem or root—from παραθήκη, ης<br>Concordance References:<br>⇒ Strong's #3866 parathēkē<br>⇒ NIV #4146 parathēkē<br>⇒ NASB #3866 parathēkē<br><br>**2 Tim. 1:12**<br>For the which cause I also suffer these things: nevertheless I am not ashamed: for I know whom I have believed, and am persuaded that he is able to keep that which I have **committed unto** him against that day. [KJV]<br>For this reason I also suffer these things, but I am not ashamed; for I know whom I have believed and I am convinced that He is able to guard what I have **entrusted to** Him until that day. [NASB]<br>That is why I am suffering as I am. Yet I am not ashamed, because I know whom I have believed, and am convinced that he is able to guard what I have **entrusted to** him for that day. [NIV]<br>For this reason I also suffer these things; nevertheless I am not ashamed, for I know whom I have believed and am persuaded that He is able to keep what I have **committed to** Him until that Day. [NKJV]<br>And that is why I am suffering here in prison. But I am not ashamed of it, for I know the one in whom I trust, and I am sure that he is able to guard what I have **entrusted to** him until the day of his return. [NLT]<br>δι' ἣν αἰτίαν καὶ ταῦτα πάσχω, ἀλλ' οὐκ | To deposit; to entrust; to commit.<br><br>**Practical Application**<br>Paul was persuaded of God's keeping power. Paul had committed both his life and work to Christ—all that Paul was as a person and all that Paul did upon earth was entrusted to Christ. The word "committed" (*parathēkēn*) means to deposit. A.T. Robertson says that Paul means, "'My deposit' as in a bank, the bank of heaven which no burglar can break (Matthew 6:19f)" (*Word Pictures in the New Testament*, Vol.4, p.614). Paul had deposited, turned everything he was and had over to Christ. Why? Because he knew that Christ could keep it and take care of it forever and ever. What exactly did Paul turn over to Christ? His life and work. Imagine!<br>⇒ Paul deposited his *life* into the hands of Christ; therefore, Christ increased his life, guided his life to bear the richest interest and the greatest return. Paul's *deposit of life was increased* to eternal life.<br>⇒ Paul deposited his *work* into the hands of Christ; therefore, Christ increased his work to bear the richest interest and the greatest return. Paul's *deposit of work was increased* to eternal responsibility and management for God. (See POSB note, Rewards—Luke 16:10-12 for more discussion.) |

# PRACTICAL WORD STUDIES
## in the NEW TESTAMENT

| ENGLISH WORD | GREEK WORD AND VERSE | THE WORD MEANS... |
|---|---|---|
| | ἐπαισχύνομαι· οἶδα γὰρ ᾧ πεπίστευκα, καὶ πέπεισμαι ὅτι δυνατός ἐστι τὴν **παραθήκην** μου φυλάξαι εἰς ἐκείνην τὴν ἡμέραν. [GNS]<br>δι᾽ ἣν αἰτίαν καὶ ταῦτα πάσχω· ἀλλ᾽ οὐκ ἐπαισχύνομαι, οἶδα γὰρ ᾧ πεπίστευκα καὶ πέπεισμαι ὅτι δυνατός ἐστιν τὴν **παραθήκην** μου φυλάξαι εἰς ἐκείνην τὴν ἡμέραν. [GNT] | |
| **#659**<br>**Committed**<br><br>**Committed**–KJV<br>Entrusting–NASB<br>Entrusted–NIV<br>**Committed**–NKJV<br>Left his case–NLT<br><br>**POSB REFERENCE**<br>(1 Pt.2:21-24; esp. v.23)<br>Note 2, point 3c | παρεδίδου = *paredidou*<br>Pronunciation: [par-ed-id'-oo]<br>Parsing (part of speech): verb<br>  Mood—indicative<br>  Tense—imperfect<br>  Voice—active<br>  Person—3rd person<br>  Number—singular<br>Stem or root—from παραδίδωμι<br>Concordance References:<br> ⇒ Strong's #3860 paradidōmi<br> ⇒ NIV #4140 paradidōmi<br> ⇒ NASB #3860 paradidōmi<br><br>**1 Peter 2:23**<br>Who, when he was reviled, reviled not again; when he suffered, he threatened not; but **committed** himself to him that judgeth righteously: [KJV]<br>And while being reviled, He did not revile in return; while suffering, He uttered no threats, but kept **entrusting** Himself to Him who judges righteously; [NASB]<br>When they hurled their insults at him, he did not retaliate; when he suffered, he made no threats. Instead, he **entrusted** himself to him who judges justly. [NIV]<br>Who, when He was reviled, did not revile in return; when He suffered, He did not threaten, but **committed** *Himself* to Him who judges righteously; [NKJV]<br>He did not retaliate when he was insulted. When he suffered, he did not threaten to get even. He **left his case** in the hands of God, who always judges fairly. [NLT]<br>ὃς λοιδορούμενος οὐκ ἀντελοιδόρει, πάσχων οὐκ ἠπείλει, **παρεδίδου** δὲ τῷ κρίνοντι δικαίως· [GNS]<br>ὃς λοιδορούμενος οὐκ ἀντελοιδόρει, πάσχων οὐκ ἠπείλει, **παρεδίδου** δὲ τῷ κρίνοντι δικαίως· [GNT] | Entrusted, committed, handed over; to deliver into the hands of.<br><br>**Practical Application**<br>Jesus Christ handed over His life to God; He delivered His life into the hands and keeping of God. Again, He did not have to suffer death, for He had the power to stop it all. But He had come to save men; therefore, he willingly suffered, committing His death and cause into the hands of God. He knew that God would raise Him up to prove His claim to be the Son of God, the Savior of the world. |
| **#660**<br>**Common Good**<br><br>Profit–KJV<br>**Common good–NASB**<br>Common good–NIV<br>Profit–NKJV<br>Helping the entire church–NLT<br><br>**POSB REFERENCE**<br>(1 Cor.12:7)<br>Note 2 | συμφέρον = *sumpheron*<br>Pronunciation: [soom-fer'-on]<br>Parsing (part of speech): verb<br>  Mood—participle<br>  Tense—present<br>  Voice—active<br>  Gender—neuter<br>  Number—singular<br>Stem or root—from συμφέρω<br>Concordance References:<br> ⇒ Strong's #4851 sumpherō<br> ⇒ NIV #5237 sumpherō<br> ⇒ NASB #4851 sumpherō<br><br>**1 Cor. 12:7**<br>But the manifestation of the Spirit is given to every man to **profit** withal. [KJV]<br>But to each one is given the manifestation of the Spirit for the **common good**. [NASB]<br>Now to each one the manifestation of the Spirit is given for the **common good**. [NIV]<br>But the manifestation of the Spirit is given to each one for the **profit** *of all:* [NKJV]<br>A spiritual gift is given to each of us as a means of **helping the entire church**. [NLT]<br>ἑκάστῳ δὲ δίδοται ἡ φανέρωσις τοῦ Πνεύματος πρὸς τὸ **συμφέρον**. [GNS]<br>ἑκάστῳ δὲ δίδοται ἡ φανέρωσις τοῦ πνεύματος πρὸς τὸ **συμφέρον**. [GNT] | Common good, edification, profit; help, advantage, benefit.<br><br>**Practical Application**<br>Believers are equipped with spiritual gifts primarily for the *benefit and edification of others*, not for themselves. The gifts are not given to believers for their own gratification or for them to revel in a sense of self-importance and super-spirituality. The believer does, of course, profit and benefit from the gift given him, but he is gifted primarily to edify and help others. This is seen in the word "manifestation." It means to be openly and publicly seen. The gifts of the Spirit are to be openly and publicly used; they are...<br>• to be manifested to the church, that is, used to edify the church.<br>• to be manifested to the world, that is, used to benefit the world (reaching the lost).<br><br>Note a crucial fact that is not always understood. The gifts of the Spirit are "given to each one." They are not given only to the educated and outstanding. Every single believer is given some spiritual gift by the Spirit of God, and it is given because it is needed within the church and the world, needed to help in ministering to people and in reaching the lost for Christ. |

## PRACTICAL WORD STUDIES in the NEW TESTAMENT

| ENGLISH WORD | GREEK WORD AND VERSE | THE WORD MEANS... |
|---|---|---|
| **#661** **Common Or Unclean** **Common or unclean**– KJV Unholy and unclean– NASB Impure or unclean– NIV **Common or unclean**– NKJV Forbidden by our Jewish laws–NLT **POSB REFERENCE** (Acts 10:11-16; esp. v.14) *Deeper Study #3* | κοινὸν καὶ ἀκάθαρτον = *koinon kai akatharton* Pronunciation: [koy-non' kah-ee ak-ath'-ar-ton] Parsing *koinon* (part of speech): pronominal adjective     Case—accusative     Gender—neuter     Number—singular     Stem or root—from κοινός, ή, όν Parsing *akatharton* (part of speech): pronominal adjective     Case—accusative     Gender—neuter     Number—singular     Stem or root—from ἀκάθαρτος, ον Concordance References: ⇒ Strong's #2839 koinos + 2532 kai + 169 akathartos ⇒ NIV #3123 koinos [impure] + 2779 kai [or] + 176 akathartos [unclean] ⇒ NASB #2839 koinos + 2532 kai + 169 akathartos **Acts 10:14** But Peter said, Not so, Lord; for I have never eaten any thing that is **common or unclean**. [KJV] But Peter said, "By no means, Lord, for I have never eaten anything **unholy and unclean**." [NASB] "Surely not, Lord!" Peter replied. "I have never eaten anything **impure or unclean**." [NIV] But Peter said, "Not so, Lord! For I have never eaten anything **common or unclean**." [NKJV] "Never, Lord," Peter declared. "I have never in all my life eaten anything **forbidden by our Jewish laws**." [NLT] ὁ δὲ Πέτρος εἶπε, Μηδαμῶς Κύριε· ὅτι οὐδέποτε ἔφαγον πᾶν **κοινὸν ἢ ἀκάθαρτον**. [GNS] ὁ δὲ Πέτρος εἶπεν, Μηδαμῶς, κύριε, ὅτι οὐδέποτε ἔφαγον πᾶν **κοινὸν καὶ ἀκάθαρτον**. [GNT] | Impure or unclean; common or unclean; unholy and unclean. **Practical Application** The words "common or unclean" (*koinon kai akatharton*) refer to being religiously or ceremonially unclean. The unclean animals were unhallowed, profaned. The Jews felt that eating them would not please God. |
| **#662** **Common To Man** **Common to man**– KJV **Common to man**– NASB **Common to man**– NIV **Common to man**– NKJV No different from what others experience–NLT **POSB REFERENCE** (1 Cor.10:11-13; esp. v.13) Note 3, point 3 | ἀνθρώπινος = *anthrōpinos* Pronunciation: [anth-ro'-pee-nos] Parsing (part of speech): adjective     Case—nominative     Gender—masculine     Number—singular     Stem or root—from ἀνθρώπινος, η, ον Concordance References: ⇒ Strong's #442 anthrōpinos ⇒ NIV #474 anthrōpinos ⇒ NASB #442 anthrōpinos **1 Cor. 10:13** There hath no temptation taken you but such as is **common to man**: but God is faithful, who will not suffer you to be tempted above that ye are able; but will with the temptation also make a way to escape, that ye may be able to bear it. [KJV] No temptation has overtaken you but such as is **common to man**; and God is faithful, who will not allow you to be tempted beyond what you are able, but with the temptation will provide the way of escape also, that you may be able to endure it. [NASB] No temptation has seized you except what is **common to man**. And God is faithful; he will not let you be tempted beyond what you can bear. But when you are tempted, he will also provide a way out so that you can stand up under it. [NIV] No temptation has overtaken you except such as is **common to man**; but God *is* faithful, who will not allow you to be tempted beyond what you are able, but with the temptation will also make the way of escape, that you may be able to bear *it.* [NKJV] But remember that the temptations that come into your | Common to man; a universal human characteristic; a human temptation that falls to the lot of man. **Practical Application** This is an amazing promise. Think about it. No temptation... • is superhuman. • is unique. • is beyond man's capacity to handle. • is terrifying in any sense of the word. Every single temptation that attacks the believer is *common to all men. All men* face the same temptation. This means a wonderful thing: some men have already overcome it. Yes, many fell, caved in to the temptation; but some demonstrated the will and energy to overcome it. |

## PRACTICAL WORD STUDIES
### in the NEW TESTAMENT

| ENGLISH WORD | GREEK WORD AND VERSE | THE WORD MEANS... |
|---|---|---|
| | life are **no different from what others experience**. And God is faithful. He will keep the temptation from becoming so strong that you can't stand up against it. When you are tempted, he will show you a way out so that you will not give in to it. [NLT]<br>πειρασμὸς ὑμᾶς οὐκ εἴληφεν εἰ μὴ **ἀνθρώπινος**· πιστὸς δὲ ὁ Θεός, ὃς οὐκ ἐάσει ὑμᾶς πειρασθῆναι ὑπὲρ ὃ δύνασθε, ἀλλὰ ποιήσει σὺν τῷ πειρασμῷ καὶ τὴν ἔκβασιν, τοῦ δύνασθαι ὑμᾶς ὑπενεγκεῖν. [GNS]<br>πειρασμὸς ὑμᾶς οὐκ εἴληφεν εἰ μὴ **ἀνθρώπινος**· πιστὸς δὲ ὁ θεός, ὃς οὐκ ἐάσει ὑμᾶς πειρασθῆναι ὑπὲρ ὃ δύνασθε ἀλλὰ ποιήσει σὺν τῷ πειρασμῷ καὶ τὴν ἔκβασιν τοῦ δύνασθαι ὑπενεγκεῖν. [GNT] | |
| **#663**<br>**Commotions**<br><br>**Commotions**–KJV<br>Disturbances–NASB<br>Revolutions–NIV<br>**Commotions**–NKJV<br>Insurrections–NLT<br><br>**POSB**<br>**REFERENCE**<br>(Lk.21:9-10; esp. v.9)<br>Note 3, point 1 | ἀκαταστασίας = akatastasias<br>Pronunciation: [ak-at-as-tah-see'-ahs]<br>Parsing (part of speech): noun<br>    Case—accusative<br>    Gender—feminine<br>    Number—plural<br>    Stem or root—from ἀκαταστασία, ας<br>Concordance References:<br>  ⇒ Strong's #181 akatastasia<br>  ⇒ NIV #189 akatastasia<br>  ⇒ NASB #181 akatastasia<br><br>**Luke 21:9**<br>But when ye shall hear of wars and **commotions**, be not terrified: for these things must first come to pass; but the end is not by and by. [KJV]<br>"And when you hear of wars and **disturbances**, do not be terrified; for these things must take place first, but the end does not follow immediately." [NASB]<br>When you hear of wars and **revolutions**, do not be frightened. These things must happen first, but the end will not come right away." [NIV]<br>But when you hear of wars and **commotions**, do not be terrified; for these things must come to pass first, but the end *will not come* immediately." [NKJV]<br>And when you hear of wars and **insurrections**, don't panic. Yes, these things must come, but the end won't follow immediately." [NLT]<br>ὅταν δὲ ἀκούσητε πολέμους καὶ **ἀκαταστασίας**, μὴ πτοηθῆτε· δεῖ γὰρ ταῦτα γενέσθαι πρῶτον, ἀλλ' οὐκ εὐθέως τὸ τέλος. [GNS]<br>ὅταν δὲ ἀκούσητε πολέμους καὶ **ἀκαταστασίας**, μὴ πτοηθῆτε· δεῖ γὰρ ταῦτα γενέσθαι πρῶτον, ἀλλ' οὐκ εὐθέως τὸ τέλος. [GNT] | Revolutions, disturbances, insurrections, commotions, anarchy, rebellion, tumults, uproars, riots, terrorism; mob violence; treason against and confusion within governments.<br><br>**Practical Application**<br>Believers can become extremely disturbed over the news. But, believers are not to be "frightened" (*ptoethete*). They are not to let their hearts "be troubled" (John 14:1). World violence can trouble people; but the believer's heart and life are to be centered upon God, trusting His presence, care, and security—eternally. |
| **#664**<br>**Communion**<br><br>**Communion**–KJV<br>Fellowship–NASB<br>Fellowship–NIV<br>**Communion**–NKJV<br>Live with–NLT<br><br>**POSB**<br>**REFERENCE**<br>(2 Cor.6:14-16; esp. v.14)<br>Note 2, point 2 | κοινωνία = koinōnia<br>Pronunciation: [koy-nohn-ee'-ah]<br>Parsing (part of speech): noun<br>    Case—nominative<br>    Gender—feminine<br>    Number—singular<br>    Stem or root—from κοινωνία, ας<br>Concordance References:<br>  ⇒ Strong's #2842 koinōnia<br>  ⇒ NIV #3126 koinōnia<br>  ⇒ NASB #2842 koinōnia<br><br>**2 Cor. 6:14**<br>Be ye not unequally yoked together with unbelievers: for what fellowship hath righteousness with unrighteousness? and what **communion** hath light with darkness? [KJV]<br>Do not be bound together with unbelievers; for what partnership have righteousness and lawlessness, or what **fellowship** has light with darkness? [NASB]<br>Do not be yoked together with unbelievers. For what do righteousness and wickedness have in common? Or what **fellowship** can light have with darkness? [NIV]<br>Do not be unequally yoked together with unbelievers. | Fellowship; communion; to live with; to share; to be in union, in partnership, in a bound fellowship; to be closely bound together; to have a close, mutual relationship.<br><br>**Practical Application**<br>It means to be so closely bound together that there is open and mutual sharing: what one has belongs to the other. The point is clear: there is no such fellowship or union between light and darkness. On the contrary, light and darkness are mutually exclusive, of different natures entirely. They cannot coexist. |

# PRACTICAL WORD STUDIES
## in the NEW TESTAMENT

| ENGLISH WORD | GREEK WORD AND VERSE | THE WORD MEANS... |
|---|---|---|
| | For what fellowship has righteousness with lawlessness? And what **communion** has light with darkness? [NKJV]<br><br>Don't team up with those who are unbelievers. How can goodness be a partner with wickedness? How can light **live with** darkness? [NLT]<br><br>Μὴ γίνεσθε ἑτεροζυγοῦντες ἀπίστοις· τίς γὰρ μετοχὴ δικαιοσύνῃ καὶ ἀνομίᾳ; τίς δὲ **κοινωνία** φωτὶ πρὸς σκότος; [GNS]<br><br>Μὴ γίνεσθε ἑτεροζυγοῦντες ἀπίστοις· τίς γὰρ μετοχὴ δικαιοσύνῃ καὶ ἀνομίᾳ, ἢ τίς **κοινωνία** φωτὶ πρὸς σκότος; [GNT] | |
| **#665**<br>**Companion**<br><br>Yokefellow–KJV<br>Comrade–NASB<br>Yokefellow–NIV<br>**Companion–NKJV**<br>Teammate–NLT<br><br>**POSB REFERENCE**<br>(Philip.4:2-3; esp. v.3)<br>Note 2, point 2 | σύζυγε = *suzuge*<br>Pronunciation: [sood'-zoo-geh]<br>Parsing (part of speech): pronominal adjective<br>    Case—vocative<br>    Gender—masculine<br>    Number—singular<br>    Stem or root—from σύζυγος, ου<br>Concordance References:<br>  ⇒ Strong's #4805 suzugos<br>  ⇒ NIV #5187 suzugos<br>  ⇒ NASB #4805 suzugos<br><br>**Philip. 4:3**<br>And I intreat thee also, true **yokefellow**, help those women which laboured with me in the gospel, with Clement also, and with other my fellowlabourers, whose names are in the book of life. [KJV]<br><br>Indeed, true **comrade**, I ask you also to help these women who have shared my struggle in the cause of the gospel, together with Clement also, and the rest of my fellow workers, whose names are in the book of life. [NASB]<br><br>Yes, and I ask you, loyal **yokefellow**, help these women who have contended at my side in the cause of the gospel, along with Clement and the rest of my fellow workers, whose names are in the book of life. [NIV]<br><br>And I urge you also, true **companion**, help these women who labored with me in the gospel, with Clement also, and the rest of my fellow workers, whose names are in the Book of Life. [NKJV]<br><br>And I ask you, my true **teammate**, to help these women, for they worked hard with me in telling others the Good News. And they worked with Clement and the rest of my co-workers, whose names are written in the Book of Life. [NLT]<br><br>καὶ ἐρωτῶ καὶ σέ, **σύζυγε** γνήσιε, συλλαμβάνου αὐταῖς, αἵτινες ἐν τῷ εὐαγγελίῳ συνήθλησάν μοι, μετὰ καὶ Κλήμεντος, καὶ τῶν λοιπῶν συνεργῶν μου, ὧν τὰ ὀνόματα ἐν βίβλῳ ζωῆς. [GNS]<br><br>ναὶ ἐρωτῶ καὶ σέ, γνήσιε **σύζυγε**, συλλαμβάνου αὐταῖς, αἵτινες ἐν τῷ εὐαγγελίῳ συνήθλησάν μοι μετὰ καὶ Κλήμεντος καὶ τῶν λοιπῶν συνεργῶν μου, ὧν τὰ ὀνόματα ἐν βίβλῳ ζωῆς. [GNT] | Yokefellow, fellow worker, comrade, teammate.<br><br>**Practical Application**<br>The need is for a true friend, a yokefellow, to step in to help any who are quarreling. The word "companion" (*suzuge*) is thought by some to be a proper name given to some Christians when they were baptized. It was a common practice for believers to be given new names at their baptism in order to symbolize their spiritual birth. Just who this yokefellow was is not known, but he must have been a man deeply respected by the people of the church. His name refers to the *yoke* or *collar* that was fitted around the neck of oxen for plowing. The collar attached the plow and held the two oxen together so that they would pull together and more quickly get the work done. Therefore, "yokefellow" means a person who pulls and works cooperatively with others. The very fact that Paul would ask him to help the two quarreling ladies shows that he was highly esteemed. Paul felt that he cared and that the two quarrelers would listen to him—that he could solve the dispute and bring about reconciliation.<br><br>Most churches have one or more yokefellows, persons...<br>• who love and care deeply for others.<br>• who are always helping and ministering to others.<br>• whom God has gifted and appointed to be ministerial helpers to the flock.<br>• who are highly respected and esteemed by most in the congregation.<br><br>The yokefellow is the person who should step in when quarrels and divisiveness begin to arouse their poisonous heads. The yokefellow is the person especially gifted by God to bring reconciliation and peace to the church. |
| **#666**<br>**Company Of Soldiers**<br><br>Band of soldiers–KJV<br>Cohort–NASB<br>**Company of soldiers–NIV**<br>Garrison–NKJV<br>Battalion–NLT<br><br>**POSB REFERENCE**<br>(Mt.27:26-38; esp. v.27)<br>Note 2, point 2 | σπεῖραν = *speiran*<br>Pronunciation: [spi'-rahn]<br>Parsing (part of speech): noun<br>    Case—accusative<br>    Gender—feminine<br>    Number—singular<br>    Stem or root—from σπεῖρα, ης<br>Concordance References:<br>  ⇒ Strong's #4686 speira<br>  ⇒ NIV #5061 speira<br>  ⇒ NASB #4686 speira<br><br>**Matthew 27:27**<br>Then the soldiers of the governor took Jesus into the common hall, and gathered unto him the whole **band of soldiers**. [KJV]<br><br>Then the soldiers of the governor took Jesus into the Praetorium and gathered the whole Roman **cohort** | A company, battalion, detachment, cohort, garrison or band of soldiers; a regiment.<br><br>**Practical Application**<br>This usually meant a company or battalion which was made up of six hundred soldiers. However, "company of soldiers" (*speiran*) sometimes meant maniple. Every company consisted of three maniples, about two hundred soldiers. Which is meant here is not known. Most believe the number of soldiers was large, certainly close to the two hundred serving in a maniple. |

# Practical Word Studies
## in the New Testament

| ENGLISH WORD | GREEK WORD AND VERSE | THE WORD MEANS... |
|---|---|---|
| | around Him. [NASB]<br>Then the governor's soldiers took Jesus into the Praetorium and gathered the whole **company of soldiers** around him. [NIV]<br>Then the soldiers of the governor took Jesus into the Praetorium and gathered the whole **garrison** around Him. [NKJV]<br>Some of the governor's soldiers took Jesus into their headquarters and called out the entire **battalion**. [NLT]<br>Τότε οἱ στρατιῶται τοῦ ἡγεμόνος παραλαβόντες τὸν Ἰησοῦν εἰς τὸ πραιτώριον συνήγαγον ἐπ' αὐτὸν ὅλην τὴν **σπεῖραν**· [GNS]<br>Τότε οἱ στρατιῶται τοῦ ἡγεμόνος παραλαβόντες τὸν Ἰησοῦν εἰς τὸ πραιτώριον συνήγαγον ἐπ' αὐτὸν ὅλην τὴν **σπεῖραν**. [GNT] | |
| **#667**<br>**Company With, Keep**<br><br>Company with–KJV<br>Associate with–NASB<br>Associate with–NIV<br>Keep company with–NKJV<br>Associate with–NLT<br><br>**POSB REFERENCE**<br>(1 Cor.5:9-10; esp. v.9)<br>Note 4 | συναναμίγνυσθαι = *sunanamignusthai*<br>Pronunciation: [soon-an-am-ig'-noos-thah-ee]<br>Parsing (part of speech): verb<br>   Mood—infinitive<br>   Tense—present<br>   Voice—middle or passive<br>   Stem or root—from συναναμίγνυμι<br>Concordance References:<br>  ⇒ Strong's #4874 sunanameignumi<br>  ⇒ NIV #5264 sunanameignumi<br>  ⇒ NASB #4874 sunanameignumi<br><br>**1 Cor. 5:9**<br>I wrote unto you in an epistle not to **company with** fornicators: [KJV]<br>I wrote you in my letter not to **associate with** immoral people; [NASB]<br>I have written you in my letter not to **associate with** sexually immoral people—[NIV]<br>I wrote to you in my epistle not to **keep company with** sexually immoral people. [NKJV]<br>When I wrote to you before, I told you not to **associate with** people who indulge in sexual sin. [NLT]<br>Ἔγραψα ὑμῖν ἐν τῇ ἐπιστολῇ μὴ **συναναμίγνυσθαι** πόρνοις· [GNS]<br>Ἔγραψα ὑμῖν ἐν τῇ ἐπιστολῇ μὴ **συναναμίγνυσθαι** πόρνοις, [GNT] | Associate with, company with; have dealings with; mix up.<br><br>**Practical Application**<br>The church and its believers cannot go out of the world; therefore, some contact with the unbelievers of the world is necessary. This is understandable to any thinking and honest person. However, it is also understandable that the church must not become *mixed up* with the shameful sinners of the world. The church and its believers must be separate in their behavior and fellowship. The church and the believers are to be holy and pure and righteous before God and to hold up the banner of holiness and purity and righteousness before the people of the world. Believers are *in the world*, but they must not be *of the world*. |
| **#668**<br>**Compassion**<br><br>Compassion–KJV<br>Compassion–NASB<br>Compassion–NIV<br>Compassion–NKJV<br>Pity–NLT<br><br>**POSB REFERENCE**<br>(Mt.9:36)<br>*Deeper Study* #2<br><br>See also POSB REF:<br>(Mt.20:34)<br>Note 6 | ἐσπλαγχνίσθη = *esplagchnisthē*<br>Pronunciation: [es-plangkh-ni'-sthee]<br>Parsing (part of speech): verb<br>   Mood—indicative<br>   Tense—aorist<br>   Voice—passive deponent<br>   Person—3rd person<br>   Number—singular<br>   Stem or root—from σπλαγχνίζομαι<br>Concordance References:<br>  ⇒ Strong's #4697 splagchnizomai<br>  ⇒ NIV #5072 splanchnizomai<br>  ⇒ NASB #4697 splagchnizomai<br><br>**Matthew 9:36**<br>But when he saw the multitudes, he was moved with **compassion** on them, because they fainted, and were scattered abroad, as sheep having no shepherd. [KJV]<br>And seeing the multitudes, He felt **compassion** for them, because they were distressed and downcast like sheep without a shepherd. [NASB]<br>When he saw the crowds, he had **compassion** on them, because they were harassed and helpless, like sheep without a shepherd. [NIV]<br>But when He saw the multitudes, He was moved with **compassion** for them, because they were weary and scattered, like sheep having no shepherd. [NKJV]<br>He felt great **pity** for the crowds that came, because their problems were so great and they didn't know where | Compassion; to be moved inwardly; to yearn with tender mercy, affection, pity, and empathy.<br><br>**Practical Application**<br>Compassion arises from the very depth of a person's affections. It is the deepest movement of emotions possible, being touched with the deepest feelings possible. |

# PRACTICAL WORD STUDIES
## in the NEW TESTAMENT

| ENGLISH WORD | GREEK WORD AND VERSE | THE WORD MEANS... |
|---|---|---|
| | to go for help. They were like sheep without a shepherd. [NLT]<br>ἰδὼν δὲ τοὺς ὄχλους, **ἐσπλαγχνίσθη** περὶ αὐτῶν, ὅτι ἦσαν ἐκλελυμένοι καὶ ἐρριμμένοι ὡσεὶ πρόβατα μὴ ἔχοντα ποιμένα. [GNS]<br>Ἰδὼν δὲ τοὺς ὄχλους **ἐσπλαγχνίσθη** περὶ αὐτῶν, ὅτι ἦσαν ἐσκυλμένοι καὶ ἐρριμμένοι ὡσεὶ πρόβατα μὴ ἔχοντα ποιμένα. [GNT] | |
| **#669**<br>**Compassion**<br><br>**Compassion–KJV**<br>**Compassion–NASB**<br>Heart went out–NIV<br>**Compassion–NKJV**<br>**Compassion–NLT**<br><br>**POSB REFERENCE**<br>(Lk.7:13)<br>*Deeper Study #1* | ἐσπλαγχνίσθη = *esplagchnisthē*<br>Pronunciation: [es-splangch-nees'-thay]<br>Parsing (part of speech): verb<br>    Mood—indicative<br>    Tense—aorist<br>    Voice—passive deponent<br>    Person—3rd person<br>    Number—singular<br>    Stem or root—from σπλαγχνίζομαι<br>Concordance References:<br>  ⇒ Strong's #4697 splagchnizomai<br>  ⇒ NIV #5072 splagchnizomai<br>  ⇒ NASB #4697 splagchnizomai<br><br>**Luke 7:13**<br>And when the Lord saw her, he had **compassion** on her, and said unto her, Weep not. [KJV]<br>And when the Lord saw her, He felt **compassion** for her, and said to her, "Do not weep." [NASB]<br>When the Lord saw her, his **heart went out** to her and he said, "Don't cry." [NIV]<br>When the Lord saw her, He had **compassion** on her and said to her, "Do not weep." [NKJV]<br>When the Lord saw her, his heart overflowed with **compassion**. "Don't cry!" he said. [NLT]<br>καὶ ἰδὼν αὐτὴν ὁ Κύριος **ἐσπλαγχνίσθη** ἐπ' αὐτῇ, καὶ εἶπεν αὐτῇ, Μὴ κλαῖε. [GNS]<br>καὶ ἰδὼν αὐτὴν ὁ κύριος **ἐσπλαγχνίσθη** ἐπ' αὐτῇ καὶ εἶπεν αὐτῇ, Μὴ κλαῖε. [GNT] | To be moved inwardly; to yearn with tender mercy, affection, pity, empathy, compassion; to have one's heart reach out.<br><br>**Practical Application**<br>It is the very seat of a man's affections. It is the deepest movement of emotions possible; being moved within the deepest part of one's being. The Lord saw and had compassion and assured the woman. Note three striking facts.<br>1. It was "the Lord" who saw her. This is the first time Luke uses the title "the Lord" by itself and it is striking. The point Luke is making is that "the Lord," the Sovereign Power of the universe, saw this woman who was utterly heartbroken. The Lord actually saw her.<br>2. It was "the Lord" who had compassion upon her. The fact is shocking, for the sovereign power of the universe actually felt compassion for a simple woman. He was not just the sovereign power of a vast universe who was way off in outer space someplace, unattached and disinterested in this earth and its inhabitants. Contrariwise, He was vitally interested, interested enough to be looking and seeing; and He was concerned about what He saw, full of compassion for the heartbroken (see POSB note—Luke 7:13).<br>3. It was "the Lord" who spoke and gave assurance. Again, the fact was shocking, for the sovereign power of the universe actually spoke and gave assurance to a simple woman. Luke is definitely stressing the staggering thought: "the Lord," the sovereign majesty of the universe speaks to men, and His Word gives great assurance. The Lord is vitally interested in the affairs of men, even in the plight of a simple woman. |
| **#670**<br>**Compassion**<br><br>Mercies–KJV<br>Mercies–NASB<br>**Compassion–NIV**<br>Mercies–NKJV<br>Every mercy–NLT<br><br>**POSB REFERENCE**<br>(2 Cor.1:3)<br>Note 1 | οἰκτιρμῶν = *oiktirmōn*<br>Pronunciation: [oyk-tir-mon]<br>Parsing (part of speech): noun<br>    Case—genitive<br>    Gender—masculine<br>    Number—plural<br>    Stem or root—from οἰκτιρμός, οῦ<br>Concordance References:<br>  ⇒ Strong's #3628 oiktirmos<br>  ⇒ NIV #3880 oiktirmos<br>  ⇒ NASB #3628 oiktirmos<br><br>**2 Cor. 1:3**<br>Blessed be God, even the Father of our Lord Jesus Christ, the Father of **mercies**, and the God of all comfort; [KJV]<br>Blessed be the God and Father of our Lord Jesus Christ, the Father of **mercies** and God of all comfort; [NASB]<br>Praise be to the God and Father of our Lord Jesus Christ, the Father of **compassion** and the God of all comfort, [NIV] | Compassion, pity, and mercy. It means looking upon people in need and having compassion and mercy upon them.<br><br>**Practical Application**<br>⇒ Note that God is not the God of compassion but the Father of compassion. His very nature and behavior toward us is that of a Father, not of a God. He is our Father, a Father who is merciful and compassionate and who showers His mercies and compassions upon us.<br>⇒ Note that the word "compassion" [see parsing] is plural. God does not show mercy just once, nor just here and there. God showers His compassion upon us continuously (cp. Romans 12:1; Phil. 2:1; Col. 3:12; Hebrews 10:28). |

# PRACTICAL WORD STUDIES
## in the NEW TESTAMENT

| ENGLISH WORD | GREEK WORD AND VERSE | THE WORD MEANS... |
|---|---|---|
| | Blessed *be* the God and Father of our Lord Jesus Christ, the Father of **mercies** and God of all comfort, [NKJV]<br>All praise to the God and Father of our Lord Jesus Christ. He is the source of **every mercy** and the God who comforts us. [NLT]<br>Εὐλογητὸς ὁ Θεὸς καὶ πατὴρ τοῦ Κυρίου ἡμῶν Ἰησοῦ Χριστοῦ, ὁ πατὴρ τῶν **οἰκτιρμῶν** καὶ Θεὸς πάσης παρακλήσεως, [GNS]<br>Εὐλογητὸς ὁ θεὸς καὶ πατὴρ τοῦ κυρίου ἡμῶν Ἰησοῦ Χριστοῦ, ὁ πατὴρ τῶν **οἰκτιρμῶν** καὶ θεὸς πάσης παρακλήσεως, [GNT] | |
| **#671**<br>**Compassion**<br><br>Mercies–KJV<br>**Compassion**–NASB<br>**Compassion**–NIV<br>Mercies–NKJV<br>Mercy–NLT<br><br>**POSB REFERENCE**<br>(Col.3:12)<br>Note 2 | οἰκτιρμοῦ = *oiktirmou*<br>Pronunciation: [oyk-tir-mon']<br>Parsing (part of speech): noun<br>    Case—genitive<br>    Gender—masculine<br>    Number—singular<br>    Stem or root—from οἰκτιρμός, οῦ<br>Concordance References:<br>  ⇒ Strong's #3628 oiktirmos<br>  ⇒ NIV #3880 oiktirmos<br>  ⇒ NASB #3628 oiktirmos<br><br>**Col. 3:12**<br>Put on therefore, as the elect of God, holy and beloved, bowels of **mercies**, kindness, humbleness of mind, meekness, longsuffering; [KJV]<br>And so, as those who have been chosen of God, holy and beloved, put on a heart of **compassion**, kindness, humility, gentleness and patience; [NASB]<br>Therefore, as God's chosen people, holy and dearly loved, clothe yourselves with **compassion**, kindness, humility, gentleness and patience. [NIV]<br>Therefore, as *the* elect of God, holy and beloved, put on tender **mercies**, kindness, humility, meekness, longsuffering; [NKJV]<br>Since God chose you to be the holy people whom he loves, you must clothe yourselves with tenderhearted **mercy**, kindness, humility, gentleness, and patience. [NLT]<br>Ἐνδύσασθε οὖν, ὡς ἐκλεκτοὶ τοῦ Θεοῦ, ἅγιοι καὶ ἠγαπημένοι, σπλάγχνα **οἰκτιρμῶν**, χρηστότητα, ταπεινοφροσύνην, πραότητα, μακροθυμίαν· [GNS]<br>Ἐνδύσασθε οὖν, ὡς ἐκλεκτοὶ τοῦ θεοῦ, ἅγιοι καὶ ἠγαπημένοι, σπλάγχνα **οἰκτιρμοῦ** χρηστότητα ταπεινοφροσύνην πραΰτητα μακροθυμίαν, [GNT] | Compassion, mercy, pity, tenderheartedness.<br><br>**Practical Application**<br>God has had so much mercy upon us, that the one thing we should do is to show mercy to others. Compassion and pity should flood our hearts for the...<br>• lost<br>• wayward<br>• lonely<br>• homeless<br>• hungry<br>• aged<br>• hurting<br>• diseased<br>• poor<br>• empty<br>• unclothed<br>• orphaned<br><br>Of course, the list could go on and on. The point is that the believer no longer has the right to overlook the needy of the world. He is now a new man. A part of the clothing of the new man is the garment of compassion; the believer is to be clothed with compassion. He is to have mercy and reach out to meet the needs of the world—reach out with all he is and has, holding back nothing so long as a single need exists. |
| **#672**<br>**Compassion**<br><br>**Compassion**–KJV<br>Sympathetic–NASB<br>Sympathetic–NIV<br>**Compassion**–NKJV<br>Sympathy–NLT<br><br>**POSB REFERENCE**<br>(1 Pt.3:8)<br>Note 2 | συμπαθεῖς = *sumpatheis*<br>Pronunciation: [soom-path-ice']<br>Parsing (part of speech): adjective<br>    Case—nominative<br>    Gender—masculine<br>    Number—plural<br>    Stem or root—from συμπαθής, ές<br>Concordance References:<br>  ⇒ Strong's #4835 sumpathēs<br>  ⇒ NIV #5218 sumpathēs<br>  ⇒ NASB #4835 sumpathēs<br><br>**1 Peter 3:8**<br>Finally, be ye all of one mind, having **compassion** one of another, love as brethren, be pitiful, be courteous: [KJV]<br>To sum up, let all be harmonious, **sympathetic**, brotherly, kindhearted, and humble in spirit; [NASB]<br>Finally, all of you, live in harmony with one another; be **sympathetic**, love as brothers, be compassionate and humble. [NIV]<br>Finally, all *of you be* of one mind, having **compassion** for one another; love as brothers, *be* tenderhearted, *be* courteous; [NKJV] | Sympathy; compassion; to actually feel with others.<br><br>**Practical Application**<br>Believers must have compassion for one another. The word compassion (*sumpatheis*) means sympathy; to actually feel with others. It means to feel for others so much that...<br>• one suffers with those who suffer.<br>• one weeps with those who weep.<br>• one rejoices when others are honored.<br>• one understands the pressure that a leader is under when he has to lead.<br>• one hurts with those who are criticized and attacked.<br>• one grieves with the sorrows of others.<br><br>Unity cannot exist unless believers feel compassion and sympathy for one another. Believers cannot be selfish and aloof; they cannot be seeking attention and seeking to get their own way if they are to be unified. Unity demands sympathy; unity demands that believers feel for one another—that they feel deeply, so deeply that they |

# Practical Word Studies in the New Testament

| ENGLISH WORD | GREEK WORD AND VERSE | THE WORD MEANS... |
|---|---|---|
| | Finally, all of you should be of one mind, full of **sympathy** toward each other, loving one another with tender hearts and humble minds. [NLT]<br>Τὸ δὲ τέλος, πάντες ὁμόφρονες, **συμπαθεῖς**, φιλάδελφοι, εὔσπλαγχνοι, φιλόφρονες· [GNS]<br>Τὸ δὲ τέλος πάντες ὁμόφρονες, **συμπαθεῖς**, φιλάδελφοι, εὔσπλαγχνοι, ταπεινόφρονες, [GNT] | actually experience what other believers experience: pain, hurt, abuse, suffering, joy, and rejoicing. |
| **#673**<br>**Compassionate**<br><br>Tenderhearted–KJV<br>Tender-hearted–NASB<br>**Compassionate–NIV**<br>Tenderhearted–NKJV<br>Tenderhearted–NLT<br><br>**POSB REFERENCE**<br>(Eph.4:32)<br>Note 7, point 2 | εὔσπλαγχνοι = eusplagchnoi<br>Pronunciation: [yoo'-splangkh-noy]<br>Parsing (part of speech): adjective<br>    Case—nominative<br>    Gender—masculine<br>    Number—plural<br>    Stem or root—from εὔσπλαγχνος, ον<br>Concordance References:<br>  ⇒ Strong's #2155 eusplagchnos<br>  ⇒ NIV #2359 eusplagchnos<br>  ⇒ NASB #2155 eusplagchnos<br><br>**Ephes. 4:32**<br>And be ye kind one to another, **tenderhearted**, forgiving one another, even as God for Christ's sake hath forgiven you. [KJV]<br>And be kind to one another, **tender-hearted**, forgiving each other, just as God in Christ also has forgiven you. [NASB]<br>Be kind and **compassionate** to one another, forgiving each other, just as in Christ God forgave you. [NIV]<br>And be kind to one another, **tenderhearted**, forgiving one another, just as God in Christ forgave you. [NKJV]<br>Instead, be kind to each other, **tenderhearted**, forgiving one another, just as God through Christ has forgiven you. [NLT]<br>γίνεσθε δὲ εἰς ἀλλήλους χρηστοί, **εὔσπλαγχνοι**, χαριζόμενοι ἑαυτοῖς, καθὼς καὶ ὁ Θεὸς ἐν Χριστῷ ἐχαρίσατο ὑμῖν. [GNS]<br>γίνεσθε [δὲ] εἰς ἀλλήλους χρηστοί, **εὔσπλαγχνοι**, χαριζόμενοι ἑαυτοῖς, καθὼς καὶ ὁ θεὸς ἐν Χριστῷ ἐχαρίσατο ὑμῖν. [GNT] | Compassionate, tenderhearted, kind. It means to show compassion, mercy, understanding, love, tenderness, and warmth.<br><br>**Practical Application**<br>It means to *be aware* of a person's hurts and sufferings, problems and difficulties, emotions and mental state, physical and spiritual condition. It means to be tenderhearted toward them. |
| **#674**<br>**Compassionate**<br><br>Pitiful–KJV<br>Kindhearted–NASB<br>**Compassionate–NIV**<br>Tenderhearted–NKJV<br>Tender hearts–NLT<br><br>**POSB REFERENCE**<br>(1 Pt.3:8)<br>Note 4 | εὔσπλαγχνοι = eusplagchnoi<br>Pronunciation: [yoo'-splangkh-noy]<br>Parsing (part of speech): adjective<br>    Case—nominative<br>    Gender—masculine<br>    Number—plural<br>    Stem or root—from εὔσπλαγχνος, ον<br>Concordance References:<br>  ⇒ Strong's #2155 eusplagchnos<br>  ⇒ NIV #2359 eusplagchnos<br>  ⇒ NASB #2155 eusplagchnos<br><br>**1 Peter 3:8**<br>Finally, be ye all of one mind, having compassion one of another, love as brethren, be **pitiful**, be courteous: [KJV]<br>To sum up, let all be harmonious, sympathetic, brotherly, **kindhearted**, and humble in spirit; [NASB]<br>Finally, all of you, live in harmony with one another; be sympathetic, love as brothers, be **compassionate** and humble. [NIV]<br>Finally, all *of you be* of one mind, having compassion for one another; love as brothers, *be* **tenderhearted**, *be* courteous; [NKJV]<br>Finally, all of you should be of one mind, full of sympathy toward each other, loving one another with **tender hearts** and humble minds. [NLT]<br>Τὸ δὲ τέλος, πάντες ὁμόφρονες, συμπαθεῖς, φιλάδελφοι, **εὔσπλαγχνοι**, φιλόφρονες· [GNS]<br>Τὸ δὲ τέλος πάντες ὁμόφρονες, συμπαθεῖς, φιλάδελφοι, **εὔσπλαγχνοι**, ταπεινόφρονες, [GNT] | To be compassionate, to pity; to be kindhearted, to have a tender heart. It means to be tenderhearted; to be sensitive and affectionate toward the needs of others; to be moved with tender feelings over the pain and sufferings of others.<br><br>**Practical Application**<br>We live in a world that desperately needs pity, a world of extreme suffering. So many suffer and continue to suffer without ever having their needs met. The means and resources to meet their needs exist, but so many within the world have become hardened to the sufferings of others. They bank, hoard, and build up asset after asset instead of sacrificing and reaching out to meet the needs of the world. But this is not to be true of the believer. Believers are to have pity upon the sufferings of others. Believers are to feel pity to the point that they are moved to act, sacrificing and reaching out to meet the needs of the suffering.<br>Again, note how compassion leaves no room for selfishness. Compassion demands that a person deny himself and help others in their desperate needs and sufferings. Note also how pity draws people together. Helping and ministering to one another binds and knits people together. Having compassion—feeling for one another |

# Practical Word Studies
## in the New Testament

| ENGLISH WORD | GREEK WORD AND VERSE | THE WORD MEANS... |
|---|---|---|
| | | and sacrificing and reaching out to help one another—unites people together. A great bond is created between the believer and those to whom he ministers. |
| **#675**<br>**Compel–**<br>**Compels**<br><br>**Compel–KJV**<br>Force–NASB<br>Forces–NIV<br>**Compels–NKJV**<br>Demands–NLT<br><br>**POSB**<br>**REFERENCE**<br>(Mt.5:39-41, esp.v.41)<br>Note 3, point.3 | ἀγγαρεύσει = aggareusei<br>Pronunciation: [ang-ar-yew'-see]<br>Parsing (part of speech): verb<br>    Mood—indicative<br>    Tense—future<br>    Voice—active<br>    Person—3rd person<br>    Number—singular<br>    Stem or root—from ἀγγαρεύω<br>Concordance References:<br>  ⇒ Strong's #29 aggareuo<br>  ⇒ NIV #30 angareuo<br>  ⇒ NASB #29 aggareuo<br><br>**Matthew 5:41**<br>And whosoever shall **compel** thee to go a mile, go with him twain. [KJV]<br>"And whoever shall **force** you to go one mile, go with him two. [NASB]<br>If someone **forces** you to go one mile, go with him two miles. [NIV]<br>And whoever **compels** you to go one mile, go with him two. [NKJV]<br>If a soldier **demands** that you carry his gear for a mile, carry it two miles. [NLT]<br>καὶ ὅστις σε **ἀγγαρεύσει** μίλιον ἕν, ὕπαγε μετ' αὐτοῦ δύο. [GNS]<br>καὶ ὅστις σε **ἀγγαρεύσει** μίλιον ἕν, ὕπαγε μετ' αὐτοῦ δύο. [GNT] | To force, compel, demand, press into service under the threat of punishment.<br><br>**Practical Application**<br>Ordinary citizens could be drafted for any task that the person in authority deemed necessary. Christ is saying that if a believer is forced to go a mile, he should go twice as far. Again, rights—even the rights of liberty—are not the primary concern of the believer. The believer's primary concern is people and their burdens—reaching and relieving their burdens in obedience to God.<br>Going a second mile is difficult. It means a person does not become bitter and resentful, grumbling and griping, complaining and criticizing, self-pitying and begrudging. It means a person forgives and serves and offers more service. He sets his mind and heart on reaching out to the offender by helping more and more. Such action will more likely reach the offender for the Kingdom of Heaven. It will certainly help bring the Kingdom of Heaven closer to this earth (see POSB *Deeper Study* #3—Matthew 19:23-24). |
| **#676**<br>**Compelled**<br><br>Laid upon–KJV<br>Under compulsion–<br>NASB<br>**Compelled–NIV**<br>Laid upon–NKJV<br>**Compelled–NLT**<br><br>**POSB**<br>**REFERENCE**<br>(1 Cor.9:16)<br>Note 1 | ἀνάγκη ἐπίκειται = anagkē epikeitai<br>Pronunciation: [an-ang-kay' ep-ik'-eh-ee-tah-ee]<br>Parsing *anagkē* (part of speech): noun<br>    Case—nominative<br>    Gender—feminine<br>    Number—singular<br>    Stem or root—from ἀνάγκη, ης<br>Parsing *epikeitai* (part of speech): verb<br>    Mood—indicative<br>    Tense—present<br>    Voice—middle or passive deponent<br>    Person—3rd person<br>    Number—singular<br>    Stem or root—from ἐπίκειμαι<br>Concordance References:<br>  ⇒ Strong's #318+1945 anagkē epikeimai<br>  ⇒ NIV #340+2130 anagkē epikeimai [compelled]<br>  ⇒ NASB #318+1945 anagkē epikeimai<br><br>**1 Cor. 9:16**<br>For though I preach the gospel, I have nothing to glory of: for necessity is **laid upon** me; yea, woe is unto me, if I preach not the gospel! [KJV]<br>For if I preach the gospel, I have nothing to boast of, for I am **under compulsion**; for woe is me if I do not preach the gospel. [NASB]<br>Yet when I preach the gospel, I cannot boast, for I am **compelled** to preach. Woe to me if I do not preach the gospel! [NIV]<br>For if I preach the gospel, I have nothing to boast of, for necessity is **laid upon** me; yes, woe is me if I do not preach the gospel! [NKJV]<br>For preaching the Good News is not something I can boast about. I am **compelled** by God to do it. How terrible for me if I didn't do it! [NLT]<br>ἐὰν γὰρ εὐαγγελίζωμαι, οὐκ ἔστι μοι καύχημα· **ἀνάγκη** γάρ μοι **ἐπίκειται**· οὐαὶ δέ μοί ἐστιν, ἐὰν μὴ | To be pressed, compelled, constrained, required; to be duty bound, gripped with a sense of duty; to preach the gospel. It means to be urged, under force, under compulsion, imposed upon.<br><br>**Practical Application**<br>God had called Paul to preach the gospel; therefore, it was his charge, his work, his business, his call in life. He could not do otherwise: he was compelled to preach. His preaching was not a matter of choice; he had not chosen to be a preacher. His preaching was a matter of duty. If he did not preach, he would be disobeying God and would miss the very purpose for his life upon earth. |

# PRACTICAL WORD STUDIES
## in the NEW TESTAMENT

| ENGLISH WORD | GREEK WORD AND VERSE | THE WORD MEANS... |
|---|---|---|
| | εὐαγγελίζωμαι. [GNS]<br>ἐὰν γὰρ εὐαγγελίζωμαι, οὐκ ἔστιν μοι καύχημα· ἀνάγκη γάρ μοι ἐπίκειται· οὐαὶ γάρ μοί ἐστιν ἐὰν μὴ εὐαγγελίσωμαι. [GNT] | |
| **#677**<br>**Compelled To Go**<br><br>Driveth–KJV<br>Impelled...to go out– NASB<br>Sent...out–NIV<br>Drove–NKJV<br>**Compelled...to go– NLT**<br><br>**POSB REFERENCE**<br>(Mk.1:12)<br>Note 2 | ἐκβάλλει = *ekballei*<br>Pronunciation: [ek-bal'-leh-ee]<br>Parsing (part of speech): verb<br>    Mood—indicative<br>    Tense—present<br>    Voice—active<br>    Person—3rd person<br>    Number—singular<br>    Stem or root—from ἐκβάλλω<br>Concordance References:<br>  ⇒ Strong's #1544 ekballō<br>  ⇒ NIV #1675 ekballō<br>  ⇒ NASB #1544 ekballō<br><br>**Mark 1:12**<br>And immediately the Spirit **driveth** him into the wilderness. [KJV]<br>And immediately the Spirit **impelled** Him **to go out** into the wilderness. [NASB]<br>At once the Spirit **sent** him **out** into the desert, [NIV]<br>Immediately the Spirit **drove** Him into the wilderness. [NKJV]<br>Immediately the Holy Spirit **compelled** Jesus **to go** into the wilderness. [NLT]<br>Καὶ εὐθὺς τὸ Πνεῦμα αὐτὸν **ἐκβάλλει** εἰς τὴν ἔρημον. [GNS]<br>Καὶ εὐθὺς τὸ πνεῦμα αὐτὸν **ἐκβάλλει** εἰς τὴν ἔρημον. [GNT] | Sent out, impelled to go out; compelled to go; to drive out; to thrust; to cast forth; to drive forth; to force.<br><br>**Practical Application**<br>Jesus was compelled with great force to go into the wilderness. He was driven by the Spirit to be tried. He was to be tried and tested not to make Him fall, but to make Him stronger and better prepared to do great things for God (see POSB note, pt.3—Matthew 4:1). |
| **#678**<br>**Compels**<br><br>Constraineth–KJV<br>Controls–NASB<br>**Compels–NIV**<br>**Compels–NKJV**<br>Controls–NLT<br><br>**POSB REFERENCE**<br>(2 Cor.5:14-16; esp. v.14)<br>Note 4 | συνέχει = *sunechei*<br>Pronunciation: [soon-ekh'-ee]<br>Parsing (part of speech): verb<br>    Mood—indicative<br>    Tense—present<br>    Voice—active<br>    Person—3rd person<br>    Number—singular<br>    Stem or root—from συνέχω<br>Concordance References:<br>  ⇒ Strong's #4912 sunechō<br>  ⇒ NIV #5309 sunechō<br>  ⇒ NASB #4912 sunechō<br><br>**2 Cor. 5:14**<br>For the love of Christ **constraineth** us; because we thus judge, that if one died for all, then were all dead: [KJV]<br>For the love of Christ **controls** us, having concluded this, that one died for all, therefore all died; [NASB]<br>For Christ's love **compels** us, because we are convinced that one died for all, and therefore all died. [NIV]<br>For the love of Christ **compels** us, because we judge thus: that if One died for all, then all died; [NKJV]<br>Whatever we do, it is because Christ's love **controls** us. Since we believe that Christ died for everyone, we also believe that we have all died to the old life we used to live. [NLT]<br>ἡ γὰρ ἀγάπη τοῦ Χριστοῦ **συνέχει** ἡμᾶς, κρίναντας τοῦτο, ὅτι εἰ εἷς ὑπὲρ πάντων ἀπέθανεν, ἄρα οἱ πάντες ἀπέθανον· [GNS]<br>ἡ γὰρ ἀγάπη τοῦ Χριστοῦ **συνέχει** ἡμᾶς, κρίναντας τοῦτο, ὅτι εἰ εἷς ὑπὲρ πάντων ἀπέθανεν, ἄρα οἱ πάντες ἀπέθανον· [GNT] | To compel; to constrain; to control; to press.<br><br>**Practical Application**<br>The love of Christ presses, compels, and stirs Paul to hold fast to the ministry. The love of Christ is the great thing that constrains Paul to minister. Note that Paul does not say that he is driven to minister because of...<br>• the great teaching of Christ.<br>• the great example of Christ.<br>• the great ministry of Christ.<br>• the great life of Christ.<br><br>All of these areas of the Lord's life are important, critically so, but they are not the foundation of our salvation and ministry. The foundation of the believer's life is the love of Christ. |
| **#679**<br>**Competes– Competes In The Games** | ἀγωνιζόμενος = *agōnizomenos*<br>Pronunciation: [ag-o-nid'-zom-eh-nos]<br>Parsing (part of speech): verb<br>    Mood—participle<br>    Tense—present | To compete in games; to compete as a highly disciplined athlete; to struggle in competition; to struggle; to make every effort. |

## PRACTICAL WORD STUDIES
## in the NEW TESTAMENT

| ENGLISH WORD | GREEK WORD AND VERSE | THE WORD MEANS... |
|---|---|---|
| Striveth–KJV<br>**Competes in the games–NASB**<br>**Competes in the games–NIV**<br>**Competes–NKJV**<br>Athletes practice–NLT<br><br>**POSB REFERENCE**<br>(1 Cor.9:25)<br>Note 2 | Voice—middle or passive deponent<br>Case—nominative<br>Gender—masculine<br>Number—singular<br>Stem or root—from ἀγωνίζομαι<br>Concordance References:<br>⇒ Strong's #75 agōnizomai<br>⇒ NIV #76 agōnizomai<br>⇒ NASB #75 agōnizomai<br><br>**1 Cor. 9:25**<br>And every man that **striveth** for the mastery is temperate in all things. Now they do it to obtain a corruptible crown; but we an incorruptible. [KJV]<br>And everyone who **competes in the games** exercises self-control in all things. They then do it to receive a perishable wreath, but we an imperishable. [NASB]<br>Everyone who **competes in the games** goes into strict training. They do it to get a crown that will not last; but we do it to get a crown that will last forever. [NIV]<br>And everyone who **competes** *for the prize* is temperate in all things. Now they *do it* to obtain a perishable crown, but we *for* an imperishable *crown*. [NKJV]<br>All **athletes practice** strict self-control. They do it to win a prize that will fade away, but we do it for an eternal prize. [NLT]<br>πᾶς δὲ ὁ **ἀγωνιζόμενος** πάντα ἐγκρατεύεται, ἐκεῖνοι μὲν οὖν ἵνα φθαρτὸν στέφανον λάβωσιν, ἡμεῖς δὲ ἄφθαρτον. [GNS]<br>πᾶς δὲ ὁ **ἀγωνιζόμενος** πάντα ἐγκρατεύεται, ἐκεῖνοι μὲν οὖν ἵνα φθαρτὸν στέφανον λάβωσιν, ἡμεῖς δὲ ἄφθαρτον. [GNT] | **Practical Application**<br>Every runner and boxer is highly disciplined in body, mind, thought, spirit, exercise, workouts, and contests. He is disciplined...<br>• in body: what he eats and how much he eats.<br>• in mind and thought: his concentration on the goal and how to best gear his body, spirit, and mind to that end.<br>• in spirit: keeping his spirit strong and motivated for the strain necessary to work out day by day and to reach his goal.<br>The minister or believer is to do no less. He must be just as disciplined as the athlete. He disciplines himself to the point of pain. And note: the discipline "goes into strict training." It covers his body, mind, and spirit, the place where God's presence actually dwells. Therefore, he does not allow anything to touch or enter his body, not anything, that is corrupt, impure, polluted, or that will cause a more rapid deterioration of the temple. |
| **#680**<br>**Complained**<br><br>Murmured–KJV<br>Grumbling–NASB<br>Grumble–NIV<br>**Complained–NKJV**<br>Murmur–NLT<br><br>**POSB REFERENCE**<br>(Jn.6:41-43; esp. v.41)<br>Note 1 | Ἐγόγγυζον = Egogguzon<br>Pronunciation: [eh-gong-good'-zon]<br>Parsing (part of speech): verb<br>  Mood—indicative<br>  Tense—imperfect<br>  Voice—active<br>  Person—3rd person<br>  Number—plural<br>  Stem or root—from γογγύζω<br>Concordance References:<br>⇒ Strong's #1111 gogguzō<br>⇒ NIV #1197 gogguzō<br>⇒ NASB #1111 gogguzō<br><br>**John 6:41**<br>The Jews then **murmured** at him, because he said, I am the bread which came down from heaven. [KJV]<br>The Jews therefore were **grumbling** about Him, because He said, "I am the bread that came down out of heaven." [NASB]<br>At this the Jews began to **grumble** about him because he said, "I am the bread that came down from heaven." [NIV]<br>The Jews then **complained** about Him, because He said, "I am the bread which came down from heaven." [NKJV]<br>Then the people began to **murmur** in disagreement because he had said, "I am the bread from heaven." [NLT]<br>Ἐγόγγυζον οὖν οἱ Ἰουδαῖοι περὶ αὐτοῦ, ὅτι εἶπεν, Ἐγώ εἰμι ὁ ἄρτος ὁ καταβὰς ἐκ τοῦ οὐρανοῦ. [GNS]<br>Ἐγόγγυζον οὖν οἱ Ἰουδαῖοι περὶ αὐτοῦ ὅτι εἶπεν, Ἐγώ εἰμι ὁ ἄρτος ὁ καταβὰς ἐκ τοῦ οὐρανοῦ, [GNT] | To grumble; to murmur against; to mutter; to whisper undertones; to grouse; to complain.<br><br>**Practical Application**<br>The Jews complained against Him. The word refers to the grumbling, the buzzing, the discontent that arises from a crowd that is upset and confused; that is, misunderstanding, rejecting, and opposing a speaker. |
| **#681**<br>**Complaining**<br><br>Murmurings–KJV<br>Grumbling–NASB<br>**Complaining–NIV** | γογγυσμῶν = goggusmōn<br>Pronunciation: [gong-goos-mown']<br>Parsing (part of speech): noun<br>  Case—genitive<br>  Gender—masculine<br>  Number—plural<br>  Stem or root—from γογγυσμός, οῦ | Complaining, murmuring, grumbling, whispering, quarreling.<br><br>**Practical Application**<br>Note: it means the quiet, soft, behind-the-back undertone of complaining and grumbling. |

# PRACTICAL WORD STUDIES
## in the NEW TESTAMENT

| ENGLISH WORD | GREEK WORD AND VERSE | THE WORD MEANS... |
|---|---|---|
| **Complaining**–NKJV<br>**Complaining**–NLT<br><br>**POSB<br>REFERENCE**<br>(Philip.2:14)<br>Note 3 | Concordance References:<br>⇒ Strong's #1112 goggusmos<br>⇒ NIV #1198 goggusmos<br>⇒ NASB #1112 goggusmos<br><br>**Philip. 2:14**<br>Do all things without **murmurings** and disputings: [KJV]<br>Do all things without **grumbling** or disputing; [NASB]<br>Do everything without **complaining** or arguing, [NIV]<br>Do all things without **complaining** and disputing, [NKJV]<br>In everything you do, stay away from **complaining** and arguing, [NLT]<br>πάντα ποιεῖτε χωρὶς **γογγυσμῶν** καὶ διαλογισμῶν, [GNS]<br>πάντα ποιεῖτε χωρὶς **γογγυσμῶν** καὶ διαλογισμῶν, [GNT] | It is the kind of criticism, dissatisfaction, fault-finding and gossip that goes on within small groups or cliques.<br>The results of complaining are far worse than people ever think. This is the primary reason God forbids complaining in no uncertain terms. Complaining...<br>• hurts<br>• damages<br>• divides<br>• tears down<br>• downs a person<br>• says "look at me"<br>• elevates selfish opinion<br>• opposes God's will<br>• hinders progress<br>• stymies growth<br>• misleads people<br>• is self-centered<br>• pushes people away from Christ and the church |
| **#682<br>Complete**<br><br>Perfect–KJV<br>Perfected–NASB<br>**Complete**–NIV<br>Perfect–NKJV<br>Perfected–NLT<br><br>**POSB<br>REFERENCE**<br>(Jn.17:23)<br>*Deeper Study #2* | τετελειωμένοι = *teteleiömenoi*<br>Pronunciation: [teh-tel-i-o'-mehn-oy]<br>Parsing (part of speech): verb<br>    Mood—participle<br>    Tense—perfect<br>    Voice—passive<br>    Case—nominative<br>    Gender—masculine<br>    Number—plural<br>    Stem or root—from τελειόω<br>Concordance References:<br>⇒ Strong's #5048 teleioo<br>⇒ NIV #5457 teleioo<br>⇒ NASB #5048 teleioo<br><br>**John 17:23**<br>I in them, and thou in me, that they may be made **perfect** in one; and that the world may know that thou hast sent me, and hast loved them, as thou hast loved me. [KJV]<br>I in them, and Thou in Me, that they may be **perfected** in unity, that the world may know that Thou didst send Me, and didst love them, even as Thou didst love Me. [NASB]<br>I in them and you in me. May they be brought to **complete** unity to let the world know that you sent me and have loved them even as you have loved me. [NIV]<br>I in them, and You in Me; that they may be made **perfect** in one, and that the world may know that You have sent Me, and have loved them as You have loved Me. [NKJV]<br>I in them and you in me, all being **perfected** into one. Then the world will know that you sent me and will understand that you love them as much as you love me. [NLT]<br>ἐγὼ ἐν αὐτοῖς καὶ σὺ ἐν ἐμοί, ἵνα ὦσι **τετελειωμένοι** εἰς ἕν, καὶ ἵνα γινώσκῃ ὁ κόσμος ὅτι σύ με ἀπέστειλας, καὶ ἠγάπησας αὐτοὺς, καθὼς ἐμὲ ἠγάπησας. [GNS]<br>ἐγὼ ἐν αὐτοῖς καὶ σὺ ἐν ἐμοί, ἵνα ὦσιν **τετελειωμένοι** εἰς ἕν, ἵνα γινώσκῃ ὁ κόσμος ὅτι σύ με ἀπέστειλας καὶ ἠγάπησας αὐτοὺς καθὼς ἐμὲ ἠγάπησας. [GNT] | To be complete; to be perfect; to finish; to accomplish some end; to reach a goal.<br><br>**Practical Application**<br>The idea of this word (*teteleiömenoi*) is perfection of purpose. It has to do with an end, an aim, a goal, a purpose. It means fit, mature, fully grown at a particular stage of growth. For example, a fully grown child is a perfect child; he has reached the height of childhood, achieved the purpose of childhood. The word "complete" does not mean completion or perfection of character, that is, being without sin. It is fitness, maturity for task and purpose. It is full development, maturity of godliness. (See POSB note—Ephes. 4:12-16; cp. Phil. 3:12; 1 John 1:8, 10.) |
| **#683<br>Complete**<br><br>Perfect–KJV<br>Adequate–NASB | ἄρτιος = *artios*<br>Pronunciation: [ar'-tee-os]<br>Parsing (part of speech): adjective<br>    Case—nominative<br>    Gender—masculine<br>    Number—singular | To be thorough; to be perfect; to be adequate; to be prepared in every way. It means complete, matured, filled. |

# PRACTICAL WORD STUDIES
## in the NEW TESTAMENT

| ENGLISH WORD | GREEK WORD AND VERSE | THE WORD MEANS... |
|---|---|---|
| Thoroughly–NIV<br>**Complete**–NKJV<br>Preparing us in every way–NLT<br><br>**POSB REFERENCE**<br>(2 Tim. 3:17)<br>Note 5 | Stem or root—from ἄρτιος, α, ον<br>Concordance References:<br>⇒ Strong's #739 artios<br>⇒ NIV #787 artios<br>⇒ NASB #739 artios<br><br>**2 Tim. 3:17**<br>That the man of God may be **perfect**, throughly furnished unto all good works. [KJV]<br>That the man of God may be **adequate**, equipped for every good work. [NASB]<br>So that the man of God may be **thoroughly** equipped for every good work. [NIV]<br>That the man of God may be **complete**, thoroughly equipped for every good work. [NKJV]<br>It is God's way of **preparing us in every way**, fully equipped for every good thing God wants us to do. [NLT]<br>ἵνα **ἄρτιος** ᾖ ὁ τοῦ Θεοῦ ἄνθρωπος, πρὸς πᾶν ἔργον ἀγαθὸν ἐξηρτισμένος. [GNS]<br>ἵνα **ἄρτιος** ᾖ ὁ τοῦ Θεοῦ ἄνθρωπος, πρὸς πᾶν ἔργον ἀγαθὸν ἐξηρτισμένος. [GNT] | **Practical Application**<br>Scripture perfects a man and equips him for every good work. "Complete" (*artios*) means, adequate, matured, perfect, filled. No person is complete or mature apart from Scripture. Man was made for God and he is to live by the Word of God. If he tries to live without God and His Word, man fails in life. He lives an incomplete, immature, and misfitted life. This is particularly true of the *man of God*, the person who claims to be a minister or teacher of God's Word. |
| **#684**<br>**Complete**<br><br>Entire–KJV<br>**Complete**–NASB<br>**Complete**–NIV<br>**Complete**–NKJV<br>Fully developed–NLT<br><br>**POSB REFERENCE**<br>(Jas 1:4)<br>Note 3, point 2 | ὁλόκληροι = *holoklēroi*<br>Pronunciation: [hol-ok'-lay-roy]<br>Parsing (part of speech): adjective<br>  Case—nominative<br>  Gender—masculine<br>  Number—plural<br>Stem or root—from ὁλόκληρος, ον<br>Concordance References:<br>⇒ Strong's #3648 holoklēros<br>⇒ NIV #3908 holoklēros<br>⇒ NASB #3648 holoklēros<br><br>**James 1:4**<br>But let patience have her perfect work, that ye may be perfect and **entire**, wanting nothing. [KJV]<br>And let endurance have its perfect result, that you may be perfect and **complete**, lacking in nothing. [NASB]<br>Perseverance must finish its work so that you may be mature and **complete**, not lacking anything. [NIV]<br>But let patience have *its* perfect work, that you may be perfect and **complete**, lacking nothing. [NKJV]<br>So let it grow, for when your endurance is **fully developed**, you will be strong in character and ready for anything. [NLT]<br>ἡ δὲ ὑπομονὴ ἔργον τέλειον ἐχέτω, ἵνα ἦτε τέλειοι καὶ **ὁλόκληροι**, ἐν μηδενὶ λειπόμενοι. [GNS]<br>ἡ δὲ ὑπομονὴ ἔργον τέλειον ἐχέτω, ἵνα ἦτε τέλειοι καὶ **ὁλόκληροι** ἐν μηδενὶ λειπόμενοι. [GNT] | Complete, entire, fully developed, whole. It means to be wholly fit, perfectly sound, complete with no weaknesses, flaws, defects, or shortcomings.<br><br>**Practical Application**<br>This means a most wonderful thing. When a person perseveres and conquers trials or temptations...<br>• he becomes more complete, more fit, more sound, and more fully developed.<br>• he also eliminates more weaknesses, more flaws, more defects, and more shortcomings.<br>Day by day—trial by trial and temptation by temptation—when a person perseveres and conquers, he becomes more and more complete. He becomes stronger and more pure and righteous—more and more like the Lord Jesus. As the last words of James 1:4 say, "not lacking anything." The believer who faces trials and temptations in the joy of Christ conquers all, and he lacks nothing.<br>⇒ He becomes more and more complete, fulfilling his task and purpose for being on earth a little bit more.<br>⇒ He becomes more and more entire and fit, eliminating more and more weaknesses and shortcomings in his life. |
| **#685**<br>**Complete In Knowledge**<br><br>Filled with all knowledge–KJV<br>Filled with all knowledge–NASB<br>**Complete in knowledge**–NIV<br>Filled with all knowledge–NKJV<br>Know these things so well–NLT<br><br>**POSB REFERENCE**<br>(Rom.15:14)<br>Note 1, point 2b | πεπληρωμένοι πάσης γνώσεως = *peplērōmenoi pasēs gnōseōs*<br>Pronunciation: [peh-play-ro'-mehn-oy pah-says gno'-seh-os]<br>Parsing *peplērōmenoi* (part of speech): verb<br>  Mood—participle<br>  Tense—perfect<br>  Voice—passive<br>  Case—nominative<br>  Gender—masculine<br>  Person—2nd person<br>  Number—plural<br>  Stem or root—from πληρόω<br>Parsing *gnōseōs* (part of speech): noun<br>  Case—genitive<br>  Gender—feminine<br>  Number—singular<br>  Stem or root—from γνῶσις, εως<br>Concordance References:<br>⇒ Strong's #3956 + 4137 pas plēroō + 1108 gnōsis<br>⇒ NIV #4246 + 4444 pas plēroō [complete] + 1194 gnōsis [knowledge]<br>⇒ NASB #3956 + 4137 pas plēroō + 1108 gnōsis | To be complete in knowledge; to be filled with all knowledge; to know [these things] very well.<br><br>**Practical Application**<br>The believers were "complete in knowledge" (*peplērōmenoi pasēs gnōseōs*): They were filled...<br>• with spiritual insight and perception.<br>• with knowledge of Christ, God, and the Holy Spirit.<br>• with spiritual truth.<br>• with the spiritual need of man and his world. |

# PRACTICAL WORD STUDIES
## in the NEW TESTAMENT

| ENGLISH WORD | GREEK WORD AND VERSE | THE WORD MEANS... |
|---|---|---|
| | **Romans 15:14**<br>And I myself also am persuaded of you, my brethren, that ye also are full of goodness, **filled with all knowledge**, able also to admonish one another. [KJV]<br>And concerning you, my brethren, I myself also am convinced that you yourselves are full of goodness, **filled with all knowledge**, and able also to admonish one another. [NASB]<br>I myself am convinced, my brothers, that you yourselves are full of goodness, **complete in knowledge** and competent to instruct one another. [NIV]<br>Now I myself am confident concerning you, my brethren, that you also are full of goodness, **filled with all knowledge**, able also to admonish one another. [NKJV]<br>I am fully convinced, dear brothers and sisters, that you are full of goodness. You **know these things so well** that you are able to teach others all about them. [NLT]<br>Πέπεισμαι δέ, ἀδελφοί μου, καὶ αὐτὸς ἐγὼ περὶ ὑμῶν, ὅτι καὶ αὐτοὶ μεστοί ἐστε ἀγαθωσύνης, **πεπληρωμένοι πάσης γνώσεως**, δυνάμενοι καὶ ἀλλήλους νουθετεῖν. [GNS]<br>Πέπεισμαι δέ, ἀδελφοί μου, καὶ αὐτὸς ἐγὼ περὶ ὑμῶν ὅτι καὶ αὐτοὶ μεστοί ἐστε ἀγαθωσύνης, **πεπληρωμένοι πάσης** [τῆς] **γνώσεως**, δυνάμενοι καὶ ἀλλήλους νουθετεῖν. [GNT] | |
| **#686**<br>**Completely**<br><br>Uttermost–KJV<br>Forever–NASB<br>**Completely–NIV**<br>Uttermost–NKJV<br>Once and forever–NLT<br><br>**POSB REFERENCE**<br>(Heb.7:25)<br>Note 1, point 3 | εἰς τὸ παντελές = *eis to panteles*<br>Pronunciation: [ice to pan-tel-ehs]<br>Parsing *panteles* (part of speech): pronominal adjective<br>  Case—accusative<br>  Gender—neuter<br>  Number—singular<br>  Stem or root—from παντελής, ές<br>Concordance References:<br>⇒ Strong's #1519+3588+3838 eis ho pantelës<br>⇒ NIV #1650+3836+4117 eis ho pantelës [completely]<br>⇒ NASB #1519+3588+3838 eis ho pantelës<br><br>**Hebrews 7:25**<br>Wherefore he is able also to save them to the **uttermost** that come unto God by him, seeing he ever liveth to make intercession for them. [KJV]<br>Hence, also, He is able to save **forever** those who draw near to God through Him, since He always lives to make intercession for them. [NASB]<br>Therefore he is able to save **completely** those who come to God through him, because he always lives to intercede for them. [NIV]<br>Therefore He is also able to save to the **uttermost** those who come to God through Him, since He always lives to make intercession for them. [NKJV]<br>Therefore he is able, **once and forever**, to save everyone who comes to God through him. He lives forever to plead with God on their behalf. [NLT]<br>ὅθεν καὶ σώζειν **εἰς τὸ παντελὲς** δύναται τοὺς προσερχομένους δι' αὐτοῦ τῷ Θεῷ, πάντοτε ζῶν εἰς τὸ ἐντυγχάνειν ὑπὲρ αὐτῶν. [GNS]<br>ὅθεν καὶ σώζειν **εἰς τὸ παντελὲς** δύναται τοὺς προσερχομένους δι' αὐτοῦ τῷ θεῷ, πάντοτε ζῶν εἰς τὸ ἐντυγχάνειν ὑπὲρ αὐτῶν. [GNT] | Completely; to the uttermost; forever, once and forever.<br><br>**Practical Application**<br><br>Jesus Christ is able to save all persons completely. What does it mean to be saved completely, to the uttermost (*panteles*)? It means to be saved "completely, perfectly, finally and for all time and eternity" (Amplified New Testament). It means that Jesus Christ presents us to God as perfect. He presents us in His righteousness as perfected forever. Therefore in Christ—because He makes intercession for us and because He stands before God as the perfect and eternal sacrifice for our sins—we become acceptable to God. But it means much more. In outline form, when Jesus Christ completely saves us, it means...<br><br>• that He saves us from sin, death and condemnation (John 5:24; Romans 8:34).<br>• that He saves us to live with God eternally (John 3:16; Romans 8:39).<br>• that He saves us to be the citizens of the new heaven and earth (2 Peter 3:10-13; Rev. 21:1f).<br>• that He saves us to rule and reign over the universe right along with Him throughout all of eternity (Luke 12:42-44; Luke 22:28-29; 1 Cor. 6:2-3). |
| **#687**<br>**Completely Cut Off From**<br><br>Destroyed–KJV<br>Utterly destroyed from–NASB<br>**Completely cut off from–NIV**<br>Utterly destroyed | ἐξολεθρευθήσεται ἐκ = *exolethreuthēsetai ek*<br>Pronunciation: [ex-ol-eth-ryoo'-thay-seh-tah-ee ek]<br>Parsing *exolethreuthēsetai* (part of speech): verb<br>  Mood—indicative or imperative<br>  Tense—future or aorist<br>  Voice—passive<br>  Person—3rd person<br>  Number—singular<br>  Stem or root—from ἐξολεθρεύω<br>Concordance References:<br>⇒ Strong's #1537 + 1842 ek exolethreuō | To be completely cut off from; to be utterly destroyed or slayed; to lose one's well-being; to be wasted and ruined and given a worthless existence.<br><br>**Practical Application**<br><br>It does not mean that a person will cease to exist. It means a person will be destroyed and devastated and condemned to a worthless existence. He will suffer waste and loss and ruin forever and ever. |

# PRACTICAL WORD STUDIES
## in the NEW TESTAMENT

| ENGLISH WORD | GREEK WORD AND VERSE | THE WORD MEANS... |
|---|---|---|
| from–NKJV<br>Cut off from–NLT<br><br>**POSB REFERENCE**<br>(Acts 3:23)<br>*Deeper Study #4* | ⇒ NIV #1666 + 2017 ek exolethreuö<br>⇒ NASB #1537 + 1842 ek exolethreuö<br><br>**Acts 3:23**<br>And it shall come to pass, that every soul, which will not hear that prophet, shall be **destroyed** from among the people. [KJV]<br>'And it shall be that every soul that does not heed that prophet shall be **utterly destroyed from** among the people.' [NASB]<br>Anyone who does not listen to him will be **completely cut off from** among his people.' [NIV]<br>*And it shall be that every soul who will not hear that Prophet shall be **utterly destroyed from** among the people.' [NKJV]<br>Then Moses said, 'Anyone who will not listen to that Prophet will be **cut off from** God's people and utterly destroyed.' [NLT]<br>ἔσται δέ, πᾶσα ψυχὴ ἥτις ἐὰν μὴ ἀκούσῃ τοῦ προφήτου ἐκείνου, **ἐξολεθρευθήσεται ἐκ** τοῦ λαοῦ. [GNS]<br>ἔσται δὲ πᾶσα ψυχὴ ἥτις ἐὰν μὴ ἀκούσῃ τοῦ προφήτου ἐκείνου **ἐξολεθρευθήσεται ἐκ** τοῦ λαοῦ. [GNT] | |
| **#688**<br>**Composed**<br><br>Tempered–KJV<br>**Composed–NASB**<br>Combined–NIV<br>**Composed–NKJV**<br>Put together–NLT<br><br>**POSB REFERENCE**<br>(1 Cor.12:24-26; esp. v.24)<br>Note 4 | συνεκέρασεν = *sunekerasen*<br>Pronunciation: [soon-eh-ker'-ahn-sehn]<br>Parsing (part of speech): verb<br>    Mood—indicative<br>    Tense—aorist<br>    Voice—active<br>    Person—3rd person<br>    Number—singular<br>    Stem or root—from συγκεράννυμι<br>Concordance References:<br>⇒ Strong's #4786 sugkerannumi<br>⇒ NIV #5166 sugkerannumi<br>⇒ NASB #4786 sugkerannumi<br><br>**1 Cor. 12:24**<br>For our comely parts have no need: but God hath **tempered** the body together, having given more abundant honour to that part which lacked: [KJV]<br>Whereas our seemly members have no need of it. But God has so **composed** the body, giving more abundant honor to that member which lacked, [NASB]<br>While our presentable parts need no special treatment. But God has **combined** the members of the body and has given greater honor to the parts that lacked it, [NIV]<br>But our presentable *parts* have no need. But God **composed** the body, having given greater honor to that *part* which lacks it, [NKJV]<br>While other parts do not require this special care. So God has **put** the body **together** in such a way that extra honor and care are given to those parts that have less dignity. [NLT]<br>τὰ δὲ εὐσχήμονα ἡμῶν οὐ χρείαν ἔχει· ἀλλ ὁ Θεὸς **συνεκέρασε** τὸ σῶμα, τῷ ὑστεροῦντι περισσοτέραν δοὺς τιμήν, [GNS]<br>τὰ δὲ εὐσχήμονα ἡμῶν οὐ χρείαν ἔχει. ἀλλὰ ὁ θεὸς **συνεκέρασεν** τὸ σῶμα τῷ ὑστερουμένῳ περισσοτέραν δοὺς τιμήν, [GNT] | To mix, combine, unite, compose; put together; arrange, and blend together.<br><br>**Practical Application**<br>God has arranged the church as it is: the gifted and less gifted mix, combine, and blend together. And He has done it in such a manner that more honor really belongs to those who are not as gifted. The prayer warrior is much more essential than the soloist who is out before the people. The lay witness for Christ is more necessary than the preacher who stands in the pulpit. The person who ministers to the sick or elderly is more honorable than the committee chairman who leads the whole congregation in administrative matters. |
| **#689**<br>**Comrade**<br><br>Yokefellow–KJV<br>**Comrade–NASB**<br>Yokefellow–NIV<br>Companion–NKJV<br>Teammate–NLT | σύζυγε = *suzuge*<br>Pronunciation: [sood'-zoo-geh]<br>Parsing (part of speech): pronominal adjective<br>    Case—vocative<br>    Gender—masculine<br>    Number—singular<br>    Stem or root—from σύζυγος, ου<br>Concordance References:<br>⇒ Strong's #4805 suzugos<br>⇒ NIV #5187 suzugos<br>⇒ NASB #4805 suzugos | Yokefellow, fellow worker, comrade, teammate.<br><br>**Practical Application**<br>The need is for a true friend, a yokefellow, to step in to help any who are quarreling. The word "comrade" (*suzuge*) is thought by some to be a proper name given to some Christians when they were baptized. It was a common practice for |

# PRACTICAL WORD STUDIES
## in the NEW TESTAMENT

| ENGLISH WORD | GREEK WORD AND VERSE | THE WORD MEANS... |
|---|---|---|
| **POSB REFERENCE** (Philip.4:2-3; esp. v.3) Note 2, point 2 | **Philip. 4:3**<br>And I intreat thee also, true **yokefellow**, help those women which laboured with me in the gospel, with Clement also, and with other my fellowlabourers, whose names are in the book of life. [KJV]<br>Indeed, true **comrade**, I ask you also to help these women who have shared my struggle in the cause of the gospel, together with Clement also, and the rest of my fellow workers, whose names are in the book of life. [NASB]<br>Yes, and I ask you, loyal **yokefellow**, help these women who have contended at my side in the cause of the gospel, along with Clement and the rest of my fellow workers, whose names are in the book of life. [NIV]<br>And I urge you also, true **companion**, help these women who labored with me in the gospel, with Clement also, and the rest of my fellow workers, whose names are in the Book of Life. [NKJV]<br>And I ask you, my true **teammate**, to help these women, for they worked hard with me in telling others the Good News. And they worked with Clement and the rest of my co-workers, whose names are written in the Book of Life. [NLT]<br>καὶ ἐρωτῶ καὶ σέ, **σύζυγε** γνήσιε, συλλαμβάνου αὐταῖς, αἵτινες ἐν τῷ εὐαγγελίῳ συνήθλησάν μοι, μετὰ καὶ Κλήμεντος, καὶ τῶν λοιπῶν συνεργῶν μου, ὧν τὰ ὀνόματα ἐν βίβλῳ ζωῆς. [GNS]<br>ναὶ ἐρωτῶ καὶ σέ, γνήσιε **σύζυγε**, συλλαμβάνου αὐταῖς, αἵτινες ἐν τῷ εὐαγγελίῳ συνήθλησάν μοι μετὰ καὶ Κλήμεντος καὶ τῶν λοιπῶν συνεργῶν μου, ὧν τὰ ὀνόματα ἐν βίβλῳ ζωῆς. [GNT] | believers to be given new names at their baptism in order to symbolize their spiritual birth. Just who this yokefellow was is not known, but he must have been a man deeply respected by the people of the church. His name refers to the *yoke* or *collar* that was fitted around the neck of oxen for plowing. The collar attached the plow and held the two oxen together so that they would pull together and more quickly get the work done. Therefore, "comrade" means a person who pulls and works cooperatively with others. The very fact that Paul would ask him to help the two quarreling ladies shows that he was highly esteemed. Paul felt that he cared and that the two quarrelers would listen to him—that he could solve the dispute and bring about reconciliation.<br>Most churches have one or more yokefellows, persons...<br>• who love and care deeply for others.<br>• who are always helping and ministering to others.<br>• whom God has gifted and appointed to be ministerial helpers to the flock.<br>• who are highly respected and esteemed by most in the congregation.<br>The yokefellow is the person who should step in when quarrels and divisiveness begin to arouse their poisonous heads. The yokefellow is the person especially gifted by God to bring reconciliation and peace to the church. |
| **#690**<br>**Conceit–Conceits**<br>Swellings–KJV<br>Arrogance–NASB<br>Arrogance–NIV<br>**Conceits–NKJV**<br>**Conceit–NLT**<br><br>**POSB REFERENCE** (2 Cor.12:19-21; esp. v.20) Note 3, point 2 | φυσιώσεις = *phusiōseis*<br>Pronunciation: [foo-see'-o-seh-ees]<br>Parsing (part of speech): noun<br>    Case—nominative<br>    Gender—feminine<br>    Number—plural<br>    Stem or root—from φυσίωσις, εως<br>Concordance References:<br>    ⇒ Strong's #5450 phusiōsis<br>    ⇒ NIV #5883 phusiōsis<br>    ⇒ NASB #5450 phusiōsis<br><br>**2 Cor. 12:20**<br>For I fear, lest, when I come, I shall not find you such as I would, and that I shall be found unto you such as ye would not: lest there be debates, envyings, wraths, strifes, backbitings, whisperings, **swellings**, tumults: [KJV]<br>For I am afraid that perhaps when I come I may find you to be not what I wish and may be found by you to be not what you wish; that perhaps there may be strife, jealousy, angry tempers, disputes, slanders, gossip, **arrogance**, disturbances; [NASB]<br>For I am afraid that when I come I may not find you as I want you to be, and you may not find me as you want me to be. I fear that there may be quarreling, jealousy, outbursts of anger, factions, slander, gossip, **arrogance** and disorder. [NIV]<br>For I fear lest, when I come, I shall not find you such as I wish, and that I shall be found by you such as you do not wish; lest there be contentions, jealousies, outbursts of wrath, selfish ambitions, backbitings, whisperings, **conceits**, tumults; [NKJV]<br>For I am afraid that when I come to visit you I won't like what I find, and then you won't like my response. I am afraid that I will find quarreling, jealousy, outbursts of anger, selfishness, backstabbing, gossip, **conceit**, and disorderly behavior. [NLT]<br>φοβοῦμαι γὰρ μή πως ἐλθὼν οὐχ οἵους θέλω εὕρω ὑμᾶς, κἀγὼ εὑρεθῶ ὑμῖν οἷον οὐ θέλετε· μή πως ἔρις, | To be conceited; to be swollen with pride; to be puffed up; arrogance.<br><br>**Practical Application**<br>The arrogant, the conceited, the proud person feels that he is better than others. Note that this is a feeling within the heart. The proud person may appear quiet and humble; but within his heart, he secretly feels better than others. God opposes the proud. |

# Practical Word Studies
## in the New Testament

| ENGLISH WORD | GREEK WORD AND VERSE | THE WORD MEANS... |
|---|---|---|
| | ζῆλοι, θυμοί, ἐριθεῖαι, καταλαλιαί, ψιθυρισμοί, **φυσιώσεις**, ἀκαταστασίαι· [GNS]<br>φοβοῦμαι γὰρ μή πως ἐλθὼν οὐχ οἵους θέλω εὕρω ὑμᾶς κἀγὼ εὑρεθῶ ὑμῖν οἷον οὐ θέλετε· μή πως ἔρις, ζῆλος, θυμοί, ἐριθεῖαι, καταλαλιαί, ψιθυρισμοί, **φυσιώσεις**, ἀκαταστασίαι· [GNT] | |
| **#691**<br>**Conceited**<br><br>Proud–KJV<br>**Conceited–NASB**<br>**Conceited–NIV**<br>Proud–NKJV<br>**Conceited–NLT**<br><br>**POSB<br>REFERENCE**<br>(1 Tim. 6:4)<br>Note 2 | τετύφωται = *tetuphōtai*<br>Pronunciation: [teh-toof-o'-tah-ee]<br>Parsing (part of speech): verb<br>    Mood—indicative<br>    Tense—perfect<br>    Voice—passive<br>    Person—3rd person<br>    Number—singular<br>    Stem or root—from τυφόομαι<br>Concordance References:<br>  ⇒ Strong's #5187 tuphoomai<br>  ⇒ NIV #5605 tuphoómai<br>  ⇒ NASB #5187 tuphoomai<br><br>**1 Tim. 6:4**<br>He is **proud**, knowing nothing, but doting about questions and strifes of words, whereof cometh envy, strife, railings, evil surmisings, [KJV]<br>He is **conceited** and understands nothing; but he has a morbid interest in controversial questions and disputes about words, out of which arise envy, strife, abusive language, evil suspicions, [NASB]<br>He is **conceited** and understands nothing. He has an unhealthy interest in controversies and quarrels about words that result in envy, strife, malicious talk, evil suspicions [NIV]<br>He is **proud**, knowing nothing, but is obsessed with disputes and arguments over words, from which come envy, strife, reviling, evil suspicions, [NKJV]<br>Anyone who teaches anything different is both **conceited** and ignorant. Such a person has an unhealthy desire to quibble over the meaning of words. This stirs up arguments ending in jealousy, fighting, slander, and evil suspicions. [NLT]<br>**τετύφωται**, μηδὲν ἐπιστάμενος, ἀλλὰ νοσῶν περὶ ζητήσεις καὶ λογομαχίας, ἐξ ὧν γίνεται φθόνος, ἔρις, βλασφημίαι, ὑπόνοιαι πονηραί, [GNS]<br>**τετύφωται**, μηδὲν ἐπιστάμενος, ἀλλὰ νοσῶν περὶ ζητήσεις καὶ λογομαχίας, ἐξ ὧν γίνεται φθόνος ἔρις βλασφημίαι, ὑπόνοιαι πονηραί, [GNT] | To be conceited; to be swollen with pride; to be puffed up.<br><br>**Practical Application**<br>The word includes the idea of folly; it lacks good sense. Rejecting the evidence that Jesus is the Lord—the Lord Jesus Christ—is the height of pride and folly. Such rejection just lacks good sense (source unknown).<br>The false teacher takes pride...<br>• in his views and ideas.<br>• in his rejection of certain portions of the Bible.<br>• in his knowledge that some of the stories and events in the Bible are what he calls fables.<br>• in his intellectual ability to dissect the truth from the falsehood about Christ.<br>• in his enlightenment—that he knows better than to believe in such things as the miracles, deity, virgin birth, incarnation, resurrection, ascension and the personal return of Christ to earth.<br>• in his new and novel concepts and ideas about Christ.<br>The list could go on and on, but all ministers have detected this pride in discussions with other ministers. And, tragically, we have all been guilty of feeling pride over our own ideas before. |
| **#692**<br>**Conceited**<br><br>Highminded–KJV<br>**Conceited–NASB**<br>**Conceited–NIV**<br>Haughty–NKJV<br>Puffed up with pride–<br>NLT<br><br>**POSB<br>REFERENCE**<br>(2 Tim. 3:2-4; esp. v.4)<br>Note 2, point 17 | τετυφωμένοι = *tetuphōmenoi*<br>Pronunciation: [teh-toof-o'-mehn-oy]<br>Parsing (part of speech): verb<br>    Mood—participle<br>    Tense—perfect<br>    Voice—passive<br>    Case—nominative<br>    Gender—masculine<br>    Number—plural<br>    Stem or root—from τυφόομαι<br>Concordance References:<br>  Strong's #5187 tuphoomai<br>  NIV #5605 tuphoomai<br>  NASB #5187 tuphoomai<br><br>**2 Tim. 3:4**<br>Traitors, heady, **highminded**, lovers of pleasures more than lovers of God; [KJV]<br>Treacherous, reckless, **conceited**, lovers of pleasure rather than lovers of God; [NASB]<br>Treacherous, rash, **conceited**, lovers of pleasure rather than lovers of God [NIV]<br>Traitors, headstrong, **haughty**, lovers of pleasure rather than lovers of God, [NKJV] | To be conceited; to be highminded; to be puffed up with pride; to be swollen with pride, having feelings of self-importance.<br><br>**Practical Application**<br>It is a person who feels so educated, so scientific, so advanced, so high in position and authority, ability, and gifts that he feels completely self-sufficient. He feels no need for God. He is above God and above most people. |

# PRACTICAL WORD STUDIES
## in the NEW TESTAMENT

| ENGLISH WORD | GREEK WORD AND VERSE | THE WORD MEANS... |
|---|---|---|
| | They will betray their friends, be reckless, be **puffed up with pride**, and love pleasure rather than God. [NLT]<br><br>προδόται, προπετεῖς, **τετυφωμένοι**, φιλήδονοι μᾶλλον ἢ φιλόθεοι, [GNS]<br><br>προδόται προπετεῖς **τετυφωμένοι**, φιλήδονοι μᾶλλον ἢ φιλόθεοι, [GNT] | |
| **#693**<br>**Conceived**<br><br>**Conceived–KJV**<br>**Conceived–NASB**<br>**Conceived–NIV**<br>**Conceived–NKJV**<br>**Conceived–NLT**<br><br>**POSB REFERENCE**<br>(Mt.1:20-21; esp. v.20)<br>Note 3 | γεννηθὲν = *gennēthen*<br>Pronunciation: [ghen-nay'-then]<br>Parsing (part of speech): verb<br>  Mood—participle<br>  Tense—aorist<br>  Voice—passive<br>  Case—nominative<br>  Gender—neuter<br>  Number—singular<br>  Stem or root—from γεννάω<br>Concordance References:<br>⇒ Strong's #1080 gennaō<br>⇒ NIV #1164 gennaō<br>⇒ NASB #1080 gennaō<br><br>**Matthew 1:20**<br>But while he thought on these things, behold, the angel of the Lord appeared unto him in a dream, saying, Joseph, thou son of David, fear not to take unto thee Mary thy wife: for that which is **conceived** in her is of the Holy Ghost. [KJV]<br>But when he had considered this, behold, an angel of the Lord appeared to him in a dream, saying, "Joseph, son of David, do not be afraid to take Mary as your wife; for that which has been **conceived** in her is of the Holy Spirit. [NASB]<br>But after he had considered this, an angel of the Lord appeared to him in a dream and said, "Joseph son of David, do not be afraid to take Mary home as your wife, because what is **conceived** in her is from the Holy Spirit. [NIV]<br>But while he thought about these things, behold, an angel of the Lord appeared to him in a dream, saying, "Joseph, son of David, do not be afraid to take to you Mary your wife, for that which is **conceived** in her is of the Holy Spirit. [NKJV]<br>As he considered this, he fell asleep, and an angel of the Lord appeared to him in a dream. "Joseph, son of David," the angel said, "do not be afraid to go ahead with your marriage to Mary. For the child within her has been **conceived** by the Holy Spirit. [NLT]<br>ταῦτα δὲ αὐτοῦ ἐνθυμηθέντος, ἰδοὺ, ἄγγελος Κυρίου κατ' ὄναρ ἐφάνη αὐτῷ, λέγων, Ἰωσὴφ, υἱὸς Δαβίδ, μὴ φοβηθῇς παραλαβεῖν Μαριὰμ τὴν γυναῖκά σου. τὸ γὰρ ἐν αὐτῇ **γεννηθὲν** ἐκ Πνεύματός ἐστιν Ἁγίου· [GNS]<br>ταῦτα δὲ αὐτοῦ ἐνθυμηθέντος ἰδοὺ ἄγγελος κυρίου κατ' ὄναρ ἐφάνη αὐτῷ λέγων, Ἰωσὴφ υἱὸς Δαυίδ, μὴ φοβηθῇς παραλαβεῖν Μαριὰμ τὴν γυναῖκά σου· τὸ γὰρ ἐν αὐτῇ **γεννηθὲν** ἐκ πνεύματός ἐστιν ἁγίου. [GNT] | To be conceived, born, begotten; to give birth to.<br><br>**Practical Application**<br>In this context, "conceived" is attributed to the Holy Spirit. In looking at the virgin birth of Christ, man needs to think deeply and honestly. Both are necessary: man must be honest, and he must engage in concentrated thought. One question needs to be asked. Why would God's Son have to enter the world through a virgin? Or more simply put, why was Christ born of a virgin? Why was a virgin birth necessary? (Note: Mary confirmed that she was a virgin, Luke 1:34.)<br>1. The birth of God's Son required a miracle. He could not be born through the natural process as other men are. If He had been born as other men, His very birth would indicate that He was no more than mere man.<br>2. The birth of God's Son required a combined act on God's part and on woman's part. If God's Son were to become a man and identify with men, He had to come through the process of conception through a woman. Why? Because man can only come through the woman. Therefore, if God willed to send His Son into the world as a man, He would have to perform a miracle, causing Mary to conceive by an act of His divine power.<br>3. The birth of God's Son required a miraculous nature—both a divine nature and a human nature.<br>⇒ He had to be born of a woman to partake of human nature. (Cp. Hebrews 2:14-18.)<br>⇒ He had to be born by a miraculous act of God so as not to partake of man's corruption.<br>4. The birth of God's Son required the birth of a perfect nature. Why? Because a perfect life needed to be lived. Righteousness, that is, perfection, needed to be secured.<br>5. The birth of God's Son required the creative Word of God. God created the world by simply speaking the Word. God always creates by the power of His Word and the power of His Word alone.<br>6. The birth of God's Son required the virgin birth because Christ is the *only begotten* Son of God. He is God's only Son, who possesses all the nature and fullness of God Himself (Phil. 2:6-7; Col. 2:9). Therefore, His birth had to be different. He had to enter the world differently from others, for He is different by the very nature of His being.<br>7. The birth of God's Son required a second Adam, a second man.<br>8. The birth of God's Son required an espoused state, and not a single or married state. Why?<br>⇒ Because a single woman would cause far more questioning and heap far more contempt upon Christ and His followers.<br>⇒ Because a married woman would not be a |

PRACTICAL WORD STUDIES
in the NEW TESTAMENT

| ENGLISH WORD | GREEK WORD AND VERSE | THE WORD MEANS... |
|---|---|---|
| | | virgin and God's Son had to be born of a virgin as indicated by the points above.<br>The espoused state provided the ideal marital relationship for God to use in sending His Son into the world (see POSB note 2—Luke 1:27). The fact that Jewish society was using the espoused relationship as a preparation for marriage shows how God was preparing the world for the coming of His Son. (See POSB *Deeper Study* #1, Fullness of Time—Galatians 4:4. See also Mt.1:20-21; esp. v.20, POSB note 3 for a more thorough discussion) |
| #694<br>**Concern, Showed**<br><br>Visit–KJV<br>Concerned–NASB<br>**Showed...concern–NIV**<br>Visited–NKJV<br>Visited–NLT<br><br>**POSB REFERENCE**<br>(Acts 15:13-21; esp. v.14)<br>Note 4, point 1 | ἐπεσκέψατο = *epeskepsato*<br>Pronunciation: [ep-eh-skep'-sah-tow]<br>Parsing (part of speech): verb<br>  Mood—indicative<br>  Tense—aorist<br>  Voice—middle dep<br>  Person—3rd person<br>  Number—singular<br>  Stem or root—from ἐπισκέπτομαι<br>Concordance References:<br> ⇒ Strong's #1980 episkeptomai<br> ⇒ NIV #2170 episkeptomai<br> ⇒ NASB #1980a episkeptomai<br><br>**Acts 15:14**<br>Simeon hath declared how God at the first did **visit** the Gentiles, to take out of them a people for his name. [KJV]<br>"Simeon has related how God first **concerned** Himself about taking from among the Gentiles a people for His name. [NASB]<br>Simon has described to us how God at first **showed** his **concern** by taking from the Gentiles a people for himself. [NIV]<br>Simon has declared how God at the first **visited** the Gentiles to take out of them a people for His name. [NKJV]<br>Peter has told you about the time God first **visited** the Gentiles to take from them a people for himself. [NLT]<br>Συμεὼν ἐξηγήσατο καθὼς πρῶτον ὁ θεὸς **ἐπεσκέψατο** λαβεῖν ἐξ ἐθνῶν λαὸν ἐπὶ τῷ ὀνόματι αὐτοῦ. [GNS]<br>Συμεὼν ἐξηγήσατο καθὼς πρῶτον ὁ θεὸς **ἐπεσκέψατο** λαβεῖν ἐξ ἐθνῶν λαὸν τῷ ὀνόματι αὐτοῦ. [GNT] | To show concern; to visit; to care for; to look after.<br><br>**Practical Application**<br>James supported Peter's great declaration. The way James worded his support is significant.<br>⇒ "God...did show His concern (*epeskepsato*) for the Gentiles."<br>⇒ "by taking *from the Gentiles* a people": to choose; to appoint; to remove them from the Gentile nations and select a chosen people. The word "people" (*laon*) is the same word used of the Jewish people (cp. Acts 10:2). The point is that God was calling out *a new people*—a new body, a new nation, a new race—to be His chosen people, just as He had done with Abraham and the Jews. (See POSB *Deeper Study* #8, pt.6—Matthew 21:43; POSB note—Ephes. 2:11-18; POSB note—Ephes. 2:14-15; POSB note—Ephes. 2:19-22; and POSB note—Ephes. 4:17-19 for more discussion.)<br>⇒ "For His name": two verses clearly show what God means by choosing a people "for His name."<br><br>*"You are my witnesses," declares the LORD, "and my servant whom I have chosen, so that you may know and believe me and understand that I am he. Before me no god was formed, nor will there be one after me. (Isaiah 43:10) [NIV]*<br><br>*For as a belt is bound around a man's waist, so I bound the whole house of Israel and the whole house of Judah to me,' declares the LORD, 'to be my people for my renown and praise and honor. But they have not listened.' (Jeremiah 13:11) [NIV]* |
| #695<br>**Concerned**<br><br>Visit–KJV<br>**Concerned–NASB**<br>Showed...concern–NIV<br>Visited–NKJV<br>Visited–NLT<br><br>**POSB REFERENCE**<br>(Acts 15:13-21; esp. v.14)<br>Note 4, point 1 | ἐπεσκέψατο = *epeskepsato*<br>Pronunciation: [ep-eh-skep'-sah-tow]<br>Parsing (part of speech): verb<br>  Mood—indicative<br>  Tense—aorist<br>  Voice—middle deponent<br>  Person—3rd person<br>  Number—singular<br>  Stem or root—from ἐπισκέπτομαι<br>Concordance References:<br> ⇒ Strong's #1980 episkeptomai<br> ⇒ NIV #2170 episkeptomai<br> ⇒ NASB #1980a episkeptomai<br><br>**Acts 15:14**<br>Simeon hath declared how God at the first did **visit** the Gentiles, to take out of them a people for his name. [KJV] | To show concern; to visit; to care for; to look after.<br><br>**Practical Application**<br>James supported Peter's great declaration. The way James worded his support is significant.<br>⇒ "God...did show concern (*epeskepsato*) for the Gentiles."<br>⇒ "to take *from among the Gentiles* a people": to choose; to appoint; to remove them from the Gentile nations and select a chosen people. The word "people" (*laon*) is the same word used of the Jewish people (cp. Acts 10:2). The point is that God was calling out *a new people*—a new body, a new nation, a new race—to be His chosen people, just as He had done with Abraham and the Jews. |

# PRACTICAL WORD STUDIES
## in the NEW TESTAMENT

| ENGLISH WORD | GREEK WORD AND VERSE | THE WORD MEANS... |
|---|---|---|
| | "Simeon has related how God first **concerned** Himself about taking from among the Gentiles a people for His name. [NASB]<br>Simon has described to us how God at first **showed** his **concern** by taking from the Gentiles a people for himself. [NIV]<br>Simon has declared how God at the first **visited** the Gentiles to take out of them a people for His name. [NKJV]<br>Peter has told you about the time God first **visited** the Gentiles to take from them a people for himself. [NLT]<br>Συμεὼν ἐξηγήσατο καθὼς πρῶτον ὁ θεὸς **ἐπεσκέψατο** λαβεῖν ἐξ ἐθνῶν λαὸν ἐπὶ τῷ ὀνόματι αὐτοῦ. [GNS]<br>Συμεὼν ἐξηγήσατο καθὼς πρῶτον ὁ θεὸς **ἐπεσκέψατο** λαβεῖν ἐξ ἐθνῶν λαὸν τῷ ὀνόματι αὐτοῦ. [GNT] | (See POSB *Deeper Study #8*, pt.6—Matthew 21:43; POSB note—Ephes. 2:11-18; POSB note—Ephes. 2:14-15; POSB note—Ephes. 2:19-22; and POSB note—Ephes. 4:17-19 for more discussion.)<br>⇒ "For His name": two verses clearly show what God means by choosing a people "for His name."<br><br>*"You are My witnesses," declares the LORD, "And My servant whom I have chosen, In order that you may know and believe Me, And understand that I am He. Before Me there was no God formed, And there will be none after Me. (Isaiah 43:10)* [NASB]<br>*"'For as the waistband clings to the waist of a man, so I made the whole household of Israel and the whole household of Judah cling to Me,' declares the LORD, 'that they might be for Me a people, for renown, for praise, and for glory; but they did not listen.' (Jeremiah 13:11)* [NASB] |
| **#696**<br>**Conclude–**<br>**Concluding**<br><br>Assuredly gathering–KJV<br>**Concluding–NASB**<br>**Concluding–NIV**<br>**Concluding–NKJV**<br>**Conclude–NLT**<br><br>**POSB**<br>**REFERENCE**<br>(Acts 16:10)<br>Note 3 | συμβιβάζοντες = *sumbibazontes*<br>Pronunciation: [soom-bib-ad'-zon-tehs]<br>Parsing (part of speech): verb<br>  Mood—participle<br>  Tense—present<br>  Voice—active<br>  Case—nominative<br>  Gender—masculine<br>  Person—1st person<br>  Number—plural<br>  Stem or root—from συμβιβάζω<br>Concordance References:<br>  ⇒ Strong's #4822 sumbibazō<br>  ⇒ NIV #5204 sumbibazō<br>  ⇒ NASB #4822 sumbibazō<br><br>**Acts 16:10**<br>And after he had seen the vision, immediately we endeavoured to go into Macedonia, **assuredly gathering** that the Lord had called us for to preach the gospel unto them. [KJV]<br>And when he had seen the vision, immediately we sought to go into Macedonia, **concluding** that God had called us to preach the gospel to them. [NASB]<br>After Paul had seen the vision, we got ready at once to leave for Macedonia, **concluding** that God had called us to preach the gospel to them. [NIV]<br>Now after he had seen the vision, immediately we sought to go to Macedonia, **concluding** that the Lord had called us to preach the gospel to them. [NKJV]<br>So we decided to leave for Macedonia at once, for we could only **conclude** that God was calling us to preach the Good News there. [NLT]<br>ὡς δὲ τὸ ὅραμα εἶδεν, εὐθέως ἐζητήσαμεν ἐξελθεῖν εἰς τὸν Μακεδονίαν, **συμβιβάζοντες** ὅτι προσκέκληται ἡμᾶς ὁ Κύριος εὐαγγελίσασθαι αὐτούς. [GNS]<br>ὡς δὲ τὸ ὅραμα εἶδεν, εὐθέως ἐζητήσαμεν ἐξελθεῖν εἰς Μακεδονίαν **συμβιβάζοντες** ὅτι προσκέκληται ἡμᾶς ὁ θεὸς εὐαγγελίσασθαι αὐτούς. [GNT] | To conclude or concluding; to prove, put together, set side by side; to bring together.<br><br>**Practical Application**<br>The picture is that of the three men's discussing and reasoning, considering all that had happened to them. They were logically setting the facts together, side by side and coming to their conclusion. |
| **#697**<br>**Concluded**<br><br>**Concluded–KJV**<br>Shut up–NASB<br>Bound over–NIV<br>Committed–NKJV<br>Imprisoned–NLT | συνέκλεισεν = *sunekleisen*<br>Pronunciation: [soon-he-kli'-sehn]<br>Parsing (part of speech): verb<br>  Mood—indicative<br>  Tense—aorist<br>  Voice—active<br>  Person—3rd person<br>  Number—singular<br>  Stem or root—from συγκλείω | To be bound over; to imprison; to shut up in a place; to close up; to lock up; to be committed to disobedience.<br><br>**Practical Application**<br>This is an unusual idea: God has taken men, both Jews and Gentiles, and concluded them all |

# PRACTICAL WORD STUDIES
## in the NEW TESTAMENT

| ENGLISH WORD | GREEK WORD AND VERSE | THE WORD MEANS... |
|---|---|---|
| **POSB REFERENCE** (Rom.11:32) Note 5 | Concordance References:<br>⇒ Strong's #4788 sugkleiö<br>⇒ NIV #5168 sugkleiö<br>⇒ NASB #4788 sugkleiö<br><br>**Romans 11:32**<br>For God hath **concluded** them all in unbelief, that he might have mercy upon all. [KJV]<br>For God has **shut up** all in disobedience that He might show mercy to all. [NASB]<br>For God has **bound** all men **over** to disobedience so that he may have mercy on them all. [NIV]<br>For God has **committed** them all to disobedience, that He might have mercy on all. [NKJV]<br>For God has **imprisoned** all people in their own disobedience so he could have mercy on everyone. [NLT]<br>συνέκλεισε γὰρ ὁ Θεὸς τοὺς πάντας εἰς ἀπείθειαν ἵνα τοὺς πάντας ἐλεήσῃ. [GNS]<br>συνέκλεισεν γὰρ ὁ θεὸς τοὺς πάντας εἰς ἀπείθειαν, ἵνα τοὺς πάντας ἐλεήσῃ. [GNT] | (*sunekleisen*) to unbelief (*apeitheian*) or disobedience. This is the judicial judgment of God (see POSB *Deeper Study* #2—Romans 11:7-10; POSB note—Romans 1:24; POSB *Deeper Study* #1—John 12:39-41). It is the picture of God's using sin and events for good. God takes sin and works it out for the good of the world. Man has chosen sin, choosing to go his own way in life, so God allows man to do his own thing. God locks man up in his own world of selfishness, allowing man to roam around in his world of sin. Why? So that man's true nature of sinfulness will be clearly seen and thereby cause the honest and thinking man to seek God. God wishes to have mercy upon all, both Jew and Gentile; but before men can come to God, they must confess two things:<br>⇒ that they are sinful and dying creatures in desperate need of God.<br>⇒ that God exists and that He will have mercy upon the person who diligently seeks Him (Heb.11:6). |
| **#698 Condemn**<br><br>Judge–KJV<br>Judge–NASB<br>**Condemn–NIV**<br>Judge–NKJV<br>**Condemn–NLT**<br><br>**POSB REFERENCE** (Rom.14:3-4; esp. v.3) Note 2 | κρινέτω = *krinetö*<br>Pronunciation: [kree'-neh-tow]<br>Parsing (part of speech): verb<br>  Mood—imperative<br>  Tense—present<br>  Voice—active<br>  Person—3rd person<br>  Number—singular<br>  Stem or root—from κρίνω<br>Concordance References:<br>⇒ Strong's #2919 krinö<br>⇒ NIV #3212 krinö<br>⇒ NASB #2919 krinö<br><br>**Romans 14:3**<br>Let not him that eateth despise him that eateth not; and let not him which eateth not **judge** him that eateth: for God hath received him. [KJV]<br>Let not him who eats regard with contempt him who does not eat, and let not him who does not eat **judge** him who eats, for God has accepted him. [NASB]<br>The man who eats everything must not look down on him who does not, and the man who does not eat everything must not **condemn** the man who does, for God has accepted him. [NIV]<br>Let not him who eats despise him who does not eat, and let not him who does not eat **judge** him who eats; for God has received him. [NKJV]<br>Those who think it is all right to eat anything must not look down on those who won't. And those who won't eat certain foods must not **condemn** those who do, for God has accepted them. [NLT]<br>ὁ ἐσθίων τὸν μὴ ἐσθίοντα μὴ ἐξουθενείτω, καὶ ὁ μὴ ἐσθίων τὸν ἐσθίοντα μὴ **κρινέτω**· ὁ Θεὸς γὰρ αὐτὸν προσελάβετο. [GNS]<br>ὁ ἐσθίων τὸν μὴ ἐσθίοντα μὴ ἐξουθενείτω, ὁ δὲ μὴ ἐσθίων τὸν ἐσθίοντα μὴ **κρινέτω**, ὁ θεὸς γὰρ αὐτὸν προσελάβετο. [GNT] | To condemn; to judge; to regard; to criticize; to censor.<br><br>**Practical Application**<br>Three reasons are given for not looking down upon and condemning one another, three reasons that stand as a warning to believers.<br>1. God Himself has accepted the strong believer. The believer who walks in the liberty of Christ and does not live a strict life has been accepted by God, no matter what the more legalistic believer may think. There may be some man-made religious rules which he does not observe, but he has trusted Christ, and he obeys the Word of God. Therefore, he is not to be criticized and judged, but he is to be accepted into the fellowship of the more legalistic believer.<br>2. No one has the *right* to judge the Lord's servant. Note: both believers belong to the Lord; both are the servants of the Lord. Therefore, the Lord alone has the right to judge them. Believers do not have the *right to play God* and to judge each other. They have no right to condemn and pass judgment upon each other's behavior and works, for they do not belong to each other. They each belong to Christ; therefore, He alone determines whether or not they stand or fall and are accepted or rejected.<br>3. God *will hold* the believer up (v.4). There is no question about the matter: the believer will be held up, for God is able to make him stand. |
| **#699 Condemn**<br><br>Beguile–KJV<br>Defrauding–NASB<br>Disqualify...for–NIV<br>Cheat–NKJV<br>**Condemn–NLT** | καταβραβευέτω = *katabrabeuetö*<br>Pronunciation: [kat-ab-rab-yoo'-eh-tow]<br>Parsing (part of speech): verb<br>  Mood—imperative<br>  Tense—present<br>  Voice—active<br>  Person—3rd person<br>  Number—singular<br>  Stem or root—from καταβραβεύω | To disqualify; to beguile; to defraud; to cheat; to condemn. It means to rob; to defraud; to cheat a person out of his reward.<br><br>**Practical Application**<br>It is possible for believers to be disqualified for their reward by false teachers. How? By following those who teach that there is another |

## PRACTICAL WORD STUDIES
### in the NEW TESTAMENT

| ENGLISH WORD | GREEK WORD AND VERSE | THE WORD MEANS... |
|---|---|---|
| **POSB REFERENCE** (Col.2:18-19; esp. v.18) Note 2 | Concordance References:<br>⇒ Strong's #2603 katabrabeuō<br>⇒ NIV #2857 katabrabeuō<br>⇒ NASB #2603 katabrabeuō<br><br>**Col. 2:18**<br>Let no man **beguile** you of your reward in a voluntary humility and worshipping of angels, intruding into those things which he hath not seen, vainly puffed up by his fleshly mind, [KJV]<br>Let no one keep **defrauding** you of your prize by delighting in self-abasement and the worship of the angels, taking his stand on visions he has seen, inflated without cause by his fleshly mind, [NASB]<br>Do not let anyone who delights in false humility and the worship of angels **disqualify** you **for** the prize. Such a person goes into great detail about what he has seen, and his unspiritual mind puffs him up with idle notions. [NIV]<br>Let no one **cheat** you of your reward, taking delight in *false* humility and worship of angels, intruding into those things which he has not seen, vainly puffed up by his fleshly mind, [NKJV]<br>Don't let anyone **condemn** you by insisting on self-denial. And don't let anyone say you must worship angels, even though they say they have had visions about this. These people claim to be so humble, but their sinful minds have made them proud. [NLT]<br>μηδεὶς ὑμᾶς **καταβραβευέτω** θέλων ἐν ταπεινοφροσύνῃ καὶ θρησκείᾳ τῶν ἀγγέλων, ἃ μὴ ἑώρακεν ἐμβατεύων, εἰκῇ φυσιούμενος ὑπὸ τοῦ νοὸς τῆς σαρκὸς αὐτοῦ, [GNS]<br>μηδεὶς ὑμᾶς **καταβραβευέτω** θέλων ἐν ταπεινοφροσύνῃ καὶ θρησκείᾳ τῶν ἀγγέλων, ἃ ἑόρακεν ἐμβατεύων, εἰκῇ φυσιούμενος ὑπὸ τοῦ νοὸς τῆς σαρκὸς αὐτοῦ, [GNT] | approach to God other than Christ. Christ is God's appointed way to approach Him, and there is no other way. |
| **#700 Condemnation**<br><br>Damnation–KJV<br>**Condemnation–NASB**<br>Judgment–NIV<br>Judgment–NKJV<br>Punishment–NLT<br><br>**POSB REFERENCE** (Rom.13:1-2; esp. v.2) Note 2, point 2<br><br>See also POSB REF: (1 Cor.11:27-30; esp. v.29) Note 4, point 2 | κρίμα = *krima*<br>Pronunciation: [kree'-mah]<br>Parsing (part of speech): noun<br>   Case—accusative<br>   Gender—neuter<br>   Number—singular<br>   Stem or root—from κρίμα, τος<br>Concordance References:<br>⇒ Strong's #2917 krima<br>⇒ NIV #3210 krima<br>⇒ NASB #2917 krima<br><br>**Romans 13:2**<br>Whosoever therefore resisteth the power, resisteth the ordinance of God: and they that resist shall receive to themselves **damnation**. [KJV]<br>Therefore he who resists authority has opposed the ordinance of God; and they who have opposed will receive **condemnation** upon themselves. [NASB]<br>Consequently, he who rebels against the authority is rebelling against what God has instituted, and those who do so will bring **judgment** on themselves. [NIV]<br>Therefore whoever resists the authority resists the ordinance of God, and those who resist will bring **judgment** on themselves. [NKJV]<br>So those who refuse to obey the laws of the land are refusing to obey God, and **punishment** will follow. [NLT]<br>ὥστε ὁ ἀντιτασσόμενος τῇ ἐξουσίᾳ, τῇ τοῦ θεοῦ διαταγῇ ἀνθέστηκεν· οἱ δὲ ἀνθεστηκότες ἑαυτοῖς **κρίμα** λήμψονται. [GNS]<br>ὥστε ὁ ἀντιτασσόμενος τῇ ἐξουσίᾳ τῇ τοῦ θεοῦ διαταγῇ ἀνθέστηκεν, οἱ δὲ ἀνθεστηκότες ἑαυτοῖς **κρίμα** λήμψονται. [GNT] | Judgment, verdict; condemnation, punishment.<br><br>**Practical Application**<br>The believer who resists the authorities will be condemned. The idea is that the disobedient believer will have to face the judgment of God if he disobeys the just laws of government. Some commentators think this refers to the judgment of the civil authorities. There is no question, if the believer is caught breaking the laws of the state, he will be punished. However, the civil authorities may never catch the believer. Yet, God knows every law broken by the believer, and by resisting the laws of the state, the believer has broken the law of God. Therefore, the believer stands guilty before God, and he will be judged by God. |
| **#701 Condemned** | κριθῶσιν = *krithōsin*<br>Pronunciation: [kree'-tho-sin]<br>Parsing (part of speech): verb<br>   Mood—subjunctive | Condemned, damned, judged, punished.<br><br>**Practical Application**<br>The followers of the antichrist are the con- |

# PRACTICAL WORD STUDIES
## in the NEW TESTAMENT

| ENGLISH WORD | GREEK WORD AND VERSE | THE WORD MEANS... |
|---|---|---|
| Damned–KJV<br>Judged–NASB<br>**Condemned–NIV**<br>**Condemned–NKJV**<br>**Condemned–NLT**<br><br>**POSB<br>REFERENCE**<br>(2 Thes.2:12)<br>Note 4 | Tense—aorist<br>Voice—passive<br>Person—3rd person<br>Number—plural<br>Stem or root—from κρίνω<br>Concordance References:<br>⇒ Strong's #2919 krinō<br>⇒ NIV #3212 krinō<br>⇒ NASB #2919 krinō<br><br>**2 Thes. 2:12**<br>That they all might be **damned** who believed not the truth, but had pleasure in unrighteousness. [KJV]<br>In order that they all may be **judged** who did not believe the truth, but took pleasure in wickedness. [NASB]<br>And so that all will be **condemned** who have not believed the truth but have delighted in wickedness. [NIV]<br>That they all may be **condemned** who did not believe the truth but had pleasure in unrighteousness. [NKJV]<br>Then they will be **condemned** for not believing the truth and for enjoying the evil they do. [NLT]<br>ἵνα **κριθῶσι** πάντες οἱ μὴ πιστεύσαντες τῇ ἀληθείᾳ, ἀλλ᾽ εὐδοκήσαντες ἐν τῇ ἀδικίᾳ. [GNS]<br>ἵνα **κριθῶσιν** πάντες οἱ μὴ πιστεύσαντες τῇ ἀληθείᾳ ἀλλὰ εὐδοκήσαντες τῇ ἀδικίᾳ. [GNT] | demned—those who take pleasure in unrighteousness. There are two reasons why the followers of the antichrist will be judged.<br>1. They will not believe the truth of the gospel, the truth of the Lord Jesus Christ. God loves His Son Jesus Christ—loves Him with a perfect love.<br>2. They will delight in wickedness. They will be people who live unrighteous lives and take pleasure in their unrighteousness. They will be people who love their sins. |
| #702<br>**Condemned Already**<br><br>Condemned already–KJV<br>Judged already–NASB<br>Condemned already–NIV<br>Condemned already–NKJV<br>Already been judged–NLT<br><br>**POSB<br>REFERENCE**<br>(Jn.3:18)<br>Note 2 | ἤδη κέκριται = ëdë kekritai<br>Pronunciation: [ay-day eh-kree'-tah-ee]<br>Parsing ëdë (part of speech): adverb adjective<br>    Stem or root—from ἤδη<br>Parsing kekritai (part of speech): verb<br>    Mood—indicative<br>    Tense—perfect<br>    Voice—passive<br>    Person—3rd person<br>    Number—singular<br>    Stem or root—from κρίνω<br>Concordance References:<br>⇒ Strong's #2235 ëdë +2919 krinō<br>⇒ NIV #2453 ëdë [already] + 3212 krinō [condemned]<br>⇒ NASB #2235 ëdë +2919 krinō<br><br>**John 3:18**<br>He that believeth on him is not condemned: but he that believeth not is **condemned already**, because he hath not believed in the name of the only begotten Son of God. [KJV]<br>"He who believes in Him is not judged; he who does not believe has been **judged already**, because he has not believed in the name of the only begotten Son of God. [NASB]<br>Whoever believes in him is not condemned, but whoever does not believe stands **condemned already** because he has not believed in the name of God's one and only Son. [NIV]<br>He who believes in Him is not condemned; but he who does not believe is **condemned already**, because he has not believed in the name of the only begotten Son of God. [NKJV]<br>"There is no judgment awaiting those who trust him. But those who do not trust him have **already been judged** for not believing in the only Son of God. [NLT]<br>ὁ πιστεύων εἰς αὐτὸν, οὐ κρίνεται· ὁ δὲ μὴ πιστεύων **ἤδη κέκριται**, ὅτι μὴ πεπίστευκεν εἰς τὸ ὄνομα τοῦ μονογενοῦς υἱοῦ τοῦ Θεοῦ. [GNS]<br>ὁ πιστεύων εἰς αὐτὸν οὐ κρίνεται· ὁ δὲ μὴ πιστεύων **ἤδη κέκριται**, ὅτι μὴ πεπίστευκεν εἰς τὸ ὄνομα τοῦ μονογενοῦς υἱοῦ τοῦ θεοῦ. [GNT] | To be condemned already; to be judged already; to have judgment passed upon; to be punished already.<br><br>**Practical Application**<br>At least three things are meant by being "condemned already":<br>1. Condemnation is a sure fact. The unbeliever's judgment is sure, so sure it is as though he has already been condemned. Nothing can change or stop the judgment from coming upon the unbeliever. Ignoring, denying, and struggling against the great day of judgment will not change one detail of the day. It is coming, and every single unbeliever will be judged.<br>2. The unbeliever is already under the present curse of sin. He is...<br>  • without Christ.<br>  • an alien or foreigner from the people of God.<br>  • a stranger to the promises of God.<br>  • without hope.<br>  • without God in the world (Ephes. 2:12).<br>3. The unbeliever already stands guilty of all the sins he has ever committed; he is already condemned. The law of God already exists. Every time a man breaks the law of God, he immediately becomes guilty and is condemned. The judgment is already pronounced. The unbeliever must pay the penalty for every transgression of God's law. He is already under the curse, the full force of the law. |

# PRACTICAL WORD STUDIES
## in the NEW TESTAMENT

| ENGLISH WORD | GREEK WORD AND VERSE | THE WORD MEANS... |
|---|---|---|
| **#703**<br>**Condemned To Die–Condemned To Death**<br><br>Appointed to death–KJV<br>**Condemned to death–NASB**<br>**Condemned to die–NIV**<br>**Condemned to death–NKJV**<br>**Condemned to die–NLT**<br><br>**POSB REFERENCE**<br>(1 Cor.4:9-10; esp. v.9)<br>Note 4, point 1 | ἐπιθανατίους = epithanatious<br>Pronunciation: [ep-ee-than-at'-ee-oos]<br>Parsing (part of speech): adjective<br>  Case—accusative<br>  Gender—masculine<br>  Number—plural<br>  Stem or root—from ἐπιθανάτιος, ον<br>Concordance References:<br>  ⇒ Strong's #1935 epithanatios<br>  ⇒ NIV #2119 epithanatios<br>  ⇒ NASB #1935 epithanatios<br><br>**1 Cor. 4:9**<br>For I think that God hath set forth us the apostles last, as it were **appointed to death**: for we are made a spectacle unto the world, and to angels, and to men. [KJV]<br>For, I think, God has exhibited us apostles last of all, as men **condemned to death**; because we have become a spectacle to the world, both to angels and to men. [NASB]<br>For it seems to me that God has put us apostles on display at the end of the procession, like men **condemned to die** in the arena. We have been made a spectacle to the whole universe, to angels as well as to men. [NIV]<br>For I think that God has displayed us, the apostles, last, as men **condemned to death**; for we have been made a spectacle to the world, both to angels and to men. [NKJV]<br>But sometimes I think God has put us apostles on display, like prisoners of war at the end of a victor's parade, **condemned to die**. We have become a spectacle to the entire world—to people and angels alike. [NLT]<br>δοκῶ γάρ, ὅτι ὁ Θεὸς ἡμᾶς τοὺς ἀποστόλους ἐσχάτους ἀπέδειξεν ὡς **ἐπιθανατίους**· ὅτι θέατρον ἐγενήθημεν τῷ κόσμῳ, καὶ ἀγγέλοις καὶ ἀνθρώποις. [GNS]<br>δοκῶ γάρ, ὁ θεὸς ἡμᾶς τοὺς ἀποστόλους ἐσχάτους ἀπέδειξεν ὡς **ἐπιθανατίους**, ὅτι θέατρον ἐγενήθημεν τῷ κόσμῳ καὶ ἀγγέλοις καὶ ἀνθρώποις. [GNT] | Condemned to die; appointed to death; sentenced to death.<br><br>**Practical Application**<br>This is the picture of a doomed gladiator. He is marched through the city streets and before the screaming mobs of the arena. He is made a spectacle before the world, and he has to endure it, for he has no choice.<br>Paul sees ministers as being spectacles. They are being marched across the scene of world history to carry on their combat as ordained by the Emperor and King. They are mere spectacles to the world and to angels and men, with few ever understanding and fully accepting them. And from among the few who do accept them, some eventually withdraw and turn against them. |
| **#704**<br>**Conduct**<br><br>Conversation–KJV<br>**Conduct–NASB**<br>**Conduct–NIV**<br>**Conduct–NKJV**<br>Live–NLT<br><br>**POSB REFERENCE**<br>(Philip.1:27)<br>Note 1 | πολιτεύεσθε = politeuesthe<br>Pronunciation: [pol-it-yoo'-ehs-theh]<br>Parsing (part of speech): verb<br>  Mood—imperative<br>  Tense—present<br>  Voice—middle or passive deponent<br>  Person—2nd person<br>  Number—plural<br>  Stem or root—from πολιτεύομαι<br>Concordance References:<br>  ⇒ Strong's #4176 politeuomai<br>  ⇒ NIV #4488 politeuomai<br>  ⇒ NASB #4176 politeuomai<br><br>**Philip. 1:27**<br>Only let your **conversation** be as it becometh the gospel of Christ: that whether I come and see you, or else be absent, I may hear of your affairs, that ye stand fast in one spirit, with one mind striving together for the faith of the gospel; [KJV]<br>Only **conduct** yourselves in a manner worthy of the gospel of Christ; so that whether I come and see you or remain absent, I may hear of you that you are standing firm in one spirit, with one mind striving together for the faith of the gospel; [NASB]<br>Whatever happens, **conduct** yourselves in a manner worthy of the gospel of Christ. Then, whether I come and see you or only hear about you in my absence, I will know that you stand firm in one spirit, contending as one man for the faith of the gospel [NIV]<br>Only let your **conduct** be worthy of the gospel of Christ, so that whether I come and see you or am absent, I may hear of your affairs, that you stand fast in one spirit, with one mind striving together for the faith of the | Behavior; conduct; to live one's life.<br><br>**Practical Application**<br>A.T. Robertson points out that this word is used only twice in the New Testament (Acts 23:1; Phil. 1:27) (*Word Pictures in the New Testament*, Vol.4, p.441). Usually, when the New Testament refers to behavior or conduct, it uses a word meaning how a person should walk about day by day (*peripatein*). But Paul switches the word in writing to the Philippians. Why? The reason is significant. Philippi was a proud Roman colony. In fact, it was famous as a miniature Rome. A city became a Roman colony by one of two ways. At first, Rome founded colonies throughout the outer reaches of the Empire to keep the peace and to guard against invasions from barbaric hordes. Veteran soldiers, ready for retirement, were usually granted citizenship if they would go out to settle these colonies. Later on, however, a city was granted the distinctive title of a Roman Colony for loyalty and service to the Empire. The distinctive thing about these colonies was their fanatic loyalty to Rome. The citizens kept all their Roman ties: the Roman language, titles, customs, affairs, and dress. They refused to allow any infiltration of local influence whatsoever. They totally rejected the influence of the world around them. They were Roman colonists within an alien environment.<br>This is the reason Paul uses the word *poli-* |

## PRACTICAL WORD STUDIES
### in the NEW TESTAMENT

| ENGLISH WORD | GREEK WORD AND VERSE | THE WORD MEANS... |
|---|---|---|
| | gospel, [NKJV]<br>But whatever happens to me, you must **live** in a manner worthy of the Good News about Christ, as citizens of heaven. Then, whether I come and see you again or only hear about you, I will know that you are standing side by side, fighting together for the Good News. [NLT]<br>μόνον ἀξίως τοῦ εὐαγγελίου τοῦ Χριστοῦ **πολιτεύεσθε**, ἵνα εἴτε ἐλθὼν καὶ ἰδὼν ὑμᾶς, εἴτε ἀπὼν, ἀκούσω τὰ περὶ ὑμῶν, ὅτι στήκετε ἐν ἑνὶ πνεύματι, μιᾷ ψυχῇ συναθλοῦντες τῇ πίστει τοῦ εὐαγγελίου, [GNS]<br>Μόνον ἀξίως τοῦ εὐαγγελίου τοῦ Χριστοῦ **πολιτεύεσθε**, ἵνα εἴτε ἐλθὼν καὶ ἰδὼν ὑμᾶς εἴτε ἀπὼν ἀκούω τὰ περὶ ὑμῶν, ὅτι στήκετε ἐν ἑνὶ πνεύματι, μιᾷ ψυχῇ συναθλοῦντες τῇ πίστει τοῦ εὐαγγελίου [GNT] | *teuesthe*. It means conduct and behavior; but more accurately, it means the conduct and behavior of *citizenship*, of a person who is the citizen of a great nation. The Philippian church knew exactly what Paul was saying: they were citizens of heaven. Therefore, they must...<br>• keep their close ties with heaven.<br>• speak the clean and pure language of heaven.<br>• bear the title of heaven, Christian, and do so proudly.<br>• bear witness to the customs of heaven.<br>• carry on the affairs of heaven.<br>• dress as a citizen of heaven.<br>• allow no infiltration of worldly influence whatsoever.<br>• live and conduct themselves as a heavenly colony within a polluted and dying environment. |
| **#705**<br>**Conduct**<br><br>Behave–KJV<br>**Conduct–NASB**<br>**Conduct–NIV**<br>**Conduct–NKJV**<br>**Conduct–NLT**<br><br>**POSB REFERENCE**<br>(1 Tim..3:14-15; esp. v.15)<br>Note 1 | ἀναστρέφεσθαι = *anastrephesthai*<br>Pronunciation: [an-as-tref'-ehs-tha-ee]<br>Parsing (part of speech): verb<br>    Mood—infinitive<br>    Tense—present<br>    Voice—passive<br>    Stem or root—from ἀναστρέφω<br>Concordance References:<br>⇒ Strong's #390 anastrephō<br>⇒ NIV #418 anastrephō<br>⇒ NASB #390 anastrephō<br><br>**1 Tim. 3:15**<br>But if I tarry long, that thou mayest know how thou oughtest to **behave** thyself in the house of God, which is the church of the living God, the pillar and ground of the truth. [KJV]<br>But in case I am delayed, I write so that you may know how one ought to **conduct** himself in the household of God, which is the church of the living God, the pillar and support of the truth. [NASB]<br>If I am delayed, you will know how people ought to **conduct** themselves in God's household, which is the church of the living God, the pillar and foundation of the truth. [NIV]<br>But if I am delayed, *I write* so that you may know how you ought to **conduct** yourself in the house of God, which is the church of the living God, the pillar and ground of the truth. [NKJV]<br>So that if I can't come for a while, you will know how people must **conduct** themselves in the household of God. This is the church of the living God, the pillar and support of the truth. [NLT]<br>ἐὰν δὲ βραδύνω, ἵνα εἰδῇς πῶς δεῖ ἐν οἴκῳ Θεοῦ **ἀναστρέφεσθαι**, ἥτις ἐστὶν ἐκκλησία Θεοῦ ζῶντος, στῦλος καὶ ἑδραίωμα τῆς ἀληθείας. [GNS]<br>ἐὰν δὲ βραδύνω, ἵνα εἰδῇς πῶς δεῖ ἐν οἴκῳ θεοῦ **ἀναστρέφεσθαι**, ἥτις ἐστὶν ἐκκλησία θεοῦ ζῶντος, στῦλος καὶ ἑδραίωμα τῆς ἀληθείας. [GNT] | To conduct; to behave; to live.<br><br>**Practical Application**<br>The word "conduct" (*anastrephesthai*) means the conduct, walk, and behavior of a person; but it especially refers to how a person relates to other people. Therefore, the great concern of the Pastoral Epistles is how believers behave in their relationships to God, to each other, and to the unbelievers of the world.<br>Remember: Timothy was in Ephesus and Paul was writing from Macedonia. Paul hoped to visit Ephesus and Timothy soon, but he was not quite sure that he would be able to leave Macedonia. Therefore, he was spelling out in some detail.<br>• how Christian believers are to conduct themselves within the church.<br>• how Christian believers are to behave and witness to a world that is lost and reeling under the weight of corruption and evil. |
| **#706**<br>**Conduct**<br><br>Conversation–KJV<br>Character–NASB<br>Lives–NIV<br>**Conduct–NKJV**<br>Not translated–NLT | τρόπος = *tropos*<br>Pronunciation: [trop'-os]<br>Parsing (part of speech): noun<br>    Case—nominative<br>    Gender—masculine<br>    Number—singular<br>    Stem or root—from τρόπος, ου<br>Concordance References:<br>⇒ Strong's #5158 tropos<br>⇒ NIV #5573 tropos<br>⇒ NASB #5158 tropos | Character, conversation, lives, ways, conduct. Thomas Hewitt points out that the Greek word for "conduct" (*tropos*) means *manner of life*, or *the way of thought and life* (*The Epistle to the Hebrews*. "Tyndale New Testament Commentaries," p.206).<br><br>**Practical Application**<br>The believer's life, yes, his very thoughts are to be free from covetousness. His thoughts are to |

# PRACTICAL WORD STUDIES
## in the NEW TESTAMENT

| ENGLISH WORD | GREEK WORD AND VERSE | THE WORD MEANS... |
|---|---|---|
| **POSB REFERENCE** (Heb.13:5-6; esp. v.5) Note 5 | **Hebrews 13:5**<br>Let your **conversation** *be* without covetousness; *and be* content with such things as ye have: for he hath said, I will never leave thee, nor forsake thee. [KJV]<br>Let your **character** be free from the love of money, being content with what you have; for He Himself has said, "I WILL NEVER DESERT YOU, NOR WILL I EVER FORSAKE YOU," [NASB]<br>Keep your **lives** free from the love of money and be content with what you have, because God has said, "Never will I leave you; never will I forsake you." [NIV]<br>*Let your* **conduct** *be* without covetousness; *be* content with such things as you have. For He Himself has said, *"I will never leave you nor forsake you."* [NKJV]<br>Stay away from the love of money; be satisfied with what you have. For God has said, "I will never fail you. I will never forsake you." [NLT]—NOT TRANSLATED<br>ἀφιλάργυρος ὁ **τρόπος**, ἀρκούμενοι τοῖς παροῦσιν· αὐτὸς γὰρ εἴρηκεν, Οὐ μή σε ἀνῶ, οὐδ' οὐ μήσε ἐγκαταλίπω. [GNS]<br>Ἀφιλάργυρος ὁ **τρόπος**, ἀρκούμενοι τοῖς παροῦσιν. αὐτὸς γὰρ εἴρηκεν, Οὐ μή σε ἀνῶ οὐδ' οὐ μή σε ἐγκαταλίπω, [GNT] | be focused upon Christ and the glorious hope of eternity, not upon this passing world and its possessions. The believer is to have no secret lust for the things of this world. |
| **#707 Confidence**<br><br>Boldness–KJV<br>**Confidence–NASB**<br>**Confidence–NIV**<br>Boldness–NKJV<br>Boldly–NLT<br><br>**POSB REFERENCE** (Heb.10:19-20; esp. v.19) Note 1 | παρρησίαν = *parrësian*<br>Pronunciation: [par-rhay-see'-ahn]<br>Parsing (part of speech): noun<br>  Case—accusative<br>  Gender—feminine<br>  Number—singular<br>  Stem or root—from παρρησία, ας<br>Concordance References:<br>⇒ Strong's #3954 *parrësia*<br>⇒ NIV #4244 *parrësia*<br>⇒ NASB #3954 *parrësia*<br><br>**Hebrews 10:19**<br>Having therefore, brethren, **boldness** to enter into the holiest by the blood of Jesus, [KJV]<br>Since therefore, brethren, we have **confidence** to enter the holy place by the blood of Jesus, [NASB]<br>Therefore, brothers, since we have **confidence** to enter the Most Holy Place by the blood of Jesus, [NIV]<br>Therefore, brethren, having **boldness** to enter the Holiest by the blood of Jesus, [NKJV]<br>And so, dear brothers and sisters, we can **boldly** enter heaven's Most Holy Place because of the blood of Jesus. [NLT]<br>Ἔχοντες οὖν, ἀδελφοί, **παρρησίαν** εἰς τὴν εἴσοδον τῶν ἁγίων ἐν τῷ αἵματι Ἰησοῦ, [GNS]<br>Ἔχοντες οὖν, ἀδελφοί, **παρρησίαν** εἰς τὴν εἴσοδον τῶν ἁγίων ἐν τῷ αἵματι 'Ιησοῦ, [GNT] | Confidence, boldness, unshakable assurance.<br><br>**Practical Application**<br>The word "confidence" (*parrësian*) means to enter God's presence freely and openly, with confidence and assurance. Just imagine...<br>• being able to enter the presence of God freely and openly.<br>• knowing God personally and intimately.<br>• fellowshipping and communing with God.<br>• having God guide and direct, look after and care for, provide and protect, strengthen and deliver us with joy, rejoicing, assurance, confidence, and victory over all the trials and temptations in life.<br>Imagine having God take care of one's life like that. This is what the new and living faith is: it is *confidence* to enter God's presence, to know God intimately and personally, experiencing His fellowship, presence, and power all the time. It is living and moving and having our being in God.<br>How is this possible? How can a person know God so personally and intimately? By the blood of Jesus Christ. The death of Jesus Christ opened up a new and living way for us to approach God. It opened up a way that brings us right into the holiest place of all, into the very presence of God. |
| **#708 Confidence–Confident**<br><br>Confidence–KJV<br>Confidence–NASB<br>Confident–NIV<br>Confidence–NKJV<br>Full of courage–NLT<br><br>**POSB REFERENCE** (1 Jn.2:28) Note 2, point 2 | σχῶμεν παρρησίαν = *schömen parrësian*<br>Pronunciation: [skho'-men par-rhay-see'-ahn]<br>Parsing *schömen* (part of speech): verb<br>  Mood—subjunctive<br>  Tense—aorist<br>  Voice—active<br>  Person—1st person<br>  Number—plural<br>  Stem or root—from ἔχω<br>Parsing *parrësian* (part of speech): noun<br>  Case—accusative<br>  Gender—feminine<br>  Number—singular<br>  Stem or root—from παρρησία, ας<br>Concordance References:<br>⇒ Strong's #2192+3954 *echö parrësia*<br>⇒ NIV #2400+4244 *echö parrësia* [confident]<br>⇒ NASB #2192+3954 *echö parrësia* | Confident, confidence; to be full of courage, boldness, assurance.<br><br>**Practical Application**<br>It has the idea of unshakable boldness and assurance. If we abide in Christ now, today, and every day hereafter, we can have unshakable confidence and assurance and even boldness when Jesus Christ returns to earth. |

# PRACTICAL WORD STUDIES
## in the NEW TESTAMENT

| ENGLISH WORD | GREEK WORD AND VERSE | THE WORD MEANS... |
|---|---|---|
| | **1 John 2:28**<br>And now, little children, abide in him; that, when he shall appear, we may have **confidence**, and not be ashamed before him at his coming. [KJV]<br>And now, little children, abide in Him, so that when He appears, we may have **confidence** and not shrink away from Him in shame at His coming. [NASB]<br>And now, dear children, continue in him, so that when he appears we may be **confident** and unashamed before him at his coming. [NIV]<br>And now, little children, abide in Him, that when He appears, we may have **confidence** and not be ashamed before Him at His coming. [NKJV]<br>And now, dear children, continue to live in fellowship with Christ so that when he returns, you will be **full of courage** and not shrink back from him in shame. [NLT]<br>καὶ νῦν, τεκνία, μένετε ἐν αὐτῷ· ἵνα ὅταν φανερωθῇ **ἔχωμεν παρρησίαν**, καὶ μὴ αἰσχυνθῶμεν ἀπ' αὐτοῦ, ἐν τῇ παρουσίᾳ αὐτοῦ. [GNS]<br>Καὶ νῦν, τεκνία, μένετε ἐν αὐτῷ, ἵνα ἐὰν φανερωθῇ **σχῶμεν παρρησίαν** καὶ μὴ αἰσχυνθῶμεν ἀπ' αὐτοῦ ἐν τῇ παρουσίᾳ αὐτοῦ. [GNT] | |
| **#709**<br>**Confident**<br><br>Trusted–KJV<br>Trusted–NASB<br>**Confident–NIV**<br>Trusted–NKJV<br>Self-confidence–NLT<br><br>**POSB REFERENCE**<br>(Lk.18:9)<br>Note 1, point 1 | πεποιθότας = *pepoithotas*<br>Pronunciation: [peh-poy-tho-tahs]<br>Parsing (part of speech): verb<br>    Mood—participle<br>    Tense—perfect<br>    Voice—active<br>    Case—accusative<br>    Gender—masculine<br>    Number—plural<br>    Stem or root—from πείθω<br>Concordance References:<br>  ⇒ Strong's #3982 peithō<br>  ⇒ NIV #4275 peithō<br>  ⇒ NASB #3982 peithō<br><br>**Luke 18:9**<br>And he spake this parable unto certain which **trusted** in themselves that they were righteous, and despised others: [KJV]<br>And He also told this parable to certain ones who **trusted** in themselves that they were righteous, and viewed others with contempt: [NASB]<br>To some who were **confident** of their own righteousness and looked down on everybody else, Jesus told this parable: [NIV]<br>Also He spoke this parable to some who **trusted** in themselves that they were righteous, and despised others: [NKJV]<br>Then Jesus told this story to some who had great **self-confidence** and scorned everyone else: [NLT]<br>Εἶπε δὲ καὶ πρός τινας τοὺς **πεποιθότας** ἐφ' ἑαυτοῖς ὅτι εἰσὶ δίκαιοι, καὶ ἐξουθενοῦντας τοὺς λοιπούς, τὴν παραβολὴν ταύτην· [GNS]<br>Εἶπεν δὲ καὶ πρός τινας τοὺς **πεποιθότας** ἐφ' ἑαυτοῖς ὅτι εἰσὶν δίκαιοι καὶ ἐξουθενοῦντας τοὺς λοιποὺς τὴν παραβολὴν ταύτην· [GNT] | To be confident; to trust in one's own self; to have self-confidence; to rely upon oneself.<br><br>**Practical Application**<br>It means those who trust in themselves; that is, those who feel they are completely self-sufficient and have no need for anyone else. They feel all they need dwells within their own bodies and minds. There is a feeling that neither God nor anyone else is really needed—not too often, if ever—as one ploughs through life. |
| **#710**<br>**Confident**<br><br>**Confident–KJV**<br>Good courage–NASB<br>**Confident–NIV**<br>**Confident–NKJV**<br>**Confident–NLT** | Θαρροῦντες = *Tharrountes*<br>Pronunciation: [thar-roon'-tehs]<br>Parsing (part of speech): verb<br>    Mood—participle<br>    Tense—present<br>    Voice—active<br>    Case—nominative<br>    Gender—masculine<br>    Person—1st person<br>    Stem or root—from θαρρέω<br>Concordance References:<br>  ⇒ Strong's #2292 tharreō | Confident, to have good courage; to act boldly; "to be cheered up" (A.T. Robertson. *Word Pictures in the New Testament*, Vol. 4, p.229).<br><br>**Practical Application**<br>The Holy Spirit stirs confidence and courage to face the present life. In this world all believers face such things as...<br>• pressure<br>• trouble<br>• sorrow |

# PRACTICAL WORD STUDIES
## in the NEW TESTAMENT

| ENGLISH WORD | GREEK WORD AND VERSE | THE WORD MEANS... |
|---|---|---|
| POSB REFERENCE (2 Cor.5:5-8; esp. v.6) Note 3 | ⇒ NIV #2509 tharreö<br>⇒ NASB #2292 tharreö<br><br>**2 Cor. 5:6**<br>Therefore we are always **confident**, knowing that, whilst we are at home in the body, we are absent from the Lord: [KJV]<br>Therefore, being always of **good courage**, and knowing that while we are at home in the body we are absent from the Lord [NASB]<br>Therefore we are always **confident** and know that as long as we are at home in the body we are away from the Lord. [NIV]<br>So *we are* always **confident**, knowing that while we are at home in the body we are absent from the Lord. [NKJV]<br>So we are always **confident**, even though we know that as long as we live in these bodies we are not at home with the Lord. [NLT]<br>Θαρροῦντες οὖν πάντοτε, καὶ εἰδότες ὅτι ἐνδημοῦντες ἐν τῷ σώματι ἐκδημοῦμεν ἀπὸ τοῦ Κυρίου, [GNS]<br>Θαρροῦντες οὖν πάντοτε καὶ εἰδότες ὅτι ἐνδημοῦντες ἐν τῷ σώματι ἐκδημοῦμεν ἀπὸ τοῦ κυρίου· [GNT] | • accident<br>• rejection<br>• loss<br>• disease<br>• death<br><br>But no matter what they face, the Holy Spirit stirs their courage to face it all. How? Again, note the word "knowing." The Holy Spirit enhances our *knowledge*...<br>• that our present home is the body, but it is temporary and passing. Therefore, all trials and problems will quickly pass away.<br>• that we are now absent from the Lord. The idea is that we are to be with Him. The Holy Spirit stirs a longing within us to be with Him. And that longing gives us courage to march on through this life. |
| #711<br>**Confident Assurance**<br><br>Substance–KJV<br>Assurance–NASB<br>Sure–NIV<br>Substance–NKJV<br>**Confident assurance–NLT**<br><br>POSB REFERENCE (Heb.11:1) Note 1 | ὑπόστασις = *hupostasis*<br>Pronunciation: [hoop-os'-tas-is]<br>Parsing (part of speech): noun<br>  Case—nominative<br>  Gender—feminine<br>  Number—singular<br>  Stem or root—from ὑπόστασις, εως<br>Concordance References:<br>⇒ Strong's #5287 hupostasis<br>⇒ NIV #5712 hupostasis<br>⇒ NASB #5287 hupostasis<br><br>**Hebrews 11:1**<br>Now faith is the **substance** of things hoped for, the evidence of things not seen. [KJV]<br>Now faith is the **assurance** of things hoped for, the conviction of things not seen. [NASB]<br>Now faith is being **sure** of what we hope for and certain of what we do not see. [NIV]<br>Now faith is the **substance** of things hoped for, the evidence of things not seen. [NKJV]<br>What is faith? It is the **confident assurance** that what we hope for is going to happen. It is the evidence of things we cannot yet see. [NLT]<br>Ἔστι δὲ πίστις ἐλπιζομένων **ὑπόστασις**, πραγμάτων ἔλεγχος οὐ βλεπομένων. ΓΝΣ<br>Ἔστιν δὲ πίστις ἐλπιζομένων **ὑπόστασις**, πραγμάτων ἔλεγχος οὐ βλεπομένων. [GNT] | The foundation, assurance, title-deed, and guarantee of things hoped for.<br><br>**Practical Application**<br>Look closely at what is being said and note that faith is being described as an act, an act of the mind and heart. That is, our hearts and minds believe something, and we have assurance and conviction that it is true. This is certainly true; faith is an act of the mind and heart. But many of the earlier interpreters understood "confident assurance" (*hupostasis*) to mean *real being, substantial nature, the real nature of a thing*. Vincent points this out and even says that it suggests the real sense, but he backs off of the meaning and concludes that faith is basically an act of what he calls "moral intelligence directed at an object" (Marvin Vincent. *Word Studies in the New Testament*, Vol. 4, p.510).<br>Now, what does all this discussion mean? It means this: faith is the substance, the actual possession, of things hoped for, the evidence and reality of things not seen. It is *both an act and a possession* of the thing believed. It is believing and trusting in that which actually exists—in that which we can possess. We may not be able to see it, but it is real and existing; and we can possess it by believing and having faith in it. We can possess it now—we cannot see it, but we can actually possess the very substance of it by believing and entrusting our lives to it.<br>⇒ Faith is trusting and possessing all that God is and says.<br>⇒ Faith is believing and possessing all that God is and says.<br>⇒ Faith is having confidence in and possessing all that God is and says.<br>⇒ Faith is *hoping for something and possessing it* because God is (exists) and has promised it.<br>Note what Biblical faith is not. It is not...<br>• "I think so; I hope so."<br>• "It may be so; it may not be so."<br>• "It might be true; it might not be true." |

# PRACTICAL WORD STUDIES
## in the NEW TESTAMENT

| ENGLISH WORD | GREEK WORD AND VERSE | THE WORD MEANS... |
|---|---|---|
| | | Biblical faith does not deal with what is unreal, imaginary, fanciful, visionary, superficial, or deceptive. Biblical faith is the knowledge, experience, and possession of things hoped for. True Biblical faith deals only with truth and reality. It is...<br>• knowing what is real.<br>• experiencing what is real.<br>• possessing what is real. |
| **#712**<br>**Confident Expectation Of Salvation**<br><br>Hope–KJV<br>Hope–NASB<br>Hope–NIV<br>Hope–NKJV<br>Confident expectation of salvation–NLT<br><br>**POSB REFERENCE**<br>(Romans 5:3-5; esp. v.4)<br>Note 5, point 3 | ἐλπίδα = elpida<br>Pronunciation: [el-pee-dah']<br>Parsing (part of speech): noun<br>  Case—accusative<br>  Gender—feminine<br>  Number—singular<br>  Stem or root—from ἐλπίς, ίδος<br>Concordance References:<br>⇒ Strong's #1680 elpis<br>⇒ NIV #1828 elpis<br>⇒ NASB #1680 elpis<br><br>**Romans 5:4**<br>And patience, experience; and experience, **hope**: [KJV]<br>and perseverance, proven character; and proven character, **hope**; [NASB]<br>Perseverance, character; and character, **hope**. [NIV]<br>And perseverance, character; and character, **hope**. [NKJV]<br>And endurance develops strength of character in us, and character strengthens our **confident expectation of salvation**. [NLT]<br>ἡ δὲ ὑπομονὴ δοκιμήν, ἡ δὲ δοκιμὴ ἐλπίδα· [GNS]<br>ἡ δὲ ὑπομονὴ δοκιμήν, ἡ δὲ δοκιμὴ ἐλπίδα. [GNT] | Hope; ground or basis of hope; what is hoped for; to expect with confidence. It means to hope; to anticipate knowing; to look and long for with surety; to desire with assurance; to rely on with certainty; to trust with the guarantee; to believe with the knowledge.<br><br>**Practical Application**<br>Note that hope is expectation, anticipation, looking and longing for, desiring, relying upon, and trusting. But it is also confidence, knowledge, surety, assurance, certainty, and a guarantee. When a justified man becomes stronger in character, he draws closer to God; and the closer he draws to God, the more he hopes for the glory of God. (See POSB note, Hope—Romans 5:2 for more discussion and verses.) |
| **#713**<br>**Confident That**<br><br>Confident that–KJV<br>Confident that–NASB<br>Convinced that–NIV<br>Confident that–NKJV<br>Convinced that–NLT<br><br>**POSB REFERENCE**<br>(Romans 2:17-20; esp. v.19)<br>Note 1, point 6 | πέποιθάς = pepoithas<br>Pronunciation: [pi'-poy-thas]<br>Parsing (part of speech): verb<br>  Mood—indicative<br>  Tense—perfect<br>  Voice—active<br>  Person—2nd person<br>  Number—singular<br>  Stem or root—from πείθω<br>Concordance References:<br>⇒ Strong's #3982 peithō<br>⇒ NIV #4275 peithō<br>⇒ NASB #3982 peithō<br><br>**Romans 2:19**<br>And art **confident that** thou thyself art a guide of the blind, a light of them which are in darkness, [KJV]<br>And are **confident that** you yourself are a guide to the blind, a light to those who are in darkness, [NASB]<br>If you are **convinced that** you are a guide for the blind, a light for those who are in the dark, [NIV]<br>And are **confident that** you yourself are a guide to the blind, a light to those who are in darkness, [NKJV]<br>You are **convinced that** you are a guide for the blind and a beacon light for people who are lost in darkness without God. [NLT]<br>πέποιθάς τε σεαυτὸν ὁδηγὸν εἶναι τυφλῶν, φῶς τῶν ἐν σκότει, [GNS]<br>πέποιθάς τε σεαυτὸν ὁδηγὸν εἶναι τυφλῶν, φῶς τῶν ἐν σκότει, [GNT] | Convinced that; confident that; to be persuaded and sure.<br><br>**Practical Application**<br>The religionist is confident that religion is true, that religion is the way men should live. He believes that a man who does not believe in God and live a religious life is blind, needing to be guided to the truth. By living a religious life, he feels...<br>• he is an example to men.<br>• he is a guide to help men find God.<br>• he can cure men of their blindness to God and religion.<br>However, being "confident that" one is a guide of the blind does not mean that one is a true guide. A person must be sure that he himself is following the truth, Jesus Christ (John 14:6). There are many guides in the world who are leading people down the wrong road. They are blind guides, the blind leading the blind (Matthew 15:14). |
| **#714**<br>**Confirm**<br><br>Confirm–KJV<br>Confirm–NASB | βεβαιώσει = bebaiōsei<br>Pronunciation: [beb-ah-yo'-see]<br>Parsing (part of speech): verb<br>  Mood—indicative<br>  Tense—future<br>  Voice—active | To confirm; to verify; to prove; to strengthen; to sustain; to keep strong. To preserve and establish, make steadfast and firm and secure.<br><br>**Practical Application**<br>Jesus Christ will preserve and secure the |

# PRACTICAL WORD STUDIES
## in the NEW TESTAMENT

| ENGLISH WORD | GREEK WORD AND VERSE | THE WORD MEANS... |
|---|---|---|
| Keep you strong–NIV<br>**Confirm–NKJV**<br>Keep you strong–NLT<br><br>**POSB<br>REFERENCE**<br>(1 Cor.1:8)<br>Note 3 | Person—3rd person<br>Number—singular<br>Stem or root—from βεβαιόω<br>Concordance References:<br>⇒ Strong's #950 bebaioō<br>⇒ NIV #1011 bebaioō<br>⇒ NASB #950 bebaioō<br><br>**1 Cor. 1:8**<br>Who shall also **confirm** you unto the end, that ye may be blameless in the day of our Lord Jesus Christ. [KJV]<br>Who shall also **confirm** you to the end, blameless in the day of our Lord Jesus Christ. [NASB]<br>He will **keep you strong** to the end, so that you will be blameless on the day of our Lord Jesus Christ. [NIV]<br>Who will also **confirm** you to the end, *that you may be* blameless in the day of our Lord Jesus Christ. [NKJV]<br>He will **keep you strong** right up to the end, and he will keep you free from all blame on the great day when our Lord Jesus Christ returns. [NLT]<br>ὃς καὶ **βεβαιώσει** ὑμᾶς ἕως τέλους, ἀνεγκλήτους ἐν τῇ ἡμέρᾳ τοῦ Κυρίου ἡμῶν Ἰησοῦ Χριστοῦ. [GNS]<br>ὃς καὶ **βεβαιώσει** ὑμᾶς ἕως τέλους ἀνεγκλήτους ἐν τῇ ἡμέρᾳ τοῦ κυρίου ἡμῶν Ἰησοῦ [Χριστοῦ]. [GNT] | believer from falling. Note the glorious reason: that the believer may be "blameless in the day of our Lord Jesus Christ." |
| **#715**<br>**Confirm**<br><br>Stablish–KJV<br>**Confirm–NASB**<br>Make...strong–NIV<br>Establish–NKJV<br>Support–NLT<br><br>**POSB<br>REFERENCE**<br>(1 Pt.5:10)<br>Note 2, point 2 | στηρίξει = stērixei<br>Pronunciation: [stay-rich'-eh-ee]<br>Parsing (part of speech): verb<br>  Mood—indicative<br>  Tense—future<br>  Voice—active<br>  Person—3rd person<br>  Number—singular<br>  Stem or root—from στηρίζω<br>Concordance References:<br>⇒ Strong's #4741 stērizō<br>⇒ NIV #5114 stērizō<br>⇒ NASB #4741 stērizō<br><br>**1 Peter 5:10**<br>But the God of all grace, who hath called us unto his eternal glory by Christ Jesus, after that ye have suffered a while, make you perfect, **stablish**, strengthen, settle you. [KJV]<br>And after you have suffered for a little while, the God of all grace, who called you to His eternal glory in Christ, will Himself perfect, **confirm**, strengthen and establish you. [NASB]<br>And the God of all grace, who called you to his eternal glory in Christ, after you have suffered a little while, will himself restore you and **make** you **strong**, firm and steadfast. [NIV]<br>But may the God of all grace, who called us to His eternal glory by Christ Jesus, after you have suffered a while, perfect, **establish**, strengthen, and settle *you*. [NKJV]<br>In his kindness God called you to his eternal glory by means of Jesus Christ. After you have suffered a little while, he will restore, **support**, and strengthen you, and he will place you on a firm foundation. [NLT]<br>ὁ δὲ Θεὸς πάσης χάριτος, ὁ καλέσας ὑμᾶς εἰς τὴν αἰώνιον αὐτοῦ δόξαν ἐν Χριστῷ Ἰησοῦ, ὀλίγον παθόντας αὐτὸς καταρτίσει ὑμᾶς, **στηρίξει**, σθενώσαι, θεμελιώσαι. [GNS]<br>Ὁ δὲ Θεὸς πάσης χάριτος, ὁ καλέσας ὑμᾶς εἰς τὴν αἰώνιον αὐτοῦ δόξαν ἐν Χριστῷ [Ἰησοῦ], ὀλίγον παθόντας αὐτὸς καταρτίσει, **στηρίξει**, σθενώσει, θεμελιώσει. [GNT] | To make steadfast, firm, strong and solid; to establish; to fix. It means to be firmly set, as firmly as if one were set in reinforced concrete. It means to be immovable.<br><br>**Practical Application**<br>God Himself uses the believer's sufferings to establish the believer. God is able to attach us to Himself to such a degree that we will be immovable, no matter how severe the attack of temptation or suffering. But remember our duty: we must resist the devil and resist him steadfastly (1 Peter 5:8). The promise is clear: if we resist the devil and draw near God, He will draw near us (James 4:7-8). |
| **#716**<br>**Confirming** | ἐπιστηρίζοντες = epistērizontes<br>Pronunciation: [ep-ee-stay-rid'-zon-tehs]<br>Parsing (part of speech): verb<br>  Mood—participle | Strengthening, making firm, confirming, establishing. |

# PRACTICAL WORD STUDIES
## in the NEW TESTAMENT

| ENGLISH WORD | GREEK WORD AND VERSE | THE WORD MEANS... |
|---|---|---|
| **Confirming–KJV**<br>Strengthening–NASB<br>Strengthening–NIV<br>Strengthening–NKJV<br>Strengthened–NLT<br><br>**POSB REFERENCE**<br>(Acts 14:21-27; esp. v.22)<br>Note 2, point 1<br><br>**See also POSB REF:**<br>(Acts 15:39-41; esp. v.41)<br>Note 3, point 3c | Tense—present<br>Voice—active<br>Case—nominative<br>Gender—masculine<br>Number—plural<br>Stem or root—from ἐπιστηρίζω<br>Concordance References:<br>⇒ Strong's #1991 epistērizō<br>⇒ NIV #2185 epistērizō<br>⇒ NASB #1991 epistērizō<br><br>**Acts 14:22**<br>**Confirming** the souls of the disciples, and exhorting them to continue in the faith, and that we must through much tribulation enter into the kingdom of God. [KJV]<br>**Strengthening** the souls of the disciples, encouraging them to continue in the faith, and saying, "Through many tribulations we must enter the kingdom of God." [NASB]<br>**Strengthening** the disciples and encouraging them to remain true to the faith. "We must go through many hardships to enter the kingdom of God," they said. [NIV]<br>**Strengthening** the souls of the disciples, exhorting *them* to continue in the faith, and *saying*, "We must through many tribulations enter the kingdom of God." [NKJV]<br>Where they **strengthened** the believers. They encouraged them to continue in the faith, reminding them that they must enter into the Kingdom of God through many tribulations. [NLT]<br>**ἐπιστηρίζοντες** τὰς ψυχὰς τῶν μαθητῶν, παρακαλοῦντες ἐμμένειν τῇ πίστει, καὶ ὅτι διὰ πολλῶν θλίψεων δεῖ ἡμᾶς εἰσελθεῖν εἰς τὴν βασιλείαν τοῦ Θεοῦ. [GNS]<br>**ἐπιστηρίζοντες** τὰς ψυχὰς τῶν μαθητῶν, παρακαλοῦντες ἐμμένειν τῇ πίστει, καὶ ὅτι διὰ πολλῶν θλίψεων δεῖ ἡμᾶς εἰσελθεῖν εἰς τὴν βασιλείαν τοῦ θεοῦ. [GNT] | **Practical Application**<br>New converts and churches always stand in danger of...<br>• wavering<br>• being lured away<br>• returning to religious tradition<br>• slipping back<br>• not praying faithfully<br>• being tempted by worldly friends<br>• not studying the Scripture consistently<br>• not witnessing |
| **#717**<br>**Conflict**<br><br>**Conflict–KJV**<br>Struggle–NASB<br>Struggling–NIV<br>**Conflict–NKJV**<br>Agonized–NLT<br><br>**POSB REFERENCE**<br>(Col.2:1)<br>Note 1 | ἀγῶνα = agōna<br>Pronunciation: [ag-on'-ah]<br>Parsing (part of speech): noun<br>Case—accusative<br>Gender—masculine<br>Number—singular<br>Stem or root—from ἀγών, ῶνος<br>Concordance References:<br>⇒ Strong's #73 agōn<br>⇒ NIV #74 agōn<br>⇒ NASB #73 agōn<br><br>**Col. 2:1**<br>For I would that ye knew what great **conflict** I have for you, and *for* them at Laodicea, and *for* as many as have not seen my face in the flesh; [KJV]<br>For I want you to know how great a **struggle** I have on your behalf, and for those who are at Laodicea, and for all those who have not personally seen my face, [NASB]<br>I want you to know how much I am **struggling** for you and for those at Laodicea, and for all who have not met me personally. [NIV]<br>For I want you to know what a great **conflict** I have for you and those in Laodicea, and *for* as many as have not seen my face in the flesh, [NKJV]<br>I want you to know how much I have **agonized** for you and for the church at Laodicea, and for many other friends who have never known me personally. [NLT]<br>Θέλω γὰρ ὑμᾶς εἰδέναι ἡλίκον **ἀγῶνα** ἔχω ὑπέρ περὶ ὑμῶν καὶ τῶν ἐν Λαοδικείᾳ, καὶ ὅσοι οὐχ ἑωράκασι τὸ πρόσωπόν μου ἐν σαρκί, [GNS]<br>Θέλω γὰρ ὑμᾶς εἰδέναι ἡλίκον **ἀγῶνα** ἔχω ὑπέρ ὑμῶν καὶ τῶν ἐν Λαοδικείᾳ καὶ ὅσοι οὐχ ἑόρακαν τὸ πρόσωπόν μου ἐν σαρκί, [GNT] | To struggle; to agonize; to fight. It means to strive, agonize, struggle, and wrestle in prayer for the believers of the churches.<br><br>**Practical Application**<br>It is the picture of an athlete's exerting every ounce of energy he has in the struggle of the contest. The idea is that Paul labored hard, toiled, strove, agonized, struggled, and wrestled in prayer. |

**PRACTICAL WORD STUDIES**
**in the NEW TESTAMENT**

| ENGLISH WORD | GREEK WORD AND VERSE | THE WORD MEANS... |
|---|---|---|
| **#718**<br>**Conform To The Pattern Of–**<br>**Conformed**<br><br>**Conformed–KJV**<br>**Conformed–NASB**<br>**Conform...to the pattern of–NIV**<br>**Conformed–NKJV**<br>Copy the behavior and customs–NLT<br><br>**POSB REFERENCE**<br>(Rom.12:2)<br>Note 3, point 1 | συσχηματίζεσθε = suschēmatizesthe<br>Pronunciation: [soos-khay-mat-id'-zehs-theh]<br>Parsing (part of speech): verb<br>    Mood—imperative<br>    Tense—present<br>    Voice—middle or passive<br>    Person—2nd person<br>    Number—plural<br>    Stem or root—from συσχηματίζομαι<br>Concordance References:<br>  ⇒ Strong's #4964 suschēmatizō<br>  ⇒ NIV #5372 suschēmatizō<br>  ⇒ NASB #4964 suschēmatizō<br><br>**Romans 12:2**<br>And be not **conformed** to this world: but be ye transformed by the renewing of your mind, that ye may prove what is that good, and acceptable, and perfect, will of God. [KJV]<br>And do not be **conformed** to this world, but be transformed by the renewing of your mind, that you may prove what the will of God is, that which is good and acceptable and perfect. [NASB]<br>Do not **conform** any longer **to the pattern of** this world, but be transformed by the renewing of your mind. Then you will be able to test and approve what God's will is—his good, pleasing and perfect will. [NIV]<br>And do not be **conformed** to this world, but be transformed by the renewing of your mind, that you may prove what *is* that good and acceptable and perfect will of God. [NKJV]<br>Don't **copy the behavior and customs** of this world, But let God transform you into a new person by changing the way you think. Then you will know what God wants you to do, and you will know how good and pleasing and perfect his will really is. [NLT]<br>καὶ μὴ **συσχηματίζεσθε** τῷ αἰῶνι τούτῳ, ἀλλὰ μεταμορφοῦσθε τῇ ἀνακαινώσει τοῦ νοός ὑμῶν, εἰς τὸ δοκιμάζειν ὑμᾶς τί τὸ θέλημα τοῦ Θεοῦ, τὸ ἀγαθὸν καὶ εὐάρεστον καὶ τέλειον. [GNS]<br>καὶ μὴ **συσχηματίζεσθε** τῷ αἰῶνι τούτῳ, ἀλλὰ μεταμορφοῦσθε τῇ ἀνακαινώσει τοῦ νοός εἰς τὸ δοκιμάζειν ὑμᾶς τί τὸ θέλημα τοῦ Θεοῦ, τὸ ἀγαθὸν καὶ εὐάρεστον καὶ τέλειον. [GNT] | To conform to the pattern of; to copy the behavior and customs of; to be shaped by; to fashion.<br><br>**Practical Application**<br>It is the outward form and appearance of a man. It is the appearance of a person that changes from day to day and year to year. A man dresses differently for work than he does for an evening out. A man looks different as a young man than he does as an older man. His *suschēmatizesthe*, his fashion, his outward appearance, differs. |
| **#719**<br>**Conformed To The Image, Likeness**<br><br>**Conformed to the image–KJV**<br>**Conformed to the image–NASB**<br>**Conformed to the likeness–NIV**<br>**Conformed to the image–NKJV**<br>To become like–NLT<br><br>**POSB REFERENCE**<br>(Rom.8:29)<br>Note 2, point 2<br>(Rom.8:29)<br>Note 2, point 2a<br>(Rom.8:29)<br>Note 2, point 2b | συμμόρφους τῆς εἰκόνος = summorphous tēs eikonos<br>Pronunciation: [soom-mor-foos' tace i-kone'-os]<br>Parsing *summorphous* (part of speech): adjective<br>    Case—accusative<br>    Gender—masculine<br>    Number—plural<br>    Stem or root—from σύμμορφος, ον<br>Parsing *eikonos* (part of speech): noun<br>    Case—genitive<br>    Gender—feminine<br>    Number—singular<br>    Stem or root—from εἰκών, όνος<br>Concordance References:<br>  ⇒ Strong's #4832 summorphos + 3588 ho + 1504 eikōn<br>  ⇒ NIV #5215 summorphos [conformed] + 3836 ho [the] + 1635 eikōn [likeness]<br>  ⇒ NASB #4832 summorphos + 3588 ho + 1504 eikōn<br><br>**Romans 8:29**<br>For whom he did foreknow, he also did predestinate to be **conformed to the image** of his Son, that he might be the firstborn among many brethren. [KJV]<br>For whom He foreknew, He also predestined to become **conformed to the image** of His Son, that He might be the first-born among many brethren; [NASB] | Conformed to the likeness, conformed to the image; to become like.<br><br>**Practical Application**<br>"Conformed" (*summorphous*) means the very same form or image as Christ. Within our nature—our being, our person—we will be made just like Christ. As He is perfect and eternal—without disease and pain, sin and death—so we will be perfected just like Him. We will be transformed into His very likeness.<br>"Image" or "likeness" (*eikonos*) means a derived or a given likeness. The image or likeness of Christ is not something which believers merit or for which they work; it is not an image that comes from their own nature or character. No man can earn or produce the perfection and eternal life possessed by Christ. The image of Christ, His perfection and life, is a gift of God. To be conformed to the image of God's Son means...<br>• to participate in the divine nature (2 Peter 1:4).<br>• to be adopted as a son of God (Ephes. 1:5).<br>• to be holy and without blame before Him |

# PRACTICAL WORD STUDIES
## in the NEW TESTAMENT

| ENGLISH WORD | GREEK WORD AND VERSE | THE WORD MEANS... |
|---|---|---|
| | For those God foreknew he also predestined to be **conformed to the likeness** of his Son, that he might be the firstborn among many brothers. [NIV]<br>For whom He foreknew, He also predestined *to be* **conformed to the image** of His Son, that He might be the firstborn among many brethren. [NKJV]<br>For God knew his people in advance, and he chose them **to become like** his Son, so that his Son would be the firstborn, with many brothers and sisters. [NLT]<br>ὅτι οὓς προέγνω, καὶ προώρισε **συμμόρφους τῆς εἰκόνος** τοῦ υἱοῦ αὐτοῦ, εἰς τὸ εἶναι αὐτὸν πρωτότοκον ἐν πολλοῖς ἀδελφοῖς· [GNS]<br>ὅτι οὓς προέγνω, καὶ προώρισεν **συμμόρφους τῆς εἰκόνος** τοῦ υἱοῦ αὐτοῦ, εἰς τὸ εἶναι αὐτὸν πρωτότοκον ἐν πολλοῖς ἀδελφοῖς· [GNT] | (Ephes. 1:4; Ephes. 4:24).<br>• to bear the image of the heavenly: which is an incorruptible, immortal body (1 Cor. 15:49-54; cp. 1 Cor. 15:42-44).<br>• to have one's body fashioned (conformed) just like His glorious body (Phil. 3:21).<br>• to be changed (transformed) into the same image of the Lord (2 Cor. 3:18).<br>• to be recreated just like Him (1 John 3:2-3). |
| **#720**<br>**Confound**<br><br>Confound–KJV<br>Shame–NASB<br>Shame–NIV<br>Shame–NKJV<br>Shame–NLT<br><br>**POSB REFERENCE**<br>(1 Cor.1:27-28; esp. v.27)<br>Note 2, point 1 | καταισχύνῃ = *kataischunë*<br>Pronunciation: [kat-ahee-skhoo'-nay]<br>Parsing (part of speech): verb<br>    Mood—subjunctive<br>    Tense—present<br>    Voice—active<br>    Person—3rd person<br>    Number—singular<br>    Stem or root—from καταισχύνω<br>Concordance References:<br>  ⇒ Strong's #2617 kataischunö<br>  ⇒ NIV #2875 kataischunö<br>  ⇒ NASB #2617 kataischunö<br><br>**1 Cor. 1:27**<br>But God hath chosen the foolish things of the world to **confound** the wise; and God hath chosen the weak things of the world to confound the things which are mighty; [KJV]<br>But God has chosen the foolish things of the world to shame the wise, and God has chosen the weak things of the world to **shame** the things which are strong, [NASB]<br>But God chose the foolish things of the world to shame the wise; God chose the weak things of the world to **shame** the strong. [NIV]<br>But God has chosen the foolish things of the world to put to **shame** the wise, and God has chosen the weak things of the world to put to shame the things which are mighty; [NKJV]<br>Instead, God deliberately chose things the world considers foolish in order to **shame** those who think they are wise. And he chose those who are powerless to shame those who are powerful. [NLT]<br>ἀλλὰ τὰ μωρὰ τοῦ κόσμου ἐξελέξατο ὁ Θεός, ἵνα τοὺς σοφούς, **καταισχύνῃ**· καὶ τὰ ἀσθενῆ τοῦ κόσμου ἐξελέξατο ὁ Θεός, ἵνα καταισχύνῃ τὰ ἰσχυρά· [GNS]<br>ἀλλὰ τὰ μωρὰ τοῦ κόσμου ἐξελέξατο ὁ θεός, ἵνα **καταισχύνῃ** τοὺς σοφούς, καὶ τὰ ἀσθενῆ τοῦ κόσμου ἐξελέξατο ὁ θεός, ἵνα καταισχύνῃ τὰ ἰσχυρά, [GNT] | To shame; to confound; to humiliate; to disgrace; to disappoint; to embarrass.<br><br>**Practical Application**<br>The wise feel self-sufficient in their education, knowledge, and wisdom. They feel little if any need for God and often question if there is a living and true God who is sovereign. Common sense and logic tell us that such an attitude of arrogance could never be acceptable to God. Not because He denies men the right to ask and think through legitimate questions, but because most of the wise of this world are not sincere enough to genuinely study the truth of God which has been revealed in Christ and in the Holy Scriptures. And, too often, the few who might seek the truth study secondary sources (books about the Bible) instead of studying the primary source, the Bible itself. Too many seek for God through what men say instead of letting God speak for Himself.<br>It is because of such pride, arrogance, and close-mindedness that God chooses few of the wise in this world. In fact, God does exactly what most men would do: He chooses those who humble themselves before Him, confessing Him to be God and asking Him to save them. The result, of course, is that the wise of this world are shamed, and their shame will become ever so visible and embarrassing when judgment comes. |
| **#721**<br>**Congregation**<br><br>Church–KJV<br>**Congregation–NASB**<br>Assembly–NIV<br>**Congregation–NKJV**<br>Assembly–NLT<br><br>**POSB REFERENCE**<br>(Acts 7:38)<br>*Deeper Study* #4 | ἐκκλησίᾳ = *ekklësia*<br>Pronunciation: [ek-klay-see'-ah]<br>Parsing (part of speech): noun<br>    Case—dative<br>    Gender—feminine<br>    Number—singular<br>    Stem or root— from ἐκκλησία<br>Concordance References:<br>  ⇒ Strong's #1577 ekklësia<br>  ⇒ NIV #1711 ekklësia<br>  ⇒ NASB #1577 ekklësia<br><br>**Acts 7:38**<br>This is he, that was in the **church** in the wilderness with the angel which spake to him in the mount Sina, and with our fathers: who received the lively oracles to give unto us: [KJV] | Assembly, church, congregation, gathering.<br><br>**Practical Application**<br>Israel was God's church, God's assembly, God's congregation in the wilderness. Israel was a type of the church in the world. |

# PRACTICAL WORD STUDIES
## in the NEW TESTAMENT

| ENGLISH WORD | GREEK WORD AND VERSE | THE WORD MEANS... |
|---|---|---|
| | "This is the one who was in the **congregation** in the wilderness together with the angel who was speaking to him on Mount Sinai, and who was with our fathers; and he received living oracles to pass on to you. [NASB]<br><br>He was in the **assembly** in the desert, with the angel who spoke to him on Mount Sinai, and with our fathers; and he received living words to pass on to us. [NIV]<br><br>This is he who was in the **congregation** in the wilderness with the Angel who spoke to him on Mount Sinai, and with our fathers, the one who received the living oracles to give to us, [NKJV]<br><br>Moses was with the **assembly** of God's people in the wilderness. He was the mediator between the people of Israel and the angel who gave him life-giving words on Mount Sinai to pass on to us. [NLT]<br><br>οὗτός ἐστιν ὁ γενόμενος ἐν τῇ **ἐκκλησίᾳ** ἐν τῇ ἐρήμῳ, μετὰ τοῦ ἀγγέλου τοῦ λαλοῦντος αὐτῷ ἐν τῷ ὄρει Σινᾶ καὶ τῶν πατέρων ἡμῶν· ὃς ἐδέξατο λόγια ζῶντα δοῦναι ἡμῖν· [GNS]<br><br>οὗτός ἐστιν ὁ γενόμενος ἐν τῇ **ἐκκλησίᾳ** ἐν τῇ ἐρήμῳ μετὰ τοῦ ἀγγέλου τοῦ λαλοῦντος αὐτῷ ἐν τῷ ὄρει Σινᾶ καὶ τῶν πατέρων ἡμῶν, ὃς ἐδέξατο λόγια ζῶντα δοῦναι ἡμῖν, [GNT] | |
| #722<br>**Consecrated**<br><br>Consecrated–KJV<br>Made perfect–NASB<br>Made perfect–NIV<br>Perfected–NKJV<br>Made perfect–NLT<br><br>POSB<br>REFERENCE<br>(Heb.7:28)<br>Note 4 | τετελειωμένον = teteleiömenon<br>Pronunciation: [teh-tel-i-o'-mehn-on]<br>Parsing (part of speech): verb<br>    Mood—participle<br>    Tense—perfect<br>    Voice—passive<br>    Case—accusative<br>    Gender—masculine<br>    Number—singular<br>    Stem or root—from τελειόω<br>Concordance References:<br>    ⇒ Strong's #5048 teleioö<br>    ⇒ NIV #5457 teleioö<br>    ⇒ NASB #5048 teleioö<br><br>**Hebrews 7:28**<br>For the law maketh men high priests which have infirmity; but the word of the oath, which was since the law, maketh the Son, who is **consecrated** for evermore. [KJV]<br><br>For the Law appoints men as high priests who are weak, but the word of the oath, which came after the Law, appoints a Son, **made perfect** forever. [NASB]<br><br>For the law appoints as high priests men who are weak; but the oath, which came after the law, appointed the Son, who has been **made perfect** forever. [NIV]<br><br>For the law appoints as high priests men who have weakness, but the word of the oath, which came after the law, *appoints* the Son who has been **perfected** forever. [NKJV]<br><br>Those who were high priests under the law of Moses were limited by human weakness. But after the law was given, God appointed his Son with an oath, and his Son has been **made perfect** forever. [NLT]<br><br>ὁ νόμος γὰρ ἀνθρώπους καθίστησιν ἀρχιερεῖς, ἔχοντας ἀσθένειαν· ὁ λόγος δὲ τῆς ὁρκωμοσίας τῆς μετὰ τὸν νόμον, υἱὸν εἰς τὸν αἰῶνα **τετελειωμένον**. [GNS]<br><br>ὁ νόμος γὰρ ἀνθρώπους ἀθίστησιν ἀρχιερεῖς ἔχοντας ἀσθένειαν, ὁ λόγος δὲ τῆς ὁρκωμοσίας τῆς μετὰ τὸν νόμον υἱὸν εἰς τὸν αἰῶνα **τετελειωμένον**. [GNT] | Perfected, consecrated; made perfect, complete.<br><br>**Practical Application**<br>Jesus Christ is the High Priest with a perfect appointment. Men—mere men—are appointed to be priests by the law. The law can appoint no one else but men with infirmities and weaknesses—men who are imperfect, frail, sinful, and dying. But the glorious message of this passage offers eternal hope for man. Why? Because God has given us two wonderful things: God has given His Word, His precious promise that He will give us a perfect and eternal High Priest to save us, and God has sworn that He will fulfill His Word. God has assured us with a double surety. Jesus Christ, the Son of God, is consecrated forever more. The word "consecrated" (*teteleiömenon*) means perfected. Jesus Christ is the perfected and eternal High Priest promised and sworn by God to save man. What greater salvation and surety could we ask than to have God send His own Son to perfect us and to give us eternal life and the glorious privilege of living forever with Him—the glorious privilege of ruling and reigning with Him throughout all of eternity. |
| #723<br>**Consecrated Bread**<br><br>Shewbread–KJV<br>**Consecrated bread–NASB** | ἄρτους τῆς προθέσεως = artous tace protheseös<br>Pronunciation: [ar'-tos tace proth'-es-eh-os]<br>Parsing *artous* (part of speech): noun<br>    Case—accusative<br>    Gender—masculine<br>    Number—plural<br>    Stem or root—from ἄρτος, ου | Consecrated bread, special bread, showbread, the bread of the face (referring to the face or Presence of God) or the bread of the Presence.<br><br>**Practical Application**<br>What the table of Consecrated bread taught:<br>1. The twelve loaves of consecrated bread repre- |

# PRACTICAL WORD STUDIES
## in the NEW TESTAMENT

| ENGLISH WORD | GREEK WORD AND VERSE | THE WORD MEANS... |
|---|---|---|
| **Consecrated bread– NIV**<br>Showbread–NKJV<br>Special bread–NLT<br><br>**POSB REFERENCE**<br>(Lk.6:4)<br>*Deeper Study #2* | Parsing *protheseōs* (part of speech): noun<br>   Case—genitive<br>   Gender—feminine<br>   Number—singular<br>   Stem or root—from πρόθεσις, εως<br>Concordance References:<br>  ⇒ Strong's #4286 prothesis +740 artos<br>  ⇒ NIV #4606 prothesis [consecrated] +788 artos [bread]<br>  ⇒ NASB #4286 prothesis +740 artos<br><br>**Luke 6:4**<br>How he went into the house of God, and did take and eat the **shewbread**, and gave also to them that were with him; which it is not lawful to eat but for the priests alone? [KJV]<br>How he entered the house of God, and took and ate the **consecrated bread** which is not lawful for any to eat except the priests alone, and gave it to his companions?" [NASB]<br>He entered the house of God, and taking the **consecrated bread**, he ate what is lawful only for priests to eat. And he also gave some to his companions." [NIV]<br>How he went into the house of God, took and ate the **showbread**, and also gave some to those with him, which is not lawful for any but the priests to eat?" [NKJV]<br>He went into the house of God, ate the **special bread** reserved for the priests alone, and then gave some to his friends. That was breaking the law, too." [NLT]<br>ὡς εἰσῆλθεν εἰς τὸν οἶκον τοῦ Θεοῦ, καὶ τοὺς **ἄρτους τῆς προθέσεως** ἔλαβε, καὶ ἔφαγε, καὶ ἔδωκε καὶ τοῖς μετ' αὐτοῦ, οὓς οὐκ ἔξεστι φαγεῖν εἰ μὴ μόνους τοὺς ἱερεῖς; [GNS]<br>[ὡς] εἰσῆλθεν εἰς τὸν οἶκον τοῦ θεοῦ καὶ τοὺς **ἄρτους τῆς προθέσεως** λαβὼν ἔφαγεν καὶ ἔδωκεν τοῖς μετ' αὐτοῦ, οὓς οὐκ ἔξεστιν φαγεῖν εἰ μὴ μόνους τοὺς ἱερεῖς; [GNT] | sented an offering from each tribe of Israel, an offering of thanksgiving to God. Each tribe was represented as thanking God for the bread and food He provided, for meeting their physical needs.<br>2. The twelve loaves also represented the people's dependence upon God. Note that the loaves sat in God's presence, before His very face. The people were to acknowledge their dependence upon God, acknowledge that they needed His provision. They needed His watchful eye upon the bread, upon them as His followers. They needed Him to continue to provide their bread and food, continue to look after and care for them. Their dependence upon God as the Provision of life was symbolized in the consecrated bread as well as their offering of thanksgiving.<br>3. The twelve loaves also acknowledged their trust of God. By setting the bread before God, they were declaring their belief and trust that He would continue to meet their physical needs.<br>4. The consecrated bread also pointed to Jesus Christ as the Bread of Life. Scripture declares that He is the Living Bread that came *out of* heaven to satisfy the hunger of a person's soul.<br>5. The consecrated bread pointed to God Himself as the nourishment that man really needs. Far too often, man tries to live his life apart from God's provision and presence.<br>6. The consecrated bread pointed to the great need of people for the bread of God's presence and worship. A constant diet of unhealthy things will cause a person to become sick and unhealthy.<br>7. The consecrated bread pointed to the bread that we all desperately need, the bread...<br>  • that satisfies the hunger of our hearts<br>  • that supplies our needs<br>  • that provides for us<br>  • that nourishes fellowship among us (cp. 1 Jn.1:3; Rev.3:20)<br>The consecrated bread pointed to the spiritual needs of man. This is seen in that the showbread sat in the Tabernacle itself, the very place where spiritual needs were met. This truth was dictated by both God and His Son, the Lord Jesus Christ. |
| **#724**<br>**Consecutive Order**<br><br>In order–KJV<br>**Consecutive order– NASB**<br>Orderly–NIV<br>Orderly–NKJV<br>Careful summary– NLT<br><br>**POSB REFERENCE**<br>(Lk.1:3)<br>Note 3, point 3 | καθεξῆς = *kathexēs*<br>Pronunciation: [kath-ex-ace']<br>Parsing (part of speech): adjective adverb<br>   Stem or root—from καθεξῆς<br>Concordance References:<br>  ⇒ Strong's #2517 kathexēs<br>  ⇒ NIV #2759 kathexēs<br>  ⇒ NASB #2517 kathexēs<br><br>**Luke 1:3**<br>It seemed good to me also, having had perfect understanding of all things from the very first, to write unto thee **in order**, most excellent Theophilus, [KJV]<br>It seemed fitting for me as well, having investigated everything carefully from the beginning, to write it out for you in **consecutive order**, most excellent Theophilus; [NASB]<br>Therefore, since I myself have carefully investigated | Orderly, in order, in consecutive order, in a careful summary, methodical, precise, correct.<br><br>**Practical Application**<br>Luke is the only writer in the New Testament to use this word (*kathexēs*). He uses it in the gospel only once and in Acts twice (Acts 11:4; Acts 18:23). The question is, what does Luke mean by orderly? Consecutive or chronological arrangement? Logical arrangement? Subject arrangement? Inspired or Spirit-led arrangement? The meaning is not clear. Perhaps he is saying that he is writing a full account of the life of Christ and that his account is a better arrangement; that is, it has more order and is better arranged than those in existence. |

# PRACTICAL WORD STUDIES
## in the NEW TESTAMENT

| ENGLISH WORD | GREEK WORD AND VERSE | THE WORD MEANS... |
|---|---|---|
| | everything from the beginning, it seemed good also to me to write an **orderly** account for you, most excellent Theophilus, [NIV]<br>It seemed good to me also, having had perfect understanding of all things from the very first, to write to you an **orderly** account, most excellent Theophilus, [NKJV]<br>Having carefully investigated all of these accounts from the beginning, I have decided to write a **careful summary** for you, [NLT]<br>ἔδοξε κἀμοὶ παρηκολουθηκότι ἄνωθεν πᾶσιν ἀκριβῶς, **καθεξῆς** σοι γράψαι, κράτιστε Θεόφιλε, [GNS]<br>ἔδοξε κἀμοὶ παρηκολουθηκότι ἄνωθεν πᾶσιν ἀκριβῶς **καθεξῆς** σοι γράψαι, κράτιστε Θεόφιλε, [GNT] | |
| **#725**<br>**Consent**<br><br>**Consent**–KJV<br>Agree–NASB<br>Agree–NIV<br>Agree–NKJV<br>Agree–NLT<br><br>**POSB REFERENCE**<br>(Rom.7:14-17; esp. v.16)<br>Note 2, point 2 | σύμφημι = *sumphēmi*<br>Pronunciation: [soom'-fay-mee]<br>Parsing (part of speech): verb<br>    Mood—indicative<br>    Tense—present<br>    Voice—active<br>    Person—1st person<br>    Number—singular<br>    Stem or root—from σύμφημι<br>Concordance References:<br>  ⇒ Strong's #4852 *sumphēmi*<br>  ⇒ NIV #5238 *sumphēmi*<br>  ⇒ NASB #4852 *sumphēmi*<br><br>**Romans 7:16**<br>If then I do that which I would not, I **consent** unto the law that *it is* good. [KJV]<br>But if I do the very thing I do not wish *to do*, I **agree** with the Law, *confessing* that it is good. [NASB]<br>And if I do what I do not want to do, I **agree** that the law is good. [NIV]<br>If, then, I do what I will not to do, I **agree** with the law that *it is* good. [NKJV]<br>I know perfectly well that what I am doing is wrong, and my bad conscience shows that I **agree** that the law is good. [NLT]<br>εἰ δὲ ὃ οὐ θέλω, τοῦτο ποιῶ, **σύμφημι** τῷ νόμῳ ὅτι καλός. [GNS]<br>εἰ δὲ ὃ οὐ θέλω τοῦτο ποιῶ, **σύμφημι** τῷ νόμῳ ὅτι καλός. [GNT] | To agree; to consent; to be in complete accord; to harmonize together like that of a symphony; to sound together; to act together in each other's nature.<br><br>**Practical Application**<br>The word "consent" (*sumphēmi*) means to agree, to say the same thing, to speak right along with the law, to prove and demonstrate that the law is right. The law proves and demonstrates that a man cannot live a perfectly righteous life. A carnal man proves the very same thing. He sins, finding himself doing exactly what the law says not to do and what he himself prefers not to do.<br>The point is this: when a carnal man sins, the law points out his sin. The law tells the carnal man the truth: he is a sinner doomed to die. Knowing this, the carnal man is able to seek the Lord and His forgiveness. Therefore, the carnal man agrees with the law; the law is very good, for it tells him that he must seek the Savior and His forgiveness. He may not actually follow through and seek the Lord, but the law has at least fulfilled its function and shown the carnal man what he needs to do. |
| **#726**<br>**Consent**<br><br>**Consent**–KJV<br>Agree with–NASB<br>Agree to–NIV<br>**Consent**–NKJV<br>Deny–NLT<br><br>**POSB REFERENCE**<br>(1 Tim.6:3)<br>Note 1, point 1 & 2 | προσέρχεται = *proserchetai*<br>Pronunciation: [pros-er'-kheh-tah-ee]<br>Parsing (part of speech): verb<br>    Mood—indicative<br>    Tense—present<br>    Voice—middle or passive deponent<br>    Person—3rd person<br>    Number—singular<br>    Stem or root—from προσέρχομαι<br>Concordance References:<br>  ⇒ Strong's #4334 *proserchomai*<br>  ⇒ NIV #4665 *proserchomai*<br>  ⇒ NASB #4334 *proserchomai*<br><br>**1 Tim. 6:3**<br>If any man teach otherwise, and **consent** not to wholesome words, even the words of our Lord Jesus Christ, and to the doctrine which is according to godliness; [KJV]<br>If anyone advocates a different doctrine, and does not **agree with** sound words, those of our Lord Jesus Christ, and with the doctrine conforming to godliness, [NASB]<br>If anyone teaches false doctrines and does not **agree to** the sound instruction of our Lord Jesus Christ and to godly teaching, [NIV]<br>If anyone teaches otherwise and does not **consent** to wholesome words, even the words of our Lord Jesus Christ, and to the doctrine which accords with godliness, [NKJV] | To agree to; to agree with; to consent.<br><br>**Practical Application**<br>The word "consent" (*proserchetai*) has the sense of "attaching oneself to" Christ (Daniel Guthrie. *The Pastoral Epistles.* "Tyndale New Testament Commentaries," p.110f).<br>1. The false teacher is just not willing to attach himself to the *Lord Jesus Christ*. He is...<br>  • not willing to confess that Jesus is the *Lord God* from heaven, the very Son of God Himself.<br>  • not willing to confess that Jesus is the Christ, the Messiah and Savior of the world.<br>2. The false teacher does not consent to the teachings of godliness. He is...<br>  • not willing to accept the righteousness of God revealed in Jesus Christ.<br>  • not willing to separate himself from the world nor to set his life wholly apart unto God.<br>One or both of these reasons are why the false teacher does not teach the wholesome words of Christ but rather chooses to teach a different doctrine and way of life. He has committed his |

# PRACTICAL WORD STUDIES
## in the NEW TESTAMENT

| ENGLISH WORD | GREEK WORD AND VERSE | THE WORD MEANS... |
|---|---|---|
| | Some false teachers may **deny** these things, but these are the sound, wholesome teachings of the Lord Jesus Christ, and they are the foundation for a godly life. [NLT]<br>Εἴ τις ἑτεροδιδασκαλεῖ, καὶ μὴ **προσέρχεται** ὑγιαίνουσι λόγοις, τοῖς τοῦ Κυρίου ἡμῶν Ἰησοῦ Χριστοῦ, καὶ τῇ κατ' εὐσέβειαν διδασκαλίᾳ, [GNS]<br>εἴ τις ἑτεροδιδασκαλεῖ καὶ μὴ **προσέρχεται** ὑγιαίνουσιν λόγοις τοῖς τοῦ κυρίου ἡμῶν Ἰησοῦ Χριστοῦ καὶ τῇ κατ' εὐσέβειαν διδασκαλίᾳ, [GNT] | life to the *profession* of the ministry...<br>• as a way to serve mankind.<br>• as a way to earn a livelihood.<br>But he is not committed to represent Christ and His Word. As a result, the person is called a false teacher by both the Holy Scriptures and Christ. |
| #727<br>**Consenting**<br><br>**Consenting–KJV**<br>Hearty agreement–NASB<br>Giving approval–NIV<br>**Consenting–NKJV**<br>Official witnesses–NLT<br><br>**POSB REFERENCE**<br>(Acts 8:1)<br>Note 1, point 1 | συνευδοκῶν = *suneudokōn*<br>Pronunciation: [soon-yoo-dok-own]<br>Parsing (part of speech): verb<br>    Mood—participle<br>    Tense—present<br>    Voice—active<br>    Case—nominative<br>    Gender—masculine<br>    Number—singular<br>    Stem or root—from συνευδοκέω<br>Concordance References:<br>  ⇒ Strong's #4909 suneudokeō<br>  ⇒ NIV #5306 suneudokeō<br>  ⇒ NASB #4909 suneudokeō<br><br>**Acts 8:1**<br>And Saul was **consenting** unto his death. And at that time there was a great persecution against the church which was at Jerusalem; and they were all scattered abroad throughout the regions of Judaea and Samaria, except the apostles. [KJV]<br>And Saul was in **hearty agreement** with putting him to death. And on that day a great persecution arose against the church in Jerusalem; and they were all scattered throughout the regions of Judea and Samaria, except the apostles. [NASB]<br>And Saul was there, **giving approval** to his death. On that day a great persecution broke out against the church at Jerusalem, and all except the apostles were scattered throughout Judea and Samaria. [NIV]<br>Now Saul was **consenting** to his death. At that time a great persecution arose against the church which was at Jerusalem; and they were all scattered throughout the regions of Judea and Samaria, except the apostles. [NKJV]<br>Saul was one of the **official witnesses** at the killing of Stephen. A great wave of persecution began that day, sweeping over the church in Jerusalem, and all the believers except the apostles fled into Judea and Samaria. [NLT]<br>Σαῦλος δὲ ἦν **συνευδοκῶν** τῇ ἀναιρέσει αὐτοῦ. Ἐγένετο δὲ ἐν ἐκείνῃ τῇ ἡμέρᾳ διωγμὸς μέγας ἐπὶ τὴν ἐκκλησίαν τὴν ἐν Ἱεροσολύμοις· πάντες τε διεσπάρησαν κατὰ τὰς χώρας τῆς Ἰουδαίας καὶ Σαμαρείας, πλὴν τῶν ἀποστόλων. [GNS]<br>Σαῦλος δὲ ἦν **συνευδοκῶν** τῇ ἀναιρέσει αὐτοῦ. Ἐγένετο δὲ ἐν ἐκείνῃ τῇ ἡμέρᾳ διωγμὸς μέγας ἐπὶ τὴν ἐκκλησίαν τὴν ἐν Ἱεροσολύμοις, πάντες δὲ διεσπάρησαν κατὰ τὰς χώρας τῆς Ἰουδαίας καὶ Σαμαρείας πλὴν τῶν ἀποστόλων. [GNT] | Giving approval; consenting; hearty agreement; to be willing; to agree with. The word means to give full consent of the will; to willingly approve; to approve with pleasure; to delight in; to applaud what is being done.<br><br>**Practical Application**<br>Saul was well-pleased with Stephen's death. An *inflamed fury* had been building up in him against the church, for he felt that the preaching of Christ threatened his religion, Judaism. In fact, Saul was the leader in persecuting the church, the one who *boiled* more than anyone else against the church. He was apparently a leader among the religionists. |
| #728<br>**Consider**<br><br>Reckon–KJV<br>**Consider–NASB**<br>Count–NIV<br>Reckon–NKJV<br>**Consider–NLT** | λογίζεσθε = *logizesthe*<br>Pronunciation: [log-id'-zehs-theh]<br>Parsing (part of speech): verb<br>    Mood—imperative<br>    Tense—present<br>    Voice—middle or passive deponent<br>    Person—2nd person<br>    Number—plural<br>    Stem or root—from λογίζομαι<br>Concordance References:<br>  ⇒ Strong's #3049 logizomai | To count; to consider; to reckon; to credit; to set to one's account; to lay to one's charge; to impute; to judge; to treat; to compute. It is an accounting word; it implies something put to a man's credit. It is used many times throughout Romans, about eleven times in Romans 4 alone. It is an extremely important idea in Scripture.<br><br>**Practical Application**<br>The believer's first step in conquering sin is |

## PRACTICAL WORD STUDIES
### in the NEW TESTAMENT

| ENGLISH WORD | GREEK WORD AND VERSE | THE WORD MEANS... |
|---|---|---|
| **POSB REFERENCE** (Rom.6:11) *Deeper Study* #1 | ⇒ NIV #3357 logizomai<br>⇒ NASB #3049 logizomai<br><br>**Romans 6:11**<br>Likewise **reckon** ye also yourselves to be dead indeed unto sin, but alive unto God through Jesus Christ our Lord. [KJV]<br>Even so **consider** yourselves to be dead to sin, but alive to God in Christ Jesus. [NASB]<br>In the same way, **count** yourselves dead to sin but alive to God in Christ Jesus. [NIV]<br>Likewise you also, **reckon** yourselves to be dead indeed to sin, but alive to God in Christ Jesus our Lord. [NKJV]<br>So you should **consider** yourselves dead to sin and able to live for the glory of God through Christ Jesus. [NLT]<br>οὕτω καὶ ὑμεῖς **λογίζεσθε** ἑαυτοὺς νεκροὺς μὲν εἶναι τῇ ἁμαρτίᾳ, ζῶντας δὲ τῷ Θεῷ ἐν Χριστῷ Ἰησοῦ τῷ Κυρίῳ ἡμῶν. [GNS]<br>οὕτως καὶ ὑμεῖς **λογίζεσθε** ἑαυτοὺς [εἶναι] νεκροὺς μὲν τῇ ἁμαρτίᾳ ζῶντας δὲ τῷ θεῷ ἐν Χριστῷ Ἰησοῦ. [GNT] | to consider himself dead to sin, but alive to God. The believer must *know and live out* his position, the glorious life God has given him in the death and resurrection of Jesus Christ our Lord. The believer who keeps his mind and thoughts upon *his position* in Christ's death and resurrection will conquer sin—every time. |
| **#729**<br>**Consider**<br><br>Behold–KJV<br>Take note–NASB<br>**Consider–NIV**<br>Look on–NKJV<br>Hear–NLT<br><br>**POSB REFERENCE** (Acts 4:29-30; esp. v.29) Note 4, point 1b | ἔπιδε ἐπί = *epide epi*<br>Pronunciation: [ep-i'-deh hep-ee]<br>Parsing *epide* (part of speech): verb<br>    Mood—imperative<br>    Tense—aorist<br>    Voice—active<br>    Person—2nd person<br>    Number—singular<br>    Stem or root—from ἐπεῖδον<br>Parsing *epi* (part of speech): preposition<br>    Case—accusative<br>    Stem or root—from ἐπι<br>Concordance References:<br>  ⇒ Strong's #1896 + 1909 epeidon epi<br>  ⇒ NIV #2078 + 2093 epeidon epi<br>  ⇒ NASB #1896 + 1909 epeidon epi<br><br>**Acts 4:29**<br>And now, Lord, **behold** their threatenings: and grant unto thy servants, that with all boldness they may speak thy word, [KJV]<br>"And now, Lord, **take note** of their threats, and grant that Thy bond-servants may speak Thy word with all confidence, [NASB]<br>Now, Lord, **consider** their threats and enable your servants to speak your word with great boldness. [NIV]<br>Now, Lord, **look on** their threats, and grant to Your servants that with all boldness they may speak Your word, [NKJV]<br>And now, O Lord, **hear** their threats, and give your servants great boldness in their preaching. [NLT]<br>καὶ τὰ νῦν, Κύριε, **ἔπιδε ἐπὶ** τὰς ἀπειλὰς αὐτῶν, καὶ δὸς τοῖς δούλοις σου μετὰ παρρησίας πάσης λαλεῖν τὸν λόγον σου, [GNS]<br>καὶ τὰ νῦν, κύριε, **ἔπιδε ἐπὶ** τὰς ἀπειλὰς αὐτῶν καὶ δὸς τοῖς δούλοις σου μετὰ παρρησίας πάσης λαλεῖν τὸν λόγον σου, [GNT] | To consider; to behold; to take note; to hear; to look upon.<br><br>**Practical Application**<br>The church was asking God to concentrate and focus upon the persecution; to deal with it and to overrule the enemy; to give whatever was necessary to endure through it all. |
| **#730**<br>**Consider**<br><br>**Consider–KJV**<br>**Consider–NASB**<br>Fix...thoughts on–NIV<br>**Consider–NKJV**<br>Think about–NLT | κατανοήσατε = *katanoësate*<br>Pronunciation: [kat-an-o-ay-sah'-teh]<br>Parsing (part of speech): verb<br>    Mood—imperative<br>    Tense—aorist<br>    Voice—active<br>    Person—2nd person<br>    Number—plural<br>    Stem or root—from κατανοέω<br>Concordance References:<br>  ⇒ Strong's #2657 katanoeö | To fix thoughts on; to consider; to think about; to observe; to look upon; to see; to fix one's thoughts and mind, attention and eyes upon Jesus Christ.<br><br>**Practical Application**<br>It means to concentrate; to seek to grasp; to focus and to be attentive in order to learn about Jesus Christ. Note: this exhortation is written to believers. |

# PRACTICAL WORD STUDIES
## in the NEW TESTAMENT

| ENGLISH WORD | GREEK WORD AND VERSE | THE WORD MEANS... |
|---|---|---|
| **POSB REFERENCE** (Heb.3:1) Note 1 | ⇒ NIV #2917 katanoeö<br>⇒ NASB #2657 katanoeö<br><br>**Hebrews 3:1**<br>Wherefore, holy brethren, partakers of the heavenly calling, **consider** the Apostle and High Priest of our profession, Christ Jesus; [KJV]<br>Therefore, holy brethren, partakers of a heavenly calling, **consider** Jesus, the Apostle and High Priest of our confession. [NASB]<br>Therefore, holy brothers, who share in the heavenly calling, **fix** your **thoughts on** Jesus, the apostle and high priest whom we confess. [NIV]<br>Therefore, holy brethren, partakers of the heavenly calling, **consider** the Apostle and High Priest of our confession, Christ Jesus, [NKJV]<br>And so, dear brothers and sisters who belong to God and are bound for heaven, **think about** this Jesus whom we declare to be God's Messenger and High Priest. [NLT]<br>Ὅθεν, ἀδελφοὶ ἅγιοι, κλήσεως ἐπουρανίου μέτοχοι, **κατανοήσατε** τὸν ἀπόστολον καὶ ἀρχιερέα τῆς ὁμολογίας ἡμῶν Χριστὸν Ἰησοῦν, [GNS]<br>Ὅθεν, ἀδελφοὶ ἅγιοι, κλήσεως ἐπουρανίου μέτοχοι, **κατανοήσατε** τὸν ἀπόστολον καὶ ἀρχιερέα τῆς ὁμολογίας ἡμῶν Ἰησοῦν, [GNT] | |
| **#731**<br>**Consider**<br><br>Consider–KJV<br>Consider–NASB<br>Consider–NIV<br>Consider–NKJV<br>Think of ways–NLT<br><br>**POSB REFERENCE** (Heb.10:24) Note 3 | κατανοῶμεν = katanoömen<br>Pronunciation: [kat-an-o-ow'-mehn]<br>Parsing (part of speech): verb<br>    Mood—subjunctive<br>    Tense—present<br>    Voice—active<br>    Person—1st person<br>    Number—plural<br>    Stem or root—from κατανοέω<br>Concordance References:<br>⇒ Strong's #2657 katanoeö<br>⇒ NIV #2917 katanoeö<br>⇒ NASB #2657 katanoeö<br><br>**Hebrews 10:24**<br>And let us **consider** one another to provoke unto love and to good works: [KJV]<br>And let us **consider** how to stimulate one another to love and good deeds, [NASB]<br>And let us **consider** how we may spur one another on toward love and good deeds. [NIV]<br>And let us **consider** one another in order to stir up love and good works, [NKJV]<br>**Think of ways** to encourage one another to outbursts of love and good deeds. [NLT]<br>καὶ **κατανοῶμεν** ἀλλήλους εἰς παροξυσμὸν ἀγάπης καὶ καλῶν ἔργων, [GNS]<br>καὶ **κατανοῶμεν** ἀλλήλους εἰς παροξυσμὸν ἀγάπης καὶ καλῶν ἔργων, [GNT] | To consider; to think of ways; to notice; to observe; to look upon; to be aware of. It means to give attention to; to fix our attention upon; to give continuous care; to watch over.<br><br>**Practical Application**<br>What an exhortation to believers!<br>⇒ Give attention to one another.<br>⇒ Fix your attention upon one another.<br>⇒ Give continuous care to one another.<br>⇒ Watch over one another.<br>How different the church would be—how much stronger we would be in Christ and in life—if we heeded this exhortation! And note what it is that we are to give attention to: to make sure that we are stirred up and living for Christ—that we are loving one another and doing good works. This simply means...<br>• that we are considerate of one another.<br>• that we show concern for one another.<br>• that we meet one another's needs.<br>• that we strengthen one another's weaknesses.<br>• that we help one another through every trial and temptation.<br>It means that we love—love in act and not in word—that we...<br>• feed the poor<br>• visit the sick and shut-ins<br>• look after the orphans and the children of broken homes and single parents<br>• become a friend to the lonely<br>• give direction to the empty and those without purpose.<br>Note the exhortation again: we give attention to one another. Why? To make sure none of us are slacking up—to stir one another to love and to do good works. This is the duty of the new, living faith Jesus Christ has wrought for us. It is not a dead faith. It is a faith that stirs us to action—that stirs us to live, truly live, live in love and good works—for the sake of a needful and sick world. |

# PRACTICAL WORD STUDIES
## in the NEW TESTAMENT

| ENGLISH WORD | GREEK WORD AND VERSE | THE WORD MEANS... |
|---|---|---|
| **#732**<br>**Consider**<br><br>**Consider**–KJV<br>**Consider**–NASB<br>**Consider**–NIV<br>**Consider**–NKJV<br>Think about–NLT<br><br>**POSB REFERENCE**<br>(Heb.12:3)<br>Note 4 | ἀναλογίσασθε = analogisasthe<br>Pronunciation: [an-al-og-i'-sahs-theh]<br>Parsing (part of speech): verb<br>    Mood—imperative<br>    Tense—aorist<br>    Voice—middle deponent<br>    Person—2nd person<br>    Number—plural<br>    Stem or root—from ἀναλογίζομαι<br>Concordance References:<br>  ⇒ Strong's #357 analogizomai<br>  ⇒ NIV #382 analogizomai<br>  ⇒ NASB #357 analogizomai<br><br>**Hebrews 12:3**<br>For **consider** him that endured such contradiction of sinners against himself, lest ye be wearied and faint in your minds. [KJV]<br>For **consider** Him who has endured such hostility by sinners against Himself, so that you may not grow weary and lose heart. [NASB]<br>**Consider** him who endured such opposition from sinful men, so that you will not grow weary and lose heart. [NIV]<br>For **consider** Him who endured such hostility from sinners against Himself, lest you become weary and discouraged in your souls. [NKJV]<br>**Think about** all he endured when sinful people did such terrible things to him, so that you don't become weary and give up. [NLT]<br>ἀναλογίσασθε γὰρ τὸν τοιαύτην ὑπομεμενηκότα ὑπὸ τῶν ἁμαρτωλῶν εἰς αὑτὸν ἀντιλογίαν, ἵνα μὴ κάμητε, ταῖς ψυχαῖς ὑμῶν ἐκλυόμενοι. [GNS]<br>ἀναλογίσασθε γὰρ τὸν τοιαύτην ὑπομεμενηκότα ὑπὸ τῶν ἁμαρτωλῶν εἰς ἑαυτὸν ἀντιλογίαν, ἵνα μὴ κάμητε ταῖς ψυχαῖς ὑμῶν ἐκλυόμενοι. [GNT] | To consider; to think about. It means to compare, reckon, count up, weigh.<br><br>**Practical Application**<br>Believers are to focus upon Jesus Christ and His sufferings and compare and weigh them against their sufferings. Christ endured so much more than we have to endure. Let any orphan, widow, criminal, prostitute, slave, or sufferer—any person whatsoever—compare himself with all this, and remember Jesus bore *all this*:<br>⇒ being born to an unwed mother (Matthew 1:18-19).<br>⇒ being born in a stable, the worst of conditions (Luke 2:7).<br>⇒ being born to poor parents (Luke 2:24).<br>⇒ having his life threatened as a baby (Matthew 2:13f).<br>⇒ being the cause of unimaginable sorrow (Matthew 2:16f).<br>⇒ having to be moved and shifted as a baby (Matthew 2:13f).<br>⇒ being reared in a despicable place, Nazareth (Luke 2:39).<br>⇒ having his father die during His youth (see POSB note, pt. 3—Matthew 13:53-58).<br>⇒ having to support His mother and brothers and sisters (see POSB note, pt. 3—Matthew 13:53-58).<br>⇒ having no home, not even a place to lay His head (Matthew 8:20; Luke 9:58).<br>⇒ being hated and opposed by religionists (Mark 14:1-2).<br>⇒ being charged with insanity (Mark 3:21).<br>⇒ being charged with demon possession (Mark 3:22).<br>⇒ being opposed by His own family (Mark 3:31-32).<br>⇒ being rejected, hated, and opposed by audiences to whom He spoke (Matthew 13:53-58; Luke 4:28-29).<br>⇒ being betrayed by a close friend (Mark 14:10-11, 18).<br>⇒ being left alone, rejected, and forsaken by all His friends (Mark 14:50).<br>⇒ being tried before the high court of the land on the charge of treason (John 18:33).<br>⇒ being executed by crucifixion, the worst possible death (John 19:16f). |
| **#733**<br>**Consider–Considered**<br><br>**Considered**–KJV<br>Contemplated–NASB<br>Faced the fact–NIV<br>**Consider**–NKJV<br>Knew–NLT<br><br>**POSB REFERENCE**<br>(Romans 4:18-22; esp. v.19)<br>Note 2, point 1a | κατενόησεν = katenoësen<br>Pronunciation: [kat-ehn-o-ay'-sehn]<br>Parsing (part of speech): verb<br>    Mood—indicative<br>    Tense—aorist<br>    Voice—active<br>    Person—3rd person<br>    Number—singular<br>    Stem or root—from κατανοέω<br>Concordance References:<br>  ⇒ Strong's #2657 katanoeō<br>  ⇒ NIV #2917 katanoeō<br>  ⇒ NASB #2657 katanoeō<br><br>**Romans 4:19**<br>And being not weak in faith, he **considered** not his own body now dead, when he was about an hundred years old, neither yet the deadness of Sarah's womb: [KJV] | To consider; to face the facts; to think upon; to contemplate; to observe; to look upon; to see through the facts; to be aware of; to pay attention to; to fix one's thoughts upon.<br><br>**Practical Application**<br>Abraham was not weak in faith despite thinking about his own physical inability. His body was "now dead"; he and Sarah were about one hundred years old. The word "dead" is a perfect participle in the Greek which means that his reproductive organs had stopped functioning and were dead forever and could never again function. Abraham could never have a son; it was not humanly possible. He and Sarah were almost one hundred years old, now sexually "dead." |

## PRACTICAL WORD STUDIES
### in the NEW TESTAMENT

| ENGLISH WORD | GREEK WORD AND VERSE | THE WORD MEANS... |
|---|---|---|
| | And without becoming weak in faith he **contemplated** his own body, now as good as dead since he was about a hundred years old, and the deadness of Sarah's womb; [NASB]<br>Without weakening in his faith, he **faced the fact** that his body was as good as dead—since he was about a hundred years old—and that Sarah's womb was also dead. [NIV]<br>And not being weak in faith, he did not **consider** his own body, already dead (since he was about a hundred years old), and the deadness of Sarah's womb. [NKJV]<br>And Abraham's faith did not weaken, even though he **knew** that he was too old to be a father at the age of one hundred and that Sarah, his wife, had never been able to have children. [NLT]<br>καὶ μὴ ἀσθενήσας τῇ πίστει, οὐ **κατενόησε** τὸ ἑαυτοῦ σῶμα ἤδη νενεκρωμένον -- ἑκατονταετής που ὑπάρχων --, καὶ τὴν νέκρωσιν τῆς μήτρας Σάρρας, [GNS]<br>καὶ μὴ ἀσθενήσας τῇ πίστει **κατενόησεν** τὸ ἑαυτοῦ σῶμα [ἤδη] νενεκρωμένον, ἑκατονταετής που ὑπάρχων, καὶ τὴν νέκρωσιν τῆς μήτρας Σάρρας· [GNT] | Abraham thought about the matter. The word "considered" (*katenoësen*) means He fixed his thoughts, his mind, his attention upon the matter. But he did not give in to the thoughts. He was not weak in faith. |
| **#734**<br>**Consider Nothing Sacred**<br><br>Unholy–KJV<br>Unholy–NASB<br>Unholy–NIV<br>Unholy–NKJV<br>**Consider nothing sacred–NLT**<br><br>**POSB REFERENCE**<br>(2 Tim. 3:2-4; esp. v.2)<br>Note 2, point 8 | ἀνόσιοι = *anosioi*<br>Pronunciation: [an-os'-ee-oy]<br>Parsing (part of speech): adjective<br>  Case—nominative<br>  Gender—masculine<br>  Number—plural<br>  Stem or root—from ἀνόσιος, ον<br>Concordance References:<br>⇒ Strong's #462 anosios<br>⇒ NIV #495 anosios<br>⇒ NASB #462 anosios<br><br>**2 Tim. 3:2**<br>For men shall be lovers of their own selves, covetous, boasters, proud, blasphemers, disobedient to parents, unthankful, **unholy**, [KJV]<br>For men will be lovers of self, lovers of money, boastful, arrogant, revilers, disobedient to parents, ungrateful, **unholy**, [NASB]<br>People will be lovers of themselves, lovers of money, boastful, proud, abusive, disobedient to their parents, ungrateful, **unholy**, [NIV]<br>For men will be lovers of themselves, lovers of money, boasters, proud, blasphemers, disobedient to parents, unthankful, **unholy**, [NKJV]<br>For people will love only themselves and their money. They will be boastful and proud, scoffing at God, disobedient to their parents, and ungrateful. They will **consider nothing sacred**. [NLT]<br>ἔσονται γὰρ οἱ ἄνθρωποι φίλαυτοι, φιλάργυροι, ἀλαζόνες, ὑπερήφανοι, βλάσφημοι, γονεῦσιν ἀπειθεῖς, ἀχάριστοι, **ἀνόσιοι**, [GNS]<br>ἔσονται γὰρ οἱ ἄνθρωποι φίλαυτοι φιλάργυροι ἀλαζόνες ὑπερήφανοι βλάσφημοι γονεῦσιν ἀπειθεῖς, ἀχάριστοι **ἀνόσιοι** [GNT] | Profane, indecent, shameless, given over to the most base passions, being blind to modesty, decency, purity, and righteousness.<br><br>**Practical Application**<br>People will "consider nothing sacred" (*anosioi*). The unholy person...<br>• is mastered by passion.<br>• seeks constant gratification of the flesh.<br>• senses little shame.<br>• is blind to decency.<br>• seeks his pleasure in the abnormal. (Just think of the abnormal sex that is flaunted today.) |
| **#735**<br>**Considerate**<br><br>Gentle–KJV<br>Gentle–NASB<br>**Considerate–NIV**<br>Gentle–NKJV<br>Gentle at all times– NLT<br><br>**POSB REFERENCE**<br>(Jas 3:17-18; esp. v.17)<br>Note 3, point 2c | ἐπιεικής = *epieikës*<br>Pronunciation: [ep-ee-i-kace']<br>Parsing (part of speech): adjective<br>  Case—nominative<br>  Gender—feminine<br>  Number—singular<br>  Stem or root—from ἐπιεικής, ές<br>Concordance References:<br>⇒ Strong's #1933 epieikës<br>⇒ NIV #2117 epieikës<br>⇒ NASB #1933 epieikës<br><br>**James 3:17**<br>But the wisdom that is from above is first pure, then peaceable, **gentle**, and easy to be intreated, full of mercy | To be considerate; to be gentle; to be gentle at all times.<br><br>**Practical Application**<br>True wisdom is "considerate" (*epieikës*). The word is difficult to translate into English. It is translated by others as gentleness, forbearance, reasonableness, consideration, agreeableness, courtesy, patience, and softness. There is the tendency to say that either forbearance or gentleness is the better translation. It means that there is *something better than mere justice*—a gracious gentleness. The wise teacher is to be gen- |

# PRACTICAL WORD STUDIES
## in the NEW TESTAMENT

| ENGLISH WORD | GREEK WORD AND VERSE | THE WORD MEANS... |
|---|---|---|
| See also POSB REF: (Tit.3:2) Note 5 (Philip.4:5) Note 4 | and good fruits, without partiality, and without hypocrisy. [KJV]<br>But the wisdom from above is first pure, then peaceable, **gentle**, reasonable, full of mercy and good fruits, unwavering, without hypocrisy. [NASB]<br>But the wisdom that comes from heaven is first of all pure; then peace-loving, **considerate**, submissive, full of mercy and good fruit, impartial and sincere. [NIV]<br>But the wisdom that is from above is first pure, then peaceable, **gentle**, willing to yield, full of mercy and good fruits, without partiality and without hypocrisy. [NKJV]<br>But the wisdom that comes from heaven is first of all pure. It is also peace loving, **gentle at all times**, and willing to yield to others. It is full of mercy and good deeds. It shows no partiality and is always sincere. [NLT]<br>ἡ δὲ ἄνωθεν σοφία πρῶτον μὲν ἁγνή ἐστιν, ἔπειτα εἰρηνική, **ἐπιεικής**, εὐπειθής, μεστὴ ἐλέους καὶ καρπῶν ἀγαθῶν, ἀδιάκριτος καὶ ἀνυπόκριτος. [GNS]<br>ἡ δὲ ἄνωθεν σοφία πρῶτον μὲν ἁγνή ἐστιν, ἔπειτα εἰρηνική, **ἐπιεικής**, εὐπειθής, μεστὴ ἐλέους καὶ καρπῶν ἀγαθῶν, ἀδιάκριτος, ἀνυπόκριτος. [GNT] | tle and forbearing in dealing with other people. |
| #736<br>**Consideration**<br><br>Meekness–KJV<br>**Consideration–NASB**<br>Humility–NIV<br>Humility–NKJV<br>Humility–NLT<br><br>**POSB REFERENCE**<br>(Tit.3:2) Note 6 | πραΰτητα = prautēta<br>Pronunciation: [prah-oo-tay'-tah]<br>Parsing (part of speech): noun<br>    Case—accusative<br>    Gender—feminine<br>    Number—singular<br>    Stem or root—from πραΰτης, ητος<br>Concordance References:<br>⇒ Strong's #4240 prautēs<br>⇒ NIV #4559 prautēs<br>⇒ NASnB #4240 prautēs<br><br>**Titus 3:2**<br>To speak evil of no man, to be no brawlers, but gentle, shewing all **meekness** unto all men. [KJV]<br>To malign no one, to be uncontentious, gentle, showing every **consideration** for all men. [NASB]<br>To slander no one, to be peaceable and considerate, and to show true **humility** toward all men. [NIV]<br>To speak evil of no one, to be peaceable, gentle, showing all **humility** to all men. [NKJV]<br>They must not speak evil of anyone, and they must avoid quarreling. Instead, they should be gentle and show true **humility** to everyone. [NLT]<br>μηδένα βλασφημεῖν, ἀμάχους εἶναι, ἐπιεικεῖς, πᾶσαν ἐνδεικνυμένους **πραότητα** πρὸς πάντας ἀνθρώπους. [GNS]<br>μηδένα βλασφημεῖν, ἀμάχους εἶναι, ἐπιεικεῖς, πᾶσαν ἐνδεικνυμένους **πραΰτητα** πρὸς πάντας ἀνθρώπους. [GNT] | Humility, meekness, consideration, gentleness. The word means to be gentle, tender, humble, mild, considerate, but strongly so.<br><br>**Practical Application**<br>The Christian citizen must show "consideration" (prautēta) to all citizens. Consideration has the strength to control and discipline, and it does so at the right time.<br>1. Humility has *a humble state of mind*. But this does not mean the person is weak, cowardly, and bowing. The humble person simply loves people and loves peace; therefore, he walks humbly among men regardless of their status and circumstance in life. Associating with the poor and lowly of this earth does not bother the humble person. He desires to be a friend to all and to help all as much as possible.<br>2. Humility has *a strong state of mind*. It looks at situations and wants justice and right to be done. It is not a weak mind that ignores and neglects evil and wrong-doing, abuse and suffering.<br>⇒ If someone is suffering, humility steps in to do what it can to help.<br>⇒ If evil is being done, humility does what it can to stop and correct it.<br>⇒ If evil is running rampant and indulging itself, humility actually strikes out in anger. However, note a crucial point: the anger is always at the right time and against the right thing.<br>3. Humility has *strong self-control*. The meek person controls his spirit and mind. He controls the lusts of his flesh. He does not give way to ill-temper, retaliation, passion, indulgence, or license. The humble person dies to himself, to what his flesh would like to do, and he does the right thing—exactly what God wants done.<br>In summary, the humble man walks in a humble, tender, but strong state of mind; denies himself, giving utmost consideration to others. He shows a control and righteous anger against injustice and evil. A humble man forgets self and lives for others because of what Christ has done for him. |

# PRACTICAL WORD STUDIES
## in the NEW TESTAMENT

| ENGLISH WORD | GREEK WORD AND VERSE | THE WORD MEANS... |
|---|---|---|
| **#737**<br>**Considered Worthy**<br><br>Counted worthy–KJV<br>**Considered worthy–NASB**<br>Counted worthy–NIV<br>Counted worthy–NKJV<br>Make...worthy–NLT<br><br>**POSB REFERENCE**<br>(2 Thes.1:4-5; esp. v.5)<br>Note 3 | καταξιωθῆναι = kataxiōthēnai<br>Pronunciation: [kat-ax-ee-o'-thay-nah-ee]<br>Parsing (part of speech): verb<br>    Mood—infinitive<br>    Tense—aorist<br>    Voice—passive<br>    Case—accusative<br>    Stem or root—from καταξιόω<br>Concordance References:<br> ⇒ Strong's #2661 kataxioō<br> ⇒ NIV #2921 kataxioō<br> ⇒ NASB #2661 kataxioō<br><br>**2 Thes. 1:5**<br>Which is a manifest token of the righteous judgment of God, that ye may be **counted worthy** of the kingdom of God, for which ye also suffer: [KJV]<br>This is a plain indication of God's righteous judgment so that you may be **considered worthy** of the kingdom of God, for which indeed you are suffering. [NASB]<br>All this is evidence that God's judgment is right, and as a result you will be **counted worthy** of the kingdom of God, for which you are suffering. [NIV]<br>Which is manifest evidence of the righteous judgment of God, that you may be **counted worthy** of the kingdom of God, for which you also suffer; [NKJV]<br>But God will use this persecution to show his justice. For he will **make** you **worthy** of his Kingdom, for which you are suffering, [NLT]<br>ἔνδειγμα τῆς δικαίας κρίσεως τοῦ Θεοῦ, εἰς τὸ **καταξιωθῆναι** ὑμᾶς τῆς βασιλείας τοῦ Θεοῦ, ὑπὲρ ἧς καὶ πάσχετε· [GNS]<br>ἔνδειγμα τῆς δικαίας κρίσεως τοῦ θεοῦ, εἰς τὸ **καταξιωθῆναι** ὑμᾶς τῆς βασιλείας τοῦ θεοῦ ὑπὲρ ἧς καὶ πάσχετε, [GNT] | Counted worthy, considered worthy, deserving and commendable.<br><br>**Practical Application**<br>It does not mean to make worthy; it means to consider, count, reckon, and declare worthy (see POSB note, Justification—Romans 5:1). A believer is not saved because he remains faithful through the sufferings of this life; he is saved because he believes in Jesus Christ as his Savior and Lord. However, when he suffers in this world and endures through the suffering, he is counted worthy of God's kingdom. He does not disappoint God. He proves his grit—that he is truly a man or a woman of God. He is worthy to enter heaven, for he has proven his faith. |
| **#738**<br>**Considering**<br><br>**Considering–KJV**<br>Looking–NASB<br>Watch–NIV<br>**Considering–NKJV**<br>Be careful–NLT<br><br>**POSB REFERENCE**<br>(Gal.6:1)<br>Note 3 | σκοπῶν = skopōn<br>Pronunciation: [skop-own]<br>Parsing (part of speech): verb<br>    Mood—participle (imperative sense)<br>    Tense—present<br>    Voice—active<br>    Case—nominative<br>    Gender—masculine<br>    Person—2nd person<br>    Number—singular<br>    Stem or root—from σκοπέω<br>Concordance References:<br> ⇒ Strong's #4648 skopeō<br> ⇒ NIV #5023 skopeō<br> ⇒ NASB #4648 skopeō<br><br>**Galatians 6:1**<br>Brethren, if a man be overtaken in a fault, ye which are spiritual, restore such an one in the spirit of meekness; **considering** thyself, lest thou also be tempted. [KJV]<br>Brethren, even if a man is caught in any trespass, you who are spiritual, restore such a one in a spirit of gentleness; each one **looking** to yourself, lest you too be tempted. [NASB]<br>Brothers, if someone is caught in a sin, you who are spiritual should restore him gently. But **watch** yourself, or you also may be tempted. [NIV]<br>Brethren, if a man is overtaken in any trespass, you who *are* spiritual restore such a one in a spirit of gentleness, **considering** yourself lest you also be tempted. [NKJV]<br>Dear brothers and sisters, if another Christian is overcome by some sin, you who are godly should gently and humbly help that person back onto the right path. And **be careful** not to fall into the same temptation yourself. [NLT] | To watch; to carefully consider; to look to oneself; to keep one's attention on; to fix eyes on; to take note of; to think about oneself and to give attention to oneself. It means to keep an attentive eye on oneself.<br><br>**Practical Application**<br>If we really watch and consider the matter, then we will reach out in love and gentleness to help our fallen brothers. We have to help them, for we are all ever so subject to being caught in a sin. |

# PRACTICAL WORD STUDIES
## in the NEW TESTAMENT

| ENGLISH WORD | GREEK WORD AND VERSE | THE WORD MEANS... |
|---|---|---|
| | Ἀδελφοί, ἐὰν καὶ προληφθῇ ἄνθρωπος ἔν τινι παραπτώματι, ὑμεῖς οἱ πνευματικοὶ καταρτίζετε τὸν τοιοῦτον ἐν πνεύματι πραότητος, **σκοπῶν** σεαυτόν, μὴ καὶ σὺ πειρασθῇς. [GNS]<br>Ἀδελφοί, ἐὰν καὶ προλημφθῇ ἄνθρωπος ἔν τινι παραπτώματι, ὑμεῖς οἱ πνευματικοὶ καταρτίζετε τὸν τοιοῦτον ἐν πνεύματι πραΰτητος, **σκοπῶν** σεαυτόν μὴ καὶ σὺ πειρασθῇς. [GNT] | |
| **#739**<br>**Consolation**<br><br>**Consolation**–KJV<br>Comfort–NASB<br>Comfort–NIV<br>**Consolation**–NKJV<br>Happiness–NLT<br><br>**POSB REFERENCE**<br>(Lk.6:24-26; esp. v.24)<br>Note 2, point 1d<br><br>See also POSB REF:<br>(Acts 15:30-35; esp. v.31)<br>Note 5, point 1 | παράκλησιν = *paraklēsin*<br>Pronunciation: [par-ak'-lay-sin]<br>Parsing (part of speech): noun<br>  Case—accusative<br>  Gender—feminine<br>  Number—singular<br>  Stem or root—from παράκλησις, εως<br>Concordance References:<br>⇒ Strong's #3874 paraklesis<br>⇒ NIV #4155 paraklēsis<br>⇒ NASB #3874 paraklesis<br><br>**Luke 6:24**<br>But woe unto you that are rich! for ye have received your **consolation**. [KJV]<br>"But woe to you who are rich, for you are receiving your **comfort** in full. [NASB]<br>"But woe to you who are rich, for you have already received your **comfort**. [NIV]<br>But woe to you who are rich,or you have received your **consolation**. [NKJV]<br>"What sorrows await you who are rich, for you have your only **happiness** now. [NLT]<br>πλὴν οὐαὶ ὑμῖν τοῖς πλουσίοις, ὅτι ἀπέχετε τὴν **παράκλησιν** ὑμῶν. [GNS]<br>Πλὴν οὐαὶ ὑμῖν τοῖς πλουσίοις, ὅτι ἀπέχετε τὴν **παράκλησιν** ὑμῶν. [GNT] | Comfort, help, aid, happiness, consolation, encouragement.<br><br>**Practical Application**<br>Their (the rich) only "consolation" is to be on this earth—the wealth they have. There will be no comfort after this life—no help, no aid, no encouragement, no cheer. They are paid in full. |
| **#740**<br>**Consolation**<br><br>**Consolation**–KJV<br>Encouragement–NASB<br>Encouraging message–NIV<br>Encouragement–NKJV<br>Encouraging message–NLT<br><br>**POSB REFERENCE**<br>(Acts 15:30-35; esp. v.31)<br>Note 5, point 1 | παρακλήσει = *paraklēsei*<br>Pronunciation: [par-ak'-lay-seh-ee]<br>Parsing (part of speech): noun<br>  Case—dative<br>  Gender—feminine<br>  Number—singular<br>  Stem or root—from παράκλησις, εως<br>Concordance References:<br>⇒ Strong's #3874 paraklēsis<br>⇒ NIV #4155 paraklēsis<br>⇒ NASB #3874 paraklēsis<br><br>**Acts 15:31**<br>Which when they had read, they rejoiced for the **consolation**. [KJV]<br>And when they had read it, they rejoiced because of its **encouragement**. [NASB]<br>The people read it and were glad for its **encouraging message**. [NIV]<br>When they had read it, they rejoiced over its **encouragement**. [NKJV]<br>And there was great joy throughout the church that day as they read this **encouraging message**. [NLT]<br>ἀναγνόντες δὲ, ἐχάρησαν ἐπὶ τῇ **παρακλήσει**. [GNS]<br>ἀναγνόντες δὲ ἐχάρησαν ἐπὶ τῇ **παρακλήσει**. [GNT] | An encouraging message; consolation, encouragement, comfort, help, appeal.<br><br>**Practical Application**<br>When the four men arrived in Antioch, the whole church was called together and the great decree on salvation was read. When it was read, four great results occurred. Note how God took the dissension and its subsequent events to work it all out for the good of the Antioch church and for the cause of Christ. The results were four-fold.<br>1. There was great "*rejoicing*" (*echaresan*): joy, gladness, rejoicing over the consolation (*paraklēsei*), that is, over the encouragement and help given by the Jerusalem church.<br>2. There was great "consolation" (v.32). Note that it was Silas and Judas who were exhorting and confirming the faith of the Antioch believers. Note also the phrase "lengthy message." They encouraged for a long time, building the believers up more and more, assuring them of their faith in the Lord Jesus. They were saved by the grace of God and His grace alone, and the two visiting preachers wanted the believers to know that the apostles and elders of the great Jerusalem church confirmed the glorious truth.<br>3. There was the discovery of the great missionary, Silas. The oldest Greek manuscripts do not include this verse (note the word "they" in Acts 15:33). Some scholars feel it was added at a later date because Silas appears with Paul in Acts 15:40. There was, of course, plenty of |

# PRACTICAL WORD STUDIES
## in the NEW TESTAMENT

| ENGLISH WORD | GREEK WORD AND VERSE | THE WORD MEANS... |
|---|---|---|
| | | time for Silas to travel to Jerusalem and report back to the church and then to return to Antioch before Paul left on his second missionary journey. Other scholars believe the verse was in the original manuscript. No matter who is accurate, Silas and his great gift from God were discovered by Paul at Antioch, and apparently Paul invited him to join the great mission thrust. (See POSB *Deeper Study* #1, Silas—Acts 15:34 for more discussion.)<br>4. A great teaching ministry grew within the church (v.35). |
| **#741**<br>**Consolation**<br><br>Comfort–KJV<br>**Consolation–NASB**<br>Comfort–NIV<br>Comfort–NKJV<br>Comforting–NLT<br><br>**POSB REFERENCE**<br>(1 Cor.14:3)<br>*Deeper Study* #1, point 3 | παραμυθίαν = *paramuthian*<br>Pronunciation: [par-am-oo-thee'-ahn]<br>Parsing (part of speech): noun<br>    Case—accusative<br>    Gender—feminine<br>    Number—singular<br>    Stem or root—from παραμυθία, ας<br>Concordance References:<br>⇒ Strong's #3889 *paramuthia*<br>⇒ NIV #4171 *paramuthia*<br>⇒ NASB #3889 *paramuthia*<br><br>**1 Cor. 14:3**<br>But he that prophesieth speaketh unto men to edification, and exhortation, and **comfort**. [KJV]<br>But one who prophesies speaks to men for edification and exhortation and **consolation**. [NASB]<br>But everyone who prophesies speaks to men for their strengthening, encouragement and **comfort**. [NIV]<br>But he who prophesies speaks edification and exhortation and **comfort** to men. [NKJV]<br>But one who prophesies is helping others grow in the Lord, encouraging and **comforting** them. [NLT]<br>ὁ δὲ προφητεύων ἀνθρώποις λαλεῖ οἰκοδομὴν καὶ παράκλησιν καὶ **παραμυθίαν**. [GNS]<br>ὁ δὲ προφητεύων ἀνθρώποις λαλεῖ οἰκοδομὴν καὶ παράκλησιν καὶ **παραμυθίαν**. [GNT] | Comfort, consolation; to give strength and hope to; to ease the grief or trouble of someone.<br><br>**Practical Application**<br>Consolation (*paramuthian*) has the idea of consoling through the most severe experiences of life, for example, through death (cp. John 11:19, 31). |
| **#742**<br>**Consolation**<br><br>**Consolation–KJV**<br>Encouragement–NASB<br>Encouragement–NIV<br>**Consolation–NKJV**<br>Encouragement–NLT<br><br>**POSB REFERENCE**<br>(Philip.2:1)<br>Note 1 | παράκλησις = *paraklēsis*<br>Pronunciation: [par-ak'-lay-sis]<br>Parsing (part of speech): noun<br>    Case—nominative<br>    Gender—feminine<br>    Number—singular<br>    Stem or root—from παράκλησις, εως<br>Concordance References:<br>⇒ Strong's #3874 *paraklēsis*<br>⇒ NIV #4155 *paraklēsis*<br>⇒ NASB #3874 *paraklēsis*<br><br>**Philip. 2:1**<br>If there be therefore any **consolation** in Christ, if any comfort of love, if any fellowship of the Spirit, if any bowels and mercies, [KJV]<br>If therefore there is any **encouragement** in Christ, if there is any consolation of love, if there is any fellowship of the Spirit, if any affection and compassion, [NASB]<br>If you have any **encouragement** from being united with Christ, if any comfort from his love, if any fellowship with the Spirit, if any tenderness and compassion, [NIV]<br>Therefore if *there is* any **consolation** in Christ, if any comfort of love, if any fellowship of the Spirit, if any affection and mercy, [NKJV]<br>Is there any **encouragement** from belonging to Christ? Any comfort from his love? Any fellowship together in the Spirit? Are your hearts tender and sympa- | The word means many things throughout Scripture; but in the present context it means encouragement, comfort, solace, exhortation, and strengthening; consolation, appeal, help.<br><br>**Practical Application**<br>Note that this trait is a characteristic of Christ Himself. The very beat of His Spirit is to encourage, comfort, and strengthen believers to be one in spirit and busy about the ministry of His church. Christ wants no murmuring, no grumbling, no disturbance, or weakening of the unity within the church. The Spirit of Christ is to take the disturbed or upset person and...<br>• console him<br>• comfort him<br>• encourage him<br>• strengthen him |

# PRACTICAL WORD STUDIES
## in the NEW TESTAMENT

| ENGLISH WORD | GREEK WORD AND VERSE | THE WORD MEANS... |
|---|---|---|
| | thetic? [NLT]<br>Εἴ τις οὖν **παράκλησις** ἐν Χριστῷ, εἴ τι παραμύθιον ἀγάπης, εἴ τις κοινωνία Πνεύματος, εἴ τινα σπλάγχνα καὶ οἰκτιρμοί, [GNS]<br>Εἴ τις οὖν **παράκλησις** ἐν Χριστῷ, εἴ τι παραμύθιον ἀγάπης, εἴ τις κοινωνία πνεύματος, εἴ τις σπλάγχνα καὶ οἰκτιρμοί, [GNT] | |
| **#743**<br>**Consolation**<br><br>Comfort–KJV<br>**Consolation–NASB**<br>Comfort–NIV<br>Comfort–NKJV<br>Comfort–NLT<br><br>**POSB REFERENCE**<br>(Philip.2:1)<br>Note 2 | παραμύθιον = *paramuthion*<br>Pronunciation: [par-am-oo'-thee-on]<br>Parsing (part of speech): noun<br>  Case—nominative<br>  Gender—feminine<br>  Number—singular<br>  Stem or root—from παράκλησις, εως<br>Concordance References:<br>⇒ Strong's #3890 paramuthion<br>⇒ NIV #4172 paramuthion<br>⇒ NASB #3890 paramuthion<br><br>**Philip. 2:1**<br>If *there be* therefore any consolation in Christ, if any **comfort** of love, if any fellowship of the Spirit, if any bowels and mercies, [KJV]<br>If therefore there is any encouragement in Christ, if there is any **consolation** of love, if there is any fellowship of the Spirit, if any affection and compassion, [NASB]<br>If you have any encouragement from being united with Christ, if any **comfort** from his love, if any fellowship with the Spirit, if any tenderness and compassion, [NIV]<br>Therefore if *there is* any consolation in Christ, if any **comfort** of love, if any fellowship of the Spirit, if any affection and mercy, [NKJV]<br>Is there any encouragement from belonging to Christ? Any **comfort** from his love? Any fellowship together in the Spirit? Are your hearts tender and sympathetic? [NLT]<br>Εἴ τις οὖν παράκλησις ἐν Χριστῷ, εἴ τι **παραμύθιον** ἀγάπης, εἴ τις κοινωνία Πνεύματος, εἴ τινα σπλάγχνα καὶ οἰκτιρμοί, [GNS]<br>Εἴ τις οὖν παράκλησις ἐν Χριστῷ, εἴ τι **παραμύθιον** ἀγάπης, εἴ τις κοινωνία πνεύματος, εἴ τις σπλάγχνα καὶ οἰκτιρμοί, [GNT] | Comfort, consolation, encouragement, help.<br><br>**Practical Application**<br>There is a consolation (*paramuthion*) of love that is in Christ. The love of Christ stirs a person to keep the unity with other believers. The word "love" is *agape love*, the love that is selfless and sacrificial. *Agape love* is the love of the mind, of the reason, and of the will. It is the love that goes so far...<br>• that it loves a person even if he does not deserve to be loved.<br>• that actually loves the person who is utterly unworthy of being loved.<br>Agape love is the love of Christ, the love which He showed when He gave and sacrificed Himself for us. We did not deserve it and were utterly unworthy of such love, yet Christ loved us despite all.<br>Imagine the spirit of unity that would exist within a church if every member would let the love of Christ flow through him. There would be no bitterness, anger, or strife—no action that would hurt another person whatsoever. If the person were wrong and deserved punishment, the church's members would sacrifice and give themselves for him. |
| **#744**<br>**Constant**<br><br>Without ceasing–KJV<br>Fervently–NASB<br>Earnestly–NIV<br>**Constant–NKJV**<br>Earnestly–NLT<br><br>**POSB REFERENCE**<br>(Acts 12:5-17; esp. v.5)<br>Note 2, point 1c | ἐκτενῶς = *ektenōs*<br>Pronunciation: [ek-ten-os']<br>Parsing (part of speech): adjective adverb<br>  Stem or root—from ἐκτενῶς<br>Concordance References:<br>⇒ Strong's #1618 ektenes<br>⇒ NIV #1757 ektenōs<br>⇒ NASB #1619 ektenos<br><br>**Acts 12:5**<br>Peter therefore was kept in prison: but prayer was made **without ceasing** of the church unto God for him. [KJV]<br>So Peter was kept in the prison, but prayer for him was being made **fervently** by the church to God. [NASB]<br>So Peter was kept in prison, but the church was **earnestly** praying to God for him. [NIV]<br>Peter was therefore kept in prison, but **constant** prayer was offered to God for him by the church. [NKJV]<br>But while Peter was in prison, the church prayed very **earnestly** for him. [NLT]<br>ὁ μὲν οὖν Πέτρος ἐτηρεῖτο ἐν τῇ φυλακῇ· προσευχὴ δὲ ἦν **ἐκτενῶς** γινομένη ὑπὸ τῆς ἐκκλησίας πρὸς τὸν Θεὸν ὑπὲρ αὐτοῦ. [GNS]<br>ὁ μὲν οὖν Πέτρος ἐτηρεῖτο ἐν τῇ φυλακῇ· προσευχὴ δὲ ἦν **ἐκτενῶς** γινομένη ὑπὸ τῆς ἐκκλησίας πρὸς τὸν θεὸν περὶ αὐτοῦ. [GNT] | Earnestly, deeply, ceaselessly, fervently, constantly.<br><br>**Practical Application**<br>The idea is intense prayer, prayer that captivates and focuses a person's concentration. The root meaning of the word is "to stretch out." The picture is that the church was stretched out, prostrate before God, earnestly and fervently crying out for God's sovereign deliverance of Peter. The church could do nothing and they knew it. Peter's only hope was God. |

# PRACTICAL WORD STUDIES
## in the NEW TESTAMENT

| ENGLISH WORD | GREEK WORD AND VERSE | THE WORD MEANS... |
|---|---|---|
| **#745**<br>**Constraineth**<br><br>Constraineth–KJV<br>Controls–NASB<br>Compels–NIV<br>Compels–NKJV<br>Controls–NLT<br><br>**POSB REFERENCE**<br>(2 Cor.5:14-16; esp. v.14)<br>Note 4 | συνέχει = sunechei<br>Pronunciation: [soon-ekh'-ee]<br>Parsing (part of speech): verb<br>    Mood—indicative<br>    Tense—present<br>    Voice—active<br>    Person—3rd person<br>    Number—singular<br>    Stem or root—from συνέχω<br>Concordance References:<br>  ⇒ Strong's #4912 sunechō<br>  ⇒ NIV #5309 sunechō<br>  ⇒ NASB #4912 sunechō<br><br>**2 Cor. 5:14**<br>For the love of Christ **constraineth** us; because we thus judge, that if one died for all, then were all dead: [KJV]<br>For the love of Christ **controls** us, having concluded this, that one died for all, therefore all died; [NASB]<br>For Christ's love **compels** us, because we are convinced that one died for all, and therefore all died. [NIV]<br>For the love of Christ **compels** us, because we judge thus: that if One died for all, then all died; [NKJV]<br>Whatever we do, it is because Christ's love **controls** us. Since we believe that Christ died for everyone, we also believe that we have all died to the old life we used to live. [NLT]<br>ἡ γὰρ ἀγάπη τοῦ Χριστοῦ **συνέχει** ἡμᾶς, κρίναντας τοῦτο, ὅτι εἰ εἷς ὑπὲρ πάντων ἀπέθανεν, ἄρα οἱ πάντες ἀπέθανον· [GNS]<br>ἡ γὰρ ἀγάπη τοῦ Χριστοῦ **συνέχει** ἡμᾶς, κρίναντας τοῦτο, ὅτι εἷς ὑπὲρ πάντων ἀπέθανεν, ἄρα οἱ πάντες ἀπέθανον· [GNT] | To compel; to constrain; to control; to press.<br><br>**Practical Application**<br>The love of Christ presses, compels, constrains and stirs Paul to hold fast to the ministry. The love of Christ is the great thing that constrains Paul to minister. Note that Paul does not say that he is driven to minister because of...<br>• the great teaching of Christ.<br>• the great example of Christ.<br>• the great ministry of Christ.<br>• the great life of Christ.<br><br>All of these areas of the Lord's life are important, critically so, but they are not the foundation of our salvation and ministry. The foundation of the believer's life is the love of Christ. |
| **#746**<br>**Consumed With Worms**<br><br>Eaten of worms–KJV<br>Eaten by worms–NASB<br>Eaten by worms–NIV<br>Eaten by worms–NKJV<br>**Consumed with worms**–NLT<br><br>**POSB REFERENCE**<br>(Acts 12:18-23; esp. v.23)<br>Note 3, point 2 | σκωληκόβρωτος = skōlēkobrōtos<br>Pronunciation: [sko-lay-kob'-ro-tos]<br>Parsing (part of speech): adjective<br>    Case—nominative<br>    Gender—masculine<br>    Number—singular<br>    Stem or root—from σκωληκόβρωτος, ον<br>Concordance References:<br>  ⇒ Strong's #4662 skōlēkobrōtos<br>  ⇒ NIV #5037 skōlēkobrōtos<br>  ⇒ NASB #4662 skōlēkobrōtos<br><br>**Acts 12:23**<br>And immediately the angel of the Lord smote him, because he gave not God the glory: and he was **eaten of worms**, and gave up the ghost. [KJV]<br>And immediately an angel of the Lord struck him because he did not give God the glory, and he was **eaten by worms** and died. [NASB]<br>Immediately, because Herod did not give praise to God, an angel of the Lord struck him down, and he was **eaten by worms** and died. [NIV]<br>Then immediately an angel of the Lord struck him, because he did not give glory to God. And he was **eaten by worms** and died. [NKJV]<br>Instantly, an angel of the Lord struck Herod with a sickness, because he accepted the people's worship instead of giving the glory to God. So he was **consumed with worms** and died. [NLT]<br>παραχρῆμα δὲ ἐπάταξεν αὐτὸν ἄγγελος Κυρίου, ἀνθ' ὧν οὐκ ἔδωκε τὴν δόξαν τῷ Θεῷ· καὶ γενόμενος **σκωληκόβρωτος**, ἐξέψυξεν. [GNS]<br>παραχρῆμα δὲ ἐπάταξεν αὐτὸν ἄγγελος κυρίου ἀνθ' ὧν οὐκ ἔδωκεν τὴν δόξαν τῷ θεῷ, καὶ γενόμενος **σκωληκόβρωτος** ἐξέψυξεν. [GNT] | To be eaten by worms; to be consumed by worms.<br><br>**Practical Application**<br>The word "*skolex*" was used by the Greeks to refer to intestinal worms. Josephus, the renowned historian of that day, reported that Herod lingered for five days, suffering great pain in the area of the stomach (Flavius Josephus. *Josephus Complete Works.* Translated by William Whiston. Grand Rapids, MI: Kregel, 1960. Ant. 19.8.2). |

## PRACTICAL WORD STUDIES in the NEW TESTAMENT

| ENGLISH WORD | GREEK WORD AND VERSE | THE WORD MEANS... |
|---|---|---|
| **#747**<br>**Contemplated**<br><br>Considered–KJV<br>**Contemplated–NASB**<br>Faced the fact–NIV<br>Consider–NKJV<br>Knew–NLT<br><br>**POSB REFERENCE**<br>(Romans 4:18-22; esp. v.19)<br>Note 2, point 1a | κατενόησεν = katenoësen<br>Pronunciation: [kat-ehn-o-ay'-sehn]<br>Parsing (part of speech): verb<br>    Mood—indicative<br>    Tense—aorist<br>    Voice—active<br>    Person—3rd person<br>    Number—singular<br>    Stem or root—from κατανοέω<br>Concordance References:<br>  ⇒ Strong's #2657 katanoeö<br>  ⇒ NIV #2917 katanoeö<br>  ⇒ NASB #2657 katanoeö<br><br>**Romans 4:19**<br>And being not weak in faith, he **considered** not his own body now dead, when he was about an hundred years old, neither yet the deadness of Sarah's womb: [KJV]<br>And without becoming weak in faith he **contemplated** his own body, now as good as dead since he was about a hundred years old, and the deadness of Sarah's womb; [NASB]<br>Without weakening in his faith, he **faced the fact** that his body was as good as dead—since he was about a hundred years old—and that Sarah's womb was also dead. [NIV]<br>And not being weak in faith, he did not **consider** his own body, already dead (since he was about a hundred years old), and the deadness of Sarah's womb. [NKJV]<br>And Abraham's faith did not weaken, even though he **knew** that he was too old to be a father at the age of one hundred and that Sarah, his wife, had never been able to have children. [NLT]<br>καὶ μὴ ἀσθενήσας τῇ πίστει, οὐ κατενόησε τὸ ἑαυτοῦ σῶμα ἤδη νενεκρωμένον -- ἑκατονταετής που ὑπάρχων --, καὶ τὴν νέκρωσιν τῆς μήτρας Σάρρας, [GNS]<br>καὶ μὴ ἀσθενήσας τῇ πίστει κατενόησεν τὸ ἑαυτοῦ σῶμα [ἤδη] νενεκρωμένον, ἑκατονταετής που ὑπάρχων, καὶ τὴν νέκρωσιν τῆς μήτρας Σάρρας· [GNT] | To consider; to think of; to notice; to observe; to see; to look; to see through; to face the fact; to be aware of; to pay attention to; to fix thoughts on.<br><br>**Practical Application**<br>Abraham was not weak in faith despite thinking about his own physical inability. His body was "now dead"; he and Sarah were about one hundred years old. The word "dead" is a perfect participle in the Greek which means that his reproductive organs had stopped functioning and were dead forever and could never again function. Abraham could never have a son; it was not humanly possible. He and Sarah were almost one hundred years old, now sexually "dead."<br>Abraham thought about the matter. The word "contemplated" (*katenoësen*) means He fixed his thoughts, his mind, his attention upon the matter. But he did not give in to the thoughts. He was not weak in faith. |
| **#748**<br>**Contempt**<br><br>Nought–KJV<br>**Contempt–NASB**<br>Ridiculed–NIV<br>**Contempt–NKJV**<br>Ridiculing–NLT<br><br>**POSB REFERENCE**<br>(Lk.23:8-11; esp. v.11)<br>Note 3, point 4 | ἐξουθενήσας = exouthenësas<br>Pronunciation: [ex-oo-then-eh'-sas]<br>Parsing (part of speech): verb<br>    Mood—participle<br>    Tense—aorist<br>    Voice—active<br>    Case—nominative<br>    Gender—masculine<br>    Number—singular<br>    Stem or root—from ἐξουθενέω<br>Concordance References:<br>  ⇒ Strong's #1848 exoutheneö<br>  ⇒ NIV #2024 exoutheneö<br>  ⇒ NASB #1848 exoutheneö<br><br>**Luke 23:11**<br>And Herod with his men of war set him at **nought**, and mocked him, and arrayed him in a gorgeous robe, and sent him again to Pilate. [KJV]<br>And Herod with his soldiers, after treating Him with **contempt** and mocking Him, dressed Him in a gorgeous robe and sent Him back to Pilate. [NASB]<br>Then Herod and his soldiers **ridiculed** and mocked him. Dressing him in an elegant robe, they sent him back to Pilate. [NIV]<br>Then Herod, with his men of war, treated Him with **contempt** and mocked *Him*, arrayed Him in a gorgeous robe, and sent Him back to Pilate. [NKJV]<br>Now Herod and his soldiers began mocking and **ridiculing** Jesus. Then they put a royal robe on him and sent him back to Pilate. [NLT]<br>ἐξουθενήσας δὲ αὐτὸν ὁ Ἡρώδης σὺν τοῖς στρατεύμασιν αὐτοῦ, καὶ ἐμπαίξας, περιβαλὼν αὐτὸν ἐσθῆτα λαμπρὰν, ἀνέπεμψεν αὐτὸν τῷ Πιλάτῳ. [GNS]<br>ἐξουθενήσας δὲ αὐτὸν [καὶ] ὁ Ἡρώδης σὺν τοῖς στρατεύμασιν αὐτοῦ καὶ ἐμπαίξας περιβαλὼν ἐσθῆτα λαμπρὰν ἀνέπεμψεν αὐτὸν τῷ Πιλάτῳ. [GNT] | To ridicule; to count as nothing; to make nothing of; to despise; to look down upon; to reject; to think something is unimportant; to count as zero—therefore, to treat with utter contempt.<br><br>**Practical Application**<br>Note the contrast in the verse. Herod sat there as King with "his soldiers" surrounding him, and Jesus stood there beaten and battered in torn, ragged clothes. Herod, judging by appearance, counted the Man who claimed to be the Son of God as nothing. This Man and His claim did not matter, not to Herod. |

# PRACTICAL WORD STUDIES
## in the NEW TESTAMENT

| ENGLISH WORD | GREEK WORD AND VERSE | THE WORD MEANS... |
|---|---|---|
| **#749**<br>**Contended**<br><br>**Contended–KJV**<br>Took issue–NASB<br>Criticized–NIV<br>**Contended–NKJV**<br>Criticized–NLT<br><br>**POSB REFERENCE**<br>(Acts 11:1-3; esp. v.2)<br>Note 1, point 2 | διεκρίνοντο = diekrinonto<br>Pronunciation: [dee-eh-kree-non-tow]<br>Parsing (part of speech): verb<br>    Mood—indicative<br>    Tense—imperfect<br>    Voice—middle<br>    Person—3rd person<br>    Number—plural<br>    Stem or root—from διακρίνω<br>Concordance References:<br>  ⇒ Strong's #1252 diakrinō<br>  ⇒ NIV #1359 diakrinō<br>  ⇒ NASB #1252 diakrinō<br><br>**Acts 11:2**<br>And when Peter was come up to Jerusalem, they that were of the circumcision **contended** with him, [KJV]<br>And when Peter came up to Jerusalem, those who were circumcised **took issue** with him, [NASB]<br>So when Peter went up to Jerusalem, the circumcised believers **criticized** him [NIV]<br>And when Peter came up to Jerusalem, those of the circumcision **contended** with him, [NKJV]<br>But when Peter arrived back in Jerusalem, some of the Jewish believers **criticized** him. [NLT]<br>καὶ ὅτε δὲ ἀνέβη Πέτρος εἰς Ἰερουσαλήμ, **διεκρίνοντο** πρὸς αὐτὸν οἱ ἐκ περιτομῆς, [GNS]<br>ὅτε δὲ ἀνέβη Πέτρος εἰς Ἰερουσαλήμ, **διεκρίνοντο** πρὸς αὐτὸν οἱ ἐκ περιτομῆς [GNT] | To criticize; to take issue with; to contend; to debate; to dispute. The word "contend" (*diekrinonto*) means to stand against, to take an opposite position, to take sides against, to oppose, to create a cleavage, a division. It is creating strife, struggle, and discord.<br><br>**Practical Application**<br>They (the circumcision, the religionists) readily and willingly opposed Peter, and the idea is that it was repeated: it went on and on; the issue was prolonged.<br>Again keep in mind the issue: Peter had carried the Word of God to the Gentiles.<br>⇒ He had allowed the non-Jews to receive the Word of God without circumcising them (Acts 11:1).<br>⇒ He had broken the law of Moses by "going to the uncircumcised [non-Jews] and eating" with them (Acts 11:3). |
| **#750**<br>**Contending As**<br><br>Striving together–KJV<br>Striving together–NASB<br>**Contending as–NIV**<br>Striving together–NKJV<br>Fighting together–NLT<br><br>**POSB REFERENCE**<br>(Philip.1:27)<br>Note 3, point 2 | συναθλοῦντες = sunathlountes<br>Pronunciation: [soon-ath-loon'-tehs]<br>Parsing (part of speech): verb<br>    Mood—participle<br>    Tense—present<br>    Voice—active<br>    Case—nominative<br>    Gender—masculine<br>    Person—2nd person<br>    Number—plural<br>    Stem or root—from συναθλέω<br>Concordance References:<br>  ⇒ Strong's #4866 sunathleō<br>  ⇒ NIV #5254 sunathleō<br>  ⇒ NASB #4866 sunathleō<br><br>**Philip. 1:27**<br>Only let your conversation be as it becometh the gospel of Christ: that whether I come and see you, or else be absent, I may hear of your affairs, that ye stand fast in one spirit, with one mind **striving together** for the faith of the gospel; [KJV]<br>Only conduct yourselves in a manner worthy of the gospel of Christ; so that whether I come and see you or remain absent, I may hear of you that you are standing firm in one spirit, with one mind **striving together** for the faith of the gospel; [NASB]<br>Whatever happens, conduct yourselves in a manner worthy of the gospel of Christ. Then, whether I come and see you or only hear about you in my absence, I will know that you stand firm in one spirit, **contending as** one man for the faith of the gospel [NIV]<br>Only let your conduct be worthy of the gospel of Christ, so that whether I come and see you or am absent, I may hear of your affairs, that you stand fast in one spirit, with one mind **striving together** for the faith of the gospel, [NKJV]<br>But whatever happens to me, you must live in a manner worthy of the Good News about Christ, as citizens of heaven. Then, whether I come and see you again or only hear about you, I will know that you are standing side by side, **fighting together** for the Good News. [NLT]<br>ὄνον ἀξίως τοῦ εὐαγγελίου τοῦ Χριστοῦ πολιτεύεσθε, | Contending as; striving together; struggling, fighting together; working together.<br><br>**Practical Application**<br>The word "contending as" (*sunathlountes*) is the word taken from an athletic contest. It is the picture of a team working and struggling together against strong opposition (compare a football team). The church—every member of it—is to strive for the faith of the gospel: strive, work, struggle, push, exert all the energy possible; everyone's cooperating together, not a single person's letting up or turning aside or walking off the field. The opposition is difficult; therefore, the faith of the gospel needs every member's working and struggling together. |

# PRACTICAL WORD STUDIES
## in the NEW TESTAMENT

| ENGLISH WORD | GREEK WORD AND VERSE | THE WORD MEANS... |
|---|---|---|
| | ἵνα εἴτε ἐλθὼν καὶ ἰδὼν ὑμᾶς, εἴτε ἀπὼν, ἀκούσω τὰ περὶ ὑμῶν, ὅτι στήκετε ἐν ἑνὶ πνεύματι, μιᾷ ψυχῇ **συναθλοῦντες** τῇ πίστει τοῦ εὐαγγελίου, [GNS]<br>Μόνον ἀξίως τοῦ εὐαγγελίου τοῦ Χριστοῦ πολιτεύεσθε, ἵνα εἴτε ἐλθὼν καὶ ἰδὼν ὑμᾶς εἴτε ἀπὼν ἀκούω τὰ περὶ ὑμῶν, ὅτι στήκετε ἐν ἑνὶ πνεύματι, μιᾷ ψυχῇ **συναθλοῦντες** τῇ πίστει τοῦ εὐαγγελίου [GNT] | |
| **#751**<br>**Content**<br><br>Content–KJV<br>Content–NASB<br>Content–NIV<br>Content–NKJV<br>How to get along happily–NLT<br><br>**POSB REFERENCE**<br>(Philip.4:11-14; esp. v.11)<br>Note 2, point 1 | αὐτάρκης = autarkēs<br>Pronunciation: [ow-tar'-kace]<br>Parsing (part of speech): adjective<br>  Case—nominative<br>  Gender—masculine<br>  Number—singular<br>  Stem or root—from αὐτάρκης, ες<br>Concordance References:<br>  ⇒ Strong's #842 autarkēs<br>  ⇒ NIV #895 autarkēs<br>  ⇒ NASB #842 autarkēs<br><br>**Philip. 4:11**<br>Not that I speak in respect of want: for I have learned, in whatsoever state I am, therewith to be **content**. [KJV]<br>Not that I speak from want; for I have learned to be **content** in whatever circumstances I am. [NASB]<br>I am not saying this because I am in need, for I have learned to be **content** whatever the circumstances. [NIV]<br>Not that I speak in regard to need, for I have learned in whatever state I am, to be **content**: [NKJV]<br>Not that I was ever in need, for I have learned **how to get along happily** whether I have much or little. [NLT]<br>οὐχ ὅτι καθ' ὑστέρησιν λέγω· ἐγὼ γὰρ ἔμαθον, ἐν οἷς εἰμι, **αὐτάρκης** εἶναι. [GNS]<br>οὐχ ὅτι καθ' ὑστέρησιν λέγω, ἐγὼ γὰρ ἔμαθον ἐν οἷς εἰμι **αὐτάρκης** εἶναι.[GNT] | To be content; to be happy; to be satisfied; to be self-sufficient; to be completely detached from circumstances.<br><br>**Practical Application**<br>Note the word "learned." It was a learning experience. Paul had to learn to conquer circumstances and not let circumstances conquer him. But note: he had learned contentment. He says three descriptive things:<br>⇒ that he knew how to live in need (to live humbly with little) and how it feels to live with plenty (to live with plenty and prosperity).<br>⇒ that he knew the *secret* to facing every situation, whether being full or going hungry.<br>⇒ that he knew how to live well fed (live in plenty) and how to live in want. |
| **#752**<br>**Contention**<br><br>Contention–KJV<br>Sharp disagreement–NASB<br>Sharp disagreement–NIV<br>Contention–NKJV<br>Disagreement–NLT<br><br>**POSB REFERENCE**<br>(Acts 15:39)<br>Note 2, point 1 | παροξυσμός = paroxusmos<br>Pronunciation: [par-ox-oos-mos']<br>Parsing (part of speech): noun<br>  Case—nominative<br>  Gender—masculine<br>  Number—singular<br>  Stem or root—from παροξυσμός, οῦ<br>Concordance References:<br>  ⇒ Strong's #3948 paroxusmos<br>  ⇒ NIV #4237 paroxusmos<br>  ⇒ NASB #3948 paroxusmos<br><br>**Acts 15:39**<br>And the **contention** was so sharp between them, that they departed asunder one from the other: and so Barnabas took Mark, and sailed unto Cyprus; [KJV]<br>And there arose such a **sharp disagreement** that they separated from one another, and Barnabas took Mark with him and sailed away to Cyprus. [NASB]<br>They had such a **sharp disagreement** that they parted company. Barnabas took Mark and sailed for Cyprus, [NIV]<br>Then the **contention** became so sharp that they parted from one another. And so Barnabas took Mark and sailed to Cyprus; [NKJV]<br>Their **disagreement** over this was so sharp that they separated. Barnabas took John Mark with him and sailed for Cyprus. [NLT]<br>ἐγένετο οὖν **παροξυσμός**, ὥστε ἀποχωρισθῆναι αὐτοὺς ἀπ' ἀλλήλων, τόν τε Βαρναβᾶν παραλαβόντα τὸν Μᾶρκον, ἐκπλεῦσαι εἰς Κύπρον· [GNS]<br>ἐγένετο δὲ **παροξυσμός** ὥστε ἀποχωρισθῆναι αὐτοὺς ἀπ' ἀλλήλων, τόν τε Βαρναβᾶν παραλαβόντα τὸν Μᾶρκον ἐκπλεῦσαι εἰς Κύπρον, [GNT] | A sharp disagreement; a contention; a debate; a struggle; a conflict.<br><br>**Practical Application**<br>The idea is that of differing to the point of suffering pain. Contrary to the picture usually painted of the conflict, the picture seems to be that both men were hurting. The difference was sharp and both hearts were cut deeply. Each man was thoroughly convinced that he was right before the Lord; therefore, each argued strongly for his position. This does not mean that they were cutting each other with sharp and ugly words. This is important to note, for sharp words should never be spoken among believers. But the opposing positions and convictions cut and hurt both hearts. They loved and respected each other, and their sharp conflict seemed irreconcilable. |

# PRACTICAL WORD STUDIES
## in the NEW TESTAMENT

| ENGLISH WORD | GREEK WORD AND VERSE | THE WORD MEANS... |
|---|---|---|
| **#753**<br>**Contentions**<br><br>**Contentions**–KJV<br>Quarrels–NASB<br>Quarrels–NIV<br>**Contentions**–NKJV<br>Arguments–NLT<br><br>**POSB<br>REFERENCE**<br>(1 Cor.1:11)<br>Note 2 | ἔριδες = *erides*<br>Pronunciation: [er'-i-des]<br>Parsing (part of speech): noun<br>    Case—nominative<br>    Gender—feminine<br>    Number—plural<br>    Stem or root—from ἔρις, ιδος<br>Concordance References:<br>  ⇒ Strong's #2054 *eris*<br>  ⇒ NIV #2251 *eris*<br>  ⇒ NASB #2054 *eris*<br><br>**1 Cor. 1:11**<br>For it hath been declared unto me of you, my brethren, by them which are of the house of Chloe, that there are **contentions** among you. [KJV]<br><br>For I have been informed concerning you, my brethren, by Chloe's people, that there are **quarrels** among you. [NASB]<br><br>My brothers, some from Chloe's household have informed me that there are **quarrels** among you. [NIV]<br><br>For it has been declared to me concerning you, my brethren, by those of Chloe's *household*, that there are **contentions** among you. [NKJV]<br><br>For some members of Chloe's household have told me about your **arguments**, dear brothers and sisters. [NLT]<br><br>ἐδηλώθη γάρ μοι περὶ ὑμῶν, ἀδελφοί μου, ὑπὸ τῶν Χλόης ὅτι **ἔριδες** ἐν ὑμῖν εἰσι. [GNS]<br><br>ἐδηλώθη γάρ μοι περὶ ὑμῶν, ἀδελφοί μου, ὑπὸ τῶν Χλόης ὅτι **ἔριδες** ἐν ὑμῖν εἰσιν. [GNT] | Wranglings, strifes, quarrels, fightings, factions, discord.<br><br>**Practical Application**<br>Note: the nature of division is more clearly defined by the word. The church was arguing and splitting into groups, contending and quarreling over something. There was a severe strife between factions and cliques in the church. |
| **#754**<br>**Contentions**<br><br>Debates–KJV<br>Strife–NASB<br>Quarreling–NIV<br>**Contentions**–NKJV<br>Quarreling–NLT<br><br>**POSB<br>REFERENCE**<br>(2 Cor.12:19-21; esp. v.20)<br>Note 3 | ἔρις = *eris*<br>Pronunciation: [er'-is]<br>Parsing (part of speech): noun<br>    Case—nominative<br>    Gender—feminine<br>    Number—singular<br>    Stem or root—from ἔρις, ιδος<br>Concordance References:<br>  ⇒ Strong's #2054 *eris*<br>  ⇒ NIV #2251 *eris*<br>  ⇒ NASB #2054 *eris*<br><br>**2 Cor. 12:20**<br>For I fear, lest, when I come, I shall not find you such as I would, and that I shall be found unto you such as ye would not: lest there be **debates**, envyings, wraths, strifes, backbitings, whisperings, swellings, tumults: [KJV]<br><br>For I am afraid that perhaps when I come I may find you to be not what I wish and may be found by you to be not what you wish; that perhaps there may be **strife**, jealousy, angry tempers, disputes, slanders, gossip, arrogance, disturbances; [NASB]<br><br>For I am afraid that when I come I may not find you as I want you to be, and you may not find me as you want me to be. I fear that there may be **quarreling**, jealousy, outbursts of anger, factions, slander, gossip, arrogance and disorder. [NIV]<br><br>For I fear lest, when I come, I shall not find you such as I wish, and *that* I shall be found by you such as you do not wish; lest *there be* **contentions**, jealousies, outbursts of wrath, selfish ambitions, backbitings, whisperings, conceits, tumults; [NKJV]<br><br>For I am afraid that when I come to visit you I won't like what I find, and then you won't like my response. I am afraid that I will find **quarreling**, jealousy, outbursts of anger, selfishness, backstabbing, gossip, conceit, and disorderly behavior. [NLT]<br><br>φοβοῦμαι γὰρ μή πως ἐλθὼν οὐχ οἵους θέλω εὕρω ὑμᾶς, κἀγὼ εὑρεθῶ ὑμῖν οἷον οὐ θέλετε· μή πως **ἔρις**, | Quarreling, debates, strife, dissension, fighting, contention, rivalry, competitiveness.<br><br>**Practical Application**<br>Paul was stricken with fear, fear lest the church fail to be what it should be and reject him and his ministry. Paul feared that the church would fail to deal with the carnal critics and continue putting up with their evil attacks against him. He lists eight evils—including "contentions" (*eris*)—that were and still are characteristic of divisive critics in the church. |

# PRACTICAL WORD STUDIES
in the NEW TESTAMENT

| ENGLISH WORD | GREEK WORD AND VERSE | THE WORD MEANS... |
|---|---|---|
| | ζῆλοι, θυμοί, ἐριθεῖαι, καταλαλιαί, ψιθυρισμοί, φυσιώσεις, ἀκαταστασίαι· [GNS]<br>φοβοῦμαι γὰρ μή πως ἐλθὼν οὐχ οἵους θέλω εὕρω ὑμᾶς κἀγὼ εὑρεθῶ ὑμῖν οἷον οὐ θέλετε· μή πως **ἔρις**, ζῆλος, θυμοί, ἐριθεῖαι, καταλαλιαί, ψιθυρισμοί, fusiώσεις, ἀκαταστασίαι· [GNT] | |
| **#755**<br>**Contentions**<br><br>Variance–KJV<br>Strife–NASB<br>Discord–NIV<br>**Contentions–NKJV**<br>Quarreling–NLT<br><br>**POSB**<br>**REFERENCE**<br>(Gal.5:19-21; esp. v.20)<br>Note 2 | **ἔρις** = eris<br>Pronunciation: [er'-is]<br>Parsing (part of speech): noun<br>    Case—nominative<br>    Gender—feminine<br>    Number—singular<br>    Stem or root—from ἔρις, ιδος<br>Concordance References:<br>  ⇒ Strong's #2054 eris<br>  ⇒ NIV #2251 eris<br>  ⇒ NASB #2054 eris<br><br>**Galatians 5:20**<br>Idolatry, witchcraft, hatred, **variance**, emulations, wrath, strife, seditions, heresies, [KJV]<br>Idolatry, sorcery, enmities, **strife**, jealousy, outbursts of anger, disputes, dissensions, factions, [NASB]<br>Idolatry and witchcraft; hatred, **discord**, jealousy, fits of rage, selfish ambition, dissensions, factions [NIV]<br>Idolatry, sorcery, hatred, **contentions**, jealousies, outbursts of wrath, selfish ambitions, dissensions, heresies, [NKJV]<br>Idolatry, participation in demonic activities, hostility, **quarreling**, jealousy, outbursts of anger, selfish ambition, divisions, the feeling that everyone is wrong except those in your own little group, [NLT]<br>εἰδωλολατρία, φαρμακεία, ἔχθραι, **ἔρεις**, ζῆλοι, θυμοί, ἐριθεῖαι, διχοστασίαι, αἱρέσεις, [GNS]<br>εἰδωλολατρία, φαρμακεία, ἔχθραι, **ἔρις**, ζῆλος, θυμοί, ἐριθεῖαι, διχοστασίαι, αἱρέσεις, [GNT] | Discord, variance, strife, quarreling, contention, fighting, struggling, dissension, wrangling, selfish rivalry.<br><br>**Practical Application**<br>It means that a person fights against another person in order to get something: position, promotion, property, honor, recognition. He deceives, doing whatever has to be done to get what he is after. |
| **#756**<br>**Contentious**<br><br>**Contentious–KJV**<br>Selfishly ambitious–NASB<br>Self-seeking–NIV<br>Self-seeking–NKJV<br>Live for themselves–NLT<br><br>**POSB**<br>**REFERENCE**<br>(Romans 2:8)<br>*Deeper Study #4* | **ἐριθείας** = eritheias<br>Pronunciation: [er-ith-i'-ahs]<br>Parsing (part of speech): noun<br>    Case—genitive<br>    Gender—feminine<br>    Number—singular<br>    Stem or root—from ἐριθεία, ας<br>Concordance References:<br>  ⇒ Strong's #1537 ek + 2052 eritheia<br>  ⇒ NIV #2249 eritheia<br>  ⇒ NASB #2052 eritheia<br><br>**Romans 2:8**<br>But unto them that are **contentious**, and do not obey the truth, but obey unrighteousness, indignation and wrath, [KJV]<br>but to those who are **selfishly ambitious** and do not obey the truth, but obey unrighteousness, wrath and indignation. [NASB]<br>But for those who are **self-seeking** and who reject the truth and follow evil, there will be wrath and anger. [NIV]<br>But to those who are **self-seeking** and do not obey the truth, but obey unrighteousness—indignation and wrath, [NKJV]<br>But he will pour out his anger and wrath on those who **live for themselves**, who refuse to obey the truth and practice evil deeds. [NLT]<br>τοῖς δὲ ἐξ **ἐριθείας**, καὶ ἀπειθοῦσι μὲν τῇ ἀληθείᾳ πειθομένοις δὲ τῇ ἀδικίᾳ, θυμός καὶ ὀργή, [GNS]<br>τοῖς δὲ ἐξ **ἐριθείας** καὶ ἀπειθοῦσι τῇ ἀληθείᾳ πειθομένοις δὲ τῇ ἀδικίᾳ ὀργὴ καὶ θυμός. [GNT] | To strive; to struggle; to fight; to quarrel; to wrangle; to argue; to debate; to be divisive, factious, contentious, argumentative, and belligerent; selfish rivalry; selfish ambition.<br><br>**Practical Application**<br>The evil-doer does not like what God says; therefore, he strives against it. He wrangles and wrestles, struggles and fights against God. He refuses to buckle under and surrender to God's will. When dealing with God, the evil-doer is contentious. |

# PRACTICAL WORD STUDIES
## in the NEW TESTAMENT

| ENGLISH WORD | GREEK WORD AND VERSE | THE WORD MEANS... |
|---|---|---|
| **#757**<br>**Contentment**<br><br>Contentment–KJV<br>Contentment–NASB<br>Contentment–NIV<br>Contentment–NKJV<br>Contentment–NLT<br><br>**POSB REFERENCE**<br>(1 Tim.6:6-8; esp. v.6)<br>Note 1 | αὐταρκείας = autarkeias<br>Pronunciation: [ow-tar'-ki-ahs]<br>Parsing (part of speech): noun<br>    Case—genitive<br>    Gender—feminine<br>    Number—singular<br>    Stem or root—from αὐτάρκεια, ας<br>Concordance References:<br>⇒ Strong's #841 autarkeia<br>⇒ NIV #894 autarkeia<br>⇒ NASB #841 autarkeia<br><br>**1 Tim. 6:6**<br>But godliness with **contentment** is great gain. [KJV]<br>But godliness actually is a means of great gain, when accompanied by **contentment**. [NASB]<br>But godliness with **contentment** is great gain. [NIV]<br>Now godliness with **contentment** is great gain. [NKJV]<br>Yet true religion with **contentment** is great wealth. [NLT]<br>ἔστι δὲ πορισμὸς μέγας ἡ εὐσέβεια μετὰ **αὐταρκείας**· [GNS]<br>ἔστιν δὲ πορισμὸς μέγας ἡ εὐσέβεια μετὰ **αὐταρκείας**·[GNT] | Contentment, satisfaction; to be *completely sufficient*, to need absolutely nothing. It means to be fulfilled, satisfied, and complete.<br><br>**Practical Application**<br>Imagine a person who feels *wholly complete and sufficient*, who lacks absolutely nothing. This is what Scripture means by contentment; this is what Scripture means by the contented person. What makes a person content? What brings such contentment to the human soul? Scripture pulls no punches; it unequivocally states that it is *godliness*. Godliness alone can make a person content. Godliness alone can take a person and make him...<br>• fulfilled<br>• satisfied<br>• complete<br>• sufficient<br>Godliness alone can give man the sense that he lacks absolutely nothing. Imagine being so contented—so fulfilled, so satisfied, so completed, so sufficient—that you sense no lack. You just sense no need whatsoever within your innermost being and soul. This is exactly what godliness does for the human soul. This is the reason Scripture declares that godliness with contentment is great gain. No greater gain could ever come to a person than contentment. |
| **#758**<br>**Continually Devoting Themselves To**<br><br>Continued with one accord–KJV<br>**Continually devoting themselves to– NASB**<br>Joined...constantly– NIV<br>Continued with one accord–NKJV<br>Met together continually–NLT<br><br>**POSB REFERENCE**<br>(Acts 1:12-15; esp. v.14)<br>Note 1, point 4 | ἦσαν προσκαρτεροῦντες = ësan proskarterountes<br>Pronunciation: [ay-sahn-pros-kar-ter-oon-tes]<br>Parsing *proskarterountes* (part of speech): verb<br>    Mood—participle<br>    Tense—present<br>    Voice—active<br>    Case—nominative<br>    Gender—masculine<br>    Number—plural<br>    Stem or root—from προσκαρτερέω<br>Concordance References:<br>⇒ Strong's #1488 eimi + 4342 proskartereö<br>⇒ NIV #1639 eimi + 4674 proskartereö<br>⇒ NASB #1488 eimi + 4342 proskartereö<br><br>**Acts 1:14**<br>These all **continued with one accord** in prayer and supplication, with the women, and Mary the mother of Jesus, and with his brethren. [KJV]<br>These all with one mind were **continually devoting themselves to** prayer, along with the women, and Mary the mother of Jesus, and with His brothers. [NASB]<br>They all **joined** together **constantly** in prayer, along with the women and Mary the mother of Jesus, and with his brothers. [NIV]<br>These all **continued with one accord** in prayer and supplication, with the women and Mary the mother of Jesus, and with His brothers. [NKJV]<br>They all **met together continually** for prayer, along with Mary the mother of Jesus, several other women, and the brothers of Jesus. [NLT]<br>οὗτοι πάντες **ἦσαν προσκαρτεροῦντες** ὁμοθυμαδὸν τῇ προσευχῇ καὶ τῇ δεήσει, σὺν γυναιξὶ καὶ Μαρίᾳ τῇ μητρὶ τοῦ Ἰησοῦ, καὶ σὺν τοῖς ἀδελφοῖς αὐτοῦ. [GNS]<br>οὗτοι πάντες **ἦσαν προσκαρτεροῦντες** ὁμοθυμαδὸν τῇ προσευχῇ σὺν γυναιξὶν καὶ Μαριὰμ τῇ μητρὶ τοῦ Ἰησοῦ καὶ τοῖς ἀδελφοῖς αὐτοῦ. [GNT] | To join constantly together; to continue with one accord; to be continually devoting themselves; to meet together continually; to be in regular attendance.<br><br>**Practical Application**<br>The word is strong. They continued, persevered, endured, persisted, stuck to praying. |
| **#759**<br>**Continually Devoting Themselves To** | ἦσαν προσκαρτεροῦντες = ësan proskarterountes<br>Pronunciation: [ay-san pros-kar-ter-oon'-tehs]<br>Parsing *proskarterountes* (part of speech): verb<br>    Mood—participle<br>    Tense—present | Devoted to; to continue; to persevere; to endure; to stick; to persist. |

# PRACTICAL WORD STUDIES
## in the NEW TESTAMENT

| ENGLISH WORD | GREEK WORD AND VERSE | THE WORD MEANS... |
|---|---|---|
| Continued steadfastly–KJV<br>**Continually devoting themselves to–NASB**<br>Devoted...to–NIV<br>Continued steadfastly–NKJV<br>Devoted themselves to–NLT<br><br>**POSB REFERENCE**<br>(Acts 2:42)<br>*Deeper Study #1* | Voice—active<br>Case—nominative<br>Gender—masculine<br>Number—plural<br>Stem or root—from προσκαρτερέω<br>Concordance References:<br>⇒ Strong's #1488 + 4342 eimi proskartereō<br>⇒ NIV #1639 + 4674 eimi proskartereō [devoted to]<br>⇒ NASB #1488 + 4342 eimi proskartereō<br><br>**Acts 2:42**<br>And they **continued stedfastly** in the apostles' doctrine and fellowship, and in breaking of bread, and in prayers. [KJV]<br>And they were **continually devoting themselves to** the apostles' teaching and to fellowship, to the breaking of bread and to prayer. [NASB]<br>They **devoted** themselves **to** the apostles' teaching and to the fellowship, to the breaking of bread and to prayer. [NIV]<br>And they **continued steadfastly** in the apostles' doctrine and fellowship, in the breaking of bread, and in prayers. [NKJV]<br>They joined with the other believers and **devoted themselves to** the apostles' teaching and fellowship, sharing in the Lord's Supper and in prayer. [NLT]<br>ἦσαν δὲ **προσκαρτεροῦντες** τῇ διδαχῇ τῶν ἀποστόλων καὶ τῇ κοινωνίᾳ, καὶ τῇ κλάσει τοῦ ἄρτου καὶ ταῖς προσευχαῖς. [GNS]<br>ἦσαν δὲ **προσκαρτεροῦντες** τῇ διδαχῇ τῶν ἀποστόλων καὶ τῇ κοινωνίᾳ, τῇ κλάσει τοῦ ἄρτου καὶ ταῖς προσευχαῖς. [GNT] | **Practical Application**<br>A person does not quit, back off, fade away, or slip back. He continues on steadfastly. |
| **#760**<br>**Continue**<br><br>Continue–KJV<br>Abide–NASB<br>Hold–NIV<br>Abide–NKJV<br>Keep obeying–NLT<br><br>**POSB REFERENCE**<br>(Jn.8:31)<br>Note 1, point 2 | μείνητε = *meinēte*<br>Pronunciation: [meen'-ay-teh]<br>Parsing (part of speech): verb<br>    Mood—subjunctive<br>    Tense—aorist<br>    Voice—active<br>    Person—2nd person plural<br>Stem or root—from μένω<br>Concordance References:<br>⇒ Strong's #3306 meno<br>⇒ NIV #3531 menō<br>⇒ NASB #3306 meno<br><br>**John 8:31**<br>Then said Jesus to those Jews which believed on him, If ye **continue** in my word, then are ye my disciples indeed; [KJV]<br>Jesus therefore was saying to those Jews who had believed Him, "If you **abide** in My word, then you are truly disciples of Mine; [NASB]<br>To the Jews who had believed him, Jesus said, "If you **hold** to my teaching, you are really my disciples. [NIV]<br>Then Jesus said to those Jews who believed Him, "If you **abide** in My word, you are My disciples indeed. [NKJV]<br>Jesus said to the people who believed in him, "You are truly my disciples if you **keep obeying** my teachings. [NLT]<br>Ἔλεγεν οὖν ὁ Ἰησοῦς πρὸς τοὺς πεπιστευκότας αὐτῷ Ἰουδαίους, Ἐὰν ὑμεῖς **μείνητε** ἐν τῷ λόγῳ τῷ ἐμῷ, ἀληθῶς μαθηταί μού ἐστε· [GNS]<br>Ἔλεγεν οὖν ὁ Ἰησοῦς πρὸς τοὺς πεπιστευκότας αὐτῷ Ἰουδαίους, Ἐὰν ὑμεῖς **μείνητε** ἐν τῷ λόγῳ τῷ ἐμῷ, ἀληθῶς μαθηταί μού ἐστε [GNT] | To hold; to continue; to abide; to remain; to keep on obeying. It means to dwell, continue, stay, sojourn, rest in or upon; to live; to rest; to nest.<br><br>**Practical Application**<br>The idea is that of dwelling, just as a person dwells at home. The Word of the Lord is the believer's dwelling place. He continues and abides in God's Word. Very simply, what Jesus was saying is this:<br>⇒ A person who really begins to believe will "continue in" or "hold on to" the Lord's Word. He will continue both to study and to do the Word (2 Tim. 2:15).<br>⇒ A person who does not really believe will not "hold on" to the Lord's Word.<br>⇒ The proof that a person "really believes" is that he does "continue" in the Lord's Word.<br>⇒ The proof that a person has made only a false or a superficial profession is that he does not "continue in" the Lord's Word. He just does not obey the Word of God. |
| **#761**<br>**Continue** | προσκαρτερεῖτε = *proskartereite*<br>Pronunciation: [pros-kar-ter-eh'-ee-teh]<br>Parsing (part of speech): verb<br>    Mood—imperative<br>    Tense—present | To devote; to continue; to be constant, persevering, and unwearied in prayer. It means to be in constant and unbroken prayer—to be in constant and unbroken fellowship and communion |

# Practical Word Studies
## in the New Testament

| ENGLISH WORD | GREEK WORD AND VERSE | THE WORD MEANS... |
|---|---|---|
| Continue–KJV<br>Devote–NASB<br>Devote–NIV<br>Continue–NKJV<br>Devote–NLT<br><br>**POSB REFERENCE**<br>(Col.4:2-4; esp. v.2)<br>Note 1, point 1 | Voice—active<br>Person—2nd person<br>Number—plural<br>Stem or root—from προσκαρτερέω<br>Concordance References:<br>⇒ Strong's #4342 proskartereö<br>⇒ NIV #4674 proskartereö<br>⇒ NASB #4342 proskartereö<br><br>**Col. 4:2**<br>**Continue** in prayer, and watch in the same with thanksgiving; [KJV]<br>**Devote** yourselves to prayer, keeping alert in it with an attitude of thanksgiving; [NASB]<br>**Devote** yourselves to prayer, being watchful and thankful. [NIV]<br>**Continue** earnestly in prayer, being vigilant in it with thanksgiving; [NKJV]<br>**Devote** yourselves to prayer with an alert mind and a thankful heart. [NLT]<br>Τῇ προσευχῇ **προσκαρτερεῖτε**, γρηγοροῦντες ἐν αὐτῇ ἐν εὐχαριστίᾳ· [GNS]<br>Τῇ προσευχῇ **προσκαρτερεῖτε**, γρηγοροῦντες ἐν αὐτῇ ἐν εὐχαριστίᾳ, [GNT] | with God. It means to walk and breathe prayer—to live and move and have our being in prayer. It means to never face a moment when we are not in prayer.<br><br>**Practical Application**<br>How is this possible? When we have so many duties and affairs that demand our attention, how can we continue and walk in unbroken prayer? What Scripture means is that we...<br>• develop an *attitude of prayer*.<br>• walk in a *spirit of prayer*.<br>• take a mental break from our work and spend a moment *in prayer*.<br>• *pray always* when our minds are not upon some duty.<br>• *arise early* and pray before daily activities begin. Spend a worship time with God in prayer. Make this a continued practice.<br>• *pray before going to bed*. Spend an extended time in prayer before going to bed. Make this a continued practice.<br>In all honesty, the vast majority of us waste minute after minute every hour in useless daydreaming and wandering thoughts—wasting precious time that could be spent in prayer. If we would learn to captivate these minutes for prayer, we would discover what it is to walk and live in prayer. Note a critical fact: this is the duty of the believer. It is not something God can do for us. We are the ones who have to discipline ourselves to pray. If we do not pray, then prayer never gets done. |
| #762<br>**Continue**<br><br>Continue–KJV<br>Persevere in–NASB<br>Persevere in–NIV<br>Continue–NKJV<br>Stay true–NLT<br><br>**POSB REFERENCE**<br>(1 Tim.4:16)<br>Note 12<br><br>See also POSB REF:<br>(Col.1:23)<br>Note 4, point 1<br>(Rom.11:22)<br>Note 4, point 2 | ἐπίμενε = epimene<br>Pronunciation: [ep-ee-men'-eh]<br>Parsing (part of speech): verb<br>  Mood—imperative<br>  Tense—present<br>  Voice—active<br>  Person—2nd person<br>  Number—singular<br>  Stem or root—from ἐπιμένω<br>Concordance References:<br>⇒ Strong's #1961 epimenö<br>⇒ NIV #2152 epimenö<br>⇒ NASB #1961 epimenö<br><br>**1 Tim. 4:16**<br>Take heed unto thyself, and unto the doctrine; **continue** in them: for in doing this thou shalt both save thyself, and them that hear thee. [KJV]<br>Pay close attention to yourself and to your teaching; **persevere in** these things; for as you do this you will insure salvation both for yourself and for those who hear you. [NASB]<br>Watch your life and doctrine closely. **Persevere in** them, because if you do, you will save both yourself and your hearers. [NIV]<br>Take heed to yourself and to the doctrine. **Continue** in them, for in doing this you will save both yourself and those who hear you. [NKJV]<br>Keep a close watch on yourself and on your teaching. **Stay true** to what is right, and God will save you and those who hear you. [NLT]<br>ἔπεχε σεαυτῷ καὶ τῇ διδασκαλίᾳ. **ἐπίμενε** αὐτοῖς· τοῦτο γὰρ ποιῶν καὶ σεαυτὸν σώσεις καὶ τοὺς ἀκούοντάς σου. [GNS]<br>ἔπεχε σεαυτῷ καὶ τῇ διδασκαλίᾳ, **ἐπίμενε** αὐτοῖς· τοῦτο γὰρ ποιῶν καὶ σεαυτὸν σώσεις καὶ τοὺς ἀκούοντάς σου.[GNT] | To continue; to persevere in; to stay true; to persist in; to remain; to keep on. The word "continue" (*epimene*) means to "stay by them," "stick to them," "see them through" (A.T. Robertson. *Word Pictures in the New Testament*, Vol.4, p.582).<br><br>**Practical Application**<br>Note what he does. He continues in the instructions of the Word of God. Why? Because by continuing in them, he saves both himself and those who hear him. |

# PRACTICAL WORD STUDIES
## in the NEW TESTAMENT

| ENGLISH WORD | GREEK WORD AND VERSE | THE WORD MEANS... |
|---|---|---|
| **#763**<br>**Continue**<br><br>**Continue–KJV**<br>**Continue–NASB**<br>**Continue–NIV**<br>**Continue–NKJV**<br>Remain faithful–NLT<br><br>**POSB**<br>**REFERENCE**<br>(2 Tim. 3:14)<br>Note 1 | μένε = mene<br>Pronunciation: [men'-ay]<br>Parsing (part of speech): verb<br>    Mood—imperative<br>    Tense—present<br>    Voice—active<br>    Person—2nd person<br>    Number—singular<br>    Stem or root—from μένω<br>Concordance References:<br>  ⇒ Strong's #3306 menö<br>  ⇒ NIV #3531 menö<br>  ⇒ NASB #3306 menö<br><br>**2 Tim. 3:14**<br>But **continue** thou in the things which thou hast learned and hast been assured of, knowing of whom thou hast learned them; [KJV]<br>You, however, **continue** in the things you have learned and become convinced of, knowing from whom you have learned them; [NASB]<br>But as for you, **continue** in what you have learned and have become convinced of, because you know those from whom you learned it, [NIV]<br>But you must **continue** in the things which you have learned and been assured of, knowing from whom you have learned *them,* [NKJV]<br>But you must **remain faithful** to the things you have been taught. You know they are true, for you know you can trust those who taught you. [NLT]<br>σὺ δὲ **μένε** ἐν οἷς ἔμαθες καὶ ἐπιστώθης, εἰδὼς παρὰ τίνος ἔμαθες [GNS]<br>σὺ δὲ **μένε** ἐν οἷς ἔμαθες καὶ ἐπιστώθης, εἰδὼς παρὰ τίνων ἔμαθες, [GNT] | To continue; to remain faithful; to abide, dwell, remain, and stay in the Scripture.<br><br>**Practical Application**<br>Simply stated, Timothy had to *live* in the Scripture—live, move, and have his being in the Scripture. And more, he had to *live out* the Scripture—continue to walk and live in the truths of the Scripture. He had to do what Scripture said. |
| **#764**<br>**Continued**<br>**Steadfastly,**<br>**Stedfastly**<br><br>**Continued stedfastly–KJV**<br>Continually devoting themselves to–NASB<br>Devoted...to–NIV<br>**Continued steadfastly–NKJV**<br>Devoted themselves to–NLT<br><br>**POSB**<br>**REFERENCE**<br>(Acts 2:42)<br>*Deeper Study #1* | ἦσαν προσκαρτεροῦντες = ësan proskarterountes<br>Pronunciation: [ay-san pros-kar-ter-oon'-tehs]<br>Parsing *proskarterountes* (part of speech): verb<br>    Mood—participle<br>    Tense—present<br>    Voice—active<br>    Case—nominative<br>    Gender—masculine<br>    Number—plural<br>    Stem or root—from προσκαρτερέω<br>Concordance References:<br>  ⇒ Strong's #1488 + 4342 eimi proskartereo<br>  ⇒ NIV #1639 + 4674 eimi proskartereö [devoted to]<br>  ⇒ NASB #1488 + 4342 eimi proskartereo<br><br>**Acts 2:42**<br>And they **continued stedfastly** in the apostles' doctrine and fellowship, and in breaking of bread, and in prayers. [KJV]<br>And they were **continually devoting themselves to** the apostles' teaching and to fellowship, to the breaking of bread and to prayer. [NASB]<br>They **devoted** themselves **to** the apostles' teaching and to the fellowship, to the breaking of bread and to prayer. [NIV]<br>And they **continued steadfastly** in the apostles' doctrine and fellowship, in the breaking of bread, and in prayers. [NKJV]<br>They joined with the other believers and **devoted themselves to** the apostles' teaching and fellowship, sharing in the Lord's Supper and in prayer. [NLT]<br>ἦσαν δὲ **προσκαρτεροῦντες** τῇ διδαχῇ τῶν ἀποστόλων καὶ τῇ κοινωνίᾳ, καὶ τῇ κλάσει τοῦ ἄρτου καὶ ταῖς προσευχαῖς. [GNS]<br>ἦσαν δὲ **προσκαρτεροῦντες** τῇ διδαχῇ τῶν ἀποστόλων καὶ τῇ κοινωνίᾳ, τῇ κλάσει τοῦ ἄρτου καὶ ταῖς προσευχαῖς. [GNT] | Devoted to; to continue, persevere, endure, stick, persist.<br><br>**Practical Application**<br>A person does not quit, back off, fade away, or slip back. He continues on steadfastly. |

## PRACTICAL WORD STUDIES
### in the NEW TESTAMENT

| ENGLISH WORD | GREEK WORD AND VERSE | THE WORD MEANS... |
|---|---|---|
| **#765**<br>**Continued With One Accord**<br><br>**Continued with one accord**–KJV<br>Continually devoting themselves to–NASB<br>Joined...constantly–NIV<br>**Continued with one accord**–NKJV<br>Met together continually–NLT<br><br>**POSB REFERENCE**<br>(Acts 1:12-15; esp. v.14)<br>Note 1, point 4 | ἦσαν προσκαρτεροῦντες = ësan proskarterountes<br>Pronunciation: [ay-sahn pros-kar-ter-oon'-tes]<br>Parsing *proskarterountes* (part of speech): verb<br>   Mood—participle<br>   Tense—present<br>   Voice—active<br>   Case—nominative<br>   Gender—masculine<br>   Number—plural<br>   Stem or root—from προσκαρτερέω<br>Concordance References:<br>  ⇒ Strong's #1488 eimi + 4342 proskartereö<br>  ⇒ NIV #1639 eimi + 4674 proskartereö<br>  ⇒ NASB #1488 eimi + 4342 proskartereö<br><br>**Acts 1:14**<br>These all **continued with one accord** in prayer and supplication, with the women, and Mary the mother of Jesus, and with his brethren. [KJV]<br>These all with one mind were **continually devoting themselves to** prayer, along with the women, and Mary the mother of Jesus, and with His brothers. [NASB]<br>They all **joined** together **constantly** in prayer, along with the women and Mary the mother of Jesus, and with his brothers. [NIV]<br>These all **continued with one accord** in prayer and supplication, with the women and Mary the mother of Jesus, and with His brothers. [NKJV]<br>They all **met together continually** for prayer, along with Mary the mother of Jesus, several other women, and the brothers of Jesus. [NLT]<br>οὗτοι πάντες **ἦσαν προσκαρτεροῦντες** ὁμοθυμαδὸν τῇ προσευχῇ καὶ τῇ δεήσει, σὺν γυναιξὶ καὶ Μαρίᾳ τῇ μητρὶ τοῦ Ἰησοῦ, καὶ σὺν τοῖς ἀδελφοῖς αὐτοῦ. [GNS]<br>οὗτοι πάντες **ἦσαν προσκαρτεροῦντες** ὁμοθυμαδὸν τῇ προσευχῇ σὺν γυναιξὶν καὶ Μαριὰμ τῇ μητρὶ τοῦ Ἰησοῦ καὶ τοῖς ἀδελφοῖς αὐτοῦ. [GNT] | Joined constantly; to continue with one accord; continually devoting themselves; met together continually; to be in regular attendance.<br><br>**Practical Application**<br>The word is strong. They continued, persevered, endured, persisted, stuck to praying. |
| **#766**<br>**Continuing Instant**<br><br>Continuing instant–KJV<br>Devoted–NASB<br>Faithful–NIV<br>Continuing steadfastly–NKJV<br>Always–NLT<br><br>**POSB REFERENCE**<br>(Romans 12:12)<br>Note 3, point 3 | προσκαρτεροῦντες = proskarterountes<br>Pronunciation: [pros-kar-ter-oon'-tehs]<br>Parsing (part of speech): verb<br>   Mood—participle (imperative sense)<br>   Tense—present<br>   Voice—active<br>   Case—nominative<br>   Gender—masculine<br>   Person—2nd person<br>   Number—plural<br>   Stem or root—from προσκαρτερέω<br>Concordance References:<br>  ⇒ Strong's #4342 proskartereö<br>  ⇒ NIV #4674 proskartereö<br>  ⇒ NASB #4342 proskartereö<br><br>**Romans 12:12**<br>Rejoicing in hope; patient in tribulation; **continuing instant** in prayer; [KJV]<br>Rejoicing in hope, persevering in tribulation, **devoted** to prayer, [NASB]<br>Be joyful in hope, patient in affliction, **faithful** in prayer. [NIV]<br>Rejoicing in hope, patient in tribulation, **continuing steadfastly** in prayer; [NKJV]<br>Be glad for all God is planning for you. Be patient in trouble, and **always** be prayerful. [NLT]<br>τῇ ἐλπίδι χαίροντες· τῇ θλίψει ὑπομένοντες· τῇ προσευχῇ **προσκαρτεροῦντες**· [GNS]<br>τῇ ἐλπίδι χαίροντες, τῇ θλίψει ὑπομένοντες, τῇ προσευχῇ **προσκαρτεροῦντες**, [GNT] | To be faithful; to be devoted and attentive to; to give constant attention to; to give unceasing care to; to wait steadfastly upon, to persevere.<br><br>**Practical Application**<br>Very simply, the believer overcomes trials by giving constant attention to God and waiting upon His delivering power. The believer stays in constant communion with his Lord, depending upon Him to supply the strength to walk through the trials of daily living. |
| **#767**<br>**Continuing Steadfastly** | προσκαρτεροῦντες = proskarterountes<br>Pronunciation: [pros-kar-ter-oon'-tehs]<br>Parsing (part of speech): verb<br>   Mood—participle (imperative sense) | To be faithful; to be devoted and attentive to; to give constant attention to; to give unceasing care to; to wait steadfastly upon, to persevere. |

## PRACTICAL WORD STUDIES
### in the NEW TESTAMENT

| ENGLISH WORD | GREEK WORD AND VERSE | THE WORD MEANS... |
|---|---|---|
| Continuing instant–KJV<br>Devoted–NASB<br>Faithful–NIV<br>**Continuing steadfastly–NKJV**<br>Always–NLT<br><br>**POSB REFERENCE**<br>(Romans 12:12)<br>Note 3, point 3 | Tense—present<br>Voice—active<br>Case—nominative<br>Gender—masculine<br>Person—2nd person<br>Number—plural<br>Stem or root—from προσκαρτερέω<br>Concordance References:<br>⇒ Strong's #4342 proskartereō<br>⇒ NIV #4674 proskartereō<br>⇒ NASB #4342 proskartereō<br><br>**Romans 12:12**<br>Rejoicing in hope; patient in tribulation; **continuing instant** in prayer; [KJV]<br>Rejoicing in hope, persevering in tribulation, **devoted** to prayer, [NASB]<br>Be joyful in hope, patient in affliction, **faithful** in prayer. [NIV]<br>Rejoicing in hope, patient in tribulation, **continuing steadfastly** in prayer; [NKJV]<br>Be glad for all God is planning for you. Be patient in trouble, and **always** be prayerful. [NLT]<br>τῇ ἐλπίδι χαίροντες· τῇ θλίψει ὑπομένοντες· τῇ προσευχῇ **προσκαρτεροῦντες**· [GNS]<br>τῇ ἐλπίδι χαίροντες, τῇ θλίψει ὑπομένοντες, τῇ προσευχῇ **προσκαρτεροῦντες**, [GNT] | **Practical Application**<br>Very simply, the believer overcomes trials by giving constant attention to God and waiting upon His delivering power. The believer stays in constant communion with his Lord, depending upon Him to supply the strength to walk through the trials of daily living. |
| **#768**<br>**Contradictions**<br><br>Oppositions–KJV<br>Opposing arguments–NASB<br>Opposing ideas–NIV<br>**Contradictions–NKJV**<br>Oppose–NLT<br><br>**POSB REFERENCE**<br>(1 Tim.6:20-21; esp. v.20)<br>Note 2, point 2b | ἀντιθέσεις = *antitheseis*<br>Pronunciation: [an-tith'-es-is]<br>Parsing (part of speech): noun<br>  Case—accusative<br>  Gender—feminine<br>  Number—plural<br>  Stem or root—from ἀντίθεσις, εως<br>Concordance References:<br>⇒ Strong's #477 antithesis<br>⇒ NIV #509 antithesis<br>⇒ NASB #477 antithesis<br><br>**1 Tim. 6:20**<br>O Timothy, keep that which is committed to thy trust, avoiding profane and vain babblings, and **oppositions** of science falsely so called: [KJV]<br>O Timothy, guard what has been entrusted to you, avoiding worldly and empty chatter and the **opposing arguments** of what is falsely called "knowledge"—[NASB]<br>Timothy, guard what has been entrusted to your care. Turn away from godless chatter and the **opposing ideas** of what is falsely called knowledge, [NIV]<br>O Timothy! Guard what was committed to your trust, avoiding the profane *and* idle babblings and **contradictions** of what is falsely called knowledge—[NKJV]<br>Timothy, guard what God has entrusted to you. Avoid godless, foolish discussions with those who **oppose** you with their so-called knowledge. [NLT]<br>Ὦ Τιμόθεε, τὴν παρακαταθήκην φύλαξον, ἐκτρεπόμενος τὰς βεβήλους κενοφωνίας καὶ **ἀντιθέσεις** τῆς ψευδωνύμου γνώσεως· [GNS]<br>Ὦ Τιμόθεε, τὴν παραθήκην φύλαξον ἐκτρεπόμενος τὰς βεβήλους κενοφωνίας καὶ **ἀντιθέσεις** τῆς ψευδωνύμου γνώσεως, [GNT] | On the contrary; in the judgment of.<br><br>**Practical Application**<br>The leaders of the church did not agree with the Judaizers as the Judaizers had hoped; on the contrary, they stood with and championed the call and gospel of Christ. They saw that God had called Paul to preach to the Gentiles (the uncircumcision) just as he had called Peter to preach to the Jews (the circumcision). They championed the truth that God gives to every man a particular task. |
| **#769**<br>**Contrariwise**<br><br>**Contrariwise–KJV**<br>On...contrary–NASB<br>On...contrary–NIV<br>On...contrary –NKJV<br>Not translated–NLT | τοὐναντίον = *tounantion*<br>Pronunciation: [too-nan-tee'-on]<br>Parsing (part of speech): adjective<br>  Type—adverb<br>  Stem or root—from ἐναντίον<br>Concordance References:<br>⇒ Strong's #5121 tounantion<br>⇒ NIV #5539 tounantion<br>⇒ NASB #5121 tounantion | Opposing ideas, oppositions, opposing arguments, contradiction; to oppose. It means antithesis, that is, to stand against some thesis, truth, or fact.<br><br>**Practical Application**<br>What is being condemned is the false knowledge of men, the things that men teach that are |

## PRACTICAL WORD STUDIES
### in the NEW TESTAMENT

| ENGLISH WORD | GREEK WORD AND VERSE | THE WORD MEANS... |
|---|---|---|
| **POSB REFERENCE** (Gal.2:7-10; esp. v.7) Note 5 | **Galatians 2:7**<br>But **contrariwise**, when they saw that the gospel of the uncircumcision was committed unto me, as the gospel of the circumcision was unto Peter; [KJV]<br>But **on** the **contrary**, seeing that I had been entrusted with the gospel to the uncircumcised, just as Peter had been to the circumcised [NASB]<br>**On** the **contrary**, they saw that I had been entrusted with the task of preaching the gospel to the Gentiles, just as Peter had been to the Jews. [NIV]<br>But **on** the **contrary**, when they saw that the gospel for the uncircumcised had been committed to me, as *the gospel* for the circumcised *was* to Peter [NKJV]<br>They saw that God had given me the responsibility of preaching the Good News to the Gentiles, just as he had given Peter the responsibility of preaching to the Jews. [NLT]—NOT TRANSLATED<br>ἀλλὰ **τοὐναντίον**, ἰδόντες ὅτι πεπίστευμαι τὸ εὐαγγέλιον τῆς ἀκροβυστίας, καθὼς Πέτρος τῆς περιτομῆς, [GNS]<br>ἀλλὰ **τοὐναντίον** ἰδόντες ὅτι πεπίστευμαι τὸ εὐαγγέλιον τῆς ἀκροβυστίας καθὼς Πέτρος τῆς περιτομῆς, [GNT] | contrary to God's glorious revelation in Christ and in the Word of God. The minister of God—in fact, any person—is a fool to stand against truth and fact, whether of God or of true science. |
| **#770 Contrary**<br><br>**Contrary**–KJV<br>**Contrary**–NASB<br>Against–NIV<br>**Contrary**–NKJV<br>Headwinds–NLT<br><br>**POSB REFERENCE** (Acts 27:4-12; esp. v.4) Note 2, point 1a | ἐναντίους = *enantious*<br>Pronunciation: [en-an-tee'-oos]<br>Parsing (part of speech): adjective<br>    Case—accusative<br>    Gender—masculine<br>    Number—plural<br>    Stem or root—from ἐναντίος<br>Concordance References:<br>  ⇒ Strong's #1727 enantios<br>  ⇒ NIV #1885 enantios<br>  ⇒ NASB #1727 enantios<br><br>**Acts 27:4**<br>And when we had launched from thence, we sailed under Cyprus, because the winds were **contrary**. [KJV]<br>And from there we put out to sea and sailed under the shelter of Cyprus because the winds were **contrary**. [NASB]<br>From there we put out to sea again and passed to the lee of Cyprus because the winds were **against** us. [NIV]<br>When we had put to sea from there, we sailed under the shelter of Cyprus, because the winds were **contrary**. [NKJV]<br>Putting out to sea from there, we encountered **headwinds** that made it difficult to keep the ship on course, so we sailed north of Cyprus between the island and the mainland. [NLT]<br>κἀκεῖθεν ἀναχθέντες ὑπεπλεύσαμεν τὴν Κύπρον, διὰ τὸ τοὺς ἀνέμους εἶναι **ἐναντίους**, [GNS]<br>κἀκεῖθεν ἀναχθέντες ὑπεπλεύσαμεν τὴν Κύπρον διὰ τὸ τοὺς ἀνέμους εἶναι **ἐναντίους**, [GNT] | Against, contrary, opposed, hostile headwinds.<br><br>**Practical Application**<br>The winds were "contrary": strong and forceful; a northwest headwind faced them. Therefore, they could not strike a straight course through the open sea. |
| **#771 Contributing**<br><br>Distributing–KJV<br>**Contributing**–NASB<br>Share with–NIV<br>Distributing–NKJV<br>Help them–NLT<br><br>**POSB REFERENCE** (Rom.12:13) Note 4, point 1 | κοινωνοῦντες = *koinōnountes*<br>Pronunciation: [koy-no-noon'-tehs]<br>Parsing (part of speech): verb<br>    Mood—participle (imperative sense)<br>    Tense—present<br>    Voice—active<br>    Case—nominative<br>    Gender—masculine<br>    Person—2nd person<br>    Number—plural<br>    Stem or root—from κοινωνέω<br>Concordance References:<br>  ⇒ Strong's #2841 koinōneō<br>  ⇒ NIV #3125 koinōneō<br>  ⇒ NASB #2841 koinōneō | To share; to help; to contribute; to give.<br><br>**Practical Application**<br>The believer is to meet the needs of people unselfishly. The believer is to give generously; to share with those in need. He is to "contribute" (*koinōnountes*), that is, to give and share in order to meet their needs. |

# PRACTICAL WORD STUDIES
## in the NEW TESTAMENT

| ENGLISH WORD | GREEK WORD AND VERSE | THE WORD MEANS... |
|---|---|---|
| | **Romans 12:13**<br>**Distributing** to the necessity of saints; given to hospitality. [KJV]<br>**Contributing** to the needs of the saints, practicing hospitality. [NASB]<br>**Share with** God's people who are in need. Practice hospitality. [NIV]<br>**Distributing** to the needs of the saints, given to hospitality. [NKJV]<br>When God's children are in need, be the one to **help them** out. And get into the habit of inviting guests home for dinner or, if they need lodging, for the night. [NLT]<br>ταῖς χρείαις τῶν ἁγίων **κοινωνοῦντες**· τὴν φιλοξενίαν διώκοντες. [GNS]<br>ταῖς χρείαις τῶν ἁγίων **κοινωνοῦντες**, τὴν φιλοξενίαν διώκοντες. [GNT] | |
| **#772**<br>**Contributing To The Needs Of Others**<br><br>Giveth–KJV<br>Gives–NASB<br>Contributing to the needs of others–NIV<br>Gives–NKJV<br>Share it–NLT<br><br>**POSB REFERENCE**<br>(Rom.12:6-8; esp. v.8)<br>Note 2, point 5 | μεταδιδοὺς = *metadidous*<br>Pronunciation: [met-ad-id'-oos]<br>Parsing (part of speech): verb<br>  Mood—participle<br>  Tense—present<br>  Voice—active<br>  Case—nominative<br>  Gender—masculine<br>  Number—singular<br>  Stem or root—from μεταδίδωμι<br>Concordance References:<br> ⇒ Strong's #3330 metadidōmi<br> ⇒ NIV #3556 metadidōmi<br> ⇒ NASB #3330 metadidōmi<br><br>**Romans 12:8**<br>Or he that exhorteth, on exhortation: he that **giveth**, let him do it with simplicity; he that ruleth, with diligence; he that sheweth mercy, with cheerfulness. [KJV]<br>Or he who exhorts, in his exhortation; he who **gives**, with liberality; he who leads, with diligence; he who shows mercy, with cheerfulness. [NASB]<br>If it is encouraging, let him encourage; if it is **contributing to the needs of others**, let him give generously; if it is leadership, let him govern diligently; if it is showing mercy, let him do it cheerfully. [NIV]<br>He who exhorts, in exhortation; he who **gives**, with liberality; he who leads, with diligence; he who shows mercy, with cheerfulness. [NKJV]<br>If your gift is to encourage others, do it! If you have money, **share it** generously. If God has given you leadership ability, take the responsibility seriously. And if you have a gift for showing kindness to others, do it gladly. [NLT]<br>εἴτε ὁ παρακαλῶν, ἐν τῇ παρακλήσει· ὁ **μεταδιδοὺς** ἐν ἁπλότητι, ὁ προϊστάμενος, ἐν σπουδῇ· ὁ ἐλεῶν ἐν ἱλαρότητι. [GNS]<br>εἴτε ὁ παρακαλῶν ἐν τῇ παρακλήσει· ὁ **μεταδιδοὺς** ἐν ἁπλότητι, ὁ προϊστάμενος ἐν σπουδῇ, ὁ ἐλεῶν ἐν ἱλαρότητι. [GNT] | To contribute to the needs of others; to give; to share; to impart.<br><br>**Practical Application**<br>There is the gift of giving (*metadidous*). This simply means the giving of one's earthly possessions such as money, clothing, and food. Note that in listing this particular gift, Scripture adds a point: it tells how the person is to give. He is to give "generously" (*haplotetes*). |
| **#773**<br>**Control**<br><br>Reign–KJV<br>Reign–NASB<br>Reign–NIV<br>Reign–NKJV<br>**Control–NLT**<br><br>**POSB REFERENCE**<br>(Rom 6:12)<br>Note 2, point 1 | βασιλευέτω = *basileuetō*<br>Pronunciation: [bas-il-yoo'-eh-tow]<br>Parsing (part of speech): verb<br>  Mood—imperative<br>  Tense—present<br>  Voice—active<br>  Person—3rd person<br>  Number—singular<br>  Stem or root—from βασιλεύω<br>Concordance References:<br> ⇒ Strong's #936 basileuō<br> ⇒ NIV #996 basileuō<br> ⇒ NASB #936 basileuō | To rule; to reign; to become like a king; to have authority; to control; to occupy; to hold sway; to prevail over.<br><br>**Practical Application**<br>The believer must resist sin. This is an imperative–a forceful command. It is up to the believer to resist sin; he is responsible for resisting it.<br>He must not let sin have control (*basileuetō*). The present tense is used, so the idea is a continuous attitude and behavior. The believer is always to keep his mind off sin. He is to keep his |

# PRACTICAL WORD STUDIES
## in the NEW TESTAMENT

| ENGLISH WORD | GREEK WORD AND VERSE | THE WORD MEANS... |
|---|---|---|
| | **Romans 6:12**<br>Let not sin therefore **reign** in your mortal body, that ye should obey it in the lusts thereof. [KJV]<br>Therefore do not let sin **reign** in your mortal body that you should obey its lusts, [NASB]<br>Therefore do not let sin **reign** in your mortal body so that you obey its evil desires. [NIV]<br>Therefore do not let sin **reign** in your mortal body, that you should obey it in its lusts. [NKJV]<br>Do not let sin **control** the way you live; do not give in to its lustful desires. [NLT]<br>Μὴ οὖν **βασιλευέτω** ἡ ἁμαρτία ἐν τῷ θνητῷ ὑμῶν σώματι, εἰς τὸ ὑπακούειν ταῖς ἐπιθυμίαις αὐτοῦ· [GNS]<br>Μὴ οὖν **βασιλευέτω** ἡ ἁμαρτία ἐν τῷ θνητῷ ὑμῶν σώματι εἰς τὸ ὑπακούειν ταῖς ἐπιθυμίαις αὐτοῦ, [GNT] | mind under control by keeping his mind off...<br>• wealth and material things<br>• position and power<br>• recognition and fame<br>• the lust of the eyes<br>• the lust of the flesh<br>• the pride of life<br>• parties and sex<br>• appearance and clothes<br>The believer is not to let sin dominate, control, and reign in his mortal body. Sin is not to dominate his thoughts and life. He is to resist sin by standing against it and by rebuking and fighting against it. He is to oppose sin with all his might. |
| **#774**<br>**Controlled By Your Own Sinful Desires**<br><br>Carnal–KJV<br>Fleshly–NASB<br>Worldly–NIV<br>Carnal–NKJV<br>Controlled by your own sinful desires–NLT<br><br>**POSB REFERENCE**<br>(1 Cor.3:1-4; esp. v.3)<br>*Deeper Study* #1 | σαρκικοί = sarkikoi<br>Pronunciation: [sar-kee-koy']<br>Parsing (part of speech): adjective<br>    Case—nominative<br>    Gender—masculine<br>    Number—plural<br>    Stem or root—from σαρκικός, ή, όν<br>Concordance References:<br>  ⇒ Strong's #4559 sarkikos<br>  ⇒ NIV #4920 sarkikos<br>  ⇒ NASB #4559 sarkikos<br><br>**1 Cor. 3:3**<br>For ye are yet **carnal**: for whereas there is among you envying, and strife, and divisions, are ye not carnal, and walk as men? [KJV]<br>For you are still **fleshly**. For since there is jealousy and strife among you, are you not fleshly, and are you not walking like mere men? [NASB]<br>You are still **worldly**. For since there is jealousy and quarreling among you, are you not worldly? Are you not acting like mere men? [NIV]<br>For you are still **carnal**. For where *there are* envy, strife, and divisions among you, are you not carnal and behaving like *mere* men? [NKJV]<br>For you are still **controlled by your own sinful desires**. You are jealous of one another and quarrel with each other. Doesn't that prove you are controlled by your own desires? You are acting like people who don't belong to the Lord. [NLT]<br>ἔτι γὰρ **σαρκικοί** ἐστε· ὅπου γὰρ ἐν ὑμῖν ζῆλος καὶ ἔρις καὶ διχοστασίαι, οὐχὶ σαρκικοί ἐστε, καὶ κατὰ ἄνθρωπον περιπατεῖτε; [GNS]<br>ἔτι γὰρ **σαρκικοί** ἐστε. ὅπου γὰρ ἐν ὑμῖν ζῆλος καὶ ἔρις, οὐχὶ σαρκικοί ἐστε καὶ κατὰ ἄνθρωπον περιπατεῖτε; [GNT] | Worldly, carnal, fleshly, sinful; controlled by your own sinful desires.<br><br>**Practical Application**<br>The ending "*ikoi*" means to be "characterized by." Paul is saying that the Corinthians were not only "made of flesh" but characterized and "dominated by the flesh." They were allowing the flesh and its passions to captivate and control their behavior. They were living on the level of the flesh, still controlled by it. |
| **#775**<br>**Controls**<br><br>Constraineth–KJV<br>**Controls–NASB**<br>Compels–NIV<br>Compels–NKJV<br>**Controls–NLT**<br><br>**POSB REFERENCE**<br>(2 Cor.5:14-16; esp. v.14)<br>Note 4 | συνέχει = sunechei<br>Pronunciation: [soon-ekh'-ee]<br>Parsing (part of speech): verb<br>    Mood—indicative<br>    Tense—present<br>    Voice—active<br>    Person—3rd person<br>    Number—singular<br>    Stem or root—from συνέχω<br>Concordance References:<br>  ⇒ Strong's #4912 sunechō<br>  ⇒ NIV #5309 sunechō<br>  ⇒ NASB #4912 sunechō<br><br>**2 Cor. 5:14**<br>For the love of Christ **constraineth** us; because we thus judge, that if one died for all, then were all dead: [KJV]<br>For the love of Christ **controls** us, having concluded | To compel; to constrain; to control; to press.<br><br>**Practical Application**<br>The love of Christ presses, compels, and stirs Paul to hold fast to the ministry. The love of Christ is the great thing that constrains Paul to minister. Note that Paul does not say that he is driven to minister because of...<br>• the great teaching of Christ.<br>• the great example of Christ.<br>• the great ministry of Christ.<br>• the great life of Christ.<br><br>All of these areas of the Lord's life are important, critically so, but they are not the foundation of our salvation and ministry. The foundation of the believer's life is the love of Christ. |

# PRACTICAL WORD STUDIES
## in the NEW TESTAMENT

| ENGLISH WORD | GREEK WORD AND VERSE | THE WORD MEANS... |
|---|---|---|
| | this, that one died for all, therefore all died; [NASB]<br>For Christ's love **compels** us, because we are convinced that one died for all, and therefore all died. [NIV]<br>For the love of Christ **compels** us, because we judge thus: that if One died for all, then all died; [NKJV]<br>Whatever we do, it is because Christ's love **controls** us. Since we believe that Christ died for everyone, we also believe that we have all died to the old life we used to live. [NLT]<br>ἡ γὰρ ἀγάπη τοῦ Χριστοῦ **συνέχει** ἡμᾶς, κρίναντας τοῦτο, ὅτι εἰ εἷς ὑπὲρ πάντων ἀπέθανεν, ἄρα οἱ πάντες ἀπέθανον· [GNS]<br>ἡ γὰρ ἀγάπη τοῦ Χριστοῦ **συνέχει** ἡμᾶς, κρίναντας τοῦτο, ὅτι εἷς ὑπὲρ πάντων ἀπέθανεν, ἄρα οἱ πάντες ἀπέθανον· [GNT] | |
| **#776**<br>**Conversation**<br><br>**Conversation–KJV**<br>Conduct–NASB<br>Conduct–NIV<br>Conduct–NKJV<br>Live–NLT<br><br>**POSB REFERENCE**<br>(Philip.1:27)<br>Note 1 | πολιτεύεσθε = politeuesthe<br>Pronunciation: [pol-it-yoo'-ehs-theh]<br>Parsing (part of speech): verb<br>   Mood—imperative<br>   Tense—present<br>   Voice—middle or passive deponent<br>   Person—2nd person<br>   Number—plural<br>   Stem or root—from πολιτεύομαι<br>Concordance References:<br>  ⇒ Strong's #4176 politeuomai<br>  ⇒ NIV #4488 politeuomai<br>  ⇒ NASB #4176 politeuomai<br><br>**Philip. 1:27**<br>Only let your **conversation** be as it becometh the gospel of Christ: that whether I come and see you, or else be absent, I may hear of your affairs, that ye stand fast in one spirit, with one mind striving together for the faith of the gospel; [KJV]<br>Only **conduct** yourselves in a manner worthy of the gospel of Christ; so that whether I come and see you or remain absent, I may hear of you that you are standing firm in one spirit, with one mind striving together for the faith of the gospel; [NASB]<br>Whatever happens, **conduct** yourselves in a manner worthy of the gospel of Christ. Then, whether I come and see you or only hear about you in my absence, I will know that you stand firm in one spirit, contending as one man for the faith of the gospel [NIV]<br>Only let your **conduct** be worthy of the gospel of Christ, so that whether I come and see you or am absent, I may hear of your affairs, that you stand fast in one spirit, with one mind striving together for the faith of the gospel, [NKJV]<br>But whatever happens to me, you must **live** in a manner worthy of the Good News about Christ, as citizens of heaven. Then, whether I come and see you again or only hear about you, I will know that you are standing side by side, fighting together for the Good News. [NLT]<br>μόνον ἀξίως τοῦ εὐαγγελίου τοῦ Χριστοῦ **πολιτεύεσθε**, ἵνα εἴτε ἐλθὼν καὶ ἰδὼν ὑμᾶς, εἴτε ἀπὼν ἀκούσω τὰ περὶ ὑμῶν, ὅτι στήκετε ἐν ἑνὶ πνεύματι, μιᾷ ψυχῇ συναθλοῦντες τῇ πίστει τοῦ εὐαγγελίου, [GNS]<br>Μόνον ἀξίως τοῦ εὐαγγελίου τοῦ Χριστοῦ **πολιτεύεσθε**, ἵνα εἴτε ἐλθὼν καὶ ἰδὼν ὑμᾶς εἴτε ἀπὼν ἀκούω τὰ περὶ ὑμῶν, ὅτι στήκετε ἐν ἑνὶ πνεύματι, μιᾷ ψυχῇ συναθλοῦντες τῇ πίστει τοῦ εὐαγγελίου [GNT] | Behavior; conduct; to live one's life.<br><br>**Practical Application**<br>A.T. Robertson points out that this word is used only twice in the New Testament (Acts 23:1; Phil. 1:27) (*Word Pictures in the New Testament*, Vol.4, p.441). Usually, when the New Testament refers to behavior or conduct, it uses a word meaning how a person should walk about day by day (*peripatein*). But Paul switches the word in writing to the Philippians. Why? The reason is significant. Philippi was a proud Roman colony. In fact, it was famous as a miniature Rome. A city became a Roman colony by one of two ways. At first, Rome founded colonies throughout the outer reaches of the Empire to keep the peace and to guard against invasions from barbaric hordes. Veteran soldiers, ready for retirement, were usually granted citizenship if they would go out to settle these colonies. Later on, however, a city was granted the distinctive title of a Roman Colony for loyalty and service to the Empire. The distinctive thing about these colonies was their fanatic loyalty to Rome. The citizens kept all their Roman ties: the Roman language, titles, customs, affairs, and dress. They refused to allow any infiltration of local influence whatsoever. They totally rejected the influence of the world around them. They were Roman colonists within an alien environment.<br>This is the reason Paul uses the word *politeuesthe*. It means conduct and behavior; but more accurately, it means the conduct and behavior of *citizenship*, of a person who is the citizen of a great nation. The Philippian church knew exactly what Paul was saying: they were citizens of heaven. Therefore, they must...<br>• keep their close ties with heaven.<br>• speak the clean and pure language of heaven.<br>• bear the title of heaven, Christian, and do so proudly.<br>• bear witness to the customs of heaven.<br>• carry on the affairs of heaven.<br>• dress as a citizen of heaven.<br>• allow no infiltration of worldly influence whatsoever.<br>• live and conduct themselves as a heavenly colony within a polluted and dying environment. |

# PRACTICAL WORD STUDIES
## in the NEW TESTAMENT

| ENGLISH WORD | GREEK WORD AND VERSE | THE WORD MEANS... |
|---|---|---|
| **#777**<br>**Conversation**<br><br>**Conversation–KJV**<br>Citizenship–NASB<br>Citizenship–NIV<br>Citizenship–NKJV<br>Citizens–NLT<br><br>**POSB REFERENCE**<br>(Philip.3:20-21; esp. v.20)<br>Note 1, point 1 | πολίτευμα = politeuma<br>Pronunciation: [pol-it'-yoo-mah]<br>Parsing (part of speech): noun<br>    Case—nominative<br>    Gender—neuter<br>    Number—singular<br>    Stem or root—from πολίτευμα, τος<br>Concordance References:<br>⇒ Strong's #4175 politeuma<br>⇒ NIV #4487 politeuma<br>⇒ NASB #4175 politeuma<br><br>**Philip. 3:20**<br>For our **conversation** is in heaven; from whence also we look for the Saviour, the Lord Jesus Christ: [KJV]<br>For our **citizenship** is in heaven, from which also we eagerly wait for a Savior, the Lord Jesus Christ; [NASB]<br>But our **citizenship** is in heaven. And we eagerly await a Savior from there, the Lord Jesus Christ, [NIV]<br>For our **citizenship** is in heaven, from which we also eagerly wait for the Savior, the Lord Jesus Christ, [NKJV]<br>But we are **citizens** of heaven, where the Lord Jesus Christ lives. And we are eagerly waiting for him to return as our Savior. [NLT]<br>ἡμῶν γὰρ τὸ **πολίτευμα** ἐν οὐρανοῖς ὑπάρχει, ἐξ οὗ καὶ Σωτῆρα ἀπεκδεχόμεθα, Κύριον Ἰησοῦν Χριστόν· [GNS]<br>ἡμῶν γὰρ τὸ **πολίτευμα** ἐν οὐρανοῖς ὑπάρχει, ἐξ οὗ καὶ σωτῆρα ἀπεκδεχόμεθα κύριον Ἰησοῦν Χριστόν, [GNT] | Citizenship; to be a citizen of; to be in the place of citizenship.<br><br>**Practical Application**<br>The believer's life is to be heaven-centered, for his conversation [citizenship] is in heaven. Remember that Philippi was a Roman colony and its citizens, although in Macedonia, were citizens of Rome. The citizens of Roman colonies lived as Romans: they dressed as Romans, spoke the Roman language, lived by the laws of Rome, engaged in Roman pleasures and social affairs, and worshipped the Roman gods. Despite the fact that they lived in Macedonia, their citizenship was in Rome. (See POSB note, Citizenship, Heavenly—Phil. 1:27 for more discussion; cp. Ephes. 2:6.)<br>The point to see is this: the Philippian believers knew exactly what it meant to live in one place and to be a citizen of another place. They knew exactly what it would mean to live upon the earth and...<br>• to dress as a citizen of heaven and not of the earth.<br>• to speak as a citizen of heaven and not of the earth.<br>• to engage in the pleasures of a citizen of heaven and not of the earth.<br>• to live by the laws of heaven as well as the laws of earth.<br>• to worship the God of heaven and not the religions and gods of this earth. |
| **#778**<br>**Conversation**<br><br>**Conversation–KJV**<br>Character–NASB<br>Lives–NIV<br>Conduct–NKJV<br>Not translated–NLT<br><br>**POSB REFERENCE**<br>(Heb.13:5-6; esp. v.5)<br>Note 5 | τρόπος = tropos<br>Pronunciation: [trop'-os]<br>Parsing (part of speech): noun<br>    Case—nominative<br>    Gender—masculine<br>    Number—singular<br>    Stem or root—from τρόπος, ου<br>Concordance References:<br>⇒ Strong's #5158 tropos<br>⇒ NIV #5573 tropos<br>⇒ NASB #5158 tropos<br><br>**Hebrews 13:5**<br>Let your **conversation** be without covetousness; and be content with such things as ye have: for he hath said, I will never leave thee, nor forsake thee. [KJV]<br>Let your **character** be free from the love of money, being content with what you have; for He Himself has said, "I will never desert you, nor will I ever forsake you," [NASB]<br>Keep your **lives** free from the love of money and be content with what you have, because God has said, "Never will I leave you; never will I forsake you." [NIV]<br>Let your **conduct** be without covetousness; be content with such things as you have. For He Himself has said, *"I will never leave you nor forsake you."* [NKJV]<br>Stay away from the love of money; be satisfied with what you have. For God has said, "I will never fail you. I will never forsake you." [NLT]—NOT TRANSLATED<br>ἀφιλάργυρος ὁ **τρόπος**, ἀρκούμενοι τοῖς παροῦσιν· αὐτὸς γὰρ εἴρηκεν, Οὐ μή σε ἀνῶ, οὐδ' οὐ μήσε ἐγκαταλίπω. [GNS]<br>Ἀφιλάργυρος ὁ **τρόπος**, ἀρκούμενοι τοῖς παροῦσιν. αὐτὸς γὰρ εἴρηκεν, Οὐ μή σε ἀνῶ οὐδ' οὐ μή σε ἐγκαταλίπω. [GNT] | Conversation, character, lives, ways, conduct. Thomas Hewitt points out that the Greek word for "conversation" (*tropos*) means *manner of life*, or *the way of thought and life* (*The Epistle to the Hebrews*. "Tyndale New Testament Commentaries," p.206).<br><br>**Practical Application**<br>The believer's very thoughts are to be free from covetousness. His thoughts are to be focused upon Christ and the glorious hope of eternity, not upon this passing world and its possessions. The believer is to have no secret lust for the things of this world. |
| **#779**<br>**Convert** | προσήλυτον = prosëluton<br>Pronunciation: [pros-ay'-loo-ton]<br>Parsing (part of speech): noun<br>    Case—accusative | A convert; a proselyte.<br><br>**Practical Application**<br>It is a person who has actually approached |

# PRACTICAL WORD STUDIES
## in the NEW TESTAMENT

| ENGLISH WORD | GREEK WORD AND VERSE | THE WORD MEANS... |
|---|---|---|
| Proselyte–KJV<br>Proselyte–NASB<br>**Convert–NIV**<br>Proselyte–NKJV<br>**Convert–NLT**<br><br>**POSB<br>REFERENCE**<br>(Mt.23:15)<br>*Deeper Study #4* | Gender—masculine<br>Number—singular<br>Stem or root—from προσήλυτος, ου<br>Concordance References:<br>⇒ Strong's #4339 prosēlutos<br>⇒ NIV #4670 prosēlutos<br>⇒ NASB #4339 prosēlutos<br><br>**Matthew 23:15**<br>Woe unto you, scribes and Pharisees, hypocrites! for ye compass sea and land to make one **proselyte**, and when he is made, ye make him twofold more the child of hell than yourselves. [KJV]<br>"Woe to you, scribes and Pharisees, hypocrites, because you travel about on sea and land to make one **proselyte**; and when he becomes one, you make him twice as much a son of hell as yourselves. [NASB]<br>"Woe to you, teachers of the law and Pharisees, you hypocrites! You travel over land and sea to win a single **convert**, and when he becomes one, you make him twice as much a son of hell as you are. [NIV]<br>Woe to you, scribes and Pharisees, hypocrites! For you travel land and sea to win one **proselyte**, and when he is won, you make him twice as much a son of hell as yourselves. [NKJV]<br>Yes, how terrible it will be for you teachers of religious law and you Pharisees. For you cross land and sea to make one **convert**, and then you turn him into twice the son of hell as you yourselves are. [NLT]<br>Οὐαὶ ὑμῖν, γραμματεῖς καὶ Φαρισαῖοι ὑποκριταί, ὅτι περιάγετε τὴν θάλασσαν καὶ τὴν ξηρὰν ποιῆσαι ἕνα **προσήλυτον**, καὶ ὅταν γένηται ποιεῖτε αὐτὸν υἱὸν γεέννης διπλότερον ὑμῶν. [GNS]<br>Οὐαὶ ὑμῖν, γραμματεῖς καὶ Φαρισαῖοι ὑποκριταί, ὅτι περιάγετε τὴν θάλασσαν καὶ τὴν ξηρὰν ποιῆσαι ἕνα **προσήλυτον**, καὶ ὅταν γένηται ποιεῖτε αὐτὸν υἱὸν γεέννης διπλότερον ὑμῶν. [GNT] | and drawn near religion, that is, adopted the beliefs of religion. Note the tragedy of this portion of Scripture: The Jewish religious leaders went after the God-fearing and devout people who had already shown interest in religion (Judaism). Some of these people were so pleased with what Judaism offered them that when one really became a convert, he became extremely zealous for Judaism. He was so indoctrinated that he was made into a fanatic, more devoted than many of the Jews themselves. Thus the false teachers caused these converts to heap damnation upon themselves.<br><br>One of the strongest lessons to be learned from the teachers of the law (scribes) and Pharisees is zeal in evangelism.<br>1. They had a willingness to go. They who held to a false religion were so willing to go. Why are we, who know the truth, so unwilling to go? Where is our zeal to reach people?<br>2. They were willing to go anyplace. They traveled worldwide to reach just one convert. Where is our willingness to go as missionaries? As witnesses? Where is our willingness to go even around the corner? |
| #780<br>**Converted**<br><br>**Converted–KJV**<br>**Converted–NASB**<br>Change–NIV<br>**Converted–NKJV**<br>Turn–NLT<br><br>**POSB<br>REFERENCE**<br>(Mt.18:3)<br>Note 2 | στραφῆτε = *straphēte*<br>Pronunciation: [stref'-ee-teh]<br>Parsing (part of speech): verb<br>  Mood—subjunctive<br>  Tense—aorist<br>  Voice—passive<br>  Person—2nd person<br>  Number—plural<br>  Stem or root—from στρέφω<br>Concordance References:<br>⇒ Strong's #4762 strephō<br>⇒ NIV #5138 strephō<br>⇒ NASB #4762 strephō<br><br>**Matthew 18:3**<br>And said, Verily I say unto you, Except ye be **converted**, and become as little children, ye shall not enter into the kingdom of heaven. [KJV]<br>And said, "Truly I say to you, unless you are **converted** and become like children, you shall not enter the kingdom of heaven. [NASB]<br>And he said: "I tell you the truth, unless you **change** and become like little children, you will never enter the kingdom of heaven. [NIV]<br>And said, "Assuredly, I say to you, unless you are **converted** and become as little children, you will by no means enter the kingdom of heaven. [NKJV]<br>Then he said, "I assure you, unless you **turn** from your sins and become as little children, you will never get into the Kingdom of Heaven. [NLT]<br>καὶ εἶπεν, Ἀμὴν λέγω ὑμῖν, ἐὰν μὴ **στραφῆτε** καὶ γένησθε ὡς τὰ παιδία, οὐ μὴ εἰσέλθητε εἰς τὴν βασιλείαν τῶν οὐρανῶν. [GNS]<br>καὶ εἶπεν, Ἀμὴν λέγω ὑμῖν, ἐὰν μὴ **στραφῆτε** καὶ γένησθε ὡς τὰ παιδία, οὐ μὴ εἰσέλθητε εἰς τὴν βασιλείαν τῶν οὐρανῶν. [GNT] | To change; to turn around; to be converted; to turn from one thing to something else.<br><br>**Practical Application**<br>How is a person changed or converted? By turning and becoming as a little child. What does it mean "to become as a little child"? When Christ *called* the child to Him, the child demonstrated exactly what Christ meant.<br>1. The child *trusted* Christ. The child responded to the call of Christ. He sensed the openness, warmth, tenderness, care, and love of Christ; so he felt free to respond and to trust Christ's call.<br>2. The child *surrendered* himself to Christ. He was willing to give up what he was doing to go to Christ, willing to surrender whatever it was that was occupying his thoughts and behavior.<br>3. The child *obeyed* Christ. He was obedient, doing exactly what Christ requested, and it was probably difficult to do so. There were at least thirteen adult men standing or sitting there, and the child was being asked to walk into the midst of these men. Note that he obeyed despite the difficulty and obeyed simply because Christ asked him.<br>4. The child *humbled* himself before Christ. All the above traits show humility. However, there is something often overlooked and abused by the adult world. Little children do not push themselves forward. They are not |

## PRACTICAL WORD STUDIES
### in the NEW TESTAMENT

| ENGLISH WORD | GREEK WORD AND VERSE | THE WORD MEANS... |
|---|---|---|
| | | interested in prominence, fame, power, wealth, or position. They do not want to be placed in the midst of a group of adults, for they prefer to be in the background, away from staring, gawking eyes. Such embarrasses them and makes them feel self-conscious. Therefore, they prefer to be left in their obscure world. They are by nature humble, knowing little if anything of the competitive world that surrounds them; that is, they know little of it until they are brought into it by adults. |
| #781 **Converted**  **Converted**–KJV  Turned again–NASB  Turned back–NIV  Returned–NKJV  Repented and turned–NLT  **POSB REFERENCE** (Lk.22:32) Note 2, point 2  See also POSB REF: (Acts 3:19) Note 7 | ἐπιστρέψας = *epistrepsas*  Pronunciation: [ep-ee-stref'-ahs]  Parsing (part of speech): verb     Mood—participle     Tense—aorist     Voice—active     Case—nominative     Gender—masculine     Person—2nd person     Number—singular     Stem or root—from ἐπιστρέφω  Concordance References:  ⇒ Strong's #1994 epistrephō  ⇒ NIV #2188 epistrephō  ⇒ NASB #1994 epistrephō  **Luke 22:32**  But I have prayed for thee, that thy faith fail not: and when thou art **converted**, strengthen thy brethren." [KJV]  But I have prayed for you, that your faith may not fail; and you, when once you have **turned again**, strengthen your brothers." [NASB]  But I have prayed for you, Simon, that your faith may not fail. And when you have **turned back**, strengthen your brothers." [NIV]  But I have prayed for you, that your faith should not fail; and when you have **returned** to *Me*, strengthen your brethren." [NKJV]  But I have pleaded in prayer for you, Simon, that your faith should not fail. So when you have **repented and turned** to me again, strengthen and build up your brothers." [NLT]  ἐγὼ δὲ ἐδεήθην περὶ σοῦ, ἵνα μὴ ἐκλείπῃ ἡ πίστις σου· καὶ σύ ποτε ἐπιστρέψας, στήριξον τοὺς ἀδελφούς σου. [GNS]  ἐγὼ δὲ ἐδεήθην περὶ σοῦ ἵνα μὴ ἐκλίπῃ ἡ πίστις σου· καὶ σύ ποτε ἐπιστρέψας στήρισον τοὺς ἀδελφούς σου. [GNT] | To turn around; to convert; to turn back to; to repent and turn; to turn again; to return.  **Practical Application**  It is a turning away from sin and turning toward God. It is a change of mind, a forsaking of sin. It is putting sin out of one's thoughts and behavior. It is resolving never to think or do a thing again. (See POSB note—Acts 17:29-30 and POSB *Deeper Study* #1, Repentance—Acts 17:29-30.) |
| #782 **Converted**  **Converted**–KJV  Return–NASB  Turn to–NIV  **Converted**–NKJV  Turn to–NLT  **POSB REFERENCE** (Acts 3:19) Note 7 | ἐπιστρέψατε = *epistrepsate*  Pronunciation: [ep-ee-stref'-ah-teh]  Parsing (part of speech): verb     Mood—imperfect     Tense—aorist     Voice—active     Person—2nd person     Number—plural     Stem or root—from ἐπιστρέφω  Concordance References:  ⇒ Strong's #1994 epistrephō  ⇒ NIV #2188 epistrephō  ⇒ NASB #1994 epistrephō  **Acts 3:19**  Repent ye therefore, and be **converted**, that your sins may be blotted out, when the times of refreshing shall come from the presence of the Lord; [KJV]  "Repent therefore and **return**, that your sins may be | Turn to; convert; return; to turn back; to turn around.  **Practical Application**  The word "converted" (*epistrepsate*) means to turn again. Men must repent and turn again to God. (See POSB note—Acts 17:29-30 and POSB *Deeper Study* #1, Repentance—Acts 17:29-30.) |

# PRACTICAL WORD STUDIES
## in the NEW TESTAMENT

| ENGLISH WORD | GREEK WORD AND VERSE | THE WORD MEANS... |
|---|---|---|
| | wiped away, in order that times of refreshing may come from the presence of the Lord; [NASB]<br>    Repent, then, and **turn to** God, so that your sins may be wiped out, that times of refreshing may come from the Lord, [NIV]<br>    Repent therefore and be **converted**, that your sins may be blotted out, so that times of refreshing may come from the presence of the Lord, [NKJV]<br>    Now turn from your sins and **turn to** God, so you can be cleansed of your sins. [NLT]<br>    ετανοήσατε οὖν καὶ **ἐπιστρέψατε**, εἰς τὸ ἐξαλειφθῆναι ὑμῶν τὰς ἁμαρτίας, [GNS]<br>    μετανοήσατε οὖν καὶ **ἐπιστρέψατε** εἰς τὸ ἐξαλειφθῆναι ὑμῶν τὰς α [GNT] | |
| **#783**<br>**Convict**<br><br>Convince–KJV<br>Refute–NASB<br>Refute–NIV<br>**Convict–NKJV**<br>Show–NLT<br><br>**POSB REFERENCE**<br>(Tit.1:9)<br>Note 4, point 2 | ἐλέγχειν = elegchein<br>Pronunciation: [el-eng'-kheen]<br>Parsing (part of speech): verb<br>    Mood—infinitive<br>    Tense—present<br>    Voice—active<br>    Stem or root—from ἐλέγχω<br>Concordance References:<br>  ⇒ Strong's #1651 elegchō<br>  ⇒ NIV #1794 elegchō<br>  ⇒ NASB #1651 elegchō<br><br>**Titus 1:9**<br>    Holding fast the faithful word as he hath been taught, that he may be able by sound doctrine both to exhort and to **convince** the gainsayers. [KJV]<br>    Holding fast the faithful word which is in accordance with the teaching, that he may be able both to exhort in sound doctrine and to **refute** those who contradict. [NASB]<br>    He must hold firmly to the trustworthy message as it has been taught, so that he can encourage others by sound doctrine and **refute** those who oppose it. [NIV]<br>    Holding fast the faithful word as he has been taught, that he may be able, by sound doctrine, both to exhort and **convict** those who contradict. [NKJV]<br>    He must have a strong and steadfast belief in the trustworthy message he was taught; then he will be able to encourage others with right teaching and **show** those who oppose it where they are wrong. [NLT]<br>    ἀντεχόμενον τοῦ κατὰ τὴν διδαχὴν πιστοῦ λόγου, ἵνα δυνατὸς ᾖ καὶ παρακαλεῖν ἐν τῇ διδασκαλίᾳ τῇ ὑγιαινούσῃ, καὶ τοὺς ἀντιλέγοντας **ἐλέγχειν**. [GNS]<br>    ἀντεχόμενον τοῦ κατὰ τὴν διδαχὴν πιστοῦ λόγου, ἵνα δυνατὸς ᾖ καὶ παρακαλεῖν ἐν τῇ διδασκαλίᾳ τῇ ὑγιαινούσῃ καὶ τοὺς ἀντιλέγοντας **ἐλέγχειν**. [GNT] | To convict of guilt; to reprove; to convince; to show a person his error; to rebuke; to refute.<br><br>**Practical Application**<br>    There is a strong reason why the bishop or minister must hold fast to the Word of God: he must be able to exhort and to convert those who oppose God and Christ.<br>  ⇒ People need to be exhorted, that is, encouraged to trust Christ and to follow Him.<br>  ⇒ People need to be convicted, especially those who stand opposed to God and curse him, refusing to surrender to Him. The word convict (*elegchein*) means "to rebuke a man in such a way that he is compelled to see and to admit the error of his ways. Trench says that it means 'to rebuke another, with such an effectual wielding of the victorious arms of the truth, as to bring him, if not always to a confession, yet at least to a conviction of his sin'....Christian rebuke means far more than 'giving a man a row'...means far more than merely speaking to him in such a way that he sees the error of his ways and accepts the truth. The aim of Christian rebuke is not to humiliate a man, but to enable him to see and recognize and admit the duty and the truth to which he has been either blind or disobedient" (William Barclay. *The Letters to Timothy, Titus, and Philemon*, p.274).<br>    Note how the minister of God is to exhort and convince people: "by sound doctrine." And note the word "able": he is to be so grounded in God's Word that he is able to exhort and convict people *out of God's Word*. |
| **#784**<br>**Convict–**<br>**Convict Of Guilt**<br><br>Reprove–KJV<br>**Convict–NASB**<br>**Convict of guilt–NIV**<br>**Convict–NKJV**<br>Convince–NLT<br><br>**POSB REFERENCE**<br>(Jn.16:8-11; esp. v.8)<br>Note 2 | ἐλέγξει = elegxei<br>Pronunciation: [el-eng'-cheh-ee]<br>Parsing (part of speech): verb<br>    Mood—indicative<br>    Tense—future<br>    Voice—active<br>    Person—3rd person<br>    Number—singular<br>    Stem or root—from ἐλέγχω<br>Concordance References:<br>  ⇒ Strong's #1651 elegcho<br>  ⇒ NIV #1794 elegcho<br>  ⇒ NASB #1651 elegcho<br><br>**John 16:8**<br>    And when he is come, he will **reprove** the world of | To convict of guilt; to reprove; to correct; to convince; to condemn; to prove guilty; to show a person his error.<br><br>**Practical Application**<br>    It means both to convict and to convince a person of his fault.<br>  ⇒ Convict means to prick a person's heart until he senses and knows he is guilty. He has done wrong or failed to do right.<br>  ⇒ Convince means to hammer and drive at a person's heart until he knows the fact is true. |

# PRACTICAL WORD STUDIES
## in the NEW TESTAMENT

| ENGLISH WORD | GREEK WORD AND VERSE | THE WORD MEANS... |
|---|---|---|
| | sin, and of righteousness, and of judgment: [KJV]<br>"And He, when He comes, will **convict** the world concerning sin, and righteousness, and judgment; [NASB]<br>When he comes, he will **convict** the world **of guilt** in regard to sin and righteousness and judgment: [NIV]<br>And when He has come, He will **convict** the world of sin, and of righteousness, and of judgment: [NKJV]<br>And when he comes, he will **convince** the world of its sin, and of God's righteousness, and of the coming judgment. [NLT]<br>καὶ ἐλθὼν ἐκεῖνος **ἐλέγξει** τὸν κόσμον περὶ ἁμαρτίας καὶ περὶ δικαιοσύνης καὶ περὶ κρίσεως. [GNS]<br>καὶ ἐλθὼν ἐκεῖνος **ἐλέγξει** τὸν κόσμον περὶ ἁμαρτίας καὶ περὶ δικαιοσύνης καὶ περὶ κρίσεως· [GNT] | |
| **#785**<br>**Convicted Them Deeply**<br><br>Pricked–KJV<br>Pierced–NASB<br>Cut to–NIV<br>Cut to–NKJV<br>**Convicted them deeply–NLT**<br><br>**POSB REFERENCE**<br>(Acts 2:37)<br>Note 1 | κατενύγησαν = *katenugēsan*<br>Pronunciation: [kat-en-oog'-ay-san]<br>Parsing (part of speech): verb<br>   Mood—indicative<br>   Tense—aorist<br>   Voice—passive<br>   Person—3rd person<br>   Number—plural<br>   Stem or root—from κατανύσσομαι<br>Concordance References:<br> ⇒ Strong's #2660 katanussomai<br> ⇒ NIV #2920 katanussomai<br> ⇒ NASB #2660 katanussomai<br><br>**Acts 2:37**<br>Now when they heard this, they were **pricked** in their heart, and said unto Peter and to the rest of the apostles, Men and brethren, what shall we do? [KJV]<br>Now when they heard this, they were **pierced** to the heart, and said to Peter and the rest of the apostles, "Brethren, what shall we do?" [NASB]<br>When the people heard this, they were **cut to** the heart and said to Peter and the other apostles, "Brothers, what shall we do?" [NIV]<br>Now when they heard *this,* they were **cut to** the heart, and said to Peter and the rest of the apostles, "Men *and* brethren, what shall we do?" [NKJV]<br>Peter's words **convicted them deeply**, and they said to him and to the other apostles, "Brothers, what should we do?" [NLT]<br>Ἀκούσαντες δὲ **κατενύγησαν** τὴν καρδίαν, εἶπόν τε πρὸς τὸν Πέτρον καὶ τοὺς λοιποὺς ἀποστόλους, Τί ποιήσομεν, ἄνδρες ἀδελφοί; [GNS]<br>Ἀκούσαντες δὲ **κατενύγησαν** τὴν καρδίαν εἶπόν τε πρὸς τὸν Πέτρον καὶ τοὺς λοιποὺς ἀποστόλους, Τί ποιήσωμεν, ἄνδρες ἀδελφοί; [GNT] | To be cut to the heart; to be pricked; to be pierced; to be convicted deeply; to be stabbed. The words "convicted them deeply" *(katenugēsan)* mean to convict, cut, sting, sense pain and hurt.<br><br>**Practical Application**<br>In this Scripture, we learn how the gospel affects the hearts of repentant sinners. The power of the gospel convicts people deeply. |
| **#786**<br>**Convince**<br><br>Reprove–KJV<br>Convict–NASB<br>Convict...of guilt–NIV<br>Convict–NKJV<br>**Convince–NLT**<br><br>**POSB REFERENCE**<br>(Jn.16:8-11; esp. v.8)<br>Note 2 | ἐλέγξει = *elegxei*<br>Pronunciation: [el-eng'-cheh-ee]<br>Parsing (part of speech): verb<br>   Mood—indicative<br>   Tense—future<br>   Voice—active<br>   Person—3rd person<br>   Number—singular<br>   Stem or root—from ἐλέγχω<br>Concordance References:<br> ⇒ Strong's #1651 elegcho<br> ⇒ NIV #1794 elegcho<br> ⇒ NASB #1651 elegcho<br><br>**John 16:8**<br>And when he is come, he will **reprove** the world of sin, and of righteousness, and of judgment: [KJV]<br>"And He, when He comes, will **convict** the world concerning sin, and righteousness, and judgment; [NASB]<br>When he comes, he will **convict** the world **of guilt** in regard to sin and righteousness and judgment: [NIV] | To convict of guilt; to reprove; to convince; to show a person his error; to rebuke; to refute.<br><br>**Practical Application**<br>It means both to convict and to convince a person of his fault.<br>⇒ Convict means to prick a person's heart until he senses and knows he is guilty. He has done wrong or failed to do right.<br>⇒ Convince means to hammer and drive at a person's heart until he knows the fact is true. |

## PRACTICAL WORD STUDIES
### in the NEW TESTAMENT

| ENGLISH WORD | GREEK WORD AND VERSE | THE WORD MEANS... |
|---|---|---|
| | And when He has come, He will **convict** the world of sin, and of righteousness, and of judgment: [NKJV]<br>And when he comes, he will **convince** the world of its sin, and of God's righteousness, and of the coming judgment. [NLT]<br>καὶ ἐλθὼν ἐκεῖνος **ἐλέγξει** τὸν κόσμον περὶ ἁμαρτίας καὶ περὶ δικαιοσύνης καὶ περὶ κρίσεως. [GNS]<br>καὶ ἐλθὼν ἐκεῖνος **ἐλέγξει** τὸν κόσμον περὶ ἁμαρτίας καὶ περὶ δικαιοσύνης καὶ περὶ κρίσεως· [GNT] | |
| #787<br>**Convince**<br><br>Reprove–KJV<br>Reprove–NASB<br>Correct–NIV<br>**Convince–NKJV**<br>Correct–NLT<br><br>**POSB REFERENCE**<br>(2 Tim. 4:2)<br>Note 2, point 3 | **ἔλεγξον** = elegxon<br>Pronunciation: [el-eng'-khon]<br>Parsing (part of speech): verb<br>  Mood—imperative<br>  Tense—aorist<br>  Voice—active<br>  Person—2nd person<br>  Number—singular<br>  Stem or root—from ἐλέγχω<br>Concordance References:<br>⇒ Strong's #1651 elegchō<br>⇒ NIV #1794 elegchō<br>⇒ NASB #1651 elegchō<br><br>**2 Tim. 4:2**<br>Preach the word; be instant in season, out of season; **reprove**, rebuke, exhort with all longsuffering and doctrine. [KJV]<br>Preach the word; be ready in season and out of season; **reprove**, rebuke, exhort, with great patience and instruction. [NASB]<br>Preach the Word; be prepared in season and out of season; **correct**, rebuke and encourage—with great patience and careful instruction. [NIV]<br>Preach the word! Be ready in season *and* out of season. **Convince**, rebuke, exhort, with all longsuffering and teaching. [NKJV]<br>Preach the word of God. Be persistent, whether the time is favorable or not. Patiently **correct**, rebuke, and encourage your people with good teaching. [NLT]<br>κήρυξον τὸν λόγον, ἐπίστηθι εὐκαίρως, ἀκαίρως, **ἔλεγξον**, ἐπιτίμησον, παρακάλεσον, ἐν πάσῃ μακροθυμίᾳ καὶ διδαχῇ. [GNS]<br>κήρυξον τὸν λόγον, ἐπίστηθι εὐκαίρως, ἀκαίρως, **ἔλεγξον**, ἐπιτίμησον, παρακάλεσον, ἐν πάσῃ μακροθυμίᾳ καὶ διδαχῇ. [GNT] | To correct; to reprove; to rebuke; to convince; to show fault; to prove guilty.<br><br>**Practical Application**<br>The word means to stir up a person to prove himself; to put a person under conviction; to lead a person to see his sin and to feel guilt over it. It means to put a person under conviction of sin and to lead him to confession and repentance. |
| #788<br>**Convince**<br><br>**Convince–KJV**<br>Refute–NASB<br>Refute–NIV<br>Convict–NKJV<br>Show–NLT<br><br>**POSB REFERENCE**<br>(Tit.1:9)<br>Note 4, point 2 | **ἐλέγχειν** = elegchein<br>Pronunciation: [el-eng'-kheen]<br>Parsing (part of speech): verb<br>  Mood—infinitive<br>  Tense—present<br>  Voice—active<br>  Stem or root—from ἐλέγχω<br>Concordance References:<br>⇒ Strong's #1651 elegchō<br>⇒ NIV #1794 elegchō<br>⇒ NASB #1651 elegchō<br><br>**Titus 1:9**<br>Holding fast the faithful word as he hath been taught, that he may be able by sound doctrine both to exhort and to **convince** the gainsayers. [KJV]<br>Holding fast the faithful word which is in accordance with the teaching, that he may be able both to exhort in sound doctrine and to **refute** those who contradict. [NASB]<br>He must hold firmly to the trustworthy message as it has been taught, so that he can encourage others by sound doctrine and **refute** those who oppose it. [NIV]<br>Holding fast the faithful word as he has been taught, that he may be able, by sound doctrine, both to exhort and | To convict of guilt; to reprove; to convince; to show a person his error; to rebuke; to refute.<br><br>**Practical Application**<br>There is a strong reason why the bishop or minister must hold fast to the Word of God: he must be able to exhort and to convert those who oppose God and Christ.<br>⇒ People need to be exhorted, that is, encouraged to trust Christ and to follow Him.<br>⇒ People need to be convicted, especially those who stand opposed to God and curse him and refuse to surrender to Him. The word convince (*elegchein*) means "*to rebuke a man in such a way that he is compelled to see and to admit the error of his ways. Trench says that it means 'to rebuke another, with such an effectual wielding of the victorious arms of the truth, as to bring him, if not always to a confession, yet at least to a conviction of his sin'....Christian rebuke means far more than 'giving a man a row'...means* |

## PRACTICAL WORD STUDIES
## in the NEW TESTAMENT

| ENGLISH WORD | GREEK WORD AND VERSE | THE WORD MEANS... |
|---|---|---|
| | **convict** those who contradict. [NKJV]<br>He must have a strong and steadfast belief in the trustworthy message he was taught; then he will be able to encourage others with right teaching and **show** those who oppose it where they are wrong. [NLT]<br>ἀντεχόμενον τοῦ κατὰ τὴν διδαχὴν πιστοῦ λόγου, ἵνα δυνατὸς ᾖ καὶ παρακαλεῖν ἐν τῇ διδασκαλίᾳ τῇ ὑγιαινούσῃ, καὶ τοὺς ἀντιλέγοντας **ἐλέγχειν**. [GNS]<br>ἀντεχόμενον τοῦ κατὰ τὴν διδαχὴν πιστοῦ λόγου, ἵνα δυνατὸς ᾖ καὶ παρακαλεῖν ἐν τῇ διδασκαλίᾳ τῇ ὑγιαινούσῃ καὶ τοὺς ἀντιλέγοντας **ἐλέγχειν**. [GNT] | *far more than merely speaking to him in such a way that he sees the error of his ways and accepts the truth. The aim of Christian rebuke is not to humiliate a man, but to enable him to see and recognize and admit the duty and the truth to which he has been either blind or disobedient*" (William Barclay. *The Letters to Timothy, Titus, and Philemon*, p.274).<br><br>Note how the minister of God is to exhort and convince people: "by sound doctrine." And note the word "able": he is to be so grounded in God's Word that he is able to exhort and convict people *out of God's Word*. |
| **#789**<br>**Convince, Trying To**<br><br>Persuaded–KJV<br>Trying to persuade–NASB<br>Trying to persuade–NIV<br>Persuaded–NKJV<br>**Trying to convince–NLT**<br><br>**POSB REFERENCE**<br>(Acts 18:4)<br>Note 4, point 2 | **ἔπειθέν** = epeithen<br>Pronunciation: [eh-peh-i'-then]<br>Parsing (part of speech): verb<br>    Mood—indicative<br>    Tense—imperfect<br>    Voice—active<br>    Person—3rd person<br>    Number—singular<br>    Stem or root—from πείθω<br>Concordance References:<br>  ⇒ Strong's #3982 peithö<br>  ⇒ NIV #4275 peithö<br>  ⇒ NASB #3982 peithö<br><br>**Acts 18:4**<br>And he reasoned in the synagogue every sabbath, and **persuaded** the Jews and the Greeks. [KJV]<br>And he was reasoning in the synagogue every Sabbath and **trying to persuade** Jews and Greeks. [NASB]<br>Every Sabbath he reasoned in the synagogue, **trying to persuade** Jews and Greeks. [NIV]<br>And he reasoned in the synagogue every Sabbath, and **persuaded** both Jews and Greeks. [NKJV]<br>Each Sabbath found Paul at the synagogue, **trying to convince** the Jews and Greeks alike. [NLT]<br>διελέγετο δὲ ἐν τῇ συναγωγῇ κατὰ πᾶν σάββατον, **ἔπειθέ** τε Ἰουδαίους καὶ Ἕλληνας. [GNS]<br>διελέγετο δὲ ἐν τῇ συναγωγῇ κατὰ πᾶν σάββατον, **ἔπειθέν** τε Ἰουδαίους καὶ Ἕλληνας. [GNT] | Trying to persuade; trying to convince; trying to win the approval; to win over.<br><br>**Practical Application**<br>It means that Paul tried; he prevailed, urged, induced, pleaded, begged, sought to move and bring about a change of heart and mind. |
| **#790**<br>**Convinced**<br><br>Believed–KJV<br>Believed–NASB<br>Believed–NIV<br>Believed–NKJV<br>**Convinced–NLT**<br><br>**POSB REFERENCE**<br>(Jn.2:23)<br>Note 1, point 1<br><br>See also POSB REF:<br>(Jn.2:23-24; esp. v.23)<br>*Deeper Study #2* | **ἐπίστευσαν** = episteusan<br>Pronunciation: [eh-pist-yoo'-sahn]<br>Parsing (part of speech): verb<br>    Mood—indicative<br>    Tense—aorist<br>    Voice—active<br>    Person—3rd person<br>    Number—plural<br>    Stem or root—from πιστεύω<br>Concordance References:<br>  ⇒ Strong's #4100 pisteuö<br>  ⇒ NIV #4409 pisteuö<br>  ⇒ NASB #4100 pisteuö<br><br>**John 2:23**<br>Now when he was in Jerusalem at the passover, in the feast day, many **believed** in his name, when they saw the miracles which he did. [KJV]<br>Now when He was in Jerusalem at the Passover, during the feast, many **believed** in His name, beholding His signs which He was doing. [NASB]<br>Now while he was in Jerusalem at the Passover Feast, many people saw the miraculous signs he was doing and **believed** in his name. [NIV]<br>Now when He was in Jerusalem at the Passover, during the feast, many **believed** in His name when they saw | To trust; to have faith in; to be persuaded; to accept; to have no doubt; to be convinced; to believe; to rely on.<br><br>**Practical Application**<br>The word "convinced" (*episteusan*) is in the Greek aorist tense, which means they believed *once-for-all*. In this Scripture, their belief was genuine, at least the belief of some. However, the belief of others was not genuine. The fact that Jesus knew "what people were really like" (all those professing belief) and did not commit Himself to them shows the inadequacy of their faith (John 2:24). |

## PRACTICAL WORD STUDIES
### in the NEW TESTAMENT

| ENGLISH WORD | GREEK WORD AND VERSE | THE WORD MEANS... |
|---|---|---|
| | the signs which He did. [NKJV]<br>Because of the miraculous signs he did in Jerusalem at the Passover celebration, many people were **convinced** that he was indeed the Messiah. [NLT]<br>Ὡς δὲ ἦν ἐν Ἱεροσολύμοις ἐν τῷ πάσχα ἐν τῇ ἑορτῇ, πολλοὶ **ἐπίστευσαν** εἰς τὸ ὄνομα αὐτοῦ, θεωροῦντες αὐτοῦ τὰ σημεῖα ἃ ἐποίει. [GNS]<br>Ὡς δὲ ἦν ἐν τοῖς Ἱεροσολύμοις ἐν τῷ πάσχα ἐν τῇ ἑορτῇ, πολλοὶ **ἐπίστευσαν** εἰς τὸ ὄνομα αὐτοῦ θεωροῦντες αὐτοῦ τὰ σημεῖα ἃ ἐποίει· [GNT] | |
| **#791**<br>**Convinced**<br><br>Convinced–KJV<br>Refuted–NASB<br>Refuted–NIV<br>Refuted–NKJV<br>Arguments–NLT<br><br>**POSB REFERENCE**<br>(Acts 18:27-28; esp. v.28)<br>Note 8, point 2b | διακατηλέγχετο = *diakatēlegcheto*<br>Pronunciation: [dee-ak-at-el-eng'-cheh-tow]<br>Parsing (part of speech): verb<br>  Mood—indicative<br>  Tense—imperfect<br>  Voice—middle or passive deponent<br>  Person—3rd person<br>  Number—singular<br>  Stem or root—from διακατελέγχομαι<br>Concordance References:<br> ⇒ Strong's #1246 diakatelegchomai<br> ⇒ NIV #1352 diakatelegchomai<br> ⇒ NASB #1246 diakatelegchomai<br><br>**Acts 18:28**<br>For he mightily **convinced** the Jews, and that publicly, shewing by the scriptures that Jesus was Christ. [KJV]<br>For he powerfully **refuted** the Jews in public, demonstrating by the Scriptures that Jesus was the Christ. [NASB]<br>For he vigorously **refuted** the Jews in public debate, proving from the Scriptures that Jesus was the Christ. [NIV]<br>For he vigorously **refuted** the Jews publicly, showing from the Scriptures that Jesus is the Christ. [NKJV]<br>He refuted all the Jews with powerful **arguments** in public debate. Using the Scriptures, he explained to them, "The Messiah you are looking for is Jesus." [NLT]<br>εὐτόνως γὰρ τοῖς Ἰουδαίοις **διακατηλέγχετο** δημοσίᾳ ἐπιδεικνὺς διὰ τῶν γραφῶν εἶναι τὸν Χριστόν, Ἰησοῦν. [GNS]<br>εὐτόνως γὰρ τοῖς Ἰουδαίοις **διακατηλέγχετο** δημοσίᾳ ἐπιδεικνὺς διὰ τῶν γραφῶν εἶναι τὸν Χριστὸν Ἰησοῦν. [GNT] | Refuted to the very last point, confronted, defeated in argument; to be argued down.<br><br>**Practical Application**<br>Apollos did it publicly. But note: he was not using human reason to argue; he was using the Scripture. And his purpose was to prove that Jesus is the Messiah. (See POSB *Deeper Study #2*—Matthew 1:18 for discussion.) |
| **#792**<br>**Convinced That**<br><br>Confident that–KJV<br>Confident that–NASB<br>**Convinced that–NIV**<br>Confident that–NKJV<br>**Convinced that–NLT**<br><br>**POSB REFERENCE**<br>(Romans 2:17-20; esp. v.19)<br>Note 1, point 6 | πέποιθάς = *pepoithas*<br>Pronunciation: [pi'-poy-thas]<br>Parsing (part of speech): verb<br>  Mood—indicative<br>  Tense—perfect<br>  Voice—active<br>  Person—2nd person<br>  Number—singular<br>  Stem or root—from πείθω<br>Concordance References:<br> ⇒ Strong's #3982 peithō<br> ⇒ NIV #4275 peithō<br> ⇒ NASB #3982 peithō<br><br>**Romans 2:19**<br>And art **confident that** thou thyself art a guide of the blind, a light of them which are in darkness, [KJV]<br>and are **confident that** you yourself are a guide to the Blind, a light to those who are in darkness, [NASB]<br>If you are **convinced that** you are a guide for the blind, a light for those who are in the dark, [NIV]<br>And are **confident that** you yourself are a guide to the blind, a light to those who are in darkness, [NKJV]<br>You are **convinced that** you are a guide for the blind and a beacon light for people who are lost in darkness without God. [NLT] | Convinced that, confident that; to be persuaded and sure.<br><br>**Practical Application**<br>The religionist is convinced that religion is true, that religion is the way men should live. He believes that a man who does not believe in God and live a religious life is blind, needing to be guided to the truth. By living a religious life, he feels...<br>• he is an example to men.<br>• he is a guide to help men find God.<br>• he can cure men of their blindness to God and religion.<br>However, being "convinced" that one is a guide of the blind does not mean that one is a true guide. A person must be sure that he himself is following the truth, Jesus Christ (John 14:6). There are many guides in the world who are leading people down the wrong road. They are blind guides, the blind leading the blind (Matthew 15:14). |

# PRACTICAL WORD STUDIES
## in the NEW TESTAMENT

| ENGLISH WORD | GREEK WORD AND VERSE | THE WORD MEANS... |
|---|---|---|
| | πέποιθάς τε σεαυτὸν ὁδηγὸν εἶναι τυφλῶν, φῶς τῶν ἐν σκότει, [GNS]<br>πέποιθάς τε σεαυτὸν ὁδηγὸν εἶναι τυφλῶν, φῶς τῶν ἐν σκότει, [GNT] | |
| **#793**<br>**Convulsed**<br><br>Torn–KJV<br>Throwing...into convulsions–NASB<br>Shook...violently–NIV<br>**Convulsed–NKJV**<br>Threw...into a convulsion–NLT<br><br>**POSB REFERENCE**<br>(Mk.1:25-26; esp. v.26)<br>Note 2, point 2 | σπαράξαν = *sparaxan*<br>Pronunciation: [spar-ach'-zahn]<br>Parsing (part of speech): verb<br>    Mood—participle<br>    Tense—aorist<br>    Voice—active<br>    Case—nominative<br>    Gender—neuter<br>    Number—singular<br>    Stem or root—from σπαράσσω<br>Concordance References:<br>  ⇒ Strong's #4682 sparassō<br>  ⇒ NIV #5057 sparassō<br>  ⇒ NASB #4682 sparassō<br><br>**Mark 1:26**<br>And when the unclean spirit had **torn** him, and cried with a loud voice, he came out of him. [KJV]<br>And **throwing** him **into convulsions**, the unclean spirit cried out with a loud voice, and came out of him. [NASB]<br>The evil spirit **shook** the man **violently** and came out of him with a shriek. [NIV]<br>And when the unclean spirit had **convulsed** him and cried out with a loud voice, he came out of him. [NKJV]<br>At that, the evil spirit screamed and **threw** the man **into a convulsion**, but then he left him. [NLT]<br>καὶ **σπαράξαν** αὐτὸν τὸ πνεῦμα τὸ ἀκάθαρτον καὶ κράξαν φωνῇ μεγάλῃ, ἐξῆλθεν ἐξ αὐτοῦ. [GNS]<br>καὶ **σπαράξαν** αὐτὸν τὸ πνεῦμα τὸ ἀκάθαρτον καὶ φωνῆσαν φωνῇ μεγάλῃ ἐξῆλθεν ἐξ αὐτοῦ. [GNT] | To be shaken violently; to be convulsed; to be thrown into convulsions; to jolt, jar, or shake up.<br><br>**Practical Application**<br>Apparently the man had a convulsion, jerking to and fro and crying out with a loud voice. |
| **#794**<br>**Convulsions, Throwing Into– Convulsion, Threw Into A**<br><br>Torn–KJV<br>**Throwing...into convulsions–NASB**<br>Shook...violently–NIV<br>Convulsed–NKJV<br>**Threw...into a convulsion–NLT**<br><br>**POSB REFERENCE**<br>(Mk.1:25-26; esp. v.26)<br>Note 2, point 2 | σπαράξαν = *sparaxan*<br>Pronunciation: [spar-ach'-zahn]<br>Parsing (part of speech): verb<br>    Mood—participle<br>    Tense—aorist<br>    Voice—active<br>    Case—nominative<br>    Gender—neuter<br>    Number—singular<br>    Stem or root—from σπαράσσω<br>Concordance References:<br>  ⇒ Strong's #4682 sparassō<br>  ⇒ NIV #5057 sparassō<br>  ⇒ NASB #4682 sparassō<br><br>**Mark 1:26**<br>And when the unclean spirit had **torn** him, and cried with a loud voice, he came out of him. [KJV]<br>And **throwing** him **into convulsions**, the unclean spirit cried out with a loud voice, and came out of him. [NASB]<br>The evil spirit **shook** the man **violently** and came out of him with a shriek. [NIV]<br>And when the unclean spirit had **convulsed** him and cried out with a loud voice, he came out of him. [NKJV]<br>At that, the evil spirit screamed and **threw** the man **into a convulsion**, but then he left him. [NLT]<br>καὶ **σπαράξαν** αὐτὸν τὸ πνεῦμα τὸ ἀκάθαρτον καὶ κράξαν φωνῇ μεγάλῃ, ἐξῆλθεν ἐξ αὐτοῦ. [GNS]<br>καὶ **σπαράξαν** αὐτὸν τὸ πνεῦμα τὸ ἀκάθαρτον καὶ φωνῆσαν φωνῇ μεγάλῃ ἐξῆλθεν ἐξ αὐτοῦ. [GNT] | To be shaken violently; to be convulsed; to be thrown into convulsions; to jolt, jar, or shake up.<br><br>**Practical Application**<br>Apparently the man had a convulsion, jerking to and fro and crying out with a loud voice. |
| **#795**<br>**Copy** | ὑποδείγματι = *hupodeigmati*<br>Pronunciation: [hoop-od'-igue-mah-tee]<br>Parsing (part of speech): noun<br>    Case—dative<br>    Gender—neuter | Copy, example, imitation, pattern, shadow; a shadowy outline; a reflection.<br><br>**Practical Application**<br>The tabernacle and sacrifices of the Old |

# PRACTICAL WORD STUDIES
## in the NEW TESTAMENT

| ENGLISH WORD | GREEK WORD AND VERSE | THE WORD MEANS... |
|---|---|---|
| Example–KJV<br>**Copy**–NASB<br>**Copy**–NIV<br>**Copy**–NKJV<br>**Copy**–NLT<br><br>**POSB<br>REFERENCE**<br>(Heb.8:4-5, esp. v.5)<br>Note 5 | Number—singular<br>Stem or root—from ὑπόδειγμα, τος<br>Concordance References:<br>⇒ Strong's #5262 hupodeigma<br>⇒ NIV #5682 hupodeigma<br>⇒ NASB #5262 hupodeigma<br><br>**Hebrews 8:5**<br>Who serve unto the **example** and shadow of heavenly things, as Moses was admonished of God when he was about to make the tabernacle: for, See, saith he, that thou make all things according to the pattern shewed to thee in the mount. [KJV]<br>Who serve a **copy** and shadow of the heavenly things, just as Moses was warned by God when he was about to erect the tabernacle; for, "See," He says, "that you make all things according to the pattern which was shown you on the mountain." [NASB]<br>They serve at a sanctuary that is a **copy** and shadow of what is in heaven. This is why Moses was warned when he was about to build the tabernacle: "See to it that you make everything according to the pattern shown you on the mountain." [NIV]<br>Who serve the **copy** and shadow of the heavenly things, as Moses was divinely instructed when he was about to make the tabernacle. For He said, *"See that you make all things according to the pattern shown you on the mountain."* [NKJV]<br>They serve in a place of worship that is only a **copy**, a shadow of the real one in heaven. For when Moses was getting ready to build the Tabernacle, God gave him this warning: "Be sure that you make everything according to the design I have shown you here on the mountain." [NLT]<br>οἵτινες **ὑποδείγματι** καὶ σκιᾷ λατρεύουσι τῶν ἐπουρανίων, καθὼς κεχρημάτισται Μωσῆς μέλλων ἐπιτελεῖν τὴν σκηνήν, Ὅρα, γάρ φησί, ποιήσῃς πάντα κατὰ τὸν τύπον τὸν δειχθέντα σοι ἐν τῷ ὄρει. [GNS]<br>οἵτινες **ὑποδείγματι** καὶ σκιᾷ λατρεύουσιν τῶν ἐπουρανίων, καθὼς κεχρημάτισται Μωϋσῆς μέλλων ἐπιτελεῖν τὴν σκηνήν, Ὅρα γάρ φησίν, ποιήσεις πάντα κατὰ τὸν τύπον τὸν δειχθέντα σοι ἐν τῷ ὄρει· [GNT] | Testament were only shadows of heavenly things. Jesus Christ is the Minister of heaven, of the real world, of the real sanctuary and tabernacle of God. The things of religion and worship upon earth are only examples and shadows, copies and sketches, shadowy outlines and reflections of heavenly worship.<br>Note: there is a real world, a heavenly world, and there is a tabernacle, a throne room in which the glorious presence of God dwells. It was the pattern from which Moses made the earthly tabernacle (cp. Exodus 25:40). God had shown Moses the real pattern of heavenly worship and told him to make a copy of it upon earth. That is what the tabernacle was that was carried around by Israel in the wilderness wanderings.<br>The point is this: earthly priests can only give us the shadow and picture of heaven. But Jesus Christ is the Priest and Minister of the heavenly worship, of the real world. Therefore, He is the One who can lead men into heaven, into the world that is real and perfect and unending. He is the One who can lead us into the very presence of God. |
| **#796<br>Copy The<br>Behavior<br>And Customs**<br><br>Conformed–KJV<br>Conformed–NASB<br>Conform...to the pattern of–NIV<br>Conformed–NKJV<br>Copy the behavior and customs–NLT<br><br>**POSB<br>REFERENCE**<br>(Rom.12:2)<br>Note 3, point 1 | *συσχηματίζεσθε* = suschēmatizesthe<br>Pronunciation: [soos-khay-mat-id'-zehs-theh]<br>Parsing (part of speech): verb<br>  Mood—imperative<br>  Tense—present<br>  Voice—middle or passive<br>  Person—2nd person<br>  Number—plural<br>Stem or root—from συσχηματίζομαι<br>Concordance References:<br>⇒ Strong's #4964 suschēmatizō<br>⇒ NIV #5372 suschēmatizō<br>⇒ NASB #4964 suschēmatizō<br><br>**Romans 12:2**<br>And be not **conformed** to this world: but be ye transformed by the renewing of your mind, that ye may prove what is that good, and acceptable, and perfect, will of God. [KJV]<br>And do not be **conformed** to this world, but be transformed by the renewing of your mind, that you may prove what the will of God is, that which is good and acceptable and perfect. [NASB]<br>Do not **conform** any longer **to the pattern of** this world, but be transformed by the renewing of your mind. Then you will be able to test and approve what God's will is—his good, pleasing and perfect will. [NIV]<br>And do not be **conformed** to this world, but be transformed by the renewing of your mind, that you may prove | To conform to the pattern of; to copy the behavior and customs of; to be shaped by; to fashion.<br><br>**Practical Application**<br>It is the outward form and appearance of a man. It is the appearance of a person that changes from day to day and year to year. A man dresses differently for work than he does for an evening out. A man looks different as a young man than he does as an older man. His *suschēmatizesthe*, his fashion, his outward appearance, differs. |

# PRACTICAL WORD STUDIES
## in the NEW TESTAMENT

| ENGLISH WORD | GREEK WORD AND VERSE | THE WORD MEANS... |
|---|---|---|
| | what *is* that good and acceptable and perfect will of God. [NKJV]<br><br>Don't **copy the behavior and customs** of this world, But let God transform you into a new person by changing the way you think. Then you will know what God wants you to do, and you will know how good and pleasing and perfect his will really is. [NLT]<br><br>καὶ μὴ **συσχηματίζεσθε** τῷ αἰῶνι τούτῳ, ἀλλὰ μεταμορφοῦσθε τῇ ἀνακαινώσει τοῦ νοός ὑμῶν, εἰς τὸ δοκιμάζειν ὑμᾶς τί τὸ θέλημα τοῦ Θεοῦ, τὸ ἀγαθὸν καὶ εὐάρεστον καὶ τέλειον. [GNS]<br><br>καὶ μὴ **συσχηματίζεσθε** τῷ αἰῶνι τούτῳ, ἀλλὰ μεταμορφοῦσθε τῇ ἀνακαινώσει τοῦ νοός εἰς τὸ δοκιμάζειν ὑμᾶς τί τὸ θέλημα τοῦ θεοῦ, τὸ ἀγαθὸν καὶ εὐάρεστον καὶ τέλειον. [GNT] | |
| **#797**<br>**Correct**<br><br>Reprove–KJV<br>Reprove–NASB<br>**Correct–NIV**<br>Convince–NKJV<br>**Correct–NLT**<br><br>**POSB REFERENCE**<br>(2 Tim. 4:2)<br>Note 2, point 3 | ἔλεγξον = *elegxon*<br>Pronunciation: [el-eng'-khon]<br>Parsing (part of speech): verb<br>    Mood—imperative<br>    Tense—aorist<br>    Voice—active<br>    Person—2nd person<br>    Number—singular<br>    Stem or root—from ἐλέγχω<br>Concordance References:<br>  ⇒ Strong's #1651 elegchō<br>  ⇒ NIV #1794 elegchō<br>  ⇒ NASB #1651 elegchō<br><br>**2 Tim. 4:2**<br>Preach the word; be instant in season, out of season; **reprove**, rebuke, exhort with all longsuffering and doctrine. [KJV]<br><br>Preach the word; be ready in season and out of season; **reprove**, rebuke, exhort, with great patience and instruction. [NASB]<br><br>Preach the Word; be prepared in season and out of season; **correct**, rebuke and encourage—with great patience and careful instruction. [NIV]<br><br>Preach the word! Be ready in season *and* out of season. **Convince**, rebuke, exhort, with all longsuffering and teaching. [NKJV]<br><br>Preach the word of God. Be persistent, whether the time is favorable or not. Patiently **correct**, rebuke, and encourage your people with good teaching. [NLT]<br><br>ἤρυξον τὸν λόγον, ἐπίστηθι εὐκαίρως, ἀκαίρως, **ἔλεγξον**, ἐπιτίμησον, παρακάλεσον, ἐν πάσῃ μακροθυμίᾳ καὶ διδαχῇ. [GNS]<br><br>κήρυξον τὸν λόγον, ἐπίστηθι εὐκαίρως ἀκαίρως, **ἔλεγξον**, ἐπιτίμησον, παρακάλεσον, ἐν πάσῃ μακροθυμίᾳ καὶ διδαχῇ. [GNT] | To correct; to reprove; to rebuke; to convince; to show fault; to prove guilty.<br><br>**Practical Application**<br>The word means to stir up a person to prove himself; to put a person under conviction; to lead a person to see his sin and to feel guilt over it. It means to put a person under conviction of sin and to lead him to confession and repentance. |
| **#798**<br>**Corrected**<br><br>Rebuke–KJV<br>Rebuke–NASB<br>Rebuke–NIV<br>Rebuke–NKJV<br>**Corrected–NLT**<br><br>**POSB REFERENCE**<br>(Mt.16:21-23; esp. v.22)<br>Note 1, point 2<br><br>See also POSB REF:<br>(2 Tim.4:2)<br>Note 2, point 4 | ἐπιτιμᾶν = *epitiman*<br>Pronunciation: [ep-ee-tee-mahn']<br>Parsing (part of speech): verb<br>    Mood—infinitive<br>    Tense—present<br>    Voice—active<br>    Stem or root—from ἐπιτιμάω<br>Concordance References:<br>  ⇒ Strong's #2008 epitimaō<br>  ⇒ NIV #2203 epitimaō<br>  ⇒ NASB #2008 epitimaō<br><br>**Matthew 16:22**<br>Then Peter took him, and began to **rebuke** him, saying, Be it far from thee, Lord: this shall not be unto thee. [KJV]<br><br>And Peter took Him aside and began to **rebuke** Him, saying, "God forbid it, Lord! This shall never happen to You." [NASB] | To rebuke; to censure; to order; to correct; to scold; to strongly disapprove of; to give a command.<br><br>**Practical Application**<br>It is not just a wish, but a forcible attempt to stop the idea of the suffering Savior. "This shall never happen to you!" This must not and cannot happen to you. God forbid it is the equivalent idea. The point is this: Peter was out to stop the cross. He was urging Christ to be the Messiah of power, fame, and sensation whom the Jews were expecting. |

# PRACTICAL WORD STUDIES
## in the NEW TESTAMENT

| ENGLISH WORD | GREEK WORD AND VERSE | THE WORD MEANS... |
|---|---|---|
| | Peter took him aside and began to **rebuke** him. "Never, Lord!" he said. "This shall never happen to you!" [NIV]<br><br>Then Peter took Him aside and began to **rebuke** Him, saying, "Far be it from You, Lord; this shall not happen to You!" [NKJV]<br><br>But Peter took him aside and **corrected** him. "Heaven forbid, Lord," he said. "This will never happen to you!" [NLT]<br><br>καὶ προσλαβόμενος αὐτὸν ὁ Πέτρος ἤρξατο **ἐπιτιμᾶν** αὐτῷ, λέγων, Ἵλεώς σοι, Κύριε· οὐ μὴ ἔσται σοι τοῦτο. [GNS]<br><br>καὶ προσλαβόμενος αὐτὸν ὁ Πέτρος ἤρξατο **ἐπιτιμᾶν** αὐτῷ λέγων, Ἵλεώς σοι, κύριε· οὐ μὴ ἔσται σοι τοῦτο. [GNT] | |
| **#799**<br>**Correctly Explains**<br><br>Rightly dividing–KJV<br>Handling accurately–NASB<br>Correctly handles–NIV<br>Rightly dividing–NKJV<br>**Correctly explains–NLT**<br><br>POSB REFERENCE<br>(2 Tim. 2:15)<br>Note 2 | ὀρθοτομοῦντα = orthotomounta<br>Pronunciation: [or-tho-tow-moon-tah]<br>Parsing (part of speech): verb<br>   Mood—participle (imperative sense)<br>   Tense—present<br>   Voice—active<br>   Case—accusative<br>   Gender—masculine<br>   Person—2nd person<br>   Number—singular<br>   Stem or root—from ὀρθοτομέω<br>Concordance References:<br>⇒ Strong's #3718 orthotomeö<br>⇒ NIV #3982 orthotomeö<br>⇒ NASB #3718 orthotomeö<br><br>**2 Tim. 2:15**<br>Study to shew thyself approved unto God, a workman that needeth not to be ashamed, **rightly dividing** the word of truth. [KJV]<br>Be diligent to present yourself approved to God as a workman who does not need to be ashamed, **handling accurately** the word of truth. [NASB]<br>Do your best to present yourself to God as one approved, a workman who does not need to be ashamed and who **correctly handles** the word of truth. [NIV]<br>Be diligent to present yourself approved to God, a worker who does not need to be ashamed, **rightly dividing** the word of truth. [NKJV]<br>Work hard so God can approve you. Be a good worker, one who does not need to be ashamed and who **correctly explains** the word of truth. [NLT]<br>σπούδασον σεαυτὸν δόκιμον παραστῆσαι τῷ Θεῷ, ἐργάτην ἀνεπαίσχυντον, **ὀρθοτομοῦντα** τὸν λόγον τῆς ἀληθείας. [GNS]<br>σπούδασον σεαυτὸν δόκιμον παραστῆσαι τῷ θεῷ, ἐργάτην ἀνεπαίσχυντον, **ὀρθοτομοῦντα** τὸν λόγον τῆς ἀληθείας. [GNT] | To correctly handle; to rightly divide; to handle accurately; to correctly explain; to interpret correctly; to cut straight.<br><br>**Practical Application**<br>Believers are to cut straight to the truth; they are not to take crooked paths and side tracks to the truth. We are to study the truth and correctly handle it. Once we have studied and learned the Word of God, we are to *accurately teach* the Word of God. We are not to teach...<br>• our own ideas.<br>• the theories of other people.<br>• what we think.<br>• what other men think.<br><br>We are not to mishandle the Word of God: twist it to fit what we think or want it to say; over emphasize or under emphasize its teachings; add to or take away from it. Any person who mishandles God's Word is not approved of God. This is the point of this verse: if we want God's approval—if we want to be acceptable to God—we must study, rush and seek to be a true teacher of God's Word. We must be *workmen* who study God's Word, workmen who study diligently: *who correctly analyze and accurately divide—rightly handle and skillfully teach—the Word of Truth* (Amplified New Testament). This is the believer who will not be ashamed when he faces the Lord Jesus Christ in the great day of judgment. |
| **#800**<br>**Correctly Handles**<br><br>Rightly dividing–KJV<br>Handling accurately–NASB<br>**Correctly handles–NIV**<br>Rightly dividing–NKJV<br>Correctly explains–NLT | ὀρθοτομοῦντα = orthotomounta<br>Pronunciation: [or-tho-tow-moon-tah]<br>Parsing (part of speech): verb<br>   Mood—participle (imperative sense)<br>   Tense—present<br>   Voice—active<br>   Case—accusative<br>   Gender—masculine<br>   Person—2nd person<br>   Number—singular<br>   Stem or root—from ὀρθοτομέω<br>Concordance References:<br>⇒ Strong's #3718 orthotomeö<br>⇒ NIV #3982 orthotomeö<br>⇒ NASB #3718 orthotomeö<br><br>**2 Tim. 2:15**<br>Study to shew thyself approved unto God, a workman | To correctly handle; to rightly divide; to handle accurately; to correctly explain; to interpret correctly; to cut straight.<br><br>**Practical Application**<br>Believers are to cut straight to the truth; they are not to take crooked paths and side tracks to the truth. We are to study the truth and correctly handle it. Once we have studied and learned the Word of God, we are to *correctly handle or accurately teach* the Word of God. We are not to teach...<br>• our own ideas.<br>• the theories of other people.<br>• what we think.<br>• what other men think. |

# PRACTICAL WORD STUDIES
## in the New Testament

| ENGLISH WORD | GREEK WORD AND VERSE | THE WORD MEANS... |
|---|---|---|
| **POSB REFERENCE** (2 Tim. 2:15) Note 2 | that needeth not to be ashamed, **rightly dividing** the word of truth. [KJV]<br>Be diligent to present yourself approved to God as a workman who does not need to be ashamed, **handling accurately** the word of truth. [NASB]<br>Do your best to present yourself to God as one approved, a workman who does not need to be ashamed and who **correctly handles** the word of truth. [NIV]<br>Be diligent to present yourself approved to God, a worker who does not need to be ashamed, **rightly dividing** the word of truth. [NKJV]<br>Work hard so God can approve you. Be a good worker, one who does not need to be ashamed and who **correctly explains** the word of truth. [NLT]<br>σπούδασον σεαυτὸν δόκιμον παραστῆσαι τῷ Θεῷ, ἐργάτην ἀνεπαίσχυντον, **ὀρθοτομοῦντα** τὸν λόγον τῆς ἀληθείας. [GNS]<br>σπούδασον σεαυτὸν δόκιμον παραστῆσαι τῷ θεῷ, ἐργάτην ἀνεπαίσχυντον, **ὀρθοτομοῦντα** τὸν λόγον τῆς ἀληθείας. [GNT] | (See **Correctly Explains** for more application). |
| **#801 Corresponding**<br><br>Figure–KJV<br>**Corresponding–NASB**<br>Symbolizes–NIV<br>Antitype–NKJV<br>Picture–NLT<br><br>**POSB REFERENCE** (1 Pt.3:21) Note 1, point 3 | ἀντίτυπον = antitupon<br>Pronunciation: [an-teet'-oo-pon]<br>Parsing (part of speech): adjective adverb OR adjective<br>    Case—nominative<br>    Gender—neuter<br>    Number—singular<br>    Stem or root—from ἀντίτυπος, ον<br>Concordance References:<br>  ⇒ Strong's #499 antitupos<br>  ⇒ NIV #531 antitupos<br>  ⇒ NASB #499 antitupos<br><br>**1 Peter 3:21**<br>The like **figure** whereunto even baptism doth also now save us (not the putting away of the filth of the flesh, but the answer of a good conscience toward God,) by the resurrection of Jesus Christ: [KJV]<br>And **corresponding** to that, baptism now saves you—not the removal of dirt from the flesh, but an appeal to God for a good conscience—through the resurrection of Jesus Christ, [NASB]<br>And this water **symbolizes** baptism that now saves you also—not the removal of dirt from the body but the pledge of a good conscience toward God. It saves you by the resurrection of Jesus Christ, [NIV]<br>There is also an **antitype** which now saves us—baptism (not the removal of the filth of the flesh, but the answer of a good conscience toward God), through the resurrection of Jesus Christ, [NKJV]<br>And this is a **picture** of baptism, which now saves you by the power of Jesus Christ's resurrection. Baptism is not a removal of dirt from your body; it is an appeal to God from a clean conscience. [NLT]<br>ᾧ καὶ ἡμᾶς **ἀντίτυπον** νῦν σῴζει βάπτισμα, οὐ σαρκὸς ἀπόθεσις ῥύπου, ἀλλὰ συνειδήσεως ἀγαθῆς ἐπερώτημα εἰς Θεόν, δι' ἀναστάσεως Ἰησοῦ Χριστοῦ, [GNS]<br>ὃ καὶ ὑμᾶς **ἀντίτυπον** νῦν σῴζει βάπτισμα, οὐ σαρκὸς ἀπόθεσις ῥύπου ἀλλὰ συνειδήσεως ἀγαθῆς ἐπερώτημα εἰς θεόν, δι' ἀναστάσεως Ἰησοῦ Χριστοῦ, [GNT] | Symbolize, figure; copy; antitype.<br><br>**Practical Application**<br>Jesus Christ saves the believer through baptism: not the baptism by water, but the baptism of a good conscience wrought by the power of the resurrection of Jesus Christ (1 Peter 3:21).<br>The water which saved Noah and his family is a type of the cleansing that saves us. The water...<br>• bore up the ark and saved them through the judgment of God.<br>• delivered them from the ridicule and mockery of evil men.<br>• delivered them from the corruption of the world and led them to a new life.<br>• put to death the old world and gave them the hope of a new world.<br>• put to death their old life and gave them a new beginning.<br>• saved the race of man and created a new people of God.<br>• delivered them from the old world right into the new world.<br><br>What is Peter saying? Note the word "corresponding" (*antitupon*). The figure or picture of baptism is just like the water that saved Noah and his family.<br>⇒ The *flooding waters* of Noah's day picture the judgment of God upon sin. The flooding waters picture how man was saved from a corruptible world and carried into a new world.<br>⇒ The *baptismal water* pictures the judgment of God upon Christ, a judgment of death that was due sinners. It pictures how man is saved from a corruptible life and world and carried into a new life and world by the resurrection of Christ. |
| **#802 Corrupt**<br><br>Corrupt–KJV<br>Peddling–NASB<br>Peddle...for profit–NIV | καπηλεύοντες = kapëleuontes<br>Pronunciation: [kap-ale-yoo'-on-tehs]<br>Parsing (part of speech): verb<br>    Mood—participle<br>    Tense—present<br>    Voice—active<br>    Case—nominative | To peddle for profit; to corrupt. It means to peddle, to adulterate, to whittle down, to contaminate, to tamper with the Word of God.<br><br>**Practical Application**<br>The qualified man does not "peddle or corrupt the word of God." The word "corrupt" |

# PRACTICAL WORD STUDIES
## in the NEW TESTAMENT

| ENGLISH WORD | GREEK WORD AND VERSE | THE WORD MEANS... |
|---|---|---|
| Peddling–NKJV<br>Hucksters–NLT<br><br>**POSB<br>REFERENCE**<br>(2 Cor.2:16-17; esp. v.17)<br>Note 4 | Gender—masculine<br>Person—1st person<br>Number—plural<br>Stem or root—from καπηλεύω<br>Concordance References:<br>⇒ Strong's #2585 kapēleuō<br>⇒ NIV #2836 kapēleuō<br>⇒ NASB #2585 kapēleuō<br><br>**2 Cor. 2:17**<br>For we are not as many, which **corrupt** the word of God: but as of sincerity, but as of God, in the sight of God speak we in Christ. [KJV]<br>For we are not like many, **peddling** the word of God, but as from sincerity, but as from God, we speak in Christ in the sight of God. [NASB]<br>Unlike so many, we do not **peddle** the word of God **for profit**. On the contrary, in Christ we speak before God with sincerity, like men sent from God. [NIV]<br>For we are not, as so many, **peddling** the word of God; but as of sincerity, but as from God, we speak in the sight of God in Christ. [NKJV]<br>You see, we are not like those **hucksters**—and there are many of them—who preach just to make money. We preach God's message with sincerity and with Christ's authority. And we know that the God who sent us is watching us. [NLT]<br>οὐ γάρ ἐσμεν ὡς οἱ πολλοί, **καπηλεύοντες** τὸν λόγον τοῦ Θεοῦ· ἀλλ' ὡς ἐξ εἰλικρινείας, ἀλλ' ὡς ἐκ Θεοῦ κατενώπιον Θεοῦ· ἀλλ' ὡς ἐξ εἰλικρινείας, ἀλλ' ὡς ἐκ Θεοῦ, κατενώπιον τοῦ Θεοῦ, ἐν Χριστῷ λαλοῦμεν. [GNS]<br>οὐ γάρ ἐσμεν ὡς οἱ πολλοί **καπηλεύοντες** τὸν λόγον τοῦ θεοῦ, ἀλλ' ὡς ἐξ εἰλικρινείας, ἀλλ' ὡς ἐκ θεοῦ κατέναντι θεοῦ ἐν Χριστῷ λαλοῦμεν. [GNT] | (*kapeleuontes*) is taken from an old word meaning huckster or peddler. It means to mix other things into the gospel, for example, personal ideas, speculations, the latest religious fads or novel ideas. |
| #803<br>**Corrupt**<br><br>Untoward–KJV<br>Perverse–NASB<br>**Corrupt–NIV**<br>Perverse–NKJV<br>Astray–NLT<br><br>**POSB<br>REFERENCE**<br>(Acts 2:40)<br>Note 5, point 2 | σκολιᾶς = *skolias*<br>Pronunciation: [skol-ee-ahs']<br>Parsing (part of speech): adjective<br>  Case—genitive<br>  Gender—feminine<br>  Number—singular<br>  Stem or root—from σκολιός, ά, όν<br>Concordance References:<br>⇒ Strong's #4646 skolios<br>⇒ NIV #5021 skolios<br>⇒ NASB #4646 skolios<br><br>**Acts 2:40**<br>And with many other words did he testify and exhort, saying, Save yourselves from this **untoward** generation. [KJV]<br>And with many other words he solemnly testified and kept on exhorting them, saying, "Be saved from this **perverse** generation!" [NASB]<br>With many other words he warned them; and he pleaded with them, "Save yourselves from this **corrupt** generation." [NIV]<br>And with many other words he testified and exhorted them, saying, "Be saved from this **perverse** generation." [NKJV]<br>Then Peter continued preaching for a long time, strongly urging all his listeners, "Save yourselves from this generation that has gone **astray**!" [NLT]<br>ἑτέροις τε λόγοις πλείοσι διεμαρτύρετο καὶ παρεκάλει, λέγων, Σώθητε ἀπὸ τῆς γενεᾶς τῆς **σκολιᾶς** ταύτης. [GNS]<br>ἑτέροις τε λόγοις πλείοσιν διεμαρτύρατο καὶ παρεκάλει αὐτοὺς λέγων, Σώθητε ἀπὸ τῆς γενεᾶς τῆς **σκολιᾶς** ταύτης. [GNT] | To be corrupt; to be harsh; to be perverse; to go astray; to be crooked or bent out of shape.<br><br>**Practical Application**<br>People are far from being straight and far from being in the shape intended by God. They are crooked and bent, unrighteous and ungodly, sinful and corrupt. |
| #804<br>**Corrupt** | σαπρός = *sapros*<br>Pronunciation: [sap-ros']<br>Parsing (part of speech): adjective<br>  Case—nominative | Rotten, foul, corrupt, abusive, putrid, bad, unwholesome, polluting. |

# Practical Word Studies
## in the New Testament

| ENGLISH WORD | GREEK WORD AND VERSE | THE WORD MEANS... |
|---|---|---|
| **Corrupt–KJV**<br>Unwholesome–NASB<br>Unwholesome–NIV<br>**Corrupt–NKJV**<br>Foul or abusive–NLT<br><br>**POSB<br>REFERENCE**<br>(Eph.4:29)<br>Note 4 | Gender—masculine<br>Number—singular<br>Stem or root—from σαπρός, ά, όν<br>Concordance References:<br>⇒ Strong's #4550 sapros<br>⇒ NIV #4911 sapros<br>⇒ NASB #4550 sapros<br><br>**Ephes. 4:29**<br>Let no **corrupt** communication proceed out of your mouth, but that which is good to the use of edifying, that it may minister grace unto the hearers. [KJV]<br>Let no **unwholesome** word proceed from your mouth, but only such a word as is good for edification according to the need of the moment, that it may give grace to those who hear. [NASB]<br>Do not let any **unwholesome** talk come out of your mouths, but only what is helpful for building others up according to their needs, that it may benefit those who listen. [NIV]<br>Let no **corrupt** word proceed out of your mouth, but what is good for necessary edification, that it may impart grace to the hearers. [NKJV]<br>Don't use **foul or abusive** language. Let everything you say be good and helpful, so that your words will be an encouragement to those who hear them. [NLT]<br>πᾶς λόγος **σαπρὸς** ἐκ τοῦ στόματος ὑμῶν μὴ ἐκπορευέσθω, ἀλλ εἴ τις ἀγαθὸς πρὸς οἰκοδομὴν τῆς χρείας, ἵνα δῷ χάριν τοῖς ἀκούουσι. [GNS]<br>πᾶς λόγος **σαπρὸς** ἐκ τοῦ στόματος ὑμῶν μὴ ἐκπορευέσθω, ἀλλὰ εἴ τις ἀγαθὸς πρὸς οἰκοδομὴν τῆς χρείας, ἵνα δῷ χάριν τοῖς ἀκούουσιν. [GNT] | **Practical Application**<br>The believer is to strip away filthy and foul talk. The word "corrupt" (*sapros*) means rotten, foul, putrid and polluting. Corrupt talk, of course, would include cursing and unholy talk and even the worthless conversation that is so often carried on by people. The Amplified New Testament has a good description.<br><br>*Let no foul or polluting language, nor evil word, nor unwholesome or worthless talk [ever] come out of your mouth (Ephes. 4:29).* |
| **#805<br>Corrupted**<br><br>**Corrupted–KJV**<br>Rotted–NASB<br>Rotted–NIV<br>**Corrupted–NKJV**<br>Rotting away–NLT<br><br>**POSB<br>REFERENCE**<br>(Jas 5:2-3)<br>Note 2 | σέσηπεν = *sesëpen*<br>Pronunciation: [seh-say'-pehn]<br>Parsing (part of speech): verb<br>    Mood—indicative<br>    Tense—perfect<br>    Voice—active<br>    Person—3rd person<br>    Number—singular<br>Stem or root—from σήπω<br>Concordance References:<br>⇒ Strong's #4595 sëpö<br>⇒ NIV #4960 sepö<br>⇒ NASB #4595 sëpö<br><br>**James 5:2**<br>Your riches are **corrupted**, and your garments are motheaten. [KJV]<br>Your riches have **rotted** and your garments have become moth-eaten. [NASB]<br>Your wealth has **rotted**, and moths have eaten your clothes. [NIV]<br>Your riches are **corrupted**, and your garments are moth-eaten. [NKJV]<br>Your wealth is **rotting away**, and your fine clothes are moth-eaten rags. [NLT]<br>ὁ πλοῦτος ὑμῶν **σέσηπε**, καὶ τὰ ἱμάτια ὑμῶν σητόβρωτα γέγονεν· [GNS]<br>ὁ πλοῦτος ὑμῶν **σέσηπεν** καὶ τὰ ἱμάτια ὑμῶν σητόβρωτα γέγονεν, [GNT] | Rotted, corrupted.<br><br>**Practical Application**<br>This would refer to such things as farm produce like wheat and vegetables or building products like wood or wallboard. Many a person gains a comfortable and lavish living and, in some cases, wealth through an industry (like farming or construction) whose products eventually rot away. |
| **#806<br>Corruption**<br><br>**Corruption–KJV**<br>Decay–NASB<br>Decay–NIV<br>**Corruption–NKJV**<br>Rot in the grave–NLT | διαφθοράν = *diaphthoran*<br>Pronunciation: [dee-af-thor-ahn']<br>Parsing (part of speech): noun<br>    Case—accusative<br>    Gender—feminine<br>    Number—singular<br>Stem or root—from διαφθορά, ᾶς<br>Concordance References:<br>⇒ Strong's #1312 diaphthora<br>⇒ NIV #1426 diaphthora<br>⇒ NASB #1312 diaphthora | Decay; corrupt; deteriorate, putrefy, perish. It speaks of the grave and the rotting of a dead body.<br><br>**Practical Application**<br>In no place does Christ promise a new body to the unbeliever, to the unsaved and lost. A person's body and flesh can be destroyed forever. (This is a fact seldom pointed out.) |

# PRACTICAL WORD STUDIES
## in the NEW TESTAMENT

| ENGLISH WORD | GREEK WORD AND VERSE | THE WORD MEANS... |
|---|---|---|
| **POSB REFERENCE** (Acts 2:25-28; esp. v.27) Note 1, point 2c<br><br>(Acts 2:27) Deeper Study #1, point 2<br><br>See also POSB REF: (Acts 13:32-37; esp. v.34) Deeper Study #4 | **Acts 2:27**<br>Because thou wilt not leave my soul in hell, neither wilt thou suffer thine Holy One to see **corruption**. [KJV]<br>Because Thou wilt not abandon my soul to Hades, Nor ALLOW Thy Holy One to UNDERGO **DECAY**. [NASB]<br>Because you will not abandon me to the grave, nor will you let your Holy One see **decay**. [NIV]<br>*For You will not leave my soul in Hades, Nor will You allow Your Holy One to see* **corruption**. [NKJV]<br>For you will not leave my soul among the dead or allow your Holy One to **rot in the grave**. [NLT]<br>ὅτι οὐκ ἐγκαταλείψεις τὴν ψυχήν μου εἰς ᾅδου, οὐδὲ δώσεις τὸν ὅσιόν σου ἰδεῖν **διαφθοράν**. [GNS]<br>ὅτι οὐκ ἐγκαταλείψεις τὴν ψυχήν μου εἰς ᾅδην οὐδὲ δώσεις τὸν ὅσιόν σου ἰδεῖν **διαφθοράν**. [GNT] | |
| **#807**<br>**Corruption**<br><br>Corruption–KJV<br>Decay–NASB<br>Decay–NIV<br>Corruption–NKJV<br>Die–NLT<br><br>**POSB REFERENCE** (Acts 13:32-37; esp. v.34) Deeper Study #4 | ὑποστρέφειν εἰς διαφθοράν = *hupostrephein eis diaphthoran*<br>Pronunciation: [who-po-streph-eh-een ice dee-ahph-tho-rahn]<br>Parsing *diaphthoran* (part of speech): noun<br>  Case—accusative<br>  Gender—feminine<br>  Number—singular<br>  Stem or root— from διαφθορά, ᾶς<br>Concordance References:<br> ⇒ Strong's #1312+1519+5290 diaphthora eis hupostrephō<br> ⇒ NIV #1426+1650+5715 diaphthora [decay] eis hupostrephō<br> ⇒ NASB #1312+1519+5290 diaphthora eis hupostrephō<br><br>**Acts 13:34**<br>And as concerning that he raised him up from the dead, now no more to return to **corruption**, he said on this wise, I will give you the sure mercies of David. [KJV]<br>"And as for the fact that He raised Him up from the dead, no more to return to **decay**, He has spoken in this way: 'I will give you the holy and sure blessings of David.' [NASB]<br>The fact that God raised him from the dead, never to **decay**, is stated in these words: " 'I will give you the holy and sure blessings promised to David.' [NIV]<br>And that He raised Him from the dead, no more to return to **corruption**, He has spoken thus: '*I will give you the sure mercies of David.*' [NKJV]<br>For God had promised to raise him from the dead, never again to **die**. This is stated in the Scripture that says, 'I will give you the sacred blessings I promised to David.' [NLT]<br>ὅτι δὲ ἀνέστησεν αὐτὸν ἐκ νεκρῶν μηκέτι μέλλοντα **ὑποστρέφειν εἰς διαφθοράν**, οὕτως εἴρηκεν ὅτι Δώσω ὑμῖν τὰ ὅσια Δαβὶδ τὰ πιστά. [GNS]<br>ὅτι δὲ ἀνέστησεν αὐτὸν ἐκ νεκρῶν μηκέτι μέλλοντα **ὑποστρέφειν εἰς διαφθοράν**, οὕτως εἴρηκεν ὅτι Δώσω ὑμῖν τὰ ὅσια Δαυὶδ τὰ πιστά. [GNT] | To decay; to die; to become corrupt.<br><br>**Practical Application**<br>In no place does Christ promise a new body to the unbeliever, to the unsaved and lost. A person's body and flesh can be destroyed forever. (This is a fact seldom pointed out.) |
| **#808**<br>**Counsel**<br><br>Counsel–KJV<br>Plan–NASB<br>Purpose–NIV<br>Purpose–NKJV<br>Plan–NLT | βουλῇ = *boulē*<br>Pronunciation: [boo-lay']<br>Parsing (part of speech): noun<br>  Case—dative<br>  Gender—feminine<br>  Number—singular<br>  Stem or root—from βουλή, ῆς<br>Concordance References:<br> ⇒ Strong's #1012 boulē<br> ⇒ NIV #1087 boulē<br> ⇒ NASB #1012 boulē | Purpose, counsel, plan, intention, motive, design, will.<br><br>**Practical Application**<br>It carries the force of being willed and determined. Since God knows exactly what would happen in every situation, He plans for the best thing to happen. God takes counsel, puts all things under advisement, and chooses the best way. |

## PRACTICAL WORD STUDIES
### in the NEW TESTAMENT

| ENGLISH WORD | GREEK WORD AND VERSE | THE WORD MEANS... |
|---|---|---|
| **POSB REFERENCE** (Acts 2:23) *Deeper Study #3, point 2* | **Acts 2:23**<br>Him, being delivered by the determinate **counsel** and foreknowledge of God, ye have taken, and by wicked hands have crucified and slain: [KJV]<br>this Man, delivered up by the predetermined **plan** and foreknowledge of God, you nailed to a cross by the hands of godless men and put Him to death. [NASB]<br>This man was handed over to you by God's set **purpose** and foreknowledge; and you, with the help of wicked men, put him to death by nailing him to the cross. [NIV]<br>Him, being delivered by the determined **purpose** and foreknowledge of God, you have taken by lawless hands, have crucified, and put to death; [NKJV]<br>But you followed God's prearranged **plan**. With the help of lawless Gentiles, you nailed him to the cross and murdered him. [NLT]<br>τοῦτον τῇ ὡρισμένῃ **βουλῇ** καὶ προγνώσει τοῦ Θεοῦ ἔκδοτον λαβόντες διὰ χειρῶν ἀνόμων προσπήξαντες ἀνείλατε, [GNS]<br>τοῦτον τῇ ὡρισμένῃ **βουλῇ** καὶ προγνώσει τοῦ θεοῦ ἔκδοτον διὰ χειρὸς ἀνόμων προσπήξαντες ἀνείλατε, [GNT] | |
| **#809 Counselor**<br>Comforter–KJV<br>Helper–NASB<br>**Counselor–NIV**<br>Helper–NKJV<br>**Counselor–NLT**<br>**POSB REFERENCE** (Jn.14:16) *Deeper Study #1* | παράκλητον = *paraklëton*<br>Pronunciation: [par-ak'-lay-ton]<br>Parsing (part of speech): noun<br>    Case—accusative<br>    Gender—masculine<br>    Number—singular<br>    Stem or root—from παράκλητος, ου<br>Concordance References:<br>⇒ Strong's #3875 parakletos<br>⇒ NIV #4156 parakletos<br>⇒ NASB #3875 parakletos<br><br>**John 14:16**<br>And I will pray the Father, and he shall give you another **Comforter**, that he may abide with you for ever; [KJV]<br>"And I will ask the Father, and He will give you another **Helper**, that He may be with you forever; [NASB]<br>And I will ask the Father, and he will give you another **Counselor** to be with you forever—[NIV]<br>And I will pray the Father, and He will give you another **Helper**, that He may abide with you forever—[NKJV]<br>And I will ask the Father, and he will give you another **Counselor**, who will never leave you. [NLT]<br>καὶ ἐγὼ ἐρωτήσω τὸν πατέρα, καὶ ἄλλον **παράκλητον** δώσει ὑμῖν, μένῃ ἵνα μεθ' ὑμῶν εἰς τὸν αἰῶνα, [GNS]<br>κἀγὼ ἐρωτήσω τὸν πατέρα καὶ ἄλλον **παράκλητον** δώσει ὑμῖν, ἵνα μεθ' ὑμῶν εἰς τὸν αἰῶνα ᾖ, [GNT] | Counselor, Comforter, Helper, Intercessor; One called in; One called to the side of another.<br><br>**Practical Application**<br>The purpose is to help in any way possible.<br>1. There is the picture of a friend called in to help a person who is troubled or distressed or confused.<br>2. There is the picture of a commander called in to help a discouraged and dispirited army.<br>3. There is the picture of a lawyer, an advocate called in to help a defendant who needs his case pleaded. There is no one word that can adequately translate *paracletos*. The word that probably comes closest is simply *Helper*. |
| **#810 Count**<br>Reckon–KJV<br>Consider–NASB<br>**Count–NIV**<br>Reckon–NKJV<br>Consider–NLT<br>**POSB REFERENCE** (Rom.6:11) *Deeper Study #1* | λογίζεσθε = *logizesthe*<br>Pronunciation: [log-id'-zehs-theh]<br>Parsing (part of speech): verb<br>    Mood—imperative<br>    Tense—present<br>    Voice—middle or passive deponent<br>    Person—2nd person<br>    Number—plural<br>    Stem or root—from λογίζομαι<br>Concordance References:<br>⇒ Strong's #3049 logizomai<br>⇒ NIV #3357 logizomai<br>⇒ NASB #3049 logizomai<br><br>**Romans 6:11**<br>Likewise **reckon** ye also yourselves to be dead indeed unto sin, but alive unto God through Jesus Christ our Lord. [KJV] | To count; to consider; to reckon; to credit; to set to one's account; to lay to one's charge; to impute; to judge; to treat; to compute. It is an accounting word; it implies something put to a man's credit. It is used many times throughout Romans, about eleven times in Romans 4 alone. It is an extremely important idea in Scripture.<br><br>**Practical Application**<br>The believer's first step in conquering sin is to count himself dead to sin, but alive to God. The believer must *know and live out* his position, the glorious life God has given him in the death and resurrection of Jesus Christ our Lord. The believer who keeps his mind and thoughts upon *his position* in Christ's death and resurrection will conquer sin—every time. |

# PRACTICAL WORD STUDIES
## in the NEW TESTAMENT

| ENGLISH WORD | GREEK WORD AND VERSE | THE WORD MEANS... |
|---|---|---|
| | Even so **consider** yourselves to be dead to sin, but alive to God in Christ Jesus. [NASB]<br>In the same way, **count** yourselves dead to sin but alive to God in Christ Jesus. [NIV]<br>Likewise you also, **reckon** yourselves to be dead indeed to sin, but alive to God in Christ Jesus our Lord. [NKJV]<br>So you should **consider** yourselves dead to sin and able to live for the glory of God through Christ Jesus. [NLT]<br>οὕτω καὶ ὑμεῖς **λογίζεσθε** ἑαυτοὺς νεκροὺς μὲν εἶναι τῇ ἁμαρτίᾳ, ζῶντας δὲ τῷ Θεῷ ἐν Χριστῷ Ἰησοῦ τῷ Κυρίῳ ἡμῶν. [GNS]<br>οὕτως καὶ ὑμεῖς **λογίζεσθε** ἑαυτοὺς [εἶναι] νεκροὺς μὲν τῇ ἁμαρτίᾳ ζῶντας δὲ τῷ θεῷ ἐν Χριστῷ Ἰησοῦ. [GNT] | |
| **#811**<br>**Counted Worthy**<br><br>Counted worthy–KJV<br>Considered worthy–NASB<br>Counted worthy–NIV<br>Counted worthy–NKJV<br>Make...worthy–NLT<br><br>**POSB REFERENCE**<br>(2 Thes.1:4-5; esp. v.5)<br>Note 3 | καταξιωθῆναι = *kataxiōthēnai*<br>Pronunciation: [kat-ax-ee-o'-thay-nah-ee]<br>Parsing (part of speech): verb<br>    Mood—infinitive<br>    Tense—aorist<br>    Voice—passive<br>    Case—accusative<br>    Stem or root—from καταξιόω<br>Concordance References:<br>  ⇒ Strong's #2661 kataxioō<br>  ⇒ NIV #2921 kataxioō<br>  ⇒ NASB #2661 kataxioō<br><br>**2 Thes. 1:5**<br>Which is a manifest token of the righteous judgment of God, that ye may be **counted worthy** of the kingdom of God, for which ye also suffer: [KJV]<br>This is a plain indication of God's righteous judgment so that you may be **considered worthy** of the kingdom of God, for which indeed you are suffering. [NASB]<br>All this is evidence that God's judgment is right, and as a result you will be **counted worthy** of the kingdom of God, for which you are suffering. [NIV]<br>Which is manifest evidence of the righteous judgment of God, that you may be **counted worthy** of the kingdom of God, for which you also suffer; [NKJV]<br>But God will use this persecution to show his justice. For he will **make** you **worthy** of his Kingdom, for which you are suffering, [NLT]<br>ἔνδειγμα τῆς δικαίας κρίσεως τοῦ Θεοῦ, εἰς τὸ **καταξιωθῆναι** ὑμᾶς τῆς βασιλείας τοῦ Θεοῦ, ὑπὲρ ἧς καὶ πάσχετε· [GNS]<br>ἔνδειγμα τῆς δικαίας κρίσεως τοῦ θεοῦ, εἰς τὸ **καταξιωθῆναι** ὑμᾶς τῆς βασιλείας τοῦ θεοῦ ὑπὲρ ἧς καὶ πάσχετε, [GNT] | Counted worthy, considered worthy, deserving and commendable.<br><br>**Practical Application**<br>It does not mean to make worthy; it means to count, reckon, and declare worthy (see POSB note, Justification—Romans 5:1). A believer is not saved because he remains faithful through the sufferings of this life; he is saved because he believes in Jesus Christ as his Savior and Lord. However, when he suffers in this world and endures through the suffering, he is counted worthy of God's kingdom. He does not disappoint God. He proves his grit—that he is truly a man or a woman of God. He is worthy to enter heaven, for he has proven his faith. |
| **#812**<br>**Counting**<br><br>Imputing–KJV<br>Counting–NASB<br>Counting–NIV<br>Imputing–NKJV<br>Counting–NLT<br><br>**POSB REFERENCE**<br>(2 Cor.5:18-19; esp. v.19)<br>Note 2, point 2 | λογιζόμενος = *logizomenos*<br>Pronunciation: [log-id-zo'-mehn-os]<br>Parsing (part of speech): verb<br>    Mood—participle<br>    Tense—present<br>    Voice—middle or passive deponent<br>    Case—nominative<br>    Gender—masculine<br>    Number—singular<br>    Stem or root—from λογίζομαι<br>Concordance References:<br>  ⇒ Strong's #3049 logizomai<br>  ⇒ NIV #3357 logizomai<br>  ⇒ NASB #3049 logizomai<br><br>**2 Cor. 5:19**<br>To wit, that God was in Christ, reconciling the world unto himself, not **imputing** their trespasses unto them; and hath committed unto us the word of reconciliation. [KJV] | To count; to reckon; to regard; to impute; to take into account; to calculate and to credit. It means to charge or put to a person's account.<br><br>**Practical Application**<br>God does not count or impute sin to men. If God does not impute or charge sin against men, then it means that He forgives their sins. When Jesus Christ died on the cross, God was in Christ dying for the sins of men. God was making it possible for men to be freed from the guilt and condemnation of their sins.<br>Picture the scene: hanging there on the cross, God in Christ was not charging men with sin. He was dying for the sins of men. God was not there upon the cross to impute sin against men; He was there making it possible for men to be forgiven their sins. |

## Practical Word Studies in the New Testament

| ENGLISH WORD | GREEK WORD AND VERSE | THE WORD MEANS... |
|---|---|---|
| | Namely, that God was in Christ reconciling the world to Himself, not **counting** their trespasses against them, and He has committed to us the word of reconciliation. [NASB]<br><br>That God was reconciling the world to himself in Christ, not **counting** men's sins against them. And he has committed to us the message of reconciliation. [NIV]<br><br>That is, that God was in Christ reconciling the world to Himself, not **imputing** their trespasses to them, and has committed to us the word of reconciliation. [NKJV]<br><br>For God was in Christ, reconciling the world to himself, no longer **counting** people's sins against them. This is the wonderful message he has given us to tell others. [NLT]<br><br>ὡς ὅτι Θεὸς ἦν ἐν Χριστῷ κόσμον καταλλάσσων ἑαυτῷ, μὴ **λογιζόμενος** αὐτοῖς τὰ παραπτώματα αὐτῶν, καὶ θέμενος ἐν ἡμῖν τὸν λόγον τῆς καταλλαγῆς. [GNS]<br><br>ὡς ὅτι Θεὸς ἦν ἐν Χριστῷ κόσμον καταλλάσσων ἑαυτῷ, μὴ **λογιζόμενος** αὐτοῖς τὰ παραπτώματα αὐτῶν καὶ θέμενος ἐν ἡμῖν τὸν λόγον τῆς καταλλαγῆς. [GNT] | |
| **#813**<br>**Countryman**<br><br>Kinsman–KJV<br>Kinsman–NASB<br>Relative–NIV<br>**Countryman–NKJV**<br>Relative–NLT<br><br>**POSB REFERENCE**<br>(Romans 16:11)<br>Note 11 | συγγενῆ = *suggenë*<br>Pronunciation: [soong-ghen-ay']<br>Parsing (part of speech): pronominal adjective<br>    Case—accusative<br>    Gender—masculine<br>    Number—singular<br>    Stem or root—from συγγενής, οῦς<br>Concordance References:<br>  ⇒ Strong's #4773 suggenës<br>  ⇒ NIV #5150 suggenës<br>  ⇒ NASB #4773 suggenës<br><br>**Romans 16:11**<br>Salute Herodion my **kinsman**. Greet them that be of the household of Narcissus, which are in the Lord. [KJV]<br><br>Greet Herodion, my **kinsman**. Greet those of the household of Narcissus, who are in the Lord. [NASB]<br><br>Greet Herodion, my **relative**. Greet those in the household of Narcissus who are in the Lord [NIV]<br><br>Greet Herodion, my **countryman**. Greet those who are of the *household* of Narcissus who are in the Lord. [NKJV]<br><br>Greet Herodion, my **relative**. Greet the Christians in the household of Narcissus. [NLT]<br><br>ἀσπάσασθε Ἡρῳδίωνα τὸν **συγγενῆ** μου. ἀσπάσασθε τοὺς ἐκ τῶν Ναρκίσσου, τοὺς ὄντας ἐν Κυρίῳ. [GNS]<br><br>ἀσπάσασθε Ἡρῳδίωνα τὸν **συγγενῆ** μου. ἀσπάσασθε τοὺς ἐκ τῶν Ναρκίσσου τοὺς ὄντας ἐν κυρίῳ. [GNT] | Relative, kinsman; fellow countryman.<br><br>**Practical Application**<br>Herodion was another relative of Paul who was a believer (cp. Romans 16:7). There is no reason for translating kinsman (*suggenë*) as fellow countryman instead of relative. Others who are mentioned were Jews, but are not called kinsmen by Paul. What effect did this relative have upon Paul's conversion? Again the answer is unknown, but the fact that we should be witnessing to our relatives is driven home to our hearts and minds. |
| **#814**<br>**Courage**<br><br>Bold–KJV<br>Boldness–NASB<br>Dared–NIV<br>Bold–NKJV<br>**Courage–NLT**<br><br>**POSB REFERENCE**<br>(1 Thes.2:2)<br>Note 2 | ἐπαρρησιασάμεθα = *eparrësiasametha*<br>Pronunciation: [ep-ar-hray-see-ahs-ah-meh-tha]<br>Parsing (part of speech): verb<br>    Mood—indicative<br>    Tense—aorist<br>    Voice—middle deponent<br>    Person—1st person<br>    Number—plural<br>    Stem or root—from παρρησιάζομαι<br>Concordance References:<br>  ⇒ Strong's #3955 parrësiazomai<br>  ⇒ NIV #4245 parrësiazomai<br>  ⇒ NASB #3955 parrësiazomai<br><br>**1 Thes. 2:2**<br>But even after that we had suffered before, and were shamefully entreated, as ye know, at Philippi, we were **bold** in our God to speak unto you the gospel of God with much contention. [KJV]<br><br>But after we had already suffered and been mistreated in Philippi, as you know, we had the **boldness** in our God to speak to you the gospel of God amid much opposition. [NASB] | Boldness, courage, daring. It means to speak boldly and freely; to speak out and to speak publicly without fear.<br><br>**Practical Application**<br>Too many fail to witness for Christ because they fear ridicule, embarrassment, mockery, and persecution. They are secret believers of Christ instead of bold witnesses for Christ. |

# PRACTICAL WORD STUDIES
## in the NEW TESTAMENT

| ENGLISH WORD | GREEK WORD AND VERSE | THE WORD MEANS... |
|---|---|---|
| | We had previously suffered and been insulted in Philippi, as you know, but with the help of our God we **dared** to tell you his gospel in spite of strong opposition. [NIV]<br><br>But even after we had suffered before and were spitefully treated at Philippi, as you know, we were **bold** in our God to speak to you the gospel of God in much conflict. [NKJV]<br><br>You know how badly we had been treated at Philippi just before we came to you and how much we suffered there. Yet our God gave us the **courage** to declare his Good News to you boldly, even though we were surrounded by many who opposed us. [NLT]<br><br>ἀλλὰ καὶ προπαθόντες καὶ ὑβρισθέντες, καθὼς οἴδατε, ἐν Φιλίπποις, **ἐπαρρησιασάμεθα** ἐν τῷ Θεῷ ἡμῶν λαλῆσαι πρὸς ὑμᾶς τὸ εὐαγγέλιον τοῦ Θεοῦ ἐν πολλῷ ἀγῶνι. [GNS]<br><br>ἀλλὰ προπαθόντες καὶ ὑβρισθέντες, καθὼς οἴδατε, ἐν Φιλίπποις **ἐπαρρησιασάμεθα** ἐν τῷ θεῷ ἡμῶν λαλῆσαι πρὸς ὑμᾶς τὸ εὐαγγέλιον, τοῦ θεοῦ ἐν πολλῷ ἀγῶνι. [GNT] | |
| **#815**<br>**Course**<br><br>Course–KJV<br>Course–NASB<br>Ways–NIV<br>Course–NKJV<br>Like the rest–NLT<br><br>**POSB REFERENCE**<br>(Eph.2:1-2; esp. v.2)<br>Note 2 | αἰῶνα = *aiöna*<br>Pronunciation: [ahee-ohn'-ah]<br>Parsing (part of speech): noun<br>  Case—accusative<br>  Gender—masculine<br>  Number—singular<br>  Stem or root—from αἰών, ῶνος<br>Concordance References:<br>  ⇒ Strong's #165 aiön<br>  ⇒ NIV #172 aiön<br>  ⇒ NASB #165 aiön<br><br>**Ephes. 2:2**<br>Wherein in time past ye walked according to the **course** of this world, according to the prince of the power of the air, the spirit that now worketh in the children of disobedience: [KJV]<br><br>In which you formerly walked according to the **course** of this world, according to the prince of the power of the air, of the spirit that is now working in the sons of disobedience. [NASB]<br><br>In which you used to live when you followed the **ways** of this world and of the ruler of the kingdom of the air, the spirit who is now at work in those who are disobedient. [NIV]<br><br>In which you once walked according to the **course** of this world, according to the prince of the power of the air, the spirit who now works in the sons of disobedience, [NKJV]<br><br>You used to live just **like the rest** of the world, full of sin, obeying Satan, the mighty prince of the power of the air. He is the spirit at work in the hearts of those who refuse to obey God. [NLT]<br><br>ἐν αἷς ποτε περιεπατήσατε κατὰ τὸν **αἰῶνα** τοῦ κόσμου τούτου, κατὰ τὸν ἄρχοντα τῆς ἐξουσίας τοῦ ἀέρος, τοῦ πνεύματος τοῦ νῦν ἐνεργοῦντος ἐν τοῖς υἱοῖς τῆς ἀπειθείας· [GNS]<br><br>ἐν αἷς ποτε περιεπατήσατε κατὰ τὸν **αἰῶνα** τοῦ κόσμου τούτου, κατὰ τὸν ἄρχοντα τῆς ἐξουσίας τοῦ ἀέρος, τοῦ πνεύματος τοῦ νῦν ἐνεργοῦντος ἐν τοῖς υἱοῖς τῆς ἀπειθείας· [GNT] | Ways, course, world order, age, universe.<br><br>**Practical Application**<br>The sinner follows the "course of this world." This simply means he follows the world in its...<br>• opinions<br>• life<br>• speculations<br>• pleasures<br>• selfishness<br>• purposes<br>• technology<br>• possessions<br>• positions<br>• popularity<br>• honor<br>• religion<br>• values<br>• science<br>• standards |
| **#816**<br>**Courteous**<br><br>Courteous–KJV<br>Humble in spirit–<br>  NASB<br>Humble–NIV | ταπεινόφρονες = *tapeinophrones*<br>Pronunciation: [tap-eh-in-o-fro'-nes]<br>Parsing (part of speech): adjective<br>  Case—nominative<br>  Gender—masculine<br>  Number—plural<br>  Stem or root—from ταπεινόφρων, ον | Humble, humble in spirit, humble in mind, courteous; to be humble minded; to be lowly in mind.<br><br>**Practical Application**<br>Believers must be "courteous" (*tapeinophrones*). It means to offer oneself as lowly and |

## PRACTICAL WORD STUDIES
### in the NEW TESTAMENT

| ENGLISH WORD | GREEK WORD AND VERSE | THE WORD MEANS... |
|---|---|---|
| **Courteous–NKJV**<br>Humble in mind–NLT<br><br>**POSB REFERENCE**<br>(1 Pt.3:8)<br>Note 5 | Concordance References:<br>⇒ Strong's #5391 philophron<br>⇒ NIV #5426 tapeinophrōn<br>⇒ NASB #5012b tapeinophrōn<br><br>**1 Peter 3:8**<br>Finally, be ye all of one mind, having compassion one of another, love as brethren, be pitiful, be **courteous**: [KJV]<br>To sum up, let all be harmonious, sympathetic, brotherly, kindhearted, and **humble in spirit**; [NASB]<br>Finally, all of you, live in harmony with one another; be sympathetic, love as brothers, be compassionate and **humble**. [NIV]<br>Finally, all *of you be* of one mind, having compassion for one another; love as brothers, *be* tenderhearted, *be* **courteous**; [NKJV]<br>Finally, all of you should be of one mind, full of sympathy toward each other, loving one another with tender hearts and **humble minds**. [NLT]<br>Τὸ δὲ τέλος, πάντες ὁμόφρονες, συμπαθεῖς, φιλάδελφοι, εὔσπλαγχνοι, **φιλόφρονες**· [GNS]<br>Τὸ δὲ τέλος πάντες ὁμόφρονες, συμπαθεῖς, φιλάδελφοι, εὔσπλαγχνοι, **ταπεινόφρονες**, [GNT] | submissive; to walk in a spirit of lowliness; *to present* oneself as lowly; to be of low degree and low rank; not to be highminded, proud, haughty, arrogant, or assertive.<br>Note: a humble person may have a high position, power, wealth, fame, and much more; but he carries himself in a spirit of lowliness and submission. He denies himself for the sake of Christ and in order to help others. |
| **#817**<br>**Covenant**<br><br>Testament–KJV<br>**Covenant–NASB**<br>**Covenant–NIV**<br>**Covenant–NKJV**<br>**Covenant–NLT**<br><br>**POSB REFERENCE**<br>(2 Cor.3:6)<br>Note 1<br><br>See also POSB REF:<br>(1 Cor.11:23-26; esp. v.25)<br>Note 3, point 2 | διαθήκης = *diathēkēs*<br>Pronunciation: [dee-ath-ay'-kays]<br>Parsing (part of speech): noun<br>    Case—genitive<br>    Gender—feminine<br>    Number—singular<br>    Stem or root—from διαθήκη, ης<br>Concordance References:<br>⇒ Strong's #1242 diathēkē<br>⇒ NIV #1347 diathēkē<br>⇒ NASB #1242 diathēkē<br><br>**2 Cor. 3:6**<br>Who also hath made us able ministers of the new **testament**; not of the letter, but of the spirit: for the letter killeth, but the spirit giveth life. [KJV]<br>Who also made us adequate as servants of a new **covenant**, not of the letter, but of the Spirit; for the letter kills, but the Spirit gives life. [NASB]<br>He has made us competent as ministers of a new **covenant**—not of the letter but of the Spirit; for the letter kills, but the Spirit gives life. [NIV]<br>Who also made us sufficient as ministers of the new **covenant**, not of the letter but of the Spirit; for the letter kills, but the Spirit gives life. [NKJV]<br>He is the one who has enabled us to represent his new **covenant**. This is a covenant, not of written laws, but of the Spirit. The old way ends in death; in the new way, the Holy Spirit gives life. [NLT]<br>ὃς καὶ ἱκάνωσεν ἡμᾶς διακόνους καινῆς **διαθήκης**, οὐ γράμματος ἀλλὰ πνεύματος· τὸ γὰρ γράμμα ἀποκτείνει, τὸ δὲ πνεῦμα ζωοποιεῖ. [GNS]<br>ὃς καὶ ἱκάνωσεν ἡμᾶς διακόνους καινῆς **διαθήκης**, οὐ γράμματος ἀλλὰ πνεύματος· τὸ γὰρ γράμμα ἀποκτέννει, τὸ δὲ πνεῦμα ζωοποιεῖ. [GNT] | Covenant, testament. It means an agreement made between two parties; a contract drawn up between two or more people; a special relationship set up and established between persons.<br><br>**Practical Application**<br>In the Old Testament period of history, God had set up an old covenant between Himself and man which is here called the covenant of the letter. This simply means a written covenant or the covenant of the law. Since Christ, God has set up a *new covenant* with man which is here called the "new covenant of the Spirit." This is simply another way of describing the covenant of grace or of the gospel (Hebrews 8:8). Vine points out that this covenant is called the "new" (Hebrews 9:15), the "second" (Hebrews 8:7), and the "better" (Hebrews 7:22) (W.E. Vine. *Expository Dictionary of New Testament Words*).<br>The point is this: God used to deal with man by law, but now He deals with man *through the Holy Spirit*. The law was the old covenant between God and man. The Spirit is the new covenant between God and man. Today, since Christ, the minister serves the new covenant of the Spirit, not the old covenant of the law. |
| **#818**<br>**Covenant**<br><br>**Covenant–KJV**<br>**Covenant–NASB**<br>**Covenant–NIV**<br>**Covenant–NKJV**<br>Not translated–NLT | διαθήκην = *diathēkēn*<br>Pronunciation: [dee-ath-ay'-kayn]<br>Parsing (part of speech): noun<br>    Case—accusative<br>    Gender—feminine<br>    Number—singular<br>    Stem or root—from διαθήκη, ης<br>Concordance References:<br>⇒ Strong's #1242 diathēkē<br>⇒ NIV #1347 diathēkē<br>⇒ NASB #1242 diathēkē | Covenant, will, testament.<br><br>**Practical Application**<br>A covenant is an agreement made between two parties, a special relationship set up and established by two or more persons. The point is that once a covenant has been made and executed, it stands: it cannot be annulled or added to. By law the promises of the covenant are sealed; both parties are bound to keep their word, their |

# PRACTICAL WORD STUDIES
## in the NEW TESTAMENT

| ENGLISH WORD | GREEK WORD AND VERSE | THE WORD MEANS... |
|---|---|---|
| **POSB REFERENCE** (Gal.3:15) Note 1 | **Galatians 3:15** Brethren, I speak after the manner of men; Though it be but a man's **covenant**, yet if it be confirmed, no man disannulleth, or addeth thereto. [KJV] <br> Brethren, I speak in terms of human relations: even though it is only a man's **covenant**, yet when it has been ratified, no one sets it aside or adds conditions to it. [NASB] <br> Brothers, let me take an example from everyday life. Just as no one can set aside or add to a human **covenant** that has been duly established, so it is in this case. [NIV] <br> Brethren, I speak in the manner of men: Though *it is* only a man's **covenant**, yet *if it is* confirmed, no one annuls or adds to it. [NKJV] <br> Dear brothers and sisters, here's an example from everyday life. Just as no one can set aside or amend an irrevocable agreement, so it is in this case. [NLT]—NOT TRANSLATED <br> Ἀδελφοί, κατὰ ἄνθρωπον λέγω· ὅμως ἀνθρώπου κεκυρωμένην **διαθήκην** οὐδεὶς ἀθετεῖ ἢ ἐπιδιατάσσεται. [GNS] <br> Ἀδελφοί, κατὰ ἄνθρωπον λέγω· ὅμως ἀνθρώπου κεκυρωμένην **διαθήκην** οὐδεὶς ἀθετεῖ ἢ ἐπιδιατάσσεται. [GNT] | promises. (See POSB note, Covenant—2 Cor. 3:6; Cp. Romans 9:4.) |
| **#819 Covenant-breakers** <br><br> Covenantbreakers–KJV <br> Untrustworthy–NASB <br> Faithless–NIV <br> Untrustworthy–NKJV <br> Break their promises–NLT <br><br> **POSB REFERENCE** (Romans 1:31) *Deeper Study* #20 | ἀσυνθέτους = *asunthetous* <br> Pronunciation: [as-oon'-thet-oos] <br> Parsing (part of speech): adjective <br>     Case—accusative <br>     Gender—masculine <br>     Number—plural <br> Stem or root—from ἀσύνθετος, ον <br> Concordance References: <br>   ⇒ Strong's #802 asunthetos <br>   ⇒ NIV #853 asunthetos <br>   ⇒ NASB #802 asunthetos <br><br> **Romans 1:31** <br> Without understanding, **covenantbreakers**, without natural affection, implacable, unmerciful: [KJV] <br> Without understanding, **untrustworthy**, unloving, unmerciful; [NASB] <br> They are senseless, **faithless**, heartless, ruthless. [NIV] <br> Undiscerning, **untrustworthy**, unloving, unforgiving, unmerciful; [NKJV] <br> They refuse to understand, **break their promises**, and are heartless and unforgiving. [NLT] <br> ἀσυνέτους, **ἀσυνθέτους**, ἀστόργους, ἀσπόνδους, ἀνελεήμονας· [GNS] <br> ἀσυνέτους **ἀσυνθέτους** ἀστόργους ἀνελεήμονας [GNT] | Faithless; covenant breakers; untrustworthy; disloyal; one who breaks his promises; disloyal breakers of promises or agreements; untruthful. <br><br> **Practical Application** <br> It is a person who tragically does not keep his word or promise. He is simply untrustworthy, not undependable. |
| **#820 Covet–Coveting** <br><br> Covet–KJV <br> Covet–NASB <br> Covet–NIV <br> Covet–NKJV <br> Coveting–NLT <br><br> **POSB REFERENCE** (Rom.13:9) Note 6 | ἐπιθυμήσεις = *epithumēseis* <br> Pronunciation: [ep-ee-thoo-may'-sees] <br> Parsing (part of speech): verb <br>     Mood—indicative or imperative <br>     Tense—future or aorist <br>     Voice—active <br>     Person—2nd person <br>     Number—singular <br> Stem or root—from ἐπιθυμέω <br> Concordance References: <br>   ⇒ Strong's #1937 epithumeö <br>   ⇒ NIV #2121 epithumeö <br>   ⇒ NASB #1937 epithumeö <br><br> **Romans 13:9** <br> For this, Thou shalt not commit adultery, Thou shalt not kill, Thou shalt not steal, Thou shalt not bear false witness, Thou shalt not **covet**; and if there be any other commandment, it is briefly comprehended in this saying, namely, Thou shalt love thy neighbour as thyself. [KJV] | To covet; to crave; to desire; to long for; to want; to eagerly desire. <br><br> **Practical Application** <br> A person can desire both good and bad things; the word can be used in both a good and bad sense (cp. 1 Cor. 14:1 for the good sense). In the present context, the believer is not to covet in an evil sense. If he loves his neighbors and fellow citizens, he will not covet. (See POSB *Deeper Study* #4, Covetousness—Romans 1:29 for the full meaning of the word.) |

# PRACTICAL WORD STUDIES
## in the NEW TESTAMENT

| ENGLISH WORD | GREEK WORD AND VERSE | THE WORD MEANS... |
|---|---|---|
| | For this, "You shall not commit adultery, You shall not murder, You shall not steal, You shall not **covet**," and if there is any other commandment, it is summed up in this saying, "You shall love your neighbor as yourself." [NASB]<br><br>The commandments, "Do not commit adultery," "Do not murder," "Do not steal," "Do not **covet**," and whatever other commandment there may be, are summed up in this one rule: "Love your neighbor as yourself." [NIV]<br><br>For the commandments, *"You shall not commit adultery," "You shall not murder," "You shall not steal," "You shall not bear false witness," "You shall not **covet**,"* and if *there is* any other commandment, are *all* summed up in this saying, namely, *"You shall love your neighbor as yourself."* [NKJV]<br><br>For the commandments against adultery and murder and stealing and **coveting**—and any other commandment—are all summed up in this one commandment: "Love your neighbor as yourself." [NLT]<br><br>τὸ γάρ, Οὐ μοιχεύσεις, οὐ φονεύσεις, οὐ κλέψεις, οὐ ψευδομαρτυρήσεις, οὐκ **ἐπιθυμήσεις**, καὶ εἴ τις ἑτέρα ἐντολή, ἐν τούτῳ τῷ λόγῳ ἀνακεφαλαιοῦται, ἐν τῷ Ἀγαπήσεις τὸν πλησίον σου ὡς σεαυτόν. [GNS]<br><br>τὸ γὰρ Οὐ μοιχεύσεις, Οὐ φονεύσεις, Οὐ κλέψεις, Οὐκ **ἐπιθυμήσεις**, καὶ εἴ τις ἑτέρα ἐντολή, ἐν τῷ λόγῳ τούτῳ ἀνακεφαλαιοῦται [ἐν τῷ] Ἀγαπήσεις τὸν πλησίον σου ὡς σεαυτόν. [GNT] | |
| **#821**<br>**Coveting**<br><br>Covetousness–KJV<br>**Coveting–NASB**<br>Greed–NIV<br>Covetousness–NKJV<br>Greed–NLT<br><br>**POSB REFERENCE**<br>(Mk.7:22)<br>*Deeper Study #8*<br><br>See also POSB REF:<br>(Rom.1:29)<br>*Deeper Study #4* | πλεονεξίαι = *pleonexiai*<br>Pronunciation: [pleh-on-ex-ee'-ah-ee]<br>Parsing (part of speech): noun<br>    Case—nominative<br>    Gender—feminine<br>    Number—plural<br>    Stem or root—from πλεονεξία, ας<br>Concordance References:<br>  ⇒ Strong's #4124 pleonexia<br>  ⇒ NIV #4432 pleonexia<br>  ⇒ NASB #4124 pleonexia<br><br>**Mark 7:22**<br>Thefts, **covetousness**, wickedness, deceit, lasciviousness, an evil eye, blasphemy, pride, foolishness: [KJV]<br><br>Deeds of **coveting** and wickedness, as well as deceit, sensuality, envy, slander, pride and foolishness. [NASB]<br><br>**Greed**, malice, deceit, lewdness, envy, slander, arrogance and folly. [NIV]<br><br>Thefts, **covetousness**, wickedness, deceit, lewdness, an evil eye, blasphemy, pride, foolishness. [NKJV]<br><br>Adultery, **greed**, wickedness, deceit, eagerness for lustful pleasure, envy, slander, pride, and foolishness. [NLT]<br><br>**πλεονεξίαι**, πονηρίαι, δόλος, ἀσέλγεια, ὀφθαλμὸς πονηρός, βλασφημία, ὑπερηφανία, ἀφροσύνη· [GNS]<br><br>μοιχεῖαι, **πλεονεξίαι**, πονηρίαι, δόλος, ἀσέλγεια, ὀφθαλμὸς πονηρός, βλασφημία, ὑπερηφανία, ἀφροσύνη· [GNT] | Greed, covetousness; to lust for more and more; to have a starving appetite for something; to have a love of possessing (2 Peter 2:14); to crave after and for.<br><br>**Practical Application**<br>It means to crave and grasp after possessions, pleasure, power, fame. Coveting or greed lacks restraint. It lacks the ability to discriminate. It wants to have in order to spend in pleasure and luxury. Coveting or greed is an insatiable lust and craving of the flesh that cannot be satisfied. It is an intense appetite for gain, a passion for the pleasure that things can bring. It is a lust and craving so deep that a person finds his happiness in things instead of in God. It is idolatry (Ephes. 5:5). |
| **#822**<br>**Covetous**<br><br>**Covetous–KJV**<br>**Covetous–NASB**<br>Greedy–NIV<br>**Covetous–NKJV**<br>Greedy–NLT<br><br>**POSB REFERENCE**<br>(1 Cor.5:9-10; esp. v.9)<br>Note 4, point 2 | πλεονέκταις = *pleonektais*<br>Pronunciation: [pleh-on-ek'-tace]<br>Parsing (part of speech): noun<br>    Case—dative<br>    Gender—masculine<br>    Number—plural<br>    Stem or root—from πλεονέκτης, ου<br>Concordance References:<br>  ⇒ Strong's #4123 pleonektēs<br>  ⇒ NIV #4431 pleonektēs<br>  ⇒ NASB #4123 pleonektēs<br><br>**1 Cor. 5:10**<br>Yet not altogether with the fornicators of this world, or | Greedy, covetous, grabbing for more and more.<br><br>**Practical Application**<br>The church was not to become mixed up with the covetous (*pleonektais*) of this world. The word means those who seek for more and more while millions within the world are dying from sin, hunger, disease, and poverty. This is a sin that is especially despised by God.<br><br>The "greedy or covetous" (*pleonektai*) are those...<br>• who always want more and more |

## PRACTICAL WORD STUDIES
### in the NEW TESTAMENT

| ENGLISH WORD | GREEK WORD AND VERSE | THE WORD MEANS... |
|---|---|---|
| See also POSB REF:<br>(1 Cor.6:10)<br>Note 3, point 2<br>(Eph.5:5-6; esp. v.5)<br>Note 5, point 1 | with the **covetous**, or extortioners, or with idolaters; for then must ye needs go out of the world. [KJV]<br><br>I did not at all mean with the immoral people of this world, or with the **covetous** and swindlers, or with idolaters; for then you would have to go out of the world. [NASB]<br><br>Not at all meaning the people of this world who are immoral, or the **greedy** and swindlers, or idolaters. In that case you would have to leave this world. [NIV]<br><br>Yet *I* certainly *did* not *mean* with the sexually immoral people of this world, or with the **covetous**, or extortioners, or idolaters, since then you would need to go out of the world. [NKJV]<br><br>But I wasn't talking about unbelievers who indulge in sexual sin, or who are **greedy** or are swindlers or idol worshipers. You would have to leave this world to avoid people like that. [NLT]<br><br>καὶ οὐ πάντως τοῖς πόρνοις τοῦ κόσμου τούτου ἢ τοῖς **πλεονέκταις**, ἢ ἅρπαξιν, ἢ εἰδωλολάτραις· ἐπεὶ ὠφείλετε ἄρα ἐκ τοῦ κόσμου ἐξελθεῖν. [GNS]<br><br>οὐ πάντως τοῖς πόρνοις τοῦ κόσμου τούτου ἢ τοῖς **πλεονέκταις** καὶ ἅρπαξιν ἢ εἰδωλολάτραις, ἐπεὶ ὠφείλετε ἄρα ἐκ τοῦ κόσμου ἐξελθεῖν. [GNT] | • who are never satisfied with what they have.<br>• who want more and more to spend in pleasure and luxury.<br>• who crave for possessions, pleasure, fame, power.<br>• who bank and store up and hoard, ignoring and neglecting the desperate needs of teeming millions who are dying from hunger, disease, poverty, and sin. (See POSB outline—Matthew 19:16-22 and POSB note—Matthew 19:16-22; POSB outline—Matthew 19:23-26; POSB outline—Luke 16:19-31; POSB note—Matthew 19:16-22 and POSB note—Matthew 19:16-22; POSB note—Matthew 19:23-26; and POSB note—Luke 16:19-31 for more discussion.) |
| **#823**<br>**Covetous**<br><br>Covetous–KJV<br>Lovers of money–NASB<br>Lovers of money–NIV<br>Lovers of money–NKJV<br>Love...their money–NLT<br><br>**POSB REFERENCE**<br>(2 Tim. 3:2-4; esp. v.2)<br>Note 2, point 2 | φιλάργυροι = *philarguroi*<br>Pronunciation: [fil-ar'-goo-roy]<br>Parsing (part of speech): adjective<br>    Case—nominative<br>    Gender—masculine<br>    Number—plural<br>    Stem or root—from φιλάργυρος, ον<br>Concordance References:<br>  ⇒ Strong's #5366 philarguros<br>  ⇒ NIV #5795 philarguros<br>  ⇒ NASB #5366 philarguros<br><br>**2 Tim. 3:2**<br>For men shall be lovers of their own selves, **covetous**, boasters, proud, blasphemers, disobedient to parents, unthankful, unholy, [KJV]<br><br>For men will be lovers of self, **lovers of money**, boastful, arrogant, revilers, disobedient to parents, ungrateful, unholy, [NASB]<br><br>People will be lovers of themselves, **lovers of money**, boastful, proud, abusive, disobedient to their parents, ungrateful, unholy, [NIV]<br><br>For men will be lovers of themselves, **lovers of money**, boasters, proud, blasphemers, disobedient to parents, unthankful, unholy, [NKJV]<br><br>For people will **love** only themselves and **their money**. They will be boastful and proud, scoffing at God, disobedient to their parents, and ungrateful. They will consider nothing sacred. [NLT]<br><br>ἔσονται γὰρ οἱ ἄνθρωποι φίλαυτοι, **φιλάργυροι**, ἀλαζόνες, ὑπερήφανοι, βλάσφημοι, γονεῦσιν ἀπειθεῖς, ἀχάριστοι, ἀνόσιοι, [GNS]<br><br>ἔσονται γὰρ οἱ ἄνθρωποι φίλαυτοι **φιλάργυροι** ἀλαζόνες ὑπερήφανοι βλάσφημοι, γονεῦσιν ἀπειθεῖς, ἀχάριστοι ἀνόσιοι [GNT] | Lovers of money; possessions.<br><br>**Practical Application**<br>People will be *covetous* (*philarguroi*): People will want more and more and bigger and bigger and better and better, and they will seldom be satisfied with what they have. In the last days people will focus upon...<br>• money, banking more and more.<br>• houses in the best neighborhoods, on the seashore, in the mountains, and by the rivers.<br>• furnishings and property.<br>• possessions—such as clothes, jewelry, antiques, art, and vehicles.<br>• travel, seeing more and more sights.<br>• property, stocks and bonds—owning more and more.<br>• power—controlling more and more.<br><br>Men will love money, what it buys and allows them to do, and they will covet more and more of it in order to buy things. Their eyes and hearts will be focused upon money instead of God. They will indulge and hoard instead of meeting the desperate needs of the poor and lost of the world. |
| **#824**<br>**Covetous Man**<br><br>Covetous man–KJV<br>Covetous man–NASB<br>Greedy person–NIV<br>Covetous man–NKJV<br>Greedy person–NLT<br><br>**POSB REFERENCE** | πλεονέκτης = *pleonektēs*<br>Pronunciation: [pleh-on-ek'-tace]<br>Parsing (part of speech): noun<br>    Case—nominative<br>    Gender—masculine<br>    Number—singular<br>    Stem or root—from πλεονέκτης, ου<br>Concordance References:<br>  ⇒ Strong's #4123 pleonektēs<br>  ⇒ NIV #4431 pleonektēs<br>  ⇒ NASB #4123 pleonektēs | Greedy person; covetous man; one who is always grasping for more and more; hoarding all one can get and still craving more.<br><br>**Practical Application**<br>It is being enslaved and held in bondage by the things of this earth: for example, food, drink, and a host of fleshly sins and self-centered behavior. |

# PRACTICAL WORD STUDIES
## in the NEW TESTAMENT

| ENGLISH WORD | GREEK WORD AND VERSE | THE WORD MEANS... |
|---|---|---|
| (Eph.5:5-6; esp. v.5)<br>Note 5, point 1 | **Ephes. 5:5**<br>For this ye know, that no whoremonger, nor unclean person, nor **covetous man**, who is an idolater, hath any inheritance in the kingdom of Christ and of God. [KJV]<br>For this you know with certainty, that no immoral or impure person or **covetous man**, who is an idolater, has an inheritance in the kingdom of Christ and God. [NASB]<br>For of this you can be sure: No immoral, impure or **greedy person**—such a man is an idolater—has any inheritance in the kingdom of Christ and of God. [NIV]<br>For this you know, that no fornicator, unclean person, nor **covetous man**, who is an idolater, has any inheritance in the kingdom of Christ and of God. [NKJV]<br>You can be sure that no immoral, impure, or greedy person will inherit the Kingdom of Christ and of God. For a **greedy person** is really an idolater who worships the things of this world. [NLT]<br>τοῦτο γὰρ ἔστε γινώσκοντες, ὅτι πᾶς πόρνος, ἢ ἀκάθαρτος, ἢ **πλεονέκτης**, ὅς ἐστιν εἰδωλολάτρης, οὐκ ἔχει κληρονομίαν ἐν τῇ βασιλείᾳ τοῦ Χριστοῦ καὶ Θεοῦ. [GNS]<br>τοῦτο γὰρ ἴστε γινώσκοντες, ὅτι πᾶς πόρνος ἢ ἀκάθαρτος ἢ **πλεονέκτης**, ὅ ἐστιν εἰδωλολάτρης, οὐκ ἔχει κληρονομίαν ἐν τῇ βασιλείᾳ τοῦ Χριστοῦ καὶ θεοῦ. [GNT] | |
| #825<br>**Covetousness**<br><br>**Covetousness–KJV**<br>Coveting–NASB<br>Greed–NIV<br>**Covetousness–NKJV**<br>Greed–NLT<br><br>**POSB<br>REFERENCE**<br>(Mk.7:22)<br>*Deeper Study #8*<br><br>See also POSB REF:<br>(Rom.1:29)<br>*Deeper Study #4* | πλεονεξίαι = *pleonexiai*<br>Pronunciation: [pleh-on-ex-ee'-ah-ee]<br>Parsing (part of speech): noun<br>    Case—nominative<br>    Gender—feminine<br>    Number—plural<br>    Stem or root—from πλεονεξία, ας<br>Concordance References:<br>⇒ Strong's #4124 pleonexia<br>⇒ NIV #4432 pleonexia<br>⇒ NASB #4124 pleonexia<br><br>**Mark 7:22**<br>Thefts, **covetousness**, wickedness, deceit, lasciviousness, an evil eye, blasphemy, pride, foolishness: [KJV]<br>Deeds of **coveting** and wickedness, as well as deceit, sensuality, envy, slander, pride and foolishness. [NASB]<br>**Greed**, malice, deceit, lewdness, envy, slander, arrogance and folly. [NIV]<br>Thefts, **covetousness**, wickedness, deceit, lewdness, an evil eye, blasphemy, pride, foolishness. [NKJV]<br>Adultery, **greed**, wickedness, deceit, eagerness for lustful pleasure, envy, slander, pride, and foolishness. [NLT]<br>**πλεονεξίαι**, πονηρίαι, δόλος, ἀσέλγεια, ὀφθαλμὸς πονηρός, βλασφημία, ὑπερηφανία, ἀφροσύνη· [GNS]<br>μοιχεῖαι, **πλεονεξίαι**, πονηρίαι, δόλος, ἀσέλγεια, ὀφθαλμὸς πονηρός, βλασφημία, ὑπερηφανία, ἀφροσύνη· [GNT] | Greed, covetousness; to lust for more and more; to have a starving appetite for something; to have a love of possessing (2 Peter 2:14); to crave after and for.<br><br>**Practical Application**<br>It means to crave and grasp after possessions, pleasure, power, fame. Covetousness or greed lacks restraint. It lacks the ability to discriminate. It wants to have in order to spend in pleasure and luxury. Covetousness or greed is an insatiable lust and craving of the flesh that cannot be satisfied. It is an intense appetite for gain, a passion for the pleasure that things can bring. It is a lust and craving so deep that a person finds his happiness in things instead of in God. It is idolatry (Ephes. 5:5). |
| #826<br>**Covetousness**<br><br>**Covetousness–KJV**<br>Greed–NASB<br>Greed–NIV<br>**Covetousness–NKJV**<br>Greedy–NLT<br><br>**POSB<br>REFERENCE**<br>(Lk.12:15)<br>*Deeper Study #1* | πλεονεξίας = *pleonexias*<br>Pronunciation: [pleh-on-ex-ee'-ah]<br>Parsing (part of speech): noun<br>    Case—genitive<br>    Gender—feminine<br>    Number—singular<br>    Stem or root—from πλεονεξία, ας<br>Concordance References:<br>⇒ Strong's #4124 pleonexia<br>⇒ NIV #4432 pleonexia<br>⇒ NASB #4124 pleonexia<br><br>**Luke 12:15**<br>And he said unto them, Take heed, and beware of **covetousness**: for a man's life consisteth not in the abundance of the things which he possesseth. [KJV] | Greed, covetousness, lust, avarice; a craving, a desire for more.<br><br>**Practical Application**<br>It is covetousness, a dissatisfaction with what is enough. It includes the cravings for both material things and fleshly indulgence. It is desiring what belongs to others; snatching at something that belongs to others; a love of having, a cry of "give me, give me" (cp. 2 Peter 2:14).<br>⇒ It is a lust so deep within a man that he finds his happiness in things instead of in God.<br>⇒ It is a greed so deep that it desires the power that things bring more than the |

# PRACTICAL WORD STUDIES
## in the NEW TESTAMENT

| ENGLISH WORD | GREEK WORD AND VERSE | THE WORD MEANS... |
|---|---|---|
| See also POSB REF: (Col.3:5-7; esp. v.5) Note 1, point 1 | And He said to them, "Beware, and be on your guard against every form of **greed**; for not even when one has an abundance does his life consist of his possessions." [NASB]<br>Then he said to them, "Watch out! Be on your guard against all kinds of **greed**; a man's life does not consist in the abundance of his possessions." [NIV]<br>And He said to them, "Take heed and beware of **covetousness**, for one's life does not consist in the abundance of the things he possesses." [NKJV]<br>Then he said, "Beware! Don't be **greedy** for what you don't have. Real life is not measured by how much we own." [NLT]<br>εἶπε δὲ πρὸς αὐτούς, Ὁρᾶτε καὶ φυλάσσεσθε ἀπὸ πάσης **πλεονεξίας**· ὅτι οὐκ ἐν τῷ περισσεύειν τινὶ ἡ ζωὴ αὐτοῦ ἐστιν ἐκ τῶν ὑπαρχόντων αὐτοῦ. [GNS]<br>ἶπεν δὲ πρὸς αὐτούς, Ὁρᾶτε καὶ φυλάσσεσθε ἀπὸ πάσης **πλεονεξίας**, ὅτι οὐκ ἐν τῷ περισσεύειν τινὶ ἡ ζωὴ αὐτοῦ ἐστιν ἐκ τῶν ὑπαρχόντων αὐτῷ. [GNT] | things themselves.<br>⇒ It is an intense appetite for gain; a passion for the pleasure that things can bring. It goes beyond the pleasure of possessing things for their own sake. |
| **#827**<br>**Covetousness, Without**<br><br>Without covetousness–KJV<br>Free from the love of money–NASB<br>Free from the love of money–NIV<br>Without covetousness–NKJV<br>Stay away from the love of money–NLT<br><br>**POSB REFERENCE**<br>(Heb.13:5-6; esp. v.5) Note 5 | Ἀφιλάργυρος = Aphilarguros<br>Pronunciation: [af-il-ar'-goo-ros]<br>Parsing (part of speech): adjective<br>    Case—nominative<br>    Gender—masculine<br>    Number—singular<br>    Stem or root—from ἀφιλάργυρος, ον<br>Concordance References:<br>⇒ Strong's #866 aphilarguros<br>⇒ NIV #921 aphilarguros<br>⇒ NASB #866 aphilarguros<br><br>**Hebrews 13:5**<br>Let your conversation be **without covetousness**; and be content with such things as ye have: for he hath said, I will never leave thee, nor forsake thee. [KJV]<br>Let your character be **free from the love of money**, being content with what you have; for He Himself has said, "I will never desert you, nor will I ever forsake you," [NASB]<br>Keep your lives **free from the love of money** and be content with what you have, because God has said, "Never will I leave you; never will I forsake you." [NIV]<br>*Let your* conduct *be* **without covetousness**; *be* content with such things as you have. For He Himself has said, *"I will never leave you nor forsake you."* [NKJV]<br>**Stay away from the love of money**; be satisfied with what you have. For God has said, "I will never fail you. I will never forsake you." [NLT]<br>ἀφιλάργυρος ὁ τρόπος, ἀρκούμενοι τοῖς παροῦσιν· αὐτὸς γὰρ εἴρηκεν, Οὐ μή σε ἀνῶ, οὐδ' οὐ μήσε ἐγκαταλίπω. [GNS]<br>Ἀφιλάργυρος ὁ τρόπος, ἀρκούμενοι τοῖς παροῦσιν. αὐτὸς γὰρ εἴρηκεν, Οὐ μή σε ἀνῶ οὐδ' οὐ μή σε ἐγκαταλίπω, [GNT] | Covetousness; a love of money; avarice; greed. It means a lover of money or possessions. A person can love money, property, estates, houses, cars—anything on earth.<br><br>**Practical Application**<br>Note what it is that brings contentment:<br>⇒ living life without covetousness.<br>⇒ being satisfied with what one has.<br>⇒ knowing God personally: experiencing His constant companionship and care, knowing that He never leaves or forsakes us. |
| **#828**<br>**Craftiness**<br><br>Craftiness–KJV<br>Craftiness–NASB<br>Deception–NIV<br>Craftiness–NKJV<br>Trick–NLT<br><br>**POSB REFERENCE**<br>(2 Cor.4:2) Note 2 | πανουργία = panourgia<br>Pronunciation: [pan-oorg-ee'-ah]<br>Parsing (part of speech): noun<br>    Case—dative<br>    Gender—feminine<br>    Number—singular<br>    Stem or root—from πανουργία, ας<br>Concordance References:<br>⇒ Strong's #3834 panourgia<br>⇒ NIV #4111 panourgia<br>⇒ NASB #3834 panourgia<br><br>**2 Cor. 4:2**<br>But have renounced the hidden things of dishonesty, not walking in **craftiness**, nor handling the word of God deceitfully; but by manifestation of the truth commending | Deception, craftiness, trickery, cunning, cleverness, shrewdness, evil design. It means a man who will do anything and use any means to get what he wants.<br><br>**Practical Application**<br>Note the believer is not to "walk" this way; he is not to walk using and misusing people, circumstances, events, and things for his own end. The believer is to walk as Jesus walked. |

**PRACTICAL WORD STUDIES
in the NEW TESTAMENT**

| ENGLISH WORD | GREEK WORD AND VERSE | THE WORD MEANS... |
|---|---|---|
| | ourselves to every man's conscience in the sight of God. [KJV]<br><br>But we have renounced the things hidden because of shame, not walking in **craftiness** or adulterating the word of God, but by the manifestation of truth commending ourselves to every man's conscience in the sight of God. [NASB]<br><br>Rather, we have renounced secret and shameful ways; we do not use **deception**, nor do we distort the word of God. On the contrary, by setting forth the truth plainly we commend ourselves to every man's conscience in the sight of God. [NIV]<br><br>But we have renounced the hidden things of shame, not walking in **craftiness** nor handling the word of God deceitfully, but by manifestation of the truth commending ourselves to every man's conscience in the sight of God. [NKJV]<br><br>We reject all shameful and underhanded methods. We do not try to **trick** anyone, and we do not distort the word of God. We tell the truth before God, and all who are honest know that. [NLT]<br><br>ἀλλ ἀπειπάμεθα τὰ κρυπτὰ τῆς αἰσχύνης, μὴ περιπατοῦντες ἐν **πανουργίᾳ** μηδὲ δολοῦντες τὸν λόγον τοῦ Θεοῦ, ἀλλὰ τῇ φανερώσει τῆς ἀληθείας συνιστῶντες ἑαυτοὺς πρὸς πᾶσαν συνείδησιν ἀνθρώπων ἐνώπιον τοῦ Θεοῦ. [GNS]<br><br>ἀλλὰ ἀπειπάμεθα τὰ κρυπτὰ τῆς αἰσχύνης, μὴ περιπατοῦντες ἐν **πανουργίᾳ** μηδὲ δολοῦντες τὸν λόγον τοῦ θεοῦ ἀλλὰ τῇ φανερώσει τῆς ἀληθείας συνιστάνοντες ἑαυτοὺς πρὸς πᾶσαν συνείδησιν ἀνθρώπων ἐνώπιον τοῦ θεοῦ. [GNT] | |
| **#829**<br>**Crave**<br><br>Desire–KJV<br>Long for–NASB<br>**Crave–NIV**<br>Desire–NKJV<br>**Crave–NLT**<br><br>**POSB REFERENCE**<br>(1 Pt.2:2-3; esp. v.2)<br>Note 2 | ἐπιποθήσατε = *epipothēsate*<br>Pronunciation: [ep-ee-poth-ay'-sah-teh]<br>Parsing (part of speech): verb<br>    Mood—imperative<br>    Tense—aorist<br>    Voice—active<br>    Person—2nd person<br>    Number—plural<br>    Stem or root—from ἐπιποθέω<br>Concordance References:<br>  ⇒ Strong's #1971 epipotheō<br>  ⇒ NIV #2160 epipotheō<br>  ⇒ NASB #1971 epipotheō<br><br>**1 Peter 2:2**<br>As newborn babes, **desire** the sincere milk of the word, that ye may grow thereby: [KJV]<br><br>Like newborn babes, **long for** the pure milk of the word, that by it you may grow in respect to salvation, [NASB]<br><br>Like newborn babies, **crave** pure spiritual milk, so that by it you may grow up in your salvation, [NIV]<br><br>As newborn babes, **desire** the pure milk of the word, that you may grow thereby, [NKJV]<br><br>You must **crave** pure spiritual milk so that you can grow into the fullness of your salvation. Cry out for this nourishment as a baby cries for milk, [NLT]<br><br>ὡς ἀρτιγέννητα βρέφη, τὸ λογικὸν ἄδολον γάλα **ἐπιποθήσατε**, ἵνα ἐν αὐτῷ αὐξηθῆτε, [GNS]<br><br>ὡς ἀρτιγέννητα βρέφη τὸ λογικὸν ἄδολον γάλα **ἐπιποθήσατε**, ἵνα ἐν αὐτῷ αὐξηθῆτε εἰς σωτηρίαν, [GNT] | To crave; to desire; to long for; to yearn for. It means to crave, yearn, and long for the Word of God.<br><br>**Practical Application**<br>The believer is to crave one thing—the milk of God's Word. The charge is an imperative, a command: "You desire, crave, and yearn for the pure spiritual milk of the Word. And the craving and yearning are to be constant." The word "crave" (*epipothēsate*) is a strong word, very strong. It paints the picture of being an absolute essential, of hungering and thirsting after the Word. If a believer is to grow, it is absolutely essential that he hunger and thirst after the milk of the Word. |
| **#830**<br>**Crazy**<br><br>Beside ourselves–KJV<br>Beside ourselves– NASB | ἐξέστημεν = *exestēmen*<br>Pronunciation: [ex-is'-tay-mehn]<br>Parsing (part of speech): verb<br>    Mood—indicative<br>    Tense—aorist<br>    Voice—active<br>    Person—1st person | To be crazy; to be beside oneself; to be out of one's mind; to be insane.<br><br>**Practical Application**<br>One of the charges against Paul was that he was crazy (*exestēmen*), that he was mad, insane. It means to act in the extreme, abnormally, |

# PRACTICAL WORD STUDIES
## in the NEW TESTAMENT

| ENGLISH WORD | GREEK WORD AND VERSE | THE WORD MEANS... |
|---|---|---|
| Out of mind–NIV<br>Beside ourselves–NKJV<br>**Crazy–NLT**<br><br>**POSB REFERENCE**<br>(2 Cor.5:13)<br>Note 3 | Number—plural<br>Stem or root—from ἐξίστημι and ἐξιστάνω<br>Concordance References:<br>⇒ Strong's #1839 existēmi<br>⇒ NIV #2014 existēmi<br>⇒ NASB #1839 existēmi<br><br>**2 Cor. 5:13**<br>For whether we be **beside ourselves**, it is to God: or whether we be sober, it is for your cause. [KJV]<br>For if we are **beside ourselves**, it is for God; if we are of sound mind, it is for you. [NASB]<br>If we are **out of** our **mind**, it is for the sake of God; if we are in our right mind, it is for you. [NIV]<br>For if we are **beside ourselves**, *it is* for God; or if we are of sound mind, *it is* for you. [NKJV]<br>If it seems that we are **crazy**, it is to bring glory to God. And if we are in our right minds, it is for your benefit. [NLT]<br>εἴτε γὰρ **ἐξέστημεν**, Θεῷ· εἴτε σωφρονοῦμεν, ὑμῖν. [GNS]<br>εἴτε γὰρ **ἐξέστημεν**, Θεῷ· εἴτε σωφρονοῦμεν, ὑμῖν. [GNT] | unlike what others act. Paul was charged with being a "fool" for Christ. Note that he accepts the charge as true. |
| **#831**<br>**Created**<br><br>Were made–KJV<br>Came into being–NASB<br>Were made–NIV<br>Were made–NKJV<br>Created–NLT<br><br>**POSB REFERENCE**<br>(Jn.1:3)<br>Note 2, point 2 | ἐγένετο = *egeneto*<br>Pronunciation: [eh-ghin'-eh-tow]<br>Parsing (part of speech): verb<br>   Mood—indicative<br>   Tense—aorist<br>   Voice—middle deponent<br>   Person—3rd person<br>   Number—singular<br>   Stem or root—from γίνομαι<br>Concordance References:<br>⇒ Strong's #1096 ginomai<br>⇒ NIV #1181 ginomai<br>⇒ NASB #1096 ginomai<br><br>**John 1:3**<br>All things **were made** by him; and without him was not any thing made that was made. [KJV]<br>All things **came into being** by Him, and apart from Him nothing came into being that has come into being. [NASB]<br>Through him all things **were made**; without him nothing was made that has been made. [NIV]<br>All things **were made** through Him, and without Him nothing was made that was made. [NKJV]<br>He **created** everything there is. Nothing exists that he didn't make. [NLT]<br>πάντα δι' αὐτοῦ **ἐγένετο**, καὶ χωρὶς αὐτοῦ ἐγένετο οὐδὲ ἕν, ὃ γέγονεν. [GNS]<br>πάντα δι' αὐτοῦ **ἐγένετο**, καὶ χωρὶς αὐτοῦ **ἐγένετο** οὐδὲ ἕν. ὃ γέγονεν [GNT] | Were made, came into being or became, created; to take place; to happen.<br><br>**Practical Application**<br>Note what this is saying. Nothing was existing—no substance, no matter whatsoever. Matter is not eternal. God did not take something outside of Himself, something less than perfect (evil) to create the world. Christ, the Word, took nothing but His will and power; and He spoke the Word and created every single thing out of nothing (*ex nihilo*). |
| **#832**<br>**Created, Were**<br><br>Were created–KJV<br>Were created–NASB<br>Were created–NIV<br>Were created–NKJV<br>Created–NLT<br><br>**POSB REFERENCE**<br>(Col.1:16)<br>Note 1, point 3 | ἐκτίσθη = *ektisthē*<br>Pronunciation: [ek-tis'-thay]<br>Parsing (part of speech): verb<br>   Mood—indicative<br>   Tense—aorist<br>   Voice—passive<br>   Person—3rd person<br>   Number—singular<br>   Stem or root—from κτίζω<br>Concordance References:<br>⇒ Strong's #2936 ktizō<br>⇒ NIV #3231 ktizō<br>⇒ NASB #2936 ktizō<br><br>**Col. 1:16**<br>For by him **were** all things **created**, that are in heaven, and that are in earth, visible and invisible, whether they be thrones, or dominions, or principalities, or pow- | Created, made; brought into being.<br><br>**Practical Application**<br>The words "were created" (*ektisthē*) are in the Greek aorist tense which simply means that creation is an historical event. Creation actually took place in this way. Jesus Christ Himself *created* the world. There was a time, a day, an hour, a moment when He spoke the Word and all things in their intricate detail came into being. |

# PRACTICAL WORD STUDIES
## in the NEW TESTAMENT

| ENGLISH WORD | GREEK WORD AND VERSE | THE WORD MEANS... |
|---|---|---|
| | ers: all things were created by him, and for him: [KJV]<br>For by Him all things **were created**, both in the heavens and on earth, visible and invisible, whether thrones or dominions or rulers or authorities—all things have been created by Him and for Him. [NASB]<br>For by him all things **were created**: things in heaven and on earth, visible and invisible, whether thrones or powers or rulers or authorities; all things were created by him and for him. [NIV]<br>For by Him all things **were created** that are in heaven and that are on earth, visible and invisible, whether thrones or dominions or principalities or powers. All things were created through Him and for Him. [NKJV]<br>Christ is the one through whom God **created** everything in heaven and earth. He made the things we can see and the things we can't see—kings, kingdoms, rulers, and authorities. Everything has been created through him and for him. [NLT]<br>ὅτι ἐν αὐτῷ **ἐκτίσθη** τὰ πάντα, τὰ ἐν τοῖς οὐρανοῖς καὶ τὰ ἐπὶ τῆς γῆς, τὰ ὁρατὰ καὶ τὰ ἀόρατα, εἴτε θρόνοι, εἴτε κυριότητες, εἴτε ἀρχαί, εἴτε ἐξουσίαι· τὰ πάντα δι᾽ αὐτοῦ καὶ εἰς αὐτὸν ἔκτισται· [GNS]<br>ὅτι ἐν αὐτῷ **ἐκτίσθη** τὰ πάντα ἐν τοῖς οὐρανοῖς καὶ ἐπὶ τῆς γῆς, τὰ ὁρατὰ καὶ τὰ ἀόρατα, εἴτε θρόνοι εἴτε κυριότητες εἴτε ἀρχαὶ εἴτε ἐξουσίαι· τὰ πάντα δι᾽ αὐτοῦ καὶ εἰς αὐτὸν ἔκτισται· [GNT] | |
| **#833**<br>**Credited**<br><br>Reckoned–KJV<br>Reckoned–NASB<br>**Credited–NIV**<br>Accounted–NKJV<br>Declared–NLT<br><br>**POSB REFERENCE**<br>(Romans 4:9)<br>Note 2 | Ἐλογίσθη = elogisthē<br>Pronunciation: [eh-log-ees'-thay]<br>Parsing (part of speech): verb<br>    Mood—indicative<br>    Tense—aorist<br>    Voice—passive<br>    Person—3rd person<br>    Number—singular<br>    Stem or root—from λογίζομαι<br>Concordance References:<br>  ⇒ Strong's #3049 logizomai<br>  ⇒ NIV #3357 logizomai<br>  ⇒ NASB #3049 logizomai<br><br>**Romans 4:9**<br>Cometh this blessedness then upon the circumcision only, or upon the uncircumcision also? for we say that faith was **reckoned** to Abraham for righteousness. [KJV]<br>Is this blessing then upon the circumcised, or upon the uncircumcised also? For we say, "Faith was **reckoned** to Abraham as righteousness." [NASB]<br>Is this blessedness only for the circumcised, or also for the uncircumcised? We have been saying that Abraham's faith was **credited** to him as righteousness. [NIV]<br>Does this blessedness then come upon the circumcised only, or upon the uncircumcised also? For we say that faith was **accounted** to Abraham for righteousness. [NKJV]<br>Now then, is this blessing only for the Jews, or is it for Gentiles, too? Well, what about Abraham? We have been saying he was **declared** righteous by God because of his faith. [NLT]<br>ὁ μακαρισμὸς οὖν οὗτος ἐπὶ τὴν περιτομὴν ἢ καὶ ἐπὶ τὴν ἀκροβυστίαν; λέγομεν γὰρ ὅτι **Ἐλογίσθη** τῷ Ἀβραὰμ ἡ πίστις εἰς δικαιοσύνην. [GNS]<br>ὁ μακαρισμὸς οὖν οὗτος ἐπὶ τὴν περιτομὴν ἢ καὶ ἐπὶ τὴν ἀκροβυστίαν; λέγομεν γάρ, **Ἐλογίσθη** τῷ Ἀβραὰμ ἡ πίστις εἰς δικαιοσύνην. [GNT] | Credited, reckoned, declared; to count; to deposit; to put to one's account; to impute; to consider; to evaluate; to calculate.<br><br>**Practical Application**<br>Abraham's faith was counted for righteousness or credited as righteousness (see POSB note, Justification—Romans 4:1-3; POSB note—Romans 4:6-8; POSB *Deeper Study* #1—Romans 4:22; POSB *Deeper Study* #2—Romans 4:22; POSB note—Romans 5:1 for more discussion).<br>Note that Abraham was justified or counted righteous by faith; he was not justified...<br>• by being religious.<br>• by performing good deeds.<br>• by doing some good work.<br>• by being good and virtuous.<br>• by submitting to a ritual.<br>• by joining some body of believers. |
| **#834**<br>**Credited**<br><br>Imputed–KJV<br>Reckoned–NASB | ἐλογίσθη = elogisthē<br>Pronunciation: [eh-log-ees'-thay]<br>Parsing (part of speech): verb<br>    Mood—indicative<br>    Tense—aorist<br>    Voice—passive | To credit; to impute; to reckon; to declare; to count; to compute; to ascribe; to deposit; to put to one's account.<br><br>**Practical Application**<br>Abraham's faith was counted for righteous- |

# PRACTICAL WORD STUDIES
## in the NEW TESTAMENT

| ENGLISH WORD | GREEK WORD AND VERSE | THE WORD MEANS... |
|---|---|---|
| **Credited–NIV**<br>Accounted–NKJV<br>Declared–NLT<br><br>**POSB REFERENCE**<br>(Romans 4:22)<br>*Deeper Study* #1 | Person—3rd person<br>Number—singular<br>Stem or root—from λογίζομαι<br>Concordance References:<br>⇒ Strong's #3049 logizomai<br>⇒ NIV #3357 logizomai<br>⇒ NASB #3049 logizomai<br><br>**Romans 4:22**<br>And therefore it was **imputed** to him for righteousness. [KJV]<br>Therefore also it was **reckoned** to him as righteousness. [NASB]<br>This is why "it was **credited** to him as righteousness." [NIV]<br>And therefore *"it was **accounted** to him for righteousness."* [NKJV]<br>And because of Abraham's faith, God **declared** him to be righteous. [NLT]<br>διὸ καὶ **ἐλογίσθη** αὐτῷ εἰς δικαιοσύνην. [GNS]<br>διὸ [καὶ] **ἐλογίσθη** αὐτῷ εἰς δικαιοσύνην. [GNT] | ness. (See *Deeper Study* #1, Reckon—Romans 6:11 for a fuller discussion.) Abraham deposited his faith with God, and God credited Abraham's faith as righteousness. |
| **#835**<br>**Credits**<br><br>Imputeth–KJV<br>Reckons–NASB<br>**Credits–NIV**<br>Imputes–NKJV<br>Declared–NLT<br><br>**POSB REFERENCE**<br>(Romans 4:6-8; esp. v.6)<br>Note 3, point 1 | λογίζεται = *logizetai*<br>Pronunciation: [log-id'-zeh-ahee]<br>Parsing (part of speech): verb<br>  Mood—indicative<br>  Tense—present<br>  Voice—middle or passive deponent<br>  Person—3rd person<br>  Number—singular<br>  Stem or root—from λογίζομαι<br>Concordance References:<br>⇒ Strong's #3049 logizomai<br>⇒ NIV #3357 logizomai<br>⇒ NASB #3049 logizomai<br><br>**Romans 4:6**<br>Even as David also describeth the blessedness of the man, unto whom God **imputeth** righteousness without works, [KJV]<br>Just as David also speaks of the blessing upon the man to whom God **reckons** righteousness apart from works: [NASB]<br>David says the same thing when he speaks of the blessedness of the man to whom God **credits** righteousness apart from works: [NIV]<br>Just as David also describes the blessedness of the man to whom God **imputes** righteousness apart from works: [NKJV]<br>King David spoke of this, describing the happiness of an undeserving sinner who is **declared** to be righteous: [NLT]<br>καθάπερ καὶ Δαβὶδ λέγει τὸν μακαρισμὸν τοῦ ἀνθρώπου, ᾧ ὁ Θεὸς **λογίζεται** δικαιοσύνην χωρὶς ἔργων, [GNS]<br>καθάπερ καὶ Δαυὶδ λέγει τὸν μακαρισμὸν τοῦ ἀνθρώπου ᾧ ὁ Θεὸς **λογίζεται** δικαιοσύνην χωρὶς ἔργων, [GNT] | To credit; to impute; to reckon; to declare; to count; to put to one's account; to deposit.<br><br>**Practical Application**<br>The blessed man is the man who is counted righteous without works. Just think for a moment. If God credits and counts a man righteous "without works," then we know something: Man is not justified by works, but by faith. (See POSB *Deeper Study* #1, Reckon—Romans 6:11 for more discussion.) |
| **#836**<br>**Cried**<br><br>Cried–KJV<br>Call out–NASB<br>Called out–NIV<br>**Cried–NKJV**<br>Called out–NLT<br><br>**POSB REFERENCE**<br>(Lk.8:5-8; esp. v.8)<br>Note 2, point 4 | ἐφώνει = *ephōnei*<br>Pronunciation: [eh-fo-neh'-ee]<br>Parsing (part of speech): verb<br>  Mood—indicative<br>  Tense—imperfect<br>  Voice—active<br>  Person—3rd person<br>  Number—singular<br>  Stem or root—from φωνέω<br>Concordance References:<br>⇒ Strong's #5455 phōneō<br>⇒ NIV #5888 phōneō<br>⇒ NASB #5455 phōneō | To call out; to cry; to summon; to call out with a loud voice.<br><br>**Practical Application**<br>In this Scripture, note what Jesus did. Immediately upon finishing the parable, He cried (*ephōnei*) with a loud shout: "He who has ears to hear, let him hear." He warned: "Hear!" He issued a strong warning. |

# PRACTICAL WORD STUDIES
## in the NEW TESTAMENT

| ENGLISH WORD | GREEK WORD AND VERSE | THE WORD MEANS... |
|---|---|---|
| | **Luke 8:8**<br>And other fell on good ground, and sprang up, and bare fruit an hundredfold. And when he had said these things, he **cried**, He that hath ears to hear, let him hear. [KJV]<br>"And other seed fell into the good soil, and grew up, and produced a crop a hundred times as great." As He said these things, He would **call out**, "He who has ears to hear, let him hear." [NASB]<br>Still other seed fell on good soil. It came up and yielded a crop, a hundred times more than was sown."When he said this, he **called out**, "He who has ears to hear, let him hear." [NIV]<br>But others fell on good ground, sprang up, and yielded a crop a hundredfold." When He had said these things He **cried**, "He who has ears to hear, let him hear!" [NKJV]<br>Still other seed fell on fertile soil. This seed grew and produced a crop one hundred times as much as had been planted." When he had said this, he **called out**, "Anyone who is willing to hear should listen and understand!" [NLT]<br>καὶ ἕτερον ἔπεσεν ἐπὶ τὴν γῆν τὴν ἀγαθήν, καὶ φυὲν ἐποίησε καρπὸν ἑκατονταπλασίονα. Ταῦτα λέγων, **ἐφώνει**, Ὁ ἔχων ὦτα ἀκούειν ἀκουέτω. [GNS]<br>καὶ ἕτερον ἔπεσεν εἰς τὴν γῆν τὴν ἀγαθὴν καὶ φυὲν ἐποίησεν καρπὸν ἑκατονταπλασίονα. ταῦτα λέγων **ἐφώνει**, Ὁ ἔχων ὦτα ἀκούειν ἀκουέτω. [GNT] | |
| **#837**<br>**Cried–**<br>**Cried Out**<br><br>**Cried–KJV**<br>**Cried out–NASB**<br>A loud voice–NIV<br>**Cried out–NKJV**<br>Shouted–NLT<br><br>**POSB**<br>**REFERENCE**<br>(Jn.7:37-39; esp. v.37)<br>Note 2 | ἔκραξεν = ekraxen<br>Pronunciation: [eh-krahd'-zehn]<br>Parsing (part of speech): verb<br>   Mood—indicative<br>   Tense—aorist<br>   Voice—active<br>   Person—3rd person<br>   Number—singular<br>   Stem or root—from κράζω<br>Concordance References:<br>⇒ Strong's #2896 krazō<br>⇒ NIV #3189 krazō<br>⇒ NASB #2896 krazō<br><br>**John 7:37**<br>In the last day, that great day of the feast, Jesus stood and **cried**, saying, If any man thirst, let him come unto me, and drink. [KJV]<br>Now on the last day, the great day of the feast, Jesus stood and **cried out**, saying, "If any man is thirsty, let him come to Me and drink. [NASB]<br>On the last and greatest day of the Feast, Jesus stood and said in **a loud voice**, "If anyone is thirsty, let him come to me and drink. [NIV]<br>On the last day, that great *day* of the feast, Jesus stood and **cried out**, saying, "If anyone thirsts, let him come to Me and drink. [NKJV]<br>On the last day, the climax of the festival, Jesus stood and **shouted** to the crowds, "If you are thirsty, come to me! [NLT]<br>Ἐν δὲ τῇ ἐσχάτῃ ἡμέρᾳ τῇ μεγάλῃ τῆς ἑορτῆς εἱστήκει ὁ Ἰησοῦς, καὶ **ἔκραξε**, λέγων, Ἐάν τις διψᾷ ἐρχέσθω πρός με, καὶ πινέτω. [GNS]<br>Ἐν δὲ τῇ ἐσχάτῃ ἡμέρᾳ τῇ μεγάλῃ τῆς ἑορτῆς εἱστήκει ὁ Ἰησοῦς καὶ **ἔκραξεν** λέγων, Ἐάν τις διψᾷ ἐρχέσθω πρός με καὶ πινέτω. [GNT] | To cry out with a loud voice; to shout in order to be heard.<br><br>**Practical Application**<br>It was on "the last day, that great day of the feast," the day when the people marched in the processional seven times that Jesus made His phenomenal claim. Some imagine Jesus' shouting His claim just as the people finished saying, "grant us success" (Psalm 118:25).<br>Imagine the scene: Jesus did two unusual things. He "stood" (a teacher always sat in that day), and He "cried out" (*ekrazen*), shouting loudly. Both actions would startle and shock the people to attention. Picture thousands of voices praying to God for the fruitful rains in the coming season, reciting: "grant us success." Then all of a sudden, piercing the air, comes the thundering cry:<br>*"If any man is thirsty, let him come to Me and drink. "He who believes in Me, as the Scripture said, 'From his innermost being shall flow rivers of living water.'" (John 7:37-38) [NASB]*<br><br>Jesus made three phenomenal claims.<br>1. Jesus Christ is the source of life: He is the One who can quench the real thirst of man's being, who can meet the desperate need of man for prosperity, the real fruit and bounty of life.<br>2. Jesus Christ is the source of abundant life. Rivers of *living water* can flow out from a person. An abundance of life can be experienced (see POSB *Deeper Study* #1—John 1:4; POSB *Deeper Study* #1—John 10:10).<br>3. Jesus Christ is the source of the Holy Spirit. Rivers of living water refer to the Holy Spirit. This is a crucial verse, for it is the only place "living waters" is defined. When Jesus spoke of giving "living water," He meant He would |

# PRACTICAL WORD STUDIES
## in the NEW TESTAMENT

| ENGLISH WORD | GREEK WORD AND VERSE | THE WORD MEANS... |
|---|---|---|
| | | give the Holy Spirit to a person. The presence of the Holy Spirit, of course, meant the experience of abundant and eternal life.<br><br>Note: it is only the believer in Christ who receives the Holy Spirit. Belief in Him is essential. Christ is the Giver of the Spirit. (See POSB note—John 4:13-14 for more discussion.) |
| **#838**<br>**Cried–**<br>**Cried Out**<br><br>**Cried**–KJV<br>**Cried out**–NASB<br>**Cried out**–NIV<br>**Cried out**–NKJV<br>Called out–NLT<br><br>**POSB**<br>**REFERENCE**<br>(Jn.7:25-31; esp. v.28)<br>Note 2 | ἔκραξεν = ekraxen<br>Pronunciation: [eh-krahd'-zehn]<br>Parsing (part of speech): verb<br>  Mood—indicative<br>  Tense—aorist<br>  Voice—active<br>  Person—3rd person<br>  Number—singular<br>  Stem or root—from κράζω<br>Concordance References:<br>  ⇒ Strong's #2896 krazo<br>  ⇒ NIV #3189 krazo<br>  ⇒ NASB #2896 krazo<br><br>**John 7:28**<br>Then **cried** Jesus in the temple as he taught, saying, Ye both know me, and ye know whence I am: and I am not come of myself, but he that sent me is true, whom ye know not. [KJV]<br><br>Jesus therefore **cried out** in the temple, teaching and saying, "You both know Me and know where I am from; and I have not come of Myself, but He who sent Me is true, whom you do not know. [NASB]<br><br>Then Jesus, still teaching in the temple courts, **cried out**, "Yes, you know me, and you know where I am from. I am not here on my own, but he who sent me is true. You do not know him, [NIV]<br><br>Then Jesus **cried out**, as He taught in the temple, saying, "You both know Me, and you know where I am from; and I have not come of Myself, but He who sent Me is true, whom you do not know. [NKJV]<br><br>While Jesus was teaching in the Temple, he **called out**, "Yes, you know me, and you know where I come from. But I represent one you don't know, and he is true. [NLT]<br><br>ἔκραξεν οὖν ἐν τῷ ἱερῷ διδάσκων ὁ Ἰησοῦς καὶ λέγων, Κἀμὲ οἴδατε, καὶ οἴδατε πόθεν εἰμί, καὶ ἀπ' ἐμαυτοῦ οὐκ ἐλήλυθα, ἀλλ' ἔστιν ἀληθινὸς ὁ πέμψας με, ὃν ὑμεῖς οὐκ οἴδατε· [GNS]<br><br>ἔκραξεν οὖν ἐν τῷ ἱερῷ διδάσκων ὁ Ἰησοῦς καὶ λέγων, Κἀμὲ οἴδατε καὶ οἴδατε πόθεν εἰμί· καὶ ἀπ' ἐμαυτοῦ οὐκ ἐλήλυθα, ἀλλ' ἔστιν ἀληθινὸς ὁ πέμψας με, ὃν ὑμεῖς οὐκ οἴδατε· [GNT] | To call out with a loud voice; to cry out with great emotion; to shout.<br><br>**Practical Application**<br>In this Scripture, we discover what Christ cried out in the temple courts:<br>1. He *is* a man, and men do know where He came from. He was born of Mary and did come from Nazareth, but that is not all. There is much, much more.<br>2. He has come *from God*. God sent Him. Note exactly what Jesus claimed.<br>  a. "I am not here on my own": His mission and message were not His own. He did not dream up nor plan them. He was not out for self glory or to build a movement and a following. What He did was not of Himself.<br>  b. "He who sent me is true." A real Person sent Jesus, and note: the Person is not only real, He is true. He is a Person who is the very embodiment of truth. (See POSB *Deeper Study* #1—John 1:9; POSB *Deeper Study* #2—John 14:6.) What Jesus was claiming and doing was exactly what He had been sent and commissioned to claim and to do.<br>  c. "You do not know Him." They did not know that Person who is truth. Jesus was saying, of course, that they did not know God. If they knew God, really knew Him, they would recognize and know that Jesus' mission and works were of God. They would know that only God's perfect love and power could speak and do as Jesus did.<br>3. "I know Him [God]." Jesus told how He knew God.<br>  a. He knew God because He was from God (see POSB *Deeper Study* #1—John 3:31 for verses of Scripture). He actually came from God's presence, from being face to face with Him.<br>  b. He knew God because He was sent by God (see POSB *Deeper Study* #3—John 3:34). While face to face with God, God commissioned Him to go forth to *proclaim* and *live* the truth before men. (See POSB *Deeper Study* #2—John 14:6.) |
| **#839**<br>**Criticized**<br><br>Contended–KJV<br>Took issue–NASB<br>**Criticized**–NIV<br>Contended–NKJV<br>**Criticized**–NLT | διεκρίνοντο = diekrinonto<br>Pronunciation: [dee-eh-kree-non-tow]<br>Parsing (part of speech): verb<br>  Mood—indicative<br>  Tense—imperfect<br>  Voice—middle<br>  Person—3rd person<br>  Number—plural<br>  Stem or root—from διακρίνω | To criticize; to contend; to debate; to dispute; to take issue with. The word "criticized" (*diekrinonto*) means to stand against, to take an opposite position, to take sides against, to oppose, to create a cleavage, a division. It is creating strife, struggle, and discord.<br><br>**Practical Application**<br>They (the circumcision, the religionists) read- |

# PRACTICAL WORD STUDIES
## in the NEW TESTAMENT

| ENGLISH WORD | GREEK WORD AND VERSE | THE WORD MEANS... |
|---|---|---|
| **POSB REFERENCE** (Acts 11:1-3; esp. v.2) Note 1, point 2 | Concordance References:<br>⇒ Strong's #1252 diakrinō<br>⇒ NIV #1359 diakrinō<br>⇒ NASB #1252 diakrinō<br><br>**Acts 11:2**<br>And when Peter was come up to Jerusalem, they that were of the circumcision **contended** with him, [KJV]<br>And when Peter came up to Jerusalem, those who were circumcised **took issue** with him, [NASB]<br>So when Peter went up to Jerusalem, the circumcised believers **criticized** him [NIV]<br>And when Peter came up to Jerusalem, those of the circumcision **contended** with him, [NKJV]<br>But when Peter arrived back in Jerusalem, some of the Jewish believers **criticized** him. [NLT]<br>καὶ ὅτε δὲ ἀνέβη Πέτρος εἰς Ἰερουσαλήμ, **διεκρίνοντο** πρὸς αὐτὸν οἱ ἐκ περιτομῆς, [GNS]<br>ὅτε δὲ ἀνέβη Πέτρος εἰς Ἰερουσαλήμ, **διεκρίνοντο** πρὸς αὐτὸν οἱ ἐκ περιτομῆς [GNT] | ily and willingly opposed Peter, and the idea is that it was repeated: it went on and on; the issue was prolonged.<br>Again keep in mind the issue: Peter had carried the Word of God to the Gentiles.<br>⇒ He had allowed the non-Jews to receive the Word of God without circumcising them (Acts 11:1).<br>⇒ He had broken the law of Moses by "going to the uncircumcised [non-Jews] and eating" with them (Acts 11:3). |
| **#840 Criticized Sharply**<br><br>Murmured against–KJV<br>Scolding–NASB<br>Rebuked...harshly–NIV<br>**Criticized...sharply–NKJV**<br>Scolded...harshly–NLT<br><br>**POSB REFERENCE** (Mk.14:4-5; esp. v.5) Note 2 | ἐνεβριμῶντο = eneboimonto<br>Pronunciation: [en-eh-brim-own'-tow]<br>Parsing (part of speech): verb<br>  Mood—indicative<br>  Tense—imperfect<br>  Voice—middle or passive deponent<br>  Person—3rd person<br>  Number—plural<br>  Stem or root—from ἐμβριμάομαι<br>Concordance References:<br>⇒ Strong's #1690 embrimaomai<br>⇒ NIV #1839 embrimaomai<br>⇒ NASB #1690 embrimaomai<br><br>**Mark 14:5**<br>For it might have been sold for more than three hundred pence, and have been given to the poor. And they **murmured against** her. [KJV]<br>"For this perfume might have been sold for over three hundred denarii, and the money given to the poor." And they were **scolding** her. [NASB]<br>It could have been sold for more than a year's wages and the money given to the poor." And they **rebuked** her **harshly**. [NIV]<br>For it might have been sold for more than three hundred denarii and given to the poor." And they **criticized** her **sharply**. [NKJV]<br>"She could have sold it for a small fortune and given the money to the poor!" And they **scolded** her **harshly**. [NLT]<br>ἠδύνατο γὰρ τοῦτο πραθῆναι ἐπάνω τριακοσίων δηναρίων, καὶ δοθῆναι τοῖς πτωχοῖς. καὶ **ἐνεβριμῶντο** αὐτῇ. [GNS]<br>ἠδύνατο γὰρ τοῦτο τὸ μύρον πραθῆναι ἐπάνω δηναρίων τριακοσίων καὶ δοθῆναι τοῖς πτωχοῖς· καὶ **ἐνεβριμῶντο** αὐτῇ. [GNT] | To growl, rebuke, murmur against, scold; to speak harshly against.<br><br>**Practical Application**<br>In this Scripture, what disturbed the disciples was not the fact that Mary anointed Jesus. Anointing Him was easy enough to understand since it was a common custom of the day. What disturbed them was the gift she gave. The gift...<br>• seemed too valuable and priceless.<br>• seemed unnecessary and thoughtless.<br>• seemed misplaced and wasted.<br>• seemed too costly and sacrificial.<br>• seemed to be a foolish and senseless act. |
| **#841 Crossed**<br><br>Went forth–KJV<br>Went forth–NASB<br>Left–NIV<br>Went out–NKJV<br>**Crossed–NLT**<br><br>**POSB REFERENCE** (Jn.18:1-3; esp. v.1) Note 1 | ἐξῆλθεν = exēlthen<br>Pronunciation: [ex-ayl'-thehn]<br>Parsing (part of speech): verb<br>  Mood—indicative<br>  Tense—aorist<br>  Voice—active<br>  Person—3rd person<br>  Number—singular<br>  Stem or root—from ἐξέρχομαι<br>Concordance References:<br>⇒ Strong's #1831 exerchomai<br>⇒ NIV #2002 exerchomai<br>⇒ NASB #1831 exerchomai | To leave; to go forth; to cross over; to go; to set out.<br><br>**Practical Application**<br>The idea being conveyed is purpose. Jesus was going forth deliberately, for a specific purpose, knowing exactly what He was doing.<br>Jesus "crossed" to prepare Himself spiritually. He was facing *the hour* to which God had called Him, the hour of His death (see POSB note, Hour—John 2:3-5; POSB *Deeper Study* #1—John 12:23-24). He knew that God's will was for Him to die for the sins of the world. He |

## PRACTICAL WORD STUDIES
### in the NEW TESTAMENT

| ENGLISH WORD | GREEK WORD AND VERSE | THE WORD MEANS... |
|---|---|---|
| | **John 18:1**<br>When Jesus had spoken these words, he **went forth** with his disciples over the brook Cedron, where was a garden, into the which he entered, and his disciples. [KJV]<br>When Jesus had spoken these words, He **went forth** with His disciples over the ravine of the Kidron, where there was a garden, into which He Himself entered, and His disciples. [NASB]<br>When he had finished praying, Jesus **left** with his disciples and crossed the Kidron Valley. On the other side there was an olive grove, and he and his disciples went into it. [NIV]<br>When Jesus had spoken these words, He **went out** with His disciples over the Brook Kidron, where there was a garden, which He and His disciples entered. [NKJV]<br>After saying these things, Jesus **crossed** the Kidron Valley with his disciples and entered a grove of olive trees. [NLT]<br>Ταῦτα εἰπὼν ὁ Ἰησοῦς **ἐξῆλθε** σὺν τοῖς μαθηταῖς αὐτοῦ πέραν τοῦ χειμάρρου τοῦ Κεδρών, ὅπου ἦν κῆπος, εἰς ὃν εἰσῆλθεν αὐτὸς καὶ οἱ μαθηταὶ αὐτοῦ. [GNS]<br>Ταῦτα εἰπὼν ὁ Ἰησοῦς **ἐξῆλθεν** σὺν τοῖς μαθηταῖς αὐτοῦ πέραν τοῦ χειμάρρου τοῦ Κεδρὼν ὅπου ἦν κῆπος, εἰς ὃν εἰσῆλθεν αὐτὸς καὶ οἱ μαθηταὶ αὐτοῦ. [GNT] | knew the awful separation from God that sin causes; therefore, He knew that He was to be cut off from God's presence, that God would have to forsake and turn His back upon Him because of sin. He was feeling the awful pressure of God's coming judgment upon sin which was to be exercised upon Him. In the flesh, He wanted to flee; He wanted another way to be chosen to save man (Matthew 26:39, 42, 44). Yet He...<br>• was *committed* to God.<br>• was totally *devoted* to His Father.<br>• *must* do God's will.<br><br>But to do God's will, He had to have God's help. He had to pray and seek God's face. He desperately needed God to meet His need in some special way. It was for this reason that He headed for the garden. He was seeking to be alone with His Father, to have His Father strengthen Him for the terrible ordeal and judgment of the cross. (SO DO I!) |
| **#842**<br>**Crowding Around**<br><br>Pressed upon–KJV<br>Pressing around–NASB<br>**Crowding around–NIV**<br>Pressed about–NKJV<br>Pressed in–NLT<br><br>**POSB REFERENCE**<br>(Lk.5:1)<br>Note 2 | ἐπικεῖσθαι = *epikeisthai*<br>Pronunciation: [ep-ik'-ees-thah-ee]<br>Parsing (part of speech): verb<br>   Mood—infinitive<br>   Tense—present<br>   Voice—middle or passive deponent<br>   Case—dative<br>   Stem or root—from ἐπίκειμαι<br>Concordance References:<br>  ⇒ Strong's #1945 epikeimai<br>  ⇒ NIV #2130 epikeimai<br>  ⇒ NASB #1945 epikeimai<br><br>**Luke 5:1**<br>And it came to pass, that, as the people **pressed upon** him to hear the word of God, he stood by the lake of Gennesaret, [KJV]<br>Now it came about that while the multitude were **pressing around** Him and listening to the word of God, He was standing by the lake of Gennesaret; [NASB]<br>One day as Jesus was standing by the Lake of Gennesaret, with the people **crowding around** him and listening to the word of God, [NIV]<br>So it was, as the multitude **pressed about** Him to hear the word of God, that He stood by the Lake of Gennesaret, [NKJV]<br>One day as Jesus was preaching on the shore of the Sea of Galilee, great crowds **pressed in** on him to listen to the word of God. [NLT]<br>Ἐγένετο δὲ ἐν τῷ τὸν ὄχλον **ἐπικεῖσθαι** αὐτῷ τοῦ ἀκούειν τὸν λόγον τοῦ Θεοῦ, καὶ αὐτὸς ἦν ἑστὼς παρὰ τὴν λίμνην Γεννησαρέτ· [GNS]<br>Ἐγένετο δὲ ἐν τῷ τὸν ὄχλον **ἐπικεῖσθαι** αὐτῷ καὶ ἀκούειν τὸν λόγον τοῦ θεοῦ καὶ αὐτὸς ἦν ἑστὼς παρὰ τὴν λίμνην Γεννησαρέτ [GNT] | To crowd around; to press in; to press around.<br><br>**Practical Application**<br>In this Scripture, the people gathered and crowded around Him. Note why: to hear the Word of God. They pressed to hear the Word of God. They had a craving, a hunger and thirst after righteousness. |
| **#843**<br>**Crown**<br><br>Crown–KJV<br>Crown–NASB<br>Crown–NIV<br>Crown–NKJV<br>Crown–NLT | στέφανος = *stephanos*<br>Pronunciation: [stef'-an-os]<br>Parsing (part of speech): noun<br>   Case—nominative<br>   Gender—masculine<br>   Number—singular<br>   Stem or root—Στέφανος, ου<br>Concordance References:<br>  ⇒ Strong's #4735 stephanos<br>  ⇒ NIV #5109 stephanos2<br>  ⇒ NASB #4735 stephanos | Crown. It is a public prize or symbol of honor.<br><br>**Practical Application**<br>Who was this rider? The rider is conquest in general, the antichrist in particular.<br>⇒ He is the deceiver; therefore, he appears in *white* (Matthew 24:5; 2 Thes. 2:11).<br>⇒ The crown he wears is different from the crown worn by Christ in Rev. 19. It is the |

# PRACTICAL WORD STUDIES
## in the New Testament

| ENGLISH WORD | GREEK WORD AND VERSE | THE WORD MEANS... |
|---|---|---|
| **POSB REFERENCE** (Rev.6:1-2; esp. v.2) Note 1, point 2 | **Rev. 6:2**<br>And I saw, and behold a white horse: and he that sat on him had a bow; and a **crown** was given unto him: and he went forth conquering, and to conquer. [KJV]<br>And I looked, and behold, a white horse, and he who sat on it had a bow; and a **crown** was given to him; and he went out conquering, and to conquer. [NASB]<br>I looked, and there before me was a white horse! Its rider held a bow, and he was given a **crown**, and he rode out as a conqueror bent on conquest. [NIV]<br>And I looked, and behold, a white horse. He who sat on it had a bow; and a **crown** was given to him, and he went out conquering and to conquer. [NKJV]<br>I looked up and saw a white horse. Its rider carried a bow, and a **crown** was placed on his head. He rode out to win many battles and gain the victory. [NLT]<br>καὶ εἶδον, καὶ ἰδοὺ, ἵππος λευκός, καὶ ὁ καθήμενος ἐπ' αὐτῷ ἔχων τόξον· καὶ ἐδόθη αὐτῷ **στέφανος**, καὶ ἐξῆλθε νικῶν, καὶ ἵνα νικήσῃ. [GNS]<br>καὶ εἶδον, καὶ ἰδοὺ ἵππος λευκός, καὶ ὁ καθήμενος ἐπ' αὐτὸν ἔχων τόξον καὶ ἐδόθη αὐτῷ **στέφανος** καὶ ἐξῆλθεν νικῶν καὶ ἵνα νικήσῃ. [GNT] | crown of the conqueror (*stephenos*) not the royal crown of a king (*diadema*).<br>In one's interpretation, it is extremely important to note this: when the rider appears upon the scene, he *already possesses a bow*. But *the crown is given* to him. After it is given, then he goes forth to conquer. This points strongly to a counterfeit Christ. Note three facts:<br>First, this rider has a bow. Christ possesses no bow; a weapon of war is not a part of His being.<br>Second, this rider is given a crown. Christ is not given a crown. One has to say that Christ has been crowned throughout all of eternity or else at His ascension.<br>Third, this rider sets out to conquer. There is no point of time at which Christ set forth to conquer the hearts of men. He has always been about the mission of salvation. Conquering men's hearts will continue to be His mission until the day of judgment appears. Thus, there is no point from which He has to move to conquer; He is conquering souls even as He has always been conquering souls. But this is not true with this rider. This horseman who sets out to conquer is one who already possesses a bow and is given a crown at some point in time. From that point, he *goes forth* to conquer. (Cp. The Little Horn of Daniel 7; The Man of Sin and the Beast and the Ruler of the Restored Roman Empire of Rev. 13; the Abomination of Desolation of Matthew 24:15.)<br>The strongest arguments seem to point toward the white riders being the antichrist. How is the antichrist going to conquer the world? Scripture tells us that it is going to be through deception. Because of the sins and evil of people, because people have chosen to go the way of sin and evil, the antichrist is going to be able to deceive them. |
| **#844**<br>**Crowns**<br><br>**Crowns–KJV**<br>Diadems–NASB<br>**Crowns–NIV**<br>**Crowns–NKJV**<br>**Crowns–NLT**<br><br>**POSB REFERENCE** (Rev.19:12) Note 2, point 2 | διαδήματα = *diadēmata*<br>Pronunciation: [dee-ad'-ay-mah-tah]<br>Parsing (part of speech): noun<br>    Case—nominative<br>    Gender—neuter<br>    Number—plural<br>    Stem or root—from διάδημα, τος<br>Concordance References:<br>  ⇒ Strong's #1238 diadēma<br>  ⇒ NIV #1343 diadēma<br>  ⇒ NASB #1238 diadēma<br><br>**Rev. 19:12**<br>His eyes were as a flame of fire, and on his head were many **crowns**; and he had a name written, that no man knew, but he himself. [KJV]<br>And His eyes are a flame of fire, and upon His head are many **diadems**; and He has a name written upon Him which no one knows except Himself. [NASB]<br>His eyes are like blazing fire, and on his head are many **crowns**. He has a name written on him that no one knows but he himself. [NIV]<br>His eyes *were* like a flame of fire, and on His head *were* many **crowns**. He had a name written that no one knew except Himself. [NKJV]<br>His eyes were bright like flames of fire, and on his head were many **crowns**. A name was written on him, and only he knew what it meant. [NLT]<br>οἱ δὲ ὀφθαλμοὶ αὐτοῦ ὡς φλὸξ πυρός, καὶ ἐπὶ τὴν | Crown, diadem.<br><br>**Practical Application**<br>Christ will be wearing many crowns (*diadēmata*), that is, the royal crowns of rule and authority over many kingdoms. He is coming to conquer all the kingdoms of the earth. |

# PRACTICAL WORD STUDIES
## in the NEW TESTAMENT

| ENGLISH WORD | GREEK WORD AND VERSE | THE WORD MEANS... |
|---|---|---|
| | κεφαλὴν αὐτοῦ **διαδήματα** πολλά· ἔχων ὄνομα γεγραμμένον, ὃ οὐδεὶς οἶδεν εἰ μὴ αὐτός, [GNS]<br>οἱ δὲ ὀφθαλμοὶ αὐτοῦ [ὡς] φλὸξ πυρός, καὶ ἐπὶ τὴν κεφαλὴν αὐτοῦ **διαδήματα** πολλά, ἔχων ὄνομα γεγραμμένον ὃ οὐδεὶς οἶδεν εἰ μὴ αὐτός, [GNT] | |
| **#845**<br>**Crucifixion**<br><br>Passion–KJV<br>Suffering–NASB<br>Suffering–NIV<br>Suffering–NKJV<br>**Crucifixion–NLT**<br><br>**POSB REFERENCE**<br>(Acts 1:3)<br>Note 3 | παθεῖν = *pathein*<br>Pronunciation: [path'-een]<br>Parsing (part of speech): verb<br>  Mood—infinitive<br>  Tense—aorist<br>  Voice—active<br>  Case—accusative<br>  Stem or root—from πάσχω<br>Concordance References:<br>⇒ Strong's #3958 paschō<br>⇒ NIV #4248 paschō<br>⇒ NASB ##3958 paschō<br><br>**Acts 1:3**<br>To whom also he shewed himself alive after his **passion** by many infallible proofs, being seen of them forty days, and speaking of the things pertaining to the kingdom of God: [KJV]<br>To these He also presented Himself alive, after His **suffering**, by many convincing proofs, appearing to them over a period of forty days, and speaking of the things concerning the kingdom of God. [NASB]<br>After his **suffering**, he showed himself to these men and gave many convincing proofs that he was alive. He appeared to them over a period of forty days and spoke about the kingdom of God. [NIV]<br>To whom He also presented Himself alive after His **suffering** by many infallible proofs, being seen by them during forty days and speaking of the things pertaining to the kingdom of God. [NKJV]<br>During the forty days after his **crucifixion**, he appeared to the apostles from time to time and proved to them in many ways that he was actually alive. On these occasions he talked to them about the Kingdom of God. [NLT]<br>οἷς καὶ παρέστησεν ἑαυτὸν ζῶντα μετὰ τὸ **παθεῖν** αὐτὸν ἐν πολλοῖς τεκμηρίοις, δι' ἡμερῶν τεσσεράκοντα ὀπτανόμενος αὐτοῖς, καὶ λέγων τὰ περὶ τῆς βασιλείας τοῦ Θεοῦ. [GNS]<br>οἷς καὶ παρέστησεν ἑαυτὸν ζῶντα μετὰ τὸ **παθεῖν** αὐτὸν ἐν πολλοῖς τεκμηρίοις, δι' ἡμερῶν τεσσεράκοντα ὀπτανόμενος αὐτοῖς καὶ λέγων τὰ περὶ τῆς βασιλείας τοῦ θεοῦ· [GNT] | Suffering, passion, crucifixion.<br><br>**Practical Application**<br>The word "crucifixion" (*pathein*) means suffering; it refers to the sufferings or death of Christ. His death and resurrection assured the salvation of man. |
| **#846**<br>**Crucify**<br><br>Crucify–KJV<br>Crucify–NASB<br>Crucify–NIV<br>Crucify–NKJV<br>Crucify–NLT<br><br>**POSB REFERENCE**<br>(Mk.15:12-14, esp. v.13)<br>Note 5, point 2 | Σταύρωσον = *staurōson*<br>Pronunciation: [stow-ro'-son]<br>Parsing (part of speech): verb<br>  Mood—imperative<br>  Tense—aorist<br>  Voice—active<br>  Person—2nd person<br>  Number—singular<br>  Stem or root—from σταυρόω<br>Concordance References:<br>⇒ Strong's #4717 stauroo<br>⇒ NIV #5090 stauroö<br>⇒ NASB #4717 stauroo<br><br>**Mark 15:13**<br>And they cried out again, **Crucify** him. [KJV]<br>And they shouted back, "**Crucify** Him!" [NASB]<br>"**Crucify** him!" they shouted. [NIV]<br>So they cried out again, "**Crucify** Him!" [NKJV]<br>They shouted back, "**Crucify** him!" [NLT]<br>οἱ δὲ πάλιν ἔκραξαν, **Σταύρωσον** αὐτόν. [GNS]<br>οἱ δὲ πάλιν ἔκραξαν, **Σταύρωσον** αὐτόν. [GNT] | To crucify; to put to death on a cross.<br><br>**Practical Application**<br>The crucifixion itself was the most horrible of deaths. The ancient writer Tacitus called it "a despicable death." Cicero called it "the most cruel and horrifying death." He simply said it was "incapable of description." There was the pain of the driven spikes forced through the flesh of His hands and feet or ankles. There was the weight of His body jolting and pulling against the spikes as the cross was lifted and rocked into place. There was the scorching sun and the unquenchable thirst gnawing away at His dry mouth and throat. There was the blood oozing from His scourged back, His thorn crowned brow, His feet, and His stick beaten head. In addition, just imagine the aggravation of flies, gnats, and other insects. There was also the piercing of the spear thrust into His side. On and on the sufferings could be described. There has never been a more cruel form of execution than crucifixion upon a cross. |

# PRACTICAL WORD STUDIES
## in the NEW TESTAMENT

| ENGLISH WORD | GREEK WORD AND VERSE | THE WORD MEANS... |
|---|---|---|
| **#847**<br>**Cruel**<br><br>Fierce–KJV<br>Brutal–NASB<br>Brutal–NIV<br>Brutal–NKJV<br>**Cruel–NLT**<br><br>**POSB REFERENCE**<br>(2 Tim. 3:2-4; esp. v.3)<br>Note 2, point 13 | ἀνήμεροι = anēmeroi<br>Pronunciation: [an-ay'-mer-oy]<br>Parsing (part of speech): adjective<br>    Case—nominative<br>    Gender—masculine<br>    Number—plural<br>    Stem or root—from ἀνήμερος, ον<br>Concordance References:<br>⇒  Strong's #434 anēmeros<br>⇒  NIV #466 anēmeros<br>⇒  NASB #434 anēmeros<br><br>**2 Tim. 3:3**<br>Without natural affection, trucebreakers, false accusers, incontinent, **fierce**, despisers of those that are good, [KJV]<br>Unloving, irreconcilable, malicious gossips, without self-control, **brutal**, haters of good, [NASB]<br>Without love, unforgiving, slanderous, without self-control, **brutal**, not lovers of the good, [NIV]<br>Unloving, unforgiving, slanderers, without self-control, **brutal**, despisers of good, [NKJV]<br>They will be unloving and unforgiving; they will slander others and have no self-control; they will be **cruel** and have no interest in what is good. [NLT]<br>ἄστοργοι, ἄσπονδοι, διάβολοι, ἀκρατεῖς, **ἀνήμεροι**, ἀφιλάγαθοι, [GNS]<br>ἄστοργοι ἄσπονδοι διάβολοι ἀκρατεῖς **ἀνήμεροι** ἀφιλάγαθοι, [GNT] | Brutal, fierce, cruel, savage, and untamed.<br><br>**Practical Application**<br>It is the word that describes the savage beast of the wild that is unrestrained in its fierceness. It is a word that should never be true of people, yet tragically it is. Never in the history of the world have men become as fierce and savage as they are today.<br>1. People no longer just murder...<br>   • they mutilate<br>   • they torture<br>   • they kill at random<br>   • they kill by twos and threes and by thousands and millions (for example, Hitler, Stalin)<br>And they take pleasure in their torture and savagery.<br>2. People no longer just correct and rebuke children, spouse, friend, neighbor, employee, or stranger...<br>   • they curse<br>   • they abuse<br>   • they attack<br>   • they maim<br>   • they act violently<br>The last days will see an increase in brutal, fierce and savage behavior. |
| **#848**<br>**Crushed–<br>Crushed And<br>Broken**<br><br>Distressed–KJV<br>**Crushed–NASB**<br>**Crushed–NIV**<br>**Crushed–NKJV**<br>**Crushed and broken–NLT**<br><br>**POSB REFERENCE**<br>(2 Cor.4:7-9; esp. v.8)<br>Note 2, point 1 | στενοχωρούμενοι = stenochōroumenoi<br>Pronunciation: [sten-okh-o'-roo-mehn-oy]<br>Parsing (part of speech): verb<br>    Mood—participle<br>    Tense—present<br>    Voice—passive<br>    Case—nominative<br>    Gender—masculine<br>    Person—1st person<br>    Number—plural<br>    Stem or root—from στενοχωρέομαι<br>Concordance References:<br>⇒  Strong's #4729 stenochōreō<br>⇒  NIV #5102 stenochōreō<br>⇒  NASB #4729 stenochōreō<br><br>**2 Cor. 4:8**<br>We are troubled on every side, yet not **distressed**; we are perplexed, but not in despair; [KJV]<br>We are afflicted in every way, but not **crushed**; perplexed, but not despairing; [NASB]<br>We are hard pressed on every side, but not **crushed**; perplexed, but not in despair; [NIV]<br>*We are* hard pressed on every side, yet not **crushed**; *we are* perplexed, but not in despair; [NKJV]<br>We are pressed on every side by troubles, but we are not **crushed and broken**. We are perplexed, but we don't give up and quit. [NLT]<br>ἐν παντὶ θλιβόμενοι, ἀλλ' οὐ **στενοχωρούμενοι**· ἀπορούμενοι ἀλλ' οὐκ ἐξαπορούμενοι. [GNS]<br>ἐν παντὶ θλιβόμενοι ἀλλ' οὐ **στενοχωρούμενοι**, ἀπορούμενοι ἀλλ' οὐκ ἐξαπορούμενοι, [GNT] | To be crushed and broken; to be kept in a narrow, cramped place.<br><br>**Practical Application**<br>Our faith, even when we are hard pressed on every side, is used by God to strengthen and encourage others in their need. Therefore, we stand strong in faith, growing stronger and stronger in faith. |
| **#849**<br>**Cry**<br><br>Wept–KJV<br>Wept–NASB<br>Wept–NIV<br>Wept–NKJV<br>**Cry–NLT** | ἔκλαυσεν = eklausen<br>Pronunciation: [eh-klah'-sehn]<br>Parsing (part of speech): verb<br>    Mood—indicative<br>    Tense—aorist<br>    Voice—active<br>    Person—3rd person<br>    Number—singular<br>    Stem or root—from κλαίω | To burst into tears; to weep out loud; to sob; to wail; to mourn.<br><br>**Practical Application**<br>Jesus was literally heartbroken over Jerusalem. Jesus was weeping while the city was engaged in the excitement of feasting and fellowshipping in a jovial, party-like spirit. The |

## PRACTICAL WORD STUDIES
### in the NEW TESTAMENT

| ENGLISH WORD | GREEK WORD AND VERSE | THE WORD MEANS... |
|---|---|---|
| **POSB REFERENCE** (Lk.19:41-42; esp. v.41) Note 1, point 1a | Concordance References:<br>⇒ Strong's #2799 klaiö<br>⇒ NIV #3081 klaiö<br>⇒ NASB #2799 klaiö<br><br>**Luke 19:41**<br>And when he was come near, he beheld the city, and **wept** over it, [KJV]<br>And when He approached, He saw the city and **wept** over it, [NASB]<br>As he approached Jerusalem and saw the city, he **wept** over it [NIV]<br>Now as He drew near, He saw the city and **wept** over it, [NKJV]<br>But as they came closer to Jerusalem and Jesus saw the city ahead, he began to **cry**. [NLT]<br>Καὶ ὡς ἤγγισεν, ἰδὼν τὴν πόλιν, **ἔκλαυσεν** ἐπ' αὐτή, [GNS]<br>Καὶ ὡς ἤγγισεν ἰδὼν τὴν πόλιν **ἔκλαυσεν** ἐπ' αὐτήν [GNT] | whole atmosphere was like that of a present-day convention. The scene can be imagined. But while the people were in such a partying mood, Jesus was off on the hillside weeping over the city and its people. |
| **#850 Cubit**<br><br>Cubit–KJV<br>Cubit–NASB<br>Hour–NIV<br>Cubit–NKJV<br>Moment–NLT<br><br>**POSB REFERENCE** (Mt.6:27) Note 4 | πῆχυν = pēchun<br>Pronunciation: [pay'-khoon]<br>Parsing (part of speech): noun<br>  Case—accusative<br>  Gender—masculine<br>  Number—singular<br>  Stem or root—from πῆχυς, εως<br>Concordance References:<br>⇒ Strong's #4083 pēchus<br>⇒ NIV #4388 pēchus<br>⇒ NASB #4083 pēchus<br><br>**Matthew 6:27**<br>Which of you by taking thought can add one **cubit** unto his stature? [KJV]<br>"And which of you by being anxious can add a single **cubit** to his life's span? [NASB]<br>Who of you by worrying can add a single **hour** to his life? [NIV]<br>Which of you by worrying can add one **cubit** to his stature? [NKJV]<br>Can all your worries add a single **moment** to your life? Of course not. [NLT]<br>τίς δὲ ἐξ ὑμῶν μεριμνῶν δύναται προσθεῖναι ἐπὶ τὴν ἡλικίαν αὐτοῦ **πῆχυν** ἕνα; [GNS]<br>τίς δὲ ἐξ ὑμῶν μεριμνῶν δύναται προσθεῖναι ἐπὶ τὴν ἡλικίαν αὐτοῦ **πῆχυν** ἕνα; [GNT] | An hour, a moment, a cubit.<br><br>**Practical Application**<br>In this Scripture, the word speaks of a time, an hour, in a person's life that is past and can never be added to. |
| **#851 Cubit**<br><br>Cubit–KJV<br>Cubit–NASB<br>Hour–NIV<br>Cubit–NKJV<br>Moment–NLT<br><br>**POSB REFERENCE** (Lk.12:22-28; esp. v.25) Note 1, point 3 | πῆχυν = pēchun<br>Pronunciation: [pay'-khoon]<br>Parsing (part of speech): noun<br>  Case—accusative<br>  Gender—masculine<br>  Number—singular<br>  Stem or root—from πῆχυς, εως<br>Concordance References:<br>⇒ Strong's #4083 pēchus<br>⇒ NIV #4388 pēchus<br>⇒ NASB #4083 pēchus<br><br>**Luke 12:25**<br>And which of you with taking thought can add to his stature one **cubit**? [KJV]<br>"And which of you by being anxious can add a single **cubit** to his life's span? [NASB]<br>Who of you by worrying can add a single **hour** to his life? [NIV]<br>And which of you by worrying can add one **cubit** to his stature? [NKJV]<br>Can all your worries add a single **moment** to your life? Of course not! [NLT] | Cubit, hour, moment. The word "cubit" literally means measure of space, or distance (approximately 18 inches); but it can also mean a measure of time or age (John 9:21). It is an age, a time of life.<br><br>**Practical Application**<br>In this context, the word speaks of a time that is past. So the verse can read either "who can add one cubit to his stature" or "a single hour or moment to his life span." |

## Practical Word Studies in the New Testament

| ENGLISH WORD | GREEK WORD AND VERSE | THE WORD MEANS... |
|---|---|---|
| | τίς δὲ ἐξ ὑμῶν μεριμνῶν δύναται προσθεῖναι ἐπὶ τὴν ἡλικίαν αὐτοῦ **πῆχυν** ἕνα; [GNS]<br>τίς δὲ ἐξ ὑμῶν μεριμνῶν δύναται προσθεῖναι ἐπὶ τὴν ἡλικίαν αὐτοῦ **πῆχυν**; [GNT] | |
| **#852**<br>**Cumbered**<br><br>**Cumbered**–KJV<br>Distracted–NASB<br>Distracted–NIV<br>Distracted–NKJV<br>Worrying–NLT<br><br>**POSB REFERENCE**<br>(Lk.10:40)<br>Note 3 | περιεσπᾶτο = *periespato*<br>Pronunciation: [per-ee-spah'-tow]<br>Parsing (part of speech): verb<br>    Mood—indicative<br>    Tense—imperfect<br>    Voice—passive<br>    Person—3rd person<br>    Number—singular<br>    Stem or root—from περισπάομαι<br>Concordance References:<br>  ⇒ Strong's #4049 perispaō<br>  ⇒ NIV #4352 perispaō<br>  ⇒ NASB #4049 perispaō<br><br>**Luke 10:40**<br>But Martha was **cumbered** about much serving, and came to him, and said, Lord, dost thou not care that my sister hath left me to serve alone? bid her therefore that she help me. [KJV]<br>But Martha was **distracted** with all her preparations; and she came up to Him, and said, "Lord, do You not care that my sister has left me to do all the serving alone? Then tell her to help me." [NASB]<br>But Martha was **distracted** by all the preparations that had to be made. She came to him and asked, "Lord, don't you care that my sister has left me to do the work by myself? Tell her to help me!" [NIV]<br>But Martha was **distracted** with much serving, and she approached Him and said, "Lord, do You not care that my sister has left me to serve alone? Therefore tell her to help me." [NKJV]<br>But Martha was **worrying** over the big dinner she was preparing. She came to Jesus and said, "Lord, doesn't it seem unfair to you that my sister just sits here while I do all the work? Tell her to come and help me." [NLT]<br>ἡ δὲ Μάρθα **περιεσπᾶτο** περὶ πολλὴν διακονίαν· ἐπιστᾶσα δὲ εἶπε, Κύριε, οὐ μέλει σοι ὅτι ἡ ἀδελφή μου μόνην με κατέλιπε διακονεῖν; εἰπὲ οὖν αὐτῇ ἵνα μοι συναντιλάβηται. [GNS]<br>ἡ δὲ Μάρθα **περιεσπᾶτο** περὶ πολλὴν διακονίαν· ἐπιστᾶσα δὲ εἶπεν, Κύριε, οὐ μέλει σοι ὅτι ἡ ἀδελφή μου μόνην με κατέλιπεν διακονεῖν; εἰπὲ οὖν αὐτῇ ἵνα μοι συναντιλάβηται. [GNT] | To be distracted; to worry; to draw around; to twist; to be drawn here and there.<br><br>**Practical Application**<br>The idea is that Martha was drawn around and twisted with anxiety and worry. She was distracted, running here and there, being drawn by the cares of this and that person. |
| **#853**<br>**Cured**<br><br>Made...whole–KJV<br>**Cured**–NASB<br>Healed–NIV<br>Made...well–NKJV<br>Healed–NLT<br><br>**POSB REFERENCE**<br>(Mt.14:36)<br>Note 6 | διεσώθησαν = *diesōthēsan*<br>Pronunciation: [dee-so'-thay-sahn]<br>Parsing (part of speech): verb<br>    Mood—indicative<br>    Tense—aorist<br>    Voice—passive<br>    Person—3rd person<br>    Number—plural<br>    Stem or root—from διασῴζω<br>Concordance References:<br>  ⇒ Strong's #1295 diasōzō<br>  ⇒ NIV #1407 diasōzō<br>  ⇒ NASB #1295 diasōzō<br><br>**Matthew 14:36**<br>And besought him that they might only touch the hem of his garment: and as many as touched were **made** perfectly **whole**. [KJV]<br>And they began to entreat Him that they might just touch the fringe of His cloak; and as many as touched it were **cured**. [NASB]<br>And begged him to let the sick just touch the edge of his cloak, and all who touched him were **healed**. [NIV] | To be healed or cured through and through; to be made whole through and through; to rescue.<br><br>**Practical Application**<br>A complete restoration takes place within the person. The person is completely cured, spiritually and inwardly, as well as physically and outwardly. |

## Practical Word Studies in the New Testament

| ENGLISH WORD | GREEK WORD AND VERSE | THE WORD MEANS... |
|---|---|---|
| | And begged Him that they might only touch the hem of His garment. And as many as touched *it* were **made** perfectly **well**. [NKJV]<br>The sick begged him to let them touch even the fringe of his robe, and all who touched it were **healed**. [NLT]<br>καὶ παρεκάλουν αὐτὸν, ἵνα μόνον ἅψωνται τοῦ κρασπέδου τοῦ ἱματίου αὐτοῦ· καὶ ὅσοι ἥψαντο **διεσώθησαν**. [GNS]<br>καὶ παρεκάλουν αὐτὸν ἵνα μόνον ἅψωνται τοῦ κρασπέδου τοῦ ἱματίου αὐτοῦ· καὶ ὅσοι ἥψαντο **διεσώθησαν**. [GNT] | |
| **#854**<br>**Curse**<br><br>Vanity–KJV<br>Futility–NASB<br>Frustration–NIV<br>Futility–NKJV<br>**Curse–NLT**<br><br>**POSB REFERENCE**<br>(Romans 8:19-22, esp. v.20)<br>Note 2, point 1 | ματαιότητι = *mataiotēti*<br>Pronunciation: [mat-ah-yot'-ay-tee]<br>Parsing (part of speech): noun<br>    Case—dative<br>    Gender—feminine<br>    Number—singular<br>    Stem or root—from ματαιότης, ητος<br>Concordance References:<br>  ⇒ Strong's #3153 *mataiotēs*<br>  ⇒ NIV #3470 *mataiotēs*<br>  ⇒ NASB #3153 *mataiotēs*<br><br>**Romans 8:20**<br>For the creature was made subject to **vanity**, not willingly, but by reason of him who hath subjected the same in hope, [KJV]<br>For the creation was subjected to **futility**, not of its own will, but because of Him who subjected it, in hope [NASB]<br>For the creation was subjected to **frustration**, not by its own choice, but by the will of the one who subjected it, in hope [NIV]<br>For the creation was subjected to **futility**, not willingly, but because of Him who subjected *it* in hope; [NKJV]<br>Against its will, everything on earth was subjected to God's **curse**. [NLT]<br>τῇ γὰρ **ματαιότητι** ἡ κτίσις ὑπετάγη, οὐχ ἑκοῦσα ἀλλὰ διὰ τὸν ὑποτάξαντα, ἐφ᾽ ἑλπίδι· [GNS]<br>τῇ γὰρ **ματαιότητι** ἡ κτίσις ὑπετάγη, οὐχ ἑκοῦσα ἀλλὰ διὰ τὸν ὑποτάξαντα, ἐφ᾽ ἑλπίδι [GNT] | Worthlessness, futility; emptiness, frustration; cursed.<br><br>**Practical Application**<br>Creation is subject to corruption. This is clearly seen by men; and what men see is constantly confirmed by such authorities as the botanist, zoologist, geologist, and astronomer of the world. All of creation, whether mineral, plant, or animal, suffers just as men do. All creation suffers hurt, damage, loss, deterioration, erosion, death, and decay—all creation struggles for life. It is "cursed" (*mataios*), that is, condemned to futility and frustration, unable to realize its purpose, subject to corruption. |
| **#855**<br>**Curse**<br><br>**Curse–KJV**<br>**Curse–NASB**<br>**Curse–NIV**<br>**Curse–NKJV**<br>**Curse–NLT**<br><br>**POSB REFERENCE**<br>(Gal.3:10-12; esp. v.10)<br>Note 3 | κατάραν = *kataran*<br>Pronunciation: [kat-ar'-ahn]<br>Parsing (part of speech): noun<br>    Case—accusative<br>    Gender—feminine<br>    Number—singular<br>    Stem or root—from κατάρα, ας<br>Concordance References:<br>  ⇒ Strong's #2671 *katara*<br>  ⇒ NIV #2932 *katara*<br>  ⇒ NASB #2671 *katara*<br><br>**Galatians 3:10**<br>For as many as are of the works of the law are under the **curse**: for it is written, Cursed is every one that continueth not in all things which are written in the book of the law to do them. [KJV]<br>For as many as are of the works of the Law are under a **curse**; for it is written, "Cursed is everyone who does not abide by all things written in the book of the law, to perform them." [NASB]<br>All who rely on observing the law are under a **curse**, for it is written: "Cursed is everyone who does not continue to do everything written in the Book of the Law." [NIV]<br>For as many as are of the works of the law are under the **curse**; for it is written, "Cursed is everyone who does not continue in all things which are written in the book of the law, to do them." [NKJV] | To curse; to be condemned and doomed to punishment by the righteous judgment of God.<br><br>**Practical Application**<br>Galatians 3:13 says that Christ bore the curse of the law for us (the sin condemnation, death, and punishment due us for having broken the law). The law carries with it a curse. A person either keeps the law or else he is cursed; that is, he is to stand before the Judge and bear the punishment of a lawbreaker. The curse (penalty or punishment) for violating the law is...<br>• the mark of death (2 Cor. 3:7).<br>• the mark of condemnation (2 Cor. 3:9). |

# PRACTICAL WORD STUDIES
## in the NEW TESTAMENT

| ENGLISH WORD | GREEK WORD AND VERSE | THE WORD MEANS... |
|---|---|---|
| | But those who depend on the law to make them right with God are under his **curse**, for the Scriptures say, "Cursed is everyone who does not observe and obey all these commands that are written in God's Book of the Law." [NLT]<br>ὅσοι γὰρ ἐξ ἔργων νόμου εἰσίν, ὑπὸ **κατάραν** εἰσί· γέγραπται γὰρ Ἐπικατάρατος πᾶς ὃς οὐκ ἐμμένει πᾶσι τοῖς γεγραμμένοις ἐν τῷ βιβλίῳ τοῦ νόμου τοῦ ποιῆσαι αὐτά. [GNS]<br>ὅσοι γὰρ ἐξ ἔργων νόμου εἰσίν, ὑπὸ **κατάραν** εἰσίν· γέγραπται γὰρ ὅτι Ἐπικατάρατος πᾶς ὃς οὐκ ἐμμένει πᾶσιν τοῖς γεγραμμένοις ἐν τῷ βιβλίῳ τοῦ νόμου τοῦ ποιῆσαι αὐτά. [GNT] | |
| **#856**<br>**Curse–**<br>**Cursed**<br><br>Anathema–KJV<br>Accursed–NASB<br>**Curse–NIV**<br>Accursed–NKJV<br>**Cursed–NLT**<br><br>**POSB REFERENCE**<br>(1 Cor.16:19-24; esp. v.22)<br>Note 6, point 2 | ἀνάθεμα = *anathema*<br>Pronunciation: [an-ath'-em-ah]<br>Parsing (part of speech): noun<br>   Case—nominative<br>   Gender—neuter<br>   Number—singular<br>   Stem or root—from ἀνάθεμα, τος<br>Concordance References:<br>  ⇒ Strong's #331 anathema<br>  ⇒ NIV #353 anathema<br>  ⇒ NASB #331 anathema<br><br>**1 Cor. 16:22**<br>If any man love not the Lord Jesus Christ, let him be **Anathema** Maranatha. [KJV]<br>If anyone does not love the Lord, let him be **accursed**. Maranatha. [NASB]<br>If anyone does not love the Lord—a **curse** be on him. Come, O Lord! [NIV]<br>If anyone does not love the Lord Jesus Christ, let him be **accursed**. O Lord, come! [NKJV]<br>If anyone does not love the Lord, that person is **cursed**. Our Lord, come! [NLT]<br>εἴ τις οὐ φιλεῖ τὸν Κύριον Ἰησοῦν Χριστόν, ἤτω **ἀνάθεμα**. Μαρὰν ἀθα. [GNS]<br>εἴ τις οὐ φιλεῖ τὸν κύριον, ἤτω **ἀνάθεμα**. Μαρανα θα. [GNT] | Curse, accursed, under the ban, cast away. It is something doomed to utter destruction.<br><br>**Practical Application**<br>There was the terrifying importance of love for Christ. Paul uses the word four times (Romans 9:3; 1 Cor. 12:3; 1 Cor. 16:22; Galatians 1:8; cp. Acts 23:14). The words "Come, O Lord" or "Our Lord, come" "*maranatha*" means the Lord comes! The idea is that any man who does not love the Lord Jesus Christ will be cursed. And the Lord is coming, therefore this person will be cursed. |
| **#857**<br>**Curse, Bound...**<br>**Under A**<br><br>**Bound...under a curse–KJV**<br>Bound...under an oath–NASB<br>Bound...with an oath–NIV<br>Bound...under an oath–NKJV<br>Bound...with an oath–NLT<br><br>**POSB REFERENCE**<br>(Acts 23:12-15; esp. v.12)<br>Note 1, point 1 | ἀνεθεμάτισαν = *anethematisan*<br>Pronunciation: [an-eth-ehm-aht-i'-sahn]<br>Parsing (part of speech): verb<br>   Mood—indicative<br>   Tense—aorist<br>   Voice—active<br>   Person—3rd person<br>   Number—plural<br>   Stem or root—from ἀναθεματίζω<br>Concordance References:<br>  ⇒ Strong's #332 anathematizō<br>  ⇒ NIV #354 anathematizō<br>  ⇒ NASB #332 anathematizō<br><br>**Acts 23:12**<br>And when it was day, certain of the Jews banded together, and **bound** themselves **under a curse**, saying that they would neither eat nor drink till they had killed Paul. [KJV]<br>And when it was day, the Jews formed a conspiracy and **bound** themselves **under an oath**, saying that they would neither eat nor drink until they had killed Paul. [NASB]<br>The next morning the Jews formed a conspiracy and **bound** themselves **with an oath** not to eat or drink until they had killed Paul. [NIV]<br>And when it was day, some of the Jews banded together and **bound** themselves **under an oath**, saying that they would neither eat nor drink till they had killed Paul. [NKJV]<br>The next morning a group of Jews got together and | To be bound with an oath; to be bound under a curse; to bind by a solemn vow.<br><br>**Practical Application**<br>The curse was what may be called a religious curse. It was an anathema; that is, they devoted themselves to God; they would not eat or drink until they had killed Paul. They actually thought they would be pleasing God by getting rid of Paul. |

# PRACTICAL WORD STUDIES
## in the NEW TESTAMENT

| ENGLISH WORD | GREEK WORD AND VERSE | THE WORD MEANS... |
|---|---|---|
| | **bound** themselves **with an oath** to neither eat nor drink until they had killed Paul. [NLT]<br><br>Γενομένης δὲ ἡμέρας, ποιήσαντες τινες τῶν Ἰουδαίων συστροφήν, **ἀνεθεμάτισαν** ἑαυτούς, λέγοντες μήτε φαγεῖν μήτε πίειν ἕως οὗ ἀποκτείνωσι τὸν Παῦλον. [GNS]<br><br>Γενομένης δὲ ἡμέρας ποιήσαντες συστροφὴν οἱ Ἰουδαῖοι **ἀνεθεμάτισαν** ἑαυτοὺς λέγοντες μήτε φαγεῖν μήτε πίειν ἕως οὗ ἀποκτείνωσιν τὸν Παῦλον. [GNT] | |
| **#858**<br>**Cursed**<br><br>Accursed–KJV<br>Accursed–NASB<br>**Cursed–NIV**<br>Accursed–NKJV<br>**Cursed–NLT**<br><br>**POSB REFERENCE**<br>(Rom.9:1-3; esp. v.3)<br>Note 1, point 3 | ἀνάθεμα = *anathema*<br>Pronunciation: [an-ath'-em-ah]<br>Parsing (part of speech): noun<br>   Case—nominative<br>   Gender—neuter<br>   Number—singular<br>   Stem or root—from ἀνάθεμα, τος<br>Concordance References:<br>  ⇒ Strong's #331 anathema<br>  ⇒ NIV #353 anathema<br>  ⇒ NASB #331 anathema<br><br>**Romans 9:3**<br>For I could wish that myself were **accursed** from Christ for my brethren, my kinsmen according to the flesh; [KJV]<br>For I could wish that I myself were **accursed**, separated from Christ for the sake of my brethren, my kinsmen according to the flesh, [NASB]<br>For I could wish that I myself were **cursed** and cut off from Christ for the sake of my brothers, those of my own race, [NIV]<br>For I could wish that I myself were **accursed** from Christ for my brethren, my countrymen according to the flesh, [NKJV]<br>For my people, my Jewish brothers and sisters. I would be willing to be forever **cursed**—cut off from Christ!—if that would save them. [NLT]<br>ηὐχόμην γὰρ αὐτὸς ἐγὼ **ἀνάθεμα** εἶναι ἀπὸ τοῦ Χριστοῦ ὑπὲρ τῶν ἀδελφῶν μου, τῶν συγγενῶν μου κατὰ σάρκα· [GNS]<br>ηὐχόμην γὰρ **ἀνάθεμα** εἶναι αὐτὸς ἐγὼ ἀπὸ τοῦ Χριστοῦ ὑπὲρ τῶν ἀδελφῶν μου τῶν συγγενῶν μου κατὰ σάρκα, [GNT] | Curse, accursed, under the ban, cast away. It is something doomed to utter destruction.<br><br>**Practical Application**<br>The picture is that of a man who had an unbelievable willingness to be sacrificed for his people. Paul could wish to be cursed (*anathema*), that is, separated from Christ if it would save his people. He could be willing to swap his salvation for their doom if it would lead to their salvation. Paul felt the deepest emotion and love and concern for his people. |
| **#859**<br>**Curtain**<br><br>Veil–KJV<br>Veil–NASB<br>**Curtain–NIV**<br>Veil–NKJV<br>**Curtain–NLT**<br><br>**POSB REFERENCE**<br>(Mk.15:38)<br>Note 15, point 1<br><br>See also POSB REF:<br>(Lk.23:45)<br>Note 13, point 1 | καταπέτασμα = *katapetasma*<br>Pronunciation: [kat-ap-et'-as-mah]<br>Parsing (part of speech): noun<br>   Case—nominative<br>   Gender—neuter<br>   Number—singular<br>   Stem or root—from καταπέτασμα, τος<br>Concordance References:<br>  ⇒ Strong's #2665 katapetasma<br>  ⇒ NIV #2925 katapetasma<br>  ⇒ NASB #2665 katapetasma<br><br>**Mark 15:38**<br>And the **veil** of the temple was rent in twain from the top to the bottom. [KJV]<br>And the **veil** of the temple was torn in two from top to bottom. [NASB]<br>The **curtain** of the temple was torn in two from top to bottom. [NIV]<br>Then the **veil** of the temple was torn in two from top to bottom. [NKJV]<br>And the **curtain** in the Temple was torn in two, from top to bottom. [NLT]<br>καὶ τὸ **καταπέτασμα** τοῦ ναοῦ ἐσχίσθη εἰς δύο ἀπὸ ἄνωθεν ἕως κάτω. [GNS]<br>Καὶ τὸ **καταπέτασμα** τοῦ ναοῦ ἐσχίσθη εἰς δύο ἀπ' ἄνωθεν ἕως κάτω. [GNT] | The curtain or veil; the curtain which separated the Holy of Holies from the Holy Place.<br><br>**Practical Application**<br>1. What the facts reveal:<br>  a. It was a curtain or veil of great beauty made with remarkable skill. Like the inner curtain, it was made of fine linen. The same striking colors of blue, purple, and scarlet were a part of this veil. The embroidered cherubim were also worked into this veil.<br>  b. It was hung with gold hooks on four posts of durable wood (acacia). The posts stood on four silver sockets or bases.<br>  c. The purpose for the inner curtain was basically to shield the ark of God from all else.<br>    1) The inner curtain was to separate the Most Holy Place from the Holy Place. This symbolized the majestic holiness and righteousness of God, the light of His perfection which no man can approach.<br>    2) The inner curtain separated the mercy seat from all else. The curtain symbolized the holiness of God, separation from the presence of God. Note what was sep- |

# PRACTICAL WORD STUDIES
## in the New Testament

| ENGLISH WORD | GREEK WORD AND VERSE | THE WORD MEANS... |
|---|---|---|
| | | arated from the Mercy Seat in the Most Holy Place:<br>⇒ The Table of Showbread: the table was placed on the north side in the Holy Place.<br>⇒ The Lampstand: the Lampstand was placed opposite the table on the south side.<br>2. What the Inner Veil or Curtain Door taught:<br>  a. God is holy and righteous, far, far removed from man and his world—totally set apart and separated from the pollution and uncleanness of man.<br>  b. God must be approached ever so carefully—in reverence, awe, and fear.<br>  c. There is only one way to God, only one door into His presence.<br>  d. Fellowship and communion with God Himself is the supreme act of worship.<br>3. How Christ fulfilled the symbolism of the veil:<br>  The *inner curtain* is rich in symbolism as it speaks of Jesus Christ. Christ fulfilled the symbolism of the inner curtain. Christ and Christ alone is the way to God, the way to know God and to experience the presence, fellowship, and communion of God. Remember what happened to the inner curtain of the temple when Christ died on the cross: it was torn from top to bottom, symbolizing that God Himself acted, took the initiative, and tore the veil. The heavenly curtain that kept man out of God's presence was torn by Christ when He suffered and died on the cross. We now have eternal access into the presence of God. The door into God's presence is wide open. |
| **#860**<br>**Cut In On**<br><br>Hinder–KJV<br>Hindered–NASB<br>**Cut in on–NIV**<br>Hindered–NKJV<br>Interfered with–NLT<br><br>**POSB REFERENCE**<br>(Gal.5:7)<br>Note 1, point 1 | ἐνέκοψεν = enekopsen<br>Pronunciation: [en-ek-op'-sen]<br>Parsing (part of speech): verb<br>  Mood—indicative<br>  Tense—aorist<br>  Voice—active<br>  Person—3rd person<br>  Number—singular<br>  Stem or root—from ἐγκόπτω<br>Concordance References:<br>  ⇒ Strong's #1465 egkoptō<br>  ⇒ NIV #1601 egkoptō<br>  ⇒ NASB #1465 egkoptō<br><br>**Galatians 5:7**<br>Ye did run well; who did **hinder** you that ye should not obey the truth? [KJV]<br>You were running well; who **hindered** you from obeying the truth? [NASB]<br>You were running a good race. Who **cut in on** you and kept you from obeying the truth? [NIV]<br>You ran well. Who **hindered** you from obeying the truth? [NKJV]<br>You were getting along so well. Who has **interfered with** you to hold you back from following the truth? [NLT]<br>ἐτρέχετε καλῶς· τίς ὑμᾶς **ἀνέοψε** τῇ ἀληθείᾳ μὴ πείθεσθαι; [GNS]<br>Ἐτρέχετε καλῶς· τίς ὑμᾶς **ἐνέκοψεν** [τῇ] ἀληθείᾳ μὴ πείθεσθαι; [GNT] | To cut in on; to hinder; to edge in; to interfere with; to detain; to obstruct.<br><br>**Practical Application**<br>While the Galatians had been running the Christian race, some had edged in on them and begun to hinder and interfere with their running. They were no longer obeying the truth. They were now trying to approach God by some other way than Christ. They were now thinking...<br>• that God accepted them because they had been *ritualized*: circumcised and baptized.<br>• that God accepted them because they tried to keep the law: tried to be as good as they could and did good deeds as opportunity arose.<br>• that God approved them because they were faithful to the church: its rituals, ceremonies, services, rules and regulations.<br>They were no longer running well. They had allowed some false teacher to hinder them and to turn them from the truth. They had a need to think about the matter, a desperate need...<br>• to think about the race they had been running.<br>• to think about who it was that was now cutting in on their running. |

## PRACTICAL WORD STUDIES
### in the NEW TESTAMENT

| ENGLISH WORD | GREEK WORD AND VERSE | THE WORD MEANS... |
|---|---|---|
| **#861**<br>**Cut Off**<br><br>Cut off–KJV<br>Cut off–NASB<br>Cut off–NIV<br>Cut off–NKJV<br>Cut off–NLT<br><br>**POSB REFERENCE**<br>(Rom.11:22)<br>Note 4, point 2 | ἐκκοπήσῃ = *ekkopësë*<br>Pronunciation: [ek-kop'-tay-say]<br>Parsing (part of speech): verb<br>    Mood—indicative<br>    Tense—future<br>    Voice—passive<br>    Person—2nd person<br>    Number—singular<br>    Stem or root—from ἐκκόπτω<br>Concordance References:<br>  ⇒ Strong's #1581 ekkoptö<br>  ⇒ NIV #1716 ekkoptö<br>  ⇒ NASB #1581 ekkoptö<br><br>**Romans 11:22**<br>Behold therefore the goodness and severity of God: on them which fell, severity; but toward thee, goodness, if thou continue in his goodness: otherwise thou also shalt be **cut off**. [KJV]<br>Behold then the kindness and severity of God; to those who fell, severity, but to you, God's kindness, if you continue in His kindness; otherwise you also will be **cut off**. [NASB]<br>Consider therefore the kindness and sternness of God: sternness to those who fell, but kindness to you, provided that you continue in his kindness. Otherwise, you also will be **cut off**. [NIV]<br>Therefore consider the goodness and severity of God: on those who fell, severity; but toward you, goodness, if you continue in *His* goodness. Otherwise you also will be **cut off**. [NKJV]<br>Notice how God is both kind and severe. He is severe to those who disobeyed, but kind to you as you continue to trust in his kindness. But if you stop trusting, you also will be **cut off**. [NLT]<br>ἴδε οὖν χρηστότητα καὶ ἀποτομίαν Θεοῦ· ἐπὶ μὲν τοὺς πεσόντας, ἀποτομίαν· ἐπὶ δὲ σέ, χρηστότητα, ἐὰν ἐπιμένῃς τῇ χρηστότητι· ἐπεὶ καὶ σὺ **ἐκκοπήσῃ**. [GNS]<br>ἴδε οὖν χρηστότητα καὶ ἀποτομίαν θεοῦ· ἐπὶ μὲν τοὺς πεσόντας ἀποτομία, ἐπὶ δὲ σὲ χρηστότης θεοῦ, ἐὰν ἐπιμένῃς τῇ χρηστότητι, ἐπεὶ καὶ σὺ **ἐκκοπήσῃ**. [GNT] | To cut off; to cut down; to remove.<br><br>**Practical Application**<br>It is the picture of a person who is remaining and abiding in the house of God's goodness. A Gentile believer must continue and abide, endure and persevere in the goodness of God. Otherwise, he too will be cut off (*ekkopësë*) just as the Jews were cut off (Romans 11:17). |
| **#862**<br>**Cut Off From**<br><br>Destroyed–KJV<br>Utterly destroyed from–NASB<br>Completely cut off from–NIV<br>Utterly destroyed from–NKJV<br>Cut off from–NLT<br><br>**POSB REFERENCE**<br>(Acts 3:23)<br>*Deeper Study #4* | ἐξολεθρευθήσεται ἐκ = *exolethreuthësetai ek*<br>Pronunciation: [ex-ol-eth-ryoo'-thay-seh-tah-ee ek]<br>Parsing *exolethreuthësetai* (part of speech): verb<br>    Mood—indicative or imperative<br>    Tense—future or aorist<br>    Voice—passive<br>    Person—3rd person<br>    Number—singular<br>    Stem or root—from ἐξολεθρεύω<br>Concordance References:<br>  ⇒ Strong's #1537 + 1842 ek exolethreuö<br>  ⇒ NIV #1666 + 2017 ek exolethreuö<br>  ⇒ NASB #1537 + 1842 ek exolethreuö<br><br>**Acts 3:23**<br>And it shall come to pass, that every soul, which will not hear that prophet, shall be **destroyed** from among the people. [KJV]<br>'And it shall be that every soul that does not heed that prophet shall be **utterly destroyed from** among the people.' [NASB]<br>Anyone who does not listen to him will be **completely cut off from** among his people.' [NIV]<br>*And it shall be that every soul who will not hear that Prophet shall be **utterly destroyed from** among the people.'* [NKJV]<br>Then Moses said, 'Anyone who will not listen to that Prophet will be **cut off from** God's people and utterly destroyed.' [NLT]<br>ἔσται δὲ, πᾶσα ψυχὴ ἥτις ἐὰν μὴ ἀκούσῃ τοῦ | To completely cut off from; to be utterly destroyed or slayed; to lose one's well-being; to be wasted and ruined and given a worthless existence.<br><br>**Practical Application**<br>It does not mean that a person will cease to exist. It means a person will be destroyed and devastated and condemned to a worthless existence. He will suffer waste and loss and ruin forever and ever. |

## PRACTICAL WORD STUDIES
### in the NEW TESTAMENT

| ENGLISH WORD | GREEK WORD AND VERSE | THE WORD MEANS... |
|---|---|---|
| | προφήτου ἐκείνου, **ἐξολεθρευθήσεται ἐκ** τοῦ λαοῦ. [GNS]<br>ἔσται δὲ πᾶσα ψυχὴ ἥτις ἐὰν μὴ ἀκούσῃ τοῦ προφήτου ἐκείνου **ἐξολεθρευθήσεται ἐκ** τοῦ λαοῦ. [GNT] | |
| **#863**<br>**Cut To**<br><br>Pricked–KJV<br>Pierced–NASB<br>**Cut to–NIV**<br>**Cut to–NKJV**<br>Convicted them deeply–NLT<br><br>**POSB REFERENCE**<br>(Acts 2:37)<br>Note 1 | κατενύγησαν = *katenugësan*<br>Pronunciation: [kat-en-oog'-ay-san]<br>Parsing (part of speech): verb<br>   Mood—indicative<br>   Tense—aorist<br>   Voice—passive<br>   Person—3rd person<br>   Number—plural<br>   Stem or root—from κατανύσσομαι<br>Concordance References:<br>  ⇒ Strong's #2660 katanussomai<br>  ⇒ NIV #2920 katanussomai<br>  ⇒ NASB #2660 katanussomai<br><br>**Acts 2:37**<br>Now when they heard this, they were **pricked** in their heart, and said unto Peter and to the rest of the apostles, Men and brethren, what shall we do? [KJV]<br>Now when they heard this, they were **pierced** to the heart, and said to Peter and the rest of the apostles, "Brethren, what shall we do?" [NASB]<br>When the people heard this, they were **cut to** the heart and said to Peter and the other apostles, "Brothers, what shall we do?" [NIV]<br>Now when they heard *this,* they were **cut to** the heart, and said to Peter and the rest of the apostles, "Men *and* brethren, what shall we do?" [NKJV]<br>Peter's words **convicted them deeply**, and they said to him and to the other apostles, "Brothers, what should we do?" [NLT]<br>Ἀκούσαντες δὲ **κατενύγησαν** τὴν καρδίαν, εἶπόν τε πρὸς τὸν Πέτρον καὶ τοὺς λοιποὺς ἀποστόλους, Τί ποιήσομεν, ἄνδρες ἀδελφοί; [GNS]<br>Ἀκούσαντες δὲ **κατενύγησαν** τὴν καρδίαν εἶπόν τε πρὸς τὸν Πέτρον καὶ τοὺς λοιποὺς ἀποστόλους, Τί ποιήσωμεν, ἄνδρες ἀδελφοί; [GNT] | To be cut to the heart; to be pricked; to be pierced; to be convicted deeply; to be stabbed. The word "cut to" (*katenugësan*) means to convict, cut, sting, sense pain and hurt.<br><br>**Practical Application**<br>In this Scripture, we learn how the gospel affects the hearts of repentant sinners. The power of the gospel convicts people deeply. |
| **#864**<br>**Cut To The Heart**<br><br>**Cut to the heart–KJV**<br>Cut to the quick–NASB<br>Furious–NIV<br>**Cut to the heart–NKJV**<br>Infuriated–NLT<br><br>**POSB REFERENCE**<br>(Acts 7:54)<br>Note 1, point 2 | διεπρίοντο ταῖς καρδίαις = *dieprionto tais kardiais*<br>Pronunciation: [dee-ehp-ree'-on-tow tace kar-dee'-ah-ees]<br>Parsing *dieprionto* (part of speech): verb<br>   Mood—indicative<br>   Tense—imperfect<br>   Voice—passive<br>   Person—3rd person<br>   Number—plural<br>   Stem or root—from διαπρίομαι<br>Parsing *kardiais* (part of speech): noun<br>   Case—dative<br>   Gender—feminine<br>   Number—plural<br>   Stem or root—from καρδία, ας<br>Concordance References:<br>  ⇒ Strong's #1282 + 2588 + 3588 diaprio kardia ho<br>  ⇒ NIV #1391 + 2840 + 3836 diaprio kardia ho<br>  ⇒ NASB #1282 + 2588 + 3588 diaprio kardia ho<br><br>**Acts 7:54**<br>When they heard these things, they were **cut to the heart**, and they gnashed on him with their teeth. [KJV]<br>Now when they heard this, they were **cut to the quick**, and they began gnashing their teeth at him. [NASB]<br>When they heard this, they were **furious** and gnashed their teeth at him. [NIV]<br>When they heard these things they were **cut to the heart**, and they gnashed at him with *their* teeth. [NKJV]<br>The Jewish leaders were **infuriated** by Stephen's | To be furious; to cut to the heart; to cut to the quick; to infuriate; to be enraged.<br><br>**Practical Application**<br>The word "*dieprionto*" means to saw asunder; to cut through. It is used to show violent reaction. The response of their hearts was anger, not godly sorrow (see POSB *Deeper Study* #1, Godly Sorrow—2 Cor. 7:10). They had no intention of confessing that they had been wrong. |

## PRACTICAL WORD STUDIES
### in the NEW TESTAMENT

| ENGLISH WORD | GREEK WORD AND VERSE | THE WORD MEANS... |
|---|---|---|
| | accusation, and they shook their fists in rage. [NLT]<br>Ἀκούοντες δὲ ταῦτα, **διεπρίοντο ταῖς καρδίαις** αὐτῶν, καὶ ἔβρυχον τοὺς ὀδόντας ἐπ' αὐτόν. [GNS]<br>Ἀκούοντες δὲ ταῦτα **διεπρίοντο ταῖς καρδίαις** αὐτῶν καὶ ἔβρυχον τοὺς ὀδόντας ἐπ' αὐτόν. [GNT] | |
| **#865**<br>**Cut To The Heart**<br><br>Cut to the heart–KJV<br>Cut to the quick–NASB<br>Furious–NIV<br>Furious–NKJV<br>Furious–NLT<br><br>**POSB REFERENCE**<br>(Acts 5:32-40; esp. v.33)<br>Note 4, point 1 | **διεπρίοντο** = *dieprionto*<br>Pronunciation: [dee-ap-ree'-on-tow]<br>Parsing (part of speech): verb<br>    Mood—indicative<br>    Tense—imperfect<br>    Voice—passive<br>    Person—3rd person<br>    Number—plural<br>    Stem or root—from **διαπρίομαι**<br>Concordance References:<br>  ⇒ Strong's #1282 diaprio<br>  ⇒ NIV #1391 dapriö<br>  ⇒ NASB #1282 diaprio<br><br>**Acts 5:33**<br>When they heard that, they were **cut to the heart**, and took counsel to slay them. [KJV]<br>But when they heard this, they were **cut to the quick** and were intending to slay them. [NASB]<br>When they heard this, they were **furious** and wanted to put them to death. [NIV]<br>When they heard *this*, they were **furious** and plotted to kill them. [NKJV]<br>At this, the high council was **furious** and decided to kill them. [NLT]<br>Οἱ δὲ ἀκούσαντες **διεπρίοντο**, καὶ ἐβούλοντο ἀνελεῖν αὐτούς. [GNS]<br>Οἱ δὲ ἀκούσαντες **διεπρίοντο** καὶ ἐβούλοντο ἀνελεῖν αὐτούς. [GNT] | To be furious; to be cut to the quick; to cut to the heart; to be enraged.<br><br>**Practical Application**<br>Their hearts were sawn in two, into two parts, through and through. The idea is they were cut to the heart, not with conviction but with anger, wrath, rage, and reaction against the apostles. |
| **#866**<br>**Cut To The Quick**<br><br>Cut to the heart–KJV<br>Cut to the quick–NASB<br>Furious–NIV<br>Furious–NKJV<br>Furious–NLT<br><br>**POSB REFERENCE**<br>(Acts 5:32-40; esp. v.33)<br>Note 4, point 1 | **διεπρίοντο** = *dieprionto*<br>Pronunciation: [dee-ap-ree'-on-tow]<br>Parsing (part of speech): verb<br>    Mood—indicative<br>    Tense—imperfect<br>    Voice—passive<br>    Person—3rd person<br>    Number—plural<br>    Stem or root—from **διαπρίομαι**<br>Concordance References:<br>  ⇒ Strong's #1282 diaprio<br>  ⇒ NIV #1391 dapriö<br>  ⇒ NASB #1282 diaprio<br><br>**Acts 5:33**<br>When they heard that, they were **cut to the heart**, and took counsel to slay them. [KJV]<br>But when they heard this, they were **cut to the quick** and were intending to slay them. [NASB]<br>When they heard this, they were **furious** and wanted to put them to death. [NIV]<br>When they heard *this*, they were **furious** and plotted to kill them. [NKJV]<br>At this, the high council was **furious** and decided to kill them. [NLT]<br>Οἱ δὲ ἀκούσαντες **διεπρίοντο**, καὶ ἐβούλοντο ἀνελεῖν αὐτούς. [GNS]<br>Οἱ δὲ ἀκούσαντες **διεπρίοντο** καὶ ἐβούλοντο ἀνελεῖν αὐτούς. [GNT] | To be furious; to be cut to the quick; to cut to the heart; to be enraged.<br><br>**Practical Application**<br>Their hearts were sawn in two, into two parts, through and through. The idea is they were cut to the heart, not with conviction but with anger, wrath, rage, and reaction against the apostles. |
| **#867**<br>**Cut To The Quick**<br><br>Cut to the heart–KJV<br>Cut to the quick– | **διεπρίοντο ταῖς καρδίαις** = *dieprionto tais kardiais*<br>Pronunciation: [dee-ehp-ree'-on-tow tace kar-dee'-ah-ees]<br>Parsing *dieprionto* (part of speech): verb<br>    Mood—indicative<br>    Tense—imperfect<br>    Voice—passive | To be furious; to cut to the heart; to cut to the quick; to infuriate; to be enraged.<br><br>**Practical Application**<br>The word "*dieprionto*" means to saw asunder; to cut through. It is used to show violent |

# PRACTICAL WORD STUDIES
## in the NEW TESTAMENT

| ENGLISH WORD | GREEK WORD AND VERSE | THE WORD MEANS... |
|---|---|---|
| **NASB**<br>Furious–NIV<br>Cut to the heart–NKJV<br>Infuriated–NLT<br><br>**POSB REFERENCE**<br>(Acts 7:54)<br>Note 1, point 2 | Person—3rd person<br>Number—plural<br>Stem or root—from διαπρίομαι<br>Parsing *kardiais* (part of speech): noun<br>    Case—dative<br>    Gender—feminine<br>    Number—plural<br>    Stem or root—from καρδία, ας<br>Concordance References:<br>  ⇒ Strong's #1282 + 2588 + 3588 diapriō kardia ho<br>  ⇒ NIV #1391 + 2840 + 3836 diapriō kardia ho<br>  ⇒ NASB #1282 + 2588 + 3588 diapriō kardia ho<br><br>**Acts 7:54**<br>When they heard these things, they were **cut to the heart**, and they gnashed on him with their teeth. [KJV]<br>Now when they heard this, they were **cut to the quick**, and they began gnashing their teeth at him. [NASB]<br>When they heard this, they were **furious** and gnashed their teeth at him. [NIV]<br>When they heard these things they were **cut to the heart**, and they gnashed at him with *their* teeth. [NKJV]<br>The Jewish leaders were **infuriated** by Stephen's accusation, and they shook their fists in rage. [NLT]<br>Ἀκούοντες δὲ ταῦτα, **διεπρίοντο ταῖς καρδίαις** αὐτῶν, καὶ ἔβρυχον τοὺς ὀδόντας ἐπ' αὐτόν. [GNS]<br>Ἀκούοντες δὲ ταῦτα **διεπρίοντο ταῖς καρδίαις** αὐτῶν καὶ ἔβρυχον τοὺς ὀδόντας ἐπ' αὐτόν. [GNT] | reaction. The response of their hearts was anger, not godly sorrow (see POSB *Deeper Study* #1, Godly Sorrow—2 Cor. 7:10). They had no intention of confessing that they had been wrong. |
| **#868**<br>**Cuts Off**<br><br>Taketh away–KJV<br>Takes away–NASB<br>**Cuts off–NIV**<br>Takes away–NKJV<br>**Cuts off–NLT**<br><br>**POSB REFERENCE**<br>(Jn.15:2)<br>Note 2, point 3 | αἴρει = *airei*<br>Pronunciation: [ah'ee-ree]<br>Parsing (part of speech): verb<br>    Mood—indicative<br>    Tense—present<br>    Voice—active<br>    Person—3rd person<br>    Number—singular<br>    Stem or root—from αἴρω<br>Concordance References:<br>  ⇒ Strong's #142 airo<br>  ⇒ NIV #149 airo<br>  ⇒ NASB #142 airo<br><br>**John 15:2**<br>Every branch in me that beareth not fruit he **taketh away**: and every branch that beareth fruit, he purgeth it, that it may bring forth more fruit. [KJV]<br>"Every branch in Me that does not bear fruit, He **takes away**; and every branch that bears fruit, He prunes it, that it may bear more fruit. [NASB]<br>He **cuts off** every branch in me that bears no fruit, while every branch that does bear fruit he prunes so that it will be even more fruitful. [NIV]<br>Every branch in Me that does not bear fruit He **takes away**; and every *branch* that bears fruit He prunes, that it may bear more fruit. [NKJV]<br>He **cuts off** every branch that doesn't produce fruit, and he prunes the branches that do bear fruit so they will produce even more. [NLT]<br>πᾶν κλῆμα ἐν ἐμοὶ μὴ φέρον καρπόν, **αἴρει** αὐτό· καὶ πᾶν τὸ καρπὸν φέρον, καθαίρει αὐτό, ἵνα πλείονα καρπὸν φέρῃ. [GNS]<br>πᾶν κλῆμα ἐν ἐμοὶ μὴ φέρον καρπὸν **αἴρει** αὐτό, καὶ πᾶν τὸ καρπὸν φέρον καθαίρει αὐτὸ ἵνα καρπὸν πλείονα φέρῃ. [GNT] | To cut off; to take away and to remove; to carry away.<br><br>**Practical Application**<br>In relation to the vine, the branch is pruned, removed, and taken away. This is a severe warning to every branch "in" the vine, to make sure his profession is genuine enough to bear fruit. |
| **#869**<br>**Cutting Deep** | διϊκνούμενος = *diiknoumenos*<br>Pronunciation: [dee-ik-noo'-mehn-os]<br>Parsing (part of speech): verb<br>    Mood—participle<br>    Tense—present | Piercing; cutting deep; penetrating.<br><br>**Practical Application**<br>The Word of God is "cutting deep" (*diiknou-* |

# PRACTICAL WORD STUDIES
## in the NEW TESTAMENT

| ENGLISH WORD | GREEK WORD AND VERSE | THE WORD MEANS... |
|---|---|---|
| Piercing–KJV<br>Piercing–NASB<br>Penetrates–NIV<br>Piercing–NKJV<br>**Cutting deep–NLT**<br><br>**POSB REFERENCE**<br>(Heb.4:11-13; esp. v.22)<br>Note 5, point 2 | Voice—middle or passive deponent<br>Case—nominative<br>Gender—masculine<br>Number—singular<br>Stem or root—from διϊκνέομαι<br>Concordance References:<br>⇒ Strong's #1338 diikneomai<br>⇒ NIV #1459 diikneomai<br>⇒ NASB #1338 diikneomai<br><br>**Hebrews 4:12**<br>For the word of God is quick, and powerful, and sharper than any twoedged sword, **piercing** even to the dividing asunder of soul and spirit, and of the joints and marrow, and is a discerner of the thoughts and intents of the heart. [KJV]<br>For the word of God is living and active and sharper than any two-edged sword, and **piercing** as far as the division of soul and spirit, of both joints and marrow, and able to judge the thoughts and intentions of the heart. [NASB]<br>For the word of God is living and active. Sharper than any double-edged sword, it **penetrates** even to dividing soul and spirit, joints and marrow; it judges the thoughts and attitudes of the heart. [NIV]<br>For the word of God *is* living and powerful, and sharper than any two-edged sword, **piercing** even to the division of soul and spirit, and of joints and marrow, and is a discerner of the thoughts and intents of the heart. [NKJV]<br>For the word of God is full of living power. It is sharper than the sharpest knife, **cutting deep** into our innermost thoughts and desires. It exposes us for what we really are. [NLT]<br>ζῶν γὰρ ὁ λόγος τοῦ Θεοῦ, καὶ ἐνεργής, καὶ τομώτερος ὑπὲρ πᾶσαν μάχαιραν δίστομον, καὶ **διϊκνούμενος**· ἄχρι μερισμοῦ ψυχῆς τὲ καὶ πνεύματος, ἁρμῶν τε καὶ μυελῶν, καὶ κριτικὸς ἐνθυμήσεων καὶ ἐννοιῶν καρδίας. [GNS]<br>Ζῶν γὰρ ὁ λόγος τοῦ θεοῦ καὶ ἐνεργὴς καὶ τομώτερος ὑπὲρ πᾶσαν μάχαιραν δίστομον καὶ **διϊκνούμενος** ἄχρι μερισμοῦ ψυχῆς καὶ πνεύματος, ἁρμῶν τε καὶ μυελῶν, καὶ κριτικὸς ἐνθυμήσεων καὶ ἐννοιῶν καρδίας· [GNT] | *menos*). It goes right through to the soul and spirit of man. It is the Word of God that takes man's earthly, soulish nature and separates it from the spiritual call and promise of God. It pierces and separates a man's soul and spirit just as a sword pierces a man's joints and marrow.<br>⇒ It separates a proud soul from a humble spirit.<br>⇒ It separates a sinful soul from a righteous spirit.<br>⇒ It separates a rebellious soul from an obedient spirit.<br>⇒ It separates an unbelieving soul from a believing spirit. |

# PRACTICAL WORD STUDIES
## in the NEW TESTAMENT

| ENGLISH WORD | GREEK WORD AND VERSE | THE WORD MEANS... |
|---|---|---|
| **#870**<br>**Damnable**<br><br>Damnable–KJV<br>Destructive–NASB<br>Destructive–NIV<br>Destructive–NKJV<br>Destructive–NLT<br><br>**POSB REFERENCE**<br>(2 Pt.2:1)<br>Note 2, point 2<br><br>See also POSB REF:<br>(2 Pt.2:3-9; esp. v.3)<br>Note 5 | ἀπωλείας = apōleias<br>Pronunciation: [ap-o'-li-ahs]<br>Parsing (part of speech): noun<br>  Case—genitive<br>  Gender—feminine<br>  Number—singular<br>  Stem or root—from ἀπώλεια, ας<br>Concordance References:<br>⇒ Strong's #684 apōleia<br>⇒ NIV #724 apōleia<br>⇒ NASB #684 apōleia<br><br>**2 Peter 2:1**<br>But there were false prophets also among the people, even as there shall be false teachers among you, who privily shall bring in **damnable** heresies, even denying the Lord that bought them, and bring upon themselves swift destruction. [KJV]<br>But false prophets also arose among the people, just as there will also be false teachers among you, who will secretly introduce **destructive** heresies, even denying the Master who bought them, bringing swift destruction upon themselves. [NASB]<br>But there were also false prophets among the people, just as there will be false teachers among you. They will secretly introduce **destructive** heresies, even denying the sovereign Lord who bought them—bringing swift destruction on themselves. [NIV]<br>But there were also false prophets among the people, even as there will be false teachers among you, who will secretly bring in **destructive** heresies, even denying the Lord who bought them, *and* bring on themselves swift destruction. [NKJV]<br>But there were also false prophets in Israel, just as there will be false teachers among you. They will cleverly teach their **destructive** heresies about God and even turn against their Master who bought them. Theirs will be a swift and terrible end. [NLT]<br>Ἐγένοντο δὲ καὶ ψευδοπροφῆται ἐν τῷ λαῷ, ὡς καὶ ἐν ὑμῖν ἔσονται ψευδοδιδάσκαλοι, οἵτινες παρεισάξουσιν αἱρέσεις **ἀπωλείας**, καὶ τὸν ἀγοράσαντα αὐτοὺς δεσπότην ἀρνούμενοι, ἐπάγοντες ἑαυτοῖς ταχινὴν ἀπώλειαν, [GNS]<br>Ἐγένοντο δὲ καὶ ψευδοπροφῆται ἐν τῷ λαῷ, ὡς καὶ ἐν ὑμῖν ἔσονται ψευδοδιδάσκαλοι, οἵτινες παρεισάξουσιν αἱρέσεις **ἀπωλείας** καὶ τὸν ἀγοράσαντα αὐτοὺς δεσπότην ἀρνούμενοι. ἐπάγοντες ἑαυτοῖς ταχινὴν ἀπώλειαν, [GNT] | Destructive, damnable. It means heresies that cause one to lose one's well being; to be ruined; to be wasted; to perish; to be destroyed; to suffer perdition.<br><br>**Practical Application**<br>Note where false teachers teach their destructive heresies: in the church, right among believers. The false teachers are not out in the world, but they are within the church. They have joined the church, and they have been outstanding members long enough to become teachers and preachers within the church. They hold leadership positions from which they can teach their destructive heresies. Note that the word "heresies" (*haireseis*) is plural. What are the heresies being referred to? Any teaching that goes contrary to the Scripture, that is, the Word of God or Bible. This is clearly what is meant, for the exhortation has just been given: "Take heed to the word of prophecy, to the Scripture" (cp. 2 Peter 1:19-21). |
| **#871**<br>**Damnation**<br><br>Damnation–KJV<br>Condemnation–NASB<br>Judgment–NIV<br>Judgment–NKJV<br>Punishment–NLT<br><br>**POSB REFERENCE**<br>(Rom.13:1-2; esp. v.2)<br>Note 2, point 2<br><br>See also POSB REF:<br>(1 Cor.11:27-30; esp. v.2)<br>Note 4, point 2 | κρίμα = krima<br>Pronunciation: [kree'-mah]<br>Parsing (part of speech): noun<br>  Case—accusative<br>  Gender—neuter<br>  Number—singular<br>  Stem or root—from κρίμα, τος<br>Concordance References:<br>⇒ Strong's #2917 krima<br>⇒ NIV #3210 krima<br>⇒ NASB #2917 krima<br><br>**Romans 13:2**<br>Whosoever therefore resisteth the power, resisteth the ordinance of God: and they that resist shall receive to themselves **damnation**. [KJV]<br>Therefore he who resists authority has opposed the ordinance of God; and they who have opposed will receive **condemnation** upon themselves. [NASB]<br>Consequently, he who rebels against the authority is rebelling against what God has instituted, and those who do so will bring **judgment** on themselves. [NIV]<br>Therefore whoever resists the authority resists the | Judgment; condemnation, punishment.<br><br>**Practical Application**<br>The believer who resists the authorities will be condemned. The idea is that the disobedient believer will have to face the judgment of God if he disobeys the just laws of government. Some commentators think this refers to the judgment of the civil authorities. There is no question, if the believer is caught breaking the laws of the state, he will be punished. However, the civil authorities may never catch the believer. Yet, God knows every law broken by the believer, and by resisting the laws of the state, the believer has broken the law of God. Therefore, the believer stands guilty before God, and he will be judged by God. |

# PRACTICAL WORD STUDIES
## in the NEW TESTAMENT

| ENGLISH WORD | GREEK WORD AND VERSE | THE WORD MEANS... |
|---|---|---|
| | ordinance of God, and those who resist will bring **judgment** on themselves. [NKJV]<br>So those who refuse to obey the laws of the land are refusing to obey God, and **punishment** will follow. [NLT]<br>ὥστε ὁ ἀντιτασσόμενος τῇ ἐξουσίᾳ, τῇ τοῦ θεοῦ διαταγῇ ἀνθέστηκεν· οἱ δὲ ἀνθεστηκότες ἑαυτοῖς **κρίμα** λήμψονται. [GNS]<br>ὥστε ὁ ἀντιτασσόμενος τῇ ἐξουσίᾳ τῇ τοῦ θεοῦ διαταγῇ ἀνθέστηκεν, οἱ δὲ ἀνθεστηκότες ἑαυτοῖς **κρίμα** λήμψονται. [GNT] | |
| **#872**<br>**Damned**<br><br>Damned–KJV<br>Judged–NASB<br>Condemned–NIV<br>Condemned–NKJV<br>Condemned–NLT<br><br>**POSB REFERENCE**<br>(2 Thes.2:12)<br>Note 4 | κριθῶσιν = *krithōsin*<br>Pronunciation: [kree'-tho-sin]<br>Parsing (part of speech): verb<br>    Mood—subjunctive<br>    Tense—aorist<br>    Voice—passive<br>    Person—3rd person<br>    Number—plural<br>    Stem or root—from κρίνω<br>Concordance References:<br>⇒ Strong's #2919 krinō<br>⇒ NIV #3212 krinō<br>⇒ NASB #2919 krinō<br><br>**2 Thes. 2:12**<br>That they all might be **damned** who believed not the truth, but had pleasure in unrighteousness. [KJV]<br>In order that they all may be **judged** who did not believe the truth, but took pleasure in wickedness. [NASB]<br>And so that all will be **condemned** who have not believed the truth but have delighted in wickedness. [NIV]<br>That they all may be **condemned** who did not believe the truth but had pleasure in unrighteousness. [NKJV]<br>Then they will be **condemned** for not believing the truth and for enjoying the evil they do. [NLT]<br>ἵνα **κριθῶσι** πάντες οἱ μὴ πιστεύσαντες τῇ ἀληθείᾳ, ἀλλ' εὐδοκήσαντες ἐν τῇ ἀδικίᾳ. [GNS]<br>ἵνα **κριθῶσιν** πάντες οἱ μὴ πιστεύσαντες τῇ ἀληθείᾳ ἀλλὰ εὐδοκήσαντες τῇ ἀδικίᾳ. [GNT] | Condemned, damned, judged, punished.<br><br>**Practical Application**<br>The followers of the antichrist are the condemned or damned—those who take pleasure in unrighteousness. There are two reasons why the followers of the antichrist will be judged.<br>1. They will not believe the truth of the gospel, the truth of the Lord Jesus Christ. God loves His Son Jesus Christ—loves Him with a perfect love.<br>2. They will delight in wickedness. They will be people who live unrighteous lives and take pleasure in their unrighteousness. They will be people who love their sins. |
| **#873**<br>**Dangerous Reefs**<br><br>Spots–KJV<br>Hidden reefs–NASB<br>Blemishes–NIV<br>Spots–NKJV<br>**Dangerous reefs–NLT**<br><br>**POSB REFERENCE**<br>(Jude 1:12)<br>Note 14 | σπιλάδες = *spilades*<br>Pronunciation: [spee-la-des']<br>Parsing (part of speech): noun<br>    Case—nominative<br>    Gender—feminine<br>    Number—plural<br>    Stem or root—from σπιλάς, άδος<br>Concordance References:<br>⇒ Strong's #4694 spilas<br>⇒ NIV #5069 spilas<br>⇒ NASB #4694 spilas<br><br>**Jude 1:12**<br>These are **spots** in your feasts of charity, when they feast with you, feeding themselves without fear: clouds they are without water, carried about of winds; trees whose fruit withereth, without fruit, twice dead, plucked up by the roots; [KJV]<br>These men are those who are **hidden reefs** in your love feasts when they feast with you without fear, caring for themselves; clouds without water, carried along by winds; autumn trees without fruit, doubly dead, uprooted; [NASB]<br>These men are **blemishes** at your love feasts, eating with you without the slightest qualm—shepherds who feed only themselves. They are clouds without rain, blown along by the wind; autumn trees, without fruit and uprooted—twice dead. [NIV]<br>These are **spots** in your love feasts, while they feast | Blemishes, spots, hidden reefs, dangerous reefs; anything that poses a dangerous threat.<br><br>**Practical Application**<br>False teachers are *dangerous reefs* upon the fellowship of the church. The Greek word for "dangerous reefs" (*spilas*) can mean *submerged rocks or hidden reefs* that can wreck a ship. False teachers are reefs within the church that can wreck the fellowship of the church. Translators differ as to which meaning Jude intended. Perhaps he meant both, for both are certainly true.<br>The *love feasts* referred to were called *love feasts* by the early church. They were fellowship meals that the church celebrated after the services on the Lord's Day. Each family brought what food they could. This, of course, meant that the wealthy brought plenty and the poor brought little or nothing. Remember that many of the believers were slaves in that day, so some of them would not be able to bring any food whatsoever. Some churches had the most joyful fellowship around the love feasts. It provided a time when the believers could share the warmth of their hearts and grow in fellowship together. It was a time when the Holy Spirit could draw the |

## PRACTICAL WORD STUDIES
## in the NEW TESTAMENT

| ENGLISH WORD | GREEK WORD AND VERSE | THE WORD MEANS... |
|---|---|---|
| | with you without fear, serving *only* themselves. *They are* clouds without water, carried about by the winds; late autumn trees without fruit, twice dead, pulled up by the roots; [NKJV]<br><br>When these people join you in fellowship meals celebrating the love of the Lord, they are like **dangerous reefs** that can shipwreck you. They are shameless in the way they care only about themselves. They are like clouds blowing over dry land without giving rain, promising much but producing nothing. They are like trees without fruit at harvesttime. They are not only dead but doubly dead, for they have been pulled out by the roots. [NLT]<br><br>οὗτοί εἰσιν ἐν ταῖς ἀγάπαις ὑμῶν **σπιλάδες**, συνευωχούμενοι ὑμῖν, ἀφόβως ἑαυτοὺς ποιμαίνοντες· νεφέλαι ἄνυδροι, ὑπὸ ἀνέμων περιφερόμεναι· δένδρα φθινοπωρινὰ, ἄκαρπα, δὶς ἀποθανόντα, ἐκριζωθέντα· [GNS]<br><br>οὗτοί εἰσιν οἱ ἐν ταῖς ἀγάπαις ὑμῶν **σπιλάδες** συνευωχούμενοι ἀφόβως, ἑαυτοὺς ποιμαίνοντες, νεφέλαι ἄνυδροι ὑπὸ ἀνέμων παραφερόμεναι, δένδρα φθινοπωρινὰ ἄκαρπα δὶς ἀποθανόντα ἐκριζωθέντα, [GNT] | hearts of believers together in love and joy and care and sharing. It was a time that the Holy Spirit could use to bind believers together in feelings for one another and in warmth and tenderness.<br><br>The point is this: fellowship among believers is a most wonderful time, a unique opportunity to grow and share together. But when false teachers are present, the scene is entirely different.<br>⇒ False teachers are spots or blemishes upon the fellowship of believers. They dirty and soil the name of Christ and the testimony of the church. They profess to be believers and are even teachers of God's Word, but they are not pure. Their false teaching disturbs genuine believers and causes division within the fellowship of the church. Those who are not rooted in Christ and in God's Word follow and support the false teacher; those who are rooted in Christ and in God's Word reject the false teacher. False teachers always spot and dirty the fellowship of the church because they cause division among the people and destroy the Spirit of Christ among them.<br>⇒ False teachers are reefs or submerged rocks that wreck the fellowship of the church. Their teaching is often injected into the church quietly and insidiously, completely unknown to the general membership. Therefore, the fellowship is subject to being shipwrecked upon the reefs of false teaching. Note that the false teachers feed themselves—that is, they fellowship with believers—without fear. There is no fear of God nor thought about the damage they are doing to the fellowship of the church. Their interest is to boost themselves forward; to be recognized as excellent teachers or preachers, persons of unusual gifts, teachers with new insights, teachers who are progressive, who are a notch above others. |
| **#874**<br>**Dared**<br><br>Bold–KJV<br>Boldness–NASB<br>**Dared–NIV**<br>Bold–NKJV<br>Courage–NLT<br><br>**POSB REFERENCE**<br>(1 Thes.2:2)<br>Note 2 | ἐπαρρησιασάμεθα = *eparrēsiasametha*<br>Pronunciation: [ep-ar-hray-see-ahs-ah-meh-tha]<br>Parsing (part of speech): verb<br>    Mood—indicative<br>    Tense—aorist<br>    Voice—middle deponent<br>    Person—1st person<br>    Number—plural<br>    Stem or root—from παρρησιάζομαι<br>Concordance References:<br>  ⇒ Strong's #3955 parrēsiazomai<br>  ⇒ NIV #4245 parrēsiazomai<br>  ⇒ NASB #3955 parrēsiazomai<br><br>**1 Thes. 2:2**<br>But even after that we had suffered before, and were shamefully entreated, as ye know, at Philippi, we were **bold** in our God to speak unto you the gospel of God with much contention. [KJV]<br><br>But after we had already suffered and been mistreated in Philippi, as you know, we had the **boldness** in our God to speak to you the gospel of God amid much opposition. [NASB]<br><br>We had previously suffered and been insulted in Philippi, as you know, but with the help of our God we **dared** to tell you his gospel in spite of strong opposition. [NIV] | Boldness, courage, daring. It means to speak boldly and freely; to speak out and to speak publicly without fear.<br><br>**Practical Application**<br>Too many fail to witness for Christ because they fear ridicule, embarrassment, mockery, and persecution. They are secret believers of Christ instead of bold witnesses for Christ. |

# PRACTICAL WORD STUDIES
## in the NEW TESTAMENT

| ENGLISH WORD | GREEK WORD AND VERSE | THE WORD MEANS... |
|---|---|---|
| | But even after we had suffered before and were spitefully treated at Philippi, as you know, we were **bold** in our God to speak to you the gospel of God in much conflict. [NKJV]<br><br>You know how badly we had been treated at Philippi just before we came to you and how much we suffered there. Yet our God gave us the **courage** to declare his Good News to you boldly, even though we were surrounded by many who opposed us. [NLT]<br><br>ἀλλὰ καὶ προπαθόντες καὶ ὑβρισθέντες, καθὼς οἴδατε, ἐν Φιλίπποις, **ἐπαρρησιασάμεθα** ἐν τῷ Θεῷ ἡμῶν λαλῆσαι πρὸς ὑμᾶς τὸ εὐαγγέλιον τοῦ Θεοῦ ἐν πολλῷ ἀγῶνι. [GNS]<br><br>ἀλλὰ προπαθόντες καὶ ὑβρισθέντες, καθὼς οἴδατε, ἐν Φιλίπποις **ἐπαρρησιασάμεθα** ἐν τῷ θεῷ ἡμῶν λαλῆσαι πρὸς ὑμᾶς τὸ εὐαγγέλιον, τοῦ θεοῦ ἐν πολλῷ ἀγῶνι. [GNT] | |
| #875<br>**Dark And Confused**<br><br>Darkened–KJV<br>Darkened–NASB<br>Darkened–NIV<br>Darkened–NKJV<br>Dark and confused–NLT<br><br>**POSB REFERENCE**<br>(Rom.1:21)<br>Note 4, point 2 | ἐσκοτίσθη = eskotisthē<br>Pronunciation: [eh-sko-tis-thay]<br>Parsing (part of speech): verb<br>    Mood—indicative<br>    Tense—aorist<br>    Voice—passive<br>    Person—3rd person<br>    Number—singular<br>    Stem or root—from σκοτίζομαι<br>Concordance References:<br>  ⇒ Strong's #4654 skotizo<br>  ⇒ NIV #5029 skotizomai<br>  ⇒ NASB #4654 skotizo<br><br>**Romans 1:21**<br>Because that, when they knew God, they glorified him not as God, neither were thankful; but became vain in their imaginations, and their foolish heart was **darkened**. [KJV]<br><br>For even though they knew God, they did not honor Him as God, or give thanks; but they became futile in their speculations, and their foolish heart was **darkened**. [NASB]<br><br>For although they knew God, they neither glorified him as God nor gave thanks to him, but their thinking became futile and their foolish hearts were **darkened**. [NIV]<br><br>Because, although they knew God, they did not glorify *Him* as God, nor were thankful, but became futile in their thoughts, and their foolish hearts were **darkened**. [NKJV]<br><br>Yes, they knew God, but they wouldn't worship him as God or even give him thanks. And they began to think up foolish ideas of what God was like. The result was that their minds became **dark and confused**. [NLT]<br><br>διότι γνόντες τὸν Θεὸν οὐχ ὡς Θεὸν ἐδόξασαν ἢ ηὐχαρίστησαν, ἀλλ' ἐματαιώθησαν ἐν τοῖς διαλογισμοῖς αὐτῶν, καὶ **ἐσκοτίσθη** ἡ ἀσύνετος αὐτῶν καρδία. [GNS]<br><br>διότι γνόντες τὸν θεὸν οὐχ ὡς θεὸν ἐδόξασαν ἢ ηὐχαρίστησαν, ἀλλ' ἐματαιώθησαν ἐν τοῖς διαλογισμοῖς αὐτῶν καὶ **ἐσκοτίσθη** ἡ ἀσύνετος αὐτῶν καρδία. [GNT] | To be or become darkened; to turn dark.<br><br>**Practical Application**<br>The words "dark and confused" mean blinded, unable to see. Note a critical point. Men suffer empty imaginations and darkened hearts because they...<br>• do not glorify God.<br>• do not offer thanks to God. |
| #876<br>**Dark– Darkness**<br><br>Darkness–KJV<br>Darkness–NASB<br>Dark–NIV<br>Darkness–NKJV<br>Darkness–NLT | σκότει = skotei<br>Pronunciation: [skot'-ee]<br>Parsing (part of speech): noun<br>    Case—dative<br>    Gender—neuter<br>    Number—singular<br>    Stem or root—from σκότος, ους<br>Concordance References:<br>  ⇒ Strong's #4655 skotos<br>  ⇒ NIV #5030 skotos<br>  ⇒ NASB #4655 skotos | Darkness; sin, evil.<br><br>**Practical Application**<br>The religionist is sure he is a light to those in darkness (Romans 2:19). The word "darkness" (*skotei*) means those who stumble about searching for the light but are unable to find it. The religionist feels he has found the light; therefore, he is a light to those who are searching for it. However, the religionist makes a serious mis- |

# PRACTICAL WORD STUDIES
## in the NEW TESTAMENT

| ENGLISH WORD | GREEK WORD AND VERSE | THE WORD MEANS... |
|---|---|---|
| **POSB REFERENCE**<br>(Rom.2:17-20; esp. v.19)<br>Note 1, point 7 | **Romans 2:19**<br>And art confident that thou thyself art a guide of the blind, a light of them which are in **darkness**, [KJV]<br>And are confident that you yourself are a guide to the blind, a light to those who are in **darkness**, [NASB]<br>If you are convinced that you are a guide for the blind, a light for those who are in the **dark**, [NIV]<br>And are confident that you yourself are a guide to the blind, a light to those who are in **darkness**, [NKJV]<br>You are convinced that you are a guide for the blind and a beacon light for people who are lost in **darkness** without God. [NLT]<br>πέποιθάς τε σεαυτὸν ὁδηγὸν εἶναι τυφλῶν, φῶς τῶν ἐν **σκότει**, [GNS]<br>πέποιθάς τε σεαυτὸν ὁδηγὸν εἶναι τυφλῶν, φῶς τῶν ἐν **σκότει**, [GNT] | take. Religion is not the light of the world—Jesus Christ is. (See POSB *Deeper Study* #1—John 8:12.) |
| **#877**<br>**Dark–**<br>**Darkness**<br><br>Darkened–KJV<br>Darkened–NASB<br>Darkened–NIV<br>Darkened–NKJV<br>Dark and confused–NLT<br><br>**POSB REFERENCE**<br>(Rom.1:21)<br>Note 4, point 2 | ἐσκοτίσθη = *eskotisthë*<br>Pronunciation: [eh-sko-tis-thay]<br>Parsing (part of speech): verb<br>    Mood—indicative<br>    Tense—aorist<br>    Voice—passive<br>    Person—3rd person<br>    Number—singular<br>    Stem or root—from σκοτίζομαι<br>Concordance References:<br>  ⇒ Strong's #4654 skotizo<br>  ⇒ NIV #5029 skotizomai<br>  ⇒ NASB #4654 skotizo<br><br>**Romans 1:21**<br>Because that, when they knew God, they glorified him not as God, neither were thankful; but became vain in their imaginations, and their foolish heart was **darkened**. [KJV]<br>For even though they knew God, they did not honor Him as God, or give thanks; but they became futile in their speculations, and their foolish heart was **darkened**. [NASB]<br>For although they knew God, they neither glorified him as God nor gave thanks to him, but their thinking became futile and their foolish hearts were **darkened**. [NIV]<br>Because, although they knew God, they did not glorify *Him* as God, nor were thankful, but became futile in their thoughts, and their foolish hearts were **darkened**. [NKJV]<br>Yes, they knew God, but they wouldn't worship him as God or even give him thanks. And they began to think up foolish ideas of what God was like. The result was that their minds became **dark and confused**. [NLT]<br>διότι γνόντες τὸν Θεὸν οὐχ ὡς Θεὸν ἐδόξασαν ἢ ηὐχαρίστησαν, ἀλλ' ἐματαιώθησαν ἐν τοῖς διαλογισμοῖς αὐτῶν, καὶ **ἐσκοτίσθη** ἡ ἀσύνετος αὐτῶν καρδία. [GNS]<br>διότι γνόντες τὸν θεὸν οὐχ ὡς θεὸν ἐδόξασαν ἢ ηὐχαρίστησαν, ἀλλ' ἐματαιώθησαν ἐν τοῖς διαλογισμοῖς αὐτῶν καὶ **ἐσκοτίσθη** ἡ ἀσύνετος αὐτῶν καρδία. [GNT] | To be or become darkened; to become dark.<br><br>**Practical Application**<br>The word "darkened" means blinded, unable to see. Note a critical point. Men suffer empty imaginations and darkened hearts because they...<br>• do not glorify God.<br>• do not offer thanks to God. |
| **#878**<br>**Darkness**<br><br>Darkness–KJV<br>Darkness–NASB<br>Darkness–NIV<br>Darkness–NKJV<br>Darkness–NLT | σκότος = *skotos*<br>Pronunciation: [skot'-os]<br>Parsing (part of speech): noun<br>    Case—accusative<br>    Gender—neuter<br>    Number—singular<br>    Stem or root—from σκότος, ους<br>Concordance References:<br>  ⇒ Strong's #4655 skotos<br>  ⇒ NIV #5030 skotos<br>  ⇒ NASB #4655 skotos | Darkness, evil, sin, wickedness.<br><br>**Practical Application**<br>The word is used in Scripture to describe both the state and the works of man. Darkness is very real in Scripture.<br>1. The darkness refers to the world of the natural man who does not know Jesus Christ (John 8:12). The natural man walks in ignorance... |

# PRACTICAL WORD STUDIES
## in the New Testament

| ENGLISH WORD | GREEK WORD AND VERSE | THE WORD MEANS... |
|---|---|---|
| **POSB REFERENCE** (2 Cor.6:14) *Deeper Study #1* | **2 Cor. 6:14**<br>Be ye not unequally yoked together with unbelievers: for what fellowship hath righteousness with unrighteousness? and what communion hath light with **darkness**? [KJV]<br>Do not be bound together with unbelievers; for what partnership have righteousness and lawlessness, or what fellowship has light with **darkness**? [NASB]<br>Do not be yoked together with unbelievers. For what do righteousness and wickedness have in common? Or what fellowship can light have with **darkness**? [NIV]<br>Do not be unequally yoked together with unbelievers. For what fellowship has righteousness with lawlessness? And what communion has light with **darkness**? [NKJV]<br>Don't team up with those who are unbelievers. How can goodness be a partner with wickedness? How can light live with **darkness**? [NLT]<br>Μὴ γίνεσθε ἑτεροζυγοῦντες ἀπίστοις· τίς γὰρ μετοχὴ δικαιοσύνῃ καὶ ἀνομίᾳ; τίς δὲ κοινωνία φωτὶ πρὸς **σκότος**; [GNS]<br>Μὴ γίνεσθε ἑτεροζυγοῦντες ἀπίστοις· τίς γὰρ μετοχὴ δικαιοσύνῃ καὶ ἀνομίᾳ, ἢ τίς κοινωνία φωτὶ πρὸς **σκότος**; [GNT] | • of Jesus Christ.<br>• of God as revealed by Jesus Christ.<br>• of the real purpose and destiny of life as shown by Jesus Christ.<br>    The natural man stumbles and gropes about in this world. He knows nothing other than the things of this world as he sees them. His only hope is the hope of living a long life before death overtakes him. He walks in darkness, ignorant of real life now and hereafter (cp. John 12:35, 46).<br>2. The darkness symbolizes unpreparedness and unwatchfulness. It symbolizes the time when evil occurs (1 Thes. 5:4-8).<br>3. The darkness is loved by men. Sinful men do their evil deeds under the cover of darkness. Men therefore hate the light because the light uncovers their evil behavior (John 3:19-20).<br>4. The darkness is hostile to light (see POSB *Deeper Study #4*—John 1:5). |
| **#879**<br>**Darkness**<br><br>Darkness–KJV<br>Darkness–NASB<br>Darkness–NIV<br>Darkness–NKJV<br>Darkness–NLT<br><br>**POSB REFERENCE** (1 Jn.1:5) *Deeper Study #1*<br><br>See also POSB REF: (Jn.8:12) *Deeper Study #2* | σκοτία = *skotia*<br>Pronunciation: [skot-ee'-ah]<br>Parsing (part of speech): noun<br>    Case—nominative<br>    Gender—feminine<br>    Number—singular<br>    Stem or root—from σκοτία, ας<br>Concordance References:<br>  ⇒ Strong's #4653 skotia<br>  ⇒ NIV #5028 skotia<br>  ⇒ NASB #4653 skotia<br><br>**1 John 1:5**<br>This then is the message which we have heard of him, and declare unto you, that God is light, and in him is no **darkness** at all. [KJV]<br>And this is the message we have heard from Him and announce to you, that God is light, and in Him there is no **darkness** at all. [NASB]<br>This is the message we have heard from him and declare to you: God is light; in him there is no **darkness** at all. [NIV]<br>This is the message which we have heard from Him and declare to you, that God is light and in Him is no **darkness** at all. [NKJV]<br>This is the message he has given us to announce to you: God is light and there is no **darkness** in him at all. [NLT]<br>Καὶ ἔστιν αὕτη ἡ ἀγγελία ἣν ἀκηκόαμεν ἀπ' αὐτοῦ καὶ ἀναγγέλλομεν ὑμῖν, ὅτι ὁ Θεὸς φῶς ἐστι, καὶ **σκοτία** ἐν αὐτῷ οὐκ ἔστιν οὐδεμία. [GNS]<br>Καὶ ἔστιν αὕτη ἡ ἀγγελία ἣν ἀκηκόαμεν ἀπ' αὐτοῦ καὶ ἀναγγέλλομεν ὑμῖν, ὅτι ὁ Θεὸς φῶς ἐστιν καὶ **σκοτία** ἐν αὐτῷ οὐκ ἔστιν οὐδεμία. [GNT] | Darkness, evil, sin, wickedness, iniquity, corruption, depravity, lightlessness or no light.<br><br>**Practical Application**<br>The word darkness describes both the state and works of a person. It symbolizes evil and sin, everything that life should not be and everything that a person should not do.<br>1. The darkness means that man is ignorant of God.<br>  ⇒ that a person is vain in his imaginations about God and foolish in his thoughts about God. (Romans 1:21).<br>  ⇒ that a person does not live and walk in the light of God and Christ. (John 8:12).<br>  ⇒ that a person is blind to the light of Christ and stumbles about through life. (John 11:9-10).<br>  ⇒ that a person does not understand the light and is powerless to extinguish the light. (John 1:5).<br>  ⇒ that a person does not see the glory of God in the face of Jesus Christ. (2 Cor. 4:6).<br>2. The darkness means evil behavior and deeds.<br>  ⇒ that a person's deeds are evil and that he hates the light. (John 3:19-21).<br>  ⇒ that a person walks in the darkness of hate and antagonism against others. (1 John 2:9-11).<br>  ⇒ that a person lives a secretive life, a life that is gripped by the hidden things of darkness, that cannot bear the light. (1 Cor. 4:5).<br>3. The darkness means man's nature, that his nature is darkness.<br>  ⇒ that a person is the very embodiment of darkness, that his very nature and character are that of darkness. (Ephes. 5:8).<br>  ⇒ that a person's eye is focused upon evil; therefore, his whole being is full of darkness or evil. (Matthew 6:22-23).<br>  ⇒ that a person is an unbeliever and has communion with darkness. (2 Cor. 6:14).<br>4. The darkness means that man is unfruitful in life. (Ephes. 5:11). |

## PRACTICAL WORD STUDIES
in the NEW TESTAMENT

| ENGLISH WORD | GREEK WORD AND VERSE | THE WORD MEANS... |
|---|---|---|
| | | 5. The darkness means that man dwells in darkness.<br>⇒ that a person dwells in darkness and is blind to the glorious day of salvation and of the Lord's return. (1 Thes. 5:4-5).<br>⇒ that a person has rejected the call of God and still dwells in darkness. (2 Peter 2:9-10).<br>6. The darkness means the influence and power of Satan.<br>⇒ that a person is under the power of Satan and is guilty of sin; that his sins are not forgiven. (Acts 26:18).<br>7. The darkness means the place of punishment and hell, the pit of darkness.<br>⇒ the place of punishment and hell where all the ungodly shall be cast in the final judgment. (Ephes. 6:12). (2 Peter 2:9). (Jude 13). |
| **#880**<br>**Day–**<br>**Day...Now**<br><br>Seasons–KJV<br>Time–NASB<br>Time–NIV<br>**Day–NKJV**<br>**Day...now–NLT**<br><br>**POSB**<br>**REFERENCE**<br>(Acts 20:18-19; esp. v.18)<br>Note 2, point 1 | χρόνον = chronon<br>Pronunciation: [khron'-on]<br>Parsing (part of speech): noun<br>   Case—accusative<br>   Gender—masculine<br>   Number—singular<br>   Stem or root—from χρόνος, ου<br>Concordance References:<br>  ⇒ Strong's #5550 chronos<br>  ⇒ NIV #5989 chronos<br>  ⇒ NASB #5550 chronos<br><br>**Acts 20:18**<br>And when they were come to him, he said unto them, Ye know, from the first day that I came into Asia, after what manner I have been with you at all **seasons**, [KJV]<br>And when they had come to him, he said to them, "You yourselves know, from the first day that I set foot in Asia, how I was with you the whole **time**, [NASB]<br>When they arrived, he said to them: "You know how I lived the whole **time** I was with you, from the first day I came into the province of Asia. [NIV]<br>And when they had come to him, he said to them: "You know, from the first **day** that I came to Asia, in what manner I always lived among you, [NKJV]<br>When they arrived he declared, "You know that from the **day** I set foot in the province of Asia until **now** [NLT]<br>ὡς δὲ παρεγένοντο πρὸς αὐτόν, εἶπεν αὐτοῖς, Ὑμεῖς ἐπίστασθε, ἀπὸ πρώτης ἡμέρας ἀφ' ἧς ἐπέβην εἰς τὴν Ἀσίαν, πῶς μεθ' ὑμῶν τὸν πάντα **χρόνον** ἐγενόμην, [GNS]<br>ὡς δὲ παρεγένοντο πρὸς αὐτὸν εἶπεν αὐτοῖς, Ὑμεῖς ἐπίστασθε, ἀπὸ πρώτης ἡμέρας ἀφ' ἧς ἐπέβην εἰς τὴν Ἀσίαν πῶς μεθ' ὑμῶν τὸν πάντα **χρόνον** ἐγενόμην, [GNT] | Time, seasons, day as in a moment of time.<br><br>**Practical Application**<br>Paul was totally devoted from "the [very] first day" (*chronon*) and in "what manner," [NKJV] that is, through all kinds of situations and circumstances. |
| **#881**<br>**Day, On That**<br><br>At that time–KJV<br>**On that day–NASB**<br>**On that day–NIV**<br>At that time–NKJV<br>At the killing of Stephen–NLT<br><br>**POSB**<br>**REFERENCE**<br>(Acts 8:1)<br>Note 1, point 2 | ἐν ἐκείνῃ τῇ ἡμέρᾳ = en ekeinë të hëmera<br>Pronunciation: [en eh-keh-ee-nay tay hay-mer'-ah]<br>Parsing *hëmera* (part of speech): noun<br>   Case—dative<br>   Gender—feminine<br>   Number—singular<br>   Stem or root—from ἡμέρα, ας<br>Concordance References:<br>  ⇒ Strong's #1722 en + 1565 ekeinos + 3588 ho + 2250 hëmera<br>  ⇒ NIV #1877 en [On] + 1697 ekeinos [that] + 3836 ho + 2465 hëmera [day]<br>  ⇒ NASB #1722 en + 1565 ekeinos + 3588 ho + 2250 hëmera | On that day; at that time.<br><br>**Practical Application**<br>The words "on that day" mean on that very same day. Saul wished to act and to act quickly in wiping out the church. The believers were frightened and on the run. He had to strike immediately to catch them before they could escape. |

# PRACTICAL WORD STUDIES
## in the NEW TESTAMENT

| ENGLISH WORD | GREEK WORD AND VERSE | THE WORD MEANS... |
|---|---|---|
| | **Acts 8:1**<br>And Saul was consenting unto his death. And **at that time** there was a great persecution against the church which was at Jerusalem; and they were all scattered abroad throughout the regions of Judaea and Samaria, except the apostles. [KJV]<br>And Saul was in hearty agreement with putting him to death. And **on that day** a great persecution arose against the church in Jerusalem; and they were all scattered throughout the regions of Judea and Samaria, except the apostles. [NASB]<br>And Saul was there, giving approval to his death. **On that day** a great persecution broke out against the church at Jerusalem, and all except the apostles were scattered throughout Judea and Samaria. [NIV]<br>Now Saul was consenting to his death. **At that time** a great persecution arose against the church which was at Jerusalem; and they were all scattered throughout the regions of Judea and Samaria, except the apostles. [NKJV]<br>Saul was one of the official witnesses **at the killing of Stephen**. A great wave of persecution began that day, sweeping over the church in Jerusalem, and all the believers except the apostles fled into Judea and Samaria. [NLT]<br>Σαῦλος δὲ ἦν συνευδοκῶν τῇ ἀναιρέσει αὐτοῦ. Ἐγένετο δὲ **ἐν ἐκείνῃ τῇ ἡμέρᾳ** διωγμὸς μέγας ἐπὶ τὴν ἐκκλησίαν τὴν ἐν Ἱεροσολύμοις· πάντες τε διεσπάρησαν κατὰ τὰς χώρας τῆς Ἰουδαίας καὶ Σαμαρείας, πλὴν τῶν ἀποστόλων. [GNS]<br>Σαῦλος δὲ ἦν συνευδοκῶν τῇ ἀναιρέσει αὐτοῦ. Ἐγένετο δὲ **ἐν ἐκείνῃ τῇ ἡμέρᾳ** διωγμὸς μέγας ἐπὶ τὴν ἐκκλησίαν τὴν ἐν Ἱεροσολύμοις, πάντες δὲ διεσπάρησαν κατὰ τὰς χώρας τῆς Ἰουδαίας καὶ Σαμαρείας πλὴν τῶν ἀποστόλων. [GNT] | |
| **#882**<br>**Dazzling**<br><br>Shining–KJV<br>Radiant–NASB<br>**Dazzling–NIV**<br>Shining–NKJV<br>**Dazzling–NLT**<br><br>**POSB REFERENCE**<br>(Mk.9:2-3; esp. v.3)<br>*Deeper Study* #2, point 1 | στίλβοντα λίαν = *stilbonta lian*<br>Pronunciation: [stil'-bon-tah lee'-an]<br>Parsing *stilbonta* (part of speech): verb<br>    Mood—participle<br>    Tense—present<br>    Voice—active<br>    Case—nominative<br>    Gender—neuter<br>    Number—plural<br>    Stem or root—from στίλβω<br>Parsing *lian* (part of speech): adjective adverb<br>    Stem or root—from λίαν<br>Concordance References:<br>  ⇒ Strong's #3029+4744 lian stilbō<br>  ⇒ NIV #3336+5118 lian stilbō<br>  ⇒ NASB #3029+4744 lian stilbō<br><br>**Mark 9:3**<br>And his raiment became **shining**, exceeding white as snow; so as no fuller on earth can white them. [KJV]<br>And His garments became **radiant** and exceedingly white, as no launderer on earth can whiten them. [NASB]<br>His clothes became **dazzling** white, whiter than anyone in the world could bleach them. [NIV]<br>His clothes became **shining**, exceedingly white, like snow, such as no launderer on earth can whiten them. [NKJV]<br>And his clothing became **dazzling** white, far whiter than any earthly process could ever make it. [NLT]<br>καὶ τὰ ἱμάτια αὐτοῦ ἐγένετο **στίλβοντα**, λευκὰ λίαν ὡς χιών, οἷα γναφεὺς ἐπὶ τῆς γῆς οὐ δύναται λευκᾶναι. [GNS]<br>καὶ τὰ ἱμάτια αὐτοῦ ἐγένετο **στίλβοντα** λευκὰ **λίαν** οἷα γναφεὺς ἐπὶ τῆς γῆς οὐ δύναται οὕτως λευκᾶναι. [GNT] | To be dazzling, radiant, brilliant, shining, awe-inspiring; to glisten very much.<br><br>**Practical Application**<br>The word "dazzling" (*stilbonta*) is a Greek participle which means the shining is active. The transfiguration was a real, active experience. It was no illusion, no dream; it was not of the imagination. It was not a reflection of the sun shining off some rock, glass, or lake. "His [own] face did shine." The glory that was "dazzling" was the glory of the Lord's inner nature, of His Godly nature actively shining right through His being. |

## PRACTICAL WORD STUDIES
## in the NEW TESTAMENT

| ENGLISH WORD | GREEK WORD AND VERSE | THE WORD MEANS... |
|---|---|---|
| **#883**<br>**Dazzling**<br><br>Glistering–KJV<br>Gleaming–NASB<br>Flash of lightning–NIV<br>Glistening–NKJV<br>**Dazzling–NLT**<br><br>**POSB REFERENCE**<br>(Lk.9:29)<br>Note 3, point 2 | ἐξαστράπτων = *exastraptōn*<br>Pronunciation: [ex-as-trap'-tone]<br>Parsing (part of speech): verb<br>  Mood—participle<br>  Tense—present<br>  Voice—active<br>  Case—nominative<br>  Gender—masculine<br>  Number—singular<br>  Stem or root—from ἐξαστράπτω<br>Concordance References:<br>⇒ Strong's #1823 exastraptō<br>⇒ NIV #1993 exastraptō<br>⇒ NASB #1823 exastraptō<br><br>**Luke 9:29**<br>And as he prayed, the fashion of his countenance was altered, and his raiment was white and **glistering**. [KJV]<br>And while He was praying, the appearance of His face became different, and His clothing became white and **gleaming**. [NASB]<br>As he was praying, the appearance of his face changed, and his clothes became as bright as a **flash of lightning**. [NIV]<br>As He prayed, the appearance of His face was altered, and His robe *became* white *and* **glistening**. [NKJV]<br>And as he was praying, the appearance of his face changed, and his clothing became **dazzling** white. [NLT]<br>καὶ ἐγένετο, ἐν τῷ προσεύχεσθαι αὐτὸν, τὸ εἶδος τοῦ προσώπου αὐτοῦ ἕτερον, καὶ ὁ ἱματισμὸς αὐτοῦ λευκὸς **ἐξαστράπτων**. [GNS]<br>καὶ ἐγένετο ἐν τῷ προσεύχεσθαι αὐτὸν τὸ εἶδος τοῦ προσώπου αὐτοῦ ἕτερον καὶ ὁ ἱματισμὸς αὐτοῦ λευκὸς **ἐξαστράπτων**. [GNT] | To flash like lightning; to gleam; to brighten; to be radiant; to dazzle.<br><br>**Practical Application**<br>Jesus was praying when these changes took place. Apparently, He was concentrating so intensely and was so wrapped up in God that God transformed Him, that is, allowed His Godly nature to shine right through Him. What is the lesson for the believer? When a genuine believer prays with intensity and heavy concentration, his countenance is sometimes changed. He experiences a precious glow, a brightness, a light about his whole countenance. |
| **#884**<br>**Deacon**<br><br>Servant–KJV<br>Servant–NASB<br>Servant–NIV<br>Servant–NKJV<br>**Deacon–NLT**<br><br>**POSB REFERENCE**<br>(Rom.16:1-2; esp. v.1)<br>Note 1, point 3 | διάκονον = *diakonon*<br>Pronunciation: [dee-ak-on-on]<br>Parsing (part of speech): noun<br>  Case—accusative<br>  Gender—feminine<br>  Number—singular<br>  Stem or root—from διάκονος, ου<br>Concordance References:<br>⇒ Strong's #1249 diakonos<br>⇒ NIV #1356 diakonos<br>⇒ NASB #1249 diakonos<br><br>**Romans 16:1**<br>I commend unto you Phebe our sister, which is a **servant** of the church which is at Cenchrea: [KJV]<br>I commend to you our sister Phoebe, who is a **servant** of the church which is at Cenchrea; [NASB]<br>I commend to you our sister Phoebe, a **servant** of the church in Cenchrea. [NIV]<br>I commend to you Phoebe our sister, who is a **servant** of the church in Cenchrea, [NKJV]<br>Our sister Phoebe, a **deacon** in the church in Cenchrea, will be coming to see you soon. [NLT]<br>Συνίστημι δὲ ὑμῖν Φοίβην τὴν ἀδελφὴν ἡμῶν, οὖσαν **διάκονον** τῆς ἐκκλησίας τῆς ἐν Κεγχρεαῖς· [GNS]<br>Συνίστημι δὲ ὑμῖν Φοίβην τὴν ἀδελφὴν ἡμῶν, οὖσαν [καὶ] **διάκονον** τῆς ἐκκλησίας τῆς ἐν Κεγχρεαῖς, [GNT] | Servant, deacon, deaconess, helper, minister.<br><br>**Practical Application**<br>Phoebe was a servant of the church at Cenchrea, which was the seaport of Corinth (see POSB *Deeper Study* #1, Cenchrea—Acts 18:18). Does this mean that Phoebe held the official office of a deacon in the early church? Note closely what the Scripture says and it seems to be saying that she did: "Phoebe, a *deacon* (deaconess) in the church." [NLT] |
| **#885**<br>**Deacons**<br><br>**Deacons–KJV**<br>**Deacons–NASB**<br>**Deacons–NIV**<br>**Deacons–NKJV**<br>**Deacons–NLT** | Διακόνους = *Diakonous*<br>Pronunciation: [dee-ak-on-oos]<br>Parsing (part of speech): noun<br>  Case—accusative<br>  Gender—masculine<br>  Number—plural<br>  Stem or root—διάκονος, ου<br>Concordance References:<br>⇒ Strong's #1249 diakonos<br>⇒ NIV #1356 diakonos<br>⇒ NASB #1249 diakonos | Deacons, deaconesses, servants, helpers, ministers.<br><br>**Practical Application**<br>The first reference to deacons is in Acts (Acts 6:1-7). Deacons were appointed to help in the ministerial and administrative duties of the church (Acts 6:2). Their function was to relieve ministers so that ministers could give themselves "continually to prayer and to the ministry of the |

# PRACTICAL WORD STUDIES
## in the NEW TESTAMENT

| ENGLISH WORD | GREEK WORD AND VERSE | THE WORD MEANS... |
|---|---|---|
| **POSB REFERENCE** (1 Tim.3:8-13 esp. v.8) *Deeper Study* #1<br><br>See also POSB REF: (Philip.1:1) Note 4, point 2 | **1 Tim. 3:8**<br>Likewise must the **deacons** be grave, not double-tongued, not given to much wine, not greedy of filthy lucre; [KJV]<br>**Deacons** likewise must be men of dignity, not double-tongued, or addicted to much wine or fond of sordid gain, [NASB]<br>**Deacons**, likewise, are to be men worthy of respect, sincere, not indulging in much wine, and not pursuing dishonest gain. [NIV]<br>Likewise **deacons** *must be* reverent, not double-tongued, not given to much wine, not greedy for money, [NKJV]<br>In the same way, **deacons** must be people who are respected and have integrity. They must not be heavy drinkers and must not be greedy for money. [NLT]<br>διακόνους ὡσαύτως σεμνούς, μὴ διλόγους, μὴ οἴνῳ πολλῷ προσέχοντας, μὴ αἰσχροκερδεῖς, [GNS]<br>Διακόνους ὡσαύτως σεμνούς, μὴ διλόγους, μὴ οἴνῳ πολλῷ προσέχοντας, μὴ αἰσχροκερδεῖς, [GNT] | Word" (Acts 6:4). In particular they were chosen to minister to the day-to-day needs of believers and to the needs of widows and widowers and the poor and sick of a church. They were to relieve ministers so the ministers could *concentrate on prayer and preaching* (Acts 6:3-4).<br><br>However, note a significant fact: this does not mean that ministers are never to meet day-to-day needs of believers nor that deacons should never share or preach the Word. In the early church both ministers and deacons served in both areas, but each *concentrated* upon their primary call and mission.<br>⇒ Preachers were sometimes called deacons, that is, servants (1 Cor. 3:5). (2 Cor. 3:6).<br>⇒ The first deacons preached as well as ministered to the needy of the church. (Acts 6:8). (Acts 8:5).<br>⇒ Deacons are closely linked to bishops. (Phil. 1:1).<br>⇒ Deacons are to be spiritually equipped for their task. (Acts 6:3; cp. 1 Tim. 3:8-13).<br>⇒ The office of the deacon was an early development in the church. (Acts 6:1-4). |
| **#886**<br>**Dead**<br><br>Hell–KJV<br>Hades–NASB<br>Grave–NIV<br>Hades–NKJV<br>Dead–NLT<br><br>**POSB REFERENCE** (Acts 2:25-28; esp. v.27) Note 1, point 2b<br><br>See also POSB REF: (Acts 2:27) *Deeper Study* #1 | ᾅδην = hadën<br>Pronunciation: [hah'-dane]<br>Parsing (part of speech): noun<br>    Case—accusative<br>    Gender—masculine<br>    Number—singular<br>    Stem or root—from ᾅδης, ου<br>Concordance References:<br>  ⇒ Strong's #86 hadës<br>  ⇒ NIV #87 hadës<br>  ⇒ NASB #86 hadës<br><br>**Acts 2:27**<br>Because thou wilt not leave my soul in **hell**, neither wilt thou suffer thine Holy One to see corruption. [KJV]<br>Because Thou wilt not abandon my soul to **Hades**, Nor ALLOW Thy Holy One to UNDERGO DECAY. [NASB]<br>Because you will not abandon my soul to the **grave**, nor will you let your Holy One see decay. [NIV]<br>*For you will not leave my soul in Hades, Nor will You allow Your Holy One to see corruption.* [NKJV]<br>For you will not leave my soul among the **dead** or allow your Holy One to rot in the grave. [NLT]<br>ὅτι οὐκ ἐγκαταλείψεις τὴν ψυχήν μου εἰς ᾅδου, οὐδὲ δώσεις τὸν ὅσιόν σου ἰδεῖν διαφθοράν. [GNS]<br>ὅτι οὐκ ἐγκαταλείψεις τὴν ψυχήν μου εἰς ᾅδην οὐδὲ δώσεις τὸν ὅσιόν σου ἰδεῖν διαφθοράν. [GNT] | Grave, hell, hades, dead; the depths; the place of death.<br><br>**Practical Application**<br>Jesus revealed that the grave or Hades is the other world, that is, the unseen world, the spiritual dimension of being (see POSB *Deeper Study* #3—Luke 16:23). Jesus said that Hades (the other world) was divided into two huge areas or sections. The two areas are separated by a great gulf that is impassable (Luke 16:26). One area is the place of sorrow (Luke 16:23-24, 28), and the other area is the place of paradise where believers go. To say that a person is dead is to say that he is in hades or in the other world. |
| **#887**<br>**Dead**<br><br>Dead–KJV<br>Dead–NASB<br>Dead–NIV<br>Dead–NKJV<br>Dead–NLT<br><br>**POSB REFERENCE** (Eph.2:1) Note 1 | νεκρούς = nekrous<br>Pronunciation: [nek-roos']<br>Parsing (part of speech): adjective<br>    Case—accusative<br>    Gender—masculine<br>    Number—plural<br>    Stem or root—from νεκρός, ά, όν<br>Concordance References:<br>  ⇒ Strong's #3498 nekros<br>  ⇒ NIV #3738 nekros<br>  ⇒ NASB #3498 nekros<br><br>**Ephes. 2:1**<br>And you hath he quickened, who were **dead** in tres- | Dead, lifeless, useless.<br><br>**Practical Application**<br>How can a man be living and yet be dead? To answer this question, we must understand what death means. The basic meaning of death (*nekrous*) is *separation*. Death never means extinction, annihilation, non-existence, or inactivity. Death simply means that a person is separated, either separated from his body or from God or from both. H.S. Miller says, "Death is the separation of a person from the purpose or use for which he was intended" (quoted by |

## PRACTICAL WORD STUDIES
### in the New Testament

| ENGLISH WORD | GREEK WORD AND VERSE | THE WORD MEANS... |
|---|---|---|
| | passes and sins; [KJV]<br>And you were **dead** in your trespasses and sins, [NASB]<br>As for you, you were **dead** in your transgressions and sins, [NIV]<br>And you *He made alive,* who were **dead** in trespasses and sins, [NKJV]<br>Once you were **dead**, doomed forever because of your many sins. [NLT]<br>Καὶ ὑμᾶς ὄντας **νεκροὺς** τοῖς παραπτώμασι, καὶ ταῖς ἁμαρτίαις, [GNS]<br>Καὶ ὑμᾶς ὄντας **νεκροὺς** τοῖς παραπτώμασιν καὶ ταῖς ἁμαρτίαις ὑμῶν, [GNT] | Lehman Strauss, *Devotional Studies in Galatians and Ephesians*, p.137). Man was created to know, fellowship, worship, and serve God; but man does not do it. If he worships at all, he worships his *own ideas and concepts of God*, creating a god to suit his own notions—a god that will allow him to go ahead and live as he wishes.<br>   The point is this: man does not fulfill his purpose on earth, not the purpose for which he was created. He has little if anything to do with God. He is *separated from and dead to* God. The Bible speaks of three deaths.<br>1. Physical death: the *separation* of a man's spirit from his body. This is what men commonly call death. It is when a person ceases to exist on this earth and is buried.<br>2. Spiritual death: the separation of a man from God while he is still living and walking upon earth. This is the *natural state* of a man on earth without Jesus Christ. Man is seen as still in his sins and dead to God.<br>  ⇒ A person may walk in life without God and Christ, rejecting, rebelling and cursing God. The man is spiritually *separated* from God; he is *dead* to God.<br>  ⇒ A person may walk in life as a religious person, worshipping a god of his own thoughts and notions, rejecting the only living and true God who was revealed by Jesus Christ. The religious person is spiritually separated from God; he is dead to God.<br>   Spiritual death speaks of a person who is dead while he still lives (1 Tim. 5:6). He is a natural man living in this present world, but he is said to be dead to the Lord Jesus Christ and to God and to spiritual matters.<br>3. Eternal death: the separation of man from God's presence forever. This is the second death, an eternal state of being *dead to God*. It is spiritual death, separation from God that is prolonged beyond the death of the body. It is called the "second death" or eternal death. |
| **#888**<br>**Dealer In Purple Cloth**<br><br>Seller of purple–KJV<br>Seller of purple fabrics–NASB<br>**Dealer in purple cloth–NIV**<br>Seller of purple–NKJV<br>Merchant of expensive purple cloth–NLT<br><br>**POSB REFERENCE**<br>(Acts 16:14)<br>Note 2 | πορφυρόπωλις = *porphuropŏlis*<br>Pronunciation: [por-foo-rop'-o-lis]<br>Parsing (part of speech): noun<br>  Case—nominative<br>  Gender—feminine<br>  Number—singular<br>  Stem or root—from πορφυρόπωλις, ιδος<br>Concordance References:<br>  ⇒ Strong's #4211 porphuropŏlis<br>  ⇒ NIV #4527 porphuropŏlis<br>  ⇒ NASB #4211 porphuropŏlis<br><br>**Acts 16:14**<br>And a certain woman named Lydia, a **seller of purple**, of the city of Thyatira, which worshipped God, heard us: whose heart the Lord opened, that she attended unto the things which were spoken of Paul. [KJV]<br>And a certain woman named Lydia, from the city of Thyatira, a **seller of purple fabrics**, a worshiper of God, was listening; and the Lord opened her heart to respond to the things spoken by Paul. [NASB]<br>One of those listening was a woman named Lydia, a **dealer in purple cloth** from the city of Thyatira, who was a worshiper of God. The Lord opened her heart to | Dealer in purple cloth; seller of purple; seller of purple fabrics; merchant of expensive purple cloth.<br><br>**Practical Application**<br>  Purple fabrics were in great demand in the Roman world. Purple was used on the toga or outer garments by the royalty of Rome. Therefore, as in every society, the lower classes desired what the upper class had. Royal purple always has been and still is a common term. |

# PRACTICAL WORD STUDIES
## in the NEW TESTAMENT

| ENGLISH WORD | GREEK WORD AND VERSE | THE WORD MEANS... |
|---|---|---|
| | respond to Paul's message. [NIV]<br>Now a certain woman named Lydia heard *us*. She was a **seller of purple** from the city of Thyatira, who worshiped God. The Lord opened her heart to heed the things spoken by Paul. [NKJV]<br>One of them was Lydia from Thyatira, a **merchant of expensive purple cloth**. She was a worshiper of God. As she listened to us, the Lord opened her heart, and she accepted what Paul was saying. [NLT]<br>καί τις γυνὴ ὀνόματι Λυδία, **πορφυρόπωλις**, πόλεως Θυατείρων σεβομένη τὸν Θεόν, ἤκουεν· ἧς ὁ Κύριος διήνοιξε τὴν καρδίαν, προσέχειν τοῖς λαλουμένοις ὑπὸ τοῦ Παύλου. [GNS]<br>καί τις γυνὴ ὀνόματι Λυδία, **πορφυρόπωλις** πόλεως Θυατείρων σεβομένη τὸν θεόν, ἤκουεν, ἧς ὁ κύριος διήνοιξεν τὴν καρδίαν προσέχειν τοῖς λαλουμένοις ὑπὸ τοῦ Παύλου. [GNT] | |
| **#889**<br>**Dear**<br><br>**Dear**–KJV<br>Highly regarded–NASB<br>Valued highly–NIV<br>**Dear**–NKJV<br>Highly valued–NLT<br><br>**POSB REFERENCE**<br>(Lk.7:2)<br>Note 2 | ἦν ἔντιμος = ën entimos<br>Pronunciation: [ayn en'-tee-mos]<br>Parsing *ën* (part of speech): verb<br>    Mood—indicative<br>    Tense—imperfect<br>    Voice—active<br>    Person—3rd person<br>    Number—singular<br>    Stem or root—from εἰμί<br>Parsing *entimos* (part of speech): adjective<br>    Case—nominative<br>    Gender—masculine<br>    Number—singular<br>    Stem or root—from ἔντιμος, ον<br>Concordance References:<br>  ⇒ Strong's #1510 eimi + 1784 entimos<br>  ⇒ NIV #1639 eimi + 1952 entimos<br>  ⇒ NASB #1510 eimi + 1784 entimos<br><br>**Luke 7:2**<br>And a certain centurion's servant, who was **dear** unto him, was sick, and ready to die. [KJV]<br>And a certain centurion's slave, who was **highly regarded** by him, was sick and about to die. [NASB]<br>There a centurion's servant, whom his master **valued highly**, was sick and about to die. [NIV]<br>And a certain centurion's servant, who was **dear** to him, was sick and ready to die. [NKJV]<br>Now the **highly valued** slave of a Roman officer was sick and near death. [NLT]<br>Ἑκατοντάρχου δέ τινος δοῦλος κακῶς ἔχων ἤμελλε τελευτᾶν, ὃς ἦν αὐτῷ **ἔντιμος**. [GNS]<br>Ἑκατοντάρχου δέ τινος δοῦλος κακῶς ἔχων ἤμελλεν τελευτᾶν, ὃς ἦν αὐτῷ **ἔντιμος**. [GNT] | Valued highly; to be highly regarded; to be held dear, esteemed, honored, distinguished, precious, prized.<br><br>**Practical Application**<br>In the society of that day, a slave was nothing, only a tool or a thing to be used as the owner wished. He had no rights whatsoever, not even the right to live. An owner could mistreat and kill a slave without having to give an account. But this soldier loved his slave. This reveals a deep concern and care for people. It would have been much less bother to dispose of the slave or to ignore him and just let him die, but not this soldier. He cared. Note how he personally looked after the slave, a person who meant nothing to the rest of society. |
| **#890**<br>**Dear**<br><br>**Dear**–KJV<br>**Dear**–NASB<br>Worth–NIV<br>**Dear**–NKJV<br>Worth–NLT<br><br>**POSB REFERENCE**<br>(Acts 20:24)<br>Note 6, point 1 | τιμίαν = timian<br>Pronunciation: [tim'-ee-ahn]<br>Parsing (part of speech): adjective<br>    Case—accusative<br>    Gender—feminine<br>    Number—singular<br>    Stem or root—from τίμιος, α, ον<br>Concordance References:<br>  ⇒ Strong's #5093 timios<br>  ⇒ NIV #5508 timios<br>  ⇒ NASB #5093 timios<br><br>**Acts 20:24**<br>But none of these things move me, neither count I my life **dear** unto myself, so that I might finish my course with joy, and the ministry, which I have received of the Lord Jesus, to testify the gospel of the grace of God. [KJV]<br>"But I do not consider my life of any account as **dear** to myself, in order that I may finish my course, and the | Precious, dear, costly, of great value, priceless, honored. It means precious and valuable, of extreme worth.<br><br>**Practical Application**<br>Paul's life was not for himself, not for his own use. His life was the precious and valuable possession of the Lord. |

## PRACTICAL WORD STUDIES
### in the NEW TESTAMENT

| ENGLISH WORD | GREEK WORD AND VERSE | THE WORD MEANS... |
|---|---|---|
| | ministry which I received from the Lord Jesus, to testify solemnly of the gospel of the grace of God. [NASB]<br><br>However, I consider my life **worth** nothing to me, if only I may finish the race and complete the task the Lord Jesus has given me—the task of testifying to the gospel of God's grace. [NIV]<br><br>But none of these things move me; nor do I count my life **dear** to myself, so that I may finish my race with joy, and the ministry which I received from the Lord Jesus, to testify to the gospel of the grace of God. [NKJV]<br><br>But my life is **worth** nothing unless I use it for doing the work assigned me by the Lord Jesus—the work of telling others the Good News about God's wonderful kindness and love. [NLT]<br><br>ἀλλ' οὐδενὸς λόγου ποιοῦμαι, οὐδὲ ἔχω τὴν ψυχήν μου **τιμίαν** ἐμαυτῷ, ὡς τελειῶσαι τὸν δρόμον μου μετὰ χαρᾶς, καὶ τὴν διακονίαν ἣν ἔλαβον παρὰ τοῦ Κυρίου Ἰησοῦ, διαμαρτύρασθαι τὸ εὐαγγέλιον τῆς χάριτος τοῦ Θεοῦ. [GNS]<br><br>ἀλλ' οὐδενὸς λόγου ποιοῦμαι τὴν ψυχὴν **τιμίαν** ἐμαυτῷ ὡς τελειῶσαι τὸν δρόμον μου καὶ τὴν διακονίαν ἣν ἔλαβον παρὰ τοῦ κυρίου Ἰησοῦ, διαμαρτύρασθαι τὸ εὐαγγέλιον τῆς χάριτος τοῦ θεοῦ. [GNT] | |
| **#891**<br>**Death**<br><br>Departure–KJV<br>Departure–NASB<br>Departure–NIV<br>Departure–NKJV<br>**Death–NLT**<br><br>**POSB REFERENCE**<br>(2 Tim. 4:6)<br>Note 1, point 2 | ἀναλύσεώς = *analuseōs*<br>Pronunciation: [an-al'-oo-seh-os]<br>Parsing (part of speech): noun<br>    Case—genitive<br>    Gender—feminine<br>    Number—singular<br>    Stem or root—from ἀνάλυσις, εως<br>Concordance References:<br>  ⇒ Strong's #359 analusis<br>  ⇒ NIV #385 analusis<br>  ⇒ NASB #359 analusis<br><br>**2 Tim. 4:6**<br>For I am now ready to be offered, and the time of my **departure** is at hand. [KJV]<br><br>For I am already being poured out as a drink offering, and the time of my **departure** has come. [NASB]<br><br>For I am already being poured out like a drink offering, and the time has come for my **departure**. [NIV]<br><br>For I am already being poured out as a drink offering, and the time of my **departure** is at hand. [NKJV]<br><br>As for me, my life has already been poured out as an offering to God. The time of my **death** is near. [NLT]<br><br>ἐγὼ γὰρ ἤδη σπένδομαι, καὶ ὁ καιρὸς τῆς ἐμῆς **ἀναλύσεώς** ἐφέστηκε. [GNS]<br><br>Ἐγὼ γὰρ ἤδη σπένδομαι, καὶ ὁ καιρὸς τῆς **ἀναλύσεώς** μου ἐφέστηκεν. [GNT] | Departure, death.<br><br>**Practical Application**<br>The word (*analuseōs*) is striking in its meaning. (The following meanings are taken from W.E. Vine. *Expository Dictionary of New Testament Words*.)<br>1. To depart is the picture of a ship hoisting the anchor and loosening the mooring ropes and departing one country for another country. Paul had been anchored and tied to this world, but the anchor and ropes of this world were now being loosed, and Paul was about to set sail for the greatest of all ports—heaven itself.<br>2. To depart is the picture of "breaking up an encampment" (W.E. Vine). Paul had been camping in this world. If any man has ever known what it is like to be unsettled and moving about from place to place, it was Paul. And unfortunately it was often not by choice. Many times the opposition to the gospel had been so violent, he had been forced to break camp and move on, sometimes fleeing for his life. But now, Paul was to break camp and depart for the last time, and what a departure it was to be. He would never again have to move. He was departing this world for his permanent residence: heaven itself.<br>3. To depart is the picture of the unyoking of an animal from the burden of the cart, plough, or millstone which it had been pulling to grind the grain. Paul was to be released from the yoke and burden of labor and toil in this life. He was being released and set free to depart for the pastures and still waters and rest of heaven and eternity. |
| **#892**<br>**Debased Mind**<br><br>Reprobate mind–KJV<br>Depraved mind–NASB | ἀδόκιμον νοῦν = *adokimon noun*<br>Pronunciation: [ad-ok'-ee-mon noon]<br>Parsing *adokimon* (part of speech): adjective<br>    Case—accusative<br>    Gender—masculine<br>    Number—singular<br>    Stem or root—from ἀδόκιμος, ον | A mind that fails to meet the test; that is disqualified, debased, worthless; a corrupted mind, (thought, reason, attitude, intention, purpose; understanding, discernment). |

# PRACTICAL WORD STUDIES
## in the NEW TESTAMENT

| ENGLISH WORD | GREEK WORD AND VERSE | THE WORD MEANS... |
|---|---|---|
| Depraved mind–NIV<br>**Debased mind–NKJV**<br>Evil minds–NLT<br><br>**POSB<br>REFERENCE**<br>(Rom.1:28-31; esp. v.28)<br>Note 4, point 1 | Parsing *noun* (part of speech): noun<br>    Case—accusative<br>    Gender—masculine<br>    Number—singular<br>    Stem or root—from νοῦς, νοός, νοΐ, νοῦν<br>Concordance References:<br>⇒ Strong's #96 adokimos + 3563 nous<br>⇒ NIV #99 adokimos [depraved] + 3808 nous [mind]<br>⇒ NASB #96 adokimos + 3563 nous<br><br>**Romans 1:28**<br>And even as they did not like to retain God in their knowledge, God gave them over to a **reprobate mind**, to do those things which are not convenient; [KJV]<br>And just as they did not see fit to acknowledge God any longer, God gave them over to a **depraved mind**, to do those things which are not proper, [NASB]<br>Furthermore, since they did not think it worthwhile to retain the knowledge of God, he gave them over to a **depraved mind**, to do what ought not to be done. [NIV]<br>And even as they did not like to retain God in *their* knowledge, God gave them over to a **debased mind**, to do those things which are not fitting; [NKJV]<br>When they refused to acknowledge God, he abandoned them to their **evil minds** and let them do things that should never be done. [NLT]<br>Καὶ καθὼς οὐκ ἐδοκίμασαν τὸν Θεὸν ἔχειν ἐν ἐπιγνώσει, παρέδωκεν αὐτοὺς ὁ Θεὸς εἰς **ἀδόκιμον νοῦν**, ποιεῖν τὰ μὴ καθήκοντα, [GNS]<br>καὶ καθὼς οὐκ ἐδοκίμασαν τὸν θεὸν ἔχειν ἐν ἐπιγνώσει, παρέδωκεν αὐτοὺς ὁ θεὸς εἰς **ἀδόκιμον νοῦν**, ποιεῖν τὰ μὴ καθήκοντα, [GNT] | **Practical Application**<br>God shows wrath by giving men up to reprobate, depraved minds. The term "evil or debased mind" (*adokimon noun*) means a mind that is rejected, disapproved, degraded, depraved; a mind that cannot stand the test of judgment.<br>The reason God gives men up to reprobate minds is because men reject God. They know God, but they do not "like to retain God in their knowledge." They...<br>• do not like to approve God.<br>• do not like to recognize God.<br>• do not like to acknowledge God.<br><br>They simply do not want God to have anything to do with their lives; therefore, they push Him out of their minds. They ignore and refuse to accept God's presence. |
| #893<br>**Debate**<br><br>Debate–KJV<br>Strife–NASB<br>Strife–NIV<br>Strife–NKJV<br>Fighting–NLT<br><br>**POSB<br>REFERENCE**<br>(Romans 1:29)<br>*Deeper Study #8* | ἔριδος = *eridos*<br>Pronunciation: [er'-i-dos]<br>Parsing (part of speech): noun<br>    Case—genitive<br>    Gender—feminine<br>    Number—singular<br>    Stem or root—from ἔρις, ιδος<br>Concordance References:<br>⇒ Strong's #2054 eris<br>⇒ NIV #2251 eris<br>⇒ NASB #2054 eris<br><br>**Romans 1:29**<br>Being filled with all unrighteousness, fornication, wickedness, covetousness, maliciousness; full of envy, murder, **debate**, deceit, malignity; whisperers, [KJV]<br>being filled with all unrighteousness, wickedness, greed, evil; full of envy, murder, **strife**, deceit, malice; they are gossips, [NASB]<br>They have become filled with every kind of wickedness, evil, greed and depravity. They are full of envy, murder, **strife**, deceit and malice. They are gossips, [NIV]<br>Being filled with all unrighteousness, sexual immorality, wickedness, covetousness, maliciousness; full of envy, murder, **strife**, deceit, evil-mindedness; *they are* whisperers, [NKJV]<br>Their lives became full of every kind of wickedness, sin, greed, hate, envy, murder, **fighting**, deception, malicious behavior, and gossip. [NLT]<br>πεπληρωμένους πάσῃ ἀδικίᾳ πορνείᾳ, πονηρίᾳ πλεονεξίᾳ κακίᾳ· μεστοὺς φθόνου, φόνου, **ἔριδος**, δόλου, κακοηθείας· [GNS]<br>πεπληρωμένους πάσῃ ἀδικίᾳ πονηρίᾳ πλεονεξίᾳ κακίᾳ, μεστοὺς φθόνου φόνου **ἔριδος** δόλου κακοηθείας, ψιθυριστάς [GNT] | Selfish rivalry; arguments. The word debate (*eridos*) means strife, discord, contention, fighting, struggling, quarreling, dissension, wrangling.<br><br>**Practical Application**<br>It means that a man fights against another person in order to get something: position, promotion, property, honor, recognition. He fights in a dishonest and evil way. |
| #894<br>**Debate** | διελέγετο = *dielegeto*<br>Pronunciation: [dee-ehl-eg'-eh-tow]<br>Parsing (part of speech): verb<br>    Mood—indicative | Reasoning, dispute, debate, discussion.<br><br>**Practical Application**<br>Paul proclaimed the gospel daily. The idea is |

# PRACTICAL WORD STUDIES
## in the NEW TESTAMENT

| ENGLISH WORD | GREEK WORD AND VERSE | THE WORD MEANS... |
|---|---|---|
| Disputed–KJV<br>Reasoning–NASB<br>Reasoned–NIV<br>Reasoned–NKJV<br>Debate–NLT<br><br>**POSB REFERENCE**<br>(Acts 17:17)<br>Note 2<br><br>See also POSB REF:<br>(Acts 18:4)<br>Note 4, point 1 | Tense—imperfect<br>Voice—middle or passive deponent<br>Person—3rd person<br>Number—singular<br>Stem or root—from διαλέγομαι<br>Concordance References:<br>⇒ Strong's #1256 dialegomai<br>⇒ NIV #1363 dialegomai<br>⇒ NASB #1256 dialegomai<br><br>**Acts 17:17**<br>Therefore **disputed** he in the synagogue with the Jews, and with the devout persons, and in the market daily with them that met with him. [KJV]<br><br>So he was **reasoning** in the synagogue with the Jews and the God-fearing Gentiles, and in the market place every day with those who happened to be present. [NASB]<br><br>So he **reasoned** in the synagogue with the Jews and the God-fearing Greeks, as well as in the marketplace day by day with those who happened to be there. [NIV]<br><br>Therefore he **reasoned** in the synagogue with the Jews and with the *Gentile* worshipers, and in the marketplace daily with those who happened to be there. [NKJV]<br><br>He went to the synagogue to **debate** with the Jews and the God-fearing Gentiles, and he spoke daily in the public square to all who happened to be there. [NLT]<br><br>**διελέγετο** μὲν οὖν ἐν τῇ συναγωγῇ τοῖς Ἰουδαίοις καὶ τοῖς σεβομένοις καὶ ἐν τῇ ἀγορᾷ κατὰ πᾶσαν ἡμέραν πρὸς τοὺς παρατυγχάνοντας. [GNS]<br><br>**διελέγετο** μὲν οὖν ἐν τῇ συναγωγῇ τοῖς Ἰουδαίοις καὶ τοῖς σεβομένοις καὶ ἐν τῇ ἀγορᾷ κατὰ πᾶσαν ἡμέραν πρὸς τοὺς παρατυγχάνοντας. [GNT] | twofold.<br>1. He was zealous, full of fervor and passion, eagerly grasping every moment and opportunity.<br>2. He knew the stakes were high. The destiny of everyone he passed and saw lay in the balance. They were all lost and doomed unless he could reach them with the gospel. Therefore, no matter the cost, he had to do all he could to reach and help them in their search for the truth. He reasoned, argued, debated for the gospel and the salvation of souls. |
| #895<br>**Debates**<br><br>Debates–KJV<br>Strife–NASB<br>Quarreling–NIV<br>Contentions–NKJV<br>Quarreling–NLT<br><br>**POSB REFERENCE**<br>(2 Cor.12:19-21; esp. v.20)<br>Note 3, point 2 | ἔρις = eris<br>Pronunciation: [er'-is]<br>Parsing (part of speech): noun<br>  Case—nominative<br>  Gender—feminine<br>  Number—singular<br>Stem or root—from ἔρις, ιδος<br>Concordance References:<br>⇒ Strong's #2054 eris<br>⇒ NIV #2251 eris<br>⇒ NASB #2054 eris<br><br>**2 Cor. 12:20**<br>For I fear, lest, when I come, I shall not find you such as I would, and that I shall be found unto you such as ye would not: lest there be **debates**, envyings, wraths, strifes, backbitings, whisperings, swellings, tumults: [KJV]<br><br>For I am afraid that perhaps when I come I may find you to be not what I wish and may be found by you to be not what you wish; that perhaps there may be **strife**, jealousy, angry tempers, disputes, slanders, gossip, arrogance, disturbances; [NASB]<br><br>For I am afraid that when I come I may not find you as I want you to be, and you may not find me as you want me to be. I fear that there may be **quarreling**, jealousy, outbursts of anger, factions, slander, gossip, arrogance and disorder. [NIV]<br><br>For I fear lest, when I come, I shall not find you such as I wish, and *that* I shall be found by you such as you do not wish; lest *there be* **contentions**, jealousies, outbursts of wrath, selfish ambitions, backbitings, whisperings, conceits, tumults; [NKJV]<br><br>For I am afraid that when I come to visit you I won't like what I find, and then you won't like my response. I am afraid that I will find **quarreling**, jealousy, outbursts of anger, selfishness, backstabbing, gossip, conceit, and | Quarreling, debate, strife, dissension, fighting, contention, rivalry, competitiveness.<br><br>**Practical Application**<br>Paul was stricken with fear, fear lest the church fail to be what it should be and reject him and his ministry. Paul feared that the church would fail to deal with the carnal critics and continue putting up with their evil attacks against him. He lists eight evils—including "debates" (*eris*)—that were and still are characteristic of divisive critics in the church. |

# Practical Word Studies in the New Testament

| ENGLISH WORD | GREEK WORD AND VERSE | THE WORD MEANS... |
|---|---|---|
| | disorderly behavior. [NLT]<br><br>φοβοῦμαι γὰρ μή πως ἐλθὼν οὐχ οἵους θέλω εὕρω ὑμᾶς, κἀγὼ εὑρεθῶ ὑμῖν οἷον οὐ θέλετε· μή πως **ἔρις**, ζῆλοι, θυμοί, ἐριθεῖαι, καταλαλιαί, ψιθυρισμοί, φυσιώσεις, ἀκαταστασίαι [GNS]<br><br>φοβοῦμαι γὰρ μή πως ἐλθὼν οὐχ οἵους θέλω εὕρω ὑμᾶς κἀγὼ εὑρεθῶ ὑμῖν οἷον οὐ θέλετε· μή πως **ἔρις**, ζῆλος, θυμοί, ἐριθεῖαι, καταλαλιαί, ψιθυρισμοί, fusiώσεις, ἀκαταστασίαι· [GNT] | |
| **#896**<br>**Debauchery**<br><br>Wantonness–KJV<br>Sensuality–NASB<br>**Debauchery–NIV**<br>Lust–NKJV<br>Immoral living–NLT<br><br>**POSB REFERENCE**<br>(Rom.13:13)<br>Note 4, point 4 | ἀσελγείαις = *aselgeiais*<br>Pronunciation: [as-elg'-i-ah-is]<br>Parsing (part of speech): noun<br>    Case—dative<br>    Gender—feminine<br>    Number—plural<br>    Stem or root—from ἀσέλγεια, ας<br>Concordance References:<br>⇒ Strong's #766 aselgeia<br>⇒ NIV #816 aselgeia<br>⇒ NASB #766 aselgeia<br><br>**Romans 13:13**<br>Let us walk honestly, as in the day; not in rioting and drunkenness, not in chambering and **wantonness**, not in strife and envying. [KJV]<br>Let us behave properly as in the day, not in carousing and drunkenness, not in sexual promiscuity and **sensuality**, not in strife and jealousy. [NASB]<br>Let us behave decently, as in the daytime, not in orgies and drunkenness, not in sexual immorality and **debauchery**, not in dissension and jealousy. [NIV]<br>Let us walk properly, as in the day, not in revelry and drunkenness, not in lewdness and **lust**, not in strife and envy. [NKJV]<br>We should be decent and true in everything we do, so that everyone can approve of our behavior. Don't participate in wild parties and getting drunk, or in adultery and **immoral living**, or in fighting and jealousy. [NLT]<br>ὡς ἐν ἡμέρᾳ, εὐσχημόνως περιπατήσωμεν, μὴ κώμοις καὶ μέθαις, μὴ κοίταις καὶ **ἀσελγείαις**, μὴ ἔριδι καὶ ζήλῳ. [GNS]<br>ὡς ἐν ἡμέρᾳ εὐσχημόνως περιπατήσωμεν, μὴ κώμοις καὶ μέθαις, μὴ κοίταις καὶ **ἀσελγείαις**, μὴ ἔριδι καὶ ζήλῳ, [GNT] | Debauchery; sensuality; lust; running wild; licentiousness; wantonness; homosexuality; lasciviousness; living a wild, partying, and immoral life.<br><br>**Practical Application**<br>It is excess lust, unbridled lust that consumes one's thoughts and behavior through...<br>• looks and dress<br>• films and pictures<br>• dances and parties<br>• suggestions and gestures<br>• books and pamphlets<br>• songs and music<br>• talk and jokes<br>• touch and behavior<br>• sensuality, indecency, and vices |
| **#897**<br>**Debauchery**<br><br>Excess–KJV<br>Dissipation–NASB<br>**Debauchery–NIV**<br>Dissipation–NKJV<br>Will ruin your life–NLT<br><br>**POSB REFERENCE**<br>(Eph.5:18)<br>Note 4 | ἀσωτία = *asōtia*<br>Pronunciation: [as-o-tee'-ah]<br>Parsing (part of speech): noun<br>    Case—nominative<br>    Gender—feminine<br>    Number—singular<br>    Stem or root—from ἀσωτία, ας<br>Concordance References:<br>⇒ Strong's #810 asōtia<br>⇒ NIV #861 asōtia<br>⇒ NASB #810 asōtia<br><br>**Ephes. 5:18**<br>And be not drunk with wine, wherein is **excess**; but be filled with the Spirit; [KJV]<br>And do not get drunk with wine, for that is **dissipation**, but be filled with the Spirit, [NASB]<br>Do not get drunk on wine, which leads to **debauchery**. Instead, be filled with the Spirit. [NIV]<br>And do not be drunk with wine, in which is **dissipation**; but be filled with the Spirit, [NKJV]<br>Don't be drunk with wine, because that **will ruin your life**. Instead, let the Holy Spirit fill and control you. [NLT]<br>καὶ μὴ μεθύσκεσθε οἴνῳ, ἐν ᾧ ἐστιν **ἀσωτία**, ἀλλὰ πληροῦσθε ἐν Πνεύματι, [GNS]<br>καὶ μὴ μεθύσκεσθε οἴνῳ, ἐν ᾧ ἐστιν **ἀσωτία**, ἀλλὰ πληροῦσθε ἐν πνεύματι, [GNT] | Debauchery, excess behavior, dissipation, reckless living, a ruined life. The word means...<br>• the dissipation and wasting away of the body.<br>• uncontrolled behavior.<br>• rioting, debauchery, wild and outrageous behavior and conduct.<br><br>**Practical Application**<br>Drunkenness is a work of the flesh and it often leads to other sins of the flesh: partying, loose behavior, immodest clothing, exposure of the body, sexual thoughts, immorality, wicked or evil and unjust behavior or violence and physical abuse, notions of grandeur, strength or power. The Bible says several things about drunkenness.<br>1. Drunkenness excludes a person from the kingdom of God.<br>2. Drunkenness leads to other forms of misbehavior and sin.<br>3. Drunkenness makes it impossible to grasp the fleeting opportunities of time. |

## Practical Word Studies in the New Testament

| ENGLISH WORD | GREEK WORD AND VERSE | THE WORD MEANS... |
|---|---|---|
| **#898**<br>**Debauchery**<br><br>Lasciviousness–KJV<br>Sensuality–NASB<br>**Debauchery–NIV**<br>Lewdness–NKJV<br>Immorality–NLT<br><br>**POSB REFERENCE**<br>(1 Pt.4:3)<br>Note 3, point 1 | ἀσελγείαις = *aselgeiais*<br>Pronunciation: [as-elg'-i-ah-is]<br>Parsing (part of speech): noun<br>    Case—dative<br>    Gender—feminine<br>    Number—plural<br>    Stem or root—from ἀσέλγεια, ας<br>Concordance References:<br>⇒ Strong's #766 *aselgeia*<br>⇒ NIV #816 *aselgeia*<br>⇒ NASB #766 *aselgeia*<br><br>**1 Peter 4:3**<br>For the time past of our life may suffice us to have wrought the will of the Gentiles, when we walked in **lasciviousness**, lusts, excess of wine, revellings, banquetings, and abominable idolatries. [KJV]<br>For the time already past is sufficient for you to have carried out the desire of the Gentiles, having pursued a course of **sensuality**, lusts, drunkenness, carousals, drinking parties and abominable idolatries. [NASB]<br>For you have spent enough time in the past doing what pagans choose to do—living in **debauchery**, lust, drunkenness, orgies, carousing and detestable idolatry. [NIV]<br>For we have spent enough of our past lifetime in doing the will of the Gentiles—when we walked in **lewdness**, lusts, drunkenness, revelries, drinking parties, and abominable idolatries. [NKJV]<br>You have had enough in the past of the evil things that godless people enjoy—their **immorality** and lust, their feasting and drunkenness and wild parties, and their terrible worship of idols. [NLT]<br>ἀρκετὸς γὰρ ἡμῖν ὁ παρεληλυθὼς χρόνος τὸ βίου τὸ θέλημα τῶν ἐθνῶν κατεργάσασθαι, πεπορευμένους ἐν **ἀσελγείαις**, ἐπιθυμίαις, οἰνοφλυγίαις, κώμοις, πότοις, καὶ ἀθεμίτοις εἰδωλολατρείαις· [GNS]<br>ἀρκετὸς γὰρ ὁ παρεληλυθὼς χρόνος τὸ βούλημα τῶν ἐθνῶν κατειργάσθαι πεπορευμένους ἐν **ἀσελγείαις**, ἐπιθυμίαις, οἰνοφλυγίαις, κώμοις, πότοις καὶ ἀθεμίτοις εἰδωλολατρίαις. [GNT] | Debauchery, lasciviousness, sensuality, immorality, vice, filthiness, indecency, shamelessness, license, lustful desire; without restraint; lewdness.<br><br>**Practical Application**<br>A chief characteristic of the behavior is open and shameless indecency. It means unrestrained evil thoughts and behavior. It is giving in to brutish and lustful desires, a readiness for any pleasure. It is a man who knows no restraint, a man who has sinned so much that he no longer cares what people say or think. It is something far more distasteful than just doing wrong. The man who misbehaves usually tries to hide his wrong, but a sensual man does not care who knows about his exploits or shame. He wants; therefore he seeks to take and gratify. Decency and opinion do not matter. Initially when he began to sin, he did as all men do: he misbehaved in secret. But eventually, the sin got the best of him—to the point that he no longer cared who saw or knew. He became the subject of a master—the master of habit, of the thing itself. |
| **#899**<br>**Debtor**<br><br>Debtor–KJV<br>Under obligation–NASB<br>Obligated–NIV<br>Debtor–NKJV<br>Great sense of obligation–NLT<br><br>**POSB REFERENCE**<br>(Rom.1:14-15; esp. v.14)<br>Note 5, point 1<br><br>See also POSB REF:<br>(Rom.8:12-13; esp. v.12)<br>Note 6, point 1 | ὀφειλέτης = *opheiletēs*<br>Pronunciation: [of-i-let'-ace]<br>Parsing (part of speech): noun<br>    Case—nominative<br>    Gender—masculine<br>    Number—singular<br>    Stem or root—from ὀφειλέτης, ου<br>Concordance References:<br>⇒ Strong's #3781 *opheiletēs*<br>⇒ NIV #4050 *opheiletēs*<br>⇒ NASB #3781 *opheiletēs*<br><br>**Romans 1:14**<br>I am **debtor** both to the Greeks, and to the Barbarians; both to the wise, and to the unwise. [KJV]<br>I am **under obligation** both to Greeks and to barbarians, both to the wise and to the foolish. [NASB]<br>I am **obligated** both to Greeks and non-Greeks, both to the wise and the foolish. [NIV]<br>I am a **debtor** both to Greeks and to barbarians, both to wise and to unwise. [NKJV]<br>For I have a **great sense of obligation** to people in our culture and to people in other cultures, to the educated and uneducated alike. [NLT]<br>Ἕλλησί τε καὶ βαρβάροις, σοφοῖς τε καὶ ἀνοήτοις **ὀφειλέτης** εἰμί· [GNS]<br>Ἕλλησίν τε καὶ βαρβάροις, σοφοῖς τε καὶ ἀνοήτοις **ὀφειλέτης** εἰμί, [GNT] | To be obligated; to be in debt; to owe; to be bound by duty; to have a great sense of obligation or debt.<br><br>**Practical Application**<br>The Greek is impossible to translate into English, for two ideas are being expressed by Paul. He was a "debtor"...<br>• because Christ had done so much for him (saved him).<br>• because Christ had called him to preach (given him a task to do).<br>The indebtedness was deeply felt by Paul. The idea is that it was intense, unwavering, unrelentless, powerful. The sense of debt just would not let Paul go. He was compelled to preach the gospel; therefore, he could do nothing else. He was obligated and duty-bound to preach it. He actually felt that he owed the gospel to the world; therefore, if he kept quiet, it would be worse than knowing the cure for the most terrible disease of history but refusing to share it. |

## Practical Word Studies
### in the New Testament

| ENGLISH WORD | GREEK WORD AND VERSE | THE WORD MEANS... |
|---|---|---|
| **#900**<br>**Debts**<br><br>Debts–KJV<br>Debts–NASB<br>Debts–NIV<br>Debts–NKJV<br>Sins–NLT<br><br>**POSB REFERENCE**<br>(Mt.6:12)<br>*Deeper Study #8* | ὀφειλήματα = *opheilēmata*<br>Pronunciation: [of-i'-lay-mah-tah]<br>Parsing (part of speech): noun<br>    Case—accusative<br>    Gender—neuter<br>    Number—plural<br>    Stem or root—from ὀφείλημα, τος<br>Concordance References:<br>  ⇒ Strong's #3783 opheilēma<br>  ⇒ NIV #4052 opheilēma<br>  ⇒ NASB #3783 opheilēma<br>          **Matthew 6:12**<br>And forgive us our **debts**, as we forgive our debtors. [KJV]<br>'And forgive us our **debts**, as we also have forgiven our debtors. [NASB]<br>Forgive us our **debts**, as we also have forgiven our debtors. [NIV]<br>And forgive us our **debts**, As we forgive our debtors. [NKJV]<br>And forgive us our **sins**, just as we have forgiven those who have sinned against us. [NLT]<br>καὶ ἄφες ἡμῖν τὰ **ὀφειλήματα** ἡμῶν, ὡς καὶ ἡμεῖς ἀφίεμεν τοῖς ὀφειλέταις ἡμῶν· [GNS]<br>καὶ ἄφες ἡμῖν τὰ **ὀφειλήματα** ἡμῶν, ὡς καὶ ἡμεῖς ἀφήκαμεν τοῖς ὀφειλέταις ἡμῶν· [GNT] | Dues, duties, sins, wrongs, debts—that which is owed, that which is legally due.<br><br>**Practical Application**<br>It means a failure to pay one's debts, one's dues; a failure to do one's duty, to keep one's responsibilities. |
| **#901**<br>**Decay**<br><br>Corruption–KJV<br>Decay–NASB<br>Decay–NIV<br>Corruption–NKJV<br>Rot in the grave–NLT<br><br>**POSB REFERENCE**<br>(Acts 2:25-28; esp. v.27)<br>Note 1, point 2c<br><br>(Acts 2:27)<br>*Deeper Study #1, point 2*<br><br>See also POSB REF:<br>(Acts.13:32-37; esp. v.34)<br>*Deeper Study #4* | διαφθοράν = *diaphthoran*<br>Pronunciation: [dee-af-thor-ahn']<br>Parsing (part of speech): noun<br>    Case—accusative<br>    Gender—feminine<br>    Number—singular<br>    Stem or root—from διαφθορά, ᾶς<br>Concordance References:<br>  ⇒ Strong's #1312 diaphthora<br>  ⇒ NIV #1426 diaphthora<br>  ⇒ NASB #1312 diaphthora<br>          **Acts 2:27**<br>Because thou wilt not leave my soul in hell, neither wilt thou suffer thine Holy One to see **corruption**. [KJV]<br>Because Thou wilt not abandon my soul to Hades, Nor ALLOW Thy Holy One to UNDERGO **DECAY**. [NASB]<br>Because you will not abandon me to the grave, nor will you let your Holy One see **decay**. [NIV]<br>*For You will not leave my soul in Hades, Nor will You allow Your oly One to see **corruption**.* [NKJV]<br>For you will not leave my soul among the dead or allow your Holy One to **rot in the grave**. [NLT]<br>ὅτι οὐκ ἐγκαταλείψεις τὴν ψυχήν μου εἰς ᾅδου, οὐδὲ δώσεις τὸν ὅσιόν σου ἰδεῖν **διαφθοράν**. [GNS]<br>ὅτι οὐκ ἐγκαταλείψεις τὴν ψυχήν μου εἰς ᾅδην οὐδὲ δώσεις τὸν ὅσιόν σου ἰδεῖν **διαφθοράν**. [GNT] | Decay; corrupt; deteriorate, putrefy, perish. It speaks of the grave and the rotting of a dead body.<br><br>**Practical Application**<br>In no place does Christ promise a new body to the unbeliever, to the unsaved and lost. A person's body and flesh can be destroyed forever. (This is a fact seldom pointed out.) |
| **#902**<br>**Decay**<br><br>Corruption–KJV<br>Decay–NASB<br>Decay–NIV<br>Corruption–NKJV<br>Die–NLT<br><br>**POSB REFERENCE**<br>(Acts 13:32-37; esp. v.34)<br>*Deeper Study #4* | ὑποστρέφειν εἰς διαφθοράν = *hupostrephein eis diaphthoran*<br>Pronunciation: [who-po-streph-eh-een ice dee-ahph-tho-rahn]<br>Parsing *diaphthoran* (part of speech): noun<br>    Case—accusative<br>    Gender—feminine<br>    Number—singular<br>    Stem or root— from διαφθορά, ᾶς<br>Concordance References:<br>  ⇒ Strong's #1312+1519+5290 diaphthora eis hupostrephō<br>  ⇒ NIV #1426+1650+5715 diaphthora [decay] eis hupostrephō<br>  ⇒ NASB #1312+1519+5290 diaphthora eis hupostrephō | To decay; to die; to become corrupt.<br><br>**Practical Application**<br>In no place does Christ promise a new body to the unsaved and lost. A person's body and flesh can be destroyed forever. (This is a fact seldom pointed out.) |

## PRACTICAL WORD STUDIES
### in the NEW TESTAMENT

| ENGLISH WORD | GREEK WORD AND VERSE | THE WORD MEANS... |
|---|---|---|
| | **Acts 13:34**<br>And as concerning that he raised him up from the dead, now no more to return to **corruption**, he said on this wise, I will give you the sure mercies of David. [KJV]<br>"And as for the fact that He raised Him up from the dead, no more to return to **decay**, He has spoken in this way: 'I will give you the holy and sure blessings of David.' [NASB]<br>The fact that God raised him from the dead, never to **decay**, is stated in these words: " 'I will give you the holy and sure blessings promised to David.' [NIV]<br>And that He raised Him from the dead, no more to return to **corruption**, He has spoken thus:'*I will give you the sure mercies of David.*' [NKJV]<br>For God had promised to raise him from the dead, never again to **die**. This is stated in the Scripture that says, 'I will give you the sacred blessings I promised to David.' [NLT]<br>ὅτι δὲ ἀνέστησεν αὐτὸν ἐκ νεκρῶν μηκέτι μέλλοντα **ὑποστρέφειν εἰς διαφθοράν**, οὕτως εἴρηκεν ὅτι Δώσω ὑμῖν τὰ ὅσια Δαβὶδ τὰ πιστά. [GNS]<br>ὅτι δὲ ἀνέστησεν αὐτὸν ἐκ νεκρῶν μηκέτι μέλλοντα **ὑποστρέφειν εἰς διαφθοράν**, οὕτως εἴρηκεν ὅτι Δώσω ὑμῖν τὰ ὅσια Δαυὶδ τὰ πιστά. [GNT] | |
| **#903**<br>**Decease**<br><br>Decease–KJV<br>Departure–NASB<br>Departure–NIV<br>Decease–NKJV<br>Dying–NLT<br><br>**POSB REFERENCE**<br>(Lk.9:30-31; esp. v.31)<br>Note 4, point 2 | ἔξοδον = *exodon*<br>Pronunciation: [ex'-od-on]<br>Parsing (part of speech): noun<br>    Case—accusative<br>    Gender—feminine<br>    Number—singular<br>    Stem or root—from ἔξοδος, ου<br>Concordance References:<br>  ⇒ Strong's #1841 exodos<br>  ⇒ NIV #2016 exodos<br>  ⇒ NASB #1841 exodos<br><br>**Luke 9:31**<br>Who appeared in glory, and spake of his **decease** which he should accomplish at Jerusalem. [KJV]<br>Who, appearing in glory, were speaking of His **departure** which He was about to accomplish at Jerusalem. [NASB]<br>Appeared in glorious splendor, talking with Jesus. They spoke about his **departure**, which he was about to bring to fulfillment at Jerusalem. [NIV]<br>Who appeared in glory and spoke of His **decease** which He was about to accomplish at Jerusalem. [NKJV]<br>They were glorious to see. And they were speaking of how he was about to fulfill God's plan by **dying** in Jerusalem. [NLT]<br>οἱ ὀφθέντες ἐν δόξῃ ἔλεγον τὴν **ἔξοδον** αὐτοῦ, ἣν ἤμελλε πληροῦν ἐν Ἰερουσαλήμ. [GNS]<br>οἱ ὀφθέντες ἐν δόξῃ ἔλεγον τὴν **ἔξοδον** αὐτοῦ, ἣν ἤμελλεν πληροῦν ἐν Ἰερουσαλήμ. [GNT] | Departure, exodus, decease; to depart; to go out; to die.<br><br>**Practical Application**<br>In this Scripture, there stood Moses sharing how God had so miraculously saved and delivered the children of Israel out of bondage and how the exodus (deliverance) was only a picture of the marvelous deliverance that He, God's Son, was to accomplish for man. Jesus was to accomplish a new exodus, a new saving deliverance; except this time, it was to be for all men. All men were to be delivered from the bondage of sin and death, from the devil and hell—delivered into the glorious liberty of God and life, both abundant and eternal life. Jesus' dying was to be well worth it, Moses and Elijah stressed. Note: the very encouragement that our Lord needed as Man was given by two who had believed and hoped in His coming. Being reminded of the marvelous deliverance (*exodon*) that had happened so long ago was bound to strengthen and lift the heart of Christ. Just seeing Moses and Elijah stand there, two who had trusted and believed and hoped, was bound to cause the Lord's spirit to rise. He was greatly encouraged and knew that He could not fail these men who had trusted and hoped in Him so much. |
| **#904**<br>**Deceit**<br><br>Deceit–KJV<br>Deceit–NASB<br>Deceit–NIV<br>Deceit–NKJV<br>Deceit–NLT<br><br>**POSB REFERENCE**<br>(Mk.7:22)<br>*Deeper Study* #10<br><br>See also POSB REF: | δόλος = *dolos*<br>Pronunciation: [dol'-os]<br>Parsing (part of speech): noun<br>    Case—nominative<br>    Gender—masculine<br>    Number—singular<br>    Stem or root—from δόλος, ου<br>Concordance References:<br>  ⇒ Strong's #1388 dolos<br>  ⇒ NIV #1515 dolos<br>  ⇒ NASB #1388 dolos<br><br>**Mark 7:22**<br>Thefts, covetousness, wickedness, **deceit**, lasciviousness, an evil eye, blasphemy, pride, foolishness: [KJV]<br>Deeds of coveting and wickedness, as well as **deceit**, sensuality, envy, slander, pride and foolishness. [NASB] | Deceit, treachery; to bait; to snare; to mislead; to beguile; to be crafty and deceitful; to mislead or give a false impression by word, act, or influence.<br><br>**Practical Application**<br>It is conniving and twisting the truth to get one's own way. A person plots and deceives, doing whatever has to be done in order to get what he or she wants. |

## PRACTICAL WORD STUDIES
### in the NEW TESTAMENT

| ENGLISH WORD | GREEK WORD AND VERSE | THE WORD MEANS... |
|---|---|---|
| (Rom.1:29)<br>*Deeper Study #9* | Greed, malice, **deceit**, lewdness, envy, slander, arrogance and folly. [NIV]<br>Thefts, covetousness, wickedness, **deceit**, lewdness, an evil eye, blasphemy, pride, foolishness. [NKJV]<br>Adultery, greed, wickedness, **deceit**, eagerness for lustful pleasure, envy, slander, pride, and foolishness. [NLT]<br>πλεονεξίαι, πονηρίαι, **δόλος**, ἀσέλγεια, ὀφθαλμὸς πονηρός, βλασφημία, ὑπερηφανία, ἀφροσύνη· [GNS]<br>μοιχεῖαι, πλεονεξίαι, πονηρίαι, **δόλος**, ἀσέλγεια, ὀφθαλμὸς πονηρός, βλασφημία, ὑπερηφανία, ἀφροσύνη· [GNT] | |
| **#905**<br>**Deceit**<br><br>Guile–KJV<br>Guile–NASB<br>False–NIV<br>**Deceit–NKJV**<br>Honest–NLT<br><br>**POSB**<br>**REFERENCE**<br>(Jn.1:47-48; esp. v.47)<br>Note 2, point 1b | **δόλος** = *dolos*<br>Pronunciation: [dol'-os]<br>Parsing (part of speech): noun<br>   Case—nominative<br>   Gender—masculine<br>   Number—singular<br>   Stem or root—from **δόλος**, ου<br>Concordance References:<br>  ⇒ Strong's #1388 dolos<br>  ⇒ NIV #1515 dolos<br>  ⇒ NASB #1388 dolos<br><br>**John 1:47**<br>Jesus saw Nathanael coming to him, and saith of him, Behold an Israelite indeed, in whom is no **guile**! [KJV]<br>Jesus saw Nathanael coming to Him, and said of him, "Behold, an Israelite indeed, in whom is no **guile**!" [NASB]<br>When Jesus saw Nathanael approaching, he said of him, "Here is a true Israelite, in whom there is nothing **false**." [NIV]<br>Jesus saw Nathanael coming toward Him, and said of him, "Behold, an Israelite indeed, in whom is no **deceit**!" [NKJV]<br>As they approached, Jesus said, "Here comes an **honest** man—a true son of Israel." [NLT]<br>εἶδεν ὁ Ἰησοῦς τὸν Ναθαναὴλ ἐρχόμενον πρὸς αὐτόν, καὶ λέγει περὶ αὐτοῦ, Ἴδε ἀληθῶς Ἰσραηλίτης, ἐν ᾧ **δόλος** οὐκ ἔστι. [GNS]<br>εἶδεν ὁ Ἰησοῦς τὸν Ναθαναὴλ ἐρχόμενον πρὸς αὐτὸν καὶ λέγει περὶ αὐτοῦ, Ἴδε ἀληθῶς Ἰσραηλίτης ἐν ᾧ **δόλος** οὐκ ἔστιν. [GNT] | False, deceit, guile, fraud, trickery, deception, treachery, an impostor, an impersonator, a fake.<br><br>**Practical Application**<br>Note that these terms did not describe Nathanael's behavior. The word "deceit" (*dolos*) means he did not deceive, bait, or mislead people. He did not hide what he thought; he said what he thought and acted what he felt. He was straightforward, open and honest, not deceptive or hypocritical. This trait had just been demonstrated in his response to Philip. He would not hide his true thoughts (John 1:46). One of the great tragedies in the legacy of persons is that they are full of guile. Many deceive, bait, and mislead others. Few are straightforward, open and honest, free of deception and hypocrisy. |
| **#906**<br>**Deceit**<br><br>Guile–KJV<br>Guile–NASB<br>**Deceit–NIV**<br>**Deceit–NKJV**<br>**Deceit–NLT**<br><br>**POSB**<br>**REFERENCE**<br>(1 Pt.2:1)<br>Note 1, point 1 | **δόλον** = *dolon*<br>Pronunciation: [dol'-on]<br>Parsing (part of speech): noun<br>   Case—accusative<br>   Gender—masculine<br>   Number—singular<br>   Stem or root—from **δόλος**, ου<br>Concordance References:<br>  ⇒ Strong's #1388 dolos<br>  ⇒ NIV #1515 dolos<br>  ⇒ NASB #1388 dolos<br><br>**1 Peter 2:1**<br>Wherefore laying aside all malice, and all **guile**, and hypocrisies, and envies, and all evil speakings, [KJV]<br>Therefore, putting aside all malice and all **guile** and hypocrisy and envy and all slander, [NASB]<br>Therefore, rid yourselves of all malice and all **deceit**, hypocrisy, envy, and slander of every kind. [NIV]<br>Therefore, laying aside all malice, all **deceit**, hypocrisy, envy, and all evil speaking, [NKJV]<br>So get rid of all malicious behavior and **deceit**. Don't just pretend to be good! Be done with hypocrisy and jealousy and backstabbing. [NLT]<br>Ἀποθέμενοι οὖν πᾶσαν κακίαν καὶ πάντα **δόλον** καὶ ὑποκρίσεις καὶ φθόνους καὶ πάσας καταλαλιάς, [GNS]<br>Ἀποθέμενοι οὖν πᾶσαν κακίαν καὶ πάντα **δόλον** καὶ ὑποκρίσεις καὶ φθόνους καὶ πάσας καταλαλιάς, [GNT] | Deceit, guile, false, treachery, trickery.<br><br>**Practical Application**<br>The word means to deceive and mislead people; to set bait so as to catch them; to bait or deceive in order to achieve one's own end. It means to be two-faced. Note that guile or deception has to do primarily with words. When a person wants something, he tries to get it...<br>• by flattery<br>• by false promises<br>• by false tales<br>• by suggestive talk<br>• by off-colored suggestions<br>• by enticing words<br>• by outright lying<br><br>When a person wants something, he looks at the other person's weakness or ignorance, and he tries to appeal to it. He appeals to it by deceiving and beguiling the person. The exhortation is strong: believers must strip off deceit or guile. We must not deceive and mislead people. |

## PRACTICAL WORD STUDIES
### in the NEW TESTAMENT

| ENGLISH WORD | GREEK WORD AND VERSE | THE WORD MEANS... |
|---|---|---|
| **#907**<br>**Deceit–**<br>**Deceitful**<br><br>Guile–KJV<br>Guile–NASB<br>**Deceitful–NIV**<br>**Deceit–NKJV**<br>Lies–NLT<br><br>**POSB**<br>**REFERENCE**<br>(1 Pt.3:10)<br>Note 1 | δόλον = *dolon*<br>Pronunciation: [dol'-on]<br>Parsing (part of speech): noun<br>    Case—accusative<br>    Gender—masculine<br>    Number—singular<br>    Stem or root—from δόλος, ου<br>Concordance References:<br>  ⇒ Strong's #1388 *dolos*<br>  ⇒ NIV #1515 *dolos*<br>  ⇒ NASB #1388 *dolos*<br><br>**1 Peter 3:10**<br>For he that will love life, and see good days, let him refrain his tongue from evil, and his lips that they speak no **guile**: [KJV]<br><br>For, "Let him who means to love life and see good days Refrain his tongue from evil and his lips from speaking **guile**. [NASB]<br><br>For, "Whoever would love life and see good days must keep his tongue from evil and his lips from **deceitful** speech. [NIV]<br><br>For "He who would love life And see good days, Let him refrain his tongue from evil, And his lips from speaking **deceit**. [NKJV]<br><br>For the Scriptures say, "If you want a happy life and good days, keep your tongue from speaking evil, and keep your lips from telling **lies**. [NLT]<br><br>Ὁ γὰρ θέλων ζωὴν ἀγαπᾶν, καὶ ἰδεῖν ἡμέρας ἀγαθὰς, παυσάτω τὴν γλῶσσαν αὐτοῦ ἀπὸ κακοῦ, καὶ χείλη αὐτοῦ τοῦ μὴ λαλῆσαι **δόλον**· [GNS]<br><br>ὁ γὰρ θέλων ζωὴν ἀγαπᾶν καὶ ἰδεῖν ἡμέρας ἀγαθὰς παυσάτω τὴν γλῶσσαν ἀπὸ κακοῦ καὶ χείλη τοῦ μὴ λαλῆσαι **δόλον**, [GNT] | Deceitful, guile, lies, trickery, treachery.<br><br>**Practical Application**<br>A deceitful tongue is...<br>• a false tongue<br>• a cheating tongue<br>• a treacherous tongue<br>• a deceptive tongue<br>• a lying tongue<br>• a mistreating tongue<br>• a beguiling tongue<br>• a flattering tongue<br><br>We deceive and smooth talk others in order to get what we are after or to protect ourselves. But note what Scripture says: the very first step to loving and enjoying life is to keep our tongues from deceiving and beguiling others. Deception leads to sin and sin destroys. Just think about the deceptive tongues that have...<br>• destroyed marriages<br>• damaged friendships<br>• caused injuries<br>• prevented promotions<br>• disturbed children<br>• ruined reputations<br>• aroused fights<br>• maimed bodies<br>• caused wars<br><br>If we wish to love and enjoy life, we must stop our tongues from doing evil and from deceiving others. We must control and discipline our tongues. |
| **#908**<br>**Deceitfully**<br><br>**Deceitfully–KJV**<br>Adulterating–NASB<br>Distort–NIV<br>**Deceitfully–NKJV**<br>Distort–NLT<br><br>**POSB**<br>**REFERENCE**<br>(2 Cor.4:2)<br>Note 2 | δολοῦντες = *dolountes*<br>Pronunciation: [dol-oon'-tehs]<br>Parsing (part of speech): verb<br>    Mood—participle<br>    Tense—present<br>    Voice—active<br>    Case—nominative<br>    Number—masculine<br>    Person—1st person<br>    Number—plural<br>    Stem or root—from δολόω<br>Concordance References:<br>  ⇒ Strong's #1389 *doloö*<br>  ⇒ NIV #1516 *doloö*<br>  ⇒ NASB #1389 *doloö*<br><br>**2 Cor. 4:2**<br>But have renounced the hidden things of dishonesty, not walking in craftiness, nor handling the word of God **deceitfully**; but by manifestation of the truth commending ourselves to every man's conscience in the sight of God. [KJV]<br><br>But we have renounced the things hidden because of shame, not walking in craftiness or **adulterating** the word of God, but by the manifestation of truth commending ourselves to every man's conscience in the sight of God. [NASB]<br><br>Rather, we have renounced secret and shameful ways; we do not use deception, nor do we **distort** the word of God. On the contrary, by setting forth the truth plainly we commend ourselves to every man's conscience in the sight of God. [NIV]<br><br>But we have renounced the hidden things of shame, not walking in craftiness nor handling the word of God **deceitfully**, but by manifestation of the truth commending ourselves to every man's conscience in the sight of | To distort; to falsify; to adulterate; to corrupt; to deceive; to ensnare.<br><br>**Practical Application**<br>The minister is not to deceitfully (*dolountes*) handle the word of God. It is "the Word *of God*"; that is, it has come from God, not man. The Author of the Word of God is God. God is the *Authority* of the Word of God. The minister is only the *spokesman* for God; therefore, he is...<br>• not to falsify the Word of God.<br>• not to adulterate the Word of God.<br>• not to corrupt the Word of God.<br>• not to deceive or ensnare people by mishandling the Word of God.<br><br>The minister is not *to add* the ideas, traditions, philosophies, or speculations of men to the Word of God. Neither is he to take away portions of Scripture, denying that they are the Word of God; nor is he to neglect, ignore, or keep silent about some part of God's Word. The minister of God is not to distort the Word of God in any form or fashion. |

## Practical Word Studies in the New Testament

| ENGLISH WORD | GREEK WORD AND VERSE | THE WORD MEANS... |
|---|---|---|
| | God. [NKJV]<br>We reject all shameful and underhanded methods. We do not try to trick anyone, and we do not **distort** the word of God. We tell the truth before God, and all who are honest know that. [NLT]<br>ἀλλ ἀπειπάμεθα τὰ κρυπτὰ τῆς αἰσχύνης, μὴ περιπατοῦντες ἐν πανουργίᾳ μηδὲ **δολοῦντες** τὸν λόγον τοῦ Θεοῦ, ἀλλὰ τῇ φανερώσει τῆς ἀληθείας συνιστῶντες ἑαυτοὺς πρὸς πᾶσαν συνείδησιν ἀνθρώπων ἐνώπιον τοῦ Θεοῦ. [GNS]<br>ἀλλὰ ἀπειπάμεθα τὰ κρυπτὰ τῆς αἰσχύνης, μὴ περιπατοῦντες ἐν πανουργίᾳ μηδὲ **δολοῦντες** τὸν λόγον τοῦ θεοῦ ἀλλὰ τῇ φανερώσει τῆς ἀληθείας συνιστάνοντες ἑαυτοὺς πρὸς πᾶσαν συνείδησιν ἀνθρώπων ἐνώπιον τοῦ θεοῦ. [GNT] | |
| **#909**<br>**Deceive**<br><br>Beguile–KJV<br>Delude–NASB<br>**Deceive–NIV**<br>**Deceive–NKJV**<br>**Deceive–NLT**<br><br>**POSB REFERENCE**<br>(Col.2:4)<br>Note 3 | παραλογίζηται = *paralogizētai*<br>Pronunciation: [par-al-og-id'-zay-tah-ee]<br>Parsing (part of speech): verb<br>    Mood—subjunctive<br>    Tense—present<br>    Voice—middle or passive deponent<br>    Person—3rd person<br>    Number—singular<br>    Stem or root—from παραλογίζομαι<br>Concordance References:<br>  ⇒ Strong's #3884 paralogizomai<br>  ⇒ NIV #4165 paralogizomai<br>  ⇒ NASB #3884 paralogizomai<br><br>**Col. 2:4**<br>And this I say, lest any man should **beguile** you with enticing words. [KJV]<br>I say this in order that no one may **delude** you with persuasive argument. [NASB]<br>I tell you this so that no one may **deceive** you by fine-sounding arguments. [NIV]<br>Now this I say lest anyone should **deceive** you with persuasive words. [NKJV]<br>I am telling you this so that no one will be able to **deceive** you with persuasive arguments. [NLT]<br>τοῦτο δὲ λέγω, ἵνα μὴ τις ὑμᾶς **παραλογίζηται** ἐν πιθανολογίᾳ. [GNS]<br>Τοῦτο λέγω ἵνα μηδεὶς ὑμᾶς **παραλογίζηται** ἐν πιθανολογίᾳ. [GNT] | To deceive; to delude; to beguile; to mislead, cheat, seduce, and lead someone astray.<br><br>**Practical Application**<br>Note how the seduction takes place: by "fine-sounding arguments" (*pithanologiai*), that is, by words that are persuasive, appealing, eloquent, flowery, and attractive. |
| **#910**<br>**Deceive**<br><br>Seduce–KJV<br>**Deceive–NASB**<br>Lead..astray–NIV<br>**Deceive–NKJV**<br>Lead..astray–NLT<br><br>**POSB REFERENCE**<br>(1 Jn.2:26)<br>Note 3 | πλανώντων = *planōntōn*<br>Pronunciation: [plan-on'-ton]<br>Parsing (part of speech): verb<br>    Mood—participle<br>    Tense—present<br>    Voice—active<br>    Case—genitive<br>    Gender—masculine<br>    Number—plural<br>    Stem or root—from πλανάω<br>Concordance References:<br>  ⇒ Strong's #4105 planaō<br>  ⇒ NIV #4414 planaō<br>  ⇒ NASB #4105 planaō<br><br>**1 John 2:26**<br>These things have I written unto you concerning them that **seduce** you. [KJV]<br>These things I have written to you concerning those who are trying to **deceive** you. [NASB]<br>I am writing these things to you about those who are trying to **lead** you **astray**. [NIV]<br>These things I have written to you concerning those who *try to* **deceive** you. [NKJV]<br>I have written these things to you because you need to be aware of those who want to **lead** you **astray**. [NLT] | To lead astray; to seduce; to deceive; to be mistaken.<br><br>**Practical Application**<br>A false teacher is one who attempts to lead us away from Jesus Christ, from the glorious truth that He is the Son of God who came to earth to die for our sins. The false teacher deceives people; that is, he teaches that man can become acceptable to God by some other way than Jesus Christ. He teaches that there are other ways to God, other approaches, other religions, other truths. He seduces and leads people astray; he deceives people into following some other teaching. Note this: the tense is continuous action in the Greek. That is, false teachers are continually teaching false doctrine. They are always teaching a false doctrine and always trying to seduce people.<br>Believers must be on constant guard against false teaching. So much is at stake: the very promise of God. We will abandon the faith if we listen to the deception and go astray. We must continue to follow Christ; we must let the gospel |

## PRACTICAL WORD STUDIES
## in the NEW TESTAMENT

| ENGLISH WORD | GREEK WORD AND VERSE | THE WORD MEANS... |
|---|---|---|
| | ταῦτα ἔγραψα ὑμῖν περὶ τῶν **πλανώντων** ὑμᾶς. [GNS] <br> Ταῦτα ἔγραψα ὑμῖν περὶ τῶν **πλανώντων** ὑμᾶς. [GNT] | abide and take up a permanent residence in our lives. |
| **#911** <br> **Deceive–** <br> **Deceivers** <br><br> Deceivers–KJV <br> Deceivers–NASB <br> Deceivers–NIV <br> Deceivers–NKJV <br> Deceive–NLT <br><br> **POSB** <br> **REFERENCE** <br> (Tit.1:10-12; esp. v.10) <br> Note 1, point 3 | φρεναπάται = phrenapatai <br> Pronunciation: [fren-ap-at'-ah-ee] <br> Parsing (part of speech): noun <br>   Case—nominative <br>   Gender—masculine <br>   Number—plural <br> Stem or root—from φρεναπάτης, ου <br> Concordance References: <br> ⇒ Strong's #5423 phrenapatēs <br> ⇒ NIV #5855 phrenapatēs <br> ⇒ NASB #5423 phrenapatēs <br><br> **Titus 1:10** <br> For there are many unruly and vain talkers and **deceivers**, specially they of the circumcision: [KJV] <br> For there are many rebellious men, empty talkers and **deceivers**, especially those of the circumcision, [NASB] <br> For there are many rebellious people, mere talkers and **deceivers**, especially those of the circumcision group. [NIV] <br> For there are many insubordinate, both idle talkers and **deceivers**, especially those of the circumcision, [NKJV] <br> For there are many who rebel against right teaching; they engage in useless talk and **deceive** people. This is especially true of those who insist on circumcision for salvation. [NLT] <br> Εἰσὶ γὰρ πολλοὶ καὶ ἀνυπότακτοι, ματαιολόγοι καὶ **φρεναπάται**, μάλιστα οἱ ἐκ τῆς περιτομῆς, [GNS] <br> Εἰσὶν γὰρ πολλοὶ [καὶ] ἀνυπότακτοι, ματαιολόγοι καὶ **φρεναπάται**, μάλιστα οἱ ἐκ τῆς περιτομῆς, [GNT] | Deceiver, cheater, conniver, swindler, impostor. <br><br> **Practical Application** <br> They were *deceivers* (*phrenapatai*): "mind-deceivers" (A.T. Robertson. *Word Pictures in the New Testament*, Vol.4, p.600), misleaders. They misled themselves and misled others away from the truth. They turned away from the truth and followed error; they followed a false belief. |
| **#912** <br> **Deceived** <br><br> Deceived–KJV <br> Deceived–NASB <br> Deceived–NIV <br> Deceived–NKJV <br> Misled by others–NLT <br><br> **POSB** <br> **REFERENCE** <br> (Tit.3:3) <br> *Deeper Study* #3 <br><br> See also POSB REF: <br> (Gal.6:7-9; esp. v.7) <br> Note 2 | πλανώμενοι = planōmenoi <br> Pronunciation: [plan-o'-mehn-oy] <br> Parsing (part of speech): verb <br>   Mood—participle <br>   Tense—present <br>   Voice—passive <br>   Case—nominative <br>   Gender—masculine <br>   Person—1st person <br>   Number—plural <br> Stem or root—from πλανάω <br> Concordance References: <br> ⇒ Strong's #4105 planaō <br> ⇒ NIV #4414 planaō <br> ⇒ NASB #4105 planaō <br><br> **Titus 3:3** <br> For we ourselves also were sometimes foolish, disobedient, **deceived**, serving divers lusts and pleasures, living in malice and envy, hateful, and hating one another. [KJV] <br> For we also once were foolish ourselves, disobedient, **deceived**, enslaved to various lusts and pleasures, spending our life in malice and envy, hateful, hating one another. [NASB] <br> At one time we too were foolish, disobedient, **deceived** and enslaved by all kinds of passions and pleasures. We lived in malice and envy, being hated and hating one another. [NIV] <br> For we ourselves were also once foolish, disobedient, **deceived**, serving various lusts and pleasures, living in malice and envy, hateful and hating one another. [NKJV] <br> Once we, too, were foolish and disobedient. We were **misled by others** and became slaves to many wicked desires and evil pleasures. Our lives were full of evil and envy. We hated others, and they hated us. [NLT] <br> ἦμεν γάρ ποτε καὶ ἡμεῖς ἀνόητοι, ἀπειθεῖς, **πλανώμενοι**, δουλεύοντες ἐπιθυμίαις καὶ ἡδοναῖς | To deceive; to be misled by others; to be led astray. <br><br> **Practical Application** <br> It means to be seduced away from God and the truth and from what is right. Man is so easily led astray that Scripture pictures him as a wandering and lost sheep. He is a sheep that must be sought after, found, and saved or else he will be destroyed by the wilderness of the world—destroyed because he was deceived and led away from the eternal pasture of God. Scripture teaches that man is *seduced and led astray* by several things. <br> ⇒ Man is seduced and led astray by immoral and seductive persons. <br> ⇒ Man is seduced and led astray by false teaching and false systems of religion. <br> ⇒ Man is seduced and led astray by self. <br> ⇒ Man is seduced and led astray by Satan. <br> ⇒ Man is seduced and led astray by evil, immoral, and unjust governments and states. <br> ⇒ Man is seduced and led astray by sin. <br> Remember the point of this verse: once we were all deceived. All of us had been led astray from God. But thanks be to God our Savior. He has found us and saved us, and He will find and save any person who will turn toward Him and call out for Him. God our Savior is searching for every person, not willing that any should perish. In fact, God is with the person at all times. All the person has to do is *turn* to God and call upon Him, and God will save him. |

# PRACTICAL WORD STUDIES
## in the NEW TESTAMENT

| ENGLISH WORD | GREEK WORD AND VERSE | THE WORD MEANS... |
|---|---|---|
| | ποικίλαις, ἐν κακίᾳ καὶ φθόνῳ διάγοντες, στυγητοί, μισοῦντες ἀλλήλους. [GNS]<br>Ἦμεν γάρ ποτε καὶ ἡμεῖς ἀνόητοι, ἀπειθεῖς, **πλανώμενοι**, δουλεύοντες ἐπιθυμίαις καὶ ἡδοναῖς ποικίλαις, ἐν κακίᾳ καὶ φθόνῳ διάγοντες, στυγητοί, μισοῦντες ἀλλήλους. [GNT] | |
| **#913**<br>**Deceived, Be Not–Deceived, Do Not**<br><br>Be not deceived–KJV<br>Do not be deceived–NASB<br>Do not be misled–NIV<br>Do not be deceived–NKJV<br>Don't be fooled–NLT<br><br>**POSB REFERENCE**<br>(1 Cor.15:33)<br>Note 3 | μὴ πλανᾶσθε = mē planasthe<br>Pronunciation: [may plan-ahs'-theh]<br>Parsing *planasthe* (part of speech): verb<br>    Mood—imperative<br>    Tense—present<br>    Voice—passive<br>    Person—2nd person<br>    Number—plural<br>    Stem or root—from πλανάω<br>Concordance References:<br>⇒ Strong's #3361 mē + 4105 planaō<br>⇒ NIV #3590 mē [Do not] + 4414 planaō [be misled]<br>⇒ NASB #3361 mē + 4105 planaō<br><br>**1 Cor. 15:33**<br>**Be not deceived**: evil communications corrupt good manners. [KJV]<br>**Do not be deceived**: "Bad company corrupts good morals." [NASB]<br>**Do not be misled**: "Bad company corrupts good character." [NIV]<br>**Do not be deceived**: "Evil company corrupts good habits." [NKJV]<br>**Don't be fooled** by those who say such things, for "bad company corrupts good character." [NLT]<br>μὴ **πλανᾶσθε**· Φθείρουσιν ἤθη χρήσθ ὁμιλίαι κακαί. [GNS]<br>μὴ **πλανᾶσθε**· Φθείρουσιν ἤθη χρηστὰ ὁμιλίαι κακαί. [GNT] | Do not be misled; do not be deceived; do not be fooled; do not be led astray, led in the error of such a false teaching; do not be mistaken.<br><br>**Practical Application**<br>There is to be a resurrection of the dead. "They" who deny the resurrection are wrong. Do not be deceived by their error. It is an utterly false teaching and it is corrupting. |
| **#914**<br>**Decent and True**<br><br>Honestly–KJV<br>Properly–NASB<br>Decently–NIV<br>Properly–NKJV<br>Decent and true–NLT<br><br>**POSB REFERENCE**<br>(Rom.13:13)<br>Note 4 | εὐσχημόνως = euschēmonōs<br>Pronunciation: [yoo-skhay-mon'-oce]<br>Parsing (part of speech): adjective adverb<br>    Stem or root—from εὐσχημόνως<br>Concordance References:<br>⇒ Strong's #2156 euschēmonōs<br>⇒ NIV #2361 euschēmonōs<br>⇒ NASB #2156 euschēmonōs<br><br>**Romans 13:13**<br>Let us walk **honestly**, as in the day; not in rioting and drunkenness, not in chambering and wantonness, not in strife and envying. [KJV]<br>Let us behave **properly** as in the day, not in carousing and drunkenness, not in sexual promiscuity and sensuality, not in strife and jealousy. [NASB]<br>Let us behave **decently**, as in the daytime, not in orgies and drunkenness, not in sexual immorality and debauchery, not in dissension and jealousy. [NIV]<br>Let us walk **properly**, as in the day, not in revelry and drunkenness, not in lewdness and lust, not in strife and envy. [NKJV]<br>We should be **decent and true** in everything we do, so that everyone can approve of our behavior. Don't participate in wild parties and getting drunk, or in adultery and immoral living, or in fighting and jealousy. [NLT]<br>ὡς ἐν ἡμέρᾳ, **εὐσχημόνως** περιπατήσωμεν, μὴ κώμοις καὶ μέθαις, μὴ κοίταις καὶ ἀσελγείαις, μὴ ἔριδι καὶ ζήλῳ. [GNS]<br>ὡς ἐν ἡμέρᾳ **εὐσχημόνως** περιπατήσωμεν, μὴ κώμοις καὶ μέθαις, μὴ κοίταις καὶ ἀσελγείαις, μὴ ἔριδι καὶ ζήλῳ, [GNT] | Decently, honestly, properly; decent and true; honorable, noble, respectable.<br><br>**Practical Application**<br>The believer is to walk in honesty before God. He is to live a life of honesty, decency, and nobility. He is to live a life of honor and honesty before God. He is to walk in the day, not hiding nor trying to hide anything. This Scripture gives six sins in particular which the believer is to cast off and turn away from—forever. |

# PRACTICAL WORD STUDIES
## in the NEW TESTAMENT

| ENGLISH WORD | GREEK WORD AND VERSE | THE WORD MEANS... |
|---|---|---|
| **#915**<br>**Decently**<br><br>Honestly–KJV<br>Properly–NASB<br>**Decently–NIV**<br>Properly–NKJV<br>Decent and true–NLT<br><br>**POSB<br>REFERENCE**<br>(Rom.13:13)<br>Note 4 | εὐσχημόνως = euschēmonōs<br>Pronunciation: [yoo-skhay-mon'-oce]<br>Parsing (part of speech): adjective adverb<br>    Stem or root—from εὐσχημόνως<br>Concordance References:<br>  ⇒ Strong's #2156 euschēmonōs<br>  ⇒ NIV #2361 euschēmonōs<br>  ⇒ NASB #2156 euschēmonōs<br><br>**Romans 13:13**<br>Let us walk **honestly**, as in the day; not in rioting and drunkenness, not in chambering and wantonness, not in strife and envying. [KJV]<br>Let us behave **properly** as in the day, not in carousing and drunkenness, not in sexual promiscuity and sensuality, not in strife and jealousy. [NASB]<br>Let us behave **decently**, as in the daytime, not in orgies and drunkenness, not in sexual immorality and debauchery, not in dissension and jealousy. [NIV]<br>Let us walk **properly**, as in the day, not in revelry and drunkenness, not in lewdness and lust, not in strife and envy. [NKJV]<br>We should be **decent and true** in everything we do, so that everyone can approve of our behavior. Don't participate in wild parties and getting drunk, or in adultery and immoral living, or in fighting and jealousy. [NLT]<br>ὡς ἐν ἡμέρᾳ, **εὐσχημόνως** περιπατήσωμεν, μὴ κώμοις καὶ μέθαις, μὴ κοίταις καὶ ἀσελγείαις, μὴ ἔριδι καὶ ζήλῳ. [GNS]<br>ὡς ἐν ἡμέρᾳ **εὐσχημόνως** περιπατήσωμεν, μὴ κώμοις καὶ μέθαις, μὴ κοίταις καὶ ἀσελγείαις, μὴ ἔριδι καὶ ζήλῳ. [GNT] | Decently, honestly, properly, decent and true, honorable, noble, respectably.<br><br>**Practical Application**<br>The believer is to walk decently before God. He is to live a life of honesty, decency, and nobility. He is to live a life of honor and honesty before God. He is to walk in the day, not hiding nor trying to hide anything. This scripture gives six sins in particular which the believer is to cast off and turn from—forever. |
| **#916**<br>**Deception**<br><br>Craftiness–KJV<br>Craftiness–NASB<br>**Deception–NIV**<br>Craftiness–NKJV<br>Trick–NLT<br><br>**POSB<br>REFERENCE**<br>(2 Cor.4:2)<br>Note 2 | πανουργία = panourgia<br>Pronunciation: [pan-oorg-ee'-ah]<br>Parsing (part of speech): noun<br>    Case—dative<br>    Gender—feminine<br>    Number—singular<br>    Stem or root—from πανουργία, ας<br>Concordance References:<br>  ⇒ Strong's #3834 panourgia<br>  ⇒ NIV #4111 panourgia<br>  ⇒ NASB #3834 panourgia<br><br>**2 Cor. 4:2**<br>But have renounced the hidden things of dishonesty, not walking in **craftiness**, nor handling the word of God deceitfully; but by manifestation of the truth commending ourselves to every man's conscience in the sight of God. [KJV]<br>But we have renounced the things hidden because of shame, not walking in **craftiness** or adulterating the word of God, but by the manifestation of truth commending ourselves to every man's conscience in the sight of God. [NASB]<br>Rather, we have renounced secret and shameful ways; we do not use **deception**, nor do we distort the word of God. On the contrary, by setting forth the truth plainly we commend ourselves to every man's conscience in the sight of God. [NIV]<br>But we have renounced the hidden things of shame, not walking in **craftiness** nor handling the word of God deceitfully, but by manifestation of the truth commending ourselves to every man's conscience in the sight of God. [NKJV]<br>We reject all shameful and underhanded methods. We do not try to **trick** anyone, and we do not distort the word of God. We tell the truth before God, and all who are honest know that. [NLT]<br>ἀλλ᾽ ἀπειπάμεθα τὰ κρυπτὰ τῆς αἰσχύνης, μὴ περιπατοῦντες ἐν **πανουργίᾳ** μηδὲ δολοῦντες τὸν λόγον τοῦ Θεοῦ, ἀλλὰ τῇ φανερώσει τῆς ἀληθείας συνιστῶντες ἑαυτοὺς πρὸς πᾶσαν συνείδησιν ἀνθρώπων ἐνώπιον τοῦ | Deception, craftiness, trickery, cunning, cleverness, shrewdness, evil design. It means a man who will do anything and use any means to get what he wants.<br><br>**Practical Application**<br>Note the believer is not to "walk" this way; he is not to walk using and misusing people, circumstances, events, and things for his own end. The believer is to walk as Jesus walked. |

# PRACTICAL WORD STUDIES
## in the NEW TESTAMENT

| ENGLISH WORD | GREEK WORD AND VERSE | THE WORD MEANS... |
|---|---|---|
| | Θεοῦ. [GNS]<br>ἀλλὰ ἀπειπάμεθα τὰ κρυπτὰ τῆς αἰσχύνης, μὴ περιπατοῦντες ἐν **πανουργίᾳ** μηδὲ δολοῦντες τὸν λόγον τοῦ θεοῦ ἀλλὰ τῇ φανερώσει τῆς ἀληθείας συνιστάνοντες ἑαυτοὺς πρὸς πᾶσαν συνείδησιν ἀνθρώπων ἐνώπιον τοῦ θεοῦ. [GNT] | |
| #917<br>**Decided**<br><br>Took counsel–KJV<br>Intending–NASB<br>Wanted–NIV<br>Plotted–NKJV<br>**Decided–NLT**<br><br>**POSB REFERENCE**<br>(Acts 5:32-40; esp. v.33)<br>Note 4, point 1 | ἐβούλοντο = *eboulonto*<br>Pronunciation: [eh-bool-on-tow]<br>Parsing (part of speech): verb<br>  Mood—indicative<br>  Tense—imperfect<br>  Voice—middle or passive deponent<br>  Person—3rd person<br>  Number—plural<br>  Stem or root—from βούλομαι<br>Concordance References:<br> ⇒ Strong's #1014 boulomai<br> ⇒ NIV #1089 boulomai<br> ⇒ NASB #1014 boulomai<br><br>**Acts 5:33**<br>When they heard that, they were cut to the heart, and **took counsel** to slay them. [KJV]<br>But when they heard this, they were cut to the quick and were **intending** to slay them. [NASB]<br>When they heard this, they were furious and **wanted** to put them to death. [NIV]<br>When they heard *this*, they were furious and **plotted** to kill them. [NKJV]<br>At this, the high council was furious and **decided** to kill them. [NLT]<br>Οἱ δὲ ἀκούσαντες διεπρίοντο, καὶ **ἐβούλοντο** ἀνελεῖν αὐτούς. [GNS]<br>Οἱ δὲ ἀκούσαντες διεπρίοντο καὶ **ἐβούλοντο** ἀνελεῖν αὐτούς. [GNT] | To want; to take counsel; to intend; to decide; to wish; to plan.<br><br>**Practical Application**<br>They were minded, were intending; were set on killing the disciples. |
| #918<br>**Declare**<br><br>**Declare–KJV**<br>Instruction–NASB<br>Directives–NIV<br>Instructions–NKJV<br>Mention–NLT<br><br>**POSB REFERENCE**<br>(1 Cor.11:17)<br>Note 1 | παραγγέλλων = *paraggellōn*<br>Pronunciation: [par-ang-gel'-lone]<br>Parsing (part of speech): verb<br>  Mood—participle<br>  Tense—present<br>  Voice—active<br>  Case—nominative<br>  Gender—masculine<br>  Person—1st person<br>  Number—singular<br>  Stem or root—from παραγγέλλω<br>Concordance References:<br> ⇒ Strong's #3853 paraggellō<br> ⇒ NIV #4133 paraggellō<br> ⇒ NASB #3853 paraggellō<br><br>**1 Cor. 11:17**<br>Now in this that I **declare** unto you I praise you not, that ye come together not for the better, but for the worse. [KJV]<br>But in giving this **instruction**, I do not praise you, because you come together not for the better but for the worse. [NASB]<br>In the following **directives** I have no praise for you, for your meetings do more harm than good. [NIV]<br>Now in giving these **instructions** I do not praise *you*, since you come together not for the better but for the worse. [NKJV]<br>But now when I **mention** this next issue, I cannot praise you. For it sounds as if more harm than good is done when you meet together. [NLT]<br>Τοῦτο δὲ **παραγγέλλων** οὐκ ἐπαινῶ, ὅτι οὐκ εἰς τὸ κρεῖττον ἀλλ' εἰς τὸ ἧττον συνέρχεσθε. [GNS]<br>Τοῦτο δὲ **παραγγέλλων** οὐκ ἐπαινῶ ὅτι οὐκ εἰς τὸ κρεῖσσον ἀλλὰ εἰς τὸ ἧσσον συνέρχεσθε. [GNT] | To command; to give strict orders; to give instructions; to charge.<br><br>**Practical Application**<br>Note how forceful Paul is: "I declare (*paraggellōn*) unto you I praise you not." His forcefulness stresses the awesome importance of the Lord's Supper, and the absolute necessity to celebrate it as it should be celebrated. |

## Practical Word Studies in the New Testament

| ENGLISH WORD | GREEK WORD AND VERSE | THE WORD MEANS... |
|---|---|---|
| **#919**<br>**Declare**<br><br>Declare–KJV<br>Make known–NASB<br>Remind–NIV<br>Declare–NKJV<br>Remind–NLT<br><br>**POSB REFERENCE**<br>(1 Cor.15:1-2; esp. v.1)<br>Note 1 | Γνωρίζω = Gnörizö<br>Pronunciation: [gno-rid'-zo]<br>Parsing (part of speech): verb<br>    Mood—indicative<br>    Tense—present<br>    Voice—active<br>    Person—1st person<br>    Number—singular<br>    Stem or root—from γνωρίζω<br>Concordance References:<br>⇒ Strong's #1107 gnörizö<br>⇒ NIV #1192 gnörizö<br>⇒ NASB #1107 gnörizö<br><br>**1 Cor. 15:1**<br>Moreover, brethren, I **declare** unto you the gospel which I preached unto you, which also ye have received, and wherein ye stand; [KJV]<br>Now I **make known** to you, brethren, the gospel which I preached to you, which also you received, in which also you stand, [NASB]<br>Now, brothers, I want to **remind** you of the gospel I preached to you, which you received and on which you have taken your stand. [NIV]<br>Moreover, brethren, I **declare** to you the gospel which I preached to you, which also you received and in which you stand, [NKJV]<br>Now let me **remind** you, dear brothers and sisters, of the Good News I preached to you before. You welcomed it then and still do now, for your faith is built on this wonderful message. [NLT]<br>Γνωρίζω δὲ ὑμῖν, ἀδελφοί, τὸ εὐαγγέλιον ὃ εὐηγγελισάμην ὑμῖν, ὃ καὶ παρελάβετε, ἐν ᾧ καὶ ἑστήκατε, [GNS]<br>Γνωρίζω δὲ ὑμῖν, ἀδελφοί, τὸ εὐαγγέλιον ὃ εὐηγγελισάμην ὑμῖν, ὃ καὶ παρελάβετε, ἐν ᾧ καὶ ἑστήκατε, [GNT] | To remind; to declare; to tell; to present; to make known.<br><br>**Practical Application**<br>Paul is not reminding the Corinthians of the gospel, he is...<br>• declaring it as though they had never heard it.<br>• proclaiming it as though they had never sat before it.<br>• making it known as though they had never known it. |
| **#920**<br>**Declare, That**<br><br>Show forth–KJV<br>Proclaim–NASB<br>That...declare–NIV<br>Proclaim–NKJV<br>Show–NLT<br><br>**POSB REFERENCE**<br>(1 Pt.2:9)<br>Note 2 | ὅπως ἐξαγγείλητε = hopös exaggeilëte<br>Pronunciation: [hop'-oce ex-ang-eel'-lay-teh]<br>Parsing *exaggeilëte* (part of speech): verb<br>    Mood—subjunctive<br>    Tense—aorist<br>    Voice—active<br>    Person—2nd person<br>    Number—plural<br>    Stem or root—from ἐξαγγέλλω<br>Concordance References:<br>⇒ Strong's #3704 hopös + 1804 exaggellö<br>⇒ NIV #3968 hopös [that] + 1972 exaggellö [declare]<br>⇒ NASB #3704 hopös + 1804 exaggellö<br><br>**1 Peter 2:9**<br>But ye are a chosen generation, a royal priesthood, an holy nation, a peculiar people; that ye should **show forth** the praises of him who hath called you out of darkness into his marvellous light: [KJV]<br>But you are a chosen race, a royal priesthood, a HOLY NATION, a people for God's own possession, that you may **proclaim** the excellencies of Him who has called you out of darkness into His marvelous light; [NASB]<br>But you are a chosen people, a royal priesthood, a holy nation, a people belonging to God, **that** you may **declare** the praises of him who called you out of darkness into his wonderful light. [NIV]<br>But you *are* a chosen generation, a royal priesthood, a holy nation, His own special people, that you may **proclaim** the praises of Him who called you out of darkness into His marvelous light; [NKJV]<br>But you are not like that, for you are a chosen people. You are a kingdom of priests, God's holy nation, his very | To declare; to show forth; to proclaim; to speak; to tell; to publish; to set forth.<br><br>**Practical Application**<br>The very task of the believer is to witness for God, to share the glorious message of God. What is that message? The message that we are to share is the glorious message of salvation. God will deliver man out of darkness into the light. This is what He has done for believers. Therefore, we are to proclaim the glorious truth that God has saved us through the Light of the world, through Jesus Christ Himself. He has saved us out of the darkness of sin and death and delivered us into the light of eternity. We shall live forever. We are to praise God, proclaim the glorious message of His marvelous light or salvation. |

# PRACTICAL WORD STUDIES
## in the NEW TESTAMENT

| ENGLISH WORD | GREEK WORD AND VERSE | THE WORD MEANS... |
|---|---|---|
| | own possession. This is so you can **show** others the goodness of God, for he called you out of the darkness into his wonderful light. [NLT]<br><br>ὑμεῖς δὲ γένος ἐκλεκτόν, βασίλειον ἱεράτευμα, ἔθνος ἅγιον, λαὸς εἰς περιποίησιν, **ὅπως** τὰς ἀρετὰς **ἐξαγγείλητε** τοῦ ἐκ σκότους ὑμᾶς καλέσαντος εἰς τὸ θαυμαστὸν αὐτοῦ φῶς [GNS]·<br><br>Ὑμεῖς δὲ γένος ἐκλεκτόν, βασίλειον ἱεράτευμα, ἔθνος ἅγιον, λαὸς εἰς περιποίησιν, **ὅπως** τὰς ἀρετὰς **ἐξαγγείλητε** τοῦ ἐκ σκότους ὑμᾶς καλέσαντος εἰς τὸ θαυμαστὸν αὐτοῦ φῶς· [GNT] | |
| **#921**<br>**Declared**<br><br>Imputeth–KJV<br>Reckons–NASB<br>Credits–NIV<br>Imputes–NKJV<br>**Declared–NLT**<br><br>**POSB REFERENCE**<br>(Romans 4:6-8; esp. v.6)<br>Note 3, point 1 | λογίζεται = logizetai<br>Pronunciation: [log-id'-zeh-ahee]<br>Parsing (part of speech): verb<br>  Mood—indicative<br>  Tense—present<br>  Voice—middle or passive deponent<br>  Person—3rd person<br>  Number—singular<br>  Stem or root—from λογίζομαι<br>Concordance References:<br>  ⇒ Strong's #3049 logizomai<br>  ⇒ NIV #3357 logizomai<br>  ⇒ NASB #3049 logizomai<br><br>**Romans 4:6**<br>Even as David also describeth the blessedness of the man, unto whom God **imputeth** righteousness without works, [KJV]<br>Just as David also speaks of the blessing upon the man to whom God **reckons** righteousness apart from works: [NASB]<br>David says the same thing when he speaks of the blessedness of the man to whom God **credits** righteousness apart from works: [NIV]<br>Just as David also describes the blessedness of the man to whom God **imputes** righteousness apart from orks: [NKJV]<br>King David spoke of this, describing the happiness of an undeserving sinner who is **declared** to be righteous: [NLT]<br><br>καθάπερ καὶ Δαβὶδ λέγει τὸν μακαρισμὸν τοῦ ἀνθρώπου, ᾧ ὁ Θεὸς **λογίζεται** δικαιοσύνην χωρὶς ἔργων, [GNS]<br>καθάπερ καὶ Δαυὶδ λέγει τὸν μακαρισμὸν τοῦ ἀνθρώπου ᾧ ὁ θεὸς **λογίζεται** δικαιοσύνην χωρὶς ἔργων, [GNT] | To credit; to impute; to reckon; to declare; to count; to put to one's account; to credit; to deposit.<br><br>**Practical Application**<br>The blessed man is the man who is counted righteous without works. Just think for a moment. If God credits and counts a man righteous "without works," then we know something: Man is not justified by works, but by faith. (See POSB *Deeper Study* #1, Reckon—Romans 6:11 for more discussion.) |
| **#922**<br>**Declared**<br><br>Reckoned–KJV<br>Reckoned–NASBR<br>Credited–NIV<br>Accounted–NKJV<br>**Declared–NLT**<br><br>**POSB REFERENCE**<br>(Romans 4:9)<br>Note 2 | Ἐλογίσθη = elogisthë<br>Pronunciation: [eh-log-ees'-thay]<br>Parsing (part of speech): verb<br>  Mood—indicative<br>  Tense—aorist<br>  Voice—passive<br>  Person—3rd person<br>  Number—singular<br>  Stem or root—from λογίζομαι<br>Concordance References:<br>  ⇒ Strong's #3049 logizomai<br>  ⇒ NIV #3357 logizomai<br>  ⇒ NASB #3049 logizomai<br><br>**Romans 4:9**<br>Cometh this blessedness then upon the circumcision only, or upon the uncircumcision also? for we say that faith was **reckoned** to Abraham for righteousness. [KJV]<br>Is this blessing then upon the circumcised, or upon the uncircumcised also? For we say, "Faith was **reckoned** to Abraham as righteousness." [NASB]<br>Is this blessedness only for the circumcised, or also for the uncircumcised? We have been saying that Abraham's faith was **credited** to him as righteousness. [NIV] | Credited, reckoned, declared; to count; to deposit; to put to one's account; to impute; to consider; to evaluate; to calculate.<br><br>**Practical Application**<br>Abraham's faith was counted for righteousness or declared as righteous (see POSB note, Justification—Romans 4:1-3; POSB note—Romans 4:6-8; POSB *Deeper Study* #1—Romans 4:22; POSB *Deeper Study* #2—Romans 4:22; POSB note—Romans 5:1 for more discussion).<br>Note that Abraham was justified or counted righteous by faith; he was not justified...<br>• by being religious.<br>• by performing good deeds.<br>• by doing some good work.<br>• by being good and virtuous.<br>• by submitting to a ritual.<br>• by joining some body of believers. |

# PRACTICAL WORD STUDIES
## in the NEW TESTAMENT

| ENGLISH WORD | GREEK WORD AND VERSE | THE WORD MEANS... |
|---|---|---|
| | *Does* this blessedness then *come* upon the circumcised *only*, or upon the uncircumcised also? For we say that faith was **accounted** to Abraham for righteousness. [NKJV]<br><br>Now then, is this blessing only for the Jews, or is it for Gentiles, too? Well, what about Abraham? We have been saying he was **declared** righteous by God because of his faith. [NLT]<br><br>ὁ μακαρισμὸς οὖν οὗτος ἐπὶ τὴν περιτομὴν η καὶ ἐπὶ τὴν ἀκροβυστίαν; λέγομεν γάρ ὅτι **Ἐλογίσθη** τῷ Ἀβραὰμ ἡ πίστις εἰς δικαιοσύνην. [GNS]<br><br>ὁ μακαρισμὸς οὖν οὗτος ἐπὶ τὴν περιτομὴν η καὶ ἐπὶ τὴν ἀκροβυστίαν; λέγομεν γάρ, **Ἐλογίσθη** τῷ Ἀβραὰμ ἡ πίστις εἰς δικαιοσύνην. [GNT] | |
| #923<br>**Declared**<br><br>Imputed–KJV<br>Reckoned–NASB<br>Credited–NIV<br>Accounted–NKJV<br>**Declared–NLT**<br><br>**POSB REFERENCE**<br>(Romans 4:22)<br>*Deeper Study #1* | ἐλογίσθη = *elogisthë*<br>Pronunciation: [eh-log-ees'-thay]<br>Parsing (part of speech): verb<br>  Mood—indicative<br>  Tense—aorist<br>  Voice—passive<br>  Person—3rd person<br>  Number—singular<br>  Stem or root—from λογίζομαι<br>Concordance References:<br>  ⇒ Strong's #3049 logizomai<br>  ⇒ NIV #3357 logizomai<br>  ⇒ NASB #3049 logizomai<br><br>**Romans 4:22**<br>And therefore it was **imputed** to him for righteousness. [KJV]<br><br>Therefore also it was **reckoned** to him as righteousness. [NASB]<br><br>This is why "it was **credited** to him as righteousness." [NIV]<br><br>And therefore "it was **accounted** to him for righteousness." [NKJV]<br><br>And because of Abraham's faith, God **declared** him to be righteous. [NLT]<br><br>διὸ καὶ **ἐλογίσθη** αὐτῷ εἰς δικαιοσύνην. [GNS]<br>διὸ [καὶ] **ἐλογίσθη** αὐτῷ εἰς δικαιοσύνην. [GNT] | To credit; to impute; to reckon; to declare; to count; to compute; to ascribe; to deposit; to put to one's account; to calculate.<br><br>**Practical Application**<br>Abraham's faith was declared to be righteous. (See *Deeper Study #1*, Reckon—Romans 6:11 for a fuller discussion.) Abraham deposited his faith with God, and God credited Abraham's faith as righteousness. |
| #924<br>**Declared**<br><br>Testifying–KJV<br>Testifying–NASB<br>**Declared–NIV**<br>Testifying–NKJV<br>Message–NLT<br><br>**POSB REFERENCE**<br>(Acts 20:20-21; esp. v.21)<br>Note 3, point 3 | διαμαρτυρόμενος = *diamarturomenos*<br>Pronunciation: [dee-am-ar-too'-rom-ehn-os]<br>Parsing (part of speech): verb<br>  Mood—participle<br>  Tense—present<br>  Voice—middle or passive deponent<br>  Case—nominative<br>  Gender—masculine<br>  Person—1st person<br>  Number—singular<br>  Stem or root—from διαμαρτύρομαι<br>Concordance References:<br>  ⇒ Strong's #1263 diamarturomai<br>  ⇒ NIV #1371 diamarturomai<br>  ⇒ NASB #1263 diamarturomai<br><br>**Acts 20:21**<br>**Testifying** both to the Jews, and also to the Greeks, repentance toward God, and faith toward our Lord Jesus Christ. [KJV]<br><br>solemnly **testifying** to both Jews and Greeks of repentance toward God and faith in our Lord Jesus Christ. [NASB]<br><br>I have **declared** to both Jews and Greeks that they must turn to God in repentance and have faith in our Lord Jesus. [NIV]<br><br>**Testifying** to Jews, and also to Greeks, repentance toward God and faith toward our Lord Jesus Christ. [NKJV]<br><br>I have had one **message** for Jews and Gentiles alike— | To declare; to testify; to warn; to give a strong, sobering message.<br><br>**Practical Application**<br>Paul taught powerfully, as a man under oath. This is seen in the word "declared" (*diamarturomenos*). He proclaimed the truth as a man of truth. He spoke with authority, as one who had the right of God Himself to testify. |

## Practical Word Studies in the New Testament

| ENGLISH WORD | GREEK WORD AND VERSE | THE WORD MEANS... |
|---|---|---|
| | the necessity of turning from sin and turning to God, and of faith in our Lord Jesus. [NLT]<br>**διαμαρτυρόμενος** Ἰουδαίοις τε καὶ Ἕλλησι τὴν εἰς Θεὸν μετάνοιαν καὶ τὴν πίστιν τὴν εἰς τὸν Κύριον ἡμῶν Ἰησοῦν Χριστόν. [GNS]<br>**διαμαρτυρόμενος** Ἰουδαίοις τε καὶ Ἕλλησιν τὴν εἰς θεὸν μετάνοιαν καὶ πίστιν εἰς τὸν κύριον ἡμῶν Ἰησοῦν. [GNT] | |
| **#925**<br>**Deeds**<br><br>Deeds–KJV<br>Deeds–NASB<br>Done–NIV<br>Deeds–NKJV<br>Done–NLT<br><br>**POSB REFERENCE**<br>(Rom.2:6-10; esp. v.6)<br>Note 3 | **ἔργα** = *erga*<br>Pronunciation: [er'-gah]<br>Parsing (part of speech): noun<br>    Case—accusative<br>    Gender—neuter<br>    Number—plural<br>    Stem or root—from ἔργον, ου<br>Concordance References:<br>⇒ Strong's #2041 ergon<br>⇒ NIV #2240 ergon<br>⇒ NASB #2041 ergon<br><br>**Romans 2:6**<br>Who will render to every man according to his **deeds**: [KJV]<br>WHO WILL RENDER TO EVERY MAN ACCORDING TO HIS DEEDS: [NASB]<br>God "will give to each person according to what he has **done**." [NIV]<br>Who *"will render to each one according to his deeds"*: [NKJV]<br>Will judge all people according to what they have **done**. [NLT]<br>ὃς ἀποδώσει ἑκάστῳ κατὰ τὰ **ἔργα** αὐτοῦ· [GNS]<br>ὃς ἀποδώσει ἑκάστῳ κατὰ τὰ **ἔργα** αὐτοῦ· [GNT] | Work, deed, action, task, occupation, undertaking, practical expression, handiwork, workmanship.<br><br>**Practical Application**<br>The judgment of God—of the only living and true God—is according to deeds (Proverbs 24:12; 2 Tim. 4:14; cp. Matthew 16:27; Rev. 22:12), and it will be universal. Every one will be either eternally rewarded or eternally punished. No one will be exempt; no one will escape.<br>Now note: judgment is to be based upon a man's "deeds" (*erga*) or works. This does not mean that faith is not necessary. Contrariwise, there is no such thing as...<br>• faith without works.<br>• righteous and acceptable works without faith. |
| **#926**<br>**Deeds Of Kindness**<br><br>Good works–KJV<br>Deeds of kindness–NASB<br>Doing good–NIV<br>Good works–NKJV<br>Doing kind things–NLT<br><br>**POSB REFERENCE**<br>(Acts 9:36-39; esp. v.36)<br>Note 2, point 1b | **ἔργων ἀγαθῶν** = *ergōn agathōn*<br>Pronunciation: [er'-gon ag-ath-on']<br>Parsing *ergōn* (part of speech): noun<br>    Case—genitive<br>    Gender—neuter<br>    Number—plural<br>    Stem or root—from ἔργον, ου<br>Parsing *agathōn* (part of speech): adjective<br>    Case—genitive<br>    Gender—neuter<br>    Number—plural<br>    Stem or root—from ἀγαθός, ή, όν<br>Concordance References:<br>⇒ Strong's #2041 ergon + 18 agathos<br>⇒ NIV #2240 ergon [doing] + 19 agathos [good]<br>⇒ NASB #2041 ergon + 18 agathos<br><br>**Acts 9:36**<br>Now there was at Joppa a certain disciple named Tabitha, which by interpretation is called Dorcas: this woman was full of **good works** and almsdeeds which she did. [KJV]<br>Now in Joppa there was a certain disciple named Tabitha (which translated in Greek is called Dorcas); this woman was abounding with **deeds of kindness** and charity, which she continually did. [NASB]<br>In Joppa there was a disciple named Tabitha (which, when translated, is Dorcas), who was always **doing good** and helping the poor. [NIV]<br>At Joppa there was a certain disciple named Tabitha, which is translated Dorcas. This woman was full of **good works** and charitable deeds which she did. [NKJV]<br>There was a believer in Joppa named Tabitha (which in Greek is Dorcas). She was always **doing kind things** for others and helping the poor. [NLT]<br>Ἐν Ἰόππῃ δέ τις ἦν μαθήτρια ὀνόματι Ταβιθά, ἣ διερμηνευομένη λέγεται Δορκάς· αὕτη ἦν πλήρης **ἀγαθῶν** | Work, deed, action; task, occupation, undertaking; practical expression; handiwork, workmanship (1 Cor 9.1); perhaps effect, result or product (Jas 1.4). It is a general term meaning all kinds of good works, serving and doing all kinds of good to all who needed help.<br><br>**Practical Application**<br>Two names are given for her: "Tabitha," which was her Jewish or Hebrew name, and "Dorcas," which was her Greek name. Her name means gazelle (or doe or deer) which is a most beautiful creature. The gazelle is known for...<br>• its slender features.<br>• its grace and loveliness.<br>• its bright eyes and tender looks.<br>The same traits were apparently characteristic of Dorcas. Note: Scripture does say the wife is to be as the loving hind and the graceful doe to her husband (Proverbs 5:19). She is to be as the beautiful creature: gracious and loving, bright eyed (joyful, excited, expectant) and tender.<br>She was deeply committed to Christ, a very faithful and devoted disciple, full of...<br>• "deeds of kindness" (*ergōn agathōn*)<br>• "charity": charitable gifts. She gave gifts to the needy. |

# PRACTICAL WORD STUDIES
## in the New Testament

| ENGLISH WORD | GREEK WORD AND VERSE | THE WORD MEANS... |
|---|---|---|
| | ἔργων καὶ ἐλεημοσυνῶν ὧν ἐποίει. [GNS]<br>Ἐν Ἰόππῃ δέ τις ἦν μαθήτρια ὀνόματι Ταβιθά, ἣ διερμηνευομένη λέγεται Δορκάς· αὕτη ἦν πλήρης **ἔργων ἀγαθῶν** καὶ ἐλεημοσυνῶν ὧν ἐποίει. [GNT] | |
| **#927**<br>**Deep–Deeply**<br><br>Fervent–KJV<br>Fervent–NASB<br>**Deeply–NIV**<br>Fervent–NKJV<br>**Deep–NLT**<br><br>**POSB REFERENCE**<br>(1 Pt.4:8)<br>Note 3 | ἐκτενή = *ektenë*<br>Pronunciation: [ek-ten-ay']<br>Parsing (part of speech): adjective<br>    Case—accusative<br>    Gender—feminine<br>    Number—singular<br>    Stem or root—from ἐκτενής, ές<br>Concordance References:<br>  ⇒ Strong's #1618 ektenës<br>  ⇒ NIV #1756 ektenës<br>  ⇒ NASB #1618 ektenës<br><br>**1 Peter 4:8**<br>And above all things have **fervent** charity among yourselves: for charity shall cover the multitude of sins. [KJV]<br>Above all, keep **fervent** in your love for one another, because love covers a multitude of sins. [NASB]<br>Above all, love each other **deeply**, because love covers over a multitude of sins. [NIV]<br>And above all things have **fervent** love for one another, for *"love will cover a multitude of sins."* [NKJV]<br>Most important of all, continue to show **deep** love for each other, for love covers a multitude of sins. [NLT]<br>πρὸ πάντων δὲ τὴν εἰς ἑαυτοὺς ἀγάπην **ἐκτενή** ἔχοντες, ὅτι ἀγάπη καλύψει πλῆθος ἁμαρτιῶν. [GNS]<br>πρὸ πάντων τὴν εἰς ἑαυτοὺς ἀγάπην **ἐκτενή** ἔχοντες, ὅτι ἀγάπη καλύπτει πλῆθος ἁμαρτιῶν. [GNT] | Deep, fervent, unfailing, constant.<br><br>**Practical Application**<br>The word (*ektenë*) is an athletic word. It means to stretch and reach out; to strain and exert to the utmost degree just like an athlete in a race. It has the idea of burning and boiling and of being passionate about loving one's brother in Christ. Note how a deep or fervent love is far more than the human love of warm feelings and attraction. It is far more than sentimental and caring feelings for a person.<br>    The believer is to love with the ultimate love, the love of fervency. And note: deep or fervent love is to be put before all else. It is the most important duty of the believer. We are to strain every ounce of energy in our minds and hearts to love. |
| **#928**<br>**Deep Grief**<br><br>Be afflicted–KJV<br>Be miserable–NASB<br>Grieve–NIV<br>Lament–NKJV<br>**Deep grief–NLT**<br><br>**POSB REFERENCE**<br>(Jas 4:9)<br>Note 3 | ταλαιπωρήσατε = *talaipörësate*<br>Pronunciation: [tal-ahee-po-ray'-sah-teh]<br>Parsing (part of speech): verb<br>    Mood—imperative<br>    Tense—aorist<br>    Voice—active<br>    Person—2nd person<br>    Number—plural<br>    Stem or root—from ταλαιπωρέω<br>Concordance References:<br>  ⇒ Strong's #5003 talaipöreö<br>  ⇒ NIV #5415 talaipöreö<br>  ⇒ NASB #5003 talaipöreö<br><br>**James 4:9**<br>**Be afflicted**, and mourn, and weep: let your laughter be turned to mourning, and your joy to heaviness. [KJV]<br>**Be miserable** and mourn and weep; let your laughter be turned into mourning, and your joy to gloom. [NASB]<br>**Grieve**, mourn and wail. Change your laughter to mourning and your joy to gloom. [NIV]<br>**Lament** and mourn and weep! Let your laughter be turned to mourning and *your* joy to gloom. [NKJV]<br>Let there be tears for the wrong things you have done. Let there be sorrow and **deep grief**. Let there be sadness instead of laughter, and gloom instead of joy. [NLT]<br>ταλαιπωρήσατε καὶ πενθήσατε καὶ κλαύσατε· ὁ γέλως ὑμῶν εἰς πένθος μετατραπήτω, καὶ ἡ χαρὰ εἰς κατήφειαν. [GNS]<br>ταλαιπωρήσατε καὶ πενθήσατε καὶ κλαύσατε. ὁ γέλως ὑμῶν εἰς πένθος μετατραπήτω καὶ ἡ χαρὰ εἰς κατήφειαν. [GNT] | To grieve; to be afflicted; to be miserable; to lament; to suffer deep grief; to endure toils (A.T. Robertson. *Word Pictures in the New Testament*, Vol. 6, p.53); to discipline and to voluntarily abstain (William Barclay. *The Letters of James and Peter*, p.127).<br><br>**Practical Application**<br>The picture is this: when temptation strikes us, it is not time...<br>• to be laughing<br>• to be joking around<br>• to be lighthearted<br>• to be complacent<br>• to be at ease<br>• to be jolly<br>• to be teasing<br>• to be unconcerned<br>• to be uncomfortable<br>• to be lying around<br><br>Temptation is affliction; therefore, it is time to be disciplined and to control the comforts and joys of life. Temptation is a time for rigorous warfare—for battle and the discipline and endurance of battle. |
| **#929**<br>**Deeply**<br><br>Fervently–KJV<br>Fervently–NASB<br>**Deeply–NIV**<br>Fervently–NKJV<br>Intensely–NLT | ἐκτενῶς = *ektenös*<br>Pronunciation: [ek-ten-oce']<br>Parsing (part of speech): adjective adverb<br>    Stem or root—from ἐκτενῶς<br>Concordance References:<br>  ⇒ Strong's #1617 ektenös<br>  ⇒ NIV #1757 ektenös<br>  ⇒ NASB #1617 ektenös | Deeply, fervently, intensely, constantly, earnestly.<br><br>**Practical Application**<br>The word (*ektenös*) "does not mean 'with warmth' but rather 'with full intensity'." It liter- |

## PRACTICAL WORD STUDIES
### in the NEW TESTAMENT

| ENGLISH WORD | GREEK WORD AND VERSE | THE WORD MEANS... |
|---|---|---|
| **POSB REFERENCE** (1 Pt.1:22-25; esp. v.22) Note 1 | **1 Peter 1:22** Seeing ye have purified your souls in obeying the truth through the Spirit unto unfeigned love of the brethren, see that ye love one another with a pure heart **fervently**: [KJV] Since you have in obedience to the truth purified your souls for a sincere love of the brethren, **fervently** love one another from the heart, [NASB] Now that you have purified yourselves by obeying the truth so that you have sincere love for your brothers, love one another **deeply**, from the heart. [NIV] Since you have purified your souls in obeying the truth through the Spirit in sincere love of the brethren, love one another **fervently** with a pure heart, [NKJV] Now you can have sincere love for each other as brothers and sisters because you were cleansed from your sins when you accepted the truth of the Good News. So see to it that you really do love each other **intensely** with all your hearts. [NLT] τὰς ψυχὰς ὑμῶν ἡγνικότες ἐν τῇ ὑπακοῇ τῆς ἀληθείας διὰ Πνεύματος εἰς φιλαδελφίαν ἀνυπόκριτον, ἐκ καθαρᾶς καρδίας ἀλλήλους ἀγαπήσατε **ἐκτενῶς**· [GNS] Τὰς ψυχὰς ὑμῶν ἡγνικότες ἐν τῇ ὑπακοῇ τῆς ἀληθείας εἰς φιλαδελφίαν ἀνυπόκριτον, ἐκ [καθαρᾶς] καρδίας ἀλλήλους ἀγαπήσατε **ἐκτενῶς** [GNT] | ally means to *stretch love fully out* or to love one another *in an all out manner* (Alan M. Stibbs. *The First Epistle General of Peter.* "The Tyndale New Testament Commentaries," p.94). |
| **#930 Deeply Moved** Groaned–KJV **Deeply moved–NASB Deeply moved–NIV** Groaned–NKJV Moved–NLT **POSB REFERENCE** (Jn.11:33-36; esp. v.33) Note 5, point 1 | ἐνεβριμήσατο = enebrimēsato Pronunciation: [en-eh-brim-ay'-sah-tow] Parsing (part of speech): verb     Mood—indicative     Tense—aorist     Voice—middle deponent     Person—3rd person     Number—singular     Stem or root—from ἐμβριμάομαι Concordance References: ⇒ Strong's #1690 embrimaomai ⇒ NIV #1839 embrimaomai ⇒ NASB #1690 embrimaomai **John 11:33** When Jesus therefore saw her weeping, and the Jews also weeping which came with her, he **groaned** in the spirit, and was troubled, [KJV] When Jesus therefore saw her weeping, and the Jews who came with her, also weeping, He was **deeply moved** in spirit, and was troubled, [NASB] When Jesus saw her weeping, and the Jews who had come along with her also weeping, he was **deeply moved** in spirit and troubled. [NIV] Therefore, when Jesus saw her weeping, and the Jews who came with her weeping, He **groaned** in the spirit and was troubled. [NKJV] When Jesus saw her weeping and saw the other people wailing with her, he was **moved** with indignation and was deeply troubled. [NLT] Ἰησοῦς οὖν ὡς εἶδεν αὐτὴν κλαίουσαν, καὶ τοὺς συνελθόντας αὐτῇ Ἰουδαίους κλαίοντας, **ἐνεβριμήσατο** τῷ πνεύματι, καὶ ἐτάραξεν ἑαυτόν, [GNS] Ἰησοῦς οὖν ὡς εἶδεν αὐτὴν κλαίουσαν καὶ τοὺς συνελθόντας αὐτῇ Ἰουδαίους κλαίοντας, **ἐνεβριμήσατο** τῷ πνεύματι καὶ ἐτάραξεν ἑαυτόν· [GNT] | To be deeply moved; to groan in the spirit; to be agitated by grief and sorrow. **Practical Application** Jesus is deeply moved in understanding and feeling and compassion for all who are hurting and suffering. In this Scripture, we see Jesus gripped with intense emotion. He was deeply moved... • by Mary, who was so broken in sorrow. • by Martha, who was gripped by pain and hurt. • by those who were really feeling the death of Lazarus and the sorrow of the family. • by the terrible tragedy of death and the pain it causes. • by the terrible price He was soon to pay conquering death. (This was certainly glimpsed by Jesus in such a scene as He was now experiencing.) |
| **#931 Deeply Troubled** Stirred–KJV Provoked–NASB | παρωξύνετο = parōxuneto Pronunciation: [par-ox-oo'-neh-tow] Parsing (part of speech): verb     Mood—indicative     Tense—imperfect     Voice—passive     Person—3rd person     Number—singular     Stem or root—from παροξύνομαι | To be greatly distressed; to be stirred; to be provoked; to be deeply troubled; to be aroused; to be agitated; to be irritated; to be greatly upset. **Practical Application** Paul in Athens, the great intellectual and cultural center of the world. Paul was alone, and no doubt he did as anyone would do–he toured the |

# PRACTICAL WORD STUDIES
## in the NEW TESTAMENT

| ENGLISH WORD | GREEK WORD AND VERSE | THE WORD MEANS... |
|---|---|---|
| Greatly distressed– NIV<br>Provoked–NKJV<br>**Deeply troubled–NLT**<br><br>**POSB REFERENCE**<br>(Acts 17:16)<br>Note 1 | Concordance References:<br>⇒ Strong's #3947 paroxunō<br>⇒ NIV #4236 paroxunō<br>⇒ NASB #3947 paroxunō<br><br>**Acts 17:16**<br>Now while Paul waited for them at Athens, his spirit was **stirred** in him, when he saw the city wholly given to idolatry. [KJV]<br>Now while Paul was waiting for them at Athens, his spirit was being **provoked** within him as he was beholding the city full of idols. [NASB]<br>While Paul was waiting for them in Athens, he was **greatly distressed** to see that the city was full of idols. [NIV]<br>Now while Paul waited for them at Athens, his spirit was **provoked** within him when he saw that the city was given over to idols. [NKJV]<br>While Paul was waiting for them in Athens, he was **deeply troubled** by all the idols he saw everywhere in the city. [NLT]<br>Ἐν δὲ ταῖς Ἀθήναις ἐκδεχομένου αὐτοὺς τοῦ Παύλου, **παρωξύνετο** τὸ πνεῦμα αὐτοῦ ἐν αὐτῷ, θεωροῦντι κατείδωλον οὖσαν τὴν πόλιν. [GNS]<br>Ἐν δὲ ταῖς Ἀθήναις ἐκδεχομένου αὐτοὺς τοῦ Παύλου **παρωξύνετο** τὸ πνεῦμα αὐτοῦ ἐν αὐτῷ θεωροῦντος κατείδωλον οὖσαν τὴν πόλιν. [GNT] | city. But note: he was not swept off his feet by the majestic buildings and splendor of the architecture. Contrariwise, what gripped him was the idolatry. The city was full of idols. Paul saw idols "everywhere in the city." Ancient writers estimate that the city had thousands and thousands of idols, one or more for every person in the city. The idols sat everywhere, lining the streets and buildings, within and without every home. Seeing such a sight "deeply disturbed" (*paröxuneto*) the spirit of Paul. Paul was aroused...<br>• over the abuse of God's glory.<br>• over the spiritual blindness of man's mind and reason.<br>• against the devil's enslavement of lives.<br>• with compassion for the souls of men.<br>Note what happened: Paul could wait no longer. He had been waiting for Silas and Timothy, but he could not swallow the scene of idolatry anymore. He began to *reason* and *discuss* the gospel with men everywhere. |
| **#932**<br>**Defense**<br><br>Answer–KJV<br>**Defense–NASB**<br>Answer–NIV<br>**Defense–NKJV**<br>Explain–NLT<br><br>**POSB REFERENCE**<br>(1 Pt.3:15)<br>Note 3 | ἀπολογίαν = *apologian*<br>Pronunciation: [ap-ol-og-ee'-ahn]<br>Parsing (part of speech): noun<br>   Case—accusative<br>   Gender—feminine<br>   Number—singular<br>   Stem or root—from ἀπολογία, ας<br>Concordance References:<br>⇒ Strong's #627 apologia<br>⇒ NIV #665 apologia<br>⇒ NASB #627 apologia<br><br>**1 Peter 3:15**<br>But sanctify the Lord God in your hearts: and be ready always to give an **answer** to every man that asketh you a reason of the hope that is in you with meekness and fear: [KJV]<br>But sanctify Christ as Lord in your hearts, always being ready to make a **defense** to everyone who asks you to give an account for the hope that is in you, yet with gentleness and reverence; [NASB]<br>But in your hearts set apart Christ as Lord. Always be prepared to give an **answer** to everyone who asks you to give the reason for the hope that you have. But do this with gentleness and respect, [NIV]<br>But sanctify the Lord God in your hearts, and always be ready to give a **defense** to everyone who asks you a reason for the hope that is in you, with meekness and fear; [NKJV]<br>Instead, you must worship Christ as Lord of your life. And if you are asked about your Christian hope, always be ready to **explain** it. [NLT]<br>Κύριον δὲ τὸν Θεὸν ἁγιάσατε ἐν ταῖς καρδίαις ὑμῶν· ἕτοιμοι δὲ ἀεὶ πρὸς **ἀπολογίαν** παντὶ τῷ αἰτοῦντι ὑμᾶς λόγον περὶ τῆς ἐν ὑμῖν ἐλπίδος, [GNS]<br>ύριον δὲ τὸν Χριστὸν ἁγιάσατε ἐν ταῖς καρδίαις ὑμῶν, ἕτοιμοι ἀεὶ πρὸς **ἀπολογίαν** παντὶ τῷ αἰτοῦντι ὑμᾶς λόγον περὶ τῆς ἐν ὑμῖν ἐλπίδος, [GNT] | To answer; to reply; to defend; to explain. It means a decision, response, discovery, solution.<br><br>**Practical Application**<br>One answer to persecution is to readily defend the hope of salvation to every man and to do so with gentleness and respect. The word "answer" or "defend" (*apologian*) means just that, to answer back or to give a defense of the believer's hope (A.T. Robertson. *Word Pictures in the New Testament*, Vol.6, p.114). |
| **#933**<br>**Defile–Defiles**<br><br>Defile–KJV<br>Destroys–NASB | φθερεῖ = *phtheirei*<br>Pronunciation: [fthee'-ree]<br>Parsing (part of speech): verb<br>   Mood—indicative<br>   Tense—future<br>   Voice—active | To destroy; to defile; to ruin; to corrupt; to lead astray.<br><br>**Practical Application**<br>The person who defiles the church will face |

## PRACTICAL WORD STUDIES in the NEW TESTAMENT

| ENGLISH WORD | GREEK WORD AND VERSE | THE WORD MEANS... |
|---|---|---|
| Destroys–NIV<br>**Defiles–NKJV**<br>Ruins–NLT<br><br>**POSB REFERENCE**<br>(1 Cor.3:17)<br>Note 7 | Person—3rd person<br>Number—singular<br>Stem or root—from φθείρω<br>Concordance References:<br>⇒ Strong's #5351 phtheirö<br>⇒ NIV #5780 phtheirö<br>⇒ NASB #5351 phtheirö<br><br>**1 Cor. 3:17**<br>If any man **defile** the temple of God, him shall God destroy; for the temple of God is holy, which temple ye are. [KJV]<br>If any man **destroys** the temple of God, God will destroy him, for the temple of God is holy, and that is what you are. [NASB]<br>If anyone **destroys** God's temple, God will destroy him; for God's temple is sacred, and you are that temple. [NIV]<br>If anyone **defiles** the temple of God, God will destroy him. For the temple of God is holy, which *temple* you are. [NKJV]<br>God will bring ruin upon anyone who **ruins** this temple. For God's temple is holy, and you Christians are that temple. [NLT]<br>εἴ τις τὸν ναὸν τοῦ Θεοῦ φθείρει, **φθερεῖ** τοῦτον ὁ Θεός· ὁ γὰρ ναὸς τοῦ Θεοῦ ἅγιός ἐστιν, οἵτινές ἐστε ὑμεῖς. [GNS]<br>εἴ τις τὸν ναὸν τοῦ θεοῦ φθείρει, **φθερεῖ** τοῦτον ὁ θεός· ὁ γὰρ ναὸς τοῦ θεοῦ ἅγιός ἐστιν, οἵτινές ἐστε ὑμεῖς. [GNT] | terrible judgment. The point is striking: the person who troubles the church will suffer the same kind of trouble himself. Whatever he sows, he is definitely going to reap. Troublemaking within the church destroys the spirit of unity and love within the church. To corrupt and destroy the church is to invite God to corrupt and destroy the troublemaker. Note that the punishment is not specifically described. It is simply made clear that he who does such a terrible thing as trouble a church will suffer a terrible punishment. He will be destroyed: wrecked, devastated. |
| **#934**<br>**Defileth–**<br>**Defiles–**<br>**Defiled**<br><br>Defileth–KJV<br>Defiles–NASB<br>Unclean–NIV<br>Defiles–NKJV<br>Defiled–NLT<br><br>**POSB REFERENCE**<br>(Mt.15:10-11, esp.v.11)<br>Note 3 | κοινοῖ = *koinoi*<br>Pronunciation: [koy-noy']<br>Parsing (part of speech): verb<br>    Mood—indicative<br>    Tense—present<br>    Voice—active<br>    Person—3rd person<br>    Number—singular<br>    Stem or root—from κοινόω<br>Concordance References:<br>⇒ Strong's #2840 koinoö<br>⇒ NIV #3124 koinoö<br>⇒ NASB #2840 koinoö<br><br>**Matthew 15:11**<br>Not that which goeth into the mouth **defileth** a man; but that which cometh out of the mouth, this **defileth** a man. [KJV]<br>"Not what enters into the mouth **defiles** the man, but what proceeds out of the mouth, this **defiles** the man." [NASB]<br>What goes into a man's mouth does not make him '**unclean**,' but what comes out of his mouth, that is what makes him '**unclean**.'" [NIV]<br>Not what goes into the mouth **defiles** a man; but what comes out of the mouth, this **defiles** a man." [NKJV]<br>You are not **defiled** by what you eat; you are **defiled** by what you say and do." [NLT]<br>οὐ τὸ εἰσερχόμενον εἰς τὸ στόμα **κοινοῖ** τὸν ἄνθρωπον· ἀλλὰ τὸ ἐκπορευόμενον ἐκ τοῦ στόματος, τοῦτο **κοινοῖ** τὸν ἄνθρωπον. [GNS]<br>οὐ τὸ εἰσερχόμενον εἰς τὸ στόμα **κοινοῖ** τὸν ἄνθρωπον, ἀλλὰ τὸ ἐκπορευόμενον ἐκ τοῦ στόματος τοῦτο **κοινοῖ** τὸν ἄνθρωπον. [GNT] | To pollute, defile, contaminate, dirty, stain; to make impure, unholy, foul, unclean.<br><br>**Practical Application**<br>Note the effects of an obscene mouth: The obscene mouth may range from off-colored humor to dirty jokes, from immoral suggestions to outright propositions. But no matter, a man with a foul mouth stinks just like an open grave; his filthiness causes corruption, the decay of character. The filth from his mouth eats and eats away at his character and at the character of his listeners so much that he becomes as offensive as that of a decayed corpse. The foul, filthy mouth kills character, its attractiveness, trust, faithfulness, morality, honor, and godliness. |
| **#935**<br>**Deformed Hand**<br><br>Withered hand–KJV<br>Withered hand–NASB | ἐξηραμμένην ἔχων τὴν χεῖρα = *exerammenen echon ten cheira*<br>Pronunciation: [ex-ay-rahm'mehn-ayn ekh'-own tayn khir-ah]<br>Parsing *exerammenen* (part of speech): verb<br>    Mood—participle<br>    Tense—perfect | To have an injured or sick hand. This phrase describes a hand that was withered, shriveled, dried up, wilted, wasted, dropped, scorched.<br><br>**Practical Application**<br>His hand had been injured or become dis- |

# PRACTICAL WORD STUDIES
## in the NEW TESTAMENT

| ENGLISH WORD | GREEK WORD AND VERSE | THE WORD MEANS... |
|---|---|---|
| Shriveled hand–NIV<br>Withered hand–NKJV<br>**Deformed hand–NLT**<br><br>**POSB REFERENCE**<br>(Mk.3:1-2; esp. v.1)<br>Note 1, point 1 | Voice—passive<br>Case—accusative<br>Gender—feminine<br>Number—singular<br>Stem or root—from ξηραίνω<br>Parsing *echon* (part of speech): verb<br>  Mood—participle<br>  Tense—present<br>  Voice—active<br>  Case—nominative<br>  Gender—masculine<br>  Number—singular<br>  Stem or root—from ἔχω<br>Parsing *ten* (part of speech): determiner [definite article]<br>  Case—accusative<br>  Gender—feminine<br>  Number—singular<br>  Stem or root—from ὁ, ἡ, τό<br>Parsing *cheira* (part of speech): noun<br>  Case—accusative<br>  Gender—feminine<br>  Number—singular<br>  Stem or root—from χείρ, χειρός<br>Concordance References:<br>⇒ Strong's #3583 xeraino + #5495 cheir<br>⇒ NIV #2400 echō [with] + 3830 xërainö [shriveled] + 5931 cheir [hand]<br>⇒ NASB #3583 xeraino + #5495 cheir<br><br>**Mark 3:1**<br>And he entered again into the synagogue; and there was a man there which had a **withered hand**. [KJV]<br>And He entered again into a synagogue; and a man was there with a **withered hand**. [NASB]<br>Another time he went into the synagogue, and a man with a **shriveled hand** was there. [NIV]<br>And He entered the synagogue again, and a man was there who had a **withered hand**. [NKJV]<br>Jesus went into the synagogue again and noticed a man with a **deformed hand**. [NLT]<br>Καὶ εἰσῆλθε πάλιν εἰς τὴν συναγωγήν, καὶ ἦν ἐκεῖ ἄνθρωπος **ἐξηραμμένην** ἔχων τὴν χεῖρα. [GNS]<br>Καὶ εἰσῆλθεν πάλιν εἰς τὴν συναγωγήν. καὶ ἦν ἐκεῖ ἄνθρωπος **ἐξηραμμένην** ἔχων τὴν χεῖρα. [GNT] | eased. He was not born with a deformed hand. His plight, of course, was desperate; for he was unable to work for a livelihood with a withered hand. Tradition says he was a stone mason who beseeched Jesus to heal him so that he might not have to beg in shame (see POSB notes—Matthew 12:9-13). |
| #936<br>**Defrauding**<br><br>Beguile–KJV<br>**Defrauding–NASB**<br>Disqualify...for–NIV<br>Cheat–NKJV<br>Condemn–NLT<br><br>**POSB REFERENCE**<br>(Col.2:18-19; esp. v.18)<br>Note 2 | καταβραβευέτω = katabrabeuetö<br>Pronunciation: [kat-ab-rab-yoo'-eh-tow]<br>Parsing (part of speech): verb<br>  Mood—imperative<br>  Tense—present<br>  Voice—active<br>  Person—3rd person<br>  Number—singular<br>  Stem or root—from καταβραβεύω<br>Concordance References:<br>⇒ Strong's #2603 katabrabeuö<br>⇒ NIV #2857 katabrabeuö<br>⇒ NASB #2603 katabrabeuö<br><br>**Col. 2:18**<br>Let no man **beguile** you of your reward in a voluntary humility and worshipping of angels, intruding into those things which he hath not seen, vainly puffed up by his fleshly mind, [KJV]<br>Let no one keep **defrauding** you of your prize by delighting in self-abasement and the worship of the angels, taking his stand on visions he has seen, inflated without cause by his fleshly mind, [NASB]<br>Do not let anyone who delights in false humility and the worship of angels **disqualify** you **for** the prize. Such a person goes into great detail about what he has seen, and his unspiritual mind puffs him up with idle notions. [NIV]<br>Let no one **cheat** you of your reward, taking delight in *false* humility and worship of angels, intruding into those | To disqualify; to beguile; to defraud; to cheat; to condemn. It means to rob; to defraud; to cheat a person out of his reward.<br><br>**Practical Application**<br>It is possible for believers to be disqualified for their reward by false teachers. How? By following those who teach that there is another approach to God other than Christ. Christ is God's appointed way to approach Him, and there is no other way. |

# PRACTICAL WORD STUDIES
## in the NEW TESTAMENT

| ENGLISH WORD | GREEK WORD AND VERSE | THE WORD MEANS... |
|---|---|---|
| | things which he has not seen, vainly puffed up by his fleshly mind, [NKJV]<br>Don't let anyone **condemn** you by insisting on self-denial. And don't let anyone say you must worship angels, even though they say they have had visions about this. These people claim to be so humble, but their sinful minds have made them proud. [NLT]<br>μηδεὶς ὑμᾶς **καταβραβευέτω** θέλων ἐν ταπεινοφροσύνῃ καὶ θρησκείᾳ τῶν ἀγγέλων, ἃ μὴ ἑώρακεν ἐμβατεύων, εἰκῇ φυσιούμενος ὑπὸ τοῦ νοὸς τῆς σαρκὸς αὐτοῦ, [GNS]<br>μηδεὶς ὑμᾶς **καταβραβευέτω** θέλων ἐν ταπεινοφροσύνῃ καὶ θρησκείᾳ τῶν ἀγγέλων, ἃ ἑόρακεν ἐμβατεύων, εἰκῇ φυσιούμενος ὑπὸ τοῦ νοὸς τῆς σαρκὸς αὐτοῦ, [GNT] | |
| **#937**<br>**Degrading Passions**<br><br>Vile affections–KJV<br>**Degrading passions– NASB**<br>Shameful lusts–NIV<br>Vile passions–NKJV<br>Shameful desires–NLT<br><br>**POSB REFERENCE**<br>(Romans 1:26-27; esp. v.26)<br>Note 3, point 1 | πάθη ἀτιμίας = pathë atimias<br>Pronunciation: [path'-ay at-ee-mee'-ahs]<br>Parsing *pathë* (part of speech): noun<br>    Case—accusative<br>    Gender—neuter<br>    Number—plural<br>    Stem or root—from πάθος, ους<br>Parsing *atimias* (part of speech): noun<br>    Case—genitive<br>    Gender—feminine<br>    Number—singular<br>    Stem or root—from ἀτιμία, ας<br>Concordance References:<br>⇒ Strong's #3806 pathos + 819 atimia<br>⇒ NIV #4079 pathos [lusts] + 871 atimia [shameful]<br>⇒ NASB #3806 pathos + 819 atimia<br><br>**Romans 1:26**<br>For this cause God gave them up unto **vile affections**: for even their women did change the natural use into that which is against nature: [KJV]<br>For this reason God gave them over to **degrading passions**; for their women exchanged the natural function for that which is unnatural, [NASB]<br>Because of this, God gave them over to **shameful lusts**. Even their women exchanged natural relations for unnatural ones. [NIV]<br>For this reason God gave them up to **vile passions**. For even their women exchanged the natural use for what is against nature. [NKJV]<br>That is why God abandoned them to their **shameful desires**. Even the women turned against the natural way to have sex and instead indulged in sex with each other. [NLT]<br>Διὰ τοῦτο παρέδωκεν αὐτοὺς ὁ Θεὸς εἰς **πάθη ἀτιμίας**· αἵ τε γὰρ θήλειαι αὐτῶν μετήλλαξαν τὴν φυσικὴν χρῆσιν εἰς τὴν παρὰ φύσιν· [GNS]<br>διὰ τοῦτο παρέδωκεν αὐτοὺς ὁ θεὸς εἰς **πάθη ἀτιμίας**, αἵ τε γὰρ θήλειαι αὐτῶν μετήλλαξαν τὴν φυσικὴν χρῆσιν εἰς τὴν παρὰ φύσιν, [GNT] | Shameful lusts, vile affections, degrading passions, shameful desires. It means to be dishonored, disgraced, shamed, and degraded. It means passions that cannot be controlled or governed, that run loose and wild, no matter how much a person tries to control them.<br><br>**Practical Application**<br>The reason God gives men up to degrading passions (*pathë atimias*) is because of their unnatural passion. Men lust and lust, craving the illegitimate and unlawful. They burn in their lust one for another. And note what Scripture is talking about: unnatural affection, that is, homosexuality.<br>⇒ Women burn and lust and exchange the "natural function for that which is unnatural." [NASB] And note, it is unnatural.<br>⇒ Men burn in their "desire toward one another, men with men committing indecent acts." (Rom.1:27) [NASB] |
| **#938**<br>**Delay, Do Not– Delay, Not– Delay, Not To**<br><br>Not delay–KJV<br>**Do not delay–NASB**<br>At once–NIV<br>**Not to delay–NKJV**<br>Come as soon as possible–NLT | Μὴ ὀκνήσῃς = Më oknëses<br>Pronunciation: [may ok-nay'-says]<br>Parsing *oknëses* (part of speech): verb<br>    Mood—subjunctive or imperative<br>    Tense—aorist<br>    Voice—active<br>    Person—2nd person<br>    Number—singular<br>    Stem or root—from ὀκνέω<br>Concordance References:<br>⇒ Strong's #3361 + 3635 më okneö<br>⇒ NIV #3590 + 3890 më okneö [at once]<br>⇒ NASB #3361 + 3635 më okneö | At once; without delay; to come as soon as possible.<br><br>**Practical Application**<br>It means not to hesitate, not to be reluctant; but to act and act now, quickly, without questioning. |

# PRACTICAL WORD STUDIES
## in the NEW TESTAMENT

| ENGLISH WORD | GREEK WORD AND VERSE | THE WORD MEANS... |
|---|---|---|
| **POSB REFERENCE** (Acts 9:36-39; esp. v.38) Note 2, point 3c | **Acts 9:38** And forasmuch as Lydda was nigh to Joppa, and the disciples had heard that Peter was there, they sent unto him two men, desiring him that he would **not delay** to come to them. [KJV] And since Lydda was near Joppa, the disciples, having heard that Peter was there, sent two men to him, entreating him, "**Do not delay** to come to us." [NASB] Lydda was near Joppa; so when the disciples heard that Peter was in Lydda, they sent two men to him and urged him, "Please come **at once**!" [NIV] And since Lydda was near Joppa, and the disciples had heard that Peter was there, they sent two men to him, imploring him **not to delay** in coming to them. [NKJV] But they had heard that Peter was nearby at Lydda, so they sent two men to beg him, "Please **come as soon as possible**!" [NLT] ἐγγὺς δὲ οὔσης Λύδδης τῇ Ἰόππῃ, οἱ μαθηταὶ ἀκούσαντες ὅτι Πέτρος ἐστὶν ἐν αὐτῇ, ἀπέστειλαν δύο ἄνδρας πρὸς αὐτὸν παρακαλοῦντες **μὴ ὀκνῆσαι** διελθεῖν ἕως αὐτῶν. [GNS] ἐγγὺς δὲ οὔσης Λύδδας τῇ Ἰόππῃ οἱ μαθηταὶ ἀκούσαντες ὅτι Πέτρος ἐστὶν ἐν αὐτῇ ἀπέστειλαν δύο ἄνδρας πρὸς αὐτὸν παρακαλοῦντες, **Μὴ ὀκνήσῃς** διελθεῖν ἕως ἡμῶν. [GNT] | |
| **#939 Deliberatly Violated** Put away–KJV Rejected–NASB Rejected–NIV Rejected–NKJV Deliberately violated–NLT **POSB REFERENCE** (1 Tim.1:19-20; esp. v.19) Note 3 | ἀπωσάμενοι = *apōsamenoi* Pronunciation: [ap-o'-sah-mehn-oy] Parsing (part of speech): verb   Mood—participle   Tense—aorist   Voice—middle deponent   Case—nominative   Gender—masculine   Number—plural   Stem or root—from ἀπωθέομαι Concordance References:   ⇒ Strong's #683 apōtheō   ⇒ NIV #723 apōtheō   ⇒ NASB #683 apōtheō **1 Tim. 1:19** Holding faith, and a good conscience; which some having **put away** concerning faith have made shipwreck: [KJV] Keeping faith and a good conscience, which some have **rejected** and suffered shipwreck in regard to their faith. [NASB] Holding on to faith and a good conscience. Some have **rejected** these and so have shipwrecked their faith. [NIV] Having faith and a good conscience, which some having **rejected**, concerning the faith have suffered shipwreck, [NKJV] Cling tightly to your faith in Christ, and always Keep your conscience clear. For some people have **deliberately violated** their consciences; as a result, their faith has been shipwrecked. [NLT] ἔχων πίστιν καὶ ἀγαθὴν συνείδησιν, ἥν τινες **ἀπωσάμενοι**, περὶ τὴν πίστιν ἐναυάγησαν· [GNS] ἔχων πίστιν καὶ ἀγαθὴν συνείδησιν, ἥν τινες **ἀπωσάμενοι** περὶ τὴν πίστιν ἐναυάγησαν, [GNT] | To reject; to put away; to deliberately violate; to push aside; to push away with force. **Practical Application** It is a willful and deliberate pushing away of conscience. Conscience says that something is wrong and should not be done, but conscience is ignored and subdued, turned away from and denied. When a person *continues to push his conscience away*, something terrible happens: his faith is shipwrecked. His faith is broken to pieces and destroyed. A person must live as Scripture dictates: righteously and godly. If he does not live righteously and godly, then he weakens his faith and soon dashes it upon the storms of evil, worldliness, and false doctrine. His faith is shipwrecked—because he pushed his conscience aside refusing to listen to its call to live righteously and godly. |
| **#940 Deliver** Deliver–KJV Deliver–NASB Rescue–NIV Deliver–NKJV Rescue–NLT | ἐξέληται = *exelētai* Pronunciation: [ex-eh-lay'-tah-ee] Parsing (part of speech): verb   Mood—subjunctive   Tense—aorist   Voice—middle   Person—3rd person   Number—singular   Stem or root—from ἐξαιρέω Concordance References:   ⇒ Strong's #1807 exaireō | To deliver; to rescue and to pluck out; to save; to set free. **Practical Application** But note the point: this was the very purpose for Jesus' death. He died to deliver us from this present evil world. The word "deliver" (*exelētai*) means to rescue and to pluck out. Jesus Christ died to rescue and to pluck us out of this present evil world. How? As stated above, "He gave |

# PRACTICAL WORD STUDIES
## in the New Testament

| ENGLISH WORD | GREEK WORD AND VERSE | THE WORD MEANS... |
|---|---|---|
| **POSB REFERENCE** (Gal.1:4-5; esp. v.4), Note 4, point 2 | ⇒ NIV #1975 exaireō<br>⇒ NASB #1807 exaireō<br><br>**Galatians 1:4**<br>Who gave himself for our sins, that he might **deliver** us from this present evil world, according to the will of God and our Father, [KJV]<br>Who gave Himself for our sins, that He might **deliver** us out of this present evil age, according to the will of our God and Father, [NASB]<br>Who gave himself for our sins to **rescue** us from the present evil age, according to the will of our God and Father, [NIV]<br>Who gave Himself for our sins, that He might **deliver** us from this present evil age, according to the will of our God and Father, [NKJV]<br>He died for our sins, just as God our Father planned, in order to **rescue** us from this evil world in which we live. [NLT]<br>τοῦ δόντος ἑαυτὸν ὑπὲρ τῶν ἁμαρτιῶν ἡμῶν ὅπως **ἐξέληται** ἡμᾶς ἐκ τοῦ ἐνεστῶτος αἰῶνος πονηροῦ, κατὰ τὸ θέλημα τοῦ Θεοῦ καὶ πατρὸς ἡμῶν· [GNS]<br>τοῦ δόντος ἑαυτὸν ὑπὲρ τῶν ἁμαρτιῶν ἡμῶν, ὅπως **ἐξέληται** ἡμᾶς ἐκ τοῦ αἰῶνος τοῦ ἐνεστῶτος πονηροῦ κατὰ τὸ θέλημα τοῦ θεοῦ καὶ πατρὸς ἡμῶν, [GNT] | Himself for our sins." He delivers or rescues us from both *the power and the fate of the world.* The believer experiences both abundant and eternal life now and forever. |
| **#941**<br>**Deliver–<br>Delivered**<br><br>Deliver–KJV<br>Delivered–NASB<br>Hand...over–NIV<br>Deliver–NKJV<br>Betrayed–NLT<br><br>**POSB REFERENCE** (Mk.10:33) Note 4 | παραδοθήσεται = *paradothesetai*<br>Pronunciation: [par-ad-o-theh-seh-tah-ee]<br>Parsing (part of speech): verb<br>    Mood—indicative<br>    Tense—future<br>    Voice—passive<br>    Person—3rd person<br>    Number—singular<br>    Stem or root—from παραδίδωμι<br>Concordance References:<br>⇒ Strong's #3860 paradidōmi<br>⇒ NIV #4140 paradidōmi<br>⇒ NASB #3860 paradidōmi<br><br>**Mark 10:33**<br>Saying, Behold, we go up to Jerusalem; and the Son of man shall be delivered unto the chief priests, and unto the scribes; and they shall condemn him to death, and shall **deliver** him to the Gentiles: [KJV]<br>Saying, "Behold, we are going up to Jerusalem, and the Son of Man will be **delivered** to the chief priests and the scribes; and they will condemn Him to death, and will deliver Him to the Gentiles. [NASB]<br>"We are going up to Jerusalem," he said, "and the Son of Man will be betrayed to the chief priests and teachers of the law. They will condemn him to death and will **hand** him **over** to the Gentiles, [NIV]<br>"Behold, we are going up to Jerusalem, and the Son of Man will be betrayed to the chief priests and to the scribes; and they will condemn Him to death and **deliver** Him to the Gentiles; [NKJV]<br>"When we get to Jerusalem," he told them, "the Son of Man will be **betrayed** to the leading priests and the teachers of religious law. They will sentence him to die and hand him over to the Romans. [NLT]<br>ὅτι Ἰδοὺ ἀναβαίνομεν εἰς Ἱεροσόλυμα· καὶ ὁ υἱὸς τοῦ ἀνθρώπου **παραδοθήσεται** τοῖς ἀρχιερεῦσι καὶ τοῖς γραμματεῦσι, καὶ κατακρινοῦσιν αὐτὸν θανάτῳ, καὶ παραδώσουσιν αὐτὸν τοῖς ἔθνεσι, [GNS]<br>ὅτι Ἰδοὺ ἀναβαίνομεν εἰς Ἱεροσόλυμα, καὶ ὁ υἱὸς τοῦ ἀνθρώπου **παραδοθήσεται** τοῖς ἀρχιερεῦσιν καὶ τοῖς γραμματεῦσιν, καὶ κατακρινοῦσιν αὐτὸν θανάτῳ καὶ παραδώσουσιν αὐτὸν τοῖς ἔθνεσιν [GNT] | To hand over; to be betrayed, to be abandoned, to be delivered over and into death.<br><br>**Practical Application**<br>It means that His death was determined, ordained, set in the plan and counsel of God. Note that Jesus said, "The Son of Man will be betrayed." His death was right before His face, ready to take place. |

# PRACTICAL WORD STUDIES
## in the NEW TESTAMENT

| ENGLISH WORD | GREEK WORD AND VERSE | THE WORD MEANS... |
|---|---|---|
| **#942**<br>**Delivered**<br><br>Shall be betrayed–KJV<br>**Will be delivered–NASB**<br>Will be betrayed–NIV<br>Will be betrayed–NKJV<br>Will be betrayed–NLT<br><br>**POSB REFERENCE**<br>(Mt.20:18)<br>Note 2, point 1<br><br>See also POSB REF:<br>(Mt.17:22)<br>Note 1, point 2<br>(Mk.9:31)<br>Note 2, point 2<br>(Lk.9:44-45; esp. v.44)<br>Note 4, point 2 | παραδοθήσεται = *paradothēsetai*<br>Pronunciation: [par-ad-o-the'-say-tai]<br>Parsing (part of speech): verb<br>    Mood—indicative<br>    Tense—future<br>    Voice—passive<br>    Person—3rd person<br>    Number—singular<br>    Stem or root—from παραδίδωμι<br>Concordance References:<br>  ⇒ Strong's #3860 paradidōmi<br>  ⇒ NIV #4140 paradidōmi<br>  ⇒ NASB #3860 paradidōmi<br><br>**Matthew 20:18**<br>Behold, we go up to Jerusalem; and the Son of man **shall be betrayed** unto the chief priests and unto the scribes, and they shall condemn him to death, [KJV]<br><br>"Behold, we are going up to Jerusalem; and the Son of Man **will be delivered** to the chief priests and scribes, and they will condemn Him to death, [NASB]<br><br>"We are going up to Jerusalem, and the Son of Man **will be betrayed** to the chief priests and the teachers of the law. They will condemn him to death [NIV]<br><br>"Behold, we are going up to Jerusalem, and the Son of Man **will be betrayed** to the chief priests and to the scribes; and they will condemn Him to death, [NKJV]<br><br>"When we get to Jerusalem," he said, "the Son of Man **will be betrayed** to the leading priests and the teachers of religious law. They will sentence him to die. [NLT]<br><br>Ἰδοὺ ἀναβαίνομεν εἰς Ἱεροσόλυμα, καὶ ὁ υἱὸς τοῦ ἀνθρώπου **παραδοθήσεται** τοῖς ἀρχιερεῦσι καὶ γραμματεῦσι· καὶ κατακρινοῦσιν αὐτὸν θανάτῳ, [GNS]<br><br>Ἰδοὺ ἀναβαίνομεν εἰς Ἱεροσόλυμα, καὶ ὁ υἱὸς τοῦ ἀνθρώπου **παραδοθήσεται** τοῖς ἀρχιερεῦσιν καὶ γραμματεῦσιν, καὶ κατακρινοῦσιν αὐτὸν θανάτῳ [GNT] | To be betrayed; to be delivered up into the power of someone else; to hand over; to give over; to be arrested.<br><br>**Practical Application**<br>This betrayal or deliverance led to the handing over of Jesus Christ to the Gentiles. He was mocked, flogged, and crucified. Was Christ taken aback by this betrayal? Was He caught off guard?<br><br>God knows every person's heart. Even a person's inner thoughts are known to God, as well as what a person does. No one can hide what He does from God, not even a thought. God knows if a man is betraying His Son. He even knows if a man is thinking about sinning and turning his back on Jesus. The more a man thinks about sinning, the more likely he is to turn back. His betrayal can be predicted.<br><br>Note: the greatest act of betrayal in all of history was conquered when Jesus Christ rose from the dead. No human betrayal can divert the purpose of God. |
| **#943**<br>**Delivered**<br><br>Delivered–KJV<br>Released–NASB<br>Released–NIV<br>Delivered–NKJV<br>Released–NLT<br><br>**POSB REFERENCE**<br>(Rom.7:6)<br>Note 4 | κατηργήθημεν = *katērgēthēmen*<br>Pronunciation: [kat-ayrg-ay'-thay-mehn]<br>Parsing (part of speech): verb<br>    Mood—indicative<br>    Tense—aorist<br>    Voice—passive<br>    Person—1st person<br>    Number—plural<br>    Stem or root—from καταργέω<br>Concordance References:<br>  ⇒ Strong's #2673 katargeō<br>  ⇒ NIV #2934 katargeō<br>  ⇒ NASB #2673 katargeō<br><br>**Romans 7:6**<br>But now we are **delivered** from the law, that being dead wherein we were held; that we should serve in newness of spirit, and not in the oldness of the letter. [KJV]<br><br>But now we have been **released** from the Law, having died to that by which we were bound, so that we serve in newness of the Spirit and not in oldness of the letter. [NASB]<br><br>But now, by dying to what once bound us, we have been **released** from the law so that we serve in the new way of the Spirit, and not in the old way of the written code. [NIV]<br><br>But now we have been **delivered** from the law, having died to what we were held by, so that we should serve in the newness of the Spirit and not *in* the oldness of the letter. [NKJV]<br><br>But now we have been **released** from the law, for we died with Christ, and we are no longer captive to its power. Now we can really serve God, not in the old way by obeying the letter of the law, but in the new way, by the Spirit. [NLT]<br><br>νυνὶ δὲ **κατηργήθημεν** ἀπὸ τοῦ νόμου, ἀποθανόντες ἐν ᾧ κατειχόμεθα, ὥστε δουλεύειν ἡμᾶς ἐν | To be released; to be delivered; to be discharged.<br><br>**Practical Application**<br>Believers are "delivered" (*katērgēthēmen*), that is, have been discharged from the law. How? By their death "in" Christ (see POSB note, Jesus Christ, Redemption—Romans 7:4 for discussion). |

# PRACTICAL WORD STUDIES
## in the NEW TESTAMENT

| ENGLISH WORD | GREEK WORD AND VERSE | THE WORD MEANS... |
|---|---|---|
| | καινότητι πνεύματος, καὶ οὐ παλαιότητι γράμματος. [GNS]<br>νυνὶ δὲ **κατηργήθημεν** ἀπὸ τοῦ νόμου ἀποθανόντες ἐν ᾧ κατειχόμεθα, ὥστε δουλεύειν ἡμᾶς ἐν καινότητι πνεύματος καὶ οὐ παλαιότητι γράμματος. [GNT] | |
| **#944**<br>**Delivered**<br><br>Delivered–KJV<br>Delivered–NASB<br>Rescued–NIV<br>Delivered–NKJV<br>Rescued–NLT<br><br>**POSB REFERENCE**<br>(Col.1:13)<br>Note 2, point 2 | ἐρρύσατο = *errusato*<br>Pronunciation: [eh-rhoo'-sah-to]<br>Parsing (part of speech): verb<br>    Mood—indicative<br>    Tense—aorist<br>    Voice—middle deponent<br>    Person—3rd person<br>    Number—singular<br>    Stem or root—from ῥύομαι<br>Concordance References:<br>⇒  Strong's #4506 hruomai<br>⇒  NIV #4861 hruomai<br>⇒  NASB #4506 hruomai<br><br>**Col. 1:13**<br>Who hath **delivered** us from the power of darkness, and hath translated *us* into the kingdom of his dear Son: [KJV]<br>For He **delivered** us from the domain of darkness, and transferred us to the kingdom of His beloved Son, [NASB]<br>For he has **rescued** us from the dominion of darkness and brought us into the kingdom of the Son he loves, [NIV]<br>He has **delivered** us from the power of darkness and conveyed *us* into the kingdom of the Son of His love, [NKJV]<br>For he has **rescued** us from the one who rules in the kingdom of darkness, and he has brought us into the Kingdom of his dear Son. [NLT]<br>ὃς **ἐρρύσατο** ἡμᾶς ἐκ τῆς ἐξουσίας τοῦ σκότους, καὶ μετέστησεν εἰς τὴν βασιλείαν τοῦ υἱοῦ τῆς ἀγάπης αὐτοῦ, [GNS]<br>ὃς **ἐρρύσατο** ἡμᾶς ἐκ τῆς ἐξουσίας τοῦ σκότους καὶ μετέστησεν εἰς τὴν βασιλείαν τοῦ υἱοῦ τῆς ἀγάπης αὐτοῦ, [GNT] | To be rescued; to be delivered; to be saved. The word "delivered" (*errusato*) means to rescue or snatch from darkness.<br><br>**Practical Application**<br>Note that it is God Himself who has delivered us from darkness. A person lost in pitch black darkness is hopeless unless someone rescues him. And note: he cannot be rescued by those who are lost in the same darkness as he is. No person who is in the world of darkness has light, or else he would use the light to get out of the darkness. This is the very reason God had to rescue man. He alone is light; therefore, He alone could reach down and snatch man from the darkness. How did He do this? The answer is given in the next paragraph.<br>God transferred us into the kingdom of His dear Son, into the kingdom of the Lord Jesus Christ. We must always remember that the kingdom of Christ already exists.<br>⇒  His rule and reign already exists in the spiritual world or spiritual dimension of being, that is, in heaven.<br>⇒  His rule and reign already exists in the hearts and lives of believers in this physical world or physical dimension of being.<br>The message of the glorious gospel is that God has transferred the believer from the power of darkness into the kingdom of His dear Son. (See POSB *Deeper Study #3*, Kingdom of Heaven—Matthew 19:23-24 for more discussion.) |
| **#945**<br>**Delude**<br><br>Beguile–KJV<br>**Delude–NASB**<br>Deceive–NIV<br>Deceive–NKJV<br>Deceive–NLT<br><br>**POSB REFERENCE**<br>(Col.2:4)<br>Note 3 | παραλογίζηται = *paralogizētai*<br>Pronunciation: [par-al-og-id'-zay-tah-ee]<br>Parsing (part of speech): verb<br>    Mood—subjunctive<br>    Tense—present<br>    Voice—middle or passive deponent<br>    Person—3rd person<br>    Number—singular<br>    Stem or root—from παραλογίζομαι<br>Concordance References:<br>⇒  Strong's #3884 paralogizomai<br>⇒  NIV #4165 paralogizomai<br>⇒  NASB #3884 paralogizomai<br><br>**Col. 2:4**<br>And this I say, lest any man should **beguile** you with enticing words. [KJV]<br>I say this in order that no one may **delude** you with persuasive argument. [NASB]<br>I tell you this so that no one may **deceive** you by fine-sounding arguments. [NIV]<br>Now this I say lest anyone should **deceive** you with persuasive words. [NKJV]<br>I am telling you this so that no one will be able to **deceive** you with persuasive arguments. [NLT]<br>τοῦτο δὲ λέγω, ἵνα μή τις ὑμᾶς **παραλογίζηται** ἐν πιθανολογίᾳ.[GNS]<br>Τοῦτο λέγω ἵνα μηδεὶς ὑμᾶς **παραλογίζηται** ἐν πιθανολογίᾳ. [GNT] | To deceive; to delude; to beguile; to mislead, cheat, seduce, and lead someone astray.<br><br>**Practical Application**<br>Note how the seduction takes place: by "persuasive argument" (*pithanologiai*), that is, by words that are persuasive, appealing, eloquent, flowery, and attractive. |

## Practical Word Studies
### in the New Testament

| ENGLISH WORD | GREEK WORD AND VERSE | THE WORD MEANS... |
|---|---|---|
| **#946**<br>**Deluding Influence**<br><br>Strong delusion–KJV<br>**Deluding influence–NASB**<br>Powerful delusion–NIV<br>Strong delusion–NKJV<br>Great deception–NLT<br><br>**POSB REFERENCE**<br>(2 Thes.2:11)<br>Note 3 | ἐνέργειαν πλάνης = *energeian planës*<br>Pronunciation: [en-erg'-i-ahn plan'-ace]<br>Parsing *energeian* (part of speech): noun<br>    Case—accusative<br>    Gender—feminine<br>    Number—singular<br>    Stem or root—from ἐνέργεια, ας<br>Parsing *planës* (part of speech): noun<br>    Case—genitive<br>    Gender—feminine<br>    Number—singular<br>    Stem or root—from πλάνη, ης<br>Concordance References:<br>  ⇒ Strong's #1753 energeia + 4106 planë<br>  ⇒ NIV #1918 energeia + 4415 planë<br>  ⇒ NASB #1753 energeia + 4106 planë<br><br>**2 Thes. 2:11**<br>And for this cause God shall send them **strong delusion**, that they should believe a lie: [KJV]<br>And for this reason God will send upon them a **deluding influence** so that they might believe what is false, [NASB]<br>For this reason God sends them a **powerful delusion** so that they will believe the lie [NIV]<br>And for this reason God will send them **strong delusion**, that they should believe the lie, [NKJV]<br>So God will send **great deception** upon them, and they will believe all these lies. [NLT]<br>καὶ διὰ τοῦτο πέμψει αὐτοῖς ὁ Θεὸς **ἐνέργειαν πλάνης**, εἰς τὸ πιστεῦσαι αὐτοὺς τῷ ψεύδει· [GNS]<br>καὶ διὰ τοῦτο πέμπει αὐτοῖς ὁ θεὸς **ἐνέργειαν πλάνης** εἰς τὸ πιστεῦσαι αὐτοὺς τῷ ψεύδει, [GNT] | Powerful delusion; strong delusion; deluding influence; great deception; great error; strong deceit; a working of error.<br><br>**Practical Application**<br>In the end time, people will work error after error, sin after sin, evil after evil. They will become stronger and stronger in their sin, harder and harder. They will become steeped in their rejection of the gospel more and more. |
| **#947**<br>**Demanded Permission**<br><br>Desired–KJV<br>**Demanded permission–NASB**<br>Asked–NIV<br>Asked–NKJV<br>Asked–NLT<br><br>**POSB REFERENCE**<br>(Lk.22:31)<br>Note 1, point 2 | ἐξῃτήσατο = *exëtësato*<br>Pronunciation: [ex-ahee-teh'-saw-tow]<br>Parsing (part of speech): verb<br>    Mood—indicative<br>    Tense—aorist<br>    Voice—middle<br>    Person—3rd person<br>    Number—singular<br>    Stem or root—from ἐξαιτέομαι<br>Concordance References:<br>  ⇒ Strong's #1809 exaiteomai<br>  ⇒ NIV #1977 exaiteö<br>  ⇒ NASB #1809 exaiteö<br><br>**Luke 22:31**<br>And the Lord said, Simon, Simon, behold, Satan hath **desired** to have you, that he may sift you as wheat: [KJV]<br>"Simon, Simon, behold, Satan has **demanded permission** to sift you like wheat; [NASB]<br>"Simon, Simon, Satan has **asked** to sift you as wheat. [NIV]<br>And the Lord said, "Simon, Simon! Indeed, Satan has **asked** for you, that he may sift *you* as wheat. [NKJV]<br>"Simon, Simon, Satan has **asked** to have all of you, to sift you like wheat. [NLT]<br>εἶπε δὲ ὁ Κύριος, Σίμων Σίμων, ἰδοὺ ὁ Σατανᾶς **ἐξῃτήσατο** ὑμᾶς, τοῦ σινιάσαι ὡς τὸν σῖτον· [GNS]<br>Σίμων Σίμων, ἰδοὺ ὁ Σατανᾶς **ἐξῃτήσατο** ὑμᾶς τοῦ σινιάσαι ὡς τὸν σῖτον· [GNT] | To beg for something; to desire; to make an appeal; to demand; to obtain by asking.<br><br>**Practical Application**<br>Jesus pictured Satan as begging permission of God to trip the disciples. It is the same picture that is found in Job (Job 1:6f). The Bible is clear in its teaching: God is sovereign; anything that goes on in the universe goes on because God allows it, even temptation. The truth to see is that...<br>• Jesus did give a glimpse into the spiritual world.<br>• Satan begged God to let him test and try the disciples.<br>• Satan is subject to God and has no right or power to tempt believers unless God allows it.<br>• The Lord's prayer does include the words "Deliver us from the evil one" (*a po tou poneron*) (see POSB *Deeper Study* #9—Matthew 6:13). |
| **#948**<br>**Demand Its Own Way**<br><br>Seeketh not her own–KJV<br>Seeks its own–NASB | ζητεῖ τὰ ἑαυτῆς = *zëtei ta heautës*<br>Pronunciation: [dzay-teh'-ee tah yoo-tace']<br>Parsing *zëtei* (part of speech): verb<br>    Mood—indicative<br>    Tense—present<br>    Voice—active<br>    Person—3rd person<br>    Number—singular<br>    Stem or root—from ζητέω | Self-seeking; demanding one's own way; to strive for one's own interest—ignoring the feelings of other people.<br><br>**Practical Application**<br>Love seeks not her own: is not selfish; does not insist upon its own rights (Charles B. Williams. *The New Testament in the Language* |

# PRACTICAL WORD STUDIES
## in the NEW TESTAMENT

| ENGLISH WORD | GREEK WORD AND VERSE | THE WORD MEANS... |
|---|---|---|
| Self-seeking–NIV<br>Seek its own–NKJV<br>**Demands its own way–NLT**<br><br>**POSB REFERENCE**<br>(1 Cor.13:4-7; esp. v.5)<br>Note 2, point 7 | Concordance References:<br>⇒ Strong's #1438+2212+3588 heautou zēteō ho<br>⇒ NIV #1571+2426+3836 heautou zēteō ho [self seeking]<br>⇒ NASB #1438+2212+3588 heautou zēteō ho<br><br>**1 Cor. 13:5**<br>Doth not behave itself unseemly, **seeketh not her own**, is not easily provoked, thinketh no evil; [KJV]<br>Does not act unbecomingly; it does not **seek its own**, is not provoked, does not take into account a wrong suffered, [NASB]<br>It is not rude, it is not **self-seeking**, it is not easily angered, it keeps no record of wrongs. [NIV]<br>Does not behave rudely, does not **seek its own**, is not provoked, thinks no evil; [NKJV]<br>Or rude. Love does not **demand its own way**. Love is not irritable, and it keeps no record of when it has been wronged. [NLT]<br>οὐκ ἀσχημονεῖ, οὐ **ζητεῖ τὰ ἑαυτῆς**, οὐ παροξύνεται, οὐ λογίζεται τὸ κακόν, [GNS]<br>οὐκ ἀσχημονεῖ, οὐ **ζητεῖ τὰ ἑαυτῆς**, οὐ παροξύνεται, οὐ λογίζεται τὸ κακόν, [GNT] | *of the People.* "The Four Translation New Testament." Printed for Decision Magazine by World Wide Publications of Minneapolis, New York, NY: Iversen Associates, 1966). Love is not focused upon who one is nor upon what one has done. Love seeks to serve, not have others serving oneself. Love is acknowledging others, not insisting that others acknowledge oneself; it is giving to others, not insisting that others give to oneself. |
| #949<br>**Demands**<br><br>Compel–KJV<br>Force–NASB<br>Forces–NIV<br>Compels–NKJV<br>**Demands–NLT**<br><br>**POSB REFERENCE**<br>(Mt.5:39-41, esp.v.41)<br>Note 3, point 3 | ἀγγαρεύσει = aggareusei<br>Pronunciation: [ang-ar-yew'-see]<br>Parsing (part of speech): verb<br>  Mood—indicative<br>  Tense—future<br>  Voice—active<br>  Person—3rd person<br>  Number—singular<br>  Stem or root—from ἀγγαρεύω<br>Concordance References:<br>⇒ Strong's #29 aggareuo<br>⇒ NIV #30 angareuo<br>⇒ NASB #29 aggareuo<br><br>**Matthew 5:41**<br>And whosoever shall **compel** thee to go a mile, go with him twain. [KJV]<br>"And whoever shall **force** you to go one mile, go with him two. [NASB]<br>If someone **forces** you to go one mile, go with him two miles. [NIV]<br>And whoever **compels** you to go one mile, go with him two. [NKJV]<br>If a soldier **demands** that you carry his gear for a mile, carry it two miles. [NLT]<br>καὶ ὅστις σε **ἀγγαρεύσει** μίλιον ἕν, ὕπαγε μετ' αὐτοῦ δύο. [GNS]<br>καὶ ὅστις σε **ἀγγαρεύσει** μίλιον ἕν, ὕπαγε μετ' αὐτοῦ δύο. [GNT] | To force; to compel; to demand; to press into service under the threat of punishment.<br><br>**Practical Application**<br>Ordinary citizens could be drafted for any task that the person in authority deemed necessary. Christ is saying that if a believer is forced to go a mile, he should go twice as far. Again, rights—even the rights of liberty—are not the primary concern of the believer. The believer's primary concern is people and their burdens—reaching and relieving their burdens in obedience to God.<br>Going a second mile is difficult. It means a person does not become bitter and resentful, grumbling and griping, complaining and criticizing, self-pitying and begrudging. It means a person forgives and serves and offers more service. He sets his mind and heart on reaching out to the offender by helping more and more. Such action will more likely reach the offender for the Kingdom of Heaven. It will certainly help bring the Kingdom of Heaven closer to this earth (see POSB DEEPER STUDY #3—Matthew 19:23-24). |
| #950<br>**Demon-Possessed**<br><br>Spirit of divination–KJV<br>Spirit of divination–NASB<br>Spirit...which...predicted the future–NIV<br>Spirit of divination–NKJV<br>**Demon-possessed–NLT** | πνεῦμα πύθωνα = pneuma puthōna<br>Pronunciation: [pnyoo'-mah poo'-thone-ah]<br>Parsing *pneuma* (part of speech): noun<br>  Case—accusative<br>  Gender—neuter<br>  Number—singular<br>  Stem or root—from πνεῦμα, τος<br>Parsing *puthōna* (part of speech): noun<br>  Case—accusative<br>  Gender—masculine<br>  Number—plural<br>  Stem or root—from πύθων, ωνος<br>Concordance References:<br>⇒ Strong's #4151 + 4436 pneuma puthōn<br>⇒ NIV #4460 + 4780 pneuma puthōn [spirit which predicted the future]<br>⇒ NASB #4151 + 4436 pneuma puthōn | Spirit which predicted the future; spirit of divination; spirit that is demon possessed; spirit of foretelling the future and fate of people; to be a fortuneteller.<br><br>**Practical Application**<br>The Greek word *"puthōna"* which is our English word python, refers to the large python serpent. In ancient myth the Greek god Apollo was said to have slain the great serpent or dragon python. As a result Apollo took both his great gift of predictions and his name. Apollo became known as "puthios Apollo" or "Python Apollo." The young slave girl is said to have the spirit of "python" *(puthōna)*; that is, the people thought she was the voice, the oracle of the great Greek god Apollo. There were also ventriloquists who |

# PRACTICAL WORD STUDIES
## in the NEW TESTAMENT

| ENGLISH WORD | GREEK WORD AND VERSE | THE WORD MEANS... |
|---|---|---|
| **POSB REFERENCE** (Acts 16:16-17; esp. v.16) Note 1, point 1 | **Acts 16:16** And it came to pass, as we went to prayer, a certain damsel possessed with a **spirit of divination** met us, which brought her masters much gain by soothsaying: [KJV]<br><br>And it happened that as we were going to the place of prayer, a certain slave-girl having a **spirit of divination** met us, who was bringing her masters much profit by fortunetelling. [NASB]<br><br>Once when we were going to the place of prayer, we were met by a slave girl who had a **spirit** by **which** she **predicted the future**. She earned a great deal of money for her owners by fortune-telling. [NIV]<br><br>Now it happened, as we went to prayer, that a certain slave girl possessed with a **spirit of divination** met us, who brought her masters much profit by fortune-telling. [NKJV]<br><br>One day as we were going down to the place of prayer, we met a **demon-possessed** slave girl. She was a fortune-teller who earned a lot of money for her masters. [NLT]<br><br>Ἐγένετο δὲ πορευομένων ἡμῶν εἰς τὴν προσευχήν, παιδίσκην τινὰ ἔχουσαν **πνεῦμα Πύθωνος** ἀπαντῆσαι ἡμῖν, ἥτις ἐργασίαν πολλὴν παρεῖχε τοῖς κυρίοις αὐτῆς μαντευομένη. [GNS]<br><br>Ἐγένετο δὲ πορευομένων ἡμῶν εἰς τὴν προσευχὴν παιδίσκην τινὰ ἔχουσαν **πνεῦμα πύθωνα** ὑπαντῆσαι ἡμῖν, ἥτις ἐργασίαν πολλὴν παρεῖχεν τοῖς κυρίοις αὐτῆς μαντευομένη. [GNT] | were thought to be empowered with the spirit of Apollo. |
| **#951 Demonstration**<br><br>Demonstration–KJV<br>Demonstration–NASB<br>Demonstration–NIV<br>Demonstration–NKJV<br>Powerful–NLT<br><br>**POSB REFERENCE** (1 Cor.2:4) Note 4, point 3 | ἀποδείξει = *apodeixei*<br>Pronunciation: [ap-od'-eek-see]<br>Parsing (part of speech): noun<br>    Case—dative<br>    Gender—feminine<br>    Number—singular<br>    Stem or root—from ἀπόδειξις, εως<br>Concordance References:<br>⇒ Strong's #585 apodeixis<br>⇒ NIV #618 apodeixis<br>⇒ NASB #585 apodeixis<br><br>**1 Cor. 2:4**<br>And my speech and my preaching was not with enticing words of man's wisdom, but in **demonstration** of the Spirit and of power: [KJV]<br><br>And my message and my preaching were not in persuasive words of wisdom, but in **demonstration** of the Spirit and of power, [NASB]<br><br>My message and my preaching were not with wise and persuasive words, but with a **demonstration** of the Spirit's power, [NIV]<br><br>And my speech and my preaching *were* not with persuasive words of human wisdom, but in **demonstration** of the Spirit and of power, [NKJV]<br><br>And my message and my preaching were very plain. I did not use wise and persuasive speeches, but the Holy Spirit was **powerful** among you. [NLT]<br><br>καὶ ὁ λόγος μου καὶ τὸ κήρυγμά μου οὐκ ἐν πειθοῖς ἀνθρωπίνης σοφίας λόγοις, ἀλλ' ἐν **ἀποδείξει** πνεύματος καὶ δυνάμεως· [GNS]<br><br>καὶ ὁ λόγος μου καὶ τὸ κήρυγμά μου οὐκ ἐν πειθοῖ[ς] σοφίας [λόγοις] ἀλλ' ἐν **ἀποδείξει** πνεύματος καὶ δυνάμεως, [GNT] | Demonstration, proof, to show forth with the most rigorous evidence and proof.<br><br>**Practical Application**<br>The idea is that the evidence is presented so strongly that the truth is clearly seen. |
| **#952 Demonstrates**<br><br>Commendeth–KJV<br>Demonstrates–NASB<br>Demonstrates–NIV | συνίστησιν = *sunistēsin*<br>Pronunciation: [soon-is-tay'-sin]<br>Parsing (part of speech): verb<br>    Mood—indicative<br>    Tense—present<br>    Voice—active<br>    Person—3rd person | Recommends; commends; gives approval to; shows, proves, demonstrates; to stand with or beside.<br><br>**Practical Application**<br>We were sinners, yet God proved His love to us. The word "demonstrates" (*sunistēsin*) means |

# PRACTICAL WORD STUDIES
## in the NEW TESTAMENT

| ENGLISH WORD | GREEK WORD AND VERSE | THE WORD MEANS... |
|---|---|---|
| **Demonstrates–NKJV**<br>Showed–NLT<br><br>**POSB REFERENCE**<br>(Rom.5:8-9; esp. v.8)<br>Note 2 | Number—singular<br>Stem or root—from συνίστημι and συνιστάνω<br>Concordance References:<br>⇒ Strong's #4921 sunistēmi<br>⇒ NIV #5319 sunistēmi<br>⇒ NASB #4921 sunistēmi<br><br>**Romans 5:8**<br>But God **commendeth** his love toward us, in that, while we were yet sinners, Christ died for us. [KJV]<br>But God **demonstrates** His own love toward us, in that while we were yet sinners, Christ died for us. [NASB]<br>But God **demonstrates** his own love for us in this: While we were still sinners, Christ died for us. [NIV]<br>But God **demonstrates** His own love toward us, in that while we were still sinners, Christ died for us. [NKJV]<br>But God **showed** his great love for us by sending Christ to die for us while we were still sinners. [NLT]<br>**συνίστησι** δὲ τὴν ἑαυτοῦ ἀγάπην εἰς ἡμᾶς ὁ Θεὸς ὅτι ἔτι ἁμαρτωλῶν ὄντων ἡμῶν Χριστὸς ὑπὲρ ἡμῶν ἀπέθανε. [GNS]<br>**συνίστησιν** δὲ τὴν ἑαυτοῦ ἀγάπην εἰς ἡμᾶς ὁ θεός, ὅτι ἔτι ἁμαρτωλῶν ὄντων ἡμῶν Χριστὸς ὑπὲρ ἡμῶν ἀπέθανεν. [GNT] | to show, prove, exhibit. It is the present tense: God is always showing and proving His love to us. |
| **#953**<br>**Deny**<br><br>Deny–KJV<br>Deny–NASB<br>Deny–NIV<br>Deny–NKJV<br>Put aside–NLT<br><br>**POSB REFERENCE**<br>(Mt.16:24)<br>Note 2, point 2<br><br>See also POSB REF:<br>(Mk.8:34)<br>*Deeper Study #2* | **ἀπαρνησάσθω** = *aparnēsasthō*<br>Pronunciation: [ap-ar-neh'-sas-tho]<br>Parsing (part of speech): verb<br>    Mood—imperative<br>    Tense—aorist<br>    Voice—middle deponent<br>    Person—3rd person<br>    Number—singular<br>    Stem or root—from ἀπαρνέομαι<br>Concordance References:<br>⇒ Strong's #533 aparneomai<br>⇒ NIV #565 aparneomai<br>⇒ NASB #533 aparneomai<br><br>**Matthew 16:24**<br>Then said Jesus unto his disciples, If any man will come after me, let him **deny** himself, and take up his cross, and follow me. [KJV]<br>Then Jesus said to His disciples, "If anyone wishes to come after Me, let him **deny** himself, and take up his cross, and follow Me. [NASB]<br>Then Jesus said to his disciples, "If anyone would come after me, he must **deny** himself and take up his cross and follow me. [NIV]<br>Then Jesus said to His disciples, "If anyone desires to come after Me, let him **deny** himself, and take up his cross, and follow Me. [NKJV]<br>Then Jesus said to the disciples, "If any of you wants to be my follower, you must **put aside** your selfish ambition, shoulder your cross, and follow me. [NLT]<br>τότε ὁ Ἰησοῦς εἶπε τοῖς μαθηταῖς αὐτοῦ, Εἴ τις θέλει ὀπίσω μου ἐλθεῖν, **ἀπαρνησάσθω** ἑαυτὸν, καὶ ἀράτω τὸν σταυρὸν αὐτοῦ καὶ ἀκολουθείτω μοι. [GNS]<br>Τότε ὁ Ἰησοῦς εἶπεν τοῖς μαθηταῖς αὐτοῦ, Εἴ τις θέλει ὀπίσω μου ἐλθεῖν, **ἀπαρνησάσθω** ἑαυτὸν καὶ ἀράτω τὸν σταυρὸν αὐτοῦ καὶ ἀκολουθείτω μοι. [GNT] | To disown, disregard, deny, put aside, forsake, renounce, reject, refuse, restrain, disclaim. It means to subdue, to disregard one's self and one's interest. Very simply, it means to say "no."<br><br>**Practical Application**<br>But note: the call is not to say "no" to some behavior or thing, but to self. A person is to deny self; and this means much more than just being negative, that is, giving up something and doing without something. It means that we are to act positively, to say "yes" to Christ and "no" to self. It means to let Christ rule and reign in our hearts and lives, to let Christ have His way completely. Of course, if a person allows Christ to rule in his life, all negative as well as positive behavior is taken care of (see POSB note and POSB *Deeper Study* #1—Mark 8:34, POSB *Deeper Study* #2—Mark 8:34, POSB *Deeper Study* #3—Mark 8:34). In the Greek, the word "deny" is an ingressive aorist which means that the person enters a new state or condition. It means, "Let him at once begin to deny self." |
| **#954**<br>**Deny**<br><br>Consent–KJV<br>Agree with–NASB<br>Agree to–NIV<br>Consent–NKJV<br>Deny–NLT | **προσέρχεται** = *proserchetai*<br>Pronunciation: [pros-er'-kheh-tah-ee]<br>Parsing (part of speech): verb<br>    Mood—indicative<br>    Tense—present<br>    Voice—middle or passive deponent<br>    Person—3rd person<br>    Number—singular<br>    Stem or root—from προσέρχομαι<br>Concordance References: | To agree to; to agree with; to consent.<br><br>**Practical Application**<br>The word "agree to" (*proserchetai*) has the sense of "attaching oneself to" Christ (Daniel Guthrie. *The Pastoral Epistles*. "Tyndale New Testament Commentaries," p.110f).<br>1. The false teacher is just not willing to attach himself to the *Lord Jesus Christ*. He is... |

## PRACTICAL WORD STUDIES
### in the NEW TESTAMENT

| ENGLISH WORD | GREEK WORD AND VERSE | THE WORD MEANS... |
|---|---|---|
| **POSB REFERENCE** (1 Tim.6:3) Note 1, point 1, 2 | ⇒ Strong's #4334 proserchomai<br>⇒ NIV #4665 proserchomai<br>⇒ NASB #4334 proserchomai<br><br>**1 Tim. 6:3**<br>If any man teach otherwise, and **consent** not to wholesome words, *even* the words of our Lord Jesus Christ, and to the doctrine which is according to godliness; [KJV]<br>If anyone advocates a different doctrine, and does not **agree with** sound words, those of our Lord Jesus Christ, and with the doctrine conforming to godliness, [NASB]<br>If anyone teaches false doctrines and does not **agree to** the sound instruction of our Lord Jesus Christ and to godly teaching, [NIV]<br>If anyone teaches otherwise and does not **consent** to wholesome words, *even* the words of our Lord Jesus Christ, and to the doctrine which accords with godliness, [NKJV]<br>Some false teachers may **deny** these things, but these are the sound, wholesome teachings of the Lord Jesus Christ, and they are the foundation for a godly life. [NLT]<br>Εἴ τις ἑτεροδιδασκαλεῖ, καὶ μὴ **προσέρχεται** ὑγιαίνουσι λόγοις, τοῖς τοῦ Κυρίου ἡμῶν Ἰησοῦ Χριστοῦ, καὶ τῇ κατ' εὐσέβειαν διδασκαλίᾳ, [GNS]<br>εἴ τις ἑτεροδιδασκαλεῖ καὶ μὴ **προσέρχεται** ὑγιαίνουσιν λόγοις τοῖς τοῦ κυρίου ἡμῶν Ἰησοῦ Χριστοῦ καὶ τῇ κατ' εὐσέβειαν διδασκαλίᾳ, [GNT] | • not willing to confess that Jesus is the *Lord God* from heaven, the very Son of God Himself.<br>• not willing to confess that Jesus is the Christ, the Messiah and Savior of the world.<br>2. The false teacher does not consent to or agree with the teachings of godliness. He is...<br>• not willing to accept the righteousness of God revealed in Jesus Christ.<br>• not willing to separate himself from the world nor to set his life wholly apart unto God.<br>One or both of these reasons are why the false teacher does not teach the wholesome words of Christ but rather chooses to teach a different doctrine and way of life. He has committed his life to the *profession* of the ministry...<br>• as a way to serve mankind.<br>• as a way to earn a livelihood.<br>But he is not committed to represent Christ and His Word. As a result, the person is called a false teacher by both the Holy Scriptures and Christ. |
| #955<br>**Deny These Things**<br><br>Teach otherwise–KJV<br>Advocates a different doctrine–NASB<br>Teaches false doctrines–NIV<br>Teaches otherwise–NKJV<br>**Deny these things–NLT**<br><br>**POSB REFERENCE** (1 Tim.6:3) Note 1 | ἑτεροδιδασκαλεῖ = *heterodidaskalei*<br>Pronunciation: [het-er-od-id-as-kal-eh'-ee]<br>Parsing (part of speech): verb<br>    Mood—indicative<br>    Tense—present<br>    Voice—active<br>    Person—3rd person<br>    Number—singular<br>    Stem or root—from ἑτεροδιδασκαλέω<br>Concordance References:<br>⇒ Strong's #2085 heterodidaskaleō<br>⇒ NIV #2281 heterodidaskaleō<br>⇒ NASB #2085 heterodidaskaleō<br><br>**1 Tim. 6:3**<br>If any man **teach otherwise**, and consent not to wholesome words, *even* the words of our Lord Jesus Christ, and to the doctrine which is according to godliness; [KJV]<br>If anyone **advocates a different doctrine**, and does not agree with sound words, those of our Lord Jesus Christ, and with the doctrine conforming to godliness, [NASB]<br>If anyone **teaches false doctrines** and does not agree to the sound instruction of our Lord Jesus Christ and to godly teaching, [NIV]<br>If anyone **teaches otherwise** and does not consent to wholesome words, *even* the words of our Lord Jesus Christ, and to the doctrine which accords with godliness, [NKJV]<br>Some false teachers may **deny these things**, but these are the sound, wholesome teachings of the Lord Jesus Christ, and they are the foundation for a godly life. [NLT]<br>Εἴ τις **ἑτεροδιδασκαλεῖ**, καὶ μὴ προσέρχεται ὑγιαίνουσι λόγοις, τοῖς τοῦ Κυρίου ἡμῶν Ἰησοῦ Χριστοῦ, καὶ τῇ κατ' εὐσέβειαν διδασκαλίᾳ, [GNS]<br>εἴ τις **ἑτεροδιδασκαλεῖ** καὶ μὴ προσέρχεται ὑγιαίνουσιν λόγοις τοῖς τοῦ κυρίου ἡμῶν Ἰησοῦ Χριστοῦ καὶ τῇ κατ' εὐσέβειαν διδασκαλίᾳ, [GNT] | Teaches false doctrines; to advocate a different doctrine.<br><br>**Practical Application**<br>The false teacher advocates a different doctrine or denies these things. He does not teach the words of the Lord Jesus Christ. This is a terrible indictment. Imagine being in the pulpit of a Christian church and claiming to be a teacher of the Lord Jesus Christ, yet not teaching His words. How many of us are guilty of this indictment? How many of us are guilty of advocating a different doctrine? |
| #956<br>**Depart** | ἀποχωρεῖτε ἀπ' = *apochōreite ap'*<br>Pronunciation: [ap-okh-o-reh'-i-teh ap]<br>Parsing (part of speech): verb<br>    Mood—imperative<br>    Tense—present | To depart from; to go away; to be cut off from; to leave a place. |

# PRACTICAL WORD STUDIES
## in the NEW TESTAMENT

| ENGLISH WORD | GREEK WORD AND VERSE | THE WORD MEANS... |
|---|---|---|
| **Depart–KJV**<br>**Depart–NASB**<br>Away from–NIV<br>**Depart–NKJV**<br>Away–NLT<br><br>**POSB REFERENCE**<br>(Mt.7:23)<br>*Deeper Study #1* | Voice—active<br>Person—2nd person<br>Number—plural<br>Stem or root—from ἀποχωρέω<br>Concordance References:<br>⇒ Strong's #672 apochōreō + 575 apo<br>⇒ NIV #713+608 apochōreō apo<br>⇒ NASB #672 apochōreō + 575 apo<br><br>**Matthew 7:23**<br>And then will I profess unto them, I never knew you: **depart** from me, ye that work iniquity. [KJV]<br>"And then I will declare to them, 'I never knew you; **depart** from Me, you who practice lawlessness.' [NASB]<br>Then I will tell them plainly, 'I never knew you. **Away from** me, you evildoers!' [NIV]<br>And then I will declare to them, 'I never knew you; **depart** from Me, you who practice lawlessness!' [NKJV]<br>But I will reply, 'I never knew you. Go **away**; the things you did were unauthorized.' [NLT]<br>καὶ τότε ὁμολογήσω αὐτοῖς, ὅτι οὐδέποτε ἔγνων ὑμᾶς· **ἀποχωρεῖτε ἀπ'** ἐμοῦ οἱ ἐργαζόμενοι τὴν ἀνομίαν. [GNS]<br>καὶ τότε ὁμολογήσω αὐτοῖς ὅτι Οὐδέποτε ἔγνων ὑμᾶς· **ἀποχωρεῖτε ἀπ'** ἐμοῦ οἱ ἐργαζόμενοι τὴν ἀνομίαν. [GNT] | **Practical Application**<br>In this Scripture, the idea is the enormous distance, the great gulf, placed between the person making a false profession and the Lord's presence. There will never be a sadder moment in a person's life than to hear Christ's command to "go away from Me, depart from Me...I never knew you!" |
| #957<br>**Depart**<br><br>**Depart–KJV**<br>**Depart–NASB**<br>**Depart–NIV**<br>**Depart–NKJV**<br>Go–NLT<br><br>**POSB REFERENCE**<br>(Philip.1:22-23; esp. v.23)<br>Note 3, points 1, 2 | ἀναλῦσαι = *analusai*<br>Pronunciation: [an-al-oo'-sah-ee]<br>Parsing (part of speech): verb<br>Mood—infinitive<br>Tense—aorist<br>Voice—active<br>Case—accusative<br>Stem or root—from ἀναλύω<br>Concordance References:<br>⇒ Strong's #360 analuō<br>⇒ NIV #386 analuō<br>⇒ NASB #360 analuō<br><br>**Philip. 1:23**<br>For I am in a strait betwixt two, having a desire to **depart**, and to be with Christ; which is far better: [KJV]<br>But I am hard-pressed from both directions, having the desire to **depart** and be with Christ, for that is very much better; [NASB]<br>I am torn between the two: I desire to **depart** and be with Christ, which is better by far; [NIV]<br>For I am hard pressed between the two, having a desire to **depart** and be with Christ, *which is* far better. [NKJV]<br>I'm torn between two desires: Sometimes I want to live, and sometimes I long to **go** and be with Christ. That would be far better for me, [NLT]<br>συνέχομαι γὰρ ἐκ τῶν δύο, τὴν ἐπιθυμίαν ἔχων εἰς τὸ **ἀναλῦσαι** καὶ σὺν Χριστῷ εἶναι, πολλῷ γὰρ μᾶλλον κρεῖσσον· [GNS]<br>συνέχομαι δὲ ἐκ τῶν δύο, τὴν ἐπιθυμίαν ἔχων εἰς τὸ **ἀναλῦσαι** καὶ σὺν Χριστῷ εἶναι, πολλῷ [γὰρ] μᾶλλον κρεῖσσον· [GNT] | To depart; to go; to return home; to come back.<br><br>**Practical Application**<br>The word "depart" (*analusai*) is descriptive. It has a twofold meaning that speaks to the believer's heart.<br>1. It means to break up; to loosen as in breaking camp and loosening the ropes of the tent. It is the picture of breaking loose; packing up; and moving on to a new location. The same picture is true of the believer when he departs this life. He is not ceasing to exist; he is simply breaking loose and moving on to a new campsite, in fact, a perfect campsite.<br>2. It means to loosen the moorings of a ship, weigh anchor, and set sail for another port. Again, the believer does not cease to exist, he simply loosens the moorings of this life, pulls the anchor up, and sets sail for God's eternal presence.<br>Paul says that he is caught between two great desires:<br>⇒ One desire is to live a life of fruitful service for the Lord Jesus Christ.<br>⇒ The other desire is to depart and go on to be with Christ which is far better.<br>The natural mind wonders and questions how a person in his right mind could ever want to go ahead and die. The reason is simply answered: the genuine believer does not die; he never tastes death. He is transferred into the presence of Christ. Immediately—quicker than the blinking of an eye—the believer is transported into the perfect world of God which is named heaven. The believer is perfected—never again to experience pain, suffering, sin, corruption, infirmity, weakness, deformity, disappointment, fear, loss, or |

# PRACTICAL WORD STUDIES
## in the New Testament

| ENGLISH WORD | GREEK WORD AND VERSE | THE WORD MEANS... |
|---|---|---|
| | | death. He will be perfected to work for Christ throughout the new heavens and earth, and he will serve and worship Christ for ever and ever. The promises of God to the believer are phenomenal; they just explode the human mind. It is for this reason that the believer can declare: "To die is gain." |
| **#958** **Departure** Decease–KJV **Departure–NASB** **Departure–NIV** Decease–NKJV Dying–NLT **POSB REFERENCE** (Lk.9:30-31; esp. v.31) Note 4, point 2 | ἔξοδον = exodon Pronunciation: [ex'-od-on] Parsing (part of speech): noun     Case—accusative     Gender—feminine     Number—singular     Stem or root—from ἔξοδος, ου Concordance References: ⇒ Strong's #1841 exodos ⇒ NIV #2016 exodos ⇒ NASB #1841 exodos **Luke 9:31** Who appeared in glory, and spake of his **decease** which he should accomplish at Jerusalem. [KJV] Who, appearing in glory, were speaking of His **departure** which He was about to accomplish at Jerusalem. [NASB] Appeared in glorious splendor, talking with Jesus. They spoke about his **departure**, which he was about to bring to fulfillment at Jerusalem. [NIV] Who appeared in glory and spoke of His **decease** which He was about to accomplish at Jerusalem. [NKJV] They were glorious to see. And they were speaking of how he was about to fulfill God's plan by **dying** in Jerusalem. [NLT] οἳ ὀφθέντες ἐν δόξῃ ἔλεγον τὴν **ἔξοδον** αὐτοῦ, ἣν ἤμελλε πληροῦν ἐν Ἰερουσαλήμ. [GNS] οἳ ὀφθέντες ἐν δόξῃ ἔλεγον τὴν **ἔξοδον** αὐτοῦ, ἣν ἤμελλεν πληροῦν ἐν Ἰερουσαλήμ. [GNT] | Departure; exodus, decease; to depart; to go out; to die. **Practical Application** In this Scripture, there stood Moses sharing how God had so miraculously saved and delivered the children of Israel out of bondage and how the exodus (deliverance) was only a picture of the marvelous deliverance that He, God's Son, was to accomplish for man. Jesus was to accomplish a new exodus, a new saving deliverance; except this time, it was to be for all men. All men were to be delivered from the bondage of sin and death, from the devil and hell—delivered into the glorious liberty of God and life, both abundant and eternal life. Jesus' dying was to be well worth it, Moses and Elijah stressed. Note: the very encouragement that our Lord needed as Man was given by two who had believed and hoped in His coming. Being reminded of the marvelous deliverance (*exodon*) that had happened so long ago was bound to strengthen and lift the heart of Christ. Just seeing Moses and Elijah stand there, two who had trusted and believed and hoped, was bound to cause the Lord's spirit to rise. He was greatly encouraged and knew that He could not fail these men who had trusted and hoped in Him so much. |
| **#959** **Departure** **Departure–KJV** **Departure–NASB** **Departure–NIV** **Departure–NKJV** Death–NLT **POSB REFERENCE** (2 Tim. 4:6) Note 1, point 2 | ἀναλύσεως = analuseōs Pronunciation: [an-al'-oo-seh-os] Parsing (part of speech): noun     Case—genitive     Gender—feminine     Number—singular     Stem or root—from ἀνάλυσις, εως Concordance References: ⇒ Strong's #359 analusis ⇒ NIV #385 analusis ⇒ NASB #359 analusis **2 Tim. 4:6** For I am now ready to be offered, and the time of my **departure** is at hand. [KJV] For I am already being poured out as a drink offering, and the time of my **departure** has come. [NASB] For I am already being poured out like a drink offering, and the time has come for my **departure**. [NIV] For I am already being poured out as a drink offering, and the time of my **departure** is at hand. [NKJV] As for me, my life has already been poured out as an offering to God. The time of my **death** is near. [NLT] ἐγὼ γὰρ ἤδη σπένδομαι, καὶ ὁ καιρὸς τῆς ἐμῆς **ἀναλύσεως** ἐφέστηκε. [GNS] Ἐγὼ γὰρ ἤδη σπένδομαι, καὶ ὁ καιρὸς τῆς **ἀναλύσεώς** μου ἐφέστηκεν. [GNT] | Departure, death. **Practical Application** The word (*analuseōs*) is striking in its meaning. (The following meanings are taken from W.E. Vine. *Expository Dictionary of New Testament Words*.) 1. To depart is the picture of a ship hoisting the anchor and loosening the mooring ropes and departing one country for another country. Paul had been anchored and tied to this world, but the anchor and ropes of this world were now being loosed, and Paul was about to set sail for the greatest of all ports—heaven itself. 2. To depart is the picture of "breaking up an encampment" (W.E. Vine). Paul had been camping in this world. If any man has ever known what it is like to be unsettled and moving about from place to place, it was Paul. And unfortunately it was often not by choice. Many times the opposition to the gospel had been so violent, he had been forced to break camp and move on, sometimes fleeing for his life. But now, Paul was to break camp and depart for the last time, and what a departure it was to be. He would never again have to move. He was departing this world for his permanent residence: heaven itself. 3. To depart is the picture of the unyoking of an animal from the burden of the cart, plough, or millstone which it had been pulling to grind the grain. Paul was to be released from the |

## Practical Word Studies in the New Testament

| ENGLISH WORD | GREEK WORD AND VERSE | THE WORD MEANS... |
|---|---|---|
| | | yoke and burden of labor and toil in this life. He was being released and set free to depart for the pastures and still waters and rest of heaven and eternity. |
| **#960** **Deposit Guaranteeing** Earnest–KJV Pledge–NASB **Deposit guaranteeing–NIV** Guarantee–NKJV Guarantee–NLT **POSB REFERENCE** (Eph.1:13-14; esp. v.14) Note 8 | ἀρραβὼν = arrabōn Pronunciation: [ar-hrab-ohn'] Parsing (part of speech): noun     Case—nominative     Gender—masculine     Number—singular     Stem or root—from ἀρραβών, ῶνος Concordance References: ⇒ Strong's #728 arrabōn ⇒ NIV #775 arrabōn ⇒ NASB #728 arrabōn **Ephes. 1:14** Which is the **earnest** of our inheritance until the redemption of the purchased possession, unto the praise of his glory. [KJV] Who is given as a **pledge** of our inheritance, with a view to the redemption of God's own possession, to the praise of His glory. [NASB] Who is a **deposit guaranteeing** our inheritance until the redemption of those who are God's possession—to the praise of his glory. [NIV] Who is the **guarantee** of our inheritance until the redemption of the purchased possession, to the praise of His glory. [NKJV] The Spirit is God's **guarantee** that he will give us everything he promised and that he has purchased us to be his own people. This is just one more reason for us to praise our glorious God. [NLT] ὅς ἐστιν **ἀρραβὼν** τῆς κληρονομίας ἡμῶν, εἰς ἀπολύτρωσιν τῆς περιποιήσεως, εἰς ἔπαινον τῆς δόξης αὐτοῦ. [GNS] ὅ ἐστιν **ἀρραβὼν** τῆς κληρονομίας ἡμῶν, εἰς ἀπολύτρωσιν τῆς περιποιήσεως, εἰς ἔπαινον τῆς δόξης αὐτοῦ. [GNT] | A deposit guaranteeing; an earnest; a pledge; a guarantee; a down payment. **Practical Application** The Holy Spirit is given to the believer to give the believer perfect assurance of his salvation. We know that we are redeemed—that we are God's cherished possession—by the Holy Spirit who lives within us. Again note: Why does God give us such a glorious guarantee as His own wonderful presence? That His glory might be praised eternally. |
| **#961** **Deposit Guaranteeing What Is To Come** Earnest–KJV Pledge–NASB **Deposit guaranteeing what is to come–NIV** Guarantee–NKJV First installment–NLT **POSB REFERENCE** (2 Cor.1:21-22; esp. v.22) Note 5 | ἀρραβῶνα = arrabōna Pronunciation: [ar-hrab-ohn'-ah] Parsing (part of speech): noun     Case—accusative     Gender—masculine     Number—singular     Stem or root—from ἀρραβών, ῶνος Concordance References: ⇒ Strong's #728 arrabōn ⇒ NIV #775 arrabōn ⇒ NASB #728 arrabōn **2 Cor. 1:22** Who hath also sealed us, and given the **earnest** of the Spirit in our hearts. [KJV] Who also sealed us and gave us the Spirit in our hearts as a **pledge**. [NASB] Set his seal of ownership on us, and put his Spirit in our hearts as a **deposit, guaranteeing what is to come**. [NIV] Who also has sealed us and given us the Spirit in our hearts as a **guarantee**. [NKJV] And he has identified us as his own by placing the Holy Spirit in our hearts as the **first installment** of everything he will give us. [NLT] ὁ καὶ σφραγισάμενος ἡμᾶς, καὶ δοὺς τὸν **ἀρραβῶνα** τοῦ Πνεύματος ἐν ταῖς καρδίαις ἡμῶν. [GNS] ὁ καὶ σφραγισάμενος ἡμᾶς καὶ δοὺς τὸν **ἀρραβῶνα** τοῦ πνεύματος ἐν ταῖς καρδίαις ἡμῶν. [GNT] | Deposit, guarantee, security, pledge, first installment (of what is to come), payment. **Practical Application** It was the first installment paid on an item to guarantee that the rest would be paid. It was the engagement ring that guaranteed the marriage. God has given the Holy Spirit as the guarantee of eternal life. The Holy Spirit is an advanced payment, a down payment, on His promise to believers. |
| **#962** **Depraved Mind** | ἀδόκιμον νοῦν = adokimon noun Pronunciation: [ad-ok'-ee-mon noon] Parsing *adokimon* (part of speech): adjective     Case—accusative | Failing to meet the test; disqualified; worthless; corrupted (mind); mind, thought, reason; attitude, intention, purpose; understanding, discernment. |

## Practical Word Studies
### in the New Testament

| ENGLISH WORD | GREEK WORD AND VERSE | THE WORD MEANS... |
|---|---|---|
| Reprobate mind–KJV<br>**Deprived mind– NASB**<br>**Depraved mind–NIV**<br>Debased mind–NKJV<br>Evil minds–NLT<br><br>**POSB REFERENCE**<br>(Rom.1:28-31; esp. v.28)<br>Note 4, point 1 | Gender—masculine<br>Number—singular<br>Stem or root—from ἀδόκιμος, ον<br>Parsing *noun* (part of speech): noun<br>    Case—accusative<br>    Gender—masculine<br>    Number—singular<br>    Stem or root—from νοῦς, νοός, νοΐ, νοῦν<br>Concordance References:<br>⇒ Strong's #96 adokimos + 3563 nous<br>⇒ NIV #99 adokimos [depraved] + 3808 nous [mind]<br>⇒ NASB #96 adokimos + 3563 nous<br><br>**Romans 1:28**<br>And even as they did not like to retain God in their knowledge, God gave them over to a **reprobate mind**, to do those things which are not convenient; [KJV]<br>And just as they did not see fit to acknowledge God any longer, God gave them over to a **depraved mind**, to do those things which are not proper, [NASB]<br>Furthermore, since they did not think it worthwhile to retain the knowledge of God, he gave them over to a **depraved mind**, to do what ought not to be done. [NIV]<br>And even as they did not like to retain God in *their* knowledge, God gave them over to a **debased mind**, to do those things which are not fitting; [NKJV]<br>When they refused to acknowledge God, he abandoned them to their **evil minds** and let them do things that should never be done. [NLT]<br>Καὶ καθὼς οὐκ ἐδοκίμασαν τὸν Θεὸν ἔχειν ἐν ἐπιγνώσει, παρέδωκεν αὐτοὺς ὁ Θεὸς εἰς **ἀδόκιμον νοῦν**, ποιεῖν τὰ μὴ καθήκοντα, [GNS]<br>καὶ καθὼς οὐκ ἐδοκίμασαν τὸν θεὸν ἔχειν ἐν ἐπιγνώσει, παρέδωκεν αὐτοὺς ὁ θεὸς εἰς **ἀδόκιμον νοῦν**, ποιεῖν τὰ μὴ καθήκοντα, [GNT] | **Practical Application**<br>God shows wrath by giving men up to reprobate, depraved minds. The term "depraved or reprobate mind" (*adokimon noun*) means a mind that is rejected, disapproved, degraded, depraved; a mind that cannot stand the test of judgment.<br>The reason God gives men up to reprobate minds is because men reject God. They know God, but they do not "like to retain God in their knowledge." They...<br>• do not like to approve God.<br>• do not like to recognize God.<br>• do not like to acknowledge God.<br><br>They simply do not want God to have anything to do with their lives; therefore, they push Him out of their minds. They ignore and refuse to accept God's presence. |
| #963<br>**Depravity**<br><br>Maliciousness–KJV<br>Evil–NASB<br>**Depravity–NIV**<br>Maliciousness–NKJV<br>Hate–NLT<br><br>**POSB REFERENCE**<br>(Rom.1:29)<br>*Deeper Study #5* | κακία = *kakia*<br>Pronunciation: [kak-ee'-ah]<br>Parsing (part of speech): noun<br>    Case—dative<br>    Gender—feminine<br>    Number—singular<br>    Stem or root—from κακία, ας<br>Concordance References:<br>⇒ Strong's #2549 kakia<br>⇒ NIV #2798 kakia<br>⇒ NASB #2549 kakia<br><br>**Romans 1:29**<br>Being filled with all unrighteousness, fornication, wickedness, covetousness, **maliciousness**; full of envy, murder, debate, deceit, malignity; whisperers, [KJV]<br>Being filled with all unrighteousness, wickedness, greed, **evil**; full of envy, murder, strife, deceit, malice; they are gossips, [NASB]<br>They have become filled with every kind of wickedness, evil, greed and **depravity**. They are full of envy, murder, strife, deceit and malice. They are gossips, [NIV]<br>Being filled with all unrighteousness, sexual immorality, wickedness, covetousness, **maliciousness**; full of envy, murder, strife, deceit, evil-mindedness; *they are* whisperers, [NKJV]<br>Their lives became full of every kind of wickedness, sin, greed, **hate**, envy, murder, fighting, deception, malicious behavior, and gossip. [NLT]<br>πεπληρωμένους πάσῃ ἀδικίᾳ πορνείᾳ, πονηρίᾳ πλεονεξίᾳ **κακίᾳ**· μεστοὺς φθόνου, φόνου, ἔριδος, δόλου, κακοηθείας· [GNS]<br>πεπληρωμένους πάσῃ ἀδικίᾳ πονηρίᾳ πλεονεξίᾳ **κακίᾳ**, μεστοὺς φθόνου φόνου ἔριδος δόλου κακοηθείας, ψιθυριστάς [GNT] | Evil; wickedness; hateful feelings; malice; viciousness; ill will; spite; a grudge; worry (Mt 6.34).<br><br>**Practical Application**<br>Depravity (*kakia*) means that a man has turned his heart completely over to evil.<br>⇒ He no longer has any good within—none whatsoever.<br>⇒ He is full of viciousness and malice.<br>⇒ He is actively pursuing evil with a vengeance. |

# PRACTICAL WORD STUDIES
## in the NEW TESTAMENT

| ENGLISH WORD | GREEK WORD AND VERSE | THE WORD MEANS... |
|---|---|---|
| **#964**<br>**Deputy**<br><br>Deputy–KJV<br>Proconsul–NASB<br>Proconsul–NIV<br>Proconsul–NKJV<br>Governor–NLT<br><br>**POSB REFERENCE**<br>(Acts 13:7)<br>Note 3 | ἀνθυπάτῳ = *anthupatō*<br>Pronunciation: [an-thoo'-pah-tow]<br>Parsing (part of speech): noun<br>    Case—dative<br>    Gender—masculine<br>    Number—singular<br>    Stem or root—from ἀνθύπατος, ου<br>Concordance References:<br>  ⇒ Strong's #446 anthupatos<br>  ⇒ NIV #478 anthupatos<br>  ⇒ NASB #446 anthupatos<br><br>**Acts 13:7**<br>Which was with the **deputy** of the country, Sergius Paulus, a prudent man; who called for Barnabas and Saul, and desired to hear the word of God. [KJV]<br><br>Who was with the **proconsul**, Sergius Paulus, a man of intelligence. This man summoned Barnabas and Saul and sought to hear the word of God. [NASB]<br><br>Who was an attendant of the proconsul, Sergius Paulus. The **proconsul**, an intelligent man, sent for Barnabas and Saul because he wanted to hear the word of God. [NIV]<br><br>Who was with the **proconsul**, Sergius Paulus, an intelligent man. This man called for Barnabas and Saul and sought to hear the word of God. [NKJV]<br><br>He had attached himself to the **governor**, Sergius Paulus, a man of considerable insight and understanding. The governor invited Barnabas and Saul to visit him, for he wanted to hear the word of God. [NLT]<br><br>ὃς ἦν σὺν τῷ **ἀνθυπάτῳ** Σεργίῳ Παύλῳ, ἀνδρὶ συνετῷ. οὗτος προσκαλεσάμενος Βαρναβᾶν καὶ Σαῦλον, ἐπεζήτησεν ἀκοῦσαι τὸν λόγον τοῦ Θεοῦ. [GNS]<br><br>ὃς ἦν σὺν τῷ **ἀνθυπάτῳ** Σεργίῳ Παύλῳ, ἀνδρὶ συνετῷ. οὗτος προσκαλεσάμενος Βαρναβᾶν καὶ Σαῦλον ἐπεζήτησεν ἀκοῦσαι τὸν λόγον τοῦ θεοῦ· [GNT] | Proconsul, deputy, governor.<br><br>**Practical Application**<br>The Roman proconsul was appointed and controlled by the Roman Senate. He was the highest ranking official, the man of power and influence on the island. |
| **#965**<br>**Desecration, Sacrilegious Object That Causes**<br><br>Abomination of desolation–KJV<br>Abomination of desolation–NASB<br>Abomination that causes desolation–NIV<br>Abomination of desolation–NKJV<br>Sacrilegious object that causes desecration–NLT<br><br>**POSB REFERENCE**<br>(Mt.24:15)<br>*Deeper Study #1*<br><br>See also POSB REF:<br>(Mk.13:14)<br>*Deeper Study #1* | βδέλυγμα ἐρημώσεως = *bdelugma erēmōseōs*<br>Pronunciation: [bdel'-oog-mah er-ay'-mo-say'-os]<br>Parsing *bdelugma* (part of speech): noun<br>    Case—accusative<br>    Gender—neuter<br>    Number—singular<br>    Stem or root—from βδέλυγμα, τος<br>Parsing *erēmōseōs* (part of speech): noun<br>    Case—genitive<br>    Gender—feminine<br>    Number—singular<br>    Stem or root—from ἐρήμωσις, εως<br>Concordance References:<br>  ⇒ Strong's #946 bdelugma + 2050 eremosis<br>  ⇒ NIV #1007 bdelugma [abomination] + 3836 ho + 2247 erēmōsis [desolation]<br>  ⇒ NASB #946 bdelugma + 2050 eremosis<br><br>**Matthew 24:15**<br>When ye therefore shall see the **abomination of desolation**, spoken of by Daniel the prophet, stand in the holy place, (whoso readeth, let him understand:) [KJV]<br><br>"Therefore when you see the **abomination of desolation** which was spoken of through Daniel the prophet, standing in the holy place (let the reader understand), [NASB]<br><br>"So when you see standing in the holy place 'the **abomination that causes desolation**,' spoken of through the prophet Daniel—let the reader understand— [NIV]<br><br>"Therefore when you see the *'**abomination of desolation**,'* spoken of by Daniel the prophet, standing in the holy place" (whoever reads, let him understand), [NKJV]<br><br>"The time will come when you will see what Daniel | To detest or detestable.<br><br>**Practical Application**<br>It is a picture of becoming sick with nausea. The sacrilegious object that causes desecration is translated three other times as "sacrilegious object" or "a gold goblet full of obscenities" in the New Testament (See Mark 13:14 and Rev.17:4-5).<br><br>The word "desecration" comes from the greek word (*erēmōsis*) and means a wilderness, a desert, and in this context, a wasted, desolate place.<br><br>**Practical Application**<br>Without the presence of God a place and person are like a wilderness, deserted and left all alone. They are left to waste away. |

# PRACTICAL WORD STUDIES
## in the NEW TESTAMENT

| ENGLISH WORD | GREEK WORD AND VERSE | THE WORD MEANS... |
|---|---|---|
| | the prophet spoke about: **the sacrilegious object that causes desecration** standing in the holy place"—reader, pay attention! [NLT]<br><br>Ὅταν οὖν ἴδητε τὸ **βδέλυγμα** τῆς **ἐρημώσεως** τὸ ῥηθὲν διὰ Δανιὴλ τοῦ προφήτου ἑστὼς ἐν τόπῳ ἁγίῳ, -- ὁ ἀναγινώσκων νοείτω, [GNS]<br><br>Ὅταν οὖν ἴδητε τὸ **βδέλυγμα** τῆς **ἐρημώσεως** τὸ ῥηθὲν διὰ Δανιὴλ τοῦ προφήτου ἑστὸς ἐν τόπῳ ἁγίῳ, ὁ ἀναγινώσκων νοείτω, [GNT] | |
| **#966**<br>**Desert**<br><br>Offended–KJV<br>Fall away–NASB<br>Fall away–NIV<br>Made to stumble–NKJV<br>**Desert–NLT**<br><br>**POSB REFERENCE**<br>(Mt.26:31)<br>*Deeper Study #1*<br><br>See also POSB REF:<br>(Mk.14:27)<br>Note 1, point 1 | **σκανδαλισθήσεσθε** = skandalisthēsesthe<br>Pronunciation: [skan-dal-is'-thay-sehs-theh]<br>Parsing (part of speech): verb<br>  Mood—indicative<br>  Tense—future<br>  Voice—passive<br>  Person—2nd person<br>  Number—plural<br>  Stem or root—from σκανδαλίζω<br>Concordance References:<br>  ⇒ Strong's #4624 skandalizō<br>  ⇒ NIV #4997 skandalizō<br>  ⇒ NASB #4624 skandalizō<br><br>**Matthew 26:31**<br>Then saith Jesus unto them, All ye shall be **offended** because of me this night: for it is written, I will smite the shepherd, and the sheep of the flock shall be scattered abroad. [KJV]<br><br>Then Jesus said to them, "You will all **fall away** because of Me this night, for it is written, 'I WILL STRIKE DOWN THE SHEPHERD, AND THE SHEEP OF THE FLOCK SHALL BE SCATTERED.' [NASB]<br><br>Then Jesus told them, "This very night you will all **fall away** on account of me, for it is written:" 'I will strike the shepherd, and the sheep of the flock will be scattered.' [NIV]<br><br>Then Jesus said to them, "All of you will be **made to stumble** because of Me this night, for it is written: '*I will strike the Shepherd, An the sheep of the flock will be scattered.*' [NKJV]<br><br>"Tonight all of you will **desert** me," Jesus told them. "For the Scriptures say, 'God will strike the Shepherd, and the sheep of the flock will be scattered.' [NLT]<br><br>Τότε λέγει αὐτοῖς ὁ Ἰησοῦς, Πάντες ὑμεῖς **σκανδαλισθήσεσθε** ἐν ἐμοὶ ἐν τῇ νυκτὶ ταύτῃ, γέγραπται γάρ, Πατάξω τὸν ποιμένα, καὶ διασκορπισθήσεται τὰ πρόβατα τῆς ποίμνης· [GNS]<br><br>Τότε λέγει αὐτοῖς ὁ Ἰησοῦς, Πάντες ὑμεῖς **σκανδαλισθήσεσθε** ἐν ἐμοὶ ἐν τῇ νυκτὶ ταύτῃ, γέγραπται γάρ, Πατάξω τὸν ποιμένα, καὶ διασκορπισθήσονται τὰ πρόβατα τῆς ποίμνης. [GNT] | To stumble; to cause to stumble; to be led into sin; to be offended; to fall (because of Christ). (See POSB *Deeper Study* #1—Matthew 26:31).<br><br>**Practical Application**<br>When facing Christ, men stumble over three things. (For a thorough discussion see POSB *Deeper Study* #9—Matthew 21:44 and POSB *Deeper Study* #10—Matthew 21:44 cp. POSB note—Luke 20:17-18.)<br>1. Men stumble over who Christ is (John 6:54-58, 60, 66).<br>2. Men stumble over the cross of Christ (1 Cor. 1:21-23, esp. 1 Cor. 1:23).<br>3. Men stumble over the cross God calls them to bear (see POSB note—Luke 9:23 and POSB *Deeper Study* #1—Luke 9:23). |
| **#967**<br>**Deserting**<br><br>Removed–KJV<br>**Deserting–NASB**<br>**Deserting–NIV**<br>Turning away–NKJV<br>Turning away–NLT<br><br>**POSB REFERENCE**<br>(Gal.1:6-7, esp. v.6)<br>Note 2, point 1 | **μετατίθεσθε ἀπὸ** = metatithesthe apo<br>Pronunciation: [met-at-ith'-ehs-the ah-po]<br>Parsing *metatithesthe* (part of speech): verb<br>  Mood—indicative<br>  Tense—present<br>  Voice—middle or passive<br>  Person—2nd person<br>  Number—plural<br>  Stem or root—from μετατίθημι<br>Parsing *apo* (part of speech): preposition<br>  Case—genitive<br>  Stem or root—from ἀπό<br>Concordance References:<br>  ⇒ Strong's #575+3346 apo metatithēmi<br>  ⇒ NIV #608+3572 apo metatithēmi [deserting]<br>  ⇒ NASB #575+3346 apo metatithēmi<br><br>**Galatians 1:6**<br>I marvel that ye are so soon **removed** from him that | To desert; to remove; to turn away; to change places; to transfer elsewhere.<br><br>**Practical Application**<br>The believers were deserting God, removing themselves away from God. The tense of the verb (*metatithesthe*) is present tense which means the Galatians were in the process of turning; they had not yet fully turned. There was still hope for them to repent and return to God. |

# Practical Word Studies
## in the New Testament

| ENGLISH WORD | GREEK WORD AND VERSE | THE WORD MEANS... |
|---|---|---|
| | called you into the grace of Christ unto another gospel: [KJV]<br><br>I am amazed that you are so quickly **deserting** Him who called you by the grace of Christ, for a different gospel; [NASB]<br><br>I am astonished that you are so quickly **deserting** the one who called you by the grace of Christ and are turning to a different gospel— [NIV]<br><br>I marvel that you are **turning away** so soon from Him who called you in the grace of Christ, to a different gospel, [NKJV]<br><br>I am shocked that you are **turning away** so soon from God, who in his love and mercy called you to share the eternal life he gives through Christ. You are already following a different way [NLT]<br><br>Θαυμάζω ὅτι οὕτω ταχέως **μετατίθεσθε ἀπὸ** τοῦ καλέσαντος ὑμᾶς ἐν χάριτι Χριστοῦ εἰς ἕτερον εὐαγγέλιον· [GNS]<br><br>Θαυμάζω ὅτι οὕτως ταχέως **μετατίθεσθε ἀπὸ** τοῦ καλέσαντος ὑμᾶς ἐν χάριτι [Χριστοῦ] εἰς ἕτερον εὐαγγέλιον, [GNT] | |
| **#968**<br>**Design–**<br>**Designed**<br><br>Device–KJV<br>Thought–NASB<br>**Design–NIV**<br>Devising–NKJV<br>**Designed–NLT**<br><br>**POSB**<br>**REFERENCE**<br>(Acts 17:29-30; esp. v.29)<br>Note 7, point 1 | ἐνθυμήσεως = enthumëseös<br>Pronunciation: [en-thoo'-may-seh-os]<br>Parsing (part of speech): noun<br>    Case—genitive<br>    Gender—feminine<br>    Number—singular<br>    Stem or root—from ἐνθύμησις, εως<br>Concordance References:<br>  ⇒  Strong's #1761 enthumësis<br>  ⇒  NIV #1927 enthumësis<br>  ⇒  NASB #1761 enthumësis<br><br>**Acts 17:29**<br>Forasmuch then as we are the offspring of God, we ought not to think that the Godhead is like unto gold, or silver, or stone, graven by art and man's **device**. [KJV]<br><br>"Being then the offspring of God, we ought not to think that the Divine Nature is like gold or silver or stone, an image formed by the art and **thought** of man. [NASB]<br><br>"Therefore since we are God's offspring, we should not think that the divine being is like gold or silver or stone—an image made by man's **design** and skill. [NIV]<br><br>Therefore, since we are the offspring of God, we ought not to think that the Divine Nature is like gold or silver or stone, something shaped by art and man's **devising**. [NKJV]<br><br>And since this is true, we shouldn't think of God as an idol **designed** by craftsmen from gold or silver or stone. [NLT]<br><br>γένος οὖν ὑπάρχοντες τοῦ Θεοῦ, οὐκ ὀφείλομεν νομίζειν χρυσῷ ἢ ἀργύρῳ ἢ λίθῳ, χαράγματι τέχνης καὶ **ἐνθυμήσεως** ἀνθρώπου, τὸ θεῖον εἶναι ὅμοιον. [GNS]<br><br>γένος οὖν ὑπάρχοντες τοῦ θεοῦ οὐκ ὀφείλομεν νομίζειν χρυσῷ ἢ ἀργύρῳ ἢ λίθῳ, χαράγματι τέχνης καὶ **ἐνθυμήσεως** ἀνθρώπου, τὸ θεῖον εἶναι ὅμοιον. [GNT] | Design, device, thought.<br><br>**Practical Application**<br>It means internal thoughts, ideas, imaginations. Every man has a concept, a thought about God. But we should not. We should seek to find the only living and true God that is revealed in Christ and in the Word of God, the Holy Scriptures of the Bible. Every person is personally responsible for forsaking the idols of this world and for finding God. |
| **#969**<br>**Desire**<br><br>**Desire–KJV**<br>Desire earnestly–NASB<br>Eagerly desire–NIV<br>**Desire–NKJV**<br>**Desire–NLT**<br><br>**POSB**<br>**REFERENCE**<br>(1 Cor.14:1)<br>Note 1, point 2 | ζηλοῦτε = zëloute<br>Pronunciation: [dzay-loo'-teh]<br>Parsing (part of speech): verb<br>    Mood—imperative<br>    Tense—present<br>    Voice—active<br>    Person—2nd person<br>    Number—plural<br>    Stem or root—from ζηλόω<br>Concordance References:<br>  ⇒  Strong's #2206 zëloö<br>  ⇒  NIV #2420 zëloö<br>  ⇒  NASB #2206 zëloö | To desire eagerly; to desire earnestly; to covet earnestly; to be zealous and ambitious for; to show a great interest in.<br><br>**Practical Application**<br>Spiritual gifts are to be desired. We are to pursue love first, but this does not mean we are not to seek the spiritual gifts of God. On the contrary, the more we love God and men, the more we covet the gifts of God so that we can minister to the world of men more effectively. |

# PRACTICAL WORD STUDIES
## in the NEW TESTAMENT

| ENGLISH WORD | GREEK WORD AND VERSE | THE WORD MEANS... |
|---|---|---|
| | **1 Cor. 14:1**<br>Follow after charity, and **desire** spiritual gifts, but rather that ye may prophesy. [KJV]<br>Pursue love, yet **desire earnestly** spiritual gifts, but especially that you may prophesy. [NASB]<br>Follow the way of love and **eagerly desire** spiritual gifts, especially the gift of prophecy. [NIV]<br>Pursue love, and **desire** spiritual *gifts*, but especially that you may prophesy. [NKJV]<br>Let love be your highest goal, but also **desire** the special abilities the Spirit gives, especially the gift of prophecy. [NLT]<br>Διώκετε τὴν ἀγάπην· **ζηλοῦτε** δὲ τὰ πνευματικά, μᾶλλον δὲ ἵνα προφητεύητε. [GNS]<br>Διώκετε τὴν ἀγάπην, **ζηλοῦτε** δὲ τὰ πνευματικά, μᾶλλον δὲ ἵνα προφητεύητε. [GNT] | |
| **#970**<br>**Desire**<br><br>**Desire–KJV**<br>**Desire–NASB**<br>**Desire–NIV**<br>**Desire–NKJV**<br>Longing–NLT<br><br>**POSB**<br>**REFERENCE**<br>(Rom.10:1-3; esp. v.1)<br>Note 1 | εὐδοκία = *eudokia*<br>Pronunciation: [yoo-dok-ee'-ah]<br>Parsing (part of speech): noun<br>    Case—nominative<br>    Gender—feminine<br>    Number—singular<br>    Stem or root—from εὐδοκία, ας<br>Concordance References:<br>  ⇒ Strong's #2107 eudokia<br>  ⇒ NIV #2306 eudokia<br>  ⇒ NASB #2107 eudokia<br><br>**Romans 10:1**<br>Brethren, my heart's **desire** and prayer to God for Israel is, that they might be saved. [KJV]<br>Brethren, my heart's **desire** and my prayer to God for them is for their salvation. [NASB]<br>Brothers, my heart's **desire** and prayer to God for the Israelites is that they may be saved. [NIV]<br>Brethren, my heart's **desire** and prayer to God for Israel is that they may be saved. [NKJV]<br>Dear brothers and sisters, the **longing** of my heart and my prayer to God is that the Jewish people might be saved. [NLT]<br>Ἀδελφοί, ἡ μὲν **εὐδοκία** τῆς ἐμῆς καρδίας καὶ ἡ δέησις πρὸς τὸν Θεὸν ὑπὲρ τοῦ Ἰσραήλ ἐστιν εἰς σωτηρίαν. [GNS]<br>Ἀδελφοί, ἡ μὲν **εὐδοκία** τῆς ἐμῆς καρδίας καὶ ἡ δέησις πρὸς τὸν θεὸν ὑπὲρ αὐτῶν εἰς σωτηρίαν. [GNT] | Good will, pleasure, favor; desire, longing; purpose, choice. The word "desire" (*eudokia*) means longing, willing, yearning, craving.<br><br>**Practical Application**<br>Paul had a burning desire for Israel's salvation. He loved his people and loved them deeply. He craved and yearned to see the salvation of his people. If he saw their salvation, his desire would be fulfilled.<br>    Note that Paul prayed for Israel's salvation. They could be saved; their rejection of Christ was not hopeless. The door of salvation is open to all men, the Jew as well as the Gentile. |
| **#971**<br>**Desire**<br><br>**Desire–KJV**<br>Long for–NASB<br>Crave–NIV<br>**Desire–NKJV**<br>Crave–NLT<br><br>**POSB**<br>**REFERENCE**<br>(1 Pt.2:2-3; esp. v.2)<br>Note 2 | ἐπιποθήσατε = *epipothēsate*<br>Pronunciation: [ep-ee-poth-ay'-sah-teh]<br>Parsing (part of speech): verb<br>    Mood—imperative<br>    Tense—aorist<br>    Voice—active<br>    Person—2nd person<br>    Number—plural<br>    Stem or root—from ἐπιποθέω<br>Concordance References:<br>  ⇒ Strong's #1971 epipotheō<br>  ⇒ NIV #2160 epipotheō<br>  ⇒ NASB #1971 epipotheō<br><br>**1 Peter 2:2**<br>As newborn babes, **desire** the sincere milk of the word, that ye may grow thereby: [KJV]<br>Like newborn babes, **long for** the pure milk of the word, that by it you may grow in respect to salvation, [NASB]<br>Like newborn babies, **crave** pure spiritual milk, so that by it you may grow up in your salvation, [NIV]<br>As newborn babes, **desire** the pure milk of the word, that you may grow thereby, [NKJV]<br>You must **crave** pure spiritual milk so that you can grow into the fullness of your salvation. Cry out for this nourishment as a baby cries for milk, [NLT] | To crave; to desire; to long for; to yearn for. It means to crave, yearn, and long for the Word of God.<br><br>**Practical Application**<br>The believer is to crave one thing—the milk of God's Word. The charge is an imperative, a command: "You desire, crave, and yearn for the pure spiritual milk of the Word. And the craving and yearning are to be constant." The word "desire" (*epipothēsate*) is a strong word, very strong. It paints the picture of being an absolute essential, of hungering and thirsting after the Word. If a believer is to grow, it is absolutely essential that he hunger and thirst after the milk of the Word. |

# PRACTICAL WORD STUDIES
## in the NEW TESTAMENT

| ENGLISH WORD | GREEK WORD AND VERSE | THE WORD MEANS... |
|---|---|---|
| | ὡς ἀρτιγέννητα βρέφη, τὸ λογικὸν ἄδολον γάλα **ἐπιποθήσατε**, ἵνα ἐν αὐτῷ αὐξηθῆτε, [GNS]<br>ὡς ἀρτιγέννητα βρέφη τὸ λογικὸν ἄδολον γάλα **ἐπιποθήσατε**, ἵνα ἐν αὐτῷ αὐξηθῆτε εἰς σωτηρίαν, [GNT] | |
| **#972**<br>**Desire–**<br>**Desires**<br><br>Lusts–KJV<br>**Desires–NASB**<br>Desire–NIV<br>Desires–NKJV<br>Evil things–NLT<br><br>**POSB**<br>**REFERENCE**<br>(Jn.8:44)<br>*Deeper Study* #1 | **ἐπιθυμίας** = *epithumias*<br>Pronunciation: [ep-ee-thoo-mee'-ahs]<br>Parsing (part of speech): noun<br>    Case—accusative<br>    Gender—feminine<br>    Number—plural<br>    Stem or root—from ἐπιθυμία, ας<br>Concordance References:<br>  ⇒ Strong's #1939 epithumia<br>  ⇒ NIV #2123 epithumia<br>  ⇒ NASB #1939 epithumia<br><br>**John 8:44**<br>Ye are of your father the devil, and the **lusts** of your father ye will do. He was a murderer from the beginning, and abode not in the truth, because there is no truth in him. When he speaketh a lie, he speaketh of his own: for he is a liar, and the father of it. [KJV]<br>"You are of your father the devil, and you want to do the **desires** of your father. He was a murderer from the beginning, and does not stand in the truth, because there is no truth in him. Whenever he speaks a lie, he speaks from his own nature; for he is a liar, and the father of lies. [NASB]<br>You belong to your father, the devil, and you want to carry out your father's **desire**. He was a murderer from the beginning, not holding to the truth, for there is no truth in him. When he lies, he speaks his native language, for he is a liar and the father of lies. [NIV]<br>You are of *your* father the devil, and the **desires** of your father you want to do. He was a murderer from the beginning, and *does not* stand in the truth, because there is no truth in him. When he speaks a lie, he speaks from his own *resources,* for he is a liar and the father of it. [NKJV]<br>For you are the children of your father the Devil, and you love to do the **evil things** he does. He was a murderer from the beginning and has always hated the truth. There is no truth in him. When he lies, it is consistent with his character; for he is a liar and the father of lies. [NLT]<br>ὑμεῖς ἐκ πατρὸς τοῦ διαβόλου ἐστὲ, καὶ τὰς **ἐπιθυμίας** τοῦ πατρὸς ὑμῶν θέλετε ποιεῖν. ἐκεῖνος ἀνθρωποκτόνος ἦν ἀπ' ἀρχῆς, καὶ ἐν τῇ ἀληθείᾳ οὐκ ἔστηκεν, ὅτι οὐκ ἔστιν ἀλήθεια ἐν αὐτῷ. ὅταν λαλῇ τὸ ψεῦδος, ἐκ τῶν ἰδίων λαλεῖ· ὅτι ψεύστης ἐστὶ καὶ ὁ πατὴρ αὐτοῦ. [GNS]<br>ὑμεῖς ἐκ τοῦ πατρὸς τοῦ διαβόλου ἐστὲ καὶ τὰς **ἐπιθυμίας** τοῦ πατρὸς ὑμῶν θέλετε ποιεῖν. ἐκεῖνος ἀνθρωποκτόνος ἦν ἀπ' ἀρχῆς καὶ ἐν τῇ ἀληθείᾳ οὐκ ἔστηκεν, ὅτι οὐκ ἔστιν ἀλήθεια ἐν αὐτῷ. ὅταν λαλῇ τὸ ψεῦδος, ἐκ τῶν ἰδίων λαλεῖ, ὅτι ψεύστης ἐστὶν καὶ ὁ πατὴρ αὐτοῦ. [GNT] | Desire; lust, long for; loving to do evil things; a strong desire, a yearning passion for, an all-consuming craving.<br><br>**Practical Application**<br>The word desire (*epithumias*) is used in a good sense three different times in Scripture (Luke 22:15; Phil. 1:23; 1 Thes. 2:17). A person is to turn his strong desires toward righteousness and godliness; however, a person has to struggle to turn away from the desire to please himself. A person's natural tendency is the desire or lust to satisfy self before others, in particular when survival and comfort are at stake.<br>1. The very nature of a person is lust, the lust of the flesh and of the mind (Ephes. 2:2-3). Sinful and evil lust show that people are by nature...<br>  • the children of wrath.<br>  • the children of disobedience.<br>  • the children of the spirit who is the prince and power of the air, that is, the devil.<br>2. The very nature of a person and of the world is lust, a tendency both to be and to get.<br>What a person discovers is that his cravings are never satisfied; they have to be controlled. There is something within a person's innermost being that craves for more and more; and as more and more is taken, the lust does not diminish, it grows. It craves for still more and more. A person's cravings are never satisfied; his only answer is to control them by the power of Christ (see POSB note, Lust—James 4:2 for a discussion of the Spirit of God's control. Cp. Galatians 5:22-23.) |
| **#973**<br>**Desire**<br>**Earnestly**<br><br>Desire–KJV<br>**Desire earnestly–**<br>**NASB**<br>Eagerly desire–NIV<br>Desire–NKJV<br>Desire–NLT | **ζηλοῦτε** = *zēloute*<br>Pronunciation: [dzay-loo'-teh]<br>Parsing (part of speech): verb<br>    Mood—imperative<br>    Tense—present<br>    Voice—active<br>    Person—2nd person<br>    Number—plural<br>    Stem or root—from ζηλόω<br>Concordance References:<br>  ⇒ Strong's #2206 zēloō<br>  ⇒ NIV #2420 zēloō<br>  ⇒ NASB #2206 zēloō | To desire eagerly; to desire earnestly; to covet earnestly; to be zealous and ambitious for; to show a great interest in.<br><br>**Practical Application**<br>Spiritual gifts are to be desired. We are to pursue love first, but this does not mean we are not to seek the spiritual gifts of God. On the contrary, the more we love God and men, the more we covet the gifts of God so that we can minister to the world of men more effectively. |

# Practical Word Studies
## in the New Testament

| ENGLISH WORD | GREEK WORD AND VERSE | THE WORD MEANS... |
|---|---|---|
| **POSB REFERENCE** (1 Cor.14:1) Note 1, point 2 | **1 Cor. 14:1**<br>Follow after charity, and **desire** spiritual gifts, but rather that ye may prophesy. [KJV]<br>Pursue love, yet **desire earnestly** spiritual gifts, but especially that you may prophesy. [NASB]<br>Follow the way of love and **eagerly desire** spiritual gifts, especially the gift of prophecy. [NIV]<br>Pursue love, and **desire** spiritual *gifts,* but especially that you may prophesy. [NKJV]<br>Let love be your highest goal, but also **desire** the special abilities the Spirit gives, especially the gift of prophecy. [NLT]<br>Διώκετε τὴν ἀγάπην· ζηλοῦτε δὲ τὰ πνευματικά, μᾶλλον δὲ ἵνα προφητεύητε. [GNS]<br>Διώκετε τὴν ἀγάπην, ζηλοῦτε δὲ τὰ πνευματικά, μᾶλλον δὲ ἵνα προφητεύητε. [GNT] | |
| **#974 Desired**<br><br>Desired–KJV<br>Demanded permission–NASB<br>Asked–NIV<br>Asked–NKJV<br>Asked–NLT<br><br>**POSB REFERENCE** (Lk.22:31) Note 1, point 2 | ἐξῃτήσατο = exētēsato<br>Pronunciation: [ex-ahee-teh'-saw-tow]<br>Parsing (part of speech): verb<br>  Mood—indicative<br>  Tense—aorist<br>  Voice—middle<br>  Person—3rd person<br>  Number—singular<br>  Stem or root—from ἐξαιτέομαι<br>Concordance References:<br>⇒ Strong's #1809 exaiteomai<br>⇒ NIV #1977 exaiteō<br>⇒ NASB #1809 exaiteō<br><br>**Luke 22:31**<br>And the Lord said, Simon, Simon, behold, Satan hath **desired** to have you, that he may sift you as wheat: [KJV]<br>"Simon, Simon, behold, Satan has **demanded permission** to sift you like wheat; [NASB]<br>"Simon, Simon, Satan has **asked** to sift you as wheat. [NIV]<br>And the Lord said, "Simon, Simon! Indeed, Satan has **asked** for you, that he may sift *you* as wheat. [NKJV]<br>"Simon, Simon, Satan has **asked** to have all of you, to sift you like wheat. [NLT]<br>εἶπε δὲ ὁ Κύριος, Σίμων Σίμων, ἰδοὺ ὁ Σατανᾶς **ἐξῃτήσατο** ὑμᾶς, τοῦ σινιάσαι ὡς τὸν σῖτον· [GNS]<br>Σίμων Σίμων, ἰδοὺ ὁ Σατανᾶς **ἐξῃτήσατο** ὑμᾶς τοῦ σινιάσαι ὡς τὸν σῖτον· [GNT] | To beg for something; to desire; to make an appeal; to demand; to obtain by asking.<br><br>**Practical Application**<br>Jesus pictured Satan as begging permission of God to trip the disciples. It is the same picture that is found in Job (Job 1:6f). The Bible is clear in its teaching: God is sovereign; anything that goes on in the universe goes on because God allows it, even temptation. The truth to see is that...<br>• Jesus did give a glimpse into the spiritual world.<br>• Satan begged God to let him test and try the disciples.<br>• Satan is subject to God and has no right or power to tempt believers unless God allows it.<br>• The Lord's prayer does include the words "*Deliver us from the evil one*" *(a po tou poneron)* (see POSB *Deeper Study* #9—Matthew 6:13). |
| **#975 Desired**<br><br>Lusts–KJV<br>Lusts–NASB<br>Sinful desires–NIV<br>Lusts–NKJV<br>**Desired–NLT**<br><br>**POSB REFERENCE** (Romans 1:24-25; esp. v.24) Note 2, point 1 | ἐπιθυμίαις = epithumiais<br>Pronunciation: [ep-ee-thoo-mee'-ah-ees]<br>Parsing (part of speech): noun<br>  Case—dative<br>  Gender—feminine<br>  Number—plural<br>  Stem or root—from ἐπιθυμία, ας<br>Concordance References:<br>⇒ Strong's #1939 epithumia<br>⇒ NIV #2123 epithumia<br>⇒ NASB #1939 epithumia<br><br>**Romans 1:24**<br>Wherefore God also gave them up to uncleanness through the **lusts** of their own hearts, to dishonour their own bodies between themselves: [KJV]<br>Therefore God gave them over in the **lusts** of their hearts to impurity, that their bodies might be dishonored among them. [NASB]<br>Therefore God gave them over in the **sinful desires** of their hearts to sexual impurity for the degrading of their bodies with one another. [NIV]<br>Therefore God also gave them up to uncleanness, in the **lusts** of their hearts, to dishonor their bodies among themselves, [NKJV]<br>So God let them go ahead and do whatever shameful | Desire, longing; lust, passion; covetousness; sinful desires.<br><br>**Practical Application**<br>Their hearts are filled with lusts or "shameful...desires" (*epithumiais*), that is, passionate cravings and urges. They long after things that displease God and that dishonor their bodies. God cares deeply about the human body, and he judges any person who abuses the body. (See POSB outline—Matthew 6:11 and POSB *Deeper Study* #6—Matthew 6:11; POSB note—1 Cor. 3:16; POSB note—1 Cor. 3:17; POSB *Deeper Study* #1—1 Cor. 6:18; POSB note—1 Cor. 6:19; POSB note—1 Cor. 6:20; cp. 1 Thes. 4:3-5 for more discussion.)<br><br>In the Greek the lusts or desires are said to be "in [*en*] their own hearts." [KJV] Sin takes place in the heart before it takes place by act. |

# PRACTICAL WORD STUDIES
## in the NEW TESTAMENT

| ENGLISH WORD | GREEK WORD AND VERSE | THE WORD MEANS... |
|---|---|---|
| | things their hearts **desired**. As a result, they did vile and degrading things with each other's bodies. [NLT]<br>Διὸ καὶ παρέδωκεν αὐτοὺς ὁ Θεὸς ἐν ταῖς **ἐπιθυμίαις** τῶν καρδιῶν αὐτῶν εἰς ἀκαθαρσίαν τοῦ ἀτιμάζεσθαι τὰ σώματα αὐτῶν ἐν αὐτοῖς· [GNS]<br>Διὸ παρέδωκεν αὐτοὺς ὁ Θεὸς ἐν ταῖς **ἐπιθυμίαις** τῶν καρδιῶν αὐτῶν εἰς ἀκαθαρσίαν τοῦ ἀτιμάζεσθαι τὰ σώματα αὐτῶν ἐν αὐτοῖς· [GNT] | |
| **#976**<br>**Desires**<br><br>Will–KJV<br>Wishes–NASB<br>Would–NIV<br>**Desires–NKJV**<br>Wants–NLT<br><br>**POSB REFERENCE**<br>(Mt.16:24)<br>Note 2, point 1 | θέλει = *thelë*<br>Pronunciation: [thel'-ee]<br>Parsing (part of speech): verb<br>    Mood—indicative<br>    Tense—present<br>    Voice—active<br>    Person—3rd person<br>    Number—singular<br>    Stem or root—from θέλω<br>Concordance References:<br>  ⇒ Strong's #2309 thelo<br>  ⇒ NIV #2527 thelö<br>  ⇒ NASB #2309 thelo<br><br>**Matthew 16:24**<br>Then said Jesus unto his disciples, If any man **will** come after me, let him deny himself, and take up his cross, and follow me. [KJV]<br>Then Jesus said to His disciples, "If anyone **wishes** to come after Me, let him deny himself, and take up his cross, and follow Me. [NASB]<br>Then Jesus said to his disciples, "If anyone **would** come after me, he must deny himself and take up his cross and follow me. [NIV]<br>Then Jesus said to His disciples, "If anyone **desires** to come after Me, let him deny himself, and take up his cross, and follow Me. [NKJV]<br>Then Jesus said to the disciples, "If any of you **wants** to be my follower, you must put aside your selfish ambition, shoulder your cross, and follow me. [NLT]<br>τότε ὁ Ἰησοῦς εἶπε τοῖς μαθηταῖς αὐτοῦ, Εἴ τις **θέλει** ὀπίσω μου ἐλθεῖν, ἀπαρνησάσθω ἑαυτὸν, καὶ ἀράτω τὸν σταυρὸν αὐτοῦ καὶ ἀκολουθείτω μοι. [GNS]<br>Τότε ὁ Ἰησοῦς εἶπεν τοῖς μαθηταῖς αὐτοῦ, Εἴ τις **θέλει** ὀπίσω μου ἐλθεῖν, ἀπαρνησάσθω ἑαυτὸν καὶ ἀράτω τὸν σταυρὸν αὐτοῦ καὶ ἀκολουθείτω μοι. [GNT] | To desire, wish, design, purpose, resolve, determine.<br><br>**Practical Application**<br>It is a deliberate willing, a deliberate choice, a determined resolve to follow Christ.<br>If a person really wills and deliberately chooses to follow Christ, then he has to do the three things mentioned. Note: the choice is voluntary; it is made by the person. |
| **#977**<br>**Desires**<br><br>Lust–KJV<br>Lust–NASB<br>Evil desire–NIV<br>**Desires–NKJV**<br>Evil desires–NLT<br><br>**POSB REFERENCE**<br>(Jas 1:14-16; esp. v.14)<br>Note 2 | ἐπιθυμίας = *epithumias*<br>Pronunciation: [ep-ee-thoo-mee'-ahs]<br>Parsing (part of speech): noun<br>    Case—genitive<br>    Gender—feminine<br>    Number—singular<br>    Stem or root—from ἐπιθυμία, ας<br>Concordance References:<br>  ⇒ Strong's #1939 epithumia<br>  ⇒ NIV #2123 epithumia<br>  ⇒ NASB #1939 epithumia<br><br>**James 1:14**<br>But every man is tempted, when he is drawn away of his own **lust**, and enticed. [KJV]<br>But each one is tempted when he is carried away and enticed by his own **lust**. [NASB]<br>But each one is tempted when, by his own **evil desire**, he is dragged away and enticed. [NIV]<br>But each one is tempted when he is drawn away by his own **desires** and enticed. [NKJV]<br>Temptation comes from the lure of our own **evil desires**. [NLT]<br>ἕκαστος δὲ πειράζεται, ὑπὸ τῆς ἰδίας **ἐπιθυμίας** ἐξελκόμενος καὶ δελεαζόμενος. [GNS]<br>ἕκαστος δὲ πειράζεται ὑπὸ τῆς ἰδίας **ἐπιθυμίας** ἐξελκόμενος καὶ δελεαζόμενος· [GNT] | Evil desire, lust, passion, longing. It means to crave either good or evil. There are good desires and bad desires.<br><br>**Practical Application**<br>Every man—there are no exceptions—is tempted when he is drawn away by his own lusts and enticed.<br>The picture is this: man has good desires, natural and normal desires. Therefore, when he begins to think about or look at something, he very naturally desires it. His desire is normal behavior. The problem arises when the thing is forbidden or is harmful. If he looks at and thinks about the forbidden or harmful thing, he begins to lust and to be enticed or lured to go after it. This is the very beginning stage of temptation. Man takes his desire and focuses it upon the forbidden or harmful thing. He begins to pay attention to what he should not look at; he begins to think about the things of the flesh and of the world. Thereby he is tempted and drawn away by his own lusts and enticements. |

## PRACTICAL WORD STUDIES
### in the NEW TESTAMENT

| ENGLISH WORD | GREEK WORD AND VERSE | THE WORD MEANS... |
|---|---|---|
| **#978** **Desires** Lusts–KJV Desires–NASB Desires–NIV Desires–NKJV Desires–NLT **POSB REFERENCE** (2 Tim. 4:3-4; esp. v.3) Note 3, point 2 | ἐπιθυμίας = epithumias Pronunciation: [ep-ee-thoo-mee'-ahs] Parsing (part of speech): noun    Case—accusative    Gender—feminine    Number—plural    Stem or root—ἐπιθυμία, ας Concordance References: ⇒ Strong's #1939 epithumia ⇒ NIV #2123 epithumia ⇒ NASB #1939 epithumia **2 Tim. 4:3** For the time will come when they will not endure sound doctrine; but after their own **lusts** shall they heap to themselves teachers, having itching ears; [KJV] For the time will come when they will not endure sound doctrine; but wanting to have their ears tickled, they will accumulate for themselves teachers in accordance to their own **desires**; [NASB] For the time will come when men will not put up with sound doctrine. Instead, to suit their own **desires**, they will gather around them a great number of teachers to say what their itching ears want to hear. [NIV] For the time will come when they will not endure sound doctrine, but according to their own **desires**, *because* they have itching ears, they will heap up for themselves teachers; [NKJV] For a time is coming when people will no longer listen to right teaching. They will follow their own **desires** and will look for teachers who will tell them whatever they want to hear. [NLT] ἔσται γὰρ καιρὸς ὅτε τῆς ὑγιαινούσης διδασκαλίας οὐκ ἀνέξονται, ἀλλὰ κατὰ τὰς **ἐπιθυμίας** τὰς ἰδίας ἑαυτοῖς ἐπισωρεύσουσι διδασκάλους, κνηθόμενοι τὴν ἀκοήν· [GNS] ἔσται γὰρ καιρὸς ὅτε τῆς ὑγιαινούσης διδασκαλίας οὐκ ἀνέξονται ἀλλὰ κατὰ τὰς ἰδίας **ἐπιθυμίας** ἑαυτοῖς ἐπισωρεύσουσιν διδασκάλους κνηθόμενοι τὴν ἀκοήν [GNT] | Desire; lust; loving to do evil things, a strong desire, a yearning passion for, an all-consuming craving. **Practical Application** People will want teachers who will allow them to live like they desire. The Greek actually says that people will be *dominated* "by their own lusts or desires" (*epithumias*). They will be living lives of lusts, cravings, and gratifications—lives that seek the gratification of the flesh through... • sex and immorality • recognition and honor • power and authority • status and position • money and possessions • image and approval • discipline and control • religion and personal righteousness • good works and benevolence Such lusts and cravings will so dominate people's lives that they will seek ministers and teachers who will tickle their ears with the message of personal development and self-image. |
| **#979** **Desires** Lusts–KJV Pleasures–NASB Desires–NIV Desires for pleasure–NKJV Desires–NLT **POSB REFERENCE** (Jas 4:1) Note 1 | ἡδονῶν = hēdonōn Pronunciation: [hay-don-own'] Parsing (part of speech): noun    Case—genitive    Gender—feminine    Number—plural    Stem or root—from ἡδονή, ῆς Concordance References: ⇒ Strong's #2237 hēdonē ⇒ NIV #2454 hēdonē ⇒ NASB #2237 hēdonē **James 4:1** From whence come wars and fightings among you? come they not hence, even of your **lusts** that war in your members? [KJV] What is the source of quarrels and conflicts among you? Is not the source your **pleasures** that wage war in your members? [NASB] What causes fights and quarrels among you? Don't they come from your **desires** that battle within you? [NIV] Where do wars and fights *come* from among you? Do *they* not *come* from your **desires for** pleasure that war in your members? [NKJV] What is causing the quarrels and fights among you? Isn't it the whole army of evil **desires** at war within you? [NLT] Πόθεν πόλεμοι καὶ μάχαι ἐν ὑμῖν; οὐκ ἐντεῦθεν, ἐκ τῶν **ἡδονῶν** ὑμῶν τῶν στρατευομένων ἐν τοῖς μέλεσιν ὑμῶν; [GNS] | Desires, lusts, pleasures, passions. It means to crave pleasure; to crave gratification. **Practical Application** This Scripture says that desires for pleasure and gratification war within our bodies. The picture is that of constant warfare, of our bodies craving, yearning, pulling, urging, desiring, and grasping after whatever will gratify our pleasure. We want and want, desire and desire, and the battle of wanting and desiring rages on and on within our bodies. Our bodies are a battlefield of wants and desires. Every person knows what it is to experience this warfare, to have his flesh yearning and yearning after something. Desires or lusts are strong and difficult to control. In fact, few people control it completely. A few people may control their desire or lust in what are called the gross and visible sins such as vengeance and murder, but they gratify their desire or lust in acceptable things such as over-eating and selfishness, in buying and hoarding more than what is needed, and in looking when they should not look. The point is this: man is a walking civil war; desire after desire or lust after lust wages war within him, seeking gratification and pleasure. Man senses desire after desire, wanting to lift the restraint and to cut loose to enjoy the pleasure of |

# PRACTICAL WORD STUDIES
## in the New Testament

| ENGLISH WORD | GREEK WORD AND VERSE | THE WORD MEANS... |
|---|---|---|
| | Πόθεν πόλεμοι καὶ πόθεν μάχαι ἐν ὑμῖν; οὐκ ἐντεῦθεν, ἐκ τῶν **ἡδονῶν** ὑμῶν τῶν στρατευομένων ἐν τοῖς μέλεσιν ὑμῶν; [GNT] | the evil desire. It may be the desire or lust for...<br>• food and more food<br>• drink and more drink<br>• drugs and more drugs<br>• sex and more sex<br>• possessions and more possessions<br>• money and more money<br>• property and more property<br>• land and more land<br>• recognition and more recognition<br>• popularity and more popularity<br>• authority and more authority<br>• vengeance and more vengeance<br>As stated, desire after desire wars within our members seeking its pleasure and gratification. Man is a civil war of lust and desire, of pleasure and gratification raging within his body and its members. |
| **#980**<br>**Desires**<br><br>Lusts–KJV<br>Lusts–NASB<br>Passions–NIV<br>Lusts–NKJV<br>**Desires–NLT**<br><br>**POSB REFERENCE**<br>(Tit.3:3)<br>Note 2<br><br>**See also POSB REF:**<br>(Tit.2:12)<br>Note 2, point 2d | ἐπιθυμίας = epithumias<br>Pronunciation: [ep-ee-thoo-mee'-ahs]<br>Parsing (part of speech): noun<br>    Case—accusative<br>    Gender—feminine<br>    Number—plural<br>    Stem or root—from ἐπιθυμία, ας<br>Concordance References:<br>  ⇒ Strong's #1939 epithumia<br>  ⇒ NIV #2123 epithumia<br>  ⇒ NASB #1939 epithumia<br><br>**Titus 3:3**<br>For we ourselves also were sometimes foolish, disobedient, deceived, serving divers **lusts** and pleasures, living in malice and envy, hateful, and hating one another. [KJV]<br>For we also once were foolish ourselves, disobedient, deceived, enslaved to various **lusts** and pleasures, spending our life in malice and envy, hateful, hating one another. [NASB]<br>At one time we too were foolish, disobedient, deceived and enslaved by all kinds of **passions** and pleasures. We lived in malice and envy, being hated and hating one another. [NIV]<br>For we ourselves were also once foolish, disobedient, deceived, serving various **lusts** and pleasures, living in malice and envy, hateful and hating one another. [NKJV]<br>Once we, too, were foolish and disobedient. We were misled by others and became slaves to many wicked **desires** and evil pleasures. Our lives were full of evil and envy. We hated others, and they hated us. [NLT]<br>ἦμεν γάρ ποτε καὶ ἡμεῖς ἀνόητοι, ἀπειθεῖς, πλανώμενοι, δουλεύοντες **ἐπιθυμίαις** καὶ ἡδοναῖς ποικίλαις, ἐν κακίᾳ καὶ φθόνῳ διάγοντες, στυγητοί, μισοῦντες ἀλλήλους. [GNS]<br>Ἦμεν γάρ ποτε καὶ ἡμεῖς ἀνόητοι, ἀπειθεῖς, πλανώμενοι, δουλεύοντες **ἐπιθυμίαις** καὶ ἡδοναῖς ποικίλαις, ἐν κακίᾳ καὶ φθόνῳ διάγοντες, στυγητοί, μισοῦντες ἀλλήλους. [GNT] | Passions, lusts, desires, pleasures. It means desire, lust, loving to do evil things, a strong desire, a yearning passion for, an all-consuming craving. The word (*epithumias*) means passionate cravings, desires, and urges.<br><br>**Practical Application**<br>Man is enslaved by the things of the world, things that damage his body—that make him greedy and selfish—that destroy his spirit and doom him to destruction.<br>But thanks be to God our Savior. He has saved us and delivered us from the enslavements of this world, the enslavements of lust and pleasure that destroy our bodies and souls. The wonderful news is that any person can be delivered from the destructive lusts and pleasures of this world. How? Through our Lord Jesus Christ. If a person will turn away from the destructive lusts and pleasures and turn to Christ, God will deliver him. God will give him the power to conquer the lusts and enslavements of this world. |
| **#981**<br>**Desires Contrary To**<br><br>Lusteth–KJV<br>Sets its desire against–NASB<br>**Desires...contrary to–NIV**<br>Lusts–NKJV<br>Loves to do evil–NLT | ἐπιθυμεῖ κατὰ = epithumei kata<br>Pronunciation: [ep-ee-thoo-mee' kat-ah']<br>Parsing *epithumei* (part of speech): verb<br>    Mood—indicative<br>    Tense—present<br>    Voice—active<br>    Person—3rd person<br>    Number—singular<br>    Stem or root—from ἐπιθυμέω<br>Parsing *kata* (part of speech): preposition<br>    Case—genitive<br>    Stem or root—from κατά | A yearning passion for; a love to do evil; to long for; to desire; to lust for.<br><br>**Practical Application**<br>The flesh fights for dominance. It lusts against the Spirit, struggles and fights to control the man. The picture is that of a tug of war (A.T. Robertson. *Word Pictures in the New Testament*, Vol.4, p.311). The flesh stands contrary to the Spirit—toe to toe, face to face—and it seeks to control man. |

## PRACTICAL WORD STUDIES in the NEW TESTAMENT

| ENGLISH WORD | GREEK WORD AND VERSE | THE WORD MEANS... |
|---|---|---|
| **POSB REFERENCE** (Gal.5:16-18; esp. v.17) Note 1 | Concordance References:<br>⇒ Strong's #1937 epithumeö + 2596 kata<br>⇒ NIV #2121 epithumeö [desires] + 2848 kata [contrary to]<br>⇒ NASB #1937 epithumeö + 2596 kata<br><br>**Galatians 5:17**<br>For the flesh **lusteth** against the Spirit, and the Spirit against the flesh: and these are contrary the one to the other: so that ye cannot do the things that ye would. [KJV]<br>For the flesh **sets its desire against** the Spirit, and the Spirit against the flesh; for these are in opposition to one another, so that you may not do the things that you please. [NASB]<br>For the sinful nature **desires** what is **contrary to** the Spirit, and the Spirit what is contrary to the sinful nature. They are in conflict with each other, so that you do not do what you want. [NIV]<br>For the flesh **lusts** against the Spirit, and the Spirit against the flesh; and these are contrary to one another, so that you do not do the things that you wish. [NKJV]<br>The old sinful nature **loves to do evil**, which is just opposite from what the Holy Spirit wants. And the Spirit gives us desires that are opposite from what the sinful nature desires. These two forces are constantly fighting each other, and your choices are never free from this conflict. [NLT]<br>ἡ γὰρ σὰρξ **ἐπιθυμεῖ κατὰ** τοῦ Πνεύματος, τὸ δὲ Πνεῦμα κατὰ τῆς σαρκός· ταῦτα δὲ ἀντίκειται ἀλλήλοις, ἵνα μὴ ἃ ἐὰν θέλητε, ταῦτα ποιῆτε. [GNS]<br>ἡ γὰρ σὰρξ **ἐπιθυμεῖ κατὰ** τοῦ πνεύματος, τὸ δὲ πνεῦμα κατὰ τῆς σαρκός, ταῦτα γὰρ ἀλλήλοις ἀντίκειται, ἵνα μὴ ἃ ἐὰν θέλητε ταῦτα ποιῆτε. [GNT] | Every person has experienced the flesh's...<br>• yearning<br>• pulling<br>• desiring<br>• wanting<br>• grasping<br>• grabbing<br>• craving<br>• hungering<br>• thirsting<br>• longing<br>• taking<br><br>Every person knows what it is to have his sinful nature lusting after something, to have it yearning and yearning to lay hold of something. The sinful nature is very strong and difficult to control. This is the first reason why a believer's only hope to control the sinful nature is the Spirit of God. |
| #982<br>**Desires For Pleasure**<br><br>Lusts–KJV<br>Pleasures–NASB<br>Desires–NIV<br>**Desires for pleasure–NKJV**<br>Desires–NLT<br><br>**POSB REFERENCE** (Jas 4:1) Note 1 | ἔρημος. = erēmos<br>Pronunciation: [er'-ay-mos]<br>Parsing (part of speech): adjective<br>    Case—nominative<br>    Gender—masculine<br>    Number—singular<br>    Stem or root—from ἔρημος, ον<br>Concordance References:<br>⇒ Strong's #2048 erēmos<br>⇒ NIV #2245 erēmos<br>⇒ NASB #2048 erēmos<br><br>ἡδονῶν = hēdonōn<br>Pronunciation: [hay-don-own']<br>Parsing (part of speech): noun<br>    Case—genitive<br>    Gender—feminine<br>    Number—plural<br>    Stem or root—from ἡδονή, ῆς<br>Concordance References:<br>⇒ Strong's #2237 hēdonē<br>⇒ NIV #2454 hēdonē<br>⇒ NASB #2237 hēdonē<br><br>**James 4:1**<br>From whence come wars and fightings among you? come they not hence, even of your **lusts** that war in your members? [KJV]<br>What is the source of quarrels and conflicts among you? Is not the source your **pleasures** that wage war in your members? [NASB]<br>What causes fights and quarrels among you? Don't they come from your **desires** that battle within you? [NIV]<br>Where do wars and fights *come* from among you? Do *they* not *come* from your ***desires for*** pleasure that war in your members? [NKJV]<br>What is causing the quarrels and fights among you? Isn't it the whole army of evil **desires** at war within you? [NLT]<br>Πόθεν πόλεμοι καὶ μάχαι ἐν ὑμῖν; οὐκ ἐντεῦθεν, ἐκ | Desires, lusts, pleasures, passions. It means to crave pleasure; to crave gratification.<br><br>**Practical Application**<br>This Scripture says that desires for pleasure and gratification war within our bodies. The picture is that of constant warfare, of our bodies craving, yearning, pulling, urging, desiring, and grasping after whatever will gratify our pleasure. We want and want, desire and desire, and the battle of wanting and desiring rages on and on within our bodies. Our bodies are a battlefield of wants and desires. Every person knows what it is to experience this warfare, to have his flesh yearning and yearning after something. Desires or lusts are strong and difficult to control. In fact, few people control it completely. A few people may control their desire or lust in what are called the gross and visible sins such as vengeance and murder, but they gratify their desire or lust in acceptable things such as over-eating and selfishness, in buying and hoarding more than what is needed, and in looking when they should not look.<br>The point is this: man is a walking civil war; desires and lusts wage war within him, seeking gratification and pleasure. Man senses one desire after another, wanting to lift the restraint and to cut loose to enjoy the pleasure of the evil desire. It may be the desire or lust for...<br>• food     • drink<br>• drugs     • sex<br>• possessions     • money<br>• property     • land<br>• recognition     • popularity<br>• authority     • vengeance |

| ENGLISH WORD | GREEK WORD AND VERSE | THE WORD MEANS... |
|---|---|---|
| | τῶν **ἡδονῶν** ὑμῶν τῶν στρατευομένων ἐν τοῖς μέλεσιν ὑμῶν; [GNS]<br>Πόθεν πόλεμοι καὶ πόθεν μάχαι ἐν ὑμῖν; οὐκ ἐντεῦθεν, ἐκ τῶν **ἡδονῶν** ὑμῶν τῶν στρατευομένων ἐν τοῖς μέλεσιν ὑμῶν; [GNT] | As stated, desire after desire wars within our members seeking its pleasure and gratification. Man is a civil war of lust and desire, of pleasure and gratification raging within his body and its members. |
| **#983**<br>**Desolate**<br><br>Desolate–KJV<br>Desolate–NASB<br>Desolate–NIV<br>Desolate–NKJV<br>Desolate–NLT<br>**POSB REFERENCE**<br>(Mt.23:38)*Deeper Study #2* | ἔρημος. = erēmos<br>Pronunciation: [er'-ay-mos]<br>Parsing (part of speech): adjective<br>    Case—nominative<br>    Gender—masculine<br>    Number—singular<br>    Stem or root—from ἔρημος, ον<br>Concordance References:<br>  ⇒ Strong's #2048 erēmos<br>  ⇒ NIV #2245 erēmos<br>  ⇒ NASB #2048 erēmos<br><br>**Matthew 23:38**<br>Behold, your house is left unto you **desolate**. [KJV]<br>"Behold, your house is being left to you **desolate**! [NASB]<br>Look, your house is left to you **desolate**. [NIV]<br>See! Your house is left to you **desolate**; [NKJV]<br>And now look, your house is left to you, empty and **desolate**. [NLT]<br>ἰδοὺ ἀφίεται ὑμῖν ὁ οἶκος ὑμῶν **ἔρημος**. [GNS]<br>ἰδοὺ ἀφίεται ὑμῖν ὁ οἶκος ὑμῶν **ἔρημος**. [GNT] | Desolate; uninhabited; lonely; remote; solitary places; to lay to waste and make into a wilderness; open country; lonely places; desert region.<br><br>**Practical Application**<br>Without the presence of God a place and person are like a wilderness, deserted and left all alone. They are left to waste away. |
| **#984**<br>**Desolate**<br><br>Desolate–KJV<br>Left alone–NASB<br>Left all alone–NIV<br>Left alone–NKJV<br>Truly alone–NLT<br>**POSB REFERENCE**<br>(1 Tim.5:4-8; esp. v.5)<br>Note 2, point 2 | μεμονωμένη = memonōmenē<br>Pronunciation: [meh-mon-o'-meh-nay]<br>Parsing (part of speech): verb<br>    Mood—participle<br>    Tense—perfect<br>    Voice—passive<br>    Case—nominative<br>    Gender—feminine<br>    Number—singular<br>    Stem or root—from μονόομαι<br>Concordance References:<br>  ⇒ Strong's #3443 monoö<br>  ⇒ NIV #3670 monoö<br>  ⇒ NASB #3443 monoö<br><br>**1 Tim. 5:5**<br>Now she that is a widow indeed, and **desolate**, trusteth in God, and continueth in supplications and prayers night and day. [KJV]<br>Now she who is a widow indeed, and who has been **left alone** has fixed her hope on God, and continues in entreaties and prayers night and day. [NASB]<br>The widow who is really in need and **left all alone** puts her hope in God and continues night and day to pray and to ask God for help. [NIV]<br>Now she who is really a widow, and **left alone**, trusts in God and continues in supplications and prayers night and day. [NKJV]<br>But a woman who is a true widow, one who is **truly alone** in this world, has placed her hope in God. Night and day she asks God for help and spends much time in prayer. [NLT]<br>ἡ δὲ ὄντως χήρα καὶ **μεμονωμένη** ἤλπικεν ἐπὶ Θεὸν, καὶ προσμένει ταῖς δεήσεσι καὶ ταῖς προσευχαῖς νυκτὸς καὶ ἡμέρας. [GNS]<br>ἡ δὲ ὄντως χήρα καὶ **μεμονωμένη** ἤλπικεν ἐπὶ θεὸν καὶ προσμένει ταῖς δεήσεσιν καὶ ταῖς προσευχαῖς νυκτὸς καὶ ἡμέρας, [GNT] | To be left all alone; to be desolate; to be truly alone.<br><br>**Practical Application**<br>Widowed parents who are true Christians are to live above reproach. Who are "widows indeed," the persons who are to be cared for by the church? The person who is "desolate" (*memonōmenē*): left completely alone without husband, children, or close kin. |
| **#985**<br>**Despairing**<br><br>In despair–KJV<br>**Despairing–NASB**<br>In despair–NIV<br>In despair–NKJV<br>Give up and quit–NLT | ἐξαπορούμενοι = exaporoumenoi<br>Pronunciation: [ex-ap-or-oo'-mehn-oy]<br>Parsing (part of speech): verb<br>    Mood—participle<br>    Tense—present<br>    Voice—middle or passive deponent<br>    Case—nominative<br>    Gender—masculine | To be in despair; to give up and quit; to be hopeless; to have no confidence or assurance; to be without any sense of security.<br><br>**Practical Application**<br>The believer is often perplexed, not understanding why this or that happened, what should be done or said, how the situation should be han- |

# PRACTICAL WORD STUDIES
## in the NEW TESTAMENT

| ENGLISH WORD | GREEK WORD AND VERSE | THE WORD MEANS... |
|---|---|---|
| **POSB REFERENCE** (2 Cor.4:7-9; esp. v.8) Note 2, point 2 | Person—1st person<br>Number—plural<br>Stem or root—from ἐξαπορέομαι<br>Concordance References:<br>⇒ Strong's #1820 exaporeō<br>⇒ NIV #1989 exaporeō<br>⇒ NASB #1820 exaporeō<br><br>**2 Cor. 4:8**<br>We are troubled on every side, yet not distressed; we are perplexed, but not **in despair**; [KJV]<br>We are afflicted in every way, but not crushed; perplexed, but not **despairing**; [NASB]<br>We are hard pressed on every side, but not crushed; perplexed, but not **in despair**; [NIV]<br>*We are* hard pressed on every side, yet not crushed; *we are* perplexed, but not **in despair**; [NKJV]<br>We are pressed on every side by troubles, but we are not crushed and broken. We are perplexed, but we don't **give up and quit**. [NLT]<br>ἐν παντὶ θλιβόμενοι, ἀλλ' οὐ στενοχωρούμενοι· ἀπορούμενοι ἀλλ' οὐκ **ἐξαπορούμενοι**· [GNS]<br>ἐν παντὶ θλιβόμενοι ἀλλ' οὐ στενοχωρούμενοι, ἀπορούμενοι ἀλλ' οὐκ **ἐξαπορούμενοι**, [GNT] | dled, and on and on. Sometimes situations become so puzzling that he is almost stymied and the threat of despair faces him. There is the danger that his confidence and assurance will be shaken. But again, the presence and power of God steps in and saves the believer from despair. God gives him hope and stirs his confidence and shows him the way out. God never allows him to be overcome by despair. |
| **#986 Despise**<br><br>Despise–KJV<br>Regard with contempt–NASB<br>Look down on–NIV<br>Despise–NKJV<br>Look down on–NLT<br><br>**POSB REFERENCE** (Romans 14:3-4, esp. v.3) Note 2 | ἐξουθενείτω = *exoutheneitō*<br>Pronunciation: [ex-oo-then-ee'-tow]<br>Parsing (part of speech): verb<br>  Mood—imperative<br>  Tense—present<br>  Voice—active<br>  Person—3rd person<br>  Number—singular<br>  Stem or root—from ἐξουθενέω<br>Concordance References:<br>⇒ Strong's #1848 exoutheneō<br>⇒ NIV #2024 exoutheneō<br>⇒ NASB #1848 exoutheneō<br><br>**Romans 14:3**<br>Let not him that eateth **despise** him that eateth not; and let not him which eateth not judge him that eateth: for God hath received him. [KJV]<br>Let not him who eats **regard with contempt** him who does not eat, and let not him who does not eat judge him who eats, for God has accepted him. [NASB]<br>The man who eats everything must not **look down on** him who does not, and the man who does not eat everything must not condemn the man who does, for God has accepted him. [NIV]<br>Let not him who eats **despise** him who does not eat, and let not him who does not eat judge him who eats; for God has received him. [NKJV]<br>Those who think it is all right to eat anything must not **look down on** those who won't. And those who won't eat certain foods must not condemn those who do, for God has accepted them. [NLT]<br>ὁ ἐσθίων τὸν μὴ ἐσθίοντα μὴ **ἐξουθενείτω**, καὶ ὁ μὴ ἐσθίων τὸν ἐσθίοντα μὴ κρινέτω· ὁ θεὸς γὰρ αὐτὸν προσελάβετο. [GNS]<br>ὁ ἐσθίων τὸν μὴ ἐσθίοντα μὴ **ἐξουθενείτω**, ὁ δὲ μὴ ἐσθίων τὸν ἐσθίοντα μὴ κρινέτω, ὁ θεὸς γὰρ αὐτὸν προσελάβετο. [GNT] | To look down on; to despise; to refuse to accept; to regard with contempt; to hold in contempt; to reject; to treat as meaningless and utterly wrong.<br><br>**Practical Application**<br>Three reasons are given for not despising and judging one another, three reasons that stand as a warning to believers.<br>1. God Himself has received the strong believer. The believer who walks in the liberty of Christ and does not live a strict life has been accepted by God, no matter what the more legalistic believer may think. There may be some man-made religious rules which he does not observe, but he has trusted Christ, and he obeys the Word of God. Therefore, he is not to be criticized and judged, but he is to be accepted into the fellowship of the more legalistic believer.<br>2. No one has the *right* to judge the Lord's servant. Note: both believers belong to the Lord; both are the servants of the Lord. Therefore, the Lord alone has the right to judge them. Believers do not have the *right to play God* by judging each other. They have no right to condemn and pass judgment upon each other's behavior and works, for they do not belong to each other. They each belong to Christ; therefore, He alone determines whether or not they stand or fall and are accepted or rejected.<br>3. God *will hold* up the believer. There is no question about the matter: the believer will be held up, for God is able to make him stand. |
| **#987 Despise, Do Not**<br><br>Despise not–KJV<br>Not regard lightly–NASB<br>Not make light of–NIV | μὴ ὀλιγώρει = *mē oligōrei*<br>Pronunciation: [may ol-ig-o-reh'-ee]<br>Parsing *oligōrei* (part of speech): verb<br>  Mood—imperative<br>  Tense—present<br>  Voice—active<br>  Person—2nd person<br>  Number—singular<br>  Stem or root—from ὀλιγωρέω<br>Concordance References:<br>⇒ Strong's #3361 mē + 3643 oligōreō | Not to make light of; not to regard lightly; not to despise; not to ignore; not to think lightly of; not to scorn; not to make little of, treat lightly.<br><br>**Practical Application**<br>When we are being taught, disciplined, or corrected, there is always the danger of...<br>• despising it<br>• scorning it<br>• making light of it |

# PRACTICAL WORD STUDIES
## in the New Testament

| ENGLISH WORD | GREEK WORD AND VERSE | THE WORD MEANS... |
|---|---|---|
| **Do not despise–NKJV**<br>Don't ignore it–NLT<br><br>**POSB REFERENCE**<br>(Heb.12:5-7; esp. v.5)<br>Note 1 | ⇒ NIV #3590 mē [not] + 3902 oligōreō [make light of]<br>⇒ NASB #3361 mē + 3643 oligōreō<br><br>**Hebrews 12:5**<br>And ye have forgotten the exhortation which speaketh unto you as unto children, My son, **despise not** thou the chastening of the Lord, nor faint when thou art rebuked of him: [KJV]<br>And you have forgotten the exhortation which is addressed to you as sons, "My son, do **not regard lightly** the discipline of the Lord, Nor FAINT WHEN YOU ARE REPROVED BY Him; [NASB]<br>And you have forgotten that word of encouragement that addresses you as sons: "My son, **do not make light of** the Lord's discipline, and do not lose heart when he rebukes you, [NIV]<br>And you have forgotten the exhortation which speaks to you as to sons: *"My son, **do not despise** the chastening of the LORD, Nor be discouraged when yu are rebuked by Him;* [NKJV]<br>And have you entirely forgotten the encouraging words God spoke to you, his children? He said, "My child, **don't ignore it** when the Lord disciplines you, and don't be discouraged when he corrects you. [NLT]<br>καὶ ἐκλέλησθε τῆς παρακλήσεως, ἥτις ὑμῖν ὡς υἱοῖς διαλέγεται, Υἱέ μου, **μὴ ὀλιγώρει** παιδείας Κυρίου, μηδὲ ἐκλύου, ὑπ' αὐτοῦ ἐλεγχόμενος· [GNS]<br>καὶ ἐκλέλησθε τῆς παρακλήσεως, ἥτις ὑμῖν ὡς υἱοῖς διαλέγεται, Υἱέ μου, **μὴ ὀλιγώρει** παιδείας κυρίου μηδὲ ἐκλύου ὑπ' αὐτοῦ ἐλεγχόμενος· [GNT] | • treating it too lightly<br>Too often, we pay little attention to the discipline and correction of God: to the tug and pull of the Spirit of God, to the little consequences and sufferings of our hearts, to the little things that happen to us. As a result, we continue right on in our little irresponsible behaviors and sins. The little flaws and sins get bigger and bigger until finally the roof caves in, and the consequences involve so much destruction and suffering that we can no longer ignore them.<br>Why do we suffer so much in this life? Because of our irresponsibilities and sins—because we do not heed the discipline and correction of God when we first begin to act irresponsibly. If we heeded the discipline of God, then we could correct our small misbehavior and no big sin would happen. This would mean that much of the great sufferings in the world would never happen.<br>The point is this: we are not to despise the discipline of God—not to scorn it nor take and treat it lightly. We are to heed it. As we do, life will be much easier, and we will be stronger and much more triumphant and victorious. |
| **#988**<br>**Despise Not**<br><br>Despise not–KJV<br>Not regard lightly–NASB<br>Not make light of–NIV<br>Not despise–NKJV<br>Don't ignore it–NLT<br><br>**POSB REFERENCE**<br>(Heb.12:5-7; esp. v.5)<br>Note 1 | **μὴ ὀλιγώρει** = mē oligōrei<br>Pronunciation: [may ol-ig-o-reh'-ee]<br>Parsing *oligōrei* (part of speech): verb<br>  Mood—imperative<br>  Tense—present<br>  Voice—active<br>  Person—2nd person<br>  Number—singular<br>  Stem or root—from ὀλιγωρέω<br>Concordance References:<br>⇒ Strong's #3361 mē + 3643 oligōreō<br>⇒ NIV #3590 mē [not] + 3902 oligōreō [make light of]<br>⇒ NASB #3361 mē + 3643 oligōreō<br><br>**Hebrews 12:5**<br>And ye have forgotten the exhortation which speaketh unto you as unto children, My son, **despise not** thou the chastening of the Lord, nor faint when thou art rebuked of him: [KJV]<br>And you have forgotten the exhortation which is addressed to you as sons, "My son, do **not regard lightly** the discipline of the Lord, Nor FAINT WHEN YOU ARE REPROVED BY Him; [NASB]<br>And you have forgotten that word of encouragement that addresses you as sons: "My son, do **not make light of** the Lord's discipline, and do not lose heart when he rebukes you, [NIV]<br>And you have forgotten the exhortation which speaks to you as to sons: *"My son, **do not despise** the chastening of the LORD , Nor be discouraged when yu are rebuked by Him;* [NKJV]<br>And have you entirely forgotten the encouraging words God spoke to you, his children? He said, "My child, **don't ignore it** when the Lord disciplines you, and don't be discouraged when he corrects you. [NLT]<br>καὶ ἐκλέλησθε τῆς παρακλήσεως, ἥτις ὑμῖν ὡς υἱοῖς διαλέγεται, Υἱέ μου, **μὴ ὀλιγώρει** παιδείας Κυρίου, μηδὲ ἐκλύου, ὑπ' αὐτοῦ ἐλεγχόμενος· [GNS]<br>καὶ ἐκλέλησθε τῆς παρακλήσεως, ἥτις ὑμῖν ὡς υἱοῖς διαλέγεται, Υἱέ μου, **μὴ ὀλιγώρει** παιδείας κυρίου μηδὲ ἐκλύου ὑπ' αὐτοῦ ἐλεγχόμενος· [GNT] | Not to make light of; not to regard lightly; not to despise; not to ignore; not to think lightly of; not to scorn; not to make little of, treat lightly.<br><br>**Practical Application**<br>When we are being taught, disciplined, or corrected, there is always the danger of...<br>• despising it<br>• scorning it<br>• making light of it<br>• treating it too lightly<br>Too often, we pay little attention to the discipline and correction of God: to the tug and pull of the Spirit of God, to the little consequences and sufferings of our hearts, to the little things that happen to us. As a result we continue right on in our little irresponsible behaviors and sins. The little flaws and sins get bigger and bigger until finally the roof caves in and the consequences involve so much destruction and suffering that we can no longer ignore them.<br>Why do we suffer so much in this life? Because of our irresponsibilities and sins—because we do not heed the discipline and correction of God when we first begin to act irresponsibly. If we heeded the discipline of God, then we could correct our small misbehavior and no big sin would happen. This would mean that much of the great sufferings in the world would never happen.<br>The point is this: we are not to despise the discipline of God—not to scorn it nor take and treat it lightly. We are to heed it. As we do, life will be much easier, and we will be stronger and much more triumphant and victorious. |

# PRACTICAL WORD STUDIES
## in the NEW TESTAMENT

| ENGLISH WORD | GREEK WORD AND VERSE | THE WORD MEANS... |
|---|---|---|
| **#989**<br>**Despised**<br><br>Despised–KJV<br>Viewed others with contempt–NASB<br>Looked down on–NIV<br>Despised–NKJV<br>Scorned–NLT<br><br>**POSB REFERENCE**<br>(Lk.18:9)<br>Note 1, point 3 | ἐξουθενοῦντας = exouthenountas<br>Pronunciation: [ex-oo-then-oon'-tas]<br>Parsing (part of speech): verb<br>    Mood—participle<br>    Tense—present<br>    Voice—active<br>    Case—accusative<br>    Gender—masculine<br>    Number—plural<br>    Stem or root—from ἐξουθενέω<br>Concordance References:<br>⇒ Strong's #1848 exoutheneö<br>⇒ NIV #2024 exoutheneö<br>⇒ NASB #1848 exoutheneö<br><br>**Luke 18:9**<br>And he spake this parable unto certain which trusted in themselves that they were righteous, and **despised** others: [KJV]<br>And He also told this parable to certain ones who trusted in themselves that they were righteous, and **viewed others with contempt**: [NASB]<br>To some who were confident of their own righteousness and **looked down on** everybody else, Jesus told this parable: [NIV]<br>Also He spoke this parable to some who trusted in themselves that they were righteous, and **despised** others: [NKJV]<br>Then Jesus told this story to some who had great self-confidence and **scorned** everyone else: [NLT]<br>Εἶπε δὲ καὶ πρός τινας τοὺς πεποιθότας ἐφ' ἑαυτοῖς ὅτι εἰσὶ δίκαιοι, καὶ **ἐξουθενοῦντας** τοὺς λοιποὺς, τὴν παραβολὴν ταύτην· [GNS]<br>Εἶπεν δὲ καὶ πρός τινας τοὺς πεποιθότας ἐφ' ἑαυτοῖς ὅτι εἰσὶν δίκαιοι καὶ **ἐξουθενοῦντας** τοὺς λοιποὺς τὴν παραβολὴν ταύτην· [GNT] | To despise; to view others with contempt; to look down on; to scorn; to set at naught; to count as nothing, as unimportant and insignificant.<br><br>**Practical Application**<br>Such persons feel and act as though they are above and better, more important and significant, than others. They shy away from, ignore and neglect, pass by and downgrade, criticize and talk about...<br>• the poor<br>• the unfortunate<br>• the poorly dressed<br>• the homeless<br>• the downcast<br>• the derelict<br>• the undernourished |
| **#990**<br>**Despisers**<br><br>Despisers–KJV<br>Scoffers–NASB<br>Scoffers–NIV<br>Despisers–NKJV<br>Mockers–NLT<br><br>**POSB REFERENCE**<br>(Acts 13:23-41; esp. v.41)<br>Note 3, point 7 | καταφρονηταί = kataphronëtai<br>Pronunciation: [kat-af-ron-ay-tah-ee]<br>Parsing (part of speech): noun<br>    Case—vocative<br>    Gender—masculine<br>    Number—plural<br>    Stem or root—from καταφρονητής, οῦ<br>Concordance References:<br>⇒ Strong's #2707 kataphronëtës<br>⇒ NIV #2970 kataphronëtës<br>⇒ NASB #2707 kataphronëtës<br><br>**Acts 13:41**<br>Behold, ye **despisers**, and wonder, and perish: for I work a work in your days, a work which ye shall in no wise believe, though a man declare it unto you. [KJV]<br>'Behold, you **scoffers**, and marvel, and perish; For I am accomplishing a work in your days, A work which you will never believe, though someone should describe it to you.'" [NASB]<br>" 'Look, you **scoffers**, wonder and perish, for I am going to do something in your days that you would never believe, even if someone told you.'" [NIV]<br>"Behold, you **despisers**, Marvel and perish! For I work a work in your days, A work which you will by no means believe, Though one wer to declare it to you.' " [NKJV]<br>'Look you **mockers**, be amazed and die! For I am doing something in your own day, something you wouldn't believe even if someone told you about it.'"[NLT]<br>Ἴδετε, οἱ **καταφρονηταί**, καὶ θαυμάσατε καὶ ἀφανίσθητε· ὅτι ἔργον ἐγὼ ἐργάζομαι ἐν ταῖς ἡμέραις ὑμῶν, ἔργον ᾧ οὐ μὴ πιστεύσητε ἐάν τις ἐκδιηγῆται | Scoffers; scorners; mockers; cynics; mimics. It means to look down upon; think lightly of; act against.<br><br>**Practical Application**<br>The Savior brings judgment upon men. Since He has come, men must beware lest what the prophet declared come upon them (Habakkuk 1:5).<br>⇒ They can be "despisers" (kataphronëtai).<br>⇒ They can wonder and perish. The idea is that a man can perish wondering if Jesus is truly the Savior and if the Word preached is true (Acts 13:38-39). (See POSB *Deeper Study* #2, Perish—John 3:16.) |

# PRACTICAL WORD STUDIES
## in the NEW TESTAMENT

| ENGLISH WORD | GREEK WORD AND VERSE | THE WORD MEANS... |
|---|---|---|
| | ὑμῖν. [GNS]<br>Ἴδετε, οἱ **καταφρονηταί**, καὶ θαυμάσατε καὶ ἀφανίσθητε, ὅτι ἔργον ἐργάζομαι ἐγὼ ἐν ταῖς ἡμέραις ὑμῶν, ἔργον ὃ οὐ μὴ πιστεύσητε ἐάν τις ἐκδιηγῆται ὑμῖν. [GNT] | |
| **#991**<br>**Despisers Of Those That Are Good**<br><br>Despisers of those that are good–KJV<br>Haters of good–NASB<br>Not lovers of good–NIV<br>Despisers of good–NKJV<br>No interest in what is good–NLT<br><br>**POSB REFERENCE**<br>(2 Tim. 3:2-4; esp. v.3)<br>Note 1, point 14 | **ἀφιλάγαθοι** = aphilagathoi<br>Pronunciation: [af-il-ag'-ath-oy]<br>Parsing (part of speech): adjective<br>    Case—nominative<br>    Gender—masculine<br>    Number—plural<br>    Stem or root—from ἀφιλάγαθος, ον<br>Concordance References:<br>  ⇒ Strong's #865 aphilagathos<br>  ⇒ NIV #920 aphilagathos<br>  ⇒ NASB #865 aphilagathos<br><br>**2 Tim. 3:3**<br>Without natural affection, trucebreakers, false accusers, incontinent, fierce, **despisers of those that are good**, [KJV]<br>Unloving, irreconcilable, malicious gossips, without self-control, brutal, **haters of good**, [NASB]<br>Without love, unforgiving, slanderous, without self-control, brutal, **not lovers of** the **good**, [NIV]<br>Unloving, unforgiving, slanderers, without self-control, brutal, **despisers of good**, [NKJV]<br>They will be unloving and unforgiving; they will slander others and have no self-control; they will be cruel and have **no interest in what is good**. [NLT]<br>ἄστοργοι, ἄσπονδοι, διάβολοι, ἀκρατεῖς, ἀνήμεροι, **ἀφιλάγαθοι**, [GNS]<br>ἄστοργοι ἄσπονδοι διάβολοι ἀκρατεῖς ἀνήμεροι **ἀφιλάγαθοι** [GNT] | Not lovers of good; despisers of those who are good; haters of good; no interest in what is good; an enemy to goodness.<br><br>**Practical Application**<br>People will be *despisers of those who are good (aphilagathoi)*: this refers to people despising both good people and good things. In the last days people will be embarrassed...<br>• to speak up for what is right.<br>• to take a stand for what is good.<br>• to be known as a good person.<br>• to be a friend to good people.<br><br>People will want to fulfill their desires and to satisfy their flesh; they will want to party, indulge, look, feel, taste, experience, possess, take, and fit in and be acceptable with the crowd. They will let morality and justice go, rejecting whatever restraint they feel. They will actually despise righteousness and want nothing to do with anyone who speaks up for what is right. |
| **#992**<br>**Despiteful**<br><br>Despiteful–KJV<br>Insolent–NASB<br>Insolent–NIV<br>Violent–NKJV<br>Insolent–NLT<br><br>**POSB REFERENCE**<br>(Romans 1:30)<br>*Deeper Study* #14 | **ὑβριστάς** = hubristas<br>Pronunciation: [hoo-bris-tahs']<br>Parsing (part of speech): noun<br>    Case—accusative<br>    Gender—masculine<br>    Number—plural<br>    Stem or root—from ὑβριστής, οῦ<br>Concordance References:<br>  ⇒ Strong's #5197 hubristēs<br>  ⇒ NIV #5616 hubristēs<br>  ⇒ NASB #5197 hubristēs<br><br>**Romans 1:30**<br>Backbiters, haters of God, **despiteful**, proud, boasters, inventors of evil things, disobedient to parents, [KJV]<br>Slanderers, haters of God, **insolent**, arrogant, boastful, inventors of evil, disobedient to parents, [NASB]<br>Slanderers, God-haters, **insolent**, arrogant and boastful; they invent ways of doing evil; they disobey their parents; [NIV]<br>Backbiters, haters of God, **violent**, proud, boasters, inventors of evil things, disobedient to parents, [NKJV]<br>They are backstabbers, haters of God, **insolent**, proud, and boastful. They are forever inventing new ways of sinning and are disobedient to their parents. [NLT]<br>ψιθυριστάς, καταλάλους, θεοστυγεῖς, **ὑβριστάς**, ὑπερηφάνους, ἀλαζόνας, ἐφευρετὰς κακῶν, γονεῦσιν ἀπειθεῖς, [GNS]<br>καταλάλους θεοστυγεῖς **ὑβριστάς** ὑπερηφάνους ἀλαζόνας, ἐφευρετὰς κακῶν, γονεῦσιν ἀπειθεῖς, [GNT] | Insolent, despiteful, insulting, and defying; a violent man.<br><br>**Practical Application**<br>It is a spirit of spite, of attack and assault, verbally or physically. It is despising and attacking, inflicting injury either by word or act. It is a man who...<br>• lives his own life as he wishes, ignoring both God and men.<br>• lives as though his rights and affairs are the only rights and affairs which matter.<br>• stands toe to toe with both God and men, acting as though he needs neither.<br>• acts so independent in life that he dares God or men to get in his way.<br>• does what he wants when he wants, even if it hurts or destroys others.<br><br>The sin of despite, of being insolent and insulting, is the spirit that hurts and harms others in order to do what one wants. |
| **#993**<br>**Destroy**<br><br>Destroy–KJV<br>Destroy–NASB | **ἀπολέσαι** = apolesai<br>Pronunciation: [ap-ol'-le-sai]<br>Parsing (part of speech): verb<br>    Mood—infinitive<br>    Tense—aorist<br>    Voice—active<br>    Stem or root—from ἀπόλλυμι | To destroy, lay waste, ruin, kill, inflict a worthless existence. It is causing the loss of one's *well-being*, not the loss of one's being.<br><br>**Practical Application**<br>"Who can destroy both soul and body in hell" |

## PRACTICAL WORD STUDIES
### in the NEW TESTAMENT

| ENGLISH WORD | GREEK WORD AND VERSE | THE WORD MEANS... |
|---|---|---|
| **Destroy–NIV**<br>**Destroy–NKJV**<br>**Destroy–NLT**<br><br>**POSB<br>REFERENCE**<br>(Mt.10:28)<br>*Deeper Study #1* | Concordance References:<br>⇒ Strong's #622 apollumi<br>⇒ NIV #660 apollumi<br>⇒ NASB #622 apollumi<br><br>**Matthew 10:28**<br>And fear not them which kill the body, but are not able to kill the soul: but rather fear him which is able to **destroy** both soul and body in hell. [KJV]<br>"And do not fear those who kill the body, but are unable to kill the soul; but rather fear Him who is able to **destroy** both soul and body in hell. [NASB]<br>Do not be afraid of those who kill the body but cannot kill the soul. Rather, be afraid of the One who can **destroy** both soul and body in hell. [NIV]<br>And do not fear those who kill the body but cannot kill the soul. But rather fear Him who is able to **destroy** both soul and body in hell. [NKJV]<br>"Don't be afraid of those who want to kill you. They can only kill your body; they cannot touch your soul. Fear only God, who can **destroy** both soul and body in hell. [NLT]<br>καὶ μὴ φοβηθῆτε ἀπὸ τῶν ἀποκτεινόντων τὸ σῶμα, τὴν δὲ ψυχὴν μὴ δυναμένων ἀποκτεῖναι. φοβηθῆτε δὲ μᾶλλον τὸν δυνάμενον καὶ ψυχὴν καὶ σῶμα **ἀπολέσαι** ἐν γεέννῃ. [GNS]<br>καὶ μὴ φοβεῖσθε ἀπὸ τῶν ἀποκτεννόντων τὸ σῶμα, τὴν δὲ ψυχὴν μὴ δυναμένων ἀποκτεῖναι· φοβεῖσθε δὲ μᾶλλον τὸν δυνάμενον καὶ ψυχὴν καὶ σῶμα **ἀπολέσαι** ἐν γεέννῃ. [GNT] | does not mean that a person would cease to exist but that he would live a worthless existence. It means the loss of a person's well-being, not his being. It means that the person would suffer waste and ruin forever and ever. |
| **#994<br>Destroy**<br><br>**Destroy–KJV**<br>**Destroy–NASB**<br>**Kill–NIV**<br>**Destroy–NKJV**<br>**Kill–NLT**<br><br>**POSB<br>REFERENCE**<br>(Lk.19:47-48; esp. v.47)<br>Note 3, point 1a<br><br>See also POSB REF:<br>(Mk.11:18)<br>Note 3 | ἀπολέσαι = *apolesai*<br>Pronunciation: [ap-ol'-ee-sah-ee]<br>Parsing (part of speech): verb<br>    Mood—infinitive<br>    Tense—aorist<br>    Voice—active<br>    Stem or root—from ἀπόλλυμι<br>Concordance References:<br>⇒ Strong's #622 apollumi<br>⇒ NIV #660 apollumi<br>⇒ NASB #622 apollumi<br><br>**Luke 19:47**<br>And he taught daily in the temple. But the chief priests and the scribes and the chief of the people sought to **destroy** him, [KJV]<br>And He was teaching daily in the temple; but the chief priests and the scribes and the leading men among the people were trying to **destroy** Him, [NASB]<br>Every day he was teaching at the temple. But the chief priests, the teachers of the law and the leaders among the people were trying to **kill** him. [NIV]<br>And He was teaching daily in the temple. But the chief priests, the scribes, and the leaders of the people sought to **destroy** Him, [NKJV]<br>After that, he taught daily in the Temple, but the leading priests, the teachers of religious law, and the other leaders of the people began planning how to **kill** him. [NLT]<br>Καὶ ἦν διδάσκων τὸ καθ' ἡμέραν ἐν τῷ ἱερῷ. οἱ δὲ ἀρχιερεῖς καὶ οἱ γραμματεῖς ἐζήτουν αὐτὸν **ἀπολέσαι**, καὶ οἱ πρῶτοι τοῦ λαοῦ· [GNS]<br>Καὶ ἦν διδάσκων τὸ καθ' ἡμέραν ἐν τῷ ἱερῷ. οἱ δὲ ἀρχιερεῖς καὶ οἱ γραμματεῖς ἐζήτουν αὐτὸν **ἀπολέσαι** καὶ οἱ πρῶτοι τοῦ λαοῦ, [GNT] | To utterly destroy; to demolish; to obliterate; to cause to perish; to bring to an end; to put to death.<br><br>**Practical Application**<br>In this Scripture, note two things:<br>1. The leaders were actively seeking to "destroy" (*apolesai*) Christ. (Imagine religious leaders being so disturbed that they sought to destroy and ruin the ministry of a person.)<br>2. The reason why the leaders were so disturbed was twofold: first, they were losing control of the temple; and second, they were losing control of the people. Jesus had invaded their temple by cleansing it; and He was teaching the true gospel of the Kingdom of God and righteousness. They were losing money because Jesus had cast out the vendors, and their own personal ideas and control were being undermined. They were unwilling to accept the truth personally and to surrender their lives to Jesus. (See POSB notes—Matthew 12:1-8; POSB note—Matthew 12:10 and POSB *Deeper Study #1*—Matthew 12:10 for more discussion.) |
| **#995<br>Destroy**<br><br>**Wasted–KJV**<br>**Destroy–NASB** | ἐπόρθουν = *eporthoun*<br>Pronunciation: [eh-por-thoon]<br>Parsing (part of speech): verb<br>    Mood—indicative<br>    Tense—imperfect<br>    Voice—active | To destroy; to get rid of; to make havoc; to utterly rack or lay waste; to devastate, destroy, ruin, or wipe out. |

# PRACTICAL WORD STUDIES
## in the NEW TESTAMENT

| ENGLISH WORD | GREEK WORD AND VERSE | THE WORD MEANS... |
|---|---|---|
| Destroy–NIV<br>Destroy–NKJV<br>Get rid of–NLT<br><br>**POSB REFERENCE**<br>(Gal.1:13-16; esp. v.13)<br>Note 3, point 1a | Person—1st person<br>Number—singular<br>Stem or root—from πορθέω<br>Concordance References:<br>⇒ Strong's #4199 portheö<br>⇒ NIV #4514 portheö<br>⇒ NASB #4199 portheö<br><br>**Galatians 1:13**<br>For ye have heard of my conversation in time past in the Jews' religion, how that beyond measure I persecuted the church of God, and **wasted** it: [KJV]<br>For you have heard of my former manner of life in Judaism, how I used to persecute the church of God beyond measure, and tried to **destroy** it; [NASB]<br>For you have heard of my previous way of life in Judaism, how intensely I persecuted the church of God and tried to **destroy** it. [NIV]<br>For you have heard of my former conduct in Judaism, how I persecuted the church of God beyond measure and *tried to* **destroy** it. [NKJV]<br>You know what I was like when I followed the Jewish religion—how I violently persecuted the Christians. I did my best to **get rid of** them. [NLT]<br>ἠκούσατε γὰρ τὴν ἐμὴν ἀναστροφήν ποτε ἐν τῷ Ἰουδαϊσμῷ, ὅτι καθ' ὑπερβολὴν ἐδίωκον τὴν ἐκκλησίαν τοῦ Θεοῦ, καὶ **ἐπόρθουν** αὐτήν· [GNS]<br>Ἠκούσατε γὰρ τὴν ἐμὴν ἀναστροφήν ποτε ἐν τῷ Ἰουδαϊσμῷ, ὅτι καθ' ὑπερβολὴν ἐδίωκον τὴν ἐκκλησίαν τοῦ θεοῦ καὶ **ἐπόρθουν** αὐτήν, [GNT] | **Practical Application**<br>The point to see is that Paul had been bent on violence; he had sought to utterly stamp out the church; to wipe believers off the face of the earth. (See POSB note, Church, Persecution of—Acts 8:3 for more discussion.) |
| #996<br>**Destroy**<br><br>Destroy–KJV<br>Render powerless–NASB<br>**Destroy–NIV**<br>**Destroy–NKJV**<br>Break–NLT<br><br>**POSB REFERENCE**<br>(Heb.2:14-16; esp. v.14)<br>Note 1, point 3 | καταργήσῃ = katargēsē<br>Pronunciation: [kat-arg-ay'-say]<br>Parsing (part of speech): verb<br>Mood—subjunctive<br>Tense—aorist<br>Voice—active<br>Person—3rd person<br>Number—singular<br>Stem or root—from καταργέω<br>Concordance References:<br>⇒ Strong's #2673 katargeö<br>⇒ NIV #2934 katargeö<br>⇒ NASB #2673 katargeö<br><br>**Hebrews 2:14**<br>Forasmuch then as the children are partakers of flesh and blood, he also himself likewise took part of the same; that through death he might **destroy** him that had the power of death, that is, the devil; [KJV]<br>Since then the children share in flesh and blood, He Himself likewise also partook of the same, that through death He might **render powerless** him who had the power of death, that is, the devil; [NASB]<br>Since the children have flesh and blood, he too shared in their humanity so that by his death he might **destroy** him who holds the power of death—that is, the devil— [NIV]<br>Inasmuch then as the children have partaken of flesh and blood, He Himself likewise shared in the same, that through death He might **destroy** him who had the power of death, that is, the devil, [NKJV]<br>Because God's children are human beings—made of flesh and blood—Jesus also became flesh and blood by being born in human form. For only as a human being could he die, and only by dying could he **break** the power of the Devil, who had the power of death. [NLT]<br>ἐπεὶ οὖν τὰ παιδία κεκοινώνηκε σαρκὸς καὶ αἵματος, καὶ αὐτὸς παραπλησίως μετέσχε τῶν αὐτῶν, ἵνα διὰ τοῦ θανάτου **καταργήσῃ** τὸν τὸ κράτος ἔχοντα τοῦ θανάτου, τοῦτ' ἔστι τὸν διάβολον, [GNS]<br>ἐπεὶ οὖν τὰ παιδία κεκοινώνηκεν αἵματος καὶ σαρκός, | To destroy; to render powerless; to break; to abolish; to render ineffective; to cancel; to nullify; to bring to nothing; to do away; to make inoperative.<br><br>**Practical Application**<br>Jesus Christ alone has broken and destroyed the power of Satan over sin and death. Satan's power over sin and death functions and operates within man, and what a power it is—the awesome power to separate men from God for eternity. But Jesus Christ has broken that power. He has made the power of Satan ineffective and inoperative. Man no longer has to be enslaved by sin and its guilt nor by death. He is delivered from death because Jesus Christ has broken Satan's power over death. |

# PRACTICAL WORD STUDIES
## in the NEW TESTAMENT

| ENGLISH WORD | GREEK WORD AND VERSE | THE WORD MEANS... |
|---|---|---|
| | καὶ αὐτὸς παραπλησίως μετέσχεν τῶν αὐτῶν, ἵνα διὰ τοῦ θανάτου **καταργήσῃ** τὸν τὸ κράτος ἔχοντα τοῦ θανάτου, τοῦτ' ἔστιν τὸν διάβολον, [GNT] | |
| #997 **Destroy Not** <br><br> Destroy not–KJV <br> Do not destroy–NASB <br> Do not...destroy–NIV <br> Do not destroy–NKJV <br> Don't...ruin–NLT <br><br> **POSB REFERENCE** <br> (Rom.14:13-15; esp. v.15) <br> Note 6, point 2 | μὴ ἀπόλλυε = mē apollue <br> Pronunciation: [may ap-ol'-loo-eh] <br> Parsing *apollue* (part of speech): verb <br>   Mood—imperative <br>   Tense—present <br>   Voice—active <br>   Person—2nd person <br>   Number—singular <br>   Stem or root—from ἀπόλλυμι <br> Concordance References: <br> ⇒ Strong's #3361 mē + 622 apollumi <br> ⇒ NIV #3590 mē [not] + 660 apollumi [destroy] <br> ⇒ NASB #3361 mē + 622 apollumi <br><br> **Romans 14:15** <br> But if thy brother be grieved with thy meat, now walkest thou not charitably. **Destroy not** him with thy meat, for whom Christ died. [KJV] <br> For if because of food your brother is hurt, you are no longer walking according to love. **Do not destroy** with your food him for whom Christ died. [NASB] <br> If your brother is distressed because of what you eat, you are no longer acting in love. **Do not** by your eating **destroy** your brother for whom Christ died. [NIV] <br> Yet if your brother is grieved because of *your* food, you are no longer walking in love. **Do not destroy** with your food the one for whom Christ died. [NKJV] <br> And if another Christian is distressed by what you eat, you are not acting in love if you eat it. **Don't** let your eating **ruin** someone for whom Christ died. [NLT] <br> εἰ δὲ διὰ βρῶμα ὁ ἀδελφός σου λυπεῖται, οὐκέτι κατὰ ἀγάπην περιπατεῖς. **μὴ** τῷ βρώματί σου ἐκεῖνον **ἀπόλλυε**, ὑπὲρ οὗ Χριστὸς ἀπέθανε. [GNS] <br> εἰ γὰρ διὰ βρῶμα ὁ ἀδελφός σου λυπεῖται, οὐκέτι κατὰ ἀγάπην περιπατεῖς· **μὴ** τῷ βρώματί σου ἐκεῖνον **ἀπόλλυε** ὑπὲρ οὗ Χριστὸς ἀπέθανεν. [GNT] | Do not destroy or ruin; not to spoil; to hurt and wound to the point of ruining. <br><br> **Practical Application** <br> We are to do nothing that would destroy a brother. This is a forceful command: "Destroy not (*mē apollue*)." Such behavior is absolutely forbidden of the Christian believer. We are to do absolutely nothing that would destroy or ruin our brother. |
| #998 **Destroy, Began To** <br><br> Havock–KJV <br> Ravaging–NASB <br> **Began to destroy–NIV** <br> Havoc–NKJV <br> Devastate–NLT <br><br> **POSB REFERENCE** <br> (Acts 8:3) <br> Note 3 | ἐλυμαίνετο = elumaineto <br> Pronunciation: [loo-mah'ee-neh-tow] <br> Parsing (part of speech): verb <br>   Mood—indicative <br>   Tense—imperfect <br>   Voice—middle <br>   Person—3rd person <br>   Number—singular <br>   Stem or root—from λυμαίνομαι <br> Concordance References: <br> ⇒ Strong's #3075 lumainomai <br> ⇒ NIV #3381 lumainō <br> ⇒ NASB #3075 lumainomai <br><br> **Acts 8:3** <br> As for Saul, he made **havock** of the church, entering into every house, and haling men and women committed them to prison. [KJV] <br> But Saul began **ravaging** the church, entering house after house; and dragging off men and women, he would put them in prison. [NASB] <br> But Saul **began to destroy** the church. Going from house to house, he dragged off men and women and put them in prison. [NIV] <br> As for Saul, he made **havoc** of the church, entering every house, and dragging off men and women, committing *them* to prison. [NKJV] <br> Saul was going everywhere to **devastate** the church. He went from house to house, dragging out both men and women to throw them into jail. [NLT] <br> Σαῦλος δὲ **ἐλυμαίνετο** τὴν ἐκκλησίαν, κατὰ τοὺς οἴκους εἰσπορευόμενος, σύρων τε ἄνδρας καὶ γυναῖκας | To destroy; to devastate; to ravage; to ruin; to wipe out. <br><br> **Practical Application** <br> The mercy and grace of God are fully demonstrated in the life of Paul. God's mercy is available to all of us, no matter how terribly we have sinned. There is hope, forgiveness, and a glorious ministry for any of us, no matter who we are or what we have done—if we will repent and surrender ourselves to the Lord Jesus, to follow and obey Him. |

# Practical Word Studies
## in the New Testament

| ENGLISH WORD | GREEK WORD AND VERSE | THE WORD MEANS... |
|---|---|---|
| | παρεδίδου εἰς φυλακήν. [GNS]<br>Σαῦλος δὲ **ἐλυμαίνετο** τὴν ἐκκλησίαν κατὰ τοὺς οἴκους εἰσπορευόμενος, σύρων τε ἄνδρας καὶ γυναῖκας παρεδίδου εἰς φυλακήν. [GNT] | |
| **#999**<br>**Destroy, Do Not**<br><br>Destroy not–KJV<br>**Do not destroy–NASB**<br>**Do not...destroy–NIV**<br>**Do not destroy–NKJV**<br>Don't...ruin–NLT<br><br>**POSB REFERENCE**<br>(Rom.14:13-15; esp. v.15)<br>Note 6, point 2 | **μὴ ἀπόλλυε** = më apollue<br>Pronunciation: [may ap-ol'-loo-eh]<br>Parsing *apollue* (part of speech): verb<br>    Mood—imperative<br>    Tense—present<br>    Voice—active<br>    Person—2nd person<br>    Number—singular<br>    Stem or root—from **ἀπόλλυμι**<br>Concordance References:<br>  ⇒ Strong's #3361 më + 622 apollumi<br>  ⇒ NIV #3590 më [not] + 660 apollumi [destroy]<br>  ⇒ NASB #3361 më + 622 apollumi<br><br>**Romans 14:15**<br>But if thy brother be grieved with thy meat, now walkest thou not charitably. **Destroy not** him with thy meat, for whom Christ died. [KJV]<br>For if because of food your brother is hurt, you are no longer walking according to love. **Do not destroy** with your food him for whom Christ died. [NASB]<br>If your brother is distressed because of what you eat, you are no longer acting in love. **Do not** by your eating **destroy** your brother for whom Christ died. [NIV]<br>Yet if your brother is grieved because of *your* food, you are no longer walking in love. **Do not destroy** with your food the one for whom Christ died. [NKJV]<br>And if another Christian is distressed by what you eat, you are not acting in love if you eat it. **Don't** let your eating **ruin** someone for whom Christ died. [NLT]<br>εἰ δὲ διὰ βρῶμα ὁ ἀδελφός σου λυπεῖται, οὐκέτι κατὰ ἀγάπην περιπατεῖς. **μὴ** τῷ βρώματί σου ἐκεῖνον **ἀπόλλυε**, ὑπὲρ οὗ Χριστὸς ἀπέθανε. [GNS]<br>εἰ γὰρ διὰ βρῶμα ὁ ἀδελφός σου λυπεῖται, οὐκέτι κατὰ ἀγάπην περιπατεῖς· **μὴ** τῷ βρώματί σου ἐκεῖνον **ἀπόλλυε** ὑπὲρ οὗ Χριστὸς ἀπέθανεν. [GNT] | Do not destroy or ruin; not to spoil; to hurt and wound to the point of ruining.<br><br>**Practical Application**<br>We are to do nothing that would destroy a brother. This is a forceful command: "Do not destroy (*më apollue*)." Such behavior is absolutely forbidden of the Christian believer. We are to do absolutely nothing that would destroy or ruin our brother. |
| **#1000**<br>**Destroyed**<br><br>**Destroyed–KJV**<br>**Destroyed–NASB**<br>**Destroyed–NIV**<br>**Destroyed–NKJV**<br>Keep going–NLT<br><br>**POSB REFERENCE**<br>(2 Cor.4:7-9; esp. v.9)<br>Note 2, point 4 | **ἀπολλύμενοι** = apollumenoi<br>Pronunciation: [ap-ol-loo'-mehn-oy]<br>Parsing (part of speech): verb<br>    Mood—participle<br>    Tense—present<br>    Voice—middle or passive<br>    Case—nominative<br>    Gender—masculine<br>    Person—1st person<br>    Stem or root—from **ἀπόλλυμι**<br>Concordance References:<br>  ⇒ Strong's #622 apollumi<br>  ⇒ NIV #660 apollumi<br>  ⇒ NASB #622 apollumi<br><br>**2 Cor. 4:9**<br>Persecuted, but not forsaken; cast down, but not **destroyed**; [KJV]<br>Persecuted, but not forsaken; struck down, but not **destroyed**; [NASB]<br>Persecuted, but not abandoned; struck down, but not **destroyed**. [NIV]<br>Persecuted, but not forsaken; struck down, but not **destroyed**— [NKJV]<br>We are hunted down, but God never abandons us. We get knocked down, but we get up again and **keep going**. [NLT]<br>διωκόμενοι, ἀλλ' οὐκ ἐγκαταλειπόμενοι, καταβαλλόμενοι ἀλλ' οὐκ **ἀπολλύμενοι**· [GNS]<br>διωκόμενοι ἀλλ' οὐκ ἐγκαταλειπόμενοι, καταβαλλόμενοι ἀλλ' οὐκ **ἀπολλύμενοι**, [GNT] | To be destroyed; to perish; to die; to strike out; to bring to an end; to be killed; to be lost.<br><br>**Practical Application**<br>The minister (or believer) may be cast down, but he is never destroyed. The minister (or believer) may be struck down, but he is never allowed to strike out; he may be knocked down, but he is never knocked out. |

# PRACTICAL WORD STUDIES
## in the NEW TESTAMENT

| ENGLISH WORD | GREEK WORD AND VERSE | THE WORD MEANS... |
|---|---|---|
| **#1001**<br>**Destroyed**<br><br>**Destroyed**–KJV<br>Utterly destroyed from–NASB<br>Completely cut off from–NIV<br>**Destroyed**–NKJV<br>Cut off from–NLT<br><br>**POSB REFERENCE**<br>(Acts 3:23)<br>*Deeper Study #4* | ἐξολεθρευθήσεται ἐκ = *exolethreuthēsetai ek*<br>Pronunciation: [ex-ol-eth-ryoo'-thay-seh-tah-ee ek]<br>Parsing *exolethreuthēsetai* (part of speech): verb<br>    Mood—indicative or imperative<br>    Tense—future or aorist<br>    Voice—passive<br>    Person—3rd person<br>    Number—singular<br>    Stem or root—from ἐξολεθρεύω<br>Concordance References:<br>⇒ Strong's #1537 + 1842 ek exolethreuō<br>⇒ николайNIV #1666 + 2017 ek exolethreuō<br>⇒ NASB #1537 + 1842 ek exolethreuō<br><br>**Acts 3:23**<br>And it shall come to pass, that every soul, which will not hear that prophet, shall be **destroyed** from among the people. [KJV]<br><br>'And it shall be that every soul that does not heed that prophet shall be **utterly destroyed from** among the people.' [NASB]<br><br>Anyone who does not listen to him will be **completely cut off from** among his people.' [NIV]<br><br>*And it shall be that every soul who will not hear that Prophet shall be utterly **destroyed** from among the people.'* [NKJV]<br><br>Then Moses said, 'Anyone who will not listen to that Prophet will be **cut off from** God's people and utterly destroyed.' [NLT]<br><br>ἔσται δέ, πᾶσα ψυχὴ ἥτις ἐὰν μὴ ἀκούσῃ τοῦ προφήτου ἐκείνου, **ἐξολεθρευθήσεται ἐκ** τοῦ λαοῦ. [GNS]<br><br>ἔσται δὲ πᾶσα ψυχὴ ἥτις ἐὰν μὴ ἀκούσῃ τοῦ προφήτου ἐκείνου **ἐξολεθρευθήσεται ἐκ** τοῦ λαοῦ. [GNT] | To be completely cut off from; to be utterly destroyed or slayed; to lose one's well-being; to be wasted and ruined and given a worthless existence.<br><br>**Practical Application**<br>It does not mean that a person will cease to exist. It means a person will be destroyed and devastated and condemned to a worthless existence. He will suffer waste and loss and ruin forever and ever. |
| **#1002**<br>**Destroys**<br><br>Defile–KJV<br>**Destroys**–NASB<br>**Destroys**–NIV<br>Defiles–NKJV<br>Ruins–NLT<br><br>**POSB REFERENCE**<br>(1 Cor.3:17)<br>Note 7 | φθερεῖ = *phtheirei*<br>Pronunciation: [fthee'-ree]<br>Parsing (part of speech): verb<br>    Mood—indicative<br>    Tense—future<br>    Voice—active<br>    Person—3rd person<br>    Number—singular<br>    Stem or root—from φθείρω<br>Concordance References:<br>⇒ Strong's #5351 phtheirō<br>⇒ NIV #5780 phtheirō<br>⇒ NASB #5351 phtheirō<br><br>**1 Cor. 3:17**<br>If any man **defile** the temple of God, him shall God destroy; for the temple of God is holy, which temple ye are. [KJV]<br><br>If any man **destroys** the temple of God, God will destroy him, for the temple of God is holy, and that is what you are. [NASB]<br><br>If anyone **destroys** God's temple, God will destroy him; for God's temple is sacred, and you are that temple. [NIV]<br><br>If anyone **defiles** the temple of God, God will destroy him. For the temple of God is holy, which *temple* you are. [NKJV]<br><br>God will bring ruin upon anyone who **ruins** this temple. For God's temple is holy, and you Christians are that temple. [NLT]<br><br>εἴ τις τὸν ναὸν τοῦ Θεοῦ φθείρει, **φθερεῖ** τοῦτον ὁ Θεός· ὁ γὰρ ναὸς τοῦ Θεοῦ ἅγιός ἐστιν, οἵτινές ἐστε ὑμεῖς. [GNS]<br><br>εἴ τις τὸν ναὸν τοῦ θεοῦ φθείρει, **φθερεῖ** τοῦτον ὁ θεός· ὁ γὰρ ναὸς τοῦ θεοῦ ἅγιός ἐστιν, οἵτινές ἐστε ὑμεῖς. [GNT] | To destroy; to defile; to ruin; to corrupt; to lead astray.<br><br>**Practical Application**<br>The person who destroys the church will face terrible judgment. The point is striking: the person who troubles the church will suffer the same kind of trouble himself. Whatever he sows, he is definitely going to reap. Troublemaking within the church destroys the spirit of unity and love within the church. To corrupt and destroy the church is to invite God to corrupt and destroy the troublemaker. Note that the punishment is not specifically described. It is simply made clear that he who does such a terrible thing as trouble a church will suffer a terrible punishment. He will be destroyed: wrecked, devastated. |

# PRACTICAL WORD STUDIES
## in the NEW TESTAMENT

| ENGLISH WORD | GREEK WORD AND VERSE | THE WORD MEANS... |
|---|---|---|
| **#1003**<br>**Destruction**<br><br>**Destruction**–KJV<br>**Destruction**–NASB<br>**Destruction**–NIV<br>**Destruction**–NKJV<br>Eternal destruction–NLT<br><br>**POSB REFERENCE**<br>(Philip.3:18-19; esp. v.19)<br>Note 2, point 1 | ἀπώλεια = apōleia<br>Pronunciation: [ap-o'-li-a]<br>Parsing (part of speech): noun<br>    Case—nominative<br>    Gender—feminine<br>    Number—singular<br>    Stem or root—from ἀπώλεια, ας<br>Concordance References:<br>⇒ Strong's #684 apōleia<br>⇒ NIV #724 apōleia<br>⇒ NASB #684 apōleia<br><br>**Philip. 3:19**<br>Whose end is **destruction**, whose God is their belly, and whose glory is in their shame, who mind earthly things.) [KJV]<br>Whose end is **destruction**, whose god is their appetite, and whose glory is in their shame, who set their minds on earthly things. [NASB]<br>Their destiny is **destruction**, their god is their stomach, and their glory is in their shame. Their mind is on earthly things. [NIV]<br>Whose end *is* **destruction**, whose god *is their* belly, and *whose* glory *is* in their shame—who set their mind on earthly things. [NKJV]<br>Their future is **eternal destruction**. Their god is their appetite, they brag about shameful things, and all they think about is this life here on earth. [NLT]<br>ὧν τὸ τέλος **ἀπώλεια**, ὧν ὁ θεὸς ἡ κοιλία, καὶ ἡ δόξα ἐν τῇ αἰσχύνῃ αὐτῶν, οἱ τὰ ἐπίγεια φρονοῦντες. [GNS]<br>ὧν τὸ τέλος **ἀπώλεια**, ὧν ὁ θεὸς ἡ κοιλία καὶ ἡ δόξα ἐν τῇ αἰσχύνῃ αὐτῶν, οἱ τὰ ἐπίγεια φρονοῦντες. [GNT] | Destruction, eternal destruction. The word means perdition, to be slayed or utterly ruined; to lose one's well-being; to be wasted and ruined and given a worthless existence. It does not mean that a person will cease to exist. It means a person will be destroyed and devastated and condemned to a worthless existence. He will suffer waste and loss and ruin forever and ever.<br><br>**Practical Application**<br>If a person stands as an enemy of the cross, he will be destroyed. It does not matter who he is, either within or without the church, he will suffer perdition, that is, utter destruction. Who is an enemy of the cross? It is the person...<br>• who rejects the cross of Christ as the only way to God.<br>• who does not accept the death of Christ as payment for his sins.<br>• who does not believe that Christ died for him, that is, as the punishment for his transgressions.<br>• who does not believe that the penalty for his imperfection was borne by Christ on the cross.<br>• who does not approach God claiming that he is coming by the death of Christ—that is, that he wants God to accept him in the death of Christ.<br>• who claims that there are other ways to approach God—ways other than the cross of Christ.<br>• who considers the cross of Christ to be foolishness.<br>• who opposes and curses Christ and His cross.<br>• who persecutes and attempts to stamp out Christ and His cross.<br>• who denies and questions that Christ died for our sins. |
| **#1004**<br>**Destruction**<br><br>Perdition–KJV<br>**Destruction**–NASB<br>Doomed to destruction–NIV<br>Perdition–NKJV<br>**Destruction**–NLT<br><br>**POSB REFERENCE**<br>(2 Thes.2:3; see v.4 for commentary)<br>Note 1, point 2c | ἀπωλείας = apōleias<br>Pronunciation: [ap-o'-li-ahs]<br>Parsing (part of speech): noun<br>    Case—genitive<br>    Gender—feminine<br>    Number—singular<br>    Stem or root—from ἀπώλεια, ας<br>Concordance References:<br>⇒ Strong's #684 apōleia<br>⇒ NIV #724 apōleia<br>⇒ NASB #684 apōleia<br><br>**2 Thes. 2:3**<br>Let no man deceive you by any means: for that day shall not come, except there come a falling away first, and that man of sin be revealed, the son of **perdition**; [KJV]<br>Let no one in any way deceive you, for it will not come unless the apostasy comes first, and the man of lawlessness is revealed, the son of **destruction**, [NASB]<br>Don't let anyone deceive you in any way, for that day will not come until the rebellion occurs and the man of lawlessness is revealed, the man **doomed to destruction**. [NIV]<br>Let no one deceive you by any means; for *that Day will not come* unless the falling away comes first, and the man of sin is revealed, the son of **perdition**, [NKJV]<br>Don't be fooled by what they say.For that day will not come until there is a great rebellion against God and the | Doomed to destruction, perdition, complete and utter ruin; doom and destruction.<br><br>**Practical Application**<br>The antichrist is the "son of destruction" or "the one who brings destruction." Judas is said to be the son of destruction. But the meaning here is that the antichrist is the very embodiment of destruction...<br>• he is the son of the most violent doom and destruction; the son of the most violent evil imaginable.<br>• the son who is more deserving of doom and destruction than anyone else who has ever lived.<br>• the son of destruction, of the devil himself, the father of doom and destruction. |

| ENGLISH WORD | GREEK WORD AND VERSE | THE WORD MEANS... |
|---|---|---|
| | man of lawlessness is revealed—the one who brings **destruction**. [NLT]<br>μή τις ὑμᾶς ἐξαπατήσῃ κατὰ μηδένα τρόπον· ὅτι ἐὰν μὴ ἔλθῃ ἡ ἀποστασία πρῶτον, καὶ ἀποκαλυφθῇ ὁ ἄνθρωπος τῆς ἁμαρτίας, ὁ υἱὸς τῆς **ἀπωλείας**, [GNS]<br>μή τις ὑμᾶς ἐξαπατήσῃ κατὰ μηδένα τρόπον. ὅτι ἐὰν μὴ ἔλθῃ ἡ ἀποστασία πρῶτον καὶ ἀποκαλυφθῇ ὁ ἄνθρωπος τῆς ἀνομίας, ὁ υἱὸς τῆς **ἀπωλείας**, [GNT] | |
| **#1005**<br>**Destructive**<br><br>Damnable–KJV<br>**Destructive–NASB**<br>**Destructive–NIV**<br>**Destructive–NKJV**<br>**Destructive–NLT**<br><br>POSB<br>REFERENCE<br>(2 Pt.2:1)<br>Note 2, point 2 | ἀπωλείας = *apōleias*<br>Pronunciation: [ap-o'-li-ahs]<br>Parsing (part of speech): noun<br>    Case—genitive<br>    Gender—feminine<br>    Number—singular<br>    Stem or root—from ἀπώλεια, ας<br>Concordance References:<br>⇒ Strong's #684 apōleia<br>⇒ NIV #724 apōleia<br>⇒ NASB #684 apōleia<br><br>**2 Peter 2:1**<br>But there were false prophets also among the people, even as there shall be false teachers among you, who privily shall bring in **damnable** heresies, even denying the Lord that bought them, and bring upon themselves swift destruction. [KJV]<br>But false prophets also arose among the people, just as there will also be false teachers among you, who will secretly introduce **destructive** heresies, even denying the Master who bought them, bringing swift destruction upon themselves. [NASB]<br>But there were also false prophets among the people, just as there will be false teachers among you. They will secretly introduce **destructive** heresies, even denying the sovereign Lord who bought them—bringing swift destruction on themselves. [NIV]<br>But there were also false prophets among the people, even as there will be false teachers among you, who will secretly bring in **destructive** heresies, even denying the Lord who bought them, *and* bring on themselves swift destruction. [NKJV]<br>But there were also false prophets in Israel, just as there will be false teachers among you. They will cleverly teach their **destructive** heresies about God and even turn against their Master who bought them. Theirs will be a swift and terrible end. [NLT]<br>Ἐγένοντο δὲ καὶ ψευδοπροφῆται ἐν τῷ λαῷ, ὡς καὶ ἐν ὑμῖν ἔσονται ψευδοδιδάσκαλοι, οἵτινες παρεισάξουσιν αἱρέσεις **ἀπωλείας**, καὶ τὸν ἀγοράσαντα αὐτοὺς δεσπότην ἀρνούμενοι, ἐπάγοντες ἑαυτοῖς ταχινὴν ἀπώλειαν, [GNS]<br>Ἐγένοντο δὲ καὶ ψευδοπροφῆται ἐν τῷ λαῷ, ὡς καὶ ἐν ὑμῖν ἔσονται ψευδοδιδάσκαλοι, οἵτινες παρεισάξουσιν αἱρέσεις **ἀπωλείας** καὶ τὸν ἀγοράσαντα αὐτοὺς δεσπότην ἀρνούμενοι. ἐπάγοντες ἑαυτοῖς ταχινὴν ἀπώλειαν, [GNT] | Destructive, damnable. It means heresies that cause one to lose one's well being; to be ruined; to be wasted; to perish; to be destroyed; to suffer perdition.<br><br>**Practical Application**<br>Note where false teachers teach their destructive heresies: in the church, right among believers. The false teachers are not out in the world, but they are within the church. They have joined the church, and they have been outstanding members long enough to become teachers and preachers within the church. They hold leadership positions from which they can teach their destructive heresies. Note that the word "heresies" (*haireseis*) is plural. What are the heresies being referred to? Any teaching that goes contrary to the Scripture, that is, the Word of God or Bible. This is clearly what is meant, for the exhortation has just been given: "Take heed to the word of prophecy, to the Scripture" (cp. 2 Peter 1:19-21). |
| **#1006**<br>**Detachment Of Soldiers, Troops**<br><br>Band–KJV<br>Cohort–NASB<br>**Detachment of soldiers–NIV**<br>**Detachment of troops–NKJV**<br>Battalion of Roman soldiers–NLT | σπεῖραν = *speiran*<br>Pronunciation: [spi'-rahn]<br>Parsing (part of speech): noun<br>    Case—accusative<br>    Gender—feminine<br>    Number—singular<br>    Stem or root—from σπεῖρα, ης<br>Concordance References:<br>⇒ Strong's #4686 speira<br>⇒ NIV #5061 speira<br>⇒ NASB #4686 speira<br><br>**John 18:3**<br>Judas then, having received a **band** of men and officers from the chief priests and Pharisees, cometh thither | A detachment; a company; a battalion; a band; a cohort of Roman soldiers; a regiment.<br><br>**Practical Application**<br>This usually meant a cohort or battalion which was made up of six hundred soldiers. However, "detachment of soldiers" (*speiran*) sometimes meant maniple. Every detachment of soldiers consisted of three maniples, about two hundred soldiers. Which is meant here is not known. Most believe the number of soldiers was large, certainly close to the two hundred serving in a maniple. |

## PRACTICAL WORD STUDIES
### in the NEW TESTAMENT

| ENGLISH WORD | GREEK WORD AND VERSE | THE WORD MEANS... |
|---|---|---|
| **POSB REFERENCE** (Jn.18:3) *Deeper Study #1* | with lanterns and torches and weapons. [KJV]<br>Judas then, having received the Roman **cohort**, and officers from the chief priests and the Pharisees, came there with lanterns and torches and weapons. [NASB]<br>So Judas came to the grove, guiding a **detachment of soldiers** and some officials from the chief priests and Pharisees. They were carrying torches, lanterns and weapons. [NIV]<br>Then Judas, having received a **detachment of troops**, and officers from the chief priests and Pharisees, came there with lanterns, torches, and weapons. [NKJV]<br>The leading priests and Pharisees had given Judas a **battalion of Roman soldiers** and Temple guards to accompany him. Now with blazing torches, lanterns, and weapons, they arrived at the olive grove. [NLT]<br>ὁ οὖν Ἰούδας, λαβὼν τὴν **σπεῖραν**, καὶ ἐκ τῶν ἀρχιερέων καὶ Φαρισαίων ὑπηρέτας ἔρχεται ἐκεῖ μετὰ φανῶν καὶ λαμπάδων καὶ ὅπλων. [GNS]<br>ὁ οὖν Ἰούδας λαβὼν τὴν **σπεῖραν** καὶ ἐκ τῶν ἀρχιερέων καὶ ἐκ τῶν Φαρισαίων ὑπηρέτας ἔρχεται ἐκεῖ μετὰ φανῶν καὶ λαμπάδων καὶ ὅπλων. [GNT] | |
| **#1007 Determinate– Determined**<br><br>**Determinate–KJV**<br>Predetermined–NASB<br>Set–NIV<br>**Determined–NKJV**<br>Prearranged–NLT<br><br>**POSB REFERENCE** (Acts 2:23) *Deeper Study #3, point 2* | ὡρισμένῃ = hōrismenē<br>Pronunciation: [hor-is'-meh-nay]<br>Parsing (part of speech): verb<br>    Mood—participle<br>    Tense—perfect<br>    Voice—passive<br>    Case—dative<br>    Gender—feminine<br>    Number—singular<br>    Stem or root—from ὁρίζω<br>Concordance References:<br>  ⇒ Strong's #3724 horizō<br>  ⇒ NIV #3988 horizō<br>  ⇒ NASB #3724 horizō<br><br>**Acts 2:23**<br>Him, being delivered by the **determinate** counsel and foreknowledge of God, ye have taken, and by wicked hands have crucified and slain: [KJV]<br>This Man, delivered up by the **predetermined** plan and foreknowledge of God, you nailed to a cross by the hands of godless men and put Him to death. [NASB]<br>This man was handed over to you by God's **set** purpose and foreknowledge; and you, with the help of wicked men, put him to death by nailing him to the cross. [NIV]<br>Him, being delivered by the **determined** purpose and foreknowledge of God, you have taken by lawless hands, have crucified, and put to death; [NKJV]<br>But you followed God's **prearranged** plan. With the help of lawless Gentiles, you nailed him to the cross and murdered him. [NLT]<br>τοῦτον τῇ **ὡρισμένῃ** βουλῇ καὶ προγνώσει τοῦ Θεοῦ ἔκδοτον λαβόντες διὰ χειρῶν ἀνόμων προσπήξαντες ἀνείλατε, [GNS]<br>τοῦτον τῇ **ὡρισμένῃ** βουλῇ καὶ προγνώσει τοῦ θεοῦ ἔκδοτον διὰ χειρὸς ἀνόμων προσπήξαντες ἀνείλατε, [GNT] | Set, predetermined, prearranged, appointed, decreed, ordained, planned, purposed.<br><br>**Practical Application**<br>It is a plan set within bounds, within a certain boundary. It is a purpose that is set, marked out, determined, decreed to happen. |
| **#1008 Devastate**<br><br>Havock–KJV<br>Ravaging–NASB<br>Began to destroy–NIV<br>Havoc–NKJV<br>**Devastate–NLT** | ἐλυμαίνετο = elumaineto<br>Pronunciation: [loo-mah'ee-neh-tow]<br>Parsing (part of speech): verb<br>    Mood—indicative<br>    Tense—imperfect<br>    Voice—middle<br>    Person—3rd person<br>    Number—singular<br>    Stem or root—from λυμαίνομαι<br>Concordance References:<br>  ⇒ Strong's #3075 lumainomai<br>  ⇒ NIV #3381 lumainō<br>  ⇒ NASB #3075 lumainomai | To destroy; to devastate; to ravage; to ruin; to wipe out.<br><br>**Practical Application**<br>The mercy and grace of God are fully demonstrated in the life of Paul. God's mercy is available to all of us, no matter how terribly we have sinned. There is hope, forgiveness, and a glorious ministry for any of us, no matter who we are or what we have done—if we will repent and surrender ourselves to the Lord Jesus, to follow and obey Him. |

# Practical Word Studies
## in the New Testament

| ENGLISH WORD | GREEK WORD AND VERSE | THE WORD MEANS... |
|---|---|---|
| **POSB REFERENCE** (Acts 8:3) Note 3 | **Acts 8:3** As for Saul, he made **havock** of the church, entering into every house, and haling men and women committed them to prison. [KJV] But Saul began **ravaging** the church, entering house after house; and dragging off men and women, he would put them in prison. [NASB] But Saul **began to destroy** the church. Going from house to house, he dragged off men and women and put them in prison. [NIV] As for Saul, he made **havoc** of the church, entering every house, and dragging off men and women, committing *them* to prison. [NKJV] Saul was going everywhere to **devastate** the church. He went from house to house, dragging out both men and women to throw them into jail. [NLT] Σαῦλος δὲ **ἐλυμαίνετο** τὴν ἐκκλησίαν, κατὰ τοὺς οἴκους εἰσπορευόμενος, σύρων τε ἄνδρας καὶ γυναῖκας παρεδίδου εἰς φυλακήν. [GNS] Σαῦλος δὲ **ἐλυμαίνετο** τὴν ἐκκλησίαν κατὰ τοὺς οἴκους εἰσπορευόμενος, σύρων τε ἄνδρας καὶ γυναῖκας παρεδίδου εἰς φυλακήν. [GNT] | |
| **#1009 Device** **Device**–KJV Thought–NASB Design–NIV Devising–NKJV Designed–NLT **POSB REFERENCE** (Acts 17:29-30; esp. v.29) Note 7, point 1 | ἐνθυμήσεως = *enthumēseōs* Pronunciation: [en-thoo'-may-seh-os] Parsing (part of speech): noun     Case—genitive     Gender—feminine     Number—singular     Stem or root—from ἐνθύμησις, εως Concordance References:   ⇒ Strong's #1761 enthumēsis   ⇒ NIV #1927 enthumēsis   ⇒ NASB #1761 enthumēsis **Acts 17:29** Forasmuch then as we are the offspring of God, we ought not to think that the Godhead is like unto gold, or silver, or stone, graven by art and man's **device**. [KJV] "Being then the offspring of God, we ought not to think that the Divine Nature is like gold or silver or stone, an image formed by the art and **thought** of man. [NASB] "Therefore since we are God's offspring, we should not think that the divine being is like gold or silver or stone—an image made by man's **design** and skill. [NIV] Therefore, since we are the offspring of God, we ought not to think that the Divine Nature is like gold or silver or stone, something shaped by art and man's **devising**. [NKJV] And since this is true, we shouldn't think of God as an idol **designed** by craftsmen from gold or silver or stone. [NLT] γένος οὖν ὑπάρχοντες τοῦ Θεοῦ, οὐκ ὀφείλομεν νομίζειν χρυσῷ ἢ ἀργύρῳ ἢ λίθῳ, χαράγματι τέχνης καὶ **ἐνθυμήσεως** ἀνθρώπου, τὸ θεῖον εἶναι ὅμοιον. [GNS] γένος οὖν ὑπάρχοντες τοῦ θεοῦ οὐκ ὀφείλομεν νομίζειν χρυσῷ ἢ ἀργύρῳ ἢ λίθῳ, χαράγματι τέχνης καὶ **ἐνθυμήσεως** ἀνθρώπου, τὸ θεῖον εἶναι ὅμοιον. [GNT] | Design, device, thought, devising. **Practical Application** It means internal thoughts, ideas, imaginations. Every man has a concept, a thought about God. But we should not. We should seek to find the only living and true God that is revealed in Christ and in the Word of God, the Holy Scriptures of the Bible. Every person is personally responsible for forsaking the idols of this world and for finding God. |
| **#1010 Devil** **Devil**–KJV **Devil**–NASB **Devil**–NIV **Devil**–NKJV **Devil**–NLT | διάβολος = *diabolos* Pronunciation: [dee-ab'-ol-os] Parsing (part of speech): pronominal adjective     Case—nominative     Gender—masculine     Number—singular     Stem or root—from διάβολος, ου, ον Concordance References:   ⇒ Strong's #1228 diabolos   ⇒ NIV #1333 diabolos   ⇒ NASB #1228 diabolos | Devil, slanderer or false accuser. **Practical Application** The devil is a malicious enemy who accuses us before God and makes false charges against us. Scripture teaches that Satan is constantly bringing up our sins and transgressions before God, that he is constantly reminding God of our disobedience. But note: the accusations against us are false. The charges are not true. How can they not be true when we are sinners, for no true |

# PRACTICAL WORD STUDIES
## in the NEW TESTAMENT

| ENGLISH WORD | GREEK WORD AND VERSE | THE WORD MEANS... |
|---|---|---|
| **POSB REFERENCE**<br>(1 Pt.5:8)<br>Note 2, point 2<br><br>See also POSB REF:<br>(Eph.4:26-27; esp. v.27)<br>Note 2, point 3 | **1 Peter 5:8**<br>Be sober, be vigilant; because your adversary the **devil**, as a roaring lion, walketh about, seeking whom he may devour: [KJV]<br>Be of sober spirit, be on the alert. Your adversary, the **devil**, prowls about like a roaring lion, seeking someone to devour. [NASB]<br>Be self-controlled and alert. Your enemy the **devil** prowls around like a roaring lion looking for someone to devour. [NIV]<br>Be sober, be vigilant; because your adversary the **devil** walks about like a roaring lion, seeking whom he may devour. [NKJV]<br>Be careful! Watch out for attacks from the **Devil**, your great enemy. He prowls around like a roaring lion, looking for some victim to devour. [NLT]<br>νήψατε, γρηγορήσατε, ὅτι ὁ ἀντίδικος ὑμῶν **διάβολος**, ὡς λέων ὠρυόμενος περιπατεῖ ζητῶν τινα καταπίῃ· [GNS]<br>Νήψατε, γρηγορήσατε. ὁ ἀντίδικος ὑμῶν **διάβολος** ὡς λέων ὠρυόμενος περιπατεῖ ζητῶν [τινα] καταπιεῖν· [GNT] | believer denies his sin? By Christ. We believe Christ and we have cast ourselves upon Christ, upon the glorious fact that He died for our sins. We have trusted Christ for forgiveness of sin; and when He forgives us, our sins are removed from us. We are no longer guilty of sin. Therefore, the accusations and charges of Satan against us are false. Why then would he accuse and charge us before God? Why would he remind God time and again of our sins? To hurt God, to cut the heart of God. He is the devil, the one who stands opposed to God and to all that God stands for. Eons ago, sometime before the world was ever created, he was apparently the highest angel in all of creation. God had created him as the highest spiritual being in the universe. At that time his name was Lucifer. But he did what all men do—rebelled against God—and he led other angelic beings to rebel with him. Therefore, God judged him, by casting him from his exalted position in heaven. From what we can glean from Scripture, this is what happened to Satan, how he became the devil, the terrible opponent to God. (See POSB *Deeper Study* #1—Rev. 12:9 for more discussion. Cp. Isaiah 14:12-17; Ezekiel 28:11-19. Also see POSB *Deeper Study* #1—2 Cor. 4:4.)<br>The point is this: the devil does all he can to cut and hurt the heart of God. Therefore, he constantly reminds God of our sins. This, of course, means that he does all he can to tempt and lead us into sin, for the more we sin the more he can hurt God. |
| **#1011**<br>**Devising**<br><br>Device–KJV<br>Thought–NASB<br>Design–NIV<br>**Devising–NKJV**<br>Designed–NLT<br><br>**POSB REFERENCE**<br>(Acts 17:29-30; esp. v.29)<br>Note 7, point 1 | ἐνθυμήσεως = enthumēseōs<br>Pronunciation: [en-thoo'-may-seh-os]<br>Parsing (part of speech): noun<br>    Case—genitive<br>    Gender—feminine<br>    Number—singular<br>    Stem or root—from ἐνθύμησις, εως<br>Concordance References:<br>⇒ Strong's #1761 enthumēsis<br>⇒ NIV #1927 enthumēsis<br>⇒ NASB #1761 enthumēsis<br><br>**Acts 17:29**<br>Forasmuch then as we are the offspring of God, we ought not to think that the Godhead is like unto gold, or silver, or stone, graven by art and man's **device**. [KJV]<br>"Being then the offspring of God, we ought not to think that the Divine Nature is like gold or silver or stone, an image formed by the art and **thought** of man. [NASB]<br>"Therefore since we are God's offspring, we should not think that the divine being is like gold or silver or stone—an image made by man's **design** and skill. [NIV]<br>Therefore, since we are the offspring of God, we ought not to think that the Divine Nature is like gold or silver or stone, something shaped by art and man's **devising**. [NKJV]<br>And since this is true, we shouldn't think of God as an idol **designed** by craftsmen from gold or silver or stone. [NLT]<br>γένος οὖν ὑπάρχοντες τοῦ Θεοῦ, οὐκ ὀφείλομεν νομίζειν χρυσῷ ἢ ἀργύρῳ ἢ λίθῳ, χαράγματι τέχνης καὶ **ἐνθυμήσεως** ἀνθρώπου, τὸ θεῖον εἶναι ὅμοιον. [GNS]<br>γένος οὖν ὑπάρχοντες τοῦ θεοῦ οὐκ ὀφείλομεν νομίζειν χρυσῷ ἢ ἀργύρῳ ἢ λίθῳ, χαράγματι τέχνης καὶ **ἐνθυμήσεως** ἀνθρώπου, τὸ θεῖον εἶναι ὅμοιον. [GNT] | Design, device, thought, devising.<br><br>**Practical Application**<br>It means internal thoughts, ideas, imaginations. Every man has a concept, a thought about God. But we should not. We should seek to find the only living and true God. Every person is personally responsible for forsaking the idols of this world and for finding God. |

# PRACTICAL WORD STUDIES
## in the NEW TESTAMENT

| ENGLISH WORD | GREEK WORD AND VERSE | THE WORD MEANS... |
|---|---|---|
| **#1012**<br>**Devote**<br><br>Continue–KJV<br>Devote–NASB<br>Devote–NIV<br>Continue–NKJV<br>Devote–NLT<br><br>**POSB REFERENCE**<br>(Col.4:2-4; esp. v.2)<br>Note 1, point 1 | προσκαρτερεῖτε = *proskartereite*<br>Pronunciation: [pros-kar-ter-eh'-ee-teh]<br>Parsing (part of speech): verb<br>  Mood—imperative<br>  Tense—present<br>  Voice—active<br>  Person—2nd person<br>  Number—plural<br>  Stem or root—from προσκαρτερέω<br>Concordance References:<br>  ⇒ Strong's #4342 proskartereō<br>  ⇒ NIV #4674 proskartereō<br>  ⇒ NASB #4342 proskartereō<br><br>**Col. 4:2**<br>**Continue** in prayer, and watch in the same with thanksgiving; [KJV]<br>**Devote** yourselves to prayer, keeping alert in it with an attitude of thanksgiving; [NASB]<br>**Devote** yourselves to prayer, being watchful and thankful. [NIV]<br>**Continue** earnestly in prayer, being vigilant in it with thanksgiving; [NKJV]<br>**Devote** yourselves to prayer with an alert mind and a thankful heart. [NLT]<br>Τῇ προσευχῇ **προσκαρτερεῖτε**, γρηγοροῦντες ἐν αὐτῇ ἐν εὐχαριστίᾳ· [GNS]<br>Τῇ προσευχῇ **προσκαρτερεῖτε**, γρηγοροῦντες ἐν αὐτῇ ἐν εὐχαριστίᾳ, [GNT] | To devote; to continue; to be constant, persevering, and unwearied in prayer. It means to be in constant and unbroken prayer—to be in constant and unbroken fellowship and communion with God. It means to walk and breathe prayer—to live and move and have our being in prayer. It means to never face a moment when we are not in prayer.<br><br>**Practical Application**<br>How is this possible? When we have so many duties and affairs that demand our attention, how can we continue and walk in unbroken prayer? What Scripture means is that we...<br>• develop an *attitude of prayer*.<br>• walk in a *spirit of prayer*.<br>• take a mental break from our work and spend a moment *in prayer*.<br>• *pray always* when our minds are not upon some duty.<br>• *arise early* and pray before daily activities begin. Spend a worship time with God in prayer. Make this a continued practice.<br>• *pray before going to bed*. Spend an extended time in prayer before going to bed. Make this a continued practice.<br>In all honesty, the vast majority of us waste minute after minute every hour in useless daydreaming and wandering thoughts—wasting precious time that could be spent in prayer. If we would learn to captivate these minutes for prayer, we would discover what it is to walk and live in prayer. Note a critical fact: this is the duty of the believer. It is not something God can do for us. We are the ones who have to discipline ourselves to pray. If we do not pray, then prayer never gets done. |
| **#1013**<br>**Devote**<br><br>Maintain–KJV<br>Engage–NASB<br>Devote–NIV<br>Maintain–NKJV<br>Do–NLT<br><br>**POSB REFERENCE**<br>(Tit.3:8)<br>Note 1 | προΐστασθαι = *proistasthai*<br>Pronunciation: [pro-is'-tahs-tha-ee]<br>Parsing (part of speech): verb<br>  Mood—infinitive<br>  Tense—present<br>  Voice—middle<br>  Stem or root—from προΐστημι<br>Concordance References:<br>  ⇒ Strong's #4291 proistēmi<br>  ⇒ NIV #4613 proistēmi<br>  ⇒ NASB #4291b proistēmi<br><br>**Titus 3:8**<br>This is a faithful saying, and these things I will that thou affirm constantly, that they which have believed in God might be careful to **maintain** good works. These things are good and profitable unto men. [KJV]<br>This is a trustworthy statement; and concerning these things I want you to speak confidently, so that those who have believed God may be careful to **engage** in good deeds. These things are good and profitable for men. [NASB]<br>This is a trustworthy saying. And I want you to stress these things, so that those who have trusted in God may be careful to **devote** themselves to doing what is good. These things are excellent and profitable for everyone. [NIV]<br>This is a faithful saying, and these things I want you to affirm constantly, that those who have believed in God should be careful to **maintain** good works. These things are good and profitable to men. [NKJV]<br>These things I have told you are all true. I want you to | To devote; to maintain; to engage; to do; to manage; to care for; to set before; to give attention to; to be forward and eager and diligent in doing good works.<br><br>**Practical Application**<br>Believers must do good works and keep on doing them. It means...<br>• to keep on doing good works.<br>• to sustain good works.<br>• to persevere in doing good works.<br>• to carry on good works.<br>It even has the idea of sustaining good works against all odds regardless of circumstances and difficulties. It means to persevere in good works even in the midst of opposition or danger. |

# PRACTICAL WORD STUDIES
## in the NEW TESTAMENT

| ENGLISH WORD | GREEK WORD AND VERSE | THE WORD MEANS... |
|---|---|---|
| | insist on them so that everyone who trusts in God will be careful to **do** good deeds all the time. These things are good and beneficial for everyone. [NLT]<br><br>ιστὸς ὁ λόγος, καὶ περὶ τούτων βούλομαί σε διαβεβαιοῦσθαι, ἵνα φροντίζωσι καλῶν ἔργων **προΐστασθαι** οἱ πεπιστευκότες τῷ Θεῷ. ταῦτά ἐστι τὰ καλὰ καὶ ὠφέλιμα τοῖς ἀνθρώποις· [GNS]<br><br>Πιστὸς ὁ λόγος· καὶ περὶ τούτων βούλομαί σε διαβεβαιοῦσθαι, ἵνα φροντίζωσιν καλῶν ἔργων **προΐστασθαι** οἱ πεπιστευκότες θεῷ· ταῦτά ἐστιν καλὰ καὶ ὠφέλιμα τοῖς ἀνθρώποις. [GNT] | |
| **#1014**<br>**Devote Ourselves**<br><br>Give ourselves–KJV<br>**Devote ourselves–NASB**<br>Give...attention–NIV<br>Give ourselves–NKJV<br>Spend our time–NLT<br><br>**POSB REFERENCE**<br>(Acts 6:4)<br>Note 4, point 2 | προσκαρτερήσομεν = proskarterēsomen<br>Pronunciation: [pros-kar-ter-eh'-so-men]<br>Parsing (part of speech): verb<br>    Mood—indicative<br>    Tense—future<br>    Voice—active<br>    Person—1st person<br>    Number—plural<br>    Stem or root—from προσκαρτερέω<br>Concordance References:<br>  ⇒ Strong's #4342 proskartereö<br>  ⇒ NIV #4674 proskartereö<br>  ⇒ NASB #4342 proskartereö<br><br>**Acts 6:4**<br>But we will **give ourselves** continually to prayer, and to the ministry of the word. [KJV]<br>"But we will **devote ourselves** to prayer, and to the ministry of the word." [NASB]<br>And will **give** our **attention** to prayer and the ministry of the word." [NIV]<br>But we will **give ourselves** continually to prayer and to the ministry of the word." [NKJV]<br>Then we can **spend our time** in prayer and preaching and teaching the word." [NLT]<br>ἡμεῖς δὲ τῇ προσευχῇ καὶ τῇ διακονίᾳ τοῦ λόγου **προσκαρτερήσομεν**. [GNS]<br>ἡμεῖς δὲ τῇ προσευχῇ καὶ τῇ διακονίᾳ τοῦ λόγου **προσκαρτερήσομεν**. [GNT] | To give attention; to give ourselves; to devote ourselves; to spend our time. It means to continue steadfastly; to persevere; to continue on and on, sticking to it.<br><br>**Practical Application**<br>The minister is to pray and pray and study and study and share and share, preaching and teaching the Word—without letting up. He is to be steadfast, persevering, continuing on and on in both prayer and in the Word. |
| **#1015**<br>**Devoted**<br><br>Addicted–KJV<br>**Devoted–NASB**<br>**Devoted–NIV**<br>**Devoted–NKJV**<br>Spending their lives–NLT<br><br>**POSB REFERENCE**<br>(1 Cor.16:15-18; esp. v.15)<br>Note 5 | ἔταξαν = etaxan<br>Pronunciation: [eh-taxs'-ahn]<br>Parsing (part of speech): verb<br>    Mood—indicative<br>    Tense—aorist<br>    Voice—active<br>    Person—3rd person<br>    Number—plural<br>    Stem or root—from τάσσω<br>Concordance References:<br>  ⇒ Strong's #5021 tassö<br>  ⇒ NIV #5435 tassö<br>  ⇒ NASB #5021 tassö<br><br>**1 Cor. 16:15**<br>I beseech you, brethren, (ye know the house of Stephanas, that it is the firstfruits of Achaia, and that they have **addicted** themselves to the ministry of the saints,) [KJV]<br>Now I urge you, brethren (you know the household of Stephanas, that they were the first fruits of Achaia, and that they have **devoted** themselves for ministry to the saints), [NASB]<br>You know that the household of Stephanas were the first converts in Achaia, and they have **devoted** themselves to the service of the saints. I urge you, brothers, [NIV]<br>I urge you, brethren—you know the household of Stephanas, that it is the firstfruits of Achaia, and *that* they have **devoted** themselves to the ministry of the saints— [NKJV] | Devoted, addicted, loyal, faithful, devout, dutiful, established; spending their lives.<br><br>**Practical Application**<br>It means they [Stephanas and his household] devoted themselves, appointed themselves, diligently gave themselves to meeting the day-to-day needs of the believers. They not only ministered to others; they were addicted to meeting the needs of believers. |

## PRACTICAL WORD STUDIES
in the NEW TESTAMENT

| ENGLISH WORD | GREEK WORD AND VERSE | THE WORD MEANS... |
|---|---|---|
| | You know that Stephanas and his household were the first to become Christians in Greece, and they are **spending their lives** in service to other Christians. I urge you, dear brothers and sisters, [NLT]<br><br>Παρακαλῶ δὲ ὑμᾶς, ἀδελφοί· -- οἴδατε τὴν οἰκίαν Στεφανᾶ, ὅτι ἐστὶν ἀπαρχὴ τῆς Ἀχαΐας, καὶ εἰς διακονίαν τοῖς ἁγίοις **ἔταξαν** ἑαυτούς [GNS]<br><br>Παρακαλῶ δὲ ὑμᾶς, ἀδελφοί· οἴδατε τὴν οἰκίαν Στεφανᾶ, ὅτι ἐστὶν ἀπαρχὴ τῆς Ἀχαΐας καὶ εἰς διακονίαν τοῖς ἁγίοις **ἔταξαν** ἑαυτούς·[GNT] | |
| **#1016**<br>**Devoted**<br><br>Kindly affectioned–KJV<br>**Devoted**–NASB<br>**Devoted**–NIV<br>Kindly affectionate–NKJV<br>Genuine affection–NLT<br><br>**POSB REFERENCE**<br>(Rom.12:9-10; esp. v.10)<br>Note 1, point 3 | φιλόστοργοι = *philostorgoi*<br>Pronunciation: [fil-os'-tor-goy]<br>Parsing (part of speech): adjective<br>    Case—nominative<br>    Gender—masculine<br>    Number—plural<br>    Stem or root—from φιλόστοργος, ον<br>Concordance References:<br> ⇒ Strong's #5387 philostorgos<br> ⇒ NIV #5816 philostorgos<br> ⇒ NASB #5387 philostorgos<br><br>**Romans 12:10**<br>Be **kindly affectioned** one to another with brotherly love; in honour preferring one another; [KJV]<br>Be **devoted** to one another in brotherly love; give preference to one another in honor; [NASB]<br>Be **devoted** to one another in brotherly love. Honor one another above yourselves. [NIV]<br>*Be* **kindly affectionate** to one another with brotherly love, in honor giving preference to one another; [NKJV]<br>Love each other with **genuine affection**, and take delight in honoring each other. [NLT]<br>τῇ φιλαδελφίᾳ εἰς ἀλλήλους **φιλόστοργοι**· τῇ τιμῇ ἀλλήλους προηγούμενοι [GNS]<br>τῇ φιλαδελφίᾳ εἰς ἀλλήλους **φιλόστοργοι**, τῇ τιμῇ ἀλλήλους προηγούμενοι, [GNT] | Loving, devoted. The word "devoted" (*philostorgoi*) means the love existing between family members.<br><br>**Practical Application**<br>The believer is to love by loving his brothers in Christ, by being kind and affectionate toward them. This charge is dealing with the Christian family, the brothers and sisters within the church. We are to love each other by being kind and affectionate. We are a family of children who have actually been adopted by God as His sons and daughters (2 Cor. 6:17-18; Galatians 4:4-6; Romans 8:16-17). Therefore, the believer is to live as a family member with his brothers and sisters; he is to live being both kind and affectionate. Note: there is no dissension or divisiveness in love. The church is to live in love, and living in love is peace. |
| **#1017**<br>**Devoted**<br><br>Continuing instant–KJV<br>**Devoted**–NASB<br>Faithful–NIV<br>Continuing steadfastly–NKJV<br>Always–NLT<br><br>**POSB REFERENCE**<br>(Romans 12:12)<br>Note 3, point 3 | προσκαρτεροῦντες = *proskarterountes*<br>Pronunciation: [pros-kar-ter-oon'-tehs]<br>Parsing (part of speech): verb<br>    Mood—participle (imperative sense)<br>    Tense—present<br>    Voice—active<br>    Case—nominative<br>    Gender—masculine<br>    Person—2nd person<br>    Number—plural<br>    Stem or root—from προσκαρτερέω<br>Concordance References:<br> ⇒ Strong's #4342 proskartereō<br> ⇒ NIV #4674 proskartereō<br> ⇒ NASB #4342 proskartereō<br><br>**Romans 12:12**<br>Rejoicing in hope; patient in tribulation; **continuing instant** in prayer; [KJV]<br>Rejoicing in hope, persevering in tribulation, **devoted** to prayer, [NASB]<br>Be joyful in hope, patient in affliction, **faithful** in prayer. [NIV]<br>Rejoicing in hope, patient in tribulation, **continuing steadfastly** in prayer; [NKJV]<br>Be glad for all God is planning for you. Be patient in trouble, and **always** be prayerful. [NLT]<br>τῇ ἐλπίδι χαίροντες· τῇ θλίψει ὑπομένοντες· τῇ προσευχῇ **προσκαρτεροῦντες** [GNS]<br>τῇ ἐλπίδι χαίροντες, τῇ θλίψει ὑπομένοντες, τῇ προσευχῇ **προσκαρτεροῦντες**, [GNT] | To be faithful; to be devoted and attentive to; to give constant attention to; to give unceasing care to; to wait steadfastly upon, to persevere.<br><br>**Practical Application**<br>Very simply, the believer overcomes trials by giving constant attention to God and waiting upon His delivering power. The believer stays in constant communion with his Lord, depending upon Him to supply the strength to walk through the trials of daily living. |

# PRACTICAL WORD STUDIES
## in the NEW TESTAMENT

| ENGLISH WORD | GREEK WORD AND VERSE | THE WORD MEANS... |
|---|---|---|
| **#1018**<br>**Devoted To–**<br>**Devoted Themselves To**<br><br>Continued stedfastly–KJV<br>Continually devoting themselves to–NASB<br>Devoted...to–NIV<br>Continued steadfastly–NKJV<br>Devoted themselves to–NLT<br><br>**POSB REFERENCE**<br>(Acts 2:42)<br>*Deeper Study #1* | ἦσαν προσκαρτεροῦντες = ësan proskarterountes<br>Pronunciation: [ay-san pros-kar-ter-oon'-tehs]<br>Parsing *proskarterountes* (part of speech): verb<br>    Mood—participle<br>    Tense—present<br>    Voice—active<br>    Case—nominative<br>    Gender—masculine<br>    Number—plural<br>    Stem or root—from προσκαρτερέω<br>Concordance References:<br>  ⇒ Strong's #1488 + 4342 eimi proskartereö<br>  ⇒ NIV #1639 + 4674 eimi proskartereö [devoted to]<br>  ⇒ NASB #1488 + 4342 eimi proskartereö<br><br>**Acts 2:42**<br>And they **continued stedfastly** in the apostles' doctrine and fellowship, and in breaking of bread, and in prayers. [KJV]<br>And they were **continually devoting themselves to** the apostles' teaching and to fellowship, to the breaking of bread and to prayer. [NASB]<br>They **devoted** themselves **to** the apostles' teaching and to the fellowship, to the breaking of bread and to prayer. [NIV]<br>And they **continued steadfastly** in the apostles' doctrine and fellowship, in the breaking of bread, and in prayers. [NKJV]<br>They joined with the other believers and **devoted themselves to** the apostles' teaching and fellowship, sharing in the Lord's Supper and in prayer. [NLT]<br>ἦσαν δὲ **προσκαρτεροῦντες** τῇ διδαχῇ τῶν ἀποστόλων καὶ τῇ κοινωνίᾳ, καὶ τῇ κλάσει τοῦ ἄρτου καὶ ταῖς προσευχαῖς. [GNS]<br>ἦσαν δὲ **προσκαρτεροῦντες** τῇ διδαχῇ τῶν ἀποστόλων καὶ τῇ κοινωνίᾳ, τῇ κλάσει τοῦ ἄρτου καὶ ταῖς προσευχαῖς. [GNT] | Devoted to; to continue; to persevere; to endure; to stick; to persist.<br><br>**Practical Application**<br>A person does not quit, back off, fade away, or slip back. He continues on steadfastly. |
| **#1019**<br>**Devotion To God**<br><br>Godly–KJV<br>Godly–NASB<br>Godly–NIV<br>Godly–NKJV<br>Devotion to God–NLT<br><br>**POSB REFERENCE**<br>(Tit.2:12)<br>Note 2, point 2c | εὐσεβῶς = eusebös<br>Pronunciation: [yoo-seb-oce']<br>Parsing (part of speech): adjective adverb<br>    Stem or root—from εὐσεβῶς<br>Concordance References:<br>  ⇒ Strong's #2153 eusebös<br>  ⇒ NIV #2357 eusebös<br>  ⇒ NASB #2153 eusebös<br><br>**Titus 2:12**<br>Teaching us that, denying ungodliness and worldly lusts, we should live soberly, righteously, and **godly**, in this present world; [KJV]<br>Instructing us to deny ungodliness and worldly desires and to live sensibly, righteously and **godly** in the present age, [NASB]<br>It teaches us to say "No" to ungodliness and worldly passions, and to live self-controlled, upright and **godly** lives in this present age, [NIV]<br>Teaching us that, denying ungodliness and worldly lusts, we should live soberly, righteously, and **godly** in the present age, [NKJV]<br>And we are instructed to turn from godless living and sinful pleasures. We should live in this evil world with self-control, right conduct, and **devotion to God**, [NLT]<br>παιδεύουσα ἡμᾶς ἵνα, ἀρνησάμενοι τὴν ἀσέβειαν καὶ τὰς κοσμικὰς ἐπιθυμίας σωφρόνως καὶ δικαίως καὶ **εὐσεβῶς** ζήσωμεν ἐν τῷ νῦν αἰῶνι, [GNS]<br>παιδεύουσα ἡμᾶς, ἵνα ἀρνησάμενοι τὴν ἀσέβειαν καὶ τὰς κοσμικὰς ἐπιθυμίας σωφρόνως καὶ δικαίως καὶ **εὐσεβῶς** ζήσωμεν ἐν τῷ νῦν αἰῶνι, [GNT] | Godly; devotion to God; to live in a godly manner; to be like God; to live as God would live on this earth; to live in the consciousnness of God.<br><br>**Practical Application**<br>It means that God lives within the very body of the believer—that the believer's body is the very temple of God. It is living and moving and having one's being in God. It is living just like God says to live, obeying Him in all things. |
| **#1020**<br>**Devotions** | τὰ σεβάσματα = ta sebasmata<br>Pronunciation: [tah seb'-as-mah-tah]<br>Parsing *sebasmata* (part of speech): noun<br>    Case—accusative | Objects of worship; altars; places of devotion and worship. |

# PRACTICAL WORD STUDIES
## in the NEW TESTAMENT

| ENGLISH WORD | GREEK WORD AND VERSE | THE WORD MEANS... |
|---|---|---|
| **Devotions–KJV**<br>Objects of...worship–NASB<br>Objects of worship–NIV<br>Objects of...worship–NKJV<br>Altars–NLT<br><br>**POSB REFERENCE**<br>(Acts 17:23)<br>Note 3, point 1 | Gender—neuter<br>Number—plural<br>Stem or root—from σέβασμα, τος<br>Concordance References:<br>⇒ Strong's #3588 ho + 4574 sebasma<br>⇒ NIV #3836 ho + 4934 sebasma<br>⇒ NASB #3588 ho + 4574 sebasma<br><br>**Acts 17:23**<br>For as I passed by, and beheld your **devotions**, I found an altar with this inscription, TO THE UNKNOWN GOD. Whom therefore ye ignorantly worship, him declare I unto you. [KJV]<br>"For while I was passing through and examining the **objects of** your **worship**, I also found an altar with this inscription, 'TO AN UNKNOWN GOD.' What therefore you worship in ignorance, this I proclaim to you. [NASB]<br>For as I walked around and looked carefully at your **objects of worship**, I even found an altar with this inscription: to an unknown god. Now what you worship as something unknown I am going to proclaim to you. [NIV]<br>For as I was passing through and considering the **objects of** your **worship**, I even found an altar with this inscription: TO THE UNKNOWN GOD. Therefore, the One whom you worship without knowing, Hm I proclaim to you: [NKJV]<br>For as I was walking along I saw your many **altars**. And one of them had this inscription on it—'To an Unknown God.' You have been worshiping him without knowing who he is, and now I wish to tell you about him. [NLT]<br>διερχόμενος γὰρ καὶ ἀναθεωρῶν τὰ σεβάσματα ὑμῶν, εὗρον καὶ βωμὸν ἐν ᾧ ἐπεγέγραπτο, Ἀγνώστῳ Θεῷ. ὃν οὖν ἀγνοοῦντες εὐσεβεῖτε, τοῦτον ἐγὼ καταγγέλλω ὑμῖν. [GNS]<br>διερχόμενος γὰρ καὶ ἀναθεωρῶν τὰ σεβάσματα ὑμῶν εὗρον καὶ βωμὸν ἐν ᾧ ἐπεγέγραπτο, Ἀγνώστῳ θεῷ. ὃ οὖν ἀγνοοῦντες εὐσεβεῖτε, τοῦτο ἐγὼ καταγγέλλω ὑμῖν. [GNT] | **Practical Application**<br>It means the objects of worship such as idols, altars, images. |
| **#1021**<br>**Devout**<br><br>**Devout–KJV**<br>**Devout–NASB**<br>**Devout–NIV**<br>**Devout–NKJV**<br>**Devout–NLT**<br><br>**POSB REFERENCE**<br>(Lk.2:25-27; esp. v.25)<br>Note 1, point 1 | εὐλαβής = eulabēs<br>Pronunciation: [yoo-lab-ace']<br>Parsing (part of speech): adjective<br>    Case—nominative<br>    Gender—masculine<br>    Number—singular<br>    Stem or root—from εὐλαβής, ές<br>Concordance References:<br>⇒ Strong's #2126 eulabēs<br>⇒ NIV #2327 eulabēs<br>⇒ NASB #2126 eulabēs<br><br>**Luke 2:25**<br>And, behold, there was a man in Jerusalem, whose name was Simeon; and the same man was just and **devout**, waiting for the consolation of Israel: and the Holy Ghost was upon him. [KJV]<br>And behold, there was a man in Jerusalem whose name was Simeon; and this man was righteous and **devout**, looking for the consolation of Israel; and the Holy Spirit was upon him. [NASB]<br>Now there was a man in Jerusalem called Simeon, who was righteous and **devout**. He was waiting for the consolation of Israel, and the Holy Spirit was upon him. [NIV]<br>And behold, there was a man in Jerusalem whose name was Simeon, and this man was just and **devout**, waiting for the Consolation of Israel, and the Holy Spirit was upon him. [NKJV]<br>Now there was a man named Simeon who lived in Jerusalem. He was a righteous man and very **devout**. He was filled with the Holy Spirit, and he eagerly expected | Cautious and careful in relation to God. It means reverence for God, being pious, devoted, devout. It means to be very careful in one's relationship with God.<br><br>**Practical Application**<br>God is our Father. He has adopted us as His children through the Lord Jesus Christ. Therefore, we are to reverence Him. We are...<br>• to honor and respect Him.<br>• to hold Him in the highest esteem.<br>• to fear lest we displease and dishonor Him and bring pain to His heart.<br><br>The point is this: if you call God "Father," then live like it. Stay true to Him. Stand against all the trials and persecutions, temptations and evils of this life. Call upon your Father; ask for His help and strength. But reverence Him; show honor and respect by living for Him. |

# PRACTICAL WORD STUDIES
## in the NEW TESTAMENT

| ENGLISH WORD | GREEK WORD AND VERSE | THE WORD MEANS... |
|---|---|---|
| | the Messiah to come and rescue Israel. [NLT]<br>καὶ ἰδοὺ ἦν ἄνθρωπος ἐν Ἰερουσαλήμ, ᾧ ὄνομα Συμεών, καὶ ὁ ἄνθρωπος οὗτος δίκαιος καὶ **εὐλαβής**, προσδεχόμενος παράκλησιν τοῦ Ἰσραήλ, καὶ Πνεῦμα Ἅγιον ἦν ἐπ' αὐτόν, [GNS]<br>Καὶ ἰδοὺ ἄνθρωπος ἦν ἐν Ἰερουσαλὴμ ᾧ ὄνομα Συμεών καὶ ὁ ἄνθρωπος οὗτος δίκαιος καὶ **εὐλαβής** προσδεχόμενος παράκλησιν τοῦ Ἰσραήλ, καὶ πνεῦμα ἦν ἅγιον ἐπ' αὐτόν· [GNT] | |
| **#1022**<br>**Devout**<br><br>**Devout–KJV**<br>**Devout–NASB**<br>God-fearing–NIV<br>**Devout–NKJV**<br>Godly–NLT<br><br>**POSB REFERENCE**<br>(Acts 2:5-11; esp. v.5)<br>Note 5, point 1 | εὐλαβεῖς = *eulabeis*<br>Pronunciation: [yoo-lab-ace']<br>Parsing (part of speech): adjective<br>    Case—nominative<br>    Gender—masculine<br>    Number—plural<br>    Stem or root—from εὐλαβής, ές<br>Concordance References:<br>  ⇒ Strong's #2126 eulabēs<br>  ⇒ NIV #2327 eulabēs<br>  ⇒ NASB #2126 eulabēs<br><br>**Acts 2:5**<br>And there were dwelling at Jerusalem Jews, **devout** men, out of every nation under heaven. [KJV]<br>Now there were Jews living in Jerusalem, **devout** men, from every nation under heaven. [NASB]<br>Now there were staying in Jerusalem **God-fearing** Jews from every nation under heaven. [NIV]<br>And there were dwelling in Jerusalem Jews, **devout** men, from every nation under heaven. [NKJV]<br>**Godly** Jews from many nations were living in Jerusalem at that time. [NLT]<br>Ἦσαν δὲ ἐν Ἰερουσαλὴμ κατοικοῦντες Ἰουδαῖοι, ἄνδρες **εὐλαβεῖς**, ἀπὸ παντὸς ἔθνους τῶν ὑπὸ τὸν οὐρανόν· [GNS]<br>Ἦσαν δὲ εἰς Ἰερουσαλὴμ κατοικοῦντες Ἰουδαῖοι, ἄνδρες **εὐλαβεῖς** ἀπὸ παντὸς ἔθνους τῶν ὑπὸ τὸν οὐρανόν. [GNT] | God-fearing, devout, reverent, worshipful, careful, godly. It means persons who handle spiritual matters carefully.<br><br>**Practical Application**<br>Devout men, Jewish pilgrims who had come from *all over the world*, had returned to Jerusalem to celebrate the "Feast of the First Fruits." Note how the groundwork for preaching is first laid by personal witnessing. (See POSB *Deeper Study #1*, Witnessing—Acts 1:8 for Scripture.) |
| **#1023**<br>**Devout**<br><br>**Devout–KJV**<br>God-fearing Gentiles–NASB<br>God-fearing Greeks–NIV<br>Gentile worshipers–NKJV<br>God-fearing Gentiles–NLT<br><br>**POSB REFERENCE**<br>(Acts 17:17)<br>Note 3 | σεβομένοις = *sebomenois*<br>Pronunciation: [seb'-om-ehn-o-ees]<br>Parsing (part of speech): verb<br>    Mood—participle<br>    Tense—present<br>    Voice—middle<br>    Case—dative<br>    Gender—masculine<br>    Number—plural<br>    Stem or root—from σέβομαι<br>Concordance References:<br>  ⇒ Strong's #4576 sebō<br>  ⇒ NIV #4936 sebō<br>  ⇒ NASB #4576 sebō<br><br>**Acts 17:17**<br>Therefore disputed he in the synagogue with the Jews, and with the **devout** persons, and in the market daily with them that met with him. [KJV]<br>So he was reasoning in the synagogue with the Jews and the **God-fearing Gentiles**, and in the market place every day with those who happened to be present. [NASB]<br>So he reasoned in the synagogue with the Jews and the **God-fearing Greeks**, as well as in the marketplace day by day with those who happened to be there. [NIV]<br>Therefore he reasoned in the synagogue with the Jews and with the **Gentile worshipers**, and in the marketplace daily with those who happened to be there. [NKJV]<br>He went to the synagogue to debate with the Jews and the **God-fearing Gentiles**, and he spoke daily in the public square to all who happened to be there. [NLT]<br>διελέγετο μὲν οὖν ἐν τῇ συναγωγῇ τοῖς Ἰουδαίοις καὶ | God-fearing Greeks or Gentiles; a worshiper of God.<br><br>**Practical Application**<br>The word "devout" (*sebomenois*) means those who worship God or the God-fearing men and women who are not Jews. |

# PRACTICAL WORD STUDIES
## in the NEW TESTAMENT

| ENGLISH WORD | GREEK WORD AND VERSE | THE WORD MEANS... |
|---|---|---|
| | τοῖς **σεβομένοις** καὶ ἐν τῇ ἀγορᾷ κατὰ πᾶσαν ἡμέραν πρὸς τοὺς παρατυγχάνοντας. [GNS]<br>διελέγετο μὲν οὖν ἐν τῇ συναγωγῇ τοῖς Ἰουδαίοις καὶ τοῖς **σεβομένοις** καὶ ἐν τῇ ἀγορᾷ κατὰ πᾶσαν ἡμέραν πρὸς τοὺς παρατυγχάνοντας. [GNT] | |
| **#1024**<br>**Diadems**<br><br>Crowns–KJV<br>**Diadems–NASB**<br>Crowns–NIV<br>Crowns–NKJV<br>Crowns–NLT<br><br>**POSB REFERENCE**<br>(Rev.19:12)<br>Note 2, point 2 | διαδήματα = *diadēmata*<br>Pronunciation: [dee-ad'-ay-mah-tah]<br>Parsing (part of speech): noun<br>    Case—nominative<br>    Gender—neuter<br>    Number—plural<br>    Stem or root—from διάδημα, τος<br>Concordance References:<br>  ⇒ Strong's #1238 diadēma<br>  ⇒ NIV #1343 diadēma<br>  ⇒ NASB #1238 diadēma<br><br>**Rev. 19:12**<br>His eyes were as a flame of fire, and on his head were many **crowns**; and he had a name written, that no man knew, but he himself. [KJV]<br>And His eyes are a flame of fire, and upon His head are many **diadems**; and He has a name written upon Him which no one knows except Himself. [NASB]<br>His eyes are like blazing fire, and on his head are many **crowns**. He has a name written on him that no one knows but he himself. [NIV]<br>His eyes *were* like a flame of fire, and on His head *were* many **crowns**. He had a name written that no one knew except Himself. [NKJV]<br>His eyes were bright like flames of fire, and on his head were many **crowns**. A name was written on him, and only he knew what it meant. [NLT]<br>οἱ δὲ ὀφθαλμοὶ αὐτοῦ ὡς φλὸξ πυρός, καὶ ἐπὶ τὴν κεφαλὴν αὐτοῦ **διαδήματα** πολλά· ἔχων ὄνομα γεγραμμένον, ὃ οὐδεὶς οἶδεν εἰ μὴ αὐτός, [GNS]<br>οἱ δὲ ὀφθαλμοὶ αὐτοῦ [ὡς] φλὸξ πυρός, καὶ ἐπὶ τὴν κεφαλὴν αὐτοῦ **διαδήματα** πολλά, ἔχων ὄνομα γεγραμμένον ὃ οὐδεὶς οἶδεν εἰ μὴ αὐτός, [GNT] | Crown, diadem.<br><br>**Practical Application**<br>Christ will be wearing many diadems (*diadēmata*), that is, the royal crowns of rule and authority over many kingdoms. He is coming to conquer all the kingdoms of the earth. |
| **#1025**<br>**Did Work In**<br><br>**Did work in–KJV**<br>At work in–NASB<br>At work in–NIV<br>At work in–NKJV<br>At work within–NLT<br><br>**POSB REFERENCE**<br>(Rom.7:5)<br>Note 1, point 1 | ἐνηργεῖτο ἐν = *enērgeito en*<br>Pronunciation: [en-ayrg-ee'-tow en]<br>Parsing *enērgeito* (part of speech): verb<br>    Mood—indicative<br>    Tense—imperfect<br>    Voice—middle<br>    Person—3rd person<br>    Number—singular<br>    Stem or root—from ἐνεργέω<br>Concordance References:<br>  ⇒ Strong's #1722 + 1754 en energeō<br>  ⇒ NIV #1877 + 1919 en energeō [at work in]<br>  ⇒ NASB #1722 + 1754 en energeō<br><br>**Romans 7:5**<br>For when we were in the flesh, the motions of sins, which were by the law, **did work in** our members to bring forth fruit unto death. [KJV]<br>For while we were in the flesh, the sinful passions, which were aroused by the Law, were **at work in** the members of our body to bear fruit for death. [NASB]<br>For when we were controlled by the sinful nature, the sinful passions aroused by the law were **at work in** our bodies, so that we bore fruit for death. [NIV]<br>For when we were in the flesh, the sinful passions which were aroused by the law were **at work in** our members to bear fruit to death. [NKJV]<br>When we were controlled by our old nature, sinful desires were **at work within** us, and the law aroused these evil desires that produced sinful deeds, resulting in death. [NLT]<br>ὅτε γὰρ ἦμεν ἐν τῇ σαρκί, τὰ παθήματα τῶν ἁμαρτιῶν | To be at work in or within; to do work in or within.<br><br>**Practical Application**<br>Sinful feelings are actually at "work in" (*enērgeito*) our bodies—did work by the statement or restriction of he law. When the law prohibits and forbids something, it actually creates within us...<br>• an interest<br>• an attraction<br>• an excitement<br>• an appeal<br>• a tug or pull<br>• a fascination<br>• a seduction<br>• an arousal<br>There is within man something that makes him want to do what he is forbidden to do. When he is restricted or fenced in, he wants to break through the restriction or fence. He wants to go beyond where he is allowed, to take control of his own life as he wishes and wills. (See POSB note—Romans 7:8 for more discussion.) |

## PRACTICAL WORD STUDIES
## in the NEW TESTAMENT

| ENGLISH WORD | GREEK WORD AND VERSE | THE WORD MEANS... |
|---|---|---|
|  | τὰ διὰ τοῦ νόμου **ἐνηργεῖτο ἐν** τοῖς μέλεσιν ἡμῶν εἰς τὸ καρποφορῆσαι τῷ θανάτῳ, [GNS]<br>ὅτε γὰρ ἦμεν ἐν τῇ σαρκί, τὰ παθήματα τῶν ἁμαρτιῶν τὰ διὰ τοῦ νόμου **ἐνηργεῖτο ἐν** τοῖς μέλεσιν ἡμῶν, εἰς τὸ καρποφορῆσαι τῷ θανάτῳ· [GNT] |  |
| **#1026**<br>**Didn't Know Where to Go**<br><br>Scattered abroad–KJV<br>Downcast–NASB<br>Helpless–NIV<br>Scattered–NKJV<br>**Didn't know where to go for help– NLT**<br><br>**POSB REFERENCE**<br>(Mt.9:36)<br>*Deeper Study #4* | ἐρριμμένοι = *errimmenoi*<br>Pronunciation: [rim-me'-noi]<br>Parsing (part of speech): verb<br>    Mood—participle<br>    Tense—perfect<br>    Voice—passive<br>    Case—nominative<br>    Gender—masculine<br>    Number—plural<br>    Stem or root—from ῥίπτω and ῥιπτέω<br>Concordance References:<br>  ⇒ Strong's #4496 hriptō<br>  ⇒ NIV #4849 hriptō<br>  ⇒ NASB #4496 hriptō<br><br>**Matthew 9:36**<br>But when he saw the multitudes, he was moved with compassion on them, because they fainted, and were **scattered abroad**, as sheep having no shepherd. [KJV]<br>And seeing the multitudes, He felt compassion for them, because they were distressed and **downcast** like sheep without a shepherd. [NASB]<br>When he saw the crowds, he had compassion on them, because they were harassed and **helpless**, like sheep without a shepherd. [NIV]<br>But when He saw the multitudes, He was moved with compassion for them, because they were weary and **scattered**, like sheep having no shepherd. [NKJV]<br>He felt great pity for the crowds that came, because their problems were so great and they **didn't know where to go for help**. They were like sheep without a shepherd. [NLT]<br>ἰδὼν δὲ τοὺς ὄχλους, ἐσπλαγχνίσθη περὶ αὐτῶν, ὅτι ἦσαν ἐκλελυμένοι καὶ **ἐρριμμένοι** ὡσεὶ πρόβατα μὴ ἔχοντα ποιμένα. [GNS]<br>Ἰδὼν δὲ τοὺς ὄχλους ἐσπλαγχνίσθη περὶ αὐτῶν, ὅτι ἦσαν ἐσκυλμένοι καὶ **ἐρριμμένοι** ὡσεὶ πρόβατα μὴ ἔχοντα ποιμένα. [GNT] | To be helpless, hopeless, scattered, downcast; to be cast out, laid low, thrown down, prostrated, dejected and hopeless.<br><br>**Practical Application**<br>Not knowing where to go for help may come from experiences such as drunkenness, or struggling and fighting within and without, or being so weary that a person is just cast down. It is being prostrated by forces within oneself or laid low by forces outside of oneself. |
| **#1027**<br>**Didn't Return**<br><br>Came not as yet–KJV<br>Came no more–NASB<br>Not return–NIV<br>Came no more–NKJV<br>**Didn't return–NLT**<br><br>**POSB REFERENCE**<br>(2 Cor.1:23)<br>Note 1<br><br>(Special note: see also 2 Cor.2:1, Note 2 for more discussion) | οὐκέτι ἦλθον = *ouketi ēlthon*<br>Pronunciation: [oo-keh-tee ale'-thon]<br>Parsing *ēlthon* (part of speech): verb<br>    Mood—indicative<br>    Tense—aorist<br>    Voice—active<br>    Person—1st person<br>    Number—singular<br>    Stem or root—from ἔρχομαι<br>Concordance References:<br>  ⇒ Strong's #3765 ouketi + 2064 erchomai<br>  ⇒ NIV #4033 ouketi [not] + 2262 erchomai [return]<br>  ⇒ NASB #3765 ouketi + 2064 erchomai<br><br>**2 Cor. 1:23**<br>Moreover I call God for a record upon my soul, that to spare you I **came not as yet** unto Corinth. [KJV]<br>But I call God as witness to my soul, that to spare you I **came no more** to Corinth. [NASB]<br>I call God as my witness that it was in order to spare you that I did **not return** to Corinth. [NIV]<br>Moreover I call God as witness against my soul, that to spare you I **came no more** to Corinth. [NKJV]<br>Now I call upon God as my witness that I am telling the truth. The reason I **didn't return** to Corinth was to spare you from a severe rebuke. [NLT]<br>Ἐγὼ δὲ μάρτυρα τὸν Θεὸν ἐπικαλοῦμαι ἐπὶ τὴν ἐμὴν | Did not return; did not make his way back; did not go back.<br><br>**Practical Application**<br>The statement, "I didn't return," can be equally translated, "I came no more to Corinth." This, too, points toward Paul's having made a quick visit to Corinth after writing his first letter, a visit that resulted in the people's rejecting him and breaking his heart (see POSB Introduction, Special Features, pt. 3— 1 Corinthians for more discussion). |

# PRACTICAL WORD STUDIES
## in the NEW TESTAMENT

| ENGLISH WORD | GREEK WORD AND VERSE | THE WORD MEANS... |
|---|---|---|
| | ψυχήν, ὅτι φειδόμενος ὑμῶν **οὐκέτι ἦλθον** εἰς Κόρινθον. [GNS]<br>Ἐγὼ δὲ μάρτυρα τὸν θεὸν ἐπικαλοῦμαι ἐπὶ τὴν ἐμὴν ψυχήν, ὅτι φειδόμενος ὑμῶν **οὐκέτι ἦλθον** εἰς Κόρινθον. [GNT] | |
| **#1028**<br>**Die**<br><br>See death–KJV<br>See death–NASB<br>See death–NIV<br>See death–NKJV<br>**Die–NLT**<br><br>**POSB REFERENCE**<br>(Jn.8:51)<br>*Deeper Study #1,*<br>point 3 | θεωρήσῃ θάνατον = *theōrēsē thanaton*<br>Pronunciation: [theh-o-ray'-say thahn'-at-on]<br>Parsing *theōrēsē* (part of speech): verb<br>    Mood—subjunctive<br>    Tense—aorist<br>    Voice—active<br>    Person—3rd person<br>    Number—singular<br>    Stem or root—from θεωρέω<br>Parsing *thanaton* (part of speech): noun<br>    Case—accusative<br>    Gender—masculine<br>    Number—singular<br>    Stem or root—θάνατος, ου<br>Concordance References:<br>⇒ Strong's #2334 theoreo +2288 thanatos<br>⇒ NIV #2555 theoreo [see] + 2505 thanatos [death]<br>⇒ NASB #2334 theoreo +2288 thanatos<br><br>**John 8:51**<br>Verily, verily, I say unto you, If a man keep my saying, he shall never **see death**. [KJV]<br>"Truly, truly, I say to you, if anyone keeps My word he shall never **see death**." [NASB]<br>I tell you the truth, if anyone keeps my word, he will never **see death**." [NIV]<br>Most assuredly, I say to you, if anyone keeps My word he shall never **see death**." [NKJV]<br>I assure you, anyone who obeys my teaching will never **die**!" [NLT]<br>ἀμὴν ἀμὴν λέγω ὑμῖν, ἐάν τις τὸν λόγον τὸν ἐμὸν τηρήσῃ, **θάνατον** οὐ μὴ **θεωρήσῃ** εἰς τὸν αἰῶνα. [GNS]<br>ἀμὴν ἀμὴν λέγω ὑμῖν, ἐάν τις τὸν ἐμὸν λόγον τηρήσῃ, **θάνατον** οὐ μὴ **θεωρήσῃ** εἰς τὸν αἰῶνα. [GNT] | To see, observe, experience death (spiritually); to die; to expose to death.<br><br>**Practical Application**<br>Note the words "die" and "never die," (John 8:52). The meaning is that a genuine follower of Christ will...<br>• never experience death nor see death.<br>• never know death nor partake of death.<br>• never face the condemnation of death.<br>• never experience the terror, the hurt, the pain, and the suffering of death.<br>• never experience the anguish of being separated from God and from the glory, beauty, perfection, and life of heaven.<br>In a flash, quicker than lightning or the blinking of an eye, the follower of Christ passes from this world into the next. He never ceases to experience life and never loses consciousness. One moment he is in this world, the next moment he is in the presence of God Himself.<br>Note the reason why the believer will never "die": it is because Jesus came "by God's grace, Jesus tasted death for everyone in all the world" (Hebrews 2:9). |
| **#1029**<br>**Die**<br><br>Taste death–KJV<br>Taste death–NASB<br>Taste death–NIV<br>Taste death–NKJV<br>**Die–NLT**<br><br>**POSB REFERENCE**<br>(Jn.8:51; esp. v.52)<br>*Deeper Study #1*<br>point 3 | γεύσηται θανάτου = *geusētai thanatou*<br>Pronunciation: [ghyoo'-say-tah-ee thahn'-at-oo]<br>Parsing *geusētai* (part of speech): verb<br>    Mood—subjunctive<br>    Tense—aorist<br>    Voice—middle deponent<br>    Person—3rd person<br>    Number—singular<br>    Stem or root—from γεύομαι<br>Parsing *thanatou* (part of speech): noun<br>    Case—genitive<br>    Gender—masculine<br>    Number—singular<br>    Stem or root—from θάνατος, ου<br>Concordance References:<br>⇒ Strong's #1089 geuomai + 2288 thanatos<br>⇒ NIV #1174 geuomai [taste] + 2505 thanatos [death]<br>⇒ NASB #1089 geuomai + 2288 thanatos<br><br>**John 8:52**<br>Then said the Jews unto him, Now we know that thou hast a devil. Abraham is dead, and the prophets; and thou sayest, If a man keep my saying, he shall never **taste of death**. [KJV]<br>The Jews said to Him, "Now we know that You have a demon. Abraham died, and the prophets also; and You say, 'If anyone keeps My word, he shall never **taste of death**.' [NASB]<br>At this the Jews exclaimed, "Now we know that you are demon-possessed! Abraham died and so did the | To taste, experience death; to die; to eat of death.<br><br>**Practical Application**<br>The meaning is that a genuine follower of Christ will...<br>• never experience death nor see death.<br>• never know death nor partake of death.<br>• never face the condemnation of death.<br>• never experience the terror, the hurt, the pain, and the suffering of death; never experience the anguish of being separated from God and from the glory, beauty, perfection, and life of heaven.<br>In a flash, quicker than lightning or the blinking of an eye, the follower of Christ passes from this world into the next. He never ceases to experience life and never loses consciousness. One moment he is in this world, the next moment he is in the presence of God Himself.<br>Note the reason why the believer will never "die": it is because Jesus came "by God's grace, Jesus tasted death for everyone in all the world" (Hebrews 2:9). |

## Practical Word Studies
## in the New Testament

| ENGLISH WORD | GREEK WORD AND VERSE | THE WORD MEANS... |
|---|---|---|
| | prophets, yet you say that if anyone keeps your word, he will never **taste death**. [NIV]<br>Then the Jews said to Him, "Now we know that You have a demon! Abraham is dead, and the prophets; and You say, 'If anyone keeps My word he shall never **taste death**.' [NKJV]<br>The people said, "Now we know you are possessed by a demon. Even Abraham and the prophets died, but you say that those who obey your teaching will never **die**! [NLT]<br>εἶπον οὖν αὐτῷ οἱ Ἰουδαῖοι, Νῦν ἐγνώκαμεν ὅτι δαιμόνιον ἔχεις· Ἀβραὰμ ἀπέθανε καὶ οἱ προφῆται, καὶ σὺ λέγεις, Ἐάν τις τὸν λόγον μου τηρήσῃ, οὐ μὴ **γεύσεται θανάτου** εἰς τὸν αἰῶνα. [GNS]<br>εἶπον [οὖν] αὐτῷ οἱ Ἰουδαῖοι, Νῦν ἐγνώκαμεν ὅτι δαιμόνιον ἔχεις. Ἀβραὰμ ἀπέθανεν καὶ οἱ προφῆται, καὶ σὺ λέγεις, Ἐάν τις τὸν λόγον μου τηρήσῃ, οὐ μὴ **γεύσηται θανάτου** εἰς τὸν αἰῶνα. [GNT] | |
| **#1030**<br>**Die**<br><br>Corruption–KJV<br>Decay–NASB<br>Decay–NIV<br>Corruption–NKJV<br>Die–NLT<br><br>**POSB REFERENCE**<br>(Acts 13:32-37; esp. v.34)<br>*Deeper Study #4* | ὑποστρέφειν εἰς διαφθοράν = *hupostrephein eis diaphthoran*<br>Pronunciation: [who-po-streph-eh-een ice dee-ahph-tho-rahn]<br>Parsing *diaphthoran* (part of speech): noun<br>    Case—accusative<br>    Gender—feminine<br>    Number—singular<br>    Stem or root— from διαφθορά, ᾶς<br>Concordance References:<br>⇒ Strong's #1312+1519+5290 *diaphthora eis hupostrephō*<br>⇒ NIV #1426+1650+5715 *diaphthora [decay] eis hupostrephō*<br>⇒ NASB #1312+1519+5290 *diaphthora eis hupostrephō*<br><br>**Acts 13:34**<br>And as concerning that he raised him up from the dead, now no more to return to **corruption**, he said on this wise, I will give you the sure mercies of David. [KJV]<br>"And as for the fact that He raised Him up from the dead, no more to return to **decay**, He has spoken in this way: 'I will give you the holy and sure blessings of David.' [NASB]<br>The fact that God raised him from the dead, never to **decay**, is stated in these words: " 'I will give you the holy and sure blessings promised to David.' [NIV]<br>And that He raised Him from the dead, no more to return to **corruption**, He has spoken thus: *'I will give you the sure mercies of David.'* [NKJV]<br>For God had promised to raise him from the dead, never again to **die**. This is stated in the Scripture that says, 'I will give you the sacred blessings I promised to David.' [NLT]<br>ὅτι δὲ ἀνέστησεν αὐτὸν ἐκ νεκρῶν μηκέτι μέλλοντα **ὑποστρέφειν εἰς διαφθοράν**, οὕτως εἴρηκεν ὅτι Δώσω ὑμῖν τὰ ὅσια Δαβὶδ τὰ πιστά. [GNS]<br>ὅτι δὲ ἀνέστησεν αὐτὸν ἐκ νεκρῶν μηκέτι μέλλοντα **ὑποστρέφειν εἰς διαφθοράν**, οὕτως εἴρηκεν ὅτι Δώσω ὑμῖν τὰ ὅσια Δαυὶδ τὰ πιστά. [GNT] | To decay; to die; to become corrupt.<br><br>**Practical Application**<br>In no place does Christ promise a new body to the unbeliever, to the unsaved and lost. A person's body and flesh can be destroyed forever. (This is a fact seldom pointed out.) |
| **#1031**<br>**Die-Dies**<br><br>Die–KJV<br>Die–NASB<br>Die–NIV<br>Die–NKJV<br>Dies–NLT | ἀποθανεῖν = *apothanein*<br>Pronunciation: [ap-oth-ahn-een]<br>Parsing (part of speech): verb<br>    Mood—infinitive<br>    Tense—aorist<br>    Voice—active<br>    Stem or root—from ἀποθνήσκω<br>Concordance References:<br>⇒ Strong's #599 *apothnēskō*<br>⇒ NIV #633 *apothnēskō*<br>⇒ NASB #599 *apothnēskō* | Death; to be at death's door; to die. The basic meaning of death is *separation*. Death never means extinction, annihilation, non-existence, or inactivity. "Death is the separation of a person from the purpose or use for which he was intended." (H.S. Miller. Quoted by Lehman Strauss. *Devotional Studies in Galatians and Ephesians*. Neptune, NJ: Loizeaux Bros. Copyright 1957 by Lehman Strauss, p.137.) |

# PRACTICAL WORD STUDIES
## in the NEW TESTAMENT

| ENGLISH WORD | GREEK WORD AND VERSE | THE WORD MEANS... |
|---|---|---|
| **POSB REFERENCE** (Heb.9:27) *Deeper Study* #1 | **Hebrews 9:27** And as it is appointed unto men once to **die**, but after this the judgment: [KJV] And inasmuch as it is appointed for men to **die** once and after this comes judgment, [NASB] Just as man is destined to **die** once, and after that to face judgment, [NIV] And as it is appointed for men to **die** once, but after this the judgment, [NKJV] And just as it is destined that each person **dies** only once and after that comes judgment, [NLT] καὶ καθ' ὅσον ἀπόκειται τοῖς ἀνθρώποις ἅπαξ **ἀποθανεῖν**, μετὰ δὲ τοῦτο κρίσις· [GNS] καὶ καθ' ὅσον ἀπόκειται τοῖς ἀνθρώποις ἅπαξ **ἀποθανεῖν**, μετὰ δὲ τοῦτο κρίσις, [GNT] | **Practical Application** The Bible speaks of three deaths. 1. Physical death: the *separation* of a man's spirit or life from the body. This is what men commonly call death. It is when a person ceases to exist on this earth and is buried (1 Cor. 15:21-22; Hebrews 9:27). 2. Spiritual death: the *separation* of man's spirit from God while he is still living and walking upon earth. This death is the *natural state* of a man on earth without Christ. Man is seen as still in his sins and *dead* to God (Ephes. 2:1; Ephes. 4:18; 1 John 5:12). Spiritual death speaks of a person who is dead while he still lives (1 Tim. 5:6). He is a natural man living in this present world, but he is said to be dead to the Lord Jesus Christ and to God and to spiritual matters.    a. A person who wastes his life in riotous living is spiritually dead (Luke 15:32).    b. A person who has not partaken of Christ is spiritually dead (John 6:53).    c. A person who does not have the spirit of Christ is said to be spiritually dead. (Romans 8:9).    d. A person who lives in sin is said to be spiritually dead (Ephes. 2:1; Col. 2:13).    e. A person who is alienated from God is said to be spiritually dead (Ephes. 4:18-19).    f. A person who sleeps in sin is spiritually dead (Ephes. 5:14).    g. A person who lives in sinful pleasure is dead while he lives (1 Tim. 5:6).    h. A person who does not have the Son of God is dead (1 John 5:12).    i. A person who does great religious works but does the wrong works is dead (Rev. 3:1). 3. Eternal death: the *separation* of man from God's presence forever. This is the second death, an eternal state of being *dead to God* (1 Cor. 6:9-10; 2 Thes. 1:9). It is spiritual death, separation from God, that is prolonged beyond the death of the body. It is called the "second death" or eternal death (Romans 6:23; Romans 8:6; 2 Thes. 1:9). |
| **#1032 Different** Another–KJV **Different–NASB** **Different–NIV** **Different–NKJV** **Different–NLT** **POSB REFERENCE** (Gal.1:6-7; esp. v.6) Note 2 | ἕτερον = heteron Pronunciation: [het'-er-on] Parsing (part of speech): adjective    Case—accusative    Gender—neuter    Number—singular    Stem or root—from ἕτερος, α, ον Concordance References:   ⇒ Strong's #2087 heteros   ⇒ NIV #2283 heteros   ⇒ NASB #2087 heteros **Galatians 1:6** I marvel that ye are so soon removed from him that called you into the grace of Christ unto **another** gospel: [KJV] I am amazed that you are so quickly deserting Him who called you by the grace of Christ, for a **different** gospel; [NASB] I am astonished that you are so quickly deserting the one who called you by the grace of Christ and are turning to a **different** gospel—[NIV] | Different, unnatural, altered in a strange way. **Practical Application** It means a different kind of gospel, not just a difference in emphasis or spirit (A.T. Robertson. *Word Pictures in the New Testament*, Vol.4, p.276). It means a different kind of gospel that presents... • a different Jesus • a different grace • a different way to be saved • a different God • a different picture of God's love But note what Scripture declares: the gospel to which the Galatians were turning was *not a different gospel*. There is no other gospel; there is only one true gospel by which men can become acceptable to God, and that is the gospel of God Himself revealed in the death of His Son, even "the grace of Christ." |

# PRACTICAL WORD STUDIES
## in the New Testament

| ENGLISH WORD | GREEK WORD AND VERSE | THE WORD MEANS... |
|---|---|---|
| | I marvel that you are turning away so soon from Him who called you in the grace of Christ, to a **different** gospel, [NKJV]<br><br>I am shocked that you are turning away so soon from God, who in his love and mercy called you to share the eternal life he gives through Christ. You are already following a **different** way [NLT]<br><br>Θαυμάζω ὅτι οὕτω ταχέως μετατίθεσθε ἀπὸ τοῦ καλέσαντος ὑμᾶς ἐν χάριτι Χριστοῦ εἰς **ἕτερον** εὐαγγέλιον· [GNS]<br><br>Θαυμάζω ὅτι οὕτως ταχέως μετατίθεσθε ἀπὸ τοῦ καλέσαντος ὑμᾶς ἐν χάριτι [Χριστοῦ] εἰς **ἕτερον** εὐαγγέλιον, [GNT] | |
| #1033<br>**Difficult**<br><br>Hard–KJV<br>**Difficult–NASB**<br>Hard–NIV<br>Hard–NKJV<br>Hard–NLT<br><br>POSB<br>REFERENCE<br>(Jn.6:59-60; esp. v.60)<br>Note 1 | Σκληρός = sklëros<br>Pronunciation: [sklay-ros']<br>Parsing (part of speech): adjective<br>    Case—nominative<br>    Gender—masculine<br>    Number—singular<br>    Stem or root—from σκληρός, ά, όν<br>Concordance References:<br>  ⇒  Strong's #4642 skleros<br>  ⇒  NIV #5017 skleros<br>  ⇒  NASB #4642 skleros<br><br>**John 6:60**<br>Many therefore of his disciples, when they had heard this, said, This is an **hard** saying; who can hear it? [KJV]<br><br>Many therefore of His disciples, when they heard this said, "This is a **difficult** statement; who can listen to it?" [NASB]<br><br>On hearing it, many of his disciples said, "This is a **hard** teaching. Who can accept it?" [NIV]<br><br>Therefore many of His disciples, when they heard *this*, said, "This is a **hard** saying; who can understand it?" [NKJV]<br><br>Even his disciples said, "This is very **hard** to understand. How can anyone accept it?" [NLT]<br><br>Πολλοὶ οὖν ἀκούσαντες ἐκ τῶν μαθητῶν αὐτοῦ εἶπον, **Σκληρός** ἐστιν οὗτος ὁ λόγος· τίς δύναται αὐτοῦ ἀκούειν; [GNS]<br><br>Πολλοὶ οὖν ἀκούσαντες ἐκ τῶν μαθητῶν αὐτοῦ εἶπαν, **Σκληρός** ἐστιν ὁ λόγος οὗτος· τίς δύναται αὐτοῦ ἀκούειν; [GNT] | Rough and harsh, hard, difficult.<br><br>**Practical Application**<br>What Jesus had said was hard and difficult to accept, but His words were clearly understood. The people's problem was not in their understanding, but in their hearts. There were three responses to the Lord's message.<br>  1. There were disciples or followers who turned back. Note that "many...withdrew, and were not walking with Him anymore." (Jn.6:66). They forsook and deserted the Lord. Why? Very simply, following Christ cost too much. It involved the cross, which meant complete denial of oneself.<br>    a. Jesus was claiming to be Lord. This meant that a man had to give all he was and had to Christ.<br>    b. Jesus was claiming to be the very Son of God, to have come down out of heaven. Some just could not receive and accept the fact.<br>    c. Jesus was demanding total allegiance and complete self-denial, and following Him would just cost too much (see POSB *Deeper Study* #1—Luke 9:23).<br>  2. There was the disciple who believed that Jesus was the Lord. Note four facts.<br>    a. Peter spoke for all the apostles. He was their leader and spokesman.<br>    b. Peter called Jesus "Lord," and he used the title in its fullest meaning (cp. John 6:68-69). Jesus was recognized to be the sovereign Lord of the universe, the One to whom all men owe their allegiance.<br>    c. Peter declared that Jesus' words were the words of eternal life. He declared that what Jesus had just proclaimed was true (John 6:63). (See POSB *Deeper Study* #2—John 1:4; POSB *Deeper Study* #1—John 10:10; POSB *Deeper Study* #1—John 17:2-3.)<br>    d. Peter proclaimed that he and the apostles both *believed* and *knew* something: Jesus was...<br>      • "the Christ, the Son of the living God" (the latest manuscripts read this).<br>      • "the Holy One of God" (the oldest manuscripts read this).<br>  3. There was the disciple who betrayed Jesus. Note these facts.<br>    a. Judas was a "chosen" man, chosen not only to be saved, but to be a minister of Christ. |

# PRACTICAL WORD STUDIES
## in the NEW TESTAMENT

| ENGLISH WORD | GREEK WORD AND VERSE | THE WORD MEANS... |
|---|---|---|
| | | b. Judas was called "a devil," a malicious gossip (2 Tim. 3:3), an adversary, an enemy of Christ.<br>c. Judas was a betrayer, a professed follower, but a hypocrite. |
| **#1034**<br>**Dignity**<br><br>Gravity–KJV<br>**Dignity–NASB**<br>Respect–NIV<br>Reverence–NKJV<br>Respect–NLT<br><br>**POSB REFERENCE**<br>(1 Tim.3:4-5; esp. v.4)<br>Note 3 | σεμνότητος = *semnotētos*<br>Pronunciation: [sem-no-tay-tos]<br>Parsing (part of speech): noun<br>    Case—genitive<br>    Gender—feminine<br>    Number—singular<br>    Stem or root—from σεμνότης, ητος<br>Concordance References:<br>  ⇒ Strong's #4587 semnotēs<br>  ⇒ NIV #4949 semnotēs<br>  ⇒ NASB #4587 semnotēs<br><br>**1 Tim. 3:4**<br>One that ruleth well his own house, having his children in subjection with all **gravity**; [KJV]<br>He must be one who manages his own household well, keeping his children under control with all **dignity** [NASB]<br>He must manage his own family well and see that his children obey him with proper **respect**. [NIV]<br>One who rules his own house well, having *his* children in submission with all **reverence** [NKJV]<br>He must manage his own family well, with children who **respect** and obey him. [NLT]<br>τοῦ ἰδίου οἴκου καλῶς προϊστάμενον, τέκνα ἔχοντα ἐν ὑποταγῇ μετὰ πάσης **σεμνότητος**· [GNS]<br>τοῦ ἰδίου οἴκου καλῶς προϊστάμενον, τέκνα ἔχοντα ἐν ὑποταγῇ, μετὰ πάσης **σεμνότητος** [GNT] | Respect, gravity, dignity, reverence, respectability, seriousness.<br><br>**Practical Application**<br>The minister must rule his home with dignity, reverence, respect, and love. As the Amplified New Testament says: "With true dignity, commanding their respect in every way and keeping them respectful."<br>As Scripture says, "But if a man does not know how to manage his own household, how will he take care of the church of God?" (1 Tim. 3:5) [NASB]. |
| **#1035**<br>**Dignity**<br><br>Grave–KJV<br>**Dignity–NASB**<br>Worthy of respect–NIV<br>Reverent–NKJV<br>Respected–NLT<br><br>**POSB REFERENCE**<br>(1 Tim.3:8)<br>Note 1, point 1<br><br>See also POSB REF:<br>(1 Tim.3:11-12)<br>Note 3<br>(Tit.2:2)<br>Note 2 | σεμνούς = *semnous*<br>Pronunciation: [sem-noos']<br>Parsing (part of speech): adjective<br>    Case—accusative<br>    Gender—masculine<br>    Number—plural<br>    Stem or root—from σεμνός, ή, όν<br>Concordance References:<br>  ⇒ Strong's #4586 semnos<br>  ⇒ NIV #4948 semnos<br>  ⇒ NASB #4586 semnos<br><br>**1 Tim. 3:8**<br>Likewise must the deacons be **grave**, not doubletongued, not given to much wine, not greedy of filthy lucre; [KJV]<br>Deacons likewise must be men of **dignity**, not double-tongued, or addicted to much wine or fond of sordid gain, [NASB]<br>Deacons, likewise, are to be men **worthy of respect**, sincere, not indulging in much wine, and not pursuing dishonest gain. [NIV]<br>Likewise deacons *must be* **reverent**, not doubletongued, not given to much wine, not greedy for money, [NKJV]<br>In the same way, deacons must be people who are **respected** and have integrity. They must not be heavy drinkers and must not be greedy for money. [NLT]<br>διακόνους ὡσαύτως **σεμνούς**, μὴ διλόγους, μὴ οἴνῳ πολλῷ προσέχοντας, μὴ αἰσχροκερδεῖς, [GNS]<br>Διακόνους ὡσαύτως **σεμνούς**, μὴ διλόγους, μὴ οἴνῳ πολλῷ προσέχοντας, μὴ αἰσχροκερδεῖς, [GNT] | Worthy of respect, grave, dignity, highly respected, serious, honorable, worthy, revered, noble.<br><br>**Practical Application**<br>It is being serious-minded, the very opposite...<br>• of being flippant.<br>• of dishonoring oneself.<br>• of being shallow by being over talkative.<br>• of having little respect because one is not grave or serious enough.<br>• of having a surface religion only.<br>However, this does not mean that the deacon is to walk around with a long face, never smiling, joking, or having fun. It simply means that he is to be serious-minded and committed to Christ and to the mission of the church: the mission of reaching the lost and meeting the desperate needs of the world. |
| **#1036**<br>**Diligence**<br><br>Business–KJV | σπουδῇ = *spoudē*<br>Pronunciation: [spoo-day']<br>Parsing (part of speech): noun<br>    Case—dative<br>    Gender—feminine<br>    Number—singular | Zeal, concern, diligence, work, business, earnestness, effort.<br><br>**Practical Application**<br>The exhortation is clear: the believer must... |

# PRACTICAL WORD STUDIES
## in the NEW TESTAMENT

| ENGLISH WORD | GREEK WORD AND VERSE | THE WORD MEANS... |
|---|---|---|
| **Diligence–NASB**<br>Zeal–NIV<br>**Diligence–NKJV**<br>Work–NLT<br><br>**POSB REFERENCE**<br>(Rom.12:11)<br>Note 2, point 1 | Stem or root—from σπουδή, ῆς<br>Concordance References:<br>⇒ Strong's #4710 spoudë<br>⇒ NIV #5082 spoudë<br>⇒ NASB #4710 spoudë<br><br>**Romans 12:11**<br>Not slothful in **business**; fervent in spirit; serving the Lord; [KJV]<br>Not lagging behind in **diligence**, fervent in spirit, serving the Lord; [NASB]<br>Never be lacking in **zeal**, but keep your spiritual fervor, serving the Lord. [NIV]<br>Not lagging in **diligence**, fervent in spirit, serving the Lord; [NKJV]<br>Never be lazy in your **work**, but serve the Lord enthusiastically. [NLT]<br>τῇ **σπουδῇ** μὴ ὀκνηροί· τῷ πνεύματι ζέοντες· τῷ Κυρίῳ δουλεύοντες· [GNS]<br>τῇ **σπουδῇ** μὴ ὀκνηροί, τῷ πνεύματι ζέοντες, τῷ κυρίῳ δουλεύοντες, [GNT] | • not be lazy or slow moving in zeal.<br>• not be sluggish or lethargic in diligence.<br>• not be hesitating or delaying in earnestness.<br><br>The believer just cannot approach life in a lackadaisical, easygoing, slow moving fashion. The world is reeling in pain, with millions starving and suffering due to man's selfishness and sin, hoarding, disease, war, death—and the list could go on and on. The believer must not give in to sluggishness and complacency. He must serve the Lord with all diligence and zeal and earnestness. He must be enthusiastic in his service. |
| **#1037**<br>**Diligence–Diligently**<br><br>Diligence–KJV<br>Diligence–NASB<br>Diligently–NIV<br>Diligence–NKJV<br>Seriously–NLT<br><br>**POSB REFERENCE**<br>(Rom.12:6-8; esp. v.8)<br>Note 2, point 6 | ἐν σπουδῇ = en spoudë<br>Pronunciation: [en spoo-day']<br>Parsing *spoudë* (part of speech): noun<br>  Case—dative<br>  Gender—feminine<br>  Number—singular<br>  Stem or root—from σπουδή, ῆς<br>Concordance References:<br>⇒ Strong's #1722 + 4710 en spoudë<br>⇒ NIV #1877 + 5082 en spoudë [diligently]<br>⇒ NASB #1722 + 4710 en spoudë<br><br>**Romans 12:8**<br>Or he that exhorteth, on exhortation: he that giveth, let him do it with simplicity; he that ruleth, with **diligence**; he that sheweth mercy, with cheerfulness. [KJV]<br>Or he who exhorts, in his exhortation; he who gives, with liberality; he who leads, with **diligence**; he who shows mercy, with cheerfulness. [NASB]<br>If it is encouraging, let him encourage; if it is contributing to the needs of others, let him give generously; if it is leadership, let him govern **diligently**; if it is showing mercy, let him do it cheerfully. [NIV]<br>He who exhorts, in exhortation; he who gives, with liberality; he who leads, with **diligence**; he who shows mercy, with cheerfulness. [NKJV]<br>If your gift is to encourage others, do it! If you have money, share it generously. If God has given you leadership ability, take the responsibility **seriously**. And if you have a gift for showing kindness to others, do it gladly. [NLT]<br>εἴτε ὁ παρακαλῶν, ἐν τῇ παρακλήσει· ὁ μεταδιδοὺς ἐν ἁπλότητι, ὁ προϊστάμενος, **ἐν σπουδῇ**· ὁ ἐλεῶν ἐν ἱλαρότητι. [GNS]<br>εἴτε ὁ παρακαλῶν ἐν τῇ παρακλήσει· ὁ μεταδιδοὺς ἐν ἁπλότητι, ὁ προϊστάμενος **ἐν σπουδῇ**, ὁ ἐλεῶν ἐν ἱλαρότητι. [GNT] | Earnestness, diligence, eagerness, zeal, effort.<br><br>**Practical Application**<br>There is the gift of ruling (*proistemi*). This means the ability of leadership, authority, administration, government. Note that this person is to lead with diligence (*spoudë*): haste, zeal, desire, and concentrated attention. There is no room for laziness, complacency, and irresponsibility in the Kingdom of God and His church. The leaders are the ones who are to blaze the path for the flock of God, and they are to do it with zeal, hard work, and iron determination. |
| **#1038**<br>**Diligent**<br><br>Diligent–KJV<br>Diligent–NASB<br>Zealous–NIV<br>Diligent–NKJV<br>Earnest–NLT | σπουδαῖον = spoudaion<br>Pronunciation: [spoo-dah'-ee-on]<br>Parsing (part of speech): adjective<br>  Case—accusative<br>  Gender—masculine<br>  Number—singular<br>  Stem or root—from σπουδαῖος, α, ον<br>Concordance References:<br>⇒ Strong's #4705 spoudaios<br>⇒ NIV #5080 spoudaios<br>⇒ NASB #4705 spoudaios | Zealous, diligent, earnest, enthusiastic, eager, devoted.<br><br>**Practical Application**<br>Men who handle collections (ushers) are diligent in many things, but especially in collections. Who this unnamed brother was is not known. Three significant points are made about him, points that should speak to the heart of every church usher and person who handles collections.<br><br>1. He was a brother, a true believer who was in |

# PRACTICAL WORD STUDIES
## in the NEW TESTAMENT

| ENGLISH WORD | GREEK WORD AND VERSE | THE WORD MEANS... |
|---|---|---|
| **POSB REFERENCE** (2 Cor.8:22) Note 4 | **2 Cor. 8:22** And we have sent with them our brother, whom we have oftentimes proved **diligent** in many things, but now much more diligent, upon the great confidence which I have in you. [KJV] <br> And we have sent with them our brother, whom we have often tested and found **diligent** in many things, but now even more diligent, because of his great confidence in you. [NASB] <br> In addition, we are sending with them our brother who has often proved to us in many ways that he is **zealous**, and now even more so because of his great confidence in you. [NIV] <br> And we have sent with them our brother whom we have often proved **diligent** in many things, but now much more diligent, because of the great confidence which *we have* in you. [NKJV] <br> And we are also sending with them another brother who has been thoroughly tested and has shown how **earnest** he is on many occasions. He is now even more enthusiastic because of his increased confidence in you. [NLT] <br> συνεπέμψαμεν δὲ αὐτοῖς τὸν ἀδελφὸν ἡμῶν, ὃν ἐδοκιμάσαμεν ἐν πολλοῖς πολλάκις **σπουδαῖον** ὄντα, νυνὶ δὲ πολὺ σπουδαιότερον πεποιθήσει πολλῇ τῇ εἰς ὑμᾶς. [GNS] <br> συνεπέμψαμεν δὲ αὐτοῖς τὸν ἀδελφὸν ἡμῶν ὃν ἐδοκιμάσαμεν ἐν πολλοῖς πολλάκις **σπουδαῖον** ὄντα, νυνὶ δὲ πολὺ σπουδαιότερον πεποιθήσει πολλῇ τῇ εἰς ὑμᾶς. [GNT] | fellowship with other believers and cooperated with the church in its mission endeavors. <br> 2. He had often "proved diligent" (*spoudaion*) when other ministries had been assigned to him. He gave himself wholeheartedly to whatever task the church gave him. <br> 3. He observed and was alert to the testimony of churches. When Paul told him about the Corinthian church—about the great revival of the church—he became excited and was more willing than ever to serve Christ in the midst of the church. |
| **#1039 Diligent** <br> Labour–KJV <br> **Diligent–NASB** <br> Make every effort–NIV <br> **Diligent–NKJV** <br> Do our best–NLT <br> **POSB REFERENCE** (Heb.4:11-13; esp. v.11) Note 5, point 1 | σπουδάσωμεν = *spoudasōmen* <br> Pronunciation: [spoo-dah'-so-mehn] <br> Parsing (part of speech): verb <br>   Mood—subjunctive <br>   Tense—aorist <br>   Voice—active <br>   Person—1st person <br>   Number—plural <br>   Stem or root—from σπουδάζω <br> Concordance References: <br> ⇒ Strong's #4704 spoudazō <br> ⇒ NIV #5079 spoudazō <br> ⇒ NASB #4704 spoudazō <br><br> **Hebrews 4:11** <br> Let us **labour** therefore to enter into that rest, lest any man fall after the same example of unbelief. [KJV] <br> Let us therefore be **diligent** to enter that rest, lest anyone fall through following the same example of disobedience. [NASB] <br> Let us, therefore, **make every effort** to enter that rest, so that no one will fall by following their example of disobedience. [NIV] <br> Let us therefore be **diligent** to enter that rest, lest anyone fall according to the same example of disobedience. [NKJV] <br> Let us **do our best** to enter that place of rest. For anyone who disobeys God, as the people of Israel did, will fall. [NLT] <br> **σπουδάσωμεν** οὖν εἰσελθεῖν εἰς ἐκείνην τὴν κατάπαυσιν, ἵνα μὴ ἐν τῷ αὐτῷ τις ὑποδείγματι πέσῃ τῆς ἀπειθείας. [GNS] <br> **σπουδάσωμεν** οὖν εἰσελθεῖν εἰς ἐκείνην τὴν κατάπαυσιν, ἵνα μὴ ἐν τῷ αὐτῷ τις ὑποδείγματι πέσῃ τῆς ἀπειθείας. [GNT] | To make every effort, labor; to be diligent, do your best, work hard, endeavor, to give all diligence, be zealous, eagerly strive, exert one's self, and make haste. <br><br> **Practical Application** <br> A person must be diligent to enter God's rest or else he will fall into unbelief. There is no place for sleepiness or laziness, complacency or lethargy. Unless a person labors with all diligence, he will fall just as Israel fell. And remember Israel's experience: the people would labor for a while and then fall back for awhile; labor again and then fall back again. Israel lived an up and down life, and the nation was not allowed to enter God's rest. There is no place for inconsistency, no place for living an up-and-down life—not in God's rest. Diligence—laboring every day—is an absolute essential. We must be diligent or else fall from God's rest as Israel fell. |
| **#1040 Diligently** <br> Diligently–KJV <br> Accurately–NASB <br> Accurately–NIV | ἀκριβῶς = *akribōs* <br> Pronunciation: [ak-ree-boce'] <br> Parsing (part of speech): adjective adverb <br>   Stem or root—from ἀκριβῶς <br> Concordance References: <br> ⇒ Strong's #199 akribōs | Accurately, diligently, with care. <br><br> **Practical Application** <br> The stress is that Apollos taught accurately (*akribōs*), that is, carefully and diligently. <br> ⇒ He was true to the Scriptures, weighing |

# PRACTICAL WORD STUDIES
## in the NEW TESTAMENT

| ENGLISH WORD | GREEK WORD AND VERSE | THE WORD MEANS... |
|---|---|---|
| Accurately–NKJV<br>Accuracy–NLT<br><br>**POSB REFERENCE**<br>(Acts 18:25)<br>Note 5 | ⇒ NIV #209 akribōs<br>⇒ NASB #199 akribōs<br><br>**Acts 18:25**<br>This man was instructed in the way of the Lord; and being fervent in the spirit, he spake and taught **diligently** the things of the Lord, knowing only the baptism of John. [KJV]<br>This man had been instructed in the way of the Lord; and being fervent in spirit, he was speaking and teaching **accurately** the things concerning Jesus, being acquainted only with the baptism of John; [NASB]<br>He had been instructed in the way of the Lord, and he spoke with great fervor and taught about Jesus **accurately**, though he knew only the baptism of John. [NIV]<br>This man had been instructed in the way of the Lord; and being fervent in spirit, he spoke and taught **accurately** the things of the Lord, though he knew only the baptism of John. [NKJV]<br>He had been taught the way of the Lord and talked to others with great enthusiasm and **accuracy** about Jesus. However, he knew only about John's baptism. [NLT]<br>οὗτος ἦν κατηχημένος τὴν ὁδὸν τοῦ Κυρίου, καὶ ζέων τῷ πνεύματι ἐλάλει καὶ ἐδίδασκεν **ἀκριβῶς** τὰ περὶ τοῦ Κύριον, ἐπιστάμενος μόνον τὸ βάπτισμα Ἰωάννου· [GNS]<br>οὗτος ἦν κατηχημένος τὴν ὁδὸν τοῦ κυρίου, καὶ ζέων τῷ πνεύματι ἐλάλει καὶ ἐδίδασκεν **ἀκριβῶς** τὰ περὶ τοῦ Ἰησοῦ, ἐπιστάμενος μόνον τὸ βάπτισμα Ἰωάννου. [GNT] | carefully what they said.<br>⇒ He proclaimed what the Scriptures taught and all that they taught. He did not neglect subjects his listeners might not like to hear.<br>⇒ He did not twist the Scriptures, adding to or taking away from them. |
| **#1041**<br>**Diligently Seek**<br><br>Diligently seek–KJV<br>Seek–NASB<br>Earnestly seek–NIV<br>Diligently seek–NKJV<br>Sincerely seek–NLT<br><br>**POSB REFERENCE**<br>(Heb.11:6)<br>Note 5, point 2b | ἐκζητοῦσιν = ekzētousin<br>Pronunciation: [ek-zay-too-sin]<br>Parsing (part of speech): verb<br>  Mood—participle<br>  Tense—present<br>  Voice—active<br>  Case—dative<br>  Gender—masculine<br>  Number—plural<br>  Stem or root—from ἐκζητέω<br>Concordance References:<br>⇒ Strong's #1567 ekzēteō<br>⇒ NIV #1699 ekzēteō<br>⇒ NASB #1567 ekzēteō<br><br>**Hebrews 11:6**<br>But without faith it is impossible to please him: for he that cometh to God must believe that he is, and that he is a rewarder of them that **diligently seek** him. [KJV]<br>And without faith it is impossible to please Him, for he who comes to God must believe that He is, and that He is a rewarder of those who **seek** Him. [NASB]<br>And without faith it is impossible to please God, because anyone who comes to him must believe that he exists and that he rewards those who **earnestly seek** him. [NIV]<br>But without faith *it is* impossible to please *Him,* for he who comes to God must believe that He is, and *that* He is a rewarder of those who **diligently seek** Him. [NKJV]<br>So, you see, it is impossible to please God without faith. Anyone who wants to come to him must believe that there is a God and that he rewards those who **sincerely seek** him. [NLT]<br>χωρὶς δὲ πίστεως ἀδύνατον εὐαρεστῆσαι· πιστεῦσαι γὰρ δεῖ τὸν προσερχόμενον τῷ Θεῷ, ὅτι ἔστι, καὶ τοῖς **ἐκζητοῦσιν** αὐτὸν μισθαποδότης γίνεται. [GNS]<br>χωρὶς δὲ πίστεως ἀδύνατον εὐαρεστῆσαι· πιστεῦσαι γὰρ δεῖ τὸν προσερχόμενον τῷ θεῷ ὅτι ἔστιν καὶ τοῖς **ἐκζητοῦσιν** αὐτὸν μισθαποδότης γίνεται. [GNT] | To earnestly seek; to diligently seek; to sincerely seek. It means to *seek out God*; to diligently seek to find Him and to follow Him.<br><br>**Practical Application**<br>God does not reward the sleepy eyed, the complacent, the non-thinker, the half-interested, the worldly-minded, the pleasure seeker. God rewards those who diligently seek to know and follow Him. The idea is that we must be in earnest and persevere, enduring to the end. What is the reward to those who diligently seek God? It is the same reward given to Abel and Enoch: righteousness and God's care in this life and deliverance from death to live eternally with God. |
| **#1042**<br>**Diligently Study** | ἐραυνᾶτε = eraunate<br>Pronunciation: [eh-rah-oon-ah'-teh]<br>Parsing (part of speech): verb<br>  Mood—indicative or imperative<br>  Tense—present | To diligently study; to search; to inquire; to investigate; to closely examine; to explore; to thoroughly search; to research; to delve into. |

# PRACTICAL WORD STUDIES
## in the NEW TESTAMENT

| ENGLISH WORD | GREEK WORD AND VERSE | THE WORD MEANS... |
|---|---|---|
| Search—KJV<br>Search—NASB<br>**Diligently study—NIV**<br>Search—NKJV<br>Search—NLT<br><br>**POSB<br>REFERENCE**<br>(Jn.5:39)<br>Note 6, point 1 | Voice—active<br>Person—2nd person<br>Number—plural<br>Stem or root—from ἐραυνάω<br>Concordance References:<br>⇒ Strong's #2045 eraunaö<br>⇒ NIV #2236 eraunaö<br>⇒ NASB #2045 eraunaö<br><br>**John 5:39**<br>**Search** the scriptures; for in them ye think ye have eternal life: and they are they which testify of me. [KJV]<br>"You **search** the Scriptures, because you think that in them you have eternal life; and it is these that bear witness of Me; [NASB]<br>You **diligently study** the Scriptures because you think that by them you possess eternal life. These are the Scriptures that testify about me, [NIV]<br>You **search** the Scriptures, for in them you think you have eternal life; and these are they which testify of Me. [NKJV]<br>"You **search** the Scriptures because you believe they give you eternal life. But the Scriptures point to me! [NLT]<br>ἐρευνᾶτε τὰς γραφάς, ὅτι ὑμεῖς δοκεῖτε ἐν αὐταῖς ζωὴν αἰώνιον ἔχειν, καὶ ἐκεῖναί εἰσιν αἱ μαρτυροῦσαι περὶ ἐμοῦ· [GNS]<br>ἐρευνᾶτε τὰς γραφάς, ὅτι ὑμεῖς δοκεῖτε ἐν αὐταῖς ζωὴν αἰώνιον ἔχειν· καὶ ἐκεῖναί εἰσιν αἱ μαρτυροῦσαι περὶ ἐμοῦ· [GNT] | **Practical Application**<br>The words "diligently study" can be either a fact, that "you diligently study the Scriptures," or a command that charges a person to "diligently study the Scriptures." It seems that the words "for you think" point toward the meaning being a statement of fact. The religionists do "diligently study the Scriptures," for they think they have eternal life "in their diligent study." But note this most important fact:<br>The Scriptures *proclaim* the message of eternal life and show us how to secure eternal life, but the Scriptures do not impart or give eternal life. Only Christ can give eternal life. A person does not secure eteral life...<br>• by reading the Scripture, no matter how much he reads.<br>• by knowing the Scripture, no matter how much he knows.<br>• by being religious, no matter how religious he is.<br>• by doing religious works, no matter how much good he does.<br>A person receives eternal life only by believing and giving his heart and life to Jesus Christ. (See POSB *Deeper Study* #2—John 2:24.) |
| **#1043<br>Diminishing**<br><br>Diminishing—KJV<br>Failure—NASB<br>Loss—NIV<br>Failure—NKJV<br>Turned down—NLT<br><br>**POSB<br>REFERENCE**<br>(Romans 11:11-12,<br>esp. v.12)<br>Note 1, point 3 | ἥττημα = hëttëma<br>Pronunciation: [hayt'-tay-mah]<br>Parsing (part of speech): noun<br>   Case—nominative<br>   Gender—neuter<br>   Number—singular<br>   Stem or root—from ἥττημα, τος<br>Concordance References:<br>⇒ Strong's #2275 hëttëma<br>⇒ NIV #2488 hëttëma<br>⇒ NASB #2275 hëttëma<br><br>**Romans 11:12**<br>Now if the fall of them *be* the riches of the world, and the **diminishing** of them the riches of the Gentiles; how much more their fulness? [KJV]<br>Now if their transgression be riches for the world and their **failure** be riches for the Gentiles, how much more will their fulfillment be! [NASB]<br>But if their transgression means riches for the world, and their **loss** means riches for the Gentiles, how much greater riches will their fullness bring! [NIV]<br>Now if their fall *is* riches for the world, and their **failure** riches for the Gentiles, how much more their fullness! [NKJV]<br>Now if the Gentiles were enriched because the Jews **turned down** God's offer of salvation, think how much greater a blessing the world will share when the Jews finally accept it. [NLT]<br>εἰ δὲ τὸ παράπτωμα αὐτῶν πλοῦτος κόσμου, καὶ τὸ ἥττημα αὐτῶν πλοῦτος ἐθνῶν, πόσῳ μᾶλλον τὸ πλήρωμα αὐτῶν; [GNS]<br>εἰ δὲ τὸ παράπτωμα αὐτῶν πλοῦτος κόσμου καὶ τὸ ἥττημα αὐτῶν πλοῦτος ἐθνῶν, πόσῳ μᾶλλον τὸ πλήρωμα αὐτῶν. [GNT] | Defeat; failure; diminishing loss; turning down, downfall.<br><br>**Practical Application**<br>God assures the glorious restoration of Israel and a rich period for the whole earth. Note the sharp contrast...<br>• between "full" and "riches."<br>• between "diminishing" and "riches."<br>The word "diminishing" (*hëttëma*) means loss, defeat, injury. It means that Israel became impoverished spiritually. Israel was spiritually injured and defeated; the Jewish people lost the blessings of salvation. Now...<br>• if the spiritual fall of Israel led to the riches of salvation being carried to the world...<br>• if the spiritual loss of Israel led to the riches of salvation being carried to the Gentiles...<br>...how much more will the fullness (the restoration of Israel) bring the blessings of God to earth? |
| **#1044<br>Direct**<br><br>**Direct—KJV<br>Direct—NASB** | κατευθύναι = kateuthunai<br>Pronunciation: [kat-yoo-thoo'-nah-ee]<br>Parsing (part of speech): verb<br>   Mood—optative<br>   Tense—aorist<br>   Voice—active | To direct; to bring; to guide; to make straight or to be straight. It means to remove obstacles out of the way or to open up. |

## PRACTICAL WORD STUDIES in the NEW TESTAMENT

| ENGLISH WORD | GREEK WORD AND VERSE | THE WORD MEANS... |
|---|---|---|
| **Direct–NIV**<br>**Direct–NKJV**<br>Bring–NLT<br><br>**POSB REFERENCE**<br>(2 Thes.3:3-5; esp. v.5)<br>Note 2, point 3 | Person—3rd person<br>Number—singular<br>Stem or root—from κατευθύνω<br>Concordance References:<br>⇒ Strong's #2720 kateuthunō<br>⇒ NIV #2985 kateuthunō<br>⇒ NASB #2720 kateuthunō<br><br>**2 Thes. 3:5**<br>And the Lord **direct** your hearts into the love of God, and into the patient waiting for Christ. [KJV]<br>And may the Lord **direct** your hearts into the love of God and into the steadfastness of Christ. [NASB]<br>May the Lord **direct** your hearts into God's love and Christ's perseverance. [NIV]<br>Now may the Lord **direct** your hearts into the love of God and into the patience of Christ. [NKJV]<br>May the Lord **bring** you into an ever deeper understanding of the love of God and the endurance that comes from Christ. [NLT]<br>ὁ δὲ Κύριος **κατευθύναι** ὑμῶν τὰς καρδίας εἰς τὴν ἀγάπην τοῦ Θεοῦ, καὶ εἰς τὴν ὑπομονὴν τοῦ Χριστοῦ. [GNS]<br>Ὁ δὲ κύριος **κατευθύναι** ὑμῶν τὰς καρδίας εἰς τὴν ἀγάπην τοῦ θεοῦ καὶ εἰς τὴν ὑπομονὴν τοῦ Χριστοῦ. [GNT] | **Practical Application**<br>The Lord Jesus Christ takes the genuine believer and opens up his heart; He straightens, directs, and focuses the believer's heart upon the love of God. The result is that the believer learns to love God more and more. His attention and focus become more and more set upon God's love. Therefore, when trials, trouble, temptation, and evil attack the believer, he is able to stand in the love of God and overcome the attack. |
| **#1045**<br>**Direct**<br><br>Rule–KJV<br>Rule–NASB<br>**Direct–NIV**<br>Rule–NKJV<br>Do their work–NLT<br><br>**POSB REFERENCE**<br>(1 Tim.5:17-18; esp. v.17)<br>Note 1 | προεστῶτες = *proestōtes*<br>Pronunciation: [pro-ehst'-o-tehs]<br>Parsing (part of speech): verb<br>  Mood—participle<br>  Tense—perfect<br>  Voice—active<br>  Case—nominative<br>  Gender—plural<br>Stem or root—from προΐστημι<br>Concordance References:<br>⇒ Strong's #4291 proistēmi<br>⇒ NIV #4613 proistēmi<br>⇒ NASB #4291 proistēmi<br><br>**1 Tim. 5:17**<br>Let the elders that **rule** well be counted worthy of double honour, especially they who labour in the word and doctrine. [KJV]<br>Let the elders who **rule** well be considered worthy of double honor, especially those who work hard at preaching and teaching. [NASB]<br>The elders who **direct** the affairs of the church well are worthy of double honor, especially those whose work is preaching and teaching. [NIV]<br>Let the elders who **rule** well be counted worthy of double honor, especially those who labor in the word and doctrine. [NKJV]<br>Elders who **do their work** well should be paid well, especially those who work hard at both preaching and teaching. [NLT]<br>Οἱ καλῶς **προεστῶτες** πρεσβύτεροι διπλῆς τιμῆς ἀξιούσθωσαν, μάλιστα οἱ κοπιῶντες ἐν λόγῳ καὶ διδασκαλίᾳ· [GNS]<br>Οἱ καλῶς **προεστῶτες** πρεσβύτεροι διπλῆς τιμῆς ἀξιούσθωσαν, μάλιστα οἱ κοπιῶντες ἐν λόγῳ καὶ διδασκαλίᾳ. [GNT] | To direct; to rule; to do their work; to be a manager; to be a leader; to have authority over. The word (*proestōtes*) is a general word meaning to oversee, supervise, and look after.<br><br>**Practical Application**<br>There is a condition attached to honoring the minister. The minister to be honored is one who "directs...well." The minister who is worthy of double honor is the minister who labors and labors and works and works. If he is to receive double honor, then he must demonstrate a double commitment to Christ and the church.<br>Note also that the whole ministerial staff is covered by this charge. All the ministers of a church staff are to be counted worthy of double honor. But there is one minister who is singled out: the minister who labors in the Word and doctrine, that is, who preaches and teaches. It is he upon whom so much responsibility lies: he is the minister who takes the lead in edifying and building up the believer and the church. He is the one who has to spend hours on his face before God and in the Word in order to preach and teach—this in addition to taking the lead in all the other duties and ministries of the church. If he is a committed minister, a minister who labors and labors for Christ and works and works for the church, then he is worthy of double honor. |
| **#1046**<br>**Directives**<br><br>Declare–KJV<br>Instruction–NASB<br>**Directives–NIV**<br>Instructions–NKJV<br>Mention–NLT | παραγγέλλων = *paraggellōn*<br>Pronunciation: [par-ang-gel'-lone]<br>Parsing (part of speech): verb<br>  Mood—participle<br>  Tense—present<br>  Voice—active<br>  Case—nominative<br>  Gender—masculine<br>  Person—1st person | To command; to give strict orders; to give instructions; to charge.<br><br>**Practical Application**<br>Note how forceful Paul is: "In the following directives (*paraggellōn*) I have no praise for you." His forcefulness stresses the awesome importance of the Lord's Supper, and the |

# PRACTICAL WORD STUDIES
## in the New Testament

| ENGLISH WORD | GREEK WORD AND VERSE | THE WORD MEANS... |
|---|---|---|
| **POSB REFERENCE** (1 Cor.11:17) Note 1 | Number—singular<br>Stem or root—from παραγγέλλω<br>Concordance References:<br>⇒ Strong's #3853 paraggellö<br>⇒ NIV #4133 paraggellö<br>⇒ NASB #3853 paraggellö<br><br>**1 Cor. 11:17**<br>Now in this that I **declare** unto you I praise you not, that ye come together not for the better, but for the worse. [KJV]<br>But in giving this **instruction**, I do not praise you, because you come together not for the better but for the worse. [NASB]<br>In the following **directives** I have no praise for you, for your meetings do more harm than good. [NIV]<br>Now in giving these **instructions** I do not praise *you*, since you come together not for the better but for the worse. [NKJV]<br>But now when I **mention** this next issue, I cannot praise you. For it sounds as if more harm than good is done when you meet together. [NLT]<br>Τοῦτο δὲ **παραγγέλλων** οὐκ ἐπαινῶ, ὅτι οὐκ εἰς τὸ κρεῖττον ἀλλ εἰς τὸ ἧττον συνέρχεσθε. [GNS]<br>Τοῦτο δὲ **παραγγέλλων** οὐκ ἐπαινῶ ὅτι οὐκ εἰς τὸ κρεῖσσον ἀλλὰ εἰς τὸ ἧσσον συνέρχεσθε. [GNT] | absolute necessity to celebrate it as it should be celebrated. |
| **#1047 Dirty Language**<br><br>Filthy communication–KJV<br>Abusive speech–NASB<br>Filthy language–NIV<br>Filthy language–NKJV<br>**Dirty language–NLT**<br><br>**POSB REFERENCE** (Col.3:8-11; esp. v.8) Note 2, point 1e | αἰσχρολογίαν = *aischrologian*<br>Pronunciation: [ahee-skhrol-og-ee'-ahn]<br>Parsing (part of speech): noun<br>    Case—accusative<br>    Gender—feminine<br>    Number—singular<br>    Stem or root—from αἰσχρολογία, ας<br>Concordance References:<br>⇒ Strong's #148 aischrologia<br>⇒ NIV #155 aischrologia<br>⇒ NASB #148 aischrologia<br><br>**Col. 3:8**<br>But now ye also put off all these; anger, wrath, malice, blasphemy, **filthy communication** out of your mouth. [KJV]<br>But now you also, put them all aside: anger, wrath, malice, slander, *and* **abusive speech** from your mouth. [NASB]<br>But now you must rid yourselves of all such things as these: anger, rage, malice, slander, and **filthy language** from your lips. [NIV]<br>But now you yourselves are to put off all these: anger, wrath, malice, blasphemy, **filthy language** out of your mouth. [NKJV]<br>But now is the time to get rid of anger, rage, malicious behavior, slander, and **dirty language**. [NLT]<br>νυνὶ δὲ ἀπόθεσθε καὶ ὑμεῖς τὰ πάντα, ὀργήν, θυμόν, κακίαν, βλασφημίαν, **αἰσχρολογίαν** ἐκ τοῦ στόματος ὑμῶν [GNS]<br>νυνὶ δὲ ἀπόθεσθε καὶ ὑμεῖς τὰ πάντα, ὀργήν, θυμόν, κακίαν, βλασφημίαν, **αἰσχρολογίαν** ἐκ τοῦ στόματος ὑμῶν·[GNT] | Filthy language; filthy communication; abusive speech; dirty language; obscene speech.<br><br>**Practical Application**<br>If a believer is to follow and imitate God, he has to be pure in speech and conversation; he has to keep his mouth or tongue clean. He cannot let his mouth become foul and polluted, filthy and vile.<br>He is never, not once, to be engaged in "dirty language" (*aischrologian*): using the mouth in obscene, shameful, foul, polluted, base, immoral conduct and conversation. What an indictment of our day—a day of sodomy and perversion. And note: the word refers to both conduct and speech. How polluted and foul-mouthed so many have become—so much so that society could easily be known as a second Sodom and Gomorrah. |
| **#1048 Disagreement**<br><br>Contention–KJV<br>Sharp disagreement–NASB<br>Sharp disagreement–NIV<br>Contention–NKJV<br>**Disagreement–NLT** | παροξυσμός = *paroxusmos*<br>Pronunciation: [par-ox-oos-mos']<br>Parsing (part of speech): noun<br>    Case—nominative<br>    Gender—masculine<br>    Number—singular<br>    Stem or root—from παροξυσμός, οῦ<br>Concordance References:<br>⇒ Strong's #3948 paroxusmos<br>⇒ NIV #4237 paroxusmos<br>⇒ NASB #3948 paroxusmos | A sharp disagreement; a contention; a debate; a struggle; a conflict.<br><br>**Practical Application**<br>The idea is that of differing to the point of suffering pain. Contrary to the picture usually painted of the conflict, the picture seems to be that both men were hurting. The difference was sharp and both hearts were cut deeply. Each man was thoroughly convinced that he was right before the Lord; therefore, each argued strongly |

## Practical Word Studies in the New Testament

| ENGLISH WORD | GREEK WORD AND VERSE | THE WORD MEANS... |
|---|---|---|
| **POSB REFERENCE** (Acts 15:39) Note 2, point 1 | **Acts 15:39** And the **contention** was so sharp between them, that they departed asunder one from the other: and so Barnabas took Mark, and sailed unto Cyprus; [KJV] And there arose such a **sharp disagreement** that they separated from one another, and Barnabas took Mark with him and sailed away to Cyprus. [NASB] They had such a **sharp disagreement** that they parted company. Barnabas took Mark and sailed for Cyprus, [NIV] Then the **contention** became so sharp that they parted from one another. And so Barnabas took Mark and sailed to Cyprus; [NKJV] Their **disagreement** over this was so sharp that they separated. Barnabas took John Mark with him and sailed for Cyprus. [NLT] ἐγένετο οὖν **παροξυσμός**, ὥστε ἀποχωρισθῆναι αὐτοὺς ἀπ' ἀλλήλων, τόν τε Βαρναβᾶν παραλαβόντα τὸν Μᾶρκον, ἐκπλεῦσαι εἰς Κύπρον· [GNS] ἐγένετο δὲ **παροξυσμός** ὥστε ἀποχωρισθῆναι αὐτοὺς ἀπ' ἀλλήλων, τόν τε Βαρναβᾶν παραλαβόντα τὸν Μᾶρκον ἐκπλεῦσαι εἰς Κύπρον, [GNT] | for his position. This does not mean that they were cutting each other with sharp and ugly words. This is important to note, for sharp words should never be spoken among believers. But the opposing positions and convictions cut and hurt both hearts. They loved and respected each other, and their sharp conflict seemed irreconcilable. |
| **#1049 Disappeared** Received–KJV Received–NASB Hid–NIV Received–NKJV **Disappeared–NLT** **POSB REFERENCE** (Acts 1:10-11; esp. v.9) Note 5, point 1 | ὑπέλαβεν = *hupelaben* Pronunciation: [hoop-eh-la-ben'] Parsing (part of speech): verb     Mood—indicative     Tense—aorist     Voice—active     Person—3rd person     Number—singular     Stem or root—from ὑπολαμβάνω Concordance References: ⇒ Strong's #5274 hupolambanō ⇒ NIV #5696 hupolambanō ⇒ NASB #5274 hupolambanō **Acts 1:9** And when he had spoken these things, while they beheld, he was taken up; and a cloud **received** him out of their sight. [KJV] And after He had said these things, He was lifted up while they were looking on, and a cloud **received** Him out of their sight. [NASB] After he said this, he was taken up before their very eyes, and a cloud **hid** him from their sight. [NIV] Now when He had spoken these things, while they watched, He was taken up, and a cloud **received** Him out of their sight. [NKJV] It was not long after he said this that he was taken up into the sky while they were watching, and he **disappeared** into a cloud. [NLT] καὶ ταῦτα εἰπών, βλεπόντων αὐτῶν ἐπήρθη, καὶ νεφέλη **ὑπέλαβεν** αὐτὸν ἀπὸ τῶν ὀφθαλμῶν αὐτῶν. [GNS] καὶ ταῦτα εἰπὼν βλεπόντων αὐτῶν ἐπήρθη, καὶ νεφέλη **ὑπέλαβεν** αὐτὸν ἀπὸ τῶν ὀφθαλμῶν αὐτῶν. [GNT] | Hid, received, disappeared. **Practical Application** The point is this: it is as though the cloud made Christ "disappear" (*hupelaben*). The cloud was apparently the Shekinah glory (see POSB note 2—John 1:14). Christ had said He would return to earth in the clouds of heaven (Matthew 24:30; Matthew 26:64; Mark 13:26; cp. Rev. 1:7). Seeing such a dramatic ascension confirmed for the disciples (and for us) that Jesus' promise of returning to earth will take place just as He said. |
| **#1050 Disappoint** Ashamed–KJV **Disappoint–NASB** **Disappoint–NIV** **Disappoint–NKJV** **Disappoint–NLT** **POSB REFERENCE** (Rom.5:3-5; esp. v.5) Note 5, point 4 | καταισχύνει = *kataischunei* Pronunciation: [kat-ahee-skhoo'-neh-ee] Parsing (part of speech): verb     Mood—indicative     Tense—present     Voice—active     Person—3rd person     Number—singular     Stem or root—from καταισχύνω Concordance References: ⇒ Strong's #2617 kataischunō ⇒ NIV #2875 kataischunō ⇒ NASB #2617 kataischunō | To disappoint; to embarrass; to make ashamed; to humiliate; to disgrace. **Practical Application** Hope never disappoints: never shames, deludes, deceives, confounds, confuses. The believer, the person who is truly justified, will never be disappointed or shamed. He will see his hope fulfilled. He will live forever in the presence of God inheriting the promises God has given in His Word. |

# PRACTICAL WORD STUDIES
## in the NEW TESTAMENT

| ENGLISH WORD | GREEK WORD AND VERSE | THE WORD MEANS... |
|---|---|---|
| | **Romans 5:5**<br>And hope maketh not **ashamed**; because the love of God is shed abroad in our hearts by the Holy Ghost which is given unto us. [KJV]<br>And hope does not **disappoint**, because the love of God has been poured out within our hearts through the Holy Spirit who was given to us. [NASB]<br>And hope does not **disappoint** us, because God has poured out his love into our hearts by the Holy Spirit, whom he has given us. [NIV]<br>Now hope does not **disappoint**, because the love of God has been poured out in our hearts by the Holy Spirit who was given to us. [NKJV]<br>And this expectation will not **disappoint** us. For we know how dearly God loves us, because he has given us the Holy Spirit to fill our hearts with his love. [NLT]<br>ἡ δὲ ἐλπὶς οὐ **καταισχύνει**, ὅτι ἡ ἀγάπη τοῦ Θεοῦ ἐκκέχυται ἐν ταῖς καρδίαις ἡμῶν διὰ Πνεύματος Ἁγίου τοῦ δοθέντος ἡμῖν, [GNS]<br>ἡ δὲ ἐλπὶς οὐ **καταισχύνει**, ὅτι ἡ ἀγάπη τοῦ θεοῦ ἐκκέχυται ἐν ταῖς καρδίαις ἡμῶν διὰ πνεύματος ἁγίου τοῦ δοθέντος ἡμῖν. [GNT] | |
| **#1051**<br>**Disbelieved**<br><br>Unbelieving–KJV<br>**Disbelieved–NASB**<br>Refused to believe–NIV<br>Unbelieving–NKJV<br>Spurned God's message–NLT<br><br>**POSB REFERENCE**<br>(Acts 14:2)<br>Note 4, point 1 | ἀπειθήσαντες = apeithēsantes<br>Pronunciation: [ap-i-thoon'-tace]<br>Parsing (part of speech): verb<br>    Mood—participle<br>    Tense—aorist<br>    Voice—active<br>    Case—nominative<br>    Gender—masculine<br>    Number—plural<br>    Stem or root—from ἀπειθέω<br>Concordance References:<br>  ⇒ Strong's #544 apeitheō<br>  ⇒ NIV #578 apeitheō<br>  ⇒ NASB #544 apeitheō<br><br>**Acts 14:2**<br>But the **unbelieving** Jews stirred up the Gentiles, and made their minds evil affected against the brethren. [KJV]<br>But the Jews who **disbelieved** stirred up the minds of the Gentiles, and embittered them against the brethren. [NASB]<br>But the Jews who **refused to believe** stirred up the Gentiles and poisoned their minds against the brothers. [NIV]<br>But the **unbelieving** Jews stirred up the Gentiles and poisoned their minds against the brethren. [NKJV]<br>But the Jews who **spurned God's message** stirred up distrust among the Gentiles against Paul and Barnabas, saying all sorts of evil things about them. [NLT]<br>οἱ δὲ **ἀπειθοῦντες** Ἰουδαῖοι ἐπήγειραν καὶ ἐκάκωσαν τὰς ψυχὰς τῶν ἐθνῶν κατὰ τῶν ἀδελφῶν. [GNS]<br>οἱ δὲ **ἀπειθήσαντες** Ἰουδαῖοι ἐπήγειραν καὶ ἐκάκωσαν τὰς ψυχὰς τῶν ἐθνῶν κατὰ τῶν ἀδελφῶν. [GNT] | Refused to believe; unbelieving; disbelieved; to spurn God's message; to be disobedient; to be an unbeliever.<br><br>**Practical Application**<br>The idea is they were unwilling to believe or be persuaded. They deliberately withheld belief, disobeying God. |
| **#1052**<br>**Discerned**<br><br>**Discerned–KJV**<br>Appraised–NASB<br>**Discerned–NIV**<br>**Discerned–NKJV**<br>Means–NLT<br><br>**POSB REFERENCE**<br>(1 Cor.2:14)<br>Note 1, point 3 | ἀνακρίνεται = anakrinetai<br>Pronunciation: [an-ak-ree'-neh-tah-ee]<br>Parsing (part of speech): verb<br>    Mood—indicative<br>    Tense—present<br>    Voice—passive<br>    Person—3rd person<br>    Number—singular<br>    Stem or root—from ἀνακρίνω<br>Concordance References:<br>  ⇒ Strong's #350 anakrinō<br>  ⇒ NIV #373 anakrinō<br>  ⇒ NASB #350 anakrinō | Discerned, investigated, judged, scrutinized, examined, appraised, estimated.<br><br>**Practical Application**<br>Spiritual things have to be discerned by a living spirit, not by a natural man—a man without the Spirit—not by a man who is primarily living by his animal nature. Spiritual things can be discerned only by a spirit that is living. Spiritual things can be...<br>• investigated only by a living spirit<br>• judged only by a living spirit<br>• examined only by a living spirit<br>• estimated and valued only by a living spirit. |

# PRACTICAL WORD STUDIES
## in the NEW TESTAMENT

| ENGLISH WORD | GREEK WORD AND VERSE | THE WORD MEANS... |
|---|---|---|
| | **1 Cor. 2:14**<br>But the natural man receiveth not the things of the Spirit of God: for they are foolishness unto him: neither can he know them, because they are spiritually **discerned**. [KJV]<br>But a natural man does not accept the things of the Spirit of God; for they are foolishness to him, and he cannot understand them, because they are spiritually **appraised**. [NASB]<br>The man without the Spirit does not accept the things that come from the Spirit of God, for they are foolishness to him, and he cannot understand them, because they are spiritually **discerned**. [NIV]<br>But the natural man does not receive the things of the Spirit of God, for they are foolishness to him; nor can he know *them*, because they are spiritually **discerned**. [NKJV]<br>But people who aren't Christians can't understand these truths from God's Spirit. It all sounds foolish to them because only those who have the Spirit can understand what the Spirit **means**. [NLT]<br>ψυχικὸς δὲ ἄνθρωπος οὐ δέχεται τὰ τοῦ Πνεύματος τοῦ Θεοῦ· μωρία γὰρ αὐτῷ ἐστι, καὶ οὐ δύναται γνῶναι, ὅτι πνευματικῶς **ἀνακρίνεται**· [GNS]<br>ψυχικὸς δὲ ἄνθρωπος οὐ δέχεται τὰ τοῦ πνεύματος τοῦ θεοῦ, μωρία γὰρ αὐτῷ ἐστιν, καὶ οὐ δύναται γνῶναι, ὅτι πνευματικῶς **ἀνακρίνεται**· [GNT] | |
| **#1053**<br>**Discerner**<br><br>**Discerner**–KJV<br>Judge–NASB<br>Judges–NIV<br>**Discerner**–NKJV<br>Exposes–NLT<br><br>**POSB REFERENCE**<br>(Heb.4:11-13; esp. v.12)<br>Note 5, point 2e | κριτικός = *kritikos*<br>Pronunciation: [krit-ee-kos']<br>Parsing (part of speech): adjective<br>    Case—nominative<br>    Gender—masculine<br>    Number—singular<br>    Stem or root—from κριτικός, ή, όν<br>Concordance References:<br>  ⇒ Strong's #2924 kritikos<br>  ⇒ NIV #3217 kritikos<br>  ⇒ NASB #2924 kritikos<br><br>**Hebrews 4:12**<br>For the word of God is quick, and powerful, and sharper than any twoedged sword, piercing even to the dividing asunder of soul and spirit, and of the joints and marrow, and is a **discerner** of the thoughts and intents of the heart. [KJV]<br>For the word of God is living and active and sharper than any two-edged sword, and piercing as far as the division of soul and spirit, of both joints and marrow, and able to **judge** the thoughts and intentions of the heart. [NASB]<br>For the word of God is living and active. Sharper than any double-edged sword, it penetrates even to dividing soul and spirit, joints and marrow; it **judges** the thoughts and attitudes of the heart. [NIV]<br>For the word of God *is* living and powerful, and sharper than any two-edged sword, piercing even to the division of soul and spirit, and of joints and marrow, and is a **discerner** of the thoughts and intents of the heart. [NKJV]<br>For the word of God is full of living power. It is sharper than the sharpest knife, cutting deep into our innermost thoughts and desires. It **exposes** us for what we really are. [NLT]<br>ζῶν γὰρ ὁ λόγος τοῦ Θεοῦ, καὶ ἐνεργής, καὶ τομώτερος ὑπὲρ πᾶσαν μάχαιραν δίστομον, καὶ διϊκνούμενος ἄχρι μερισμοῦ ψυχῆς τὲ καὶ πνεύματος, ἁρμῶν τε καὶ μυελῶν, καὶ **κριτικὸς** ἐνθυμήσεων καὶ ἐννοιῶν καρδίας. [GNS]<br>Ζῶν γὰρ ὁ λόγος τοῦ θεοῦ καὶ ἐνεργὴς καὶ τομώτερος ὑπὲρ πᾶσαν μάχαιραν δίστομον καὶ διϊκνούμενος ἄχρι μερισμοῦ ψυχῆς καὶ πνεύματος, ἁρμῶν τε καὶ μυελῶν, καὶ **κριτικὸς** ἐνθυμήσεων καὶ ἐννοιῶν καρδίας· [GNT] | To judge; to discern; to expose; to sift and analyze.<br><br>**Practical Application**<br>The Word of God "discerns the thoughts and intents [purpose] of the heart."[KJV] "The Word of God is able to penetrate into the furthermost recesses of a person's spiritual being, sifting out and analyzing the thoughts and intents of the heart" (Kenneth Wuest. *Hebrews*, Vol. 2, p.89).<br>God's Word sees whether a person believes or does not believe His promise of rest. God's Word actually sees through the thoughts and purposes of a person. |

# PRACTICAL WORD STUDIES
## in the NEW TESTAMENT

| ENGLISH WORD | GREEK WORD AND VERSE | THE WORD MEANS... |
|---|---|---|
| **#1054**<br>**Discerning**<br><br>**Discerning–KJV**<br>Judge rightly–NASB<br>Recognizing–NIV<br>**Discerning–NKJV**<br>Honoring–NLT<br><br>**POSB**<br>**REFERENCE**<br>(1 Cor.11:27-30; esp. v.29)<br>Note 4, point 2 | διακρίνων = *diakrinōn*<br>Pronunciation: [dee-ak-ree'-noan]<br>Parsing (part of speech): verb<br>   Mood—participle<br>   Tense—present<br>   Voice—active<br>   Case—nominative<br>   Gender—masculine<br>   Number—singular<br>   Stem or root—from διακρίνω<br>Concordance References:<br>⇒ Strong's #1252 diakrinō<br>⇒ NIV #1359 diakrinō<br>⇒ NASB #1252 diakrinō<br><br>**1 Cor. 11:29**<br>For he that eateth and drinketh unworthily, eateth and drinketh damnation to himself, not **discerning** the Lord's body. [KJV]<br>For he who eats and drinks, eats and drinks judgment to himself, if he does not **judge** the body **rightly**. [NASB]<br>For anyone who eats and drinks without **recognizing** the body of the Lord eats and drinks judgment on himself. [NIV]<br>For he who eats and drinks in an unworthy manner eats and drinks judgment to himself, not **discerning** the Lord's body. [NKJV]<br>For if you eat the bread or drink the cup unworthily, not **honoring** the body of Christ, you are eating and drinking God's judgment upon yourself. [NLT]<br>ὁ γὰρ ἐσθίων καὶ πίνων ἀναξίως, κρίμα ἑαυτῷ ἐσθίει καὶ πίνει, μὴ **διακρίνων** τὸ σῶμα τοῦ Κυρίου. [GNS]<br>ὁ γὰρ ἐσθίων καὶ πίνων κρίμα ἑαυτῷ ἐσθίει καὶ πίνει μὴ **διακρίνων** τὸ σῶμα. [GNT] | To recognize; to discriminate; to distinguish; to evaluate, to judge rightly.<br><br>**Practical Application**<br>The person who eats the bread and drinks the cup unworthily just fails to think about what he is doing. He fails to discriminate and discern the seriousness of his act. If he thought about the matter, he would not partake of the Lord's Supper with unconfessed sin in his life, for such irreverence of the body and blood of the Lord stirs the judgment of God. |
| **#1055**<br>**Discernment**<br><br>Judgment–KJV<br>**Discernment–NASB**<br>Insight–NIV<br>**Discernment–NKJV**<br>Understanding–NLT<br><br>**POSB**<br>**REFERENCE**<br>(Philip.1:9-10; esp. v.9)<br>Note 7 | αἰσθήσει = *aisthēsei*<br>Pronunciation: [ah'ee-sthay-seh-ee]<br>Parsing (part of speech): noun<br>   Case—dative<br>   Gender—feminine<br>   Number—singular<br>   Stem or root—from αἴσθησις, εως<br>Concordance References:<br>⇒ Strong's #144 aisthēsis<br>⇒ NIV #151 aisthēsis<br>⇒ NASB #144 aisthēsis<br><br>**Philip. 1:9**<br>And this I pray, that your love may abound yet more and more in knowledge and *in* all **judgment**; [KJV]<br>And this I pray, that your love may abound still more and more in real knowledge and all **discernment**, [NASB]<br>And this is my prayer: that your love may abound more and more in knowledge and depth of **insight**, [NIV]<br>And this I pray, that your love may abound still more and more in knowledge and all **discernment**, [NKJV]<br>I pray that your love for each other will overflow more and more, and that you will keep on growing in your knowledge and **understanding**. [NLT]<br>καὶ τοῦτο προσεύχομαι, ἵνα ἡ ἀγάπη ὑμῶν ἔτι μᾶλλον καὶ μᾶλλον περισσεύῃ ἐν ἐπιγνώσει καὶ πάσῃ **αἰσθήσει**, [GNS]<br>καὶ τοῦτο προσεύχομαι, ἵνα ἡ ἀγάπη ὑμῶν ἔτι μᾶλλον καὶ μᾶλλον περισσεύῃ ἐν ἐπιγνώσει καὶ πάσῃ **αἰσθήσει** [GNT] | Insight, judgment, discernment, understanding, intelligence.<br><br>**Practical Application**<br>Love in the Bible never focuses upon *good feelings*. Feelings may and usually do come to the person who truly loves another person, but feelings are never the focus—not with true love. What then is the focus?<br>⇒ The focus of love is knowledge. If we truly love someone, we want to know that person. In fact, we want to know all we can about the person.<br>⇒ The force of love is discernment (*aisthēsei*). If we truly love someone, we not only want to know a person but we want to learn all we can about the person. We want to gather all the intelligence and facts possible and discern them so that we can please the person. |
| **#1056**<br>**Disciples,**<br>**Made Many** | μαθητεύσαντες ἱκανούς = *mathēteusantes hikanous*<br>Pronunciation: [math-ayt-yoo'-san-tehs hik-an-oos']<br>Parsing *mathēteusantes* (part of speech): verb<br>   Mood—participle<br>   Tense—aorist | Won a large number of disciples; taught many; made many disciples. |

# PRACTICAL WORD STUDIES
## in the NEW TESTAMENT

| ENGLISH WORD | GREEK WORD AND VERSE | THE WORD MEANS... |
|---|---|---|
| Taught many–KJV<br>**Made many disciples**–NASB<br>Won a large number of disciples–NIV<br>**Made many disciples**–NKJV<br>Making many disciples–NLT<br><br>**POSB REFERENCE**<br>(Acts 14:21)<br>Note 1, point 2 | Voice—active<br>Case—nominative<br>Gender—masculine<br>Number—plural<br>Stem or root—from μαθητεύω<br>Parsing *hikanous* (part of speech): pronominal adjective<br>    Case—accusative<br>    Gender—masculine<br>    Number—plural<br>    Stem or root—from ἱκανός, ή, όν<br>Concordance References:<br>⇒ Strong's #3100 mathēteuō + 2425 hikanos<br>⇒ NIV #3411 mathēteuō [won disciples]+ 2653 hikanos [large number]<br>⇒ NASB #3100 mathēteuō + 2425 hikanos<br><br>**Acts 14:21**<br>And when they had preached the gospel to that city, and had **taught many**, they returned again to Lystra, and to Iconium, and Antioch, [KJV]<br>And after they had preached the gospel to that city and had **made many disciples**, they returned to Lystra and to Iconium and to Antioch, [NASB]<br>They preached the good news in that city and **won a large number of disciples**. Then they returned to Lystra, Iconium and Antioch, [NIV]<br>And when they had preached the gospel to that city and **made many disciples**, they returned to Lystra, Iconium, and Antioch, [NKJV]<br>After preaching the Good News in Derbe and **making many disciples**, Paul and Barnabas returned again to Lystra, Iconium, and Antioch of Pisidia, [NLT]<br>εὐαγγελισάμενοί τε τὴν πόλιν ἐκείνην καὶ **μαθητεύσαντες ἱκανούς**, ὑπέστρεψαν εἰς τὴν Λύστραν καὶ Ἰκόνιον καὶ Ἀντιόχειαν, [GNS]<br>Εὐαγγελισάμενοί τε τὴν πόλιν ἐκείνην καὶ **μαθητεύσαντες ἱκανούς** ὑπέστρεψαν εἰς τὴν Λύστραν καὶ εἰς Ἰκόνιον καὶ εἰς Ἀντιόχειαν, [GNT] | **Practical Application**<br>The ministry of the preachers (Paul and Barnabas) was to make disciples. They not only preached, but they had taken the believers and made disciples out of them (see POSB note, Discipleship—Acts 13:5-6 for discussion). |
| **#1057**<br>**Disciples, Making Many**<br><br>Taught many–KJV<br>Made many disciples–NASB<br>Won a large number of disciples–NIV<br>Made many disciples–NKJV<br>**Making many disciples**–NLT<br><br>**POSB REFERENCE**<br>(Acts 14:21)<br>Note 1, point 2 | μαθητεύσαντες ἱκανούς = *mathēteusantes hikanous*<br>Pronunciation: [math-ayt-yoo'-san-tehs hik-an-oos']<br>Parsing *mathēteusantes* (part of speech): verb<br>    Mood—participle<br>    Tense—aorist<br>    Voice—active<br>    Case—nominative<br>    Gender—masculine<br>    Number—plural<br>    Stem or root—from μαθητεύω<br>Parsing *hikanous* (part of speech): pronominal adjective<br>    Case—accusative<br>    Gender—masculine<br>    Number—plural<br>    Stem or root—from ἱκανός, ή, όν<br>Concordance References:<br>⇒ Strong's #3100 mathēteuō + 2425 hikanos<br>⇒ NIV #3411 mathēteuō [won disciples]+ 2653 hikanos [large number]<br>⇒ NASB #3100 mathēteuō + 2425 hikanos<br><br>**Acts 14:21**<br>And when they had preached the gospel to that city, and had **taught many**, they returned again to Lystra, and to Iconium, and Antioch, [KJV]<br>And after they had preached the gospel to that city and had **made many disciples**, they returned to Lystra and to Iconium and to Antioch, [NASB]<br>They preached the good news in that city and **won a large number of disciples**. Then they returned to Lystra, Iconium and Antioch, [NIV]<br>And when they had preached the gospel to that city and **made many disciples**, they returned to Lystra, Iconium, and Antioch, [NKJV] | Won a large number of disciples; taught many; made many disciples.<br><br>**Practical Application**<br>The ministry of the preachers (Paul and Barnabas) was to make disciples. They not only preached, but they had taken the believers and made disciples out of them (see POSB note, Discipleship—Acts 13:5-6 for discussion). |

# PRACTICAL WORD STUDIES
## in the New Testament

| ENGLISH WORD | GREEK WORD AND VERSE | THE WORD MEANS... |
|---|---|---|
| | After preaching the Good News in Derbe and **making many disciples**, Paul and Barnabas returned again to Lystra, Iconium, and Antioch of Pisidia. [NLT]<br><br>εὐαγγελισάμενοί τε τὴν πόλιν ἐκείνην καὶ **μαθητεύσαντες ἱκανοὺς**, ὑπέστρεψαν εἰς τὴν Λύστραν καὶ Ἰκόνιον καὶ Ἀντιόχειαν, [GNS]<br><br>Εὐαγγελισάμενοί τε τὴν πόλιν ἐκείνην καὶ **μαθητεύσαντες ἱκανοὺς** ὑπέστρεψαν εἰς τὴν Λύστραν καὶ εἰς Ἰκόνιον καὶ εἰς Ἀντιόχειαν [GNT] | |
| **#1058**<br>**Discipline**<br><br>Nurture–KJV<br>**Discipline**–NASB<br>Training–NIV<br>Training–NKJV<br>**Discipline**–NLT<br><br>**POSB REFERENCE**<br>(Eph.6:4)<br>Note 2, point 2 | παιδείᾳ = paideia<br>Pronunciation: [pahee-di'-ah]<br>Parsing (part of speech): noun<br>   Case—dative<br>   Gender—feminine<br>   Number—singular<br>   Stem or root—from παιδεία, ας<br>Concordance References:<br>⇒ Strong's #3809 paideia<br>⇒ NIV #4082 paideia<br>⇒ NASB #3809 paideia<br><br>**Ephes. 6:4**<br>And, ye fathers, provoke not your children to wrath: but bring them up in the **nurture** and admonition of the Lord. [KJV]<br><br>And, fathers, do not provoke your children to anger; but bring them up in the **discipline** and instruction of the Lord. [NASB]<br><br>Fathers, do not exasperate your children; instead, bring them up in the **training** and instruction of the Lord. [NIV]<br><br>And you, fathers, do not provoke your children to wrath, but bring them up in the **training** and admonition of the Lord. [NKJV]<br><br>And now a word to you fathers. Don't make your children angry by the way you treat them. Rather, bring them up with the **discipline** and instruction approved by the Lord. [NLT]<br><br>καὶ οἱ πατέρες, μὴ παροργίζετε τὰ τέκνα ὑμῶν, ἀλλ᾽ ἐκτρέφετε αὐτὰ ἐν **παιδείᾳ** καὶ νουθεσίᾳ Κυρίου. [GNS]<br><br>Καὶ οἱ πατέρες, μὴ παροργίζετε τὰ τέκνα ὑμῶν ἀλλὰ ἐκτρέφετε αὐτὰ ἐν **παιδείᾳ** καὶ νουθεσίᾳ κυρίου. [GNT] | To train; to nurture; to discipline. The word discipline (*paideia*) means "the whole training and education of children which [involves]...the cultivation of mind and morals...commands and admonitions...reproof and punishment...correcting mistakes and curbing the passions...the increase of virtue" (*Thayers Greek-English Lexicon of the New Testament*. New York: American Book Co.).<br><br>**Practical Application**<br>A parent is to bring up a child in the ways of the Lord, in the nurture and admonition of the Lord. |
| **#1059**<br>**Discipline**<br><br>Exercise–KJV<br>**Discipline**–NASB<br>Training–NIV<br>Exercise–NKJV<br>Exercise–NLT<br><br>**POSB REFERENCE**<br>(1 Tim.4:8)<br>Note 4, point 1 | γυμνασία = gumnasia<br>Pronunciation: [goom-nas-ee'-ah]<br>Parsing (part of speech): noun<br>   Case—nominative<br>   Gender—feminine<br>   Number—singular<br>   Stem or root—from γυμνασία, ας<br>Concordance References:<br>⇒ Strong's #1129 gumnasia<br>⇒ NIV #1215 gumnasia<br>⇒ NASB #1129 gumnasia<br><br>**1 Tim. 4:8**<br>For bodily **exercise** profiteth little: but godliness is profitable unto all things, having promise of the life that now is, and of that which is to come. [KJV]<br><br>For bodily **discipline** is only of little profit, but godliness is profitable for all things, since it holds promise for the present life and also for the life to come. [NASB]<br><br>For physical **training** is of some value, but godliness has value for all things, holding promise for both the present life and the life to come. [NIV]<br><br>For bodily **exercise** profits a little, but godliness is profitable for all things, having promise of the life that now is and of that which is to come. [NKJV]<br><br>Physical **exercise** has some value, but spiritual exercise is much more important, for it promises a reward in both this life and the next. [NLT] | Training, exercise, discipline.<br><br>**Practical Application**<br>The minister is to discipline (*gumnasia*) himself in godliness as much as an Olympic athlete exercises his body. How much energy, effort, time, and dedication does an Olympic athlete put into his training? His sport is his life—unequivocally so. So it is with the minister: godliness is to be his life. All of his energy, effort, time, and dedication are to be given over to godliness. The minister is to know *no discipline* but the discipline of godliness. |

# PRACTICAL WORD STUDIES
## in the New Testament

| ENGLISH WORD | GREEK WORD AND VERSE | THE WORD MEANS... |
|---|---|---|
| | ἡ γὰρ σωματικὴ **γυμνασία** πρὸς ὀλίγον ἐστὶν ὠφέλιμος· ἡ δὲ εὐσέβεια πρὸς πάντα ὠφέλιμός ἐστιν, ἐπαγγελίαν ἔχουσα ζωῆς τῆς νῦν καὶ τῆς μελλούσης. [GNS]<br><br>ἡ γὰρ σωματικὴ **γυμνασία** πρὸς ὀλίγον ἐστὶν ὠφέλιμος, ἡ δὲ εὐσέβεια πρὸς πάντα ὠφέλιμός ἐστιν, ἐπαγγελίαν ἔχουσα ζωῆς τῆς νῦν καὶ τῆς μελλούσης. [GNT] | |
| **#1060**<br>**Discipline**<br><br>Sound mind–KJV<br>**Discipline–NASB**<br>Self-discipline–NIV<br>Sound mind–NKJV<br>Self-discipline–NLT<br><br>**POSB REFERENCE**<br>(2 Tim. 1:7)<br>Note 2, point 3 | σωφρονισμοῦ = söphronismou<br>Pronunciation: [so-fron-is-moo']<br>Parsing (part of speech): noun<br>    Case—genitive<br>    Gender—masculine<br>    Number—singular<br>Stem or root—from σωφρονισμός, οῦ<br>Concordance References:<br>  ⇒ Strong's #4995 söphronismos<br>  ⇒ NIV #5406 söphronismos<br>  ⇒ NASB #4995 söphronismos<br><br>**2 Tim. 1:7**<br>For God hath not given us the spirit of fear; but of power, and of love, and of a **sound mind**. [KJV]<br>For God has not given us a spirit of timidity, but of power and love and **discipline**. [NASB]<br>For God did not give us a spirit of timidity, but a spirit of power, of love and of **self-discipline**. [NIV]<br>For God has not given us a spirit of fear, but of power and of love and of a **sound mind**. [NKJV]<br>For God has not given us a spirit of fear and timidity, but of power, love, and **self-discipline**. [NLT]<br>οὐ γὰρ ἔδωκεν ἡμῖν ὁ Θεὸς πνεῦμα δειλίας, ἀλλὰ δυνάμεως καὶ ἀγάπης καὶ **σωφρονισμοῦ**. [GNS]<br>οὐ γὰρ ἔδωκεν ἡμῖν ὁ Θεὸς πνεῦμα δειλίας ἀλλὰ δυνάμεως καὶ ἀγάπης καὶ **σωφρονισμοῦ**. [GNT] | Self-discipline, sound mind, discipline, self-control; the ability to control one's emotions, feelings, and thoughts in the midst of trials and circumstances, no matter how severe and stressful; to have sound judgment.<br><br>**Practical Application**<br>The Holy Spirit infuses a discipline into the believer's spirit. It is just as the verse says, a sound mind—the mastery over one's mind, over one's heart and life despite the trial or opposition. When the believer begins to live and bear testimony for Christ, the Holy Spirit gives him a sound mind—a most glorious gift. |
| **#1061**<br>**Disciplined**<br><br>Watch–KJV<br>Sober spirit–NASB<br>Self-controlled–NIV<br>Watchful–NKJV<br>**Disciplined–NLT**<br><br>**POSB REFERENCE**<br>(1 Pt.4:7)<br>Note 2<br><br>See also POSB REF:<br>(1 Pt.1:13)<br>Note 1, point 2 | νήψατε = nëpsate<br>Pronunciation: [nay'-psah-teh]<br>Parsing (part of speech): verb<br>    Mood—imperative<br>    Tense—aorist<br>    Voice—active<br>    Person—2nd person<br>    Number—plural<br>Stem or root—from νήφω<br>Concordance References:<br>  ⇒ Strong's #3525 nëphö<br>  ⇒ NIV #3768 nëphö<br>  ⇒ NASB #3525 nëphö<br><br>**1 Peter 4:7**<br>But the end of all things is at hand: be ye therefore sober, and **watch** unto prayer. [KJV]<br>The end of all things is at hand; therefore, be of sound judgment and **sober spirit** for the purpose of prayer. [NASB]<br>The end of all things is near. Therefore be clear minded and **self-controlled** so that you can pray. [NIV]<br>But the end of all things is at hand; therefore be serious and **watchful** in your prayers. [NKJV]<br>The end of the world is coming soon. Therefore, be earnest and **disciplined** in your prayers. [NLT]<br>Πάντων δὲ τὸ τέλος ἤγγικε· σωφρονήσατε οὖν καὶ **νήψατε** εἰς τὰς προσευχάς· [GNS]<br>Πάντων δὲ τὸ τέλος ἤγγικεν. σωφρονήσατε οὖν καὶ **νήψατε** εἰς προσευχάς· [GNT] | To be self-controlled; to watch; to have a sober spirit; to be disciplined; to stay sober and alert and awake at all times.<br><br>**Practical Application**<br>This says two things.<br>1. The believer is to keep his mind disciplined, always watching. He is not to drink intoxicating beverages or take drugs or do anything else that numbs his mind. He is to keep his mind sober and alert at all times. He is not to be escaping reality; he is to be grasping reality. He is to be always praying for all things, and he cannot be praying if his mind is numb because of drink and drugs.<br>2. The believer is to keep his mind alert, keep it from being sleepy-eyed and lazy and wandering about. The mind is always thinking; it is always upon something; it is never without thought. Therefore, the believer is to keep his mind alert and active. He is to control his thoughts even to the point of captivating every thought (2 Cor.10:4-5). Every moment that his thoughts are not engaged with the necessary activities of life, he is to focus his thoughts upon prayer. Even while carrying on the activities of life, he needs to flicker his thoughts to prayer here and there. He needs to acknowledge God in all His ways. This is what it means to watch and pray. The believer is to keep his mind disciplined and alert to every opportunity to pray. |

# PRACTICAL WORD STUDIES
## in the New Testament

| ENGLISH WORD | GREEK WORD AND VERSE | THE WORD MEANS... |
|---|---|---|
| **#1062**<br>**Disciplines**<br><br>Chasteneth–KJV<br>**Disciplines–NASB**<br>**Disciplines–NIV**<br>Chastens–NKJV<br>**Disciplines–NLT**<br><br>**POSB REFERENCE**<br>(Heb.12:5-13; esp. v.6)<br>Introduction | παιδεύει = *paideuei*<br>Pronunciation: [pahee-dyoo'-eh-ee]<br>Parsing (part of speech): verb<br>   Mood—indicative<br>   Tense—present<br>   Voice—active<br>   Person—3rd person<br>   Number—singular<br>   Stem or root—from παιδεύω<br>Concordance References:<br>  ⇒ Strong's #3811 paideuō<br>  ⇒ NIV #4084 paideuō<br>  ⇒ NASB #3811 paideuō<br><br>**Hebrews 12:6**<br>For whom the Lord loveth he **chasteneth**, and scourgeth every son whom he receiveth. [KJV]<br><br>For those WHOM THE Lord loves He **disciplines**, And He scourges every son whom He receives." [NASB]<br><br>Because the Lord **disciplines** those he loves, and he punishes everyone he accepts as a son." [NIV]<br><br>*For whom the* LORD *loves He* **chastens**, *And scourges every son whom He receives."* [NKJV]<br><br>For the Lord **disciplines** those he loves, and he punishes those he accepts as his children." [NLT]<br><br>ὃν γὰρ ἀγαπᾷ Κύριος **παιδεύει**· μαστιγοῖ δὲ πάντα υἱὸν ὃν παραδέχεται. [GNS]<br><br>ὃν γὰρ ἀγαπᾷ κύριος **παιδεύει**, μαστιγοῖ δὲ πάντα υἱὸν ὃν παραδέχεται. [GNT] | To discipline; to chasten; to correct; to train; to instruct; to teach; to beat; to whip.<br><br>**Practical Application**<br>God does not cause bad and evil in life. God loves man and loves this world. Therefore, God's concern is not to cause problems and pain for us; His concern is to deliver us through all the trouble and pain on earth and to save us for heaven and eternity. How does God do this? By disciplining us. What does disciplining (*paideuei*) mean? When we think of discipline, we usually think of chastisement and correction and it does mean this. But it also means to train and teach and instruct a person. Both meanings are included in the Biblical word *discipline and chastisement* (cp. A.T. Robertson. *Word Pictures in the New Testament*, Vol. 5, p.435). God does two things with us:<br>1. First, when we face some trial and sin in life, God stirs us to stand fast and to conquer the trial or to turn away from the sin. He guides, directs, teaches, trains, and instructs us all along the way, making us stronger and stronger in life and drawing us closer and closer to Him. God does not want the trials and sins of life to defeat and engulf us; He wants them to strengthen us. He wants to use them to discipline and teach us more and more endurance and He wants to teach us to trust and depend upon Him more and more. But note this: we have to let God work in our hearts to use the trials to strengthen us. We cannot wallow around in self-pity or react against the trials and problems that attack us. We must turn to God—truly turn to God—and ask Him for help and strength and let Him help us.<br>    An illustration is this. A small innocent baby who is crippled in an automobile accident by a drunkard is not being chastised or corrected by God. The child has done nothing for which to be chastised. The child is crippled because of a sinful man who followed the path of Satan, crippled because he lives in a corruptible world. God loves the child, and God will look after the child as the child grows if the child will look to God for help. God will use the child's sufferings...<br>  God will teach and discipline the *growing child* to endure more and more, making him stronger and stronger.<br>  God will teach and discipline the *growing* child to trust and depend upon Christ more and more and to fellowship and commune with Christ more and more.<br>  God will use the endurance and faith of the *growing* child as a testimony to the love and care of God—as a testimony to the living reality and delivering power of God that can conquer all the trials and sorrows of life, even that of death.<br>2. Second, when we fail and cave in to the trial and sin, God lets us reap what we have sown. We bear the results of our sin; but even during sin and failure, God loves us. He loves and works with us, convicting us by His |

# PRACTICAL WORD STUDIES
## in the NEW TESTAMENT

| ENGLISH WORD | GREEK WORD AND VERSE | THE WORD MEANS... |
|---|---|---|
| | | Spirit to repent. He then uses the suffering of the sin to stir us to think of Him and our failure. God takes the sufferings that are caused by trials and sins, using them to correct and discipline us. This is the key statement, and it is what we must always remember when dealing with all the bad and evil things upon earth. God does not cause them; we cause them, and the corruptible world in which we live causes them, and the archenemy Satan causes them. God loves us and has nothing in mind for us except love and the very best of everything. Therefore, God takes all the bad and evil—all the suffering of bad and evil— and He uses it all to make us think about Him and our failure. He uses the suffering caused by sin and trials to correct and discipline us, to stir us to draw near Him in trust, dependence, and love, and to live like we should. |
| #1063 **Disclose** Manifest–KJV **Disclose–NASB** Show–NIV Manifest–NKJV Reveal–NLT **POSB REFERENCE** (Jn.14:21) *Deeper Study #3* | ἐμφανίσω = *emphanisō* Pronunciation: [em-fahn-ee'-so] Parsing (part of speech): verb  Mood—indicative  Tense—future  Voice—active  Person—1st person  Number—singular  Stem or root—from ἐμφανίζω Concordance References: ⇒ Strong's #1718 emphanizo ⇒ NIV #1872 emphanizo ⇒ NASB #1718 emphanizo  **John 14:21** He that hath my commandments, and keepeth them, he it is that loveth me: and he that loveth me shall be loved of my Father, and I will love him, and will **manifest** myself to him. [KJV] "He who has My commandments and keeps them, he it is who loves Me; and he who loves Me shall be loved by My Father, and I will love him, and will **disclose** Myself to him." [NASB] Whoever has my commands and obeys them, he is the one who loves me. He who loves me will be loved by my Father, and I too will love him and **show** myself to him." [NIV] He who has My commandments and keeps them, it is he who loves Me. And he who loves Me will be loved by My Father, and I will love him and **manifest** Myself to him." [NKJV] Those who obey my commandments are the ones who love me. And because they love me, my Father will love them, and I will love them. And I will **reveal** myself to each one of them." [NLT] ὁ ἔχων τὰς ἐντολάς μου καὶ τηρῶν αὐτάς, ἐκεῖνός ἐστιν ὁ ἀγαπῶν με· ὁ δὲ ἀγαπῶν με, ἀγαπηθήσεται ὑπὸ τοῦ πατρός μου· καὶ ἐγὼ ἀγαπήσω αὐτόν, καὶ **ἐμφανίσω** αὐτῷ ἐμαυτόν. [GNS] ὁ ἔχων τὰς ἐντολάς μου καὶ τηρῶν αὐτὰς ἐκεῖνός ἐστιν ὁ ἀγαπῶν με· ὁ δὲ ἀγαπῶν με ἀγαπηθήσεται ὑπὸ τοῦ πατρός μου, κἀγὼ ἀγαπήσω αὐτὸν καὶ **ἐμφανίσω** αὐτῷ ἐμαυτόν. [GNT] | To show; to manifest; to disclose; to reveal; to appear; to make known. **Practical Application** When "disclose" (*emphanisō*) is used in the sense of an unveiling or revelation, it suggests that a new thing has come to light, that something never known by man before is made known. Some mystery has now been revealed. It is something that cannot be discovered by man's reason or wisdom. It is a mystery that is hidden from man and beyond his grasp. Here in John 14:21-22, it means that Jesus' presence is revealed (brought to light), illuminated, manifested, quickened in the life of the believer. It means that He manifests Himself to His disciples in a very special way. He discloses His person, His nature, His goodness. He illuminates Himself within their hearts and lives. He gives a very special consciousness within their souls. (See POSB note—John 14:21-22; POSB *Deeper Study #1*—Acts 2:1-4.) |
| #1064 **Discord** Variance–KJV Strife–NASB **Discord–NIV** Contentions–NKJV Quarreling–NLT | ἔρις = *eris* Pronunciation: [er'-is] Parsing (part of speech): noun  Case—nominative  Gender—feminine  Number—singular  Stem or root—from ἔρις, ιδος | Discord, variance, strife, quarreling, contention, fighting, struggling, dissension, wrangling, selfish rivalry. **Practical Application** It means that a person fights against another person in order to get something: position, pro- |

# PRACTICAL WORD STUDIES
## in the NEW TESTAMENT

| ENGLISH WORD | GREEK WORD AND VERSE | THE WORD MEANS... |
|---|---|---|
| **POSB REFERENCE** (Gal.5:19-21; esp. v.20) Note 2 | Concordance References:<br>⇒ Strong's #2054 eris<br>⇒ NIV #2251 eris<br>⇒ NASB #2054 eris<br><br>**Galatians 5:20**<br>Idolatry, witchcraft, hatred, **variance**, emulations, wrath, strife, seditions, heresies, [KJV]<br>Idolatry, sorcery, enmities, **strife**, jealousy, outbursts of anger, disputes, dissensions, factions, [NASB]<br>Idolatry and witchcraft; hatred, **discord**, jealousy, fits of rage, selfish ambition, dissensions, factions [NIV]<br>Idolatry, sorcery, hatred, **contentions**, jealousies, outbursts of wrath, selfish ambitions, dissensions, heresies, [NKJV]<br>Idolatry, participation in demonic activities, hostility, **quarreling**, jealousy, outbursts of anger, selfish ambition, divisions, the feeling that everyone is wrong except those in your own little group, [NLT] εἰδωλολατρία, φαρμακεία, ἔχθραι, **ἔρεις**, ζῆλοι, θυμοί, ἐριθείαι, διχοστασίαι, αἱρέσεις, [GNS]<br>εἰδωλολατρία, φαρμακεία, ἔχθραι, **ἔρις**, ζῆλος, θυμοί, ἐριθείαι, διχοστασίαι, αἱρέσεις, [GNT] | motion, property, honor, recognition. He deceives, doing whatever has to be done to get what he is after. |
| **#1065**<br>**Discouraged**<br><br>Faint–KJV<br>Faint–NASB<br>Lose heart–NIV<br>**Discouraged–NKJV**<br>**Discouraged–NLT**<br><br>**POSB REFERENCE** (Heb.12:5-7, esp. v.5) Note 1, point 2 | ἐκλύου = ekluou<br>Pronunciation: [ek-loo'-oo]<br>Parsing (part of speech): verb<br>  Mood—imperative<br>  Tense—present<br>  Voice—passive<br>  Person—2nd person<br>  Number—singular<br>  Stem or root—from ἐκλύομαι<br>Concordance References:<br>⇒ Strong's #1590 ekluö<br>⇒ NIV #1725 ekluö<br>⇒ NASB #1590 ekluö<br><br>**Hebrews 12:5**<br>And ye have forgotten the exhortation which speaketh unto you as unto children, My son, despise not thou the chastening of the Lord, nor **faint** when thou art rebuked of him: [KJV]<br>And you have forgotten the exhortation which is addressed to you as sons, "My son, do not regard lightly the discipline of the Lord, Nor **FAINT** WHEN YOU ARE REPROVED BY Him; [NASB]<br>And you have forgotten that word of encouragement that addresses you as sons: "My son, do not make light of the Lord's discipline, and do not **lose heart** when he rebukes you, [NIV]<br>And you have forgotten the exhortation which speaks to you as to sons:"My son, do not despise the chastening of the LORD,Nor be **discouraged** when yu are rebuked by Him; [NKJV]<br>And have you entirely forgotten the encouraging words God spoke to you, his children? He said, "My child, don't ignore it when the Lord disciplines you,and don't be **discouraged** when he corrects you. [NLT]<br>καὶ ἐκλέλησθε τῆς παρακλήσεως, ἥτις ὑμῖν ὡς υἱοῖς διαλέγεται, Υἱέ μου, μὴ ὀλιγώρει παιδείας Κυρίου, μηδὲ **ἐκλύου**, ὑπ' αὐτοῦ ἐλεγχόμενος· [GNS]<br>καὶ ἐκλέλησθε τῆς παρακλήσεως, ἥτις ὑμῖν ὡς υἱοῖς διαλέγεται, Υἱέ μου, μὴ ὀλιγώρει παιδείας κυρίου μηδὲ **ἐκλύου** ὑπ' αὐτοῦ ἐλεγχόμενος· [GNT] | To lose heart; to be faint; to be discouraged; to give up; to give out; to lose heart; to collapse; to buckle under; to lose courage; to weaken.<br><br>**Practical Application**<br>The trials and sufferings of this world can become extremely heavy and painful—sometimes almost too much to bear. The rebuking hand of God that convicts us to repent and to correct our behavior becomes almost unbearable.<br>In either case, we are not to faint or give up. We are to turn totally to God in trust and dependence, asking for His help and strength. We have the glorious assurance that He will deliver us victoriously through all. He will make us stronger and make us a much greater witness for Him. God will save us and live within our hearts and lives—save us both now and eternally—save us even through death itself so that we may live with Him forever and ever in the new heavens and earth (1 Peter 3:10-13; Rev. 21:1f). |
| **#1066**<br>**Discreet**<br><br>Discreet–KJV<br>Sensible–NASB<br>Self-controlled–NIV | σώφρονας = söphronas<br>Pronunciation: [so'-frone-ahs]<br>Parsing (part of speech): adjective<br>  Case—accusative<br>  Gender—feminine<br>  Number—plural<br>  Stem or root—from σώφρων, ον<br>Concordance References: | To be self-controlled; to be discreet; to be sensible; to be careful; to live wisely; to be modest.<br><br>**Practical Application**<br>Young women are to be self-controlled or discreet (söphronas): this is the same Greek |

# PRACTICAL WORD STUDIES
## in the NEW TESTAMENT

| ENGLISH WORD | GREEK WORD AND VERSE | THE WORD MEANS... |
|---|---|---|
| **Discreet–NKJV**<br>Live wisely–NLT<br><br>**POSB REFERENCE**<br>(Tit.2:4-5; esp. v.5)<br>Note 4, point 4 | ⇒ Strong's #4998 söphrön<br>⇒ NIV #5409 söphrön<br>⇒ NASB #4998 söphrön<br><br>**Titus 2:5**<br>To be **discreet**, chaste, keepers at home, good, obedient to their own husbands, that the word of God be not blasphemed. [KJV]<br>To be **sensible**, pure, workers at home, kind, being subject to their own husbands, that the word of God may not be dishonored. [NASB]<br>To be **self-controlled** and pure, to be busy at home, to be kind, and to be subject to their husbands, so that no one will malign the word of God. [NIV]<br>To be **discreet**, chaste, homemakers, good, obedient to their own husbands, that the word of God may not be blasphemed. [NKJV]<br>To **live wisely** and be pure, to take care of their homes, to do good, and to be submissive to their husbands. Then they will not bring shame on the word of God. [NLT]<br>σώφρονας, ἁγνάς, οἰκουργούς ἀγαθάς, ὑποτασσομένας τοῖς ἰδίοις ἀνδράσιν, ἵνα μὴ ὁ λόγος τοῦ Θεοῦ βλασφημῆται [GNS]<br>σώφρονας ἁγνάς οἰκουργούς ἀγαθάς, ὑποτασσομένας τοῖς ἰδίοις ἀνδράσιν, ἵνα μὴ ὁ λόγος τοῦ θεοῦ βλασφημῆ͵αι. [GNT] | word translated *temperate* in Titus 2:2. (See POSB note, pt.3—Titus 2:2 for discussion and verses.) Simply stated, young women are not to live a life of license within the home or out in public: partying, drinking, overeating, indulging in any sense of the word. They are to curb their desires and emotions. |
| **#1067**<br>**Discussed It**<br><br>Reasoned–KJV<br>Reasoning–NASB<br>**Discussed it–NIV**<br>Reasoned–NKJV<br>Talked it over–NLT<br><br>**POSB REFERENCE**<br>(Mk.11:29-32; esp. v.31)<br>Note 3, point 2 | διελογίζοντο = *dielogizonto*<br>Pronunciation: [di-eh-log-id'-zon-tow]<br>Parsing (part of speech): verb<br>   Mood—indicative<br>   Tense—imperfect<br>   Voice—middle or passive deponent<br>   Person—3rd person<br>   Number—plural<br>   Stem or root—from διαλογίζομαι<br>Concordance References:<br>⇒ Strong's #3049 logizomai<br>⇒ NIV #1368 dialogizomai<br>⇒ NASB #1260 dialogizomai<br><br>**Mark 11:31**<br>And they **reasoned** with themselves, saying, If we shall say, From heaven; he will say, Why then did ye not believe him? [KJV]<br>And they began **reasoning** among themselves, saying, "If we say, 'From heaven,' He will say, 'Then why did you not believe him?' [NASB]<br>They **discussed it** among themselves and said, "If we say, 'From heaven,' he will ask, 'Then why didn't you believe him?' [NIV]<br>And they **reasoned** among themselves, saying, "If we say, 'From heaven,' He will say, 'Why then did you not believe him?' [NKJV]<br>They **talked it over** among themselves. "If we say it was from heaven, he will ask why we didn't believe him. [NLT]<br>καὶ ἐλογίζοντο πρὸς ἑαυτοὺς, λέγοντες, Ἐὰν εἴπωμεν, Ἐξ οὐρανοῦ, ἐρεῖ, Διατί οὖν οὐκ ἐπιστεύσατε αὐτῷ; [GNS]<br>καὶ διελογίζοντο πρὸς ἑαυτοὺς λέγοντες, Ἐὰν εἴπωμεν, Ἐξ οὐρανοῦ, ἐρεῖ, Διὰ τί [οὖν] οὐκ ἐπιστεύσατε αὐτῷ; [GNT] | To discuss; to reason; to talk over; to calculate something in the presence of others, to think through or reason aloud what is in the mind.<br><br>**Practical Application**<br>They [the chief priests, the teachers of the law, and the elders] discussed their answer among themselves. They did not just discuss it among (*en*) themselves, with each left to his own thoughts. This was a planned attack against Jesus, a deliberate rejection of Jesus. |
| **#1068**<br>**Discussing**<br><br>Disputed–KJV<br>**Discussing–NASB**<br>Arguing about–NIV<br>Disputed–NKJV<br>**Discussing–NLT** | διελογίζεσθε = *dielogizesthe*<br>Pronunciation: [dee-el-og-id'-zehs-theh]<br>Parsing (part of speech): verb<br>   Mood—indicative<br>   Tense—imperfect<br>   Voice—middle or passive deponent<br>   Person—2nd person<br>   Number—plural | To dispute, to discuss. It is arguing, complaining, questioning, contesting, hairsplitting, nit-picking, and bickering as well as reasoning.<br><br>**Practical Application**<br>In this Scripture, the word pictures an intense debate between the disciples of Christ. They |

# PRACTICAL WORD STUDIES
## in the New Testament

| ENGLISH WORD | GREEK WORD AND VERSE | THE WORD MEANS... |
|---|---|---|
| **POSB REFERENCE** (Mk.9:33) Note 1 | Stem or root—from διαλογίζομαι<br>Concordance References:<br>⇒ Strong's #1260 dialogizomai<br>⇒ NIV #1368 dialogizomai<br>⇒ NASB #1260 dialogizomai<br><br>**Mark 9:33**<br>And he came to Capernaum: and being in the house he asked them, What was it that ye **disputed** among yourselves by the way? [KJV]<br>And they came to Capernaum; and when He was in the house, He began to question them, "What were you **discussing** on the way?" [NASB]<br>They came to Capernaum. When he was in the house, he asked them, "What were you **arguing about** on the road?" [NIV]<br>Then He came to Capernaum. And when He was in the house He asked them, "What was it you **disputed** among yourselves on the road?" [NKJV]<br>After they arrived at Capernaum, Jesus and his disciples settled in the house where they would be staying. Jesus asked them, "What were you **discussing** out on the road?" [NLT]<br>Καὶ ἦλθεν εἰς Καπερναούμ· καὶ ἐν τῇ οἰκίᾳ γενόμενος, ἐπηρώτα αὐτούς, Τί ἐν τῇ ὁδῷ πρὸς ἑαυτοὺς **διελογίζεσθε**; [GNS]<br>Καὶ ἦλθον εἰς Καφαρναούμ. καὶ ἐν τῇ οἰκίᾳ γενόμενος ἐπηρώτα αὐτούς, Τί ἐν τῇ ὁδῷ **διελογίζεσθε**; [GNT] | argued over which of them would be the greatest in the kingdom of Christ. |
| **#1069**<br>**Discussing**<br><br>Hearing–KJV<br>Listening–NASB<br>Listening–NIV<br>Listening–NKJV<br>**Discussing–NLT**<br><br>**POSB REFERENCE** (Lk.2:46-47; esp. v.46) Note 3, point 2a | ἀκούοντα = akouonta<br>Pronunciation: [ah-koo'-on-tah]<br>Parsing (part of speech): verb<br>    Mood—participle<br>    Tense—present<br>    Voice—active<br>    Case—accusative<br>    Gender—masculine<br>    Number—singular<br>    Stem or root—from ἀκούω<br>Concordance References:<br>⇒ Strong's #191 akouō<br>⇒ NIV #201 akouō<br>⇒ NASB #191 akouō<br><br>**Luke 2:46**<br>And it came to pass, that after three days they found him in the temple, sitting in the midst of the doctors, both **hearing** them, and asking them questions. [KJV]<br>And it came about that after three days they found Him in the temple, sitting in the midst of the teachers, both **listening** to them, and asking them questions. [NASB]<br>After three days they found him in the temple courts, sitting among the teachers, **listening** to them and asking them questions. [NIV]<br>Now so it was *that* after three days they found Him in the temple, sitting in the midst of the teachers, both **listening** to them and asking them questions. [NKJV]<br>Three days later they finally discovered him. He was in the Temple, sitting among the religious teachers, **discussing** deep questions with them. [NLT]<br>καὶ ἐγένετο, μεθ' ἡμέρας τρεῖς εὗρον αὐτὸν ἐν τῷ ἱερῷ, καθεζόμενον ἐν μέσῳ τῶν διδασκάλων, καὶ **ἀκούοντα** αὐτῶν, καὶ ἐπερωτῶντα αὐτούς. [GNS]<br>καὶ ἐγένετο μετὰ ἡμέρας τρεῖς εὗρον αὐτὸν ἐν τῷ ἱερῷ καθεζόμενον ἐν μέσῳ τῶν διδασκάλων καὶ **ἀκούοντα** αὐτῶν καὶ ἐπερωτῶντα αὐτούς· [GNT] | To listen to; to hear; to attend; to harken; to perceive; to receive news of; to give heed to.<br><br>**Practical Application**<br>In this Scripture, Jesus was "hearing" what the teachers said. He listened closely, attentively, with rapt attention |
| **#1070**<br>**Discussing Deep Questions** | ἐπερωτῶντα = eperōtōnta<br>Pronunciation: [ep-er-o-town'-tah]<br>Parsing (part of speech): verb<br>    Mood—participle<br>    Tense—passive | To ask questions; to interrogate; to demand; to inquire; to examine; to discuss deep questions. |

## PRACTICAL WORD STUDIES
### in the New Testament

| ENGLISH WORD | GREEK WORD AND VERSE | THE WORD MEANS... |
|---|---|---|
| Asking...questions–KJV<br>Asking...questions–NASB<br>Asking...questions–NIV<br>Asking...questions–NKJV<br>**Discussing deep questions–NLT**<br><br>**POSB REFERENCE**<br>(Lk.2:46-47; esp. v.46)<br>Note 3, point 2b | Voice—active<br>Case—accusative<br>Gender—masculine<br>Number—singular<br>Stem or root—from ἐπερωτάω<br>Concordance References:<br>⇒ Strong's #1905 eperōtaō<br>⇒ NIV #2089 eperōtaō<br>⇒ NASB #1905 eperōtaō<br><br>**Luke 2:46**<br>And it came to pass, that after three days they found him in the temple, sitting in the midst of the doctors, both hearing them, and **asking** them **questions**. [KJV]<br>And it came about that after three days they found Him in the temple, sitting in the midst of the teachers, both listening to them, and **asking** them **questions**. [NASB]<br>After three days they found him in the temple courts, sitting among the teachers, listening to them and **asking** them **questions**. [NIV]<br>Now so it was *that* after three days they found Him in the temple, sitting in the midst of the teachers, both listening to them and **asking** them **questions**. [NKJV]<br>Three days later they finally discovered him. He was in the Temple, sitting among the religious teachers, **discussing deep questions** with them. [NLT]<br>καὶ ἐγένετο, μεθ' ἡμέρας τρεῖς εὗρον αὐτὸν ἐν τῷ ἱερῷ, καθεζόμενον ἐν μέσῳ τῶν διδασκάλων, καὶ ἀκούοντα αὐτῶν, καὶ **ἐπερωτῶντα** αὐτούς. [GNS]<br>καὶ ἐγένετο μετὰ ἡμέρας τρεῖς εὗρον αὐτὸν ἐν τῷ ἱερῷ καθεζόμενον ἐν μέσῳ τῶν διδασκάλων καὶ ἀκούοντα αὐτῶν καὶ **ἐπερωτῶντα** αὐτούς· [GNT] | **Practical Application**<br>In this Scripture, Christ was "discussing deep questions." He wanted answers, more understanding. He thirsted for truth and sought it. |
| #1071<br>**Disguise**<br><br>Transformed–KJV<br>**Disguise–NASB**<br>Masquerade–NIV<br>Transform–NKJV<br>Pretending–NLT<br><br>**POSB REFERENCE**<br>(2 Cor.11:13-15; esp. v.15)<br>Note 6 | μετασχηματίζονται = *metaschēmatizontai*<br>Pronunciation: [met-askh-ay-mat-id'-zon-tah-ee]<br>Parsing (part of speech): verb<br>  Mood—indicative<br>  Tense—present<br>  Voice—middle<br>  Person—3rd person<br>  Number—plural<br>  Stem or root—from μετασχηματίζω<br>Concordance References:<br>⇒ Strong's #3345 metaschēmatizō<br>⇒ NIV #3571 metaschēmatizō<br>⇒ NASB #3345 metaschēmatizō<br><br>**2 Cor. 11:15**<br>Therefore it is no great thing if his ministers also be **transformed** as the ministers of righteousness; whose end shall be according to their works. [KJV]<br>Therefore it is not surprising if his servants also **disguise** themselves as servants of righteousness; whose end shall be according to their deeds. [NASB]<br>It is not surprising, then, if his servants **masquerade** as servants of righteousness. Their end will be what their actions deserve. [NIV]<br>Therefore *it is* no great thing if his ministers also **transform** themselves into ministers of righteousness, whose end will be according to their works. [NKJV]<br>So it is no wonder his servants can also do it by **pretending** to be godly ministers. In the end they will get every bit of punishment their wicked deeds deserve. [NLT]<br>οὐ μέγα οὖν εἰ καὶ οἱ διάκονοι αὐτοῦ **μετασχηματίζονται** ὡς διάκονοι δικαιοσύνης, ὧν τὸ τέλος ἔσται κατὰ τὰ ἔργα αὐτῶν. [GNS]<br>οὐ μέγα οὖν εἰ καὶ οἱ διάκονοι αὐτοῦ **μετασχηματίζονται** ὡς διάκονοι δικαιοσύνης· ὧν τὸ τέλος ἔσται κατὰ τὰ ἔργα αὐτῶν. [GNT] | To masquerade; to disguise; to pretend; to transform; to fashion; to change one's outward appearance.<br><br>**Practical Application**<br>They pose as "gentlemen of the cloth," but they are nothing but cloth (A.T. Robertson. *Word Pictures in the New Testament*, Vol. 4, p.259). They are false ministers. |

# PRACTICAL WORD STUDIES
## in the NEW TESTAMENT

| ENGLISH WORD | GREEK WORD AND VERSE | THE WORD MEANS... |
|---|---|---|
| **#1072**<br>**Dishonest Gain, Not For**<br><br>Not for filthy lucre– KJV<br>Not for sordid gain– NASB<br>Not greedy for money–NIV<br>**Not for dishonest gain–NKJV**<br>Not grudgingly–NLT<br><br>**POSB REFERENCE**<br>(1 Pt.5:2-3; esp. v.2)<br>Note 2, point 2 | μηδὲ αἰσχροκερδῶς = mēde aischrokerdōs<br>Pronunciation: [may-deh' ahee-skhrok-er-doce']<br>Parsing *aischrokerdōs* (part of speech): adjective<br>    Type—adverb<br>    Stem or root—from αἰσχροκερδῶς<br>Concordance References:<br>⇒ Strong's #3366 mēde + 147 aischrokerdōs<br>⇒ NIV #3593 mēde [not] +154 aischrokerdōs [greedy for money]<br>⇒ NASB #3366 mēde + 147 aischrokerdōs<br><br>**1 Peter 5:2**<br>Feed the flock of God which is among you, taking the oversight thereof, not by constraint, but willingly; **not for filthy lucre**, but of a ready mind; [KJV]<br>Shepherd the flock of God among you, exercising oversight not under compulsion, but voluntarily, according to the will of God; and **not for sordid gain**, but with eagerness; [NASB]<br>Be shepherds of God's flock that is under your care, serving as overseers—not because you must, but because you are willing, as God wants you to be; **not greedy for money**, but eager to serve; [NIV]<br>Shepherd the flock of God which is among you, serving as overseers, not by compulsion but willingly, **not for dishonest gain** but eagerly; [NKJV]<br>Care for the flock of God entrusted to you. Watch over it willingly, **not grudgingly**—not for what you will get out of it, but because you are eager to serve God. [NLT]<br>ποιμάνατε τὸ ἐν ὑμῖν ποίμνιον τοῦ Θεοῦ, ἐπισκοποῦντες μὴ ἀναγκαστῶς, ἀλλ᾽ ἑκουσίως· **μηδὲ αἰσχροκερδῶς**, ἀλλὰ προθύμως, [GNS]<br>ποιμάνατε τὸ ἐν ὑμῖν ποίμνιον τοῦ θεοῦ [ἐπισκοποῦντες] μὴ ἀναγκαστῶς ἀλλὰ ἑκουσίως κατὰ θεόν, **μηδὲ αἰσχροκερδῶς** ἀλλὰ προθύμως, [GNT] | Not greedy for money; not greedy for sordid gain; not grudgingly; not greedy for material gain.<br><br>**Practical Application**<br>The elder or minister must take the oversight of the flock not for personal profit and gain, but with a ready mind. The Greek says that no person is to enter the ministry for "dishonest gain" (*mēde aischrokerdōs*), that is, for base gain, or for some soiled and dirty advantage. No person should ever enter the ministry...<br>• as a profession.<br>• as a means of livelihood.<br>• as a means to serve mankind.<br>• because people say he has the gifts for it.<br>• because people say he would make a good minister.<br>• because family and friends encourage him to enter the ministry.<br>All of these reasons usually surround a person's entrance into the ministry. But they must never be *the reasons* why a person enters the ministry and cares for God's people. The ministry is a *call from God*, and no person dare enter the ministry without a personal call to the ministry. But note: when the call comes, the person is to have a ready mind. He is to minister to God's people; he is to readily feed the flock of God. |
| **#1073**<br>**Dishonesty**<br><br>Dishonesty–KJV<br>Shame–NASB<br>Shameful–NIV<br>Shame–NKJV<br>Shameful–NLT<br><br>**POSB REFERENCE**<br>(2 Cor.4:2)<br>Note 2 | αἰσχύνης = aischunēs<br>Pronunciation: [ahee-skhoo'-nays]<br>Parsing (part of speech): noun<br>    Case—genitive<br>    Gender—feminine<br>    Number—singular<br>    Stem or root—from αἰσχύνη, ης<br>Concordance References:<br>⇒ Strong's #152 aischunē<br>⇒ NIV #158 aischunē<br>⇒ NASB #152 aischunē<br><br>**2 Cor. 4:2**<br>But have renounced the hidden things of **dishonesty**, not walking in craftiness, nor handling the word of God deceitfully; but by manifestation of the truth commending ourselves to every man's conscience in the sight of God. [KJV]<br>But we have renounced the things hidden because of **shame**, not walking in craftiness or adulterating the word of God, but by the manifestation of truth commending ourselves to every man's conscience in the sight of God. [NASB]<br>Rather, we have renounced secret and **shameful** ways; we do not use deception, nor do we distort the word of God. On the contrary, by setting forth the truth plainly we commend ourselves to every man's conscience in the sight of God. [NIV]<br>But we have renounced the hidden things of **shame**, not walking in craftiness nor handling the word of God deceitfully, but by manifestation of the truth commending ourselves to every man's conscience in the sight of God. [NKJV]<br>We reject all **shameful** and underhanded methods. We do not try to trick anyone, and we do not distort the word of God. We tell the truth before God, and all who are | Shame, shameful, disgrace, humiliate; scandal.<br><br>**Practical Application**<br>The ministry demands honesty and integrity in life and ministry. The hidden or secret things that shame and disgrace men, that cause scandals, are to have no part in the minister's life. |

# PRACTICAL WORD STUDIES
## in the NEW TESTAMENT

| ENGLISH WORD | GREEK WORD AND VERSE | THE WORD MEANS... |
|---|---|---|
| | honest know that. [NLT]<br>ἀλλ ἀπειπάμεθα τὰ κρυπτὰ τῆς **αἰσχύνης**, μὴ περιπατοῦντες ἐν πανουργίᾳ μηδὲ δολοῦντες τὸν λόγον τοῦ Θεοῦ, ἀλλὰ τῇ φανερώσει τῆς ἀληθείας συνιστῶντες ἑαυτοὺς πρὸς πᾶσαν συνείδησιν ἀνθρώπων ἐνώπιον τοῦ Θεοῦ. [GNS]<br>ἀλλὰ ἀπειπάμεθα τὰ κρυπτὰ τῆς **αἰσχύνης**, μὴ περιπατοῦντες ἐν πανουργίᾳ μηδὲ δολοῦντες τὸν λόγον τοῦ θεοῦ ἀλλὰ τῇ φανερώσει τῆς ἀληθείας συνιστάνοντες ἑαυτοὺς πρὸς πᾶσαν συνείδησιν ἀνθρώπων ἐνώπιον τοῦ θεοῦ. [GNT] | |
| **#1074**<br>**Dismissed, You Are Going To Be**<br><br>No longer–KJV<br>For you can no longer–NASB<br>Because [you] cannot–NIV<br>For you can no longer–NKJV<br>**You are going to be dismissed–NLT**<br><br>**POSB REFERENCE**<br>(Lk.16:1-7; esp. v.2)<br>Note 1, point 2a | οὐ γὰρ δύνῃ = ou gar dunē<br>Pronunciation: [oo gar doo-nay]<br>Parsing *dunē* (part of speech): verb<br>  Mood—indicative<br>  Tense—present<br>  Voice—middle or passive deponent<br>  Person—2nd person<br>  Number—singular<br>  Stem or root—from δύναμαι<br>Concordance References:<br>⇒ Strong's #1063 gar + dunamai 1410 + 3756 ou<br>⇒ NIV #1142 gar [because] + 1538 dunamai + 4024 ou [cannot]<br>⇒ NASB #1063 gar + dunamai 1410 + 3756 ou<br><br>**Luke 16:2**<br>And he called him, and said unto him, How is it that I hear this of thee? give an account of thy stewardship; for thou mayest be **no longer** steward. [KJV]<br>"And he called him and said to him, 'What is this I hear about you? Give an account of your stewardship, **for you can no longer** be steward.' [NASB]<br>So he called him in and asked him, 'What is this I hear about you? Give an account of your management, **because you cannot** be manager any longer.' [NIV]<br>So he called him and said to him, 'What is this I hear about you? Give an account of your stewardship, **for you can no longer** be steward.' [NKJV]<br>So his employer called him in and said, 'What's this I hear about your stealing from me? Get your report in order, because **you are going to be dismissed.**' [NLT]<br>καὶ φωνήσας αὐτόν, εἶπεν αὐτῷ, Τί τοῦτο ἀκούω περὶ σοῦ; ἀπόδος τὸν λόγον τῆς οἰκονομίας σου· **οὐ γὰρ δυνήσῃ** ἔτι οἰκονομεῖν. [GNS]<br>καὶ φωνήσας αὐτὸν εἶπεν αὐτῷ, Τί τοῦτο ἀκούω περὶ σοῦ; ἀπόδος τὸν λόγον τῆς οἰκονομίας σου, **οὐ γὰρ δύνῃ** ἔτι οἰκονομεῖν. [GNT] | Because you cannot; for you can no longer; you are going to be dismissed; not capable of; cannot do; not able to do.<br><br>**Practical Application**<br>In this Scripture, the manager is required to give an account of his actions, to prepare a final accounting. Note two important facts:<br>1. The Lord hears that the manager has been misusing His "possessions" (cp. Lk.16:1). The Lord had only heard about the embezzlement. The full evidence against the manager was not yet fully known. The Lord gave the manager a chance to prove his trust and faithfulness. The accounting did not mean that the manager would be dismissed from the Lord's estate (heaven, Kingdom of God), only that he must prove his trust and faithfulness. Of course, if the manager had not been faithful in looking after the Lord's goods, then he would be dismissed.<br>2. The final accounting is at death (Hebrews 9:27). If the manager is found to have been untrustworthy, he will be dismissed and discharged from the Lord's estate (kingdom, heaven, eternal life. See POSB *Deeper Study* #3—Matthew 19:23-24.) |
| **#1075**<br>**Disobedience**<br><br>Unbelief–KJV<br>**Disobedience–NASB**<br>**Disobedience–NIV**<br>**Disobedience–NKJV**<br>**Disobedience–NLT**<br><br>**POSB REFERENCE**<br>(Rom.11:32)<br>Note 5 | ἀπείθειαν = apeitheian<br>Pronunciation: [ap-i'-thi-ahn]<br>Parsing (part of speech): noun<br>  Case—accusative<br>  Gender—feminine<br>  Number—singular<br>  Stem or root—from ἀπείθεια, ας<br>Concordance References:<br>⇒ Strong's #543 apeitheia<br>⇒ NIV #577 apeitheia<br>⇒ NASB #543 apeitheia<br><br>**Romans 11:32**<br>For God hath concluded them all in **unbelief**, that he might have mercy upon all. [KJV]<br>For God has shut up all in **disobedience** that He might show mercy to all. [NASB]<br>For God has bound all men over to **disobedience** so that he may have mercy on them all. [NIV]<br>For God has committed them all to **disobedience**, that He might have mercy on all. [NKJV]<br>For God has imprisoned all people in their own **disobedience** so he could have mercy on everyone. [NLT] | Unbelief, disobedience, insubordination, defiance, disregard.<br><br>**Practical Application**<br>God has taken men, both Jews and Gentiles, and shut them up to disobedience (*apeitheian*). This is the judicial judgment of God (see POSB *Deeper Study* #2—Romans 11:7-10; POSB note—Romans 1:24; POSB *Deeper Study* #1—John 12:39-41). It is the picture of God's using sin and events for good. God takes sin and works it out for the good of the world. Man has chosen sin, choosing to go his own way in life, so God allows man to do his own thing. God locks man up in his own world of selfishness, allowing man to roam around in his world of sin. Why? So that man's true nature of sinfulness will be clearly seen, and thereby cause the honest and thinking man to seek God. God wishes to and will have mercy upon all, both Jew and Gentile; but before men can come to God, they must confess two |

# PRACTICAL WORD STUDIES
## in the NEW TESTAMENT

| ENGLISH WORD | GREEK WORD AND VERSE | THE WORD MEANS... |
|---|---|---|
| | συνέκλεισε γὰρ ὁ Θεὸς τοὺς πάντας εἰς **ἀπείθειαν** ἵνα τοὺς πάντας ἐλεήσῃ. [GNS]<br>συνέκλεισεν γὰρ ὁ Θεὸς τοὺς πάντας εἰς **ἀπείθειαν**, ἵνα τοὺς πάντας ἐλεήσῃ. [GNT] | things:<br>⇒ that they are sinful and dying creatures in desperate need of God.<br>⇒ that God exists and that He will have mercy upon the person who diligently seeks Him. |
| #1076<br>**Disobedience**<br><br>Disobedience–KJV<br>Disobedience–NASB<br>Disobedience–NIV<br>Disobedience–NKJV<br>Disobedience–NLT<br><br>**POSB REFERENCE**<br>(Heb.2:2)<br>Note 2 | **παρακοή** = *parakoē*<br>Pronunciation: [par-ak-o-ay']<br>Parsing (part of speech): noun<br>    Case—nominative<br>    Gender—feminine<br>    Number—singular<br>    Stem or root—from παρακοή, ῆς<br>Concordance References:<br>⇒ Strong's #3876 parakoē<br>⇒ NIV #4157 parakoē<br>⇒ NASB #3876 parakoē<br><br>**Hebrews 2:2**<br>For if the word spoken by angels was stedfast, and every transgression and **disobedience** received a just recompence of reward; [KJV]<br>For if the word spoken through angels proved unalterable, and every transgression and **disobedience** received a just recompense, [NASB]<br>For if the message spoken by angels was binding, and every violation and **disobedience** received its just punishment, [NIV]<br>For if the word spoken through angels proved steadfast, and every transgression and **disobedience** received a just reward, [NKJV]<br>The message God delivered through angels has always proved true, and the people were punished for every violation of the law and every act of **disobedience**. [NLT]<br>εἰ γὰρ ὁ δι' ἀγγέλων λαληθεὶς λόγος ἐγένετο βέβαιος, καὶ πᾶσα παράβασις καὶ **παρακοὴ** ἔλαβεν ἔνδικον μισθαποδοσίαν, [GNS]<br>εἰ γὰρ ὁ δι' ἀγγέλων λαληθεὶς λόγος ἐγένετο βέβαιος καὶ πᾶσα παράβασις καὶ **παρακοὴ** ἔλαβεν ἔνδικον μισθαποδοσίαν, [GNT] | Disobedience, disloyalty. It means to neglect, refuse, and fail to obey the law of God.<br><br>**Practical Application**<br>To disobey God is sin, and the disobedient are to be punished. The great danger was to deliberately reject the law of God. If a person deliberately rejected God's law, he was sentenced to die, and the punishment was irrevocable. |
| #1077<br>**Disobedient**<br><br>Believed not–KJV<br>**Disobedient–NASB**<br>Refused to believe–NIV<br>Did not believe–NKJV<br>Rejected–NLT<br><br>**POSB REFERENCE**<br>(Acts 19:2-9; esp. v.9)<br>Note 2, point 2d | **ἠπείθουν** = *ēpeithoun*<br>Pronunciation: [ap-i-thoon']<br>Parsing (part of speech): verb<br>    Mood—indicative<br>    Tense—imperfect<br>    Voice—active<br>    Person—3rd person<br>    Number—plural<br>    Stem or root—from ἀπειθέω<br>Concordance References:<br>⇒ Strong's #544 apeitheō<br>⇒ NIV #578 apeitheō<br>⇒ NASB #544 apeitheō<br><br>**Acts 19:9**<br>But when divers were hardened, and **believed not**, but spake evil of that way before the multitude, he departed from them, and separated the disciples, disputing daily in the school of one Tyrannus. [KJV]<br>But when some were becoming hardened and **disobedient**, speaking evil of the Way before the multitude, he withdrew from them and took away the disciples, reasoning daily in the school of Tyrannus. [NASB]<br>But some of them became obstinate; they **refused to believe** and publicly maligned the Way. So Paul left them. He took the disciples with him and had discussions daily in the lecture hall of Tyrannus. [NIV]<br>But when some were hardened and **did not believe**, but spoke evil of the Way before the multitude, he departed from them and withdrew the disciples, reasoning daily | To refuse to believe; to be disobedient; to reject.<br><br>**Practical Application**<br>Take note of this, for rejecting the gospel is not just unbelief. It is much worse: it is disobeying God. God demands that men believe in His Son Jesus Christ. Refusing to believe is outright disobedience, an affront to God, an act of rebellion and hostility against His commandment. |

## PRACTICAL WORD STUDIES
### in the NEW TESTAMENT

| ENGLISH WORD | GREEK WORD AND VERSE | THE WORD MEANS... |
|---|---|---|
| | in the school of Tyrannus. [NKJV]<br>But some **rejected** his message and publicly spoke against the Way, so Paul left the synagogue and took the believers with him. Then he began preaching daily at the lecture hall of Tyrannus. [NLT]<br>ὡς δέ τινες ἐσκληρύνοντο καὶ **ἠπείθουν**, κακολογοῦντες τὴν ὁδὸν ἐνώπιον τοῦ πλήθους, ἀποστὰς ἀπ' αὐτῶν ἀφώρισε τοὺς μαθητάς, καθ' ἡμέραν διαλεγόμενος ἐν τῇ σχολῇ τυράννου τινός. [GNS]<br>ὡς δέ τινες ἐσκληρύνοντο καὶ **ἠπείθουν** κακολογοῦντες τὴν ὁδὸν ἐνώπιον τοῦ πλήθους, ἀποστὰς ἀπ' αὐτῶν ἀφώρισεν τοὺς μαθητὰς καθ' ἡμέραν διαλεγόμενος ἐν τῇ σχολῇ Τυράννου. [GNT] | |
| **#1078**<br>**Disobedient**<br><br>Believed not–KJV<br>**Disobedient–NASB**<br>Disobeyed–NIV<br>Did not obey–NKJV<br>Disobeyed–NLT<br><br>**POSB<br>REFERENCE**<br>(Heb.3:13-19; esp. v.18)<br>Note 3, point 7 | **ἀπειθήσασιν** = apeithēsasin<br>Pronunciation: [ap-i-thay'-sah-sin]<br>Parsing (part of speech): verb<br>    Mood—participle<br>    Tense—aorist<br>    Voice—active<br>    Case—dative<br>    Gender—masculine<br>    Number—plural<br>    Stem or root—from ἀπειθέω<br>Concordance References:<br>⇒ Strong's #544 apeitheō<br>⇒ NIV #578 apeitheō<br>⇒ NASB #544 apeitheō<br><br>**Hebrews 3:18**<br>And to whom sware he that they should not enter into his rest, but to them that **believed not**? [KJV]<br>And to whom did He swear that they should not enter His rest, but to those who were **disobedient**? [NASB]<br>And to whom did God swear that they would never enter his rest if not to those who **disobeyed**? [NIV]<br>And to whom did He swear that they would not enter His rest, but to those who **did not obey**? [NKJV]<br>And to whom was God speaking when he vowed that they would never enter his place of rest? He was speaking to those who **disobeyed** him. [NLT]<br>τίσι δὲ ὤμοσε μὴ εἰσελεύσεσθαι εἰς τὴν κατάπαυσιν αὐτοῦ, εἰ μὴ τοῖς **ἀπειθήσασι**; [GNS]<br>τίσιν δὲ ὤμοσεν μὴ εἰσελεύσεσθαι εἰς τὴν κατάπαυσιν αὐτοῦ εἰ μὴ τοῖς **ἀπειθήσασιν**; [GNT] | To disobey; to fail to believe; to be disobedient; to refuse to be persuaded; to refuse to believe; to withhold belief.<br><br>**Practical Application**<br>It is a person who just refuses to be persuaded despite the evidence that Jesus Christ is truly the Savior of the world; the kind of person who chooses to continue living for the world and self despite the fact of coming judgment. The unbeliever will not be allowed to enter God's promised land of heaven nor God's eternal rest. |
| **#1079**<br>**Disobedient**<br><br>Disobedient–KJV<br>Disobedient–NASB<br>Disobedient–NIV<br>Disobedient–NKJV<br>Disobedient–NLT<br><br>**POSB<br>REFERENCE**<br>(Tit.3:3)<br>*Deeper Study #2* | **ἀπειθεῖς** = apeitheis<br>Pronunciation: [ap-i-thees]<br>Parsing (part of speech): adjective<br>    Case—nominative<br>    Gender—masculine<br>    Number—plural<br>    Stem or root—<br>Concordance References:<br>⇒ Strong's #545 apeithēs<br>⇒ NIV #579 apeithēs<br>⇒ NASB #545 apeithēs<br><br>**Titus 3:3**<br>For we ourselves also were sometimes foolish, **disobedient**, deceived, serving divers lusts and pleasures, living in malice and envy, hateful, and hating one another. [KJV]<br>For we also once were foolish ourselves, **disobedient**, deceived, enslaved to various lusts and pleasures, spending our life in malice and envy, hateful, hating one another. [NASB]<br>At one time we too were foolish, **disobedient**, deceived and enslaved by all kinds of passions and pleasures. We lived in malice and envy, being hated and hating one another. [NIV]<br>For we ourselves were also once foolish, **disobedient**, deceived, serving various lusts and pleasures, living | Disobedient, rebellious. The word means to refuse to obey by not doing what one should; to rebel against and to reject instruction; to refuse to be persuaded; to be obstinate, stubborn against authority.<br><br>**Practical Application**<br>Note a most significant fact: the charge is that man is disobedient in general; that is, he disobeys all authority.<br>He disobeys parents, civil authorities, civil laws, and the natural laws of nature—polluting and misusing everything surrounding him.<br>⇒ He disobeys the laws of personal duty as he walks day by day at home, in the workplace, and throughout his community.<br>⇒ He disobeys God and His Word, the very Person who can save him and who has laid down the commandments of life for man This is the most tragic of all—in fact, the cause of all other disobedience.<br>Man just comes short, disobeying all the laws and duties of life—not all the time, but sometimes. By nature, when a person wants something that is forbidden, he is drawn to go after it |

# PRACTICAL WORD STUDIES
## in the NEW TESTAMENT

| ENGLISH WORD | GREEK WORD AND VERSE | THE WORD MEANS... |
|---|---|---|
| | in malice and envy, hateful and hating one another. [NKJV]<br>Once we, too, were foolish and **disobedient**. We were misled by others and became slaves to many wicked desires and evil pleasures. Our lives were full of evil and envy. We hated others, and they hated us. [NLT]<br>ἦμεν γάρ ποτε καὶ ἡμεῖς ἀνόητοι, **ἀπειθεῖς**, πλανώμενοι, δουλεύοντες ἐπιθυμίαις καὶ ἡδοναῖς ποικίλαις, ἐν κακίᾳ καὶ φθόνῳ διάγοντες, στυγητοί, μισοῦντες ἀλλήλους. [GNS]<br>Ἦμεν γάρ ποτε καὶ ἡμεῖς ἀνόητοι, **ἀπειθεῖς**, πλανώμενοι, δουλεύοντες ἐπιθυμίαις καὶ ἡδοναῖς ποικίλαις, ἐν κακίᾳ καὶ φθόνῳ διάγοντες, στυγητοί, μισοῦντες ἀλλήλους. [GNT] | despite the fact that it is wrong and disobedient. He is simply drawn to disobey the law of God or the law of the land and the restriction of the parent.<br>The point is this: all of us—believers and unbelievers—have walked in disobedience. We have all disobeyed all authority; we have been lawless and transgressed all authority ranging from parents over to God. We have come short—far short—of what we should have done.<br>But thanks be to God our Savior, for He has provided the way for us to be forgiven. Our guilt and punishment for having broken the law of God and of man can be completely removed from us. How? Through the Lord Jesus Christ. No matter how disobedient we have been—no matter how lawless we have been—God our Savior will forgive our transgressions. He will forgive them if we genuinely believe that His Son, the Lord Jesus Christ, paid the punishment of our transgression when He died upon the cross. |
| **#1080**<br>**Disobedient To Parents, To Their Parents**<br><br>Disobedient to parents–KJV<br>Disobedient to parents–NASB<br>Disobedient to their parents–NIV<br>Disobedient to parents–NKJV<br>Disobedient to their parents–NLT<br><br>**POSB REFERENCE**<br>(2 Tim. 3:2-4; esp. v.2) Note 2, point 6<br><br>See also POSB REF:<br>(Rom.1:30)<br>*Deeper Study* #18 | γονεῦσιν ἀπειθεῖς = goneusin apeitheis<br>Pronunciation: [gon-yoo-sin' hap-i-theh-ees]<br>Parsing *goneusin* (part of speech): noun<br>  Case—dative<br>  Gender—masculine<br>  Number—plural<br>  Stem or root—from γονεύς, έως<br>Parsing *apeitheis* (part of speech): adjective<br>  Case—nominative<br>  Gender—masculine<br>  Number—plural<br>  Stem or root—from ἀπειθής, ές<br>Concordance References:<br>⇒ Strong's #1118 goneus + 545 apeithēs<br>⇒ NIV #1204 goneus [parents] + 579 apeithēs [disobedient]<br>⇒ NASB #1118 goneus + 545 apeithēs<br><br>**2 Tim. 3:2**<br>For men shall be lovers of their own selves, covetous, boasters, proud, blasphemers, **disobedient to parents**, unthankful, unholy, [KJV]<br>For men will be lovers of self, lovers of money, boastful, arrogant, revilers, **disobedient to parents**, ungrateful, unholy, [NASB]<br>People will be lovers of themselves, lovers of money, boastful, proud, abusive, **disobedient to their parents**, ungrateful, unholy, [NIV]<br>For men will be lovers of themselves, lovers of money, boasters, proud, blasphemers, **disobedient to parents**, unthankful, unholy, [NKJV]<br>For people will love only themselves and their money. They will be boastful and proud, scoffing at God, **disobedient to their parents**, and ungrateful. They will consider nothing sacred. [NLT]<br>ἔσονται γὰρ οἱ ἄνθρωποι φίλαυτοι, φιλάργυροι, ἀλαζόνες, ὑπερήφανοι, βλάσφημοι, **γονεῦσιν ἀπειθεῖς**, ἀχάριστοι, ἀνόσιοι, [GNS]<br>ἔσονται γὰρ οἱ ἄνθρωποι φίλαυτοι φιλάργυροι ἀλαζόνες ὑπερήφανοι βλάσφημοι, **γονεῦσιν ἀπειθεῖς**, ἀχάριστοι ἀνόσιοι [GNT] | To be disobedient or rebellious against parents. It means refusing to do what one's parents say; rebelling against one's parents; showing disrespect to parents; rejecting parental instruction; dishonoring parental example.<br><br>**Practical Application**<br>If a child will not honor and respect his mother and father, who will he respect? If a child will mistreat his parents—those who are the closest to him—who else will he mistreat? If a child will not obey his parents, those who love and care for him most, who then will he obey? Parents are the ones who gave birth, loved and cared for the children of the world. If the children are not loyal to them, then the children will not be loyal to anyone. The home, society, and civilization will crumble. |
| **#1081**<br>**Disobeyed**<br><br>Believed not–KJV<br>Disobedient–NASB<br>**Disobeyed–NIV** | ἀπειθήσασιν = apeithēsasin<br>Pronunciation: [ap-i-thay'-sah-sin]<br>Parsing (part of speech): verb<br>  Mood—participle<br>  Tense—aorist<br>  Voice—active<br>  Case—dative | To disobey; to fail to believe; to be disobedient; to refuse to be persuaded; to refuse to believe; to withhold belief.<br><br>**Practical Application**<br>It is a person who just refuses to be persuad- |

# PRACTICAL WORD STUDIES
## in the NEW TESTAMENT

| ENGLISH WORD | GREEK WORD AND VERSE | THE WORD MEANS... |
|---|---|---|
| Did not obey–NKJV<br>**Disobeyed**–NLT<br><br>**POSB REFERENCE**<br>(Heb.3:13-19; esp. v.18)<br>Note 3, point 7 | Gender—masculine<br>Number—plural<br>Stem or root—from ἀπειθέω<br>Concordance References:<br>⇒ Strong's #544 apeitheō<br>⇒ NIV #578 apeitheō<br>⇒ NASB #544 apeitheō<br><br>**Hebrews 3:18**<br>And to whom sware he that they should not enter into his rest, but to them that **believed not**? [KJV]<br>And to whom did He swear that they should not enter His rest, but to those who were **disobedient**? [NASB]<br>And to whom did God swear that they would never enter his rest if not to those who **disobeyed**? [NIV]<br>And to whom did He swear that they would not enter His rest, but to those who **did not obey**? [NKJV]<br>And to whom was God speaking when he vowed that they would never enter his place of rest? He was speaking to those who **disobeyed** him. [NLT]<br>τίσι δὲ ὤμοσε μὴ εἰσελεύσεσθαι εἰς τὴν κατάπαυσιν αὐτοῦ, εἰ μὴ τοῖς **ἀπειθήσασι**; [GNS]<br>τίσιν δὲ ὤμοσεν μὴ εἰσελεύσεσθαι εἰς τὴν κατάπαυσιν αὐτοῦ εἰ μὴ τοῖς **ἀπειθήσασιν**; [GNT] | ed despite the evidence that Jesus Christ is truly the Savior of the world; the kind of person who chooses to continue living for the world and self despite the fact of coming judgment. The unbeliever will not be allowed to enter God's promised land of heaven nor God's eternal rest. |
| #1082<br>**Disorder**<br><br>Tumults–KJV<br>Disturbances–NASB<br>**Disorder**–NIV<br>Tumults–NKJV<br>Disorderly behavior–NLT<br><br>**POSB REFERENCE**<br>(2 Cor.12:19-21; esp. v.20)<br>Note 3, point 2 | ἀκαταστασίαι = akatastasiai<br>Pronunciation: [ak-at-as-tah-see'-ah-ee]<br>Parsing (part of speech): noun<br>Case—nominative<br>Gender—feminine<br>Number—plural<br>Stem or root—from ἀκαταστασία, ας<br>Concordance References:<br>⇒ Strong's #181 akatastasia<br>⇒ NIV #189 akatastasia<br>⇒ NASB #181 akatastasia<br><br>**2 Cor. 12:20**<br>For I fear, lest, when I come, I shall not find you such as I would, and that I shall be found unto you such as ye would not: lest there be debates, envyings, wraths, strifes, backbitings, whisperings, swellings, **tumults**: [KJV]<br>For I am afraid that perhaps when I come I may find you to be not what I wish and may be found by you to be not what you wish; that perhaps there may be strife, jealousy, angry tempers, disputes, slanders, gossip, arrogance, **disturbances**; [NASB]<br>For I am afraid that when I come I may not find you as I want you to be, and you may not find me as you want me to be. I fear that there may be quarreling, jealousy, outbursts of anger, factions, slander, gossip, arrogance and **disorder**. [NIV]<br>For I fear lest, when I come, I shall not find you such as I wish, and *that* I shall be found by you such as you do not wish; lest *there be* contentions, jealousies, outbursts of wrath, selfish ambitions, backbitings, whisperings, conceits, **tumults**; [NKJV]<br>For I am afraid that when I come to visit you I won't like what I find, and then you won't like my response. I am afraid that I will find quarreling, jealousy, outbursts of anger, selfishness, backstabbing, gossip, conceit, and **disorderly behavior**. [NLT]<br>φοβοῦμαι γὰρ μή πως ἐλθὼν οὐχ οἵους θέλω εὕρω ὑμᾶς, κἀγὼ εὑρεθῶ ὑμῖν οἷον οὐ θέλετε· μή πως ἔρις, ζῆλοι, θυμοί, ἐριθεῖαι, καταλαλιαί, ψιθυρισμοί, φυσιώσεις, **ἀκαταστασίαι**· [GNS]<br>φοβοῦμαι γὰρ μή πως ἐλθὼν οὐχ οἵους θέλω εὕρω ὑμᾶς κἀγὼ εὑρεθῶ ὑμῖν οἷον οὐ θέλετε· μή πως ἔρις, ζῆλος, θυμοί, ἐριθεῖαι, καταλαλιαί, ψιθυρισμοί, φυσιώσεις, **ἀκαταστασίαι**· [GNT] | Disorder, tumults, disturbances, disorderly behavior, insurrection, anarchy, confusion.<br><br>**Practical Application**<br>Paul was stricken with fear, fear lest the church fail to be what it should be and reject him and his ministry. Paul feared that the church would fail to deal with the carnal critics and continue putting up with their evil attacks against him. He lists eight evils, including "disorder" (*akatastasiai*), that were and still are characteristic of divisive critics in the church. |

## PRACTICAL WORD STUDIES
### in the NEW TESTAMENT

| ENGLISH WORD | GREEK WORD AND VERSE | THE WORD MEANS... |
|---|---|---|
| **#1083**<br>**Disorderly Behavior**<br><br>Tumults–KJV<br>Disturbances–NASB<br>Disorder–NIV<br>Tumults–NKJV<br>**Disorderly behavior–NLT**<br><br>**POSB REFERENCE**<br>(2 Cor.12:19-21; esp. v.20)<br>Note 3, point 2 | ἀκαταστασίαι = akatastasiai<br>Pronunciation: [ak-at-as-tah-see'-ah-ee]<br>Parsing (part of speech): noun<br>    Case—nominative<br>    Gender—feminine<br>    Number—plural<br>    Stem or root—from ἀκαταστασία, ας<br>Concordance References:<br>  ⇒ Strong's #181 akatastasia<br>  ⇒ NIV #189 akatastasia<br>  ⇒ NASB #181 akatastasia<br><br>**2 Cor. 12:20**<br>For I fear, lest, when I come, I shall not find you such as I would, and that I shall be found unto you such as ye would not: lest there be debates, envyings, wraths, strifes, backbitings, whisperings, swellings, **tumults**; [KJV]<br>For I am afraid that perhaps when I come I may find you to be not what I wish and may be found by you to be not what you wish; that perhaps there may be strife, jealousy, angry tempers, disputes, slanders, gossip, arrogance, **disturbances**; [NASB]<br>For I am afraid that when I come I may not find you as I want you to be, and you may not find me as you want me to be. I fear that there may be quarreling, jealousy, outbursts of anger, factions, slander, gossip, arrogance and **disorder**. [NIV]<br>For I fear lest, when I come, I shall not find you such as I wish, and *that* I shall be found by you such as you do not wish; lest *there be* contentions, jealousies, outbursts of wrath, selfish ambitions, backbitings, whisperings, conceits, **tumults**; [NKJV]<br>For I am afraid that when I come to visit you I won't like what I find, and then you won't like my response. I am afraid that I will find quarreling, jealousy, outbursts of anger, selfishness, backstabbing, gossip, conceit, and **disorderly behavior**. [NLT]<br>φοβοῦμαι γὰρ μή πως ἐλθὼν οὐχ οἵους θέλω εὕρω ὑμᾶς, κἀγὼ εὑρεθῶ ὑμῖν οἷον οὐ θέλετε· μή πως ἔρις, ζῆλοι, θυμοί, ἐριθείαι, καταλαλιαί, ψιθυρισμοί, φυσιώσεις, **ἀκαταστασίαι**· [GNS]<br>φοβοῦμαι γὰρ μή πως ἐλθὼν οὐχ οἵους θέλω εὕρω ὑμᾶς, κἀγὼ εὑρεθῶ ὑμῖν οἷον οὐ θέλετε· μή πως ἔρις, ζῆλος, θυμοί, ἐριθείαι, καταλαλιαί, ψιθυρισμοί, φυσιώσεις, **ἀκαταστασίαι**· [GNT] | Disorder, tumults, disturbances, disorderly behavior, insurrection, anarchy, confusion.<br><br>**Practical Application**<br>Paul was stricken with fear, fear lest the church fail to be what it should be and reject him and his ministry. Paul feared that the church would fail to deal with the carnal critics and continue putting up with their evil attacks against him. He lists eight evils, including "disorderly behavior" (*akatastasiai*), that was and still is characteristic of divisive critics in the church. |
| **#1084**<br>**Dispensation**<br><br>**Dispensation–KJV**<br>Stewardship–NASB<br>Trust–NIV<br>Stewardship–NKJV<br>Sacred trust–NLT<br><br>**POSB REFERENCE**<br>(1 Cor.9:16-17; esp. v.17)<br>Note 2 | οἰκονομίαν = oikonomian<br>Pronunciation: [oy-kon-om-ee'-ahn]<br>Parsing (part of speech): noun<br>    Case—accusative<br>    Gender—feminine<br>    Number—singular<br>    Stem or root—from οἰκονομία, ας<br>Concordance References:<br>  ⇒ Strong's #3622 oikonomia<br>  ⇒ NIV #3873 oikonomia<br>  ⇒ NASB #3622 oikonomia<br><br>**1 Cor. 9:17**<br>For if I do this thing willingly, I have a reward: but if against my will, a **dispensation** of the gospel is committed unto me. [KJV]<br>For if I do this voluntarily, I have a reward; but if against my will, I have a **stewardship** entrusted to me. [NASB]<br>If I preach voluntarily, I have a reward; if not voluntarily, I am simply discharging the **trust** committed to me. [NIV]<br>For if I do this willingly, I have a reward; but if against my will, I have been entrusted with a **stewardship**. [NKJV]<br>If I were doing this of my own free will, then I would | A stewardship; a sacred trust; a commission; a responsibility.<br><br>**Practical Application**<br>The steward was the manager of a large household or estate. The minister of God is the manager of God's household and estate (church).<br>Once God had called Paul to preach, the stewardship and trust of preaching was his. Whether he followed through and preached did not matter; he was still responsible for preaching. There was no release from the call and duty. He would stand accountable for preaching the gospel, or he would stand accountable for not preaching the gospel.<br>The call to preach the gospel is an awesome responsibility. God places the stewardship of the gospel into the hands of the person He calls. Just think about it: whatever these persons do with the gospel is all that will be done with the gospel—nothing more, nothing less. God has placed His gospel—the stewardship of it—into the hands of the persons He calls. Only what |

# PRACTICAL WORD STUDIES
## in the NEW TESTAMENT

| ENGLISH WORD | GREEK WORD AND VERSE | THE WORD MEANS... |
|---|---|---|
| | deserve payment. But God has chosen me and given me this **sacred trust**, and I have no choice. [NLT]<br>εἰ γὰρ ἑκὼν τοῦτο πράσσω, μισθὸν ἔχω· εἰ δὲ ἄκων, **οἰκονομίαν** πεπίστευμαι. [GNS]<br>εἰ γὰρ ἑκὼν τοῦτο πράσσω, μισθὸν ἔχω· εἰ δὲ ἄκων, **οἰκονομίαν** πεπίστευμαι· [GNT] | they do with the gospel will be done. What an awesome responsibility! |
| **#1085**<br>**Dispensation**<br><br>**Dispensation**–KJV<br>Administration–NASB<br>Put into effect–NIV<br>**Dispensation**–NKJV<br>This is his plan–NLT<br><br>**POSB**<br>**REFERENCE**<br>(Eph.1:9-10; esp. v.10)<br>Note 6, point 3 | **οἰκονομίαν** = oikonomian<br>Pronunciation: [oy-kon-om-ee'-ahn]<br>Parsing (part of speech): noun<br>    Case—accusative<br>    Gender—feminine<br>    Number—singular<br>    Stem or root—from οἰκονομία, ας<br>Concordance References:<br>⇒ Strong's #3622 oikonomia<br>⇒ NIV #3873 oikonomia<br>⇒ NASB #3622 oikonomia<br><br>**Ephes. 1:10**<br>That in the **dispensation** of the fulness of times he might gather together in one all things in Christ, both which are in heaven, and which are on earth; even in him: [KJV]<br>With a view to an **administration** suitable to the fulness of the times, that is, the summing up of all things in Christ, things in the heavens and things upon the earth. In Him [NASB]<br>To be **put into effect** when the times will have reached their fulfillment—to bring all things in heaven and on earth together under one head, even Christ. [NIV]<br>That in the **dispensation** of the fullness of the times He might gather together in one all things in Christ, both which are in heaven and which are on earth—in Him. [NKJV]<br>And **this is his plan**: At the right time he will bring everything together under the authority of Christ—everything in heaven and on earth. [NLT]<br>εἰς **οἰκονομίαν** τοῦ πληρώματος τῶν καιρῶν, ἀνακεφαλαιώσασθαι τὰ πάντα ἐν τῷ Χριστῷ, τά τε ἐν τοῖς οὐρανοῖς καὶ τὰ ἐπὶ τῆς γῆς· ἐν αὐτῷ, [GNS]<br>εἰς **οἰκονομίαν** τοῦ πληρώματος τῶν καιρῶν, ἀνακεφαλαιώσασθαι τὰ πάντα ἐν τῷ Χριστῷ, τὰ ἐπὶ τοῖς οὐρανοῖς καὶ τὰ ἐπὶ τῆς γῆς ἐν αὐτῷ. [GNT] | To put into effect; administration; to have a plan. The word Paul uses literally means "household arrangement."<br><br>**Practical Application**<br>The idea is that the universe is a house under the management of God. God is handling, planning, arranging, and administering all things toward a climactic consummation for Christ and His followers. In that climactic day all disharmony and division and evil will be subjected and harmonized (*anakephalaioo*) under Christ. A new and perfect and eternal creation will be established for the Lord and His followers throughout the universe. |
| **#1086**<br>**Dispensation**<br><br>**Dispensation**–KJV<br>Stewardship–NASB<br>Administration–NIV<br>**Dispensation**–NKJV<br>Special ministry–NLT<br><br>**POSB**<br>**REFERENCE**<br>(Eph.3:2)<br>Note 1, point 2 | **οἰκονομίαν** = oikonomian<br>Pronunciation: [oy-kon-om-ee'-ahn]<br>Parsing (part of speech): noun<br>    Case—accusative<br>    Gender—feminine<br>    Number—singular<br>    Stem or root—from οἰκονομία, ας<br>Concordance References:<br>⇒ Strong's #3622 oikonomia<br>⇒ NIV #3873 oikonomia<br>⇒ NASB #3622 oikonomia<br><br>**Ephes. 3:2**<br>If ye have heard of the **dispensation** of the grace of God which is given me to youward: [KJV]<br>If indeed you have heard of the **stewardship** of God's grace which was given to me for you; [NASB]<br>Surely you have heard about the **administration** of God's grace that was given to me for you, [NIV]<br>If indeed you have heard of the **dispensation** of the grace of God which was given to me for you, [NKJV]<br>As you already know, God has given me this **special ministry** of announcing his favor to you Gentiles. [NLT]<br>εἴγε ἠκούσατε τὴν **οἰκονομίαν** τῆς χάριτος τοῦ Θεοῦ τῆς δοθείσης μοι εἰς ὑμᾶς, [GNS]<br>εἴ γε ἠκούσατε τὴν **οἰκονομίαν** τῆς χάριτος τοῦ θεοῦ τῆς δοθείσης μοι εἰς ὑμᾶς, [GNT] | Administration, stewardship, management, ownership; to have a special ministry.<br><br>**Practical Application**<br>Paul existed to be a steward of God. Paul was given the duty to oversee and administer the grace of God to the world. |

# PRACTICAL WORD STUDIES
## in the New Testament

| ENGLISH WORD | GREEK WORD AND VERSE | THE WORD MEANS... |
|---|---|---|
| **#1087**<br>**Dispensation**<br><br>Dispensation–KJV<br>Stewardship–NASB<br>Commission–NIV<br>Stewardship–NKJV<br>Responsibility–NLT<br><br>**POSB REFERENCE**<br>(Col.1:25)<br>Note 2 | οἰκονομίαν = *oikonomian*<br>Pronunciation: [oy-kon-om-ee'-ahn]<br>Parsing (part of speech): noun<br>    Case—accusative<br>    Gender—feminine<br>    Number—singular<br>    Stem or root—from οἰκονομία, ας<br>Concordance References:<br>  ⇒ Strong's #3622 oikonomia<br>  ⇒ NIV #3873 oikonomia<br>  ⇒ NASB #3622 oikonomia<br><br>**Col. 1:25**<br>Whereof I am made a minister, according to the **dispensation** of God which is given to me for you, to fulfil the word of God; [KJV]<br>Of this church I was made a minister according to the **stewardship** from God bestowed on me for your benefit, that I might fully carry out the preaching of the word of God, [NASB]<br>I have become its servant by the **commission** God gave me to present to you the word of God in its fullness—[NIV]<br>Of which I became a minister according to the **stewardship** from God which was given to me for you, to fulfill the word of God, [NKJV]<br>God has given me the **responsibility** of serving his church by proclaiming his message in all its fullness to you Gentiles. [NLT]<br>ἧς ἐγενόμην ἐγὼ διάκονος, κατὰ τὴν **οἰκονομίαν** τοῦ Θεοῦ τὴν δοθεῖσάν μοι εἰς ὑμᾶς, πληρῶσαι τὸν λόγον τοῦ Θεοῦ, [GNS]<br>ἧς ἐγενόμην ἐγὼ διάκονος κατὰ τὴν **οἰκονομίαν** τοῦ θεοῦ τὴν δοθεῖσάν μοι εἰς ὑμᾶς πληρῶσαι τὸν λόγον τοῦ θεοῦ, [GNT] | Commission, dispensation, stewardship, responsibility; management of; responsibility of, duty of.<br><br>**Practical Application**<br>The word "dispensation" (*oikonomian*) refers to the steward who oversees the household and property of the owner. The minister is the steward of God, the person chosen to oversee the house or church of God. This fact is almost unbelievable, but it is true: God has actually chosen some persons to oversee His affairs for Him. The minister has actually been chosen by God to be the steward of His world and church and people. God has literally taken His church and people and placed them into the hands of His ministers, into...<br><br>• their stewardship<br>• their supervision<br>• their administration<br>• their ministry<br>• their responsibility<br>• their management<br>• their care<br>• their lives<br>• their love<br><br>What an enormous call and responsibility, yet it comes from God; therefore, it must be fulfilled. |
| **#1088**<br>**Dispersed Abroad**<br><br>Scattered abroad–KJV<br>Dispersed abroad–NASB<br>Scattered among the nations–NIV<br>Scattered abroad–NKJV<br>Scattered among the nations–NLT<br><br>**POSB REFERENCE**<br>(Jas 1:1)<br>Note 2, point 2<br><br>See also POSB REF:<br>(Jn.7:35-36; esp. v.35)<br>Note 3, point 1 | διασπορᾷ = *diaspora*<br>Pronunciation: [dee-as-por-ah']<br>Parsing (part of speech): noun<br>    Case—dative<br>    Gender—feminine<br>    Number—singular<br>    Stem or root—from διασπορά, ᾶς<br>Concordance References:<br>  ⇒ Strong's #1290 diaspora<br>  ⇒ NIV #1402 diaspora<br>  ⇒ NASB #1290 diaspora<br><br>**James 1:1**<br>James, a servant of God and of the Lord Jesus Christ, to the twelve tribes which are **scattered abroad**, greeting. [KJV]<br>James, a bond-servant of God and of the Lord Jesus Christ, to the twelve tribes who are **dispersed abroad**, greetings. [NASB]<br>James, a servant of God and of the Lord Jesus Christ, To the twelve tribes **scattered among the nations**: Greetings. [NIV]<br>James, a bondservant of God and of the Lord Jesus Christ, To the twelve tribes which are **scattered abroad**: Greetings. [NKJV]<br>This letter is from James, a slave of God and of the Lord Jesus Christ.It is written to Jewish Christians **scattered among the nations**.Greetings! [NLT]<br>Ἰάκωβος, Θεοῦ καὶ Κυρίου Ἰησοῦ Χριστοῦ δοῦλος, ταῖς δώδεκα φυλαῖς ταῖς ἐν τῇ **διασπορᾷ**, χαίρειν. [GNS]<br>Ἰάκωβος θεοῦ καὶ κυρίου Ἰησοῦ Χριστοῦ δοῦλος ταῖς δώδεκα φυλαῖς ταῖς ἐν τῇ **διασπορᾷ** χαίρειν. [GNT] | Scattered among the nations, scattered abroad, dispersed abroad. *Diaspora* is simply a Greek word that means all the millions of Jews scattered all over the world.<br><br>**Practical Application**<br>James loved his people with an unusual love. They were deeply rooted in his heart, and he felt a strong calling to reach and exhort them in the Lord. This is the very reason he was writing them. Just think what an awesome task it must have been to draw up the plans by which his letter could be passed from church to church and from synagogue to synagogue all over the world. James either laid out the plans and followed through in seeing that the plans were carried out or else the Holy Spirit gave him assurance that his letter would be spread to all the Jews scattered all over the world. James had some indication that he would be reaching all Jews—the twelve tribes scattered all over. His heart longed to reach the millions of the *diaspora*.<br><br>The point to see is the love and the evangelistic heart that James had for his people. True, he is writing primarily to Jewish believers, but he is also doing what he says: sending greetings to the twelve tribes of the diaspora—all the millions who are scattered all over the world. What he says is applicable to all believers of all generations.<br><br>What a dynamic example in love and evangelism for us. What would happen if our hearts beat with the same degree of love and evangelism—the compassion to reach the lost and suffering people of our communities, cities, and nations? |

## PRACTICAL WORD STUDIES
### in the NEW TESTAMENT

| ENGLISH WORD | GREEK WORD AND VERSE | THE WORD MEANS... |
|---|---|---|
| **#1089**<br>**Display Of [God's] Power**<br><br>Mighty power–KJV<br>Greatness–NASB<br>Greatness–NIV<br>Majesty–NKJV<br>Display of [God's] power–NLT<br><br>**POSB REFERENCE**<br>(Lk.9:42-43; esp. v.43)<br>Note 3, point 2 | μεγαλειότητι = megaleiotēti<br>Pronunciation: [meg-al-i-ot'-ay-tee]<br>Parsing (part of speech): noun<br>    Case—dative<br>    Gender—feminine<br>    Number—singular<br>Stem or root—from μεγαλειότης, ητος<br>Concordance References:<br>  ⇒ Strong's #3168 megaleiotēs<br>  ⇒ NIV #3484 megaleiotēs<br>  ⇒ NASB #3168 megaleiotēs<br><br>**Luke 9:43**<br>And they were all amazed at the **mighty power** of God. But while they wondered every one at all things which Jesus did, he said unto his disciples, [KJV]<br>And they were all amazed at the **greatness** of God. But while everyone was marveling at all that He was doing, He said to His disciples, [NASB]<br>And they were all amazed at the **greatness** of God.While everyone was marveling at all that Jesus did, he said to his disciples, [NIV]<br>And they were all amazed at the **majesty** of God. But while everyone marveled at all the things which Jesus did, He said to His disciples, [NKJV]<br>Awe gripped the people as they saw this **display of God's power**. While everyone was marveling over all the wonderful things he was doing, Jesus said to his disciples, [NLT]<br>ἐξεπλήσσοντο δὲ πάντες ἐπὶ τῇ **μεγαλειότητι** τοῦ Θεοῦ. Πάντων δὲ θαυμαζόντων ἐπὶ πᾶσιν οἷς ἐποίει ὁ Ἰησοῦς, εἶπε πρὸς τοὺς μαθητὰς αὐτοῦ, [GNS]<br>ἐξεπλήσσοντο δὲ πάντες ἐπὶ τῇ **μεγαλειότητι** τοῦ θεοῦ. Πάντων δὲ θαυμαζόντων ἐπὶ πᾶσιν οἷς ἐποίει εἶπεν πρὸς τοὺς μαθητὰς αὐτοῦ, [GNT] | Majesty, greatness, glory, mighty power; a display of God's glory and power.<br><br>**Practical Application**<br>They marveled at "this display of God's power." Note that Jesus brought honor to God, not to Himself. |
| **#1090**<br>**Displayed**<br><br>Set forth–KJV<br>Exhibited–NASB<br>Put...on display–NIV<br>Displayed–NKJV<br>Put...on display–NLT<br><br>**POSB REFERENCE**<br>(1 Cor.4:9-10; esp. v.9)<br>Note 4 | ἀπέδειξεν = apedeixen<br>Pronunciation: [ap-ed'-eek-zehn]<br>Parsing (part of speech): verb<br>    Mood—indicative<br>    Tense—aorist<br>    Voice—active<br>    Person—3rd person<br>    Number—singular<br>Stem or root—from ἀποδείκνυμι<br>Concordance References:<br>  ⇒ Strong's #584 apodeiknumi<br>  ⇒ NIV #617 apodeiknumi<br>  ⇒ NASB #584 apodeiknumi<br><br>**1 Cor. 4:9**<br>For I think that God hath **set forth** us the apostles last, as it were appointed to death: for we are made a spectacle unto the world, and to angels, and to men. [KJV]<br>For, I think, God has **exhibited** us apostles last of all, as men condemned to death; because we have become a spectacle to the world, both to angels and to men. [NASB]<br>For it seems to me that God has **put** us apostles **on display** at the end of the procession, like men condemned to die in the arena. We have been made a spectacle to the whole universe, to angels as well as to men. [NIV]<br>For I think that God has **displayed** us, the apostles, last, as men condemned to death; for we have been made a spectacle to the world, both to angels and to men. [NKJV]<br>But sometimes I think God has **put** us apostles **on display**, like prisoners of war at the end of a victor's parade, condemned to die. We have become a spectacle to the entire world—to people and angels alike. [NLT]<br>δοκῶ γάρ, ὅτι ὁ Θεὸς ἡμᾶς τοὺς ἀποστόλους ἐσχάτους **ἀπέδειξεν** ὡς ἐπιθανατίους· ὅτι θέατρον ἐγενήθημεν τῷ | To put on display; to set forth; to exhibit; to proclaim; to prove.<br><br>**Practical Application**<br>The word "displayed" (*apedeixen*) means more than to be seen or exhibited. The picture is that of doomed gladiators being taken to the arena. God has displayed the minister as a doomed gladiator to serve the world no matter the cost. |

## PRACTICAL WORD STUDIES
## in the NEW TESTAMENT

| ENGLISH WORD | GREEK WORD AND VERSE | THE WORD MEANS... |
|---|---|---|
| | κόσμῳ, καὶ ἀγγέλοις καὶ ἀνθρώποις. [GNS]<br>δοκῶ γάρ, ὁ θεὸς ἡμᾶς τοὺς ἀποστόλους ἐσχάτους **ἀπέδειξεν** ὡς ἐπιθανατίους, ὅτι θέατρον ἐγενήθημεν τῷ κόσμῳ καὶ ἀγγέλοις καὶ ἀνθρώποις. [GNT] | |
| **#1091**<br>**Displayed Publicly**<br><br>Set forth–KJV<br>Displayed publicly–NASB<br>Presented–NIV<br>Set forth–NKJV<br>Sent–NLT<br><br>**POSB REFERENCE**<br>(Romans 3:25)<br>Note 4, point 1a | **προέθετο** = proetheto<br>Pronunciation: [pro-eth'-eh-tow]<br>Parsing (part of speech): verb<br>   Mood—indicative<br>   Tense—aorist<br>   Voice—middle<br>   Person—3rd person<br>   Number—singular<br>   Stem or root—from προτίθεμαι<br>Concordance References:<br>  ⇒ Strong's #4388 protithēmi<br>  ⇒ NIV #4729 protithēmi<br>  ⇒ NASB #4388 protithēmi<br><br>**Romans 3:25**<br>Whom God hath **set forth** to be a propitiation through faith in his blood, to declare his righteousness for the remission of sins that are past, through the forbearance of God; [KJV]<br><br>Whom God **displayed publicly** as a propitiation in His blood through faith. This was to demonstrate His righteousness, because in the forbearance of God He passed over the sins previously committed; [NASB]<br><br>God **presented** him as a sacrifice of atonement, through faith in his blood. He did this to demonstrate his justice, because in his forbearance he had left the sins committed beforehand unpunished—[NIV]<br><br>Whom God **set forth** as a propitiation by His blood, through faith, to demonstrate His righteousness, because in His forbearance God had passed over the sins that were previously committed, [NKJV]<br><br>For God **sent** Jesus to take the punishment for our sins and to satisfy God's anger against us. We are made right with God when we believe that Jesus shed his blood, sacrificing his life for us. God was being entirely fair and just when he did not punish those who sinned in former times. [NLT]<br><br>ὃν **προέθετο** ὁ Θεὸς ἱλαστήριον διὰ τῆς πίστεως, ἐν τῷ αὐτοῦ αἵματι, εἰς ἔνδειξιν τῆς δικαιοσύνης αὐτοῦ διὰ τὴν πάρεσιν τῶν προγεγονότων ἁμαρτημάτων [GNS]<br><br>ὃν **προέθετο** ὁ Θεὸς ἱλαστήριον διὰ [τῆς] πίστεως ἐν τῷ αὐτοῦ αἵματι εἰς ἔνδειξιν τῆς δικαιοσύνης αὐτοῦ διὰ τὴν πάρεσιν τῶν προγεγονότων ἁμαρτημάτων [GNT] | To set forth; to send; to display publicly; to present; to plan; to purpose; to intend.<br><br>**Practical Application**<br>God is the One who appointed Christ to be *publicly displayed* (*proetheto*) as the propitiation for man's sins.<br>God purposed to *publicly display* Christ: God determined, resolved, ordained Christ to be the propitiation or the sacrifice for man's sins.<br>God set Christ "before" (*pro*) the world as the propitiation for the world's sins. The *pro* in the Greek word *proetheto* (display publicly) indicates this fact.<br>⇒ God set Christ before Himself, purposed that He be the propitiation or the sacrifice for man's sin.<br>⇒ God set Christ publicly before the world, showing that He is definitely the propitiation for the world's sins. |
| **#1092**<br>**Displeased**<br><br>**Displeased–KJV**<br>Indignant–NASB<br>Indignant–NIV<br>**Displeased–NKJV**<br>**Displeased–NLT**<br><br>**POSB REFERENCE**<br>(Mk.10:14)<br>Deeper Study #2 | **ἠγανάκτησεν** = ēganaktēsen<br>Pronunciation: [ayg-ahn-ak-tay'-sehn]<br>Parsing (part of speech): verb<br>   Mood—indicative<br>   Tense—aorist<br>   Voice—active<br>   Person—3rd person<br>   Number—singular<br>   Stem or root—from ἀγανακτέω<br>Concordance References:<br>  ⇒ Strong's #234 aganakteō<br>  ⇒ NIV #24 aganakteō<br>  ⇒ NASB #234 aganakteō<br><br>**Mark 10:14**<br>But when Jesus saw it, he was much **displeased**, and said unto them, Suffer the little children to come unto me, and forbid them not: for of such is the kingdom of God. [KJV]<br><br>But when Jesus saw this, He was **indignant** and said to them, "Permit the children to come to Me; do not hinder them; for the kingdom of God belongs to such as | To be indignant; to be moved with indignation; to feel pain; to be angry; to grieve; to be displeased, sore displeased, and much displeased (cp. 2 Cor. 7:11).<br><br>**Practical Application**<br>The word is very strong, expressing deep, even violent emotion. The Lord was moved with indignation toward the disciples for what they were doing. Note two facts indicated by this experience.<br>1. Strong indignation against sin and injustice is sometimes justified.<br>2. Not being moved with indignation toward sin and injustice is sometimes a gross wrong. |

## PRACTICAL WORD STUDIES in the NEW TESTAMENT

| ENGLISH WORD | GREEK WORD AND VERSE | THE WORD MEANS... |
|---|---|---|
| | these. [NASB]<br>When Jesus saw this, he was **indignant**. He said to them, "Let the little children come to me, and do not hinder them, for the kingdom of God belongs to such as these. [NIV]<br>But when Jesus saw *it*, He was greatly **displeased** and said to them, "Let the little children come to Me, and do not forbid them; for of such is the kingdom of God. [NKJV]<br>But when Jesus saw what was happening, he was very **displeased** with his disciples. He said to them, "Let the children come to me. Don't stop them! For the Kingdom of God belongs to such as these. [NLT]<br>ἰδὼν δὲ ὁ Ἰησοῦς **ἠγανάκτησε**, καὶ εἶπεν αὐτοῖς, Ἄφετε τὰ παιδία ἔρχεσθαι πρός με, καὶ μὴ κωλύετε αὐτά. τῶν γὰρ τοιούτων ἐστὶν ἡ βασιλεία τοῦ Θεοῦ. [GNS]<br>ἰδὼν δὲ ὁ Ἰησοῦς **ἠγανάκτησεν** καὶ εἶπεν αὐτοῖς, Ἄφετε τὰ παιδία ἔρχεσθαι πρός με, μὴ κωλύετε αὐτά, τῶν γὰρ τοιούτων ἐστὶν ἡ βασιλεία τοῦ θεοῦ. [GNT] | |
| **#1093**<br>**Displeased, Was**<br><br>Was...displeased– KJV<br>Was very angry– NASB<br>Had been quarreling– NIV<br>Had been very angry– NKJV<br>Was very angry–NLT<br><br>**POSB REFERENCE**<br>(Acts 12:18-23; esp. v.20)<br>Note 3, point 1 | Ἦν θυμομαχῶν = Ēn thumomachōn<br>Pronunciation: [ayne thoo-mom-ach-on]<br>Parsing *thumomachōn* (part of speech): verb<br>  Mood—participle<br>  Tense—present<br>  Voice—active<br>  Case—nominative<br>  Gender—masculine<br>  Number—singular<br>  Stem or root—from θυμομαχέω<br>Concordance References:<br>  ⇒ Strong's #1488 eimi + 2371 thumomacheō<br>  ⇒ NIV #1639 eimi [been] + 2595 thumomacheō [quarreling]<br>  ⇒ NASB #1488 eimi + 237 1thumomacheō<br><br>**Acts 12:20**<br>And Herod **was** highly **displeased** with them of Tyre and Sidon: but they came with one accord to him, and, having made Blastus the king's chamberlain their friend, desired peace; because their country was nourished by the king's country. [KJV]<br>Now he **was very angry** with the people of Tyre and Sidon; and with one accord they came to him, and having won over Blastus the king's chamberlain, they were asking for peace, because their country was fed by the king's country. [NASB]<br>He **had been quarreling** with the people of Tyre and Sidon; they now joined together and sought an audience with him. Having secured the support of Blastus, a trusted personal servant of the king, they asked for peace, because they depended on the king's country for their food supply. [NIV]<br>Now Herod **had been very angry** with the people of Tyre and Sidon; but they came to him with one accord, and having made Blastus the king's personal aide their friend, they asked for peace, because their country was supplied with food by the king's *country*. [NKJV]<br>Now Herod **was very angry** with the people of Tyre and Sidon. So they sent a delegation to make peace with him because their cities were dependent upon Herod's country for their food. They made friends with Blastus, Herod's personal assistant, [NLT]<br>Ἦν δὲ ὁ Ἡρώδης **θυμομαχῶν** Τυρίοις καὶ Σιδωνίοις· τὴν ὁμοθυμαδὸν δὲ παρῆσαν πρὸς αὐτόν, καὶ πείσαντες Βλάστον τὸν ἐπὶ τοῦ κοιτῶνος τοῦ βασιλέως, ἠτοῦντο εἰρήνην, διὰ τὸ τρέφεσθαι αὐτῶν τὴν χώραν ἀπὸ τῆς βασιλικῆς. [GNS]<br>Ἦν δὲ **θυμομαχῶν** Τυρίοις καὶ Σιδωνίοις· ὁμοθυμαδὸν δὲ παρῆσαν πρὸς αὐτόν καὶ πείσαντες Βλάστον, τὸν ἐπὶ τοῦ κοιτῶνος τοῦ βασιλέως, ἠτοῦντο εἰρήνην διὰ τὸ τρέφεσθαι αὐτῶν τὴν χώραν ἀπὸ τῆς βασιλικῆς. [GNT] | To be very angry; to be displeased; to quarrel in an irate way.<br><br>**Practical Application**<br>Herod's nature is seen in the word "displeased" (*Ēn thumomachōn*). The word means to be inflamed, to be filled with violent hostility. It is very hot anger, an emotion that should never characterize the leader of a nation. |

PRACTICAL WORD STUDIES
in the NEW TESTAMENT

| ENGLISH WORD | GREEK WORD AND VERSE | THE WORD MEANS... |
|---|---|---|
| **#1094**<br>**Dispute**<br><br>Strife–KJV<br>**Dispute**–NASB<br>**Dispute**–NIV<br>**Dispute**–NKJV<br>Argue–NLT<br><br>**POSB<br>REFERENCE**<br>(Lk.22:24)<br>Note 1, point 1 | φιλονεικία = philoneikia<br>Pronunciation: [fil-on-i-kee'-ah]<br>Parsing (part of speech): noun<br>    Case—nominative<br>    Gender—feminine<br>    Number—singular<br>    Stem or root—from φιλονεικία, ας<br>Concordance References:<br>  ⇒  Strong's #5379 philoneikia<br>  ⇒  NIV #5808 philoneikia<br>  ⇒  NASB #5379 philoneikia<br><br>**Luke 22:24**<br>And there was also a **strife** among them, which of them should be accounted the greatest. [KJV]<br>And there arose also a **dispute** among them as to which one of them was regarded to be greatest. [NASB]<br>Also a **dispute** arose among them as to which of them was considered to be greatest. [NIV]<br>Now there was also a **dispute** among them, as to which of them should be considered the greatest. [NKJV]<br>And they began to **argue** among themselves as to who would be the greatest in the coming Kingdom. [NLT]<br>Ἐγένετο δὲ καὶ **φιλονεικία** ἐν αὐτοῖς τὸ, τίς αὐτῶν δοκεῖ εἶναι μείζων. [GNS]<br>Ἐγένετο δὲ καὶ **φιλονεικία** ἐν αὐτοῖς, τὸ τίς αὐτῶν δοκεῖ εἶναι μείζων. [GNT] | Being eager and ready to argue, debate and contend; being alert to strive for one's position.<br><br>**Practical Application**<br>It conveys the idea of giving no ground, of standing up no matter what, of being stubborn, of resisting regardless of circumstances. |
| **#1095**<br>**Disputed**<br><br>**Disputed**–KJV<br>Discussing–NASB<br>Arguing about–NIV<br>**Disputed**–NKJV<br>Discussing–NLT<br><br>**POSB<br>REFERENCE**<br>(Mk.9:33)<br>Note 1 | διελογίζεσθε = dielogizesthe<br>Pronunciation: [dee-el-og-id'-zehs-theh]<br>Parsing (part of speech): verb<br>    Mood—indicative<br>    Tense—imperfect<br>    Voice—middle or passive deponent<br>    Person—2nd person<br>    Number—plural<br>    Stem or root—from διαλογίζομαι<br>Concordance References:<br>  ⇒  Strong's #1260 dialogizomai<br>  ⇒  NIV #1368 dialogizomai<br>  ⇒  NASB #1260 dialogizomai<br><br>**Mark 9:33**<br>And he came to Capernaum: and being in the house he asked them, What was it that ye **disputed** among yourselves by the way? [KJV]<br>And they came to Capernaum; and when He was in the house, He began to question them, "What were you **discussing** on the way?" [NASB]<br>They came to Capernaum. When he was in the house, he asked them, "What were you **arguing about** on the road?" [NIV]<br>Then He came to Capernaum. And when He was in the house He asked them, "What was it you **disputed** among yourselves on the road?" [NKJV]<br>After they arrived at Capernaum, Jesus and his disciples settled in the house where they would be staying. Jesus asked them, "What were you **discussing** out on the road?" [NLT]<br>Καὶ ἦλθεν εἰς Καπερναούμ· καὶ ἐν τῇ οἰκίᾳ γενόμενος, ἐπηρώτα αὐτούς, Τί ἐν τῇ ὁδῷ πρὸς ἑαυτοὺς **διελογίζεσθε**; [GNS]<br>Καὶ ἦλθον εἰς Καφαρναούμ. καὶ ἐν τῇ οἰκίᾳ γενόμενος ἐπηρώτα αὐτούς, Τί ἐν τῇ ὁδῷ **διελογίζεσθε**; [GNT] | To dispute; to discuss. It is arguing, complaining, questioning, contesting, hairsplitting, nit-picking, and bickering as well as reasoning.<br><br>**Practical Application**<br>In this Scripture, the word pictures an intense debate between the disciples of Christ. They argued over which of them would be the greatest in the kingdom of Christ. |
| **#1096**<br>**Disputed**<br><br>**Disputed**–KJV<br>Reasoning–NASB | διελέγετο = dielegeto<br>Pronunciation: [dee-ehl-eg'-ch-tow]<br>Parsing (part of speech): verb<br>    Mood—indicative<br>    Tense—imperfect<br>    Voice—middle or passive deponent | Reasoning, addressing, dispute, debate, discussion.<br><br>**Practical Application**<br>Paul proclaimed the gospel daily. The idea is twofold. |

# PRACTICAL WORD STUDIES
## in the NEW TESTAMENT

| ENGLISH WORD | GREEK WORD AND VERSE | THE WORD MEANS... |
|---|---|---|
| Reasoned–NIV<br>Reasoned–NKJV<br>Debate–NLT<br><br>**POSB<br>REFERENCE**<br>(Acts 17:17)<br>Note 2<br><br>See also POSB REF:<br>(Acts 18:4)<br>Note 4, point 1 | Person—3rd person<br>Number—singular<br>Stem or root—from διαλέγομαι<br>Concordance References:<br>⇒ Strong's #1256 dialegomai<br>⇒ NIV #1363 dialegomai<br>⇒ NASB #1256 dialegomai<br><br>**Acts 17:17**<br>Therefore **disputed** he in the synagogue with the Jews, and with the devout persons, and in the market daily with them that met with him. [KJV]<br>So he was **reasoning** in the synagogue with the Jews and the God-fearing Gentiles, and in the market place every day with those who happened to be present. [NASB]<br>So he **reasoned** in the synagogue with the Jews and the God-fearing Greeks, as well as in the marketplace day by day with those who happened to be there. [NIV]<br>Therefore he **reasoned** in the synagogue with the Jews and with the *Gentile* worshipers, and in the marketplace daily with those who happened to be there. [NKJV]<br>He went to the synagogue to **debate** with the Jews and the God-fearing Gentiles, and he spoke daily in the public square to all who happened to be there. [NLT]<br>διελέγετο μὲν οὖν ἐν τῇ συναγωγῇ τοῖς Ἰουδαίοις καὶ τοῖς σεβομένοις καὶ ἐν τῇ ἀγορᾷ κατὰ πᾶσαν ἡμέραν πρὸς τοὺς παρατυγχάνοντας. [GNS]<br>διελέγετο μὲν οὖν ἐν τῇ συναγωγῇ τοῖς Ἰουδαίοις καὶ τοῖς σεβομένοις καὶ ἐν τῇ ἀγορᾷ κατὰ πᾶσαν ἡμέραν πρὸς τοὺς παρατυγχάνοντας. [GNT] | 1. He was zealous, full of fervor and passion, eagerly grasping every moment and opportunity.<br>2. He knew the stakes were high. The destiny of everyone he passed and saw lay in the balance. They were all lost and doomed unless he could reach them with the gospel. Therefore, no matter the cost, he had to do all he could to reach and help them in their search for the truth. He reasoned, argued, debated for the gospel and the salvation of souls. |
| #1097<br>**Disputes**<br><br>Strifes–KJV<br>**Disputes**–NASB<br>Factions–NIV<br>Selfish ambitions–NKJV<br>Selfishness–NLT<br><br>**POSB<br>REFERENCE**<br>(2 Cor.12:19-21; esp. v.20)<br>Note 3, point 2<br><br>See also POSB REF:<br>(Gal.5:19-21; esp. v.20)<br>Note 2 | ἐριθεῖαι = *eritheiai*<br>Pronunciation: [er-ith-i'-ah-ee]<br>Parsing (part of speech): noun<br>   Case—nominative<br>   Gender—feminine<br>   Number—plural<br>   Stem or root—from ἐριθεία, ας<br>Concordance References:<br>⇒ Strong's #2052 eritheia<br>⇒ NIV #2249 eritheia<br>⇒ NASB #2052 eritheia<br><br>**2 Cor. 12:20**<br>For I fear, lest, when I come, I shall not find you such as I would, and that I shall be found unto you such as ye would not: lest there be debates, envyings, wraths, **strifes**, backbitings, whisperings, swellings, tumults: [KJV]<br>For I am afraid that perhaps when I come I may find you to be not what I wish and may be found by you to be not what you wish; that perhaps there may be strife, jealousy, angry tempers, **disputes**, slanders, gossip, arrogance, disturbances; [NASB]<br>For I am afraid that when I come I may not find you as I want you to be, and you may not find me as you want me to be. I fear that there may be quarreling, jealousy, outbursts of anger, **factions**, slander, gossip, arrogance and disorder. [NIV]<br>For I fear lest, when I come, I shall not find you such as I wish, and *that* I shall be found by you such as you do not wish; lest *there be* contentions, jealousies, outbursts of wrath, **selfish ambitions**, backbitings, whisperings, conceits, tumults; [NKJV]<br>For I am afraid that when I come to visit you I won't like what I find, and then you won't like my response. I am afraid that I will find quarreling, jealousy, outbursts of anger, **selfishness**, backstabbing, gossip, conceit, and disorderly behavior. [NLT]<br>φοβοῦμαι γὰρ μή πως ἐλθὼν οὐχ οἵους θέλω εὕρω ὑμᾶς, κἀγὼ εὑρεθῶ ὑμῖν οἷον οὐ θέλετε· μή πως ἔρις, | Factions, envying, disputes, selfishness; selfish ambitions; an envious spirit or clique that stands as a rival to others; a factious spirit caused by selfishness or self-seeking.<br><br>**Practical Application**<br>Paul was stricken with fear, fear lest the church fail to be what it should be and reject him and his ministry. Paul feared that the church would fail to deal with the carnal critics and continue putting up with their evil attacks against him. He lists eight evils—including "disputes" (*eritheiai*)—that were and still are characteristic of divisive critics in the church. |

# PRACTICAL WORD STUDIES
## in the NEW TESTAMENT

| ENGLISH WORD | GREEK WORD AND VERSE | THE WORD MEANS... |
|---|---|---|
| | ζῆλοι, θυμοί, **ἐριθεῖαι**, καταλαλιαί, ψιθυρισμοί, φυσιώσεις, ἀκαταστασίαι· [GNS]<br>φοβοῦμαι γὰρ μή πως ἐλθὼν οὐχ οἵους θέλω εὕρω ὑμᾶς κἀγὼ εὑρεθῶ ὑμῖν οἷον οὐ θέλετε· μή πως ἔρις, ζῆλος, θυμοί, **ἐριθεῖαι**, καταλαλιαί, ψιθυρισμοί, φυσιώσεις, ἀκαταστασίαι· [GNT] | |
| **#1098**<br>**Disputes**<br><br>Seditions–KJV<br>**Disputes–NASB**<br>Dissensions–NIV<br>Dissensions–NKJV<br>Divisions–NLT<br><br>**POSB REFERENCE**<br>(Gal.5:19-21; esp. v.20)<br>Note 2 | διχοστασίαι = *dichostasiai*<br>Pronunciation: [dee-khos-tas-ee'-ah-ee]<br>Parsing (part of speech): noun<br>    Case—nominative<br>    Gender—feminine<br>    Number—plural<br>    Stem or root—from διχοστασία, ας<br>Concordance References:<br>  ⇒ Strong's #1370 dichostasia<br>  ⇒ NIV #1496 dichostasia<br>  ⇒ NASB #1370 dichostasia<br><br>**Galatians 5:20**<br>Idolatry, witchcraft, hatred, variance, emulations, wrath, strife, **seditions**, heresies, [KJV]<br>Idolatry, sorcery, enmities, strife, jealousy, outbursts of anger, **disputes**, dissensions, factions, [NASB]<br>Idolatry and witchcraft; hatred, discord, jealousy, fits of rage, selfish ambition, **dissensions**, factions [NIV]<br>Idolatry, sorcery, hatred, contentions, jealousies, outbursts of wrath, selfish ambitions, **dissensions**, heresies, [NKJV]<br>Idolatry, participation in demonic activities, hostility, quarreling, jealousy, outbursts of anger, selfish ambition, **divisions**, the feeling that everyone is wrong except those in your own little group, [NLT]<br>εἰδωλολατρία, φαρμακεία, ἔχθραι, ἔρεις, ζῆλοι, θυμοί, ἐριθεῖαι, **διχοστασίαι**, αἱρέσεις, [GNS]<br>εἰδωλολατρία, φαρμακεία, ἔχθραι, ἔρις, ζῆλος, θυμοί, ἐριθεῖαι, **διχοστασίαι**, αἱρέσεις, [GNT] | Dissensions, seditions, disputes, divisions, rebellions, standing against others, splitting off from others.<br><br>**Practical Application**<br>Despising authority within society is dangerous. It often leads to rebellion.<br>What happens is that those in power create human laws that favor themselves, the rich and the powerful. Human law is not enough for man, for man cannot create a law higher than himself. Therefore, whoever is in power will always be influenced by some selfishness. He will seldom, if ever, give all he is and has to be perfectly just and equal to all. Therefore, God's law is necessary. Man must have a law that is above and beyond himself. Man must have a law that controls and governs all men. And more than this, man must have a living Lord who can give him the power and who can motivate him to live like he should. This is the reason the Lord Jesus Christ, who reveals and fulfills the law of God perfectly, must be proclaimed. He must be exalted and not denied. The only hope for man is to deny himself and give all he is and has to meet the desperate needs of *all the people and not of just a few*. |
| **#1099**<br>**Disputing**<br><br>**Disputing–KJV**<br>Reasoning–NASB<br>Arguing–NIV<br>Reasoning–NKJV<br>Arguing–NLT<br><br>**POSB REFERENCE**<br>(Acts 19:2-9; esp. v.8)<br>Note 2, point 2a | διαλεγόμενος = *dialegomenos*<br>Pronunciation: [dee-al-eg'-om-ehn-os]<br>Parsing (part of speech): verb<br>    Mood—participle<br>    Tense—present<br>    Voice—middle or passive deponent<br>    Case—nominative<br>    Gender—masculine<br>    Number—singular<br>    Stem or root—from διαλέγομαι<br>Concordance References:<br>  ⇒ Strong's #1256 dialegomai<br>  ⇒ NIV #1363 dialegomai<br>  ⇒ NASB #1256 dialegomai<br><br>**Acts 19:8**<br>And he went into the synagogue, and spake boldly for the space of three months, **disputing** and persuading the things concerning the kingdom of God. [KJV]<br>And he entered the synagogue and continued speaking out boldly for three months, **reasoning** and persuading them about the kingdom of God. [NASB]<br>Paul entered the synagogue and spoke boldly there for three months, **arguing** persuasively about the kingdom of God. [NIV]<br>And he went into the synagogue and spoke boldly for three months, **reasoning** and persuading concerning the things of the kingdom of God. [NKJV]<br>Then Paul went to the synagogue and preached boldly for the next three months, **arguing** persuasively about the Kingdom of God. [NLT]<br>Εἰσελθὼν δὲ εἰς τὴν συναγωγὴν, ἐπαρρησιάζετο, ἐπὶ μῆνας τρεῖς **διαλεγόμενος**, καὶ πείθων τὰ περὶ τῆς βασιλείας τοῦ Θεοῦ. [GNS]<br>Εἰσελθὼν δὲ εἰς τὴν συναγωγὴν ἐπαρρησιάζετο ἐπὶ μῆνας τρεῖς **διαλεγόμενος** καὶ πείθων [τὰ] περὶ τῆς βασιλείας τοῦ θεοῦ. [GNT] | To argue; to dispute; to reason; to discuss; to convince; to debate; to answer questions.<br><br>**Practical Application**<br>Paul preached boldly in the synagogue of the Jews. He discussed the gospel, asking and answering questions, convincing all who were willing to be convinced. |

## PRACTICAL WORD STUDIES
### in the NEW TESTAMENT

| ENGLISH WORD | GREEK WORD AND VERSE | THE WORD MEANS... |
|---|---|---|
| **#1100**<br>**Disqualified**<br><br>Castaway–KJV<br>**Disqualified–NASB**<br>**Disqualified–NIV**<br>**Disqualified –NKJV**<br>**Disqualified–NLT**<br><br>**POSB<br>REFERENCE**<br>(1 Cor.9:27)<br>Note 6, point 2 | ἀδόκιμος = *adokimos*<br>Pronunciation: [ad-ok'-ee-mos]<br>Parsing (part of speech): adjective<br>    Case—nominative<br>    Gender—masculine<br>    Number—singular<br>    Stem or root—from ἀδόκιμος, ον<br>Concordance References:<br>  ⇒ Strong's #96 adokimos<br>  ⇒ NIV #99 adokimos<br>  ⇒ NASB #96 adokimos<br><br>**1 Cor. 9:27**<br>But I keep under my body, and bring it into subjection: lest that by any means, when I have preached to others, I myself should be a **castaway**. [KJV]<br>But I buffet my body and make it my slave, lest possibly, after I have preached to others, I myself should be **disqualified**. [NASB]<br>No, I beat my body and make it my slave so that after I have preached to others, I myself will not be **disqualified** for the prize. [NIV]<br>But I discipline my body and bring *it* into subjection, lest, when I have preached to others, I myself should become **disqualified**. [NKJV]<br>I discipline my body like an athlete, training it to do what it should. Otherwise, I fear that after preaching to others I myself might be **disqualified**. [NLT]<br>ἀλλὰ ὑπωπιάζω μου τὸ σῶμα καὶ δουλαγωγῶ, μήπως, ἄλλοις κηρύξας αὐτὸς **ἀδόκιμος** γένωμαι. [GNS]<br>ἀλλὰ ὑπωπιάζω μου τὸ σῶμα καὶ δουλαγωγῶ, μή πως ἄλλοις κηρύξας αὐτὸς **ἀδόκιμος** γένωμαι. [GNT] | Disqualified, reprobate, worthless, rejected, disapproved, depraved, unfit; failing to stand the test.<br><br>**Practical Application**<br>What does Paul mean? Most writers think that Paul is referring to salvation, that when he comes to the end of the race, he sees the possibility of being rejected—if he has not *lived* what he has preached to others.<br>The very fact that most writers understand Paul to be dealing with salvation clearly speaks to all ministers of the gospel: we must heed the Scripture.<br>Now, what does Paul mean? Five things are sure about Paul's teaching in Scripture.<br>**First**, Paul definitely pictured himself in a life-long struggle for salvation. The great Greek scholar A.T. Robertson says that Paul alone uses the Greek word *adokimos* in a moral sense in the New Testament, and Paul definitely says that he subjects his body and keeps it under control lest he be *disqualified*. Look at Paul's use of the word. It stands as a beneficial warning to us all—to live what we preach, to profess and live it with the utmost diligence and effort. (*Word Pictures in the New Testament*, Vol. 4, p.150.)<br>**Second**, Paul definitely pictured himself as having to struggle against sin throughout life, and he struggled against sin for two reasons:<br>⇒ to attain to the resurrection of the dead (Philip.3:11).<br>⇒ to conquer the flesh, the sinful nature.<br>**Third**, Paul was perfectly assured of his salvation; he was perfectly assured that he would run the race and run it well. He was persuaded of two things:<br>⇒ that nothing in heaven or earth, in fact, nothing present and nothing to come, could ever separate him from the love of God (Ro.8:35-39).<br>⇒ that the Lord was able to *keep him* until the day of redemption.<br>**Fourth**, Paul was convinced that only those who walked in the Spirit and were committed to a deadly struggle against sin were saved and given the absolute assurance of their salvation (see POSB outline—Romans 8:1-17 and POSB notes—Romans 8:1-17).<br>**Fifth**, Paul was not perfect, and he confessed the fact, confessing that he was far from perfect. Therefore, until he was made perfect, he was going to struggle, follow, press, and strive for perfection; that is, to be conformed to the image of Christ (Ro.8:29; Philip.3:10-11). |
| **#1101**<br>**Disqualified**<br><br>Reprobates–KJV<br>Fail the test–NASB<br>Fail the test–NIV<br>**Disqualified–NKJV**<br>Failed the test–NLT | ἀδόκιμοί ἐστε = *adokimoi este*<br>Pronunciation: [ad-ok'-ee-moy es-teh]<br>Parsing *adokimoi* (part of speech): adjective<br>    Case—nominative<br>    Gender—masculine<br>    Number—plural<br>    Stem or root—from ἀδόκιμος, ον<br>Concordance References:<br>  ⇒ Strong's #96 adokimos + 1510 eimi<br>  ⇒ NIV #99+1639 adokimos eimi [fail the test]<br>  ⇒ NASB #96b adokimos + 1510 eimi | To fail the test; to be a reprobate; to be tested and found worthless; to be tested and disqualified and rejected; to be found unfit and disapproved; to be doomed and condemned to perdition.<br><br>**Practical Application**<br>The believers had to examine themselves to make sure they were in the faith.<br>⇒ They needed to make sure they were gen- |

# PRACTICAL WORD STUDIES
## in the NEW TESTAMENT

| ENGLISH WORD | GREEK WORD AND VERSE | THE WORD MEANS... |
|---|---|---|
| **POSB REFERENCE** (2 Cor.13:1-6; esp. v.5) Note 1, point 3 | **2 Cor. 13:5**<br>Examine yourselves, whether ye be in the faith; prove your own selves. Know ye not your own selves, how that Jesus Christ is in you, except ye be **reprobates**? [KJV]<br>Test yourselves to see if you are in the faith; examine yourselves! Or do you not recognize this about yourselves, that Jesus Christ is in you— unless indeed you **fail the test**? [NASB]<br>Examine yourselves to see whether you are in the faith; test yourselves. Do you not realize that Christ Jesus is in you—unless, of course, you **fail the test**? [NIV]<br>Examine yourselves *as to* whether you are in the faith. Test yourselves. Do you not know yourselves, that Jesus Christ is in you?—unless indeed you are **disqualified**. [NKJV]<br>Examine yourselves to see if your faith is really genuine. Test yourselves. If you cannot tell that Jesus Christ is among you, it means you have **failed the test**. [NLT]<br>ἑαυτοὺς πειράζετε εἰ ἐστὲ ἐν τῇ πίστει, ἑαυτοὺς δοκιμάζετε. ἢ οὐκ ἐπιγινώσκετε ἑαυτοὺς ὅτι Ἰησοῦς Χριστὸς ἐν ὑμῖν; εἰ μή τι **ἀδόκιμοί ἐστε**. [GNS]<br>Ἑαυτοὺς πειράζετε εἰ ἐστὲ ἐν τῇ πίστει, ἑαυτοὺς δοκιμάζετε· ἢ οὐκ ἐπιγινώσκετε ἑαυτοὺς ὅτι Ἰησοῦς Χριστὸς ἐν ὑμῖν; εἰ μήτι **ἀδόκιμοί ἐστε**. [GNT] | uine. Living in sin makes a person's faith suspect. Some were living in sin: "Examine yourselves *as to* whether you are in the faith. Test yourselves."<br>⇒ They needed to make sure that *Jesus Christ was in them* and that they were *not* "disqualified" (*adokimoi este*). (see POSB note, Castaway—1 Cor. 9:27—for more discussion.)<br>⇒ They needed to know that Paul was not disqualified.<br><br>The only way the Corinthians could know these things was to examine themselves. |
| **#1102**<br>**Disqualify For**<br><br>Beguile–KJV<br>Defrauding–NASB<br>**Disqualify for–NIV**<br>Cheat–NKJV<br>Condemn–NLT<br><br>**POSB REFERENCE** (Col.2:18-19; esp. v.18) Note 2 | καταβραβευέτω = *katabrabeuetō*<br>Pronunciation: [kat-ab-rab-yoo'-eh-tow]<br>Parsing (part of speech): verb<br>  Mood—imperative<br>  Tense—present<br>  Voice—active<br>  Person—3rd person<br>  Number—singular<br>  Stem or root—from καταβραβεύω<br>Concordance References:<br>⇒ Strong's #2603 katabrabeuō<br>⇒ NIV #2857 katabrabeuō<br>⇒ NASB #2603 katabrabeuō<br><br>**Col. 2:18**<br>Let no man **beguile** you of your reward in a voluntary humility and worshipping of angels, intruding into those things which he hath not seen, vainly puffed up by his fleshly mind, [KJV]<br>Let no one keep **defrauding** you of your prize by delighting in self-abasement and the worship of the angels, taking his stand on visions he has seen, inflated without cause by his fleshly mind, [NASB]<br>Do not let anyone who delights in false humility and the worship of angels **disqualify** you **for** the prize. Such a person goes into great detail about what he has seen, and his unspiritual mind puffs him up with idle notions. [NIV]<br>Let no one **cheat** you of your reward, taking delight in *false* humility and worship of angels, intruding into those things which he has not seen, vainly puffed up by his fleshly mind, [NKJV]<br>Don't let anyone **condemn** you by insisting on self-denial. And don't let anyone say you must worship angels, even though they say they have had visions about this. These people claim to be so humble, but their sinful minds have made them proud. [NLT]<br>μηδεὶς ὑμᾶς **καταβραβευέτω** θέλων ἐν ταπεινοφροσύνῃ καὶ θρησκείᾳ τῶν ἀγγέλων, ἃ μὴ ἑώρακεν ἐμβατεύων, εἰκῇ φυσιούμενος ὑπὸ τοῦ νοὸς τῆς σαρκὸς αὐτοῦ, [GNS]<br>μηδεὶς ὑμᾶς **καταβραβευέτω** θέλων ἐν ταπεινοφροσύνῃ καὶ θρησκείᾳ τῶν ἀγγέλων, ἃ ἑόρακεν ἐμβατεύων, εἰκῇ φυσιούμενος ὑπὸ τοῦ νοὸς τῆς σαρκὸς αὐτοῦ, [GNT] | To disqualify; to beguile; to defraud; to cheat; to condemn. It means to rob; to defraud; to cheat a person out of his reward.<br><br>**Practical Application**<br>It is possible for believers to be disqualified for their reward by false teachers. How? By following those who teach that there is another approach to God other than Christ. Christ is God's appointed way to approach Him, and there is no other way. |

# PRACTICAL WORD STUDIES
## in the NEW TESTAMENT

| ENGLISH WORD | GREEK WORD AND VERSE | THE WORD MEANS... |
|---|---|---|
| **#1103**<br>**Dissension**<br><br>Strife–KJV<br>Strife–NASB<br>**Dissension–NIV**<br>Strife–NKJV<br>Fighting–NLT<br><br>**POSB REFERENCE**<br>(Rom.13:13)<br>Note 4, point 5 | ἔριδι = *eridi*<br>Pronunciation: [er'-i-di]<br>Parsing (part of speech): noun<br>    Case—dative<br>    Gender—feminine<br>    Number—singular<br>    Stem or root—from ἔρις, ιδος<br>Concordance References:<br>⇒ Strong's #2054 eris<br>⇒ NIV #2251 eris<br>⇒ NASB #2054 eris<br><br>**Romans 13:13**<br>    Let us walk honestly, as in the day; not in rioting and drunkenness, not in chambering and wantonness, not in **strife** and envying. [KJV]<br>    Let us behave properly as in the day, not in carousing and drunkenness, not in sexual promiscuity and sensuality, not in **strife** and jealousy. [NASB]<br>    Let us behave decently, as in the daytime, not in orgies and drunkenness, not in sexual immorality and debauchery, not in **dissension** and jealousy. [NIV]<br>    Let us walk properly, as in the day, not in revelry and drunkenness, not in lewdness and lust, not in **strife** and envy. [NKJV]<br>    We should be decent and true in everything we do, so that everyone can approve of our behavior. Don't participate in wild parties and getting drunk, or in adultery and immoral living, or in **fighting** and jealousy. [NLT]<br>    ὡς ἐν ἡμέρᾳ, εὐσχημόνως περιπατήσωμεν, μὴ κώμοις καὶ μέθαις, μὴ κοίταις καὶ ἀσελγείαις, μὴ **ἔριδι** καὶ ζήλῳ. [GNS]<br>    ὡς ἐν ἡμέρᾳ εὐσχημόνως περιπατήσωμεν, μὴ κώμοις καὶ μέθαις, μὴ κοίταις καὶ ἀσελγείαις, μὴ **ἔριδι** καὶ ζήλῳ, [GNT] | Dissension, strife, fighting, selfish rivalry, contention, quarreling, arguing, striving.<br><br>**Practical Application**<br>    It is the restless craving deep within a person that wants recognition, honor, position, and authority. It is a spirit that is in constant competition with others, that will push one forward...<br>• by putting others down<br>• by bypassing others<br>• by ignoring others<br>• by holding others back<br>• by blaming others<br>• by neglecting others |
| **#1104**<br>**Dissensions**<br><br>Divisions–KJV<br>**Dissensions–NASB**<br>Divisions–NIV<br>Divisions–NKJV<br>Divisions–NLT<br><br>**POSB REFERENCE**<br>(Rom.16:17-18; esp. v.17)<br>Note 1, point 1 | διχοστασίας = *dichostasias*<br>Pronunciation: [dee-khos-tas-ee'-ahs]<br>Parsing (part of speech): noun<br>    Case—accusative<br>    Gender—feminine<br>    Number—plural<br>    Stem or root—from διχοστασία, ας<br>Concordance References:<br>⇒ Strong's #1370 dichostasia<br>⇒ NIV #1496 dichostasia<br>⇒ NASB #1370 dichostasia<br><br>**Romans 16:17**<br>    Now I beseech you, brethren, mark them which cause **divisions** and offences contrary to the doctrine which ye have learned; and avoid them. [KJV]<br>    Now I urge you, brethren, keep your eye on those who cause **dissensions** and hindrances contrary to the teaching which you learned, and turn away from them. [NASB]<br>    I urge you, brothers, to watch out for those who cause **divisions** and put obstacles in your way that are contrary to the teaching you have learned. Keep away from them. [NIV]<br>    Now I urge you, brethren, note those who cause **divisions** and offenses, contrary to the doctrine which you learned, and avoid them. [NKJV]<br>    And now I make one more appeal, my dear brothers and sisters. Watch out for people who cause **divisions** and upset people's faith by teaching things that are contrary to what you have been taught. Stay away from them. [NLT]<br>    Παρακαλῶ δὲ ὑμᾶς, ἀδελφοί, σκοπεῖν τοὺς τὰς **διχοστασίας** καὶ τὰ σκάνδαλα, παρὰ τὴν διδαχὴν ἣν ὑμεῖς ἐμάθετε, ποιοῦντας· καὶ ἐκκλίνατε ἀπ' αὐτῶν. [GNS] | Divisions, dissensions, disputes, rebellion; splitting off from the others. It means standing apart, being separate, causing cleavage.<br><br>**Practical Application**<br>    A divisive person causes division and lays stumbling blocks in the way of growth. Note exactly what is said: a divisive person acts "contrary to the teaching which [believers] learned." He causes "dissensions and divisions." |

# Practical Word Studies
## in the New Testament

| ENGLISH WORD | GREEK WORD AND VERSE | THE WORD MEANS... |
|---|---|---|
| | Παρακαλῶ δὲ ὑμᾶς, ἀδελφοί, σκοπεῖν τοὺς τὰς **διχοστασίας** καὶ τὰ σκάνδαλα παρὰ τὴν διδαχὴν ἣν ὑμεῖς ἐμάθετε ποιοῦντας, καὶ ἐκκλίνετε ἀπ' αὐτῶν· [GNT] | |
| **#1105**<br>**Dissensions**<br><br>Seditions–KJV<br>Disputes–NASB<br>**Dissensions–NIV**<br>**Dissensions–NKJV**<br>Divisions–NLT<br><br>**POSB REFERENCE**<br>(Gal.5:19-21; esp. v.20)<br>Note 2 | διχοστασίαι = *dichostasiai*<br>Pronunciation: [dee-khos-tas-ee'-ah-ee]<br>Parsing (part of speech): noun<br>    Case—nominative<br>    Gender—feminine<br>    Number—plural<br>    Stem or root—from διχοστασία, ας<br>Concordance References:<br>  ⇒ Strong's #1370 dichostasia<br>  ⇒ NIV #1496 dichostasia<br>  ⇒ NASB #1370 dichostasia<br><br>**Galatians 5:20**<br>Idolatry, witchcraft, hatred, variance, emulations, wrath, strife, **seditions**, heresies, [KJV]<br>Idolatry, sorcery, enmities, strife, jealousy, outbursts of anger, **disputes**, dissensions, factions, [NASB]<br>Idolatry and witchcraft; hatred, discord, jealousy, fits of rage, selfish ambition, **dissensions**, factions [NIV]<br>Idolatry, sorcery, hatred, contentions, jealousies, outbursts of wrath, selfish ambitions, **dissensions**, heresies, [NKJV]<br>Idolatry, participation in demonic activities, hostility, quarreling, jealousy, outbursts of anger, selfish ambition, **divisions**, the feeling that everyone is wrong except those in your own little group, [NLT]<br>εἰδωλολατρία, φαρμακεία, ἔχθραι, ἔρεις, ζῆλοι, θυμοί, ἐριθεῖαι, **διχοστασίαι**, αἱρέσεις, [GNS]<br>εἰδωλολατρία, φαρμακεία, ἔχθραι, ἔρις, ζῆλος, θυμοί, ἐριθεῖαι, **διχοστασίαι**, αἱρέσεις, [GNT] | Dissensions, seditions, disputes, divisions, rebellions, standing against others, splitting off from others.<br><br>**Practical Application**<br>Despising authority within society is dangerous. It often leads to rebellion.<br>What happens is that those in power create human laws that favor themselves, the rich and the powerful. Human law is not enough for man, for man cannot create a law higher than himself. Therefore, whoever is in power will always be influenced by some selfishness. He will seldom, if ever, give all he is and has to be perfectly just and equal to all. Therefore, God's law is necessary. Man must have a law that is above and beyond himself. Man must have a law that controls and governs all men. And more than this, man must have a living Lord who can give him the power and who can motivate him to live like he should. This is the reason the Lord Jesus Christ, who reveals and fulfills the law of God perfectly, must be proclaimed. He must be exalted and not denied. The only hope for man is to deny himself and give all he is and has to meet the desperate needs of *all the people and not of just a few.* |
| **#1106**<br>**Dissimulation, Without**<br><br>**Without dissimulation**–KJV<br>Without hypocrisy–NASB<br>Sincere–NIV<br>Without hypocrisy–NKJV<br>Don't just pretend–NLT<br><br>**POSB REFERENCE**<br>(Rom.12:9-10; esp. v.9)<br>Note 1<br><br>See also POSB REF:<br>(1 Pt.1:22-25; esp. v.22)<br>Note 1<br>(Jas 3:17-18; esp. v.17)<br>Note 3 | ἀνυπόκριτος = *anupokritos*<br>Pronunciation: [an-oo-pok'-ree-tos]<br>Parsing (part of speech): adjective<br>    Case—nominative<br>    Gender—feminine<br>    Number—singular<br>    Stem or root—from ἀνυπόκριτος, ον<br>Concordance References:<br>  ⇒ Strong's #505 anupokritos<br>  ⇒ NIV #537 anupokritos<br>  ⇒ NASB #505 anupokritos<br><br>**Romans 12:9**<br>Let love be **without dissimulation**. Abhor that which is evil; cleave to that which is good. [KJV]<br>Let love be **without hypocrisy**. Abhor what is evil; cling to what is good. [NASB]<br>Love must be **sincere**. Hate what is evil; cling to what is good. [NIV]<br>*Let* love *be* **without hypocrisy**. Abhor what is evil. Cling to what is good. [NKJV]<br>**Don't just pretend** that you love others. Really love them. Hate what is wrong. Stand on the side of the good. [NLT]<br>Ἡ ἀγάπη **ἀνυπόκριτος**. ἀποστυγοῦντες τὸ πονηρόν, κολλώμενοι τῷ ἀγαθῷ. [GNS]<br>Ἡ ἀγάπη **ἀνυπόκριτος**. ἀποστυγοῦντες τὸ πονηρόν, κολλώμενοι τῷ ἀγαθῷ, [GNT] | To be sincere; to be genuine. It means without hypocrisy, without play-acting. This means to be free from insincerity, hypocrisy, play-acting, and wearing a mask.<br><br>**Practical Application**<br>The believer is to love sincerely without hypocrisy or dissimulation. It means that a person does not just say "I love you," but he actually loves. He sincerely loves; he honestly and truthfully loves. The love being spoken about is love for all men and not only for believers. The believer must never pretend, be hypocritical, play-act, or have an ulterior motive when dealing with others. He must show love and respect, interest and attention, care and concern; but he must not show it from an impure motive. |
| **#1107**<br>**Dissipation**<br><br>Surfeiting–KJV<br>**Dissipation–NASB**<br>**Dissipation–NIV**<br>Carousing–NKJV<br>Careless ease–NLT | κραιπάλη = *kraipalē*<br>Pronunciation: [krahee-pal'-ay]<br>Parsing (part of speech): noun<br>    Case—dative<br>    Gender—feminine<br>    Number—singular<br>    Stem or root—from κραιπάλη, ης<br>Concordance References:<br>  ⇒ Strong's #2897 kraipalē | Dissipation, surfeiting, careless ease; to be light hearted, silly, frivolous, giddy.<br><br>**Practical Application**<br>Medically, it referred to drunken nausea or headaches. It is the kind of light heartedness, silliness, frivolity, and giddiness that comes from partying and drinking. It is the loose, giddy, |

# Practical Word Studies
## in the New Testament

| ENGLISH WORD | GREEK WORD AND VERSE | THE WORD MEANS... |
|---|---|---|
| **POSB REFERENCE** (Lk.21:34-35; esp. v.34) Note 1, point 1 | ⇒ NIV #3190 kraipalë<br>⇒ NASB #2897 kraipalë<br><br>**Luke 21:34**<br>And take heed to yourselves, lest at any time your hearts be overcharged with **surfeiting**, and drunkenness, and cares of this life, and so that day come upon you unawares. [KJV]<br>"Be on guard, that your hearts may not be weighted down with **dissipation** and drunkenness and the worries of life, and that day come on you suddenly like a trap; [NASB]<br>"Be careful, or your hearts will be weighed down with **dissipation**, drunkenness and the anxieties of life, and that day will close on you unexpectedly like a trap. [NIV]<br>"But take heed to yourselves, lest your hearts be weighed down with **carousing**, drunkenness, and cares of this life, and that Day come on you unexpectedly. [NKJV]<br>"Watch out! Don't let me find you living in **careless ease** and drunkenness, and filled with the worries of this life. Don't let that day catch you unaware, [NLT]<br>Προσέχετε δὲ ἑαυτοῖς, μήποτε βαρυνθῶσιν ὑμῶν αἱ καρδίαι ἐν **κραιπάλῃ** καὶ μέθῃ καὶ μερίμναις βιωτικαῖς, καὶ αἰφνίδιος ἐφ' ὑμᾶς ἐπιστῇ ἡ ἡμέρα ἐκείνη· [GNS]<br>Προσέχετε δὲ ἑαυτοῖς μήποτε βαρηθῶσιν ὑμῶν αἱ καρδίαι ἐν **κραιπάλῃ** καὶ μέθῃ καὶ μερίμναις βιωτικαῖς καὶ ἐπιστῇ ἐφ' ὑμᾶς αἰφνίδιος ἡ ἡμέρα ἐκείνη [GNT] | suggestive movements and talk that take place...<br>• at parties<br>• at social gatherings<br>• on dates<br>• behind closed doors<br>• at luncheons & dinner engagements<br>• at dances<br>• at clubs<br>• on business trips<br>• in the dark |
| **#1108**<br>**Dissipation**<br><br>Excess–KJV<br>**Dissipation**–NASB<br>Debauchery–NIV<br>**Dissipation**–NKJV<br>Will ruin your life–NLT<br><br>**POSB REFERENCE** (Eph.5:18) Note 4 | ἀσωτία = asōtia<br>Pronunciation: [as-o-tee'-ah]<br>Parsing (part of speech): noun<br>    Case—nominative<br>    Gender—feminine<br>    Number—singular<br>    Stem or root—from ἀσωτία, ας<br>Concordance References:<br>⇒ Strong's #810 asōtia<br>⇒ NIV #861 asōtia<br>⇒ NASB #810 asōtia<br><br>**Ephes. 5:18**<br>And be not drunk with wine, wherein is **excess**; but be filled with the Spirit; [KJV]<br>And do not get drunk with wine, for that is **dissipation**, but be filled with the Spirit, [NASB]<br>Do not get drunk on wine, which leads to **debauchery**. Instead, be filled with the Spirit. [NIV]<br>And do not be drunk with wine, in which is **dissipation**; but be filled with the Spirit, [NKJV]<br>Don't be drunk with wine, because that **will ruin your life**. Instead, let the Holy Spirit fill and control you. [NLT]<br>καὶ μὴ μεθύσκεσθε οἴνῳ, ἐν ᾧ ἐστιν **ἀσωτία**, ἀλλὰ πληροῦσθε ἐν Πνεύματι, [GNS]<br>καὶ μὴ μεθύσκεσθε οἴνῳ, ἐν ᾧ ἐστιν **ἀσωτία**, ἀλλὰ πληροῦσθε ἐν πνεύματι, [GNT] | Debauchery, excess behavior, dissipation, reckless living, a ruined life. The word means...<br>• the dissipation and wasting away of the body.<br>• uncontrolled behavior.<br>• rioting, debauchery, wild and outrageous behavior and conduct.<br><br>**Practical Application**<br>Drunkenness is a work of the flesh and it often leads to other sins of the flesh: partying, loose behavior, immodest clothing, exposure of the body, sexual thoughts, immorality, wicked or evil and unjust behavior or violence and physical abuse, notions of grandeur, strength or power. The Bible says several things about drunkenness.<br>1. Drunkenness excludes a person from the kingdom of God.<br>2. Drunkenness leads to other forms of misbehavior and sin.<br>3. Drunkenness makes it impossible to grasp the fleeting opportunities of time. |
| **#1109**<br>**Distort**<br><br>Deceitfully–KJV<br>Adulterating–NASB<br>**Distort**–NIV<br>Deceitfully–NKJV<br>**Distort**–NLT | δολοῦντες = dolountes<br>Pronunciation: [dol-oon'-tehs]<br>Parsing (part of speech): verb<br>    Mood—participle<br>    Tense—present<br>    Voice—active<br>    Case—nominative<br>    Number—masculine<br>    Person—1st person<br>    Number—plural<br>    Stem or root—from δολόω<br>Concordance References:<br>⇒ Strong's #1389 doloō | To distort; to falsify; to adulterate; to corrupt; to deceive; to ensnare.<br><br>**Practical Application**<br>The minister is not to distort (*dolountes*) the word of God." It is "the Word *of God*"; that is, it has come from God, not man. The Author of the Word of God is God. God is the *Authority* of the Word of God. The minister is only the *spokesman* for God; therefore, he is...<br>• not to falsify the Word of God. |

# PRACTICAL WORD STUDIES
## in the NEW TESTAMENT

| ENGLISH WORD | GREEK WORD AND VERSE | THE WORD MEANS... |
|---|---|---|
| **POSB REFERENCE** (2 Cor.4:2) Note 2 | ⇒ NIV #1516 doloö<br>⇒ NASB #1389 doloö<br><br>**2 Cor. 4:2**<br>But have renounced the hidden things of dishonesty, not walking in craftiness, nor handling the word of God **deceitfully**; but by manifestation of the truth commending ourselves to every man's conscience in the sight of God. [KJV]<br>But we have renounced the things hidden because of shame, not walking in craftiness or **adulterating** the word of God, but by the manifestation of truth commending ourselves to every man's conscience in the sight of God. [NASB]<br>Rather, we have renounced secret and shameful ways; we do not use deception, nor do we **distort** the word of God. On the contrary, by setting forth the truth plainly we commend ourselves to every man's conscience in the sight of God. [NIV]<br>But we have renounced the hidden things of shame, not walking in craftiness nor handling the word of God **deceitfully**, but by manifestation of the truth commending ourselves to every man's conscience in the sight of God. [NKJV]<br>We reject all shameful and underhanded methods. We do not try to trick anyone, and we do not **distort** the word of God. We tell the truth before God, and all who are honest know that. [NLT]<br>ἀλλ ἀπειπάμεθα τὰ κρυπτὰ τῆς αἰσχύνης, μὴ περιπατοῦντες ἐν πανουργίᾳ μηδὲ **δολοῦντες** τὸν λόγον τοῦ Θεοῦ, ἀλλὰ τῇ φανερώσει τῆς ἀληθείας συνιστῶντες ἑαυτοὺς πρὸς πᾶσαν συνείδησιν ἀνθρώπων ἐνώπιον τοῦ Θεοῦ. [GNS]<br>ἀλλὰ ἀπειπάμεθα τὰ κρυπτὰ τῆς αἰσχύνης, μὴ περιπατοῦντες ἐν πανουργίᾳ μηδὲ **δολοῦντες** τὸν λόγον τοῦ θεοῦ ἀλλὰ τῇ φανερώσει τῆς ἀληθείας συνιστάνοντες ἑαυτοὺς πρὸς πᾶσαν συνείδησιν ἀνθρώπων ἐνώπιον τοῦ θεοῦ. [GNT] | • not to adulterate the Word of God.<br>• not to corrupt the Word of God.<br>• not to deceive or ensnare people by mishandling the Word of God.<br>The minister is not *to add* the ideas, traditions, philosophies, or speculations of men to the Word of God. Neither is he to take away portions of Scripture, denying that they are the Word of God; nor is he to neglect, ignore, or keep silent about some part of God's Word. The minister of God is not to distort the Word of God in any form or fashion. |
| **#1110**<br>**Distort**<br><br>Pervert–KJV<br>**Distort–NASB**<br>Pervert–NIV<br>Pervert–NKJV<br>Twist and change–NLT<br><br>**POSB REFERENCE** (Gal.1:6-7; esp. v.7) Note 2 | μεταστρέψαι = metastrepsai<br>Pronunciation: [met-as-tref´-sah-ee]<br>Parsing (part of speech): verb<br>    Mood—infinitive<br>    Tense—aorist<br>    Voice—active<br>    Stem or root—from μεταστρέφω<br>Concordance References:<br>⇒ Strong's #3344 metastrephö<br>⇒ NIV #3570 metastrephö<br>⇒ NASB #3344 metastrephö<br><br>**Galatians 1:7**<br>Which is not another; but there be some that trouble you, and would **pervert** the gospel of Christ. [KJV]<br>Which is really not another; only there are some who are disturbing you, and want to **distort** the gospel of Christ. [NASB]<br>Which is really no gospel at all. Evidently some people are throwing you into confusion and are trying to **pervert** the gospel of Christ. [NIV]<br>Which is not another; but there are some who trouble you and want to **pervert** the gospel of Christ. [NKJV]<br>That pretends to be the Good News but is not the Good News at all. You are being fooled by those who **twist and change** the truth concerning Christ. [NLT]<br>ὃ οὐκ ἔστιν ἄλλο, εἰ μή τινές εἰσιν οἱ ταράσσοντες ὑμᾶς καὶ θέλοντες **μεταστρέψαι** τὸ εὐαγγέλιον τοῦ Χριστοῦ. [GNS]<br>ὃ οὐκ ἔστιν ἄλλο, εἰ μή τινές εἰσιν οἱ ταράσσοντες ὑμᾶς καὶ θέλοντες **μεταστρέψαι** τὸ εὐαγγέλιον τοῦ Χριστοῦ. [GNT] | To distort; to turn about; to pervert; to change completely; to twist and change; to alter.<br><br>**Practical Application**<br>The false teachers were taking the gospel of God's love as demonstrated in His Son, Jesus Christ, and changing it. The false teachers claimed to be Christians, followers of Christ. They even believed with Paul...<br>• that God did love the world and sent His Son into the world.<br>• that Jesus Christ was the Son of God who did actually come to earth.<br>• that Jesus Christ did die and arise from the dead.<br>However, the false teachers were adding to and taking away from the gospel, twisting its meaning and making it say something entirely different from the Holy Scripture. |

## PRACTICAL WORD STUDIES
### in the NEW TESTAMENT

| ENGLISH WORD | GREEK WORD AND VERSE | THE WORD MEANS... |
|---|---|---|
| **#1111**<br>**Distort The Truth**<br><br>Speaking perverse things–KJV<br>Speaking perverse things–NASB<br>**Distort the truth–NIV**<br>Speaking perverse things–NKJV<br>**Distort the truth–NLT**<br><br>**POSB REFERENCE**<br>(Acts 20:29-30; esp. v.30)<br>*Deeper Study #2,* point 3 | λαλοῦντες διεστραμμένα = *lalountes diestrammena*<br>Pronunciation: [lal-oon'-tehs dee-as-tram'-mehn-ah]<br>Parsing *lalountes* (part of speech): verb<br>    Mood—participle<br>    Tense—present<br>    Voice—active<br>    Case—nominative<br>    Gender—masculine<br>    Number—plural<br>    Stem or root—from λαλέω<br>Parsing *diestrammena* (part of speech): verb<br>    Mood—participle<br>    Tense—perfect<br>    Voice—passive<br>    Case—accusative<br>    Gender—neuter<br>    Number—plural<br>    Stem or root—from διαστρέφω<br>Concordance References:<br>⇒ Strong's #1294 + 2980 diastrephō laleō<br>⇒ NIV #1406 + 3281 diastrephō laleō [distort the truth]<br>⇒ NASB #1294 + 2980 diastrephō laleō<br><br>**Acts 20:30**<br>Also of your own selves shall men arise, **speaking perverse things**, to draw away disciples after them. [KJV]<br>and from among your own selves men will arise, **speaking perverse things**, to draw away the disciples after them. [NASB]<br>Even from your own number men will arise and **distort the truth** in order to draw away disciples after them. [NIV]<br>Also from among yourselves men will rise up, **speaking perverse things**, to draw away the disciples after themselves. [NKJV]<br>Even some of you will **distort the truth** in order to draw a following. [NLT]<br>καὶ ἐξ ὑμῶν αὐτῶν ἀναστήσονται ἄνδρες **λαλοῦντες διεστραμμένα**, τοῦ ἀποσπᾶν τοὺς μαθητὰς ὀπίσω αὐτῶν. [GNS]<br>καὶ ἐξ ὑμῶν αὐτῶν ἀναστήσονται ἄνδρες **λαλοῦντες διεστραμμένα** τοῦ ἀποσπᾶν τοὺς μαθητὰς ὀπίσω αὐτῶν. [GNT] | To distort the truth; to speak perverse things; to pervert; to turn away; to mislead; to lead astray.<br><br>**Practical Application**<br>The term "distort the truth" (*lalountes diestrammena*) means turned aside, twisted, distorted. What the false teachers teach has some truth and some error. They take the truth and pervert it, coming up with a twisted truth. They teach "distorted truth" that is not of God, not of His Word or will. (See POSB note—Matthew 7:17; POSB note—Matthew 7:18 for more discussion.) |
| **#1112**<br>**Distracted**<br><br>Cumbered–KJV<br>**Distracted–NASB**<br>**Distracted–NIV**<br>**Distracted–NKJV**<br>Worrying–NLT<br><br>**POSB REFERENCE**<br>(Lk.10:40)<br>Note 3 | περιεσπᾶτο = *periespato*<br>Pronunciation: [per-ee-spah'-tow]<br>Parsing (part of speech): verb<br>    Mood—indicative<br>    Tense—imperfect<br>    Voice—passive<br>    Person—3rd person<br>    Number—singular<br>    Stem or root—from περισπάομαι<br>Concordance References:<br>⇒ Strong's #4049 perispaō<br>⇒ NIV #4352 perispaō<br>⇒ NASB #4049 perispaō<br><br>**Luke 10:40**<br>But Martha was **cumbered** about much serving, and came to him, and said, Lord, dost thou not care that my sister hath left me to serve alone? bid her therefore that she help me. [KJV]<br>But Martha was **distracted** with all her preparations; and she came up to Him, and said, "Lord, do You not care that my sister has left me to do all the serving alone? Then tell her to help me." [NASB]<br>But Martha was **distracted** by all the preparations that had to be made. She came to him and asked, "Lord, don't you care that my sister has left me to do the work by | To be distracted; to worry; to draw around; to twist; to be drawn here and there.<br><br>**Practical Application**<br>The idea is that Martha was drawn around and twisted with anxiety and worry. She was distracted, running here and there, being drawn by the cares of this and that person. |

# PRACTICAL WORD STUDIES
## in the NEW TESTAMENT

| ENGLISH WORD | GREEK WORD AND VERSE | THE WORD MEANS... |
|---|---|---|
| | myself? Tell her to help me!" [NIV]<br><br>But Martha was **distracted** with much serving, and she approached Him and said, "Lord, do You not care that my sister has left me to serve alone? Therefore tell her to help me." [NKJV]<br><br>But Martha was **worrying** over the big dinner she was preparing. She came to Jesus and said, "Lord, doesn't it seem unfair to you that my sister just sits here while I do all the work? Tell her to come and help me." [NLT]<br><br>ἡ δὲ Μάρθα **περιεσπᾶτο** περὶ πολλὴν διακονίαν· ἐπιστᾶσα δὲ εἶπε, Κύριε, οὐ μέλει σοι ὅτι ἡ ἀδελφή μου μόνην με κατέλιπε διακονεῖν; εἰπὲ οὖν αὐτῇ ἵνα μοι συναντιλάβηται. [GNS]<br><br>ἡ δὲ Μάρθα **περιεσπᾶτο** περὶ πολλὴν διακονίαν· ἐπιστᾶσα δὲ εἶπεν, Κύριε, οὐ μέλει σοι ὅτι ἡ ἀδελφή μου μόνην με κατέλιπεν διακονεῖν; εἰπὲ οὖν αὐτῇ ἵνα μοι συναντιλάβηται. [GNT] | |
| **#1113**<br>**Distress**<br><br>Anguish–KJV<br>**Distress**–NASB<br>**Distress**–NIV<br>Anguish–NKJV<br>Calamity–NLT<br><br>**POSB REFERENCE**<br>(Rom.2:9)<br>*Deeper Study #9* | στενοχωρία = stenochōria<br>Pronunciation: [sten-okh-o-ree'-ah]<br>Parsing (part of speech): noun<br>    Case—nominative<br>    Gender—feminine<br>    Number—singular<br>    Stem or root—from στενοχωρία, ας<br>Concordance References:<br>  ⇒ Strong's #4730 stenochōria<br>  ⇒ NIV #5103 stenochōria<br>  ⇒ NASB #4730 stenochōria<br><br>**Romans 2:9**<br>Tribulation and **anguish**, upon every soul of man that doeth evil, of the Jew first, and also of the Gentile; [KJV]<br><br>There will be tribulation and **distress** for every soul of man who does evil, of the Jew first and also of the Greek, [NASB]<br><br>There will be trouble and **distress** for every human being who does evil: first for the Jew, then for the Gentile; [NIV]<br><br>Tribulation and **anguish**, on every soul of man who does evil, of the Jew first and also of the Greek; [NKJV]<br><br>There will be trouble and **calamity** for everyone who keeps on sinning—for the Jew first and also for the Gentile. [NLT]<br><br>θλῖψις καὶ **στενοχωρία** ἐπὶ πᾶσαν ψυχὴν ἀνθρώπου τοῦ κατεργαζομένου τὸ κακόν, Ἰουδαίου τε πρῶτον καὶ Ἕλληνος· [GNS]<br><br>θλῖψις καὶ **στενοχωρία** ἐπὶ πᾶσαν ψυχὴν ἀνθρώπου τοῦ κατεργαζομένου τὸ κακόν, Ἰουδαίου τε πρῶτον καὶ Ἕλληνος· [GNT] | Distress, anguish, calamity, trouble, hardship, difficulty. It means to be put into a narrow place; to be compressed together; to experience extreme pain, sorrow, and affliction.<br><br>**Practical Application**<br>Every evil-doer is to be judged, both Jew and Gentile. No evil-doer will escape. Every soul of man that does evil will suffer, and the judgment will be severe and terrible. His judgment will involve indignation and wrath, tribulation and anguish (see POSB *Deeper Study #6*—Romans 2:8; POSB *Deeper Study #7*—Romans 2:8; POSB *Deeper Study #8*—Romans 2:9; and POSB *Deeper Study #9*—Romans 2:9 for discussion). |
| **#1114**<br>**Distressed**<br><br>Fainted–KJV<br>**Distressed**–NASB<br>Harassed–NIV<br>Weary–NKJV<br>Problems were so great–NLT<br><br>**POSB REFERENCE**<br>(Mt.9:36)<br>*Deeper Study #3* | ἐσκυλμένοι = eskulmenoi<br>Pronunciation: [es-kool-me'-noi]<br>Parsing (part of speech): verb<br>    Mood—participle<br>    Tense—perfect<br>    Voice—passive<br>    Case—nominative<br>    Gender—masculine<br>    Number—plural<br>    Stem or root—from σκύλλω<br>Concordance References:<br>  ⇒ Strong's #4660 skullō<br>  ⇒ NIV #5035 skullō<br>  ⇒ NASB #4660 skullō<br><br>**Matthew 9:36**<br>But when he saw the multitudes, he was moved with compassion on them, because they **fainted**, and were scattered abroad, as sheep having no shepherd. [KJV]<br><br>And seeing the multitudes, He felt compassion for them, because they were **distressed** and downcast like sheep without a shepherd. [NASB] | To be harassed; to faint; to grow weary; to be troubled; to lose heart; to lack courage; to be distressed, fainthearted, bewildered. It means to be completely overwhelmed with problems.<br><br>**Practical Application**<br>The word is used when a person has struggled and struggled against sin, or stood against the barrage of insult after insult until he can stand no more. It means that a person has undergone trial after trial until he is ready to collapse (Heb.12:3). |

# Practical Word Studies
## in the New Testament

| ENGLISH WORD | GREEK WORD AND VERSE | THE WORD MEANS... |
|---|---|---|
| | When he saw the crowds, he had compassion on them, because they were **harassed** and helpless, like sheep without a shepherd. [NIV]<br><br>But when He saw the multitudes, He was moved with compassion for them, because they were **weary** and scattered, like sheep having no shepherd. [NKJV]<br><br>He felt great pity for the crowds that came, because their **problems were so great** and they didn't know where to go for help. They were like sheep without a shepherd. [NLT]<br><br>Ἰδὼν δὲ τοὺς ὄχλους, ἐσπλαγχνίσθη περὶ αὐτῶν, ὅτι ἦσαν **ἐκλελυμένοι** καὶ ἐρριμμένοι ὡσεὶ πρόβατα μὴ ἔχοντα ποιμένα. [GNS]<br><br>Ἰδὼν δὲ τοὺς ὄχλους ἐσπλαγχνίσθη περὶ αὐτῶν, ὅτι ἦσαν **ἐσκυλμένοι** καὶ ἐρριμμένοι ὡσεὶ πρόβατα μὴ ἔχοντα ποιμένα. [GNT] | |
| **#1115**<br>**Distressed**<br><br>Distressed–KJV<br>Crushed–NASB<br>Crushed–NIV<br>Crushed–NKJV<br>Crushed and broken–NLT<br><br>**POSB REFERENCE**<br>(2 Cor.4:7-9; esp. v.8)<br>Note 2, point 1 | στενοχωρούμενοι = stenochōroumenoi<br>Pronunciation: [sten-okh-o'-roo-mehn-oy]<br>Parsing (part of speech): verb<br>    Mood—participle<br>    Tense—present<br>    Voice—passive<br>    Case—nominative<br>    Gender—masculine<br>    Person—1st person<br>    Number—plural<br>    Stem or root—from στενοχωρέομαι<br>Concordance References:<br>  ⇒ Strong's #4729 stenochōreō<br>  ⇒ NIV #5102 stenochōreō<br>  ⇒ NASB #4729 stenochōreō<br><br>**2 Cor. 4:8**<br>We are troubled on every side, yet not **distressed**; we are perplexed, but not in despair; [KJV]<br><br>We are afflicted in every way, but not **crushed**; perplexed, but not despairing; [NASB]<br><br>We are hard pressed on every side, but not **crushed**; perplexed, but not in despair; [NIV]<br><br>*We are* hard pressed on every side, yet not **crushed**; *we are* perplexed, but not in despair; [NKJV]<br><br>We are pressed on every side by troubles, but we are not **crushed and broken**. We are perplexed, but we don't give up and quit. [NLT]<br><br>ἐν παντὶ θλιβόμενοι, ἀλλ' οὐ **στενοχωρούμενοι**· ἀπορούμενοι ἀλλ' οὐκ ἐξαπορούμενοι [GNS]<br><br>ἐν παντὶ θλιβόμενοι ἀλλ' οὐ **στενοχωρούμενοι**, ἀπορούμενοι ἀλλ' οὐκ ἐξαπορούμενοι, [GNT] | To be crushed and broken; to be kept in a narrow, cramped place.<br><br>**Practical Application**<br>Our faith, even when we are hard pressed on every side, is used by God to strengthen and encourage others in their need. Therefore, we stand strong in faith, growing stronger and stronger in faith. |
| **#1116**<br>**Distressed**<br><br>Heaviness–KJV<br>**Distressed**–NASB<br>Suffer grief–NIV<br>Grieved–NKJV<br>Endure–NLT<br><br>**POSB REFERENCE**<br>(1 Pt.1:6)<br>Note 1, point 2 | λυπηθέντες = lupēthentes<br>Pronunciation: [loo-pay'-then-tehs]<br>Parsing (part of speech): verb<br>    Mood—participle<br>    Tense—aorist<br>    Voice—passive<br>    Case—nominative<br>    Gender—masculine<br>    Person—2nd person<br>    Number—plural<br>    Stem or root—from λυπέω<br>Concordance References:<br>  ⇒ Strong's #3076 lupeō<br>  ⇒ NIV #3382 lupeō<br>  ⇒ NASB #3076 lupeō<br><br>**1 Peter 1:6**<br>Wherein ye greatly rejoice, though now for a season, if need be, ye are in **heaviness** through manifold temptations: [KJV]<br><br>In this you greatly rejoice, even though now for a little while, if necessary, you have been **distressed** by various trials, [NASB] | To suffer grief, heaviness; to be distressed, sorrowful; to be hurt; to be made sorry; to be sad; to be grieving; to suffer sorrow, stress, pressure, and mental anguish.<br><br>**Practical Application**<br>Trials and temptations cause a heaviness within us. We all know what it is to feel heavy and weighed down with grief; to suffer stress and pressure; to be mentally in anguish, wondering, questioning, and suffering under the weight of trial or temptation. |

## PRACTICAL WORD STUDIES
## in the NEW TESTAMENT

| ENGLISH WORD | GREEK WORD AND VERSE | THE WORD MEANS... |
|---|---|---|
| | In this you greatly rejoice, though now for a little while you may have had to **suffer grief** in all kinds of trials. [NIV]<br>In this you greatly rejoice, though now for a little while, if need be, you have been **grieved** by various trials, [NKJV]<br>So be truly glad! There is wonderful joy ahead, even though it is necessary for you to **endure** many trials for a while. [NLT]<br>ἐν ᾧ ἀγαλλιᾶσθε ὀλίγον ἄρτι, εἰ δέον ἐστί, **λυπηθέντες** ἐν ποικίλοις πειρασμοῖς, [GNS]<br>ἐν ᾧ ἀγαλλιᾶσθε, ὀλίγον ἄρτι εἰ δέον [ἐστὶν] **λυπηθέντες** ἐν ποικίλοις πειρασμοῖς, [GNT] | |
| **#1117**<br>**Distressed–**<br>**Distress, Deep–**<br>**Deeply**<br>**Distressed**<br><br>Very heavy–KJV<br>**Distressed**–NASB<br>Troubled–NIV<br>**Deeply distressed**–NKJV<br>**Deep distress**–NLT<br><br>**POSB**<br>**REFERENCE**<br>(Mt.26:37)<br>*Deeper Study* #3<br><br>See also POSB REF:<br>(Mk.14:33-34; esp. v.33)<br>Note 2 | ἀδημονεῖν = adēmonein<br>Pronunciation: [ad-ay-mon-een]<br>Parsing (part of speech): verb<br>   Mood—infinitive<br>   Tense—present<br>   Voice—active<br>   Stem or root—from ἀδημονέω<br>Concordance References:<br>⇒ Strong's #85 adēmoneō<br>⇒ NIV #86 adēmoneō<br>⇒ NASB #85 adēmoneō<br><br>**Matthew 26:37**<br>And he took with him Peter and the two sons of Zebedee, and began to be sorrowful and **very heavy**. [KJV]<br>And He took with Him Peter and the two sons of Zebedee, and began to be grieved and **distressed**. [NASB]<br>He took Peter and the two sons of Zebedee along with him, and he began to be sorrowful and **troubled**. [NIV]<br>And He took with Him Peter and the two sons of Zebedee, and He began to be sorrowful and **deeply distressed**. [NKJV]<br>He took Peter and Zebedee's two sons, James and John, and he began to be filled with anguish and **deep distress**. [NLT]<br>καὶ παραλαβὼν τὸν Πέτρον καὶ τοὺς δύο υἱοὺς Ζεβεδαίου, ἤρξατο λυπεῖσθαι καὶ **ἀδημονεῖν**. [GNS]<br>καὶ παραλαβὼν τὸν Πέτρον καὶ τοὺς δύο υἱοὺς Ζεβεδαίου ἤρξατο λυπεῖσθαι καὶ **ἀδημονεῖν**. [GNT] | To be troubled, dismayed, disturbed. It means to be *gripped* with intense heaviness of soul.<br><br>**Practical Application**<br>*Troubled, very heavy,* or *distressed* pictures the trouble and dismay that is caused by an *unexpected calamity*. It is consternation, a heaviness that drives a man to be alone, for he is unfit for company. He desperately needs quiet, and he needs a few companions who understand and can help bear the trouble. |
| **#1118**<br>**Distressed,**<br>**Deeply**<br><br>Grieved–KJV<br>Grieved–NASB<br>**Deeply distressed**–NIV<br>Grieved–NKJV<br>Deeply disturbed–NLT<br><br>**POSB**<br>**REFERENCE**<br>(Mk.3:5)<br>*Deeper Study* #1 | συλλυπούμενος = sullupoumenos<br>Pronunciation: [sool-loop-oo'-mehn-os]<br>Parsing (part of speech): verb<br>   Mood—participle<br>   Tense—present<br>   Voice—middle or passive deponent<br>   Case—nominative<br>   Gender—masculine<br>   Number—singular<br>   Stem or root—from συλλυπέομαι<br>Concordance References:<br>⇒ Strong's #4818 sullupeō<br>⇒ NIV #5200 sullupeō<br>⇒ NASB #4818 sullupeō<br><br>**Mark 3:5**<br>And when he had looked round about on them with anger, being **grieved** for the hardness of their hearts, he saith unto the man, Stretch forth thine hand. And he stretched it out: and his hand was restored whole as the other. [KJV]<br>And after looking around at them with anger, **grieved** at their hardness of heart, He said to the man, "Stretch out your hand." And he stretched it out, and his hand was restored. [NASB]<br>He looked around at them in anger and, **deeply distressed** at their stubborn hearts, said to the man, "Stretch | To sense grief, sorrow, empathy; to suffer with a person because they are injured; to be deeply distressed or disturbed.<br><br>**Practical Application**<br>In this particular passage, Jesus' anger was combined with grief over people who harmed themselves. The anger of Jesus was a grieving anger over obstinate unbelief. The people who closed their minds—who just remained obstinate in unbelief despite the evidence aroused a grieving anger within Him. |

# PRACTICAL WORD STUDIES
## in the NEW TESTAMENT

| ENGLISH WORD | GREEK WORD AND VERSE | THE WORD MEANS... |
|---|---|---|
| | out your hand." He stretched it out, and his hand was completely restored. [NIV]<br>And when He had looked around at them with anger, being **grieved** by the hardness of their hearts, He said to the man, "Stretch out your hand." And he stretched *it* out, and his hand was restored as whole as the other. [NKJV]<br>He looked around at them angrily, because he was **deeply disturbed** by their hard hearts. Then he said to the man, "Reach out your hand." The man reached out his hand, and it became normal again! [NLT]<br>καὶ περιβλεψάμενος αὐτοὺς μετ' ὀργῆς, **συλλυπούμενος** ἐπὶ τῇ πωρώσει τῆς καρδίας αὐτῶν, λέγει τῷ ἀνθρώπῳ, Ἔκτεινον τὴν χεῖρα σου. καὶ ἐξέτεινε, καὶ ἀποκατεστάθη ἡ χεὶρ αὐτοῦ ὑγιὴς ὡς ἡ ἄλλη. [GNS]<br>καὶ περιβλεψάμενος αὐτοὺς μετ' ὀργῆς, **συλλυπούμενος** ἐπὶ τῇ πωρώσει τῆς καρδίας αὐτῶν λέγει τῷ ἀνθρώπῳ, Ἔκτεινον τὴν χεῖρα. καὶ ἐξέτεινεν καὶ ἀπεκατεστάθη ἡ χεὶρ αὐτοῦ. [GNT] | |
| **#1119**<br>**Distressed, Deeply-Distressed, Very**<br><br>Sore amazed–KJV<br>Very distressed–NASB<br>Deeply distressed–NIV<br>Deeply distressed–NKJV<br>Filled with horror–NLT<br><br>**POSB REFERENCE**<br>(Mk.14:33-34; esp. v.33)<br>Note 2 | ἐκθαμβεῖσθαι = *ekthambeisthai*<br>Pronunciation: [ek-tham-be-ees-tha-ee]<br>Parsing (part of speech): verb<br>  Mood—infinitive<br>  Tense—present<br>  Voice—passive<br>  Stem or root—from ἐκθαμβέομαι<br>Concordance References:<br>  ⇒ Strong's #1568 ekthambeō<br>  ⇒ NIV #1701 ekthambeō<br>  ⇒ NASB #1568 ekthambeō<br><br>**Mark 14:33**<br>And he taketh with him Peter and James and John, and began to be **sore amazed**, and to be very heavy; [KJV]<br>And He took with Him Peter and James and John, and began to be **very distressed** and troubled. [NASB]<br>He took Peter, James and John along with him, and he began to be **deeply distressed** and troubled. [NIV]<br>And He took Peter, James, and John with Him, and He began to be troubled and **deeply distressed**. [NKJV]<br>He took Peter, James, and John with him, and he began to be **filled with horror** and deep distress. [NLT]<br>καὶ παραλαμβάνει τὸν Πέτρον καὶ τὸν Ἰάκωβον καὶ Ἰωάννην μετ' αὐτοῦ, καὶ ἤρξατο **ἐκθαμβεῖσθαι** καὶ ἀδημονεῖν. [GNS]<br>καὶ παραλαμβάνει τὸν Πέτρον καὶ [τὸν] Ἰάκωβον καὶ [τὸν] Ἰωάννην μετ' αὐτοῦ καὶ ἤρξατο **ἐκθαμβεῖσθαι** καὶ ἀδημονεῖν [GNT] | To be deeply distressed; to be filled with utter and extreme fright, horror, terror, bewilderment, and amazement.<br><br>**Practical Application**<br>Jesus "began" to experience extreme agony and pressure beyond imagination. The words "deeply distressed" (*ekthambeisthai*) are very strong words in the Greek. Jesus was staggering under the "horror of great darkness," something like what fell upon Abraham, except Jesus' horror was much, much worse (Genesis 15:12). |
| **#1120**<br>**Distresses**<br><br>Distresses–KJV<br>Distresses–NASB<br>Distresses–NIV<br>Distresses–NKJV<br>Calamaties–NLT<br><br>**POSB REFERENCE**<br>(2 Cor.6:4-5; esp. v.4)<br>Note 3 | στενοχωρίαις = *stenochōriais*<br>Pronunciation: [sten-okh-o-ree'-ah-ees]<br>Parsing (part of speech): noun<br>  Case—dative<br>  Gender—feminine<br>  Number—plural<br>  Stem or root—from στενοχωρία, ας<br>Concordance References:<br>  ⇒ Strong's #4730 stenochōria<br>  ⇒ NIV #5103 stenochōria<br>  ⇒ NASB #4730 stenochōria<br><br>**2 Cor. 6:4**<br>But in all things approving ourselves as the ministers of God, in much patience, in afflictions, in necessities, in **distresses**, [KJV]<br>But in everything commending ourselves as servants of God, in much endurance, in afflictions, in hardships, in **distresses**, [NASB]<br>Rather, as servants of God we commend ourselves in every way: in great endurance; in troubles, hardships and **distresses**; [NIV]<br>But in all *things* we commend ourselves as ministers | Distresses, difficulties, troubles, straits, calamities, tight places, inescapable situations.<br><br>**Practical Application**<br>It is the picture of being cornered and being unable to escape; a picture of having no room or place to turn, of being forced to confront the situation or else being utterly devastated and defeated. When the minister or servant is cornered by temptation or trial—when there seems to be no escape—his only resource is endurance. He must steadfastly endure lest he offend the gospel and become a stumbling block to others. |

# Practical Word Studies in the New Testament

| ENGLISH WORD | GREEK WORD AND VERSE | THE WORD MEANS... |
|---|---|---|
| | of God: in much patience, in tribulations, in needs, in **distresses**. [NKJV]<br>In everything we do we try to show that we are true ministers of God. We patiently endure troubles and hardships and **calamities** of every kind. [NLT]<br>ἀλλ' ἐν παντὶ συνίσταντες ἑαυτοὺς ὡς Θεοῦ διάκονοι, ἐν ὑπομονῇ πολλῇ, ἐν θλίψεσιν, ἐν ἀνάγκαις, ἐν **στενοχωρίαις**, [GNS]<br>ἀλλ' ἐν παντὶ συνίσταντες ἑαυτοὺς ὡς θεοῦ διάκονοι, ἐν ὑπομονῇ πολλῇ, ἐν θλίψεσιν, ἐν ἀνάγκαις, ἐν **στενοχωρίαις**, [GNT] | |
| **#1121**<br>**Distributing**<br><br>**Distributing**–KJV<br>Contributing–NASB<br>Share with–NIV<br>**Distributing**–NKJV<br>Help them–NLT<br><br>**POSB REFERENCE**<br>(Rom.12:13)<br>Note 4, point 1 | κοινωνοῦντες = *koinōnountes*<br>Pronunciation: [koy-no-noon'-tehs]<br>Parsing (part of speech): verb<br>    Mood—participle (imperative sense)<br>    Tense—present<br>    Voice—active<br>    Case—nominative<br>    Gender—masculine<br>    Person—2nd person<br>    Number—plural<br>    Stem or root—from κοινωνέω<br>Concordance References:<br>  ⇒ Strong's #2841 koinōneō<br>  ⇒ NIV #3125 koinōneō<br>  ⇒ NASB #2841 koinōneō<br><br>**Romans 12:13**<br>**Distributing** to the necessity of saints; given to hospitality. [KJV]<br>**Contributing** to the needs of the saints, practicing hospitality. [NASB]<br>**Share with** God's people who are in need. Practice hospitality. [NIV]<br>**Distributing** to the needs of the saints, given to hospitality. [NKJV]<br>When God's children are in need, be the one to **help them** out. And get into the habit of inviting guests home for dinner or, if they need lodging, for the night. [NLT]<br>ταῖς χρείαις τῶν ἁγίων **κοινωνοῦντες**· τὴν φιλοξενίαν διώκοντες. [GNS]<br>ταῖς χρείαις τῶν ἁγίων **κοινωνοῦντες**, τὴν φιλοξενίαν διώκοντες. [GNT] | To share; to help; to contribute; to give.<br><br>**Practical Application**<br>The believer is to meet the needs of people unselfishly. The believer is to give generously, to share with those in need. He is to "distribute" (*koinōnountes*), that is, to give and share in order to meet their needs. |
| **#1122**<br>**Distributing**<br><br>Cloven–KJV<br>**Distributing**–NASB<br>Separated–NIV<br>Divided–NKJV<br>Not translated–NLT<br><br>**POSB REFERENCE**<br>(Acts 2:2-4; esp. v.3)<br>Note 4, point 2 | διαμεριζόμεναι = *diamerizomenai*<br>Pronunciation: [dee-am-er-id'-zo-men-ah-ee]<br>Parsing (part of speech): verb<br>    Mood—participle<br>    Tense—present<br>    Voice—middle or passive<br>    Case—nominative<br>    Gender—feminine<br>    Number—plural<br>    Stem or root—from διαμερίζω<br>Concordance References:<br>  ⇒ Strong's #1266 diamerizō<br>  ⇒ NIV #1374 diamcrizō<br>  ⇒ NASB #1266 diamerizō<br><br>**Acts 2:3**<br>And there appeared unto them **cloven** tongues like as of fire, and it sat upon each of them. [KJV]<br>And there appeared to them tongues as of fire **distributing** themselves, and they rested on each one of them. [NASB]<br>They saw what seemed to be tongues of fire that **separated** and came to rest on each of them. [NIV]<br>Then there appeared to them **divided** tongues, as of fire, and *one* sat upon each of them. [NKJV]<br>Then, what looked like flames or tongues of fire appeared and settled on each of them. [NLT]—not translated | Separated, distributed; divided.<br><br>**Practical Application**<br>The Greek means a tongue that was cloven, that is, parted asunder. The idea is that a single tongue appeared and then began to split and divide itself, resting upon each of the disciples. |

# Practical Word Studies
## in the New Testament

| ENGLISH WORD | GREEK WORD AND VERSE | THE WORD MEANS... |
|---|---|---|
| | καὶ ὤφθησαν αὐτοῖς **διαμεριζόμεναι** γλῶσσαι ὡσεὶ πυρός, καὶ ἐκάθισε τε ἐφ' ἕνα ἕκαστο αὐτῶν. [GNS]<br>καὶ ὤφθησαν αὐτοῖς **διαμεριζόμεναι** γλῶσσαι ὡσεὶ πυρός καὶ ἐκάθισεν ἐφ' ἕνα ἕκαστον αὐτῶν, [GNT] | |
| **#1123**<br>**Disturbances**<br><br>Commotions–KJV<br>**Disturbances–NASB**<br>Revolutions–NIV<br>Commotions–NKJV<br>Insurrections–NLT<br><br>**POSB REFERENCE**<br>(Lk.21:9-10; esp. v.9)<br>Note 3, point 1 | ἀκαταστασίας = *akatastasias*<br>Pronunciation: [ak-at-as-tah-see'-ahs]<br>Parsing (part of speech): noun<br>    Case—accusative<br>    Gender—feminine<br>    Number—plural<br>    Stem or root—from ἀκαταστασία, ας<br>Concordance References:<br>  ⇒ Strong's #181 akatastasia<br>  ⇒ NIV #189 akatastasia<br>  ⇒ NASB #181 akatastasia<br><br>**Luke 21:9**<br>But when ye shall hear of wars and **commotions**, be not terrified: for these things must first come to pass; but the end is not by and by. [KJV]<br>"And when you hear of wars and **disturbances**, do not be terrified; for these things must take place first, but the end does not follow immediately." [NASB]<br>When you hear of wars and **revolutions**, do not be frightened. These things must happen first, but the end will not come right away." [NIV]<br>But when you hear of wars and **commotions**, do not be terrified; for these things must come to pass first; but the end *will not come* immediately." [NKJV]<br>And when you hear of wars and **insurrections**, don't panic. Yes, these things must come, but the end won't follow immediately." [NLT]<br>ὅταν δὲ ἀκούσητε πολέμους καὶ **ἀκαταστασίας**, μὴ πτοηθῆτε· δεῖ γὰρ ταῦτα γενέσθαι πρῶτον, ἀλλ' οὐκ εὐθέως τὸ τέλος. [GNS]<br>ὅταν δὲ ἀκούσητε πολέμους καὶ **ἀκαταστασίας**, μὴ πτοηθῆτε· δεῖ γὰρ ταῦτα γενέσθαι πρῶτον, ἀλλ' οὐκ εὐθέως τὸ τέλος. [GNT] | Revolutions, disturbances, insurrections, commotions, anarchy, rebellion, tumults, uproars, riots, terrorism; mob violence; treason against and confusion within governments.<br><br>**Practical Application**<br>Believers can become extremely disturbed over the news. But, believers are not to be "distressed" (*ptoethete*). They are not to let their hearts "be troubled" (John 14:1). World violence can trouble people; but the believer's heart and life are to be centered upon God, trusting His presence, care, and security—eternally. |
| **#1124**<br>**Disturbances**<br><br>Tumults–KJV<br>**Disturbances–NASB**<br>Disorder–NIV<br>Tumults–NKJV<br>Disorderly behavior–NLT<br><br>**POSB REFERENCE**<br>(2 Cor.12:19-21; esp. v.20)<br>Note 3, point 2 | ἀκαταστασίαι = *akatastasiai*<br>Pronunciation: [ak-at-as-tah-see'-ah-ee]<br>Parsing (part of speech): noun<br>    Case—nominative<br>    Gender—feminine<br>    Number—plural<br>    Stem or root—from ἀκαταστασία, ας<br>Concordance References:<br>  ⇒ Strong's #181 akatastasia<br>  ⇒ NIV #189 akatastasia<br>  ⇒ NASB #181 akatastasia<br><br>**2 Cor. 12:20**<br>For I fear, lest, when I come, I shall not find you such as I would, and that I shall be found unto you such as ye would not: lest there be debates, envyings, wraths, strifes, backbitings, whisperings, swellings, **tumults**: [KJV]<br>For I am afraid that perhaps when I come I may find you to be not what I wish and may be found by you to be not what you wish; that perhaps there may be strife, jealousy, angry tempers, disputes, slanders, gossip, arrogance, **disturbances**; [NASB]<br>For I am afraid that when I come I may not find you as I want you to be, and you may not find me as you want me to be. I fear that there may be quarreling, jealousy, outbursts of anger, factions, slander, gossip, arrogance and **disorder**. [NIV]<br>For I fear lest, when I come, I shall not find you such as I wish, and *that* I shall be found by you such as you do not wish; lest *there be* contentions, jealousies, outbursts of wrath, selfish ambitions, backbitings, whisperings, conceits, **tumults**; [NKJV] | Disorder, tumults, results, riots, disturbances, disorderly behavior, insurrection, anarchy, confusion.<br><br>**Practical Application**<br>Paul was stricken with fear, fear lest the church fail to be what it should be and reject him and his ministry. Paul feared that the church would fail to deal with the carnal critics and continue putting up with their evil attacks against him. He lists eight evils, including "disturbances" (*akatastasiai*), that were and still are characteristic of divisive critics in the church. |

# PRACTICAL WORD STUDIES
## in the NEW TESTAMENT

| ENGLISH WORD | GREEK WORD AND VERSE | THE WORD MEANS... |
|---|---|---|
| | For I am afraid that when I come to visit you I won't like what I find, and then you won't like my response. I am afraid that I will find quarreling, jealousy, outbursts of anger, selfishness, backstabbing, gossip, conceit, and **disorderly behavior**. [NLT]<br>φοβοῦμαι γὰρ μή πως ἐλθὼν οὐχ οἵους θέλω εὕρω ὑμᾶς, κἀγὼ εὑρεθῶ ὑμῖν οἷον οὐ θέλετε· μή πως ἔρις, ζῆλοι, θυμοί, ἐριθεῖαι, καταλαλιαί, ψιθυρισμοί, φυσιώσεις, **ἀκαταστασίαι**· [GNS]<br>φοβοῦμαι γὰρ μή πως ἐλθὼν οὐχ οἵους θέλω εὕρω ὑμᾶς κἀγὼ εὑρεθῶ ὑμῖν οἷον οὐ θέλετε· μή πως ἔρις, ζῆλος, θυμοί, ἐριθεῖαι, καταλαλιαί, ψιθυρισμοί, φυσιώσεις, **ἀκαταστασίαι**· [GNT] | |
| **#1125**<br>**Disturbed**<br><br>Troubled–KJV<br>**Disturbed–NASB**<br>**Disturbed–NIV**<br>Troubled–NKJV<br>Troubled–NLT<br><br>**POSB REFERENCE**<br>(Acts 15:24)<br>Note 2, point 1 | ἐτάραξαν = etaraxan<br>Pronunciation: [eh-tar-axs'-sahn]<br>Parsing (part of speech): verb<br>    Mood—indicative<br>    Tense—aorist<br>    Voice—active<br>    Person—3rd person<br>    Number—plural<br>    Stem or root—from ταράσσω<br>Concordance References:<br>  ⇒ Strong's #5015 tarassō<br>  ⇒ NIV #5429 tarassō<br>  ⇒ NASB #5015 tarassō<br><br>**Acts 15:24**<br>Forasmuch as we have heard, that certain which went out from us have **troubled** you with words, subverting your souls, saying, Ye must be circumcised, and keep the law: to whom we gave no such commandment: [KJV]<br>"Since we have heard that some of our number to whom we gave no instruction have **disturbed** you with their words, unsettling your souls, [NASB]<br>We have heard that some went out from us without our authorization and **disturbed** you, troubling your minds by what they said. [NIV]<br>Since we have heard that some who went out from us have **troubled** you with words, unsettling your souls, saying, "You must be circumcised and keep the law"—to whom we gave no such commandment— [NKJV]<br>"We understand that some men from here have **troubled** you and upset you with their teaching, but they had no such instructions from us. [NLT]<br>Ἐπειδὴ ἠκούσαμεν ὅτι τινὲς ἐξ ἡμῶν ἐξελθόντες **ἐτάραξαν** ὑμᾶς λόγοις, ἀνασκευάζοντες τὰς ψυχὰς ὑμῶν, λέγοντες περιτέμνεσθαι καὶ τηρεῖν τὸν νόμον, οἷς οὐ διεστειλάμεθα· [GNS]<br>Ἐπειδὴ ἠκούσαμεν ὅτι τινὲς ἐξ ἡμῶν [ἐξελθόντες] **ἐτάραξαν** ὑμᾶς λόγοις ἀνασκευάζοντες τὰς ψυχὰς ὑμῶν οἷς οὐ διεστειλάμεθα, [GNT] | Disturbed; troubled; terrified; startled; upset; frightened; stirred up; thrown into turmoil.<br><br>**Practical Application**<br>The picture is that of words heaped upon words, false words that "disturb," agitate, trouble, and shake violently. |
| **#1126**<br>**Disturbed, Deeply**<br><br>Grieved–KJV<br>Grieved–NASB<br>Deeply distressed–NIV<br>Grieved–NKJV<br>**Deeply disturbed–NLT**<br><br>**POSB REFERENCE**<br>(Mk.3:5)<br>*Deeper Study #1* | συλλυπούμενος = sullupoumenos<br>Pronunciation: [sool-loop-oo'-mehn-os]<br>Parsing (part of speech): verb<br>    Mood—participle<br>    Tense—present<br>    Voice—middle or passive deponent<br>    Case—nominative<br>    Gender—masculine<br>    Number—singular<br>    Stem or root—from συλλυπέομαι<br>Concordance References:<br>  ⇒ Strong's #4818 sullupeō<br>  ⇒ NIV #5200 sullupeō<br>  ⇒ NASB #4818 sullupeō<br><br>**Mark 3:5**<br>And when he had looked round about on them with anger, being **grieved** for the hardness of their hearts, he saith unto the man, Stretch forth thine hand. And he | To sense grief, sorrow, empathy; to suffer with a person because they are injured; to be deeply distressed or disturbed.<br><br>**Practical Application**<br>In this particular passage, Jesus' anger was combined with grief over people who harmed themselves. The anger of Jesus was a grieving anger over obstinate unbelief. The people who closed their minds—who just remained obstinate in unbelief despite the evidence—aroused a grieving anger within Him. |

# PRACTICAL WORD STUDIES
## in the NEW TESTAMENT

| ENGLISH WORD | GREEK WORD AND VERSE | THE WORD MEANS... |
|---|---|---|
| | stretched it out: and his hand was restored whole as the other. [KJV]<br>    And after looking around at them with anger, **grieved** at their hardness of heart, He said to the man, "Stretch out your hand." And he stretched it out, and his hand was restored. [NASB]<br>    He looked around at them in anger and, **deeply distressed** at their stubborn hearts, said to the man, "Stretch out your hand." He stretched it out, and his hand was completely restored. [NIV]<br>    And when He had looked around at them with anger, being **grieved** by the hardness of their hearts, He said to the man, "Stretch out your hand." And he stretched *it* out, and his hand was restored as whole as the other. [NKJV]<br>    He looked around at them angrily, because he was **deeply disturbed** by their hard hearts. Then he said to the man, "Reach out your hand." The man reached out his hand, and it became normal again! [NLT]<br>    καὶ περιβλεψάμενος αὐτοὺς μετ' ὀργῆς, **συλλυπούμενος** ἐπὶ τῇ πωρώσει τῆς καρδίας αὐτῶν, λέγει τῷ ἀνθρώπῳ, Ἔκτεινον τὴν χεῖρά σου. καὶ ἐξέτεινε, καὶ ἀποκατεστάθη ἡ χεὶρ αὐτοῦ ὑγιὴς ὡς ἡ ἄλλη. [GNS]<br>    καὶ περιβλεψάμενος αὐτοὺς μετ' ὀργῆς, **συλλυπούμενος** ἐπὶ τῇ πωρώσει τῆς καρδίας αὐτῶν λέγει τῷ ἀνθρώπῳ, Ἔκτεινον τὴν χεῖρα. καὶ ἐξέτεινεν καὶ ἀπεκατεστάθη ἡ χεὶρ αὐτοῦ. [GNT] | |
| **#1127**<br>**Divided**<br><br>Cloven–KJV<br>Distributing–NASB<br>Separated–NIV<br>**Divided–NKJV**<br>Not translated–NLT<br><br>**POSB**<br>**REFERENCE**<br>(Acts 2:2-4; esp. v.3)<br>Note 4, point 2 | διαμεριζόμεναι = *diamerizomenai*<br>Pronunciation: [dee-am-er-id'-zo-men-ah-ee]<br>Parsing (part of speech): verb<br>    Mood—participle<br>    Tense—present<br>    Voice—middle or passive<br>    Case—nominative<br>    Gender—feminine<br>    Number—plural<br>    Stem or root—from διαμερίζω<br>Concordance References:<br>  ⇒ Strong's #1266 diamerizō<br>  ⇒ NIV #1374 diamerizō<br>  ⇒ NASB #1266 diamerizō<br><br>                   **Acts 2:3**<br>    And there appeared unto them **cloven** tongues like as of fire, and it sat upon each of them. [KJV]<br>    And there appeared to them tongues as of fire **distributing** themselves, and they rested on each one of them. [NASB]<br>    They saw what seemed to be tongues of fire that **separated** and came to rest on each of them. [NIV]<br>    Then there appeared to them **divided** tongues, as of fire, and *one* sat upon each of them. [NKJV]<br>    Then, what looked like flames or tongues of fire appeared and settled on each of them. [NLT]—NOT TRANSLATED<br>    καὶ ὤφθησαν αὐτοῖς **διαμεριζόμεναι** γλῶσσαι ὡσεὶ πυρός, καὶ ἐκάθισε τε ἐφ' ἕνα ἕκαστο αὐτῶν. [GNS]<br>    καὶ ὤφθησαν αὐτοῖς **διαμεριζόμεναι** γλῶσσαι ὡσεὶ πυρός καὶ ἐκάθισεν ἐφ' ἕνα ἕκαστον αὐτῶν, [GNT] | Separated, distributed; divided.<br><br>**Practical Application**<br>    The Greek means a tongue that was cloven, that is, parted asunder. The idea is that a single tongue appeared and then began to split and divide itself, resting upon each of the disciples. |
| **#1128**<br>**Divisions**<br><br>Divisions–KJV<br>Divisions–NASB<br>Divisions–NIV<br>Divisions–NKJV<br>Divisions–NLT<br><br>**POSB**<br>**REFERENCE** | σχίσματα = *schismata*<br>Pronunciation: [skhis'-mah-tah]<br>Parsing (part of speech): noun<br>    Case—nominative<br>    Gender—neuter<br>    Number—plural<br>    Stem or root—from σχίσμα, τος<br>Concordance References:<br>  ⇒ Strong's #4978 schisma<br>  ⇒ NIV #5388 schisma<br>  ⇒ NASB #4978 schisma | To split, to rend, to tear apart; to divide.<br><br>**Practical Application**<br>    Note the words "among you." The division or dissension is not outside the church; it is not out in the world. It is inside the church. The divisive church is not working to bring peace, love, and brotherhood to the world; the divisive church is not seen out in the world ministering to the starving, diseased, and lost masses of the world. The divisive church is seen fuming and fighting. |

# PRACTICAL WORD STUDIES
## in the New Testament

| ENGLISH WORD | GREEK WORD AND VERSE | THE WORD MEANS... |
|---|---|---|
| (1 Cor.1:10) Note 1 | **1 Cor. 1:10**<br>Now I beseech you, brethren, by the name of our Lord Jesus Christ, that ye all speak the same thing, and that there be no **divisions** among you; but that ye be perfectly joined together in the same mind and in the same judgment. [KJV]<br>Now I exhort you, brethren, by the name of our Lord Jesus Christ, that you all agree, and there be no **divisions** among you, but you be made complete in the same mind and in the same judgment. [NASB]<br>I appeal to you, brothers, in the name of our Lord Jesus Christ, that all of you agree with one another so that there may be no **divisions** among you and that you may be perfectly united in mind and thought. [NIV]<br>Now I plead with you, brethren, by the name of our Lord Jesus Christ, that you all speak the same thing, and *that* there be no **divisions** among you, but *that* you be perfectly joined together in the same mind and in the same judgment. [NKJV]<br>Now, dear brothers and sisters, I appeal to you by the authority of the Lord Jesus Christ to stop arguing among yourselves. Let there be real harmony so there won't be **divisions** in the church. I plead with you to be of one mind, united in thought and purpose. [NLT]<br>Παρακαλῶ δὲ ὑμᾶς, ἀδελφοί, διὰ τοῦ ὀνόματος τοῦ Κυρίου ἡμῶν Ἰησοῦ Χριστοῦ, ἵνα τὸ αὐτὸ λέγητε πάντες, καὶ μὴ ᾖ ἐν ὑμῖν **σχίσματα**, ἦτε δὲ κατηρτισμένοι ἐν τῷ αὐτῷ νοῒ καὶ ἐν τῇ αὐτῇ γνώμῃ. [GNS]<br>Παρακαλῶ δὲ ὑμᾶς, ἀδελφοί, διὰ τοῦ ὀνόματος τοῦ κυρίου ἡμῶν Ἰησοῦ Χριστοῦ, ἵνα τὸ αὐτὸ λέγητε πάντες καὶ μὴ ᾖ ἐν ὑμῖν **σχίσματα**, ἦτε δὲ κατηρτισμένοι ἐν τῷ αὐτῷ νοῒ καὶ ἐν τῇ αὐτῇ γνώμῃ. [GNT] | The sinful and devastating problems of dissension are within the divisive church. The divisive church is splitting, rending, and tearing itself apart. |
| #1129<br>**Divisions**<br><br>**Divisions–KJV**<br>Dissensions–NASB<br>**Divisions–NIV**<br>**Divisions–NKJV**<br>**Divisions–NLT**<br><br>**POSB REFERENCE**<br>(Rom.16:17-18; esp. v.17)<br>Note 1, point 1 | διχοστασίας = dichostasias<br>Pronunciation: [dee-khos-tas-ee'-ahs]<br>Parsing (part of speech): noun<br>    Case—accusative<br>    Gender—feminine<br>    Number—plural<br>    Stem or root—from διχοστασία, ας<br>Concordance References:<br>  ⇒ Strong's #1370 dichostasia<br>  ⇒ NIV #1496 dichostasia<br>  ⇒ NASB #1370 dichostasia<br><br>**Romans 16:17**<br>Now I beseech you, brethren, mark them which cause **divisions** and offences contrary to the doctrine which ye have learned; and avoid them. [KJV]<br>Now I urge you, brethren, keep your eye on those who cause **dissensions** and hindrances contrary to the teaching which you learned, and turn away from them. [NASB]<br>I urge you, brothers, to watch out for those who cause **divisions** and put obstacles in your way that are contrary to the teaching you have learned. Keep away from them. [NIV]<br>Now I urge you, brethren, note those who cause **divisions** and offenses, contrary to the doctrine which you learned, and avoid them. [NKJV]<br>And now I make one more appeal, my dear brothers and sisters. Watch out for people who cause **divisions** and upset people's faith by teaching things that are contrary to what you have been taught. Stay away from them. [NLT]<br>Παρακαλῶ δὲ ὑμᾶς, ἀδελφοί, σκοπεῖν τοὺς τὰς **διχοστασίας** καὶ τὰ σκάνδαλα, παρὰ τὴν διδαχὴν ἣν ὑμεῖς ἐμάθετε, ποιοῦντας· καὶ ἐκκλίνατε ἀπ' αὐτῶν. [GNS] | Divisions, dissensions, disputes, rebellion; splitting off from the others. It means standing apart, being separate, causing cleavage.<br><br>**Practical Application**<br>A divisive person causes division and lays stumbling blocks in the way of growth. Note exactly what is said: a divisive person acts "contrary to the doctrine which [believers] have learned." He causes "divisions and dissensions." |

# PRACTICAL WORD STUDIES
## in the NEW TESTAMENT

| ENGLISH WORD | GREEK WORD AND VERSE | THE WORD MEANS... |
|---|---|---|
| | Παρακαλῶ δὲ ὑμᾶς, ἀδελφοί, σκοπεῖν τοὺς τὰς **διχοστασίας** καὶ τὰ σκάνδαλα παρὰ τὴν διδαχὴν ἣν ὑμεῖς ἐμάθετε ποιοῦντας, καὶ ἐκκλίνετε ἀπ' αὐτῶν· [GNT] | |
| **#1130**<br>**Divisions**<br><br>Seditions–KJV<br>Disputes–NASB<br>Dissensions–NIV<br>Selfish ambitions–NKJV<br>**Divisions–NLT**<br><br>**POSB REFERENCE**<br>(Gal.5:19-21; esp. v.20)<br>Note 2 | **διχοστασίαι** = *dichostasiai*<br>Pronunciation: [dee-khos-tas-ee'-ah-ee]<br>Parsing (part of speech): noun<br>    Case—nominative<br>    Gender—feminine<br>    Number—plural<br>    Stem or root—from **διχοστασία**, ας<br>Concordance References:<br>  ⇒ Strong's #1370 dichostasia<br>  ⇒ NIV #1496 dichostasia<br>  ⇒ NASB #1370 dichostasia<br><br>**Galatians 5:20**<br>Idolatry, witchcraft, hatred, variance, emulations, wrath, strife, **seditions**, heresies, [KJV]<br>Idolatry, sorcery, enmities, strife, jealousy, outbursts of anger, **disputes**, dissensions, factions, [NASB]<br>Idolatry and witchcraft; hatred, discord, jealousy, fits of rage, selfish ambition, **dissensions**, factions [NIV]<br>Idolatry, sorcery, hatred, contentions, jealousies, outbursts of wrath, **selfish ambitions**, dissensions, heresies, [NKJV]<br>Idolatry, participation in demonic activities, hostility, quarreling, jealousy, outbursts of anger, selfish ambition, **divisions**, the feeling that everyone is wrong except those in your own little group, [NLT]<br>εἰδωλολατρία, φαρμακεία, ἔχθραι, ἔρεις, ζῆλοι, θυμοί, ἐριθεῖαι, **διχοστασίαι**, αἱρέσεις, [GNS]<br>εἰδωλολατρία, φαρμακεία, ἔχθραι, ἔρις, ζῆλος, θυμοί, ἐριθεῖαι, **διχοστασίαι**, αἱρέσεις, [GNT] | Dissensions, seditions, disputes, divisions, rebellions, standing against others, splitting off from others.<br><br>**Practical Application**<br>Despising authority within society is dangerous. It often leads to rebellion.<br>What happens is that those in power create human laws that favor themselves, the rich and the powerful. Human law is not enough for man, for man cannot create a law higher than himself. Therefore, whoever is in power will always be influenced by some selfishness. He will seldom, if ever, give all he is and has to be perfectly just and equal to all. Therefore, God's law is necessary. Man must have a law that is above and beyond himself. Man must have a law that controls and governs all men. And more than this, man must have a living Lord who can give him the power and who can motivate him to live like he should. This is the reason the Lord Jesus Christ, who reveals and fulfills the law of God perfectly, must be proclaimed. He must be exalted and not denied. The only hope for man is to deny himself and give all he is and has to meet the desperate needs of *all the people and not of just a few*. |
| **#1131**<br>**Divisions**<br><br>Heretick–KJV<br>Factious–NASB<br>Divisive–NIV<br>Divisive–NKJV<br>**Divisions–NLT**<br><br>**POSB REFERENCE**<br>(Tit.3:10-11; esp. v.10)<br>Note 3 | **αἱρετικὸν** = *hairetikon*<br>Pronunciation: [ahee-ret-ee-kon']<br>Parsing (part of speech): adjective<br>    Case—accusative<br>    Gender—masculine<br>    Number—singular<br>    Stem or root—from **αἱρετικός**, ή, όν<br>Concordance References:<br>  ⇒ Strong's #141 hairetikos<br>  ⇒ NIV #148 hairetikos<br>  ⇒ NASB #141 hairetikos<br><br>**Titus 3:10**<br>A man that is an **heretick** after the first and second admonition reject; [KJV]<br>Reject a **factious** man after a first and second warning, [NASB]<br>Warn a **divisive** person once, and then warn him a second time. After that, have nothing to do with him. [NIV]<br>Reject a **divisive** man after the first and second admonition, [NKJV]<br>If anyone is causing **divisions** among you, give a first and second warning. After that, have nothing more to do with that person. [NLT]<br>**αἱρετικὸν** ἄνθρωπον μετὰ μίαν καὶ δευτέραν νουθεσίαν παραιτοῦ, [GNS]<br>**αἱρετικὸν** ἄνθρωπον μετὰ μίαν καὶ δευτέραν νουθεσίαν παραιτοῦ, [GNT] | Divisive, heretic, factious, divisions. The Greek word heretic (*hairetikon*) is interesting. It means to take for oneself; to choose for oneself.<br><br>**Practical Application**<br>Therefore, a heretic is a person who chooses what he is to believe. He rejects all authority no matter what it is: God, Christ, the Word of God, the church, man. He himself chooses what he is to believe. He and he alone is his authority; he and he alone determines truth—what is and what is not truth.<br>Note that this heretic is in the church; he associates with believers. This is the picture of most heretics. Few reject all the teachings of Christ and of the Bible. Most heretics remain in the church, holding to some basic teachings but rejecting those doctrines that they do not like. The Scripture is clear: believers are to reach out to the heretic or false teacher. He is not to be lambasted, rejected, and expelled from the church. An attempt is to be made to reach him for Christ. In fact, two strong attempts are to be made to reach him. He is to be shown love and care and admonished to repent and confess the truth of Christ and His Word. But note: there is a limit. On the third try, if he does not repent, he is to be rejected, that is, expelled from the church. He is not to be allowed to lead other believers astray. (See POSB outline—Matthew 18:15-20 and POSB notes—Matthew 18:15-20 for more detailed discussion on church discipline as taught by Christ.) |

# PRACTICAL WORD STUDIES
## in the NEW TESTAMENT

| ENGLISH WORD | GREEK WORD AND VERSE | THE WORD MEANS... |
|---|---|---|
| **#1132**<br>**Divisive**<br><br>Heretick–KJV<br>Factious–NASB<br>**Divisive–NIV**<br>**Divisive–NKJV**<br>Divisions–NLT<br><br>**POSB REFERENCE**<br>(Tit.3:10-11; esp. v.10)<br>Note 3 | αἱρετικὸν = *hairetikon*<br>Pronunciation: [ahee-ret-ee-kon']<br>Parsing (part of speech): adjective<br>    Case—accusative<br>    Gender—masculine<br>    Number—singular<br>    Stem or root—from αἱρετικός, ή, όν<br>Concordance References:<br>  ⇒ Strong's #141 hairetikos<br>  ⇒ NIV #148 hairetikos<br>  ⇒ NASB #141 hairetikos<br><br>**Titus 3:10**<br>A man that is an **heretick** after the first and second admonition reject; [KJV]<br>Reject a **factious** man after a first and second warning, [NASB]<br>Warn a **divisive** person once, and then warn him a second time. After that, have nothing to do with him. [NIV]<br>Reject a **divisive** man after the first and second admonition, [NKJV]<br>If anyone is causing **divisions** among you, give a first and second warning. After that, have nothing more to do with that person. [NLT]<br>αἱρετικὸν ἄνθρωπον μετὰ μίαν καὶ δευτέραν νουθεσίαν παραιτοῦ, [GNS]<br>αἱρετικὸν ἄνθρωπον μετὰ μίαν καὶ δευτέραν νουθεσίαν παραιτοῦ, [GNT] | Divisive, heretic, factious, divisions. The Greek word divisive (*hairetikon*) is interesting. It means to take for oneself; to choose for oneself.<br><br>**Practical Application**<br>Therefore, a heretic is a person who chooses what he is to believe. He rejects all authority no matter what it is: God, Christ, the Word of God, the church, man. He himself chooses what he is to believe. He and he alone is his authority; he and he alone determines truth—what is and what is not truth.<br>Note that this heretic is in the church; he associates with believers. This is the picture of most heretics. Few reject all the teachings of Christ and of the Bible. Most heretics remain in the church, holding to some basic teachings but rejecting those doctrines that they do not like. The Scripture is clear: believers are to reach out to the heretic or false teacher. He is not to be lambasted, rejected, and expelled from the church. An attempt is to be made to reach him for Christ. In fact, two strong attempts are to be made to reach him. He is to be shown love and care and admonished to repent and confess the truth of Christ and His Word. But note: there is a limit. On the third try, if he does not repent, he is to be rejected, that is, expelled from the church. He is not to be allowed to lead other believers astray. (See POSB outline—Matthew 18:15-20 and POSB notes—Matthew 18:15-20 for more detailed discussion on church discipline as taught by Christ.) |
| **#1133**<br>**Do**<br><br>Maintain–KJV<br>Engage–NASB<br>Devote–NIV<br>Maintain–NKJV<br>**Do–NLT**<br><br>**POSB REFERENCE**<br>(Tit.3:8)<br>Note 1 | προΐστασθαι = *proistasthai*<br>Pronunciation: [pro-is'-tahs-tha-ee]<br>Parsing (part of speech): verb<br>    Mood—infinitive<br>    Tense—present<br>    Voice—middle<br>    Stem or root—from προΐστημι<br>Concordance References:<br>  ⇒ Strong's #4291 proistēmi<br>  ⇒ NIV #4613 proistēmi<br>  ⇒ NASB #4291b proistēmi<br><br>**Titus 3:8**<br>This is a faithful saying, and these things I will that thou affirm constantly, that they which have believed in God might be careful to **maintain** good works. These things are good and profitable unto men. [KJV]<br>This is a trustworthy statement; and concerning these things I want you to speak confidently, so that those who have believed God may be careful to **engage** in good deeds. These things are good and profitable for men. [NASB]<br>This is a trustworthy saying. And I want you to stress these things, so that those who have trusted in God may be careful to **devote** themselves to doing what is good. These things are excellent and profitable for everyone. [NIV]<br>This is a faithful saying, and these things I want you to affirm constantly, that those who have believed in God should be careful to **maintain** good works. These things are good and profitable to men. [NKJV]<br>These things I have told you are all true. I want you to insist on them so that everyone who trusts in God will be careful to **do** good deeds all the time. These things are good and beneficial for everyone. [NLT] | To devote; to maintain; to engage; to do; to manage; to care for; to set before; to give attention to; to be forward and eager and diligent in doing good works.<br><br>**Practical Application**<br>Believers must do good works and keep on doing them. It means...<br>- to keep on doing good works.<br>- to sustain good works.<br>- to persevere in doing good works.<br>- to carry on good works.<br><br>It even has the idea of sustaining good works against all odds regardless of circumstances and difficulties. It means to persevere in good works even in the midst of opposition or danger. |

# Practical Word Studies
## in the New Testament

| ENGLISH WORD | GREEK WORD AND VERSE | THE WORD MEANS... |
|---|---|---|
| | πιστὸς ὁ λόγος, καὶ περὶ τούτων βούλομαί σε διαβεβαιοῦσθαι, ἵνα φροντίζωσι καλῶν ἔργων **προΐστασθαι** οἱ πεπιστευκότες τῷ Θεῷ. ταῦτά ἐστι τὰ καλὰ καὶ ὠφέλιμα τοῖς ἀνθρώποις· [GNS]<br><br>Πιστὸς ὁ λόγος· καὶ περὶ τούτων βούλομαί σε διαβεβαιοῦσθαι, ἵνα φροντίζωσιν καλῶν ἔργων **προΐστασθαι** οἱ πεπιστευκότες θεῷ. ταῦτά ἐστιν καλὰ καὶ ὠφέλιμα τοῖς ἀνθρώποις. [GNT] | |
| **#1134**<br>**Do Business**<br><br>Occupy–KJV<br>**Do business–NASB**<br>Put to work–NIV<br>**Do business–NKJV**<br>Invest–NLT<br><br>**POSB REFERENCE**<br>(Lk.19:13)<br>Note 3, point 2<br>*Deeper Study #2* | *Πραγματεύσασθε* = *Pragmateusasthe*<br>Pronunciation: [prag-mat-yoo'-sahs-theh]<br>Parsing (part of speech): verb<br>   Mood—imperative<br>   Tense—aorist<br>   Voice—middle deponent<br>   Person—2nd person<br>   Number—plural<br>   Stem or root—from πραγματεύομαι<br>Concordance References:<br>  ⇒ Strong's #4231 pragmateuomai<br>  ⇒ NIV #4549 pragmateuomai<br>  ⇒ NASB #4231 pragmateuomai<br><br>**Luke 19:13**<br>And he called his ten servants, and delivered them ten pounds, and said unto them, **Occupy** till I come. [KJV]<br>"And he called ten of his slaves, and gave them ten minas, and said to them, '**Do business** with this until I come back.' [NASB]<br>So he called ten of his servants and gave them ten minas. '**Put** this money **to work**,' he said, 'until I come back.' [NIV]<br>So he called ten of his servants, delivered to them ten minas, and said to them, '**Do business** till I come.' [NKJV]<br>Before he left, he called together ten servants and gave them ten pounds of silver to **invest** for him while he was gone. [NLT]<br>καλέσας δὲ δέκα δούλους ἑαυτοῦ, ἔδωκεν αὐτοῖς δέκα μνᾶς, καὶ εἶπε πρὸς αὐτούς, **Πραγματεύσασθε** ἕως ἔρχομαι. [GNS]<br>καλέσας δὲ δέκα δούλους ἑαυτοῦ ἔδωκεν αὐτοῖς δέκα μνᾶς καὶ εἶπεν πρὸς αὐτούς, **Πραγματεύσασθε** ἐν ᾧ ἔρχομαι. [GNT] | To invest; to do business; to put to work; to trade; to occupy.<br><br>**Practical Application**<br>The words "do business" are words of diligent action. It is from the root word meaning to walk, to set in motion, and to continue in motion. The servant is to labor diligently, never letting up but using all the Lord has given him to look after. This is the only time the word *Pragmateusasthe* is used in the New Testament (cp. Isaiah 35:3; Hebrews 12:28; Hebrews 12:12). |
| **#1135**<br>**Do Not Cling To Me–Don't Cling To Me**<br><br>Touch me not–KJV<br>Stop clinging to Me–NASB<br>Do not hold on to me–NIV<br>**Do not cling to Me–NKJV**<br>Don't cling to me–NLT<br><br>**POSB REFERENCE**<br>(Jn.20:17-18; esp. v.17)<br>Note 4 | *Μή μου ἅπτου* = *mē mou haptou*<br>Pronunciation: [may moo hap-too]<br>Parsing *haptou* (part of speech): verb<br>   Mood—imperative<br>   Tense—present<br>   Voice—middle<br>   Person—2nd person<br>   Number—singular<br>   Stem or root—from ἅπτω<br>Concordance References:<br>  ⇒ Strong's #3361 me + 1473 ego + 680 hapto<br>  ⇒ NIV #3590 me [not] + 1609 ego [me] + 721 hapto [hold on to]<br>  ⇒ NASB #3361 me + 1473 ego + 680 hapto<br><br>**John 20:17**<br>Jesus saith unto her, **Touch me not**; for I am not yet ascended to my Father: but go to my brethren, and say unto them, I ascend unto my Father, and your Father; and to my God, and your God. [KJV]<br>Jesus said to her, "**Stop clinging to Me**, for I have not yet ascended to the Father; but go to My brethren, and say to them, 'I ascend to My Father and your Father, and My God and your God.'" [NASB]<br>Jesus said, "**Do not hold on to me**, for I have not yet returned to the Father. Go instead to my brothers and tell them, 'I am returning to my Father and your Father, to my God and your God.'"[NIV] | To not hold on to; to stop clinging; to resist touching; not to physically reach out and touch the body of Christ.<br><br>**Practical Application**<br>The words are present action, stop clinging to Me—do not cling to Me. Mary's great love seemingly had one flaw. She wanted to revel in her love for the Lord and in the fellowship that that love brought her. She was reaching out to clutch and to cling to His body (physically), but in doing so, she was missing the point: His cross and resurrection had created a totally new relationship. He was no longer just her Rabboni, her Master. He was her LORD and God (cp. John 20:28). He was soon to ascend back to the Father, so she must not waste time clutching and clinging. She must run to tell her great discovery. The Master was now her LORD and God, for He had created a new spiritual relationship with people. |

# PRACTICAL WORD STUDIES
## in the NEW TESTAMENT

| ENGLISH WORD | GREEK WORD AND VERSE | THE WORD MEANS... |
|---|---|---|
| | Jesus said to her, "**Do not cling to Me**, for I have not yet ascended to My Father; but go to My brethren and say to them, 'I am ascending to My Father and your Father, and *to* My God and your God.' " [NKJV]<br><br>"**Don't cling to me**," Jesus said, "for I haven't yet ascended to the Father. But go find my brothers and tell them that I am ascending to my Father and your Father, my God and your God." [NLT]<br><br>λέγει αὐτῇ ὁ Ἰησοῦς, **Μή μου ἅπτου**, οὔπω γὰρ ἀναβέβηκα πρὸς τὸν πατέρα μου· πορεύου δὲ πρὸς τοὺς ἀδελφούς μου, καὶ εἰπὲ αὐτοῖς, Ἀναβαίνω πρὸς τὸν πατέρα μου καὶ πατέρα ὑμῶν, καὶ Θεόν μου καὶ Θεὸν ὑμῶν. [GNS]<br><br>λέγει αὐτῇ Ἰησοῦς, **Μή μου ἅπτου**, οὔπω γὰρ ἀναβέβηκα πρὸς τὸν πατέρα· πορεύου δὲ πρὸς τοὺς ἀδελφούς μου καὶ εἰπὲ αὐτοῖς, Ἀναβαίνω πρὸς τὸν πατέρα μου καὶ πατέρα ὑμῶν καὶ θεόν μου καὶ θεὸν ὑμῶν. [GNT] | |
| **#1136**<br>**Do Not Hold On To Me**<br><br>Touch me not–KJV<br>Stop clinging to Me–NASB<br>**Do not hold on to me– NIV**<br>Do not cling to Me–NKJV<br>Stop clinging to Me–NLT<br><br>**POSB REFERENCE**<br>(Jn.20:17-18; esp. v.17)<br>Note 4 | **Μή μου ἅπτου** = mē mou haptou<br>Pronunciation: [may moo hap-too]<br>Parsing *haptou* (part of speech): verb<br>   Mood—imperative<br>   Tense—present<br>   Voice—middle<br>   Person—2nd person<br>   Number—singular<br>   Stem or root—from ἅπτω<br>Concordance References:<br>⇒ Strong's #3361 me + 1473 ego + 680 hapto<br>⇒ NIV #3590 me [not] + 1609 ego [me] + 721 hapto [hold on to]<br>⇒ NASB #3361 me + 1473 ego + 680 hapto<br><br>### John 20:17<br>Jesus saith unto her, **Touch me not**; for I am not yet ascended to my Father: but go to my brethren, and say unto them, I ascend unto my Father, and your Father; and to my God, and your God. [KJV]<br><br>Jesus said to her, "**Stop clinging to Me**, for I have not yet ascended to the Father; but go to My brethren, and say to them, 'I ascend to My Father and your Father, and My God and your God.'" [NASB]<br><br>Jesus said, "**Do not hold on to me**, for I have not yet returned to the Father. Go instead to my brothers and tell them, 'I am returning to my Father and your Father, to my God and your God.'" [NIV]<br><br>Jesus said to her, "**Do not cling to Me**, for I have not yet ascended to My Father; but go to My brethren and say to them, 'I am ascending to My Father and your Father, and *to* My God and your God.'" [NKJV]<br><br>"**Don't cling to me**," Jesus said, "for I haven't yet ascended to the Father. But go find my brothers and tell them that I am ascending to my Father and your Father, my God and your God." [NLT]<br><br>λέγει αὐτῇ ὁ Ἰησοῦς, **Μή μου ἅπτου**, οὔπω γὰρ ἀναβέβηκα πρὸς τὸν πατέρα μου· πορεύου δὲ πρὸς τοὺς ἀδελφούς μου, καὶ εἰπὲ αὐτοῖς, Ἀναβαίνω πρὸς τὸν πατέρα μου καὶ πατέρα ὑμῶν, καὶ Θεόν μου καὶ Θεὸν ὑμῶν. [GNS]<br><br>λέγει αὐτῇ Ἰησοῦς, **Μή μου ἅπτου**, οὔπω γὰρ ἀναβέβηκα πρὸς τὸν πατέρα· πορεύου δὲ πρὸς τοὺς ἀδελφούς μου καὶ εἰπὲ αὐτοῖς, Ἀναβαίνω πρὸς τὸν πατέρα μου καὶ πατέρα ὑμῶν καὶ θεόν μου καὶ θεὸν ὑμῶν. [GNT] | To not hold on to; to stop clinging; to resist touching; not to physically reach out and touch the body of Christ.<br><br>### Practical Application<br>The words are present action, stop clinging to Me—do not hold on to Me. Mary's great love seemingly had one flaw. She wanted to revel in her love for the Lord and in the fellowship that that love brought her. She was reaching out to clutch and to cling to His body (physically), but in doing so, she was missing the point: His cross and resurrection had created a totally new relationship. He was no longer just her Rabboni, her Master. He was her LORD and God (cp. John 20:28). He was soon to ascend back to the Father, so she must not waste time clutching and clinging. She must run to tell her great discovery. The Master was now her LORD and God, for He had created a new spiritual relationship with people. |
| **#1137**<br>**Do Our Best**<br><br>Labour–KJV<br>Diligent–NASB<br>Make every effort–NIV | σπουδάσωμεν = spoudasōmen<br>Pronunciation: [spoo-dah'-so-mehn]<br>Parsing (part of speech): verb<br>   Mood—subjunctive<br>   Tense—aorist<br>   Voice—active<br>   Person—1st person | To make every effort; to labor; to be diligent; to do one's best; to work hard; to endeavor, to give all diligence, be zealous, strive eagerly, exert one's self, and make haste. |

## PRACTICAL WORD STUDIES
### in the New Testament

| ENGLISH WORD | GREEK WORD AND VERSE | THE WORD MEANS... |
|---|---|---|
| Diligent–NKJV<br>Do our best–NLT<br><br>**POSB<br>REFERENCE**<br>(Heb.4:11-13; esp. v.11)<br>Note 5, point 1 | Number—plural<br>Stem or root—from σπουδάζω<br>Concordance References:<br>⇒ Strong's #4704 spoudazō<br>⇒ NIV #5079 spoudazō<br>⇒ NASB #4704 spoudazō<br><br>**Hebrews 4:11**<br>Let us **labour** therefore to enter into that rest, lest any man fall after the same example of unbelief. [KJV]<br>Let us therefore be **diligent** to enter that rest, lest anyone fall through following the same example of disobedience. [NASB]<br>Let us, therefore, **make every effort** to enter that rest, so that no one will fall by following their example of disobedience. [NIV]<br>Let us therefore be **diligent** to enter that rest, lest anyone fall according to the same example of disobedience. [NKJV]<br>Let us **do our best** to enter that place of rest. For anyone who disobeys God, as the people of Israel did, will fall. [NLT]<br>**σπουδάσωμεν** οὖν εἰσελθεῖν εἰς ἐκείνην τὴν κατάπαυσιν, ἵνα μὴ ἐν τῷ αὐτῷ τις ὑποδείγματι πέσῃ τῆς ἀπειθείας.<br>**σπουδάσωμεν** οὖν εἰσελθεῖν εἰς ἐκείνην τὴν κατάπαυσιν, ἵνα μὴ ἐν τῷ αὐτῷ τις ὑποδείγματι πέσῃ τῆς ἀπειθείας. [GNT] | **Practical Application**<br>A person must do his best or labor to enter God's rest or else he will fall into unbelief. There is no place for sleepiness or laziness, complacency or lethargy. Unless a person does his best or labors with all diligence, he will fall just as Israel fell. And remember Israel's experience: the people would labor for a while and then fall back for a while; labor again and then fall back again. Israel lived an up and down life, and the nation was not allowed to enter God's rest. There is no place for inconsistency, no place for living an up-and-down life—not in God's rest. Diligence—laboring every day—is an absolute essential. We must labor or else fall from God's rest as Israel fell. |
| **#1138**<br>**Do Their Work**<br><br>Rule–KJV<br>Rule–NASB<br>Direct–NIV<br>Rule–NKJV<br>Do their work–NLT<br><br>**POSB<br>REFERENCE**<br>(1 Tim.5:17-18; esp. v.17)<br>Note 1 | προεστῶτες = *proestōtes*<br>Pronunciation: [pro-ehst'-o-tehs]<br>Parsing (part of speech): verb<br>    Mood—participle<br>    Tense—perfect<br>    Voice—active<br>    Case—nominative<br>    Gender—plural<br>Stem or root—from προΐστημι<br>Concordance References:<br>⇒ Strong's #4291 proistēmi<br>⇒ NIV #4613 proistēmi<br>⇒ NASB #4291 proistēmi<br><br>**1 Tim. 5:17**<br>Let the elders that **rule** well be counted worthy of double honour, especially they who labour in the word and doctrine. [KJV]<br>Let the elders who **rule** well be considered worthy of double honor, especially those who work hard at preaching and teaching. [NASB]<br>The elders who **direct** the affairs of the church well are worthy of double honor, especially those whose work is preaching and teaching. [NIV]<br>Let the elders who **rule** well be counted worthy of double honor, especially those who labor in the word and doctrine. [NKJV]<br>Elders who **do their work** well should be paid well, especially those who work hard at both preaching and teaching. [NLT]<br>Οἱ καλῶς **προεστῶτες** πρεσβύτεροι διπλῆς τιμῆς ἀξιούσθωσαν, μάλιστα οἱ κοπιῶντες ἐν λόγῳ καὶ διδασκαλίᾳ· [GNS]<br>Οἱ καλῶς **προεστῶτες** πρεσβύτεροι διπλῆς τιμῆς ἀξιούσθωσαν, μάλιστα οἱ κοπιῶντες ἐν λόγῳ καὶ διδασκαλίᾳ. [GNT] | To direct; to rule; to do their work; to be a manager; to be a leader; to have authority over. The word *proestōtes* is a general word meaning to oversee, supervise, and look after.<br><br>**Practical Application**<br>There is a condition attached to honoring the minister. The minister to be honored is one who "rules well." The minister who is worthy of double honor is the minister who labors and labors and works and works. If he is to receive double honor, then he must demonstrate a double commitment to Christ and the church.<br>Note also that the whole ministerial staff is covered by this charge. All the ministers of a church staff are to be counted worthy of double honor. But there is one minister who is singled out: the minister who labors in the Word and doctrine, that is, who preaches and teaches. It is he upon whom so much responsibility lies: he is the minister who takes the lead in edifying and building up the believer and the church. He is the one who has to spend hours on his face before God and in the Word in order to preach and teach—this in addition to taking the lead in all the other duties and ministries of the church. If he is a committed minister, a minister who labors and labors for Christ and works and works for the church, then he is worthy of double honor. |
| **#1139**<br>**Do Things In<br>Such A Way**<br><br>Provide–KJV<br>Respect–NASB | προνοούμενοι = *pronooumenoi*<br>Pronunciation: [pro-no-oo-meh'-noy]<br>Parsing (part of speech): verb<br>    Mood—participle (imperative sense)<br>    Tense—present<br>    Voice—middle<br>    Case—nominative | To be careful; to provide; to respect; to do things in such a way; to take care of; to think before acting; to take pains.<br>The believer is to demonstrate good behavior in the sight of all men. The phrase "do things in |

# PRACTICAL WORD STUDIES
## in the NEW TESTAMENT

| ENGLISH WORD | GREEK WORD AND VERSE | THE WORD MEANS... |
|---|---|---|
| Careful–NIV<br>Have regard–NKJV<br>**Do things in such a way**–NLT<br><br>**POSB REFERENCE**<br>(Rom.12:17)<br>Note 4, point 2 | Gender—masculine<br>Person—2nd person<br>Number—plural<br>Stem or root—from προνοέω<br>Concordance References:<br>⇒ Strong's #4306 pronoeö<br>⇒ NIV #4629 pronoeö<br>⇒ NASB #4306 pronoeö<br><br>**Romans 12:17**<br>Recompense to no man evil for evil. **Provide** things honest in the sight of all men. [KJV]<br>Never pay back evil for evil to anyone. **Respect** what is right in the sight of all men. [NASB]<br>Do not repay anyone evil for evil. Be **careful** to do what is right in the eyes of everybody. [NIV]<br>Repay no one evil for evil. **Have regard** for good things in the sight of all men. [NKJV]<br>Never pay back evil for evil to anyone. **Do things in such a way** that everyone can see you are honorable. [NLT]<br>μηδενὶ κακὸν ἀντὶ κακοῦ ἀποδιδόντες, **προνοούμενοι** καλὰ ἐνώπιον πάντων ἀνθρώπων. [GNS]<br>μηδενὶ κακὸν ἀντὶ κακοῦ ἀποδιδόντες, **προνοούμενοι** καλὰ ἐνώπιον πάντων ἀνθρώπων· [GNT] | such a way" (*pronooumenoi*) means to think before acting.<br><br>**Practical Application**<br>The idea is this: when someone does evil against the believer, the believer is to think before he acts. He is to think and pray through his behavior. Why? So that he can respond in the right and proper way. The believer needs to do what is right and noble, and the only way to do it is to think through the situation. |
| #1140<br>**Do Well**<br><br>Do well–KJV<br>Do well–NASB<br>Do well–NIV<br>Do well–NKJV<br>Do well–NLT<br><br>**POSB REFERENCE**<br>(Acts 15:28-29; esp. v.29)<br>Note 4, point 2 | εὖ πράξετε = *eu praxete*<br>Pronunciation: [yoo prahx-eh-teh]<br>Parsing *eu* (part of speech): adjective adverb<br>    Stem or root—from εὖ<br>Parsing *praxete* (part of speech): verb<br>    Mood—indicative<br>    Tense—future<br>    Voice—active<br>    Person—2nd person<br>    Number—plural<br>    Stem or root—from πράσσω<br>Concordance References:<br>⇒ Strong's #2095 eu + 4238 + prassö<br>⇒ NIV #2292 eu + 4556 prassö<br>⇒ NASB #2095 eu + 4238 + prassö<br><br>**Acts 15:29**<br>That ye abstain from meats offered to idols, and from blood, and from things strangled, and from fornication: from which if ye keep yourselves, ye shall **do well**. Fare ye well. [KJV]<br>That you abstain from things sacrificed to idols and from blood and from things strangled and from fornication; if you keep yourselves free from such things, you will **do well**. Farewell." [NASB]<br>You are to abstain from food sacrificed to idols, from blood, from the meat of strangled animals and from sexual immorality. You will **do well** to avoid these things. Farewell. [NIV]<br>That you abstain from things offered to idols, from blood, from things strangled, and from sexual immorality. If you keep yourselves from these, you will **do well**. Farewell. [NKJV]<br>You must abstain from eating food offered to idols, from consuming blood or eating the meat of strangled animals, and from sexual immorality. If you do this, you will **do well**. Farewell." [NLT]<br>ἀπέχεσθαι εἰδωλοθύτων καὶ αἵματος καὶ πνικτῶν καὶ πορνείας· ἐξ ὧν διατηροῦντες ἑαυτοὺς **εὖ πράξετε**. ἔρρωσθε. [GNS]<br>ἀπέχεσθαι εἰδωλοθύτων καὶ αἵματος καὶ πνικτῶν καὶ πορνείας, ἐξ ὧν διατηροῦντες ἑαυτοὺς **εὖ πράξετε**. Ἔρρωσθε. [GNT] | To do well; to do a splendid job; to put into practice.<br><br>**Practical Application**<br>It means to fare well and experience good—love, joy, peace—both within their own hearts and lives and between themselves and other believers. (See POSB note, pt.4—Acts 15:13-21 for discussion of the four necessary rules.) |
| #1141<br>**Doctrine** | διδαχῇ = *didachë*<br>Pronunciation: [did-akh-ay']<br>Parsing (part of speech): noun<br>    Case—dative | Teaching, doctrine, instruction, principle, training. |

# PRACTICAL WORD STUDIES
## in the New Testament

| ENGLISH WORD | GREEK WORD AND VERSE | THE WORD MEANS... |
|---|---|---|
| **Doctrine**–KJV<br>Teaching–NASB<br>Teaching–NIV<br>**Doctrine**–NKJV<br>Teaching–NLT<br><br>**POSB<br>REFERENCE**<br>(Acts 2:42)<br>*Deeper Study* #2 | Gender—feminine<br>Number—singular<br>Stem or root—from διδαχή, ῆς<br>Concordance References:<br>⇒ Strong's #1322 didachē<br>⇒ NIV #1439 didachē<br>⇒ NASB #1322 didachē<br><br>**Acts 2:42**<br>And they continued stedfastly in the apostles' **doctrine** and fellowship, and in breaking of bread, and in prayers. [KJV]<br>And they were continually devoting themselves to the apostles' **teaching** and to fellowship, to the breaking of bread and to prayer. [NASB]<br>They devoted themselves to the apostles' **teaching** and to the fellowship, to the breaking of bread and to prayer. [NIV]<br>And they continued steadfastly in the apostles' **doctrine** and fellowship, in the breaking of bread, and in prayers. [NKJV]<br>They joined with the other believers and devoted themselves to the apostles' **teaching** and fellowship, sharing in the Lord's Supper and in prayer. [NLT]<br>ἦσαν δὲ προσκαρτεροῦντες τῇ **διδαχῇ** τῶν ἀποστόλων καὶ τῇ κοινωνίᾳ, καὶ τῇ κλάσει τοῦ ἄρτου καὶ ταῖς προσευχαῖς. [GNS]<br>ἦσαν δὲ προσκαρτεροῦντες τῇ **διδαχῇ** τῶν ἀποστόλων καὶ τῇ κοινωνίᾳ, τῇ κλάσει τοῦ ἄρτου καὶ ταῖς προσευχαῖς. [GNT] | **Practical Application**<br>It is the doctrine or teaching, the instruction of the apostles. This would include both what Christ taught and His death, resurrection, ascension, or exaltation. It would be the same doctrine and instructions...<br>• that are shared in the New Testament.<br>• that the disciples wrote to various churches and bodies of believers.<br>The doctrine or teaching would be no different. There is only one message, only one Word that saves and grounds people in the Lord—the Word of God Himself, the message of the New Testament. On the day of Pentecost, the persons who were saved needed to be grounded in the faith. And the only message that could ground them was the message found in the New Testament. It was that message, that doctrine they were taught. |
| #1142<br>**Doesn't Know Much**<br><br>Unskillful–KJV<br>Not accustomed to–NASB<br>Not acquainted with–NIV<br>Unskilled–NKJV<br>**Doesn't know much**–NLT<br><br>**POSB<br>REFERENCE**<br>(Heb.5:13)<br>Note 3 | ἄπειρος = apeiros<br>Pronunciation: [ap'-i-ros]<br>Parsing (part of speech): adjective<br>    Case—nominative<br>    Gender—masculine<br>    Number—singular<br>Stem or root—from ἄπειρος, ον<br>Concordance References:<br>⇒ Strong's #552 apeiros<br>⇒ NIV #586 apeiros<br>⇒ NASB #552 apeiros<br><br>**Hebrews 5:13**<br>For every one that useth milk is **unskilful** in the word of righteousness: for he is a babe. [KJV]<br>For everyone who partakes only of milk is **not accustomed to** the word of righteousness, for he is a babe. [NASB]<br>Anyone who lives on milk, being still an infant, is **not acquainted with** the teaching about righteousness. [NIV]<br>For everyone who partakes *only* of milk *is* **unskilled** in the word of righteousness, for he is a babe. [NKJV]<br>And a person who is living on milk isn't very far along in the Christian life and **doesn't know much** about doing what is right. [NLT]<br>πᾶς γὰρ ὁ μετέχων γάλακτος **ἄπειρος** λόγου δικαιοσύνης· νήπιος γάρ ἐστι. [GNS]<br>πᾶς γὰρ ὁ μετέχων γάλακτος **ἄπειρος** λόγου δικαιοσύνης, νήπιος γάρ ἐστιν· [GNT] | Not acquainted with; unskillful; not accustomed to; does not know much; inexperienced in.<br><br>**Practical Application**<br>A person becomes immature because of being unskilled in the Word. The Hebrew believers remained unskillful in the Word of righteousness. They professed Christ and His righteousness, but they had never grasped or experienced Him—not fully—not in a mature sense. Note the verse: although this person is a church member, "he is a babe." |
| #1143<br>**Dogs**<br><br>Dogs–KJV<br>Dogs–NASB<br>Dogs–NIV<br>Dogs–NKJV<br>Dogs–NLT | κύνας = kunas<br>Pronunciation: [koo'-nahs]<br>Parsing (part of speech): noun<br>    Case—accusative<br>    Gender—masculine<br>    Number—plural<br>Stem or root—from κύων, κυνός<br>Concordance References:<br>⇒ Strong's #2965 kuōn | Dogs. The word "dogs" was the lowest title possible to convey contempt and ridicule. Dog does not refer to the house pet of today, but to the wild dogs that roamed in the forests by day and the city streets by night. They were scavengers and snarlers who could be very vicious and dangerous. |

# PRACTICAL WORD STUDIES
## in the NEW TESTAMENT

| ENGLISH WORD | GREEK WORD AND VERSE | THE WORD MEANS... |
|---|---|---|
| **POSB REFERENCE** (Philip.3:2) Note 3, point 1 | ⇒ NIV #3264 kuōn<br>⇒ NASB #2965 kuōn<br><br>**Philip. 3:2**<br>Beware of **dogs**, beware of evil workers, beware of the concision. [KJV]<br>Beware of the **dogs**, beware of the evil workers, beware of the false circumcision; [NASB]<br>Watch out for those **dogs**, those men who do evil, those mutilators of the flesh. [NIV]<br>Beware of **dogs**, beware of evil workers, beware of the mutilation! [NKJV]<br>Watch out for those **dogs**, those wicked men and their evil deeds, those mutilators who say you must be circumcised to be saved. [NLT]<br>βλέπετε τοὺς **κύνας**, βλέπετε τοὺς κακοὺς ἐργάτας, βλέπετε τὴν κατατομήν· [GNS]<br>Βλέπετε τοὺς **κύνας**, βλέπετε τοὺς κακοὺς ἐργάτας, βλέπετε τὴν κατατομήν. [GNT] | **Practical Application**<br>It should be noted that both Jew and Gentile called each other dogs as a term of contempt.<br>The point is descriptive: there are some false teachers who are just like wild dogs.<br>⇒ They are scavengers who seek out all whom they can consume with their false teaching.<br>⇒ And if any person steps forward to defend the sheep and the truth, they snarl and often become vicious and dangerous, ready to attack the defender and destroy him. |
| **#1144**<br>**Doing Good**<br><br>Good works–KJV<br>Deeds of kindness–NASB<br>**Doing good–NIV**<br>Good works–NKJV<br>Doing kind things–NLT<br><br>**POSB REFERENCE** (Acts 9:36-39; esp. v.36) Note 2, point 1b | ἔργων ἀγαθῶν = ergōn agathōn<br>Pronunciation: [er'-gon ag-ath-on']<br>Parsing *ergōn* (part of speech): noun<br>  Case—genitive<br>  Gender—neuter<br>  Number—plural<br>  Stem or root—from ἔργον, ου<br>Parsing *agathōn* (part of speech): adjective<br>  Case—genitive<br>  Gender—neuter<br>  Number—plural<br>  Stem or root—from ἀγαθός, ή, όν<br>Concordance References:<br>⇒ Strong's #2041 ergon + 18 agathos<br>⇒ NIV #2240 ergon [doing] + 19 agathos [good]<br>⇒ NASB #2041 ergon + 18 agathos<br><br>**Acts 9:36**<br>Now there was at Joppa a certain disciple named Tabitha, which by interpretation is called Dorcas: this woman was full of **good works** and almsdeeds which she did. [KJV]<br>Now in Joppa there was a certain disciple named Tabitha (which translated in Greek is called Dorcas); this woman was abounding with **deeds of kindness** and charity, which she continually did. [NASB]<br>In Joppa there was a disciple named Tabitha (which, when translated, is Dorcas), who was always **doing good** and helping the poor. [NIV]<br>At Joppa there was a certain disciple named Tabitha, which is translated Dorcas. This woman was full of **good works** and charitable deeds which she did. [NKJV]<br>There was a believer in Joppa named Tabitha (which in Greek is Dorcas). She was always **doing kind things** for others and helping the poor. [NLT]<br>Ἐν Ἰόππῃ δέ τις ἦν μαθήτρια ὀνόματι Ταβιθά, ἡ διερμηνευομένη λέγεται Δορκάς· αὕτη ἦν πλήρης **ἀγαθῶν ἔργων** καὶ ἐλεημοσυνῶν ὧν ἐποίει. [GNS]<br>Ἐν Ἰόππῃ δέ τις ἦν μαθήτρια ὀνόματι Ταβιθά, ἡ διερμηνευομένη λέγεται Δορκάς· αὕτη ἦν πλήρης **ἔργων ἀγαθῶν** καὶ ἐλεημοσυνῶν ὧν ἐποίει. [GNT] | Work, deed, action; task, occupation, undertaking; practical expression; handiwork, workmanship (1 Cor 9.1); perhaps effect, result or product (Jas 1.4). It is a general term meaning all kinds of good works, serving and doing all kinds of good to all who needed help.<br><br>**Practical Application**<br>Two names are given for her: "Tabitha," which was her Jewish or Hebrew name, and "Dorcas," which was her Greek name. Her name means gazelle (or doe or deer) which is a most beautiful creature. The gazelle is known for...<br>• its slender features.<br>• its grace and loveliness.<br>• its bright eyes and tender looks.<br>The same traits were apparently characteristic of Dorcas. Note: Scripture does say the wife is to be as the loving doe and the graceful deer to her husband (Proverbs 5:19). She is to be as the beautiful creature: gracious and loving, bright eyed (joyful, excited, expectant) and tender.<br>She was deeply committed to Christ, a very faithful and devoted disciple, full of...<br>• "doing good" (*ergōn agathōn*)<br>• "charitable deeds": charitable gifts. She gave gifts to the needy. |
| **#1145**<br>**Doing Kind Things**<br><br>Good works–KJV<br>Deeds of kindness–NASB<br>Doing good–NIV<br>Good works–NKJV<br>**Doing kind things–NLT** | ἔργων ἀγαθῶν = ergōn agathōn<br>Pronunciation: [er'-gon ag-ath-on']<br>Parsing *ergōn* (part of speech): noun<br>  Case—genitive<br>  Gender—neuter<br>  Number—plural<br>  Stem or root—from ἔργον, ου<br>Parsing *agathōn* (part of speech): adjective<br>  Case—genitive<br>  Gender—neuter<br>  Number—plural<br>  Stem or root—from ἀγαθός, ή, όν | Work, deed, action; task, occupation, undertaking; practical expression; handiwork, workmanship (1 Cor 9.1); perhaps effect, result or product (Jas 1.4). It is a general term meaning all kinds of good works, serving and doing all kinds of good to all who needed help.<br><br>**Practical Application**<br>Two names are given for her: "Tabitha," which was her Jewish or Hebrew name, and "Dorcas," which was her Greek name. Her name |

# PRACTICAL WORD STUDIES
## in the NEW TESTAMENT

| ENGLISH WORD | GREEK WORD AND VERSE | THE WORD MEANS... |
|---|---|---|
| **POSB REFERENCE** (Acts 9:36-39; esp. v.36) Note 2, point 1b | Concordance References:<br>⇒ Strong's #2041 ergon + 18 agathos<br>⇒ NIV #2240 ergon [doing] + 19 agathos [good]<br>⇒ NASB #2041 ergon + 18 agathos<br><br>**Acts 9:36**<br>Now there was at Joppa a certain disciple named Tabitha, which by interpretation is called Dorcas: this woman was full of **good works** and almsdeeds which she did. [KJV]<br>Now in Joppa there was a certain disciple named Tabitha (which translated in Greek is called Dorcas); this woman was abounding with **deeds of kindness** and charity, which she continually did. [NASB]<br>In Joppa there was a disciple named Tabitha (which, when translated, is Dorcas), who was always **doing good** and helping the poor. [NIV]<br>At Joppa there was a certain disciple named Tabitha, which is translated Dorcas. This woman was full of **good works** and charitable deeds which she did. [NKJV]<br>There was a believer in Joppa named Tabitha (which in Greek is Dorcas). She was always **doing kind things** for others and helping the poor. [NLT]<br>Ἐν Ἰόππῃ δέ τις ἦν μαθήτρια ὀνόματι Ταβιθά, ἣ διερμηνευομένη λέγεται Δορκάς· αὕτη ἦν πλήρης **ἀγαθῶν ἔργων** καὶ ἐλεημοσυνῶν ὧν ἐποίει. [GNS]<br>Ἐν Ἰόππῃ δέ τις ἦν μαθήτρια ὀνόματι Ταβιθά, ἣ διερμηνευομένη λέγεται Δορκάς· αὕτη ἦν πλήρης **ἔργων ἀγαθῶν** καὶ ἐλεημοσυνῶν ὧν ἐποίει. [GNT] | means gazelle (or doe or deer) which is a most beautiful creature. The gazelle is known for...<br>• its slender features.<br>• its grace and loveliness.<br>• its bright eyes and tender looks.<br>The same traits were apparently characteristic of Dorcas. Note: Scripture does say the wife is to be as the loving doe and the graceful deer to her husband (Proverbs 5:19). She is to be as the beautiful creature: gracious and loving, bright eyed (joyful, excited, expectant) and tender.<br>She was deeply committed to Christ, a very faithful and devoted disciple, full of...<br>• "doing kind things" (*ergōn agathōn*)<br>• "helping the poor": charitable gifts. She gave gifts to the needy. |
| **#1146**<br>**Don't Be Afraid Of Suffering For The Lord**<br><br>Endure afflictions– KJV<br>Endure hardship– NASB<br>Endure hardship–NIV<br>Endure afflictions– NKJV<br>Don't be afraid of suffering for the Lord–NLT<br><br>**POSB REFERENCE** (2 Tim. 4:5) Note 4, point 2 | κακοπάθησον = *kakopathēson*<br>Pronunciation: [kak-op-ath-ay'-son]<br>Parsing (part of speech): verb<br>   Mood—imperative<br>   Tense—aorist<br>   Voice—active<br>   Person—2nd person<br>   Number—singular<br>   Stem or root—from κακοπαθέω<br>Concordance References:<br>⇒ Strong's #2553 kakopatheō<br>⇒ NIV #2802 kakopatheō<br>⇒ NASB #2553 kakopatheō<br><br>**2 Tim. 4:5**<br>But watch thou in all things, **endure afflictions**, do the work of an evangelist, make full proof of thy ministry. [KJV]<br>But you, be sober in all things, **endure hardship**, do the work of an evangelist, fulfill your ministry. [NASB]<br>But you, keep your head in all situations, **endure hardship**, do the work of an evangelist, discharge all the duties of your ministry. [NIV]<br>But you be watchful in all things, **endure afflictions**, do the work of an evangelist, fulfill your ministry. [NKJV]<br>But you should keep a clear mind in every situation. **Don't be afraid of suffering for the Lord**. Work at bringing others to Christ. Complete the ministry God has given you. [NLT]<br>σὺ δὲ νῆφε ἐν πᾶσι, **κακοπάθησον**, ἔργον ποίησον εὐαγγελιστοῦ, τὴν διακονίαν σου πληροφόρησον. [GNS]<br>σὺ δὲ νῆφε ἐν πᾶσιν, **κακοπάθησον**, ἔργον ποίησον εὐαγγελιστοῦ, τὴν διακονίαν σου πληροφόρησον. [GNT] | To endure hardship, afflictions; not to be afraid of suffering for the Lord; to suffer hardships, troubles, problems, difficulties, and evils.<br><br>**Practical Application**<br>Kenneth Wuest gives an excellent discussion of this point, a discussion that merits attention by every minister who has any concern for people whatsoever.<br><br>"The verb [don't be afraid of suffering for the Lord] is aorist imperative. It is a sharp command given with military snap and curtness. Timothy needed just that. He was not cast in a heroic mold. How we in the ministry of the Word need that injunction today. What 'softies' we sometimes are, afraid to come out clearly in our proclamation of the truth and our stand as to false doctrine, fearing the ostracism of our fellows, the ecclesiastical displeasure of our superiors, or the cutting off of our immediate financial income. I would rather walk a lonely road with Jesus than be without His fellowship in the crowd, wouldn't you? I would rather live in a cottage and eat simple food, and have Him as Head of my house and the Unseen Guest at every meal, than to live in royal style in a mansion without Him" (*The Pastoral Epistles*, Vol.2, p.159). |
| **#1147**<br>**Don't Care Anymore About Right And Wrong** | ἀπηλγηκότες = *apēlgēkotes*<br>Pronunciation: [ap-ayl'-gay'-ko-tehs]<br>Parsing (part of speech): verb<br>   Mood—participle<br>   Tense—perfect<br>   Voice—active<br>   Case—nominative<br>   Gender—masculine | To lose all sensitivity; to be past feeling; to become callous; not to care anymore about right and wrong; to become insensible, hardened.<br><br>**Practical Application**<br>Unbelievers reach a point where they no longer have feelings for God and His standard of |

# Practical Word Studies
## in the New Testament

| ENGLISH WORD | GREEK WORD AND VERSE | THE WORD MEANS... |
|---|---|---|
| Past feeling–KJV<br>Having become callous–NASB<br>Lost all sensitivity–NIV<br>Past feeling–NKJV<br>**Don't care anymore about right and wrong–NLT**<br><br>**POSB REFERENCE**<br>(Eph.4:17-19; esp. v.19)<br>Note 1, point 4 | Number—plural<br>Stem or root—from ἀπαλγέω<br>Concordance References:<br>⇒ Strong's #524 apalgeō<br>⇒ NIV #556 apalgeō<br>⇒ NASB #524 apalgeō<br><br>**Ephes. 4:19**<br>Who being **past feeling** have given themselves over unto lasciviousness, to work all uncleanness with greediness. [KJV]<br>And they, **having become callous**, have given themselves over to sensuality, for the practice of every kind of impurity with greediness. [NASB]<br>Having **lost all sensitivity**, they have given themselves over to sensuality so as to indulge in every kind of impurity, with a continual lust for more. [NIV]<br>Who, being **past feeling**, have given themselves over to lewdness, to work all uncleanness with greediness. [NKJV]<br>They **don't care anymore about right and wrong**, and they have given themselves over to immoral ways. Their lives are filled with all kinds of impurity and greed. [NLT]<br>οἵτινες **ἀπηλγηκότες** ἑαυτοὺς παρέδωκαν τῇ ἀσελγείᾳ, εἰς ἐργασίαν ἀκαθαρσίας πάσης ἐν πλεονεξίᾳ. [GNS]<br>οἵτινες **ἀπηλγηκότες** ἑαυτοὺς παρέδωκαν τῇ ἀσελγείᾳ εἰς ἐργασίαν ἀκαθαρσίας πάσης ἐν πλεονεξίᾳ. [GNT] | morality. The more a person walks without God the more callous a person becomes to God. The more a person walks in sin, the more callous his conscience becomes to righteousness. Sin becomes more and more acceptable. The person's conscience no longer bothers him. He reaches a point of being *past feeling*. The believer is not to return to sin. He is not to walk as other men walk—in sin, becoming callous and insensitive to God. |
| **#1148**<br>**Don't Ignore It**<br><br>Despise not–KJV<br>Not regard lightly–NASB<br>Not make light of–NIV<br>Not despise–NKJV<br>**Don't ignore it–NLT**<br><br>**POSB REFERENCE**<br>(Heb.12:5-7; esp. v.5)<br>Note 1 | μὴ ὀλιγώρει = mē oligōrei<br>Pronunciation: [may ol-ig-o-reh'-ee]<br>Parsing *oligōrei* (part of speech): verb<br>    Mood—imperative<br>    Tense—present<br>    Voice—active<br>    Person—2nd person<br>    Number—singular<br>    Stem or root—from ὀλιγωρέω<br>Concordance References:<br>⇒ Strong's #3361 mē + 3643 oligōreō<br>⇒ NIV #3590 mē [not] + 3902 oligōreō [make light of]<br>⇒ NASB #3361 mē + 3643 oligōreō<br><br>**Hebrews 12:5**<br>And ye have forgotten the exhortation which speaketh unto you as unto children, My son, **despise not** thou the chastening of the Lord, nor faint when thou art rebuked of him: [KJV]<br>And you have forgotten the exhortation which is addressed to you as sons, "My son, do **not regard lightly** the discipline of the Lord, Nor FAINT WHEN YOU ARE REPROVED BY Him; [NASB]<br>And you have forgotten that word of encouragement that addresses you as sons: "My son, do **not make light of** the Lord's discipline, and do not lose heart when he rebukes you, [NIV]<br>And you have forgotten the exhortation which speaks to you as to sons:"*My son, **do not despise** the chastening of the Lord,Nor be discouraged when yu are rebuked by Him;* [NKJV]<br>And have you entirely forgotten the encouraging words God spoke to you, his children? He said, "My child, **don't ignore it** when the Lord disciplines you,and don't be discouraged when he corrects you. [NLT]<br>καὶ ἐκλέλησθε τῆς παρακλήσεως, ἥτις ὑμῖν ὡς υἱοῖς διαλέγεται, Υἱέ μου, **μὴ ὀλιγώρει** παιδείας Κυρίου, μηδὲ ἐκλύου, ὑπ' αὐτοῦ ἐλεγχόμενος· [GNS]<br>καὶ ἐκλέλησθε τῆς παρακλήσεως, ἥτις ὑμῖν ὡς υἱοῖς διαλέγεται, Υἱέ μου, **μὴ ὀλιγώρει** παιδείας κυρίου μηδὲ ἐκλύου ὑπ' αὐτοῦ ἐλεγχόμενος· [GNT] | Not to make light of; not to regard lightly; not to despise; not to ignore; not to think lightly of; not to scorn; not to make little of, treat lightly.<br><br>**Practical Application**<br>When we are being taught, disciplined, or corrected, there is always the danger of...<br>• despising it<br>• scorning it<br>• making light of it<br>• treating it too lightly<br>Too often, we pay little attention to the discipline and correction of God: to the tug and pull of the Spirit of God, to the little consequences and sufferings of our hearts, to the little things that happen to us. As a result we continue right on in our little irresponsible behaviors and sins. The little flaws and sins get bigger and bigger until finally the roof caves in and the consequences involve so much destruction and suffering that we can no longer ignore them.<br>Why do we suffer so much in this life? Because of our irresponsibilities and sins—because we do not heed the discipline and correction of God when we first begin to act irresponsibly. If we heeded the discipline of God, then we could correct our small misbehavior and no big sin would happen. This would mean that much of the great sufferings in the world would never happen.<br>The point is this: we are not to despise the discipline of God—not to scorn it nor take and treat it lightly. We are to heed it. As we do, life will be much easier and stronger and much more triumphant and victorious. |

## PRACTICAL WORD STUDIES
### in the NEW TESTAMENT

| ENGLISH WORD | GREEK WORD AND VERSE | THE WORD MEANS... |
|---|---|---|
| **#1149**<br>**Don't Let**<br><br>Beware–KJV<br>See to it–NASB<br>See to it–NIV<br>Beware–NKJV<br>**Don't let–NLT**<br><br>**POSB**<br>**REFERENCE**<br>(Col.2:8)<br>Note 1<br><br>See also POSB REF:<br>(Heb.12:25-29; esp. v.25)<br>Introduction | βλέπετε = blepete<br>Pronunciation: [blep'-eh-teh]<br>Parsing (part of speech): verb<br>  Mood—imperative<br>  Tense—present<br>  Voice—active<br>  Person—2nd person<br>  Number—plural<br>  Stem or root—from βλέπω<br>Concordance References:<br> ⇒ Strong's #991 blepō<br> ⇒ NIV #1063 blepö<br> ⇒ NASB #991 blepö<br><br>**Col. 2:8**<br>**Beware** lest any man spoil you through philosophy and vain deceit, after the tradition of men, after the rudiments of the world, and not after Christ. [KJV]<br>**See to it** that no one takes you captive through philosophy and empty deception, according to the tradition of men, according to the elementary principles of the world, rather than according to Christ. [NASB]<br>**See to it** that no one takes you captive through hollow and deceptive philosophy, which depends on human tradition and the basic principles of this world rather than on Christ. [NIV]<br>**Beware** lest anyone cheat you through philosophy and empty deceit, according to the tradition of men, according to the basic principles of the world, and not according to Christ. [NKJV]<br>**Don't let** anyone lead you astray with empty philosophy and high-sounding nonsense that come from human thinking and from the evil powers of this world, and not from Christ. [NLT]<br>βλέπετε μή τις ὑμᾶς ἔσται ὁ συλαγωγῶν διὰ τῆς φιλοσοφίας καὶ κενῆς ἀπάτης, κατὰ τὴν παράδοσιν τῶν ἀνθρώπων, κατὰ τὰ στοιχεῖα τοῦ κόσμου, καὶ οὐ κατὰ Χριστόν· [GNS]<br>βλέπετε μή τις ὑμᾶς ἔσται ὁ συλαγωγῶν διὰ τῆς φιλοσοφίας καὶ κενῆς ἀπάτης κατὰ τὴν παράδοσιν τῶν ἀνθρώπων, κατὰ τὰ στοιχεῖα τοῦ κόσμου καὶ οὐ κατὰ Χριστόν· [GNT] | To see to it, to beware of; to not let; to take heed, look out, guard yourself.<br><br>**Practical Application**<br>Why is this important, "That no one takes you captive through hollow and deceptive philosophy?"<br>⇒ Some men are in a genuine search for truth and reality. They seek to learn the truth and reality of the universe and the problems that face them, but they limit themselves to the universe.<br>⇒ Other persons have novel ideas or philosophies about truth and reality, but they become more interested in their position than the truth. They need others to accept their positions or else their ideas die. Therefore, they have to present and persuade people of their ideas and philosophies whether they are sound or not.<br>Believers must, therefore, beware to guard against worldly philosophies and ideas lest they become ensnared and enslaved. |
| **#1150**<br>**Don't Ruin**<br><br>Destroy not–KJV<br>Do not destroy–NASB<br>Do not destroy–NIV<br>Do not destroy–NKJV<br>**Don't ruin–NLT**<br><br>**POSB**<br>**REFERENCE**<br>(Rom.14:13-15; esp. v.15)<br>Note 6, point 2 | μὴ ἀπόλλυε = më apollue<br>Pronunciation: [may ap-ol'-loo-eh]<br>Parsing *apollue* (part of speech): verb<br>  Mood—imperative<br>  Tense—present<br>  Voice—active<br>  Person—2nd person<br>  Number—singular<br>  Stem or root—from ἀπόλλυμι<br>Concordance References:<br> ⇒ Strong's #3361 më + 622 apollumi<br> ⇒ NIV #3590 më [not] + 660 apollumi [destroy]<br> ⇒ NASB #3361 më + 622 apollumi<br><br>**Romans 14:15**<br>But if thy brother be grieved with thy meat, now walkest thou not charitably. **Destroy not** him with thy meat, for whom Christ died. [KJV]<br>For if because of food your brother is hurt, you are no longer walking according to love. **Do not destroy** with your food him for whom Christ died. [NASB]<br>If your brother is distressed because of what you eat, you are no longer acting in love. **Do not** by your eating **destroy** your brother for whom Christ died. [NIV]<br>Yet if your brother is grieved because of *your* food, you are no longer walking in love. **Do not destroy** with your food the one for whom Christ died. [NKJV]<br>And if another Christian is distressed by what you eat, you are not acting in love if you eat it. **Don't** let your eat- | Do not destroy or ruin; not to spoil, hurt and wound to the point of ruining.<br><br>**Practical Application**<br>We are to do nothing that would destroy a brother. This is a forceful command: "Don't ruin (*më apollue*) someone." Such behavior is absolutely forbidden of the Christian believer. We are to do absolutely nothing that would destroy or ruin our brother. |

## PRACTICAL WORD STUDIES
## in the NEW TESTAMENT

| ENGLISH WORD | GREEK WORD AND VERSE | THE WORD MEANS... |
|---|---|---|
| | ing **ruin** someone for whom Christ died. [NLT]<br>εἰ δὲ διὰ βρῶμα ὁ ἀδελφός σου λυπεῖται, οὐκέτι κατὰ ἀγάπην περιπατεῖς. **μὴ** τῷ βρώματί σου ἐκεῖνον **ἀπόλλυε**, ὑπὲρ οὗ Χριστὸς ἀπέθανε. [GNS]<br>εἰ γὰρ διὰ βρῶμα ὁ ἀδελφός σου λυπεῖται, οὐκέτι κατὰ ἀγάπην περιπατεῖς· **μὴ** τῷ βρώματί σου ἐκεῖνον **ἀπόλλυε** ὑπὲρ οὗ Χριστὸς ἀπέθανεν. [GNT] | |
| #1151<br>**Done**<br><br>Wrought–KJV<br>Wrought–NASB<br>**Done–NIV**<br>**Done–NKJV**<br>Wants–NLT<br><br>**POSB<br>REFERENCE**<br>(Jn.3:21)<br>Note 4, point 3 | ἔστιν εἰργασμένα = estin eirgasmena<br>Pronunciation: [eh-stin eerg-ahs-mehn-ah]<br>Parsing *estin* (part of speech): verb<br>   Mood—indicative<br>   Tense—present<br>   Voice—active<br>   Person—3rd person<br>   Number—singular<br>   Stem or root—from εἰμί<br>Parsing *eirgasmena* (part of speech): verb<br>   Mood—participle<br>   Tense—perfect<br>   Voice—passive<br>   Case—nominative<br>   Gender—neuter<br>   Number—plural<br>   Stem or root—from ἐργάζομαι<br>Concordance References:<br>  ⇒ Strong's #1488+2038 eimi ergazomai<br>  ⇒ NIV #1639+2237 eimi ergazomai<br>  ⇒ NASB #1488+2038 eimi ergazomai<br><br>**John 3:21**<br>But he that doeth truth cometh to the light, that his deeds may be made manifest, that they are **wrought** in God. [KJV]<br>"But he who practices the truth comes to the light, that his deeds may be manifested as having been **wrought** in God." [NASB]<br>But whoever lives by the truth comes into the light, so that it may be seen plainly that what he has done has been **done** through God." [NIV]<br>But he who does the truth comes to the light, that his deeds may be clearly seen, that they have been **done** in God." [NKJV]<br>But those who do what is right come to the light gladly, so everyone can see that they are doing what God **wants**." [NLT]<br>ὁ δὲ ποιῶν τὴν ἀλήθειαν, ἔρχεται πρὸς τὸ φῶς, ἵνα φανερωθῇ αὐτοῦ τὰ ἔργα, ὅτι ἐν Θεῷ **ἐστιν εἰργασμένα**. [GNS]<br>ὁ δὲ ποιῶν τὴν ἀλήθειαν ἔρχεται πρὸς τὸ φῶς, ἵνα φανερωθῇ αὐτοῦ τὰ ἔργα ὅτι ἐν θεῷ **ἐστιν εἰργασμένα**. [GNT] | To work, produce, perform, originate, and fashion from something.<br><br>**Practical Application**<br>The idea is that the person comes to Christ (the Light) so that his works will be "done," originated, and worked in and of God. The person who comes to Christ lives close to God. He walks and talks and listens to God (His Word), and he does what God says (cp. 2 Cor. 1:12). |
| #1152<br>**Done**<br><br>Deeds–KJV<br>Deeds–NASB<br>**Done–NIV**<br>Deeds–NKJV<br>**Done–NLT**<br><br>**POSB<br>REFERENCE**<br>(Rom.2:6-10; esp. v.6)<br>Note 3 | ἔργα = erga<br>Pronunciation: [er'-gah]<br>Parsing (part of speech): noun<br>   Case—accusative<br>   Gender—neuter<br>   Number—plural<br>   Stem or root—from ἔργον, ου<br>Concordance References:<br>  ⇒ Strong's #2041 ergon<br>  ⇒ NIV #2240 ergon<br>  ⇒ NASB #2041 ergon<br><br>**Romans 2:6**<br>Who will render to every man according to his **deeds**: [KJV]<br>Who will render to every man according to his **deeds**: [NASB]<br>God "will give to each person according to what he has **done**." [NIV]<br>Who *"will render to each one according to his* | Work, deed, action, task, occupation, undertaking, practical expression, handiwork, workmanship.<br><br>**Practical Application**<br>The judgment of God—of the only living and true God—is according to what each person has done (Proverbs 24:12; 2 Tim. 4:14; cp. Matthew 16:27; Rev. 22:12), and it will be universal. Every one will be either eternally rewarded or eternally punished. No one shall be exempt; no one will escape.<br>Now note: judgment is to be based upon "what he [a person] has done" (*erga*) or works. This does not mean that faith is not necessary. Contrariwise, there is no such thing as...<br>• faith without works.<br>• righteous and acceptable works without faith. |

## Practical Word Studies in the New Testament

| ENGLISH WORD | GREEK WORD AND VERSE | THE WORD MEANS... |
|---|---|---|
| | *deeds"*: [NKJV]<br>Will judge all people according to what they have **done**. [NLT]<br>ὃς ἀποδώσει ἑκάστῳ κατὰ τὰ **ἔργα** αὐτοῦ· [GNS]<br>ὃς ἀποδώσει ἑκάστῳ κατὰ τὰ **ἔργα** αὐτοῦ· [GNT] | |
| **#1153**<br>**Done The Lord's Work**<br><br>Serving the Lord–KJV<br>Serving the Lord–NASB<br>Served the Lord–NIV<br>Serving the Lord–NKJV<br>**Done the Lord's work–NLT**<br><br>**POSB REFERENCE**<br>(Acts 20:18-19; esp. v.19)<br>Note 2, point 2 | δουλεύων τῷ κυρίῳ = *douleuōn tō kuriō*<br>Pronunciation: [dool-yoo'-own tow koo'-ree-o]<br>Parsing *douleuōn* (part of speech): verb<br>    Mood—participle<br>    Tense—present<br>    Voice—active<br>    Case—nominative<br>    Gender—masculine<br>    Person—1st person<br>    Number—singular<br>    Stem or root—from δουλεύω<br>Concordance References:<br>⇒ Strong's #1398 *douleuō* +3588 *ho* + 2962 *kurios*<br>⇒ NIV #1526 *douleuō* [served] + 3836 *ho* [the] + 3261 *kurios* [Lord]<br>⇒ NASB #1398 *douleuō* +3588 *ho* +2962 *kurios*<br><br>**Acts 20:19**<br>**Serving the Lord** with all humility of mind, and with many tears, and temptations, which befell me by the lying in wait of the Jews: [KJV]<br>**serving the Lord** with all humility and with tears and with trials which came upon me through the plots of the Jews; [NASB]<br>I **served the Lord** with great humility and with tears, although I was severely tested by the plots of the Jews. [NIV]<br>**Serving the Lord** with all humility, with many tears and trials which happened to me by the plotting of the Jews; [NKJV]<br>I have **done the Lord's work** humbly—yes, and with tears. I have endured the trials that came to me from the plots of the Jews. [NLT]<br>δουλεύων τῷ Κυρίῳ μετὰ πάσης ταπεινοφροσύνης καὶ δακρύων καὶ πολλῶν πειρασμῶν τῶν συμβάντων μοι ἐν ταῖς ἐπιβουλαῖς τῶν Ἰουδαίων· [GNS]<br>δουλεύων τῷ κυρίῳ μετὰ πάσης ταπεινοφροσύνης καὶ δακρύων καὶ πειρασμῶν τῶν συμβάντων μοι ἐν ταῖς ἐπιβουλαῖς τῶν Ἰουδαίων, [GNT] | To have served the Lord; to have done the Lord's work; to have served as a slave.<br><br>**Practical Application**<br>The phrase "done the Lord's work" (*douleuōn tō kuriō*) is taken from the word bond-slave (*doulos*). Paul constantly called himself the slave of Jesus Christ (see POSB note—Romans 1:1 for discussion). |
| **#1154**<br>**Doomed To Destruction**<br><br>Perdition–KJV<br>Destruction–NASB<br>**Doomed to destruction–NIV**<br>Perdition–NKJV<br>Destruction–NLT<br><br>**POSB REFERENCE**<br>(2 Thes.2:3; see v.4 for commentary)<br>Note 1, point 2c | ἀπωλείας = *apōleias*<br>Pronunciation: [ap-o'-li-ahs]<br>Parsing (part of speech): noun<br>    Case—genitive<br>    Gender—feminine<br>    Number—singular<br>    Stem or root—from ἀπώλεια, ας<br>Concordance References:<br>⇒ Strong's #684 *apōleia*<br>⇒ NIV #724 *apōleia*<br>⇒ NASB #684 *apōleia*<br><br>**2 Thes. 2:3**<br>Let no man deceive you by any means: for that day shall not come, except there come a falling away first, and that man of sin be revealed, the son of **perdition**; [KJV]<br>Let no one in any way deceive you, for it will not come unless the apostasy comes first, and the man of lawlessness is revealed, the son of **destruction**, [NASB]<br>Don't let anyone deceive you in any way, for that day will not come until the rebellion occurs and the man of lawlessness is revealed, the man **doomed to destruction**. [NIV]<br>Let no one deceive you by any means; for *that Day will not* come unless the falling away comes first, and the man of sin is revealed, the son of **perdition**, [NKJV]<br>Don't be fooled by what they say. For that day will not | Doomed to destruction, perdition, complete and utter ruin, doom and destruction.<br><br>**Practical Application**<br>The antichrist is the "man doomed to destruction." Judas is said to be the man of destruction. But the meaning here is that the antichrist is the very embodiment of destruction...<br>• he is the son of the most violent doom and destruction; the son of the most violent evil imaginable.<br>• the son who is more deserving of doom and destruction than anyone else who has ever lived.<br>• the man doomed to destruction, of the devil himself, the father of doom and destruction. |

# PRACTICAL WORD STUDIES
## in the NEW TESTAMENT

| ENGLISH WORD | GREEK WORD AND VERSE | THE WORD MEANS... |
|---|---|---|
| | come until there is a great rebellion against God and the man of lawlessness is revealed—the one who brings **destruction**. [NLT]<br>ἥ τις ὑμᾶς ἐξαπατήσῃ κατὰ μηδένα τρόπον· ὅτι ἐὰν μὴ ἔλθῃ ἡ ἀποστασία πρῶτον, καὶ ἀποκαλυφθῇ ὁ ἄνθρωπος τῆς ἁμαρτίας, ὁ υἱὸς τῆς **ἀπωλείας**, [GNS]<br>μὴ τις ὑμᾶς ἐξαπατήσῃ κατὰ μηδένα τρόπον καὶ ἀποκαλυφθῇ ὁ ἄνθρωπος τῆς ἀνομίας, ὁ υἱὸς τῆς **ἀπωλείας**, [GNT] | |
| **#1155**<br>**Doubt**<br><br>Doubt–KJV<br>Perplexity–NASB<br>Perplexed–NIV<br>Perplexed–NKJV<br>Perplexed–NLT<br><br>**POSB REFERENCE**<br>(Acts 2:12-13; esp. v.12)<br>Note 6, point 1 | διηπόρουν = diëporoun<br>Pronunciation: [dee-ayp-or-oon]<br>Parsing (part of speech): verb<br>   Mood—indicative<br>   Tense—imperfect<br>   Voice—active<br>   Person—3rd person<br>   Number—plural<br>   Stem or root—from διαπορέω<br>Concordance References:<br>  ⇒ Strong's #1280 diaporeö<br>  ⇒ NIV #1389 diaporeö<br>  ⇒ NASB #1280 diaporeö<br><br>**Acts 2:12**<br>And they were all amazed, and were in **doubt**, saying one to another, What meaneth this? [KJV]<br>And they all continued in amazement and great **perplexity**, saying to one another, "What does this mean?" [NASB]<br>Amazed and **perplexed**, they asked one another, "What does this mean?" [NIV]<br>So they were all amazed and **perplexed**, saying to one another, "Whatever could this mean?" [NKJV]<br>They stood there amazed and **perplexed**. "What can this mean?" they asked each other. [NLT]<br>ἐξίσταντο δὲ πάντες καὶ **διηπόρουν**, ἄλλος πρὸς ἄλλον λέγοντες, Τί ἂν θέλει τοῦτο εἶναι; [GNS]<br>ἐξίσταντο δὲ πάντες καὶ **διηπόρουν**, ἄλλος πρὸς ἄλλον λέγοντες, Τί θέλει τοῦτο εἶναι; [GNT] | To be perplexed; to doubt; to be extremely confused; to wonder about; to be puzzled.<br><br>**Practical Application**<br>Some were attracted, perplexed and wondering, at a loss as to what was happening. But they were attracted to seek meaning in it all. |
| **#1156**<br>**Doubted**<br><br>Doubted–KJV<br>Perplexed–NASB<br>Puzzled–NIV<br>Wondered–NKJV<br>Perplexed–NLT<br><br>**POSB REFERENCE**<br>(Acts 5:21-25; esp. v.24)<br>Note 4, point 3 | διηπόρουν = diëporoun<br>Pronunciation: [dee-ap-or-oon]<br>Parsing (part of speech): verb<br>   Mood—indicative<br>   Tense—imperfect<br>   Voice—active<br>   Person—3rd person<br>   Number—plural<br>   Stem or root—from διαπορέω<br>Concordance References:<br>  ⇒ Strong's #1280 diaporeö<br>  ⇒ NIV #1389 diaporeö<br>  ⇒ NASB #1280 diaporeö<br><br>**Acts 5:24**<br>Now when the high priest and the captain of the temple and the chief priests heard these things, they **doubted** of them whereunto this would grow. [KJV]<br>Now when the captain of the temple guard and the chief priests heard these words, they were greatly **perplexed** about them as to what would come of this. [NASB]<br>On hearing this report, the captain of the temple guard and the chief priests were **puzzled**, wondering what would come of this. [NIV]<br>Now when the high priest, the captain of the temple, and the chief priests heard these things, they **wondered** what the outcome would be. [NKJV]<br>When the captain of the Temple guard and the leading priests heard this, they were **perplexed**, wondering where it would all end. [NLT]<br>ὡς δὲ ἤκουσαν τοὺς λόγους τούτους ὅ τε ἱερεὺς καὶ | To be puzzled; to be perplexed; to be completely baffled; to be at a loss; to wonder about.<br><br>**Practical Application**<br>They could not understand how the disciples could be delivered "out of their hand." They were apprehensive about the growth of the *new movement*.<br>In the present situation, the authorities probably thought some of the guards had either willfully released the prisoners or else been careless while on duty. |

## PRACTICAL WORD STUDIES
### in the NEW TESTAMENT

| ENGLISH WORD | GREEK WORD AND VERSE | THE WORD MEANS... |
|---|---|---|
| | ὁ στρατηγὸς τοῦ ἱεροῦ καὶ οἱ ἀρχιερεῖς, **διηπόρουν** περὶ αὐτῶν, τί ἂν γένοιτο τοῦτο. [GNS]<br>ὡς δὲ ἤκουσαν τοὺς λόγους τούτους ὅ τε στρατηγὸς τοῦ ἱεροῦ καὶ οἱ ἀρχιερεῖς, **διηπόρουν** περὶ αὐτῶν τί ἂν γένοιτο τοῦτο. [GNT] | |
| **#1157**<br>**Doubting Nothing**<br><br>Nothing doubting–KJV<br>Without misgivings–NASB<br>No hesitation–NIV<br>**Doubting nothing–NKJV**<br>Not to worry about–NLT<br><br>**POSB REFERENCE**<br>(Acts 11:4-15; esp. v.12)<br>Note 2, point 3 | μηδὲν διακρίναντα = mēden diakrinanta<br>Pronunciation: [may-dehn' dee-ak-ree'-nahn-tah]<br>Parsing *diakrinanta* (part of speech): verb<br>    Mood—participle<br>    Tense—aorist<br>    Voice—active<br>    Case—accusative<br>    Gender—masculine<br>    Person—1st person<br>    Number—singular<br>    Stem or root—from διακρίνω<br>Concordance References:<br>  ⇒ Strong's #3367 mēdeis + 1252 diakrinō<br>  ⇒ NIV #3594 mēdeis [no] + 1359 diakrinō [hesitation]<br>  ⇒ NASB #3367 mēdeis + 1252 diakrinō<br><br>**Acts 11:12**<br>And the spirit bade me go with them, **nothing doubting**. Moreover these six brethren accompanied me, and we entered into the man's house: [KJV]<br>"And the Spirit told me to go with them **without misgivings**. And these six brethren also went with me, and we entered the man's house. [NASB]<br>The Spirit told me to have **no hesitation** about going with them. These six brothers also went with me, and we entered the man's house. [NIV]<br>Then the Spirit told me to go with them, **doubting nothing**. Moreover these six brethren accompanied me, and we entered the man's house. [NKJV]<br>The Holy Spirit told me to go with them and **not to worry about** their being Gentiles. These six brothers here accompanied me, and we soon arrived at the home of the man who had sent for us. [NLT]<br>εἶπε δέ μοι τὸ Πνεῦμά συνελθεῖν αὐτοῖς, **μηδὲν διακρινόμενον**. ἦλθον δὲ σὺν ἐμοὶ καὶ οἱ ἓξ ἀδελφοὶ οὗτοι, καὶ εἰσήλθομεν εἰς τὸν οἶκον τοῦ ἀνδρός· [GNS]<br>εἶπεν δὲ τὸ πνεῦμά μοι συνελθεῖν αὐτοῖς **μηδὲν διακρίναντα**. ἦλθον δὲ σὺν ἐμοὶ καὶ οἱ ἓξ ἀδελφοὶ οὗτοι καὶ εἰσήλθομεν εἰς τὸν οἶκον τοῦ ἀνδρός. [GNT] | Not to hesitate; not to have misgivings; not to worry about; not to doubt.<br><br>**Practical Application**<br>It means that they were to make no distinction. God tells Peter in no uncertain terms, "Go with them [the Gentiles] making no distinctions."<br>The same command is given to all believers of all generations. Believers are not to make distinctions, not to discriminate in proclaiming the gospel. What an indictment against so many! How many *withdraw* from the poor? How many do not reach out to people of other races and social classes? |
| **#1158**<br>**Doubting, Stop**<br><br>Be not faithless–KJV<br>Be not unbelieving–NASB<br>**Stop doubting–NIV**<br>Do not be unbelieving–NKJV<br>Don't be faithless any longer–NLT<br><br>**POSB REFERENCE**<br>(Jn.20:26-28; esp. v.27)<br>Note 3, point 1b | μὴ γίνου ἄπιστος = mē ginou apistos<br>Pronunciation: [may ghen-oo ha-pis-tos]<br>Parsing *ginou* (part of speech): verb<br>    Mood—imperative<br>    Tense—present<br>    Voice—middle or passive deponent<br>    Person—2nd person<br>    Number—singular<br>    Stem or root—from γίνομαι<br>Parsing *apistos* (part of speech): adjective<br>    Case—nominative<br>    Gender—masculine<br>    Number—singular<br>    Stem or root—from ἄπιστος, ον<br>Concordance References:<br>  ⇒ Strong's #3361 me + 571+1096 apistos ginomai<br>  ⇒ NIV #3590 mē [Stop] + 603+1181 apistos ginomai [doubting]<br>  ⇒ NASB #3361 me + 571+1096 apistos ginomai<br><br>**John 20:27**<br>Then saith he to Thomas, reach hither thy finger, and behold my hands; and reach hither thy hand, and thrust it into my side: and **be not faithless**, but believing. [KJV]<br>Then He said to Thomas, "Reach here your finger, and see My hands; and reach your hand, and put it into | To stop doubting; to stop being faithless; to stop becoming an unbeliever.<br><br>**Practical Application**<br>In this Scripture, Jesus warned and called for belief. Thomas had been walking down a dangerous road. The disciples had witnessed to him time and again, but he had refused time and again to accept their testimony. Note the Lord's strong charge:<br>⇒ "Stop doubting" (*mē ginou apistos*): stop becoming an unbeliever. You are running the risk of *becoming faithless* and unbelieving, beyond the point of believing. You have carried your unbelief too far. It is now time to stop the foolishness. The others have been witnessing and witnessing the truth to you. Stop the stiff-necked, obstinate unbelief. You are in danger. |

## PRACTICAL WORD STUDIES
### in the NEW TESTAMENT

| ENGLISH WORD | GREEK WORD AND VERSE | THE WORD MEANS... |
|---|---|---|
| | My side; and **be not unbelieving**, but believing." [NASB]<br><br>Then he said to Thomas, "Put your finger here; see my hands. Reach out your hand and put it into my side. **Stop doubting** and believe." [NIV]<br><br>Then He said to Thomas, "Reach your finger here, and look at My hands; and reach your hand *here*, and put *it* into My side. **Do not be unbelieving**, but believing." [NKJV]<br><br>Then he said to Thomas, "Put your finger here and see my hands. Put your hand into the wound in my side. **Don't be faithless any longer**. Believe!" [NLT]<br><br>εἶτα λέγει τῷ Θωμᾷ, Φέρε τὸν δάκτυλόν σου ὧδε, καὶ ἴδε τὰς χεῖράς μου. καὶ φέρε τὴν χεῖρά σου καὶ βάλε εἰς τὴν πλευράν μου· καὶ **μὴ γίνου ἄπιστος** ἀλλὰ πιστός. [GNS]<br><br>εἶτα λέγει τῷ Θωμᾷ, Φέρε τὸν δάκτυλόν σου ὧδε καὶ ἴδε τὰς χεῖράς μου, καὶ φέρε τὴν χεῖρά σου καὶ βάλε εἰς τὴν πλευράν μου, καὶ **μὴ γίνου ἄπιστος** ἀλλὰ πιστός. [GNT] | |
| **#1159**<br>**Downcast**<br><br>Scattered abroad–KJV<br>**Downcast–NASB**<br>Helpless–NIV<br>Scattered–NKJV<br>Didn't know where to go for help–NLT<br><br>**POSB REFERENCE**<br>(Mt.9:36)<br>*Deeper Study #4* | ἐρριμμένοι = *errimmenoi*<br>Pronunciation: [rim-me'-noi]<br>Parsing (part of speech): verb<br>    Mood—participle<br>    Tense—perfect<br>    Voice—passive<br>    Case—nominative<br>    Gender—masculine<br>    Number—plural<br>    Stem or root—from ῥίπτω and ῥιπτέω<br>Concordance References:<br>⇒ Strong's #4496 hriptö<br>⇒ NIV #4849 hriptö<br>⇒ NASB #4496 hriptö<br><br>**Matthew 9:36**<br>But when he saw the multitudes, he was moved with compassion on them, because they fainted, and were **scattered abroad**, as sheep having no shepherd. [KJV]<br><br>And seeing the multitudes, He felt compassion for them, because they were distressed and **downcast** like sheep without a shepherd. [NASB]<br><br>When he saw the crowds, he had compassion on them, because they were harassed and **helpless**, like sheep without a shepherd. [NIV]<br><br>But when He saw the multitudes, He was moved with compassion for them, because they were weary and **scattered**, like sheep having no shepherd. [NKJV]<br><br>He felt great pity for the crowds that came, because their problems were so great and they **didn't know where to go for help**. They were like sheep without a shepherd. [NLT]<br><br>Ἰδὼν δὲ τοὺς ὄχλους, ἐσπλαγχνίσθη περὶ αὐτῶν, ὅτι ἦσαν ἐκλελυμένοι καὶ **ἐρριμμένοι** ὡσεὶ πρόβατα μὴ ἔχοντα ποιμένα. [GNS]<br><br>Ἰδὼν δὲ τοὺς ὄχλους ἐσπλαγχνίσθη περὶ αὐτῶν, ὅτι ἦσαν ἐσκυλμένοι καὶ **ἐρριμμένοι** ὡσεὶ πρόβατα μὴ ἔχοντα ποιμένα. [GNT] | To be helpless, hopeless, scattered, downcast; to be cast out, laid low, thrown down, prostrated, dejected and hopeless.<br><br>**Practical Application**<br>Being helpless may come from experiences such as drunkenness, or struggling and fighting within and without, or being so weary that a person is just cast down. It is being prostrated by forces within oneself or laid low by forces outside of oneself. |
| **#1160**<br>**Downcast**<br><br>Sad–KJV<br>Sad–NASB<br>**Downcast–NIV**<br>Sad–NKJV<br>Sadness–NLT | σκυθρωποί = *skuthröpoi*<br>Pronunciation: [skoo-thro-po-ee']<br>Parsing (part of speech): adjective<br>    Case—nominative<br>    Gender—masculine<br>    Number—plural<br>    Stem or root—from σκυθρωπός, ή, όν<br>Concordance References:<br>⇒ Strong's #4659 skuthröpos<br>⇒ NIV #5034 skuthröpos<br>⇒ NASB #4659 skuthröpos | Sad, downcast, gloomy, dejected, despondent, sullen, overcast, grim, helpless.<br><br>**Practical Application**<br>Jesus could see sadness and despair written all over their faces. Why were these two so downcast? Cleopas was surprised that the stranger did not know. "How could anyone be in Jerusalem and not know why we are sad and despairing?" he asked. Terrible things had happened. These two were seeking to understand the death and empty tomb of Christ. Christ was the |

# PRACTICAL WORD STUDIES
## in the NEW TESTAMENT

| ENGLISH WORD | GREEK WORD AND VERSE | THE WORD MEANS... |
|---|---|---|
| **POSB REFERENCE** (Lk.24:15-27; esp. v.17) Note 2, point 1 | **Luke 24:17**<br>And he said unto them, What manner of communications are these that ye have one to another, as ye walk, and are **sad**? [KJV]<br>And He said to them, "What are these words that you are exchanging with one another as you are walking?" And they stood still, looking **sad**. [NASB]<br>He asked them, "What are you discussing together as you walk along?"They stood still, their faces **downcast**. [NIV]<br>And He said to them, "What kind of conversation *is* this that you have with one another as you walk and are **sad**?" [NKJV]<br>"You seem to be in a deep discussion about something," he said. "What are you so concerned about?"They stopped short, **sadness** written across their faces. [NLT]<br>εἶπε δὲ πρὸς αὐτούς, Τίνες οἱ λόγοι οὗτοι οὓς ἀντιβάλλετε πρὸς ἀλλήλους περιπατοῦντες, καὶ ἐστὲ **σκυθρωποί**; [GNS]<br>εἶπεν δὲ πρὸς αὐτούς, Τίνες οἱ λόγοι οὗτοι οὓς ἀντιβάλλετε πρὸς ἀλλήλους περιπατοῦντες; καὶ ἐστάθησαν **σκυθρωποί**. [GNT] | subject of their conversation. They were seeking the truth; therefore, Christ drew near them. |
| **#1161 Dragged**<br><br>Drew–KJV<br>**Dragged–NASB**<br>**Dragged–NIV**<br>**Dragged–NKJV**<br>**Dragged–NLT**<br><br>**POSB REFERENCE** (Acts 16:19-24; esp. v.19) Note 3, point 1 | εἵλκυσαν = *heilkusan*<br>Pronunciation: [eel-koo'-sahn]<br>Parsing (part of speech): verb<br>    Mood—indicative<br>    Tense—aorist<br>    Voice—active<br>    Person—3rd person<br>    Number—plural<br>    Stem or root—from ἕλκω<br>Concordance References:<br>⇒ Strong's #1670 helkuō<br>⇒ NIV #1816 helkuō<br>⇒ NASB #1670 helkuō<br><br>**Acts 16:19**<br>And when her masters saw that the hope of their gains was gone, they caught Paul and Silas, and **drew** them into the marketplace unto the rulers, [KJV]<br>But when her masters saw that their hope of profit was gone, they seized Paul and Silas and **dragged** them into the market place before the authorities, [NASB]<br>When the owners of the slave girl realized that their hope of making money was gone, they seized Paul and Silas and **dragged** them into the marketplace to face the authorities. [NIV]<br>But when her masters saw that their hope of profit was gone, they seized Paul and Silas and **dragged** *them* into the marketplace to the authorities. [NKJV]<br>Her masters' hopes of wealth were now shattered, so they grabbed Paul and Silas and **dragged** them before the authorities at the marketplace. [NLT]<br>ἰδόντες δὲ οἱ κύριοι αὐτῆς ὅτι ἐξῆλθεν ἡ ἐλπὶς τῆς ἐργασίας αὐτῶν, ἐπιλαβόμενοι τὸν Παῦλον καὶ τὸν Σιλᾶν, **εἵλκυσαν** εἰς τὴν ἀγορὰν ἐπὶ τοὺς ἄρχοντας, [GNS]<br>ἰδόντες δὲ οἱ κύριοι αὐτῆς ὅτι ἐξῆλθεν ἡ ἐλπὶς τῆς ἐργασίας αὐτῶν, ἐπιλαβόμενοι τὸν Παῦλον καὶ τὸν Σιλᾶν **εἵλκυσαν** εἰς τὴν ἀγορὰν ἐπὶ τοὺς ἄρχοντας [GNT] | To drag; to haul in; to draw.<br><br>**Practical Application**<br>The idea is to use physical force violently. The great tragedy of so many in the world is that they put selfishness, greed, and money before people. It is because of selfishness that so many influential people attack genuine believers. But Christ changes lives. He changes...<br>• the immoral to the moral<br>• the unjust to the just<br>• the dishonest to the honest<br>• the prideful to the humble<br>• the powerful to the servant<br>• the wealthy to the benevolent<br>• the authoritarian to the helpful<br>So many of the influential, wealthy, and powerful are unwilling to become servants of mankind—servants who sacrifice all they are and have for the needy. They are unwilling to truly sacrifice themselves and their money to help the desperate of the world. Therefore, they oppose anything that requires them to *sacrifice* their selfishness. They will give and help enough to salve their consciences, but not sacrificially. |
| **#1162 Dragged**<br><br>Drew–KJV<br>Swept–NASB<br>Swept–NIV<br>Drew–NKJV<br>**Dragged–NLT** | σύρει = *surei*<br>Pronunciation: [soo'-reh-ee]<br>Parsing (part of speech): verb<br>    Mood—indicative<br>    Tense—present<br>    Voice—active<br>    Person—3rd person<br>    Number—singular<br>    Stem or root—from σύρω<br>Concordance References:<br>⇒ Strong's #4951 surō | Swept, drew, dragged; to sweep; to drag down.<br><br>**Practical Application**<br>There is the origin of the dragon or devil. This statement is telling where Satan came from. This is clearly seen in the Greek tense of the statement. His tail "drug" (*surei*, present tense) a third part of heaven. That is, Satan draws, pulls, and drags a third of the stars, that is, angels of heaven. |

# PRACTICAL WORD STUDIES
## in the NEW TESTAMENT

| ENGLISH WORD | GREEK WORD AND VERSE | THE WORD MEANS... |
|---|---|---|
| **POSB REFERENCE** (Rev.12:3-4; esp.v.4) Note 2, point 2 | ⇒ NIV #5359 surö<br>⇒ NASB #4951 surö<br><br>**Rev. 12:4**<br>And his tail **drew** the third part of the stars of heaven, and did cast them to the earth: and the dragon stood before the woman which was ready to be delivered, for to devour her child as soon as it was born. [KJV]<br>And his tail **swept** away a third of the stars of heaven, and threw them to the earth. And the dragon stood before the woman who was about to give birth, so that when she gave birth he might devour her child. [NASB]<br>His tail **swept** a third of the stars out of the sky and flung them to the earth. The dragon stood in front of the woman who was about to give birth, so that he might devour her child the moment it was born. [NIV]<br>His tail **drew** a third of the stars of heaven and threw them to the earth. And the dragon stood before the woman who was ready to give birth, to devour her Child as soon as it was born. [NKJV]<br>His tail **dragged** down one-third of the stars, which he threw to the earth. He stood before the woman as she was about to give birth to her child, ready to devour the baby as soon as it was born. [NLT]<br>καὶ ἡ οὐρὰ αὐτοῦ **σύρει** τὸ τρίτον τῶν ἀστέρων τοῦ οὐρανοῦ, καὶ ἔβαλεν αὐτοὺς εἰς τὴν γῆν· καὶ ὁ δράκων ἔστηκεν ἐνώπιον τῆς γυναικὸς τῆς μελλούσης τεκεῖν, ἵνα, ὅταν τέκῃ τὸ τέκνον αὐτῆς, καταφάγῃ. [GNS]<br>καὶ ἡ οὐρὰ αὐτοῦ **σύρει** τὸ τρίτον τῶν ἀστέρων τοῦ οὐρανοῦ καὶ ἔβαλεν αὐτοὺς εἰς τὴν γῆν. καὶ ὁ δράκων ἔστηκεν ἐνώπιον τῆς γυναικὸς τῆς μελλούσης τεκεῖν, ἵνα ὅταν τέκῃ τὸ τέκνον αὐτῆς καταφάγῃ. [GNT] | |
| **#1163 Dragged Away**<br><br>Caught–KJV<br>**Dragged...away–NASB**<br>Seized–NIV<br>Seized–NKJV<br>Brought–NLT<br><br>**POSB REFERENCE** (Acts 6:11-14; esp. v.12) Note 3, point 3 | συνήρπασαν = sunërpasan<br>Pronunciation: [soon-ayr-pa'-sahn]<br>Parsing (part of speech): verb<br>    Mood—indicative<br>    Tense—aorist<br>    Voice—active<br>    Person—3rd person<br>    Number—plural<br>    Stem or root—from συναρπάζω<br>Concordance References:<br>⇒ Strong's #4884 sunarpazo<br>⇒ NIV #5275 sunarpazö<br>⇒ NASB #4884 sunarpazo<br><br>**Acts 6:12**<br>And they stirred up the people, and the elders, and the scribes, and came upon him, and **caught** him, and brought him to the council, [KJV]<br>And they stirred up the people, the elders and the scribes, and they came upon him and **dragged** him **away**, and brought him before the Council. [NASB]<br>So they stirred up the people and the elders and the teachers of the law. They **seized** Stephen and brought him before the Sanhedrin. [NIV]<br>And they stirred up the people, the elders, and the scribes; and they came upon *him*, **seized** him, and brought *him* to the council. [NKJV]<br>Naturally, this roused the crowds, the elders, and the teachers of religious law. So they arrested Stephen and **brought** him before the high council. [NLT]<br>συνεκίνησάν τε τὸν λαὸν καὶ τοὺς πρεσβυτέρους καὶ τοὺς γραμματεῖς, καὶ ἐπιστάντες **συνήρπασαν** αὐτόν, καὶ ἤγαγον εἰς τὸ συνέδριον, [GNS]<br>συνεκίνησάν τε τὸν λαὸν καὶ τοὺς πρεσβυτέρους καὶ τοὺς γραμματεῖς, καὶ ἐπιστάντες **συνήρπασαν** αὐτὸν καὶ ἤγαγον εἰς τὸ συνέδριον, [GNT] | To seize; to catch; to drag away; to bring.<br><br>**Practical Application**<br>The word "dragged...away" (*sunërpasan*) means to seize with violence. The picture is that they seized and literally dragged him to court (cp. Luke 8:29; Acts 19:29; Acts 27:15). |

# PRACTICAL WORD STUDIES
## in the NEW TESTAMENT

| ENGLISH WORD | GREEK WORD AND VERSE | THE WORD MEANS... |
|---|---|---|
| **#1164**<br>**Dragged Off–**<br>**Dragging Off–**<br>**Dragging Out**<br><br>Haling–KJV<br>Dragging off–NASB<br>Dragged off–NIV<br>Dragging off–NKJV<br>Dragging out–NLT<br><br>**POSB**<br>**REFERENCE**<br>(Acts 8:3)<br>Note 3, point 2 | σύρων = surōn<br>Pronunciation: [soo'-rown]<br>Parsing (part of speech): verb<br>  Mood—participle<br>  Tense—present<br>  Voice—active<br>  Case—nominative<br>  Gender—masculine<br>  Number—singular<br>  Stem or root—from σύρω<br>Concordance References:<br>  ⇒ Strong's #4951 surō<br>  ⇒ NIV #5359 surō<br>  ⇒ NASB #4951 surō<br><br>**Acts 8:3**<br>As for Saul, he made havock of the church, entering into every house, and **haling** men and women committed them to prison. [KJV]<br>But Saul began ravaging the church, entering house after house; and **dragging off** men and women, he would put them in prison. [NASB]<br>But Saul began to destroy the church. Going from house to house, he **dragged off** men and women and put them in prison. [NIV]<br>As for Saul, he made havoc of the church, entering every house, and **dragging off** men and women, committing *them* to prison. [NKJV]<br>Saul was going everywhere to devastate the church. He went from house to house, **dragging out** both men and women to throw them into jail. [NLT]<br>Σαῦλος δὲ ἐλυμαίνετο τὴν ἐκκλησίαν, κατὰ τοὺς οἴκους εἰσπορευόμενος, **σύρων** τε ἄνδρας καὶ γυναῖκας παρεδίδου εἰς φυλακήν. [GNS]<br>Σαῦλος δὲ ἐλυμαίνετο τὴν ἐκκλησίαν κατὰ τοὺς οἴκους εἰσπορευόμενος, **σύρων** τε ἄνδρας καὶ γυναῖκας παρεδίδου εἰς φυλακήν. [GNT] | To drag off; to drag away using force; to be swept.<br><br>**Practical Application**<br>It means constraining and dragging them, using whatever force was necessary to arrest and subdue them. The picture is that of forcibly dragging them from their homes through the city streets. |
| **#1165**<br>**Draw–**<br>**Draw Away**<br><br>Draw away–KJV<br>Draw away–NASB<br>Draw away–NIV<br>Draw–NKJV<br>Draw–NLT<br><br>**POSB**<br>**REFERENCE**<br>(Acts 20:29-30; esp. v.30)<br>*Deeper Study* #2, point 4 | τοῦ ἀποσπᾶν = tou apospan<br>Pronunciation: [too ap-os-pahn']<br>Parsing *apospan* (part of speech): verb<br>  Mood—infinitive<br>  Tense—present<br>  Voice—active<br>  Case—genitive<br>  Stem or root—from ἀποσπάω<br>Concordance References:<br>  ⇒ Strong's #3588 ho + 645 apospaō<br>  ⇒ NIV #3836 ho + 685 apospaō<br>  ⇒ NASB #3588 ho + 645 apospaō<br><br>**Acts 20:30**<br>Also of your own selves shall men arise, speaking perverse things, to **draw away** disciples after them. [KJV]<br>And from among your own selves men will arise, speaking perverse things, to **draw away** the disciples after them. [NASB]<br>Even from your own number men will arise and distort the truth in order to **draw away** disciples after them. [NIV]<br>Also from among yourselves men will rise up, speaking perverse things, to **draw** away the disciples after themselves. [NKJV]<br>Even some of you will distort the truth in order to **draw** a following. [NLT]<br>καὶ ἐξ ὑμῶν αὐτῶν ἀναστήσονται ἄνδρες λαλοῦντες διεστραμμένα, **τοῦ ἀποσπᾶν** τοὺς μαθητὰς ὀπίσω αὐτῶν. [GNS]<br>καὶ ἐξ ὑμῶν αὐτῶν ἀναστήσονται ἄνδρες λαλοῦντες διεστραμμένα **τοῦ ἀποσπᾶν** τοὺς μαθητὰς ὀπίσω αὐτῶν. [GNT] | To draw away; to draw out. The phrase means to separate, to drag and tear away.<br><br>**Practical Application**<br>False teachers draw people away from the truth in three different ways.<br>1. They attack the believers themselves: sowing discord and mischief among them.<br>2. They teach error, perverting and distorting the truth, either taking away or adding to the Word of God.<br>3. They attack the genuine leaders: defaming their characters and ministries, and stirring up believers against them. |

# PRACTICAL WORD STUDIES
## in the NEW TESTAMENT

| ENGLISH WORD | GREEK WORD AND VERSE | THE WORD MEANS... |
|---|---|---|
| **#1166**<br>**Draw–Draws**<br><br>Draw–KJV<br>Draws–NASB<br>Draws–NIV<br>Draws–NKJV<br>Draws–NLT<br><br>**POSB REFERENCE**<br>(Jn.6:44-46; esp. v.44)<br>Note 2, point 1 | ἑλκύσῃ = *helkusë*<br>Pronunciation: [el-koo'-say]<br>Parsing (part of speech): verb<br>    Mood—subjunctive<br>    Tense—aorist<br>    Voice—active<br>    Person—3rd person<br>    Number—singular<br>    Stem or root—from ἕλκω<br>Concordance References:<br>⇒ Strong's #1670 *helkuō*<br>⇒ NIV #1816 *helkuō*<br>⇒ NASB #1670 *helkuō*<br><br>**John 6:44**<br>No man can come to me, except the Father which hath sent me **draw** him: and I will raise him up at the last day. [KJV]<br>"No one can come to Me, unless the Father who sent Me **draws** him; and I will raise him up on the last day. [NASB]<br>"No one can come to me unless the Father who sent me **draws** him, and I will raise him up at the last day. [NIV]<br>No one can come to Me unless the Father who sent Me **draws** him; and I will raise him up at the last day. [NKJV]<br>For people can't come to me unless the Father who sent me **draws** them to me, and at the last day I will raise them from the dead. [NLT]<br>οὐδεὶς δύναται ἐλθεῖν πρός με ἐὰν μὴ ὁ πατὴρ ὁ πέμψας με **ἑλκύσῃ** αὐτόν, κἀγὼ ἀναστήσω αὐτὸν τῇ ἐσχάτῃ ἡμέρᾳ. [GNS]<br>οὐδεὶς δύναται ἐλθεῖν πρός με ἐὰν μὴ ὁ πατὴρ ὁ πέμψας με **ἑλκύσῃ** αὐτόν, κἀγὼ ἀναστήσω αὐτὸν ἐν τῇ ἐσχάτῃ ἡμέρᾳ. [GNT] | To draw; to invite; to attract; to entice; to lure; to allure.<br><br>**Practical Application**<br>The word "draws" has the idea of both initiative and rebellion, of constraint and resistance. For example, the pulling in of a net loaded with fish involves both actions of pulling and resistance (cp. John 21:6); a person being dragged to court encounters both actions of pulling and resistance (Acts 16:19).<br>How God draws a person is clearly stated. He draws by teaching (John 6:45). The teaching may come from the voice of a preacher, the observation of nature, the reading of Scripture or from a myriad of other sources. But one thing is always common: the movement of God's Spirit upon the human heart, teaching the need for God and drawing the heart toward God for salvation. The Spirit of God teaches a person and moves upon the heart of a person. |
| **#1167**<br>**Dress**<br><br>Adorn–KJV<br>Adorn–NASB<br>Dress–NIV<br>Adorn–NKJV<br>Wear–NLT<br><br>**POSB REFERENCE**<br>(1 Tim.2:9-10; esp. v.9)<br>Note 1 | κοσμεῖν = *kosmein*<br>Pronunciation: [kos-meh'-in]<br>Parsing (part of speech): verb<br>    Mood—infinitive<br>    Tense—present<br>    Voice—active<br>    Stem or root—from κοσμέω<br>Concordance References:<br>⇒ Strong's #2885 *kosmeō*<br>⇒ NIV #3175 *kosmeō*<br>⇒ NASB #2885 *kosmeō*<br><br>**1 Tim. 2:9**<br>In like manner also, that women **adorn** themselves in modest apparel, with shamefacedness and sobriety; not with broided hair, or gold, or pearls, or costly array; [KJV]<br>Likewise, I want women to **adorn** themselves with proper clothing, modestly and discreetly, not with braided hair and gold or pearls or costly garments; [NASB]<br>I also want women to **dress** modestly, with decency and propriety, not with braided hair or gold or pearls or expensive clothes, [NIV]<br>In like manner also, that the women **adorn** themselves in modest apparel, with propriety and moderation, not with braided hair or gold or pearls or costly clothing, [NKJV]<br>And I want women to be modest in their appearance. They should **wear** decent and appropriate clothing and not draw attention to themselves by the way they fix their hair or by wearing gold or pearls or expensive clothes. [NLT]<br>ὡσαύτως καὶ τὰς γυναῖκας ἐν καταστολῇ κοσμίῳ, μετὰ αἰδοῦς καὶ σωφροσύνης, **κοσμεῖν** ἑαυτάς, μὴ ἐν πλέγμασιν, ἢ χρυσῷ, ἢ μαργαρίταις, ἢ ἱματισμῷ πολυτελεῖ, [GNS] | To dress; to adorn; to wear.<br><br>**Practical Application**<br>The word "dress" (*kosmein*) is really a better translation of what Scripture means. The word means the dress, ornaments, and arrangement of clothing upon the body. But the word *dress* also refers to behavior and demeanor, that is, the way a woman carries herself, walks, moves, and behaves in public. Remember: this passage is being written to genuine Christian women—women who truly believe in the Lord and wish to honor the Lord and to have a strong testimony for Him. The Christian woman wants to guard her clothing in order to dress modestly; she wants to watch the way she dresses, walks, moves, and behaves in public. She wants to bring honor to the Lord and to build a strong testimony—a testimony that she loves the Lord and has committed her life...<br>• to help people, not to seduce them.<br>• to serve people, not to destroy them.<br>• to point people to Jesus, not to attract them to herself.<br>• to teach people righteous behavior, not fleshly and worldly behavior. |

**PRACTICAL WORD STUDIES**
in the NEW TESTAMENT

| ENGLISH WORD | GREEK WORD AND VERSE | THE WORD MEANS... |
|---|---|---|
| | ὡσαύτως [καὶ] γυναῖκας ἐν καταστολῇ κοσμίῳ μετὰ αἰδοῦς καὶ σωφροσύνης **κοσμεῖν** ἑαυτάς, μὴ ἐν πλέγμασιν καὶ χρυσίῳ ἢ μαργαρίταις ἢ ἱματισμῷ πολυτελεῖ, [GNT] | |
| #1168<br>**Drew**<br><br>Drew–KJV<br>Dragged–NASB<br>Dragged–NIV<br>Dragged–NKJV<br>Dragged–NLT<br><br>**POSB<br>REFERENCE**<br>(Acts 16:19-24; esp. v.19)<br>Note 3, point 1 | εἵλκυσαν = *heilkusan*<br>Pronunciation: [eel-koo'-sahn]<br>Parsing (part of speech): verb<br>    Mood—indicative<br>    Tense—aorist<br>    Voice—active<br>    Person—3rd person<br>    Number—plural<br>    Stem or root—from ἕλκω<br>Concordance References:<br>⇒ Strong's #1670 helkuō<br>⇒ NIV #1816 helkuō<br>⇒ NASB #1670 helkuō<br><br>**Acts 16:19**<br>And when her masters saw that the hope of their gains was gone, they caught Paul and Silas, and **drew** them into the marketplace unto the rulers, [KJV]<br>But when her masters saw that their hope of profit was gone, they seized Paul and Silas and **dragged** them into the market place before the authorities, [NASB]<br>When the owners of the slave girl realized that their hope of making money was gone, they seized Paul and Silas and **dragged** them into the marketplace to face the authorities. [NIV]<br>But when her masters saw that their hope of profit was gone, they seized Paul and Silas and **dragged** *them* into the marketplace to the authorities. [NKJV]<br>Her masters' hopes of wealth were now shattered, so they grabbed Paul and Silas and **dragged** them before the authorities at the marketplace. [NLT]<br>ἰδόντες δὲ οἱ κύριοι αὐτῆς ὅτι ἐξῆλθεν ἡ ἐλπὶς τῆς ἐργασίας αὐτῶν, ἐπιλαβόμενοι τὸν Παῦλον καὶ τὸν Σιλᾶν, **εἵλκυσαν** εἰς τὴν ἀγορὰν ἐπὶ τοὺς ἄρχοντας, [GNS]<br>ἰδόντες δὲ οἱ κύριοι αὐτῆς ὅτι ἐξῆλθεν ἡ ἐλπὶς τῆς ἐργασίας αὐτῶν, ἐπιλαβόμενοι τὸν Παῦλον καὶ τὸν Σιλᾶν **εἵλκυσαν** εἰς τὴν ἀγορὰν ἐπὶ τοὺς ἄρχοντας [GNT] | To drag; to haul in; to draw.<br><br>**Practical Application**<br>The idea is to use physical force violently. The great tragedy of so many in the world is that they put selfishness, greed, and money before people. It is because of selfishness that so many influential people attack genuine believers. But Christ changes lives. He changes...<br>• the immoral to the moral<br>• the unjust to the just<br>• the dishonest to the honest<br>• the prideful to the humble<br>• the powerful to the servant<br>• the wealthy to the benevolent<br>• the authoritarian to the helpful<br>So many of the influential, wealthy, and powerful are unwilling to become servants of mankind—servants who sacrifice all they are and have for the needy. They are unwilling to truly sacrifice themselves and their money to help the desperate of the world. Therefore, they oppose anything that requires them to *sacrifice* their selfishness. They will give and help enough to salve their consciences, but not sacrificially. |
| #1169<br>**Drew**<br><br>Drew–KJV<br>Swept–NASB<br>Swept–NIV<br>Drew–NKJV<br>Dragged–NLT<br><br>**POSB<br>REFERENCE**<br>(Rev.12:3-4; esp.v.4)<br>Note 2, point 2 | σύρει = *surei*<br>Pronunciation: [soo'-reh-ee]<br>Parsing (part of speech): verb<br>    Mood—indicative<br>    Tense—present<br>    Voice—active<br>    Person—3rd person<br>    Number—singular<br>    Stem or root—from σύρω<br>Concordance References:<br>⇒ Strong's #4951 surō<br>⇒ NIV #5359 surō<br>⇒ NASB #4951 surō<br><br>**Rev. 12:4**<br>And his tail **drew** the third part of the stars of heaven, and did cast them to the earth: and the dragon stood before the woman which was ready to be delivered, for to devour her child as soon as it was born. [KJV]<br>And his tail **swept** away a third of the stars of heaven, and threw them to the earth. And the dragon stood before the woman who was about to give birth, so that when she gave birth he might devour her child. [NASB]<br>His tail **swept** a third of the stars out of the sky and flung them to the earth. The dragon stood in front of the woman who was about to give birth, so that he might devour her child the moment it was born. [NIV]<br>His tail **drew** a third of the stars of heaven and threw them to the earth. And the dragon stood before the woman | Swept, drew, dragged; to sweep; to drag down.<br><br>**Practical Application**<br>There is the origin of the dragon or devil. This statement is telling where Satan came from. This is clearly seen in the Greek tense of the statement. His tail "draws" (*surei*, present tense) a third part of heaven. That is, Satan draws, pulls, and drags a third of the stars, that is, angels of heaven. |

# PRACTICAL WORD STUDIES
## in the NEW TESTAMENT

| ENGLISH WORD | GREEK WORD AND VERSE | THE WORD MEANS... |
|---|---|---|
| | who was ready to give birth, to devour her Child as soon as it was born. [NKJV]<br>His tail **dragged** down one-third of the stars, which he threw to the earth. He stood before the woman as she was about to give birth to her child, ready to devour the baby as soon as it was born. [NLT]<br>καὶ ἡ οὐρὰ αὐτοῦ **σύρει** τὸ τρίτον τῶν ἀστέρων τοῦ οὐρανοῦ, καὶ ἔβαλεν αὐτοὺς εἰς τὴν γῆν· καὶ ὁ δράκων ἔστηκεν ἐνώπιον τῆς γυναικὸς τῆς μελλούσης τεκεῖν, ἵνα, ὅταν τέκῃ τὸ τέκνον αὐτῆς, καταφάγῃ. [GNS]<br>καὶ ἡ οὐρὰ αὐτοῦ **σύρει** τὸ τρίτον τῶν ἀστέρων τοῦ οὐρανοῦ καὶ ἔβαλεν αὐτοὺς εἰς τὴν γῆν. καὶ ὁ δράκων ἔστηκεν ἐνώπιον τῆς γυναικὸς τῆς μελλούσης τεκεῖν, ἵνα ὅταν τέκῃ τὸ τέκνον αὐτῆς καταφάγῃ. [GNT] | |
| **#1170**<br>**Dries Up**<br><br>Withered–KJV<br>**Dries up–NASB**<br>Withers–NIV<br>Withered–NKJV<br>Withers–NLT<br><br>**POSB REFERENCE**<br>(Jn.15:4-6; esp. v.6)<br>Note 4, point 4b | ἐξηράνθη = exëranthë<br>Pronunciation: [ex-ay-rah'n-thay]<br>Parsing (part of speech): verb<br>    Mood—indicative<br>    Tense—aorist<br>    Voice—passive<br>    Person—3rd person<br>    Number—singular<br>    Stem or root—from ξηραίνω<br>Concordance References:<br>⇒ Strong's #3583 xërainö<br>⇒ NIV #3830 xërainö<br>⇒ NASB #3583 xërainö<br><br>**John 15:6**<br>If a man abide not in me, he is cast forth as a branch, and is **withered**; and men gather them, and cast them into the fire, and they are burned. [KJV]<br>"If anyone does not abide in Me, he is thrown away as a branch, and **dries up**; and they gather them, and cast them into the fire, and they are burned. [NASB]<br>If anyone does not remain in me, he is like a branch that is thrown away and **withers**; such branches are picked up, thrown into the fire and burned. [NIV]<br>If anyone does not abide in Me, he is cast out as a branch and is **withered**; and they gather them and throw *them* into the fire, and they are burned. [NKJV]<br>Anyone who parts from me is thrown away like a useless branch and **withers**. Such branches are gathered into a pile to be burned. [NLT]<br>ἐὰν μή τις μείνῃ ἐν ἐμοί, ἐβλήθη ἔξω ὡς τὸ κλῆμα, καὶ **ἐξηράνθη**, καὶ συνάγουσιν αὐτὰ, καὶ εἰς πῦρ βάλλουσι, καὶ καίεται. [GNS]<br>ἐὰν μή τις μένῃ ἐν ἐμοί, ἐβλήθη ἔξω ὡς τὸ κλῆμα καὶ **ἐξηράνθη** καὶ συνάγουσιν αὐτὰ καὶ εἰς τὸ πῦρ βάλλουσιν καὶ καίεται. [GNT] | To be dried up, wrinkled, withered, peeled; to become sapless and bare; to lose energy and strength.<br><br>**Practical Application**<br>The unattached branch experiences everything withering away—its...<br>• gifts and abilities<br>• life and body<br>• family and friends<br>• fate and destiny<br>• hopes and dreams<br>• confidence and assurance<br>• purpose and meaning |
| **#1171**<br>**Drift Away**<br><br>Slip–KJV<br>**Drift away–NASB**<br>**Drift away–NIV**<br>**Drift away–NKJV**<br>**Drift away–NLT**<br><br>**POSB REFERENCE**<br>(Heb.2:1)<br>Note 1 | παραρυῶμεν = pararuömen<br>Pronunciation: [par-ar-oo-o'-mehn]<br>Parsing (part of speech): verb<br>    Mood—subjunctive<br>    Tense—aorist<br>    Voice—passive<br>    Person—1st person<br>    Number—plural<br>    Stem or root—from παραρρέω<br>Concordance References:<br>⇒ Strong's #3901 pararreö<br>⇒ NIV #4184 pararreö<br>⇒ NASB #3901 pararreö<br><br>**Hebrews 2:1**<br>Therefore we ought to give the more earnest heed to the things which we have heard, lest at any time we should let them **slip**. [KJV]<br>For this reason we must pay much closer attention to what we have heard, lest we **drift away** from it. [NASB]<br>We must pay more careful attention, therefore, to what | To drift away; to slip; to flow past; to glide by; to slip past.<br><br>**Practical Application**<br>What does it mean to slip or drift away from the gospel of salvation? It is the picture...<br>• of a ring slipping off the finger.<br>• of some truth slipping out of the mind and being forgotten. The person is unable to remember it.<br>• of some liquid in a container—water, gas, fluid—that has leaked out and gone away.<br><br>William Barclay says, "It is regularly used of something which has carelessly or thoughtlessly been allowed to slip away and become lost" (*The Letter to the Hebrews*. "The Daily Study Bible." Philadelphia, PA: The Westminster Press, 1955, p.13). But there is another meaning to the word |

# PRACTICAL WORD STUDIES
## in the NEW TESTAMENT

| ENGLISH WORD | GREEK WORD AND VERSE | THE WORD MEANS... |
|---|---|---|
|  | we have heard, so that we do not **drift away**. [NIV]<br>Therefore we must give the more earnest heed to the things we have heard, lest we **drift away**. [NKJV]<br>So we must listen very carefully to the truth we have heard, or we may **drift away** from it. [NLT]<br>Διὰ τοῦτο δεῖ περισσοτέρως ἡμᾶς προσέχειν τοῖς ἀκουσθεῖσι, μή ποτε **παραρρυῶμεν**. [GNS]<br>Διὰ τοῦτο δεῖ περισσοτέρως προσέχειν ἡμᾶς τοῖς ἀκουσθεῖσιν, μήποτε **παραρυῶμεν**. [GNT] | *slip* that is even more descriptive. *Slip* can mean to drift by or to drift past. It is the picture of a ship that drifts past the harbor. It drifts by the harbor because of the captain's...<br>• miscalculations<br>• lethargy and complacency<br>• sleepiness<br>• carelessness<br>• inattentiveness<br>• drunkenness<br>An innumerable list of things could be given as to why the captain would drift away from the safety of the harbor. But the point is well made: we must all anchor our lives to the truths of salvation. We must earnestly heed them. We must heed them lest the ship of our lives drift away from the safety of salvation. |
| **#1172**<br>**Drinking**<br><br>Drinking–KJV<br>Drinking–NASB<br>Drinking–NIV<br>Drinking–NKJV<br>Parties–NLT<br><br>**POSB REFERENCE**<br>(Mt.24:38)<br>*Deeper Study* #4 | πίνοντες = *pinontes*<br>Pronunciation: [pee'-non-tes]<br>Parsing (part of speech): verb<br>   Mood—participle<br>   Tense—present<br>   Voice—active<br>   Case—nominative<br>   Gender—masculine<br>   Number—plural<br>   Stem or root— from πίνω<br>Concordance References:<br>⇒ Strong's #4095 pinō<br>⇒ NIV #4403 pinō<br>⇒ NASB #4095 pinō<br><br>**Matthew 24:38**<br>For as in the days that were before the flood they were eating and **drinking**, marrying and giving in marriage, until the day that Noe entered into the ark, [KJV]<br>"For as in those days which were before the flood they were eating and **drinking**, they were marrying and giving in marriage, until the day that Noah entered the ark, [NASB]<br>For in the days before the flood, people were eating and **drinking**, marrying and giving in marriage, up to the day Noah entered the ark; [NIV]<br>For as in the days before the flood, they were eating and **drinking**, marrying and giving in marriage, until the day that Noah entered the ark, [NKJV]<br>In those days before the Flood, the people were enjoying banquets and **parties** and weddings right up to the time Noah entered his boat. [NLT]<br>ὥσπερ γὰρ ἦσαν ἐν ταῖς ἡμέραις ταῖς πρὸ τοῦ κατακλυσμοῦ τρώγοντες καὶ **πίνοντες**, γαμοῦντες καὶ ἐκγαμίζοντες, ἄχρι ἧς ἡμέρας εἰσῆλθε Νῶε εἰς τὴν κιβωτόν, [GNS]<br>ὡς γὰρ ἦσαν ἐν ταῖς ἡμέραις [ἐκείναις] ταῖς πρὸ τοῦ κατακλυσμοῦ τρώγοντες καὶ **πίνοντες**, γαμοῦντες καὶ γαμίζοντες, ἄχρι ἧς ἡμέρας εἰσῆλθεν Νῶε εἰς τὴν κιβωτόν, [GNT] | To drink; to participate in the partying spirit of drink; to participate in the abomination of drinking.<br><br>**Practical Application**<br>The idea is a habitual practice, drinking to excess (cp. Galatians 5:21; cp. Ephes. 5:18). The teaching from Scripture is clear:<br>Drunkards "will not inherit the kingdom of God." (cp. 1 Cor.6:10). "Drunkards" (*methusoi*) are people who take drink and drugs to affect their senses for lust and pleasure; who seek to be tipsy or intoxicated; who seek to loosen their moral restraints for the sake of bodily pleasure. |
| **#1173**<br>**Drinking Parties**<br><br>Banquetings–KJV<br>**Drinking parties– NASB**<br>Carousing–NIV<br>**Drinking parties– NKJV**<br>Wild parties–NLT | πότοις = *potois*<br>Pronunciation: [pot'-oys]<br>Parsing (part of speech): noun<br>   Case—dative<br>   Gender—masculine<br>   Number—plural<br>   Stem or root—from πότος, ου<br>Concordance References:<br>⇒ Strong's #4224 potos<br>⇒ NIV #4542 potos<br>⇒ NASB #4224 potos | Carousing, banquetings, drunkenness; drinking parties; wild parties; partying and getting drunk; a drunken orgy.<br><br>**Practical Application**<br>The believer's life is divided into two parts: *his old life and his new life*. Note the force of this verse: in his *old life*, he sinned enough. He has already followed the desires and lusts of the ungodly (Gentiles) enough. He has already worked the will of the ungodly. He has walked after them, walked just as they walk, and enough |

# PRACTICAL WORD STUDIES
## in the NEW TESTAMENT

| ENGLISH WORD | GREEK WORD AND VERSE | THE WORD MEANS... |
|---|---|---|
| **POSB REFERENCE** (1 Pt.4:3) Note 3, point 5 | **1 Peter 4:3**<br>For the time past of *our* life may suffice us to have wrought the will of the Gentiles, when we walked in lasciviousness, lusts, excess of wine, revellings, **banquetings**, and abominable idolatries. [KJV]<br>For the time already past is sufficient *for you* to have carried out the desire of the Gentiles, having pursued a course of sensuality, lusts, drunkenness, carousals, **drinking parties** and abominable idolatries. [NASB]<br>For you have spent enough time in the past doing what pagans choose to do—living in debauchery, lust, drunkenness, orgies, **carousing** and detestable idolatry. [NIV]<br>For we *have spent* enough of our past lifetime in doing the will of the Gentiles—when we walked in lewdness, lusts, drunkenness, revelries, **drinking parties**, and abominable idolatries. [NKJV]<br>You have had enough in the past of the evil things that godless people enjoy—their immorality and lust, their feasting and drunkenness and **wild parties**, and their terrible worship of idols. [NLT]<br>ἀρκετὸς γὰρ ἡμῖν ὁ παρεληλυθὼς χρόνος τὸ βίου τὸ θέλημα τῶν ἐθνῶν κατεργάσασθαι, πεπορευμένους ἐν ἀσελγείαις, ἐπιθυμίαις, οἰνοφλυγίαις, κώμοις, **πότοις**, καὶ ἀθεμίτοις εἰδωλολατρείαις· [GNS]<br>ἀρκετὸς γὰρ ὁ παρεληλυθὼς χρόνος τὸ βούλημα τῶν ἐθνῶν κατειργάσθαι πεπορευμένους ἐν ἀσελγείαις, ἐπιθυμίαις, οἰνοφλυγίαις, κώμοις, **πότοις** καὶ ἀθεμίτοις εἰδωλολατρίαις. [GNT] | is enough. The believer is no longer to fulfill the desires of the flesh. |
| **#1174**<br>**Driven Out**<br><br>Cast out–KJV<br>Cast out–NASB<br>**Driven out–NIV**<br>Cast out–NKJV<br>Cast out–NLT<br><br>**POSB REFERENCE** (Jn.12:31) *Deeper Study #3*, point 3 | ἐκβληθήσεται ἔξω = ekblēthēsetai exō<br>Pronunciation: [ek-blay-thay-seh-tah-ee ex-o]<br>Parsing *ekblēthēsetai* (part of speech): verb<br>    Mood—indicative<br>    Tense—future<br>    Voice—passive<br>    Person—3rd person<br>    Number—singular<br>    Stem or root—from ἐκβάλλω<br>Parsing *exō* (part of speech): adjective adverb<br>    Stem or root— from ἔξω<br>Concordance References:<br>    ⇒ Strong's #1544 ekballo + 1854 exō<br>    ⇒ NIV #1675 ekballo [driven] + 2032 exō [out]<br>    ⇒ NASB #1544 ekballo + 1854 exō<br><br>**John 12:31**<br>Now is the judgment of this world: now shall the prince of this world be **cast out**. [KJV]<br>"Now judgment is upon this world; now the ruler of this world shall be **cast out**. [NASB]<br>Now is the time for judgment on this world; now the prince of this world will be **driven out**. [NIV]<br>Now is the judgment of this world; now the ruler of this world will be **cast out**. [NKJV]<br>The time of judgment for the world has come, when the prince of this world will be **cast out**. [NLT]<br>νῦν κρίσις ἐστὶ τοῦ κόσμου τούτου· νῦν ὁ ἄρχων τοῦ κόσμου τούτου **ἐκβληθήσεται ἔξω**. [GNS]<br>νῦν κρίσις ἐστὶν τοῦ κόσμου τούτου, νῦν ὁ ἄρχων τοῦ κόσμου τούτου **ἐκβληθήσεται ἔξω**· [GNT] | To drive out; to cast out; to cast from or forth; to reject; to expel; to exclude; to cast clean out (*exō*) of a place; to throw out; to pluck out; to put outside.<br><br>**Practical Application**<br>Note the words "driven out" (*ekblēthēsetai exō*, future passive of ekballo which means a sure fact lying in the future). The words mean Satan in all his power, rule, and reign is driven out by the death of Christ. His power, rule, and reign over lives is now broken. |
| **#1175**<br>**Driveth**<br><br>**Driveth–KJV**<br>Impelled...to go out–NASB<br>Sent...out–NIV<br>Drove–NKJV<br>Compelled...to go–NLT | ἐκβάλλει = ekballei<br>Pronunciation: [ek-bal'-leh-ee]<br>Parsing (part of speech): verb<br>    Mood—indicative<br>    Tense—present<br>    Voice—active<br>    Person—3rd person<br>    Number—singular<br>    Stem or root—from ἐκβάλλω<br>Concordance References:<br>    ⇒ Strong's #1544 ekballō<br>    ⇒ NIV #1675 ekballō<br>    ⇒ NASB #1544 ekballō | Sent out, compelled to go; impelled to go out; to drive out; to thrust; to cast forth; to drive forth; to force.<br><br>**Practical Application**<br>Jesus was driven out with great force to go into the wilderness. He was driven by the Spirit to be tried. He was to be tried and tested not to make Him fall, but to make Him stronger and better prepared to do great things for God (see POSB note, pt.3—Matthew 4:1). |

## PRACTICAL WORD STUDIES
## in the NEW TESTAMENT

| ENGLISH WORD | GREEK WORD AND VERSE | THE WORD MEANS... |
|---|---|---|
| POSB REFERENCE (Mk.1:12) Note 2 | **Mark 1:12**<br>And immediately the Spirit **driveth** him into the wilderness. [KJV]<br>And immediately the Spirit **impelled** Him *to go* out into the wilderness. [NASB]<br>At once the Spirit **sent** him **out** into the desert, [NIV]<br>Immediately the Spirit **drove** Him into the wilderness. [NKJV]<br>Immediately the Holy Spirit **compelled** Jesus *to go* into the wilderness. [NLT]<br>Καὶ εὐθὺς τὸ Πνεῦμα αὐτὸν **ἐκβάλλει** εἰς τὴν ἔρημον. [GNS]<br>Καὶ εὐθὺς τὸ πνεῦμα αὐτὸν **ἐκβάλλει** εἰς τὴν ἔρημον. [GNT] | |
| #1176<br>**Drops**<br><br>Great drops–KJV<br>**Drops–NASB**<br>**Drops–NIV**<br>**Drops–NKJV**<br>Great drops–NLT<br><br>**POSB REFERENCE** (Lk.22:43-44; esp. v.44) Note 4, point 3 | θρόμβοι = thromboi<br>Pronunciation: [throm'-bo-ee]<br>Parsing (part of speech): noun<br>    Case—nominative<br>    Gender—masculine<br>    Number—plural<br>    Stem or root—from θρόμβος, ου<br>Concordance References:<br>  ⇒ Strong's #2361 thrombos<br>  ⇒ NIV #2584 thrombos<br>  ⇒ NASB #2361 thrombos<br><br>**Luke 22:44**<br>And being in an agony he prayed more earnestly: and his sweat was as it were **great drops** of blood falling down to the ground. [KJV]<br>And being in agony He was praying very fervently; and His sweat became like **drops** of blood, falling down upon the ground. [NASB]<br>And being in anguish, he prayed more earnestly, and his sweat was like **drops** of blood falling to the ground. [NIV]<br>And being in agony, He prayed more earnestly. Then His sweat became like great **drops** of blood falling down to the ground. [NKJV]<br>He prayed more fervently, and he was in such agony of spirit that his sweat fell to the ground like **great drops** of blood. [NLT]<br>καὶ γενόμενος ἐν ἀγωνίᾳ, ἐκτενέστερον προσηύχετο. ἐγένετο δὲ ὁ ἱδρὼς αὐτοῦ ὡσεὶ **θρόμβοι** αἵματος καταβαίνοντος ἐπὶ τὴν γῆν. [GNS]<br>καὶ γενόμενος ἐν ἀγωνίᾳ ἐκτενέστερον προσηύχετο· καὶ ἐγένετο ὁ ἱδρὼς αὐτοῦ ὡσεὶ **θρόμβοι** αἵματος καταβαίνοντος ἐπὶ τὴν γῆν. [GNT] | Drops, great drops, thick clots of blood.<br><br>**Practical Application**<br>Apparently, Jesus was under so much pressure the capillary veins right under the skin burst and the blood, mingling with sweat, poured through the enlarged pores. What Jesus was experiencing can never be known (see POSB *Deeper Study* #2, Jesus Christ, Suffering—Luke 22:43-44). |
| #1177<br>**Drove**<br><br>Driveth–KJV<br>Impelled to go out–NASB<br>Sent out–NIV<br>**Drove–NKJV**<br>Compelled to go–NLT<br><br>**POSB REFERENCE** (Mk.1:12) Note 2 | ἐκβάλλει = ekballei<br>Pronunciation: [ek-bal'-leh-ee]<br>Parsing (part of speech): verb<br>    Mood—indicative<br>    Tense—present<br>    Voice—active<br>    Person—3rd person<br>    Number—singular<br>    Stem or root—from ἐκβάλλω<br>Concordance References:<br>  ⇒ Strong's #1544 ekballō<br>  ⇒ NIV #1675 ekballō<br>  ⇒ NASB #1544 ekballō<br><br>**Mark 1:12**<br>And immediately the Spirit **driveth** him into the wilderness. [KJV]<br>And immediately the Spirit **impelled** Him *to go* out into the wilderness. [NASB]<br>At once the Spirit **sent** him **out** into the desert, [NIV]<br>Immediately the Spirit **drove** Him into the wilderness. [NKJV]<br>Immediately the Holy Spirit **compelled** Jesus *to go* | Sent out, compelled to go; impelled to go out, to drive out; to thrust; to cast forth; to drive forth; to force.<br><br>**Practical Application**<br>Jesus was driven out with great force to go into the wilderness. He was driven by the Spirit to be tried. He was to be tried and tested not to make Him fall, but to make Him stronger and better prepared to do great things for God (see POSB note, pt.3—Matthew 4:1). |

# PRACTICAL WORD STUDIES
## in the NEW TESTAMENT

| ENGLISH WORD | GREEK WORD AND VERSE | THE WORD MEANS... |
|---|---|---|
| | into the wilderness. [NLT]<br>Καὶ εὐθὺς τὸ Πνεῦμα αὐτὸν **ἐκβάλλει** εἰς τὴν ἔρημον. [GNS]<br>Καὶ εὐθὺς τὸ πνεῦμα αὐτὸν **ἐκβάλλει** εἰς τὴν ἔρημον. [GNT] | |
| **#1178**<br>**Drowsy**<br><br>Slumbered–KJV<br>**Drowsy–NASB**<br>**Drowsy–NIV**<br>Slumbered–NKJV<br>Lay down–NLT<br><br>**POSB REFERENCE**<br>(Mt.25:5)<br>*Deeper Study #3* | ἐνύσταξαν = enustaxan<br>Pronunciation: [eh-noos-tadz'-an]<br>Parsing (part of speech): verb<br>    Mood—indicative<br>    Tense—aorist<br>    Voice—active<br>    Person—3rd person<br>    Number—plural<br>    Stem or root—from νυστάζω<br>Concordance References:<br>⇒ Strong's #3573 nustazō<br>⇒ NIV #3818 nustazō<br>⇒ NASB #3573 nustazō<br><br>**Matthew 25:5**<br>While the bridegroom tarried, they all **slumbered** and slept. [KJV]<br>"Now while the bridegroom was delaying, they all got **drowsy** and began to sleep. [NASB]<br>The bridegroom was a long time in coming, and they all became **drowsy** and fell asleep. [NIV]<br>But while the bridegroom was delayed, they all **slumbered** and slept. [NKJV]<br>When the bridegroom was delayed, they all **lay down** and slept. [NLT]<br>χρονίζοντος δὲ τοῦ νυμφίου **ἐνύσταξαν** πᾶσαι καὶ ἐκάθευδον. [GNS]<br>χρονίζοντος δὲ τοῦ νυμφίου **ἐνύσταξαν** πᾶσαι καὶ ἐκάθευδον. [GNT] | To grow drowsy; to slumber; to lay down to sleep; to nod; to nap; to drift off to sleep.<br><br>**Practical Application**<br>Note that the virgins allowed themselves to become drowsy, then the drowsiness led to sleep. We must guard against becoming drowsy, against cooling off. A little drowsiness will lead to a cooling of fervor. A little loss of fervor may not seem too serious; but the first step, as small as it may seem, leads to heavy eyelids. |
| **#1179**<br>**Drunkards**<br><br>Drunkards–KJV<br>Drunkards–NASB<br>Drunkards–NIV<br>Drunkards–NKJV<br>Drunkards–NLT<br><br>**POSB REFERENCE**<br>(1 Cor.6:10)<br>Note 3, point 3 | μέθυσοι = methusoi<br>Pronunciation: [meth'-oo-soy-ee]<br>Parsing (part of speech): noun<br>    Case—nominative<br>    Gender—masculine<br>    Number—plural<br>    Stem or root—from μέθυσος, ου<br>Concordance References:<br>⇒ Strong's #3183 methusos<br>⇒ NIV #3500 methusos<br>⇒ NASB #3183 methusos<br><br>**1 Cor. 6:10**<br>Nor thieves, nor covetous, nor **drunkards**, nor revilers, nor extortioners, shall inherit the kingdom of God. [KJV]<br>Nor thieves, nor the covetous, nor **drunkards**, nor revilers, nor swindlers, shall inherit the kingdom of God. [NASB]<br>Nor thieves nor the greedy nor **drunkards** nor slanderers nor swindlers will inherit the kingdom of God. [NIV]<br>Nor thieves, nor covetous, nor **drunkards**, nor revilers, nor extortioners will inherit the kingdom of God. [NKJV]<br>Thieves, greedy people, **drunkards**, abusers, and swindlers—none of these will have a share in the Kingdom of God. [NLT]<br>οὔτε κλέπται, οὔτε πλεονέκται, οὐ **μέθυσοι**, οὐ λοίδοροι, οὐχ ἅρπαγες, βασιλείαν Θεοῦ οὐ κληρονομήσουσι. [GNS]<br>οὔτε κλέπται οὔτε πλεονέκται, οὐ **μέθυσοι**, οὐ λοίδοροι, οὐχ ἅρπαγες βασιλείαν θεοῦ κληρονομήσουσιν. [GNT] | Drunkards, alcoholics, boozers, heavy drinkers. It describes the person who is intoxicated, stoned, inebriated.<br><br>**Practical Application**<br>Drunkards (*methusoi*) are people who take drink and drugs to affect their senses for lust and pleasure; who seek to be tipsy or intoxicated; who seek to loosen their moral restraints for the sake of bodily pleasure. |
| **#1180**<br>**Drunkenness** | μέθη = methē<br>Pronunciation: [meth'-ay]<br>Parsing (part of speech): noun<br>    Case—dative | Drunkenness, excess, overindulgence, insobriety, debauchery, intemperance; to be drunk with wine (or any other strong drink or drug); to be intoxicated. The word comes from the word |

# PRACTICAL WORD STUDIES
## in the NEW TESTAMENT

| ENGLISH WORD | GREEK WORD AND VERSE | THE WORD MEANS... |
|---|---|---|
| Drunkenness–KJV<br>Drunkenness–NASB<br>Drunkenness–NIV<br>Drunkenness–NKJV<br>Drunkenness–NLT<br><br>**POSB REFERENCE**<br>(Lk.21:34-35; esp. v.34)<br>Note 1, point 2<br><br>See also POSB REF:<br>(Rom.13:13)<br>Note 4, point 2<br>(Gal.5:19-21; esp. v.21)<br>Note 2 | Gender—feminine<br>Number—singular<br>Stem or root—from μέθη, ης<br>Concordance References:<br>⇒ Strong's #3178 methē<br>⇒ NIV #3494 methē<br>⇒ NASB #3178 methē<br><br>**Luke 21:34**<br>And take heed to yourselves, lest at any time your hearts be overcharged with surfeiting, and **drunkenness**, and cares of this life, and so that day come upon you unawares. [KJV]<br>"Be on guard, that your hearts may not be weighted down with dissipation and **drunkenness** and the worries of life, and that day come on you suddenly like a trap; [NASB]<br>"Be careful, or your hearts will be weighed down with dissipation, **drunkenness** and the anxieties of life, and that day will close on you unexpectedly like a trap. [NIV]<br>"But take heed to yourselves, lest your hearts be weighed down with carousing, **drunkenness**, and cares of this life, and that Day come on you unexpectedly. [NKJV]<br>"Watch out! Don't let me find you living in careless ease and **drunkenness**, and filled with the worries of this life. Don't let that day catch you unaware, [NLT]<br>Προσέχετε δὲ ἑαυτοῖς, μήποτε βαρυνθῶσιν ὑμῶν αἱ καρδίαι ἐν κραιπάλῃ καὶ **μέθῃ** καὶ μερίμναις βιωτικαῖς, καὶ αἰφνίδιος ἐφ' ὑμᾶς ἐπιστῇ ἡ ἡμέρα ἐκείνη· [GNS]<br>Προσέχετε δὲ ἑαυτοῖς μήποτε βαρηθῶσιν ὑμῶν αἱ καρδίαι ἐν κραιπάλῃ καὶ **μέθῃ** καὶ μερίμναις βιωτικαῖς καὶ ἐπιστῇ ἐφ' ὑμᾶς αἰφνίδιος ἡ ἡμέρα ἐκείνη [GNT] | meaning wine (*methu*).<br><br>**Practical Application**<br>Becoming drunk with wine (or any other strong drink or drug) has several bad effects:<br>⇒ It indulges the lust, the appetite of the flesh.<br>⇒ It loosens up a person's moral restraints and allows the indulging of sexual and immoral cravings.<br>⇒ It dulls the mind to responsibility.<br>⇒ It burdens the heart and conscience and causes guilt, at least until a person becomes hardened in his sin.<br>⇒ It deadens feelings for spouses and loved ones, causing distance and withdrawal (such is seldom, if ever, regained).<br>⇒ It harms the body. |
| #1181<br>**Drunkenness**<br><br>Excess of wine–KJV<br>Drunkenness–NASB<br>Drunkenness–NIV<br>Drunkenness–NKJV<br>Drunkenness–NLT<br><br>**POSB REFERENCE**<br>(1 Pt.4:3)<br>Note 3, point 3 | οἰνοφλυγίαις = oinophlugiais<br>Pronunciation: [oy-nof-loog-ee'-ah-ees]<br>Parsing (part of speech): noun<br>  Case—dative<br>  Gender—feminine<br>  Number—plural<br>Stem or root—from οἰνοφλυγία, ας<br>Concordance References:<br>⇒ Strong's #3632 oinophlugia<br>⇒ NIV #3886 oinophlugia<br>⇒ NASB #3632 oinophlugia<br><br>**1 Peter 4:3**<br>For the time past of our life may suffice us to have wrought the will of the Gentiles, when we walked in lasciviousness, lusts, **excess of wine**, revellings, banquetings, and abominable idolatries: [KJV]<br>For the time already past is sufficient for you to have carried out the desire of the Gentiles, having pursued a course of sensuality, lusts, **drunkenness**, carousals, drinking parties and abominable idolatries. [NASB]<br>For you have spent enough time in the past doing what pagans choose to do—living in debauchery, lust, **drunkenness**, orgies, carousing and detestable idolatry. [NIV]<br>For we *have spent* enough of our past lifetime in doing the will of the Gentiles—when we walked in lewdness, lusts, **drunkenness**, revelries, drinking parties, and abominable idolatries. [NKJV]<br>You have had enough in the past of the evil things that godless people enjoy—their immorality and lust, their feasting and **drunkenness** and wild parties, and their terrible worship of idols. [NLT]<br>ἀρκετὸς γὰρ ἡμῖν ὁ παρεληλυθὼς χρόνος τὸ βίου τὸ θέλημα τῶν ἐθνῶν κατεργάσασθαι, πεπορευμένους ἐν ἀσελγείαις, ἐπιθυμίαις, **οἰνοφλυγίαις**, κώμοις, πότοις, | Drunkenness, excess, overindulgence, insobriety, debauchery, intemperance; excess of wine, winebibbing.<br><br>**Practical Application**<br>It would include taking drink or drugs to affect one's senses for lust or pleasure; becoming tipsy or intoxicated; partaking of drugs; seeking to loosen moral restraint for bodily pleasure. |

# PRACTICAL WORD STUDIES
## in the NEW TESTAMENT

| ENGLISH WORD | GREEK WORD AND VERSE | THE WORD MEANS... |
|---|---|---|
| | καὶ ἀθεμίτοις εἰδωλολατρείαις· [GNS]<br>ἀρκετὸς γὰρ ὁ παρεληλυθὼς χρόνος τὸ βούλημα τῶν ἐθνῶν κατειργάσθαι πεπορευμένους ἐν ἀσελγείαις, ἐπιθυμίαις, **οἰνοφλυγίαις**, κώμοις, πότοις καὶ ἀθεμίτοις εἰδωλολατρίαις. [GNT] | |
| **#1182**<br>**Due**<br><br>Due–KJV<br>His duty–NASB<br>His marital duty–NIV<br>Due–NKJV<br>Sexual intimacy–NLT<br><br>**POSB REFERENCE**<br>(1 Cor.7:3)<br>Note 3 | τὴν ὀφειλὴν = tēn opheilēn<br>Pronunciation: [tayn of-i'-layn]<br>Parsing *opheilēn* (part of speech): noun<br>    Case—accusative<br>    Gender—feminine<br>    Number—singular<br>    Stem or root—from ὀφειλή, ῆς<br>Concordance References:<br>⇒ Strong's #3588 ho + 3784 opheilo<br>⇒ NIV #3836 ho [his] + 4051 opheilē [marital duty]<br>⇒ NASB #3588 ho + 3782 opheilē<br><br>**1 Cor. 7:3**<br>Let the husband render unto the wife **due** benevolence: and likewise also the wife unto the husband. [KJV]<br>Let the husband fulfill **his duty** to his wife, and likewise also the wife to her husband. [NASB]<br>The husband should fulfill **his marital duty** to his wife, and likewise the wife to her husband. [NIV]<br>Let the husband render to his wife the affection **due** her, and likewise also the wife to her husband. [NKJV]<br>The husband should not deprive his wife of **sexual intimacy**, which is her right as a married woman, nor should the wife deprive her husband. [NLT]<br>τῇ γυναικὶ ὁ ἀνὴρ **τὴν ὀφειλομένην** εὔνοιαν ἀποδιδότω· ὁμοίως δὲ καὶ ἡ γυνὴ τῷ ἀνδρί. [GNS]<br>τῇ γυναικὶ ὁ ἀνὴρ **τὴν ὀφειλὴν** ἀποδιδότω, ὁμοίως δὲ καὶ ἡ γυνὴ τῷ ἀνδρί. [GNT] | Marital duty; the debt; to owe; to render what is due.<br><br>**Practical Application**<br>The husband and wife owe some things to the other.<br>⇒ Both have rights; each can expect to receive some things from the other.<br>⇒ Both have the responsibility to pay to the other exactly what is due. |
| **#1183**<br>**Due Time**<br><br>Due time–KJV<br>Right time–NASB<br>Right time–NIV<br>Due time–NKJV<br>Right time–NLB<br><br>**POSB REFERENCE**<br>(Romans (5:6-7; esp. v.6)<br>Note 1, point 3 | κατὰ καιρὸν = kata kairon<br>Pronunciation: [ah-tah kahee-ron']<br>Parsing *kairon* (part of speech): noun<br>    Case—accusative<br>    Gender—masculine<br>    Number—singular<br>    Stem or root—from καιρός, οῦ<br>Concordance References:<br>⇒ Strong's #2596 kata + 2540 kairos<br>⇒ NIV #2848 kata [at] + 2789 kairos [right time]<br>⇒ NASB #2596 kata + 2540 kairos<br><br>**Romans 5:6**<br>For when we were yet without strength, in **due time** Christ died for the ungodly. [KJV]<br>For while we were still helpless, at the **right time** Christ died for the ungodly. [NASB]<br>You see, at just the **right time**, when we were still powerless, Christ died for the ungodly. [NIV]<br>For when we were still without strength, in **due time** Christ died for the ungodly. [NKJV]<br>When we were utterly helpless, Christ came at just the **right time** and died for us sinners. [NLT]<br>ἔτι γὰρ Χριστὸς ὄντων ἡμῶν ἀσθενῶν, ἔτι **κατὰ καιρὸν** ὑπὲρ ἀσεβῶν ἀπέθανε. [GNS]<br>ἔτι γὰρ Χριστὸς ὄντων ἡμῶν ἀσθενῶν ἔτι **κατὰ καιρὸν** ὑπὲρ ἀσεβῶν ἀπέθανεν. [GNT] | Appointed or proper time, season, age opportunity; the last times<br><br>**Practical Application**<br>It was in "due time" (*kata kairon*) that Christ died for us. It was in God's appointed time: His destined time, appropriate time. Men had to be prepared for Christ before God could send Him into the world. Men had to learn that they were without strength and ungodly, that they needed a Savior. (This was the purpose of the Old Testament and the law, to show men that they were sinful. See POSB outline—Romans 4:14-15 and POSB note—Romans 4:14-15.) |
| **#1184**<br>**Dull**<br><br>Dull–KJV<br>Dull–NASB<br>Slow–NIV<br>Dull–NKJV<br>Hard–NLT | νωθροί = nōthroi<br>Pronunciation: [no-throy']<br>Parsing (part of speech): adjective<br>    Case—nominative<br>    Gender—masculine<br>    Number—plural<br>    Stem or root—from νωθρός, ά, όν<br>Concordance References:<br>Strong's #3576 nōthros<br>NIV #3821 nōthros | Slow, dull, hard of hearing. It means sluggish, slow, lazy, lethargic, forgetful.<br><br>**Practical Application**<br>A person becomes immature because of dull hearing. The writer to the Hebrews had much that he wanted to teach, especially about the Lord Jesus Christ and His Priestly ministry, but he was unable. Why? Because the Christian |

# Practical Word Studies
## in the New Testament

| ENGLISH WORD | GREEK WORD AND VERSE | THE WORD MEANS... |
|---|---|---|
| **POSB REFERENCE** (Heb.5:11) Note 1 | NASB #3576 nōthros<br><br>**Hebrews 5:11**<br>Of whom we have many things to say, and hard to be uttered, seeing ye are **dull** of hearing. [KJV]<br>Concerning him we have much to say, and it is hard to explain, since you have become **dull** of hearing. [NASB]<br>We have much to say about this, but it is hard to explain because you are **slow** to learn. [NIV]<br>Of whom we have much to say, and hard to explain, since you have become **dull** of hearing. [NKJV]<br>There is so much more we would like to say about this. But you don't seem to listen, so it's **hard** to make you understand. [NLT]<br>Περὶ οὗ πολὺς ἡμῖν ὁ λόγος καὶ δυσερμήνευτος λέγειν, ἐπεὶ **νωθροὶ** γεγόνατε ταῖς ἀκοαῖς. [GNS]<br>Περὶ οὗ πολὺς ἡμῖν ὁ λόγος καὶ δυσερμήνευτος λέγειν, ἐπεὶ **νωθροὶ** γεγόνατε ταῖς ἀκοαῖς. [GNT] | faith—the Word of God and the Bible—is difficult to understand. No person can grasp the Word of God and its truths by simply reading it. A person must study, meditate, and practice the Word of God in order to understand it.<br>   The Hebrew believers had become mentally lazy and sluggish and spiritually complacent and slothful. Even though they were sitting and listening to the preachers and teachers and reading the Scriptures, they were not listening or paying attention. Their minds, wandering about, were unwilling to exert the energy to concentrate and study.<br>   Note: some of the Hebrew believers were already dull of hearing. Some had already become immature; they had already fallen and were no longer growing spiritually. |
| **#1185**<br>**Dwell**<br><br>Dwell–KJV<br>Dwell–NASB<br>Dwell–NIV<br>Dwell–NKJV<br>More and more at home–NLT<br><br>**POSB REFERENCE** (Eph.3:17) Note 3<br><br>See also POSB REF: (Col.1:19) Note 5 | κατοικῆσαι = katoikēsai<br>Pronunciation: [kat-oy-kay'-sah-ee]<br>Parsing (part of speech): verb<br>  Mood—infinitive<br>  Tense—aorist<br>  Voice—active<br>  Stem or root—from κατοικέω<br>Concordance References:<br>  ⇒ Strong's #2730 katoikeō<br>  ⇒ NIV #2997 katoikeō<br>  ⇒ NASB #2730 katoikeō<br><br>**Ephes. 3:17**<br>That Christ may **dwell** in your hearts by faith; that ye, being rooted and grounded in love, [KJV]<br>So that Christ may **dwell** in your hearts through faith; and that you, being rooted and grounded in love, [NASB]<br>So that Christ may **dwell** in your hearts through faith. And I pray that you, being rooted and established in love, [NIV]<br>That Christ may **dwell** in your hearts through faith; that you, being rooted and grounded in love, [NKJV]<br>And I pray that Christ will be **more and more at home** in your hearts as you trust in him. May your roots go down deep into the soil of God's marvelous love. [NLT]<br>**κατοικῆσαι** τὸν Χριστὸν διὰ τῆς πίστεως ἐν ταῖς καρδίαις ὑμῶν· ἐν ἀγάπῃ ἐρριζωμένοι καὶ τεθεμελιωμένοι [GNS]<br>**κατοικῆσαι** τὸν Χριστὸν διὰ τῆς πίστεως ἐν ταῖς καρδίαις ὑμῶν, ἐν ἀγάπῃ ἐρριζωμένοι καὶ τεθεμελιωμένοι, [GNT] | To dwell; to live in; to inhabit; to be more and more at home. It means a permanent not a temporary dwelling. It means to take up permanent residence; to live in a home; to enter, settle down, and be at home.<br><br>**Practical Application**<br>   When a person believes in Jesus Christ for the first time, Christ enters his life. Therefore, the believer is not praying for Christ to enter the hearts and lives of believers; Christ is already in their hearts and lives. What then does this request mean? Just what the verse says:<br>⇒ that Christ would be at home and live in a permanent sense within the believer.<br>⇒ that the believer would be aware and conscious of Christ within his heart—always aware and conscious that Christ has taken up residence within him.<br>⇒ that the believer would let Christ control and guide his life—permanently and constantly—because Christ is at home in his heart.<br>   It is the presence of Christ within that motivates the believer to follow Christ. The more the believer is aware and conscious of Christ within him, the more he will *walk and live* in Christ. |
| **#1186**<br>**Dwell–<br>Dwelleth<br>Dwells**<br><br>Dwelleth–KJV<br>Dwell–NASB<br>Lives–NIV<br>Dwells–NKJV<br>Lives–NLT<br><br>**POSB REFERENCE** (Col.2:9-10; esp. v.9) Note 2, point 1 | κατοικεῖ = katoikei<br>Pronunciation: [kat-oy-keh'-ee]<br>Parsing (part of speech): verb<br>  Mood—indicative<br>  Tense—present<br>  Voice—active<br>  Person—3rd person<br>  Number—singular<br>  Stem or root—from κατοικέω<br>Concordance References:<br>  ⇒ Strong's #2730 katoikeō<br>  ⇒ NIV #2997 katoikeō<br>  ⇒ NASB #2730 katoikeō<br><br>**Col. 2:9**<br>For in him **dwelleth** all the fulness of the Godhead bodily. [KJV]<br>For in Him all the fulness of Deity **dwells** in bodily form, [NASB]<br>For in Christ all the fulness of the Deity **lives** in bodily form, [NIV] | Lives, dwells; to live in; to inhabit; to stay. The word "dwells" (katoikei) means to be at home, to be permanently settled and present.<br><br>**Practical Application**<br>This tells us...<br>• that the fullness of God has always dwelt in Christ, even before He came to earth (John 1:1, 18; John 17:5, 24; Phil. 2:6).<br>• that the fullness of God dwelt in Christ when Christ was walking upon earth in a human body (John 1:14, 18; 1 John 1:1-3).<br>• that the fullness of God was not just a temporary gift to Christ.<br>What does all this mean to us in practical day to day living? It means two wonderful things.<br>   1. First, God is not far off in outer space someplace. God is not unconcerned with the world. God has not just created the world and |

# PRACTICAL WORD STUDIES
## in the NEW TESTAMENT

| ENGLISH WORD | GREEK WORD AND VERSE | THE WORD MEANS... |
|---|---|---|
| | For in Him **dwells** all the fullness of the Godhead bodily; [NKJV]<br>For in Christ the fullness of God **lives** in a human body, [NLT]<br>ὅτι ἐν αὐτῷ **κατοικεῖ** πᾶν τὸ πλήρωμα τῆς θεότητος σωματικῶς, [GNS]<br>ὅτι ἐν αὐτῷ **κατοικεῖ** πᾶν τὸ πλήρωμα τῆς θεότητος σωματικῶς, [GNT] | wound it up and left it on its own to fly throughout space with man making out the best he can. God is interested and concerned with the world—so much so that He has come to earth to show how vitally concerned He is.<br>2. God is love, not evil. Only a God of evil would leave man in the dark where he would have to grope and gasp and stumble about in order to find God. A God of love would reveal Himself and show man...<br>• the way to God.<br>• the truth of God, man, and his world.<br>• the life that man is to live (John 14:6). |
| **#1187**<br>**Dwell–**<br>**Dwell In**<br><br>Dwell–KJV<br>Dwell–NASB<br>Dwell in–NIV<br>Dwell in–NKJV<br>Live–NLT<br><br>**POSB**<br>**REFERENCE**<br>(Col.3:16)<br>Note 2, point 1 | ἐνοικείτω ἐν = enoikeitō en<br>Pronunciation: [en-oy-keh'-o en]<br>Parsing (part of speech): verb<br>  Mood—imperative<br>  Tense—present<br>  Voice—active<br>  Person—3rd person<br>  Number—singular<br>  Stem or root—from ἐνοικέω<br>Concordance References:<br>  ⇒ Strong's #1722+1774 en enoikeö<br>  ⇒ NIV #1877+1940 en enoikeö [dwell in]<br>  ⇒ NASB #1722+1774 en enoikeö<br><br>**Col. 3:16**<br>Let the word of Christ **dwell** in you richly in all wisdom; teaching and admonishing one another in psalms and hymns and spiritual songs, singing with grace in your hearts to the Lord. [KJV]<br>Let the word of Christ richly **dwell** within you, with all wisdom teaching and admonishing one another with psalms and hymns and spiritual songs, singing with thankfulness in your hearts to God. [NASB]<br>Let the word of Christ **dwell in** you richly as you teach and admonish one another with all wisdom, and as you sing psalms, hymns and spiritual songs with gratitude in your hearts to God. [NIV]<br>Let the word of Christ **dwell in** you richly in all wisdom, teaching and admonishing one another in psalms and hymns and spiritual songs, singing with grace in your hearts to the Lord. [NKJV]<br>Let the words of Christ, in all their richness, **live** in your hearts and make you wise. Use his words to teach and counsel each other. Sing psalms and hymns and spiritual songs to God with thankful hearts. [NLT]<br>ὁ λόγος τοῦ Χριστοῦ **ἐνοικείτω ἐν** ὑμῖν πλουσίως, ἐν πάσῃ σοφίᾳ· διδάσκοντες καὶ νουθετοῦντες ἑαυτοὺς ψαλμοῖς, καὶ ὕμνοις, καὶ ᾠδαῖς πνευματικαῖς, ἐν χάριτι ᾄδοντες ἐν τῇ καρδίᾳ ὑμῶν τῷ Κυρίῳ. [GNS]<br>ὁ λόγος τοῦ Χριστοῦ **ἐνοικείτω ἐν** ὑμῖν πλουσίως, ἐν πάσῃ σοφίᾳ διδάσκοντες καὶ νουθετοῦντες ἑαυτούς, ψαλμοῖς ὕμνοις ᾠδαῖς πνευματικαῖς ἐν [τῇ] χάριτι ᾄδοντες ἐν ταῖς καρδίαις ὑμῶν τῷ θεῷ. [GNT] | To dwell; to live; to be at home or to make a home; to abide or dwell within.<br><br>**Practical Application**<br>The choice is up to the believer: the Word of Christ does not naturally dwell within the believer's heart. The believer must make room within his heart for the Word of Christ. He must let the Word of Christ enter his heart and make a home within his life. He must let the Word of Christ dwell and abide in his heart. The believer must clean out all the old furnishings of his life and let the Word of Christ settle down as the permanent resident within his heart. |
| **#1188**<br>**Dwell–Dwells**<br><br>Dwell–KJV<br>Dwells–NASB<br>Lives–NIV<br>Dwells–NKJV<br>Living–NLT | οἰκεῖ = oikei<br>Pronunciation: [oy-keh'-ee]<br>Parsing (part of speech): verb<br>  Mood—indicative<br>  Tense—present<br>  Voice—active<br>  Person—3rd person<br>  Number—singular<br>  Stem or root—from οἰκέω<br>Concordance References:<br>  ⇒ Strong's #3611 oikeö | Lives, dwells; lives in (1 Tim.6.16).<br><br>**Practical Application**<br>The Spirit lives or dwells within the believer, putting the Spirit of Christ within him.<br>The power of the Spirit is seen in the word "dwells" (*oikei*). The word "dwells" is the picture of a home (*oikei*). The Holy Spirit lives within the believer: He makes His home, takes up residence, and lives within the believer just as we live in our homes. |

## PRACTICAL WORD STUDIES
## in the NEW TESTAMENT

| ENGLISH WORD | GREEK WORD AND VERSE | THE WORD MEANS... |
|---|---|---|
| **POSB REFERENCE** (Romans 8:9) Note 4, point 1 | ⇒ NIV #3861 oikeö<br>⇒ NASB #3611 oikeö<br><br>**Romans 8:9**<br>But ye are not in the flesh, but in the Spirit, if so be that the Spirit of God **dwell** in you. Now if any man have not the Spirit of Christ, he is none of his. [KJV]<br>However, you are not in the flesh but in the Spirit, if indeed the Spirit of God **dwells** in you. But if anyone does not have the Spirit of Christ, he does not belong to Him. [NASB]<br>You, however, are controlled not by the sinful nature but by the Spirit, if the Spirit of God **lives** in you. And if anyone does not have the Spirit of Christ, he does not belong to Christ. [NIV]<br>But you are not in the flesh but in the Spirit, if indeed the Spirit of God **dwells** in you. Now if anyone does not have the Spirit of Christ, he is not His. [NKJV]<br>But you are not controlled by your sinful nature. You are controlled by the Spirit if you have the Spirit of God **living** in you. (And remember that those who do not have the Spirit of Christ living in them are not Christians at all. [NLT]<br>ὑμεῖς δὲ οὐκ ἐστὲ ἐν σαρκὶ, ἀλλὰ ἐν πνεύματι, εἴπερ Πνεῦμα Θεοῦ **οἰκεῖ** ἐν ὑμῖν. εἰ δέ τις Πνεῦμα Χριστοῦ οὐκ ἔχει, οὗτος οὐκ ἔστιν αὐτοῦ. [GNS]<br>ὑμεῖς δὲ οὐκ ἐστὲ ἐν σαρκὶ ἀλλὰ ἐν πνεύματι, εἴπερ πνεῦμα θεοῦ **οἰκεῖ** ἐν ὑμῖν. εἰ δέ τις πνεῦμα Χριστοῦ οὐκ ἔχει, οὗτος οὐκ ἔστιν αὐτοῦ. [GNT] | |
| **#1189 Dwell In**<br><br>Rest upon–KJV<br>**Dwell in–NASB**<br>Rest on–NIV<br>Rest upon–NKJV<br>Work through–NLT<br><br>**POSB REFERENCE** (2 Cor.12:7-10; esp. v.9) Note 3, point 3b | ἐπισκηνώσῃ ἐπ' = *episkënösë ep'*<br>Pronunciation: [ep-ee-skay-no'-say ep]<br>Parsing *episkënösë* (part of speech): verb<br>    Mood—subjunctive<br>    Tense—aorist<br>    Voice—active<br>    Person—3rd person<br>    Number—singular<br>    Stem or root—from ἐπισκηνόω<br>Concordance References:<br>⇒ Strong's #1909+1981 epi episkënoö<br>⇒ NIV #2093+2172 epi episkënoö [rest on]<br>⇒ NASB #1909+1981 epi episkënoö<br><br>**2 Cor. 12:9**<br>And he said unto me, My grace is sufficient for thee: for my strength is made perfect in weakness. Most gladly therefore will I rather glory in my infirmities, that the power of Christ may **rest upon** me. [KJV]<br>And He has said to me, "My grace is sufficient for you, for power is perfected in weakness." Most gladly, therefore, I will rather boast about my weaknesses, that the power of Christ may **dwell in** me. [NASB]<br>But he said to me, "My grace is sufficient for you, for my power is made perfect in weakness." Therefore I will boast all the more gladly about my weaknesses, so that Christ's power may **rest on** me. [NIV]<br>And He said to me, "My grace is sufficient for you, for My strength is made perfect in weakness." Therefore most gladly I will rather boast in my infirmities, that the power of Christ may **rest upon** me. [NKJV]<br>Each time he said, "My gracious favor is all you need. My power works best in your weakness." So now I am glad to boast about my weaknesses, so that the power of Christ may **work through** me. [NLT]<br>καὶ εἴρηκέ μοι, Ἀρκεῖ σοι ἡ χάρις μου· ἡ γὰρ δύναμις μου ἐν ἀσθενείᾳ τελειοῦται. ἥδιστα οὖν μᾶλλον καυχήσομαι ἐν ταῖς ἀσθενείαις μου, ἵνα **ἐπισκηνώσῃ ἐπ'** ἐμὲ ἡ δύναμις τοῦ Χριστοῦ. [GNS]<br>καὶ εἴρηκέν μοι· Ἀρκεῖ σοι ἡ χάρις μου, ἡ γὰρ δύναμις ἐν ἀσθενείᾳ τελεῖται. ἥδιστα οὖν μᾶλλον καυχήσομαι ἐν ταῖς ἀσθενείαις μου, ἵνα **ἐπισκηνώσῃ ἐπ'** ἐμὲ ἡ δύναμις τοῦ Χριστοῦ. [GNT] | To rest on; to rest upon; to dwell in; to live in; to work through; to fix a tent upon.<br><br>**Practical Application**<br>The idea is that the power of Christ rests upon the suffering believer just as the Shekinah glory dwelt in the holy place of the tabernacle. What a glorious thought! The strength of Christ fixes itself upon and dwells within the believer—filling him with the Shekinah glory of God—when he suffers. |

# PRACTICAL WORD STUDIES
## in the NEW TESTAMENT

| ENGLISH WORD | GREEK WORD AND VERSE | THE WORD MEANS... |
|---|---|---|
| **#1190**<br>**Dwell With**<br><br>**Dwell with**–KJV<br>Live with–NASB<br>Live with–NIV<br>**Dwell with**–NKJV<br>Give honor–NLT<br><br>**POSB REFERENCE**<br>(1 Pt.3:7)<br>Note 1 | συνοικοῦντες = sunoikountes<br>Pronunciation: [soon-oy-koon-tehs]<br>Parsing (part of speech): verb<br>  Mood—participle (imperative sense)<br>  Tense—present<br>  Voice—active<br>  Case—nominative<br>  Gender—masculine<br>  Person—2nd person<br>  Number—plural<br>  Stem or root—from συνοικέω<br>Concordance References:<br>  ⇒ Strong's #4924 sunoikeō<br>  ⇒ NIV #5324 sunoikeō<br>  ⇒ NASB #4924 sunoikeō<br><br>**1 Peter 3:7**<br>Likewise, ye husbands, **dwell with** them according to knowledge, giving honour unto the wife, as unto the weaker vessel, and as being heirs together of the grace of life; that your prayers be not hindered. [KJV]<br>You husbands likewise, **live with** your wives in an understanding way, as with a weaker vessel, since she is a woman; and grant her honor as a fellow heir of the grace of life, so that your prayers may not be hindered. [NASB]<br>Husbands, in the same way be considerate as you **live with** your wives, and treat them with respect as the weaker partner and as heirs with you of the gracious gift of life, so that nothing will hinder your prayers. [NIV]<br>Husbands, likewise, **dwell with** *them* with understanding, giving honor to the wife, as to the weaker vessel, and as *being* heirs together of the grace of life, that your prayers may not be hindered. [NKJV]<br>In the same way, you husbands must **give honor** to your wives. Treat her with understanding as you live together. She may be weaker than you are, but she is your equal partner in God's gift of new life. If you don't treat her as you should, your prayers will not be heard. [NLT]<br>Οἱ ἄνδρες ὁμοίως, **συνοικοῦντες** κατὰ γνῶσιν, ὡς ἀσθενεστέρῳ σκεύει τῷ γυναικείῳ ἀπονέμοντες τιμήν, ὡς καὶ συγκληρονόμοι χάριτος ζωῆς, εἰς τὸ μὴ ἐκκόπτεσθαι τὰς προσευχὰς ὑμῶν. [GNS]<br>Οἱ ἄνδρες ὁμοίως, **συνοικοῦντες** κατὰ γνῶσιν ὡς ἀσθενεστέρῳ σκεύει τῷ γυναικείῳ, ἀπονέμοντες τιμήν ὡς καὶ συγκληρονόμοις χάριτος ζωῆς εἰς τὸ μὴ ἐγκόπτεσθαι τὰς προσευχὰς ὑμῶν. [GNT] | To live with; to dwell with; to remain with; to reside with; to dwell together; to give honor.<br><br>**Practical Application**<br>Alan Stibbs points out that it is a word that is often used in the Greek for sexual intercourse. It is similar to the Hebrew verb *to know* which means that a man and woman *know* each other sexually (cp. Genesis 4:1; Matthew 1:25). (*The First Epistle General of Peter.* "The Tyndale New Testament Commentaries," p.127).<br>The point is this: the husband is to *dwell with his wife* and with no one else. He is not to *know* anyone else; he is not to have sexual intercourse with any other woman. The husband has a wife and he is to dwell with her in purity, righteousness, and holiness, and not as an adulterer.<br>Note one other fact as well: to dwell with his wife means that he is not to be gone all of the time. He stays at home and dwells with her: he is a close and supportive companion. He is not out and away from the home all of the time pursuing his own interests and hobbies. A good husband dwells at home; he is close to his wife and he is supportive of her in all of life. In fact, the term *dwell with* actually means to dwell together. The husband and wife are a team; they are as one body, one body that dwells and lives and moves together. This is not to do away with individuality. But individuality never has been and never will be the problem within a marriage of normal people. The problem with normal people will always be denying self and sacrificially giving oneself to one's spouse. *Husbands* must always remember this: they are to dwell with—to live and move and have their being with—their wives. |
| **#1191**<br>**Dwellest, Where**<br><br>Where dwellest–KJV<br>Where...staying–NASB<br>Where...staying–NIV<br>Where...staying–NKJV<br>Where...staying–NLT<br><br>**POSB REFERENCE**<br>(Jn.1:38-39; esp. v.38)<br>Note 2, point 2 | ποῦ μένεις = pou meneis<br>Pronunciation: [poo mehn'-ice]<br>Parsing *pou* (part of speech): adjective adverb<br>  Type—interrogative<br>  Stem or root—from ποῦ<br>Parsing *meneis* (part of speech): verb<br>  Mood—indicative<br>  Tense—present<br>  Voice—active<br>  Person—2nd person<br>  Number—singular<br>  Stem or root—from μένω<br>Concordance References:<br>  ⇒ Strong's #4226 pou + 3306 meno<br>  ⇒ NIV #4544 pou [where] + 3531 menō [staying]<br>  ⇒ NASB #4226 pou + 3306 meno<br><br>**John 1:38**<br>Then Jesus turned, and saw them following, and saith unto them, What seek ye? They said unto him, Rabbi, (which is to say, being interpreted, Master,) **where dwellest** thou? [KJV]<br>And Jesus turned, and beheld them following, and said to them, "What do you seek?" And they said to Him, "Rabbi (which translated means Teacher), **where** are You | Where are you staying; where are you dwelling, living, residing.<br><br>**Practical Application**<br>Jesus asked the basic question of life: "What do you want?" He did not ask, "Whom do you seek?" but "What do you want?" "What are you after?"<br>They had never met Jesus before, yet they called Him Master or Teacher, acknowledging His position as their Teacher. They were not asking for a simple conversation by the side of the road. They were asking to join Him in the quiet of His home, to open and pour out their hearts to Him and for Him to become their teacher. They wanted Him to meet the crying need of their heart and to do such in the quiet confines of His dwelling. |

# PRACTICAL WORD STUDIES
## in the NEW TESTAMENT

| ENGLISH WORD | GREEK WORD AND VERSE | THE WORD MEANS... |
|---|---|---|
| | staying?" [NASB]<br>Turning around, Jesus saw them following and asked, "What do you want?"They said, "Rabbi" (which means Teacher), "**where** are you **staying**?" [NIV]<br>Then Jesus turned, and seeing them following, said to them, "What do you seek?" They said to Him, "Rabbi" (which is to say, when translated, Teacher), "**where** are You **staying**?" [NKJV]<br>Jesus looked around and saw them following. "What do you want?" he asked them.They replied, "Rabbi" (which means Teacher), "**where** are you **staying**?" [NLT]<br>Στραφεὶς δὲ ὁ Ἰησοῦς, καὶ θεασάμενος αὐτοὺς ἀκολουθοῦντας, λέγει αὐτοῖς, Τί ζητεῖτε; οἱ δὲ εἶπον αὐτῷ, Ῥαββί -- ὃ λέγεται ἑρμηνευόμενον, Διδάσκαλε -- , **ποῦ μένεις**; [GNS]<br>στραφεὶς δὲ ὁ Ἰησοῦς καὶ θεασάμενος αὐτοὺς ἀκολουθοῦντας λέγει αὐτοῖς, Τί ζητεῖτε; οἱ δὲ εἶπαν αὐτῷ, Ῥαββί (ὃ λέγεται μεθερμηνευόμενον Διδάσκαλε), **ποῦ μένεις**; [GNT] | |
| **#1192**<br>**Dwelleth**<br><br>Dwelleth–KJV<br>Abides–NASB<br>Remains–NIV<br>Abides–NKJV<br>Remain–NLT<br><br>**POSB<br>REFERENCE**<br>(Jn.6:56)<br>Note 4 | μένει = menei<br>Pronunciation: [mehn'-ee]<br>Parsing (part of speech): verb<br>  Mood—indicative<br>  Tense—present<br>  Voice—active<br>  Number—3rd person singular<br>  Stem or root—from μένω<br>Concordance References:<br>  ⇒ Strong's #3306 meno<br>  ⇒ NIV #3531 menö<br>  ⇒ NASB #3306 meno<br><br>**John 6:56**<br>He that eateth my flesh, and drinketh my blood, **dwelleth** in me, and I in him. [KJV]<br>"He who eats My flesh and drinks My blood **abides** in Me, and I in him. [NASB]<br>Whoever eats my flesh and drinks my blood **remains** in me, and I in him. [NIV]<br>He who eats My flesh and drinks My blood **abides** in Me, and I in him. [NKJV]<br>All who eat my flesh and drink my blood **remain** in me, and I in them. [NLT]<br>ὁ τρώγων μου τὴν σάρκα, καὶ πίνων μου τὸ αἷμα, ἐν ἐμοὶ **μένει**, κἀγὼ ἐν αὐτῷ. [GNS]<br>ὁ τρώγων μου τὴν σάρκα καὶ πίνων μου τὸ αἷμα ἐν ἐμοὶ **μένει** κἀγὼ ἐν αὐτῷ. [GNT] | To hold; to continue; to abide; to remain; to keep on obeying. It means to dwell, stay, sojourn, rest in or upon; to live; to rest; to nest.<br><br>**Practical Application**<br>It is being fixed and set and remaining there, continuing on and on. Such is the state and condition and being of the person who receives Christ. The person receives Christ into his being, and Christ enters the person's life and abides within him. The person is also taken and placed into Christ, that is, placed with all other believers into the spiritual body of Christ. |
| **#1193**<br>**Dwelling Place, His**<br><br>His habitation–KJV<br>His homestead–NASB<br>His place–NIV<br>**His dwelling place–NKJV**<br>His home–NLT<br><br>**POSB<br>REFERENCE**<br>(Acts 1:16-20; esp. v.20)<br>Note 2, point 6a | ἡ ἔπαυλις αὐτοῦ = hē epaulis autou<br>Pronunciation: [ey ep'-ow-lis aw-too]<br>Parsing *epaulis* (part of speech): noun<br>  Case—nominative<br>  Gender—feminine<br>  Number—singular<br>  Stem or root—from ἔπαυλις, εως<br>Concordance References:<br>  ⇒ Strong's #3588 ho + 1886 epaulis + 846 autos<br>  ⇒ NIV #3836 ho [Not in English] + 2068 epaulis [place] + 899 autos [his]<br>  ⇒ NASB #3588 ho + 1886 epaulis + 846 autos<br><br>**Acts 1:20**<br>For it is written in the book of Psalms, Let **his habitation** be desolate, and let no man dwell therein: and his bishoprick let another take. [KJV]<br>"For it is written in the book of Psalms, 'Let **his homestead** be made desolate, And let no man dwell in it'; and, 'His OFFICE LET ANOTHER MAN TAKE.' [NASB]<br>"For," said Peter, "it is written in the book of Psalms, "'May **his place** be deserted; let there be no one to dwell | His place; His habitation; His homestead; His home.<br><br>**Practical Application**<br>The phrase "His dwelling place" (*hē epaulis autou*) is descriptive. It means a farm house or a place for sheep such as a pasture or sheep yard. The idea is that Judas would never again be allowed to be the farmer (husbandman) or shepherd for God. |

# PRACTICAL WORD STUDIES
## in the New Testament

| ENGLISH WORD | GREEK WORD AND VERSE | THE WORD MEANS... |
|---|---|---|
| | in it,' and, "'May another take his place of leadership.' [NIV]<br>"For it is written in the book of Psalms: 'Let **his dwelling place** be desolate, And let no one live in it'; and, 'Let another take his office.' [NKJV]<br>Peter continued, "This was predicted in the book of Psalms, where it says, 'Let **his home** become desolate, with no one living in it.' And again, 'Let his position be given to someone else.' [NLT]<br>γέγραπται γὰρ ἐν βίβλῳ Ψαλμῶν, Γενηθήτω ἡ **ἔπαυλις αὐτοῦ** ἔρημος, καὶ μὴ ἔστω ὁ κατοικῶν ἐν αὐτῇ· καί, Τὴν ἐπισκοπὴν αὐτοῦ λαβέοι ἕτερος. [GNS]<br>Γέγραπται γὰρ ἐν βίβλῳ ψαλμῶν, Γενηθήτω ἡ **ἔπαυλις αὐτοῦ** ἔρημος καὶ μὴ ἔστω ὁ κατοικῶν ἐν αὐτῇ, καί, Τὴν ἐπισκοπὴν αὐτοῦ λαβέτω ἕτερος. [GNT] | |
| **#1194**<br>**Dwelling Places**<br><br>Mansions–KJV<br>**Dwelling places–NASB**<br>Rooms–NIV<br>Mansions–NKJV<br>Rooms–NLT<br><br>**POSB REFERENCE**<br>(Jn.14:2)<br>Note 2, point 3 | μοναί = *monai*<br>Pronunciation: [mon-ah-ee']<br>Parsing (part of speech): noun<br>  Case—nominative<br>  Gender—feminine<br>  Number—plural<br>  Stem or root—from μονή, ῆς<br>Concordance References:<br>  ⇒ Strong's #3438 mone<br>  ⇒ NIV #3665 mone<br>  ⇒ NASB #3438 mone<br><br>**John 14:2**<br>In my Father's house are many **mansions**: if it were not so, I would have told you. I go to prepare a place for you. [KJV]<br>"In My Father's house are many **dwelling places**; if it were not so, I would have told you; for I go to prepare a place for you. [NASB]<br>In my Father's house are many **rooms**; if it were not so, I would have told you. I am going there to prepare a place for you. [NIV]<br>In My Father's house are many **mansions**; if *it were not so,* I would have told you. I go to prepare a place for you. [NKJV]<br>There are many **rooms** in my Father's home, and I am going to prepare a place for you. If this were not so, I would tell you plainly. [NLT]<br>ἐν τῇ οἰκίᾳ τοῦ πατρός μου **μοναί** πολλαί εἰσιν· εἰ δὲ μή, εἶπον ἂν ὑμῖν· πορεύομαι ἑτοιμάσαι τόπον ὑμῖν. [GNS]<br>ἐν τῇ οἰκίᾳ τοῦ πατρός μου **μοναί** πολλαί εἰσιν· εἰ δὲ μή, εἶπον ἂν ὑμῖν ὅτι πορεύομαι ἑτοιμάσαι τόπον ὑμῖν; [GNT] | Rooms, mansions, dwelling places, abiding places. It means places, residences, dwellings, areas, spaces for living, homes.<br><br>**Practical Application**<br>What a glorious hope! How much clearer could Jesus be: *a place* for every one of us—a place for every believer to dwell and live. Just as we have dwellings and homes here on earth, so Jesus promises us dwellings and homes (dwelling places) in heaven.<br>And note: there is no shortage. There are "*many dwelling places.*" (In the other gospels, Jesus talks a great deal about believers inheriting huge areas or places, even whole realms and kingdoms, which probably mean the heavenly bodies all throughout the universe that will be recreated in the new heavens and earth; 2 Peter 3:10-13; Rev. 21:1. See POSB note—Matthew 19:28; POSB note—Matthew 24:45-47; POSB note—Matthew 25:20-23.)<br>Note how Jesus stressed the truth and reality of "God's house" and its "dwelling places": "If it were not so, I would have told you." Jesus did not lie. He told only the truth. Note something else: one thing is essential to inherit these dwelling places—belief in Christ (John 14:1). |
| **#1195**<br>**Dying**<br><br>Decease–KJV<br>Departure–NASB<br>Departure–NIV<br>Decease–NKJV<br>**Dying–NLT**<br><br>**POSB REFERENCE**<br>(Lk.9:30-31; esp. v.31)<br>Note 4, point 2 | ἔξοδον = *exodon*<br>Pronunciation: [ex'-od-on]<br>Parsing (part of speech): noun<br>  Case—accusative<br>  Gender—feminine<br>  Number—singular<br>  Stem or root—from ἔξοδος, ου<br>Concordance References:<br>  ⇒ Strong's #1841 exodos<br>  ⇒ NIV #2016 exodos<br>  ⇒ NASB #1841 exodos<br><br>**Luke 9:31**<br>Who appeared in glory, and spake of his **decease** which he should accomplish at Jerusalem. [KJV]<br>Who, appearing in glory, were speaking of His **departure** which He was about to accomplish at Jerusalem. [NASB]<br>Appeared in glorious splendor, talking with Jesus. They spoke about his **departure**, which he was about to bring to fulfillment at Jerusalem. [NIV] | Departure; exodus, decease; to depart; to go out; to die.<br><br>**Practical Application**<br>In this Scripture, there stood Moses sharing how God had so miraculously saved and delivered the children of Israel out of bondage and how the exodus (deliverance) was only a picture of the marvelous deliverance that He, God's Son, was to accomplish for man. Jesus was to accomplish a new exodus, a new saving deliverance; except this time, it was to be for all men. All men were to be delivered from the bondage of sin and death, from the devil and hell—delivered into the glorious liberty of God and life, both abundant and eternal life. Jesus' dying was to be well worth it, Moses and Elijah stressed. Note: the very encouragement that our Lord needed as Man was given by two who had believed and hoped in His coming. Being |

| ENGLISH WORD | GREEK WORD AND VERSE | THE WORD MEANS |
|---|---|---|
| | Who appeared in glory and spoke of His **decease** which He was about to accomplish at Jerusalem. [NKJV]<br>They were glorious to see. And they were speaking of how he was about to fulfill God's plan by **dying** in Jerusalem. [NLT]<br>οἳ ὀφθέντες ἐν δόξῃ ἔλεγον τὴν **ἔξοδον** αὐτοῦ, ἣν ἤμελλε πληροῦν ἐν Ἰερουσαλήμ. [GNS]<br>οἳ ὀφθέντες ἐν δόξῃ ἔλεγον τὴν **ἔξοδον** αὐτοῦ, ἣν ἤμελλεν πληροῦν ἐν Ἰερουσαλήμ. [GNT] | reminded of the marvelous deliverance (*exodon*) that had happened so long ago was bound to strengthen and lift the heart of Christ. Just seeing Moses and Elijah stand there, two who had trusted and believed and hoped, was bound to cause the Lord's spirit to rise. He was greatly encouraged and knew that He could not fail these men who had trusted and hoped in Him so much. |

## PRACTICAL WORD STUDIES
### in the NEW TESTAMENT

| ENGLISH WORD | GREEK WORD AND VERSE | THE WORD MEANS... |
|---|---|---|
| **#1196**<br>**Eager**<br><br>Ready–KJV<br>**Eager**–NASB<br>**Eager**–NIV<br>Ready–NKJV<br>**Eager**–NLT<br><br>**POSB REFERENCE**<br>(Romans 1:14-15; esp. v.15)<br>Note 5, point 2 | πρόθυμον = prothumon<br>Pronunciation: [proth'-oo-mon]<br>Parsing (part of speech): pronominal adjective<br>    Case—nominative<br>    Gender—neuter<br>    Number—singular<br>    Stem or root—from πρόθυμος, ον<br>Concordance References:<br>  ⇒ Strong's #4289 prothumos<br>  ⇒ NIV #4609 prothumos<br>  ⇒ NASB #4289 prothumos<br><br>**Romans 1:15**<br>So, as much as in me is, I am **ready** to preach the gospel to you that are at Rome also. [KJV]<br>Thus, for my part, I am **eager** to preach the gospel to you also who are in Rome. [NASB]<br>That is why I am so **eager** to preach the gospel also to you who are at Rome. [NIV]<br>So, as much as is in me, *I am* **ready** to preach the gospel to you who are in Rome also. [NKJV]<br>So I am **eager** to come to you in Rome, too, to preach God's Good News. [NLT]<br>οὕτω τὸ κατ' ἐμὲ **πρόθυμον** καὶ ὑμῖν τοῖς ἐν Ῥώμῃ εὐαγγελίσασθαι. [GNS]<br>οὕτως τὸ κατ' ἐμὲ **πρόθυμον** καὶ ὑμῖν τοῖς ἐν Ῥώμῃ εὐαγγελίσασθαι. [GNT] | Willing; eager, prepared, equipped, set. The word "eager" means an urgent willingness.<br><br>**Practical Application**<br>Paul experienced both a willingness and an urgency to preach the gospel. Note the words, "as much as in me is." Paul wanted to take all that was in him and pour it into people—all the energy and effort, all the truth and knowledge of the gospel. There was nothing that could keep him from sharing the gospel, not if he had a chance to share it. He allowed no hindrance to enter his life that would affect his message. He was possessed and obsessed with a readiness to preach the glorious message of the living Lord. |
| **#1197**<br>**Eager**<br><br>Followers–KJV<br>Zealous–NASB<br>**Eager**–NIV<br>Followers–NKJV<br>**Eager**–NLT<br><br>**POSB REFERENCE**<br>(1 Pt.3:13-14; esp. v.13)<br>Note 1 | ζηλωταὶ = zēlōtai<br>Pronunciation: [dzay-lo-tah-ee]<br>Parsing (part of speech): noun<br>    Case—nominative<br>    Gender—masculine<br>    Number—plural<br>    Stem or root—from ζηλωτής, οῦ<br>Concordance References:<br>  ⇒ Strong's #3402 mimetes<br>  ⇒ NIV #2421 zēlōtēs<br>  ⇒ NASB #2207 zēlōtēs<br><br>**1 Peter 3:13**<br>And who is he that will harm you, if ye be **followers** of that which is good? [KJV]<br>And who is there to harm you if you prove **zealous** for what is good? [NASB]<br>Who is going to harm you if you are **eager** to do good? [NIV]<br>And who *is* he who will harm you if you become **followers** of what is good? [NKJV]<br>Now, who will want to harm you if you are **eager** to do good? [NLT]<br>Καὶ τίς ὁ κακώσων ὑμᾶς, ἐὰν τοῦ ἀγαθοῦ **μιμηταὶ** γένησθε; [GNS]<br>Καὶ τίς ὁ κακώσων ὑμᾶς ἐὰν τοῦ ἀγαθοῦ **ζηλωταὶ** γένησθε; [GNT] | To be eager; to be a follower, a strongly committed follower; to be zealous; to be a Zealot.<br><br>**Practical Application**<br>Note the verse: it actually says to be "eager to do good." The believer is to be so zealous for what is right that he is actually known as a zealot for good. Imagine being gripped with so much passion and zeal for good that one becomes known as a zealot! This is the challenge of this passage. Several attitudes toward doing good permeate society.<br>⇒ Some persons have a *"care less"* attitude toward goodness. Doing what is right and good matters little. What is right and good is rebelled against, ignored, cursed, and rejected. The person has little conscience about right and wrong. His values are ever so weak. He could care less if he does what is right and good.<br>⇒ Some persons have a *selfish attitude* toward goodness. If doing what is right and good benefits them, then they do it. If it helps them, meets their need and enlarges their holdings, then they do what is right. But if it costs them, demands discipline and control, and takes away from their pleasure and holdings, then they reject the good and refuse to do what is right.<br>⇒ Some persons have a *surface or sentimental attitude* to what is good and right. They readily profess to believe in what is good and right and want to be known as moral and upright. But behind the scenes, they go ahead and live like they want, doing their own thing.<br>⇒ Some persons, of course, have a zealous attitude toward what is right and good. They have committed their lives to seeking and doing what they should. This is exactly what Scripture is saying: "Be a zealot—be a fanatic—be a passionate follower—after that which is good and right." |

## PRACTICAL WORD STUDIES
### in the NEW TESTAMENT

| ENGLISH WORD | GREEK WORD AND VERSE | THE WORD MEANS... |
|---|---|---|
| **#1198**<br>**Eager Expectation**<br><br>Earnest expectation–KJV<br>Earnest expectation–NASB<br>Eagerly expect–NIV<br>Earnest expectation–NKJV<br>**Eager expectation–NLT**<br><br>**POSB REFERENCE**<br>(Philip.1:20)<br>Note 1, point 1 | ἀποκαραδοκίαν = *apokaradokian*<br>Pronunciation: [ap-ok-ar-ad-ok-ee'-ahn]<br>Parsing (part of speech): noun<br>    Case—accusative<br>    Gender—feminine<br>    Number—singular<br>    Stem or root—from ἀποκαραδοκία, ας<br>Concordance References:<br>⇒ Strong's #603 apokaradokia<br>⇒ NIV #638 apokaradokia<br>⇒ NASB #603 apokaradokia<br><br>**Philip. 1:20**<br>According to my **earnest expectation** and my hope, that in nothing I shall be ashamed, but that with all boldness, as always, so now also Christ shall be magnified in my body, whether it be by life, or by death. [KJV]<br>According to my **earnest expectation** and hope, that I shall not be put to shame in anything, but that with all boldness, Christ shall even now, as always, be exalted in my body, whether by life or by death. [NASB]<br>I **eagerly expect** and hope that I will in no way be ashamed, but will have sufficient courage so that now as always Christ will be exalted in my body, whether by life or by death. [NIV]<br>According to my **earnest expectation** and hope that in nothing I shall be ashamed, but with all boldness, as always, so now also Christ will be magnified in my body, whether by life or by death. [NKJV]<br>For I live in **eager expectation** and hope that I will never do anything that causes me shame, but that I will always be bold for Christ, as I have been in the past, and that my life will always honor Christ, whether I live or I die. [NLT]<br>κατὰ τὴν **ἀποκαραδοκίαν** καὶ ἐλπίδα μου, ὅτι ἐν οὐδενὶ αἰσχυνθήσομαι, ἀλλ' ἐν πάσῃ παρρησίᾳ, ὡς πάντοτε, καὶ νῦν μεγαλυνθήσεται Χριστὸς ἐν τῷ σώματί μου, εἴτε διὰ ζωῆς, εἴτε διὰ θανάτου. [GNS]<br>κατὰ τὴν **ἀποκαραδοκίαν** καὶ ἐλπίδα μου, ὅτι ἐν οὐδενὶ αἰσχυνθήσομαι ἀλλ' ἐν πάσῃ παρρησίᾳ ὡς πάντοτε καὶ νῦν μεγαλυνθήσεται Χριστὸς ἐν τῷ σώματί μου, εἴτε διὰ ζωῆς εἴτε διὰ θανάτου. [GNT] | To eagerly expect; to have an earnest expectation; to have an eager expectation; to have a deep desire.<br><br>**Practical Application**<br>It means to gaze into the distance with the head erect and outstretched just like a watchman on a tower. It is aiming one's attention at an object with concentration, eagerness, and intensity. It is turning the eyes away from everything else and focusing upon one object and one object alone. It is total concentration upon a person's desire. |
| **#1199**<br>**Eager Expectation For**<br><br>Earnest expectation of–KJV<br>Anxious longing of–NASB<br>**Eager expectation for–NIV**<br>Earnest expectation of–NKJV<br>Waiting eagerly for–NLT<br><br>**POSB REFERENCE**<br>(Romans 8:19-22; esp. v.19)<br>Note 2 | ἀποκαραδοκία = *apokaradokia*<br>Pronunciation: [ap-ok-ar-ad-ok-ee'-ah]<br>Parsing (part of speech): noun<br>    Case—nominative<br>    Gender—feminine<br>    Number—singular<br>    Stem or root—from ἀποκαραδοκία, ας<br>Concordance References:<br>⇒ Strong's #603 apokaradokia<br>⇒ NIV #638 apokaradokia<br>⇒ NASB #603 apokaradokia<br><br>**Romans 8:19**<br>For the **earnest expectation of** the creature waiteth for the manifestation of the sons of God. [KJV]<br>For the **anxious longing of** the creation waits eagerly for the revealing of the sons of God. [NASB]<br>The creation waits in **eager expectation for** the sons of God to be revealed. [NIV]<br>For the **earnest expectation of** the creation eagerly waits for the revealing of the sons of God. [NKJV]<br>For all creation is **waiting eagerly for** that future day when God will reveal who his children really are. [NLT]<br>ἡ γὰρ **ἀποκαραδοκία** τῆς κτίσεως τὴν ἀποκάλυψιν τῶν υἱῶν τοῦ Θεοῦ ἀπεκδέχεται· [GNS]<br>ἡ γὰρ **ἀποκαραδοκία** τῆς κτίσεως τὴν ἀποκάλυψιν τῶν υἱῶν τοῦ θεοῦ ἀπεκδέχεται. [GNT] | Eager longing; deep desire; eager expectation for; earnest expectation.<br><br>**Practical Application**<br>The creation suffers and struggles for deliverance from corruption. The word "creation" refers to everything under man: animal, plant, and mineral. All creation is pictured as living and waiting expectantly for the day when the sons of God will be glorified. The words "eager expectation for" (*apokaradokia*) mean to watch with the neck outstretched and the head erect. It is a persistent, unswerving expectation, an expectation that does not give up but keeps looking until the event happens. |

# PRACTICAL WORD STUDIES
## in the NEW TESTAMENT

| ENGLISH WORD | GREEK WORD AND VERSE | THE WORD MEANS... |
|---|---|---|
| **#1200**<br>**Eagerly**<br><br>With all readiness of mind–KJV<br>With great eagerness–NASB<br>With great eagerness–NIV<br>With all readiness–NKJV<br>Eagerly–NLT<br><br>**POSB REFERENCE**<br>(Acts 17:11)<br>Note 5 | μετὰ πάσης προθυμίας = meta pasës prothumias<br>Pronunciation: [meh-tah pah-sace thro-thoo-me-ahs ]<br>Parsing *pasës* (part of speech): adjective<br>   Case—genitive<br>   Gender—feminine<br>   Number—singular<br>   Stem or root—from πᾶς, πᾶσα, πᾶν<br>Parsing *prothumias* (part of speech): noun<br>   Case—genitive<br>   Gender—feminine<br>   Number—singular<br>   Stem or root—from προθυμία, ας<br>Concordance References:<br>  ⇒ Strong's #3326 meta +3956 pas + 4288 prothumia<br>  ⇒ NIV #3552 meta [with] +4246 pas [great] + 4608 prothumia [eagerness]<br>  ⇒ NASB #3326 meta +3956 pas + 4288 prothumia<br><br>**Acts 17:11**<br>These were more noble than those in Thessalonica, in that they received the word **with all readiness of mind**, and searched the scriptures daily, whether those things were so. [KJV]<br>Now these were more noble-minded than those in Thessalonica, for they received the word **with great eagerness**, examining the Scriptures daily, to see whether these things were so. [NASB]<br>Now the Bereans were of more noble character than the Thessalonians, for they received the message **with great eagerness** and examined the Scriptures every day to see if what Paul said was true. [NIV]<br>These were more fair-minded than those in Thessalonica, in that they received the word **with all readiness**, and searched the Scriptures daily *to find out* whether these things were so. [NKJV]<br>And the people of Berea were more open-minded than those in Thessalonica, and they listened **eagerly** to Paul's message. They searched the Scriptures day after day to check up on Paul and Silas, to see if they were really teaching the truth. [NLT]<br>οὗτοι δὲ ἦσαν εὐγενέστεροι τῶν ἐν Θεσσαλονίκῃ, οἵτινες ἐδέξαντο τὸν λόγον **μετὰ πάσης προθυμίας**, τὸ καθ' ἡμέραν ἀνακρίνοντες τὰς γραφὰς, εἰ ἔχοι ταῦτα οὕτως. [GNS]<br>οὗτοι δὲ ἦσαν εὐγενέστεροι τῶν ἐν Θεσσαλονίκῃ, οἵτινες ἐδέξαντο τὸν λόγον **μετὰ πάσης προθυμίας** καθ' ἡμέραν ἀνακρίνοντες τὰς γραφὰς εἰ ἔχοι ταῦτα οὕτως. [GNT] | With great eagerness; with all readiness of mind; eagerly; with zeal. It means to have a willing desire, an eagerness, a hunger, a thirst to know the truth.<br><br>**Practical Application**<br>A noble people are an honest, thinking and searching people. They investigate, study, and seek to verify the message of truth. Note: the Bereans sought "eagerly" (*meta pasës prothumias*): a willing desire, an eagerness, a hunger, a thirst to know the truth. A noble people do not shut their minds or hearts; they do not refuse to listen or consider.<br>Note another fact: a noble people do not just accept and swallow whatever is said. Paul himself was the authority proclaiming the truth, but the Bereans studied, investigated, and searched the Scriptures for the truth themselves. And they searched daily. The truth of God and His Word has no end; it is unfathomable. Discovering the truth is a daily responsibility. God has made it so (Luke 9:23). |
| **#1201**<br>**Eagerly Await, Wait–Eagerly Waiting**<br><br>Look–KJV<br>Eagerly wait–NASB<br>Eagerly await–NIV<br>Eagerly wait–NKJV<br>Eagerly waiting–NLT<br><br>**POSB REFERENCE**<br>(Philip.3:20-21; esp. v.20)<br>Note 3, point 2 | ἀπεκδεχόμεθα = apekdechometha<br>Pronunciation: [ap-ek-dekh'-om-ethh-ah]<br>Parsing (part of speech): verb<br>   Mood—indicative<br>   Tense—present<br>   Voice—middle or passive deponent<br>   Person—1st person<br>   Number—plural<br>   Stem or root—from ἀπεκδέχομαι<br>Concordance References:<br>  ⇒ Strong's #553 apekdechomai<br>  ⇒ NIV #587 apekdechomai<br>  ⇒ NASB #553 apekdechomai<br><br>**Philip. 3:20**<br>For our conversation is in heaven; from whence also we **look** for the Saviour, the Lord Jesus Christ: [KJV]<br>For our citizenship is in heaven, from which also we **eagerly wait** for a Savior, the Lord Jesus Christ; [NASB]<br>But our citizenship is in heaven. And we **eagerly await** a Savior from there, the Lord Jesus Christ, [NIV] | To eagerly await; to look; to await expectantly. It means to yearn, to eagerly look and wait for the coming of the Lord Jesus to take His dear people to heaven.<br><br>**Practical Application**<br>The believer's life is to be focused upon the return of Christ. He is to be looking for the Lord's return—constantly looking—looking every day of his life.<br>Kenneth Wuest points out that the Greek words "eagerly await" or "eagerly wait" (*apekdechometha*) is made up of three words put together. There is...<br>• the word "receive" which speaks of welcoming as the welcoming of a guest. It also has the idea of preparation for the guest.<br>• the word "off" which speaks of withdrawing one's attention from other objects.<br>• the word "out" which has the idea of waiting for, of stretching out the neck and wait- |

| ENGLISH WORD | GREEK WORD AND VERSE | THE WORD MEANS... |
|---|---|---|
| | For our citizenship is in heaven, from which we also **eagerly wait** for the Savior, the Lord Jesus Christ, [NKJV]<br>But we are citizens of heaven, where the Lord Jesus Christ lives. And we are **eagerly waiting** for him to return as our Savior. [NLT]<br>ἡμῶν γὰρ τὸ πολίτευμα ἐν οὐρανοῖς ὑπάρχει, ἐξ οὗ καὶ Σωτῆρα ἀπεκδεχόμεθα, Κύριον Ἰησοῦν Χριστόν· [GNS]<br>ἡμῶν γὰρ τὸ πολίτευμα ἐν οὐρανοῖς ὑπάρχει, ἐξ οὗ καὶ σωτῆρα **ἀπεκδεχόμεθα** κύριον Ἰησοῦν Χριστόν, [GNT] | ing out or for the return of Christ. (*Philippians*, Vol.1, p.102). |
| **#1202**<br>**Eagerly For, Waiting**<br><br>Earnest expectation of–KJV<br>Anxious longing of–NASB<br>Eager expectation for–NIV<br>Earnest expectation of–NKJV<br>**Waiting eagerly for–NLT**<br><br>**POSB REFERENCE**<br>(Romans 8:19-22; esp. v.19)<br>Note 2 | ἀποκαραδοκία* *apokaradokia*<br>Pronunciation: [ap-ok-ar-ad-ok-ee'-ah]<br>Parsing (part of speech): noun<br>    Case—nominative<br>    Gender—feminine<br>    Number—singular<br>    Stem or root—from ἀποκαραδοκία, ας<br>Concordance References:<br>  ⇒ Strong's #603 apokaradokia<br>  ⇒ NIV #638 apokaradokia<br>  ⇒ NASB #603 apokaradokia<br><br>**Romans 8:19**<br>For the **earnest expectation of** the creature waiteth for the manifestation of the sons of God. [KJV]<br>For the **anxious longing of** the creation waits eagerly for the revealing of the sons of God. [NASB]<br>The creation waits in **eager expectation for** the sons of God to be revealed. [NIV]<br>For the **earnest expectation of** the creation eagerly waits for the revealing of the sons of God. [NKJV]<br>For all creation is **waiting eagerly for** that future day when God will reveal who his children really are. [NLT]<br>ἡ γὰρ **ἀποκαραδοκία** τῆς κτίσεως τὴν ἀποκάλυψιν τῶν υἱῶν τοῦ Θεοῦ ἀπεκδέχεται· [GNS]<br>ἡ γὰρ **ἀποκαραδοκία** τῆς κτίσεως τὴν ἀποκάλυψιν τῶν υἱῶν τοῦ θεοῦ ἀπεκδέχεται. [GNT] | Eager longing; deep desire; eager expectation for; earnest expectation.<br><br>**Practical Application**<br>The creation suffers and struggles for deliverance from corruption. The word "creation" refers to everything under man: animal, plant, and mineral. All creation is pictured as living and waiting expectantly for the day when the sons of God will be glorified. The words "waiting eagerly for" (*apokaradokia*) mean to watch with the neck outstretched and the head erect. It is a persistent, unswerving expectation, an expectation that does not give up but keeps looking until the event happens. |
| **#1203**<br>**Eagerly Desire**<br><br>Desire–KJV<br>Desire earnestly–NASB<br>**Eagerly desire–NIV**<br>Desire spiritual–NKJV<br>Desire–NLT<br><br>**POSB REFERENCE**<br>(1 Cor.14:1)<br>Note 1, point 2 | ζηλοῦτε = *zēloute*<br>Pronunciation: [dzay-loo'-teh]<br>Parsing (part of speech): verb<br>    Mood—imperative<br>    Tense—present<br>    Voice—active<br>    Person—2nd person<br>    Number—plural<br>    Stem or root—from ζηλόω<br>Concordance References:<br>  ⇒ Strong's #2206 zēloō<br>  ⇒ NIV #2420 zēloō<br>  ⇒ NASB #2206 zēloō<br><br>**1 Cor. 14:1**<br>Follow after charity, and **desire** spiritual gifts, but rather that ye may prophesy. [KJV]<br>Pursue love, yet **desire earnestly** spiritual gifts, but especially that you may prophesy. [NASB]<br>Follow the way of love and **eagerly desire** spiritual gifts, especially the gift of prophecy. [NIV]<br>Pursue love, and **desire spiritual** *gifts*, but especially that you may prophesy. [NKJV]<br>Let love be your highest goal, but also **desire** the special abilities the Spirit gives, especially the gift of prophecy. [NLT]<br>Διώκετε τὴν ἀγάπην· **ζηλοῦτε** δὲ τὰ πνευματικά, μᾶλλον δὲ ἵνα προφητεύητε. [GNS]<br>Διώκετε τὴν ἀγάπην, **ζηλοῦτε** δὲ τὰ πνευματικά, μᾶλλον δὲ ἵνα προφητεύητε. [GNT] | To desire eagerly; to desire earnestly; to covet earnestly; to be zealous and ambitious for; to show a great interest in.<br><br>**Practical Application**<br>Spiritual gifts are to be desired. We are to pursue love first, but this does not mean we are not to seek the spiritual gifts of God. On the contrary, the more we love God and men, the more we covet the gifts of God so that we can minister to the world of men more effectively. |

## PRACTICAL WORD STUDIES
### in the NEW TESTAMENT

| ENGLISH WORD | GREEK WORD AND VERSE | THE WORD MEANS... |
|---|---|---|
| **#1204**<br>**Eagerly Expect**<br><br>Earnest expectation–KJV<br>Earnest expectation–NASB<br>**Eagerly expect–NIV**<br>Earnest expectation–NKJV<br>Eager expectation–NLT<br><br>**POSB REFERENCE**<br>(Philip.1:20)<br>Note 1, point 1 | ἀποκαραδοκίαν = apokaradokian<br>Pronunciation: [ap-ok-ar-ad-ok-ee'-ahn]<br>Parsing (part of speech): noun<br>    Case—accusative<br>    Gender—feminine<br>    Number—singular<br>    Stem or root—from ἀποκαραδοκία, ας<br>Concordance References:<br>  ⇒ Strong's #603 apokaradokia<br>  ⇒ NIV #638 apokaradokia<br>  ⇒ NASB #603 apokaradokia<br><br>**Philip. 1:20**<br>According to my **earnest expectation** and my hope, that in nothing I shall be ashamed, but that with all boldness, as always, so now also Christ shall be magnified in my body, whether it be by life, or by death. [KJV]<br>According to my **earnest expectation** and hope, that I shall not be put to shame in anything, but that with all boldness, Christ shall even now, as always, be exalted in my body, whether by life or by death. [NASB]<br>I **eagerly expect** and hope that I will in no way be ashamed, but will have sufficient courage so that now as always Christ will be exalted in my body, whether by life or by death. [NIV]<br>According to my **earnest expectation** and hope that in nothing I shall be ashamed, but with all boldness, as always, so now also Christ will be magnified in my body, whether by life or by death. [NKJV]<br>For I live in **eager expectation** and hope that I will never do anything that causes me shame, but that I will always be bold for Christ, as I have been in the past, and that my life will always honor Christ, whether I live or I die. [NLT]<br>κατὰ τὴν **ἀποκαραδοκίαν** καὶ ἐλπίδα μου, ὅτι ἐν οὐδενὶ αἰσχυνθήσομαι, ἀλλ' ἐν πάσῃ παρρησίᾳ, ὡς πάντοτε, καὶ νῦν μεγαλυνθήσεται Χριστὸς ἐν τῷ σώματί μου, εἴτε διὰ ζωῆς, εἴτε διὰ θανάτου. [GNS]<br>κατὰ τὴν **ἀποκαραδοκίαν** καὶ ἐλπίδα μου, ὅτι ἐν οὐδενὶ αἰσχυνθήσομαι ἀλλ' ἐν πάσῃ παρρησίᾳ ὡς πάντοτε καὶ νῦν μεγαλυνθήσεται Χριστὸς ἐν τῷ σώματί μου, εἴτε διὰ ζωῆς εἴτε διὰ θανάτου. [GNT] | To eagerly expect; to have an earnest expectation; to have an eager expectation; to have a deep desire.<br><br>**Practical Application**<br>It means to gaze into the distance with the head erect and outstretched just like a watchman on a tower. It is aiming one's attention at an object with concentration, eagerness, and intensity. It is turning the eyes away from everything else and focusing upon one object and one object alone. It is total concentration upon a person's desire. |
| **#1205**<br>**Eagerly Look Forward**<br><br>Hope–KJV<br>Hope–NASB<br>Hope–NIV<br>Hope–NKJV<br>**Eagerly look forward–NLT**<br><br>**POSB REFERENCE**<br>(Romans 8:24-25, esp. v.24)<br>*Deeper Study* #1 | ἐλπίδι = elpidi<br>Pronunciation: [el-pee-dee']<br>Parsing (part of speech): noun<br>    Case—dative<br>    Gender—feminine<br>    Number—singular<br>    Stem or root—from ἐλπίς, ίδος<br>Concordance References:<br>  ⇒ Strong's #1680 elpis<br>  ⇒ NIV #1828 elpis<br>  ⇒ NASB #1680 elpis<br><br>**Romans 8:24**<br>For we are saved by **hope**: but hope that is seen is not hope: for what a man seeth, why doth he yet hope for? [KJV]<br>For in **hope** we have been saved, but hope that is seen is not hope; for why does one also hope for what he sees? [NASB]<br>For in this **hope** we were saved. But hope that is seen is no hope at all. Who hopes for what he already has? [NIV]<br>For we were saved in this **hope**, but hope that is seen is not hope; for why does one still hope for what he sees? [NKJV]<br>Now that we are saved, we **eagerly look forward** to this freedom. For if you already have something, you don't need to hope for it. [NLT]<br>τῇ γὰρ **ἐλπίδι** ἐσώθημεν· ἐλπὶς δὲ βλεπομένη οὐκ | Eagerly look forward to; assured expectation, confident knowledge, inward possession, spiritual surety, hope.<br><br>**Practical Application**<br>Note the statements of definition again, for they are packed full of meaning. The believer's hope cannot be defined as the world defines hope. The believer's hope is entirely different from the world's hope or desire or wish. The world desires and wishes for what it can see, and they may or may not be able to get what they long for.<br>The believer's hope is entirely different in that it deals with spiritual things, and the believer will unquestionably get what he hopes for. The believer's hope is based on the inward experience and witness of God's Spirit. The believer knows that God's Spirit lives within him, and he actually experiences the things of the Spirit now. Granted, his experience is but a taste; the things of the Spirit are not yet perfected in his life, but they do exist, and they are present in his body. He already possesses the things of God while in the flesh. His hope of salvation is a present experience—he is saved now—he already has a taste of salvation. The believer's hope to be saved is a |

## Practical Word Studies in the New Testament

| English Word | Greek Word and Verse | The Word Means... |
|---|---|---|
| | ἔστιν ἐλπίς· ὃ γὰρ βλέπει τίς, τί καὶἐλπίζει; [GNS]<br>τῇ γὰρ **ἐλπίδι** ἐσώθημεν· ἐλπὶς δὲ βλεπομένη οὐκ ἔστιν ἐλπίς· ὃ γὰρ βλέπει τίς ἐλπίζει; [GNT] | living reality now; therefore, his hope is a sure hope. To the genuine believer, hope is the absolute assurance of things promised, but not yet seen.<br><br>He has absolute assurance because he already experiences the things of God. They are already an inward possession, a spiritual surety, an assured expectation, a confident knowledge. |
| **#1206**<br>**Eagerness For Lustful Pleasure**<br><br>Lasciviousness–KJV<br>Sensuality–NASB<br>Lewdness–NIV<br>Lewdness–NKJV<br>Eagerness for lustful pleasure–NLT<br><br>**POSB REFERENCE**<br>(Mk.7:22)<br>*Deeper Study* #11<br><br>See also POSB REF:<br>(2 Cor.12:19-21; esp. v.21)<br>Note 3, point 2<br>(Gal.5:19-21; esp. v.19)<br>Note 2<br>(1 Pt.4:3)<br>Note 3, point 1 | ἀσέλγεια = aselgeia<br>Pronunciation: [as-elg'-i-a]<br>Parsing (part of speech): noun<br>  Case—nominative<br>  Gender—feminine<br>  Number—singular<br>  Stem or root—from ἀσέλγεια, ας<br>Concordance References:<br>⇒ Strong's #766 aselgeia<br>⇒ NIV #816 aselgeia<br>⇒ NASB #766 aselgeia<br><br>**Mark 7:22**<br>Thefts, covetousness, wickedness, deceit, **lasciviousness**, an evil eye, blasphemy, pride, foolishness: [KJV]<br>Deeds of coveting and wickedness, as well as deceit, **sensuality**, envy, slander, pride and foolishness. [NASB]<br>Greed, malice, deceit, **lewdness**, envy, slander, arrogance and folly. [NIV]<br>Thefts, covetousness, wickedness, deceit, **lewdness**, an evil eye, blasphemy, pride, foolishness. [NKJV]<br>Adultery, greed, wickedness, deceit, **eagerness for lustful pleasure**, envy, slander, pride, and foolishness. [NLT]<br>πλεονεξίαι, πονηρίαι, δόλος, **ἀσέλγεια**, ὀφθαλμὸς πονηρός, βλασφημία, ὑπερηφανία, ἀφροσύνη· [GNS]<br>μοιχεῖαι, πλεονεξίαι, πονηρίαι, δόλος, **ἀσέλγεια**, ὀφθαλμὸς πονηρός, βλασφημία, ὑπερηφανία, ἀφροσύνη· [GNT] | Debauchery; lasciviousness; lewdness; eagerness for lustful pleasure; sensuality and indecency; shamelessness; uncontrolled, undisciplined, and unrestrained lust and passion.<br><br>**Practical Application**<br>A chief characteristic of the behavior is open and shameless indecency. It means unrestrained evil thoughts and behavior. It is giving in to brutish and lustful desires, a readiness for any pleasure. It is a person who knows no restraint, an individual man who has sinned so much that he no longer cares what people say or think. It is something far more distasteful than just doing wrong. The person who misbehaves usually tries to hide his wrong, but a man with an *eagerness for lustful pleasure* does not care who knows about his exploits or shame. He wants; therefore, he seeks to take and gratify. Decency and opinion do not matter. When he initially began to sin, he did as all people men do: he misbehaved in secret. But eventually, the sin got the best of him—to the point that he no longer cared who saw or knew. He became the subject of a master—the master of habit, of the thing itself. People become the slaves of such things as unbridled lust, wantonness, licentiousness, outrageousness, shamelessness, insolence (Mark 7:22), wanton manners, filthy words, indecent body movements, immoral handling of males and females (Romans 13:13), carnality, gluttony, and sexual immorality (1 Peter 4:3; 2 Peter 2:2, 18). (Cp. 2 Cor. 12:21; Galatians 5:19; Ephes. 4:19; 2 Peter 2:7.) |
| **#1207**<br>**Eagerness, With Great**<br><br>With all readiness of mind–KJV<br>With great eagerness–NASB<br>With great eagerness–NIV<br>With all readiness–NKJV<br>Eagerly–NLT<br><br>**POSB REFERENCE**<br>(Acts 17:11)<br>Note 5 | μετὰ πάσης προθυμίας = meta pasēs prothumias<br>Pronunciation: [meh-tah pah-sace thro-thoo-me-ahs]<br>Parsing *pasēs* (part of speech): adjective<br>  Case—genitive<br>  Gender—feminine<br>  Number—singular<br>  Stem or root—from πᾶς, πᾶσα, πᾶν<br>Parsing *prothumias* (part of speech): noun<br>  Case—genitive<br>  Gender—feminine<br>  Number—singular<br>  Stem or root—from προθυμία, ας<br>Concordance References:<br>⇒ Strong's #3326 meta +3956 pas + 4288 prothumia<br>⇒ NIV #3552 meta [with] +4246 pas [great] + 4608 prothumia [eagerness]<br>⇒ NASB #3326 meta +3956 pas + 4288 prothumia<br><br>**Acts 17:11**<br>These were more noble than those in Thessalonica, in that they received the word **with all readiness of mind**, and searched the scriptures daily, whether those things were so. [KJV]<br>Now these were more noble-minded than those in Thessalonica, for they received the word **with great eagerness**, examining the Scriptures daily, to see | With great eagerness; with all readiness of mind; with willingness; with zeal. It means to have a willing desire, an eagerness, a hunger, a thirst to know the truth.<br><br>**Practical Application**<br>A noble people are an honest, thinking and searching people. They investigate, study, and seek to verify the message of truth. Note: the Bereans sought "with great eagerness" (*meta pasēs prothumias*): a willing desire, an eagerness, a hunger, a thirst to know the truth. A noble people do not shut their minds or hearts; they do not refuse to listen or consider.<br><br>Note another fact: a noble people do not just accept and swallow whatever is said. Paul himself was the authority proclaiming the truth, but the Bereans studied, investigated, and searched the Scriptures for the truth themselves. And they searched daily. The truth of God and His Word has no end; it is unfathomable. Discovering the truth is a daily responsibility. God has made it so (Luke 9:23). |

# PRACTICAL WORD STUDIES
## in the NEW TESTAMENT

| ENGLISH WORD | GREEK WORD AND VERSE | THE WORD MEANS... |
|---|---|---|
| | whether these things were so. [NASB]<br>　Now the Bereans were of more noble character than the Thessalonians, for they received the message **with great eagerness** and examined the Scriptures every day to see if what Paul said was true. [NIV]<br>　These were more fair-minded than those in Thessalonica, in that they received the word **with all readiness**, and searched the Scriptures daily *to find out* whether these things were so. [NKJV]<br>　And the people of Berea were more open-minded than those in Thessalonica, and they listened **eagerly** to Paul's message. They searched the Scriptures day after day to check up on Paul and Silas, to see if they were really teaching the truth. [NLT]<br>　οὗτοι δὲ ἦσαν εὐγενέστεροι τῶν ἐν Θεσσαλονίκῃ, οἵτινες ἐδέξαντο τὸν λόγον **μετὰ πάσης προθυμίας**, τὸ καθ᾽ ἡμέραν ἀνακρίνοντες τὰς γραφάς, εἰ ἔχοι ταῦτα οὕτως. [GNS]<br>　οὗτοι δὲ ἦσαν εὐγενέστεροι τῶν ἐν Θεσσαλονίκῃ, οἵτινες ἐδέξαντο τὸν λόγον **μετὰ πάσης προθυμίας** καθ᾽ ἡμέραν ἀνακρίνοντες τὰς γραφὰς εἰ ἔχοι ταῦτα οὕτως. [GNT] | |
| **#1208**<br>**Eagles, The**<br><br>**The eagles**–KJV<br>The vultures–NASB<br>The vultures–NIV<br>**The eagles**–NKJV<br>Vultures–NLT<br><br>**POSB REFERENCE**<br>(Lk.17:37)<br>Note 8 | οἱ ἀετοί = *hoi aetoi*<br>Pronunciation: [hoi ah-et-o-ee]<br>Parsing *aetoi* (part of speech): noun<br>　Case—nominative<br>　Gender—masculine<br>　Number—plural<br>　Stem or root—from ἀετός, οῦ<br>Concordance References:<br>　⇒ Strong's #3588 ho + 105 aetos<br>　⇒ NIV #3836 ho [the] + 108 aetos [vultures]<br>　⇒ NASB #3588 ho + 105 aetos<br><br>**Luke 17:37**<br>　And they answered and said unto him, Where, Lord? And he said unto them, Wheresoever the body is, thither will **the eagles** be gathered together. [KJV]<br>　And answering they said to Him, "Where, Lord?" And He said to them, "Where the body is, there also will **the vultures** be gathered." [NASB]<br>　"Where, Lord?" they asked. He replied, "Where there is a dead body, there **the vultures** will gather." [NIV]<br>　And they answered and said to Him, "Where, Lord?" So He said to them, "Wherever the body is, there **the eagles** will be gathered together." [NKJV]<br>　"Lord, where will this happen?" the disciples asked. Jesus replied, "Just as the gathering of **vultures** shows there is a carcass nearby, so these signs indicate that the end is near." [NLT]<br>　καὶ ἀποκριθέντες λέγουσιν αὐτῷ, Ποῦ, Κύριε; ὁ δὲ εἶπεν αὐτοῖς, Ὅπου τὸ σῶμα, ἐκεῖ συναχθήσονται **οἱ ἀετοί**. [GNS]<br>　καὶ ἀποκριθέντες λέγουσιν αὐτῷ, Ποῦ, κύριε; ὁ δὲ εἶπεν αὐτοῖς, Ὅπου τὸ σῶμα, ἐκεῖ καὶ **οἱ ἀετοὶ** ἐπισυναχθήσονται. [GNT] | Eagle or vulture.<br><br>**Practical Application**<br>　It probably should be translated vulture here, for they are the ones who gather universally as scavengers over dead bodies. Vultures gather where the dead are and feast upon them. Since death is universal, vultures are found everywhere. |
| **#1209**<br>**Early**<br><br>Beginning–KJV<br>Beginning–NASB<br>First–NIV<br>Beginning–NKJV<br>**Early**–NLT<br><br>**POSB REFERENCE**<br>(Lk.1:2-3, esp. v.2)<br>Note 3, point 2 | ἀρχῆς = *archēs*<br>Pronunciation: [ar-khays']<br>Parsing (part of speech): noun<br>　Case—genitive<br>　Gender—feminine<br>　Number—singular<br>　Stem or root—from ἀρχή, ῆς<br>Concordance References:<br>　⇒ Strong's #746 archē<br>　⇒ NIV #794 archē<br>　⇒ NASB #746 archē<br><br>**Luke 1:2**<br>　Even as they delivered them unto us, which from the **beginning** were eyewitnesses, and ministers of the word; [KJV] | The beginning, the first of all, the origin, the genesis, the dawn, the conception, the start, the commencement.<br><br>**Practical Application**<br>　In the context of this Scripture, Luke notes that the ministers of the Word were eyewitnesses from the beginning, from the first. They were "early" eyewitnesses of every event and word of Christ, eyewitnesses of His life day by day. |

# PRACTICAL WORD STUDIES
## in the NEW TESTAMENT

| ENGLISH WORD | GREEK WORD AND VERSE | THE WORD MEANS... |
|---|---|---|
| | Just as those who from the **beginning** were eyewitnesses and servants of the word have handed them down to us, [NASB]<br>Just as they were handed down to us by those who from the **first** were eyewitnesses and servants of the word. [NIV]<br>Just as those who from the **beginning** were eyewitnesses and ministers of the word delivered them to us, [NKJV]<br>They used as their source material the reports circulating among us from the **early** disciples and other eyewitnesses of what God has done in fulfillment of his promises. [NLT]<br>καθὼς παρέδοσαν ἡμῖν οἱ ἀπ' **ἀρχῆς** αὐτόπται καὶ ὑπηρέται γενόμενοι τοῦ λόγου, [GNS]<br>καθὼς παρέδοσαν ἡμῖν οἱ ἀπ' **ἀρχῆς** αὐτόπται καὶ ὑπηρέται γενόμενοι τοῦ λόγου, [GNT] | |
| **#1210**<br>**Earnest**<br><br>**Earnest**–KJV<br>Pledge–NASB<br>Deposit guaranteeing what is to come–NIV<br>Guarantee–NKJV<br>First installment–NLT<br><br>**POSB REFERENCE**<br>(2 Cor.1:21-22; esp. v.22)<br>Note 5 | ἀρραβῶνα = *arrabōna*<br>Pronunciation: [ar-hrab-ohn'-ah]<br>Parsing (part of speech): noun<br>  Case—accusative<br>  Gender—masculine<br>  Number—singular<br>  Stem or root—from ἀρραβών, ῶνος<br>Concordance References:<br>  ⇒ Strong's #728 arrabōn<br>  ⇒ NIV #775 arrabōn<br>  ⇒ NASB #728 arrabōn<br><br>**2 Cor. 1:22**<br>Who hath also sealed us, and given the **earnest** of the Spirit in our hearts. [KJV]<br>Who also sealed us and gave us the Spirit in our hearts as a **pledge**. [NASB]<br>Set his seal of ownership on us, and put his Spirit in our hearts as a **deposit, guaranteeing what is to come**. [NIV]<br>Who also has sealed us and given us the Spirit in our hearts as a **guarantee**. [NKJV]<br>And he has identified us as his own by placing the Holy Spirit in our hearts as the **first installment** of everything he will give us. [NLT]<br>ὁ καὶ σφραγισάμενος ἡμᾶς, καὶ δοὺς τὸν **ἀρραβῶνα** τοῦ Πνεύματος ἐν ταῖς καρδίαις ἡμῶν. [GNS]<br>ὁ καὶ σφραγισάμενος ἡμᾶς καὶ δοὺς τὸν **ἀρραβῶνα** τοῦ πνεύματος ἐν ταῖς καρδίαις ἡμῶν. [GNT] | Deposit, guarantee, security, pledge, first installment (of what is to come), payment.<br><br>**Practical Application**<br>It was the first installment paid on an item to guarantee that the rest would be paid. It was the engagement ring that guaranteed the marriage. God has given the Holy Spirit as the guarantee of eternal life. The Holy Spirit is an advanced payment, a down payment, on His promise to believers. |
| **#1211**<br>**Earnest**<br><br>Diligent–KJV<br>Diligent–NASB<br>Zealous–NIV<br>Diligent–NKJV<br>**Earnest**–NLT<br><br>**POSB REFERENCE**<br>(2 Cor.8:22)<br>Note 4 | σπουδαῖον = *spoudaion*<br>Pronunciation: [spoo-dah'-ee-on]<br>Parsing (part of speech): adjective<br>  Case—accusative<br>  Gender—masculine<br>  Number—singular<br>  Stem or root—from σπουδαῖος, α, ον<br>Concordance References:<br>  ⇒ Strong's #4705 spoudaios<br>  ⇒ NIV #5080 spoudaios<br>  ⇒ NASB #4705 spoudaios<br><br>**2 Cor. 8:22**<br>And we have sent with them our brother, whom we have oftentimes proved **diligent** in many things, but now much more diligent, upon the great confidence which I have in you. [KJV]<br>And we have sent with them our brother, whom we have often tested and found **diligent** in many things, but now even more diligent, because of his great confidence in you. [NASB]<br>In addition, we are sending with them our brother who has often proved to us in many ways that he is **zealous**, and now even more so because of his great confidence | Zealous, diligent, earnest, enthusiastic, eager, devoted.<br><br>**Practical Application**<br>Men who handle collections (ushers) are diligent in many things, but especially in collections. Who this unnamed brother was is not known. Three significant points are made about him, points that should speak to the heart of every church usher and person who handles collections.<br>1. He was a brother, a true believer who was in fellowship with other believers and cooperated with the church in its mission endeavors.<br>2. He had often shown how "earnest" (*spoudaion*) he was when other ministries had been assigned to him. He gave himself wholeheartedly to whatever task the church gave him.<br>3. He observed and was alert to the testimony of churches. When Paul told him about the Corinthian church—about the great revival of |

# PRACTICAL WORD STUDIES
## in the NEW TESTAMENT

| ENGLISH WORD | GREEK WORD AND VERSE | THE WORD MEANS... |
|---|---|---|
| | you. [NIV]<br>And we have sent with them our brother whom we have often proved **diligent** in many things, but now much more diligent, because of the great confidence which *we have* in you. [NKJV]<br>And we are also sending with them another brother who has been thoroughly tested and has shown how **earnest** he is on many occasions. He is now even more enthusiastic because of his increased confidence in you. [NLT]<br>συνεπέμψαμεν δὲ αὐτοῖς τὸν ἀδελφὸν ἡμῶν, ὃν ἐδοκιμάσαμεν ἐν πολλοῖς πολλάκις **σπουδαῖον**, ὄντα, νυνὶ δὲ πολὺ σπουδαιότερον πεποιθήσει πολλῇ τῇ εἰς ὑμᾶς. [GNS]<br>συνεπέμψαμεν δὲ αὐτοῖς τὸν ἀδελφὸν ἡμῶν ὃν ἐδοκιμάσαμεν ἐν πολλοῖς πολλάκις **σπουδαῖον** ὄντα, νυνὶ δὲ πολὺ σπουδαιότερον πεποιθήσει πολλῇ τῇ εἰς ὑμᾶς. [GNT] | the church—he became excited and was more willing than ever to serve Christ in the midst of the church. |
| **#1212**<br>**Earnest**<br><br>Earnest–KJV<br>Pledge–NASB<br>Deposit guaranteeing–NIV<br>Guarantee–NKJV<br>Guarantee–NLT<br><br>**POSB REFERENCE**<br>(Eph.1:13-14; esp. v.14)<br>Note 8 | ἀρραβών = *arrabōn*<br>Pronunciation: [ar-hrab-ohn']<br>Parsing (part of speech): noun<br>   Case—nominative<br>   Gender—masculine<br>   Number—singular<br>   Stem or root—from ἀρραβών, ῶνος<br>Concordance References:<br>  ⇒ Strong's #728 arrabōn<br>  ⇒ NIV #775 arrabōn<br>  ⇒ NASB #728 arrabōn<br><br>**Ephes. 1:14**<br>Which is the **earnest** of our inheritance until the redemption of the purchased possession, unto the praise of his glory. [KJV]<br>Who is given as a **pledge** of our inheritance, with a view to the redemption of God's own possession, to the praise of His glory. [NASB]<br>Who is a **deposit guaranteeing** our inheritance until the redemption of those who are God's possession—to the praise of his glory. [NIV]<br>Who is the **guarantee** of our inheritance until the redemption of the purchased possession, to the praise of His glory. [NKJV]<br>The Spirit is God's **guarantee** that he will give us everything he promised and that he has purchased us to be his own people. This is just one more reason for us to praise our glorious God. [NLT]<br>ὅς ἐστιν **ἀρραβών** τῆς κληρονομίας ἡμῶν, εἰς ἀπολύτρωσιν τῆς περιποιήσεως, εἰς ἔπαινον τῆς δόξης αὐτοῦ. [GNS]<br>ὅ ἐστιν **ἀρραβών** τῆς κληρονομίας ἡμῶν, εἰς ἀπολύτρωσιν τῆς περιποιήσεως, εἰς ἔπαινον τῆς δόξης αὐτοῦ. [GNT] | A deposit guaranteeing; an earnestness; a pledge; a guarantee; a down payment.<br><br>**Practical Application**<br>The Holy Spirit is given to the believer to give the believer perfect assurance of his salvation. We know that we are redeemed—that we are God's cherished possession—by the Holy Spirit who lives within us.<br>Again note: Why does God give us such a glorious guarantee as His own wonderful presence? That His glory might be praised eternally. |
| **#1213**<br>**Earnest**<br><br>Sober–KJV<br>Sound judgment–NASB<br>Clear minded–NIV<br>Serious–NKJV<br>**Earnest–NLT**<br><br>**POSB REFERENCE**<br>(1 Pt.4:7)<br>Note 1 | σωφρονήσατε = *sōphronēsate*<br>Pronunciation: [so-fron-ay'-sah-teh]<br>Parsing (part of speech): verb<br>   Mood—imperative<br>   Tense—aorist<br>   Voice—active<br>   Person—2nd person<br>   Number—plural<br>   Stem or root—from σωφρονέω<br>Concordance References:<br>  ⇒ Strong's #4993 sōphroneō<br>  ⇒ NIV #5404 sōphroneō<br>  ⇒ NASB #4993 sōphroneō<br><br>**1 Peter 4:7**<br>But the end of all things is at hand: be ye therefore **sober**, and watch unto prayer. [KJV]<br>The end of all things is at hand; therefore, be of **sound** | To be clear minded; to be sober; to exhibit sound judgment; to be earnest. This means to be serious and to have a sound mind; to be in control of oneself and to be self-restrained; to be calm and sensible.<br><br>**Practical Application**<br>The believer lives under the climax of history; he keeps his mind upon the return of Christ by doing three things.<br>1. He is earnest about everything. He is not a jolly, back-slapping, frivolous type of person. He takes life seriously, knowing that man has a purpose for being on earth, that life is the most meaningful and significant possession that man has. Therefore, he measures the importance of things. He measures all things |

# PRACTICAL WORD STUDIES
## in the NEW TESTAMENT

| ENGLISH WORD | GREEK WORD AND VERSE | THE WORD MEANS... |
|---|---|---|
| | **judgment** and sober spirit for the purpose of prayer. [NASB]<br><br>The end of all things is near. Therefore be **clear minded** and self-controlled so that you can pray. [NIV]<br><br>But the end of all things is at hand; therefore be **serious** and watchful in your prayers. [NKJV]<br><br>The end of the world is coming soon. Therefore, be **earnest** and disciplined in your prayers. [NLT]<br><br>Πάντων δὲ τὸ τέλος ἤγγικε· **σωφρονήσατε** οὖν καὶ νήψατε εἰς τὰς προσευχάς· [GNS]<br><br>Πάντων δὲ τὸ τέλος ἤγγικεν. **σωφρονήσατε** οὖν καὶ νήψατε εἰς προσευχάς· [GNT] | in light of eternity as well as time. He considers the future as well as the present. He knows that his life could be snatched from him overnight by some accident or by the news of some disease. The believer who keeps his mind upon the climax of history, upon the return of the Lord Jesus Christ, is a sober person; he is a serious-and sound-minded person.<br>2. He controls and restrains his desires and lusts and appetites. He never gives in to excess—to the lust for more and more. He controls sex and uses it for marriage. He controls desire for food and uses it for health. He controls the desire for material possessions and uses it to meet the needs of his family and the desperate needs of the world.<br>3. He is calm and sensible about all things. He is not overly shaken by trouble, problems, or circumstances that arise within his family, employment, society, or world. Family problems and world events just do not shake him. He is concerned but not shaken. He does not get overly excited with recreation, sports, or any other happening of life. He enjoys the happenings and experiences of life, but he keeps a sensible perspective of all things and gives each thing its proper place. |
| #1214<br>**Earnest Expecation**<br><br>**Earnest expectation– KJV**<br>**Earnest expectation– NASB**<br>Eagerly expect–NIV<br>**Earnest expectation– NKJV**<br>Eager expectation– NLT<br><br>**POSB REFERENCE**<br>(Philip.1:20)<br>Note 1, point 1 | **ἀποκαραδοκίαν** = apokaradokian<br>Pronunciation: [ap-ok-ar-ad-ok-ee'-ahn]<br>Parsing (part of speech): noun<br>  Case—accusative<br>  Gender—feminine<br>  Number—singular<br>  Stem or root—from **ἀποκαραδοκία**, ας<br>Concordance References:<br>⇒ Strong's #603 apokaradokia<br>⇒ NIV #638 apokaradokia<br>⇒ NASB #603 apokaradokia<br><br>**Philip. 1:20**<br>According to my **earnest expectation** and my hope, that in nothing I shall be ashamed, but that with all boldness, as always, so now also Christ shall be magnified in my body, whether it be by life, or by death. [KJV]<br><br>According to my **earnest expectation** and hope, that I shall not be put to shame in anything, but that with all boldness, Christ shall even now, as always, be exalted in my body, whether by life or by death. [NASB]<br><br>I **eagerly expect** and hope that I will in no way be ashamed, but will have sufficient courage so that now as always Christ will be exalted in my body, whether by life or by death. [NIV]<br><br>According to my **earnest expectation** and hope that in nothing I shall be ashamed, but with all boldness, as always, so now also Christ will be magnified in my body, whether by life or by death. [NKJV]<br><br>For I live in **eager expectation** and hope that I will never do anything that causes me shame, but that I will always be bold for Christ, as I have been in the past, and that my life will always honor Christ, whether I live or I die. [NLT]<br><br>κατὰ τὴν **ἀποκαραδοκίαν** καὶ ἐλπίδα μου, ὅτι ἐν οὐδενὶ αἰσχυνθήσομαι, ἀλλ' ἐν πάσῃ παρρησίᾳ, ὡς πάντοτε, καὶ νῦν μεγαλυνθήσεται Χριστὸς ἐν τῷ σώματί μου, εἴτε διὰ ζωῆς, εἴτε διὰ θανάτου. [GNS]<br><br>κατὰ τὴν **ἀποκαραδοκίαν** καὶ ἐλπίδα μου, ὅτι ἐν οὐδενὶ αἰσχυνθήσομαι ἀλλ' ἐν πάσῃ παρρησίᾳ ὡς πάντοτε καὶ νῦν μεγαλυνθήσεται Χριστὸς ἐν τῷ σώματί μου, εἴτε διὰ ζωῆς εἴτε διὰ θανάτου. [GNT] | Eager longing; deep desire; eager expectation for; earnest expectation.<br><br>**Practical Application**<br>It means to gaze into the distance with the head erect and outstretched just like a watchman on a tower. It is aiming one's attention at an object with concentration, eagerness, and intensity. It is turning the eyes away from everything else and focusing upon one object and one object alone. It is total concentration upon a person's desire. |

# PRACTICAL WORD STUDIES
## in the NEW TESTAMENT

| ENGLISH WORD | GREEK WORD AND VERSE | THE WORD MEANS... |
|---|---|---|
| **#1215**<br>**Earnest Expectation Of**<br><br>Earnest expectation of–KJV<br>Anxious longing of–NASB<br>Eager expectation for–NIV<br>Earnest expectation of–NKJV<br>Waiting eagerly for–NLT<br><br>**POSB REFERENCE**<br>(Romans 8:19-22; esp. v.19)<br>Note 2 | ἀποκαραδοκία = apokaradokia<br>Pronunciation: [ap-ok-ar-ad-ok-ee'-ah]<br>Parsing (part of speech): noun<br>    Case—nominative<br>    Gender—feminine<br>    Number—singular<br>    Stem or root—from ἀποκαραδοκία, ας<br>Concordance References:<br>  ⇒ Strong's #603 apokaradokia<br>  ⇒ NIV #638 apokaradokia<br>  ⇒ NASB #603 apokaradokia<br><br>**Romans 8:19**<br>For the **earnest expectation of** the creature waiteth for the manifestation of the sons of God. [KJV]<br>For the **anxious longing of** the creation waits eagerly for the revealing of the sons of God. [NASB]<br>The creation waits in **eager expectation for** the sons of God to be revealed. [NIV]<br>For the **earnest expectation of** the creation eagerly waits for the revealing of the sons of God. [NKJV]<br>For all creation is **waiting eagerly for** that future day when God will reveal who his children really are. [NLT]<br>ἡ γὰρ **ἀποκαραδοκία** τῆς κτίσεως τὴν ἀποκάλυψιν τῶν υἱῶν τοῦ Θεοῦ ἀπεκδέχεται· [GNS]<br>ἡ γὰρ **ἀποκαραδοκία** τῆς κτίσεως τὴν ἀποκάλυψιν τῶν υἱῶν τοῦ θεοῦ ἀπεκδέχεται. [GNT] | To have an eager longing; to have a deep desire; to have an earnest expectation; to have an anxious longing for.<br><br>**Practical Application**<br>The creation suffers and struggles for deliverance from corruption. The word "creation" refers to everything under man: animal, plant, and mineral. All creation is pictured as living and waiting expectantly for the day when the sons of God will be glorified. The words "earnest expectation" (*apokaradokia*) mean to watch with the neck outstretched and the head erect. It is a persistent, unswerving expectation, an expectation that does not give up but keeps looking until the event happens. |
| **#1216**<br>**Earnest Heed**<br><br>Earnest heed–KJV<br>Pay...attention to–NASB<br>Pay...attention...to–NIV<br>Earnest heed–NKJV<br>Listen...to–NLT<br><br>**POSB REFERENCE**<br>(Heb.2:1)<br>Note 1 | προσέχειν = prosechein<br>Pronunciation: [pros-ekh'-een]<br>Parsing (part of speech): verb<br>    Mood—infinitive<br>    Tense—present<br>    Voice—active<br>    Stem or root—from προσέχω<br>Concordance References:<br>  ⇒ Strong's #4337 prosechō<br>  ⇒ NIV #4668 prosechō<br>  ⇒ NASB #4337 prosechō<br><br>**Hebrews 2:1**<br>Therefore we ought to give the more **earnest heed** to the things which we have heard, lest at any time we should let them slip. [KJV]<br>For this reason we must **pay** much closer **attention to** what we have heard, lest we drift away from it. [NASB]<br>We must **pay** more careful **attention**, therefore, **to** what we have heard, so that we do not drift away. [NIV]<br>Therefore we must give the more **earnest heed** to the things we have heard, lest we drift away. [NKJV]<br>So we must **listen** very carefully **to** the truth we have heard, or we may drift away from it. [NLT]<br>Διὰ τοῦτο δεῖ περισσοτέρως ἡμᾶς **προσέχειν** τοῖς ἀκουσθεῖσι, μή ποτε παραρρυῶμεν. [GNS]<br>Διὰ τοῦτο δεῖ περισσοτέρως **προσέχειν** ἡμᾶς τοῖς ἀκουσθεῖσιν, μήποτε παραρυῶμεν. [GNT] | To pay attention; to heed; to listen to; to listen very carefully; to be careful; to be on guard.<br><br>**Practical Application**<br>Note how intense the warning is: we must pay attention to the gospel. We *must pay more careful attention* to the gospel. We are to pay the utmost attention to the gospel of salvation:<br>⇒ to listen more closely than ever before.<br>⇒ to pay more attention than ever before. |
| **#1217**<br>**Earnestly**<br><br>Without ceasing–KJV<br>Fervently–NASB<br>**Earnestly–NIV**<br>Constant–NKJV<br>**Earnestly–NLT**<br><br>**POSB REFERENCE**<br>(Acts 12:5-17; esp. v.5)<br>*Note 2, point 1c | ἐκτενῶς = ektenōs<br>Pronunciation: [ek-ten-os']<br>Parsing (part of speech): adjective adverb<br>    Stem or root—from ἐκτενῶς<br>Concordance References:<br>  ⇒ Strong's #1618 ektenes<br>  ⇒ NIV #1757 ektenōs<br>  ⇒ NASB #1619 ektenos<br><br>**Acts 12:5**<br>Peter therefore was kept in prison: but prayer was made **without ceasing** of the church unto God for him. [KJV]<br>So Peter was kept in the prison, but prayer for him was | Earnestly; deeply; ceaselessly; fervently; constantly.<br><br>**Practical Application**<br>The idea is intense prayer, prayer that captivates and focuses a person's concentration. The root meaning of the word is "to stretch out." The picture is that the church was stretched out, prostrate before God, earnestly and fervently crying out for God's sovereign deliverance of Peter. The church could do nothing and they knew it. Peter's only hope was God. |

# PRACTICAL WORD STUDIES
## in the NEW TESTAMENT

| ENGLISH WORD | GREEK WORD AND VERSE | THE WORD MEANS... |
|---|---|---|
| | being made **fervently** by the church to God. [NASB]<br>So Peter was kept in prison, but the church was **earnestly** praying to God for him. [NIV]<br>Peter was therefore kept in prison, but **constant** prayer was offered to God for him by the church. [NKJV]<br>But while Peter was in prison, the church prayed very **earnestly** for him. [NLT]<br>ὁ μὲν οὖν Πέτρος ἐτηρεῖτο ἐν τῇ φυλακῇ· προσευχὴ δὲ ἦν **ἐκτενῶς** γινομένη ὑπὸ τῆς ἐκκλησίας πρὸς τὸν Θεὸν ὑπὲρ αὐτοῦ. [GNS]<br>ὁ μὲν οὖν Πέτρος ἐτηρεῖτο ἐν τῇ φυλακῇ· προσευχὴ δὲ ἦν **ἐκτενῶς** γινομένη ὑπὸ τῆς ἐκκλησίας πρὸς τὸν θεὸν περὶ αὐτοῦ. [GNT] | |
| #1218<br>**Earnestly Seek**<br><br>Diligently seek–KJV<br>Seek–NASB<br>**Earnestly seek–NIV**<br>Seek–NKJV<br>Sincerely seek–NLT<br><br>**POSB REFERENCE**<br>(Heb.11:6)<br>Note 5, point 2b | ἐκζητοῦσιν = ekzētousin<br>Pronunciation: [ek-zay-too-sin]<br>Parsing (part of speech): verb<br>    Mood—participle<br>    Tense—present<br>    Voice—active<br>    Case—dative<br>    Gender—masculine<br>    Number—plural<br>    Stem or root—from ἐκζητέω<br>Concordance References:<br>  ⇒ Strong's #1567 ekzēteō<br>  ⇒ NIV #1699 ekzēteō<br>  ⇒ NASB #1567 ekzēteō<br><br>**Hebrews 11:6**<br>But without faith it is impossible to please him: for he that cometh to God must believe that he is, and that he is a rewarder of them that **diligently seek** him. [KJV]<br>And without faith it is impossible to please Him, for he who comes to God must believe that He is, and that He is a rewarder of those who **seek** Him. [NASB]<br>And without faith it is impossible to please God, because anyone who comes to him must believe that he exists and that he rewards those who **earnestly seek** him. [NIV]<br>But without faith *it is* impossible to please *Him,* for he who comes to God must believe that He is, and *that* He is a rewarder of those who diligently **seek** Him. [NKJV]<br>So, you see, it is impossible to please God without faith. Anyone who wants to come to him must believe that there is a God and that he rewards those who **sincerely seek** him. [NLT]<br>χωρὶς δὲ πίστεως ἀδύνατον εὐαρεστῆσαι· πιστεῦσαι γὰρ δεῖ τὸν προσερχόμενον τῷ Θεῷ, ὅτι ἐστι, καὶ τοῖς **ἐκζητοῦσιν** αὐτὸν μισθαποδότης γίνεται. [GNS]<br>χωρὶς δὲ πίστεως ἀδύνατον εὐαρεστῆσαι· πιστεῦσαι γὰρ δεῖ τὸν προσερχόμενον τῷ θεῷ ὅτι ἔστιν καὶ τοῖς **ἐκζητοῦσιν** αὐτὸν μισθαποδότης γίνεται. [GNT] | To earnestly seek; to diligently seek; to sincerely seek. It means to *seek out God*; to diligently seek to find Him and to follow Him.<br><br>**Practical Application**<br>God does not reward the sleepy eyed, the complacent, the non-thinker, the half-interested, the worldly-minded, the pleasure seeker. God rewards those who diligently seek to know and follow Him. The idea is that we must be in earnest and persevere, enduring to the end. What is the reward to those who diligently seek God? It is the same reward given to Abel and Enoch: righteousness and God's care in this life and deliverance from death to live eternally with God. |
| #1219<br>**Easily Angered**<br><br>Easily provoked–KJV<br>Provoked–NASB<br>**Easily angered–NIV**<br>Provoked–NKJV<br>Irritable–NLT<br><br>**POSB REFERENCE**<br>(1 Cor.13:4-7; esp. v.5)<br>Note 2, point 8 | παροξύνεται = paroxunetai<br>Pronunciation: [par-ox-oo'-neh-tah-ee]<br>Parsing (part of speech): verb<br>    Mood—indicative<br>    Tense—present<br>    Voice—passive<br>    Person—3rd person<br>    Number—singular<br>    Stem or root—from παροξύνομαι<br>Concordance References:<br>  ⇒ Strong's #3947 paroxunō<br>  ⇒ NIV #4236 paroxunō<br>  ⇒ NASB #3947 paroxunō<br><br>**1 Cor. 13:5**<br>Doth not behave itself unseemly, seeketh not her own, is not **easily provoked**, thinketh no evil; [KJV]<br>Does not act unbecomingly; it does not seek its own, is not **provoked**, does not take into account a wrong suffered, [NASB] | To be easily angered; to be easily provoked; to be greatly distressed; to be irritable; to be greatly upset.<br><br>**Practical Application**<br>Love is not easily angered (*paroxunetai*): not easily provoked; not ready to take offense; not quick tempered; not touchy. It is not easily aroused to anger; does not become "exasperated" (William Barclay). Love controls the emotions and never becomes angry without a cause (Romans 12:18). |

# PRACTICAL WORD STUDIES
## in the NEW TESTAMENT

| ENGLISH WORD | GREEK WORD AND VERSE | THE WORD MEANS... |
|---|---|---|
|  | It is not rude, it is not self-seeking, it is not **easily angered**, it keeps no record of wrongs. [NIV]<br>Does not behave rudely, does not seek its own, is not **provoked**, thinks no evil; [NKJV]<br>Or rude. Love does not demand its own way. Love is not **irritable**, and it keeps no record of when it has been wronged. [NLT]<br>οὐκ ἀσχημονεῖ, οὐ ζητεῖ τὰ ἑαυτῆς, οὐ **παροξύνεται**, οὐ λογίζεται τὸ κακόν, [GNS]<br>οὐκ ἀσχημονεῖ, οὐ ζητεῖ τὰ ἑαυτῆς, οὐ **παροξύνεται**, οὐ λογίζεται τὸ Κακόν. [GNT] |  |
| **#1220**<br>**Easily Beset**<br><br>Easily beset–KJV<br>Easily entangles–NASB<br>Easily entangles–NIV<br>Ensnares–NKJV<br>Slows us down–NLT<br><br>**POSB REFERENCE**<br>(Heb.12:1)<br>Note 2, point 1b | εὐπερίστατον = euperistaton<br>Pronunciation: [yoo-per-is'-taht-on]<br>Parsing (part of speech): adjective<br>    Case—accusative<br>    Gender—feminine<br>    Number—singular<br>    Stem or root—from εὐπερίστατος, ον<br>Concordance References:<br>⇒ Strong's #2139 euperistatos<br>⇒ NIV #2342 euperistatos<br>⇒ NASB #2139 euperistatos<br><br>**Hebrews 12:1**<br>Wherefore seeing we also are compassed about with so great a cloud of witnesses, let us lay aside every weight, and the sin which doth so **easily beset** us, and let us run with patience the race that is set before us, [KJV]<br>Therefore, since we have so great a cloud of witnesses surrounding us, let us also lay aside every encumbrance, and the sin which so **easily entangles** us, and let us run with endurance the race that is set before us, [NASB]<br>Therefore, since we are surrounded by such a great cloud of witnesses, let us throw off everything that hinders and the sin that so **easily entangles**, and let us run with perseverance the race marked out for us. [NIV]<br>Therefore we also, since we are surrounded by so great a cloud of witnesses, let us lay aside every weight, and the sin which so easily **ensnares** us, and let us run with endurance the race that is set before us, [NKJV]<br>Therefore, since we are surrounded by such a huge crowd of witnesses to the life of faith, let us strip off every weight that **slows us down**, especially the sin that so easily hinders our progress. And let us run with endurance the race that God has set before us. [NLT]<br>Τοιγαροῦν καὶ ἡμεῖς τοσοῦτον ἔχοντες περικείμενον ἡμῖν νέφος μαρτύρων, ὄγκον ἀποθέμενοι πάντα καὶ τὴν **εὐπερίστατον** ἁμαρτίαν, δι' ὑπομονῆς τρέχωμεν τὸν προκείμενον ἡμῖν ἀγῶνα, [GNS]<br>Τοιγαροῦν καὶ ἡμεῖς τοσοῦτον ἔχοντες περικείμενον ἡμῖν νέφος μαρτύρων, ὄγκον ἀποθέμενοι πάντα καὶ τὴν **εὐπερίστατον** ἁμαρτίαν, δι' ὑπομονῆς τρέχωμεν τὸν προκείμενον ἡμῖν ἀγῶνα [GNT] | To easily entangle, easily beset, slow us down. The words "easily beset" (*euperistaton*) mean the sin that clings, distracts, entangles, and trips up the Christian runner.<br><br>**Practical Application**<br>The Christian runner must strip off the sin which so easily trips or besets him. It is the picture of clothing's flapping around a person while he is running: it entangles and trips him, causing him to fall. What is the sin that entangles and trips believers? Various sins have been suggested as common to all believers. However, the exhortation speaks strongly to any *particular sin* that entangles and throws that believer. Each one of us must ask: What is the sin that so easily trips me? Pleasure, indulgence, the tongue, the flesh, pride, possessions, worldly friends, television, sports—what is it that consumes my energy, keeping me from following God fully and wholly—that trips me up far, far too often. We must strip it off or else it will entangle us and trip us up, and we will never finish the race. |
| **#1221**<br>**Easily Entangles**<br><br>Easily beset–KJV<br>**Easily entangles–NASB**<br>**Easily entangles–NIV**<br>Ensnares–NKJV<br>Slows us down–NLT<br><br>**POSB REFERENCE**<br>(Heb.12:1)<br>Note 2, point 1b | εὐπερίστατον = euperistaton<br>Pronunciation: [yoo-per-is'-taht-on]<br>Parsing (part of speech): adjective<br>    Case—accusative<br>    Gender—feminine<br>    Number—singular<br>    Stem or root—from εὐπερίστατος, ον<br>Concordance References:<br>⇒ Strong's #2139 euperistatos<br>⇒ NIV #2342 euperistatos<br>⇒ NASB #2139 euperistatos<br><br>**Hebrews 12:1**<br>Wherefore seeing we also are compassed about with so great a cloud of witnesses, let us lay aside every weight, and the sin which doth so **easily beset** us, and let us run with patience the race that is set before us, [KJV] | Easily entangles, easily beset, slows us down. The words "easily entangles" (*euperistaton*) mean the sin which clings, distracts, entangles, and trips up the Christian runner.<br><br>**Practical Application**<br>The Christian runner must strip off the sin which so easily trips or entangles him. It is the picture of clothing's flapping around a person while he is running: it entangles and trips him, causing him to fall. What is the sin that entangles and trips believers? Various sins have been suggested as common to all believers. However, the exhortation speaks strongly to every believer and to the *particular sin* that entangles and |

# PRACTICAL WORD STUDIES
## in the NEW TESTAMENT

| ENGLISH WORD | GREEK WORD AND VERSE | THE WORD MEANS... |
|---|---|---|
| | Therefore, since we have so great a cloud of witnesses surrounding us, let us also lay aside every encumbrance, and the sin which so **easily entangles** us, and let us run with endurance the race that is set before us, [NASB]<br><br>Therefore, since we are surrounded by such a great cloud of witnesses, let us throw off everything that hinders and the sin that so **easily entangles**, and let us run with perseverance the race marked out for us. [NIV]<br><br>Therefore we also, since we are surrounded by so great a cloud of witnesses, let us lay aside every weight, and the sin which so easily **ensnares us**, and let us run with endurance the race that is set before us, [NKJV]<br><br>Therefore, since we are surrounded by such a huge crowd of witnesses to the life of faith, let us strip off every weight that **slows us down**, especially the sin that so easily hinders our progress. And let us run with endurance the race that God has set before us. [NLT]<br><br>Τοιγαροῦν καὶ ἡμεῖς τοσοῦτον ἔχοντες περικείμενον ἡμῖν νέφος μαρτύρων, ὄγκον ἀποθέμενοι πάντα καὶ τὴν **εὐπερίστατον** ἁμαρτίαν, δι' ὑπομονῆς τρέχωμεν τὸν προκείμενον ἡμῖν ἀγῶνα, [GNS]<br><br>Τοιγαροῦν καὶ ἡμεῖς τοσοῦτον ἔχοντες περικείμενον ἡμῖν νέφος μαρτύρων, ὄγκον ἀποθέμενοι πάντα καὶ τὴν **εὐπερίστατον** ἁμαρτίαν, δι' ὑπομονῆς τρέχωμεν τὸν προκείμενον ἡμῖν ἀγῶνα [GNT] | throws that believer. Each one of us must ask: What is the sin that so easily traps me? Pleasure, indulgence, the tongue, the flesh, pride, possessions, worldly friends, television, sports—what is it that consumes my energy, keeping me from following God fully and wholly—that trips me up far, far too often. We must strip it off or else it will entangle us and trip us up, and we will never finish the race. |
| **#1222**<br>**Easily Provoked**<br><br>Easily provoked–KJV<br>Provoked–NASB<br>Easily angered–NIV<br>Provoked–NKJV<br>Irritable–NLT<br><br>**POSB REFERENCE**<br>(1 Cor.13:4-7; esp. v.5)<br>Note 2, point 8 | παροξύνεται = *paroxunetai*<br>Pronunciation: [par-ox-oo'-neh-tah-ee]<br>Parsing (part of speech): verb<br>   Mood—indicative<br>   Tense—present<br>   Voice—passive<br>   Person—3rd person<br>   Number—singular<br>   Stem or root—from παροξύνομαι<br>Concordance References:<br>  ⇒ Strong's #3947 paroxunō<br>  ⇒ NIV #4236 paroxunō<br>  ⇒ NASB #3947 paroxunō<br><br>**1 Cor. 13:5**<br>Doth not behave itself unseemly, seeketh not her own, is not **easily provoked**, thinketh no evil; [KJV]<br><br>Does not act unbecomingly; it does not seek its own, is not **provoked**, does not take into account a wrong suffered, [NASB]<br><br>It is not rude, it is not self-seeking, it is not **easily angered**, it keeps no record of wrongs. [NIV]<br><br>Does not behave rudely, does not seek its own, is not **provoked**, thinks no evil; [NKJV]<br><br>Or rude. Love does not demand its own way. Love is not **irritable**, and it keeps no record of when it has been wronged. [NLT]<br><br>οὐκ ἀσχημονεῖ, οὐ ζητεῖ τὰ ἑαυτῆς, οὐ **παροξύνεται**, οὐ λογίζεται τὸ κακόν, [GNS]<br><br>οὐκ ἀσχημονεῖ, οὐ ζητεῖ τὰ ἑαυτῆς, οὐ **παροξύνεται**, οὐ λογίζεται τὸ Κακόν, [GNT] | To be easily angered; to be easily provoked; to be greatly distressed; to be irritable; to be greatly upset.<br><br>**Practical Application**<br>Love is not easily provoked (*paroxunetai*): not easily angered; not ready to take offense; not quick tempered; not "touchy" (Phillips, as quoted by Leon Morris). It is not easily aroused to anger; does not become "exasperated" (Barclay). Love controls the emotions, and never becomes angry without a cause (Romans 12:18). |
| **#1223**<br>**Easy**<br><br>Easy–KJV<br>Easy–NASB<br>Easy–NIV<br>Easy–NKJV<br>Fits perfectly–NLT<br><br>**POSB REFERENCE**<br>(Mt.11:29-30; esp.v.30)<br>Note 2, point 1 | χρηστός = *chrēstos*<br>Pronunciation: [khrase-tos']<br>Parsing (part of speech): adjective<br>   Case—nominative<br>   Gender—masculine<br>   Number—singular<br>   Stem or root—from χρηστός, ή, όν<br>Concordance References:<br>  ⇒ Strong's #5543 chrēstos<br>  ⇒ NIV #5982 chrēstos<br>  ⇒ NASB #5543 chrēstos<br><br>**Matthew 11:30**<br>For my yoke is **easy**, and my burden is light. [KJV]<br><br>"For My yoke is **easy**, and My load is light." [NASB] | To be easy, well-fitting, good, kind, better.<br><br>**Practical Application**<br>In this Scripture, Christ is saying that His yoke, His life and task, are fitted to a person. It is just what a person needs, and it is easy, the easiest life and task the person could live and undertake. |

## PRACTICAL WORD STUDIES
### in the NEW TESTAMENT

| ENGLISH WORD | GREEK WORD AND VERSE | THE WORD MEANS... |
|---|---|---|
| | For my yoke is **easy** and my burden is light." [NIV]<br>For My yoke *is* **easy** and My burden is light." [NKJV]<br>For my yoke **fits perfectly**, and the burden I give you is light." [NLT]<br>ὁ γὰρ ζυγός μου **χρηστός**, καὶ τὸ φορτίον μου ἐλαφρόν ἐστιν. [GNS]<br>ὁ γὰρ ζυγός μου **χρηστός** καὶ τὸ φορτίον μου ἐλαφρόν ἐστιν. [GNT] | |
| **#1224**<br>**Easy To Be Intreated**<br><br>Easy to be intreated–KJV<br>Reasonable–NASB<br>Sumissive–NIV<br>Willing to yield–NKJV<br>Willing to yield to others–NLT<br><br>**POSB REFERENCE**<br>(Jas.3:17-18; esp. v.17)<br>Note 3, point 2d | εὐπειθής = *eupeithēs*<br>Pronunciation: [yoo-pi-thace']<br>Parsing (part of speech): adjective<br>    Case—nominative<br>    Gender—feminine<br>    Number—singular<br>    Stem or root—from εὐπειθής, ές<br>Concordance References:<br>  ⇒ Strong's #2138 *eupeithēs*<br>  ⇒ NIV #2340 *eupeithēs*<br>  ⇒ NASB #2138 *eupeithēs*<br><br>**James 3:17**<br>But the wisdom that is from above is first pure, then peaceable, gentle, and **easy to be intreated**, full of mercy and good fruits, without partiality, and without hypocrisy. [KJV]<br>But the wisdom from above is first pure, then peaceable, gentle, **reasonable**, full of mercy and good fruits, unwavering, without hypocrisy. [NASB]<br>But the wisdom that comes from heaven is first of all pure; then peace-loving, considerate, **submissive**, full of mercy and good fruit, impartial and sincere. [NIV]<br>But the wisdom that is from above is first pure, then peaceable, gentle, **willing to yield**, full of mercy and good fruits, without partiality and without hypocrisy. [NKJV]<br>But the wisdom that comes from heaven is first of all pure. It is also peace loving, gentle at all times, and **willing to yield to others**. It is full of mercy and good deeds. It shows no partiality and is always sincere. [NLT]<br>ἡ δὲ ἄνωθεν σοφία πρῶτον μὲν ἁγνή ἐστιν, ἔπειτα εἰρηνική, ἐπιεικής, εὐπειθής, μεστὴ ἐλέους καὶ καρπῶν ἀγαθῶν, ἀδιάκριτος καὶ ἀνυπόκριτος. [GNS]<br>ἡ δὲ ἄνωθεν σοφία πρῶτον μὲν ἁγνή ἐστιν, ἔπειτα εἰρηνική, ἐπιεικής, **εὐπειθής**, μεστὴ ἐλέους καὶ καρπῶν ἀγαθῶν, ἀδιάκριτος, ἀνυπόκριτος. [GNT] | To be submissive; to be reasonable; to be willing to yield to others, easy to be entreated, open to reason. The word means being willing to listen to reason and to appeal; being willing to change when one is wrong.<br><br>**Practical Application**<br>True wisdom is not stubborn or hard. The wise teacher listens to the voice and reasoning of God and of his fellow believers; and when he is wrong, he changes his behavior. |
| **#1225**<br>**Eat–Eats**<br><br>Eat–KJV<br>Eat–NASB<br>Eat–NIV<br>Eat–NKJV<br>Eats–NLT<br><br>**POSB REFERENCE**<br>(Jn.6:47-51; esp. v.50)<br>Note 3, point 2b | φάγῃ = *phagē*<br>Pronunciation: [fahg'-ay]<br>Parsing (part of speech): verb<br>    Mood—subjunctive<br>    Tense—aorist<br>    Voice—active<br>    Person—3rd person<br>    Number—singular<br>    Stem or root—from ἐσθίω and ἔσθω<br>Concordance References:<br>  ⇒ Strong's #2068 *esthiō*<br>  ⇒ NIV #2266 *esthiō*<br>  ⇒ NASB #2068 *esthiō*<br><br>**John 6:50**<br>This is the bread which cometh down from heaven, that a man may **eat** thereof, and not die. [KJV]<br>"This is the bread which comes down out of heaven, so that one may **eat** of it and not die. [NASB]<br>But here is the bread that comes down from heaven, which a man may **eat** and not die. [NIV]<br>This is the bread which comes down from heaven, that one may **eat** of it and not die. [NKJV]<br>However, the bread from heaven gives eternal life to everyone who **eats** it. [NLT] | To spiritually eat or drink; to partake; to consume Christ; to have a feast.<br><br>**Practical Application**<br>What does it mean to the person who "eats" Christ? It means to receive, accept, partake, appropriate, assimilate, absorb, and to make part of oneself. A person can actually receive and partake of Christ in the closest and most intimate and nourishing sense of his being (flesh and blood). The receiving and partaking can be just as intimate and nourishing as eating and drinking.<br>The point is this: a person must receive Christ into his heart, into his innermost being if he wishes to live. In fact, he is dead spiritually and eternally unless he so receives Christ.<br>Note: the word "eat" is in the Greek aorist tense. This means that a person eats and partakes (receives) of Christ once-for-all. It is a one time experience. |

## PRACTICAL WORD STUDIES in the NEW TESTAMENT

| ENGLISH WORD | GREEK WORD AND VERSE | THE WORD MEANS... |
|---|---|---|
| | οὗτός ἐστιν ὁ ἄρτος ὁ ἐκ τοῦ οὐρανοῦ καταβαίνων, ἵνα τις ἐξ αὐτοῦ **φάγῃ** καὶ μὴ ἀποθάνῃ. [GNS]<br>οὗτός ἐστιν ὁ ἄρτος ὁ ἐκ τοῦ οὐρανοῦ καταβαίνων, ἵνα τις ἐξ αὐτοῦ **φάγῃ** καὶ μὴ ἀποθάνῃ. [GNT] | |
| **#1226**<br>**Eaten By Worms–Eaten Of Worms**<br><br>Eaten of worms–KJV<br>Eaten by worms–NASB<br>Eaten by worms–NIV<br>Eaten by worms–NKJV<br>Consumed with worms–NLT<br><br>**POSB REFERENCE**<br>(Acts 12:18-23; esp. v.23)<br>Note 3, point 2 | σκωληκόβρωτος = *skōlēkobrōtos*<br>Pronunciation: [sko-lay-kob'-ro-tos]<br>Parsing (part of speech): adjective<br>    Case—nominative<br>    Gender—masculine<br>    Number—singular<br>    Stem or root—from σκωληκόβρωτος, ον<br>Concordance References:<br>  ⇒ Strong's #4662 *skōlēkobrōtos*<br>  ⇒ NIV #5037 *skōlēkobrōtos*<br>  ⇒ NASB #4662 *skōlēkobrōtos*<br><br>**Acts 12:23**<br>And immediately the angel of the Lord smote him, because he gave not God the glory: and he **was eaten of worms**, and gave up the ghost. [KJV]<br>And immediately an angel of the Lord struck him because he did not give God the glory, and he **was eaten by worms** and died. [NASB]<br>Immediately, because Herod did not give praise to God, an angel of the Lord struck him down, and he **was eaten by worms** and died. [NIV]<br>Then immediately an angel of the Lord struck him, because he did not give glory to God. And he **was eaten by worms** and ied. [NKJV]<br>Instantly, an angel of the Lord struck Herod with a sickness, because he accepted the people's worship instead of giving the glory to God. So he **was consumed with worms** and died. [NLT]<br>παραχρῆμα δὲ ἐπάταξεν αὐτὸν ἄγγελος Κυρίου, ἀνθ' ὧν οὐκ ἔδωκε τὴν δόξαν τῷ Θεῷ· καὶ γενόμενος **σκωληκόβρωτος**, ἐξέψυξεν. [GNS]<br>παραχρῆμα δὲ ἐπάταξεν αὐτὸν ἄγγελος κυρίου ἀνθ' ὧν οὐκ ἔδωκεν τὴν δόξαν τῷ θεῷ, καὶ γενόμενος **σκωληκόβρωτος** ἐξέψυξεν. [GNT] | To be eaten by worms; to be consumed by worms.<br><br>**Practical Application**<br>The word *skolex* was used by the Greeks to refer to intestinal worms. Josephus, the renowned historian of that day, reported that Herod lingered for five days, suffering great pain in the area of the stomach (Flavius Josephus. *Josephus Complete Works*. Translated by William Whiston. Grand Rapids, MI: Kregel, 1960. Ant. 19.8.2). |
| **#1227**<br>**Eating**<br><br>Eating–KJV<br>Eating–NASB<br>Eating–NIV<br>Eating–NKJV<br>Enjoying banquets–NLT<br><br>**POSB REFERENCE**<br>(Mt.24:38)<br>*Deeper Study #3* | τρώγοντες = *trōgontes*<br>Pronunciation: [tro'-gon-tes]<br>    Parsing (part of speech): verb<br>    Mood—participle<br>    Tense—present<br>    Voice—active<br>    Case—nominative<br>    Gender—masculine<br>    Number—plural<br>    Stem or root—from τρώγω<br>Concordance References:<br>  ⇒ Strong's #5176 *trōgō*<br>  ⇒ NIV #5592 *trōgō*<br>  ⇒ NASB #5176 *trōgō*<br><br>**Matthew 24:38**<br>For as in the days that were before the flood they were **eating** and drinking, marrying and giving in marriage, until the day that Noah entered into the ark, [KJV]<br>"For as in those days which were before the flood they were **eating** and drinking, they were marrying and giving in marriage, until the day that Noah entered the ark [NASB]<br>For in the days before the flood, people were **eating** and drinking, marrying and giving in marriage, up to the day Noah entered the ark; [NIV]<br>For a in the days before the flood, they were **eating** and drinking, marrying and giving in marriage, until the day that Noah entered the ark, [NKJV]<br>In those days before the Flood, the people were **enjoying banquets** and parties and weddings right up | To eat; to gnaw; to chew; to feed on. It has the idea of grabbing and gnawing greedily like a hungry dog.<br><br>**Practical Application**<br>Here it means the habitual practice of eating with a gluttonous appetite, eating excessively.<br>The gluttonous, the well fed, are those who are filled with all that the world has to offer; in essence they are full of themselves, their own desires, urges, and cravings. They have no hunger for righteousness at all. Scripture identifies the full as those...<br>• who fill their bellies with the husks of the world (Luke 15:16).<br>• who serve their own bellies and not the Lord Jesus Christ (Romans 16:18).<br>• who indulge in the meats (things, sins) of the world (1 Cor. 6:13; cp. 1 Cor. 6:9-13).<br>• who make their god their belly (1 Cor. 3:19).<br>• who "[are] filled with all unrighteousness, [such as] fornication, wickedness, covetousness, maliciousness; full of envy, murder, debate, deceit, malignity; whisperers, backbiters, haters of God, despiteful, proud, boasters, inventors of evil things, disobedient to parents, without understanding, covenant breakers, without natural affection, implacable, unmerciful: who knowing the judgment of God, that they which commit such things |

**PRACTICAL WORD STUDIES**
in the NEW TESTAMENT

| ENGLISH WORD | GREEK WORD AND VERSE | THE WORD MEANS... |
|---|---|---|
| | to the time Noah entered his boat. [NLT]<br><br>ὥσπερ γὰρ ἦσαν ἐν ταῖς ἡμέραις ταῖς πρὸ τοῦ κατακλυσμοῦ **τρώγοντες** καὶ πίνοντες, γαμοῦντες καὶ ἐκγαμίζοντες, ἄχρι ἧς ἡμέρας εἰσῆλθε Νῶε εἰς τὴν κιβωτόν, [GNS]<br><br>ὡς γὰρ ἦσαν ἐν ταῖς ἡμέραις [ἐκείναις] ταῖς πρὸ τοῦ κατακλυσμοῦ **τρώγοντες** καὶ πίνοντες, γαμοῦντες καὶ γαμίζοντες, ἄχρι ἧς ἡμέρας εἰσῆλθεν Νῶε εἰς τὴν κιβωτόν, [GNT] | are worthy of death, not only do the same, but have pleasure in them that do them" (Romans 1:29-32). [KJV]<br><br>The judgment of the full will be hunger. This means they...<br>• will leave all that filled them behind when they die (Luke 12:20; Luke 16:25).<br>• will have no desires filled after this life.<br>• will have no delights fulfilled throughout eternity.<br>• will hunger for good things (righteous things) throughout eternity. |
| **#1228**<br>**Eats–**<br>**Eateth–**<br>**Eat**<br><br>Eateth–KJV<br>Eats–NASB<br>Eats–NIV<br>Eats–NKJV<br>Eat–NLT<br><br>**POSB**<br>**REFERENCE**<br>(Jn.6:54)<br>Note 2, point 1 | τρώγων = *trōgōn*<br>Pronunciation: [tro'-gon]<br>Parsing (part of speech): verb<br>    Mood—participle<br>    Tense—present<br>    Voice—active<br>    Case—nominative<br>    Gender—masculine<br>    Number—singular<br>    Stem or root—from τρώγω<br>Concordance References:<br>  ⇒ Strong's #5176 trogo<br>  ⇒ NIV #5592 trogo<br>  ⇒ NASB #5176 trogo<br><br>**John 6:54**<br>Whoso **eateth** my flesh, and drinketh my blood, hath eternal life; and I will raise him up at the last day. [KJV]<br>"He who **eats** My flesh and drinks My blood has eternal life, and I will raise him up on the last day. [NASB]<br>Whoever **eats** my flesh and drinks my blood has eternal life, and I will raise him up at the last day. [NIV]<br>Whoever **eats** My flesh and drinks My blood has eternal life, and I will raise him up at the last day. [NKJV]<br>But those who **eat** my flesh and drink my blood have eternal life, and I will raise them at the last day. [NLT]<br>ὁ **τρώγων** μου τὴν σάρκα καὶ πίνων μου τὸ αἷμα, ἔχει ζωὴν αἰώνιον, καὶ ἐγὼ ἀναστήσω αὐτὸν τῇ ἐσχάτῃ ἡμέρᾳ. [GNS]<br>ὁ **τρώγων** μου τὴν σάρκα καὶ πίνων μου τὸ αἷμα ἔχει ζωὴν αἰώνιον, κἀγὼ ἀναστήσω αὐτὸν τῇ ἐσχάτῃ ἡμέρᾳ. [GNT] | To eat eagerly, to grasp at chunks; to eat with pleasure; to chew.<br><br>**Practical Application**<br>It is the picture of hungering after Christ and eagerly wanting to feed and feast on Him. This word is in the present tense, which means continuous action. A person must continue to eat and to develop and grow into the habit of feasting upon Christ. Christian growth day by day is the picture.<br>    Now note the point. A genuine believer, a person who really receives Christ, is a person who partakes of Him continually. Day by day the person will feast upon Christ. |
| **#1229**<br>**Edification**<br><br>**Edification–KJV**<br>**Edification–NASB**<br>Strengthening–NIV<br>**Edification–NKJV**<br>Helping others grow in the Lord–NLT<br><br>**POSB**<br>**REFERENCE**<br>(1 Cor.14:3)<br>*Deeper Study* #1, point 1 | οἰκοδομὴν = *oikodomēn*<br>Pronunciation: [oy-kod-om-ayn']<br>Parsing (part of speech): noun<br>    Case—accusative<br>    Gender—feminine<br>    Number—singular<br>    Stem or root—from οἰκοδομή, ῆς<br>Concordance References:<br>  ⇒ Strong's #3619 oikodomē<br>  ⇒ NIV #3869 oikodomē<br>  ⇒ NASB #3619 oikodomē<br><br>**1 Cor. 14:3**<br>But he that prophesieth speaketh unto men to **edification**, and exhortation, and comfort. [KJV]<br>But one who prophesies speaks to men for **edification** and exhortation and consolation. [NASB]<br>But everyone who prophesies speaks to men for their **strengthening**, encouragement and comfort. [NIV]<br>But he who prophesies speaks **edification** and exhortation and comfort to men. [NKJV]<br>But one who prophesies is **helping others grow in the Lord**, encouraging and comforting them. [NLT] | To strengthen; to build up; to edify; to help others grow in the Lord; to encourage.<br><br>**Practical Application**<br>*Edification* (*oikodomēn*) is a construction word referring to constructing some building. The first purpose of prophecy is to build up people. |

## PRACTICAL WORD STUDIES
### in the NEW TESTAMENT

| ENGLISH WORD | GREEK WORD AND VERSE | THE WORD MEANS... |
|---|---|---|
| | ὁ δὲ προφητεύων ἀνθρώποις λαλεῖ **οἰκοδομὴν** καὶ παράκλησιν καὶ παραμυθίαν. [GNS]<br>ὁ δὲ προφητεύων ἀνθρώποις λαλεῖ **οἰκοδομὴν** καὶ παράκλησιν καὶ παραμυθίαν. [GNT] | |
| **#1230**<br>**Edified**<br><br>**Edified–KJV**<br>Being built up–NASB<br>Strengthened–NIV<br>**Edified–NKJV**<br>Grew in strength–NLT<br><br>**POSB REFERENCE**<br>(Acts 9:31)<br>Note 2 | **οἰκοδομουμένη** = *oikodomoumenë*<br>Pronunciation: [oy-kod-om-oo'-mehn-ah-ee]<br>Parsing (part of speech): verb<br>  Mood—participle<br>  Tense—present<br>  Voice—passive<br>  Case—nominative<br>  Gender—feminine<br>  Number—singular<br>  Stem or root—from **οἰκοδομέω**<br>Concordance References:<br>  ⇒ Strong's #3618 oikodomeö<br>  ⇒ NIV #3868 oikodomeö<br>  ⇒ NASB #3618 oikodomeö<br><br>**Acts 9:31**<br>Then had the churches rest throughout all Judaea and Galilee and Samaria, and were **edified**; and walking in the fear of the Lord, and in the comfort of the Holy Ghost, were multiplied. [KJV]<br>So the church throughout all Judea and Galilee and Samaria enjoyed peace, **being built up**; and, going on in the fear of the Lord and in the comfort of the Holy Spirit, it continued to increase. [NASB]<br>Then the church throughout Judea, Galilee and Samaria enjoyed a time of peace. It was **strengthened**; and encouraged by the Holy Spirit, it grew in numbers, living in the fear of the Lord. [NIV]<br>Then the churches throughout all Judea, Galilee, and Samaria had peace and were **edified**. And walking in the fear of the Lord and in the comfort of the Holy Spirit, they were multiplied. [NKJV]<br>The church then had peace throughout Judea, Galilee, and Samaria, and it **grew in strength** and numbers. The believers were walking in the fear of the Lord and in the comfort of the Holy Spirit. [NLT]<br>Αἱ μὲν οὖν ἐκκλησίαι καθ' ὅλης τῆς Ἰουδαίας καὶ Γαλιλαίας καὶ Σαμαρείας εἶχον εἰρήνην, **οἰκοδομούμεναι** καὶ πορευόμεναι τῷ φόβῳ τοῦ Κυρίου, καὶ τῇ παρακλήσει τοῦ Ἁγίου Πνεύματος ἐπληθύνετο. [GNS]<br>Ἡ μὲν οὖν ἐκκλησία καθ' ὅλης τῆς Ἰουδαίας καὶ Γαλιλαίας καὶ Σαμαρείας εἶχεν εἰρήνην **οἰκοδομουμένη** καὶ πορευομένη τῷ φόβῳ τοῦ κυρίου καὶ τῇ παρακλήσει τοῦ ἁγίου πνεύματος ἐπληθύνετο. [GNT] | To be strengthened; to be edified; to build; to encourage; to restore; to help others grow in Christ.<br><br>**Practical Application**<br>The word means to build up; to grow spiritually; to promote spiritual growth; to strengthen; to establish; to confirm in the faith. The tense is continuous action. |
| **#1231**<br>**Edify**<br><br>**Edify–KJV**<br>Build up–NASB<br>Build...up–NIV<br>**Edify–NKJV**<br>Build Up–NLT<br><br>**POSB REFERENCE**<br>(1 Thes.5:11)<br>Note 4 | **οἰκοδομεῖτε** = *oikodomeite*<br>Pronunciation: [oy-kod-om-eh'-ee-teh]<br>Parsing (part of speech): verb<br>  Mood—imperative<br>  Tense—present<br>  Voice—active<br>  Person—2nd person<br>  Number—plural<br>  Stem or root—from **οἰκοδομέω**<br>Concordance References:<br>  ⇒ Strong's #3618 oikodomeö<br>  ⇒ NIV #3868 oikodomeö<br>  ⇒ NASB #3618 oikodomeö<br><br>**1 Thes. 5:11**<br>Wherefore comfort yourselves together, and **edify** one another, even as also ye do. [KJV]<br>Therefore encourage one another, and **build up** one another, just as you also are doing. [NASB]<br>Therefore encourage one another and **build** each other **up**, just as in fact you are doing. [NIV]<br>Therefore comfort each other and **edify** one another, | To build up; to edify; to strengthen; to encourage; to restore; to erect; to rebuild.<br><br>**Practical Application**<br>We are to "*edify*" (*oikodomeite*) one another: strengthen and build one another up. The believer is to speak only that which is good and which will edify or build up people. Speech is for the purpose...<br>  • of sharing good things.<br>  • of building up and strengthening people.<br>  • of ministering grace (favor, blessings) and helping one another as we plow through life. |

## PRACTICAL WORD STUDIES
## in the NEW TESTAMENT

| ENGLISH WORD | GREEK WORD AND VERSE | THE WORD MEANS... |
|---|---|---|
| | just as you also are doing. [NKJV]<br>So encourage each other and **build** each other **up**, just as you are already doing. [NLT]<br>διὸ παρακαλεῖτε ἀλλήλους, καὶ **οἰκοδομεῖτε** εἰς τὸν ἕνα, καθὼς καὶ ποιεῖτε. [GNS]<br>Διὸ παρακαλεῖτε ἀλλήλους καὶ **οἰκοδομεῖτε** εἰς τὸν ἕνα, καθὼς καὶ ποιεῖτε. [GNT] | |
| **#1232**<br>**Effeminate**<br><br>Effeminate–KJV<br>Effeminate–NASB<br>Male prostitutes–NIV<br>Homosexuals–NKJV<br>Male prostitutes–NLT<br><br>**POSB REFERENCE**<br>(1 Cor.6:9)<br>Note 2, point 4 | μαλακοὶ = *malakoi*<br>Pronunciation: [mal-ak-oy-ee']<br>Parsing (part of speech): pronominal adjective<br>    Case—nominative<br>    Gender—masculine<br>    Number—plural<br>    Stem or root—from μαλακός, ή, όν<br>Concordance References:<br>  ⇒ Strong's #3120 malakos<br>  ⇒ NIV #3434 malakos<br>  ⇒ NASB #3120 malakos<br><br>**1 Cor. 6:9**<br>Know ye not that the unrighteous shall not inherit the kingdom of God? Be not deceived: neither fornicators, nor idolaters, nor adulterers, nor **effeminate**, nor abusers of themselves with mankind, [KJV]<br>Or do you not know that the unrighteous shall not inherit the kingdom of God? Do not be deceived; neither fornicators, nor idolaters, nor adulterers, nor **effeminate**, nor homosexuals, [NASB]<br>Do you not know that the wicked will not inherit the kingdom of God? Do not be deceived: Neither the sexually immoral nor idolaters nor adulterers nor **male prostitutes** nor homosexual offenders [NIV]<br>Do you not know that the unrighteous will not inherit the kingdom of God? Do not be deceived. Neither fornicators, nor idolaters, nor adulterers, nor **homosexuals**, nor sodomites, [NKJV]<br>Don't you know that those who do wrong will have no share in the Kingdom of God? Don't fool yourselves. Those who indulge in sexual sin, who are idol worshipers, adulterers, **male prostitutes**, homosexuals, [NLT]<br>ἢ οὐκ οἴδατε ὅτι ἄδικοι βασιλείαν Θεοῦ οὐ κληρονομήσουσι; μὴ πλανᾶσθε· οὔτε πόρνοι, οὔτε εἰδωλολάτραι, οὔτε μοιχοί, οὔτε **μαλακοί**, οὔτε ἀρσενοκοῖται, [GNS]<br>ἢ οὐκ οἴδατε ὅτι ἄδικοι θεοῦ βασιλείαν οὐ κληρονομήσουσιν; μὴ πλανᾶσθε· οὔτε πόρνοι οὔτε εἰδωλολάτραι οὔτε μοιχοὶ οὔτε **μαλακοὶ** οὔτε ἀρσενοκοῖται [GNT] | Male prostitutes; effeminate; a homosexual pervert; gay.<br><br>**Practical Application**<br>The sin of homosexuality takes place in the heart. Men and women *burn within*, crave the sin before they commit the act. It is their burning, their lusting, their craving that sets them aflame to pursue the shameful act. Their heart burns after other men and women, not after God. Therefore, they stand condemned, and God is forced to judge them. They "will not inherit the kingdom of God. Do not be deceived." |
| **#1233**<br>**Eight Hundred Gallons**<br><br>Hundred measures–KJV<br>Hundred measures–NASB<br>**Eight hundred gallons–NIV**<br>Hundred measures–NKJV<br>**Eight hundred gallons–NLT**<br><br>**POSB REFERENCE**<br>(Lk.16:6-7; esp. v.6)<br>Deeper Study #1 | Ἑκατὸν βάτους = *hekaton batous*<br>Pronunciation: [hek-at-on bat'-oos]<br>Parsing *hekaton* (part of speech): adjective<br>    Type—cardinal<br>    Case—accusative<br>    Gender—masculine<br>    Number—plural<br>    Stem or root—from ἑκατόν<br>Parsing *batous* (part of speech): noun<br>    Case—accusative<br>    Gender—masculine<br>    Number—plural<br>    Stem or root—from βάτος, ου<br>Concordance References:<br>  ⇒ Strong's #1540 hekaton + 943 batos<br>  ⇒ NIV #1004 batos2+1669 hekaton [eight hundred gallons]<br>  ⇒ NASB #1540 hekaton + 943 batos<br><br>**Luke 16:6**<br>And he said, An **hundred measures** of oil. And he said unto him, Take thy bill, and sit down quickly, and write fifty. [KJV] | Eight hundred gallons or a hundred measures. The word (*hekaton*) means hundred or hundreds. The word (*batous*) means a liquid measure of 65 pints or approximately 8 gallons.<br><br>**Practical Application**<br>A measure of oil was about 8 ¾ gallons. Therefore, the payment was a sizable 800 gallons. |

# PRACTICAL WORD STUDIES
## in the NEW TESTAMENT

| ENGLISH WORD | GREEK WORD AND VERSE | THE WORD MEANS... |
|---|---|---|
| | "And he said, 'A **hundred measures** of oil.' And he said to him, 'Take your bill, and sit down quickly and write fifty.' [NASB]<br>"'**Eight hundred gallons** of olive oil,' he replied."The manager told him, 'Take your bill, sit down quickly, and make it four hundred.' [NIV]<br>And he said, 'A **hundred measures** of oil.' So he said to him, 'Take your bill, and sit down quickly, and write fifty.' [NKJV]<br>The man replied, 'I owe him **eight hundred gallons** of olive oil.' So the manager told him, 'Tear up that bill and write another one for four hundred gallons.' [NLT]<br>ὁ δὲ εἶπεν, Ἑκατὸν βάτους ἐλαίου. καὶ εἶπεν αὐτῷ, Δέξαι σου τὰ γράμμα, καὶ καθίσας ταχέως γράψον πεντήκοντα. [GNS]<br>ὁ δὲ εἶπεν, Ἑκατὸν βάτους ἐλαίου. ὁ δὲ εἶπεν αὐτῷ, Δέξαι σου τὰ γράμματα καὶ καθίσας ταχέως γράψον πεντήκοντα. [GNT] | |
| **#1234**<br>**Elders**<br><br>Overseers–KJV<br>Overseers–NASB<br>Overseers–NIV<br>Overseers–NKJV<br>**Elders–NLT**<br><br>**POSB REFERENCE**<br>(Acts 20:28-31; esp. v.28)<br>Note 2, point 2 | ἐπισκόπους = episkopous<br>Pronunciation: [ep-is'-kop-oos]<br>Parsing (part of speech): noun<br>    Case—accusative<br>    Gender—masculine<br>    Number—plural<br>    Stem or root—from ἐπίσκοπος, ου<br>Concordance References:<br>  ⇒ Strong's #1985 episkopos<br>  ⇒ NIV #2176 episkopos<br>  ⇒ NASB #1985 episkopos<br><br>**Acts 20:28**<br>Take heed therefore unto yourselves, and to all the flock, over the which the Holy Ghost hath made you **overseers**, to feed the church of God, which he hath purchased with his own blood. [KJV]<br>"Be on guard for yourselves and for all the flock, among which the Holy Spirit has made you **overseers**, to shepherd the church of God which He purchased with His own blood. [NASB]<br>Keep watch over yourselves and all the flock of which the Holy Spirit has made you **overseers**. Be shepherds of the church of God, which he bought with his own blood. [NIV]<br>Therefore take heed to yourselves and to all the flock, among which the Holy Spirit has made you **overseers**, to shepherd the church of God which He purchased with His own blood. [NKJV]<br>"And now beware! Be sure that you feed and shepherd God's flock—his church, purchased with his blood—over whom the Holy Spirit has appointed you as **elders**. [NLT]<br>προσέχετε οὖν ἑαυτοῖς καὶ παντὶ τῷ ποιμνίῳ, ἐν ᾧ ὑμᾶς τὸ Πνεῦμα τὸ Ἅγιον ἔθετο **ἐπισκόπους**, ποιμαίνειν τὴν ἐκκλησίαν τοῦ Θεοῦ, ἣν περιεποιήσατο διὰ τοῦ ἰδίου αἵματος. [GNS]<br>προσέχετε ἑαυτοῖς καὶ παντὶ τῷ ποιμνίῳ, ἐν ᾧ ὑμᾶς τὸ πνεῦμα τὸ ἅγιον ἔθετο **ἐπισκόπους** ποιμαίνειν τὴν ἐκκλησίαν τοῦ θεοῦ, ἣν περιεποιήσατο διὰ τοῦ αἵματος τοῦ ἰδίου. [GNT] | Overseers, elders, guardians, bishops.<br><br>**Practical Application**<br>Note the terms are used interchangeably: elder (Acts 20:17), bishop (Acts 20:28), overseer or *episkopate* (Acts 20:28), and shepherd (feed, Acts 20:28). (See POSB *Deeper Study* #1, Elder—Titus 1:5-9 for discussion.) |
| **#1235**<br>**Elders**<br><br>Bishops–KJV<br>Overseers–NASB<br>Overseers–NIV<br>Bishops–NKJV<br>**Elders–NLT** | ἐπισκόποις = episkopois<br>Pronunciation: [ep-is'-kop-oys]<br>Parsing (part of speech): noun<br>    Case—dative<br>    Gender—masculine<br>    Number—plural<br>    Stem or root—from ἐπίσκοπος, ου<br>Concordance References:<br>  ⇒ Strong's #1985 episkopos<br>  ⇒ NIV #2176 episkopos<br>  ⇒ NASB #1985 episkopos | To oversee; to look after; to manage; to guard; to be an elder, a bishop.<br><br>**Practical Application**<br>The bishops (*episkopois*) were apparently the same as the elders (*presbuteros*) or ministers of a church. The two words are used interchangeably to refer to the same men (Acts 20:17, 28; Titus 1:5, 7).<br>The instructions in the *Epistle of Titus* say that his duties included primarily exhortation and overseeing the lives of the believers. The |

# PRACTICAL WORD STUDIES
## in the NEW TESTAMENT

| ENGLISH WORD | GREEK WORD AND VERSE | THE WORD MEANS... |
|---|---|---|
| **POSB REFERENCE** (Philip.1:1) Note 4, point 1 | **Philip. 1:1**<br>Paul and Timotheus, the servants of Jesus Christ, to all the saints in Christ Jesus which are at Philippi, with the **bishops** and deacons: [KJV]<br>Paul and Timothy, bond-servants of Christ Jesus, to all the saints in Christ Jesus who are in Philippi, including the **overseers** and deacons: [NASB]<br>Paul and Timothy, servants of Christ Jesus, To all the saints in Christ Jesus at Philippi, together with the **overseers** and deacons: [NIV]<br>Paul and Timothy, bondservants of Jesus Christ, To all the saints in Christ Jesus who are in Philippi, with the **bishops** and deacons: [NKJV]<br>This letter is from Paul and Timothy, slaves of Christ Jesus.It is written to all of God's people in Philippi, who believe in Christ Jesus, and to the **elders** and deacons. [NLT]<br>Παῦλος καὶ Τιμόθεος δοῦλοι Ἰησοῦ Χριστοῦ, πᾶσι τοῖς ἁγίοις ἐν Χριστῷ Ἰησοῦ τοῖς οὖσιν ἐν Φιλίπποις, σὺν **ἐπισκόποις** καὶ διακόνοις· [GNS]<br>Παῦλος καὶ Τιμόθεος δοῦλοι Χριστοῦ Ἰησοῦ πᾶσιν τοῖς ἁγίοις ἐν Χριστῷ Ἰησοῦ τοῖς οὖσιν ἐν Φιλίπποις, σὺν **ἐπισκόποις** καὶ διακόνοις, [GNT] | overseer was the person whom we call the minister of the church. (See POSB *Deeper Study* #1—Titus 1:5-9 for full discussion.) |
| **#1236**<br>**Elders**<br><br>Elders–KJV<br>Elders–NASB<br>Elders–NIV<br>Elders–NKJV<br>Elders–NLT<br><br>**POSB REFERENCE** (Tit.1:5-9; esp. v.5) Deeper Study #1 | πρεσβυτέρους = *presbuterous*<br>Pronunciation: [pres-boo'-ter-oos]<br>Parsing (part of speech): pronominal adjective<br>    Case—accusative<br>    Gender—masculine<br>    Number—plural<br>    Stem or root—from πρεσβύτερος, α, ον<br>Concordance References:<br>⇒ Strong's #4245 presbuteros<br>⇒ NIV #4565 presbuteros<br>⇒ NASB #4245 presbuteros<br><br>**Titus 1:5**<br>For this cause left I thee in Crete, that thou shouldest set in order the things that are wanting, and ordain **elders** in every city, as I had appointed thee: [KJV]<br>For this reason I left you in Crete, that you might set in order what remains, and appoint **elders** in every city as I directed you, [NASB]<br>The reason I left you in Crete was that you might straighten out what was left unfinished and appoint **elders** in every town, as I directed you. [NIV]<br>For this reason I left you in Crete, that you should set in order the things that are lacking, and appoint **elders** in every city as I commanded you [NKJV]<br>I left you on the island of Crete so you could complete our work there and appoint **elders** in each town as I instructed you. [NLT]<br>Τούτου χάριν κατέλιπόν σε ἐν Κρήτῃ, ἵνα τὰ λείποντα ἐπιδιορθώσῃ, καὶ καταστήσῃς κατὰ πόλιν **πρεσβυτέρους**, ὡς ἐγώ σοι διεταξάμην· [GNS]<br>Τούτου χάριν ἀπέλιπόν σε ἐν Κρήτῃ, ἵνα τὰ λείποντα ἐπιδιορθώσῃ καὶ καταστήσῃς κατὰ πόλιν **πρεσβυτέρους**, ὡς ἐγώ σοι διεταξάμην, [GNT] | Elder, overseer, bishop. Note the term elder (*presbuterous*) and bishop (*episkopos*) are used interchangeably in this passage (Titus 1:5, 7). (See POSB outline—1 Tim. 3:1-7 and POSB notes—1 Tim. 3:1-7 for more discussion.)<br><br>**Practical Application**<br>The elder or bishop was probably the same office as the pastor-teacher or minister of a church. The gift of pastor-teacher refers to only one gift which is given to the same person (Ephes. 4:11). The focus of the gift is to *pastor*, *oversee*, and *shepherd* believers in the local church. William Barclay points out that elder was more of a Jewish name and bishop was more of a Greek name, each referring to the same office (*The Letters to Timothy, Titus, and Philemon*, p.80-81). The word *elder* was used to refer to the man, to his standing, to his years of faithfulness and service. The word *bishop* (*episkopas*—overseer) and the gift *pastor-teacher* were used to refer to the man's duties and his work of overseeing and supervising the church. In comparison, a man today is often called minister, pastor, preacher, or reverend. Usually reverend is used to refer to the man personally and minister, pastor, or preacher is used to refer to the man's functions.<br>The pastoral gift is the gift that is directly ascribed to the Lord Jesus. He called Himself the Good Shepherd (John 10:11, 14). Others called Him the Great Shepherd of the sheep (Hebrews 13:20), the Shepherd of men's souls (1 Peter 2:25), and the Chief Shepherd (1 Peter 5:4). The pastoral gift is an ordained office; the elder is the basic office of the church.<br>1. Elders are called and set apart by the Holy Spirit (Acts 20:28; Acts 13:2).<br>2. Elders are ordained officers (Acts 14:23; Titus 1:5).<br>3. Elders shepherd and oversee the flock of God (Acts 20:28-29; 1 Peter 5:2-3).<br>4. Elders are to guard and preach the Word (Titus 1:9).<br>5. Elders have a healing ministry through |

# PRACTICAL WORD STUDIES
## in the NEW TESTAMENT

| ENGLISH WORD | GREEK WORD AND VERSE | THE WORD MEANS... |
|---|---|---|
| | | prayers and the anointing with oil (James 5:14).<br>6. Elders took a leading part in the decisions of the Jerusalem Council. They are identified along with the apostles as the chief authorities of the church (Acts 15:2; Acts 16:4).<br>7. Elders are the ones to whom Paul reports when returning from his third missionary journey, and they are the ones who advise him how to combat the Judaizers (Acts 21:18-25).<br>8. Elders are the ones to whom Paul delivers the offering that had been taken for the Jerusalem Church during the great famine (Acts 11:30). |
| #1237<br>**Elect**<br><br>Elect–KJV<br>Elect–NASB<br>Elect–NIV<br>Elect–NKJV<br>Chosen ones–NLT<br><br>**POSB REFERENCE**<br>(Mt.24:31)<br>Note 6 | ἐκλεκτοὺς = eklektous<br>Pronunciation: [ek-lek-toos']<br>    Parsing (part of speech): pronominal adjective<br>        Case—accusative<br>        Gender—masculine<br>        Number—plural<br>    Stem or root—from ἐκλεκτός, ή, όν<br>Concordance References:<br>  ⇒ Strong's #1588 eklektos<br>  ⇒ NIV #1723 eklektos<br>  ⇒ NASB #1588 eklektos<br><br>**Matthew 24:31**<br>And he shall send his angels with a great sound of a trumpet, and they shall gather together his **elect** from the four winds, from one end of heaven to the other. [KJV]<br>"And He will send forth His angels with a great trumpet and they will gather together His **elect** from the four winds, from one end of the sky to the other. [NASB]<br>And he will send his angels with a loud trumpet call, and they will gather his **elect** from the four winds, from one end of the heavens to the other. [NIV]<br>And He will send His angels with a great sound of a trumpet, and they will gather together His **elect** from the four winds, from one end of heaven to the ther. [NKJV]<br>And he will send forth his angels with the sound of a mighty trumpet blast, and they will gather together his **chosen ones** from the farthest ends of the earth and heaven. [NLT]<br>καὶ ἀποστελεῖ τοὺς ἀγγέλους αὐτοῦ μετὰ σάλπιγγος φωνῆς μεγάλης, καὶ ἐπισυνάξουσι τοὺς **ἐκλεκτοὺς** αὐτοῦ ἐκ τῶν τεσσάρων ἀνέμων ἀπ' ἄκρων οὐρανῶν ἕως ἄκρων αὐτῶν. [GNS]<br>καὶ ἀποστελεῖ τοὺς ἀγγέλους αὐτοῦ μετὰ σάλπιγγος μεγάλης, καὶ ἐπισυνάξουσιν τοὺς **ἐκλεκτοὺς** αὐτοῦ ἐκ τῶν τεσσάρων ἀνέμων ἀπ' ἄκρων οὐρανῶν ἕως [τῶν] ἄκρων αὐτῶν. [GNT] | To be chosen; to be elected; the chosen ones; to be selected; those who are the recipients of the eternal, saving, atoning, grace of God.<br><br>**Practical Application**<br>Who are the elect?<br>⇒ They are the people who cry (pray, converse, share) day and night unto God (Luke 18:7).<br>⇒ They are the people who are justified by God (Romans 8:33).<br>⇒ They are the people who are "holy and dearly loved," who "clothe themselves with compassion, kindness, humility, gentleness, and patience" (Col. 3:12)—[NIV] |
| #1238<br>**Elect**<br><br>Elect–KJV<br>Elect–NASB<br>Chosen–NIV<br>Elect–NKJV<br>Chosen–NLT<br><br>**POSB REFERENCE**<br>(Lk.18:7)<br>Deeper Study #1 | ἐκλεκτῶν = eklektōn<br>Pronunciation: [ek-lek-ton]<br>Parsing (part of speech): pronominal adjective<br>        Case—genitive<br>        Gender—masculine<br>        Number—plural<br>    Stem or root—from ἐκλεκτός, ή, όν<br>Concordance References:<br>  ⇒ Strong's #1588 eklektos<br>  ⇒ NIV #1723 eklektos<br>  ⇒ NASB #1588 eklektos<br><br>**Luke 18:7**<br>And shall not God avenge his own **elect**, which cry day and night unto him, though he bear long with them? [KJV]<br>Now shall not God bring about justice for His **elect**, who cry to Him day and night, and will He delay long over them? [NASB] | The chosen, the elect, the selected, the favored, the choice, the person picked out.<br><br>**Practical Application**<br>The chosen or elect are the believers, the disciples of Christ, the people who genuinely belong to God (Matthew 24:22, 24, 31; Mark 13:20, 22, 27; Romans 8:33; Col. 3:12; 2 Tim. 2:10; Titus 1:1; 1 Peter 1:1; 1 Peter 2:9. Also cp. where the word is translated "chosen," Matthew 20:16; Matthew 22:14; Romans 16:13; 2 John 1:1, 13; Rev. 17:14, KJV only.)<br>The focus of the word is upon God's choice. There is no doubt about this, for the word itself means that God does the choosing and the picking out. But note: the choosing is for service, not for salvation or position (John 15:16). The |

# PRACTICAL WORD STUDIES
## in the New Testament

| ENGLISH WORD | GREEK WORD AND VERSE | THE WORD MEANS... |
|---|---|---|
| | And will not God bring about justice for his **chosen** ones, who cry out to him day and night? Will he keep putting them off? [NIV]<br>And shall God not avenge His own **elect** who cry out day and night to Him, though He bears long with them? [NKJV]<br>Even he rendered a just decision in the end, so don't you think God will surely give justice to his **chosen** people who plead with him day and night? Will he keep putting them off? [NLT]<br>ὁ δὲ Θεὸς οὐ μὴ ποιήσει τὴν ἐκδίκησιν τῶν **ἐκλεκτῶν** αὐτοῦ τῶν βοώντων πρὸς αὐτῷ ἡμέρας καὶ νυκτός, καὶ μακροθυμῶν ἐπ' αὐτοῖς; [GNS]<br>ὁ δὲ θεὸς οὐ μὴ ποιήσῃ τὴν ἐκδίκησιν τῶν **ἐκλεκτῶν** αὐτοῦ τῶν βοώντων αὐτῷ ἡμέρας καὶ νυκτός, καὶ μακροθυμεῖ ἐπ' αὐτοῖς; [GNT] | believer is chosen to bear fruit (see POSB *Deeper Study* #1—John 15:1-8). |
| **#1239**<br>**Elect**<br><br>**Elect**–KJV<br>Chosen–NASB<br>**Elect**–NIV<br>**Elect**–NKJV<br>Chosen–NLT<br><br>**POSB REFERENCE**<br>(Tit.1:1)<br>Note 2 | **ἐκλεκτῶν** = *eklektōn*<br>Pronunciation: [ek-lek-ton']<br>Parsing (part of speech): pronominal adjective<br>   Case—genitive<br>   Gender—masculine<br>   Number—plural<br>   Stem or root—from ἐκλεκτός, ή, όν<br>Concordance References:<br>  ⇒ Strong's #1588 eklektos<br>  ⇒ NIV #1723 eklektos<br>  ⇒ NASB #1588 eklektos<br><br>**Titus 1:1**<br>Paul, a servant of God, and an apostle of Jesus Christ, according to the faith of God's **elect**, and the acknowledging of the truth which is after godliness; [KJV]<br>Paul, a bond-servant of God, and an apostle of Jesus Christ, for the faith of those **chosen** of God and the knowledge of the truth which is according to godliness, [NASB]<br>Paul, a servant of God and an apostle of Jesus Christ for the faith of God's **elect** and the knowledge of the truth that leads to godliness—[NIV]<br>Paul, a bondservant of God and an apostle of Jesus Christ, according to the faith of God's **elect** and the acknowledgment of the truth which accords with godliness, [NKJV]<br>This letter is from Paul, a slave of God and an apostle of Jesus Christ. I have been sent to bring faith to those God has **chosen** and to teach them to know the truth that shows them how to live godly lives. [NLT]<br>Παῦλος, δοῦλος Θεοῦ, ἀπόστολος δὲ Ἰησοῦ Χριστοῦ, κατὰ πίστιν **ἐκλεκτῶν** Θεοῦ καὶ ἐπίγνωσιν ἀληθείας τῆς κατ' εὐσέβειαν, [GNS]<br>Παῦλος δοῦλος θεοῦ, ἀπόστολος δὲ Ἰησοῦ Χριστοῦ κατὰ πίστιν **ἐκλεκτῶν** θεοῦ καὶ ἐπίγνωσιν ἀληθείας τῆς κατ' εὐσέβειαν [GNT] | The chosen, the elect, the selected, the person picked out. It means to be chosen by God; separated or set apart.<br><br>**Practical Application**<br>The purpose of God's servant is to stir believers. Note that believers are called "those chosen of God" (*eklektōn*). They are the persons whom God has chosen to be His "holy and beloved" people.<br>God called believers out of the world and away from the old life it offered, the old life of sin and death. He called believers to be separated and set apart unto Himself and the new life He offers, the new life of righteousness and eternity. |
| **#1240**<br>**Elect**<br><br>**Elect**–KJV<br>Chosen–NASB<br>Chosen–NIV<br>**Elect**–NKJV<br>Chosen–NLT<br><br>**POSB REFERENCE**<br>(2 Jn.1:1)<br>Note 1 | **ἐκλεκτῇ** = *eklektē*<br>Pronunciation: [ek-lek-tay']<br>Parsing (part of speech): adjective<br>   Case—dative<br>   Gender—feminine<br>   Number—singular<br>   Stem or root—from ἐκλεκτός, ή, όν<br>Concordance References:<br>  ⇒ Strong's #1588 eklektos<br>  ⇒ NIV #1723 eklektos<br>  ⇒ NASB #1588 eklektos<br><br>**2 John 1:1**<br>The elder unto the **elect** lady and her children, whom I love in the truth; and not I only, but also all they that have known the truth; [KJV]<br>The elder to the **chosen** lady and her children, whom I love in truth; and not only I, but also all who know the truth, [NASB] | Chosen, elected, selected. It means to be chosen by God.<br><br>**Practical Application**<br>It means to be one of God's *holy and beloved* followers. This dear mother was elected or chosen by God to be one of His chosen, one of His *holy and beloved* followers. |

# PRACTICAL WORD STUDIES
## in the NEW TESTAMENT

| ENGLISH WORD | GREEK WORD AND VERSE | THE WORD MEANS... |
|---|---|---|
| | The elder, To the **chosen** lady and her children, whom I love in the truth—and not I only, but also all who know the truth—[NIV]<br>The Elder, To the **elect** lady and her children, whom I love in truth, and not only I, but also all those who have known the truth, [NKJV]<br>This letter is from John the Elder. It is written to the **chosen** lady and to her children, whom I love in the truth, as does everyone else who knows God's truth—[NLT]<br>Ὁ πρεσβύτερος **ἐκλεκτῇ** κυρίᾳ, καὶ τοῖς τέκνοις αὐτῆς, οὓς ἐγὼ ἀγαπῶ ἐν ἀληθείᾳ, καὶ οὐκ ἐγὼ μόνος ἀλλὰ καὶ πάντες οἱ ἐγνωκότες τὴν ἀλήθειαν, [GNS]<br>Ὁ πρεσβύτερος **ἐκλεκτῇ** κυρίᾳ καὶ τοῖς τέκνοις αὐτῆς, οὓς ἐγὼ ἀγαπῶ ἐν ἀληθείᾳ, καὶ οὐκ ἐγὼ μόνος ἀλλὰ καὶ πάντες οἱ ἐγνωκότες τὴν ἀλήθειαν, [GNT] | |
| #1241<br>**Elementary Principles**<br><br>Rudiments–KJV<br>**Elementary principles–NASB**<br>Basic principles–NIV<br>Basic principles–NKJV<br>Evil powers–NLT<br><br>**POSB REFERENCE**<br>(Col.2:20)<br>Note 1 | στοιχείων = stoicheiön<br>Pronunciation: [stoy-khi'-on]<br>Parsing (part of speech): noun<br>   Case—genitive<br>   Gender—neuter<br>   Number—plural<br>   Stem or root—from στοιχεῖα, ων<br>Concordance References:<br>  ⇒ Strong's #4747 stoicheion<br>  ⇒ NIV #5122 stoicheion<br>  ⇒ NASB #4747 stoicheion<br><br>**Col. 2:20**<br>Wherefore if ye be dead with Christ from the **rudiments** of the world, why, as though living in the world, are ye subject to ordinances, [KJV]<br>If you have died with Christ to the **elementary principles** of the world, why, as if you were living in the world, do you submit yourself to decrees, such as, [NASB]<br>Since you died with Christ to the **basic principles** of this world, why, as though you still belonged to it, do you submit to its rules: [NIV]<br>Therefore, if you died with Christ from the **basic principles** of the world, why, as though living in the world, do you subject yourselves to regulations—[NKJV]<br>You have died with Christ, and he has set you free from the **evil powers** of this world. So why do you keep on following rules of the world, such as, [NLT]<br>Εἰ οὖν ἀπεθάνετε σὺν τῷ Χριστῷ, ἀπὸ τῶν **στοιχείων** τοῦ κόσμου, τί ὡς ζῶντες ἐν κόσμῳ δογματίζεσθε, [GNS]<br>Εἰ ἀπεθάνετε σὺν Χριστῷ ἀπὸ τῶν **στοιχείων** τοῦ κόσμου, τί ὡς ζῶντες ἐν κόσμῳ δογματίζεσθε; [GNT] | Basic principles; rudiments; elements; elementary principles; first lessons; evil powers.<br><br>**Practical Application**<br>The term "elementary principles" (stoicheiön) means two things and Christ saves us from both. (See POSB note, Philosophy—Col. 2:8 for more discussion.)<br>1. *Elementary principles* means crude notions of men about the universe—that is, about God, reality, and truth. It is man's ideas and philosophies, their elementary or rudimentary teachings, their ABC understanding of God and the universe, reality, and truth. When men think of God, they come up with all kinds of ways and laws to reach Him and to secure His approval and acceptance. However, there are three basic problems with man's approach to God.<br>a. First, we cannot keep rules and laws—not in a perfect sense. No matter what way we choose to reach God, we cannot walk a straight path to Him.<br>b. Second, once we have broken a rule or law, we stand guilty before God. Therefore, we must be judged, condemned, and punished for having broken the law. A law-breaker is guilty and unacceptable and the punishment must be borne. Therefore, rules and laws cannot make us acceptable to God. They can only lead to guilt and condemnation.<br>c. Third, we die; we do not live forever. Moreover, there is no law or force on this earth that can give us the energy and power to live forever. Rules and laws only condemn us when we break them. They have no power to save us from death nor to give us eternal life. Because of this, rules and laws cannot be the way to approach God.<br>How then can we approach God? If the best thinking of men about the universe and God are not the way to approach God, what is the way? The answer will be discussed in a moment, but first look at the second meaning of the term *elementary principles*.<br>2. *Elementary principles* means the basic elements or materials of the universe, the things that men say lie behind the universe or at the very base of reality. Down through the centuries men have posed all kinds of forces, energies, powers, principalities, spirits, angels, and beings as standing behind the uni- |

# Practical Word Studies in the New Testament

| ENGLISH WORD | GREEK WORD AND VERSE | THE WORD MEANS... |
|---|---|---|
| | | verse and life. As a result men have committed their lives to and worshipped all sorts of creatures and forces or elements and materials. However, there is a critical problem with this approach to God, a problem that dooms all who seek truth and who approach God through the elements of this universe or through the spirits of the spiritual world.<br>a. First, there is the problem of corruption. Everything in the universe is corruptible, aging, dying, deteriorating, and decaying. Therefore, there is nothing in the universe that can save man, for the way of all things—all elements and all materials—is the way of change and death.<br>b. Second, there is a problem with seeking truth and God through the spirits or angels of a spiritual world.<br>⇒ First, man cannot penetrate the spiritual world. He is physical, and the physical just cannot move over into the world of the spiritual no matter what any person claims. If the spiritual world is ever to be known, then the spiritual has to reveal itself to us.<br>⇒ Second, any person who claims to have been given visions or revelations by the spiritual world still has the same problems that everyone else has: the problems of imperfection (unrighteousness), death, and eternal life. No angel, spirit, or any other intermediary has ever taken care of the problem of sin and death and of eternal life for us. We have already sinned, and we are already imperfect. Therefore, someone, someplace must *bear our sin* or punishment for us or else we have to pay for it ourselves. And, in addition, someone has to go through the experience of death to conquer it to tell us how to do the same or else we are going to die and never reach God.<br>This is the glorious message of the gospel. God is love, eternal and infinite love, so He has done all this for us. He did it through His Son, Jesus Christ. |
| **#1242**<br>**Elementary Principles**<br><br>First principles–KJV<br>**Elementary principles–NASB**<br>Elementary truths–NIV<br>First principles–NKJV<br>Basic things–NLT<br><br>**POSB REFERENCE**<br>(Heb.5:12)<br>Note 2 | στοιχεῖα τῆς ἀρχῆς = *stoicheia tēs archēs*<br>Pronunciation: [stoy-khi'-eh-ee tays ar-khays']<br>Parsing *stoicheia* (part of speech): noun<br>    Case—accusative<br>    Gender—neuter<br>    Number—plural<br>    Stem or root—from στοιχεῖα, ων<br>Parsing *archēs* (part of speech): noun<br>    Case—genitive<br>    Number—feminine<br>    Number—singular<br>    Stem or root—from ἀρχή, ῆς<br>Concordance References:<br>⇒ Strong's #746+3588+4747 archē ho stoicheion<br>⇒ NIV #794+3836+5122 archē ho stoicheion [elementary truths]<br>⇒ NASB #746+3588+4747 archē ho stoicheion<br><br>**Hebrews 5:12**<br>For when for the time ye ought to be teachers, ye have need that one teach you again which be the **first principles** of the oracles of God; and are become such as have | Elementary truths, first principles, elementary principles, basic things, first things. It means the basic principles of God's Word, the elementary teachings, the ABC's of God's Word.<br><br>**Practical Application**<br>A person becomes immature because he refuses to grow up spiritually. The Hebrew believers refused to move beyond the elementary principles of God's Word. They (*stoicheia tēs archēs*) are the very basic teachings of salvation and of spiritual growth, such teachings as...<br>• a person should be saved<br>• a person should grow spiritually<br>• a person should live righteously<br>• a person should worship<br>• a person should keep the rituals and ceremonies of religion |

# PRACTICAL WORD STUDIES
## in the NEW TESTAMENT

| ENGLISH WORD | GREEK WORD AND VERSE | THE WORD MEANS... |
|---|---|---|
| | need of milk, and not of strong meat. [KJV]<br><br>For though by this time you ought to be teachers, you have need again for someone to teach you the **elementary principles** of the oracles of God, and you have come to need milk and not solid food. [NASB]<br><br>In fact, though by this time you ought to be teachers, you need someone to teach you the **elementary truths** of God's word all over again. You need milk, not solid food! [NIV]<br><br>For though by this time you ought to be teachers, you need *someone* to teach you again the **first principles** of the oracles of God; and you have come to need milk and not solid food. [NKJV]<br><br>You have been Christians a long time now, and you ought to be teaching others. Instead, you need someone to teach you again the **basic things** a beginner must learn about the Scriptures. You are like babies who drink only milk and cannot eat solid food. [NLT]<br><br>καὶ γὰρ ὀφείλοντες εἶναι διδάσκαλοι, διὰ τὸν χρόνον, πάλιν χρείαν ἔχετε τοῦ διδάσκειν ὑμᾶς, τινὰ τὰ **στοιχεῖα τῆς ἀρχῆς** τῶν λογίων τοῦ Θεοῦ· καὶ γεγόνατε χρείαν ἔχοντες γάλακτος, καὶ οὐ στερεᾶς τροφῆς. [GNS]<br><br>καὶ γὰρ ὀφείλοντες εἶναι διδάσκαλοι διὰ τὸν χρόνον, πάλιν χρείαν ἔχετε τοῦ διδάσκειν ὑμᾶς τινὰ τὰ **στοιχεῖα τῆς ἀρχῆς** τῶν λογίων τοῦ θεοῦ καὶ γεγόνατε χρείαν ἔχοντες γάλακτος [καὶ] οὐ στερεᾶς τροφῆς. [GNT] | Such basic truths as these are the milk of God's Word. They are truths that are to be preached and taught, but they are the truths for the unsaved and for young believers, for babes in Christ. They are to be learned and learned quickly by the believers, and then he is to move on to maturity. Note that the Christian life is compared to physical growth. A young believer is said to be a babe in Christ, and the elementary principles of God's Word are said to be the milk upon which he is to feed. A young believer is to feed upon the milk of the Word, the elementary principles, but he is expected to grow until he is feeding upon the meat of the Word—studying and growing a mature understanding of the Christian life. |
| **#1243**<br>**Elementary Truths**<br><br>First principles–KJV<br>Elementary principles–NASB<br>**Elementary truths–NIV**<br>First principles–NKJV<br>Basic things–NLT<br><br>**POSB REFERENCE**<br>(Heb.5:12)<br>Note 2 | στοιχεῖα τῆς ἀρχῆς = *stoicheia tēs archēs*<br>Pronunciation: [stoy-khi'-eh-ee tays ar-khays']<br>Parsing *stoicheia* (part of speech): noun<br>  Case—accusative<br>  Gender—neuter<br>  Number—plural<br>  Stem or root—from στοιχεῖα, ων<br>Parsing *archēs* (part of speech): noun<br>  Case—genitive<br>  Number—feminine<br>  Number—singular<br>  Stem or root—from ἀρχή, ῆς<br>Concordance References:<br>  ⇒ Strong's #746+3588+4747 archē ho stoicheion<br>  ⇒ NIV #794+3836+5122 archē ho stoicheion [elementary truths]<br>  ⇒ NASB #746+3588+4747 archē ho stoicheion<br><br>**Hebrews 5:12**<br>For when for the time ye ought to be teachers, ye have need that one teach you again which be the **first principles** of the oracles of God; and are become such as have need of milk, and not of strong meat. [KJV]<br><br>For though by this time you ought to be teachers, you have need again for someone to teach you the **elementary principles** of the oracles of God, and you have come to need milk and not solid food. [NASB]<br><br>In fact, though by this time you ought to be teachers, you need someone to teach you the **elementary truths** of God's word all over again. You need milk, not solid food! [NIV]<br><br>For though by this time you ought to be teachers, you need *someone* to teach you again the **first principles** of the oracles of God; and you have come to need milk and not solid food. [NKJV]<br><br>You have been Christians a long time now, and you ought to be teaching others. Instead, you need someone to teach you again the **basic things** a beginner must learn about the Scriptures. You are like babies who drink only milk and cannot eat solid food. [NLT]<br><br>καὶ γὰρ ὀφείλοντες εἶναι διδάσκαλοι, διὰ τὸν χρόνον, πάλιν χρείαν ἔχετε τοῦ διδάσκειν ὑμᾶς, τινὰ τὰ **στοιχεῖα τῆς ἀρχῆς** τῶν λογίων τοῦ Θεοῦ· καὶ γεγόνατε χρείαν ἔχοντες γάλακτος, καὶ οὐ στερεᾶς τροφῆς. [GNS] | Elementary truths, first principles, elementary principles, basic things, first things. It means the basic principles of God's Word, the elementary teachings, the ABC's of God's Word.<br><br>**Practical Application**<br>A person becomes immature because he refuses to grow up spiritually. The Hebrew believers refused to move beyond the first elementary truths of God's Word. They (*stoicheia tēs archēs*) are the very basic teachings of salvation and of spiritual growth, such teachings as...<br>• a person should be saved<br>• a person should grow spiritually<br>• a person should live righteously<br>• a person should worship<br>• a person should keep the rituals and ceremonies of religion<br><br>Such basic truths as these are the milk of God's Word. They are truths that are to be preached and taught, but they are the truths for the unsaved and for young believers, for babes in Christ. They are to be learned and learned quickly by the believers, and then he is to move on to maturity. Note that the Christian life is compared to physical growth. A young believer is said to be a babe in Christ, and the first elementary truths of God's Word are said to be the milk upon which he is to feed. A young believer is to feed upon the milk of the Word, the first elementary truths, but he is expected to grow until he is feeding upon the meat of the Word—studying and growing a mature understanding of the Christian life. |

# PRACTICAL WORD STUDIES
## in the NEW TESTAMENT

| ENGLISH WORD | GREEK WORD AND VERSE | THE WORD MEANS... |
|---|---|---|
| | καὶ γὰρ ὀφείλοντες εἶναι διδάσκαλοι διὰ τὸν χρόνον, πάλιν χρείαν ἔχετε τοῦ διδάσκειν ὑμᾶς τινὰ τὰ **στοιχεῖα τῆς ἀρχῆς** τῶν λογίων τοῦ θεοῦ καὶ γεγόνατε χρείαν ἔχοντες γάλακτος [καὶ] οὐ στερεᾶς τροφῆς. [GNT] | |
| **#1244**<br>**Eloquence Or Superior Wisdom**<br><br>Excellency of speech or of wisdom–KJV<br>Superiority of speech or of wisdom–NASB<br>**Eloquence or superior wisdom–NIV**<br>Excellence of speech or of wisdom–NKJV<br>Lofty words and brilliant ideas–NLT<br><br>**POSB REFERENCE**<br>(1 Cor.2:1)<br>Note 1, point 1 | ὑπεροχὴν λόγου ἢ σοφίας = *huperochēn logou ē sophias*<br>Pronunciation: [hoop-er-okh-ayn' log'-oo hey sof-ee'-ahs]<br>Parsing *huperochēn* (part of speech): noun<br>  Case—accusative<br>  Gender—feminine<br>  Number—singular<br>  Stem or root—from ὑπεροχή, ῆς<br>Parsing *logou* (part of speech): noun<br>  Case—genitive<br>  Gender—masculine<br>  Number—singular<br>  Stem or root—from λόγος, ου<br>Parsing *sophias* (part of speech): noun<br>  Case—genitive<br>  Gender—feminine<br>  Number—singular<br>  Stem or root—from σοφία, ας<br>Concordance References:<br>⇒ Strong's #3056 logos + 2228 ē + 4678+5247 sophia huperochē<br>⇒ NIV #3364 logos [eloquence] + 2445 ē [or] + 5053+5667 sophia huperochē [superior wisdom]<br>⇒ NASB #3056 logos + 2228 ē + 4678+5247 sophia huperochē<br><br>**1 Cor. 2:1**<br>And I, brethren, when I came to you, came not with **excellency of speech or of wisdom**, declaring unto you the testimony of God. [KJV]<br>And when I came to you, brethren, I did not come with **superiority of speech or of wisdom**, proclaiming to you the testimony of God. [NASB]<br>When I came to you, brothers, I did not come with **eloquence or superior wisdom** as I proclaimed to you the testimony about God. [NIV]<br>And I, brethren, when I came to you, did not come with **excellence of speech or of wisdom** declaring to you the testimony of God. [NKJV]<br>Dear brothers and sisters, when I first came to you I didn't use **lofty words and brilliant ideas** to tell you God's message. [NLT]<br>Κἀγὼ ἐλθὼν πρὸς ὑμᾶς, ἀδελφοί, ἦλθον οὐ καθ' **ὑπεροχὴν λόγου ἢ σοφίας** καταγγέλλων ὑμῖν τὸ μυστήριον τοῦ Θεοῦ. [GNS]<br>Κἀγὼ ἐλθὼν πρὸς ὑμᾶς, ἀδελφοί, ἦλθον οὐ καθ' **ὑπεροχὴν λόγου ἢ σοφίας** καταγγέλλων ὑμῖν τὸ μυστήριον τοῦ θεοῦ. [GNT] | Eloquent words; superior, elevated, preeminent words; words that rise above.<br><br>**Practical Application**<br>Remember Paul is speaking about words, not so much about himself, although the behavior of a person could be involved. Paul did not try to sound more superior, more elevated, and more eloquent in his preaching than did others. He was not concerned in the least with his preaching's rising above and being more preeminent and recognized than the preaching of others. Paul did not seek to impress the Corinthians with superior wisdom or brilliant ideas. |
| **#1245**<br>**Eloquent Man**<br><br>**Eloquent man–KJV**<br>**Eloquent man–NASB**<br>Learned man–NIV<br>**Eloquent man–NKJV**<br>Eloquent speaker–NLT<br><br>**POSB REFERENCE**<br>(Acts 18:24)<br>Note 2 | ἀνὴρ λόγιος = *anēr logios*<br>Pronunciation: [an'-ayr log'-ee-os]<br>Parsing *anēr* (part of speech): noun<br>  Case—nominative<br>  Gender—masculine<br>  Number—singular<br>  Stem or root—from ἀνήρ, ἀνδρός<br>Parsing *logios* (part of speech): adjective<br>  Case—nominative<br>  Gender—masculine<br>  Number—singular<br>  Stem or root—from λόγιος, α, ον<br>Concordance References:<br>⇒ Strong's #435 anēr + 3052 logios<br>⇒ NIV #467 anēr [man] + 3360 logios [learned]<br>⇒ NASB #435 anēr + 3052 logios | Learned man; wise man; eloquent man or speaker.<br><br>**Practical Application**<br>The term "learned man" or "eloquent man" can mean either learned or eloquent. In this case it probably means both. But note the point: it was the Scriptures that Apollos...<br>• learned so well.<br>• spoke forth so eloquently or forcefully. |

# PRACTICAL WORD STUDIES
## in the NEW TESTAMENT

| ENGLISH WORD | GREEK WORD AND VERSE | THE WORD MEANS... |
|---|---|---|
| | **Acts 18:24**<br>And a certain Jew named Apollos, born at Alexandria, an **eloquent man**, and mighty in the scriptures, came to Ephesus. [KJV]<br>Now a certain Jew named Apollos, an Alexandrian by birth, an **eloquent man**, came to Ephesus; and he was mighty in the Scriptures. [NASB]<br>Meanwhile a Jew named Apollos, a native of Alexandria, came to Ephesus. He was a **learned man**, with a thorough knowledge of the Scriptures. [NIV]<br>Now a certain Jew named Apollos, born at Alexandria, an **eloquent man** and mighty in the Scriptures, came to Ephesus. [NKJV]<br>Meanwhile, a Jew named Apollos, an **eloquent speaker** who knew the Scriptures well, had just arrived in Ephesus from Alexandria in Egypt. [NLT]<br>Ἰουδαῖος δέ τις Ἀπολλῶς ὀνόματι, Ἀλεξανδρεὺς τῷ γένει, **ἀνὴρ λόγιος**, κατήντησεν εἰς Ἔφεσον, δυνατὸς ὢν ἐν ταῖς γραφαῖς· [GNS]<br>Ἰουδαῖος δέ τις Ἀπολλῶς ὀνόματι, Ἀλεξανδρεὺς τῷ γένει, **ἀνὴρ λόγιος**, κατήντησεν εἰς Ἔφεσον, δυνατὸς ὢν ἐν ταῖς γραφαῖς. [GNT] | |
| **#1246**<br>**Eloquent Speaker**<br><br>Eloquent man–KJV<br>Eloquent man–NASB<br>Learned man–NIV<br>Eloquent man–NKJV<br>**Eloquent speaker– NLT**<br><br>**POSB REFERENCE**<br>(Acts 18:24)<br>Note 2 | **ἀνὴρ λόγιος** = *anēr logios*<br>Pronunciation: [an'-ayr log'-ee-os]<br>Parsing *anēr* (part of speech): noun<br>    Case—nominative<br>    Gender—masculine<br>    Number—singular<br>    Stem or root—from ἀνήρ, ἀνδρός<br>Parsing *logios* (part of speech): adjective<br>    Case—nominative<br>    Gender—masculine<br>    Number—singular<br>    Stem or root—from λόγιος, α, ον<br>Concordance References:<br>⇒ Strong's #435 anēr + 3052 logios<br>⇒ NIV #467 anēr [man] + 3360 logios [learned]<br>⇒ NASB #435 anēr + 3052 logios<br><br>**Acts 18:24**<br>And a certain Jew named Apollos, born at Alexandria, an **eloquent man**, and mighty in the scriptures, came to Ephesus. [KJV]<br>Now a certain Jew named Apollos, an Alexandrian by birth, an **eloquent man**, came to Ephesus; and he was mighty in the Scriptures. [NASB]<br>Meanwhile a Jew named Apollos, a native of Alexandria, came to Ephesus. He was a **learned man**, with a thorough knowledge of the Scriptures. [NIV]<br>Now a certain Jew named Apollos, born at Alexandria, an **eloquent man** and mighty in the Scriptures, came to Ephesus. [NKJV]<br>Meanwhile, a Jew named Apollos, an **eloquent speaker** who knew the Scriptures well, had just arrived in Ephesus from Alexandria in Egypt. [NLT]<br>Ἰουδαῖος δέ τις Ἀπολλῶς ὀνόματι, Ἀλεξανδρεὺς τῷ γένει, **ἀνὴρ λόγιος**, κατήντησεν εἰς Ἔφεσον, δυνατὸς ὢν ἐν ταῖς γραφαῖς· [GNS]<br>Ἰουδαῖος δέ τις Ἀπολλῶς ὀνόματι, Ἀλεξανδρεὺς τῷ γένει, **ἀνὴρ λόγιος**, κατήντησεν εἰς Ἔφεσον, δυνατὸς ὢν ἐν ταῖς γραφαῖς. [GNT] | Learned man; eloquent man or speaker.<br><br>**Practical Application**<br>The term "learned man" or "eloquent speaker" can mean either learned or eloquent. In this case it probably means both. But note the point: it was the Scriptures that Apollos...<br>• learned so well.<br>• spoke forth so eloquently or forcefully. |
| **#1247**<br>**Embraced**<br><br>**Embraced–KJV**<br>Welcomed–NASB<br>Welcomed–NIV<br>**Embraced–NKJV**<br>Welcomed–NLT | **ἀσπασάμενοι** = *aspasamenoi*<br>Pronunciation: [as-pas'-ah-mehn-oy]<br>Parsing (part of speech): verb<br>    Mood—participle<br>    Tense—aorist<br>    Voice—middle deponent<br>    Case—nominative<br>    Gender—masculine<br>    Number—plural<br>    Stem or root—from ἀσπάζομαι | To welcome; to embrace; to receive with warmth and respect.<br><br>**Practical Application**<br>Those who died in faith had a *growing faith*.<br>⇒ They saw the promise of God and were thankful to God for the privilege of seeing it.<br>⇒ They were persuaded of the promises of |

# PRACTICAL WORD STUDIES
## in the NEW TESTAMENT

| ENGLISH WORD | GREEK WORD AND VERSE | THE WORD MEANS... |
|---|---|---|
| **POSB REFERENCE** (Heb.11:13-15; esp. v.13) Note 1, point 2 | Concordance References:<br>⇒ Strong's #782 aspazomai<br>⇒ NIV #832 aspazomai<br>⇒ NASB #782 aspazomai<br><br>**Hebrews 11:13**<br>These all died in faith, not having received the promises, but having seen them afar off, and were persuaded of them, and **embraced** them, and confessed that they were strangers and pilgrims on the earth. [KJV]<br>All these died in faith, without receiving the promises, but having seen them and having **welcomed** them from a distance, and having confessed that they were strangers and exiles on the earth. [NASB]<br>All these people were still living by faith when they died. They did not receive the things promised; they only saw them and **welcomed** them from a distance. And they admitted that they were aliens and strangers on earth. [NIV]<br>These all died in faith, not having received the promises, but having seen them afar off were assured of them, **embraced** *them* and confessed that they were strangers and pilgrims on the earth. [NKJV]<br>All these faithful ones died without receiving what God had promised them, but they saw it all from a distance and **welcomed** the promises of God. They agreed that they were no more than foreigners and nomads here on earth. [NLT]<br>Κατὰ πίστιν ἀπέθανον οὗτοι πάντες, μὴ λαβόντες τὰς ἐπαγγελίας, ἀλλὰ πόρρωθεν αὐτὰς ἰδόντες, καὶ πεισθέντες, καὶ **ἀσπασάμενοι**, καὶ ὁμολογήσαντες ὅτι ξένοι καὶ παρεπίδημοί εἰσιν ἐπὶ τῆς γῆς. [GNS]<br>Κατὰ πίστιν ἀπέθανον οὗτοι πάντες, μὴ λαβόντες τὰς ἐπαγγελίας ἀλλὰ πόρρωθεν αὐτὰς ἰδόντες καὶ **ἀσπασάμενοι** καὶ ὁμολογήσαντες ὅτι ξένοι καὶ παρεπίδημοί εἰσιν ἐπὶ τῆς γῆς. [GNT] | God. They believed that the promises were true, that there was a promised land and that God was going to give it to them. They believed in God and that what God promised He was going to fulfill.<br>⇒ They embraced (*aspasamenoi*) the promises. They were ever so thankful and appreciative to God for such a glorious hope as the promised land. They rejoiced and loved the promise, setting their eyes upon it and not looking away. |
| **#1248**<br>**Emmanuel**<br><br>Emmanuel–KJV<br>Immanuel–NASB<br>Immanuel–NIV<br>Immanuel–NKJV<br>Immanuel–NLT<br><br>**POSB REFERENCE** (Mt.1:23)<br>*Deeper Study* #9 | Ἐμμανουήλ = *Emmanouël*<br>Pronunciation: [em-man-oo-ale']<br>Parsing (part of speech): noun<br>   Case—accusative<br>   Gender—masculine<br>   Number—singular<br>   Stem or root—from Ἐμμανουήλ<br>Concordance References:<br>⇒ Strong's #1694 Emmanouël<br>⇒ NIV #1842 Emmanouël<br>⇒ NASB #1694 Emmanouël<br><br>**Matthew 1:23**<br>Behold, a virgin shall be with child, and shall bring forth a son, and they shall call his name **Emmanuel**, which being interpreted is, God with us. [KJV]<br>"Behold, the virgin shall be with CHILD, AND SHALL BEAR A Son, and they shall call His name **Immanuel**," which translated means, "God with us." [NASB]<br>"The virgin will be with child and will give birth to a son, and they will call him **Immanuel**"—which means, "God with us." [NIV]<br>"Behold, the virgin shall be with child, and bear a Son, and they shall call His name **Immanuel**," which is translated, "God with us." [NKJV]<br>"Look! The virgin will conceive a child! She will give birth to a son, and he will be called **Immanuel** (meaning, God is with us)." [NLT]<br>Ἰδοὺ, ἡ παρθένος ἐν γαστρὶ ἕξει καὶ τέξεται υἱόν, καὶ καλέσουσι τὸ ὄνομα αὐτοῦ **Ἐμμανουήλ**, ὅ ἐστι μεθερμηνευόμενον, Μεθ' ἡμῶν ὁ Θεός. [GNS]<br>Ἰδοὺ ἡ παρθένος ἐν γαστρὶ ἕξει καὶ τέξεται υἱόν, καὶ καλέσουσιν τὸ ὄνομα αὐτοῦ **Ἐμμανουήλ**, ὅ ἐστιν μεθερμηνευόμενον Μεθ' ἡμῶν ὁ θεός. [GNT] | God with us. Jesus Christ is God manifest in human flesh.<br><br>**Practical Application**<br>The word "*Emmanouël*" is not a name or a title. It is a descriptive term. It characterizes a person. Jesus Christ is Emmanuel: God with us, God revealed in human flesh (cp. Isaiah 1:26; Isaiah 9:6; Jn.1:1, 14; 2 Cor. 5:19; 1 Jn.1:2). |

## PRACTICAL WORD STUDIES
### in the NEW TESTAMENT

| ENGLISH WORD | GREEK WORD AND VERSE | THE WORD MEANS... |
|---|---|---|
| #1249 **Emptied**<br><br>Reputation–KJV<br>**Emptied**–NASB<br>Made...nothing–NIV<br>Reputation–NKJV<br>Made...nothing–NLT<br><br>**POSB REFERENCE**<br>(Philip.2:7)<br>Note 3, point 1 | ἐκένωσεν = ekenōsen<br>Pronunciation: [eh-ken-o'-sehn]<br>Parsing (part of speech): verb<br>  Mood—indicative<br>  Tense—aorist<br>  Voice—active<br>  Person—3rd person<br>  Number—singular<br>  Stem or root—from κενόω<br>Concordance References:<br> ⇒ Strong's #2758 kenoö<br> ⇒ NIV #3033 kenoö<br> ⇒ NASB #2758 kenoö<br><br>**Philip. 2:7**<br>But made himself of no **reputation**, and took upon him the form of a servant, and was made in the likeness of men: [KJV]<br>But **emptied** Himself, taking the form of a bond-servant, and being made in the likeness of men. [NASB]<br>But **made** himself **nothing**, taking the very nature of a servant, being made in human likeness. [NIV]<br>But made Himself of no **reputation**, taking the form of a bondservant, *and* coming in the likeness of men. [NKJV]<br>He **made** himself **nothing**; he took the humble position of a slave and appeared in human form. [NLT]<br>ἀλλ ἑαυτὸν **ἐκένωσε**, μορφὴν δούλου λαβών, ἐν ὁμοιώματι ἀνθρώπων γενόμενος· καὶ σχήματι εὑρεθεὶς ὡς ἄνθρωπος, [GNS]<br>ἀλλὰ ἑαυτὸν **ἐκένωσεν** μορφὴν δούλου λαβών, ἐν ὁμοιώματι ἀνθρώπων γενόμενος· καὶ σχήματι εὑρεθεὶς ὡς ἄνθρωπος [GNT] | Made [himself] nothing; to have no reputation; to empty oneself; to be completely empty.<br><br>**Practical Application**<br>Jesus Christ made Himself of no *reputation*; that is, He *emptied Himself*. It is the picture of pouring water out of a glass until it is empty or of dumping something until it is all removed (William Barclay. *The Letters to the Philippians, Colossians, and Thessalonians*, p.44). The very picture of being completely empty stirs a feeling of just how far Christ went in humbling Himself for us. What was it that was poured or emptied out of Jesus Christ when He left heaven and came to earth? (This is what theologians call the *kenosis theory*.) Note that this passage does not say. It only says that Christ *emptied Himself*. Other Scriptures, however, give some indication. (See POSB note, pt.4—Mark 13:32 for more discussion.)<br>1. Christ did not lay aside His deity when He came to earth. He could not cease to be who He was: God. No person can ever cease to be who he is. A person may take on different traits and behave differently; a person may change his behavior and looks, but he is the same person in being, nature, and essence. Jesus Christ is God; therefore, He is always God—He always possesses the nature of God (See POSB notes—John 1:1-2 for more discussion.)<br>2. Christ laid aside some of His rights as God:<br> ⇒ He laid aside His right *to experience only the glory* and majesty, honor and worship of heaven. In coming to earth as a man, He was to experience anything but glory and majesty, honor and worship. Men would treat Him far differently than they would a heavenly being.<br> ⇒ He laid aside His right *to appear only in heaven* and to appear only as the Sovereign God of heaven. In coming to earth as a man, He was, of course, to appear as a man on earth. |
| #1250 **Empty**<br><br>Vain–KJV<br>Vain–NASB<br>Useless–NIV<br>**Empty**–NKJV<br>Useless–NLT<br><br>**POSB REFERENCE**<br>(1 Cor.15:13-15; esp. v.14)<br>Note 2, point 2 | κενὸν = kenon<br>Pronunciation: [ken-on']<br>Parsing (part of speech): adjective<br>  Case—nominative<br>  Gender—neuter<br>  Number—singular<br>  Stem or root—from κενός, ή, όν<br>Concordance References:<br> ⇒ Strong's #2756 kenos<br> ⇒ NIV #3031 kenos<br> ⇒ NASB #2756 kenos<br><br>**1 Cor. 15:14**<br>And if Christ be not risen, then *is* our preaching **vain**, and your faith *is* also vain. [KJV]<br>And if Christ has not been raised, then our preaching is **vain**, your faith also is vain. [NASB]<br>And if Christ has not been raised, our preaching is **useless** and so is your faith. [NIV]<br>And if Christ is not risen, then our preaching *is* **empty** and your faith *is* also empty. [NKJV]<br>And if Christ was not raised, then all our preaching is **useless**, and your trust in God is useless. [NLT]<br>εἰ δὲ Χριστὸς οὐκ ἐγήγερται, **κενὸν** ἄρα τὸ κήρυγμα | Useless, vain, empty, senseless, groundless, foolish, void of all truth and meaning.<br><br>**Practical Application**<br>How does denying the resurrection of the body make our preaching meaningless? There are two ways.<br>1. The message we preach is the gospel (*good news*) of the resurrected Lord who has been raised to give us the glorious privilege:<br> ⇒ of living forever in the presence of God.<br> ⇒ of having a personal face-to-face relationship with God.<br> ⇒ of being made perfect and serving God face to face in a new heavens and earth.<br>There is no way *disembodied spirits* can serve God. What is a disembodied spirit anyway? It takes a *body*, a whole and real person to serve God. If we are not to be whole and real persons then we cannot be alive and serving God. The only way we can live with God eternally is for God to resurrect our bodies |

# PRACTICAL WORD STUDIES
## in the NEW TESTAMENT

| ENGLISH WORD | GREEK WORD AND VERSE | THE WORD MEANS... |
|---|---|---|
| | ἡμῶν, κενὴ δὲ καὶ ἡ πίστις ὑμῶν, [GNS]<br>εἰ δὲ Χριστὸς οὐκ ἐγήγερται, **κενὸν** ἄρα [καὶ] τὸ κήρυγμα ἡμῶν, κενὴ καὶ ἡ πίστις ὑμῶν· [GNT] | and make them perfect by changing their corruptible nature into an incorruptible nature.<br>    Therefore, to deny the resurrection of Christ or of believers is to deny what we preach. Our preaching of the resurrected Lord and of our living forever is empty and meaningless. We may as well be doing something else; there is no need to preach a false hope.<br>2. The message we preach is that Jesus Christ is the Son of God who died for our sins and rose again conquering death for us. The fact that God raised Him from the dead is the glorious proof that He is the Son of God, the proof that God accepted His sacrifice for our sins (Romans 1:4). If Christ did not arise, then it means that God left Him in the grave, that He is no more than what other men are, a man doomed to die and remain in the grave forever with all other men. But if God did raise Christ up from the grave, then it means that death is conquered and that He will raise us up to live forever with Him.<br>    The point is this: if there is no resurrection—no resurrection of Christ and no resurrection of us—then the consequence is terrible. Jesus Christ is not the Son of God. What we are preaching is useless and meaningless. We may as well keep quiet. |
| **#1251**<br>**Empty Chatter**<br><br>Vain babblings–KJV<br>**Empty chatter–NASB**<br>Chatter–NIV<br>Idle babblings–NKJV<br>Foolish discussions–NLT<br><br>**POSB REFERENCE**<br>(1 Tim.6:20)<br>Note 2, point 2a | κενοφωνίας = *kenophōnias*<br>Pronunciation: [ken-of-o-nee'-ahs]<br>Parsing (part of speech): noun<br>    Case—accusative<br>    Gender—feminine<br>    Number—plural<br>    Stem or root—from κενοφωνία, ας<br>Concordance References:<br>⇒ Strong's #2757 kenophōnia<br>⇒ NIV #3032 kenophōnia<br>⇒ NASB #2757 kenophōnia<br><br>**1 Tim. 6:20**<br>O Timothy, keep that which is committed to thy trust, avoiding profane and **vain babblings**, and oppositions of science falsely so called: [KJV]<br>O Timothy, guard what has been entrusted to you, avoiding worldly and **empty chatter** and the opposing arguments of what is falsely called "knowledge"—[NASB]<br>Timothy, guard what has been entrusted to your care. Turn away from godless **chatter** and the opposing ideas of what is falsely called knowledge, [NIV]<br>O Timothy! Guard what was committed to your trust, avoiding the profane *and* **idle babblings** and contradictions of what is falsely called knowledge—[NKJV]<br>Timothy, guard what God has entrusted to you. Avoid godless, **foolish discussions** with those who oppose you with their so-called knowledge. [NLT]<br>Ὦ Τιμόθεε, τὴν παρακαταθήκην φύλαξον, ἐκτρεπόμενος τὰς βεβήλους **κενοφωνίας** καὶ ἀντιθέσεις τῆς ψευδωνύμου γνώσεως· [GNS]<br>Ὦ Τιμόθεε, τὴν παρακαταθήκην φύλαξον ἐκτρεπόμενος τὰς βεβήλους **κενοφωνίας** καὶ ἀντιθέσεις τῆς ψευδωνύμου γνώσεως, [GNT] | Chatter; vain babblings; idle babblings; empty chatter, foolish discussions, foolish talk.<br><br>**Practical Application**<br>The charge is to take all *empty talk* and turn away from it. Have absolutely nothing to do with common, irreverent, godless, and *empty voices*—no matter who is sounding forth the words. This would, of course, include...<br>• false claims to truth<br>• worldly philosophy<br>• cursing<br>• criticism<br>• suggestive talk<br>• all forms of false teaching<br>• novel ideas of religion<br>• gossip<br>• off-colored jokes |
| **#1252**<br>**Empty Talkers**<br><br>Vain talkers–KJV<br>**Empty talkers–NASB** | ματαιολόγοι = *mataiologoi*<br>Pronunciation: [mat-ah-yol-og'-oy]<br>Parsing (part of speech): pronominal adjective<br>    Case—nominative<br>    Gender—masculine<br>    Number—plural | Mere talkers, vain talkers, empty talkers, useless talkers.<br><br>**Practical Application**<br>They were saying and teaching things that |

# PRACTICAL WORD STUDIES
## in the New Testament

| ENGLISH WORD | GREEK WORD AND VERSE | THE WORD MEANS... |
|---|---|---|
| Mere talkers–NIV<br>Idle talkers–NKJV<br>Useless talk–NLT<br><br>**POSB REFERENCE**<br>(Tit.1:10-12; esp. v.10)<br>Note 1, point 2 | Stem or root—from ματαιολόγος, ου<br>Concordance References:<br>⇒ Strong's #3151 mataiologos<br>⇒ NIV #3468 mataiologos<br>⇒ NASB #3151 mataiologos<br><br>**Titus 1:10**<br>For there are many unruly and **vain talkers** and deceivers, specially they of the circumcision: [KJV]<br>For there are many rebellious men, **empty talkers** and deceivers, especially those of the circumcision, [NASB]<br>For there are many rebellious people, **mere talkers** and deceivers, especially those of the circumcision group. [NIV]<br>For there are many insubordinate, both **idle talkers** and deceivers, especially those of the circumcision, [NKJV]<br>For there are many who rebel against right teaching; they engage in **useless talk** and deceive people. This is especially true of those who insist on circumcision for salvation. [NLT]<br>Εἰσὶ γὰρ πολλοὶ καὶ ἀνυπότακτοι, **ματαιολόγοι** καὶ φρεναπάται, μάλιστα οἱ ἐκ τῆς περιτομῆς, [GNS]<br>Εἰσὶν γὰρ πολλοὶ [καὶ] ἀνυπότακτοι, **ματαιολόγοι** καὶ φρεναπάται, μάλιστα οἱ ἐκ τῆς περιτομῆς, [GNT] | amounted to nothing and were worthless. Their teaching helped no one—not permanently and not eternally. Their teaching was not able to overcome sin and death—not able to bring true forgiveness of sin and eternal life to a person. |
| **#1253**<br>**Emulations**<br><br>Emulations–KJV<br>Jealousy–NASB<br>Jealousy–NIV<br>Jealousies–NKJV<br>Jealousy–NLT<br><br>**POSB REFERENCE**<br>(Gal.5:19-21; esp. v.20)<br>Note 2, point 9 | ζῆλος = zēlos<br>Pronunciation: [dzay'-los]<br>Parsing (part of speech): noun<br>  Case—nominative<br>  Gender—masculine or neuter<br>  Number—singular<br>Stem or root—from ζῆλος, ου<br>Concordance References:<br>⇒ Strong's #2205 zēlos<br>⇒ NIV #2419 zēlos<br>⇒ NASB #2205 zēlos<br><br>**Galatians 5:20**<br>Idolatry, witchcraft, hatred, variance, **emulations**, wrath, strife, seditions, heresies, [KJV]<br>Idolatry, sorcery, enmities, strife, **jealousy**, outbursts of anger, disputes, dissensions, factions, [NASB]<br>Idolatry and witchcraft; hatred, discord, **jealousy**, fits of rage, selfish ambition, dissensions, factions [NIV]<br>Idolatry, sorcery, hatred, contentions, **jealousies**, outbursts of wrath, selfish ambitions, dissensions, heresies, [NKJV]<br>Idolatry, participation in demonic activities, hostility, quarreling, **jealousy**, outbursts of anger, selfish ambition, divisions, the feeling that everyone is wrong except those in your own little group, [NLT]<br>εἰδωλολατρία, φαρμακεία, ἔχθραι, ἔρεις, **ζῆλοι**, θυμοί, ἐριθεῖαι, διχοστασίαι, αἱρέσεις, [GNS]<br>εἰδωλολατρία, φαρμακεία, ἔχθραι, ἔρις, **ζῆλος**, θυμοί, ἐριθεῖαι, διχοστασίαι, αἱρέσεις, [GNT] | Jealousy, emulations, zeal, wanting and desiring to have what someone else has. It may be material things, recognition, honor, or position.<br><br>**Practical Application**<br>The works of the flesh—including "emulations" (*zēlos*)—are the fruit of indwelling sin, and sin originates in the heart not in the flesh. The sins of the flesh listed in this passage are clearly seen throughout society. Tragically they are not only seen on the daily newscasts of every city, but within every community, home, and life on planet earth. The very presence of such fleshly sins shows just how strong the flesh is and how helpless man is to control his flesh. |
| **#1254**<br>**Enabled**<br><br>Enabled–KJV<br>Strengthened–NASB<br>Given strength–NIV<br>Enabled–NKJV<br>Not translated–NLT<br><br>**POSB REFERENCE**<br>(1 Tim.1:12-14; esp. v.12)<br>Note 1, point 1 | ἐνδυναμώσαντί = endunamōsanti<br>Pronunciation: [en-doo-nam-o'-sahn-tee]<br>Parsing (part of speech): verb<br>  Mood—participle<br>  Tense—aorist<br>  Voice—active<br>  Case—dative<br>  Gender—masculine<br>  Number—singular<br>Stem or root—from ἐνδυναμόω<br>Concordance References:<br>⇒ Strong's #1743 endunamoō<br>⇒ NIV #1904 endunamoō<br>⇒ NASB #1743 endunamoō | To be given strength; to be strengthened, enabled; to make strong; to strengthen and give power to.<br><br>**Practical Application**<br>Christ Jesus *enabled* Paul. The power of Paul's ministry came from Christ. Christ gave him the strength to minister. Paul's strength and power to minister did not come from his...<br>• trying to stir up power within himself.<br>• talking about the results and power in his ministry.<br>• trying to program strength and power into |

# PRACTICAL WORD STUDIES
## in the NEW TESTAMENT

| ENGLISH WORD | GREEK WORD AND VERSE | THE WORD MEANS... |
|---|---|---|
| | **1 Tim. 1:12**<br>And I thank Christ Jesus our Lord, who hath **enabled** me, for that he counted me faithful, putting me into the ministry; [KJV]<br>I thank Christ Jesus our Lord, who has **strengthened** me, because He considered me faithful, putting me into service; [NASB]<br>I thank Christ Jesus our Lord, who has **given me strength**, that he considered me faithful, appointing me to his service. [NIV]<br>And I thank Christ Jesus our Lord who has **enabled** me, because He counted me faithful, putting *me* into the ministry, [NKJV]<br>How thankful I am to Christ Jesus our Lord for considering me trustworthy and appointing me to serve him, [NLT]—NOT TRANSLATED<br>Καὶ χάριν ἔχω τῷ **ἐνδυναμώσαντί** με Χριστῷ Ἰησοῦτῷ Κυρίῳ ἡμῶν, ὅτι πιστόν με ἡγήσατο, θέμενος εἰς διακονίαν, [GNS]<br>Χάριν ἔχω τῷ **ἐνδυναμώσαντί** με Χριστῷ Ἰησοῦ τῷ κυρίῳ ἡμῶν, ὅτι πιστόν με ἡγήσατο θέμενος εἰς διακονίαν [GNT] | his ministry.<br>• trying to shout power into his preaching.<br><br>Christ Himself put Paul into the ministry; therefore, Christ Himself strengthened and empowered Paul for the ministry. No person has the power to do spiritual warfare; no person can penetrate the spirits of other people. If a person is to minister to people, he must be empowered by Christ, for only Christ can penetrate the spirits of people. Therefore, the minister must possess the power of Christ. |
| **#1255**<br>**Encourage**<br><br>Exhortation–KJV<br>Exhortation–NASB<br>**Encourage–NIV**<br>Exhortation–NKJV<br>**Encourage–NLT**<br><br>**POSB REFERENCE**<br>(Romans 12:6-8, esp. v.8)<br>Note 2<br><br>See also POSB REF:<br>(1 Cor.14:3)<br>*Deeper Study* #1, point 2 | παρακλήσει = *paraklēsei*<br>Pronunciation: [par-ak'-lay-see]<br>Parsing (part of speech): noun<br>   Case—dative<br>   Gender—feminine<br>   Number—singular<br>   Stem or root—from παράκλησις, εως<br>Concordance References:<br>  ⇒ Strong's #3874 paraklēsis<br>  ⇒ NIV #4155 paraklēsis<br>  ⇒ NASB #3874 paraklēsis<br><br>**Romans 12:8**<br>Or he that exhorteth, on **exhortation**: he that giveth, let him do it with simplicity; he that ruleth, with diligence; he that sheweth mercy, with cheerfulness. [KJV]<br>Or he who exhorts, in his **exhortation**; he who gives, with liberality; he who leads, with diligence; he who shows mercy, with cheerfulness. [NASB]<br>If it is encouraging, let him **encourage**; if it is contributing to the needs of others, let him give generously; if it is leadership, let him govern diligently; if it is showing mercy, let him do it cheerfully. [NIV]<br>He who exhorts, in **exhortation**; he who gives, with liberality; he who leads, with diligence; he who shows mercy, with cheerfulness. [NKJV]<br>If your gift is to **encourage** others, do it! If you have money, share it generously. If God has given you leadership ability, take the responsibility seriously. And if you have a gift for showing kindness to others, do it gladly. [NLT]<br>εἴτε ὁ παρακαλῶν, ἐν τῇ **παρακλήσει**· ὁ μεταδιδοὺς ἐν ἁπλότητι, ὁ προϊστάμενος, ἐν σπουδῇ· ὁ ἐλεῶν ἐν ἱλαρότητι. [GNS]<br>εἴτε ὁ παρακαλῶν ἐν τῇ **παρακλήσει**· ὁ μεταδιδοὺς ἐν ἁπλότητι, ὁ προϊστάμενος ἐν σπουδῇ, ὁ ἐλεῶν ἐν ἱλαρότητι. [GNT] | Encouragement, help, comfort, consolation, appeal, request.<br><br>**Practical Application**<br>There is the gift of encouragement (*paraklēsei*). This is the very special ability to excite, motivate, advise, exhort, encourage, comfort, and warn people. The dominant factor would be the motivation and encouragement of people, the ability to stir people to make a decision for Christ and to grow in Him. It is the gift that arouses people to get up and get busy fulfilling their task for the Lord. |
| **#1256**<br>**Encourage**<br><br>Comfort–KJV<br>Comfort–NASB<br>**Encourage–NIV**<br>Comfort–NKJV<br>Comfort–NLT | παρακαλέσαι = *parakalesai*<br>Pronunciation: [par-ak-al-eh'-sah-ee]<br>Parsing (part of speech): verb<br>   Mood—optative<br>   Tense—aorist<br>   Voice—active<br>   Person—3rd person<br>   Number—singular<br>   Stem or root—from παρακαλέω | To encourage; to comfort; to console; to cheer up. The word means exhortation, encouragement, admonition, comfort.<br><br>**Practical Application**<br>Note that God and Christ are the Ones who can comfort, exhort, and encourage the believer to live like they should. When the believer comes to Christ for strength, Christ will comfort and encourage him. |

# PRACTICAL WORD STUDIES
## in the NEW TESTAMENT

| ENGLISH WORD | GREEK WORD AND VERSE | THE WORD MEANS... |
|---|---|---|
| **POSB REFERENCE** (2 Thes.2:16-17; esp. v.17) Note 5, point 4 | Concordance References:<br>⇒ Strong's #3870 parakaleō<br>⇒ NIV #4151 parakaleō<br>⇒ NASB #3870 parakaleō<br><br>**2 Thes. 2:17**<br>**Comfort** your hearts, and stablish you in every good word and work. [KJV]<br>**Comfort** and strengthen your hearts in every good work and word. [NASB]<br>**Encourage** your hearts and strengthen you in every good deed and word. [NIV]<br>**Comfort** your hearts and establish you in every good word and work. [NKJV]<br>**Comfort** your hearts and give you strength in every good thing you do and say. [NLT]<br>παρακαλέσαι ὑμῶν τὰς καρδίας, καὶ στηρίξαι ὑμᾶς ἐν παντὶ λόγῳ καὶ ἔργῳ ἀγαθῷ. [GNS]<br>παρακαλέσαι ὑμῶν τὰς καρδίας καὶ στηρίξαι ἐν παντὶ ἔργῳ καὶ λόγῳ ἀγαθῷ. [GNT] | |
| **#1257 Encourage**<br><br>Exhort–KJV<br>Exhort–NASB<br>**Encourage–NIV**<br>Exhort–NKJV<br>**Encourage–NLT**<br><br>**POSB REFERENCE** (2 Tim. 4:2) Note 2, point 5<br><br>See also POSB REF: (1 Tim.2:1) Note 1 | παρακάλεσον = *parakaleson*<br>Pronunciation: [par-ak-al-eh'-son]<br>Parsing (part of speech): verb<br>  Mood—imperative<br>  Tense—aorist<br>  Voice—active<br>  Person—2nd person<br>  Number—singular<br>  Stem or root—from παρακαλέω<br>Concordance References:<br>⇒ Strong's #3870 parakaleō<br>⇒ NIV #4151 parakaleō<br>⇒ NASB #3870 parakaleō<br><br>**2 Tim. 4:2**<br>Preach the word; be instant in season, out of season; reprove, rebuke, **exhort** with all longsuffering and doctrine. [KJV]<br>Preach the word; be ready in season and out of season; reprove, rebuke, **exhort**, with great patience and instruction. [NASB]<br>Preach the Word; be prepared in season and out of season; correct, rebuke and **encourage**—with great patience and careful instruction. [NIV]<br>Preach the word! Be ready in season *and* out of season. Convince, rebuke, **exhort**, with all longsuffering and teaching. [NKJV]<br>Preach the word of God. Be persistent, whether the time is favorable or not. Patiently correct, rebuke, and **encourage** your people with good teaching. [NLT]<br>κήρυξον τὸν λόγον, ἐπίστηθι εὐκαίρως, ἀκαίρως, ἔλεγξον, ἐπιτίμησον, **παρακάλεσον**, ἐν πάσῃ μακροθυμίᾳ καὶ διδαχῇ. [GNS]<br>κήρυξον τὸν λόγον, ἐπίστηθι εὐκαίρως ἀκαίρως, ἔλεγξον, ἐπιτίμησον, **παρακάλεσον**, ἐν πάσῃ μακροθυμίᾳ καὶ διδαχῇ. [GNT] | To encourage; to exhort; to console; to plead with. It means to beseech, encourage, comfort, and help. The word "encourage" (*parakaleson*) has the idea of "please, I beg of you, I urge you" (Kenneth Wuest. *The Pastoral Epistles*, Vol.2, p.155).<br><br>**Practical Application**<br>It is not enough to reprove and rebuke people. The minister must encourage and comfort, help and carry the person to Christ. Note how crucial this point is.<br>1. The minister must "encourage (*makrothumia*) with great patience." The idea is that the minister patiently endures in exhorting people—no matter the circumstances. He encourages and encourages, exhorts and exhorts. He suffers a long, long time with people...<br>• enduring whatever weaknesses and failings they have.<br>• enduring whatever evil and injury is done.<br>  The minister suffers a long, long time without resentment or anger, and he never gives up for he knows the power of Christ to change lives.<br>2. The minister "encourages with careful instruction or teaching." He does not teach bits and pieces of God's Word. He does not focus upon subjects...<br>• that are popular.<br>• that are favorites.<br>• that arouse curiosity.<br>• that he thinks are needed.<br>  He focuses upon all the instructions or doctrines of God—the whole counsel of God. He encourages people in all the instruction or doctrines of God. |
| **#1258 Encourage**<br><br>Exhort–KJV<br>**Encourage–NASB**<br>**Encourage–NIV**<br>Exhort–NKJV<br>Warn–NLT | παρακαλεῖτε = *parakaleite*<br>Pronunciation: [par-ak-al-eh'-ee-teh]<br>Parsing (part of speech): verb<br>  Mood—imperative<br>  Tense—present<br>  Voice—active<br>  Person—2nd person<br>  Number—plural<br>  Stem or root—from παρακαλέω | To encourage; to exhort; to warn; to plead with; to console. The word "encourage" (*parakaleite*) means to "beg, entreat, beseech, exhort" (Kenneth Wuest. *Hebrews*, Vol. 2, p.79).<br><br>**Practical Application**<br>It is from the same word that the Comforter or Paraclete (the Holy Spirit) is taken. This means that the word "encourage" also includes comfort, the kind of comfort that will "strengthen |

## PRACTICAL WORD STUDIES
### in the NEW TESTAMENT

| ENGLISH WORD | GREEK WORD AND VERSE | THE WORD MEANS... |
|---|---|---|
| **POSB REFERENCE** (Heb.3:13-19; esp. v.13) Note 3<br><br>See also POSB REF: (Lk.3:18) Note 7 | Concordance References:<br>⇒ Strong's #3870 parakaleō<br>⇒ NIV #4151 parakaleō<br>⇒ NASB #3870 parakaleō<br><br>**Hebrews 3:13**<br>But **exhort** one another daily, while it is called Today; lest any of you be hardened through the deceitfulness of sin. [KJV]<br>But **encourage** one another day after day, as long as it is still called "Today," lest any one of you be hardened by the deceitfulness of sin. [NASB]<br>But **encourage** one another daily, as long as it is called Today, so that none of you may be hardened by sin's deceitfulness. [NIV]<br>But **exhort** one another daily, while it is called "Today," lest any of you be hardened through the deceitfulness of sin. [NKJV]<br>You must **warn** each other every day, as long as it is called "today," so that none of you will be deceived by sin and hardened against God. [NLT]<br>ἀλλὰ **παρακαλεῖτε** ἑαυτοὺς καθ' ἑκάστην ἡμέραν, ἄχρις οὗ τὸ Σήμερον καλεῖται, ἵνα μὴ σκληρυνθῇ τις ἐξ ὑμῶν ἀπάτῃ τῆς ἁμαρτίας· [GNS]<br>ἀλλὰ **παρακαλεῖτε** ἑαυτοὺς καθ' ἑκάστην ἡμέραν, ἄχρις οὗ τὸ Σήμερον καλεῖται, ἵνα μὴ σκληρυνθῇ τις ἐξ ὑμῶν ἀπάτῃ τῆς ἁμαρτίας· [GNT] | and encourage the believer each single day so that when a crises arises he may be able to stand fast" (Thomas Hewitt. *The Epistle to the Hebrews*. "Tyndale New Testament Commentaries." Grand Rapids, MI: Eerdmans, 1960, p.83). Believers are to constantly encourage one another to guard themselves against unbelief and sin. |
| **#1259**<br>**Encourage-Encouraged**<br><br>Exhorted–KJV<br>Encourage–NASB<br>Encouraged–NIV<br>Encouraged–NKJV<br>Encouraged–NLT<br><br>**POSB REFERENCE**<br>(Acts 11:19-30; esp. v.23)<br>*Deeper Study* #2, point 3 | **παρεκάλει** = *parekalei*<br>Pronunciation: [par-ek-al-eh-ee]<br>Parsing (part of speech): verb<br>  Mood—indicative<br>  Tense—imperfect<br>  Voice—active<br>  Person—3rd person<br>  Number—singular<br>  Stem or root—from παρακαλέω<br>Concordance References:<br>⇒ Strong's #3870 parakaleō<br>⇒ NIV #4151 parakaleō<br>⇒ NASB #3870 parakaleō<br><br>**Acts 11:23**<br>Who, when he came, and had seen the grace of God, was glad, and **exhorted** them all, that with purpose of heart they would cleave unto the Lord. [KJV]<br>Then when he had come and witnessed the grace of God, he rejoiced and began to **encourage** them all with resolute heart to remain true to the Lord; [NASB]<br>When he arrived and saw the evidence of the grace of God, he was glad and **encouraged** them all to remain true to the Lord with all their hearts. [NIV]<br>When he came and had seen the grace of God, he was glad, and **encouraged** them all that with purpose of heart they should continue with the Lord. [NKJV]<br>When he arrived and saw this proof of God's favor, he was filled with joy, and he **encouraged** the believers to stay true to the Lord. [NLT]<br>ὃς παραγενόμενος καὶ ἰδὼν τὴν χάριν τοῦ Θεοῦ, ἐχάρη, καὶ **παρεκάλει** πάντας τῇ προθέσει τῆς καρδίας προσμένειν τῷ κυρίῳ, [GNS]<br>ὃς παραγενόμενος καὶ ἰδὼν τὴν χάριν [τὴν] τοῦ θεοῦ, ἐχάρη καὶ **παρεκάλει** πάντας τῇ προθέσει τῆς καρδίας προσμένειν τῷ κυρίῳ, [GNT] | To encourage; to exhort; to console; to appease; to plead with. This word means to admonish, advise, challenge, entreat, call upon, beseech, urge, warn, comfort, and encourage.<br><br>**Practical Application**<br>The message was...<br>• "with resolute heart" [NIV]: a determined, set, focused, purpose, steady, purposed heart.<br>• to "remain true to the Lord" [NIV]: to continue; to be constant, loyal, steadfast, persistent, persevering, faithful. |
| **#1260**<br>**Encourage Each Other**<br><br>Be of good comfort–KJV<br>Be comforted–NASB | **παρακαλεῖσθε** = *parakaleisthe*<br>Pronunciation: [par-ak-al-eehs'-the]<br>Parsing (part of speech): verb<br>  Mood—imperative<br>  Tense—present<br>  Voice—passive<br>  Person—2nd person<br>  Number—plural<br>  Stem or root—from παρακαλέω | To be comforted; to encourage each other; to cheer up; to be assured, consoled. The word could also mean "be exhorted"; that is, listen and heed what I have said.<br><br>**Practical Application**<br>If the believers of the church would do these four things... |

# PRACTICAL WORD STUDIES
## in the NEW TESTAMENT

| ENGLISH WORD | GREEK WORD AND VERSE | THE WORD MEANS... |
|---|---|---|
| Listen to...appeal–NIV<br>Be of good comfort–NKJV<br>**Encourage each other–NLT**<br><br>**POSB REFERENCE**<br>(2 Cor.13:11-13; esp. v.11)<br>Note 3 | Concordance References:<br>⇒ Strong's #3870 parakaleō<br>⇒ NIV #4151 parakaleō<br>⇒ NASB #3870 parakaleō<br><br>**2 Cor. 13:11**<br>Finally, brethren, farewell. Be perfect, **be of good comfort**, be of one mind, live in peace; and the God of love and peace shall be with you. [KJV]<br>Finally, brethren, rejoice, be made complete, **be comforted**, be like-minded, live in peace; and the God of love and peace shall be with you. [NASB]<br>Finally, brothers, good-by. Aim for perfection, **listen to** my **appeal**, be of one mind, live in peace. And the God of love and peace will be with you. [NIV]<br>Finally, brethren, farewell. Become complete. **Be of good comfort**, be of one mind, live in peace; and the God of love and peace will be with you. [NKJV]<br>Dear brothers and sisters, I close my letter with these last words: Rejoice. Change your ways. **Encourage each other**. Live in harmony and peace. Then the God of love and peace will be with you. [NLT]<br>Λοιπόν, ἀδελφοί, χαίρετε· καταρτίζεσθε, **παρακαλεῖσθε**, τὸ αὐτὸ φρονεῖτε, εἰρηνεύετε· καὶ ὁ Θεὸς τῆς ἀγάπης καὶ εἰρήνης ἔσται μεθ' ὑμῶν. [GNS]<br>Λοιπόν, ἀδελφοί, χαίρετε, καταρτίζεσθε, **παρακαλεῖσθε**, τὸ αὐτὸ φρονεῖτε, εἰρηνεύετε, καὶ ὁ Θεὸς τῆς ἀγάπης καὶ εἰρήνης ἔσται μεθ' ὑμῶν. [GNT] | • change one's ways<br>• encourage each other<br>• live in harmony<br>• live in peace<br><br>...then the God of love and peace would be with them. Note that God is the Author, the Giver of love and peace. Therefore, if a man wishes to know true love and true peace, he must accept the challenge to live accordingly. |
| #1261<br>**Encouragement**<br><br>Consolation–KJV<br>**Encouragement–NASB**<br>Encouraging message–NIV<br>**Encouragement–NKJV**<br>Encouraging message–NLT<br><br>**POSB REFERENCE**<br>(Acts 15:30-35; esp. v.31)<br>Note 5, point 1 | παρακλήσει = *paraklēsei*<br>Pronunciation: [par-ak'-lay-seh-ee]<br>Parsing (part of speech): noun<br>  Case—dative<br>  Gender—feminine<br>  Number—singular<br>  Stem or root—from παράκλησις, εως<br>Concordance References:<br>⇒ Strong's #3874 paraklēsis<br>⇒ NIV #4155 paraklēsis<br>⇒ NASB #3874 paraklēsis<br><br>**Acts 15:31**<br>Which when they had read, they rejoiced for the **consolation**. [KJV]<br>And when they had read it, they rejoiced because of its **encouragement**. [NASB]<br>The people read it and were glad for its **encouraging message**. [NIV]<br>When they had read it, they rejoiced over its **encouragement**. [NKJV]<br>And there was great joy throughout the church that day as they read this **encouraging message**. [NLT]<br>ἀναγνόντες δὲ, ἐχάρησαν ἐπὶ τῇ **παρακλήσει**. [GNS]<br>ἀναγνόντες δὲ ἐχάρησαν ἐπὶ τῇ **παρακλήσει**. [GNT] | An encouraging message; consolation, encouragement, comfort, help, appeal.<br><br>**Practical Application**<br>When the four men arrived in Antioch, the whole church was called together and the great decree on salvation was read. When it was read, four great results occurred. Note how God took the dissension and its subsequent events to work it all out for the good of the Antioch church and for the cause of Christ. The results were fourfold.<br>1. There was great "*rejoicing*" (*echaresan*): joy, gladness, rejoicing over the encouragement (*paraklēsei*), that is, over the encouragement and help given by the Jerusalem church.<br>2. There was great "*encouragement*" (v.32). Note that it was Silas and Judas who were exhorting and confirming the faith of the Antioch believers. Note also the phrase "lengthy message." They encouraged for a long time, building the believers up more and more, assuring them of their faith in the Lord Jesus. They were saved by the grace of God and His grace alone, and the two visiting preachers wanted the believers to know that the apostles and elders of the great Jerusalem church confirmed the glorious truth.<br>3. There was the discovery of the great missionary, Silas. The oldest Greek manuscripts do not include this verse (note the word "they" in Acts 15:33). Some scholars feel it was added at a later date because Silas appears with Paul in Acts 15:40. There was, of course, plenty of time for Silas to travel to Jerusalem and report back to the church, and then to return to Antioch before Paul left on his second missionary journey. Other scholars believe the verse was in the original manuscript. No matter who is accurate, Silas and his great gift |

### PRACTICAL WORD STUDIES
in the NEW TESTAMENT

| ENGLISH WORD | GREEK WORD AND VERSE | THE WORD MEANS... |
|---|---|---|
| | | from God were discovered by Paul at Antioch, and apparently Paul invited him to join the great mission thrust. (See POSB *Deeper Study* #1, Silas—Acts 15:34 for more discussion.)<br>4. A great teaching ministry grew within the church (v.35). |
| **#1262**<br>**Encouragement**<br><br>Consolation–KJV<br>**Encouragement–**<br>**NASB**<br>**Encouragement–NIV**<br>Consolation–NKJV<br>**Encouragement–NLT**<br><br>**POSB**<br>**REFERENCE**<br>(Philip.2:1)<br>Note 1 | παράκλησις = *paraklēsis*<br>Pronunciation: [par-ak'-lay-sis]<br>Parsing (part of speech): noun<br>  Case—nominative<br>  Gender—feminine<br>  Number—singular<br>  Stem or root—from παράκλησις, εως<br>Concordance References:<br> ⇒ Strong's #3874 *paraklēsis*<br> ⇒ NIV #4155 *paraklēsis*<br> ⇒ NASB #3874 *paraklēsis*<br><br>**Philip. 2:1**<br>If there be therefore any **consolation** in Christ, if any comfort of love, if any fellowship of the Spirit, if any bowels and mercies, [KJV]<br>If therefore there is any **encouragement** in Christ, if there is any consolation of love, if there is any fellowship of the Spirit, if any affection and compassion, [NASB]<br>If you have any **encouragement** from being united with Christ, if any comfort from his love, if any fellowship with the Spirit, if any tenderness and compassion, [NIV]<br>Therefore if *there is* any **consolation** in Christ, if any comfort of love, if any fellowship of the Spirit, if any affection and mercy, [NKJV]<br>Is there any **encouragement** from belonging to Christ? Any comfort from his love? Any fellowship together in the Spirit? Are your hearts tender and sympathetic? [NLT]<br>Εἴ τις οὖν **παράκλησις** ἐν Χριστῷ, εἴ τι παραμύθιον ἀγάπης, εἴ τις κοινωνία Πνεύματος, εἴ τινα σπλάγχνα καὶ οἰκτιρμοί, [GNS]<br>Εἴ τις οὖν **παράκλησις** ἐν Χριστῷ, εἴ τι παραμύθιον ἀγάπης, εἴ τις κοινωνία πνεύματος, εἴ τις σπλάγχνα καὶ οἰκτιρμοί, [GNT] | The word means many things throughout Scripture; but in the present context it means encouragement, comfort, solace, exhortation, and strengthening; consolation, appeal, help.<br><br>**Practical Application**<br>Note that this trait is a characteristic of Christ Himself. The very beat of His Spirit is to encourage, comfort, and strengthen believers to be one in spirit and busy about the ministry of His church. Christ wants no murmuring, no grumbling, no disturbance, or weakening of the unity within the church. The Spirit of Christ is to take the disturbed or upset person and...<br>• console him<br>• comfort him<br>• encourage him<br>• strengthen him |
| **#1263**<br>**Encouraged**<br><br>Comfort–KJV<br>Comfort–NASB<br>**Encouraged–NIV**<br>Comfort–NKJV<br>Comfort–NLT<br><br>**POSB**<br>**REFERENCE**<br>(Acts 9:31)<br>Note 3, point 2<br><br>**See also POSB REF:**<br>(Rom.15:4)<br>Note 2, point 2b | παρακλήσει = *paraklēsei*<br>Pronunciation: [par-ak'-lay-seh-ee]<br>Parsing (part of speech): noun<br>  Case—dative<br>  Gender—feminine<br>  Number—singular<br>  Stem or root—from παράκλησις, εως<br>Concordance References:<br> ⇒ Strong's #3874 *paraklēsis*<br> ⇒ NIV #4155 *paraklēsis*<br> ⇒ NASB #3874 *paraklēsis*<br><br>**Acts 9:31**<br>Then had the churches rest throughout all Judaea and Galilee and Samaria, and were edified; and walking in the fear of the Lord, and in the **comfort** of the Holy Ghost, were multiplied. [KJV]<br>So the church throughout all Judea and Galilee and Samaria enjoyed peace, being built up; and, going on in the fear of the Lord and in the **comfort** of the Holy Spirit, it continued to increase. [NASB]<br>Then the church throughout Judea, Galilee and Samaria enjoyed a time of peace. It was strengthened; and **encouraged** by the Holy Spirit, it grew in numbers, living in the fear of the Lord. [NIV]<br>Then the churches throughout all Judea, Galilee, and Samaria had peace and were edified. And walking in the | Encouragement, comfort, help.<br><br>**Practical Application**<br>The word "encouraged" (*paraklēsei*) means paraclete, the very title by which Christ called the Holy Spirit. It means comforter, advisor, helper, encourager, exhorter. The picture is that of One who is called to stand by the believer's side (just as Jesus did). |

# PRACTICAL WORD STUDIES
## in the NEW TESTAMENT

| ENGLISH WORD | GREEK WORD AND VERSE | THE WORD MEANS... |
|---|---|---|
| | fear of the Lord and in the **comfort** of the Holy Spirit, they were multiplied. [NKJV]<br><br>The church then had peace throughout Judea, Galilee, and Samaria, and it grew in strength and numbers. The believers were walking in the fear of the Lord and in the **comfort** of the Holy Spirit. [NLT]<br><br>Αἱ μὲν οὖν ἐκκλησίαι καθ' ὅλης τῆς Ἰουδαίας καὶ Γαλιλαίας καὶ Σαμαρείας εἶχον εἰρήνην, οἰκοδομουμέναι καὶ πορευομέναι τῷ φόβῳ τοῦ Κυρίου, καὶ τῇ **παρακλήσει** τοῦ Ἁγίου Πνεύματος ἐπληθύνετο. [GNS]<br><br>Ἡ μὲν οὖν ἐκκλησία καθ' ὅλης τῆς Ἰουδαίας καὶ Γαλιλαίας καὶ Σαμαρείας εἶχεν εἰρήνην οἰκοδομουμένη καὶ πορευομένη τῷ φόβῳ τοῦ κυρίου καὶ τῇ **παρακλήσει** τοῦ ἁγίου πνεύματος ἐπληθύνετο. [GNT] | |
| **#1264**<br>**Encouraged**<br><br>Comforted–KJV<br>**Encouraged–NASB**<br>**Encouraged–NIV**<br>**Encouraged–NKJV**<br>**Encouraged–NLT**<br><br>**POSB REFERENCE**<br>(Col.2:2-3; esp. v.2)<br>Note 2 | **παρακληθῶσιν** = *paraklēthōsin*<br>Pronunciation: [par-ak-lay-tho'-sin]<br>Parsing (part of speech): verb<br>    Mood—subjunctive<br>    Tense—aorist<br>    Voice—passive<br>    Person—3rd person<br>    Number—plural<br>    Stem or root—from **παρακαλέω**<br>Concordance References:<br>    ⇒ Strong's #3870 parakaleō<br>    ⇒ NIV #4151 parakaleō<br>    ⇒ NASB #3870 parakaleō<br><br>**Col. 2:2**<br>That their hearts might be **comforted**, being knit together in love, and unto all riches of the full assurance of understanding, to the acknowledgement of the mystery of God, and of the Father, and of Christ; [KJV]<br><br>That their hearts may be **encouraged**, having been knit together in love, and attaining to all the wealth that comes from the full assurance of understanding, resulting in a true knowledge of God's mystery, that is, Christ Himself, [NASB]<br><br>My purpose is that they may be **encouraged** in heart and united in love, so that they may have the full riches of complete understanding, in order that they may know the mystery of God, namely, Christ, [NIV]<br><br>That their hearts may be **encouraged**, being knit together in love, and *attaining* to all riches of the full assurance of understanding, to the knowledge of the mystery of God, both of the Father and of Christ, [NKJV]<br><br>My goal is that they will be **encouraged** and knit together by strong ties of love. I want them to have full confidence because they have complete understanding of God's secret plan, which is Christ himself. [NLT]<br><br>ἵνα **παρακληθῶσιν** αἱ καρδίαι αὐτῶν, συμβιβασθέντων ἐν ἀγάπῃ, καὶ εἰς πᾶν πλοῦτον τῆς πληροφορίας τῆς συνέσεως, εἰς ἐπίγνωσιν τοῦμυστηρίου τοῦ Θεοῦ καὶ πατρὸς καὶ τοῦ Χριστοῦ, [GNS]<br><br>ἵνα **παρακληθῶσιν** αἱ καρδίαι αὐτῶν, συμβιβασθέντες ἐν ἀγάπῃ καὶ εἰς πᾶν πλοῦτος τῆς πληροφορίας τῆς συνέσεως, εἰς ἐπίγνωσιν τοῦ μυστηρίου τοῦ θεοῦ, Χριστοῦ, [GNT] | To be encouraged; to be comforted; to be consoled; to be appeased; to urge; to plead with. The word "encouraged" (*paraklēthōsin*) means to be strong, strengthened, established and braced (Marvin Vincent. *Word Studies in the New Testament*, Vol.3, p.482).<br><br>**Practical Application**<br>It is the kind of strength...<br>• that stirs confidence and assurance.<br>• that braces a person to withstand the onslaught of false teaching, trials, and temptations.<br>• that comforts and builds assurance and confidence in life, both now and eternally.<br>The human heart aches for such strength, for this kind of confidence, assurance, and comfort. |
| **#1265**<br>**Encouraged By Yours**<br><br>Comforted together–KJV<br><br>Encouraged together–NASB<br><br>Mutually encouraged–NIV<br><br>Encouraged together–NKJV | **συμπαρακληθῆναι** = *sumparaklēthēnai*<br>Pronunciation: [soom-par-ak-leh'-thay-nah-ee]<br>Parsing (part of speech): verb<br>    Mood—infinitive<br>    Tense—aorist<br>    Voice—passive<br>    Case—accusative<br>    Stem or root—from **συμπαρακαλέομαι**<br>Concordance References:<br>    ⇒ Strong's #4837 sumparakaleō<br>    ⇒ NIV #5220 sumparakaleō<br>    ⇒ NASB #4837 sumparakaleō | To be encouraged together; to be mutually encouraged; to be strengthened and consoled together.<br><br>**Practical Application**<br>Paul wished to be encouraged together with other believers. Paul expected to be taught and strengthened by the believers as well as to teach and to strengthen them. There was to be a mutual sharing among all. Paul expected all believers to be actively sharing the gospel. He even |

## PRACTICAL WORD STUDIES
### in the NEW TESTAMENT

| ENGLISH WORD | GREEK WORD AND VERSE | THE WORD MEANS... |
|---|---|---|
| **Encouraged by yours–NLT**<br><br>**POSB REFERENCE**<br>(Romans 1:10-13; esp. v.12)<br>Note 4, point 2 | **Romans 1:12**<br>That is, that I may be **comforted together** with you by the mutual faith both of you and me. [KJV]<br>That is, that I may be **encouraged together** with you while among you, each of us by the other's faith, both yours and mine. [NASB]<br>That is, that you and I may be **mutually encouraged** by each other's faith. [NIV]<br>That is, that I may be **encouraged together** with you by the mutual faith both of you and me. [NKJV]<br>I'm eager to encourage you in your faith, but I also want to be **encouraged by yours**. In this way, each of us will be a blessing to the other. [NLT]<br>τοῦτο δέ ἐστι, **συμπαρακληθῆναι** ἐν ὑμῖν διὰ τῆς ἐν ἀλλήλοις πίστεως ὑμῶν τε καὶ ἐμοῦ. [GNS]<br>τοῦτο δέ ἐστιν **συμπαρακληθῆναι** ἐν ὑμῖν διὰ τῆς ἐν ἀλλήλοις πίστεως ὑμῶν τε καὶ ἐμοῦ. [GNT] | expected them to share with him so that he might grow and be more firmly rooted in the faith. |
| **#1266**<br>**Encouraged Together**<br><br>Comforted together–KJV<br>**Encouraged together–NASB**<br>**Mutually encouraged–NIV**<br>**Encouraged together–NKJV**<br>Encouraged by yours–NLT<br><br>**POSB REFERENCE**<br>(Romans 1:10-13; esp. v.12)<br>Note 4, point 2 | συμπαρακληθῆναι = *sumparaklēthēnai*<br>Pronunciation: [soom-par-ak-leh'-thay-nah-ee]<br>Parsing (part of speech): verb<br>    Mood—infinitive<br>    Tense—aorist<br>    Voice—passive<br>    Case—accusative<br>    Stem or root—from συμπαρακαλέομαι<br>Concordance References:<br>  ⇒ Strong's #4837 sumparakaleō<br>  ⇒ NIV #5220 sumparakaleō<br>  ⇒ NASB #4837 sumparakaleō<br><br>**Romans 1:12**<br>That is, that I may be **comforted together** with you by the mutual faith both of you and me. [KJV]<br>That is, that I may be **encouraged together** with you while among you, each of us by the other's faith, both yours and mine. [NASB]<br>That is, that you and I may be **mutually encouraged** by each other's faith. [NIV]<br>that is, that I may be **encouraged together** with you by the mutual faith both of you and me. [NKJV]<br>I'm eager to encourage you in your faith, but I also want to be **encouraged by yours**. In this way, each of us will be a blessing to the other. [NLT]<br>τοῦτο δέ ἐστι, **συμπαρακληθῆναι** ἐν ὑμῖν διὰ τῆς ἐν ἀλλήλοις πίστεως ὑμῶν τε καὶ ἐμοῦ. [GNS]<br>τοῦτο δέ ἐστιν **συμπαρακληθῆναι** ἐν ὑμῖν διὰ τῆς ἐν ἀλλήλοις πίστεως ὑμῶν τε καὶ ἐμοῦ. [GNT] | To be encouraged together; to be mutually encouraged; to be strengthened and consoled together.<br><br>**Practical Application**<br>Paul wished to be encouraged together with other believers. Paul expected to be taught and strengthened by the believers as well as to teach and to strengthen them. There was to be a mutual sharing among all. Paul expected all believers to be actively sharing the gospel. He even expected them to share with him so that he might grow and be more firmly rooted in the faith. |
| **#1267**<br>**Encouraging Message**<br><br>Consolation–KJV<br>Encouragement–NASB<br>**Encouraging message–NIV**<br>Encouragement–NKJV<br>**Encouraging message–NLT**<br><br>**POSB REFERENCE**<br>(Acts 15:30-35; esp. v.31)<br>Note 5, point 1 | παρακλήσει = *paraklēsei*<br>Pronunciation: [par-ak'-lay-seh-ee]<br>Parsing (part of speech): noun<br>    Case—dative<br>    Gender—feminine<br>    Number—singular<br>    Stem or root—from παράκλησις, εως<br>Concordance References:<br>  ⇒ Strong's #3874 paraklēsis<br>  ⇒ NIV #4155 paraklēsis<br>  ⇒ NASB #3874 paraklēsis<br><br>**Acts 15:31**<br>Which when they had read, they rejoiced for the **consolation**. [KJV]<br>And when they had read it, they rejoiced because of its **encouragement**. [NASB]<br>The people read it and were glad for its **encouraging message**. [NIV]<br>When they had read it, they rejoiced over its **encouragement**. [NKJV]<br>And there was great joy throughout the church that day as they read this **encouraging message**. [NLT] | An encouraging message; consolation, exhortation, appeal, encouragement, comfort, help.<br><br>**Practical Application**<br>When the four men arrived in Antioch, the whole church was called together and the great decree on salvation was read. When it was read, four great results occurred. Note how God took the dissension and its subsequent events and worked it all out for the good of the Antioch church and for the cause of Christ. The results were fourfold.<br>1. There was great "gladness" (*echaresan*): joy, rejoicing over the encouraging message (*paraklēsei*), that is, over the encouragement and help given by the Jerusalem church.<br>2. There was great "encouragement." Note that it was Silas and Judas who were encouraging and confirming the faith of the Antioch believers." They encouraged for a long time, building the believers up more and more, assuring them of their faith in the Lord Jesus. |

# PRACTICAL WORD STUDIES
## in the NEW TESTAMENT

| ENGLISH WORD | GREEK WORD AND VERSE | THE WORD MEANS... |
|---|---|---|
| | ἀναγνόντες δὲ, ἐχάρησαν ἐπὶ τῇ **παρακλήσει**. [GNS]<br>ἀναγνόντες δὲ ἐχάρησαν ἐπὶ τῇ **παρακλήσει**. [GNT] | They were saved by the grace of God and His grace alone, and the two visiting preachers wanted the believers to know that the apostles and elders of the great Jerusalem church confirmed the glorious truth.<br>3. There was the discovery of the great missionary, Silas. The oldest Greek manuscripts do not include this verse (note the word "they" in Acts 15:33). Some scholars feel it was added at a later date because Silas appears with Paul in Acts 15:40. There was, of course, plenty of time for Silas to travel to Jerusalem and report back to the church and then to return to Antioch before Paul left on his second missionary journey. Other scholars believe the verse was in the original manuscript. No matter who is accurate, Silas and his great gift from God were discovered by Paul at Antioch, and apparently Paul invited him to join the great mission thrust. (See POSB *Deeper Study* #1, Silas—Acts 15:34 for more discussion.)<br>4. A great teaching ministry grew within the church (v.35). |
| **#1268**<br>**End**<br><br>End–KJV<br>End–NASB<br>End–NIV<br>End–NKJV<br>End–NLT<br><br>**POSB REFERENCE**<br>(1 Cor.15:24-28; esp. v.24)<br>Note 2 | τέλος = *telos*<br>Pronunciation: [tel'-os]<br>Parsing (part of speech): noun<br>    Case—nominative<br>    Gender—neuter<br>    Number—singular<br>    Stem or root—from τέλος, ους<br>Concordance References:<br>  ⇒ Strong's #5056 telos<br>  ⇒ NIV #5465 telos<br>  ⇒ NASB #5056 telos<br><br>**1 Cor. 15:24**<br>Then cometh the **end**, when he shall have delivered up the kingdom to God, even the Father; when he shall have put down all rule and all authority and power. [KJV]<br>Then comes the **end**, when He delivers up the kingdom to the God and Father, when He has abolished all rule and all authority and power. [NASB]<br>Then the **end** will come, when he hands over the kingdom to God the Father after he has destroyed all dominion, authority and power. [NIV]<br>Then *comes* the **end**, when He delivers the kingdom to God the Father, when He puts an end to all rule and all authority and power. [NKJV]<br>After that the **end** will come, when he will turn the Kingdom over to God the Father, having put down all enemies of every kind. [NLT]<br>εἶτα τὸ **τέλος**, ὅταν παραδῷ τὴν βασιλείαν τῷ Θεῷ καὶ πατρί, ὅταν καταργήσῃ πᾶσαν ἀρχὴν καὶ πᾶσαν ἐξουσίαν καὶ δύναμιν. [GNS]<br>εἶτα τὸ **τέλος**, ὅταν παραδιδῷ τὴν βασιλείαν τῷ θεῷ καὶ πατρί, ὅταν καταργήσῃ πᾶσαν ἀρχὴν καὶ πᾶσαν ἐξουσίαν καὶ δύναμιν. [GNT] | The purposed end; the determined goal; the destined climax; the sought after consummation; the fulfillment; the result; the outcome; the last; the full extent of the termination; accomplished the whole purpose.<br><br>**Practical Application**<br>After Christ has resurrected believers, He will then move to deliver the kingdom to God. This clearly points to the end of time, the climax and consummation of human history. Note three significant facts:<br>⇒ The length of time between the resurrection of Christ and believers (1 Cor. 15:23) has already been millenniums.<br>⇒ The length of time between the resurrection of believers and Christ's delivering the kingdom to God is not given.<br>⇒ The words "then" (*eita*) and "when" (*hotan*) both indicate indefinite periods of time, long intervals of time.<br>These facts clearly indicate that great events and generations of time can occur between the resurrection of believers and the end of the world, for example, the one thousand year millennial reign of Christ. |
| **#1269**<br>**End**<br><br>End–KJV<br>End–NASB<br>End–NIV<br>End–NKJV<br>Accomplished the whole purpose– NLT | τέλος = *telos*<br>Pronunciation: [tel'-os]<br>Parsing (part of speech): noun<br>    Case—nominative<br>    Gender—neuter<br>    Number—singular<br>    Stem or root—from τέλος, ους<br>Concordance References:<br>  ⇒ Strong's #5056 telos<br>  ⇒ NIV #5465 telos<br>  ⇒ NASB #5056 telos | The purposed end; the determined goal; the destined climax; the sought after consummation; the fulfillment; the result; the outcome; the last; the full extent of the termination; accomplished the whole purpose.<br><br>**Practical Application**<br>Jesus Christ is the One who puts an end (*telos*) to man having to seek righteousness through the law. Man no longer has to work and |

# PRACTICAL WORD STUDIES
## in the NEW TESTAMENT

| ENGLISH WORD | GREEK WORD AND VERSE | THE WORD MEANS... |
|---|---|---|
| **POSB REFERENCE** (Romans 10:4) Note 2 | **Romans 10:4**<br>For Christ is the **end** of the law for righteousness to every one that believeth. [KJV]<br>For Christ is the **end** of the law for righteousness to everyone who believes. [NASB]<br>Christ is the **end** of the law so that there may be righteousness for everyone who believes. [NIV]<br>For Christ *is* the **end** of the law for righteousness to everyone who believes. [NKJV]<br>For Christ has **accomplished the whole purpose** of the law. All who believe in him are made right with God. [NLT]<br>τέλος γὰρ νόμου Χριστὸς εἰς δικαιοσύνην παντὶ τῷ πιστεύοντι. [GNS]<br>τέλος γὰρ νόμου Χριστὸς εἰς δικαιοσύνην παντὶ τῷ πιστεύοντι. [GNT] | work to be acceptable to God, to work and work knowing full well that he is coming ever so short of God's glory and demand. Man no longer has to live under the enslaving power of sin, under its guilt and shame and punishment. Man no longer has to live under the weight and pressure of failing and of being ever so unworthy and hopeless, lonely and alienated. Man can now be set free, knowing full well that he is acceptable to God. Man can now have a heart that swells with assurance and confidence, the perfect knowledge that he is God's and God is his. Man can know that he is accepted as righteous before God. How? Through the righteousness of Jesus Christ. |
| **#1270**<br>**Endeavouring**<br><br>Endeavouring–KJV<br>Being diligent–NASB<br>Make every effort– NIV<br>**Endeavoring**–NKJV<br>Always keep yourselves–NLT<br><br>**POSB REFERENCE** (Eph.4:3) Note 2 | σπουδάζοντες = *spoudazontes*<br>Pronunciation: [spoo-dad'-zon-tes]<br>Parsing (part of speech): verb<br>    Mood—participle (imperative sense)<br>    Tense—present<br>    Voice—active<br>    Case—nominative<br>    Gender—masculine<br>    Person—2nd person<br>    Number—plural<br>    Stem or root—from σπουδάζω<br>Concordance References:<br>⇒ Strong's #4704 spoudazō<br>⇒ NIV #5079 spoudazō<br>⇒ NASB #4704 spoudazō<br><br>**Ephes. 4:3**<br>**Endeavouring** to keep the unity of the Spirit in the bond of peace. [KJV]<br>**Being diligent** to preserve the unity of the Spirit in the bond of peace. [NASB]<br>**Make every effort** to keep the unity of the Spirit through the bond of peace. [NIV]<br>**Endeavoring** to keep the unity of the Spirit in the bond of peace. [NKJV]<br>**Always keep yourselves** united in the Holy Spirit, and bind yourselves together with peace. [NLT]<br>σπουδάζοντες τηρεῖν τὴν ἑνότητα τοῦ Πνεύματος ἐν τῷ συνδέσμῳ τῆς εἰρήνης. [GNS]<br>σπουδάζοντες τηρεῖν τὴν ἑνότητα τοῦ πνεύματος ἐν τῷ συνδέσμῳ τῆς εἰρήνης· [GNT] | To make every effort; to work hard; to be eager; to do one's best, being diligent, to work at, taking care and doing one's very best, and to make haste to do it.<br><br>**Practical Application**<br>The only way to walk worthy of God's great calling is to work at keeping the peace and unity which God has given us. Nothing cuts the heart of God like divisiveness between His people, divisiveness which tears apart His church. The very thing God is doing is creating a new body of people to live together in the love and unity of His Son. He is going to create a new heavens and earth in which there will be no other spirit. Therefore, He expects us to live in the love and unity of His Spirit now. |
| **#1271**<br>**Endorsed**<br><br>Approved–KJV<br>Attested–NASB<br>Accredited–NIV<br>Attested–NKJV<br>**Endorsed–NLT**<br><br>**POSB REFERENCE** (Acts 2:22-24; esp. v.22)<br>Note 3, point 1 | ἀποδεδειγμένον = *apodedeigmenon*<br>Pronunciation: [ap-od-eh-deeng-meh'-non]<br>Parsing (part of speech): verb<br>    Mood—participle<br>    Tense—perfect<br>    Voice—passive<br>    Case—accusative<br>    Gender—masculine<br>    Number—singular<br>    Stem or root—from ἀποδείκνυμι<br>Concordance References:<br>⇒ Strong's #584 apodeiknumi<br>⇒ NIV #617 apodeiknumi<br>⇒ NASB #584 apodeiknumi<br><br>**Acts 2:22**<br>Ye men of Israel, hear these words; Jesus of Nazareth, a man **approved** of God among you by miracles and wonders and signs, which God did by him in the midst of you, as ye yourselves also know: [KJV]<br>"Men of Israel, listen to these words: Jesus the Nazarene, a man **attested** to you by God with miracles and wonders and signs which God performed through Him in your midst, just as you yourselves know— [NASB] | To accredit; to approve; to endorse; to point out; to display; to show; to attest; to sanction; to certify.<br><br>**Practical Application**<br>God put His stamp of approval upon Jesus. He demonstrated and showed all men that Jesus is perfectly acceptable to Him. Jesus of Nazareth had God's approval, His perfect acceptance. |

# PRACTICAL WORD STUDIES
## in the NEW TESTAMENT

| ENGLISH WORD | GREEK WORD AND VERSE | THE WORD MEANS... |
|---|---|---|
| | "Men of Israel, listen to this: Jesus of Nazareth was a man **accredited** by God to you by miracles, wonders and signs, which God did among you through him, as you yourselves know. [NIV]<br><br>"Men of Israel, hear these words: Jesus of Nazareth, a Man **attested** by God to you by miracles, wonders, and signs which God did through Him in your midst, as you yourselves also know—[NKJV]<br><br>"People of Israel, listen! God publicly **endorsed** Jesus of Nazareth by doing wonderful miracles, wonders, and signs through him, as you well know. [NLT]<br><br>ἄνδρες Ἰσραηλῖται, ἀκούσατε τοὺς λόγους τούτους· Ἰησοῦν τὸν Ναζωραῖον, ἄνδρα ἀπὸ τοῦ Θεοῦ **ἀποδεδειγμένον** εἰς ὑμᾶς δυνάμεσι καὶ τέρασι καὶ σημείοις, οἷς ἐποίησε δι' αὐτοῦ ὁ Θεὸς ἐν μέσῳ ὑμῶν, καθὼς καὶ αὐτοὶ οἴδατε, [GNS]<br><br>Ἄνδρες Ἰσραηλῖται, ἀκούσατε τοὺς λόγους τούτους· Ἰησοῦν τὸν Ναζωραῖον, ἄνδρα **ἀποδεδειγμένον** ἀπὸ τοῦ θεοῦ εἰς ὑμᾶς δυνάμεσι καὶ τέρασι καὶ σημείοις οἷς ἐποίησεν δι' αὐτοῦ ὁ θεὸς ἐν μέσῳ ὑμῶν καθὼς αὐτοὶ οἴδατε, [GNT] | |
| **#1272**<br>**Endued With**<br><br>Endued with–KJV<br>Clothed with–NASB<br>Clothed with–NIV<br>Endued with–NKJV<br>Comes and fills–NLT<br><br>**POSB REFERENCE**<br>(Lk.24:44-49; esp. v.49)<br>Note 2, point 4 | ἐνδύσησθε = endusësthe<br>Pronunciation: [en-doo'-sees-thay]<br>Parsing (part of speech): verb<br>    Mood—subjunctive<br>    Tense—aorist<br>    Voice—middle<br>    Person—2nd person<br>    Number—plural<br>    Stem or root—from ἐνδύω<br>Concordance References:<br>  ⇒ Strong's #1746 enduō<br>  ⇒ NIV #1907 enduō<br>  ⇒ NASB #1746 enduō<br><br>**Luke 24:49**<br>And, behold, I send the promise of my Father upon you: but tarry ye in the city of Jerusalem, until ye be **endued with** power from on high. [KJV]<br><br>"And behold, I am sending forth the promise of My Father upon you; but you are to stay in the city until you are **clothed with** power from on high." [NASB]<br><br>I am going to send you what my Father has promised; but stay in the city until you have been **clothed with** power from on high." [NIV]<br><br>Behold, I send the Promise of My Father upon you; but tarry in the city of Jerusalem until you are **endued with** power from on high." [NKJV]<br><br>"And now I will send the Holy Spirit, just as my Father promised. But stay here in the city until the Holy Spirit **comes and fills** you with power from heaven." [NLT]<br><br>καὶ ἰδοὺ ἐγὼ ἀποστέλλω τὴν ἐπαγγελίαν τοῦ πατρός μου ἐφ' ὑμᾶς· ὑμεῖς δὲ καθίσατε ἐν τῇ πόλει Ἰερουσαλήμ, ἕως οὗ **ἐνδύσησθε** δύναμιν ἐξ ὕψους. [GNS]<br><br>καὶ [ἰδοὺ] ἐγὼ ἀποστέλλω τὴν ἐπαγγελίαν τοῦ πατρός μου ἐφ' ὑμᾶς· ὑμεῖς δὲ καθίσατε ἐν τῇ πόλει ἕως οὗ **ἐνδύσησθε** ἐξ ὕψους δύναμιν. [GNT] | To put on a garment; to be clothed with; to wear; to dress.<br><br>**Practical Application**<br>In this Scripture, we find that the source of the Spirit and power was God.<br>⇒ Christ was to send the promise.<br>⇒ The promise was from the Father. God gave the promise.<br>⇒ Believers had to stay; to tarry; that is, to wait upon the Lord and pray for the promise.<br>⇒ The promise was to come from "on high." God Himself was the Source of power for all evangelism. |
| **#1273**<br>**Endurance**<br><br>Patience–KJV<br>Steadfastness–NASB<br>**Endurance–NIV**<br>Patience–NKJV<br>**Endurance–NLT** | ὑπομονήν = hupomonēn<br>Pronunciation: [hoop-om-on-ayn']<br>Parsing (part of speech): noun<br>    Case—accusative<br>    Gender—feminine<br>    Number—singular<br>    Stem or root—from ὑπομονή, ῆς<br>Concordance References:<br>  ⇒ Strong's #5281 hupomonē<br>  ⇒ NIV #5705 hupomonē<br>  ⇒ NASB #5281 hupomonē | Endurance, patience, steadfastness, fortitude, constancy, perseverance.<br><br>**Practical Application**<br>The word (*hupomonēn*) is not passive; it is active. It is not the spirit that sits back and puts up with the trials of life, taking whatever may come. Rather, it is the spirit that stands up and faces the trials of life, that actively goes about conquering and overcoming them. When trials confront a person who is truly justified, he is stirred to arise and face the trials head on. He |

# PRACTICAL WORD STUDIES
## in the New Testament

| ENGLISH WORD | GREEK WORD AND VERSE | THE WORD MEANS... |
|---|---|---|
| **POSB REFERENCE** (Col.1:11) Note 3, point 1<br><br>**See also POSB REF:** (2 Tim. 3:10) Note 1, point 7<br>(2 Thes.1:4-5; esp. v.4) Note 6<br>(1 Tim.6:11) Note 2, point 5<br>(Heb.12:11) Note 2, point 2 | **Col. 1:11**<br>Strengthened with all might, according to his glorious power, unto all **patience** and longsuffering with joyfulness; [KJV]<br>Strengthened with all power, according to His glorious might, for the attaining of all **steadfastness** and patience; joyously [NASB]<br>Being strengthened with all power according to his glorious might so that you may have great **endurance** and patience, and joyfully [NIV]<br>Strengthened with all might, according to His glorious power, for all **patience** and longsuffering with joy; [NKJV]<br>We also pray that you will be strengthened with his glorious power so that you will have all the patience and **endurance** you need. May you be filled with joy, [NLT]<br>ἐν πάσῃ δυνάμει δυναμούμενοι κατὰ τὸ κράτος τῆς δόξης αὐτοῦ, εἰς πᾶσαν **ὑπομονὴν** καὶ μακροθυμίαν, μετὰ χαρᾶς· [GNS]<br>ἐν πάσῃ δυνάμει δυναμούμενοι κατὰ τὸ κράτος τῆς δόξης αὐτοῦ εἰς πᾶσαν **ὑπομονὴν** καὶ μακροθυμίαν. μετὰ χαρᾶς [GNT] | immediately sets out to conquer and overcome them. He knows that God is allowing the trials in order to teach him more and more patience (endurance).<br><br>The godly person follows the example of those who are actively patient, who endure by walking through the trials of life, conquering all for Christ. |
| **#1274**<br>**Endurance**<br><br>Patience–KJV<br>**Endurance**–NASB<br>To persevere–NIV<br>**Endurance**–NKJV<br>Patient endurance– NLT<br><br>**POSB REFERENCE** (Heb.10:32-39; esp. v.36) Note 4 | **ὑπομονῆς** = *hupomonēs*<br>Pronunciation: [hoop-om-on-ays']<br>Parsing (part of speech): noun<br>    Case—genitive<br>    Gender—feminine<br>    Number—singular<br>    Stem or root—from ὑπομονή, ῆς<br>Concordance References:<br>  ⇒ Strong's #5281 hupomonē<br>  ⇒ NIV #5705 hupomonē<br>  ⇒ NASB #5281 hupomonē<br><br>**Hebrews 10:36**<br>For ye have need of **patience**, that, after ye have done the will of God, ye might receive the promise. [KJV]<br>For you have need of **endurance**, so that when you have done the will of God, you may receive what was promised. [NASB]<br>You need **to persevere** so that when you have done the will of God, you will receive what he has promised. [NIV]<br>For you have need of **endurance**, so that after you have done the will of God, you may receive the promise: [NKJV]<br>**Patient endurance** is what you need now, so you will continue to do God's will. Then you will receive all that he has promised. [NLT]<br>**ὑπομονῆς** γὰρ ἔχετε χρείαν, ἵνα τὸ θέλημα τοῦ Θεοῦ ποιήσαντες, κομίσησθε τὴν ἐπαγγελίαν. [GNS]<br>**ὑπομονῆς** γὰρ ἔχετε χρείαν ἵνα τὸ θέλημα τοῦ θεοῦ ποιήσαντες κομίσησθε τὴν ἐπαγγελίαν. [GNT] | To persevere; to be patient; to have endurance; to be steadfast in doing the will of God.<br><br>**Practical Application**<br>The verses (Hebrews 10:35-37) state it well: endure and you will receive the promise of God's reward. For in just a little while Christ is coming, and He will not tarry. His coming is assured; and when He comes, He will come with His reward. |
| **#1275**<br>**Endurance**<br><br>Patience–KJV<br>**Endurance**–NASB<br>Perseverance–NIV<br>**Endurance**–NKJV<br>**Endurance**–NLT<br><br>**POSB REFERENCE** (Heb.12:1) Note 2, point 2 | **ὑπομονῆς** = *hupomonēs*<br>Pronunciation: [hoop-om-on-ays']<br>Parsing (part of speech): noun<br>    Case—genitive<br>    Gender—feminine<br>    Number—singular<br>    Stem or root—from ὑπομονή, ῆς<br>Concordance References:<br>  ⇒ Strong's #5281 hupomonē<br>  ⇒ NIV #5705 hupomonē<br>  ⇒ NASB #5281 hupomonē<br><br>**Hebrews 12:1**<br>Wherefore seeing we also are compassed about with so great a cloud of witnesses, let us lay aside every weight, and the sin which doth so easily beset us, and let us run with **patience** the race that is set before us, [KJV]<br>Therefore, since we have so great a cloud of witnesses | To persevere; to be patient; to have endurance; to be steadfast in doing the will of God.<br><br>**Practical Application**<br>The word *endurance* is not passive; it is active. It is not the spirit that just sits back and puts up with the trials of life, taking whatever may come. Rather, it is the spirit that stands up and faces the trials of life, that actively goes about conquering and overcoming them. When trials confront a man who is truly justified, he is stirred to arise and face the trials head on. He immediately sets out to conquer and overcome them. He knows that God is allowing the trials in order to teach him more and more endurance (patience). |

# PRACTICAL WORD STUDIES
## in the NEW TESTAMENT

| ENGLISH WORD | GREEK WORD AND VERSE | THE WORD MEANS... |
|---|---|---|
| | surrounding us, let us also lay aside every encumbrance, and the sin which so easily entangles us, and let us run with **endurance** the race that is set before us, [NASB]<br><br>Therefore, since we are surrounded by such a great cloud of witnesses, let us throw off everything that hinders and the sin that so easily entangles, and let us run with **perseverance** the race marked out for us. [NIV]<br><br>Therefore we also, since we are surrounded by so great a cloud of witnesses, let us lay aside every weight, and the sin which so easily ensnares *us,* and let us run with **endurance** the race that is set before us, [NKJV]<br><br>Therefore, since we are surrounded by such a huge crowd of witnesses to the life of faith, let us strip off every weight that slows us down, especially the sin that so easily hinders our progress. And let us run with **endurance** the race that God has set before us. [NLT]<br><br>Τοιγαροῦν καὶ ἡμεῖς τοσοῦτον ἔχοντες περικείμενον ἡμῖν νέφος μαρτύρων, ὄγκον ἀποθέμενοι πάντα καὶ τὴν εὐπερίστατον ἁμαρτίαν, δι' **ὑπομονῆς** τρέχωμεν τὸν προκείμενον ἡμῖν ἀγῶνα, [GNS]<br><br>Τοιγαροῦν καὶ ἡμεῖς τοσοῦτον ἔχοντες περικείμενον ἡμῖν νέφος μαρτύρων, ὄγκον ἀποθέμενοι πάντα καὶ τὴν εὐπερίστατον ἁμαρτίαν, δι' **ὑπομονῆς** τρέχωμεν τὸν προκείμενον ἡμῖν ἀγῶνα [GNT] | |
| **#1276**<br>**Endurance**<br><br>Patience–KJV<br>**Endurance–NASB**<br>Perseverance–NIV<br>Patience–NKJV<br>**Endurance–NLT**<br><br>**POSB REFERENCE**<br>(Jas.1:2-4; esp. v.3)<br>Note 2, point 1<br><br>See also POSB REF:<br>(Heb.10:32-39; esp. v.36)<br>Note 4<br>(2 Cor.6:4)<br>Note 2<br>(Rom.5:3-5; esp. v.3)<br>Note 5, point 1<br>(2 Pt.1:5-7; esp. v.6)<br>Note 1, point 4 | ὑπομονήν = *hupomonēn*<br>Pronunciation: [hoop-om-on-ayn']<br>Parsing (part of speech): noun<br>    Case—accusative<br>    Gender—feminine<br>    Number—singular<br>    Stem or root—from ὑπομονή, ῆς<br>Concordance References:<br>  ⇒ Strong's #5281 hupomonē<br>  ⇒ NIV #5705 hupomonē<br>  ⇒ NASB #5281 hupomonē<br><br>**James 1:3**<br>Knowing this, that the trying of your faith worketh **patience**. [KJV]<br>Knowing that the testing of your faith produces **endurance**. [NASB]<br>Because you know that the testing of your faith develops **perseverance**. [NIV]<br>Knowing that the testing of your faith produces **patience**. [NKJV]<br>For when your faith is tested, your **endurance** has a chance to grow. [NLT]<br>γινώσκοντες ὅτι τὸ δοκίμιον ὑμῶν τῆς πίστεως κατεργάζεται **ὑπομονήν**· [GNS]<br>γινώσκοντες ὅτι τὸ δοκίμιον ὑμῶν τῆς πίστεως κατεργάζεται **ὑπομονήν**. [GNT] | Perseverance, patience, endurance, steadfastness.<br><br>**Practical Application**<br>We must know something: know that testings and temptations produce endurance (James 1:3). Trials and temptations are not to defeat and discourage us, but to prove us, to make us much stronger and more pure and righteous. The believer is to know that the trials and temptations of life will make him more steadfast, more persevering, and more enduring. They will make him much stronger, not weaker. They will make him strong just like Jesus, and they will give him a pure and righteous character just like Jesus. When the believer keeps this fact in his mind, he can face trials and temptations much more positively. He can then begin to move toward the spirit of living joyfully in the face of trials and temptations. |
| **#1277**<br>**Endurance–Endure**<br><br>Patience–KJV<br>**Endurance–NASB**<br>**Endurance–NIV**<br>Patience–NKJV<br>**Endure–NLT**<br><br>**POSB REFERENCE**<br>(2 Cor.6:4)<br>Note 2 | ὑπομονῇ = *hupomonē*<br>Pronunciation: [hoop-om-on-ay']<br>Parsing (part of speech): noun<br>    Case—dative<br>    Gender—feminine<br>    Number—singular<br>    Stem or root—from ὑπομονή, ῆς<br>Concordance References:<br>  ⇒ Strong's #5281 hupomonē<br>  ⇒ NIV #5705 hupomonē<br>  ⇒ NASB #5281 hupomonē<br><br>**2 Cor. 6:4**<br>But in all things approving ourselves as the ministers of God, in much **patience**, in afflictions, in necessities, in distresses, [KJV]<br>But in everything commending ourselves as servants of God, in much **endurance**, in afflictions, in hardships, in distresses, [NASB]<br>Rather, as servants of God we commend ourselves in | Endurance; steadfast endurance; patient endurance; perseverance; constancy; to stand firm.<br><br>**Practical Application**<br>Endurance is the supreme quality, the very backbone of consistency. Unless a man endures, he will never be consistent, not in a corruptible and sinful world. A corruptible and sinful world presents obstacle after obstacle and sin after sin that have to be *endured and overcome* if a person is to live a consistent life. Steadfast endurance is the basic ingredient and force that a person must have to live a consistent life for the Lord Jesus. When trials, fatigue, temptations, or opposition confront the minister of God (or the believer), he must do all he can to endure. |

# PRACTICAL WORD STUDIES
## in the NEW TESTAMENT

| ENGLISH WORD | GREEK WORD AND VERSE | THE WORD MEANS... |
|---|---|---|
| | every way: in great **endurance**; in troubles, hardships and distresses; [NIV]<br>But in all *things* we commend ourselves as ministers of God: in much **patience**, in tribulations, in needs, in distresses, [NKJV]<br>In everything we do we try to show that we are true ministers of God. We patiently **endure** troubles and hardships and calamities of every kind. [NLT]<br>ἀλλ' ἐν παντὶ συνίσταντες ἑαυτοὺς ὡς Θεοῦ διάκονοι, ἐν **ὑπομονῇ** πολλῇ, ἐν θλίψεσιν, ἐν ἀνάγκαις, ἐν στενοχωρίαις, [GNS]<br>ἀλλ' ἐν παντὶ συνίσταντες ἑαυτοὺς ὡς θεοῦ διάκονοι, ἐν **ὑπομονῇ** πολλῇ, ἐν θλίψεσιν, ἐν ἀνάγκαις, ἐν στενοχωρίαις, [GNT] | |
| **#1278**<br>**Endure**<br><br>Heaviness–KJV<br>Distressed–NASB<br>Suffer grief–NIV<br>Grieved–NKJV<br>**Endure–NLT**<br><br>**POSB REFERENCE**<br>(1 Pt.1:6)<br>Note 1, point 2 | λυπηθέντες = *lupēthentes*<br>Pronunciation: [loo-pay'-then-tehs]<br>Parsing (part of speech): verb<br>  Mood—participle<br>  Tense—aorist<br>  Voice—passive<br>  Case—nominative<br>  Gender—masculine<br>  Person—2nd person<br>  Number—plural<br>  Stem or root—from λυπέω<br>Concordance References:<br>  ⇒ Strong's #3076 lupeō<br>  ⇒ NIV #3382 lupeō<br>  ⇒ NASB #3076 lupeō<br><br>**1 Peter 1:6**<br>Wherein ye greatly rejoice, though now for a season, if need be, ye are in **heaviness** through manifold temptations: [KJV]<br>In this you greatly rejoice, even though now for a little while, if necessary, you have been **distressed** by various trials, [NASB]<br>In this you greatly rejoice, though now for a little while you may have had to **suffer grief** in all kinds of trials. [NIV]<br>In this you greatly rejoice, though now for a little while, if need be, you have been **grieved** by various trials, [NKJV]<br>So be truly glad! There is wonderful joy ahead, even though it is necessary for you to **endure** many trials for a while. [NLT]<br>ἐν ᾧ ἀγαλλιᾶσθε ὀλίγον ἄρτι, εἰ δέον ἐστί, **λυπηθέντες** ἐν ποικίλοις πειρασμοῖς, [GNS]<br>ἐν ᾧ ἀγαλλιᾶσθε, ὀλίγον ἄρτι εἰ δέον [ἐστὶν] **λυπηθέντες** ἐν ποικίλοις πειρασμοῖς, [GNT] | To suffer grief, heaviness; to be distressed, sorrowful; to be hurt; to be made sorry; to be sad; to be grieving; to suffer sorrow, stress, pressure, and mental anguish.<br><br>**Practical Application**<br>Trials and temptations cause a heaviness within us. We all know what it is to feel heavy and weighed down with grief; to suffer stress and pressure; to be mentally in anguish, wondering, questioning, and suffering under the weight of trial or temptation. |
| **#1279**<br>**Endure–<br>Endures**<br><br>Endure–KJV<br>Endures–NASB<br>Stands firm–NIV<br>Endures–NKJV<br>**Endure–NLT**<br><br>**POSB REFERENCE**<br>(Mk.13:13)<br>Note 9, point 1<br><br>See also POSB REF:<br>(Mt.24:13)<br>Note 9 | ὑπομείνας = *upomeinas*<br>Pronunciation: [hoop-om-en'-ahs]<br>Parsing (part of speech): verb<br>  Mood—participle<br>  Tense—aorist<br>  Voice—active<br>  Case—nominative<br>  Gender—masculine<br>  Number—singular<br>  Stem or root—from ὑπομένω<br>Concordance References:<br>  ⇒ Strong's #5278 hupomenō<br>  ⇒ NIV #5702 hupomenō<br>  ⇒ NASB #5278 hupomenō<br><br>**Mark 13:13**<br>And ye shall be hated of all men for my name's sake: but he that shall **endure** unto the end, the same shall be saved. [KJV]<br>"And you will be hated by all on account of My name, but the one who **endures** to the end, he shall be saved. [NASB] | To stand firm; to endure; to bear up under suffering, to stand firm, to be courageous in suffering, to persevere and endure patiently—but actively, not passively.<br><br>**Practical Application**<br>It is enduring, actively bearing intense suffering. The believer is to stand firm through all forms of persecution and abuse, even if it leads to inhuman torture and death. |

# PRACTICAL WORD STUDIES
## in the NEW TESTAMENT

| ENGLISH WORD | GREEK WORD AND VERSE | THE WORD MEANS... |
|---|---|---|
| | All men will hate you because of me, but he who **stands firm** to the end will be saved. [NIV]<br><br>And you will be hated by all for My name's sake. But he who **endures** to the end shall be saved. [NKJV]<br><br>And everyone will hate you because of your allegiance to me. But those who **endure** to the end will be saved. [NLT]<br><br>καὶ ἔσεσθε μισούμενοι ὑπὸ πάντων διὰ τὸ ὄνομά μου. ὁ δὲ **ὑπομείνας** εἰς τέλος, οὗτος σωθήσεται. [GNS]<br><br>καὶ ἔσεσθε μισούμενοι ὑπὸ πάντων διὰ τὸ ὄνομά μου. ὁ δὲ **ὑπομείνας** εἰς τέλος οὗτος σωθή [GNT] | |
| **#1280**<br>**Endure Afflictions**<br><br>**Endure afflictions–** KJV<br>Endure hardship– NASB<br>Endure hardship–NIV<br>**Endure afflictions– NKJV**<br>Don't be afraid of suffering for the Lord–NLT<br><br>**POSB REFERENCE**<br>(2 Tim. 4:5)<br>Note 4, point 2 | κακοπάθησον = kakopathēson<br>Pronunciation: [kak-op-ath-ay'-son]<br>Parsing (part of speech): verb<br>   Mood—imperative<br>   Tense—aorist<br>   Voice—active<br>   Person—2nd person<br>   Number—singular<br>   Stem or root—from κακοπαθέω<br>Concordance References:<br>  ⇒ Strong's #2553 kakopatheō<br>  ⇒ NIV #2802 kakopatheō<br>  ⇒ NASB #2553 kakopatheō<br><br>**2 Tim. 4:5**<br>But watch thou in all things, **endure afflictions**, do the work of an evangelist, make full proof of thy ministry. [KJV]<br><br>But you, be sober in all things, **endure hardship**, do the work of an evangelist, fulfill your ministry. [NASB]<br><br>But you, keep your head in all situations, **endure hardship**, do the work of an evangelist, discharge all the duties of your ministry. [NIV]<br><br>But you be watchful in all things, **endure afflictions**, do the work of an evangelist, fulfill your ministry. [NKJV]<br><br>But you should keep a clear mind in every situation. **Don't be afraid of suffering for the Lord**. Work at bringing others to Christ. Complete the ministry God has given you. [NLT]<br><br>σὺ δὲ νῆφε ἐν πᾶσι, **κακοπάθησον**, ἔργον ποίησον εὐαγγελιστοῦ, τὴν διακονίαν σου πληροφόρησον. [GNS]<br><br>σὺ δὲ νῆφε ἐν πᾶσιν, **κακοπάθησον**, ἔργον ποίησον εὐαγγελιστοῦ, τὴν διακονίαν σου πληροφόρησον. [GNT] | To endure hardship, afflictions; not to be afraid of suffering for the Lord; to suffer hardships, troubles, problems, difficulties, and evils.<br><br>**Practical Application**<br>Kenneth Wuest gives an excellent discussion of this point, a discussion that merits attention by every minister who has any concern for people whatsoever.<br><br>*"The verb [endure afflictions] is aorist imperative. It is a sharp command given with military snap and curtness. Timothy needed just that. He was not cast in a heroic mold. How we in the ministry of the Word need that injunction today. What 'softies' we sometimes are, afraid to come out clearly in our proclamation of the truth and our stand as to false doctrine, fearing the ostracism of our fellows, the ecclesiastical displeasure of our superiors, or the cutting off of our immediate financial income. I would rather walk a lonely road with Jesus than be without His fellowship in the crowd, wouldn't you? I would rather live in a cottage and eat simple food, and have Him as Head of my house and the Unseen Guest at every meal, than to live in royal style in a mansion without Him"* (The Pastoral Epistles, Vol.2, p.159). |
| **#1281**<br>**Endure Hardship**<br><br>Endure afflictions– KJV<br>**Endure hardship– NASB**<br>**Endure hardship– NIV**<br>Endure afflictions– NKJV<br>Don't be afraid of suffering for the Lord–NLT<br><br>**POSB REFERENCE**<br>(2 Tim. 4:5)<br>Note 4, point 2 | κακοπάθησον = kakopathēson<br>Pronunciation: [kak-op-ath-ay'-son]<br>Parsing (part of speech): verb<br>   Mood—imperative<br>   Tense—aorist<br>   Voice—active<br>   Person—2nd person<br>   Number—singular<br>   Stem or root—from κακοπαθέω<br>Concordance References:<br>  ⇒ Strong's #2553 kakopatheō<br>  ⇒ NIV #2802 kakopatheō<br>  ⇒ NASB #2553 kakopatheō<br><br>**2 Tim. 4:5**<br>But watch thou in all things, **endure afflictions**, do the work of an evangelist, make full proof of thy ministry. [KJV]<br><br>But you, be sober in all things, **endure hardship**, do the work of an evangelist, fulfill your ministry. [NASB]<br><br>But you, keep your head in all situations, **endure hardship**, do the work of an evangelist, discharge all the duties of your ministry. [NIV]<br><br>But you be watchful in all things, **endure afflic-** | To endure hardship, afflictions; not to be afraid of suffering for the Lord; to suffer hardships, troubles, problems, difficulties, and evils.<br><br>**Practical Application**<br>Kenneth Wuest gives an excellent discussion of this point, a discussion that merits attention by every minister who has any concern for people whatsoever.<br><br>*"The verb [endure hardship] is aorist imperative. It is a sharp command given with military snap and curtness. Timothy needed just that. He was not cast in a heroic mold. How we in the ministry of the Word need that injunction today. What 'softies' we sometimes are, afraid to come out clearly in our proclamation of the truth and our stand as to false doctrine, fearing the ostracism of our fellows, the ecclesiastical displeasure of our superiors, or the cutting off of our immediate financial income. I would rather walk a lonely road with Jesus than be without His fellowship in the crowd, wouldn't you? I* |

## Practical Word Studies in the New Testament

| ENGLISH WORD | GREEK WORD AND VERSE | THE WORD MEANS... |
|---|---|---|
| | **tions**, do the work of an evangelist, fulfill your ministry. [NKJV]<br>But you should keep a clear mind in every situation. **Don't be afraid of suffering for the Lord**. Work at bringing others to Christ. Complete the ministry God has given you. [NLT]<br>σὺ δὲ νῆφε ἐν πᾶσι, **κακοπάθησον**, ἔργον ποίησον εὐαγγελιστοῦ, τὴν διακονίαν σου πληροφόρησον. [GNS]<br>σὺ δὲ νῆφε ἐν πᾶσιν, **κακοπάθησον**, ἔργον ποίησον εὐαγγελιστοῦ, τὴν διακονίαν σου πληροφόρησον. [GNT] | would rather live in a cottage and eat simple food, and have Him as Head of my house and the Unseen Guest at every meal, than to live in royal style in a mansion without Him" (*The Pastoral Epistles*, Vol.2, p.159). |
| **#1282**<br>**Endures–Endureth**<br><br>Endureth–KJV<br>Endures–NASB<br>Perseveres–NIV<br>Endures–NKJV<br>Endures–NLT<br><br>**POSB REFERENCE**<br>(1 Cor.13:4-7; esp. v.7)<br>Note 2, point 15 | ὑπομένει = hupomenei<br>Pronunciation: [hoop-om-en'-ee]<br>Parsing (part of speech): verb<br>  Mood—indicative<br>  Tense—present<br>  Voice—active<br>  Person—3rd person<br>  Number—singular<br>  Stem or root—from ὑπομένω<br>Concordance References:<br>  ⇒ Strong's #5278 hupomenō<br>  ⇒ NIV #5702 hupomenō<br>  ⇒ NASB #5278 hupomenō<br><br>**1 Cor. 13:7**<br>Beareth all things, believeth all things, hopeth all things, **endureth** all things. [KJV]<br>Bears all things, believes all things, hopes all things, **endures** all things. [NASB]<br>It always protects, always trusts, always hopes, always **perseveres**. [NIV]<br>Bears all things, believes all things, hopes all things, **endures** all things. [NKJV]<br>Love never gives up, never loses faith, is always hopeful, and **endures** through every circumstance. [NLT]<br>πάντα στέγει, πάντα πιστεύει, πάντα ἐλπίζει, πάντα **ὑπομένει**. [GNS]<br>πάντα στέγει, πάντα πιστεύει, πάντα ἐλπίζει, πάντα **ὑπομένει**. [GNT] | To persevere; to endure; to be patient; to hold out; to stand firm; to stand ground; to put up with; to press on through opposition. The word "endures" (*huopmenei*) is a military word meaning to stand against the attack of an enemy.<br><br>**Practical Application**<br>Love actively fights and endures all attacks. Love is strong, full of fortitude and fight, and it struggles against any and every assault to buckle in to an unloving spirit. Love conquers and triumphs—always—because it endures all things. No matter what attacks love, named or unnamed, it endures the attack and continues to love. |
| **#1283**<br>**Enemies**<br><br>Enemies–KJV<br>Enemies–NASB<br>Enemies–NIV<br>Enemies–NKJV<br>Enemies–NLT<br><br>**POSB REFERENCE**<br>(Romans 11:28-29, esp. v. 28)<br>Note 3, point 1 | ἐχθροί = echthroi<br>Pronunciation: [ekh-throy']<br>Parsing (part of speech): adjective<br>  Case—nominative<br>  Gender—masculine<br>  Number—plural<br>  Stem or root—from ἐχθρός, ή, όν<br>Concordance References:<br>  ⇒ Strong's #2190 echthros<br>  ⇒ NIV #2398 echthros<br>  ⇒ NASB #2190 echthros<br><br>**Romans 11:28**<br>As concerning the gospel, they are **enemies** for your sakes: but as touching the election, they are beloved for the fathers' sakes. [KJV]<br>From the standpoint of the gospel they are **enemies** for your sake, but from the standpoint of God's choice they are beloved for the sake of the fathers; [NASB]<br>As far as the gospel is concerned, they are **enemies** on your account; but as far as election is concerned, they are loved on account of the patriarchs, [NIV]<br>Concerning the gospel *they are* **enemies** for your sake, but concerning the election *they are* beloved for the sake of the fathers. [NKJV]<br>Many of the Jews are now **enemies** of the Good News. But this has been to your benefit, for God has given his gifts to you Gentiles. Yet the Jews are still his chosen people because of his promises to Abraham, Isaac, and Jacob. [NLT]<br>κατὰ μὲν τὸ εὐαγγέλιον, **ἐχθροὶ** δι' ὑμᾶς· κατὰ δὲ τὴν ἐκλογὴν, ἀγαπητοὶ διὰ τοὺς πατέρας· [GNS]<br>κατὰ μὲν τὸ εὐαγγέλιον **ἐχθροὶ** δι' ὑμᾶς, κατὰ δὲ τὴν ἐκλογὴν ἀγαπητοὶ διὰ τοὺς πατέρας· [GNT] | Enemies, foes, adversaries, traitors, rebels.<br><br>**Practical Application**<br>The statement "they [the Jews] are enemies for your sakes" sounds as though God predestinated Israel's rejection. However, God does not cause sin (James 1:13-14); God does not cause people to reject His Son and His will. What the statement means is this: the word "enemy" (*echthroi*) has both an active and passive meaning. It means either hostile or hated by, and it means either hating or being hated. It is possible that in this particular passage it is to be read both ways. The Jews were hostile to God; they had refused the offer of God's righteousness in Jesus Christ, and they had refused to be the missionary force for God's Son. Therefore, they had aroused God's displeasure. They hated God; consequently, God was displeased with them. |

# PRACTICAL WORD STUDIES
## in the NEW TESTAMENT

| ENGLISH WORD | GREEK WORD AND VERSE | THE WORD MEANS... |
|---|---|---|
| **#1284**<br>**Enemies**<br><br>**Enemies**–KJV<br>Hostile–NASB<br>**Enemies**–NIV<br>**Enemies**–NKJV<br>**Enemies**–NLT<br><br>**POSB**<br>**REFERENCE**<br>(Col.1:21-22; esp. v.21)<br>Note 2, point 2 | ἐχθρούς = *echthrous*<br>Pronunciation: [ekh-throos']<br>Parsing (part of speech): pronominal adjective<br>    Case—accusative<br>    Gender—masculine<br>    Number—plural<br>    Stem or root—from ἐχθρός, ή, όν<br>Concordance References:<br>  ⇒ Strong's #2190 echthros<br>  ⇒ NIV #2398 echthros<br>  ⇒ NASB #2190 echthros<br><br>**Col. 1:21**<br>And you, that were sometime alienated and **enemies** in your mind by wicked works, yet now hath he reconciled [KJV]<br><br>And although you were formerly alienated and **hostile** in mind, engaged in evil deeds, [NASB]<br><br>Once you were alienated from God and were **enemies** in your minds because of your evil behavior. [NIV]<br><br>And you, who once were alienated and **enemies** in your mind by wicked works, yet now He has reconciled [NKJV]<br><br>This includes you who were once so far away from God. You were his **enemies**, separated from him by your evil thoughts and actions, [NLT]<br><br>καὶ ὑμᾶς ποτε ὄντας ἀπηλλοτριωμένους καὶ **ἐχθρούς** τῇ διανοίᾳ ἐν τοῖς ἔργοις τοῖς πονηροῖς, [GNS]<br><br>Καὶ ὑμᾶς ποτε ὄντας ἀπηλλοτριωμένους καὶ **ἐχθρούς** τῇ διανοίᾳ ἐν τοῖς ἔργοις τοῖς πονηροῖς, [GNT] | Enemies, hostile, hateful, rebellious.<br><br>**Practical Application**<br>Believers had been "enemies" (*echthrous*) of God. Just think for a moment: think about how men act toward God. They...<br>• ignore Him<br>• curse Him<br>• blaspheme Him<br>• mock Him<br>• falsely profess Him<br>• deny Him, His very existence<br>• disobey Him<br>• neglect Him<br>• half heartedly serve Him<br><br>Note where rebellion takes place: in the mind and in the thoughts. A man thinks about doing something, and he knows it is against God's will and Word. But the thought is planted in his mind, and he harbors the thought. It is the thought, the mind, that leads to wicked works. And any behavior or act that is not in accordance with God's will is rebellion. When the human heart is aroused to disobey God, it acts against God. And acting against the King of kings is insurrection. It is going contrary to the *explicit orders* of the King of kings. The terrible tragedy is that every person has rebelled, and too often, does rebel against God. Every human being has stood or is standing upon the earth as an enemy of God, an enemy who is in open defiance against God. Every human being has refused to obey the commandments of the King, and every human being who is open and honest knows it. The great task of man...<br>• is not to disprove the charge that he is an enemy of God.<br>• is not to prove that he is good enough to be acceptable to God.<br>• is not to deny and disprove God (denial and disproof can never eliminate truth and fact).<br><br>The fact of man's alienation—that he is an enemy of God—is clearly seen. The great task of man is to seek how to be reconciled to God. |
| **#1285**<br>**Enemy**<br><br>Adversary–KJV<br>Adversary–NASB<br>**Enemy**–NIV<br>Adversary–NKJV<br>**Enemy**–NLT<br><br>**POSB**<br>**REFERENCE**<br>(1 Pt.5:8)<br>Note 2 | ἀντίδικος = *antidikos*<br>Pronunciation: [an-tid'-ee-kos]<br>Parsing (part of speech): noun<br>    Case—nominative<br>    Gender—masculine<br>    Number—singular<br>    Stem or root—from ἀντίδικος, ου<br>Concordance References:<br>  ⇒ Strong's #476 antidikos<br>  ⇒ NIV #508 antidikos<br>  ⇒ NASB #476 antidikos<br><br>**1 Peter 5:8**<br>Be sober, be vigilant; because your **adversary** the devil, as a roaring lion, walketh about, seeking whom he may devour: [KJV]<br><br>Be of sober spirit, be on the alert. Your **adversary**, the devil, prowls about like a roaring lion, seeking someone to devour. [NASB]<br><br>Be self-controlled and alert. Your **enemy** the devil prowls around like a roaring lion looking for someone to devour. [NIV]<br><br>Be sober, be vigilant; because your **adversary** the | Enemy, adversary, opponent; an adversary who is seeking to take one to court.<br><br>**Practical Application**<br>The Greek word means a legal opponent such as an opponent in a lawsuit. It also means a common day-to-day opponent like a neighbor who opposes and stands as an enemy against us. The picture is that of the devil opposing us in every conceivable way.<br>⇒ It is the picture of Satan standing in a law court, standing as an adversary in the court of God and accusing us before God.<br>⇒ It is the picture of Satan standing here on earth, standing against us and doing all he can to trip us up and to defeat and to destroy us. |

# Practical Word Studies in the New Testament

| ENGLISH WORD | GREEK WORD AND VERSE | THE WORD MEANS... |
|---|---|---|
| | devil walks about like a roaring lion, seeking whom he may devour. [NKJV]<br><br>Be careful! Watch out for attacks from the Devil, your great **enemy**. He prowls around like a roaring lion, looking for some victim to devour. [NLT]<br><br>νήψατε, γρηγορήσατε, ὅτι ὁ **ἀντίδικος** ὑμῶν διάβολος, ὡς λέων ὠρυόμενος περιπατεῖ ζητῶν τινα καταπίῃ [GNS]<br><br>Νήψατε, γρηγορήσατε. ὁ **ἀντίδικος** ὑμῶν διάβολος ὡς λέων ὠρυόμενος περιπατεῖ ζητῶν [τινα] καταπιεῖν· [GNT] | |
| **#1286**<br>**Energy**<br><br>Working–KJV<br>Power–NASB<br>**Energy–NIV**<br>Working–NKJV<br>Power–NLT<br><br>**POSB REFERENCE**<br>(Col.1:29)<br>Note 5, point 2 | ἐνέργειαν = energeian<br>Pronunciation: [en-erg'-i-ahn]<br>Parsing (part of speech): noun<br>    Case—accusative<br>    Gender—feminine<br>    Number—singular<br>    Stem or root—from ἐνέργεια, ας<br>Concordance References:<br>  ⇒ Strong's #1753 energeia<br>  ⇒ NIV #1918 energeia<br>  ⇒ NASB #1753 energeia<br><br>**Col. 1:29**<br>Whereunto I also labour, striving according to his **working**, which worketh in me mightily. [KJV]<br><br>And for this purpose also I labor, striving according to His **power**, which mightily works within me. [NASB]<br><br>To this end I labor, struggling with all his **energy**, which so powerfully works in me. [NIV]<br><br>To this *end* I also labor, striving according to His **working** which works in me mightily. [NKJV]<br><br>I work very hard at this, as I depend on Christ's mighty **power** that works within me. [NLT]<br><br>εἰς ὃ καὶ κοπιῶ, ἀγωνιζόμενος κατὰ τὴν **ἐνέργειαν** αὐτοῦ, τὴν ἐνεργουμένην ἐν ἐμοὶ ἐν δυνάμει. [GNS]<br><br>εἰς ὃ καὶ κοπιῶ ἀγωνιζόμενος κατὰ τὴν **ἐνέργειαν** αὐτοῦ τὴν ἐνεργουμένην ἐν ἐμοὶ ἐν δυνάμει. [GNT] | Energy, working, power. The word "energy" (*energeian*) means energy and efficiency and is only used of superhuman power (Wuest, *Ephesians and Colossians,* Vol.1, p.195). In this case, it is the power of Christ.<br><br>**Practical Application**<br>When the minister has gone as far as he can, Christ steps in to infuse energy and power into his body—an energy and power that works in him powerfully. The minister who has truly labored to the point of exhaustion and experienced the energy and power of Christ knows how glorious the experience is. It is just tragic that there are too few who so labor and even fewer who consistently labor to the point that Christ has to step in with His energy and power. We seem to forget too easily:<br>⇒ as long as we have physical strength and energy left to labor, the energy and power of Christ are not needed.<br><br>The only way we can experience the physical energy and power of Christ is to use up all of our own strength. When we are completely empty, then Christ has to step in or else leave us and abandon us and disregard the promise of His Word. And this He will never do. Therefore, when we have no more strength to walk and labor, it is then that He infuses us with His own supernatural energy and power. |
| **#1287**<br>**Engage**<br><br>Maintain–KJV<br>**Engage–NASB**<br>Devote–NIV<br>Maintain–NKJV<br>Do–NLT<br><br>**POSB REFERENCE**<br>(Tit.3:8)<br>Note 1 | προΐστασθαι = proistasthai<br>Pronunciation: [pro-is'-tahs-tha-ee]<br>Parsing (part of speech): verb<br>    Mood—infinitive<br>    Tense—present<br>    Voice—middle<br>    Stem or root—from προΐστημι<br>Concordance References:<br>  ⇒ Strong's #4291 proistēmi<br>  ⇒ NIV #4613 proistēmi<br>  ⇒ NASB #4291b proistēmi<br><br>**Titus 3:8**<br>This is a faithful saying, and these things I will that thou affirm constantly, that they which have believed in God might be careful to **maintain** good works. These things are good and profitable unto men. [KJV]<br><br>This is a trustworthy statement; and concerning these things I want you to speak confidently, so that those who have believed God may be careful to **engage** in good deeds. These things are good and profitable for men. [NASB]<br><br>This is a trustworthy saying. And I want you to stress these things, so that those who have trusted in God may be careful to **devote** themselves to doing what is good. These things are excellent and profitable for everyone. [NIV]<br><br>This is a faithful saying, and these things I want you to | To devote; to maintain; to engage; to do; to manage; to care for; to set before; to give attention to; to be forward and eager and diligent in doing good works.<br><br>**Practical Application**<br>Believers must do good works and keep on doing them. It means...<br>• to keep on doing good works.<br>• to sustain good works.<br>• to persevere in doing good works.<br>• to carry on good works.<br><br>It even has the idea of sustaining good works against all odds regardless of circumstances and difficulties. It means to persevere in good works even in the midst of opposition or danger. |

# PRACTICAL WORD STUDIES
## in the NEW TESTAMENT

| ENGLISH WORD | GREEK WORD AND VERSE | THE WORD MEANS... |
|---|---|---|
| | affirm constantly, that those who have believed in God should be careful to **maintain** good works. These things are good and profitable to men. [NKJV]<br><br>These things I have told you are all true. I want you to insist on them so that everyone who trusts in God will be careful to **do** good deeds all the time. These things are good and beneficial for everyone. [NLT]<br><br>πιστὸς ὁ λόγος, καὶ περὶ τούτων βούλομαί σε διαβεβαιοῦσθαι, ἵνα φροντίζωσι καλῶν ἔργων **προΐστασθαι** οἱ πεπιστευκότες τῷ Θεῷ. ταῦτά ἐστι τὰ καλὰ καὶ ὠφέλιμα τοῖς ἀνθρώποις· [GNS]<br><br>Πιστὸς ὁ λόγος· καὶ περὶ τούτων βούλομαί σε διαβεβαιοῦσθαι, ἵνα φροντίζωσιν καλῶν ἔργων **προΐστασθαι** οἱ πεπιστευκότες θεῷ· ταῦτά ἐστιν καλὰ καὶ ὠφέλιμα τοῖς ἀνθρώποις. [GNT] | |
| **#1288**<br>**Engrafted**<br><br>Engrafted–KJV<br>Implanted–NASB<br>Planted in–NIV<br>Implanted–NKJV<br>Planted in–NLT<br><br>**POSB REFERENCE**<br>(Jas.1:19-21; esp. v.21)<br>Note 1 | ἔμφυτον = emphuton<br>Pronunciation: [em'-foo-ton]<br>Parsing (part of speech): adjective<br>    Case—accusative<br>    Gender—masculine<br>    Number—singular<br>    Stem or root—from ἔμφυτος, ον<br>Concordance References:<br>  ⇒ Strong's #1721 emphutos<br>  ⇒ NIV #1875 emphutos<br>  ⇒ NASB #1721 emphutos<br><br>**James 1:21**<br>Wherefore lay apart all filthiness and superfluity of naughtiness, and receive with meekness the **engrafted** word, which is able to save your souls. [KJV]<br><br>Therefore putting aside all filthiness and all that remains of wickedness, in humility receive the word **implanted**, which is able to save your souls. [NASB]<br><br>Therefore, get rid of all moral filth and the evil that is so prevalent and humbly accept the word **planted in** you, which can save you. [NIV]<br><br>Therefore lay aside all filthiness and overflow of wickedness, and receive with meekness the **implanted** word, which is able to save your souls. [NKJV]<br><br>So get rid of all the filth and evil in your lives, and humbly accept the message God has **planted in** your hearts, for it is strong enough to save your souls. [NLT]<br><br>διὸ ἀποθέμενοι πᾶσαν ῥυπαρίαν καὶ περισσείαν κακίας, ἐν πραΰτητι δέξασθε τὸν **ἔμφυτον** λόγον, τὸν δυνάμενον σῶσαι τὰς ψυχὰς ὑμῶν. [GNS]<br><br>διὸ ἀποθέμενοι πᾶσαν ῥυπαρίαν καὶ περισσείαν κακίας ἐν πραΰτητι, δέξασθε τὸν **ἔμφυτον** λόγον τὸν δυνάμενον σῶσαι τὰς ψυχὰς ὑμῶν. [GNT] | To be planted in; to be engrafted; to be implanted; to be born within.<br><br>**Practical Application**<br>When a person really listens to the Word of God, it is planted within his heart and life. What God says is actually born within his heart, and the man hears exactly what God says. The Word of God is born within his heart and life, and the person's soul is saved. He conquers and triumphs over all temptation, including the terrible temptation of rejecting God and doing his own thing and living like he wants. He is saved to live eternally with God. This is the first preparation that a person must make to withstand temptation: he must be quick to hear the Word of God. |
| **#1289**<br>**Enjoy Having Guests In His Home**<br><br>Hospitality–KJV<br>Hospitable–NASB<br>Hospitable–NIV<br>Hospitable–NKJV<br>**Enjoy having guests in his home–NLT**<br><br>**POSB REFERENCE**<br>(1 Tim.3:2-3; esp. v.2)<br>Note 2, point 6 | φιλόξενον = philoxenon<br>Pronunciation: [fil-ox'-en-on]<br>Parsing (part of speech): adjective<br>    Case—accusative<br>    Gender—masculine<br>    Number—singular<br>    Stem or root—from φιλόξενος, ον<br>Concordance References:<br>  Strong's #5382 philoxenos<br>  NIV #5811 philoxenos<br>  NASB #5382 philoxenos<br><br>**1 Tim. 3:2**<br>A bishop then must be blameless, the husband of one wife, vigilant, sober, of good behaviour, given to **hospitality**, apt to teach; [KJV]<br><br>An overseer, then, must be above reproach, the husband of one wife, temperate, prudent, respectable, **hospitable**, able to teach, [NASB]<br><br>Now the overseer must be above reproach, the husband of but one wife, temperate, self-controlled, respectable, **hospitable**, able to teach, [NIV]<br><br>A bishop then must be blameless, the husband of one | Hospitable, hospitality, enjoy having guests in one's home. It means to have an open heart and home; "showing love or being a friend to the believers, especially strangers or foreigners" (Amplified New Testament).<br><br>**Practical Application**<br>The minister helps and entertains as much as he can. He does not open his heart, home, time, or money to the things of the world; but he uses what resources he has to help and minister to people. |

## Practical Word Studies
### in the New Testament

| ENGLISH WORD | GREEK WORD AND VERSE | THE WORD MEANS... |
|---|---|---|
| | wife, temperate, sober-minded, of good behavior, **hospitable**, able to teach; [NKJV]<br><br>For an elder must be a man whose life cannot be spoken against. He must be faithful to his wife. He must exhibit self-control, live wisely, and have a good reputation. He must **enjoy having guests in his home** and must be able to teach. [NLT]<br><br>δεῖ οὖν τὸν ἐπίσκοπον ἀνεπίλημπτον εἶναι, μιᾶς γυναικὸς ἄνδρα, νηφάλιον, σώφρονα, κόσμιον, **φιλόξενον**, διδακτικόν· [GNS]<br><br>δεῖ οὖν τὸν ἐπίσκοπον ἀνεπίλημπτον εἶναι, μιᾶς γυναικὸς ἄνδρα, νηφάλιον σώφρονα κόσμιον **φιλόξενον** διδακτικόν, [GNT] | |
| #1290<br>**Enmities**<br><br>Hatred–KJV<br>**Enmities**–NASB<br>Hatred–NIV<br>Hatred–NKJV<br>Hostility–NLT<br><br>**POSB REFERENCE**<br>(Gal.5:19-21; esp. v.20)<br>Note 2 | ἔχθραι = echthrai<br>Pronunciation: [ekh'-thrah-ee]<br>Parsing (part of speech): noun<br>    Case—nominative<br>    Gender—feminine<br>    Number—plural<br>    Stem or root—from ἔχθρα, ας<br>Concordance References:<br>  ⇒ Strong's #2189 echthra<br>  ⇒ NIV #2397 echthra<br>  ⇒ NASB #2189 echthra<br><br>**Galatians 5:20**<br>Idolatry, witchcraft, **hatred**, variance, emulations, wrath, strife, seditions, heresies, [KJV]<br>Idolatry, sorcery, **enmities**, strife, jealousy, outbursts of anger, disputes, dissensions, factions, [NASB]<br>Idolatry and witchcraft; **hatred**, discord, jealousy, fits of rage, selfish ambition, dissensions, factions [NIV]<br>Idolatry, sorcery, **hatred**, contentions, jealousies, outbursts of wrath, selfish ambitions, dissensions, heresies, [NKJV]<br>Idolatry, participation in demonic activities, **hostility**, quarreling, jealousy, outbursts of anger, selfish ambition, divisions, the feeling that everyone is wrong except those in your own little group, [NLT]<br><br>εἰδωλολατρία, φαρμακεία, **ἔχθραι**, ἔρεις, ζῆλοι, θυμοί, ἐριθεῖαι, διχοστασίαι, αἱρέσεις, [GNS]<br>εἰδωλολατρία, φαρμακεία, **ἔχθραι**, ἔρις, ζῆλος, θυμοί, ἐριθεῖαι, διχοστασίαι, αἱρέσεις, [GNT] | Hatred, hostility, ill will, enmity, hostility, animosity.<br><br>**Practical Application**<br>It is the hatred that lingers and is held for a long, long time; a hatred that is deep within. |
| #1291<br>**Ensnares, Easily**<br><br>Easily beset–KJV<br>Easily entangles–NASB<br>Easily entangles–NIV<br>**Easily ensnares**–NKJV<br>Slows us down–NLT<br><br>**POSB REFERENCE**<br>(Heb.12:1)<br>Note 2, point 1b | εὐπερίστατον = euperistaton<br>Pronunciation: [yoo-per-is'-taht-on]<br>Parsing (part of speech): adjective<br>    Case—accusative<br>    Gender—feminine<br>    Number—singular<br>    Stem or root—from εὐπερίστατος, ον<br>Concordance References:<br>  ⇒ Strong's #2139 euperistatos<br>  ⇒ NIV #2342 euperistatos<br>  ⇒ NASB #2139 euperistatos<br><br>**Hebrews 12:1**<br>Wherefore seeing we also are compassed about with so great a cloud of witnesses, let us lay aside every weight, and the sin which doth so **easily beset** us, and let us run with patience the race that is set before us, [KJV]<br>Therefore, since we have so great a cloud of witnesses surrounding us, let us also lay aside every encumbrance, and the sin which so **easily entangles** us, and let us run with endurance the race that is set before us, [NASB]<br>Therefore, since we are surrounded by such a great cloud of witnesses, let us throw off everything that hinders and the sin that so **easily entangles**, and let us run with perseverance the race marked out for us. [NIV]<br>Therefore we also, since we are surrounded by so great a cloud of witnesses, let us lay aside every weight, and the sin which so **easily ensnares** *us,* and let us run with endurance the race that is set before us, [NKJV] | Easily entangles, easily beset, slows us down. The word "ensnares" (*euperistaton*) means the sin which clings, distracts, entangles, and trips up the Christian runner.<br><br>**Practical Application**<br>The Christian runner must strip off the sin which so easily trips or besets him. It is the picture of clothing's flapping around a person while he is running: it ensnares and trips him, causing him to fall. What is the sin that entangles and trips believers? Various sins have been suggested as common to all believers. However, the exhortation speaks strongly to every believer and to the *particular sin* that entangles and throws the believer. Each one of us must ask: What is the sin that so easily traps me? Pleasure, indulgence, the tongue, the flesh, pride, possessions, worldly friends, television, sports—what is it that consumes my energy, keeping me from following God fully and wholly—that trips me up far, far too often. We must strip it off or else it will entangle us and trip us up, and we will never finish the race. |

## PRACTICAL WORD STUDIES
## in the NEW TESTAMENT

| ENGLISH WORD | GREEK WORD AND VERSE | THE WORD MEANS... |
|---|---|---|
| | Therefore, since we are surrounded by such a huge crowd of witnesses to the life of faith, let us strip off every weight that **slows us down**, especially the sin that so easily hinders our progress. And let us run with endurance the race that God has set before us. [NLT]<br><br>Τοιγαροῦν καὶ ἡμεῖς τοσοῦτον ἔχοντες περικείμενον ἡμῖν νέφος μαρτύρων, ὄγκον ἀποθέμενοι πάντα καὶ τὴν **εὐπερίστατον** ἁμαρτίαν, δι' ὑπομονῆς τρέχωμεν τὸν προκείμενον ἡμῖν ἀγῶνα, [GNS]<br><br>Τοιγαροῦν καὶ ἡμεῖς τοσοῦτον ἔχοντες περικείμενον ἡμῖν νέφος μαρτύρων, ὄγκον ἀποθέμενοι πάντα καὶ τὴν **εὐπερίστατον** ἁμαρτίαν, δι' ὑπομονῆς τρέχωμεν τὸν προκείμενον ἡμῖν ἀγῶνα [GNT] | |
| **#1292**<br>**Ensue**<br><br>Ensue–KJV<br>Pursue–NASB<br>Pursue–NIV<br>Pursue–NKJV<br>Work hard–NLT<br><br>**POSB**<br>**REFERENCE**<br>(1 Pt.3:11)<br>Note 3 | διωξάτω = *diöxatö*<br>Pronunciation: [dee-o'-kaht-o']<br>Parsing (part of speech): verb<br>   Mood—imperative<br>   Tense—aorist<br>   Voice—active<br>   Person—3rd person<br>   Number—singular<br>   Stem or root—from διώκω<br>Concordance References:<br>⇒ Strong's #1377 diökö<br>⇒ NIV #1503 diökö<br>⇒ NASB #1377 diökö<br><br>**1 Peter 3:11**<br>Let him eschew evil, and do good; let him seek peace, and **ensue** it. [KJV]<br>"And let him turn away from evil and do good; Let him seek peace and **pursue** it. [NASB]<br>He must turn from evil and do good; he must seek peace and **pursue** it. [NIV]<br>Let him turn away from evil and do good; Let him seek peace and **pursue** it. [NKJV]<br>Turn away from evil and do good. **Work hard** at living in peace with others. [NLT]<br><br>ἐκκλινάτω ἀπὸ κακοῦ, καὶ ποιησάτω ἀγαθόν· ζητησάτω εἰρήνην, καὶ **διωξάτω** αὐτήν. [GNS]<br>ἐκκλινάτω δὲ ἀπὸ κακοῦ καὶ ποιησάτω ἀγαθόν, ζητησάτω εἰρήνην καὶ **διωξάτω** αὐτήν· [GNT] | To pursue; to ensue; to work hard; to strive for; to seek after. The word "ensue" (*diöxatö*) means to run after, chase after, press after, and to pursue. It has the idea of swiftness and endurance—of hotly pursuing and staying after peace.<br><br>**Practical Application**<br>Believers are not only to desire peace, but they are to actively pursue and go after it. We live in a world that is full of corruptible and evil people who could care less about peace and holiness just so they get what they are after. However, the believer must not give up, for peace is the very reason he is on earth.<br>The believer is to follow after peace (*eirenen*) with all men. The fact that he has to follow after peace means that peace is not always possible.<br>⇒ Some persons within the church are troublemakers: grumblers, complainers, gossipers, criticizers; some are self-centered leaders full of pride; some people within the church are just selfish and self-centered and care more about pushing themselves forward and getting their own way than they do about peace. Self is put before Christ and the church and its mission.<br>⇒ Some persons within the world are troublemakers who cause great trouble for the believer. They oppose the believer: ridicule, mock, poke fun at, curse, abuse, persecute, ignore, and isolate him.<br>⇒ Some persons within the world are troublemakers for the world at large: dissenters, dividers, fighters, egotists, power-builders, and warmongers. Some people have no interest in peace whatever unless they can have their own way.<br>The point is this: the believer is to follow after peace with *all men*—no matter who they are. The very purpose for the believer's being on earth is to bring peace between men and God and between men and all other men. Therefore, the believer is to do all he can to live at peace with everyone and to lead others to live in peace. |
| **#1293**<br>**Enthusiastically**<br><br>Fervent–KJV<br>Fervent–NASB<br>Fervor–NIV<br>Fervent–NKJV<br>Enthusiastically–NLT | ζέοντες = *zeontes*<br>Pronunciation: [dzeh'-on-tehs]<br>Parsing (part of speech): verb<br>   Mood—participle (imperative sense)<br>   Tense—present<br>   Voice—active<br>   Case—nominative<br>   Gender—masculine<br>   Person—2nd person<br>   Number—plural<br>   Stem or root—from ζέω | Fervent in spirit; with a heart full of devotion; with great fervor. The word "enthusiastically" (*zeontes*) means to be hot; to boil; to set aflame.<br><br>**Practical Application**<br>The believer's spirit is to be hot, that is, boiling and flaming for Christ. The believer must have a holy zeal for Christ. He must be aflame in his service for Christ. Why? The world is reeling under the weight of desperate need, dying with- |

# PRACTICAL WORD STUDIES
## in the NEW TESTAMENT

| ENGLISH WORD | GREEK WORD AND VERSE | THE WORD MEANS... |
|---|---|---|
| **POSB REFERENCE** (Rom.12:11) Note 2, point 2 | Concordance References:<br>⇒ Strong's #2204 zeö<br>⇒ NIV #2417 zeö<br>⇒ NASB #2204 zeö<br><br>**Romans 12:11**<br>Not slothful in business; **fervent** in spirit; serving the Lord; [KJV]<br>Not lagging behind in diligence, **fervent** in spirit, serving the Lord; [NASB]<br>Never be lacking in zeal, but keep your spiritual **fervor**, serving the Lord. [NIV]<br>Not lagging in diligence, **fervent** in spirit, serving the Lord; [NKJV]<br>Never be lazy in your work, but serve the Lord **enthusiastically**. [NLT]<br>τῇ σπουδῇ μὴ ὀκνηροί· τῷ πνεύματι **ζέοντες**· τῷ Κυρίῳ δουλεύοντες· [GNS]<br>τῇ σπουδῇ μὴ ὀκνηροί, τῷ πνεύματι **ζέοντες**, τῷ κυρίῳ δουλεύοντες, [GNT] | out Christ and being doomed to an eternity separated from God. |
| **#1294 Enticed**<br><br>Enticed–KJV<br>Enticed–NASB<br>Enticed–NIV<br>Enticed–NKJV<br>Lure–NLT<br><br>**POSB REFERENCE** (Jas.1:14-16; esp. v.14) Note 2, point 1 | δελεαζόμενος = *deleazomenos*<br>Pronunciation: [del-eh-ad'-zo-mehn-os]<br>Parsing (part of speech): verb<br>  Mood—participle<br>  Tense—present<br>  Voice—passive<br>  Case—nominative<br>  Gender—masculine<br>  Number—singular<br>  Stem or root—from δελεάζω<br>Concordance References:<br>⇒ Strong's #1185 deleazö<br>⇒ NIV #1284 deleazö<br>⇒ NASB #1185 deleazö<br><br>**James 1:14**<br>But every man is tempted, when he is drawn away of his own lust, and **enticed**. [KJV]<br>But each one is tempted when he is carried away and **enticed** by his own lust. [NASB]<br>But each one is tempted when, by his own evil desire, he is dragged away and **enticed**. [NIV]<br>But each one is tempted when he is drawn away by his own desires and **enticed**. [NKJV]<br>Temptation comes from the **lure** of our own evil desires. [NLT]<br>ἕκαστος δὲ πειράζεται, ὑπὸ τῆς ἰδίας ἐπιθυμίας ἐξελκόμενος καὶ **δελεαζόμενος**. [GNS]<br>ἕκαστος δὲ πειράζεται ὑπὸ τῆς ἰδίας ἐπιθυμίας ἐξελκόμενος καὶ **δελεαζόμενος**· [GNT] | To entice, lure, trap, catch, seduce. It means to lure and bait just as a person lures and baits a fish.<br><br>**Practical Application**<br>Every man—there are no exceptions—is tempted when he is drawn away by his own lusts and enticed.<br>The picture is this: man has good desires, natural and normal desires. Therefore, when he begins to think about or look at something, he very naturally desires it. His desire is normal behavior. The problem arises when the thing is forbidden or is harmful. If he looks at and thinks about the forbidden or harmful thing, he begins to lust and is enticed or lured to go after it. This is the very beginning stage of temptation. Man focuses his desire upon the forbidden or harmful thing. He begins to pay attention to what he should not look at; he begins to think about the things of the flesh and of the world. Thereby, he is tempted and drawn away by his own lusts and enticements. |
| **#1295 Enticing**<br><br>Enticing–KJV<br>Persuasive–NASB<br>Persuasive–NIV<br>Persuasive–NKJV<br>Persuasive–NLT<br><br>**POSB REFERENCE** (1 Cor.2:4) Note 4, point 2 | πειθοῖ[ς] = *peithois*<br>Pronunciation: [pee-thoys']<br>Parsing (part of speech): adjective<br>  Case—dative<br>  Gender—masculine<br>  Number—plural<br>OR<br>Parsing (part of speech): noun<br>  Case—dative<br>  Gender—feminine<br>  Number—singular<br>  Stem or root—from πειθός, ή, όν<br>Concordance References:<br>⇒ Strong's #3981 peithos<br>⇒ NIV #4273 peithos<br>⇒ NASB #3981 peithos<br><br>**1 Cor. 2:4**<br>And my speech and my preaching *was* not with **enticing** words of man's wisdom, but in demonstration of the Spirit and of power: [KJV]<br>And my message and my preaching were not in per- | Persuasive, enticing, plausible, skillful.<br><br>**Practical Application**<br>Paul's witnessing and preaching were not based upon the enticing, persuasive, plausible arguments of man's wisdom and philosophy. |

## PRACTICAL WORD STUDIES
### in the NEW TESTAMENT

| ENGLISH WORD | GREEK WORD AND VERSE | THE WORD MEANS... |
|---|---|---|
| | **suasive** words of wisdom, but in demonstration of the Spirit and of power, [NASB]<br>My message and my preaching were not with wise and **persuasive** words, but with a demonstration of the Spirit's power, [NIV]<br>And my speech and my preaching *were* not with **persuasive** words of human wisdom, but in demonstration of the Spirit and of power, [NKJV]<br>And my message and my preaching were very plain. I did not use wise and **persuasive** speeches, but the Holy Spirit was powerful among you. [NLT]<br>καὶ ὁ λόγος μου καὶ τὸ κήρυγμά μου οὐκ ἐν **πειθοῖς** ἀνθρωπίνης σοφίας λόγοις, ἀλλ' ἐν ἀποδείξει πνεύματος καὶ δυνάμεως· [GNS]<br>καὶ ὁ λόγος μου καὶ τὸ κήρυγμά μου οὐκ ἐν **πειθοῖ[ς]** σοφίας [λόγοις] ἀλλ' ἐν ἀποδείξει πνεύματος καὶ δυνάμεως, [GNT] | |
| **#1296**<br>**Enticing Words**<br><br>Enticing words–KJV<br>Persuasive argument–NASB<br>Fine sounding arguments–NIV<br>Persuasive words–NKJV<br>Persuasive arguments–NLT<br><br>**POSB REFERENCE**<br>(Col.2:4)<br>Note 3 | πιθανολογίᾳ = *pithanologia*<br>Pronunciation: [pith-an-ol-og-ee'-ah]<br>Parsing (part of speech): noun<br>    Case—dative<br>    Gender—feminine<br>    Number—singular<br>    Stem or root—from πιθανολογία, ας<br>Concordance References:<br>  ⇒ Strong's #4086 pithanologia<br>  ⇒ NIV #4391 pithanologia<br>  ⇒ NASB #4086 pithanologia<br><br>**Col. 2:4**<br>And this I say, lest any man should beguile you with **enticing words**. [KJV]<br>I say this in order that no one may delude you with **persuasive argument**. [NASB]<br>I tell you this so that no one may deceive you by **fine-sounding arguments**. [NIV]<br>Now this I say lest anyone should deceive you with **persuasive words**. [NKJV]<br>I am telling you this so that no one will be able to deceive you with **persuasive arguments**. [NLT]<br>τοῦτο δὲ λέγω, ἵνα μη τις ὑμᾶς παραλογίζηται ἐν **πιθανολογίᾳ**. [GNS]<br>Τοῦτο λέγω ἵνα μηδεὶς ὑμᾶς παραλογίζηται ἐν **πιθανολογίᾳ**. [GNT] | Fine-sounding arguments; enticing words; persuasive arguments.<br><br>**Practical Application**<br>A mature person resists seduction and deception. The word "beguile" (*paralogizetai*) means to mislead, delude, deceive, cheat, seduce, and lead someone astray. Note how the seduction takes place: by "enticing words" (*pithanologia*), that is, by words that are persuasive, appealing, eloquent, flowery, and attractive. |
| **#1297**<br>**Entire**<br><br>Entire–KJV<br>Complete–NASB<br>Complete–NIV<br>Complete–NKJV<br>Fully developed–NLT<br><br>**POSB REFERENCE**<br>(Jas.1:4)<br>Note 3, point 2 | ὁλόκληροι = *holoklēroi*<br>Pronunciation: [hol-ok'-lay-roy]<br>Parsing (part of speech): adjective<br>    Case—nominative<br>    Gender—masculine<br>    Number—plural<br>    Stem or root—from ὁλόκληρος, ον<br>Concordance References:<br>  ⇒ Strong's #3648 holoklēros<br>  ⇒ NIV #3908 holoklēros<br>  ⇒ NASB #3648 holoklēros<br><br>**James 1:4**<br>But let patience have her perfect work, that ye may be perfect and **entire**, wanting nothing. [KJV]<br>And let endurance have its perfect result, that you may be perfect and **complete**, lacking in nothing. [NASB]<br>Perseverance must finish its work so that you may be mature and **complete**, not lacking anything. [NIV]<br>But let patience have *its* perfect work, that you may be perfect and **complete**, lacking nothing. [NKJV]<br>So let it grow, for when your endurance is **fully developed**, you will be strong in character and ready for anything. [NLT]<br>ἡ δὲ ὑπομονὴ ἔργον τέλειον ἐχέτω, ἵνα ἦτε τέλειοι καὶ **ὁλόκληροι**, ἐν μηδενὶ λειπόμενοι. [GNS]<br>ἡ δὲ ὑπομονὴ ἔργον τέλειον ἐχέτω, ἵνα ἦτε τέλειοι καὶ **ὁλόκληροι** ἐν μηδενὶ λειπόμενοι. [GNT] | Complete, entire, fully developed, whole. It means to be wholly fit, perfectly sound, complete with no weaknesses, flaws, defects, or shortcomings.<br><br>**Practical Application**<br>This means a most wonderful thing. When a person perseveres and conquers trials or temptations...<br>• he becomes more entire, more fit, more sound, and more complete.<br>• he also eliminates more weaknesses, more flaws, more defects, and more shortcomings.<br>Day by day—trial by trial and temptation by temptation—when a person perseveres and conquers, he becomes more and more entire. He becomes stronger and more pure and righteous—more and more like the Lord Jesus. As the last words of James 1:4 say, "wanting nothing." The believer who faces trials and temptations in the joy of Christ conquers all, and he lacks nothing.<br>⇒ He becomes more and more complete, fulfilling his task and purpose for being on earth a little bit more. |

# PRACTICAL WORD STUDIES
## in the NEW TESTAMENT

| ENGLISH WORD | GREEK WORD AND VERSE | THE WORD MEANS... |
|---|---|---|
| | | ⇒ He becomes more and more entire and fit, eliminating more and more weaknesses and shortcomings in his life. |
| #1298<br>**Entreated**<br><br>Besought–KJV<br>**Entreated–NASB**<br>Pleaded...with–NIV<br>Begged–NKJV<br>Pleading with–NLT<br><br>**POSB REFERENCE**<br>(Mk.5:22-24; esp. v.23)<br>Note 2 point 3 | παρακαλεῖ = *parakalei*<br>Pronunciation: [par-ak-al-eh'-ee]<br>Parsing (part of speech): verb<br>  Mood—indicative<br>  Tense—present<br>  Voice—active<br>  Person—3rd person<br>  Number—singular<br>  Stem or root—from παρακαλέω<br>Concordance References:<br>  ⇒ Strong's #3870 parakaleō<br>  ⇒ NIV #4151 parakaleō<br>  ⇒ NASB #3870 parakaleō<br><br>**Mark 5:23**<br>And **besought** him greatly, saying, My little daughter lieth at the point of death: I pray thee, come and lay thy hands on her, that she may be healed; and she shall live. [KJV]<br>And **entreated** Him earnestly, saying, "My little daughter is at the point of death; please come and lay Your hands on her, that she may get well and live." [NASB]<br>And **pleaded** earnestly **with** him, "My little daughter is dying. Please come and put your hands on her so that she will be healed and live." [NIV]<br>And **begged** Him earnestly, saying, "My little daughter lies at the point of death. Come and lay Your hands on her, that she may be healed, and she will live." [NKJV]<br>**Pleading with** him to heal his little daughter. "She is about to die," he said in desperation. "Please come and place your hands on her; heal her so she can live." [NLT]<br>καὶ **παρακαλεῖ** αὐτὸν πολλά, λέγων ὅτι Τὸ θυγάτριόν μου ἐσχάτως ἔχει· ἵνα ἐλθὼν ἐπιθῇς αὐτῇ τὰς χεῖρας, ὅπως σωθῇ καὶ ζήσεται. [GNS]<br>καὶ **παρακαλεῖ** αὐτὸν πολλὰ λέγων ὅτι Τὸ θυγάτριόν μου ἐσχάτως ἔχει, ἵνα ἐλθὼν ἐπιθῇς τὰς χεῖρας αὐτῇ ἵνα σωθῇ καὶ ζήσῃ. [GNT] | To plead with; to entreat; to beseech; to call to one's side for help; to beg; to urge; to appeal to; to request.<br><br>**Practical Application**<br>In this Scripture, the ruler had a pleading attitude. He pleaded with and entreated Jesus to come and heal his daughter. |
| #1299<br>**Entreaties**<br><br>Supplications–KJV<br>**Entreaties–NASB**<br>Requests–NIV<br>Supplications–NKJV<br>Requests–NLT<br><br>**POSB REFERENCE**<br>(1 Tim.2:1)<br>Note 1, point 1 | δεήσεις = *deēseis*<br>Pronunciation: [deh'-ay-seh-is]<br>Parsing (part of speech): noun<br>  Case—accusative<br>  Gender—feminine<br>  Number—plural<br>  Stem or root—from δέησις, εως<br>Concordance References:<br>  ⇒ Strong's #1162 deēsis<br>  ⇒ NIV #1255 deēsis<br>  ⇒ NASB #1162 deēsis<br><br>**1 Tim. 2:1**<br>I exhort therefore, that, first of all, **supplications**, prayers, intercessions, and giving of thanks, be made for all men; [KJV]<br>First of all, then, I urge that **entreaties** and prayers, petitions and thanksgivings, be made on behalf of all men, [NASB]<br>I urge, then, first of all, that **requests**, prayers, intercession and thanksgiving be made for everyone—[NIV]<br>Therefore I exhort first of all that **supplications**, prayers, intercessions, *and* giving of thanks be made for all men, [NKJV]<br>I urge you, first of all, to pray for all people. As you make your **requests**, plead for God's mercy upon them, and give thanks. [NLT]<br>Παρακαλῶ οὖν πρῶτον πάντων ποιεῖσθαι **δεήσεις**, | Requests, supplications, entreaties, petitions, specific prayers.<br><br>**Practical Application**<br>This refers to the prayers that focus upon special needs—deep and intense needs. When we see special needs in the life of a person, we are to supplicate for them. That is, we are to be carrying the needs before God with a great sense of urgency and plead and beg for the person or persons. The idea is that of intense and deep brokenness before God in behalf of another person—that God would help and save the person. |

# Practical Word Studies
## in the New Testament

| ENGLISH WORD | GREEK WORD AND VERSE | THE WORD MEANS... |
|---|---|---|
| | προσευχάς, ἐντεύξεις, εὐχαριστίας, ὑπὲρ πάντων ἀνθρώπων· [GNS]<br><br>Παρακαλῶ οὖν πρῶτον πάντων ποιεῖσθαι **δεήσεις** προσευχάς ἐντεύξεις εὐχαριστίας ὑπὲρ πάντων ἀνθρώπων, [GNT] | |
| **#1300**<br>**Entrust**<br><br>Commend—KJV<br>Commend—NASB<br>Commit—NIV<br>Commend—NKJV<br>**Entrust—NLT**<br><br>**POSB REFERENCE**<br>(Acts 20:32)<br>Note 3 | **παρατίθεμαι** = *paratithemai*<br>Pronunciation: [par-at-ith'-eh-mah-ee]<br>Parsing (part of speech): verb<br>  Mood—indicative<br>  Tense—present<br>  Voice—middle<br>  Person—1st person<br>  Number—singular<br>  Stem or root—from **παρατίθημι**<br>Concordance References:<br>⇒ Strong's #3908 paratithēmi<br>⇒ NIV #4192 paratithēmi<br>⇒ NASB #3908 paratithēmi<br><br>**Acts 20:32**<br>And now, brethren, I **commend** you to God, and to the word of his grace, which is able to build you up, and to give you an inheritance among all them which are sanctified. [KJV]<br><br>"And now I **commend** you to God and to the word of His grace, which is able to build you up and to give you the inheritance among all those who are sanctified. [NASB]<br><br>"Now I **commit** you to God and to the word of his grace, which can build you up and give you an inheritance among all those who are sanctified. [NIV]<br><br>So now, brethren, I **commend** you to God and to the word of His grace, which is able to build you up and give you an inheritance among all those who are sanctified. [NKJV]<br><br>"And now I **entrust** you to God and the word of his grace—his message that is able to build you up and give you an inheritance with all those he has set apart for himself. [NLT]<br><br>καὶ τὰ νῦν **παρατίθεμαι** ὑμᾶς, ἀδελφοί, τῷ Θεῷ καὶ τῷ λόγῳ τῆς χάριτος αὐτοῦ τῷ δυναμένῳ ἐποικοδομῆσαι, καὶ δοῦναι ὑμῖν κληρονομίαν ἐν τοῖς ἡγιασμένοις πᾶσιν. [GNS]<br><br>καὶ τὰ νῦν **παρατίθεμαι** ὑμᾶς τῷ θεῷ καὶ τῷ λόγῳ τῆς χάριτος αὐτοῦ, τῷ δυναμένῳ οἰκοδομῆσαι καὶ δοῦναι τὴν κληρονομίαν ἐν τοῖς ἡγιασμένοις πᾶσιν. [GNT] | To commit; to commend; to entrust.<br><br>**Practical Application**<br>The believer is to be committed to God's Word; that is, he is to place, commit, entrust, fix, lay, and deposit his life with God and His Word. Very simply, the church leader is to totally entrust his life to God and His Word, laying himself completely upon both. |
| **#1301**<br>**Entrust**<br><br>Commit—KJV<br>**Entrust—NASB**<br>Commit—NIV<br>Commit—NKJV<br>Trust—NLT<br><br>**POSB REFERENCE**<br>(1 Pt.4:19)<br>Note 7 | **παρατιθέσθωσαν** = *paratithesthōsan*<br>Pronunciation: [par-at-ith'-ehs-tho'-sahn]<br>Parsing (part of speech): verb<br>  Mood—imperative<br>  Tense—present<br>  Voice—middle<br>  Person—3rd person<br>  Number—plural<br>  Stem or root—from **παρατίθημι**<br>Concordance References:<br>⇒ Strong's #3908 paratithēmi<br>⇒ NIV #4192 paratithēmi<br>⇒ NASB #3908 paratithēmi<br><br>**1 Peter 4:19**<br>Wherefore let them that suffer according to the will of God **commit** the keeping of their souls to him in well doing, as unto a faithful Creator. [KJV]<br><br>Therefore, let those also who suffer according to the will of God **entrust** their souls to a faithful Creator in doing what is right. [NASB]<br><br>So then, those who suffer according to God's will should **commit** themselves to their faithful Creator and continue to do good. [NIV]<br><br>Therefore let those who suffer according to the will of | To commit; to entrust; to trust; to deposit; to entrust into the hands of a trusted banker or friend.<br><br>**Practical Application**<br>God can be trusted; He will not fail the believer. He will either deliver the believer through the suffering or else take him home to be with Christ forever. God will save the believer's soul. The believer can trust God, trust Him far more than any friend on earth, for God never fails. God is a faithful Creator. He has created us to be with Him eternally, and His plan will not be defeated. If we commit our souls to Him, no matter what men may do to us, God will save us. He will fulfill His plan and purpose in our lives. |

# PRACTICAL WORD STUDIES
## in the NEW TESTAMENT

| ENGLISH WORD | GREEK WORD AND VERSE | THE WORD MEANS... |
|---|---|---|
| | God **commit** their souls to Him in doing good, as to a faithful reator. [NKJV]<br><br>So if you are suffering according to God's will, keep on doing what is right, and **trust** yourself to the God who made you, for he will never fail you. [NLT]<br><br>ὥστε καὶ οἱ πάσχοντες κατὰ τὸ θέλημα τοῦ Θεοῦ, ὡς πιστῷ κτίστῃ **παρατιθέσθωσαν** τὰς ψυχὰς ἑαυτῶν ἐν ἀγαθοποιΐᾳ. [GNS]<br><br>ὥστε καὶ οἱ πάσχοντες κατὰ τὸ θέλημα τοῦ θεοῦ πιστῷ κτίστῃ **παρατιθέσθωσαν** τὰς ψυχὰς αὐτῶν ἐν ἀγαθοποιΐᾳ. [GNT] | |
| **#1302**<br>**Entrust–**<br>**Entrusting**<br><br>Commit–KJV<br>**Entrusting–NASB**<br>**Entrust–NIV**<br>Commit–NKJV<br>Trust–NLT<br><br>**POSB**<br>**REFERENCE**<br>(Jn.2:24)<br>*Deeper Study* #2 | ἐπίστευεν = *episteuen*<br>Pronunciation: [eh-pist-yoo'-ehn]<br>Parsing (part of speech): verb<br>    Mood—indicative<br>    Tense—imperfect<br>    Voice—active<br>    Person—3rd person<br>    Number—singular<br>    Stem or root—from πιστεύω<br>Concordance References:<br>⇒ Strong's #4100 pisteuō<br>⇒ NIV #4409 pisteuō<br>⇒ NASB #4100 pisteuō<br><br>**John 2:24**<br>But Jesus did not **commit** himself unto them, because he knew all men, [KJV]<br>But Jesus, on His part, was not **entrusting** Himself to them, for He knew all men, [NASB]<br>But Jesus would not **entrust** himself to them, for he knew all men. [NIV]<br>But Jesus did not **commit** Himself to them, because He knew all *men*, [NKJV]<br>But Jesus didn't **trust** them, because he knew what people were really like. [NLT]<br>αὐτὸς δὲ ὁ Ἰησοῦς οὐκ **ἐπίστευεν** ἑαυτὸν αὐτοῖς, διὰ τὸ αὐτὸν γινώσκειν πάντας, [GNS]<br>αὐτὸς δὲ Ἰησοῦς οὐκ **ἐπίστευεν** αὐτὸν αὐτοῖς διὰ τὸ αὐτὸν γινώσκειν πάντας [GNT] | To entrust; to commit; to trust; to believe; to have faith in; to confide in; to have confidence in.<br><br>**Practical Application**<br>The Greek word "entrust" is the very same word "believe" (cp. John 2:23). This gives an excellent picture of saving faith, of what genuine faith is—of the kind of faith that really saves a person. Note the circumstances behind this Scripture.<br>Jesus did not trust nor believe in the people; He did not commit Himself into their lives or hands. The verb is continuous action: Jesus kept on refusing to trust men, kept on refusing to commit Himself into their lives. Two reasons are given for this continuing attitude of Jesus.<br>1. Jesus knew all men. The idea is that He knew every single man personally. Not a person escaped His knowledge.<br>2. Jesus knew what was in man. No one needed to tell Him about man. He knew man's nature: his depravity, evil, deception, and fickleness. He knew the men He could trust and could not trust. He knew every man who professed to believe, yet would...<br>• betray Him.<br>• deny his faith under pressure.<br>• forsake Him, turning back to the world.<br>• slip and fall back into sin.<br>• be weak and easily influenced, tossed to and fro.<br>• prove untrustworthy.<br>• lack zeal and genuine commitment.<br>• lack courage to stand.<br>    Jesus knew all this about every man. Nothing was hid from Him. Therefore, He was not able to commit Himself and His blessings to some men despite the fact that they professed to believe. |
| **#1303**<br>**Entrusted–**<br>**Entrusting**<br><br>Committed–KJV<br>**Entrusting–NASB**<br>**Entrusted–NIV**<br>Committed–NKJV<br>Left his case–NLT<br><br>**POSB**<br>**REFERENCE**<br>(1 Pt.2:21-24; esp. v.23)<br>Note 2, point 3c | παρεδίδου = *paredidou*<br>Pronunciation: [par-ed-id'-oo]<br>Parsing (part of speech): verb<br>    Mood—indicative<br>    Tense—imperfect<br>    Voice—active<br>    Person—3rd person<br>    Number—singular<br>    Stem or root—from παραδίδωμι<br>Concordance References:<br>⇒ Strong's #3860 paradidōmi<br>⇒ NIV #4140 paradidōmi<br>⇒ NASB #3860 paradidōmi | Entrusted, committed, handed over; to deliver into the hands of.<br><br>**Practical Application**<br>Jesus Christ handed over His life to God; He delivered His life into the hands and keeping of God. Again, He did not have to suffer death, for He had the power to stop it all. But He had come to save men; therefore, he willingly suffered, committing His death and cause into the hands of God. He knew that God would raise Him up to prove His claim to be the Son of God, the Savior of the world. |

# PRACTICAL WORD STUDIES
## in the NEW TESTAMENT

| ENGLISH WORD | GREEK WORD AND VERSE | THE WORD MEANS... |
|---|---|---|
| | **1 Peter 2:23**<br>Who, when he was reviled, reviled not again; when he suffered, he threatened not; but **committed** himself to him that judgeth righteously; [KJV]<br>And while being reviled, He did not revile in return; while suffering, He uttered no threats, but kept **entrusting** Himself to Him who judges righteously; [NASB]<br>When they hurled their insults at him, he did not retaliate; when he suffered, he made no threats. Instead, he **entrusted** himself to him who judges justly. [NIV]<br>Who, when He was reviled, did not revile in return; when He suffered, He did not threaten, but **committed** Himself to Him who judges righteously; [NKJV]<br>He did not retaliate when he was insulted. When he suffered, he did not threaten to get even. He **left his case** in the hands of God, who always judges fairly. [NLT]<br>ὃς λοιδορούμενος οὐκ ἀντελοιδόρει, πάσχων οὐκ ἠπείλει, **παρεδίδου** δὲ τῷ κρίνοντι δικαίως· [GNS]<br>ὃς λοιδορούμενος οὐκ ἀντελοιδόρει, πάσχων οὐκ ἠπείλει, **παρεδίδου** δὲ τῷ κρίνοντι δικαίως· [GNT] | |
| **#1304**<br>**Entrusted To**<br><br>Committed unto–KJV<br>**Entrusted to–NASB**<br>**Entrusted to–NIV**<br>Committed to–NKJV<br>**Entrusted to–NLT**<br><br>**POSB REFERENCE**<br>(2 Tim. 1:11-12 esp. v.12)<br>Note 5, point 2b | **παραθήκην** = parathëkën<br>Pronunciation: [par-ath-ay'-kayn]<br>Parsing (part of speech): noun<br>   Case—accusative<br>   Gender—feminine<br>   Number—singular<br>   Stem or root—from παραθήκη, ης<br>Concordance References:<br>  ⇒ Strong's #3866 parathëkë<br>  ⇒ NIV #4146 parathëkë<br>  ⇒ NASB #3866 parathëkë<br><br>**2 Tim. 1:12**<br>For the which cause I also suffer these things: nevertheless I am not ashamed: for I know whom I have believed, and am persuaded that he is able to keep that which I have **committed unto** him against that day. [KJV]<br>For this reason I also suffer these things, but I am not ashamed; for I know whom I have believed and I am convinced that He is able to guard what I have **entrusted to** Him until that day. [NASB]<br>That is why I am suffering as I am. Yet I am not ashamed, because I know whom I have believed, and am convinced that he is able to guard what I have **entrusted to** him for that day. [NIV]<br>For this reason I also suffer these things; nevertheless I am not ashamed, for I know whom I have believed and am persuaded that He is able to keep what I have **committed to** Him until that Day. [NKJV]<br>And that is why I am suffering here in prison. But I am not ashamed of it, for I know the one in whom I trust, and I am sure that he is able to guard what I have **entrusted to** him until the day of his return. [NLT]<br>δι' ἣν αἰτίαν καὶ ταῦτα πάσχω, ἀλλ' οὐκ ἐπαισχύνομαι· οἶδα γὰρ ᾧ πεπίστευκα, καὶ πέπεισμαι ὅτι δυνατός ἐστι τὴν **παραθήκην** μου φυλάξαι εἰς ἐκείνην τὴν ἡμέραν. [GNS]<br>δι' ἣν αἰτίαν καὶ ταῦτα πάσχω· ἀλλ' οὐκ ἐπαισχύνομαι, οἶδα γὰρ ᾧ πεπίστευκα καὶ πέπεισμαι ὅτι δυνατός ἐστιν τὴν **παραθήκην** μου φυλάξαι εἰς ἐκείνην τὴν ἡμέραν. [GNT] | To deposit; to entrust; to commit.<br><br>**Practical Application**<br>Paul was persuaded of God's keeping power. Paul had committed both his life and work to Christ—all that Paul was as a person and all that Paul did upon earth was entrusted to Christ. A.T. Robertson says that Paul means, "'My deposit' as in a bank, the bank of heaven which no burglar can break (Matthew 6:19f)" (*Word Pictures in the New Testament*, Vol.4, p.614). Paul had deposited, turned everything he was and had over to Christ. Why? Because he knew that Christ could keep it and take care of it forever and ever. What exactly did Paul turn over to Christ? His life and work. Imagine!<br>⇒ Paul deposited his life into the hands of Christ; therefore, Christ *increased* his life, guided his life to bear the richest interest and the greatest return. Paul's *deposit of life was increased* to eternal life.<br>⇒ Paul deposited his work into the hands of Christ; therefore, Christ increased his work to bear the richest interest and the greatest return. Paul's *deposit of work was increased* to eternal responsibility and management for God. (See POSB note, Rewards—Luke 16:10-12 for more discussion.) |
| **#1305**<br>**Entrusted To**<br><br>Heritage–KJV<br>Allotted to–NASB<br>**Entrusted to–NIV**<br>**Entrusted to–NKJV**<br>Assigned to–NLT | **κλήρων** = klërön<br>Pronunciation: [klay'-rown]<br>Parsing (part of speech): noun<br>   Case—genitive<br>   Gender—masculine<br>   Number—plural<br>   Stem or root—from κλῆρος, ου<br>Concordance References:<br>  ⇒ Strong's #2819 klëros | Entrusted to; allotted to; assigned to.<br><br>**Practical Application**<br>This is the word that was used of Israel in the Old Testament. It means that the Jews were the people who were set apart and allotted and assigned to God. They were His very special allotment and assignment—His treasures—the |

# PRACTICAL WORD STUDIES
## in the NEW TESTAMENT

| ENGLISH WORD | GREEK WORD AND VERSE | THE WORD MEANS... |
|---|---|---|
| **POSB REFERENCE** (1 Pt.5:2-3; esp. v.3) Note 2, point 3 | ⇒ NIV #3102 klēros<br>⇒ NASB #2819 klēros<br><br>**1 Peter 5:3**<br>Neither as being lords over God's **heritage**, but being ensamples to the flock. [KJV]<br>Nor yet as lording it over those **allotted to** your charge, but proving to be examples to the flock. [NASB]<br>Not lording it over those **entrusted to** you, but being examples to the flock. [NIV]<br>Nor as being lords over those **entrusted to** you, but being examples to the flock; [NKJV]<br>Don't lord it over the people **assigned to** your care, but lead them by your good example. [NLT]<br>μηδ' ὡς κατακυριεύοντες τῶν **κλήρων**, ἀλλὰ τύποι γινόμενοι τοῦ ποιμνίου. [GNS]<br>μηδ' ὡς κατακυριεύοντες τῶν **κλήρων** ἀλλὰ τύποι γινόμενοι τοῦ ποιμνίου· [GNT] | people charged to His care and oversight. This is the picture painted of the elder or minister and the flock of God. God has given the minister a very special heritage or allotment and assignment: the minister has been assigned to feed the heritage of God, the very flock that belongs to God Himself.<br><br>Now note how the minister is to lead God's flock. He is not to lord it over them, but he is to lead by example. The minister...<br>• is not to be a dictator but an example.<br>• is not to preach one thing and do something else.<br><br>The minister is to lead people by living for Christ. He is to preach and teach Christ, but he is to first of all live a pure and righteous life just like Christ lived. The minister is to live exactly what he preaches. He is to be a pattern and model for Christ, a pattern and model of just what God wants His people to be. |
| **#1306**<br>**Envy**<br><br>An evil eye–KJV<br>**Envy–NASB**<br>**Envy–NIV**<br>An evil eye–NKJV<br>**Envy–NLT**<br><br>**POSB REFERENCE** (Mk.7:22)<br>*Deeper Study* #12 | ὀφθαλμὸς πονηρός = *aphthalmos poneros*<br>Pronunciation: [of-thal-mos' pon-ay-ros']<br>Parsing *aphthalmos* (part of speech): noun<br>  Case—nominative<br>  Gender—masculine<br>  Number—singular<br>  Stem or root—from ὀφθαλμός, οῦ<br>Parsing *poneros* (part of speech): adjective<br>  Case—nominative<br>  Gender—masculine<br>  Number—singular<br>  Stem or root—from πονηρός, ά, όν<br>Concordance References:<br>⇒ Strong's #3788 ophthalmos +4190 poneros<br>⇒ NIV #4057+4505 ophthalmos ponēros [envy]<br>⇒ NASB #3788 ophthalmos +4190 poneros<br><br>**Mark 7:22**<br>Thefts, covetousness, wickedness, deceit, lasciviousness, **an evil eye**, blasphemy, pride, foolishness: [KJV]<br>Deeds of coveting and wickedness, as well as deceit, sensuality, **envy**, slander, pride and foolishness. [NASB]<br>Greed, malice, deceit, lewdness, **envy**, slander, arrogance and folly. [NIV]<br>Thefts, covetousness, wickedness, deceit, lewdness, **an evil eye**, blasphemy, pride, foolishness. [NKJV]<br>Adultery, greed, wickedness, deceit, eagerness for lustful pleasure, **envy**, slander, pride, and foolishness. [NLT]<br>πλεονεξίαι, πονηρίαι, δόλος, ἀσέλγεια, **ὀφθαλμὸς πονηρός**, βλασφημία, ὑπερηφανία, ἀφροσύνη· [GNS]<br>μοιχεῖαι, πλεονεξίαι, πονηρίαι, δόλος, ἀσέλγεια, **ὀφθαλμὸς πονηρός**, βλασφημία, ὑπερηφανία, ἀφροσύνη· [GNT] | To look where one should not; to lust after what one should not; to envy, covet, crave and desire by looking; to use the eye in an evil way; to satisfy one's lusts and desires by looking.<br><br>**Practical Application**<br>This word goes beyond jealousy. It is the spirit...<br>• that wants not only the things that another person has but begrudges the fact that the person has them.<br>• that wants not only the things to be taken away from the person but wants him to suffer through the loss of them. |
| **#1307**<br>**Envy**<br><br>**Envy–KJV**<br>**Envy–NASB**<br>**Envy–NIV**<br>**Envy–NKJV**<br>**Envy–NLT**<br><br>**POSB REFERENCE** (Tit.3:3)<br>*Deeper Study* #5 | φθόνῳ = *phthonō*<br>Pronunciation: [fthon'-o']<br>Parsing (part of speech): noun<br>  Case—dative<br>  Gender—masculine<br>  Number—singular<br>  Stem or root—from φθόνος, ου<br>Concordance References:<br>⇒ Strong's #5355 phthonos<br>⇒ NIV #5784 phthonos<br>⇒ NASB #5355 phthonos<br><br>**Titus 3:3**<br>For we ourselves also were sometimes foolish, disobedient, deceived, serving divers lusts and pleasures, living in malice and **envy**, hateful, and hating one another. [KJV] | Envy, jealousy, spite. The word means that a person covets what someone else has, covets it so much that he wants it even if it means that it has to be taken away from the other person. He may even wish that the other person did not have it or had not received it.<br><br>**Practical Application**<br>We may look at people and envy their...<br>• money<br>• position<br>• looks<br>• social status<br>• recognition<br>• possessions |

# PRACTICAL WORD STUDIES
## in the New Testament

| ENGLISH WORD | GREEK WORD AND VERSE | THE WORD MEANS... |
|---|---|---|
| See also POSB REF: (Rom.1:29) *Deeper Study #6* (Gal.5:19-21; esp. v.21) Note 2 (1 Pt.2:1) Note 1 | For we also once were foolish ourselves, disobedient, deceived, enslaved to various lusts and pleasures, spending our life in malice and **envy**, hateful, hating one another. [NASB]<br><br>At one time we too were foolish, disobedient, deceived and enslaved by all kinds of passions and pleasures. We lived in malice and **envy**, being hated and hating one another. [NIV]<br><br>For we ourselves were also once foolish, disobedient, deceived, serving various lusts and pleasures, living in malice and **envy**, hateful and hating one another. [NKJV]<br><br>Once we, too, were foolish and disobedient. We were misled by others and became slaves to many wicked desires and evil pleasures. Our lives were full of evil and **envy**. We hated others, and they hated us. [NLT]<br><br>ἦμεν γάρ ποτε καὶ ἡμεῖς ἀνόητοι, ἀπειθεῖς, πλανώμενοι, δουλεύοντες ἐπιθυμίαις καὶ ἡδοναῖς ποικίλαις, ἐν κακίᾳ καὶ **φθόνῳ** διάγοντες, στυγητοί, μισοῦντες ἀλλήλους. [GNS]<br><br>Ἦμεν γάρ ποτε καὶ ἡμεῖς ἀνόητοι, ἀπειθεῖς, πλανώμενοι, δουλεύοντες ἐπιθυμίαις καὶ ἡδοναῖς ποικίλαις, ἐν κακίᾳ καὶ **φθόνῳ** διάγοντες, στυγητοί, μισοῦντες ἀλλήλους. [GNT] | • popularity<br>• clothes<br>• authority<br><br>The results of envy are terrible; envy takes a terrible toll upon the life and body of a person.<br><br>⇒ A person who envies *does not have peace or happiness*. He is dissatisfied with what he is and has and is always wanting more and more of what others have.<br><br>⇒ In addition to this, envy often drives a person into *crime and lawlessness* in order to get what he craves.<br><br>⇒ Furthermore, envy often leads to *physical problems* such as migraine headaches, high blood pressure, and ulcers.<br><br>⇒ Envy also causes *emotional problems* ranging from mild neurosis of depression to psychotic behavior.<br><br>But thanks to be to God our Savior. He saves and delivers us from envy. Through Christ He gives us life, real life, and He satisfies our hearts and lives with pleasures forevermore (Psalm 16:11). |
| **#1308**<br>**Envy–Envieth**<br><br>Envieth–KJV<br>Jealous–NASB<br>Envy–NIV<br>Envy–NKJV<br>Jealous–NLT<br><br>**POSB REFERENCE**<br>(1 Cor.13:4-7; esp. v.4) Note 2, point 3<br><br>See also POSB REF: (Acts 7:9) *Deeper Study #2* | ζηλοῖ = zēloi<br>Pronunciation: [dzay-loy'ee]<br>Parsing (part of speech): verb<br>   Mood—indicative<br>   Tense—present<br>   Voice—active<br>   Person—3rd person<br>   Number—singular<br>   Stem or root—from ζηλόω<br>Concordance References:<br>  ⇒ Strong's #2206 zēloō<br>  ⇒ NIV #2420 zēloō<br>  ⇒ NASB #2206 zēloō<br><br>**1 Cor. 13:4**<br>Charity suffereth long, and is kind; charity **envieth** not; charity vaunteth not itself, is not puffed up, [KJV]<br><br>Love is patient, love is kind, and is not **jealous**; love does not brag and is not arrogant, [NASB]<br><br>Love is patient, love is kind. It does not **envy**, it does not boast, it is not proud. [NIV]<br><br>Love suffers long *and* is kind; love does not **envy**; love does not parade itself, is not puffed up; [NKJV]<br><br>Love is patient and kind. Love is not **jealous** or boastful or proud [NLT]<br><br>ἡ ἀγάπη μακροθυμεῖ, χρηστεύεται· ἡ ἀγάπη, οὐ **ζηλοῖ**· ἡ ἀγάπη οὐ περπερεύεται, οὐ φυσιοῦται, [GNS]<br><br>Ἡ ἀγάπη μακροθυμεῖ, χρηστεύεται ἡ ἀγάπη, οὐ **ζηλοῖ**, [ἡ ἀγάπη] οὐ περπερεύεται, οὐ φυσιοῦται, [GNT] | To be jealous; to envy; to eagerly desire; to covet; to be zealous for.<br><br>**Practical Application**<br>Love does not envy (*zēloi*): is not jealous; does not have feelings against others because of what they have, such as gifts, position, friends, recognition, possessions, popularity, abilities. Love does not begrudge or attack or downplay the abilities and success of others. Love shares and joys and rejoices in the experience and good of others. |
| **#1309**<br>**Envyings**<br><br>Envyings–KJV<br>Jealousy–NASB<br>Jealousy–NIV<br>Jealousies–NKJV<br>Jealousy–NLT<br><br>**POSB REFERENCE**<br>(2 Cor.12:19-21; esp. v.20) Note 3, point 2 | ζῆλος = zēlos<br>Pronunciation: [dzay'-los]<br>Parsing (part of speech): noun<br>   Case—nominative<br>   Gender—masculine or neuter<br>   Number—singular<br>   Stem or root—from ζῆλος, ου<br>Concordance References:<br>  ⇒ Strong's #2205 zēlos<br>  ⇒ NIV #2419 zēlos<br>  ⇒ NASB #2205 zēlos<br><br>**2 Cor. 12:20**<br>For I fear, lest, when I come, I shall not find you such as I would, and that I shall be found unto you such as ye would not: lest there be debates, **envyings**, wraths, strifes, backbitings, whisperings, swellings, tumults: [KJV] | Jealousy; envyings; begrudging what others have, whether position, abilities, recognition, acceptance, loyalty, wealth, or anything else.<br><br>**Practical Application**<br>Paul was stricken with fear, fear lest the church fail to be what it should be and reject him and his ministry. Paul feared that the church would fail to deal with the carnal critics and continue putting up with their evil attacks against him. He lists eight evils including "envyings" (*zēlos*) that were and still are characteristic of divisive critics in the church. |

# PRACTICAL WORD STUDIES
## in the NEW TESTAMENT

| ENGLISH WORD | GREEK WORD AND VERSE | THE WORD MEANS... |
|---|---|---|
| See also POSB REF: (Rom.13:13) Note 4, point 6 | For I am afraid that perhaps when I come I may find you to be not what I wish and may be found by you to be not what you wish; that perhaps there may be strife, **jealousy**, angry tempers, disputes, slanders, gossip, arrogance, disturbances; [NASB]<br><br>For I am afraid that when I come I may not find you as I want you to be, and you may not find me as you want me to be. I fear that there may be quarreling, **jealousy**, outbursts of anger, factions, slander, gossip, arrogance and disorder. [NIV]<br><br>For I fear lest, when I come, I shall not find you such as I wish, and *that* I shall be found by you such as you do not wish; lest *there be* contentions, **jealousies**, outbursts of wrath, selfish ambitions, backbitings, whisperings, conceits, tumults; [NKJV]<br><br>For I am afraid that when I come to visit you I won't like what I find, and then you won't like my response. I am afraid that I will find quarreling, **jealousy**, outbursts of anger, selfishness, backstabbing, gossip, conceit, and disorderly behavior. [NLT]<br><br>φοβοῦμαι γὰρ μή πως ἐλθὼν οὐχ οἵους θέλω εὕρω ὑμᾶς, κἀγὼ εὑρεθῶ ὑμῖν οἷον οὐ θέλετε· μή πως ἔρις, **ζῆλοι**, θυμοί, ἐριθεῖαι, καταλαλιαί, ψιθυρισμοί, φυσιώσεις, ἀκαταστασίαι· [GNS]<br><br>φοβοῦμαι γὰρ μή πως ἐλθὼν οὐχ οἵους θέλω εὕρω ὑμᾶς κἀγὼ εὑρεθῶ ὑμῖν οἷον οὐ θέλετε· μή πως ἔρις, **ζῆλος**, θυμοί, ἐριθεῖαι, καταλαλιαί, ψιθυρισμοί, φυσιώσεις, ἀκαταστασίαι· [GNT] | |
| **#1310**<br>**Equal–**<br>**Equality**<br><br>Equal–KJV<br>Equality–NASB<br>Equality–NIV<br>Equal–NKJV<br>Rights–NLT<br><br>**POSB REFERENCE**<br>(Philip.2:6)<br>Note 2, point 3 | τὸ εἶναι ἴσα = *to einai isa*<br>Pronunciation: [to i-nah-ee' ee'-sah]<br>Parsing *einai* (part of speech): verb<br>    Mood—infinitive<br>    Tense—present<br>    Voice—active<br>    Case—accusative<br>    Stem or root—from εἰμί<br>Parsing *isa* (part of speech): adjective<br>    Type—adverb<br>    Stem or root—from ἴσος, η, ον<br>Concordance References:<br>  ⇒ Strong's #1510+2470+3588 eimi isos ho<br>  ⇒ NIV #1639+2698+3836 eimi isos ho [equality]<br>  ⇒ NASB #1510+2470+3588 eimi isos ho<br><br>**Philip. 2:6**<br>Who, being in the form of God, thought it not robbery to be **equal** with God: [KJV]<br>Who, although He existed in the form of God, did not regard **equality** with God a thing to be grasped, [NASB]<br>Who, being in very nature God, did not consider **equality** with God something to be grasped, [NIV]<br>Who, being in the form of God, did not consider it robbery to be **equal** with God, [NKJV]<br>Though he was God, he did not demand and cling to his **rights** as God. [NLT]<br>ὃς ἐν μορφῇ θεοῦ ὑπάρχων, οὐχ ἁρπαγμὸν ἡγήσατο τὸ εἶναι ἴσα θεῷ, [GNS]<br>ὃς ἐν μορφῇ θεοῦ ὑπάρχων οὐχ ἁρπαγμὸν ἡγήσατο τὸ εἶναι ἴσα θεῷ, [GNT] | Equal, equality, same. Jesus Christ is "equal with God" (Greek). It means to be *on an equal basis with God*; to possess all the being, qualities and attributes of God Himself.<br><br>**Practical Application**<br>Note also the word "robbery" [KJV, NKJV] (*arpagmon*). It is the picture of a thief's seeking to snatch or take something that is not his. When Jesus Christ was on earth, He was constantly claiming...<br>• to be God.<br>• to be the Son of God.<br>• to have the nature of God.<br>• to be one with God.<br>• to be *on an equal basis with God*.<br><br>Was He a thief? Was He robbing and snatching the title of God or was He truly God?<br>The answer is a most glorious truth. Jesus Christ did not have to rob or snatch at equality with God. He did not have to rob and grasp after the deity of God; He was already on an equal basis with God. |
| **#1311**<br>**Equip–**<br>**Equipping**<br><br>Perfecting–KJV<br>**Equipping–NASB**<br>Prepare–NIV<br>**Equipping–NKJV**<br>Equip–NLT | καταρτισμὸν = *katartismon*<br>Pronunciation: [kat-ar-tis-mon']<br>Parsing (part of speech): noun<br>    Case—accusative<br>    Gender—masculine<br>    Number—singular<br>    Stem or root—from καταρτισμός, οῦ<br>Concordance References:<br>  ⇒ Strong's #2677 katartismos<br>  ⇒ NIV #2938 katartismos<br>  ⇒ NASB #2677 katartismos | To prepare; to perfect; to equip; to train; to equip for service and ministry.<br><br>**Practical Application**<br>There is an immediate purpose for the professional or office-bearing gifts in the church and among God's people. It is to equip believers to do the work of the ministry. This is critical to see, for the office bearer in the church is not to be the only one who goes about doing the work |

# PRACTICAL WORD STUDIES
## in the NEW TESTAMENT

| ENGLISH WORD | GREEK WORD AND VERSE | THE WORD MEANS... |
|---|---|---|
| **POSB REFERENCE** (Eph.4:12-16; esp. v.12) Note 4, point 1 | **Ephes. 4:12** <br> For the **perfecting** of the saints, for the work of the ministry, for the edifying of the body of Christ: [KJV] <br> For the **equipping** of the saints for the work of service, to the building up of the body of Christ; [NASB] <br> To **prepare** God's people for works of service, so that the body of Christ may be built up [NIV] <br> For the **equipping** of the saints for the work of ministry, for the edifying of the body of Christ, [NKJV] <br> Their responsibility is to **equip** God's people to do his work and build up the church, the body of Christ, [NLT] <br> πρὸς τὸν **καταρτισμὸν** τῶν ἁγίων, εἰς ἔργον διακονίας, εἰς οἰκοδομὴν τοῦ σώματος τοῦ Χριστοῦ· [GNS] <br> πρὸς τὸν **καταρτισμὸν** τῶν ἁγίων εἰς ἔργον διακονίας, εἰς οἰκοδομὴν τοῦ σώματος τοῦ Χριστοῦ, [GNT] | of the ministry. In fact, his *primary task* is to be an equipper, a person who makes disciples and prepares others to serve Christ (see POSB note, Discipleship—Matthew 28:19-20). <br> Note another critical point: the very purpose for equipping laymen is so that the body of Christ, the church, may be built up. This is a significant point, for it means that the church cannot be built up without the members themselves doing the work of the ministry. All believers within a church must be involved in the work of the ministry. As Wuest says: "This is an order that the Body of Christ, the Church might be built up, by additions to its membership in lost souls being saved, and by the building up of individual saints." (Kenneth Wuest. *Ephesians and Colossians,* Vol.1, p.101). |
| #1312 **Establish** <br><br> Stablish–KJV <br> **Establish–NASB** <br> **Establish–NIV** <br> **Establish–NKJV** <br> Make...strong–NLT <br><br> **POSB REFERENCE** (Rom.16:25-27, esp. v.25) Introduction | στηρίξαι = stērixai <br> Pronunciation: [stay-rich'-ah-ee] <br> Parsing (part of speech): verb <br>     Mood—infinitive <br>     Tense—aorist <br>     Voice—active <br>     Stem or root—from στηρίζω <br> Concordance References: <br> ⇒ Strong's #4741 stērizō <br> ⇒ NIV #5114 stērizō <br> ⇒ NASB #4741 stērizō <br><br> **Romans 16:25** <br> Now to him that is of power to **stablish** you according to my gospel, and the preaching of Jesus Christ, according to the revelation of the mystery, which was kept secret since the world began, [KJV] <br> Now to Him who is able to **establish** you according to my gospel and the preaching of Jesus Christ, according to the revelation of the mystery which has been kept secret for long ages past, [NASB] <br> Now to him who is able to **establish** you by my gospel and the proclamation of Jesus Christ, according to the revelation of the mystery hidden for long ages past, [NIV] <br> Now to Him who is able to **establish** you according to my gospel and the preaching of Jesus Christ, according to the revelation of the mystery kept secret since the world began [NKJV] <br> God is able to **make** you **strong**, just as the Good News says. It is the message about Jesus Christ and his plan for you Gentiles, a plan kept secret from the beginning of time. [NLT] <br> Τῷ δὲ δυναμένῳ ὑμᾶς **στηρίξαι** κατὰ τὸ εὐαγγέλιόν μου καὶ τὸ κήρυγμα Ἰησοῦ Χριστοῦ, κατὰ ἀποκάλυψιν μυστηρίου χρόνοις αἰωνίοις σεσιγημένου [GNS] <br> [Τῷ δὲ δυναμένῳ ὑμᾶς **στηρίξαι** κατὰ τὸ εὐαγγέλιόν μου καὶ τὸ κήρυγμα Ἰησοῦ Χριστοῦ, κατὰ ἀποκάλυψιν μυστηρίου χρόνοις αἰωνίοις σεσιγημένου, [GNT] | To strengthen; to make firm; to establish; to fix; to set up. It means to strengthen, secure, make stable, set fast, and make firm. <br><br> **Practical Application** <br> God is able to establish the believer. The one thing people long for is to be secure, strong, and firmly established in life. God is able to fulfill this longing. God is able to establish and strengthen people and to give them a strong life. |
| #1313 **Establish** <br><br> Settle–KJV <br> **Establish–NASB** <br> Steadfast–NIV <br> **Settle–NKJV** <br> Place you on a firm foundation–NLT | θεμελιώσει = themeliōsei <br> Pronunciation: [them-el-ee-o'-seh-ee] <br> Parsing (part of speech): verb <br>     Mood—indicative <br>     Tense—future <br>     Voice—active <br>     Person—3rd person <br>     Number—singular <br>     Stem or root—from θεμελιόω <br> Concordance References: <br> ⇒ Strong's #2311 themelioō | To be steadfast; to settle; to establish; to place on a firm foundation; to secure as in a foundation; to ground with security. <br><br> **Practical Application** <br> God Himself will *establish us*. God is able to make us secure through all the sufferings of life, no matter what they are. He is able to settle and secure our nerves, thoughts, and fears—all the uneasy and unnerving emotions that disturb us. |

**PRACTICAL WORD STUDIES**
**in the NEW TESTAMENT**

| ENGLISH WORD | GREEK WORD AND VERSE | THE WORD MEANS... |
|---|---|---|
| **POSB REFERENCE** (1 Pt.5:10) Note 2, point 4 | ⇒ NIV #2530 themelioö<br>⇒ NASB #2311 themelioö<br>**1 Peter 5:10**<br>But the God of all grace, who hath called us unto his eternal glory by Christ Jesus, after that ye have suffered a while, make you perfect, stablish, strengthen, **settle** you. [KJV]<br>And after you have suffered for a little while, the God of all grace, who called you to His eternal glory in Christ, will Himself perfect, confirm, strengthen and **establish** you. [NASB]<br>And the God of all grace, who called you to his eternal glory in Christ, after you have suffered a little while, will himself restore you and make you strong, firm and **steadfast**. [NIV]<br>But may the God of all grace, who called us to His eternal glory by Christ Jesus, after you have suffered a while, perfect, establish, strengthen, and **settle** you. [NKJV]<br>In his kindness God called you to his eternal glory by means of Jesus Christ. After you have suffered a little while, he will restore, support, and strengthen you, and he will **place you on a firm foundation**. [NLT]<br>ὁ δὲ Θεὸς πάσης χάριτος, ὁ καλέσας ὑμᾶς εἰς τὴν αἰώνιον αὐτοῦ δόξαν ἐν Χριστῷ Ἰησοῦ, ὀλίγον παθόντας αὐτὸς καταρτίσει ὑμᾶς, στηρίξει, σθενώσαι, **θεμελιώσαι**. [GNS]<br>Ὁ δὲ Θεὸς πάσης χάριτος, ὁ καλέσας ὑμᾶς εἰς τὴν αἰώνιον αὐτοῦ δόξαν ἐν Χριστῷ [Ἰησοῦ], ὀλίγον παθόντας αὐτὸς καταρτίσει, στηρίξει, σθενώσει, **θεμελιώσει**. [GNT] | God can settle us if we will only do one thing: resist the devil and draw near to Him. |
| **#1314**<br>**Establish**<br><br>Stablish–KJV<br>Strengthen–NASB<br>Stand firm–NIV<br>**Establish–NKJV**<br>Take courage–NLT<br><br>**POSB REFERENCE**<br>(James 5:7-9; esp. v.8) Note 2, point 1 | στηρίξατε τὰς καρδίας = stērixate tas kardias<br>Pronunciation: [stay-rid'-zah-teh tas kar-dee'-ahs]<br>Parsing *stērixate* (part of speech): verb<br>    Mood—imperative<br>    Tense—aorist<br>    Voice—active<br>    Person—2$^{nd}$ person<br>    Number—plural<br>    Stem or root— from στηρίζω<br>Parsing *kardias* (part of speech): noun<br>    Case—accusative<br>    Gender—feminine<br>    Number—plural<br>    Stem or root—from καρδία, ας<br>Concordance References:<br>⇒ Strong's #2588+3588+4741 kardia ho sterizō<br>⇒ NIV #2840+3836+5114 kardia ho sterizō [stand firm]<br>⇒ NASB #2588+3588+4741 kardia ho sterizō<br>**James 5:8**<br>Be ye also patient; **stablish** your hearts: for the coming of the Lord draweth nigh. [KJV]<br>You too be patient; **strengthen** your hearts, for the coming of the Lord is at hand. [NASB]<br>You too, be patient and **stand firm**, because the Lord's coming is near. [NIV]<br>You also be patient. **Establish** your hearts, for the coing of the Lord is at hand. [NKJV]<br>You, too, must be patient. And **take courage**, for the coming of the Lord is near. [NLT]<br>μακροθυμήσατε καὶ ὑμεῖς, **στηρίξατε τὰς καρδίας** ὑμῶν, ὅτι ἡ παρουσία τοῦ Κυρίου ἤγγικε. [GNS]<br>μακροθυμήσατε καὶ ὑμεῖς, **στηρίξατε τὰς καρδίας** ὑμῶν, ὅτι ἡ παρουσία τοῦ κυρίου ἤγγικεν. [GNT] | To stand firm; to stablish; to strengthen; to take courage; to stand firm in one's mind, his inner self, his heart.<br><br>**Practical Application**<br>Believers must "establish" (*stērixate*) their hearts. The word means to set upon; to fix upon; to make fast (W.E. Vine. *Expository Dictionary of New Testament Words*, p.41). We must set our hearts upon the Lord's coming, for His coming is near. The idea is that it is drawing ever so close and can happen at any moment. We must focus and set our hearts upon His return—be looking for it every day just as the farmer looks for his great day of harvest. Looking for the great day of redemption—for the Lord's glorious return—will stir us to combat temptation and trial step by step. It will stir us to patiently endure no matter the situation, and by patiently enduring we shall gain the victory over all—no matter how bad the situation may be. |
| **#1315**<br>**Establish** | στηρίξει = stērixei<br>Pronunciation: [stay-rich'-eh-ee]<br>Parsing (part of speech): veerb<br>    Mood—indicative | To make steadfast, firm, strong and solid; to establish; to fix. It means to be firmly set, as firmly as if one were set in reinforced concrete. |

# PRACTICAL WORD STUDIES
## in the NEW TESTAMENT

| ENGLISH WORD | GREEK WORD AND VERSE | THE WORD MEANS... |
|---|---|---|
| Stablish–KJV<br>Confirm–NASB<br>Make...strong–NIV<br>**Establish–NKJV**<br>Support–NLT<br><br>**POSB REFERENCE**<br>(1 Pt.5:10)<br>Note 2, point 2 | Tense—future<br>Voice—active<br>Person—3rd person<br>Number—singular<br>Stem or root—from στηρίζω<br>Concordance References:<br>⇒ Strong's #4741 stērizō<br>⇒ NIV #5114 stērizō<br>⇒ NASB #4741 stērizō<br><br>**1 Peter 5:10**<br>But the God of all grace, who hath called us unto his eternal glory by Christ Jesus, after that ye have suffered a while, make you perfect, **stablish**, strengthen, settle you. [KJV]<br>And after you have suffered for a little while, the God of all grace, who called you to His eternal glory in Christ, will Himself perfect, **confirm**, strengthen and establish you. [NASB]<br>And the God of all grace, who called you to his eternal glory in Christ, after you have suffered a little while, will himself restore you and **make** you **strong**, firm and steadfast. [NIV]<br>But may the God of all grace, who called us to His eternal glory by Christ Jesus, after you have suffered a while, perfect, **establish**, strengthen, and settle *you*. [NKJV]<br>In his kindness God called you to his eternal glory by means of Jesus Christ. After you have suffered a little while, he will restore, **support**, and strengthen you, and he will place you on a firm foundation. [NLT]<br>ὁ δὲ Θεὸς πάσης χάριτος, ὁ καλέσας ὑμᾶς εἰς τὴν αἰώνιον αὐτοῦ δόξαν ἐν Χριστῷ Ἰησοῦ, ὀλίγον παθόντας αὐτὸς καταρτίσει ὑμᾶς, **στηρίξει**, σθενώσαι, θεμελιώσαι. [GNS]<br>Ὁ δὲ Θεὸς πάσης χάριτος, ὁ καλέσας ὑμᾶς εἰς τὴν αἰώνιον αὐτοῦ δόξαν ἐν Χριστῷ [Ἰησοῦ], ὀλίγον παθόντας αὐτὸς καταρτίσει, **στηρίξει**, σθενώσει, θεμελιώσει. [GNT] | It means to be immovable.<br><br>**Practical Application**<br>God Himself uses the believer's sufferings to establish the believer. God is able to attach us to Himself to such a degree that we will be immovable, no matter how severe the attack of temptation or suffering. But remember our duty: we must resist the devil and resist him steadfastly (1 Peter 5:8). The promise is clear: if we resist the devil and draw near God, He will draw near us (James 4:7-8). |
| #1316<br>**Established**<br><br>Established–KJV<br>Established–NASB<br>Make...strong–NIV<br>**Established–NKJV**<br>Grow strong–NLT<br><br>**POSB REFERENCE**<br>(Rom.1:10-13; esp. v.11)<br>Note 4, point 1 | στηριχθῆναι = stērichthēnai<br>Pronunciation: [stay-rix'-thay-nah-ee]<br>Parsing (part of speech): verb<br>Mood—infinitive<br>Tense—aorist<br>Voice—passive<br>Case—accusative<br>Stem or root—from στηρίζω<br>Concordance References:<br>⇒ Strong's #4741 stērizō<br>⇒ NIV #5114 stērizō<br>⇒ NASB #4741 stērizō<br><br>**Romans 1:11**<br>For I long to see you, that I may impart unto you some spiritual gift, to the end ye may be **established**; [KJV]<br>For I long to see you in order that I may impart some spiritual gift to you, that you may be **established**; [NASB]<br>I long to see you so that I may impart to you some spiritual gift to **make** you **strong**—[NIV]<br>For I long to see you, that I may impart to you some spiritual gift, so that you may be **established**—[NKJV]<br>For I long to visit you so I can share a spiritual blessing with you that will help you **grow strong** in the Lord. [NLT]<br>ἐπιποθῶ γὰρ ἰδεῖν ὑμᾶς, ἵνα τι μεταδῶ χάρισμα ὑμῖν πνευματικὸν εἰς τὸ **στηριχθῆναι** ὑμᾶς, [GNS]<br>ἐπιποθῶ γὰρ ἰδεῖν ὑμᾶς, ἵνα τι μεταδῶ χάρισμα ὑμῖν πνευματικὸν εἰς τὸ **στηριχθῆναι** ὑμᾶς, [GNT] | To make firm; to make strong; to establish; to fix; to make fast; to strengthen; to set.<br><br>**Practical Application**<br>Paul wished to *impart some spiritual gift* to the believers. Why? So that they might be more deeply established in the faith. The term spiritual gift (*charisma*) means a gift of grace. The term often refers to specific gifts given by the Holy Spirit (Romans 12:6-8), but here it means *the truths* of the grace of God, of His spiritual blessings to man revealed in Christ Jesus our Lord. Very simply, Paul longed to share the truths of the gospel with the believers at Rome. God's spiritual blessings were overflowing in his heart, and he was aching to share the gift of God's blessings. |

# PRACTICAL WORD STUDIES
## in the NEW TESTAMENT

| ENGLISH WORD | GREEK WORD AND VERSE | THE WORD MEANS... |
|---|---|---|
| **#1317**<br>**Established**<br><br>Grounded–KJV<br>**Established–NASB**<br>**Established–NIV**<br>Grounded–NKJV<br>Stand in it–NLT<br><br>**POSB**<br>**REFERENCE**<br>(Col.1:23)<br>Note 4, point 1 | τεθεμελιωμένοι = tethemeliōmenoi<br>Pronunciation: [teh-them-el-ee-o'-mehn-oy]<br>Parsing (part of speech): verb<br>    Mood—participle<br>    Tense—perfect<br>    Voice—passive<br>    Case—nominative<br>    Gender—masculine<br>    Person—2nd person<br>    Number—plural<br>    Stem or root—from θεμελιόω<br>Concordance References:<br>  ⇒ Strong's #2311 themelioō<br>  ⇒ NIV #2530 themelioō<br>  ⇒ NASB #2311 themelioō<br><br>**Col. 1:23**<br>If ye continue in the faith **grounded** and settled, and be not moved away from the hope of the gospel, which ye have heard, and which was preached to every creature which is under heaven; whereof I Paul am made a minister; [KJV]<br><br>If indeed you continue in the faith firmly **established** and steadfast, and not moved away from the hope of the gospel that you have heard, which was proclaimed in all creation under heaven, and of which I, Paul, was made a minister. [NASB]<br><br>If you continue in your faith, **established** and firm, not moved from the hope held out in the gospel. This is the gospel that you heard and that has been proclaimed to every creature under heaven, and of which I, Paul, have become a servant. [NIV]<br><br>If indeed you continue in the faith, **grounded** and steadfast, and are not moved away from the hope of the gospel which you heard, which was preached to every creature under heaven, of which I, Paul, became a minister. [NKJV]<br><br>But you must continue to believe this truth and **stand in it** firmly. Don't drift away from the assurance you received when you heard the Good News. The Good News has been preached all over the world, and I, Paul, have been appointed by God to proclaim it. [NLT]<br><br>εἴγε ἐπιμένετε τῇ πίστει **τεθεμελιωμένοι** καὶ ἑδραῖοι, καὶ μὴ μετακινούμενοι ἀπὸ τῆς ἐλπίδος τοῦ εὐαγγελίου οὗ ἠκούσατε, τοῦ κηρυχθέντος ἐν πάσῃ τῇ κτίσει τῇ ὑπὸ τὸν οὐρανόν, οὗ ἐγενόμην ἐγὼ Παῦλος διάκονος. [GNS]<br><br>εἴ γε ἐπιμένετε τῇ πίστει **τεθεμελιωμένοι** καὶ ἑδραῖοι καὶ μὴ μετακινούμενοι ἀπὸ τῆς ἐλπίδος τοῦεὐαγγελίου οὗ ἠκούσατε, τοῦ κηρυχθέντος ἐν πάσῃ κτίσει τῇ ὑπὸ τὸν οὐρανόν, οὗ ἐγενόμην ἐγὼ Παῦλος διάκονος. [GNT] | To be established; to be grounded; to be rooted; to make strong; to be fixed. It means to be grounded in Christ like the firm, solid foundation of a building.<br><br>**Practical Application**<br>This is the word that pictures the foundation of a building, the solid foundation that gives the greatest stability possible to a building. The believer must be so grounded in Christ that he can withstand the severest storms of life. |
| **#1318**<br>**Establishes**<br><br>Stablisheth–KJV<br>**Establishes–NASB**<br>Makes...stand firm–NIV<br>**Establishes–NKJV**<br>Stand firm–NLT<br><br>**POSB**<br>**REFERENCE**<br>(2 Cor.1:21-22; esp. v.21)<br>Note 5 | βεβαιῶν = bebaiōn<br>Pronunciation: [beb-ah-yi'-own]<br>Parsing (part of speech): verb<br>    Mood—participle<br>    Tense—present<br>    Voice—active<br>    Case—nominative<br>    Gender—masculine<br>    Number—singular<br>    Stem or root—from βεβαιόω<br>Concordance References:<br>  ⇒ Strong's #950 bebaioō<br>  ⇒ NIV #1011 bebaioō<br>  ⇒ NASB #950 bebaioō<br><br>**2 Cor. 1:21**<br>Now he which **stablisheth** us with you in Christ, and hath anointed us, is God; [KJV]<br><br>Now He who **establishes** us with you in Christ and | To establish; to confirm; to sustain; to keep strong; to strengthen; to make firm, steadfast, and constant.<br><br>**Practical Application**<br>The word "us" refers primarily to Paul. He is comparing himself with the Corinthians, and he is also including those who oppose him. In no uncertain terms, Paul says that the same God who has worked in the Corinthians has also worked in him. |

# PRACTICAL WORD STUDIES
## in the NEW TESTAMENT

| ENGLISH WORD | GREEK WORD AND VERSE | THE WORD MEANS... |
|---|---|---|
| | anointed us is God, [NASB]<br>Now it is God who **makes** both us and you **stand firm** in Christ. He anointed us, [NIV]<br>Now He who **establishes** us with you in Christ and has anointed us *is* God, [NKJV]<br>It is God who gives us, along with you, the ability to **stand firm** for Christ. He has commissioned us, [NLT]<br>ὁ δὲ **βεβαιῶν** ἡμᾶς σὺν ὑμῖν εἰς Χριστόν, καὶ χρίσας ἡμᾶς, Θεός, [GNS]<br>ὁ δὲ **βεβαιῶν** ἡμᾶς σὺν ὑμῖν εἰς Χριστὸν καὶ χρίσας ἡμᾶς θεός, [GNT] | |
| **#1319**<br>**Eternal**<br><br>Eternal–KJV<br>Eternal–NASB<br>Eternal–NIV<br>Eternal–NKJV<br>Eternal–NLT<br><br>**POSB<br>REFERENCE**<br>(Jn.17:2-3; esp. v.3)<br>*Deeper Study* #1 | αἰώνιος = aiōnios<br>Pronunciation: [ahee-o'-nee-os]<br>Parsing (part of speech): adjective<br>    Case—nominative<br>    Gender—feminine<br>    Number—singular<br>    Stem or root—from αἰώνιος, ον<br>Concordance References:<br>  ⇒ Strong's #166 aionios<br>  ⇒ NIV #173 aionios<br>  ⇒ NASB #166 aionios<br><br>**John 17:3**<br>And this is life **eternal**, that they might know thee the only true God, and Jesus Christ, whom thou hast sent. [KJV]<br>"And this is **eternal** life, that they may know Thee, the only true God, and Jesus Christ whom Thou hast sent. [NASB]<br>Now this is **eternal** life: that they may know you, the only true God, and Jesus Christ, whom you have sent. [NIV]<br>And this is **eternal** life, that they may know You, the only true God, and Jesus Christ whom You have sent. [NKJV]<br>And this is the way to have **eternal** life—to know you, the only true God, and Jesus Christ, the one you sent to earth. [NLT]<br>αὕτη δέ ἐστιν ἡ **αἰώνιος** ζωή, ἵνα γινώσκωσι σὲ τὸν μόνον ἀληθινὸν Θεόν, καὶ ὃν ἀπέστειλας Ἰησοῦν Χριστόν. [GNS]<br>αὕτη δέ ἐστιν ἡ **αἰώνιος** ζωή ἵνα γινώσκωσιν σὲ τὸν μόνον ἀληθινὸν θεὸν καὶ ὃν ἀπέστειλας Ἰησοῦν Χριστόν. [GNT] | Eternal, perpetual, forever, endless, ageless, dateless, timeless, everlasting, infinite, permanent, ceaseless. It means a quality of life that is not bound to the limitation of time. It describes life, real life.<br><br>**Practical Application**<br>What kind of life is "eternal (*aiōnios*)?" It is the very life of God Himself. It is the very energy, force, being, essence, principle, and power of life. It has more to do with quality and with what life really is than with duration. To live forever in the present world is not necessarily a good thing. The world and man's body need changing. That changed life is found only in eternal life. The only being who can be said to be eternal is God. Therefore, life—supreme life—is found only in God. To possess eternal life is to know God. Once a person knows God and Jesus Christ whom He has sent, that person has eternal life—he will live forever. But more essential, the person has the supreme quality of life, the very life of God Himself. (See POSB *Deeper Study* #2—John 1:4; POSB *Deeper Study* #1—John 10:10.) |
| **#1320**<br>**Eternal<br>Comfort**<br><br>Everlasting consolation–KJV<br>**Eternal comfort–NASB**<br>Eternal encouragement–NIV<br>Everlasting consolation–NKJV<br>Everlasting comfort–NLT<br><br>**POSB<br>REFERENCE**<br>(2 Thes. 2:16-17, esp. v.16)<br>Note 5, point 2 | παράκλησιν αἰωνίαν = *paraklēsin aiōnian*<br>Pronunciation: [par-ak'-lay-sin ah-ee-o'-nee-ahn]<br>Parsing *paraklēsin* (part of speech): noun<br>    Case—accusative<br>    Gender—feminine<br>    Number—singular<br>    Stem or root—from παράκλησις, εως<br>Parsing *aiōnian* (part of speech): adjective<br>    Case—accusative<br>    Gender—feminine<br>    Number—singular<br>    Stem or root—from αἰώνιος, ον<br>Concordance References:<br>  ⇒ Strong's #3874 paraklēsis + 166 aiōnios<br>  ⇒ NIV #4155 paraklēsis [encouragement] + 173 aiōnios [eternal]<br>  ⇒ NASB #3874 paraklēsis + 166 aiōnios<br><br>**2 Thes. 2:16**<br>Now our Lord Jesus Christ himself, and God, even our Father, which hath loved us, and hath given us **everlasting consolation** and good hope through grace, [KJV]<br>Now may our Lord Jesus Christ Himself and God our Father, who has loved us and given us **eternal comfort** and good hope by grace, [NASB]<br>May our Lord Jesus Christ himself and God our | Eternal encouragement; everlasting consolation; eternal comfort; everlasting comfort.<br><br>**Practical Application**<br>The person who is saved receives eternal comfort (*paraklēsin aiōnian*). It is a comfort and strength that cannot be shaken by anything—no matter what it is—either now or in eternity. |

# PRACTICAL WORD STUDIES
## in the NEW TESTAMENT

| ENGLISH WORD | GREEK WORD AND VERSE | THE WORD MEANS... |
|---|---|---|
| | Father, who loved us and by his grace gave us **eternal encouragement** and good hope, [NIV]<br><br>Now may our Lord Jesus Christ Himself, and our God and Father, who has loved us and given *us* **everlasting consolation** and good hope by grace, [NKJV]<br><br>May our Lord Jesus Christ and God our Father, who loved us and in his special favor gave us **everlasting comfort** and good hope, [NLT]<br><br>Αὐτὸς δὲ ὁ Κύριος ἡμῶν Ἰησοῦς Χριστὸς, καὶ ὁ Θεὸς καὶ πατὴρ ἡμῶν ὁ ἀγαπήσας ἡμᾶς, καὶ δοὺς **παράκλησιν αἰωνίαν** καὶ ἐλπίδα ἀγαθὴν ἐν χάριτι, [GNS]<br><br>Αὐτὸς δὲ ὁ κύριος ἡμῶν Ἰησοῦς Χριστὸς καὶ [ὁ] θεὸς ὁ πατὴρ ἡμῶν, ὁ ἀγαπήσας ἡμᾶς καὶ δοὺς **παράκλησιν αἰωνίαν** καὶ ἐλπίδα ἀγαθὴν ἐν χάριτι, [GNT] | |
| **#1321**<br>**Eternal Destruction**<br><br>Destruction–KJV<br>Destruction–NASB<br>Destruction–NIV<br>Destruction–NKJV<br>**Eternal destruction–NLT**<br><br>**POSB REFERENCE**<br>(Philip.3:18-19; esp. v.19)<br>Note 2, point 1 | ἀπώλεια = apōleia<br>Pronunciation: [ap-o'-li-a]<br>Parsing (part of speech): noun<br>  Case—nominative<br>  Gender—feminine<br>  Number—singular<br>  Stem or root—from ἀπώλεια, ας<br>Concordance References:<br>⇒ Strong's #684 apōleia<br>⇒ NIV #724 apōleia<br>⇒ NASB #684 apōleia<br><br>**Philip. 3:19**<br>Whose end is **destruction**, whose God is their belly, and whose glory is in their shame, who mind earthly things. [KJV]<br>Whose end is **destruction**, whose god is their appetite, and whose glory is in their shame, who set their minds on earthly things. [NASB]<br>Their destiny is **destruction**, their god is their stomach, and their glory is in their shame. Their mind is on earthly things. [NIV]<br>Whose end *is* **destruction**, whose god *is their* belly, and *whose* glory *is* in their shame—who set their mind on earthly things. [NKJV]<br>Their future is **eternal destruction**. Their god is their appetite, they brag about shameful things, and all they think about is this life here on earth. [NLT]<br>ὧν τὸ τέλος **ἀπώλεια**, ὧν ὁ θεὸς ἡ κοιλία, καὶ ἡ δόξα ἐν τῇ αἰσχύνῃ αὐτῶν, οἱ τὰ ἐπίγεια φρονοῦντες. [GNS]<br>ὧν τὸ τέλος **ἀπώλεια**, ὧν ὁ θεὸς ἡ κοιλία καὶ ἡ δόξα ἐν τῇ αἰσχύνῃ αὐτῶν, οἱ τὰ ἐπίγεια φρονοῦντες. [GNT] | Destruction, eternal destruction. The word means perdition; to be slayed or utterly ruined; to lose one's well-being; to be wasted and ruined and given a worthless existence. It does not mean that a person will cease to exist. It means a person will be destroyed and devastated and condemned to a worthless existence. He will suffer waste and loss and ruin forever and ever.<br><br>**Practical Application**<br>If a person stands as an enemy of the cross, he will be destroyed. It does not matter who he is, either within or without the church, he will suffer perdition, that is, utter destruction. Who is an enemy of the cross? It is the person...<br>• who rejects the cross of Christ as the only way to God.<br>• who does not accept the death of Christ as payment for his sins.<br>• who does not believe that Christ died for him, that is, as the punishment for his transgressions.<br>• who does not believe that the penalty for his imperfection was borne by Christ on the cross.<br>• who does not approach God claiming that he is coming by the death of Christ—that is, that he wants God to accept him in the death of Christ.<br>• who claims that there are other ways to approach God—ways other than the cross of Christ.<br>• who considers the cross of Christ to be foolishness.<br>• who opposes and curses Christ and His cross.<br>• who persecutes and attempts to stamp out Christ and His cross.<br>• who denies and questions that Christ died for our sins. |
| **#1322**<br>**Eternal Destruction**<br><br>Everlasting destruction–KJV<br>**Eternal destruction–NASB**<br>Everlasting destruction–NIV<br>Everlasting destruction–NKJV<br>Everlasting destruction–NLT | ὄλεθρον αἰώνιον = olethron aiōnion<br>Pronunciation: [ol'-eth-ron ahee-o'-nee-on]<br>Parsing *olethron* (part of speech): noun<br>  Case—accusative<br>  Gender—masculine<br>  Number—singular<br>  Stem or root—from ὄλεθρος, ου<br>Parsing *aiōnion* (part of speech): adjective<br>  Case—accusative<br>  Gender—masculine<br>  Number—singular<br>  Stem or root—from αἰώνιος, ον | Everlasting destruction, eternal destruction, ruin. The words "eternal destruction" (*olethron aiōnion*) do not mean annihilation or ceasing to exist. They mean exactly what they say in this verse: to be separated from the face of the Lord and from the glory of His power—an eternity of woe (A.T. Robertson. *Word Pictures in the New Testament*, Vol.4, p.44). They mean complete ruin and loss; to be cut off, excluded, removed, separated, extinguished, deprived, abhorred, and banished from all the good things of life. |

# PRACTICAL WORD STUDIES
## in the NEW TESTAMENT

| ENGLISH WORD | GREEK WORD AND VERSE | THE WORD MEANS... |
|---|---|---|
| **POSB REFERENCE** (2 Thes.1:9) Note 4, point 3 | Concordance References:<br>⇒ Strong's #3639 olethros + 166 aiönios<br>⇒ NIV #3897 olethros [destruction] + 173 aiönios [everlasting]<br>⇒ NASB #3639 olethros + 166 aiönios<br><br>**2 Thes. 1:9**<br>Who shall be punished with **everlasting destruction** from the presence of the Lord, and from the glory of his power; [KJV]<br>And these will pay the penalty of **eternal destruction**, away from the presence of the Lord and from the glory of His power, [NASB]<br>They will be punished with **everlasting destruction** and shut out from the presence of the Lord and from the majesty of his power [NIV]<br>These shall be punished with **everlasting destruction** from the presence of the Lord and from the glory of His power, [NKJV]<br>They will be punished with **everlasting destruction**, forever separated from the Lord and from his glorious power [NLT]<br>οἵτινες δίκην τίσουσιν, **ὄλεθρον αἰώνιον** ἀπὸ προσώπου τοῦ Κυρίου καὶ ἀπὸ τῆς δόξης τῆς ἰσχύος αὐτοῦ, [GNS]<br>οἵτινες δίκην τίσουσιν **ὄλεθρον αἰώνιον** ἀπὸ προσώπου τοῦ κυρίου καὶ ἀπὸ τῆς δόξης τῆς ἰσχύος αὐτοῦ, [GNT] | **Practical Application**<br>What do the words "eternal destruction" (*olethron aiönion*) mean?<br>⇒ *Complete ruin and loss*: from all that life should be.<br>⇒ *Cut off*: from the presence of God and from the glory of His power and of heaven.<br>⇒ *Excluded*: from all joy, pleasure and satisfaction. It is utter emptiness.<br>⇒ *Removed*: from all companionship and associations and from all possessions. It is being left all alone and left with nothing. It is utter loneliness.<br>⇒ *Separated*: from the presence of all goodness and righteousness—from God and from all those who sought after righteousness. And there is no prospect of the separation ever ending, not even for an hour.<br>⇒ *Extinguished*: from love and affection. It is a hell of passion let loose.<br>⇒ *Deprived*: from the Holy Spirit's restraining the force of evil. It is a hell of lawlessness.<br>⇒ *Abhorred*: from the bodies of glory. It is a decayed carcass (Isaiah 66:23-24).<br>⇒ *Banished*: from all hope. It is being eternally lost forever, and there is no prospect of the banishment ever ending—not even for one hour. |
| #1323<br>**Eternal Encouragement**<br><br>Everlasting consolation–KJV<br>Eternal comfort–NASB<br>**Eternal encouragement–NIV**<br>Everlasting consolation–NKJV<br>Everlasting comfort–NLT<br><br>**POSB REFERENCE** (2 Thes.2:16-17; esp. v.16) Note 5, point 2 | παράκλησιν αἰωνίαν = *paraklësin aiönian*<br>Pronunciation: [par-ak'-lay-sin ah-ee-o'-nee-ahn]<br>Parsing *paraklësin* (part of speech): noun<br>    Case—accusative<br>    Gender—feminine<br>    Number—singular<br>    Stem or root—from παράκλησις, εως<br>Parsing *aiönian* (part of speech): adjective<br>    Case—accusative<br>    Gender—feminine<br>    Number—singular<br>    Stem or root—from αἰώνιος, ον<br>Concordance References:<br>⇒ Strong's #3874 paraklësis + 166 aiönios<br>⇒ NIV #4155 paraklësis [encouragement] + 173 aiönios [eternal]<br>⇒ NASB #3874 paraklësis + 166 aiönios<br><br>**2 Thes. 2:16**<br>Now our Lord Jesus Christ himself, and God, even our Father, which hath loved us, and hath given us **everlasting consolation** and good hope through grace, [KJV]<br>Now may our Lord Jesus Christ Himself and God our Father, who has loved us and given us **eternal comfort** and good hope by grace, [NASB]<br>May our Lord Jesus Christ himself and God our Father, who loved us and by his grace gave us **eternal encouragement** and good hope, [NIV]<br>Now may our Lord Jesus Christ Himself, and our God and Father, who has loved us and given *us* **everlasting consolation** and good hope by grace, [NKJV]<br>May our Lord Jesus Christ and God our Father, who loved us and in his special favor gave us **everlasting comfort** and good hope, [NLT]<br>Αὐτὸς δὲ ὁ Κύριος ἡμῶν Ἰησοῦς Χριστός, καὶ ὁ Θεὸς καὶ πατὴρ ἡμῶν ὁ ἀγαπήσας ἡμᾶς, καὶ δοὺς **παράκλησιν αἰωνίαν** καὶ ἐλπίδα ἀγαθὴν ἐν χάριτι, [GNS]<br>Αὐτὸς δὲ ὁ κύριος ἡμῶν Ἰησοῦς Χριστὸς καὶ [ὁ] θεὸς ὁ πατὴρ ἡμῶν, ὁ ἀγαπήσας ἡμᾶς καὶ δοὺς **παράκλησιν αἰωνίαν** καὶ ἐλπίδα ἀγαθὴν ἐν χάριτι, [GNT] | Eternal encouragement; everlasting consolation; eternal comfort; everlasting comfort.<br><br>**Practical Application**<br>The person who is saved receives eternal encouragement (*paraklësin aiönian*). It is an encouragement and strength that cannot be shaken by anything—no matter what it is—either now or in eternity. |

# PRACTICAL WORD STUDIES
## in the NEW TESTAMENT

| ENGLISH WORD | GREEK WORD AND VERSE | THE WORD MEANS... |
|---|---|---|
| **#1324**<br>**Eternal Fire**<br><br>Everlasting fire–KJV<br>**Eternal fire–NASB**<br>**Eternal fire–NIV**<br>Everlasting fire–NKJV<br>Unquenchable fire–NLT<br><br>**POSB REFERENCE**<br>(Mt.18:8)<br>*Deeper Study #1*<br><br>See also POSB REF:<br>(Mt.25:41)<br>*Deeper Study #3* | πῦρ τὸ αἰώνιον = *pur to aiōnion*<br>Pronunciation: [poor tow ahee-o'-nee-on]<br>Parsing *pur* (part of speech): noun<br>   Case—accusative<br>   Gender—neuter<br>   Number—singular<br>   Stem or root—from πῦρ, ός<br>Parsing *aiōnion* (part of speech): adjective<br>   Case—accusative<br>   Gender—neuter<br>   Number—singular<br>   Stem or root—from αἰώνιος, ον<br>Concordance References:<br>  ⇒ Strong's #4442 pur + 166 aionios<br>  ⇒ NIV #4786 pur [fire] + 173 aiōnios [eternal]<br>  ⇒ NASB #4442 pur + 166 aionios<br><br>**Matthew 18:8**<br>Wherefore if thy hand or thy foot offend thee, cut them off, and cast them from thee: it is better for thee to enter into life halt or maimed, rather than having two hands or two feet to be cast into **everlasting fire**. [KJV]<br>"And if your hand or your foot causes you to stumble, cut it off and throw it from you; it is better for you to enter life crippled or lame, than having two hands or two feet, to be cast into the **eternal fire**. [NASB]<br>If your hand or your foot causes you to sin cut it off and throw it away. It is better for you to enter life maimed or crippled than to have two hands or two feet and be thrown into **eternal fire**. [NIV]<br>If your hand or foot causes you to sin, cut it off and cast it from you. It is better for you to enter into life lame or maimed, rather than having two hands or two feet, to be cast into the **everlasting fire**. [NKJV]<br>So if your hand or your foot causes you to sin, cut it off and throw it away. It is better to enter heaven crippled or lame than to be thrown into the **unquenchable fire** with both of your hands and feet. [NLT]<br>εἰ δὲ ἡ χείρ σου η ὁ πούς σου σκανδαλίζει σε, ἔκκοψον αὐτὰ καὶ βάλε ἀπὸ σοῦ· καλόν σοί ἐστιν εἰσελθεῖν εἰς τὴν ζωὴν χωλόν η κυλλόν, η δύο χεῖρας η δύο πόδας ἔχοντα βληθῆναι εἰς τὸ **πῦρ τὸ αἰώνιον**. [GNS]<br>Εἰ δὲ ἡ χείρ σου η ὁ πούς σου σκανδαλίζει σε, ἔκκοψον αὐτὸν καὶ βάλε ἀπὸ σοῦ· καλόν ἐστιν εἰσελθεῖν εἰς τὴν ζωὴν κυλλόν η χωλόν η δύο χεῖρας η δύο πόδας ἔχοντα βληθῆναι εἰς τὸ **πῦρ τὸ αἰώνιον**. [GNT] | Eternal fire, everlasting fire, unquenchable fire, a fire without end.<br><br>**Practical Application**<br>This is the first time the words *eternal fire* are used. The words point to an awful fate, a terrible and horrible eternity. Everlasting means for the duration, on and on without end. The fact that the unforgiven sinner is to suffer so great a punishment should cause all sinners to cease from being stumbling blocks. It should stir them to become stepping stones to God (see POSB *Deeper Study #2*—Matthew 5:22; POSB *Deeper Study #3*—Luke 16:23; POSB *Deeper Study #4*—Luke 16:24). |
| **#1325**<br>**Evangelists**<br><br>Evangelists–KJV<br>Evangelists–NASB<br>Evangelists–NIV<br>Evangelists–NKJV<br>Evangelists–NLT<br><br>**POSB REFERENCE**<br>(Eph.4:11)<br>Note 3, point 3 | εὐαγγελιστάς = *euaggelistas*<br>Pronunciation: [yoo-ang-ghel-is-tahs]<br>Parsing (part of speech): noun<br>   Case—accusative<br>   Gender—masculine<br>   Number—plural<br>   Stem or root—from εὐαγγελιστής, οῦ<br>Concordance References:<br>  ⇒ Strong's #2099 euaggelistēs<br>  ⇒ NIV #2296 euaggelistēs<br>  ⇒ NASB #2099 euaggelistēs<br><br>**Ephes. 4:11**<br>And he gave some, apostles; and some, prophets; and some, **evangelists**; and some, pastors and teachers; [KJV]<br>And He gave some as apostles, and some as prophets, and some as **evangelists**, and some as pastors and teachers, [NASB]<br>It was he who gave some to be apostles, some to be prophets, some to be **evangelists**, and some to be pastors and teachers, [NIV]<br>And He Himself gave some *to be* apostles, some prophets, some **evangelists**, and some pastors and teachers, [NKJV]<br>He is the one who gave these gifts to the church: the apostles, the prophets, the **evangelists**, and the pastors | Evangelist, a preacher of good news.<br><br>**Practical Application**<br>This is the gift of carrying the gospel all over the world. It is the gift that specializes in proclaiming the gospel to the lost of the world. It would include both what we call the evangelist and the missionary. |

# Practical Word Studies in the New Testament

| ENGLISH WORD | GREEK WORD AND VERSE | THE WORD MEANS... |
|---|---|---|
| | and teachers. [NLT]<br>καὶ αὐτὸς ἔδωκε τοὺς μὲν, ἀποστόλους, τοὺς δὲ, προφήτας, τοὺς δὲ, **εὐαγγελιστάς**, τοὺς δὲ, ποιμένας καὶ διδασκάλους, [GNS]<br>καὶ αὐτὸς ἔδωκεν τοὺς μὲν ἀποστόλους, τοὺς δὲ προφήτας, τοὺς δὲ **εὐαγγελιστάς**, τοὺς δὲ ποιμένας καὶ διδασκάλους, [GNT] | |
| #1326<br>**Even If He Dies**<br><br>Though he were dead–KJV<br>**Even if he dies–NASB**<br>Though he dies–NIV<br>Though he may die–NKJV<br>Though they die–NLT<br><br>**POSB REFERENCE**<br>(Jn.11:25-27; esp. v.25)<br>Note 4, point 2a | κἂν ἀποθάνῃ = kan apothanë<br>Pronunciation: [kahn ah-po-thah-nay]<br>Parsing *kan* (part of speech): adjective<br>    Type—adverb<br>AND<br>Parsing *kan* (part of speech): conjunction<br>    Type—subordinating<br>    Stem or root—from κἂν<br>Parsing *apothanë* (part of speech): verb<br>    Mood—subjunctive<br>    Tense—aorist<br>    Voice—active<br>    Person—3rd person<br>    Number—singular<br>    Stem or root—from ἀποθνῄσκω<br>Concordance References:<br>⇒ Strong's #2579 kan + 599 apothnesko<br>⇒ NIV #2829 kan [even though] + 633 apothnesko [dies]<br>⇒ NASB #2579 kan + 599 apothnesko<br><br>**John 11:25**<br>Jesus said unto her, I am the resurrection, and the life: he that believeth in me, **though he were dead**, yet shall he live: [KJV]<br>Jesus said to her, "I am the resurrection and the life; he who believes in Me shall live **even if he dies**, [NASB]<br>Jesus said to her, "I am the resurrection and the life. He who believes in me will live, even **though he dies**; [NIV]<br>Jesus said to her, "I am the resurrection and the life. He who believes in Me, **though he may die**, he shall live. [NKJV]<br>Jesus told her, "I am the resurrection and the life. Those who believe in me, even **though they die** like everyone else, will live again. [NLT]<br>εἶπεν αὐτῇ ὁ Ἰησοῦς, Ἐγώ εἰμι ἡ ἀνάστασις καὶ ἡ ζωή· ὁ πιστεύων εἰς ἐμὲ **κἂν ἀποθάνῃ**, ζήσεται· [GNS]<br>εἶπεν αὐτῇ ὁ Ἰησοῦς, Ἐγώ εἰμι ἡ ἀνάστασις καὶ ἡ ζωή· ὁ πιστεύων εἰς ἐμὲ **κἂν ἀποθάνῃ** ζήσεται, [GNT] | Though He dies; though He were dead; even if He dies.<br><br>**Practical Application**<br>Note Jesus' great promise: "He who believes in me, will live, even if he dies (*kan apothanë*)." He lives in the other world: in heaven, in the spiritual dimension of being, in the very presence of God Himself. The believer who has passed from this world is not some place...<br>• in a semi-conscious state.<br>• in a deep sleep, locked up in a compartment someplace.<br>• in space moving about and floating around on a fluffy cloud.<br><br>The believer is fully alive: he lives in heaven, in the other world, in the very presence of God Himself. Another world exists just as this world exists. It is not a world that lies out in the future; it is a world that exists now—a spiritual world, a spiritual dimension—a world that the Bible calls heaven. It is the spiritual world and dimension where God and Christ and angels and all those who have gone on before now live.<br>The point is this: when a person who has *believed in Jesus Christ* dies, he goes to live in heaven, in the spiritual world where God and Christ and the heavenly hosts live. *Hallelujah!* Only the word "hallelujah" can express the hope and joy that fills the soul of the true believer. |
| #1327<br>**Event Of Great Significance**<br><br>Wonder–KJV<br>Sign–NASB<br>Wondrous sign–NIV<br>Sign–NKJV<br>**Event of great significance–NLT**<br><br>**POSB REFERENCE**<br>(Rev.12:1-2; esp.v.1)<br>Note 1 | σημεῖον = sëmeion<br>Pronunciation: [say-mi'-on]<br>Parsing (part of speech): noun<br>    Case—nominative<br>    Gender—neuter<br>    Number—singular<br>    Stem or root—from σημεῖον, ου<br>Concordance References:<br>⇒ Strong's #4592 sëmeion<br>⇒ NIV #4956 sëmeion<br>⇒ NASB #4592 sëmeion<br><br>**Rev. 12:1**<br>And there appeared a great **wonder** in heaven; a woman clothed with the sun, and the moon under her feet, and upon her head a crown of twelve stars: [KJV]<br>And a great **sign** appeared in heaven: a woman clothed with the sun, and the moon under her feet, and on her head a crown of twelve stars; [NASB]<br>A great and **wondrous sign** appeared in heaven: a woman clothed with the sun, with the moon under her feet and a crown of twelve stars on her head. [NIV]<br>Now a great **sign** appeared in heaven: a woman clothed with the sun, with the moon under her feet, and on | A wondrous sign; a wonder; a sign; an event of great significance; a miraculous sign.<br><br>**Practical Application**<br>Note how the woman bursts upon the scene. She is said to be an "event of great significance" (*sëmeion*) or a great sign in heaven. Note also that she is in heaven. This means that she is the heavenly representative of some earthly people. |

# Practical Word Studies in the New Testament

| ENGLISH WORD | GREEK WORD AND VERSE | THE WORD MEANS... |
|---|---|---|
| | her head a garland of twelve stars. [NKJV]<br>Then I witnessed in heaven an **event of great significance**. I saw a woman clothed with the sun, with the moon beneath her feet, and a crown of twelve stars on her head. [NLT]<br>Καὶ **σημεῖον** μέγα ὤφθη ἐν τῷ οὐρανῷ, γυνὴ περιβεβλημένη τὸν ἥλιον, καὶ ἡ σελήνη ὑποκάτω τῶν ποδῶν αὐτῆς, καὶ ἐπὶ τῆς κεφαλῆς αὐτῆς στέφανος ἀστέρων δώδεκα· [GNS]<br>Καὶ **σημεῖον** μέγα ὤφθη ἐν τῷ οὐρανῷ, γυνὴ περιβεβλημένη τὸν ἥλιον, καὶ ἡ σελήνη ὑποκάτω τῶν ποδῶν αὐτῆς καὶ ἐπὶ τῆς κεφαλῆς αὐτῆς στέφανος ἀστέρων δώδεκα, [GNT] | |
| **#1328**<br>**Ever-living**<br><br>Uncorruptible–KJV<br>Incorruptible–NASB<br>Immortal–NIV<br>Incorruptible–NKJV<br>**Ever-living–NLT**<br><br>**POSB REFERENCE**<br>(Romans 1:22-23; esp. v.23)<br>Note 5, point 2a | ἀφθάρτου = *aphthartou*<br>Pronunciation: [af'-thar-too]<br>Parsing (part of speech): adjective<br>  Case—genitive<br>  Gender—masculine<br>  Number—singular<br>  Stem or root—from ἄφθαρτος, ον<br>Concordance References:<br>⇒ Strong's #862 aphthartos<br>⇒ NIV #915 aphthartos<br>⇒ NASB #862a aphthartos<br><br>**Romans 1:23**<br>And changed the glory of the **uncorruptible** God into an image made like to corruptible man, and to birds, and fourfooted beasts, and creeping things. [KJV]<br>And exchanged the glory of the **incorruptible** God for an image in the form of corruptible man and of birds and four-footed animals and crawling creatures. [NASB]<br>And exchanged the glory of the **immortal** God for images made to look like mortal man and birds and animals and reptiles. [NIV]<br>And changed the glory of the **incorruptible** God into an image made like corruptible man—and birds and four-footed animals and creeping things. [NKJV]<br>And instead of worshiping the glorious, **ever-living** God, they worshiped idols made to look like mere people, or birds and animals and snakes. [NLT]<br>καὶ ἤλλαξαν τὴν δόξαν τοῦ **ἀφθάρτου** Θεοῦ ἐν ὁμοιώματι εἰκόνος φθαρτοῦ ἀνθρώπου καὶ πετεινῶν καὶ τετραπόδων καὶ ἑρπετῶν. [GNS]<br>καὶ ἤλλαξαν τὴν δόξαν τοῦ **ἀφθάρτου** θεοῦ ἐν ὁμοιώματι εἰκόνος φθαρτοῦ ἀνθρώπου καὶ πετεινῶν καὶ τετραπόδων καὶ ἑρπετῶν. [GNT] | Imperishable; immortal; last forever; ever-living; incorruptible. God is said to be "ever-living" (*aphthartou*), which means non-decaying, imperishable, unchanging, and unaging.<br><br>**Practical Application**<br>Ever-living or incorruptible means that God is not subject to passing away; He is eternal. God always has been and always will be: God will always exist. |
| **#1329**<br>**Everlasting Comfort**<br><br>Everlasting consolation–KJV<br>Eternal comfort–NASB<br>Eternal encouragement–NIV<br>Everlasting consolation–NKJV<br>**Everlasting comfort–NLT**<br><br>**POSB REFERENCE**<br>(2 Thes.2:16-17; esp. v.16)<br>Note 5, point 2 | παράκλησιν αἰωνίαν = *paraklēsin aiōnian*<br>Pronunciation: [par-ak'-lay-sin ah-ee-o'-nee-ahn]<br>Parsing *paraklēsin* (part of speech): noun<br>  Case—accusative<br>  Gender—feminine<br>  Number—singular<br>  Stem or root—from παράκλησις, εως<br>Parsing *aiōnian* (part of speech): adjective<br>  Case—accusative<br>  Gender—feminine<br>  Number—singular<br>  Stem or root—from αἰώνιος, ον<br>Concordance References:<br>⇒ Strong's #3874 paraklēsis + 166 aiōnios<br>⇒ NIV #4155 paraklēsis [encouragement] + 173 aiōnios [eternal]<br>⇒ NASB #3874 paraklēsis + 166 aiōnios<br><br>**2 Thes. 2:16**<br>Now our Lord Jesus Christ himself, and God, even our Father, which hath loved us, and hath given us **everlasting consolation** and good hope through grace, [KJV]<br>Now may our Lord Jesus Christ Himself and God our Father, who has loved us and given us **eternal comfort** | Eternal encouragement; everlasting consolation; eternal comfort; everlasting comfort.<br><br>**Practical Application**<br>The person who is saved receives everlasting comfort (*paraklēsin aiōnian*). It is an everlasting comfort and strength that cannot be shaken by anything—no matter what it is—either now or in eternity. |

## PRACTICAL WORD STUDIES
## in the NEW TESTAMENT

| ENGLISH WORD | GREEK WORD AND VERSE | THE WORD MEANS... |
|---|---|---|
| | and good hope by grace, [NASB]<br>May our Lord Jesus Christ himself and God our Father, who loved us and by his grace gave us **eternal encouragement** and good hope, [NIV]<br>Now may our Lord Jesus Christ Himself, and our God and Father, who has loved us and given us **everlasting consolation** and good hope by grace, [NKJV]<br>May our Lord Jesus Christ and God our Father, who loved us and in his special favor gave us **everlasting comfort** and good hope, [NLT]<br>Αὐτὸς δὲ ὁ Κύριος ἡμῶν Ἰησοῦς Χριστός, καὶ ὁ Θεὸς καὶ πατὴρ ἡμῶν ὁ ἀγαπήσας ἡμᾶς, καὶ δοὺς **παράκλησιν αἰωνίαν** καὶ ἐλπίδα ἀγαθὴν ἐν χάριτι, [GNS]<br>Αὐτὸς δὲ ὁ κύριος ἡμῶν Ἰησοῦς Χριστὸς καὶ [ὁ] θεὸς ὁ πατὴρ ἡμῶν, ὁ ἀγαπήσας ἡμᾶς καὶ δοὺς **παράκλησιν αἰωνίαν** καὶ ἐλπίδα ἀγαθὴν ἐν χάριτι, [GNT] | |
| **#1330**<br>**Everlasting Consolation**<br><br>Everlasting consolation–KJV<br>Eternal comfort–NASB<br>Eternal encouragement–NIV<br>**Everlasting consolation–NKJV**<br>Everlasting comfort–NLT<br><br>**POSB REFERENCE**<br>(2 Thes.2:16-17; esp. v.16)<br>Note 5, point 2 | παράκλησιν αἰωνίαν = paraklēsin aiōnian<br>Pronunciation: [par-ak'-lay-sin ah-ee-o'-nee-ahn]<br>Parsing *paraklēsin* (part of speech): noun<br>    Case—accusative<br>    Gender—feminine<br>    Number—singular<br>    Stem or root—from παράκλησις, εως<br>Parsing *aiōnian* (part of speech): adjective<br>    Case—accusative<br>    Gender—feminine<br>    Number—singular<br>    Stem or root—from αἰώνιος, ον<br>Concordance References:<br>⇒ Strong's #3874 paraklēsis + 166 aiōnios<br>⇒ NIV #4155 paraklēsis [encouragement] + 173 aiōnios [eternal]<br>⇒ NASB #3874 paraklēsis + 166 aiōnios<br><br>**2 Thes. 2:16**<br>Now our Lord Jesus Christ himself, and God, even our Father, which hath loved us, and hath given us **everlasting consolation** and good hope through grace, [KJV]<br>Now may our Lord Jesus Christ Himself and God our Father, who has loved us and given us **eternal comfort** and good hope by grace, [NASB]<br>May our Lord Jesus Christ himself and God our Father, who loved us and by his grace gave us **eternal encouragement** and good hope, [NIV]<br>Now may our Lord Jesus Christ Himself, and our God and Father, who has loved us and given us **everlasting consolation** and good hope by grace, [NKJV]<br>May our Lord Jesus Christ and God our Father, who loved us and in his special favor gave us **everlasting comfort** and good hope, [NLT]<br>Αὐτὸς δὲ ὁ Κύριος ἡμῶν Ἰησοῦς Χριστός, καὶ ὁ Θεὸς καὶ πατὴρ ἡμῶν ὁ ἀγαπήσας ἡμᾶς, καὶ δοὺς **παράκλησιν αἰωνίαν** καὶ ἐλπίδα ἀγαθὴν ἐν χάριτι, [GNS]<br>Αὐτὸς δὲ ὁ κύριος ἡμῶν Ἰησοῦς Χριστὸς καὶ [ὁ] θεὸς ὁ πατὴρ ἡμῶν, ὁ ἀγαπήσας ἡμᾶς καὶ δοὺς **παράκλησιν αἰωνίαν** καὶ ἐλπίδα ἀγαθὴν ἐν χάριτι, [GNT] | Eternal encouragement; everlasting consolation; eternal comfort; everlasting comfort.<br><br>**Practical Application**<br>The person who is saved receives everlasting consolation (*paraklēsin aiōnian*). It is a consolation and strength that cannot be shaken by anything—no matter what it is—either now or in eternity. |
| **#1331**<br>**Everlasting Destruction**<br><br>Everlasting destruction–KJV<br>Eternal destruction–NASB<br>Everlasting destruction–NIV<br>Everlasting destruction–NKJV<br>Everlasting destruction–NLT | ὄλεθρον αἰώνιον = olethron aiōnion<br>Pronunciation: [ol'-eth-ron ahee-o'-nee-on]<br>Parsing *olethron* (part of speech): noun<br>    Case—accusative<br>    Gender—masculine<br>    Number—singular<br>    Stem or root—from ὄλεθρος, ου<br>Parsing *aiōnion* (part of speech): adjective<br>    Case—accusative<br>    Gender—masculine<br>    Number—singular<br>    Stem or root—from αἰώνιος, ον<br>Concordance References:<br>⇒ Strong's #3639 olethros + 166 aiōnios<br>⇒ NIV #3897 olethros [destruction] + 173 aiōnios | Everlasting destruction, eternal destruction, ruin. The words "everlasting destruction" (*olethron aiōnion*) do not mean annihilation or ceasing to exist. They mean exactly what they say in this verse: to be separated from the face of the Lord and from the glory of His power—an eternity of woe (A.T. Robertson. *Word Pictures in the New Testament*, Vol.4, p.44). They mean complete ruin and loss; to be cut off, excluded, removed, separated, extinguished, deprived, abhorred, and banished from all the good things of life. |

# PRACTICAL WORD STUDIES
## in the New Testament

| ENGLISH WORD | GREEK WORD AND VERSE | THE WORD MEANS... |
|---|---|---|
| **POSB REFERENCE** (2 Thes.1:9) Note 4, point 3 | [everlasting]<br>⇒ NASB #3639 olethros + 166 aiōnios<br><br>**2 Thes. 1:9**<br>Who shall be punished with **everlasting destruction** from the presence of the Lord, and from the glory of his power; [KJV]<br>And these will pay the penalty of **eternal destruction**, away from the presence of the Lord and from the glory of His power, [NASB]<br>They will be punished with **everlasting destruction** and shut out from the presence of the Lord and from the majesty of his power [NIV]<br>These shall be punished with **everlasting destruction** from the presence of the Lord and from the glory of His power, [NKJV]<br>They will be punished with **everlasting destruction**, forever separated from the Lord and from his glorious power [NLT]<br>οἵτινες δίκην τίσουσιν, **ὄλεθρον αἰώνιον** ἀπὸ προσώπου τοῦ Κυρίου καὶ ἀπὸ τῆς δόξης τῆς ἰσχύος αὐτοῦ, [GNS]<br>οἵτινες δίκην τίσουσιν **ὄλεθρον αἰώνιον** ἀπὸ προσώπου τοῦ κυρίου καὶ ἀπὸ τῆς δόξης τῆς ἰσχύοςαὐτοῦ, [GNT] | **Practical Application**<br>What do the words "everlasting destruction" (*olethron aiōnion*) mean?<br>⇒ *Complete ruin and loss*: from all that life should be.<br>⇒ *Cut off*: from the presence of God and from the glory of His power and of heaven.<br>⇒ *Excluded*: from all joy, pleasure and satisfaction. It is utter emptiness.<br>⇒ *Removed*: from all companionship and associations and from all possessions. It is being left all alone and left with nothing. It is utter loneliness.<br>⇒ *Separated*: from the presence of all goodness and righteousness—from God and from all those who sought after righteousness. And there is no prospect of the separation ever ending, not even for an hour.<br>⇒ *Extinguished*: from love and affection. It is a hell of passion let loose.<br>⇒ *Deprived*: from the Holy Spirit's restraining the force of evil. It is a hell of lawlessness.<br>⇒ *Abhorred*: from the bodies of glory. It is a decayed carcass (Isaiah 66:23-24).<br>⇒ *Banished*: from all hope. It is being eternally lost forever, and there is no prospect of the banishment ever ending—not even for one hour. |
| #1332<br>**Everlasting Fire**<br><br>**Everlasting fire**–KJV<br>Eternal fire–NASB<br>Eternal fire–NIV<br>**Everlasting fire**–NKJV<br>Unquenchable fire–NLT<br><br>**POSB REFERENCE** (Mt.18:8) *Deeper Study #1*<br><br>See also POSB REF: (Mt.25:41) *Deeper Study #3* | πῦρ τὸ αἰώνιον = *pur to aiōnion*<br>Pronunciation: [poor tow ahee-o'-nee-on]<br>Parsing *pur* (part of speech): noun<br>  Case—accusative<br>  Gender—neuter<br>  Number—singular<br>  Stem or root—from πῦρ, ός<br>Parsing *aiōnion* (part of speech): adjective<br>  Case—accusative<br>  Gender—neuter<br>  Number—singular<br>  Stem or root—from αἰώνιος, ον<br>Concordance References:<br>⇒ Strong's #4442 pur + 166 aiōnios<br>⇒ NIV #4786 pur [fire] + 173 aiōnios [eternal]<br>⇒ NASB #4442 pur + 166 aionios<br><br>**Matthew 18:8**<br>Wherefore if thy hand or thy foot offend thee, cut them off, and cast them from thee: it is better for thee to enter into life halt or maimed, rather than having two hands or two feet to be cast into **everlasting fire**. [KJV]<br>"And if your hand or your foot causes you to stumble, cut it off and throw it from you; it is better for you to enter life crippled or lame, than having two hands or two feet, to be cast into the **eternal fire**. [NASB]<br>If your hand or your foot causes you to sin cut it off and throw it away. It is better for you to enter life maimed or crippled than to have two hands or two feet and be thrown into **eternal fire**. [NIV]<br>If your hand or foot causes you to sin, cut it off and cast it from you. It is better for you to enter into life lame or maimed, rather than having two hands or two feet, to be cast into the **everlasting fire**. [NKJV]<br>So if your hand or foot causes you to sin, cut it off and throw it away. It is better to enter heaven crippled or lame than to be thrown into the **unquenchable fire** with both of your hands and feet. [NLT]<br>εἰ δὲ ἡ χείρ σου η ὁ πούς σου σκανδαλίζει σε, ἔκκοψον αὐτὰ καὶ βάλε ἀπὸ σοῦ· καλόν σοί ἐστιν εἰσελθεῖν εἰς τὴν ζωὴν χωλόν η κυλλόν, η δύο χεῖρας η | Eternal fire; everlasting fire; unquenchable fire; a fire without end.<br><br>**Practical Application**<br>This is the first time the words *everlasting fire* are used. The words point to an awful fate, a terrible and horrible eternity. Everlasting means for the duration, on and on without end. The fact that the unforgiven sinner is to suffer so great a punishment should cause all sinners to cease from being stumbling blocks. It should stir them to become stepping stones to God (see POSB *Deeper Study* #2—Matthew 5:22; POSB *Deeper Study* #3—Luke 16:23; POSB *Deeper Study* #4—Luke 16:24). |

# PRACTICAL WORD STUDIES
## in the NEW TESTAMENT

| ENGLISH WORD | GREEK WORD AND VERSE | THE WORD MEANS... |
|---|---|---|
| | δύο πόδας ἔχοντα βληθῆναι εἰς τὸ **πῦρ τὸ αἰώνιον**. [GNS]<br><br>Εἰ δὲ ἡ χείρ σου ἡ ὁ πούς σου σκανδαλίζει σε, ἔκκοψον αὐτὸν καὶ βάλε ἀπὸ σοῦ· καλόν σοί ἐστιν εἰσελθεῖν εἰς τὴν ζωὴν κυλλὸν ἢ χωλὸν ἢ δύο χεῖρας ἢ δύο πόδας ἔχοντα βληθῆναι εἰς τὸ **πῦρ τὸ αἰώνιον**. [GNT] | |
| **#1333**<br>**Every Encumbrance**<br><br>Every weight–KJV<br>**Every encumbrance–NASB**<br>Everything that hinders–NIV<br>Every weight–NKJV<br>Every weight–NLT<br><br>**POSB REFERENCE**<br>(Heb.12:1)<br>Note 2, point 1a | ὄγκον πάντα = ogkon panta<br>Pronunciation: [ong'-kon pahn-tah]<br>Parsing ogkon (part of speech): noun<br>  Case—accusative<br>  Gender—masculine<br>  Number—singular<br>  Stem or root—from ὄγκος, ου<br>Parsing panta (part of speech): adjective<br>  Case—accusative<br>  Gender—masculine<br>  Number—singular<br>  Stem or root—from πᾶς, πᾶσα, πᾶν<br>Concordance References:<br>  ⇒ Strong's #3591 ogkos + 3956 pas<br>  ⇒ NIV #3839 ogkos [hinders] + 4246 pas [everything]<br>  ⇒ NASB #3591 ogkos + 3956 pas<br><br>**Hebrews 12:1**<br>Wherefore seeing we also are compassed about with so great a cloud of witnesses, let us lay aside **every weight**, and the sin which doth so easily beset us, and let us run with patience the race that is set before us, [KJV]<br><br>Therefore, since we have so great a cloud of witnesses surrounding us, let us also lay aside **every encumbrance**, and the sin which so easily entangles us, and let us run with endurance the race that is set before us, [NASB]<br><br>Therefore, since we are surrounded by such a great cloud of witnesses, let us throw off **everything that hinders** and the sin that so easily entangles, and let us run with perseverance the race marked out for us. [NIV]<br><br>Therefore we also, since we are surrounded by so great a cloud of witnesses, let us lay aside **every weight**, and the sin which so easily ensnares *us,* and let us run with endurance the race that is set before us, [NKJV]<br><br>Therefore, since we are surrounded by such a huge crowd of witnesses to the life of faith, let us strip off **every weight** that slows us down, especially the sin that so easily hinders our progress. And let us run with endurance the race that God has set before us. [NLT]<br><br>Τοιγαροῦν καὶ ἡμεῖς τοσοῦτον ἔχοντες περικείμενον ἡμῖν νέφος μαρτύρων, **ὄγκον** ἀποθέμενοι **πάντα** καὶ τὴν εὐπερίστατον ἁμαρτίαν, δι' ὑπομονῆς τρέχωμεν τὸν προκείμενον ἡμῖν ἀγῶνα, [GNS]<br><br>Τοιγαροῦν καὶ ἡμεῖς τοσοῦτον ἔχοντες περικείμενον ἡμῖν νέφος μαρτύρων, **ὄγκον** ἀποθέμενοι **πάντα** καὶ τὴν εὐπερίστατον ἁμαρτίαν, δι' ὑπομονῆς τρέχωμεν τὸν προκείμενον ἡμῖν ἀγῶνα [GNT] | Everything that hinders; every weight; every encumbrance; every impediment.<br><br>**Practical Application**<br>The Christian runner must strip off "every encumbrance" (*ogkon panta*). This means any excess weight and bulk of body. All serious athletes train and strain to remove all excess weight. This refers to things that may be legitimate and innocent in and of themselves, but they hinder the Christian runner. They hamper and slow him down instead of helping him run faster. What kind of things would these be? What are some legitimate and innocent things, things that do not help us as believers to grow and run the race as fast as we can?<br>⇒ Seeking entertainment instead of fellowshipping and communing with God—instead of praying and reading our Bibles, instead of worshipping and witnessing. Recreation is sometimes needed, but the problem with most of us is that we relax and rest far more than we need, and we neglect our fellowship and communion with God and our intercessory prayer for others. Too many of us do not even know how to spend long times *keeping our minds* upon God and communing with Him.<br>⇒ Seeking the possessions and things of this world instead of *seeking* God.<br>⇒ Listening to music and other sounds that do not build up our spirits nor focus our minds upon the truth and God.<br>⇒ Watching films and television that fail to strengthen us.<br><br>We could go on and on, but the thrust is edification. Anything that does not build us up and make us stronger is excess weight that slows us down. The Christian runner must do exactly what the Olympic runner does: strain to remove all excess weight. Do nothing—absolutely nothing—that hinders or hampers him from running at full speed. He must strip off all unnecessary weight. |
| **#1334**<br>**Every Proud Argument**<br><br>Imaginations–KJV<br>Speculations–NASB<br>Arguments–NIV<br>Arguments–NKJV<br>**Every proud argument–NLT** | λογισμοὺς = logismous<br>Pronunciation: [log-is-moos']<br>Parsing (part of speech): noun<br>  Case—accusative<br>  Gender—masculine<br>  Number—plural<br>  Stem or root—from λογισμός, οῦ<br>**Note: this comes from verse 4 in the Greek, but is translated in the English Bible in verse 5**<br><br>Concordance References:<br>  ⇒ Strong's #3053 logismos<br>  ⇒ NIV #3361 logismos<br>  ⇒ NASB #3053 logismos | Arguments, speculations, false reasoning.<br><br>**Practical Application**<br>The believer is to *demolish or break down every proud argument*: thoughts and imaginations that are uncontrolled, wild, evil, lustful, immoral, unjust, wrong, untrue, devilish, and set against God. |

# PRACTICAL WORD STUDIES
## in the NEW TESTAMENT

| ENGLISH WORD | GREEK WORD AND VERSE | THE WORD MEANS... |
|---|---|---|
| **POSB REFERENCE** (2 Cor.10:3-5; esp. v.5) Note 2 | **2 Cor. 10:5**<br>Casting down **imaginations**, and every high thing that exalteth itself against the knowledge of God, and bringing into captivity every thought to the obedience of Christ; [KJV]<br>We are destroying **speculations** and every lofty thing raised up against the knowledge of God, and we are taking every thought captive to the obedience of Christ, [NASB]<br>We demolish **arguments** and every pretension that sets itself up against the knowledge of God, and we take captive every thought to make it obedient to Christ. [NIV]<br>Casting down **arguments** and every high thing that exalts itself against the knowledge of God, bringing every thought into captivity to the obedience of Christ, [NKJV]<br>With these weapons we break down **every proud argument** that keeps people from knowing God. With these weapons we conquer their rebellious ideas, and we teach them to obey Christ. [NLT]<br>τὰ γὰρ ὅπλα τῆς στρατείας ἡμῶν οὐ σαρκικά, ἀλλὰ δυνατὰ τῷ Θεῷ πρὸς καθαίρεσιν ὀχυρωμάτων --, **λογισμοὺς** καθαιροῦντες **2 Cor. 10:4** [GNS]<br>καὶ πᾶν ὕψωμα ἐπαιρόμενον κατὰ τῆς γνώσεως τοῦ Θεοῦ, καὶ αἰχμαλωτίζοντες πᾶν νόημα εἰς τὴν ὑπακοὴν τοῦ Χριστοῦ, **2 Cor. 10:5** [GNS]<br>τὰ γὰρ ὅπλα τῆς στρατείας ἡμῶν οὐ σαρκικὰ ἀλλὰ δυνατὰ τῷ θεῷ πρὸς καθαίρεσιν ὀχυρωμάτων, **λογισμοὺς** καθαιροῦντες **2 Cor. 10:4** [GNT]<br>καὶ πᾶν ὕψωμα ἐπαιρόμενον κατὰ τῆς γνώσεως τοῦ θεοῦ, καὶ αἰχμαλωτίζοντες πᾶν νόημα εἰvj τὴν ὑπακοὴν τοῦ Χριστοῦ, **2 Cor. 10:5** [GNT] | |
| **#1335**<br>**Every Weight**<br><br>Every weight–KJV<br>Every encumbrance–NASB<br>Everything that hinders–NIV<br>Every weight–NKJV<br>Every weight–NLT<br><br>**POSB REFERENCE** (Heb.12:1) Note 2, point 1a | ὄγκον πάντα = ogkon panta<br>Pronunciation: [ong'-kon pahn-tah]<br>Parsing *ogkon* (part of speech): noun<br>    Case—accusative<br>    Gender—masculine<br>    Number—singular<br>    Stem or root—from ὄγκος, ου<br>Parsing *panta* (part of speech): adjective<br>    Case—accusative<br>    Gender—masculine<br>    Number—singular<br>    Stem or root—from πᾶς, πᾶσα, πᾶν<br>Concordance References:<br>⇒ Strong's #3591 ogkos + 3956 pas<br>⇒ NIV #3839 ogkos [hinders] + 4246 pas [everything]<br>⇒ NASB #3591 ogkos + 3956 pas<br><br>**Hebrews 12:1**<br>Wherefore seeing we also are compassed about with so great a cloud of witnesses, let us lay aside **every weight**, and the sin which doth so easily beset us, and let us run with patience the race that is set before us, [KJV]<br>Therefore, since we have so great a cloud of witnesses surrounding us, let us also lay aside **every encumbrance**, and the sin which so easily entangles us, and let us run with endurance the race that is set before us, [NASB]<br>Therefore, since we are surrounded by such a great cloud of witnesses, let us throw off **everything that hinders** and the sin that so easily entangles, and let us run with perseverance the race marked out for us. [NIV]<br>Therefore we also, since we are surrounded by so great a cloud of witnesses, let us lay aside **every weight**, and the sin which so easily ensnares *us,* and let us run with endurance the race that is set before us, [NKJV]<br>Therefore, since we are surrounded by such a huge crowd of witnesses to the life of faith, let us strip off **every weight** that slows us down, especially the sin that | Everything that hinders; every weight; every encumbrance; every impediment.<br><br>**Practical Application**<br>The Christian runner must strip off "every weight" (*ogkon panta*). This means any excess weight and bulk of body. All serious athletes train and strain to remove all excess weight. This refers to things that may be legitimate and innocent in and of themselves, but they hinder the Christian runner. They hamper and slow him down instead of helping him run faster. What kind of things would these be? What are some legitimate and innocent things, things that do not help us as believers to grow and run the race as fast as we can?<br>⇒ Seeking entertainment instead of fellowshipping and communing with God—instead of praying and reading our Bibles, instead of worshipping and witnessing. Recreation is sometimes needed, but the problem with most of us is that we relax and rest far more than we need, and we neglect our fellowship and communion with God and our intercessory prayer for others. Too many of us do not even know how to spend long times *keeping our minds* upon God and communing with Him.<br>⇒ Seeking the possessions and things of this world instead of *seeking* God.<br>⇒ Listening to music and other sounds that do not build up our spirits nor focus our minds upon the truth and God.<br>⇒ Watching films and television that fail to strengthen us. |

## PRACTICAL WORD STUDIES
### in the NEW TESTAMENT

| ENGLISH WORD | GREEK WORD AND VERSE | THE WORD MEANS... |
|---|---|---|
| | so easily hinders our progress. And let us run with endurance the race that God has set before us. [NLT]<br><br>Τοιγαροῦν καὶ ἡμεῖς τοσοῦτον ἔχοντες περικείμενον ἡμῖν νέφος μαρτύρων, **ὄγκον** ἀποθέμενοι **πάντα** καὶ τὴν εὐπερίστατον ἁμαρτίαν, δι' ὑπομονῆς τρέχωμεν τὸν προκείμενον ἡμῖν ἀγῶνα, [GNS]<br><br>Τοιγαροῦν καὶ ἡμεῖς τοσοῦτον ἔχοντες περικείμενον ἡμῖν νέφος μαρτύρων, **ὄγκον** ἀποθέμενοι **πάντα** καὶ τὴν εὐπερίστατον ἁμαρτίαν, δι' ὑπομονῆς τρέχωμεν τὸν προκείμενον ἡμῖν ἀγῶνα [GNT] | We could go on and on, but the thrust is edification. Anything that does not build us up and make us stronger is excess weight that slows us down. The Christian runner must do exactly what the Olympic runner does: strain to remove all excess weight. Do nothing—absolutely nothing—that hinders or hampers him from running at full speed. He must strip off all unnecessary weight. |
| **#1336**<br>**Everyone, Christ Died For**<br><br>One died for all–KJV<br>One died for all–NASB<br>One died for all–NIV<br>One died for all–NKJV<br>**Christ died for everyone–NLT**<br><br>**POSB REFERENCE**<br>(2 Cor.5:14-16; esp. v.14)<br>Note 4, point 1 | εἷς ὑπὲρ πάντων ἀπέθανεν = heis huper pantōn apethanen<br>Pronunciation: [ice who-pare pawn-town hap-eh-tha-nehn]<br>Parsing *pantōn* (part of speech): pronominal adjective<br>  Case—genitive<br>  Gender—masculine<br>  Number—plural<br>  Stem or root—from πᾶς, πᾶσα, πᾶν<br>Concordance References:<br>⇒ Strong's #1520 heis + 599 apothnēskō + 5228 huper + 3956 pas<br>⇒ NIV #1651 heis [one] + 633 apothnēskō [died] +5642 huper [for] + 4246 pas [all]<br>⇒ NASB #1520 heis + 599 apothnēskō + 5228 huper + 3956 pas<br><br>**2 Cor. 5:14**<br>For the love of Christ constraineth us; because we thus judge, that if **one died for all**, then were all dead: [KJV]<br>For the love of Christ controls us, having concluded this, that **one died for all**, therefore all died; [NASB]<br>For Christ's love compels us, because we are convinced that **one died for all**, and therefore all died. [NIV]<br>For the love of Christ compels us, because we judge thus: that if **One died for all**, then all died; [NKJV]<br>Whatever we do, it is because Christ's love controls us. Since we believe that **Christ died for everyone**, we also believe that we have all died to the old life we used to live. [NLT]<br><br>ἡ γὰρ ἀγάπη τοῦ Χριστοῦ συνέχει ἡμᾶς, κρίναντας τοῦτο, ὅτι εἰ **εἷς ὑπὲρ πάντων ἀπέθανεν**, ἄρα οἱ πάντες ἀπέθανον· [GNS]<br>ἡ γὰρ ἀγάπη τοῦ Χριστοῦ συνέχει ἡμᾶς, κρίναντας τοῦτο, ὅτι **εἷς ὑπὲρ πάντων ἀπέθανεν**, ἄρα οἱ πάντες ἀπέθανον· [GNT] | One died for *all*; Christ died for *everyone*.<br><br>**Practical Application**<br>Christ died that everyone might die *in Him*. In the Greek this verse says:<br>⇒ "Christ died for everyone" (*heis huper pantōn apethanen*).<br>⇒ "all died to the old life we used to live" (*ara hoi pantes apethanon*).<br>Note the exact words: "Since we believe that Christ died for everyone, we also believe that we have all died to the old life we used to live." Paul is saying...<br>• that Jesus Christ died for all men; therefore all men died when He died.<br>• that since Christ died for everyone, then it follows that all men died in Him.<br>• that everyone was represented in Christ when He died.<br>• that all men are counted as having died when Christ died.<br>• that Jesus Christ died the ideal death, the death that stands for all men.<br>Of course, this is simply saying the same thing in different ways so that we can more easily grasp exactly what Paul is saying. But note: the word "everyone" is not teaching universal salvation, that is, that every human being is saved by the death of Christ. This passage has to be kept in context with the rest of Scripture; therefore, "*all*" means all who are redeemed by faith in the death of Christ. |
| **#1337**<br>**Everything That Hinders**<br><br>Every weight–KJV<br>Every encumbrance–NASB<br>**Everything that hinders–NIV**<br>Every weight–NKJV<br>Every weight–NLT<br><br>**POSB REFERENCE**<br>(Heb.12:1)<br>Note 2, point 1a | ὄγκον πάντα = ogkon panta<br>Pronunciation: [ong'-kon pahn-tah]<br>Parsing *ogkon* (part of speech): noun<br>  Case—accusative<br>  Gender—masculine<br>  Number—singular<br>  Stem or root—from ὄγκος, ου<br>Parsing *panta* (part of speech): adjective<br>  Case—accusative<br>  Gender—masculine<br>  Number—singular<br>  Stem or root—from πᾶς, πᾶσα, πᾶν<br>Concordance References:<br>⇒ Strong's #3591 ogkos + 3956 pas<br>⇒ NIV #3839 ogkos [hinders] + 4246 pas [everything]<br>⇒ NASB #3591 ogkos + 3956 pas<br><br>**Hebrews 12:1**<br>Wherefore seeing we also are compassed about with so great a cloud of witnesses, let us lay aside **every weight**, and the sin which doth so easily beset us, and let us run with patience the race that is set before us, [KJV]<br>Therefore, since we have so great a cloud of witnesses | Everything that hinders; every weight; every encumbrance; every impediment.<br><br>**Practical Application**<br>The Christian runner must strip off "every that hinders" (*ogkon panta*). This means any excess weight and bulk of body. All serious athletes train and strain to remove all excess weight. This refers to things that may be legitimate and innocent in and of themselves, but they hinder the Christian runner. They hamper and slow him down instead of helping him run faster. What kind of things would these be? What are some legitimate and innocent things, things that do not help us as believers to grow and run the race as fast as we can?<br>⇒ Seeking entertainment instead of fellowshipping and communing with God—instead of praying and reading our Bibles, instead of worshipping and witnessing. Recreation is sometimes needed, but the problem with most of us is that we relax and rest far more |

# PRACTICAL WORD STUDIES
## in the NEW TESTAMENT

| ENGLISH WORD | GREEK WORD AND VERSE | THE WORD MEANS... |
|---|---|---|
| | surrounding us, let us also lay aside **every encumbrance**, and the sin which so easily entangles us, and let us run with endurance the race that is set before us, [NASB]<br><br>Therefore, since we are surrounded by such a great cloud of witnesses, let us throw off **everything that hinders** and the sin that so easily entangles, and let us run with perseverance the race marked out for us. [NIV]<br><br>Therefore we also, since we are surrounded by so great a cloud of witnesses, let us lay aside **every weight**, and the sin which so easily ensnares *us*, and let us run with endurance the race that is set before us, [NKJV]<br><br>Therefore, since we are surrounded by such a huge crowd of witnesses to the life of faith, let us strip off **every weight** that slows us down, especially the sin that so easily hinders our progress. And let us run with endurance the race that God has set before us. [NLT]<br><br>Τοιγαροῦν καὶ ἡμεῖς τοσοῦτον ἔχοντες περικείμενον ἡμῖν νέφος μαρτύρων, **ὄγκον** ἀποθέμενοι **πάντα** καὶ τὴν εὐπερίστατον ἁμαρτίαν, δι' ὑπομονῆς τρέχωμεν τὸν προκείμενον ἡμῖν ἀγῶνα, [GNS]<br><br>Τοιγαροῦν καὶ ἡμεῖς τοσοῦτον ἔχοντες περικείμενον ἡμῖν νέφος μαρτύρων, **ὄγκον** ἀποθέμενοι **πάντα** καὶ τὴν εὐπερίστατον ἁμαρτίαν, δι' ὑπομονῆς τρέχωμεν τὸν προκείμενον ἡμῖν ἀγῶνα, [GNT] | than we need, and we neglect our fellowship and communion with God and our intercessory prayer for others. Too many of us do not even know how to spend long times *keeping our minds* upon God and communing with Him.<br>⇒ Seeking the possessions and things of this world instead of *seeking* God.<br>⇒ Listening to music and other sounds that do not build up our spirits nor focus our minds upon the truth and God.<br>⇒ Watching films and television that fail to strengthen us.<br>We could go on and on, but the thrust is edification. Anything that does not build us up and make us stronger is excess weight that slows us down. The Christian runner must do exactly what the Olympic runner does: strain to remove all excess weight. Do nothing—absolutely nothing—that hinders or hampers him from running at full speed. He must strip off all unnecessary weight. |
| **#1338**<br>**Everything There Is**<br><br>All things–KJV<br>All things–NASB<br>All things–NIV<br>All things–NKJV<br>**Everything there is**–NLT<br><br>**POSB REFERENCE**<br>(Jn.1:3)<br>Note 2, point 1<br><br>See also POSB REF:<br>(Col.1:16)<br>Note 1, point 2 | πάντα = *panta*<br>Pronunciation: [pahn-tah]<br>Parsing (part of speech): pronominal adjective<br>    Case—nominative<br>    Gender—neuter<br>    Number—plural<br>    Stem or root—from πᾶς, πᾶσα, πᾶν<br>Concordance References:<br>   ⇒ Strong's #3956 pas<br>   ⇒ NIV #4246 pas<br>   ⇒ NASB #3956 pas<br><br>**John 1:3**<br>**All things** were made by him; and without him was not any thing made that was made. [KJV]<br>**All things** came into being by Him, and apart from Him nothing came into being that has come into being. [NASB]<br>Through him **all things** were made; without him nothing was made that has been made. [NIV]<br>**All things** were made through Him, and without Him nothing was made that was made. [NKJV]<br>He created **everything there is**. Nothing exists that he didn't make. [NLT]<br>**πάντα** δι' αὐτοῦ ἐγένετο, καὶ χωρὶς αὐτοῦ ἐγένετο οὐδὲ ἕν, ὃ γέγονεν. [GNS]<br>**πάντα** δι' αὐτοῦ ἐγένετο, καὶ χωρὶς αὐτοῦ ἐγένετο οὐδὲ ἕν. ὃ γέγονεν. [GNT] | All things; everything there is; every detail of creation—not creation as a whole, but every single detail.<br><br>**Practical Application**<br>Each element and thing, each being and person—whether material or spiritual, angelic or human—has come into being by Christ. The words "everything there is" (*panta*) are very significant. They mean...<br>• "all things" collectively, that is, all the things within the universe were created by Christ.<br>• "all things" individually, that is, every single detail of creation, was created by Christ. Each particle and thing, each being and element has come into being by Christ and by Him alone.<br><br>The point is that nothing exists that was not created by Christ. All things were made by Him, even the very details of every single thing. |
| **#1339**<br>**Evil**<br><br>Unclean–KJV<br>Unclean–NASB<br>**Evil**–NIV<br>Unclean–NKJV<br>Not translated–NLT<br><br>**POSB REFERENCE**<br>(Lk.4:33-37; esp. v.33)<br>Note 3, point 2 | ἀκαθάρτου = *akathartou*<br>Pronunciation: [ak-ath'-ar-too]<br>Parsing (part of speech): adjective<br>    Case—genitive<br>    Gender—neuter<br>    Number—singular<br>    Stem or root—from ἀκάθαρτος, ον<br>Concordance References:<br>   ⇒ Strong's #169 akathartos<br>   ⇒ NIV #176 akathartos<br>   ⇒ NASB #169 akathartos<br><br>**Luke 4:33**<br>And in the synagogue there was a man, which had a spirit of an **unclean** devil, and cried out with a loud voice, [KJV]<br>And there was a man in the synagogue possessed by | To be evil, unclean, dirty, tainted, desecrated.<br><br>**Practical Application**<br>It refers to an evil, unclean, polluted, defiled devil or demon. It means that the man was both morally and ceremonially unclean, dirty, disheveled, filthy. He was worshipping, but he was morally unclean and corrupt; his life was all disheveled. |

## PRACTICAL WORD STUDIES
## in the NEW TESTAMENT

| ENGLISH WORD | GREEK WORD AND VERSE | THE WORD MEANS... |
|---|---|---|
| | the spirit of an **unclean** demon, and he cried out with a loud voice, [NASB]<br>In the synagogue there was a man possessed by a demon, an **evil** spirit. He cried out at the top of his voice, [NIV]<br>Now in the synagogue there was a man who had a spirit of an **unclean** demon. And he cried out with a loud voice, [NKJV]<br>Once when he was in the synagogue, a man possessed by a demon began shouting at Jesus, [NLT]—NOT TRANSLATED<br>καὶ ἐν τῇ συναγωγῇ ἦν ἄνθρωπος ἔχων πνεῦμα δαιμονίου **ἀκαθάρτου**, καὶ ἀνέκραξε φωνῇ μεγάλῃ, λέγων, [GNS]<br>καὶ ἐν τῇ συναγωγῇ ἦν ἄνθρωπος ἔχων πνεῦμα δαιμονίου **ἀκαθάρτου** καὶ ἀνέκραξεν φωνῇ μεγάλῃ, [GNT] | |
| **#1340**<br>**Evil**<br><br>Wickedness–KJV<br>Wickedness–NASB<br>Wickedness–NIV<br>Wickedness–NKJV<br>Evil–NLT<br><br>**POSB REFERENCE**<br>(1 Cor.5:8)<br>Note 3 | πονηρίας = ponërias<br>Pronunciation: [pon-ay-ree'-ahs]<br>Parsing (part of speech): noun<br>    Case—genitive<br>    Gender—feminine<br>    Number—singular<br>    Stem or root—from πονηρία, ας<br>Concordance References:<br>  ⇒ Strong's #4189 ponëria<br>  ⇒ NIV #4504 ponëria<br>  ⇒ NASB #4189 ponëria<br><br>**1 Cor. 5:8**<br>Therefore let us keep the feast, not with old leaven, neither with the leaven of malice and **wickedness**; but with the unleavened bread of sincerity and truth. [KJV]<br>Let us therefore celebrate the feast, not with old leaven, nor with the leaven of malice and **wickedness**, but with the unleavened bread of sincerity and truth. [NASB]<br>Therefore let us keep the Festival, not with the old yeast, the yeast of malice and **wickedness**, but with bread without yeast, the bread of sincerity and truth. [NIV]<br>Therefore let us keep the feast, not with old leaven, nor with the leaven of malice and **wickedness**, but with the unleavened *bread* of sincerity and truth. [NKJV]<br>So let us celebrate the festival, not by eating the old bread of wickedness and **evil**, but by eating the new bread of purity and truth. [NLT]<br>ὥστε ἑορτάζωμεν, μὴ ἐν ζύμῃ παλαιᾷ, μηδὲ ἐν ζύμῃ κακίας καὶ **πονηρίας**, ἀλλ' ἐν ἀζύμοις εἰλικρινείας καὶ ἀληθείας. [GNS]<br>ὥστε ἑορτάζωμεν μὴ ἐν ζύμῃ παλαιᾷ μηδὲ ἐν ζύμῃ κακίας καὶ **πονηρίας** ἀλλ' ἐν ἀζύμοις εἰλικρινείας καὶ ἀληθείας. [GNT] | Wickedness, evil.<br><br>**Practical Application**<br>The word "evil" (*ponërias*) means more than just sin and coming short. It means taking pleasure in evil. The church must purge itself of its pride in prestigious men who are living in shameful sin. Such wickedness must be purged out. |
| **#1341**<br>**Evil**<br><br>Iniquity–KJV<br>Unrighteousness–NASB<br>**Evil–NIV**<br>Iniquity–NKJV<br>Injustice–NLT<br><br>**POSB REFERENCE**<br>(1 Cor.13:4-7; esp. v.6)<br>Note 2, point 10<br><br>**See also POSB REF:**<br>(Rom.2:8)<br>*Deeper Study #5* | ἀδικίᾳ = adikia<br>Pronunciation: [ad-ee-kee'-ah]<br>Parsing (part of speech): noun<br>    Case—dative<br>    Gender—feminine<br>    Number—singular<br>    Stem or root—from ἀδικία, ας<br>Concordance References:<br>  ⇒ Strong's #93 adikia<br>  ⇒ NIV #94 adikia<br>  ⇒ NASB #93 adikia<br><br>**1 Cor. 13:6**<br>Rejoiceth not in **iniquity**, but rejoiceth in the truth; [KJV]<br>Does not rejoice in **unrighteousness**, but rejoices with the truth; [NASB]<br>Love does not delight in **evil** but rejoices with the truth. [NIV]<br>Does not rejoice in **iniquity**, but rejoices in the truth; [NKJV] | Evil, iniquity, wickedness, sin, unrighteousness, wrong-doing, harmful injustice.<br><br>**Practical Application**<br>Love does not take pleasure in the unrighteousness and sin of others; it does not feed upon sin and wrong, nor does it pass along the stories of sin and wrong. Man's nature is too often fed the tragedy of evil, whether personal sin or natural disaster (cp. the daily news reports and the subjects of conversation between so many people). |

## PRACTICAL WORD STUDIES
### in the NEW TESTAMENT

| ENGLISH WORD | GREEK WORD AND VERSE | THE WORD MEANS... |
|---|---|---|
| | It is never glad about **injustice** but rejoices whenever the truth wins out. [NLT]<br>οὐ χαίρει ἐπὶ τῇ **ἀδικίᾳ**, συγχαίρει δὲ τῇ ἀληθείᾳ· [GNS]<br>οὐ χαίρει ἐπὶ τῇ **ἀδικίᾳ**, συγχαίρει δὲ τῇ ἀληθείᾳ· [GNT] | |
| #1342<br>**Evil**<br><br>Maliciousness–KJV<br>**Evil**–NASB<br>Depravity–NIV<br>Maliciousness–NKJV<br>Hate–NLT<br><br>**POSB REFERENCE**<br>(Rom.1:29)<br>*Deeper Study #5* | κακία  *kakia*<br>Pronunciation: [kak-ee'-ah]<br>Parsing (part of speech): noun<br>   Case—dative<br>   Gender—feminine<br>   Number—singular<br>   Stem or root—from κακία, ας<br>Concordance References:<br>  ⇒ Strong's #2549 kakia<br>  ⇒ NIV #2798 kakia<br>  ⇒ NASB #2549 kakia<br><br>**Romans 1:29**<br>Being filled with all unrighteousness, fornication, wickedness, covetousness, **maliciousness**; full of envy, murder, debate, deceit, malignity; whisperers, [KJV]<br>Being filled with all unrighteousness, wickedness, greed, **evil**; full of envy, murder, strife, deceit, malice; they are gossips, [NASB]<br>They have become filled with every kind of wickedness, evil, greed and **depravity**. They are full of envy, murder, strife, deceit and malice. They are gossips, [NIV]<br>Being filled with all unrighteousness, sexual immorality, wickedness, covetousness, **maliciousness**; full of envy, murder, strife, deceit, evil-mindedness; *they are* whisperers, [NKJV]<br>Their lives became full of every kind of wickedness, sin, greed, **hate**, envy, murder, fighting, deception, malicious behavior, and gossip. [NLT]<br>πεπληρωμένους πάσῃ ἀδικίᾳ πορνείᾳ, πονηρίᾳ πλεονεξίᾳ **κακίᾳ**· μεστοὺς φθόνου, φόνου, ἔριδος, δόλου, κακοηθείας· [GNS]<br>πεπληρωμένους πάσῃ ἀδικίᾳ πονηρίᾳ πλεονεξίᾳ **κακίᾳ**, μεστοὺς φθόνου φόνου ἔριδος δόλου κακοηθείας, ψιθυριστάς [GNT] | Evil; wickedness; hateful feelings; malice; viciousness; ill will; spite; a grudge; worry (Mt. 6.34).<br><br>**Practical Application**<br>It means that a man has turned his heart completely over to evil.<br>⇒ He no longer has any good within—none whatsoever.<br>⇒ He is full of viciousness and malice.<br>⇒ He is actively pursuing evil with a vengeance. |
| #1343<br>**Evil**<br><br>Wickedness–KJV<br>**Evil**–NASB<br>**Evil**–NIV<br>Wickedness–NKJV<br>Sin–NLT<br><br>**POSB REFERENCE**<br>(Rom.1:29)<br>*Deeper Study #3* | πονηρία = *ponëria*<br>Pronunciation: [pon-ay-ree'-ah]<br>Parsing (part of speech): noun<br>   Case—dative<br>   Gender—feminine<br>   Number—singular<br>   Stem or root—from πονηρία, ας<br>Concordance References:<br>  ⇒ Strong's #4189 ponëria<br>  ⇒ NIV #4504 ponëria<br>  ⇒ NASB #4189 ponëria<br><br>**Romans 1:29**<br>Being filled with all unrighteousness, fornication, **wickedness**, covetousness, maliciousness; full of envy, murder, debate, deceit, malignity; whisperers, [KJV]<br>Being filled with all unrighteousness, wickedness, greed, **evil**; full of envy, murder, strife, deceit, malice; they are gossips, [NASB]<br>They have become filled with every kind of wickedness, **evil**, greed and depravity. They are full of envy, murder, strife, deceit and malice. They are gossips, [NIV]<br>Being filled with all unrighteousness, sexual immorality, **wickedness**, covetousness, maliciousness; full of envy, murder, strife, deceit, evil-mindedness; *they are* whisperers, [NKJV]<br>Their lives became full of every kind of wickedness, **sin**, greed, hate, envy, murder, fighting, deception, malicious behavior, and gossip. [NLT] | To be depraved; to be actively evil; to do mischief; to trouble others and cause harm; to be malicious; to be dangerous and destructive. It is malice, wickedness, sin, hatred, evil intention and ill will.<br><br>**Practical Application**<br>It is an active evil or wickedness, a desire within the heart to do harm and to corrupt people. It is a person who actually pursues others to seduce or to injure them. |

## PRACTICAL WORD STUDIES
### in the NEW TESTAMENT

| ENGLISH WORD | GREEK WORD AND VERSE | THE WORD MEANS... |
|---|---|---|
| | πεπληρωμένους πάση ἀδικίᾳ **πορνείᾳ**, πονηρίᾳ πλεονεξίᾳ κακίᾳ· μεστοὺς φθόνου, φόνου, ἔριδος, δόλου, κακοηθείας· [GNS]<br><br>πεπληρωμένους πάσῃ ἀδικίᾳ **πονηρίᾳ** πλεονεξίᾳ κακίᾳ, μεστοὺς φθόνου φόνου ἔριδος δόλου κακοηθείας, ψιθυριστάς [GNT] | |
| **#1344**<br>**Evil**<br><br>Evil–KJV<br>Evil–NASB<br>Evil–NIV<br>Evil–NKJV<br>Evil–NLT<br><br>**POSB<br>REFERENCE**<br>(2 Thes.3:3-5, esp. v.3)<br>Note 2, point 1 | **πονηροῦ** = *ponērou*<br>Pronunciation: [pon-ay-roo']<br>Parsing (part of speech): pronominal adjective<br>    Case—genitive<br>    Gender—masculine OR neuter<br>    Number—singular<br>    Stem or root—from πονηρός, ά, όν<br>Concordance References:<br>  ⇒ Strong's #4190 ponēros<br>  ⇒ NIV #4505 ponēros<br>  ⇒ NASB #4190 ponēros<br><br>**2 Thes. 3:3**<br>But the Lord is faithful, who shall stablish you, and keep you from **evil**. [KJV]<br>But the Lord is faithful, and He will strengthen and protect you from the **evil** one. [NASB]<br>But the Lord is faithful, and he will strengthen and protect you from the **evil** one. [NIV]<br>But the Lord is faithful, who will establish you and guard *you* from the **evil** one. [NKJV]<br>But the Lord is faithful; he will make you strong and guard you from the **evil** one. [NLT]<br>πιστὸς δέ ἐστι ὁ Κύριος, ὃς στηρίξει ὑμᾶς καὶ φυλάξει ἀπὸ τοῦ **πονηροῦ**. [GNS]<br>πιστὸς δέ ἐστιν ὁ κύριος, ὃς στηρίξει ὑμᾶς καὶ φυλάξει ἀπὸ τοῦ **πονηροῦ**. [GNT] | Evil, wicked, sinful, bad; the evil one.<br><br>**Practical Application**<br>The word "evil" (*ponērou*) can refer both to evil behavior and to the evil one, that is, Satan. The point is this: the Lord is faithful, even if we fail to help one another. God will strengthen and guard us against Satan and his evil followers. In fact, the Lord will strengthen and guard us against all evil no matter what it is. Even if the evil seems to be conquering us, it will not—not in the final analysis. |
| **#1345**<br>**Evil**<br><br>Malice–KJV<br>Malice–NASB<br>Malice–NIV<br>Malice–NKJV<br>Evil–NLT<br><br>**POSB<br>REFERENCE**<br>(Tit.3:3)<br>*Deeper Study* #4 | **κακίᾳ** = *kakia*<br>Pronunciation: [kak-ee'-ah]<br>Parsing (part of speech): noun<br>    Case—dative<br>    Gender—feminine<br>    Number—singular<br>    Stem or root—from κακία, ας<br>Concordance References:<br>  ⇒ Strong's #2549 kakia<br>  ⇒ NIV #2798 kakia<br>  ⇒ NASB #2549 kakia<br><br>**Titus 3:3**<br>For we ourselves also were sometimes foolish, disobedient, deceived, serving divers lusts and pleasures, living in **malice** and envy, hateful, and hating one another. [KJV]<br>For we also once were foolish ourselves, disobedient, deceived, enslaved to various lusts and pleasures, spending our life in **malice** and envy, hateful, hating one another. [NASB]<br>At one time we too were foolish, disobedient, deceived and enslaved by all kinds of passions and pleasures. We lived in **malice** and envy, being hated and hating one another. [NIV]<br>For we ourselves were also once foolish, disobedient, deceived, serving various lusts and pleasures, living in **malice** and envy, hateful and hating one another. [NKJV]<br>Once we, too, were foolish and disobedient. We were misled by others and became slaves to many wicked desires and evil pleasures. Our lives were full of **evil** and envy. We hated others, and they hated us. [NLT]<br>ἦμεν γάρ ποτε καὶ ἡμεῖς ἀνόητοι, ἀπειθεῖς, πλανώμενοι, δουλεύοντες ἐπιθυμίαις καὶ ἡδοναῖς ποικίλαις, ἐν **κακίᾳ** καὶ φθόνῳ διάγοντες, στυγητοί, μισοῦντες ἀλλήλους. [GNS] | Malice, evil, wickedness. The word means evil disposition or evil in nature. It is a spirit full of evil and malice and injury, a character that is as evil as it can be. It is a person who always looks for the worst in other people and always passes on the worst about them. It is the person who so often ruins other people both in reputation and body and in mind and spirit. It is a person so full of evil that he is always ruining others either by word or violence.<br><br>**Practical Application**<br>There are some people who would never actively strike or harm a person, yet they have experienced feelings against another person. The feelings arose from some argument or difference within the family, with a neighbor, or at work, school, or play. And the feelings were strong, so strong that the person could care less if something bad happened to the other person. And most people have even had feelings...<br>• that wished something bad upon others.<br>• that downgraded and tore down others.<br><br>Tragically, these feelings even occur within families. People hold malice within their hearts; they are unconcerned about something bad happening to others. But thanks be to God our Savior, who has provided forgiveness for this terrible sin—both forgiveness and deliverance. And He will forgive and deliver any person who turns away from his malice and bitterness against others and turns to Him. |

# PRACTICAL WORD STUDIES
## in the NEW TESTAMENT

| ENGLISH WORD | GREEK WORD AND VERSE | THE WORD MEANS... |
|---|---|---|
| | Ἦμεν γάρ ποτε καὶ ἡμεῖς ἀνόητοι, ἀπειθεῖς, πλανώμενοι, δουλεύοντες ἐπιθυμίαις καὶ ἡδοναῖς ποικίλαις, ἐν **κακίᾳ** καὶ φθόνῳ διάγοντες, στυγητοί, μισοῦντες ἀλλήλους. [GNT] | |
| **#1346** **Evil Concupiscence** Evil concupiscence– KJV Evil desire–NASB Evil desires–NIV Evil desire–NKJV Shameful desires–NLT **POSB REFERENCE** (Col.3:5-7; esp. v.5) Note 1, point 1d | ἐπιθυμίαν κακήν = *epithumian kakën* Pronunciation: [ep-ee-thoo-mee'-ahn kak-ayn'] Parsing *epithumian* (part of speech): noun  Case—accusative  Gender—feminine  Number—singular  Stem or root—from ἐπιθυμία, ας Parsing *kakën* (part of speech): adjective  Case—accusative  Gender—feminine  Number—plural  Stem or root—from κακός, ή, όν Concordance References:  ⇒ Strong's #2556 kakos + 1939 epithumia  ⇒ NIV #2805 kakos [evil] + 2123 epithumia [desires]  ⇒ NASB #2556 kakos + 1939 epithumia **Col. 3:5** Mortify therefore your members which are upon the earth; fornication, uncleanness, inordinate affection, **evil concupiscence**, and covetousness, which is idolatry: [KJV] Therefore consider the members of your earthly body as dead to immorality, impurity, passion, **evil desire**, and greed, which amounts to idolatry. [NASB] Put to death, therefore, whatever belongs to your earthly nature: sexual immorality, impurity, lust, **evil desires** and greed, which is idolatry. [NIV] Therefore put to death your members which are on the earth: fornication, uncleanness, passion, **evil desire**, and covetousness, which is idolatry. [NKJV] So put to death the sinful, earthly things lurking within you. Have nothing to do with sexual sin, impurity, lust, and **shameful desires**. Don't be greedy for the good things of this life, for that is idolatry. [NLT] Νεκρώσατε οὖν τὰ μέλη ὑμῶν τὰ ἐπὶ τῆς γῆς, πορνείαν, ἀκαθαρσίαν, πάθος, **ἐπιθυμίαν κακήν**, καὶ τὴν πλεονεξίαν, ἥτις ἐστὶν εἰδωλολατρεία, [GNS] Νεκρώσατε οὖν τὰ μέλη τὰ ἐπὶ τῆς γῆς, πορνείαν ἀκαθαρσίαν πάθος **ἐπιθυμίαν κακήν**, καὶ τὴν πλεονεξίαν, ἥτις ἐστὶν εἰδωλολατρία, [GNT] | Evil desires, evil concupiscence, shameful desires, passions, lusts, a yearning and an aching for all kinds of evil. **Practical Application** It is that within a person that pulls him to desire, grasp, grab, and take hold of all forms of evil that give pleasure to the body and its members. It is that which drives the man to... • look and look • feel and feel • touch and touch • listen and listen • smell and smell • seek and seek |
| **#1347** **Evil Desire– Evil Desires** Lust–KJV Lust–NASB Evil desire–NIV Desires–NKJV Evil desires–NLT **POSB REFERENCE** (Jas.1:14-16; esp. v.14) Note 2 | ἐπιθυμίας = *epithumias* Pronunciation: [ep-ee-thoo-mee'-ahs] Parsing (part of speech): noun  Case—genitive  Gender—feminine  Number—singular  Stem or root—from ἐπιθυμία, ας Concordance References:  ⇒ Strong's #1939 epithumia  ⇒ NIV #2123 epithumia  ⇒ NASB #1939 epithumia **James 1:14** But every man is tempted, when he is drawn away of his own **lust**, and enticed. [KJV] But each one is tempted when he is carried away and enticed by his own **lust**. [NASB] But each one is tempted when, by his own **evil desire**, he is dragged away and enticed. [NIV] But each one is tempted when he is drawn away by his own **desires** and enticed. [NKJV] Temptation comes from the lure of our own **evil desires**. [NLT] ἕκαστος δὲ πειράζεται, ὑπὸ τῆς ἰδίας **ἐπιθυμίας** ἐξελκόμενος καὶ δελεαζόμενος. [GNS] ἕκαστος δὲ πειράζεται ὑπὸ τῆς ἰδίας **ἐπιθυμίας** ἐξελκόμενος καὶ δελεαζόμενος· [GNT] | Evil desire, lust, passion, longing. It means to crave either good or evil. There are good desires and bad desires. **Practical Application** Every man—there are no exceptions—is tempted when by his own evil desire, he is dragged away and enticed. The picture is this: man has good desires, natural and normal desires. Therefore, when he begins to think about or look at something, he very naturally desires it. His desire is normal behavior. The problem arises when the thing is forbidden or is harmful. If he looks at and thinks about the forbidden or harmful thing, he begins to lust and to be enticed or lured to go after it. This is the very beginning stage of temptation. Man focuses his desire upon the forbidden or harmful thing. He begins to pay attention to what he should not look at; he begins to think about the things of the flesh and of the world. Thereby he is tempted and drawn away by his own lusts and enticements. |

# Practical Word Studies
## in the New Testament

| English Word | Greek Word and Verse | The Word Means... |
|---|---|---|
| **#1348**<br>**Evil Desires**<br><br>Lusts–KJV<br>Lusts–NASB<br>**Evil desires–NIV**<br>Lusts–NKJV<br>Lust–NLT<br><br>**POSB**<br>**REFERENCE**<br>(2 Tim. 2:22)<br>Note 1<br><br>See also POSB REF:<br>(Rom.6:12)<br>Note 2, point 2<br>(Rom.1:24-25; esp. v.24)<br>Note 2, point 1 | ἐπιθυμίας = epithumias<br>Pronunciation: [ep-ee-thoo-mee'-ahs]<br>Parsing (part of speech): noun<br>    Case—accusative<br>    Gender—feminine<br>    Number—plural<br>    Stem or root—from ἐπιθυμία, ας<br>Concordance References:<br>  ⇒ Strong's #1939 epithumia<br>  ⇒ NIV #2123 epithumia<br>  ⇒ NASB #1939 epithumia<br><br>**2 Tim. 2:22**<br>Flee also youthful **lusts**: but follow righteousness, faith, charity, peace, with them that call on the Lord out of a pure heart. [KJV]<br>Now flee from youthful **lusts**, and pursue righteousness, faith, love and peace, with those who call on the Lord from a pure heart. [NASB]<br>Flee the **evil desires** of youth, and pursue righteousness, faith, love and peace, along with those who call on the Lord out of a pure heart. [NIV]<br>Flee also youthful **lusts**; but pursue righteousness, faith, love, peace with those who call on the Lord out of a pure heart. [NKJV]<br>Run from anything that stimulates youthful **lust**. Follow anything that makes you want to do right. Pursue faith and love and peace, and enjoy the companionship of those who call on the Lord with pure hearts. [NLT]<br>τὰς δὲ νεωτερικὰς **ἐπιθυμίας** φεῦγε· δίωκε δὲ δικαιοσύνην, πίστιν, ἀγάπην, εἰρήνην μετὰ τῶν ἐπικαλουμένων τὸν Κύριον ἐκ καθαρᾶς καρδίας. [GNS]<br>τὰς δὲ νεωτερικὰς **ἐπιθυμίας** φεῦγε, δίωκε δὲ δικαιοσύνην πίστιν ἀγάπην εἰρήνην μετὰ τῶν ἐπικαλουμένων τὸν κύριον ἐκ καθαρᾶς καρδίας. [GNT] | Evil desires, lusts. It means passionate desires and cravings. It can mean either good or bad desires, and its meaning is always to be determined by the context (Wuest).<br><br>**Practical Application**<br>The point is this: passionate desire and craving is normal and natural. God made us to desire and crave. It is when we use our passions to hurt and damage that they become evil. What are the *evil desires* of youth?<br>⇒ *The desires of the eye*: youths desire to have and possess. To have and possess are normal desires, but the normal desire can lead to the lust for possessions and people.<br>⇒ *The desires of the flesh*: youths desire the companionship of the opposite sex. Attraction is normal and leads to marriage and the carrying on of the human race. However, the normal desire can lead to illicit sex and immorality.<br>⇒ *The desire for acceptance*: youths want friends. They want to fit in with their peers. They want approval, and they want to be recognized. This is normal, but it can lead to compromise—the compromise of one's values and morality and of the truth. It can also lead to rebellion against authority.<br>⇒ *The desire to achieve*: youths desire to be successful, to find their place in the world. However, this can lead to seeking authority and power over people and to the manipulation and using of people for one's own ends.<br>⇒ *The desire for recognition*: youths desire to be the *top gun*, the star, the best looking, the smartest, the most popular. They constantly picture themselves as winning the game in the last second, winning the beauty pageant, winning the contest being the one most recognized; and a host of other daydreams. This can lead to either pride and arrogance or to a sense of inferiority and low self-image. It can lead either to the hurting of the less gifted or to the downing of oneself.<br>⇒ *The desire to act and to act now*: youths, bursting with energy and idealism, want to see things done now. This can lead to impatience and to the mistreatment of people: bypassing and disregarding the peace and security of other people.<br>⇒ *The desire to be original and creative*: youths want to have the new and fresh idea, the better thought, and the better way for doing things. This can lead to a critical and argumentative spirit. It can also lead to cheating in order to be recognized. It can lead to the restating and rewording of things and ideas and claiming that they are creative ideas.<br>The charge to youth is direct and forceful: flee youthful lusts. |
| **#1349**<br>**Evil Desires**<br><br>Fleshly lusts–KJV<br>Fleshly lusts–NASB<br>Sinful desires–NIV | σαρκικῶν ἐπιθυμιῶν = sarkikōn epithumiōn<br>Pronunciation: [sar-kee-kon' hep-ee-thoo-mee'-own]<br>Parsing *sarkikōn* (part of speech): adjective<br>    Case—genitive<br>    Gender—feminine<br>    Number—plural<br>    Stem or root—from σαρκικός, ή, όν | Sinful desires, fleshly lusts, evil desires. The term "evil desires" (*sarkikōn epithumiōn*) means the urges, passions, and lusts of the flesh. It means to have a yearning passion for the things of the flesh. |

## PRACTICAL WORD STUDIES
## in the NEW TESTAMENT

| ENGLISH WORD | GREEK WORD AND VERSE | THE WORD MEANS... |
|---|---|---|
| Fleshly lusts–NKJV<br>Evil desires–NLT<br><br>**POSB<br>REFERENCE**<br>(1 Pt.2:11)<br>Note 2 | Parsing *epithumiōn* (part of speech): noun<br>    Case—genitive<br>    Gender—feminine<br>    Number—plural<br>    Stem or root—from ἐπιθυμία, ας<br>Concordance References:<br>⇒ Strong's #4559 sarkikos + 1939 epithumia<br>⇒ NIV #4920 sarkikos [sinful] + 2123 epithumia [desires]<br>⇒ NASB #4559 sarkikos + 1939 epithumia<br><br>**1 Peter 2:11**<br>Dearly beloved, I beseech you as strangers and pilgrims, abstain from **fleshly lusts**, which war against the soul; [KJV]<br>Beloved, I urge you as aliens and strangers to abstain from **fleshly lusts**, which wage war against the soul. [NASB]<br>Dear friends, I urge you, as aliens and strangers in the world, to abstain from **sinful desires**, which war against your soul. [NIV]<br>Beloved, I beg *you* as sojourners and pilgrims, abstain from **fleshly lusts** which war against the soul, [NKJV]<br>Dear brothers and sisters, you are foreigners and aliens here. So I warn you to keep away from **evil desires** because they fight against your very souls. [NLT]<br>Ἀγαπητοί, παρακαλῶ ὡς παροίκους καὶ παρεπιδήμους ἀπέχεσθαι τῶν **σαρκικῶν ἐπιθυμιῶν**, αἵτινες στρατεύονται κατὰ τῆς ψυχῆς· [GNS]<br>Ἀγαπητοί, παρακαλῶ ὡς παροίκους καὶ παρεπιδήμους ἀπέχεσθαι τῶν **σαρκικῶν ἐπιθυμιῶν** αἵτινες στρατεύονται κατὰ τῆς ψυχῆς· [GNT] | **Practical Application**<br>Every person has experienced the flesh's...<br>• yearning<br>• pulling<br>• desiring<br>• wanting<br>• grasping<br>• grabbing<br>• craving<br>• hungering<br>• thirsting<br>• longing<br>• taking<br><br>Every person knows what it is to have his flesh lusting after something, to have it yearning and yearning to lay hold of something. The flesh is strong and difficult to control, and it never lets up its assault against the will. |
| #1350<br>**Evil Desire–<br>Evil Desires**<br><br>Evil concupiscence–KJV<br>**Evil desire–NASB**<br>**Evil desires–NIV**<br>**Evil desire–NKJV**<br>Shameful desires–NLT<br><br>**POSB<br>REFERENCE**<br>(Col.3:5-7; esp. v.5)<br>Note 1, point 1d | ἐπιθυμίαν κακήν = epithumian kakēn<br>Pronunciation: [ep-ee-thoo-mee'-ahn kak-ayn']<br>Parsing *epithumian* (part of speech): noun<br>    Case—accusative<br>    Gender—feminine<br>    Number—singular<br>    Stem or root—from ἐπιθυμία, ας<br>Parsing *kakēn* (part of speech): adjective<br>    Case—accusative<br>    Gender—feminine<br>    Number—plural<br>    Stem or root—from κακός, ή, όν<br>Concordance References:<br>⇒ Strong's #2556 kakos + 1939 epithumia<br>⇒ NIV #2805 kakos [evil] + 2123 epithumia [desires]<br>⇒ NASB #2556 kakos + 1939 epithumia<br><br>**Col. 3:5**<br>Mortify therefore your members which are upon the earth; fornication, uncleanness, inordinate affection, **evil concupiscence**, and covetousness, which is idolatry: [KJV]<br>Therefore consider the members of your earthly body as dead to immorality, impurity, passion, **evil desire**, and greed, which amounts to idolatry. [NASB]<br>Put to death, therefore, whatever belongs to your earthly nature: sexual immorality, impurity, lust, **evil desires** and greed, which is idolatry. [NIV]<br>Therefore put to death your members which are on the earth: fornication, uncleanness, passion, **evil desire**, and covetousness, which is idolatry. [NKJV]<br>So put to death the sinful, earthly things lurking within you. Have nothing to do with sexual sin, impurity, lust, and **shameful desires**. Don't be greedy for the good things of this life, for that is idolatry. [NLT]<br>Νεκρώσατε οὖν τὰ μέλη ὑμῶν τὰ ἐπὶ τῆς γῆς, πορνείαν, ἀκαθαρσίαν, πάθος, **ἐπιθυμίαν κακήν**, καὶ | Evil desires, evil concupiscence, shameful desires, passions, lusts, a yearning and an aching for all kinds of evil.<br><br>**Practical Application**<br>It is that within a person that pulls him to desire, grasp, grab, and take hold of all forms of evil that give pleasure to the body and its members. It is that which drives the man to...<br>• look and look<br>• feel and feel<br>• touch and touch<br>• listen and listen<br>• smell and smell<br>• seek and seek |

## Practical Word Studies in the New Testament

| ENGLISH WORD | GREEK WORD AND VERSE | THE WORD MEANS... |
|---|---|---|
| | τὴν πλεονεξίαν, ἥτις ἐστὶν εἰδωλολατρεία, [GNS]<br>Νεκρώσατε οὖν τὰ μέλη τὰ ἐπὶ τῆς γῆς, πορνείαν ἀκαθαρσίαν πάθος **ἐπιθυμίαν κακήν**, καὶ τὴν πλεονεξίαν, ἥτις ἐστὶν εἰδωλολατρία, [GNT] | |
| #1351<br>**Evil Eye, An**<br><br>An evil eye–KJV<br>Envy–NASB<br>Envy–NIV<br>An evil eye–NKJV<br>Envy–NLT<br><br>**POSB REFERENCE**<br>(Mk.7:22)<br>*Deeper Study* #12 | ὀφθαλμὸς πονηρός = aphthalmos poneros<br>Pronunciation: [of-thal-mos' pon-ay-ros']<br>Parsing *aphthalmos* (part of speech): noun<br>   Case—nominative<br>   Gender—masculine<br>   Number—singular<br>   Stem or root—from ὀφθαλμός, οῦ<br>Parsing *poneros* (part of speech): adjective<br>   Case—nominative<br>   Gender—masculine<br>   Number—singular<br>   Stem or root—from πονηρός, ά, όν<br>Concordance References:<br> ⇒ Strong's #3788 ophthalmos +4190 ponēros<br> ⇒ NIV #4057+4505 ophthalmos ponēros [envy]<br> ⇒ NASB #3788 ophthalmos +4190 ponēros<br><br>**Mark 7:22**<br>Thefts, covetousness, wickedness, deceit, lasciviousness, **an evil eye**, blasphemy, pride, foolishness: [KJV]<br>Deeds of coveting and wickedness, as well as deceit, sensuality, **envy**, slander, pride and foolishness. [NASB]<br>Greed, malice, deceit, lewdness, **envy**, slander, arrogance and folly. [NIV]<br>Thefts, covetousness, wickedness, deceit, lewdness, **an evil eye**, blasphemy, pride, foolishness. [NKJV]<br>Adultery, greed, wickedness, deceit, eagerness for lustful pleasure, **envy**, slander, pride, and foolishness. [NLT]<br>πλεονεξίαι, πονηρίαι, δόλος, ἀσέλγεια, **ὀφθαλμὸς πονηρός**, βλασφημία, ὑπερηφανία, ἀφροσύνη· [GNS]<br>μοιχεῖαι, πλεονεξίαι, πονηρίαι, δόλος, ἀσέλγεια, **ὀφθαλμὸς πονηρός**, βλασφημία, ὑπερηφανία, ἀφροσύνη· [GNT] | To look where one should not; to lust after what one should not; to envy, covet, crave and desire by looking; to use the eye in an evil way; to satisfy one's lusts and desires by looking.<br><br>**Practical Application**<br>This phrase goes beyond jealousy. It is the spirit...<br>• that wants not only the things that another person has but begrudges the fact that the person has them.<br>• that wants not only the things to be taken away from the person but wants him to suffer through the loss of them. |
| #1352<br>**Evil- Mindedness**<br><br>Malignity–KJV<br>Malice–NASB<br>Malice–NIV<br>Evil-mindedness–NKJV<br>Malicious behavior–NLT<br><br>**POSB REFERENCE**<br>(Romans 1:29)<br>*Deeper Study* #10 | κακοηθείας° kakoëtheias<br>Pronunciation: [kak-o-ay'-thee-ahs]<br>Parsing (part of speech): noun<br>   Case—genitive<br>   Gender—feminine<br>   Number—singular<br>   Stem or root—from κακοήθεια, ας<br>Concordance References:<br> ⇒ Strong's #2550 kakoëtheia<br> ⇒ NIV #2799 kakoëtheia<br> ⇒ NASB #2550 kakoëtheia<br><br>**Romans 1:29**<br>Being filled with all unrighteousness, fornication, wickedness, covetousness, maliciousness; full of envy, murder, debate, deceit, **malignity**; whisperers, [KJV]<br>Being filled with all unrighteousness, wickedness, greed, evil; full of envy, murder, strife, deceit, **malice**; they are gossips, [NASB]<br>They have become filled with every kind of wickedness, evil, greed and depravity. They are full of envy, murder, strife, deceit and **malice**. They are gossips, [NIV]<br>Being filled with all unrighteousness, sexual immorality, wickedness, covetousness, maliciousness; full of envy, murder, strife, deceit, **evil-mindedness**; *they are* whisperers, [NKJV]<br>Their lives became full of every kind of wickedness, sin, greed, hate, envy, murder, fighting, deception, **malicious behavior**, and gossip. [NLT]<br>πεπληρωμένους πάσῃ ἀδικίᾳ πορνείᾳ, πονηρίᾳ πλεονεξίᾳ κακίᾳ· μεστοὺς φθόνου, φόνου, ἔριδος, δόλου, **κακοηθείας**· [GNS]<br>πεπληρωμένους πάσῃ ἀδικίᾳ πονηρίᾳ πλεονεξίᾳ κακίᾳ, μεστοὺς φθόνου φόνου ἔριδος δόλου **κακοηθείας**, ψιθυριστάς [GNT] | Malignity, malice, meanness; evil disposition; evil in nature; evil done for the sake of evil.<br><br>**Practical Application**<br>It is a spirit full of evil and malice and injury, a character that is as evil as he can be. It is a person who always looks for the worst in other people and always passes on the worst about them. It is the person who so often ruins other people both in reputation and body and in mind and spirit. It is a person so full of evil that he is always ruining others either by word or violence. |

## Practical Word Studies in the New Testament

| ENGLISH WORD | GREEK WORD AND VERSE | THE WORD MEANS... |
|---|---|---|
| **#1353**<br>**Evil Minds**<br><br>Reprobate mind–KJV<br>Depraved mind–NASB<br>Depraved mind–NIV<br>Debased mind–NKJV<br>**Evil minds–NLT**<br><br>**POSB REFERENCE**<br>(Rom.1:28-31; esp. v.28)<br>Note 4, point 1 | ἀδόκιμον νοῦν = *adokimon noun*<br>Pronunciation: [ad-ok'-ee-mon noon]<br>Parsing *adokimon* (part of speech): adjective<br>    Case—accusative<br>    Gender—masculine<br>    Number—singular<br>    Stem or root—from ἀδόκιμος, ον<br>Parsing *noun* (part of speech): noun<br>    Case—accusative<br>    Gender—masculine<br>    Number—singular<br>    Stem or root—from νοῦς, νοός, νοΐ, νοῦν<br>Concordance References:<br>  ⇒ Strong's #96 adokimos + 3563 nous<br>  ⇒ NIV #99 adokimos [depraved] + 3808 nous [mind]<br>  ⇒ NASB #96 adokimos + 3563 nous<br><br>**Romans 1:28**<br>And even as they did not like to retain God in their knowledge, God gave them over to a **reprobate mind**, to do those things which are not convenient; [KJV]<br>And just as they did not see fit to acknowledge God any longer, God gave them over to a **depraved mind**, to do those things which are not proper, [NASB]<br>Furthermore, since they did not think it worthwhile to retain the knowledge of God, he gave them over to a **depraved mind**, to do what ought not to be done. [NIV]<br>And even as they did not like to retain God in *their* knowledge, God gave them over to a **debased mind**, to do those things which are not fitting; [NKJV]<br>When they refused to acknowledge God, he abandoned them to their **evil minds** and let them do things that should never be done. [NLT]<br>Καὶ καθὼς οὐκ ἐδοκίμασαν τὸν Θεὸν ἔχειν ἐν ἐπιγνώσει, παρέδωκεν αὐτοὺς ὁ Θεὸς εἰς **ἀδόκιμον** νοῦν, ποιεῖν τὰ μὴ καθήκοντα, [GNS]<br>καὶ καθὼς οὐκ ἐδοκίμασαν τὸν θεὸν ἔχειν ἐν ἐπιγνώσει, παρέδωκεν αὐτοὺς ὁ θεὸς εἰς **ἀδόκιμον** νοῦν, ποιεῖν τὰ μὴ καθήκοντα, [GNT] | Failing to meet the test; disqualified; worthless; corrupted (mind); mind, thought, reason; attitude, intention, purpose; understanding, discernment.<br><br>**Practical Application**<br>God shows wrath by giving men up to reprobate, depraved minds. The term "evil minds" (*adokimon noun*) means a mind that is rejected, disapproved, degraded, depraved; a mind that cannot stand the test of judgment.<br>The reason God gives men up to reprobate minds is because men reject God. They know God, but they "refuse to acknowledge God." They...<br>• do not like to approve God.<br>• do not like to recognize God.<br>• do not like to acknowledge God.<br><br>They simply do not want God to have anything to do with their lives; therefore, they push Him out of their minds. They ignore and refuse to accept God's presence. |
| **#1354**<br>**Evil Powers**<br><br>Rudiments–KJV<br>Elementary principles–NASB<br>Basic principles–NIV<br>Basic principles–NKJV<br>**Evil powers–NLT**<br><br>**POSB REFERENCE**<br>(Col.2:20)<br>Note 1 | στοιχείων = *stoicheiön*<br>Pronunciation: [stoy-khi'-on]<br>Parsing (part of speech): noun<br>    Case—genitive<br>    Gender—neuter<br>    Number—plural<br>    Stem or root—from στοιχεῖα, ων<br>Concordance References:<br>  ⇒ Strong's #4747 stoicheion<br>  ⇒ NIV #5122 stoicheion<br>  ⇒ NASB #4747 stoicheion<br><br>**Col. 2:20**<br>Wherefore if ye be dead with Christ from the **rudiments** of the world, why, as though living in the world, are ye subject to ordinances, [KJV]<br>If you have died with Christ to the **elementary principles** of the world, why, as if you were living in the world, do you submit yourself to decrees, such as, [NASB]<br>Since you died with Christ to the **basic principles** of this world, why, as though you still belonged to it, do you submit to its rules: [NIV]<br>Therefore, if you died with Christ from the **basic principles** of the world, why, as though living in the world, do you subject yourselves to regulations— [NKJV]<br>You have died with Christ, and he has set you free from the **evil powers** of this world. So why do you keep on following rules of the world, such as, [NLT]<br>Εἰ οὖν ἀπεθάνετε σὺν τῷ Χριστῷ, ἀπὸ τῶν | Basic principles; rudiments; elements; elementary principles; first lessons; evil powers.<br><br>**Practical Application**<br>The term "evil powers" (*stoicheiön*) means two things and Christ saves us from both. (See POSB note, Philosophy—Col. 2:8 for more discussion.)<br>1. *Evil powers* means crude notions of men about the universe—that is, about God, reality, and truth. It is man's ideas and philosophies, their elementary or rudimentary teachings, their ABC understanding of God and the universe, reality, and truth. When men think of God, they come up with all kinds of ways and laws to reach Him and to secure His approval and acceptance. However, there are three basic problems with man's approach to God.<br>  a. First, we cannot keep rules and laws—not in a perfect sense. No matter what way we choose to reach God, we cannot walk a straight path to Him.<br>  b. Second, once we have broken a rule or law, we stand guilty before God. Therefore, we must be judged, condemned, and punished for having broken the law. A law breaker is guilty and unacceptable and the punishment must be borne. Therefore, rules and laws cannot |

| ENGLISH WORD | GREEK WORD AND VERSE | THE WORD MEANS... |
|---|---|---|
| | στοιχείων τοῦ κόσμου, τί ὡς ζῶντες ἐν κόσμῳ δογματίζεσθε, [GNS]<br>Εἰ ἀπεθάνετε σὺν Χριστῷ ἀπὸ τῶν **στοιχείων** τοῦ κόσμου, τί ὡς ζῶντες ἐν κόσμῳ δογματίζεσθε; [GNT] | make us acceptable to God. They can only lead to guilt and condemnation.<br>c. Third, we die; we do not live forever. Moreover, there is no law or force on this earth that can give us the energy and power to live forever. Rules and laws only condemn us when we break them. They have no power to save us from death nor to give us eternal life. Because of this, rules and laws cannot be the way to approach God.<br>  How then can we approach God? If the best thinking of men about the universe and God are not the way to approach God, what is the way? The answer will be discussed in a moment, but first look at the second meaning of the term e*vil powers*.<br>2. *Evil powers* means the basic elements or materials of the universe, the things that men say lie behind the universe or at the very base of reality. Down through the centuries men have posed all kinds of forces, energies, powers, principalities, spirits, angels, and beings as standing behind the universe and life. As a result, men have committed their lives to and worshipped all sorts of creatures and forces or elements and materials. However, there is a critical problem with this approach to God, a problem that dooms all who seek truth and who approach God through the elements of this universe or through the spirits of the spiritual world.<br>  a. First, there is the problem of corruption. Everything in the universe is corruptible, aging, dying, deteriorating, and decaying. Therefore, there is nothing in the universe that can save man, for the way of all things—all elements and all materials—is the way of change and death.<br>  b. Second, there is a problem with seeking truth and God through the spirits or angels of a spiritual world.<br>    ⇒ First, man cannot penetrate the spiritual world. He is physical, and the physical just cannot move over into the world of the spiritual no matter what any person claims. If the spiritual world is ever to be known, then the spiritual has to reveal itself to us.<br>    ⇒ Second, any person who claims to have been given visions or revelations by the spiritual world still has the same problems that everyone else has: the problems of imperfection (unrighteousness), death, and eternal life. No angel, spirit, or any other intermediary has ever taken care of the problem of sin and death and of eternal life for us. We have already sinned, and we are already imperfect. Therefore, someone, someplace must *bear our sin* or punishment for us or else we have to pay for it ourselves. And, in addition, someone has to go through the experience of death to conquer it to tell us how to do the same or else we are going to die and never reach God. |

# PRACTICAL WORD STUDIES
## in the New Testament

| ENGLISH WORD | GREEK WORD AND VERSE | THE WORD MEANS... |
|---|---|---|
| | | This is the glorious message of the gospel. God is love, eternal and infinite love, so He has done all this for us. He did it through His Son, Jesus Christ. |
| **#1355**<br>**Evil Rulers**<br><br>Principalities–KJV<br>Rulers–NASB<br>Rulers–NIV<br>Principalities–NKJV<br>**Evil rulers–NLT**<br><br>**POSB REFERENCE**<br>(Eph.6:12)<br>Note 3, point 5 | ἀρχάς = archas<br>Pronunciation: [ar-khas']<br>Parsing (part of speech): noun<br>  Case—accusative<br>  Gender—feminine<br>  Number—plural<br>  Stem or root—from ἀρχή, ῆς<br>Concordance References:<br>⇒ Strong's #746 archë<br>⇒ NIV #794 archë<br>⇒ NASB #746 archë<br><br>**Ephes. 6:12**<br>For we wrestle not against flesh and blood, but against **principalities**, against powers, against the rulers of the darkness of this world, against spiritual wickedness in high places. [KJV]<br>For our struggle is not against flesh and blood, but against the **rulers**, against the powers, against the world forces of this darkness, against the spiritual forces of wickedness in the heavenly places. [NASB]<br>For our struggle is not against flesh and blood, but against the **rulers**, against the authorities, against the powers of this dark world and against the spiritual forces of evil in the heavenly realms. [NIV]<br>For we do not wrestle against flesh and blood, but against **principalities**, against powers, against the rulers of the darkness of this age, against spiritual *hosts* of wickedness in the heavenly *places*. [NKJV]<br>For we are not fighting against people made of flesh and blood, but against the **evil rulers** and authorities of the unseen world, against those mighty powers of darkness who rule this world, and against wicked spirits in the heavenly realms. [NLT]<br>ὅτι οὐκ ἔστιν ἡμῖν ἡ πάλη πρὸς αἷμα καὶ σάρκα, ἀλλὰ πρὸς τὰς **ἀρχάς**, πρὸς τὰς ἐξουσίας, πρὸς τοὺς κοσμοκράτορας τοῦ σκότους τοῦ αἰῶνος τούτου, πρὸς τὰ πνευματικὰ τῆς πονηρίας ἐν τοῖς ἐπουρανίοις. [GNS]<br>ὅτι οὐκ ἔστιν ἡμῖν ἡ πάλη πρὸς αἷμα καὶ σάρκα, ἀλλὰ πρὸς τὰς **ἀρχάς**, πρὸς τὰς ἐξουσίας, πρὸς τοὺς κοσμοκράτορας τοῦ σκότους τούτου, πρὸς τὰ πνευματικὰ τῆς πονηρίας ἐν τοῖς ἐπουρανίοις. [GNT] | Rulers, principalities, evil rulers, ruling powers.<br><br>**Practical Application**<br>The great Greek scholar Kenneth Wuest identifies the forces of evil as follows:<br>⇒ The *evil rulers* (*archas*): "the first ones, preeminent ones, leaders."<br>⇒ The *powers* (*exousias*): "the authorities," the demons of Satan in the lower atmosphere who constitute his kingdom in the air."<br>⇒ The *rulers of the darkness of this world* (*kosmokrator*): Satan and his demons.<br>⇒ The *spiritual wickedness in high places* (*pneumatika tes ponerias*): Satan and all his demonic forces.<br>(*Ephesians and Colossians*, Vol.1, p.141.) |
| **#1356**<br>**Evil Speaking**<br><br>**Evil speaking–KJV**<br>Slander–NASB<br>Slander–NIV<br>**Evil speaking–NKJV**<br>Slander–NLT<br><br>**POSB REFERENCE**<br>(Eph.4:31)<br>Note 6, point 5 | βλασφημία = blasphëmia<br>Pronunciation: [blas-fay-me'-ah]<br>Parsing (part of speech): noun<br>  Case—nominative<br>  Gender—feminine<br>  Number—singular<br>  Stem or root—from βλασφημία, ας<br>Concordance References:<br>⇒ Strong's #988 blasphëmia<br>⇒ NIV #1060 blasphëmia<br>⇒ NASB #988 blasphëmia<br><br>**Ephes. 4:31**<br>Let all bitterness, and wrath, and anger, and clamour, and **evil speaking**, be put away from you, with all malice: [KJV]<br>Let all bitterness and wrath and anger and clamor and **slander** be put away from you, along with all malice. [NASB]<br>Get rid of all bitterness, rage and anger, brawling and **slander**, along with every form of malice. [NIV]<br>Let all bitterness, wrath, anger, clamor, and **evil speaking** be put away from you, with all malice. [NKJV] | Slander; evil speaking; blasphemy; malicious talk; to speak against God; to insult. It is hurtful, injurious speech.<br><br>**Practical Application**<br>The Christian citizen is *to speak evil of no person*. No citizen is to be slandered or verbally abused and torn down. God's ideal for society is this: all citizens working to build up and enrich the lives of each other and their community and nation. If a person, ruler or citizen, is working to build us up, why would we speak evil of him? We know that in day-to-day practical living, we live in an evil world where some citizens are selfish and greedy and others commit some terrible and atrocious acts. It is this that causes chaos in society.<br>But note: the Christian citizen is not to speak evil against any citizen, not even an evil ruler. The answer to reaching evil people is not cursing, reviling, slandering, criticizing, and tearing them down. Verbal abuse only causes more |

# PRACTICAL WORD STUDIES
## in the NEW TESTAMENT

| ENGLISH WORD | GREEK WORD AND VERSE | THE WORD MEANS... |
|---|---|---|
| | Get rid of all bitterness, rage, anger, harsh words, and **slander**, as well as all types of malicious behavior. [NLT]<br><br>πᾶσα πικρία καὶ θυμὸς καὶ ὀργὴ καὶ κραυγὴ καὶ **βλασφημία** ἀρθήτω ἀφ' ὑμῶν, σὺν πάσῃ κακίᾳ· [GNS]<br><br>πᾶσα πικρία καὶ θυμὸς καὶ ὀργὴ καὶ κραυγὴ καὶ **βλασφημία** ἀρθήτω ἀφ' ὑμῶν σὺν πάσῃ κακίᾳ. [GNT] | evil—active retaliation. The only answer to reaching an evil citizen is to reach out to him in kindness, trying to lead him to change and live the way he should as a contributing citizen to the community. But note this: reaching out to evil people and not speaking evil against them does not mean that we do not use firm, strong, and warning words. We are never to give license to evil, nor to indulge the selfish and sinful acts of people. We are to speak with authority and strength against evil and untruth. We are to warn, and the community is to back up the warning with *just control*, even if it means imprisonment.<br><br>The point is this; there is no place in a just society for citizens speaking evil against each other. Cursing, reviling, slandering, and railing at each other is not the way to help those in rebellion against God, government, and man. The way to help is to reach out with kindness; and then if kindness fails, to reach out with strong, authoritative warnings—and then back up the warning. There is never a place for evil speaking. Christian citizens are to take the lead in speaking kind and strong words, words that warn against selfish and evil behavior. |
| **#1357**<br>**Evil Spirit, By**<br><br>With unclean spirit–KJV<br>With unclean spirit–NASB<br>**By evil spirit–NIV**<br>With unclean spirit–NKJV<br>**By evil spirit–NLT**<br><br>**POSB REFERENCE**<br>(Mk.1:23-24; esp. v.23)<br>Note 1 | ἐν πνεύματι ἀκαθάρτῳ = *en pneumati akatharto*<br>Pronunciation: [en pnyoo'-mah-tee ak-ath'-ar-to]<br>Parsing *pneumati* (part of speech): noun<br>    Case—dative<br>    Gender—neuter<br>    Number—singular<br>    Stem or root—from πνεῦμα, τος<br>Parsing *akatharto* (part of speech): adjective<br>    Case—dative<br>    Gender—neuter<br>    Number—singular<br>    Stem or root—from ἀκάθαρτος, ον<br>Concordance References:<br>⇒ Strong's #169 akathartos + #4151 pneuma<br>⇒ NIV #1877 en (by) + 176 akathartos [evil] +4460 pneuma [spirit]<br>⇒ NASB #169 akathartos + #4151 pneuma<br><br>**Mark 1:23**<br>And there was in their synagogue a man **with an unclean spirit**; and he cried out, [KJV]<br>And just then there was in their synagogue a man **with an unclean spirit**; and he cried out, [NASB]<br>Just then a man in their synagogue who was possessed **by an evil spirit** cried out, [NIV]<br>Now there was a man in their synagogue **with an unclean spirit**. And he cried out, [NKJV]<br>A man possessed **by an evil spirit** was in the synagogue, [NLT]<br>καὶ ἦν ἐν τῇ συναγωγῇ αὐτῶν ἄνθρωπος ἐν πνεύματι ἀκαθάρτῳ, καὶ ἀνέκραξε, [GNS]<br>καὶ εὐθὺς ἦν ἐν τῇ συναγωγῇ αὐτῶν ἄνθρωπος ἐν πνεύματι ἀκαθάρτῳ καὶ ἀνέκραξεν [GNT] | Evil spirit, unclean spirit; to be evil, unclean, dirty, tainted, desecrated. It refers to an evil, unclean, polluted, defiled devil or demon. These two words [*akatharto* (evil) + *pneumati* (spirit)] should be translated "in" (*en*) an evil or unclean spirit.<br><br>**Practical Application**<br>The man was in the grasp, in the possession of the unclean spirit. He was in the grip, captivated by the unclean spirit. He was under the spell, the will of the unclean spirit. To better understand the meaning, think of all the evil in the world, all the evil that occurs every hour and every day. Then note John's words, "The whole world is under the control of the evil one" (1 Jn.5:19). |
| **#1358**<br>**Evil Things**<br><br>Lusts–KJV<br>Desires–NASB<br>Desire–NIV<br>Desires–NKJV<br>**Evil things–NLT** | ἐπιθυμίας = *epithumias*<br>Pronunciation: [ep-ee-thoo-mee'-ahs]<br>Parsing (part of speech): noun<br>    Case—accusative<br>    Gender—feminine<br>    Number—plural<br>    Stem or root—from ἐπιθυμία, ας<br>Concordance References:<br>⇒ Strong's #1939 epithumia<br>⇒ NIV #2123 epithumia<br>⇒ NASB #1939 epithumia | Desire, lust, cravings, loving to do evil things, a strong desire, a yearning passion for, an all-consuming craving.<br><br>**Practical Application**<br>The word is used in a good sense three different times in Scripture (Luke 22:15; Phil. 1:23; 1 Thes. 2:17). A person is to turn his strong desires toward righteousness and godliness; however, a person has to struggle to turn away |

## PRACTICAL WORD STUDIES
### in the NEW TESTAMENT

| ENGLISH WORD | GREEK WORD AND VERSE | THE WORD MEANS... |
|---|---|---|
| **POSB REFERENCE** (Jn.8:44) *Deeper Study #1* | **John 8:44**<br>Ye are of your father the devil, and the **lusts** of your father ye will do. He was a murderer from the beginning, and abode not in the truth, because there is no truth in him. When he speaketh a lie, he speaketh of his own: for he is a liar, and the father of it. [KJV]<br>"You are of your father the devil, and you want to do the **desires** of your father. He was a murderer from the beginning, and does not stand in the truth, because there is no truth in him. Whenever he speaks a lie, he speaks from his own nature; for he is a liar, and the father of lies. [NASB]<br>You belong to your father, the devil, and you want to carry out your father's **desire**. He was a murderer from the beginning, not holding to the truth, for there is no truth in him. When he lies, he speaks his native language, for he is a liar and the father of lies. [NIV]<br>You are of *your* father the devil, and the **desires** of your father you want to do. He was a murderer from the beginning, and *does not* stand in the truth, because there is no truth in him. When he speaks a lie, he speaks from his own *resources,* for he is a liar and the father of it. [NKJV]<br>For you are the children of your father the Devil, and you love to do the **evil things** he does. He was a murderer from the beginning and has always hated the truth. There is no truth in him. When he lies, it is consistent with his character; for he is a liar and the father of lies. [NLT]<br>ὑμεῖς ἐκ πατρὸς τοῦ διαβόλου ἐστὲ, καὶ τὰς **ἐπιθυμίας** τοῦ πατρὸς ὑμῶν θέλετε ποιεῖν. ἐκεῖνος ἀνθρωποκτόνος ἦν ἀπ' ἀρχῆς, καὶ ἐν τῇ ἀληθείᾳ οὐκ ἔστηκεν, ὅτι οὐκ ἔστιν ἀλήθεια ἐν αὐτῷ. ὅταν λαλῇ τὸ ψεῦδος, ἐκ τῶν ἰδίων λαλεῖ· ὅτι ψεύστης ἐστὶ καὶ ὁ πατὴρ αὐτοῦ. [GNS]<br>ὑμεῖς ἐκ τοῦ πατρὸς τοῦ διαβόλου ἐστὲ καὶ τὰς **ἐπιθυμίας** τοῦ πατρὸς ὑμῶν θέλετε ποιεῖν. ἐκεῖνος ἀνθρωποκτόνος ἦν ἀπ' ἀρχῆς καὶ ἐν τῇ ἀληθείᾳ οὐκ ἔστηκεν, ὅτι οὐκ ἔστιν ἀλήθεια ἐν αὐτῷ. ὅταν λαλῇ τὸ ψεῦδος, ἐκ τῶν ἰδίων λαλεῖ, ὅτι ψεύστης ἐστὶν καὶ ὁ πατὴρ αὐτοῦ. [GNT] | from the desire to please himself. A person's natural tendency is the desire or lust to satisfy self before others, in particular when survival and comfort are at stake.<br>1. The very nature of a person is lust, the lust of the flesh and of the mind (Ephes. 2:2-3). Sinful and evil lust show that people are by nature...<br>• the children of wrath.<br>• the children of disobedience.<br>• the children of the spirit who is the prince and power of the air, that is, the devil.<br>2. The very nature of a person and of the world is lust, a tendency both to be and to get.<br><br>What a person discovers is that his cravings are never satisfied; they have to be controlled. There is something within a person's innermost being that craves for more and more; but as more and more is taken, the lust does not diminish, it grows. It craves for still more and more. A person's cravings are never satisfied; his only answer is to control them by the power of Christ (see POSB note, Lust—James 4:2 for a discussion of the Spirit of God's control. Cp. Galatians 5:22-23.) |
| **#1359**<br>**Evil Thoughts**<br><br>Evil thoughts–KJV<br>Evil thoughts–NASB<br>Evil thoughts–NIV<br>Evil thoughts–NKJV<br>Evil thoughts–NLT<br><br>**POSB REFERENCE** (Mk.7:21) *Deeper Study #3* | διαλογισμοὶ οἱ κακοὶ = *dialogismoi hoi kakoi*<br>Pronunciation: [dee-al-og-is-moy' oy kak-oy']<br>Parsing *dialogismoi* (part of speech): noun<br>    Case—nominative<br>    Gender—masculine<br>    Number—plural<br>    Stem or root—from διαλογισμός, οῦ<br>Parsing *kakoi* (part of speech): adjective<br>    Case—nominative<br>    Gender—masculine<br>    Number—plural<br>    Stem or root—from κακός, ή, όν<br>Concordance References:<br>⇒ Strong's #2556 kakos + #1261 dialogismos<br>⇒ NIV #2805 kakos [evil] + 1369 dialogismos [thoughts]<br>⇒ NASB #2556 kakos + #1261 dialogismos<br><br>**Mark 7:21**<br>For from within, out of the heart of men, proceed **evil thoughts**, adulteries, fornications, murders, [KJV]<br>"For from within, out of the heart of men, proceed the **evil thoughts**, fornications, thefts, murders, adulteries, [NASB]<br>For from within, out of men's hearts, come **evil thoughts**, sexual immorality, theft, murder, adultery, [NIV]<br>For from within, out of the heart of men, proceed **evil thoughts**, adulteries, fornications, murders, [NKJV]<br>For from within, out of a person's heart, come **evil thoughts**, sexual immorality, theft, murder, [NLT]<br>ἔσωθεν γὰρ ἐκ τῆς καρδίας τῶν ἀνθρώπων οἱ | Evil thoughts, evil reasonings, bad motives, wrong opinions.<br><br>### Practical Application<br>These words (*dialogismoi hoi kakoi*) describe thoughts and imaginations and ideas and concepts that are evil, base, wrong, wicked, immoral, unjust, reprehensible; thoughts that are not what they should be; thoughts that are not moral, clean and pure; thoughts that are not just and equitable; thoughts that are not uplifting and edifying; thoughts that are not spiritual, but carnal. (Cp. Romans 8:6; 2 Cor. 10:5; Phil. 4:8. Cp. Matthew 5:28.) Evil thoughts are a sin against all the commandments (Exodus 20:1f). |

# PRACTICAL WORD STUDIES
## in the NEW TESTAMENT

| ENGLISH WORD | GREEK WORD AND VERSE | THE WORD MEANS... |
|---|---|---|
| | διαλογισμοὶ οἱ κακοὶ ἐκπορεύονται, μοιχεῖαι, πορνεῖαι, φόνοι, κλοπαί, [GNS]<br>ἔσωθεν γὰρ ἐκ τῆς καρδίας τῶν ἀνθρώπων οἱ διαλογισμοὶ οἱ κακοὶ ἐκπορεύονται, πορνεῖαι, κλοπαί, φόνοι, [GNT] | |
| **#1360**<br>**Exact Representation**<br><br>Express image–KJV<br>**Exact representation–NASB**<br>**Exact representation–NIV**<br>Express image–NKJV<br>Represents God exactly–NLT<br><br>**POSB EFERENCE**<br>(Heb.1:3)<br>Note 5 | χαρακτὴρ = *charaktër*<br>Pronunciation: [khar-ak-tare']<br>Parsing (part of speech): noun<br>  Case—nominative<br>  Gender—masculine<br>  Number—singular<br>  Stem or root—from χαρακτήρ, ῆρος<br>Concordance References:<br>  ⇒ Strong's #5481 charaktër<br>  ⇒ NIV #5917 charaktër<br>  ⇒ NASB #5481 charaktër<br><br>**Hebrews 1:3**<br>Who being the brightness of his glory, and the **express image** of his person, and upholding all things by the word of his power, when he had by himself purged our sins, sat down on the right hand of the Majesty on high; [KJV]<br>And He is the radiance of His glory and the **exact representation** of His nature, and upholds all things by the word of His power. When He had made purification of sins, He sat down at the right hand of the Majesty on high; [NASB]<br>The Son is the radiance of God's glory and the **exact representation** of his being, sustaining all things by his powerful word. After he had provided purification for sins, he sat down at the right hand of the Majesty in heaven. [NIV]<br>Who being the brightness of *His* glory and the **express image** of His person, and upholding all things by the word of His power, when He had by Himself purged our sins, sat down at the right hand of the Majesty on high, [NKJV]<br>The Son reflects God's own glory, and everything about him **represents God exactly**. He sustains the universe by the mighty power of his command. After he died to cleanse us from the stain of sin, he sat down in the place of honor at the right hand of the majestic God of heaven. [NLT]<br>ὃς ὢν ἀπαύγασμα τῆς δόξης, καὶ **χαρακτὴρ** τῆς ὑποστάσεως αὐτοῦ, φέρων τε τὰ πάντα τῷ ῥήματι τῆς δυνάμεως αὐτοῦ, δι' ἑαυτοῦ καθαρισμὸν ποιησάμενος τῶν ἁμαρτιῶν ἡμῶν, ἐκάθισεν ἐν δεξιᾷ τῆςμεγαλωσύνης ἐν ὑψηλοῖς, [GNS]<br>ὃς ὢν ἀπαύγασμα τῆς δόξης καὶ **χαρακτὴρ** τῆς ὑποστάσεως αὐτοῦ, φέρων τε τὰ πάντα τῷ ῥήματι τῆς δυνάμεως αὐτοῦ, καθαρισμὸν τῶν ἁμαρτιῶν ποιησάμενος ἐκάθισεν ἐν δεξιᾷ τῆς μεγαλωσύνης ἐν ὑψηλοῖς, [GNT] | Exact representation, express image; an exact likeness represents God exactly. The word "exact" (*charaktër*) means the very stamp, mark, and impression—the very reproduction of God.<br><br>**Practical Application**<br>Jesus Christ is "the perfect imprint and very image of [God's] nature." Jesus Christ is the express image of God. When Jesus Christ came to earth, men were able to see God, to see exactly what God is like:<br>  ⇒ loving, compassionate, caring<br>  ⇒ healing, restoring, saving<br>  ⇒ correcting, disciplining, controlling<br>  ⇒ holy, righteous, just<br><br>A person could look at Jesus Christ and see exactly what God is like. |
| **#1361**<br>**Exacting**<br><br>Austere–KJV<br>**Exacting–NASB**<br>Hard–NIV<br>Austere–NKJV<br>Tough–NLT<br><br>**POSB REFERENCE**<br>(Lk.19:15-23; esp. v.22)<br>Note 5, point 6b | αὐστηρός = *austëros*<br>Pronunciation: [ow-stay-ros']<br>Parsing (part of speech): adjective<br>  Case—nominative<br>  Gender—masculine<br>  Number—singular<br>  Stem or root—from αὐστηρός, ά, όν<br>Concordance References:<br>  ⇒ Strong's #840 austeros<br>  ⇒ NIV #893 austëros<br>  ⇒ NASB #840 austeros<br><br>**Luke 19:22**<br>And he saith unto him, Out of thine own mouth will I judge thee, thou wicked servant. Thou knewest that I was an **austere** man, taking up that I laid not down, and reaping that I did not sow: [KJV] | Sharp, hard, exacting, tough, austere, stringent.<br><br>**Practical Application**<br>In this Scripture, the unfaithful servant accused the Lord of being too hard. He felt that the Lord was too demanding and strict; and if he committed himself to the Lord's affairs, he would lose out on too much of the pleasures and comforts of life. But note: this was merely an excuse for his failure. He had chosen to live a life of selfishness and comfort and worldliness in the kingdom of the Lord without paying the price of helping to build it. He had been complacent and idle, doing very little. He had to cover up his failure or else face judgment, but his |

# PRACTICAL WORD STUDIES
## in the NEW TESTAMENT

| ENGLISH WORD | GREEK WORD AND VERSE | THE WORD MEANS... |
|---|---|---|
| | "He said to him, 'By your own words I will judge you, you worthless slave. Did you know that I am an **exacting** man, taking up what I did not lay down, and reaping what I did not sow? [NASB]<br><br>"His master replied, 'I will judge you by your own words, you wicked servant! You knew, did you, that I am a **hard** man, taking out what I did not put in, and reaping what I did not sow? [NIV]<br><br>And he said to him, 'Out of your own mouth I will judge you, you wicked servant. You knew that I was an **austere** man, collecting what I did not deposit and reaping what I did not sow. [NKJV]<br><br>"'You wicked servant!' the king roared. 'Hard, am I? If you knew so much about me and how **tough** I am, [NLT]<br><br>λέγει δὲ αὐτῷ, Ἐκ τοῦ στόματός σου κρίνω σε, πονηρὲ δοῦλε. ᾔδεις ὅτι ἐγὼ ἄνθρωπος **αὐστηρός** εἰμι, αἴρων ὃ οὐκ ἔθηκα, καὶ θερίζων ὃ οὐκ ἔσπειρα· [GNS]<br><br>λέγει αὐτῷ, Ἐκ τοῦ στόματός σου κρινῶ σε, πονηρὲ δοῦλε. ᾔδεις ὅτι ἐγὼ ἄνθρωπος **αὐστηρός** εἰμι, αἴρων ὃ οὐκ ἔθηκα καὶ θερίζων ὃ οὐκ ἔσπειρα; [GNT] | excuse was unacceptable. Perfect justice was executed: "By your own words I will judge you." The very excuse, as well as the life, of the unfaithful servant determined his judgment. |
| **#1362**<br>**Exalting God**<br><br>Magnify God–KJV<br>**Exalting God–NASB**<br>Praising God–NIV<br>Magnify God–NKJV<br>Praising God–NLT<br><br>**POSB REFERENCE**<br>(Acts 10:46)<br>Note 2 | μεγαλυνόντων τὸν θεόν = megalunontön ton theon<br>Pronunciation: [meh-gah-loon-on-toan ton they-on]<br>Parsing *megalunontön* (part of speech): verb<br>    Mood—participle<br>    Tense—present<br>    Voice—active<br>    Case—genitive<br>    Gender-masculine<br>    Number—plural<br>    Stem or root—from μεγαλύνω<br>Concordance References:<br>⇒ Strong's #3170 megalunö + 3588 ho + 2316 theos<br>⇒ NIV #3486 megalunö + 3836 ho + 2536 theos<br>⇒ NASB #3170 megalunö + 3588 ho + 2316 theos<br><br>**Acts 10:46**<br>For they heard them speak with tongues, and **magnify God**. Then answered Peter, [KJV]<br><br>For they were hearing them speaking with tongues and **exalting God**. Then Peter answered, [NASB]<br><br>For they heard them speaking in tongues and **praising God**. Then Peter said, [NIV]<br><br>For they heard them speak with tongues and **magnify God**. Then Peter answered, [NKJV]<br><br>And there could be no doubt about it, for they heard them speaking in tongues and **praising God**. Then Peter asked, [NLT]<br><br>ἤκουον γὰρ αὐτῶν λαλούντων γλώσσαις, καὶ **μεγαλυνόντων τὸν Θεόν**. τότε ἀπεκρίθη ὁ Πέτρος, [GNS]<br><br>ἤκουον γὰρ αὐτῶν λαλούντων γλώσσαις καὶ **μεγαλυνόντων τὸν θεόν**. τότε ἀπεκρίθη Πέτρος, [GNT] | To praise God; to magnify God; to exalt God.<br><br>**Practical Application**<br>Note: the speaking in tongues led the Gentile believers into a glorious and joyful praise of God. They *exalted God* (*megalunontön ton theon*). They were caught up in an ecstatic praise of the Lord. The "speaking with tongues" seems to be the sign that the Holy Spirit had fallen upon the Gentiles. Both Peter and the Jewish believers needed a sign, a sign that would leave no doubt that the Gentiles were saved. Speaking in tongues, that is, breaking out in an ecstatic praise of God, was such a sign. It was the sign that would leave no doubt whatsoever. Note: it is this that utterly shocked the Jewish believers who were with Peter; for the Gentiles were, as Peter says, receiving "the Holy Spirit *as well as we*" (Acts 10:47. See POSB *Deeper Study #1*—Acts 2:1-4. Also see POSB *Deeper Study #4*, Tongues—Acts 2:4 for more discussion.) |
| **#1363**<br>**Exalts**<br><br>Magnify–KJV<br>**Exalts–NASB**<br>Glorifies–NIV<br>Magnifies–NKJV<br>Praise–NLT<br><br>**POSB REFERENCE**<br>(Lk.1:46)<br>Note 1, point 2 | Μεγαλύνει = Megalunei<br>Pronunciation: [meg-al-oo'-neh-ee]<br>Parsing (part of speech): verb<br>    Mood—indicative<br>    Tense—present<br>    Voice—active<br>    Person—3rd person<br>    Number—singular<br>    Stem or root—from μεγαλύνω<br>Concordance References:<br>⇒ Strong's #3170 megalunö<br>⇒ NIV #3486 megalunö<br>⇒ NASB #3170 megalunö<br><br>**Luke 1:46**<br>And Mary said, My soul doth **magnify** the Lord, [KJV]<br>And Mary said: "My soul **exalts** the Lord, [NASB]<br>And Mary said: "My soul **glorifies** the Lord [NIV] | To exalt; to magnify; to highly regard; to glorify; to praise; to declare the greatness of.<br><br>**Practical Application**<br>The idea is habitual; that is, it was the habit of Mary's soul to magnify or glorify the Lord. |

## PRACTICAL WORD STUDIES
### in the NEW TESTAMENT

| ENGLISH WORD | GREEK WORD AND VERSE | THE WORD MEANS... |
|---|---|---|
| | And Mary said: "My soul **magnifies** the Lord, [NKJV]<br>Mary responded, "Oh, how I **praise** the Lord. [NLT]<br>Καὶ εἶπε Μαριάμ, [GNS]—**Luke 1:46**<br>**Μεγαλύνει** ἡ ψυχή μου τὸν Κύριον, καὶ ἠγαλλίασε τὸ πνεῦμά μου ἐπὶ τῷ Θεῷ τῷ σωτῆρί μου, [GNS]—**Luke 1:47**<br>Καὶ εἶπεν Μαριάμ, [GNT]—**Luke 1:46**<br>**Μεγαλύνει** ἡ ψυχή μου τὸν κύριον, καὶ ἠγαλλίασεν τὸ πνεῦμά μου ἐπὶ τῷ θεῷ τῷ σωτῆρί μου, [GNT]—**Luke 1:47**<br>NOTE: This greek word (**Μεγαλύνει**) in verse 47 is translated in verse 46 in English Bibles. | |
| **#1364**<br>**Examined**<br><br>Judged–KJV<br>**Examined–NASB**<br>Judged–NIV<br>Judged–NKJV<br>Thinks–NLT<br><br>**POSB REFERENCE**<br>(1 Cor.4:3)<br>Note 2 | ἀνακρίνω = anakrinō<br>Pronunciation: [an-ak-ree'-no]<br>Parsing (part of speech): verb<br>  Mood—subjunctive<br>  Tense—aorist<br>  Voice—passive<br>  Person—1st person<br>  Number—singular<br>  Stem or root—from ἀνακρίνω<br>Concordance References:<br> ⇒ Strong's #350 anakrinō<br> ⇒ NIV #373 anakrinō<br> ⇒ NASB #350 anakrinō<br><br>**1 Cor. 4:3**<br>But with me it is a very small thing that I should be **judged** of you, or of man's judgment: yea, I judge not mine own self. [KJV]<br>But to me it is a very small thing that I should be **examined** by you, or by any human court; in fact, I do not even examine myself. [NASB]<br>I care very little if I am **judged** by you or by any human court; indeed, I do not even judge myself. [NIV]<br>But with me it is a very small thing that I should be **judged** by you or by a human court. In fact, I do not even judge myself. [NKJV]<br>What about me? Have I been faithful? Well, it matters very little what you or anyone else **thinks**. I don't even trust my own judgment on this point. [NLT]<br>ἐμοὶ δὲ εἰς ἐλάχιστόν ἐστιν ἵνα ὑφ' ὑμῶν ἀνακριθῶ, ἢ ὑπὸ ἀνθρωπίνης ἡμέρας· ἀλλ' οὐδὲ ἐμαυτὸν **ἀνακρίνω**. [GNS]<br>ἐμοὶ δὲ εἰς ἐλάχιστόν ἐστιν, ἵνα ὑφ' ὑμῶν ἀνακριθῶ ἢ ὑπὸ ἀνθρωπίνης ἡμέρας· ἀλλ' οὐδὲ ἐμαυτὸν **ἀνακρίνω**. [GNT] | To judge; to examine; to evaluate; to discern; to closely study; to scrutinize; to investigate; to question; and to cross-examine.<br><br>**Practical Application**<br>  Note this: Paul does not even judge himself. Paul knew precisely what every honest and thinking person knows.<br>⇒ No minister can honestly judge his own ministry: its true success; his motives for every single thing he has done; how much fruit he has really borne in people's lives and how much should have been borne.<br>⇒ A person who begins to judge his own works either begins to think too highly of himself or too lowly. To varying degrees, he becomes prideful or discouraged. |
| **#1365**<br>**Example**<br><br>Followers–KJV<br>Imitators–NASB<br>Imitate–NIV<br>Imitate–NKJV<br>**Example–NLT**<br><br>**POSB REFERENCE**<br>(1 Cor.4:16)<br>Note 3 | μιμηταί γίνεσθε. = mimētai ginesthe<br>Pronunciation: [mim-ay-tace']<br>Parsing *mimētai* (part of speech): noun<br>  Case—nominative<br>  Gender—masculine<br>  Number—plural<br>  Stem or root—from μιμητής, οῦ<br>Parsing *ginesthe* (part of speech): verb<br>  Mood—imperative<br>  Tense—present<br>  Voice—middle or passive deponent<br>  Person—2nd person<br>  Number—plural<br>  Stem or root—from γίνομαι<br>Concordance References:<br> ⇒ Strong's #1096+3402 ginomai mimētēs<br> ⇒ NIV #1181+3629 ginomai mimētēs [imitate]<br> ⇒ NASB #1096+3402 ginomai mimētēs<br><br>**1 Cor. 4:16**<br>Wherefore I beseech you, be ye **followers** of me. [KJV]<br>I exhort you therefore, be **imitators** of me. [NASB]<br>Therefore I urge you to **imitate** me. [NIV] | Imitate, followers, example; to copy; to impersonate; to emulate; to duplicate.<br><br>**Practical Application**<br>  Every father should live such a life that his children could follow in his steps. This is what Paul was saying. He had lived a life of commitment and self-denial for the Lord Jesus Christ. He had given all he was and had to Christ. He was saying: "Follow me—imitate me! Commit your life to Christ; deny yourself completely—give all you are and have to Him. Help me in evangelizing and meeting the desperate needs of the world for Him. The world is starving and dying from sin, hunger, disease, cold, heat, loneliness, and purposelessness; and they are doomed to die in both this world and the next. Follow me! Help me to reach this world for Christ Jesus our Lord." |

# PRACTICAL WORD STUDIES
## in the NEW TESTAMENT

| ENGLISH WORD | GREEK WORD AND VERSE | THE WORD MEANS... |
|---|---|---|
| | Therefore I urge you, **imitate** me. [NKJV]<br>So I ask you to follow my **example** and do as I do. [NLT]<br>παρακαλῶ οὖν ὑμᾶς, **μιμηταί** μου γίνεσθε. [GNS]<br>παρακαλῶ οὖν ὑμᾶς, **μιμηταί** μου γίνεσθε. [GNT] | |
| **#1366**<br>**Example**<br><br>Followers–KJV<br>Imitators–NASB<br>Imitators–NIV<br>Imitators–NKJV<br>Example–NLT<br><br>**POSB REFERENCE**<br>(Eph.5:1)<br>Note 1 | **μιμηταί** = *mimētai*<br>Pronunciation: [mim-ay-tah-ee']<br>Parsing (part of speech): noun<br>    Case—nominative<br>    Gender—masculine<br>    Number—plural<br>    Stem or root—from μιμητής, οῦ<br>Concordance References:<br>  ⇒ Strong's #3402 mimētēs<br>  ⇒ NIV #3629 mimētēs<br>  ⇒ NASB #3402 mimētēs<br><br>**Ephes. 5:1**<br>Be ye therefore **followers** of God, as dear children; [KJV]<br>Therefore be **imitators** of God, as beloved children; [NASB]<br>Be **imitators** of God, therefore, as dearly loved children [NIV]<br>Therefore be **imitators** of God as dear children. [NKJV]<br>Follow God's **example** in everything you do, because you are his dear children. [NLT]<br>Γίνεσθε οὖν **μιμηταί** τοῦ Θεοῦ, ὡς τέκνα ἀγαπητά· [GNS]<br>γίνεσθε οὖν **μιμηταί** τοῦ θεοῦ ὡς τέκνα ἀγαπητά [GNT] | Imitators, followers, examples.<br><br>**Practical Application**<br>Some prefer the translation that we are to become *imitators* of God. Note the phrase "because you are his dear children." Just as children learn by imitating their parents, so we are to learn by imitating God. The very idea that we are to be *followers and imitators* of God is a bold idea. Just imagine, Scripture boldly proclaims that we are to become *like God!*<br>⇒ Christ said: "Be ye therefore perfect, even as your Father which is in heaven is perfect" (Matthew 5:48).<br>⇒ God demanded: "Ye shall be holy: for I the LORD your God am holy" (Leviticus 19:2).<br>⇒ Paul declared: "But we all...are changed into the same image [of Christ] from glory to glory" (2 Cor. 4:18).<br>⇒ Peter charged: "But as he which hath called you is holy, so be ye holy in all manner of conversation; because it is written, Be ye holy; for I am holy" (1 Peter 1:15-16)<br>⇒ The early church saint, Clement of Alexandria said: "The Christian practices being God" (Quoted by William Barclay, *The Letters to the Galatians* and *Ephesians*, p.190). |
| **#1367**<br>**Example**<br><br>Example–KJV<br>Example–NASB<br>Example–NIV<br>Example–NKJV<br>Example–NLT<br><br>**POSB REFERENCE**<br>(1 Pt.2:21)<br>Note 1 | **ὑπογραμμόν** = *hupogrammon*<br>Pronunciation: [hoop-og-ram-mon']<br>Parsing (part of speech): noun<br>    Case—accusative<br>    Gender—masculine<br>    Number—singular<br>    Stem or root—from ὑπογραμμός, οῦ<br>Concordance References:<br>  ⇒ Strong's #5261 hupogrammos<br>  ⇒ NIV #5681 hupogrammos<br>  ⇒ NASB #5261 hupogrammos<br><br>**1 Peter 2:21**<br>For even hereunto were ye called: because Christ also suffered for us, leaving us an **example**, that ye should follow his steps: [KJV]<br>For you have been called for this purpose, since Christ also suffered for you, leaving you an **example** for you to follow in His steps, [NASB]<br>To this you were called, because Christ suffered for you, leaving you an **example**, that you should follow in his steps. [NIV]<br>For to this you were called, because Christ also suffered for us, leaving us an **example**, that you should follow His steps: [NKJV]<br>This suffering is all part of what God has called you to. Christ, who suffered for you, is your **example**. Follow in his steps. [NLT]<br>εἰς τοῦτο γὰρ ἐκλήθητε, ὅτι καὶ Χριστὸς ἔπαθεν ὑπὲρ ὑμῶν, ὑμῖν ὑπολιμπάνων **ὑπογραμμόν**, ἵνα ἐπακολουθήσητε τοῖς ἴχνεσιν αὐτοῦ· [GNS]<br>εἰς τοῦτο γὰρ ἐκλήθητε, ὅτι καὶ Χριστὸς ἔπαθεν ὑπὲρ ὑμῶν ὑμῖν ὑπολιμπάνων **ὑπογραμμόν** ἵνα ἐπακολουθήσητε τοῖς ἴχνεσιν αὐτοῦ, [GNT] | Example. The word means the pattern of some picture or letter that a teacher gives to the pupil.<br><br>**Practical Application**<br>The pattern is to be copied or reproduced. The idea is that an exact copy is to be made; every detail of the pattern is to be reproduced. The exhortation is that we are to be an exact copy of Christ; we are to follow the pattern of Christ in every detail. |

# PRACTICAL WORD STUDIES
## in the NEW TESTAMENT

| ENGLISH WORD | GREEK WORD AND VERSE | THE WORD MEANS... |
|---|---|---|
| **#1368**<br>**Example**<br><br>**Example–KJV**<br>Copy–NASB<br>Copy–NIV<br>Copy–NKJV<br>Copy–NLT<br><br>**POSB REFERENCE**<br>(Heb.8:4-5, esp. v.5)<br>Note 5 | ὑποδείγματι = *hupodeigmati*<br>Pronunciation: [hoop-od'-igue-mah-tee]<br>Parsing (part of speech): noun<br>    Case—dative<br>    Gender—neuter<br>    Number—singular<br>    Stem or root—from ὑπόδειγμα, τος<br>Concordance References:<br>  ⇒ Strong's #5262 hupodeigma<br>  ⇒ NIV #5682 hupodeigma<br>  ⇒ NASB #5262 hupodeigma<br><br>**Hebrews 8:5**<br>Who serve unto the **example** and shadow of heavenly things, as Moses was admonished of God when he was about to make the tabernacle: for, See, saith he, that thou make all things according to the pattern shewed to thee in the mount. [KJV]<br><br>Who serve a **copy** and shadow of the heavenly things, just as Moses was warned by God when he was about to erect the tabernacle; for, "See," He says, "that you make all things according to the pattern which was shown you on the mountain." [NASB]<br><br>They serve at a sanctuary that is a **copy** and shadow of what is in heaven. This is why Moses was warned when he was about to build the tabernacle: "See to it that you make everything according to the pattern shown you on the mountain." [NIV]<br><br>Who serve the **copy** and shadow of the heavenly things, as Moses was divinely instructed when he was about to make the tabernacle. For He said, *"See that you make all things according to the pattern shown you on the mountain."* [NKJV]<br><br>They serve in a place of worship that is only a **copy**, a shadow of the real one in heaven. For when Moses was getting ready to build the Tabernacle, God gave him this warning: "Be sure that you make everything according to the design I have shown you here on the mountain." [NLT]<br><br>οἵτινες **ὑποδείγματι** καὶ σκιᾷ λατρεύουσι τῶν ἐπουρανίων, καθὼς κεχρημάτισται Μωσῆς μέλλων ἐπιτελεῖν τὴν σκηνήν, Ὅρα, γάρ φησι, ποιήσης πάντα κατὰ τὸν τύπον τὸν δειχθέντα σοι ἐν τῷ ὄρει. [GNS]<br><br>οἵτινες **ὑποδείγματι** καὶ σκιᾷ λατρεύουσιν τῶν ἐπουρανίων, καθὼς κεχρημάτισται Μωϋσῆς μέλλων ἐπιτελεῖν τὴν σκηνήν, Ὅρα γάρ φησιν, ποιήσεις πάντα κατὰ τὸν τύπον τὸν δειχθέντα σοι ἐν τῷ ὄρει· [GNT] | Copy, example, imitation, pattern, shadow; a shadowy outline; a reflection.<br><br>**Practical Application**<br>The tabernacle and sacrifices of the Old Testament were only shadows of heavenly things. Jesus Christ is the Minister of heaven, of the real world, of the real sanctuary and tabernacle of God. The things of religion and worship upon earth are only examples and shadows, copies and sketches, shadowy outlines and reflections of heavenly worship.<br><br>Note: there is a real world, a heavenly world, and there is a tabernacle, a throne room in which the glorious presence of God dwells. It was the pattern from which Moses made the earthly tabernacle (cp. Exodus 25:40). God had shown Moses the real pattern of heavenly worship and told him to make a copy of it upon earth. That is what the tabernacle was that was carried around by Israel in the wilderness wanderings.<br><br>The point is this: earthly priests can only give us the shadow and picture of heaven. But Jesus Christ is the Priest and Minister of the heavenly worship, of the real world. Therefore, He is the One who can lead men into heaven, into the world that is real and perfect and unending. He is the One who can lead us into the very presence of God. |
| **#1369**<br>**Example**<br><br>Pattern–KJV<br>**Example–NASB**<br>**Example–NIV**<br>Pattern–NKJV<br>**Example–NLT**<br><br>**POSB REFERENCE**<br>(Tit.2:7-8; esp. v.7)<br>Note 6, point 1<br><br>**See also POSB REF:**<br>(Philip.3:17)<br>Note 1 | τύπον = *tupon*<br>Pronunciation: [too'-pon]<br>Parsing (part of speech): noun<br>    Case—accusative<br>    Gender—masculine<br>    Number—singular<br>    Stem or root—from τύπος, ου<br>Concordance References:<br>  ⇒ Strong's #5179 tupos<br>  ⇒ NIV #5596 tupos<br>  ⇒ NASB #5179 tupos<br><br>**Titus 2:7**<br>In all things shewing thyself a **pattern** of good works: in doctrine shewing uncorruptness, gravity, sincerity, [KJV]<br><br>In all things show yourself to be an **example** of good deeds, with purity in doctrine, dignified, [NASB]<br><br>In everything set them an **example** by doing what is good. In your teaching show integrity, seriousness [NIV]<br><br>In all things showing yourself *to be* a **pattern** of good works; in doctrine *showing* integrity, reverence, incorruptibility, [NKJV]<br><br>And you yourself must be an **example** to them by | Example, pattern, model, standard, image. The word "example" (*tupon*) literally means to make an impression with a die, to mould or form, to strike an impression.<br><br>**Practical Application**<br>Young ministers and teachers are to be a pattern, a model of good works. This can be forcefully stated in several ways:<br>⇒ He must live what he preaches.<br>⇒ His behavior must match his teaching.<br>⇒ His life must not tear down what his words build up.<br>⇒ His deeds must show the light which he proclaims.<br>⇒ His example must be his first concern; his instruction must be his second concern.<br><br>Teaching others is a necessity, but being an example to others is an *absolute* essential. Words mean nothing without the behavior to back up the words. When people see a life that is strong and full of love, joy, peace, and righteousness, |

## Practical Word Studies
### in the New Testament

| ENGLISH WORD | GREEK WORD AND VERSE | THE WORD MEANS... |
|---|---|---|
| | doing good deeds of every kind. Let everything you do reflect the integrity and seriousness of your teaching. [NLT]<br><br>περὶ πάντα σεαυτὸν παρεχόμενος **τύπον** καλῶν ἔργων, ἐν τῇ διδασκαλίᾳ ἀδιαφθορίαν, σεμνότητα, ἀφθαρσιαν, [GNS]<br><br>περὶ πάντα, σεαυτὸν παρεχόμενος **τύπον** καλῶν ἔργων, ἐν τῇ διδασκαλίᾳ ἀφθορίαν, σεμνότητα, [GNT] | they are far more likely to receive Christ and to live righteous lives themselves. |
| **#1370**<br>**Exasperate**<br><br>Provoke–KJV<br>Provoke–NASB<br>**Exasperate–NIV**<br>Provoke–NKJV<br>Treat–NLT<br><br>**POSB REFERENCE**<br>(Eph.6:4)<br>Note 2 | παροργίζετε = *parorgizete*<br>Pronunciation: [par-org-id'-zeh-teh]<br>Parsing (part of speech): verb<br>    Mood—imperative<br>    Tense—present<br>    Voice—active<br>    Person—2nd person<br>    Number—plural<br>    Stem or root—from παροργίζω<br>Concordance References:<br>  ⇒ Strong's #3949 parorgizō<br>  ⇒ NIV #4239 parorgizō<br>  ⇒ NASB #3949 parorgizō<br><br>**Ephes. 6:4**<br>And, ye fathers, **provoke** not your children to wrath: but bring them up in the nurture and admonition of the Lord. [KJV]<br><br>And, fathers, do not **provoke** your children to anger; but bring them up in the discipline and instruction of the Lord. [NASB]<br><br>Fathers, do not **exasperate** your children; instead, bring them up in the training and instruction of the Lord. [NIV]<br><br>And you, fathers, do not **provoke** your children to wrath, but bring them up in the training and admonition of the Lord. [NKJV]<br><br>And now a word to you fathers. Don't make your children angry by the way you **treat** them. Rather, bring them up with the discipline and instruction approved by the Lord. [NLT]<br><br>καὶ οἱ πατέρες, μὴ **παροργίζετε** τὰ τέκνα ὑμῶν, ἀλλ' ἐκτρέφετε αὐτὰ ἐν παιδείᾳ καὶ νουθεσίᾳ Κυρίου. [GNS]<br><br>Καὶ οἱ πατέρες, μὴ **παροργίζετε** τὰ τέκνα ὑμῶν ἀλλὰ ἐκτρέφετε αὐτὰ ἐν παιδείᾳ καὶ νουθεσίᾳ κυρίου. [GNT] | To exasperate; to provoke; to treat wrongly; to anger. The word "exasperate" (*parorgizete*) means to arouse to wrath or anger, to provoke to the point of utter exasperation and resentment.<br><br>**Practical Application**<br>Parents are not to exasperate their children to wrath. Parents are bound to upset and irritate their children sometimes; we all upset and irritate people sometimes. Discipline, correction, and reproof are seldom enjoyable experiences. Their very nature is that of disturbance and irritation. This is not what this instruction means. Four things will provoke a child.<br>1. Failing to accept the fact that things do change. Time and generations do change. This does not mean that a child should participate in nor be allowed to do everything that his generation does. But it does mean that parents need to be alert to the changes between generations and allow the child to be a part of his own generation instead of trying to conform the child to the parent's childhood generation. The parent's childhood generation does not exist nor will it ever exist again.<br>2. Overcontrolling a child will also provoke a child to wrath. Overcontrol ranges all the way from stern restriction and discipline to child abuse. Disciplining and restricting a child too much will either stifle the growth of a child or stir him to react and rebel, causing the child to flee from the parent. What is too much discipline? How much should a child be restricted? Should he be allowed to do everything he wants? No! There is a limit, and the limit must be placed upon the child and discipline must be exercised when the limit is crossed over.<br>3. Undercontrolling a child can provoke a child. It should be noted that this is the most prevalent problem in an industrialized society. There is a tendency for those with plenty or with wealth to pamper, indulge, and give a child everything imaginable—well beyond what a child needs and what is really best for him.<br>4. Living an inconsistent life before a child can provoke a child. A parent who tells a child one thing and then turns around and does the opposite thing himself is full of hypocrisy and false profession. Yet, how common! How many children are doing things because their parents do them:<br>⇒ drinking alcohol.<br>⇒ taking drugs.<br>⇒ watching sexual scenes on television or movies.<br>⇒ reading immoral stories.<br>⇒ looking at magazines exposing the human body. |

# PRACTICAL WORD STUDIES
## in the NEW TESTAMENT

| ENGLISH WORD | GREEK WORD AND VERSE | THE WORD MEANS... |
|---|---|---|
| | | ⇒ eating too much.<br>⇒ wasting time.<br>⇒ dressing or exposing the body to attract attention.<br>⇒ attending socials or parties that are loose on decency, morality, marital faithfulness, and on and on.<br><br>Seeing an inconsistent life in a parent can provoke children. |
| **#1371**<br>**Exasperated**<br><br>Grieved–KJV<br>Annoyed–NASB<br>Troubled–NIV<br>Annoyed–NKJV<br>**Exasperated–NLT**<br><br>**POSB REFERENCE**<br>(Acts 16:18)<br>Note 2, point 2 | διαπονηθείς = *diaponëtheis*<br>Pronunciation: [dee-ap-on-ay'-theh-ees]<br>Parsing (part of speech): verb<br>    Mood—participle<br>    Tense—aorist<br>    Voice—passive deponent<br>    Case—nominative<br>    Gender—masculine<br>    Number—singular<br>    Stem or root—from διαπονέομαι<br>Concordance References:<br>  ⇒ Strong's #1278 diaponeomai<br>  ⇒ NIV #1387 diaponeomai<br>  ⇒ NASB #1278 diaponeomai<br><br>**Acts 16:18**<br>And this did she many days. But Paul, being **grieved**, turned and said to the spirit, I command thee in the name of Jesus Christ to come out of her. And he came out the same hour. [KJV]<br><br>And she continued doing this for many days. But Paul was greatly **annoyed**, and turned and said to the spirit, "I command you in the name of Jesus Christ to come out of her!" And it came out at that very moment. [NASB]<br><br>She kept this up for many days. Finally Paul became so **troubled** that he turned around and said to the spirit, "In the name of Jesus Christ I command you to come out of her!" At that moment the spirit left her. [NIV]<br><br>And this she did for many days. But Paul, greatly **annoyed**, turned and said to the spirit, "I command you in the name of Jesus Christ to come out of her." And he came out that very hour. [NKJV]<br><br>This went on day after day until Paul got so **exasperated** that he turned and spoke to the demon within her. "I command you in the name of Jesus Christ to come out of her," he said. And instantly it left her. [NLT]<br><br>τοῦτο δὲ ἐποίει ἐπὶ πολλὰς ἡμέρας. διαπονηθείς δὲ ὁ Παῦλος, καὶ ἐπιστρέψας, τῷ πνεύματι εἶπε, Παραγγέλλω σοι ἐν τῷ ὀνόματι Ἰησοῦ Χριστοῦ, ἐξελθεῖν ἀπ' αὐτῆς. Καὶ ἐξῆλθεν αὐτῇ τῇ ὥρᾳ. [GNS]<br><br>τοῦτο δὲ ἐποίει ἐπὶ πολλὰς ἡμέρας. διαπονηθείς δὲ Παῦλος καὶ ἐπιστρέψας τῷ πνεύματι εἶπεν, Παραγγέλλω σοι ἐν ὀνόματι Ἰησοῦ Χριστοῦ ἐξελθεῖν ἀπ' αὐτῆς· καὶ ἐξῆλθεν αὐτῇ τῇ ὥρᾳ. [GNT] | Troubled, grieved, annoyed, exasperated. The word means pained, deeply troubled, worked up, annoyed, and angry (a righteous anger).<br><br>**Practical Application**<br>Paul was troubled and hurting...<br>• over the girl's being enslaved by sin.<br>• over the girl's being so used by greedy and lustful men.<br>• over the false witness to the Lord's name.<br>• over the mockery and ridicule of his ministry as the servant of Christ. |
| **#1372**<br>**Exceeding**<br><br>**Exceeding–KJV**<br>Surpassing–NASB<br>Incomparably–NIV<br>**Exceeding–NKJV**<br>Incredible–NLT<br><br>**POSB REFERENCE**<br>(Eph.1:19)<br>Note 1 | ὑπερβάλλον = *huperballon*<br>Pronunciation: [hoop-er-bal'-lon]<br>Parsing (part of speech): verb<br>    Mood—participle<br>    Tense—present<br>    Voice—active<br>    Case—nominative<br>    Gender—neuter<br>    Number—singular<br>    Stem or root—from ὑπερβάλλω<br>Concordance References:<br>  ⇒ Strong's #5235 huperballō<br>  ⇒ NIV #5650 huperballō<br>  ⇒ NASB #5235 huperballō | Incomparable, incredible, surpassing, unlimited, immeasurable, beyond imagination.<br><br>**Practical Application**<br>When a believer really knows God, he experiences power—the power of God Himself. The thing to note is that God's power is to us who believe; that is, God takes His power and extends it, presents it, makes it available to the believer. How do we know this? Because of what God did for Christ. What God did for Christ He will do for us. God's power is demonstrated by what He did for Christ. |

# PRACTICAL WORD STUDIES
## in the NEW TESTAMENT

| ENGLISH WORD | GREEK WORD AND VERSE | THE WORD MEANS... |
|---|---|---|
| | **Ephes. 1:19**<br>And what is the **exceeding** greatness of his power to us-ward who believe, according to the working of his mighty power, [KJV]<br>And what is the **surpassing** greatness of His power toward us who believe. These are in accordance with the working of the strength of His might [NASB]<br>And his **incomparably** great power for us who believe. That power is like the working of his mighty strength, [NIV]<br>And what *is* the **exceeding** greatness of His power toward us who believe, according to the working of His mighty power [NKJV]<br>I pray that you will begin to understand the **incredible** greatness of his power for us who believe him. This is the same mighty power [NLT]<br>καὶ τί τὸ **ὑπερβάλλον** μέγεθος τῆς δυνάμεως αὐτοῦ εἰς ἡμᾶς τοὺς πιστεύοντας κατὰ τὴν ἐνέργειαν τοῦ κράτους τῆς ἰσχύος αὐτοῦ [GNS]<br>καὶ τί τὸ **ὑπερβάλλον** μέγεθος τῆς δυνάμεως αὐτοῦ εἰς ἡμᾶς τοὺς πιστεύοντας κατὰ τὴν ἐνέργειαν τοῦ κράτους τῆς ἰσχύος αὐτοῦ. [GNT] | |
| #1373<br>**Exceedingly**<br><br>**Exceedingly**–KJV<br>Greatly enlarged–NASB<br>Growing more and more–NIV<br>**Exceedingly**–NKJV<br>Flourishing–NLT<br><br>**POSB REFERENCE**<br>(2 Thes.1:3)<br>Note 4 | ὑπεραυξάνει = *huperauxanei*<br>Pronunciation: [hoop-er-owx-ahn'-eh-ee]<br>Parsing (part of speech): verb<br>    Mood—indicative<br>    Tense—present<br>    Voice—active<br>    Person—3rd person<br>    Number—singular<br>    Stem or root—from ὑπεραυξάνω<br>Concordance References:<br>  ⇒ Strong's #5232 huperauxanō<br>  ⇒ NIV #5647 huperauxanō<br>  ⇒ NASB #5232 huperauxanō<br><br>**2 Thes. 1:3**<br>We are bound to thank God always for you, brethren, as it is meet, because that your faith groweth **exceedingly**, and the charity of every one of you all toward each other aboundeth; [KJV]<br>We ought always to give thanks to God for you, brethren, as is only fitting, because your faith is **greatly enlarged**, and the love of each one of you toward one another grows ever greater; [NASB]<br>We ought always to thank God for you, brothers, and rightly so, because your faith is **growing more and more**, and the love every one of you has for each other is increasing. [NIV]<br>We are bound to thank God always for you, brethren, as it is fitting, because your faith grows **exceedingly**, and the love of every one of you all abounds toward each other, [NKJV]<br>Dear brothers and sisters, we always thank God for you, as is right, for we are thankful that your faith is **flourishing** and you are all growing in love for each other. [NLT]<br>Εὐχαριστεῖν ὀφείλομεν τῷ Θεῷ πάντοτε περὶ ὑμῶν, ἀδελφοί, καθὼς ἄξιόν ἐστιν, ὅτι **ὑπεραυξάνει** ἡ πίστις ὑμῶν, καὶ πλεονάζει ἡ ἀγάπη ἑνὸς ἑκάστου πάντων ὑμῶν εἰς ἀλλήλους· [GNS]<br>Εὐχαριστεῖν ὀφείλομεν τῷ θεῷ πάντοτε περὶ ὑμῶν, ἀδελφοί, καθὼς ἄξιόν ἐστιν, ὅτι **ὑπεραυξάνει** ἡ πίστις ὑμῶν καὶ πλεονάζει ἡ ἀγάπη ἑνὸς ἑκάστου πάντων ὑμῶν εἰς ἀλλήλους, [GNT] | Growing more and more; exceedingly; greatly enlarged; flourishing; to grow abundantly; to grow beyond measure; to grow far beyond what would be expected.<br><br>**Practical Application**<br>What a glorious testimony! Faith that just grows and grows more and more. Imagine a church full of believers whose faith in Christ Jesus grows explosively—beyond measure—beyond what we could ever imagine. And remember: the church was growing in faith while they were in the midst of savage persecution. This is the reason Paul says: "We are bound to thank God always for you." |
| #1374<br>**Excellence** | ἀρετή = *aretē*<br>Pronunciation: [ar-et-ay']<br>Parsing (part of speech): noun<br>    Case—nominative<br>    Gender—feminine | Excellent; virtue, excellence, goodness, praises.<br><br>**Practical Application**<br>Positive thinking is the answer to peace for |

# Practical Word Studies
## in the New Testament

| ENGLISH WORD | GREEK WORD AND VERSE | THE WORD MEANS... |
|---|---|---|
| Virtue–KJV<br>**Excellence–NASB**<br>Excellent–NIV<br>Virtue–NKJV<br>Excellent–NLT<br><br>**POSB<br>REFERENCE**<br>(Philip.4:8-9; esp. v.8)<br>Note 2, point 1g | Number—singular<br>Stem or root—from ἀρετή, ῆς<br>Concordance References:<br>⇒ Strong's #703 aretē<br>⇒ NIV #746 aretë<br>⇒ NASB #703 aretē<br><br>**Philip. 4:8**<br>Finally, brethren, whatsoever things are true, whatsoever things are honest, whatsoever things are just, whatsoever things are pure, whatsoever things are lovely, whatsoever things are of good report; if there be any **virtue**, and if there be any praise, think on these things. [KJV]<br>Finally, brethren, whatever is true, whatever is honorable, whatever is right, whatever is pure, whatever is lovely, whatever is of good repute, if there is any **excellence** and if anything worthy of praise, let your mind dwell on these things. [NASB]<br>Finally, brothers, whatever is true, whatever is noble, whatever is right, whatever is pure, whatever is lovely, whatever is admirable—if anything is **excellent** or praiseworthy—think about such things. [NIV]<br>Finally, brethren, whatever things are true, whatever things *are* noble, whatever things *are* just, whatever things *are* pure, whatever things *are* lovely, whatever things *are* of good report, if *there is* any **virtue** and if *there is* anything praiseworthy—meditate on these things. [NKJV]<br>And now, dear brothers and sisters, let me say one more thing as I close this letter. Fix your thoughts on what is true and honorable and right. Think about things that are pure and lovely and admirable. Think about things that are **excellent** and worthy of praise. [NLT]<br>Τὸ λοιπόν, ἀδελφοί, ὅσα ἐστὶν ἀληθῆ, ὅσα σεμνά, ὅσα δίκαια, ὅσα ἁγνά, ὅσα προσφιλῆ, ὅσα εὔφημα, εἴ τις **ἀρετὴ** καὶ εἴ τις ἔπαινος, ταῦτα λογίζεσθε· [GNS]<br>Τὸ λοιπόν, ἀδελφοί, ὅσα ἐστὶν ἀληθῆ, ὅσα σεμνά, ὅσα δίκαια, ὅσα ἁγνά, ὅσα προσφιλῆ, ὅσα εὔφημα, εἴ τις **ἀρετὴ** καὶ εἴ τις ἔπαινος, ταῦτα λογίζεσθε· [GNT] | the Christian believer. The truth is:<br>⇒ what we think is what we become.<br>⇒ where we have kept our minds is where we are.<br>⇒ our thoughts shape our behavior.<br>⇒ what we do is what we think.<br><br>William Barclay says, *"...it is a law of life that, if a man thinks of something often enough and long enough, he will come to the stage when he cannot stop thinking about it. His thoughts will be quite literally in a groove out of which he cannot jerk them"* (*The Letters to the Philippians, Colossians, and Thessalonians*, p.97).<br><br>A person who centers his thoughts upon the world and its things will live for the world and its things: money, wealth, lands, property, houses, possessions, position, power, recognition, honor, social standing, fame, and a host of other worldly pursuits. |
| **#1375<br>Excellencies**<br><br>Praises–KJV<br>**Excellencies–NASB**<br>Praises–NIV<br>Praises–NKJV<br>Goodness–NLT<br><br>**POSB<br>REFERENCE**<br>(1 Pt.2:9)<br>Note 2 | ἀρετάς = aretas<br>Pronunciation: [ar-et-ahs']<br>Parsing (part of speech): noun<br>   Case—accusative<br>   Gender—feminine<br>   Number—plural<br>   Stem or root—from ἀρετή, ῆς<br>Concordance References:<br>⇒ Strong's #703 aretē<br>⇒ NIV #746 aretē<br>⇒ NASB #703 aretē<br><br>**1 Peter 2:9**<br>But ye are a chosen generation, a royal priesthood, an holy nation, a peculiar people; that ye should shew forth the **praises** of him who hath called you out of darkness into his marvellous light: [KJV]<br>But you are a chosen race, a royal priesthood, a HOLY NATION, a people for God's own possession, that you may proclaim the **excellencies** of Him who has called you out of darkness into His marvelous light; [NASB]<br>But you are a chosen people, a royal priesthood, a holy nation, a people belonging to God, that you may declare the **praises** of him who called you out of darkness into his wonderful light. [NIV]<br>But you *are* a chosen generation, a royal priesthood, a holy nation, His own special people, that you may proclaim the **praises** of Him who called you out of darkness into His marvelous light; [NKJV]<br>But you are not like that, for you are a chosen people. | Goodness. The word "excellencies" (*aretas*) means virtues, praises, and the supreme and eminent qualities of God (Alan Stibbs. *The First Epistle General of Peter.* "The Tyndale New Testament Commentaries," p.104).<br><br>**Practical Application**<br>The very task of the believer is to witness for God, to share the glorious message of God. What is that message? Note the verse: "the praises of Him who has called you out of darkness into His marvelous light." The message that we are to share is the glorious message of salvation. God will deliver man out of darkness into the light. This is what He has done for believers. Therefore, we are to proclaim the glorious truth that God has saved us through the Light of the world, through Jesus Christ Himself. He has saved us out of the darkness of sin and death to deliver us into the light of eternity. We will live forever. We are to praise God, proclaiming the glorious message of His marvelous light or salvation. |

## PRACTICAL WORD STUDIES
### in the NEW TESTAMENT

| ENGLISH WORD | GREEK WORD AND VERSE | THE WORD MEANS... |
|---|---|---|
| | You are a kingdom of priests, God's holy nation, his very own possession. This is so you can show others the **goodness** of God, for he called you out of the darkness into his wonderful light. [NLT]<br><br>ὑμεῖς δὲ γένος ἐκλεκτόν, βασίλειον ἱεράτευμα, ἔθνος ἅγιον, λαὸς εἰς περιποίησιν, ὅπως τὰς **ἀρετὰς** ἐξαγγείλητε τοῦ ἐκ σκότους ὑμᾶς καλέσαντος εἰς τὸ θαυμαστὸν αὐτοῦ φῶς· [GNS]<br><br>Ὑμεῖς δὲ γένος ἐκλεκτόν, βασίλειον ἱεράτευμα, ἔθνος ἅγιον, λαὸς εἰς περιποίησιν, ὅπως τὰς **ἀρετὰς** ἐξαγγείλητε τοῦ ἐκ σκότους ὑμᾶς καλέσαντος εἰς τὸ θαυμαστὸν αὐτοῦ φῶς· [GNT] | |
| **#1376**<br>**Excellence Of Speech Or Of Wisdom**<br><br>Excellency of speech or of wisdom–KJV<br>Superiority of speech or of wisdom–NASB<br>Eloquence or superior wisdom–NIV<br>**Excellence of speech or of wisdom– NKJV**<br>Lofty words and brilliant ideas–NLT<br><br>**POSB REFERENCE**<br>(1 Cor. 2:1)<br>Note 1, point 1 | ὑπεροχὴν λόγου ἡ σοφίας = huperochēn logou ē sophias<br>Pronunciation: [hoop-er-okh-ayn' log'-oo hey sof-ee'-ahs]<br>Parsing *huperochēn* (part of speech): noun<br>    Case–accusative<br>    Gender–feminine<br>    Number–singular<br>    Stem or root–from ὑπεροχή, ῆς<br>Parsing *logou* (part of speech): noun<br>    Case–genitive<br>    Gender–masculine<br>    Number–singular<br>    Stem or root–from λόγος, ου<br>Parsing *sophias* (part of speech): noun<br>    Case–genitive<br>    Gender–feminine<br>    Number–singular<br>    Stem or root–from σοφία, ας<br>Concordance References:<br>    Strong's #3056 logos + 2228 ē + 4678+5247 sophia huperochē<br>    NIV #3364 logos [eloquence] + 2445 ē [or] + 5053+5667 sophia huperochē [superior wisdom]<br>    NASB #3056 logos + 2228 ē + 4678+5247 sophia huperochē<br><br>**1 Cor. 2:1**<br>And I, brethren, when I came to you, came not with **excellency of speech or of wisdom**, declaring unto you the testimony of God. [KJV]<br>And when I came to you, brethren, I did not come with **superiority of speech or of wisdom**, proclaiming to you the testimony of God. [NASB]<br>When I came to you, brothers, I did not come with **eloquence or superior wisdom** as I proclaimed to you the testimony about God. [NIV]<br>And I, brethren, when I came to you, did not come with **excellence of speech or of wisdom** declaring to you the testimony of God. [NKJV]<br>Dear brothers and sisters, when I first came to you I didn't use **lofty words and brilliant ideas** to tell you God's message. [NLT]<br><br>Κἀγὼ ἐλθὼν πρὸς ὑμᾶς, ἀδελφοί, ἦλθον οὐ καθ' **ὑπεροχὴν λόγου ἡ σοφίας** καταγγέλλων ὑμῖν τὸ μυστήριον τοῦ Θεοῦ. [GNS]<br><br>Κἀγὼ ἐλθὼν πρὸς ὑμᾶς, ἀδελφοί, ἦλθον οὐ καθ' **ὑπεροχὴν λόγου ἡ σοφίας** καταγγέλλων ὑμῖν τὸ μυστήριον τοῦ θεοῦ. [GNT] | Eloquent words; superior, elevated, preeminent words; words that rise above.<br><br>**Practical Application**<br>Remember Paul is speaking about words, not so much about himself, although the behavior of a person could be involved. Paul did not try to sound more superior, more elevated, and more eloquent in his preaching than did others. He was not concerned in the least with his preaching's rising above and being more preeminent and more recognized than the preaching of others. Paul did not seek to impress the Corinthians with superior wisdom or brilliant ideas. |
| **#1377**<br>**Excellency Of Speech Or Of Wisdom**<br><br>Excellency of speech or of wisdom– KJV | ὑπεροχὴν λόγου ἡ σοφίας = huperochēn logou ē sophias<br>Pronunciation: [hoop-er-okh-ayn' log'-oo hey sof-ee'-ahs]<br>Parsing *logou* (part of speech): noun<br>    Case–genitive<br>    Gender–masculine<br>    Number–singular<br>    Stem or root–from λόγος, ου<br>Parsing *huperochēn* (part of speech): noun<br>    Case–accusative | Eloquent words; superior, elevated, preeminent words; words that rise above.<br><br>**Practical Application**<br>Remember Paul is speaking about words, not so much about himself, although the behavior of a person could be involved. Paul did not try to sound more superior, more elevated, and more eloquent in his preaching than did others. He |

# Practical Word Studies
## in the New Testament

| ENGLISH WORD | GREEK WORD AND VERSE | THE WORD MEANS... |
|---|---|---|
| Superiority of speech or of wisdom–NASB<br>Eloquence or superior wisdom–NIV<br>Excellence of speech or of wisdom–NKJV<br>Lofty words and brilliant ideas–NLT<br><br>**POSB REFERENCE**<br>(1 Cor.2:1)<br>Note 1, point 1 | Gender—feminine<br>Number—singular<br>Stem or root—from ὑπεροχή, ῆς<br>Parsing *sophias* (part of speech): noun<br>  Case—genitive<br>  Gender—feminine<br>  Number—singular<br>  Stem or root—from σοφία, ας<br>Concordance References:<br>⇒ Strong's #3056 logos + 2228 ë + 4678+5247 sophia huperochë<br>⇒ NIV #3364 logos [eloquence] + 2445 ë [or] + 5053+5667 sophia huperochë [superior wisdom]<br>⇒ NASB #3056 logos + 2228 ë + 4678+5247 sophia huperochë<br><br>**1 Cor. 2:1**<br>And I, brethren, when I came to you, came not with **excellency of speech or of wisdom**, declaring unto you the testimony of God. [KJV]<br>And when I came to you, brethren, I did not come with **superiority of speech or of wisdom**, proclaiming to you the testimony of God. [NASB]<br>When I came to you, brothers, I did not come with **eloquence or superior wisdom** as I proclaimed to you the testimony about God. [NIV]<br>And I, brethren, when I came to you, did not come with **excellence of speech or of wisdom** declaring to you the testimony of God. [NKJV]<br>Dear brothers and sisters, when I first came to you I didn't use **lofty words and brilliant ideas** to tell you God's message. [NLT]<br>Κἀγὼ ἐλθὼν πρὸς ὑμᾶς, ἀδελφοί, ἦλθον οὐ καθ' **ὑπεροχὴν λόγου ἢ σοφίας** καταγγέλλων ὑμῖν τὸ μυστήριον τοῦ Θεοῦ. [GNS]<br>Κἀγὼ ἐλθὼν πρὸς ὑμᾶς, ἀδελφοί, ἦλθον οὐ καθ' **ὑπεροχὴν λόγου ἢ σοφίας** καταγγέλλων ὑμῖν τὸ μυστήριον τοῦ Θεοῦ. [GNT] | was not concerned in the least with his preaching's rising above and being more preeminent and more recognized than the preaching of others. Paul did not seek to impress the Corinthians with superior wisdom or brilliant ideas. |
| #1378<br>**Excellent**<br><br>Virtue–KJV<br>Excellence–NASB<br>**Excellent–NIV**<br>Virtue–NKJV<br>**Excellent–NLT**<br><br>**POSB REFERENCE**<br>(Philip.4:8-9; esp. v.8)<br>Note 2, point 1g | ἀρετή = *aretë*<br>Pronunciation: [ar-et-ay']<br>Parsing (part of speech): noun<br>  Case—nominative<br>  Gender—feminine<br>  Number—singular<br>  Stem or root—from ἀρετή, ῆς<br>Concordance References:<br>⇒ Strong's #703 aretë<br>⇒ NIV #746 aretë<br>⇒ NASB #703 aretë<br><br>**Philip. 4:8**<br>Finally, brethren, whatsoever things are true, whatsoever things are honest, whatsoever things are just, whatsoever things are pure, whatsoever things are lovely, whatsoever things are of good report; if there be any **virtue**, and if there be any praise, think on these things. [KJV]<br>Finally, brethren, whatever is true, whatever is honorable, whatever is right, whatever is pure, whatever is lovely, whatever is of good repute, if there is any **excellence** and if anything worthy of praise, let your mind dwell on these things. [NASB]<br>Finally, brothers, whatever is true, whatever is noble, whatever is right, whatever is pure, whatever is lovely, whatever is admirable—if anything is **excellent** or praiseworthy—think about such things. [NIV]<br>Finally, brethren, whatever things are true, whatever things *are* noble, whatever things *are* just, whatever things *are* pure, whatever things *are* lovely, whatever things *are* of good report, if *there is* any **virtue** and if *there is* anything praiseworthy—meditate on these things. [NKJV] | Excellent, virtue, goodness, praises.<br><br>**Practical Application**<br>Positive thinking is the answer to peace for the Christian believer. The truth is:<br>⇒ what we think is what we become.<br>⇒ where we have kept our minds is where we are.<br>⇒ our thoughts shape our behavior.<br>⇒ what we do is what we think.<br><br>William Barclay says, *"...it is a law of life that, if a man thinks of something often enough and long enough, he will come to the stage when he cannot stop thinking about it. His thoughts will be quite literally in a groove out of which he cannot jerk them"* (The Letters to the Philippians, Colossians, and Thessalonians, p.97).<br><br>A person who centers his thoughts upon the world and its things will live for the world and its things: money, wealth, lands, property, houses, possessions, position, power, recognition, honor, social standing, fame, and a host of other worldly pursuits. |

## PRACTICAL WORD STUDIES
### in the NEW TESTAMENT

| ENGLISH WORD | GREEK WORD AND VERSE | THE WORD MEANS... |
|---|---|---|
| | And now, dear brothers and sisters, let me say one more thing as I close this letter. Fix your thoughts on what is true and honorable and right. Think about things that are pure and lovely and admirable. Think about things that are **excellent** and worthy of praise. [NLT]<br><br>Τὸ λοιπόν, ἀδελφοί, ὅσα ἐστὶν ἀληθῆ, ὅσα σεμνά, ὅσα δίκαια, ὅσα ἁγνά, ὅσα προσφιλῆ, ὅσα εὔφημα, εἴ τις **ἀρετὴ** καὶ εἴ τις ἔπαινος, ταῦτα λογίζεσθε· [GNS]<br><br>Τὸ λοιπόν, ἀδελφοί, ὅσα ἐστὶν ἀληθῆ, ὅσα σεμνά, ὅσα δίκαια, ὅσα ἁγνά, ὅσα προσφιλῆ, ὅσα εὔφημα, εἴ τις **ἀρετὴ** καὶ εἴ τις ἔπαινος, ταῦτα λογίζεσθε· [GNT] | |
| **#1379**<br>**Excellent**<br><br>Honest–KJV<br>**Excellent**–NASB<br>Good–NIV<br>Honorable–NKJV<br>Be careful how you live–NLT<br><br>**POSB REFERENCE**<br>(1 Pt.2:12)<br>Note 3 | καλήν = *kalën*<br>Pronunciation: [kal-ayn']<br>Parsing (part of speech): adjective<br>    Case—accusative<br>    Gender—feminine<br>    Number—singular<br>    Stem or root—from καλός, ή, όν<br>Concordance References:<br>  ⇒ Strong's #2570 kalos<br>  ⇒ NIV #2819 kalos<br>  ⇒ NASB #2570 kalos<br><br>**1 Peter 2:12**<br>Having your conversation **honest** among the Gentiles: that, whereas they speak against you as evildoers, they may by your good works, which they shall behold, glorify God in the day of visitation. [KJV]<br><br>Keep your behavior **excellent** among the Gentiles, so that in the thing in which they slander you as evildoers, they may on account of your good deeds, as they observe them, glorify God in the day of visitation. [NASB]<br><br>Live such **good** lives among the pagans that, though they accuse you of doing wrong, they may see your good deeds and glorify God on the day he visits us. [NIV]<br><br>Having your conduct **honorable** among the Gentiles, that when they speak against you as evildoers, they may, by *your* good works which they observe, glorify God in the day of visitation. [NKJV]<br><br>**Be careful how you live** among your unbelieving neighbors. Even if they accuse you of doing wrong, they will see your honorable behavior, and they will believe and give honor to God when he comes to judge the world. [NLT]<br><br>τὴν ἀναστροφὴν ὑμῶν ἐν τοῖς ἔθνεσιν ἔχοντες **καλήν**, ἵνα, ἐν ᾧ καταλαλοῦσιν ὑμῶν ὡς κακοποιῶν, ἐκ τῶν καλῶν ἔργων ἐποπτεύσαντες δοξάσωσι τὸν Θεὸν ἐν ἡμέρᾳ ἐπισκοπῆς. [GNS]<br><br>τὴν ἀναστροφὴν ὑμῶν ἐν τοῖς ἔθνεσιν ἔχοντες **καλήν**, ἵνα, ἐν ᾧ καταλαλοῦσιν ὑμῶν ὡς κακοποιῶν ἐκ τῶν καλῶν ἔργων ἐποπτεύοντες δοξάσωσιν τὸν θεὸν ἐν ἡμέρᾳ ἐπισκοπῆς. [GNT] | Good, honest, excellent; honorable, proper; to be careful how one lives.<br><br>**Practical Application**<br>The word "excellent" (*kalën*) means a good life, a life that is honorable, righteous, pure, lovely, decent, excellent, upright, and noble. It means a life that is without blame, that cannot be justly or accurately blamed with any sin or evil. The world watches a genuine believer to see if he really lives what he professes. Therefore, we must live good lives, honest lives, lives that are just what we profess: holy, righteous, and pure. |
| **#1380**<br>**Excess**<br><br>Excess–KJV<br>Dissipation–NASB<br>Debauchery–NIV<br>Dissipation–NKJV<br>Will ruin your life–NLT<br><br>**POSB REFERENCE**<br>(Eph.5:18)<br>Note 4 | ἀσωτία = *asōtia*<br>Pronunciation: [as-o-tee'-ah]<br>Parsing (part of speech): noun<br>    Case—nominative<br>    Gender—feminine<br>    Number—singular<br>    Stem or root—from ἀσωτία, ας<br>Concordance References:<br>  ⇒ Strong's #810 asōtia<br>  ⇒ NIV #861 asōtia<br>  ⇒ NASB #810 asōtia<br><br>**Ephes. 5:18**<br>And be not drunk with wine, wherein is **excess**; but be filled with the Spirit; [KJV]<br><br>And do not get drunk with wine, for that is **dissipation**, but be filled with the Spirit, [NASB] | Debauchery, excess behavior, wild, dissipation, reckless living, a ruined life. The word means...<br>• the dissipation and wasting away of the body.<br>• uncontrolled behavior.<br>• rioting, debauchery, wild and outrageous behavior and conduct.<br><br>**Practical Application**<br>Drunkenness is a work of the flesh that often leads to other sins of the flesh: partying, loose behavior, immodest clothing, exposure of the body, sexual thoughts, immorality, wicked or evil and unjust behavior or violence and physical abuse, notions of grandeur, strength or power. |

## PRACTICAL WORD STUDIES
### in the NEW TESTAMENT

| ENGLISH WORD | GREEK WORD AND VERSE | THE WORD MEANS... |
|---|---|---|
| | Do not get drunk on wine, which leads to **debauchery**. Instead, be filled with the Spirit. [NIV]<br>And do not be drunk with wine, in which is **dissipation**; but be filled with the Spirit, [NKJV]<br>Don't be drunk with wine, because that **will ruin your life**. Instead, let the Holy Spirit fill and control you. [NLT]<br>καὶ μὴ μεθύσκεσθε οἴνῳ, ἐν ᾧ ἐστιν **ἀσωτία**, ἀλλὰ πληροῦσθε ἐν Πνεύματι, [GNS]<br>καὶ μὴ μεθύσκεσθε οἴνῳ, ἐν ᾧ ἐστιν **ἀσωτία**, ἀλλὰ πληροῦσθε ἐν πνεύματι, [GNT] | The Bible says several things about drunkenness.<br>1. Drunkenness excludes a person from the kingdom of God.<br>2. Drunkenness leads to other forms of misbehavior and sin.<br>3. Drunkenness makes it impossible to grasp the fleeting opportunities of time. |
| #1381<br>**Excess Of Wine**<br><br>Excess of wine–KJV<br>Drunkenness–NASB<br>Drunkenness–NIV<br>Drunkenness–NKJV<br>Drunkenness–NLT<br><br>**POSB REFERENCE**<br>(1 Pt.4:3)<br>Note 3, point 3 | **οἰνοφλυγίαις** = *oinophlugiais*<br>Pronunciation: [oy-nof-loog-ee'-ah-ees]<br>Parsing (part of speech): noun<br>    Case—dative<br>    Gender—feminine<br>    Number—plural<br>    Stem or root—from οἰνοφλυγία, ας<br>Concordance References:<br>  ⇒ Strong's #3632 oinophlugia<br>  ⇒ NIV #3886 oinophlugia<br>  ⇒ NASB #3632 oinophlugia<br><br>**1 Peter 4:3**<br>For the time past of our life may suffice us to have wrought the will of the Gentiles, when we walked in lasciviousness, lusts, **excess of wine**, revellings, banquetings, and abominable idolatries: [KJV]<br>For the time already past is sufficient for you to have carried out the desire of the Gentiles, having pursued a course of sensuality, lusts, **drunkenness**, carousals, drinking parties and abominable idolatries. [NASB]<br>For you have spent enough time in the past doing what pagans choose to do—living in debauchery, lust, **drunkenness**, orgies, carousing and detestable idolatry. [NIV]<br>For we *have spent* enough of our past lifetime in doing the will of the Gentiles—when we walked in lewdness, lusts, **drunkenness**, revelries, drinking parties, and abominable idolatries. [NKJV]<br>You have had enough in the past of the evil things that godless people enjoy—their immorality and lust, their feasting and **drunkenness** and wild parties, and their terrible worship of idols. [NLT]<br>ἀρκετὸς γὰρ ἡμῖν ὁ παρεληλυθὼς χρόνος τὸ βίου τὸ θέλημα τῶν ἐθνῶν κατεργάσασθαι, πεπορευμένους ἐν ἀσελγείαις, ἐπιθυμίαις, **οἰνοφλυγίαις**, κώμοις, πότοις, καὶ ἀθεμίτοις εἰδωλολατρείαις· [GNS]<br>ἀρκετὸς γὰρ ὁ παρεληλυθὼς χρόνος τὸ βούλημα τῶν ἐθνῶν κατειργάσθαι πεπορευμένους ἐν ἀσελγείαις, ἐπιθυμίαις, **οἰνοφλυγίαις**, κώμοις, πότοις καὶ ἀθεμίτοις εἰδωλολατρίαις. [GNT] | Drunkenness, excess, overindulgence, insobriety, debauchery, intemperance; excess of wine, winebibbing.<br><br>**Practical Application**<br>It would include taking drink or drugs to affect one's senses for lust or pleasure; becoming tipsy or intoxicated; partaking of drugs; seeking to loosen moral restraint for bodily pleasure. |
| #1382<br>**Exercise**<br><br>Exercise–KJV<br>Best–NASB<br>Strive–NIV<br>Strive–NKJV<br>Try–NLT<br><br>**POSB REFERENCE**<br>(Acts 24:14-16; esp. v.16)<br>Note 3, point 4a | **ἀσκῶ** = *askō*<br>Pronunciation: [as-ko']<br>Parsing (part of speech): verb<br>    Mood—indicative<br>    Tense—present<br>    Voice—active<br>    Person—1st person<br>    Number—singular<br>    Stem or root—from ἀσκέω<br>Concordance References:<br>  ⇒ Strong's #778 askeō<br>  ⇒ NIV #828 askeō<br>  ⇒ NASB #778 askeō<br><br>**Acts 24:16**<br>And herein do I **exercise** myself, to have always a conscience void of offence toward God, and toward men. [KJV]<br>"In view of this, I also do my **best** to maintain always | To strive; to exercise; to try; to endeavor; to give one's best.<br><br>**Practical Application**<br>Paul exercised himself—actively trained, disciplined, practiced, labored, strove, struggled, even to the point of pain—to keep a pure conscience. |

# PRACTICAL WORD STUDIES
## in the NEW TESTAMENT

| ENGLISH WORD | GREEK WORD AND VERSE | THE WORD MEANS... |
|---|---|---|
| | a blameless conscience both before God and before men. [NASB]<br><br>So I **strive** always to keep my conscience clear before God and man. [NIV]<br><br>This *being* so, I myself always **strive** to have a conscience without offense toward God and men. [NKJV]<br><br>Because of this, I always **try** to maintain a clear conscience before God and everyone else. [NLT]<br><br>ἐν τούτῳ δὲ αὐτὸς **ἀσκῶ**, ἀπρόσκοπον συνείδησιν ἔχειν πρὸς τὸν Θεὸν καὶ τοὺς ἀνθρώπους διὰ παντός. [GNS]<br><br>ἐν τούτῳ καὶ αὐτὸς **ἀσκῶ** ἀπρόσκοπον συνείδησιν ἔχειν πρὸς τὸν θεὸν καὶ τοὺς ἀνθρώπους διὰ παντός. [GNT] | |
| **#1383**<br>**Exercise**<br><br>**Exercise–KJV**<br>Discipline–NASB<br>Training–NIV<br>**Exercise–NKJV**<br>**Exercise–NLT**<br><br>**POSB REFERENCE**<br>(1 Tim.4:8)<br>Note 4, point 1 | γυμνασία = *gumnasia*<br>Pronunciation: [goom-nas-ee'-ah]<br>Parsing (part of speech): noun<br>    Case—nominative<br>    Gender—feminine<br>    Number—singular<br>    Stem or root—from γυμνασία, ας<br>Concordance References:<br>  ⇒ Strong's #1129 gumnasia<br>  ⇒ NIV #1215 gumnasia<br>  ⇒ NASB #1129 gumnasia<br><br>**1 Tim. 4:8**<br>For bodily **exercise** profiteth little: but godliness is profitable unto all things, having promise of the life that now is, and of that which is to come. [KJV]<br><br>For bodily **discipline** is only of little profit, but godliness is profitable for all things, since it holds promise for the present life and also for the life to come. [NASB]<br><br>For physical **training** is of some value, but godliness has value for all things, holding promise for both the present life and the life to come. [NIV]<br><br>For bodily **exercise** profits a little, but godliness is profitable for all things, having promise of the life that now is and of that which is to come. [NKJV]<br><br>Physical **exercise** has some value, but spiritual exercise is much more important, for it promises a reward in both this life and the next. [NLT]<br><br>ἡ γὰρ σωματικὴ **γυμνασία** πρὸς ὀλίγον ἐστὶν ὠφέλιμος· ἡ δὲ εὐσέβεια πρὸς πάντα ὠφέλιμός ἐστιν, ἐπαγγελίαν ἔχουσα ζωῆς τῆς νῦν καὶ τῆς μελλούσης. [GNS]<br><br>ἡ γὰρ σωματικὴ **γυμνασία** πρὸς ὀλίγον ἐστὶν ὠφέλιμος, ἡ δὲ εὐσέβεια πρὸς πάντα ὠφέλιμός ἐστιν ἐπαγγελίαν ἔχουσα ζωῆς τῆς νῦν καὶ τῆς μελλούσης. [GNT] | Training, exercise, discipline.<br><br>**Practical Application**<br>The minister is to exercise (*gumnasia*) himself in godliness as much as an Olympic athlete exercises his body. How much energy, effort, time, and dedication does an Olympic athlete put into his training? His sport is his life—unequivocally so. So it is with the minister: godliness is to be his life. All of his energy, effort, time, and dedication are to be given over to godliness. The minister is to know *no exercise* but the exercise of godliness. |
| **#1384**<br>**Exercise Self-Control**<br><br>Sober–KJV<br>Temperate–NASB<br>Temperate–NIV<br>Sober–NKJV<br>**Exercise self-control–NLT**<br><br>**POSB REFERENCE**<br>(Tit.2:2)<br>Note 2, point 1 | νηφαλίους = *nēphalious*<br>Pronunciation: [nay-fal'-ee'-oos]<br>Parsing (part of speech): adjective<br>    Case—accusative<br>    Gender—masculine<br>    Number—plural<br>    Stem or root—from νηφάλιος, α, ον<br>Concordance References:<br>  ⇒ Strong's #3524 nēphalios<br>  ⇒ NIV #3767 nēphalios<br>  ⇒ NASB #3524 nēphalios<br><br>**Titus 2:2**<br>That the aged men be **sober**, grave, temperate, sound in faith, in charity, in patience. [KJV]<br><br>Older men are to be **temperate**, dignified, sensible, sound in faith, in love, in perseverance. [NASB]<br><br>Teach the older men to be **temperate**, worthy of respect, self-controlled, and sound in faith, in love and in endurance. [NIV]<br><br>That the older men be **sober**, reverent, temperate, sound in faith, in love, in patience; [NKJV] | To be temperate; to be sober; to exercise self-control; to be moderate.<br><br>**Practical Application**<br>It is the opposite of over indulgence in anything such as eating, drinking, recreation, or whatever. |

## PRACTICAL WORD STUDIES
## in the NEW TESTAMENT

| ENGLISH WORD | GREEK WORD AND VERSE | THE WORD MEANS... |
|---|---|---|
| | Teach the older men to **exercise self-control**, to be worthy of respect, and to live wisely. They must have strong faith and be filled with love and patience. [NLT]<br>πρεσβύτας **νηφαλίους** εἶναι, σεμνούς, σώφρονας, ὑγιαίνοντας τῇ πίστει, τῇ ἀγάπῃ, τῇ ὑπομονῇ· [GNS]<br>πρεσβύτας **νηφαλίους** εἶναι, σεμνούς, σώφρονας, ὑγιαίνοντας τῇ πίστει, τῇ ἀγάπῃ, τῇ ὑπομονῇ· [GNT] | |
| **#1385**<br>**Exhibit Self Control**<br><br>Vigilant–KJV<br>Temperate–NASB<br>Temperate–NIV<br>Temperate–NKJV<br>**Exhibit self control–NLT**<br><br>**POSB REFERENCE**<br>(1 Tim.3:2-3; esp. v.2)<br>Note 2 | **νηφάλιον** = nēphalion<br>Pronunciation: [nay-fal'-ee-on]<br>Parsing (part of speech): adjective<br>    Case—accusative<br>    Gender—masculine<br>    Number—singular<br>    Stem or root—from νηφάλιος, α, ον<br>Concordance References:<br>  ⇒ Strong's #3524 nēphalios<br>  ⇒ NIV #3767 nēphalios<br>  ⇒ NASB #3524 nēphalios<br><br>**1 Tim. 3:2**<br>A bishop then must be blameless, the husband of one wife, **vigilant**, sober, of good behaviour, given to hospitality, apt to teach; [KJV]<br>An overseer, then, must be above reproach, the husband of one wife, **temperate**, prudent, respectable, hospitable, able to teach, [NASB]<br>Now the overseer must be above reproach, the husband of but one wife, **temperate**, self-controlled, respectable, hospitable, able to teach, [NIV]<br>A bishop then must be blameless, the husband of one wife, **temperate**, sober-minded, of good behavior, hospitable, able to teach; [NKJV]<br>For an elder must be a man whose life cannot be spoken against. He must be faithful to his wife. He must **exhibit self-control**, live wisely, and have a good reputation. He must enjoy having guests in his home and must be able to teach. [NLT]<br>δεῖ οὖν τὸν ἐπίσκοπον ἀνεπίλημπτον εἶναι, μιᾶς γυναικὸς ἄνδρα, **νηφάλιον**, σώφρονα, κόσμιον, φιλόξενον, διδακτικόν· [GNS]<br>δεῖ οὖν τὸν ἐπίσκοπον ἀνεπίλημπτον εἶναι, μιᾶς γυναικὸς ἄνδρα, **νηφάλιον** σώφρονα κόσμιον φιλόξενον διδακτικόν, [GNT] | Temperate, vigilant, sober; to exhibit self control.<br><br>**Practical Application**<br>The minister or bishop must exhibit self control (*nēphalion*). He must be temperate, self-controlled, and watchful. He must be vigilant, watch over, and control his own life and the lives of his dear people. |
| **#1386**<br>**Exhibited**<br><br>Set forth–KJV<br>**Exhibited–NASB**<br>Put...on display–NIV<br>Displayed–NKJV<br>Put...on display–NLT<br><br>**POSB REFERENCE**<br>(1 Cor.4:9-10; esp. v.9)<br>Note 4 | ἀπέδειξεν = apedeixen<br>Pronunciation: [ap-ed'-eek-zehn]<br>Parsing (part of speech): verb<br>    Mood—indicative<br>    Tense—aorist<br>    Voice—active<br>    Person—3rd person<br>    Number—singular<br>    Stem or root—from ἀποδείκνυμι<br>Concordance References:<br>  ⇒ Strong's #584 apodeiknumi<br>  ⇒ NIV #617 apodeiknumi<br>  ⇒ NASB #584 apodeiknumi<br><br>**1 Cor. 4:9**<br>For I think that God hath **set forth** us the apostles last, as it were appointed to death: for we are made a spectacle unto the world, and to angels, and to men. [KJV]<br>For, I think, God has **exhibited** us apostles last of all, as men condemned to death; because we have become a spectacle to the world, both to angels and to men. [NASB]<br>For it seems to me that God has **put** us apostles **on display** at the end of the procession, like men condemned to die in the arena. We have been made a spectacle to the whole universe, to angels as well as to men. [NIV]<br>For I think that God has **displayed** us, the apostles, | To put on display; to set forth; to prove; to exhibit; to proclaim.<br><br>**Practical Application**<br>The word "exhibited" (*apedeixen*) means more than to be seen or exhibited. The picture is that of doomed gladiators being taken to the arena. God has put on display the minister as a doomed gladiator to serve the world no matter the cost. |

**PRACTICAL WORD STUDIES**
in the NEW TESTAMENT

| ENGLISH WORD | GREEK WORD AND VERSE | THE WORD MEANS... |
|---|---|---|
| | last, as men condemned to death; for we have been made a spectacle to the world, both to angels and to men. [NKJV]<br>But sometimes I think God has **put** us apostles **on display**, like prisoners of war at the end of a victor's parade, condemned to die. We have become a spectacle to the entire world—to people and angels alike. [NLT]<br>δοκῶ γάρ, ὅτι ὁ Θεὸς ἡμᾶς τοὺς ἀποστόλους ἐσχάτους **ἀπέδειξεν** ὡς ἐπιθανατίους· ὅτι θέατρον ἐγενήθημεν τῷ κόσμῳ, καὶ ἀγγέλοις καὶ ἀνθρώποις. [GNS]<br>δοκῶ γάρ, ὁ θεὸς ἡμᾶς τοὺς ἀποστόλους ἐσχάτους **ἀπέδειξεν** ὡς ἐπιθανατίους, ὅτι θέατρον ἐγενήθημεν τῷ κόσμῳ καὶ ἀγγέλοις καὶ ἀνθρώποις. [GNT] | |
| **#1387**<br>**Exhort**<br><br>Beseech–KJV<br>**Exhort–NASB**<br>Appeal–NIV<br>Plead–NKJV<br>Appeal–NLT<br><br>**POSB REFERENCE**<br>(1 Cor.1:10)<br>Note 1<br><br>See also POSB REF:<br>(1 Tim.5:1-2; esp. v.1)<br>Introduction | Παρακαλῶ = Parakalō<br>Pronunciation: [par-ak-al-o']<br>Parsing (part of speech): verb<br>  Mood—indicative<br>  Tense—present<br>  Voice—active<br>  Person—1st person<br>  Number—singular<br>  Stem or root—from παρακαλέω<br>Concordance References:<br>  ⇒ Strong's #3870 parakaleō<br>  ⇒ NIV #4151 parakaleō<br>  ⇒ NASB #3870 parakaleō<br><br>**1 Cor. 1:10**<br>Now I **beseech** you, brethren, by the name of our Lord Jesus Christ, that ye all speak the same thing, and that there be no divisions among you; but that ye be perfectly joined together in the same mind and in the same judgment. [KJV]<br>Now I **exhort** you, brethren, by the name of our Lord Jesus Christ, that you all agree, and there be no divisions among you, but you be made complete in the same mind and in the same judgment. [NASB]<br>I **appeal** to you, brothers, in the name of our Lord Jesus Christ, that all of you agree with one another so that there may be no divisions among you and that you may be perfectly united in mind and thought. [NIV]<br>Now I **plead** with you, brethren, by the name of our Lord Jesus Christ, that you all speak the same thing, and that there be no divisions among you, but that you be perfectly joined together in the same mind and in the same judgment. [NKJV]<br>Now, dear brothers and sisters, **I appeal** to you by the authority of the Lord Jesus Christ to stop arguing among yourselves. Let there be real harmony so there won't be divisions in the church. I plead with you to be of one mind, united in thought and purpose. [NLT]<br>**Παρακαλῶ** δὲ ὑμᾶς, ἀδελφοί, διὰ τοῦ ὀνόματος τοῦ Κυρίου ἡμῶν Ἰησοῦ Χριστοῦ, ἵνα τὸ αὐτὸ λέγητε πάντες, καὶ μὴ ᾖ ἐν ὑμῖν σχίσματα, ἦτε δὲ κατηρτισμένοι ἐν τῷ αὐτῷ νοΐ καὶ ἐν τῇ αὐτῇ γνώμῃ. [GNS]<br>**Παρακαλῶ** δὲ ὑμᾶς, ἀδελφοί, διὰ τοῦ ὀνόματος τοῦ κυρίου ἡμῶν Ἰησοῦ Χριστοῦ, ἵνα τὸ αὐτὸ λέγητε πάντες καὶ μὴ ᾖ ἐν ὑμῖν σχίσματα, ἦτε δὲ κατηρτισμένοι ἐν τῷ αὐτῷ νοΐ καὶ ἐν τῇ αὐτῇ γνώμῃ. [GNT] | To appeal; to ask; to exhort; to encourage; to beseech; to beg; to urge; to request; to summon; to call to one's side.<br><br>**Practical Application**<br>Paul says, "I call you to my side; come, let's share together, talk the matter over. I ask, plead, beg—hear what I have to say." |
| **#1388**<br>**Exhort**<br><br>Exhort–KJV<br>**Exhort–NASB**<br>Encourage–NIV<br>**Exhort–NKJV**<br>Encourage–NLT | παρακάλεσον = parakaleson<br>Pronunciation: [par-ak-al-eh'-son]<br>Parsing (part of speech): verb<br>  Mood—imperative<br>  Tense—aorist<br>  Voice—active<br>  Person—2nd person<br>  Number—singular<br>  Stem or root—from παρακαλέω<br>Concordance References:<br>  ⇒ Strong's #3870 parakaleō | To encourage; to exhort; to console. It means to beseech, encourage, comfort, and help. The word "exhort" (*parakaleson*) has the idea of "please, I beg of you, I urge you" (Kenneth Wuest. *The Pastoral Epistles*, Vol.2, p.155).<br><br>**Practical Application**<br>It is not enough to reprove and rebuke people. The minister must encourage and comfort, help and carry the person to Christ. Note how crucial |

# PRACTICAL WORD STUDIES
## in the NEW TESTAMENT

| ENGLISH WORD | GREEK WORD AND VERSE | THE WORD MEANS... |
|---|---|---|
| **POSB REFERENCE** (2 Tim. 4:2) Note 2, point 5  See also POSB REF: (1 Tim.2:1) Note 1 | ⇒ NIV #4151 parakaleö<br>⇒ NASB #3870 parakaleö<br><br>**2 Tim. 4:2**<br>Preach the word; be instant in season, out of season; reprove, rebuke, **exhort** with all longsuffering and doctrine. [KJV]<br>Preach the word; be ready in season and out of season; reprove, rebuke, **exhort**, with great patience and instruction. [NASB]<br>Preach the Word; be prepared in season and out of season; correct, rebuke and **encourage**—with great patience and careful instruction. [NIV]<br>Preach the word! Be ready in season *and* out of season. Convince, rebuke, **exhort**, with all longsuffering and teaching. [NKJV]<br>Preach the word of God. Be persistent, whether the time is favorable or not. Patiently correct, rebuke, and **encourage** your people with good teaching. [NLT]<br>κήρυξον τὸν λόγον, ἐπίστηθι εὐκαίρως, ἀκαίρως, ἔλεγξον, ἐπιτίμησον, **παρακάλεσον**, ἐν πάσῃ μακροθυμίᾳ καὶ διδαχῇ. [GNS]<br>κήρυξον τὸν λόγον, ἐπίστηθι εὐκαίρως ἀκαίρως, ἔλεγξον, ἐπιτίμησον, **παρακάλεσον**, ἐν πάσῃ μακροθυμίᾳ καὶ διδαχῇ. [GNT] | this point is.<br>1. The minister must "exhort with all longsuffering" (*makrothumia*). The idea is that the minister patiently endures in exhorting people—no matter the circumstances. He exhorts and exhorts, encourages and encourages. He suffers a long, long time with people...<br>• enduring whatever weaknesses and failings they have.<br>• enduring whatever evil and injury is done.<br><br>The minister suffers a long, long time without resentment or anger, and he never gives up for he knows the power of Christ to change lives.<br>2. The minister "exhorts with all doctrine." He does not teach bits and pieces of God's Word. He does not focus upon subjects...<br>• that are popular.<br>• that are favorites.<br>• that arouse curiosity.<br>• that he thinks are needed.<br><br>He focuses upon all the doctrines of God—the whole counsel of God. He exhorts people in all the doctrines of God. |
| **#1389 Exhort**<br><br>Exhort–KJV<br>Encourage–NASB<br>Encourage–NIV<br>Exhort–NKJV<br>Warn–NLT<br><br>**POSB REFERENCE** (Heb.3:13-19; esp. v.13) Note 3<br><br>See also POSB REF: (Lk.3:18) Note 7 | παρακαλεῖτε = *parakaleite*<br>Pronunciation: [par-ak-al-eh'-ee-teh]<br>Parsing (part of speech): verb<br>  Mood—imperative<br>  Tense—present<br>  Voice—active<br>  Person—2nd person<br>  Number—plural<br>  Stem or root—from παρακαλέω<br>Concordance References:<br>⇒ Strong's #3870 parakaleö<br>⇒ NIV #4151 parakaleö<br>⇒ NASB #3870 parakaleö<br><br>**Hebrews 3:13**<br>But **exhort** one another daily, while it is called To day; lest any of you be hardened through the deceitfulness of sin. [KJV]<br>But **encourage** one another day after day, as long as it is still called "Today," lest any one of you be hardened by the deceitfulness of sin. [NASB]<br>But **encourage** one another daily, as long as it is called Today, so that none of you may be hardened by sin's deceitfulness. [NIV]<br>But **exhort** one another daily, while it is called *"Today,"* lest any of you be hardened through the deceitfulness of sin. [NKJV]<br>You must **warn** each other every day, as long as it is called "today," so that none of you will be deceived by sin and hardened against God. [NLT]<br>ἀλλὰ **παρακαλεῖτε** ἑαυτοὺς καθ᾽ ἑκάστην ἡμέραν, ἄχρις οὗ τὸ Σήμερον καλεῖται, ἵνα μὴ σκληρυνθῇ τις ἐξ ὑμῶν ἀπάτῃ τῆς ἁμαρτίας· [GNS]<br>ἀλλὰ **παρακαλεῖτε** ἑαυτοὺς καθ᾽ ἑκάστην ἡμέραν, ἄχρις οὗ τὸ Σήμερον καλεῖται, ἵνα μὴ σκληρυνθῇ τις ἐξ ὑμῶν ἀπάτῃ τῆς ἁμαρτίας· [GNT] | To encourage; to exhort; to warn; to plead with; to console. The word "exhort" (*parakaleite*) means to "beg, entreat, beseech, exhort" (Kenneth Wuest. *Hebrews*, Vol. 2, p.79).<br><br>**Practical Application**<br>It is from the same word that the Comforter or Paraclete (the Holy Spirit) is taken. This means that the word "exhort" also includes comfort, the kind of comfort that will "strengthen and encourage the believer each single day so that when a crises arises he may be able to stand fast" (Thomas Hewitt. *The Epistle to the Hebrews*. "Tyndale New Testament Commentaries." Grand Rapids, MI: Eerdmans, 1960, p.83). Believers are to constantly exhort one another to guard themselves against unbelief and sin. |
| **#1390 Exhortation**<br><br>Exhortation–KJV<br>Exhortation–NASB<br>Encourage–NIV<br>Exhortation–NKJV<br>Encourage–NLT | παρακλήσει = *paraklēsei*<br>Pronunciation: [par-ak'-lay-see]<br>Parsing (part of speech): noun<br>  Case—dative<br>  Gender—feminine<br>  Number—singular<br>  Stem or root—from παράκλησις, εως | Encouragement, help, comfort, consolation, appeal, request.<br><br>**Practical Application**<br>There is the gift of exhortation (*paraklēsei*). This is the very special ability to excite, motivate, advise, encourage, comfort, and warn peo- |

# PRACTICAL WORD STUDIES
## in the NEW TESTAMENT

| ENGLISH WORD | GREEK WORD AND VERSE | THE WORD MEANS... |
|---|---|---|
| **POSB REFERENCE** (Romans 12:6-8, esp. v.8) Note 2<br><br>See also POSB REF: (1 Cor.14:3) *Deeper Study #1*, point 2 | Concordance References:<br>⇒ Strong's #3874 paraklēsis<br>⇒ NIV #4155 paraklēsis<br>⇒ NASB #3874 paraklēsis<br><br>**Romans 12:8**<br>Or he that exhorteth, on **exhortation**: he that giveth, let him do it with simplicity; he that ruleth, with diligence; he that sheweth mercy, with cheerfulness. [KJV]<br>Or he who exhorts, in his **exhortation**; he who gives, with liberality; he who leads, with diligence; he who shows mercy, with cheerfulness. [NASB]<br>If it is encouraging, let him **encourage**; if it is contributing to the needs of others, let him give generously; if it is leadership, let him govern diligently; if it is showing mercy, let him do it cheerfully. [NIV]<br>He who exhorts, in **exhortation**; he who gives, with liberality; he who leads, with diligence; he who shows mercy, with cheerfulness. [NKJV]<br>If your gift is to **encourage** others, do it! If you have money, share it generously. If God has given you leadership ability, take the responsibility seriously. And if you have a gift for showing kindness to others, do it gladly. [NLT]<br>εἴτε ὁ παρακαλῶν, ἐν τῇ **παρακλήσει**· ὁ μεταδιδοὺς ἐν ἁπλότητι, ὁ προϊστάμενος, ἐν σπουδῇ· ὁ ἐλεῶν ἐν ἱλαρότητι. [GNS]<br>εἴτε ὁ παρακαλῶν ἐν τῇ **παρακλήσει**· ὁ μεταδιδοὺς ἐν ἁπλότητι, ὁ προϊστάμενος ἐν σπουδῇ, ὁ ἐλεῶν ἐν ἱλαρότητι. [GNT] | ple. The dominant factor would be the motivation and encouragement of people, the ability to stir people to make a decision for Christ and to grow in Him. It is the gift that arouses people to get up and get busy fulfilling their task for the Lord. |
| **#1391**<br>**Exhorted**<br><br>Exhorted–KJV<br>Encourage–NASB<br>Encouraged–NIV<br>Encouraged–NKJV<br>Encouraged–NLT<br><br>**POSB REFERENCE** (Acts 11:19-30; esp. v.23) *Deeper Study #2*, point 3 | παρεκάλει = *parekalei*<br>Pronunciation: [par-ek-al-eh-ee]<br>Parsing (part of speech): verb<br>    Mood—indicative<br>    Tense—imperfect<br>    Voice—active<br>    Person—3rd person<br>    Number—singular<br>    Stem or root—from παρακαλέω<br>Concordance References:<br>⇒ Strong's #3870 parakaleō<br>⇒ NIV #4151 parakaleō<br>⇒ NASB #3870 parakaleō<br><br>**Acts 11:23**<br>Who, when he came, and had seen the grace of God, was glad, and **exhorted** them all, that with purpose of heart they would cleave unto the Lord. [KJV]<br>Then when he had come and witnessed the grace of God, he rejoiced and began to **encourage** them all with resolute heart to remain true to the Lord; [NASB]<br>When he arrived and saw the evidence of the grace of God, he was glad and **encouraged** them all to remain true to the Lord with all their hearts. [NIV]<br>When he came and had seen the grace of God, he was glad, and **encouraged** them all that with purpose of heart they should continue with the Lord. [NKJV]<br>When he arrived and saw this proof of God's favor, he was filled with joy, and he **encouraged** the believers to stay true to the Lord. [NLT]<br>ὃς παραγενόμενος καὶ ἰδὼν τὴν χάριν τοῦ Θεοῦ, ἐχάρη, καὶ **παρεκάλει** πάντας τῇ προθέσει τῆς καρδίας προσμένειν τῷ κυρίῳ, [GNS]<br>ὃς παραγενόμενος καὶ ἰδὼν τὴν χάριν [τὴν] τοῦ θεοῦ, ἐχάρη καὶ **παρεκάλει** πάντας τῇ προθέσει τῆς καρδίας προσμένειν τῷ κυρίῳ, [GNT] | To encourage; to exhort; to console; to appease; to plead with. This word means to admonish, advise, challenge, entreat, call upon, beseech, urge, warn, comfort, and encourage.<br><br>**Practical Application**<br>The message was...<br>• "with purpose of heart" [KJV]: a determined, set, focused, purpose, steady, purposed heart.<br>• to "cleave unto the Lord" [KJV]: to continue; to be constant, loyal, steadfast, persistent, persevering, faithful. |
| **#1392**<br>**Existed** | ὑπάρχων = *huparchōn*<br>Pronunciation: [hoop-ar'-khown]<br>Parsing (part of speech): verb<br>    Mood—participle | Being, existed, was. The word "existed" (*huparchōn*) means existence, what a person is within and without. |

# PRACTICAL WORD STUDIES
## in the NEW TESTAMENT

| ENGLISH WORD | GREEK WORD AND VERSE | THE WORD MEANS... |
|---|---|---|
| Being–KJV<br>**Existed–NASB**<br>Being–NIV<br>Being–NKJV<br>Was–NLT<br><br>**POSB<br>REFERENCE**<br>(Philip.2:6)<br>Note 2, point 1 | Tense—present<br>Voice—active<br>Case—nominative<br>Gender—masculine<br>Number—singular<br>Stem or root—from ὑπάρχω<br>Concordance References:<br>⇒ Strong's #5225 huparchō<br>⇒ NIV #5639 huparchō<br>⇒ NASB #5225 huparchō<br><br>**Philip. 2:6**<br>Who, **being** in the form of God, thought it not robbery to be equal with God: [KJV]<br>Who, although He **existed** in the form of God, did not regard equality with God a thing to be grasped, [NASB]<br>Who, **being** in very nature God, did not consider equality with God something to be grasped, [NIV]<br>Who, **being** in the form of God, did not consider it robbery to be equal with God, [NKJV]<br>Though he **was** God, he did not demand and cling to his rights as God. [NLT]<br>ὃς ἐν μορφῇ θεοῦ **ὑπάρχων**, οὐχ ἁρπαγμὸν ἡγήσατο τὸ εἶναι ἴσα θεῷ, [GNS]<br>ὃς ἐν μορφῇ θεοῦ **ὑπάρχων** οὐχ ἁρπαγμὸν ἡγήσατο τὸ εἶναι ἴσα θεῷ, [GNT] | **Practical Application**<br>It is the very essence of a person, what a person is; that part of a person that cannot be changed. It is who a person is and all that he is.<br>This is a most glorious truth because it means that *Jesus Christ is God*; He is the very *being of God*. |
| #1393<br>**Existed Before<br>Me, Long<br>Before I Did**<br><br>Was before me–KJV<br>**Existed before me–<br>NASB**<br>Was before me–NIV<br>Was before me–NKJV<br>**Existed long before I<br>did–NLT**<br><br>**POSB<br>REFERENCE**<br>(Jn.1:15)<br>Note 3 | ὅτι πρῶτός μου = *hoti prōtos mou*<br>Pronunciation: [ho-tee pro-tos moo]<br>Parsing *hoti* (part of speech): conjunction<br>  Type—subordinating<br>  Stem or root—from ὅτι<br>Parsing *prōtos* (part of speech): adjective<br>  Type—ordinal<br>  Case—nominative<br>  Gender—masculine<br>  Number—singular<br>  Stem or root—from πρῶτος, η, ον<br>Parsing *mou* (part of speech): noun<br>  Type—pronoun<br>  Case—genitive<br>  Person—1st person<br>  Number—singular<br>  Stem or root—from ἐγώ<br>Concordance References:<br>⇒ Strong's #3754 hoti +4413 protos + 1473 ego<br>⇒ NIV #4022 hoti [was] + 4755 prōtos [before] + 1609 egō [me]<br>⇒ NASB #3754 hoti +4413 protos + 1473 ego<br><br>**John 1:15**<br>John bare witness of him, and cried, saying, This was he of whom I spake, He that cometh after me is preferred before me: for he **was before me**. [KJV]<br>John bore witness of Him, and cried out, saying, "This was He of whom I said, 'He who comes after me has a higher rank than I, for He **existed before me**.'" [NASB]<br>John testifies concerning him. He cries out, saying, "This was he of whom I said, 'He who comes after me has surpassed me because he **was before me**.'" [NIV]<br>John bore witness of Him and cried out, saying, "This was He of whom I said, 'He who comes after me is preferred before me,' for He **was before me**.'" [NKJV]<br>John pointed him out to the people. He shouted to the crowds, "This is the one I was talking about when I said, 'Someone is coming who is far greater than I am, for he **existed long before I did**.'" [NLT]<br>Ἰωάννης μαρτυρεῖ περὶ αὐτοῦ καὶ κέκραγε λέγων, Οὗτος ἦν ὃν εἶπον, Ὁ ὀπίσω μου ἐρχόμενος ἔμπροσθέν μου γέγονεν· **ὅτι πρῶτός μου** ἦν. [GNS]<br>Ἰωάννης μαρτυρεῖ περὶ αὐτοῦ καὶ κέκραγεν λέγων, Οὗτος ἦν ὃν εἶπον, Ὁ ὀπίσω μου ἐρχόμενος ἔμπροσθέν μου γέγονεν, **ὅτι πρῶτός μου** ἦν. [GNT] | Was before me; existed before me; existed long before I did; literally first to me or first of me.<br><br>**Practical Application**<br>It refers both to time and importance. Jesus Christ was first in time, existing before John. He existed "in the beginning"—throughout all eternity. John proclaimed, "He was before me": He always existed; He was the First; He was the very cause for John's existence. John also declared that Jesus was first in importance. He was first in superiority, Being, Person. His very name is the First and the Last, the Alpha and the Omega, the Beginning and the End. |

# PRACTICAL WORD STUDIES
## in the NEW TESTAMENT

| ENGLISH WORD | GREEK WORD AND VERSE | THE WORD MEANS... |
|---|---|---|
| **#1394**<br>**Expedient**<br><br>**Expedient–KJV**<br>Profitable–NASB<br>Beneficial–NIV<br>Helpful–NKJV<br>Good for you–NLT<br><br>**POSB REFERENCE**<br>(1 Cor.6:12)<br>Note 1, point 1 | συμφέρει = sumpherei<br>Pronunciation: [soom-fer'-eh-ee]<br>Parsing (part of speech): verb<br>    Mood—indicative<br>    Tense—present<br>    Voice—active<br>    Person—3rd person<br>    Number—singular<br>    Stem or root—from συμφέρω<br>Concordance References:<br>⇒ Strong's #4851 sumpherö<br>⇒ NIV #5237 sumpherö<br>⇒ NASB #4851 sumpherö<br><br>**1 Cor. 6:12**<br>All things are lawful unto me, but all things are not **expedient**: all things are lawful for me, but I will not be brought under the power of any. [KJV]<br>All things are lawful for me, but not all things are **profitable**. All things are lawful for me, but I will not be mastered by anything. [NASB]<br>"Everything is permissible for me"—but not everything is **beneficial**. "Everything is permissible for me"—but I will not be mastered by anything. [NIV]<br>All things are lawful for me, but all things are not **helpful**. All things are lawful for me, but I will not be brought under the power of any. [NKJV]<br>You may say, "I am allowed to do anything." But I reply, "Not everything is **good for you**." And even though "I am allowed to do anything," I must not become a slave to anything. [NLT]<br>Πάντα μοι ἔξεστιν, ἀλλ' οὐ πάντα **συμφέρει**· πάντα μοι ἔξεστιν, ἀλλ' οὐκ ἐγὼ ἐξουσιασθήσομαι ὑπό τινος. [GNS]<br>Πάντα μοι ἔξεστιν ἀλλ' οὐ πάντα **συμφέρει**. πάντα μοι ἔξεστιν ἀλλ' οὐκ ἐγὼ ἐξουσιασθήσομαι ὑπό τινος. [GNT] | Beneficial, expedient, useful, helpful, worthwhile, advisable, profitable, good for you.<br><br>**Practical Application**<br>For example, it is beneficial to eat fish; it is unprofitable to eat poisonous berries. It is advisable to keep active for the sake of the body; it is harmful to lie around and become inactive. Note that doing some activities is lawful, but others are not good and profitable. |
| **#1395**<br>**Experience**<br><br>**Experience–KJV**<br>Proven character–NASB<br>Character–NIV<br>Character–NKJV<br>Strength of character–NLT<br><br>**POSB REFERENCE**<br>(Romans 5:3-5; esp. v.4)<br>Note 5, point 2 | δοκιμήν = dokimën<br>Pronunciation: [dok-ee-mayn']<br>Parsing (part of speech): noun<br>    Case—accusative<br>    Gender—feminine<br>    Number—singular<br>    Stem or root—from δοκιμή, ῆς<br>Concordance References:<br>⇒ Strong's #1382 dokimë<br>⇒ NIV #1509 dokimë<br>⇒ NASB #1382 dokimë<br><br>**Romans 5:4**<br>And patience, **experience**; and experience, hope: [KJV]<br>And perseverance, **proven character**; and proven character, hope; [NASB]<br>Perseverance, **character**; and character, hope. [NIV]<br>And perseverance, **character**; and character, hope. [NKJV]<br>And endurance develops **strength of character** in us, and character strengthens our confident expectation of salvation. [NLT]<br>ἡ δὲ ὑπομονὴ **δοκιμήν**, ἡ δὲ δοκιμὴ ἐλπίδα· [GNS]<br>ἡ δὲ ὑπομονὴ **δοκιμήν**, ἡ δὲ δοκιμὴ ἐλπί. [GNT] | Character, experience, proven character, strength of character, integrity, strength. The idea is that of proven experience, of gaining strength through the trials of life; therefore, the word is more accurately translated "character."<br><br>**Practical Application**<br>When a justified man endures trials, he comes out of it stronger than ever before. He is a man of much stronger character and integrity. He knows much more about the presence and strength of God. |
| **#1396**<br>**Experienced**<br><br>Tasted–KJV<br>Tasted–NASB<br>Tasted–NIV<br>Tasted–NKJV<br>**Experienced–NLT** | γευσαμένους = geusamenous<br>Pronunciation: [ghyoo'-ahm-eh-noos]<br>Parsing (part of speech): verb<br>    Mood—participle<br>    Tense—aorist<br>    Voice—middle deponent<br>    Case—accusative<br>    Gender—masculine<br>    Number—plural<br>    Stem or root—from γεύομαι | To taste; to experience; to eat. The word "experienced" (*geusamenous*) means to partake of; to take in; to come to know. The Greek scholar Marvin Vincent says that it means to "have consciously partaken of" (*Word Studies in the New Testament*, Vol. 4, p.445).<br><br>**Practical Application**<br>The Greek Scripture definitely uses the aorist |

# Practical Word Studies in the New Testament

| ENGLISH WORD | GREEK WORD AND VERSE | THE WORD MEANS... |
|---|---|---|
| **POSB REFERENCE** (Heb.6:4-5, esp. v.4) Note 1 | Concordance References:<br>⇒ Strong's #1089 geuomai<br>⇒ NIV #1174 geuomai<br>⇒ NASB #1089 geuomai<br><br>**Hebrews 6:4**<br>For it is impossible for those who were once enlightened, and have **tasted** of the heavenly gift, and were made partakers of the Holy Ghost, [KJV]<br>For in the case of those who have once been enlightened and have **tasted** of the heavenly gift and have been made partakers of the Holy Spirit, [NASB]<br>It is impossible for those who have once been enlightened, who have **tasted** the heavenly gift, who have shared in the Holy Spirit, [NIV]<br>For *it is* impossible for those who were once enlightened, and have **tasted** the heavenly gift, and have become partakers of the Holy Spirit, [NKJV]<br>For it is impossible to restore to repentance those who were once enlightened—those who have **experienced** the good things of heaven and shared in the Holy Spirit, [NLT]<br>ἀδύνατον γὰρ τοὺς ἅπαξ φωτισθέντας, **γευσαμένους** τε τῆς δωρεᾶς τῆς ἐπουρανίου, καὶ μετόχους γενηθέντας Πνεύματος Ἁγίου, [GNS]<br>Ἀδύνατον γὰρ τοὺς ἅπαξ φωτισθέντας, **γευσαμένους** τε τῆς δωρεᾶς τῆς ἐπουρανίου καὶ μετόχους γενηθέντας πνεύματος ἁγίου [GNT] | tense which means that the person had a *once-for-all* experience, an experience that was once-for-all completed, fulfilled, and finished. How could this apply to anyone else other than a believer? Note how each of these read in the aorist tense: the person...<br>• *was once-for-all* enlightened.<br>• *had once-for-all* tasted of the heavenly gift.<br>• *was once-for-all* made a partaker of the Holy Spirit.<br>• *had once-for-all* tasted of the good Word of God.<br>• *had once-for-all* tasted of the power of the world to come.<br><br>The very same word is used of Christ when it said that He "tasted death" for us (Hebrews 2:9). And one thing is sure: Christ tasted, that is, *consciously experienced*, death for us. Therefore, this passage must mean that this person *fully tasted and fully experienced* salvation. As stated, it seems that we have to twist Scripture to make it say any less than a conscious and full experience. Note the glorious experiences and privileges these persons received in Christ. |
| **#1397 Expert Builder**<br><br>Masterbuilder–KJV<br>Master builder–NASB<br>**Expert builder–NIV**<br>Master builder–NKJV<br>**Expert builder–NLT**<br><br>**POSB REFERENCE** (1 Cor.3:10) Note 1 | ἀρχιτέκτων = architektōn<br>Pronunciation: [ar-khee-tek'-tone]<br>Parsing (part of speech): noun<br>    Case—nominative<br>    Gender—masculine<br>    Number—singular<br>    Stem or root—from ἀρχιτέκτων, ονος<br>Concordance References:<br>⇒ Strong's #753 architektōn<br>⇒ NIV #802 architektōn<br>⇒ NASB #753 architektōn<br><br>**1 Cor. 3:10**<br>According to the grace of God which is given unto me, as a wise **masterbuilder**, I have laid the foundation, and another buildeth thereon. But let every man take heed how he buildeth thereupon. [KJV]<br>According to the grace of God which was given to me, as a wise **master builder** I laid a foundation, and another is building upon it. But let each man be careful how he builds upon it. [NASB]<br>By the grace God has given me, I laid a foundation as an **expert builder**, and someone else is building on it. But each one should be careful how he builds. [NIV]<br>According to the grace of God which was given to me, as a wise **master builder** I have laid the foundation, and another builds on it. But let each one take heed how he builds on it. [NKJV]<br>Because of God's special favor to me, I have laid the foundation like an **expert builder**. Now others are building on it. But whoever is building on this foundation must be very careful. [NLT]<br>Κατὰ τὴν χάριν τοῦ Θεοῦ τὴν δοθεῖσάν μοι, ὡς σοφὸς **ἀρχιτέκτων** θεμέλιον τέθεικα, ἄλλος δὲ ἐποικοδομεῖ. ἕκαστος δὲ βλεπέτω πῶς ἐποικοδομεῖ. [GNS]<br>Κατὰ τὴν χάριν τοῦ θεοῦ τὴν δοθεῖσάν μοι ὡς σοφὸς **ἀρχιτέκτων** θεμέλιον ἔθηκα, ἄλλος δὲ ἐποικοδομεῖ. ἕκαστος δὲ βλεπέτω πῶς ἐποικοδομεῖ. [GNT] | Expert builder, master builder. It means the superintendent or architect of the building project.<br><br>**Practical Application**<br>Paul says that he was the one who planned the church at Corinth. He was the one who laid the foundation, who began and superintended the founding of the church. |
| **#1398 Expert In The Law– Expert In Religious Law** | νομικός = nomikos<br>Pronunciation: [nom-ik-os']<br>Parsing (part of speech): pronominal adjective<br>    Case—nominative<br>    Gender—masculine<br>    Number—singular<br>    Stem or root—from νομικός, ή, όν | An expert in the law, an expert in religious law, a lawyer, a profession of laymen who studied, taught, interpreted, and dealt with the practical questions of Jewish law. |

## PRACTICAL WORD STUDIES
### in the NEW TESTAMENT

| ENGLISH WORD | GREEK WORD AND VERSE | THE WORD MEANS... |
|---|---|---|
| Lawyer–KJV<br>Lawyer–NASB<br>**Expert in the law–NIV**<br>Lawyer–NKJV<br>**Expert in religious law–NLT**<br><br>**POSB REFERENCE**<br>(Mt.22:35)<br>*Deeper Study #1* | Concordance References:<br>⇒ Strong's #3544 nomikos<br>⇒ NIV #3788 nomikos<br>⇒ NASB #3544 nomikos<br><br>**Matthew 22:35**<br>Then one of them, which was a **lawyer**, asked him a question, tempting him, and saying, [KJV]<br>And one of them, a **lawyer**, asked Him a question, testing Him, [NASB]<br>One of them, an **expert in the law**, tested him with this question: [NIV]<br>Then one of them, a **lawyer**, asked Him a question, testing Him, and saying, [NKJV]<br>One of them, an **expert in religious law**, tried to trap him with this question: [NLT]<br>καὶ ἐπηρώτησεν εἷς ἐξ αὐτῶν **νομικὸς** πειράζων αὐτόν, [GNS]<br>καὶ ἐπηρώτησεν εἷς ἐξ αὐτῶν [**νομικὸς**] πειράζων αὐτόν, [GNT] | **Practical Application**<br>They were a special group within the profession commonly called Scribes (cp. Mark 12:28). They functioned both in the court and synagogues (cp. Luke 7:30; Luke 10:25; Luke 11:45, 46, 52; Luke 14:3; Titus 3:13). They apparently dealt with the study and interpretation of the law. |
| #1399<br>**Explain**<br><br>Put...in remembrance–KJV<br>Pointing out–NASB<br>Point...out–NIV<br>Instruct–NKJV<br>Explain–NLT<br><br>**POSB REFERENCE**<br>(1 Tim.4:6)<br>Note 1 | ὑποτιθέμενος = *hupotithemenos*<br>Pronunciation: [hoop-ot-ith'-eh-mehn-os]<br>Parsing (part of speech): verb<br>  Mood—participle<br>  Tense—present<br>  Voice—middle<br>  Case—nominative<br>  Gender—masculine<br>  Person—2nd person<br>  Number—singular<br>  Stem or root—from ὑποτίθημι<br>Concordance References:<br>⇒ Strong's #5294 hupotithēmi<br>⇒ NIV #5719 hupotithēmi<br>⇒ NASB #5294 hupotithēmi<br><br>**1 Tim. 4:6**<br>If thou **put** the brethren **in remembrance** of these things, thou shalt be a good minister of Jesus Christ, nourished up in the words of faith and of good doctrine, whereunto thou hast attained. [KJV]<br>In **pointing out** these things to the brethren, you will be a good servant of Christ Jesus, constantly nourished on the words of the faith and of the sound doctrine which you have been following. [NASB]<br>If you **point** these things **out** to the brothers, you will be a good minister of Christ Jesus, brought up in the truths of the faith and of the good teaching that you have followed. [NIV]<br>If you **instruct** the brethren in these things, you will be a good minister of Jesus Christ, nourished in the words of faith and of the good doctrine which you have carefully followed. [NKJV]<br>If you **explain** this to the brothers and sisters, you will be doing your duty as a worthy servant of Christ Jesus, one who is fed by the message of faith and the true teaching you have followed. [NLT]<br>Ταῦτα **ὑποτιθέμενος** τοῖς ἀδελφοῖς καλὸς ἔσῃ διάκονος Ἰησοῦ Χριστοῦ, ἐντρεφόμενος τοῖς λόγοις τῆς πίστεως, καὶ τῆς καλῆς διδασκαλίας ᾗ παρηκολούθηκας. [GNS]<br>Ταῦτα **ὑποτιθέμενος** τοῖς ἀδελφοῖς καλὸς ἔσῃ διάκονος Χριστοῦ Ἰησοῦ, ἐντρεφόμενος τοῖς λόγοις τῆς πίστεως καὶ τῆς καλῆς διδασκαλίας ᾗ παρηκολούθηκας· [GNT] | To point out; to put in remembrance; to explain; to teach. The Greek word "explain" (*hupotithemenos*) means to place under, suggest, counsel, advise.<br><br>**Practical Application**<br>The point is this: false teaching is such a threat to the church and believers that the good minister of Jesus Christ will use every method of communication he can to instruct and protect his flock from being seduced by false teachers. |
| #1400<br>**Explain**<br><br>Answer–KJV<br>Defense–NASB<br>Answer–NIV | ἀπολογίαν = *apologian*<br>Pronunciation: [ap-ol-og-ee'-ahn]<br>Parsing (part of speech): noun<br>  Case—accusative<br>  Gender—feminine<br>  Number—singular<br>  Stem or root—from ἀπολογία, ας | To answer; to reply; to defend; to explain. It means a decision, response, discovery, solution.<br><br>**Practical Application**<br>One answer to persecution is to readily defend the hope of salvation to every man and to |

# PRACTICAL WORD STUDIES
## in the New Testament

| ENGLISH WORD | GREEK WORD AND VERSE | THE WORD MEANS... |
|---|---|---|
| Defense–NKJV<br>Explain–NLT<br><br>**POSB REFERENCE**<br>(1 Pt.3:15)<br>Note 3 | Concordance References:<br>⇒ Strong's #627 apologia<br>⇒ NIV #665 apologia<br>⇒ NASB #627 apologia<br><br>**1 Peter 3:15**<br>But sanctify the Lord God in your hearts: and be ready always to give an **answer** to every man that asketh you a reason of the hope that is in you with meekness and fear: [KJV]<br>But sanctify Christ as Lord in your hearts, always being ready to make a **defense** to everyone who asks you to give an account for the hope that is in you, yet with gentleness and reverence; [NASB]<br>But in your hearts set apart Christ as Lord. Always be prepared to give an **answer** to everyone who asks you to give the reason for the hope that you have. But do this with gentleness and respect, [NIV]<br>But sanctify the Lord God in your hearts, and always be ready to give a **defense** to everyone who asks you a reason for the hope that is in you, with meekness and fear; [NKJV]<br>Instead, you must worship Christ as Lord of your life. And if you are asked about your Christian hope, always be ready to **explain** it. [NLT]<br>Κύριον δὲ τὸν Θεὸν ἁγιάσατε ἐν ταῖς καρδίαις ὑμῶν· ἕτοιμοι δὲ ἀεὶ πρὸς **ἀπολογίαν** παντὶ τῷ αἰτοῦντι ὑμᾶς λόγον περὶ τῆς ἐν ὑμῖν ἐλπίδος, [GNS]<br>ύριον δὲ τὸν Χριστὸν ἁγιάσατε ἐν ταῖς καρδίαις ὑμῶν, ἕτοιμοι ἀεὶ πρὸς **ἀπολογίαν** παντὶ τῷ αἰτοῦντι ὑμᾶς λόγον περὶ τῆς ἐν ὑμῖν ἐλπίδος , [GNT] | do so with gentleness and respect. The word "explain" (*apologian*) means just that, to explain, to answer back, or to give a defense of the believer's hope (A.T. Robertson. *Word Pictures in the New Testament*, Vol.6, p.114). |
| **#1401**<br>**Explicitly**<br><br>Expressly–KJV<br>**Explicitly–NASB**<br>Clearly–NIV<br>Expressly–NKJV<br>Clearly–NLT<br><br>**POSB REFERENCE**<br>(1 Tim.4:1)<br>Note 1 | ῥητῶς = *hrētōs*<br>Pronunciation: [hray-toce']<br>Parsing (part of speech): adjective adverb<br>Stem or root—from ῥητῶς<br>Concordance References:<br>⇒ Strong's #4490 hrētōs<br>⇒ NIV #4843 hrētōs<br>⇒ NASB #4490 hrētōs<br><br>**1 Tim. 4:1**<br>Now the Spirit speaketh **expressly**, that in the latter times some shall depart from the faith, giving heed to seducing spirits, and doctrines of devils; [KJV]<br>But the Spirit **explicitly** says that in later times some will fall away from the faith, paying attention to deceitful spirits and doctrines of demons, [NASB]<br>The Spirit **clearly** says that in later times some will abandon the faith and follow deceiving spirits and things taught by demons. [NIV]<br>Now the Spirit **expressly** says that in latter times some will depart from the faith, giving heed to deceiving spirits and doctrines of demons, [NKJV]<br>Now the Holy Spirit tells us **clearly** that in the last times some will turn away from what we believe; they will follow lying spirits and teachings that come from demons. [NLT]<br>Τὸ δὲ Πνεῦμα **ῥητῶς** λέγει, ὅτι ἐν ὑστέροις καιροῖς ἀποστήσονταί τινες τῆς πίστεως, προσέχοντες πνεύμασι πλάνοις καὶ διδασκαλίαις δαιμονίων, [GNS]<br>Τὸ δὲ πνεῦμα **ῥητῶς** λέγει ὅτι ἐν ὑστέροις καιροῖς ἀποστήσονταί τινες τῆς πίστεως προσέχοντες πνεύμασιν πλάνοις καὶ διδασκαλίαις δαιμονίων, [GNT] | Clearly, expressly, explicitly, specifically.<br><br>**Practical Application**<br>The Spirit has spoken "explicity" (*hrētōs*), that is, in specific terms, in plain words, distinctly, so that there can be no question about what is being said. False teachers will arise in the latter times. |
| **#1402**<br>**Expose**<br><br>Reprove–KJV<br>**Expose–NASB**<br>**Expose–NIV**<br>**Expose–NKJV**<br>**Expose–NLT** | ἐλέγχετε = *elegchete*<br>Pronunciation: [el-eng'-kheh-teh]<br>Parsing (part of speech): verb<br>    Mood—imperative<br>    Tense—present<br>    Voice—active<br>    Person—2nd person<br>    Number—plural<br>    Stem or root—from ἐλέγχω | To expose; to reprove; to rebuke; to condemn; to convict; to prove guilty.<br><br>**Practical Application**<br>The believer's task on earth is striking: he is not to fellowship with the works of darkness; he is to live in so much light that his life exposes (*elegchete*, that is, reproves, rebukes, and |

## Practical Word Studies in the New Testament

| ENGLISH WORD | GREEK WORD AND VERSE | THE WORD MEANS... |
|---|---|---|
| **POSB REFERENCE** (Eph.5:11-12; esp. v.11) Note 4, point 2 | Concordance References:<br>⇒ Strong's #1651 elegchō<br>⇒ NIV #1794 elegchō<br>⇒ NASB #1651 elegchō<br><br>**Ephes. 5:11**<br>And have no fellowship with the unfruitful works of darkness, but rather **reprove** them. [KJV]<br>And do not participate in the unfruitful deeds of darkness, but instead even **expose** them; [NASB]<br>Have nothing to do with the fruitless deeds of darkness, but rather **expose** them. [NIV]<br>And have no fellowship with the unfruitful works of darkness, but rather **expose** them. [NKJV]<br>Take no part in the worthless deeds of evil and darkness; instead, rebuke and **expose** them. [NLT]<br>καὶ μὴ συγκοινωνεῖτε τοῖς ἔργοις τοῖς ἀκάρποις τοῦ σκότους, μᾶλλον δὲ καὶ **ἐλέγχετε**· [GNS]<br>καὶ μὴ συγκοινωνεῖτε τοῖς ἔργοις τοῖς ἀκάρποις τοῦ σκότους, μᾶλλον δὲ καὶ **ἐλέγχετε**. [GNT] | convicts) people of their sins or dark works.<br><br>Sin is never to be taken lightly. The very fact that we are charged to expose it is clear evidence. Our task is to reflect so much light that all the works of darkness around us are exposed and expelled. Remember when light appears, the darkness is always extinguished. But if the light leaves or is turned off, the darkness reappears. |
| **#1403**<br>**Exposes**<br><br>Discerner–KJV<br>Judge–NASB<br>Judges–NIV<br>Discerner–NKJV<br>**Exposes–NLT**<br><br>**POSB REFERENCE** (Heb.4:11-13; esp. v.12) Note 5, point 2e | κριτικός = *kritikos*<br>Pronunciation: [krit-ee-kos']<br>Parsing (part of speech): adjective<br>    Case—nominative<br>    Gender—masculine<br>    Number—singular<br>    Stem or root—from κριτικός, ή, όν<br>Concordance References:<br>⇒ Strong's #2924 kritikos<br>⇒ NIV #3217 kritikos<br>⇒ NASB #2924 kritikos<br><br>**Hebrews 4:12**<br>For the word of God is quick, and powerful, and sharper than any twoedged sword, piercing even to the dividing asunder of soul and spirit, and of the joints and marrow, and is a **discerner** of the thoughts and intents of the heart. [KJV]<br>For the word of God is living and active and sharper than any two-edged sword, and piercing as far as the division of soul and spirit, of both joints and marrow, and able to **judge** the thoughts and intentions of the heart. [NASB]<br>For the word of God is living and active. Sharper than any double-edged sword, it penetrates even to dividing soul and spirit, joints and marrow; it **judges** the thoughts and attitudes of the heart. [NIV]<br>For the word of God *is* living and powerful, and sharper than any two-edged sword, piercing even to the division of soul and spirit, and of joints and marrow, and is a **discerner** of the thoughts and intents of the heart. [NKJV]<br>For the word of God is full of living power. It is sharper than the sharpest knife, cutting deep into our innermost thoughts and desires. It **exposes** us for what we really are. [NLT]<br>ζῶν γὰρ ὁ λόγος τοῦ Θεοῦ, καὶ ἐνεργὴς, καὶ τομώτερος ὑπὲρ πᾶσαν μάχαιραν δίστομον, καὶ διϊκνούμενος· ἄχρι μερισμοῦ ψυχῆς τὲ καὶ πνεύματος, ἁρμῶν τε καὶ μυελῶν, καὶ **κριτικὸς** ἐνθυμήσεων καὶ ἐννοιῶν καρδίας. [GNS]<br>Ζῶν γὰρ ὁ λόγος τοῦ θεοῦ καὶ ἐνεργὴς καὶ τομώτερος ὑπὲρ πᾶσαν μάχαιραν δίστομον καὶ διϊκνούμενος ἄχρι μερισμοῦ ψυχῆς καὶ πνεύματος, ἁρμῶν τε καὶ μυελῶν, καὶ **κριτικὸς** ἐνθυμήσεων καὶ ἐννοιῶν καρδίας· [GNT] | To judge; to discern; to expose; to sift and analyze.<br><br>**Practical Application**<br>The Word of God "discerns the thoughts and intents [purpose] of the heart."[KJV] "The Word of God is able to penetrate into the furthermost recesses of a person's spiritual being, sifting out and analyzing the thoughts and intents of the heart" (Kenneth Wuest. *Hebrews*, Vol. 2, p.89).<br>God's Word sees whether a person believes or does not believe His promise of rest. God's Word actually sees through the thoughts and purposes of a person. |
| **#1404**<br>**Express Image**<br><br>**Express image–KJV**<br>Exact representation–NASB | χαρακτήρ = *charaktēr*<br>Pronunciation: [khar-ak-tare']<br>Parsing (part of speech): noun<br>    Case—nominative<br>    Gender—masculine<br>    Number—singular<br>    Stem or root—from χαρακτήρ, ῆρος | Exact representation, express image; an exact likeness represents God exactly. The word "express" (*charaktēr*) means the very stamp, mark, and impression—the very reproduction of God. |

# PRACTICAL WORD STUDIES
## in the NEW TESTAMENT

| ENGLISH WORD | GREEK WORD AND VERSE | THE WORD MEANS... |
|---|---|---|
| Exact representation–NIV<br>**Express image–NKJV**<br>Represents God exactly–NLT<br><br>**POSB REFERENCE**<br>(Heb.1:3)<br>Note 5 | Concordance References:<br>⇒ Strong's #5481 charaktër<br>⇒ NIV #5917 charaktër<br>⇒ NASB #5481 charaktër<br><br>**Hebrews 1:3**<br>Who being the brightness of his glory, and the **express image** of his person, and upholding all things by the word of his power, when he had by himself purged our sins, sat down on the right hand of the Majesty on high; [KJV]<br>And He is the radiance of His glory and the **exact representation** of His nature, and upholds all things by the word of His power. When He had made purification of sins, He sat down at the right hand of the Majesty on high; [NASB]<br>The Son is the radiance of God's glory and the **exact representation** of his being, sustaining all things by his powerful word. After he had provided purification for sins, he sat down at the right hand of the Majesty in heaven. [NIV]<br>Who being the brightness of *His* glory and the **express image** of His person, and upholding all things by the word of His power, when He had by Himself purged our sins, sat down at the right hand of the Majesty on high, [NKJV]<br>The Son reflects God's own glory, and everything about him **represents God exactly**. He sustains the universe by the mighty power of his command. After he died to cleanse us from the stain of sin, he sat down in the place of honor at the right hand of the majestic God of heaven. [NLT]<br>ὃς ὢν ἀπαύγασμα τῆς δόξης, καὶ **χαρακτὴρ** τῆς ὑποστάσεως αὐτοῦ, φέρων τε τὰ πάντα τῷ ῥήματι τῆς δυνάμεως αὐτοῦ, δι᾽ ἑαυτοῦ καθαρισμὸν ποιησάμενος τῶν ἁμαρτιῶν ἡμῶν, ἐκάθισεν ἐν δεξιᾷ τῆς μεγαλωσύνης ἐν ὑψηλοῖς, [GNS]<br>ὃς ὢν ἀπαύγασμα τῆς δόξης καὶ **χαρακτὴρ** τῆς ὑποστάσεως αὐτοῦ, φέρων τε τὰ πάντα τῷ ῥήματι τῆς δυνάμεως αὐτοῦ, καθαρισμὸν τῶν ἁμαρτιῶν ποιησάμενος ἐκάθισεν ἐν δεξιᾷ τῆς μεγαλωσύνης ἐν ὑψηλοῖς, [GNT] | **Practical Application**<br>Jesus Christ is "the perfect imprint and very image of [God's] nature." Jesus Christ is the express image of God. When Jesus Christ came to earth, men were able to see God, to see exactly what God is like:<br>⇒ healing, restoring, saving<br>⇒ correcting, disciplining, controlling<br>⇒ holy, righteous, just<br><br>A person could look at Jesus Christ and see exactly what God is like. |
| #1405<br>**Expressly**<br><br>Expressly–KJV<br>Explicitly–NASB<br>Clearly–NIV<br>**Expressly–NKJV**<br>Clearly–NLT<br><br>**POSB REFERENCE**<br>(1 Tim.4:1)<br>Note 1 | ῥητῶς = hrētōs<br>Pronunciation: [hray-toce']<br>Parsing (part of speech): adjective adverb<br>   Stem or root—from ῥητῶς<br>Concordance References:<br>⇒ Strong's #4490 hrētōs<br>⇒ NIV #4843 hrētōs<br>⇒ NASB #4490 hrētōs<br><br>**1 Tim. 4:1**<br>Now the Spirit speaketh **expressly**, that in the latter times some shall depart from the faith, giving heed to seducing spirits, and doctrines of devils; [KJV]<br>But the Spirit **explicitly** says that in later times some will fall away from the faith, paying attention to deceitful spirits and doctrines of demons, [NASB]<br>The Spirit **clearly** says that in later times some will abandon the faith and follow deceiving spirits and things taught by demons. [NIV]<br>Now the Spirit **expressly** says that in latter times some will depart from the faith, giving heed to deceiving spirits and doctrines of demons, [NKJV]<br>Now the Holy Spirit tells us **clearly** that in the last times some will turn away from what we believe; they will follow lying spirits and teachings that come from demons. [NLT]<br>Τὸ δὲ Πνεῦμα **ῥητῶς** λέγει, ὅτι ἐν ὑστέροις καιροῖς ἀποστήσονταί τινες τῆς πίστεως, προσέχοντες | Clearly, expressly, explicitly, specifically.<br><br>**Practical Application**<br>The Spirit has spoken "expressly" (hrētōs), that is, in specific terms, in plain words, distinctly, so that there can be no question about what is being said. False teachers will arise in the latter times. |

## PRACTICAL WORD STUDIES
### in the NEW TESTAMENT

| ENGLISH WORD | GREEK WORD AND VERSE | THE WORD MEANS... |
|---|---|---|
| | πνεύμασι πλάνοις καὶ διδασκαλίαις δαιμονίων, [GNS]<br>Τὸ δὲ πνεῦμα **ῥητῶς** λέγει ὅτι ἐν ὑστέροις καιροῖς ἀποστήσονταί τινες τῆς πίστεως προσέχοντες πνεύμασιν πλάνοις καὶ διδασκαλίαις δαιμονίων, [GNT] | |
| **#1406**<br>**Extort Money**<br><br>Violence–KJV<br>Take money...by force–NASB<br>**Extort money–NIV**<br>Intimidate–NKJV<br>**Extort money–NLT**<br><br>**POSB REFERENCE**<br>(Lk.3:10-14; esp. v.14)<br>Note 5, point 3a | διασείσητε = *diaseisēte*<br>Pronunciation: [dee-as-i'-say-teh]<br>Parsing (part of speech): verb<br>  Mood—subjunctive OR imperative<br>  Tense—aorist<br>  Voice—active<br>  Person—2nd person<br>  Number—plural<br>  Stem or root—from διασείω<br>Concordance References:<br>  Strong's #1286 diaseiō<br>  NIV #1398 diaseiō<br>  NASB #1286 diaseiō<br><br>**Luke 3:14**<br>And the soldiers likewise demanded of him, saying, And what shall we do? And he said unto them, Do **violence** to no man, neither accuse any falsely; and be content with your wages. [KJV]<br>And some soldiers were questioning him, saying, "And what about us, what shall we do?" And he said to them, "Do not **take money** from anyone **by force**, or accuse anyone falsely, and be content with your wages." [NASB]<br>Then some soldiers asked him, "And what should we do?" He replied, "Don't **extort money** and don't accuse people falsely—be content with your pay." [NIV]<br>Likewise the soldiers asked him, saying, "And what shall we do?" So he said to them, "Do not **intimidate** anyone or accuse falsely, and be content with your wages." [NKJV]<br>"What should we do?" asked some soldiers. John replied, "Don't **extort money**, and don't accuse people of things you know they didn't do. And be content with your pay." [NLT]<br>ἐπηρώτων δὲ αὐτὸν καὶ στρατευόμενοι, λέγοντες, Καὶ ἡμεῖς τί ποιήσομεν; καὶ εἶπε πρὸς αὐτοῖς, Μηδένα **διασείσητε** μηδὲ συκοφαντήσητε· καὶ ἀρκεῖσθε τοῖς ὀψωνίοις ὑμῶν. [GNS]<br>ἐπηρώτων δὲ αὐτὸν καὶ στρατευόμενοι λέγοντες, Τί ποιήσωμεν καὶ ἡμεῖς; καὶ εἶπεν αὐτοῖς, Μηδένα **διασείσητε** μηδὲ συκοφαντήσητε καὶ ἀρκεῖσθε τοῖς ὀψωνίοις ὑμῶν. [GNT] | To extort money; to take money by force; to shake violently, agitate, terrify.<br><br>**Practical Application**<br>The thought is that some persons extorted money by terrifying people. Roman soldiers were, of course, posted to protect the interests of Rome. It was common for soldiers to allow illegal things to go on for a bribe. |
| **#1407**<br>**Extortioners**<br><br>Extortioners–KJV<br>Swindlers–NASB<br>Swindlers–NIV<br>**Extortioners–NKJV**<br>Swindlers–NLT<br><br>**POSB REFERENCE**<br>(1 Cor.5:9-10; esp. v.9)<br>Note 4, point 3 | ἅρπαξιν = *harpaxin*<br>Pronunciation: [har'-pax-in]<br>Parsing (part of speech): pronominal adjective<br>  Case—dative<br>  Gender—masculine<br>  Number—plural<br>  Stem or root—from ἅρπαξ, αγος<br>Concordance References:<br>  ⇒ Strong's #727 harpax<br>  ⇒ NIV #774 harpax<br>  ⇒ NASB #727 harpax<br><br>**1 Cor. 5:10**<br>Yet not altogether with the fornicators of this world, or with the covetous, or **extortioners**, or with idolaters; for then must ye needs go out of the world. [KJV]<br>I did not at all mean with the immoral people of this world, or with the covetous and **swindlers**, or with idolaters; for then you would have to go out of the world. [NASB]<br>Not at all meaning the people of this world who are immoral, or the greedy and **swindlers**, or idolaters. In that case you would have to leave this world. [NIV] | Swindlers; extortioners; a person who is as savage as a wolf.<br><br>**Practical Application**<br>These are the thieves, hijackers, grafters, and those who take advantage of the poor in order to get more gain for themselves. Again, these are especially despised by God because of their unreal view of the world, a world that reels under the weight of so many gripped by poverty, disease, sin, and death. |

# Practical Word Studies
## in the New Testament

| ENGLISH WORD | GREEK WORD AND VERSE | THE WORD MEANS... |
|---|---|---|
| | Yet *I* certainly *did* not *mean* with the sexually immoral people of this world, or with the covetous, or **extortioners**, or idolaters, since then you would need to go out of the world. [NKJV]<br>But I wasn't talking about unbelievers who indulge in sexual sin, or who are greedy or are **swindlers** or idol worshipers. You would have to leave this world to avoid people like that. [NLT]<br>καὶ οὐ πάντως τοῖς πόρνοις τοῦ κόσμου τούτου η τοῖς πλεονέκταις, η **ἅρπαξιν**, η εἰδωλολάτραις· ἐπεὶ ὠφείλετε ἄρα ἐκ τοῦ κόσμου ἐξελθεῖν. [GNS]<br>οὐ πάντως τοῖς πόρνοις τοῦ κόσμου τούτου η τοῖς πλεονέκταις καὶ **ἅρπαξιν** η εἰδωλολάτραις, ἐπεὶ ὠφείλετε ἄρα ἐκ τοῦ κόσμου ἐξελθεῖν. [GNT] | |
| **#1408**<br>**Extortioners**<br><br>**Extortioners**–KJV<br>Swindlers–NASB<br>Swindlers–NIV<br>**Extortioners**–NKJV<br>Swindlers–NLT<br><br>**POSB REFERENCE**<br>(1 Cor.6:10)<br>Note 3, point 5 | ἅρπαγες = *harpages*<br>Pronunciation: [har'-pah-gehs]<br>Parsing (part of speech): pronominal adjective<br>    Case—nominative<br>    Gender—masculine<br>    Number—plural<br>    Stem or root—from ἅρπαξ, αγος<br>Concordance References:<br>  ⇒ Strong's #727 harpax<br>  ⇒ NIV #774 harpax<br>  ⇒ NASB #727 harpax<br><br>**1 Cor. 6:10**<br>Nor thieves, nor covetous, nor drunkards, nor revilers, nor **extortioners**, shall inherit the kingdom of God. [KJV]<br>Nor thieves, nor the covetous, nor drunkards, nor revilers, nor **swindlers**, shall inherit the kingdom of God. [NASB]<br>Nor thieves nor the greedy nor drunkards nor slanderers nor **swindlers** will inherit the kingdom of God. [NIV]<br>Nor thieves, nor covetous, nor drunkards, nor revilers, nor **extortioners** will inherit the kingdom of God. [NKJV]<br>Thieves, greedy people, drunkards, abusers, and **swindlers**—none of these will have a share in the Kingdom of God. [NLT]<br>οὔτε κλέπται, οὔτε πλεονέκται, οὐ μέθυσοι, οὐ λοίδοροι, οὐχ **ἅρπαγες**, βασιλείαν Θεοῦ οὐ κληρονομήσουσι. [GNS]<br>οὔτε κλέπται οὔτε πλεονέκται, οὐ μέθυσοι, οὐ λοίδοροι, οὐχ **ἅρπαγες** βασιλείαν θεοῦ κληρονομήσουσιν. [GNT] | Swindlers, extortioners, savage like a wolf.<br><br>**Practical Application**<br>Extortioners (*harpages*) are persons who take money and things from others either by scheme or force. They take advantage of the poor, the ignorant, the innocent, the unsuspecting, and sometimes even family and friends. They use whoever and whatever they can to get what they want. They grasp to get more and more. |
| **#1409**<br>**Extraordinary Miracles**<br><br>Special miracles–KJV<br>**Extraordinary miracles**–NASB<br>**Extraordinary miracles**–NIV<br>Unusual miracles–NKJV<br>Unusual miracles–NLT<br><br>**POSB REFERENCE**<br>(Acts 19:10-20; esp. v.11)<br>Note 3, point 2 | Δυνάμεις τε οὐ τὰς τυχούσας = *Dunameis te ou tas tuchousas*<br>Pronunciation: [doo'-nam-eh-is the oo tahs too-choo'-sahs]<br>Parsing *Dunameis* (part of speech): noun<br>    Case—accusative<br>    Gender—feminine<br>    Number—plural<br>    Stem or root—from δύναμις, εως<br>Parsing *tuchousas* (part of speech): verb<br>    Mood—participle<br>    Tense—aorist<br>    Voice—active<br>    Case—accusative<br>    Gender—feminine<br>    Number—plural<br>    Stem or root—from τυγχάνω<br>Concordance References:<br>  ⇒ Strong's #1411 dunamis + 5037 te + 3588 + 3756 + 5177 ho ou tugchanō<br>  ⇒ NIV #1539 dunamis [miracles] + 5445 te + 3836 + 4024 + 5593 ho ou tugchanō [extraordinary]<br>  ⇒ NASB #1411 dunamis + 5037 te + 3588 + 3756 + 5177 ho ou tugchanō | Extraordinary miracles; special miracles; unusual miracles; supernatural miracles.<br><br>**Practical Application**<br>The phrase actually means two things:<br>⇒ They were miracles, powers that were not regular happenings; powers that were not the day-to-day experiences of men.<br>⇒ They were miracles that were extraordinary; that were usually not seen; that were uncommon; that were usually not performed. Even the disciples had not witnessed such miracles, not on a regular basis. |

**PRACTICAL WORD STUDIES**
**in the NEW TESTAMENT**

| ENGLISH WORD | GREEK WORD AND VERSE | THE WORD MEANS... |
|---|---|---|
| | **Acts 19:11**<br>And God wrought **special miracles** by the hands of Paul: [KJV]<br>And God was performing **extraordinary miracles** by the hands of Paul, [NASB]<br>God did **extraordinary miracles** through Paul, [NIV]<br>Now God worked **unusual miracles** by the ands of Paul, [NKJV]<br>God gave Paul the power to do **unusual miracles**, [NLT]<br>δυνάμεις τε οὐ τὰς τυχούσας ἐποίει ὁ Θεὸς διὰ τῶν χειρῶν Παύλου, [GNS]<br>Δυνάμεις τε οὐ τὰς τυχούσας ὁ Θεὸς ἐποίει διὰ τῶν χειρῶν Παύλου, [GNT] | |
| **#1410**<br>**Exulted**<br><br>Glad–KJV<br>**Exulted–NASB**<br>Rejoices–NIV<br>Glad–NKJV<br>Shouts his praises– NLT<br><br>**POSB REFERENCE**<br>(Acts 2:25-28; esp. v.26)<br>Note 1, point 1b | ἠγαλλιάσατο = ëgalliasato<br>Pronunciation: [ahg-al-lee-ah'-sah-tow]<br>Parsing (part of speech): verb<br>    Mood—indicative<br>    Tense—aorist<br>    Voice—middle<br>    Person—3rd person<br>    Number—singular<br>    Stem or root—from ἀγαλλιάω<br>Concordance References:<br>  ⇒ Strong's #21 agalliaö<br>  ⇒ NIV #22 agalliaö<br>  ⇒ NASB #21 agalliaö<br><br>**Acts 2:26**<br>Therefore did my heart rejoice, and my tongue was **glad**; moreover also my flesh shall rest in hope: [KJV]<br>'Therefore my heart was glad and my tongue **exulted**; Moreover my flesh also will abide in hope; [NASB]<br>Therefore my heart is glad and my tongue **rejoices**; my body also will live in hope, [NIV]<br>Therefore my heart rejoiced, and my tongue was **glad**; Moreover my flesh also will rest in hope. [NKJV]<br>No wonder my heart is filled with joy, and my mouth **shouts his praises**! My body rests in hope. [NLT]<br>Διὰ τοῦτο εὐφράνθη ἡ καρδία μου, καὶ **ἠγαλλιάσατο** ἡ γλῶσσά μου· ἔτι δὲ καὶ ἡ σάρξ μου κατασκηνώσει ἐπ' ἐλπίδι· [GNS]<br>διὰ τοῦτο ηὐφράνθη ἡ καρδία μου καὶ **ἠγαλλιάσατο** ἡ γλῶσσά μου, ἔτι δὲ καὶ ἡ σάρξ μου κατασκηνώσει ἐπ' ἐλπίδι, [GNT] | Rejoices, glad, exulting, rejoicing, filled with joy; greatly rejoicing; to shout God's praises; to be extremely joyful. It means to leap for joy and break forth with praise and song.<br><br>**Practical Application**<br>Peter said that "David [spoke] concerning Christ" (Psalm 16:8-11). What David said was a prophecy of the Lord's experience upon earth (Acts 2:25-28). David's prophecy concerned Jesus' daily experience or life.<br>1. Jesus experienced God's constant presence and power.<br>  ⇒Jesus always saw God before His face. Jesus looked and kept His gaze upon God. He thought upon God, focused His mind and attention upon God. He concentrated and stayed His mind upon Him. The idea is that Jesus always practiced and was always conscious of God's presence—"captivating every thought" (cp. 2 Cor. 10:5).<br>  ⇒Jesus always had God on His right hand, that He should not be moved. God was right there as an advocate and as a protector and defender. God was a provider looking after Christ, strengthening, guiding, upholding, seeing that He was not moved nor shaken. The picture is that of a defender in court or of a soldier on the battlefield standing at a person's right hand, protecting, looking after, and providing for his welfare. (Cp. Psalm 109:31 for this picture.)<br>2. Jesus' heart rejoiced and His tongue praised God. Such a consciousness of God's presence was bound to cause...<br>  • the heart to rejoice (ëuphranthë): to be joyful and full of euphoria, full of God's presence and glory.<br>  • the tongue to be glad (ëgalliasato): to leap for joy and break forth with praise and song.<br>3. Jesus' flesh rested in hope. The phrase "will rest" or "abide" (kataskenosei) means *shall tabernacle* or pitch a tent. Jesus' *flesh* rested, tabernacled, pitched its tent, encamped and made its abode upon hope—the hope of conquering death, of being resurrected. Hope of living forever was the basis and foundation of Jesus' life, that for which He lived. He focused His whole life and being upon the hope of the glorious resurrection (cp. Paul's testimony—Phil. 3:7-16, esp. Phil. 3:11). |

## PRACTICAL WORD STUDIES
### in the NEW TESTAMENT

| ENGLISH WORD | GREEK WORD AND VERSE | THE WORD MEANS... |
|---|---|---|
| **#1411**<br>**Fables**<br><br>**Fables**–KJV<br>Myths–NASB<br>Myths–NIV<br>**Fables**–NKJV<br>Myths–NLT<br><br>**POSB<br>REFERENCE**<br>(1 Tim.1:4)<br>Note 2, point 1 | μύθοις = *muthois*<br>Pronunciation: [moo'-thoys]<br>Parsing (part of speech): noun<br>    Case—dative<br>    Gender—masculine<br>    Number—plural<br>    Stem or root—from μῦθος, ου<br>Concordance References:<br>  ⇒ Strong's #3454 *muthos*<br>  ⇒ NIV #3680 *muthos*<br>  ⇒ NASB #3454 *muthos*<br><br>**1 Tim. 1:4**<br>Neither give heed to **fables** and endless genealogies, which minister questions, rather than godly edifying which is in faith: so do. [KJV]<br>Nor to pay attention to **myths** and endless genealogies, which give rise to mere speculation rather than furthering the administration of God which is by faith. [NASB]<br>Nor to devote themselves to **myths** and endless genealogies. These promote controversies rather than God's work—which is by faith. [NIV]<br>Nor give heed to **fables** and endless genealogies, which cause disputes rather than godly edification which is in faith. [NKJV]<br>Don't let people waste time in endless speculation over **myths** and spiritual pedigrees. For these things only cause arguments; they don't help people live a life of faith in God. [NLT]<br>μηδὲ προσέχειν **μύθοις** καὶ γενεαλογίαις ἀπεράντοις, αἵτινες ζητήσεις παρέχουσι μᾶλλον ἢ οἰκοδομίαν Θεοῦ τὴν ἐν πίστει-. [GNS]<br>μηδὲ προσέχειν **μύθοις** καὶ γενεαλογίαις ἀπεράντοις, αἵτινες ἐκζητήσεις παρέχουσιν μᾶλλον ἢ οἰκονομίαν θεοῦ τὴν ἐν πίστει. [GNT] | Myths, fables, stories. The word "fables" (*muthois*) refers to *all forms* of false and fictional teaching or doctrine.<br><br>**Practical Application**<br>It means the *false ideas* and speculations of men about God and Christ and the teachings of God's Word. The doctrines of men are only speculations, fables, narratives, stories, fictions, and falsehoods (A.T. Robertson. *Word Pictures in the New Testament*, Vol.4, p.561). |
| **#1412**<br>**Faced Angry<br>Mobs**<br><br>Tumults–KJV<br>Tumults–NASB<br>Riots–NIV<br>Tumults–NKJV<br>**Faced angry mobs**–<br>NLT<br><br>**POSB<br>REFERENCE**<br>(2 Cor.6:4-5; esp. v.5)<br>Note 3 | ἀκαταστασίαις = *akatastasiais*<br>Pronunciation: [ak-at-as-tah-see'-ah-ees]<br>Parsing (part of speech): noun<br>    Case—dative<br>    Gender—feminine<br>    Number—plural<br>    Stm or root—from ἀκαταστασία, ας<br>Concordance References:<br>  ⇒ Strong's #181 *akatastasia*<br>  ⇒ NIV #189 *akatastasia*<br>  ⇒ NASB #181 *akatastasia*<br><br>**2 Cor. 6:5**<br>In stripes, in imprisonments, in **tumults**, in labours, in watchings, in fastings; [KJV]<br>In beatings, in imprisonments, in **tumults**, in labors, in sleeplessness, in hunger, [NASB]<br>In beatings, imprisonments and **riots**; in hard work, sleepless nights and hunger; [NIV]<br>In stripes, in imprisonments, in **tumults**, in labors, in sleeplessness, in fastings; [NKJV]<br>We have been beaten, been put in jail, **faced angry mobs**, worked to exhaustion, endured sleepless nights, and gone without food. [NLT]<br>ἐν πληγαῖς, ἐν φυλακαῖς, ἐν **ἀκαταστασίαις**, ἐν κόποις, ἐν ἀγρυπνίαις, ἐν νηστείαις, [GNS]<br>ἐν πληγαῖς, ἐν φυλακαῖς, ἐν **ἀκαταστασίαις**, ἐν κόποις, ἐν ἀγρυπνίαις, ἐν νηστείαις, [GNT] | Riots, tumults, disorder, revolutions, insurrection; to face angry mob uprisings and attacks.<br><br>**Practical Application**<br>Paul often faced angered mobs: at Antioch of Pisidia (Acts 13:50); Lystra (Acts 14:19); Philippi (Acts 16:19); Ephesus (Acts 19:29); and at Jerusalem (Acts 21:30). Mob uprisings present one of the most difficult and frightening situations imaginable for a believer, for a mob cannot be controlled by reason. The believer is unable to be heard, so speech is useless. Believers often face the abuse and ridicule of crowds because of the righteous lives they live and because they refuse to join in the worldly pleasures and indulgences of life. At such times the believer must be consistent in his testimony—no matter the temptation to go along with the crowd. The true believer, layman and minister alike, must steadfastly endure. |
| **#1413**<br>**Faced The Fact**<br><br>Considered–KJV<br>Contemplated–NASB<br>**Faced the fact**–NIV | κατενόησεν = *katenoësen*<br>Pronunciation: [kat-ehn-o-ay'-sehn]<br>Parsing (part of speech): verb<br>    Mood—indicative<br>    Tense—aorist<br>    Voice—active<br>    Person—3rd person | To consider; to face the facts; to think upon; to contemplate; to observe; to look upon; to see through the facts; to be aware of; to pay attention to; to fix one's thoughts upon. |

# PRACTICAL WORD STUDIES
## in the NEW TESTAMENT

| ENGLISH WORD | GREEK WORD AND VERSE | THE WORD MEANS... |
|---|---|---|
| Consider–NKJV<br>Knew–NLT<br><br>**POSB REFERENCE**<br>(Romans 4:18-22; esp. v.19)<br>Note 2, point 1a | Number—singular<br>Stem or root—from κατανοέω<br>Concordance References:<br>⇒ Strong's #2657 katanoeö<br>⇒ NIV #2917 katanoeö<br>⇒ NASB #2657 katanoeö<br><br>**Romans 4:19**<br>And being not weak in faith, he **considered** not his own body now dead, when he was about an hundred years old, neither yet the deadness of Sarah's womb: [KJV]<br>And without becoming weak in faith he **contemplated** his own body, now as good as dead since he was about a hundred years old, and the deadness of Sarah's womb; [NASB]<br>Without weakening in his faith, he **faced the fact** that his body was as good as dead—since he was about a hundred years old—and that Sarah's womb was also dead. [NIV]<br>And not being weak in faith, he did not **consider** his own body, already dead (since he was about a hundred years old), and the deadness of Sarah's womb. [NKJV]<br>And Abraham's faith did not weaken, even though he **knew** that he was too old to be a father at the age of one hundred and that Sarah, his wife, had never been able to have children. [NLT]<br>καὶ μὴ ἀσθενήσας τῇ πίστει, οὐ **κατενόησε** τὸ ἑαυτοῦ σῶμα ἤδη νενεκρωμένον -- ἑκατονταετής που ὑπάρχων --, καὶ τὴν νέκρωσιν τῆς μήτρας Σάρρας, [GNS]<br>καὶ μὴ ἀσθενήσας τῇ πίστει **κατενόησεν** τὸ ἑαυτοῦ σῶμα [ἤδη] νενεκρωμένον, ἑκατονταετής που ὑπάρχων, καὶ τὴν νέκρωσιν τῆς μήτρας Σάρρας· [GNT] | **Practical Application**<br>Abraham was not weak in faith despite thinking about his own physical inability. His body was "now dead"; he and Sarah were about one hundred years old. The word "dead" is a perfect participle in the Greek which means that his reproductive organs had stopped functioning and were dead forever and could never again function. Abraham could never have a son; it was not humanly possible. He and Sarah were almost one hundred years old, now sexually "dead."<br>Abraham thought about the matter. The words "faced the fact" (*katenoësen*) means He fixed his thoughts, his mind, his attention upon the matter. But he did not give in to the thoughts. He was not weak in faith. |
| **#1414**<br>**Factions**<br><br>Strifes–KJV<br>Disputes–NASB<br>**Factions–NIV**<br>Selfish ambitions–NKJV<br>Selfishness–NLT<br><br>**POSB REFERENCE**<br>(2 Cor.12:19-21; esp. v.20)<br>Note 3, point 2<br><br>See also POSB REF:<br>(Gal.5:19-21; esp. v.20) | ἐριθεῖαι = *eritheiai*<br>Pronunciation: [er-ith-i'-ah-ee]<br>Parsing (part of speech): noun<br>Case—nominative<br>Gender—feminine<br>Number—plural<br>Stem or root—from ἐριθεία, ας<br>Concordance References:<br>⇒ Strong's #2052 eritheia<br>⇒ NIV #2249 eritheia<br>⇒ NASB #2052 eritheia<br><br>**2 Cor. 12:20**<br>For I fear, lest, when I come, I shall not find you such as I would, and that I shall be found unto you such as ye would not: lest there be debates, envyings, wraths, **strifes**, backbitings, whisperings, swellings, tumults: [KJV]<br>For I am afraid that perhaps when I come I may find you to be not what I wish and may be found by you to be not what you wish; that perhaps there may be strife, jealousy, angry tempers, **disputes**, slanders, gossip, arrogance, disturbances; [NASB]<br>For I am afraid that when I come I may not find you as I want you to be, and you may not find me as you want me to be. I fear that there may be quarreling, jealousy, outbursts of anger, **factions**, slander, gossip, arrogance and disorder. [NIV]<br>For I fear lest, when I come, I shall not find you such as I wish, and *that* I shall be found by you such as you do not wish; lest *there be* contentions, jealousies, outbursts of wrath, **selfish ambitions**, backbitings, whisperings, conceits, tumults; [NKJV]<br>For I am afraid that when I come to visit you I won't like what I find, and then you won't like my response. I am afraid that I will find quarreling, jealousy, outbursts of anger, **selfishness**, backstabbing, gossip, conceit, and disorderly behavior. [NLT] | Factions, envying, disputes, selfishness; selfish ambitions; an envious spirit or clique that stands as a rival to others; a factious spirit caused by selfishness or self-seeking; to pay attention to; to fix thoughts on; to look more closely.<br><br>**Practical Application**<br>Paul was stricken with fear, fear lest the church fail to be what it should be and reject him and his ministry. Paul feared that the church would fail to deal with the carnal critics and continue putting up with their evil attacks against him. He lists eight evils—including factions (*eritheiai*) that were and still are characteristic of divisive critics in the church. |

# Practical Word Studies
## in the New Testament

| ENGLISH WORD | GREEK WORD AND VERSE | THE WORD MEANS... |
|---|---|---|
| | φοβοῦμαι γὰρ μή πως ἐλθὼν οὐχ οἵους θέλω εὕρω ὑμᾶς, κἀγὼ εὑρεθῶ ὑμῖν οἷον οὐ θέλετε· μή πως ἔρις, ζῆλοι, θυμοί, **ἐριθεῖαι**, καταλαλιαί, ψιθυρισμοί, φυσιώσεις, ἀκαταστασίαι· [GNS]<br><br>φοβοῦμαι γὰρ μή πως ἐλθὼν οὐχ οἵους θέλω εὕρω ὑμᾶς κἀγὼ εὑρεθῶ ὑμῖν οἷον οὐ θέλετε· μή πως ἔρις, ζῆλος, θυμοί, **ἐριθεῖαι**, καταλαλιαί, ψιθυρισμοί, φυσιώσεις, ἀκαταστασίαι· [GNT] | |
| **#1415**<br>**Factions**<br><br>Heresies–KJV<br>**Factions–NASB**<br>**Factions–NIV**<br>Heresies–NKJV<br>Feeling that everyone is wrong except those in your own little group–NLT<br><br>**POSB REFERENCE**<br>(Gal.5:19-21; esp. v.20)<br>Note 2 | αἱρέσεις = *haireseis*<br>Pronunciation: [ah'ee-res-ee-is]<br>Parsing (part of speech): noun<br>    Case—nominative<br>    Gender—feminine<br>    Number—plural<br>    Stem or root—from αἵρεσις, εως<br>Concordance References:<br> ⇒ Strong's #139 hairesis<br> ⇒ NIV #146 hairesis<br> ⇒ NASB #139 hairesis<br><br>**Galatians 5:20**<br>Idolatry, witchcraft, hatred, variance, emulations, wrath, strife, seditions, **heresies**, [KJV]<br>Idolatry, sorcery, enmities, strife, jealousy, outbursts of anger, disputes, dissensions, **factions**, [NASB]<br>Idolatry and witchcraft; hatred, discord, jealousy, fits of rage, selfish ambition, dissensions, **factions** [NIV]<br>Idolatry, sorcery, hatred, contentions, jealousies, outbursts of wrath, selfish ambitions, dissensions, **heresies**, [NKJV]<br>Idolatry, participation in demonic activities, hostility, quarreling, jealousy, outbursts of anger, selfish ambition, divisions, the **feeling that everyone is wrong except those in your own little group**, [NLT]<br>εἰδωλολατρία, φαρμακεία, ἔχθραι, ἔρεις, ζῆλοι, θυμοί, ἐριθεῖαι, διχοστασίαι, **αἱρέσεις**, [GNS]<br>εἰδωλολατρία, φαρμακεία, ἔχθραι, ἔρις, ζῆλος, θυμοί, ἐριθεῖαι, διχοστασίαι, **αἱρέσεις**, [GNT] | Factions; differences; heresies; feeling that everyone is wrong except in one's own little group; inner circle; non conformists.<br><br>**Practical Application**<br>It is rejecting the fundamental beliefs of God, Christ, the Scriptures, and the church; believing and holding to some teaching other than the truth. |
| **#1416**<br>**Factious**<br><br>Heretick–KJV<br>**Factious–NASB**<br>Divisive–NIV<br>Divisive–NKJV<br>Divisions–NLT<br><br>**POSB REFERENCE**<br>(Tit.3:10-11; esp. v.10)<br>Note 3 | αἱρετικὸν = *hairetikon*<br>Pronunciation: [ahee-ret-ee-kon']<br>Parsing (part of speech): adjective<br>    Case—accusative<br>    Gender—masculine<br>    Number—singular<br>    Stem or root—from αἱρετικός, ή, όν<br>Concordance References:<br> ⇒ Strong's #141 hairetikos<br> ⇒ NIV #148 hairetikos<br> ⇒ NASB #141 hairetikos<br><br>**Titus 3:10**<br>A man that is an **heretick** after the first and second admonition reject; [KJV]<br>Reject a **factious** man after a first and second warning, [NASB]<br>Warn a **divisive** person once, and then warn him a second time. After that, have nothing to do with him. [NIV]<br>Reject a **divisive** man after the first and second admonition, [NKJV]<br>If anyone is causing **divisions** among you, give a first and second warning. After that, have nothing more to do with that person. [NLT]<br>**αἱρετικὸν** ἄνθρωπον μετὰ μίαν καὶ δευτέραν νουθεσίαν παραιτοῦ, [GNS]<br>**αἱρετικὸν** ἄνθρωπον μετὰ μίαν καὶ δευτέραν νουθεσίαν παραιτοῦ, [GNT] | Divisive, heretic, factious, divisions. The Greek word factions (*hairetikon*) is interesting. It means to take for oneself; to choose for oneself.<br><br>**Practical Application**<br>A factious man is one who chooses what he is to believe. He rejects all authority no matter what it is: God, Christ, the Word of God, the church, man. He himself chooses what he is to believe. He and he alone is his authority; he and he alone determines truth—what is and what is not truth.<br>Note that this factious man is in the church; he associates with believers. This is the picture of most factious men. Few reject all the teachings of Christ and of the Bible. Most heretics remain in the church, holding to some basic teachings but rejecting those doctrines that they do not like. The Scripture is clear: believers are to reach out to the heretic or false teacher. He is not to be lambasted, rejected, and expelled from the church. An attempt is to be made to reach him for Christ. In fact, two strong attempts are to be made to reach him. He is to be shown love and care and admonished to repent and confess the truth of Christ and His Word. But note: there is a limit. On the third try, if he does not repent, he is to be rejected, that is, expelled from the church. He is not to be allowed to lead other |

## PRACTICAL WORD STUDIES
### in the NEW TESTAMENT

| ENGLISH WORD | GREEK WORD AND VERSE | THE WORD MEANS... |
|---|---|---|
| | | believers astray. (See POSB outline—Matthew 18:15-20 and POSB notes—Matthew 18:15-20 for more detailed discussion on church discipline as taught by Christ.) |
| **#1417**<br>**Fade (Never)–**<br>**Fade Away,**<br>**Not–**<br>**Fadeth Not**<br>**Away**<br><br>Fadeth not away–KJV<br>Not fade away–NASB<br>Fade, never–NIV<br>Not fade away–NKJV<br>Beyond the reach–NLT<br><br>**POSB**<br>**REFERENCE**<br>(1 Pt.1:4)<br>Note 2, point 3 | ἀμίαντον = amaranton<br>Pronunciation: [am-ar'-an-ton]<br>Parsing (part of speech): adjective<br>    Case—accusative<br>    Gender—feminine<br>    Number—singular<br>    Stem or root—from ἀμάραντος, ον<br>Concordance References:<br>  ⇒ Strong's #96 adokimos + 1510 eimi<br>  ⇒ NIV #99+1639 adokimos eimi [fail the test]<br>  ⇒ NASB #96b adokimos + 1510 eimi<br><br>**1 Peter 1:4**<br>To an inheritance incorruptible, and undefiled, and that **fadeth not away**, reserved in heaven for you, [KJV]<br>To obtain an inheritance which is imperishable and undefiled and will **not fade away**, reserved in heaven for you, [NASB]<br>And into an inheritance that can **never** perish, spoil or **fade**—kept in heaven for you, [NIV]<br>To an inheritance incorruptible and undefiled and that does **not fade away**, reserved in heaven for you, [NKJV]<br>For God has reserved a priceless inheritance for his children. It is kept in heaven for you, pure and undefiled, **beyond the reach** of change and decay. [NLT]<br>εἰς κληρονομίαν ἄφθαρτον καὶ ἀμίαντον καὶ ἀμάραντον, τετηρημένην ἐν οὐρανοῖς εἰς ὑμᾶς [GNS]<br>εἰς κληρονομίαν ἄφθαρτον καὶ ἀμίαντον καὶ ἀμάραντον, τετηρημένην ἐν οὐρανοῖς εἰς ὑμᾶς [GNT] | To not fade away; to be unfading; to be permanent.<br><br>**Practical Application**<br>Our inheritance *can never fade away* (*amaranton*). It will last forever and ever. The splendor and beauty of it all—of life and of all the positions and possessions which God will give us—none of the splendor and beauty will fade or diminish whatsoever. Nothing, not even our energy and bodies, will wear out or waste away. |
| **#1418**<br>**Fail The Test–**<br>**Failed The Test**<br><br>Reprobates–KJV<br>Fail the test–NASB<br>Fail the test–NIV<br>Disqualified–NKJV<br>Failed the test–NLT<br><br>**POSB**<br>**REFERENCE**<br>(2 Cor.13:1-6; esp. v.5)<br>Note 1 | ἀδόκιμοί ἐστε = adokimoi este<br>Pronunciation: [ad-ok'-ee-moy es-teh]<br>Parsing *adokimoi* (part of speech): adjective<br>    Case—nominative<br>    Gender—masculine<br>    Number—plural<br>    Stem or root—from ἀδόκιμος, ον<br>Concordance References:<br>  ⇒ Strong's #96 adokimos<br>  ⇒ NIV #99+1639 adokimos eimi [fail the test]<br>  ⇒ NASB #96b adokimos<br><br>**2 Cor. 13:5**<br>Examine yourselves, whether ye be in the faith; prove your own selves. Know ye not your own selves, how that Jesus Christ is in you, except ye be **reprobates**? [KJV]<br>Test yourselves to see if you are in the faith; examine yourselves! Or do you not recognize this about yourselves, that Jesus Christ is in you— unless indeed you **fail the test**? [NASB]<br>Examine yourselves to see whether you are in the faith; test yourselves. Do you not realize that Christ Jesus is in you—unless, of course, you **fail the test**? [NIV]<br>Examine yourselves *as to* whether you are in the faith. Test yourselves. Do you not know yourselves, that Jesus Christ is in you?—unless indeed you are **disqualified**. [NKJV]<br>Examine yourselves to see if your faith is really genuine. Test yourselves. If you cannot tell that Jesus Christ is among you, it means you have **failed the test**. [NLT]<br>ἑαυτοὺς πειράζετε εἰ ἐστὲ ἐν τῇ πίστει, ἑαυτοὺς δοκιμάζετε. ἢ οὐκ ἐπιγινώσκετε ἑαυτοὺς ὅτι Ἰησοῦς Χριστὸς ἐν ὑμῖν; εἰ μή τι **ἀδόκιμοί ἐστε**. [GNS]<br>Ἑαυτοὺς πειράζετε εἰ ἐστὲ ἐν τῇ πίστει, ἑαυτοὺς δοκιμάζετε· ἢ οὐκ ἐπιγινώσκετε ἑαυτοὺς ὅτι Ἰησοῦς Χριστὸς ἐν ὑμῖν; εἰ μήτι **ἀδόκιμοί ἐστε**. [GNT] | To fail the test; to be a reprobate; to be tested and found worthless; to be tested and disqualified and rejected; to be found unfit and disapproved; to be doomed and condemned to perdition.<br><br>**Practical Application**<br>The believers had to examine themselves to make sure they were in the faith.<br>⇒ They needed to make sure they were genuine. Living in sin makes a person's faith suspect. Some were living in sin: "Examine yourselves *as to* whether you are in the faith. Test yourselves."<br>⇒ They needed to make sure that *Jesus Christ was in them* and that they did not *"fail the test"* (*adokimoi este*). (see POSB note, Castaway—1 Cor. 9:27—for more discussion.)<br>⇒ They needed to know that Paul was not disqualified.<br>The only way the Corinthians could know these things was to examine themselves. |

## Practical Word Studies
in the New Testament

| ENGLISH WORD | GREEK WORD AND VERSE | THE WORD MEANS... |
|---|---|---|
| **#1419**<br>**Failure**<br><br>Diminishing–KJV<br>**Failure**–NASB<br>Loss–NIV<br>**Failure**–NKJV<br>Turned down–NLT<br><br>**POSB REFERENCE**<br>(Romans 11:11-12, esp. v.12)<br>Note 1, point 3 | ἥττημα = hèttèma<br>Pronunciation: [hayt'-tay-mah]<br>Parsing (part of speech): noun<br>   Case—nominative<br>   Gender—neuter<br>   Number—singular<br>   Stem or root—from ἥττημα, τος<br>Concordance References:<br>  ⇒ Strong's #2275 hèttèma<br>  ⇒ NIV #2488 hèttèma<br>  ⇒ NASB #2275 hèttèma<br><br>**Romans 11:12**<br>Now if the fall of them be the riches of the world, and the **diminishing** of them the riches of the Gentiles; how much more their fulness? [KJV]<br>Now if their transgression be riches for the world and their **failure** be riches for the Gentiles, how much more will their fulfillment be! [NASB]<br>But if their transgression means riches for the world, and their **loss** means riches for the Gentiles, how much greater riches will their fullness bring! [NIV]<br>Now if their fall *is* riches for the world, and their **failure** riches for the Gentiles, how much more their fullness! [NKJV]<br>Now if the Gentiles were enriched because the Jews **turned down** God's offer of salvation, think how much greater a blessing the world will share when the Jews finally accept it. [NLT]<br>εἰ δὲ τὸ παράπτωμα αὐτῶν πλοῦτος κόσμου, καὶ τὸ ἥττημα αὐτῶν πλοῦτος ἐθνῶν, πόσῳ μᾶλλον τὸ πλήρωμα αὐτῶν; [GNS]<br>εἰ δὲ τὸ παράπτωμα αὐτῶν πλοῦτος κόσμου καὶ τὸ ἥττημα αὐτῶν πλοῦτος ἐθνῶν, πόσῳ μᾶλλον τὸ πλήρωμα αὐτῶν. [GNT] | Defeat; failure; diminishing loss; turning down, downfall.<br><br>**Practical Application**<br>God assures the glorious restoration of Israel and a rich period for the whole earth. Note the sharp contrast.<br>• between "full" and "riches."<br>• between "diminishing" and "riches."<br><br>It means that Israel became impoverished spiritually. Israel was spiritually injured and defeated; the Jewish people lost the blessings of salvation. Now...<br>• if the spiritual fall of Israel led to the riches of salvation being carried to the world...<br>• if the spiritual failure of Israel led to the riches of salvation being carried to the Gentiles...<br>...how much more will the fullness (the restoration of Israel) bring the blessings of God to earth? |
| **#1420**<br>**Faint**<br><br>Faint–KJV<br>Faint–NASB<br>Lose heart–NIV<br>Discouraged–NKJV<br>Discouraged–NLT<br><br>**POSB REFERENCE**<br>(Heb.12:5-7, esp. v.5)<br>Note 1, point 2 | ἐκλύου = ekluou<br>Pronunciation: [ek-loo'-oo]<br>Parsing (part of speech): verb<br>   Mood—imperative<br>   Tense—present<br>   Voice—passive<br>   Person—2nd person<br>   Number—singular<br>   Stem or root—from ἐκλύομαι<br>Concordance References:<br>  ⇒ Strong's #1590 ekluō<br>  ⇒ NIV #1725 ekluō<br>  ⇒ NASB #1590 ekluō<br><br>**Hebrews 12:5**<br>And ye have forgotten the exhortation which speaketh unto you as unto children, My son, despise not thou the chastening of the Lord, nor **faint** when thou art rebuked of him: [KJV]<br>And you have forgotten the exhortation which is addressed to you as sons, "My son, do not regard lightly the discipline of the Lord, Nor **FAINT** WHEN YOU ARE REPROVED BY Him; [NASB]<br>And you have forgotten that word of encouragement that addresses you as sons: "My son, do not make light of the Lord's discipline, and do not **lose heart** when he rebukes you, [NIV]<br>And you have forgotten the exhortation which speaks to you as to sons: "My son, do not despise the chastening of the Lord, Nor be **discouraged** when you are rebuked by Him; [NKJV]<br>And have you entirely forgotten the encouraging words God spoke to you, his children? He said, "My child, don't ignore it when the Lord disciplines you, and don't be **discouraged** when he corrects you [NLT]<br>καὶ ἐκλέλησθε τῆς παρακλήσεως, ἥτις ὑμῖν ὡς υἱοῖς | To lose heart; to be faint; to be discouraged; to give up; to give out; to lose heart; to collapse; to buckle under; to lose courage; to weaken.<br><br>**Practical Application**<br>The trials and sufferings of this world can become extremely heavy and painful—sometimes almost too much to bear. The rebuking hand of God that convicts us to repent and to correct our behavior becomes almost unbearable.<br>In either case, we are not to faint or give up. We are to turn totally to God in trust and dependence, asking for His help and strength. We have the glorious assurance that He will deliver us victoriously through all. He will make us stronger and make us a much greater witness for Him. God will save us and live within our hearts and lives—save us both now and eternally—save us even through death itself so that we may live with Him forever and ever in the new heavens and earth (1 Peter 3:10-13; Rev. 21:1f). |

# PRACTICAL WORD STUDIES
## in the New Testament

| ENGLISH WORD | GREEK WORD AND VERSE | THE WORD MEANS... |
|---|---|---|
| | διαλέγεται, Υἱέ μου, μὴ ὀλιγώρει παιδείας Κυρίου, μηδὲ ἐκλύου, ὑπ' αὐτοῦ ἐλεγχόμενος· [GNS]<br>καὶ ἐκλέλησθε τῆς παρακλήσεως, ἥτις ὑμῖν ὡς υἱοῖς διαλέγεται, Υἱέ μου, μὴ ὀλιγώρει παιδείας κυρίου μηδὲ ἐκλύου ὑπ' αὐτοῦ ἐλεγχόμενος. [GNT] | |
| **#1421**<br>**Faint Not**<br><br>Faint not–KJV<br>Not lose heart–NASB<br>Not lose heart–NIV<br>Not lose heart–NKJV<br>Never give up–NLT<br><br>**POSB REFERENCE**<br>(2 Cor.4:1)<br>Note 1 | οὐκ ἐγκακοῦμεν = *ouk egkakoumen*<br>Pronunciation: [ook eg-kak-oo'-mehn]<br>Parsing *egkakoumen* (part of speech): verb<br>    Mood—indicative<br>    Tense—present<br>    Voice—active<br>    Person—1st person<br>    Number—plural<br>    Stem or root—from ἐγκακέω<br>Concordance References:<br>  ⇒ Strong's #3756 ou + 1573 egkakeö<br>  ⇒ NIV #4024 ou [not] +1591 egkakeö [lose heart]<br>  ⇒ NASB #3756 ou + 1573 egkakeö<br><br>**2 Cor. 4:1**<br>Therefore seeing we have this ministry, as we have received mercy, we **faint not**; [KJV]<br>Therefore, since we have this ministry, as we received mercy, we do **not lose heart**, [NASB]<br>Therefore, since through God's mercy we have this ministry, we do **not lose heart**. [NIV]<br>Therefore, since we have this ministry, as we have received mercy, we do **not lose heart**. [NKJV]<br>And so, since God in his mercy has given us this wonderful ministry, we **never give up**. [NLT]<br>Διὰ τοῦτο ἔχοντες τὴν διακονίαν ταύτην, καθὼς ἠλεήθημεν, **οὐκ ἐκκακοῦμεν**· [GNS]<br>Διὰ τοῦτο, ἔχοντες τὴν διακονίαν ταύτην καθὼς ἠλεήθημεν, **οὐκ ἐγκακοῦμεν** [GNT] | Not to lose heart; not to tire of; not to faint; not to become weary; never give up; not become discouraged, spiritless, fainthearted, despondent, or discouraged.<br><br>**Practical Application**<br>The ministry demands constancy, demands that one never faint. Paul did not quit or give up for any reason, not even because of persecution or weariness and exhaustion. |
| **#1422**<br>**Faint, Not To**<br><br>Not to faint–KJV<br>Not to lose heart–NASB<br>Not give up–NIV<br>Not lose heart–NKJV<br>Never give up–NLT<br><br>**POSB REFERENCE**<br>(Lk.18:1)<br>Note 1, point 4 | μὴ ἐγκακεῖν = *mē egkakein*<br>Pronunciation: [may eg-kak-eh'-een]<br>Parsing *egkakein* (part of speech): verb<br>    Mood—infinitive<br>    Tense—present<br>    Voice—active<br>    Stem or root—from ἐγκακέω<br>Concordance References:<br>  ⇒ Strong's #3361 me +1573 egkakeo<br>  ⇒ NIV #3590 mē [not] + 1591 egkakeö [give up]<br>  ⇒ NASB #3361 me +1573 egkakeo<br><br>**Luke 18:1**<br>And he spake a parable unto them to this end, that men ought always to pray, and **not to faint**; [KJV]<br>Now He was telling them a parable to show that at all times they ought to pray and **not to lose heart**, [NASB]<br>Then Jesus told his disciples a parable to show them that they should always pray and **not give up**. [NIV]<br>Then He spoke a parable to them, that men always ought to pray and **not lose heart**, [NKJV]<br>One day Jesus told his disciples a story to illustrate their need for constant prayer and to show them that they must **never give up**. [NLT]<br>Ἔλεγε δὲ καὶ παραβολὴν αὐτοῖς πρὸς τὸ δεῖν πάντοτε προσεύχεσθαι, καὶ **μὴ ἐκκακεῖν**, [GNS]<br>Ἔλεγεν δὲ παραβολὴν αὐτοῖς πρὸς τὸ δεῖν πάντοτε προσεύχεσθαι αὐτοὺς καὶ **μὴ ἐγκακεῖν**, [GNT] | Not to lose heart; not to faint; not to tire of; not to become discouraged; not to turn coward, or give up, or give in to evil.<br><br>**Practical Application**<br>There is need for perseverance in prayer, for praying over a long period of time and not giving in and becoming discouraged. God's people are to pray and keep on praying until Christ returns, no matter how long He may be delayed. |
| **#1423**<br>**Fainted**<br><br>Fainted–KJV<br>Distressed–NASB<br>Harassed–NIV<br>Weary–NKJV<br>Problems were so great–NLT | ἐσκυλμένοι = *eskulmenoi*<br>Pronunciation: [es-kool-me'-noi]<br>Parsing (part of speech): verb<br>    Mood—participle<br>    Tense—perfect<br>    Voice—passive<br>    Case—nominative<br>    Gender—masculine<br>    Number—plural<br>    Stem or root—from σκύλλω | To be harassed; to faint; to grow weary; to be troubled; to lose heart; to lack courage; to be distressed, fainthearted, bewildered. It means to be completely overwhelmed with problems.<br><br>**Practical Application**<br>The word is used when a person has struggled and struggled against sin, or stood against the barrage of insult after insult until he can stand no more. It means that a person has undergone trial |

# PRACTICAL WORD STUDIES
## in the NEW TESTAMENT

| ENGLISH WORD | GREEK WORD AND VERSE | THE WORD MEANS... |
|---|---|---|
| **POSB REFERENCE** (Mt.9:36) *Deeper Study* #3 | Concordance References:<br>⇒ Strong's #4660 skullö<br>⇒ NIV #5035 skullö<br>⇒ NASB #4660 skullö<br><br>**Matthew 9:36**<br>But when he saw the multitudes, he was moved with compassion on them, because they **fainted**, and were scattered abroad, as sheep having no shepherd. [KJV]<br>And seeing the multitudes, He felt compassion for them, because they were **distressed** and downcast like sheep without a shepherd. [NASB]<br>When he saw the crowds, he had compassion on them, because they were **harassed** and helpless, like sheep without a shepherd. [NIV]<br>But when He saw the multitudes, He was moved with compassion for them, because they were **weary** and scattered, like sheep having no shepherd. [NKJV]<br>He felt great pity for the crowds that came, because their **problems were so great** and they didn't know where to go for help. They were like sheep without a shepherd. [NLT]<br>ἰδὼν δὲ τοὺς ὄχλους, ἐσπλαγχνίσθη περὶ αὐτῶν, ὅτι ἦσαν **ἐκλελυμένοι** καὶ ἐρριμμένοι ὡσεὶ πρόβατα μὴ ἔχοντα ποιμένα. [GNS]<br>Ἰδὼν δὲ τοὺς ὄχλους ἐσπλαγχνίσθη περὶ αὐτῶν, ὅτι ἦσαν **ἐσκυλμένοι** καὶ ἐρριμμένοι ὡσεὶ πρόβατα μὴ ἔχοντα ποιμένα. [GNT] | after trial until he is ready to collapse (Heb.12:3). |
| **#1424 Fair**<br>Just–KJV<br>Just–NASB<br>Upright–NIV<br>Just–NKJV<br>Fair–NLT<br><br>**POSB REFERENCE** (Tit.1:7-8; esp. v.8) Note 3, point 2d | δίκαιον = *dikaion*<br>Pronunciation: [dik'-ah-ee-on]<br>Parsing (part of speech): adjective<br>    Case—accusative<br>    Gender—masculine<br>    Number—singular<br>    Stem or root—from δίκαιος, α, ον<br>Concordance References:<br>⇒ Strong's #1342 dikaios<br>⇒ NIV #1465 dikaios<br>⇒ NASB #1342 dikaios<br><br>**Titus 1:8**<br>But a lover of hospitality, a lover of good men, sober, **just**, holy, temperate; [KJV]<br>But hospitable, loving what is good, sensible, **just**, devout, self-controlled, [NASB]<br>Rather he must be hospitable, one who loves what is good, who is self-controlled, **upright**, holy and disciplined. [NIV]<br>But hospitable, a lover of what is good, sober-minded, **just**, holy, self-controlled, [NKJV]<br>He must enjoy having guests in his home and must love all that is good. He must live wisely and be **fair**. He must live a devout and disciplined life. [NLT]<br>ἀλλὰ φιλόξενον, φιλάγαθον, σώφρονα, **δίκαιον**, ὅσιον, ἐγκρατῆ, [GNS]<br>ἀλλὰ φιλόξενον φιλάγαθον σώφρονα **δίκαιον** ὅσιον ἐγκρατῆ, [GNT] | Upright, just, fair, honest, innocent, proper, above board in his behavior and dealings with both God and man.<br><br>**Practical Application**<br>There is no deception, lying, cheating, stealing, meanness, misbehavior, or irresponsibility whatsoever in the minister's dealings—not with men nor with God. |
| **#1425 Faith**<br>Faith–KJV<br>Faith–NASB<br>Faith–NIV<br>Faith–NKJV<br>Faith–NLT<br><br>**POSB REFERENCE** (Mk.2:5) Note 3, point 1 | πίστιν = *pistin*<br>Pronunciation: [pis'-tin]<br>Parsing (part of speech): noun<br>    Case—accusative<br>    Gender—feminine<br>    Number—singular<br>    Stem or root—from πίστις, εως<br>Concordance References:<br>⇒ Strong's #4102 pistis<br>⇒ NIV #4411 pistis<br>⇒ NASB #4102 pistis<br><br>**Mark 2:5**<br>When Jesus saw their **faith**, he said unto the sick of the palsy, Son, thy sins be forgiven thee. [KJV]<br>And Jesus seeing their **faith** said to the paralytic, "My | To believe; to fully trust in; to have confidence; to have assurance; to have reliance; to have conviction. Faith means both to believe and to be faithful to the belief.<br><br>**Practical Application**<br>⇒ The believer seeks faith: to learn to trust God more and more; to be a man of faith, a man of great faith and belief. He wants to believe, trust, and depend upon God—to grow more and more in believing God.<br>⇒ The believer seeks to be faithful: be faithful to God more and more. He wants to be loyal, obedient, and attached to God. He |

## PRACTICAL WORD STUDIES
### in the NEW TESTAMENT

| ENGLISH WORD | GREEK WORD AND VERSE | THE WORD MEANS... |
|---|---|---|
| See also POSB REF: (1 Tim.6:11) Note 3 | son, your sins are forgiven." [NASB]<br>When Jesus saw their **faith**, he said to the paralytic, "Son, your sins are forgiven." [NIV]<br>When Jesus saw their **faith**, He said to the paralytic, "Son, your sins are forgiven you." [NKJV]<br>Seeing their **faith**, Jesus said to the paralyzed man, "My son, your sins are forgiven." [NLT]<br>ἰδὼν δὲ ὁ Ἰησοῦς τὴν **πίστιν** αὐτῶν, λέγει τῷ παραλυτικῷ, Τέκνον, ἀφέωνταί σοι αἱ ἁμαρτίαι σου. [GNS]<br>καὶ ἰδὼν ὁ Ἰησοῦς τὴν **πίστιν** αὐτῶν λέγει τῷ παραλυτικῷ, Τέκνον, ἀφίενταί σου αἱ ἁμαρτίαι. [GNT] | wants to please God in all that he does.<br>In this Scripture, Jesus saw their faith—the faith of the man himself and the faith of the four men who brought him. The faith of the friends played a large part in the man's being healed and in his receiving forgiveness of sins. (See POSB note—Matthew 9:2; POSB note—Mark 11:23.) |
| **#1426**<br>**Faith**<br><br>Faith–KJV<br>Faithfulness–NASB<br>Faithfulness–NIV<br>Faithfulness–NKJV<br>Faithfulness–NLT<br><br>**POSB REFERENCE**<br>(Gal.5:22-23; esp. v.22)<br>Note 1 | πίστις = *pistis*<br>Pronunciation: [pis'-tis]<br>Parsing (part of speech): noun<br>  Case—nominative<br>  Gender—feminine<br>  Number—singular<br>  Stem or root—from πίστις, εως<br>Concordance References:<br>  ⇒ Strong's #4102 pistis<br>  ⇒ NIV #4411 pistis<br>  ⇒ NASB #4102 pistis<br><br>**Galatians 5:22**<br>But the fruit of the Spirit is love, joy, peace, longsuffering, gentleness, goodness, **faith**, [KJV]<br>But the fruit of the Spirit is love, joy, peace, patience, kindness, goodness, **faithfulness**, [NASB]<br>But the fruit of the Spirit is love, joy, peace, patience, kindness, goodness, **faithfulness**, [NIV]<br>But the fruit of the Spirit is love, joy, peace, longsuffering, kindness, goodness, **faithfulness**, [NKJV]<br>But when the Holy Spirit controls our lives, he will produce this kind of fruit in us: love, joy, peace, patience, kindness, goodness, **faithfulness**, [NLT]<br>ὁ δὲ καρπὸς τοῦ Πνεύματός ἐστιν ἀγάπη, χαρά, εἰρήνη, μακροθυμία, χρηστότης, ἀγαθωσύνη, **πίστις**, [GNS]<br>Ὁ δὲ καρπὸς τοῦ πνεύματός ἐστιν ἀγάπη χαρά εἰρήνη, μακροθυμία, χρηστότης ἀγαθωσύνη, **πίστις** [GNT] | Faith, faithfulness. It means to be faithful and trustworthy; to be loyal and steadfast in devotion and allegiance. It means to be constant, staunch, and enduring.<br><br>**Practical Application**<br>A faithful person denies and sacrifices himself—all he is and has—and trusts God. He believes God and knows that God will work all things out for good. Therefore, he casts himself totally upon God and becomes faithful to God.<br>⇒ Faith does not doubt God—not His salvation, provision, or strength to help.<br>⇒ Faith does not begin with God then back off and give up.<br>⇒ Faith does not walk with God then give in to the lusts of the flesh.<br>Faithfulness begins with God and continues with God. Faithfulness continues on and on; it never slackens or surrenders. |
| **#1427**<br>**Faithful**<br><br>Continuing instant–KJV<br>Devoted–NASB<br>**Faithful**–NIV<br>Continuing steadfastly–NKJV<br>Always–NLT<br><br>**POSB REFERENCE**<br>(Romans 12:12)<br>Note 3, point 3 | προσκαρτεροῦντες = *proskarterountes*<br>Pronunciation: [pros-kar-ter-oon'-tehs]<br>Parsing (part of speech): verb<br>  Mood—participle (imperative sense)<br>  Tense—present<br>  Voice—active<br>  Case—nominative<br>  Gender—masculine<br>  Person—2nd person<br>  Number—plural<br>  Stem or root—from προσκαρτερέω<br>Concordance References:<br>  ⇒ Strong's #4342 proskartereō<br>  ⇒ NIV #4674 proskartereō<br>  ⇒ NASB #4342 proskartereō<br><br>**Romans 12:12**<br>Rejoicing in hope; patient in tribulation; **continuing instant** in prayer; [KJV]<br>Rejoicing in hope, persevering in tribulation, **devoted** to prayer, [NASB]<br>Be joyful in hope, patient in affliction, **faithful** in prayer. [NIV]<br>Rejoicing in hope, patient in tribulation, **continuing steadfastly** in prayer; [NKJV]<br>Be glad for all God is planning for you. Be patient in trouble, and **always** be prayerful. [NLT]<br>τῇ ἐλπίδι χαίροντες· τῇ θλίψει ὑπομένοντες· τῇ προσευχῇ **προσκαρτεροῦντες**· [GNS]<br>τῇ ἐλπίδι χαίροντες, τῇ θλίψει ὑπομένοντες, τῇ προσευχῇ **προσκαρτεροῦντες**, [GNT] | To be faithful; to be devoted and attentive to; to give constant attention to; to give unceasing care to; to wait steadfastly upon; to persevere.<br><br>**Practical Application**<br>Very simply, the believer overcomes trials by giving constant attention to God and waiting upon His delivering power. The believer stays in constant communion with his Lord, depending upon Him to supply the strength to walk through the trials of daily living. |

# PRACTICAL WORD STUDIES
## in the NEW TESTAMENT

| ENGLISH WORD | GREEK WORD AND VERSE | THE WORD MEANS... |
|---|---|---|
| **#1428**<br>**Faithful**<br><br>Faithful–KJV<br>Faithful–NASB<br>Faithful–NIV<br>Faithful–NKJV<br>Faithful–NLT<br><br>**POSB<br>REFERENCE**<br>(Eph.1:1-2; esp. v.1)<br>Note 2, point 1b | πιστοῖς = *pistois*<br>Pronunciation: [pis-toys']<br>Parsing (part of speech): adjective<br>    Case—dative<br>    Gender—masculine<br>    Number—plural<br>    Stem or root— from πιστός, ή, όν<br>Concordance References:<br>  ⇒ Strong's #4103 pistos<br>  ⇒ NIV #4412 pistos<br>  ⇒ NASB #4103 pistos<br><br>**Ephes. 1:1**<br><br>Paul, an apostle of Jesus Christ by the will of God, to the saints which are at Ephesus, and to the **faithful** in Christ Jesus: [KJV]<br>Paul, an apostle of Christ Jesus by the will of God, to the saints who are at Ephesus, and who are **faithful** in Christ Jesus: [NASB]<br>Paul, an apostle of Christ Jesus by the will of God, To the saints in Ephesus, the **faithful** in Christ Jesus: [NIV]<br>Paul, an apostle of Jesus Christ by the will of God, To the saints who are in Ephesus, and **faithful** in Christ Jesus: [NKJV]<br>This letter is from Paul, chosen by God to be an apostle of Christ Jesus. It is written to God's holy people in Ephesus, who are **faithful** followers of Christ Jesus. [NLT]<br>Παῦλος ἀπόστολος Ἰησοῦ Χριστοῦ διὰ θελήματος Θεοῦ, τοῖς ἁγίοις τοῖς οὖσιν ἐν Ἐφέσῳ, καὶ **πιστοῖς** ἐν Χριστῷ Ἰησοῦ [GNS]<br>Παῦλος ἀπόστολος Χριστοῦ Ἰησοῦ διὰ θελήματος θεοῦ τοῖς ἁγίοις τοῖς οὖσιν [ἐν Ἐφέσῳ] καὶ **πιστοῖς** ἐν Χριστῷ Ἰησοῦ, [GNT] | Faithful, trustworthy, reliable, believing. The word "faithful" (*pistois*) means a person who has placed his faith in the Lord Jesus Christ.<br><br>**Practical Application**<br>The faithful person is a person who has looked upon the Lord Jesus Christ and...<br>• believed that Christ could and would save him.<br>• counted Christ worthy of his trust.<br>• placed his confidence in Christ and His Word.<br>• entrusted his salvation into the hands of Christ.<br>• committed his life to Christ.<br><br>Very simply, the faithful are those who have surrendered and set their lives apart to Jesus Christ, trusting Him to save them. This is the very first call God gives to people: to be the saints and the faithful of the Lord Jesus Christ. |
| **#1429**<br>**Faithful**<br><br>Faithful–KJV<br>Faithful–NASB<br>Reliable–NIV<br>Faithful–NKJV<br>Trustworthy–NLT<br><br>**POSB<br>REFERENCE**<br>(2 Tim. 2:2)<br>Note 2, point 2 | πιστοῖς = *pistois*<br>Pronunciation: [pis-toys']<br>Parsing (part of speech): adjective<br>    Case—dative<br>    Gender—masculine<br>    Number—plural<br>    Stem or root— from πιστός, ή, όν<br>Concordance References:<br>  ⇒ Strong's #4103 pistos<br>  ⇒ NIV #4412 pistos<br>  ⇒ NASB #4103 pistos<br><br>**2 Tim. 2:2**<br><br>And the things that thou hast heard of me among many witnesses, the same commit thou to **faithful** men, who shall be able to teach others also. [KJV]<br>And the things which you have heard from me in the presence of many witnesses, these entrust to **faithful** men, who will be able to teach others also. [NASB]<br>And the things you have heard me say in the presence of many witnesses entrust to **reliable** men who will also be qualified to teach others. [NIV]<br>And the things that you have heard from me among many witnesses, commit these to **faithful** men who will be able to teach others also. [NKJV]<br>You have heard me teach many things that have been confirmed by many reliable witnesses. Teach these great truths to **trustworthy** people who are able to pass them on to others. [NLT]<br>καὶ ἃ ἤκουσας παρ' ἐμοῦ διὰ πολλῶν μαρτύρων, ταῦτα παράθου **πιστοῖς** ἀνθρώποις, οἵτινες ἱκανοὶ ἔσονται καὶ ἑτέρους διδάξαι. [GNS]<br>καὶ ἃ ἤκουσας παρ' ἐμοῦ διὰ πολλῶν μαρτύρων, ταῦτα παράθου **πιστοῖς** ἀνθρώποις, οἵτινες ἱκανοὶ ἔσονται καὶ ἑτέρους διδάξαι. [GNT] | Reliable, faithful, trustworthy, unfailing.<br><br>**Practical Application**<br>By faithful (*pistois*) is meant a person...<br>• who *believes* in Christ and in the Word of God.<br>• who is loyal, reliable, dependable, and trustworthy.<br><br>Naturally, a person who does not believe in God or in God's Word cannot be said to be faithful to God. He is unfaithful and disloyal. God cannot trust or rely on him.<br>The point is this: a strong teacher will not commit the truth to an unfaithful person. The strong teacher will look for faithful people and commit the truth to them. |

## PRACTICAL WORD STUDIES
### in the NEW TESTAMENT

| ENGLISH WORD | GREEK WORD AND VERSE | THE WORD MEANS... |
|---|---|---|
| **#1430**<br>**Faithful**<br><br>Undefiled–KJV<br>Undefiled–NASB<br>Pure–NIV<br>Undefiled–NKJV<br>**Faithful–NLT**<br><br>**POSB**<br>**REFERENCE**<br>(Heb.13:4)<br>Note 4 | ἀμίαντος = amiantos<br>Pronunciation: [am-ee'-ahn-tos]<br>Parsing (part of speech): adjective<br>    Case—nominative<br>    Gender—feminine<br>    Number—singular<br>    Stem or root—from ἀμίαντος, ον<br>Concordance References:<br>  ⇒ Strong's #283 amiantos<br>  ⇒ NIV #299 amiantos<br>  ⇒ NASB #283 amiantos<br><br>**Hebrews 13:4**<br>Marriage is honourable in all, and the bed **undefiled**: but whoremongers and adulterers God will judge. [KJV]<br><br>Let marriage be held in honor among all, and let the marriage bed be **undefiled**; for fornicators and adulterers God will judge. [NASB]<br><br>Marriage should be honored by all, and the marriage bed kept **pure**, for God will judge the adulterer and all the sexually immoral. [NIV]<br><br>Marriage *is* honorable among all, and the bed **undefiled**; but fornicators and adulterers God will judge. [NKJV]<br><br>Give honor to marriage, and remain **faithful** to one another in marriage. God will surely judge people who are immoral and those who commit adultery. [NLT]<br><br>τίμιος ὁ γάμος ἐν πᾶσι, καὶ ἡ κοίτη **ἀμίαντος**· πόρνους δὲ καὶ μοιχοὺς κρινεῖ ὁ Θεός. [GNS]<br><br>Τίμιος ὁ γάμος ἐν πᾶσιν καὶ ἡ κοίτη **ἀμίαντος**, πόρνους γὰρ καὶ μοιχοὺς κρινεῖ ὁ θεός. [GNT] | Pure, undefiled, faithful, faultless, unstained, devoted, reliable, constant, unswerving, allegiant, unwavering, scrupulous.<br><br>**Practical Application**<br>The word "faithful" (*amiantos*) means that the bed is unstained by sin, absolutely free from all moral impurity, uncleanness, and defilement. This is saying at least three things.<br>⇒ First, husband and wife are free and encouraged to be close in bed. Closeness and intimacy are a gift from God; it is even a type of the church (cp. Eph. 5:22f).<br>⇒ Second, the closeness in bed between husband and wife will prevent unfaithfulness.<br>⇒ Third, the bed is to be kept undefiled. Only husband and wife are to be close in bed, and only with each other. There is absolutely no place for anyone else in the bed.<br><br>The importance of the bed in marriage cannot be overemphasized. God's Word says that it is so important that husband and wife are not to separate for any period of time except for fasting and prayer, and even then separation is not to occur unless it is by mutual consent. |
| **#1431**<br>**Faithfulness**<br><br>Faith–KJV<br>**Faithfulness–NASB**<br>**Faithfulness–NIV**<br>**Faithfulness–NKJV**<br>**Faithfulness–NLT**<br><br>**POSB**<br>**REFERENCE**<br>(Gal.5:22-23; esp. v.22)<br>Note 1 | πίστις = pistis<br>Pronunciation: [pis'-tis]<br>Parsing (part of speech): noun<br>    Case—nominative<br>    Gender—feminine<br>    Number—singular<br>    Stem or root—from πίστις, εως<br>Concordance References:<br>  ⇒ Strong's #4102 pistis<br>  ⇒ NIV #4411 pistis<br>  ⇒ NASB #4102 pistis<br><br>**Galatians 5:22**<br>But the fruit of the Spirit is love, joy, peace, longsuffering, gentleness, goodness, **faith**, [KJV]<br><br>But the fruit of the Spirit is love, joy, peace, patience, kindness, goodness, **faithfulness**, [NASB]<br><br>But the fruit of the Spirit is love, joy, peace, patience, kindness, goodness, **faithfulness**, [NIV]<br><br>But the fruit of the Spirit is love, joy, peace, longsuffering, kindness, goodness, **faithfulness**, [NKJV]<br><br>But when the Holy Spirit controls our lives, he will produce this kind of fruit in us: love, joy, peace, patience, kindness, goodness, **faithfulness**, [NLT]<br><br>ὁ δὲ καρπὸς τοῦ Πνεύματός ἐστιν ἀγάπη, χαρά, εἰρήνη, μακροθυμία, χρηστότης, ἀγαθωσύνη, **πίστις**, [GNS]<br><br>Ὁ δὲ καρπὸς τοῦ πνεύματός ἐστιν ἀγάπη χαρά εἰρήνη, μακροθυμία, χρηστότης ἀγαθωσύνη **πίστις** [GNT] | Faith, faithfulness. It means to be faithful and trustworthy; to be loyal and steadfast in devotion and allegiance. It means to be constant, staunch, and enduring.<br><br>**Practical Application**<br>A faithful person denies and sacrifices himself—all he is and has—and trusts God. He believes God and knows that God will work all things out for good. Therefore, he casts himself totally upon God and becomes faithful to God.<br>⇒ Faith does not doubt God—not His salvation, provision, or strength to help.<br>⇒ Faith does not begin with God then back off and give up.<br>⇒ Faith does not walk with God then give in to the lusts of the flesh.<br><br>Faithfulness begins with God and continues with God. Faithfulness continues on and on; it never slackens or surrenders. |
| **#1432**<br>**Faithless**<br><br>**Faithless–KJV**<br>Unbelieving–NASB<br>Unbelieving–NIV<br>**Faithless–NKJV**<br>**Faithless–NLT** | ἄπιστος = apistos<br>Pronunciation: [ap'-is-tos]<br>Parsing (part of speech): adjective<br>    Case—vocative<br>    Gender—feminine<br>    Number—singular<br>    Stem or root—from ἄπιστος, ον<br>Concordance References:<br>  ⇒ Strong's #571 apistos<br>  ⇒ NIV #603 apistos<br>  ⇒ NASB #571 apistos | Faithless; unbelieving; disbelieving; doubting; being without faith; being out of faith; not keeping faith (cp. Titus 1:15).<br><br>**Practical Application**<br>What is unbelief or being faithless?<br>1. Unbelief or being faithless is doubting Christ Himself, the object of one's faith. It is questioning the power of Christ. Is He really strong enough to do what is needed: to save, |

# PRACTICAL WORD STUDIES
## in the NEW TESTAMENT

| ENGLISH WORD | GREEK WORD AND VERSE | THE WORD MEANS... |
|---|---|---|
| **POSB REFERENCE** (Lk.9:41) *Deeper Study #2* | **Luke 9:41**<br>And Jesus answering said, O **faithless** and perverse generation, how long shall I be with you, and suffer you? Bring thy son hither. [KJV]<br>And Jesus answered and said, "O **unbelieving** and perverted generation, how long shall I be with you, and put up with you? Bring your son here." [NASB]<br>"O **unbelieving** and perverse generation," Jesus replied, "how long shall I stay with you and put up with you? Bring your son here." [NIV]<br>Then Jesus answered and said, "O **faithless** and perverse generation, how long shall I be with you and bear with you? Bring your son here." [NKJV]<br>"You stubborn, **faithless** people," Jesus said, "how long must I be with you and put up with you? Bring him here." [NLT]<br>ἀποκριθεὶς δὲ ὁ Ἰησοῦς εἶπεν, Ὦ γενεὰ **ἄπιστος** καὶ διεστραμμένη, ἕως πότε ἔσομαι πρὸς ὑμᾶς, καὶ ἀνέξομαι ὑμῶν; προσάγαγε ὧδε τὸν υἱόν σου. [GNS]<br>ἀποκριθεὶς δὲ ὁ Ἰησοῦς εἶπεν, Ὦ γενεὰ **ἄπιστος** καὶ διεστραμμένη, ἕως πότε ἔσομαι πρὸς ὑμᾶς καὶ ἀνέξομαι ὑμῶν; προσάγαγε ὧδε τὸν υἱόν σου. [GNT] | deliver, heal, and help; and to remove evil empires, entrenched wickedness, destructive greed, and the threat of wars?<br>2. Unbelief or being faithless is doubting the power of the Lord within oneself. It is questioning if one is close enough to Christ for Him to hear and answer or to grant enough power to meet the need.<br>3. Unbelief or being faithless is doubting one's own faith. It is questioning the strength of one's own dependence and confidence in Christ.<br>4. Unbelief or being faithless is doubting if the thing needed is God's will. It is questioning if one should be seeking such a thing or if God is willing to do what is needed. |
| **#1433 Faithless**<br><br>Covenantbreakers–KJV<br>Untrustworthy–NASB<br>**Faithless–NIV**<br>Untrustworthy–NKJV<br>Break their promises–NLT<br><br>**POSB REFERENCE** (Romans 1:31) *Deeper Study #20* | ἀσυνθέτους = *asunthetous*<br>Pronunciation: [as-oon'-thet-oos]<br>Parsing (part of speech): adjective<br>  Case—accusative<br>  Gender—masculine<br>  Number—plural<br>  Stem or root—from ἀσύνθετος, ον<br>Concordance References:<br>  ⇒ Strong's #802 asunthetos<br>  ⇒ NIV #853 asunthetos<br>  ⇒ NASB #802 asunthetos<br><br>**Romans 1:31**<br>Without understanding, **covenantbreakers**, without natural affection, implacable, unmerciful: [KJV]<br>Without understanding, **untrustworthy**, unloving, unmerciful; [NASB]<br>They are senseless, **faithless**, heartless, ruthless. [NIV]<br>Undiscerning, **untrustworthy**, unloving, unforgiving, unmerciful; [NKJV]<br>They refuse to understand, **break their promises**, and are heartless and unforgiving. [NLT]<br>ἀσυνέτους, **ἀσυνθέτους**, ἀστόργους, ἀσπόνδους, ἀνελεήμονας· [GNS]<br>ἀσυνέτους **ἀσυνθέτους** ἀστόργους ἀνελεήμονας· [GNT] | Faithless, untrustworthy, disloyal, covenant breakers, breakers of promises or agreements.<br><br>**Practical Application**<br>It is a person who tragically does not keep his word or promise. He is simply untrustworthy, not dependable. |
| **#1434 Faithless, Be Not**<br><br>**Be not faithless–KJV**<br>Be not unbelieving–NASB<br>Stop doubting–NIV<br>Do not be unbelieving–NKJV<br>Don't be faithless any longer–NLT<br><br>**POSB REFERENCE** (Jn.20:26-28; esp. v.27) Note 3, point 1b | μὴ γίνου ἄπιστος = *mē ginou apistos*<br>Pronunciation: [may ghen-oo ah-pis-tos]<br>Parsing *ginou* (part of speech): verb<br>  Mood—imperative<br>  Tense—present<br>  Voice—middle or passive deponent<br>  Person—2nd person<br>  Number—singular<br>  Stem or root—from γίνομαι<br>Parsing *apistos* (part of speech): adjective<br>  Case—nominative<br>  Gender—masculine<br>  Number—singular<br>  Stem or root—from ἄπιστος, ον<br>Concordance References:<br>  ⇒ Strong's #3361 me + 571+1096 apistos ginomai<br>  ⇒ NIV #3590 mē [Stop] + 603+1181 apistos ginomai [doubting]<br>  ⇒ NASB #3361 me + 571+1096 apistos ginomai<br><br>**John 20:27**<br>Then saith he to Thomas, reach hither thy finger, and behold my hands; and reach hither thy hand, and thrust it | To stop doubting; to stop being faithless; to stop becoming an unbeliever.<br><br>**Practical Application**<br>In this Scripture, Jesus warned and called for belief. Thomas had been walking down a dangerous road. The disciples had witnessed to him time and again, but he had refused time and again to accept their testimony. Note the Lord's strong charge:<br>⇒ "Be not faithless" (*mē ginou apistos*): stop becoming an unbeliever. You are running the risk of *becoming faithless* and unbelieving, beyond the point of believing. You have carried your unbelief too far. It is now time to stop the foolishness. The others have been witnessing and witnessing the truth to you. Stop the stiff-necked, obstinate unbelief. You are in danger. |

# PRACTICAL WORD STUDIES
## in the NEW TESTAMENT

| ENGLISH WORD | GREEK WORD AND VERSE | THE WORD MEANS... |
|---|---|---|
| | into my side: and **be not faithless**, but believing. [KJV]<br><br>Then He said to Thomas, "Reach here your finger, and see My hands; and reach here your hand, and put it into My side; and **be not unbelieving**, but believing." [NASB]<br><br>Then he said to Thomas, "Put your finger here; see my hands. Reach out your hand and put it into my side. **Stop doubting** and believe." [NIV]<br><br>Then He said to Thomas, "Reach your finger here, and look at My hands; and reach your hand *here*, and put *it* into My side. **Do not be unbelieving**, but believing." [NKJV]<br><br>Then he said to Thomas, "Put your finger here and see my hands. Put your hand into the wound in my side. **Don't be faithless any longer**. Believe!" [NLT]<br><br>εἶτα λέγει τῷ Θωμᾷ, Φέρε τὸν δάκτυλόν σου ὧδε, καὶ ἴδε τὰς χεῖράς μου. καὶ φέρε τὴν χεῖρά σου καὶ βάλε εἰς τὴν πλευράν μου· καὶ **μὴ γίνου ἄπιστος** ἀλλὰ πιστός. [GNS]<br><br>εἶτα λέγει τῷ Θωμᾷ, Φέρε τὸν δάκτυλόν σου ὧδε καὶ ἴδε τὰς χεῖράς μου, καὶ φέρε τὴν χεῖρά σου καὶ βάλε εἰς τὴν πλευράν μου, καὶ **μὴ γίνου ἄπιστος** ἀλλὰ πιστός. [GNT] | |
| #1435<br>**Faithless, Don't Be Any Longer**<br><br>Be not faithless–KJV<br>Be not unbelieving–NASB<br>Stop doubting–NIV<br>Do not be unbelieving–NKJV<br>**Don't be faithless any longer**–NLT<br><br>**POSB REFERENCE**<br>(Jn.20:26-28; esp. v.27)<br>Note 3, point 1b | **μὴ γίνου ἄπιστος** = *më ginou apistos*<br>Pronunciation: [may ghen-oo ah-pis-tos]<br>Parsing *ginou* (part of speech): verb<br>  Mood—imperative<br>  Tense—present<br>  Voice—middle or passive deponent<br>  Person—2nd person<br>  Number—singular<br>  Stem or root—from γίνομαι<br>Parsing *apistos* (part of speech): adjective<br>  Case—nominative<br>  Gender—masculine<br>  Number—singular<br>  Stem or root—from ἄπιστος, ον<br>Concordance References:<br>⇒ Strong's #3361 me + 571+1096 apistos ginomai<br>⇒ NIV #3590 më [Stop] + 603+1181 apistos ginomai [doubting]<br>⇒ NASB #3361 me + 571+1096 apistos ginomai<br><br>**John 20:27**<br>Then saith he to Thomas, reach hither thy finger, and behold my hands; and reach hither thy hand, and thrust it into my side: and **be not faithless**, but believing. [KJV]<br><br>Then He said to Thomas, "Reach here your finger, and see My hands; and reach here your hand, and put it into My side; and **be not unbelieving**, but believing." [NASB]<br><br>Then he said to Thomas, "Put your finger here; see my hands. Reach out your hand and put it into my side. **Stop doubting** and believe." [NIV]<br><br>Then He said to Thomas, "Reach your finger here, and look at My hands; and reach your hand *here*, and put *it* into My side. **Do not be unbelieving,** but believing." [NKJV]<br><br>Then he said to Thomas, "Put your finger here and see my hands. Put your hand into the wound in my side. **Don't be faithless any longer**. Believe!" [NLT]<br><br>εἶτα λέγει τῷ Θωμᾷ, Φέρε τὸν δάκτυλόν σου ὧδε, καὶ ἴδε τὰς χεῖράς μου. καὶ φέρε τὴν χεῖρά σου καὶ βάλε εἰς τὴν πλευράν μου· καὶ **μὴ γίνου ἄπιστος** ἀλλὰ πιστός. [GNS]<br><br>εἶτα λέγει τῷ Θωμᾷ, Φέρε τὸν δάκτυλόν σου ὧδε καὶ ἴδε τὰς χεῖράς μου, καὶ φέρε τὴν χεῖρά σου καὶ βάλε εἰς τὴν πλευράν μου, καὶ **μὴ γίνου ἄπιστος** ἀλλὰ πιστός. [GNT] | To stop doubting; to stop being faithless; to stop becoming an unbeliever.<br><br>**Practical Application**<br>In this Scripture, Jesus warned and called for belief. Thomas had been walking down a dangerous road. The disciples had witnessed to him time and again, but he had refused time and again to accept their testimony. Note the Lord's strong charge:<br>⇒ "Don't be faithless any longer" (*më ginou apistos*): stop becoming an unbeliever. You are running the risk of *becoming faithless* and unbelieving, beyond the point of believing. You have carried your unbelief too far. It is now time to stop the foolishness. The others have been witnessing and witnessing the truth to you. Stop the stiff-necked, obstinate unbelief. You are in danger. |

# PRACTICAL WORD STUDIES
## in the New Testament

| ENGLISH WORD | GREEK WORD AND VERSE | THE WORD MEANS... |
|---|---|---|
| **#1436**<br>**Fall Away**<br><br>Offended–KJV<br>**Fall away–NASB**<br>**Fall away–NIV**<br>Stumble–NKJV<br>Desert–NLT<br><br>**POSB REFERENCE**<br>(Mt.26:31)<br>*Deeper Study* #1<br><br>See also POSB REF:<br>(Mk.14:27)<br>Note 1, point 1 | σκανδαλισθήσεσθε = skandalisthēsesthe<br>Pronunciation: [skan-dal-is'-thay-sehs-theh]<br>Parsing (part of speech): verb<br>    Mood—indicative<br>    Tense—future<br>    Voice—passive<br>    Person—2nd person<br>    Number—plural<br>    Stem or root—from σκανδαλίζω<br>Concordance References:<br>⇒ Strong's #4624 skandalizō<br>⇒ NIV #4997 skandalizō<br>⇒ NASB #4624 skandalizō<br><br>**Matthew 26:31**<br>Then saith Jesus unto them, All ye shall be **offended** because of me this night: for it is written, I will smite the shepherd, and the sheep of the flock shall be scattered abroad. [KJV]<br>Then Jesus said to them, "You will all **fall away** because of Me this night, for it is written, 'I WILL STRIKE DOWN THE SHEPHERD, AND THE SHEEP OF THE FLOCK SHALL BE SCATTERED.' [NASB]<br>Then Jesus told them, "This very night you will all **fall away** on account of me, for it is written:" 'I will strike the shepherd, and the sheep of the flock will be scattered.' [NIV]<br>Then Jesus said to them, "All of you will be made to **stumble** because of Me this night, for it is written: 'I will strike the Shepherd, And the sheep of the flock will be scattered.' [NKJV]<br>"Tonight all of you will **desert** me," Jesus told them. "For the Scriptures say, 'God will strike the Shepherd, and the sheep of the flock will be scattered.'" [NLT]<br>Τότε λέγει αὐτοῖς ὁ Ἰησοῦς, Πάντες ὑμεῖς **σκανδαλισθήσεσθε** ἐν ἐμοὶ ἐν τῇ νυκτὶ ταύτῃ, γέγραπται γάρ, Πατάξω τὸν ποιμένα, καὶ διασκορπισθήσεται τὰ πρόβατα τῆς ποίμνης· [GNS]<br>Τότε λέγει αὐτοῖς ὁ Ἰησοῦς, Πάντες ὑμεῖς **σκανδαλισθήσεσθε** ἐν ἐμοὶ ἐν τῇ νυκτὶ ταύτῃ, γέγραπται γάρ, Πατάξω τὸν ποιμένα, καὶ διασκορπισθήσονται τὰ πρόβατα τῆς ποίμνης. [GNT] | To stumble; to cause to stumble; to be led into sin; to be offended; to fall (because of Christ). (See POSB *Deeper Study* #1—Matthew 26:31).<br><br>**Practical Application**<br>When facing Christ, men stumble over three things. (For a thorough discussion see POSB *Deeper Study* #9—Matthew 21:44 and POSB *Deeper Study* #10—Matthew 21:44 cp. POSB note—Luke 20:17-18.)<br>1. Men stumble over who Christ is (John 6:54-58, 60, 66).<br>2. Men stumble over the cross of Christ (1 Cor. 1:21-23, esp. 1 Cor. 1:23).<br>3. Men stumble over the cross God calls them to bear (see POSB note—Luke 9:23 and POSB *Deeper Study* #1—Luke 9:23). |
| **#1437**<br>**Fall Away**<br><br>Offended–KJV<br>Stumbling–NASB<br>Go astray–NIV<br>Stumble–NKJV<br>**Fall away–NLT**<br><br>**POSB REFERENCE**<br>(Jn.16:1)<br>Note 1 | σκανδαλισθῆτε = skandalisthēte<br>Pronunciation: [skan-dal-is'-thay-teh]<br>Parsing (part of speech): verb<br>    Mood—subjunctive<br>    Tense—aorist<br>    Voice—passive<br>    Person—2nd person<br>    Number—plural<br>    Stem or root—from σκανδαλίζω<br>Concordance References:<br>⇒ Strong's #4624 skandalizo<br>⇒ NIV #4997 skandalizo<br>⇒ NASB #4624 skandalizo<br><br>**John 16:1**<br>These things have I spoken unto you, that ye should not be **offended**. [KJV]<br>"These things I have spoken to you, that you may be kept from **stumbling**. [NASB]<br>"All this I have told you so that you will not **go astray**. [NIV]<br>"These things I have spoken to you, that you should not be made to **stumble**. [NKJV]<br>"I have told you these things so that you won't **fall away**. [NLT]<br>Ταῦτα λελάληκα ὑμῖν, ἵνα μὴ **σκανδαλισθῆτε**· [GNS]<br>Ταῦτα λελάληκα ὑμῖν ἵνα μὴ**σκανδαλισθῆτε**. [GNT] | To go astray; to fall away; to cause to stumble or sin; to be offended; to stumble and to trip.<br><br>**Practical Application**<br>Jesus warned the believer that religionists would persecute His followers. Jesus warned the believer because He wants to prevent the believer from slipping away. The believer can stumble and fall over persecution. Persecution can...<br>• cause a believer to question his beliefs.<br>• cause a believer to weaken and return to the way of false religion.<br>• silence a believer and his witness.<br>• cause a believer to deny Jesus. |

# Practical Word Studies
## in the New Testament

| ENGLISH WORD | GREEK WORD AND VERSE | THE WORD MEANS... |
|---|---|---|
| **#1438**<br>**Fall Away–**<br>**Fallen Away**<br><br>Fall away–KJV<br>Fallen away–NASB<br>Fall away–NIV<br>Fall away–NKJV<br>Turn away–NLT<br><br>**POSB**<br>**REFERENCE**<br>(Heb.6:6)<br>Note 2 | παραπεσόντας = *parapesontas*<br>Pronunciation: [par-ap-ehs-on'-tahs]<br>Parsing (part of speech): verb<br>    Mood—participle<br>    Tense—aorist<br>    Voice—active<br>    Case—accusative<br>    Gender—masculine<br>    Number—plural<br>    Stem or root—from παραπίπτω<br>Concordance References:<br>⇒ Strong's #3895 parapiptō<br>⇒ NIV #4178 parapiptō<br>⇒ NASB #3895 parapiptō<br><br>**Hebrews 6:6**<br>If they shall **fall away**, to renew them again unto repentance; seeing they crucify to themselves the Son of God afresh, and put him to an open shame. [KJV]<br><br>And then have **fallen away**, it is impossible to renew them again to repentance, since they again crucify to themselves the Son of God, and put Him to open shame. [NASB]<br><br>If they **fall away**, to be brought back to repentance, because to their loss they are crucifying the Son of God all over again and subjecting him to public disgrace. [NIV]<br><br>If they **fall away,** to renew them again to repentance, since they crucify again for themselves the Son of God, and put *Him* to an open shame. [NKJV]<br><br>And who then **turn away** from God. It is impossible to bring such people to repentance again because they are nailing the Son of God to the cross again by rejecting him, holding him up to public shame. [NLT]<br><br>καὶ **παραπεσόντας**, πάλιν ἀνακαινίζειν εἰς μετάνοιαν, ἀνασταυροῦντας ἑαυτοῖς τὸν υἱὸν τοῦ Θεοῦ καὶ παραδειγματίζοντας· [GNS]<br><br>καὶ **παραπεσόντας**, πάλιν ἀνακαινίζειν εἰς μετάνοιαν, ἀνασταυροῦντας ἑαυτοῖς τὸν υἱὸν τοῦ θεοῦ καὶ παραδειγματίζοντας. [GNT] | To fall away; to turn away; to commit apostasy. This means to turn aside; to deviate.<br><br>**Practical Application**<br>It means...<br>• to turn aside from Christ.<br>• to turn away from Christ.<br>• to deviate from Christ. |
| **#1439**<br>**Fallen–Fall**<br><br>Fall–KJV<br>Fallen–NASB<br>Fallen–NIV<br>Fallen–NKJV<br>Fallen–NLT<br><br>**POSB**<br>**REFERENCE**<br>(Rev.9:1)<br>Note 2 | πεπτωκότα = *peptōkota*<br>Pronunciation: [pip'-tow-koh-tah]<br>Parsing (part of speech): verb<br>    Mood—participle<br>    Tense—perfect<br>    Voice—active<br>    Case—accusative<br>    Gender—masculine<br>    Number—singular<br>    Stem or root— from πίπτω<br>Concordance References:<br>⇒ Strong's #4098 piptō<br>⇒ NIV #4406 piptō<br>⇒ NASB #4098 piptō<br><br>**Rev. 9:1**<br>And the fifth angel sounded, and I saw a star **fall** from heaven unto the earth: and to him was given the key of the bottomless pit. [KJV]<br><br>And the fifth angel sounded, and I saw a star from heaven which had **fallen** to the earth; and the key of the bottomless pit was given to him. [NASB]<br><br>The fifth angel sounded his trumpet, and I saw a star that had **fallen** from the sky to the earth. The star was given the key to the shaft of the Abyss. [NIV]<br><br>Then the fifth angel sounded: And I saw a star **fallen** from heaven to the earth. To him was given the key to the bottomless pit. [NKJV]<br><br>Then the fifth angel blew his trumpet, and I saw a star that had **fallen** to earth from the sky, and he was given the key to the shaft of the bottomless pit. [NLT]<br><br>Καὶ ὁ πέμπτος ἄγγελος ἐσάλπισε, καὶ εἶδον ἀστέρα ἐκ τοῦ οὐρανοῦ **πεπτωκότα** εἰς τὴν γῆν, καὶ ἐδόθη αὐτῷ ἡ | Fall; fallen; fall down; fall to one's ruin or destruction; fall to one's knees; to collapse; be done away with, come to an end.<br><br>**Practical Application**<br>A star is said to fall from heaven. What is this star? Note that the pronoun *him* [KJV, NASB, NKJV] is used to refer to this star. It is a person. The word *star* is used in its symbolic way to refer to a person of fame or of high position. Who is this person? Note these facts.<br>⇒ He is said to be a star "fallen" (*peptōkota*) from heaven to earth. This is perfect tense which indicates past action. It means that he was already fallen when God gave him the key to the bottomless pit. |

# PRACTICAL WORD STUDIES
## in the New Testament

| ENGLISH WORD | GREEK WORD AND VERSE | THE WORD MEANS... |
|---|---|---|
| | κλεὶς τοῦ φρέατος τῆς ἀβύσσου. [GNS]<br>Καὶ ὁ πέμπτος ἄγγελος ἐσάλπισεν· καὶ εἶδον ἀστέρα ἐκ τοῦ οὐρανοῦ **πεπτωκότα** εἰς τὴν γῆν, καὶ ἐδόθη αὐτῷ ἡ κλεὶς τοῦ φρέατος τῆς ἀβύσσου [GNT] | |
| **#1440**<br>**False**<br><br>Guile–KJV<br>Guile–NASB<br>**False–NIV**<br>Deceit–NKJV<br>Honest–NLT<br><br>**POSB REFERENCE**<br>(Jn.1:47-48; esp. v.47)<br>Note 2, point 1b | δόλος = *dolos*<br>Pronunciation: [dol'-os]<br>Parsing (part of speech): noun<br>  Case—nominative<br>  Gender—masculine<br>  Number—singular<br>  Stem or root—from δόλος, ου<br>Concordance References:<br>⇒ Strong's #1388 dolos<br>⇒ NIV #1515 dolos<br>⇒ NASB #1388 dolos<br><br>**John 1:47**<br>Jesus saw Nathanael coming to him, and saith of him, Behold an Israelite indeed, in whom is no **guile**! [KJV]<br>Jesus saw Nathanael coming to Him, and said of him, "Behold, an Israelite indeed, in whom is no **guile**!" [NASB]<br>When Jesus saw Nathanael approaching, he said of him, "Here is a true Israelite, in whom there is nothing **false**." [NIV]<br>Jesus saw Nathanael coming toward Him, and said of him, "Behold, an Israelite indeed, in whom is no **deceit**!" [NKJV]<br>As they approached, Jesus said, "Here comes an **honest** man—a true son of Israel." [NLT]<br>εἶδεν ὁ Ἰησοῦς τὸν Ναθαναὴλ ἐρχόμενον πρὸς αὐτόν, καὶ λέγει περὶ αὐτοῦ, Ἴδε ἀληθῶς Ἰσραηλίτης, ἐν ᾧ **δόλος** οὐκ ἔστι. [GNS]<br>εἶδεν ὁ Ἰησοῦς τὸν Ναθαναὴλ ἐρχόμενον πρὸς αὐτόν καὶ λέγει περὶ αὐτοῦ, Ἴδε ἀληθῶς Ἰσραηλίτης ἐν ᾧ **δόλος** οὐκ ἔστιν. [GNT] | False, deceit, guile, fraud, trickery, deception, treachery, an impostor, an impersonator, a fake.<br><br>**Practical Application**<br>Note that these terms did not describe Nathanael's behavior. The words "nothing false" (*dolos*) means he did not deceive, bait, or mislead people. He did not hide what he thought; he said what he thought and acted what he felt. He was straightforward, open and honest, not deceptive or hypocritical. This trait had just been demonstrated in his response to Philip. He would not hide his true thoughts (John 1:46). One of the great tragedies in the legacy of persons is that they are full of guile. Many deceive, bait, and mislead others. Few are straightforward, open and honest, free of deception and hypocrisy. |
| **#1441**<br>**False Accusers**<br><br>**False accusers–KJV**<br>Malicious gossips–NASB<br>Slanderers–NIV<br>Slanderers–NKJV<br>Speaking evil of others–NLT<br><br>**POSB REFERENCE**<br>(Tit.2:3)<br>Note 3, point 2<br><br>**See also POSB REF:**<br>(2 Tim. 3:2-4; esp. v.3)<br>Note 2, point 11 | διαβόλους = *diabolous*<br>Pronunciation: [dee-ab'-ol-oos]<br>Parsing (part of speech): adjective<br>  Case—accusative<br>  Gender—feminine<br>  Number—plural<br>  Stem or root—from διάβολος, ου<br>Concordance References:<br>⇒ Strong's #1228 diabolos<br>⇒ NIV #1333 diabolos<br>⇒ NASB #1228 diabolos<br><br>**Titus 2:3**<br>The aged women likewise, that they be in behaviour as becometh holiness, not **false accusers**, not given to much wine, teachers of good things; [KJV]<br>Older women likewise are to be reverent in their behavior, not **malicious gossips**, nor enslaved to much wine, teaching what is good, [NASB]<br>Likewise, teach the older women to be reverent in the way they live, not to be **slanderers** or addicted to much wine, but to teach what is good. [NIV]<br>The older women likewise, that they be reverent in behavior, not **slanderers**, not given to much wine, teachers of good things—[NKJV]<br>Similarly, teach the older women to live in a way that is appropriate for someone serving the Lord. They must not go around **speaking evil of others** and must not be heavy drinkers. Instead, they should teach others what is good. [NLT]<br>Πρεσβύτιδας ὡσαύτως ἐν καταστήματι ἱεροπρεπεῖς, μὴ **διαβόλους**, μὴ οἴνῳ πολλῷ δεδουλωμένας, καλοδιδασκάλους, [GNS]<br>πρεσβύτιδας ὡσαύτως ἐν καταστήματι ἱεροπρεπεῖς, μὴ **διαβόλους** μηδὲ οἴνῳ πολλῷ δεδουλωμένας, καλοδιδασκάλους, [GNT] | Slanderers, false accusers, malicious gossips, speaking evil of others, talebearers, gossipers, a person who goes about talking about others, stirring up mischief and disturbance.<br><br>**Practical Application**<br>This is so terrible a sin that the devil himself is called *the false accuser* (*diabolous*). This—slanderer (*diabolous*)—is one of the very names of the devil. |

## PRACTICAL WORD STUDIES
### in the NEW TESTAMENT

| ENGLISH WORD | GREEK WORD AND VERSE | THE WORD MEANS... |
|---|---|---|
| **#1442**<br>**Falsehood**<br><br>Lying–KJV<br>**Falsehood**–NASB<br>**Falsehood**–NIV<br>Lying–NKJV<br>**Falsehood**–NLT<br><br>**POSB REFERENCE**<br>(Eph.4:25)<br>Note 1 | ψεῦδος = pseudos<br>Pronunciation: [psyoo'-dos]<br>Parsing (part of speech): noun<br>    Case—accusative<br>    Gender—neuter<br>    Number—singular<br>    Stem or root—from ψεῦδος, ους<br>Concordance References:<br>  ⇒ Strong's #5579 pseudos<br>  ⇒ NIV #6022 pseudos<br>  ⇒ NASB #5579 pseudos<br><br>**Ephes. 4:25**<br>Wherefore putting away **lying**, speak every man truth with his neighbour: for we are members one of another. [KJV]<br>Therefore, laying aside **falsehood**, speak truth, each one of you, with his neighbor, for we are members of one another. [NASB]<br>Therefore each of you must put off **falsehood** and speak truthfully to his neighbor, for we are all members of one body. [NIV]<br>Therefore, putting away **lying**, "Let each one of you speak truth with his neighbor," for we are members of one another. [NKJV]<br>So put away all **falsehood** and "tell your neighbor the truth" because we belong to each other. [NLT]<br>Διὸ ἀποθέμενοι τὸ **ψεῦδος** λαλεῖτε ἀλήθειαν ἕκαστος μετὰ τοῦ πλησίον αὐτοῦ· ὅτι ἐσμὲν ἀλλήλων μέλη. [GNS]<br>Διὸ ἀποθέμενοι τὸ **ψεῦδος** λαλεῖτε ἀλήθειαν ἕκαστος μετὰ τοῦ πλησίον αὐτοῦ, ὅτι ἐσμὲν ἀλλήλων μέλη. [GNT] | Falsehood, lying, distortion, fabrication, fib, untruth. It is untruthfulness, deception, lying, misrepresentation, exaggeration.<br><br>**Practical Application**<br>A lie or falsehood does at least three things.<br>1. Lying or falsehood misrepresents the truth. It camouflages and hides the truth. The person lied to does not know the truth; therefore, he has to act or live upon a lie. If the lie is serious, it can be very damaging:<br>  ⇒ A lie about a business deal can cost money and cause terrible loss.<br>  ⇒ A lie about the salvation of the gospel can cost a person the hope of eternal life.<br>  ⇒ A lie about loving someone can stir emotions that lead to destruction.<br>2. Lying deceives a person. It leads a person astray. A person deceives...<br>  • to get what he wants.<br>  • to seduce someone.<br>  • to cover up or hide something.<br>  • to cause harm or hurt.<br>The point to see is that lying is a deception, and deception eventually causes misunderstanding, disappointment, bewilderment, helplessness, and emotional upheaval.<br>3. Lying builds a wrong relationship, a relationship built upon sinking sand. Two people cannot possibly be friends or live together if the relationship is based upon lies. Lying destroys...<br>  • confidence<br>  • assurance<br>  • security<br>  • love<br>  • trust<br>  • hope |
| **#1443**<br>**Fan**<br><br>**Fan**–KJV<br>Winnowing fork–NASB<br>Winnowing fork–NIV<br>Winnowing fan–NKJV<br>Winnowing fork–NLT<br><br>**POSB REFERENCE**<br>(Lk.3:15-17; esp.v.17)<br>Note 6, point 3a | πτύον = ptuon<br>Pronunciation: [ptoo'-on]<br>Parsing (part of speech): noun<br>    Case—nominative<br>    Gender—neuter<br>    Number—singular<br>    Stem or root—from πτύον, ου<br>Concordance References:<br>  ⇒ Strong's #4425 ptuon<br>  ⇒ NIV #4768 ptuon<br>  ⇒ NASB #4425 ptuon<br><br>**Luke 3:17**<br>Whose **fan** is in his hand, and he will throughly purge his floor, and will gather the wheat into his garner; but the chaff he will burn with fire unquenchable. [KJV]<br>"And His **winnowing fork** is in His hand to thoroughly clear His threshing floor, and to gather the wheat into His barn; but He will burn up the chaff with unquenchable fire." [NASB]<br>His **winnowing fork** is in his hand to clear his threshing floor and to gather the wheat into his barn, but he will burn up the chaff with unquenchable fire." [NIV]<br>His **winnowing fan** is in His hand, and He will thoroughly clean out His threshing floor, and gather the wheat into His barn; but the chaff He will burn with unquenchable fire." [NKJV]<br>He is ready to separate the chaff from the grain with his **winnowing fork**. Then he will clean up the threshing area, storing the grain in his barn but burning the chaff | A winnowing fork, fan, or shovel that was used to throw grain up in the air to separate the wheat from the chaff.<br><br>**Practical Application**<br>In this Scripture, the winnowing fork or fan is the Messiah's power to pick up both the wheat and the chaff. |

# PRACTICAL WORD STUDIES
## in the NEW TESTAMENT

| ENGLISH WORD | GREEK WORD AND VERSE | THE WORD MEANS... |
|---|---|---|
| | with never-ending fire." [NLT]<br>οὗτο **πτύον** ἐν τῇ χειρὶ αὐτοῦ, διακαθαριεῖ τὴν ἅλωνα αὐτοῦ, καὶ συναξεῖ τὸν σῖτον εἰς τὴν ἀποθήκην αὐτοῦ, τὸ δὲ ἄχυρον κατακαύσει πυρὶ ἀσβέστῳ. [GNS]<br>οὗ τὸ **πτύον** ἐν τῇ χειρὶ αὐτοῦ διακαθᾶραι τὴν ἅλωνα αὐτοῦ καὶ συναγαγεῖν τὸν σῖτον εἰς τὴν ἀποθήκην αὐτοῦ, τὸ δὲ ἄχυρον κατακαύσει πυρὶ ἀσβέστῳ. [GNT] | |
| **#1444**<br>**Fan Into Flame–**<br>**Fan Into Flames**<br><br>Stir up–KJV<br>Kindle afresh–NASB<br>Fan into flame–NIV<br>Stir up–NKJV<br>Fan into flames–NLT<br><br>**POSB REFERENCE**<br>(2 Tim.1:6)<br>Note 1 | ἀναζωπυρεῖν = anazōpurein<br>Pronunciation: [an-ad-zo-poor-eh'-een]<br>Parsing (part of speech): verb<br>   Mood—infinitive<br>   Tense—present<br>   Voice—active<br>   Stem or root—from ἀναζωπυρέω<br>Concordance References:<br>  ⇒ Strong's #329 anazōpureō<br>  ⇒ NIV #351 anazōpureō<br>  ⇒ NASB #329 anazōpureō<br><br>**2 Tim. 1:6**<br>Wherefore I put thee in remembrance that thou **stir up** the gift of God, which is in thee by the putting on of my hands. [KJV]<br>And for this reason I remind you to **kindle afresh** the gift of God which is in you through the laying on of my hands. [NASB]<br>For this reason I remind you to **fan into flame** the gift of God, which is in you through the laying on of my hands. [NIV]<br>Therefore I remind you to **stir up** the gift of God which is in you through the laying on of my hands. [NKJV]<br>This is why I remind you to **fan into flames** the spiritual gift God gave you when I laid my hands on you. [NLT]<br>δι᾽ ἣν αἰτίαν ἀναμιμνῄσκω σε **ἀναζωπυρεῖν** τὸ χάρισμα τοῦ Θεοῦ, ὅ ἐστιν ἐν σοὶ διὰ τῆς ἐπιθέσεως τῶν χειρῶν μου. [GNS]<br>δι᾽ ἣν αἰτίαν ἀναμιμνῄσκω σε **ἀναζωπυρεῖν** τὸ χάρισμα τοῦ θεοῦ, ὅ ἐστιν ἐν σοὶ διὰ τῆς ἐπιθέσεως τῶν χειρῶν μου. [GNT] | To fan into flame; to stir up; to kindle afresh; to stir into flame. The phrase "fan into flame" (*anazōpurein*) can mean to keep blazing and to keep the flame of the fire burning. But it can also mean to rekindle and to restir the flame, indicating that the flame was about to go out.<br><br>**Practical Application**<br>Which is meant here? No doubt Timothy faced what we sometimes face: times when he needed to be restirred and rekindled. But there is no indication that Timothy's flame was about to go out.<br>Keep this is mind: Paul was facing death; he was about to be executed. He clearly states this fact (2 Tim. 4:6-8). Therefore, Paul sensed the need to give Timothy charge after charge. One of the very first things Timothy needed to do was to keep his spiritual gifts blazing and burning to the hottest point possible. The idea is present tense, which means it is progressive and continuous action. The believer is to *keep on* fanning the flame of his gift, never letting its flame lose any of its intensity. He is to use his gift to minister and minister, never slacking up nor losing his zeal. God has gifted the believer to minister, gifted him in a very, very special way; therefore, he must minister. He must do exactly what God has gifted him to do. |
| **#1445**<br>**Fashion**<br><br>Fashion–KJV<br>Form–NASB<br>Present form–NIV<br>Form–NKJV<br>All it contains–NLT<br><br>**POSB REFERENCE**<br>(1 Cor.7:29-31; esp. v.31)<br>Note 3 | σχῆμα = schēma<br>Pronunciation: [skhay'-mah]<br>Parsing (part of speech): noun<br>   Case—nominative<br>   Gender—neuter<br>   Number—singular<br>   Stem or root—from σχῆμα, τος<br>Concordance References:<br>  ⇒ Strong's #4976 schēma<br>  ⇒ NIV #5386 schēma [present form]<br>  ⇒ NASB #4976 schēma<br><br>**1 Cor. 7:31**<br>And they that use this world, as not abusing it: for the **fashion** of this world passeth away. [KJV]<br>And those who use the world, as though they did not make full use of it; for the **form** of this world is passing away. [NASB]<br>Those who use the things of the world, as if not engrossed in them. For this world in its **present form** is passing away. [NIV]<br>And those who use this world as not misusing *it*. For the **form** of this world is passing away. [NKJV]<br>Those in frequent contact with the things of the world should make good use of them without becoming attached to them, for this world and **all it contains** will pass away. [NLT]<br>καὶ οἱ χρώμενοι τῳ κόσμῳ τοῦτῳ, ὡς μὴ καταχρώμενοι· παράγει γὰρ τὸ **σχῆμα** τοῦ κόσμου τούτου. [GNS]<br>καὶ οἱ χρώμενοι τὸν κόσμον ὡς μὴ καταχρώμενοι· παράγει γὰρ τὸ **σχῆμα** τοῦ κόσμου τούτου. [GNT] | Present form, fashion, likeness, appearance, nature, all it [the world] contains.<br><br>**Practical Application**<br>It is a word taken from the theater. The world is nothing more than the passing scenes of a film that will soon end. The world is destined to end in its present form or fashion. The present state of things will cease just as the scenes of a film cease. The believer must keep this in mind; he must not live for the passing fashion of this world. He must live for eternity, keeping before his mind that time is short, ever so short. |

# PRACTICAL WORD STUDIES
## in the New Testament

| ENGLISH WORD | GREEK WORD AND VERSE | THE WORD MEANS... |
|---|---|---|
| **#1446**<br>**Fashion**<br><br>Fashion–KJV<br>Pattern–NASB<br>Pattern–NIV<br>Pattern–NKJV<br>Plan–NLT<br><br>**POSB REFERENCE**<br>(Acts 7:42-53; esp. v.44)<br>Note 6, point 3a | τύπον = tupon<br>Pronunciation: [too'-pon]<br>Parsing (part of speech): noun<br>  Case—accusative<br>  Gender—masculine<br>  Number—singular<br>  Stem or root—from τύπος, ου<br>Concordance References:<br>  ⇒ Strong's #5179 tupos<br>  ⇒ NIV #5596 tupos<br>  ⇒ NASB #5179 tupos<br><br>**Acts 7:44**<br>Our fathers had the tabernacle of witness in the wilderness, as he had appointed, speaking unto Moses, that he should make it according to the **fashion** that he had seen. [KJV]<br>"Our fathers had the tabernacle of testimony in the wilderness, just as He who spoke to Moses directed him to make it according to the **pattern** which he had seen. [NASB]<br>"Our forefathers had the tabernacle of the Testimony with them in the desert. It had been made as God directed Moses, according to the **pattern** he had seen. [NIV]<br>"Our fathers had the tabernacle of witness in the wilderness, as He appointed, instructing Moses to make it according to the **pattern** that he had seen, [NKJV]<br>"Our ancestors carried the Tabernacle with them through the wilderness. It was constructed in exact accordance with the **plan** shown to Moses by God. [NLT]<br>ἡ σκηνὴ τοῦ μαρτυρίου ἦν ἐν τοῖς πατράσιν ἡμῶν ἐν τῇ ἐρήμῳ, καθὼς διετάξατο ὁ λαλῶν τῷ Μωσῇ, ποιῆσαι αὐτὴν κατὰ τὸν **τύπον** ὃν ἑωράκει, [GNS]<br>Ἡ σκηνὴ τοῦ μαρτυρίου ἦν τοῖς πατράσιν ἡμῶν ἐν τῇ ἐρήμῳ καθὼς διετάξατο ὁ λαλῶν τῷ Μωϋσῇ ποιῆσαι αὐτὴν κατὰ τὸν **τύπον** ὃν ἑωράκει· [GNT] | A Pattern; a fashion; a plan; a form; a figure; a picture; an example; a model; a standard.<br><br>**Practical Application**<br>The people were inexcusable. Why? Because they were greatly blessed (Acts 7:44-47). God had blessed them with three particular things.<br>1. God had blessed the people with the tabernacle of His presence and testimony. Note that God had shown Moses a "fashion" (*tupon*), that is, a figure, a pattern, a picture of the tabernacle; and Moses had constructed it after the picture God had shown him.<br>2. God had blessed the people with leaders. Joshua and David and Solomon are mentioned. All three had the favor and blessings of God upon their lives. Therefore, the people were greatly blessed through these leaders.<br>3. God had blessed the people with the temple. David had desired to build the temple, but it was Solomon whom God appointed to construct it. (Cp. 1 Kings 6-8.) When the Jews returned from captivity to Jerusalem, Zerubbabel rebuilt the temple (516 B.C.). Sometime later, around 20 B.C., Herod the Great rebuilt the temple, making it one of the wonders of the world. It was this temple in which the Jews gloried.<br>The point is this: by being so blessed, the people (Israel) were inexcusable in their rejection of God. They had every opportunity available, yet they still chose the world instead of God. |
| **#1447**<br>**Fast–**<br>**Fasting–**<br>**Fasted**<br><br>Fast–KJV<br>Fasting–NASB<br>Fasting–NIV<br>Fasting–NKJV<br>Fasted–NLT<br><br>**POSB REFERENCE**<br>(Mk.2:18)<br>Note 1 | ἦσαν νηστεύοντες. = esan nesteuontes<br>Pronunciation: [ay'-sahn nace-tyoo'-o-tehs]<br>Parsing *esan* (part of speech): verb<br>  Mood—indicative<br>  Tense—imperfect<br>  Voice—active<br>  Person—3rd person<br>  Number—plural<br>  Stem or root—from εἰμί<br>Parsing *nesteuontes* (part of speech): verb<br>  Mood—participle<br>  Tense—present<br>  Voice—active<br>  Case—nominative<br>  Gender—masculine<br>  Number—plural<br>  Stem or root—from νηστεύω<br>Concordance References:<br>  ⇒ Strong's #1510 eimi + 3522 nesteuo<br>  ⇒ NIV #1639 eimi [were] + 3764 nësteuö [fasting]<br>  ⇒ NASB #1510 eimi + 3522 nesteuo<br><br>**Mark 2:18**<br>And the disciples of John and of the Pharisees used to **fast**: and they come and say unto him, Why do the disciples of John and of the Pharisees fast, but thy disciples fast not? [KJV]<br>And John's disciples and the Pharisees were **fasting**; and they came and said to Him, "Why do John's disciples and the disciples of the Pharisees fast, but Your disciples do not fast?" [NASB]<br>Now John's disciples and the Pharisees were **fasting**. Some people came and asked Jesus, "How is it that John's disciples and the disciples of the Pharisees are fasting, but yours are not?" [NIV] | To do without food, to abstain from eating, to refrain from eating for a specified amount of time for spiritual reasons.<br><br>**Practical Application**<br>In this Scripture, these words are more accurately translated "are fasting." The disciples of John and of the Pharisees were actually fasting when they asked Jesus this question. |

## PRACTICAL WORD STUDIES
### in the NEW TESTAMENT

| ENGLISH WORD | GREEK WORD AND VERSE | THE WORD MEANS... |
|---|---|---|
| | The disciples of John and of the Pharisees were **fasting**. Then they came and said to Him, "Why do the disciples of John and of the Pharisees fast, but Your disciples do not fast?" [NKJV]<br><br>John's disciples and the Pharisees sometimes **fasted**. One day some people came to Jesus and asked, "Why do John's disciples and the Pharisees fast, but your disciples don't fast?" [NLT]<br><br>Καὶ ἦσαν οἱ μαθηταὶ Ἰωάννου καὶ οἱ Φαρισαίων **νηστεύοντες**· καὶ ἔρχονται, καὶ λέγουσιν αὐτῷ, Διατί οἱ μαθηταὶ Ἰωάννου καὶ οἱ τῶν Φαρισαίων νηστεύουσιν, οἱ δὲ σοὶ μαθηταὶ οὐ νηστεύουσι; [GNS]<br><br>Καὶ ἦσαν οἱ μαθηταὶ Ἰωάννου καὶ οἱ Φαρισαῖοι **νηστεύοντες**. καὶ ἔρχονται καὶ λέγουσιν αὐτῷ, Διὰ τί οἱ μαθηταὶ Ἰωάννου καὶ οἱ μαθηταὶ τῶν Φαρισαίων νηστεύουσιν, οἱ δὲ σοὶ μαθηταὶ οὐ νηστεύουσιν; [GNT] | |
| **#1448**<br>**Fastings**<br><br>Fastings–KJV<br>Hunger–NASB<br>Hunger–NIV<br>Fastings–NKJV<br>Gone without food–NLT<br><br>**POSB REFERENCE**<br>(2 Cor.6:5)<br>Note 4 | νηστείαις = *nēsteiais*<br>Pronunciation: [nace-ti'-ah-ees]<br>Parsing (part of speech): noun<br>  Case—dative<br>  Gender—feminine<br>  Number—plural<br>  Stem or root—from νηστεία, ας<br>Concordance References:<br>  ⇒ Strong's #3521 nēsteia<br>  ⇒ NIV #3763 nēsteia<br>  ⇒ NASB #3521 nēsteia<br><br>**2 Cor. 6:5**<br>In stripes, in imprisonments, in tumults, in labours, in watchings, in **fastings**; [KJV]<br>In beatings, in imprisonments, in tumults, in labors, in sleeplessness, in **hunger**, [NASB]<br>In beatings, imprisonments and riots; in hard work, sleepless nights and **hunger**; [NIV]<br>In stripes, in imprisonments, in tumults, in labors, in sleeplessness, in **fastings**; [NKJV]<br>We have been beaten, been put in jail, faced angry mobs, worked to exhaustion, endured sleepless nights, and **gone without food**. [NLT]<br>ἐν πληγαῖς, ἐν φυλακαῖς, ἐν ἀκαταστασίαις, ἐν κόποις, ἐν ἀγρυπνίαις, ἐν **νηστείαις**, [GNS]<br>ἐν πληγαῖς, ἐν φυλακαῖς, ἐν ἀκαταστασίαις, ἐν κόποις, ἐν ἀγρυπνίαις, ἐν **νηστείαις**, [GNT] | Hunger, fasting, starvation; to go without food.<br><br>**Practical Application**<br>This means not only deliberate fastings, but being so involved in his work that Paul forgot to eat or else chose to keep working instead of eating. |
| **#1449**<br>**Father**<br><br>Father–KJV<br>Father–NASB<br>Father–NIV<br>Father–NKJV<br>Father–NLT<br><br>**POSB REFERENCE**<br>(Lk.22:41-42; esp. v.42)<br>Note 3, point 2 | Πάτερ = *Patēr*<br>Pronunciation: [pat-ayr']<br>Parsing (part of speech): noun<br>  Case—vocative<br>  Gender—masculine<br>  Number—singular<br>  Stem or root—from πατήρ, πατρός<br>Concordance References:<br>  ⇒ Strong's #3962 patēr<br>  ⇒ NIV #4252 patēr<br>  ⇒ NASB #3962 patēr<br><br>**Luke 22:42**<br>Saying, **Father**, if thou be willing, remove this cup from me: nevertheless not my will, but thine, be done. [KJV]<br>Saying, "**Father**, if Thou art willing, remove this cup from Me; yet not My will, but Thine be done." [NASB]<br>"**Father**, if you are willing, take this cup from me; yet not my will, but yours be done." [NIV]<br>Saying, "**Father**, if it is Your will, take this cup away from Me; nevertheless not My will, but Yours, be done." [NKJV]<br>"**Father**, if you are willing, please take this cup of suffering away from me. Yet I want your will, not mine." [NLT]<br>λέγων, **Πάτερ**, εἰ βούλει παρένεγκε τὸ ποτήριον | Father.<br><br>**Practical Application**<br>It is the address of a child's love and dependency and trust. The child knows that His father will hear and turn to him when he calls "Father."<br>When a person genuinely says "Father," he is surrendering to God. He is...<br>• denying humanism, self-sufficiency, and all other gods.<br>• surrendering himself to the Father of the Lord Jesus Christ.<br>• acknowledging the Father of the Lord Jesus Christ to be his own Father. |

# PRACTICAL WORD STUDIES
## in the NEW TESTAMENT

| ENGLISH WORD | GREEK WORD AND VERSE | THE WORD MEANS... |
|---|---|---|
| | τοῦτο ἀπ' ἐμοῦ· πλὴν μὴ τὸ θέλημά μου, ἀλλὰ τὸ σὸν γενέσθω. [GNS]<br>λέγων, Πάτερ, εἰ βούλει παρένεγκε τοῦτο τὸ ποτήριον ἀπ' ἐμοῦ· πλὴν μὴ τὸ θέλημά μου ἀλλὰ τὸ σὸν γινέσθω. [GNT] | |
| **#1450**<br>**Fault, Without**<br><br>Without blame–KJV<br>Blameless–NASB<br>Blameless–NIV<br>Without blame–NKJV<br>**Without fault–NLT**<br><br>**POSB**<br>**REFERENCE**<br>(Eph.1:4)<br>Note 2, point 2 | ἀμώμους = amōmous<br>Pronunciation: [am'-o-moos]<br>Parsing (part of speech): adjective<br>    Case—accusative<br>    Gender—masculine<br>    Number—plural<br>    Stem or root—from ἄμωμος, ον<br>Concordance References:<br>  ⇒ Strong's #299 amōmos<br>  ⇒ NIV #320 amōmos<br>  ⇒ NASB #299 amōmos<br><br>**Ephes. 1:4**<br>According as he hath chosen us in him before the foundation of the world, that we should be holy and **without blame** before him in love: [KJV]<br>Just as He chose us in Him before the foundation of the world, that we should be holy and **blameless** before Him. In love [NASB]<br>For he chose us in him before the creation of the world to be holy and **blameless** in his sight. In love [NIV]<br>Just as He chose us in Him before the foundation of the world, that we should be holy and **without blame** before Him in love, [NKJV]<br>Long ago, even before he made the world, God loved us and chose us in Christ to be holy and **without fault** in his eyes. [NLT]<br>καθὼς ἐξελέξατο ἡμᾶς ἐν αὐτῷ πρὸ καταβολῆς κόσμου, εἶναι ἡμᾶς ἁγίους, καὶ **ἀμώμους** κατενώπιον αὐτοῦ ἐν ἀγάπῃ, [GNS]<br>καθὼς ἐξελέξατο ἡμᾶς ἐν αὐτῷ πρὸ καταβολῆς κόσμου εἶναι ἡμᾶς ἁγίους καὶ **ἀμώμους** κατενώπιον αὐτοῦ ἐν ἀγάπῃ, [GNT] | To be blameless; to be without blame; to be faultless; to be unblemished.<br><br>**Practical Application**<br>The words "without fault" (*amōmous*) mean to be free from sin, dirt, and filth; to be above reproach and without blemish; to be without fault and defilement. |
| **#1451**<br>**Faultless**<br><br>**Faultless–KJV**<br>Blameless–NASB<br>Without fault–NIV<br>**Faultless–NKJV**<br>Innocent of sin–NLT<br><br>**POSB**<br>**REFERENCE**<br>(Jude 1:24-25; esp. v.24)<br>Note 4, point 2 | ἀμώμους = amōmous<br>Pronunciation: [am'-o-moos]<br>Parsing (part of speech): adjective<br>    Case—accusative<br>    Gender—masculine<br>    Number—plural<br>    Stem or root—from ἄμωμος, ον<br>Concordance References:<br>  ⇒ Strong's #299 amōmos<br>  ⇒ NIV #320 amōmos<br>  ⇒ NASB #299b amōmos<br><br>**Jude 1:24**<br>Now unto him that is able to keep you from falling, and to present you **faultless** before the presence of his glory with exceeding joy, [KJV]<br>Now to Him who is able to keep you from stumbling, and to make you stand in the presence of His glory **blameless** with great joy, [NASB]<br>To him who is able to keep you from falling and to present you before his glorious presence **without fault** and with great joy—[NIV]<br>Now to Him who is able to keep you from stumbling, And to present you **faultless** before the presence of His glory with exceeding joy, [NKJV]<br>And now, all glory to God, who is able to keep you from stumbling, and who will bring you into his glorious presence **innocent of sin** and with great joy. [NLT]<br>Τῷ δὲ δυναμένῳ φυλάξαι ὑμᾶς ἀπταίστους, καὶ στῆσαι κατενώπιον τῆς δόξης αὐτοῦ **ἀμώμους** ἐν ἀγαλλιάσει, [GNS]<br>Τῷ δὲ δυναμένῳ φυλάξαι ὑμᾶς ἀπταίστους καὶ στῆσαι κατενώπιον τῆς δόξης αὐτοῦ **ἀμώμους** ἐν ἀγαλλιάσει, [GNT] | To be without fault, blameless; to be innocent of sin; to be faultless, without blemish; to be spotless and pure, without any defilement whatsoever.<br><br>**Practical Application**<br>God is *able to present us faultless* when we come face to face with Him. God is able to accept us in Jesus Christ, the spotless Lamb of God. If we will continue to approach God in Christ—in the name of Christ and His death—then God will accept us and count our faith as righteousness. He will accept us in the righteousness of His Son, the Lord Jesus Christ. God is able to do this, and He will do it if we will draw near Him *in Christ*. |

# PRACTICAL WORD STUDIES
## in the New Testament

| ENGLISH WORD | GREEK WORD AND VERSE | THE WORD MEANS... |
|---|---|---|
| **#1452**<br>**Fear**<br><br>Fear–KJV<br>Fear–NASB<br>Afraid–NIV<br>Fear–NKJV<br>Fear–NLT<br><br>**POSB REFERENCE**<br>(Mt.10:29)<br>*Deeper Study #2*<br>[Note: the word **FEAR** is used in Mt.10:26, 28, 31] | φοβεῖσθε = phobeisthe<br>Pronunciation: [fob-ees-the]<br>Parsing (part of speech): verb<br>    Mood—imperative<br>    Tense—present<br>    Voice—middle or passive deponent<br>    Person—2nd person<br>    Number—plural<br>    Stem or root—from φοβέομαι<br>Concordance References:<br>  ⇒ Strong's #5399 phobeo<br>  ⇒ NIV #5828 phobeo<br>  ⇒ NASB #5399 phobeo<br><br>**Matthew 10:28**<br>And fear not them which kill the body, but are not able to kill the soul: but rather **fear** him which is able to destroy both soul and body in hell. [KJV]<br><br>"And do not fear those who kill the body, but are unable to kill the soul; but rather **fear** Him who is able to destroy both soul and body in hell. [NASB]<br><br>Do not be afraid of those who kill the body but cannot kill the soul. Rather, be **afraid of** the One who can destroy both soul and body in hell. [NIV]<br><br>And do not fear those who kill the body but cannot kill the soul. But rather **fear** Him who is able to destroy both soul and body in hell. [NKJV]<br><br>"Don't be afraid of those who want to kill you. They can only kill your body; they cannot touch your soul. **Fear** only God, who can destroy both soul and body in hell. [NLT]<br><br>καὶ μὴ φοβηθῆτε ἀπὸ τῶν ἀποκτεινόντων τὸ σῶμα, τὴν δὲ ψυχὴν μὴ δυναμένων ἀποκτεῖναι. φοβηθῆτε δὲ μᾶλλον τὸν δυνάμενον καὶ ψυχὴν καὶ σῶμα ἀπολέσαι ἐν γεέννῃ. [GNS]<br><br>καὶ μὴ φοβεῖσθε ἀπὸ τῶν ἀποκτεννόντων τὸ σῶμα, τὴν δὲ ψυχὴν μὴ δυναμένων ἀποκτεῖναι· φοβεῖσθε δὲ μᾶλλον τὸν δυνάμενον καὶ ψυχὴν καὶ σῶμα ἀπολέσαι ἐν γεέννῃ. [GNT] | Fear, fright, alarm, dread, terror.<br><br>**Practical Application**<br>In relation to God it means to fear; to show reverence, to sense a reverential fear; to stand in awe because of a holy fear. It means we fear God because He is God: holy, righteous, pure, and just. It means that we fear and stand in awe and reverence of God who will reveal His holiness when he executes His justice in some future day of judgment.<br><br>*[Handwritten notes:]*<br>Hebrew "Yirah" (Strongs H3374)<br>Fear, Terror, Awe, Respectful<br>Greek version<br>fear, dread, terror<br>(Strongs G5401)<br><br>"The fear of the Lord means to fear him."<br>"fear of the Lord" or "fear the Lord" occurs 110 times in the Bible and the word meanings are CONSISTENT! |
| **#1453**<br>**Fear**<br><br>Fear–KJV<br>Fear–NASB<br>Awe–NIV<br>Fear–NKJV<br>Wonder–NLT<br><br>**POSB REFERENCE**<br>(Lk.1:64-66; esp. v.65)<br>Note 3, point 2<br><br>See also POSB REF:<br>(Acts 2:43)<br>Note 3<br>(Acts 9:31)<br>*Deeper Study #1* | φόβος = phobos<br>Pronunciation: [fob'-os]<br>Parsing (part of speech): noun<br>    Case—nominative<br>    Gender—masculine<br>    Number—singular<br>    Stem or root—from φόβος, ου<br>Concordance References:<br>  ⇒ Strong's #5401 phobos<br>  ⇒ NIV #5832 phobos<br>  ⇒ NASB #5401 phobos<br><br>**Luke 1:65**<br>And **fear** came on all that dwelt round about them: and all these sayings were noised abroad throughout all the hill country of Judaea. [KJV]<br><br>And **fear** came on all those living around them; and all these matters were being talked about in all the hill country of Judea. [NASB]<br><br>The neighbors were all filled with **awe**, and throughout the hill country of Judea people were talking about all these things. [NIV]<br><br>Then **fear** came on all who dwelt around them; and all these sayings were discussed throughout all the hill country of Judea. [NKJV]<br><br>**Wonder** fell upon the whole neighborhood, and the news of what had happened spread throughout the Judean hills. [NLT]<br><br>καὶ ἐγένετο ἐπὶ πάντας φόβος τοὺς περιοικοῦντας αὐτούς· καὶ ἐν ὅλῃ τῇ ὀρεινῇ τῆς Ἰουδαίας διελαλεῖτο πάντα τὰ ῥήματα ταῦτα, [GNS]<br><br>καὶ ἐγένετο ἐπὶ πάντας φόβος τοὺς περιοικοῦντας αὐτούς, καὶ ἐν ὅλῃ τῇ ὀρεινῇ τῆς Ἰουδαίας διελαλεῖτο πάντα τὰ ῥήματα ταῦτα. [GNT] | Awe, fear, wonder. *NOTE:*<br><br>**Practical Application**<br>It does not mean to fear God's presence, to shrink and withdraw from Him. To the contrary, it means that a person reverences and stands in awe of Him, wanting to approach and know Him because He is the majestic and sovereign Being of the universe. It means that a person does not fear...<br>• to trust and believe Him.<br>• to approach and worship Him.<br>• to do His will.<br>• to serve Him.<br><br>*[Handwritten: Come boldly to the Throne of GRACE!]*<br><br>Fear does not mean terror or fright. It means...<br>• a godly fear, a fear of God, of His displeasure and judgment.<br>• a holy sense of God's presence.<br>• a consciousness that God is working.<br>• a reverence for God and for what is happening.<br>• a sense of awe and wonder. |

## PRACTICAL WORD STUDIES
### in the NEW TESTAMENT

| ENGLISH WORD | GREEK WORD AND VERSE | THE WORD MEANS... |
|---|---|---|
| **#1454**<br>**Fear**<br><br>Fear–KJV<br>Fear–NASB<br>Reverent fear–NIV<br>Fear–NKJV<br>Reverent fear–NLT<br><br>**POSB REFERENCE**<br>(1 Pt.1:17)<br>Note 2 | φόβῳ = *phobō*<br>Pronunciation: [fob'-o']<br>Parsing (part of speech): noun<br>  Case—dative<br>  Gender—masculine<br>  Number—singular<br>  Stem or root—from φόβος, ου<br>Concordance References:<br>  ⇒ Strong's #5401 phobos<br>  ⇒ NIV #5832 phobos<br>  ⇒ NASB #5401 phobos<br><br>**1 Peter 1:17**<br>And if ye call on the Father, who without respect of persons judgeth according to every man's work, pass the time of your sojourning here in **fear**: [KJV]<br>And if you address as Father the One who impartially judges according to each man's work, conduct yourselves in **fear** during the time of your stay upon earth; [NASB]<br>Since you call on a Father who judges each man's work impartially, live your lives as strangers here in **reverent fear**. [NIV]<br>And if you call on the Father, who without partiality judges according to each one's work, conduct yourselves throughout the time of your stay *here* in **fear**; [NKJV]<br>And remember that the heavenly Father to whom you pray has no favorites when he judges. He will judge or reward you according to what you do. So you must live in **reverent fear** of him during your time as foreigners here on earth. [NLT]<br>καὶ εἰ πατέρα ἐπικαλεῖσθε τὸν ἀπροσωπολήμπτως κρίνοντα κατὰ τὸ ἑκάστου ἔργον, ἐν **φόβῳ** τὸν τῆς παροικίας ὑμῶν χρόνον ἀναστράφητε· [GNS]<br>καὶ εἰ πατέρα ἐπικαλεῖσθε τὸν ἀπροσωπολήμπτως κρίνοντα κατὰ τὸ ἑκάστου ἔργον, ἐν **φόβῳ** τὸν τῆς παροικίας ὑμῶν χρόνον ἀναστράφητε, [GNT] | Fear; reverent fear; respect; awe; wonder; amazement.<br><br>**Practical Application**<br>Believers are to reverence God because *God will judge the world*. Note that the word "fear" (*phobō*) is used. It means to hold God in reverence and awe. The judgment of God should strike fear, dread and terror within us, for it is to be the most fearful, dreaded and terrorizing experience imaginable. In fact, the human mind cannot even picture how awful and frightening it will be to be judged and cut off from God for eternity. Two things are said about the judgment of God.<br>1. Every person is going to be judged. No one will escape. Every person will come to the day when he will stand all alone in a private interview with God. In that moment, he will stand face to face with God for one purpose and one purpose alone: to be judged.<br>2. It is the works of a person that are to be judged. No false profession will stand in that day. When God reveals the person's works, his works will show that he never really trusted in Christ. He only said that he believed Christ, but his life and works will prove differently. It will be seen that he lived a lie. His life and works will show that he lived for the world and its possessions and pleasure. |
| **#1455**<br>**Fear**<br><br>Fear–KJV<br>Reverence–NASB<br>Holy fear–NIV<br>Godly fear–NKJV<br>Obeyed–NLT<br><br>**POSB REFERENCE**<br>(Heb.11:7)<br>Note 1, point 1 | εὐλαβηθείς = *eulabētheis*<br>Pronunciation: [yoo-lab-ay'-theh-ees]<br>Parsing (part of speech): verb<br>  Mood—participle<br>  Tense—aorist<br>  Voice—passive deponent<br>  Case—nominative<br>  Gender—masculine<br>  Number—singular<br>  Stem or root—from εὐλαβέομαι<br>Concordance References:<br>  ⇒ Strong's #2125 eulabeomai<br>  ⇒ NIV #2326 eulabeomai<br>  ⇒ NASB #2125 eulabeomai<br><br>**Hebrews 11:7**<br>By faith Noah, being warned of God of things not seen as yet, moved with **fear**, prepared an ark to the saving of his house; by the which he condemned the world, and became heir of the righteousness which is by faith. [KJV]<br>By faith Noah, being warned by God about things not yet seen, in **reverence** prepared an ark for the salvation of his household, by which he condemned the world, and became an heir of the righteousness which is according to faith. [NASB]<br>By faith Noah, when warned about things not yet seen, in **holy fear** built an ark to save his family. By his faith he condemned the world and became heir of the righteousness that comes by faith. [NIV]<br>By faith Noah, being divinely warned of things not yet seen, moved with godly **fear**, prepared an ark for the saving of his household, by which he condemned the world and became heir of the righteousness which is according to faith. [NKJV]<br>It was by faith that Noah built an ark to save his fami- | Fear, holy fear; to reverence; to obey; to be moved with fear. The word "fear" (*eulabētheis*) means with godly fear (A.T. Robertson. *Word Pictures in the New Testament*, Vol. 5, p.421). It has the idea of...<br>• reverence.<br>• standing in awe of God and His warning.<br>• taking heed lest one fall under God's judgment.<br>• diligently taking God at His Word.<br>• immediately acting upon what God says.<br><br>**Practical Application**<br>There was a time in world history when the earth had become so wicked that it was filled with corruption and violence. It was so corrupt that every imagination of man's heart was corrupt and evil. Man had reached the point of no return; he would never repent and return to God. God was left with no choice: the earth had to be destroyed. But there was one man on earth who was godly—Noah. Noah worshipped and honored God in his life. Therefore, God warned Noah of the coming judgment upon the earth.<br>⇒ God told Noah to prepare an ark and the ark would save him, his family, and two of every animal.<br>⇒ God also told Noah to warn the world of coming judgment.<br>Noah believed God's warning of coming judgment, and he began to build the ark with a godly fear and reverence, knowing that what God said would come true. God's judgment |

# Practical Word Studies in the New Testament

| ENGLISH WORD | GREEK WORD AND VERSE | THE WORD MEANS... |
|---|---|---|
| | ly from the flood. He **obeyed** God, who warned him about something that had never happened before. By his faith he condemned the rest of the world and was made right in God's sight. [NLT]<br><br>πίστει χρηματισθεὶς Νῶε περὶ τῶν μηδέπω βλεπομένων, **εὐλαβηθεὶς**, κατεσκεύασε κιβωτὸν εἰς σωτηρίαν τοῦ οἴκου αὐτοῦ· δι' ἧς κατέκρινε τὸν κόσμον, καὶ τῆς κατὰ πίστιν δικαιοσύνης ἐγένετο κληρονόμος. [GNS]<br><br>Πίστει χρηματισθεὶς Νῶε περὶ τῶν μηδέπω βλεπομένων, **εὐλαβηθεὶς** κατεσκεύασεν κιβωτὸν εἰς σωτηρίαν τοῦ οἴκου αὐτοῦ δι' ἧς κατέκρινεν τὸν κόσμον, καὶ τῆς κατὰ πίστιν δικαιοσύνης ἐγένετο κληρονόμος. [GNT] | would fall upon the earth; Noah believed it and knew it by faith. |
| **#1456**<br>**Fear–**<br>**Fear, Great**<br><br>Fear–KJV<br>Fear–NASB<br>Filled with awe–NIV<br>Fear–NKJV<br>Great fear–NLT<br><br>**POSB REFERENCE**<br>(Lk.7:16-17; esp. v.16)<br>Note 4 | ἔλαβεν φόβος = elaben phobos<br>Pronunciation: [eh-la-behn' fob'-os]<br>Parsing *elaben* (part of speech): verb<br>  Mood—indicative<br>  Tense—aorist<br>  Voice—active<br>  Person—3rd person<br>  Number—singular<br>  Stem or root—from λαμβάνω<br>Parsing *phobos* (part of speech): noun<br>  Case—nominative<br>  Gender—masculine<br>  Number—singular<br>  Stem or root—from φόβος, ου<br>Concordance References:<br>⇒ Strong's #2983 lambanō + 5401 phobos<br>⇒ NIV #3284 lambanō [filled with] + 5832 phobos [awe]<br>⇒ NASB #2983 lambanō + 5401 phobos<br><br>**Luke 7:16**<br>And there came a **fear** on all: and they glorified God, saying, That a great prophet is risen up among us; and, That God hath visited his people. [KJV]<br>And **fear** gripped them all, and they began glorifying God, saying, "A great prophet has arisen among us!" and, "God has visited His people!" [NASB]<br>They were all **filled with awe** and praised God. "A great prophet has appeared among us," they said. "God has come to help his people." [NIV]<br>Then **fear** came upon all, and they glorified God, saying, "A great prophet has risen up among us"; and, "God has visited His people." [NKJV]<br>**Great fear** swept the crowd, and they praised God, saying, "A mighty prophet has risen among us," and "We have seen the hand of God at work today." [NLT]<br>Ἔλαβε δὲ φόβος ἅπαντας, καὶ ἐδόξαζον τὸν Θεὸν, λέγοντες, ὅτι Προφήτης μέγας ἐγήγερται ἐν ἡμῖν, καὶ ὅτι Ἐπεσκέψατο ὁ Θεὸς τὸν λαὸν αὐτοῦ. [GNS]<br>Ἔλαβεν δὲ φόβος πάντας καὶ ἐδόξαζον τὸν θεὸν λέγοντες ὅτι Προφήτης μέγας ἠγέρθη ἐν ἡμῖν καὶ ὅτι Ἐπεσκέψατο ὁ θεὸς τὸν λαὸν αὐτοῦ. [GNT] | To be filled with awe; to fear; to wonder; to be amazed; to be astonished; to respect; to have a great fear, reverence and awe. It is fear, dread, terror.<br><br>**Practical Application**<br>In relation to God, it means to be afraid; to show reverence, to sense a reverential fear; to stand in awe because of a holy fear. It means we fear God because He is God: holy, righteous, pure, just. It means that we fear and stand in awe and reverence of God who will reveal His holiness and execute His justice in some future day of judgment. |
| **#1457**<br>**Fear Not–**<br>**Fear, Do Not**<br><br>Fear not–KJV<br>Do not fear–NASB<br>Don't [be] afraid–NIV<br>Do not be afraid–NKJV<br>Don't be afraid–NLT | Μὴ φοβοῦ = mē phobou<br>Pronunciation: [may fob-oo']<br>Parsing (part of speech): verb<br>  Mood—imperative<br>  Tense—present<br>  Voice—middle or passive deponent<br>  Person—2nd person<br>  Number—singular<br>  Stem or root—from φοβέομαι<br>Concordance References:<br>⇒ Strong's #3361 me + 5399 phobou<br>⇒ NIV #3590 mē + 5828 phobou<br>⇒ NASB #3361 me + 5399 phobou<br><br>**Luke 5:10**<br>And so was also James, and John, the sons of Zebedee, | Do not have fear, dread, terror; do not be afraid.<br><br>**Practical Application**<br>The words "Fear not" indicate that Peter was actually scared and frightened. Jesus was calming him, telling him to trust and stop fearing. |

## Practical Word Studies in the New Testament

| ENGLISH WORD | GREEK WORD AND VERSE | THE WORD MEANS... |
|---|---|---|
| **POSB REFERENCE**<br>(Lk.5:10)<br>Note 7, point 1<br><br>See also POSB REF:<br>(Lk.8:49-56; esp. v.50)<br>Note 4, point 2 | which were partners with Simon. And Jesus said unto Simon, **Fear not**; from henceforth thou shalt catch men. [KJV]<br>And so also James and John, sons of Zebedee, who were partners with Simon. And Jesus said to Simon, "**Do not fear**, from now on you will be catching men." [NASB]<br>And so were James and John, the sons of Zebedee, Simon's partners. Then Jesus said to Simon, "**Don't be afraid**; from now on you will catch men." [NIV]<br>And so also were James and John, the sons of Zebedee, who were partners with Simon. And Jesus said to Simon, "**Do not be afraid**. From now on you will catch men." [NKJV]<br>His partners, James and John, the sons of Zebedee, were also amazed. Jesus replied to Simon, "**Don't be afraid**! From now on you'll be fishing for people!" [NLT]<br>ὁμοίως δὲ καὶ Ἰάκωβον καὶ Ἰωάννην, υἱοὺς Ζεβεδαίου, οἳ ἦσαν κοινωνοὶ τῷ Σίμωνι. καὶ εἶπε πρὸς τὸν Σίμωνα ὁ Ἰησοῦς, **Μὴ φοβοῦ**· ἀπὸ τοῦ νῦν ἀνθρώπους ἔσῃ ζωγρῶν. [GNS]<br>ὁμοίως δὲ καὶ Ἰάκωβον καὶ Ἰωάννην υἱοὺς Ζεβεδαίου, οἳ ἦσαν κοινωνοὶ τῷ Σίμωνι. καὶ εἶπεν πρὸς τὸν Σίμωνα ὁ Ἰησοῦς, **Μὴ φοβοῦ**· ἀπὸ τοῦ νῦν ἀνθρώπους ἔσῃ ζωγρῶν. [GNT] | |
| **#1458**<br>**Feast, Let Us Keep The**<br><br>Let us keep the feast–KJV<br>Let us therefore celebrate the feast–NASB<br>Let us keep the Festival–NIV<br>Let us keep the feast–NKJV<br>Let us celebrate the festival–NLT<br><br>**POSB REFERENCE**<br>(1 Cor.5:8)<br>Note 3, point 5 | ἑορτάζωμεν = heortazōmen<br>Pronunciation: [eh-or-tad'-zo-mehn]<br>Parsing (part of speech): verb<br>  Mood—subjunctive<br>  Tense—present<br>  Voice—active<br>  Person—1st person<br>  Number—plural<br>  Stem or root—from ἑορτάζω<br>Concordance References:<br> ⇒ Strong's #1858 heortazō<br> ⇒ NIV #2037 heortazō<br> ⇒ NASB #1858 heortazō<br><br>**1 Cor. 5:8**<br>Therefore **let us keep the feast**, not with old leaven, neither with the leaven of malice and wickedness; but with the unleavened bread of sincerity and truth. [KJV]<br>**Let us therefore celebrate the feast**, not with old leaven, nor with the leaven of malice and wickedness, but with the unleavened bread of sincerity and truth. [NASB]<br>Therefore **let us keep the Festival**, not with the old yeast, the yeast of malice and wickedness, but with bread without yeast, the bread of sincerity and truth. [NIV]<br>Therefore **let us keep the feast**, not with old leaven, nor with the leaven of malice and wickedness, but with the unleavened *bread* of sincerity and truth. [NKJV]<br>So **let us celebrate the festival**, not by eating the old bread of wickedness and evil, but by eating the new bread of purity and truth. [NLT]<br>ὥστε **ἑορτάζωμεν**, μὴ ἐν ζύμῃ παλαιᾷ, μηδὲ ἐν ζύμῃ κακίας καὶ πονηρίας, ἀλλ' ἐν ἀζύμοις εἰλικρινείας καὶ ἀληθείας. [GNS]<br>ὥστε **ἑορτάζωμεν** μὴ ἐν ζύμῃ παλαιᾷ μηδὲ ἐν ζύμῃ κακίας καὶ πονηρίας ἀλλ' ἐν ἀζύμοις εἰλικρινείας καὶ ἀληθείας. [GNT] | Let us keep the festival or feast; let us celebrate the festival or feast; let us observe the festival or feast. The words "let us keep" are in the present tense, which means continuous action.<br><br>**Practical Application**<br>The church *must continue* to *keep* the feast, continue to purge out the old yeast of sin and its corrupting influences. It must not only discipline itself and the man who is living in shameful sin, it must continue to keep itself pure, to continue celebrating the feast of purity before God. |
| **#1459**<br>**Feast, Let Us Therefore Celebrate The**<br><br>Let us keep the feast–KJV | ἑορτάζωμεν = heortazōmen<br>Pronunciation: [eh-or-tad'-zo-mehn]<br>Parsing (part of speech): verb<br>  Mood—subjunctive<br>  Tense—present<br>  Voice—active<br>  Person—1st person<br>  Number—plural<br>  Stem or root—from ἑορτάζω | Let us keep the festival or feast; let us celebrate the festival or feast; let us observe the festival or feast. The words "let us keep" are in the present tense, which means continuous action.<br><br>**Practical Application**<br>The church *must continue* to *celebrate* the feast, continue to purge out the old yeast of sin |

# Practical Word Studies in the New Testament

| ENGLISH WORD | GREEK WORD AND VERSE | THE WORD MEANS... |
|---|---|---|
| **Let us therefore celebrate the feast–NASB**<br>Let us keep the Festival–NIV<br>Let us keep the feast–NKJV<br>Let us celebrate the festival–NLT<br><br>**POSB REFERENCE**<br>(1 Cor.5:8)<br>Note 3, point 5 | Concordance References:<br>⇒ Strong's #1858 heortazō<br>⇒ NIV #2037 heortazō<br>⇒ NASB #1858 heortazō<br><br>**1 Cor. 5:8**<br>Therefore **let us keep the feast**, not with old leaven, neither with the leaven of malice and wickedness; but with the unleavened bread of sincerity and truth. [KJV]<br>**Let us therefore celebrate the feast**, not with old leaven, nor with the leaven of malice and wickedness, but with the unleavened bread of sincerity and truth. [NASB]<br>Therefore **let us keep the Festival**, not with the old yeast, the yeast of malice and wickedness, but with bread without yeast, the bread of sincerity and truth. [NIV]<br>Therefore **let us keep the feast**, not with old leaven, nor with the leaven of malice and wickedness, but with the unleavened *bread* of sincerity and truth. [NKJV]<br>So **let us celebrate the festival**, not by eating the old bread of wickedness and evil, but by eating the new bread of purity and truth. [NLT]<br>ὥστε **ἑορτάζωμεν**, μὴ ἐν ζύμῃ παλαιᾷ, μηδὲ ἐν ζύμῃ κακίας καὶ πονηρίας, ἀλλ' ἐν ἀζύμοις εἰλικρινείας καὶ ἀληθείας. [GNS]<br>ὥστε **ἑορτάζωμεν** μὴ ἐν ζύμῃ παλαιᾷ μηδὲ ἐν ζύμῃ κακίας καὶ πονηρίας ἀλλ' ἐν ἀζύμοις εἰλικρινείας καὶ ἀληθείας. [GNT] | and its corrupting influences. It must not only discipline itself and the man who is living in shameful sin, it must continue to keep itself pure, to continue celebrating the feast of purity before God. |
| **#1460**<br>**Feasting**<br><br>Revellings–KJV<br>Carousals–NASB<br>Orgies–NIV<br>Revelries–NKJV<br>**Feasting–NLT**<br><br>**POSB REFERENCE**<br>(1 Pt.4:3)<br>Note 3, point 4 | **κώμοις** = kōmois<br>Pronunciation: [ko'-moys]<br>Parsing (part of speech): noun<br>    Case—dative<br>    Gender—masculine<br>    Number—plural<br>    Stem or root—from κῶμος, ου<br>Concordance References:<br>⇒ Strong's #2970 kōmos<br>⇒ NIV #3269 kōmos<br>⇒ NASB #2970 kōmos<br><br>**1 Peter 4:3**<br>For the time past of our life may suffice us to have wrought the will of the Gentiles, when we walked in lasciviousness, lusts, excess of wine, **revellings**, banquetings, and abominable idolatries: [KJV]<br>For the time already past is sufficient for you to have carried out the desire of the Gentiles, having pursued a course of sensuality, lusts, drunkenness, **carousals**, drinking parties and abominable idolatries. [NASB]<br>For you have spent enough time in the past doing what pagans choose to do—living in debauchery, lust, drunkenness, **orgies**, carousing and detestable idolatry. [NIV]<br>For we *have spent* enough of our past lifetime in doing the will of the Gentiles—when we walked in lewdness, lusts, drunkenness, **revelries**, drinking parties, and abominable idolatries. [NKJV]<br>You have had enough in the past of the evil things that godless people enjoy—their immorality and lust, their **feasting** and drunkenness and wild parties, and their terrible worship of idols. [NLT]<br>ἀρκετὸς γὰρ ἡμῖν ὁ παρεληλυθὼς χρόνος τὸ βίου τὸ θέλημα τῶν ἐθνῶν κατεργάσασθαι, πεπορευμένους ἐν ἀσελγείαις, ἐπιθυμίαις, οἰνοφλυγίαις, **κώμοις**, πότοις, καὶ ἀθεμίτοις εἰδωλολατρείαις· [GNS]<br>ἀρκετὸς γὰρ ὁ παρεληλυθὼς χρόνος τὸ βούλημα τῶν ἐθνῶν κατειργάσθαι πεπορευμένους ἐν ἀσελγείαις, ἐπιθυμίαις, οἰνοφλυγίαις, **κώμοις**, πότοις καὶ ἀθεμίτοις εἰδωλολατρίαις. [GNT] | Orgies, revelings, carousals; feasting, uncontrolled license, indulgence, and pleasure; taking part in wild parties or in drinking parties or in orgies; lying around indulging in feeding the lusts of the flesh, the desires of the sinful nature.<br><br>**Practical Application**<br>It is a graphic picture of a life that is out of control, a life that has cast off reason and pursued a course of carousals. |

# Practical Word Studies
## in the New Testament

| ENGLISH WORD | GREEK WORD AND VERSE | THE WORD MEANS... |
|---|---|---|
| **#1461**<br>**Feeble**<br><br>Feeble–KJV<br>Weaker–NASB<br>Weaker–NIV<br>Weaker–NKJV<br>Weakest and least important–NLT<br><br>**POSB REFERENCE**<br>(1 Cor.12:21-23; esp. v.22)<br>Note 3 | ἀσθενέστερα = asthenestera<br>Pronunciation: [as-then-ehs'-teh-rah]<br>Parsing (part of speech): adjective<br>    Type—comparative<br>    Case—nominative<br>    Gender—neuter<br>    Number—plural<br>    Stem or root—from ἀσθενής, ές<br>Concordance References:<br>  ⇒ Strong's #772 asthenēs<br>  ⇒ NIV #822 asthenēs<br>  ⇒ NASB #772 asthenēs<br><br>**1 Cor. 12:22**<br>Nay, much more those members of the body, which seem to be more **feeble**, are necessary: [KJV]<br>On the contrary, it is much truer that the members of the body which seem to be **weaker** are necessary; [NASB]<br>On the contrary, those parts of the body that seem to be **weaker** are indispensable, [NIV]<br>No, much rather, those members of the body which seem to be **weaker** are necessary. [NKJV]<br>In fact, some of the parts that seem **weakest and least important** are really the most necessary. [NLT]<br>ἀλλὰ πολλῷ μᾶλλον τὰ δοκοῦντα μέλη τοῦ σώματος **ἀσθενέστερα** ὑπάρχειν, ἀναγκαῖά ἐστι· [GNS]<br>ἀλλὰ πολλῷ μᾶλλον τὰ δοκοῦντα μέλη τοῦ σώματος **ἀσθενέστερα** ὑπάρχειν ἀναγκαῖά ἐστιν, [GNT] | Feeble, sick, sickly, weak, delicate, fragile, helpless.<br><br>**Practical Application**<br>In appearance the lesser parts of the body may seem unimportant, but they are not; they are essential. In fact, they are actually more necessary. The average layman who serves as a personal worker, although he is never seen by the crowds, is much more essential to decisions for Christ than the evangelist who is in the center of the scene. The dear saint who has become a *prayer warrior* is much more essential to the strength of the church than the most eloquent preacher who ever fills the pulpit. |
| **#1462**<br>**Feed**<br><br>Feed–KJV<br>Tend–NASB<br>Feed–NIV<br>Feed–NKJV<br>Feed–NLT<br><br>**POSB REFERENCE**<br>(Jn.21:16; cp. Jn.21:15, 17)<br>Note 3, point 3 | Βόσκε = Boske<br>Pronunciation: [bos'-keh]<br>Parsing (part of speech): verb<br>    Mood—imperative<br>    Tense—present<br>    Voice—active<br>    Person—2nd person<br>    Number—singular<br>    Stem or root—from βόσκω<br>Concordance References:<br>  ⇒ Strong's #1006 bosko<br>  ⇒ NIV #1081 bosko<br>  ⇒ NASB #1006 bosko<br><br>**John 21:15**<br>So when they had dined, Jesus saith to Simon Peter, Simon, son of Jonas, lovest thou me more than these? He saith unto him, Yea, Lord; thou knowest that I love thee. He saith unto him, **Feed** my lambs. [KJV]<br>So when they had finished breakfast, Jesus said to Simon Peter, "Simon, son of John, do you love Me more than these?" He said to Him, "Yes, Lord; You know that I love You." He said to him, "**Tend** My lambs." [NASB]<br>When they had finished eating, Jesus said to Simon Peter, "Simon son of John, do you truly love me more than these?" "Yes, Lord," he said, "you know that I love you." Jesus said, "**Feed** my lambs." [NIV]<br>So when they had eaten breakfast, Jesus said to Simon Peter, "Simon, *son* of Jonah, do you love Me more than these?" He said to Him, "Yes, Lord; You know that I love You." He said to him, "**Feed** My lambs." [NKJV]<br>After breakfast Jesus said to Simon Peter, "Simon son of John, do you love me more than these?" "Yes, Lord," Peter replied, "you know I love you." "Then **feed** my lambs," Jesus told him. [NLT]<br>Ὅτε οὖν ἠρίστησαν, λέγει τῷ Σίμωνι Πέτρῳ ὁ Ἰησοῦς, Σίμων Ἰωνᾶ, ἀγαπᾷς με πλέον τούτων; λέγει αὐτῷ, Ναί Κύριε· σὺ οἶδας ὅτι φιλῶ σε. λέγει αὐτῷ, **Βόσκε** τὰ ἀρνία μου. [GNS]<br>Ὅτε οὖν ἠρίστησαν λέγει τῷ Σίμωνι Πέτρῳ ὁ Ἰησοῦς, Σίμων Ἰωάννου, ἀγαπᾷς με πλέον τούτων; λέγει αὐτῷ, Ναί, κύριε, σὺ οἶδας ὅτι φιλῶ σε. λέγει αὐτῷ, **Βόσκε** τὰ ἀρνία μου. [GNT] | To feed; to tend; to nourish; to support; to sustain; to provide for.<br><br>**Practical Application**<br>Note that the word used for feeding (*Boske*) is the word used for both the lambs (John 21:15) and the sheep (John 21:17). Both the lambs and sheep are to be fed on the same Word and fed in the same way. The ministry to the flock or church is twofold.<br>1. The first ministry is to feed (*boske*, John 21:15, 17).<br>  ⇒ To give food, teaching both the milk and meat of the Word. (1 Peter 2:2-3; Hebrews 5:12-14).<br>  ⇒ To guide into the study of the Word—showing oneself approved to God. (2 Tim. 2:15).<br>2. The second ministry is to shepherd (*poimaine*, John 21:16). Shepherding involves all the works of the ministry. |

# PRACTICAL WORD STUDIES
## in the NEW TESTAMENT

| ENGLISH WORD | GREEK WORD AND VERSE | THE WORD MEANS... |
|---|---|---|
| | **NOTE ALSO THIS SCRIPTURE...**<br>**John 21:17**<br>He saith unto him the third time, Simon, *son* of Jonas, lovest thou me? Peter was grieved because he said unto him the third time, Lovest thou me? And he said unto him, Lord, thou knowest all things; thou knowest that I love thee. Jesus saith unto him, **Feed** my sheep. [KJV]<br>He said to him the third time, "Simon, *son* of John, do you love Me?" Peter was grieved because He said to him the third time, "Do you love Me?" And he said to Him, "Lord, You know all things; You know that I love You." Jesus said to him, "**Tend** My sheep. [NASB]<br>The third time he said to him, "Simon son of John, do you love me?" Peter was hurt because Jesus asked him the third time, "Do you love me?" He said, "Lord, you know all things; you know that I love you." Jesus said, "**Feed** my sheep. [NIV]<br>He said to him the third time, "Simon, *son* of Jonah, do you love Me?" Peter was grieved because He said to him the third time, "Do you love Me?" And he said to Him, "Lord, You know all things; You know that I love You." Jesus said to him, "**Feed** My sheep. [NKJV]<br>Once more he asked him, "Simon son of John, do you love me?" Peter was grieved that Jesus asked the question a third time. He said, "Lord, you know everything. You know I love you." Jesus said, "Then **feed** my sheep. [NLT]<br>λέγει αὐτῷ τὸ τρίτον, Σίμων Ἰωνᾶ, φιλεῖς με; ἐλυπήθη ὁ Πέτρος, ὅτι εἶπεν αὐτῷ τὸ τρίτον, φιλεῖς με; καὶ εἶπεν αὐτῷ, Κύριε, σὺ πάντα οἶδας· σὺ γινώσκεις ὅτι φιλῶ σε. λέγει αὐτῷ ὁ Ἰησοῦς, **Βόσκε** τὰ πρόβατά μου. [GNS]<br>λέγει αὐτῷ τὸ τρίτον, Σίμων Ἰωάννου, φιλεῖς με; ἐλυπήθη ὁ Πέτρος ὅτι εἶπεν αὐτῷ τὸ τρίτον, Φιλεῖς με; καὶ λέγει αὐτῷ, Κύριε, πάντα σὺ οἶδας, σὺ γινώσκεις ὅτι φιλῶ σε. λέγει αὐτῷ [ὁ Ἰησοῦς], **Βόσκε** τὰ πρόβατά μου. [GNT] | |
| **#1463**<br>**Feed**<br><br>Feed–KJV<br>Shepherd–NASB<br>Take care of–NIV<br>Tend–NKJV<br>Take care of–NLT<br><br>**POSB REFERENCE**<br>(Jn.21:16; cp. Jn.21:15, 17)<br>Note 3, point 3 | Ποίμαινε = poimaine<br>Pronunciation: [poy-mah'ee-neh]<br>Parsing (part of speech): verb<br>   Mood—imperative<br>   Tense—present<br>   Voice—active<br>   Person—2nd person<br>   Number—singular<br>   Stem or root—from ποιμαίνω<br>Concordance References:<br> ⇒ Strong's #4165 poimaino<br> ⇒ NIV #4477 poimaino<br> ⇒ NASB #4165 poimaino<br><br>**John 21:16**<br>He saith to him again the second time, Simon, son of Jonas, lovest thou me? He saith unto him, Yea, Lord; thou knowest that I love thee. He saith unto him, **Feed** my sheep. [KJV]<br>He said to him again a second time, "Simon, son of John, do you love Me?" He said to Him, "Yes, Lord; You know that I love You." He said to him, "**Shepherd** My sheep." [NASB]<br>Again Jesus said, "Simon son of John, do you truly love me?" He answered, "Yes, Lord, you know that I love you." Jesus said, "**Take care of** my sheep." [NIV]<br>He said to him again a second time, "Simon, *son* of Jonah, do you love Me?" He said to Him, "Yes, Lord; You know that I love You." He said to him, "**Tend** My sheep." [NKJV]<br>Jesus repeated the question: "Simon son of John, do you love me?" "Yes, Lord," Peter said, "you know I love you." "Then **take care of** my sheep," Jesus said. [NLT] | To take care of; to feed; to shepherd; to rule.<br><br>**Practical Application**<br>What is the responsibility of the Shepherd to the sheep? The Shepherd leads and shepherds the sheep. He loves them as His own; therefore, He must lead them to the green pastures and still waters. He must see that they are nourished and protected and given the very best care possible. (See POSB note—Mark 6:34 for more discussion, what happens to sheep without a Shepherd.)<br>1. He feeds the sheep even if He has to gather them in His arms to carry them to the feeding pasture (Isaiah 40:11).<br>2. He guides the sheep to the pasture and away from the rough places and precipices (Psalm 23:1-4).<br>3. He seeks and saves the sheep who get lost (Matthew 18:11-12; Ezekiel 34:16).<br>4. He protects the sheep. He even sacrifices His life for the sheep (John 10:11; Hebrews 13:20).<br>5. He restores the sheep who go astray and return (1 Peter 2:25).<br>6. He rewards the sheep for obedience and faithfulness (1 Peter 5:4).<br>7. He shall keep the sheep separate from the goats (Matthew 25:32-33). |

# PRACTICAL WORD STUDIES
## in the NEW TESTAMENT

| ENGLISH WORD | GREEK WORD AND VERSE | THE WORD MEANS... |
|---|---|---|
| | λέγει αὐτῷ πάλιν δεύτερον, Σίμων Ἰωνᾶ ἀγαπᾷς με; Λέγει αὐτῷ, Ναί, Κύριε· σὺ οἶδας ὅτι φιλῶ σε. λέγει αὐτῷ, **Ποίμαινε** τὰ πρόβατά μου. [GNS]<br>λέγει αὐτῷ πάλιν δεύτερον, Σίμων Ἰωάννου, ἀγαπᾷς με; λέγει αὐτῷ, Ναί, κύριε, σὺ οἶδας ὅτι φιλῶ σε. λέγει αὐτῷ, **Ποίμαινε** τὰ πρόβατά μου. [GNT] | |
| **#1464**<br>**Feed The Flock Of God**<br><br>Feed the flock of God—KJV<br>Shepherd the flock of God—NASB<br>Be shepherds of—NIV<br>Shepherd the flock of God—NKJV<br>Care for the flock of God—NLT<br><br>**POSB REFERENCE**<br>(1 Pt.5:2-3)<br>Note 2<br><br>See also POSB REF:<br>(Acts 20:28-31; esp. v.28)<br>Note 2 | ποιμάνατε = *poimanate*<br>Pronunciation: [poy-mah'nah-teh]<br>Parsing (part of speech): verb<br>  Mood—imperative<br>  Tense—aorist<br>  Voice—active<br>  Person—2nd person<br>  Number—plural<br>  Stem or root—from ποιμαίνω<br>Concordance References:<br>  ⇒ Strong's #4165 poimainō<br>  ⇒ NIV #4477 poimainō<br>  ⇒ NASB #4165 poimainō<br><br>**1 Peter 5:2**<br>**Feed the flock of God** which is among you, taking the oversight thereof, not by constraint, but willingly; not for filthy lucre, but of a ready mind; [KJV]<br>**Shepherd the flock of God** among you, exercising oversight not under compulsion, but voluntarily, according to the will of God; and not for sordid gain, but with eagerness; [NASB]<br>**Be shepherds of** God's flock that is under your care, serving as overseers—not because you must, but because you are willing, as God wants you to be; not greedy for money, but eager to serve; [NIV]<br>**Shepherd the flock of God** which is among you, serving as overseers, not by compulsion but willingly, not for dishonest gain but eagerly; [NKJV]<br>**Care for the flock of God** entrusted to you. Watch over it willingly, not grudgingly—not for what you will get out of it, but because you are eager to serve God. [NLT]<br>**ποιμάνατε** τὸ ἐν ὑμῖν ποίμνιον τοῦ Θεοῦ, ἐπισκοποῦντες μὴ ἀναγκαστῶς, ἀλλ᾽ ἑκουσίως· μηδὲ αἰσχροκερδῶς, ἀλλὰ προθύμως," [GNS]<br>**ποιμάνατε** τὸ ἐν ὑμῖν ποίμνιον τοῦ θεοῦ [ἐπισκοποῦντες] μὴ ἀναγκαστῶς ἀλλὰ ἑκουσίως κατὰ θεόν, μηδὲ αἰσχροκερδῶς ἀλλὰ προθύμως, [GNT] | Be shepherds of, to feed the flock of God; to shepherd the flock of God; to care for the flock of God.<br><br>**Practical Application**<br>The word "feed" (*poimanate*) is an all-inclusive word that covers all the duties of the minister. It means not only to preach and teach the Word of God but to tend and shepherd the flock. It means to act like a shepherd, to carry out the duties of a shepherd. The duties of the shepherd are several fold (see POSB *Deeper Study* #2—1 Peter 2:25 for more discussion):<br>⇒ to feed the sheep even if he has to gather them in his arms to carry them to the pasture.<br>⇒ to guide the sheep to the pasture and away from the rough places and precipices.<br>⇒ to seek and save the sheep who get lost.<br>⇒ to protect the sheep, even to sacrifice His life for the sheep, if necessary.<br>⇒ to restore the sheep who go astray and return.<br>⇒ to reward the sheep for obedience and faithfulness.<br>⇒ to keep the sheep separate from the goats.<br><br>But note this: in all the duties of tending and looking after the flock of God, we must never forget what the great Greek scholar W.E. Vine stresses:<br>*"In the spiritual care of God's children, the feeding of the flock from the Word of God is the constant and regular necessity; it is to have the foremost place. The tending (which includes this) consists of other acts, of discipline, authority, restoration, material assistance of individuals, but they are incidental in comparison with the feeding"* (Expository Dictionary of New Testament Words). |
| **#1465**<br>**Feeds**<br><br>Nourisheth—KJV<br>Nourishes—NASB<br>**Feeds**—NIV<br>Nourishes—NKJV<br>Cares—NLT<br><br>**POSB REFERENCE**<br>(Eph.5:25-33; esp. v.29)<br>Note 2, point 2 | ἐκτρέφει = *ektrephei*<br>Pronunciation: [ek-tref'-eh-ee]<br>Parsing (part of speech): verb<br>  Mood—indicative<br>  Tense—present<br>  Voice—active<br>  Person—3rd person<br>  Number—singular<br>  Stem or root—from ἐκτρέφω<br>Concordance References:<br>  ⇒ Strong's #1625 ektrephō<br>  ⇒ NIV #1763 ektrephō<br>  ⇒ NASB #1625 ektrephō<br><br>**Ephes. 5:29**<br>For no man ever yet hated his own flesh; but **nourisheth** and cherisheth it, even as the Lord the church: [KJV]<br>For no one ever hated his own flesh, but **nourishes** and cherishes it, just as Christ also does the church, [NASB]<br>After all, no one ever hated his own body, but he **feeds** and cares for it, just as Christ does the church—[NIV] | To feed; to clothe; to nurture; to look after until she is mature in the marriage and then to continue nourishing her as long as she lives.<br><br>**Practical Application**<br>The love which the husband is to have for his wife is the very same love he has for his own body. This is a startling statement. Note again what it says: the husband is to love his wife just as much as he loves *his own body*. This means that he is to care for his wife as he does his own body.<br>What a difference would exist in marriage if the husband just *cares for* his wife as he does his own body. Think through the meaning of the two words for just a moment and imagine the difference that could exist. |

# PRACTICAL WORD STUDIES
## in the NEW TESTAMENT

| ENGLISH WORD | GREEK WORD AND VERSE | THE WORD MEANS... |
|---|---|---|
| | For no one ever hated his own flesh, but **nourishes** and cherishes it, just as the Lord *does* the church. [NKJV]<br><br>No one hates his own body but lovingly **cares** for it, just as Christ cares for his body, which is the church. [NLT]<br><br>οὐδεὶς γάρ ποτε τὴν ἑαυτοῦ σάρκα ἐμίσησεν, ἀλλ **ἐκτρέφει** καὶ θάλπει αὐτήν, καθὼς καὶ ὁ Κύριος τὴν ἐκκλησίαν· [GNS]<br><br>οὐδεὶς γάρ ποτε τὴν ἑαυτοῦ σάρκα ἐμίσησεν ἀλλὰ **ἐκτρέφει** καὶ θάλπει αὐτήν, καθὼς καὶ ὁ Χριστὸς τὴν ἐκκλησίαν, [GNT] | |
| **#1466**<br>**Feeling That Everyone Is Wrong Except Those In Your Own Little Group**<br><br>Heresies–KJV<br>Factions–NASB<br>Factions–NIV<br>Heresies–NKJV<br>Feeling that everyone is wrong except those in your own little group–NLT<br><br>**POSB REFERENCE**<br>(Gal.5:19-21; esp. v.20)<br>Note 2 | αἱρέσεις = *haireseis*<br>Pronunciation: [ah'ee-res-ee-is]<br>Parsing (part of speech): noun<br>   Case—nominative<br>   Gender—feminine<br>   Number—plural<br>   Stem or root—from αἵρεσις, εως<br>Concordance References:<br> ⇒ Strong's #139 hairesis<br> ⇒ NIV #146 hairesis<br> ⇒ NASB #139 hairesis<br><br>**Galatians 5:20**<br>Idolatry, witchcraft, hatred, variance, emulations, wrath, strife, seditions, **heresies**, [KJV]<br>Idolatry, sorcery, enmities, strife, jealousy, outbursts of anger, disputes, dissensions, **factions**, [NASB]<br>Idolatry and witchcraft; hatred, discord, jealousy, fits of rage, selfish ambition, dissensions, **factions** [NIV]<br>Idolatry, sorcery, hatred, contentions, jealousies, outbursts of wrath, selfish ambitions, dissensions, **heresies**, [NKJV]<br>Idolatry, participation in demonic activities, hostility, quarreling, jealousy, outbursts of anger, selfish ambition, divisions, the **feeling that everyone is wrong except those in your own little group**, [NLT]<br>εἰδωλολατρία, φαρμακεία, ἔχθραι, ἔρεις, ζῆλοι, θυμοί, ἐριθεῖαι, διχοστασίαι, **αἱρέσεις**, [GNS]<br>εἰδωλολατρία, φαρμακεία, ἔχθραι, ἔρις, ζῆλος, θυμοί, ἐριθεῖαι, διχοστασίαι, **αἱρέσεις**, [GNT] | Factions; differences; heresies; feeling that everyone is wrong except in one's own little group; inner circle; non conformists.<br><br>**Practical Application**<br>It is rejecting the fundamental beliefs of God, Christ, the Scriptures, and the church; believing and holding to some teaching other than the truth. |
| **#1467**<br>**Fell Into Trance**<br><br>Fell into [a] trance–KJV<br>Fell into [a] trance–NASB<br>Fell into [a] trance–NIV<br>Fell into [a] trance –NKJV<br>Fell into [a] trance–NLT<br><br>**POSB REFERENCE**<br>Acts 10:9-22; esp. v.10)<br>Note 2, point 3 | ἐγένετο ἐπ' ἔκστασις = *egeneto ep' ekstasis*<br>Pronunciation: [eg-ehn-eh-to ep-ee' ek'-stas-is]<br>Parsing *egeneto* (part of speech): verb<br>   Mood—indicative<br>   Tense—aorist<br>   Voice—middle deponent<br>   Person—3rd person<br>   Number—singular<br>   Stem or root—from γίνομαι<br>Parsing *ekstasis* (part of speech): noun<br>   Case—nominative<br>   Gender—feminine<br>   Number—singular<br>   Stem or root—from ἔκστασις, εως<br>Concordance References:<br> ⇒ Strong's #1096 + 1611 + 1909 ginomai ekstasis epi<br> ⇒ NIV #1181 + 1749 + 2093 ginomai ekstasis epi<br> ⇒ NASB #1096 + 1611 + 1909 ginomai ekstasis epi<br><br>**Acts 10:10**<br>And he became very hungry, and would have eaten: but while they made ready, he **fell into** a **trance**, [KJV]<br>And he became hungry, and was desiring to eat; but while they were making preparations, he **fell into** a **trance**; [NASB]<br>He became hungry and wanted something to eat, and while the meal was being prepared, he **fell into** a **trance**. [NIV] | To fall into a trance, a dreamlike state, a deep relaxation.<br><br>**Practical Application**<br>The Greek says that "a trance [an ecstasy] came upon him"; that is, he was transported out of himself (*ekstasis*). His mind was so concentrated, so focused that Peter lost all sense of the world around him. He was swallowed up in the thoughts of God, transported mentally out of this world. It is something like a daydream, but a daydream so concentrated and focused that all contact with one's surroundings is completely lost. It is a time of ecstasy in the presence of the Lord, receiving His Word, whatever He has to say to one's heart. |

## PRACTICAL WORD STUDIES
### in the NEW TESTAMENT

| ENGLISH WORD | GREEK WORD AND VERSE | THE WORD MEANS... |
|---|---|---|
| | Then he became very hungry and wanted to eat; but while they made ready, he **fell into** a trance [NKJV]<br>And he was hungry. But while lunch was being prepared, he **fell into** a trance. [NLT]<br>ἐγένετο δὲ πρόσπεινος, καὶ ἤθελε γεύσασθαι· παρασκευαζόντων δὲ ἐκείνων, ἐπέπεσεν **ἐπ'** αὐτὸν **ἔκστασις**, [GNS]<br>ἐγένετο δὲ πρόσπεινος καὶ ἤθελεν γεύσασθαι, παρασκευαζόντων δὲ αὐτῶν ἐγένετο **ἐπ'** αὐτὸν **ἔκστασις** [GNT] | |
| **#1468**<br>**Fell On–**<br>**Fell Upon**<br><br>Fell on–KJV<br>Fell upon–NASB<br>Came on–NIV<br>Fell upon–NKJV<br>Fell upon–NLT<br><br>**POSB**<br>**REFERENCE**<br>(Acts 10:44-45; esp. v.44)<br>Note 1, point 3 | ἐπέπεσεν ἐπὶ = epepesen epi<br>Pronunciation: [eh-pehp-ehs-en ehp-ee]<br>Parsing *epepesen* (part of speech): verb<br>    Mood—indicative<br>    Tense—aorist<br>    Voice—active<br>    Person—3rd person<br>    Number—singular<br>    Stem or root—from ἐπιπίπτω<br>Parsing *epi* (part of speech): preposition<br>    Case—accusative<br>    Stem or root—from ἐπί<br>Concordance References:<br>  ⇒ Strong's #1909 + 1968 epi epipiptō<br>  ⇒ NIV #2093 + 2158 epi epipiptō<br>  ⇒ NASB #1909 + 1968 epi epipiptō<br><br>**Acts 10:44**<br>While Peter yet spake these words, the Holy Ghost **fell on** all them which heard the word. [KJV]<br>While Peter was still speaking these words, the Holy Spirit **fell upon** all those who were listening to the message. [NASB]<br>While Peter was still speaking these words, the Holy Spirit **came on** all who heard the message. [NIV]<br>While Peter was still speaking these words, the Holy Spirit **fell upon** all those who heard the word. [NKJV]<br>Even as Peter was saying these things, the Holy Spirit **fell upon** all who had heard the message. [NLT]<br>Ἔτι λαλοῦντος τοῦ Πέτρου τὰ ῥήματα ταῦτα, **ἐπέπεσε** τὸ Πνεῦμα τὸ Ἅγιον **ἐπὶ** πάντας τοὺς ἀκούοντας τὸν λόγον. [GNS]<br>Ἔτι λαλοῦντος τοῦ Πέτρου τὰ ῥήματα ταῦτα **ἐπέπεσεν** τὸ πνεῦμα τὸ ἅγιον **ἐπὶ** πάντας τοὺς ἀκούοντας τὸν λόγον. [GNT] | Came upon; fell upon; fell on.<br><br>**Practical Application**<br>Peter was still preaching; he had not finished his message when the Holy Spirit fell. God and God alone caused the Holy Spirit to fall upon the Gentile believers, not the hands of Peter...<br>• anointing them<br>• being laid upon them<br>• baptizing them<br>• placing them into water<br><br>No man had anything to do with God's pouring His Spirit upon these believers. The gift of the Spirit was the act of God and God alone. |
| **#1469**<br>**Fellowship**<br><br>Fellowship–KJV<br>Partnership–NASB<br>In common–NIV<br>Fellowship–NKJV<br>Partner–NLT<br><br>**POSB**<br>**REFERENCE**<br>(2 Cor.6:14-16; esp. v.14)<br>Note 2, point 1c | μετοχή = metochē<br>Pronunciation: [met-okh-ay']<br>Parsing (part of speech): noun<br>    Case—nominative<br>    Gender—feminine<br>    Number—singular<br>    Stem or root—from μετοχή, ῆς<br>Concordance References:<br>  ⇒ Strong's #3352 metochē<br>  ⇒ NIV #3580 metochē<br>  ⇒ NASB #3352 metochē<br><br>**2 Cor. 6:14**<br>Be ye not unequally yoked together with unbelievers: for what **fellowship** hath righteousness with unrighteousness? and what communion hath light with darkness? [KJV]<br>Do not be bound together with unbelievers; for what **partnership** have righteousness and lawlessness, or what fellowship has light with darkness? [NASB]<br>Do not be yoked together with unbelievers. For what do righteousness and wickedness have **in common**? Or what fellowship can light have with darkness? [NIV]<br>Do not be unequally yoked together with unbelievers. For what **fellowship** has righteousness with lawlessness? And what communion has light with darkness? | In common, sharing fellowship, partnership, and participation.<br><br>**Practical Application**<br>How can a believer who focuses his life upon the righteousness of Jesus Christ share and participate with unbelievers, unbelievers who care little if anything about Jesus Christ and His call to righteousness?<br>Unbelievers do not obey God. They live and do as they wish, not as God says. They reject God and what God says and go about doing their own thing. They rebel against God and His commandments, living lawless and unrighteous lives. |

## PRACTICAL WORD STUDIES in the NEW TESTAMENT

| ENGLISH WORD | GREEK WORD AND VERSE | THE WORD MEANS... |
|---|---|---|
| | [NKJV]<br>Don't team up with those who are unbelievers. How can goodness be a **partner** with wickedness? How can light live with darkness? [NLT]<br>Μὴ γίνεσθε ἑτεροζυγοῦντες ἀπίστοις· τίς γὰρ **μετοχὴ** δικαιοσύνῃ καὶ ἀνομίᾳ; τίς δὲ κοινωνία φωτὶ πρὸς σκότος; [GNS]<br>Μὴ γίνεσθε ἑτεροζυγοῦντες ἀπίστοις· τίς γὰρ **μετοχὴ** δικαιοσύνῃ καὶ ἀνομίᾳ, ἢ τίς κοινωνία φωτὶ πρὸς σκότος; [GNT] | |
| **#1470**<br>**Fellowship**<br><br>Communion–KJV<br>**Fellowship–NASB**<br>**Fellowship–NIV**<br>**Fellowship–NKJV**<br>Live with–NLT<br><br>**POSB REFERENCE**<br>(2 Cor.6:14-16; esp. v.14)<br>Note 2, point 2 | κοινωνία = *koinōnia*<br>Pronunciation: [koy-nohn-ee'-ah]<br>Parsing (part of speech): noun<br>    Case—nominative<br>    Gender—feminine<br>    Number—singular<br>    Stem or root—from κοινωνία, ας<br>Concordance References:<br>  ⇒ Strong's #2842 koinōnia<br>  ⇒ NIV #3126 koinōnia<br>  ⇒ NASB #2842 koinōnia<br><br>**2 Cor. 6:14**<br>Be ye not unequally yoked together with unbelievers: for what fellowship hath righteousness with unrighteousness? and what **communion** hath light with darkness? [KJV]<br>Do not be bound together with unbelievers; for what partnership have righteousness and lawlessness, or what **fellowship** has light with darkness? [NASB]<br>Do not be yoked together with unbelievers. For what do righteousness and wickedness have in common? Or what **fellowship** can light have with darkness? [NIV]<br>Do not be unequally yoked together with unbelievers. For what **fellowship** has righteousness with lawlessness? And what communion has light with darkness? [NKJV]<br>Don't team up with those who are unbelievers. How can goodness be a partner with wickedness? How can light **live with** darkness? [NLT]<br>Μὴ γίνεσθε ἑτεροζυγοῦντες ἀπίστοις· τίς γὰρ μετοχὴ δικαιοσύνῃ καὶ ἀνομίᾳ; τίς δὲ **κοινωνία** φωτὶ πρὸς σκότος; [GNS]<br>Μὴ γίνεσθε ἑτεροζυγοῦντες ἀπίστοις· τίς γὰρ μετοχὴ δικαιοσύνῃ καὶ ἀνομίᾳ, ἢ τίς **κοινωνία** φωτὶ πρὸς σκότος; [GNT] | Fellowship; communion; to live with; to share; to be in union, in partnership, in a bound fellowship; to be closely bound together; to have a close, mutual relationship.<br><br>**Practical Application**<br>It means to be so closely bound together that there is open and mutual sharing: what one has belongs to the other. The point is clear: there is no such fellowship or union between light and darkness. On the contrary, light and darkness are mutually exclusive, of different natures entirely. They cannot coexist. |
| **#1471**<br>**Fervent**<br><br>**Fervent–KJV**<br>**Fervent–NASB**<br>Fervor–NIV<br>**Fervent–NKJV**<br>Enthusiastically–NLT<br><br>**POSB REFERENCE**<br>(Romans 12:11)<br>Note 2, point 2 | ζέοντες = *zeontes*<br>Pronunciation: [dzeh'-on-tehs]<br>Parsing (part of speech): verb<br>    Mood—participle (imperative sense)<br>    Tense—present<br>    Voice—active<br>    Case—nominative<br>    Gender—masculine<br>    Person—2nd person<br>    Number—plural<br>    Stem or root—from ζέω<br>Concordance References:<br>  ⇒ Strong's #2204 zeō<br>  ⇒ NIV #2417 zeō<br>  ⇒ NASB #2204 zeō<br><br>**Romans 12:11**<br>Not slothful in business; **fervent** in spirit; serving the Lord; [KJV]<br>Not lagging behind in diligence, **fervent** in spirit, serving the Lord; [NASB]<br>Never be lacking in zeal, but keep your spiritual **fervor**, serving the Lord. [NIV]<br>Not lagging in diligence, **fervent** in spirit, serving the Lord; Romans [NKJV] | Fervent in spirit, boil; with enthusiasm; with a heart full of devotion. The word "fervent" (*zeontes*) means to be hot, to boil, to set aflame.<br><br>**Practical Application**<br>The believer's spirit is to be hot, that is, boiling and flaming for Christ. The believer must have a holy zeal for Christ. He must be aflame in his service for Christ. Why? The world is reeling under the weight of desperate need and dying without Christ and being doomed to an eternity separated from God. |

## PRACTICAL WORD STUDIES in the NEW TESTAMENT

| ENGLISH WORD | GREEK WORD AND VERSE | THE WORD MEANS... |
|---|---|---|
| | Never be lazy in your work, but serve the Lord **enthusiastically**. [NLT]<br>τῇ σπουδῇ μὴ ὀκνηροί· τῷ πνεύματι **ζέοντες**· τῷ Κυρίῳ δουλεύοντες· [GNS]<br>τῇ σπουδῇ μὴ ὀκνηροί, τῷ πνεύματι **ζέοντες**, τῷ κυρίῳ δουλεύοντες, [GNT] | |
| **#1472**<br>**Fervent**<br><br>**Fervent**–KJV<br>**Fervent**–NASB<br>Deeply–NIV<br>**Fervent**–NKJV<br>Deep–NLT<br><br>**POSB REFERENCE**<br>(1 Pt.4:8)<br>Note 3 | ἐκτενῆ = ektenë<br>Pronunciation: [ek-ten-ay']<br>Parsing (part of speech): adjective<br>    Case—accusative<br>    Gender—feminine<br>    Number—singular<br>    Stem or root—from ἐκτενής, ές<br>Concordance References:<br>  ⇒ Strong's #1618 ektenës<br>  ⇒ NIV #1756 ektenës<br>  ⇒ NASB #1618 ektenës<br><br>**1 Peter 4:8**<br>And above all things have **fervent** charity among yourselves: for charity shall cover the multitude of sins. [KJV]<br>Above all, keep **fervent** in your love for one another, because love covers a multitude of sins. [NASB]<br>Above all, love each other **deeply**, because love covers over a multitude of sins. [NIV]<br>And above all things have **fervent** love for one another, for *"love will cover a multitude of sins."* [NKJV]<br>Most important of all, continue to show **deep** love for each other, for love covers a multitude of sins. [NLT]<br>πρὸ πάντων δὲ τὴν εἰς ἑαυτοὺς ἀγάπην **ἐκτενῆ** ἔχοντες, ὅτι ἀγάπη καλύψει πλῆθος ἁμαρτιῶν· [GNS]<br>πρὸ πάντων τὴν εἰς ἑαυτοὺς ἀγάπην **ἐκτενῆ** ἔχοντες, ὅτι ἀγάπη καλύπτει πλῆθος ἁμαρτιῶν. [GNT] | Deep, fervent, unfailing, constant.<br><br>**Practical Application**<br>The word (*ektenë*) is an athletic word. It means to stretch and reach out; to strain and exert to the utmost degree just like an athlete in a race. It has the idea of burning and boiling and of being passionate about loving one's brother in Christ. Note how a deep or fervent love is far more than the human love of warm feelings and attraction. It is far more than sentimental and caring feelings for a person.<br>The believer is to love with the ultimate love, the love of fervency. And note: deep or fervent love is to be put before all else. It is the most important duty of the believer. We are to strain every ounce of energy in our minds and hearts to love. |
| **#1473**<br>**Fervent In Spirit, In The Spirit**<br><br>**Fervent in the spirit**–KJV<br>**Fervent in spirit**–NASB<br>With great fervor–NIV<br>**Fervent in spirit**–NKJV<br>With great enthusiasm–NLT<br><br>**POSB REFERENCE**<br>(Acts 18:25)<br>Note 4 | ζέων τῷ πνεύματι = zeön tö pneumati<br>Pronunciation: [dzeh'-own tow pnyoo'-mah-tee]<br>Parsing *zeön* (part of speech): verb<br>    Mood—participle<br>    Tense—present<br>    Voice—active<br>    Case—nominative<br>    Gender—masculine<br>    Number—singular<br>    Stem or root—from ζέω<br>Parsing *pneumati* (part of speech): noun<br>    Case—dative<br>    Gender—neuter<br>    Number—singular<br>    Stem or root—from πνεῦμα, τος<br>Concordance References:<br>  ⇒ Strong's #2204 + 3588 + 4151 zeö ho pneuma<br>  ⇒ NIV #2417 + 3836 + 4460 zeö ho pneuma<br>  ⇒ NASB #2204 + 3588 + 4151 zeö ho pneuma<br><br>**Acts 18:25**<br>This man was instructed in the way of the Lord; and being **fervent in the spirit**, he spake and taught diligently the things of the Lord, knowing only the baptism of John. [KJV]<br>This man had been instructed in the way of the Lord; and being **fervent in spirit**, he was speaking and teaching accurately the things concerning Jesus, being acquainted only with the baptism of John; [NASB]<br>He had been instructed in the way of the Lord, and he spoke **with great fervor** and taught about Jesus accurately, though he knew only the baptism of John. [NIV]<br>This man had been instructed in the way of the Lord; and being **fervent in spirit**, he spoke and taught accurately the things of the Lord, though he knew only the baptism of John. [NKJV]<br>He had been taught the way of the Lord and talked to | With great fervor; to be fervent in spirit; with great enthusiasm. The word means to be boiling, glowing, burning, passionate.<br><br>**Practical Application**<br>Apollos' spirit was set aflame, filled with all fervency and zeal for God. He was burning with a holy fire to proclaim the glorious promise that Jesus is the promised Messiah, the Lamb of God. |

## PRACTICAL WORD STUDIES
### in the New Testament

| ENGLISH WORD | GREEK WORD AND VERSE | THE WORD MEANS... |
|---|---|---|
| | others **with great enthusiasm** and accuracy about Jesus. However, he knew only about John's baptism. [NLT]<br><br>οὗτος ἦν κατηχημένος τὴν ὁδὸν τοῦ Κυρίου, καὶ **ζέων τῷ πνεύματι** ἐλάλει καὶ ἐδίδασκεν ἀκριβῶς τὰ περὶ τοῦ Κύριον, ἐπιστάμενος μόνον τὸ βάπτισμα Ἰωάννου· [GNS]<br><br>οὗτος ἦν κατηχημένος τὴν ὁδὸν τοῦ κυρίου καὶ **ζέων τῷ πνεύματι** ἐλάλει καὶ ἐδίδασκεν ἀκριβῶς τὰ περὶ τοῦ Ἰησοῦ, ἐπιστάμενος μόνον τὸ βάπτισμα Ἰωάννου· [GNT] | |
| **#1474**<br>**Fervently**<br><br>Without ceasing–KJV<br>**Fervently–NASB**<br>Earnestly–NIV<br>Constant–NKJV<br>Earnestly–NLT<br><br>**POSB**<br>**REFERENCE**<br>(Acts 12:5-17; esp. v.5)<br>Note 2, point 1c | ἐκτενῶς = ektenōs<br>Pronunciation: [ek-ten-os']<br>Parsing (part of speech): adjective adverb<br>   Stem or root—from ἐκτενῶς<br>Concordance References:<br>  ⇒ Strong's #1618 ektenes<br>  ⇒ NIV #1757 ektenōs<br>  ⇒ NASB #1619 ektenōs<br><br>**Acts 12:5**<br>Peter therefore was kept in prison: but prayer was made **without ceasing** of the church unto God for him. [KJV]<br>So Peter was kept in the prison, but prayer for him was being made **fervently** by the church to God. [NASB]<br>So Peter was kept in prison, but the church was **earnestly** praying to God for him. [NIV]<br>Peter was therefore kept in prison, but **constant** prayer was offered to God for him by the church. [NKJV]<br>But while Peter was in prison, the church prayed very **earnestly** for him. [NLT]<br>ὁ μὲν οὖν Πέτρος ἐτηρεῖτο ἐν τῇ φυλακῇ· προσευχὴ δὲ ἦν **ἐκτενῶς** γινομένη ὑπὸ τῆς ἐκκλησίας πρὸς τὸν Θεὸν ὑπὲρ αὐτοῦ. [GNS]<br>ὁ μὲν οὖν Πέτρος ἐτηρεῖτο ἐν τῇ φυλακῇ· προσευχὴ δὲ ἦν **ἐκτενῶς** γινομένη ὑπὸ τῆς ἐκκλησίας πρὸς τὸν θεὸν περὶ αὐτοῦ. [GNT] | Earnestly; deeply; ceaselessly; fervently; constantly.<br><br>**Practical Application**<br>The idea is intense prayer, prayer that captivates and focuses a person's concentration. The root meaning of the word is "to stretch out." The picture is that the church was stretched out, prostrate before God, earnestly and fervently crying out for God's sovereign deliverance of Peter. The church could do nothing and they knew it. Peter's only hope was God. |
| **#1475**<br>**Fervently**<br><br>**Fervently–KJV**<br>**Fervently–NASB**<br>Deeply–NIV<br>**Fervently–NKJV**<br>Intensely–NLT<br><br>**POSB**<br>**REFERENCE**<br>(1 Pt.1:22-25; esp. v.22)<br>Note 1 | ἐκτενῶς = ektenōs<br>Pronunciation: [ek-ten-oce']<br>Parsing (part of speech): adjective adverb<br>   Stem or root—from ἐκτενῶς<br>Concordance References:<br>  ⇒ Strong's #1619 ektenōs<br>  ⇒ NIV #1757 ektenōs<br>  ⇒ NASB #1619 ektenōs<br><br>**1 Peter 1:22**<br>Seeing ye have purified your souls in obeying the truth through the Spirit unto unfeigned love of the brethren, see that ye love one another with a pure heart **fervently**: [KJV]<br>Since you have in obedience to the truth purified your souls for a sincere love of the brethren, **fervently** love one another from the heart, [NASB]<br>Now that you have purified yourselves by obeying the truth so that you have sincere love for your brothers, love one another **deeply**, from the heart. [NIV]<br>Since you have purified your souls in obeying the truth through the Spirit in sincere love of the brethren, love one another **fervently** with a pure heart, [NKJV]<br>Now you can have sincere love for each other as brothers and sisters because you were cleansed from your sins when you accepted the truth of the Good News. So see to it that you really do love each other **intensely** with all your hearts. [NLT]<br>τὰς ψυχὰς ὑμῶν ἡγνικότες ἐν τῇ ὑπακοῇ τῆς ἀληθείας διὰ Πνεύματος εἰς φιλαδελφίαν ἀνυπόκριτον, ἐκ καθαρᾶς καρδίας ἀλλήλους ἀγαπήσατε **ἐκτενῶς**· [GNS]<br>Τὰς ψυχὰς ὑμῶν ἡγνικότες ἐν τῇ ὑπακοῇ τῆς ἀληθείας εἰς φιλαδελφίαν ἀνυπόκριτον, ἐκ [καθαρᾶς] καρδίας ἀλλήλους ἀγαπήσατε **ἐκτενῶς** [GNT] | Deeply, fervently, intensely, constantly, earnestly.<br><br>**Practical Application**<br>The word "fervently" (*ektenōs*) "does not mean 'with warmth' but rather 'with full intensity'." It literally means to *stretch love fully out* or to love one another *in an all-out manner* (Alan M. Stibbs. *The First Epistle General of Peter.* "The Tyndale New Testament Commentaries," p.94). |

# PRACTICAL WORD STUDIES
in the NEW TESTAMENT

| ENGLISH WORD | GREEK WORD AND VERSE | THE WORD MEANS... |
|---|---|---|
| **#1476**<br>**Fervor**<br><br>Fervent–KJV<br>Fervent–NASB<br>**Fervor–NIV**<br>Fervent–NKJV<br>Enthusiastically–NLT<br><br>**POSB<br>REFERENCE**<br>(Romans 12:11)<br>Note 2, point 2 | ζέοντες = zeontes<br>Pronunciation: [dzeh'-on-tehs]<br>Parsing (part of speech): verb<br>    Mood—participle (imperative sense)<br>    Tense—present<br>    Voice—active<br>    Case—nominative<br>    Gender—masculine<br>    Person—2nd person<br>    Number—plural<br>    Stem or root—from ζέω<br>Concordance References:<br>  ⇒ Strong's #2204 zeō<br>  ⇒ NIV #2417 zeō<br>  ⇒ NASB #2204 zeō<br><br>**Romans 12:11**<br>Not slothful in business; **fervent** in spirit; serving the Lord; [KJV]<br>Not lagging behind in diligence, **fervent** in spirit, serving the Lord; [NASB]<br>Never be lacking in zeal, but keep your spiritual **fervor**, serving the Lord. [NIV]<br>Not lagging in diligence, **fervent** in spirit, serving the Lord; [NKJV]<br>Never be lazy in your work, but serve the Lord **enthusiastically**. [NLT]<br>τῇ σπουδῇ μὴ ὀκνηροί· τῷ πνεύματι **ζέοντες**· τῷ Κυρίῳ δουλεύοντες· [GNS]<br>τῇ σπουδῇ μὴ ὀκνηροί, τῷ πνεύματι **ζέοντες**, τῷ κυρίῳ δουλεύοντες, [GNT] | Be fervent in spirit; boil; with enthusiasm; with a heart full of devotion. The word "fervor" (*zeontes*) means to be hot, to boil, to set aflame.<br><br>**Practical Application**<br>The believer's spirit is to be hot, that is, boiling and flaming for Christ. The believer must have a holy zeal for Christ. He must be aflame in his service for Christ. Why? The world is reeling under the weight of desperate need and dying without Christ, being doomed to an eternity separated from God. |
| **#1477**<br>**Festival, Let Us Celebrate The**<br><br>Let us keep the feast–KJV<br>Let us therefore celebrate the feast–NASB<br>Let us keep the Festival–NIV<br>Let us keep the feast–NKJV<br>**Let us celebrate the festival–NLT**<br><br>**POSB<br>REFERENCE**<br>(1 Cor. 5:8)<br>Note 3, point 5 | ἑορτάζωμεν = heortazōmen<br>Pronunciation: [eh-or-tad'-zo-mehn]<br>Parsing (part of speech): verb<br>    Mood—subjunctive<br>    Tense—present<br>    Voice—active<br>    Person—1st person<br>    Number—plural<br>    Stem or root—from ἑορτάζω<br>Concordance References:<br>  ⇒ Strong's #1858 heortazō<br>  ⇒ NIV #2037 heortazō<br>  ⇒ NASB #1858 heortazō<br><br>**1 Cor. 5:8**<br>Therefore **let us keep the feast**, not with old leaven, neither with the leaven of malice and wickedness; but with the unleavened bread of sincerity and truth. [KJV]<br>**Let us therefore celebrate the feast**, not with old leaven, nor with the leaven of malice and wickedness, but with the unleavened bread of sincerity and truth. [NASB]<br>Therefore **let us keep the Festival**, not with the old yeast, the yeast of malice and wickedness, but with bread without yeast, the bread of sincerity and truth. [NIV]<br>Therefore **let us keep the feast**, not with old leaven, nor with the leaven of malice and wickedness, but with the unleavened bread of sincerity and truth. [NKJV]<br>So **let us celebrate the festival**, not by eating the old bread of wickedness and evil, but by eating the new bread of purity and truth. [NLT]<br>ὥστε **ἑορτάζωμεν**, μὴ ἐν ζύμῃ παλαιᾷ, μηδὲ ἐν ζύμῃ κακίας καὶ πονηρίας, ἀλλ' ἐν ἀζύμοις εἰλικρινείας καὶ ἀληθείας. [GNS]<br>ὥστε **ἑορτάζωμεν** μὴ ἐν ζύμῃ παλαιᾷ μηδὲ ἐν ζύμῃ κακίας καὶ πονηρίας ἀλλ' ἐν ἀζύμοις εἰλικρινείας καὶ ἀληθείας. [GNT] | Let us keep the festival or feast; let us celebrate the festival or feast; let us observe the festival or feast. The words "let us celebrate" are in the present tense, which means continuous action.<br><br>**Practical Application**<br>The church *must continue* to *celebrate* the festival, continue to purge out the old yeast of sin and its corrupting influences. It must not only discipline itself and the man who is living in shameful sin, but it must also continue to keep itself pure, to continue celebrating the feast of purity before God. |
| **#1478**<br>**Festival, Let Us Keep The** | ἑορτάζωμεν = heortazōmen<br>Pronunciation: [eh-or-tad'-zo-mehn]<br>Parsing (part of speech): verb<br>    Mood—subjunctive | Let us keep the festival or feast; let us celebrate the festival or feast; let us observe the festival or feast. The words "let us keep" are in the present tense, which means continuous action. |

# PRACTICAL WORD STUDIES
## in the NEW TESTAMENT

| ENGLISH WORD | GREEK WORD AND VERSE | THE WORD MEANS... |
|---|---|---|
| Let us keep the feast– KJV<br>Let us therefore celebrate the feast– NASB<br>**Let us keep the Festival–NIV**<br>Let us keep the feast– NKJV<br>Let us celebrate the festival–NLT<br><br>**POSB REFERENCE**<br>(1 Cor.5:8)<br>Note 3, point 5 | Tense—present<br>Voice—active<br>Person—1st person<br>Number—plural<br>Stem or root—from ἑορτάζω<br>Concordance References:<br>⇒ Strong's #1858 heortazö<br>⇒ NIV #2037 heortazö<br>⇒ NASB #1858 heortazö<br><br>**1 Cor. 5:8**<br>Therefore **let us keep the feast**, not with old leaven, neither with the leaven of malice and wickedness; but with the unleavened bread of sincerity and truth. [KJV]<br>**Let us therefore celebrate the feast**, not with old leaven, nor with the leaven of malice and wickedness, but with the unleavened bread of sincerity and truth. [NASB]<br>Therefore **let us keep the Festival**, not with the old yeast, the yeast of malice and wickedness, but with bread without yeast, the bread of sincerity and truth. [NIV]<br>Therefore **let us keep the feast**, not with old leaven, nor with the leaven of malice and wickedness, but with the unleavened *bread* of sincerity and truth. [NKJV]<br>So **let us celebrate the festival**, not by eating the old bread of wickedness and evil, but by eating the new bread of purity and truth. [NLT]<br>ὥστε **ἑορτάζωμεν**, μὴ ἐν ζύμῃ παλαιᾷ, μηδὲ ἐν ζύμῃ κακίας καὶ πονηρίας, ἀλλ' ἐν ἀζύμοις εἰλικρινείας καὶ ἀληθείας. [GNS]<br>ὥστε **ἑορτάζωμεν** μὴ ἐν ζύμῃ παλαιᾷ μηδὲ ἐν ζύμῃ κακίας καὶ πονηρίας ἀλλ' ἐν ἀζύμοις εἰλικρινείας καὶ ἀληθείας. [GNT] | **Practical Application**<br>The church *must continue* to *keep* the Festival, continue to purge out the old yeast of sin and its corrupting influences. It must not only discipline itself and the man who is living in shameful sin, but it must also continue to keep itself pure, to continue celebrating the feast of purity before God. |
| **#1479**<br>**Few Days**<br><br>Certain days–KJV<br>Several days–NASB<br>Several days–NIV<br>Some days–NKJV<br>**Few days–NLT**<br><br>**POSB REFERENCE**<br>(Acts 9:19)<br>Note 2 | ἡμέρας τινάς = hēmeras tinas<br>Pronunciation: [ay-mer'-ahs ti'-nahs]<br>Parsing *hēmeras* (part of speech): noun<br>   Case—accusative<br>   Gender—feminine<br>   Number—plural<br>   Stem or root—from ἡμέρα, ας<br>Parsing *tinas* (part of speech): adjective<br>   Type—indefinite<br>   Case—accusative<br>   Gender—feminine<br>   Number—plural<br>   Stem or root—from τὶς, τὶ<br>Concordance References:<br>⇒ Strong's #2250 hēmera + 5100 tis<br>⇒ NIV #2465 hēmera [days] + 5516 tis [several]<br>⇒ NASB #2250 hēmera + 5100 tis<br><br>**Acts 9:19**<br>And when he had received meat, he was strengthened. Then was Saul **certain days** with the disciples which were at Damascus. [KJV]<br>And he took food and was strengthened. Now for **several days** he was with the disciples who were at Damascus, [NASB]<br>And after taking some food, he regained his strength. Saul spent **several days** with the disciples in Damascus. [NIV]<br>So when he had received food, he was strengthened. Then Saul spent **some days** with the disciples at Damascus. [NKJV]<br>Afterward he ate some food and was strengthened. Saul stayed with the believers in Damascus for a **few days**. [NLT]<br>καὶ λαβὼν τροφὴν ἐνίσχυσεν. Ἐγένετο δὲ ὁ Σαῦλος μετὰ τῶν ἐν Δαμασκῷ μαθητῶν **ἡμέρας τινάς**. [GNS]<br>καὶ λαβὼν τροφὴν ἐνίσχυσεν. Ἐγένετο δὲ μετὰ τῶν ἐν Δαμασκῷ μαθητῶν **ἡμέρας τινάς** [GNT] | Several days; a few days; certain days. It is a term indicating a short time.<br><br>**Practical Application**<br>Paul joined and became associated and identified with other believers. What happened is important to note, for it holds a much needed lesson for every generation. Paul joined the other believers at Damascus because he was a *true* believer. His old nature, the old man, had truly died; and he now had the new nature of believers. He was *bound* to join those who had the same nature as he. It was their presence he desired. He wanted to share in...<br>• their companionship and fellowship (see POSB *Deeper Study #3*—Acts 2:42 for more discussion).<br>• their love, concern, and care.<br>• their beliefs and principles.<br>• their study of the Word.<br>• their growth in Christ.<br>• their edifying and building up of each other.<br>• their witness and service.<br>Saul (or Paul) associated and became identified with the church so that the world might know that he was a believer. He wanted to openly and publicly declare that he was now...<br>• a new creature in Christ Jesus.<br>• a follower of "the Way" which he had opposed and persecuted.<br>• a true disciple of the Lord Jesus. |

# PRACTICAL WORD STUDIES
## in the NEW TESTAMENT

| ENGLISH WORD | GREEK WORD AND VERSE | THE WORD MEANS... |
|---|---|---|
| **#1480**<br>**Fierce**<br><br>Fierce–KJV<br>Brutal–NASB<br>Brutal–NIV<br>Brutal–NKJV<br>Cruel–NLT<br><br>**POSB REFERENCE**<br>(2 Tim. 3:2-4; esp. v.3)<br>Note 2, point 13 | ἀνήμεροι = anēmeroi<br>Pronunciation: [an-ay'-mer-oy]<br>Parsing (part of speech): adjective<br>    Case—nominative<br>    Gender—masculine<br>    Number—plural<br>    Stem or root—from ἀνήμερος, ον<br>Concordance References:<br>  ⇒ Strong's #434 anēmeros<br>  ⇒ NIV #466 anēmeros<br>  ⇒ NASB #434 anēmeros<br><br>**2 Tim. 3:3**<br>Without natural affection, trucebreakers, false accusers, incontinent, **fierce**, despisers of those that are good, [KJV]<br>Unloving, irreconcilable, malicious gossips, without self-control, **brutal**, haters of good, [NASB]<br>Without love, unforgiving, slanderous, without self-control, **brutal**, not lovers of the good, [NIV]<br>Unloving, unforgiving, slanderers, without self-control, **brutal**, despisers of good, [NKJV]<br>They will be unloving and unforgiving; they will slander others and have no self-control; they will be **cruel** and have no interest in what is good. [NLT]<br>ἄστοργοι, ἄσπονδοι, διάβολοι, ἀκρατεῖς, **ἀνήμεροι**, ἀφιλάγαθοι, [GNS]<br>ἄστοργοι ἄσπονδοι διάβολοι ἀκρατεῖς **ἀνήμεροι** ἀφιλάγαθοι [GNT] | Brutal, fierce, cruel, savage, and untamed.<br><br>**Practical Application**<br>It is the word that describes the savage beast of the wild that is unrestrained in its fierceness. It is a word that should never be true of people, yet tragically it is. Never in the history of the world have men become as fierce and savage as they are today.<br>1. People no longer just murder...<br>  • they mutilate<br>  • they torture<br>  • they kill at random<br>  • they kill by twos and threes and by thousands and millions (for example, Hitler, Stalin)<br>And they take pleasure in their torture and savagery.<br>2. People no longer just correct and rebuke children, spouse, friend, neighbor, employee, or stranger...<br>  • they curse<br>  • they abuse<br>  • they attack<br>  • they maim<br>  • they act violently<br>The last days will see an increase in brutal, fierce and savage behavior. |
| **#1481**<br>**Fight**<br><br>Fight–KJV<br>Fight–NASB<br>Fight–NIV<br>Fight–NKJV<br>Fight–NLT<br><br>**POSB REFERENCE**<br>(1 Tim.6:12)<br>Note 3 | ἀγωνίζου = agōnizomai<br>Pronunciation: [ag-own'-idz-o-mah-ee]<br>Parsing (part of speech): verb<br>    Mood—imperative<br>    Tense—present<br>    Voice—middle or passive deponent<br>    Person—2nd person<br>    Number—singular<br>    Stem or root—from ἀγωνίζομαι<br>Concordance References:<br>  ⇒ Strong's #75 agōnizou<br>  ⇒ NIV #76 agōnizou<br>  ⇒ NASB #75 agōnizou<br><br>**1 Tim. 6:12**<br>**Fight** the good fight of faith, lay hold on eternal life, whereunto thou art also called, and hast professed a good profession before many witnesses. [KJV]<br>**Fight** the good fight of faith; take hold of the eternal life to which you were called, and you made the good confession in the presence of many witnesses. [NASB]<br>**Fight** the good fight of the faith. Take hold of the eternal life to which you were called when you made your good confession in the presence of many witnesses. [NIV]<br>**Fight** the good fight of faith, lay hold on eternal life, to which you were also called and have confessed the good confession in the presence of many witnesses. [NKJV]<br>**Fight** the good fight for what we believe. Hold tightly to the eternal life that God has given you, which you have confessed so well before many witnesses. [NLT]<br>ἀγωνίζου τὸν καλὸν ἀγῶνα τῆς πίστεως, ἐπιλαβοῦ τῆς αἰωνίου ζωῆς, εἰς ἣν ἐκλήθης, καὶ ὡμολόγησας τὴν καλὴν ὁμολογίαν ἐνώπιον πολλῶν μαρτύρων. [GNS]<br>ἀγωνίζου τὸν καλὸν ἀγῶνα τῆς πίστεως, ἐπιλαβοῦ τῆς αἰωνίου ζωῆς, εἰς ἣν ἐκλήθης καὶ ὡμολόγησας τὴν καλὴν ὁμολογίαν ἐνώπιον πολλῶν μαρτύρων. [GNT] | To fight; to struggle; to agonize, battle, contend, and fight for the prize. It is the idea of a *desperate effort and struggle*. This is a picture of an athletic contest.<br><br>**Practical Application**<br>The believer is in a desperate struggle for eternal life. Laying hold on the prize of eternal life is the struggle. Eternal life is the goal for which the man of God is fighting. Matthew Henry described it well:<br>*"Those who will get to heaven must fight their way there. There must be a conflict with corruption and temptations and...the power of darkness. Observe. It is a good fight, it is a good cause, and it will have a good [end and purpose]... Observe...*<br>*"Eternal life is the crown proposed to us, forever encouragement to war, and to fight...*<br>*"This we must lay hold on [eternal life], as those that are afraid of coming short of it and losing it. Lay hold, and take heed of losing your hold....*<br>*"We are called to the fight, and to lay hold on eternal life"* (Matthew Henry's Commentary, Vol.6, p.830). |

# PRACTICAL WORD STUDIES
## in the NEW TESTAMENT

| ENGLISH WORD | GREEK WORD AND VERSE | THE WORD MEANS... |
|---|---|---|
| **#1482**<br>**Fighting**<br><br>Tossed–KJV<br>Battered–NASB<br>Buffeted–NIV<br>Tossed–NKJV<br>Fighting–NLT<br><br>**POSB REFERENCE**<br>(Mt.14:24-27, esp.v.24)<br>Note 2, point 1 | βασανιζόμενον = basanizomenon<br>Pronunciation: [bas-an-id'-zo-me-non]<br>Parsing (part of speech): verb<br>    Mood—participle<br>    Tense—present<br>    Voice—passive<br>    Case—nominative<br>    Gender—neuter<br>    Number—singular<br>    Stem or root—from βασανίζω<br>Concordance References:<br>  ⇒ Strong's #928 basanizō<br>  ⇒ NIV #989 basanizō<br>  ⇒ NASB #928 basanizō<br><br>**Matthew 14:24**<br>But the ship was now in the midst of the sea, **tossed** with waves: for the wind was contrary. [KJV]<br>But the boat was already many stadia away from the land, **battered** by the waves; for the wind was contrary. [NASB]<br>But the boat was already a considerable distance from land, **buffeted** by the waves because the wind was against it. [NIV]<br>But the boat was now in the middle of the sea, **tossed** by the waves, for the wind was contrary. [NKJV]<br>Meanwhile, the disciples were in trouble far away from land, for a strong wind had risen, and they were **fighting** heavy waves. [NLT]<br>τὸ δὲ πλοῖον ἤδη μέσον τῆς θαλάσσης ἦν, **βασανιζόμενον** ὑπὸ τῶν κυμάτων· ἦν γὰρ ἐναντίος ὁ ἄνεμος. [GNS]<br>τὸ δὲ πλοῖον ἤδη σταδίους πολλοὺς ἀπὸ τῆς γῆς ἀπεῖχεν **βασανιζόμενον** ὑπὸ τῶν κυμάτων, ἦν γὰρ ἐναντίος ὁ ἄνεμος. [GNT] | To be buffeted, beaten, battered, or tossed about with great force; to be tormented; to be tortured.<br><br>**Practical Application**<br>In this Scripture, it is a picture of being completely at the mercy of a force greater than any possible human resistance. It is a picture of the awesome power of unleashed nature and mankind's inability to resist its effects. |
| **#1483**<br>**Fighting**<br><br>Debate–KJV<br>Strife–NASB<br>Strife–NIV<br>Strife–NKJV<br>Fighting–NLT<br><br>**POSB REFERENCE**<br>(Romans 1:29)<br>*Deeper Study #8* | ἔριδος = eridos<br>Pronunciation: [er'-i-dos]<br>Parsing (part of speech): noun<br>    Case—genitive<br>    Gender—feminine<br>    Number—singular<br>    Stem or root—from ἔρις, ιδος<br>Concordance References:<br>  ⇒ Strong's #2054 eris<br>  ⇒ NIV #2251 eris<br>  ⇒ NASB #2054 eris<br><br>**Romans 1:29**<br>Being filled with all unrighteousness, fornication, wickedness, covetousness, maliciousness; full of envy, murder, **debate**, deceit, malignity; whisperers, [KJV]<br>Being filled with all unrighteousness, wickedness, greed, evil; full of envy, murder, **strife**, deceit, malice; they are gossips, [NASB]<br>They have become filled with every kind of wickedness, evil, greed and depravity. They are full of envy, murder, **strife**, deceit and malice. They are gossips, [NIV]<br>Being filled with all unrighteousness, sexual immorality, wickedness, covetousness, maliciousness; full of envy, murder, **strife**, deceit, evil-mindedness; *they are* whisperers, [NKJV]<br>Their lives became full of every kind of wickedness, sin, greed, hate, envy, murder, **fighting**, deception, malicious behavior, and gossip. [NLT]<br>πεπληρωμένους πάσῃ ἀδικίᾳ πορνείᾳ, πονηρίᾳ πλεονεξίᾳ κακίᾳ· μεστοὺς φθόνου, φόνου, **ἔριδος**, δόλου, κακοηθείας· [GNS]<br>πεπληρωμένους πάσῃ ἀδικίᾳ πονηρίᾳ πλεονεξίᾳ κακίᾳ, μεστοὺς φθόνου φόνου **ἔριδος** δόλου κακοηθείας, ψιθυριστάς [GNT] | Selfish rivalry; arguments. The word fighting (*eridos*) means debate, strife, discord, contention, struggling, quarreling, dissension, wrangling.<br><br>**Practical Application**<br>It means that a man fights against another person in order to get something: position, promotion, property, honor, recognition. He fights in a dishonest and evil way. |

# Practical Word Studies
## in the New Testament

| ENGLISH WORD | GREEK WORD AND VERSE | THE WORD MEANS... |
|---|---|---|
| **#1484**<br>**Fighting**<br><br>Strife–KJV<br>Strife–NASB<br>Dissension–NIV<br>Strife–NKJV<br>**Fighting–NLT**<br><br>**POSB REFERENCE**<br>(Rom.13:13)<br>Note 4, point 5 | ἔριδι = eridi<br>Pronunciation: [er'-i-di]<br>Parsing (part of speech): noun<br>    Case—dative<br>    Gender—feminine<br>    Number—singular<br>    Stem or root—from ἔρις, ιδος<br>Concordance References:<br>  ⇒ Strong's #2054 eris<br>  ⇒ NIV #2251 eris<br>  ⇒ NASB #2054 eris<br><br>**Romans 13:13**<br>Let us walk honestly, as in the day; not in rioting and drunkenness, not in chambering and wantonness, not in **strife** and envying. [KJV]<br><br>Let us behave properly as in the day, not in carousing and drunkenness, not in sexual promiscuity and sensuality, not in **strife** and jealousy. [NASB]<br><br>Let us behave decently, as in the daytime, not in orgies and drunkenness, not in sexual immorality and debauchery, not in **dissension** and jealousy. [NIV]<br><br>Let us walk properly, as in the day, not in revelry and drunkenness, not in lewdness and lust, not in **strife** and envy. [NKJV]<br><br>We should be decent and true in everything we do, so that everyone can approve of our behavior. Don't participate in wild parties and getting drunk, or in adultery and immoral living, or in **fighting** and jealousy. [NLT]<br><br>ὡς ἐν ἡμέρᾳ, εὐσχημόνως περιπατήσωμεν, μὴ κώμοις καὶ μέθαις, μὴ κοίταις καὶ ἀσελγείαις, μὴ **ἔριδι** καὶ ζήλῳ. [GNS]<br><br>ὡς ἐν ἡμέρᾳ εὐσχημόνως περιπατήσωμεν, μὴ κώμοις καὶ μέθαις, μὴ κοίταις καὶ ἀσελγείαις, μὴ **ἔριδι** καὶ ζήλῳ. [GNT] | Dissension, strife, fighting, selfish rivalry, contention, quarreling, arguing, striving.<br><br>**Practical Application**<br>It is the restless craving deep within a person that wants recognition, honor, position, and authority. It is a spirit that is in constant competition with others, that will push one forward...<br>• by putting others down<br>• by bypassing others<br>• by ignoring others<br>• by holding others back<br>• by blaming others<br>• by neglecting others |
| **#1485**<br>**Fighting Against**<br><br>Wrestle–KJV<br>Struggle–NASB<br>Struggle–NIV<br>Wrestle–NKJV<br>**Fighting against–NLT**<br><br>**POSB REFERENCE**<br>(Eph.6:12)<br>Note 3 | πάλη = palë<br>Pronunciation: [pal'-ay]<br>Parsing (part of speech): noun<br>    Case—nominative<br>    Gender—feminine<br>    Number—singular<br>    Stem or root—from πάλη, ης<br>Concordance References:<br>  ⇒ Strong's #3823 palë<br>  ⇒ NIV #4097 palë<br>  ⇒ NASB #3823 palë<br><br>**Ephes. 6:12**<br>For we **wrestle** not against flesh and blood, but against principalities, against powers, against the rulers of the darkness of this world, against spiritual wickedness in high places. [KJV]<br><br>For our **struggle** is not against flesh and blood, but against the rulers, against the powers, against the world forces of this darkness, against the spiritual forces of wickedness in the heavenly places. [NASB]<br><br>For our **struggle** is not against flesh and blood, but against the rulers, against the authorities, against the powers of this dark world and against the spiritual forces of evil in the heavenly realms. [NIV]<br><br>For we do not **wrestle** against flesh and blood, but against principalities, against powers, against the rulers of the darkness of this age, against spiritual *hosts* of wickedness in the heavenly *places*. [NKJV]<br><br>For we are not **fighting against** people made of flesh and blood, but against the evil rulers and authorities of the unseen world, against those mighty powers of darkness who rule this world, and against wicked spirits in the heavenly realms. [NLT]<br><br>ὅτι οὐκ ἔστιν ἡμῖν ἡ **πάλη** πρὸς αἷμα καὶ σάρκα, ἀλλὰ πρὸς τὰς ἀρχάς, πρὸς τὰς ἐξουσίας, πρὸς τοὺς | To struggle; to wrestle; to fight against, grapple, scuffle, tussle.<br><br>**Practical Application**<br>The warfare is not human or physical, but spiritual. Kenneth Wuest has a descriptive picture of the believer's great spiritual struggle:<br>"In the word 'wrestle' [pale], Paul uses a Greek athletic term. Thayer defines as follows: 'a contest between two in which each endeavors to throw the other, and which is decided when the victor is able to press and hold down his prostate antagonist, namely, hold him down with his hand upon his neck.' When we consider that the loser in a Greek wrestling contest had his eyes gouged out with resulting blindness for the rest of his days, we can form some conception of the Ephesian Greek's reaction to Paul's illustration. The Christian's wrestling against the powers of darkness is no less desperate and fateful" (*Ephesians and Colossians*, Vol.1, p.141).<br><br>The point to see is that the believer's struggle is not against flesh and blood. His foes are not human or physical: they are spiritual—spiritual forces that possess unbelievable power. Note exactly what is said: the believer fights...<br>• against principalities<br>• against power<br>• against the rulers of darkness<br>• against spiritual wickedness |

# PRACTICAL WORD STUDIES
## in the NEW TESTAMENT

| ENGLISH WORD | GREEK WORD AND VERSE | THE WORD MEANS... |
|---|---|---|
| | κοσμοκράτορας τοῦ σκότους τοῦ αἰῶνος τούτου, πρὸς τὰ πνευματικὰ τῆς πονηρίας ἐν τοῖς ἐπουρανίοις. [GNS]<br>ὅτι οὐκ ἔστιν ἡμῖν ἡ **πάλη** πρὸς αἷμα καὶ σάρκα, ἀλλὰ πρὸς τὰς ἀρχάς, πρὸς τὰς ἐξουσίας, πρὸς τοὺς κοσμοκράτορας τοῦ σκότους τούτου, πρὸς τὰπνευματικὰ τῆς πονηρίας ἐν τοῖς ἐπουρανίοις. [GNT] | |
| #1486<br>**Fighting Together**<br><br>Striving together–KJV<br>Striving together–NASB<br>Contending as–NIV<br>Striving together–NKJV<br>**Fighting together–NLT**<br><br>**POSB REFERENCE**<br>(Philip.1:27)<br>Note 3, point 2 | συναθλοῦντες = sunathlountes<br>Pronunciation: [soon-ath-loon'-tehs]<br>Parsing (part of speech): verb<br>  Mood—participle<br>  Tense—present<br>  Voice—active<br>  Case—nominative<br>  Gender—masculine<br>  Person—2nd person<br>  Number—plural<br>  Stem or root—from συναθλέω<br>Concordance References:<br>  ⇒ Strong's #4866 sunathleō<br>  ⇒ NIV #5254 sunathleō<br>  ⇒ NASB #4866 sunathleō<br><br>**Philip. 1:27**<br>Only let your conversation be as it becometh the gospel of Christ: that whether I come and see you, or else be absent, I may hear of your affairs, that ye stand fast in one spirit, with one mind **striving together** for the faith of the gospel; [KJV]<br>Only conduct yourselves in a manner worthy of the gospel of Christ; so that whether I come and see you or remain absent, I may hear of you that you are standing firm in one spirit, with one mind **striving together** for the faith of the gospel; [NASB]<br>Whatever happens, conduct yourselves in a manner worthy of the gospel of Christ. Then, whether I come and see you or only hear about you in my absence, I will know that you stand firm in one spirit, **contending as** one man for the faith of the gospel [NIV]<br>Only let your conduct be worthy of the gospel of Christ, so that whether I come and see you or am absent, I may hear of your affairs, that you stand fast in one spirit, with one mind **striving together** for the faith of the gospel, [NKJV]<br>But whatever happens to me, you must live in a manner worthy of the Good News about Christ, as citizens of heaven. Then, whether I come and see you again or only hear about you, I will know that you are standing side by side, **fighting together** for the Good News. [NLT]<br>μόνον ἀξίως τοῦ εὐαγγελίου τοῦ Χριστοῦ πολιτεύεσθε, ἵνα εἴτε ἐλθὼν καὶ ἰδὼν ὑμᾶς, εἴτε ἀπών, ἀκούσω τὰ περὶ ὑμῶν, ὅτι στήκετε ἐν ἑνὶ πνεύματι, μιᾷ ψυχῇ **συναθλοῦντες** τῇ πίστει τοῦ εὐαγγελίου, [GNS]<br>Μόνον ἀξίως τοῦ εὐαγγελίου τοῦ Χριστοῦ πολιτεύεσθε, ἵνα εἴτε ἐλθὼν καὶ ἰδὼν ὑμᾶς εἴτε ἀπὼν ἀκούω τὰ περὶ ὑμῶν, ὅτι στήκετε ἐν ἑνὶ πνεύματι, μιᾷ ψυχῇ **συναθλοῦντες** τῇ πίστει τοῦ εὐαγγελίου [GNT] | Contending as; striving together; struggling, fighting together; working together.<br><br>**Practical Application**<br>The word "fighting together" (*sunathlountes*) is the word taken from an athletic contest. It is the picture of a team working and struggling together against strong opposition (compare a football team). The church—every member of it—is to strive for the faith of the gospel: strive, work, struggle, push, exert all the energy possible; everyone's cooperating together, not a single person's letting up or turning aside or walking off the field. The opposition is difficult; therefore, the faith of the gospel needs every member's working and struggling together. |
| #1487<br>**Figure**<br><br>**Figure–KJV**<br>Corresponding–NASB<br>Symbolizes–NIV<br>Antitype–NKJV<br>Picture–NLT<br><br>**POSB REFERENCE**<br>(1 Pt.3:21)<br>Note 1, point 3 | ἀντίτυπον = antitupon<br>Pronunciation: [an-teet'-oo-pon]<br>Parsing (part of speech): adjective adverb OR adjective<br>  Case—nominative<br>  Gender—neuter<br>  Number—singular<br>  Stem or root—from ἀντίτυπος, ον<br>Concordance References:<br>  ⇒ Strong's #499 antitupos<br>  ⇒ NIV #531 antitupos<br>  ⇒ NASB #499 antitupos<br><br>**1 Peter 3:21**<br>The like **figure** whereunto even baptism doth also now save us (not the putting away of the filth of the flesh, | Symbolize, figure, corresponding, picture, copy; antitype.<br><br>**Practical Application**<br>Jesus Christ saves the believer through baptism: not the baptism by water, but the baptism of a good conscience wrought by the power of the resurrection of Jesus Christ (1 Peter 3:21).<br>The water which saved Noah and his family is a type of the cleansing that saves us. The water...<br>• bore up the ark and saved them through the judgment of God. |

# PRACTICAL WORD STUDIES
## in the NEW TESTAMENT

| ENGLISH WORD | GREEK WORD AND VERSE | THE WORD MEANS... |
|---|---|---|
| | but the answer of a good conscience toward God,) by the resurrection of Jesus Christ: [KJV]<br>And **corresponding** to that, baptism now saves you—not the removal of dirt from the flesh, but an appeal to God for a good conscience—through the resurrection of Jesus Christ, [NASB]<br>And this water **symbolizes** baptism that now saves you also—not the removal of dirt from the body but the pledge of a good conscience toward God. It saves you by the resurrection of Jesus Christ, [NIV]<br>There is also an **antitype** which now saves us—baptism (not the removal of the filth of the flesh, but the answer of a good conscience toward God), through the resurrection of Jesus Christ, [NKJV]<br>And this is a **picture** of baptism, which now saves you by the power of Jesus Christ's resurrection. Baptism is not a removal of dirt from your body; it is an appeal to God from a clean conscience. [NLT]<br>ᾧ καὶ ἡμᾶς **ἀντίτυπον** νῦν σῴζει βάπτισμα, οὐ σαρκὸς ἀπόθεσις ῥύπου, ἀλλὰ συνειδήσεως ἀγαθῆς ἐπερώτημα εἰς Θεόν, δι' ἀναστάσεως Ἰησοῦ Χριστοῦ, [GNS]<br>ὃ καὶ ὑμᾶς **ἀντίτυπον** νῦν σῴζει βάπτισμα, οὐ σαρκὸς ἀπόθεσις ῥύπου ἀλλὰ συνειδήσεως ἀγαθῆς ἐπερώτημα εἰς Θεόν, δι' ἀναστάσεως Ἰησοῦ Χριστοῦ, [GNT] | • delivered them from the ridicule and mockery of evil men.<br>• delivered them from the corruption of the world and led them to a new life.<br>• put to death the old world and gave them the hope of a new world.<br>• put to death their old life and gave them a new beginning.<br>• saved the race of man and created a new people of God.<br>• delivered them from the old world right into the new world.<br><br>What is Peter saying? Note the word "figure" (*antitupon*). The figure or picture of baptism is just like the water that saved Noah and his family.<br>⇒ The *flooding waters* of Noah's day picture the judgment of God upon sin. The flooding waters picture how man was saved from a corruptible world and carried into a new world.<br>⇒ The *baptismal water* pictures the judgment of God upon Christ, a judgment of death that was due sinners. It pictures how man is saved from a corruptible life and world to be carried into a new life and world by the resurrection of Christ. |
| #1488<br>**Filled With**<br><br>Overcharged–KJV<br>Weighted down–NASB<br>Weighed down–NIV<br>Weighed down–NKJV<br>Filled with–NLT<br><br>**POSB REFERENCE**<br>(Lk.21:34-35, esp. v.34) Note 1 | βαρηθῶσιν = *barēthōsin*<br>Pronunciation: [ba-ray'-tho-sin]<br>Parsing (part of speech): verb<br>  Mood—subjunctive<br>  Tense—aorist<br>  Voice—passive<br>  Person—3rd person<br>  Number—plural<br>  Stem or root—from βαρέω<br>Concordance References:<br>⇒ Strong's #925 baruno or #916 bareō<br>⇒ NIV #976 bareō<br>⇒ NASB #916 bareō<br><br>**Luke 21:34**<br>And take heed to yourselves, lest at any time your hearts be **overcharged** with surfeiting, and drunkenness, and cares of this life, and so that day come upon you unawares. [KJV]<br>"Be on guard, that your hearts may not be **weighted down** with dissipation and drunkenness and the worries of life, and that day come on you suddenly like a trap; [NASB]<br>"Be careful, or your hearts will be **weighed down** with dissipation, drunkenness and the anxieties of life, and that day will close on you unexpectedly like a trap. [NIV]<br>"But take heed to yourselves, lest your hearts be **weighed down** with carousing, drunkenness, and cares of this life, and that Day come on you unexpectedly. [NKJV]<br>"Watch out! Don't let me find you living in careless ease and drunkenness, and **filled with** the worries of this life. Don't let that day catch you unaware, [NLT]<br>Προσέχετε δὲ ἑαυτοῖς, μήποτε **βαρυνθῶσιν** ὑμῶν αἱ καρδίαι ἐν κραιπάλῃ καὶ μέθῃ καὶ μερίμναις βιωτικαῖς, καὶ αἰφνίδιος ἐφ' ὑμᾶς ἐπιστῇ ἡ ἡμέρα ἐκείνη· [GNS]<br>Προσέχετε δὲ ἑαυτοῖς μήποτε **βαρηθῶσιν** ὑμῶν αἱ καρδίαι ἐν κραιπάλῃ καὶ μέθῃ καὶ μερίμναις βιωτικαῖς καὶ ἐπιστῇ ἐφ' ὑμᾶς αἰφνίδιος ἡ ἡμέρα ἐκείνη [GNT] | Heavy, weighed down, burdened, overloaded, filled up, indulged.<br><br>**Practical Application**<br>The believer's heart is not to be filled with the worldliness described in this verse. Three worldly acts in particular are mentioned.<br>1. Careless case (*kraipale*). The word means to be light-hearted, silly, frivolous, giddy. Medically, it referred to drunken nausea or headaches. It is the kind of light-heartedness, silliness, frivolity, and giddiness that comes from partying and drinking.<br>2. Drunkenness (*methei*). The word comes from the word meaning wine (*methu*). It means to be drunk with wine (or any other strong drink or drug), to be intoxicated.<br>3. Worries of this life. This means to indulge one's cravings for more and more of the things of this world. Man too often gives his attention and focuses his mind upon more and more of this world. He desires far more than what he needs, more...<br>• food and delicacies<br>• clothes and the latest styles<br>• houses and furnishings<br>• property and holdings<br>• cars and other vehicles<br>• free time and recreation<br>• money and wealth<br>• recognition and esteem |

# PRACTICAL WORD STUDIES
## in the NEW TESTAMENT

| ENGLISH WORD | GREEK WORD AND VERSE | THE WORD MEANS... |
|---|---|---|
| **#1489**<br>**Filled With All Knowledge**<br><br>Filled with all knowledge–KJV<br>Filled with all knowledge–NASB<br>Complete in knowledge–NIV<br>Filled with all knowledge–NKJV<br>Know these things so well–NLT<br><br>**POSB REFERENCE**<br>(Rom.15:14)<br>Note 1, point 2b | πεπληρωμένοι πάσης γνώσεως = *peplërömenoi pasës gnöseös*<br>Pronunciation: [peh-play-ro'-mehn-oy pah-says gno'-seh-os]<br>Parsing *peplërömenoi* (part of speech): verb<br>  Mood—participle<br>  Tense—perfect<br>  Voice—passive<br>  Case—nominative<br>  Gender—masculine<br>  Person—2nd person<br>  Number—plural<br>  Stem or root—from πληρόω<br>Parsing *gnöseös* (part of speech): noun<br>  Case—genitive<br>  Gender—feminine<br>  Number—singular<br>  Stem or root—from γνῶσις, εως<br>Concordance References:<br>⇒ Strong's #3956 + 4137 pas plëroö + 1108 gnösis<br>⇒ NIV #4246 + 4444 pas plëroö [complete] + 1194 gnösis [knowledge]<br>⇒ NASB #3956 + 4137 pas plëroö + 1108 gnösis<br><br>**Romans 15:14**<br>And I myself also am persuaded of you, my brethren, that ye also are full of goodness, **filled with all knowledge**, able also to admonish one another. [KJV]<br>And concerning you, my brethren, I myself also am convinced that you yourselves are full of goodness, **filled with all knowledge**, and able also to admonish one another. [NASB]<br>I myself am convinced, my brothers, that you yourselves are full of goodness, **complete in knowledge** and competent to instruct one another. [NIV]<br>Now I myself am confident concerning you, my brethren, that you also are full of goodness, **filled with all knowledge**, able also to admonish one another. [NKJV]<br>I am fully convinced, dear brothers and sisters, that you are full of goodness. You **know these things so well** that you are able to teach others all about them. [NLT]<br>Πέπεισμαι δέ, ἀδελφοί μου, καὶ αὐτὸς ἐγὼ περὶ ὑμῶν, ὅτι καὶ αὐτοὶ μεστοί ἐστε ἀγαθωσύνης, **πεπληρωμένοι πάσης γνώσεως**, δυνάμενοι καὶ ἀλλήλους νουθετεῖν. [GNS]<br>Πέπεισμαι δέ, ἀδελφοί μου, καὶ αὐτὸς ἐγὼ περὶ ὑμῶν ὅτι καὶ αὐτοὶ μεστοί ἐστε ἀγαθωσύνης, **πεπληρωμένοι πάσης** [τῆς] **γνώσεως**, δυνάμενοι καὶ ἀλλήλους νουθετεῖν. [GNT] | To be complete in knowledge; to be filled with all knowledge; to know [these things] very well.<br><br>**Practical Application**<br>The believers were "filled with all knowledge" (*pases gnoseos*): They were filled...<br>• with spiritual insight and perception.<br>• with knowledge of Christ, God, and the Holy Spirit.<br>• with spiritual truth.<br>• with the spiritual need of man and his world. |
| **#1490**<br>**Filled With Awe**<br><br>Fear–KJV<br>Fear–NASB<br>**Filled with awe–NIV**<br>Fear–NKJV<br>Great fear–NLT<br><br>**POSB REFERENCE**<br>(Lk.7:16-17; esp. v.16)<br>Note 4 | ἔλαβεν φόβος = *elaben phobos*<br>Pronunciation: [eh-la-behn' fob'-os]<br>Parsing *elaben* (part of speech): verb<br>  Mood—indicative<br>  Tense—aorist<br>  Voice—active<br>  Person—3rd person<br>  Number—singular<br>  Stem or root—from λαμβάνω<br>Parsing *phobos* (part of speech): noun<br>  Case—nominative<br>  Gender—masculine<br>  Number—singular<br>  Stem or root—from φόβος, ου<br>Concordance References:<br>⇒ Strong's #2983 lambanö + 5401 phobos<br>⇒ NIV #3284 lambanö [filled with] + 5832 phobos [awe]<br>⇒ NASB #2983 lambanö + 5401 phobos | To be filled with awe; to fear; to wonder; to be amazed; to be astonished; to respect; to have a great fear, reverence and awe. It is fear, dread, terror.<br><br>**Practical Application**<br>In relation to God, it means to be afraid; to show reverence, to sense a reverential fear; to stand in awe because of a holy fear. It means we fear God because He is God: holy, righteous, pure, just. It means that we fearfully stand in awe and reverence of God who will reveal His holiness and execute His justice in some future day of judgment. |

## Practical Word Studies
### in the New Testament

| ENGLISH WORD | GREEK WORD AND VERSE | THE WORD MEANS... |
|---|---|---|
| | **Luke 7:16**<br>And there came a **fear** on all: and they glorified God, saying, That a great prophet is risen up among us; and, That God hath visited his people. [KJV]<br>And **fear** gripped them all, and they began glorifying God, saying, "A great prophet has arisen among us!" and, "God has visited His people!" [NASB]<br>They were all **filled with awe** and praised God. "A great prophet has appeared among us," they said. "God has come to help his people." [NIV]<br>Then **fear** came upon all, and they glorified God, saying, "A great prophet has risen up among us"; and, "God has visited His people." [NKJV]<br>**Great fear** swept the crowd, and they praised God, saying, "A mighty prophet has risen among us," and "We have seen the hand of God at work today." [NLT]<br>Ἔλαβε δὲ φόβος ἅπαντας, καὶ ἐδόξαζον τὸν Θεόν, λέγοντες, ὅτι Προφήτης μέγας ἐγήγερται ἐν ἡμῖν, καὶ ὅτι Ἐπεσκέψατο ὁ Θεὸς τὸν λαὸν αὐτοῦ. [GNS]<br>Ἔλαβεν δὲ φόβος πάντας καὶ ἐδόξαζον τὸν θεὸν λέγοντες ὅτι Προφήτης μέγας ἠγέρθη ἐν ἡμῖν καὶ ὅτι Ἐπεσκέψατο ὁ θεὸς τὸν λαὸν αὐτοῦ. [GNT] | |
| **#1491**<br>**Filled With Grief**<br><br>Mourned–KJV<br>Mourned–NASB<br>**Filled with grief–NIV**<br>Mourned–NKJV<br>Mourning–NLT<br><br>**POSB REFERENCE**<br>(1 Cor.5:2)<br>Note 2 | ἐπενθήσατε = epenthēsate<br>Pronunciation: [eh-pen-thay'-sah-teh]<br>Parsing (part of speech): verb<br>   Mood—indicative<br>   Tense—aorist<br>   Voice—active<br>   Person—2nd person<br>   Number—plural<br>   Stem or root—from πενθέω<br>Concordance References:<br>  ⇒ Strong's #3996 pentheō<br>  ⇒ NIV #4291 pentheō<br>  ⇒ NASB #3996 pentheō<br><br>**1 Cor. 5:2**<br>And ye are puffed up, and have not rather **mourned**, that he that hath done this deed might be taken away from among you. [KJV]<br>And you have become arrogant, and have not **mourned** instead, in order that the one who had done this deed might be removed from your midst. [NASB]<br>And you are proud! Shouldn't you rather have been **filled with grief** and have put out of your fellowship the man who did this? [NIV]<br>And you are puffed up, and have not rather **mourned**, that he who has done this deed might be taken away from among you. [NKJV]<br>And you are so proud of yourselves! Why aren't you **mourning** in sorrow and shame? And why haven't you removed this man from your fellowship? [NLT]<br>καὶ ὑμεῖς πεφυσιωμένοι ἐστέ, καὶ οὐχὶ μᾶλλον **ἐπενθήσατε**, ἵνα ἐξαρθῇ ἐκ μέσου ὑμῶν ὁ τὸ ἔργον τοῦτο ποιήσας. [GNS]<br>καὶ ὑμεῖς πεφυσιωμένοι ἐστέ καὶ οὐχὶ μᾶλλον **ἐπενθήσατε**, ἵνα ἀρθῇ ἐκ μέσου ὑμῶν ὁ τὸ ἔργον τοῦτο πράξας; [GNT] | To be filled with grief; to mourn; to grieve over; to experience sorrow.<br><br>**Practical Application**<br>The phrase "filled with grief" (*epenthēsate*) is the word used for grieving and mourning over the dead. The people in this Scripture should have been so grieved that they were driven to prayer. Their need was not to be glorying in their so-called spirituality and strength as a church; their need was to mourn over the sin in their midst, begging God to help them restore the fallen brother or to remove him and the sin from their fellowship through love and correction. |
| **#1492**<br>**Filled With Horror**<br><br>Sore amazed–KJV<br>Very distressed–NASB<br>Deeply distressed–NIV<br>Deeply distressed–NKJV<br>**Filled with horror–NLT** | ἐκθαμβεῖσθαι = ekthambeisthai<br>Pronunciation: [ek-tham-be-ees-tha-ee]<br>Parsing (part of speech): verb<br>   Mood—infinitive<br>   Tense—present<br>   Voice—passive<br>   Stem or root—from ἐκθαμβέομαι<br>Concordance References:<br>  ⇒ Strong's #1568 ekthambeō<br>  ⇒ NIV #1701 ekthambeō<br>  ⇒ NASB #1568 ekthambeō | To be deeply distressed; to be filled with utter and extreme fright, horror, terror, bewilderment, and amazement.<br><br>**Practical Application**<br>Jesus "began" to experience extreme agony and pressure beyond imagination. The words "filled with horror" (*ekthambeisthai*) are very strong words in the Greek. Jesus was staggering under the "horror of great darkness," something like what fell upon Abraham, except Jesus' horror was much, much greater (Genesis 15:12). |

# PRACTICAL WORD STUDIES
## in the New Testament

| ENGLISH WORD | GREEK WORD AND VERSE | THE WORD MEANS... |
|---|---|---|
| **POSB REFERENCE**<br>(Mk.14:33-34; esp. v.33)<br>Note 2 | **Mark 14:33**<br>And he taketh with him Peter and James and John, and began to be **sore amazed**, and to be very heavy; [KJV]<br>And He took with Him Peter and James and John, and began to be **very distressed** and troubled. [NASB]<br>He took Peter, James and John along with him, and he began to be **deeply distressed** and troubled. [NIV]<br>And He took Peter, James, and John with Him, and He began to be troubled and **deeply distressed**. [NKJV]<br>He took Peter, James, and John with him, and he began to be **filled with horror** and deep distress. [NLT]<br>καὶ παραλαμβάνει τὸν Πέτρον καὶ τὸν Ἰάκωβον καὶ Ἰωάννην μετ' αὐτοῦ, καὶ ἤρξατο **ἐκθαμβεῖσθαι** καὶ ἀδημονεῖν. [GNS]<br>καὶ παραλαμβάνει τὸν Πέτρον καὶ [τὸν] Ἰάκωβον καὶ [τὸν] Ἰωάννην μετ' αὐτοῦ καὶ ἤρξατο **ἐκθαμβεῖσθαι** καὶ ἀδημονεῖν [GNT] | |
| **#1493**<br>**Filled With Lies**<br>Used deceit–KJV<br>Keep deceiving–NASB<br>Practice deceit–NIV<br>Practiced deceit–NKJV<br>Filled with lies–NLT<br>**POSB REFERENCE**<br>(Rom.3:13-14; esp. v.13)<br>Note 3, point 2 | ἐδολιοῦσαν = *edoliousan*<br>Pronunciation: [eh-dol-ee-oo'-sahn]<br>Parsing (part of speech): verb<br>  Mood—indicative<br>  Tense—imperfect<br>  Voice—active<br>  Person—3rd person<br>  Number—plural<br>  Stem or root—from δολιόω<br>Concordance References:<br>  ⇒ Strong's #1387 *dolioō*<br>  ⇒ NIV #1514 *dolioō*<br>  ⇒ NASB #1387 *dolioō*<br><br>**Romans 3:13**<br>Their throat is an open sepulchre; with their tongues they have **used deceit**; the poison of asps is under their lips: [KJV]<br>"Their throat is an open grave, With their tongues they **keep deceiving**," "The poison of asps is under their lips"; [NASB]<br>"Their throats are open graves; their tongues **practice deceit**." "The poison of vipers is on their lips." [NIV]<br>"Their throat is an open tomb; With their tongues they have **practiced deceit**"; "The poison of asps is under their lips"; [NKJV]<br>"Their talk is foul, like the stench from an open grave. Their speech is **filled with lies**." "The poison of a deadly snake drips from their lips." [NLT]<br>τάφος ἀνεῳγμένος ὁ λάρυγξ αὐτῶν, ταῖς γλώσσαις αὐτῶν **ἐδολιοῦσαν**· ἰὸς ἀσπίδων ὑπὸ τὰ χείλη αὐτῶν· [GNS]<br>τάφος ἀνεῳγμένος ὁ λάρυγξ αὐτῶν, ταῖς γλώσσαις αὐτῶν **ἐδολιοῦσαν**, ἰὸς ἀσπίδων ὑπὸ τὰ χείλη αὐτῶν· [GNT] | To deceive; to be treacherous; to mislead; to betray; to cheat; to bamboozle; to practice deceit.<br><br>**Practical Application**<br>A sinful tongue is deceitful (Romans 3:13; cp. Psalm 5:9): "They have used deceit." The Hebrew says, "They make smooth their tongue." A deceitful person has...<br>• a false tongue<br>• a lying tongue<br>• a cheating tongue<br>• a deluding tongue<br>• a flattering tongue<br>• a misleading tongue<br>• a treacherous tongue<br>• a beguiling tongue<br>• a smooth-talking tongue<br><br>The phrase "filled with lies" (*edoliousan*) is continuous action: "Their speech is filled with lies." Man is not only guilty of deceiving, but of constantly deceiving. He is constantly hiding and camouflaging his true thoughts and feelings and behavior, seeking to protect himself or to get whatever he is after. |
| **#1494**<br>**Filth–Filthiness**<br>Filthiness–KJV<br>Filthiness–NASB<br>Moral filth–NIV<br>Filthiness–NKJV<br>Filth–NLT<br>**POSB REFERENCE**<br>(Jas.1:19-21; esp. v.21)<br>Note 1, point 3 | ῥυπαρίαν = *hruparian*<br>Pronunciation: [hroo-par-ee'-ahn]<br>Parsing (part of speech): noun<br>  Case—accusative<br>  Gender—feminine<br>  Number—singular<br>  Stem or root—from ῥυπαρία, ας<br>Concordance References:<br>  ⇒ Strong's #4507 *hruparia*<br>  ⇒ NIV #4864 *hruparia*<br>  ⇒ NASB #4507 *hruparia*<br><br>**James 1:21**<br>Wherefore lay apart all **filthiness** and superfluity of naughtiness, and receive with meekness the engrafted word, which is able to save your souls. [KJV]<br>Therefore putting aside all **filthiness** and *all* that remains of wickedness, in humility receive the word implanted, which is able to save your souls. [NASB] | Moral filth, filthiness, impurity.<br><br>**Practical Application**<br>The picture is that of *taking off* a dirty garment and putting it aside. A person must put off every dirty thing and lay it off to the side away from himself. If he enjoys the dirt and filth, then his mind is going to be on it. His mind will not be clear, not enough to hear the Word of God. William Barclay makes the point that the Greek word for "filthiness" (*hruparian*) is taken from the Greek word *rupos*. The word is sometimes used to refer to *wax in the ear* (*The Letters of James and Peter*, p.66). The picture is descriptive: a person with wax in the ear cannot hear the Word of God, not clearly. Therefore, he must take the wax out of his ear and put it away or else he will be deaf to the Word of God. |

# PRACTICAL WORD STUDIES
## in the NEW TESTAMENT

| ENGLISH WORD | GREEK WORD AND VERSE | THE WORD MEANS... |
|---|---|---|
| | Therefore, get rid of all **moral filth** and the evil that is so prevalent and humbly accept the word planted in you, which can save you. [NIV]<br><br>Therefore lay aside all **filthiness** and overflow of wickedness, and receive with meekness the implanted word, which is able to save your souls. [NKJV]<br><br>So get rid of all the **filth** and evil in your lives, and humbly accept the message God has planted in your hearts, for it is strong enough to save your souls. [NLT]<br><br>διὸ ἀποθέμενοι πᾶσαν **ῥυπαρίαν** καὶ περισσείαν κακίας, ἐν πραΰτητι δέξασθε τὸν ἔμφυτον λόγον, τὸν δυνάμενον σῶσαι τὰς ψυχὰς ὑμῶν. [GNS]<br><br>διὸ ἀποθέμενοι πᾶσαν **ῥυπαρίαν** καὶ περισσείαν κακίας ἐν πραΰτητι, δέξασθε τὸν ἔμφυτον λόγον τὸν δυνάμενον σῶσαι τὰς ψυχὰς ὑμῶν. [GNT] | |
| **#1495**<br>**Filthiness**<br><br>Filthiness–KJV<br>Filthiness–NASB<br>Obscenity–NIV<br>Filthiness–NKJV<br>Obscene stories–NLT<br><br>**POSB REFERENCE**<br>(Eph.5:4)<br>Note 4, point 1 | αἰσχρότης = aischrotēs<br>Pronunciation: [ah-hee-skhrot'-ace]<br>Parsing (part of speech): noun<br>    Case—nominative<br>    Gender—feminine<br>    Number—singular<br>    Stem or root—from αἰσχρότης, ητος<br>Concordance References:<br>⇒ Strong's #151 aischrotēs<br>⇒ NIV #157 aischrotēs<br>⇒ NASB #151 aischrotēs<br><br>**Ephes. 5:4**<br>Neither **filthiness**, nor foolish talking, nor jesting, which are not convenient: but rather giving of thanks. [KJV]<br><br>And *there must be no* **filthiness** and silly talk, or coarse jesting, which are not fitting, but rather giving of thanks. [NASB]<br><br>Nor should there be **obscenity**, foolish talk or coarse joking, which are out of place, but rather thanksgiving. [NIV]<br><br>Neither **filthiness**, nor foolish talking, nor coarse jesting, which are not fitting, but rather giving of thanks. [NKJV]<br><br>**Obscene stories**, foolish talk, and coarse jokes—these are not for you. Instead, let there be thankfulness to God. [NLT]<br><br>καὶ **αἰσχρότης**, καὶ μωρολογία, ἡ εὐτραπελία, τὰ οὐκ ἀνήκοντα· ἀλλὰ μᾶλλον εὐχαριστία. [GNS]<br><br>καὶ **αἰσχρότης** καὶ μωρολογία ἡ εὐτραπελία, ἃ οὐκ ἀνῆκεν, ἀλλὰ μᾶλλον εὐχαριστία. [GNT] | Obscenity, filthiness; to tell obscene stories; to display indecent behavior<br><br>**Practical Application**<br>The believer is never, not once, to be engaged in "filthiness" (*aischrotēs*): using the mouth in obscene, shameful, foul, polluted, base, immoral conduct and conversation. What an indictment of our day—a day of sodomy and perversion. And note: the word refers to both conduct and speech. How polluted and foul mouthed so many have become—so much so that society could easily be known as a second Sodom and Gomorrah. |
| **#1496**<br>**Filthy Communication**<br><br>Filthy communication–KJV<br>Abusive speech–NASB<br>Filthy language–NIV<br>Filthy language–NKJV<br>Dirty language–NLT<br><br>**POSB REFERENCE**<br>(Col.3:8-11; esp. v.8)<br>Note 2, point 1e | αἰσχρολογίαν = aischrologian<br>Pronunciation: [ahee-skhrol-og-ee'-ahn]<br>Parsing (part of speech): noun<br>    Case—accusative<br>    Gender—feminine<br>    Number—singular<br>    Stem or root—from αἰσχρολογία, ας<br>Concordance References:<br>⇒ Strong's #148 aischrologia<br>⇒ NIV #155 aischrologia<br>⇒ NASB #148 aischrologia<br><br>**Col. 3:8**<br>But now ye also put off all these; anger, wrath, malice, blasphemy, **filthy communication** out of your mouth. [KJV]<br><br>But now you also, put them all aside: anger, wrath, malice, slander, *and* **abusive speech** from your mouth. [NASB]<br><br>But now you must rid yourselves of all such things as these: anger, rage, malice, slander, and **filthy language** from your lips. [NIV]<br><br>But now you yourselves are to put off all these: anger, wrath, malice, blasphemy, **filthy language** out of your | Filthy language, filthy communication, abusive speech, dirty language, obscene speech.<br><br>**Practical Application**<br>If a believer is to follow and imitate God, he has to be pure in speech and conversation; he has to keep his mouth or tongue clean. He cannot let his mouth become foul and polluted, filthy and vile.<br><br>He is never, not once, to be engaged in "filthy communication" (*aischrologian*): using the mouth in obscene, shameful, foul, polluted, base, immoral conduct and conversation. What an indictment of our day—a day of sodomy and perversion. And note: the word refers to both conduct and speech. How polluted and foul mouthed so many have become—so much so that society could easily be known as a second Sodom and Gomorrah. |

| ENGLISH WORD | GREEK WORD AND VERSE | THE WORD MEANS... |
|---|---|---|
| | mouth. [NKJV]<br>But now is the time to get rid of anger, rage, malicious behavior, slander, and **dirty language**. [NLT]<br>νυνὶ δὲ ἀπόθεσθε καὶ ὑμεῖς τὰ πάντα, ὀργήν, θυμόν, κακίαν, βλασφημίαν, **αἰσχρολογίαν** ἐκ τοῦ στόματος ὑμῶν· [GNS]<br>νυνὶ δὲ ἀπόθεσθε καὶ ὑμεῖς τὰ πάντα, ὀργήν, θυμόν, κακίαν, βλασφημίαν, **αἰσχρολογίαν** ἐκ τοῦ στόματος ὑμῶν· [GNT] | |
| **#1497**<br>**Filthy Language**<br><br>Filthy communication–KJV<br>Abusive speech–NASB<br>**Filthy language–NIV**<br>**Filthy language–NKJV**<br>Dirty language–NLT<br><br>**POSB REFERENCE**<br>(Col.3:8-11; esp. v.8)<br>Note 2, point 1e | αἰσχρολογίαν = aischrologian<br>Pronunciation: [ahee-skhrol-og-ee'-ahn]<br>Parsing (part of speech): noun<br>    Case—accusative<br>    Gender—feminine<br>    Number—singular<br>    Stem or root—from αἰσχρολογία, ας<br>Concordance References:<br>  ⇒ Strong's #148 aischrologia<br>  ⇒ NIV #155 aischrologia<br>  ⇒ NASB #148 aischrologia<br><br>**Col. 3:8**<br>But now ye also put off all these; anger, wrath, malice, blasphemy, **filthy communication** out of your mouth. [KJV]<br>But now you also, put them all aside: anger, wrath, malice, slander, *and* **abusive speech** from your mouth. [NASB]<br>But now you must rid yourselves of all such things as these: anger, rage, malice, slander, and **filthy language** from your lips. [NIV]<br>But now you yourselves are to put off all these: anger, wrath, malice, blasphemy, **filthy language** out of your mouth. [NKJV]<br>But now is the time to get rid of anger, rage, malicious behavior, slander, and **dirty language**. [NLT]<br>νυνὶ δὲ ἀπόθεσθε καὶ ὑμεῖς τὰ πάντα, ὀργήν, θυμόν, κακίαν, βλασφημίαν, **αἰσχρολογίαν** ἐκ τοῦ στόματος ὑμῶν· [GNS]<br>νυνὶ δὲ ἀπόθεσθε καὶ ὑμεῖς τὰ πάντα, ὀργήν, θυμόν, κακίαν, βλασφημίαν, **αἰσχρολογίαν** ἐκ τοῦ στόματος ὑμῶν·[GNT] | Filthy language, filthy communication, abusive speech, dirty language, obscene speech.<br><br>**Practical Application**<br>If a believer is to follow and imitate God, he has to be pure in speech and conversation; he has to keep his mouth or tongue clean. He cannot let his mouth become foul and polluted, filthy and vile.<br>He is never, not once, to be engaged in "filthy language" (*aischrologian*): using the mouth in obscene, shameful, foul, polluted, base, immoral conduct and conversation. What an indictment of our day—a day of sodomy and perversion. And note: the word refers to both conduct and speech. How polluted and foulmouthed so many have become—so much so that society could easily be known as a second Sodom and Gomorrah. |
| **#1498**<br>**Filthy Lucre, Not For**<br><br>**Not for filthy lucre–KJV**<br>Not for sordid gain–NASB<br>Not greedy for money–NIV<br>Not for dishonest gain–NKJV<br>Not grudgingly–NLT<br><br>**POSB REFERENCE**<br>(1 Pt.5:2-3; esp. v.2)<br>Note 2, point 2 | μηδὲ αἰσχροκερδῶς = mēde aischrokerdōs<br>Pronunciation: [may-deh' ahee-skhrok-er-doce']<br>Parsing aischrokerdōs (part of speech):<br>    adjective<br>    Type—adverb<br>    Stem or root—from αἰσχροκερδῶς<br>Concordance References:<br>  ⇒ Strong's #3366 mēde + 147 aischrokerdōs<br>  ⇒ NIV #3593 mēde [not] +154 aischrokerdōs [greedy for money]<br>  ⇒ NASB #3366 mēde + 147 aischrokerdōs<br><br>**1 Peter 5:2**<br>Feed the flock of God which is among you, taking the oversight *thereof*, not by constraint, but willingly; **not for filthy lucre**, but of a ready mind; [KJV]<br>Shepherd the flock of God among you, exercising oversight not under compulsion, but voluntarily, according to *the will of* God; and **not for sordid gain**, but with eagerness; [NASB]<br>Be shepherds of God's flock that is under your care, serving as overseers—not because you must, but because you are willing, as God wants you to be; **not greedy for money**, but eager to serve; [NIV]<br>Shepherd the flock of God among you, exercising Shepherd the flock of God which is among you, serving as overseers, not by compulsion but willingly, **not for dishonest gain** but eagerly; [NKJV]<br>Care for the flock of God entrusted to you. Watch over | Not greedy for money; not for filthy lucre; not greedy for sordid gain; not grudgingly; not greedy for material gain.<br><br>**Practical Application**<br>The elder or minister must take the oversight of the flock not for personal profit and gain, but with a ready mind. The Greek says that no person is to enter the ministry for "filthy lucre" (*mēde aischrokerdōs*), that is, for base gain, or for some soiled and dirty advantage. No person should ever enter the ministry...<br>• as a profession.<br>• as a means of livelihood.<br>• as a means to serve mankind.<br>• because people say he has the gifts for it.<br>• because people say he would make a good minister.<br>• because family and friends encourage him to enter the ministry.<br><br>All of these reasons usually surround a person's entrance into the ministry. But they must never be *the reasons* why a person enters the ministry and cares for God's people. The ministry is a *call from God*, and no person dare enter the ministry without a personal call to the min- |

# PRACTICAL WORD STUDIES
## in the NEW TESTAMENT

| ENGLISH WORD | GREEK WORD AND VERSE | THE WORD MEANS... |
|---|---|---|
| | it willingly, **not grudgingly**—not for what you will get out of it, but because you are eager to serve God. [NLT]<br>ποιμάνατε τὸ ἐν ὑμῖν ποίμνιον τοῦ Θεοῦ, ἐπισκοποῦντες μὴ ἀναγκαστῶς, ἀλλ ἑκουσίως· **μηδὲ αἰσχροκερδῶς,** ἀλλὰ προθύμως, [GNS]<br>ποιμάνατε τὸ ἐν ὑμῖν ποίμνιον τοῦ θεοῦ [ἐπισκοποῦντες] μὴ ἀναγκαστῶς ἀλλὰ ἑκουσίως κατὰ θεόν, **μηδὲ αἰσχροκερδῶς** ἀλλὰ προθύμως, [GNT] | istry. But note: when the call comes, the person is to have a ready mind. He is to minister to God's people; he is to readily feed the flock of God. |
| #1499<br>**Find**<br><br>Seek–KJV<br>Look for–NASB<br>Look for–NIV<br>Seek–NKJV<br>**Find–NLT**<br><br>**POSB REFERENCE**<br>(Acts 11:25-26; esp. v.25)<br>Note 3 | ἀναζητῆσαι = anazēteō<br>Pronunciation: [an-ad-zay-teh'-sah-ee]<br>Parsing (part of speech): verb<br>   Mood—infinitive<br>   Tense—aorist<br>   Voice—active<br>   Stem or root—from ἀναζητέω<br>Concordance References:<br>  ⇒ Strong's #327 anazēteō<br>  ⇒ NIV #349 anazēteō<br>  ⇒ NASB #327 anazēteō<br><br>**Acts 11:25**<br>Then departed Barnabas to Tarsus, for to **seek** Saul: [KJV]<br>And he left for Tarsus to **look for** Saul; [NASB]<br>Then Barnabas went to Tarsus to **look for** Saul, [NIV]<br>Then Barnabas departed for Tarsus to **seek** Saul. [NKJV]<br>Then Barnabas went on to Tarsus to **find** Saul. [NLT]<br>ἐξῆλθε δὲ εἰς Ταρσὸν ὁ Βαρνάβας **ἀναζητῆσαι** Σαῦλον, [GNS]<br>ἐξῆλθεν δὲ εἰς Ταρσὸν **ἀναζητῆσαι** Σαῦλον, [GNT] | To look for; to seek; to find; to search after. It means to search for; to search back and forth, up and down; to make a thorough search.<br><br>**Practical Application**<br>The church sought additional staff—to have an adequate teaching staff. Barnabas is the one who is the focus of attention in this point, but the church was bound to have sensed the need for additional staff and given its approval. The point is this: the need was sensed and the decision was made to seek for help. The only question was who should be secured. A unique person was needed, a person who not only had a Jewish background but who knew the Greek language and culture and could relate to both Gentile and Jew alike. The person also needed to be fearless and bold in his witness for Christ because of the godless, immoral society of Antioch.<br>Barnabas knew such a man: Saul of Tarsus. So he set out to find him. Paul had been busy throughout Syria and Cilicia preaching Christ (Galatians 1:21). Apparently, Barnabas had difficulty finding him. But note: he knew God's will, so he did not give up the search. He kept searching until he found God's choice. What a dynamic lesson for all churches in seeking help and in building a church staff! |
| #1500<br>**Fine**<br><br>Good–KJV<br>**Fine–NASB**<br>Noble–NIV<br>Good–NKJV<br>Honorable–NLT<br><br>**POSB REFERENCE**<br>(1 Tim.3:1)<br>Note 1 | καλοῦ = kalou<br>Pronunciation: [kal-oo']<br>Parsing (part of speech): adjective<br>   Case—genitive<br>   Gender—neuter<br>   Number—singular<br>   Stem or root—from καλός, ή, όν<br>Concordance References:<br>  ⇒ Strong's #2570 kalos<br>  ⇒ NIV #2819 kalos<br>  ⇒ NASB #2570 kalos<br><br>**1 Tim. 3:1**<br>This is a true saying, If a man desire the office of a bishop, he desireth a **good** work. [KJV]<br>It is a trustworthy statement: if any man aspires to the office of overseer, it is a **fine** work he desires to do. [NASB]<br>Here is a trustworthy saying: If anyone sets his heart on being an overseer, he desires a **noble** task. [NIV]<br>This *is* a faithful saying: If a man desires the position of a bishop, he desires a **good** work. [NKJV]<br>It is a true saying that if someone wants to be an elder, he desires an **honorable** responsibility. [NLT]<br>Πιστὸς ὁ λόγος· Εἴ τις ἐπισκοπῆς ὀρέγεται, **καλοῦ** ἔργου ἐπιθυμεῖ· [GNS]<br>πιστὸς ὁ λόγος. Εἴ τις ἐπισκοπῆς ὀρέγεται, **καλοῦ** ἔργου ἐπιθυμεῖ. [GNT] | Noble, good, fine, honorable, honest, proper, right, excellent, beneficial, productive.<br><br>**Practical Application**<br>The office of an overseer is a "fine work." Note that the position of the ministry is not what is stressed, but the work of the ministry. The emphasis is not the esteem and honor of the profession. The emphasis is upon the work of the ministry. It is the work that is honorable, excellent, beneficial, and productive. The work of the ministry is a "fine work." |
| #1501<br>**Fine-Sounding Arguments** | πιθανολογία = pithanologia<br>Pronunciation: [pith-an-ol-og-ee'-ah]<br>Parsing (part of speech): noun<br>   Case—dative<br>   Gender—feminine | Fine-sounding arguments, enticing words, persuasive arguments. |

## PRACTICAL WORD STUDIES
### in the NEW TESTAMENT

| ENGLISH WORD | GREEK WORD AND VERSE | THE WORD MEANS... |
|---|---|---|
| Enticing words–KJV<br>Persuasive argument–NASB<br>**Fine-sounding arguments–NIV**<br>Persuasive words–NKJV<br>Persuasive arguments–NLT<br><br>**POSB REFERENCE**<br>(Col.2:4)<br>Note 3 | Number—singular<br>Stem or root—from πιθανολογία, ας<br>Concordance References:<br>⇒ Strong's #4086 pithanologia<br>⇒ NIV #4391 pithanologia<br>⇒ NASB #4086 pithanologia<br><br>**Col. 2:4**<br>And this I say, lest any man should beguile you with **enticing words**. [KJV]<br>I say this in order that no one may delude you with **persuasive argument**. [NASB]<br>I tell you this so that no one may deceive you by **fine-sounding arguments**. [NIV]<br>Now this I say lest anyone should deceive you with **persuasive words**. [NKJV]<br>I am telling you this so that no one will be able to deceive you with **persuasive arguments**. [NLT]<br>τοῦτο δὲ λέγω, ἵνα μὴ τις ὑμᾶς παραλογίζηται ἐν πιθανολογίᾳ. [GNS]<br>Τοῦτο λέγω ἵνα μηδεὶς ὑμᾶς παραλογίζηται ἐν πιθανολογίᾳ. [GNT] | **Practical Application**<br>A mature person resists seduction and deception. The word "deceive" (*paralogizetai*) means to mislead, delude, deceive, cheat, seduce, and lead someone astray. Note how the seduction takes place: by "fine-sounding arguments" (*pithanologia*), that is, by words that are persuasive, appealing, eloquent, flowery, and attractive. |
| #1502<br>**Finish–Finisher**<br><br>Finisher–KJV<br>Perfecter–NASB<br>Perfecter–NIV<br>Finisher–NKJV<br>Finish–NLT<br><br>**POSB REFERENCE**<br>(Heb.12:2)<br>Note 3 | τελειωτὴν = *teleiōtēn*<br>Pronunciation: [tel-i-o'-tayn]<br>Parsing (part of speech): noun<br>    Case—accusative<br>    Gender—masculine<br>    Number—singular<br>Stem or root—from τελειωτής, οῦ<br>Concordance References:<br>⇒ Strong's #5051 teleiōtēs OR #5047 teleiōtēs<br>⇒ NIV #5460 teleiōtēs<br>⇒ NASB #5051 teleiōtēs<br><br>**Hebrews 12:2**<br>Looking unto Jesus the author and **finisher** of our faith; who for the joy that was set before him endured the cross, despising the shame, and is set down at the right hand of the throne of God. [KJV]<br>Fixing our eyes on Jesus, the author and **perfecter** of faith, who for the joy set before Him endured the cross, despising the shame, and has sat down at the right hand of the throne of God. [NASB]<br>Let us fix our eyes on Jesus, the author and **perfecter** of our faith, who for the joy set before him endured the cross, scorning its shame, and sat down at the right hand of the throne of God. [NIV]<br>Looking unto Jesus, the author and **finisher** of our faith, who for the joy that was set before Him endured the cross, despising the shame, and has sat down at the right hand of the throne of God. [NKJV]<br>We do this by keeping our eyes on Jesus, on whom our faith depends from start to **finish**. He was willing to die a shameful death on the cross because of the joy he knew would be his afterward. Now he is seated in the place of highest honor beside God's throne in heaven. [NLT]<br>ἀφορῶντες εἰς τὸν τῆς πίστεως ἀρχηγὸν καὶ **τελειωτὴν** Ἰησοῦν, ὃς ἀντὶ τῆς προκειμένης αὐτῷ χαρᾶς, ὑπέμεινε σταυρὸν, αἰσχύνης καταφρονήσας, ἐν δεξιᾷ τε τοῦ θρόνου τοῦ Θεοῦ ἐκάθισεν. [GNS]<br>ἀφορῶντες εἰς τὸν τῆς πίστεως ἀρχηγὸν καὶ **τελειωτὴν** Ἰησοῦν, ὃς ἀντὶ τῆς προκειμένης αὐτῷ χαρᾶς ὑπέμεινεν σταυρὸν αἰσχύνης καταφρονήσας ἐν δεξιᾷ τε τοῦ θρόνου τοῦ Θεοῦ κεκάθικεν. [GNT] | Perfecter, finisher; to finish. It means that He perfected, completed, and consummated the race. He ran the race to the finish.<br><br>**Practical Application**<br>The idea is that Jesus Christ ran the course of life perfectly. He was sinless, perfectly righteous, always obeying God in everything. He ran the race of faith—of utter obedience and trust in God—all through His life upon earth. He finished His course living a perfect and righteous life upon earth. Therefore, He created and authored and completed the Christian race for all believers. He is the blazing example of faith in God—of utter dependence and obedience—for the believer. The believer is always to be looking to Jesus the Author and Finisher of faith. |
| #1503<br>**Finished**<br><br>Finished–KJV<br>Finished–NASB<br>Finished–NIV | Τετέλεσται = *Tetelestai*<br>Pronunciation: [teh-tel-ehs'-tah-ee]<br>Parsing (part of speech): verb<br>    Mood—indicative<br>    Tense—perfect<br>    Voice—passive<br>    Person—3rd person | To finish; to complete a predetermined goal; to initiate, implement, and accomplish a perfect plan.<br><br>**Practical Application**<br>The Greek word (*Tetelestai*) is the shout of |

# PRACTICAL WORD STUDIES
## in the NEW TESTAMENT

| ENGLISH WORD | GREEK WORD AND VERSE | THE WORD MEANS... |
|---|---|---|
| **Finished–NKJV**<br>**Finished–NLT**<br><br>**POSB**<br>**REFERENCE**<br>(Jn.19:30)<br>Note 7, point 1 | Number—singular<br>Stem or root—from τελέω<br>Concordance References:<br>⇒ Strong's #5055 teleo<br>⇒ NIV #5464 teleo<br>⇒ NASB #5055 teleo<br><br>**John 19:30**<br>When Jesus therefore had received the vinegar, he said, It is **finished**: and he bowed his head, and gave up the ghost. [KJV]<br>When Jesus therefore had received the sour wine, He said, "It is **finished**!" And He bowed His head, and gave up His spirit. [NASB]<br>When he had received the drink, Jesus said, "It is **finished**." With that, he bowed his head and gave up his spirit. [NIV]<br>So when Jesus had received the sour wine, He said, "It is **finished**!" And bowing His head, He gave up His spirit. [NKJV]<br>When Jesus had tasted it, he said, "It is **finished**!" Then he bowed his head and gave up his spirit. [NLT]<br>ὅτε οὖν ἔλαβε τὸ ὄξος ὁ Ἰησοῦς εἶπε, **Τετέλεσται**· καὶ κλίνας τὴν κεφαλὴν, παρέδωκε τὸ πνεῦμα. [GNS]<br>ὅτε οὖν ἔλαβεν τὸ ὄξος [ὁ] Ἰησοῦς εἶπεν, **Τετέλεσται**, καὶ κλίνας τὴν κεφαλὴν παρέδωκεν τὸ πνεῦμα. [GNT] | victorious purpose. Jesus had completed His work, His mission, and His task. He was not crying the cry of a defeated martyr. He was crying the cry of a victorious conqueror. |
| **#1504**<br>**Fire, Unquench-**<br>**able–**<br>**Fire, Never**<br>**Ending**<br><br>Fire unquenchable–<br>KJV<br>Unquenchable fire–<br>NASB<br>Unquenchable fire–<br>NIV<br>Unquenchable fire–<br>NKJV<br>Never ending fire–<br>NLT<br><br>**POSB**<br>**REFERENCE**<br>(Lk.3:17)<br>*Deeper Study #2* | πυρὶ ἀσβέστῳ = puri asbesto<br>Pronunciation: [poo-ree has'-bes-tow]<br>Parsing *puri* (part of speech): noun<br>  Case—dative<br>  Gender—neuter<br>  Number—singular<br>  Stem or root—from πῦρ, ός<br>Parsing *asbesto* (part of speech): adjective<br>  Case—dative<br>  Gender—neuter<br>  Number—singular<br>  Stem or root—from ἄσβεστος, ον<br>Concordance References:<br>⇒ Strong's #762 asbestos +4442 pur<br>⇒ NIV #812 asbestos [unquenchable] + 4786 pur [fire]<br>⇒ NASB #762 asbestos +4442 pur<br><br>**Luke 3:17**<br>Whose fan is in his hand, and he will throughly purge his floor, and will gather the wheat into his garner; but the chaff he will burn with **fire unquenchable**. [KJV]<br>"And His winnowing fork is in His hand to thoroughly clear His threshing floor, and to gather the wheat into His barn; but He will burn up the chaff with **unquenchable fire**." [NASB]<br>His winnowing fork is in his hand to clear his threshing floor and to gather the wheat into his barn, but he will burn up the chaff with **unquenchable fire**." [NIV]<br>His winnowing fan is in His hand, and He will thoroughly clean out His threshing floor, and gather the wheat into His barn; but the chaff He will burn with **unquenchable fire**." [NKJV]<br>He is ready to separate the chaff from the grain with his winnowing fork. Then he will clean up the threshing area, storing the grain in his barn but burning the chaff with **never-ending fire**." [NLT]<br>οὗτο πτύον ἐν τῇ χειρὶ αὐτοῦ, διακαθαριεῖ τὴν ἅλωνα αὐτοῦ, καὶ συνάξει τὸν σῖτον εἰς τὴν ἀποθήκην αὐτοῦ, τὸ δὲ ἄχυρον κατακαύσει **πυρὶ ἀσβέστῳ**. [GNS]<br>οὗ τὸ πτύον ἐν τῇ χειρὶ αὐτοῦ διακαθᾶραι τὴν ἅλωνα αὐτοῦ καὶ συναγαγεῖν τὸν σῖτον εἰς τὴν ἀποθήκην αὐτοῦ, τὸ δὲ ἄχυρον κατακαύσει **πυρὶ ἀσβέστῳ**. [GNT] | Fire unquenchable, never ending fire; all ablaze.<br><br>**Practical Application**<br>It is fire that cannot be quenched, snuffed out, extinguished. The idea is that the fire is eternal, burning on and on and never ending (see POSB *Deeper Study #3*—Matthew 25:41). |

## PRACTICAL WORD STUDIES
## in the NEW TESTAMENT

| ENGLISH WORD | GREEK WORD AND VERSE | THE WORD MEANS... |
|---|---|---|
| **#1505**<br>**Firm**<br><br>Stedfastness–KJV<br>Stability–NASB<br>**Firm–NIV**<br>Steadfastness–NKJV<br>Strong–NLT<br><br>**POSB REFERENCE**<br>(Col.2:5)<br>Note 4 | στερέωμα = stereōma<br>Pronunciation: [ster-eh´-o-mah]<br>Parsing (part of speech): noun<br>   Case—accusative<br>   Gender—neuter<br>   Number—singular<br>   Stem or root—from στερέωμα, τος<br>Concordance References:<br>  ⇒ Strong's #4733 stereōma<br>  ⇒ NIV #5106 stereōma<br>  ⇒ NASB #4733 stereōma<br><br>**Col. 2:5**<br><br>For though I be absent in the flesh, yet am I with you in the spirit, joying and beholding your order, and the **stedfastness** of your faith in Christ. [KJV]<br><br>For even though I am absent in body, nevertheless I am with you in spirit, rejoicing to see your good discipline and the **stability** of your faith in Christ. [NASB]<br><br>For though I am absent from you in body, I am present with you in spirit and delight to see how orderly you are and how **firm** your faith in Christ is. [NIV]<br><br>For though I am absent in the flesh, yet I am with you in spirit, rejoicing to see your *good* order and the **steadfastness** of your faith in Christ. [NKJV]<br><br>For though I am far away from you, my heart is with you. And I am very happy because you are living as you should and because of your **strong** faith in Christ. [NLT]<br><br>εἰ γὰρ καὶ τῇ σαρκὶ ἄπειμι, ἀλλὰ τῷ πνεύματι σὺν ὑμῖν εἰμι, χαίρων καὶ βλέπων ὑμῶν τὴν τάξιν καὶ τὸ **στερέωμα** τῆς εἰς Χριστὸν πίστεως ὑμῶν. [GNS]<br><br>εἰ γὰρ καὶ τῇ σαρκὶ ἄπειμι, ἀλλὰ τῷ πνεύματι σὺν ὑμῖν εἰμι, χαίρων καὶ βλέπων ὑμῶν τὴν τάξιν καὶ τὸ **στερέωμα** τῆς εἰς Χριστὸν πίστεως ὑμῶν. [GNT] | To be firm, steadfast, stable, strong. It means to stand fast and persevere; to be immovable, steady, and unyielding; to never crack, give in, or back up.<br><br>**Practical Application**<br>A mature people maintain discipline—order and steadfastness.<br><br>⇒ The word "orderly" (*taxin*) means to maintain military discipline, array, and arrangement; to hold a solid front (The Amplified New Testament); to hold the military line unbroken and intact (A.T. Robertson, *Word Pictures in the New Testament*, Vol.4, p.489).<br><br>⇒ The word "firm" (*stereōma*) is also a military word. A.T. Robertson says that it is "the solid part of the line which can and does stand the attack" of the seduction.<br><br>Note that the believers of the Colossian church were being attacked by false teaching even as Paul was writing to them. But they were responding like a victorious army. They were maintaining their discipline and holding their order and standing fast. Note also the importance of the minister's encouragement: Paul says that he was with them *in spirit*, joying and watching them gain the victory over the false teachers. |
| **#1506**<br>**Firm**<br><br>Strengthen–KJV<br>Strengthen–NASB<br>**Firm–NIV**<br>Strengthen–NKJV<br>Strengthen–NLT<br><br>**POSB REFERENCE**<br>(1 Pt.5:10)<br>Note 2, point 3 | σθενώσει = sthenōsei<br>Pronunciation: [sthen-o´-seh-ee]<br>Parsing (part of speech): verb<br>   Mood—indicative<br>   Tense—future<br>   Voice—active<br>   Person—3rd person<br>   Number—singular<br>   Stem or root—from σθενόω<br>Concordance References:<br>  ⇒ Strong's #4599 sthenoō<br>  ⇒ NIV #4964 sthenoō<br>  ⇒ NASB #4599 sthenoō<br><br>**1 Peter 5:10**<br><br>But the God of all grace, who hath called us unto his eternal glory by Christ Jesus, after that ye have suffered a while, make you perfect, stablish, **strengthen**, settle you. [KJV]<br><br>And after you have suffered for a little while, the God of all grace, who called you to His eternal glory in Christ, will Himself perfect, confirm, **strengthen** and establish you. [NASB]<br><br>And the God of all grace, who called you to his eternal glory in Christ, after you have suffered a little while, will himself restore you and make you strong, **firm** and steadfast. [NIV]<br><br>But may the God of all grace, who called us to His eternal glory by Christ Jesus, after you have suffered a while, perfect, establish, **strengthen**, and settle *you*. [NKJV]<br><br>In his kindness God called you to his eternal glory by means of Jesus Christ. After you have suffered a little while, he will restore, support, and **strengthen** you, and he will place you on a firm foundation. [NLT]<br><br>ὁ δὲ Θεὸς πάσης χάριτος, ὁ καλέσας ὑμᾶς εἰς τὴν αἰώνιον αὐτοῦ δόξαν ἐν Χριστῷ Ἰησοῦ, ὀλίγον παθόντας | Firm, strength, solid, established; to give energy, power, vigor and might.<br><br>**Practical Application**<br>God Himself will make us "firm" (*sthenōsei*). This is the only time this word is used in the New Testament. Most translators say that it means strength. It would, therefore, mean to be filled with all strength, with all the strength necessary to overcome all the trials and temptations and sufferings of life. Again, remember that it is only God Himself who can give us such enormous strength. And He will, if we will only draw near Him. |

## Practical Word Studies in the New Testament

| ENGLISH WORD | GREEK WORD AND VERSE | THE WORD MEANS... |
|---|---|---|
| | αὐτὸς καταρτίσει ὑμᾶς, στηρίξει, **σθενώσαι**, θεμελιώσαι. [GNS]<br>Ὁ δὲ θεὸς πάσης χάριτος, ὁ καλέσας ὑμᾶς εἰς τὴν αἰώνιον αὐτοῦ δόξαν ἐν Χριστῷ [Ἰησοῦ], ὀλίγον παθόντας αὐτὸς καταρτίσει, στηρίξει, **σθενώσει**, θεμελιώσει. [GNT] | |
| **#1507**<br>**Firm–Firmly**<br><br>Settled–KJV<br>Steadfast–NASB<br>**Firm–NIV**<br>Steadfast–NKJV<br>**Firmly–NLT**<br><br>**POSB REFERENCE**<br>(Col.1:23)<br>Note 4, point 1 | ἑδραῖοι = *hedraioi*<br>Pronunciation: [ed-rah'-ee-oy]<br>Parsing (part of speech): adjective<br>    Case—nominative<br>    Gender—masculine<br>    Number—plural<br>    Stem or root—from ἑδραῖος, α, ον<br>Concordance References:<br>  ⇒ Strong's #1476 *hedraios*<br>  ⇒ NIV #1612 *hedraios*<br>  ⇒ NASB #1476 *hedraios*<br><br>**Col. 1:23**<br>If ye continue in the faith grounded and **settled**, and be not moved away from the hope of the gospel, which ye have heard, and which was preached to every creature which is under heaven; whereof I Paul am made a minister; [KJV]<br>If indeed you continue in the faith firmly established and **steadfast**, and not moved away from the hope of the gospel that you have heard, which was proclaimed in all creation under heaven, and of which I, Paul, was made a minister. [NASB]<br>If you continue in your faith, established and **firm**, not moved from the hope held out in the gospel. This is the gospel that you heard and that has been proclaimed to every creature under heaven, and of which I, Paul, have become a servant. [NIV]<br>If indeed you continue in the faith, grounded and **steadfast**, and are not moved away from the hope of the gospel which you heard, which was preached to every creature under heaven, of which I, Paul, became a minister. [NKJV]<br>But you must continue to believe this truth and stand in it **firmly**. Don't drift away from the assurance you received when you heard the Good News. The Good News has been preached all over the world, and I, Paul, have been appointed by God to proclaim it. [NLT]<br>εἴγε ἐπιμένετε τῇ πίστει τεθεμελιωμένοι καὶ **ἑδραῖοι**, καὶ μὴ μετακινούμενοι ἀπὸ τῆς ἐλπίδος τοῦ εὐαγγελίου οὗ ἠκούσατε, τοῦ κηρυχθέντος ἐν πάσῃ τῇ κτίσει τῇ ὑπὸ τὸν οὐρανόν, οὗ ἐγενόμην ἐγὼ Παῦλος διάκονος. [GNS]<br>εἴ γε ἐπιμένετε τῇ πίστει τεθεμελιωμένοι καὶ **ἑδραῖοι** καὶ μὴ μετακινούμενοι ἀπὸ τῆς ἐλπίδος τοῦ εὐαγγελίου οὗ ἠκούσατε, τοῦ κηρυχθέντος ἐν πάσῃ κτίσει τῇ ὑπὸ τὸν οὐρανόν, οὗ ἐγενόμην ἐγὼ Παῦλος διάκονος. [GNT] | To be firm; to be settled; to be steadfast; to stand firm.<br><br>**Practical Application**<br>The believer must stand firm and continue on. He must be steadfast if he wishes to be presented perfect before God. |
| **#1508**<br>**Firmly Believe It**<br><br>Keep in memory–KJV<br>Hold fast–NASB<br>Hold firmly–NIV<br>Hold fast–NKJV<br>**Firmly believe it–NLT**<br><br>**POSB REFERENCE**<br>(1 Cor.15:1-2; esp. v.2)<br>Note 1, point 3 | κατέχετε = *katechete*<br>Pronunciation: [kat-ekh'-eh-teh]<br>Parsing (part of speech): verb<br>    Mood—indicative<br>    Tense—present<br>    Voice—active<br>    Person—2nd person<br>    Number—plural<br>    Stem or root—from κατέχω<br>Concordance References:<br>  ⇒ Strong's #2722 *katechō*<br>  ⇒ NIV #2988 *katechō*<br>  ⇒ NASB #2722 *katechō*<br><br>**1 Cor. 15:2**<br>By which also ye are saved, if ye **keep in memory** what I preached unto you, unless ye have believed in vain. [KJV] | To hold firm; to firmly believe; to hold fast; to keep; to retain.<br><br>**Practical Application**<br>In order to be saved, a person must hold firmly to the gospel. No person who denies the gospel could ever expect to be saved. |

# Practical Word Studies in the New Testament

| ENGLISH WORD | GREEK WORD AND VERSE | THE WORD MEANS... |
|---|---|---|
| | By which also you are saved, if you **hold fast** the word which I preached to you, unless you believed in vain. [NASB]<br>By this gospel you are saved, if you **hold firmly** to the word I preached to you. Otherwise, you have believed in vain. [NIV]<br>By which also you are saved, if you **hold fast** that word which I preached to you—unless you believed in vain. [NKJV]<br>And it is this Good News that saves you if you **firmly believe it**—unless, of course, you believed something that was never true in the first place. [NLT]<br>δι᾽ οὗ καὶ σώζεσθε· τίνι λόγῳ εὐηγγελισάμην ὑμῖν, εἰ **κατέχετε**, ἐκτὸς εἰ μὴ εἰκῇ ἐπιστεύσατε. [GNS]<br>δι᾽ οὗ καὶ σώζεσθε, τίνι λόγῳ εὐηγγελισάμην ὑμῖν εἰ **κατέχετε**, ἐκτὸς εἰ μὴ εἰκῇ ἐπιστεύσατε. [GNT] | |
| **#1509**<br>**First**<br><br>Chief–KJV<br>**First–NASB**<br>**First–NIV**<br>**First–NKJV**<br>**First–NLT**<br><br>**POSB REFERENCE**<br>(Mt.20:23-28; esp. v.27)<br>Note 3, point 3 | πρῶτος = *prōtos*<br>Pronunciation: [pro'-tos]<br>Parsing (part of speech): adjective<br>    Type—ordinal<br>    Case—nominative<br>    Gender—masculine<br>    Number—singular<br>    Stem or root—from πρῶτος, η, ον<br>Concordance References:<br>  ⇒ Strong's #4413 prōtos<br>  ⇒ NIV #4755 prōtos<br>  ⇒ NASB #4413 prōtos<br><br>**Matthew 20:27**<br>And whosoever will be **chief** among you, let him be your servant: [KJV]<br>And whoever wishes to be **first** among you shall be your slave; [NASB]<br>And whoever wants to be **first** must be your slave— [NIV]<br>And whoever desires to be **first** among you, let him be your slave— [NKJV]<br>And whoever wants to be **first** must become your slave. [NLT]<br>καὶ ὃς ἐὰν θέλῃ ἐν ὑμῖν εἶναι **πρῶτος** ἔστω ὑμῶν δοῦλος· [GNS]<br>καὶ ὃς ἂν θέλῃ ἐν ὑμῖν εἶναι **πρῶτος** ἔσται ὑμῶν δοῦλος· [GNT] | To be first in importance, chief, foremost, prominent, to be "in charge."<br><br>**Practical Application**<br>If a person wants to be first, what essential thing must be done? This person must learn to become a great servant. The word servant (*doulos*) means far more than just a servant. It means a slave totally possessed by the master. It is a *bondservant* bound by law to a master.<br>A look at the slave market of the New Testament day shows clearly what it meant to be a "slave or servant of Jesus Christ."<br>1. The slave was owned by his master; he was totally possessed by his master. The New Testament believer was purchased and possessed by Christ.<br>2. The slave existed for his master, and he had no other reason for existence. He had no personal rights whatsoever. The same was true of the New Testament believer: he existed only for Christ. His rights were the rights of Christ only.<br>3. The slave served his master, and he existed only for the purpose of service. He was at the master's disposal any hour of the day. So it was with the New Testament believer: he lived only to serve Christ—hour by hour and day by day.<br>4. The slave's will belonged to his master. He was allowed no will and no ambition other than the will and ambition of the master. He was completely subservient to the Master and owed total obedience to the will of the master. The New Testament believer belonged to Christ.<br>5. There is a fifth and most precious thing that the New Testament believer meant by "a slave of Jesus Christ." He meant that he had the highest and most honored and kingly profession in all the world. Men of God, the greatest men of history, have always been called *the servants of God*. It was the highest title of honor. The believer's slavery to Jesus Christ is no cringing, cowardly, shameful subjection. It is the position of honor—the honor that bestows upon a man the privileges and responsibilities of serving the King of kings and Lord of lords. |

# PRACTICAL WORD STUDIES
## in the NEW TESTAMENT

| ENGLISH WORD | GREEK WORD AND VERSE | THE WORD MEANS... |
|---|---|---|
| **#1510**<br>**First**<br><br>Beginning–KJV<br>Beginning–NASB<br>**First–NIV**<br>Beginning–NKJV<br>Early–NLT<br><br>**POSB<br>REFERENCE**<br>(Lk.1:2-3, esp. v.2)<br>Note 3, point 2 | ἀρχῆς = archës<br>Pronunciation: [ar-khays']<br>Parsing (part of speech): noun<br>    Case—genitive<br>    Gender—feminine<br>    Number—singular<br>    Stem or root—from ἀρχή, ῆς<br>Concordance References:<br>⇒ Strong's #746 archë<br>⇒ NIV #794 archë<br>⇒ NASB #746 archë<br><br>**Luke 1:2**<br>Even as they delivered them unto us, which from the **beginning** were eyewitnesses, and ministers of the word; [KJV]<br><br>Just as those who from the **beginning** were eyewitnesses and servants of the word have handed them down to us, [NASB]<br><br>Just as they were handed down to us by those who from the **first** were eyewitnesses and servants of the word. [NIV]<br><br>Just as those who from the **beginning** were eyewitnesses and ministers of the word delivered them to us, [NKJV]<br><br>They used as their source material the reports circulating among us from the **early** disciples and other eyewitnesses of what God has done in fulfillment of his promises. [NLT]<br><br>καθὼς παρέδοσαν ἡμῖν οἱ ἀπ' ἀρχῆς αὐτόπται καὶ ὑπηρέται γενόμενοι τοῦ λόγου, [GNS]<br><br>καθὼς παρέδοσαν ἡμῖν οἱ ἀπ' ἀρχῆς αὐτόπται καὶ ὑπηρέται γενόμενοι τοῦ λόγου, [GNT] | The beginning, the first of all, the origin, the genesis, the dawn, the conception, the start, the commencement.<br><br>**Practical Application**<br>In the context of this Scripture, Luke notes that the ministers of the Word were eyewitnesses "from the first." They were eyewitnesses of every event and word of Christ, eyewitnesses of His life day by day. |
| **#1511**<br>**First–<br>First, From The<br>Very**<br><br>First–KJV<br>Beginning–NASB<br>From the beginning–NIV<br>**From the very first–NKJV**<br>Beginning–NLT<br><br>**POSB<br>REFERENCE**<br>(Lk.1:3)<br>Note 3, point 2 | ἄνωθεν = anöthen<br>Pronunciation: [an'-o-then]<br>Parsing (part of speech): adjective adverb<br>    Stem or root—from ἄνωθεν<br>Concordance References:<br>⇒ Strong's #509 anöthen<br>⇒ NIV #540 anöthen<br>⇒ NASB #509 anöthen<br><br>**Luke 1:3**<br>It seemed good to me also, having had perfect understanding of all things from the very **first**, to write unto thee in order, most excellent Theophilus, [KJV]<br><br>It seemed fitting for me as well, having investigated everything carefully from the **beginning**, to write it out for you in consecutive order, most excellent Theophilus; [NASB]<br><br>Therefore, since I myself have carefully investigated everything **from the beginning**, it seemed good also to me to write an orderly account for you, most excellent Theophilus, [NIV]<br><br>It seemed good to me also, having had perfect understanding of all things **from the very first**, to write to you an orderly account, most excellent Theophilus, [NKJV]<br><br>Having carefully investigated all of these accounts from the **beginning**, I have decided to write a careful summary for you, [NLT]<br><br>ἔδοξε κἀμοὶ παρηκολουθηκότι ἄνωθεν πᾶσιν ἀκριβῶς, καθεξῆς σοι γράψαι, κράτιστε Θεόφιλε, [GNS]<br><br>ἔδοξε κἀμοὶ παρηκολουθηκότι ἄνωθεν πᾶσιν ἀκριβῶς καθεξῆς σοι γράψαι, κράτιστε Θεόφιλε, [GNT] | From the beginning, from the first, from above, from a higher place (heaven). The words "beginning or first" can and often do mean from above.<br><br>**Practical Application**<br>Some understand Luke to be saying that he had investigated the things from above. Several things point to this translation.<br>1. If Luke meant from the first or beginning, why does he not use the same word (*arches*) which he used in verse 2? It seems to be much more accurate to say he chooses a different word (*anöthen*) because he is saying something different, from above.<br>2. The prophets are said to have proclaimed things from above. They are said to "have inquired and searched diligently, who prophesied of the grace that should come unto you: searching what, or what manner of time the Spirit of Christ which was in them did signify, when it testified beforehand the sufferings of Christ, and the glory that should follow. Unto whom it was revealed, that not unto themselves, but unto us they did minister the things, which are now reported unto you by them that have preached the gospel unto you with the Holy Ghost sent down from heaven; which things the angels desire to look into" (1 Peter 1:10-12). Scripture also says, "For the prophecy came not in old time by the will of man: but holy men of God spake as they were moved by the Holy Ghost" (2 Peter 1:21).<br>3. Luke is certainly recording all things from above, investigating and searching diligently |

# PRACTICAL WORD STUDIES
## in the NEW TESTAMENT

| ENGLISH WORD | GREEK WORD AND VERSE | THE WORD MEANS... |
|---|---|---|
| | | to write what "the Spirit of Christ which was in [him] did signify" (1 Peter 1:11). He is certainly speaking as a holy man of God "moved by the Holy Spirit" (2 Peter 1:21). He is certainly proclaiming the gospel of the Lord Jesus Christ, the good news of Him who came from above. |
| #1512<br>**First Installment**<br><br>Earnest–KJV<br>Pledge–NASB<br>Deposit guaranteeing what is to come–NIV<br>Guarantee–NKJV<br>**First installment–NLT**<br><br>**POSB REFERENCE**<br>(2 Cor.1:21-22; esp. v.22)<br>Note 5 | ἀρραβῶνα = arrabōna<br>Pronunciation: [ar-hrab-ohn'-ah]<br>Parsing (part of speech): noun<br>  Case—accusative<br>  Gender—masculine<br>  Number—singular<br>  Stem or root—from ἀρραβών, ῶνος<br>Concordance References:<br>⇒ Strong's #728 arrabōn<br>⇒ NIV #775 arrabōn<br>⇒ NASB #728 arrabōn<br><br>**2 Cor. 1:22**<br>Who hath also sealed us, and given the **earnest** of the Spirit in our hearts. [KJV]<br>Who also sealed us and gave us the Spirit in our hearts as a **pledge**. [NASB]<br>Set his seal of ownership on us, and put his Spirit in our hearts as a **deposit, guaranteeing what is to come**. [NIV]<br>Who also has sealed us and given us the Spirit in our hearts as a **guarantee**. [NKJV]<br>And he has identified us as his own by placing the Holy Spirit in our hearts as the **first installment** of everything he will give us. [NLT]<br>ὁ καὶ σφραγισάμενος ἡμᾶς, καὶ δοὺς τὸν **ἀρραβῶνα** τοῦ Πνεύματος ἐν ταῖς καρδίαις ἡμῶν. [GNS]<br>ὁ καὶ σφραγισάμενος ἡμᾶς καὶ δοὺς τὸν **ἀρραβῶνα** τοῦ πνεύματος ἐν ταῖς καρδίαις ἡμῶν. [GNT] | Deposit, guarantee, security, pledge, first installment (of what is to come), payment.<br><br>**Practical Application**<br>It was the first installment paid on an item to guarantee that the rest would be paid. It was the engagement ring that guaranteed the marriage. God has given the Holy Spirit as the guarantee of eternal life. The Holy Spirit is an advanced payment, a down payment, on His promise to believers. |
| #1513<br>**First Of All**<br><br>Beginning–KJV<br>Beginning–NASB<br>Beginning–NIV<br>Beginning–NKJV<br>**First of all–NLT**<br><br>**POSB REFERENCE**<br>(Col.1:18)<br>Note 2 | ἀρχή = archë<br>Pronunciation: [ar-khay']<br>Parsing (part of speech): noun<br>  Case—nominative<br>  Gender—feminine<br>  Number—singular<br>  Stem or root—from ἀρχή, ῆς<br>Concordance References:<br>⇒ Strong's #746 archë<br>⇒ NIV #794 archë<br>⇒ NASB #746 archë<br><br>**Col. 1:18**<br>And he is the head of the body, the church: who is the **beginning**, the firstborn from the dead; that in all things he might have the preeminence. [KJV]<br>He is also head of the body, the church; and He is the **beginning**, the first-born from the dead; so that He Himself might come to have first place in everything. [NASB]<br>And he is the head of the body, the church; he is the **beginning** and the firstborn from among the dead, so that in everything he might have the supremacy. [NIV]<br>And He is the head of the body, the church, who is the **beginning**, the firstborn from the dead, that in all things He may have the preeminence. [NKJV]<br>Christ is the head of the church, which is his body. He is the **first of all** who will rise from the dead, so he is first in everything. [NLT]<br>καὶ αὐτός ἐστιν ἡ κεφαλὴ τοῦ σώματος, τῆς ἐκκλησίας· ὅς ἐστιν **ἀρχή**, πρωτότοκος ἐκ τῶν νεκρῶν, ἵνα γένηται ἐν πᾶσιν αὐτὸς πρωτεύων· [GNS]<br>καὶ αὐτός ἐστιν ἡ κεφαλὴ τοῦ σώματος τῆς ἐκκλησίας· ὅς ἐστιν **ἀρχή**, πρωτότοκος ἐκ τῶν νεκρῶν, ἵνα γένηται ἐν πᾶσιν αὐτὸς πρωτεύων, [GNT] | Beginning, first of all, origin, the genesis, the dawn, the conception, the start, the commencement.<br><br>**Practical Application**<br>The word "beginning" (archë) has a twofold idea.<br>1. "Beginning" means creative power. When something first begins, it is created or brought into being by some person or thing greater than itself. Jesus Christ was the Person who gave birth to the church. He is greater than the church; therefore, He had the power to create the church and bring it into existence.<br>⇒ The church is the idea of His mind: He was the One who dreamed of the church, thought it up, and saw the great purpose it could accomplish upon earth.<br>⇒ The church is the plan of His heart: He saw how the church could be founded and built upon the earth, and His heart wanted it.<br>⇒ The church is the desire of His will: He desired and longed for the church; therefore, He willed to create it.<br>⇒ The church is the activity of His hands and life. Jesus Christ came to earth and gave birth to the church (see POSB outline and note—Matthew 16:18; and POSB *Deeper Study* #1, Church—Matthew 16:18).<br>⇒ The church is the result of His love: He loved the world; therefore, He founded |

| ENGLISH WORD | GREEK WORD AND VERSE | THE WORD MEANS... |
|---|---|---|
| | | His church and He reaches out to the world through His church.<br>⇒ The church is the subject of His care. He looks after and oversees the welfare of His church, making sure that it fulfills its purpose on earth. Even the very gates of hell cannot prevail against the church because of His love and care (Matthew 16:18).<br>    The point is this: Jesus Christ began the church. He is the beginning, the creative power who founded and gave birth to the church.<br>2. "Beginning" means *first in time*. Jesus Christ was the first Person of the church. He began the church; therefore, He was the first member, the great and glorious Founder of the church. All others who come into the church follow Him. |
| #1514<br>**First Principles**<br><br>**First principles**–KJV<br>Elementary principles– NASB<br>Elementary truths– NIV<br>**First principles**– NKJV<br>Basic things–NLT<br><br>**POSB REFERENCE**<br>(Heb.5:12)<br>Note 2 | στοιχεῖα τῆς ἀρχῆς = *stoicheia tës archës*<br>Pronunciation: [stoy-khi'-eh-ee tays har-khays']<br>Parsing *stoicheia* (part of speech): noun<br>    Case—accusative<br>    Gender—neuter<br>    Number—plural<br>    Stem or root—from στοιχεῖα, ων<br>Parsing *archës* (part of speech): noun<br>    Case—genitive<br>    Number—feminine<br>    Number—singular<br>    Stem or root—from ἀρχή, ῆς<br>Concordance References:<br>⇒ Strong's #746+3588+4747 archë ho stoicheion<br>⇒ NIV #794+3836+5122 archë ho stoicheion [elementary truths]<br>⇒ NASB #746+3588+4747 archë ho stoicheion<br><br>**Hebrews 5:12**<br>For when for the time ye ought to be teachers, ye have need that one teach you again which be the **first principles** of the oracles of God; and are become such as have need of milk, and not of strong meat. [KJV]<br>    For though by this time you ought to be teachers, you have need again for someone to teach you the **elementary principles** of the oracles of God, and you have come to need milk and not solid food. [NASB]<br>    In fact, though by this time you ought to be teachers, you need someone to teach you the **elementary truths** of God's word all over again. You need milk, not solid food! [NIV]<br>    For though by this time you ought to be teachers, you need *someone* to teach you again the **first principles** of the oracles of God; and you have come to need milk and not solid food. [NKJV]<br>    You have been Christians a long time now, and you ought to be teaching others. Instead, you need someone to teach you again the **basic things** a beginner must learn about the Scriptures. You are like babies who drink only milk and cannot eat solid food. [NLT]<br>καὶ γὰρ ὀφείλοντες εἶναι διδάσκαλοι, διὰ τὸν χρόνον, πάλιν χρείαν ἔχετε τοῦ διδάσκειν ὑμᾶς, τινὰ τὰ **στοιχεῖα τῆς ἀρχῆς** τῶν λογίων τοῦ Θεοῦ· καὶ γεγόνατε χρείαν ἔχοντες γάλακτος, καὶ οὐ στερεᾶς τροφῆς. [GNS]<br>καὶ γὰρ ὀφείλοντες εἶναι διδάσκαλοι διὰ τὸν χρόνον, πάλιν χρείαν ἔχετε τοῦ διδάσκειν ὑμᾶς τινὰ τὰ **στοιχεῖα τῆς ἀρχῆς** τῶν λογίων τοῦ θεοῦ καὶ γεγόνατε χρείαν ἔχοντες γάλακτος [καὶ] οὐ στερεᾶς τροφῆς. [GNT] | Elementary truths, first principles, elementary principles, basic things, first things. It means the basic principles of God's Word, the elementary teachings, the ABC's of God's Word.<br><br>**Practical Application**<br>    A person becomes immature because he refuses to grow up spiritually. The Hebrew believers refused to move beyond the first principles of God's Word. They (*stoicheia tës archës*) are the very basic teachings of salvation and of spiritual growth, such teachings as...<br>• a person should be saved<br>• a person should grow spiritually<br>• a person should live righteously<br>• a person should worship<br>• a person should keep the rituals and ceremonies of religion<br>Such basic truths as these are the milk of God's Word. They are truths that are to be preached and taught, but they are the truths for the unsaved and for young believers, for babes in Christ. They are to be learned and learned quickly by the believers, and then he is to move on to maturity. Note that the Christian life is compared to physical growth. A young believer is said to be a babe in Christ, and the first principles of God's Word are said to be the milk upon which he is to feed. A young believer is to feed upon the milk of the Word, the first principles, but he is expected to grow until he is feeding upon the meat of the Word—studying and growing a mature understanding of the Christian life. |

# PRACTICAL WORD STUDIES
## in the NEW TESTAMENT

| ENGLISH WORD | GREEK WORD AND VERSE | THE WORD MEANS... |
|---|---|---|
| **#1515**<br>**Firstbegotten**<br><br>**Firstbegotten–KJV**<br>First-born–NASB<br>Firstborn–NIV<br>Firstborn–NKJV<br>Honored Son–NLT<br><br>**POSB REFERENCE**<br>(Heb.1:4-6; esp. v.6)<br>Note 1, point 3 | πρωτότοκον = prōtotokon<br>Pronunciation: [pro-tot-ok'-on]<br>Parsing (part of speech): pronominal adjective<br>    Case—accusative<br>    Gender—masculine<br>    Number—singular<br>    Stem or root—from πρωτότοκος, ον<br>Concordance References:<br>⇒ Strong's #4416 prōtotokos<br>⇒ NIV #4758 prōtotokos<br>⇒ NASB #4416 prōtotokos<br><br>**Hebrews 1:6**<br>And again, when he bringeth in the **firstbegotten** into the world, he saith, And let all the angels of God worship him. [KJV]<br>And when He again brings the **first-born** into the world, He says, "And let all the angels of God worship Him." [NASB]<br>And again, when God brings his **firstborn** into the world, he says, "Let all God's angels worship him." [NIV]<br>But when He again brings the **firstborn** into the world, He says: "Let all the angels of God worship Him." [NKJV]<br>And then, when he presented his **honored Son** to the world, God said, "Let all the angels of God worship him." [NLT]<br>ὅταν δὲ πάλιν εἰσαγάγῃ τὸν **πρωτότοκον** εἰς τὴν οἰκουμένην, λέγει, Καὶ προσκυνησάτωσαν αὐτῷ πάντες ἄγγελοι Θεοῦ. [GNS]<br>ὅταν δὲ πάλιν εἰσαγάγῃ τὸν **πρωτότοκον** εἰς τὴν οἰκουμένην, λέγει, Καὶ προσκυνησάτωσαν αὐτῷ πάντες ἄγγελοι θεοῦ. [GNT] | Firstborn, firstbegotten, honored son. It means *first* in the sense of priority and superiority, of being above someone else. It is a word that shows dignity, honor, worth; that someone deserves praise.<br><br>**Practical Application**<br>Jesus Christ is the One who is to be worshipped and praised, not angels.<br>⇒ When Jesus Christ was born into this world, He was attended and worshipped by angels. (Luke 2:13f).<br>⇒ When Jesus Christ was taken into the world above, at His resurrection and ascension, He was attended and worshipped by angels (Acts 1:10f).<br>⇒ When Jesus Christ returns to this earth again, He shall be attended and worshipped by angels (Matthew 13:41; Matthew 16:27; Matthew 24:31).<br><br>Jesus Christ is the Person who entered the world as Man, to save man. He is the Person who was raised from the dead and who ascended into heaven to conquer death forever. He is the Person who is to return and take us home to heaven to be with God eternally. Angels did not do this. Therefore our worship—our hope and attention and praise—is to be upon Christ. We are to be seeking Christ as our way to God, not angels or some other intermediary. Jesus Christ has a name that is far more excellent than that of angels. |
| **#1516**<br>**Firstborn**<br><br>Firstbegotten–KJV<br>**First-born–NASB**<br>**Firstborn–NIV**<br>Firstborn–NKJV<br>Honored Son–NLT<br><br>**POSB REFERENCE**<br>(Heb.1:4-6; esp. v.6)<br>Note 1, point 3 | πρωτότοκον = prōtotokon<br>Pronunciation: [pro-tot-ok'-on]<br>Parsing (part of speech): pronominal adjective<br>    Case—accusative<br>    Gender—masculine<br>    Number—singular<br>    Stem or root—from πρωτότοκος, ον<br>Concordance References:<br>⇒ Strong's #4416 prōtotokos<br>⇒ NIV #4758 prōtotokos<br>⇒ NASB #4416 prōtotokos<br><br>**Hebrews 1:6**<br>And again, when he bringeth in the **firstbegotten** into the world, he saith, And let all the angels of God worship him. [KJV]<br>And when He again brings the **first-born** into the world, He says, "And let all the angels of God worship Him." [NASB]<br>And again, when God brings his **firstborn** into the world, he says, "Let all God's angels worship him." [NIV]<br>But when He again brings the **firstborn** into the world, He says: "Let all the angels of God worship Him." [NKJV]<br>And then, when he presented his **honored Son** to the world, God said, "Let all the angels of God worship him." [NLT]<br>ὅταν δὲ πάλιν εἰσαγάγῃ τὸν **πρωτότοκον** εἰς τὴν οἰκουμένην, λέγει, Καὶ προσκυνησάτωσαν αὐτῷ πάντες ἄγγελοι Θεοῦ. [GNS]<br>ὅταν δὲ πάλιν εἰσαγάγῃ τὸν **πρωτότοκον** εἰς τὴν οἰκουμένην, λέγει, Καὶ προσκυνησάτωσαν αὐτῷ πάντες ἄγγελοι θεοῦ. [GNT] | Firstborn, firstbegotten, honored son. It means *first* in the sense of priority and superiority, of being above someone else. It is a word that shows dignity, honor, worth; that someone deserves praise.<br><br>**Practical Application**<br>Jesus Christ is the One who is to be worshipped and praised, not angels.<br>⇒ When Jesus Christ was born into this world, He was attended and worshipped by angels. (Luke 2:13f).<br>⇒ When Jesus Christ was taken into the world above, at His resurrection and ascension, He was attended and worshipped by angels (Acts 1:10f).<br>⇒ When Jesus Christ returns to this earth again, He will be attended and worshipped by angels (Matthew 13:41; Matthew 16:27; Matthew 24:31).<br>Jesus Christ is the Person who entered the world as Man, to save man. He is the Person who was raised from the dead and who ascended into heaven to conquer death forever. He is the Person who is to return and take us home to heaven to be with God eternally. Angels did not do this. Therefore our worship—our hope and attention and praise—is to be upon Christ. We are to be seeking Christ as our way to God, not angels or some other intermediary. Jesus Christ has a name that is far more excellent than that of angels. |

# PRACTICAL WORD STUDIES
## in the New Testament

| ENGLISH WORD | GREEK WORD AND VERSE | THE WORD MEANS... |
|---|---|---|
| **#1517**<br>**Fishing**<br><br>Catch–KJV<br>Catching–NASB<br>Catch–NIV<br>Catch–NKJV<br>**Fishing–NLT**<br><br>**POSB**<br>**REFERENCE**<br>(Lk.5:10)<br>Note 7, point 2 | ἔσῃ ζωγρῶν = esë zögrön<br>Pronunciation: [es-ee dzogue-rohn']<br>Parsing *esë* (part of speech): verb<br>    Mood—indicative<br>    Tense—future<br>    Voice—middle deponent<br>    Person—2nd person<br>    Number—singular<br>    Stem or root—from εἰμί<br>Parsing *zögrön* (part of speech): verb<br>    Mood—participle<br>    Tense—present<br>    Voice—active<br>    Case—nominative<br>    Gender—masculine<br>    Person—2nd person<br>    Number—singular<br>    Stem or root—from ζωγρέω<br>Concordance References:<br>  ⇒ Strong's #1488 eimi +2221 zögreö<br>  ⇒ NIV #1639 eimi +2436 zögreö<br>  ⇒ NASB #1488 eimi +2221 zögreö<br><br>**Luke 5:10**<br>And so *was* also James, and John, the sons of Zebedee, which were partners with Simon. And Jesus said unto Simon, Fear not; from henceforth thou shalt **catch** men. [KJV]<br>And so also James and John, sons of Zebedee, who were partners with Simon. And Jesus said to Simon, "Do not fear, from now on you will be **catching** men." [NASB]<br>And so were James and John, the sons of Zebedee, Simon's partners. Then Jesus said to Simon, "Don't be afraid; from now on you will **catch** men." [NIV]<br>And so also *were* James and John, the sons of Zebedee, who were partners with Simon. And Jesus said to Simon, "Do not be afraid. From now on you will **catch** men." [NKJV]<br>His partners, James and John, the sons of Zebedee, were also amazed. Jesus replied to Simon, "Don't be afraid! From now on you'll be **fishing** for people!" [NLT]<br>ὁμοίως δὲ καὶ Ἰάκωβον καὶ Ἰωάννην, υἱοὺς Ζεβεδαίου, οἳ ἦσαν κοινωνοὶ τῷ Σίμωνι. καὶ εἶπε πρὸς τὸν Σίμωνα ὁ Ἰησοῦς, Μὴ φοβοῦ· ἀπὸ τοῦ νῦν ἀνθρώπους **ἔσῃ ζωγρῶν**. [GNS]<br>ὁμοίως δὲ καὶ Ἰάκωβον καὶ Ἰωάννην υἱοὺς Ζεβεδαίου, οἳ ἦσαν κοινωνοὶ τῷ Σίμωνι. καὶ εἶπεν πρὸς τὸν Σίμωνα ὁ Ἰησοῦς, Μὴ φοβοῦ· ἀπὸ τοῦ νῦν ἀνθρώπους **ἔσῃ ζωγρῶν**. [GNT] | To catch alive or to catch for life; to capture; to nab; to fish; to seize; to snare; to grab; to take.<br><br>**Practical Application**<br>The idea is that Peter was no longer to catch (fish) for death, but he was to catch (men) for life. |
| **#1518**<br>**Fit–Fitting**<br><br>Fit–KJV<br>**Fitting–NASB**<br>**Fitting–NIV**<br>**Fitting–NKJV**<br>**Fitting–NLT**<br><br>**POSB**<br>**REFERENCE**<br>(Col.3:18)<br>Note 1, point 2 | ἀνῆκεν = anëken<br>Pronunciation: [an-ay'-ken]<br>Parsing (part of speech): verb<br>    Mood—indicative<br>    Tense—imperfect<br>    Voice—active<br>    Person—3rd person<br>    Number—singular<br>    Stem or root—from ἀνήκει<br>Concordance References:<br>  ⇒ Strong's #433 anëkö<br>  ⇒ NIV #465 anëkö<br>  ⇒ NASB #433 anëkö<br><br>**Col. 3:18**<br>Wives, submit yourselves unto your own husbands, as it is **fit** in the Lord. [KJV]<br>Wives, be subject to your husbands, as is **fitting** in the Lord. [NASB]<br>Wives, submit to your husbands, as is **fitting** in the Lord. [NIV]<br>Wives, submit to your own husbands, as is **fitting** in | Fitting, fit; to do what is proper. The word "fitting" (*anëken*) means the right thing to do.<br><br>**Practical Application**<br>Christian wives must submit because it is the only fitting thing to do. Why is it the only fitting and right thing to do? Not because the husband is superior and the wife is inferior as a human being. The reason is the wife is *in the Lord* because she has surrendered her life to live in the Lord and to love and follow Him. She then becomes a witness for Him by *living just as He says to live*. Therefore, when the Lord says that it is His will for her to submit to her husband, she submits. She submits because the Lord tells her that submission is the way He wants her to live with her husband. Again, submission is simply...<br>• God's order for the family.<br>• the relationship, cooperation, and partner- |

## PRACTICAL WORD STUDIES
### in the NEW TESTAMENT

| ENGLISH WORD | GREEK WORD AND VERSE | THE WORD MEANS... |
|---|---|---|
| | the Lord. [NKJV]<br>You wives must submit to your husbands, as is **fitting** for those who belong to the Lord. [NLT]<br>Αἱ γυναῖκες, ὑποτάσσεσθε τοῖς ἰδίοις ἀνδράσιν, ὡς **ἀνῆκεν** ἐν Κυρίῳ. [GNS]<br>Αἱ γυναῖκες, ὑποτάσσεσθε τοῖς ἀνδράσιν ὡς **ἀνῆκεν** ἐν κυρίῳ. [GNT] | ship that is to exist between the wife and husband. |
| **#1519**<br>**Fits Of Rage**<br><br>Wrath–KJV<br>Outbursts of anger–NASB<br>**Fits of rage–NIV**<br>Outbursts of wrath–NKJV<br>Outbursts of anger–NLT<br><br>**POSB REFERENCE**<br>(Gal.5:19-21; esp. v.20)<br>Note 2 | θυμοί = *thumoi*<br>Pronunciation: [thoo-moy']<br>Parsing (part of speech): noun<br>    Case—nominative<br>    Gender—masculine<br>    Number—plural<br>    Stem or root—from θυμός, ου<br>Concordance References:<br>  ⇒ Strong's #2372 thumos<br>  ⇒ NIV #2596 thumos<br>  ⇒ NASB #2372 thumos<br><br>**Galatians 5:20**<br>Idolatry, witchcraft, hatred, variance, emulations, **wrath**, strife, seditions, heresies, [KJV]<br>Idolatry, sorcery, enmities, strife, jealousy, **outbursts of anger**, disputes, dissensions, factions, [NASB]<br>Idolatry and witchcraft; hatred, discord, jealousy, **fits of rage**, selfish ambition, dissensions, factions [NIV]<br>Idolatry, sorcery, hatred, contentions, jealousies, **outbursts of wrath**, selfish ambitions, dissensions, heresies, [NKJV]<br>Idolatry, participation in demonic activities, hostility, quarreling, jealousy, **outbursts of anger**, selfish ambition, divisions, the feeling that everyone is wrong except those in your own little group, [NLT]<br>εἰδωλολατρία, φαρμακεία, ἔχθραι, ἔρεις, ζῆλοι, **θυμοί**, ἐριθεῖαι, διχοστασίαι, αἱρέσεις, [GNS]<br>εἰδωλολατρία, φαρμακεία, ἔχθραι, ἔρις, ζῆλος, **θυμοί**, ἐριθεῖαι, διχοστασίαι, αἱρέσεις, [GNT] | Fits of rage; outbursts of anger; fury; wrath; an intense feeling of indignation.<br><br>**Practical Application**<br>It is a violent, explosive temper; quick-tempered explosive reactions that arise from stirred and boiling emotions. But it is anger which fades away just as quickly as it arose. It is not anger that lasts. |
| **#1520**<br>**Fits Perfectly**<br><br>Easy–KJV<br>Easy–NASB<br>Easy–NIV<br>Easy–NKJV<br>**Fits perfectly–NLT**<br><br>**POSB REFERENCE**<br>(Mt.11:29-30, esp.v.30)<br>Note 2, point 1 | χρηστός = *chrēstos*<br>Pronunciation: [khrase-tos']<br>Parsing (part of speech): adjective<br>    Case—nominative<br>    Gender—masculine<br>    Number—singular<br>    Stem or root—from χρηστός, ή, όν<br>Concordance References:<br>  ⇒ Strong's #5543 chrēstos<br>  ⇒ NIV #5982 chrēstos<br>  ⇒ NASB #5543 chrēstos<br><br>**Matthew 11:30**<br>For my yoke is **easy**, and my burden is light. [KJV]<br>"For My yoke is **easy**, and My load is light." [NASB]<br>For my yoke is **easy** and my burden is light." [NIV]<br>For My yoke is **easy** and My burden is light." [NKJV]<br>For my yoke **fits perfectly**, and the burden I give you is light." [NLT]<br>ὁ γὰρ ζυγός μου **χρηστὸς**, καὶ τὸ φορτίον μου ἐλαφρόν ἐστιν. [GNS]<br>ὁ γὰρ ζυγός μου **χρηστὸς** καὶ τὸ φορτίον μου ἐλαφρόν ἐστιν. [GNT] | To be easy, well-fitting, good, kind, better.<br><br>**Practical Application**<br>In this Scripture, Christ is saying that His yoke, His life and task, are fitted to a person. It is just what a person needs, and it is easy, the easiest life and task the person could live and undertake. |
| **#1521**<br>**Fix Eyes–Fixing Eyes**<br><br>Looking–KJV<br>**Fixing eyes–NASB**<br>**Fix eyes–NIV**<br>Looking–NKJV<br>Keeping eyes–NLT | ἀφορῶντες = *aphorōntes*<br>Pronunciation: [af-or-own'-tehs]<br>Parsing (part of speech): verb<br>    Mood—participle<br>    Tense—present<br>    Voice—active<br>    Case—nominative<br>    Gender—masculine<br>    Person—1st person<br>    Number—plural<br>    Stem or root—from ἀφοράω | To fix one's eyes on; to keep one's eyes on; to look. The phrase "fix eyes" (*aphorōntes*) means to fix your eyes upon Jesus. It also means to fix your mind upon Him (Kenneth Wuest. *Hebrews*, Vol. 2, p.214).<br><br>**Practical Application**<br>We may and should look at the example of other believers, but we should always be *fixing our eyes on Jesus*. The Christian runner is to |

# PRACTICAL WORD STUDIES
## in the NEW TESTAMENT

| ENGLISH WORD | GREEK WORD AND VERSE | THE WORD MEANS... |
|---|---|---|
| **POSB REFERENCE**<br>(Heb.12:2)<br>Note 3 | Concordance References:<br>⇒ Strong's #872 aphoraö<br>⇒ NIV #927 aphoraö<br>⇒ NASB #872 aphoraö<br><br>**Hebrews 12:2**<br>**Looking** unto Jesus the author and finisher of our faith; who for the joy that was set before him endured the cross, despising the shame, and is set down at the right hand of the throne of God. [KJV]<br>**Fixing** our **eyes** on Jesus, the author and perfecter of faith, who for the joy set before Him endured the cross, despising the shame, and has sat down at the right hand of the throne of God. [NASB]<br>Let us **fix** our **eyes** on Jesus, the author and perfecter of our faith, who for the joy set before him endured the cross, scorning its shame, and sat down at the right hand of the throne of God. [NIV]<br>**Looking** unto Jesus, the author and finisher of *our* faith, who for the joy that was set before Him endured the cross, despising the shame, and has sat down at the right hand of the throne of God. [NKJV]<br>We do this by **keeping** our **eyes** on Jesus, on whom our faith depends from start to finish. He was willing to die a shameful death on the cross because of the joy he knew would be his afterward. Now he is seated in the place of highest honor beside God's throne in heaven. [NLT]<br>**ἀφορῶντες** εἰς τὸν τῆς πίστεως ἀρχηγὸν καὶ τελειωτὴν Ἰησοῦν, ὃς ἀντὶ τῆς προκειμένης αὐτῷ χαρᾶς, ὑπέμεινε σταυρὸν, αἰσχύνης καταφρονήσας, ἐν δεξιᾷ τε τοῦ θρόνου τοῦ Θεοῦ ἐκάθισεν. [GNS]<br>**ἀφορῶντες** εἰς τὸν τῆς πίστεως ἀρχηγὸν καὶ τελειωτὴν Ἰησοῦν, ὃς ἀντὶ τῆς προκειμένης αὐτῷ χαρᾶς ὑπέμεινεν σταυρὸν αἰσχύνης καταφρονήσας ἐν δεξιᾷ τε τοῦ θρόνου τοῦ θεοῦ κεκάθικεν. [GNT] | focus his eyes and mind upon Jesus Christ. Why? Because Jesus Christ Himself ran the race of faith when He was upon earth, and He shows us exactly how to run it. |
| **#1523**<br>**Fix Thoughts On**<br><br>Consider–KJV<br>Consider–NASB<br>**Fix...thoughts on**–NIV<br>Consider–NKJV<br>Think about–NLT<br><br>**POSB REFERENCE**<br>(Heb.3:1)<br>Note 1 | **κατανοήσατε** = *katanoësate*<br>Pronunciation: [kat-an-o-ay-sah'-teh]<br>Parsing (part of speech): verb<br>  Mood—imperative<br>  Tense—aorist<br>  Voice—active<br>  Person—2nd person<br>  Number—plural<br>  Stem or root—from κατανοέω<br>Concordance References:<br>⇒ Strong's #2657 katanoeö<br>⇒ NIV #2917 katanoeö<br>⇒ NASB #2657 katanoeö<br><br>**Hebrews 3:1**<br>Wherefore, holy brethren, partakers of the heavenly calling, **consider** the Apostle and High Priest of our profession, Christ Jesus; [KJV]<br>Therefore, holy brethren, partakers of a heavenly calling, **consider** Jesus, the Apostle and High Priest of our confession. [NASB]<br>Therefore, holy brothers, who share in the heavenly calling, **fix** your **thoughts on** Jesus, the apostle and high priest whom we confess. [NIV]<br>Therefore, holy brethren, partakers of the heavenly calling, **consider** the Apostle and High Priest of our confession, Christ Jesus, [NKJV]<br>And so, dear brothers and sisters who belong to God and are bound for heaven, **think about** this Jesus whom we declare to be God's Messenger and High Priest. [NLT]<br>Ὅθεν, ἀδελφοὶ ἅγιοι, κλήσεως ἐπουρανίου μέτοχοι, **κατανοήσατε** τὸν ἀπόστολον καὶ ἀρχιερέα τῆς ὁμολογίας ἡμῶν Χριστὸν Ἰησοῦν, [GNS]<br>Ὅθεν, ἀδελφοὶ ἅγιοι, κλήσεως ἐπουρανίου μέτοχοι, **κατανοήσατε** τὸν ἀπόστολον καὶ ἀρχιερέα τῆς ὁμολογίας ἡμῶν Ἰησοῦν, [GNT] | To fix thoughts on; to consider; to think about; to observe; to look upon; to see; to fix one's thoughts and mind, attention and eyes upon Jesus Christ.<br><br>**Practical Application**<br>It means to concentrate; to seek to grasp; to focus and to be attentive in order to learn about Jesus Christ. Note: this exhortation is written to believers. |

## PRACTICAL WORD STUDIES
### in the NEW TESTAMENT

| ENGLISH WORD | GREEK WORD AND VERSE | THE WORD MEANS... |
|---|---|---|
| **#1522**<br>**Fix [Our] Eyes On**<br><br>Look–KJV<br>Look–NASB<br>**Fix [our] eyes...on–NIV**<br>Look–NKJV<br>Look–NLT<br><br>**POSB REFERENCE**<br>(2 Cor.4:17-18; esp. v.18)<br>Note 8, point 2 | σκοπούντων = skopountōn<br>Pronunciation: [skop-oon'-tone]<br>Parsing (part of speech): verb<br>    Mood—participle<br>    Tense—present<br>    Voice—active<br>    Case—genitive<br>    Gender—masculine<br>    Person—1st person<br>    Number—plural<br>    Stem or root—from σκοπέω<br>Concordance References:<br>  ⇒ Strong's #4648 skopeō<br>  ⇒ NIV #5023 skopeō<br>  ⇒ NASB #4648 skopeō<br><br>**2 Cor. 4:18**<br>While we **look** not at the things which are seen, but at the things which are not seen: for the things which are seen are temporal; but the things which are not seen are eternal. [KJV]<br>While we **look** not at the things which are seen, but at the things which are not seen; for the things which are seen are temporal, but the things which are not seen are eternal. [NASB]<br>So we **fix our eyes** not **on** what is seen, but on what is unseen. For what is seen is temporary, but what is unseen is eternal. [NIV]<br>While we do not **look** at the things which are seen, but at the things which are not seen. For the things which are seen *are* temporary, but the things which are not seen *are* eternal. [NKJV]<br>So we don't **look** at the troubles we can see right now; rather, we look forward to what we have not yet seen. For the troubles we see will soon be over, but the joys to come will last forever. [NLT]<br>μὴ **σκοπούντων** ἡμῶν τὰ βλεπόμενα, ἀλλὰ τὰ μὴ βλεπόμενα· τὰ γὰρ βλεπόμενα πρόσκαιρα, τὰ δὲ μὴ βλεπόμενα αἰώνια. [GNS]<br>μὴ **σκοπούντων** ἡμῶν τὰ βλεπόμενα ἀλλὰ τὰ μὴ βλεπόμενα· τὰ γὰρ βλεπόμενα πρόσκαιρα, τὰ δὲ μὴ βλεπόμενα αἰώνια. [GNT] | To focus one's eyes and attention on a set goal or end; to look on with undistracted focus.<br><br>**Practical Application**<br>The goal, of course, is spending eternity with God in the new heavens and earth. The minister does not look at the things which are seen (the physical and corruptible), but at things which are not seen (the spiritual and incorruptible).<br>The reason is strikingly clear: the things which are seen are temporal (brief, temporary, fading, passing, fleeting, transient) but the things which are not seen are eternal (lasting, endless, forever, permanent, immortal, glorious). |
| **#1524**<br>**Fixing His Gaze Upon**<br><br>Looked on–KJV<br>**Fixing his gaze upon–NASB**<br>Stared at–NIV<br>Observed him–NKJV<br>Stared at–NLT<br><br>**POSB REFERENCE**<br>(Acts 10:1-8; esp. v.4)<br>Note 1, point 3c | ἀτενίσας = atenisas<br>Pronunciation: [ah-ten-i'-sahs]<br>Parsing (part of speech): verb<br>    Mood—participle<br>    Tense—aorist<br>    Voice—active<br>    Case—nominative<br>    Gender—masculine<br>    Number—singular<br>    Stem or root—from ἀτενίζω<br>Concordance References:<br>  ⇒ Strong's #816 atenizō<br>  ⇒ NIV #867 atenizō<br>  ⇒ NASB #816 atenizō<br><br>**Acts 10:4**<br>And when he **looked on** him, he was afraid, and said, What is it, Lord? And he said unto him, Thy prayers and thine alms are come up for a memorial before God. [KJV]<br>And **fixing his gaze upon** him and being much alarmed, he said, "What is it, Lord?" And he said to him, "Your prayers and alms have ascended as a memorial before God. [NASB]<br>Cornelius **stared at** him in fear. "What is it, Lord?" he asked. The angel answered, "Your prayers and gifts to the poor have come up as a memorial offering before God. [NIV]<br>And when he **observed him**, he was afraid, and said, "What is it, lord?" So he said to him, "Your prayers and | To stare at; to look on; to fix one's gaze upon; to look straight at.<br><br>**Practical Application**<br>Cornelius was "fixing his gaze upon" that is, fastening his eyes, gazing, focusing his attention; he was startled, frightened. |

# PRACTICAL WORD STUDIES
## in the NEW TESTAMENT

| ENGLISH WORD | GREEK WORD AND VERSE | THE WORD MEANS... |
|---|---|---|
| | your alms have come up for a memorial before God. [NKJV]<br>Cornelius **stared at** him in terror. "What is it, sir?" he asked the angel. And the angel replied, "Your prayers and gifts to the poor have not gone unnoticed by God! [NLT]<br>ὁ δὲ **ἀτενίσας** αὐτῷ καὶ ἔμφοβος γενόμενος εἶπε, Τί ἐστι, Κύριε; εἶπε δὲ αὐτῷ, Αἱ προσευχαί σου καὶ αἱ τε ἐλεημοσύναι σου ἀνέβησαν εἰς μνημόσυνον ἐνώπιον τοῦ Θεοῦ. [GNS]<br>ὁ δὲ **ἀτενίσας** αὐτῷ καὶ ἔμφοβος γενόμενος εἶπεν, Τί ἐστιν, κύριε; εἶπεν δὲ αὐτῷ, Αἱ προσευχαί σου καὶ αἱ ἐλεημοσύναι σου ἀνέβησαν εἰς μνημόσυνον ἔμπροσθεν τοῦ θεοῦ. [GNT] | |
| **#1525**<br>**Flash**<br><br>Moment–KJV<br>Moment–NASB<br>**Flash–NIV**<br>Moment–NKJV<br>Moment–NLT<br><br>**POSB REFERENCE**<br>(1 Cor.15:51-52; esp. v.52)<br>Note 2, point 2 | **ἀτόμῳ** = atomō<br>Pronunciation: [at'-om-o]<br>Parsing (part of speech): pronominal adjective<br>   Case—dative<br>   Gender—neuter<br>   Number—singular<br>   Stem or root—from ἄτομος, ον<br>Concordance References:<br>  ⇒ Strong's #823 atomos<br>  ⇒ NIV #875 atomos<br>  ⇒ NASB #823 atomos<br><br>**1 Cor. 15:52**<br>In a **moment**, in the twinkling of an eye, at the last trump: for the trumpet shall sound, and the dead shall be raised incorruptible, and we shall be changed. [KJV]<br>In a **moment**, in the twinkling of an eye, at the last trumpet; for the trumpet will sound, and the dead will be raised imperishable, and we shall be changed. [NASB]<br>In a **flash**, in the twinkling of an eye, at the last trumpet. For the trumpet will sound, the dead will be raised imperishable, and we will be changed. [NIV]<br>In a **moment**, in the twinkling of an eye, at the last trumpet. For the trumpet will sound, and the dead will be raised incorruptible, and we shall be changed. [NKJV]<br>It will happen in a **moment**, in the blinking of an eye, when the last trumpet is blown. For when the trumpet sounds, the Christians who have died will be raised with transformed bodies. And then we who are living will be transformed so that we will never die. [NLT]<br>ἐν **ἀτόμῳ**, ἐν ῥιπῇ ὀφθαλμοῦ, ἐν τῇ ἐσχάτῃ σάλπιγγι· σαλπίσει γάρ, καὶ οἱ νεκροὶ ἐγερθήσονται ἄφθαρτοι, καὶ ἡμεῖς ἀλλαγησόμεθα. [GNS]<br>ἐν **ἀτόμῳ**, ἐν ῥιπῇ ὀφθαλμοῦ, ἐν τῇ ἐσχάτῃ σάλπιγγι· σαλπίσει γάρ καὶ οἱ νεκροὶ ἐγερθήσονται ἄφθαρτοι καὶ ἡμεῖς ἀλλαγησόμεθα. [GNT] | In a flash; in a moment; indivisible, that which cannot be cut.<br><br>**Practical Application**<br>The resurrection will be a quick, sudden change. It (*atomō*) is the word from which we get the English word *atom*. The idea is that the resurrection will take place so quickly...<br>• that one could not divide the time into two moments.<br>• that one could not blink an eye. |
| **#1526**<br>**Flash Of Lightning**<br><br>Glistering–KJV<br>Gleaming–NASB<br>**Flash of lightning– NIV**<br>Glistering–NKJV<br>Dazzling–NLT<br><br>**POSB REFERENCE**<br>(Lk.9:29)<br>Note 3, point 2 | **ἐξαστράπτων** = exastraptōn<br>Pronunciation: [ex-as-trap'-tone]<br>Parsing (part of speech): verb<br>   Mood—participle<br>   Tense—present<br>   Voice—active<br>   Case—nominative<br>   Gender—masculine<br>   Number—singular<br>   Stem or root—from ἐξαστράπτω<br>Concordance References:<br>  ⇒ Strong's #1823 exastraptō<br>  ⇒ NIV #1993 exastraptō<br>  ⇒ NASB #1823 exastraptō<br><br>**Luke 9:29**<br>And as he prayed, the fashion of his countenance was altered, and his raiment was white and **glistering**. [KJV]<br>And while He was praying, the appearance of His face became different, and His clothing became white and **gleaming**. [NASB]<br>As he was praying, the appearance of his face | To flash like lightning; to gleam; to brighten; to be radiant; to dazzle.<br><br>**Practical Application**<br>Jesus was praying when these changes took place. Apparently, He was concentrating so intensely and was so wrapped up in God that God transformed Him, that is, allowed His Godly nature to shine right through Him. What is the lesson for the believer? When a genuine believer prays with intensity and heavy concentration, his countenance is sometimes changed. He experiences a precious glow, a brightness, a light about his whole countenance. |

## PRACTICAL WORD STUDIES
### in the NEW TESTAMENT

| ENGLISH WORD | GREEK WORD AND VERSE | THE WORD MEANS... |
|---|---|---|
| | changed, and his clothes became as bright as a **flash of lightning**. [NIV]<br><br>As He prayed, the appearance of His face was altered, and His robe became white and **glistening**. [NKJV]<br><br>And as he was praying, the appearance of his face changed, and his clothing became **dazzling** white. [NLT]<br><br>καὶ ἐγένετο, ἐν τῷ προσεύχεσθαι αὐτὸν, τὸ εἶδος τοῦ προσώπου αὐτοῦ ἕτερον, καὶ ὁ ἱματισμὸς αὐτοῦ λευκὸς **ἐξαστράπτων**. [GNS]<br><br>καὶ ἐγένετο ἐν τῷ προσεύχεσθαι αὐτὸν τὸ εἶδος τοῦ προσώπου αὐτοῦ ἕτερον καὶ ὁ ἱματισμὸς αὐτοῦ λευκὸς **ἐξαστράπτων**. [GNT] | |
| #1527<br>**Fled**<br><br>Scattered abroad–KJV<br>Scattered–NASB<br>Scattered–NIV<br>Scattered–NKJV<br>Fled–NLT<br><br>**POSB REFERENCE**<br>(Acts 8:4)<br>Note 4, point 1 | διασπαρέντες = *diasparentes*<br>Pronunciation: [dee-as-pah'-rehn-tehs]<br>Parsing (part of speech): verb<br>  Mood—participle<br>  Tense—aorist<br>  Voice—passive<br>  Case—nominative<br>  Number—plural<br>  Stem or root—from διασπείρω<br>Concordance References:<br>  ⇒ Strong's #1289 diaspeirō<br>  ⇒ NIV #1401 diaspeirō<br>  ⇒ NASB #1289 diaspeirō<br><br>**Acts 8:4**<br>Therefore they that were **scattered abroad** went every where preaching the word. [KJV]<br><br>Therefore, those who had been **scattered** went about preaching the word. [NASB]<br><br>Those who had been **scattered** preached the word wherever they went. [NIV]<br><br>Therefore those who were **scattered** went everywhere preaching the word. [NKJV]<br><br>But the believers who had **fled** Jerusalem went everywhere preaching the Good News about Jesus. [NLT]<br><br>οἱ μὲν οὖν **διασπαρέντες** διῆλθον, εὐαγγελιζόμενοι τὸν λόγον [GNS]<br><br>Οἱ μὲν οὖν **διασπαρέντες** διῆλθον εὐαγγελιζόμενοι τὸν λόγον. [GNT] | To scatter; to scatter abroad; to broadcast; to flee.<br><br>**Practical Application**<br>The believers "fled," dispersed, were scattered about just as seed is sown or scattered throughout a field. |
| #1528<br>**Fled**<br><br>Fled for refuge–KJV<br>Fled for refuge–NASB<br>**Fled–NIV**<br>Fled for refuge–NKJV<br>Fled for refuge–NLT<br><br>**POSB REFERENCE**<br>(Heb.6:18-20; esp. v.18)<br>Note 6, point 1 | καταφυγόντες = *kataphugontes*<br>Pronunciation: [kat-af-yoo'-gon-tehs]<br>Parsing (part of speech): verb<br>  Mood—participle<br>  Tense—aorist<br>  Voice—active<br>  Case—nominative<br>  Gender—masculine<br>  Person—1st person<br>  Number—plural<br>  Stem or root—from καταφεύγω<br>Concordance References:<br>  ⇒ Strong's #2703 katapheugō<br>  ⇒ NIV #2966 katapheugō<br>  ⇒ NASB #2703 katapheugō<br><br>**Hebrews 6:18**<br>That by two immutable things, in which it was impossible for God to lie, we might have a strong consolation, who have **fled for refuge** to lay hold upon the hope set before us: [KJV]<br><br>In order that by two unchangeable things, in which it is impossible for God to lie, we may have strong encouragement, we who have **fled for refuge** in laying hold of the hope set before us. [NASB]<br><br>God did this so that, by two unchangeable things in which it is impossible for God to lie, we who have **fled** to take hold of the hope offered to us may be greatly encouraged. [NIV]<br><br>That by two immutable things, in which it *is* imposs- | Fled, fled for refuge; to flee for safety. The word "fled" (*kataphugontes*) means shelter and protection from danger, distress, or some enemy.<br><br>**Practical Application**<br>Our hope in God is a refuge for the believer. It is the picture of a ship caught in a violent storm-tossed sea and desperately seeking the refuge of a haven or harbor. Believers are persons who have fled...<br>• from the violent storms of this world.<br>• from the distress of sin and shame in this world.<br>• from the dangerous enemy of this world (Satan).<br><br>Believers are persons who have fled to the refuge of God's hope—His hope of the promised land of heaven. It is the promised land of God that gives us safety from all the storms, dangers, and enemies of this world. No other property and no other land—no matter how valuable on this earth—is permanent. It all ends; it all caves in to the storms and distress of economic slumps, personal accidents, disease, and eventually death. All land is eventually turned over to someone else. Therefore, to take refuge in any promised land or any other promised wealth other than the |

# PRACTICAL WORD STUDIES
## in the NEW TESTAMENT

| ENGLISH WORD | GREEK WORD AND VERSE | THE WORD MEANS... |
|---|---|---|
| | ble for God to lie, we might have strong consolation, who have **fled for refuge** to lay hold of the hope set before us. [NKJV]<br><br>So God has given us both his promise and his oath. These two things are unchangeable because it is impossible for God to lie. Therefore, we who have **fled to him for refuge** can take new courage, for we can hold on to his promise with confidence. [NLT]<br><br>ἵνα διὰ δύο πραγμάτων ἀμεταθέτων, ἐν οἷς ἀδύνατον ψεύσασθαι Θεόν, ἰσχυρὰν παράκλησιν ἔχωμεν οἱ **καταφυγόντες** κρατῆσαι τῆς προκειμένης ἐλπίδος· [GNS]<br><br>ἵνα διὰ δύο πραγμάτων ἀμεταθέτων, ἐν οἷς ἀδύνατον ψεύσασθαι [τὸν] θεόν, ἰσχυρὰν παράκλησιν ἔχωμεν οἱ **καταφυγόντες** κρατῆσαι τῆς προκειμένης ἐλπίδος· [GNT] | promised land of God is a very foolish act. The only true refuge is the hope of God, the eternal land of heaven promised by Him. God's hope—hoping in God and His promise of salvation and eternal life—is a refuge for the believer, the only true and lasting refuge. |
| **#1529**<br>**Fled For Refuge**<br><br>Fled for refuge–KJV<br>Fled for refuge–NASB<br>Fled–NIV<br>Fled for refuge–NKJV<br>Fled for refuge–NLT<br><br>**POSB REFERENCE**<br>(Heb.6:18-20; esp. v.18)<br>Note 6, point 1 | καταφυγόντες = *kataphugontes*<br>Pronunciation: [kat-af-yoo'-gon-tehs]<br>Parsing (part of speech): verb<br>  Mood—participle<br>  Tense—aorist<br>  Voice—active<br>  Case—nominative<br>  Gender—masculine<br>  Person—1st person<br>  Number—plural<br>  Stem or root—from καταφεύγω<br>Concordance References:<br>  ⇒ Strong's #2703 katapheugö<br>  ⇒ NIV #2966 katapheugö<br>  ⇒ NASB #2703 katapheugö<br><br>**Hebrews 6:18**<br>That by two immutable things, in which it was impossible for God to lie, we might have a strong consolation, who have **fled for refuge** to lay hold upon the hope set before us: [KJV]<br><br>In order that by two unchangeable things, in which it is impossible for God to lie, we may have strong encouragement, we who have **fled for refuge** in laying hold of the hope set before us. [NASB]<br><br>God did this so that, by two unchangeable things in which it is impossible for God to lie, we who have **fled** to take hold of the hope offered to us may be greatly encouraged. [NIV]<br><br>That by two immutable things, in which it *is* impossible for God to lie, we might have strong consolation, who have **fled for refuge** to lay hold of the hope set before *us*. [NKJV]<br><br>So God has given us both his promise and his oath. These two things are unchangeable because it is impossible for God to lie. Therefore, we who have **fled to him for refuge** can take new courage, for we can hold on to his promise with confidence. [NLT]<br><br>ἵνα διὰ δύο πραγμάτων ἀμεταθέτων, ἐν οἷς ἀδύνατον ψεύσασθαι Θεόν, ἰσχυρὰν παράκλησιν ἔχωμεν οἱ **καταφυγόντες** κρατῆσαι τῆς προκειμένης ἐλπίδος· [GNS]<br><br>ἵνα διὰ δύο πραγμάτων ἀμεταθέτων, ἐν οἷς ἀδύνατον ψεύσασθαι [τὸν] θεόν, ἰσχυρὰν παράκλησιν ἔχωμεν οἱ **καταφυγόντες** κρατῆσαι τῆς προκειμένης ἐλπίδος· [GNT] | Fled, fled for refuge; to flee for safety. The word "refuge" (*kataphugontes*) means shelter and protection from danger, distress, or some enemy.<br><br>**Practical Application**<br>Our hope in God is a refuge for the believer. It is the picture of a ship caught in a violent storm-tossed sea and desperately seeking the refuge of a haven or harbor. Believers are persons who have fled...<br>• from the violent storms of this world.<br>• from the distress of sin and shame in this world.<br>• from the dangerous enemy of this world (Satan).<br><br>Believers are persons who have fled to the refuge of God's hope—His hope of the promised land of heaven. It is the promised land of God that gives us safety from all the storms, dangers, and enemies of this world. No other property and no other land—no matter how valuable on this earth—is permanent. It all ends; it all caves in to the storms and distress of economic slumps, personal accidents, disease, and eventually death. All land is eventually turned over to someone else. Therefore, to take refuge in any promised land or any other promised wealth other than the promised land of God is a very foolish act. The only true refuge is the hope of God, the eternal land of heaven promised by Him. God's hope—hoping in God and His promise of salvation and eternal life—is a refuge for the believer, the only true and lasting refuge. |
| **#1530**<br>**Flesh**<br><br>Flesh–KJV<br>Flesh–NASB<br>Flesh–NIV<br>Flesh–NKJV<br>Human–NLT | σάρξ = *sarx*<br>Pronunciation: [sarx]<br>Parsing (part of speech): noun<br>  Case—nominative<br>  Gender—feminine<br>  Number—singular<br>  Stem or root—from σάρξ, σαρκός<br>Concordance References:<br>  ⇒ Strong's #4561 sarx<br>  ⇒ NIV #4922 sarx<br>  ⇒ NASB #4561 sarx | Flesh, human. It is the physical human body that every person needs in order to live upon earth.<br><br>**Practical Application**<br>The word "flesh" (*sarx*) is the same word that Paul used to describe man's nature with all of its weakness and tendency to sin. This is a staggering thought. Jesus Christ is God—fully God, yet Jesus Christ is man—fully man. (Cp. 1 John 4:2-3.)<br>What does the Bible mean by "flesh"? And |

# PRACTICAL WORD STUDIES
## in the NEW TESTAMENT

| ENGLISH WORD | GREEK WORD AND VERSE | THE WORD MEANS... |
|---|---|---|
| **POSB REFERENCE** (Jn.1:14) Note 1 | **John 1:14** <br> And the Word was made **flesh**, and dwelt among us, (and we beheld his glory, the glory as of the only begotten of the Father,) full of grace and truth. [KJV] <br><br> And the Word became **flesh**, and dwelt among us, and we beheld His glory, glory as of the only begotten from the Father, full of grace and truth. [NASB] <br><br> The Word became **flesh** and made his dwelling among us. We have seen his glory, the glory of the One and Only, who came from the Father, full of grace and truth. [NIV] <br><br> And the Word became **flesh** and dwelt among us, and we beheld His glory, the glory as of the only begotten of the Father, full of grace and truth. [NKJV] <br><br> So the Word became **human** and lived here on earth among us. He was full of unfailing love and faithfulness. And we have seen his glory, the glory of the only Son of the Father. [NLT] <br><br> καὶ ὁ λόγος **σὰρξ** ἐγένετο, καὶ ἐσκήνωσεν ἐν ἡμῖν, -- καὶ ἐθεασάμεθα τὴν δόξαν αὐτοῦ, δόξαν ὡς μονογενοῦς παρὰ πατρός -- , πλήρης χάριτος καὶ ἀληθείας. [GNS] <br><br> Καὶ ὁ λόγος **σὰρξ** ἐγένετο καὶ ἐσκήνωσεν ἐν ἡμῖν, καὶ ἐθεασάμεθα τὴν δόξαν αὐτοῦ, δόξαν ὡς μονογενοῦς παρὰ πατρός, πλήρης χάριτος καὶ ἀληθείας. [GNT] | why did Jesus Christ have to become flesh? The best description of the flesh is probably found in 1 Cor. 15:42-44. (See POSB outline—Romans 5:12-21 and POSB note—Romans 5:12-21; POSB note—Romans 8:1f; POSB *Deeper Study* #1—1 Cor. 3:1-4). <br> 1. The flesh is corruptible. <br>   a. The flesh is tainted, debased, ruined and depraved by sin (lust, 2 Peter 1:4). There is a seed of corruption within human flesh; therefore, the flesh sins (lusts) and thereby ages, dies, deteriorates and decays. It does not live beyond a few years on this earth. <br>   b. Christ (the Word) became flesh to correct and to counteract the corruption of flesh. (2 Peter 1:4; 1 Peter 1:18-19, 23-25; John 3:16). <br> 2. The flesh is dishonorable. <br>   a. The flesh is not what God created it to be. It does not exist in the image of God that God intended. It does not hold the glory, the honor, nor the prestige it once did when God created it. It is disgraced and shamed, and it is reproached by sin and lust. It is held in the grip of sin and fear, and subject to being held in bondage—even the bondage of death. <br>   b. Jesus Christ became flesh to correct and counteract the dishonor of the flesh. (Hebrews 2:14-15; cp. Hebrews 2:14-18; Romans 5:8-10). <br> 3. The flesh is weak. <br>   a. The flesh is impotent. It is feeble, frail, fragile, infirmed, and decrepit because of sin (lust). It has no strength to please God nor to save itself. (Romans 8:8; Romans 3:20; Galatians 2:16; John 6:63). <br>   b. Jesus Christ became flesh to correct and counteract the weakness of the flesh. (Romans 5:6; Romans 8:3). <br> 4. The flesh is a natural body. <br>   a. The flesh is of the earth and is part of the earth; it is made up of the chemicals and substances of the earth. It is physical, material, animal. It is "the earthly house," the "tabernacle," the "tent," which houses the human soul and spirit (2 Cor. 5:1). It is neither spirit nor spiritual; therefore, it cannot live beyond the strength of the chemicals and substances that form its flesh. It cannot live beyond its *natural life*. (1 Cor. 15:50; Luke 24:39; 1 Cor. 15:44, 49). <br>   b. Jesus Christ became flesh to counteract the natural body of the flesh. He became flesh in order to become "a quickening spirit," the Savior who could quicken and make alive all those who would trust Him (1 Cor. 15:45). |
| **#1531** <br> **Flesh** <br><br> Carnal–KJV <br> **Flesh**–NASB <br> Unspiritual–NIV <br> Carnal–NKJV | σάρκινος = *sarkinos* <br> Pronunciation: [sahr-kee-nos'] <br> Parsing (part of speech): adjective <br>   Case — nominative <br>   Gender — masculine <br>   Number — singular <br>   Stem or root — from σάρκινος, η, ον | Unspiritual, carnal, human, worldly, fleshly; by sinful nature; to belong to this world; to be made of flesh; to consist of flesh; to have a body of flesh and blood. It means the flesh with which a man is born, the fleshly nature one inherits from his parents when he is born. |

# PRACTICAL WORD STUDIES
## in the NEW TESTAMENT

| ENGLISH WORD | GREEK WORD AND VERSE | THE WORD MEANS... |
|---|---|---|
| With me–NLT<br><br>**POSB REFERENCE**<br>(Rom.7:14-17; esp. v.14)<br>Note 2 | Concordance References:<br>⇒ Strong's #4559 sarkinos<br>⇒ NIV #4921 sarkinos<br>⇒ NASB #4560 sarkinos<br><br>**Romans 7:14**<br>For we know that the law is spiritual: but I am **carnal**, sold under sin. [KJV]<br>For we know that the Law is spiritual; but I am of **flesh**, sold into bondage to sin. [NASB]<br>We know that the law is spiritual; but I am **unspiritual**, sold as a slave to sin. [NIV]<br>For we know that the law is spiritual, but I am **carnal**, sold under sin. [NKJV]<br>The law is good, then. The trouble is not with the law but **with me**, because I am sold into slavery, with sin as my master. [NLT]<br>οἴδαμεν γὰρ ὅτι ὁ νόμος πνευματικός ἐστιν· ἐγὼ δὲ **σάρκικός** εἰμι, πεπραμένος ὑπὸ τὴν ἁμαρτίαν. [GNS]<br>οἴδαμεν γὰρ ὅτι ὁ νόμος πνευματικός ἐστιν, ἐγὼ δὲ **σάρκινός** εἰμι πεπραμένος ὑπὸ τὴν ἁμαρτίαν. [GNT] | **Practical Application**<br>The word flesh also means to be given up to the flesh, that is, to live a fleshly, sensual life; to be given over to animal appetites; to be controlled by one's sinful nature. (See POSB *Deeper Study* #1, Carnal—1 Cor. 3:1-4 for more discussion.) |
| #1532<br>**Flesh**<br><br>**Flesh–KJV**<br>**Flesh–NASB**<br>Sinful nature–NIV<br>**Flesh–NKJV**<br>Sinful nature–NLT<br><br>**POSB REFERENCE**<br>(Rom.7:18-20; esp. v.18)<br>Note 3 | σαρκί = sarki<br>Pronunciation: [sar-kee]<br>Parsing (part of speech): noun<br>    Case—dative<br>    Gender—feminine<br>    Number—singular<br>    Stem or root—from σάρξ, σαρκός<br>Concordance References:<br>⇒ Strong's #4561 sarx<br>⇒ NIV #4922 sarx<br>⇒ NASB #4561 sarx<br><br>**Romans 7:18**<br>For I know that in me (that is, in my **flesh**,) dwelleth no good thing: for to will is present with me; but how to perform that which is good I find not. [KJV]<br>For I know that nothing good dwells in me, that is, in my **flesh**; for the wishing is present in me, but the doing of the good is not. [NASB]<br>I know that nothing good lives in me, that is, in my **sinful nature**. For I have the desire to do what is good, but I cannot carry it out. [NIV]<br>For I know that in me (that is, in my **flesh**) nothing good dwells; for to will is present with me, but *how* to perform what is good I do not find. [NKJV]<br>I know I am rotten through and through so far as my old **sinful nature** is concerned. No matter which way I turn, I can't make myself do right. I want to, but I can't. [NLT]<br>οἶδα γὰρ ὅτι οὐκ οἰκεῖ ἐν ἐμοί, τοῦτ' ἔστιν ἐν τῇ **σαρκί** μου, ἀγαθόν· τὸ γὰρ θέλειν παράκειταί μοι, τὸ δὲ κατεργάζεσθαι τὸ καλὸν οὐχ εὑρίσκο. [GNS]<br>οἶδα γὰρ ὅτι οὐκ οἰκεῖ ἐν ἐμοί, τοῦτ' ἔστιν ἐν τῇ **σαρκί** μου, ἀγαθόν· τὸ γὰρ θέλειν παράκειταί μοι, τὸ δὲ κατεργάζεσθαι τὸ καλὸν οὔ· [GNT] | Flesh; physical body; human nature; earthly descent; the sinful human, earthly life and realm of existence.<br><br>**Practical Application**<br>Paul declares: there is no "good thing" in his flesh. This does not mean that he never did any good thing or work. It means that his flesh...<br>• is unable to please the goodness of God.<br>• is unable to be as good as it should be.<br>• is unable to be perfectly good.<br>• is unable to conquer the tendency and push toward sin.<br>• is unable to be conformed to the image of Christ.<br>• is corrupted and short of God's glory.<br>• is contaminated and diseased by sin.<br>• is incapable of reaching God on its own and by itself.<br>• is aging and deteriorating, dying and decaying.<br>• is condemned to face the judgment of God. |
| #1533<br>**Fleshly**<br><br>Carnal–KJV<br>**Fleshly–NASB**<br>Worldly–NIV<br>Carnal–NKJV<br>Controlled by your own sinful desires–NLT<br><br>**POSB REFERENCE**<br>(1 Cor.3:1-4; esp. v.3)<br>*Deeper Study* #1 | εσαρκικοί = sarkikoi<br>Pronunciation: [sar-kee-koy']<br>Parsing (part of speech): adjective<br>    Case—nominative<br>    Gender—masculine<br>    Number—plural<br>    Stem or root—from σαρκικός, ή, όν<br>Concordance References:<br>⇒ Strong's #4559 sarkikos<br>⇒ NIV #4920 sarkikos<br>⇒ NASB #4559 sarkikos<br><br>**1 Cor. 3:3**<br>For ye are yet **carnal**: for whereas there is among you envying, and strife, and divisions, are ye not carnal, and walk as men? [KJV] | Worldly, carnal, fleshly, sinful; controlled by your own sinful desires.<br><br>**Practical Application**<br>The ending "ikoi" means to be "characterized by." Paul is saying that the Corinthians were not only "made of flesh" but characterized and "dominated by the flesh." They were allowing the flesh and its passions to captivate and control their behavior. They were living on the level of the flesh, dominated by it. |

# PRACTICAL WORD STUDIES
## in the NEW TESTAMENT

| ENGLISH WORD | GREEK WORD AND VERSE | THE WORD MEANS... |
|---|---|---|
| | For you are still **fleshly**. For since there is jealousy and strife among you, are you not fleshly, and are you not walking like mere men? [NASB]<br><br>You are still **worldly**. For since there is jealousy and quarreling among you, are you not worldly? Are you not acting like mere men? [NIV]<br><br>For you are still **carnal**. For where *there are* envy, strife, and divisions among you, are you not carnal and behaving like *mere* men? [NKJV]<br><br>For you are still **controlled by your own sinful desires**. You are jealous of one another and quarrel with each other. Doesn't that prove you are controlled by your own desires? You are acting like people who don't belong to the Lord. [NLT]<br><br>ἔτι γὰρ **σαρκικοί** ἐστε· ὅπου γὰρ ἐν ὑμῖν ζῆλος καὶ ἔρις καὶ διχοστασίαι, οὐχὶ σαρκικοί ἐστε, καὶ κατὰ ἄνθρωπον περιπατεῖτε; [GNS]<br><br>ἔτι γὰρ **σαρκικοί** ἐστε. ὅπου γὰρ ἐν ὑμῖν ζῆλος καὶ ἔρις, οὐχὶ σαρκικοί ἐστε καὶ κατὰ ἄνθρωπον περιπατεῖτε; [GNT] | |
| **#1534**<br>**Fleshly Lusts**<br><br>Fleshly lusts–KJV<br>Fleshly lusts–NASB<br>Sinful desires–NIV<br>Fleshly lusts–NKJV<br>Evil desires–NLT<br><br>**POSB REFERENCE**<br>(1 Pt.2:11)<br>Note 2 | σαρκικῶν ἐπιθυμιῶν = sarkikōn epithumiōn<br>Pronunciation: [sar-kee-kon' ep-ee-thoo-mee'-own]<br>Parsing *sarkikōn* (part of speech): adjective<br>    Case—genitive<br>    Gender—feminine<br>    Number—plural<br>    Stem or root—from σαρκικός, ή, όν<br>Parsing *epithumiōn* (part of speech): noun<br>    Case—genitive<br>    Gender—feminine<br>    Number—plural<br>    Stem or root—from ἐπιθυμία, ας<br>Concordance References:<br>  ⇒ Strong's #4559 sarkikos + 1939 epithumia<br>  ⇒ NIV #4920 sarkikos [sinful] + 2123 epithumia [desires]<br>  ⇒ NASB #4559 sarkikos + 1939 epithumia<br><br>**1 Peter 2:11**<br>Dearly beloved, I beseech you as strangers and pilgrims, abstain from **fleshly lusts**, which war against the soul; [KJV]<br><br>Beloved, I urge you as aliens and strangers to abstain from **fleshly lusts**, which wage war against the soul. [NASB]<br><br>Dear friends, I urge you, as aliens and strangers in the world, to abstain from **sinful desires**, which war against your soul. [NIV]<br><br>Beloved, I beg *you* as sojourners and pilgrims, abstain from **fleshly lusts** which war against the soul, [NKJV]<br><br>Dear brothers and sisters, you are foreigners and aliens here. So I warn you to keep away from **evil desires** because they fight against your very souls. [NLT]<br><br>Ἀγαπητοί, παρακαλῶ ὡς παροίκους καὶ παρεπιδήμους ἀπέχεσθαι τῶν **σαρκικῶν ἐπιθυμιῶν**, αἵτινες στρατεύονται κατὰ τῆς ψυχῆς· [GNS]<br><br>Ἀγαπητοί, παρακαλῶ ὡς παροίκους καὶ παρεπιδήμους ἀπέχεσθαι τῶν **σαρκικῶν ἐπιθυμιῶν** αἵτινες στρατεύονται κατὰ τῆς ψυχῆς· [GNT] | Sinful desires, fleshly lusts, evil desires. The term "fleshly lusts" (*sarkikōn epithumiōn*) means the evil desires, urges, passions, and lusts of the flesh. It means to have a yearning passion for the things of the flesh.<br><br>**Practical Application**<br>Every person has experienced the flesh...<br>• yearning<br>• pulling<br>• desiring<br>• wanting<br>• grasping<br>• grabbing<br>• craving<br>• hungering<br>• thirsting<br>• longing<br>• taking<br><br>Every person knows what it is to have his flesh lusting after something, to have it yearning and yearning to lay hold of something. The flesh is strong and difficult to control, and it never lets up its assault against the will. |
| **#1535**<br>**Flogged, Had...**<br><br>Scourged–KJV<br>Scourged–NASB<br>Had...flogged–NIV<br>Scourged–NKJV<br>Flogged–NLT | φραγελλώσας = phragellōsas<br>Pronunciation: [frag-el-lo'-sahs]<br>Parsing (part of speech): verb<br>    Mood—participle<br>    Tense—aorist<br>    Voice—active<br>    Case—nominative<br>    Gender—masculine<br>    Number—singular<br>    Stem or root—from φραγελλόω<br>Concordance References:<br>  ⇒ Strong's #5417 phragelloo | To flog; to scourge; to lash or beat with a whip.<br><br>**Practical Application**<br>The whip that was used to flog Jesus was made of leather straps with two small balls attached to the end of each strap. The balls of rough lead or sharp bones or spikes would cut deeply into the flesh. His hands were tied to a post above His head as He was scourged (John 19:1). It was the custom for the prisoner to be |

PRACTICAL WORD STUDIES
in the NEW TESTAMENT

| ENGLISH WORD | GREEK WORD AND VERSE | THE WORD MEANS... |
|---|---|---|
| POSB REFERENCE (Mt.27:26-38; esp. v.26) Note 2, point 1 | ⇒ NIV #5849 phragelloö<br>⇒ NASB #5417 phragelloo<br><br>**Matthew 27:26**<br>Then released he Barabbas unto them: and when he had **scourged** Jesus, he delivered him to be crucified. [KJV]<br>Then he released Barabbas for them; but after having Jesus **scourged**, he delivered Him to be crucified. [NASB]<br>Then he released Barabbas to them. But he **had** Jesus **flogged**, and handed him over to be crucified. [NIV]<br>Then he released Barabbas to them; and when he had **scourged** Jesus, he delivered Him to be crucified. [NKJV]<br>So Pilate released Barabbas to them. He ordered Jesus **flogged** with a lead-tipped whip, then turned him over to the Roman soldiers to crucify him. [NLT]<br>τότε ἀπέλυσεν αὐτοῖς τὸν Βαραββᾶν· τὸν δὲ Ἰησοῦν **φραγελλώσας** παρέδωκεν ἵνα σταυρωθῇ. [GNS]<br>τότε ἀπέλυσεν αὐτοῖς τὸν Βαραββᾶν, τὸν δὲ Ἰησοῦν **φραγελλώσας** παρέδωκεν ἵνα σταυρωθῇ. [GNT] | lashed until He was judged near death by the presiding centurion (Jewish trials allowed only forty lashes [Dt.25:2-3] less one, cp. 2 Cor.11:24). The criminal's back was, of course, nothing more than an unrecognizable mass of torn flesh. |
| #1536<br>**Flourished Again**<br><br>Flourished again–KJV<br>Revived–NASB<br>Renewed–NIV<br>Flourished again–NKJV<br>Again–NLT<br><br>POSB REFERENCE (Philip.4:10) Note 1 | ἀνεθάλετε = anethalete<br>Pronunciation: [an-ath-al'-eh-teh]<br>Parsing (part of speech): verb<br>  Mood—indicative<br>  Tense—aorist<br>  Voice—active<br>  Person—2nd person<br>  Number—plural<br>  Stem or root—from ἀναθάλλω<br>Concordance References:<br>  ⇒ Strong's #330 anathallö<br>  ⇒ NIV #352 anathallö<br>  ⇒ NASB #330 anathallö<br><br>**Philip. 4:10**<br>But I rejoiced in the Lord greatly, that now at the last your care of me hath **flourished again**; wherein ye were also careful, but ye lacked opportunity. [KJV]<br>But I rejoiced in the Lord greatly, that now at last you have **revived** your concern for me; indeed, you were concerned *before*, but you lacked opportunity. [NASB]<br>I rejoice greatly in the Lord that at last you have **renewed** your concern for me. Indeed, you have been concerned, but you had no opportunity to show it. [NIV]<br>But I rejoiced in the Lord greatly that now at last your care for me has **flourished again**; though you surely did care, but you lacked opportunity. [NKJV]<br>How grateful I am, and how I praise the Lord that you are concerned about me *again*. I know you have always been concerned for me, but for a while you didn't have the chance to help me. [NLT]<br>Ἐχάρην δὲ ἐν Κυρίῳ μεγάλως, ὅτι ἤδη ποτὲ **ἀνεθάλετε** τὸ ὑπὲρ ἐμοῦ φρονεῖν,, ἐφ' ᾧ καὶ ἐφρονεῖτε, ἠκαιρεῖσθε δέ. [GNS]<br>Ἐχάρην δὲ ἐν κυρίῳ μεγάλως ὅτι ἤδη ποτὲ **ἀνεθάλετε** τὸ ὑπὲρ ἐμοῦ φρονεῖν, ἐφ' ᾧ καὶ ἐφρονεῖτε, ἠκαιρεῖσθε δέ. [GNT] | To renew; to flourish again; to revive again.<br><br>**Practical Application**<br>It is the picture of plants and flowers sprouting, shooting up, and blossoming *again*. The key word is *again*. When the church had been founded, the believers had supported Paul and his mission work on a regular basis. But for some reason, they had dropped their mission support. That had probably been over ten to twelve years before (Strauss). Why they had stopped sending support to Paul is not known. However, the point is the glorious revival of mission support that took place in the church. They picked up the support of Paul once again, and their giving flourished and blossomed anew. The joy and rejoicing of Paul's heart can just be imagined. He says, "I rejoiced greatly in the Lord." |
| #1537<br>**Flourishing**<br><br>Exceedingly–KJV<br>Greatly enlarged–NASB<br>Growing more and more–NIV<br>Exceedingly–NKJV<br>Flourishing–NLT | ὑπεραυξάνει = huperauxanei<br>Pronunciation: [hoop-er-owx-ahn'-eh-ee]<br>Parsing (part of speech): verb<br>  Mood—indicative<br>  Tense—present<br>  Voice—active<br>  Person—3rd person<br>  Number—singular<br>  Stem or root—from ὑπεραυξάνω<br>Concordance References:<br>  ⇒ Strong's #5232 huperauxanö<br>  ⇒ NIV #5647 huperauxanö<br>  ⇒ NASB #5232 huperauxanö | Growing more and more; exceedingly; greatly enlarged; flourishing; to grow abundantly; to grow beyond measure; to grow far beyond what would be expected.<br><br>**Practical Application**<br>What a glorious testimony! Faith that just grows and grows more and more. Imagine a church full of believers whose faith in Christ Jesus grows explosively—beyond measure—beyond what we could ever imagine. And remember: the church was growing in faith |

# PRACTICAL WORD STUDIES
## in the NEW TESTAMENT

| ENGLISH WORD | GREEK WORD AND VERSE | THE WORD MEANS... |
|---|---|---|
| **POSB REFERENCE** (2 Thes.1:3) Note 4 | **2 Thes. 1:3** <br> We are bound to thank God always for you, brethren, as it is meet, because that your faith groweth **exceedingly**, and the charity of every one of you all toward each other aboundeth; [KJV] <br> We ought always to give thanks to God for you, brethren, as is only fitting, because your faith is **greatly enlarged**, and the love of each one of you toward one another grows ever greater; [NASB] <br> We ought always to thank God for you, brothers, and rightly so, because your faith is **growing more and more**, and the love every one of you has for each other is increasing. [NIV] <br> We are bound to thank God always for you, brethren, as it is fitting, because your faith grows **exceedingly**, and the love of every one of you all abounds toward each other, [NKJV] <br> Dear brothers and sisters, we always thank God for you, as is right, for we are thankful that your faith is **flourishing** and you are all growing in love for each other. [NLT] <br> Εὐχαριστεῖν ὀφείλομεν τῷ Θεῷ πάντοτε περὶ ὑμῶν, ἀδελφοί, καθὼς ἄξιόν ἐστιν, ὅτι **ὑπεραυξάνει** ἡ πίστις ὑμῶν, καὶ πλεονάζει ἡ ἀγάπη ἑνὸς ἑκάστου πάντων ὑμῶν εἰς ἀλλήλους· [GNS] <br> Εὐχαριστεῖν ὀφείλομεν τῷ θεῷ πάντοτε περὶ ὑμῶν, ἀδελφοί, καθὼς ἄξιόν ἐστιν, ὅτι **ὑπεραυξάνει** ἡ πίστις ὑμῶν καὶ πλεονάζει ἡ ἀγάπη ἑνὸς ἑκάστου πάντων ὑμῶν εἰς ἀλλήλους, [GNT] | while they were in the midst of savage persecution. This is the reason Paul says: "We are bound to thank God always for you." |
| **#1538** <br> **Flung** <br><br> Cast–KJV <br> Threw–NASB <br> **Flung–NIV** <br> Threw–NKJV <br> Threw–NLT <br><br> **POSB REFERENCE** (Rev.12:3-4; esp.v.4) Note 2 | **ἔβαλεν** = *ebalen* <br> Pronunciation: [eh-bal'-lehn] <br> Parsing (part of speech): verb <br>   Mood—indicative <br>   Tense—aorist <br>   Voice—active <br>   Person—3rd person <br>   Number—singular <br>   Stem or root—from βάλλω <br> Concordance References: <br> ⇒ Strong's #906 ballō <br> ⇒ NIV #965 ballō <br> ⇒ NASB #906 ballō <br><br> **Rev. 12:4** <br> And his tail drew the third part of the stars of heaven, and did **cast** them to the earth: and the dragon stood before the woman which was ready to be delivered, for to devour her child as soon as it was born. [KJV] <br> And his tail swept away a third of the stars of heaven, and **threw** them to the earth. And the dragon stood before the woman who was about to give birth, so that when she gave birth he might devour her child. [NASB] <br> His tail swept a third of the stars out of the sky and **flung** them to the earth. The dragon stood in front of the woman who was about to give birth, so that he might devour her child the moment it was born. [NIV] <br> His tail drew a third of the stars of heaven and **threw** them to the earth. And the dragon stood before the woman who was ready to give birth, to devour her Child as soon as it was born. [NKJV] <br> His tail dragged down one-third of the stars, which he **threw** to the earth. He stood before the woman as she was about to give birth to her child, ready to devour the baby as soon as it was born. [NLT] <br> καὶ ἡ οὐρὰ αὐτοῦ σύρει τὸ τρίτον τῶν ἀστέρων τοῦ οὐρανοῦ, καὶ **ἔβαλεν** αὐτοὺς εἰς τὴν γῆν· καὶ ὁ δράκων ἕστηκεν ἐνώπιον τῆς γυναικὸς τῆς μελλούσης τεκεῖν, ἵνα, ὅταν τέκῃ τὸ τέκνον αὐτῆς. καταφάγῃ. [GNS] <br> καὶ ἡ οὐρὰ αὐτοῦ σύρει τὸ τρίτον τῶν ἀστέρων τοῦ οὐρανοῦ καὶ **ἔβαλεν** αὐτοὺς εἰς τὴν γῆν. καὶ ὁ δράκων ἕστηκεν ἐνώπιον τῆς γυναικὸς τῆς μελλούσης τεκεῖν, ἵνα ὅταν τέκῃ τὸ τέκνον αὐτῆς καταφάγῃ. [GNT] | To fling; to throw; to hurl; to chuck; to toss. <br><br> **Practical Application** <br> He "flung" (*ebalen*) them down or threw them down. This is aorist tense which means a once-for-all act; that is, it tells us what Satan did long ago. <br> The point is this: today, in the present moment, Satan has authority over one third of the stars or angels of heaven. How? Because in the past, he cast them down with himself. |

PRACTICAL WORD STUDIES
in the NEW TESTAMENT

| ENGLISH WORD | GREEK WORD AND VERSE | THE WORD MEANS... |
|---|---|---|
| **#1539**<br>**Flute**<br><br>Pipe–KJV<br>**Flute–NASB**<br>**Flute–NIV**<br>**Flute–NKJV**<br>**Flute–NLT**<br><br>**POSB**<br>**REFERENCE**<br>(1 Cor.14:6-14 esp. v.7)<br>Note 3 | αὐλός = aulos<br>Pronunciation: [ow-los']<br>Parsing (part of speech): noun<br>   Case—nominative<br>   Gender—masculine<br>   Number—singular<br>   Stem or root—from αὐλός, οῦ<br>Concordance References:<br>  ⇒ Strong's #836 aulos<br>  ⇒ NIV #888 aulos<br>  ⇒ NASB #836 aulos<br><br>**1 Cor. 14:7**<br>And even things without life giving sound, whether **pipe** or harp, except they give a distinction in the sounds, how shall it be known what is piped or harped? [KJV]<br>Yet even lifeless things, either **flute** or harp, in producing a sound, if they do not produce a distinction in the tones, how will it be known what is played on the flute or on the harp? [NASB]<br>Even in the case of lifeless things that make sounds, such as the **flute** or harp, how will anyone know what tune is being played unless there is a distinction in the notes? [NIV]<br>Even things without life, whether **flute** or harp, when they make a sound, unless they make a distinction in the sounds, how will it be known what is piped or played? [NKJV]<br>Even musical instruments like the **flute** or the harp, though they are lifeless, are examples of the need for speaking in plain language. For no one will recognize the melody unless the notes are played clearly. [NLT]<br>ὅμως τὰ ἄψυχα φωνὴν διδόντα, εἴτε **αὐλός**, εἴτε κιθάρα, ἐὰν διαστολὴν τοῖς φθόγγοις μὴ δῷ, πῶς γνωσθήσεται τὸ αὐλούμενον ἢ τὸ κιθαριζόμενον; [GNS]<br>ὅμως τὰ ἄψυχα φωνὴν διδόντα, εἴτε **αὐλός** εἴτε κιθάρα, ἐὰν διαστολὴν τοῖς φθόγγοις μὴ δῷ, πῶς γνωσθήσεται τὸ αὐλούμενον ἢ τὸ κιθαριζόμενον; [GNT] | Flute, pipe; wind instrument.<br><br>**Practical Application**<br>Flutes (*aulos*, wind instruments) and harps (*kithara*, string instruments) must have a distinctive sound or else their sound is meaningless, confused, and nonsense—just not understood. Musical instruments must communicate or else the music is unknown and fails to inspire the listeners. The point is striking: the believer who is zealous of spiritual gifts is to seek for the gifts that edify the church. Note: a believer's zeal is not to be dampened even if he has been misinformed and emphasizes the wrong gift. He is to straighten out his emphasis, keep his zeal, and direct his energy to edifying the church. The important gifts are those that build up people for Christ. |
| **#1540**<br>**Folded**<br>  **Together–**<br>**Folded Up**<br><br>Wrapped together–KJV<br>Rolled up–NASB<br>**Folded up–NIV**<br>**Folded together–NKJV**<br>**Folded up–NLT**<br><br>**POSB**<br>**REFERENCE**<br>(Jn.20:7-10; esp. v.7)<br>Note 3, point 1 | ἐντετυλιγμένον = entetuligmenon<br>Pronunciation: [en-teh-too-lig-meh'n-on]<br>Parsing (part of speech): verb<br>   Mood—participle<br>   Tense—perfect<br>   Voice—passive<br>   Case—accusative<br>   Gender—neuter<br>   Number—singular<br>   Stem or root—from ἐντυλίσσω<br>Concordance References:<br>  ⇒ Strong's #1794 entulisso<br>  ⇒ NIV #1962 entulisso<br>  ⇒ NASB #1794 entulisso<br><br>**John 20:7**<br>And the napkin, that was about his head, not lying with the linen clothes, but **wrapped together** in a place by itself. [KJV]<br>And the face-cloth, which had been on His head, not lying with the linen wrappings, but **rolled up** in a place by itself. [NASB]<br>As well as the burial cloth that had been around Jesus' head. The cloth was **folded up** by itself, separate from the linen. [NIV]<br>And the handkerchief that had been around His head, not lying with the linen cloths, but **folded together** in a place by itself. [NKJV]<br>while the cloth that had covered Jesus' head was **folded up** and lying to the side. [NLT]<br>καὶ τὸ σουδάριον, ὃ ἦν ἐπὶ τῆς κεφαλῆς αὐτοῦ, οὐ μετὰ τῶν ὀθονίων κείμενον, ἀλλὰ χωρὶς | Folded up, wrapped together, rolled up.<br><br>**Practical Application**<br>The Greek word "folded together" (*entetuligmenon*) is the verb which is used for actually winding the linens around a body for burial. The Greek word is saying that the linens were "still in their fold," wrapped just like they would be wrapped around a body—as if the body had just evaporated. They were not disheveled or disarranged. This says at least four things.<br>1. It would be impossible to extract a body from its wrappings and leave them in such good order.<br>2. The wrappings would have been taken with the body if the body had been removed.<br>3. The wrappings would have been disheveled and disarranged and scattered if thieves had ransacked the tomb.<br>4. The wrappings (under any circumstances that might be conceived in removing the body) could never be placed in the exact spot on the rock slab where the body lay. Yet, this is just how they were lying according to the Greek text. It was this that led John to an immediate belief. |

## Practical Word Studies
in the New Testament

| ENGLISH WORD | GREEK WORD AND VERSE | THE WORD MEANS... |
|---|---|---|
| | ἐντετυλιγμένον εἰς ἕνα τόπον. [GNS]<br>καὶ τὸ σουδάριον, ὃ ἦν ἐπὶ τῆς κεφαλῆς αὐτοῦ, οὐ μετὰ τῶν ὀθονίων κείμενον ἀλλὰ χωρὶς **ἐντετυλιγμένον** εἰς ἕνα τόπον. [GNT] | |
| **#1541**<br>**Follow**<br><br>Follow–KJV<br>Follow–NASB<br>Follow–NIV<br>Follow–NKJV<br>Follow–NLT<br><br>**POSB**<br>**REFERENCE**<br>(Mt.16:24)<br>Note 2, point 4<br><br>See also POSB REF:<br>(Mk.8:34)<br>*Deeper Study* #3 | ἀκολουθείτω = *akoloutheitō*<br>Pronunciation: [ak-ol-oo-theh'-ee-tow]<br>Parsing (part of speech): verb<br>    Mood—imperative<br>    Tense—present<br>    Voice—active<br>    Person—3rd person<br>    Number—singular<br>    Stem or root—from ἀκολουθέω<br>Concordance References:<br>  ⇒ Strong's #190 akoloutheō<br>  ⇒ NIV #199 akoloutheö<br>  ⇒ NASB #190 akoloutheō<br><br>**Matthew 16:24**<br>Then said Jesus unto his disciples, If any man will come after me, let him deny himself, and take up his cross, and **follow** me. [KJV]<br>Then Jesus said to His disciples, "If anyone wishes to come after Me, let him deny himself, and take up his cross, and **follow** Me. [NASB]<br>Then Jesus said to his disciples, "If anyone would come after me, he must deny himself and take up his cross and **follow** me. [NIV]<br>Then Jesus said to His disciples, "If anyone desires to come after Me, let him deny himself, and take up his cross, and **follow** Me. [NKJV]<br>Then Jesus said to the disciples, "If any of you wants to be my follower, you must put aside your selfish ambition, shoulder your cross, and **follow** me. [NLT]<br>τότε ὁ Ἰησοῦς εἶπε τοῖς μαθηταῖς αὐτοῦ, Εἴ τις θέλει ὀπίσω μου ἐλθεῖν, ἀπαρνησάσθω ἑαυτὸν, καὶ ἀράτω τὸν σταυρὸν αὐτοῦ καὶ **ἀκολουθείτω** μοι. [GNS]<br>Τότε ὁ Ἰησοῦς εἶπεν τοῖς μαθηταῖς αὐτοῦ, Εἴ τις θέλει ὀπίσω μου ἐλθεῖν, ἀπαρνησάσθω ἑαυτὸν καὶ ἀράτω τὸν σταυρὸν αὐτοῦ καὶ **ἀκολουθείτω** μοι. [GNT] | To be a follower or companion; to be a disciple; to accompany; to come or go with.<br><br>**Practical Application**<br>To follow has the idea of seeking to be in union with and in the likeness of. It is following Christ, seeking to be just like Him. Again, this is not a passive behavior, but an active commitment and walk. It is energy and effort, action and work. It is going after Christ with zeal and energy, struggling and seeking to follow in His footsteps, no matter the cost. |
| **#1542**<br>**Follow**<br><br>Follow–KJV<br>Follow–NASB<br>Follow–NIV<br>Follow–NKJV<br>Come–NLT<br><br>**POSB**<br>**REFERENCE**<br>(Jn.1:43)<br>*Deeper Study* #1 | Ἀκολούθει = *akolouthei*<br>Pronunciation: [ak-ol-oo-theh'-ee]<br>Parsing (part of speech): verb<br>    Mood—imperative<br>    Tense—present<br>    Voice—active<br>    Person—2nd person<br>    Number—singular<br>    Stem or root—from ἀκολουθέω<br>Concordance References:<br>  ⇒ Strong's #190 akoloutheō<br>  ⇒ NIV #199 akoloutheö<br>  ⇒ NASB #190 akoloutheō<br><br>**John 1:43**<br>The day following Jesus would go forth into Galilee, and findeth Philip, and saith unto him, **Follow** me. [KJV]<br>The next day He purposed to go forth into Galilee, and He found Philip. And Jesus said to him, "**Follow** Me." [NASB]<br>The next day Jesus decided to leave for Galilee. Finding Philip, he said to him, "**Follow** me." [NIV]<br>The following day Jesus wanted to go to Galilee, and He found Philip and said to him, "**Follow** Me." [NKJV]<br>The next day Jesus decided to go to Galilee. He found Philip and said to him, "**Come**, be my disciple." [NLT]<br>Τῇ ἐπαύριον ἠθέλησεν ὁ Ἰησοῦς ἐξελθεῖν εἰς τὴν Γαλιλαίαν, καὶ εὑρίσκει Φίλιππον, καὶ λέγει αὐτῷ, **Ἀκολούθει** μοι. [GNS]<br>Τῇ ἐπαύριον ἠθέλησεν ἐξελθεῖν εἰς τὴν Γαλιλαίαν καὶ εὑρίσκει Φίλιππον. καὶ λέγει αὐτῷ ὁ Ἰησοῦς, **Ἀκολούθει** μοι. [GNT] | To follow; to come; to accompany; to press on; to become a close companion, a close follower, a disciple; to go running after.<br><br>**Practical Application**<br>Two significant ideas are in the word: union and likeness, or cleaving and conformity. To follow Christ means...<br>• to cleave, to be united to Him, to be in close union with Him.<br>• to become like Him, to be conformed to Him. |

# PRACTICAL WORD STUDIES
## in the NEW TESTAMENT

| ENGLISH WORD | GREEK WORD AND VERSE | THE WORD MEANS... |
|---|---|---|
| **#1543**<br>**Follow**<br><br>Follow–KJV<br>Pursue–NASB<br>Follow–NIV<br>Pursue–NKJV<br>Highest goal–NLT<br><br>**POSB REFERENCE**<br>(1 Cor.14:1)<br>Note 1 | Διώκετε = *Diōkete*<br>Pronunciation: [dee-o'-keh-teh]<br>Parsing (part of speech): verb<br>    Mood—imperative<br>    Tense—present<br>    Voice—active<br>    Person—2nd person<br>    Number—plural<br>    Stem or root—from διώκω<br>Concordance References:<br>  ⇒ Strong's #1377 diōkō<br>  ⇒ NIV #1503 diōkō<br>  ⇒ NASB #1377 diōkō<br><br>**1 Cor. 14:1**<br>  **Follow** after charity, and desire spiritual gifts, but rather that ye may prophesy. [KJV]<br>  **Pursue** love, yet desire earnestly spiritual gifts, but especially that you may prophesy. [NASB]<br>  **Follow** the way of love and eagerly desire spiritual gifts, especially the gift of prophecy. [NIV]<br>  **Pursue** love, and desire spiritual *gifts,* but especially that you may prophesy. [NKJV]<br>  Let love be your **highest goal**, but also desire the special abilities the Spirit gives, especially the gift of prophecy. [NLT]<br>  Διώκετε τὴν ἀγάπην· ζηλοῦτε δὲ τὰ πνευματικά, μᾶλλον δὲ ἵνα προφητεύητε. [GNS]<br>  Διώκετε τὴν ἀγάπην, ζηλοῦτε δὲ τὰ πνευματικά, μᾶλλον δὲ ἵνα προφητεύητε. [GNT] | To follow; to pursue; to press on; to persist; to seek after; to strive for; to continue on and on, never giving up until love is possessed; to go running after.<br><br>**Practical Application**<br>  Love is to be followed above all else in life. Gifts, abilities, and service are important; but they pale into insignificance in comparison with love. Love is the greatest need and the supreme answer to all the needs of men. It is when we love a person that we meet the needs of a person. In fact, if we truly love a person, then we will do all we can to meet all the needs of that person. |
| **#1544**<br>**Follow**<br><br>Be–KJV<br>Be–NASB<br>Be–NIV<br>Be–NKJV<br>Follow–NLT<br><br>**POSB REFERENCE**<br>(Eph.5:1)<br>Note 1 | γίνεσθε = *ginesthe*<br>Pronunciation: [ghen-ehs-theh]<br>Parsing (part of speech): verb<br>    Mood—imperative<br>    Tense—present<br>    Voice—middle or passive dep<br>    Person—2nd person<br>    Number—plural<br>    Stem or root—from γίνομαι<br>Concordance References:<br>  ⇒ Strong's #1096 ginomai<br>  ⇒ NIV #1181 ginomai<br>  ⇒ NASB #1096 ginomai<br><br>**Ephes. 5:1**<br>  **Be** ye therefore followers of God, as dear children; [KJV]<br>  Therefore **be** imitators of God, as beloved children; [NASB]<br>  **Be** imitators of God, therefore, as dearly loved children [NIV]<br>  Therefore **be** imitators of God as dear children. [NKJV]<br>  **Follow** God's example in everything you do, because you are his dear children. [NLT]<br>  Γίνεσθε οὖν μιμηταὶ τοῦ Θεοῦ, ὡς τέκνα ἀγαπητά· [GNS]<br>  γίνεσθε οὖν μιμηταὶ τοῦ θεοῦ ὡς τέκνα ἀγαπητά [GNT] | To be; to follow; to become.<br><br>**Practical Application**<br>  It means *to become* a follower of God. The idea is that of commitment, attachment, devotion, allegiance, attention. Before a person can be a follower of God, he must commit and attach himself to God. He must surrender and devote his life to God and then begin to follow after God. |
| **#1545**<br>**Follow**<br><br>Follow–KJV<br>Pursue–NASB<br>Pursue–NIV<br>Pursue–NKJV<br>Pursue–NLT<br><br>**POSB REFERENCE**<br>(1 Tim.6:11)<br>Note 2, point 2 | δίωκε = *diōke*<br>Pronunciation: [dee-o'-keh]<br>Parsing (part of speech): verb<br>    Mood—imperative<br>    Tense—present<br>    Voice—active<br>    Person—2nd person<br>    Number—singular<br>    Stem or root—from διώκω<br>Concordance References:<br>  ⇒ Strong's #1377 diōkō<br>  ⇒ NIV #1503 diōkō<br>  ⇒ NASB #1377 diōkō | To pursue; to follow; to seek after; to press on. The word "follow" (*diōke*) is strong. It means to run after; to run swiftly after; to hotly pursue; to seek eagerly and earnestly.<br><br>**Practical Application**<br>  It has the idea of aiming at and pursuing until something is gained; of never giving up until we have reached our goal. |

## PRACTICAL WORD STUDIES
in the NEW TESTAMENT

| ENGLISH WORD | GREEK WORD AND VERSE | THE WORD MEANS... |
|---|---|---|
| See also POSB REF: (Heb.12:14) Note 1 | **1 Tim. 6:11**<br>But thou, O man of God, flee these things; and **follow** after righteousness, godliness, faith, love, patience, meekness. [KJV]<br>But flee from these things, you man of God; and **pursue** righteousness, godliness, faith, love, perseverance and gentleness. [NASB]<br>But you, man of God, flee from all this, and **pursue** righteousness, godliness, faith, love, endurance and gentleness. [NIV]<br>But you, O man of God, flee these things and **pursue** righteousness, godliness, faith, love, patience, gentleness. [NKJV]<br>But you, Timothy, belong to God; so run from all these evil things, and follow what is right and good. **Pursue** a godly life, along with faith, love, perseverance, and gentleness. [NLT]<br>Σὺ δέ ὦ ἄνθρωπε τοῦ Θεοῦ, ταῦτα φεῦγε· **δίωκε** δὲ δικαιοσύνην, εὐσέβειαν, πίστιν, ἀγάπην, ὑπομονήν, πραόπατητα· [GNS]<br>Σὺ δέ, ὦ ἄνθρωπε θεοῦ, ταῦτα φεῦγε· **δίωκε** δὲ δικαιοσύνην εὐσέβειαν πίστιν, ἀγάπην ὑπομονήν πραϋπαθίαν. [GNT] | |
| **#1546 Follow**<br><br>Follow–KJV<br>Follow–NASB<br>Follow–NIV<br>Follow–NKJV<br>Follow–NLT<br><br>**POSB REFERENCE** (1 Pt.2:21) Note 1 | ἐπακολουθήσητε = *epakolouthēsēte*<br>Pronunciation: [ep-ak-ol-oo-thay'-say-teh]<br>Parsing (part of speech): verb<br>  Mood—subjunctive<br>  Tense—aorist<br>  Voice—active<br>  Person—2nd person<br>  Number—plural<br>  Stem or root—from ἐπακολουθέω<br>Concordance References:<br>  ⇒ Strong's #1872 epakoloutheō<br>  ⇒ NIV #2051 epakoloutheō<br>  ⇒ NASB #1872 epakoloutheō<br><br>**1 Peter 2:21**<br>For even hereunto were ye called: because Christ also suffered for us, leaving us an example, that ye should **follow** his steps: [KJV]<br>For you have been called for this purpose, since Christ also suffered for you, leaving you an example for you to follow in His steps, [NASB]<br>To this you were called, because Christ suffered for you, leaving you an example, that you should **follow** in his steps. [NIV]<br>For to this you were called, because Christ also suffered for us, leaving us an example, that you should **follow** His steps: [NKJV]<br>This suffering is all part of what God has called you to. Christ, who suffered for you, is your example. **Follow** in his steps. [NLT]<br>ἰς τοῦτο γὰρ ἐκλήθητε, ὅτι καὶ Χριστὸς ἔπαθεν ὑπὲρ ὑμῶν, ὑμῖν ὑπολιμπάνων ὑπογραμμὸν, ἵνα **ἐπακολουθήσητε** τοῖς ἴχνεσιν αὐτοῦ· [GNS]<br>εἰς τοῦτο γὰρ ἐκλήθητε, ὅτι καὶ Χριστὸς ἔπαθεν ὑπὲρ ὑμῶν ὑμῖν ὑπολιμπάνων ὑπογραμμὸν ἵνα **ἐπακολουθήσητε** τοῖς ἴχνεσιν αὐτοῦ, [GNT] | To follow; to trail behind; to ensue; to accompany.<br><br>**Practical Application**<br>The word "follow" (*epakolouthēsēte*) is the picture of a guide leading us along a most difficult and rocky path, so difficult that we must actually put our feet in his footprints (B.C. Coffin. *First Peter*. "The Pulpit Commentary," Vol.22, p.75.). We are to follow Christ step by step, moment by moment, and day by day.<br><br>Remember the point: Christ has given us a great call—to follow Him and to suffer for Him and His cause even as He suffered for us. What is His cause? To love God supremely by living a holy life and to love the lost and dying of the world by meeting their desperate needs. |
| **#1547 Followed**<br><br>Followed–KJV<br>Followed–NASB<br>Followed–NIV<br>Followed–NKJV<br>Followed–NLT | ἠκολούθησαν = *ēkolouthēsan*<br>Pronunciation: [ayk-ol-oo-theh'-sahn]<br>Parsing (part of speech): verb<br>  Mood—indicative<br>  Tense—aorist<br>  Voice—active<br>  Person—3rd person<br>  Number—plural<br>  Stem or root—from ἀκολουθέω<br>Concordance References:<br>  ⇒ Strong's #190 akoloutheō<br>  ⇒ NIV #199 akoloutheō<br>  ⇒ NASB #190 akoloutheō | To accompany; to serve; to go with; to be a disciple.<br><br>**Practical Application**<br>The word "followed" (*ēkolouthēsan*) is in the Greek aorist tense, meaning a once-for-all act. Andrew was turning to Jesus, ready to make a commitment to Him. He wanted to become a disciple of Jesus. |

# PRACTICAL WORD STUDIES
## in the NEW TESTAMENT

| ENGLISH WORD | GREEK WORD AND VERSE | THE WORD MEANS... |
|---|---|---|
| **POSB REFERENCE** (Jn.1:35-37; esp. v.37) Note 1, point 3 | **John 1:37**<br>And the two disciples heard him speak, and they **followed** Jesus. [KJV]<br>And the two disciples heard him speak, and they **followed** Jesus. [NASB]<br>When the two disciples heard him say this, they **followed** Jesus. [NIV]<br>The two disciples heard him speak, and they **followed** Jesus. [NKJV]<br>Then John's two disciples turned and **followed** Jesus. [NLT]<br>Καὶ ἤκουσαν αὐτοῦ οἱ δύο μαθηταὶ λαλοῦντος, καὶ **ἠκολούθησαν** τῷ Ἰησοῦ. [GNS]<br>καὶ ἤκουσαν οἱ δύο μαθηταὶ αὐτοῦ λαλοῦντος καὶ **ἠκολούθησαν** τῷ Ἰησοῦ. [GNT] | |
| **#1548 Followed**<br><br>Fully known–KJV<br>Followed–NASB<br>Know all about–NIV<br>Followed–NKJV<br>Know–NLT<br><br>**POSB REFERENCE** (2 Tim. 3:10) Note 1 | **παρηκολούθησάς** = *parēkolouthēsas*<br>Pronunciation: [par-ayk-ol-oo-thay'-sahs]<br>Parsing (part of speech): verb<br>  Mood—indicative<br>  Tense—aorist<br>  Voice—active<br>  Person—2nd person<br>  Number—singular<br>  Stem or root—from παρακολουθέω<br>Concordance References:<br>  ⇒ Strong's #3877 parakoloutheō<br>  ⇒ NIV #4158 parakoloutheō<br>  ⇒ NASB #3877 parakoloutheō<br><br>**2 Tim. 3:10**<br>But thou hast **fully known** my doctrine, manner of life, purpose, faith, longsuffering, charity, patience, [KJV]<br>But you **followed** my teaching, conduct, purpose, faith, patience, love, perseverance, [NASB]<br>You, however, **know all about** my teaching, my way of life, my purpose, faith, patience, love, endurance, [NIV]<br>But you have carefully **followed** my doctrine, manner of life, purpose, faith, longsuffering, love, perseverance, [NKJV]<br>But you **know** what I teach, Timothy, and how I live, and what my purpose in life is. You know my faith and how long I have suffered. You know my love and my patient endurance. [NLT]<br>ὺ δὲ **παρηκολούθηκάς** μου τῇ διδασκαλίᾳ, τῇ ἀγωγῇ, τῇ προθέσει, τῇ πίστει, τῇ μακροθυμίᾳ, τῇ ἀγάπῃ, τῇ ὑπομονῇ, [GNS]<br>Σὺ δὲ **παρηκολούθησάς** μου τῇ διδασκαλίᾳ, τῇ ἀγωγῇ, τῇ προθέσει, τῇ πίστει, τῇ μακροθυμίᾳ, τῇ ἀγάπῃ, τῇ ὑπομονῇ, [GNT] | To know; to know all about; to fully know; to follow; to give full attention to. Kenneth Wuest points out that the Greek word means to follow a person so closely that one is always by the person's side, conforming his life to the person (*The Pastoral Epistles*, p.148). It means to join oneself to the person, to become his disciple and to follow his example.<br><br>**Practical Application**<br>A godly person follows a godly example. This is a sharp contrast from the godless marks of false teachers (2 Tim. 3:1-9). Timothy followed (*parēkolouthēsas*) and had closely observed and followed the godly example of Paul. Paul had lived a godly life, and Timothy had followed in his footsteps. |
| **#1549 Followed– Following**<br><br>Followed–KJV<br>Following–NASB<br>Followed–NIV<br>Followed–NKJV<br>Followed–NLT<br><br>**POSB REFERENCE** (Jn.6:1-6; esp. v.2) Note 1 | **ἠκολούθει** = *ēkolouthei*<br>Pronunciation: [ayk-ol-oo-theh'-ee]<br>Parsing (part of speech): verb<br>  Mood—indicative<br>  Tense—imperfect<br>  Voice—active<br>  Person—3rd person<br>  Number—singular<br>  Stem or root—from ἀκολουθέω<br>Concordance References:<br>  ⇒ Strong's #190 akoloutheō<br>  ⇒ NIV #199 akoloutheō<br>  ⇒ NASB #190 akoloutheō<br><br>**John 6:2**<br>And a great multitude **followed** him, because they saw his miracles which he did on them that were diseased. [KJV]<br>And a great multitude was **following** Him, because they were seeing the signs which He was performing on those who were sick. [NASB] | To follow; to tag along; to keep on following; to be a disciple.<br><br>**Practical Application**<br>The picture in this Scripture is that of Jesus sitting on the mountainside, lifting up His eyes from resting upon His knees and seeing "a great company," thousands streaming across the fields and up the mountain toward Him. The "great company" included both those who had followed Him around the lake and pilgrims who were caught up in the excitement of hearing about Jesus, the proclaimed Messiah.<br>Jesus used the occasion to demonstrate two concerns.<br>1. His concern for meeting the needs of man, even the most minute need of missing a meal. There is no need that Jesus does not want to meet. The multitude that had been following |

# PRACTICAL WORD STUDIES
## in the NEW TESTAMENT

| ENGLISH WORD | GREEK WORD AND VERSE | THE WORD MEANS... |
|---|---|---|
| | And a great crowd of people **followed** him because they saw the miraculous signs he had performed on the sick. [NIV]<br>Then a great multitude **followed** Him, because they saw His signs which He performed on those who were diseased. [NKJV]<br>And a huge crowd kept **following** him wherever he went, because they saw his miracles as he healed the sick. [NLT]<br>καὶ **ἠκολούθει** αὐτῷ ὄχλος πολύς, ὅτι ἑώρων αὐτοῦ τὰ σημεῖα ἃ ἐποίει ἐπὶ τῶν ἀσθενούντων. [GNS]<br>**ἠκολούθει** δὲ αὐτῷ ὄχλος πολύς, ὅτι ἐθεώρουν τὰ σημεῖα ἃ ἐποίει ἐπὶ τῶν ἀσθενούντων. [GNT] | Him for days had just made a nine mile journey, having rushed ("followed," *ëkolouthei*) to keep from losing Him. They were not only hungry and apparently out of food, but they were in mountainous country, an area without any possibility of purchasing food. The point is this: the people were so desperate to find and keep up with Him that they just forgot about eating. As usual, Jesus was filled with compassion for those who so desperately sought Him out. He used the occasion to teach the great lesson: He will meet even the most minute need of men. He asked His disciples, "Where shall we buy bread, that these may eat?"<br>2. His concern to strengthen the disciples. He knew what He was going to do, but He used the occasion to test and strengthen the disciples, teaching them a tremendous lesson on faith. They were as we are, full of needs; and their greatest need was the same as ours, to grow in faith. |
| **#1550**<br>**Followers**<br><br>**Followers–KJV**<br>Imitators–NASB<br>Imitate–NIV<br>Imitate–NKJV<br>Example–NLT<br><br>**POSB REFERENCE**<br>(1 Cor.4:16)<br>Note 3 | μιμηταί γίνεσθε. = *mimëtai ginesthe*<br>Pronunciation: [mim-ay-tace']<br>Parsing *mimëtai* (part of speech): noun<br>  Case—nominative<br>  Gender—masculine<br>  Number—plural<br>  Stem or root—from μιμητής, οῦ<br>Parsing *ginesthe* (part of speech): verb<br>  Mood—imperative<br>  Tense—present<br>  Voice—middle or passive deponent<br>  Person—2nd person<br>  Number—plural<br>  Stem or root—from γίνομαι<br>Concordance References:<br>⇒ Strong's #1096+3402 ginomai mimëtës<br>⇒ NIV #1181+3629 ginomai mimëtës [imitate]<br>⇒ NASB #1096+3402 ginomai mimëtës<br><br>**1 Cor. 4:16**<br>Wherefore I beseech you, be ye **followers** of me. [KJV]<br>I exhort you therefore, be **imitators** of me. [NASB]<br>Therefore I urge you to **imitate** me. [NIV]<br>Therefore I urge you, **imitate** me. [NKJV]<br>So I ask you to follow my **example** and do as I do. [NLT]<br>παρακαλῶ οὖν ὑμᾶς, **μιμηταί** μου γίνεσθε. [GNS]<br>παρακαλῶ οὖν ὑμᾶς, **μιμηταί** μου γίνεσθε. [GNT] | Imitate, follow, example; to copy; mimic; to impersonate; to emulate; to duplicate.<br><br>**Practical Application**<br>Every father should live such a life that his children could follow in his steps. This is what Paul was saying. He had lived a life of commitment and self-denial for the Lord Jesus Christ. He had given all he was and had to Christ. He was saying: "Follow me—imitate me! Commit your life to Christ; deny yourself completely—give all you are and have to Him. Help me in evangelizing and meeting the desperate needs of the world for Him. The world is starving and dying from sin, hunger, disease, cold, heat, loneliness, and purposelessness; and they are doomed to die in both this world and the next. Follow me! Help me to reach this world for Christ Jesus our Lord." |
| **#1551**<br>**Followers**<br><br>**Followers–KJV**<br>Imitators–NASB<br>Imitators–NIV<br>Imitators–NKJV<br>Example–NLT<br><br>**POSB REFERENCE**<br>(Eph.5:1)<br>Note 1 | μιμηταί = *mimëtai*<br>Pronunciation: [mim-ay-tah-ee']<br>Parsing (part of speech): noun<br>  Case—nominative<br>  Gender—masculine<br>  Number—plural<br>  Stem or root—from μιμητής, οῦ<br>Concordance References:<br>⇒ Strong's #3402 mimëtës<br>⇒ NIV #3629 mimëtës<br>⇒ NASB #3402 mimëtës<br><br>**Ephes. 5:1**<br>Be ye therefore **followers** of God, as dear children; [KJV]<br>Therefore be **imitators** of God, as beloved children; [NASB]<br>Be **imitators** of God, therefore, as dearly loved children [NIV]<br>Therefore be **imitators** of God as dear children. [NKJV] | Imitators, followers, examples.<br><br>**Practical Application**<br>Some prefer the translation that we are to become *imitators* of God. Note the phrase "as dear children." Just as children learn by imitating their parents, so we are to learn by imitating God. The very idea that we are to be *followers and imitators* of God is a bold idea. Just imagine, Scripture boldly proclaims that we are to become *like God!*<br>⇒ Christ said: "Be ye therefore perfect, even as your Father which is in heaven is perfect" (Matthew 5:48).<br>⇒ God demanded: "Ye shall be holy: for I the LORD your God am holy" (Leviticus 19:2).<br>⇒ Paul declared: "But we all...are changed into the same image [of Christ] from glory to glory" (2 Cor. 4:18). |

# PRACTICAL WORD STUDIES
## in the NEW TESTAMENT

| ENGLISH WORD | GREEK WORD AND VERSE | THE WORD MEANS... |
|---|---|---|
| | Follow God's **example** in everything you do, because you are his dear children. [NLT]<br>ίνεσθε οὖν **μιμηταί** τοῦ Θεοῦ, ὡς τέκνα ἀγαπητά· [GNS]<br>γίνεσθε οὖν **μιμηταί** τοῦ θεοῦ ὡς τέκνα ἀγαπητά [GNT] | ⇒ Peter charged: "But as he which hath called you is holy, so be ye holy in all manner of conversation; because it is written, Be ye holy; for I am holy" (1 Peter 1:15-16).<br>⇒ The early church saint Clement of Alexandria said: "The Christian practices being God" (Quoted by William Barclay, *The Letters to the Galatians and Ephesians*, p.190). |
| #1552<br>**Followers**<br><br>**Followers**–KJV<br>Zealous–NASB<br>Eager–NIV<br>**Followers**–NKJV<br>Eager–NLT<br><br>**POSB REFERENCE**<br>(1 Pt.3:13-14; esp. v.13)<br>Note 1 | ζηλωταί = zēlōtai<br>Pronunciation: [dzay-lo-tah-ee]<br>Parsing (part of speech): noun<br>    Case—nominative<br>    Gender—masculine<br>    Number—plural<br>    Stem or root—from ζηλωτής, οῦ<br>Concordance References:<br>  ⇒ Strong's #3402 mimetes<br>  ⇒ NIV #2421 zēlotēs<br>  ⇒ NASB #2207 zēlotēs<br><br>**1 Peter 3:13**<br>And who is he that will harm you, if ye be **followers** of that which is good? [KJV]<br>And who is there to harm you if you prove **zealous** for what is good? [NASB]<br>Who is going to harm you if you are **eager** to do good? [NIV]<br>And who *is* he who will harm you if you become **followers** of what is good? [NKJV]<br>Now, who will want to harm you if you are **eager** to do good? [NLT]<br>Καὶ τίς ὁ κακώσων ὑμᾶς, ἐὰν τοῦ ἀγαθοῦ **μιμηταὶ** γέγενσθε; [GNS]<br>Καὶ τίς ὁ κακώσων ὑμᾶς ἐὰν τοῦ ἀγαθοῦ **ζηλωταὶ** γένησθε; [GNT] | To be eager; to be a follower, a strongly committed follower; to be zealous; to be a Zealot.<br><br>**Practical Application**<br>Note the verse: it actually says to become "a follower of that which is good." The believer is to be so zealous for what is right that he is actually known as a zealot for good. Imagine being gripped with so much passion and zeal for good that one becomes known as a zealot! This is the challenge of this passage. Several attitudes toward doing good permeate society.<br>⇒ Some persons have a *"care less" attitude* toward goodness. Doing what is right and good matters little. What is right and good is rebelled against, ignored, cursed, and rejected. The person has little conscience about right and wrong. His values are ever so weak. He could not care less if he does what is right and good.<br>⇒ Some persons have a *selfish attitude* toward goodness. If doing what is right and good benefits them, then they do it. If it helps them, meets their need and enlarges their holdings, then they do what is right. But if it costs them, demands discipline and control, and takes away from their pleasure and holdings, then they reject the good, refusing to do what is right.<br>⇒ Some persons have a *surface or sentimental attitude* to what is good and right. They readily profess to believe in what is good and right in an effort to be known as moral and upright. But behind the scenes, they go ahead and live like they want and doing their own thing.<br>⇒ Some persons, of course, have a zealous attitude toward what is right and good. They have committed their lives to seeking and doing what they should. This is exactly what Scripture is saying: "Be a zealot—be a fanatic—be a passionate follower—after that which is good and right." |
| #1553<br>**Folly**<br><br>Foolishness–KJV<br>Foolishness–NASB<br>**Folly**–NIV<br>Foolishness–NKJV<br>Foolishness–NLT<br><br>**POSB REFERENCE**<br>(Mk.7:22)<br>*Deeper Study* #15 | ἀφροσύνη = aphrosune<br>Pronunciation: [af-ros-oo'-nay]<br>Parsing (part of speech): noun<br>    Case—nominative<br>    Gender—feminine<br>    Number—singular<br>    Stem or root—from ἀφροσύνη, ης<br>Concordance References:<br>  ⇒ Strong's #877 aphrosunē<br>  ⇒ NIV #932 aphrosunē<br>  ⇒ NASB #877 aphrosunē<br><br>**Mark 7:22**<br>Thefts, covetousness, wickedness, deceit, lasciviousness, an evil eye, blasphemy, pride, **foolishness**: [KJV] | Moral senselessness, foolishness, folly, recklessness, craziness, absurdity, insanity, thoughtlessness.<br><br>**Practical Application**<br>It is a person who acts foolishly in morals and duty, behavior and thought. It is the foolish person who chooses to focus upon oneself and one's own pleasure and flesh instead of upon God and other people. This person seeks...<br>• to put oneself before others: wife, husband, parent, child, friend, neighbor, God.<br>• to put one's own will before God's will. |

## PRACTICAL WORD STUDIES in the NEW TESTAMENT

| ENGLISH WORD | GREEK WORD AND VERSE | THE WORD MEANS... |
|---|---|---|
| | Deeds of coveting and wickedness, as well as deceit, sensuality, envy, slander, pride and **foolishness**. [NASB]<br>Greed, malice, deceit, lewdness, envy, slander, arrogance and **folly**. [NIV]<br>Thefts, covetousness, wickedness, deceit, lewdness, an evil eye, blasphemy, pride, **foolishness**. [NKJV]<br>Adultery, greed, wickedness, deceit, eagerness for lustful pleasure, envy, slander, pride, and **foolishness**. [NLT]<br>πλεονεξίαι, πονηρίαι, δόλος, ἀσέλγεια, ὀφθαλμὸς πονηρός, βλασφημία, ὑπερηφανία, **ἀφροσύνη**· [GNS]<br>μοιχεῖαι, πλεονεξίαι, πονηρίαι, δόλος, ἀσέλγεια, ὀφθαλμὸς πονηρός, βλασφημία, ὑπερηφανία, **ἀφροσύνη**· [GNT] | • to seek one's own desires without considering others.<br>• to go after what one wants even if it is unwise and hurts others.<br>• to feel that everyone and everything should revolve around oneself.<br>• to focus upon one's own pleasure and flesh, ignoring the crying needs of the desperate and dying. |
| **#1554**<br>**Fooled, Don't be**<br><br>Be not deceived–KJV<br>Be not deceived–NASB<br>Do not be misled–NIV<br>Do not be deceived–NKJV<br>**Don't be fooled–NLT**<br><br>**POSB REFERENCE**<br>(1 Cor.15:33)<br>Note 3 | μὴ πλανᾶσθε = mē planasthe<br>Pronunciation: [may plan-ahs'-theh]<br>Parsing *planasthe* (part of speech): verb<br>   Mood—imperative<br>   Tense—present<br>   Voice—passive<br>   Person—2nd person<br>   Number—plural<br>   Stem or root—from πλανάω<br>Concordance References:<br>⇒ Strong's #3361 mē + 4105 planaō<br>⇒ NIV #3590 mē [Do not] + 4414 planaō [be misled]<br>⇒ NASB #3361 mē + 4105 planaō<br><br>**1 Cor. 15:33**<br>**Be not deceived**: evil communications corrupt good manners. [KJV]<br>**Do not be deceived**: "Bad company corrupts good morals." [NASB]<br>**Do not be misled**: "Bad company corrupts good character." [NIV]<br>**Do not be deceived**: "Evil company corrupts good habits." [NKJV]<br>**Don't be fooled** by those who say such things, for "bad company corrupts good character." [NLT]<br>μὴ πλανᾶσθε· Φθείρουσιν ἤθη χρησθ ὁμιλίαι κακαί. [GNS]<br>μὴ πλανᾶσθε· Φθείρουσιν ἤθη χρηστὰ ὁμιλίαι κακαί. [GNT] | Do not be misled; do not be deceived; do not be fooled; do not be led astray, led in the error of such a false teaching; do not be mistaken.<br><br>**Practical Application**<br>There is to be a resurrection of the dead. "They" who deny the resurrection are wrong. Do not be deceived by their error. It is an utterly false teaching that corrupts. |
| **#1555**<br>**Foolish**<br><br>Vain–KJV<br>Futile–NASB<br>Futile–NIV<br>Futile–NKJV<br>**Foolish–NLT**<br><br>**POSB REFERENCE**<br>(Romans 1:21)<br>Note 4, point 1 | ἐματαιώθησαν = emataiōthēsan<br>Pronunciation: [eh-mat-ah-i'-o-thay-sahn]<br>Parsing (part of speech): verb<br>   Mood—indicative<br>   Tense—aorist<br>   Voice—passive<br>   Person—3rd person<br>   Number—plural<br>   Stem or root—from ματαιόομαι<br>Concordance References:<br>⇒ Strong's #3154 mataioō<br>⇒ NIV #3471 mataioō<br>⇒ NASB #3154 mataioō<br><br>**Romans 1:21**<br>Because that, when they knew God, they glorified him not as God, neither were thankful; but became **vain** in their imaginations, and their foolish heart was darkened. [KJV]<br>For even though they knew God, they did not honor Him as God, or give thanks; but they became **futile** in their speculations, and their foolish heart was darkened. [NASB]<br>For although they knew God, they neither glorified him as God nor gave thanks to him, but their thinking became **futile** and their foolish hearts were darkened. [NIV] | To be given to worthless or futile speculation. The word vain means empty, futile, unsuccessful, senseless, worthless.<br><br>**Practical Application**<br>The mind of man has been affected by sin. It desperately needs to be renewed. The mind is far from perfect. It is *basically worldly*, that is...<br>• selfish<br>• self-centered<br>• self-seeking<br>• centered on this world<br>• centered on the flesh<br>• centered on this life<br><br>Scripture is clear about the corruption of man's mind. The human mind has been tragically corrupted by man's selfishness and sin. |

## PRACTICAL WORD STUDIES
## in the NEW TESTAMENT

| ENGLISH WORD | GREEK WORD AND VERSE | THE WORD MEANS... |
|---|---|---|
| | Because, although they knew God, they did not glorify Him as God, nor were thankful, but became **futile** in their thoughts, and their foolish hearts were darkened. [NKJV]<br><br>Yes, they knew God, but they wouldn't worship him as God or even give him thanks. And they began to think up **foolish** ideas of what God was like. The result was that their minds became dark and confused. [NLT]<br><br>διότι γνόντες τὸν Θεὸν οὐχ ὡς Θεὸν ἐδόξασαν ἢ ηὐχαρίστησαν, ἀλλ' **ἐματαιώθησαν** ἐν τοῖς διαλογισμοῖς αὐτῶν, καὶ ἐσκοτίσθη ἡ ἀσύνετος αὐτῶν καρδία. [GNS]<br><br>διότι γνόντες τὸν Θεὸν οὐχ ὡς Θεὸν ἐδόξασαν ἢ ηὐχαρίστησαν, ἀλλ' **ἐματαιώθησαν** ἐν τοῖς διαλογισμοῖς αὐτῶν καὶ ἐσκοτίσθη ἡ ἀσύνετος αὐτῶν καρδία. [GNT] | |
| #1556<br>**Foolish**<br><br>Foolish–KJV<br>Foolish–NASB<br>Foolish–NIV<br>Foolish–NKJV<br>Foolish—NLT<br><br>**POSB REFERENCE**<br>(Romans 1:21)<br>Note 4, point 2 | ἀσύνετος = asunetos<br>Pronunciation: [as-oon'-ay-tos]<br>Parsing (part of speech): adjective<br>    Case—nominative<br>    Gender—feminine<br>    Number—singular<br>    Stem or root—from ἀσύνετος, ον<br>Concordance References:<br>  ⇒ Strong's #801 asunetos<br>  ⇒ NIV #852 asunetos<br>  ⇒ NASB #801 asunetos<br><br>**Romans 1:21**<br>Because that, when they knew God, they glorified him not as God, neither were thankful; but became vain in their imaginations, and their **foolish** heart was darkened. [KJV]<br><br>For even though they knew God, they did not honor Him as God, or give thanks; but they became futile in their speculations, and their **foolish** heart was darkened. [NASB]<br><br>For although they knew God, they neither glorified him as God nor gave thanks to him, but their thinking became futile and their **foolish** hearts were darkened. [NIV]<br><br>Because, although they knew God, they did not glorify *Him* as God, nor were thankful, but became futile in their thoughts, and their **foolish** hearts were darkened. [NKJV]<br><br>Yes, they knew God, but they wouldn't worship him as God or even give him thanks. And they began to think up **foolish** ideas of what God was like. The result was that their minds became dark and confused. [NLT]<br><br>διότι γνόντες τὸν Θεὸν οὐχ ὡς Θεὸν ἐδόξασαν ἢ ηὐχαρίστησαν, ἀλλ' ἐματαιώθησαν ἐν τοῖς διαλογισμοῖς αὐτῶν, καὶ ἐσκοτίσθη ἡ **ἀσύνετος** αὐτῶν καρδία. [GNS]<br><br>διότι γνόντες τὸν Θεὸν οὐχ ὡς Θεὸν ἐδόξασαν ἢ ηὐχαρίστησαν, ἀλλ' ἐματαιώθησαν ἐν τοῖς διαλογισμοῖς αὐτῶν καὶ ἐσκοτίσθη ἡ **ἀσύνετος** αὐτῶν καρδία. [GNT] | Foolish. It means senseless, without understanding, unintelligent, and dull.<br><br>**Practical Application**<br>Man's "foolish heart is darkened." Man's heart is...<br>• foolish<br>• senseless<br>• without understanding<br>• unintelligent<br>• dull |
| #1557<br>**Foolish**<br><br>Foolish–KJV<br>Foolish–NASB<br>Foolish–NIV<br>Foolish–NKJV<br>Ignorant–NLT | ἀφρόνων = aphronōn<br>Pronunciation: [af'-rone-own]<br>Parsing (part of speech): pronominal adjective<br>    Case—genitive<br>    Gender—masculine<br>    Number—plural<br>    Stem or root—from ἄφρων, ον<br>Concordance References:<br>  ⇒ Strong's #878 aphrōn<br>  ⇒ NIV #933 aphrōn<br>  ⇒ NASB #878 aphrōn | Foolish, ignorant, thoughtless, senseless, undirected.<br><br>**Practical Application**<br>It refers to people who walk through life giving no thought to life's purpose, as to...<br>• where they have come from.<br>• why they are here.<br>• where they are going.<br><br>The religionist is persuaded that religion answers all these questions, the basic questions |

# PRACTICAL WORD STUDIES
## in the NEW TESTAMENT

| ENGLISH WORD | GREEK WORD AND VERSE | THE WORD MEANS... |
|---|---|---|
| **POSB REFERENCE** (Romans 2:17-20; esp. v.20) Note 1, point 8 | **Romans 2:20** An instructor of the **foolish**, a teacher of babes, which hast the form of knowledge and of the truth in the law. [KJV] A corrector of the **foolish**, a teacher of the immature, having in the Law the embodiment of knowledge and of the truth, [NASB] An instructor of the **foolish**, a teacher of infants, because you have in the law the embodiment of knowledge and truth— [NIV] An instructor of the **foolish**, a teacher of babes, having the form of knowledge and truth in the law. [NKJV] You think you can instruct the **ignorant** and teach children the ways of God. For you are certain that in God's law you have complete knowledge and truth. [NLT] παιδευτὴν **ἀφρόνων**, διδάσκαλον νηπίων, ἔχοντα τὴν μόρφωσιν τῆς γνώσεως καὶ τῆς ἀληθείας ἐν τῷ νόμῳ· [GNS] παιδευτὴν **ἀφρόνων**, διδάσκαλον νηπίων, ἔχοντα τὴν μόρφωσιν τῆς γνώσεως καὶ τῆς ἀληθείας ἐν τῷ νόμῳ· [GNT] | of life. Therefore, he can help the foolish discover meaning and purpose and significance in life. The critical point for the instructor or the religionist is to make sure that his instruction is true. What he instructs must be the truth or else it is all for naught. |
| **#1558 Foolish** Foolish–KJV Foolish–NASB Foolish–NIV Foolish–NKJV Foolish–NLT **POSB REFERENCE** (Gal.3:1) Note 1 See also POSB REF: (Lk.24:15-27; esp. v.25) Note 2, point 3a (Tit.3:3) Note 1 *Deeper Study #1* | ἀνόητοι = *anoētoi* Pronunciation: [an-oh'-ay-toy] Parsing (part of speech): adjective     Case—vocative     Gender—masculine     Number—plural Stem or root—from ἀνόητος, ον Concordance References: ⇒ Strong's #453 anoētos ⇒ NIV #485 anoētos ⇒ NASB #453 anoētos **Galatians 3:1** O **foolish** Galatians, who hath bewitched you, that ye should not obey the truth, before whose eyes Jesus Christ hath been evidently set forth, crucified among you? [KJV] You **foolish** Galatians, who has bewitched you, before whose eyes Jesus Christ was publicly portrayed as crucified? [NASB] You **foolish** Galatians! Who has bewitched you? Before your very eyes Jesus Christ was clearly portrayed as crucified. [NIV] O **foolish** Galatians! Who has bewitched you that you should not obey the truth, before whose eyes Jesus Christ was clearly portrayed among you as crucified? [NKJV] Oh, **foolish** Galatians! What magician has cast an evil spell on you? For you used to see the meaning of Jesus Christ's death as clearly as though I had shown you a signboard with a picture of Christ dying on the cross. [NLT] Ὦ **ἀνόητοι** Γαλάται, τίς ὑμᾶς ἐβάσκανε τῇ ἀληθείᾳ μὴ πείθεσθαι, οἷς κατ' ὀφθαλμοὺς Ἰησοῦς Χριστὸς προεγράφη ἐν ὑμῖν ἐσταυρωμένος; [GNS] Ὦ **ἀνόητοι** Γαλάται, τίς ὑμᾶς ἐβάσκανεν, οἷς κατ' ὀφθαλμοὺς Ἰησοῦς Χριστὸς προεγράφη ἐσταυρωμένος; [GNT] | Foolish, ignorant, misunderstanding, thoughtless, and unthinking. The word means to be thoughtless, dull, senseless, and without understanding in spiritual matters; to be ignorant of God and unwise in dealing with God. **Practical Application** The Galatians were listening to false teaching and passively drinking it in. They were not thinking through what was being taught. They were lazily sitting and soaking it up, not applying their minds to see if what was being taught was true or not. They were *foolish*, acting like senseless people who were incapable of thinking. Note that men sometimes call each other *fools*, using the word as a term of reproach. But believers are forbidden to call other persons fools; God wants no person reproached. But this is not the way the word is being used in the present passage. Scripture is simply saying that a person who denies, ignores, or neglects God is acting foolishly, very unwisely. ⇒ He is thoughtless: not applying his thoughts to God; not thinking through the truth about God. ⇒ He is dull: not being sharp in his thoughts about God. He is being sleepy-minded, slow, and sluggish toward God. ⇒ He is senseless: not using good common sense about God. He is acting contrary to good common sense. He is deficient in his thoughts about God. ⇒ He is without understanding: he does not grasp or comprehend God; he does not have the right ideas or thoughts about God. ⇒ He is ignorant of God: he does not know God. He has not learned God—has not looked at, thought about, studied, nor met, walked and fellowshipped with God. ⇒ He is unwise: he is acting contrary to wisdom; he is acting dangerously and foolishly Scripture is clear: the person who walks upon earth without God is foolish. And remember: we were one time foolish—all of us—every believer. We walked upon earth most unwisely, think- |

# PRACTICAL WORD STUDIES
## in the NEW TESTAMENT

| ENGLISH WORD | GREEK WORD AND VERSE | THE WORD MEANS... |
|---|---|---|
| | | ing little if any about God, ignoring and neglecting Him; and some of us even cursed and denied Him.<br><br>But thanks be to God our Savior. He has saved us, and He will save any person no matter how foolish and ignorant of God he is. No matter how foolish and far away from God a person is, God will save him if he will call upon the name of the Lord Jesus Christ. |
| **#1559**<br>**Foolish**<br><br>**Foolish–KJV**<br>**Foolish–NASB**<br>**Foolish–NIV**<br>**Foolish–NKJV**<br>**Foolish–NLT**<br><br>**POSB REFERENCE**<br>(Tit.3:9)<br>Note 2, point 1 | μωρὰς = mōras<br>Pronunciation: [mo-rahs']<br>Parsing (part of speech): adjective<br>    Case—accusative<br>    Gender—feminine<br>    Number—plural<br>    Stem or root—from μωρός, ά, όν<br>Concordance References:<br>⇒ Strong's #3474 mōros<br>⇒ NIV #3704 mōros<br>⇒ NASB #3474 mōros<br><br>**Titus 3:9**<br>But avoid **foolish** questions, and genealogies, and contentions, and strivings about the law; for they are unprofitable and vain. [KJV]<br><br>But shun **foolish** controversies and genealogies and strife and disputes about the Law; for they are unprofitable and worthless. [NASB]<br><br>But avoid **foolish** controversies and genealogies and arguments and quarrels about the law, because these are unprofitable and useless. [NIV]<br><br>But avoid **foolish** disputes, genealogies, contentions, and strivings about the law; for they are unprofitable and useless. [NKJV]<br><br>Do not get involved in **foolish** discussions about spiritual pedigrees or in quarrels and fights about obedience to Jewish laws. These kinds of things are useless and a waste of time. [NLT]<br><br>μωρὰς δὲ ζητήσεις καὶ γενεαλογίας καὶ ἔρεις καὶ μάχας νομικὰς περιΐστασο· εἰσὶ γὰρ ἀνωφελεῖς καὶ μάταιοι. [GNS]<br><br>μωρὰς δὲ ζητήσεις καὶ γενεαλογίας καὶ ἔρεις καὶ μάχας νομικὰς περιΐστασο· εἰσὶν γὰρ ἀνωφελεῖς καὶ μάταιοι. [GNT] | To be foolish, senseless, crazy, absurd, irrational.<br><br>**Practical Application**<br>Believers must turn away from foolish and controversial discussions and from false trusts. There were some who were spending their time sitting and discussing foolish (*mōras*), useless, and stupid questions—discussions that accomplished nothing for the cause of Christ or for the welfare of humanity. William Barclay has a very descriptive discussion of this point that we all need to heed:<br><br>*It has been said that there is a danger that a man may think himself religious because he discusses religious questions. There is a kind of discussion group which argues simply for the sake of arguing. There is a kind of group which will argue for hours about theological questions. It is much easier to discuss theological questions than it is to be kind and considerate and helpful at home, or efficient and diligent and honest at work. There is no virtue in sitting discussing deep theological questions when the simple tasks of the Christian life are waiting to be done. It is indeed true that such discussion can be nothing other than an evasion of Christian duties.*<br><br>*Paul was quite certain that the real task of the Christian lay in Christian action. That is by no means to say that there is no place for Christian discussions; but it is to say that the discussion which does not end in action is very largely wasted time.* |
| **#1560**<br>**Foolish Discussions**<br><br>Vain babblings–KJV<br>Empty chatter–NASB<br>Chatter–NIV<br>Idle babblings–NKJV<br>**Foolish discussions–NLT**<br><br>**POSB REFERENCE**<br>(1 Tim.6:20)<br>Note 2, point 2a | κενοφωνίας = kenophōnias<br>Pronunciation: [ken-of-o-nee'-ahs]<br>Parsing (part of speech): noun<br>    Case—accusative<br>    Gender—feminine<br>    Number—plural<br>    Stem or root—from κενοφωνία, ας<br>Concordance References:<br>⇒ Strong's #2757 kenophōnia<br>⇒ NIV #3032 kenophōnia<br>⇒ NASB #2757 kenophōnia<br><br>**1 Tim. 6:20**<br>O Timothy, keep that which is committed to thy trust, avoiding profane and **vain babblings**, and oppositions of science falsely so called: [KJV]<br><br>O Timothy, guard what has been entrusted to you, avoiding worldly and **empty chatter** and the opposing arguments of what is falsely called "knowledge"—[NASB]<br><br>Timothy, guard what has been entrusted to your care. Turn away from godless **chatter** and the opposing ideas of what is falsely called knowledge, [NIV]<br><br>O Timothy! Guard what was committed to your trust, avoiding the profane *and* **idle babblings** and | Chatter; vain babbling; idle babblings; empty chatter; foolish discussions; foolish talk.<br><br>**Practical Application**<br>The charge is to take all *foolish* talk and turn away from it. Have absolutely nothing to do with common, irreverent, godless, and *empty voices*—no matter who is sounding forth the words. This would, of course, include...<br>⇒ false claims to truth<br>⇒ worldly philosophy<br>⇒ cursing<br>⇒ criticism<br>⇒ suggestive talk<br>⇒ all forms of false teaching<br>⇒ novel ideas of religion<br>⇒ gossip<br>⇒ off-colored jokes |

## PRACTICAL WORD STUDIES
## in the NEW TESTAMENT

| ENGLISH WORD | GREEK WORD AND VERSE | THE WORD MEANS... |
|---|---|---|
| | contradictions of what is falsely called knowledge—[NKJV]<br><br>Timothy, guard what God has entrusted to you. Avoid godless, **foolish discussions** with those who oppose you with their so-called knowledge. [NLT]<br><br>Ὦ Τιμόθεε, τὴν παρακαταθήκην φύλαξον, ἐκτρεπόμενος τὰς βεβήλους **κενοφωνίας** καὶ ἀντιθέσεις τῆς ψευδωνύμου γνώσεως· [GNS]<br><br>Ὦ Τιμόθεε, τὴν παραθήκην φύλαξον ἐκτρεπόμενος τὰς βεβήλους **κενοφωνίας** καὶ ἀντιθέσεις τῆς ψευδωνύμου γνώσεως, [GNT] | |
| **#1561**<br>**Foolish Talk, Talking**<br><br>Foolish talking–KJV<br>Silly talk–NASB<br>Foolish talk–NIV<br>Foolish talking–NKJV<br>Foolish talk–NLT<br><br>**POSB REFERENCE**<br>(Eph.5:4)<br>Note 4, point 21 | μωρολογία = mōrologia<br>Pronunciation: [mo-rol-og-ee'-ah]<br>Parsing (part of speech): noun<br>  Case—nominative<br>  Gender—feminine<br>  Number—singular<br>  Stem or root—from μωρολογία, ας<br>Concordance References:<br>  ⇒ Strong's #3473 mōrologia<br>  ⇒ NIV #3703 mōrologia<br>  ⇒ NASB #3473 mōrologia<br><br>**Ephes. 5:4**<br>Neither filthiness, nor **foolish talking**, nor jesting, which are not convenient: but rather giving of thanks. [KJV]<br><br>And there must be no filthiness and **silly talk**, or coarse jesting, which are not fitting, but rather giving of thanks. [NASB]<br><br>Nor should there be obscenity, **foolish talk** or coarse joking, which are out of place, but rather thanksgiving. [NIV]<br><br>Neither filthiness, nor **foolish talking**, nor coarse jesting, which are not fitting, but rather giving of thanks. [NKJV]<br><br>Obscene stories, **foolish talk**, and coarse jokes—these are not for you. Instead, let there be thankfulness to God. [NLT]<br><br>καὶ αἰσχρότης, καὶ **μωρολογία**, ἡ εὐτραπελία, τὰ οὐκ ἀνήκοντα· ἀλλὰ μᾶλλον εὐχαριστία. [GNS]<br><br>καὶ αἰσχρότης καὶ **μωρολογία** ἡ εὐτραπελία, ἃ οὐκ ἀνῆκεν, ἀλλὰ μᾶλλον εὐχαριστία. [GNT] | Foolish talk, silly talk.<br><br>**Practical Application**<br>The believer is never once to engage in "foolish talking" (*mōrologia*): empty, unthoughtful, senseless, wasted, idle, aimless, or purposeless talk; talk that fritters away and wastes time, that has absolutely no purpose to it. It also means sinful, foolish, silly and corrupt talk. |
| **#1562**<br>**Foolish Things**<br><br>Foolish things–KJV<br>Foolish things–NASB<br>Foolish things–NIV<br>Foolish things–NKJV<br>Things the world considers foolish–NLT<br><br>**POSB REFERENCE**<br>(1 Cor.1:27-28; esp. v.27)<br>Note 2, point 1 | μωρά = mōra<br>Pronunciation: [mo-rah']<br>Parsing (part of speech): pronominal adjective<br>  Case—accusative<br>  Gender—neuter<br>  Number—plural<br>  Stem or root—from μωρός, ά, όν<br>Concordance References:<br>  ⇒ Strong's #3474 mōros<br>  ⇒ NIV #3704 mōros [foolish things]<br>  ⇒ NASB #3474 mōros<br><br>**1 Cor. 1:27**<br>But God hath chosen the **foolish things** of the world to confound the wise; and God hath chosen the weak things of the world to confound the things which are mighty; [KJV]<br><br>But God has chosen the **foolish things** of the world to shame the wise, and God has chosen the weak things of the world to shame the things which are strong, [NASB]<br><br>But God chose the **foolish things** of the world to shame the wise; God chose the weak things of the world to shame the strong. [NIV]<br><br>But God has chosen the **foolish things** of the world to put to shame the wise, and God has chosen the weak things of the world to put to shame the things which are mighty; [NKJV]<br><br>Instead, God deliberately chose **things the world** | Foolish things, foolishness; things the world considers foolish.<br><br>**Practical Application**<br>God chooses the "foolish things [people] of this world to shame the wise." Note the term *"foolish things"* is used instead of "foolish people."<br><br>Many of the wise in the world look upon those who have little or nothing as things. They look upon them as nothing more than tools for the rich and powerful to use as they wish. God chooses the ignorant, the unlearned, and the disadvantaged over the wise of the world. |

## PRACTICAL WORD STUDIES
## in the New Testament

| ENGLISH WORD | GREEK WORD AND VERSE | THE WORD MEANS... |
|---|---|---|
| | **considers foolish** in order to shame those who think they are wise. And he chose those who are powerless to shame those who are powerful. [NLT]<br><br>ἀλλὰ τὰ **μωρὰ** τοῦ κόσμου ἐξελέξατο ὁ Θεός, ἵνα τοὺς σοφούς, καταισχύνῃ· καὶ τὰ ἀσθενῆ τοῦ κόσμου ἐξελέξατο ὁ Θεὸς, ἵνα καταισχύνῃ τὰ ἰσχυρά· [GNS]<br><br>ἀλλὰ τὰ **μωρὰ** τοῦ κόσμου ἐξελέξατο ὁ θεός, ἵνα καταισχύνῃ τοὺς σοφούς, καὶ τὰ ἀσθενῆ τοῦ κόσμου ἐξελέξατο ὁ θεός, ἵνα καταισχύνῃ τὰ ἰσχυρά, [GNT] | |
| **#1563**<br>**Foolishness**<br><br>**Foolishness–KJV**<br>**Foolishness–NASB**<br>Folly–NIV<br>**Foolishness–NKJV**<br>**Foolishness–NLT**<br><br>**POSB<br>REFERENCE**<br>(Mk.7:22)<br>*Deeper Study* #15 | ἀφροσύνη = *aphrosune*<br>Pronunciation: [af-ros-oo'-nay]<br>Parsing (part of speech): noun<br>   Case—nominative<br>   Gender—feminine<br>   Number—singular<br>   Stem or root—from ἀφροσύνη, ης<br>Concordance References:<br>  ⇒ Strong's #877 aphrosunë<br>  ⇒ NIV #932 aphrosunë<br>  ⇒ NASB #877 aphrosunë<br><br>**Mark 7:22**<br>Thefts, covetousness, wickedness, deceit, lasciviousness, an evil eye, blasphemy, pride, **foolishness**: [KJV]<br>Deeds of coveting and wickedness, as well as deceit, sensuality, envy, slander, pride and **foolishness**. [NASB]<br>Greed, malice, deceit, lewdness, envy, slander, arrogance and **folly**. [NIV]<br>Thefts, covetousness, wickedness, deceit, lewdness, an evil eye, blasphemy, pride, **foolishness**. [NKJV]<br>Adultery, greed, wickedness, deceit, eagerness for lustful pleasure, envy, slander, pride, and **foolishness**. [NLT]<br><br>πλεονεξίαι, πονηρίαι, δόλος, ἀσέλγεια, ὀφθαλμὸς πονηρός, βλασφημία, ὑπερηφανία, **ἀφροσύνη**· [GNS]<br>μοιχεῖαι, πλεονεξίαι, πονηρίαι, δόλος, ἀσέλγεια, ὀφθαλμὸς πονηρός, βλασφημία, ὑπερηφανία, **ἀφροσύνη**· [GNT] | Moral senselessness, foolishness, folly, recklessness, craziness, absurdity, insanity, thoughtlessness.<br><br>**Practical Application**<br>It is a person who acts foolishly in morals and duty, behavior and thought. It is the foolish person who chooses to focus upon oneself and one's own pleasure and flesh instead of upon God and other people. This person seeks...<br>• to put oneself before others: wife, husband, parent, child, friend, neighbor, God.<br>• to put one's own will before God's will.<br>• to seek one's own desires without considering others.<br>• to go after what one wants even if it is unwise and hurts others.<br>• to feel that everyone and everything should revolve around oneself.<br>• to focus upon one's own pleasure and flesh, ignoring the crying needs of the desperate and dying. |
| **#1564**<br>**Foolishness**<br><br>**Foolishness–KJV**<br>**Foolishness–NASB**<br>**Foolishness–NIV**<br>**Foolishness–NKJV**<br>Sounds foolish–NLT<br><br>**POSB<br>REFERENCE**<br>(1 Cor.2:14)<br>Note 1, point 2 | μωρία = *möria*<br>Pronunciation: [mo-ree'-ah]<br>Parsing (part of speech): noun<br>   Case—nominative<br>   Gender—feminine<br>   Number—singular<br>   Stem or root—from μωρία, ας<br>Concordance References:<br>  ⇒ Strong's #3472 möria<br>  ⇒ NIV #3702 möria<br>  ⇒ NASB #3472 möria<br><br>**1 Cor. 2:14**<br>But the natural man receiveth not the things of the Spirit of God: for they are **foolishness** unto him: neither can he know them, because they are spiritually discerned. [KJV]<br>But a natural man does not accept the things of the Spirit of God; for they are **foolishness** to him, and he cannot understand them, because they are spiritually appraised. [NASB]<br>The man without the Spirit does not accept the things that come from the Spirit of God, for they are **foolishness** to him, and he cannot understand them, because they are spiritually discerned. [NIV]<br>But the natural man does not receive the things of the Spirit of God, for they are **foolishness** to him; nor can he know *them*, because they are spiritually discerned. [NKJV]<br>But people who aren't Christians can't understand these truths from God's Spirit. It all **sounds foolish** to them because only those who have the Spirit can under- | Foolishness, dull, absurd, distasteful.<br><br>**Practical Application**<br>Remember the man without the Spirit lives primarily for the animal part of his nature: he lives primarily for what...<br>• looks good<br>• feels good<br>• tastes good<br>• sounds good<br><br>He lives primarily for his animal senses, primarily for what turns him on. It may be position, money, wealth, possessions, recognition, fame, influence, power, family, house, cars, sex, food, dress, popularity—an endless number of worldly and material things could be listed—anything that attracts and appeals to the animal nature within us as human beings. The man who gives in to these instincts and urges is the person who lives as the natural man. To him the things of God are secondary, of less importance. Why? Because he cannot see, feel, taste, hear, or prove spiritual things—not with his physical senses. Therefore, to his mind, it is utterly foolish to put spiritual things first. |

# PRACTICAL WORD STUDIES
## in the NEW TESTAMENT

| ENGLISH WORD | GREEK WORD AND VERSE | THE WORD MEANS... |
|---|---|---|
| | stand what the Spirit means. [NLT]<br>ψυχικὸς δὲ ἄνθρωπος οὐ δέχεται τὰ τοῦ Πνεύματος τοῦ Θεοῦ· **μωρία** γὰρ αὐτῷ ἐστι, καὶ οὐ δύναται γνῶναι, ὅτι πνευματικῶς ἀνακρίνεται· [GNS]<br>ψυχικὸς δὲ ἄνθρωπος οὐ δέχεται τὰ τοῦ πνεύματος τοῦ θεοῦ, **μωρία** γὰρ αὐτῷ ἐστιν, καὶ οὐ δύναται γνῶναι, ὅτι πνευματικῶς ἀνακρίνεται· [GNT] | |
| **#1565**<br>**For**<br><br>For–KJV<br>For–NASB<br>For–NIV<br>For–NKJV<br>For–NLT<br><br>**POSB REFERENCE**<br>(Jn.10:11)<br>*Deeper Study #2*<br><br>See also POSB REF:<br>(Romans 5:6-7; esp. v.6)<br>Note 1, point 4<br>(Gal.1:4-5; esp. v.4)<br>Note 4<br>(1 Pt.2:21-24; esp. v.21)<br>Note 2<br>(Tit.2:14)<br>Note 4 | ὑπέρ = *huper*<br>Pronunciation: [who-pehr]<br>Parsing (part of speech): preposition<br>    Case—genitive<br>    Stem or root—from ὑπέρ<br>Concordance References:<br>  ⇒ Strong's #5228 huper<br>  ⇒ NIV #5642 huper<br>  ⇒ NASB #5228 huper<br><br>**John 10:11**<br>I am the good shepherd: the good shepherd giveth his life **for** the sheep. [KJV]<br>"I am the good shepherd; the good shepherd lays down His life **for** the sheep. [NASB]<br>"I am the good shepherd. The good shepherd lays down his life **for** the sheep. [NIV]<br>I am the good shepherd. The good shepherd gives His life **for** the sheep. [NKJV]<br>"I am the good shepherd. The good shepherd lays down his life **for** the sheep. [NLT]<br>ἐγώ εἰμι ὁ ποιμὴν ὁ καλός· ὁ ποιμὴν ὁ καλὸς τὴν ψυχὴν αὐτοῦ τίθησιν **ὑπὲρ** τῶν προβάτων. [GNS]<br>Ἐγώ εἰμι ὁ ποιμὴν ὁ καλός· ὁ ποιμὴν ὁ καλὸς τὴν ψυχὴν αὐτοῦ τίθησιν **ὑπὲρ** τῶν προβάτων· [GNT] | For the sake of; for the great benefit of; for the care of; on account of.<br><br>**Practical Application**<br>The word "for" (*huper*) is a simple word with profound meaning when used with the death of Christ. It proclaims the most wonderful truth known to man. Note this striking truth: it does not mean that Christ died only as an example for us, showing us how we should be willing to die for the truth or for some great cause. What it means is that Christ died in our place, in our stead, in our room, as our substitute. This meaning is unquestionably clear.<br>Jesus Christ took our sins upon Himself and paid the penalty for them. He bore...<br>⇒ the verdict of sin, the pronouncement of *guilty* for us.<br>⇒ the condemnation of our sins for us.<br>⇒ the punishment of our sins for us.<br><br>What was the verdict, the condemnation, and the punishment which He bore for us? The guilt of our sins, which is death. Jesus Christ died for us. He died as our substitute; He died for us, and because He died for us we never have to die. This is what Scripture means when it says that Jesus Christ gave Himself for us. This is how God demonstrated His grace to the world: He gave His Son to die for the sins of men. (See POSB note—Ephes. 5:2; POSB *Deeper Study #1*—1 Peter 2:21-25 for more discussion.) |
| **#1566**<br>**For Sins**<br><br>For sins–KJV<br>For sins–NASB<br>For sins–NIV<br>For sins–NKJV<br>For...sins–NLT<br><br>**POSB REFERENCE**<br>(1 Pt.3:18)<br>Note 1, point 1 | περὶ ἁμαρτιῶν = *peri hamartiōn*<br>Pronunciation: [per-ee' am-ar-tee'-own]<br>Parsing *hamartiōn* (part of speech): noun<br>    Case—genitive<br>    Gender—feminine<br>    Number—plural<br>    Stem or root—from ἁμαρτία, ας<br>Concordance References:<br>  ⇒ Strong's #4012 peri + 266 hamartia<br>  ⇒ NIV #4309 peri [for] + 281 hamartia [sins]<br>  ⇒ NASB #4012 peri + 266 hamartia<br><br>**1 Peter 3:18**<br>For Christ also hath once suffered **for sins**, the just for the unjust, that he might bring us to God, being put to death in the flesh, but quickened by the Spirit: [KJV]<br>For Christ also died **for sins** once for all, the just for the unjust, in order that He might bring us to God, having been put to death in the flesh, but made alive in the spirit; [NASB]<br>For Christ died **for sins** once for all, the righteous for the unrighteous, to bring you to God. He was put to death in the body but made alive by the Spirit, [NIV]<br>For Christ also suffered once **for sins**, the just for the unjust, that He might bring us to God, being put to death in the flesh but made alive by the Spirit, [NKJV]<br>Christ also suffered when he died **for** our **sins** once for all time. He never sinned, but he died for sinners that he might bring us safely home to God. He suffered | For sins, a sin offering.<br><br>**Practical Application**<br>Christ died once for sins. It was for the sins of man that He died. Man is sinful; he is guilty before God,...<br>• guilty of disbelieving God. Just think how often people do not believe God, how often they do not take God and His Word seriously.<br>• guilty of disobeying God. Just think how often people transgress and break the law of God.<br>• guilty of cursing God. Just think how often people curse and blaspheme the name of God.<br>• guilty of rebelling against God. Just think how often people choose to go their own way and do their own thing instead of doing what God says.<br>• guilty of rejecting God. Just think how many people reject God.<br>Note the words "for sins" (*peri hamartiōn*). These words are the very words used in the Old Testament for the sin offering (Leviticus 5:7; Leviticus 6:30; cp. Romans 8:3; Hebrews 10:6, 8). The point is clear: Jesus Christ offered Himself *for sin*; He was the fulfillment of the |

## PRACTICAL WORD STUDIES
### in the NEW TESTAMENT

| ENGLISH WORD | GREEK WORD AND VERSE | THE WORD MEANS... |
|---|---|---|
| | physical death, but he was raised to life in the Spirit. [NLT]<br><br>ὅτι καὶ Χριστὸς ἅπαξ **περὶ ἁμαρτιῶν** ἔπαθε, δίκαιος ὑπὲρ ἀδίκων, ἵνα ὑμᾶς προσαγάγῃ τῷ Θεῷ, θανατωθεὶς μὲν σαρκὶ, ζωοποιηθεὶς δὲ τῷ πνεύματι, [GNS]<br><br>ὅτι καὶ Χριστὸς ἅπαξ **περὶ ἁμαρτιῶν** ἔπαθεν, δίκαιος ὑπὲρ ἀδίκων, ἵνα ὑμᾶς προσαγάγῃ τῷ θεῷ θανατωθεὶς μὲν σαρκὶ ζωοποιηθεὶς δὲ πνεύματι· [GNT] | sin-offering itself. This means a most wonderful thing: we can now become acceptable to God. We no longer have to stand before God guilty of sin, for Jesus Christ has died for our sin. If we trust His death to cover us, then sin and its guilt have been removed from us. *In Christ* we stand acceptable to God. |
| **#1567**<br>**For You**<br><br>For you–KJV<br>For you–NASB<br>For you–NIV<br>For you–NKJV<br>For you–NLT<br><br>**POSB REFERENCE**<br>(1 Cor.11:23-26; esp. v.24)<br>Note 3, point 1b | ὑπὲρ ὑμῶν = huper humōn<br>Pronunciation: [hoop-er' who-mown]<br>Parsing *huper* (part of speech): preposition<br>    Case—genitive<br>    Stem or root—from ὑπέρ<br>Parsing *humōn* (part of speech): noun<br>    Type—pronoun<br>    Case—genitive<br>    Person—2nd person<br>    Number—plural<br>    Stem or root—from σύ<br>Concordance References:<br>⇒ Strong's #5228 huper + 4771 su<br>⇒ NIV #5642 huper [for] + 5148 su [you]<br>⇒ NASB #5228 huper + *4771 su* (a word not included in Concordance).<br><br>**1 Cor. 11:24**<br>And when he had given thanks, he brake it, and said, Take, eat: this is my body, which is broken **for you**: this do in remembrance of me. [KJV]<br><br>And when He had given thanks, He broke it, and said, "This is My body, which is **for you**; do this in remembrance of Me." [NASB]<br><br>And when he had given thanks, he broke it and said, "This is my body, which is **for you**; do this in remembrance of me." [NIV]<br><br>And when He had given thanks, He broke it and said, "Take, eat; this is My body which is broken **for you**; do this in remembrance of Me." [NKJV]<br><br>And when he had given thanks, he broke it and said, "This is my body, which is given **for you**. Do this in remembrance of me." [NLT]<br><br>καὶ εὐχαριστήσας ἔκλασε, καὶ εἶπε, Λάβετε, φάγετε, τοῦτό μού ἐστι τὸ σῶμα τὸ **ὑπὲρ ὑμῶν** κλώμενον· τοῦτο ποιεῖτε εἰς τὴν ἐμὴν ἀνάμνησιν. [GNS]<br><br>καὶ εὐχαριστήσας ἔκλασεν καὶ εἶπεν, Τοῦτό μού ἐστιν τὸ σῶμα τὸ **ὑπὲρ ὑμῶν**· τοῦτο ποιεῖτε εἰς τὴν ἐμὴν ἀνάμνησιν. [GNT] | For you; on your behalf; in your stead; in your place.<br><br>**Practical Application**<br>The words "for you" (*huper humōn*) points to the substitutionary nature of Jesus' death. He died for us, as our substitute. |
| **#1568**<br>**Forbearance**<br><br>Forbearance–KJV<br>Forbearance–NASB<br>Tolerance–NIV<br>Forbearance–NKJV<br>Tolerant–NLT<br><br>**POSB REFERENCE**<br>(Romans 2:2-5; esp. v.4)<br>Note 2, point 2 | ἀνοχῆς = anochēs<br>Pronunciation: [an-okh-ays']<br>Parsing (part of speech): noun<br>    Case—genitive<br>    Gender—feminine<br>    Number—singular<br>    Stem or root—from ἀνοχή, ῆς<br>Concordance References:<br>⇒ Strong's #463 anochē<br>⇒ NIV #496 anochē<br>⇒ NASB #463 anochē<br><br>**Romans 2:4**<br>Or despisest thou the riches of his goodness and **forbearance** and longsuffering; not knowing that the goodness of God leadeth thee to repentance? [KJV]<br><br>Or do you think lightly of the riches of His kindness and **forbearance** and patience, not knowing that the kindness of God leads you to repentance? [NASB]<br><br>Or do you show contempt for the riches of his kindness, **tolerance** and patience, not realizing that God's kindness leads you toward repentance? [NIV]<br><br>Or do you despise the riches of His goodness, **for-** | Forbearance, tolerance...<br>⇒ of God's forbearance (*anochēs*): His refraining, holding back, abstaining and controlling His justice.<br>⇒ of God's long-suffering: His suffering a long time, being patient and slow in judging sin.<br><br>**Practical Application**<br>God, of course, is all this and much more. What the moralist fails to see is that God's goodness...<br>• is not a blank check for sin.<br>• does not give license to sin.<br>• does not condone sin.<br>• does not indulge sin.<br>• does not overlook sin. |

# PRACTICAL WORD STUDIES
## in the NEW TESTAMENT

| ENGLISH WORD | GREEK WORD AND VERSE | THE WORD MEANS... |
|---|---|---|
| | **bearance**, and longsuffering, not knowing that the goodness of God leads you to repentance? [NKJV]<br><br>Don't you realize how kind, **tolerant**, and patient God is with you? Or don't you care? Can't you see how kind he has been in giving you time to turn from your sin? [NLT]<br><br>ἡ τοῦ πλούτου τῆς χρηστότητος αὐτοῦ καὶ τῆς **ἀνοχῆς** καὶ τῆς μακροθυμίας καταφρονεῖς, ἀγνοῶν ὅτι τὸ χρηστὸν τοῦ Θεοῦ εἰς μετάνοιάν σε ἄγει; [GNS]<br><br>ἡ τοῦ πλούτου τῆς χρηστότητος αὐτοῦ καὶ τῆς **ἀνοχῆς** καὶ τῆς μακροθυμίας καταφρονεῖς, ἀγνοῶν ὅτι τὸ χρηστὸν τοῦ θεοῦ εἰς μετάνοιάν σε ἄγει; [GNT] | |
| **#1569**<br>**Forbearing**<br><br>**Forbearing**–KJV<br>Bearing with–NASB<br>Bear with–NIV<br>Bearing with–NKJV<br>Make allowance–NLT<br><br>**POSB REFERENCE**<br>(Col.3:13)<br>Note 7 | ἀνεχόμενοι = anechomenoi<br>Pronunciation: [an-ekh'-om-ehn-oy]<br>Parsing (part of speech): verb<br>  Mood—participle (imperative sense)<br>  Tense—present<br>  Voice—middle<br>  Case—nominative<br>  Gender—masculine<br>  Person—2nd person<br>  Number—plural<br>  Stem or root—from ἀνέχομαι<br>Concordance References:<br>  ⇒ Strong's #430 anechomai<br>  ⇒ NIV #462 anechomai<br>  ⇒ NASB #430 anechomai<br><br>**Col. 3:13**<br><br>**Forbearing** one another, and forgiving one another, if any man have a quarrel against any: even as Christ forgave you, so also do ye. [KJV]<br>**Bearing with** one another, and forgiving each other, whoever has a complaint against anyone; just as the Lord forgave you, so also should you. [NASB]<br>**Bear with** each other and forgive whatever grievances you may have against one another. Forgive as the Lord forgave you. [NIV]<br>**Bearing with** one another, and forgiving one another, if anyone has a complaint against another; even as Christ forgave you, so you also must do. [NKJV]<br>You must **make allowance** for each other's faults and forgive the person who offends you. Remember, the Lord forgave you, so you must forgive others. [NLT]<br><br>ἀνεχόμενοι ἀλλήλων, καὶ χαριζόμενοι ἑαυτοῖς ἐάν τις πρός τινα ἔχῃ μομφήν· καθὼς καὶ ὁ Χριστὸς ἐχαρίσατο ὑμῖν, οὕτω καὶ ὑμεῖς·[GNS]<br>ἀνεχόμενοι ἀλλήλων καὶ χαριζόμενοι ἑαυτοῖς ἐάν τις πρός τινα ἔχῃ μομφήν· καθὼς καὶ ὁ κύριος ἐχαρίσατο ὑμῖν, οὕτως καὶ ὑμεῖς· [GNT] | To bear with; to be patient with; to make allowance for; forbearance; to hold back; to put up with; to refrain; to endure; to control.<br><br>**Practical Application**<br>People have to put up with a great deal of things when dealing with us. There is a reason for this: everyone of us is guilty of...<br>• some weakness<br>• some unattractive behavior<br>• some wrong behavior<br>• some mistreatment<br>• some neglect<br>• some failure<br>• some bad habit<br>• some irritating behavior<br><br>There are some things about us that just turn some people off. None of us escapes this fact. In addition, everyone of us does things that irritate some people. Again, there is no escaping the fact. Every person has flaws and weaknesses that are readily apparent to anyone who looks at him carefully.<br>But note: this is not what Scripture says to do. Scripture says that the believer is to put on the clothing of forbearance. The believer is to forbear the flaws of others. He is to put up with and bear with the weaknesses of other believers. |
| **#1570**<br>**Forbid**<br><br>**Forbid**–KJV<br>Hinder–NASB<br>Hinder–NIV<br>**Forbid**–NKJV<br>Stop–NLT<br><br>**POSB REFERENCE**<br>(Mk.10:14)<br>Deeper Study #3 | κωλύετε = kōluete<br>Pronunciation: [ko-loo'-eh-teh]<br>Parsing (part of speech): verb<br>  Mood—imperative<br>  Tense—present<br>  Voice—active<br>  Person—2nd person<br>  Number—plural<br>  Stem or root—from κωλύω<br>Concordance References:<br>  ⇒ Strong's #2967 kōluō<br>  ⇒ NIV #3266 kōluō<br>  ⇒ NASB #2967 kōluō<br><br>**Mark 10:14**<br><br>But when Jesus saw it, he was much displeased, and said unto them, Suffer the little children to come unto me, and **forbid** them not: for of such is the kingdom of God. [KJV]<br>But when Jesus saw this, He was indignant and said to | To hinder, forbid, stop, prevent, obstruct, block, impede, encumber, restrain, withhold, hamper.<br><br>**Practical Application**<br>The tense is a present imperative, a continuous command: stop hindering, stop preventing the children from coming to Me. In this case His own disciples were hindering the children, continuously preventing their coming to Jesus. |

# PRACTICAL WORD STUDIES
## in the NEW TESTAMENT

| ENGLISH WORD | GREEK WORD AND VERSE | THE WORD MEANS... |
|---|---|---|
| | them, "Permit the children to come to Me; do not **hinder** them; for the kingdom of God belongs to such as these." [NASB]<br><br>When Jesus saw this, he was indignant. He said to them, "Let the little children come to me, and do not **hinder** them, for the kingdom of God belongs to such as these." [NIV]<br><br>But when Jesus saw it, He was greatly displeased and said to them, "Let the little children come to Me, and do not **forbid** them; for of such is the kingdom of God. [NKJV]<br><br>But when Jesus saw what was happening, he was very displeased with his disciples. He said to them, "Let the children come to me. Don't **stop** them! For the Kingdom of God belongs to such as these. [NLT]<br><br>ἰδὼν δὲ ὁ Ἰησοῦς ἠγανάκτησε, καὶ εἶπεν αὐτοῖς, Ἄφετε τὰ παιδία ἔρχεσθαι πρός με, καὶ μὴ **κωλύετε** αὐτά. τῶν γὰρ τοιούτων ἐστὶν ἡ βασιλεία τοῦ Θεοῦ. [GNS]<br><br>ἰδὼν δὲ ὁ Ἰησοῦς ἠγανάκτησεν καὶ εἶπεν αὐτοῖς, Ἄφετε τὰ παιδία ἔρχεσθαι πρός με, μὴ **κωλύετε** αὐτά, τῶν γὰρ τοιούτων ἐστὶν ἡ βασιλεία τοῦ θεοῦ. [GNT] | |
| **#1571**<br>**Forbidden By Our Jewish Laws**<br><br>Common or unclean–KJV<br>Unholy and unclean–NASB<br>Impure or unclean–NIV<br>Common or unclean–NKJV<br>**Forbidden by our Jewish laws–NLT**<br><br>**POSB REFERENCE**<br>(Acts 10:11-16; esp. v.14)<br>*Deeper Study* #3 | κοινὸν καὶ ἀκάθαρτον = *koinon kai akatharton*<br>Pronunciation: [koy-non' kah-ee ak-ath'-ar-ton]<br>Parsing *koinon* (part of speech):<br>adjective pronoun<br>    Case—accusative<br>    Gender—neuter<br>    Number—singular<br>    Stem or root—from κοινός, ή, όν<br>Parsing *akatharton* (part of speech): pronominal adjective<br>    Case—accusative<br>    Gender—neuter<br>    Number—singular<br>    Stem or root—from ἀκάθαρτος, ον<br>Concordance References:<br>  ⇒ Strong's #2839 koinos + 2532 kai + 169 akathartos<br>  ⇒ NIV #3123 koinos [impure] + 2779 kai [or] + 176 akathartos [unclean]<br>  ⇒ NASB #2839 koinos + 2532 kai + 169 akathartos<br><br>**Acts 10:14**<br>But Peter said, Not so, Lord; for I have never eaten any thing that is **common or unclean**. [KJV]<br><br>But Peter said, "By no means, Lord, for I have never eaten anything **unholy and unclean**." [NASB]<br><br>"Surely not, Lord!" Peter replied. "I have never eaten anything **impure or unclean**." [NIV]<br><br>But Peter said, "Not so, Lord! For I have never eaten anything **common or unclean**." [NKJV]<br><br>"Never, Lord," Peter declared. "I have never in all my life eaten anything **forbidden by our Jewish laws**." [NLT]<br><br>ὁ δὲ Πέτρος εἶπε, Μηδαμῶς Κύριε· ὅτι οὐδέποτε ἔφαγον πᾶν **κοινὸν** ἢ **ἀκάθαρτον**. [GNS]<br><br>ὁ δὲ Πέτρος εἶπεν, Μηδαμῶς, κύριε, ὅτι οὐδέποτε ἔφαγον πᾶν **κοινὸν καὶ ἀκάθαρτον**. [GNT] | Impure or unclean; common or unclean; unholy and unclean.<br><br>**Practical Application**<br>The words "forbidden by Jewish laws" (*koinon kai akatharton*) refer to being religiously or ceremonially unclean. The unclean animals were unhallowed, profaned. The Jews felt that eating them would not please God. |
| **#1572**<br>**Force–Forces**<br><br>Compel–KJV<br>**Force–NASB**<br>**Forces–NIV**<br>Compels–NKJV<br>Demands–NLT | ἀγγαρεύσει = *aggareusei*<br>Pronunciation: [ang-ar-yew'-see]<br>Parsing (part of speech): verb<br>    Mood—indicative<br>    Tense—future<br>    Voice—active<br>    Person—3rd person<br>    Number—singular<br>    Stem or root—from ἀγγαρεύω<br>Concordance References:<br>  ⇒ Strong's #29 aggareuo<br>  ⇒ NIV #30 angareuo<br>  ⇒ NASB #29 aggareuo | To force, compel, demand, press into service under the threat of punishment.<br><br>**Practical Application**<br>Ordinary citizens could be drafted for any task that the person in authority deemed necessary. Christ is saying that if a believer is forced to go a mile, he should go twice as far. Again, rights—even the rights of liberty—are not the primary concern of the believer. The believer's primary concern is people and their burdens— |

# PRACTICAL WORD STUDIES
## in the NEW TESTAMENT

| ENGLISH WORD | GREEK WORD AND VERSE | THE WORD MEANS... |
|---|---|---|
| **POSB REFERENCE** (Mt.5:39-41, esp.v.41) Note 3, point 3 | **Matthew 5:41**<br>And whosoever shall **compel** thee to go a mile, go with him twain. [KJV]<br>"And whoever shall **force** you to go one mile, go with him two. [NASB]<br>If someone **forces** you to go one mile, go with him two miles. [NIV]<br>And whoever **compels** you to go one mile, go with him two. [NKJV]<br>If a soldier **demands** that you carry his gear for a mile, carry it two miles. [NLT]<br>καὶ ὅστις σε **ἀγγαρεύσει** μίλιον ἕν, ὕπαγε μετ'αὐτοῦ δύο. [GNS]<br>καὶ ὅστις σε **ἀγγαρεύσει** μίλιον ἕν, ὕπαγε μετ' αὐτοῦ δύο. [GNT] | reaching and relieving their burdens in obedience to God.<br>Going a second mile is difficult. It means a person does not become bitter and resentful, grumbling and griping, complaining and criticizing, self-pitying and begrudging. It means a person forgives and serves and offers more service. He sets his mind and heart on reaching out to the offender by helping more and more. Such action will more likely reach the offender for the Kingdom of Heaven. It will certainly help bring the Kingdom of Heaven closer to this earth (see POSB *Deeper Study* #3—Matthew 19:23-24). |
| **#1573 Foreigner**<br><br>Stranger–KJV<br>**Foreigner–NASB**<br>**Foreigner–NIV**<br>**Foreigner–NKJV**<br>**Foreigner–NLT**<br><br>**POSB REFERENCE** (Lk.17:15-19; esp. v.18) Note 3, point 4 | ἀλλογενής = *allogenēs*<br>Pronunciation: [al-log-en-ace']<br>Parsing (part of speech): pronominal adjective<br>    Case—nominative<br>    Gender—masculine<br>    Number—singular<br>    Stem or root—from ἀλλογενής, οῦς<br>Concordance References:<br>⇒ Strong's #241 allogenēs<br>⇒ NIV #254 allogenēs<br>⇒ NASB #241 allogenēs<br><br>**Luke 17:18**<br>There are not found that returned to give glory to God, save this **stranger**. [KJV]<br>"Was no one found who turned back to give glory to od, except this **foreigner**?" [NASB]<br>Was no one found to return and give praise to God except this **foreigner**? [NIV]<br>Were there not any found who returned to give glory to God except this **foreigner**?" [NKJV]<br>Does only this **foreigner** return to give glory to God?" [NLT]<br>οὐχ εὑρέθησαν ὑποστρέψαντες δοῦναι δόξαν τῷ Θεῷ, εἰ μὴ ὁ **ἀλλογενής** οὗτος; [GNS]<br>οὐχ εὑρέθησαν ὑποστρέψαντες δοῦναι δόξαν τῷ θεῷ εἰ μὴ ὁ **ἀλλογενής** οὗτος; [GNT] | A person who was a foreigner or stranger, a person from another nation.<br><br>**Practical Application**<br>The most rejected was the most thankful. In the context of this Scripture, it means that he was a "foreigner to the covenants of the promise, without hope and without God in the world." (Ephes. 2:12) [NIV]. |
| **#1574 Foreigners**<br><br>Strangers–KJV<br>Strangers–NASB<br>**Foreigners–NIV**<br>Strangers–NKJV<br>Strangers–NLT<br><br>**POSB REFERENCE** (Eph.2:19) Note 1, point 1 | ξένοι = *xenoi*<br>Pronunciation: [xen'-oy]<br>Parsing (part of speech): adjective<br>    Case—nominative<br>    Gender—masculine<br>    Number—plural<br>    Stem or root—from ξένος, η, ον<br>Concordance References:<br>⇒ Strong's #3581 xenos<br>⇒ NIV #3828 xenos<br>⇒ NASB #3581 xenos<br><br>**Ephes. 2:19**<br>Now therefore ye are no more **strangers** and foreigners, but fellowcitizens with the saints, and of the household of God; [KJV]<br>So then you are no longer **strangers** and aliens, but you are fellow citizens with the saints, and are of God's household, [NASB]<br>Consequently, you are no longer **foreigners** and aliens, but fellow citizens with God's people and members of God's household, [NIV]<br>Now, therefore, you are no longer **strangers** and foreigners, but fellow citizens with the saints and members of the household of God, [NKJV]<br>So now you Gentiles are no longer **strangers** and foreigners. You are citizens along with all of God's holy people. You are members of God's family. [NLT] | Foreigners; strangers; an outsider; an alien; an unknown person; a person who does not belong.<br><br>**Practical Application**<br>There was a time when we...<br>• were outside God and His kingdom.<br>• were unknown to God and His kingdom.<br>• did not belong to God and His kingdom.<br>• were sojourners, living outside God and outside His kingdom.<br>• were alien to God and to His kingdom.<br>• were migrants, not belonging to God nor to His kingdom.<br>• were exiles to God and to His kingdom.<br><br>There was a time when we were as strangers and foreigners to God, when we were not citizens of God's kingdom. We had no relationship and no fellowship with God and no home and no rights to citizenship in His kingdom.<br>But note the glorious news: we are no longer strangers and foreigners to God. Jesus Christ has brought us to God (see POSB outline—Ephes. 2:13-18 and POSB notes—Ephes. 2:13-18). We are now *fellow citizens* with all of God's people. We now have a home and all the rights of citizenship in God's kingdom. |

# PRACTICAL WORD STUDIES
## in the NEW TESTAMENT

| ENGLISH WORD | GREEK WORD AND VERSE | THE WORD MEANS... |
|---|---|---|
| | ἄρα οὖν οὐκέτι ἐστὲ ξένοι καὶ πάροικοι, ἀλλὰ συμπολῖται τῶν ἁγίων καὶ οἰκεῖοι τοῦ Θεοῦ, [GNS]<br>ἄρα οὖν οὐκέτι ἐστὲ ξένοι καὶ πάροικοι ἀλλὰ ἐστὲ συμπολῖται τῶν ἁγίων καὶ οἰκεῖοι τοῦ Θεοῦ, [GNT] | |
| #1575<br>**Foreigners**<br><br>**Foreigners**–KJV<br>Aliens–NASB<br>Aliens–NIV<br>**Foreigners**–NKJV<br>**Foreigners**–NLT<br><br>**POSB<br>REFERENCE**<br>(Eph.2:19)<br>Note 1<br><br>**See also POSB REF:**<br>(1 Pt.2:11)<br>Note 1 | πάροικοι = paroikoi<br>Pronunciation: [par'-oy-koy]<br>Parsing (part of speech): adjective<br>    Case—nominative<br>    Gender—masculine<br>    Number—plural<br>    Stem or root—from πάροικος, ου<br>Concordance References:<br>  ⇒ Strong's #3941 paroikos<br>  ⇒ NIV #4230 paroikos<br>  ⇒ NASB #3941 paroikos<br><br>**Ephes. 2:19**<br>Now therefore ye are no more strangers and **foreigners**, but fellowcitizens with the saints, and of the household of God; [KJV]<br>So then you are no longer strangers and **aliens**, but you are fellow citizens with the saints, and are of God's household, [NASB]<br>Consequently, you are no longer foreigners and **aliens**, but fellow citizens with God's people and members of God's household, [NIV]<br>Now, therefore, you are no longer strangers and **foreigners**, but fellow citizens with the saints and members of the household of God, [NKJV]<br>So now you Gentiles are no longer strangers and **foreigners**. You are citizens along with all of God's holy people. You are members of God's family. [NLT]<br>ἄρα οὖν οὐκέτι ἐστὲ ξένοι καὶ **πάροικοι**, ἀλλὰ συμπολῖται τῶν ἁγίων καὶ οἰκεῖοι τοῦ Θεοῦ, [GNS]<br>ἄρα οὖν οὐκέτι ἐστὲ ξένοι καὶ **πάροικοι** ἀλλὰ ἐστὲ συμπολῖται τῶν ἁγίων καὶ οἰκεῖοι τοῦ Θεοῦ, [GNT] | An alien; a sojourner; a migrant; a stranger; a foreigner; an exile.<br><br>**Practical Application**<br>It is the picture of an alien or foreigner who is in a country for a while, long enough to rent or lease a house, but he is not a permanent resident. He has no legal rights or status. He is a stranger, an exile or a foreigner who dwells in a strange land (B.C. Coffin. *First Peter.* "The Pulpit Commentary," Vol.22, p.72). There was a time when we...<br>• were outside God and His kingdom.<br>• were unknown to God and His kingdom.<br>• did not belong to God and His kingdom.<br>• were sojourners, living outside God and outside His kingdom.<br>• were alien to God and to His kingdom.<br>• were migrants, not belonging to God nor to His kingdom.<br>• were exiles to God and to His kingdom.<br><br>There was a time when we were as strangers and aliens or foreigners to God, when we were not citizens of God's kingdom. We had no relationship and no fellowship with God and no home and no rights to citizenship in His kingdom.<br>But note the glorious news: we are no longer strangers and aliens or foreigners to God. Jesus Christ has brought us to God (see POSB outline and notes—Ephes. 2:13-18). We are now *fellow citizens* with all of God's people. We now have a home and all the rights of citizenship in God's kingdom. |
| #1576<br>**Foreigners**<br><br>Strangers–KJV<br>Aliens–NASB<br>Strangers–NIV<br>Pilgrims–NKJV<br>**Foreigners**–NLT<br><br>**POSB<br>REFERENCE**<br>(1 Pt.1:1)<br>Note 1<br><br>**See also POSB REF:**<br>(1 Pt.2:11)<br>Note 1, point 2 | παρεπιδήμοις = parepidēmois<br>Pronunciation: [par-ep-id'-ay-moys]<br>Parsing (part of speech): pronominal adjective<br>    Case—dative<br>    Gender—masculine<br>    Number—plural<br>    Stem or root—from παρεπίδημος, ου<br>Concordance References:<br>  ⇒ Strong's #3927 parepidēmos<br>  ⇒ NIV #4215 parepidēmos<br>  ⇒ NASB #3927 parepidēmos<br><br>**1 Peter 1:1**<br>Peter, an apostle of Jesus Christ, to the **strangers** scattered throughout Pontus, Galatia, Cappadocia, Asia, and Bithynia, [KJV]<br>Peter, an apostle of Jesus Christ, to those who reside as **aliens**, scattered throughout Pontus, Galatia, Cappadocia, Asia, and Bithynia, who are chosen [NASB]<br>Peter, an apostle of Jesus Christ, To God's elect, **strangers** in the world, scattered throughout Pontus, Galatia, Cappadocia, Asia and Bithynia, [NIV]<br>Peter, an apostle of Jesus Christ, To the **pilgrims** of the Dispersion in Pontus, Galatia, Cappadocia, Asia, and Bithynia, [NKJV]<br>This letter is from Peter, an apostle of Jesus Christ. I am writing to God's chosen people who are living as **foreigners** in the lands of Pontus, Galatia, Cappadocia, the province of Asia, and Bithynia. [NLT] | Strangers, aliens, pilgrims, foreigners. The word means pilgrim, sojourner, refugee, visitor, or exile.<br><br>**Practical Application**<br>The chosen are believers, believers who are only strangers scattered over the earth. This is the descriptive picture being painted in 1 Peter 1:1. Believers are only foreigners (*parepidēmois*) on earth. The idea is that of a person visiting a place for a while, but he is not a permanent resident. Believers are citizens of heaven; their home is in heaven *with God*, not on earth with the rulers of this world. The rulers and people of this earth may persecute believers, but believers are here on earth only temporarily—only as strangers, pilgrims, sojourners, and exiles. |

# PRACTICAL WORD STUDIES
## in the NEW TESTAMENT

| ENGLISH WORD | GREEK WORD AND VERSE | THE WORD MEANS... |
|---|---|---|
| | Πέτρος, ἀπόστολος Ἰησοῦ Χριστοῦ, ἐκλεκτοῖς **παρεπιδήμοις** διασπορᾶς Πόντου, Γαλατίας, Καππαδοκίας, Ἀσίας, καὶ Βιθυνίας, [GNS]<br>Πέτρος, ἀπόστολος Ἰησοῦ Χριστοῦ ἐκλεκτοῖς **παρεπιδήμοις** διασπορᾶς Πόντου, Γαλατίας, Καππαδοκίας, Ἀσίας καὶ Βιθυνίας, [GNT] | |
| **#1577**<br>**Foreigners**<br><br>Sojourning–KJV<br>Stay–NASB<br>Strangers–NIV<br>Stay–NKJV<br>**Foreigners–NLT**<br><br>**POSB REFERENCE**<br>(1 Pt.1:17)<br>Note 3 | **παροικίας** = *paroikias*<br>Pronunciation: [par-oy-kee'-ahs]<br>Parsing (part of speech): noun<br>    Case—genitive<br>    Gender—feminine<br>    Number—singular<br>    Stem or root—from παροικία, ας<br>Concordance References:<br>  ⇒ Strong's #3940 paroikia<br>  ⇒ NIV #4229 paroikia<br>  ⇒ NASB #3940 paroikia<br><br>**1 Peter 1:17**<br><br>And if ye call on the Father, who without respect of persons judgeth according to every man's work, pass the time of your **sojourning** here in fear: [KJV]<br>And if you address as Father the One who impartially judges according to each man's work, conduct yourselves in fear during the time of your **stay** upon earth; [NASB]<br>Since you call on a Father who judges each man's work impartially, live your lives as **strangers** here in reverent fear. [NIV]<br>And if you call on the Father, who without partiality judges according to each one's work, conduct yourselves throughout the time of your **stay** here in fear; [NKJV]<br>And remember that the heavenly Father to whom you pray has no favorites when he judges. He will judge or reward you according to what you do. So you must live in reverent fear of him during your time as **foreigners** here on earth. [NLT]<br>καὶ εἰ πατέρα ἐπικαλεῖσθε τὸν ἀπροσωπολήπτως κρίνοντα κατὰ τὸ ἑκάστου ἔργον, ἐν φόβῳ τὸν τῆς **παροικίας** ὑμῶν χρόνον ἀναστράφητε· [GNS]<br>Καὶ εἰ πατέρα ἐπικαλεῖσθε τὸν ἀπροσωπολήμπτως κρίνοντα κατὰ τὸ ἑκάστου ἔργον, ἐν φόβῳ τὸν τῆς **παροικίας** ὑμῶν χρόνον ἀναστράφητε, [GNT] | Strangers, foreigners, sojourning, staying. The word "foreigners" (*paroikias*) means to dwell alongside; to be passing by.<br><br>**Practical Application**<br><br>It is the picture of a pilgrim or stranger who is in a foreign country and is only dwelling there or passing by for a brief time. This is the believer here on earth. He is not a permanent resident on earth. He is only passing through the earth to a better world. This means a most wonderful thing: when a person is a stranger or pilgrim in a foreign land, his mind and heart are home. He lives in a consciousness of home. So it is with the believer: his thoughts are upon home. He lives and walks in the consciousness of being in heaven with God. This is his attitude and his thoughts as he walks through his pilgrimage upon earth. He travels through life with his mind and heart upon heaven, his permanent home. |
| **#1578**<br>**Foreknew**<br><br>Foreknow–KJV<br>Foreknew–NASB<br>Foreknew–NIV<br>Foreknew–NKJV<br>Knew...in advance–NLT<br><br>**POSB REFERENCE**<br>(Romans 8:29)<br>Note 2, point 3 | **προέγνω** = *proegnō*<br>Pronunciation: [pro-ehg-no]<br>Parsing (part of speech): verb<br>    Mood—indicative<br>    Tense—aorist<br>    Voice—active<br>    Person—3rd person<br>    Number—singular<br>    Stem or root—from προγινώσκω<br>Concordance References:<br>  ⇒ Strong's #4267 proginōskō<br>  ⇒ NIV #4589 proginōskō<br>  ⇒ NASB #4267 proginōskō<br><br>**Romans 8:29**<br><br>For whom he did **foreknow**, he also did predestinate to be conformed to the image of his Son, that he might be the firstborn among many brethren. [KJV]<br>For whom He **foreknew**, He also predestined to become conformed to the image of His Son, that He might be the first-born among many brethren; [NASB]<br>For those God **foreknew** he also predestined to be conformed to the likeness of his Son, that he might be the firstborn among many brothers. [NIV] | The foreknowledge of God; to know in advance; to be chosen before; to be already known.<br><br>**Practical Application**<br><br>The word "foreknow" or "foreknew" (*proegnō*) is used three different ways in Scripture. It means...<br>• to know something beforehand, ahead of time.<br>• to know something intimately by loving and accepting and approving it.<br>• to elect, foreordain, and predetermine something.<br><br>The present passage is interpreted differently by scholars. Note that the second and third meanings are much the same. When a person is loved and approved, selection or election is involved. The person becomes a very special or select person.<br>The point is not the pure logic of the theological or philosophical argument. This is not God's |

# PRACTICAL WORD STUDIES
## in the NEW TESTAMENT

| ENGLISH WORD | GREEK WORD AND VERSE | THE WORD MEANS... |
|---|---|---|
| | For whom He **foreknew**, He also predestined *to be* conformed to the image of His Son, that He might be the firstborn among many brethren. [NKJV]<br><br>For God **knew** his people **in advance**, and he chose them to become like his Son, so that his Son would be the firstborn, with many brothers and sisters. [NLT]<br><br>ὅτι οὓς **προέγνω**, καὶ προώρισε συμμόρφους τῆς εἰκόνος τοῦ υἱοῦ αὐτοῦ, εἰς τὸ εἶναι αὐτὸν πρωτότοκον ἐν πολλοῖς ἀδελφοῖς· [GNS]<br><br>ὅτι οὓς **προέγνω**, καὶ προώρισεν συμμόρφους τῆς εἰκόνος τοῦ υἱοῦ αὐτοῦ, εἰς τὸ εἶναι αὐτὸν πρωτότοκον ἐν πολλοῖς ἀδελφοῖς· [GNT] | purpose in this passage. God's purpose is to assure the believer: the believer is going to be conformed to the image of Christ, and nothing can stop the glorious process. God foreknew the fact, saw it even before the world was ever founded. He has always loved and approved the believer, electing and ordaining him from the very beginning. (See POSB *Deeper Study* #3, Foreknowledge—Acts 2:23 for more detailed discussion.) |
| **#1579**<br>**Foreknow**<br><br>Foreknow–KJV<br>Foreknew–NASB<br>Foreknew–NIV<br>Foreknew–NKJV<br>Knew in advance–NLT<br><br>**POSB REFERENCE**<br>(Romans 8:29)<br>Note 2, point 3 | προέγνω = *proegnō*<br>Pronunciation: [pro-ehg-no]<br>Parsing (part of speech): verb<br>    Mood—indicative<br>    Tense—aorist<br>    Voice—active<br>    Person—3rd person<br>    Number—singular<br>    Stem or root—from προγινώσκω<br>Concordance References:<br>    Strong's #4267 proginōskō<br>    NIV #4589 proginōskō<br>    NASB #4267 proginōskō<br><br>**Romans 8:29**<br>For whom he did **foreknow**, he also did predestinate to be conformed to the image of his Son, that he might be the firstborn among many brethren. [KJV]<br><br>For whom He **foreknew**, He also predestined to become conformed to the image of His Son, that He might be the first-born among many brethren; [NASB]<br><br>For those God **foreknew** he also predestined to be conformed to the likeness of his Son, that he might be the firstborn among many brothers. [NIV]<br><br>For whom He **foreknew**, He also predestined *to be* conformed to the image of His Son, that He might be the firstborn among many brethren. [NKJV]<br><br>For God **knew** his people **in advance**, and he chose them to become like his Son, so that his Son would be the firstborn, with many brothers and sisters. [NLT]<br><br>ὅτι οὓς **προέγνω**, καὶ προώρισε συμμόρφους τῆς εἰκόνος τοῦ υἱοῦ αὐτοῦ, εἰς τὸ εἶναι αὐτὸν πρωτότοκον ἐν πολλοῖς ἀδελφοῖς· [GNS]<br><br>ὅτι οὓς **προέγνω**, καὶ προώρισεν συμμόρφους τῆς εἰκόνος τοῦ υἱοῦ αὐτοῦ, εἰς τὸ εἶναι αὐτὸν πρωτότοκον ἐν πολλοῖς ἀδελφοῖς· [GNT] | The foreknowledge of God; to know in advance; to be chosen before; to be already known.<br><br>**Practical Application**<br>The word "foreknow" (*proegnō*) is used three different ways in Scripture. It means...<br>  to know something beforehand, ahead of time.<br>  to know something intimately by loving and accepting and approving it.<br>  to elect, foreordain, and predetermine something.<br><br>The present passage is interpreted differently by scholars. Note that the second and third meanings are much the same. When a person is loved and approved, selection or election is involved. The person becomes a very special or select person.<br><br>The point is not the pure logic of the theological or philosophical argument. This is not God's purpose in this passage. God's purpose is to assure the believer: the believer is going to be conformed to the image of Christ, and nothing can stop the glorious process. God foreknew the fact, saw it even before the world was ever founded. He has always loved and approved the believer, electing and ordaining him from the very beginning. (See POSB *Deeper Study* #3, Foreknowledge—Acts 2:23 for more detailed discussion.) |
| **#1580**<br>**Foreknowledge**<br><br>Foreknowledge–KJV<br>Foreknowledge–NASB<br>Foreknowledge–IV<br>Foreknowledge–NKJV<br>Chose you long ago–NLT<br><br>**POSB REFERENCE**<br>(1 Pt.1:2)<br>*Deeper Study* #1 | πρόγνωσιν = *prognōsin*<br>Pronunciation: [prog'-no-sin]<br>Parsing (part of speech): noun<br>    Case—accusative<br>    Gender—feminine<br>    Number—singular<br>    Stem or root—from πρόγνωσις, εως<br>Concordance References:<br>  ⇒ Strong's #4268 prognōsis<br>  ⇒ NIV #4590 prognōsis<br>  ⇒ NASB #4268 prognōsis<br><br>**1 Peter 1:2**<br>Elect according to the **foreknowledge** of God the Father, through sanctification of the Spirit, unto obedience and sprinkling of the blood of Jesus Christ: Grace unto you, and peace, be multiplied. [KJV]<br><br>According to the **foreknowledge** of God the Father, by the sanctifying work of the Spirit, that you may obey Jesus Christ and be sprinkled with His blood: May grace and peace be yours in fullest measure. [NASB]<br><br>Who have been chosen according to the **foreknowledge** of God the Father, through the sanctifying work of | To see before; to know beforehand; to see and know the future; to foreordain.<br><br>**Practical Application**<br>God is God; therefore He sees the future. No matter how far a person looks into the future, God sees it. God knows...<br>• exactly what *will* happen, every single event and its consequences.<br>• exactly what *could* happen (but will not), every single possibility and its consequences.<br>Therefore God knows...<br>• exactly what man *will* do, every single act and its consequences.<br>• exactly what man *could* do (but will not), every single possibility and its consequences.<br>God is God. He is eternal and omniscient (knowing all). He knows the past, the present, |

# PRACTICAL WORD STUDIES
## in the New Testament

| ENGLISH WORD | GREEK WORD AND VERSE | THE WORD MEANS... |
|---|---|---|
| | the Spirit, for obedience to Jesus Christ and sprinkling by his blood: Grace and peace be yours in abundance. [NIV]<br>Elect according to the **foreknowledge** of God the Father, in sanctification of the Spirit, for obedience and sprinkling of the blood of Jesus Chris:Grace to you and peace be multiplied. [NKJV]<br>God the Father **chose you long ago**, and the Spirit has made you holy. As a result, you have obeyed Jesus Christ and are cleansed by his blood. May you have more and more of God's special favor and wonderful peace. [NLT]<br>κατὰ **πρόγνωσιν** Θεοῦ πατρός, ἐν ἁγιασμῷ Πνεύματος, εἰς ὑπακοὴν καὶ ῥαντισμὸν αἵματος Ἰησοῦ Χριστοῦ· χάρις ὑμῖν καὶ εἰρήνη πληθυνθείη. [GNS]<br>κατὰ **πρόγνωσιν** θεοῦ πατρὸς ἐν ἁγιασμῷ πνεύματος εἰς ὑπακοὴν καὶ ῥαντισμὸν αἵματος Ἰησοῦ Χριστοῦ, χάρις ὑμῖν καὶ εἰρήνη πληθυνθείη. [GNT] | and the future. And note: He knows it all eternally, forever. God knew...<br>• every event of world history before the foundation of the world.<br>• every event of a person's life before the *foundation of the world* (cp. Ephes. 1:4). |
| **#1581**<br>**Foreknown**<br><br>Foreordained–KJV<br>**Foreknown–NASB**<br>Chosen before–NIV<br>Foreordained–NKJV<br>Chose him for this pupose long before–NLT<br><br>**POSB REFERENCE**<br>(1 Pt.1:18-20; esp. v.20)<br>Note 4, point 3b | προεγνωσμένου πρὸ = *proegnösmenou pro*<br>Pronunciation: [pro-ehg-noce'-men-oo pro]<br>Parsing *proegnösmenou* (part of speech): verb<br>    Mood—participle<br>    Tense—perfect<br>    Voice—passive<br>    Case—genitive<br>    Gender—masculine<br>    Number—singular<br>    Stem or root—from προγινώσκω<br>Concordance References:<br>⇒ Strong's #4253+4267 pro proginöskö<br>⇒ NIV #4574+4589 pro proginöskö [chosen before]<br>⇒ NASB #4253+4267 pro proginöskö<br><br>**1 Peter 1:20**<br>Who verily was **foreordained** before the foundation of the world, but was manifest in these last times for you, [KJV]<br>For He was **foreknown** before the foundation of the world, but has appeared in these last times for the sake of you [NASB]<br>He was **chosen before** the creation of the world, but was revealed in these last times for your sake. [NIV]<br>He indeed was **foreordained** before the foundation of the world, but was manifest in these last times for you Peter [NKJV]<br>God **chose him for this purpose long before** the world began, but now in these final days, he was sent to the earth for all to see. And he did this for you. [NLT]<br>προεγνωσμένου μὲν πρὸ καταβολῆς κόσμου, φανερωθέντος δὲ ἐπ᾽ ἐσχάτων τῶν χρόνων δι᾽ ὑμᾶς, [GNS]<br>προεγνωσμένου μὲν πρὸ καταβολῆς κόσμου φανερωθέντος δὲ ἐπ᾽ ἐσχάτου τῶν χρόνων δι᾽ ὑμᾶς [GNT] | Chosen before, foreordained, foreknown; already known.<br><br>**Practical Application**<br>God foreordained that Christ redeem us by His blood, foreordained it even before the foundation of the world. The word (*proegnösmenou*) is used three different ways in Scripture:<br>⇒ to know something beforehand, ahead of time.<br>⇒ to know something immediately by loving and accepting and approving it.<br>⇒ to elect, foreordain, and predetermine something.<br><br>Note that all three meanings are at work in this passage. Before the world was ever created, God knew, approved, and predestined Christ to redeem man by coming to earth and dying for man. (See POSB *Deeper Study* #1, Foreknowledge—1 Peter 1:2 for more discussion.) |
| **#1582**<br>**Foreordained**<br><br>**Foreordained–KJV**<br>Foreknown–NASB<br>Chosen before–NIV<br>**Foreordained–NKJV**<br>Chose him for this pupose long before–NLT<br><br>**POSB REFERENCE**<br>(1 Pt.1:18-20; esp. v.20)<br>Note 4, point 3b | προεγνωσμένου πρὸ = *proegnösmenou pro*<br>Pronunciation: [pro-ehg-noce'-men-oo pro]<br>Parsing *proegnösmenou* (part of speech): verb<br>    Mood—participle<br>    Tense—perfect<br>    Voice—passive<br>    Case—genitive<br>    Gender—masculine<br>    Number—singular<br>    Stem or root—from προγινώσκω<br>Concordance References:<br>⇒ Strong's #4253+4267 pro proginöskö<br>⇒ NIV #4574+4589 pro proginöskö [chosen before]<br>⇒ NASB #4253+4267 pro proginöskö<br><br>**1 Peter 1:20**<br>Who verily was **foreordained** before the foundation of the world, but was manifest in these last times for you, [KJV] | Chosen before, foreordained, foreknown; already known.<br><br>**Practical Application**<br>God foreordained that Christ redeem us by His blood, foreordained it even before the foundation of the world. The word (*proegnösmenou*) is used three different ways in Scripture:<br>⇒ to know something beforehand, ahead of time.<br>⇒ to know something immediately by loving and accepting and approving it.<br>⇒ to elect, foreordain, and predetermine something.<br><br>Note that all three meanings are at work in this passage. Before the world was ever created, |

## PRACTICAL WORD STUDIES
### in the NEW TESTAMENT

| ENGLISH WORD | GREEK WORD AND VERSE | THE WORD MEANS... |
|---|---|---|
| | For He was **foreknown** before the foundation of the world, but has appeared in these last times for the sake of you [NASB]<br>He was **chosen before** the creation of the world, but was revealed in these last times for your sake. [NIV]<br>He indeed was **foreordained** before the foundation of the world, but was manifest in these last times for you Peter [NKJV]<br>God **chose him for this purpose long before** the world began, but now in these final days, he was sent to the earth for all to see. And he did this for you. [NLT]<br>προεγνωσμένου μὲν πρὸ καταβολῆς κόσμου, φανερωθέντος δὲ ἐπ᾽ ἐσχάτων τῶν χρόνων δι᾽ ὑμᾶς, [GNS]<br>προεγνωσμένου μὲν πρὸ καταβολῆς κόσμου φανερωθέντος δὲ ἐπ᾽ ἐσχάτου τῶν χρόνων δι᾽ ὑμᾶς [GNT] | God knew, approved, and predestined Christ to redeem man by coming to earth and dying for man. (See POSB *Deeper Study* #1, Foreknowledge—1 Peter 1:2 for more discussion.) |
| **#1583**<br>**Forest**<br><br>Matter–KJV<br>**Forest–NASB**<br>**Forest–NIV**<br>**Forest–NKJV**<br>**Forest–NLT**<br><br>**POSB<br>REFERENCE**<br>(Jas. 3:5-6; esp. v.5)<br>Note 4 | ὕλην = *hulën*<br>Pronunciation: [hoo-layn']<br>Parsing (part of speech): noun<br>   Case—accusative<br>   Gender—feminine<br>   Number—singular<br>   Stem or root—from ὕλη, ης<br>Concordance References:<br> ⇒ Strong's #5208 hulë<br> ⇒ NIV #5627 hulë<br> ⇒ NASB #5208 hulë<br><br>**James 3:5**<br>Even so the tongue is a little member, and boasteth great things. Behold, how great a **matter** a little fire kindleth! [KJV]<br>So also the tongue is a small part of the body, and yet it boasts of great things. Behold, how great a **forest** is set aflame by such a small fire! [NASB]<br>Likewise the tongue is a small part of the body, but it makes great boasts. Consider what a great **forest** is set on fire by a small spark. [NIV]<br>Even so the tongue is a little member and boasts great things. See how great a **forest** a little fire kindles! [NKJV]<br>So also, the tongue is a small thing, but what enormous damage it can do. A tiny spark can set a great **forest** on fire. [NLT]<br>οὕτω καὶ ἡ γλῶσσα μικρὸν μέλος ἐστί, καὶ μεγαλαυχεῖ. ἰδού, ὀλίγον πῦρ ἡλίκην **ὕλην** ἀνάπτει. [GNS]<br>οὕτως καὶ ἡ γλῶσσα μικρὸν μέλος ἐστὶν καὶ μεγάλα αὐχεῖ. Ἰδοὺ ἡλίκον πῦρ ἡλίκην **ὕλην** ἀνάπτει· [GNT] | Forest, wood, matter. The word "forest" (*hulën*) means wood or a forest, hence the matter or raw material of a thing (Marvin Vincent. *Word Studies in the New Testament*, Vol. 1, p.747f). Therefore, it means that a great forest is set on fire by only a little spark of fire.<br><br>**Practical Application**<br>So it is with the tongue. The tongue is a fire that can set a whole forest of lives and relationships on fire, consuming and destroying all that lies in its path. It is a world of iniquity; it can cause what seems to be a world of sin and destruction when it is set ablaze. Just think about the great and terrible damage that has been done by the fire of words, rumors, talebearing, and sharp or cutting remarks. Think about the...<br>• marriages destroyed<br>• children disturbed<br>• friendships damaged<br>• reputations ruined<br>• wars fought<br>• fights aroused<br>• injuries caused<br>• bodies maimed<br>• promotions denied<br><br>The list could go on and on, but the point is well made. The tongue can be a little fire that sets ablaze and consumes a whole forest of people and relationships. |
| **#1584**<br>**Forever**<br><br>Uttermost–KJV<br>**Forever–NASB**<br>Completely–NIV<br>Uttermost–NKJV<br>Once and forever–<br>NLT<br><br>**POSB<br>REFERENCE**<br>(Heb.7:25)<br>Note 1, point 3 | εἰς τὸ παντελές = *eis to panteles*<br>Pronunciation: [ice to pan-tel-ehs]<br>Parsing *panteles* (part of speech): pronominal adjective<br>   Case—accusative<br>   Gender—neuter<br>   Number—singular<br>   Stem or root—from παντελής, ές<br>Concordance References:<br> ⇒ Strong's #1519+3588+3838 eis ho pantelës<br> ⇒ NIV #1650+3836+4117 eis ho pantelës [completely]<br> ⇒ NASB #1519+3588+3838 eis ho pantelës<br><br>**Hebrews 7:25**<br>Wherefore he is able also to save them to the **uttermost** that come unto God by him, seeing he ever liveth to make intercession for them. [KJV]<br>Hence, also, He is able to save **forever** those who draw near to God through Him, since He always lives to make intercession for them. [NASB]<br>Therefore he is able to save **completely** those who | Completely; to the uttermost; forever, once and forever.<br><br>**Practical Application**<br>Jesus Christ is able to save all persons completely. What does it mean to be saved completely, forever (*panteles*)? It means to be saved "completely, perfectly, finally and for all time and eternity" (Amplified New Testament). It means that Jesus Christ presents us to God as perfect. He presents us in His righteousness as perfected forever. Therefore in Christ—because He makes intercession for us and because He stands before God as the perfect and eternal sacrifice for our sins—we become acceptable to God. But it means much more. In outline form, when Jesus Christ saves us forever, it means...<br>• that He saves us from sin, death and condemnation (John 5:24; Romans 8:34). |

## PRACTICAL WORD STUDIES
## in the NEW TESTAMENT

| ENGLISH WORD | GREEK WORD AND VERSE | THE WORD MEANS... |
|---|---|---|
| | come to God through him, because he always lives to intercede for them. [NIV]<br>    Therefore He is also able to save to the **uttermost** those who come to God through Him, since He always lives to make intercession for them. [NKJV]<br>    Therefore he is able, **once and forever**, to save everyone who comes to God through him. He lives forever to plead with God on their behalf. [NLT]<br>    ὅθεν καὶ σώζειν **εἰς τὸ παντελὲς** δύναται τοὺς προσερχομένους δι' αὐτοῦ τῷ Θεῷ, πάντοτε ζῶν εἰς τὸ ἐντυγχάνειν ὑπὲρ αὐτῶν. [GNS]<br>    ὅθεν καὶ σώζειν **εἰς τὸ παντελὲς** δύναται τοὺς προσερχομένους δι' αὐτοῦ τῷ θεῷ, πάντοτε ζῶν εἰς τὸ ἐν τυγχάνειν ὑπὲρ αὐτῶν. [GNT] | • that He saves us to live with God eternally (John 3:16; Romans 8:39).<br>• that He saves us to be the citizens of the new heaven and earth (2 Peter 3:10-13; Rev. 21:1f).<br>• that He saves us to rule and reign over the universe right along with Him throughout all of eternity (Luke 12:42-44; Luke 22:28-29; 1 Cor. 6:2-3). |
| **#1585**<br>**Forfeit–<br>Forfeits**<br><br>Cast away–KJV<br>**Forfeits**–NASB<br>**Forfeit**–NIV<br>Lost–NKJV<br>**Forfeit**–NLT<br><br>**POSB<br>REFERENCE**<br>(Lk.9:25)<br>*Deeper Study #2* | ζημιωθείς = *zēmiōtheis*<br>Pronunciation: [dzay-mee-o'-thace]<br>Parsing (part of speech): verb<br>    Mood—participle<br>    Tense—aorist<br>    Voice—passive<br>    Case—nominative<br>    Gender—masculine<br>    Number—singular<br>    Stem or root—from ζημιόω<br>Concordance References:<br>  ⇒ Strong's #2210 zēmioō<br>  ⇒ NIV #2423 zēmioō<br>  ⇒ NASB #2210 zēmioō<br><br>**Luke 9:25**<br>    For what is a man advantaged, if he gain the whole world, and lose himself, or be **cast away**? [KJV]<br>    "For what is a man profited if he gains the whole world, and loses or **forfeits** himself? [NASB]<br>    What good is it for a man to gain the whole world, and yet lose or **forfeit** his very self? [NIV]<br>    For what profit is it to a man if he gains the whole world, and is himself destroyed or **lost**? [NKJV]<br>    And how do you benefit if you gain the whole world but lose or **forfeit** your own soul in the process? [NLT]<br>    τί γὰρ ὠφελεῖται ἄνθρωπος, κερδήσας τὸν κόσμον ὅλον, ἑαυτὸν δὲ ἀπολέσας, ἢ **ζημιωθείς**; [GNS]<br>    τί γὰρ ὠφελεῖται ἄνθρωπος κερδήσας τὸν κόσμον ὅλον ἑαυτὸν δὲ ἀπολέσας ἢ **ζημιωθείς**; [GNT] | To forfeit; to cast away; to harm; to suffer the loss of; to lose what is of greatest value; to be punished by forfeiting and losing.<br><br>**Practical Application**<br>    Note that this is a stated fact, an inevitable and sure result. The person who seeks to please himself is doomed to "lose or forfeit his very self." He tried to find himself here on earth, but he never did. He lost himself. He lost the greatest things in all the world: certainty, assurance, confidence, and satisfaction of knowing that he is eternally secure and destined to live and serve God forever. |
| **#1586**<br>**Forgive–<br>Forgiving**<br><br>Forgiving–KJV<br>**Forgiving**–NASB<br>**Forgive**–NIV<br>Forgiving–NKJV<br>**Forgive**–NLT<br><br>**POSB<br>REFERENCE**<br>(Col.3:13)<br>Note 8<br><br>See also POSB REF:<br>(Eph.4:32)<br>Note 7, point 3 | χαριζόμενοι = *charizomenoi*<br>Pronunciation: [khar-id'-zom-ehn-oy]<br>Parsing (part of speech): verb<br>    Mood—participle (imperative sense)<br>    Tense—present<br>    Voice—middle or passive deponent<br>    Case—nominative<br>    Gender—masculine<br>    Person—2nd person<br>    Number—plural<br>    Stem or root—from χαρίζομαι<br>Concordance References:<br>  ⇒ Strong's #5483 charizomai<br>  ⇒ NIV #5919 charizomai<br>  ⇒ NASB #5483 charizomai<br><br>**Col. 3:13**<br>    Forbearing one another, and **forgiving** one another, if any man have a quarrel against any: even as Christ forgave you, so also do ye. [KJV]<br>    Bearing with one another, and **forgiving** each other, whoever has a complaint against anyone; just as the Lord forgave you, so also should you. [NASB]<br>    Bear with each other and **forgive** whatever grievances you may have against one another. Forgive as the Lord forgave you. [NIV]<br>    Bearing with one another, and **forgiving** one another, | Forgiveness; granting pardon. The word means to be gracious to a person; to cancel a debt; to pardon him for some wrong done.<br><br>**Practical Application**<br>    The believer must put on the garment of *forgiveness*; he must be forgiving (*charizomenoi*). Note: a quarrel or some difference has taken place. A person has hurt us and brought pain to us. But no matter what they have done, we are to have a forgiving spirit clothing us. We are to be so clothed with the spirit of forgiveness that no difference or quarrel can shake us.<br>    Note why: because Christ has forgiven us. No matter how much wrong a person has done against us, it cannot match the wrong we have done against Christ. Yet, Christ has forgiven us. Therefore, we are to forgive those who have done wrong against us—no matter how great the wrong is. |

## PRACTICAL WORD STUDIES
## in the NEW TESTAMENT

| ENGLISH WORD | GREEK WORD AND VERSE | THE WORD MEANS... |
|---|---|---|
| | if anyone has a complaint against another; even as Christ forgave you, so you also must *do*. [NKJV]<br><br>You must make allowance for each other's faults and **forgive** the person who offends you. Remember, the Lord forgave you, so you must forgive others. [NLT]<br><br>ἀνεχόμενοι ἀλλήλων, καὶ **χαριζόμενοι** ἑαυτοῖς ἐάν τις πρός τινα ἔχῃ μομφήν· καθὼς καὶ ὁ Χριστὸς ἐχαρίσατο ὑμῖν, οὕτω καὶ ὑμεῖς· [GNS]<br><br>ἀνεχόμενοι ἀλλήλων, καὶ **χαριζόμενοι** ἑαυτοῖς ἐάν τις πρός τινα ἔχῃ μομφήν· καθὼς καὶ ὁ κύριος ἐχαρίσατο ὑμῖν, οὕτως καὶ ὑμεῖς· [GNT] | |
| #1587<br>**Forgive–**<br>**Forgiveness**<br><br>Remission–KJV<br>**Forgiveness–NASB**<br>**Forgiveness–NIV**<br>Remission–NKJV<br>**Forgive–NLT**<br><br>**POSB**<br>**REFERENCE**<br>(Mt.26:28)<br>*Deeper Study #4*<br><br>See also POSB REF:<br>(Acts 2:38)<br>*Deeper Study #2* | ἄφεσιν = aphesin<br>Pronunciation: [af'-es-in]<br>Parsing (part of speech): noun<br>   Case—accusative<br>   Gender—feminine<br>   Number—singular<br>   Stem or root—from ἄφεσις, εως<br>Concordance References:<br>  ⇒ Strong's #859 aphesis<br>  ⇒ NIV #912 aphesis<br>  ⇒ NASB #859 aphesis<br><br>**Matthew 26:28**<br>For this is my blood of the new testament, which is shed for many for the **remission** of sins. [KJV]<br><br>For this is My blood of the covenant, which is poured out for many for **forgiveness** of sins. [NASB]<br><br>This is my blood of the covenant, which is poured out for many for the **forgiveness** of sins. [NIV]<br><br>For this is My blood of the new covenant, which is shed for many for the **remission** of sins. [NKJV]<br><br>For this is my blood, which seals the covenant between God and his people. It is poured out to **forgive** the sins of many. [NLT]<br><br>τοῦτο γάρ ἐστι τὸ αἷμά μου, τὸ τῆς καινῆς διαθήκης, τὸ περὶ πολλῶν ἐκχυννόμενον εἰς **ἄφεσιν** ἁμαρτιῶν. [GNS]<br><br>τοῦτο γάρ ἐστιν τὸ αἷμά μου τῆς διαθήκης τὸ περὶ πολλῶν ἐκχυννόμενον εἰς **ἄφεσιν** ἁμαρτιῶν. [GNT] | Forgiveness, remission; to forgive; to send off; to send away. The wrong is cut out, sent off, and sent away from the wrongdoer. The sin is separated from the sinner.<br><br>**Practical Application**<br>There are four main ideas in the Biblical concept of forgiveness.<br>1. There is the idea of why forgiveness is needed. Forgiveness is needed because of wrongdoing and guilt and the penalty arising from both (cp. Romans 3:23; Romans 6:23; Romans 8:1).<br>2. There is the idea of a *once-for-all* forgiveness, a total forgiveness. A man is *once-for-all* forgiven when he receives Jesus Christ as his Savior. Belief in Jesus Christ is the only condition for being forgiven *once-for-all* (Ephes. 1:7; Romans 4:5-8).<br>3. There is the idea of forgiveness that maintains fellowship. Fellowship exists between God as Father and the believer as His child. When the child does wrong, the fellowship is disturbed and broken. The condition for restoring the fellowship is confessing and forsaking the sin (Psalm 66:18; Proverbs 28:13; 1 John 1:7).<br>4. There is the idea of a *releasing from guilt*. This is one of the differences between man's forgiving a man and God's forgiving a man. A man may forgive a person for wronging him, but he can never remove the guilt that his friend feels. And often he cannot remove the resentment he feels within his own heart. Only God can remove the guilt and assure the removal of resentment, and God does both. God forgives and erases the guilt and resentment (Psalm 51:2, 7-12; Psalm 103:12; 1 John 1:9). |
| #1588<br>**Forgiveness–**<br>**Forgiven**<br><br>Forgiveness–KJV<br>**Forgiveness–NASB**<br>**Forgiveness–NIV**<br>**Forgiveness–NKJV**<br>**Forgiven–NLT**<br><br>**POSB**<br>**REFERENCE**<br>(Eph.1:7)<br>*Deeper Study #1* | ἄφεσιν = aphesin<br>Pronunciation: [af'-es-in]<br>Parsing (part of speech): noun<br>   Case—accusative<br>   Gender—feminine<br>   Number—singular<br>   Stem or root—from ἄφεσις, εως<br>Concordance References:<br>  ⇒ Strong's #859 aphesis<br>  ⇒ NIV #912 aphesis<br>  ⇒ NASB #859 aphesis<br><br>**Ephes. 1:7**<br>In whom we have redemption through his blood, the **forgiveness** of sins, according to the riches of his grace; [KJV]<br><br>In Him we have redemption through His blood, the **forgiveness** of our trespasses, according to the riches of | Forgiveness; to send off; to send away; to release; to let go.<br><br>**Practical Application**<br>All men stand guilty of having broken the law of God, and the penalty for breaking the law is death. However, the blood of Jesus Christ brings forgiveness to men. How? Jesus Christ died for man. He took the penalty of sins and bore the punishment Himself. He was able to do this because He was the Perfect and Ideal Man; and as the Ideal Man, He could stand for and represent all men. When He died, He died as the Ideal Man, as the Representative for all men. Any person who really believes that Jesus Christ died for him is forgiven his sins. God takes his faith and counts it as the death of Jesus Christ. God sees |

## PRACTICAL WORD STUDIES
### in the NEW TESTAMENT

| ENGLISH WORD | GREEK WORD AND VERSE | THE WORD MEANS... |
|---|---|---|
| | His grace, [NASB]<br>In him we have redemption through his blood, the **forgiveness** of sins, in accordance with the riches of God's grace [NIV]<br>In Him we have redemption through His blood, the **forgiveness** of sins, according to the riches of His grace [NKJV]<br>He is so rich in kindness that he purchased our freedom through the blood of his Son, and our sins are **forgiven**. [NLT]<br>ἐν ᾧ ἔχομεν τὴν ἀπολύτρωσιν διὰ τοῦ αἵματος αὐτοῦ, τὴν **ἄφεσιν** τῶν παραπτωμάτων, κατὰ τὸ πλοῦτον τῆς χάριτος αὐτοῦ, [GNS]<br>ἐν ᾧ ἔχομεν τὴν ἀπολύτρωσιν διὰ τοῦ αἵματος αὐτοῦ, τὴν **ἄφεσιν** τῶν παραπτωμάτων, κατὰ τὸ πλοῦτος τῆς χάριτος αὐτοῦ. [GNT] | the man as being *in Jesus Christ*, as being in the death of Jesus Christ. God counts the death of Jesus Christ for the death of the man. Therefore, the guilt and penalty for breaking God's laws are completely removed. The man's sins and guilt are sent away or washed away by the blood of Jesus Christ. |
| #1589<br>**Form**<br><br>Fashion–KJV<br>**Form**–NASB<br>Present form–NIV<br>**Form**–NKJV<br>All it contains–NLT<br><br>**POSB<br>REFERENCE**<br>(1 Cor.7:29-31; esp. v.31)<br>Note 3 | σχῆμα = *schēma*<br>Pronunciation: [skhay'-mah]<br>Parsing (part of speech): noun<br>    Case—nominative<br>    Gender—neuter<br>    Number—singular<br>Stem or root—from σχῆμα, τος<br>Concordance References:<br>  ⇒ Strong's #4976 schēma<br>  ⇒ NIV #5386 schēma [present form]<br>  ⇒ NASB #4976 schēma<br><br>**1 Cor. 7:31**<br>And they that use this world, as not abusing it: for the **fashion** of this world passeth away. [KJV]<br>And those who use the world, as though they did not make full use of it; for the **form** of this world is passing away. [NASB]<br>Those who use the things of the world, as if not engrossed in them. For this world in its **present form** is passing away. [NIV]<br>And those who use this world as not misusing it. For the **form** of this world is passing away. [NKJV]<br>Those in frequent contact with the things of the world should make good use of them without becoming attached to them, for this world and **all it contains** will pass away. [NLT]<br>καὶ οἱ χρώμενοι τῷ κόσμῳ τοπύτῳ, ὡς μὴ καταχρώμενοι· παράγει γὰρ τὸ **σχῆμα** τοῦ κόσμου τούτου. [GNS]<br>καὶ οἱ χρώμενοι τὸν κόσμον ὡς μὴ καταχρώμενοι· παράγει γὰρ τὸ **σχῆμα** τοῦ κόσμου τούτου. [GNT] | Present form, fashion, likeness, appearance, nature, all it [the world] contains.<br><br>**Practical Application**<br>It is a word taken from the theater. The world is nothing more than the passing scenes of a film that will soon end. The world is destined to end in its present form or fashion. The present state of things will cease just as the scenes of a film cease. The believer must keep this in mind; he must not live for the passing fashion of this world. He must live for eternity, keeping before his mind that time is short, ever so short. |
| #1590<br>**Form**<br><br>Form–KJV<br>Form–NASB<br>Nature–NIV<br>Form–NKJV<br>Not translated–NLT<br><br>**POSB<br>REFERENCE**<br>(Philip.2:6)<br>Note 2, point 2 | μορφῇ = *morphē*<br>Pronunciation: [mor-fay']<br>Parsing (part of speech): noun<br>    Case—dative<br>    Gender—feminine<br>    Number—singular<br>Stem or root—from μορφή, ῆς<br>Concordance References:<br>  ⇒ Strong's #3444 morphē<br>  ⇒ NIV #3671 morphē<br>  ⇒ NASB #3444 morphē<br><br>**Philip. 2:6**<br>Who, being in the **form** of God, thought it not robbery to be equal with God: [KJV]<br>Who, although He existed in the **form** of God, did not regard equality with God a thing to be grasped, [NASB]<br>Who, being in very **nature** God, did not consider equality with God something to be grasped, [NIV]<br>Who, being in the **form** of God, did not consider it robbery to be equal with God, [NKJV]<br>Though he was God, he did not demand and cling to his rights as God. [NLT]—NOT TRANSLATED | Nature, form, appearance, model. The word form (*morphē*) means the permanent, constant being of a person. It is the very essence of a person, that part of him that never changes. It is the unchangeable being.<br><br>**Practical Application**<br>Jesus Christ is *in the form of God*. William Barclay points out that there is another Greek word translated "form" (*schema*). In contrast, it means the fleeting, outward form of a person that is always changing. For example, a man is always changing (*schema*) in looks because of age and fashion. But his manhood (*morphē*) never changes. (*The Letters to the Philippians, Colossians, and Thessalonians*, p.44.)<br>This means a most glorious thing. Jesus is of the very essence and being and image of God. He is the divine, unchangeable God Himself. He dwells in the very perfection and essence of God; He possesses the very attributes of God Himself. |

## PRACTICAL WORD STUDIES in the NEW TESTAMENT

| ENGLISH WORD | GREEK WORD AND VERSE | THE WORD MEANS... |
|---|---|---|
| | ὃς ἐν **μορφῇ** Θεοῦ ὑπάρχων, οὐχ ἁρπαγμὸν ἡγήσατο τὸ εἶναι ἴσα Θεῷ, [GNS]<br>ὃς ἐν **μορφῇ** θεοῦ ὑπάρχων οὐχ ἁρπαγμὸν ἡγήσατο τὸ εἶναι ἴσα θεῷ, [GNT] | *Who being the brightness of his glory, and the express image of his person, and upholding all things by the word of his power, when he had by himself purged our sins, sat down on the right hand of the Majesty on high (Hebrews 1:3).*<br>*Who is the image of the invisible God, the firstborn of every creature (Col. 1:15).* |
| #1591<br>**Fornication**<br><br>**Fornication**–KJV<br>Immorality–NASB<br>Sexual immorality–NIV<br>**Fornication**–NKJV<br>Sexual immorality–NLT<br><br>**POSB REFERENCE**<br>(Gal.5:19-21; esp. v.19)<br>Note 2<br><br>See also POSB REF:<br>(Mk.7:21)<br>*Deeper Study* #5<br>(2 Cor.12:19-21; esp. v.21)<br>Note 3, point 2<br>(Col.3:5-7; esp. v.5)<br>Note 1<br>(Rev.9:20-21; esp.v.21)<br>Note 4, point 2d | πορνεία = *porneia*<br>Pronunciation: [por-ni'-ah]<br>Parsing (part of speech): noun<br>   Case—nominative<br>   Gender—feminine<br>   Number—singular<br>   Stem or root—from πορνεία, ας<br>Concordance References:<br>  ⇒ Strong's #4202 porneia<br>  ⇒ NIV #4518 porneia<br>  ⇒ NASB #4202 porneia<br><br>**Galatians 5:19**<br>Now the works of the flesh are manifest, which are these; Adultery, **fornication**, uncleanness, lasciviousness, [KJV]<br>Now the deeds of the flesh are evident, which are: **immorality**, impurity, sensuality, [NASB]<br>The acts of the sinful nature are obvious: **sexual immorality**, impurity and debauchery; [NIV]<br>Now the works of the flesh are evident, which are: adultery, **fornication**, uncleanness, lewdness, [NKJV]<br>When you follow the desires of your sinful nature, your lives will produce these evil results: **sexual immorality**, impure thoughts, eagerness for lustful pleasure, [NLT]<br>φανερὰ δέ ἐστι τὰ ἔργα τῆς σαρκός, ἅτινά ἐστι μοιχεία, **πορνεία**, ἀκαθαρσία, ἀσέλγεια, [GNS]<br>φανερὰ δέ ἐστιν τὰ ἔργα τῆς σαρκός, ἅτινά ἐστιν **πορνεία**, ἀκαθαρσία, ἀσέλγεια, [GNT] | Sexual sin; immorality; sexual immorality; sexual vice; sexual unfaithfulness; premarital sex; adultery; fornication.<br><br>**Practical Application**<br>This a broad word including all forms of immoral and sexual acts. It is pre-marital sex and adultery; it is abnormal sex, all kinds of sexual vice. |
| #1592<br>**Fornication**<br><br>**Fornication**–KJV<br>Immorality–NASB<br>Adulteries–NIV<br>**Fornication**–NKJV<br>Immorality–NLT<br><br>**POSB REFERENCE**<br>(Rev.18:2-7; esp. v.3)<br>Note 2 | πορνείας = *porneias*<br>Pronunciation: [por-ni'-ahs]<br>Parsing (part of speech): noun<br>   Case—genitive<br>   Gender—feminine<br>   Number—singular<br>   Stem or root—from πορνεία, ας<br>Concordance References:<br>  ⇒ Strong's #4202 porneia<br>  ⇒ NIV #4518 porneia<br>  ⇒ NASB #4202 porneia<br><br>**Rev. 18:3**<br>For all nations have drunk of the wine of the wrath of her **fornication**, and the kings of the earth have committed fornication with her, and the merchants of the earth are waxed rich through the abundance of her delicacies. [KJV]<br>"For all the nations have drunk of the wine of the passion of her **immorality**, and the kings of the earth have committed acts of immorality with her, and the merchants of the earth have become rich by the wealth of her sensuality." [NASB]<br>For all the nations have drunk the maddening wine of her **adulteries**. The kings of the earth committed adultery with her, and the merchants of the earth grew rich from her excessive luxuries." [NIV]<br>For all the nations have drunk of the wine of the wrath of her **fornication**, the kings of the earth have committed fornication with her, and the merchants of the earth have become rich through the abundance of her luxury." [NKJV] | Adulteries; immorality; sexual sin; spiritual fornication, the rejection of God and the turning to other gods.<br><br>**Practical Application**<br>The world of the end time will be days of secularism, humanism, and materialism. Man will worship himself and his secular society. He will focus his life around...<br>• technology<br>• pleasures<br>• science<br>• recreation<br>• education<br>• comforts<br><br>Babylon, the capital of the world, will take the lead in the secular society. The city will have economic wealth that will literally intoxicate the world. The businessmen and merchants of the world will grow rich because of Babylon's wealth. Its wealth will be so vast that it will be able to control nations and leaders and businessmen all over the world.<br>The point is this: the capital city will use its influence for evil, for secularism and power. The city will manipulate the nations and leaders of the world to follow its own evil purposes. Those evil purposes will be a secular society, a worship |

# PRACTICAL WORD STUDIES
## in the NEW TESTAMENT

| ENGLISH WORD | GREEK WORD AND VERSE | THE WORD MEANS... |
|---|---|---|
| | For all the nations have drunk the wine of her passionate **immorality**. The rulers of the world have committed adultery with her, and merchants throughout the world have grown rich as a result of her luxurious living." [NLT]<br><br>ὅτι ἐκ τοῦ οἴνου τοῦ θυμοῦ τῆς **πορνείας** αὐτῆς πέπωκε πάντα τὰ ἔθνη, καὶ οἱ βασιλεῖς τῆς γῆς μετ' αὐτῆς ἐπόρνευσαν, καὶ οἱ ἔμποροι τῆς γῆς ἐκ τῆς δυνάμεως τοῦ στρήνους αὐτῆς ἐπλούτησαν. [GNS]<br><br>ὅτι ἐκ τοῦ οἴνου τοῦ θυμοῦ τῆς **πορνείας** αὐτῆς πέπωκαν πάντα τὰ ἔθνη καὶ οἱ βασιλεῖς τῆς γῆς μετ' αὐτῆς ἐπόρνευσαν καὶ οἱ ἔμποροι τῆς γῆς ἐκ τῆς δυνάμεως τοῦ στρήνους αὐτῆς ἐπλούτησαν. [GNT] | of the state and its leader as the answer to the utopian society, that is, to meeting the needs of the people. The city will lead the nations to exterminate the Jews, Christian believers, and the faithful of all other religions who refuse to give their first loyalty to the state. Babylon will be able to seduce the nations and leaders to follow in this evil plot because of its wealth. (See POSB pt.6—Rev. 13:4-8 for more discussion.) |
| **#1593**<br>**Fornication**<br><br>Fornication–KJV<br>Not translated–NASB<br>Not translated–NIV<br>Sexual immorality–NKJV<br>Not translated–NLT<br><br>**POSB REFERENCE**<br>(Romans 1:29)<br>*Deeper Study #2* | πορνεία = *porneiai*<br>Pronunciation: [por-ni'-ah]<br>(Special Note: KJV & NKJV term only)<br>Parsing (part of speech): noun<br>    Case—dative<br>    Gender—feminine<br>    Number—singular<br>    Stem or root—from πονηρία, ας<br>Concordance References:<br>⇒ Strong's #4202 porneiai<br>⇒ NIV #Not Translated<br>⇒ NASB #Not Translated<br><br>**Romans 1:29**<br>Being filled with all unrighteousness, **fornication**, wickedness, covetousness, maliciousness; full of envy, murder, debate, deceit, malignity; whisperers, [KJV]<br>Being filled with all unrighteousness, wickedness, greed, evil; full of envy, murder, strife, deceit, malice; they are gossips, [NASB]–NOT TRANSLATED<br>They have become filled with every kind of wickedness, evil, greed and depravity. They are full of envy, murder, strife, deceit and malice. They are gossips, [NIV]–NOT TRANSLATED<br>Being filled with all unrighteousness, **sexual immorality**, wickedness, covetousness, maliciousness; full of envy, murder, strife, deceit, evil-mindedness; *they are* whisperers, [NKJV]<br>Their lives became full of every kind of wickedness, sin, greed, hate, envy, murder, fighting, deception, malicious behavior, and gossip. [NLT]—NOT TRANSLATED<br><br>πεπληρωμένους πάσῃ ἀδικίᾳ **πορνείᾳ**, πονηρίᾳ πλεονεξίᾳ κακίᾳ· μεστοὺς φθόνου, φόνου, ἔριδος, δόλου, κακοηθείας·[GNS]<br><br>πεπληρωμένους πάσῃ ἀδικίᾳ πονηρίᾳ πλεονεξίᾳ κακίᾳ, μεστοὺς φθόνου φόνου ἔριδος δόλου κακοηθείας, ψιθυριστάς [GNT] | Fornication, sexual immorality, wickedness.<br><br>**Practical Application**<br>This is a broad word including all forms and kinds of immoral and sexual acts. It is pre-marital sex, adultery, and abnormal sex—all kinds of sexual vice. |
| **#1594**<br>**Fornicator**<br><br>Fornicator–KJV<br>Immoral–NASB<br>Sexually immoral–NIV<br>Fornicator–NKJV<br>Immoral–NLT<br><br>**POSB REFERENCE**<br>(Heb.12:15-17; esp. v.16)<br>Note 2, point 3<br><br>See also POSB REF:<br>(1 Cor.6:9)<br>Note 2 | πόρνος = *pornos*<br>Pronunciation: [por'-nos]<br>Parsing (part of speech): noun<br>    Case—nominative<br>    Gender—masculine<br>    Number—singular<br>    Stem or root—from πόρνος, ου<br>Concordance References:<br>⇒ Strong's #4205 pornos<br>⇒ NIV #4521 pornos<br>⇒ NASB #4205 pornos<br><br>**Hebrews 12:16**<br>Lest there be any **fornicator**, or profane person, as Esau, who for one morsel of meat sold his birthright. [KJV]<br>That there be no **immoral** or godless person like Esau, who sold his own birthright for a single meal. [NASB]<br>See that no one is **sexually immoral**, or is godless like Esau, who for a single meal sold his inheritance rights | To be sexually immoral; to be a fornicator; to be an adulterer. The word is a broad word including all forms of immoral and sexual acts. It is premarital sex and adultery; it is homosexuality and abnormal sex; it is all kinds of sexual vice, whether married or unmarried.<br><br>**Practical Application**<br>Immorality is not only committed by the act. A person is guilty of immorality when he looks in order to lust. Looking at and lusting after the opposite sex—whether in person, in magazines, in books, on beaches, or anywhere else—is committing fornication. Imagining and lusting within the mind is the very same as committing the act in the eyes of God. |

# PRACTICAL WORD STUDIES
## in the NEW TESTAMENT

| ENGLISH WORD | GREEK WORD AND VERSE | THE WORD MEANS... |
|---|---|---|
| | as the oldest son. [NIV]<br>Lest there *be* any **fornicator** or profane person like Esau, who for one morsel of food sold his birthright. [NKJV]<br>Make sure that no one is **immoral** or godless like Esau. He traded his birthright as the oldest son for a single meal. [NLT]<br>μή τις **πόρνος** η βέβηλος, ὡς 'Ησαῦ, ὃς ἀντὶ βρώσεως μιᾶς ἀπέδετο τὰ πρωτοτόκια ἀτοῦ. [GNS]<br>μή τις **πόρνος** η βέβηλος ὡς 'Ησαῦ, ὃς ἀντὶ βρώσεως μιᾶς ἀπέδετο τὰ πρωτοτόκια ἑαυτοῦ. [GNT] | |
| **#1595**<br>**Fornicators**<br><br>Fornicators–KJV<br>Immoral people–NASB<br>Sexually immoral people–NIV<br>Sexually immoral–NKJV<br>People who indulge in sexual sin–NLT<br><br>**POSB REFERENCE**<br>(1 Cor.5:9-10; esp. v.9)<br>Note 4 | πόρνοις = *pornois*<br>Pronunciation: [por'-noys]<br>Parsing (part of speech): noun<br>    Case—dative<br>    Gender—masculine<br>    Number—plural<br>    Stem or root—from πόρνος, ου<br>Concordance References:<br>  ⇒ Strong's #4205 pornos<br>  ⇒ NIV #4521 pornos<br>  ⇒ NASB #4205 pornos<br><br>**1 Cor. 5:9**<br>I wrote unto you in an epistle not to company with **fornicators**: [KJV]<br>I wrote you in my letter not to associate with **immoral people**; [NASB]<br>I have written you in my letter not to associate with **sexually immoral people**—[NIV]<br>I wrote to you in my epistle not to keep company with **sexually immoral** people. [NKJV]<br>When I wrote to you before, I told you not to associate with **people who indulge in sexual sin**. [NLT]<br>Ἔγραψα ὑμῖν ἐν τῇ ἐπιστολῇ μὴ συναναμίγνυσθαι πόρνοις· [GNS]<br>Ἔγραψα ὑμῖν ἐν τῇ ἐπιστολῇ μὴ συναναμίγνυσθαι πόρνοις, [GNT] | Sexually immoral people, fornicators, adulterers; people who indulge in sexual sin.<br><br>**Practical Application**<br>The word "*pornois*" means all kinds of immoral sexual acts. It includes adultery, premarital sex, homosexuality, and all forms of sexual deviation. Those who practice immorality are not to be part of the fellowship of the church. Believers are not to keep close fellowship with them. |
| **#1596**<br>**Forsake, To**<br><br>To forsake–KJV<br>To forsake–NASB<br>To turn away from–NIV<br>To forsake–NKJV<br>To turn their backs on–NLT<br><br>**POSB REFERENCE**<br>(Acts 21:20-26; esp. v.21)<br>Note 3, point 2 | ἀποστασίαν ἀπό = *apostasian apo*<br>Pronunciation: [ap-os-tahs-ee'-ahn hapo']<br>Parsing *apostasian* (part of speech): noun<br>    Case—accusative<br>    Gender—feminine<br>    Number—singular<br>    Stem or root—from ἀποστασία, ας<br>Parsing *apo* (part of speech): preposition<br>    Case—genitive<br>    Stem or root—from ἀπό<br>Concordance References:<br>  ⇒ Strong's #575 + 646 apo apostasia<br>  ⇒ NIV #608 + 686 apo apostasia<br>  ⇒ NASB #575 + 646 apo apostasia<br><br>**Acts 21:21**<br>And they are informed of thee, that thou teachest all the Jews which are among the Gentiles **to forsake** Moses, saying that they ought not to circumcise their children, neither to walk after the customs. [KJV]<br>And they have been told about you, that you are teaching all the Jews who are among the Gentiles **to forsake** Moses, telling them not to circumcise their children nor to walk according to the customs. [NASB]<br>They have been informed that you teach all the Jews who live among the Gentiles **to turn away from** Moses, telling them not to circumcise their children or live according to our customs. [NIV]<br>But they have been informed about you that you teach all the Jews who are among the Gentiles **to forsake** Moses, saying that they ought not to circumcise *their* children nor to walk according to the customs. [NKJV]<br>Our Jewish Christians here at Jerusalem have been | To turn away from; to forsake; to turn one's back on. It means apostasy and rebellion.<br><br>**Practical Application**<br>The word "forsake" (*apostasian*) is the word for apostasy. This is the most serious accusation possible to a Jew, apostasy from Moses and the law of circumcision. Of course, Paul never said this. He said that...<br>• a person could be circumcised and keep the customs of the law if he wished.<br>• a person, however, did not have to be circumcised or keep the law *to be saved*. The law is not what saves a person. Christ alone saves. (See POSB note, Salvation vs. Ritual—Acts 15:1-3; POSB outline—Acts 15:6-22 and POSB notes—Acts 15:6-22 for more discussion.) |

# PRACTICAL WORD STUDIES
## in the NEW TESTAMENT

| ENGLISH WORD | GREEK WORD AND VERSE | THE WORD MEANS... |
|---|---|---|
| | told that you are teaching all the Jews living in the Gentile world **to turn their backs on** the laws of Moses. They say that you teach people not to circumcise their children or follow other Jewish customs. [NLT]<br>κατηχήθησαν δὲ περὶ σοῦ, ὅτι **ἀποστασίαν** διδάσκεις **ἀπὸ** Μωσέως τοὺς κατὰ τὰ ἔθνη πάντας Ἰουδαίους, λέγων μὴ περιτέμνειν αὐτοὺς τὰ τέκνα, μηδὲ τοῖς ἔθεσι περιπατεῖν. [GNS]<br>κατηχήθησαν δὲ περὶ σοῦ ὅτι **ἀποστασίαν** διδάσκεις **ἀπὸ** Μωϋσέως τοὺς κατὰ τὰ ἔθνη πάντας Ἰουδαίους λέγων μὴ περιτέμνειν αὐτοὺς τὰ τέκνα μηδὲ τοῖς ἔθεσιν περιπατεῖν. [GNT] | |
| **#1597**<br>**Forsaken**<br><br>**Forsaken**–KJV<br>**Forsaken**–NASB<br>Abandoned–NIV<br>**Forsaken**–NKJV<br>Abandons–NLT<br><br>**POSB REFERENCE**<br>(2 Cor.4:7-9; esp. v.9)<br>Note 2, point 3 | ἐγκαταλειπόμενοι = egkataleipomenoi<br>Pronunciation: [eng-kat-al-i'-po-mehn-oy]<br>Parsing (part of speech): verb<br>    Mood—participle<br>    Tense—present<br>    Voice—passive<br>    Case—nominative<br>    Gender—masculine<br>    Person—1st person<br>    Number—plural<br>    Stem or root—from ἐγκαταλείπω<br>Concordance References:<br>⇒ Strong's #1459 egkataleipō<br>⇒ NIV #1593 egkataleipō<br>⇒ NASB #1459 egkataleipō<br><br>**2 Cor. 4:9**<br>Persecuted, but not **forsaken**; cast down, but not destroyed; [KJV]<br>Persecuted, but not **forsaken**; struck down, but not destroyed; [NASB]<br>Persecuted, but not **abandoned**; struck down, but not destroyed. [NIV]<br>Persecuted, but not **forsaken**; struck down, but not destroyed—[NKJV]<br>We are hunted down, but God never **abandons** us. We get knocked down, but we get up again and keep going. [NLT]<br>διωκόμενοι, ἀλλ' οὐκ **ἐγκαταλειπόμενοι**, καταβαλλόμενοι ἀλλ' οὐκ ἀπολλύμενοι· [GNS]<br>διωκόμενοι ἀλλ' οὐκ **ἐγκαταλειπόμενοι**, καταβαλλόμενοι ἀλλ' οὐκ ἀπολλύμενοι, [GNT] | To leave behind; to neglect; to desert; to give up; to utterly forsake and abandon. It is a strong word indicating a permanent state.<br><br>**Practical Application**<br>God never forsakes, abandons, or deserts his dear servant. God never leaves him alone. The companionship of God, His presence and power, is always with His dear servant. |
| **#1598**<br>**Foul Or Abusive**<br><br>Corrupt–KJV<br>Unwholesome–NASB<br>Unwholesome–NIV<br>Corrupt–NKJV<br>**Foul or abusive**–NLT<br><br>**POSB REFERENCE**<br>(Eph.4:29)<br>Note 4 | σαπρός = sapros<br>Pronunciation: [sap-ros']<br>Parsing (part of speech): adjective<br>    Case—nominative<br>    Gender—masculine<br>    Number—singular<br>    Stem or root—from σαπρός, ά, όν<br>Concordance References:<br>⇒ Strong's #4550 sapros<br>⇒ NIV #4911 sapros<br>⇒ NASB #4550 sapros<br><br>**Ephes. 4:29**<br>Let no **corrupt** communication proceed out of your mouth, but that which is good to the use of edifying, that it may minister grace unto the hearers. [KJV]<br>Let no **unwholesome** word proceed from your mouth, but only such a word as is good for edification according to the need of the moment, that it may give grace to those who hear. [NASB]<br>Do not let any **unwholesome** talk come out of your mouths, but only what is helpful for building others up according to their needs, that it may benefit those who listen. [NIV]<br>Let no **corrupt** word proceed out of your mouth, but what is good for necessary edification, that it may impart grace to the hearers. [NKJV] | Rotten, foul, corrupt, abusive, putrid, bad, unwholesome, polluting.<br><br>**Practical Application**<br>The believer is to strip away filthy and foul talk. Corrupt talk, of course, would include cursing and unholy talk and even the worthless conversation that is so often carried on by people. The Amplified New Testament has a good description.<br><br>*Let no foul or polluting language, nor evil word, nor unwholesome or worthless talk [ever] come out of your mouth (Ephes. 4:29).* |

# PRACTICAL WORD STUDIES
## in the NEW TESTAMENT

| ENGLISH WORD | GREEK WORD AND VERSE | THE WORD MEANS... |
|---|---|---|
| | Don't use **foul or abusive** language. Let everything you say be good and helpful, so that your words will be an encouragement to those who hear them. [NLT]<br><br>πᾶς λόγος **σαπρὸς** ἐκ τοῦ στόματος ὑμῶν μὴ ἐκπορευέσθω, ἀλλ εἴ τις ἀγαθὸς πρὸς οἰκοδομὴν τῆς χρείας, ἵνα δῷ χάριν τοῖς ἀκούουσι. [GNS]<br><br>πᾶς λόγος **σαπρὸς** ἐκ τοῦ στόματος ὑμῶν μὴ ἐκπορευέσθω, ἀλλὰ εἴ τις ἀγαθὸς πρὸς οἰκοδομὴν τῆς χρείας, ἵνα δῷ χάριν τοῖς ἀκούουσιν. [GNT] | |
| **#1599**<br>**Fraud**<br><br>Mischief–KJV<br>**Fraud–NASB**<br>Trickery–NIV<br>**Fraud–NKJV**<br>Trickery–NLT<br><br>**POSB REFERENCE**<br>(Acts 13:8-11; esp. v.10)<br>Note 4, point 3 | ῥᾳδιουργίας = *hradiourgias*<br>Pronunciation: [hrad-ee-oorg-ee'-ahs]<br>Parsing (part of speech): noun<br>    Case—genitive<br>    Gender—feminine<br>    Number—singular<br>    Stem or root—from ῥᾳδιουργία, ας<br>Concordance References:<br>  ⇒ Strong's #4468 hradiourgia<br>  ⇒ NIV #4816 hradiourgia<br>  ⇒ NASB #4468 hradiourgia<br><br>**Acts 13:10**<br>And said, O full of all subtilty and all **mischief**, thou child of the devil, thou enemy of all righteousness, wilt thou not cease to pervert the right ways of the Lord? [KJV]<br><br>And said, "You who are full of all deceit and **fraud**, you son of the devil, you enemy of all righteousness, will you not cease to make crooked the straight ways of the Lord? [NASB]<br><br>"You are a child of the devil and an enemy of everything that is right! You are full of all kinds of deceit and **trickery**. Will you never stop perverting the right ways of the Lord? [NIV]<br><br>And said, "O full of all deceit and all **fraud**, *you* son of the devil, *you* enemy of all righteousness, will you not cease perverting the straight ways of the Lord? [NKJV]<br><br>"You son of the Devil, full of every sort of **trickery** and villainy, enemy of all that is good, will you never stop perverting the true ways of the Lord? [NLT]<br><br>εἶπεν, Ὦ πλήρης παντὸς δόλου καὶ πάσης **ῥᾳδιουργίας**, υἱὲ διαβόλου, ἐχθρὲ πάσης δικαιοσύνης, οὐ παύσῃ διαστρέφων τὰς ὁδοὺς Κυρίου τὰς εὐθείας; [GNS]<br><br>εἶπεν, Ὦ πλήρης παντὸς δόλου καὶ πάσης **ῥᾳδιουργίας**, υἱὲ διαβόλου, ἐχθρὲ πάσης δικαιοσύνης, οὐ παύσῃ διαστρέφων τὰς ὁδοὺς [τοῦ] κυρίου τὰς εὐθείας; [GNT] | Trickery, mischief, fraud, unscrupulousness. It means to be full of all wickedness, fraud, villainy, and sleight of hand; moving about with ease and working against good; doing all kinds and forms of evil.<br><br>**Practical Application**<br>The judgment is from the Holy Spirit, not from Paul. What Paul did was not of himself: not of his emotions, not of personal resentment. The judgment came from the Holy Spirit. God had tolerated enough of the man's sin, hostility, and destruction. His sins were great. There was...<br>• the sin of all deceit (*pantos dolou*): full of all craftiness, guile, trickery, deceit, treachery, seeking to bait and catch, to enslave in error and untruth.<br>• the sin of all fraud (*pases rhaidiourgias*).<br>• the sin of being a son of the devil: being possessed and controlled by the devil; doing and working the will and works of the devil (cp. John 8:44; 1 John 3:10).<br>• the enemy of all righteousness: opposing all that is right and honest and just; all that is pure and moral and clean.<br>• the one who "makes crooked the straight ways of the Lord": distorting, twisting, adding to and taking away from the character of God and His Word, the Holy Scriptures. (Paul is quoting Hosea 14:9. Cp. Isaiah 40:4; Isaiah 42:16; Luke 3:5.) The man was taking the "straight ways" of God and making them crooked. |
| **#1600**<br>**Free**<br><br>Redeem–KJV<br>Redeem–NASB<br>Redeem–NIV<br>Redeem–NKJV<br>**Free–NLT**<br><br>**POSB REFERENCE**<br>(Tit.2:14)<br>Note 4, point 1 | λυτρώσηται = *lutrōsētai*<br>Pronunciation: [loo-tro'-say-tah-ee]<br>Parsing (part of speech): verb<br>    Mood—subjunctive<br>    Tense—aorist<br>    Voice—middle<br>    Person—3rd person<br>    Number—singular<br>    Stem or root—from λυτρόομαι<br>Concordance References:<br>  ⇒ Strong's #3084 lutroö<br>  ⇒ NIV #3390 lutroö<br>  ⇒ NASB #3084 lutroö<br><br>**Titus 2:14**<br>Who gave himself for us, that he might **redeem** us from all iniquity, and purify unto himself a peculiar people, zealous of good works. [KJV]<br><br>Who gave Himself for us, that He might **redeem** us from every lawless deed and purify for Himself a people for His own possession, zealous for good deeds. [NASB]<br><br>Who gave himself for us to **redeem** us from all wickedness and to purify for himself a people that are his very own, eager to do what is good. [NIV]<br><br>Who gave Himself for us, that He might **redeem** us | Note the word "all." The false prophet was totally depraved, giving himself over to *all sin*. To redeem; to free; to liberate.<br><br>**Practical Application**<br>Christ died to redeem us from all iniquity. We are guilty of iniquity, that is, of what has just been covered—of ungodliness and worldly lusts, of lawlessness, of disobeying and transgressing the law of God. We are sinners—short of God's glory—and we cannot keep from sinning and being short of God's glory. We have been kidnapped, captured, and captivated by lawlessness and imperfection. Therefore, we need to be free (*lutrōsētai*), that is, set free and delivered. The ransom needs to be paid so that we can be delivered and set free. This is why Jesus Christ gave Himself for us: to redeem us. The death of Jesus Christ was our ransom. His death sets us free from sin. How? God accepts His death for our death. When we believe that Christ died for us—really believe—God accepts our belief as the death of Jesus Christ. God takes our belief and |

## PRACTICAL WORD STUDIES
## in the NEW TESTAMENT

| ENGLISH WORD | GREEK WORD AND VERSE | THE WORD MEANS... |
|---|---|---|
| | from every lawless deed and purify for Himself *His* own special people, zealous for good works. [NKJV]<br>He gave his life to **free** us from every kind of sin, to cleanse us, and to make us his very own people, totally committed to doing what is right. [NLT]<br>ὃς ἔδωκεν ἑαυτὸν ὑπὲρ ἡμῶν, ἵνα **λυτρώσηται** ἡμᾶς ἀπὸ πάσης ἀνομίας, καὶ καθαρίσῃ ἑαυτῷ λαὸν περιούσιον, ζηλωτὴν καλῶν ἔργων. [GNS]<br>ὃς ἔδωκεν ἑαυτὸν ὑπὲρ ἡμῶν ἵνα **λυτρώσηται** ἡμᾶς ἀπὸ πάσης ἀνομίας καὶ καθαρίσῃ ἑαυτῷ λαὸν περιούσιον, ζηλωτὴν καλῶν ἔργων. [GNT] | counts it as the death of Jesus Christ. This means that we have already died, that we actually died with Christ when He died. God identifies us with Christ, with His death. Therefore, we are set free from sin and its penalty. We are delivered from the penalty of sin which is death. By faith in Jesus Christ we are redeemed, that is, set free from sin and death. (See POSB note, Redemption—Ephes. 1:7 for more discussion.) |
| **#1601**<br>**Free From Accusation**<br><br>Unreproveable–KJV<br>Beyond reproach–NASB<br>**Free from accusation–NIV**<br>Above reproach–NKJV<br>Without a single fault–NLT<br><br>**POSB REFERENCE**<br>(Col.1:22)<br>Note 3, point 3 | ἀνεγκλήτους = anegklētous<br>Pronunciation: [an-eng'-klay-toos]<br>Parsing (part of speech): adjective<br>    Case—accusative<br>    Gender—masculine<br>    Number—plural<br>    Stem or root—from ἀνέγκλητος, ον<br>Concordance References:<br>⇒ Strong's #410 anegklētos<br>⇒ NIV #441 anegklētos<br>⇒ NASB #410 anegklētos<br><br>**Col. 1:22**<br>In the body of his flesh through death, to present you holy and unblameable and **unreproveable** in his sight: [KJV]<br>Yet He has now reconciled you in His fleshly body through death, in order to present you before Him holy and blameless and **beyond reproach**—[NASB]<br>But now he has reconciled you by Christ's physical body through death to present you holy in his sight, without blemish and **free from accusation**—[NIV]<br>In the body of His flesh through death, to present you holy, and blameless, and **above reproach** in His sight—[NKJV]<br>Yet now he has brought you back as his friends. He has done this through his death on the cross in his own human body. As a result, he has brought you into the very presence of God, and you are holy and blameless as you stand before him **without a single fault**. [NLT]<br>νυνὶ δὲ ἀποκατήλλαξεν ἐν τῷ σώματι τῆς σαρκὸς αὐτοῦ διὰ τοῦ θανάτου, παραστῆσαι ὑμᾶς ἁγίους καὶ ἀμώμους καὶ **ἀνεγκλήτους** κατενώπιον αὐτοῦ· [GNS]<br>νυνὶ δὲ ἀποκατήλλαξεν ἐν τῷ σώματι τῆς σαρκὸς αὐτοῦ διὰ τοῦ θανάτου παραστῆσαι ὑμᾶς ἁγίους καὶ ἀμώμους καὶ **ἀνεγκλήτους** κατενώπιον αὐτοῦ, [GNT] | To be free from accusation; to be beyond reproach; to have nothing against him; to be without a single fault, unreproveable, blameless, unchargeable.<br><br>**Practical Application**<br>Imagine standing before God holy, unblameable, and beyond reproach. Imagine how pleased God would be! How He would joy and rejoice in us—that we had honored Christ, His only Son, by trusting Him so much! As we are presented to God, what would He say? What would His first words be to us? We would be speechless, no doubt. But what a day of coronation, of glory, of greatness—standing face to face with our Father, the God of all glory, the Sovereign Majesty of the whole universe.<br>This is God's one great purpose in reconciliation: to present us perfect before Him. |
| **#1602**<br>**Free From All Blame**<br><br>Blameless–KJV<br>Blameless–NASB<br>Blameless–NIV<br>Blameless–NKJV<br>**Free from all blame–NLT**<br><br>**POSB REFERENCE**<br>(1 Cor.1:8)<br>Note 3 | ἀνεγκλήτους = anegklētous<br>Pronunciation: [an-eng'-klay-toos]<br>Parsing (part of speech): adjective<br>    Case—accusative<br>    Gender—masculine<br>    Number—plural<br>    Stem or root—from ἀνέγκλητος, ον<br>Concordance References:<br>⇒ Strong's #410 anegklētos<br>⇒ NIV #441 anegklētos<br>⇒ NASB #410 anegklētos<br><br>**1 Cor. 1:8**<br>Who shall also confirm you unto the end, that ye may be **blameless** in the day of our Lord Jesus Christ. [KJV]<br>Who shall also confirm you to the end, **blameless** in the day of our Lord Jesus Christ. [NASB]<br>He will keep you strong to the end, so that you will be **blameless** on the day of our Lord Jesus Christ. [NIV]<br>Who will also confirm you to the end, that you may be **blameless** in the day of our Lord Jesus Christ. [NKJV]<br>He will keep you strong right up to the end, and he will keep you **free from all blame** on the great day when our Lord Jesus Christ returns. [NLT] | Blameless; beyond reproach; unreprovable; without fault; guiltless; to have nothing against us; free from accusation.<br><br>**Practical Application**<br>It means that no one will be able to accuse or bring any accusation against the believer when he stands before Christ in the day of judgment. The day "when our Lord Jesus Christ returns" will bring about the judgment seat of Christ. Only those who are preserved by the blood and power of Jesus Christ will be counted blameless (1 Cor. 1:8). |

## PRACTICAL WORD STUDIES in the NEW TESTAMENT

| ENGLISH WORD | GREEK WORD AND VERSE | THE WORD MEANS... |
|---|---|---|
| | ὃς καὶ βεβαιώσει ὑμᾶς ἕως τέλους, **ἀνεγκλήτους** ἐν τῇ ἡμέρᾳ τοῦ Κυρίου ἡμῶν Ἰησοῦ Χριστοῦ. [GNS]<br>ὃς καὶ βεβαιώσει ὑμᾶς ἕως τέλους **ἀνεγκλήτους** ἐν τῇ ἡμέρᾳ τοῦ κυρίου ἡμῶν Ἰησοῦ [Χριστοῦ]. [GNT] | |
| **#1603**<br>**Free From The Love Of Money**<br><br>Without covetousness–KJV<br>**Free from the love of money**–NASB<br>**Free from the love of money**–NIV<br>Without covetousness–NKJV<br>Stay away from the love of money–NLT<br><br>**POSB REFERENCE**<br>(Heb.13:5-6; esp. v.5)<br>Note 5, point 1<br><br>See also POSB REF:<br>(1 Tim.3:2-3; esp. v.3)<br>Note 2, point 13 | ᾽Αφιλάργυρος = Aphilarguros<br>Pronunciation: [af-il-ar'-goo-ros]<br>Parsing (part of speech): adjective<br>    Case—nominative<br>    Gender—masculine<br>    Number—singular<br>    Stem or root—from ἀφιλάργυρος, ον<br>Concordance References:<br>  ⇒ Strong's #866 aphilarguros<br>  ⇒ NIV #921 aphilarguros<br>  ⇒ NASB #866 aphilarguros<br><br>**Hebrews 13:5**<br>Let your conversation be **without covetousness**; and be content with such things as ye have: for he hath said, I will never leave thee, nor forsake thee. [KJV]<br>Let your character be **free from the love of money**, being content with what you have; for He Himself has said, "I will never desert you, nor will I ever forsake you," [NASB]<br>Keep your lives **free from the love of money** and be content with what you have, because God has said, "Never will I leave you; never will I forsake you." [NIV]<br>Let *your* conduct *be* **without covetousness**; *be* content with such things as you have. For He Himself has said, *"I will never leave you nor forsake you."* [NKJV]<br>**Stay away from the love of money**; be satisfied with what you have. For God has said, "I will never fail you. I will never forsake you." [NLT]<br>**ἀφιλάργυρος** ὁ τρόπος, ἀρκούμενοι τοῖς παροῦσιν· αὐτὸς γὰρ εἴρηκεν, Οὐ μή σε ἀνῶ, οὐδ' οὐ μήσε ἐγκαταλίπω. [GNS]<br>᾽Αφιλάργυρος ὁ τρόπος, ἀρκούμενοι τοῖς παροῦσιν. αὐτὸς γὰρ εἴρηκεν, Οὐ μή σε ἀνῶ οὐδ' οὐ μή σε ἐγκαταλίπω, [GNT] | Covetousness; a love of money; avarice; greed. It means a lover of money or possessions. A person can love money, property, estates, houses, cars—anything on earth.<br><br>**Practical Application**<br>Note what it is that brings contentment:<br>⇒ living life being free from the love of money.<br>⇒ being satisfied with what one has.<br>⇒ knowing God personally: experiencing His constant companionship and care, knowing that He never leaves nor forsakes us. |
| **#1604**<br>**Freed**<br><br>Washed–KJV<br>Released–NASB<br>**Freed**–NIV<br>Washed–NKJV<br>**Freed**–NLT<br><br>**POSB REFERENCE**<br>(Rev.1:5-6; esp.v.5)<br>Note 2, point 4 | λύσαντι = lusanti<br>Pronunciation: [loo'-sahn-tee]<br>Parsing (part of speech): verb<br>    Mood—participle<br>    Tense—aorist<br>    Voice—active<br>    Case—dative<br>    Gender—masculine<br>    Number—singular<br>    Stem or root—from λύω<br>Concordance References:<br>  ⇒ Strong's #3089 luō<br>  ⇒ NIV #3395 luō<br>  ⇒ NASB #3089 luō<br><br>**Rev. 1:5**<br>And from Jesus Christ, who is the faithful witness, and the first begotten of the dead, and the prince of the kings of the earth. Unto him that loved us, and **washed** us from our sins in his own blood, [KJV]<br>And from Jesus Christ, the faithful witness, the firstborn of the dead, and the ruler of the kings of the earth. To Him who loves us, and **released** us from our sins by His blood, [NASB]<br>And from Jesus Christ, who is the faithful witness, the firstborn from the dead, and the ruler of the kings of the earth. To him who loves us and has **freed** us from our sins by his blood, [NIV]<br>And from Jesus Christ, the faithful witness, the firstborn from the dead, and the ruler over the kings of the earth. To Him who loved us and **washed** us from our sins in His own blood, [NKJV] | To be freed, washed, loosed, set free, and released from sin.<br><br>**Practical Application**<br>Jesus Christ has redeemed us. He *"loves us and has freed us from our sins by his own blood"* (Rev. 1:5). The word *love* is in the present tense in the Greek. This means that Jesus Christ *always loves* us. He loves us today just as He has loved us in the past. How did the blood of Jesus Christ set us free from sin?<br>Jesus Christ took our sins and died for them. He had lived a sinless and perfect life as a Man upon earth. Therefore, He was able to present Himself as the Ideal and Perfect Man before God. He was able to die as the Ideal and Perfect Sacrifice. He was able to take our sins—the guilt and the judgment of our sins—upon Himself to bear the punishment for them. He was the Ideal and Perfect Man; therefore, God is able to accept His death as the Ideal and Perfect Sacrifice for sin.<br>The point is this: Jesus Christ died for our sins. He actually took our sins off of us, removed them, and died for them. Therefore, we are free and loosed from sin. Sin has been removed from us. We stand before God free of sin and acceptable to Him. But remember how: by the shed blood of Jesus Christ upon the cross. It is the |

## PRACTICAL WORD STUDIES
## in the NEW TESTAMENT

| ENGLISH WORD | GREEK WORD AND VERSE | THE WORD MEANS... |
|---|---|---|
| | And from Jesus Christ, who is the faithful witness to these things, the first to rise from the dead, and the commander of all the rulers of the world. All praise to him who loves us and has **freed** us from our sins by shedding his blood for us. [NLT]<br>καὶ ἀπὸ Ἰησοῦ Χριστοῦ, ὁ μάρτυς ὁ πιστός, ὁ πρωτότοκος τῶν νεκρῶν καὶ ὁ ἄρχων τῶν βασιλέων τῆς γῆς. τῷ ἀγαπήσαντι ἡμᾶς, καὶ **λούσαντι** ἡμᾶς ἀπὸ τῶν ἁμαρτιῶν ἡμῶν ἐν τῷ αἵματι αὐτοῦ· [GNS]<br>καὶ ἀπὸ Ἰησοῦ Χριστοῦ, ὁ μάρτυς ὁ πιστός, ὁ πρωτότοκος τῶν νεκρῶν καὶ ὁ ἄρχων τῶν βασιλέων τῆς γῆς. Τῷ ἀγαπῶντι ἡμᾶς καὶ **λύσαντι** ἡμᾶς ἐκ τῶν ἁμαρτιῶν ἡμῶν ἐν τῷ αἵματι αὐτοῦ, [GNT] | shed blood of Christ upon the cross—His dying for our sins—that frees us from sin. |
| **#1605**<br>**Freed Us By Taking Away Our Sins**<br><br>Redemption–KJV<br>Redemption–NASB<br>Redemption–NIV<br>Redemption–NKJV<br>Freed us by taking away our sins–NLT<br><br>**POSB REFERENCE**<br>(Romans 3:24)<br>*Deeper Study #2* | ἀπολυτρώσεως = *apolutrōseōs*<br>Pronunciation: [ap-ol-oo'-tro-seh-os]<br>Parsing (part of speech): noun<br>  Case—genitive<br>  Gender—feminine<br>  Number—singular<br>  Stem or root—from ἀπολύτρωσις, εως<br>Concordance References:<br>  ⇒ Strong's #629 apolutrōsis<br>  ⇒ NIV #667 apolutrōsis<br>  ⇒ NASB #629 apolutrōsis<br><br>**Romans 3:24**<br>Being justified freely by his grace through the **redemption** that is in Christ Jesus: [KJV]<br>Being justified as a gift by His grace through the **redemption** which is in Christ Jesus; [NASB]<br>And are justified freely by his grace through the **redemption** that came by Christ Jesus. [NIV]<br>Being justified freely by His grace through the **redemption** that is in Christ Jesus, [NKJV]<br>Yet now God in his gracious kindness declares us not guilty. He has done this through Christ Jesus, who has **freed us by taking away our sins**. [NLT]<br>δικαιούμενοι δωρεὰν τῇ αὐτοῦ χάριτι διὰ τῆς **ἀπολυτρώσεως** τῆς ἐν Χριστῷ Ἰησοῦ· [GNS]<br>δικαιούμενοι δωρεὰν τῇ αὐτοῦ χάριτι διὰ τῆς **ἀπολυτρώσεως** τῆς ἐν Χριστῷ Ἰησοῦ· [GNT] | Redemption; to deliver by paying a price; to set free, deliver, release; to be freed by taking away sins.<br><br>**Practical Application**<br>The phrase "freed us by taking away our sins" (*apolutrōseōs*) is used three ways in the New Testament.<br>1. It means to redeem (*agorazo*): to deliver; to set free from the slave market of sin, death, and hell.<br>2. It means to redeem out of (*exagorazo*): to deliver out of the enslavement to sin, death, and hell. It means to be delivered out of and never returned.<br>3. It means to redeem (*lutroo*): to deliver by paying a price; to buy. |
| **#1606**<br>**Friends Of The People**<br><br>Benefactors–KJV<br>Benefactors–NASB<br>Benefactors–NIV<br>Benefactors–NKJV<br>Friends of the people–NLT<br><br>**POSB REFERENCE**<br>(Lk.22:25)<br>Note 2, point 2 | εὐεργέται = *euergetai*<br>Pronunciation: [yoo-erg-et'-ah-ee]<br>Parsing (part of speech): noun<br>  Case—nominative<br>  Gender—masculine<br>  Number—plural<br>  Stem or root—from εὐεργέτης, ου<br>Concordance References:<br>  ⇒ Strong's #2110 euergetēs<br>  ⇒ NIV #2309 euergetēs<br>  ⇒ NASB #2110 euergetēs<br><br>**Luke 22:25**<br>And he said unto them, The kings of the Gentiles exercise lordship over them; and they that exercise authority upon them are called **benefactors**. [KJV]<br>And He said to them, "The kings of the Gentiles lord it over them; and those who have authority over them are called '**Benefactors**.' [NASB]<br>Jesus said to them, "The kings of the Gentiles lord it over them; and those who exercise authority over them call themselves **Benefactors**. [NIV]<br>And He said to them, "The kings of the Gentiles exercise lordship over them, and those who exercise authority over them are called '**benefactors**.' [NKJV]<br>Jesus told them, "In this world the kings and great men order their people around, and yet they are called '**friends of the people**.' [NLT]<br>ὁ δὲ εἶπεν αὐτοῖς, Οἱ βασιλεῖς τῶν ἐθνῶν κυριεύουσιν αὐτῶν, καὶ οἱ ἐξουσιάζοντες αὐτῶν, | Benefactor; a friend of people; a person who gives and helps others.<br><br>**Practical Application**<br>The friends of the people want to be known and called a benefactor, recognized and honored for his help and contribution. He desires to be known as a great person, a friend of the people, a person who is generous, thoughtful, concerned, honorable. |

## PRACTICAL WORD STUDIES
## in the NEW TESTAMENT

| ENGLISH WORD | GREEK WORD AND VERSE | THE WORD MEANS... |
|---|---|---|
| | εὐεργέται καλοῦνται. [GNS]<br>ὁ δὲ εἶπεν αὐτοῖς, Οἱ βασιλεῖς τῶν ἐθνῶν κυριεύουσιν αὐτῶν καὶ οἱ ἐξουσιάζοντες αὐτῶν εὐεργέται καλοῦνται. [GNT] | |
| **#1607**<br>**Frightened**<br><br>Terrified–KJV<br>Terrified–NASB<br>**Frightened–NIV**<br>Terrified–NKJV<br>Panic–NLT<br><br>**POSB**<br>**REFERENCE**<br>(Lk.21:9-10; esp. v.9)<br>Note 3, point 2 | πτοηθῆτε = ptoëthëte<br>Pronunciation: [pto-eh'-thay-teh]<br>Parsing (part of speech): verb<br>    Mood—subjunctive OR imperative<br>    Tense—aorist<br>    Voice—passive<br>    Person—2nd person<br>    Number—plural<br>    Stem or root—from πτοέομαι<br>Concordance References:<br>  ⇒ Strong's #4422 ptoeö<br>  ⇒ NIV #4765 ptoeö<br>  ⇒ NASB #4422 ptoeö<br><br>**Luke 21:9**<br>But when ye shall hear of wars and commotions, be not **terrified**: for these things must first come to pass; but the end is not by and by. [KJV]<br>"And when you hear of wars and disturbances, do not be **terrified**; for these things must take place first, but the end does not follow immediately." [NASB]<br>When you hear of wars and revolutions, do not be **frightened**. These things must happen first, but the end will not come right away." [NIV]<br>But when you hear of wars and commotions, do not be **terrified**; for these things must come to pass first, but the end *will not come* immediately." [NKJV]<br>And when you hear of wars and insurrections, don't **panic**. Yes, these things must come, but the end won't follow immediately." [NLT]<br>ὅταν δὲ ἀκούσητε πολέμους καὶ ἀκαταστασίας, μὴ **πτοηθῆτε**· δεῖ γὰρ ταῦτα γενέσθαι πρῶτον, ἀλλ' οὐκ εὐθέως τὸ τέλος. [GNS]<br>ὅταν δὲ ἀκούσητε πολέμους καὶ ἀκαταστασίας, μὴ **πτοηθῆτε**· δεῖ γὰρ ταῦτα γενέσθαι πρῶτον, ἀλλ' οὐκ εὐθέως τὸ τέλος. [GNT] | To be terrified; to be frightened; to panic; to be scared; to be startled.<br><br>**Practical Application**<br>Believers are not to be "frightened" (*ptoëthëte*). They are not to let their hearts "be troubled" (John 14:1). World violence can trouble people; but the believer's heart and life are to be centered upon God, trusting His presence, care, and security—eternally. |
| **#1608**<br>**Frightened, Not**<br><br>Not troubled–KJV<br>**Not frightened–**<br>**NASB**<br>Not alarmed–NIV<br>Not troubled–NKJV<br>Don't panic–NLT<br><br>**POSB**<br>**REFERENCE**<br>(Mt.24:6-7; esp. v.6)<br>Note 3, point 2<br><br>**See also POSB REF:**<br>(Mk.13:7-8; esp. v.7)<br>Note 3, point 2 | μὴ θροεῖσθε = më throeisthe<br>Pronunciation: [meh-thro-eis'-the]<br>Parsing *throeisthe* (part of speech): verb<br>    Mood—imperfect<br>    Tense—present<br>    Voice—passive<br>    Person—2nd person<br>    Number—plural<br>    Stem or root—from θροέομαι<br>Concordance References:<br>  ⇒ Strong's #2360 throeo<br>  ⇒ NIV # 3590 më + 2583 throeö<br>  ⇒ NASB #2360 throeo<br><br>**Matthew 24:6**<br>And ye shall hear of wars and rumours of wars: see that ye be **not troubled**: for all these things must come to pass, but the end is not yet. [KJV]<br>"And you will be hearing of wars and rumors of wars; see that you are **not frightened**, for those things must take place, but that is not yet the end. [NASB]<br>You will hear of wars and rumors of wars, but see to it that you are **not alarmed**. Such things must happen, but the end is still to come. [NIV]<br>And you will hear of wars and rumors of wars. See that you are **not troubled**; for all these things must come to pass, but the end is not yet. [NKJV]<br>And wars will break out near and far, but **don't panic**. Yes, these things must come, but the end won't follow immediately. [NLT]<br>μελλήσετε δὲ ἀκούειν πολέμους καὶ ἀκοὰς πολέμων· | Not to be disturbed, startled, frightened, alarmed, panicked, troubled, or confused.<br><br>**Practical Application**<br>World violence can disturb and frighten. It can lead us into confusion and commotion; to cry out within our inner being. But Christ says this is not to be the case with His disciples. Our hearts are to be fixed upon God, trusting His presence, care, and security (Matthew 10:28; Luke 12:4).<br>Three things can happen to the believer in looking at world-wide trouble.<br>1. The believer can become overly affected by the news of world affairs and turmoil. Such news can become so interesting and captivating that it can dominate the believer's life. He begins to live and thrive on the news.<br>2. The believer can become overly apprehensive about the personal safety of himself and his family. He can begin to fear so much that he forgets that his security is in God, not in this world. Fear over world affairs tends to emphasize the importance of the earth over the importance of God; it tends to emphasize the worldly over the spiritual. The world, of course, is important; but what needs to be stressed is the spiritual. And it is the believer's responsibility to stress the spiritual, the |

# PRACTICAL WORD STUDIES
## in the NEW TESTAMENT

| ENGLISH WORD | GREEK WORD AND VERSE | THE WORD MEANS... |
|---|---|---|
| | ὁρᾶτε, μὴ θροεῖσθε· δεῖ γὰρ γενέσθαι· ἀλλ' οὔπω ἐστὶ τὸ τέλος. [GNS]<br>μελλήσετε δὲ ἀκούειν πολέμους καὶ ἀκοὰς πολέμων· ὁρᾶτε μὴ θροεῖσθε· δεῖ γὰρ γενέσθαι, ἀλλ' οὔπω ἐστὶν τὸ τέλος. [GNT] | security and peace of heart that is found in Christ.<br>3. The believer can become so troubled over world affairs that he neglects his spiritual duties. The believer is naturally concerned over the world, as all men should be. But he is not to allow world affairs to interfere with his witnessing for Christ. He is to be at peace and to be secure with God, and he is to demonstrate the peace and security of God, going about his daily duties as much as possible within a turbulent world. The point is, the believer is to be witnessing for Christ no matter the turbulence of the world. |
| #1609<br>**From**<br><br>From–KJV<br>Out of–NASB<br>From–NIV<br>From–NKJV<br>From–NLT<br><br>**POSB REFERENCE**<br>(Jn.6:33)<br>Note 3, point 1a<br><br>See also POSB REF:<br>(Jn.3:13)<br>Note 6, point 1 | ἐκ = ek<br>Pronunciation: [ek]<br>Parsing (part of speech): preposition<br>    Case—genitive<br>    Stem or root—from ἐκ<br>Concordance References:<br>  ⇒ Strong's #1537 ek<br>  ⇒ NIV #1666 ek<br>  ⇒ NASB #1537 ek<br><br>**John 6:33**<br>For the bread of God is he which cometh down **from** heaven, and giveth life unto the world. [KJV]<br>"For the bread of God is that which comes down **out of** heaven, and gives life to the world." [NASB]<br>For the bread of God is he who comes down **from** heaven and gives life to the world." [NIV]<br>For the bread of God is He who comes down **from** heaven and gives life to the world." [NKJV]<br>The true bread of God is the one who comes down **from** heaven and gives life to the world." [NLT]<br>ὁ γὰρ ἄρτος τοῦ Θεοῦ ἐστιν ὁ καταβαίνων ἐκ τοῦ οὐρανοῦ, καὶ ζωὴν διδοὺς τῷ κόσμῳ. [GNS]<br>ὁ γὰρ ἄρτος τοῦ θεοῦ ἐστιν ὁ καταβαίνων ἐκ τοῦ οὐρανοῦ καὶ ζωὴν διδοὺς τῷ κόσμῳ. [GNT] | From, out of.<br><br>**Practical Application**<br>Jesus came out of (*ek*) the spiritual world into the physical world, out of the heavenly dimension of being into the earthly dimension of being. Jesus came out of...<br>• the incorruptible world into the corruptible world.<br>• the glorious world into the dishonorable world.<br>• the powerful world into the weak world.<br>• the spiritual world into the natural world. (Cp. 1 Cor. 15:42-44).<br><br>He came down from (out of) heaven. No man can ascend up into heaven; no man can penetrate the spiritual world. Flesh is flesh, that is, born of the earth; therefore, it is earthly (1 Cor. 15:47). However, Jesus Christ was different from all other men. His origin was out of heaven, out of the spiritual world and dimension of being. (See POSB *Deeper Study* #1—John 3:31; POSB note—John 1:18; POSB *Deeper Study* #1—John 14:6, POSB *Deeper Study* #2—John 14:6, POSB *Deeper Study* #3—John 14:6 for discussion.) |
| #1610<br>**From Above**<br><br>From above–KJV<br>From above–NASB<br>From above–NIV<br>From above–NKJV<br>From above–NLT<br><br>**POSB REFERENCE**<br>(Jn.3:31)<br>*Deeper Study* #1 | ἄνωθεν = anöthen<br>Pronunciation: [an'-o-then]<br>Parsing (part of speech): adjective<br>    Type—adverb<br>    Stem or root—from ἄνωθεν<br>Concordance References:<br>  ⇒ Strong's #509 anöthen<br>  ⇒ NIV #540 anöthen<br>  ⇒ NASB #509 anöthen<br><br>**John 3:31**<br>He that cometh **from above** is above all: he that is of the earth is earthly, and speaketh of the earth: he that cometh from heaven is above all. [KJV]<br>"He who comes **from above** is above all, he who is of the earth is from the earth and speaks of the earth. He who comes from heaven is above all. [NASB]<br>"The one who comes **from above** is above all; the one who is from the earth belongs to the earth, and speaks as one from the earth. The one who comes from heaven is above all. [NIV]<br>He who comes **from above** is above all; he who is of the earth is earthly and speaks of the earth. He who comes from heaven is above all. [NKJV]<br>"He has come **from above** and is greater than anyone else. I am of the earth, and my understanding is limited to the things of earth, but he has come from heaven. [NLT]<br>Ὁ ἄνωθεν ἐρχόμενος ἐπάνω πάντων ἐστίν. ὁ ὢν ἐκ | From above; out of (*ek*) the spiritual world into the physical world; out of the heavenly dimension of being into the earthly dimension of being.<br><br>**Practical Application**<br>Jesus was born from above (*anöthen*) or from heaven; that is, He was born of God as well as of Mary. Therefore, Jesus is not only Man, but He is also God. He is the God-Man. Think of it this way. A man is born of the earth, from beneath: he is born of his father and his mother. Both are of this earth, of human flesh only. Therefore, a man is only a man; he is only human flesh and blood just like his mother and father.<br>However, this is not true with Jesus. Jesus is Man, but He is also God. He is Man through the flesh of His mother, and He is the eternal Son of God by the miraculous act of the Holy Spirit through Mary. God incarnated His Son in human flesh and sent Him into the world through Mary. (Cp. John 8:12-59, esp. John 8:14, 23, 42, 57-58. POSB *Deeper Study* #3—Matthew 1:16.)<br>This means something critical. The only messiah and utopia that man can find is of this world, of the physical dimension. Therefore, man's messiah and utopia fail; they waste away, |

# PRACTICAL WORD STUDIES
## in the NEW TESTAMENT

| ENGLISH WORD | GREEK WORD AND VERSE | THE WORD MEANS... |
|---|---|---|
| | τῆς γῆς, ἐκ τῆς γῆς ἐστι, καὶ ἐκ τῆς γῆς λαλεῖ· ὁ ἐκ τοῦ οὐρανοῦ ἐρχόμενος, ἐπάνω πάντων ἐστί. [GNS]<br>Ὁ **ἄνωθεν** ἐρχόμενος ἐπάνω πάντων ἐστίν· ὁ ὢν ἐκ τῆς γῆς ἐκ τῆς γῆς ἐστιν καὶ ἐκ τῆς γῆς λαλεῖ. ὁ ἐκ τοῦ οὐρανοῦ ἐρχόμενος [ἐπάνω πάντων ἐστίν·] [GNT] | deteriorate, decay, and die. But not Christ and His utopia. He is "from heaven," from the spiritual world and eternal dimension. Therefore, He and His utopia last forever. (See POSB notes, Corruption—Matthew 6:19-20; POSB *Deeper Study* #2—Matthew 8:17; POSB *Deeper Study* #1—2 Peter 1:4.) |
| **#1611**<br>**From God**<br><br>From God–KJV<br>From God–NASB<br>From God–NIV<br>From God–NKJV<br>Not translated–NLT<br><br>**POSB REFERENCE**<br>(Jn.1:6)<br>Note 1, point 2b | παρὰ θεοῦ = *para theou*<br>Pronunciation: [par-ah theh'-oo]<br>Parsing *para* (part of speech): preposition<br>    Case—genitive<br>    Stem or root—from παρά<br>Parsing *theou* (part of speech): noun<br>    Case—genitive<br>    Gender—masculine<br>    Number—singular<br>    Stem or root—from θεός, οῦ<br>Concordance References:<br>  ⇒ Strong's #3844 para + 2316 theos<br>  ⇒ NIV #4123 para [from] + 2536 theos [God]<br>  ⇒ NASB #3844 para + 2316 theos<br><br>**John 1:6**<br>There was a man sent **from God**, whose name was John. [KJV]<br>There came a man, sent **from God**, whose name was John. [NASB]<br>There came a man who was sent **from God**; his name was John. [NIV]<br>There was a man sent **from God**, whose name *was* John. [NKJV]<br>**God** sent John the Baptist [NLT]<br>ἐγένετο ἄνθρωπος ἀπεσταλμένος **παρὰ θεοῦ**, ὄνομα αὐτῷ Ἰωάννης· [GNS]<br>Ἐγένετο ἄνθρωπος ἀπεσταλμένος **παρὰ θεοῦ**, ὄνομα αὐτῷ Ἰωάννης· [GNT] | From God; from beside God; sent from God.<br><br>**Practical Application**<br>John was not only sent by God, He was sent from the very side and heart of God. He was only a man, but a man of high calling and mission, of enormous responsibility and accountability. He was a man sent by God, not by man. |
| **#1612**<br>**From Your Heart, The Heart**<br><br>From the heart–KJV<br>From the heart–NASB<br>From your heart–NIV<br>From the heart–NKJV<br>With all your heart–NLT<br><br>**POSB REFERENCE**<br>(Eph.6:5-8; esp. v.6)<br>Note 1, point 4<br><br>See also POSB REF:<br>(Col.3:22-25; esp. v.23)<br>Note 1, point 4 | ἐκ ψυχῆς = *ek psuchës*<br>Pronunciation: [ek psoo-khays']<br>Parsing *ek* (part of speech): preposition<br>    Case—genitive<br>    Stem or root—from ἐκ<br>Parsing *psuchës* (part of speech): noun<br>    Case—genitive<br>    Gender—feminine<br>    Number—singular<br>    Stem or root—from ψυχή, ῆς<br>Concordance References:<br>  ⇒ Strong's #1537 ek + 5590 psuchë<br>  ⇒ NIV #1666 ek [from] + 6034 psuchë [heart]<br>  ⇒ NASB #1537 ek + 5590 psuchë<br><br>**Ephes. 6:6**<br>Not with eyeservice, as menpleasers; but as the servants of Christ, doing the will of God **from the heart**; [KJV]<br>Not by way of eyeservice, as men-pleasers, but as slaves of Christ, doing the will of God **from the heart**. [NASB]<br>Obey them not only to win their favor when their eye is on you, but like slaves of Christ, doing the will of God **from your heart**. [NIV]<br>Not with eyeservice, as men-pleasers, but as bondservants of Christ, doing the will of God **from the heart**, [NKJV]<br>Work hard, but not just to please your masters when they are watching. As slaves of Christ, do the will of God **with all your heart**. [NLT]<br>μὴ κατ' ὀφθαλμοδουλείαν ὡς ἀνθρωπάρεσκοι, ἀλλ' ὡς δοῦλοι τοῦ Χριστοῦ, ποιοῦντες τὸ θέλημα τοῦ Θεοῦ **ἐκ ψυχῆς**, [GNS]<br>μὴ κατ' ὀφθαλμοδουλίαν ὡς ἀνθρωπάρεσκοι ἀλλ' ὡς δοῦλοι Χριστοῦ ποιοῦντες τὸ θέλημα τοῦ θεοῦ **ἐκ ψυχῆς**, [GNT] | From your heart; from the heart; with all your heart; out of the soul; with interest and energy.<br><br>**Practical Application**<br>The Christian workman is to work as the servant of Christ doing the will of God *from his heart*. It is the opposite of routineness and listlessness, of having no energy or heart for the work. The Christian workman must always remember this: even if the boss is not looking, Christ sees what kind of work he is doing. Therefore, he must work as though he is working for Christ. In fact, the very drive of his heart and life must be to work for Christ. He must work...<br>• to serve Christ<br>• to do the will of God<br>• to do both *from the heart* |

## PRACTICAL WORD STUDIES
## in the NEW TESTAMENT

| ENGLISH WORD | GREEK WORD AND VERSE | THE WORD MEANS... |
|---|---|---|
| **#1613**<br>**Frustrate**<br><br>**Frustrate**–KJV<br>Nullify–NASB<br>Set aside–NIV<br>Set aside–NKJV<br>Meaningless–NLT<br><br>**POSB**<br>**REFERENCE**<br>(Gal.2:19-21; esp. v.21)<br>Note 5 | ἀθετῶ = athetō<br>Pronunciation: [ath-eh-to]<br>Parsing (part of speech): verb<br>    Mood—indicative<br>    Tense—present<br>    Voice—active<br>    Person—1st person<br>    Number—singular<br>    Stem or root—from ἀθετέω<br>Concordance References:<br>  ⇒ Strong's #114 athetō<br>  ⇒ NIV #119 athetō<br>  ⇒ NASB #114 athetō<br><br>**Galatians 2:21**<br>I do not **frustrate** the grace of God: for if righteousness come by the law, then Christ is dead in vain. [KJV]<br>"I do not **nullify** the grace of God; for if righteousness comes through the Law, then Christ died needlessly." [NASB]<br>I do not **set aside** the grace of God, for if righteousness could be gained through the law, Christ died for nothing!" [NIV]<br>I do not **set aside** the grace of God; for if righteousness *comes* through the law, then Christ died in vain." [NKJV]<br>I am not one of those who treats the grace of God as **meaningless**. For if we could be saved by keeping the law, then there was no need for Christ to die. [NLT]<br>οὐκ **ἀθετῶ** τὴν χάριν τοῦ Θεοῦ· εἰ γὰρ διὰ νόμου δικαιοσύνη, ἄρα Χριστὸς δωρεὰν ἀπέθανεν. [GNS]<br>οὐκ **ἀθετῶ** τὴν χάριν τοῦ θεοῦ· εἰ γὰρ διὰ νόμου δικαιοσύνη, ἄρα Χριστὸς δωρεὰν ἀπέθανεν. [GNT] | To set aside, void, invalidate, ignore, make ineffective, and nullify; to frustrate; to reject; to refuse; to be meaningless.<br><br>**Practical Application**<br>If a man sets aside the grace of God and seeks righteousness by the law, then Christ died in vain. The person who preaches that a man can be good enough—that he can work enough and keep enough law—to become righteous and acceptable to God...<br>• voids and does away with the love and grace of God.<br>• makes the death of Christ empty and meaningless.<br>The only way a man can live for God is by trusting the grace and love of God, that is, by trusting the death of Jesus Christ for His righteousness. |
| **#1614**<br>**Frustration**<br><br>Vanity–KJV<br>Futility–NASB<br>**Frustration–NIV**<br>Futility–NKJV<br>Curse–NLT<br><br>**POSB**<br>**REFERENCE**<br>(Romans 8:19-22, esp. v.20)<br>Note 2, point 1 | ματαιότητι = mataiotēti<br>Pronunciation: mat-ah-yot'-ay-tee]<br>Parsing (part of speech): noun<br>    Case—dative<br>    Gender—feminine<br>    Number—singular<br>    Stem or root—from ματαιότης, ητος<br>Concordance References:<br>  ⇒ Strong's #3153 mataiotēs<br>  ⇒ NIV #3470 mataiotēs<br>  ⇒ NASB #3153 mataiotēs<br><br>**Romans 8:20**<br>For the creature was made subject to **vanity**, not willingly, but by reason of him who hath subjected the same in hope, [KJV]<br>For the creation was subjected to **futility**, not of its own will, but because of Him who subjected it, in hope [NASB]<br>For the creation was subjected to **frustration**, not by its own choice, but by the will of the one who subjected it, in hope [NIV]<br>For the creation was subjected to **futility**, not willingly, but because of Him who subjected *it* in hope; [NKJV]<br>Against its will, everything on earth was subjected to God's **curse**. [NLT]<br>τῇ γὰρ **ματαιότητι** ἡ κτίσις ὑπετάγη, οὐχ ἑκοῦσα ἀλλὰ διὰ τὸν ὑποτάξαντα, ἐφ' ἑλπίδι· [GNS]<br>τῇ γὰρ **ματαιότητι** ἡ κτίσις ὑπετάγη, οὐχ ἑκοῦσα ἀλλὰ διὰ τὸν ὑποτάξαντα, ἐφ' ἑλπίδι [GNT] | Worthlessness, futility; emptiness, frustration; cursed.<br><br>**Practical Application**<br>Creation is subject to corruption. This is clearly seen by men; and what men see is constantly confirmed by such authorities as the botanist, zoologist, geologist, and astronomer of the world. All of creation, whether mineral, plant, or animal, suffers just as men do. All creation suffers hurt, damage, loss, deterioration, erosion, death, and decay—all creation struggles for life. It is full of "frustration" (*mataiotēti*), that is, condemned to futility and frustration, unable to realize its purpose, subject to corruption. |
| **#1615**<br>**Fulfilled**<br><br>Most surely<br>  believed–KJV<br>Accomplished–NASB<br>**Fulfilled–NIV** | πεπληροφορημένων* = peplērophorēmenōn<br>Pronunciation: [pe-play-rof-or-ee-men-own]<br>Parsing (part of speech): verb<br>    Mood—participle<br>    Tense—perfect<br>    Voice—passive<br>    Case—genitive<br>    Gender—neuter | To fill; to fill up; to make full; to come to an end; to bring to completion; to finish. It means things that were fulfilled, that were accomplished, that were actually performed, or that had run their full course (cp. 2 Tim. 4:5). |

# PRACTICAL WORD STUDIES
## in the NEW TESTAMENT

| ENGLISH WORD | GREEK WORD AND VERSE | THE WORD MEANS... |
|---|---|---|
| Fulfilled–NKJV<br>Took place–NLT<br><br>**POSB<br>REFERENCE**<br>(Lk.1:1)<br>Note 1, point 2<br><br>See also POSB REF:<br>(Lk.21:24)<br>Note 5, point 1 | Number—plural<br>Stem or root—from πληροφορέω<br>Concordance References:<br>⇒ Strong's #4135 pleromoreo<br>⇒ NIV #4442 plērophoreō<br>⇒ NASB #4135 pleromoreo<br><br>**Luke 1:1**<br>Forasmuch as many have taken in hand to set forth in order a declaration of those things which are **most surely believed** among us, [KJV]<br>Inasmuch as many have undertaken to compile an account of the things **accomplished** among us, [NASB]<br>Many have undertaken to draw up an account of the things that have been **fulfilled** among us, [NIV]<br>Inasmuch as many have taken in hand to set in order a narrative of those things which have been **fulfilled** among us, [NKJV]<br>Most honorable Theophilus: Many people have written accounts about the events that **took place** among us. [NLT]<br>Ἐπειδήπερ πολλοὶ ἐπεχείρησαν ἀνατάξασθαι διήγησιν περὶ τῶν **πεπληροφορημένων** ἐν ἡμῖν πραγμάτων, [GNS]<br>Ἐπειδήπερ πολλοὶ ἐπεχείρησαν ἀνατάξασθαι διήγησιν περὶ τῶν **πεπληροφορημένων** ἐν ἡμῖν πραγμάτων, [GNT] | **Practical Application**<br>Luke is saying that the *things of Christ* were not only believed, but they were also accomplished or fulfilled among the believers of that day. The *things* (events, matters) of Christ actually took place; they were purposeful; they were destined to be accomplished and fulfilled.<br><br>The point is this: the things of Christ are a record of historical events, things that actually happened and that actually fulfilled the purpose of God. Therefore, the things are "most surely believed among us [believers]." What are the *things* accomplished and believed? Both the things of the New Testament and of the Old Testament. The whole Bible is a record of "those things" |
| #1616<br>**Fulfilled**<br><br>Fulfilled–KJV<br>Fulfilled–NASB<br>Fulfilled–NIV<br>Fulfilled–NKJV<br>Comes to an end–NLT<br><br>**POSB<br>REFERENCE**<br>(Lk.21:24)<br>Note 5, point 1<br><br>See also POSB REF:<br>(Col.2:9-10; esp. v.9)<br>Note 2, point 1 | πληρωθῶσιν = plērōthōsin<br>Pronunciation: [play-ro'-tho-sin]<br>Parsing (part of speech): verb<br>    Mood—subjunctive<br>    Tense—aorist<br>    Voice—passive<br>    Person—3rd person<br>    Number—plural<br>    Stem or root—from πληρόω<br>Concordance References:<br>⇒ Strong's #4137 plēroō<br>⇒ NIV #4444 plēroō<br>⇒ NASB #4137 plēroō<br><br>**Luke 21:24**<br>And they shall fall by the edge of the sword, and shall be led away captive into all nations: and Jerusalem shall be trodden down of the Gentiles, until the times of the Gentiles be **fulfilled**. [KJV]<br>And they will fall by the edge of the sword, and will be led captive into all the nations; and Jerusalem will be trampled under foot by the Gentiles until the times of the Gentiles be **fulfilled**. [NASB]<br>They will fall by the sword and will be taken as prisoners to all the nations. Jerusalem will be trampled on by the Gentiles until the times of the Gentiles are **fulfilled**. [NIV]<br>And they will fall by the edge of the sword, and be led away captive into all nations. And Jerusalem will be trampled by Gentiles until the times of the Gentiles are **fulfilled**. [NKJV]<br>They will be brutally killed by the sword or sent away as captives to all the nations of the world. And Jerusalem will be conquered and trampled down by the Gentiles until the age of the Gentiles **comes to an end**. [NLT]<br>καὶ πεσοῦνται στόματι μαχαίρης, καὶ αἰχμαλωτισθήσονται εἰς πάντα τὰ ἔθνη· καὶ Ἰερουσαλὴμ ἔσται πατουμένη ὑπὸ ἐθνῶν, ἄχρι **πληρωθῶσι** καιροὶ ἐθνῶν. [GNS]<br>καὶ πεσοῦνται στόματι μαχαίρης καὶ αἰχμαλωτισθήσονται εἰς τὰ ἔθνη πάντα, καὶ Ἰερουσαλὴμ ἔσται πατουμένη ὑπὸ ἐθνῶν, ἄχρι οὗ **πληρωθῶσιν** καιροὶ ἐθνῶν. [GNT] | To fill; to fill up; to make full; to come to an end; to bring to completion; to finish.<br><br>**Practical Application**<br>It means that God is in control of the times. There is a purpose to "the times of the Gentiles" and to what has happened and is yet to happen to Israel. God is in control of history. |

# PRACTICAL WORD STUDIES
## in the New Testament

| ENGLISH WORD | GREEK WORD AND VERSE | THE WORD MEANS... |
|---|---|---|
| **#1617 Fulfillment**<br><br>Fulness–KJV<br>**Fulfillment–NASB**<br>Fullness–NIV<br>Fullness–NKJV<br>Greater a blessing–NLT<br><br>**POSB REFERENCE**<br>(Romans 11:11-12)<br>Note 1, point 3<br><br>**See also POSB REF:**<br>(Col.2:9-10; esp. v.9)<br>Note 2, pt. 1 | πλήρωμα = plërōma<br>Pronunciation: [play'-ro-mah]<br>Parsing (part of speech): noun<br>  Case—nominative<br>  Gender—neuter<br>  Number—singular<br>  Stem or root—from πλήρωμα, τος<br>Concordance References:<br>  ⇒ Strong's #4138 plërōma<br>  ⇒ NIV #4445 plërōma<br>  ⇒ NASB #4138 plërōma<br><br>**Romans 11:12**<br>Now if the fall of them be the riches of the world, and the diminishing of them the riches of the Gentiles; how much more their **fulness**? [KJV]<br>Now if their transgression be riches for the world and their failure be riches for the Gentiles, how much more will their **fulfillment** be! [NASB]<br>But if their transgression means riches for the world, and their loss means riches for the Gentiles, how much greater riches will their **fullness** bring! [NIV]<br>Now if their fall *is* riches for the world, and their failure riches for the Gentiles, how much more their **fullness**! [NKJV]<br>Now if the Gentiles were enriched because the Jews turned down God's offer of salvation, think how much **greater a blessing** the world will share when the Jews finally accept it. [NLT]<br>εἰ δὲ τὸ παράπτωμα αὐτῶν πλοῦτος κόσμου, καὶ τὸ ἥττημα αὐτῶν πλοῦτος ἐθνῶν, πόσῳ μᾶλλον τὸ **πλήρωμα** αὐτῶν; [GNS]<br>εἰ δὲ τὸ παράπτωμα αὐτῶν πλοῦτος κόσμου καὶ τὸ ἥττημα αὐτῶν πλοῦτος ἐθνῶν, πόσῳ μᾶλλον τὸ **πλήρωμα** αὐτῶν. [GNT] | Fullness, completeness; full measure.<br><br>**Practical Application**<br>The idea is that the day is coming when God's plan and purpose for Israel will be completed and perfectly fulfilled. That day, the day of Israel's restoration, will cause even a greater blessing to spread out across the world. |
| **#1618 Fulfillment– Fulfillment, Reaching [Its]**<br><br>Have an end–KJV<br>**Fulfillment–NASB**<br>Reaching [its] fulfillment–NIV<br>Have an end–NKJV<br>Will come true–NLT<br><br>**POSB REFERENCE**<br>(Lk.22:33-37; esp. v.37)<br>Note 3, point 4c | τέλος ἔχει = telos echei<br>Pronunciation: [tel'-os ex-eh-ee]<br>Parsing *telos* (part of speech): noun<br>  Case—accusative<br>  Gender—neuter<br>  Number—singular<br>  Stem or root—from τέλος, ους<br>Parsing *echei* (part of speech): verb<br>  Mood—indicative<br>  Tense—present<br>  Voice—active<br>  Person—3rd person<br>  Number—singular<br>  Stem or root—from ἔχω<br>Concordance References:<br>  ⇒ Strong's #2192 echō + 5056 telos<br>  ⇒ NIV #2400 echō [reaching] + 5465 telos [fulfillment]<br>  ⇒ NASB #2192 echō + 5056 telos<br><br>**Luke 22:37**<br>For I say unto you, that this that is written must yet be accomplished in me, And he was reckoned among the transgressors: for the things concerning me **have an end**. [KJV]<br>"For I tell you, that this which is written must be fulfilled in Me, 'And He was numbered with transgressors'; for that which refers to Me has its **fulfillment**." [NASB]<br>It is written: 'And he was numbered with the transgressors'; and I tell you that this must be fulfilled in me. Yes, what is written about me is **reaching its fulfillment**." [NIV]<br>For I say to you that this which is written must still be accomplished in Me: 'And He was numbered with the transgressors.' For the things concerning Me **have an end**." [NKJV] | Reaching an end, an accomplishment, fulfillment, completion.<br><br>**Practical Application**<br>It means that The Suffering Servant of God would fulfill Isaiah 53 and man's salvation would be finally settled, finished. He was to proclaim upon the cross, "It is finished," and then bow His head and give up the ghost. |

## PRACTICAL WORD STUDIES
## in the NEW TESTAMENT

| ENGLISH WORD | GREEK WORD AND VERSE | THE WORD MEANS... |
|---|---|---|
| | For the time has come for this prophecy about me to be fulfilled: 'He was counted among those who were rebels.' Yes, everything written about me by the prophets **will come true.**" [NLT]<br><br>λέγω γὰρ ὑμῖν ὅτι ἔτι τοῦτο τὸ γεγραμμένον δεῖ τελεσθῆναι ἐν ἐμοί, τὸ Καὶ μετὰ ἀνόμων ἐλογίσθη· καὶ γὰρ τὰ περὶ ἐμοῦ **τέλος ἔχει.** [GNS]<br><br>λέγω γὰρ ὑμῖν ὅτι τοῦτο τὸ γεγραμμένον δεῖ τελεσθῆναι ἐν ἐμοί, τὸ Καὶ μετὰ ἀνόμων ἐλογίσθη· καὶ γὰρ τὸ περὶ ἐμοῦ **τέλος ἔχει.** [GNT] | |
| **#1619**<br>**Full Of Courage**<br><br>Confidence–KJV<br>Confidence–NASB<br>Confident–NIV<br>Confidence–NKJV<br>**Full of courage–NLT**<br><br>**POSB REFERENCE**<br>(1 Jn.2:28)<br>Note 2, point 2 | σχῶμεν παρρησίαν = *schōmen parrēsian*<br>Pronunciation: [skho'-men par-rhay-see'-ahn]<br>Parsing *schōmen* (part of speech): verb<br>    Mood—subjunctive<br>    Tense—aorist<br>    Voice—active<br>    Person—1st person<br>    Number—plural<br>    Stem or root—from ἔχω<br>Parsing *parrēsian* (part of speech): noun<br>    Case—accusative<br>    Gender—feminine<br>    Number—singular<br>    Stem or root—from παρρησία, ας<br>Concordance References:<br>  ⇒ Strong's #2192+3954 echō parrēsia<br>  ⇒ NIV #2400+4244 echō parrēsia [confident]<br>  ⇒ NASB #2192+3954 echō parrēsia<br><br>**1 John 2:28**<br>And now, little children, abide in him; that, when he shall appear, we may have **confidence**, and not be ashamed before him at his coming. [KJV]<br>And now, little children, abide in Him, so that when He appears, we may have **confidence** and not shrink away from Him in shame at His coming. [NASB]<br>And now, dear children, continue in him, so that when he appears we may be **confident** and unashamed before him at his coming. [NIV]<br>And now, little children, abide in Him, that when He appears, we may have **confidence** and not be ashamed before Him at His coming. [NKJV]<br>And now, dear children, continue to live in fellowship with Christ so that when he returns, you will be **full of courage** and not shrink back from him in shame. [NLT]<br><br>καὶ νῦν, τεκνία, μένετε ἐν αὐτῷ· ἵνα ὅταν φανερωθῇ **ἔχωμεν παρρησίαν**, καὶ μὴ αἰσχυνθῶμεν ἀπ' αὐτοῦ, ἐν τῇ παρουσίᾳ αὐτοῦ. [GNS]<br>Καὶ νῦν, τεκνία, μένετε ἐν αὐτῷ, ἵνα ἐὰν φανερωθῇ **σχῶμεν παρρησίαν** καὶ μὴ αἰσχυνθῶμεν ἀπ' αὐτοῦ ἐν τῇ παρουσίᾳ αὐτοῦ. [GNT] | Confident; confidence; to be full of courage; boldness; assurance.<br><br>**Practical Application**<br>It has the idea of unshakable boldness and assurance. If we abide in Christ now, today, and every day hereafter, we can have unshakable confidence and assurance and even boldness when Jesus Christ returns to earth. |
| **#1620**<br>**Full Rights Of Sons**<br><br>Adoption of sons–KJV<br>Adoption as sons–NASB<br>**Full rights of sons–NIV**<br>Adoption as sons–NKJV<br>Adopt us as his very own children–NLT<br><br>**POSB REFERENCE**<br>(Gal.4:5-6; esp. v.5)<br>*Deeper Study #2* | υἱοθεσίαν = *huiothesian*<br>Pronunciation: [hwee-oth-es-ee'-ahn]<br>Parsing (part of speech): noun<br>    Case—accusative<br>    Gender—feminine<br>    Number—singular<br>    Stem or root—from υἱοθεσία, ας<br>Concordance References:<br>  ⇒ Strong's #5206 huiothesia<br>  ⇒ NIV #5625 huiothesia<br>  ⇒ NASB #5206 huiothesia<br><br>**Galatians 4:5**<br>To redeem them that were under the law, that we might receive the **adoption of sons.** [KJV]<br>In order that He might redeem those who were under the Law, that we might receive the **adoption as sons.** [NASB]<br>To redeem those under law, that we might receive the **full rights of sons.** [NIV] | Full rights of sons; to place as a son; adoption as sons; to adopt us as His very own children; sonship.<br><br>**Practical Application**<br>The picture of adoption is a beautiful picture of what God does for the Christian. In the ancient world the family was based on a Roman law called "*patria potestas*," the father's power. The law gave the father absolute authority over his children so long as the father lived. He could work, enslave, sell and, if he wished, pronounce the death penalty on them. Regardless of the child's adult age, the father held all power over personal and property rights.<br>Therefore, adoption was a serious matter. Yet, it was a common practice to ensure that a family would not become extinct by having no male children. And when a child was adopted, three |

| ENGLISH WORD | GREEK WORD AND VERSE | THE WORD MEANS... |
|---|---|---|
| | To redeem those who were under the law, that we might receive the **adoption as sons**. [NKJV]<br>God sent him to buy freedom for us who were slaves to the law, so that he could **adopt us as his very own children**. [NLT]<br>ἵνα τοὺς ὑπὸ νόμον ἐξαγοράσῃ, ἵνα τὴν **υἱοθεσίαν** ἀπολάβωμεν. [GNS]<br>ἵνα τοὺς ὑπὸ νόμον ἐξαγοράσῃ, ἵνα τὴν **υἱοθεσίαν** ἀπολάβωμεν. [GNT] | legal steps were taken.<br>1. The adopted son was adopted permanently. He could not be adopted today and disinherited tomorrow. He became a son of the father—forever. He was eternally secure as a son.<br>2. The adopted son immediately had all the rights of a legitimate son in the new family.<br>3. The adopted son completely lost all rights in his old family. The adopted son was looked upon as a new person—so new that old debts and obligations connected with his former family were cancelled and abolished as if they never existed.<br>The Bible says several things about the believer's adoption as a son of God.<br>1. The believer's adoption establishes a new relationship with God—forever. He is eternally secure as a child of God. But the new relationship is established only when a person comes to Christ through faith (Galatians 3:26; Galatians 4:4-5).<br>2. The believer's adoption establishes a new relationship with God as father. The believer has all the rights and privileges of a genuine son of God (Romans 8:16-17; 1 John 3:1-2).<br>3. The believer's adoption establishes a new dynamic experience with God as father, a moment-by-moment access into His very presence (Romans 8:14, 16; Galatians 4:6).<br>4. The believer's adoption gives him a very special relationship with other children of God—a family relationship that binds him with others in an unparalleled spiritual union (see POSB note—Ephes. 2:11-18; POSB note—Ephes. 2:19-22; POSB note—Ephes. 3:6; POSB note—Ephes. 4:4-6; and POSB note—Ephes. 4:17-19. Cp. Acts 2:42. See POSB outline—Matthew 12:46-50 and POSB notes—Matthew 12:46-50.)<br>5. The believer's adoption makes him a new person. The believer has been taken out from under the authority and power of the world and its sin. The believer is placed as a son into the family and authority of God. The old life with all of its debts and obligations are cancelled and wiped out (2 Cor. 5:17; Galatians 3:23-27; 2 Peter 1:4. See POSB *Deeper Study* #1—Ephes. 4:22; POSB *Deeper Study* #3—Ephes. 4:24.)<br>6. The believer's adoption is to be fully realized in the future at the return of Jesus Christ (Romans 8:19; Ephes. 1:14; 1 Thes. 4:14-17; 1 John 3:2).<br>7. The believer's adoption and its joy will be shared by all creation on a cosmic scale (Romans 8:21). There is to be a new heavens and earth (2 Peter 3:12-14; Rev. 21:1-7). |
| #1621<br>**Fullness**<br><br>Fullness–KJV<br>Fullness–NASB<br>Fullness–NIV<br>Fullness–NKJV | πληρώματος = *plērōmatos*<br>Pronunciation: [play'-ro-mah-tos]<br>Parsing (part of speech): noun<br>    Case—genitive<br>    Gender—neuter<br>    Number—singular<br>    Stem or root—from πλήρωμα, τος<br>Concordance References: | Fullness, that which fills, the sum total, the totality. It is the sum total of all that is in God (Col. 1:19). It is rich blessings from God.<br><br>**Practical Application**<br>All that Christ is, the very fullness of His being, is given to us who believe—all His "love, joy, peace, patience, kindness, goodness, faith- |

# PRACTICAL WORD STUDIES
## in the NEW TESTAMENT

| ENGLISH WORD | GREEK WORD AND VERSE | THE WORD MEANS... |
|---|---|---|
| Rich blessing–NLT<br><br>**POSB REFERENCE**<br>(Jn.1:16-17; esp. v.16)<br>Note 4 | ⇒ Strong's #4138 plërōma<br>⇒ NIV #4445 plërōma<br>⇒ NASB #4138 plërōma<br><br>**John 1:16**<br>And of his **fulness** have all we received, and grace for grace. [KJV]<br>For of His **fulness** we have all received, and grace upon grace. [NASB]<br>From the **fullness** of his grace we have all received one blessing after another. [NIV]<br>And of His **fullness** we have all received, and grace for grace. [NKJV]<br>We have all benefited from the **rich blessings** he brought to us—one gracious blessing after another. [NLT]<br>καὶ ἐκ τοῦ **πληρώματος** αὐτοῦ ἡμεῖς πάντες ἐλάβομεν, καὶ χάριν ἀντὶ χάριτος· [GNS]<br>ὅτι ἐκ τοῦ **πληρώματος** αὐτοῦ ἡμεῖς πάντες ἐλάβομεν καὶ χάριν ἀντὶ χάριτος· [GNT] | fulness, gentleness, self-control" (Galatians 5:22-23). We are complete in Him. |
| #1622<br>**Fullness–<br>Fulness**<br><br>**Fulness–KJV**<br>Fulfillment–NASB<br>**Fullness–NIV**<br>**Fullness–NKJV**<br>Greater a blessing–NLT<br><br>**POSB REFERENCE**<br>(Romans 11:11-12)<br>Note 1, point 3<br><br>See also POSB REF:<br>(Col.2:9-10; esp. v.9)<br>Note 2, point 1 | πλήρωμα = plërōma<br>Pronunciation: [play'-ro-mah]<br>Parsing (part of speech): noun<br>    Case—nominative<br>    Gender—neuter<br>    Number—singular<br>    Stem or root—from πλήρωμα, τος<br>Concordance References:<br>⇒ Strong's #4138 plërōma<br>⇒ NIV #4445 plërōma<br>⇒ NASB #4138 plërōma<br><br>**Romans 11:12**<br>Now if the fall of them be the riches of the world, and the diminishing of them the riches of the Gentiles; how much more their **fulness**? [KJV]<br>Now if their transgression be riches for the world and their failure be riches for the Gentiles, how much more will their **fulfillment** be! [NASB]<br>But if their transgression means riches for the world, and their loss means riches for the Gentiles, how much greater riches will their **fullness** bring! [NIV]<br>Now if their fall *is* riches for the world, and their failure riches for the Gentiles, how much more their **fullness**! [NKJV]<br>Now if the Gentiles were enriched because the Jews turned down God's offer of salvation, think how much **greater a blessing** the world will share when the Jews finally accept it. [NLT]<br>εἰ δὲ τὸ παράπτωμα αὐτῶν πλοῦτος κόσμου, καὶ τὸ ἥττημα αὐτῶν πλοῦτος ἐθνῶν, πόσῳ μᾶλλον τὸ **πλήρωμα** αὐτῶν; [GNS]<br>εἰ δὲ τὸ παράπτωμα αὐτῶν πλοῦτος κόσμου καὶ τὸ ἥττημα αὐτῶν πλοῦτος ἐθνῶν, πόσῳ μᾶλλον τὸ **πλήρωμα** αὐτῶν. [GNT] | Fullness, completeness; full measure.<br><br>**Practical Application**<br>The idea is that the day is coming when God's plan and purpose for Israel will be completed and perfectly fulfilled. That day, the day of Israel's restoration, will cause even a greater blessing to spread out across the world. |
| #1623<br>**Fully<br>Developed**<br><br>Entire–KJV<br>Complete–NASB<br>Complete–NIV<br>Complete–NKJV<br>**Fully developed–NLT**<br><br>**POSB REFERENCE**<br>(Jas. 1:4)<br>Note 3, point 2 | ὁλόκληροι = holoklëroi<br>Pronunciation: [hol-ok'-lay-roy]<br>Parsing (part of speech): adjective<br>    Case—nominative<br>    Gender—masculine<br>    Number—plural<br>    Stem or root—from ὁλόκληρος, ον<br>Concordance References:<br>⇒ Strong's #3648 holoklëros<br>⇒ NIV #3908 holoklëros<br>⇒ NASB #3648 holoklëros<br><br>**James 1:4**<br>But let patience have her perfect work, that ye may be perfect and **entire**, wanting nothing. [KJV]<br>And let endurance have its perfect result, that you may be perfect and **complete**, lacking in nothing. [NASB] | Complete, entire, fully developed, whole. It means to be wholly fit, perfectly sound, complete with no weaknesses, flaws, defects, or shortcomings.<br><br>**Practical Application**<br>This means a most wonderful thing. When a person perseveres and conquers trials or temptations...<br><br>• he becomes more complete, more fit, more sound, and more fully developed.<br>• he also eliminates more weaknesses, more flaws, more defects, and more shortcomings. |

## PRACTICAL WORD STUDIES
### in the NEW TESTAMENT

| ENGLISH WORD | GREEK WORD AND VERSE | THE WORD MEANS... |
|---|---|---|
| | Perseverance must finish its work so that you may be mature and **complete**, not lacking anything. [NIV]<br>But let patience have *its* perfect work, that you may be perfect and **complete**, lacking nothing. [NKJV]<br>So let it grow, for when your endurance is **fully developed**, you will be strong in character and ready for anything. [NLT]<br>ἡ δὲ ὑπομονὴ ἔργον τέλειον ἐχέτω, ἵνα ἦτε τέλειοι καὶ **ὁλόκληροι**, ἐν μηδενὶ λειπόμενοι. [GNS]<br>ἡ δὲ ὑπομονὴ ἔργον τέλειον ἐχέτω, ἵνα ἦτε τέλειοι καὶ **ὁλόκληροι** ἐν μηδενὶ λειπόμενοι. [GNT] | Day by day—trial by trial and temptation by temptation—when a person perseveres and conquers, he becomes more and more complete. He becomes stronger and more pure and righteous—more and more like the Lord Jesus. As the last words of James 1:4 say, "not lacking anything." The believer who faces trials and temptations in the joy of Christ conquers all, and he lacks nothing.<br>⇒ He becomes more and more complete, fulfilling his task and purpose for being on earth a little bit more.<br>⇒ He becomes more and more entire and fit, eliminating more and more weaknesses and shortcomings in his life. |
| #1624<br>**Fully Developed**<br><br>Perfect–KJV<br>Perfect–NASB<br>Mature–NIV<br>Perfect–NKJV<br>Fully developed–NLT<br><br>**POSB REFERENCE**<br>(Jas. 1:4)<br>Note 3<br><br>See also POSB REF:<br>(1 Cor.2:6)<br>Note 1 | τέλειοι = *teleioi*<br>Pronunciation: [tel'-i-oy]<br>Parsing (part of speech): adjective<br>    Case—nominative<br>    Gender—masculine<br>    Number—plural<br>    Stem or root—from τέλειος, α, ον<br>Concordance References:<br>  ⇒ Strong's #5046 teleios<br>  ⇒ NIV #5455 teleios<br>  ⇒ NASB #5046 teleios<br><br>**James 1:4**<br>But let patience have her perfect work, that ye may be **perfect** and entire, wanting nothing. [KJV]<br>And let endurance have its perfect result, that you may be **perfect** and complete, lacking in nothing. [NASB]<br>Perseverance must finish its work so that you may be **mature** and complete, not lacking anything. [NIV]<br>But let patience have *its* perfect work, that you may be **perfect** and complete, lacking nothing. [NKJV]<br>So let it grow, for when your endurance is **fully developed**, you will be strong in character and ready for anything. [NLT]<br>ἡ δὲ ὑπομονὴ ἔργον τέλειον ἐχέτω, ἵνα ἦτε **τέλειοι** καὶ ὁλόκληροι, ἐν μηδενὶ λειπόμενοι. [GNS]<br>ἡ δὲ ὑπομονὴ ἔργον τέλειον ἐχέτω, ἵνα ἦτε **τέλειοι** καὶ ὁλόκληροι ἐν μηδενὶ λειπόμενοι. [GNT] | Mature, perfect, fully developed; full grown, complete, whole.<br><br>**Practical Application**<br>A person becomes more fully developed (*teleioi*). The word does not mean perfect in the sense of becoming a perfect person. The word means *perfection of purpose*. It has to do with an end, an aim, a goal, a purpose. It means fit, mature, fully grown at a particular stage of growth. For example, a fully grown child is a perfect child; he has reached his childhood and achieved the purpose of childhood. It does not mean perfection of character, that is, being without sin. It is fitness, maturity for task and purpose. It is full development, maturity of godliness. (See POSB note—Ephes. 4:12-13; cp. Phil. 3:12; 1 John 1:8, 10.)<br>When a person stands against trials and temptations and conquers them...<br>• he perfects the purpose God intended. That is, he becomes a stronger and more pure person—a person who is a little more like Jesus.<br>• he perfects his task and purpose for being on earth a little bit more.<br>God has a twofold purpose for every believer: to become more and more like Jesus and to do a specific task or job while on earth. When the believer perseveres against and conquers trials or temptations, he perfects both purposes a little bit more. He becomes more like Jesus, and he finishes his task a little more. |
| #1625<br>**Fully Known**<br><br>Fully known–KJV<br>Followed–NASB<br>Know all about–NIV<br>Followed–NKJV<br>Know–NLT<br><br>**POSB REFERENCE**<br>(2 Tim. 3:10)<br>Note 1 | παρηκολούθησάς = *parëkolouthësas*<br>Pronunciation: [par-ayk-ol-oo-thay'-sahs]<br>Parsing (part of speech): verb<br>    Mood—indicative<br>    Tense—aorist<br>    Voice—active<br>    Person—2nd person<br>    Number—singular<br>    Stem or root—from παρακολουθέω<br>Concordance References:<br>  ⇒ Strong's #3877 parakoloutheö<br>  ⇒ NIV #4158 parakoloutheö<br>  ⇒ NASB #3877 parakoloutheö<br><br>**2 Tim. 3:10**<br>But thou hast **fully known** my doctrine, manner of life, purpose, faith, longsuffering, charity, patience, [KJV]<br>But you **followed** my teaching, conduct, purpose, faith, patience, love, perseverance, [NASB]<br>You, however, **know all about** my teaching, my way | To to know; to know all about; to fully know; to follow; to give full attention to. Kenneth Wuest points out that the Greek word means to follow a person so closely that one is always by the person's side, conforming his life to the person (*The Pastoral Epistles*, p.148). It means to join oneself to the person, to become his disciple and to follow his example.<br><br>**Practical Application**<br>A godly person follows a godly example. This is a sharp contrast from the godless marks of false teachers (2 Tim. 3:1-9). Timothy had known (*parëkolouthësas*) and had closely observed and followed the godly example of Paul. Paul had lived a godly life, and Timothy had followed in his footsteps. |

## PRACTICAL WORD STUDIES
### in the NEW TESTAMENT

| ENGLISH WORD | GREEK WORD AND VERSE | THE WORD MEANS... |
|---|---|---|
| | of life, my purpose, faith, patience, love, endurance, [NIV]<br><br>But you have carefully **followed** my doctrine, manner of life, purpose, faith, longsuffering, love, perseverance, [NKJV]<br><br>But you **know** what I teach, Timothy, and how I live, and what my purpose in life is. You know my faith and how long I have suffered. You know my love and my patient endurance. [NLT]<br><br>σὺ δὲ **παρηκολούθηκάς** μου τῇ διδασκαλίᾳ, τῇ ἀγωγῇ, τῇ προθέσει, τῇ πίστει, τῇ μακροθυμίᾳ, τῇ ἀγάπῃ, τῇ ὑπομονῇ, [GNS]<br><br>Σὺ δὲ **παρηκολούθησάς** μου τῇ διδασκαλίᾳ, τῇ ἀγωγῇ, τῇ προθέσει, τῇ πίστει, τῇ μακροθυμίᾳ, τῇ ἀγάπῃ, τῇ ὑπομονῇ, [GNT] | |
| **#1626**<br>**Fully Trained**<br><br>Perfect–KJV<br>**Fully trained–NASB**<br>**Fully trained–NIV**<br>Perfectly trained–NKJV<br>Works hard–NLT<br><br>**POSB REFERENCE**<br>(Lk.6:40)<br>Note 2, point 1 | κατηρτισμένος = katērtismenos<br>Pronunciation: [kat-tayr-tis'-me-nos]<br>Parsing (part of speech): verb<br>   Mood—participle<br>   Tense—perfect<br>   Voice—passive<br>   Case—nominative<br>   Gender—masculine<br>   Number—singular<br>   Stem or root—from καταρτίζω<br>Concordance References:<br>  ⇒ Strong's #2675 katartizō<br>  ⇒ NIV #2936 katartizō<br>  ⇒ NASB #2675 katartizō<br><br>**Luke 6:40**<br>The disciple is not above his master: but every one that is **perfect** shall be as his master. [KJV]<br>"A pupil is not above his teacher; but everyone, after he has been **fully trained**, will be like his teacher. [NASB]<br>A student is not above his teacher, but everyone who is **fully trained** will be like his teacher. [NIV]<br>A disciple is not above his teacher, but everyone who is **perfectly trained** will be like his teacher. [NKJV]<br>A student is not greater than the teacher. But the student who **works hard** will become like the teacher. [NLT]<br>οὐκ ἔστι μαθητὴς ὑπὲρ τὸν διδάσκαλον αὐτοῦ· **κατηρτισμένος** δὲ πᾶς ἔσται ὡς ὁ διδάσκαλος αὐτοῦ. [GNS]<br>οὐκ ἔστιν μαθητὴς ὑπὲρ τὸν διδάσκαλον· **κατηρτισμένος** δὲ πᾶς ἔσται ὡς ὁ διδάσκαλος αὐτοῦ. [GNT] | To be fully trained; to work hard; to be prepared; to be equipped. It means to complete, render fit, mend. It is a common word often used for mending, repairing, or restoring broken things such as nets (Matthew 4:21) or men (Galatians 6:1).<br><br>**Practical Application**<br>The point is forceful: "the student is not above his teacher" (see POSB note, pt.1—Matthew 10:24-25). The disciple is not better than his Lord; therefore, he cannot expect to be treated better, nor can he expect to receive more in this world than his Lord. The disciple cannot expect to be better by having more honor, praise, recognition, or esteem. He cannot expect to have more comfort, rest, or pleasure. The Lord suffered, humbled, and denied Himself for the sake of the world and its needs. The disciple, as a follower of the Lord, does the same; he denies himself in order to reach the world for his Lord (see POSB note—Luke 9:23 and POSB *Deeper Study* #1—Luke 9:23). |
| **#1627**<br>**Function**<br><br>Office–KJV<br>**Function–NASB**<br>**Function–NIV**<br>**Function–NKJV**<br>**Function—NLT**<br><br>**POSB REFERENCE**<br>(Romans 12:3-5, esp.v.4)<br>Note 1, point 2 | πρᾶξιν = praxin<br>Pronunciation: [prax'-in]<br>Parsing (part of speech): noun<br>   Case—accusative<br>   Gender—feminine<br>   Number—singular<br>   Stem or root—from πρᾶξις, εως<br>Concordance References:<br>  ⇒ Strong's #4234 praxis<br>  ⇒ NIV #4552 praxis<br>  ⇒ NASB #4234 praxis<br><br>**Romans 12:4**<br>For as we have many members in one body, and all members have not the same **office**: [KJV]<br>For just as we have many members in one body and all the members do not have the same **function**, [NASB]<br>Just as each of us has one body with many members, and these members do not all have the same **function**, [NIV]<br>For as we have many members in one body, but all the members do not have the same **function**, [NKJV] | What one does; deed, action, practice, function.<br><br>**Practical Application**<br>The point is clearly stated: all members do not have the same function (*praxin*) or office. God has set the believer in the world for a specific purpose, and God has gifted the believer with whatever measure of faith is needed to fulfill his function. The believer is a member or a part of the whole body, with each member having his task to perform. There is no room for self-exaltation, pride, or arrogance—no room for thinking too highly of oneself. The believer does not stand alone in the world. Every believer has a measure of faith to do his task, and every member is needed to get the task done. Therefore, no believer has the right to think of himself more highly than any other believer. Every single believer is important to the body of Christ. Every |

# Practical Word Studies
## in the New Testament

| ENGLISH WORD | GREEK WORD AND VERSE | THE WORD MEANS... |
|---|---|---|
| | Just as our bodies have many parts and each part has a special **function**. [NLT]<br>καθάπερ γὰρ ἐν ἑνὶ σώματι μέλη πολλὰ ἔχομεν, τὰ δὲ μέλη πάντα οὐ τὴν αὐτὴν ἔχει **πρᾶξιν**· [GNS]<br>καθάπερ γὰρ ἐν ἑνὶ σώματι πολλὰ μέλη ἔχομεν, τὰ δὲ μέλη πάντα οὐ τὴν αὐτὴν ἔχει **πρᾶξιν**, [GNT] | believer is needed to complete, fulfill, and perfect the body. The body becomes handicapped without the active functioning of every member. Every member is very important. |
| **#1628**<br>**Furious**<br><br>Filled with madness–KJV<br>Filled with rage–NASB<br>**Furious–NIV**<br>Filled with rage–NKJV<br>Wild with rage–NLT<br><br>**POSB REFERENCE**<br>(Lk.6:6-11; esp. v.11)<br>Note 3, point 5 | ἐπλήσθησαν ἀνοίας = *eplēsthēsan anoias*<br>Pronunciation: [eh-playce'-thay-san' an-oy-ahs]<br>Parsing *eplēsthēsan* (part of speech): verb<br>    Mood—indicative<br>    Tense—aorist<br>    Voice—passive<br>    Person—3rd person<br>    Number—plural<br>    Stem or root—from πίμπλημι<br>Parsing *anoias* (part of speech): noun<br>    Case—genitive<br>    Gender—feminine<br>    Number—singular<br>    Stem or root—from ἄνοια, ας<br>Concordance References:<br>⇒ Strong's #454+4130 anoia pletho<br>⇒ NIV #486+4398 anoia pimplēmi [furious]<br>⇒ NASB #454+4130 anoia pletho<br><br>**Luke 6:11**<br>And they were **filled with madness**; and communed one with another what they might do to Jesus. [KJV]<br>But they themselves were **filled with rage**, and discussed together what they might do to Jesus. [NASB]<br>But they were **furious** and began to discuss with one another what they might do to Jesus. [NIV]<br>But they were **filled with rage**, and discussed with one another what they might do to Jesus. [NKJV]<br>At this, the enemies of Jesus were **wild with rage** and began to discuss what to do with him. [NLT]<br>αὐτοὶ δὲ **ἐπλήσθησαν ἀνοίας**· καὶ διελάλουν πρὸς ἀλλήλους, τί ἂν ποιήσειαν τῷ Ἰησοῦ. [GNS]<br>αὐτοὶ δὲ **ἐπλήσθησαν ἀνοίας** καὶ διελάλουν πρὸς ἀλλήλους τί ἂν ποιήσαιεν τῷ Ἰησοῦ. [GNT] | To be furious; to be filled with wild, insane rage; to be controlled by foolishness, stupidity.<br><br>**Practical Application**<br>Jesus had confronted the religionists with the truth. They had been shown unmistakably what true religion is. They were now faced with the dilemma: they had to either accept true religion, Jesus and His teaching, or else oppose Him. They chose to oppose Him, but they needed political help, so they formed an alliance with the Herodians (see POSB *Deeper Study #2*—Matthew 22:16). Note a significant fact: despite enormous philosophical differences, there was no difference between the religious and political leaders in behavior (the Pharisees and the Herodians). Position, power, and security had corrupted their hearts and minds. They both plotted to destroy a person (Jesus) who opposed them. |
| **#1629**<br>**Furious**<br><br>Cut to the heart–KJV<br>Cut to the quick–NASB<br>**Furious–NIV**<br>**Furious–NKJV**<br>**Furious–NLT**<br><br>**POSB REFERENCE**<br>(Acts 5:32-40; esp. v.33)<br>Note 4, point 1 | διεπρίοντο = *dieprionto*<br>Pronunciation: [dee-ap-ree'-on-tow]<br>Parsing (part of speech): verb<br>    Mood—indicative<br>    Tense—imperfect<br>    Voice—passive<br>    Person—3rd person<br>    Number—plural<br>    Stem or root—from διαπρίομαι<br>Concordance References:<br>⇒ Strong's #1282 diapriō<br>⇒ NIV #1391 diapriö<br>⇒ NASB #1282 diaprio<br><br>**Acts 5:33**<br>When they heard that, they were **cut to the heart**, and took counsel to slay them. [KJV]<br>But when they heard this, they were **cut to the quick** and were intending to slay them. [NASB]<br>When they heard this, they were **furious** and wanted to put them to death. [NIV]<br>When they heard this, they were **furious** and plotted to kill them. [NKJV]<br>At this, the high council was **furious** and decided to kill them. [NLT]<br>Οἱ δὲ ἀκούσαντες **διεπρίοντο**, καὶ ἐβούλοντο ἀνελεῖν αὐτούς. [GNS]<br>Οἱ δὲ ἀκούσαντες **διεπρίοντο** καὶ ἐβούλοντο ἀνελεῖν αὐτούς. [GNT] | To be furious; to be cut to the quick; to cut to the heart; to be enraged.<br><br>**Practical Application**<br>Their hearts were sawn in two, into two parts, through and through. The idea is they were cut to the heart not with conviction—but with anger, wrath, rage, and reaction against the apostles. |

# PRACTICAL WORD STUDIES
## in the NEW TESTAMENT

| ENGLISH WORD | GREEK WORD AND VERSE | THE WORD MEANS... |
|---|---|---|
| **#1630**<br>**Furious**<br><br>Cut to the heart–KJV<br>Cut to the quick–NASB<br>**Furious–NIV**<br>Cut to the heart–NKJV<br>Infuriated–NLT<br><br>**POSB REFERENCE**<br>(Acts 7:54)<br>Note 1, point 2 | διεπρίοντο ταῖς καρδίαις = *dieprionto tais kardiais*<br>Pronunciation: [dee-ehp-ree'-on-tow tace kar-dee'-ah-ees]<br>Parsing *dieprionto* (part of speech): verb<br>    Mood—indicative<br>    Tense—imperfect<br>    Voice—passive<br>    Person—3rd person<br>    Number—plural<br>    Stem or root—from διαπρίομαι<br>Parsing *kardiais* (part of speech): noun<br>    Case—dative<br>    Gender—feminine<br>    Number—plural<br>    Stem or root—from καρδία, ας<br>Concordance References:<br>  ⇒ Strong's #1282 + 2588 + 3588 diapriō kardia ho<br>  ⇒ NIV #1391 + 2840 + 3836 diapriō kardia ho<br>  ⇒ NASB #1282 + 2588 + 3588 diapriō kardia ho<br><br>**Acts 7:54**<br>When they heard these things, they were **cut to the heart**, and they gnashed on him with their teeth. [KJV]<br>Now when they heard this, they were **cut to the quick**, and they began gnashing their teeth at him. [NASB]<br>When they heard this, they were **furious** and gnashed their teeth at him. [NIV]<br>When they heard these things they were **cut to the heart**, and they gnashed at him with *their* teeth. [NKJV]<br>The Jewish leaders were **infuriated** by Stephen's accusation, and they shook their fists in rage. [NLT]<br>Ἀκούοντες δὲ ταῦτα, **διεπρίοντο ταῖς καρδίαις** αὐτῶν, καὶ ἔβρυχον τοὺς ὀδόντας ἐπ' αὐτόν. [GNS]<br>Ἀκούοντες δὲ ταῦτα **διεπρίοντο ταῖς καρδίαις** αὐτῶν καὶ ἔβρυχον τοὺς ὀδόντας ἐπ' αὐτόν. [GNT] | To be furious; to cut to the heart; to cut to the quick; to infuriate; to be enraged.<br><br>**Practical Application**<br>The word "*dieprionto*" means to saw asunder; to cut through. It is used to show violent reaction. The response of their hearts was anger, not godly sorrow (see POSB *Deeper Study* #1, Godly Sorrow—2 Cor. 7:10). They had no intention of confessing that they had been wrong. |
| **#1631**<br>**Futile**<br><br>Vain–KJV<br>Worthless–NASB<br>**Futile–NIV**<br>**Futile–NKJV**<br>Useless–NLT<br><br>**POSB REFERENCE**<br>(1 Cor.15:16-19; esp. v.17)<br>Note 3, point 2 | ματαία = *matzaia*<br>Pronunciation: [mat'-ah-ee-ah]<br>Parsing (part of speech): adjective<br>    Case—nominative<br>    Gender—feminine<br>    Number—singular<br>    Stem or root—from μάταιος, α, ον<br>Concordance References:<br>  ⇒ Strong's #3152 mataios<br>  ⇒ NIV #3469 mataios<br>  ⇒ NASB #3152 mataios<br><br>**1 Cor. 15:17**<br>And if Christ be not raised, your faith is **vain**; ye are yet in your sins. [KJV]<br>And if Christ has not been raised, your faith is **worthless**; you are still in your sins. [NASB]<br>And if Christ has not been raised, your faith is **futile**; you are still in your sins. [NIV]<br>And if Christ is not risen, your faith *is* **futile**; you are still in your sins! [NKJV]<br>And if Christ has not been raised, then your faith is **useless**, and you are still under condemnation for your sins. [NLT]<br>εἰ δὲ Χριστὸς οὐκ ἐγήγερται, **ματαία** ἡ πίστις ὑμῶν· ἔτι ἐστὲ ἐν ταῖς ἁμαρτίαις ὑμῶν. [GNS]<br>εἰ δὲ Χριστὸς οὐκ ἐγήγερται, **ματαία** ἡ πίστις ὑμῶν, ἔτι ἐστὲ ἐν ταῖς ἁμαρτίαις ὑμῶν, [GNT] | Fruitless or futile; that is, we are still in our sins; worthless; useless.<br><br>**Practical Application**<br>To deny the resurrection (either of Christ or of us) means that our faith is futile (*matzaia*). If Jesus Christ has not risen from the dead, then He is still dead, still in the grave; therefore, there is no redemption, no forgiveness of sins. |
| **#1632**<br>**Futile**<br><br>Vain–KJV<br>**Futile–NASB** | ἐματαιώθησαν = *emataiōthēsan*<br>Pronunciation: [eh-mat-ah-i'-o-thay-sahn]<br>Parsing (part of speech): verb<br>    Mood—indicative<br>    Tense—aorist<br>    Voice—passive | Be given to worthless or futile speculation. The word futile means, empty, vain, unsuccessful, senseless, worthless. |

# PRACTICAL WORD STUDIES
## in the NEW TESTAMENT

| ENGLISH WORD | GREEK WORD AND VERSE | THE WORD MEANS... |
|---|---|---|
| **Futile**–NIV<br>**Futile**–NKJV<br>Foolish–NLT<br><br>**POSB<br>REFERENCE**<br>(Romans 1:21)<br>Note 4, point 1 | Person—3rd person<br>Number—plural<br>Stem or root—from ματαιόομαι<br>Concordance References:<br>⇒ Strong's #3154 mataioö<br>⇒ NIV #3471 mataioö<br>⇒ NASB #3154 mataioö<br><br>**Romans 1:21**<br>Because that, when they knew God, they glorified him not as God, neither were thankful; but became **vain** in their imaginations, and their foolish heart was darkened. [KJV]<br>For even though they knew God, they did not honor Him as God, or give thanks; but they became **futile** in their speculations, and their foolish heart was darkened. [NASB]<br>For although they knew God, they neither glorified him as God nor gave thanks to him, but their thinking became **futile** and their foolish hearts were darkened. [NIV]<br>Because, although they knew God, they did not glorify *Him* as God, nor were thankful, but became **futile** in their thoughts, and their foolish hearts were darkened. [NKJV]<br>Yes, they knew God, but they wouldn't worship him as God or even give him thanks. And they began to think up **foolish** ideas of what God was like. The result was that their minds became dark and confused. [NLT]<br>διότι γνόντες τὸν Θεὸν οὐχ ὡς Θεὸν ἐδόξασαν ἢ ηὐχαρίστησαν, ἀλλ' **ἐματαιώθησαν** ἐν τοῖς διαλογισμοῖς αὐτῶν, καὶ ἐσκοτίσθη ἡ ἀσύνετος αὐτῶν καρδία. [GNS]<br>διότι γνόντες τὸν θεὸν οὐχ ὡς θεὸν ἐδόξασαν ηηὐχαρίστησαν, ἀλλ' **ἐματαιώθησαν** ἐν τοῖς διαλογιδμοῖς αὐτῶν καὶ ἐσκοτίσθη ἡ ἀσύνετος αὐτῶν καρδία. [GNT] | **Practical Application**<br>When men push God out of their minds, their minds are void and empty of God. God is not in their thoughts. (Cp. Psalm 10:4.) Their minds are ready to be *filled* with some other *god* or *supremacy*. |
| **#1633<br>Futility**<br><br>Vanity–KJV<br>**Futility**–NASB<br>Frustration–NIV<br>**Futility**–NKJV<br>Curse–NLT<br><br>**POSB<br>REFERENCE**<br>(Romans 8:19-22, esp. v.20)<br>Note 2, point 1 | ματαιότητι = *mataiotēti*<br>Pronunciation: [mat-ah-yot'-ay-tee]<br>Parsing (part of speech): noun<br>  Case—dative<br>  Gender—feminine<br>  Number—singular<br>Stem or root—from ματαιότης, ητος<br>Concordance References:<br>⇒ Strong's #3153 mataiotēs<br>⇒ NIV #3470 mataiotēs<br>⇒ NASB #3153 mataiotēs<br><br>**Romans 8:20**<br>For the creature was made subject to **vanity**, not willingly, but by reason of him who hath subjected the same in hope, [KJV]<br>For the creation was subjected to **futility**, not of its own will, but because of Him who subjected it, in hope [NASB]<br>For the creation was subjected to **frustration**, not by its own choice, but by the will of the one who subjected it, in hope [NIV]<br>For the creation was subjected to **futility**, not willingly, but because of Him who subjected *it* in hope; [NKJV]<br>Against its will, everything on earth was subjected to God's **curse**. [NLT]<br>τῇ γὰρ **ματαιότητι** ἡ κτίσις ὑπετάγη, οὐχ ἑκοῦσα ἀλλὰ διὰ τὸν ὑποτάξαντα, ἐφ' ἑλπίδι· [GNS]<br>τῇ γὰρ **ματαιότητι** ἡ κτίσις ὑπετάγη, οὐχ ἑκοῦσα ἀλλὰ διὰ τὸν ὑποτάξαντα, ἐφ' ἑλπίδι [GNT] | Worthlessness, futility; emptiness, frustration; cursed.<br><br>**Practical Application**<br>Creation is subject to corruption. This is clearly seen by men; and what men see is constantly confirmed by such authorities as the botanist, zoologist, geologist, and astronomer of the world. All of creation, whether mineral, plant, or animal, suffers just as men do. All creation suffers hurt, damage, loss, deterioration, erosion, death, and decay—all creation struggles for life. It is full of "futility" (*mataiotēti*), that is, condemned to futility and frustration, unable to realize its purpose, subject to corruption. |
| **#1634<br>Futility**<br><br>Vanity–KJV<br>**Futility**–NASB | ματαιότητι = *mataiotēti*<br>Pronunciation: [mat-ah-yot'-ay-tee]<br>Parsing (part of speech): noun<br>  Case—dative<br>  Gender—feminine<br>  Number—singular | Futility, vanity; emptiness; frustration; to be hopelessly confused; to be empty, futile, senseless, aimless, unsuccessful, worthless. |

# Practical Word Studies
## in the New Testament

| ENGLISH WORD | GREEK WORD AND VERSE | THE WORD MEANS... |
|---|---|---|
| **Futility–NIV** <br> **Futility–NKJV** <br> Hopelessly confused–NLT <br><br> **POSB REFERENCE** <br> (Eph.4:17-19; esp. v.17) <br> Note 1, point 1 | Stem or root—from ματαιότης, ητος <br> Concordance References: <br> ⇒ Strong's #3153 mataiotēs <br> ⇒ NIV #3470 mataiotēs <br> ⇒ NASB #3153 mataiotēs <br><br> **Ephes. 4:17** <br> This I say therefore, and testify in the Lord, that ye henceforth walk not as other Gentiles walk, in the **vanity** of their mind, [KJV] <br> This I say therefore, and affirm together with the Lord, that you walk no longer just as the Gentiles also walk, in the **futility** of their mind, [NASB] <br> So I tell you this, and insist on it in the Lord, that you must no longer live as the Gentiles do, in the **futility** of their thinking. [NIV] <br> This I say, therefore, and testify in the Lord, that you should no longer walk as the rest of the Gentiles walk, in the **futility** of their mind, [NKJV] <br> With the Lord's authority let me say this: Live no longer as the ungodly do, for they are **hopelessly confused**. [NLT] <br> Τοῦτο οὖν λέγω καὶ μαρτύρομαι ἐν Κυρίῳ, μηκέτι ὑμᾶς περιπατεῖν καθὼς καὶ τὰ λοιπὰ ἔθνη περιπατεῖ, ἐν **ματαιότητι** τοῦ νοὸς αὐτῶν, [GNS] <br> Τοῦτο οὖν λέγω καὶ μαρτύρομαι ἐν κυρίῳ, μηκέτι ὑμᾶς περιπατεῖν, καθὼς καὶ τὰ ἔθνη περιπατεῖ ἐν **ματαιότητι** τοῦ νοὸς αὐτῶν, [GNT] | **Practical Application** <br> When men push God out of their minds, their minds are void and empty of God, of His truth and morality. *God is not in their thoughts.* Their minds are ready to be filled with some other god or supremacy, that is, with the things of the world: <br> ⇒ worldly pleasures <br> ⇒ worldly possessions <br> ⇒ worldly power <br> ⇒ worldly position <br> ⇒ worldly religions <br> ⇒ worldly ideas <br> ⇒ worldly honor <br> ⇒ worldly gods |

**PRACTICAL WORD STUDIES**
in the NEW TESTAMENT

| ENGLISH WORD | GREEK WORD AND VERSE | THE WORD MEANS... |
|---|---|---|
| **#1635**<br>**Gabriel**<br><br>Gabriel–KJV<br>Gabriel–NASB<br>Gabriel–NIV<br>Gabriel–NKJV<br>Gabriel–NLT<br><br>**POSB REFERENCE**<br>(Lk.1:19)<br>*Deeper Study #1* | Γαβριὴλ = *Gabriël*<br>Pronunciation: [gab-ree-ayle']<br>Parsing (part of speech): noun<br>  Case—nominative<br>  Gender—masculine<br>  Number—singular<br>  Stem or root—from Γαβριήλ<br>Concordance References:<br>⇒ Strong's #1043 *Gabriël*<br>⇒ NIV #1120 *Gabriël*<br>⇒ NASB #1043 *Gabriël*<br><br>**Luke 1:19**<br>And the angel answering said unto him, I am **Gabriel**, that stand in the presence of God; and am sent to speak unto thee, and to shew thee these glad tidings. [KJV]<br><br>And the angel answered and said to him, "I am **Gabriel**, who stands in the presence of God; and I have been sent to speak to you, and to bring you this good news. [NASB]<br><br>The angel answered, "I am **Gabriel**. I stand in the presence of God, and I have been sent to speak to you and to tell you this good news. [NIV]<br><br>And the angel answered and said to him, "I am **Gabriel**, who stands in the presence of God, and was sent to speak to you and bring you these glad tidings. [NKJV]<br><br>Then the angel said, "I am **Gabriel**! I stand in the very presence of God. It was he who sent me to bring you this good news! [NLT]<br><br>καὶ ἀποκριθεὶς ὁ ἄγγελος εἶπεν αὐτῷ, Ἐγώ εἰμι Γαβριὴλ ὁ παρεστηκὼς ἐνώπιον τοῦ Θεοῦ· καὶ ἀπεστάλην λαλῆσαι πρὸς σέ, καὶ εὐαγγελίσασθαί σοι ταῦτα. [GNS]<br><br>καὶ ἀποκριθεὶς ὁ ἄγγελος εἶπεν αὐτῷ, Ἐγώ εἰμι Γαβριὴλ ὁ παρεστηκὼς ἐνώπιον τοῦ θεοῦ καὶ ἀπεστάλην λαλῆσαι πρὸς σε καὶ εὐαγγελίσασθαί σοι ταῦτα· [GNT] | The *man of God*, the *hero of God* or the *mighty one of God*.<br><br>**Practical Application**<br>Note that Gabriel said two things about himself...<br>1. He is the one who actually stands in the presence of God.<br>2. He is the one who brings good news to men.<br>  ⇒ He shared the restoration of Israel with Daniel (Daniel 8:16; Daniel 9:21f).<br>  ⇒ He shared the birth of the forerunner with Zacharias (Luke 1:13f).<br>  ⇒ He shared the birth of the Messiah with Mary (Luke 1:26f). |
| **#1636**<br>**Garrison**<br><br>Band of soldiers–KJV<br>Cohort–NASB<br>Company of soldiers–NIV<br>**Garrison–NKJV**<br>Battalion–NLT<br><br>**POSB REFERENCE**<br>(Mt.27:26-38; esp. v.27)<br>Note 2, point 2 | σπεῖραν = *speiran*<br>Pronunciation: [spi'-rahn]<br>Parsing (part of speech): noun<br>  Case—accusative<br>  Gender—feminine<br>  Number—singular<br>  Stem or root—from σπεῖρά ης<br>Concordance References:<br>⇒ Strong's #4686 *speira*<br>⇒ NIV #5061 *speira*<br>⇒ NASB #4686 *speira*<br><br>**Matthew 27:27**<br>Then the soldiers of the governor took Jesus into the common hall, and gathered unto him the whole **band of soldiers**. [KJV]<br><br>Then the soldiers of the governor took Jesus into the Praetorium and gathered the whole Roman **cohort** around Him. [NASB]<br><br>Then the governor's soldiers took Jesus into the Praetorium and gathered the whole **company of soldiers** around him. [NIV]<br><br>Then the soldiers of the governor took Jesus into the Praetorium and gathered the whole **garrison** around Him. [NKJV]<br><br>Some of the governor's soldiers took Jesus into their headquarters and called out the entire **battalion**. [NLT]<br><br>Τότε οἱ στρατιῶται τοῦ ἡγεμόνος παραλαβόντες τὸν Ἰησοῦν εἰς τὸ πραιτώριον συνήγαγον ἐπ' αὐτὸν ὅλην τὴν σπεῖραν· [GNS]<br><br>Τότε οἱ στρατιῶται τοῦ ἡγεμόνος παραλαβόντες τὸν Ἰησοῦν εἰς τὸ πραιτώριον συνήγαγον ἐπ' αὐτὸν ὅλην τὴν σπεῖραν. [GNT] | A company, battalion, detachment, cohort, garrison or band of soldiers; a regiment.<br><br>**Practical Application**<br>This usually meant a garrison which was made up of six hundred soldiers. However, "garrison" (*speiran*) sometimes meant maniple. Every garrison consisted of three maniples, about two hundred soldiers. Which is meant here is not known. Most believe the number of soldiers was large, certainly close to the two hundred serving in a maniple. |

# Practical Word Studies in the New Testament

| English Word | Greek Word and Verse | The Word Means... |
|---|---|---|
| **#1637**<br>**Gather–**<br>**Gathered**<br><br>**Gather**–KJV<br>**Gather**–NASB<br>**Picked up**–NIV<br>**Gather**–NKJV<br>**Gathered**–NLT<br><br>**POSB**<br>**REFERENCE**<br>(Jn.15:4-6; esp. v.6)<br>Note 4, point 4c | συνάγουσιν = sunagousin<br>Pronunciation: [soon-ahg'-oo-sin]<br>Parsing (part of speech): verb<br>    Mood—indicative<br>    Tense—present<br>    Voice—active<br>    Person—3rd person<br>    Number—plural<br>    Stem or root—from συνάγω<br>Concordance References:<br>  ⇒ Strong's #4863 sunago<br>  ⇒ NIV #5251 sunago<br>  ⇒ NASB #4863 sunago<br><br>**John 15:6**<br>If a man abide not in me, he is cast forth as a branch, and is withered; and men **gather** them, and cast them into the fire, and they are burned. [KJV]<br>"If anyone does not abide in Me, he is thrown away as a branch, and dries up; and they **gather** them, and cast them into the fire, and they are burned. [NASB]<br>If anyone does not remain in me, he is like a branch that is thrown away and withers; such branches are **picked up**, thrown into the fire and burned. [NIV]<br>If anyone does not abide in Me, he is cast out as a branch and is withered; and they **gather** them and throw *them* into the fire, and they are burned. [NKJV]<br>Anyone who parts from me is thrown away like a useless branch and withers. Such branches are **gathered** into a pile to be burned. [NLT]<br>ἐὰν μή τις μείνῃ ἐν ἐμοί, ἐβλήθη ἔξω ὡς τὸ κλῆμα, καὶ ἐξηράνθη, καὶ **συνάγουσιν** αὐτά, καὶ εἰς πῦρ βάλλουσι, καὶ καίεται. [GNS]<br>ἐὰν μή τις μένῃ ἐν ἐμοί, ἐβλήθη ἔξω ὡς τὸ κλῆμα καὶ ἐξηράνθη καὶ **συνάγουσιν** αὐτὰ καὶ εἰς τὸ πῦρ βάλλουσιν καὶ καίεται. [GNT] | To pick up; to gather; to collect; to assemble; to bring together; to invite in.<br><br>**Practical Application**<br>Note the purpose for picking up the branches: the day of judgment arrived. In the Greek text, the person who picks up or gathers is not given. The Greek simply says, "gathered." This is probably God having His angels gather all the unattached branches, "all things that offend, and them which do iniquity" (cp. Matthew 13:41). [KJV] |
| **#1638**<br>**Gather**<br>**Together In**<br>**One All**<br>**Things**<br><br>**Gather together in**<br>**one all things**–<br>KJV<br>Summing up of all<br>things–NASB<br>Bring...together under<br>one head–NIV<br>**Gather together in**<br>**one all things**–<br>NKJV<br>Bring everything<br>together–NLT<br><br>**POSB**<br>**REFERENCE**<br>(Eph.1:9-10; esp. v.10)<br>Note 6, point 3 | ἀνακεφαλαιώσασθαι = anakephalaiösasthai<br>Pronunciation: [an-ak-ef-al-ah'ee-o-sahs-tha-ee]<br>Parsing (part of speech): verb<br>    Mood—infinitive<br>    Tense—aorist<br>    Voice—middle deponent<br>    Stem or root—from ἀνακεφαλαιόω<br>Concordance References:<br>  ⇒ Strong's #346 anakephalaioö<br>  ⇒ NIV #368 anakephalaioö<br>  ⇒ NASB #346 anakephalaioö<br><br>**Ephes. 1:10**<br>That in the dispensation of the fulness of times he might **gather together in one all things** in Christ, both which are in heaven, and which are on earth; even in him: [KJV]<br>With a view to an administration suitable to the fulness of the times, that is, the **summing up of all things** in Christ, things in the heavens and things upon the earth. In Him [NASB]<br>To be put into effect when the times will have reached their fulfillment—to **bring** all things in heaven and on earth **together under one head**, even Christ. [NIV]<br>That in the dispensation of the fullness of the times He might **gather together in one all things** in Christ, both which are in heaven and which are on earth—in Him. [NKJV]<br>And this is his plan: At the right time he will **bring everything together** under the authority of Christ—everything in heaven and on earth. [NLT]<br>εἰς οἰκονομίαν τοῦ πληρώματος τῶν καιρῶν, **ἀνακεφαλαιώσασθαι** τὰ πάντα ἐν τῷ Χριστῷ, τά τε ἐν τοῖς οὐρανοῖς καὶ τὰ ἐπὶ τῆς γῆς· ἐν αὐτῷ, [GNS]<br>εἰς οἰκονομίαν τοῦ πληρώματος τῶν καιρῶν, **ἀνακεφαλαιώσασθαι** τὰ πάντα ἐν τῷ Χριστῷ, τὰ ἐπὶ τοῖς οὐρανοῖς καὶ τὰ ἐπὶ τῆς γῆς ἐν αὐτῷ. [GNT] | To bring together under one head; to gather together in one all things; to sum up all things; to bring everything together; to unite.<br><br>**Practical Application**<br>There is to be a consummation, a climax of history—a *fullness of time*, a new order—in which all things will be unified and harmonized and brought to a peaceful state under the authority of Jesus Christ. History is in the hands of God.<br>God is handling, planning, arranging, and administering all things toward a climactic consummation for Christ and His followers. In that climactic day all disharmony and division and evil will be subjected and harmonized (*anakephalaiösasthai*) under Christ. A new and perfect and eternal creation will be established for the Lord and His followers throughout the universe. |

# PRACTICAL WORD STUDIES
## in the NEW TESTAMENT

| ENGLISH WORD | GREEK WORD AND VERSE | THE WORD MEANS... |
|---|---|---|
| **#1639**<br>**Gathered–**<br>**Gathered**<br>**Together**<br><br>Assembled–KJV<br>**Gathered together–**<br>**NASB**<br>Came together–NIV<br>Assembled–NKJV<br>**Gathered–NLT**<br><br>**POSB**<br>**REFERENCE**<br>(Mk.14:53)<br>Note 1 | συνέρχονται = sunerchontai<br>Pronunciation: [soon-er'-khon-tah-ee]<br>Parsing (part of speech): verb<br>   Mood—indicative<br>   Tense—present<br>   Voice—middle or passive deponent<br>   Person—3rd person<br>   Number—plural<br>   Stem or root—from συνέρχομαι<br>Concordance References:<br>⇒ Strong's #4905 sunerchomai<br>⇒ NIV #5302 sunerchomai<br>⇒ NASB #4905 sunerchomai<br><br>**Mark 14:53**<br>And they led Jesus away to the high priest: and with him were **assembled** all the chief priests and the elders and the scribes. [KJV]<br>And they led Jesus away to the high priest; and all the chief priests and the elders and the scribes **gathered together**. [NASB]<br>They took Jesus to the high priest, and all the chief priests, elders and teachers of the law **came together**. [NIV]<br>And they led Jesus away to the high priest; and with him were **assembled** all the chief priests, the elders, and the scribes. [NKJV]<br>Jesus was led to the high priest's home where the leading priests, other leaders, and teachers of religious law had **gathered**. [NLT]<br>Καὶ ἀπήγαγον τὸν Ἰησοῦν πρὸς τὸν ἀρχιερέα· καὶ **συνέρχονται** αὐτῷ πάντες οἱ ἀρχιερεῖς καὶ οἱ πρεσβύτεροι καὶ οἱ γραμματεῖς. [GNS]<br>Καὶ ἀπήγαγον τὸν Ἰησοῦν πρὸς τὸν ἀρχιερέα, καὶ **συνέρχονται** πάντες οἱ ἀρχιερεῖς καὶ οἱ πρεσβύτεροι καὶ οἱ γραμματεῖς. [GNT] | To assemble; to gather; to draw together; to come together; to flock together; to resort; to meet with.<br><br>**Practical Application**<br>The word also has the idea of accompanying one another. The picture is that of the Jewish leaders flocking or herding together around Jesus, of being called to accompany one another to their respective seats, ready to pounce on Jesus. |
| **#1640**<br>**Gathering**<br>**Together**<br><br>Abode–KJV<br>**Gathering together–**<br>**NASB**<br>Came together–NIV<br>Staying–NKJV<br>Returned–NLT<br><br>**POSB**<br>**REFERENCE**<br>(Mt.17:22)<br>Note 1, point 1 | Συστρεφομένων = Sustrephomenōn<br>Pronunciation: [sus-tref'-o-me'-known]<br>Parsing (part of speech): verb<br>   Mood—participle<br>   Tense—present<br>   Voice—passive<br>   Case—genitive<br>   Gender—masculine<br>   Person—plural<br>   Stem or root—from συστρέφω<br>Concordance References:<br>⇒ Strong's #390 anastrephō<br>⇒ NIV #5370 sustrephō<br>⇒ NASB #390 anastrephō<br><br>**Matthew 17:22**<br>And while they **abode** in Galilee, Jesus said unto them, The Son of man shall be betrayed into the hands of men: [KJV]<br>And while they were **gathering together** in Galilee, Jesus said to them, "The Son of Man is going to be delivered into the hands of men; [NASB]<br>When they **came together** in Galilee, he said to them, "The Son of Man is going to be betrayed into the hands of men. [NIV]<br>Now while they were **staying** in Galilee, Jesus said to them, "The Son of Man is about to be betrayed into the hands of men, [NKJV]<br>One day after they had **returned** to Galilee, Jesus told them, "The Son of Man is going to be betrayed. [NLT]<br>Ἀνατρεφομένων δὲ αὐτῶν ἐν τῇ Γαλιλαίᾳ εἶπεν αὐτοῖς ὁ Ἰησοῦς, Μέλλει ὁ υἱὸς τοῦ ἀνθρώπου παραδίδοσθαι εἰς χεῖρας ἀνθρώπων, [GNS]<br>**Συστρεφομένων** δὲ αὐτῶν ἐν τῇ Γαλιλαίᾳ εἶπεν αὐτοῖς ὁ Ἰησοῦς, Μέλλει ὁ υἱὸς τοῦ ἀνθρώπου παραδίδοσθαι εἰς χεῖρας ἀνθρώπων, [GNT] | To have gathered; to come together; to abiode; to return; to go to and fro; a picture of having gathered military troops for a review.<br><br>**Practical Application**<br>The force of this word takes on a fresh meaning when the context of this Scripture is understood.<br>Jesus Christ was preparing the "troops"—His disciples—for the time when He would no longer be with them. He was drilling into them the fact that He was to be killed and raised from the dead. Jesus had to continue talking about His death and resurrection because it was so hard to understand. There were three primary reasons why the disciples had difficulty in grasping the fact.<br>1. The Messiah's death and resurrection were new experiences, new happenings. History was to be made. The talk of a literal death and resurrection was bound to be understood in symbolic and spiritual language (see POSB note—Matthew 18:1-2). (How like so many to spiritualize the two events—even though the events really took place and are so strongly proclaimed by the disciples.) (Cp. 1 Cor. 15:3-8. See POSB note—Mark 9:32; POSB note—Mark 9:34.)<br>2. The Messiah's death and resurrection were thought to be impossible. How could God die? Most men proclaim that God cannot die. Of course, the disciples had not yet seen what death really is—basically separation from |

# PRACTICAL WORD STUDIES
## in the NEW TESTAMENT

| ENGLISH WORD | GREEK WORD AND VERSE | THE WORD MEANS... |
|---|---|---|
| | | God (see POSB *Deeper Study* #1—Hebrews 9:27). They had to learn that God was dealing with spiritual and eternal life (and death), not just with physical and temporal life (and death) on this earth.<br>3. The Messiah's death and resurrection were contrary to all their hopes and expectations. It was different from all the disciples had ever heard or been taught. The Messiah was thought to be a Messiah of power and sovereign rule not a Messiah who had to suffer and die in order to save man. (See POSB note—Matthew 1:1; POSB *Deeper Study* #2—Matthew 1:18; POSB *Deeper Study* #2—Matthew 3:11; POSB note—Matthew 11:1-6; POSB note—Matthew 11:2-3; POSB *Deeper Study* #1—Matthew 11:5; POSB *Deeper Study* #2—Matthew 11:6; POSB *Deeper Study* #1—Matthew 12:16; POSB note—Matthew 22:42; POSB note—Luke 7:21-23.) |
| **#1641**<br>**Gave**<br><br>Gave–KJV<br>Gave–NASB<br>Gave–NIV<br>Gave–NKJV<br>Gave–NLT<br><br>**POSB REFERENCE**<br>(Jn.3:16)<br>Note 2, point 2 | ἔδωκεν = *edöken*<br>Pronunciation: [eh-dow'-kehn]<br>Parsing (part of speech): verb<br>   Mood—indicative<br>   Tense—aorist<br>   Voice—active<br>   Person—3rd person<br>   Number—singular<br>   Stem or root—from δίδωμι<br>Concordance References:<br>⇒ Strong's #1325 didömi<br>⇒ NIV #1443 didömi<br>⇒ NASB #1325 didömi<br><br>**John 3:16**<br>For God so loved the world, that he **gave** his only begotten Son, that whosoever believeth in him should not perish, but have everlasting life. [KJV]<br>"For God so loved the world, that He **gave** His only begotten Son, that whoever believes in Him should not perish, but have eternal life. [NASB]<br>"For God so loved the world that he **gave** his one and only Son, that whoever believes in him shall not perish but have eternal life. [NIV]<br>For God so loved the world that He **gave** His only begotten Son, that whoever believes in Him should not perish but have everlasting life. [NKJV]<br>"For God so loved the world that he **gave** his only Son, so that everyone who believes in him will not perish but have eternal life. [NLT]<br>Οὕτω γὰρ ἠγάπησεν ὁ Θεὸς τὸν κόσμον, ὥστε τὸν υἱὸν αὐτοῦ τὸν μονογενῆ **ἔδωκεν**, ἵνα πᾶς ὁ πιστεύων εἰς αὐτὸν μὴ ἀπόληται ἀλλ' ἔχῃ ζωὴν αἰώνιον. [GNS]<br>Οὕτως γὰρ ἠγάπησεν ὁ θεὸς τὸν κόσμον, ὥστε τὸν υἱὸν τὸν μονογενῆ **ἔδωκεν**, ἵνα πᾶς ὁ πιστεύων εἰς αὐτὸν μὴ ἀπόληται ἀλλ' ἔχῃ ζωὴν αἰώνιον. [GNT] | To give in spite of great cost; to bestow upon; to present.<br><br>**Practical Application**<br>In this Scripture, the word "gave" (*edöken*) has a twofold meaning. God gave His Son to the world, and He gave His Son to die. The idea of sacrifice, of great cost, is in both acts. It cost God dearly to give His Son up to the world and up to the cross. |
| **#1642**<br>**Gave [Them] Orders**<br><br>Charged–KJV<br>**Gave [them] orders–NASB**<br>Commanded–NIV<br>Commanded–NKJV<br>Told–NLT | διεστείλατο = *diesteilato*<br>Pronunciation: [dee-es-teel'-ah-tow]<br>Parsing (part of speech): verb<br>   Mood—indicative<br>   Tense—aorist<br>   Voice—middle<br>   Person—3rd person<br>   Number—singular<br>   Stem or root—from διαστέλλω<br>Concordance References:<br>⇒ Strong's #1291 diastellomai<br>⇒ NIV #1403 diastellö<br>⇒ NASB #1291 diastellö | To charge; to give a command; to give orders; to tell someone what to do or what not to do; to warn.<br><br>**Practical Application**<br>The word for "gave them orders" (*diesteilato*) is strong. The order was clearly given. The reason is not known, but there is a lesson on humility in the command. Jesus was not after the applause or praise of peoplemen. The miracles were not done for that reason. All that He was and all that He had done was to help peoplemen and point them to God. People were lost, and He |

# PRACTICAL WORD STUDIES
## in the NEW TESTAMENT

| ENGLISH WORD | GREEK WORD AND VERSE | THE WORD MEANS... |
|---|---|---|
| **POSB REFERENCE** (Mk.7:36) Note 5 | **Mark 7:36**<br>And he **charged** them that they should tell no man: but the more he charged them, so much the more a great deal they published it; [KJV]<br>And He **gave them orders** not to tell anyone; but the more He ordered them, the more widely they continued to proclaim it. [NASB]<br>Jesus **commanded** them not to tell anyone. But the more he did so, the more they kept talking about it. [NIV]<br>Then He **commanded** them that they should tell no one; but the more He commanded them, the more widely they proclaimed it. [NKJV]<br>Jesus **told** the crowd not to tell anyone, but the more he told them not to, the more they spread the news, [NLT]<br>καὶ **διεστείλατο** αὐτοῖς ἵνα μηδενὶ εἴπωσιν· ὅσον δὲ αὐτὸς αὐτοῖς διεστέλλετο μᾶλλον περισσότερον ἐκήρυσσον· [GNS]<br>καὶ **διεστείλατο** αὐτοῖς ἵνα μηδενὶ λέγωσιν· ὅσον δὲ αὐτοῖς διεστέλλετο, αὐτοὶ μᾶλλον περισσότερον ἐκήρυσσον. [GNT] | had come to seek and save the lost, not to win their applause (cp. Luke 19:10). |
| **#1643**<br>**Gave Heed**<br><br>Gave heed–KJV<br>Giving attention–NASB<br>Paid close attention–NIV<br>Heeded–NKJV<br>Listened intently–NLT<br><br>**POSB REFERENCE** (Acts 8:6) Note 2, point 2 | προσεῖχον = *proseichon*<br>Pronunciation: [pros-eekh'-on]<br>Parsing (part of speech): verb<br>  Mood—indicative<br>  Tense—imperfect<br>  Voice—active<br>  Person—3rd person<br>  Number—plural<br>  Stem or root—from προσέχω<br>Concordance References:<br>⇒ Strong's #4337 *prosechō*<br>⇒ NIV #4668 *prosechō*<br>⇒ NASB #4337 *prosechō*<br><br>**Acts 8:6**<br>And the people with one accord **gave heed** unto those things which Philip spake, hearing and seeing the miracles which he did. [KJV]<br>And the multitudes with one accord were **giving attention** to what was said by Philip, as they heard and saw the signs which he was performing. [NASB]<br>When the crowds heard Philip and saw the miraculous signs he did, they all **paid close attention** to what he said. [NIV]<br>And the multitudes with one accord **heeded** the things spoken by Philip, hearing and seeing the miracles which he did. [NKJV]<br>Crowds **listened intently** to what he had to say because of the miracles he did. [NLT]<br>**προσεῖχον** τε οἱ ὄχλοι τοῖς λεγομένοις ὑπὸ τοῦ Φιλίππου ὁμοθυμαδὸν, ἐν τῷ ἀκούειν αὐτοὺς καὶ βλέπειν τὰ σημεῖα ἃ ἐποίει. [GNS]<br>**προσεῖχον** δὲ οἱ ὄχλοι τοῖς λεγομένοις ὑπὸ τοῦ Φιλίππου ὁμοθυμαδὸν ἐν τῷ ἀκούειν αὐτοὺς καὶ βλέπειν τὰ σημεῖα ἃ ἐποίει· [GNT] | To pay close attention; to give attention; to listen intently; to heed.<br><br>**Practical Application**<br>The believer must "give heed"; must pay close attention, keep his mind and heart upon the message. |
| **#1644**<br>**Gave Himself**<br><br>Gave himself–KJV<br>Gave Himself–NASB<br>Gave himself–NIV<br>Gave Himself–NKJV<br>He died–NLT<br><br>**POSB REFERENCE** (Gal.1:4-5; esp. v.4) Note 4, point 1 | δόντος ἑαυτὸν = *dontos heauton*<br>Pronunciation: [don'-tos eh-ow-ton]<br>Parsing *dontos* (part of speech): verb<br>  Mood—participle<br>  Tense—aorist<br>  Voice—active<br>  Case—genitive<br>  Gender—masculine<br>  Number—singular<br>  Stem or root—from δίδωμι<br>Parsing *heauton* (part of speech): noun<br>  Type—pronoun<br>  Case—accusative<br>  Gender—masculine<br>  Person—3rd person<br>  Number—singular<br>  Stem or root—from ἑαυτοῦ, ῆς, οῦ | To give; to grant; to allow; to permit Himself. The phrase "gave Himself" (*dontos heauton*) means that He sacrificed Himself for us. He gave His life for the sinner's life.<br><br>**Practical Application**<br>Jesus Christ...<br>• offered Himself to God as the sacrifice for our sin.<br>• offered Himself as the sin-offering, the offering that was to stand as the substitute for our sin.<br>• accepted the judgment and condemnation of sin for us.<br>• bore the punishment of God's justice against sin for us. |

## Practical Word Studies in the New Testament

| ENGLISH WORD | GREEK WORD AND VERSE | THE WORD MEANS... |
|---|---|---|
| | Concordance References:<br>⇒ Strong's #1325 didōmi + 1438 heautou<br>⇒ NIV #1443 didōmi [gave] + 1571 heautou [himself]<br>⇒ NASB #1325 didōmi + 1438 heautou<br><br>**Galatians 1:4**<br>Who **gave himself** for our sins, that he might deliver us from this present evil world, according to the will of God and our Father: [KJV]<br>Who **gave Himself** for our sins, that He might deliver us out of this present evil age, according to the will of our God and Father, [NASB]<br>Who **gave himself** for our sins to rescue us from the present evil age, according to the will of our God and Father, [NIV]<br>Who **gave Himself** for our sins, that He might deliver us from this present evil age, according to the will of our God and Father, [NKJV]<br>**He died** for our sins, just as God our Father planned, in order to rescue us from this evil world in which we live. [NLT]<br>τοῦ **δόντος ἑαυτὸν** ὑπὲρ τῶν ἁμαρτιῶν ἡμῶν ὅπως ἐξέληται ἡμᾶς ἐκ τοῦ ἐνεστῶτος αἰῶνος πονηροῦ, κατὰ τὸ θέλημα τοῦ Θεοῦ καὶ πατρὸς ἡμῶν· [GNS]<br>τοῦ **δόντος ἑαυτὸν** ὑπὲρ τῶν ἁμαρτιῶν ἡμῶν, ὅπως ἐξέληται ἡμᾶς ἐκ τοῦ αἰῶνος τοῦ ἐνεστῶτος πονηροῦ κατὰ τὸ θέλημα τοῦ θεοῦ καὶ πατρὸς ἡμῶν, [GNT] | |
| **#1645**<br>**Gave It**<br><br>Gave it–KJV<br>Gave it–NASB<br>Offered–NIV<br>Gave it–NKJV<br>Gave it–NLT<br><br>**POSB REFERENCE**<br>(Mk.14:23-24; esp. v.23)<br>Note 2, point 3 | ἔδωκεν = *edoken*<br>Pronunciation: [eh-dow'-kehn]<br>Parsing (part of speech): verb<br>    Mood—indicative<br>    Tense—aorist<br>    Voice—active<br>    Person—3rd person<br>    Number—singular<br>    Stem or root—from δίδωμι<br>Concordance References:<br>⇒ Strong's #1325 didōmi<br>⇒ NIV #1443 didōmi<br>⇒ NASB #1325 didōmi<br><br>**Mark 14:23**<br>And he took the cup, and when he had given thanks, he **gave it** to them: and they all drank of it. [KJV]<br>And when He had taken a cup, and given thanks, He **gave it** to them; and they all drank from it. [NASB]<br>Then he took the cup, gave thanks and **offered** it to them, and they all drank from it. [NIV]<br>Then He took the cup, and when He had given thanks He **gave** *it* to them, and they all drank from it. [NKJV]<br>And he took a cup of wine and gave thanks to God for it. He **gave it** to them, and they all drank from it. [NLT]<br>καὶ λαβὼν τὸ ποτήριον, εὐχαριστήσας **ἔδωκεν** αὐτοῖς· καὶ ἔπιον ἐξ αὐτοῦ πάντες. [GNS]<br>καὶ λαβὼν ποτήριον εὐχαριστήσας **ἔδωκεν** αὐτοῖς, καὶ ἔπιον ἐξ αὐτοῦ πάντες. [GNT] | To offer; to give to; to present; to show.<br><br>**Practical Application**<br>Christ offered the cup once for all. Note the word "offered" or "gave it" (*edoken*) is in the Greek aorist tense. He died once and only once (Romans 6:10), and man partakes of His death once and only once (Romans 6:6). |
| **#1646**<br>**Gave Orders**<br><br>Commanded–KJV<br>Ordered–NASB<br>Ordered–NIV<br>Commanded–NKJV<br>Gave orders–NLT<br><br>**POSB REFERENCE**<br>(Acts 10:48)<br>Note 4 | προσέταξεν = *prosetaxen*<br>Pronunciation: [pros-eh'-tahxs-ehn]<br>Parsing (part of speech): verb<br>    Mood—indicative<br>    Tense—aorist<br>    Voice—active<br>    Person—3rd person<br>    Number—singular<br>    Stem or root—from προστάσσω<br>Concordance References:<br>⇒ Strong's #4367 prostassō<br>⇒ NIV #4705 prostassō<br>⇒ NASB #4367 prostassō | To order; to give a command; to give orders.<br><br>**Practical Application**<br>Peter "gave orders" (*prosetaxen*) for the Gentile believers to be baptized. Evidently, he commanded the six Jewish brothers to baptize them. Note: the Gentiles...<br>• had "heard the Word" (Acts 10:44).<br>• "believed on the Lord Jesus Christ" (Acts 11:17).<br>• experienced "the Holy Spirit" falling (Acts 10:44), and being "poured" upon them (Acts 10:45). They had "received the Holy |

# PRACTICAL WORD STUDIES
## in the NEW TESTAMENT

| ENGLISH WORD | GREEK WORD AND VERSE | THE WORD MEANS... |
|---|---|---|
| | **Acts 10:48**<br>And he **commanded** them to be baptized in the name of the Lord. Then prayed they him to tarry certain days. [KJV]<br>And he **ordered** them to be baptized in the name of Jesus Christ. Then they asked him to stay on for a few days. [NASB]<br>So he **ordered** that they be baptized in the name of Jesus Christ. Then they asked Peter to stay with them for a few days. [NIV]<br>And he **commanded** them to be baptized in the name of the Lord. Then they asked him to stay a few days. [NKJV]<br>So he **gave orders** for them to be baptized in the name of Jesus Christ. Afterward Cornelius asked him to stay with them for several days. [NLT]<br>προσέταξε τε αὐτοὺς βαπτισθῆναι ἐν τῷ ὀνόματι τοῦ Κυρίου. τότε ἠρώτησαν αὐτὸν ἐπιμεῖναι ἡμέρας τινάς. [GNS]<br>προσέταξεν δὲ αὐτοὺς ἐν τῷ ὀνόματι Ἰησοῦ Χριστοῦ βαπτισθῆναι. τότε ἠρώτησαν αὐτὸν ἐπιμεῖναι ἡμέρας τινάς. [GNT] | Spirit" (Acts 10:47).<br>• were "baptized in the name of the Lord" (Acts 10:48). |
| **#1647**<br>**Gave Up His Spirit**<br><br>Yielded up the ghost– KJV<br>Yielded up His Spirit– NASB<br>Gave up his spirit– NIV<br>Yielded up His spirit– NKJV<br>Gave up his spirit– NLT<br><br>**POSB REFERENCE**<br>(Mt.27:50)<br>Note 3, point 2 | ἀφῆκεν τὸ πνεῦμα = *aphēken to pneuma*<br>Pronunciation: [af-ee'-ken to pnyoo'-mah]<br>Parsing *aphēken* (part of speech): verb<br>  Mood—indicative<br>  Tense—aorist<br>  Voice—active<br>  Person—3rd person<br>  Number—singular<br>  Stem or root—from ἀφίημι<br>Parsing *pneuma* (part of speech): noun<br>  Case—accusative<br>  Gender—neuter<br>  Number—singular<br>  Stem or root—from πνεῦμα, τος<br>Concordance References:<br>⇒ Strong's #863 aphiemi + 4151 pneuma<br>⇒ NIV #918 aphiēmi [gave up] + 3836 ho [his] + 4460 pneuma [spirit]<br>⇒ NASB #863 aphiemi + 4151 pneuma<br><br>**Matthew 27:50**<br>Jesus, when he had cried again with a loud voice, **yielded up the ghost**. [KJV]<br>And Jesus cried out again with a loud voice, and **yielded up His spirit**. [NASB]<br>And when Jesus had cried out again in a loud voice, he **gave up his spirit**. [NIV]<br>And Jesus cried out again with a loud voice, and **yielded up His spirit**. [NKJV]<br>Then Jesus shouted out again, and he **gave up his spirit**. [NLT]<br>ὁ δὲ Ἰησοῦς πάλιν κράξας φωνῇ μεγάλῃ ἀφῆκε τὸ πνεῦμα. [GNS]<br>ὁ δὲ Ἰησοῦς πάλιν κράξας φωνῇ μεγάλῃ ἀφῆκεν τὸ πνεῦμα. [GNT] | Christ willingly yielded and gave up His spirit.<br><br>**Practical Application**<br>It must always be remembered that Jesus willingly died. He willingly came to this moment of yielding and giving up His spirit to death.<br>His death was the supreme act of obedience. It was voluntary; He willingly died. No man took His life; He sacrificed it Himself. The power to take it was His and His alone.<br>Note the critical point: this "commandment" to die was of God (cp. John 10:17-18). This gives a higher meaning to the death of Jesus than just meeting man's need. It means that Jesus did not die just because of sin, but because He wished to glorify and honor God. He wished above all else to show His love and adoration for God.<br>This is an aspect of Jesus' death that is often overlooked—an aspect that rises far above the mere meeting of our need. For in giving Himself as an "offering to God," Christ was looking beyond our need to the majestic responsibility of glorifying God. This means that His first purpose was the glory of God. He was concerned primarily with doing the will of God, with obeying God. God had been terribly dishonored by the first man, Adam, and by all those who followed after him. Jesus Christ wished to honor God by showing that at least one man thought more of God's glory than of anything else. Jesus wished to show that God's will meant more than any personal desire or ambition which He might have. |
| **#1648**<br>**Gave Us Life**<br><br>Quickened together with–KJV<br>Made alive together with–NASB<br>Made alive with–NIV<br>Made us alive together | συνεζωοποίησεν = *sunezōopoiēsen*<br>Pronunciation: [soon-ehd-zo-op-oy-ee'-sehn]<br>Parsing (part of speech): verb<br>  Mood—indicative<br>  Tense—aorist<br>  Voice—active<br>  Person—3rd person<br>  Number—singular<br>  Stem or root— from συζωοποιέω | To make alive; to quicken; to give life.<br><br>**Practical Application**<br>We were dead in trespasses and sins, but God has made us alive. Why has God made us alive? Because of His very nature. God does not have a nature like most men picture: distant, disinterested, unconcerned, vengeful, and fearful. |

# PRACTICAL WORD STUDIES
## in the NEW TESTAMENT

| ENGLISH WORD | GREEK WORD AND VERSE | THE WORD MEANS... |
|---|---|---|
| with–NKJV<br>**Gave us life–NLT**<br><br>**POSB<br>REFERENCE**<br>(Eph.2:4-5; esp. v.5)<br>Note 1, point 2b | Concordance References:<br>⇒ Strong's #4806 suzōopoieō<br>⇒ NIV #5188 suzōopoieō<br>⇒ NASB #4806 suzōopoieō<br><br>**Ephes. 2:5**<br>Even when we were dead in sins, hath **quickened** us **together with** Christ, (by grace ye are saved;) [KJV]<br>Even when we were dead in our transgressions, **made** us **alive together with** Christ (by grace you have been saved), [NASB]<br>**Made** us **alive with** Christ even when we were dead in transgressions—it is by grace you have been saved. [NIV]<br>Even when we were dead in trespasses, **made** us **alive together with** Christ (by grace you have been saved), [NKJV]<br>That even while we were dead because of our sins, he **gave us life** when he raised Christ from the dead. (It is only by God's special favor that you have been saved!) [NLT]<br>καὶ ὄντας ἡμᾶς νεκροὺς τοῖς παραπτώμασι **συνεζωοποίησε** τῷ Χριστῷ· -- χάριτί ἐστε σεσῳσμένοι· -- [GNS]<br>καὶ ὄντας ἡμᾶς νεκροὺς τοῖς παραπτώμασιν **συνεζωοποίησεν** τῷ Χριστῷ, χάριτί ἐστε σεσῳσμένοι [GNT] | |
| **#1649<br>Gazing Intently,<br>Were**<br><br>While they looked stedfastly–KJV<br>**Were gazing intently–NASB**<br>Were looking intently up–NIV<br>While they looked steadfastly–NKJV<br>Were straining their eyes–NLT<br><br>**POSB<br>REFERENCE**<br>(Acts 1:9-10; esp. v.10)<br>Note 4 | ἀτενίζοντες ἦσαν = atenizontes ēsan<br>Pronunciation: [at-en-id'-zon-tes ay-san]<br>Parsing *atenizontes* (part of speech): verb<br>  Mood—participle<br>  Tense—present<br>  Voice—active<br>  Case—nominative<br>  Gender—masculine<br>  Number—plural<br>  Stem or root—from ἀτενίζω<br>Concordance References:<br>⇒ Strong's #1510 eimi + 816 atenizō<br>⇒ NIV #1639 eimi [were] + 867 atenizō [looking intently up]<br>⇒ NASB #1510 eimi + 816 atenizō<br><br>**Acts 1:10**<br>And **while they looked stedfastly** toward heaven as he went up, behold, two men stood by them in white apparel; [KJV]<br>And as they **were gazing intently** into the sky while He was departing, behold, two men in white clothing stood beside them; [NASB]<br>They **were looking intently up** into the sky as he was going, when suddenly two men dressed in white stood beside them. [NIV]<br>And **while they looked steadfastly** toward heaven as He went up, behold, two men stood by them in white apparel, [NKJV]<br>As they **were straining their eyes** to see him, two white-robed men suddenly stood there among them. [NLT]<br>καὶ ὡς **ἀτενίζοντες ἦσαν** εἰς τὸν οὐρανὸν πορευομένου αὐτοῦ, καὶ ἰδοὺ ἄνδρες δύο παρειστήκεισαν αὐτοῖς ἐν ἐσθῆτι λευκῇ, [GNS]<br>καὶ ὡς **ἀτενίζοντες ἦσαν** εἰς τὸν οὐρανὸν πορευομένου αὐτοῦ, καὶ ἰδοὺ ἄνδρες δύο παρειστήκεισαν αὐτοῖς ἐν ἐσθήσεσι λευκαῖς, [GNT] | Were looking intently up; while they looked steadfastly; were gazing intently; were straining their eyes; to fix one's eyes on; to stare; to look directly at.<br><br>**Practical Application**<br>The Lord ascended somewhat slowly in a dramatic, spectacular fashion. Why depart in this way? For the sake of the disciples. There are several significant reasons why they needed such a dramatic departure. (See POSB note, Jesus Christ, Exaltation—Acts 2:33-36 for more discussion.)<br>1. Christ needed to dramatize and enforce His final departure.<br>2. Christ needed to dramatize and enforce His claim upon the disciples.<br>3. Christ needed to dramatize and enforce His return to earth, that it would take place exactly as He said. (See POSB note—Acts 1:10-11 for discussion.)<br>4. Christ needed to dramatize and enforce that the disciples were not to be standing around "looking intently up into the sky." They were to get to the business at hand. They were to return to the upper room and...<br>• "wait" and pray for the presence and power of the Holy Spirit.<br>• move out witnessing to a world lost and reeling in desperate need.<br>(See POSB note—Acts 1:9-10 for a detailed discussion of this topic.)<br><br>(See **Looking Intently Up,** for additional discussion.) |
| **#1650<br>Genealogy**<br><br>Generation–KJV<br>**Genealogy–NASB**<br>**Genealogy–NIV**<br>**Genealogy–NKJV** | γενέσεως = geneseōs<br>Pronunciation: [ghen'-es-ee-os]<br>Parsing (part of speech): noun<br>  Case—genitive<br>  Gender—feminine<br>  Number—singular<br>  Stem or root—from γένεσις, εως<br>Concordance References: | To be or to become. It is a record of ancestors, of a person's lineage.<br><br>**Practical Application**<br>This word pictures the idea of origin, beginning, and birth. The two genealogies of Christ are recorded in the gospels of Matthew and Luke. |

# PRACTICAL WORD STUDIES
## in the NEW TESTAMENT

| ENGLISH WORD | GREEK WORD AND VERSE | THE WORD MEANS... |
|---|---|---|
| Record of ancestors–NLT<br><br>**POSB REFERENCE**<br>(Mt.1:1)<br>Note 1 | ⇒ Strong's #1078 genesis<br>⇒ NIV #1161 genesis<br>⇒ NASB #1078 genesis<br><br>**Matthew 1:1**<br>The book of the **generation** of Jesus Christ, the son of David, the son of Abraham. [KJV]<br>The book of the **genealogy** of Jesus Christ, the son of David, the son of Abraham. [NASB]<br>A record of the **genealogy** of Jesus Christ the son of David, the son of Abraham: [NIV]<br>The book of the **genealogy** of Jesus Christ, the Son of David, the Son of Abraham: [NKJV]<br>This is a **record of the ancestors** of Jesus the Messiah, a descendant of King David and of Abraham: [NLT]<br>Βίβλος **γενέσεως** Ἰησοῦ Χριστοῦ, υἱοῦ Δαβὶδ, υἱοῦ Ἀβραάμ. [GNS]<br>Βίβλος **γενέσεως** Ἰησοῦ Χριστοῦ υἱοῦ Δαυὶδ υἱοῦ Ἀβραάμ. [GNT] | |
| **#1651**<br>**Generation**<br><br>Generation–KJV<br>Genealogy–NASB<br>Genealogy–NIV<br>Genealogy–NKJV<br>Record of ancestors–NLT<br><br>**POSB REFERENCE**<br>(Mt.1:1)<br>Note 1 | γενέσεως = *geneseōs*<br>Pronunciation: [ghen'-es-ee-os]<br>Parsing (part of speech): noun<br>  Case—genitive<br>  Gender—feminine<br>  Number—singular<br>  Stem or root—from γένεσις, εως<br>Concordance References:<br>⇒ Strong's #1078 genesis<br>⇒ NIV #1161 genesis<br>⇒ NASB #1078 genesis<br><br>**Matthew 1:1**<br>The book of the **generation** of Jesus Christ, the son of David, the son of Abraham. [KJV]<br>The book of the **genealogy** of Jesus Christ, the son of David, the son of Abraham. [NASB]<br>A record of the **genealogy** of Jesus Christ the son of David, the son of Abraham: [NIV]<br>The book of the **genealogy** of Jesus Christ, the Son of David, the Son of Abraham: [NKJV]<br>This is a **record of the ancestors** of Jesus the Messiah, a descendant of King David and of Abraham: [NLT]<br>Βίβλος **γενέσεως** Ἰησοῦ Χριστοῦ, υἱοῦ Δαβὶδ, υἱοῦ Ἀβραάμ. [GNS]<br>Βίβλος **γενέσεως** Ἰησοῦ Χριστοῦ υἱοῦ Δαυὶδ υἱοῦ Ἀβραάμ. [GNT] | To be or to become. It is a record of ancestors, of a person's lineage.<br><br>**Practical Application**<br>This word pictures the idea of origin, beginning, and birth. The two genealogies of Christ are recorded in the gospels of Matthew and Luke. |
| **#1652**<br>**Generosity**<br><br>Liberality–KJV<br>Liberality–NASB<br>**Generosity–NIV**<br>Liberality–NKJV<br>**Generosity–NLT**<br><br>**POSB REFERENCE**<br>(2 Cor.8:1-5; esp. v.2)<br>Note 1, point 1 | ἁπλότητος = *haplotētos*<br>Pronunciation: [hap-lot'-ay-tos]<br>Parsing (part of speech): noun<br>  Case—genitive<br>  Gender—feminine<br>  Number—singular<br>  Stem or root—from ἁπλότης, ητος<br>Concordance References:<br>⇒ Strong's #572 haplotēs<br>⇒ NIV #605 haplotēs<br>⇒ NASB #572 haplotēs<br><br>**2 Cor. 8:2**<br>How that in a great trial of affliction the abundance of their joy and their deep poverty abounded unto the riches of their **liberality**. [KJV]<br>That in a great ordeal of affliction their abundance of joy and their deep poverty overflowed in the wealth of their **liberality**. [NASB]<br>Out of the most severe trial, their overflowing joy and their extreme poverty welled up in rich **generosity**. [NIV]<br>That in a great trial of affliction the abundance of their | Generosity, liberality, singleness of mind; sincerely, with an open and free heart.<br><br>**Practical Application**<br>The churches of Macedonia determined to give, to open their hearts and give all they could. The point is this: they knew the Lord—really knew Him—and they were committed to living for the Lord. Therefore, when someone needed help, they were ready to help. They gave liberally. They gave with great generosity. |

877

# PRACTICAL WORD STUDIES
## in the New Testament

| ENGLISH WORD | GREEK WORD AND VERSE | THE WORD MEANS... |
|---|---|---|
| | joy and their deep poverty abounded in the riches of their **liberality**. [NKJV]<br>Though they have been going through much trouble and hard times, their wonderful joy and deep poverty have overflowed in rich **generosity**. [NLT]<br>ὅτι ἐν πολλῇ δοκιμῇ θλίψεως ἡ περισσεία τῆς χαρᾶς αὐτῶν καὶ ἡ κατὰ βάθους πτωχεία αὐτῶν ἐπερίσσευσεν εἰς τὸ πλοῦτον τῆς **ἁπλότητος** αὐτῶν. [GNS]<br>ὅτι ἐν πολλῇ δοκιμῇ θλίψεως ἡ περισσεία τῆς χαρᾶς αὐτῶν καὶ ἡ κατὰ βάθους πτωχεία αὐτῶν ἐπερίσσευσεν εἰς τὸ πλοῦτος τῆς **ἁπλότητος** αὐτῶν [GNT] | |
| **#1653**<br>**Generosity**<br>Singleness–KJV<br>Sincerity–NASB<br>Sincere–NIV<br>Simplicity–NKJV<br>**Generosity–NLT**<br>**POSB REFERENCE**<br>(Acts 2:46-47; esp. v.46)<br>Note 6, point 3 | ἀφελότητι = aphelotēti<br>Pronunciation: [af-el-ot'-ay-tee]<br>Parsing (part of speech): noun<br>  Case—dative<br>  Gender—feminine<br>  Number—singular<br>  Stem or root—from ἀφελότης, ητος<br>Concordance References:<br>  ⇒ Strong's #858 aphelotēs<br>  ⇒ NIV #911 aphelotēs<br>  ⇒ NASB #858 aphelotēs<br><br>**Acts 2:46**<br>And they, continuing daily with one accord in the temple, and breaking bread from house to house, did eat their meat with gladness and **singleness** of heart, [KJV]<br>And day by day continuing with one mind in the temple, and breaking bread from house to house, they were taking their meals together with gladness and **sincerity** of heart, [NASB]<br>Every day they continued to meet together in the temple courts. They broke bread in their homes and ate together with glad and **sincere** hearts, [NIV]<br>So continuing daily with one accord in the temple, and breaking bread from house to house, they ate their food with gladness and **simplicity** of heart, [NKJV]<br>They worshiped together at the Temple each day, met in homes for the Lord's Supper, and shared their meals with great joy and **generosity**—[NLT]<br>καθ' ἡμέραν τε προσκαρτεροῦντες ὁμοθυμαδὸν ἐν τῷ ἱερῷ, κλῶντές τε κατ' οἶκον ἄρτον, μετελάμβανον τροφῆς ἐν ἀγαλλιάσει καὶ **ἀφελότητι** καρδίας, [GNS]<br>καθ' ἡμέραν τε προσκαρτεροῦντες ὁμοθυμαδὸν ἐν τῷ ἱερῷ, κλῶντές τε κατ' οἶκον ἄρτον, μετελάμβανον τροφῆς ἐν ἀγαλλιάσει καὶ **ἀφελότητι** καρδίας, [GNT] | To be sincere, without hardness; to be generous.<br><br>**Practical Application**<br>Their hearts were soft and tender, easily touched and giving. There was no selfishness or withholding on their part. Where there was need, they gave. |
| **#1654**<br>**Generous Gifts**<br>Grace–KJV<br>Grace–NASB<br>Grace–NIV<br>Grace–NKJV<br>**Generous gifts–NLT**<br>**POSB REFERENCE**<br>(1 Cor.1:4)<br>Deeper Study #1 | χάριτι = chariti<br>Pronunciation: [khar'-ee-tee]<br>Parsing (part of speech): noun<br>  Case—dative<br>  Gender—feminine<br>  Number—singular<br>  Stem or root—from χάρις, ιτος<br>Concordance References:<br>  ⇒ Strong's #5485 charis<br>  ⇒ NIV #5921 charis<br>  ⇒ NASB #5485 charis<br><br>**1 Cor. 1:4**<br>I thank my God always on your behalf, for the **grace** of God which is given you by Jesus Christ; [KJV]<br>I thank my God always concerning you, for the **grace** of God which was given you in Christ Jesus, [NASB]<br>I always thank God for you because of his **grace** given you in Christ Jesus. [NIV]<br>I thank my God always concerning you for the **grace** of God which was given to you by Christ Jesus, [NKJV]<br>I can never stop thanking God for all the **generous gifts** he has given you, now that you belong to Christ Jesus. [NLT] | The favor and blessings of God; the undeserved and unmerited favor and blessings of God; the depth and richness of the heart and mind of God; the kindness and love that dwells within the very nature of God. God's grace covers all of life.<br><br>**Practical Application**<br>1. Generous gifts means the kindness and love that God freely gives to those who have acted against Him. It is the favor of God showered upon men who do not deserve His favor, men who are...<br>• "helpless" (Romans 5:6).<br>• "sinners" (Romans 5:6, 8).<br>• "enemies" (Romans 5:10).<br><br>No other word so expresses the depth and richness of the heart and mind of God. This is the distinctive difference between God's grace and man's grace. Whereas man sometimes does favors for his friends and thereby can be said to |

## Practical Word Studies in the New Testament

| ENGLISH WORD | GREEK WORD AND VERSE | THE WORD MEANS... |
|---|---|---|
| | Εὐχαριστῶ τῷ Θεῷ μου πάντοτε περὶ ὑμῶν, ἐπὶ τῇ **χάριτι** τοῦ Θεοῦ τῇ δοθείσῃ ὑμῖν ἐν Χριστῷ Ἰησοῦ· [GNS]<br><br>Εὐχαριστῶ τῷ Θεῷ μου πάντοτε περὶ ὑμῶν, ἐπὶ τῇ **χάριτι** τοῦ Θεοῦ τῇ δοθείσῃ ὑμῖν ἐν Χριστῷ Ἰησοῦ, [GNT] | be gracious, God has done a thing unheard of among men: He has given His very own Son to die for His enemies (see POSB outline—Romans 5:6-11 and notes—Romans 5:6-11. Also see POSB notes, Love—John 21:15-17; Grace—Ephes. 2:8-9.)<br>  a. God's grace is not earned. It is something completely undeserved and umerited.<br>  b. God's grace is the free gift of God. God extends His grace out toward man.<br>  c. God's grace is the only way man can be saved.<br>2. Generous gifts means all the favors and gifts of God. It means all the good and perfect gifts of God, all the good and beneficial things He gives us and does for us, whether physical, material, or spiritual (James 1:17). |
| **#1655**<br>**Generously**<br><br>Simplicity–KJV<br>Liberality–NASB<br>**Generously–NIV**<br>Liberality–NKJV<br>**Generously–NLT**<br><br>**POSB<br>REFERENCE**<br>(Rom.12:6-8; esp. v.8)<br>Note 2, point 5 | ἐν ἁπλότητι = *en haplotēti*<br>Pronunciation: [en hap-lot'-ay-tee]<br>Parsing *haplotēti* (part of speech): noun<br>  Case—dative<br>  Gender—feminine<br>  Number—from ἁπλότης, ητος<br>Concordance References:<br>  ⇒ Strong's #572 + 1722 haplotēs en<br>  ⇒ NIV #605 + 1877 haplotēs en [generously]<br>  ⇒ NASB #572 + 1722 haplotēs en<br><br>**Romans 12:8**<br>Or he that exhorteth, on exhortation: he that giveth, let him do it with **simplicity**; he that ruleth, with diligence; he that sheweth mercy, with cheerfulness. [KJV]<br>Or he who exhorts, in his exhortation; he who gives, with **liberality**; he who leads, with diligence; he who shows mercy, with cheerfulness. [NASB]<br>If it is encouraging, let him encourage; if it is contributing to the needs of others, let him give **generously**; if it is leadership, let him govern diligently; if it is showing mercy, let him do it cheerfully. [NIV]<br>He who exhorts, in exhortation; he who gives, with **liberality**; he who leads, with diligence; he who shows mercy, with cheerfulness. [NKJV]<br>If your gift is to encourage others, do it! If you have money, share it **generously**. If God has given you leadership ability, take the responsibility seriously. And if you have a gift for showing kindness to others, do it gladly. [NLT]<br>εἴτε ὁ παρακαλῶν, ἐν τῇ παρακλήσει· ὁ μεταδιδοὺς ἐν **ἁπλότητι**, ὁ προϊστάμενος, ἐν σπουδῇ· ὁ ἐλεῶν ἐν ἱλαρότητι. [GNS]<br>εἴτε ὁ παρακαλῶν ἐν τῇ παρακλήσει· ὁ μεταδιδοὺς ἐν **ἁπλότητι**, ὁ προϊστάμενος ἐν σπουδῇ, ὁ ἐλεῶν ἐν ἱλαρότητι. [GNT] | Generosity; simplicity; sincerity; singlehearted devotion<br><br>**Practical Application**<br>The word has several ideas. It means...<br>• to give with sincerity and in simplicity.<br>• to give with singleness of heart and without show.<br>• to give liberally and generously.<br><br>The point is this: God gives some persons the special gift to make money in order to have plenty to help others and to spread the gospel around the world. These persons...<br>• must give generously. God gave them the gift of making money in order to have enough to fulfill the will of God for the world. Therefore, they must give liberally.<br>• must not hoard and bank and misuse their gift of wealth.<br>• must not give grudgingly and complaining about having to give.<br>• must not give to attract attention or to heap honor upon themselves.<br>• must not give to boost their own egos and pride. |
| **#1656**<br>**Gentile<br>Worshipers**<br><br>Devout–KJV<br>God-fearing Gentiles–NASB<br>God-fearing Greeks–NIV<br>**Gentile worhipers–NKJV**<br>God-fearing Gentiles–NLT | σεβομένοις = *sebomenois*<br>Pronunciation: [seb'-om-ehn-o-ees]<br>Parsing (part of speech): verb<br>  Mood—participle<br>  Tense—present<br>  Voice—middle<br>  Case—dative<br>  Gender—masculine<br>  Number—plural<br>  Stem or root—from σέβομαι<br>Concordance References:<br>  ⇒ Strong's #4576 sebō<br>  ⇒ NIV #4936 sebō<br>  ⇒ NASB #4576 sebō | God-fearing Greeks or Gentiles; a worshiper of God.<br><br>**Practical Application**<br>The phrase "Gentile worshipers" (*sebomenois*) means those who worship God or the God-fearing men and women who are not Jews. |

# PRACTICAL WORD STUDIES
## in the NEW TESTAMENT

| ENGLISH WORD | GREEK WORD AND VERSE | THE WORD MEANS... |
|---|---|---|
| **POSB REFERENCE** (Acts 17:17) Note 3 | **Acts 17:17**<br>Therefore disputed he in the synagogue with the Jews, and with the **devout** persons, and in the market daily with them that met with him. [KJV]<br>So he was reasoning in the synagogue with the Jews and the **God-fearing Gentiles**, and in the market place every day with those who happened to be present. [NASB]<br>So he reasoned in the synagogue with the Jews and the **God-fearing Greeks**, as well as in the marketplace day by day with those who happened to be there. [NIV]<br>Therefore he reasoned in the synagogue with the Jews and with the *Gentile worshipers*, and in the marketplace daily with those who happened to be there. [NKJV]<br>He went to the synagogue to debate with the Jews and the **God-fearing Gentiles**, and he spoke daily in the public square to all who happened to be there. [NLT]<br>διελέγετο μὲν οὖν ἐν τῇ συναγωγῇ τοῖς Ἰουδαίοις καὶ τοῖς **σεβομένοις** καὶ ἐν τῇ ἀγορᾷ κατὰ πᾶσαν ἡμέραν πρὸς τοὺς παρατυγχάνοντας. [GNS]<br>διελέγετο μὲν οὖν ἐν τῇ συναγωγῇ τοῖς Ἰουδαίοις καὶ τοῖς **σεβομένοις** καὶ ἐν τῇ ἀγορᾷ κατὰ πᾶσαν ἡμέραν πρὸς τοὺς παρατυγχάνοντας. [GNT] | |
| **#1657**<br>**Gentle**<br>Patient–KJV<br>**Gentle–NASB**<br>**Gentle–NIV**<br>**Gentle–NKJV**<br>**Gentle–NLT**<br>**POSB REFERENCE** (1 Tim.3:3; esp. v.3) Note 2, point 11 | ἐπιεικῆ = *epieikë*<br>Pronunciation: [ep-eh-ee-kayn']<br>Parsing (part of speech): adjective<br>    Case—accusative<br>    Gender—masculine<br>    Number—singular<br>    Stem or root—from ἐπιεικής, ές<br>Concordance References:<br>    ⇒ Strong's #1933 epieikēs<br>    ⇒ NIV #2117 epieikēs<br>    ⇒ NASB #1933 epieikēs<br><br>**1 Tim. 3:3**<br>Not given to wine, no striker, not greedy of filthy lucre; but **patient**, not a brawler, not covetous; [KJV]<br>Not addicted to wine or pugnacious, but **gentle**, uncontentious, free from the love of money. [NASB]<br>Not given to drunkenness, not violent but **gentle**, not quarrelsome, not a lover of money. [NIV]<br>Not given to wine, not violent, not greedy for money, but **gentle**, not quarrelsome, not covetous; [NKJV]<br>He must not be a heavy drinker or be violent. He must be **gentle**, peace loving, and not one who loves money. [NLT]<br>μὴ πάροινον, μὴ πλήκτην, μὴ αἰσχροκερδῆ, ἀλλ **ἐπιεικῆ**, ἄμαχον, ἀφιλάργυρον· [GNS]<br>μὴ πάροινον μὴ πλήκτην, ἀλλὰ **ἐπιεικῆ** ἄμαχον ἀφιλάργυρον, [GNT] | Gentle, patient, gracious, kind, forbearing, reasonable, soft, considerate, and tender.<br><br>**Practical Application**<br>The minister or bishop must be "gentle" (*epieikë*). The word goes beyond treating someone with justice: it treats a person graciously and tenderly. It reaches beyond justice and touches the person with a gentle hand. (See POSB note, Gentleness—Phil. 4:5 for more discussion.) |
| **#1658**<br>**Gentle**<br>**Gentle–KJV**<br>Kind–NASB<br>Kind–NIV<br>**Gentle–NKJV**<br>Kind–NLT<br>**POSB REFERENCE** (2 Tim. 2:24-26 esp. v.24) Note 4 | ἤπιον = *ēpion*<br>Pronunciation: [ay'-pee-on]<br>Parsing (part of speech): adjective<br>    Gender—accusative<br>    Gender—masculine<br>    Number—singular<br>    Stem or root—from ἤπιος, α, ον<br>Concordance References:<br>    ⇒ Strong's #2261 ēpios<br>    ⇒ NIV #2473 ēpios<br>    ⇒ NASB #2261 ēpios<br><br>**2 Tim. 2:24**<br>And the servant of the Lord must not strive; but be **gentle** unto all men, apt to teach, patient, [KJV]<br>And the Lord's bond-servant must not be quarrelsome, but be **kind** to all, able to teach, patient when wronged, [NASB]<br>And the Lord's servant must not quarrel; instead, he must be **kind** to everyone, able to teach, not resentful. [NIV] | Kind, gentle, reasonable, considerate, soft, tender.<br><br>**Practical Application**<br>Do not argue or fight with others. This charge is to "the servant of the Lord"—the person who really wishes to serve the Lord. We cannot argue and fight and at the same time serve the Lord. A person who argues and fights is not serving the Lord, no matter what he may claim. The charge is clear: "the servant of the Lord must not strive." He must be gentle or kind (*ēpion*):<br>⇒ When people oppose him, he does not react, he reaches out in gentleness.<br>⇒ When he has to correct people by pointing out their weaknesses, he is not mean but gentle. |

## PRACTICAL WORD STUDIES in the NEW TESTAMENT

| ENGLISH WORD | GREEK WORD AND VERSE | THE WORD MEANS... |
|---|---|---|
| | And a servant of the Lord must not quarrel but be **gentle** to all, able to teach, patient, [NKJV]<br>The Lord's servants must not quarrel but must be **kind** to everyone. They must be able to teach effectively and be patient with difficult people. [NLT]<br>δοῦλον δὲ Κυρίου οὐ δεῖ μάχεσθαι, ἀλλ **ἤπιον** εἶναι πρὸς πάντας, διδακτικόν, ἀνεξίκακον, [GNS]<br>δοῦλον δὲ κυρίου οὐ δεῖ μάχεσθαι ἀλλὰ **ἤπιον** εἶναι πρὸς πάντας, διδακτικόν, ἀνεξίκακον, [GNT] | |
| **#1659**<br>**Gentle**<br><br>Gentle–KJV<br>Gentle–NASB<br>Considerate–NIV<br>Gentle–NKJV<br>Gentle at all times–NLT<br><br>**POSB REFERENCE**<br>(Jas. 3:17-18; esp. v.17)<br>Note 3, point 2c<br><br>See also POSB REF:<br>(Tit.3:2)<br>Note 5<br>(Philip.4:5)<br>Note 4 | ἐπιεικής = epieikēs<br>Pronunciation: [ep-ee-i-kace']<br>Parsing (part of speech): adjective<br>    Case—nominative<br>    Gender—feminine<br>    Number—singular<br>    Stem or root—from ἐπιεικής, ές<br>Concordance References:<br>  ⇒ Strong's #1933 epieikēs<br>  ⇒ NIV #2117 epieikēs<br>  ⇒ NASB #1933 epieikēs<br><br>**James 3:17**<br>But the wisdom that is from above is first pure, then peaceable, **gentle**, and easy to be intreated, full of mercy and good fruits, without partiality, and without hypocrisy. [KJV]<br>But the wisdom from above is first pure, then peaceable, **gentle**, reasonable, full of mercy and good fruits, unwavering, without hypocrisy. [NASB]<br>But the wisdom that comes from heaven is first of all pure; then peace-loving, **considerate**, submissive, full of mercy and good fruit, impartial and sincere. [NIV]<br>But the wisdom that is from above is first pure, then peaceable, **gentle**, willing to yield, full of mercy and good fruits, without partiality and without hypocrisy. [NKJV]<br>But the wisdom that comes from heaven is first of all pure. It is also peace loving, **gentle at all times**, and willing to yield to others. It is full of mercy and good deeds. It shows no partiality and is always sincere. [NLT]<br>ἡ δὲ ἄνωθεν σοφία πρῶτον μὲν ἁγνή ἐστιν, ἔπειτα εἰρηνική, **ἐπιεικής**, εὐπειθής, μεστὴ ἐλέους καὶ καρπῶν ἀγαθῶν, ἀδιάκριτος καὶ ἀνυπόκριτος. [GNS]<br>ἡ δὲ ἄνωθεν σοφία πρῶτον μὲν ἁγνή ἐστιν, ἔπειτα εἰρηνική, **ἐπιεικής**, εὐπειθής, μεστὴ ἐλέους καὶ καρπῶν ἀγαθῶν, ἀδιάκριτος, ἀνυπόκριτος. [GNT] | To be considerate; to be gentle; to be gentle at all times.<br><br>**Practical Application**<br>True wisdom is "gentle" (*epieikēs*). The word is difficult to translate into English. It is translated by others as gentleness, forbearance, reasonableness, consideration, agreeableness, courtesy, patience, and softness. There is the tendency to say that either forbearance or gentleness is the better translation. It means that there is *something better than mere justice*—a gracious gentleness. The wise teacher is to be gentle and forbearing in dealing with other people. |
| **#1660**<br>**Gentle–**<br>**Gentle And**<br>**Lowly**<br><br>Meek–KJV<br>Gentle–NASB<br>Meek–NIV<br>Meek–NKJV<br>Gentle and lowly–NLT<br><br>**POSB REFERENCE**<br>(Mt.5:5)<br>Note 4 | πραεῖς = praeis<br>Pronunciation: [prah-ees']<br>Parsing (part of speech): pronominal adjective<br>    Case—nominative<br>    Gender—masculine<br>    Number—plural<br>    Stem or root—from πραΰς, πραεῖα, πραΰ<br>Concordance References:<br>  ⇒ Strong's #4239 prau`s<br>  ⇒ NIV #4558 praus<br>  ⇒ NASB #4239b praus<br><br>**Matthew 5:5**<br>Blessed are the **meek**: for they shall inherit the earth. [KJV]<br>"Blessed are the **gentle**, for they shall inherit the earth. [NASB]<br>Blessed are the **meek**, for they will inherit the earth. [NIV]<br>Blessed *are* the **meek**, for they shall nherit the earth. [NKJV]<br>God blesses those who are **gentle and lowly**, for the whole earth will belong to them. [NLT]<br>Μακάριοι οἱ **πραεῖς**, ὅτι αὐτοὶ κληρονομήσουσι τὴν γῆν. [GNS]<br>μακάριοι οἱ **πραεῖς**, ὅτι αὐτοὶ κληρονομήσουσιν τὴν γῆν. [GNT] | To be meek or gentle; to have a strong, but tender and humble, life.<br><br>**Practical Application**<br>It is a strong yet teachable spirit. It is not being weak, bowing or spineless. It is a man who is strong, very strong, yet he is humble and tender. It is a man with all the emotions and ability to take and conquer, but he is able to control himself. It is discipline—a man disciplined because he is God-controlled. The opposite of meekness is arrogance or pride. In too many persons there is an air of sufficiency and superiority. A meek person knows that he has needs and does not have all the answers. |

# PRACTICAL WORD STUDIES
## in the NEW TESTAMENT

| ENGLISH WORD | GREEK WORD AND VERSE | THE WORD MEANS... |
|---|---|---|
| **#1661**<br>**Gentle At All Times**<br><br>Gentle–KJV<br>Gentle–NASB<br>Considerate–NIV<br>Gentle–NKJV<br>**Gentle at all times–NLT**<br><br>**POSB REFERENCE**<br>(Jas. 3:17-18; esp. v.17)<br>Note 3, point 2c<br><br>See also POSB REF:<br>(Philip.4:5)<br>Note 4<br>(Tit.3:2)<br>Note 5 | ἐπιεικής = epieikēs<br>Pronunciation: [ep-ee-i-kace']<br>Parsing (part of speech): adjective<br>    Case—nominative<br>    Gender—feminine<br>    Number—singular<br>    Stem or root—from ἐπιεικής, ές<br>Concordance References:<br>  ⇒ Strong's #1933 epieikēs<br>  ⇒ NIV #2117 epieikēs<br>  ⇒ NASB #1933 epieikēs<br><br>**James 3:17**<br>But the wisdom that is from above is first pure, then peaceable, **gentle**, and easy to be intreated, full of mercy and good fruits, without partiality, and without hypocrisy. [KJV]<br><br>But the wisdom from above is first pure, then peaceable, **gentle**, reasonable, full of mercy and good fruits, unwavering, without hypocrisy. [NASB]<br><br>But the wisdom that comes from heaven is first of all pure; then peace-loving, **considerate**, submissive, full of mercy and good fruit, impartial and sincere. [NIV]<br><br>But the wisdom that is from above is first pure, then peaceable, **gentle**, willing to yield, full of mercy and good fruits, without partiality and without hypocrisy. [NKJV]<br><br>But the wisdom that comes from heaven is first of all pure. It is also peace loving, **gentle at all times**, and willing to yield to others. It is full of mercy and good deeds. It shows no partiality and is always sincere. [NLT]<br><br>ἡ δὲ ἄνωθεν σοφία πρῶτον μὲν ἁγνή ἐστιν, ἔπειτα εἰρηνική, **ἐπιεικής**, εὐπειθής, μεστὴ ἐλέους καὶ καρπῶν ἀγαθῶν, ἀδιάκριτος καὶ ἀνυπόκριτος. [GNS]<br><br>ἡ δὲ ἄνωθεν σοφία πρῶτον μὲν ἁγνή ἐστιν, ἔπειτα εἰρηνική, **ἐπιεικής**, εὐπειθής, μεστὴ ἐλέους καὶ καρπῶν ἀγαθῶν, ἀδιάκριτος, ἀνυπόκριτος. [GNT] | To be considerate; to be gentle; to be gentle at all times.<br><br>**Practical Application**<br>True wisdom is "gentle at all times" (*epieikēs*). The word is difficult to translate into English. It is translated by others as considerate, forbearance, reasonableness, consideration, agreeableness, courtesy, patience, and softness. There is the tendency to say that either forbearance or gentleness is the better translation. It means that there is *something better than mere justice*—a gracious gentleness. The wise teacher is to be gentle and forbearing in dealing with other people. |
| **#1662**<br>**Gentleness**<br><br>**Gentleness–KJV**<br>Kindness–NASB<br>Kindness–NIV<br>Kindness–NKJV<br>Kindness–NLT<br><br>**POSB REFERENCE**<br>(Gal.5:22-23; esp. v.22)<br>Note 1, point 5 | χρηστότης = chrēstotēs<br>Pronunciation: [khray-stot'-ace]<br>Parsing (part of speech): noun<br>    Case—nominative<br>    Gender—feminine<br>    Number—singular<br>    Stem or root—from χρηστότης, ητος<br>Concordance References:<br>  ⇒ Strong's #5544 chrēstotēs<br>  ⇒ NIV #5983 chrēstotēs<br>  ⇒ NASB #5544 chrēstotēs<br><br>**Galatians 5:22**<br>But the fruit of the Spirit is love, joy, peace, longsuffering, **gentleness**, goodness, faith, [KJV]<br><br>But the fruit of the Spirit is love, joy, peace, patience, **kindness**, goodness, faithfulness, [NASB]<br><br>But the fruit of the Spirit is love, joy, peace, patience, **kindness**, goodness, faithfulness, [NIV]<br><br>But the fruit of the Spirit is love, joy, peace, longsuffering, **kindness**, goodness, faithfulness, [NKJV]<br><br>But when the Holy Spirit controls our lives, he will produce this kind of fruit in us: love, joy, peace, patience, **kindness**, goodness, faithfulness, [NLT]<br><br>ὁ δὲ καρπὸς τοῦ Πνεύματός ἐστιν ἀγάπη, χαρά, εἰρήνη, μακροθυμία, **χρηστότης**, ἀγαθωσύνη, πίστις, [GNS]<br><br>Ὁ δὲ καρπὸς τοῦ πνεύματός ἐστιν ἀγάπη χαρά εἰρήνη, μακροθυμία, **χρηστότης** ἀγαθωσύνη, πίστις [GNT] | Gentleness, kindness, meekness, courtesy, favor, service, mildness, tenderness.<br><br>**Practical Application**<br>There is the fruit of "gentleness" (*chrēstotēs*): it is being kind and good, useful and helpful, gentle and sweet, considerate and gracious through all situations, no matter the circumstances. A person who is gentle does not act...<br>• hard<br>• indifferent<br>• harsh<br>• unconcerned<br>• too busy<br>• bitter<br><br>Gentleness cares for the feelings of others and feels with them. It experiences the full depth of sympathy and empathy. It shows care and gets right into the situation with a person. Gentleness suffers with those who suffer, and struggles with those who struggle, and works and those who work. |

# PRACTICAL WORD STUDIES
## in the NEW TESTAMENT

| ENGLISH WORD | GREEK WORD AND VERSE | THE WORD MEANS... |
|---|---|---|
| **#1663** **Gentleness**<br><br>Meekness–KJV<br>**Gentleness**–NASB<br>**Gentleness**–NIV<br>**Gentleness**–NKJV<br>**Gentleness**–NLT<br><br>**POSB REFERENCE**<br>(Gal.5:22-23; esp. v.23)<br>Note 1, point 8<br><br>See also POSB REF:<br>(Jas.3:13)<br>Note 1, point 2 | πραΰτης = prautës<br>Pronunciation: [prah-ot'-ace]<br>Parsing (part of speech): noun<br>  Case—nominative<br>  Gender—feminine<br>  Number—singular<br>  Stem or root—from πραΰτης, ητος<br>Concordance References:<br>  ⇒ Strong's #4240 prautës<br>  ⇒ NIV #4559 prautës<br>  ⇒ NASB #4240 prautës<br><br>**Galatians 5:23**<br>**Meekness**, temperance: against such there is no law. [KJV]<br>**Gentleness**, self-control; against such things there is no law. [NASB]<br>**Gentleness** and self-control. Against such things there is no law. [NIV]<br>**Gentleness**, self-control. Against such there is no law. [NKJV]<br>**Gentleness**, and self-control. Here there is no conflict with the law. [NLT]<br>πραΰτης, ἐγκράτεια· κατὰ τῶν τοιούτων οὐκ ἔστι νόμος. [GNS]<br>πραΰτης ἐγκράτεια· κατὰ τῶν τοιούτων οὐκ ἔστιν νόμος. [GNT] | Gentleness, meekness. It means to be gentle, tender, humble, mild, considerate, but strongly so.<br><br>**Practical Application**<br>Gentleness has the strength to control and discipline, and it does so at the right time.<br>1. Gentleness has *a humble state of mind*. But this does not mean the person is weak, cowardly, and bowing. The gentle person simply loves people and loves peace; therefore, he walks humbly among men regardless of their status and circumstance in life. Associating with the poor and lowly of this earth does not bother the gentle person. He desires to be a friend to all and to help all as much as possible.<br>2. Gentleness has *a strong state of mind*. It looks at situations and wants justice and right to be done. It is not a weak mind that ignores and neglects evil and wrong-doing, abuse and suffering.<br>  ⇒ If someone is suffering, gentleness steps in to do what it can to help.<br>  ⇒ If evil is being done, gentleness does what it can to stop and correct it.<br>  ⇒ If evil is running rampant and indulging itself, gentleness actually strikes out in anger. However, note a crucial point: the anger is always at the right time and against the right thing.<br><br>3. Gentleness has *strong self-control*. The gentle person controls his spirit and mind. He controls the lusts of his sinful nature. He does not give way to ill-temper, retaliation, passion, indulgence, or license. The gentle person dies to himself, to what his sinful nature (his flesh) would like to do, and he does the right thing—exactly what God wants done. |
| **#1664** **Gentleness**<br><br>Meekness–KJV<br>**Gentleness**–NASB<br>Humility–NIV<br>Meekness–NKJV<br>Don't brag–NLT<br><br>**POSB REFERENCE**<br>(Jas.3:13)<br>Note 1, point 2<br><br>See also POSB REF:<br>(Tit.3:2)<br>Note 6 | πραΰτητι = prautëti<br>Pronunciation: [prah-oo'-tay-tee]<br>Parsing (part of speech): noun<br>  Case—dative<br>  Gender—feminine<br>  Number—singular<br>  Stem or root—from πραΰτης, ητος<br>Concordance References:<br>  ⇒ Strong's #4240 prautës<br>  ⇒ NIV #4559 prautës<br>  ⇒ NASB #4240 prautës<br><br>**James 3:13**<br>Who is a wise man and endued with knowledge among you? let him show out of a good conversation his works with **meekness** of wisdom. [KJV]<br>Who among you is wise and understanding? Let him show by his good behavior his deeds in the **gentleness** of wisdom. [NASB]<br>Who is wise and understanding among you? Let him show it by his good life, by deeds done in the **humility** that comes from wisdom. [NIV]<br>Who is wise and understanding among you? Let him show by good conduct that his works are done in the **meekness** of wisdom. [NKJV]<br>If you are wise and understand God's ways, live a life of steady goodness so that only good deeds will pour forth. And if you **don't brag** about the good you do, then you will be truly wise! [NLT] | Humility, meekness, gentleness; to be gentle, tender, humble, mild, considerate, but strongly so.<br><br>**Practical Application**<br>Humility has the strength to control and discipline; and it does so at the right time.<br>1. Humility has *a humble state of mind*. But this does not mean the teacher is weak, cowardly, and bowing. The meek teacher simply loves people and loves peace; therefore, he walks humbly among men regardless of their status and circumstance in life. Associating with the poor and lowly of this earth does not bother the meek teacher. He desires to be a friend to all and to help all as much as possible.<br>2. Humility has *a strong state of mind*. It looks at situations and wants justice and right to be done. It is not a weak mind that ignores and neglects evil and wrongdoing, abuse and suffering.<br>  ⇒ If someone is suffering, humility steps in to do what it can to help.<br>  ⇒ If evil is being done, humility does what it can to stop and correct it.<br>  ⇒ If evil is running rampant and indulging itself, humility actually strikes out in anger. However, note a crucial point: the |

## PRACTICAL WORD STUDIES
### in the NEW TESTAMENT

| ENGLISH WORD | GREEK WORD AND VERSE | THE WORD MEANS... |
|---|---|---|
| | Τίς σοφὸς καὶ ἐπιστήμων ἐν ὑμῖν; δειξάτω ἐκ τῆς καλῆς ἀναστροφῆς τὰ ἔργα αὐτοῦ ἐν **πραΰτητι** σοφίας. [GNS]<br><br>Τίς σοφὸς καὶ ἐπιστήμων ἐν ὑμῖν; δειξάτω ἐκ τῆς καλῆς ἀναστροφῆς τὰ ἔργα αὐτοῦ ἐν **πραΰτητι** σοφίας. [GNT] | anger is always at the right time and against the right thing.<br>3. Humility has *strong self-control*. The humble teacher controls his spirit and mind. He controls the lusts of his flesh. He does not give way to ill-temper, retaliation, passion, indulgence, or license. The meek teacher dies to himself, to what his flesh would like to do, and he does the right thing—exactly what God wants done.<br><br>In summary, the humble man walks in a humble, tender, but strong state of mind; denies himself, giving utmost consideration to others. He shows a control and righteous anger against injustice and evil. A humble man forgets and lives for others because of what Christ has done for him. |
| **#1665**<br>**Gentleness**<br><br>Meekness–KJV<br>**Gentleness–NASB**<br>**Gentleness–NIV**<br>**Gentleness–NKJV**<br>**Gentleness–NLT**<br><br>**POSB**<br>**REFERENCE**<br>(1 Tim.6:11)<br>Note 2, point 6 | πραϋπαθίαν = *praupathian*<br>Pronunciation: [prauh-pah'-thee-ahn]<br>Parsing (part of speech): noun<br>    Case—accusative<br>    Gender—feminine<br>    Number—singular<br>    Stem or root—from πραϋπάθεια, ας<br>Concordance References:<br>  ⇒ Strong's #4236 praupathia<br>  ⇒ NIV #4557 praupathia<br>  ⇒ NASB #4236 praupathia<br><br>**1 Tim. 6:11**<br>But thou, O man of God, flee these things; and follow after righteousness, godliness, faith, love, patience, **meekness**. [KJV]<br>But flee from these things, you man of God; and pursue righteousness, godliness, faith, love, perseverance and **gentleness**. [NASB]<br>But you, man of God, flee from all this, and pursue righteousness, godliness, faith, love, endurance and **gentleness**. [NIV]<br>But you, O man of God, flee these things and pursue righteousness, godliness, faith, love, patience, **gentleness**. [NKJV]<br>But you, Timothy, belong to God; so run from all these evil things, and follow what is right and good. Pursue a godly life, along with faith, love, perseverance, and **gentleness**. [NLT]<br>Σὺ δέ ὦ ἄνθρωπε τοῦ Θεοῦ, ταῦτα φεῦγε· δίωκε δὲ δικαιοσύνην, εὐσέβειαν, πίστιν, ἀγάπην, ὑπομονήν, **πρᾳόπατητα**· [GNS]<br>Σὺ δέ, ὦ ἄνθρωπε θεοῦ, ταῦτα φεῦγε· δίωκε δὲ δικαιοσύνην εὐσέβειαν πίστιν, ἀγάπην ὑπομονήν **πραϋπαθίαν**. [GNT] | Gentleness, meekness, humility. Gentleness means to be gentle, tender, humble, mild, considerate, but strongly so. Gentleness has the strength to control and discipline, and it does so at the right time.<br><br>**Practical Application**<br>1. Gentleness has *a humble state of mind*. But this does not mean the person is weak, cowardly, and bowing. The gentle person simply loves people and loves peace; therefore, he walks humbly among men regardless of their status and circumstance in life. Associating with the poor and lowly of this earth does not bother the gentle person. He desires to be a friend to all and to help all as much as possible.<br>2. Gentleness has *a strong state of mind*. It looks at situations and wants justice and right to be done. It is not a weak mind that ignores and neglects evil and wrong-doing, abuse and suffering.<br>  ⇒ If someone is suffering, gentleness steps in to do what it can to help.<br>  ⇒ If evil is being done, gentleness does what it can to stop and correct it.<br>  ⇒ If evil is running rampant and indulging itself, gentleness actually strikes out in anger. However, note a crucial point: the anger is always at the right time and against the right thing.<br>3. Gentleness has *strong self-control*. The gentle person controls his spirit and mind. He controls the lusts of his flesh. He does not give way to ill-temper, retaliation, passion, indulgence, or license. The gentle person dies to himself, to what his flesh would like to do, and he does the right thing—exactly what God wants done. |
| **#1666**<br>**Genuine–**<br>**Genuinely**<br><br>Naturally–KJV<br>**Genuinely–NASB** | γνησίως = *gnēsiōs*<br>Pronunciation: [gnay'-see-os]<br>Parsing (part of speech): adjective<br>    Type—adverb<br>    Stem or root—from γνησίως<br>Concordance References:<br>  ⇒ Strong's #1104 gnēsiōs | Genuine, naturally, sincere, authentic, real, actual, certified.<br><br>**Practical Application**<br>Timothy had a kindred, brotherly spirit in caring for others. In fact, he was unequaled. There were many excellent ministers of the gospel, but |

# Practical Word Studies
## in the New Testament

| ENGLISH WORD | GREEK WORD AND VERSE | THE WORD MEANS... |
|---|---|---|
| **Genuine–NIV**<br>Sincerely–NKJV<br>**Genuinely–NLT**<br><br>**POSB<br>REFERENCE**<br>(Philip.2:20)<br>Note 1 | ⇒ NIV #1189 gnēsiōs<br>⇒ NASB #1104 gnēsiōs<br><br>**Philip. 2:20**<br>For I have no man likeminded, who will **naturally** care for your state. [KJV]<br>For I have no one else of kindred spirit who will **genuinely** be concerned for your welfare. [NASB]<br>I have no one else like him, who takes a **genuine** interest in your welfare. [NIV]<br>For I have no one like-minded, who will **sincerely** care for your state. [NKJV]<br>I have no one else like Timothy, who **genuinely** cares about your welfare. [NLT]<br>οὐδένα γὰρ ἔχω ἰσόψυχον, ὅστις **γνησίως** τὰ περὶ ὑμῶν μεριμνήσει, [GNS]<br>οὐδένα γὰρ ἔχω ἰσόψυχον, ὅστις **γνησίως** τὰ περὶ ὑμῶν μεριμνήσει· [GNT] | Timothy's spirit came closest to Paul's than all the others. Timothy cared for the churches and their believers just as Paul cared. His heart was genuine (*gnēsiōs*). His care or interest arose from deep within: it was natural and sincere—the same kind of care that a genuine brother would have. Timothy's ministry—his care and concern for the believers—would be deep and genuine, a true concern. |
| **#1667<br>Genuine<br>Affection**<br><br>Kindly affectioned–KJV<br>Devoted–NASB<br>Devoted–NIV<br>Kindly affectionate–NKJV<br>**Genuine affection–<br>NLT**<br><br>**POSB<br>REFERENCE**<br>(Rom.12:9-10; esp. v.10)<br>Note 1, point 3 | φιλόστοργοι = *philostorgoi*<br>Pronunciation: [fil-os'-tor-goy]<br>Parsing (part of speech): adjective<br>    Case—nominative<br>    Gender—masculine<br>    Number—plural<br>Stem or root—from φιλόστοργος, ον<br>Concordance References:<br>⇒ Strong's #5387 philostorgos<br>⇒ NIV #5816 philostorgos<br>⇒ NASB #5387 philostorgos<br><br>**Romans 12:10**<br>Be **kindly affectioned** one to another with brotherly love; in honour preferring one another; [KJV]<br>Be **devoted** to one another in brotherly love; give preference to one another in honor; [NASB]<br>Be **devoted** to one another in brotherly love. Honor one another above yourselves. [NIV]<br>*Be **kindly affectionate*** to one another with brotherly love, in honor giving preference to one another; [NKJV]<br>Love each other with **genuine affection**, and take delight in honoring each other. [NLT]<br>τῇ φιλαδελφίᾳ εἰς ἀλλήλους **φιλόστοργοι**· τῇ τιμῇ ἀλλήλους προηγούμενοι· [GNS]<br>τῇ φιλαδελφίᾳ εἰς ἀλλήλους **φιλόστοργοι**, τῇ τιμῇ ἀλλήλους προηγούμενοι, [GNT] | Loving, devoted; genuine affection; devout; loyal, faithful. The word "affectionate" (*philostorgoi*) means the love existing between family members.<br><br>**Practical Application**<br>The believer is to love his brothers in Christ, by being kind and affectionate toward them. This charge is dealing with the Christian family, the brothers and sisters within the church. We are to love each other by being kind and affectionate. We are a family of children who have actually been adopted by God as His sons and daughters (2 Cor. 6:17-18; Galatians 4:4-6; Romans 8:16-17). Therefore, the believer is to live as a family member with his brothers and sisters; he is to live being both kind and affectionate. Note: there is no dissension or divisiveness in love. The church is to live in love, and living in love is peace. |
| **#1668<br>Get Rid Of**<br><br>Wasted–KJV<br>Destroy–NASB<br>Destroy–NIV<br>Destroy–NKJV<br>**Get rid of–NLT**<br><br>**POSB<br>REFERENCE**<br>(Gal.1:13-16; esp. v.13)<br>Note 3, point 1a | ἐπόρθουν = *eporthoun*<br>Pronunciation: [eh-por-thoon]<br>Parsing (part of speech): verb<br>    Mood—indicative<br>    Tense—imperfect<br>    Voice—active<br>    Person—1st person<br>    Number—singular<br>Stem or root—from πορθέω<br>Concordance References:<br>⇒ Strong's #4199 portheō<br>⇒ NIV #4514 portheō<br>⇒ NASB #4199 portheō<br><br>**Galatians 1:13**<br>For ye have heard of my conversation in time past in the Jews' religion, how that beyond measure I persecuted the church of God, and **wasted** it: [KJV]<br>For you have heard of my former manner of life in Judaism, how I used to persecute the church of God beyond measure, and tried to **destroy** it; [NASB]<br>For you have heard of my previous way of life in Judaism, how intensely I persecuted the church of God | To destroy; to get rid of; to make havoc; to utterly rack or lay waste; to devastate, destroy, ruin, or wipe out.<br><br>**Practical Application**<br>The point is that Paul had been bent on violence; he had sought to utterly stamp out the church; to wipe believers off the face of the earth. (See POSB note, Church, Persecution of—Acts 8:3 for more discussion.) |

# PRACTICAL WORD STUDIES
in the NEW TESTAMENT

| ENGLISH WORD | GREEK WORD AND VERSE | THE WORD MEANS... |
|---|---|---|
| | and tried to **destroy** it. [NIV]<br><br>For you have heard of my former conduct in Judaism, how I persecuted the church of God beyond measure and *tried to* **destroy** it. [NKJV]<br><br>You know what I was like when I followed the Jewish religion—how I violently persecuted the Christians. I did my best to **get rid of** them. [NLT]<br><br>ἠκούσατε γὰρ τὴν ἐμὴν ἀναστροφήν ποτε ἐν τῷ Ἰουδαϊσμῷ, ὅτι καθ' ὑπερβολὴν ἐδίωκον τὴν ἐκκλησίαν τοῦ Θεοῦ, καὶ **ἐπόρθουν** αὐτήν· [GNS]<br><br>Ἠκούσατε γὰρ τὴν ἐμὴν ἀναστροφήν ποτε ἐν τῷ Ἰουδαϊσμῷ, ὅτι καθ' ὑπερβολὴν ἐδίωκον τὴν ἐκκλησίαν τοῦ Θεοῦ καὶ **Ἐπόρθουν** αὐτήν, [GNT] | |
| **#1669**<br>**Gethsemane**<br><br>Gethsemane–KJV<br>Gethsemane–NASB<br>Gethsemane–NIV<br>Gethsemane–NKJV<br>Gethsemane–NLT<br><br>**POSB<br>REFERENCE**<br>(Mt.26:36)<br>*Deeper Study #1* | Γεθσημανί = *Gethsëmani*<br>Pronunciation: [gheth-say-mahn-ee']<br>Parsing (part of speech): noun<br>    Case—accusative<br>    Gender—neuter<br>    Number—singular<br>    Stem or root—from Γεθσημανί<br>Concordance References:<br>  ⇒ Strong's #1068 Gethsemane<br>  ⇒ NIV #1149 Gethsëmani<br>  ⇒ NASB #1068 Gethsëmani<br><br>**Matthew 26:36**<br>Then cometh Jesus with them unto a place called **Gethsemane**, and saith unto the disciples, Sit ye here, while I go and pray yonder. [KJV]<br><br>Then Jesus came with them to a place called **Gethsemane**, and said to His disciples, "Sit here while I go over there and pray." [NASB]<br><br>Then Jesus went with his disciples to a place called **Gethsemane**, and he said to them, "Sit here while I go over there and pray." [NIV]<br><br>Then Jesus came with them to a place called **Gethsemane**, and said to the disciples, "Sit here while I go and pray over there." [NKJV]<br><br>Then Jesus brought them to an olive grove called **Gethsemane**, and he said, "Sit here while I go on ahead to pray." [NLT]<br><br>Τότε ἔρχεται μετ' αὐτῶν ὁ Ἰησοῦς εἰς χωρίον λεγόμενον **Γεθσημανῆ**, καὶ λέγει τοῖς μαθηταῖς, Καθίσατε αὐτοῦ, ἕως οὗ ἀπελθὼν προσεύξωμαι ἐκεῖ. [GNS]<br><br>Τότε ἔρχεται μετ' αὐτῶν ὁ Ἰησοῦς εἰς χωρίον λεγόμενον **Γεθσημανί**, καὶ λέγει τοῖς μαθηταῖς, Καθίσατε αὐτοῦ ἕως [οὗ] ἀπελθὼν ἐκεῖ προσεύξωμαι. [GNT] | Oil press or olive press.<br><br>**Practical Application**<br>Gethsemane was a garden sitting on the Mount of Olives. It was probably a garden of olive trees, beautifully situated on the slopes of the mountain overlooking all the surrounding area including the city of Jerusalem. Private and public gardens on the surrounding mountains were common because of the beauty of the mountains and because of the lack of space within the city. It was to such a garden that Christ withdrew in His desperate hour of need. |
| **#1670**<br>**Getting Drunk**<br><br>Drunkenness–KJV<br>Drunkenness–NASB<br>Drunkenness–NIV<br>Drunkenness–NKJV<br>Getting drunk–NLT<br><br>**POSB<br>REFERENCE**<br>(Rom.13:13)<br>Note 4, point 2 | μέθαις = *methais*<br>Pronunciation: [meth'-ays]<br>Parsing (part of speech): noun<br>    Case—dative<br>    Gender—feminine<br>    Number—plural<br>    Stem or root—from μέθη, ης<br>Concordance References:<br>  ⇒ Strong's #3178 methë<br>  ⇒ NIV #3494 methë<br>  ⇒ NASB #3178 methë<br><br>**Romans 13:13**<br>Let us walk honestly, as in the day; not in rioting and **drunkenness**, not in chambering and wantonness, not in strife and envying. [KJV]<br><br>Let us behave properly as in the day, not in carousing and **drunkenness**, not in sexual promiscuity and sensuality, not in strife and jealousy. [NASB]<br><br>Let us behave decently, as in the daytime, not in orgies | Drunkenness; excess; overindulgence; debauchery; insobriety; alcoholism; intemperance; getting drunk.<br><br>**Practical Application**<br>Getting drunk (*methais*) is to take intoxicating drink or drugs to affect the senses and faculties; to become intoxicated for the purpose of lust or pleasure; to seek to be tipsy or intoxicated; to seek to loosen moral restraint for the sake of bodily pleasure. |

# PRACTICAL WORD STUDIES
## in the NEW TESTAMENT

| ENGLISH WORD | GREEK WORD AND VERSE | THE WORD MEANS... |
|---|---|---|
| | and **drunkenness**, not in sexual immorality and debauchery, not in dissension and jealousy. [NIV]<br><br>Let us walk properly, as in the day, not in revelry and **drunkenness**, not in lewdness and lust, not in strife and envy. [NKJV]<br><br>We should be decent and true in everything we do, so that everyone can approve of our behavior. Don't participate in wild parties and **getting drunk**, or in adultery and immoral living, or in fighting and jealousy. [NLT]<br><br>ὡς ἐν ἡμέρᾳ, εὐσχημόνως περιπατήσωμεν, μὴ κώμοις καὶ **μέθαις**, μὴ κοίταις καὶ ἀσελγείαις, μὴ ἔριδι καὶ ζήλῳ. [GNS]<br><br>ὡς ἐν ἡμέρᾳ εὐσχημόνως περιπατήσωμεν, μὴ κώμοις καὶ **μέθαις**, μὴ κοίταις καὶ ἀσελγείαις, μὴ ἔριδι καὶ ζήλῳ, [GNT] | |
| **#1671**<br>**Gift**<br><br>Gift–KJV<br>Gift–NASB<br>Gift–NIV<br>Gift–NKJV<br>Blessing–NLT<br><br>**POSB REFERENCE**<br>(Romans 1:10-13; esp. v.11)<br>Note 4, point 1 | χάρισμα = charisma<br>Pronunciation: [khar'-is-mah]<br>Parsing (part of speech): noun<br>   Case—accusative<br>   Gender—neuter<br>   Number—singular<br>Stem or root—from χάρισμα, τος<br>Concordance References:<br>  ⇒ Strong's #5486 charisma<br>  ⇒ NIV #5922 charisma<br>  ⇒ NASB #5486 charisma<br><br>**Romans 1:11**<br>For I long to see you, that I may impart unto you some spiritual **gift**, to the end ye may be established; [KJV]<br><br>For I long to see you in order that I may impart some spiritual **gift** to you, that you may be established; [NASB]<br><br>I long to see you so that I may impart to you some spiritual **gift** to make you strong— [NIV]<br><br>For I long to see you, that I may impart to you some spiritual **gift**, so that you may be established— [NKJV]<br><br>For I long to visit you so I can share a spiritual **blessing** with you that will help you grow strong in the Lord. [NLT]<br><br>ἐπιποθῶ γὰρ ἰδεῖν ὑμᾶς, ἵνα τι μεταδῶ **χάρισμα** ὑμῖν πνευματικὸν εἰς τὸ στηριχθῆναι ὑμᾶς, [GNS]<br><br>ἐπιποθῶ γὰρ ἰδεῖν ὑμᾶς, ἵνα τι μεταδῶ **χάρισμα** ὑμῖν πνευματικὸν εἰς τὸ στηριχθῆναι ὑμᾶς, [GNT] | A gift; a divine blessing; a gift of grace.<br><br>**Practical Application**<br>The term often refers to specific gifts given by the Holy Spirit (Romans 12:6-8), but here it means the truths of the grace of God, of His spiritual blessings to man revealed in Christ Jesus our Lord. Very simply, Paul longed to share the truths of the gospel with the believers at Rome. God's spiritual blessings were overflowing in his heart, and he was aching to share the gift of God's blessings. |
| **#1672**<br>**Gift–Gifts**<br><br>Gift–KJV<br>Gift–NASB<br>Gift–NIV<br>Gift–NKJV<br>Gifts–NLT<br><br>**POSB REFERENCE**<br>(1 Pt.4:10-11; esp. v. 10)<br>Note 5 | χάρισμα = charisma<br>Pronunciation: [khar'-is-mah]<br>Parsing (part of speech): noun<br>   Case—accusative<br>   Gender—neuter<br>   Number—singular<br>Stem or root—from χάρισμα, τος<br>Concordance References:<br>  ⇒ Strong's #5486 charisma<br>  ⇒ NIV #5922 charisma<br>  ⇒ NASB #5486 charisma<br><br>**1 Peter 4:10**<br>As every man hath received the **gift**, even so minister the same one to another, as good stewards of the manifold grace of God. [KJV]<br><br>As each one has received a special **gift**, employ it in serving one another, as good stewards of the manifold grace of God. [NASB]<br><br>Each one should use whatever **gift** he has received to serve others, faithfully administering God's grace in its various forms. [NIV]<br><br>As each one has received a **gift**, minister it to one another, as good stewards of the manifold grace of God. [NKJV]<br><br>God has given gifts to each of you from his great vari- | Gift, spiritual gift. The word "gift" (charisma) means the very special ability given to the believer by God.<br><br>**Practical Application**<br>How do we live under the climax of history? We use our gifts ministering as good stewards of God. Note that the gift is from God; it is not a natural talent. The believer could not have attained nor secured the ability himself. It is a spiritual gift; that is, it is given by the Spirit of God for spiritual purposes. It is given to the believer so that he can fulfill his task on earth. |

## Practical Word Studies in the New Testament

| ENGLISH WORD | GREEK WORD AND VERSE | THE WORD MEANS... |
|---|---|---|
| | ety of spiritual **gifts**. Manage them well so that God's generosity can flow through you. [NLT]<br><br>ἕκαστος καθὼς ἔλαβε **χάρισμα**, εἰς ἑαυτοὺς αὐτὸ διακονοῦντες, ὡς καλοὶ οἰκονόμοι ποικίλης χάριτος Θεοῦ· [GNS]·<br><br>ἕκαστος καθὼς ἔλαβεν **χάρισμα** εἰς ἑαυτοὺς αὐτὸ διακονοῦντες ὡς καλοὶ οἰκονόμοι ποικίλης χάριτος θεοῦ. [GNT] | |
| **#1673**<br>**Gift Of Special Knowledge**<br><br>Word of knowledge–KJV<br>Word of knowledge–NASB<br>Message of knowledge–NIV<br>Word of knowledge–NKJV<br>**Gift of special knowledge–NLT**<br><br>**POSB REFERENCE**<br>(1 Cor.12:8-10; esp. v.8)<br>Note 3, point 2 | λόγος γνώσεως = *logos gnōseōs*<br>Pronunciation: [gno'-seh-os]<br>Parsing *gnōseōs* (part of speech): noun<br>    Case—genitive<br>    Gender—feminine<br>    Number—singular<br>    Stem or root—from γνῶσις, εως<br>Concordance References:<br>⇒ Strong's #3056 logos + 1108 gnōsis<br>⇒ NIV #3364 logos [message of] + 1194 gnōsis [knowledge]<br>⇒ NASB #3056 logos + 1108 gnōsis<br><br>**1 Cor. 12:8**<br>For to one is given by the Spirit the word of wisdom; to another the **word of knowledge** by the same Spirit; [KJV]<br>For to one is given the word of wisdom through the Spirit, and to another the **word of knowledge** according to the same Spirit; [NASB]<br>To one there is given through the Spirit the message of wisdom, to another the **message of knowledge** by means of the same Spirit, [NIV]<br>For to one is given the word of wisdom through the Spirit, to another the **word of knowledge** through the same Spirit, [NKJV]<br>To one person the Spirit gives the ability to give wise advice; to another he gives the **gift of special knowledge**. [NLT]<br><br>ᾧ μὲν γὰρ διὰ τοῦ Πνεύματος δίδοται λόγος σοφίας, ἄλλῳ δὲ **λόγος γνώσεως**, κατὰ τὸ αὐτὸ Πνεῦμα· [GNS]<br>ᾧ μὲν γὰρ διὰ τοῦ πνεύματος δίδοται λόγος σοφίας, ἄλλῳ δὲ **λόγος γνώσεως** κατὰ τὸ αὐτὸ πνεῦμα, [GNT] | Message, word of knowledge; a gift of practical knowledge.<br><br>**Practical Application**<br>This is practical knowledge. It is knowing what to do in the day-to-day situations that arise. It is knowing how to apply the wisdom that one has to daily living. It is being able to make practical application of truth to life. It does no good to know truth unless a person knows how to use the truth.<br><br>The *gift of special knowledge* is the gift to share with others how they should live; the ability to apply truth to their lives in day-to-day living; the ability to make practical application of truth to life. |
| **#1674**<br>**Gifts**<br><br>Gifts–KJV<br>Gifts–NASB<br>Gifts–NIV<br>Gifts–NKJV<br>Ability–NLT<br><br>**POSB REFERENCE**<br>(Rom.12:6-8; esp. v.6)<br>Note 2 | χαρίσματα = *charismata*<br>Pronunciation: [khar'-is-mah-tah]<br>Parsing (part of speech): noun<br>    Case—accusative<br>    Gender—neuter<br>    Number—plural<br>    Stem or root—from χάρισμα, τος<br>Concordance References:<br>⇒ Strong's #5486 charisma<br>⇒ NIV #5922 charisma<br>⇒ NASB #5486 charisma<br><br>**Romans 12:6**<br>Having then **gifts** differing according to the grace that is given to us, whether prophecy, let us prophesy according to the proportion of faith; [KJV]<br>And since we have **gifts** that differ according to the grace given to us, let each exercise them accordingly: if prophecy, according to the proportion of his faith; [NASB]<br>We have different **gifts**, according to the grace given us. If a man's gift is prophesying, let him use it in proportion to his faith. [NIV]<br>Having then **gifts** differing according to the grace that is given to us, *let us use them:* if prophecy, *let us prophesy* in proportion to our faith; [NKJV]<br>God has given each of us the **ability** to do certain things well. So if God has given you the ability to prophesy, speak out when you have faith that God is speaking | Gifts, ability. It means the very special ability given to the believer by God.<br><br>**Practical Application**<br>Note that the gift is from God; it is not a natural talent. The believer could not have attained nor secured the ability himself. It is a spiritual gift; that is, it is given by the Spirit of God for spiritual purposes. It is given to the believer so that he can fulfill his task on earth.<br>Note also that the gifts are said to be given "according to the grace that is given to us." This means that the gifts are given after we come to know the grace of God. This is part of our heritage in Christ, the glorious privilege...<br>• of being given a very special task upon earth.<br>• of being given purpose and meaning and significance in life.<br>• of being given a very special gift or gifts to fulfill our task on earth. |

# PRACTICAL WORD STUDIES
## in the NEW TESTAMENT

| ENGLISH WORD | GREEK WORD AND VERSE | THE WORD MEANS... |
|---|---|---|
| | through you. [NLT]<br>ἔχοντες δὲ **χαρίσματα** κατὰ τὴν χάριν τὴν δοθεῖσαν ἡμῖν διάφορα, εἴτε προφητείαν κατὰ τὴν ἀναλογίαν τῆς πίστεως· [GNS]<br>ἔχοντες δὲ **χαρίσματα** κατὰ τὴν χάριν τὴν δοθεῖσαν ἡμῖν διάφορα, εἴτε προφητείαν κατὰ τὴν ἀναλογίαν τῆς πίστεως, [GNT] | |
| **#1675**<br>**Give Attention**<br><br>Give ourselves–KJV<br>Devote ourselves–NASB<br>**Give...attention–NIV**<br>Give ourselves–NKJV<br>Spend our time–NLT<br><br>**POSB REFERENCE**<br>(Acts 6:4)<br>Note 4, point 2 | προσκαρτερήσομεν = *proskarterēsomen*<br>Pronunciation: [pros-kar-ter-eh'-so-men]<br>Parsing (part of speech): verb<br>  Mood—indicative<br>  Tense—future<br>  Voice—active<br>  Person—1st person<br>  Number—plural<br>  Stem or root—from προσκαρτερέω<br>Concordance References:<br>  ⇒ Strong's #4342 proskartereō<br>  ⇒ NIV #4674 proskartereō<br>  ⇒ NASB #4342 proskartereō<br><br>**Acts 6:4**<br>But we will **give ourselves** continually to prayer, and to the ministry of the word. [KJV]<br>"But we will **devote ourselves** to prayer, and to the ministry of the word." [NASB]<br>And will **give** our **attention** to prayer and the ministry of the word." [NIV]<br>But we will **give ourselves** continually to prayer and to the ministry of the word." [NKJV]<br>Then we can **spend our time** in prayer and preaching and teaching the word." [NLT]<br>ἡμεῖς δὲ τῇ προσευχῇ καὶ τῇ διακονίᾳ τοῦ λόγου **προσκαρτερήσομεν**. [GNS]<br>ἡμεῖς δὲ τῇ προσευχῇ καὶ τῇ διακονίᾳ τοῦ λόγου **προσκαρτερήσομεν**. [GNT] | To give attention; to give ourselves; to devote ourselves; to spend our time. It means to continue steadfastly; to persevere; to continue on and on, sticking to it.<br><br>**Practical Application**<br>The minister is to pray and pray and study and study and share and share, preaching and teaching the Word—without letting up. He is to be steadfast, persevering, continuing on and on in both prayer and in the Word. |
| **#1676**<br>**Give Honor**<br><br>Dwell with–KJV<br>Live with–NASB<br>Live with–NIV<br>Dwell with–NKJV<br>**Give honor–NLT**<br><br>**POSB REFERENCE**<br>(1 Pt.3:7)<br>Note 1 | συνοικοῦντες = *sunoikountes*<br>Pronunciation: [soon-oy-koon-tehs]<br>Parsing (part of speech): verb<br>  Mood—participle (imperative sense)<br>  Tense—present<br>  Voice—active<br>  Case—nominative<br>  Gender—masculine<br>  Person—2nd person<br>  Number—plural<br>  Stem or root—from συνοικέω<br>Concordance References:<br>  ⇒ Strong's #4924 sunoikeō<br>  ⇒ NIV #5324 sunoikeō<br>  ⇒ NASB #4924 sunoikeō<br><br>**1 Peter 3:7**<br>Likewise, ye husbands, **dwell with** them according to knowledge, giving honour unto the wife, as unto the weaker vessel, and as being heirs together of the grace of life; that your prayers be not hindered. [KJV]<br>You husbands likewise, **live with** your wives in an understanding way, as with a weaker vessel, since she is a woman; and grant her honor as a fellow heir of the grace of life, so that your prayers may not be hindered. [NASB]<br>Husbands, in the same way be considerate as you **live with** your wives, and treat them with respect as the weaker partner and as heirs with you of the gracious gift of life, so that nothing will hinder your prayers. [NIV]<br>Husbands, likewise, **dwell with** them with understanding, giving honor to the wife, as to the weaker vessel, and as being heirs together of the grace of life, that your rayers may not be hindered. [NKJV]<br>In the same way, you husbands must **give honor** to your wives. Treat her with understanding as you live | To live with; to dwell with; to remain with; to reside with; to dwell together; to give honor.<br><br>**Practical Application**<br>Alan Stibbs points out that it is a word that is often used in the Greek for sexual intercourse. It is similar to the Hebrew verb *to know* which means that a man and woman *know* each other sexually (cp. Genesis 4:1; Matthew 1:25). (*The First Epistle General of Peter.* "The Tyndale New Testament Commentaries," p.127).<br>The point is this: the husband is to *give honor to his wife*. He is not to *know* anyone else; he is not to have sexual intercourse with any other woman. The husband has a wife and he is to honor her in purity, righteousness, and holiness, and not as an adulterer.<br>Note one other fact as well: to give honor to his wife means that he is not to be gone all of the time. He stays at home and lives with her: he is a close and supportive companion. He is not out and away from the home all of the time pursuing his own interests and hobbies. A good husband dwells at home; he is close to his wife and he is supportive of her in all of life. In fact, the term *give honor* actually means to live together. The husband and wife are a team; they are as one body, one body that lives and dwells and moves together. This is not to do away with individuality. But individuality never has been and never will be the problem within a marriage of normal people. The problem with normal people will always be denying self and sacrificially giving |

# PRACTICAL WORD STUDIES
## in the New Testament

| ENGLISH WORD | GREEK WORD AND VERSE | THE WORD MEANS... |
|---|---|---|
| | make your requests, plead for God's mercy upon them, and **give thanks**. [NLT]<br><br>Παρακαλῶ οὖν πρῶτον πάντων ποιεῖσθαι δεήσεις, προσευχάς, ἐντεύξεις, **εὐχαριστίας**, ὑπὲρ πάντων ἀνθρώπων· [GNS]<br><br>Παρακαλῶ οὖν πρῶτον πάντων ποιεῖσθαι δεήσεις προσευχάς ἐντεύξεις **εὐχαριστίας** ὑπὲρ πάντων ἀνθρώπων, [GNT] | |
| **#1681**<br>**Give Up And Quit**<br><br>In despair–KJV<br>Despairing–NASB<br>In despair–NIV<br>In despair–NKJV<br>Give up and quit–NLT<br><br>**POSB REFERENCE**<br>(2 Cor.4:7-9; esp. v.8)<br>Note 2, point 2 | ἐξαπορούμενοι = exaporoumenoi<br>Pronunciation: [ex-ap-or-oo'-mehn-oy]<br>Parsing (part of speech): verb<br>    Mood—participle<br>    Tense—present<br>    Voice—middle or passive deponent<br>    Case—nominative<br>    Gender—masculine<br>    Person—1st person<br>    Number—plural<br>    Stem or root—from ἐξαπορέομαι<br>Concordance References:<br>⇒ Strong's #1820 exaporeō<br>⇒ NIV #1989 exaporeō<br>⇒ NASB #1820 exaporeō<br><br>**2 Cor. 4:8**<br>We are troubled on every side, yet not distressed; we are perplexed, but not **in despair**; [KJV]<br>We are afflicted in every way, but not crushed; perplexed, but not **despairing**; [NASB]<br>We are hard pressed on every side, but not crushed; perplexed, but not **in despair**; [NIV]<br>*We are* hard pressed on every side, yet not crushed; *we are* perplexed, but not **in despair**; [NKJV]<br>We are pressed on every side by troubles, but we are not crushed and broken. We are perplexed, but we don't **give up and quit**. [NLT]<br>ἐν παντὶ θλιβόμενοι, ἀλλ' οὐ στενοχωρούμενοι· ἀπορούμενοι ἀλλ' οὐκ **ἐξαπορούμενοι**· [GNS]<br>ἐν παντὶ θλιβόμενοι ἀλλ' οὐ στενοχωρούμενοι, ἀπορούμενοι ἀλλ' οὐκ **ἐξαπορούμενοι**, [GNT] | To be in despair; to give up and quit; to be hopeless; to have no confidence or assurance; to be without any sense of security.<br><br>**Practical Application**<br>The believer is often perplexed, not understanding why this or that happened, what should be done or said, how the situation should be handled, and on and on. Sometimes situations become so puzzling that the chrisitan is almost stymied and the threat of despair faces him. There is the danger that his confidence and assurance will be shaken. But again, the presence and power of God step in to save the believer from despair. God showing him the way out gives him hope and stirs his confidence. God never allows him to be overcome by despair. |
| **#1682**<br>**Give Up, Not–**<br>**Give Up, Never**<br><br>Not to faint–KJV<br>Not to lose heart–NASB<br>**Not give up–NIV**<br>Not lose heart–NKJV<br>**Never give up–NLT**<br><br>**POSB REFERENCE**<br>(Lk.18:1)<br>Note 1, point 4 | μὴ ἐγκακεῖν = mē egkakein<br>Pronunciation: [may eng-kak-eh'-een]<br>Parsing *egkakein* (part of speech): verb<br>    Mood—infinitive<br>    Tense—present<br>    Voice—active<br>    Stem or root—from ἐγκακέω<br>Concordance References:<br>⇒ Strong's #3361 me +1573 egkakeo<br>⇒ NIV #3590 mē [not] + 1591 egkakeō [give up]<br>⇒ NASB #3361 me +1573 egkakeo<br><br>**Luke 18:1**<br>And he spake a parable unto them to this end, that men ought always to pray, and **not to faint**; [KJV]<br>Now He was telling them a parable to show that at all times they ought to pray and **not to lose heart**, [NASB]<br>Then Jesus told his disciples a parable to show them that they should always pray and **not give up**. [NIV]<br>Then He spoke a parable to them, that men always ought to pray and **not lose heart**, [NKJV]<br>One day Jesus told his disciples a story to illustrate their need for constant prayer and to show them that they must **never give up**. [NLT]<br>Ἔλεγε δὲ καὶ παραβολὴν αὐτοῖς πρὸς τὸ δεῖν πάντοτε προσεύχεσθαι, καὶ **μὴ ἐκκακεῖν**, [GNS]<br>Ἔλεγεν δὲ παραβολὴν αὐτοῖς πρὸς τὸ δεῖν πάντοτε προσεύχεσθαι αὐτοὺς καὶ **μὴ ἐγκακεῖν**, [GNT] | Not to lose heart; not to faint; not to become discouraged; not to turn coward, or give up, or give in to evil; not to tire of.<br><br>**Practical Application**<br>There is need for perseverance in prayer, for praying over a long period of time and not giving in and becoming discouraged. God's people are to pray and keep on praying until Christ returns, no matter how long He may be delayed. |

# PRACTICAL WORD STUDIES
## in the NEW TESTAMENT

| ENGLISH WORD | GREEK WORD AND VERSE | THE WORD MEANS... |
|---|---|---|
| **#1683**<br>Give, From Now On–<br>Give, Evermore–<br>Give…Every Day<br>Give…Always<br><br>Evermore give–KJV<br>Evermore give–NASB<br>From now on give–NIV<br>Give…always–NKJV<br>Give…every day–NLT<br><br>**POSB REFERENCE**<br>(Jn.6:34-35; esp. v.34)<br>Note 4, point 1 | πάντοτε δός = *pantote dos*<br>Pronunciation: [pan'-tot-eh dos']<br>Parsing *pantote* (part of speech): adjective<br>    Type—adverb<br>    Stem or root—from πάντοτε<br>Parsing *dos* (part of speech): verb<br>    Mood—imperative<br>    Tense—aorist<br>    Voice—active<br>    Person—2nd person<br>    Number—singular<br>    Stem or root—from πάντοτε<br>Concordance References:<br>⇒ Strong's #3842 pantote + 1325 didömi<br>⇒ NIV #4121 pantote [from now on] + 1443 didömi [give]<br>⇒ NASB #3842 pantote + 1325 didömi<br><br>**John 6:34**<br>Then said they unto him, Lord, **evermore give** us this bread. [KJV]<br>They said therefore to Him, "Lord, **evermore give** us this bread." [NASB]<br>"Sir," they said, "**from now on give** us this bread." [NIV]<br>Then they said to Him, "Lord, **give** us this bread **always**." [NKJV]<br>"Sir," they said, "**give** us that bread **every day** of our lives." [NLT]<br>εἶπον οὖν πρὸς αὐτόν, Κύριε, πάντοτε δὸς ἡμῖν τὸν ἄρτον τοῦτον. [GNS]<br>Εἶπον οὖν πρὸς αὐτόν, Κύριε, πάντοτε δὸς ἡμῖν τὸν ἄρτον τοῦτον. [GNT] | From now on give; evermore give; give every day; to grant always.<br><br>**Practical Application**<br>Note that the people requested, "from now on give (*pantote dos*) us this bread." This was a once-for-all request (the Greek aorist tense). The people wanted this Bread of God once for all, so that they might have a permanent provision. The Bible is again clear on this point. Salvation, that is, partaking of the Bread of Life, is to be a permanent experience. It is to be a once-for-all experience. |
| **#1684**<br>**Given A Trust**<br><br>Stewards–KJV<br>Stewards–NASB<br>**Given a trust–NIV**<br>Stewards–NKJV<br>Put in charge as a manager–NLT<br><br>**POSB REFERENCE**<br>(1 Cor.4:1-2; esp. v.2)<br>Note 1, point 2 | ἐν οἰκονόμοις = *en oikonomois*<br>Pronunciation: [en oy-kon-om'-oys]<br>Parsing *oikonomois* (part of speech): noun<br>    Case—dative<br>    Gender—masculine<br>    Number—plural<br>    Stem or root—from οἰκονόμος, ου<br>Concordance References:<br>⇒ Strong's #1722+3623 en oikonomos<br>⇒ NIV #1877+3874 en oikonomos [given a trust]<br>⇒ NASB #1722+3623 en oikonomos<br><br>**1 Cor. 4:2**<br>Moreover it is required in **stewards**, that a man be found faithful. [KJV]<br>In this case, moreover, it is required of **stewards** that one be found trustworthy. [NASB]<br>Now it is required that those who have been **given a trust** must prove faithful. [NIV]<br>Moreover it is required in **stewards** that one be found faithful. [NKJV]<br>Now, a person who is **put in charge as a manager** must be faithful. [NLT]<br>ὃ δὲ λοιπόν, ζητεῖται ἐν τοῖς οἰκονόμοις, ἵνα πιστός τις εὑρεθῇ. [GNS]<br>ὧδε λοιπὸν ζητεῖται ἐν οἰκονόμοις, ἵνα πιστός τις εὑρεθῇ. [GNT] | To be given a trust; to be put in charge as a manager; to be a steward; to be a trustee; to be the overseer of an estate.<br><br>**Practical Application**<br>The steward or manager was always a slave, subject to a master, but he was *given a trust* or *placed in charge* of the other slaves throughout the master's house or estate. He controlled the staff and ran the whole operation for the master. He was set over others, yet he himself was still a slave of the master. His work was not closely supervised; therefore, he had to be trustworthy and responsible. Note what the minister is given a trust over: the mysteries of God. A mystery is not something hard to understand. Rather, it is something that has been hidden and kept secret. It is something that was undiscoverable by human reason, but now is revealed by God. It is crystal clear to those to whom it is revealed, but it is completely alien to those who do not receive it. What are the mysteries of God? They are the truths—the glorious truths—of God's Word. Who are the ones to whom the mysteries are revealed? The stewards, the ministers, the believing servants or managers of Christ. |
| **#1685**<br>**Given Fullness**<br><br>Complete–KJV<br>Complete–NASB<br>**Given fullness–NIV**<br>Complete–NKJV<br>Complete–NLT | ἐστὲ πεπληρωμένοι = *este peplēromenoi*<br>Pronunciation: [es-teh' peh-play-ro'-mehn-oy]<br>Parsing *este* (part of speech): verb<br>    Mood—indicative<br>    Tense—present<br>    Voice—active<br>    Person—2nd person<br>    Number—plural<br>    Stem or root—from εἰμί<br>Parsing *peplēromenoi* (part of speech): verb<br>    Mood—participle | To be given fullness; to be complete; to be made full; to fully accomplish.<br><br>**Practical Application**<br>Believers are complete in Christ. The Greek actually says, "In Him you are full." When a person truly believes and partakes of Christ, he receives the fullness of Christ. Just what is the fullness of Christ which believers receive? Scripture describes it in several ways. |

# PRACTICAL WORD STUDIES
## in the NEW TESTAMENT

| ENGLISH WORD | GREEK WORD AND VERSE | THE WORD MEANS... |
|---|---|---|
| **POSB REFERENCE** (Col.2:9-10; esp. v.10) Note 2, point 2 | Tense—perfect<br>Voice—passive<br>Case—nominative<br>Gender—masculine<br>Person—2nd person<br>Number—plural<br>Stem or root—from πληρόω<br>Concordance References:<br>⇒ Strong's #1510+4137 eimi plēroō<br>⇒ NIV #1639+4444 eimi plēroō [given fullness]<br>⇒ NASB #1510+4137 eimi plēroō<br><br>**Col. 2:10**<br>And ye are **complete** in him, which is the head of all principality and power: [KJV]<br>And in Him you have been made **complete**, and He is the head over all rule and authority; [NASB]<br>And you have been **given fullness** in Christ, who is the head over every power and authority. [NIV]<br>And you are **complete** in Him, who is the head of all principality and power. [NKJV]<br>And you are **complete** through your union with Christ. He is the Lord over every ruler and authority in the universe. [NLT]<br>καὶ **ἐστὲ** ἐν αὐτῷ **πεπληρωμένοι**, ὅς ἐστιν ἡ κεφαλὴ πάσης ἀρχῆς καὶ ἐξουσίας· [GNS]<br>καὶ **ἐστὲ** ἐν αὐτῷ **πεπληρωμένοι**, ὅς ἐστιν ἡ κεφαλὴ πάσης ἀρχῆς καὶ ἐξουσίας, [GNT] | 1. Believers receive wisdom, righteousness, sanctification, and redemption.<br>⇒ *Wisdom* means that we understand God, the world, and man: the origin, purpose, and end of creation.<br>⇒ *Righteousness* means that we understand the evil in the world, both sin and death, and that we know the only way to attain righteousness is through Christ.<br>⇒ *Sanctification* means that we have set our lives apart unto God to live for Him and to serve Him.<br>⇒ *Redemption* means that we have been saved from corruption and death and given eternal life.<br>2. Believers receive the fullness of Christ's nature. The divine nature of God is actually placed in believers and they become new creatures in Christ.<br>3. Believers receive fullness of life now. From the time believers receive Christ, they should lack nothing. If a believer ever lacks anything—any fullness of life—it is because he has taken his eyes off Christ and has slipped away.<br>4. Believers receive the fullness of life eternal.<br>5. Believers receive the fullness of the knowledge of God's will. |
| **#1686**<br>**Given Strength**<br><br>Enabled–KJV<br>Strengthened–NASB<br>**Given strength–NIV**<br>Enabled–NKJV<br>Not translated–NLT<br><br>**POSB REFERENCE** (1 Tim.1:12-14; esp. v.12) Note 1, point 1 | ἐνδυναμώσαντί = endunamōsanti<br>Pronunciation: [en-doo-nam-o'-sahn-tee]<br>Parsing (part of speech): verb<br>  Mood—participle<br>  Tense—aorist<br>  Voice—active<br>  Case—dative<br>  Gender—masculine<br>  Number—singular<br>  Stem or root—from ἐνδυναμόω<br>Concordance References:<br>⇒ Strong's #1743 endunamoō<br>⇒ NIV #1904 endunamoō<br>⇒ NASB #1743 endunamoō<br><br>**1 Tim. 1:12**<br>And I thank Christ Jesus our Lord, who hath **enabled** me, for that he counted me faithful, putting me into the ministry; [KJV]<br>I thank Christ Jesus our Lord, who has **strengthened** me, because He considered me faithful, putting me into service; [NASB]<br>I thank Christ Jesus our Lord, who has **given me strength**, that he considered me faithful, appointing me to his service. [NIV]<br>And I thank Christ Jesus our Lord who has **enabled** me, because He counted me faithful, putting *me* into the ministry, [NKJV]<br>How thankful I am to Christ Jesus our Lord for considering me trustworthy and appointing me to serve him, [NLT]—NOT TRANSLATED<br>Καὶ χάριν ἔχω τῷ **ἐνδυναμώσαντί** με Χριστῷ Ἰησοῦ Κυρίῳ ἡμῶν, ὅτι πιστόν με ἡγήσατο, θέμενος εἰς διακονίαν, [GNS]<br>Χάριν ἔχω τῷ **ἐνδυναμώσαντί**, με Χριστῷ Ἰησοῦ τῷ κυρίῳ ἡμῶν, ὅτι πιστόν με ἡγήσατο θέμενος εἰς διακονίαν [GNT] | To be given strength; to be strengthened, enabled; to make strong; to strengthen and give power to.<br><br>**Practical Application**<br>Christ Jesus gave Paul strength. The power of Paul's ministry came from Christ. Christ gave him the strength to minister. Paul's strength and power to minister did not come from his...<br>• trying to stir up power within himself.<br>• talking about the results and power in his ministry.<br>• trying to program strength and power into his ministry.<br>• trying to shout power into his preaching.<br><br>Christ Himself put Paul into the ministry; therefore, Christ Himself strengthened and empowered Paul for the ministry. No person has the power to do spiritual warfare; no person can penetrate the spirits of other people. If a person is to minister to people, he must be empowered by Christ because only Christ can penetrate the spirits of people. Therefore, the minister must possess the power of Christ. |
| **#1687**<br>**Gives–Giveth** | μεταδιδούς = metadidous<br>Pronunciation: [met-ad-id'-oos]<br>Parsing (part of speech): verb<br>  Mood—participle<br>  Tense—present | To contribute to the needs of others; to give; to share; to impart. |

# PRACTICAL WORD STUDIES
## in the NEW TESTAMENT

| ENGLISH WORD | GREEK WORD AND VERSE | THE WORD MEANS... |
|---|---|---|
| **Giveth–KJV** <br> **Gives–NASB** <br> Contributing to the needs of others– NIV <br> **Gives–NKJV** <br> Share it–NLT <br><br> **POSB REFERENCE** <br> (Rom.12:6-8; esp. v.8) <br> Note 2, point 5 | Voice—active <br> Case—nominative <br> Gender—masculine <br> Number—singular <br> Stem or root—from μεταδίδωμι <br> Concordance References: <br> ⇒ Strong's #3330 metadidōmi <br> ⇒ NIV #3556 metadidōmi <br> ⇒ NASB #3330 metadidōmi <br><br> **Romans 12:8** <br> Or he that exhorteth, on exhortation: he that **giveth**, let him do it with simplicity; he that ruleth, with diligence; he that sheweth mercy, with cheerfulness. [KJV] <br> Or he who exhorts, in his exhortation; he who **gives**, with liberality; he who leads, with diligence; he who shows mercy, with cheerfulness. [NASB] <br> If it is encouraging, let him encourage; if it is **contributing to the needs of others**, let him give generously; if it is leadership, let him govern diligently; if it is showing mercy, let him do it cheerfully. [NIV] <br> He who exhorts, in exhortation; he who **gives**, with liberality; he who leads, with diligence; he who shows mercy, with cheerfulness. [NKJV] <br> If your gift is to encourage others, do it! If you have money, **share it** generously. If God has given you leadership ability, take the responsibility seriously. And if you have a gift for showing kindness to others, do it gladly. [NLT] <br> εἴτε ὁ παρακαλῶν, ἐν τῇ παρακλήσει· ὁ **μεταδιδοὺς** ἐν ἁπλότητι, ὁ προϊστάμενος, ἐν σπουδῇ· ὁ ἐλεῶν ἐν ἱλαρότητι. [GNS] <br> εἴτε ὁ παρακαλῶν ἐν τῇ παρακλήσει· ὁ **μεταδιδοὺς** ἐν ἁπλότητι, ὁ προϊστάμενος ἐν σπουδῇ, ὁ ἐλεῶν ἐν ἱλαρότητι. [GNT] | **Practical Application** <br> There is the gift of giving (*metadidous*). This simply means the giving of one's earthly possessions such as money, clothing, and food. Note that in listing this particular gift, Scripture adds a point: it tells how the person is to give. He is to give "generously" (*haplotetes*). |
| #1688 <br> **Gives Life To** <br><br> Quickeneth–KJV <br> **Gives life to–NASB** <br> **Gives life to–NIV** <br> **Gives life to–NKJV** <br> **Gives life to–NLT** <br><br> **POSB REFERENCE** <br> (1 Tim.6:13-16; esp. v.13) <br> Note 4, point 1 | ζῳογονοῦντος = zōogonountos <br> Pronunciation: [dzo-og-on-oon'-tos] <br> Parsing (part of speech): verb <br>   Mood—participle <br>   Tense—present <br>   Voice—active <br>   Case—genitive <br>   Gender—masculine <br>   Number—singular <br> Stem or root—from ζῳογονέω <br> Concordance References: <br> ⇒ Strong's #2225 zōogoneō <br> ⇒ NIV #2441 zōogoneō <br> ⇒ NASB #2225 zōogoneō <br><br> **1 Tim. 6:13** <br> I give thee charge in the sight of God, who **quickeneth** all things, and before Christ Jesus, who before Pontius Pilate witnessed a good confession; [KJV] <br> I charge you in the presence of God, who **gives life to** all things, and of Christ Jesus, who testified the good confession before Pontius Pilate, [NASB] <br> In the sight of God, who **gives life to** everything, and of Christ Jesus, who while testifying before Pontius Pilate made the good confession, I charge you [NIV] <br> I urge you in the sight of God who **gives life to** all things, and *before* Christ Jesus who witnessed the good confession before Pontius Pilate, [NKJV] <br> And I command you before God, who **gives life to** all, and before Christ Jesus, who gave a good testimony before Pontius Pilate, [NLT] <br> παραγγέλλω σοι ἐνώπιον τοῦ Θεοῦ τοῦ **ζῳοποιοῦντος** τὰ πάντα, καὶ Χριστοῦ Ἰησοῦ τοῦ μαρτυρήσαντος ἐπὶ Ποντίου Πιλάτου τὴν καλὴν ὁμολογίαν, [GNS] <br> παραγγέλλω [σοι] ἐνώπιον τοῦ θεοῦ τοῦ **ζῳογονοῦντος** τὰ πάντα καὶ Χριστοῦ Ἰησοῦ τοῦ μαρτυρήσαντος ἐπὶ Ποντίου Πιλάτου τὴν καλὴν ὁμολογίαν, [GNT] | Gives life to; to quicken; to preserve; to bring forth alive (Robertson). <br><br> **Practical Application** <br> God has the power to quicken all things. God is life; He possesses the very energy and power of life within Himself. Therefore, God actually has the power to inject and infuse *eternal life* into us. There is no greater reason for keeping the commandments of God. If we keep His commandments, He will quicken us to live forever; He will give us eternal life. |

# PRACTICAL WORD STUDIES
## in the NEW TESTAMENT

| ENGLISH WORD | GREEK WORD AND VERSE | THE WORD MEANS... |
|---|---|---|
| **#1689**<br>**Giving Approval**<br><br>Consenting–KJV<br>Hearty agreement–NASB<br>**Giving approval–NIV**<br>Consenting–NKJV<br>Official witnesses–NLT<br><br>**POSB REFERENCE**<br>(Acts 8:1)<br>Note 1, point 1 | συνευδοκῶν = *suneudokōn*<br>Pronunciation: [soon-yoo-dok-own]<br>Parsing (part of speech): verb<br>   Mood—participle<br>   Tense—present<br>   Voice—active<br>   Case—nominative<br>   Gender—masculine<br>   Number—singular<br>   Stem or root—from συνευδοκέω<br>Concordance References:<br>  ⇒ Strong's #4909 suneudokeō<br>  ⇒ NIV #5306 suneudokeō<br>  ⇒ NASB #4909 suneudokeō<br><br>**Acts 8:1**<br>And Saul was **consenting** unto his death. And at that time there was a great persecution against the church which was at Jerusalem; and they were all scattered abroad throughout the regions of Judaea and Samaria, except the apostles. [KJV]<br><br>And Saul was in **hearty agreement** with putting him to death. And on that day a great persecution arose against the church in Jerusalem; and they were all scattered throughout the regions of Judea and Samaria, except the apostles. [NASB]<br><br>And Saul was there, **giving approval** to his death. On that day a great persecution broke out against the church at Jerusalem, and all except the apostles were scattered throughout Judea and Samaria. [NIV]<br><br>Now Saul was **consenting** to his death. At that time a great persecution arose against the church which was at Jerusalem; and they were all scattered throughout the regions of Judea and Samaria, except the apostles. [NKJV]<br><br>Saul was one of the **official witnesses** at the killing of Stephen. A great wave of persecution began that day, sweeping over the church in Jerusalem, and all the believers except the apostles fled into Judea and Samaria. [NLT]<br><br>Σαῦλος δὲ ἦν **συνευδοκῶν** τῇ ἀναιρέσει αὐτοῦ. Ἐγένετο δὲ ἐν ἐκείνῃ τῇ ἡμέρᾳ διωγμὸς μέγας ἐπὶ τὴν ἐκκλησίαν τὴν ἐν Ἱεροσολύμοις· πάντες τε διεσπάρησαν κατὰ τὰς χώρας τῆς Ἰουδαίας καὶ Σαμαρείας, πλὴν τῶν ἀποστόλων. [GNS]<br><br>Σαῦλος δὲ ἦν **συνευδοκῶν** τῇ ἀναιρέσει αὐτοῦ. Ἐγένετο δὲ ἐν ἐκείνῃ τῇ ἡμέρᾳ διωγμὸς μέγας ἐπὶ τὴν ἐκκλησίαν τὴν ἐν Ἱεροσολύμοις, πάντες δὲ διεσπάρησαν κατὰ τὰς χώρας τῆς Ἰουδαίας καὶ Σαμαρείας πλὴν τῶν ἀποστόλων. [GNT] | Giving approval; consenting; hearty agreement; to be willing; to agree with. The word means to give approval of the will; to willingly approve; to approve with pleasure; to delight in; to applaud what is being done.<br><br>**Practical Application**<br>Saul was well-pleased with Stephen's death. An *inflamed fury* had been building up in him against the church, for he felt that the preaching of Christ threatened his religion, Judaism. In fact, Saul was the leader in persecuting the church, the one who *boiled* more than anyone else against the church. He was apparently a leader among the religionists. |
| **#1690**<br>**Giving Attention**<br><br>Gave heed–KJV<br>**Giving attention–NASB**<br>Paid close attention–NIV<br>Heeded–NKJV<br>Listened intently–NLT<br><br>**POSB REFERENCE**<br>(Acts 8:6)<br>Note 2, point 2 | προσεῖχον = *proseichon*<br>Pronunciation: [pros-eekh'-on]<br>Parsing (part of speech): verb<br>   Mood—indicative<br>   Tense—imperfect<br>   Voice—active<br>   Person—3rd person<br>   Number—plural<br>   Stem or root—from προσέχω<br>Concordance References:<br>  ⇒ Strong's #4337 prosechō<br>  ⇒ NIV #4668 prosechō<br>  ⇒ NASB #4337 prosechō<br><br>**Acts 8:6**<br>And the people with one accord **gave heed** unto those things which Philip spake, hearing and seeing the miracles which he did. [KJV]<br><br>And the multitudes with one accord were **giving attention** to what was said by Philip, as they heard and saw the signs which he was performing. [NASB]<br><br>When the crowds heard Philip and saw the miraculous | To pay close attention; to give attention; to listen intently; to consider carefully; to follow; to keep watch over.<br><br>**Practical Application**<br>The believer must be "giving attention"; must keep his mind and heart upon the message. |

| ENGLISH WORD | GREEK WORD AND VERSE | THE WORD MEANS... |
|---|---|---|
| | signs he did, they all **paid close attention** to what he said. [NIV]<br>And the multitudes with one accord **heeded** the things spoken by Philip, hearing and seeing the miracles which he did. [NKJV]<br>Crowds **listened intently** to what he had to say because of the miracles he did. [NLT]<br>προσεῖχον τε οἱ ὄχλοι τοῖς λεγομένοις ὑπὸ τοῦ Φιλίππου ὁμοθυμαδὸν, ἐν τῷ ἀκούειν αὐτοὺς καὶ βλέπειν τὰ σημεῖα ἃ ἐποίει. [GNS]<br>προσεῖχον δὲ οἱ ὄχλοι τοῖς λεγομένοις ὑπὸ τοῦ Φιλίππου ὁμοθυμαδὸν ἐν τῷ ἀκούειν αὐτοὺς καὶ βλέπειν τὰ σημεῖα ἃ ἐποίει· [GNT] | |
| **#1691**<br>**Giving Of Thanks**<br><br>Giving of thanks–KJV<br>Thanksgivings–NASB<br>Thanksgiving–NIV<br>Giving of thanks–NKJV<br>Give thanks–NLT<br><br>**POSB REFERENCE**<br>(1 Tim.2:1)<br>Note 1<br><br>See also POSB REF:<br>(Philip.4:6-7; esp. v.6)<br>Note 1, point 2 | εὐχαριστίας = eucharistias<br>Pronunciation: [yoo-khar-is-tee'-ahs]<br>Parsing (part of speech): noun<br>  Case—accusative<br>  Gender—accusative<br>  Number—feminine<br>  Number—plural<br>  Stem or root—from εὐχαριστία, ας<br>Concordance References:<br>  ⇒ Strong's #2169 eucharistia<br>  ⇒ NIV #2374 eucharistia<br>  ⇒ NASB #2169 eucharistia<br><br>**1 Tim. 2:1**<br>I exhort therefore, that, first of all, supplications, prayers, intercessions, and **giving of thanks**, be made for all men; [KJV]<br>First of all, then, I urge that entreaties and prayers, petitions and **thanksgivings**, be made on behalf of all men, [NASB]<br>I urge, then, first of all, that requests, prayers, intercession and **thanksgiving** be made for everyone— [NIV]<br>Therefore I exhort first of all that supplications, prayers, intercessions, and **giving of thanks** be made for all men, [NKJV]<br>I urge you, first of all, to pray for all people. As you make your requests, plead for God's mercy upon them, and **give thanks**. [NLT]<br>Παρακαλῶ οὖν πρῶτον πάντων ποιεῖσθαι δεήσεις, προσευχάς, ἐντεύξεις, **εὐχαριστίας**, ὑπὲρ πάντων ἀνθρώπων· [GNS]<br>Παρακαλῶ οὖν πρῶτον πάντων ποιεῖσθαι δεήσεις προσευχάς ἐντεύξεις **εὐχαριστίας** ὑπὲρ πάντων ἀνθρώπων, [GNT] | Thanksgiving, thankfulness, gratitude, giving of thanks; to give thanks.<br><br>**Practical Application**<br>This means that we thank God for hearing and answering our prayers–thank Him for what He has done and is going to do for all men. We are to give thanks in all things. How can we thank God for terrible trials such as accidents and death and sin? We can not; this is not what Scripture means. What God means is to thank Him for His presence and power as we walk through such trials. In Christ Jesus there is victory and triumph over all, no matter how terrible. Therefore, *in* everything (not *for* everything)–as we walk through all–thank God for the victory He has given us through Christ. |
| **#1692**<br>**Giving Preference**<br><br>Preferring–KJV<br>Give preference–NASB<br>Above–NIV<br>Giving preference–NKJV<br>Take delight–NLT<br><br>**POSB REFERENCE**<br>(Rom.12:9-10; esp. v.10)<br>Note 1, point 4 | προηγούμενοι = proëgoumenoi<br>Pronunciation: [pro-ay-goo'-mehn-oy]<br>Parsing (part of speech): verb<br>  Mood—participle (imperative sense)<br>  Tense—present<br>  Voice—middle or passive deponent<br>  Case—nominative<br>  Gender—masculine<br>  Person—2nd person<br>  Number—plural<br>  Stem or root—from προηγέομαι<br>Concordance References:<br>  ⇒ Strong's #4285 proëgeomai<br>  ⇒ NIV #4605 proëgeomai<br>  ⇒ NASB #4285 proëgeomai<br><br>**Romans 12:10**<br>Be kindly affectioned one to another with brotherly love; in honour **preferring** one another; [KJV]<br>Be devoted to one another in brotherly love; **give preference** to one another in honor; [NASB]<br>Be devoted to one another in brotherly love. Honor one another **above** yourselves. [NIV] | Above, preferring; giving preference; to take delight; to go before; to lead; to set an example.<br><br>**Practical Application**<br>The charge is clear: the believer is to take the lead in esteeming and expressing respect for others. Imagine a church full of believers with each taking the lead in esteeming and honoring the other. What a picture of true love and care, of real warmth and tenderness, of great strength and manliness. |

# PRACTICAL WORD STUDIES
## in the New Testament

| ENGLISH WORD | GREEK WORD AND VERSE | THE WORD MEANS... |
|---|---|---|
| | Be kindly affectionate to one another with brotherly love, in honor **giving preference** to one another; [NKJV]<br>Love each other with genuine affection, and **take delight** in honoring each other. [NLT]<br>τῇ φιλαδελφίᾳ εἰς ἀλλήλους φιλόστοργοι· τῇ τιμῇ ἀλλήλους **προηγούμενοι**· [GNS]<br>τῇ φιλαδελφίᾳ εἰς ἀλλήλους φιλόστοργοι, τῇ τιμῇ ἀλλήλους **προηγούμενοι**, [GNT] | |
| #1693<br>**Glad**<br><br>Rejoice–KJV<br>Rejoiced–NASB<br>**Glad–NIV**<br>Rejoice–NKJV<br>Happy–NLT<br><br>**POSB**<br>**REFERENCE**<br>(Jn.14:28-29; esp. v.28)<br>Note 2 | ἐχάρητε = *echarēte*<br>Pronunciation: [eh-chah'-ray-teh]<br>Parsing (part of speech): verb<br>    Mood—indicative<br>    Tense—aorist<br>    Voice—passive deponent<br>    Person—2nd person<br>    Number—plural<br>    Stem or root—from χαίρω<br>Concordance References:<br>⇒ Strong's #5463 chairo<br>⇒ NIV #5897 chairo<br>⇒ NASB #5463 chairo<br><br>**John 14:28**<br>Ye have heard how I said unto you, I go away, and come again unto you. If ye loved me, ye would **rejoice**, because I said, I go unto the Father: for my Father is greater than I. [KJV]<br>"You heard that I said to you, 'I go away, and I will come to you.' If you loved Me, you would have **rejoiced**, because I go to the Father; for the Father is greater than I. [NASB]<br>"You heard me say, 'I am going away and I am coming back to you.' If you loved me, you would be **glad** that I am going to the Father, for the Father is greater than I. [NIV]<br>You have heard Me say to you, 'I am going away and coming *back* to you.' If you loved Me, you would **rejoice** because I said, 'I am going to the Father,' for My Father is greater than I. [NKJV]<br>Remember what I told you: I am going away, but I will come back to you again. If you really love me, you will be very **happy** for me, because now I can go to the Father, who is greater than I am. [NLT]<br>ἠκούσατε ὅτι ἐγὼ εἶπον ὑμῖν, Ὑπάγω καὶ ἔρχομαι πρὸς ὑμᾶς. εἰ ἠγαπᾶτέ με, **ἐχάρητε** ἂν ὅτι εἶπον, Πορεύομαι πρὸς τὸν πατέρα· ὅτι ὁ πατήρ μού μείζων ἐστί. [GNS]<br>ἠκούσατε ὅτι ἐγὼ εἶπον ὑμῖν, Ὑπάγω καὶ ἔρχομαι πρὸς ὑμᾶς. εἰ ἠγαπᾶτέ με **ἐχάρητε** ἂν ὅτι πορεύομαι πρὸς τὸν πατέρα, ὅτι ὁ πατὴρ μείζων μού ἐστιν. [GNT] | To rejoice; to have great joy; to be glad; to be delighted; to be satisfied. Joy (*chara*) and rejoicing (*echarete*, the same root word as joy) mean an inner gladness and a deep seated pleasure. It is a depth of assurance and confidence that ignites a cheerful heart. It is a cheerful heart that leads to cheerful behavior.<br><br>**Practical Application**<br>The source of joy is threefold. (See POSB *Deeper Study* #1–John 15:11 for more discussion.)<br>1. The return of Jesus to the Father causes believers to be glad. "I am going away, and I am coming back to you" is a reference to His death, resurrection, and ascension.<br>  a. The death or cross of Christ attracts and causes men to joy and rejoice. The cross is the source of their deliverance from sin, death, and hell (see POSB *Deeper Study* #4–John 12:32).<br>  b. The resurrection and ascension of Christ attracts and causes men to joy and rejoice. The resurrection and ascension are the sources of their new life and hope for eternity (see POSB notes, Resurrection–John 14:6; POSB note–John 7:33-34; POSB note–Mark 16:19-20).<br>2. The Father's greatness causes believers to be glad. The Father demonstrated His great love and power by releasing Jesus ...<br>• from the flesh: in all its limitations and weaknesses.<br>• from the world: in all its trials and tensions.<br>• from the devil: in all his oppressions and attacks.<br>• from the pressure of men: in all their needful demands and, in some cases, terrible threats and attacks.<br>The Father took Jesus home, back from where He had come; and He restored Him to His seat of glory, exalting Him above every name that is named (Phil. 2:9-11). The believer joys and rejoices in the phenomenal power of the Father's greatness.<br>3. A confirmed faith causes believers to be glad. The claims of Jesus have been proven and verified. Just as He told His disciples, all that He predicted has come to pass.<br>⇒ He did leave (die).<br>⇒ He did go to His Father (the ascension).<br>⇒ He did return (the resurrection).<br>⇒ He did send the Holy Spirit.<br>Note: by foretelling these things, Jesus strengthened the faith of believers enormously. (In fact, think about it: He could have chosen no better way to strengthen the faith of believers.) |

# PRACTICAL WORD STUDIES
## in the NEW TESTAMENT

| ENGLISH WORD | GREEK WORD AND VERSE | THE WORD MEANS... |
|---|---|---|
| **#1694**<br>**Glad**<br><br>Rejoice–KJV<br>**Glad**–NASB<br>**Glad**–NIV<br>Rejoiced–NKJV<br>Joy–NLT<br><br>**POSB REFERENCE**<br>(Acts 2:25-28; esp. v.26)<br>Note 1, point 1b | ηὐφράνθη = ëuphranthë<br>Pronunciation: [yoo-frahn'-thay]<br>Parsing (part of speech): verb<br>    Mood—indicative<br>    Tense—aorist<br>    Voice—passive<br>    Person—3rd person<br>    Number—singular<br>    Stem or root—from εὐφραίνω<br>Concordance References:<br>  ⇒ Strong's #2165 euphrainö<br>  ⇒ NIV #2370 euphrainö<br>  ⇒ NASB #2165 euphrainö<br><br>**Acts 2:26**<br>Therefore did my heart **rejoice**, and my tongue was glad; moreover also my flesh shall rest in hope: [KJV]<br>'Therefore my heart was **glad** and my tongue exulted; Moreover my flesh also will abide in hope; [NASB]<br>Therefore my heart is **glad** and my tongue rejoices; my body also will live in hope, [NIV]<br>*Therefore my heart rejoiced, and my tongue was glad;Moreover my flesh also will rest in hope.* [NKJV]<br>No wonder my heart is filled with **joy**, and my mouth shouts his praises! My body rests in hope. [NLT]<br>Διὰ τοῦτο εὐφράνθη ἡ καρδία μου, καὶ ἠγαλλιάσατο ἡ γλῶσσά μου· ἔτι δὲ καὶ ἡ σάρξ μου κατασκηνώσει ἐπ' ἐλπίδι· [GNS]<br>διὰ τοῦτο **ηὐφράνθη** ἡ καρδία μου καὶ ἠγαλλιάσατο ἡ γλῶσσά μου, ἔτι δὲ καὶ ἡ σάρξ μου κατασκηνώσει ἐπ' ἐλπίδι, [GNT] | To be glad; to rejoice; to celebrate; to be merry. It means to be joyful and full of euphoria, full of God's presence and glory.<br><br>**Practical Application**<br>Peter said that "David [spoke] concerning Christ" (Psalm 16:8-11). What David said was a prophecy of the Lord's experience upon earth (Acts 2:25-28). David's prophecy concerned Jesus' daily experience or life.<br>1. Jesus experienced God's constant presence and power.<br>  ⇒ Jesus always saw God before His face. Jesus looked and kept His gaze upon God. He thought upon God, focused His mind and attention upon God. He concentrated and stayed His mind upon Him. The idea is that Jesus always practiced and was always conscious of God's presence–"captivating every thought" (cp. 2 Cor. 10:5).<br>  ⇒ Jesus always had God on His right hand, that He should not be moved. God was right there as an advocate and as a protector and defender. God was a provider looking after Christ, strengthening, guiding, upholding, seeing that He was not moved nor shaken. The picture is that of a defender in court or of a soldier on the battlefield standing at a person's right hand, protecting, looking after, and providing for his welfare. (Cp. Psalm 109:31 for this picture.)<br>2. Jesus' heart rejoiced, and His tongue praised God. Such a consciousness of God's presence was bound to cause...<br>  • the heart to be glad (*ëuphranthë*): to be joyful and full of euphoria, full of God's presence and glory.<br>  • the tongue to rejoice (*egalliasato*): to leap for joy and break forth with praise and song.<br>3. Jesus' flesh rested in hope. The phrase "will live" (*kataskenosei*) means *shall tabernacle* or pitch a tent. Jesus' *flesh* rested, tabernacled, pitched its tent, encamped and made its abode upon hope–the hope of conquering death, of being resurrected. Hope of living forever was the basis and foundation of Jesus' life, that for which He lived. He focused His whole life and being upon the hope of the glorious resurrection (cp. Paul's testimony–Phil. 3:7-16, esp. Phil. 3:11). |
| **#1695**<br>**Glad**<br><br>Rejoiced–KJV<br>Rejoiced–NASB<br>**Glad**–NIV<br>Rejoiced–NKJV<br>Great joy–NLT<br><br>**POSB REFERENCE**<br>(Acts 15:30-35; esp. v.31)<br>Note 5, point 1 | ἐχάρησαν = echarësan<br>Pronunciation: [eh-chah'ray-sahn]<br>Parsing (part of speech): verb<br>    Mood—indicative<br>    Tense—aorist<br>    Voice—passive deponent<br>    Person—3rd person<br>    Number—plural<br>    Stem or root—from χαίρω<br>Concordance References:<br>  ⇒ Strong's #5463 chairö<br>  ⇒ NIV #5897 chairö<br>  ⇒ NASB #5463 chairö | Gladness; rejoiced; to have great joy; to be delighted; to be happy.<br><br>**Practical Application**<br>When the four men arrived in Antioch, the whole church was called together and the great decree on salvation was read. When it was read, four great results occurred. Note how God took the dissension and its subsequent events to work it all out for the good of the Antioch church and for the cause of Christ. The results were fourfold.<br>1. There was "gladness" (*echarësan*).<br>2. There was great "*encouragement*" (v.32). |

# PRACTICAL WORD STUDIES
## in the NEW TESTAMENT

| ENGLISH WORD | GREEK WORD AND VERSE | THE WORD MEANS... |
|---|---|---|
| | **Acts 15:31**<br>Which when they had read, they **rejoiced** for the consolation. [KJV]<br>And when they had read it, they **rejoiced** because of its encouragement. [NASB]<br>The people read it and were **glad** for its encouraging message. [NIV]<br>When they had read it, they **rejoiced** over its encouragement. [NKJV]<br>And there was **great joy** throughout the church that day as they read this encouraging message. [NLT]<br>ἀναγνόντες δὲ, **ἐχάρησαν** ἐπὶ τῇ παρακλήσει. [GNS]<br>ἀναγνόντες δὲ **ἐχάρησαν** ἐπὶ τῇ παρακλήσει. [GNT] | 3. There was the discovery of the great missionary, Silas (v.32).<br>4. There was the beginning of a great teaching ministry within the church (v.35). |
| **#1696**<br>**Glad**<br><br>**Glad**–KJV<br>Exulted–NASB<br>Rejoices–NIV<br>**Glad**–NKJV<br>Shouts his praises–NLT<br><br>**POSB REFERENCE**<br>(Acts 2:25-28; esp. v.26)<br>Note 1, point 1b | **ἠγαλλιάσατο** = ēgalliasato<br>Pronunciation: [ag-al-lee-ah'-sah-tow]<br>Parsing (part of speech): verb<br>    Mood—indicative<br>    Tense—aorist<br>    Voice—middle<br>    Person—3rd person<br>    Number—singular<br>    Stem or root—from ἀγαλλιάω<br>Concordance References:<br>  ⇒ Strong's #21 agalliaō<br>  ⇒ NIV #22 agalliaō<br>  ⇒ NASB #21 agalliaō<br><br>**Acts 2:26**<br>Therefore did my heart rejoice, and my tongue was **glad**; moreover also my flesh shall rest in hope: [KJV]<br>'Therefore my heart was glad and my tongue **exulted**; Moreover my flesh also will abide in hope; [NASB]<br>Therefore my heart is glad and my tongue **rejoices**; my body also will live in hope, [NIV]<br>Therefore my heart rejoiced, and my tongue was **glad**; Moreover my flesh also will rest in hope. [NKJV]<br>No wonder my heart is filled with joy, and my mouth **shouts his praises**! My body rests in hope. [NLT]<br>Διὰ τοῦτο εὐφράνθη ἡ καρδία μου, καὶ **ἠγαλλιάσατο** ἡ γλῶσσά μου· ἔτι δὲ καὶ ἡ σάρξ μου κατασκηνώσει ἐπ' ἐλπίδι· [GNS]<br>διὰ τοῦτο ηὐφράνθη ἡ καρδία μου καὶ **Ἠγαλλιάσατο** ἡ γλῶσσά μου, ἔτι δὲ καὶ ἡ σάρξ μου κατασκηνώσει ἐπ' ἐλπίδι, [GNT] | Rejoices, glad, exulting, rejoicing, filled with joy; greatly rejoicing; to shout God's praises; to be extremely joyful. It means to leap for joy and break forth with praise and song.<br><br>**Practical Application**<br>Peter said that "David [spoke] concerning Christ" (Psalm 16:8-11). What David said was a prophecy of the Lord's experience upon earth (Acts 2:25-28). David's prophecy concerned Jesus' daily experience or life.<br>1. Jesus experienced God's constant presence and power.<br>  ⇒ Jesus always saw God before His face. Jesus looked and kept His gaze upon God. He thought upon God, focused His mind and attention upon God. He concentrated and stayed His mind upon Him. The idea is that Jesus always practiced and was always conscious of God's presence–"captivating every thought" (cp. 2 Cor. 10:5).<br>  ⇒ Jesus always had God on His right hand, that He should not be moved. God was right there as an advocate and as a protector and defender. God was a provider looking after Christ, strengthening, guiding, upholding, seeing that He was not moved nor shaken. The picture is that of a defender in court or of a soldier on the battlefield standing at a person's right hand, protecting, looking after, and providing for his welfare. (Cp. Psalm 109:31 for this picture.)<br>2. Jesus' heart rejoiced and His tongue praised God. Such a consciousness of God's presence was bound to cause...<br>  • the heart to rejoice (*ëuphranthë*): to be joyful and full of euphoria, full of God's presence and glory.<br>  • the tongue to be glad (*ēgalliasato*): to leap for joy and break forth with praise and song.<br>3. Jesus' flesh rested in hope. The phrase "will rest" or "abide" (*kataskenosei*) means *shall tabernacle* or pitch a tent. Jesus' *flesh* rested, tabernacled, pitched its tent, encamped and made its abode upon hope–the hope of conquering death, of being resurrected. Hope of living forever was the basis and foundation of Jesus' life, that for which He lived. He focused His whole life and being upon the hope of the glorious resurrection (cp. Paul's testimony–Phil. 3:7-16, esp. Phil. 3:11). |

# PRACTICAL WORD STUDIES
## in the NEW TESTAMENT

| ENGLISH WORD | GREEK WORD AND VERSE | THE WORD MEANS... |
|---|---|---|
| **#1697**<br>**Gladly**<br><br>Cheerfulness–KJV<br>Cheerfulness–NASB<br>Cheerfully–NIV<br>Cheerfulness–NKJV<br>**Gladly–NLT**<br><br>**POSB**<br>**REFERENCE**<br>(Rom.12:6-8; esp. v.8)<br>Note 2, point 7 | ἐν ἱλαρότητι = en hilarotēti<br>Pronunciation: [en hil-ar-ot'-ay-tee]<br>Parsing *hilarotēti* (part of speech): noun<br>  Case—dative<br>  Gender—feminine<br>  Number—singular<br>  Stem or root—from ἱλαρότης, ητος<br>Concordance References:<br>⇒ Strong's #1722 + 2432 en hilarotēs<br>⇒ NIV #1877 + 2660 en hilarotēs [cheerfully]<br>⇒ NASB #1722 + 2432 en hilarotēs<br><br>**Romans 12:8**<br>Or he that exhorteth, on exhortation: he that giveth, let him do it with simplicity; he that ruleth, with diligence; he that sheweth mercy, with **cheerfulness**. [KJV]<br><br>Or he who exhorts, in his exhortation; he who gives, with liberality; he who leads, with diligence; he who shows mercy, with **cheerfulness**. [NASB]<br><br>If it is encouraging, let him encourage; if it is contributing to the needs of others, let him give generously; if it is leadership, let him govern diligently; if it is showing mercy, let him do it **cheerfully**. [NIV]<br><br>He who exhorts, in exhortation; he who gives, with liberality; he who leads, with diligence; he who shows mercy, with **cheerfulness**. [NKJV]<br><br>If your gift is to encourage others, do it! If you have money, share it generously. If God has given you leadership ability, take the responsibility seriously. And if you have a gift for showing kindness to others, do it **gladly**. [NLT]<br><br>εἴτε ὁ παρακαλῶν, ἐν τῇ παρακλήσει· ὁ μεταδιδοὺς ἐν ἁπλότητι, ὁ προϊστάμενος, ἐν σπουδῇ· ὁ ἐλεῶν ἐν ἱλαρότητι. [GNS]<br><br>εἴτε ὁ παρακαλῶν ἐν τῇ παρακλήσει· ὁ μεταδιδοὺς ἐν ἁπλότητι, ὁ προϊστάμενος ἐν σπουδῇ, ὁ ἐλεῶν **ἐν ἱλαρότητι**. [GNT] | Cheerfully; cheerfulness; joyful; happy; gladly; merry.<br><br>**Practical Application**<br>There is the gift of kindness (*eleon*). This is a person who is full of forgiveness and compassion, pity and kindness toward others. Note that the kind person is to show kindness with a glad (*hilarotēti*) heart. The person with the gift of kindness...<br>• is not to forgive grudgingly.<br>• is not to hesitate in forgiving others.<br>• is not to show kindness in an annoyed spirit.<br>• is not to show kindness in a spirit of criticism and rebuke toward the person who needs help. (This often happens when the person is down and out because of unemployment, lack of education, or some other unfortunate circumstance.)<br><br>The believer who has the spirit of kindness is to show kindness with a cheerful and joyful heart, doing all he can to lift up the person needing kindness. |
| **#1698**<br>**Gleaming**<br><br>Glistering–KJV<br>**Gleaming–NASB**<br>Flash of lightning–NIV<br>Glistening–NKJV<br>Dazzling–NLT<br><br>**POSB**<br>**REFERENCE**<br>(Lk.9:29)<br>Note 3, point 2 | ἐξαστράπτων = exastraptōn<br>Pronunciation: [ex-as-trap'-tone]<br>Parsing (part of speech): verb<br>  Mood—participle<br>  Tense—present<br>  Voice—active<br>  Case—nominative<br>  Gender—masculine<br>  Number—singular<br>  Stem or root—from ἐξαστράπτω<br>Concordance References:<br>⇒ Strong's #1823 exastraptō<br>⇒ NIV #1993 exastraptō<br>⇒ NASB #1823 exastraptō<br><br>**Luke 9:29**<br>And as he prayed, the fashion of his countenance was altered, and his raiment was white and **glistering**. [KJV]<br><br>And while He was praying, the appearance of His face became different, and His clothing became white and **gleaming**. [NASB]<br><br>As he was praying, the appearance of his face changed, and his clothes became as bright as a **flash of lightning**. [NIV]<br><br>As He prayed, the appearance of His face was altered, and His robe *became* white *and* **glistening**. [NKJV]<br><br>And as he was praying, the appearance of his face changed, and his clothing became **dazzling** white. [NLT]<br><br>καὶ ἐγένετο, ἐν τῷ προσεύχεσθαι αὐτὸν, τὸ εἶδος τοῦ προσώπου αὐτοῦ ἕτερον, καὶ ὁ ἱματισμὸς αὐτοῦ λευκὸς ἐξαστράπτων. [GNS]<br><br>καὶ ἐγένετο ἐν τῷ προσεύχεσθαι αὐτὸν τὸ εἶδος τοῦ προσώπου αὐτοῦ ἕτερον καὶ ὁ ἱματισμὸς αὐτοῦ λευκὸς ἐξαστράπτων. [GNT] | To flash like lightning; to gleam; to brighten; to be radiant; to dazzle.<br><br>**Practical Application**<br>Jesus was praying when these changes took place. Apparently, He was concentrating so intensely and was so wrapped up in God that God transformed Him, that is, allowed His Godly nature to shine right through Him. What is the lesson for the believer? When a genuine believer prays with intensity and heavy concentration, his countenance is sometimes changed. He experiences a precious glow, a brightness, a light about his whole countenance. |

# PRACTICAL WORD STUDIES
## in the New Testament

| ENGLISH WORD | GREEK WORD AND VERSE | THE WORD MEANS... |
|---|---|---|
| **#1699**<br>**Glistening–**<br>**Glistering**<br><br>Glistering–KJV<br>Gleaming–NASB<br>Flash of lightning–NIV<br>**Glistening**–NKJV<br>Dazzling–NLT<br><br>**POSB**<br>**REFERENCE**<br>(Lk.9:29)<br>Note 3, point 2 | ἐξαστράπτων = *exastraptōn*<br>Pronunciation: [ex-as-trap'-tone]<br>Parsing (part of speech): verb<br>  Mood—participle<br>  Tense—present<br>  Voice—active<br>  Case—nominative<br>  Gender—masculine<br>  Number—singular<br>  Stem or root—from ἐξαστράπτω<br>Concordance References:<br>  ⇒ Strong's #1823 *exastraptō*<br>  ⇒ NIV #1993 *exastraptō*<br>  ⇒ NASB #1823 *exastraptō*<br><br>**Luke 9:29**<br>And as he prayed, the fashion of his countenance was altered, and his raiment was white and **glistering**. [KJV]<br>And while He was praying, the appearance of His face became different, and His clothing became white and **gleaming**. [NASB]<br>As he was praying, the appearance of his face changed, and his clothes became as bright as a **flash of lightning**. [NIV]<br>As He prayed, the appearance of His face was altered, and His robe *became* white *and* **glistening**. [NKJV]<br>And as he was praying, the appearance of his face changed, and his clothing became **dazzling** white. [NLT]<br>καὶ ἐγένετο, ἐν τῷ προσεύχεσθαι αὐτὸν, τὸ εἶδος τοῦ προσώπου αὐτοῦ ἕτερον, καὶ ὁ ἱματισμὸς αὐτοῦ λευκὸς **ἐξαστράπτων**. [GNS]<br>καὶ ἐγένετο ἐν τῷ προσεύχεσθαι αὐτὸν τὸ εἶδος τοῦ προσώπου αὐτοῦ ἕτερον καὶ ὁ ἱματισμὸς αὐτοῦ λευκὸς **ἐξαστράπτων**. [GNT] | To flash like lightning; to gleam; to brighten; to be radiant; to dazzle.<br><br>**Practical Application**<br>Jesus was praying when these changes took place. Apparently, He was concentrating so intensely and was so wrapped up in God that God transformed Him, that is, allowed His Godly nature to shine right through Him. What is the lesson for the believer? When a genuine believer prays with intensity and heavy concentration, his countenance is sometimes changed. He experiences a precious glow, a brightness, a light about his whole countenance. |
| **#1700**<br>**Glorified God–**<br>**Glorifying God**<br><br>Glorified God–KJV<br>Glorifying God–NASB<br>Praised God–NIV<br>**Glorified God**–NKJV<br>Praised God–NLT<br><br>**POSB**<br>**REFERENCE**<br>(Lk.7:16-17; esp. v.16)<br>Note 4, point 1<br><br>See also POSB REF:<br>(Acts 4:21-22; esp. v.21)<br>Note 8 | ἐδόξαζον τὸν θεὸν = *edoxazon ton theon*<br>Pronunciation: [eh-dox-ad'-zon ton theh'-on]<br>Parsing *edoxazon* (part of speech): verb<br>  Mood—indicative<br>  Tense—imperfect<br>  Voice—active<br>  Person—3rd person<br>  Number—plural<br>  Stem or root—from δοξάζω<br>Parsing *theon* (part of speech): noun<br>  Case—accusative<br>  Gender—masculine<br>  Number—singular<br>  Stem or root—from θεός, οῦ<br>Concordance References:<br>  ⇒ Strong's #1392 *doxazō* + 2316 *theos*<br>  ⇒ NIV #1519 *doxazō* [praised] + 2536 *theos* [God]<br>  ⇒ NASB #1392 *doxazō* + 2316 *theos*<br><br>**Luke 7:16**<br>And there came a fear on all: and they **glorified God**, saying, That a great prophet is risen up among us; and, That God hath visited his people. [KJV]<br>And fear gripped them all, and they began **glorifying God**, saying, "A great prophet has arisen among us!" and, "God has visited His people!" [NASB]<br>They were all filled with awe and **praised God**. "A great prophet has appeared among us," they said. "God has come to help his people." [NIV]<br>Then fear came upon all, and they **glorified God**, saying, "A great prophet has risen up among us"; and, "God has visited His people." [NKJV]<br>Great fear swept the crowd, and they **praised God**, saying, "A mighty prophet has risen among us," and "We have seen the hand of God at work today." [NLT]<br>ἔλαβε δὲ φόβος ἅπαντας, καὶ **ἐδόξαζον τὸν θεὸν**, λέγοντες, ὅτι Προφήτης μέγας ἐγήγερται ἐν ἡμῖν, καὶ ὅτι Ἐπεσκέψατο ὁ θεὸς τὸν λαὸν αὐτοῦ. [GNS]<br>ἔλαβεν δὲ φόβος πάντας καὶ **ἐδόξαζον τὸν θεὸν** λέγοντες ὅτι Προφήτης μέγας ἠγέρθη ἐν ἡμῖν καὶ ὅτι Ἐπεσκέψατο ὁ θεὸς τὸν λαὸν αὐτοῦ. [GNT] | To glorify God; to praise God; to honor God; to exalt God.<br><br>**Practical Application**<br>The tense is imperfect active; "they began to glorify God" and continued to glorify God. Mary was greatly blessed by God, yet she did not slip into the sin of pride, nor did she think that she was a favorite of God. The more we are blessed by God, the more dangerous the sin of pride becomes. We must learn to live praising God more and more. The more He blesses us, the more we must learn to praise Him. |

# PRACTICAL WORD STUDIES
## in the NEW TESTAMENT

| ENGLISH WORD | GREEK WORD AND VERSE | THE WORD MEANS... |
|---|---|---|
| **#1701**<br>**Glorifies**<br><br>Magnify–KJV<br>Exalts–NASB<br>**Glorifies–NIV**<br>Magnifies–NKJV<br>Praise–NLT<br><br>**POSB REFERENCE**<br>(Lk.1:46)<br>Note 1, point 2 | Μεγαλύνει = *Megalunei*<br>Pronunciation: [meg-al-oo'-neh-ee]<br>Parsing (part of speech): verb<br>   Mood—indicative<br>   Tense—present<br>   Voice—active<br>   Person—3rd person<br>   Number—singular<br>   Stem or root—from μεγαλύνω<br>Concordance References:<br>⇒ Strong's #3170 megalunō<br>⇒ NIV #3486 megalunō<br>⇒ NASB #3170 megalunō<br><br>**Luke 1:46**<br>And Mary said, My soul doth **magnify** the Lord, [KJV]<br>And Mary said: "My soul **exalts** the Lord, [NASB]<br>And Mary said: "My soul **glorifies** the Lord [NIV]<br>And Mary said: "My soul **magnifies** the Lord, [NKJV]<br>Mary responded, "Oh, how I **praise** the Lord. [NLT]<br>Καὶ εἶπε Μαριάμ, [GNS]—**Luke 1:46**<br>Μεγαλύνει ἡ ψυχή μου τὸν Κύριον, καὶ ἠγαλλίασε τὸ πνεῦμά μου ἐπὶ τῷ Θεῷ τῷ σωτῆρί μου, [GNS]—**Luke 1:47**<br>Καὶ εἶπεν Μαριάμ, [GNT]—**Luke 1:46**<br>Μεγαλύνει ἡ ψυχή μου τὸν κύριον, καὶ ἠγαλλίασεν τὸ πνεῦμά μου ἐπὶ τῷ Θεῷ τῷ σωτῆρί μου, [GNT]—**Luke 1:47**<br>NOTE: This Greek word (Μεγαλύνει) in verse 47 is translated in verse 46 in English Bibles. | To exalt; to magnify; to glorify; to praise; to declare the greatness of; to highly regard.<br><br>**Practical Application**<br>The idea is habitual; that is, it was the habit of Mary's soul to magnify or glorify the Lord. |
| **#1702**<br>**Glorious God**<br><br>The God of glory–KJV<br>The God of glory–NASB<br>The God of glory–NIV<br>The God of glory–NKJV<br>**Glorious God–NLT**<br><br>**POSB REFERENCE**<br>(Acts 7:2)<br>Deeper Study #1 | Ὁ Θεὸς τῆς δόξης = *Ho theos tēs doxēs*<br>Pronunciation: [ha they-os tace dox-ace]<br>Parsing *doxēs* (part of speech): noun<br>   Case—genitive<br>   Gender—feminine<br>   Number—singular<br>   Stem or root—from δόξα, ης<br>Concordance References:<br>⇒ Strong's #3588 ho + 2316 theos + 3588 ho + 1391 doxa<br>⇒ NIV #3836 ho [The] + 2536 theos [God] + 3836 ho [Not in English] + 1518 doxa [glory]<br>⇒ NASB #3588 ho + 2316 theos + 3588 ho + 1391 doxa<br><br>**Acts 7:2**<br>And he said, Men, brethren, and fathers, hearken; **The God of glory** appeared unto our father Abraham, when he was in Mesopotamia, before he dwelt in Charran, [KJV]<br>And he said, "Hear me, brethren and fathers! **The God of glory** appeared to our father Abraham when he was in Mesopotamia, before he lived in Haran, [NASB]<br>To this he replied: "Brothers and fathers, listen to me! **The God of glory** appeared to our father Abraham while he was still in Mesopotamia, before he lived in Haran. [NIV]<br>And he said, "Brethren and fathers, listen: **The God of glory** appeared to our father Abraham when he was in Mesopotamia, before he dwelt in Haran, [NKJV]<br>This was Stephen's reply: "Brothers and honorable fathers, listen to me. Our **glorious God** appeared to our ancestor Abraham in Mesopotamia before he moved to Haran. [NLT]<br>ὁ δὲ ἔφη, Ἄνδρες ἀδελφοὶ καὶ πατέρες, ἀκούσατε. ὁ Θεὸς τῆς δόξης ὤφθη τῷ πατρὶ ἡμῶν Ἀβραὰμ ὄντι ἐν τῇ Μεσοποταμίᾳ, πρὶν ἢ κατοικῆσαι αὐτὸν ἐν Χαρράν, [GNS]<br>ὁ δὲ ἔφη, Ἄνδρες ἀδελφοὶ καὶ πατέρες, ἀκούσατε. Ὁ θεὸς τῆς δόξης ὤφθη τῷ πατρὶ ἡμῶν Ἀβραὰμ ὄντι ἐν τῇ Μεσοποταμίᾳ πρὶν ἢ κατοικῆσαι αὐτὸν ἐν Χαρράν [GNT] | God of glory; glorious God; God who possesses and manifests glory; God of the manifested glory, of the outward and visible glory; God who reveals glory.<br><br>**Practical Application**<br>It is the Shekinah glory, the visible splendor, radiance, and brilliance of God's Person that bursts forth from His Supreme Being. The idea is that God appeared to reveal His glory to Abraham. (See POSB note, Shekinah Glory–Matthew 17:5-8. Note: this throws some light on how God went about calling Abraham. It must have been a visible appearance of God's glory just as Moses and Isaiah and others received.) |

# PRACTICAL WORD STUDIES
## in the NEW TESTAMENT

| ENGLISH WORD | GREEK WORD AND VERSE | THE WORD MEANS... |
|---|---|---|
| **#1703**<br>**Glorious Power**<br><br>Glory–KJV<br>Glory–NASB<br>Glory–NIV<br>Glory–NKJV<br>**Glorious power–NLT**<br><br>**POSB REFERENCE**<br>(Rom.6:3-5; esp. v.4)<br>Note 2, point 2a<br><br>See also POSB REF:<br>(2 Thes.2:14)<br>Note 3 | δόξης = *doxës*<br>Pronunciation: [dox'-ace]<br>Parsing (part of speech): noun<br>    Case—genitive<br>    Gender—feminine<br>    Number—singular<br>    Stem or root—from δόξα, ης<br>Concordance References:<br>  ⇒ Strong's #1391 doxa<br>  ⇒ NIV #1518 doxa<br>  ⇒ NASB #1391 doxa<br><br>**Romans 6:4**<br>Therefore we are buried with him by baptism into death: that like as Christ was raised up from the dead by the **glory** of the Father, even so we also should walk in newness of life. [KJV]<br><br>Therefore we have been buried with Him through baptism into death, in order that as Christ was raised from the dead through the **glory** of the Father, so we too might walk in newness of life. [NASB]<br><br>We were therefore buried with him through baptism into death in order that, just as Christ was raised from the dead through the **glory** of the Father, we too may live a new life. [NIV]<br><br>Therefore we were buried with Him through baptism into death, that just as Christ was raised from the dead by the **glory** of the Father, even so we also should walk in newness of life. [NKJV]<br><br>For we died and were buried with Christ by baptism. And just as Christ was raised from the dead by the **glorious power** of the Father, now we also may live new lives. [NLT]<br><br>συνετάφημεν οὖν αὐτῷ διὰ τοῦ βαπτίσματος εἰς τὸν θάνατον· ἵνα ὥσπερ ἠγέρθη Χριστὸς ἐκ νεκρῶν διὰ τῆς **δόξης** τοῦ πατρός, οὕτως καὶ ἡμεῖς ἐν καινότητι ζωῆς περιπατήσωμεν. [GNS]<br><br>συνετάφημεν οὖν αὐτῷ διὰ τοῦ βαπτίσματος εἰς τὸν θάνατον, ἵνα ὥσπερ ἠγέρθη Χριστὸς ἐκ νεκρῶν διὰ τῆς **δόξης** τοῦ πατρός, οὕτως καὶ ἡμεῖς ἐν καινότητι ζωῆς περιπατήσωμεν. [GNT] | Glory, splendor, brilliance; glorious power; that which dwells. It means to possess and to be full of perfect light; to dwell in perfect light, brilliance, splendor, brightness, luster, and magnificence with God. The "glory" (*doxës*) of God means all the excellence of God; all that He is in His might and power, love and grace, compassion and mercy. It means all His attributes: His omnipotence (all power), omniscience (all knowing), omnipresence (being everywhere), and sovereignty.<br><br>**Practical Application**<br>Christ was raised up from the dead by the glory of the Father. This tells how our position in Christ happened. It happened by the glory and the power of God. In this particular passage, it refers primarily to His glorious power. It was the glory of His might and power that raised up Jesus from the dead, and it is by the glory of His might and power that he places and positions us in Christ. |
| **#1704**<br>**Glory**<br><br>Glory–KJV<br>Glory–NASB<br>Glory–NIV<br>Glory–NKJV<br>Glory–NLT<br><br>**POSB REFERENCE**<br>(Jn.1:14)<br>Note 2, point 1a<br><br>See also POSB REF:<br>(Rom.2:7)<br>*Deeper Study #1* | δόξαν = *doxan*<br>Pronunciation: [dox'-ahn]<br>Parsing (part of speech): noun<br>    Case—accusative<br>    Gender—feminine<br>    Number—singular<br>    Stem or root—from δόξα, ης<br>Concordance References:<br>  ⇒ Strong's #1391 doxa<br>  ⇒ NIV #1518 doxa<br>  ⇒ NASB #1391 doxa<br><br>**John 1:14**<br>And the Word was made flesh, and dwelt among us, (and we beheld his **glory**, the **glory** as of the only begotten of the Father,) full of grace and truth. [KJV]<br><br>And the Word became flesh, and dwelt among us, and we beheld His **glory**, **glory** as of the only begotten from the Father, full of grace and truth. [NASB]<br><br>The Word became flesh and made his dwelling among us. We have seen his **glory**, the **glory** of the One and Only, who came from the Father, full of grace and truth. [NIV]<br><br>And the Word became flesh and dwelt among us, and we beheld His **glory**, the **glory** as of the only begotten of the Father, full of grace and truth. [NKJV]<br><br>So the Word became human and lived here on earth among us. He was full of unfailing love and faithfulness. And we have seen his **glory**, the **glory** of the only Son of the Father. [NLT] | Glory, glorious power, that which dwells. It means to possess and to be full of perfect light; to dwell in perfect light, brilliance, splendor, brightness, luster, and magnificence with God. The "glory" (*doxan*) of God means all the excellence of God; all that He is in His might and power, love and grace, compassion and mercy. It means all His attributes: His omnipotence (all power), omniscience (all knowing), omnipresence (being everywhere), and sovereignty.<br><br>**Practical Application**<br>It refers to the bright cloud that God used to guide Israel out of Egypt and that rested upon the tabernacle and above the mercy seat in the Most Holy Place (Exodus 40:34-38). The cloud symbolized God's presence, and that is just what John was saying. "We beheld," actually saw, the Shekinah glory, God's very presence "dwelling among us." |

## PRACTICAL WORD STUDIES
### in the NEW TESTAMENT

| ENGLISH WORD | GREEK WORD AND VERSE | THE WORD MEANS... |
|---|---|---|
| | καὶ ὁ λόγος σὰρξ ἐγένετο, καὶ ἐσκήνωσεν ἐν ἡμῖν, -- καὶ ἐθεασάμεθα τὴν **δόξαν** αὐτοῦ, **δόξαν** ὡς μονογενοῦς παρὰ πατρός --, πλήρης χάριτος καὶ ἀληθείας. [GNS]<br><br>Καὶ ὁ λόγος σὰρξ ἐγένετο καὶ ἐσκήνωσεν ἐν ἡμῖν, καὶ ἐθεασάμεθα τὴν **δόξαν** αὐτοῦ, **δόξαν** ὡς μονογενοῦς παρὰ πατρός, πλήρης χάριτος καὶ ἀληθείας. [GNT] | |
| **#1705**<br>**Glory**<br><br>Glory–KJV<br>Glory–NASB<br>Glory–NIV<br>Glory–NKJV<br>Glorious power–NLT<br><br>**POSB REFERENCE**<br>(Rom.6:3-5; esp. v.4)<br>Note 2, point 2a<br><br>See also POSB REF:<br>(2 Thes.2:14)<br>Note 3 | δόξης = *doxës*<br>Pronunciation: [dox'-ace]<br>Parsing (part of speech): noun<br>   Case—genitive<br>   Gender—feminine<br>   Number—singular<br>   Stem or root—from δόξα, ης<br>Concordance References:<br>  ⇒ Strong's #1391 doxa<br>  ⇒ NIV #1518 doxa<br>  ⇒ NASB #1391 doxa<br><br>**Romans 6:4**<br>Therefore we are buried with him by baptism into death: that like as Christ was raised up from the dead by the **glory** of the Father, even so we also should walk in newness of life. [KJV]<br>  Therefore we have been buried with Him through baptism into death, in order that as Christ was raised from the dead through the **glory** of the Father, so we too might walk in newness of life. [NASB]<br>  We were therefore buried with him through baptism into death in order that, just as Christ was raised from the dead through the **glory** of the Father, we too may live a new life. [NIV]<br>  Therefore we were buried with Him through baptism into death, that just as Christ was raised from the dead by the **glory** of the Father, even so we also should walk in newness of life. [NKJV]<br>  For we died and were buried with Christ by baptism. And just as Christ was raised from the dead by the **glorious power** of the Father, now we also may live new lives. [NLT]<br>  συνετάφημεν οὖν αὐτῷ διὰ τοῦ βαπτίσματος εἰς τὸν θάνατον· ἵνα ὥσπερ ἠγέρθη Χριστὸς ἐκ νεκρῶν διὰ τῆς **δόξης** τοῦ πατρός, οὕτως καὶ ἡμεῖς ἐν καινότητι ζωῆς περιπατήσωμεν. [GNS]<br>  συνετάφημεν οὖν αὐτῷ διὰ τοῦ βαπτίσματος εἰς τὸν θάνατον, ἵνα ὥσπερ ἠγέρθη Χριστὸς ἐκ νεκρῶν διὰ τῆς **δόξης** τοῦ πατρός, οὕτως καὶ ἡμεῖς ἐν καινότητι ζωῆς περιπατήσωμεν. [GNT] | Glory, glorious power, that which dwells. It means to possess and to be full of perfect light; to dwell in perfect light, brilliance, splendor, brightness, luster, and magnificence with God. The "glory" (*doxës*) of God means all the excellence of God; all that He is in His might and power, love and grace, compassion and mercy. It means all His attributes: His omnipotence (all power), omniscience (all knowing), omnipresence (being everywhere), and sovereignty.<br><br>**Practical Application**<br>Christ was raised up from the dead by the glory of the Father. This tells how our glorious position in Christ happened. It happened by the glory and the power of God. In this particular passage it refers primarily to His glorious power. It was the glory of His might and power that raised up Jesus from the dead, and it is by the glory of His might and power that he places and positions us in Christ. |
| **#1706**<br>**Glorying**<br><br>Glorying–KJV<br>Boasting–NASB<br>Boasting–NIV<br>Glorying–NKJV<br>Boast–NLT<br><br>**POSB REFERENCE**<br>(1 Cor.5:6)<br>Note 1 | καύχημα = *kauchëma*<br>Pronunciation: [kow'-khay-mah]<br>Parsing (part of speech): noun<br>   Case—nominative<br>   Gender—neuter<br>   Number—singular<br>   Stem or root—from καύχημα, τος<br>Concordance References:<br>  ⇒ Strong's #2745 kauchëma<br>  ⇒ NIV #3017 kauchëma<br>  ⇒ NASB #2745 kauchëma<br><br>**1 Cor. 5:6**<br>Your **glorying** is not good. Know ye not that a little leaven leaveneth the whole lump? [KJV]<br>  Your **boasting** is not good. Do you not know that a little leaven leavens the whole lump of dough? [NASB]<br>  Your **boasting** is not good. Don't you know that a little yeast works through the whole batch of dough? [NIV]<br>  Your **glorying** is not good. Do you not know that a little leaven leavens the whole lump? [NKJV]<br>  How terrible that you should **boast** about your spirituality, and yet you let this sort of thing go on. Don't you realize that if even one person is allowed to go on sinning, | Boasting, glorying, taking pride in.<br><br>**Practical Application**<br>It means that some believers in the Corinthian Church were boasting, glorying, and taking pride in the man despite the known fact of his sin. Perhaps he was a man of outstanding leadership in the community or the city of Corinth. Perhaps he had become a leader of one of the factions in the church. Whatever the case, the church overlooked his sin and took great pride in the fact that a man of his stature would join and become a part of their fellowship. |

# PRACTICAL WORD STUDIES
## in the NEW TESTAMENT

| ENGLISH WORD | GREEK WORD AND VERSE | THE WORD MEANS... |
|---|---|---|
| | soon all will be affected? [NLT]<br>Οὐ καλὸν τὸ **καύχημα** ὑμῶν. οὐκ οἴδατε ὅτι μικρὰ ζύμη ὅλον τὸ φύραμα ζυμοῖ; [GNS]<br>Οὐ καλὸν τὸ **Καύχημα** ὑμῶν. οὐκ οἴδατε ὅτι μικρὰ ζύμη ὅλον τὸ φύραμα ζυμοῖ; [GNT] | |
| **#1707**<br>**Gnashed–**<br>**Gnashing**<br><br>**Gnashed–KJV**<br>**Gnashing–NASB**<br>**Gnashed–NIV**<br>**Gnashed–NKJV**<br>Shook–NLT<br><br>**POSB**<br>**REFERENCE**<br>(Acts 7:54)<br>Note 1, point 3 | ἔβρυχον = ebruchon<br>Pronunciation: [eh-broo'-khon]<br>Parsing (part of speech): verb<br>   Mood—indicative<br>   Tense—imperfect<br>   Voice—active<br>   Person—3rd person<br>   Number—plural<br>   Stem or root—from βρύχω<br>Concordance References:<br> ⇒ Strong's #1031 bruchö<br> ⇒ NIV #1107 bruchö<br> ⇒ NASB #1031 bruchö<br><br>**Acts 7:54**<br>When they heard these things, they were cut to the heart, and they **gnashed** on him with their teeth. [KJV]<br>Now when they heard this, they were cut to the quick, and they began **gnashing** their teeth at him. [NASB]<br>When they heard this, they were furious and **gnashed** their teeth at him. [NIV]<br>When they heard these things they were cut to the heart, and they **gnashed** at him with *their* teeth. [NKJV]<br>The Jewish leaders were infuriated by Stephen's accusation, and they **shook** their fists in rage. [NLT]<br>Ἀκούοντες δὲ ταῦτα, διεπρίοντο ταῖς καρδίαις αὐτῶν, καὶ **ἔβρυχον** τοὺς ὀδόντας ἐπ' αὐτόν. [GNS]<br>Ἀκούοντες δὲ ταῦτα διεπρίοντο ταῖς καρδίαις αὐτῶν καὶ **ἔβρυχον** τοὺς ὀδόντας ἐπ' αὐτόν. [GNT] | To gnash, grind, shake, oppress.<br><br>**Practical Application**<br>The word means to bite, to grind, to gnash the teeth just like a pack of snarling dogs. The people were in a rage, filled with anger and malice, ready to do violence, ready to unleash the fury of their emotions. |
| **#1708**<br>**Gnashing**<br><br>**Gnashing–KJV**<br>**Gnashing–NASB**<br>**Gnashing–NIV**<br>**Gnashing–NKJV**<br>**Gnashing–NLT**<br><br>**POSB**<br>**REFERENCE**<br>(Mt.8:12)<br>Note 3, point 3<br><br>See also POSB REF:<br>(Lk.13:28)<br>*Deeper Study* #2 | βρυγμός = brugmos<br>Pronunciation: [broog-mos']<br>Parsing (part of speech): noun<br>   Case—nominative<br>   Gender—masculine<br>   Number—singular<br>   Stem or root—from βρυγμός, οῦ<br>Concordance References:<br> ⇒ Strong's #1030 brugmos<br> ⇒ NIV #1106 brugmos<br> ⇒ NASB #1030 brugmos<br><br>**Matthew 8:12**<br>But the children of the kingdom shall be cast out into outer darkness: there shall be weeping and **gnashing** of teeth. [KJV]<br>But the sons of the kingdom shall be cast out into the outer darkness; in that place there shall be weeping and **gnashing** of teeth." [NASB]<br>But the subjects of the kingdom will be thrown outside, into the darkness, where there will be weeping and **gnashing** of teeth." [NIV]<br>But the sons of the kingdom will be cast out into outer darkness. There will be weeping and **gnashing** of teeth." [NKJV]<br>But many Israelites—those for whom the Kingdom was prepared—will be cast into outer darkness, where there will be weeping and **gnashing** of teeth." [NLT]<br>οἱ δὲ υἱοὶ τῆς βασιλείας ἐκβληθήσονται εἰς τὸ σκότος τὸ ἐξώτερον· ἐκεῖ ἔσται ὁ κλαυθμὸς καὶ ὁ **βρυγμὸς** τῶν ὀδόντων. [GNS]<br>οἱ δὲ υἱοὶ τῆς βασιλείας ἐκβληθήσονται εἰς τὸ σκότος τὸ ἐξώτερον· ἐκεῖ ἔσται ὁ κλαυθμὸς καὶ ὁ **βρυγμὸς** τῶν ὀδόντων. [GNT] | Grinding; gnashing; biting in hostility and bitterness and indignation; spitefully snapping the teeth. It is rage, fury, and despair because nothing can be done.<br><br>**Practical Application**<br>In this Scripture, a person's state is permanently determined–eternal damnation in hell.<br>The fire of hell, whatever its nature and qualities, is spiritual and eternal. It never ends. And men must face this; they must not shrink from the truth of hell. Why? Because hell, that is, separation from God, is much worse than any experience here on earth. It will be much worse than any physical experience imaginable. This is the teaching of Scripture. This is the point Jesus was making. Man absolutely must flee from hell. Man absolutely must flee to Christ for salvation. |

## Practical Word Studies
### in the New Testament

| ENGLISH WORD | GREEK WORD AND VERSE | THE WORD MEANS... |
|---|---|---|
| **#1709**<br>**Go**<br><br>Depart–KJV<br>Depart–NASB<br>Depart–NIV<br>Depart–NKJV<br>**Go–NLT**<br><br>**POSB REFERENCE**<br>(Philip.1:22-23; esp. v.23)<br>Note 3, points 1, 2 | ἀναλῦσαι = analusai<br>Pronunciation: [an-al-oo'-sah-ee]<br>Parsing (part of speech): verb<br>    Mood—infinitive<br>    Tense—aorist<br>    Voice—active<br>    Case—accusative<br>    Stem or root—from ἀναλύω<br>Concordance References:<br>  ⇒ Strong's #360 analuō<br>  ⇒ NIV #386 analuō<br>  ⇒ NASB #360 analuō<br><br>**Philip. 1:23**<br>For I am in a strait betwixt two, having a desire to **depart**, and to be with Christ; which is far better: [KJV]<br>But I am hard-pressed from both directions, having the desire to **depart** and be with Christ, for that is very much better; [NASB]<br>I am torn between the two: I desire to **depart** and be with Christ, which is better by far; [NIV]<br>For I am hard pressed between the two, having a desire to **depart** and be with Christ, *which is* far better. [NKJV]<br>I'm torn between two desires: Sometimes I want to live, and sometimes I long to **go** and be with Christ. That would be far better for me, [NLT]<br>συνέχομαι γὰρ ἐκ τῶν δύο, τὴν ἐπιθυμίαν ἔχων εἰς τὸ **ἀναλῦσαι** καὶ σὺν Χριστῷ εἶναι, πολλῷ γὰρ μᾶλλον κρεῖσσον· [GNS]<br>συνέχομαι δὲ ἐκ τῶν δύο, τὴν ἐπιθυμίαν ἔχων εἰς τὸ **ἀναλῦσαι** καὶ σὺν Χριστῷ εἶναι, πολλῷ [γὰρ] μᾶλλον κρεῖσσον· [GNT] | To depart; to go; to return home; to come back.<br>**Practical Application**<br>The word "go" (*analusai*) is descriptive. It has a twofold meaning that speaks to the believer's heart.<br>1. It means to break up; to loosen as in breaking camp and loosening the ropes of the tent. It is the picture of breaking loose, packing up, and moving on to a new location. The same picture is true of the believer when he departs this life. He is not ceasing to exist; he is simply breaking loose and moving on to a new campsite, in fact, a perfect campsite.<br>2. It means to loosen the moorings of a ship, weigh anchor, and set sail for another port. Again, the believer does not cease to exist, he simply loosens the moorings of this life, pulls the anchor up, and sets sail for God's eternal presence.<br>Paul says that he is caught between two great desires:<br>⇒ One desire is to live a life of fruitful service for the Lord Jesus Christ.<br>⇒ The other desire is to depart and go on to be with Christ which is far better.<br>The natural mind wonders and questions how a person in his right mind could ever want to go ahead and die. The reason is simply answered: the genuine believer does not die; he never tastes death. He is transferred into the presence of Christ. Immediately–quicker than the blinking of an eye–the believer is transported into the perfect world of God which is named heaven. The believer is perfected–never again to experience pain, suffering, sin, corruption, infirmity, weakness, deformity, disappointment, fear, loss, or death. He will be perfected to work for Christ throughout the new heavens and earth, and he will serve and worship Christ for ever and ever. The promises of God to the believer are phenomenal; they just explode the human mind. It is for this reason that the believer can declare: "Dying is even better." |
| **#1710**<br>**Go Astray**<br><br>Offended–KJV<br>Stumbling–NASB<br>**Go astray–NIV**<br>Stumble–NKJV<br>Fall away–NLT<br><br>**POSB REFERENCE**<br>(Jn.16:1)<br>Note 1 | σκανδαλισθῆτε = skandalisthēte<br>Pronunciation: [skan-dal-is'-thay-teh]<br>Parsing (part of speech): verb<br>    Mood—subjunctive<br>    Tense—aorist<br>    Voice—passive<br>    Person—2nd person<br>    Number—plural<br>    Stem or root—from σκανδαλίζω<br>Concordance References:<br>  ⇒ Strong's #4624 skandalizo<br>  ⇒ NIV #4997 skandalizo<br>  ⇒ NASB #4624 skandalizo<br><br>**John 16:1**<br>These things have I spoken unto you, that ye should not be **offended**. [KJV]<br>"These things I have spoken to you, that you may be kept from **stumbling**. [NASB]<br>"All this I have told you so that you will not **go astray**. [NIV]<br>"These things I have spoken to you, that you should not be made to **stumble**. [NKJV]<br>"I have told you these things so that you won't **fall away**. [NLT]<br>αὐτὰ λελάληκα ὑμῖν, ἵνα μὴ **σκανδαλισθῆτε**· [GNS]<br>Ταῦτα λελάληκα ὑμῖν ἵνα μὴ **Σκανδαλισθῆτε** [GNT] | To go astray; to fall away; to cause to stumble or sin; to be offended; to stumble and to trip.<br>**Practical Application**<br>Jesus warned the believer that religionists would persecute His followers. Jesus warned the believer because He wants to prevent the believer from slipping away. The believer can go astray and fall over persecution. Persecution can...<br>• cause a believer to question his beliefs.<br>• cause a believer to weaken and return to the way of false religion.<br>• silence a believer and his witness.<br>• cause a believer to deny Jesus. |

# PRACTICAL WORD STUDIES
## in the NEW TESTAMENT

| ENGLISH WORD | GREEK WORD AND VERSE | THE WORD MEANS... |
|---|---|---|
| **#1711**<br>**God**<br><br>God–KJV<br>God–NASB<br>God–NIV<br>God–NKJV<br>God–NLT<br><br>**POSB REFERENCE**<br>(Jn.1:1-2; esp. v.1)<br>Note 1, point 3 | θεός = *theos*<br>Pronunciation: [theh'-os]<br>Parsing (part of speech): noun<br>    Case—nominative<br>    Gender—masculine<br>    Number—singular<br>    Stem or root—from θεός, οῦ<br>Concordance References:<br>  ⇒ Strong's #2316 theos<br>  ⇒ NIV #2536 theos<br>  ⇒ NASB #2316 theos<br><br>**John 1:1**<br>In the beginning was the Word, and the Word was with God, and the Word was **God**. [KJV]<br>In the beginning was the Word, and the Word was with God, and the Word was **God**. [NASB]<br>In the beginning was the Word, and the Word was with God, and the Word was **God**. [NIV]<br>In the beginning was the Word, and the Word was with God, and the Word was **God**. [NKJV]<br>In the beginning the Word already existed. He was with God, and he was **God**. [NLT]<br>Ἐν ἀρχῇ ἦν ὁ λόγος, καὶ ὁ λόγος ἦν πρὸς τὸν Θεόν, καὶ **Θεὸς** ἦν ὁ λόγος. [GNS]<br>Ἐν ἀρχῇ ἦν ὁ λόγος, καὶ ὁ λόγος ἦν πρὸς τὸν θεόν, καὶ **θεὸς** ἦν ὁ λόγος. [GNT] | God; one of the many names for the One true God.<br><br>**Practical Application**<br>In this Scripture note how the word "Theos" is used in relation to Jesus Christ.<br>  John did not say that "the Word" was the God (*ho Theos*). He says "the Word" was God. He omits the definite article. John was saying that "the Word," Jesus Christ...<br>• is of the very nature and character of God the Father, but He is not the identical person of God the Father.<br>• is a distinct person from God the Father, but He is of the very being and essence (perfection) of God the Father.<br>When a man sees Christ, he sees a distinct person, but he sees a person who is of the very substance and character of God in all of His perfect being. |
| **#1712**<br>**God**<br><br>Person–KJV<br>Nature–NASB<br>Being–NIV<br>Person–NKJV<br>God–NLT<br><br>**POSB REFERENCE**<br>(Heb.1:3)<br>Note 5 | ὑποστάσεως = *hupostaseös*<br>Pronunciation: [hoop-os'-tas-eh-os]<br>Parsing (part of speech): noun<br>    Case—genitive<br>    Gender—feminine<br>    Number—singular<br>    Stem or root—from ὑπόστασις, εως<br>Concordance References:<br>  ⇒ Strong's #5287 hupostasis<br>  ⇒ NIV #5712 hupostasis<br>  ⇒ NASB #5287 hupostasis<br><br>**Hebrews 1:3**<br>Who being the brightness of his glory, and the express image of his **person**, and upholding all things by the word of his power, when he had by himself purged our sins, sat down on the right hand of the Majesty on high; [KJV]<br>And He is the radiance of His glory and the exact representation of His **nature**, and upholds all things by the word of His power. When He had made purification of sins, He sat down at the right hand of the Majesty on high; [NASB]<br>The Son is the radiance of God's glory and the exact representation of his **being**, sustaining all things by his powerful word. After he had provided purification for sins, he sat down at the right hand of the Majesty in heaven. [NIV]<br>Who being the brightness of *His* glory and the express image of His **person**, and upholding all things by the word of His power, when He had by Himself purged our sins, sat down at the right hand of the Majesty on high, [NKJV]<br>The Son reflects God's own glory, and everything about him represents **God** exactly. He sustains the universe by the mighty power of his command. After he died to cleanse us from the stain of sin, he sat down in the place of honor at the right hand of the majestic God of heaven. [NLT]<br>ὃς ὢν ἀπαύγασμα τῆς δόξης, καὶ χαρακτὴρ τῆς **ὑποστάσεως** αὐτοῦ, φέρων τε τὰ πάντα τῷ ῥήματι τῆς δυνάμεως αὐτοῦ, δι' ἑαυτοῦ καθαρισμὸν ποιησάμενος τῶν ἁμαρτιῶν ἡμῶν, ἐκάθισεν ἐν δεξιᾷ τῆς μεγαλωσύνης ἐν ὑψηλοῖς, [GNS]<br>ὃς ὢν ἀπαύγασμα τῆς δόξης καὶ χαρακτὴρ τῆς **ὑποστάσεως** αὐτοῦ, φέρων τε τὰ πάντα τῷ ῥήματι τῆς δυνάμεως αὐτοῦ, καθαρισμὸν τῶν ἁμαρτιῶν ποιησάμενος ἐκάθισεν ἐν δεξιᾷ τῆς μεγαλωσύνης ἐν ὑψηλοῖς, [GNT] | Being, person, image, nature, substance.<br><br>**Practical Application**<br>Jesus Christ is the very substance, the very Being, Person, and embodiment of God. |

# PRACTICAL WORD STUDIES
## in the NEW TESTAMENT

| ENGLISH WORD | GREEK WORD AND VERSE | THE WORD MEANS... |
|---|---|---|
| **#1713**<br>**God's Holy People**<br><br>Saints–KJV<br>Saints–NASB<br>Saints–NIV<br>Saints–NKJV<br>God's holy people– NLT<br><br>**POSB REFERENCE**<br>(Eph.1:1-2; esp. v.1)<br>Note 2<br><br>See also POSB REF:<br>(Philip.4:21-22; esp. v.21)<br>Note 2 | ἁγίοις = hagiois<br>Pronunciation: [hag'-ee-oys]<br>Parsing (part of speech): pronominal adjective<br>   Case—dative<br>   Gender—masculine<br>   Number—plural<br>   Stem or root—from ἅγιος, α, ον<br>Concordance References:<br>  ⇒ Strong's #40 hagios<br>  ⇒ NIV #41 hagios<br>  ⇒ NASB #40 hagios<br><br>**Ephes. 1:1**<br>Paul, an apostle of Jesus Christ by the will of God, to the **saints** which are at Ephesus, and to the faithful in Christ Jesus: [KJV]<br>Paul, an apostle of Christ Jesus by the will of God, to the **saints** who are at Ephesus, and who are faithful in Christ Jesus: [NASB]<br>Paul, an apostle of Christ Jesus by the will of God, to the **saints** in Ephesus, the faithful in Christ Jesus: [NIV]<br>Paul, an apostle of Jesus Christ by the will of God, To the **saints** who are in Ephesus, ad faithful in Christ Jesus: [NKJV]<br>This letter is from Paul, chosen by God to be an apostle of Christ Jesus. It is written to **God's holy people** in Ephesus, who are faithful followers of Christ Jesus. [NLT]<br>Παῦλος ἀπόστολος Ἰησοῦ Χριστοῦ διὰ θελήματος Θεοῦ, τοῖς **ἁγίοις** τοῖς οὖσιν ἐν Ἐφέσῳ, καὶ πιστοῖς ἐν Χριστῷ Ἰησοῦ· [GNS]<br>Παῦλος ἀπόστολος Χριστοῦ Ἰησοῦ διὰ θελήματος θεοῦ τοῖς **ἁγίοις** τοῖς οὖσιν [ἐν Ἐφέσῳ] καὶ πιστοῖς ἐν Χριστῷ Ἰησοῦ, [GNT] | Saint; to be God's holy people; to be set apart; to be consecrated, sacred, devoted and holy.<br><br>**Practical Application**<br>In the Bible the phrase "God's holy people" does not refer to just a few people who have done great works for God. It refers to all people.<br>God's holy people are followers of the Lord Jesus Christ who has been set apart to live for God. The saint has given himself to live a consecrated, sacred, and holy life–all for the glory of God. Note that believers are *God's holy people* in both senses:<br>⇒ Believers are *God's holy people* in the sense that they have been given a new heart by God: a heart that is renewed and recreated in righteousness and true holiness.<br>⇒ Believers are *God's holy people* in the sense that they are set apart to live consecrated and holy lives in this world. |
| **#1714**<br>**God's Holy People**<br><br>Saints–KJV<br>Saints–NASB<br>Holy–NIV<br>Saints–NKJV<br>God's holy people– NLT<br><br>**POSB REFERENCE**<br>(Col.1:2)<br>Note 3, point 1<br><br>See also POSB REF:<br>(Eph.1:4)<br>Note 2, point 1<br>(Eph.5:25-33; esp. v.25)<br>Note 2, point 1<br>(Col.1:22)<br>Note 3, point 1<br>(Col.3:12-14; esp. v.12)<br>Note 1 | ἁγίοις = hagiois<br>Pronunciation: [hag'-ee-oys]<br>Parsing (part of speech): adjective<br>   Case—dative<br>   Gender—masculine<br>   Number—plural<br>   Stem or root—from ἅγιος, α, ον<br>Concordance References:<br>  ⇒ Strong's #40 hagios<br>  ⇒ NIV #41 hagios<br>  ⇒ NASB #40 hagios<br><br>**Col. 1:2**<br>To the **saints** and faithful brethren in Christ which are at Colosse: Grace be unto you, and peace, from God our Father and the Lord Jesus Christ. [KJV]<br>To the **saints** and faithful brethren in Christ who are at Colossae: Grace to you and peace from God our Father. [NASB]<br>To the **holy** and faithful brothers in Christ at Colosse: Grace and peace to you from God our Father. [NIV]<br>To the **saints** and faithful brethren in Christ who are in Colosse: Grace to you and peace from God our Father and the Lord Jesus Christ. [NKJV]<br>It is written to **God's holy people** in the city of Colosse, who are faithful brothers and sisters in Christ.May God our Father give you grace and peace. [NLT]<br>τοῖς ἐν Κολοσσαῖς **ἁγίοις** καὶ πιστοῖς ἀδελφοῖς ἐν Χριστῷ· χάρις ὑμῖν καὶ εἰρήνη ἀπὸ Θεοῦ πατρὸς ἡμῶν καὶ Κυρίου Ἰησοῦ Χριστοῦ. [GNS]<br>τοῖς ἐν Κολοσσαῖς **ἁγίοις** καὶ πιστοῖς ἀδελφοῖς ἐν Χριστῷ, χάρις ὑμῖν καὶ εἰρήνη ἀπὸ θεοῦ πατρὸς ἡμῶν. [GNT] | To be holy; to be morally pure. It means to be set apart and consecrated to God.<br><br>**Practical Application**<br>There are the *carnal saints or believers* within the church. This refers to those who in the past had set their lives apart to follow the Lord Jesus. They *had separated* themselves from the world and *had turned* to the Lord Jesus to save them. However, a saint or believer may or may not *continue on* with the Lord Jesus. Some in the Colossian church *were not continuing on*. They were not fully committed. Their commitment to the Lord Jesus Christ was lacking. Therefore, they were running the risk of falling into the error of false teaching and turning away from Christ. The point is this: a person can be a carnal believer or carnal "saint" within the church. Just because a person has made a profession and given some semblance of following Christ does not mean he is safe and secure forever—that he is automatically mature in Christ. When a person truly comes to know Christ, he is just beginning a journey with Christ, a journey that has a much higher level of spiritual growth to reach.<br>There are faithful saints or believers in the church. This refers to those who had set their lives apart to Christ and had continued on. They were loyal and steadfast in their allegiance and they held firm against the attacks of worldliness and false teaching. They were not shaken by the temptations of the devil nor by the urges of the flesh. They were faithful against all foes.<br>The point is this: once a person has become a saint, that is, set his life apart to follow Christ, he |

PRACTICAL WORD STUDIES
in the NEW TESTAMENT

| ENGLISH WORD | GREEK WORD AND VERSE | THE WORD MEANS... |
|---|---|---|
| | | is to be faithful. And he is to grow in his faithfulness. In fact, the highest level of spiritual maturity is that of faithfulness. Being faithful or obedient to Christ is the one thing that pleases Christ above all else.<br>⇒ We must live lives that are set apart to Christ, to the belief that He died for our reconciliation and that His death covers us.<br>⇒ We must live lives that are separated from worldliness and selfishness and from the flesh and its sins.<br>⇒ We must live lives that are set apart and consecrated to God and His service, lives that live for His cause. |
| #1715<br>**God's Special Favor**<br><br>Grace–KJV<br>Grace–NASB<br>Grace–NIV<br>Grace–NKJV<br>God's special favor–NLT<br><br>**POSB REFERENCE**<br>(1 Pt.1:2)<br>Note 5, point 1 | χάρις = charis<br>Pronunciation: [khar'-ece]<br>Parsing (part of speech): noun<br>  Case—nominative<br>  Gender—feminine<br>  Number—singular<br>  Stem or root—from χάρις, ιτος<br>Concordance References:<br>⇒ Strong's #5485 charis<br>⇒ NIV #5921 charis<br>⇒ NASB #5485 charis<br><br>**1 Peter 1:2**<br>Elect according to the foreknowledge of God the Father, through sanctification of the Spirit, unto obedience and sprinkling of the blood of Jesus Christ: **Grace** unto you, and peace, be multiplied. [KJV]<br>According to the foreknowledge of God the Father, by the sanctifying work of the Spirit, that you may obey Jesus Christ and be sprinkled with His blood: May **grace** and peace be yours in fullest measure. [NASB]<br>Who have been chosen according to the foreknowledge of God the Father, through the sanctifying work of the Spirit, for obedience to Jesus Christ and sprinkling by his blood: **Grace** and peace be yours in abundance. [NIV]<br>Elect according to the foreknowledge of God the Father, in sanctification of the Spirit, for obedience and sprinkling of the blood of Jesus Christ: **Grace** to you and peace be multiplied. [NKJV]<br>God the Father chose you long ago, and the Spirit has made you holy. As a result, you have obeyed Jesus Christ and are cleansed by his blood. May you have more and more of **God's special favor** and wonderful peace. [NLT]<br>κατὰ πρόγνωσιν Θεοῦ πατρός, ἐν ἁγιασμῷ Πνεύματος, εἰς ὑπακοὴν καὶ ῥαντισμὸν αἵματος Ἰησοῦ Χριστοῦ· **χάρις** ὑμῖν καὶ εἰρήνη πληθυνθείη. [GNS]<br>κατὰ πρόγνωσιν θεοῦ πατρός ἐν ἁγιασμῷ πνεύματος εἰς ὑπακοὴν καὶ ῥαντισμὸν αἵματος Ἰησοῦ Χριστοῦ, **χάρις** ὑμῖν καὶ εἰρήνη πληθυνθείη. [GNT] | Grace, God's special favor, a special expression of God's divine presence. Grace (charis) means the *undeserved favor and blessings* of God. (See POSB notes–Romans 4:16; POSB *Deeper Study* #1–1 Cor. 1:4; POSB *Deeper Study* #1–Titus 2:11-15.)<br><br>**Practical Application**<br>The word *undeserved* is the key to understanding God's special favor. Man does not deserve God's favor; he cannot earn God's approval and blessings. God is too high and man too low for man to deserve anything from God. Man is imperfect and God is perfect; therefore, man cannot expect anything from God. (See POSB *Deeper Study* #1, Justification–Galatians 2:15-16 for more discussion.) Man has reacted against God too much. Man has...<br>• rejected God<br>• rebelled against God<br>• ignored God<br>• neglected God<br>• cursed God<br>• sinned against God<br>• disobeyed God<br>• denied God<br>• questioned God<br>Man deserves nothing from God except judgment, condemnation, and punishment. But God is love–perfect and absolute love. Therefore, God makes it possible for man to experience His special favor, in particular the favor and blessing of salvation which is in His Son, Jesus Christ. (See POSB *Deeper Study* #1, Grace–1 Cor. 1:4 for more discussion.) |
| #1716<br>**God Alone Made It Possible**<br><br>Of him–KJV<br>By His doing–NASB<br>Because of him–NIV<br>Of Him–NKJV<br>God alone made it possible–NLT | ἐξ αὐτοῦ = ex autou<br>Pronunciation: [ex ow-too']<br>Parsing *autou* (part of speech): noun<br>  Type—pronoun<br>  Case—genitive<br>  Gender—masculine<br>  Person—3rd person<br>  Number—singular<br>  Stem or root—from αὐτός, ή, ό<br>Concordance References:<br>⇒ Strong's #1537 ek + 846 autos<br>⇒ NIV #1666 ek [because of] + 899 autos [him]<br>⇒ NASB #1537 ek + 846 autos | Because of (God); out of God; out of His nature (of love and salvation); by God's doing.<br><br>**Practical Application**<br>God chooses the believer to be in Christ (see POSB *Deeper Study* #1, Position in Christ–Romans 8:1 for discussion). The stress is that it is God who saves a person; the person does not save himself, no matter how capable he is nor how much good he may do. How is God able to save people? By Christ. God presented Christ to the world as the wisdom and righteousness of God. |

# Practical Word Studies
## in the New Testament

| ENGLISH WORD | GREEK WORD AND VERSE | THE WORD MEANS... |
|---|---|---|
| **POSB REFERENCE** (1 Cor.1:30-31; esp. v.30) Note 4 | **1 Cor. 1:30**<br>But **of him** are ye in Christ Jesus, who of God is made unto us wisdom, and righteousness, and sanctification, and redemption: [KJV]<br>But **by His doing** you are in Christ Jesus, who became to us wisdom from God, and righteousness and sanctification, and redemption, [NASB]<br>It is **because of him** that you are in Christ Jesus, who has become for us wisdom from God—that is, our righteousness, holiness and redemption. [NIV]<br>But **of Him** you are in Christ Jesus, who became for us wisdom from God—and righteousness and sanctification and redemption— [NKJV]<br>**God alone made it possible** for you to be in Christ Jesus. For our benefit God made Christ to be wisdom itself. He is the one who made us acceptable to God. He made us pure and holy, and he gave himself to purchase our freedom. [NLT]<br>ἐξ αὐτοῦ δὲ ὑμεῖς ἐστε ἐν Χριστῷ Ἰησοῦ, ὃς ἐγενήθη ἡμῖν σοφία ἀπὸ Θεοῦ, δικαιοσύνη τε καὶ ἁγιασμός, καὶ ἀπολύτρωσις, [GNS]<br>ἐξ αὐτοῦ δὲ ὑμεῖς ἐστε ἐν Χριστῷ Ἰησοῦ, ὃς ἐγενήθη σοφία ἡμῖν ἀπὸ Θεοῦ, δικαιοσύνη τε καὶ ἁγιασμὸς καὶ ἀπολύτρωσις, [GNT] | |
| **#1717 God Breathed**<br><br>Inspiration of God–KJV<br>Inspired by God–NASB<br>**God breathed–NIV**<br>Inspiration of God–NKJV<br>Inspired by God–NLT<br><br>**POSB REFERENCE** (2 Tim. 3:16) Note 3, point 2 | θεόπνευστος = theopneustos<br>Pronunciation: [theh-op'-nyoo-stos]<br>Parsing (part of speech): adjective<br>  Case—nominative<br>  Gender—feminine<br>  Number—singular<br>  Stem or root—from θεόπνευστος, ον<br>Concordance References:<br>  ⇒ Strong's #2315 theopneustos<br>  ⇒ NIV #2535 theopneustos<br>  ⇒ NASB #2315 theopneustos<br><br>**2 Tim. 3:16**<br>All scripture is given by **inspiration of God**, and is profitable for doctrine, for reproof, for correction, for instruction in righteousness: [KJV]<br>All Scripture is **inspired by God** and profitable for teaching, for reproof, for correction, for training in righteousness; [NASB]<br>All Scripture is **God-breathed** and is useful for teaching, rebuking, correcting and training in righteousness, [NIV]<br>All Scripture *is* given by **inspiration of God**, and *is* profitable for doctrine, for reproof, for correction, for instruction in righteousness, [NKJV]<br>All Scripture is **inspired by God** and is useful to teach us what is true and to make us realize what is wrong in our lives. It straightens us out and teaches us to do what is right. [NLT]<br>πᾶσα γραφὴ **θεόπνευστος** καὶ ὠφέλιμος πρὸς διδασκαλίαν, πρὸς ἔλεγχον, πρὸς ἐπανόρθωσιν, πρὸς παιδείαν τὴν ἐν δικαιοσύνῃ· [GNS]<br>πᾶσα γραφὴ **θεόπνευστος** καὶ ὠφέλιμος πρὸς διδασκαλίαν, πρὸς ἐλεγμόν, πρὸς ἐπανόρθωσιν, πρὸς παιδείαν τὴν ἐν δικαιοσύνῃ, [GNT] | God breathed; inspiration of God; inspiration by God.<br><br>**Practical Application**<br>What does this mean? What does it mean to say that *God breathed* the Holy Scriptures? No one can say for sure, but this much can be said.<br>⇒ The idea is that God breathed out the Scripture or God produced the Scripture somewhat like He did creation.<br>⇒ "By the word of the LORD were the heavens made; and all the host of them by the breath of his mouth" (Psalm 33:6).<br>Note: it is the Scripture that is inspired, not the man. The Bible does not claim to be written by inspired men. It does claim that the writing is supernaturally given or breathed by God. The Scripture is *breathed out by God, not breathed into by God*. The meaning is this: the writing is supernaturally given or breathed by God. The Bible claims to be the Word given by the creative breath of God.<br>The Greek scholar A.T. Robertson says: "God-breathed...[this] is in contrast to the commandments of men" (*Word Pictures in the New Testament*, Vol.4, p.627).<br>The great Bible expositor Matthew Henry says: "It [Scripture] is a divine revelation, which we may depend upon as infallibly true. The same Spirit that breathed reason into us breathes revelation among us: 'For the prophecy came not in old time by the will of man, but holy men of God spoke as they were moved or carried forth by the Holy Ghost,' 2 Peter 1:21. The prophets and apostles did not speak from themselves, but what they received of the Lord that they delivered unto us" (*Matthew Henry's Commentary*, Vol.5, p.846f). |
| **#1718 God Forbid**<br><br>**God forbid–KJV**<br>May it never be–NASB | μὴ γένοιτο = mē genoito<br>Pronunciation: [may ghin'-oy-tow]<br>Parsing *genoito* (part of speech): verb<br>  Mood—optative<br>  Tense—aorist<br>  Voice—middle deponent | God forbid, not at all, may it never be, certainly not.<br><br>**Practical Application**<br>The question is, "If you say some Jews do not |

# PRACTICAL WORD STUDIES
## in the NEW TESTAMENT

| ENGLISH WORD | GREEK WORD AND VERSE | THE WORD MEANS... |
|---|---|---|
| Not at all–NIV<br>Certainly not!–NKJV<br>Of course not–NLT<br><br>**POSB REFERENCE**<br>(Romans 3:3-4; esp. v.4)<br>Note 2, point 1<br><br>See also POSB REF:<br>(Romans 11:1)<br>Note 1 | Person—3rd person<br>Number—singular<br>Stem or root—from γίνομαι<br>Concordance References:<br>⇒ Strong's #1096 + 3361 ginomai mē<br>⇒ NIV #1181 + 3590 ginomai mē [Not at all]<br>⇒ NASB #1096+ 3361 ginomai mē<br><br>**Romans 3:4**<br>**God forbid**: yea, let God be true, but every man a liar; as it is written, That thou mightest be justified in thy sayings, and mightest overcome when thou art judged. [KJV]<br>**May it never be**! Rather, let God be found true, though every man *be found* a liar, as it is written, "THAT THOU MIGHTEST BE JUSTIFIED IN THY WORDS, AND MIGHTEST PREVAIL WHEN THOU ART JUDGED." [NASB]<br>**Not at all**! Let God be true, and every man a liar. As it is written: "So that you may be proved right when you speak and prevail when you judge." [NIV]<br>**Certainly not!** Indeed, let God be true but every man a liar. As it is written: *"That You may be justified in Your words, And may overcome when You are judged."* [NKJV]<br>**Of course not**! Though everyone else in the world is a liar, God is true. As the Scriptures say, "He will be proved right in what he says, and he will win his case in court." [NLT]<br>μὴ γένοιτο· γινέσθω δὲ ὁ Θεὸς ἀληθής, πᾶς δὲ ἄνθρωπος ψεύστης, καθὼς γέγραπται, "Οπως ἂν δικαιωθῇς ἐν τοῖς λόγοις σου, καὶ νικήσεις ἐν τῷ κρίνεσθαί σε. [GNS]<br>μὴ γένοιτο· γινέσθω δὲ ὁ Θεὸς ἀληθής, πᾶς δὲ ἄνθρωπος ψεύστης, καθὼς γέγραπται, "Οπως ἂν δικαιωθῇς ἐν τοῖς λόγοις σου καὶ νικήσεις ἐν τῷ κρίνεσθαί σε. [GNT] | believe and are condemned, doesn't that void God's promises and make God a liar?" Or to say it another way, "What if some disbelieve and reject God's Word, will their unbelief cause God to void His Word and promises? God promised the Jews a special place and special privileges through Abraham and his seed (see POSB *Deeper Study #1*–John 4:22). If some Jews do not believe God's promises and God condemns them, isn't He breaking His promise to Abraham and his seed? Isn't He voiding His Word and Covenant and making Himself a liar? God's Word could not be based on heart religion and on moral character alone. There has to be something else, something outward–a rite (circumcision, baptism, church membership)–that shows we are religious (Jews). If we go through the rite or ritual, then God is bound to accept us. He has so promised to accept us. He is not going to break His Word."<br>The application of this question concerns every religionist. The thinking religionist poses the same objection and question: "If you say some religionists do not believe and are condemned, doesn't that void God's Word and make God a liar? God's Word promises the religious person special privileges and the hope of eternal life. His Word tells us to believe Christ and to possess His Word, to be baptized and join the fellowship of the church. If we do that and God still condemns us, is He not voiding His Word and becoming a liar?"<br>⇒ God forbid.<br>⇒ God will be faithful. His Word and promise of salvation will stand even if *every* man lies about believing and lies about giving his heart to serve Jesus.<br>⇒ God will prove His Word: He will be justified and proven faithful in what He has said. He will still save *any person* who obediently gives his heart to Jesus.<br>⇒ In fact, God will overcome; He will prove His Word another way. He will judge all who make a false profession and who judge Him and His Word, who accuse Him of being unfaithful and voiding His Word. David himself said that God would judge the unfaithful or disobedient man (Psalm 51:4). David had sinned greatly, not keeping the commandments of God, so God judged David and charged him with sin. David did the right thing: he confessed his sin and repented and began to live righteously. But David did something else: he declared that God's charge and judgment against him were *just*, that God was perfectly justified. And God was, for God is always just, and He is always justified in what He says and does. |
| **#1719**<br>**God Of Glory, The**<br><br>The God of glory–KJV<br>The God of glory–NASB | Ὁ Θεὸς τῆς δόξης = *Ho theos tēs doxēs*<br>Pronunciation: [ha they-os tace dox-ace]<br>Parsing *doxēs* (part of speech): noun<br>    Case—genitive<br>    Gender—feminine<br>    Number—singular<br>    Stem or root—from δόξα, ης | God of glory; glorious God; God who possesses and manifests glory; God of the manifested glory, of the outward and visible glory; God who reveals glory.<br><br>**Practical Application**<br>It is the Shekinah glory, the visible splendor, radiance, and brilliance of God's Person that |

# PRACTICAL WORD STUDIES
## in the NEW TESTAMENT

| ENGLISH WORD | GREEK WORD AND VERSE | THE WORD MEANS... |
|---|---|---|
| **The God of glory–NIV**<br>**The God of glory–NKJV**<br>Glorious God–NLT<br><br>**POSB REFERENCE**<br>(Acts 7:2)<br>*Deeper Study #1* | Concordance References:<br>⇒ Strong's #3588 ho + 2316 theos + 3588 ho + 1391 doxa<br>⇒ NIV #3836 ho [The] + 2536 theos [God] + 3836 ho [Not in English] + 1518 doxa [glory]<br>⇒ NASB #3588 ho + 2316 theos + 3588 ho + 1391 doxa<br><br>**Acts 7:2**<br>And he said, Men, brethren, and fathers, hearken; **The God of glory** appeared unto our father Abraham, when he was in Mesopotamia, before he dwelt in Charran, [KJV]<br>And he said, "Hear me, brethren and fathers! **The God of glory** appeared to our father Abraham when he was in Mesopotamia, before he lived in Haran, [NASB]<br>To this he replied: "Brothers and fathers, listen to me! **The God of glory** appeared to our father Abraham while he was still in Mesopotamia, before he lived in Haran. [NIV]<br>And he said, "Brethren and fathers, listen: **The God of glory** appeared to our father Abraham when he was in Mesopotamia, before he dwelt in Haran, [NKJV]<br>This was Stephen's reply: "Brothers and honorable fathers, listen to me. Our **glorious God** appeared to our ancestor Abraham in Mesopotamia before he moved to Haran. [NLT]<br><br>ὁ δὲ ἔφη, Ἄνδρες ἀδελφοὶ καὶ πατέρες, ἀκούσατε. ὁ **Θεὸς τῆς δόξης** ὤφθη τῷ πατρὶ ἡμῶν Ἀβραὰμ ὄντι ἐν τῇ Μεσοποταμίᾳ, πρὶν ἢ κατοικῆσαι αὐτὸν ἐν Χαρράν, [GNS]<br><br>ὁ δὲ ἔφη, Ἄνδρες ἀδελφοὶ καὶ πατέρες, ἀκούσατε. Ὁ **Θεὸς τῆς δόξης** ὤφθη τῷ πατρὶ ἡμῶν Ἀβραὰμ ὄντι ἐν τῇ Μεσοποταμίᾳ πρὶν ἢ κατοικῆσαι αὐτὸν ἐν Χαρράν [GNT] | bursts forth from His Supreme Being. The idea is that God appeared to reveal His glory to Abraham. (See POSB note, Shekinah Glory–Matthew 17:5-8. Note: this throws some light on how God went about calling Abraham. It must have been a visible appearance of God's glory just as Moses and Isaiah and others received.) |
| **#1720**<br>**God-Fearing**<br><br>Devout–KJV<br>Devout–NASB<br>**God-fearing–NIV**<br>Devout–NKJV<br>Godly–NLT<br><br>**POSB REFERENCE**<br>(Acts 2:5-11; esp. v.5)<br>Note 5, point 1 | εὐλαβεῖς = *eulabeis*<br>Pronunciation: [yoo-lab-ace']<br>Parsing (part of speech): adjective<br>  Case—nominative<br>  Gender—masculine<br>  Number—plural<br>  Stem or root—from εὐλαβής, ές<br>Concordance References:<br>⇒ Strong's #2126 eulabēs<br>⇒ NIV #2327 eulabēs<br>⇒ NASB #2126 eulabēs<br><br>**Acts 2:5**<br>And there were dwelling at Jerusalem Jews, **devout** men, out of every nation under heaven. [KJV]<br>Now there were Jews living in Jerusalem, **devout** men, from every nation under heaven. [NASB]<br>Now there were staying in Jerusalem **God-fearing** Jews from every nation under heaven. [NIV]<br>And there were dwelling in Jerusalem Jews, **devout** men, from every nation under heaven. [NKJV]<br>**Godly** Jews from many nations were living in Jerusalem at that time. [NLT]<br><br>Ἦσαν δὲ ἐν Ἰερουσαλὴμ κατοικοῦντες Ἰουδαῖοι, ἄνδρες **εὐλαβεῖς**, ἀπὸ παντὸς ἔθνους τῶν ὑπὸ τὸν οὐρανόν· [GNS]<br><br>Ἦσαν δὲ εἰς Ἰερουσαλὴμ κατοικοῦντες Ἰουδαῖοι, ἄνδρες **εὐλαβεῖς** ἀπὸ παντὸς ἔθνους τῶν ὑπὸ τὸν οὐρανόν. [GNT] | God-fearing, devout, reverent, worshipful, careful, godly. It means persons who handle spiritual matters carefully.<br><br>**Practical Application**<br>They were devout men, Jewish pilgrims who had come from *all over the world*, had returned to Jerusalem to celebrate the "Feast of the First Fruits." Note how the groundwork for preaching is first laid by personal witnessing. (See POSB *Deeper Study* #1, Witnessing—Acts 1:8 for Scripture.) |
| **#1721**<br>**God-Fearing Gentiles**<br><br>Devout–KJV<br>**God-fearing Gentiles– NASB** | σεβομένοις = *sebomenois*<br>Pronunciation: [seb'-om-ehn-o-ees]<br>Parsing (part of speech): verb<br>  Mood—participle<br>  Tense—present<br>  Voice—middle<br>  Case—dative<br>  Gender—masculine | God-fearing Greeks or Gentiles; a worshiper of God.<br><br>**Practical Application**<br>The phrase "God-fearing Gentiles" (*sebomenois*) means those who worship God or the God-fearing men and women who are not Jews. |

# PRACTICAL WORD STUDIES
## in the NEW TESTAMENT

| ENGLISH WORD | GREEK WORD AND VERSE | THE WORD MEANS... |
|---|---|---|
| God-fearing Greeks– NIV<br>Gentile worshipers– NKJV<br>**God-fearing Gentiles– NLT**<br><br>**POSB REFERENCE**<br>(Acts 17:17)<br>Note 3 | Number—plural<br>Stem or root—from σέβομαι<br>Concordance References:<br>⇒ Strong's #4576 sebō<br>⇒ NIV #4936 sebō<br>⇒ NASB #4576 sebō<br><br>### Acts 17:17<br>Therefore disputed he in the synagogue with the Jews, and with the **devout** persons, and in the market daily with them that met with him. [KJV]<br>So he was reasoning in the synagogue with the Jews and the **God-fearing Gentiles**, and in the market place every day with those who happened to be present. [NASB]<br>So he reasoned in the synagogue with the Jews and the **God-fearing Greeks**, as well as in the marketplace day by day with those who happened to be there. [NIV]<br>Therefore he reasoned in the synagogue with the Jews and with the *Gentile* **worshipers**, and in the marketplace daily with those who happened to be there. [NKJV]<br>He went to the synagogue to debate with the Jews and the **God-fearing Gentiles**, and he spoke daily in the public square to all who happened to be there. [NLT]<br>διελέγετο μὲν οὖν ἐν τῇ συναγωγῇ τοῖς Ἰουδαίοις καὶ τοῖς **σεβομένοις** καὶ ἐν τῇ ἀγορᾷ κατὰ πᾶσαν ἡμέραν πρὸς τοὺς παρατυγχάνοντας. [GNS]<br>διελέγετο μὲν οὖν ἐν τῇ συναγωγῇ τοῖς Ἰουδαίοις καὶ τοῖς **σεβομένοις** καὶ ἐν τῇ ἀγορᾷ κατὰ πᾶσαν ἡμέραν πρὸς τοὺς παρατυγχάνοντας. [GNT] | |
| #1722<br>**God-Fearing Greeks**<br><br>Devout–KJV<br>God-fearing *G*entiles– NASB<br>**God-fearing Greeks– NIV**<br>Gentile worshipers– NKJV<br>God-fearing Gentiles– NLT<br><br>**POSB REFERENCE**<br>(Acts 17:17)<br>Note 3 | σεβομένοις = *sebomenois*<br>Pronunciation: [seb'-om-ehn-o-ees]<br>Parsing (part of speech): verb<br>  Mood—participle<br>  Tense—present<br>  Voice—middle<br>  Case—dative<br>  Gender—masculine<br>  Number—plural<br>  Stem or root—from σέβομαι<br>Concordance References:<br>⇒ Strong's #4576 sebō<br>⇒ NIV #4936 sebō<br>⇒ NASB #4576 sebō<br><br>### Acts 17:17<br>Therefore disputed he in the synagogue with the Jews, and with the **devout** persons, and in the market daily with them that met with him. [KJV]<br>So he was reasoning in the synagogue with the Jews and the **God-fearing Gentiles**, and in the market place every day with those who happened to be present. [NASB]<br>So he reasoned in the synagogue with the Jews and the **God-fearing Greeks**, as well as in the marketplace day by day with those who happened to be there. [NIV]<br>Therefore he reasoned in the synagogue with the Jews and with the *Gentile* **worshipers**, and in the marketplace daily with those who happened to be there. [NKJV]<br>He went to the synagogue to debate with the Jews and the **God-fearing Gentiles**, and he spoke daily in the public square to all who happened to be there. [NLT]<br>διελέγετο μὲν οὖν ἐν τῇ συναγωγῇ τοῖς Ἰουδαίοις καὶ τοῖς **σεβομένοις** καὶ ἐν τῇ ἀγορᾷ κατὰ πᾶσαν ἡμέραν πρὸς τοὺς παρατυγχάνοντας. [GNS]<br>διελέγετο μὲν οὖν ἐν τῇ συναγωγῇ τοῖς Ἰουδαίοις καὶ τοῖς **σεβομένοις** καὶ ἐν τῇ ἀγορᾷ κατὰ πᾶσαν ἡμέραν πρὸς τοὺς παρατυγχάνοντας. [GNT] | God-fearing Greeks or Gentiles; a worshiper of God.<br><br>**Practical Application**<br>The phrase "God-fearing Greeks" (*sebomenois*) means those who worship God or the God-fearing men and women who are not Jews. |

# PRACTICAL WORD STUDIES
## in the NEW TESTAMENT

| ENGLISH WORD | GREEK WORD AND VERSE | THE WORD MEANS... |
|---|---|---|
| **#1723**<br>**God-Haters**<br><br>Haters of God–KJV<br>Haters of God–NASB<br>**God-haters–NIV**<br>Haters of God–NKJV<br>Haters of God–NLT<br><br>**POSB REFERENCE**<br>(Romans 1:30)<br>*Deeper Study* #13 | θεοστυγεῖς = *theostugeis*<br>Pronunciation: [theh-os-too-gees']<br>Parsing (part of speech): pronominal adjective<br>    Case—accusative<br>    Gender—masculine<br>    Number—plural<br>    Stem or root—from θεοστυγής, ές<br>Concordance References:<br>  ⇒ Strong's #2319 *theostugēs*<br>  ⇒ NIV #2539 *theostugēs*<br>  ⇒ NASB #2319 *theostugēs*<br><br>**Romans 1:30**<br>Backbiters, **haters of God**, despiteful, proud, boasters, inventors of evil things, disobedient to parents, [KJV]<br>Slanderers, **haters of God**, insolent, arrogant, boastful, inventors of evil, disobedient to parents, [NASB]<br>Slanderers, **God-haters**, insolent, arrogant and boastful; they invent ways of doing evil; they disobey their parents; [NIV]<br>Backbiters, **haters of God**, violent, proud, boasters, inventors of evil things, disobedient to parents, [NKJV]<br>They are backstabbers, **haters of God**, insolent, proud, and boastful. They are forever inventing new ways of sinning and are disobedient to their parents. [NLT]<br>ψιθυριστάς, καταλάλους, **θεοστυγεῖς**, ὑβριστάς, ὑπερηφάνους, ἀλαζόνας, ἐφευρετὰς κακῶν, γονεῦσιν ἀπειθεῖς, [GNS]<br>καταλάλους **θεοστυγεῖς**j ὑβριστάς ὑπερηφάνους ἀλαζόνας, ἐφευρετὰς κακῶν, γονεῦσιν ἀπειθεῖς, [GNT] | Hating God; to be hateful to God.<br><br>**Practical Application**<br>It is a person...<br>• who dislikes the commandments and restraints of God.<br>• who wants nothing to do with God and His restrictions and laws.<br>• who wants the license to do exactly as he wishes.<br>• who wants to be the god of his own life, doing his own thing as he wishes, determining both what he should and should not do. |
| **#1724**<br>**Godless**<br><br>Profane–KJV<br>Worldly–NASB<br>**Godless–NIV**<br>Profane–NKJV<br>**Godless–NLT**<br><br>**POSB REFERENCE**<br>(1 Tim.6:20-21; esp. v.20)<br>Note 2, point 2<br><br>See also POSB REF:<br>(2 Tim. 2:16-18, esp. v.16)<br>Note 3<br>(Heb.12:15-17; esp. v.16)<br>Note 2, point 4 | βεβήλους = *bebēlous*<br>Pronunciation: [beb'-ay-loos]<br>Parsing (part of speech): adjective<br>    Case—accusative<br>    Gender—feminine<br>    Number—plural<br>    Stem or root—from βέβηλός ον<br>Concordance References:<br>  ⇒ Strong's #952 *bebēlos*<br>  ⇒ NIV #1013 *bebēlos*<br>  ⇒ NASB #952 *bebēlos*<br><br>**1 Tim. 6:20**<br>O Timothy, keep that which is committed to thy trust, avoiding **profane** and vain babblings, and oppositions of science falsely so called: [KJV]<br>O Timothy, guard what has been entrusted to you, avoiding **worldly** and empty chatter and the opposing arguments of what is falsely called "knowledge"—[NASB]<br>Timothy, guard what has been entrusted to your care. Turn away from **godless** chatter and the opposing ideas of what is falsely called knowledge, [NIV]<br>O Timothy! Guard what was committed to your trust, avoiding the **profane** *and* idle babblings and contradictions of what is falsely called knowledge— [NKJV]<br>Timothy, guard what God has entrusted to you. Avoid **godless**, foolish discussions with those who oppose you with their so-called knowledge. [NLT]<br>Ὦ Τιμόθεε, τὴν παρακαταθήκην φύλαξον, ἐκτρεπόμενος τὰς **βεβήλους** κενοφωνίας καὶ ἀντιθέσεις τῆς ψευδωνύμου γνώσεως· [GNS]<br>Ὦ Τιμόθεε, τὴν παραθήκην φύλαξον ἐκτρεπόμενος τὰς **βεβήλους** κενοφωνίας καὶ ἀντιθέσεις τῆς ψευδωνύμου γνώσεως, [GNT] | Godless, profane, worldly, irreligious. It means common, irreverent, and godless talk. The word "godless" (*bebēlous*) means to be unhallowed and sensual; to be neglectful of spiritual things and a lover of the world and its things.<br><br>**Practical Application**<br>The minister is to turn away from false teaching. The description of false teaching is graphic.<br>1. False teaching is described as godless chatter.<br>2. False teaching is described as "knowledge," but as "knowledge falsely called."<br><br>The charge is strong, very strong: turn away from men and their teachings when they stand against Christ and the teachings of God's Word; have nothing to do with the false knowledge of men. The men and their false teachings may concern philosophy, psychology, education, sociology, religion–any area of knowledge–but turn away from them if they are false. How do you tell if they are false? By the Word of God, the revelation and record of Christ and of the truth of God. If the knowledge stands in opposition to the Word of God, turn away from it.<br><br>The charge is direct and forceful: avoid, shun, keep away from godless and empty talk. What are some examples of talk that is godless and empty? There is such talk as...<br>• false teaching<br>• worldly philosophy<br>• cursing<br>• theological theories<br>• criticism<br>• gossip<br>• off-colored conversations<br>• indecent insinuations<br>• immoral suggestions<br>• suggestive enticements |

# PRACTICAL WORD STUDIES
## in the New Testament

| ENGLISH WORD | GREEK WORD AND VERSE | THE WORD MEANS... |
|---|---|---|
| **#1725**<br>**Godless Living**<br><br>Ungodliness–KJV<br>Ungodliness–NASB<br>Ungodliness–NIV<br>Ungodliness–NKJV<br>**Godless living–NLT**<br><br>**POSB**<br>**REFERENCE**<br>(Tit.2:12)<br>Note 2, point 1 | ἀσέβειαν = asebeian<br>Pronunciation: [as-eb'-i-ahn]<br>Parsing (part of speech): noun<br>    Case—accusative<br>    Gender—feminine<br>    Number—singular<br>    Stem or root—from ἀσέβεια, ας<br>Concordance References:<br>⇒ Strong's #763 asebeia<br>⇒ NIV #813 asebeia<br>⇒ NASB #763 asebeia<br><br>**Titus 2:12**<br>Teaching us that, denying **ungodliness** and worldly lusts, we should live soberly, righteously, and godly, in this present world; [KJV]<br>Instructing us to deny **ungodliness** and worldly desires and to live sensibly, righteously and godly in the present age, [NASB]<br>It teaches us to say "No" to **ungodliness** and worldly passions, and to live self-controlled, upright and godly lives in this present age, [NIV]<br>Teaching us that, denying **ungodliness** and worldly lusts, we should live soberly, righteously, and godly in the present age, [NKJV]<br>And we are instructed to turn from **godless living** and sinful pleasures. We should live in this evil world with self-control, right conduct, and devotion to God, [NLT]<br>παιδεύουσα ἡμᾶς ἵνα, ἀρνησάμενοι τὴν **ἀσέβειαν** καὶ τὰς κοσμικὰς ἐπιθυμίας σωφρόνως καὶ δικαίως καὶ εὐσεβῶς ζήσωμεν ἐν τῷ νῦν αἰῶνι, [GNS]<br>παιδεύουσα ἡμᾶς, ἵνα ἀρνησάμενοι τὴν **ἀσέβειαν** καὶ τὰς κοσμικὰς ἐπιθυμίας σωφρόνως καὶ δικαίως καὶ εὐσεβῶς ζήσωμεν ἐν τῷ νῦν αἰῶνι, [GNT] | Ungodliness; godless living; wickedness; anything that is not like God; not holy, righteous or pure; anything that does not honor God by word or deed, that does not show reverence and worship toward God; anything that does not obey God, that violates God's commandments and goes against His will.<br><br>**Practical Application**<br>God's grace—demonstrated in the Lord Jesus Christ—teaches us to deny ungodliness and worldly lusts, that is, to reject, renounce, give up, and have nothing to do with ungodliness and worldly lusts. God's grace teaches us "to say 'no' to ungodliness [godless living] and worldly lusts" [sinful pleasures] (William F. Beck. *The New Testament in the Language of Today.* "The Four Translation New Testament." Printed for decision Magazine by World Wide Publications of Minneapolis. New York, NY: Iversen Associates, 1966). |
| **#1726**<br>**Godlessness**<br><br>Ungodliness–KJV<br>Ungodliness–NASB<br>**Godlessness–NIV**<br>Ungodliness–NKJV<br>Sinful–NLT<br><br>**POSB**<br>**REFERENCE**<br>(Rom.1:18)<br>Note 1, point 3a | ἀσέβειαν = asebeian<br>Pronunciation: [as-eb'-i-ahn]<br>Parsing (part of speech): noun<br>    Case—accusative<br>    Gender—feminine<br>    Number—singular<br>    Stem or root—from ἀσέβεια, ας<br>Concordance References:<br>⇒ Strong's #763 asebeia<br>⇒ NIV #813 asebeia<br>⇒ NASB #763 asebeia<br><br>**Romans 1:18**<br>For the wrath of God is revealed from heaven against all **ungodliness** and unrighteousness of men, who hold the truth in unrighteousness; [KJV]<br>For the wrath of God is revealed from heaven against all **ungodliness** and unrighteousness of men, who suppress the truth in unrighteousness, [NASB]<br>The wrath of God is being revealed from heaven against all the **godlessness** and wickedness of men who suppress the truth by their wickedness, [NIV]<br>For the wrath of God is revealed from heaven against all **ungodliness** and unrighteousness of men, who suppress the truth in unrighteousness, [NKJV]<br>But God shows his anger from heaven against all **sinful**, wicked people who push the truth away from themselves. [NLT]<br>Ἀποκαλύπτεται γὰρ ὀργὴ Θεοῦ ἀπ' οὐρανοῦ ἐπὶ πᾶσαν **ἀσέβειαν** καὶ ἀδικίαν ἀνθρώπων τῶν τὴν ἀλήθειαν ἐν ἀδικίᾳ κατεχόντων, [GNS]<br>Ἀποκαλύπτεται γὰρ ὀργὴ θεοῦ ἀπ' οὐρανοῦ ἐπὶ πᾶσαν **ἀσέβειαν** καὶ ἀδικίαν ἀνθρώπων τῶν τὴν ἀλήθειαν ἐν ἀδικίᾳ κατεχόντων, [GNT] | Godlessness, ungodliness; sinful, wicked behavior that is contrary to God's nature.<br><br>**Practical Application**<br>The godless (*asebeian*) fail to love and obey God. They are those who do not live as God lives. They are not like God, not holy and righteous and pure. They do not work at developing a godly nature, do not honor God by word or deed, do not worship and obey God as the only living and true God, do not reverence Him by doing what He says. On the contrary, the ungodly are those who do what they want when they want, who may give lip service to God, but who ignore Him in their day-to-day lives. |

# PRACTICAL WORD STUDIES
## in the NEW TESTAMENT

| ENGLISH WORD | GREEK WORD AND VERSE | THE WORD MEANS... |
|---|---|---|
| **#1727**<br>**Godliness**<br><br>**Godliness–KJV**<br>**Godliness–NASB**<br>**Godliness–NIV**<br>**Godliness–NKJV**<br>Godly life–NLT<br><br>**POSB**<br>**REFERENCE**<br>(1 Tim.6:11)<br>Note 2, point 2<br><br>See also POSB REF:<br>(2 Pt.1:3)<br>Note 1, point 4<br>(2 Pt.1:5-7; esp. v.6)<br>Note 1 | εὐσέβειαν = eusebeian<br>Pronunciation: [yoo-seb'-i-ahn]<br>Parsing (part of speech): noun<br>    Case—accusative<br>    Gender—feminine<br>    Number—singular<br>    Stem or root—from εὐσέβεια, ας<br>Concordance References:<br>⇒ Strong's #2150 eusebeia<br>⇒ NIV #2354 eusebeia<br>⇒ NASB #2150 eusebeia<br><br>**1 Tim. 6:11**<br>But thou, O man of God, flee these things; and follow after righteousness, **godliness**, faith, love, patience, meekness. [KJV]<br>But flee from these things, you man of God; and pursue righteousness, **godliness**, faith, love, perseverance and gentleness. [NASB]<br>But you, man of God, flee from all this, and pursue righteousness, **godliness**, faith, love, endurance and gentleness. [NIV]<br>But you, O man of God, flee these things and pursue righteousness, **godliness**, faith, love, patience, gentleness. [NKJV]<br>But you, Timothy, belong to God; so run from all these evil things, and follow what is right and good. Pursue a **godly life**, along with faith, love, perseverance, and gentleness. [NLT]<br>Σὺ δὲ ὦ ἄνθρωπε τοῦ Θεοῦ, ταῦτα φεῦγε· δίωκε δὲ δικαιοσύνην, **εὐσέβειαν**, πίστιν, ἀγάπην, ὑπομονήν, πραόπατητα· [GNS]<br>Σὺ δέ, ὦ ἄνθρωπε θεοῦ, ταῦτα φεῦγε· δίωκε δὲ δικαιοσύνην **εὐσέβειαν** πίστιν, ἀγάπην ὑπομονὴν πραϋπαθίαν. [GNT] | Godliness, godly life, godly living. Godliness means to live in the reverence and awe of God; to be *so conscious* of God's presence that one lives just as God would live if He were walking upon earth. It means to live seeking to be like God; to seek to possess the very character, nature, and behavior of God.<br><br>**Practical Application**<br>The man of God pursues godliness (*eusebeian*). The man of God follows and runs after godliness. He seeks to gain a consciousness of God's presence–a consciousness so intense that he actually lives as God would live if He were on earth. |
| **#1728**<br>**Godly**<br><br>Devout–KJV<br>Devout–NASB<br>God-fearing–NIV<br>Devout–NKJV<br>**Godly–NLT**<br><br>**POSB**<br>**REFERENCE**<br>(Acts 2:5-11; esp. v.5)<br>Note 5, point 1 | εὐλαβεῖς = eulabeis<br>Pronunciation: [yoo-lab-ace']<br>Parsing (part of speech): adjective<br>    Case—nominative<br>    Gender—masculine<br>    Number—plural<br>    Stem or root—from εὐλαβής, ές<br>Concordance References:<br>⇒ Strong's #2126 eulabēs<br>⇒ NIV #2327 eulabēs<br>⇒ NASB #2126 eulabēs<br><br>**Acts 2:5**<br>And there were dwelling at Jerusalem Jews, **devout** men, out of every nation under heaven. [KJV]<br>Now there were Jews living in Jerusalem, **devout** men, from every nation under heaven. [NASB]<br>Now there were staying in Jerusalem **God-fearing** Jews from every nation under heaven. [NIV]<br>And there were dwelling in Jerusalem Jews, **devout** men, from every nation under heaven. [NKJV]<br>**Godly** Jews from many nations were living in Jerusalem at that time. [NLT]<br>Ἦσαν δὲ ἐν Ἱερουσαλὴμ κατοικοῦντες Ἰουδαῖοι, ἄνδρες **εὐλαβεῖς**, ἀπὸ παντὸς ἔθνους τῶν ὑπὸ τὸν οὐρανόν· [GNS]<br>Ἦσαν δὲ εἰς Ἰερουσαλὴμ κατοικοῦντες Ἰουδαῖοι, ἄνδρες **εὐλαβεῖς** ἀπὸ παντὸς ἔθνους τῶν ὑπὸ τὸν οὐρανόν. [GNT] | God-fearing, devout, reverent, worshipful, careful, godly. It means persons who handle spiritual matters carefully.<br><br>**Practical Application**<br>They were devout men, Jewish pilgrims who had come from *all over the world*, had returned to Jerusalem to celebrate the "Feast of the First Fruits." Note how the groundwork for preaching is first laid by personal witnessing. (See POSB *Deeper Study* #1, Witnessing—Acts 1:8 for Scripture.) |
| **#1729**<br>**Godly**<br><br>**Godly–KJV**<br>**Godly–NASB**<br>**Godly–NIV**<br>**Godly–NKJV**<br>Devotion to God–NLT | εὐσεβῶς = eusebōs<br>Pronunciation: [yoo-seb-oce']<br>Parsing (part of speech): adjective adverb<br>    Stem or root—from εὐσεβῶς<br>Concordance References:<br>⇒ Strong's #2153 eusebōs<br>⇒ NIV #2357 eusebōs<br>⇒ NASB #2153 eusebōs | Godly; devotion to God; to live in a godly manner; to be like God; to live as God would live on this earth; to live in the consciousness of God.<br><br>**Practical Application**<br>It means that God lives within the very body |

# PRACTICAL WORD STUDIES
## in the NEW TESTAMENT

| ENGLISH WORD | GREEK WORD AND VERSE | THE WORD MEANS... |
|---|---|---|
| **POSB REFERENCE** (Tit.2:12) Note 2, point 2c | **Titus 2:12** <br> Teaching us that, denying ungodliness and worldly lusts, we should live soberly, righteously, and **godly**, in this present world; [KJV] <br> Instructing us to deny ungodliness and worldly desires and to live sensibly, righteously and **godly** in the present age, [NASB] <br> It teaches us to say "No" to ungodliness and worldly passions, and to live self-controlled, upright and **godly** lives in this present age, [NIV] <br> Teaching us that, denying ungodliness and worldly lusts, we should live soberly, righteously, and **godly** in the present age, [NKJV] <br> And we are instructed to turn from godless living and sinful pleasures. We should live in this evil world with self-control, right conduct, and **devotion to God**, [NLT] <br> παιδεύουσα ἡμᾶς ἵνα, ἀρνησάμενοι τὴν ἀσέβειαν καὶ τὰς κοσμικὰς ἐπιθυμίας σωφρόνως καὶ δικαίως καὶ **εὐσεβῶς** ζήσωμεν ἐν τῷ νῦν αἰῶνι, [GNS] <br> παιδεύουσα ἡμᾶς, ἵνα ἀρνησάμενοι τὴν ἀσέβειαν καὶ τὰς κοσμικὰς ἐπιθυμίας σωφρόνως καὶ δικαίως καὶ **Εὐσεβῶς** ζήσωμεν ἐν τῷ νῦν αἰῶνι, [GNT] | of the believer–that the believer's body is the very temple of God It is living and moving and having one's being in God. It is living just like God says to live, obeying Him in all things. |
| #1730 **Godly Fear** <br><br> Fear–KJV <br> Reverence–NASB <br> Holy fear–NIV <br> **Godly fear–NKJV** <br> Obeyed–NLT <br><br> **POSB REFERENCE** (Heb.11:7) Note 1, point 1 | **εὐλαβηθείς** = eulabētheis <br> Pronunciation: [yoo-lab-ay'-theh-ees] <br> Parsing (part of speech): verb <br>   Mood—participle <br>   Tense—aorist <br>   Voice—passive deponent <br>   Case—nominative <br>   Gender—masculine <br>   Number—singular <br>   Stem or root—from εὐλαβέομαι <br> Concordance References: <br>   ⇒ Strong's #2125 eulabeomai <br>   ⇒ NIV #2326 eulabeomai <br>   ⇒ NASB #2125 eulabeomai <br><br> **Hebrews 11:7** <br> By faith Noah, being warned of God of things not seen as yet, moved with **fear**, prepared an ark to the saving of his house; by the which he condemned the world, and became heir of the righteousness which is by faith. [KJV] <br> By faith Noah, being warned by God about things not yet seen, in **reverence** prepared an ark for the salvation of his household, by which he condemned the world, and became an heir of the righteousness which is according to faith. [NASB] <br> By faith Noah, when warned about things not yet seen, in **holy fear** built an ark to save his family. By his faith he condemned the world and became heir of the righteousness that comes by faith. [NIV] <br> By faith Noah, being divinely warned of things not yet seen, moved with **godly fear**, prepared an ark for the saving of his household, by which he condemned the world and became heir of the righteousness which is according to faith. [NKJV] <br> It was by faith that Noah built an ark to save his family from the flood. He **obeyed** God, who warned him about something that had never happened before. By his faith he condemned the rest of the world and was made right in God's sight. [NLT] <br> πίστει χρηματισθεὶς Νῶε περὶ τῶν μηδέπω βλεπομένων, **εὐλαβηθείς**, κατεσκεύασε κιβωτὸν εἰς σωτηρίαν τοῦ οἴκου αὐτοῦ· δι' ἧς κατέκρινε τὸν κόσμον, καὶ τῆς κατὰ πίστιν δικαιοσύνης ἐγένετο κληρονόμος. [GNS] <br> Πίστει χρηματισθεὶς Νῶε περὶ τῶν μηδέπω βλεπομένων, **εὐλαβηθείς** κατεσκεύασεν κιβωτὸν εἰς σωτηρίαν τοῦ οἴκου αὐτοῦ δι' ἧς κατέκρινεν τὸν κόσμον, καὶ τῆς κατὰ πίστιν δικαιοσύνης ἐγένετο κληρονόμος. [GNT] | Fear, holy fear; to reverence; to obey; to be moved with fear; to have godly fear. It has the idea of... <br> • reverence. <br> • standing in awe of God and His warning. <br> • taking heed lest one fall under God's judgment. <br> • diligently taking God at His Word. <br> • immediately acting upon what God says. <br><br> **Practical Application** <br> There was a time in world history when the earth had become so wicked that it was filled with corruption and violence. It was so corrupt that every imagination of man's heart was corrupt and evil. Man had reached the point of no return; he would never repent and return to God. God was left with no choice: the earth had to be destroyed. But there was one man on earth who was godly—Noah. Noah worshipped and honored God in his life. Therefore, God warned Noah of the coming judgment upon the earth. <br> ⇒ God told Noah to prepare an ark and the ark would save him, his family, and two of every animal. <br> ⇒ God also told Noah to warn the world of coming judgment. <br><br> Noah believed God's warning of coming judgment, and he began to build the ark with a godly fear and reverence, knowing that what God said would come true. God's judgment would fall upon the earth; Noah believed it and knew it by faith. |

# PRACTICAL WORD STUDIES
## in the NEW TESTAMENT

| ENGLISH WORD | GREEK WORD AND VERSE | THE WORD MEANS... |
|---|---|---|
| **#1731**<br>**Godly Fear**<br><br>Godly fear–KJV<br>Awe–NASB<br>Awe–NIV<br>**Godly fear–NKJV**<br>Awe–NLT<br><br>**POSB REFERENCE**<br>(Heb.12:28-29; esp. v.28)<br>Note 3, point 2 | δέους = *deous*<br>Pronunciation: [dee'-oos]<br>Parsing (part of speech): noun<br>   Case—genitive<br>   Gender—neuter<br>   Number—singular<br>   Stem or root—from δέος, ους<br>Concordance References:<br>  ⇒ Strong's #127 aidos<br>  ⇒ NIV #1290 deos<br>  ⇒ NASB #1190a dcos<br><br>**Hebrews 12:28**<br>Wherefore we receiving a kingdom which cannot be moved, let us have grace, whereby we may serve God acceptably with reverence and **godly fear**: [KJV]<br>Therefore, since we receive a kingdom which cannot be shaken, let us show gratitude, by which we may offer to God an acceptable service with reverence and **awe**; [NASB]<br>Therefore, since we are receiving a kingdom that cannot be shaken, let us be thankful, and so worship God acceptably with reverence and **awe**, [NIV]<br>Therefore, since we are receiving a kingdom which cannot be shaken, let us have grace, by which we may serve God acceptably with reverence and **godly fear**. [NKJV]<br>Since we are receiving a kingdom that cannot be destroyed, let us be thankful and please God by worshiping him with holy fear and **awe**. [NLT]<br>διὸ βασιλείαν ἀσάλευτον παραλαμβάνοντες, ἔχωμεν χάριν δι' ἧς λατρεύωμεν εὐαρέστως τῷ Θεῷ μετὰ **αἰδοῦς** καὶ εὐλαβείας· [GNS]<br>Διὸ βασιλείαν ἀσάλευτον παραλαμβάνοντες ἔχωμεν χάριν, δι' ἧς λατρεύωμεν εὐαρέστως τῷ θεῷ μετὰ εὐλαβείας καὶ **δέους**· [GNT] | Awe, reverence, godly fear. It means being apprehensive because some danger can lurk over the horizon.<br><br>**Practical Application**<br>A person must do exactly what this verse says: *serve God acceptably* with reverence and godly fear. God must be feared, for He is Lord. A person must serve God in an acceptable way. |
| **#1732**<br>**Godly Life**<br><br>Godliness–KJV<br>Godliness–NASB<br>Godliness–NIV<br>Godliness–NKJV<br>**Godly life–NLT**<br><br>**POSB REFERENCE**<br>(1 Tim.6:11)<br>Note 2, point 2 | εὐσέβειαν = *eusebeian*<br>Pronunciation: [yoo-seb'-i-ahn]<br>Parsing (part of speech): noun<br>   Case—accusative<br>   Gender—feminine<br>   Number—singular<br>   Stem or root—from εὐσέβεια, ας<br>Concordance References:<br>  ⇒ Strong's #2150 eusebeia<br>  ⇒ NIV #2354 eusebeia<br>  ⇒ NASB #2150 eusebeia<br><br>**1 Tim. 6:11**<br>But thou, O man of God, flee these things; and follow after righteousness, **godliness**, faith, love, patience, meekness. [KJV]<br>But flee from these things, you man of God; and pursue righteousness, **godliness**, faith, love, perseverance and gentleness. [NASB]<br>But you, man of God, flee from all this, and pursue righteousness, **godliness**, faith, love, endurance and gentleness. [NIV]<br>But you, O man of God, flee these things and pursue righteousness, **godliness**, faith, love, patience, gentleness. [NKJV]<br>But you, Timothy, belong to God; so run from all these evil things, and follow what is right and good. Pursue a **godly life**, along with faith, love, perseverance, and gentleness. [NLT]<br>Σὺ δέ ὦ ἄνθρωπε τοῦ Θεοῦ, ταῦτα φεῦγε· δίωκε δὲ δικαιοσύνην, **εὐσέβειαν**, πίστιν, ἀγάπην, ὑπομονήν, πρᾳόπατητα· [GNS]<br>Σὺ δέ, ὦ ἄνθρωπε θεοῦ, ταῦτα φεῦγε· δίωκε δὲ δικαιοσύνην **εὐσέβειαν** πίστιν, ἀγάπην ὑπομονὴν πραϋπαθίαν. [GNT] | Godliness, godly life, godly living. Godliness means to live in the reverence and awe of God; to be *so conscious* of God's presence that one lives just as God would live if He were walking upon earth. It means to live seeking to be like God; to seek to possess the very character, nature, and behavior of God.<br><br>**Practical Application**<br>The man of God pursues a godly life (*eusebeian*). The man of God follows and runs after godliness. He seeks to gain a consciousness of God's presence–a consciousness so intense that he actually lives as God would live if He were on earth. |

# PRACTICAL WORD STUDIES
## in the NEW TESTAMENT

| ENGLISH WORD | GREEK WORD AND VERSE | THE WORD MEANS... |
|---|---|---|
| **#1733**<br>**Godly Sincerity**<br><br>**Godly sincerity–KJV**<br>**Godly sincerity–NASB**<br>Sincerity from God–NIV<br>**Godly sincerity–NKJV**<br>Sincere–NLT<br><br>**POSB REFERENCE**<br>(2 Cor.1:12)<br>Note 1 | εἰλικρινείᾳ τοῦ θεοῦ = *eilikrineia too theou*<br>Pronunciation: [hi-lik-ree'-ni-ah too theh-oo]<br>Parsing *eilikrineia* (part of speech): noun<br>    Case—dative<br>    Gender—feminine<br>    Number—singular<br>    Stem or root—from εἰλικρίνεια, ας<br>Concordance References:<br>⇒ Strong's #1505 *eilikrineia*<br>⇒ NIV #1636 *eilikrineia* [sincerity]<br>⇒ NASB #1505 *eilikrineia*<br><br>**2 Cor. 1:12**<br>    For our rejoicing is this, the testimony of our conscience, that in simplicity and **godly sincerity**, not with fleshly wisdom, but by the grace of God, we have had our conversation in the world, and more abundantly to you-ward. [KJV]<br>    For our proud confidence is this, the testimony of our conscience, that in holiness and **godly sincerity**, not in fleshly wisdom but in the grace of God, we have conducted ourselves in the world, and especially toward you. [NASB]<br>    Now this is our boast: Our conscience testifies that we have conducted ourselves in the world, and especially in our relations with you, in the holiness and **sincerity** that are **from God**. We have done so not according to worldly wisdom but according to God's grace. [NIV]<br>    For our boasting is this: the testimony of our conscience that we conducted ourselves in the world in simplicity and **godly sincerity**, not with fleshly wisdom but by the grace of God, and more abundantly toward you. [NKJV]<br>    We can say with confidence and a clear conscience that we have been honest and **sincere** in all our dealings. We have depended on God's grace, not on our own earthly wisdom. That is how we have acted toward everyone, and especially toward you. [NLT]<br>    Ἡ γὰρ καύχησις ἡμῶν αὕτη ἐστί, τὸ μαρτύριον τῆς συνειδήσεως ἡμῶν, ὅτι ἐν ἁπλότητι καὶ **εἰλικρινείᾳ Θεοῦ**, οὐκ ἐν σοφίᾳ σαρκικῇ ἀλλ' ἐν χάριτι Θεοῦ, ἀνεστράφημεν ἐν τῷ κόσμῳ, περισσοτέρως δὲ πρὸς ὑμᾶς. [GNS]<br>    Ἡ γὰρ καύχησις ἡμῶν αὕτη ἐστίν, τὸ μαρτύριον τῆς συνειδήσεως ἡμῶν, ὅτι ἐν ἁπλότητι καὶ **εἰλικρινείᾳ τοῦ θεοῦ**, [καὶ] οὐκ ἐν σοφίᾳ σαρκικῇ ἀλλ' ἐν χάριτι θεοῦ, ἀνεστράφημεν ἐν τῷ κόσμῳ, περισσοτέρως δὲ πρὸς ὑμᾶς. [GNT] | Godly sincerity, purity. It is the unadulterated, the pure that has been shaken and rolled through a sieve. It means the unadulterated, the pure that shows up unstained and untainted when examined in the sunlight.<br><br>**Practical Application**<br>    Paul is saying that he is pure, unstained, untainted, unadulterated in his conduct and behavior. 1 Cor. 5:8 is the only other time Paul uses this word in his writings. |
| **#1734**<br>**Golgotha**<br><br>**Golgotha–KJV**<br>**Golgotha–NASB**<br>**Golgotha–NIV**<br>**Golgotha–NKJV**<br>**Golgotha–NLT**<br><br>**POSB REFERENCE**<br>(Mk.15:22)<br>Note 4 | Γολγοθᾶν = *Golgothan*<br>Pronunciation: [gol-goth-ahn']<br>Parsing (part of speech): noun<br>    Case—accusative<br>    Gender—feminine<br>    Number—singular<br>    Stem or root—from Γολγοθᾶ<br>Concordance References:<br>⇒ Strong's #1115 *Golgotha*<br>⇒ NIV #1201 *Golgotha*<br>⇒ NASB #1115 *Golgotha*<br><br>**Mark 15:22**<br>    And they bring him unto the place **Golgotha**, which is, being interpreted, The place of a skull. [KJV]<br>    And they brought Him to the place **Golgotha**, which is translated, Place of a Skull. [NASB]<br>    They brought Jesus to the place called **Golgotha** (which means The Place of the Skull). [NIV]<br>    And they brought Him to the place **Golgotha**, which is translated, Place of a Skull. [NKJV]<br>    And they brought Jesus to a place called **Golgotha** (which means Skull Hill). [NLT]<br>    καὶ φέρουσιν αὐτὸν ἐπὶ **Γολγοθᾶ** τόπον, ὅ ἐστι μεθερμηνευόμενον, Κρανίου Τόπος. [GNS]<br>    καὶ φέρουσιν αὐτὸν ἐπὶ τὸν **Γολγοθᾶν** τόπον, ὅ ἐστιν μεθερμηνευόμενον Κρανίου Τόπος. [GNT] | Golgotha, the place of a skull.<br><br>**Practical Application**<br>    Golgotha was a hill outside Jerusalem. It was known as a place of death, a place where executions took place. It stirred the thoughts of death and corruption. The very place where Jesus was crucified symbolized death itself. |

# PRACTICAL WORD STUDIES
## in the NEW TESTAMENT

| ENGLISH WORD | GREEK WORD AND VERSE | THE WORD MEANS... |
|---|---|---|
| **#1735**<br>**Gone Without Food**<br><br>Fastings–KJV<br>Hunger–NASB<br>Hunger–NIV<br>Fastings–NKJV<br>Gone without food–NLT<br><br>**POSB REFERENCE**<br>(2 Cor.6:5)<br>Note 4 | νηστείαις = nēsteiais<br>Pronunciation: [nace-ti'-ah-ees]<br>Parsing (part of speech): noun<br>    Case—dative<br>    Gender—feminine<br>    Number—plural<br>    Stem or root—from νηστεία, ας<br>Concordance References:<br>  ⇒ Strong's #3521 nēsteia<br>  ⇒ NIV #3763 nēsteia<br>  ⇒ NASB #3521 nēsteia<br><br>**2 Cor. 6:5**<br>In stripes, in imprisonments, in tumults, in labours, in watchings, in **fastings**; [KJV]<br>In beatings, in imprisonments, in tumults, in labors, in sleeplessness, in **hunger**, [NASB]<br>In beatings, imprisonments and riots; in hard work, sleepless nights and **hunger**; [NIV]<br>In stripes, in imprisonments, in tumults, in labors, in sleeplessness, in **fastings**; [NKJV]<br>We have been beaten, been put in jail, faced angry mobs, worked to exhaustion, endured sleepless nights, and **gone without food**. [NLT]<br>ἐν πληγαῖς, ἐν φυλακαῖς, ἐν ἀκαταστασίαις, ἐν κόποις, ἐν ἀγρυπνίαις, ἐν **νηστείαις**, [GNS]<br>ἐν πληγαῖς, ἐν φυλακαῖς, ἐν ἀκαταστασίαις, ἐν κόποις, ἐν ἀγρυπνίαις, ἐν **νηστείαις**, [GNT] | Hunger, fasting, starvation; to go without food.<br><br>**Practical Application**<br>This means not only deliberate fastings, but being so involved in his [Paul] work that he forgot to eat or else chose to keep working instead of eating. |
| **#1736**<br>**Gone Wrong**<br><br>Become unprofitable–KJV<br>Become useless–NASB<br>Become worthless–NIV<br>Become unprofitable–NKJV<br>Gone wrong–NLT<br><br>**POSB REFERENCE**<br>(Romans 3:10-12; esp. v.12)<br>Note 2, point 5 | ἠχρεώθησαν = ēchreōthēsan<br>Pronunciation: [aykh-ri-o'-thay-sahn]<br>Parsing (part of speech): verb<br>    Mood—indicative<br>    Tense—aorist<br>    Voice—passive<br>    Person—3rd person<br>    Number—plural<br>    Stem or root—from ἀχρειόομαι<br>Concordance References:<br>  ⇒ Strong's #889 achreioō<br>  ⇒ NIV #946 achreioō<br>  ⇒ NASB #889 achreioō<br><br>**Romans 3:12**<br>They are all gone out of the way, they are together **become unprofitable**; there is none that doeth good, no, not one. [KJV]<br>All have turned aside, together they have **become useless**; There is none who does good, There is not even one." [NASB]<br>All have turned away, they have together **become worthless**; there is no one who does good, not even one." [NIV]<br>They have all turned aside; They have together **become unprofitable**; There is none who does good, no, not one." [NKJV]<br>All have turned away from God; all have **gone wrong**. No one does good, not even one." [NLT]<br>πάντες ἐξέκλιναν, ἅμα **ἠχρεώθησαν**· οὐκ ἔστι ὁ ποιῶν χρηστότητα, οὐκ ἔστιν ἕως ἑνός. [GNS]<br>πάντες ἐξέκλιναν ἅμα **ἠχρεώθησαν**· οὐκ ἔστιν ὁ ποιῶν χρηστότητα, [οὐκ ἔστιν] ἕως ἑνός. [GNT] | To become worthless; unprofitable, useless, sour, bad, debased. (Cp. sour milk.) It means to go wrong.<br><br>**Practical Application**<br>A sinful nature is worthless (Romans 3:12; cp. Psalm 14:3): All men without Christ are worthless, useless, sour, bad. |
| **#1737**<br>**Good**<br><br>Blessed–KJV<br>Blessed–NASB<br>Good–NIV<br>Blessed–NKJV<br>Special favor–NLT | μακάριοι = makarioi<br>Pronunciation: [mak-ar'-ee-o-ee]<br>Parsing (part of speech): adjective<br>    Case—nominative<br>    Gender—masculine<br>    Number—plural<br>    Stem or root—from μακάριος, α, ον<br>Concordance References:<br>  ⇒ Strong's #3107 makarios<br>  ⇒ NIV #3421 makarios<br>  ⇒ NASB #3107 makarios | Good, blessed; to have special favor; to pronounce a person happy, fortunate or blessed.<br><br>**Practical Application**<br>It is a judgment that affirms a person's condition as being "good." The idea is that Christ is going to bestow special favor upon the believer to make him happy and blessed. Happiness and blessedness will become a state of being, the constant experience of the believer. |

## PRACTICAL WORD STUDIES
## in the NEW TESTAMENT

| ENGLISH WORD | GREEK WORD AND VERSE | THE WORD MEANS... |
|---|---|---|
| **POSB REFERENCE**<br>(Lk.12:35-40; esp. v.37)<br>Note 1, point 3 | **Luke 12:37**<br>**Blessed** are those servants, whom the lord when he cometh shall find watching: verily I say unto you, that he shall gird himself, and make them to sit down to meat, and will come forth and serve them. [KJV]<br>"**Blessed** are those slaves whom the master shall find on the alert when he comes; truly I say to you, that he will gird himself to serve, and have them recline at the table, and will come up and wait on them. [NASB]<br>It will be **good** for those servants whose master finds them watching when he comes. I tell you the truth, he will dress himself to serve, will have them recline at the table and will come and wait on them. [NIV]<br>**Blessed** *are* those servants whom the master, when he comes, will find watching. Assuredly, I say to you that he will gird himself and have them sit down *to eat,* and will come and serve them. [NKJV]<br>There will be **special favor** for those who are ready and waiting for his return. I tell you, he himself will seat them, put on an apron, and serve them as they sit and eat! [NLT]<br>μακάριοι οἱ δοῦλοι ἐκεῖνοι, οὓς ἐλθὼν ὁ κύριος εὑρήσει γρηγοροῦντας· ἀμὴν λέγω ὑμῖν ὅτι περιζώσεται καὶ ἀνακλινεῖ αὐτοὺς, καὶ παρελθὼν διακονήσει αὐτοῖς. [GNS]<br>μακάριοι οἱ δοῦλοι ἐκεῖνοι, οὓς ἐλθὼν ὁ κύριος εὑρήσει γρηγοροῦντας· ἀμὴν λέγω ὑμῖν ὅτι περιζώσεται καὶ ἀνακλινεῖ αὐτοὺς, καὶ παρελθὼν διακονήσει αὐτοῖς. [GNT] | |
| **#1738**<br>**Good**<br><br>Good–KJV<br>Good–NASB<br>Good–NIV<br>Good–NKJV<br>Good–NLT<br><br>**POSB REFERENCE**<br>(Lk.8:11-15; esp. v.15)<br>Note 4, point 4b<br><br>See also POSB REF:<br>(Mt.7:11)<br>*Deeper Study* #4 | ἀγαθῇ = *agathë*<br>Pronunciation: [ag-ah-thay']<br>Parsing (part of speech): adjective<br>    Case—dative<br>    Gender—feminine<br>    Number—singular<br>    Stem or root—from ἀγαθός, ή, όν<br>Concordance References:<br>⇒ Strong's #18 agathos<br>⇒ NIV #19 agathos<br>⇒ NASB #18 agathos<br><br>**Luke 8:15**<br>But that on the good ground are they, which in an honest and **good** heart, having heard the word, keep it, and bring forth fruit with patience. [KJV]<br>"And the seed in the good soil, these are the ones who have heard the word in an honest and **good** heart, and hold it fast, and bear fruit with perseverance. [NASB]<br>But the seed on good soil stands for those with a noble and **good** heart, who hear the word, retain it, and by persevering produce a crop. [NIV]<br>But the ones *that* fell on the good ground are those who, having heard the word with a noble and **good** heart, keep *it* and bear fruit with patience. [NKJV]<br>But the good soil represents honest, **good**-hearted people who hear God's message, cling to it, and steadily produce a huge harvest. [NLT]<br>τὸ δὲ ἐν τῇ καλῇ γῇ, οὗτοί εἰσιν οἵτινες ἐν καρδίᾳ καλῇ καὶ **ἀγαθῇ**, ἀκούσαντες τὸν λόγον, κατέχουσι, καὶ καρποφοροῦσιν ἐν ὑπομονῇ. [GNS]<br>τὸ δὲ ἐν τῇ καλῇ γῇ, οὗτοί εἰσιν οἵτινες ἐν καρδίᾳ καλῇ καὶ **ἀγαθῇ** ἀκούσαντες τὸν λόγον κατέχουσιν καὶ καρποφοροῦσιν ἐν ὑπομονῇ. [GNT] | Good, useful, beneficial, the best, excellent, of extraordinary character. It means devoted, committed, given over to the truth. Once they know the truth, they hold fast to it.<br><br>**Practical Application**<br>What are the marks of the people whose lives are like the good ground?<br>1. Their hearts are "noble" (*kalei*). The word means fair, noble, and just. It has the idea of holding fast. These people are honest and fair; they are noble people in listening and considering the Word. They honestly seek to learn and know the truth, spiritually as well as physically.<br>2. Their hearts are "good" (*agathë*), meaning devoted, committed, given over to the truth. Once they know the truth, they hold fast to it.<br>3. They keep the Word. They do not let the devil snatch it, nor the trials and temptations of life scorch it, nor the cares and riches and pleasures of this life choke it.<br>4. They bear fruit with patience. They endure and study, grow and serve more and more. They constantly water and pluck the weeds and thorns, and they continue to do so until the fruit is fully grown and plucked and taken home to the Master of the house. |
| **#1739**<br>**Good**<br><br>Good–KJV<br>Good–NASB<br>Good–NIV | καλὸν = *kalon*<br>Pronunciation: [kal-on']<br>Parsing (part of speech): adjective<br>    Case—nominative<br>    Gender—neuter<br>    Number—singular<br>    Stem or root—from καλός, ή, όν | Good, fine, right, proper.<br><br>**Practical Application**<br>The word "good" (*kalon*) means advisable, advantageous, expedient, profitable, wholesome. There are times when it is wise not to marry and to take on the responsibilities of mar- |

# PRACTICAL WORD STUDIES
## in the NEW TESTAMENT

| ENGLISH WORD | GREEK WORD AND VERSE | THE WORD MEANS... |
|---|---|---|
| Good–NKJV<br>Good–NLT<br><br>**POSB REFERENCE**<br>(1 Cor.7:1)<br>Note 1<br><br>See also POSB REF:<br>(2 Tim. 4:7)<br>Note 2 | Concordance References:<br>⇒ Strong's #2570 kalos<br>⇒ NIV #2819 kalos<br>⇒ NASB #2570 kalos<br><br>**1 Cor. 7:1**<br>Now concerning the things whereof ye wrote unto me: It is **good** for a man not to touch a woman. [KJV]<br>Now concerning the things about which you wrote, it is **good** for a man not to touch a woman. [NASB]<br>Now for the matters you wrote about: It is **good** for a man not to marry. [NIV]<br>Now concerning the things of which you wrote to me: *It is* **good** for a man not to touch a woman. [NKJV]<br>Now about the questions you asked in your letter. Yes, it is **good** to live a celibate life. [NLT]<br>Περὶ δὲ ὧν ἐγράψατέ μοι, **καλὸν** ἀνθρώπῳ γυναικὸς μὴ ἅπτεσθαι. [GNS]<br>Περὶ δὲ ὧν ἐγράψατε, **καλὸν** ἀνθρώπῳ γυναικὸς μὴ ἅπτεσθαι [GNT] | riage. There are *special situations* for not marrying. There are situations that require celibacy. |
| **#1740**<br>**Good**<br><br>Good–KJV<br>Good–NASB<br>Good–NIV<br>Good–NKJV<br>Good–NLT<br><br>**POSB REFERENCE**<br>(Romans 3:10-12; esp. v.12)<br>Note 2, point 6 | χρηστότητα = *chrēstotēta*<br>Pronunciation: [khray-stot'-ay-tah]<br>Parsing (part of speech): noun<br>  Case—accusative<br>  Gender—feminine<br>  Number—singular<br>  Stem or root—from χρηστότης, ητος<br>Concordance References:<br>⇒ Strong's #5544 chrēstotēs<br>⇒ NIV #5983 chrēstotēs<br>⇒ NASB #5544 chrēstotēs<br><br>**Romans 3:12**<br>They are all gone out of the way, they are together become unprofitable; there is none that doeth **good**, no, not one. [KJV]<br>All have turned aside, together they have become useless; There is none who does **good**, There is not even one." [NASB]<br>All have turned away, they have together become worthless; there is no one who does **good**, not even one." [NIV]<br>*They have all turned aside;They have together become unprofitable; There is none who does* **good**, *n*o, not one." [NKJV]<br>All have turned away from God; all have gone wrong. No one does **good**, not even one." [NLT]<br>πάντες ἐξέκλιναν, ἅμα ἠχρειώθησαν· οὐκ ἔστι ὁ ποιῶν **χρηστότητα**, οὐκ ἔστιν ἕως ἑνός. [GNS]<br>πάντες ἐξέκλιναν ἅμα ἠχρεώθησαν· οὐκ ἔστιν ὁ ποιῶν **χρηστότητα**, [οὐκ ἔστιν] ἕως ἑνός. [GNT] | Goodness, mercy; what is right. It means moral goodness, kindness, graciousness, gentleness, justice.<br><br>**Practical Application**<br>A sinful nature is evil (Romans 3:12; cp. Psalm 14:3): "There is none that doeth good, no, not one." All men fail in being good toward God and their neighbor, in being...<br>• kind<br>• gracious<br>• gentle<br>• just<br><br>Men come short–too often, too much. "There is none that doeth good [not always, not perfectly], no, not one." |
| **#1741**<br>**Good**<br><br>Spiritual–KJV<br>Spiritual–NASB<br>Spiritual–NIV<br>Spiritual–NKJV<br>Good–NLT<br><br>**POSB REFERENCE**<br>(Rom.7:14)<br>Note 1, point 1 | πνευματικός *pneumatikos*<br>Pronunciation: [pnyoo-mat-ik-os']<br>Parsing (part of speech): adjective<br>  Case—nominative<br>  Gender—masculine<br>  Number—singular<br>  Stem or root—from πνευματικός, ή, όν<br>Concordance References:<br>⇒ Strong's #4152 pneumatikos<br>⇒ NIV #4461 pneumatikos<br>⇒ NASB #4152 pneumatikos<br><br>**Romans 7:14**<br>For we know that the law is **spiritual**: but I am carnal, sold under sin. [KJV]<br>For we know that the Law is **spiritual**; but I am of flesh, sold into bondage to sin. [NASB]<br>We know that the law is **spiritual**; but I am unspiritual, sold as a slave to sin. [NIV]<br>For we know that the law is **spiritual**, but I am carnal, sold under sin. [NKJV] | Spiritual; good; pertaining to the spirit.<br><br>**Practical Application**<br>The law is spiritual. It is spiritual in at least three senses.<br>1. The law was given to man by the Spirit of God (*pneumatikos*). The Greek word used is the very name of the Holy Spirit. The Holy Spirit is the source of the law.<br>2. The law is the expression of the will and nature of God. The law is spiritual because it describes the will of God and tells man just what God is like. The rules of the law reveal both the mind and nature of God.<br>3. The law is spiritual because of its purposes (see POSB note, Law, Purpose—Romans 7:12 for discussion. Also cp. POSB outline—Romans 7:7-13 and POSB notes—Romans 7:7-13 for more discussion.) |

# PRACTICAL WORD STUDIES
## in the NEW TESTAMENT

| ENGLISH WORD | GREEK WORD AND VERSE | THE WORD MEANS... |
|---|---|---|
| | The law is **good**, then. The trouble is not with the law but with me, because I am sold into slavery, with sin as my master. [NLT]<br><br>οἴδαμεν γὰρ ὅτι ὁ νόμος **πνευματικός** ἐστιν· ἐγὼ δὲ σάρκικός εἰμι, πεπραμένος ὑπὸ τὴν ἁμαρτίαν. [GNS]<br><br>οἴδαμεν γὰρ ὅτι ὁ νόμος **πνευματικός** ἐστιν, ἐγὼ δὲ σάρκινός εἰμι πεπραμένος ὑπὸ τὴν ἁμαρτίαν. [GNT] | |
| **#1742**<br>**Good**<br><br>**Good–KJV**<br>**Good–NASB**<br>**Good–NIV**<br>**Good–NKJV**<br>**Good–NLT**<br><br>**POSB REFERENCE**<br>(Rom.8:28)<br>Note 1, point 3<br><br>See also POSB REF:<br>(Rom.12:2)<br>Note 4, point 2<br>(Acts 11:22-24; esp. v.24)<br>Note 2, point 2b | ἀγαθόν = *agathon*<br>Pronunciation: [ag-ath-on']<br>Parsing (part of speech): pronominal adjective<br>    Case—accusative<br>    Gender—neuter<br>    Number—singular<br>    Stem or root—from ἀγαθός, ή, όν<br>Concordance References:<br>⇒ Strong's #18 agathos<br>⇒ NIV #19 agathos<br>⇒ NASB #18 agathos<br><br>**Romans 8:28**<br>And we know that all things work together for **good** to them that love God, to them who are the called according to his purpose. [KJV]<br><br>And we know that God causes all things to work together for **good** to those who love God, to those who are called according to His purpose. [NASB]<br><br>And we know that in all things God works for the **good** of those who love him, who have been called according to his purpose. [NIV]<br><br>And we know that all things work together for **good** to those who love God, to those who are the called according to *His* purpose. [NKJV]<br><br>And we know that God causes everything to work together for the **good** of those who love God and are called according to his purpose for them. [NLT]<br><br>οἴδαμεν δὲ ὅτι τοῖς ἀγαπῶσι τὸν Θεὸν πάντα συνεργεῖ εἰς **ἀγαθόν**, τοῖς κατὰ πρόθεσιν κλητοῖς οὖσιν. [GNS]<br><br>οἴδαμεν δὲ ὅτι τοῖς ἀγαπῶσιν τὸν θεὸν πάντα συνεργεῖ εἰς **ἀγαθόν**, τοῖς κατὰ πρόθεσιν κλητοῖς οὖσιν. [GNT] | Good. The word "good" (*agathon*) means for the ultimate good.<br><br>**Practical Application**<br>We cannot see the future; we cannot take a single event and see all the lines and ramifications that run from it. We cannot see all the things that result from one single event, much less see the results of every event. But God does; therefore, God takes all the events of our lives and works them out for our ultimate good. |
| **#1743**<br>**Good**<br><br>**Good–KJV**<br>Fine–NASB<br>Noble–NIV<br>**Good–NKJV**<br>Honorable–NLT<br><br>**POSB REFERENCE**<br>(1 Tim.3:1)<br>Note 1 | καλοῦ = *kalou*<br>Pronunciation: [kal-oo']<br>Parsing (part of speech): adjective<br>    Case—genitive<br>    Gender—neuter<br>    Number—singular<br>    Stem or root—from καλός, ή, όν<br>Concordance References:<br>⇒ Strong's #2570 kalos<br>⇒ NIV #2819 kalos<br>⇒ NASB #2570 kalos<br><br>**1 Tim. 3:1**<br>This is a true saying, If a man desire the office of a bishop, he desireth a **good** work. [KJV]<br><br>It is a trustworthy statement: if any man aspires to the office of overseer, it is a **fine** work he desires to do. [NASB]<br><br>Here is a trustworthy saying: If anyone sets his heart on being an overseer, he desires a **noble** task. [NIV]<br><br>This *is* a faithful saying: If a man desires the position of a bishop, he desires a **good** work. [NKJV]<br><br>It is a true saying that if someone wants to be an elder, he desires an **honorable** responsibility. [NLT]<br><br>Πιστὸς ὁ λόγος· Εἴ τις ἐπισκοπῆς ὀρέγεται, **καλοῦ** ἔργου ἐπιθυμεῖ· [GNS]<br><br>πιστὸς ὁ λόγος. Εἴ τις ἐπισκοπῆς ὀρέγεται, **καλοῦ** ἔργου ἐπιθυμεῖ. [GNT] | Noble, good, fine, honorable, honest, proper, right, excellent, beneficial, productive.<br><br>**Practical Application**<br>The office of minister or bishop is a "good work." Note that the position of the ministry is not what is stressed, but the work of the ministry. The emphasis is not the esteem and honor of the profession. The emphasis is upon the work of the ministry. It is the work that is honorable, excellent, beneficial, and productive. The work of the ministry is a "good work." |

# PRACTICAL WORD STUDIES
## in the NEW TESTAMENT

| ENGLISH WORD | GREEK WORD AND VERSE | THE WORD MEANS... |
|---|---|---|
| **#1744**<br>**Good**<br><br>Honest–KJV<br>Excellent–NASB<br>**Good–NIV**<br>Honorable–NKJV<br>Be careful how you live–NLT<br><br>**POSB REFERENCE**<br>(1 Pt.2:12)<br>Note 3 | καλήν = *kalën*<br>Pronunciation: [kal-ayn']<br>Parsing (part of speech): adjective<br>    Case—accusative<br>    Gender—feminine<br>    Number—singular<br>    Stem or root—from καλός, ή, όν<br>Concordance References:<br>  ⇒ Strong's #2570 kalos<br>  ⇒ NIV #2819 kalos<br>  ⇒ NASB #2570 kalos<br><br>**1 Peter 2:12**<br>Having your conversation **honest** among the Gentiles: that, whereas they speak against you as evildoers, they may by your good works, which they shall behold, glorify God in the day of visitation. [KJV]<br><br>Keep your behavior **excellent** among the Gentiles, so that in the thing in which they slander you as evildoers, they may on account of your good deeds, as they observe them, glorify God in the day of visitation. [NASB]<br><br>Live such **good** lives among the pagans that, though they accuse you of doing wrong, they may see your good deeds and glorify God on the day he visits us. [NIV]<br><br>Having your conduct **honorable** among the Gentiles, that when they speak against you as evildoers, they may, by *your* good works which they observe, glorify God in the day of visitation. [NKJV]<br><br>**Be careful how you live** among your unbelieving neighbors. Even if they accuse you of doing wrong, they will see your honorable behavior, and they will believe and give honor to God when he comes to judge the world. [NLT]<br><br>τὴν ἀναστροφὴν ὑμῶν ἐν τοῖς ἔθνεσιν ἔχοντες **καλήν**, ἵνα, ἐν ᾧ καταλαλοῦσιν ὑμῶν ὡς κακοποιῶν, ἐκ τῶν καλῶν ἔργων ἐποπτεύσαντες δοξάσωσι τὸν Θεὸν ἐν ἡμέρᾳ ἐπισκοπῆς. [GNS]<br><br>τὴν ἀναστροφὴν ὑμῶν ἐν τοῖς ἔθνεσιν ἔχοντες **καλήν**, ἵνα, ἐν ᾧ καταλαλοῦσιν ὑμῶν ὡς κακοποιῶν ἐκ τῶν καλῶν ἔργων ἐποπτεύοντες δοξάσωσιν τὸν θεὸν ἐν ἡμέρᾳ ἐπισκοπῆς. [GNT] | Good, honest, right, excellent; honorable, proper; to be careful how one lives.<br><br>**Practical Application**<br>The word "good" (*kalën*) means a good life, a life that is honorable, righteous, pure, lovely, decent, excellent, upright, and noble. It means a life that is without blame, that cannot be justly or accurately blamed with any sin or evil. The world watches a genuine believer to see if he really lives what he professes. Therefore, we must live good lives, honest lives, lives that are just what we profess: holy, righteous, and pure. |
| **#1745**<br>**Good**<br><br>Good–KJV<br>Kind–NASB<br>Kind–NIV<br>**Good–NKJV**<br>**Good–NLT**<br><br>**POSB REFERENCE**<br>(Tit.2:4-5; esp. v.5)<br>Note 4 , point 7 | ἀγαθάς = *agathas*<br>Pronunciation: [ag-ath-ahs']<br>Parsing (part of speech): adjective<br>    Case—accusative<br>    Gender—feminine<br>    Number—plural<br>    Stem or root—from ἀγαθός, ή, όν<br>Concordance References:<br>  ⇒ Strong's #18 agathos<br>  ⇒ NIV #19 agathos<br>  ⇒ NASB #18 agathos<br><br>**Titus 2:5**<br>To be discreet, chaste, keepers at home, **good**, obedient to their own husbands, that the word of God be not blasphemed. [KJV]<br><br>To be sensible, pure, workers at home, **kind**, being subject to their own husbands, that the word of God may not be dishonored. [NASB]<br><br>To be self-controlled and pure, to be busy at home, to be **kind**, and to be subject to their husbands, so that no one will malign the word of God. [NIV]<br><br>To be discreet, chaste, homemakers, **good**, obedient to their own husbands, that the word of God may not be blasphemed. [NKJV]<br><br>To live wisely and be pure, to take care of their homes, to do **good**, and to be submissive to their husbands. Then they will not bring shame on the word of God. [NLT]<br><br>σώφρονας, ἁγνάς, οἰκουργούς **ἀγαθάς**, ὑποτασσομένας τοῖς ἰδίοις ἀνδράσιν, ἵνα μὴ ὁ λόγος τοῦ Θεοῦ βλασφημῆται· [GNS]<br><br>σώφρονας ἁγνάς οἰκουργούς **ἀγαθάς**, ὑποτασσομένας τοῖς ἰδίοις ἀνδράσιν, ἵνα μὴ ὁ λόγος τοῦ θεοῦ βλασφημῆται. [GNT] | Kind, good, useful, sound; of the highest quality and character; virtuous through and through; good natured and caring.<br><br>**Practical Application**<br>A young woman is to be *good* (*agathas*): There is no vice, no dirt or pollution in her life; she is pure and clean, of the highest character. And she is good to people, that is, kind and caring. She is not an idle person, going from house to house being a gossiper and busy body. She is purposeful, moving in and among people doing good, showing care and kindness, helping people wherever she can (cp. 1 Tim. 5:13). |

# PRACTICAL WORD STUDIES
## in the NEW TESTAMENT

| ENGLISH WORD | GREEK WORD AND VERSE | THE WORD MEANS... |
|---|---|---|
| **#1746**<br>**Good And Right**<br><br>Righteousness–KJV<br>Righteousness–NASB<br>Righteousness–NIV<br>Righteousness–NKJV<br>Good and right–NLT<br><br>**POSB REFERENCE**<br>(Eph.5:9)<br>*Deeper Study* #1<br><br>See also POSB REF:<br>(1 Tim.6:11-16; esp. v.11)<br>Note 2, point 1 | δικαιοσύνη = dikaiosunë<br>Pronunciation: [dik-ah-yos-oo'-nay]<br>Parsing (part of speech): noun<br>   Case—dative<br>   Gender—feminine<br>   Number—singular<br>   Stem or root—from δικαιοσύνη, ης<br>Concordance References:<br>  ⇒ Strong's #1343 dikaiosunë<br>  ⇒ NIV #1466 dikaiosunë<br>  ⇒ NASB #1343 dikaiosunë<br><br>**Ephes. 5:9**<br>(For the fruit of the Spirit is in all goodness and **righteousness** and truth;) [KJV]<br>(For the fruit of the light consists in all goodness and **righteousness** and truth), [NASB]<br>(For the fruit of the light consists in all goodness, **righteousness** and truth) [NIV]<br>(For the fruit of the Spirit *is* in all goodness, **righteousness**, and truth), [NKJV]<br>For this light within you produces only what is **good and right** and true. [NLT]<br>-- ὁ γὰρ καρπὸς τοῦ Πνεύματος ἐν πάσῃ ἀγαθωσύνῃ καὶ **δικαιοσύνῃ** καὶ ἀληθείᾳ [GNS]<br>-ὁ γὰρ καρπὸς τοῦ φωτὸς ἐν πάσῃ ἀγαθωσύνῃ καὶ **δικαιοσύνῃ** καὶ ἀληθείᾳ [GNT] | Righteousness; good and right. It means two simple but profound things. It means both *to be right and to do right*. (See *Deeper Study* #5, Righteousness–Matthew 5:6 for more discussion.)<br><br>**Practical Application**<br>1. There are those who stress *being good and right but neglect doing righteousness*. This leads to two serious errors.<br>a. False security. It causes a person to stress that he is saved and acceptable to God because he has *believed in* Jesus Christ. But he neglects doing good and living as he should. He neglects obeying God and serving man.<br>b. Loose living. It allows one to go out and do pretty much as he desires. He feels secure and comfortable in his *faith in Christ*. He knows that what he does may affect his fellowship with God and other believers, but he thinks his behavior will not affect his salvation. He thinks that no matter what he does he is still acceptable to God.<br>   The problem with this stress is that it is a false righteousness. Righteousness in the Bible means *being righteous*, but it also means *doing righteousness*. The Bible knows nothing about being righteous without living righteously.<br>2. There are those who stress *doing good and right but neglect being righteous*. This also leads to two serious errors.<br>a. Self-righteousness and legalism. It causes a person to stress that he is saved and acceptable to God because he does good. He works and behaves morally and keeps certain rules and regulations. He does the things a Christian should do by obeying the main laws of God. But he neglects the basic law: the law of love and acceptance–that God does not love him and accept him because he does good, but because he loves and trusts the righteousness of Christ (see POSB *Deeper Study* #5–Matthew 5:6).<br>b. Being judgmental and fault-finding. A person who stresses that he is righteous (acceptable to God) because he keeps certain laws often judges and finds fault with others. He feels that rules and regulations can be kept, he keeps them. Therefore, anyone who fails to keep them is judged, criticized, and censored.<br>   The problem with this stress is that it, too, is a false righteousness. Again, righteousness in the Bible is *being righteous as well as doing righteousness*. The Bible knows nothing of being acceptable to God without *being made righteous in Christ Jesus* (see POSB *Deeper Study* #5–Matthew 5:6; POSB note–Romans 5:1 for more discussion. Cp. 2 Cor. 5:21.) |
| **#1747**<br>**Good Behaviour**<br><br>Good behaviour–KJV<br>Respectable–NASB<br>Respectable–NIV | κόσμιον = kosmion<br>Pronunciation: [kos'-mee-on]<br>Parsing (part of speech): adjective<br>   Case—accusative<br>   Gender—masculine<br>   Number—singular<br>   Stem or root—from κόσμιος, ον<br>Concordance References:<br>  ⇒ Strong's #2887 kosmios<br>  ⇒ NIV #3177 kosmios<br>  ⇒ NASB #2887 kosmios | Respectable; good behavior; good reputation; well-behaved; modest; orderly; composed; solid; and honest.<br><br>**Practical Application**<br>The minister or bishop must be of "good behavior" (*kosmion*). It is a person who has good conduct, whose character and behavior stands as the ideal and pattern for others. |

PRACTICAL WORD STUDIES
in the NEW TESTAMENT

| ENGLISH WORD | GREEK WORD AND VERSE | THE WORD MEANS... |
|---|---|---|
| **Good behavior–NKJV**<br>Good reputation–NLT<br><br>**POSB REFERENCE**<br>(1 Tim.3:2-3; esp. v.2)<br>Note 2, point 5 | **1 Tim. 3:2**<br>A bishop then must be blameless, the husband of one wife, vigilant, sober, of **good behaviour**, given to hospitality, apt to teach; [KJV]<br>An overseer, then, must be above reproach, the husband of one wife, temperate, prudent, **respectable**, hospitable, able to teach, [NASB]<br>Now the overseer must be above reproach, the husband of but one wife, temperate, self-controlled, **respectable**, hospitable, able to teach, [NIV]<br>A bishop then must be blameless, the husband of one wife, temperate, sober-minded, of **good behavior**, hospitable, able to teach; [NKJV]<br>For an elder must be a man whose life cannot be spoken against. He must be faithful to his wife. He must exhibit self-control, live wisely, and have a **good reputation**. He must enjoy having guests in his home and must be able to teach. [NLT]<br>δεῖ οὖν τὸν ἐπίσκοπον ἀνεπίλημπτον εἶναι, μιᾶς γυναικὸς ἄνδρα, νηφάλιον, σώφρονα, **κόσμιον**, φιλόξενον, διδακτικόν· [GNS]<br>δεῖ οὖν τὸν ἐπίσκοπον ἀνεπίλημπτον εἶναι, μιᾶς γυναικὸς ἄνδρα, νηφάλιον σώφρονα **κόσμιον** φιλόξενον διδακτικόν, [GNT] | |
| **#1748**<br>**Good Cheer**<br><br>Good cheer–KJV<br>Take courage–NASB<br>Take courage–NIV<br>Good cheer–NKJV<br>Be encouraged–NLT<br><br>**POSB REFERENCE**<br>(Acts 23:11)<br>Note 5 | Θάρσει = *Tharsei*<br>Pronunciation: [thar-seh'-ee]<br>Parsing (part of speech): verb<br>  Mood—imperfect<br>  Tense—present<br>  Voice—active<br>  Person—2nd person<br>  Number—singular<br>  Stem or root—from θαρσέω<br>Concordance References:<br>  ⇒ Strong's #2293 tharseō<br>  ⇒ NIV #2510 tharseō<br>  ⇒ NASB #2293 tharseō<br><br>**Acts 23:11**<br>And the night following the Lord stood by him, and said, Be of **good cheer**, Paul: for as thou hast testified of me in Jerusalem, so must thou bear witness also at Rome. [KJV]<br>But on the night immediately following, the Lord stood at his side and said, "**Take courage**; for as you have solemnly witnessed to My cause at Jerusalem, so you must witness at Rome also." [NASB]<br>The following night the Lord stood near Paul and said, "**Take courage**! As you have testified about me in Jerusalem, so you must also testify in Rome." [NIV]<br>But the following night the Lord stood by him and said, "Be of **good cheer**, Paul; for as you have testified for Me in Jerusalem, so you must also bear witness at Rome." [NKJV]<br>That night the Lord appeared to Paul and said, "**Be encouraged**, Paul. Just as you have told the people about me here in Jerusalem, you must preach the Good News in Rome." [NLT]<br>Τῇ δὲ ἐπιούσῃ νυκτὶ ἐπιστὰς αὐτῷ ὁ Κύριος εἶπε, **Θάρσει** Παῦλε· ὡς γὰρ διεμαρτύρω τὰ περὶ ἐμοῦ εἰς Ἰερουσαλήμ, οὕτω σε δεῖ καὶ εἰς Ῥώμην μαρτυρῆσαι. [GNS]<br>Τῇ δὲ ἐπιούσῃ νυκτὶ ἐπιστὰς αὐτῷ ὁ κύριος εἶπεν, **Θάρσει** ὡς γὰρ διεμαρτύρω τὰ περὶ ἐμοῦ εἰς Ἰερουσαλήμ, οὕτω σε δεῖ καὶ εἰς Ῥώμην μαρτυρῆσαι. [GNT] | To take courage; to be of good cheer; to be encouraged; to cheer up; to take heart.<br><br>**Practical Application**<br>The Lord wishes His servants to always be encouraged (*Tharsei*) and courageous and full of cheer, no matter the trial. The life of His servant is under the care and leadership of the Lord. |
| **#1749**<br>**Good Courage**<br><br>Confident–KJV<br>Good courage–NASB | Θαρροῦντες = *Tharrountes*<br>Pronunciation: [thar-roon'-tehs]<br>Parsing (part of speech): verb<br>  Mood—participle<br>  Tense—present<br>  Voice—active | Confident, to have good courage; to act boldly; "to be cheered up" (A.T. Robertson. *Word Pictures in the New Testament*, Vol. 4, p.229).<br><br>**Practical Application**<br>The Holy Spirit stirs confidence and courage |

# PRACTICAL WORD STUDIES
## in the NEW TESTAMENT

| ENGLISH WORD | GREEK WORD AND VERSE | THE WORD MEANS... |
|---|---|---|
| Confident–NIV<br>Confident–NKJV<br>Confident–NLT<br><br>**POSB<br>REFERENCE**<br>(2 Cor.5:5-8; esp. v.6)<br>Note 3 | Case—nominative<br>Gender—masculine<br>Person—1st person<br>Stem or root—from θαρρέω<br>Concordance References:<br>⇒ Strong's #2292 tharreō<br>⇒ NIV #2509 tharreō<br>⇒ NASB #2292 tharreō<br><br>**2 Cor. 5:6**<br>Therefore we are always **confident**, knowing that, whilst we are at home in the body, we are absent from the Lord: [KJV]<br>Therefore, being always of **good courage**, and knowing that while we are at home in the body we are absent from the Lord—[NASB]<br>Therefore we are always **confident** and know that as long as we are at home in the body we are away from the Lord. [NIV]<br>So *we are* always **confident**, knowing that while we are at home in the body we are absent from the Lord. [NKJV]<br>So we are always **confident**, even though we know that as long as we live in these bodies we are not at home with the Lord. [NLT]<br>Θαρροῦντες οὖν πάντοτε, καὶ εἰδότες ὅτι ἐνδημοῦντες ἐν τῷ σώματι ἐκδημοῦμεν ἀπὸ τοῦ Κυρίου, [GNS]<br>Θαρροῦντες οὖν πάντοτε καὶ εἰδότες ὅτι ἐνδημοῦντες ἐν τῷ σώματι ἐκδημοῦμεν ἀπὸ τοῦ κυρίου· [GNT] | to face the present life. In this world all believers face such things as...<br>• pressure<br>• trouble<br>• sorrow<br>• accident<br>• rejection<br>• loss<br>• disease<br>• death<br><br>But no matter what they face, the Holy Spirit stirs the courage to face it all. How? Again, note the word "knowing." The Holy Spirit enhances our *knowledge*...<br>• that our present home is the body, but it is temporary and passing. Therefore, all trials and problems will quickly pass away.<br>• that we are now absent from the Lord. The idea is that we are to be with Him. The Holy Spirit stirs a longing within us to be with Him. And that longing gives us courage to march on through this life. |
| #1750<br>**Good Deeds**<br><br>Good fruits–KJV<br>Good fruits–NASB<br>Good fruit–NIV<br>Good fruits–NKJV<br>**Good deeds–NLT**<br><br>**POSB<br>REFERENCE**<br>(Jas.3:17-18; esp. v.17)<br>Note 3, point 2f | καρπῶν ἀγαθῶν = karpōn agathōn<br>Pronunciation: [kar-pon' ag-ath-own']<br>Parsing *karpōn* (part of speech): noun<br>  Case—genitive<br>  Gender—masculine<br>  Number—plural<br>  Stem or root—from Κάρπος, ου<br>Parsing *agathōn* (part of speech): adjective<br>  Case—genitive<br>  Gender—masculine<br>  Number—plural<br>  Stem or root—from ἀγαθός, ή, όν<br>Concordance References:<br>⇒ Strong's #2590 karpos + 18 agathos<br>⇒ NIV #2843 karpos [fruit] + 19 agathos [good]<br>⇒ NASB #2590 karpos + 18 agathos<br><br>**James 3:17**<br>But the wisdom that is from above is first pure, then peaceable, gentle, and easy to be intreated, full of mercy and **good fruits**, without partiality, and without hypocrisy. [KJV]<br>But the wisdom from above is first pure, then peaceable, gentle, reasonable, full of mercy and **good fruits**, unwavering, without hypocrisy. [NASB]<br>But the wisdom that comes from heaven is first of all pure; then peace-loving, considerate, submissive, full of mercy and **good fruit**, impartial and sincere. [NIV]<br>But the wisdom that is from above is first pure, then peaceable, gentle, willing to yield, full of mercy and **good fruits**, without partiality and without hypocrisy. [NKJV]<br>But the wisdom that comes from heaven is first of all pure. It is also peace loving, gentle at all times, and willing to yield to others. It is full of mercy and **good deeds**. It shows no partiality and is always sincere. [NLT]<br>ἡ δὲ ἄνωθεν σοφία πρῶτον μὲν ἁγνή ἐστιν, ἔπειτα εἰρηνική, ἐπιεικής, εὐπειθής, μεστὴ ἐλέους καὶ **καρπῶν ἀγαθῶν**, ἀδιάκριτος καὶ ἀνυπόκριτος. [GNS]<br>ἡ δὲ ἄνωθεν σοφία πρῶτον μὲν ἁγνή ἐστιν, ἔπειτα εἰρηνική, ἐπιεικής, εὐπειθής, μεστὴ ἐλέους καὶ **καρπῶν ἀγαθῶν**, ἀδιάκριτος, ἀνυπόκριτος. [GNT] | Good fruits, good deeds.<br><br>**Practical Application**<br>True wisdom is full of good deeds (*karpōn agathōn*). This means that the wise teacher actually reaches out to help those in trouble. He does not experience feelings of compassion and then push them out of his mind. He acts; he meets needs; he helps the suffering, the shut-in, the prisoner, the widow and widower, the orphan, the single parent and child, the grieving, the poor, the destitute, the homeless, the hungry, the sinner, the backslidden, the lost, and the wicked. The teacher of true wisdom reaches out and leads his followers to reach out to the needy of their community, city, state, nation, and world. The wise teacher does all he can to meet the desperate of our world. In fact, he gives all he is and has—every dime he has–sacrificing everything beyond the needs of his own family–to meet the needs of the lost and destitute of our world. The teacher of true wisdom is totally committed to good deeds and works in order to reach people for Christ and to help them through all the problems and troubles of life. |

# PRACTICAL WORD STUDIES
## in the NEW TESTAMENT

| ENGLISH WORD | GREEK WORD AND VERSE | THE WORD MEANS... |
|---|---|---|
| **#1751**<br>**Good Deeds Done**<br><br>Righteousness–KJV<br>Righteous acts–NASB<br>Righteous acts–NIV<br>Righteous acts–NKJV<br>Good deeds done–NLT<br><br>**POSB REFERENCE**<br>(Rev.19:7-8; esp.v.8)<br>Note 3, point 2 | δικαιώματα = dikaiömata<br>Pronunciation: [dik-ah'-ee-yo-mah-tah]<br>Parsing (part of speech): noun<br>    Case—nominative<br>    Gender—neuter<br>    Number—plural<br>    Stem or root—from δικαίωμα, τος<br>Concordance References:<br>  ⇒ Strong's #1345 dikaiöma<br>  ⇒ NIV #1468 dikaiöma<br>  ⇒ NASB #1345 dikaiöma<br><br>**Rev. 19:8**<br>And to her was granted that she should be arrayed in fine linen, clean and white: for the fine linen is the **righteousness** of saints. [KJV]<br><br>And it was given to her to clothe herself in fine linen, bright and clean; for the fine linen is the **righteous acts** of the saints. [NASB]<br><br>Fine linen, bright and clean, was given her to wear." (Fine linen stands for the **righteous acts** of the saints.) [NIV]<br><br>And to her it was granted to be arrayed in fine linen, clean and bright, for the fine linen is the **righteous acts** of the saints. [NKJV]<br><br>She is permitted to wear the finest white linen." (Fine linen represents the **good deeds done** by the people of God.) [NLT]<br><br>καὶ ἐδόθη αὐτῇ ἵνα περιβάληται βύσσινον καθαρὸν καὶ λαμπρόν· τὸ γὰρ βύσσινον τὰ **δικαιώματα** ἐστι τῶν ἁγίων. [GNS]<br><br>καὶ ἐδόθη αὐτῇ ἵνα περιβάληται βύσσινον λαμπρὸν καθαρόν· τὸ γὰρ βύσσινον τὰ **δικαιώματα** τῶν ἁγίων ἐστίν. [GNT] | Righteous acts; righteousness; good deeds done.<br>**Practical Application**<br>A believer prepares himself by doing good deeds for the LORD (Rev. 19:8). This would mean two things.<br>1. The believer acts righteously, *does the right thing* when he receives Jesus Christ as his Savior. It is then that God accepts the belief of the person *as righteousness*. God actually takes a person's faith in His Son and *counts his faith as righteousness*. Why? Because the person believes that the sacrifice of the Lamb, the death of the Lord Jesus Christ, was for the sins of the world. The person believes that Jesus Christ died for his sins, as his sacrifice, as his substitute. He believes that the penalty and judgment of his sins have been paid for by Christ. Therefore, he is free of sin and made acceptable to God. God takes his faith and *counts his faith as righteousness*. God counts him righteous in the righteousness of Jesus Christ. This is what is called *imputed* righteousness, righteousness that is given or put to one's account before God. It is a righteousness that is counted and credited to the believer. Therefore, when the believer is ready to attend the great *Marriage Supper of the Lamb*, he will be given the clean and white clothing necessary to enter the supper. Note: the fine clothing is actually said to be the righteousness or righteous deeds of the saints.<br>   Now, this is the first righteous deed that a person is to do. If he does this righteous deed, then he will be accepted into the great *Marriage Supper of the Lamb*.<br>2. The believer is also to do other good deeds. He is to serve the Lamb of God to the fullest degree possible. Every believer is aware that not all believers do this; not all believers serve God with all their heart, soul, and body. In fact, some believers do little for Christ. Therefore, note verse eight carefully: the bride of Christ–all believers–will be in heaven. They will be accepted and made perfect in the righteousness of Christ. They have robes that are white and pure. But note: when they get ready to attend the great *Marriage Supper of the Lamb*, God will give believers another garment that is made of fine linen that will be clean and white. What is the other garment? It is...<br>• the garment of righteous deeds and acts.<br>• the garment of reward.<br>• the garment that shows position and responsibility.<br>• the garment that rewards one for faithfulness. |
| **#1752**<br>**Good Discipline**<br><br>Order–KJV<br>Good discipline–NASB | τάξιν = taxin<br>Pronunciation: [tax'-in]<br>Parsing (part of speech): noun<br>    Case—accusative<br>    Gender—feminine<br>    Number—singular<br>    Stem or root—from τάξις, εως | Orderly, good discipline, living as one should. The words "good discipline" (*taxin*) mean to maintain military discipline, array, and arrangement; to hold a solid front (The Amplified New Testament); to hold the military line unbroken and intact (A.T. Robertson, *Word Pictures in the New Testament*, Vol.4, p.489). |

# PRACTICAL WORD STUDIES
## in the NEW TESTAMENT

| ENGLISH WORD | GREEK WORD AND VERSE | THE WORD MEANS... |
|---|---|---|
| Orderly–NIV<br>Good order–NKJV<br>Living as you should–NLT<br><br>**POSB REFERENCE**<br>(Col.2:5)<br>Note 4 | Concordance References:<br>⇒ Strong's #5010 taxis<br>⇒ NIV #5423 taxis<br>⇒ NASB #5010 taxis<br><br>**Col. 2:5**<br>For though I be absent in the flesh, yet am I with you in the spirit, joying and beholding your **order**, and the stedfastness of your faith in Christ. [KJV]<br>For even though I am absent in body, nevertheless I am with you in spirit, rejoicing to see your **good discipline** and the stability of your faith in Christ. [NASB]<br>For though I am absent from you in body, I am present with you in spirit and delight to see how **orderly** you are and how firm your faith in Christ is. [NIV]<br>For though I am absent in the flesh, yet I am with you in spirit, rejoicing to see your **good order** and the stedfastness of your faith in Christ. [NKJV]<br>For though I am far away from you, my heart is with you. And I am very happy because you are **living as you should** and because of your strong faith in Christ. [NLT]<br>εἰ γὰρ καὶ τῇ σαρκὶ ἄπειμι, ἀλλὰ τῷ πνεύματι σὺν ὑμῖν εἰμι, χαίρων καὶ βλέπων ὑμῶν τὴν **τάξιν** καὶ τὸ στερέωμα τῆς εἰς Χριστὸν πίστεως ὑμῶν. [GNS]<br>εἰ γὰρ καὶ τῇ σαρκὶ ἄπειμι, ἀλλὰ τῷ πνεύματι σὺν ὑμῖν εἰμι, χαίρων καὶ βλέπων ὑμῶν τὴν **τάξιν** καὶ τὸ στερέωμα τῆς εἰς Χριστὸν πίστεως ὑμῶν. [GNT] | **Practical Application**<br>Note that the believers of the Colossian church were being attacked by false teaching even as Paul was writing to them. But they were responding like a victorious army. They were maintaining their discipline and holding their order and standing fast. Note also the importance of the minister's encouragement: Paul says that he was with them *in spirit*, joying and watching them gain the victory over the false teachers. |
| **#1753**<br>**Good For You**<br><br>Expedient–KJV<br>Profitable–NASB<br>Beneficial–NIV<br>Helpful–NKJV<br>**Good for you–NLT**<br><br>**POSB REFERENCE**<br>(1 Cor.6:12)<br>Note 1, point 1 | συμφέρει = sumpherei<br>Pronunciation: [soom-fer'-eh-ee]<br>Parsing (part of speech): verb<br>  Mood—indicative<br>  Tense—present<br>  Voice—active<br>  Person—3rd person<br>  Number—singular<br>  Stem or root—from συμφέρω<br>Concordance References:<br>⇒ Strong's #4851 sumpherō<br>⇒ NIV #5237 sumpherō<br>⇒ NASB #4851 sumpherō<br><br>**1 Cor. 6:12**<br>All things are lawful unto me, but all things are not **expedient**: all things are lawful for me, but I will not be brought under the power of any. [KJV]<br>All things are lawful for me, but not all things are **profitable**. All things are lawful for me, but I will not be mastered by anything. [NASB]<br>"Everything is permissible for me"—but not everything is **beneficial**. "Everything is permissible for me"—but I will not be mastered by anything. [NIV]<br>All things are lawful for me, but all things are not **helpful**. All things are lawful for me, but I will not be brought under the power of any. [NKJV]<br>You may say, "I am allowed to do anything." But I reply, "Not everything is **good for you**." And even though "I am allowed to do anything," I must not become a slave to anything. [NLT]<br>Πάντα μοι ἔξεστιν, ἀλλ' οὐ πάντα **συμφέρει**· πάντα μοι ἔξεστιν, ἀλλ' οὐκ ἐγὼ ἐξουσιασθήσομαι ὑπό τινος. [GNS]<br>Πάντα μοι ἔξεστιν ἀλλ' οὐ πάντα **συμφέρει**. πάντα μοι ἔξεστιν ἀλλ' οὐκ ἐγὼ ἐξουσιασθήσομαι ὑπό τινος. [GNT] | Beneficial, expedient, useful, helpful, worthwhile, advisable, profitable, good for you.<br><br>**Practical Application**<br>For example, it is good for you to eat fish; it is unprofitable to eat poisonous berries. It is advisable to keep active for the sake of the body; it is harmful to lie around and become inactive. Note that doing some activities is lawful, but others are not good and profitable. |
| **#1754**<br>**Good Fruit-Good Fruits**<br><br>Good fruits–KJV<br>Good fruits–NASB<br>Good fruit–NIV | καρπῶν ἀγαθῶν = karpōn agathōn<br>Pronunciation: [kar-pon' ag-ath-own']<br>Parsing *karpōn* (part of speech): noun<br>  Case—genitive<br>  Gender—masculine<br>  Number—plural<br>  Stem or root—from Κάρπος, ου<br>Parsing *agathōn* (part of speech): adjective<br>  Case—genitive | Good fruits; good deeds.<br><br>**Practical Application**<br>True wisdom is full of good fruits (*karpōn agathōn*). This means that the wise teacher actually reaches out to help those in trouble. He does not experience feelings of compassion and then push them out of his mind. He acts; he meets |

## PRACTICAL WORD STUDIES
### in the NEW TESTAMENT

| ENGLISH WORD | GREEK WORD AND VERSE | THE WORD MEANS... |
|---|---|---|
| **Good fruits–NKJV**<br>Good deeds–NLT<br><br>**POSB REFERENCE**<br>(Jas.3:17-18; esp. v.17)<br>Note 3, point 2f | Gender—masculine<br>Number—plural<br>Stem or root—from Κάρπος, ου<br>Concordance References:<br>⇒ Strong's #2590 karpos + 18 agathos<br>⇒ NIV #2843 karpos [fruit] + 19 agathos [good]<br>⇒ NASB #2590 karpos + 18 agathos<br><br>**James 3:17**<br>But the wisdom that is from above is first pure, then peaceable, gentle, and easy to be intreated, full of mercy and **good fruits**, without partiality, and without hypocrisy. [KJV]<br>But the wisdom from above is first pure, then peaceable, gentle, reasonable, full of mercy and **good fruits**, unwavering, without hypocrisy. [NASB]<br>But the wisdom that comes from heaven is first of all pure; then peace-loving, considerate, submissive, full of mercy and **good fruit**, impartial and sincere. [NIV]<br>But the wisdom that is from above is first pure, then peaceable, gentle, willing to yield, full of mercy and **good fruits**, without partiality and without hypocrisy. [NKJV]<br>But the wisdom that comes from heaven is first of all pure. It is also peace loving, gentle at all times, and willing to yield to others. It is full of mercy and **good deeds**. It shows no partiality and is always sincere. [NLT]<br>ἡ δὲ ἄνωθεν σοφία πρῶτον μὲν ἁγνή ἐστιν, ἔπειτα εἰρηνική, ἐπιεικής, εὐπειθής, μεστὴ ἐλέους καὶ **καρπῶν ἀγαθῶν**, ἀδιάκριτος καὶ ἀνυπόκριτος. [GNS]<br>ἡ δὲ ἄνωθεν σοφία πρῶτον μὲν ἁγνή ἐστιν, ἔπειτα εἰρηνική, ἐπιεικής, εὐπειθής, μεστὴ ἐλέους καὶ **καρπῶν ἀγαθῶν**, ἀδιάκριτος, ἀνυπόκριτος. [GNT] | needs; he helps the suffering, the shut-in, the prisoner, the widow and widower, the orphan, the single parent and child, the grieving, the poor, the destitute, the homeless, the hungry, the sinner, the backslidden, the lost, and the wicked. The teacher of true wisdom reaches out and leads his followers to reach out to the needy of their community, city, state, nation, and world. The wise teacher does all he can to meet the desperate of our world. In fact, he gives all he is and has–every dime he has–sacrificing everything beyond the needs of his own family–to meet the needs of the lost and destitute of our world. The teacher of true wisdom is totally committed to good deeds and works in order to reach people for Christ and to help them through all the problems and troubles of life. |
| **#1755**<br>**Good News**<br><br>Gospel–KJV<br>Gospel–NASB<br>**Good news–NIV**<br>Gospel–NKJV<br>**Good News–NLT**<br><br>**POSB REFERENCE**<br>(Mt.4:23)<br>Note 2<br><br>See also POSB REF:<br>(1 Cor.15:1-11; esp. v.1)<br>*Deeper Study #1* | εὐαγγέλιον = euaggelion<br>Pronunciation: [yoo-ang-ghel'-ee-on]<br>Parsing (part of speech): noun<br>    Case—accusative<br>    Gender—neuter<br>    Number—singular<br>    Stem or root—from εὐαγγέλιον, ου<br>Concordance References:<br>⇒ Strong's #2098 euaggelion<br>⇒ NIV #2295 euaggelion<br>⇒ NASB #2098 euaggelion<br><br>**Matthew 4:23**<br>And Jesus went about all Galilee, teaching in their synagogues, and preaching the **gospel** of the kingdom, and healing all manner of sickness and all manner of disease among the people. [KJV]<br>And Jesus was going about in all Galilee, teaching in their synagogues, and proclaiming the **gospel** of the kingdom, and healing every kind of disease and every kind of sickness among the people. [NASB]<br>Jesus went throughout Galilee, teaching in their synagogues, preaching the **good news** of the kingdom, and healing every disease and sickness among the people. [NIV]<br>And Jesus went about all Galilee, teaching in their synagogues, preaching the **gospel** of the kingdom, and healing all kinds of sickness and all kinds of disease among the people. [NKJV]<br>Jesus traveled throughout Galilee teaching in the synagogues, preaching everywhere the **Good News** about the Kingdom. And he healed people who had every kind of sickness and disease. [NLT]<br>Καὶ περιῆγεν ὅλην τῇ Γαλιλαίᾳ ὁ Ἰησοῦς, διδάσκων ἐν ταῖς συναγωγαῖς αὐτῶν, καὶ κηρύσσων τὸ **εὐαγγέλιον** τῆς βασιλείας, καὶ θεραπεύων πᾶσαν νόσον καὶ πᾶσαν μαλακίαν ἐν τῷ λαῷ. [GNS]<br>Καὶ περιῆγεν ἐν ὅλῃ τῇ Γαλιλαίᾳ διδάσκων ἐν ταῖς συναγωγαῖς αὐτῶν καὶ κηρύσσων τὸ **εὐαγγέλιον** τῆς βασιλείας καὶ θεραπεύων πᾶσαν νόσον καὶ πᾶσαν μαλακίαν ἐν τῷ λαῷ. [GNT] | Gospel or Good News.<br><br>**Practical Application**<br>Throughout Scripture there is only one gospel, but it is described in different ways. It is called...<br>• the "good news of the kingdom" (Mt.4:23; Mark 1:14).<br>• the "gospel of God's grace" (Acts 20:24).<br>• the "gospel of God" (Ro.1:1).<br>• the "gospel about Jesus Christ" (Mark 1:1; Ro.1:16; 2 Cor. 4:4; 2 Cor. 10:14).<br>• the "gospel of the glory of Christ" (2 Cor. 4:4; 1 Tim. 1:11).<br>• the "eternal gospel" (Rev. 14:6). |

## PRACTICAL WORD STUDIES in the NEW TESTAMENT

| ENGLISH WORD | GREEK WORD AND VERSE | THE WORD MEANS... |
|---|---|---|
| **#1756**<br>**Good Order**<br><br>Order–KJV<br>Good discipline–NASB<br>Orderly–NIV<br>**Good order–NKJV**<br>Living as you should–NLT<br><br>**POSB REFERENCE**<br>(Col.2:5)<br>Note 4 | τάξιν = taxin<br>Pronunciation: [tax'-in]<br>Parsing (part of speech): noun<br>   Case—accusative<br>   Gender—feminine<br>   Number—singular<br>   Stem or root—from τάξις, εως<br>Concordance References:<br>  ⇒ Strong's #5010 taxis<br>  ⇒ NIV #5423 taxis<br>  ⇒ NASB #5010 taxis<br><br>**Col. 2:5**<br>For though I be absent in the flesh, yet am I with you in the spirit, joying and beholding your **order**, and the stedfastness of your faith in Christ. [KJV]<br><br>For even though I am absent in body, nevertheless I am with you in spirit, rejoicing to see your **good discipline** and the stability of your faith in Christ. [NASB]<br><br>For though I am absent from you in body, I am present with you in spirit and delight to see how **orderly** you are and how firm your faith in Christ is. [NIV]<br><br>For though I am absent in the flesh, yet I am with you in spirit, rejoicing to see your ***good* order** and the stedfastness of your faith in Christ. [NKJV]<br><br>For though I am far away from you, my heart is with you. And I am very happy because you are **living as you should** and because of your strong faith in Christ. [NLT]<br><br>εἰ γὰρ καὶ τῇ σαρκὶ ἄπειμι, ἀλλὰ τῷ πνεύματι σὺν ὑμῖν εἰμι, χαίρων καὶ βλέπων ὑμῶν τὴν **τάξιν**, καὶ τὸ στερέωμα τῆς εἰς Χριστὸν πίστεως ὑμῶν. [GNS]<br><br>εἰ γὰρ καὶ τῇ σαρκὶ ἄπειμι, ἀλλὰ τῷ πνεύματι σὺν ὑμῖν εἰμι, χαίρων καὶ βλέπων ὑμῶν τὴν **τάξιν** καὶ τὸ στερέωμα τῆς εἰς Χριστὸν πίστεως ὑμῶν. [GNT] | Orderly, good discipline, living as one should. The words "good order" (*taxin*) mean to maintain military discipline, array, and arrangement; to hold a solid front (The Amplified New Testament); to hold the military line unbroken and intact (A.T. Robertson, *Word Pictures in the New Testament,* Vol.4, p.489).<br><br>**Practical Application**<br>Note that the believers of the Colossian church were being attacked by false teaching even as Paul was writing to them. But they were responding like a victorious army. They were maintaining their discipline and holding their order and standing fast. Note also the importance of the minister's encouragement: Paul says that he was with them *in spirit*, joying and watching them gain the victory over the false teachers. |
| **#1757**<br>**Good Report**<br><br>**Good report–KJV**<br>Good repute–NASB<br>Admirable–NIV<br>**Good report–NKJV**<br>Admirable–NLT<br><br>**POSB REFERENCE**<br>(Philip.4:8-9; esp. v.8)<br>Note 2, point 1f | εὔφημα = euphēma<br>Pronunciation: [yoo'-fay-mah]<br>Parsing (part of speech): adjective<br>   Case—nominative<br>   Gender—neuter<br>   Number—plural<br>   Stem or root—from εὔφημος, ον<br>Concordance References:<br>  ⇒ Strong's #2163 euphēmos<br>  ⇒ NIV #2368 euphēmos<br>  ⇒ NASB #2163 euphēmos<br><br>**Philip. 4:8**<br>Finally, brethren, whatsoever things are true, whatsoever things *are* honest, whatsoever things *are* just, whatsoever things *are* pure, whatsoever things *are* lovely, whatsoever things *are* of **good report**; if *there be* any virtue, and if *there be* any praise, think on these things. [KJV]<br><br>Finally, brethren, whatever is true, whatever is honorable, whatever is right, whatever is pure, whatever is lovely, whatever is of **good repute**, if there is any excellence and if anything worthy of praise, let your mind dwell on these things. [NASB]<br><br>Finally, brothers, whatever is true, whatever is noble, whatever is right, whatever is pure, whatever is lovely, whatever is **admirable**—if anything is excellent or praiseworthy—think about such things. [NIV]<br><br>Finally, brethren, whatever things are true, whatever things *are* noble, whatever things *are* just, whatever things *are* pure, whatever things *are* lovely, whatever things *are* of **good report**, if *there is* any virtue and if *there is* anything praiseworthy—meditate on these things. [NKJV]<br><br>And now, dear brothers and sisters, let me say one more thing as I close this letter. Fix your thoughts on what | Admirable; of good repute; of good report. It means worthy of praise, reputable, high-toned, things of the highest quality.<br><br>**Practical Application**<br>The believer is to think only upon worthy things. He is not to listen to *bad reports*, no matter how juicy they may seem. Neither is he to fill his mind with junk, whether through rumor, radio, television, music, off-colored jokes, or by whatever source. His thoughts are to be focused only upon worthy things—only upon that which is admirable. |

# PRACTICAL WORD STUDIES
## in the NEW TESTAMENT

| ENGLISH WORD | GREEK WORD AND VERSE | THE WORD MEANS... |
|---|---|---|
| | is true and honorable and right. Think about things that are pure and lovely and **admirable**. Think about things that are excellent and worthy of praise. [NLT]<br>Τὸ λοιπόν, ἀδελφοί, ὅσα ἐστὶν ἀληθῆ, ὅσα σεμνά, ὅσα δίκαια, ὅσα ἁγνά, ὅσα προσφιλῆ, ὅσα **εὔφημα**, εἴ τις ἀρετὴ καὶ εἴ τις ἔπαινος, ταῦτα λογίζεσθε· [GNS]<br>Τὸ λοιπόν, ἀδελφοί, ὅσα ἐστὶν ἀληθῆ, ὅσα δίκαια, ὅσα ἁγνά, ὅσα προσφιλῆ, ὅσα **εὔφημα**, εἴ τις ἀρετὴ καὶ εἴ τις ἔπαινος, ταῦτα λογίζεσθε· [GNT] | |
| **#1758**<br>**Good Reputation**<br><br>Honest report–KJV<br>**Good reputation**–NASB<br>Known–NIV<br>**Good reputation**–NKJV<br>Well respected–NLT<br><br>**POSB REFERENCE**<br>(Acts 6:3)<br>Note 3, point 1 | μαρτυρουμένους = *marturoumenous*<br>Pronunciation: [mar-too-roo'-men-oos]<br>Parsing (part of speech): verb<br>    Mood—participle<br>    Tense—present<br>    Voice—passive<br>    Case—accusative<br>    Gender—masculine<br>    Number—plural<br>    Stem or root—from μαρτυρέω<br>Concordance References:<br>⇒ Strong's #3140 martureo<br>⇒ NIV #3455 martureö<br>⇒ NASB #3140 martureo<br><br>**Acts 6:3**<br>Wherefore, brethren, look ye out among you seven men of **honest report**, full of the Holy Ghost and wisdom, whom we may appoint over this business. [KJV]<br>"But select from among you, brethren, seven men of **good reputation**, full of the Spirit and of wisdom, whom we may put in charge of this task. [NASB]<br>Brothers, choose seven men from among you who are **known** to be full of the Spirit and wisdom. We will turn this responsibility over to them [NIV]<br>Therefore, brethren, seek out from among you seven men of **good reputation**, full of the Holy Spirit and wisdom, whom we may appoint over this business; [NKJV]<br>"Now look around among yourselves, brothers, and select seven men who are **well respected** and are full of the Holy Spirit and wisdom. We will put them in charge of this business. [NLT]<br>ἐπισκέψασθε οὖν, ἀδελφοί, ἄνδρας ἐξ ὑμῶν **μαρτυρουμένους** ἑπτά, πλήρεις Πνεύματος Ἁγίου καὶ σοφίας, οὓς καταστήσομεν ἐπὶ τῆς χρείας ταύτης. [GNS]<br>ἐπισκέψασθε δέ, ἀδελφοί, ἄνδρας ἐξ ὑμῶν **μαρτυρουμένους** ἑπτά, πλήρεις πνεύματος καὶ σοφίας, οὓς καταστήσομεν ἐπὶ τῆς χρείας ταύτης, [GNT] | To be known; to have a good reputation; well respected; well attested; well reported of; bearing a good witness.<br><br>**Practical Application**<br>The deacon's character was to be proven beyond reproach. They were to be men of integrity, faithful and trustworthy; moral and upright, men trusted by all. |
| **#1759**<br>**Good Reputation**<br><br>Good behaviour–KJV<br>Respectable–NASB<br>Respectable–NIV<br>Good behavior–NKJV<br>**Good reputation**–NLT<br><br>**POSB REFERENCE**<br>(1 Tim. 3:2-3; esp. v.2)<br>Note 2, point 5 | κόσμιον = *kosmion*<br>Pronunciation: [kos'-mee-on]<br>Parsing (part of speech): adjective<br>    Case—accusative<br>    Gender—masculine<br>    Number—singular<br>    Stem or root—from κόσμιος, ον<br>Concordance References:<br>⇒ Strong's #2887 kosmios<br>⇒ NIV #3177 kosmios<br>⇒ NASB #2887 kosmios<br><br>**1 Tim. 3:2**<br>A bishop then must be blameless, the husband of one wife, vigilant, sober, of **good behaviour**, given to hospitality, apt to teach; [KJV]<br>An overseer, then, must be above reproach, the husband of one wife, temperate, prudent, **respectable**, hospitable, able to teach, [NASB]<br>Now the overseer must be above reproach, the husband of but one wife, temperate, self-controlled, **respectable**, hospitable, able to teach, [NIV]<br>A bishop then must be blameless, the husband of one wife, temperate, sober-minded, of **good behavior**, hos- | Respectable; good behavior; good reputation; well-behaved; modest; orderly; composed; solid; honest.<br><br>**Practical Application**<br>The minister or bishop must be of "good reputation" (*kosmion*). It is a person who has good conduct, whose character and behavior stand as the ideal and pattern for others. |

| ENGLISH WORD | GREEK WORD AND VERSE | THE WORD MEANS... |
|---|---|---|
| | pitable, able to teach; [NKJV]<br>For an elder must be a man whose life cannot be spoken against. He must be faithful to his wife. He must exhibit self-control, live wisely, and have a **good reputation**. He must enjoy having guests in his home and must be able to teach. [NLT]<br>δεῖ οὖν τὸν ἐπίσκοπον ἀνεπίλημπτον εἶναι, μιᾶς γυναικὸς ἄνδρα, νηφάλιον, σώφρονα, **κόσμιον**, φιλόξενον, διδακτικόν· [GNS]<br>δεῖ οὖν τὸν ἐπίσκοπον ἀνεπίλημπτον εἶναι, μιᾶς γυναικὸς ἄνδρα, νηφάλιον σώφρονα **κόσμιον** φιλόξενον διδακτικόν, [GNT] | |
| **#1760**<br>**Good Repute**<br><br>Good report–KJV<br>**Good repute–NASB**<br>Admirable–NIV<br>Good report–NKJV<br>Admirable–NLT<br><br>**POSB<br>REFERENCE**<br>(Philip.4:8-9; esp. v.8)<br>Note 2, point 1f | εὔφημα = *euphēma*<br>Pronunciation: [yoo'-fay-mah]<br>Parsing (part of speech): adjective<br>    Case—nominative<br>    Gender—neuter<br>    Number—plural<br>    Stem or root—from εὔφημος, ον<br>Concordance References:<br>⇒ Strong's #2163 *euphēmos*<br>⇒ NIV #2368 *euphēmos*<br>⇒ NASB #2163 *euphēmos*<br><br>**Philip. 4:8**<br>Finally, brethren, whatsoever things are true, whatsoever things *are* honest, whatsoever things *are* just, whatsoever things *are* pure, whatsoever things *are* lovely, whatsoever things *are* of **good report**; if *there be* any virtue, and if *there be* any praise, think on these things. [KJV]<br>Finally, brethren, whatever is true, whatever is honorable, whatever is right, whatever is pure, whatever is lovely, whatever is of **good repute**, if there is any excellence and if anything worthy of praise, let your mind dwell on these things. [NASB]<br>Finally, brothers, whatever is true, whatever is noble, whatever is right, whatever is pure, whatever is lovely, whatever is **admirable**—if anything is excellent or praiseworthy—think about such things. [NIV]<br>Finally, brethren, whatever things are true, whatever things *are* noble, whatever things *are* just, whatever things *are* pure, whatever things *are* lovely, whatever things *are* of **good report**, if *there is* any virtue and if *there is* anything praiseworthy—meditate on these things. [NKJV]<br>And now, dear brothers and sisters, let me say one more thing as I close this letter. Fix your thoughts on what is true and honorable and right. Think about things that are pure and lovely and **admirable**. Think about things that are excellent and worthy of praise. [NLT]<br>Τὸ λοιπόν, ἀδελφοί, ὅσα ἐστὶν ἀληθῆ, ὅσα σεμνά, ὅσα δίκαια, ὅσα ἁγνά, ὅσα προσφιλῆ, ὅσα **εὔφημα**, εἴ τις ἀρετὴ καὶ εἴ τις ἔπαινος, ταῦτα λογίζεσθε·[GNS]<br>Τὸ λοιπόν, ἀδελφοί, ὅσα ἐστὶν ἀληθῆ, ὅσα σεμνά, ὅσα δίκαια, ὅσα ἁγνά, ὅσα προσφιλῆ, ὅσα **εὔφημα**, εἴ τις ἀρετὴ καὶ εἴ τις ἔπαινος, ταῦτα λογίζεσθε· [GNT] | Admirable; of good repute; of good report. It means worthy of praise, reputable, high-toned, things of the highest quality.<br><br>**Practical Application**<br>The believer is to think only upon worthy things. He is not to listen to *bad reports*, no matter how juicy they may seem. Neither is he to fill his mind with junk, whether through rumor, radio, television, music, off-colored jokes, or by whatever source. His thoughts are to be focused only upon worthy things—only upon that which is admirable. |
| **#1761**<br>**Good Works**<br><br>**Good works–KJV**<br>Deeds of kindness–<br>  NASB<br>Doing good–NIV<br>**Good works–NKJV**<br>Doing kind things–<br>  NLT | ἔργων ἀγαθῶν = *ergōn agathōn*<br>Pronunciation: [er'-gon ag-ath-on']<br>Parsing *ergōn* (part of speech): noun<br>    Case—genitive<br>    Gender—neuter<br>    Number—plural<br>    Stem or root—from ἔργον, ου<br>Parsing *agathōn* (part of speech): adjective<br>    Case—genitive<br>    Gender—neuter<br>    Number—plural<br>    Stem or root—from ἀγαθός, ή, όν<br>Concordance References:<br>⇒ Strong's #2041 *ergon* + 18 *agathos* | Work, deed, action; task, occupation, undertaking; practical expression; handiwork, workmanship (1 Cor 9.1); perhaps effect, result or product (Jas 1.4). It is a general term meaning all kinds of good works, serving and doing all kinds of good to all who needed help.<br><br>**Practical Application**<br>Two names are given for her: "Tabitha," which was her Jewish or Hebrew name, and "Dorcas," which was her Greek name. Her name means gazelle (or doe or deer) which is a most beautiful creature. The gazelle is known for... |

# PRACTICAL WORD STUDIES
## in the NEW TESTAMENT

| ENGLISH WORD | GREEK WORD AND VERSE | THE WORD MEANS... |
|---|---|---|
| **POSB REFERENCE** (Acts 9:36-39; esp. v.36) Note 2, point 1b | ⇒ NIV #2240 ergon [doing] + 19 agathos [good]<br>⇒ NASB #2041 ergon + 18 agathos<br><br>**Acts 9:36**<br>Now there was at Joppa a certain disciple named Tabitha, which by interpretation is called Dorcas: this woman was full of **good works** and almsdeeds which she did. [KJV]<br>Now in Joppa there was a certain disciple named Tabitha (which translated in Greek is called Dorcas); this woman was abounding with **deeds of kindness** and charity, which she continually did. [NASB]<br>In Joppa there was a disciple named Tabitha (which, when translated, is Dorcas), who was always **doing good** and helping the poor. [NIV]<br>At Joppa there was a certain disciple named Tabitha, which is translated Dorcas. This woman was full of **good works** and charitable deeds which she did. [NKJV]<br>There was a believer in Joppa named Tabitha (which in Greek is Dorcas). She was always **doing kind things** for others and helping the poor. [NLT]<br>Ἐν Ἰόππῃ δέ τις ἦν μαθήτρια ὀνόματι Ταβιθά, ἣ διερμηνευομένη λέγεται Δορκάς· αὕτη ἦν πλήρης **ἀγαθῶν ἔργων** καὶ ἐλεημοσυνῶν ὧν ἐποίει. [GNS]<br>Ἐν Ἰόππῃ δέ τις ἦν μαθήτρια ὀνόματι Ταβιθά, ἣ διερμηνευομένη λέγεται Δορκάς· αὕτη ἦν πλήρης **ἔργων ἀγαθῶν** καὶ ἐλεημοσυνῶν ὧν ἐποίει. [GNT] | • its slender features.<br>• its grace and loveliness.<br>• its bright eyes and tender looks.<br><br>The same traits were apparently characteristic of Dorcas. Note: Scripture does say the wife is to be as the loving hind and the pleasant doe to her husband (Proverbs 5:19). She is to be as the beautiful creature: gracious and loving, bright eyed (joyful, excited, expectant) and tender.<br>She was deeply committed to Christ, a very faithful and devoted disciple, full of...<br>• "good works" (*ergōn agathōn*)<br>• "charitable deeds": charitable gifts. She gave gifts to the needy. |
| **#1762 Goodness**<br><br>Goodness–KJV<br>Kindness–NASB<br>Kindness–NIV<br>Goodness–NKJV<br>Kind–NLT<br><br>**POSB REFERENCE** (Romans 2:2-5; esp. v.4) Note 2, point 2 | χρηστὸν = *chrēston*<br>Pronunciation: [khrase-ton']<br>Parsing (part of speech): pronominal adjective<br>   Case—nominative<br>   Gender—neuter<br>   Number—singular<br>   Stem or root—from χρηστός, ή, όν<br>Concordance References:<br>⇒ Strong's #5543 chrēstos<br>⇒ NIV #5982 chrēstos<br>⇒ NASB #5543 chrēstos<br><br>**Romans 2:4**<br>Or despisest thou the riches of his **goodness** and forbearance and longsuffering; not knowing that the goodness of God leadeth thee to repentance? [KJV]<br>Or do you think lightly of the riches of His **kindness** and forbearance and patience, not knowing that the kindness of God leads you to repentance? [NASB]<br>Or do you show contempt for the riches of his **kindness**, tolerance and patience, not realizing that God's kindness leads you toward repentance? [NIV]<br>Or do you despise the riches of His **goodness**, forbearance, and longsuffering, not knowing that the **goodness** of God leads you to repentance? [NKJV]<br>Don't you realize how **kind**, tolerant, and patient God is with you? Or don't you care? Can't you see how kind he has been in giving you time to turn from your sin? [NLT]<br>ἢ τοῦ πλούτου τῆς χρηστότητος αὐτοῦ καὶ τῆς ἀνοχῆς καὶ τῆς μακροθυμίας καταφρονεῖς, ἀγνοῶν ὅτι τὸ **χρηστὸν** τοῦ θεοῦ εἰς μετάνοιάν σε ἄγει; [GNS]<br>ἢ τοῦ πλούτου τῆς χρηστότητος αὐτοῦ καὶ τῆς ἀνοχῆς καὶ τῆς μακροθυμίας καταφρονεῖς, ἀγνοῶν ὅτι τὸ **χρηστὸν** τοῦ θεοῦ εἰς μετάνοιάν σε ἄγει; [GNT] | Kindness, goodness, mercy.<br><br>**Practical Application**<br>The moralist thinks God is too good to punish. When he thinks of God, he thinks of the riches...<br>• of God's goodness (*chrēston*): His kindness and grace and love.<br>• of God's forbearance (*anochē*): His refraining, holding back, abstaining and controlling His justice.<br>• of God's long suffering: His suffering a long time, being patient and slow in judging sin.<br>God, of course, is all this and much more. What the moralist fails to see is that God's goodness is not a blank check for sin. God's goodness does not...<br>• give license to sin.<br>• condone sin.<br>• indulge sin.<br>• overlook sin.<br>God's goodness is to lead men to repentance, not to sin. The fact that God *will* forgive sin should stir men to seek forgiveness and to please God. If a man sins thinking that God will just overlook and forgive his sin, he is despising God's goodness. He is taking God's goodness and making it a sham, a mockery, a joke, a thing of indulgence. The man who *despises* God's goodness–who sins thinking God will just overlook and forgive his sin–is wrong. He is mistaken. God does not just overlook and forgive his sin; He does not condone, indulge, nor give license to his sin. God will judge him and the judgment will be according to the truth. |
| **#1763 Goodness** | ἀγαθωσύνη = *agathōsunē*<br>Pronunciation: [ag-ath-o-soo'-nay]<br>Parsing (part of speech): noun<br>   Case—nominative<br>   Gender—feminine | Goodness, generosity. It is being full of virtue and excellence, kindness and helpfulness, peace and consideration. It means that a person is full of all good and he does all good. It means...<br>• that he has a good heart and good behavior. |

# PRACTICAL WORD STUDIES
## in the NEW TESTAMENT

| ENGLISH WORD | GREEK WORD AND VERSE | THE WORD MEANS... |
|---|---|---|
| Goodness—KJV<br>Goodness—NASB<br>Goodness—NIV<br>Goodness—NKJV<br>Goodness—NLT<br><br>**POSB REFERENCE**<br>(Gal.5:22-23; esp. v.22)<br>Note 1 | Number—singular<br>Stem or root—from ἀγαθωσύνη, ης<br>Concordance References:<br>⇒ Strong's #19 agathōsunē<br>⇒ NIV #20 agathōsunē<br>⇒ NASB #19 agathōsunē<br><br>**Galatians 5:22**<br>But the fruit of the Spirit is love, joy, peace, longsuffering, gentleness, **goodness**, faith, [KJV]<br>But the fruit of the Spirit is love, joy, peace, patience, kindness, **goodness**, faithfulness, [NASB]<br>But the fruit of the Spirit is love, joy, peace, patience, kindness, **goodness**, faithfulness, [NIV]<br>But the fruit of the Spirit is love, joy, peace, longsuffering, kindness, **goodness**, faithfulness, [NKJV]<br>But when the Holy Spirit controls our lives, he will produce this kind of fruit in us: love, joy, peace, patience, kindness, **goodness**, faithfulness, [NLT]<br>ὁ δὲ καρπὸς τοῦ Πνεύματός ἐστιν ἀγάπη, χαρά, εἰρήνη, μακροθυμία, χρηστότης, **ἀγαθωσύνη**, πίστις, [GNS]<br>Ὁ δὲ καρπὸς τοῦ πνεύματός ἐστιν ἀγάπη χαρά εἰρήνη, μακροθυμία, χρηστότης **ἀγαθωσύνη**, πίστις [GNT] | • that he is good and does good.<br>• that he is a quality person.<br><br>**Practical Application**<br>Note that a good person lives and treats everyone just as they should be treated. He does not take advantage of any person nor does he stand by and let others take advantage. He stands up and lives for what is right and good and just. This means that goodness involves discipline and rebuke, correction and instruction as well as love and care, peace and conciliation. A good person will not give license to evil, will not let evil run rampant. He will not allow evil to indulge itself and treat others unjustly. He will not allow others to suffer evil. Goodness steps forward to do what it can to stop and control evil. |
| **#1764**<br>**Goodness**<br><br>Praises—KJV<br>Excellencies—NASB<br>Praises—NIV<br>Praises—NKJV<br>Goodness—NLT<br><br>**POSB REFERENCE**<br>(1 Pt.2:9)<br>Note 2 | ἀρετάς = aretas<br>Pronunciation: [ar-et-ahs']<br>Parsing (part of speech): noun<br>    Case—accusative<br>    Gender—feminine<br>    Number—plural<br>Stem or root—from ἀρετή, ῆς<br>Concordance References:<br>⇒ Strong's #703 aretē<br>⇒ NIV #746 aretē<br>⇒ NASB #703 aretē<br><br>**1 Peter 2:9**<br>But ye are a chosen generation, a royal priesthood, an holy nation, a peculiar people; that ye should shew forth the **praises** of him who hath called you out of darkness into his marvellous light: [KJV]<br>But you are a chosen race, a royal priesthood, a HOLY NATION, a people for God's own possession, that you may proclaim the **excellencies** of Him who has called you out of darkness into His marvelous light; [NASB]<br>But you are a chosen people, a royal priesthood, a holy nation, a people belonging to God, that you may declare the **praises** of him who called you out of darkness into his wonderful light. [NIV]<br>But you *are* a chosen generation, a royal priesthood, a holy nation, His own special people, that you may proclaim the **praises** of Him who called you out of darkness into His marvelous light; [NKJV]<br>But you are not like that, for you are a chosen people. You are a kingdom of priests, God's holy nation, his very own possession. This is so you can show others the **goodness** of God, for he called you out of the darkness into his wonderful light. [NLT]<br>ὑμεῖς δὲ γένος ἐκλεκτόν, βασίλειον ἱεράτευμα, ἔθνος ἅγιον, λαὸς εἰς περιποίησιν, ὅπως τὰς **ἀρετὰς** ἐξαγγείλητε τοῦ ἐκ σκότους ὑμᾶς καλέσαντος εἰς τὸ θαυμαστὸν αὐτοῦ φῶς· [GNS]<br>Ὑμεῖς δὲ γένος ἐκλεκτόν, βασίλειον ἱεράτευμα, ἔθνος ἅγιον, λαὸς εἰς περιποίησιν, ὅπως τὰς **ἀρετὰς** ἐξαγγείλητε τοῦ ἐκ σκότους ὑμᾶς καλέσαντος εἰς τὸ θαυμαστὸν αὐτοῦ φῶς· [GNT] | Goodness, praises. The word "goodness" (*aretas*) means virtues, excellencies, and the supreme and eminent qualities of God (Alan Stibbs. *The First Epistle General of Peter*. "The Tyndale New Testament Commentaries," p.104).<br><br>**Practical Application**<br>The very task of the believer is to witness for God, to share the glorious message of God. What is that message? Note the verse: "the goodness of God, for he called you out of the darkness into his wonderful light." The message that we are to share is the glorious message of salvation. God will deliver man out of darkness into the light. This is what He has done for believers. Therefore, we are to proclaim the glorious truth that God has saved us through the Light of the world, through Jesus Christ Himself. He has saved us out of the darkness of sin and death to deliver us into the light of eternity. We shall live forever. We are to praise God, proclaiming the glorious message of His wonderful light or salvation. |
| **#1765**<br>**Goodness** | ἀρετήν = aretēn<br>Pronunciation: [ar-et-ayn']<br>Parsing (part of speech): noun<br>    Case—accusative<br>    Gender—feminine | Goodness, virtue; moral excellence and goodness of character; moral strength and moral courage. |

# PRACTICAL WORD STUDIES
## in the NEW TESTAMENT

| ENGLISH WORD | GREEK WORD AND VERSE | THE WORD MEANS... |
|---|---|---|
| Virtue–KJV<br>Moral excellence–NASB<br>**Goodness–NIV**<br>Virtue–NKJV<br>Moral excellence–NLT<br><br>**POSB REFERENCE**<br>(2 Pt.1:5-7; esp. v.5)<br>Note 1, point 1 | Number—singular<br>Stem or root—from ἀρετή, ῆς<br>Concordance References:<br>⇒ Strong's #703 aretë<br>⇒ NIV #746 aretë<br>⇒ NASB #703 aretë<br><br>**2 Peter 1:5**<br>And beside this, giving all diligence, add to your faith **virtue**; and to virtue knowledge; [KJV]<br>Now for this very reason also, applying all diligence, in your faith supply **moral excellence**, and in your moral excellence, knowledge; [NASB]<br>For this very reason, make every effort to add to your faith **goodness**; and to goodness, knowledge; [NIV]<br>But also for this very reason, giving all diligence, add to your faith **virtue**, to virtue knowledge, [NKJV]<br>So make every effort to apply the benefits of these promises to your life. Then your faith will produce a life of **moral excellence**. A life of moral excellence leads to knowing God better. [NLT]<br>καὶ αὐτὸ τοῦτο δὲ σπουδὴν πᾶσαν παρεισενέγκαντες, ἐπιχορηγήσατε ἐν τῇ πίστει ὑμῶν τὴν **ἀρετήν**, ἐν δὲ τῇ ἀρετῇ τὴν γνῶσιν, [GNS]<br>καὶ αὐτὸ τοῦτο δὲ σπουδὴν πᾶσαν παρεισενέγκαντες ἐπιχορηγήσατε ἐν τῇ πίστει ὑμῶν τὴν **ἀρετήν**, ἐν δὲ τῇ ἀρετῇ τὴν γνῶσιν, [GNT] | **Practical Application**<br>It means manliness; being an excellent person in life, a real man or a real woman in life; living life just like one should, in the most excellent way. It means always choosing the excellent way. |
| #1766<br>**Gospel**<br><br>Gospel–KJV<br>Gospel–NASB<br>Good news–NIV<br>Gospel–NKJV<br>"Good news"–NLT<br><br>**POSB REFERENCE**<br>(Mt.4:23)<br>Note 2<br><br>See also POSB REF:<br>(1 Cor.15:1-11; esp. v.1)<br>*Deeper Study #1* | εὐαγγέλιον = euaggelion<br>Pronunciation: [yoo-ang-ghel'-ee-on]<br>Parsing (part of speech): noun<br>    Case—accusative<br>    Gender—neuter<br>    Number—singular<br>    Stem or root—from εὐαγγέλιον, ου<br>Concordance References:<br>⇒ Strong's #2098 euaggelion<br>⇒ NIV #2295 euaggelion<br>⇒ NASB #2098 euaggelion<br><br>**Matthew 4:23**<br>And Jesus went about all Galilee, teaching in their synagogues, and preaching the **gospel** of the kingdom, and healing all manner of sickness and all manner of disease among the people. [KJV]<br>And Jesus was going about in all Galilee, teaching in their synagogues, and proclaiming the **gospel** of the kingdom, and healing every kind of disease and every kind of sickness among the people. [NASB]<br>Jesus went throughout Galilee, teaching in their synagogues, preaching the **good news** of the kingdom, and healing every disease and sickness among the people. [NIV]<br>And Jesus went about all Galilee, teaching in their synagogues, preaching the **gospel** of the kingdom, and healing all kinds of sickness and all kinds of disease among the people. [NKJV]<br>Jesus traveled throughout Galilee teaching in the synagogues, preaching everywhere the **Good News** about the Kingdom. And he healed people who had every kind of sickness and disease. [NLT]<br>Καὶ περιῆγεν ὅλην τῇ Γαλιλαίᾳ ὁ Ἰησοῦς, διδάσκων ἐν ταῖς συναγωγαῖς αὐτῶν, καὶ κηρύσσων τὸ **εὐαγγέλιον** τῆς βασιλείας, καὶ θεραπεύων πᾶσαν νόσον καὶ πᾶσαν μαλακίαν ἐν τῷ λαῷ. [GNS]<br>Καὶ περιῆγεν ἐν ὅλῃ τῇ Γαλιλαίᾳ διδάσκων ἐν ταῖς συναγωγαῖς αὐτῶν καὶ κηρύσσων τὸ **εὐαγγέλιον** τῆς βασιλείας καὶ θεραπεύων πᾶσαν νόσον καὶ πᾶσαν μαλακίαν ἐν τῷ λαῷ. [GNT] | Gospel or Good News.<br><br>**Practical Application**<br>Throughout Scripture there is only one gospel, but it is described in different ways. It is called...<br>• the "gospel of the kingdom of God" (Mt.4:23; Mark 1:14).<br>• the "gospel of the Grace of God" (Acts 20:24).<br>• the "gospel of God" (Ro.1:1).<br>• the "gospel of Christ" (Mark 1:1; Ro.1:16; 2 Cor. 4:4; 2 Cor. 10:14).<br>• the "glorious gospel" (2 Cor. 4:4; 1 Tim. 1:11).<br>• the "Everlasting gospel" (Rev. 14:6). |

# PRACTICAL WORD STUDIES
## in the NEW TESTAMENT

| ENGLISH WORD | GREEK WORD AND VERSE | THE WORD MEANS... |
|---|---|---|
| **#1767**<br>**Gossip**<br><br>Whisperings–KJV<br>**Gossip**–NASB<br>**Gossip**–NIV<br>Whisperings–NKJV<br>**Gossip**–NLT<br><br>**POSB REFERENCE**<br>(2 Cor.12:19-21; esp. v.20)<br>Note 3, point 2 | ψιθυρισμοί = *psithurismoi*<br>Pronunciation: [psith-oo-ris-moy']<br>Parsing (part of speech): noun<br>    Case—nominative<br>    Gender—masculine<br>    Number—plural<br>    Stem or root—from ψιθυρισμός, οῦ<br>Concordance References:<br>  ⇒ Strong's #5587 psithurismos<br>  ⇒ NIV #6030 psithurismos<br>  ⇒ NASB #5587 psithurismos<br><br>**2 Cor. 12:20**<br>    For I fear, lest, when I come, I shall not find you such as I would, and that I shall be found unto you such as ye would not: lest there be debates, envyings, wraths, strifes, backbitings, **whisperings**, swellings, tumults: [KJV]<br>    For I am afraid that perhaps when I come I may find you to be not what I wish and may be found by you to be not what you wish; that perhaps there may be strife, jealousy, angry tempers, disputes, slanders, **gossip**, arrogance, disturbances; [NASB]<br>    For I am afraid that when I come I may not find you as I want you to be, and you may not find me as you want me to be. I fear that there may be quarreling, jealousy, outbursts of anger, factions, slander, **gossip**, arrogance and disorder. [NIV]<br>    For I fear lest, when I come, I shall not find you such as I wish, and *that* I shall be found by you such as you do not wish; lest *there be* contentions, jealousies, outbursts of wrath, selfish ambitions, backbitings, **whisperings**, conceits, tumults; [NKJV]<br>    For I am afraid that when I come to visit you I won't like what I find, and then you won't like my response. I am afraid that I will find quarreling, jealousy, outbursts of anger, selfishness, backstabbing, **gossip**, conceit, and disorderly behavior. [NLT]<br>    φοβοῦμαι γὰρ μή πως ἐλθὼν οὐχ οἵους θέλω εὕρω ὑμᾶς, κἀγὼ εὑρεθῶ ὑμῖν οἷον οὐ θέλετε· μή πως ἔρις, ζῆλοι, θυμοί, ἐριθεῖαι, καταλαλιαί, **ψιθυρισμοί**, φυσιώσεις, ἀκαταστασίαι· [GNS]<br>    φοβοῦμαι γὰρ μή πως ἐλθὼν οὐχ οἵους θέλω εὕρω ὑμᾶς κἀγὼ εὑρεθῶ ὑμῖν οἷον οὐ θέλετε· μή πως ἔρις, ζῆλος, θυμοί, ἐριθεῖαι, καταλαλιαί, **ψιθυρισμοί**, φυσιώσεις, ἀκαταστασίαι· [GNT] | Gossip, whisperings, behind-the-back talk, spicy rumor.<br><br>**Practical Application**<br>    Paul was stricken with fear, fear lest the church fail to be what it should be and reject him and his ministry. Paul feared that the church would fail to deal with the carnal critics and continue putting up with their evil attacks against him. He lists eight evils, including gossip (*psithurismoi*), that were and still are characteristic of divisive critics in the church. |
| **#1768**<br>**Gossip–**<br>**Gossips**<br><br>Whisperers–KJV<br>**Gossips**–NASB<br>**Gossips**–NIV<br>Whisperers–NKJV<br>**Gossip**–NLT<br><br>**POSB REFERENCE**<br>(Romans 1:29)<br>*Deeper Study* #11 | ψιθυριστάς = *psithuristas*<br>Pronunciation: [psith-u-ris-tahs']<br>Parsing (part of speech): noun<br>    Case—accusative<br>    Gender—masculine<br>    Number—plural<br>    Stem or root—from ψιθυριστής, οῦ<br>Concordance References:<br>  ⇒ Strong's #5588 psithuristēs<br>  ⇒ NIV #6031 psithuristēs<br>  ⇒ NASB #5588 psithuristēs<br><br>**Romans 1:29**<br>    Being filled with all unrighteousness, fornication, wickedness, covetousness, maliciousness; full of envy, murder, debate, deceit, malignity; **whisperers**, [KJV]<br>    Being filled with all unrighteousness, wickedness, greed, evil; full of envy, murder, strife, deceit, malice; they are **gossips**, [NASB]<br>    They have become filled with every kind of wickedness, evil, greed and depravity. They are full of envy, murder, strife, deceit and malice. They are **gossips**, [NIV]<br>    Being filled with all unrighteousness, sexual immorality, wickedness, covetousness, maliciousness; full of envy, murder, strife, deceit, evil-mindedness; *they are* **whisperers**, [NKJV] | Gossips, whisperers, slanderers, backbiters, murmurers, tale bearers.<br><br>**Practical Application**<br>It is a person...<br>• who gossips behind another person's back, chewing and tearing him up.<br>• who passes on tales about others, whether true or not.<br>• who destroys the reputation of others. |

# PRACTICAL WORD STUDIES
## in the NEW TESTAMENT

| ENGLISH WORD | GREEK WORD AND VERSE | THE WORD MEANS... |
|---|---|---|
| | Their lives became full of every kind of wickedness, sin, greed, hate, envy, murder, fighting, deception, malicious behavior, and **gossip**. [NLT]<br><br>πεπληρωμένους πάσῃ ἀδικίᾳ πορνείᾳ, πονηρίᾳ πλεονεξίᾳ κακίᾳ· μεστοὺς φθόνου, φόνου, ἔριδος, δόλου, κακοηθείας· [GNS]<br><br>**ψιθυριστάς,** καταλάλους, θεοστυγεῖς, ὑβριστάς, ὑπερηφάνους, ἀλαζόνας, ἐφευρετὰς κακῶν, γονεῦσιν ἀπειθεῖς, [GNS]<br><br>πεπληρωμένους πάσῃ ἀδικίᾳ πονηρίᾳ πλεονεξίᾳ κακίᾳ, μεστοὺς φθόνου φόνου ἔριδος δόλου κακοηθείας, **ψιθυριστάς** [GNT]<br><br>καταλάλους θεοστυγεῖς ὑβριστὰς ὑπερηφάνους ἀλαζόνας, ἐφευρετὰς κακῶν, γονεῦσιν ἀπειθεῖς, [GNT] | |
| **#1769**<br>**Government Official**<br><br>Nobleman–KJV<br>Royal official–NASB<br>Royal official–NIV<br>Nobleman–NKJV<br>**Government official–NLT**<br><br>**POSB REFERENCE**<br>(Jn.4:46-47; esp. v.46)<br>Note 1 | βασιλικός = *basilikos*<br>Pronunciation: [bas-il-ee-kos']<br>Parsing (part of speech): pronominal adjective<br>    Case—nominative<br>    Gender—masculine<br>    Number—singular<br>    Stem or root—from βασιλικός, ή, όν<br>Concordance References:<br>⇒ Strong's #937 basilikos<br>⇒ NIV #997 basilikos<br>⇒ NASB #937 basilikos<br><br>**John 4:46**<br>So Jesus came again into Cana of Galilee, where he made the water wine. And there was a certain **nobleman**, whose son was sick at Capernaum. [KJV]<br><br>He came therefore again to Cana of Galilee where He had made the water wine. And there was a certain **royal official**, whose son was sick at Capernaum. [NASB]<br><br>Once more he visited Cana in Galilee, where he had turned the water into wine. And there was a certain **royal official** whose son lay sick at Capernaum. [NIV]<br><br>So Jesus came again to Cana of Galilee where He had made the water wine. And there was a certain **nobleman** whose son was sick at Capernaum. [NKJV]<br><br>In the course of his journey through Galilee, he arrived at the town of Cana, where he had turned the water into wine. There was a **government official** in the city of Capernaum whose son was very sick. [NLT]<br><br>Ἦλθεν οὖν ὁ Ἰησοῦς πάλιν εἰς τὴν Κανὰ τῆς Γαλιλαίας, ὅπου ἐποίησε τὸ ὕδωρ οἶνον. καὶ ἦν τις **βασιλικός,** οὗ ὁ υἱὸς ἠσθένει ἐν Καπερναούμ· [GNS]<br><br>Ἦλθεν οὖν πάλιν εἰς τὴν Κανὰ τῆς Γαλιλαίας, ὅπου ἐποίησεν τὸ ὕδωρ οἶνον. καὶ ἦν τις **βασιλικός** οὗ ὁ υἱὸς ἠσθένει ἐν Καφαρναούμ. [GNT] | A royal official; a nobleman; a government official; a secular leader. This man was an official of the King's royal court.<br><br>**Practical Application**<br>Needs confront every human being. Eventually the severe needs arising from accident, illness, disease, suffering, and death strike everyone. No one is exempt. One may be an official in government or even the King himself–it does not matter. The day eventually comes when every person needs help. The severe disasters of life are beyond any person's control. |
| **#1770**<br>**Governments**<br><br>**Governments–KJV**<br>Administrations–NASB<br>Those with gifts of administration–NIV<br>Administrations–NKJV<br>Those who can get others to work together–NLT<br><br>**POSB REFERENCE**<br>(1 Cor.12:27-30; esp. v.28)<br>Note 5, point 1g | κυβερνήσεις = *kubernēseis*<br>Pronunciation: [koo-ber'-nay-sees]<br>Parsing (part of speech): noun<br>    Case—accusative<br>    Gender—feminine<br>    Number—plural<br>    Stem or root—from κυβέρνησις, εως<br>Concordance References:<br>⇒ Strong's #2941 kubernēsis<br>⇒ NIV #3236 kubernēsis<br>⇒ NASB #2941 kubernēsis<br><br>**1 Cor. 12:28**<br>And God hath set some in the church, first apostles, secondarily prophets, thirdly teachers, after that miracles, then gifts of healings, helps, **governments**, diversities of tongues. [KJV]<br><br>And God has appointed in the church, first apostles, second prophets, third teachers, then miracles, then gifts of healings, helps, **administrations**, various kinds of tongues. [NASB]<br><br>And in the church God has appointed first of all apos- | Those with gifts of administration; those who can get others to work together; a God-given ability to lead.<br><br>**Practical Application**<br>The Greek word is descriptive (*kubernēseis*). It refers to the pilot of a ship, the person who steers the ship through the dangerous channels of the oceans. The church, of course, needs such persons who can give it direction as it moves along on its journey to reach the destination God has appointed for it. |

## PRACTICAL WORD STUDIES in the NEW TESTAMENT

| ENGLISH WORD | GREEK WORD AND VERSE | THE WORD MEANS... |
|---|---|---|
| | tles, second prophets, third teachers, then workers of miracles, also those having gifts of healing, those able to help others, **those with gifts of administration**, and those speaking in different kinds of tongues. [NIV]<br><br>And God has appointed these in the church: first apostles, second prophets, third teachers, after that miracles, then gifts of healings, helps, **administrations**, varieties of tongues. [NKJV]<br><br>Here is a list of some of the members that God has placed in the body of Christ: first are apostles, second are prophets, third are teachers, then those who do miracles, those who have the gift of healing, those who can help others, **those who can get others to work together**, those who speak in unknown languages. [NLT]<br><br>καὶ οὓς μὲν ἔθετο ὁ Θεὸς ἐν τῇ ἐκκλησίᾳ πρῶτον ἀποστόλους, δεύτερον προφήτας, τρίτον διδασκάλους, ἔπειτα δυνάμεις, εἶτα χαρίσματα ἰαμάτων, ἀντιλήψεις, **κυβερνήσεις**, γένη γλωσσῶν. [GNS]<br><br>καὶ οὓς μὲν ἔθετο ὁ Θεὸς ἐν τῇ ἐκκλησίᾳ πρῶτον ἀποστόλους, δεύτερον προφήτας, τρίτον διδασκάλους, ἔπειτα δυνάμεις, ἔπειτα χαρίσματα ἰαμάτων, ἀντιλήμψεις, **κυβερνήσεις**, γένη γλωσσῶν. [GNT] | |
| **#1771**<br>**Governor**<br><br>Deputy–KJV<br>Proconsul–NASB<br>Proconsul–NIV<br>Proconsul–NKJV<br>**Governor–NLT**<br><br>**POSB REFERENCE**<br>(Acts 13:7)<br>Note 3 | ἀνθυπάτῳ = *anthupatō*<br>Pronunciation: [an-thoo'-pah-tow]<br>Parsing (part of speech): noun<br>    Case—dative<br>    Gender—masculine<br>    Number—singular<br>    Stem or root—from ἀνθύπατος, ου<br>Concordance References:<br>  ⇒ Strong's #446 anthupatos<br>  ⇒ NIV #478 anthupatos<br>  ⇒ NASB #446 anthupatos<br><br>**Acts 13:7**<br>Which was with the **deputy** of the country, Sergius Paulus, a prudent man; who called for Barnabas and Saul, and desired to hear the word of God. [KJV]<br><br>Who was with the **proconsul**, Sergius Paulus, a man of intelligence. This man summoned Barnabas and Saul and sought to hear the word of God. [NASB]<br><br>Who was an attendant of the proconsul, Sergius Paulus. The **proconsul**, an intelligent man, sent for Barnabas and Saul because he wanted to hear the word of God. [NIV]<br><br>Who was with the **proconsul**, Sergius Paulus, an intelligent man. This man called for Barnabas and Saul and sought to hear the word of God. [NKJV]<br><br>He had attached himself to the **governor**, Sergius Paulus, a man of considerable insight and understanding. The governor invited Barnabas and Saul to visit him, for he wanted to hear the word of God. [NLT]<br><br>ὃς ἦν σὺν τῷ **ἀνθυπάτῳ** Σεργίῳ Παύλῳ, ἀνδρὶ συνετῷ. οὗτος προσκαλεσάμενος Βαρναβᾶν καὶ Σαῦλον, ἐπεζήτησεν ἀκοῦσαι τὸν λόγον τοῦ Θεοῦ. [GNS]<br><br>ὃς ἦν σὺν τῷ **ἀνθυπάτῳ** Σεργίῳ Παύλῳ, ἀνδρὶ συνετῷ. οὗτος προσκαλεσάμενος Βαρναβᾶν καὶ Σαῦλον ἐπεζήτησεν ἀκοῦσαι τὸν λόγον τοῦ θεοῦ· [GNT] | Proconsul, deputy, governor.<br><br>**Practical Application**<br>The Roman governor was appointed and controlled by the Roman Senate. He was the highest ranking official, the man of power and influence on the island. |
| **#1772**<br>**Grace**<br><br>Grace–KJV<br>Grace–NASB<br>Grace–NIV<br>Grace–NKJV<br>Highest privilege–NLT | χάριν = *charin*<br>Pronunciation: [khar'-in]<br>Parsing (part of speech): noun<br>    Case—accusative<br>    Gender—feminine<br>    Number—singular<br>    Stem or root—from χάρις, ιτος<br>Concordance References:<br>  ⇒ Strong's #5485 charis<br>  ⇒ NIV #5921 charis<br>  ⇒ NASB #5485 charis | Grace, highest privilege. It means a gift or a favor, an unmerited and undeserved gift or favor (see POSB notes, Grace–Romans 4:16; POSB *Deeper Study* #1–Titus 2:11-15 for more discussion.)<br><br>**Practical Application**<br>In the present passage, grace is looked upon as a place or a position. Grace is a place to which we are brought, a position into which we are placed. It is the place of God's presence, the position of salvation. The person who is justified... |

# PRACTICAL WORD STUDIES
## in the NEW TESTAMENT

| ENGLISH WORD | GREEK WORD AND VERSE | THE WORD MEANS... |
|---|---|---|
| **POSB REFERENCE** (Romans 5:2) Note 3, point 1 | **Romans 5:2** By whom also we have access by faith into this **grace** wherein we stand, and rejoice in hope of the glory of God. [KJV] Through whom also we have obtained our introduction by faith into this **grace** in which we stand; and we exult in hope of the glory of God. [NASB] Through whom we have gained access by faith into this **grace** in which we now stand. And we rejoice in the hope of the glory of God. [NIV] Through whom also we have access by faith into this **grace** in which we stand, and rejoice in the hope of the glory of God. [NKJV] Because of our faith, Christ has brought us into this place of **highest privilege** where we now stand, and we confidently and joyfully look forward to sharing God's glory. [NLT] δι' οὗ καὶ τὴν προσαγωγὴν ἐσχήκαμεν τῇ πίστει εἰς τὴν **χάριν** ταύτην ἐν ᾗ ἑστήκαμεν, καὶ καυχώμεθα ἐπ' ἐλπίδι τῆς δόξης τοῦ θεοῦ. [GNS] δι' οὗ καὶ τὴν προσαγωγὴν ἐσχήκαμεν [τῇ πίστει] εἰς τὴν **χάριν** ταύτην ἐν ᾗ ἑστήκαμεν καὶ καυχώμεθα ἐπ' ἐλπίδι τῆς δόξης τοῦ θεοῦ. [GNT] | • stands in God's presence. <br>• stands before God saved. <br>• stands in the favor of God. <br>• stands in the privileges of God. <br>• stands in the promises of God. |
| **#1773 Grace** <br><br>Grace–KJV <br>Grace–NASB <br>Grace–NIV <br>Grace–NKJV <br>Generous gifts–NLT <br><br>**POSB REFERENCE** (1 Cor.1:4) *Deeper Study #1* | χάριτι = *chariti* <br>Pronunciation: [khar'-ee-tee] <br>Parsing (part of speech): noun <br>   Case—dative <br>   Gender—feminine <br>   Number—singular <br>   Stem or root—from χάρις, ιτος <br>Concordance References: <br>  ⇒ Strong's #5485 charis <br>  ⇒ NIV #5921 charis <br>  ⇒ NASB #5485 charis <br><br>**1 Cor. 1:4** <br>I thank my God always on your behalf, for the **grace** of God which is given you by Jesus Christ; [KJV] <br>I thank my God always concerning you, for the **grace** of God which was given you in Christ Jesus, [NASB] <br>I always thank God for you because of his **grace** given you in Christ Jesus. [NIV] <br>I thank my God always concerning you for the **grace** of God which was given to you by Christ Jesus, [NKJV] <br>I can never stop thanking God for all the **generous gifts** he has given you, now that you belong to Christ Jesus. [NLT] <br>Εὐχαριστῶ τῷ Θεῷ μου πάντοτε περὶ ὑμῶν, ἐπὶ τῇ **χάριτι** τοῦ Θεοῦ τῇ δοθείσῃ ὑμῖν ἐν Χριστῷ Ἰησοῦ· [GNS] <br>Εὐχαριστῶ τῷ θεῷ μου πάντοτε περὶ ὑμῶν ἐπὶ τῇ **χάριτι** τοῦ θεοῦ τῇ δοθείσῃ ὑμῖν ἐν Χριστῷ Ἰησοῦ, [GNT] | The favor and blessings of God; the undeserved and unmerited favor and blessings of God; the depth and richness of the heart and mind of God; the kindness and love that dwells within the very nature of God. God's grace covers all of life. <br><br>**Practical Application** <br>1. Grace means the kindness and love that God freely gives to those who have acted against Him. It is the favor of God showered upon men who do not deserve His favor, men who are... <br>  • "helpless" (Romans 5:6). <br>  • "sinners" (Romans 5:6, 8). <br>  • "enemies" (Romans 5:10). <br>No other word so expresses the depth and richness of the heart and mind of God. This is the distinctive difference between God's grace and man's grace. Whereas man sometimes does favors for his friends and thereby can be said to be gracious, God has done a thing unheard of among men: He has given His very own Son to die for His enemies (see POSB outline—Romans 5:6-11 and notes—Romans 5:6-11. Also see POSB notes, Love—John 21:15-17; Grace—Ephes. 2:8-9.) <br>  a. God's grace is not earned. It is something completely undeserved and unmerited. <br>  b. God's grace is the free gift of God. God extends His grace out toward man. <br>  c. God's grace is the only way man can be saved. <br>2. Grace means all the favors and gifts of God. It means all the good and perfect gifts of God, all the good and beneficial things He gives us and does for us, whether physical, material, or spiritual (James 1:17). |
| **#1774 Grace** <br><br>Grace–KJV <br>Grace–NASB <br>Grace–NIV | χάρις = *charis* <br>Pronunciation: [khar'-ece] <br>Parsing (part of speech): noun <br>   Case—nominative <br>   Gender—feminine <br>   Number—singular <br>   Stem or root—from χάρις, ιτος | Grace, kindness, mercy, goodwill; the underserved favor and blessings of God. It means the favor and blessings of God; the undeserved and unmerited favor and blessings of God; the depth and richness of the heart and mind of God; the kindness and love that dwells within the very nature of God. God's grace covers all of life. |

PRACTICAL WORD STUDIES
in the NEW TESTAMENT

| ENGLISH WORD | GREEK WORD AND VERSE | THE WORD MEANS... |
|---|---|---|
| **Grace–NKJV**<br>**Grace–NLT**<br><br>**POSB REFERENCE**<br>(Eph.1:2)<br>*Deeper Study #1*<br><br>**See also POSB REF:**<br>(1 Cor.1:4)<br>*Deeper Study #1* | Concordance References:<br>⇒ Strong's #5485 charis<br>⇒ NIV #5921 charis<br>⇒ NASB #5485 charis<br><br>**Ephes. 1:2**<br>**Grace** be to you, and peace, from God our Father, and from the Lord Jesus Christ. [KJV]<br>**Grace** to you and peace from God our Father and the Lord Jesus Christ. [NASB]<br>**Grace** and peace to you from God our Father and the Lord Jesus Christ. [NIV]<br>**Grace** to you and peace from God our Father and the Lord Jesus Christ. [NKJV]<br>May **grace** and peace be yours, sent to you from God our Father and Jesus Christ our Lord. [NLT]<br>χάρις ὑμῖν καὶ εἰρήνη ἀπὸ Θεοῦ πατρὸς ἡμῶν, καὶ Κυρίου Ἰησοῦ Χριστοῦ. [GNS]<br>χάρις ὑμῖν καὶ εἰρήνη ἀπὸ θεοῦ πατρὸς ἡμῶν καὶ κυρίου Ἰησοῦ Χριστοῦ. [GNT] | **Practical Application**<br>Grace (*charis*) is probably the most meaningful word in the language of men. The Bible means something far more than men mean by grace. To men the word "grace" means three things.<br>⇒ Grace is that something, that quality within a thing, that is beautiful or joyful. It may be the fragrance of a flower, the rich green of the grass, the beauty of a lovely person.<br>⇒ Grace is anything that has loveliness. It may be a thought, an act, a word, a person.<br>⇒ Grace is a gift, a favor that someone might extend to a friend. The favor is always freely done, expecting nothing in return, and the favor is always done for a friend.<br><br>In light of this, grace means two very significant things.<br>1. Grace means all the favors and gifts of God. It means all the good and perfect gifts of God, all the good and beneficial things He gives us and does for us, whether physical, material, or spiritual (James 1:17).<br>2. Grace means the favor of God showered upon men–men who did not deserve His favor. When the early Christians looked at what God had done for men, they had to add a deeper and much richer meaning to the word *grace*. For God had saved sinners, those who had acted against Him. Grace became the kindness and love that God freely gives to His *enemies*–men who are...<br>• "still powerless" (Romans 5:6).<br>• "ungodly" (Romans 5:6).<br>• "sinners" (Romans 5:8).<br>• "enemies" (Romans 5:10).<br><br>No other word so expresses the depth and richness of the heart and mind of God. This is the distinctive difference between God's grace and man's grace. Whereas man sometimes does favors for his friends and thereby can be said to be gracious, God has done a thing unheard of among men: He has given His very own Son to die for His enemies (Romans 5:8-10). (See POSB note–John 21:15-17; POSB note–Ephes. 2:8-10.) |
| **#1775**<br>**Grace**<br><br>**Grace–KJV**<br>**Grace–NASB**<br>**Grace–NIV**<br>**Grace–NKJV**<br>God's special favor–NLT<br><br>**POSB REFERENCE**<br>(1 Pt.1:2)<br>Note 5, point 1<br><br>**See also POSB REF:**<br>(2 Pt.1:2)<br>Note 3 | χάρις = *charis*<br>Pronunciation: [khar'-ece]<br>Parsing (part of speech): noun<br>  Case—nominative<br>  Gender—feminine<br>  Number—singular<br>  Stem or root—from χάρις, ιτος<br>Concordance References:<br>⇒ Strong's #5485 charis<br>⇒ NIV #5921 charis<br>⇒ NASB #5485 charis<br><br>**1 Peter 1:2**<br>Elect according to the foreknowledge of God the Father, through sanctification of the Spirit, unto obedience and sprinkling of the blood of Jesus Christ: **Grace** unto you, and peace, be multiplied. [KJV]<br>According to the foreknowledge of God the Father, by the sanctifying work of the Spirit, that you may obey | Grace; God's special favor; a special expression of God's divine presence. Grace (*charis*) means the *undeserved favor and blessings* of God. (See POSB notes–Romans 4:16; POSB *Deeper Study* #1–1 Cor. 1:4; POSB *Deeper Study* #1–Titus 2:11-15.)<br><br>**Practical Application**<br>The word *undeserved* is the key to understanding grace. Man does not deserve God's favor; he cannot earn God's approval and blessings. God is too high and man too low for man to deserve anything from God. Man is imperfect and God is perfect; therefore, man cannot expect anything from God. (See POSB *Deeper Study* #1, Justification–Galatians 2:15-16 for more discussion.) Man has reacted against God too much. Man has... |

# PRACTICAL WORD STUDIES
## in the NEW TESTAMENT

| ENGLISH WORD | GREEK WORD AND VERSE | THE WORD MEANS... |
|---|---|---|
| (2 Jn.1:3)<br>*Deeper Study #1*<br>(Gal.1:3<br>Note 3<br>(Tit.2:11-15; esp. v.11)<br>*Deeper Study #1* | Jesus Christ and be sprinkled with His blood: May **grace** and peace be yours in fullest measure. [NASB]<br><br>Who have been chosen according to the foreknowledge of God the Father, through the sanctifying work of the Spirit, for obedience to Jesus Christ and sprinkling by his blood: **Grace** and peace be yours in abundance. [NIV]<br><br>Eelect according to the foreknowledge of God the Father, in sanctification of the Spirit, for obedience and sprinkling of the blood of Jesus Christ: **Grace** to you and eace be multiplied. [NKJV]<br><br>God the Father chose you long ago, and the Spirit has made you holy. As a result, you have obeyed Jesus Christ and are cleansed by his blood. May you have more and more of **God's special favor** and wonderful peace. [NLT]<br><br>κατὰ πρόγνωσιν Θεοῦ πατρός, ἐν ἁγιασμῷ Πνεύματος, εἰς ὑπακοὴν καὶ ῥαντισμὸν αἵματος Ἰησοῦ Χριστοῦ· **χάρις** ὑμῖν καὶ εἰρήνη πληθυνθείη. [GNS]<br><br>κατὰ πρόγνωσιν θεοῦ πατρός ἐν ἁγιασμῷ πνεύματος εἰς ὑπακοὴν καὶ ῥαντισμὸν αἵματος Ἰησοῦ Χριστοῦ, **χάρις** ὑμῖν καὶ εἰρήνη πληθυνθείη. [GNT] | - rejected God<br>- rebelled against God<br>- ignored God<br>- neglected God<br>- cursed God<br>- sinned against God<br>- disobeyed God<br>- denied God<br>- questioned God<br><br>Man deserves nothing from God except judgment, condemnation, and punishment. But God is love–perfect and absolute love. Therefore, God makes it possible for man to experience His grace, in particular the favor and blessing of salvation which is in His Son, Jesus Christ. (See POSB *Deeper Study #1*, Grace–1 Cor. 1:4 for more discussion.) |
| #1776<br>**Gracious**<br><br>With grace–KJV<br>With grace–NASB<br>Full of grace–NIV<br>With grace–NKJV<br>**Gracious–NLT**<br><br>**POSB REFERENCE**<br>(Col.4:6)<br>Note 3 | ἐν χάριτι = *en chariti*<br>Pronunciation: [en khar'-ih-tee]<br>Parsing *en* (part of speech): preposition<br>  Case—dative<br>  Stem or root—from ἐν<br>Parsing *chariti* (part of speech): noun<br>  Case—dative<br>  Gender—feminine<br>  Number—singular<br>  Stem or root—from χάρις, ιτος<br>Concordance References:<br>  ⇒ Strong's #1722 en + 5485 charis<br>  ⇒ NIV #1877 en [full of] + 5921 charis [grace]<br>  ⇒ NASB #1722 en + 5485 charis<br><br>**Col. 4:6**<br>Let your speech be alway **with grace**, seasoned with salt, that ye may know how ye ought to answer every man. [KJV]<br><br>Let your speech always be **with grace**, seasoned, as it were, with salt, so that you may know how you should respond to each person. [NASB]<br><br>Let your conversation be always **full of grace**, seasoned with salt, so that you may know how to answer everyone. [NIV]<br><br>Let your speech always be **with grace**, seasoned with salt, that you may know how you ought to answer each one. [NKJV]<br><br>Let your conversation be **gracious** and effective so that you will have the right answer for everyone. [NLT]<br><br>ὁ λόγος ὑμῶν πάντοτε **ἐν χάριτι**, ἅλατι ἠρτυμένος, εἰδέναι πῶς δεῖ ὑμᾶς ἑνὶ ἑκάστῳ ἀποκρίνεσθαι. [GNS]<br><br>ὁ λόγος ὑμῶν πάντοτε **ἐν χάριτι**, ἅλατι ἠρτυμένος, εἰδέναι πῶς δεῖ ὑμᾶς ἑνὶ ἑκάστῳ ἀποκρίνεσθαι. [GNT] | To be full of grace; to be with grace; to be gracious; to be kind; to be courteous.<br><br>**Practical Application**<br>As a believer, you must speak always with grace, answering and sharing what it is that makes your life different. What an expectation God has of us: to be living a life so different and righteous that men ask us what it is that makes us different. How many live a life that is that different? That godly and righteous? Note exactly what is said.<br><br>When we are walking among unbelievers, we are to guard our speech and conversation. We are...<br><br>- to make sure that we speak graciously (*en chariti*), that is, with kindness, courtesy, and graciousness.<br>- to season our conversation with salt; that is, we are to flavor and turn the conversation to tasteful and enjoyable subjects and away from corruptible and tasteless subjects.<br><br>What happens when this is done is striking: unbelievers will begin to notice our lives and conversation—that we are different in a good and wholesome way. And some will ask us what it is that gives us such peace and security and assurance in life. Then it is that we have a unique opportunity to witness. Then it is that we can reach out and bring in those who are so tragically without Christ, lost and doomed in despair and hopelessness forever. |
| #1777<br>**Grave**<br><br>Corruption–KJV<br>Decay–NASB<br>Decay–NIV<br>Corruption–NKJV<br>**Grave–NLT**<br><br>**POSB REFERENCE**<br>(Acts 2:25-28; esp. v.27)<br>Note 1, point 2c | διαφθοράν = *diaphthoran*<br>Pronunciation: [dee-af-thor-ahn']<br>Parsing (part of speech): noun<br>  Case—accusative<br>  Gender—feminine<br>  Number—singular<br>  Stem or root—from διαφθορά, ᾶς<br>Concordance References:<br>  ⇒ Strong's #1312 diaphthora<br>  ⇒ NIV #1426 diaphthora<br>  ⇒ NASB #1312 diaphthora<br><br>**Acts 2:27**<br>Because thou wilt not leave my soul in hell, neither wilt thou suffer thine Holy One to see **corruption**. [KJV] | To decay; to corrupt; to deteriorate, putrefy, destroy, perish. It speaks of the grave and the rotting of a dead body.<br><br>**Practical Application**<br>In no place does Christ promise a new body to the unbeliever, to the unsaved and lost. A person's body and flesh can be destroyed forever. (This is a fact seldom pointed out.) |

# PRACTICAL WORD STUDIES
## in the NEW TESTAMENT

| ENGLISH WORD | GREEK WORD AND VERSE | THE WORD MEANS... |
|---|---|---|
| *See also POSB REF:* (Acts 2:27) *Deeper Study #1,* point 2 | Because Thou wilt not abandon my soul to Hades, Nor ALLOW Thy Holy One to UNDERGO **DECAY**. [NASB]<br>Because you will not abandon me to the grave, nor will you let your Holy One see **decay**. [NIV]<br>*For You will not leave my soul in Hades, Nor will You allow Yur Holy One to see* **corruption**. [NKJV]<br>For you will not leave my soul among the dead or allow your Holy One to rot in the **grave**. [NLT]<br>ὅτι οὐκ ἐγκαταλείψεις τὴν ψυχήν μου εἰς ᾅδου, οὐδὲ δώσεις τὸν ὅσιόν σου ἰδεῖν **διαφθοράν**. [GNS]<br>ὅτι οὐκ ἐγκαταλείψεις τὴν ψυχήν μου εἰς ᾅδην οὐδὲ δώσεις τὸν ὅσιόν σου ἰδεῖν **διαφθοράν**. [GNT] | |
| **#1778** **Grave**<br><br>Hell–KJV<br>Hades–NASB<br>**Grave–NIV**<br>Hades–NKJV<br>Dead–NLT<br><br>**POSB REFERENCE**<br>(Acts 2:25-28; esp. v.27)<br>Note 1, point 2b<br><br>*See also POSB REF:*<br>(Acts 2:27)<br>*Deeper Study #1* | ᾅδην = hadën<br>Pronunciation: [hah'-dane]<br>Parsing (part of speech): noun<br>  Case—accusative<br>  Gender—masculine<br>  Number—singular<br>  Stem or root—from ᾅδης, ου<br>Concordance References:<br>⇒ Strong's #86 hadës<br>⇒ NIV #87 hadës<br>⇒ NASB #86 hadës<br><br>**Acts 2:27**<br>Because thou wilt not leave my soul in **hell**, neither wilt thou suffer thine Holy One to see corruption. [KJV]<br>Because Thou wilt not abandon my soul to **Hades**, Nor ALLOW Thy Holy One to UNDERGO DECAY. [NASB]<br>Because you will not abandon me to the **grave**, nor will you let your Holy One see decay. [NIV]<br>*For You will not leave my soul in* **Hades**, *Nor will You allow Yur Holy One to see corruption.* [NKJV]<br>For you will not leave my soul among the **dead** or allow your Holy One to rot in the grave. [NLT]<br>ὅτι οὐκ ἐγκαταλείψεις τὴν ψυχήν μου εἰς **ᾅδου**, οὐδὲ δώσεις τὸν ὅσιόν σου ἰδεῖν διαφθοράν. [GNS]<br>ὅτι οὐκ ἐγκαταλείψεις τὴν ψυχήν μου εἰς **ᾅδην** οὐδὲ δώσεις τὸν ὅσιόν σου ἰδεῖν διαφθοράν. [GNT] | Grave, hell, hades, dead; the place of death.<br><br>**Practical Application**<br>Jesus revealed that the grave or Hades is the other world, that is, the unseen world, the spiritual dimension of being (see POSB *Deeper Study* #3–Luke 16:23). Jesus said that Hades or the grave (the other world) was divided into two huge areas or sections. The two areas are separated by a great gulf that is impassable (Luke 16:26). One area is the place of sorrow (Luke 16:23-24, 28), and the other area is the place of paradise where believers go. To say that one is dead is to say that one is in hades or in the other world. |
| **#1779** **Grave**<br><br>**Grave–KJV**<br>Dignity–NASB<br>Worthy of respect– NIV<br>Reverent–NKJV<br>Respected–NLT<br><br>**POSB REFERENCE**<br>(1 Tim.3:8)<br>Note 1, point 1<br><br>*See also POSB REF:*<br>(1 Tim.3:11-12)<br>Note 3<br>(Tit.2:2)<br>Note 2 | σεμνούς = semnous<br>Pronunciation: [sem-noos']<br>Parsing (part of speech): adjective<br>  Case—accusative<br>  Gender—masculine<br>  Number—plural<br>  Stem or root—from σεμνός, ή, όν<br>Concordance References:<br>⇒ Strong's #4586 semnos<br>⇒ NIV #4948 semnos<br>⇒ NASB #4586 semnos<br><br>**1 Tim. 3:8**<br>Likewise *must* the deacons *be* **grave**, not doubletongued, not given to much wine, not greedy of filthy lucre; [KJV]<br>Deacons likewise *must be* men of **dignity**, not double-tongued, or addicted to much wine or fond of sordid gain, [NASB]<br>Deacons, likewise, are to be men **worthy of respect**, sincere, not indulging in much wine, and not pursuing dishonest gain. [NIV]<br>Likewise deacons *must be* **reverent**, not double-tongued, not given to much wine, not greedy for money, [NKJV]<br>In the same way, deacons must be people who are **respected** and have integrity. They must not be heavy drinkers and must not be greedy for money. [NLT]<br>διακόνους ὡσαύτως **σεμνούς**, μὴ διλόγους, μὴ οἴνῳ πολλῷ προσέχοντας, μὴ αἰσχροκερδεῖς, [GNS]<br>Διακόνους ὡσαύτως **σεμνούς**, μὴ διλόγους, μὴ οἴνῳ πολλῷ προσέχοντας, μὴ αἰσχροκερδεῖς, [GNT] | Worthy of respect, grave, dignity, highly respected, serious, honorable, worthy, revered, noble.<br><br>**Practical Application**<br>It is being serious minded, the very opposite...<br>• of being flippant.<br>• of dishonoring oneself.<br>• of being shallow by being over talkative.<br>• of having little respect because one is not grave or serious enough.<br>• of having a surface religion only.<br><br>However, this does not mean that the deacon is to walk around with a long face, never smiling, joking, or having fun. It simply means that he is serious minded and committed to Christ and to the mission of the church: the mission of reaching the lost and meeting the desperate needs of the world. |

# PRACTICAL WORD STUDIES
## in the NEW TESTAMENT

| ENGLISH WORD | GREEK WORD AND VERSE | THE WORD MEANS... |
|---|---|---|
| **#1780**<br>**Gravity**<br><br>Gravity–KJV<br>Dignity–NASB<br>Respect–NIV<br>Reverence–NKJV<br>Respect–NLT<br><br>**POSB REFERENCE**<br>(1 Tim.3:4-5; esp. v.4)<br>Note 3 | σεμνότητος = semnotētos<br>Pronunciation: [sem-no-tay-tos]<br>Parsing (part of speech): noun<br>    Case—genitive<br>    Gender—feminine<br>    Number—singular<br>    Stem or root—from σεμνότης, ητος<br>Concordance References:<br>  ⇒ Strong's #4587 semnotēs<br>  ⇒ NIV #4949 semnotēs<br>  ⇒ NASB #4587 semnotēs<br><br>**1 Tim. 3:4**<br>One that ruleth well his own house, having his children in subjection with all **gravity**; [KJV]<br>He must be one who manages his own household well, keeping his children under control with all **dignity** [NASB]<br>He must manage his own family well and see that his children obey him with proper **respect**. [NIV]<br>One who rules his own house well, having *his* children in submission with all **reverence** [NKJV]<br>He must manage his own family well, with children who **respect** and obey him. [NLT]<br>τοῦ ἰδίου οἴκου καλῶς προϊστάμενον, τέκνα ἔχοντα ἐν ὑποταγῇ μετὰ πάσης **σεμνότητος**· [GNS]<br>τοῦ ἰδίου οἴκου καλῶς προϊστάμενον, τέκνα ἔχοντα ἐν ὑποταγῇ, μετὰ πάσης **σεμνότητος** [GNT] | Respect, gravity, dignity, respectability, seriousness.<br><br>**Practical Application**<br>The minister must rule his home with dignity, respect, and love. As the Amplified New Testament says: "With true dignity, commanding their respect in every way and keeping them respectful."<br>As Scripture says, "For if a man know not how to rule his own house, how shall he take care of the church of God?" (1 Tim. 3:5). [KJV] |
| **#1781**<br>**Great**<br><br>Great–KJV<br>Great–NASB<br>Large–NIV<br>Great–NKJV<br>Large–NLT<br><br>**POSB REFERENCE**<br>(Mk.4:1-2; esp. v.1)<br>Note 1 | πλεῖστος = pleistos<br>Pronunciation: [plees-tos]<br>Parsing (part of speech): adjective<br>    Type—superlative<br>    Case—nominative<br>    Gender—masculine<br>    Number—singular<br>    Stem or root—from πολύς, πολλή, πολύ<br>Concordance References:<br>  ⇒ Strong's #4183 polus<br>  ⇒ NIV #4498 polus<br>  ⇒ NASB #4183 polus<br><br>**Mark 4:1**<br>And he began again to teach by the sea side: and there was gathered unto him a **great** multitude, so that he entered into a ship, and sat in the sea; and the whole multitude was by the sea on the land. [KJV]<br>And He began to teach again by the sea. And such a very **great** multitude gathered to Him that He got into a boat in the sea and sat down; and the whole multitude was by the sea on the land. [NASB]<br>Again Jesus began to teach by the lake. The crowd that gathered around him was so **large** that he got into a boat and sat in it out on the lake, while all the people were along the shore at the water's edge. [NIV]<br>And again He began to teach by the sea. And a **great** multitude was gathered to Him, so that He got into a boat and sat in it on the sea; and the whole multitude was on the land facing the sea. [NKJV]<br>Once again Jesus began teaching by the lakeshore. There was such a **large** crowd along the shore that he got into a boat and sat down and spoke from there. [NLT]<br>Καὶ πάλιν ἤρξατο διδάσκειν παρὰ τὴν θάλασσαν, καὶ συνήχθη πρὸς αὐτὸν ὄχλος **πολύς**, ὥστε αὐτὸν ἐμβάντα εἰς τὸ πλοῖον καθῆσθαι ἐν τῇ θαλάσσῃ, καὶ πᾶς ὁ ὄχλος πρὸς τὴν θάλασσαν ἐπὶ τῆς γῆς ἦν. [GNS]<br>Καὶ πάλιν ἤρξατο διδάσκειν παρὰ τὴν θάλασσαν· καὶ συνάγεται πρὸς αὐτὸν ὄχλος **πλεῖστος**, ὥστε αὐτὸν εἰς πλοῖον ἐμβάντα καθῆσθαι ἐν τῇ θαλάσσῃ, καὶ πᾶς ὁ ὄχλος πρὸς τὴν θάλασσαν ἐπὶ τῆς γῆς ἦσαν. [GNT] | Large, numerous, many, abundant, very great; a great deal of, a large number of, plenty of.<br><br>**Practical Application**<br>The multitude was so great that they overflowed the seashore, and they pressed in upon Jesus so much that He was forced into a boat. |

## PRACTICAL WORD STUDIES
### in the NEW TESTAMENT

| ENGLISH WORD | GREEK WORD AND VERSE | THE WORD MEANS... |
|---|---|---|
| **#1782**<br>**Great–**<br>**Greatness**<br><br>Greatness–KJV<br>Greatness–NASB<br>Great–NIV<br>Greatness–NKJV<br>Greatness–NLT<br><br>**POSB**<br>**REFERENCE**<br>(Eph.1:19)<br>Note 1 | μέγεθος = *megethos*<br>Pronunciation: [meg'-eth-os]<br>Parsing (part of speech): noun<br>    Case—nominative<br>    Gender—neuter<br>    Number—singular<br>    Stem or root—from μέγεθος<br>Concordance References:<br>  ⇒ Strong's #3174 megethos<br>  ⇒ NIV #3490 megethos<br>  ⇒ NASB #3174 megethos<br><br>**Ephes. 1:19**<br>And what is the exceeding **greatness** of his power to us-ward who believe, according to the working of his mighty power, [KJV]<br>And what is the surpassing **greatness** of His power toward us who believe. These are in accordance with the working of the strength of His might [NASB]<br>And his incomparably **great** power for us who believe. That power is like the working of his mighty strength, [NIV]<br>And what *is* the exceeding **greatness** of His power toward us who believe, according to the working of His mighty power [NKJV]<br>I pray that you will begin to understand the incredible **greatness** of his power for us who believe him. This is the same mighty power [NLT]<br>καὶ τί τὸ ὑπερβάλλον **μέγεθος** τῆς δυνάμεως αὐτοῦ εἰς ἡμᾶς τοὺς πιστεύοντας κατὰ τὴν ἐνέργειαν τοῦ κράτους τῆς ἰσχύος αὐτοῦ [GNS]<br>καὶ τί τὸ ὑπερβάλλον **μέγεθος** τῆς δυνάμεως αὐτοῦ εἰς ἡμᾶς τοὺς πιστεύοντας κατὰ τὴν ἐνέργειαν τοῦ κράτους τῆς ἰσχύος αὐτοῦ [GNT] | Great, greatness, mighty, explosive, beyond measure.<br><br>**Practical Application**<br>This is the word from which we get the English word *megathon* which measures atomic explosives. Imagine the great explosive power of God! |
| **#1783**<br>**Great**<br>**Deception**<br><br>Strong delusion–KJV<br>Deluding influence–<br>  NASB<br>Powerful delusion–<br>  NIV<br>Strong delusion–<br>  NKJV<br>**Great deception–NLT**<br><br>**POSB**<br>**REFERENCE**<br>(2 Thes.2:11)<br>Note 3 | ἐνέργειαν πλάνης = *energeian planēs*<br>Pronunciation: [en-erg'-i-ahn plan'-ace]<br>Parsing (part of speech): noun<br>    Case—accusative<br>    Gender—feminine<br>    Number—singular<br>    Stem or root—from ἐνέργεια, ας<br>Parsing (part of speech): noun<br>    Case—genitive<br>    Gender—feminine<br>    Number—singular<br>    Stem or root—from πλάνη, ης<br>Concordance References:<br>  ⇒ Strong's #1753 energeia + 4106 planē<br>  ⇒ NIV #1918 energeia + 4415 planē<br>  ⇒ NASB #1753 energeia + 4106 planē<br><br>**2 Thes. 2:11**<br>And for this cause God shall send them **strong delusion**, that they should believe a lie: [KJV]<br>And for this reason God will send upon them a **deluding influence** so that they might believe what is false, [NASB]<br>For this reason God sends them a **powerful delusion** so that they will believe the lie [NIV]<br>And for this reason God will send them **strong delusion**, that they should believe the lie, [NKJV]<br>So God will send **great deception** upon them, and they will believe all these lies. [NLT]<br>καὶ διὰ τοῦτο πέμψει αὐτοῖς ὁ Θεὸς **ἐνέργειαν πλάνης**, εἰς τὸ πιστεῦσαι αὐτοὺς τῷ ψεύδει· [GNS]<br>καὶ διὰ τοῦτο πέμπει αὐτοῖς ὁ θεὸς **ἐνέργειαν πλάνης** εἰς τὸ πιστεῦσαι αὐτοὺς τῷ ψεύδει, [GNT] | Powerful delusion, strong delusion, deluding influence, great deception, great error, strong deceit, a working of error.<br><br>**Practical Application**<br>In the end time, people will work error after error, sin after sin, evil after evil. They will become stronger and stronger in their sin, harder and harder. They will become steeped in their rejection of the gospel more and more. |

# PRACTICAL WORD STUDIES
## in the NEW TESTAMENT

| ENGLISH WORD | GREEK WORD AND VERSE | THE WORD MEANS... |
|---|---|---|
| **#1784**<br>**Great Drops**<br><br>Great drops–KJV<br>Drops–NASB<br>Drops–NIV<br>Great drops–NKJV<br>Great drops–NLT<br><br>**POSB REFERENCE**<br>(Lk.22:43-44; esp. v.44)<br>Note 4, point 3 | θρόμβοι = thromboi<br>Pronunciation: [throm'-bo-ee]<br>Parsing (part of speech): noun<br>    Case—nominative<br>    Gender—masculine<br>    Number—plural<br>    Stem or root—from θρόμβος, ου<br>Concordance References:<br>  ⇒ Strong's #2361 thrombos<br>  ⇒ NIV #2584 thrombos<br>  ⇒ NASB #2361 thrombos<br><br>**Luke 22:44**<br>And being in an agony he prayed more earnestly: and his sweat was as it were **great drops** of blood falling down to the ground. [KJV]<br>And being in agony He was praying very fervently; and His sweat became like **drops** of blood, falling down upon the ground. [NASB]<br>And being in anguish, he prayed more earnestly, and his sweat was like **drops** of blood falling to the ground. [NIV]<br>And being in agony, He prayed more earnestly. Then His sweat became like **great drops** of blood falling down to the ground. [NKJV]<br>He prayed more fervently, and he was in such agony of spirit that his sweat fell to the ground like **great drops** of blood. [NLT]<br>καὶ γενόμενος ἐν ἀγωνίᾳ, ἐκτενέστερον προσηύχετο. ἐγένετο δὲ ὁ ἱδρὼς αὐτοῦ ὡσεὶ **θρόμβοι** αἵματος καταβαίνοντος ἐπὶ τὴν γῆν. [GNS]<br>καὶ γενόμενος ἐν ἀγωνίᾳ ἐκτενέστερον προσηύχετο· καὶ ἐγένετο ὁ ἱδρὼς αὐτοῦ ὡσεὶ **θρόμβοι** αἵματος καταβαίνοντος ἐπὶ τὴν γῆν. [GNT] | Drops, great drops, thick clots of blood.<br><br>**Practical Application**<br>Apparently, Jesus was under so much pressure that the capillary veins right under the skin burst causing the blood to mingle with sweat and pour through the enlarged pores. What Jesus was experiencing can never be known (see POSB *Deeper Study* #2, Jesus Christ, Suffering—Luke 22:43-44). |
| **#1785**<br>**Great Enthusiasm, With**<br><br>Fervent in the spirit–KJV<br>Fervent in spirit–NASB<br>With great fervor–NIV<br>Fervent in spirit–NKJV<br>With great enthusiasm–NLT<br><br>**POSB REFERENCE**<br>(Acts 18:25)<br>Note 4 | ζέων τῷ πνεύματι = zeön tö pneumati<br>Pronunciation: [dzeh'-own tow pnyoo'-mah-tee]<br>Parsing *zeön* (part of speech): verb<br>    Mood—participle<br>    Tense—present<br>    Voice—active<br>    Case—nominative<br>    Gender—masculine<br>    Number—singular<br>    Stem or root—from ζέω<br>Parsing *pneumati* (part of speech): noun<br>    Case—dative<br>    Gender—neuter<br>    Number—singular<br>    Stem or root—from πνεῦμα, τος<br>Concordance References:<br>  ⇒ Strong's #2204 + 3588 + 4151 zeö ho pneuma<br>  ⇒ NIV #2417 + 3836 + 4460 zeö ho pneuma<br>  ⇒ NASB #2204 + 3588 + 4151 zeö ho pneuma<br><br>**Acts 18:25**<br>This man was instructed in the way of the Lord; and being **fervent in the spirit**, he spake and taught diligently the things of the Lord, knowing only the baptism of John. [KJV]<br>This man had been instructed in the way of the Lord; and being **fervent in spirit**, he was speaking and teaching accurately the things concerning Jesus, being acquainted only with the baptism of John; [NASB]<br>He had been instructed in the way of the Lord, and he spoke **with great fervor** and taught about Jesus accurately, though he knew only the baptism of John. [NIV]<br>This man had been instructed in the way of the Lord; and being **fervent in spirit**, he spoke and taught accurately the things of the Lord, though he knew only the baptism of John. [NKJV]<br>He had been taught the way of the Lord and talked to | With great fervor; to be fervent in spirit; with great enthusiasm. The word means to be boiling, glowing, burning, passionate.<br><br>**Practical Application**<br>Apollos' spirit was set aflame, filled with all fervency and zeal for God. He was burning with a holy fire to proclaim the glorious promise that Jesus is the promised Messiah, the Lamb of God. |

# PRACTICAL WORD STUDIES
## in the NEW TESTAMENT

| ENGLISH WORD | GREEK WORD AND VERSE | THE WORD MEANS... |
|---|---|---|
| | others **with great enthusiasm** and accuracy about Jesus. However, he knew only about John's baptism. [NLT]<br><br>οὗτος ἦν κατηχημένος τὴν ὁδὸν τοῦ Κυρίου, καὶ **ζέων τῷ πνεύματι** ἐλάλει καὶ ἐδίδασκεν ἀκριβῶς τὰ περὶ τοῦ Κυρίου, ἐπιστάμενος μόνον τὸ βάπτισμα Ἰωάννου· [GNS]<br><br>οὗτος ἦν κατηχημένος τὴν ὁδὸν τοῦ κυρίου καὶ **ζέων τῷ πνεύματι** ἐλάλει καὶ ἐδίδασκεν ἀκριβῶς τὰ περὶ τοῦ Ἰησοῦ, ἐπιστάμενος μόνον τὸ βάπτισμα Ἰωάννου· [GNT] | |
| **#1786**<br>**Great Fervor, With**<br><br>Fervent in the spirit–KJV<br>Fervent in spirit–NASB<br>**With great fervor–NIV**<br>Fervent in spirit–NKJV<br>With great enthusiasm–NLT<br><br>**POSB REFERENCE**<br>(Acts 18:25)<br>Note 4 | ζέων τῷ πνεύματι = zeön tō pneumati<br>Pronunciation: [dzeh'-own tow pnyoo'-mah-tee]<br>Parsing zeön (part of speech): verb<br>    Mood—participle<br>    Tense—present<br>    Voice—active<br>    Case—nominative<br>    Gender—masculine<br>    Number—singular<br>    Stem or root—from ζέω<br>Parsing pneumati (part of speech): noun<br>    Case—dative<br>    Gender—neuter<br>    Number—singular<br>    Stem or root—from πνεῦμα, τος<br>Concordance References:<br>  ⇒ Strong's #2204 + 3588 + 4151 zeō ho pneuma<br>  ⇒ NIV #2417 + 3836 + 4460 zeō ho pneuma<br>  ⇒ NASB #2204 + 3588 + 4151 zeō ho pneuma<br><br>**Acts 18:25**<br>This man was instructed in the way of the Lord; and being **fervent in the spirit**, he spake and taught diligently the things of the Lord, knowing only the baptism of John. [KJV]<br><br>This man had been instructed in the way of the Lord; and being **fervent in spirit**, he was speaking and teaching accurately the things concerning Jesus, being acquainted only with the baptism of John; [NASB]<br><br>He had been instructed in the way of the Lord, and he spoke **with great fervor** and taught about Jesus accurately, though he knew only the baptism of John. [NIV]<br><br>This man had been instructed in the way of the Lord; and being **fervent in spirit**, he spoke and taught accurately the things of the Lord, though he knew only the baptism of John. [NKJV]<br><br>He had been taught the way of the Lord and talked to others **with great enthusiasm** and accuracy about Jesus. However, he knew only about John's baptism. [NLT]<br><br>οὗτος ἦν κατηχημένος τὴν ὁδὸν τοῦ Κυρίου, καὶ **ζέων τῷ πνεύματι** ἐλάλει καὶ ἐδίδασκεν ἀκριβῶς τὰ περὶ τοῦ Κυρίου, ἐπιστάμενος μόνον τὸ βάπτισμα Ἰωάννου· [GNS]<br><br>οὗτος ἦν κατηχημένος τὴν ὁδὸν τοῦ κυρίου καὶ **ζέων τῷ πνεύματι** ἐλάλει καὶ ἐδίδασκεν ἀκριβῶς τὰ περὶ τοῦ Ἰησοῦ, ἐπιστάμενος μόνον τὸ βάπτισμα Ἰωάννου· [GNT] | With great fervor; to be fervent in spirit; with great enthusiasm. The word means to be boiling, glowing, burning, passionate.<br><br>**Practical Application**<br>Apollos' spirit was set aflame, filled with all fervency and zeal for God. He was burning with a holy fire to proclaim the glorious promise that Jesus is the promised Messiah, the Lamb of God. |
| **#1787**<br>**Great Help**<br><br>Succourer–KJV<br>Helper–NASB<br>**Great help–NIV**<br>Helper–NKJV<br>Helped–NLT<br><br>**POSB REFERENCE**<br>(Rom.16:1-2; esp. v.2)<br>Note 1, point 4b | προστάτις = prostatis<br>Pronunciation: [pros-tat'-is]<br>Parsing (part of speech): noun<br>    Case—nominative<br>    Gender—feminine<br>    Number—singular<br>    Stem or root—from προστάτις, ιδος<br>Concordance References:<br>  ⇒ Strong's #4368 prostatis<br>  ⇒ NIV #4706 prostatis<br>  ⇒ NASB #4368 prostatis<br><br>**Romans 16:2**<br>That ye receive her in the Lord, as becometh saints, and that ye assist her in whatsoever business she hath | Great help, succourer, helper, helped, aided.<br><br>**Practical Application**<br>Phoebe had been a "great help" (*prostatis*) to many, including Paul himself. The word means that she protected, helped, looked after, and provided for people. Phoebe was a woman who ministered to the needs of many. Apparently, she helped and looked after the welfare of any who had need. |

# PRACTICAL WORD STUDIES
## in the NEW TESTAMENT

| ENGLISH WORD | GREEK WORD AND VERSE | THE WORD MEANS... |
|---|---|---|
| | need of you: for she hath been a **succourer** of many, and of myself also. [KJV]<br>That you receive her in the Lord in a manner worthy of the saints, and that you help her in whatever matter she may have need of you; for she herself has also been a **helper** of many, and of myself as well. [NASB]<br>I ask you to receive her in the Lord in a way worthy of the saints and to give her any help she may need from you, for she has been a **great help** to many people, including me. [NIV]<br>That you may receive her in the Lord in a manner worthy of the saints, and assist her in whatever business she has need of you; for indeed she has been a **helper** of many and of myself also. [NKJV]<br>Receive her in the Lord, as one who is worthy of high honor. Help her in every way you can, for she has **helped** many in their needs, including me. [NLT]<br>ἵνα αὐτὴν προσδέξησθε ἐν Κυρίῳ ἀξίως τῶν ἁγίων, καὶ παραστῆτε αὐτῇ ἐν ᾧ ἂν ὑμῶν χρῄζῃ πράγματι· καὶ γὰρ αὐτὴ **προστάτις** πολλῶν ἐγενήθη, καὶ αὐτοῦ ἐμοῦ. [GNS]<br>ἵνα αὐτὴν προσδέξησθε ἐν κυρίῳ ἀξίως τῶν ἁγίων καὶ παραστῆτε αὐτῇ ἐν ᾧ ἂν ὑμῶν χρῄζῃ πράγματι· καὶ γὰρ αὐτὴ **προστάτις** πολλῶν ἐγενήθη καὶ ἐμοῦ αὐτοῦ. [GNT] | |
| **#1788**<br>**Great Joy**<br><br>Rejoiced–KJV<br>Rejoiced–NASB<br>Glad–NIV<br>Rejoiced–NKJV<br>**Great joy–NLT**<br><br>**POSB REFERENCE**<br>(Acts 15:30-35; esp. v.31)<br>Note 5, point 1 | ἐχάρησαν = *echarēsan*<br>Pronunciation: [eh-chah'ray-sahn]<br>Parsing (part of speech): verb<br>  Mood—indicative<br>  Tense—aorist<br>  Voice—passive deponent<br>  Person—3rd person<br>  Number—plural<br>  Stem or root—from χαίρω<br>Concordance References:<br>  ⇒ Strong's #5463 chairō<br>  ⇒ NIV #5897 chairō<br>  ⇒ NASB #5463 chairō<br><br>**Acts 15:31**<br>Which when they had read, they **rejoiced** for the consolation. [KJV]<br>And when they had read it, they **rejoiced** because of its encouragement. [NASB]<br>The people read it and were **glad** for its encouraging message. [NIV]<br>When they had read it, they **rejoiced** over its encouragement. [NKJV]<br>And there was **great joy** throughout the church that day as they read this encouraging message. [NLT]<br>ἀναγνόντες δέ, **ἐχάρησαν** ἐπὶ τῇ παρακλήσει. [GNS]<br>ἀναγνόντες δὲ **Ἐχάρησαν** ἐπὶ τῇ παρακλήσει. [GNT] | Gladness; rejoiced; to have great joy; to be delighted; to be happy.<br><br>**Practical Application**<br>When the four men arrived in Antioch, the whole church was called together and the great decree on salvation was read. When it was read, four great results occurred. Note how God took the dissension and its subsequent events to work it all out for the good of the Antioch church and for the cause of Christ. The results were fourfold.<br>1. There was "great joy" (*echarēsan*).<br>2. There was great "encouragment" (v.32).<br>3. There was the discovery of the great missionary, Silas (v.32).<br>4. There was the beginning of a great teaching ministry within the church (v.35). |
| **#1789**<br>**Great Patience**<br><br>All longsuffering–KJV<br>**Great patience–NASB**<br>**Great patience–NIV**<br>All longsuffering–NKJV<br>Patiently–NLT<br><br>**POSB REFERENCE**<br>(2 Tim. 4:2)<br>Note 2, point 5a | πάσῃ μακροθυμίᾳ = *pasē makrothumia*<br>Pronunciation: [pas-ay mak-roth-oo-mee'-ah]<br>Parsing *pasē* (part of speech): adjective<br>  Case—dative<br>  Gender—feminine<br>  Number—singular<br>  Stem or root—from πᾶς, πᾶσα, πᾶν<br>Parsing *makrothumia* (part of speech): noun<br>  Case—dative<br>  Gender—feminine<br>  Number—singular<br>  Stem or root—from μακροθυμία, ας<br>Concordance References:<br>  ⇒ Strong's #3115+3956 makrothumia pas<br>  ⇒ NIV #3429+4246 makrothumia pas [great patience]<br>  ⇒ NASB #3115+3956 makrothumia pas | Great patience; all long-suffering; patiently; great endurance; calmness.<br><br>**Practical Application**<br>The minister must "encourage, with great patience" (*pasē makrothumia*). The idea is that the minister patiently endures in encouraging people–no matter the circumstances. He exhorts and exhorts, encourages and encourages. He suffers a long, long time with people...<br>• enduring whatever weaknesses and failings they have.<br>• enduring whatever evil and injury is done.<br><br>The minister suffers a long, long time without resentment or anger; and he never gives up, for he knows the power of Christ to change lives. |

# PRACTICAL WORD STUDIES
## in the NEW TESTAMENT

| ENGLISH WORD | GREEK WORD AND VERSE | THE WORD MEANS... |
|---|---|---|
| | **2 Tim. 4:2**<br>Preach the word; be instant in season, out of season; reprove, rebuke, exhort with **all longsuffering** and doctrine. [KJV]<br>Preach the word; be ready in season and out of season; reprove, rebuke, exhort, with **great patience** and instruction. [NASB]<br>Preach the Word; be prepared in season and out of season; correct, rebuke and encourage—with **great patience** and careful instruction. [NIV]<br>Preach the word! Be ready in season *and* out of season. Convince, rebuke, exhort, with **all longsuffering** and teaching. [NKJV]<br>Preach the word of God. Be persistent, whether the time is favorable or not. **Patiently** correct, rebuke, and encourage your people with good teaching. [NLT]<br>κήρυξον τὸν λόγον, ἐπίστηθι εὐκαίρως, ἀκαίρως, ἔλεγξον, ἐπιτίμησον, παρακάλεσον, ἐν **πάσῃ μακροθυμίᾳ** καὶ διδαχῇ. [GNS]<br>κήρυξον τὸν λόγον, ἐπίστηθι εὐκαίρως ἀκαίρως, ἔλεγξον, ἐπιτίμησον, παρακάλεσον, ἐν **πάσῃ μακροθυμίᾳ** καὶ διδαχῇ. [GNT] | |
| #1790<br>**Great Persecution**<br><br>Great persecution–KJV<br>Great persecution–NASB<br>Great persecution–NIV<br>Great persecution–NKJV<br>Great wave of persecution–NLT<br><br>**POSB REFERENCE**<br>(Acts 8:1)<br>Note 1, point 3 | **διωγμὸς μέγας** = *diōgmos megas*<br>Pronunciation: [dee-ogue-mos' meg'-as]<br>Parsing *diōgmos* (part of speech): noun<br>    Case—nominative<br>    Gender—masculine<br>    Number—singular<br>    Stem or root—from διωγμός, οῦ<br>Parsing *megas* (part of speech): adjective<br>    Case—nominative<br>    Gender—masculine<br>    Number—singular<br>    Stem or root—from μέγας, μεγάλη, μέγα<br>Concordance References:<br>  ⇒ Strong's #1375 diōgmos + 3173 megas<br>  ⇒ NIV #1501 diōgmos [persecution] + 3489 megas [great]<br>  ⇒ NASB #1375 diōgmos + 3173 megas<br><br>**Acts 8:1**<br>And Saul was consenting unto his death. And at that time there was a **great persecution** against the church which was at Jerusalem; and they were all scattered abroad throughout the regions of Judaea and Samaria, except the apostles. [KJV]<br>And Saul was in hearty agreement with putting him to death.And on that day a **great persecution** arose against the church in Jerusalem; and they were all scattered throughout the regions of Judea and Samaria, except the apostles. [NASB]<br>And Saul was there, giving approval to his death.On that day a **great persecution** broke out against the church at Jerusalem, and all except the apostles were scattered throughout Judea and Samaria. [NIV]<br>Now Saul was consenting to his death. At that time a **great persecution** arose against the church which was at Jerusalem; and they were all scattered throughout the regions of Judea and Samaria, except the apostles. [NKJV]<br>Saul was one of the official witnesses at the killing of Stephen. A **great wave of persecution** began that day, sweeping over the church in Jerusalem, and all the believers except the apostles fled into Judea and Samaria. [NLT]<br>Σαῦλος δὲ ἦν συνευδοκῶν τῇ ἀναιρέσει αὐτοῦ. Ἐγένετο δὲ ἐν ἐκείνῃ τῇ ἡμέρᾳ **διωγμὸς μέγας** ἐπὶ τὴν ἐκκλησίαν τὴν ἐν Ἱεροσολύμοις· πάντες τε διεσπάρησαν κατὰ τὰς χώρας τῆς Ἰουδαίας καὶ Σαμαρείας, πλὴν τῶν ἀποστόλων. [GNS]<br>Σαῦλος δὲ ἦν συνευδοκῶν τῇ ἀναιρέσει αὐτοῦ. Ἐγένετο δὲ ἐν ἐκείνῃ τῇ ἡμέρᾳ **διωγμὸς μέγας** ἐπὶ τὴν ἐκκλησίαν τὴν ἐν Ἱεροσολύμοις, πάντες δὲ διεσπάρησαν κατὰ τὰς χώρας τῆς Ἰουδαίας καὶ Σαμαρείας πλὴν τῶν ἀποστόλων. [GNT] | Great persecution, great wave of persecution; great suppression; great oppression.<br><br>**Practical Application**<br>The idea is that Saul hotly pursued, chased, and hunted down the believers. He was bent on violence, utterly determined to stamp out the church. |

# Practical Word Studies in the New Testament

| ENGLISH WORD | GREEK WORD AND VERSE | THE WORD MEANS... |
|---|---|---|
| **#1791**<br>**Great Sense Of Obligation**<br><br>Debtor–KJV<br>Under obligation–NASB<br>Obligated–NIV<br>Debtor–NKJV<br>Great sense of obligation–NLT<br><br>**POSB REFERENCE**<br>(Rom.1:14-15; esp. v.14)<br>Note 5, point 1<br><br>See also POSB REF:<br>(Rom.8:12-13; esp. v.12)<br>Note 6, point 1 | ὀφειλέτης = *opheiletēs*<br>Pronunciation: [of-i-let'-ace]<br>Parsing (part of speech): noun<br>    Case—nominative<br>    Gender—masculine<br>    Number—singular<br>    Stem or root—from ὀφειλέτης, ου<br>Concordance References:<br>⇒ Strong's #3781 opheiletēs<br>⇒ NIV #4050 opheiletēs<br>⇒ NASB #3781 opheiletēs<br><br>**Romans 1:14**<br>I am **debtor** both to the Greeks, and to the Barbarians; both to the wise, and to the unwise. [KJV]<br>I am **under obligation** both to Greeks and to barbarians, both to the wise and to the foolish. [NASB]<br>I am **obligated** both to Greeks and non-Greeks, both to the wise and the foolish. [NIV]<br>I am a **debtor** both to Greeks and to barbarians, both to wise and to unwise. [NKJV]<br>For I have a **great sense of obligation** to people in our culture and to people in other cultures, to the educated and uneducated alike. [NLT]<br>Ἕλλησί τε καὶ βαρβάροις, σοφοῖς τε καὶ ἀνοήτοις ὀφειλέτης εἰμί [GNS]<br>Ἕλλησίν τε καὶ βαρβάροις, σοφοῖς τε καὶ ἀνοήτοις ὀφειλέτης εἰμί, [GNT] | To be obligated; to be in debt; to be under obligation; to have a great sense of obligation; to owe; to be bound by duty.<br><br>**Practical Application**<br>The Greek is impossible to translate into English, for two ideas are being expressed by Paul. He was "under a great sense of obligation"...<br>• because Christ had done so much for him (saved him).<br>• because Christ had called him to preach (given him a task to do).<br>The indebtedness was deeply felt by Paul. The idea is that it was intense, unwavering, unrelentless, powerful. The sense of debt just would not let Paul go. He was compelled to preach the gospel; therefore, he could do nothing else. He was obligated and duty-bound to preach it. He actually felt that he owed the gospel to the world; therefore, if he kept quiet, it would be worse than knowing the cure for the most terrible disease of history but refusing to share it. |
| **#1792**<br>**Great Wave Of Persecution**<br><br>Great persecution–KJV<br>Great persecution–NASB<br>Great persecution–NIV<br>Great persecution–NKJV<br>Great wave of persecution–NLT<br><br>**POSB REFERENCE**<br>(Acts 8:1)<br>Note 1, point 3 | διωγμὸς μέγας = *diōgmos megas*<br>Pronunciation: [dee-ogue-mos' meg'-as]<br>Parsing *diōgmos* (part of speech): noun<br>    Case—nominative<br>    Gender—masculine<br>    Number—singular<br>    Stem or root—from διωγμός, οῦ<br>Parsing *megas* (part of speech): adjective<br>    Case—nominative<br>    Gender—masculine<br>    Number—singular<br>    Stem or root—from μέγας, μεγάλη, μέγα<br>Concordance References:<br>⇒ Strong's #1375 diōgmos + 3173 megas<br>⇒ NIV #1501 diōgmos [persecution] + 3489 megas [great]<br>⇒ NASB #1375 diōgmos + 3173 megas<br><br>**Acts 8:1**<br>And Saul was consenting unto his death. And at that time there was a **great persecution** against the church which was at Jerusalem; and they were all scattered abroad throughout the regions of Judaea and Samaria, except the apostles. [KJV]<br>And Saul was in hearty agreement with putting him to death. And on that day a **great persecution** arose against the church in Jerusalem; and they were all scattered throughout the regions of Judea and Samaria, except the apostles. [NASB]<br>And Saul was there, giving approval to his death. On that day a **great persecution** broke out against the church at Jerusalem, and all except the apostles were scattered throughout Judea and Samaria. [NIV]<br>Now Saul was consenting to his death. At that time a **great persecution** arose against the church which was at Jerusalem; and they were all scattered throughout the regions of Judea and Samaria, except the apostles. [NKJV]<br>Saul was one of the official witnesses at the killing of Stephen. A **great wave of persecution** began that day, sweeping over the church in Jerusalem, and all the believers except the apostles fled into Judea and Samaria. [NLT]<br>Σαῦλος δὲ ἦν συνευδοκῶν τῇ ἀναιρέσει αὐτοῦ. | Great persecution, great wave of persecution; great suppression; great oppression.<br><br>**Practical Application**<br>The idea is that Saul hotly pursued, chased, and hunted down the believers. He was bent on violence, utterly determined to stamp out the church. |

# Practical Word Studies in the New Testament

| ENGLISH WORD | GREEK WORD AND VERSE | THE WORD MEANS... |
|---|---|---|
| | Ἐγένετο δὲ ἐν ἐκείνῃ τῇ ἡμέρᾳ **διωγμὸς μέγας** ἐπὶ τὴν ἐκκλησίαν τὴν ἐν Ἱεροσολύμοις· πάντες τε διεσπάρησαν κατὰ τὰς χώρας τῆς Ἰουδαίας καὶ Σαμαρείας, πλὴν τῶν ἀποστόλων. [GNS]<br>Σαῦλος δὲ ἦν συνευδοκῶν τῇ ἀναιρέσει αὐτοῦ. Ἐγένετο δὲ ἐν ἐκείνῃ τῇ ἡμέρᾳ **διωγμὸς μέγας** ἐπὶ τὴν ἐκκλησίαν τὴν ἐν Ἱεροσολύμοις, πάντες δὲ διεσπάρησαν κατὰ τὰς χώρας τῆς Ἰουδαίας καὶ Σαμαρείας πλὴν τῶν ἀποστόλων. [GNT] | |
| **#1793**<br>**Greater A Blessing**<br><br>Fulness–KJV<br>Fulfillment–NASB<br>Fullness–NIV<br>Fullness–NKJV<br>Greater a blessing–NLT<br><br>**POSB REFERENCE**<br>(Romans 11:11-12)<br>Note 1, point 3<br><br>See also POSB REF:<br>(Col.2:9-10; esp. v.9)<br>Note 2, point 1 | πλήρωμα = plērōma<br>Pronunciation: [play'-ro-mah]<br>Parsing (part of speech): noun<br>   Case—nominative<br>   Gender—neuter<br>   Number—singular<br>   Stem or root—from πλήρωμα, τος<br>Concordance References:<br>⇒ Strong's #4138 plērōma<br>⇒ NIV #4445 plērōma<br>⇒ NASB #4138 plērōma<br><br>**Romans 11:12**<br>Now if the fall of them be the riches of the world, and the diminishing of them the riches of the Gentiles; how much more their **fulness**? [KJV]<br>Now if their transgression be riches for the world and their failure be riches for the Gentiles, how much more will their **fulfillment** be! [NASB]<br>But if their transgression means riches for the world, and their loss means riches for the Gentiles, how much greater riches will their **fullness** bring! [NIV]<br>Now if their fall *is* riches for the world, and their failure riches for the Gentiles, how much more their **fullness**! [NKJV]<br>Now if the Gentiles were enriched because the Jews turned down God's offer of salvation, think how much **greater a blessing** the world will share when the Jews finally accept it. [NLT]<br>εἰ δὲ τὸ παράπτωμα αὐτῶν πλοῦτος κόσμου, καὶ τὸ ἥττημα αὐτῶν πλοῦτος ἐθνῶν, πόσῳ μᾶλλον τὸ **πλήρωμα** αὐτῶν; [GNS]<br>εἰ δὲ τὸ παράπτωμα αὐτῶν πλοῦτος κόσμου καὶ τὸ ἥττημα αὐτῶν πλοῦτος ἐθνῶν, πόσῳ μᾶλλον τὸ **Πλήρωμα** αὐτῶν. [GNT] | Fullness, completeness; full measure.<br><br>**Practical Application**<br>The idea is that the day is coming when God's plan and purpose for Israel will be completed and perfectly fulfilled. That day, the day of Israel's restoration, will cause even a greater blessing to spread out across the world. |
| **#1794**<br>**Greatly Amazed**<br><br>Greatly amazed–KJV<br>Amazed–NASB<br>Overwhelmed with wonder–NIV<br>Greatly amazed–NKJV<br>In awe–NLT<br><br>**POSB REFERENCE**<br>(Mk.9:15)<br>Deeper Study #1 | ἐξεθαμβήθησαν = exethambēthēsan<br>Pronunciation: [ek-eh-tham-bayth'-ay-sahn]<br>Parsing (part of speech): verb<br>   Mood—indicative<br>   Tense—aorist<br>   Voice—passive<br>   Person—3rd person<br>   Number—plural<br>   Stem or root—from ἐκθαμβέομαι<br>Concordance References:<br>⇒ Strong's #1568 ekthambeō<br>⇒ NIV #1701 ekthambeō<br>⇒ NASB #1568 ekthambeō<br><br>**Mark 9:15**<br>And straightway all the people, when they beheld him, were **greatly amazed**, and running to *him* saluted him. [KJV]<br>And immediately, when the entire crowd saw Him, they were **amazed**, and *began* running up to greet Him. [NASB]<br>As soon as all the people saw Jesus, they were **overwhelmed with wonder** and ran to greet him. [NIV]<br>Immediately, when they saw Him, all the people were greatly **amazed**, and running to *Him*, greeted Him. [NKJV]<br>The crowd watched Jesus **in awe** as he came toward | To be filled with wonder, to be overwhelmed with wonder and awe, to be amazed—greatly amazed.<br><br>**Practical Application**<br>What amazed the people when they "saw" Jesus?<br>1. Perhaps Jesus retained some of the glory of the transfiguration. The people may have seen a glow, a majestic countenance about Jesus. (cp. Exodus 34:29 when Moses came down from the mountain after having been with God).<br>2. Perhaps Jesus came at such an opportune time that the people were amazed to see Him, as though His timing was destined. He arrived just when His disciples needed help.<br>3. Perhaps Jesus walked with a renewed air, a more authoritative and decisive countenance than before. Just coming from the transfiguration was bound to instill a renewed confidence and authority within Him. |

## PRACTICAL WORD STUDIES
### in the New Testament

| ENGLISH WORD | GREEK WORD AND VERSE | THE WORD MEANS... |
|---|---|---|
| | them, and then they ran to greet him. [NLT]<br>καὶ εὐθέως πᾶς ὁ ὄχλος ἰδὼν αὐτὸν **ἐξεθαμβήθη**, καὶ προστρέχοντες ἠσπάζοντο αὐτόν. [GNS]<br>καὶ εὐθὺς πᾶς ὁ ὄχλος ἰδόντες αὐτὸν **ἐξεθαμβήθησαν** καὶ προστρέχοντες ἠσπάζοντο αὐτόν. [GNT] | |
| **#1795**<br>**Greatly Distressed**<br><br>Stirred–KJV<br>Provoked–NASB<br>**Greatly distressed– NIV**<br>Provoked–NKJV<br>Deeply troubled–NLT<br><br>**POSB REFERENCE**<br>(Acts 17:16)<br>Note 1 | παρωξύνετο = *paröxuneto*<br>Pronunciation: [par-ox-oo'-neh-tow]<br>Parsing (part of speech): verb<br>  Mood—indicative<br>  Tense—imperfect<br>  Voice—passive<br>  Person—3rd person<br>  Number—singular<br>  Stem or root—from ὑπεραυξάνω<br>Concordance References:<br>  ⇒ Strong's #3947 paroxunö<br>  ⇒ NIV #4236 paroxunö<br>  ⇒ NASB #3947 paroxunö<br><br>**Acts 17:16**<br>Now while Paul waited for them at Athens, his spirit was **stirred** in him, when he saw the city wholly given to idolatry. [KJV]<br>Now while Paul was waiting for them at Athens, his spirit was being **provoked** within him as he was beholding the city full of idols. [NASB]<br>While Paul was waiting for them in Athens, he was **greatly distressed** to see that the city was full of idols. [NIV]<br>Now while Paul waited for them at Athens, his spirit was **provoked** within him when he saw that the city was given over to idols. [NKJV]<br>While Paul was waiting for them in Athens, he was **deeply troubled** by all the idols he saw everywhere in the city. [NLT]<br>Ἐν δὲ ταῖς Ἀθήναις ἐκδεχομένου αὐτοὺς τοῦ Παύλου, **παρωξύνετο** τὸ πνεῦμα αὐτοῦ ἐν αὐτῷ, θεωροῦντι κατείδωλον οὖσαν τὴν πόλιν. [GNS]<br>Ἐν δὲ ταῖς Ἀθήναις ἐκδεχομένου αὐτοὺς τοῦ Παύλου **παρωξύνετο** τὸ πνεῦμα αὐτοῦ ἐν αὐτῷ θεωροῦντος κατείδωλον οὖσαν τὴν πόλιν. [GNT] | To be greatly distressed; to be stirred; to be provoked; to be deeply troubled; to be aroused; to be agitated; to be irritated; to be greatly upset.<br><br>**Practical Application**<br>Paul was in Athens, the great intellectual and cultural center of the world. Paul was alone, and no doubt he did as anyone would do–he toured the city. But note: he was not swept off his feet by the majestic buildings and splendor of the architecture. Contrariwise, what gripped him was the idolatry. The city was "full of idols." Ancient writers estimate that the city had thousands and thousands of idols, one or more for every person in the city. The idols sat everywhere, lining the streets and buildings, within and without every home. Seeing such a sight "greatly distressed" (*paröxuneto*) the spirit of Paul. Paul was aroused...<br>• over the abuse of God's glory.<br>• over the spiritual blindness of man's mind and reason.<br>• against the devil's enslavement of lives.<br>• with compassion for the souls of men.<br><br>Note what happened: Paul could wait no longer. He had been waiting for Silas and Timothy, but he could not swallow the scene of idolatry anymore. He began to *reason* and *discuss* the gospel with men everywhere. |
| **#1796**<br>**Greatly Enlarged**<br><br>Exceedingly–KJV<br>**Greatly enlarged– NASB**<br>Growing more and more–NIV<br>Exceedingly–NKJV<br>Flourishing–NLT<br><br>**POSB REFERENCE**<br>(2 Thes.1:3)<br>Note 4 | ὑπεραυξάνει = *huperauxanei*<br>Pronunciation: [hoop-er-owx-ahn'-eh-ee]<br>Parsing (part of speech): verb<br>  Mood—indicative<br>  Tense—present<br>  Voice—active<br>  Person—3rd person<br>  Number—singular<br>  Stem or root—from ὑπεραυξάνω<br>Concordance References:<br>  ⇒ Strong's #5232 huperauxanö<br>  ⇒ NIV #5647 huperauxanö<br>  ⇒ NASB #5232 huperauxanö<br><br>**2 Thes. 1:3**<br>We are bound to thank God always for you, brethren, as it is meet, because that your faith groweth **exceedingly**, and the charity of every one of you all toward each other aboundeth; [KJV]<br>We ought always to give thanks to God for you, brethren, as is only fitting, because your faith is **greatly enlarged**, and the love of each one of you toward one another grows ever greater; [NASB]<br>We ought always to thank God for you, brothers, and rightly so, because your faith is **growing more and more**, and the love every one of you has for each other is increasing. [NIV]<br>We are bound to thank God always for you, brethren, as it is fitting, because your faith grows **exceedingly**, and the love of every one of you all abounds toward each other, [NKJV] | Grow more and more, exceedingly, greatly enlarged, flourishing; to grow abundantly; to grow beyond measure; to grow far beyond what would be expected.<br><br>**Practical Application**<br>What a glorious testimony! Faith that just grows and grows more and more. Imagine a church full of believers whose faith in Christ Jesus grows explosively–beyond measure–beyond what we could ever imagine. And remember: the church was growing in faith while they were in the midst of savage persecution. This is the reason Paul says: "We ought always to give thanks to God for you." |

## PRACTICAL WORD STUDIES in the NEW TESTAMENT

| ENGLISH WORD | GREEK WORD AND VERSE | THE WORD MEANS... |
|---|---|---|
| | Dear brothers and sisters, we always thank God for you, as is right, for we are thankful that your faith is **flourishing** and you are all growing in love for each other. [NLT]<br><br>Εὐχαριστεῖν ὀφείλομεν τῷ Θεῷ πάντοτε περὶ ὑμῶν, ἀδελφοί, καθὼς ἄξιόν ἐστιν, ὅτι **ὑπεραυξάνει** ἡ πίστις ὑμῶν, καὶ πλεονάζει ἡ ἀγάπη ἑνὸς ἑκάστου πάντων ὑμῶν εἰς ἀλλήλους· [GNS]<br><br>Εὐχαριστεῖν ὀφείλομεν τῷ θεῷ πάντοτε περὶ ὑμῶν, ἀδελφοί, καθὼς ἄξιόν ἐστιν, ὅτι **ὑπεραυξάνει** ἡ πίστις ὑμῶν καὶ πλεονάζει ἡ ἀγάπη ἑνὸς ἑκάστου πάντων ὑμῶν εἰς ἀλλήλους, [GNT] | |
| **#1797**<br>**Greatness**<br><br>Mighty power–KJV<br>**Greatness–NASB**<br>**Greatness–NIV**<br>Majesty–NKJV<br>Display of [God's] power–NLT<br><br>**POSB REFERENCE**<br>(Lk.9:42-43; esp. v.43)<br>Note 3, point 2 | μεγαλειότητι = *megaleiotēti*<br>Pronunciation: [meg-al-i-ot'-ay-tee]<br>Parsing (part of speech): noun<br>  Case—dative<br>  Gender—feminine<br>  Number—singular<br>  Stem or root—from μεγαλειότης, ητος<br>Concordance References:<br>  ⇒ Strong's #3168 megaleiotēs<br>  ⇒ NIV #3484 megaleiotēs<br>  ⇒ NASB #3168 megaleiotēs<br><br>**Luke 9:43**<br>And they were all amazed at the **mighty power** of God. But while they wondered every one at all things which Jesus did, he said unto his disciples, [KJV]<br>And they were all amazed at the **greatness** of God. But while everyone was marveling at all that He was doing, He said to His disciples, [NASB]<br>And they were all amazed at the **greatness** of God. While everyone was marveling at all that Jesus did, he said to his disciples, [NIV]<br>And they were all amazed at the **majesty** of God. But while everyone marveled at all the things which Jesus did, He said to His disciples, [NKJV]<br>Awe gripped the people as they saw this **display of God's power**. While everyone was marveling over all the wonderful things he was doing, Jesus said to his disciples, [NLT]<br>ἐξεπλήσσοντο δὲ πάντες ἐπὶ τῇ **μεγαλειότητι** τοῦ Θεοῦ. Πάντων δὲ θαυμαζόντων ἐπὶ πᾶσιν οἷς ἐποίει ὁ Ἰησοῦς, εἶπε πρὸς τοὺς μαθητὰς αὐτοῦ, [GNS]<br>ἐξεπλήσσοντο δὲ πάντες ἐπὶ τῇ **μεγαλειότητι** τοῦ θεοῦ. Πάντων δὲ θαυμαζόντων ἐπὶ πᾶσιν οἷς ἐποίει εἶπεν πρὸς τοὺς μαθητὰς αὐτοῦ, [GNT] | Majesty, greatness, glory, mighty power, a display of God's glory and power.<br><br>**Practical Application**<br>They marveled at "the greatness of God." Note that Jesus brought honor to God, not to Himself. |
| **#1798**<br>**Greed**<br><br>Covetousness–KJV<br>Coveting–NASB<br>**Greed–NIV**<br>Covetousness–NKJV<br>**Greed–NLT**<br><br>**POSB REFERENCE**<br>(Mk.7:22)<br>*Deeper Study #8*<br><br>See also POSB REF:<br>(Rom.1:29)<br>*Deeper Study #4* | πλεονεξίαι = *pleonexiai*<br>Pronunciation: [pleh-on-ex-ee'-ah-ee]<br>Parsing (part of speech): noun<br>  Case—nominative<br>  Gender—feminine<br>  Number—plural<br>  Stem or root—from πλεονεξία, ας<br>Concordance References:<br>  ⇒ Strong's #4124 pleonexia<br>  ⇒ NIV #4432 pleonexia<br>  ⇒ NASB #4124 pleonexia<br><br>**Mark 7:22**<br>Thefts, **covetousness**, wickedness, deceit, lasciviousness, an evil eye, blasphemy, pride, foolishness: [KJV]<br>Deeds of **coveting** and wickedness, as well as deceit, sensuality, envy, slander, pride and foolishness. [NASB]<br>**Greed**, malice, deceit, lewdness, envy, slander, arrogance and folly. [NIV]<br>Thefts, **covetousness**, wickedness, deceit, lewdness, an evil eye, blasphemy, pride, foolishness. [NKJV]<br>Adultery, **greed**, wickedness, deceit, eagerness for lustful pleasure, envy, slander, pride, and foolishness. [NLT]<br>**πλεονεξίαι**, πονηρίαι, δόλοι, ἀσέλγεια, ὀφθαλμὸς πονηρός, βλασφημία, ὑπερηφανία, ἀφροσύνη· [GNS]<br>μοιχεῖαι, **πλεονεξίαι**, πονηρίαι, δόλος, ἀσέλγεια, ὀφθαλμὸς πονηρός, βλασφημία, ὑπερηφανία, ἀφροσύνη· [GNT] | Greed, covetousness; to lust for more and more; to have a starving appetite for something; to have a love of possessing (2 Peter 2:14); to crave after and for.<br><br>**Practical Application**<br>It means to crave and grasp after possessions, pleasure, power, fame. Covetousness or greed lacks restraint. It lacks the ability to discriminate. It wants to have in order to spend in pleasure and luxury. Covetousness or greed is an insatiable lust and craving of the flesh that cannot be satisfied. It is an intense appetite for gain, a passion for the pleasure that things can bring. It is a lust and craving so deep that a person finds his happiness in things instead of in God. It is idolatry (Ephes. 5:5). |

# PRACTICAL WORD STUDIES
## in the NEW TESTAMENT

| ENGLISH WORD | GREEK WORD AND VERSE | THE WORD MEANS... |
|---|---|---|
| **#1799**<br>**Greed**<br><br>Ravening–KJV<br>Robbery–NASB<br>**Greed–NIV**<br>**Greed–NKJV**<br>**Greed–NLT**<br><br>**POSB REFERENCE**<br>(Lk.11:39-41; esp. v.39)<br>Note 2, point 1 | ἁρπαγῆς = *harpagës*<br>Pronunciation: [har-pag-ays']<br>Parsing (part of speech): noun<br>  Case—genitive<br>  Gender—feminine<br>  Number—singular<br>  Stem or root—from ἁρπαγή, ῆς<br>Concordance References:<br>  ⇒ Strong's #724 harpagē<br>  ⇒ NIV #771 harpagē<br>  ⇒ NASB #724 harpagē<br><br>**Luke 11:39**<br>And the Lord said unto him, Now do ye Pharisees make clean the outside of the cup and the platter; but your inward part is full of **ravening** and wickedness. [KJV]<br>But the Lord said to him, "Now you Pharisees clean the outside of the cup and of the platter; but inside of you, you are full of **robbery** and wickedness. [NASB]<br>Then the Lord said to him, "Now then, you Pharisees clean the outside of the cup and dish, but inside you are full of **greed** and wickedness. [NIV]<br>Then the Lord said to him, "Now you Pharisees make the outside of the cup and dish clean, but your inward part is full of **greed** and wickedness. [NKJV]<br>Then the Lord said to him, "You Pharisees are so careful to clean the outside of the cup and the dish, but inside you are still filthy—full of **greed** and wickedness! [NLT]<br>εἶπε δὲ ὁ Κύριος πρὸς αὐτόν, Νῦν ὑμεῖς οἱ Φαρισαῖοι τὸ ἔξωθεν τοῦ ποτηρίου καὶ τοῦ πίνακος καθαρίζετε, τὸ δὲ ἔσωθεν ὑμῶν γέμει **ἁρπαγῆς** καὶ πονηρίας. [GNS]<br>εἶπεν δὲ ὁ κύριος πρὸς αὐτόν, Νῦν ὑμεῖς οἱ Φαρισαῖοι τὸ ἔξωθεν τοῦ ποτηρίου καὶ τοῦ πίνακος καθαρίζετε, τὸ δὲ ἔσωθεν ὑμῶν γέμει **ἁρπαγῆς** καὶ πονηρίας. [GNT] | Greed, robbery; a spirit of taking by violent force; plunder, seizing, extortion.<br><br>**Practical Application**<br>What did Jesus mean? A religionist is plundering the way of God, trying to seize God's kingdom his own way instead of following the way of God. He is committing extortion against God by robbing God of the salvation He has set up. |
| **#1800**<br>**Greed–Greediness**<br><br>Greediness–KJV<br>Greediness–NASB<br>Lust for more–NIV<br>Greediness–NKJV<br>Greed–NLT<br><br>**POSB REFERENCE**<br>(Eph.4:17-19; esp. v.19)<br>Note 1, point 7 | πλεονεξία = *pleonexia*<br>Pronunciation: [pleh-on-ex-ee'-ah]<br>Parsing (part of speech): noun<br>  Case—dative<br>  Gender—feminine<br>  Number—singular<br>  Stem or root—from πλεονεξία, ας<br>Concordance References:<br>  ⇒ Strong's #4124 pleonexia<br>  ⇒ NIV #4432 pleonexia<br>  ⇒ NASB #4124 pleonexia<br><br>**Ephes. 4:19**<br>Who being past feeling have given themselves over unto lasciviousness, to work all uncleanness with **greediness**. [KJV]<br>And they, having become callous, have given themselves over to sensuality, for the practice of every kind of impurity with **greediness**. [NASB]<br>Having lost all sensitivity, they have given themselves over to sensuality so as to indulge in every kind of impurity, with a continual **lust for more**. [NIV]<br>Who, being past feeling, have given themselves over to lewdness, to work all uncleanness with **greediness**. [NKJV]<br>They don't care anymore about right and wrong, and they have given themselves over to immoral ways. Their lives are filled with all kinds of impurity and **greed**. [NLT]<br>οἵτινες ἀπηλγηκότες ἑαυτοὺς παρέδωκαν τῇ ἀσελγείᾳ, εἰς ἐργασίαν ἀκαθαρσίας πάσης ἐν **πλεονεξίᾳ**. [GNS]<br>οἵτινες ἀπηλγηκότες ἑαυτοὺς παρέδωκαν τῇ ἀσελγείᾳ εἰς ἐργασίαν ἀκαθαρσίας πάσης ἐν **πλεονεξίᾳ** [GNT] | To lust for more; to be greedy. It means avarice, coveting, craving, grasping, desiring to have more and more; hoarding all one can get and still craving more.<br><br>**Practical Application**<br>It is being enslaved and held in bondage by the things of this earth: for example, food, drink, and a host of fleshly sins and self-centered behavior. Believers are not to walk in such a life. They are not to walk as other men walk. |

# PRACTICAL WORD STUDIES
## in the NEW TESTAMENT

| ENGLISH WORD | GREEK WORD AND VERSE | THE WORD MEANS... |
|---|---|---|
| **#1801**<br>**Greed–**<br>**Greedy**<br><br>Covetousness–KJV<br>Greed–NASB<br>Greed–NIV<br>Covetousness–NKJV<br>Greedy–NLT<br><br>**POSB**<br>**REFERENCE**<br>(Lk.12:15)<br>*Deeper Study* #1<br><br>See also POSB REF:<br>(Col.3:5-7; esp. v.5)<br>Note 1, point 1 | πλεονεξίας = *pleonexias*<br>Pronunciation: [pleh-on-ex-ee'-ah]<br>Parsing (part of speech): noun<br>    Case—genitive<br>    Gender—feminine<br>    Number—singular<br>    Stem or root—from πλεονεξία, ας<br>Concordance References:<br>  ⇒ Strong's #4124 pleonexia<br>  ⇒ NIV #4432 pleonexia<br>  ⇒ NASB #4124 pleonexia<br><br>**Luke 12:15**<br>And he said unto them, Take heed, and beware of **covetousness**: for a man's life consisteth not in the abundance of the things which he possesseth. [KJV]<br>And He said to them, "Beware, and be on your guard against every form of **greed**; for not even when one has an abundance does his life consist of his possessions." [NASB]<br>Then he said to them, "Watch out! Be on your guard against all kinds of **greed**; a man's life does not consist in the abundance of his possessions." [NIV]<br>And He said to them, "Take heed and beware of **covetousness**, for one's life does not consist in the abundance of the things he possesses." [NKJV]<br>Then he said, "Beware! Don't be **greedy** for what you don't have. Real life is not measured by how much we own." [NLT]<br>εἶπε δὲ πρὸς αὐτούς, Ὁρᾶτε καὶ φυλάσσεσθε ἀπὸ πάσης **πλεονεξίας**· ὅτι οὐκ ἐν τῷ περισσεύειν τινὶ ἡ ζωὴ αὐτοῦ ἐστιν ἐκ τῶν ὑπαρχόντων αὐτοῦ. [GNS]<br>ἶπεν δὲ πρὸς αὐτούς, Ὁρᾶτε καὶ φυλάσσεσθε ἀπὸ πάσης **πλεονεξίας**, ὅτι οὐκ ἐν τῷ περισσεύειν τινὶ ἡ ζωὴ αὐτοῦ ἐστιν ἐκ τῶν ὑπαρχόντων αὐτῷ. [GNT] | Greed, covetousness, lust, avarice; a craving, a desire for more.<br><br>**Practical Application**<br>It is greediness, a dissatisfaction with what is enough. It includes the cravings for both material things and fleshly indulgence. It is desiring what belongs to others; snatching at something that belongs to others; a love of having, a cry of "give me, give me" (cp. 2 Peter 2:14).<br>⇒ It is a lust so deep within a man that he finds his happiness in things instead of in God.<br>⇒ It is a greed so deep that it desires the power that things bring more than the things themselves.<br>⇒ It is an intense appetite for gain; a passion for the pleasure that things can bring. It goes beyond the pleasure of possessing things for their own sake. |
| **#1802**<br>**Greedy**<br><br>Covetous–KJV<br>Covetous–NASB<br>Greedy–NIV<br>Covetous–NKJV<br>Greedy–NLT<br><br>**POSB**<br>**REFERENCE**<br>(1 Cor.5:9-10; esp. v.9)<br>Note 4, point 2<br><br>See also POSB REF:<br>(1 Cor.6:10)<br>Note 3, point 2<br>(Eph.5:5-6; esp. v.5)<br>Note 5, point 1 | πλεονέκταις = *pleonektais*<br>Pronunciation: [pleh-on-ek'-tace]<br>Parsing (part of speech): noun<br>    Case—dative<br>    Gender—masculine<br>    Number—plural<br>    Stem or root—from πλεονέκτης, ου<br>Concordance References:<br>  ⇒ Strong's #4123 pleonektēs<br>  ⇒ NIV #4431 pleonektēs<br>  ⇒ NASB #4123 pleonektēs<br><br>**1 Cor. 5:10**<br>Yet not altogether with the fornicators of this world, or with the **covetous**, or extortioners, or with idolaters; for then must ye needs go out of the world. [KJV]<br>I did not at all mean with the immoral people of this world, or with the **covetous** and swindlers, or with idolaters; for then you would have to go out of the world. [NASB]<br>Not at all meaning the people of this world who are immoral, or the **greedy** and swindlers, or idolaters. In that case you would have to leave this world. [NIV]<br>Yet *I* certainly *did* not *mean* with the sexually immoral people of this world, or with the **covetous**, or extortioners, or idolaters, since then you would need to go out of the world. [NKJV]<br>But I wasn't talking about unbelievers who indulge in sexual sin, or who are **greedy** or are swindlers or idol worshipers. You would have to leave this world to avoid people like that. [NLT]<br>καὶ οὐ πάντως τοῖς πόρνοις τοῦ κόσμου τούτου ἢ τοῖς **πλεονέκταις**, ἢ ἅρπαξιν, ἢ εἰδωλολάτραις· ἐπεὶ ὠφείλετε ἄρα ἐκ τοῦ κόσμου ἐξελθεῖν. [GNS]<br>οὐ πάντως τοῖς πόρνοις τοῦ κόσμου τούτου ἢ τοῖς **πλεονέκταις** καὶ ἅρπαξιν ἢ εἰδωλολάτραις, ἐπεὶ ὠφείλετε ἄρα ἐκ τοῦ κόσμου ἐξελθεῖν. [GNT] | Greedy, covetous, grabbing for more and more.<br><br>**Practical Application**<br>The church was not to become mixed up with the greedy (*pleonektais*) of this world. The word means those who seek for more and more while millions within the world are dying from sin, hunger, disease, and poverty. This is a sin that is especially despised by God.<br>The "greedy" (*pleonektai*) are those...<br>• who always want more and more.<br>• who are never satisfied with what they have.<br>• who want more and more to spend in pleasure and luxury.<br>• who crave for possessions, pleasure, fame, power.<br>• who bank and store up and hoard, ignoring and neglecting the desperate needs of teeming millions who are dying from hunger, disease, poverty, and sin. (See POSB outline—Matthew 19:16-22 and POSB note—Matthew 19:16-22; POSB outline—Matthew 19:23-26; POSB outline—Luke 16:19-31; POSB note—Matthew 19:16-22 and POSB note—Matthew 19:16-22; POSB note—Matthew 19:23-26; and POSB note—Luke 16:19-31 for more discussion.) |

# PRACTICAL WORD STUDIES
## in the NEW TESTAMENT

| ENGLISH WORD | GREEK WORD AND VERSE | THE WORD MEANS... |
|---|---|---|
| **#1803**<br>**Greedy For Money, Not**<br><br>Not for filthy lucre–KJV<br>Not for sordid gain–NASB<br>**Not greedy for money– NIV**<br>Not for dishonest gain–NKJV<br>Not grudgingly–NLT<br><br>**POSB REFERENCE**<br>(1 Pt.5:2-3; esp. v.2)<br>Note 2, point 2 | μηδὲ αἰσχροκερδῶς = mëde aischrokerdös<br>Pronunciation: [may-deh' ahee-skhrok-er-doce']<br>Parsing aischrokerdös (part of speech): adjective<br>   Type—adverb<br>   Stem or root—from αἰσχροκερδῶς<br>Concordance References:<br>⇒ Strong's #3366 mëde + 147 aischrokerdös<br>⇒ NIV #3593 mëde [not] +154 aischrokerdös [greedy for money]<br>⇒ NASB #3366 mëde + 147 aischrokerdös<br><br>**1 Peter 5:2**<br>Feed the flock of God which is among you, taking the oversight thereof, not by constraint, but willingly; **not for filthy lucre**, but of a ready mind; [KJV]<br>Shepherd the flock of God among you, exercising oversight not under compulsion, but voluntarily, according to the will of God; and **not for sordid gain**, but with eagerness; [NASB]<br>Be shepherds of God's flock that is under your care, serving as overseers—not because you must, but because you are willing, as God wants you to be; **not greedy for money**, but eager to serve; [NIV]<br>Shepherd the flock of God which is among you, serving as overseers, not by compulsion but willingly, **not for dishonest gain** but eagerly; [NKJV]<br>Care for the flock of God entrusted to you. Watch over it willingly, **not grudgingly**—not for what you will get out of it, but because you are eager to serve God. [NLT]<br>ποιμάνατε τὸ ἐν ὑμῖν ποίμνιον τοῦ Θεοῦ, ἐπισκοποῦντες μὴ ἀναγκαστῶς, ἀλλ ἑκουσίως· **μηδὲ αἰσχροκερδῶς**, ἀλλὰ προθύμως, [GNS]<br>ποιμάνατε τὸ ἐν ὑμῖν ποίμνιον τοῦ θεοῦ [ἐπισκοποῦντες] μὴ ἀναγκαστῶς ἀλλὰ ἑκουσίως κατὰ θεόν, **μηδὲ αἰσχροκερδῶς** ἀλλὰ προθύμως, [GNT] | Not greedy for money; not greedy for sordid gain; not grudgingly; not greedy for material gain.<br><br>**Practical Application**<br>The elder or minister must take the oversight of the flock not for personal profit and gain, but with a ready mind. The Greek says that no person is to enter the ministry for "money" (*mëde aischrokerdös*), that is, for base gain, or for some soiled and dirty advantage. No person should ever enter the ministry...<br>• as a profession.<br>• as a means of livelihood.<br>• as a means to serve mankind.<br>• because people say he has the gifts for it.<br>• because people say he would make a good minister.<br>• because family and friends encourage him to enter the ministry.<br><br>All of these reasons usually surround a person's entrance into the ministry. But they must never be *the reasons* why a person enters the ministry of caring for God's people. The ministry is a *call from God*, and no person dare enter the ministry without a personal call to the ministry. But note: when the call comes, the person is to have a ready mind. He is to minister to God's people; he is to readily feed the flock of God. |
| **#1804**<br>**Greedy Person**<br><br>Covetous man–KJV<br>Covetous man–NASB<br>**Greedy person–NIV**<br>Covetous man–NKJV<br>**Greedy person–NLT**<br><br>**POSB REFERENCE**<br>(Eph.5:5-6; esp. v.5)<br>Note 5, point 1 | πλεονέκτης = pleonektës<br>Pronunciation: [pleh-on-ek'-tace]<br>Parsing (part of speech): noun<br>   Case—nominative<br>   Gender—masculine<br>   Number—singular<br>   Stem or root—from πλεονέκτης, ου<br>Concordance References:<br>⇒ Strong's #4123 pleonektës<br>⇒ NIV #4431 pleonektës<br>⇒ NASB #4123 pleonektës<br><br>**Ephes. 5:5**<br>For this ye know, that no whoremonger, nor unclean person, nor **covetous man**, who is an idolater, hath any inheritance in the kingdom of Christ and of God. [KJV]<br>For this you know with certainty, that no immoral or impure person or **covetous man**, who is an idolater, has an inheritance in the kingdom of Christ and God. [NASB]<br>For of this you can be sure: No immoral, impure or **greedy person**—such a man is an idolater—has any inheritance in the kingdom of Christ and of God. [NIV]<br>For this you know, that no fornicator, unclean person, nor **covetous man**, who is an idolater, has any inheritance in the kingdom of Christ and God. [NKJV]<br>You can be sure that no immoral, impure, or greedy person will inherit the Kingdom of Christ and of God. For a **greedy person** is really an idolater who worships the things of this world. [NLT]<br>τοῦτο γὰρ ἔστε γινώσκοντες, ὅτι πᾶς πόρνος, ἢ ἀκάθαρτος, ἢ **πλεονέκτης**, ὅς ἐστιν εἰδωλολάτρης, οὐκ ἔχει κληρονομίαν ἐν τῇ βασιλείᾳ τοῦ Χριστοῦ καὶ Θεοῦ. [GNS]<br>τοῦτο γὰρ ἴστε γινώσκοντες, ὅτι πᾶς πόρνος ἢ ἀκάθαρτος ἢ **πλεονέκτης**, ὅ ἐστιν εἰδωλολάτρης, οὐκ ἔχει κληρονομίαν ἐν τῇ βασιλείᾳ τοῦ Χριστοῦ καὶ θεοῦ. [GNT] | Greedy person; covetous man; one who is always grasping for more and more; hoarding all one can get and still craving more.<br><br>**Practical Application**<br>It is being enslaved and held in bondage by the things of this earth: for example, food, drink, and a host of fleshly sins and self-centered behavior. |

# PRACTICAL WORD STUDIES
## in the NEW TESTAMENT

| ENGLISH WORD | GREEK WORD AND VERSE | THE WORD MEANS... |
|---|---|---|
| **#1805**<br>**Greeted–**<br>**Greetings**<br><br>Hail–KJV<br>**Greeted**–NASB<br>**Greetings**–NIV<br>Rejoice–NKJV<br>**Greetings**–NLT<br><br>**POSB**<br>**REFERENCE**<br>(Mt.28:9)<br>*Deeper Study #2* | Χαίρετε. = *Chairete*<br>Pronunciation: [khah'ee-reh-teh]<br>Parsing (part of speech): verb<br>    Mood—imperative<br>    Tense—present<br>    Voice—active<br>    Person—2nd person<br>    Number—plural<br>    Stem or root—from χαίρω<br>OR<br>Parsing (part of speech): particle<br>    Type—sentence<br>    Stem or root—from χαίρω<br>Concordance References:<br>  ⇒ Strong's #5463 chairö<br>  ⇒ NIV #5897 chairö<br>  ⇒ NASB #5463 chairö<br><br>**Matthew 28:9**<br>And as they went to tell his disciples, behold, Jesus met them, saying, All **hail**. And they came and held him by the feet, and worshipped him. [KJV]<br>And behold, Jesus met them and **greeted** them. And they came up and took hold of His feet and worshiped Him. [NASB]<br>Suddenly Jesus met them. "**Greetings**," he said. They came to him, clasped his feet and worshiped him. [NIV]<br>And as they went to tell His disciples, behold, Jesus met them, saying, "**Rejoice**!" So they came and held Him by the feet and worshiped Him. [NKJV]<br>And as they went, Jesus met them. "**Greetings**!" he said. And they ran to him, held his feet, and worshiped him. [NLT]<br>ὡς δὲ ἐπορεύοντο ἀπαγγεῖλαι τοῖς μαθηταῖς αὐτοῦ, καὶ ἰδοὺ, ὁ Ἰησοῦς ἀπήντησεν αὐταῖς, λέγων, **Χαίρετε**. αἱ δὲ προσελθοῦσαι ἐκράτησαν αὐτοῦ τοὺς πόδας καὶ προσεκύνησαν αὐτῷ. [GNS]<br>καὶ ἰδοὺ Ἰησοῦς ὑπήντησεν αὐταῖς λέγων, **Χαίρετε**. αἱ δὲ προσελθοῦσαι ἐκράτησαν αὐτοῦ τοὺς πόδας καὶ προσεκύνησαν αὐτῷ. [GNT] | To be greeted, to rejoice; hailed.<br><br>**Practical Application**<br>It is significant that the risen Christ used this every day, common greeting to proclaim the extraordinary news of His resurrection. |
| **#1806**<br>**Grew**<br><br>Increased–KJV<br>Increasing–NASB<br>**Grew**–NIV<br>Increased–NKJV<br>**Grew**–NLT<br><br>**POSB**<br>**REFERENCE**<br>(Lk.2:52)<br>*Deeper Study #1* | προέκοπτεν = *proekopten*<br>Pronunciation: [pro-eh'-kop-ten]<br>Parsing (part of speech): verb<br>    Mood—indicative<br>    Tense—imperfect<br>    Voice—active<br>    Person—3rd person<br>    Number—singular<br>    Stem or root—from προκόπτω<br>Concordance References:<br>  ⇒ Strong's #4298 prokoptö<br>  ⇒ NIV #4621 prokoptö<br>  ⇒ NASB #4298 prokoptö<br><br>**Luke 2:52**<br>And Jesus **increased** in wisdom and stature, and in favour with God and man. [KJV]<br>And Jesus kept **increasing** in wisdom and stature, and in favor with God and men. [NASB]<br>And Jesus **grew** in wisdom and stature, and in favor with God and men. [NIV]<br>And Jesus **increased** in wisdom and stature, and in favor with God and men. [NKJV]<br>So Jesus **grew** both in height and in wisdom, and he was loved by God and by all who knew him. [NLT]<br>Καὶ Ἰησοῦς **προέκοπτε** σοφίᾳ καὶ ἡλικίᾳ, καὶ χάριτι παρὰ Θεῷ καὶ ἀνθρώποις. [GNS]<br>Καὶ Ἰησοῦς **προέκοπτεν** [ἐν τῇ] σοφίᾳ καὶ ἡλικίᾳ καὶ χάριτι παρὰ θεῷ καὶ ἀνθρώποις. [GNT] | To grow steadily; to increase; to progress; to keep advancing.<br><br>**Practical Application**<br>The picture is that of Jesus' cutting His way through the advancing years just as a pioneer cuts through the wilderness to reach his destination. |

# Practical Word Studies
## in the New Testament

| ENGLISH WORD | GREEK WORD AND VERSE | THE WORD MEANS... |
|---|---|---|
| **#1807**<br>**Grew And Multiplied**<br><br>Grew and multiplied–KJV<br>Grow and to be multiplied–NASB<br>Increase and spread–NIV<br>Grew and multiplied–NKJV<br>Spreading rapidly–NLT<br><br>**POSB REFERENCE**<br>(Acts 12:24-25; esp. v.24)<br>Note 4, point 1 | ηὔξανεν καὶ ἐπληθύνετο = ëuxanen kai eplëthuneto<br>Pronunciation: [ayoowx-ahn'-ehn ky eh-play-thoo'-neh-tow]<br>Parsing ëuxanen (part of speech): verb<br>  Mood—indicative<br>  Tense—imperfect<br>  Voice—active<br>  Person—3rd person<br>  Number—singular<br>  Stem or root—from αὐξάνω and αὔξω<br>Parsing eplëthuneto (part of speech): verb<br>  Mood—indicative<br>  Tense—imperfect<br>  Voice—passive<br>  Person—3rd person<br>  Number—singular<br>  Stem or root—from πληθύνω<br>Concordance References:<br>⇒ Strong's #837 auxanö + 2532 kai + 4129 plëthunö<br>⇒ NIV #889 auxanö [increase] + 2779 kai [and] + 4437 plëthunö [spread]<br>⇒ NASB #837 auxanö + 2532 kai + 4129 plëthunö<br><br>**Acts 12:24**<br>But the word of God **grew and multiplied**. [KJV]<br>But the word of the Lord continued to **grow and to be multiplied**. [NASB]<br>But the word of God continued to **increase and spread**. [NIV]<br>But the word of God **grew and multiplied**. [NKJV]<br>But God's Good News was **spreading rapidly**, and there were many new believers. [NLT]<br>Ὁ δὲ λόγος τοῦ Θεοῦ ηὔξανε καὶ ἐπληθύνετο. [GNS]<br>Ὁ δὲ λόγος τοῦ θεοῦ ηὔξανεν καὶ ἐπληθύνετο. [GNT] | To increase and spread; to grow and multiply; to spread rapidly.<br><br>**Practical Application**<br>The words "grew and multiplied" (*ëuxanen kai eplëthuneto*) mean that the church kept on growing and multiplying. The progress of God's Word could not be stopped. Men and governments might try to stop it. They might persecute, imprison, and kill those who proclaim God's Word; but their efforts to silence the Word will always be to no avail. God overrules all and always will. |
| **#1808**<br>**Grew In Strength**<br><br>Edified–KJV<br>Being built up–NASB<br>Strengthened–NIV<br>Edified–NKJV<br>Grew in strength–NLT<br><br>**POSB REFERENCE**<br>(Acts 9:31)<br>Note 2 | οἰκοδομουμένη = oikodomoumenë<br>Pronunciation: [oy-kod-om-oo'-mehn-ah-ee]<br>Parsing (part of speech): verb<br>  Mood—participle<br>  Tense—present<br>  Voice—passive<br>  Case—nominative<br>  Gender—feminine<br>  Number—singular<br>  Stem or root—from οἰκοδομέω<br>Concordance References:<br>⇒ Strong's #3618 oikodomeö<br>⇒ NIV #3868 oikodomeö<br>⇒ NASB #3618 oikodomeö<br><br>**Acts 9:31**<br>Then had the churches rest throughout all Judaea and Galilee and Samaria, and were **edified**; and walking in the fear of the Lord, and in the comfort of the Holy Ghost, were multiplied. [KJV]<br>So the church throughout all Judea and Galilee and Samaria enjoyed peace, **being built up**; and, going on in the fear of the Lord and in the comfort of the Holy Spirit, it continued to increase. [NASB]<br>Then the church throughout Judea, Galilee and Samaria enjoyed a time of peace. It was **strengthened**; and encouraged by the Holy Spirit, it grew in numbers, living in the fear of the Lord. [NIV]<br>Then the churches throughout all Judea, Galilee, and Samaria had peace and were **edified**. And walking in the fear of the Lord and in the comfort of the Holy Spirit, they were multiplied. [NKJV]<br>The church then had peace throughout Judea, Galilee, and Samaria, and it **grew in strength** and numbers. The believers were walking in the fear of the Lord and in the | To be strengthened; to be edified; to build; to encourage; to restore.<br><br>**Practical Application**<br>The word means to build up, to grow spiritually, to promote spiritual growth, to strengthen, to establish, to confirm in the faith. The tense is continuous action. |

## PRACTICAL WORD STUDIES
### in the NEW TESTAMENT

| ENGLISH WORD | GREEK WORD AND VERSE | THE WORD MEANS... |
|---|---|---|
| | comfort of the Holy Spirit. [NLT]<br>Αἱ μὲν οὖν ἐκκλησίαι καθ' ὅλης τῆς Ἰουδαίας καὶ Γαλιλαίας καὶ Σαμαρείας εἶχον εἰρήνην, **οἰκοδομούμεναι** καὶ πορευόμεναι τῷ φόβῳ τοῦ Κυρίου, καὶ τῇ παρακλήσει τοῦ Ἁγίου Πνεύματος ἐπληθύνετο. [GNS]<br>Ἡ μὲν οὖν ἐκκλησία καθ' ὅλης τῆς Ἰουδαίας καὶ Γαλιλαίας καὶ Σαμαρείας εἶχεν εἰρήνην **οἰκοδομουμένη** καὶ πορευομένη τῷ φόβῳ τοῦ κυρίου καὶ τῇ παρακλήσει τοῦ ἁγίου πνεύματος ἐπληθύνετο. [GNT] | |
| **#1809**<br>**Grief**<br><br>Sorrow–KJV<br>**Grief–NASB**<br>Anguish–NIV<br>**Grief–NKJV**<br>**Grief–NLT**<br><br>**POSB REFERENCE**<br>(Rom.9:1-3; esp. v.2)<br>Note 1, point 2 | ὀδύνη = odunē<br>Pronunciation: [od-oo'-nay]<br>Parsing (part of speech): noun<br>  Case—nominative<br>  Gender—feminine<br>  Number—singular<br>  Stem or root—from ὀδύνη, ης<br>Concordance References:<br>⇒ Strong's #3601 odunē<br>⇒ NIV #3850 odunē<br>⇒ NASB #3601 odunē<br><br>**Romans 9:2**<br>That I have great heaviness and continual **sorrow** in my heart. [KJV]<br>That I have great sorrow and unceasing **grief** in my heart. [NASB]<br>I have great sorrow and unceasing **anguish** in my heart. [NIV]<br>That I have great sorrow and continual **grief** in my heart. [NKJV]<br>My heart is filled with bitter sorrow and unending **grief** [NLT]<br>ὅτι λύπη μοί ἐστι μεγάλη, καὶ ἀδιάλειπτος **ὀδύνη** τῇ καρδίᾳ μου. [GNS]<br>ὅτι λύπη μοί ἐστιν μεγάλη καὶ ἀδιάλειπτος **ὀδύνη** τῇ καρδίᾳ μου. [GNT] | Intense anguish, sorrow, grief, pain, torment.<br><br>**Practical Application**<br>Note this is continuous and unceasing anguish. Paul was always bearing pain for the salvation of his kinsmen. The depth of Paul's love and concern is graphically seen in what he said. |
| **#1810**<br>**Grief-Stricken**<br><br>Lamented–KJV<br>Lamenting–NASB<br>Wailed for–NIV<br>Lamented–NKJV<br>**Grief-stricken–NLT**<br><br>**POSB REFERENCE**<br>(Lk.23:27)<br>Note 2 | ἐθρήνουν = ethrēnoun<br>Pronunciation: [eh-thray-noon]<br>Parsing (part of speech): verb<br>  Mood—indicative<br>  Tense—imperfect<br>  Voice—active<br>  Person—3rd person<br>  Number—plural<br>  Stem or root—from θρηνέω<br>Concordance References:<br>⇒ Strong's #2354 thrēneō<br>⇒ NIV #2577 thrēneō<br>⇒ NASB #2354 thrēneō<br><br>**Luke 23:27**<br>And there followed him a great company of people, and of women, which also bewailed and **lamented** him. [KJV]<br>And there were following Him a great multitude of the people, and of women who were mourning and **lamenting** Him. [NASB]<br>A large number of people followed him, including women who mourned and **wailed for** him. [NIV]<br>And a great multitude of the people followed Him, and women who also mourned and **lamented** Him. [NKJV]<br>Great crowds trailed along behind, including many **grief-stricken** women. [NLT]<br>Ἠκολούθει δὲ αὐτῷ πολὺ πλῆθος τοῦ λαοῦ, καὶ γυναικῶν αἳ καὶ ἐκόπτοντο καὶ **ἐθρήνουν** αὐτόν. [GNS]<br>Ἠκολούθει δὲ αὐτῷ πολὺ πλῆθος τοῦ λαοῦ καὶ γυναικῶν αἳ ἐκόπτοντο καὶ **ἐθρήνουν** αὐτόν. [GNT] | To be grief-stricken; to lament; to wail; to cry out loud; to mourn; to groan; to weep for; to sing out a dirge.<br><br>**Practical Application**<br>In this Scripture, the women were crying out, unable to hold back the pain cutting their hearts. Some of the people, of course, had been followers of Jesus for a long time and were feeling the depth of their Lord's sufferings. Other onlookers, as in any crowd witnessing severe suffering, felt only a natural tenderness and lament over one suffering so much. |

# PRACTICAL WORD STUDIES
## in the NEW TESTAMENT

| ENGLISH WORD | GREEK WORD AND VERSE | THE WORD MEANS... |
|---|---|---|
| **#1811**<br>**Grief-Stricken**<br><br>Bewailed–KJV<br>Mourning–NASB<br>Mourned–NIV<br>Mourned–NKJV<br>Grief-stricken–NLT<br><br>**POSB REFERENCE**<br>(Lk.23:27)<br>Note 2 | ἐκόπτοντο = ekoptonto<br>Pronunciation: [eh-kop'-tawn-tow]<br>Parsing (part of speech): verb<br>   Mood—indicative<br>   Tense—imperfect<br>   Voice—middle<br>   Person—3rd person<br>   Number—plural<br>   Stem or root—from κόπτω<br>Concordance References:<br>⇒ Strong's #2875 koptō<br>⇒ NIV #3164 koptō<br>⇒ NASB #2875 koptō<br><br>**Luke 23:27**<br>And there followed him a great company of people, and of women, which also **bewailed** and lamented him. [KJV]<br>And there were following Him a great multitude of the people, and of women who were **mourning** and lamenting Him. [NASB]<br>A large number of people followed him, including women who **mourned** and wailed for him. [NIV]<br>And a great multitude of the people followed Him, and women who also **mourned** and lamented Him. [NKJV]<br>Great crowds trailed along behind, including many **grief-stricken** women. [NLT]<br>Ἠκολούθει δὲ αὐτῷ πολὺ πλῆθος τοῦ λαοῦ, καὶ γυναικῶν αἳ καὶ **ἐκόπτοντο** καὶ ἐθρήνουν αὐτόν. [GNS]<br>Ἠκολούθει δὲ αὐτῷ πολὺ πλῆθος τοῦ λαοῦ καὶ γυναικῶν αἳ **ἐκόπτοντο** καὶ ἐθρήνουν αὐτόν. [GNT] | To mourn; to be grief-stricken; to lament; to wail; to cut, strike, smite, beat.<br><br>**Practical Application**<br>They were cut to the core of their hearts, actually feeling pain for Jesus. A natural response to the Lord's sufferings is not enough. A person must understand why Christ suffered and must feel a godly sorrow over Christ's having to bear the sins of the world (see POSB *Deeper Study* #1–2 Cor. 7:10). |
| **#1812**<br>**Grieve**<br><br>Grieve–KJV<br>Grieve–NASB<br>Grieve–NIV<br>Grieve–NKJV<br>Bring sorrow–NLT<br><br>**POSB REFERENCE**<br>(Eph.4:30)<br>Note 5 | λυπεῖτε = lupeite<br>Pronunciation: [loo-peh'-ee-teh]<br>Parsing (part of speech): verb<br>   Mood—imperative<br>   Tense—present<br>   Voice—active<br>   Person—2nd person<br>   Number—plural<br>   Stem or root—from λυπέω<br>Concordance References:<br>⇒ Strong's #3076 lupeō<br>⇒ NIV #3382 lupeō<br>⇒ NASB #3076 lupeō<br><br>**Ephes. 4:30**<br>And **grieve** not the holy Spirit of God, whereby ye are sealed unto the day of redemption. [KJV]<br>And do not **grieve** the Holy Spirit of God, by whom you were sealed for the day of redemption. [NASB]<br>And do not **grieve** the Holy Spirit of God, with whom you were sealed for the day of redemption. [NIV]<br>And do not **grieve** the Holy Spirit of God, by whom you were sealed for the day of redemption. [NKJV]<br>And do not **bring sorrow** to God's Holy Spirit by the way you live. Remember, he is the one who has identified you as his own, guaranteeing that you will be saved on the day of redemption. [NLT]<br>καὶ μὴ **λυπεῖτε** τὸ Πνεῦμα τὸ Ἅγιον τοῦ Θεοῦ, ἐν ᾧ ἐσφραγίσθητε εἰς ἡμέραν ἀπολυτρώσεως. [GNS]<br>καὶ μὴ **λυπεῖτε** τὸ πνεῦμα τὸ ἅγιον τοῦ θεοῦ, ἐν ᾧ ἐσφραγίσθητε εἰς ἡμέραν ἀπολυτρώσεως. [GNT] | To grieve; to bring sorrow; to distress; to pain; to offend; to vex; to injure; to sadden the Holy Spirit.<br><br>**Practical Application**<br>When a child acts contrary to the counsel of his parents, he hurts and grieves them. So when a person acts contrary to the counsel of the Holy Spirit, he hurts and grieves Him. Note three points.<br>1. The command is forceful, very forceful. This is seen in the name of the Holy Spirit. He is not only called the Holy Spirit here, He is called both the Holy Spirit and "the Spirit of God"–a double reference.<br>2. There are at least four ways the Holy Spirit can be grieved.<br>  a. He is *grieved* when believers allow impure things to penetrate their lives or thoughts.<br>  b. He is *grieved* when believers behave immorally.<br>  c. He is *grieved* when believers act unjustly.<br>  d. He is *grieved* when believers participate in anything contrary to the nature of the Holy Spirit. Note the context of this passage: the command to "grieve not the Spirit" is surrounded by a series of negative commands.<br>3. The reason we should not grieve the Spirit of God is because of His great ministry to us: He has sealed us until the day of redemption (see POSB note, Holy Spirit, Seal–Ephes. 1:13-14 for discussion). |

# PRACTICAL WORD STUDIES
## in the NEW TESTAMENT

| ENGLISH WORD | GREEK WORD AND VERSE | THE WORD MEANS... |
|---|---|---|
| **#1813**<br>**Grieve**<br><br>Be afflicted–KJV<br>Be miserable–NASB<br>**Grieve–NIV**<br>Lament–NKJV<br>Deep grief–NLT<br><br>**POSB<br>REFERENCE**<br>(Jas.4:9)<br>Note 3 | ταλαιπωρήσατε = talaipōrēsate<br>Pronunciation: [tal-ahee-po-ray'-sah-teh]<br>Parsing (part of speech): verb<br>    Mood—imperative<br>    Tense—aorist<br>    Voice—active<br>    Person—2nd person<br>    Number—plural<br>    Stem or root—from ταλαιπωρέω<br>Concordance References:<br>  ⇒ Strong's #5003 talaipōreō<br>  ⇒ NIV #5415 talaipōreō<br>  ⇒ NASB #5003 talaipōreō<br><br>**James 4:9**<br>**Be afflicted**, and mourn, and weep: let your laughter be turned to mourning, and your joy to heaviness. [KJV]<br>**Be miserable** and mourn and weep; let your laughter be turned into mourning, and your joy to gloom. [NASB]<br>**Grieve**, mourn and wail. Change your laughter to mourning and your joy to gloom. [NIV]<br>**Lament** and mourn and weep! Let your laughter be turned to mourning and *your* joy to gloom. [NKJV]<br>Let there be tears for the wrong things you have done. Let there be sorrow and **deep grief**. Let there be sadness instead of laughter, and gloom instead of joy. [NLT]<br>ταλαιπωρήσατε καὶ πενθήσατε καὶ κλαύσατε· ὁ γέλως ὑμῶν εἰς πένθος μετατραπήτω, καὶ ἡ χαρὰ εἰς κατήφειαν. [GNS]<br>ταλαιπωρήσατε καὶ πενθήσατε καὶ κλαύσατε. ὁ γέλως ὑμῶν εἰς πένθος μετατραπήτω καὶ ἡ χαρὰ εἰς κατήφειαν. [GNT] | To grieve; to be afflicted; to be miserable; to suffer deep grief; to endure toils (A.T. Robertson. *Word Pictures in the New Testament*, Vol. 6, p.53); to discipline and to voluntarily abstain (William Barclay. *The Letters of James and Peter*, p.127).<br><br>**Practical Application**<br>How can we overcome temptation? Endure. Be deeply and mournfully concerned. Note how descriptive this verse is:<br><br>*Grieve, mourn and wail. Change your laughter to mourning and your joy to gloom (James 4:9).* [NIV]<br><br>The picture is this: when temptation strikes us, it is not time...<br>• to be laughing<br>• to be joking around<br>• to be lighthearted<br>• to be complacent<br>• to be at ease<br>• to be jolly<br>• to be teasing<br>• to be unconcerned<br>• to be uncomfortable<br>• to be lying around<br><br>Temptation is affliction; therefore, it is time to discipline one's self to control the comforts and joys of life. Temptation is a time for rigorous warfare–for battle and the disciplined endurance of battle. |
| **#1814**<br>**Grieved**<br><br>Sorrowful–KJV<br>**Grieved–NASB**<br>Sorrowful–NIV<br>Sorrowful–NKJV<br>Anguish–NLT<br><br>**POSB<br>REFERENCE**<br>(Mt.26:37)<br>*Deeper Study #3* | λυπεῖσθαι = lupeisthai<br>Pronunciation: [loo-pehs'-thigh]<br>Parsing (part of speech): verb<br>    Mood—infinitive<br>    Tense—present<br>    Voice—passive<br>    Stem or root—from λυπέω<br>Concordance References:<br>  ⇒ Strong's #3076 lupeō<br>  ⇒ NIV #3382 lupeō<br>  ⇒ NASB #3076 lupeō<br><br>**Matthew 26:37**<br>And he took with him Peter and the two sons of Zebedee, and began to be **sorrowful** and very heavy. [KJV]<br>And He took with Him Peter and the two sons of Zebedee, and began to be **grieved** and distressed. [NASB]<br>He took Peter and the two sons of Zebedee along with him, and he began to be **sorrowful** and troubled. [NIV]<br>And He took with Him Peter and the two sons of Zebedee, and He began to be **sorrowful** and deeply distressed. [NKJV]<br>He took Peter and Zebedee's two sons, James and John, and he began to be filled with **anguish** and deep distress. [NLT]<br>καὶ παραλαβὼν τὸν Πέτρον καὶ τοὺς δύο υἱοὺς Ζεβεδαίου, ἤρξατο **λυπεῖσθαι** καὶ ἀδημονεῖν. [GNS]<br>καὶ παραλαβὼν τὸν Πέτρον καὶ τοῦ" δύο υἱοὺς Ζεβεδαίου ἤρξατο **λυπεῖσθαι** καὶ αςδμονεῖν [GNT] | To be distressed; to be grieved; to be saddened; to be hurt; to be pained with great anguish. It means to be *consumed* with intense sorrow of heart.<br><br>**Practical Application**<br>What was the source behind this great grief that Christ experienced? Apparently all that Christ had been through and was about to go through was opened up to His mind. His whole being was now focusing on the suffering He had to experience as the sin-bearer for the world. The mental vision literally compressed His physical body, almost to the point of crushing Him. (See POSB *Deeper Study #2*–Matthew 26:37-38.) |

# PRACTICAL WORD STUDIES
## in the NEW TESTAMENT

| ENGLISH WORD | GREEK WORD AND VERSE | THE WORD MEANS... |
|---|---|---|
| **#1815**<br>**Grieved**<br><br>Grieved–KJV<br>Grieved–NASB<br>Deeply distressed–NIV<br>Grieved–NKJV<br>Deeply disturbed–NLT<br><br>**POSB REFERENCE**<br>(Mk.3:5)<br>*Deeper Study #1* | συλλυπούμενος = *sullupoumenos*<br>Pronunciation: [sool-loop-oo'-mehn-os]<br>Parsing (part of speech): verb<br>    Mood—participle<br>    Tense—present<br>    Voice—middle or passive deponent<br>    Case—nominative<br>    Gender—masculine<br>    Number—singular<br>    Stem or root—from συλλυπέομαι<br>Concordance References:<br>  ⇒ Strong's #4818 sullupeō<br>  ⇒ NIV #5200 sullupeō<br>  ⇒ NASB #4818 sullupeō<br><br>**Mark 3:5**<br>And when he had looked round about on them with anger, being **grieved** for the hardness of their hearts, he saith unto the man, Stretch forth thine hand. And he stretched it out: and his hand was restored whole as the other. [KJV]<br><br>And after looking around at them with anger, **grieved** at their hardness of heart, He said to the man, "Stretch out your hand." And he stretched it out, and his hand was restored. [NASB]<br><br>He looked around at them in anger and, **deeply distressed** at their stubborn hearts, said to the man, "Stretch out your hand." He stretched it out, and his hand was completely restored. [NIV]<br><br>And when He had looked around at them with anger, being **grieved** by the hardness of their hearts, He said to the man, "Stretch out your hand." And he stretched *it* out, and his hand was restored as whole as the other. [NKJV]<br><br>He looked around at them angrily, because he was **deeply disturbed** by their hard hearts. Then he said to the man, "Reach out your hand." The man reached out his hand, and it became normal again! [NLT]<br><br>καὶ περιβλεψάμενος αὐτοὺς μετ' ὀργῆς, **συλλυπούμενος** ἐπὶ τῇ πωρώσει τῆς καρδίας αὐτῶν, λέγει τῷ ἀνθρώπῳ, Ἔκτεινον τὴν χεῖρά σου. καὶ ἐξέτεινε, καὶ ἀποκατεστάθη ἡ χεὶρ αὐτοῦ ὑγιὴς ὡς ἡ ἄλλη. [GNS]<br><br>καὶ περιβλεψάμενος αὐτοὺς μετ' ὀργῆς, **συλλυπούμενος** ἐπὶ τῇ πωρώσει τῆς καρδίας αὐτῶν λέγει τῷ ἀνθρώπῳ, Ἔκτεινον τὴν χεῖρα. καὶ ἐξέτεινεν καὶ ἀπεκατεστάθη ἡ χεὶρ αὐτοῦ. [GNT] | To sense grief, sorrow, empathy; to suffer with a person because they are injured; to be deeply distressed or disturbed.<br><br>**Practical Application**<br>In this particular passage, Jesus' anger was combined with grief over people who harmed themselves. The anger of Jesus was a grieving anger over obstinate unbelief. The people who closed their minds–who just remained obstinate in unbelief despite the evidence–aroused a grieving anger within Him. |
| **#1816**<br>**Grieved**<br><br>Grieved–KJV<br>Annoyed–NASB<br>Troubled–NIV<br>Annoyed–NKJV<br>Exasperated–NLT<br><br>**POSB REFERENCE**<br>(Acts 16:18)<br>Note 2, point 2 | διαπονηθείς = *diaponētheis*<br>Pronunciation: [dee-ap-on-ay'-theh-ees]<br>Parsing (part of speech): verb<br>    Mood—participle<br>    Tense—aorist<br>    Voice—passive deponent<br>    Case—nominative<br>    Gender—masculine<br>    Number—singular<br>    Stem or root—from διαπονέομαι<br>Concordance References:<br>  ⇒ Strong's #1278 diaponeomai<br>  ⇒ NIV #1387 diaponeomai<br>  ⇒ NASB #1278 diaponeomai<br><br>**Acts 16:18**<br>And this did she many days. But Paul, being **grieved**, turned and said to the spirit, I command thee in the name of Jesus Christ to come out of her. And he came out the same hour. [KJV]<br><br>And she continued doing this for many days. But Paul was greatly **annoyed**, and turned and said to the spirit, "I command you in the name of Jesus Christ to come out of her!" And it came out at that very moment. [NASB]<br><br>She kept this up for many days. Finally Paul became | Troubled, grieved, annoyed, exasperated. The word means pained, deeply troubled, worked up, annoyed, and angry (a righteous anger).<br><br>**Practical Application**<br>Paul was troubled and hurting...<br>• over the girl's being enslaved by sin.<br>• over the girl's being so used by greedy and lustful men.<br>• over the false witness to the Lord's name.<br>• over the mockery and ridicule of his ministry as the servant of Christ. |

# PRACTICAL WORD STUDIES
## in the NEW TESTAMENT

| ENGLISH WORD | GREEK WORD AND VERSE | THE WORD MEANS... |
|---|---|---|
| | so **troubled** that he turned around and said to the spirit, "In the name of Jesus Christ I command you to come out of her!" At that moment the spirit left her. [NIV]<br><br>And this she did for many days. But Paul, greatly **annoyed**, turned and said to the spirit, "I command you in the name of Jesus Christ to come out of her." And he came out that very hour. [NKJV]<br><br>This went on day after day until Paul got so **exasperated** that he turned and spoke to the demon within her. "I command you in the name of Jesus Christ to come out of her," he said. And instantly it left her. [NLT]<br><br>τοῦτο δὲ ἐποίει ἐπὶ πολλὰς ἡμέρας. **διαπονηθεὶς** δὲ ὁ Παῦλος, καὶ ἐπιστρέψας, τῷ πνεύματι εἶπε, Παραγγέλλω σοι ἐν τῷ ὀνόματι Ἰησοῦ Χριστοῦ, ἐξελθεῖν ἀπ' αὐτῆς. Καὶ ἐξῆλθεν αὐτῇ τῇ ὥρᾳ. [GNS]<br><br>τοῦτο δὲ ἐποίει ἐπὶ πολλὰς ἡμέρας. **διαπονηθεὶς** δὲ Παῦλος καὶ ἐπιστρέψας τῷ πνεύματι εἶπεν, Παραγγέλλω σοι ἐν ὀνόματι Ἰησοῦ Χριστοῦ ἐξελθεῖν ἀπ' αὐτῆς· καὶ ἐξῆλθεν αὐτῇ τῇ ὥρᾳ. [GNT] | |
| **#1817**<br>**Grieved**<br><br>Heaviness–KJV<br>Distressed–NASB<br>Suffer grief–NIV<br>**Grieved–NKJV**<br>Endure–NLT<br><br>**POSB REFERENCE**<br>(1 Pt.1:6)<br>Note 1, point 2 | λυπηθέντες = lupēthentes<br>Pronunciation: [loo-pay'-then-tehs]<br>Parsing (part of speech): verb<br>  Mood—participle<br>  Tense—aorist<br>  Voice—passive<br>  Case—nominative<br>  Gender—masculine<br>  Person—2nd person<br>  Number—plural<br>  Stem or root—from λυπέω<br>Concordance References:<br>  ⇒ Strong's #3076 lupeö<br>  ⇒ NIV #3382 lupeö<br>  ⇒ NASB #3076 lupeö<br><br>**1 Peter 1:6**<br>Wherein ye greatly rejoice, though now for a season, if need be, ye are in **heaviness** through manifold temptations: [KJV]<br><br>In this you greatly rejoice, even though now for a little while, if necessary, you have been **distressed** by various trials, [NASB]<br><br>In this you greatly rejoice, though now for a little while you may have had to **suffer grief** in all kinds of trials. [NIV]<br><br>In this you greatly rejoice, though now for a little while, if need be, you have been **grieved** by various trials, [NKJV]<br><br>So be truly glad! There is wonderful joy ahead, even though it is necessary for you to **endure** many trials for a while. [NLT]<br><br>ἐν ᾧ ἀγαλλιᾶσθε ὀλίγον ἄρτι, εἰ δέον ἐστί, **λυπηθέντες** ἐν ποικίλοις πειρασμοῖς, [GNS]<br><br>ἐν ᾧ ἀγαλλιᾶσθε, ὀλίγον ἄρτι εἰ δέον [ἐστὶν] **λυπηθέντες** ἐν ποικίλοις πειρασμοῖς, [GNT] | To suffer grief, heaviness; to be distressed; to be sorrowful; to be sad; to be grieving; to suffer sorrow, stress, pressure, and mental anguish.<br><br>**Practical Application**<br>Trials and temptations cause a heaviness within us. We all know what it is to feel heavy and weighed down with grief; to suffer stress and pressure; to be in mental anguish, wondering, questioning, and suffering under the weight of trial or temptation. |
| **#1818**<br>**Groaned**<br><br>**Groaned–KJV**<br>Deeply moved–NASB<br>Deeply moved–NIV<br>**Groaned–NKJV**<br>Moved–NLT<br><br>**POSB REFERENCE**<br>(Jn.11:33-36; esp. v.33)<br>Note 5, point 1 | ἐνεβριμήσατο = enebrimēsato<br>Pronunciation: [en-eh-brim-ay'-sah-tow]<br>Parsing (part of speech): verb<br>  Mood—indicative<br>  Tense—aorist<br>  Voice—middle deponent<br>  Person—3rd person<br>  Number—singular<br>  Stem or root—from ἐμβριμάομαι<br>Concordance References:<br>  ⇒ Strong's #1690 embrimaomai<br>  ⇒ NIV #1839 embrimaomai<br>  ⇒ NASB #1690 embrimaomai<br><br>**John 11:33**<br>When Jesus therefore saw her weeping, and the Jews | To be deeply moved; to groan in the spirit; to be agitated by grief and sorrow.<br><br>**Practical Application**<br>Jesus groans in understanding and feeling and compassion for all who are hurting and suffering. In this Scripture, we see Jesus gripped with intense emotion. He was deeply moved...<br>• by Mary, who was so broken in sorrow.<br>• by Martha, who was gripped by pain and hurt.<br>• by those who were really feeling the death of Lazarus and the sorrow of the family.<br>• by the terrible tragedy of death and the pain it causes. |

# PRACTICAL WORD STUDIES
## in the NEW TESTAMENT

| ENGLISH WORD | GREEK WORD AND VERSE | THE WORD MEANS... |
|---|---|---|
| | also weeping which came with her, he **groaned** in the spirit, and was troubled, [KJV]<br><br>When Jesus therefore saw her weeping, and the Jews who came with her, also weeping, He was **deeply moved** in spirit, and was troubled, [NASB]<br><br>When Jesus saw her weeping, and the Jews who had come along with her also weeping, he was **deeply moved** in spirit and troubled. [NIV]<br><br>Therefore, when Jesus saw her weeping, and the Jews who came with her weeping, He **groaned** in the spirit and was troubled. [NKJV]<br><br>When Jesus saw her weeping and saw the other people wailing with her, he was **moved** with indignation and was deeply troubled. [NLT]<br><br>Ἰησοῦς οὖν ὡς εἶδεν αὐτὴν κλαίουσαν, καὶ τοὺς συνελθόντας αὐτῇ Ἰουδαίους κλαίοντας, **ἐνεβριμήσατο** τῷ πνεύματι, καὶ ἐτάραξεν ἑαυτόν, [GNS]<br><br>Ἰησοῦς οὖν ὡς εἶδεν αὐτὴν κλαίουσαν καὶ τοὺς συνελθόντας αὐτῇ Ἰουδαίους κλαίοντας, **ἐνεβριμήσατο** τῷ πνεύματι καὶ ἐτάραξεν ἑαυτόν· [GNT] | • by the terrible price He was soon to pay conquering death. (This was certainly glimpsed by Jesus in such a scene as He was now experiencing.) |
| **#1819**<br>**Grounded**<br><br>**Grounded**–KJV<br>Established–NASB<br>Established–NIV<br>**Grounded**–NKJV<br>Stand in it–NLT<br><br>**POSB REFERENCE**<br>(Col.1:23)<br>Note 4, point 1 | τεθεμελιωμένοι = tethemeliōmenoi<br>Pronunciation: [teh-them-el-ee-o'-mehn-oy]<br>Parsing (part of speech): verb<br>    Mood—participle<br>    Tense—perfect<br>    Voice—passive<br>    Case—nominative<br>    Gender—masculine<br>    Person—2nd person<br>    Number—plural<br>    Stem or root—from θεμελιόω<br>Concordance References:<br>  ⇒ Strong's #2311 themelioō<br>  ⇒ NIV #2530 themelioō<br>  ⇒ NASB #2311 themelioō<br><br>**Col. 1:23**<br>If ye continue in the faith **grounded** and settled, and be not moved away from the hope of the gospel, which ye have heard, and which was preached to every creature which is under heaven; whereof I Paul am made a minister; [KJV]<br><br>If indeed you continue in the faith firmly **established** and steadfast, and not moved away from the hope of the gospel that you have heard, which was proclaimed in all creation under heaven, and of which I, Paul, was made a minister. [NASB]<br><br>If you continue in your faith, **established** and firm, not moved from the hope held out in the gospel. This is the gospel that you heard and that has been proclaimed to every creature under heaven, and of which I, Paul, have become a servant. [NIV]<br><br>If indeed you continue in the faith, **grounded** and steadfast, and are not moved away from the hope of the gospel which you heard, which was preached to every creature under heaven, of which I, Paul, became a minister. [NKJV]<br><br>But you must continue to believe this truth and **stand in it** firmly. Don't drift away from the assurance you received when you heard the Good News. The Good News has been preached all over the world, and I, Paul, have been appointed by God to proclaim it. [NLT]<br><br>εἴγε ἐπιμένετε τῇ πίστει **τεθεμελιωμένοι** καὶ ἑδραῖοι, καὶ μὴ μετακινούμενοι ἀπὸ τῆς ἐλπίδος τοῦ εὐαγγελίου οὗ ἠκούσατε, τοῦ κηρυχθέντος ἐν πάσῃ τῇ κτίσει τῇ ὑπὸ τὸν οὐρανόν, οὗ ἐγενόμην ἐγὼ Παῦλος διάκονος." [GNS]<br><br>εἴ γε ἐπιμένετε τῇ πίστει **τεθεμελιωμένοι** καὶ ἑδραῖοι καὶ μὴ μετακινούμενοι ἀπὸ τῆς ἐλπίδος τοῦ εὐαγγελίου οὗ ἠκούσατε, τοῦ κηρυχθέντος ἐν πάσῃ κτίσει τῇ ὑπὸ τὸν οὐρανόν, οὗ ἐγενόμην ἐγὼ Παῦλος διάκονος. [GNT] | To be established; to be grounded; to be rooted; to make strong; to be fixed. It means to be grounded in Christ like the firm, solid foundation of a building.<br><br>**Practical Application**<br>This is the word that pictures the foundation of a building, the solid foundation that gives the greatest stability possible to a building. The believer must be so grounded in Christ that he can withstand the severest storms of life. |

# PRACTICAL WORD STUDIES
## in the NEW TESTAMENT

| ENGLISH WORD | GREEK WORD AND VERSE | THE WORD MEANS... |
|---|---|---|
| **#1820**<br>**Grow And To Be Multiplied**<br><br>Grew and multiplied–KJV<br>**Grow and to be multiplied**–NASB<br>Increase and spread–NIV<br>Grew and multiplied–NKJV<br>Spreading rapidly–NLT<br><br>**POSB REFERENCE**<br>(Acts 12:24-25; esp. v.24)<br>Note 4, point 1 | ηὔξανεν καὶ ἐπληθύνετο = ëuxanen kai eplëthuneto<br>Pronunciation: [ayoowx-ahn'-ehn ky eh-play-thoo'-neh-tow]<br>Parsing *ëuxanen* (part of speech): verb<br>    Mood—indicative<br>    Tense—imperfect<br>    Voice—active<br>    Person—3rd person<br>    Number—singular<br>    Stem or root—from αὐξάνω and αὔξω<br>Parsing *eplëthuneto* (part of speech): verb<br>    Mood—indicative<br>    Tense—imperfect<br>    Voice—passive<br>    Person—3rd person<br>    Number—singular<br>    Stem or root—from πληθύνω<br>Concordance References:<br>  ⇒ Strong's #837 auxanö + 2532 kai + 4129 plëthunö<br>  ⇒ NIV #889 auxanö [increase] + 2779 kai [and] + 4437 plëthunö [spread]<br>  ⇒ NASB #837 auxanö + 2532 kai + 4129 plëthunö<br><br>**Acts 12:24**<br>But the word of God **grew and multiplied**. [KJV]<br>But the word of the Lord continued to **grow and to be multiplied**. [NASB]<br>But the word of God continued to **increase and spread**. [NIV]<br>But the word of God **grew and multiplied**. [NKJV]<br>But God's Good News was **spreading rapidly**, and there were many new believers. [NLT]<br>Ὁ δὲ λόγος τοῦ Θεοῦ ηὔξανε καὶ ἐπληθύνετο. [GNS]<br>Ὁ δὲ λόγος τοῦ θεοῦ ηὔξανεν καὶ Ἐπληθύνετο. [GNT] | To increase and spread; to grow and multiply; to spread rapidly.<br><br>**Practical Application**<br>The words "grow and to be multiplied" (*ëuxanen kai eplëthuneto*) mean that the church kept on growing and multiplying. The progress of God's Word could not be stopped. Men and governments might try to stop it. They might persecute, imprison, and kill those who proclaim God's Word, but their efforts to silence the Word will always be to no avail. God overrules all and always will. |
| **#1821**<br>**Grow Strong**<br><br>Established–KJV<br>Established–NASB<br>Make...strong–NIV<br>Established–NKJV<br>**Grow strong**–NLT<br><br>**POSB REFERENCE**<br>(Romans 1:10-13; esp. v.11)<br>Note 4, point 1, thought 1 | στηριχθῆναι = stërichthënai<br>Pronunciation: [stay-rix'-thay-nah-ee]<br>Parsing (part of speech): verb<br>    Mood—infinitive<br>    Tense—aorist<br>    Voice—passive<br>    Case—accusative<br>    Stem or root—from στηρίζω<br>Concordance References:<br>  ⇒ Strong's #4741 stërizö<br>  ⇒ NIV #5114 stërizö<br>  ⇒ NASB #4741 stërizö<br><br>**Romans 1:11**<br>For I long to see you, that I may impart unto you some spiritual gift, to the end ye may be **established**; [KJV]<br>For I long to see you in order that I may impart some spiritual gift to you, that you may be **established**; [NASB]<br>I long to see you so that I may impart to you some spiritual gift to **make** you **strong**— [NIV]<br>For I long to see you, that I may impart to you some spiritual gift, so that you may be **established**— [NKJV]<br>For I long to visit you so I can share a spiritual blessing with you that will help you **grow strong** in the Lord. [NLT]<br>ἐπιποθῶ γὰρ ἰδεῖν ὑμᾶς, ἵνα τι μεταδῶ χάρισμα ὑμῖν πνευματικὸν εἰς τὸ **στηριχθῆναι** ὑμᾶς, [GNS]<br>ἐπιποθῶ γὰρ ἰδεῖν ὑμᾶς, ἵνα τι μεταδῶ χάρισμα ὑμῖν πνευματικὸν εἰς τὸ **στηριχθῆναι** ὑμᾶς, [GNT] | To make firm; to make strong; to establish; to fix; to make fast; to strengthen; to set.<br><br>**Practical Application**<br>Paul wished to *impart some spiritual gift* to the believers. Why? So that they might be more deeply established in the faith. The term spiritual gift (*charisma*) means a gift of grace. The term often refers to specific gifts given by the Holy Spirit (Romans 12:6-8), but here it means *the truths* of the grace of God, of His spiritual blessings to man revealed in Christ Jesus our Lord. Very simply, Paul longed to share the truths of the gospel with the believers at Rome. God's spiritual blessings were overflowing in his heart, and he was aching to share the gift of God's blessings. |

# PRACTICAL WORD STUDIES
## in the NEW TESTAMENT

| ENGLISH WORD | GREEK WORD AND VERSE | THE WORD MEANS... |
|---|---|---|
| **#1822**<br>**Growing More and More**<br><br>Exceedingly–KJV<br>Greatly enlarged–NASB<br>**Growing more and more–NIV**<br>Grows exceedingly–NKJV<br>Flourishing–NLT<br><br>**POSB REFERENCE**<br>(2 Thes.1:3)<br>Note 4 | ὑπεραυξάνει = *huperauxanei*<br>Pronunciation: [hoop-er-owx-ahn'-eh-ee]<br>Parsing (part of speech): verb<br>  Mood—indicative<br>  Tense—present<br>  Voice—active<br>  Person—3rd person<br>  Number—singular<br>  Stem or root—from ὑπεραυξάνω<br>Concordance References:<br> ⇒ Strong's #5232 huperauxanō<br> ⇒ NIV #5647 huperauxanō<br> ⇒ NASB #5232 huperauxanō<br><br>**2 Thes. 1:3**<br>We are bound to thank God always for you, brethren, as it is meet, because that your faith groweth **exceedingly**, and the charity of every one of you all toward each other aboundeth; [KJV]<br><br>We ought always to give thanks to God for you, brethren, as is only fitting, because your faith is **greatly enlarged**, and the love of each one of you toward one another grows ever greater; [NASB]<br><br>We ought always to thank God for you, brothers, and rightly so, because your faith is **growing more and more**, and the love every one of you has for each other is increasing. [NIV]<br><br>We are bound to thank God always for you, brethren, as it is fitting, because your faith **grows exceedingly**, and the love of every one of you all abounds toward other, [NKJV]<br><br>Dear brothers and sisters, we always thank God for you, as is right, for we are thankful that your faith is **flourishing** and you are all growing in love for each other. [NLT]<br><br>Εὐχαριστεῖν ὀφείλομεν τῷ Θεῷ πάντοτε περὶ ὑμῶν, ἀδελφοί, καθὼς ἄξιόν ἐστιν, ὅτι **ὑπεραυξάνει** ἡ πίστις ὑμῶν, καὶ πλεονάζει ἡ ἀγάπη ἑνὸς ἑκάστου πάντων ὑμῶν εἰς ἀλλήλους· [GNS]<br><br>Εὐχαριστεῖν ὀφείλομεν τῷ θεῷ πάντοτε περὶ ὑμῶν, ἀδελφοί, καθὼς ἄξιόν ἐστιν, ὅτι **ὑπεραυξάνει** ἡ πίστις ὑμῶν, καὶ πλεονάζει ἡ ἀγάπη ἑνὸς ἑκάστου πάντων ὑμῶν εἰς ἀλλήλους, [GNT] | Growing more and more; exceedingly; greatly enlarged; flourishing; to grow abundantly; to grow beyond measure; to grow far beyond what would be expected.<br><br>**Practical Application**<br>What a glorious testimony! Faith that just grows and grows more and more. Imagine a church full of believers whose faith in Christ Jesus grows explosively–beyond measure–beyond what we could ever imagine. And remember: the church was growing in faith while they were in the midst of savage persecution. This is the reason Paul says: "We are bound to thank God always for you." |
| **#1823**<br>**Grudgingly, Not**<br><br>Not for filthy lucre–KJV<br>Not for sordid gain–NASB<br>Not greedy for money–NIV<br>Not for dishonest gain–NKJV<br>**Not grudgingly–NLT**<br><br>**POSB REFERENCE**<br>(1 Pt.5:2-3; esp. v.2)<br>Note 2, point 2 | μηδὲ αἰσχροκερδῶς = *mēde aischrokerdōs*<br>Pronunciation: [may-deh' ahee-skhrok-er-doce']<br>Parsing *aischrokerdōs* (part of speech): adjective<br>  Type—adverb<br>  Stem or root—from αἰσχροκερδῶς<br>Concordance References:<br> ⇒ Strong's #3366 mēde + 147 aischrokerdōs<br> ⇒ NIV #3593 mēde [not] +154 aischrokerdōs [greedy for money]<br> ⇒ NASB #3366 mēde + 147 aischrokerdōs<br><br>**1 Peter 5:2**<br>Feed the flock of God which is among you, taking the oversight thereof, not by constraint, but willingly; **not for filthy lucre**, but of a ready mind; [KJV]<br><br>Shepherd the flock of God among you, exercising oversight not under compulsion, but voluntarily, according to the will of God; and **not for sordid gain**, but with eagerness; [NASB]<br><br>Be shepherds of God's flock that is under your care, serving as overseers—not because you must, but because you are willing, as God wants you to be; **not greedy for money**, but eager to serve; [NIV]<br><br>Shepherd the flock of God which is among you, serving as overseers, not by compulsion but willingly, **not for dishonest gain** but eagerly; [NKJV]<br><br>Care for the flock of God entrusted to you. Watch over it willingly, **not grudgingly**—not for what you will get | Not greedy for money; not for filthy lucre; not for sordid gain; not grudgingly; not for greediness for material gain.<br><br>**Practical Application**<br>The elder or minister must take the oversight of the flock not for personal profit and gain, but of a ready mind. The Greek says that no person is to enter the ministry "grudgingly" (*mēde aischrokerdōs*), that is, for base gain, or for some soiled and dirty advantage. No person should ever enter the ministry...<br>• as a profession.<br>• as a means of livelihood.<br>• as a means to serve mankind.<br>• because people say he has the gifts for it.<br>• because people say he would make a good minister.<br>• because family and friends encourage him to enter the ministry.<br><br>All of these reasons usually surround a person's entrance into the ministry. But they must never be *the reasons* why a person enters the ministry and cares for God's people. The ministry is a *call from God*, and no person dare enter |

## PRACTICAL WORD STUDIES
### in the NEW TESTAMENT

| ENGLISH WORD | GREEK WORD AND VERSE | THE WORD MEANS... |
|---|---|---|
| | out of it, but because you are eager to serve God. [NLT]<br>ποιμάνατε τὸ ἐν ὑμῖν ποίμνιον τοῦ Θεοῦ, ἐπισκοποῦντες μὴ ἀναγκαστῶς, ἀλλ' ἑκουσίως· **μηδὲ αἰσχροκερδῶς**, ἀλλὰ προθύμως, [GNS]<br>ποιμάνατε τὸ ἐν ὑμῖν ποίμνιον τοῦ θεοῦ [ἐπισκοποῦντες] μὴ ἀναγκαστῶς ἀλλὰ ἑκουσίως κατὰ θεόν, **μηδὲ αἰσχροκερδῶς** ἀλλὰ προθύμως, [GNT] | the ministry without a personal call to the ministry. But note: when the call comes, the person is to have a ready mind. He is to minister to God's people; he is to readily feed the flock of God. |
| **#1824**<br>**Grumble–**<br>**Grumbling**<br><br>Murmured–KJV<br>**Grumbling–NASB**<br>**Grumble–NIV**<br>Complained–NKJV<br>Murmur–NLT<br><br>**POSB**<br>**REFERENCE**<br>(Jn.6:41-43; esp. v.41)<br>Note 1 | Ἐγόγγυζον = *Egogguzon*<br>Pronunciation: [eh-gong-good'-zon]<br>Parsing (part of speech): verb<br>   Mood—indicative<br>   Tense—imperfect<br>   Voice—active<br>   Person—3rd person<br>   Number—plural<br>   Stem or root—from γογγύζω<br>Concordance References:<br>  ⇒ Strong's #1111 gogguzō<br>  ⇒ NIV #1197 gogguzō<br>  ⇒ NASB #1111 gogguzō<br><br>**John 6:41**<br>The Jews then **murmured** at him, because he said, I am the bread which came down from heaven. [KJV]<br>The Jews therefore were **grumbling** about Him, because He said, "I am the bread that came down out of heaven." [NASB]<br>At this the Jews began to **grumble** about him because he said, "I am the bread that came down from heaven." [NIV]<br>The Jews then **complained** about Him, because He said, "I am the bread which came down from heaven." [NKJV]<br>Then the people began to **murmur** in disagreement because he had said, "I am the bread from heaven." [NLT]<br>Ἐγόγγυζον οὖν οἱ Ἰουδαῖοι περὶ αὐτοῦ, ὅτι εἶπεν, Ἐγώ εἰμι ὁ ἄρτος ὁ καταβὰς ἐκ τοῦ οὐρανοῦ. [GNS]<br>Ἐγόγγυζον οὖν οἱ Ἰουδαῖοι περὶ αὐτοῦ ὅτι εἶπεν, Ἐγώ εἰμι ὁ ἄρτος ὁ καταβὰς ἐκ τοῦ οὐρανοῦ, [GNT] | To grumble; to murmur against; to mutter; to whisper undertones; to grouse; to complain.<br><br>**Practical Application**<br>The Jews grumbled against Him. The word refers to the murmuring, the buzzing, the discontent that arises from a crowd that is upset and confused; that is, misunderstanding, rejecting, and opposing a speaker. |
| **#1825**<br>**Grumbling**<br><br>Murmurings–KJV<br>**Grumbling–NASB**<br>Complaining–NIV<br>Complaining–NKJV<br>Complaining–NLT<br><br>**POSB**<br>**REFERENCE**<br>(Philip.2:14)<br>Note 3 | γογγυσμῶν = *goggusmōn*<br>Pronunciation: [gong-goos-mown']<br>Parsing (part of speech): noun<br>   Case—genitive<br>   Gender—masculine<br>   Number—plural<br>   Stem or root—from γογγυσμός, οῦ<br>Concordance References:<br>  ⇒ Strong's #1112 goggusmos<br>  ⇒ NIV #1198 goggusmos<br>  ⇒ NASB #1112 goggusmos<br><br>**Philip. 2:14**<br>Do all things without **murmurings** and disputings: [KJV]<br>Do all things without **grumbling** or disputing; [NASB]<br>Do everything without **complaining** or arguing, [NIV]<br>Do all things without **complaining** and disputing, [NKJV]<br>In everything you do, stay away from **complaining** and arguing, [NLT]<br>πάντα ποιεῖτε χωρὶς **γογγυσμῶν** καὶ διαλογισμῶν, [GNS]<br>πάντα ποιεῖτε χωρὶς **γογγυσμῶν** καὶ διαλογισμῶν, [GNT] | Complaining, murmuring, grumbling, whispering, quarreling.<br><br>**Practical Application**<br>Note: it means the quiet, soft, behind-the-back undertone of complaining and grumbling. It is the kind of criticism, dissatisfaction, faultfinding and gossip that goes on within small groups or cliques.<br>The results of grumbling are far worse than people ever think. This is the primary reason God forbids grumbling in no uncertain terms. Grumbling...<br>• hurts<br>• damages<br>• divides<br>• tears down<br>• downs a person<br>• says "look at me"<br>• elevates selfish opinion<br>• opposes God's will<br>• hinders progress<br>• stymies growth<br>• misleads people<br>• is self-centered<br>• pushes people away from Christ and the church |

# PRACTICAL WORD STUDIES
## in the NEW TESTAMENT

| ENGLISH WORD | GREEK WORD AND VERSE | THE WORD MEANS... |
|---|---|---|
| **#1826**<br>**Guarantee**<br><br>Earnest–KJV<br>Pledge–NASB<br>Deposit guaranteeing what is to come–NIV<br>**Guarantee–NKJV**<br>First installment–NLT<br><br>**POSB REFERENCE**<br>(2 Cor.1:21-22; esp. v.22)<br>Note 5 | ἀρραβῶνα = *arrabōna*<br>Pronunciation: [ar-hrab-ohn'-ah]<br>Parsing (part of speech): noun<br>    Case—accusative<br>    Gender—masculine<br>    Number—singular<br>    Stem or root—from ἀρραβῶν, ῶνος<br>Concordance References:<br>  ⇒ Strong's #728 *arrabōn*<br>  ⇒ NIV #775 *arrabōn*<br>  ⇒ NASB #728 *arrabōn*<br><br>**2 Cor. 1:22**<br>Who hath also sealed us, and given the **earnest** of the Spirit in our hearts. [KJV]<br>Who also sealed us and gave us the Spirit in our hearts as a **pledge**. [NASB]<br>Set his seal of ownership on us, and put his Spirit in our hearts as a **deposit, guaranteeing what is to come**. [NIV]<br>Who also has sealed us and given us the Spirit in our hearts as a **guarantee**. [NKJV]<br>And he has identified us as his own by placing the Holy Spirit in our hearts as the **first installment** of everything he will give us. [NLT]<br>ὁ καὶ σφραγισάμενος ἡμᾶς, καὶ δοὺς τὸν **ἀρραβῶνα** τοῦ Πνεύματος ἐν ταῖς καρδίαις ἡμῶν. [GNS]<br>ὁ καὶ σφραγισάμενος ἡμᾶς καὶ δοὺς τὸν **ἀρραβῶνα** τοῦ πνεύματος ἐν ταῖς καρδίαις ἡμῶν. [GNT] | Deposit, guarantee, security, pledge, first installment (of what is to come), payment.<br><br>**Practical Application**<br>It was the first installment paid on an item to guarantee that the rest would be paid. It was the engagement ring that guaranteed the marriage. God has given the Holy Spirit as the guarantee of eternal life. The Holy Spirit is an advanced payment, a down payment on His promise to believers. |
| **#1827**<br>**Guarantee**<br><br>Earnest–KJV<br>Pledge–NASB<br>Deposit guaranteeing–NIV<br>**Guarantee–NKJV**<br>**Guarantee–NLT**<br><br>**POSB REFERENCE**<br>(Eph.1:13-14; esp. v.14)<br>Note 8 | ἀρραβῶν = *arrabōn*<br>Pronunciation: [ar-hrab-ohn']<br>Parsing (part of speech): noun<br>    Case—nominative<br>    Gender—masculine<br>    Number—singular<br>    Stem or root—from ἀρραβῶν, ῶνος<br>Concordance References:<br>  ⇒ Strong's #728 *arrabōn*<br>  ⇒ NIV #775 *arrabōn*<br>  ⇒ NASB #728 *arrabōn*<br><br>**Ephes. 1:14**<br>Which is the **earnest** of our inheritance until the redemption of the purchased possession, unto the praise of his glory. [KJV]<br>Who is given as a **pledge** of our inheritance, with a view to the redemption of God's own possession, to the praise of His glory. [NASB]<br>Who is a **deposit guaranteeing** our inheritance until the redemption of those who are God's possession—to the praise of his glory. [NIV]<br>Who is the **guarantee** of our inheritance until the redemption of the purchased possession, to the praise of His glory. [NKJV]<br>The Spirit is God's **guarantee** that he will give us everything he promised and that he has purchased us to be his own people. This is just one more reason for us to praise our glorious God. [NLT]<br>ὅς ἐστιν **ἀρραβῶν** τῆς κληρονομίας ἡμῶν, εἰς ἀπολύτρωσιν τῆς περιποιήσεως, εἰς ἔπαινον τῆς δόξης αὐτοῦ. [GNS]<br>ὅ ἐστιν **ἀρραβῶν** τῆς κληρονομίας ἡμῶν, εἰς ἀπολύτρωσιν τῆς περιποιήσεως, εἰς ἔπαινον τῆς δόξης αὐτοῦ. [GNT] | A deposit guaranteeing; an earnest; a pledge; a guarantee; a down payment.<br><br>**Practical Application**<br>The Holy Spirit is given to the believer to give the believer perfect assurance of his salvation. We know that we are redeemed–that we are God's cherished possession–by the Holy Spirit who lives within us.<br>Again note: Why does God give us such a glorious guarantee as His own wonderful presence? That His glory might be praised eternally. |
| **#1828**<br>**Guard**<br><br>Keep–KJV<br>**Guard–NASB**<br>**Guard–NIV** | φρουρήσει = *phrourēsei*<br>Pronunciation: [froo-ray'-seh-ee]<br>Parsing (part of speech): verb<br>    Mood—indicative<br>    Tense—future<br>    Voice—active<br>    Person—3rd person | To protect; to keep; to guard; to defend; to preserve; to cover; to insulate; to safeguard.<br><br>**Practical Application**<br>The word "guard" (*phrourēsei*) is a military word meaning to garrison, to keep guard and |

# PRACTICAL WORD STUDIES
## in the New Testament

| ENGLISH WORD | GREEK WORD AND VERSE | THE WORD MEANS... |
|---|---|---|
| **Guard**–NKJV<br>**Guard**–NLT<br><br>**POSB<br>REFERENCE**<br>(Philip.4:6-7; esp. v.7)<br>Note 1, point 3b | Number—singular<br>Stem or root—from φρουρέω<br>Concordance References:<br>⇒ Strong's #5432 phroureō<br>⇒ NIV #5864 phroureō<br>⇒ NASB #5432 phroureō<br><br>**Philip. 4:7**<br>And the peace of God, which passeth all understanding, shall **keep** your hearts and minds through Christ Jesus. [KJV]<br>And the peace of God, which surpasses all comprehension, shall **guard** your hearts and your minds in Christ Jesus. [NASB]<br>And the peace of God, which transcends all understanding, will **guard** your hearts and your minds in Christ Jesus. [NIV]<br>And the peace of God, which surpasses all understanding, will **guard** your hearts and minds through Christ Jesus. [NKJV]<br>If you do this, you will experience God's peace, which is far more wonderful than the human mind can understand. His peace will **guard** your hearts and minds as you live in Christ Jesus. [NLT]<br>καὶ ἡ εἰρήνη τοῦ Θεοῦ ἡ ὑπερέχουσα πάντα νοῦν, **φρουρήσει** τὰς καρδίας ὑμῶν καὶ τὰ νοήματα ὑμῶν ἐν Χριστῷ Ἰησοῦ. [GNS]<br>καὶ ἡ εἰρήνη τοῦ Θεοῦ ἡ ὑπερέχουσα πάντα νοῦν **φρουρήσει** τὰς καρδίας ὑμῶν καὶ τὰ νοήματα ὑμῶν ἐν Χριστῷ Ἰησοῦ. [GNT] | protect. The peace of God is like a most elite soldier who guards and protects the most precious possession of God: the believer's heart and mind.<br>However, note that God can guard us only as we are "in Christ Jesus." We can know the peace of God only if we have trusted Christ as our Lord and Savior and only if we walk in fellowship with Him. To be in Christ means to walk in Christ–to live, move and have our being in Him. |
| **#1829<br>Guard**<br><br>Keep–KJV<br>Protect–NASB<br>Protect–NIV<br>**Guard**–NKJV<br>**Guard**–NLT<br><br>**POSB<br>REFERENCE**<br>(2 Thes.3:3-5; esp. v.3)<br>Note 2, point 1 | φυλάξει = *phulaxei*<br>Pronunciation: [foo-lax'-eh-ee]<br>Parsing (part of speech): verb<br>  Mood—indicative<br>  Tense—future<br>  Voice—active<br>  Person—3rd person<br>  Number—singular<br>Stem or root—from φυλάσσω<br>Concordance References:<br>⇒ Strong's #5442 phulassō<br>⇒ NIV #5875 phulassō<br>⇒ NASB #5442 phulassō<br><br>**2 Thes. 3:3**<br>But the Lord is faithful, who shall stablish you, and **keep** you from evil. [KJV]<br>But the Lord is faithful, and He will strengthen and **protect** you from the evil one. [NASB]<br>But the Lord is faithful, and he will strengthen and **protect** you from the evil one. [NIV]<br>But the Lord is faithful, who will establish you and **guard** *you* from the evil one. [NKJV]<br>But the Lord is faithful; he will make you strong and **guard** you from the evil one. [NLT]<br>πιστὸς δέ ἐστι ὁ Κύριος, ὃς στηρίξει ὑμᾶς καὶ **φυλάξει** ἀπὸ τοῦ πονηροῦ. [GNS]<br>πιστὸς δέ ἐστιν ὁ κύριος, ὃς στηρίξει ὑμᾶς καὶ **φυλάξει** ἀπὸ τοῦ πονηροῦ. [GNT] | To protect; to keep; to guard; to defend; to preserve; to cover; to insulate; to safeguard.<br><br>**Practical Application**<br>The point is this: the Lord is faithful, even if we fail to help one another. God will strengthen and guard us against Satan and his evil followers. In fact, the Lord will strengthen and guard us against all evil no matter what it is. Even if the evil seems to be conquering us, it will not—not in the final analysis. |
| **#1830<br>Guardian**<br><br>Bishop–KJV<br>**Guardian**–NASB<br>Overseer–NIV<br>Overseer–NKJV<br>**Guardian**–NLT | ἐπίσκοπον = *episkopon*<br>Pronunciation: [ep-is'-kop-on]<br>Parsing (part of speech): noun<br>  Case—accusative<br>  Gender—masculine<br>  Number—singular<br>Stem or root—from ἐπίσκοπος, ου<br>Concordance References:<br>⇒ Strong's #1985 episkopos<br>⇒ NIV #2176 episkopos<br>⇒ NASB #1985 episkopos | Overseer and caretaker, guardian, protector, guide, and director (William Barclay. *The Letters of James and Peter*, p.258).<br><br>**Practical Application**<br>It is the picture of Christ's watching over our souls and looking after them with the greatest of care. Jesus Christ is our Overseer, Caretaker, Guardian, Protector, Guide, and Director. When we come to Him, He takes complete charge of our lives. |

# PRACTICAL WORD STUDIES
## in the New Testament

| ENGLISH WORD | GREEK WORD AND VERSE | THE WORD MEANS... |
|---|---|---|
| **POSB REFERENCE** (1 Pt.2:25) Note 3, point 2 | **1 Peter 2:25** For ye were as sheep going astray; but are now returned unto the Shepherd and **Bishop** of your souls. [KJV] For you were continually straying like sheep, but now you have returned to the Shepherd and **Guardian** of your souls. [NASB] For you were like sheep going astray, but now you have returned to the Shepherd and **Overseer** of your souls. [NIV] For you were like sheep going astray, but have now returned to the Shepherd and **Overseer** of your souls. [NKJV] Once you were wandering like lost sheep. But now you have turned to your Shepherd, the **Guardian** of your souls. [NLT] ἦτε γὰρ ὡς πρόβατα πλανώμενα· ἀλλ᾽ ἐπεστράφητε νῦν ἐπὶ τὸν ποιμένα καὶ **ἐπίσκοπον** τῶν ψυχῶν ὑμῶν. [GNS] ἦτε γὰρ ὡς πρόβατα πλανώμενοι, ἀλλὰ ἐπεστράφητε νῦν ἐπὶ τὸν ποιμένα καὶ **ἐπίσκοπον** τῶν ψυχῶν ὑμῶν. [GNT] | |
| **#1831 Guardian And Teacher** Schoolmaster–KJV Tutor–NASB Put in charge to lead– NIV Tutor–NKJV **Guardian and teacher–NLT** **POSB REFERENCE** (Gal.3:23-25; esp. v.24) Note 1 See also POSB REF: (1 Cor.4:15) Note 2 | παιδαγωγός = *paidagōgos* Pronunciation: [pahee-dag-o-gos'] Parsing (part of speech): noun    Case—nominative    Gender—masculine    Number—singular    Stem or root—from παιδαγωγός, οῦ Concordance References:   ⇒ Strong's #3807 paidagōgos   ⇒ NIV #4080 paidagōgos   ⇒ NASB #3807 paidagōgos **Galatians 3:24** Wherefore the law was our **schoolmaster** to bring us unto Christ, that we might be justified by faith. [KJV] Therefore the Law has become our **tutor** to lead us to Christ, that we may be justified by faith. [NASB] So the law was **put in charge to lead** us to Christ that we might be justified by faith. [NIV] Therefore the law was our **tutor** *to bring us* to Christ, that we might be justified by faith. [NKJV] Let me put it another way. The law was our **guardian and teacher** to lead us until Christ came. So now, through faith in Christ, we are made right with God. [NLT] ὥστε ὁ νόμος **παιδαγωγὸς** ἡμῶν γέγονεν εἰς Χριστόν, ἵνα ἐκ πίστεως δικαιωθῶμεν· [GNS] ὥστε ὁ νόμος **παιδαγωγὸς** ἡμῶν γέγονεν εἰς Χριστόν, ἵνα ἐκ πίστεως δικαιωθῶμεν· [GNT] | Put in charge to lead, tutor, teacher, instructor, guide. **Practical Application** The law was man's guardian and teacher to lead him to see his need for Christ. The *paidagōgos* was usually a trusted slave who was in charge of a child's moral welfare, but he had one particular duty to which Paul was referring. Every day the guardian took the child to school to deliver him to the teacher. And then at the end of the day, he returned for the child and brought him safely back home. This was what the law was to do. The law is to lead man to Christ, the true Teacher. The law does this by showing man that he is utterly unable to secure righteousness by himself. He must look to Christ, the real Teacher, for righteousness and acceptance by God, that is, for justification by faith. And once Christ (faith in Him) has come, there is no need for the law nor for any other guardian, for Jesus Christ brings us face to face with God. |
| **#1832 Guardians** Instructers–KJV Tutors–NASB **Guardians–NIV** Instructors–NKJV To teach–NLT **POSB REFERENCE** (1 Cor.4:15) Note 2 | παιδαγωγούς = *paidagōgous* Pronunciation: [pahee-dag-o-goos'] Parsing (part of speech): noun    Case—accusative    Gender—masculine    Number—plural    Stem or root—from παιδαγωγός, οῦ Concordance References:   ⇒ Strong's #3807 paidagōgos   ⇒ NIV #4080 paidagōgos   ⇒ NASB #3807 paidagōgos **1 Cor. 4:15** For though ye have ten thousand **instructers** in Christ, yet *have ye* not many fathers: for in Christ Jesus I have begotten you through the gospel. [KJV] For if you were to have countless **tutors** in Christ, yet *you would* not *have* many fathers; for in Christ Jesus I became your father through the gospel. [NASB] Even though you have ten thousand **guardians** in Christ, you do not have many fathers, for in Christ Jesus I | Guardian, instructor, tutor. **Practical Application** The "guardian" (*paidagogous*) of Paul's day was a trusted slave who was placed in complete charge of a child's welfare and growth. He was even in charge of escorting the child to school and seeing that no harm came to him. He was responsible for the growth and development of the child until he was grown. Paul says that the Corinthian church had an unlimited number of capable instructors and teachers, but he alone was their spiritual father. He was the one who brought them to Christ Jesus for life and gave birth to the church. He was the one whom God had been using and was still using to oversee the growth of the church. Paul was stressing that he as the minister of the church bore more concern, tenderness, and care for the church than others. |

# PRACTICAL WORD STUDIES
## in the NEW TESTAMENT

| ENGLISH WORD | GREEK WORD AND VERSE | THE WORD MEANS... |
|---|---|---|
| | became your father through the gospel. [NIV]<br>For though you might have ten thousand **instructors** in Christ, yet you *do* not *have* many fathers; for in Christ Jesus I have begotten you through the gospel. [NKJV]<br>For even if you had ten thousand others **to teach** you about Christ, you have only one spiritual father. For I became your father in Christ Jesus when I preached the Good News to you. [NLT]<br>ἐὰν γὰρ μυρίους **παιδαγωγοὺς** ἔχητε ἐν Χριστῷ, ἀλλ' οὐ πολλοὺς πατέρας· ἐν γὰρ Χριστῷ Ἰησοῦ διὰ τοῦ εὐαγγελίου ἐγὼ ὑμᾶς ἐγέννησα. [GNS]<br>ἐὰν γὰρ μυρίους **παιδαγωγοὺς** ἔχητε ἐν Χριστῷ ἀλλ' οὐ πολλοὺς πατέρας· ἐν γὰρ Χριστῷ Ἰησοῦ διὰ τοῦ εὐαγγελίου ἐγὼ ὑμᾶς ἐγέννησα. [GNT] | |
| **#1833**<br>**Guile**<br><br>**Guile**–KJV<br>**Guile**–NASB<br>False–NIV<br>Deceit–NKJV<br>Honest–NLT<br><br>**POSB REFERENCE**<br>(Jn.1:47-48; esp. v.47)<br>Note 2, point 1b | δόλος = *dolos*<br>Pronunciation: [dol'-os]<br>Parsing (part of speech): noun<br>  Case—nominative<br>  Gender—masculine<br>  Number—singular<br>  Stem or root—from δόλος ου<br>Concordance References:<br>  ⇒ Strong's #1388 dolos<br>  ⇒ NIV #1515 dolos<br>  ⇒ NASB #1388 dolos<br><br>**John 1:47**<br>Jesus saw Nathanael coming to him, and saith of him, Behold an Israelite indeed, in whom is no **guile**! [KJV]<br>Jesus saw Nathanael coming to Him, and said of him, "Behold, an Israelite indeed, in whom is no **guile**!" [NASB]<br>When Jesus saw Nathanael approaching, he said of him, "Here is a true Israelite, in whom there is nothing **false**." [NIV]<br>Jesus saw Nathanael coming toward Him, and said of him, "Behold, an Israelite indeed, in whom is no **deceit**!" [NKJV]<br>As they approached, Jesus said, "Here comes an **honest** man—a true son of Israel." [NLT]<br>εἶδεν ὁ Ἰησοῦς τὸν Ναθαναὴλ ἐρχόμενον πρὸς αὐτόν, καὶ λέγει περὶ αὐτοῦ, Ἴδε ἀληθῶς Ἰσραηλίτης, ἐν ᾧ **δόλος** οὐκ ἔστι. [GNS]<br>εἶδεν ὁ Ἰησοῦς τὸν Ναθαναὴλ ἐρχόμενον πρὸς αὐτὸν καὶ λέγει περὶ αὐτοῦ, Ἴδε ἀληθῶς Ἰσραηλίτης ἐν ᾧ **δόλος** οὐκ ἔστιν. [GNT] | False, deceit, guile, fraud, deception, treachery; an impostor, an impersonator, a fake.<br><br>**Practical Application**<br>Note that these terms did not describe Nathanael's behavior. The word "guile" (*dolos*) means he did not deceive, bait, or mislead people. He did not hide what he thought; he said what he thought and acted what he felt. He was straightforward, open and honest, not deceptive or hypocritical. This trait had just been demonstrated in his response to Philip. He would not hide his true thoughts (John 1:46). One of the great tragedies in the legacy of persons is that they are full of guile. Many deceive, bait, and mislead others. Few are straightforward, open and honest, free of deception and hypocrisy. |
| **#1834**<br>**Guile**<br><br>**Guile**–KJV<br>**Guile**–NASB<br>Deceit–NIV<br>Deceit–NKJV<br>Deceit–NLT<br><br>**POSB REFERENCE**<br>(1 Pt.2:1)<br>Note 1, point 1 | δόλον = *dolon*<br>Pronunciation: [dol'-on]<br>Parsing (part of speech): noun<br>  Case—accusative<br>  Gender—masculine<br>  Number—singular<br>  Stem or root—from δόλος, ου<br>Concordance References:<br>  ⇒ Strong's #1388 dolos<br>  ⇒ NIV #1515 dolos<br>  ⇒ NASB #1388 dolos<br><br>**1 Peter 2:1**<br>Wherefore laying aside all malice, and all **guile**, and hypocrisies, and envies, and all evil speakings, [KJV]<br>Therefore, putting aside all malice and all **guile** and hypocrisy and envy and all slander, [NASB]<br>Therefore, rid yourselves of all malice and all **deceit**, hypocrisy, envy, and slander of every kind. [NIV]<br>Therefore, laying aside all malice, all **deceit**, hypocrisy, envy, and all evil speaking, [NKJV]<br>So get rid of all malicious behavior and **deceit**. Don't just pretend to be good! Be done with hypocrisy and jealousy and backstabbing. [NLT]<br>Ἀποθέμενοι οὖν πᾶσαν κακίαν καὶ πάντα **δόλον** καὶ ὑποκρίσεις καὶ φθόνους καὶ πάσας καταλαλιάς, [GNS]<br>Ἀποθέμενοι οὖν πᾶσαν κακίαν καὶ πάντα **δόλον** καὶ ὑποκρίσεις καὶ φθόνους καὶ πάσας καταλαλιάς, [GNT] | Deceit, guile, false, treachery, trickery.<br><br>**Practical Application**<br>The word means to deceive and mislead people; to set bait so as to catch them; to bait or deceive in order to achieve one's own end. It means to be two-faced. Note that guile or deception has to do primarily with words. When the person wants something, he tries to get it...<br>• by flattery<br>• by false promises<br>• by false tales<br>• by suggestive talk<br>• by off-colored suggestions<br>• by enticing words<br>• by outright lying<br><br>When the person wants something, he looks at the other person's weakness or ignorance, and he tries to appeal to it. He appeals to it by deceiving and beguiling the person. The exhortation is strong: believers must strip off deceit or guile. We must not deceive and mislead people. |

## PRACTICAL WORD STUDIES
### in the New Testament

| ENGLISH WORD | GREEK WORD AND VERSE | THE WORD MEANS... |
|---|---|---|
| **#1835**<br>**Guile**<br><br>Guile–KJV<br>Guile–NASB<br>Deceitful–NIV<br>Deceit–NKJV<br>Lies–NLT<br><br>**POSB REFERENCE**<br>(1 Pt.3:10)<br>Note 1 | δόλον = dolon<br>Pronunciation: [dol'-on]<br>Parsing (part of speech): noun<br>    Case—accusative<br>    Gender—masculine<br>    Number—singular<br>    Stem or root—from δόλος ου<br>Concordance References:<br>  ⇒ Strong's #1388 dolos<br>  ⇒ NIV #1515 dolos<br>  ⇒ NASB #1388 dolos<br><br>**1 Peter 3:10**<br>For he that will love life, and see good days, let him refrain his tongue from evil, and his lips that they speak no **guile**: [KJV]<br>For, "Let him who means to love life and see good days Refrain his tongue from evil and his lips from speaking **guile**. [NASB]<br>For, "Whoever would love life and see good days must keep his tongue from evil and his lips from **deceitful** speech. [NIV]<br>For "*He who would love life, And see good days, Let him refrain his tongue from evil, And his lis from speaking deceit*. [NKJV]<br>For the Scriptures say, "If you want a happy life and good days, keep your tongue from speaking evil, and keep your lips from telling **lies**. [NLT]<br>Ὁ γὰρ θέλων ζωὴν ἀγαπᾶν, καὶ ἰδεῖν ἡμέρας ἀγαθάς, παυσάτω τὴν γλῶσσαν αὐτοῦ ἀπὸ κακοῦ, καὶ χείλη αὐτοῦ τοῦ μὴ λαλῆσαι **δόλον**· [GNS]<br>ὁ γὰρ θέλων ζωὴν ἀγαπᾶν καὶ ἰδεῖν ἡμέρας ἀγαθὰς παυσάτω τὴν γλῶσσαν ἀπὸ κακοῦ καὶ χείλη τοῦ μὴ λαλῆσαι **δόλον**, [GNT] | Deceitful, guile, lies, treachery.<br><br>**Practical Application**<br>A deceitful tongue is...<br>• a false tongue<br>• a cheating tongue<br>• a treacherous tongue<br>• a deceptive tongue<br>• a lying tongue<br>• a mistreating tongue<br>• a beguiling tongue<br>• a flattering tongue<br><br>We deceive and smooth talk others in order to get what we are after or to protect ourselves. But note what Scripture says: the very first step to loving and enjoying life is to keep our tongues from deceiving and beguiling others. Deception leads to sin and sin destroys. Just think about the deceptive tongues that have...<br>• destroyed marriages<br>• damaged friendships<br>• caused injuries<br>• prevented promotions<br>• disturbed children<br>• ruined reputations<br>• aroused fights<br>• maimed bodies<br>• caused wars<br><br>If we wish to love and enjoy life, we must stop our tongues from doing evil and from deceiving others. We must control and discipline our tongues. |
| **#1836**<br>**Gullible Women**<br><br>Silly women–KJV<br>Weak women–NASB<br>Weak-willed women–NIV<br>Gullible women–NKJV<br>Vulnerable women–NLT<br><br>**POSB REFERENCE**<br>(2 Tim. 3:6-9; esp. v.6)<br>Note 4, point 1 | γυναικάρια = gunaikaria<br>Pronunciation: [goo-nahee-kar'-ee-ah]<br>Parsing (part of speech): noun<br>    Case—accusative<br>    Gender—neuter<br>    Number—plural<br>    Stem or root—from γυναικάριον, ου<br>Concordance References:<br>  ⇒ Strong's #1133 gunaikarion<br>  ⇒ NIV #1220 gunaikarion<br>  ⇒ NASB #1133 gunaikarion<br><br>**2 Tim. 3:6**<br>For of this sort are they which creep into houses, and lead captive **silly women** laden with sins, led away with divers lusts, [KJV]<br>For among them are those who enter into households and captivate **weak women** weighed down with sins, led on by various impulses, [NASB]<br>They are the kind who worm their way into homes and gain control over **weak-willed women**, who are loaded down with sins and are swayed by all kinds of evil desires, [NIV]<br>For of this sort are those who creep into households and make captives of **gullible women** loaded down with sins, led away by various lusts, [NKJV]<br>They are the kind who work their way into people's homes and win the confidence of **vulnerable women** who are burdened with the guilt of sin and controlled by many desires. [NLT]<br>ἐκ τούτων γάρ εἰσιν οἱ ἐνδύνοντες εἰς τὰς οἰκίας, καὶ αἰχμαλωτεύοντες τὰ **γυναικάρια** σεσωρευμένα ἁμαρτίαις, ἀγόμενα ἐπιθυμίαις ποικίλαις, [GNS]<br>ἐκ τούτων γάρ εἰσιν οἱ ἐνδύνοντες εἰς τὰς οἰκίας καὶ αἰχμαλωτίζοντες **γυναικάρια** σεσωρευμένα ἁμαρτίαις, ἀγόμενα ἐπιθυμίαις ποικίλαις, [GNT] | Weak-willed women, silly women, vulnerable women, morally weak women. The Greek word means *little women*, *little* in the sense of being spiritually dead, weak, immature, and unstable. However, it should always be remembered that men are just as gullible as women, just as spiritually dead, weak, immature, and unstable.<br><br>**Practical Application**<br>The present passage zeros in on women because of the local situation in Ephesus; some of the women in the Ephesian church were following the corrupt ministers. But the warning is applicable to us all: both men and women must guard against corrupt ministers.<br>Note what the corrupt minister does. He seeks after people...<br>• who are laden or burdened down with sins and guilt.<br>• who are easily swayed and led away by all kinds of desires and lusts.<br>• who are seeking after truth—who are listening and learning all they can from anybody who claims to have the truth.<br><br>This is the person the false minister goes after and eventually captivates. When a person begins to seek the truth because he senses a need in his life, senses that he has been living only for his own selfish desires and lusts—that person is wide open for a corrupt minister to step in and lead him astray. Unfortunately, this is exactly what happens ever too often. And note the great tragedy: the person never comes to the knowledge of the truth. Why? Because he never seeks the truth in Christ. He only seeks a "form of godliness," not true godliness. True godliness is found in Christ alone and nowhere else. |

# PRACTICAL WORD STUDIES
## in the NEW TESTAMENT

| ENGLISH WORD | GREEK WORD AND VERSE | THE WORD MEANS... |
|---|---|---|
| **#1837**<br>**Habitation, His**<br><br>His habitation–KJV<br>His homestead–NASB<br>His place–NIV<br>His dwelling place–NKJV<br>His home–NLT<br><br>**POSB REFERENCE**<br>(Acts 1:16-20; esp. v.20)<br>Note 2, point 6a | ἡ ἔπαυλις αὐτοῦ = hë epaulis autou<br>Pronunciation: [ay ep'-ow-lis aw-too]<br>Parsing *epaulis* (part of speech): noun<br>   Case—nominative<br>   Gender—feminine<br>   Number—singular<br>   Stem or root—from ἔπαυλις, εως<br>Concordance References:<br>  ⇒ Strong's #3588 ho + 1886 epaulis + 846 autos<br>  ⇒ NIV #3836 ho [Not in English] + 2068 epaulis [place] + 899 autos [his]<br>  ⇒ NASB #3588 ho + 1886 epaulis + 846 autos<br><br>**Acts 1:20**<br>For it is written in the book of Psalms, Let **his habitation** be desolate, and let no man dwell therein: and his bishoprick let another take. [KJV]<br>"For it is written in the book of Psalms, 'Let **his homestead** be made desolate, And let no man dwell in it'; and, 'His OFFICE LET ANOTHER MAN TAKE.' [NASB]<br>"For," said Peter, "it is written in the book of Psalms, "'May **his place** be deserted; let there be no one to dwell in it,' and, "'May another take his place of leadership.' [NIV]<br>"For it is written in the book of Psalms: 'Let **his dwelling place** be desolate, And let no one live in it'; and, 'Let another take his office.' [NKJV]<br>Peter continued, "This was predicted in the book of Psalms, where it says, 'Let **his home** become desolate, with no one living in it.' And again, 'Let his position be given to someone else.' [NLT]<br>γέγραπται γὰρ ἐν βίβλῳ Ψαλμῶν, Γενηθήτω ἡ **ἔπαυλις αὐτοῦ** ἔρημος, καὶ μὴ ἔστω ὁ κατοικῶν ἐν αὐτῇ· καί, Τὴν ἐπισκοπὴν αὐτοῦ λάβοι ἕτερος. [GNS]<br>Γέγραπται γὰρ ἐν βίβλῳ ψαλμῶν, Γενηθήτω ἡ **ἔπαυλις αὐτοῦ** ἔρημος καὶ μὴ ἔστω ὁ κατοικῶν ἐν αὐτῇ, καί, Τὴν ἐπισκοπὴν αὐτοῦ λαβέτω ἕτερος. [GNT] | His place; His habitation; His homestead; His home.<br><br>**Practical Application**<br>The phrase "his habitation" (*hë epaulis autou*) is descriptive. It means a farm house or a place for sheep such as a pasture or sheep yard. The idea is that Judas would never again be allowed to be the farmer (husbandman) or shepherd for God. |
| **#1838**<br>**Had To**<br><br>Must–KJV<br>Must–NASB<br>Must–NIV<br>Must–NKJV<br>Had to–NLT<br><br>**POSB REFERENCE**<br>(Mt.16:21-23; esp. v.21)<br>Note 1<br><br>See also POSB REF:<br>(Lk.9:21-22; esp. v.22)<br>Note 4, point 2<br>(Lk.13:31-33 esp. v.33)<br>Note 2, point 2<br>(Lk.24:44-49 esp. v.44)<br>Note 2, point 2<br>(Jn.3:4-8; esp. v.7)<br>Note 3, point 4<br>(Jn.4:1-9; esp. v.4)<br>Note 1, point 1<br>(Jn.9:4)<br>Note 2, point 3a | δεῖ = *dei*<br>Pronunciation: [die]<br>Parsing (part of speech): verb<br>   Mood—indicative<br>   Tense—present<br>   Voice—active<br>   Person—3rd person<br>   Number—singular<br>   Stem or root—from δεῖ<br>Concordance References:<br>  ⇒ Strong's #1163 dei<br>  ⇒ NIV #1256 dei<br>  ⇒ NASB #1163 dei<br><br>**Matthew 16:21**<br>From that time forth began Jesus to shew unto his disciples, how that he **must** go unto Jerusalem, and suffer many things of the elders and chief priests and scribes, and be killed, and be raised again the third day. [KJV]<br>From that time Jesus Christ began to show His disciples that He **must** go to Jerusalem, and suffer many things from the elders and chief priests and scribes, and be killed, and be raised up on the third day. [NASB]<br>From that time on Jesus began to explain to his disciples that he **must** go to Jerusalem and suffer many things at the hands of the elders, chief priests and teachers of the law, and that he must be killed and on the third day be raised to life. [NIV]<br>From that time Jesus began to show to His disciples that He **must** go to Jerusalem, and suffer many things from the elders and chief priests and scribes, and be killed, and be raised the third day. [NKJV]<br>From then on Jesus began to tell his disciples plainly that he **had to** go to Jerusalem, and he told them what | Must go; to be compelled; to consider no other options; ought; should; had to go, an absolute necessity, an imperative, a compulsion, destiny.<br><br>**Practical Application**<br>The words "had to [*dei*]" are strong: a constraint, an imperative, a necessity was laid upon Christ. He had no choice. His death and resurrection had been planned and willed by God through all eternity. The prophets had predicted it: He must fulfill the will of God, for God had ordained His death (cp. Matthew 26:54; Luke 24:26, 46).<br>The entire life and ministry of Jesus Christ was governed by what He "must" do. The same must be true for the believer also. We must...<br>• be born again (John 3:7).<br>• become less as He becomes greater (John 3:30).<br>• worship God in spirit and in truth (John 4:24).<br>• do the work of God who sent Christ (John 6:28).<br>• follow Christ if we are going to serve Him (John 12:26).<br>• love one another (John 13:34).<br>• remain in the vine—connected to Christ—if we are to bear fruit (John 15:4). |

# PRACTICAL WORD STUDIES
## in the NEW TESTAMENT

| ENGLISH WORD | GREEK WORD AND VERSE | THE WORD MEANS... |
|---|---|---|
| (Jn.10:14-16; esp. v.16) Note 2, point 4c | would happen to him there. He would suffer at the hands of the leaders and the leading priests and the teachers of religious law. He would be killed, and he would be raised on the third day. [NLT]<br><br>Ἀπὸ τότε ἤρξατο ὁ Ἰησοῦς δεικνύειν τοῖς μαθηταῖς αὐτοῦ ὅτι **δεῖ** αὐτὸν ἀπελθεῖν εἰς Ἱεροσόλυμα, καὶ πολλὰ παθεῖν ἀπὸ τῶν πρεσβυτέρων καὶ ἀρχιερέων καὶ γραμματέων, καὶ ἀποκτανθῆναι, καὶ τῇ τρίτῃ ἡμέρᾳ ἐγερθῆναι. [GNS]<br><br>Ἀπὸ τότε ἤρξατο ὁ Ἰησοῦς δεικνύειν τοῖς μαθηταῖς αὐτοῦ ὅτι **δεῖ** αὐτὸν εἰς Ἱεροσόλυμα ἀπελθεῖν καὶ πολλὰ παθεῖν ἀπὸ τῶν πρεσβυτέρων καὶ ἀρχιερέων καὶ γραμματέων καὶ ἀποκτανθῆναι καὶ τῇ τρίτῃ ἡμέρᾳ ἐγερθῆναι. [GNT] | |
| **#1839**<br>**Hades**<br><br>Hell–KJV<br>**Hades–NASB**<br>Hell–NIV<br>**Hades–NKJV**<br>The place of the dead–NLT<br><br>**POSB REFERENCE**<br>(Lk.16:23)<br>*Deeper Study #3* | ᾅδῃ = hadë<br>Pronunciation: [hah'-day]<br>Parsing (part of speech): noun<br>  Case—dative<br>  Gender—masculine<br>  Number—singular<br>  Stem or root—from ᾅδης, ου<br>Concordance References:<br>⇒ Strong's #86 hadës<br>⇒ NIV #87 hadës<br>⇒ NASB #86 hadës<br><br>**Luke 16:23**<br>And in **hell** he lift up his eyes, being in torments, and seeth Abraham afar off, and Lazarus in his bosom. [KJV]<br>"And in **Hades** he lifted up his eyes, being in torment, and saw Abraham far away, and Lazarus in his bosom. [NASB]<br>In **hell**, where he was in torment, he looked up and saw Abraham far away, with Lazarus by his side. [NIV]<br>And being in torments in **Hades**, he lifted up his eyes and saw Abraham afar off, and Lazarus in his bosom. [NKJV]<br>And his soul went to **the place of the dead**. There, in torment, he saw Lazarus in the far distance with Abraham. [NLT]<br><br>καὶ ἐν τῷ **ᾅδῃ** ἐπάρας τοὺς ὀφθαλμοὺς αὐτοῦ, ὑπάρχων ἐν βασάνοις, ὁρᾷ τὸν Ἀβραὰμ ἀπὸ μακρόθεν, καὶ Λάζαρον ἐν τοῖς κόλποις αὐτοῦ. [GNS]<br><br>καὶ ἐν τῷ **ᾅδῃ** ἐπάρας τοὺς ὀφθαλμοὺς αὐτοῦ, ὑπάρχων ἐν βασάνοις, ὁρᾷ Ἀβραὰμ ἀπὸ μακρόθεν καὶ Λάζαρον ἐν τοῖς κόλποις αὐτοῦ. [GNT] | Hades; hell; the place of the dead; the place of final and eternal punishment. The Greek word Hades is the same as the Hebrew word Sheol (see POSB *Deeper Study #3*—Genesis 37:35).<br><br>**Practical Application**<br>The picture of Hades revealed by Jesus is that of the other world: the unseen world, the spiritual world, the spiritual dimension of being.<br>Jesus says that Hades is a place which is divided into two huge areas or sections or compartments. The two areas are separated by a great gulf that is impassable (Luke 16:26). One area is the place of sorrow (Luke 16:23-24, 28). The other area is the place of Paradise where believers go. To say that a person is dead is to say that he is in Hades, in the other world. |
| **#1840**<br>**Hades**<br><br>Hell–KJV<br>**Hades–NASB**<br>Grave–NIV<br>**Hades–NKJV**<br>Dead–NLT<br><br>**POSB REFERENCE**<br>(Acts 2:25-28; esp. v.27)<br>Note 1, point 2b<br><br>See also POSB REF:<br>(Acts 2:27)<br>*Deeper Study #1* | ᾅδην = hadën<br>Pronunciation: [hah'-dane]<br>Parsing (part of speech): noun<br>  Case—accusative<br>  Gender—masculine<br>  Number—singular<br>  Stem or root—from ᾅδης, ου<br>Concordance References:<br>⇒ Strong's #86 hadës<br>⇒ NIV #87 hadës<br>⇒ NASB #86 hadës<br><br>**Acts 2:27**<br>Because thou wilt not leave my soul in **hell**, neither wilt thou suffer thine Holy One to see corruption. [KJV]<br>Because Thou wilt not abandon my soul to **Hades**, Nor ALLOW Thy Holy One to UNDERGO DECAY. [NASB]<br>Because you will not abandon me to the **grave**, nor will you let your Holy One see decay. [NIV]<br>For You will not leave my soul in **Hades**, Nor will You allow Your Holy One to see corruption. [NKJV]<br>For you will not leave my soul among the **dead** or allow your Holy One to rot in the grave. [NLT] | Grave, hell, hades, dead; the place of death.<br><br>**Practical Application**<br>Jesus revealed that the grave or Hades is the other world, that is, the unseen world, the spiritual dimension of being (see POSB *Deeper Study #3*—Luke 16:23). Jesus said that Hades (the other world) was divided into two huge areas or sections. The two areas are separated by a great gulf that is impassable (Luke 16:26). One area is the place of sorrow (Luke 16:23-24, 28), and the other area is the place of paradise where believers go. To say that one is dead is to say that one is in hades or in the other world. |

# PRACTICAL WORD STUDIES
## in the NEW TESTAMENT

| ENGLISH WORD | GREEK WORD AND VERSE | THE WORD MEANS... |
|---|---|---|
| | ὅτι οὐκ ἐγκαταλείψεις τὴν ψυχήν μου εἰς ᾅδου, οὐδὲ δώσεις τὸν ὅσιόν σου ἰδεῖν διαφθοράν. [GNS]<br>ὅτι οὐκ ἐγκαταλείψεις τὴν ψυχήν μου εἰς ᾅδην οὐδὲ δώσεις τὸν ὅσιόν σου ἰδεῖν διαφθοράν. [GNT] | |
| **#1841**<br>**Hail**<br><br>Hail–KJV<br>Greeted–NASB<br>Greetings–NIV<br>Rejoice–NKJV<br>Greetings–NLT<br><br>**POSB<br>REFERENCE**<br>(Mt.28:9)<br>*Deeper Study #2* | Χαίρετε. = *Chairete*<br>Pronunciation: [khah'ee-reh-teh]<br>Parsing (part of speech): verb<br>    Mood—imperative<br>    Tense—present<br>    Voice—active<br>    Person—2nd person<br>    Number—plural<br>    Stem or root—from χαίρω<br>OR<br>Parsing (part of speech): particle<br>    Type—sentence<br>    Stem or root—from χαίρω<br>Concordance References:<br>  ⇒ Strong's #5463 chairö<br>  ⇒ NIV #5897 chairö<br>  ⇒ NASB #5463 chairö<br><br>**Matthew 28:9**<br>And as they went to tell his disciples, behold, Jesus met them, saying, All **hail**. And they came and held him by the feet, and worshipped him. [KJV]<br>And behold, Jesus met them and **greeted** them. And they came up and took hold of His feet and worshiped Him. [NASB]<br>Suddenly Jesus met them. "**Greetings**," he said. They came to him, clasped his feet and worshiped him. [NIV]<br>And as they went to tell His disciples, behold, Jesus met them, saying, "**Rejoice**!" So they came and held Him by the feet and worshiped Him. [NKJV]<br>And as they went, Jesus met them. "**Greetings**!" he said. And they ran to him, held his feet, and worshiped him. [NLT]<br>ὡς δὲ ἐπορεύοντο ἀπαγγεῖλαι τοῖς μαθηταῖς αὐτοῦ, καὶ ἰδού, ὁ Ἰησοῦς ἀπήντησεν αὐταῖς, λέγων, **Χαίρετε**. αἱ δὲ προσελθοῦσαι ἐκράτησαν αὐτοῦ τοὺς πόδας καὶ προσεκύνησαν αὐτῷ. [GNS]<br>καὶ ἰδοὺ Ἰησοῦς ὑπήντησεν αὐταῖς λέγων, **Χαίρετε**. αἱ δὲ προσελθοῦσαι ἐκράτησαν αὐτοῦ τοὺς πόδας καὶ προσεκύνησαν αὐτῷ. [GNT] | To be greeted, to rejoice; hailed.<br><br>**Practical Application**<br>It is significant that the risen Christ used this every day, common greeting to proclaim the extraordinary news of His resurrection. |
| **#1842**<br>**Haling**<br><br>Haling–KJV<br>Dragging off–NASB<br>Dragged off–NIV<br>Dragging off–NKJV<br>Dragging out–NLT<br><br>**POSB<br>REFERENCE**<br>(Acts 8:3)<br>Note 3, point 2 | σύρων = *surön*<br>Pronunciation: [soo'-rown]<br>Parsing (part of speech): verb<br>    Mood—participle<br>    Tense—present<br>    Voice—active<br>    Case—nominative<br>    Gender—masculine<br>    Number—singular<br>    Stem or root—from σύρω<br>Concordance References:<br>  ⇒ Strong's #4951 surö<br>  ⇒ NIV #5359 surö<br>  ⇒ NASB #4951 surö<br><br>**Acts 8:3**<br>As for Saul, he made havock of the church, entering into every house, and **haling** men and women committed them to prison. [KJV]<br>But Saul began ravaging the church, entering house after house; and **dragging off** men and women, he would put them in prison. [NASB]<br>But Saul began to destroy the church. Going from house to house, he **dragged off** men and women and put them in prison. [NIV]<br>As for Saul, he made havoc of the church, entering every house, and **dragging off** men and women, committing them to prison. [NKJV] | To drag off; to drag away using force; to be swept.<br><br>**Practical Application**<br>It means constraining and dragging them, using whatever force was necessary to arrest and subdue them. The picture is that of forcibly dragging them from their homes through the city streets. |

## PRACTICAL WORD STUDIES
### in the NEW TESTAMENT

| ENGLISH WORD | GREEK WORD AND VERSE | THE WORD MEANS... |
|---|---|---|
| | Saul was going everywhere to devastate the church. He went from house to house, **dragging out** both men and women to throw them into jail. [NLT]<br><br>Σαῦλος δὲ ἐλυμαίνετο τὴν ἐκκλησίαν, κατὰ τοὺς οἴκους εἰσπορευόμενος, **σύρων** τε ἄνδρας καὶ γυναῖκας παρεδίδου εἰς φυλακήν. [GNS]<br><br>Σαῦλος δὲ ἐλυμαίνετο τὴν ἐκκλησίαν κατὰ τοὺς οἴκους εἰσπορευόμενος, **σύρων** τε ἄνδρας καὶ γυναῖκας παρεδίδου εἰς φυλακήν. [GNT] | |
| #1843<br>**Hallowed**<br><br>Hallowed–KJV<br>Hallowed–NASB<br>Hallowed–NIV<br>Hallowed–NKJV<br>Honored–NLT<br><br>**POSB REFERENCE**<br>(Mt.6:9)<br>*Deeper Study #4* | ἁγιασθήτω = *hagiasthētō*<br>Pronunciation: [ag-ee-as'-thee-tow]<br>Parsing (part of speech): verb<br>    Mood—imperative<br>    Tense—aorist<br>    Voice—passive<br>    Person—3rd person<br>    Number—singular<br>    Stem or root—from ἁγιάζω<br>Concordance References:<br> ⇒ Strong's #37 hagiazō<br> ⇒ NIV #39 hagiazō<br> ⇒ NASB #37 hagiazō<br><br>**Matthew 6:9**<br>After this manner therefore pray ye: Our Father which art in heaven, **Hallowed** be thy name. [KJV]<br><br>"Pray, then, in this way:' Our Father who art in heaven, **Hallowed** be Thy name. [NASB]<br><br>"This, then, is how you should pray: "'Our Father in heaven, **hallowed** be your name, [NIV]<br><br>In this manner, therefore, pray: Our Father in heaven, **Hallowed** be Your name. [NKJV]<br><br>Pray like this: Our Father in heaven, may your name be **honored**. [NLT]<br><br>οὕτως οὖν προσεύχεσθε ὑμεῖς· Πάτερ ἡμῶν ὁ ἐν τοῖς οὐρανοῖς, **ἁγιασθήτω** τὸ ὄνομά σου· [GNS]<br><br>Οὕτως οὖν προσεύχεσθε ὑμεῖς· Πάτερ ἡμῶν ὁ ἐν τοῖς οὐρανοῖς, **ἁγιασθήτω** τὸ ὄνομά σου· [GNT] | To be counted and treated as holy; to be sanctified, set apart as holy; to be consecrated; to be honored and esteemed; to be made distinctive, distinguished, and different from all else; to be counted and treated as distinctive and different.<br><br>**Practical Application**<br>God is holy. He is the very embodiment and perfection of absolute holiness (see POSB *Deeper Study #1*, Holy—1 Peter 1:15-16 for more discussion).<br>⇒ God is the embodiment of absolute righteousness, purity, sinlessness, and godliness.<br>⇒ God is the very embodiment of absolute perfection, completeness, and fulfillment.<br>⇒ God is the very embodiment of absolute separation—set apart, different and separated from all else. |
| #1844<br>**Hand Over**<br><br>Deliver–KJV<br>Delivered–NASB<br>Hand...over–NIV<br>Deliver–NKJV<br>Betrayed–NLT<br><br>**POSB REFERENCE**<br>(Mk.10:33)<br>Note 4 | παραδοθήσεται = *paradothesetai*<br>Pronunciation: [par-ad-o-theh-seh-tah-ee]<br>Parsing (part of speech): verb<br>    Mood—indicative<br>    Tense—future<br>    Voice—passive<br>    Person—3rd person<br>    Number—singular<br>    Stem or root—from παραδίδωμι<br>Concordance References:<br> ⇒ Strong's #3860 paradidōmi<br> ⇒ NIV #4140 paradidōmi<br> ⇒ NASB #3860 paradidōmi<br><br>**Mark 10:33**<br>Saying, Behold, we go up to Jerusalem; and the Son of man shall be delivered unto the chief priests, and unto the scribes; and they shall condemn him to death, and shall **deliver** him to the Gentiles: [KJV]<br><br>Saying, "Behold, we are going up to Jerusalem, and the Son of Man will be **delivered** to the chief priests and the scribes; and they will condemn Him to death, and will deliver Him to the Gentiles. [NASB]<br><br>"We are going up to Jerusalem," he said, "and the Son of Man will be betrayed to the chief priests and teachers of the law. They will condemn him to death and will **hand** him **over** to the Gentiles, [NIV]<br><br>"Behold, we are going up to Jerusalem, and the Son of Man will be betrayed to the chief priests and to the scribes; and they will condemn Him to death and **deliver** Him to the Gentiles; [NKJV]<br><br>"When we get to Jerusalem," he told them, "the Son of | To hand over; to be betrayed; to be abandoned; to be delivered over and into death.<br><br>**Practical Application**<br>It means that His death was determined, ordained, set in the plan and counsel of God. Note that Jesus said, "The Son of Man will be handed over." His death was right before His face, ready to take place. |

# PRACTICAL WORD STUDIES
## in the NEW TESTAMENT

| ENGLISH WORD | GREEK WORD AND VERSE | THE WORD MEANS... |
|---|---|---|
| | Man will be **betrayed** to the leading priests and the teachers of religious law. They will sentence him to die and hand him over to the Romans. [NLT]<br>ὅτι Ἰδοὺ ἀναβαίνομεν εἰς Ἱεροσόλυμα· καὶ ὁ υἱὸς τοῦ ἀνθρώπου **παραδοθήσεται** τοῖς ἀρχιερεῦσι καὶ τοῖς γραμματεῦσι, καὶ κατακρινοῦσιν αὐτὸν θανάτῳ, καὶ παραδώσουσιν αὐτὸν τοῖς ἔθνεσι, [GNS]<br>ὅτι Ἰδοὺ ἀναβαίνομεν εἰς Ἱεροσόλυμα, καὶ ὁ υἱὸς τοῦ ἀνθρώπου **παραδοθήσεται** τοῖς ἀρχιερεῦσιν καὶ τοῖς γραμματεῦσιν, καὶ κατακρινοῦσιν αὐτὸν θανάτῳ καὶ παραδώσουσιν αὐτὸν τοῖς ἔθνεσιν [GNT] | |
| **#1845**<br>**Hand, Withered**<br><br>Withered hand–KJV<br>Withered hand–NASB<br>Shriveled hand–NIV<br>Withered hand–NKJV<br>Deformed hand–NLT<br><br>**POSB REFERENCE**<br>(Mk.3:1-2; esp. v.1)<br>Note 1, point 1 | ἐξηραμμένην ἔχων τὴν χεῖρα = *exerammenen echon ten cheira*<br>Pronunciation: [ex-ay-rahm'mehn-ayn ekh'-own tayn khir-ah]<br>Parsing *exerammenen* (part of speech): verb<br>  Mood—participle<br>  Tense—perfect<br>  Voice—passive<br>  Case—accusative<br>  Gender—feminine<br>  Number—singular<br>  Stem or root—from ξηραίνω<br>Parsing *econ* (part of speech): verb<br>  Mood—participle<br>  Tense—present<br>  Voice—active<br>  Case—nominative<br>  Gender—masculine<br>  Number—singular<br>  Stem or root—from ἔχω<br>Parsing *ten* (part of speech): determiner [definite article]<br>  Case—accusative<br>  Gender—feminine<br>  Number—singular<br>  Stem or root—from ὁ, ἡ, τό<br>Parsing *cheira* (part of speech): noun<br>  Case—accusative<br>  Gender—feminine<br>  Number—singular<br>  Stem or root—from χείρ, χειρός<br>Concordance References:<br>  ⇒ Strong's #3583 xeraino + #5495 cheir<br>  ⇒ NIV #2400 echō [with] + 3830 xērainō [shriveled] + 5931 cheir [hand]<br>  ⇒ NASB #3583 xeraino + #5495 cheir<br><br>**Mark 3:1**<br>And he entered again into the synagogue; and there was a man there which had a **withered hand**. [KJV]<br>And He entered again into a synagogue; and a man was there with a **withered hand**. [NASB]<br>Another time he went into the synagogue, and a man with a **shriveled hand** was there. [NIV]<br>And He entered the synagogue again, and a man was there who had a **withered hand**. [NKJV]<br>Jesus went into the synagogue again and noticed a man with a **deformed hand**. [NLT]<br>Καὶ εἰσῆλθε πάλιν εἰς τὴν συναγωγήν, καὶ ἦν ἐκεῖ ἄνθρωπος **ἐξηραμμένην ἔχων τὴν χεῖρα**. [GNS]<br>Καὶ εἰσῆλθεν πάλιν εἰς τὴν συναγωγήν. καὶ ἦν ἐκεῖ ἄνθρωπος **ἐξηραμμένην ἔχων τὴν χεῖρα**. [GNT] | To have an injured or sick hand. This phrase describes a hand that was withered, shriveled, dried up, wilted, wasted, dropped, scorched.<br><br>**Practical Application**<br>His hand had been injured or become diseased. He was not born with a withered hand. His plight, of course, was desperate; for he was unable to work for a livelihood with a withered hand. Tradition says he was a stone mason who beseeched Jesus to heal him so that he might not have to beg in shame (see POSB notes—Matthew 12:9-13). |
| **#1846**<br>**Handled**<br><br>Handled–KJV<br>Handled–NASB<br>Touched–NIV<br>Handled–NKJV<br>Touched–NLT | ἐψηλάφησαν = *epsëlaphësan*<br>Pronunciation: [epsay-laf-ay'-sahn]<br>Parsing (part of speech): erb<br>  Mood—indicative<br>  Tense—aorist<br>  Voice—active<br>  Person—3rd person<br>  Number—plural<br>  Stem or root—from ψηλαφάω | In a general sense to touch; to handle; to feel.<br><br>**Practical Application**<br>The word "handled" (*epsëlaphësan*) means more than just touching. It means to grope and grasp after in order to understand; to handle in order to examine closely (John RW Stott. *The Epistles of John.* "Tyndale New Testament |

# PRACTICAL WORD STUDIES
## in the New Testament

| ENGLISH WORD | GREEK WORD AND VERSE | THE WORD MEANS... |
|---|---|---|
| **POSB REFERENCE** (1 Jn.1:1) Note 2, point 4 | Concordance References:<br>⇒ Strong's #5584 psëlaphaō<br>⇒ NIV #6027 psëlaphaō<br>⇒ NASB #5584 psëlaphaō<br><br>**1 John 1:1**<br>That which was from the beginning, which we have heard, which we have seen with our eyes, which we have looked upon, and our hands have **handled**, of the Word of life; [KJV]<br>What was from the beginning, what we have heard, what we have seen with our eyes, what we beheld and our hands **handled**, concerning the Word of Life— [NASB]<br>That which was from the beginning, which we have heard, which we have seen with our eyes, which we have looked at and our hands have **touched**—this we proclaim concerning the Word of life. [NIV]<br>That which was from the beginning, which we have heard, which we have seen with our eyes, which we have looked upon, and our hands have **handled**, concerning the Word of life— [NKJV]<br>The one who existed from the beginning is the one we have heard and seen. We saw him with our own eyes and **touched** him with our own hands. He is Jesus Christ, the Word of life. [NLT]<br>"Ὃ ἦν ἀπ' ἀρχῆς, ὃ ἀκηκόαμεν, ὃ ἑωράκαμεν τοῖς ὀφθαλμοῖς ἡμῶν, ὃ ἐθεασάμεθα, καὶ αἱ χεῖρες ἡμῶν **ἐψηλάφησαν**, περὶ τοῦ λόγου τῆς ζωῆς [GNS]<br>"Ὃ ἦν ἀπ' ἀρχῆς, ὃ ἀκηκόαμεν, ὃ ἑωράκαμεν τοῖς ὀφθαλμοῖς ἡμῶν, ὃ ἐθεασάμεθα καὶ αἱ χεῖρες ἡμῶν **ἐψηλάφησαν** περὶ τοῦ λόγου τῆς ζωῆς [GNT] | Commentary," p.60). A.T. Robertson, the Greek scholar, says that it is a graphic word, the very same word that Jesus used to prove that He was not a spirit after His resurrection (*Word Pictures in the New Testament*, Vol.6, p.205). |
| #1847<br>**Handling Accurately**<br><br>Rightly dividing–KJV<br>**Handling accurately–NASB**<br>Correctly handles–NIV<br>Rightly dividing–NKJV<br>Correctly explains–NLT<br><br>**POSB REFERENCE** (2 Tim. 2:15) Note 2 | ὀρθοτομοῦντα = *orthotomounta*<br>Pronunciation: [or-tho-tow-moon-tah]<br>Parsing (part of speech): verb<br>  Mood—participle (imperative sense)<br>  Tense—present<br>  Voice—active<br>  Case—accusative<br>  Gender—masculine<br>  Person—2nd person<br>  Number—singular<br>  Stem or root—from ὀρθοτομέω<br>Concordance References:<br>⇒ Strong's #3718 orthotomeō<br>⇒ NIV #3982 orthotomeō<br>⇒ NASB #3718 orthotomeō<br><br>**2 Tim. 2:15**<br>Study to shew thyself approved unto God, a workman that needeth not to be ashamed, **rightly dividing** the word of truth. [KJV]<br>Be diligent to present yourself approved to God as a workman who does not need to be ashamed, **handling accurately** the word of truth. [NASB]<br>Do your best to present yourself to God as one approved, a workman who does not need to be ashamed and who **correctly handles** the word of truth. [NIV]<br>Be diligent to present yourself approved to God, a worker who does not need to be ashamed, **rightly dividing** the word of truth. [NKJV]<br>Work hard so God can approve you. Be a good worker, one who does not need to be ashamed and who **correctly explains** the word of truth. [NLT]<br>σπούδασον σεαυτὸν δόκιμον παραστῆσαι τῷ Θεῷ, ἐργάτην ἀνεπαίσχυντον, **ὀρθοτομοῦντα** τὸν λόγον τῆς ἀληθείας. [GNS]<br>σπούδασον σεαυτὸν δόκιμον παραστῆσαι τῷ θεῷ, ἐργάτην ἀνεπαίσχυντον, **ὀρθοτομοῦντα** τὸν λόγον τῆς ἀληθείας. [GNT] | To correctly handle; to rightly divide; to handle accurately; to correctly explain; to interpret correctly; to cut straight.<br><br>**Practical Application**<br>Believers are to cut straight to the truth; they are not to take crooked paths and side tracks to the truth. We are to study the truth and correctly handle it. Once we have studied and learned the Word of God, we are to *accurately teach* the Word of God. We are not to teach....<br>• our own ideas.<br>• the theories of other people.<br>• what we think.<br>• what other men think.<br><br>We are not to mishandle the Word of God: twist it to fit what we think or want it to say; over emphasize or under emphasize its teachings; add to or take away from it. Any person who mishandles God's Word is not approved of God. This is the point of this verse: if we want God's approval—if we want to be acceptable to God—we must study, rush and seek to be a true teacher of God's Word. We must be *workmen* who study God's Word, workmen who study diligently: *who correctly analyze and accurately divide—rightly handle and skillfully teach—the Word of Truth* (Amplified New Testament). This is the believer who will not be ashamed when he faces the Lord Jesus Christ in the great day of judgment. |

# PRACTICAL WORD STUDIES
## in the NEW TESTAMENT

| ENGLISH WORD | GREEK WORD AND VERSE | THE WORD MEANS... |
|---|---|---|
| **#1848**<br>**Handmaid**<br><br>Handmaid–KJV<br>Bondslave–NASB<br>Servant–NIV<br>Maidservant–NKJV<br>Servant–NLT<br><br>**POSB REFERENCE**<br>(Lk.1:38)<br>Note 8 | δούλη = doulē<br>Pronunciation: [doo'-lay]<br>Parsing (part of speech): noun<br>    Case—nominative<br>    Gender—feminine<br>    Number—singular<br>    Stem or root—from δούλη, ης<br>Concordance References:<br>  ⇒ Strong's #1399 doulē<br>  ⇒ NIV #1527 doulē<br>  ⇒ NASB #1399 doulē<br><br>**Luke 1:38**<br>And Mary said, Behold the **handmaid** of the Lord; be it unto me according to thy word. And the angel departed from her. [KJV]<br>And Mary said, "Behold, the **bondslave** of the Lord; be it done to me according to your word." And the angel departed from her. [NASB]<br>"I am the Lord's **servant**," Mary answered. "May it be to me as you have said." Then the angel left her. [NIV]<br>Then Mary said, "Behold the **maidservant** of the Lord! Let it be to me according to your word." And the angel departed from her. [NKJV]<br>Mary responded, "I am the Lord's **servant**, and I am willing to accept whatever he wants. May everything you have said come true." And then the angel left. [NLT]<br>εἶπε δὲ Μαριάμ, Ἰδοὺ ἡ **δούλη** Κυρίου· γένοιτό μοι κατὰ τὸ ῥῆμά σου. καὶ ἀπῆλθεν ἀπ' αὐτῆς ὁ ἄγγελος. [GNS]<br>εἶπεν δὲ Μαριάμ, Ἰδοὺ ἡ **δούλη** κυρίου· γένοιτό μοι κατὰ τὸ ῥῆμά σου. καὶ ἀπῆλθεν ἀπ' αὐτῆς ὁ ἄγγελος. [GNT] | A slave girl; a handmaid; a female servant; a bondslave.<br><br>**Practical Application**<br>Mary was saying that she was a bondslave, willing to sell herself out completely to God. She would possess herself no longer but would give herself completely to God. |
| **#1849**<br>**Handwriting**<br><br>Handwriting–KJV<br>Certificate of debt–NASB<br>Written code–NIV<br>Handwriting–NKJV<br>Record–NLT<br><br>**POSB REFERENCE**<br>(Col.2:14)<br>Note 2, point 1 | χειρόγραφον = cheirographon<br>Pronunciation: [khi-rog'-raf-on]<br>Parsing (part of speech): noun<br>    Case—accusative<br>    Gender—neuter<br>    Number—singular<br>    Stem or root—from χειρόγραφον, ου<br>Concordance References:<br>  ⇒ Strong's #5498 cheirographon<br>  ⇒ NIV #5934 cheirographon<br>  ⇒ NASB #5498 cheirographon<br><br>**Col. 2:14**<br>Blotting out the **handwriting** of ordinances that was against us, which was contrary to us, and took it out of the way, nailing it to his cross; [KJV]<br>Having canceled out the **certificate of debt** consisting of decrees against us and which was hostile to us; and He has taken it out of the way, having nailed it to the cross. [NASB]<br>Having canceled the **written code**, with its regulations, that was against us and that stood opposed to us; he took it away, nailing it to the cross. [NIV]<br>Having wiped out the **handwriting** of requirements that was against us, which was contrary to us. And He has taken it out of the way, having nailed it to the cross. [NKJV]<br>He canceled the **record** that contained the charges against us. He took it and destroyed it by nailing it to Christ's cross. [NLT]<br>ἐξαλείψας τὸ καθ' ἡμῶν **χειρόγραφον** τοῖς δόγμασιν, ὃ ἦν ὑπεναντίον ἡμῖν· καὶ αὐτὸ ἦρκεν ἐκ τοῦ μέσου, προσηλώσας αὐτὸ τῷ σταυρῷ· [GNS]<br>ἐξαλείψας τὸ καθ' ἡμῶν **χειρόγραφον** τοῖς δόγμασιν ὃ ἦν ὑπεναντίον ἡμῖν, καὶ αὐτὸ ἦρκεν ἐκ τοῦ μέσου προσηλώσας αὐτὸ τῷ σταυρῷ· [GNT] | Written code, handwriting, certificate of debt, record of one's debts. It actually means a legal note or debt, what William Barclay calls *a charge list* or a list of charges against man (*The Letters to the Philippians, Colossians, and Thessalonians*, p.170).<br><br>**Practical Application**<br>Man's concept of the law is twofold.<br>1. Some men see the law as a list of rules that God has led great religious men to write down in either the Bible or other religious books.<br>2. Other men see the laws of God as unwritten laws that are rooted in the nature of man and the world. Man just instinctively senses what is right and wrong, and he is to live as his instinct tells him (cp. Romans 2:14-15).<br>Man just senses the handwriting of laws against him—laws that condemn him when he goes contrary to what they say or what he senses. The point is this: man senses the list of charges against him. And he should sense the wrong he has done, for it is his violation of God's law that condemns him to eternal death. Only as he senses and acknowledges his transgressions will he ever turn to God to save him. |

# PRACTICAL WORD STUDIES
## in the NEW TESTAMENT

| ENGLISH WORD | GREEK WORD AND VERSE | THE WORD MEANS... |
|---|---|---|
| **#1850**<br>**Hanging Upon**<br><br>Attentive–KJV<br>**Hanging upon–NASB**<br>Hung on–NIV<br>Attentive–NKJV<br>Hung on–NLT<br><br>**POSB REFERENCE**<br>(Lk.19:47-48; esp. v.48)<br>Note 3, point 2 | ἐξεκρέματο = exekremato<br>Pronunciation: [ex-e-krem'-ah-tow]<br>Parsing (part of speech): verb<br>  Mood—indicative<br>  Tense—aorist<br>  Voice—middle<br>  Person—3rd person<br>  Number—singular<br>  Stem or root—from ἐκκρέμαμαι<br>Concordance References:<br>⇒ Strong's #1582 ekkremannumi<br>⇒ NIV #1717 ekkremannumi<br>⇒ NASB #1582 ekkremannumi<br><br>**Luke 19:48**<br>And could not find what they might do: for all the people were very **attentive** to hear him. [KJV]<br>And they could not find anything that they might do, for all the people were **hanging upon** His words. [NASB]<br>Yet they could not find any way to do it, because all the people **hung on** his words. [NIV]<br>And were unable to do anything; for all the people were very **attentive** to hear Him. [NKJV]<br>But they could think of nothing, because all the people **hung on** every word he said. [NLT]<br>καὶ οὐχ εὕρισκον τὸ τί ποιήσωσιν· ὁ λαὸς γὰρ ἅπας **ἐξεκρέματο** αὐτοῦ ἀκούων. [GNS]<br>οὐχ ὅτι καθ' ὑστέρησιν λέγω, ἐγὼ γὰρ ἔμαθον ἐν οἷς εἰμι αὐτάρκης εἶναι.[GNT] | To be attentive; to pay close attention; to hang on the words of someone speaking.<br><br>**Practical Application**<br>The word means that they hung upon Jesus, gave Him rapt attention, were struck by Him. |
| **#1851**<br>**Happily, How To Get Along**<br><br>Content–KJV<br>Content–NASB<br>Content–NIV<br>Content–NKJV<br>**How to get along happily–NLT**<br><br>**POSB REFERENCE**<br>(Philip.4:11-14; esp. v.11)<br>Note 2, point 1 | αὐτάρκης = autarkēs<br>Pronunciation: [ow-tar'-kace]<br>Parsing (part of speech): adjective<br>  Case—nominative<br>  Gender—masculine<br>  Number—singular<br>  Stem or root—from αὐτάρκης, ες<br>Concordance References:<br>⇒ Strong's #842 autarkēs<br>⇒ NIV #895 autarkēs<br>⇒ NASB #842 autarkēs<br><br>**Philip. 4:11**<br>Not that I speak in respect of want: for I have learned, in whatsoever state I am, therewith to be **content**. [KJV]<br>Not that I speak from want; for I have learned to be **content** in whatever circumstances I am. [NASB]<br>I am not saying this because I am in need, for I have learned to be **content** whatever the circumstances. [NIV]<br>Not that I speak in regard to need, for I have learned in whatever state I am, to be **content**: [NKJV]<br>Not that I was ever in need, for I have learned **how to get along happily** whether I have much or little. [NLT]<br>οὐχ ὅτι καθ' ὑστέρησιν λέγω· ἐγὼ γὰρ ἔμαθον, ἐν οἷς εἰμι, **αὐτάρκης** εἶναι. [GNS]<br>οὐχ ὅτι καθ' ὑστέρησιν λέγω, ἐγὼ γὰρ ἔμαθον ἐν οἷς εἰμι **αὐτάρκης** εἶναι.[GNT] | To be content; to be happy; to be satisfied; to be self-sufficient; to be completely detached from circumstances.<br><br>**Practical Application**<br>Note the word "learned." It was a learning experience. Paul had to learn to conquer circumstances and not let circumstances conquer him. But note: he had learned contentment. He says three descriptive things:<br>⇒ that he knew how to live in need (to live humbly with little) and how it feels to live with plenty (to live with plenty and prosperity).<br>⇒ that he knew the *secret* to facing every situation, whether being full or going hungry.<br>⇒ that he knew how to live well fed (live in plenty) and how to live in want. |
| **#1852**<br>**Happiness**<br><br>Consolation–KJV<br>Comfort–NASB<br>Comfort–NIV<br>Consolation–NKJV<br>**Happiness–NLT**<br><br>**POSB REFERENCE**<br>(Lk.6:24-26; esp. v.24)<br>Note 2, point 1d | παράκλησιν = paraklēsin<br>Pronunciation: [par-ak'-lay-sin]<br>Parsing (part of speech): noun<br>  Case—accusative<br>  Gender—feminine<br>  Number—singular<br>  Stem or root—from παράκλησις, εως<br>Concordance References:<br>⇒ Strong's #3874 paraklēsis<br>⇒ NIV #4155 paraklēsis<br>⇒ NASB #3874 paraklēsis | Comfort, help, aid, happiness, consolation, encouragement.<br><br>**Practical Application**<br>Their (the rich) only "happiness" is to be on this earth—the wealth they have. There will be no comfort after this life—no help, no aid, no encouragement, no cheer. They are paid in full. |

# PRACTICAL WORD STUDIES
## in the NEW TESTAMENT

| ENGLISH WORD | GREEK WORD AND VERSE | THE WORD MEANS... |
|---|---|---|
| See also POSB REF: (Acts 15:30-35; esp. v.31) Note 5, point 1 | **Luke 6:24**<br>But woe unto you that are rich! for ye have received your **consolation**. [KJV]<br>"But woe to you who are rich, for you are receiving your **comfort** in full. [NASB]<br>"But woe to you who are rich, for you have already received your **comfort**. [NIV]<br>But woe to you who are rich, For you have received your **consolation**. [NKJV]<br>"What sorrows await you who are rich, for you have your only **happiness** now. [NLT]<br>πλὴν οὐαὶ ὑμῖν τοῖς πλουσίοις, ὅτι ἀπέχετε τὴν **παράκλησιν** ὑμῶν. [GNS]<br>Πλὴν οὐαὶ ὑμῖν τοῖς πλουσίοις, ὅτι ἀπέχετε τὴν **παράκλησιν** ὑμῶν. [GNT] | |
| #1853<br>**Happy**<br><br>Rejoice–KJV<br>Rejoiced–NASB<br>Glad–NIV<br>Rejoice–NKJV<br>**Happy–NLT**<br><br>**POSB REFERENCE**<br>(Jn.14:28-29; esp. v.28)<br>Note 2 | ἐχάρητε = echarēte<br>Pronunciation: [eh-chah'-ray-teh]<br>Parsing (part of speech): verb<br>    Mood—indicative<br>    Tense—aorist<br>    Voice—passive deponent<br>    Person—2nd person<br>    Number—plural<br>    Stem or root—from χαίρω<br>Concordance References:<br>⇒ Strong's #5463 chairo<br>⇒ NIV #5897 chairo<br>⇒ NASB #5463 chairo<br><br>**John 14:28**<br>Ye have heard how I said unto you, I go away, and come again unto you. If ye loved me, ye would **rejoice**, because I said, I go unto the Father: for my Father is greater than I. [KJV]<br>"You heard that I said to you, 'I go away, and I will come to you.' If you loved Me, you would have **rejoiced**, because I go to the Father; for the Father is greater than I. [NASB]<br>"You heard me say, 'I am going away and I am coming back to you.' If you loved me, you would be **glad** that I am going to the Father, for the Father is greater than I. [NIV]<br>You have heard Me say to you, 'I am going away and coming *back* to you.' If you loved Me, you would **rejoice** because I said, 'I am going to the Father,' for My Father is greater than I. [NKJV]<br>Remember what I told you: I am going away, but I will come back to you again. If you really love me, you will be very **happy** for me, because now I can go to the Father, who is greater than I am. [NLT]<br>ἠκούσατε ὅτι ἐγὼ εἶπον ὑμῖν, Ὑπάγω καὶ ἔρχομαι πρὸς ὑμᾶς. εἰ ἠγαπᾶτέ με, **ἐχάρητε** ἂν ὅτι εἶπον, Πορεύομαι πρὸς τὸν πατέρα· ὅτι ὁ πατήρ μού μείζων ἐστι. [GNS]<br>ἠκούσατε ὅτι ἐγὼ εἶπον ὑμῖν, Ὑπάγω καὶ ἔρχομαι πρὸς ὑμᾶς. εἰ ἠγαπᾶτέ με **ἐχάρητε** ἂν ὅτι πορεύομαι πρὸς τὸν πατέρα, ὅτι ὁ πατὴρ μείζων μού ἐστιν. [GNT] | To rejoice; to have great joy; to be glad; to be delighted; to be satisfied. Joy (chara) and happiness (echarēte, the same root word as joy) mean an inner gladness and a deep seated pleasure. It is a depth of assurance and confidence that ignites a cheerful heart. It is a cheerful heart that leads to cheerful behavior.<br><br>**Practical Application**<br>The source of joy is threefold. (See POSB *Deeper Study* #1—John 15:11 for more discussion.)<br>1. The return of Jesus to the Father causes believers to joy and rejoice. "I am going away, and I am coming back to you" is a reference to His death, resurrection, and ascension.<br>  a. The death or cross of Christ attracts and causes men to joy and rejoice. The cross is the source of their deliverance from sin, death, and hell (see POSB *Deeper Study* #4—John 12:32).<br>  b. The resurrection and ascension of Christ attracts and causes men to joy and rejoice. The resurrection and ascension are the sources of their new life and hope for eternity (see POSB notes, Resurrection—John 14:6; POSB note—John 7:33-34; POSB note—Mark 16:19-20).<br>2. The Father's greatness causes believers to joy and rejoice. The Father demonstrated His great love and power by releasing Jesus...<br>• from the flesh: in all its limitations and weaknesses.<br>• from the world: in all its trials and tensions.<br>• from the devil: in all his oppressions and attacks.<br>• from the pressure of men: in all their needful demands and, in some cases, terrible threats and attacks.<br><br>The Father took Jesus home, back from where He had come; and He restored Him to His seat of glory, exalting Him above every name that is named (Phil. 2:9-11). The believer joys and rejoices in the phe-nomenal power of the Father's greatness.<br>3. A confirmed faith causes believers to joy and rejoice. The claims of Jesus have been proven and verified. Just as He told His disciples, all that He predicted has come to pass.<br>⇒ He did leave (die).<br>⇒ He did go to His Father (the ascension).<br>⇒ He did return (the resurrection).<br>⇒ He did send the Holy Spirit.<br><br>Note: by foretelling these things, Jesus |

# PRACTICAL WORD STUDIES
## in the New Testament

| ENGLISH WORD | GREEK WORD AND VERSE | THE WORD MEANS... |
|---|---|---|
| | | strengthened the faith of believers enormously. (In fact, think about it: He could have chosen no better way to strengthen the faith of believers.) |
| **#1854**<br>**Happy**<br><br>Joy–KJV<br>Joy–NASB<br>Joy–NIV<br>Joy–NKJV<br>**Happy–NLT**<br><br>**POSB REFERENCE**<br>(Rom. 15:13)<br>Note 5, point 1 | χαρᾶς = *charas*<br>Pronunciation: [khar-ahs']<br>Parsing (part of speech): noun<br>    Case—genitive<br>    Gender—feminine<br>    Number—singular<br>    Stem or root—from χαρά, ᾶς<br>Concordance References:<br>  ⇒ Strong's #5479 chara<br>  ⇒ NIV #5915 chara<br>  ⇒ NASB #5479 chara<br><br>**Romans 15:13**<br>Now the God of hope fill you with all **joy** and peace in believing, that ye may abound in hope, through the power of the Holy Ghost. [KJV]<br>Now may the God of hope fill you with all **joy** and peace in believing, that you may abound in hope by the power of the Holy Spirit. [NASB]<br>May the God of hope fill you with all **joy** and peace as you trust in him, so that you may overflow with hope by the power of the Holy Spirit. [NIV]<br>Now may the God of hope fill you with all **joy** and peace in believing, that you may abound in hope by the power of the Holy Spirit. [NKJV]<br>So I pray that God, who gives you hope, will keep you **happy** and full of peace as you believe in him. May you overflow with hope through the power of the Holy Spirit. [NLT]<br>ὁ δὲ Θεὸς τῆς ἐλπίδος πληρώσαι ὑμᾶς πάσης **χαρᾶς** καὶ εἰρήνης ἐν τῷ πιστεύειν, εἰς τὸ περισσεύειν ὑμᾶς ἐν τῇ ἐλπίδι ἐν δυνάμει Πνεύματος Ἁγίου. [GNS]<br>ὁ δὲ Θεὸς τῆς ἐλπίδος πληρώσαι ὑμᾶς πάσης **χαρᾶς** καὶ εἰρήνης ἐν τῷ πιστεύειν, εἰς τὸ περισσεύειν ὑμᾶς ἐν τῇ ἐλπίδι ἐν δυνάμει πνεύματος ἁγίου. [GNT] | Joy, gladness, happiness; cause or object of joy.<br><br>**Practical Application**<br>There is happiness (*charas*): an inner gladness; a deep seated pleasure. It is a depth of assurance and confidence that ignites a cheerful heart. It is a cheerful heart that leads to cheerful behavior. |
| **#1855**<br>**Harass**<br><br>Vex–KJV<br>Mistreat–NASB<br>Persecute–NIV<br>**Harass–NKJV**<br>Persecute–NLT<br><br>**POSB REFERENCE**<br>(Acts 12:1-4; esp. v.1)<br>Note 1, point 1 | κακῶσαί = *kakōsai*<br>Pronunciation: [kak-o'-sah-ee]<br>Parsing (part of speech): verb<br>    Mood—infinitive<br>    Tense—aorist<br>    Voice—active<br>    Stem or root—from κακόω<br>Concordance References:<br>  ⇒ Strong's #2559 kakoö<br>  ⇒ NIV #2808 kakoö<br>  ⇒ NASB #2559 kakoö<br><br>**Acts 12:1**<br>Now about that time Herod the king stretched forth *his* hands to **vex** certain of the church. [KJV]<br>Now about that time Herod the king laid hands on some who belonged to the church, in order to **mistreat** them. [NASB]<br>It was about this time that King Herod arrested some who belonged to the church, intending to **persecute** them. [NIV]<br>Now about that time Herod the king stretched out *his* hand to **harass** some from the church. [NKJV]<br>About that time King Herod Agrippa began to **persecute** some believers in the church. [NLT]<br>Κατ' ἐκεῖνον δὲ τὸν καιρὸν ἐπέβαλεν Ἡρῴδης ὁ βασιλεὺς τὰς χεῖρας **κακῶσαί** τινας τῶν ἀπὸ τῆς ἐκκλησίας. [GNS]<br>Κατ' ἐκεῖνον δὲ τὸν καιρὸν ἐπέβαλεν Ἡρῴδης ὁ βασιλεὺς τὰς χεῖρας **κακῶσαί** τινας τῶν ἀπὸ τῆς ἐκκλησίας. [GNT] | To persecute; to mistreat; to vex; to harass; to oppress, torment, do evil against, harm; to be cruel.<br><br>**Practical Application**<br>Certain leaders in the church were arrested and imprisoned and apparently tortured. A person can just imagine believers being man-handled and molested as the persecuted of every generation so often are, their homes and property being destroyed and confiscated or stolen. |

## PRACTICAL WORD STUDIES
### in the NEW TESTAMENT

| ENGLISH WORD | GREEK WORD AND VERSE | THE WORD MEANS... |
|---|---|---|
| **#1856**<br>**Harassed**<br><br>Fainted–KJV<br>Distressed–NASB<br>**Harassed–NIV**<br>Weary–NKJV<br>Problems were so great–NLT<br><br>**POSB REFERENCE**<br>(Mt.9:36)<br>*Deeper Study #3* | ἐσκυλμένοι = *eskulmenoi*<br>Pronunciation: [es-kool-me'-noi]<br>Parsing (part of speech): verb<br>    Mood—participle<br>    Tense—perfect<br>    Voice—passive<br>    Case—nominative<br>    Gender—masculine<br>    Number—plural<br>    Stem or root—from σκύλλω<br>Concordance References:<br>⇒ Strong's #4660 skullö<br>⇒ NIV #5035 skullö<br>⇒ NASB #4660 skullö<br><br>**Matthew 9:36**<br>But when he saw the multitudes, he was moved with compassion on them, because they **fainted**, and were scattered abroad, as sheep having no shepherd. [KJV]<br>And seeing the multitudes, He felt compassion for them, because they were **distressed** and downcast like sheep without a shepherd. [NASB]<br>When he saw the crowds, he had compassion on them, because they were **harassed** and helpless, like sheep without a shepherd. [NIV]<br>But when He saw the multitudes, He was moved with compassion for them, because they were **weary** and scattered, like sheep having no shepherd. [NKJV]<br>He felt great pity for the crowds that came, because their **problems were so great** and they didn't know where to go for help. They were like sheep without a shepherd. [NLT]<br>Ἰδὼν δὲ τοὺς ὄχλους, ἐσπλαγχνίσθη περὶ αὐτῶν, ὅτι ἦσαν **ἐκλελυμένοι** καὶ ἐρριμμένοι ὡσεὶ πρόβατα μὴ ἔχοντα ποιμένα. [GNS]<br>Ἰδὼν δὲ τοὺς ὄχλους ἐσπλαγχνίσθη περὶ αὐτῶν, ὅτι ἦσαν **ἐσκυλμένοι** καὶ ἐρριμμένοι ὡσεὶ πρόβατα μὴ ἔχοντα ποιμένα. [GNT] | To be harassed; to faint; to grow weary; to be troubled; to lose heart; to lack courage; to be distressed, fainthearted, bewildered. It means to be completely overwhelmed with problems.<br><br>**Practical Application**<br>The word is used when a person has struggled and struggled against sin or stood against the barrage of insult after insult until he can stand no more. It means that a person has undergone trial after trial until he is ready to collapse (Heb.12:3). |
| **#1857**<br>**Hard**<br><br>Austere–KJV<br>Exacting–NASB<br>**Hard–NIV**<br>Austere–NKJV<br>Tough–NLT<br><br>**POSB REFERENCE**<br>(Lk.19:15-23; esp. v.22)<br>Note 5, point 6b | αὐστηρός = *austēros*<br>Pronunciation: [ow-stay-ros']<br>Parsing (part of speech): adjective<br>    Case—nominative<br>    Gender—masculine<br>    Number—singular<br>    Stem or root—from αὐστηρός, ά, όν<br>Concordance References:<br>⇒ Strong's #840 austēros<br>⇒ NIV #893 austēros<br>⇒ NASB #840 austēros<br><br>**Luke 19:22**<br>And he saith unto him, Out of thine own mouth will I judge thee, thou wicked servant. Thou knewest that I was an **austere** man, taking up that I laid not down, and reaping that I did not sow: [KJV]<br>"He said to him, 'By your own words I will judge you, you worthless slave. Did you know that I am an **exacting** man, taking up what I did not lay down, and reaping what I did not sow? [NASB]<br>"His master replied, 'I will judge you by your own words, you wicked servant! You knew, did you, that I am a **hard** man, taking out what I did not put in, and reaping what I did not sow? [NIV]<br>And he said to him, 'Out of your own mouth I will judge you, you wicked servant. You knew that I was an **austere** man, collecting what I did not deposit and reaping what I did not sow. [NKJV]<br>"'You wicked servant!' the king roared. 'Hard, am I? If you knew so much about me and how **tough** I am, [NLT]<br>λέγει δὲ αὐτῷ, Ἐκ τοῦ στόματός σου κρίνω σε, | Sharp, hard, exacting, tough, austere, stringent.<br><br>**Practical Application**<br>In this Scripture, the unfaithful servant accused the Lord of being too hard. He felt that the Lord was too demanding and strict; and if he committed himself to the Lord's affairs, he would lose out on too much of the pleasures and comforts of life. But note: this was merely an excuse for his failure. He had chosen to live a life of selfishness and comfort and worldliness in the kingdom of the Lord without paying the price of helping to build it. He had been complacent and idle, doing very little. He had to cover up his failure or else face judgment, but his excuse was unacceptable. Perfect justice was executed: "Out of your own mouth I will judge you." The very excuse, as well as the life, of the unfaithful servant determined his judgment. |

# PRACTICAL WORD STUDIES
## in the NEW TESTAMENT

| ENGLISH WORD | GREEK WORD AND VERSE | THE WORD MEANS... |
|---|---|---|
| | πονηρὲ δοῦλε. ᾔδεις ὅτι ἐγὼ ἄνθρωπος **αὐστηρός** εἰμι, αἴρων ὃ οὐκ ἔθηκα, καὶ θερίζων ὃ οὐκ ἔσπειρα· [GNS]<br>λέγει αὐτῷ, Ἐκ τοῦ στόματός σου κρινῶ σε, πονηρὲ δοῦλε. ᾔδεις ὅτι ἐγὼ ἄνθρωπος **αὐστηρός** εἰμι, αἴρων ὃ οὐκ ἔθηκα καὶ θερίζων ὃ οὐκ ἔσπειρα; [GNT] | |
| **#1858**<br>**Hard**<br><br>Hard–KJV<br>Difficult–NASB<br>Hard–NIV<br>Hard–NKJV<br>Hard–NLT<br><br>**POSB REFERENCE**<br>(Jn.6:59-60; esp. v.60)<br>Note 1 | Σκληρός = sklēros<br>Pronunciation: [sklay-ros']<br>Parsing (part of speech): adjective<br>  Case—nominative<br>  Gender—masculine<br>  Number—singular<br>Stem or root—from σκληρός, ά, όν<br>Concordance References:<br> ⇒ Strong's #4642 skleros<br> ⇒ NIV #5017 skleros<br> ⇒ NASB #4642 skleros<br><br>**John 6:60**<br>Many therefore of his disciples, when they had heard this, said, This is an **hard** saying; who can hear it? [KJV]<br>Many therefore of His disciples, when they heard this said, "This is a **difficult** statement; who can listen to it?" [NASB]<br>On hearing it, many of his disciples said, "This is a **hard** teaching. Who can accept it?" [NIV]<br>Therefore many of His disciples, when they heard *this*, said, "This is a **hard** saying; who can understand it?" [NKJV]<br>Even his disciples said, "This is very **hard** to understand. How can anyone accept it?" [NLT]<br>Πολλοὶ οὖν ἀκούσαντες ἐκ τῶν μαθητῶν αὐτοῦ εἶπον, **Σκληρός** ἐστιν οὗτος ὁ λόγος· τίς δύναται αὐτοῦ ἀκούειν; [GNS]<br>Πολλοὶ οὖν ἀκούσαντες ἐκ τῶν μαθητῶν αὐτοῦ εἶπαν, **Σκληρός** ἐστιν ὁ λόγος οὗτος· τίς δύναται αὐτοῦ ἀκούειν; [GNT] | Rough, harsh, hard, difficult, complicated, severe.<br><br>**Practical Application**<br>What Jesus had said was hard and difficult to accept, but His words were clearly understood. The people's problem was not in their understanding, but in their hearts. There were three responses to the Lord's message.<br>1. There were disciples or followers who turned back. Note that "many...turned back, and no longer followed Him" (Jn.6:66). They forsook and deserted the Lord. Why? Very simply, following Christ cost too much. It involved the cross, which meant complete denial of oneself.<br>  a. Jesus was claiming to be Lord. This meant that a man had to give all he was and had to Christ.<br>  b. Jesus was claiming to be the very Son of God, to have come down out of heaven. Some just could not receive and accept the fact.<br>  c. Jesus was demanding total allegiance and complete self-denial, and following Him would just cost too much (see POSB *Deeper Study* #1—Luke 9:23).<br>2. There was the disciple who believed that Jesus was the Lord. Note four facts.<br>  a. Peter spoke for all the apostles. He was their leader and spokesman.<br>  b. Peter called Jesus "Lord," and he used the title in its fullest meaning (cp. John 6:68-69). Jesus was recognized to be the sovereign Lord of the universe, the One to whom all men owe their allegiance.<br>  c. Peter declared that Jesus' words were the words of eternal life. He declared that what Jesus had just proclaimed was true (John 6:63). (See POSB *Deeper Study* #2—John 1:4; POSB *Deeper Study* #1—John 10:10; POSB *Deeper Study* #1—John 17:2-3.)<br>  d. Peter proclaimed that he and the apostles both *believed* and *knew* something: Jesus was...<br>    • "the Christ, the Son of the living God" (the latest manuscripts read this).<br>    • "the Holy One of God" (the oldest manuscripts read this).<br>3. There was the disciple who betrayed Jesus. Note these facts.<br>  a. Judas was a "chosen" man, chosen not only to be saved, but to be a minister of Christ.<br>  b. Judas was called "a devil," a false accuser (2 Tim. 3:3), an adversary, an enemy of Christ.<br>  c. Judas was a betrayer, a professed follower, but a hypocrite. |

## PRACTICAL WORD STUDIES
### in the NEW TESTAMENT

| ENGLISH WORD | GREEK WORD AND VERSE | THE WORD MEANS... |
|---|---|---|
| **#1859**<br>**Hard**<br><br>Dull–KJV<br>Dull–NASB<br>Slow–NIV<br>Dull–NKJV<br>Hard–NLT<br><br>**POSB REFERENCE**<br>(Heb.5:11)<br>Note 1 | νωθροί = nōthroi<br>Pronunciation: [no-throy']<br>Parsing (part of speech): adjective<br>    Case—nominative<br>    Gender—masculine<br>    Number—plural<br>    Stem or root—from νωθρός, ά, όν<br>Concordance References:<br>  ⇒ Strong's #3576 nōthros<br>  ⇒ NIV #3821 nōthros<br>  ⇒ NASB #3576 nōthros<br><br>**Hebrews 5:11**<br>Of whom we have many things to say, and hard to be uttered, seeing ye are **dull** of hearing. [KJV]<br>Concerning him we have much to say, and it is hard to explain, since you have become **dull** of hearing. [NASB]<br>We have much to say about this, but it is hard to explain because you are **slow** to learn. [NIV]<br>Of whom we have much to say, and hard to explain, since you have become **dull** of hearing. [NKJV]<br>There is so much more we would like to say about this. But you don't seem to listen, so it's **hard** to make you understand. [NLT]<br>Περὶ οὗ πολὺς ἡμῖν ὁ λόγος καὶ δυσερμήνευτος λέγειν, ἐπεὶ **νωθροί** γεγόνατε ταῖς ἀκοαῖς. [GNS]<br>Περὶ οὗ πολὺς ἡμῖν ὁ λόγος καὶ δυσερμήνευτος λέγειν, ἐπεὶ **νωθροί** γεγόνατε ταῖς ἀκοαῖς. [GNT] | Slow, dull, hard of hearing. It means sluggish, slow, lazy, lethargic, forgetful.<br><br>**Practical Application**<br>A person becomes immature because of hard hearing. The writer to the Hebrews had much that he wanted to teach, especially about the Lord Jesus Christ and His Priestly ministry, but he was unable. Why? Because the Christian faith—the Word of God and the Bible—is difficult to understand. No person can grasp the Word of God and its truths by simply reading it. A person must study, meditate, and practice the Word of God in order to understand it.<br>The Hebrew believers had become mentally lazy and sluggish and spiritually complacent and slothful. Even though they were sitting and listening to the preachers and teachers and reading the Scriptures, they were not listening or paying attention. Their minds, wandering about, were unwilling to exert the energy to concentrate and study.<br>Note: some of the Hebrew believers were already hard of hearing. Some had already become immature; they had already fallen and were no longer growing spiritually. |
| **#1860**<br>**Hard–Hardly**<br><br>Hardly–KJV<br>Hard–NASB<br>Hard–NIV<br>Hard–NKJV<br>Hard–NLT<br><br>**POSB REFERENCE**<br>(Mt.19:23)<br>*Deeper Study* #1 | δυσκόλως = duskolōs<br>Pronunciation: [doos-kol'-oce]<br>Parsing (part of speech): adjective<br>    Type—adverb<br>    Stem or root—from δυσκόλως<br>Concordance References:<br>  ⇒ Strong's #1423 duskolōs<br>  ⇒ NIV #1552 duskolōs<br>  ⇒ NASB #1423 duskolōs<br><br>**Matthew 19:23**<br>Then said Jesus unto his disciples, Verily I say unto you, That a rich man shall **hardly** enter into the kingdom of heaven. [KJV]<br>And Jesus said to His disciples, "Truly I say to you, it is **hard** for a rich man to enter the kingdom of heaven. [NASB]<br>Then Jesus said to his disciples, "I tell you the truth, it is **hard** for a rich man to enter the kingdom of heaven. [NIV]<br>Then Jesus said to His disciples, "Assuredly, I say to you that it is **hard** for a rich man to enter the kingdom of heaven. [NKJV]<br>Then Jesus said to his disciples, "I tell you the truth, it is very **hard** for a rich person to get into the Kingdom of Heaven. [NLT]<br>Ὁ δὲ Ἰησοῦς εἶπε τοῖς μαθηταῖς αὐτοῦ, Ἀμὴν λέγω ὅτι **δυσκόλως** πλούσιος εἰσελεύσεται εἰς τὴν βασιλείαν τῶν οὐρανῶν. [GNS]<br>Ὁ δὲ Ἰησοῦς εἶπεν τοῖς μαθηταῖς αὐτοῦ, Ἀμὴν λέγω ὑμῖν ὅτι πλούσιος **δυσκόλως** εἰσελεύσεται εἰς τὴν βασιλείαν τῶν οὐρανῶν. [GNT] | Hard, hardly, barely or with great difficulty.<br><br>**Practical Application**<br>In this Scripture, we learn that it is difficult, very difficult for a rich man to enter heaven. Why? In one simple sentence: it is hard for a rich man to give all that he has to help the needy—to give all that has been so pleasing, so comfortable, so ego boosting, and so rewarding in possessions and position and self-esteem. |
| **#1861**<br>**Hard–Hard Pressed**<br><br>Troubled–KJV<br>Afflicted–NASB<br>**Hard pressed**–NIV<br>Hard–NKJV<br>Pressed–NLT | θλιβόμενοι = thlibomenoi<br>Pronunciation: [thlee'-bo-mehn-oy]<br>Parsing (part of speech): verb<br>    Mood—participle<br>    Tense—present<br>    Voice—passive<br>    Case—nominative<br>    Gender—masculine<br>    Person—1st person<br>    Number—plural<br>    Stem or root—from θλίβω | To be hard pressed, troubled, afflicted, squeezed, oppressed, hedged in; to have difficulty; to be pressured.<br><br>**Practical Application**<br>The power of God sustains the minister. The minister (or believer) of God faces all kinds of trouble and difficult situations in life. However, he has one great resource: the presence and power of God within him. God never forsakes |

# Practical Word Studies
## in the New Testament

| ENGLISH WORD | GREEK WORD AND VERSE | THE WORD MEANS... |
|---|---|---|
| **POSB REFERENCE** (2 Cor.4:7-9; esp. v.8) Note 2 | Concordance References:<br>⇒ Strong's #2346 thlibō<br>⇒ NIV #2567 thlibō<br>⇒ NASB #2346 thlibō<br><br>**2 Cor. 4:8**<br>We are **troubled** on every side, yet not distressed; we are perplexed, but not in despair; [KJV]<br>We are **afflicted** in every way, but not crushed; perplexed, but not despairing; [NASB]<br>We are **hard pressed** on every side, but not crushed; perplexed, but not in despair; [NIV]<br>*We are* **hard** pressed on every side, yet not crushed; we are perplexed, but not in despair; [NKJV]<br>We are **pressed** on every side by troubles, but we are not crushed and broken. We are perplexed, but we don't give up and quit. [NLT]<br>ἐν παντὶ **θλιβόμενοι**, ἀλλ' οὐ στενοχωρούμενοι· ἀπορούμενοι ἀλλ' οὐκ ἐξαπορούμενοι· [GNS]<br>ἐν παντὶ **θλιβόμενοι** ἀλλ' οὐ στενοχωρούμενοι, ἀπορούμενοι ἀλλ' οὐκ ἐξαπορούμενοι, [GNT] | him; God saves and delivers him through every situation and trial, no matter how difficult. The minister (or believer) may be hard pressed on every side, but God's power saves him from distress. |
| **#1862**<br>**Hard Work**<br><br>Labours–KJV<br>Labors–NASB<br>**Hard work–NIV**<br>Labors–NKJV<br>Worked to exhaustion–NLT<br><br>**POSB REFERENCE** (2 Cor.6:5) Note 4 | κόποις = *kopois*<br>Pronunciation: [kop'-oys]<br>Parsing (part of speech): noun<br>    Case—dative<br>    Gender—masculine<br>    Number—plural<br>    Stem or root—from κόπος, ου<br>Concordance References:<br>⇒ Strong's #2873 kopos<br>⇒ NIV #3160 kopos<br>⇒ NASB #2873 kopos<br><br>**2 Cor. 6:5**<br>In stripes, in imprisonments, in tumults, in **labours**, in watchings, in fastings; [KJV]<br>In beatings, in imprisonments, in tumults, in **labors**, in sleeplessness, in hunger, [NASB]<br>In beatings, imprisonments and riots; in **hard work**, sleepless nights and hunger; [NIV]<br>In stripes, in imprisonments, in tumults, in **labors**, in sleeplessness, in fastings; [NKJV]<br>We have been beaten, been put in jail, faced angry mobs, **worked to exhaustion**, endured sleepless nights, and gone without food. [NLT]<br>ἐν πληγαῖς, ἐν φυλακαῖς, ἐν ἀκαταστασίαις, ἐν **κόποις**, ἐν ἀγρυπνίαις, ἐν νηστείαις, [GNS]<br>ἐν πληγαῖς, ἐν φυλακαῖς, ἐν ἀκαταστασίαις, ἐν **κόποις**, ἐν ἀγρυπνίαις, ἐν νηστείαις, [GNT] | Hard work, labors, toil, laborious work to the point of exhaustion.<br><br>**Practical Application**<br>As we study the life of Paul, one striking characteristic about Paul's ministry becomes clear: he never stopped preaching, teaching, or ministering—not until he just had to have rest. He was not lazy, lethargic, slothful, or complacent. He got up in the mornings and put his hand to the plow: working, praying, studying, ministering, and witnessing—just as God had called him. |
| **#1863**<br>**Hard Work**<br><br>Labour–KJV<br>Toil–NASB<br>**Hard work–NIV**<br>Labor–NKJV<br>**Hard work–NLT**<br><br>**POSB REFERENCE** (Rev.2:2-3; esp. v.2) Note 3, point 1 | κόπον = *kopon*<br>Pronunciation: [kop'-on]<br>Parsing (part of speech): noun<br>    Case—accusative<br>    Gender—masculine<br>    Number—singular<br>    Stem or root—from κόπος, ου<br>Concordance References:<br>⇒ Strong's #2873 kopos<br>⇒ NIV #3160 kopos<br>⇒ NASB #2873 kopos<br><br>**Rev. 2:2**<br>I know thy works, and thy **labour**, and thy patience, and how thou canst not bear them which are evil: and thou hast tried them which say they are apostles, and are not, and hast found them liars: [KJV]<br>'I know your deeds and your **toil** and perseverance, and that you cannot endure evil men, and you put to the test those who call themselves apostles, and they are not, and you found them to be false; [NASB]<br>I know your deeds, your **hard work** and your perse- | Hard work; to labor; to toil; to labor to the point of weariness, sweat, and exhaustion; to work and labor to the limit of one's ability.<br><br>**Practical Application**<br>The church *worked* and labored for Christ. The church was a working church, a laboring church, a church committed to serve Christ and to serve Him to the fullest. |

## PRACTICAL WORD STUDIES
### in the NEW TESTAMENT

| ENGLISH WORD | GREEK WORD AND VERSE | THE WORD MEANS... |
|---|---|---|
| | verance. I know that you cannot tolerate wicked men, that you have tested those who claim to be apostles but are not, and have found them false. [NIV]<br>　I know your works, your **labor**, your patience, and that you cannot bear those who are evil. And you have tested those who say they are apostles and are not, and have found them liars; [NKJV]<br>　"I know all the things you do. I have seen your **hard work** and your patient endurance. I know you don't tolerate evil people. You have examined the claims of those who say they are apostles but are not. You have discovered they are liars. [NLT]<br>　Οἶδα τὰ ἔργα σου, καὶ τὸν **κόπον** σου, καὶ τὴν ὑπομονήν σου, καὶ ὅτι οὐ δύνῃ βαστάσαι κακούς, καὶ ἐπειράσω τοὺς φάσκοντας εἶναι ἀποστόλους καὶ οὐκ εἰσί, καὶ εὗρες αὐτοὺς ψευδεῖς, [GNS]<br>　Οἶδα τὰ ἔργα σου καὶ τὸν **κόπον** καὶ τὴν ὑπομονήν σου καὶ ὅτι οὐ δύνῃ βαστάσαι κακούς, καὶ ἐπείρασας τοὺς λέγοντας ἑαυτοὺς ἀποστόλους καὶ οὐκ εἰσίν καὶ εὗρες αὐτοὺς ψευδεῖς, [GNT] | |
| **#1864**<br>**Hard Working–**<br>**Hardworking**<br><br>Laboureth–KJV<br>**Hard-working–**<br>**NASB**<br>**Hardworking–NIV**<br>**Hard-working–**<br>**NKJV**<br>**Hardworking–NLT**<br><br>**POSB**<br>**REFERENCE**<br>(2 Tim. 2:6)<br>Note 5 | κοπιῶντα = *kopiönta*<br>Pronunciation: [kop-ee-own'-tah]<br>Parsing (part of speech): verb<br>　　Mood—participle<br>　　Tense—present<br>　　Voice—active<br>　　Gender—masculine<br>　　Number—singular<br>　　Stem or root—from κοπιάω<br>Concordance References:<br>　⇒ Strong's #2872 kopiaō<br>　⇒ NIV #3159 kopiaō<br>　⇒ NASB #2872 kopiaō<br><br>**2 Tim. 2:6**<br>　The husbandman that **laboureth** must be first partaker of the fruits. [KJV]<br>　The **hard-working** farmer ought to be the first to receive his share of the crops. [NASB]<br>　The **hardworking** farmer should be the first to receive a share of the crops. [NIV]<br>　The **hard-working** farmer must be first to partake of the crops. [NKJV]<br>　**Hardworking** farmers are the first to enjoy the fruit of their labor. [NLT]<br>　τὸν **κοπιῶντα** γεωργὸν δεῖ πρῶτον τῶν καρπῶν μεταλαμβάνειν. [GNS]<br>　τὸν **κοπιῶντα** γεωργὸν δεῖ πρῶτον τῶν καρπῶν μεταλαμβάνειν. [GNT] | Hardworking; to labor; to work hard; to become very weary and tired. It means labor that is diligent, laborious, exhausting.<br><br>**Practical Application**<br>　It is the picture of a farmer who toils to the point of becoming weary, so tired that he cannot put one foot in front of the other.<br>　Note a most significant point: it is the diligent farmer who arduously labors—who labors to the point of exhaustion—that will be the *first* to partake of the fruit. The slothful farmer...<br>• is the last to receive the reward of his harvest and fruit.<br>• never bears a full harvest and never receives the reward of a full harvest.<br><br>　The reason is that the slothful farmer either plants less seed or plants later than he should. And he never weeds or harvests the fields like he should. Note the point: it is the diligent farmer who will be the first to be rewarded. He will be the first to partake of the fruit of the harvest.<br>　The point is true of the Christian believer as well. The diligent believer will be rewarded first by God; that is, he will be given a greater reward by God. |
| **#1865**<br>**Hardened**<br><br>Hardened–KJV<br>Hardened–NASB<br>Obstinate–NIV<br>Hardened–NKJV<br>Rejected–NLT<br><br>**POSB**<br>**REFERENCE**<br>(Acts 19:2-9; esp. v.9)<br>Note 2, point 2d | ἐσκληρύνοντο = *esklērunonto*<br>Pronunciation: [es-sklay-roo'-non-tow]<br>Parsing (part of speech): verb<br>　　Mood—indicative<br>　　Tense—imperfect<br>　　Voice—passive<br>　　Person—3rd person<br>　　Number—plural<br>　　Stem or root—from σκληρύνω<br>Concordance References:<br>　⇒ Strong's #4645 sklērunō<br>　⇒ NIV #5020 sklērunō<br>　⇒ NASB #4645 sklērunō<br><br>**Acts 19:9**<br>　But when divers were **hardened**, and believed not, but spake evil of that way before the multitude, he departed from them, and separated the disciples, disputing daily in the school of one Tyrannus. [KJV]<br>　But when some were becoming **hardened** and disobedient, speaking evil of the Way before the multitude, he withdrew from them and took away the disciples, rea- | To be obstinate; to be hardened; to be rejected; to be stubborn. It means to be as hard as a stone; to be unfeeling and difficult, standing in opposition.<br><br>**Practical Application**<br>　Many were hardened and did not believe, being disobedient to the call of God to salvation. |

# PRACTICAL WORD STUDIES
## in the NEW TESTAMENT

| ENGLISH WORD | GREEK WORD AND VERSE | THE WORD MEANS... |
|---|---|---|
| | soning daily in the school of Tyrannus. [NASB]<br><br>But some of them became **obstinate**; they refused to believe and publicly maligned the Way. So Paul left them. He took the disciples with him and had discussions daily in the lecture hall of Tyrannus. [NIV]<br><br>But when some were **hardened** and did not believe, but spoke evil of the Way before the multitude, he departed from them and withdrew the disciples, reasoning daily in the school of Tyrannus. [NKJV]<br><br>But some **rejected** his message and publicly spoke against the Way, so Paul left the synagogue and took the believers with him. Then he began preaching daily at the lecture hall of Tyrannus. [NLT]<br><br>ὡς δέ τινες **ἐσκληρύνοντο** καὶ ἠπείθουν, κακολογοῦντες τὴν ὁδὸν ἐνώπιον τοῦ πλήθους, ἀποστὰς ἀπ' αὐτῶν ἀφώρισε τοὺς μαθητάς, καθ' ἡμέραν διαλεγόμενος ἐν τῇ σχολῇ τυράννου τινός. [GNS]<br><br>ὡς δέ τινες **ἐσκληρύνοντο** καὶ ἠπείθουν κακολογοῦντες τὴν ὁδὸν ἐνώπιον τοῦ πλήθους, ἀποστὰς ἀπ' αὐτῶν ἀφώρισεν τοὺς μαθητὰς καθ' ἡμέραν διαλεγόμενος ἐν τῇ σχολῇ Τυράννου. [GNT] | |
| **#1866**<br>**Hardening–Hardness**<br><br>Blindness–KJV<br>**Hardness–NASB**<br>**Hardening–NIV**<br>Blindness–NKJV<br>Shut their minds and hardened–NLT<br><br>**POSB REFERENCE**<br>(Eph.4:17-19; esp. v.18)<br>Note 1, point 3 | πώρωσιν = *pōrōsin*<br>Pronunciation: [po'-ro-sin]<br>Parsing (part of speech): noun<br>  Case—accusative<br>  Gender—feminine<br>  Number—singular<br>  Stem or root—from πώρωσις, εως<br>Concordance References:<br>  ⇒ Strong's #4457 pōrōsis<br>  ⇒ NIV #4801 pōrōsis<br>  ⇒ NASB #4457 pōrōsis<br><br>**Ephes. 4:18**<br>Having the understanding darkened, being alienated from the life of God through the ignorance that is in them, because of the **blindness** of their heart: [KJV]<br><br>Being darkened in their understanding, excluded from the life of God, because of the ignorance that is in them, because of the **hardness** of their heart; [NASB]<br><br>They are darkened in their understanding and separated from the life of God because of the ignorance that is in them due to the **hardening** of their hearts. [NIV]<br><br>Having their understanding darkened, being alienated from the life of God, because of the ignorance that is in them, because of the **blindness** of their heart; [NKJV]<br><br>Their closed minds are full of darkness; they are far away from the life of God because they have **shut their minds and hardened** their hearts against him. [NLT]<br><br>ἐσκοτισμένοι τῇ διανοίᾳ ὄντες ἀπηλλοτριωμένοι τῆς ζωῆς τοῦ Θεοῦ διὰ τὴν ἄγνοιαν τὴν οὖσαν ἐν αὐτοῖς, διὰ τὴν **πώρωσιν** τῆς καρδίας αὐτῶν· [GNS]<br><br>ἐσκοτωμένοι τῇ διανοίᾳ ὄντες, ἀπηλλοτριωμένοι τῆς ζωῆς τοῦ θεοῦ διὰ τὴν ἄγνοιαν τὴν οὖσαν ἐν αὐτοῖς, διὰ τὴν **πώρωσιν** τῆς καρδίας αὐτῶν, [GNT] | Hardening, hardness. It is a stubbornness, a numbing, a lack of feeling.<br><br>**Practical Application**<br>Unbelievers are alienated from God because of their own willful ignorance and hardness of heart. Note the words "in them." The cause is "in them":<br><br>⇒ They choose to be ignorant within their minds—choose to be ignorant of God.<br>⇒ They choose to harden their own hearts.<br><br>Unbelievers are responsible for their own death. God has provided the fountain of youth for man, the way for man to live forever. God had given His life, that is, eternal life, to man. The only way man can ever miss God's gift of eternal life is to reject God and His gift. |
| **#1867**<br>**Hardships**<br><br>Necessities–KJV<br>**Hardships–NASB**<br>**Hardships–NIV**<br>Needs–NKJV<br>**Hardships–NLT**<br><br>**POSB REFERENCE**<br>(2 Cor.6:4-5; esp. v.4)<br>Note 3 | ἀνάγκαις = *anagkais*<br>Pronunciation: [an-ang-kah-ees]<br>Parsing (part of speech): noun<br>  Case—dative<br>  Gender—feminine<br>  Number—plural<br>  Stem or root—from ἀνάγκη, ης<br>Concordance References:<br>  ⇒ Strong's #318 anagkē<br>  ⇒ NIV #340 anagkē<br>  ⇒ NASB #318 anagkē<br><br>**2 Cor. 6:4**<br>But in all things approving ourselves as the ministers of God, in much patience, in afflictions, in **necessities**, in distresses, [KJV] | Hardships; inescapable hardships, difficulties; the privation, distress, trouble, and pain suffered in life.<br><br>**Practical Application**<br>William Barclay points out that the word literally means "the necessities of life" (*The Letters to the Corinthians*, p.238). A minister or servant is called upon to face the hardships of life: he has to eat and drink, clothe and shelter himself and his family; and he has to face the sorrows and struggles and pains of life, including death itself—sometimes beyond what the average citizen has to face. Only one thing can |

## PRACTICAL WORD STUDIES
### in the NEW TESTAMENT

| ENGLISH WORD | GREEK WORD AND VERSE | THE WORD MEANS... |
|---|---|---|
| | But in everything commending ourselves as servants of God, in much endurance, in afflictions, in **hardships**, in distresses, [NASB]<br>Rather, as servants of God we commend ourselves in every way: in great endurance; in troubles, **hardships** and distresses; [NIV]<br>But in all *things* we commend ourselves as ministers of God: in much patience, in tribulations, in **needs**, in distresses, [NKJV]<br>In everything we do we try to show that we are true ministers of God. We patiently endure troubles and **hardships** and calamities of every kind. [NLT]<br>ἀλλ' ἐν παντὶ συνίσταντες ἑαυτοὺς ὡς Θεοῦ διάκονοι, ἐν ὑπομονῇ πολλῇ, ἐν θλίψεσιν, ἐν **ἀνάγκαις**, ἐν στενοχωρίαις, [GNS]<br>ἀλλ' ἐν παντὶ συνίσταντες ἑαυτοὺς ὡς θεοῦ διάκονοι, ἐν ὑπομονῇ πολλῇ, ἐν θλίψεσιν, ἐν **ἀνάγκαις**, ἐν στενοχωρίαις, [GNT] | carry the minister or servant through the hardships and experiences of life: endurance. He must steadfastly endure for the sake of the Lord Jesus Christ and His ministry. |
| **#1868**<br>**Harming**<br><br>Injurious–KJV<br>Violent aggressor–NASB<br>Violent man–NIV<br>Insolent man–NKJV<br>**Harming–NLT**<br><br>**POSB REFERENCE**<br>(1 Tim.1:12-14; esp. v.13)<br>Note 1, point 3 | ὑβριστήν = hubristēn<br>Pronunciation: [hoo-bris-tayn']<br>Parsing (part of speech): noun<br>  Case—accusative<br>  Gender—masculine<br>  Number—singular<br>  Stem or root—from ὑβριστής, οῦ<br>Concordance References:<br>⇒ Strong's #5197 hubristēs<br>⇒ NIV #5616 hubristēs<br>⇒ NASB #5197 hubristēs<br><br>**1 Tim. 1:13**<br>Who was before a blasphemer, and a persecutor, and **injurious**: but I obtained mercy, because I did it ignorantly in unbelief. [KJV]<br>Even though I was formerly a blasphemer and a persecutor and a **violent aggressor**. And yet I was shown mercy, because I acted ignorantly in unbelief; [NASB]<br>Even though I was once a blasphemer and a persecutor and a **violent man**, I was shown mercy because I acted in ignorance and unbelief. [NIV]<br>Although I was formerly a blasphemer, a persecutor, and an **insolent man**; but I obtained mercy because I did *it* ignorantly in unbelief. [NKJV]<br>Even though I used to scoff at the name of Christ. I hunted down his people, **harming** them in every way I could. But God had mercy on me because I did it in ignorance and unbelief. [NLT]<br>τὸν πρότερον ὄντα βλάσφημον καὶ διώκτην καὶ **ὑβριστήν**· ἀλλ' ἠλεήθην, ὅτι ἀγνοῶν ἐποίησα ἐν ἀπιστίᾳ· [GNS]<br>τὸ πρότερον ὄντα βλάσφημον καὶ διώκτην καὶ **ὑβριστήν**, ἀλλὰ ἠλεήθην, ὅτι ἀγνοῶν ἐποίησα ἐν ἀπιστίᾳ· [GNT] | A violent man; a violent aggressor; injurious, harmful; an insulting person; insolent; to treat and use others despitefully; to enjoy being brutal and violent; to be in a fiery rage and to inflict it upon others.<br><br>**Practical Application**<br>William Barclay says that the word "indicates a kind of arrogant sadism; it describes the man who is out to inflict pain and injury for the sheer joy of inflicting it....that is what Paul was once like in regard to the Christian Church. Not content with words of insult, he went to the limit of legal persecution. Not content with legal persecution, he went to the limit of sadistic brutality in his attempt to stamp out the Christian faith" (*The Letters to Timothy, Titus, and Philemon*, p.52).<br>However, despite all this evil, God had mercy upon Paul. Paul had not known that Christ was really the true Messiah. He thought that he knew God and that his religion was the true religion. He felt that any religion that stood against his religion was to be stamped out. Therefore, when Paul attacked Christ and His followers, he did it ignorantly in unbelief. He just did not believe that Jesus Christ could possibly be the Messiah.<br>The point is this: God had mercy upon Paul. He took pity upon Paul despite his terrible sins (see POSB *Deeper Study* #2, Mercy—1 Tim. 1:2). |
| **#1869**<br>**Harmless**<br><br>Harmless–KJV<br>Innocent–NASB<br>Blameless–NIV<br>**Harmless–NKJV**<br>Blameless–NLT<br><br>**POSB REFERENCE**<br>(Heb.7:26)<br>Note 2, point 2 | ἄκακος = akakos<br>Pronunciation: [ak'-ak-os]<br>Parsing (part of speech): adjective<br>  Case—nominative<br>  Gender—masculine<br>  Number—singular<br>  Stem or root—from ἄκακος, ον<br>Concordance References:<br>⇒ Strong's #172 akakos<br>⇒ NIV #179 akakos<br>⇒ NASB #172 akakos<br><br>**Hebrews 7:26**<br>For such an high priest became us, who is holy, **harmless**, undefiled, separate from sinners, and made higher than the heavens; [KJV]<br>For it was fitting that we should have such a high | Blameless, harmless, innocent, unsuspecting, naive; free from all guile, deception, envy, and malice against anyone.<br><br>**Practical Application**<br>William Barclay says that "Jesus *never hurt any man*" (*The Letter to the Hebrews*, p.89). We might say that Jesus Christ was so good that there was nothing but good in Him. There was nothing but the goodness and love of God in Him, and that was all that He ever shared with man. Jesus Christ is absolutely *harmless and blameless*. |

# PRACTICAL WORD STUDIES
## in the NEW TESTAMENT

| ENGLISH WORD | GREEK WORD AND VERSE | THE WORD MEANS... |
|---|---|---|
| | priest, holy, **innocent**, undefiled, separated from sinners and exalted above the heavens; [NASB]<br>Such a high priest meets our need—one who is holy, **blameless**, pure, set apart from sinners, exalted above the heavens. [NIV]<br>For such a High Priest was fitting for us, who is holy, **harmless**, undefiled, separate from sinners, and has become higher than the heavens; [NKJV]<br>He is the kind of high priest we need because he is holy and **blameless**, unstained by sin. He has now been set apart from sinners, and he has been given the highest place of honor in heaven. [NLT]<br>Τοιοῦτος γὰρ ἡμῖν ἔπρεπεν ἀρχιερεύς, ὅσιος, **ἄκακος**, ἀμίαντος, κεχωρισμένος ἀπὸ τῶν ἁμαρτωλῶν, καὶ ὑψηλότερος τῶν οὐρανῶν γενόμενος· [GNS]<br>Τοιοῦτος γὰρ ἡμῖν καὶ ἔπρεπεν ἀρχιερεύς, ὅσιος **ἄκακος** ἀμίαντος, κεχωρισμένος ἀπὸ τῶν ἁμαρτωλῶν καὶ ὑψηλότερος τῶν οὐρανῶν γενόμενος, [GNT] | |
| #1870<br>**Harmless**<br><br>**Harmless**–KJV<br>Innocent–NASB<br>Pure–NIV<br>**Harmless**–NKJV<br>Clean–NLT<br><br>**POSB<br>REFERENCE**<br>(Philip.2:15)<br>Note 4, point 2 | ἀκέραιοι = *akeraioi*<br>Pronunciation: [ak-er'-ah-ee-oy]<br>Parsing (part of speech): adjective<br>    Case—nominative<br>    Gender—masculine<br>    Number—plural<br>    Stem or root—from ἀκέραιος, ον<br>Concordance References:<br>  ⇒ Strong's #185 akeraios<br>  ⇒ NIV #193 akeraios<br>  ⇒ NASB #185 akeraios<br><br>**Philip. 2:15**<br>That ye may be blameless and **harmless**, the sons of God, without rebuke, in the midst of a crooked and perverse nation, among whom ye shine as lights in the world; [KJV]<br>That you may prove yourselves to be blameless and **innocent**, children of God above reproach in the midst of a crooked and perverse generation, among whom you appear as lights in the world, [NASB]<br>So that you may become blameless and **pure**, children of God without fault in a crooked and depraved generation, in which you shine like stars in the universe [NIV]<br>That you may become blameless and **harmless**, children of God without fault in the midst of a crooked and perverse generation, among whom you shine as lights in the world, [NKJV]<br>So that no one can speak a word of blame against you. You are to live **clean**, innocent lives as children of God in a dark world full of crooked and perverse people. Let your lives shine brightly before them. [NLT]<br>ἵνα γένησθε ἄμεμπτοι καὶ **ἀκέραιοι**, τέκνα Θεοῦ ἀμώμητα ἐν μέσῳ γενεᾶς σκολιᾶς καὶ διεστραμμένης, ἐν οἷς φαίνεσθε ὡς φωστῆρες ἐν κόσμῳ, [GNS]<br>ἵνα γένησθε ἄμεμπτοι καὶ **ἀκέραιοι**, τέκνα θεοῦ ἄμωμα μέσον γενεᾶς σκολιᾶς καὶ διεστραμμένης, ἐν οἷς φαίνεσθε ὡς φωστῆρες ἐν κόσμῳ, [GNT] | Pure, harmless, innocent, clean, without guile, unmixed and unadulterated.<br><br>**Practical Application**<br>Believers are to work at being harmless (*akeraioi*). It is the idea of flour or grain passing through a sieve to separate the pure from the impure. It means that our thoughts and lives...<br>• are not to be polluted by watching, reading, and listening to worldly and sexual attractions.<br>• are not to be given over to worldly and sexual attractions.<br><br>Our thoughts and lives are to be pure, clean, uncontaminated, and unpolluted. |
| #1871<br>**Harmonious**<br><br>One mind–KJV<br>**Harmonious**–NASB<br>Live in harmony with–NIV<br>One mind–NKJV<br>One mind–NLT<br><br>**POSB<br>REFERENCE**<br>(1 Pt.3:8)<br>Note 1 | ὁμόφρονες = *homophrones*<br>Pronunciation: [hom-of'-ron-ehs]<br>Parsing (part of speech): adjective<br>    Case—nominative<br>    Gender—masculine<br>    Number—plural<br>    Stem or root—from ὁμόφρων, ον<br>Concordance References:<br>  ⇒ Strong's #3675 homophrōn<br>  ⇒ NIV #3939 homophrōn<br>  ⇒ NASB #3675 homophrōn<br><br>**1 Peter 3:8**<br>Finally, be ye all of **one mind**, having compassion | To live in harmony; to be of one mind; to be harmonious; to be like-minded; to be of the same mind.<br><br>**Practical Application**<br>Believers must live in harmony (*homophrones*). Believers must keep their minds on the same things. They must focus their minds upon Jesus Christ and His mission. |

# PRACTICAL WORD STUDIES
## in the NEW TESTAMENT

| ENGLISH WORD | GREEK WORD AND VERSE | THE WORD MEANS... |
|---|---|---|
| | one of another, love as brethren, be pitiful, be courteous: [KJV]<br>　To sum up, let all be **harmonious**, sympathetic, brotherly, kindhearted, and humble in spirit; [NASB]<br>　Finally, all of you, **live in harmony with** one another; be sympathetic, love as brothers, be compassionate and humble. [NIV]<br>　Finally, all of you be of **one mind**, having compassion for one another; love as brothers, be tenderhearted, be courteous; [NKJV]<br>　Finally, all of you should be of **one mind**, full of sympathy toward each other, loving one another with tender hearts and humble minds. [NLT]<br>　Τὸ δὲ τέλος, πάντες **ὁμόφρονες**, συμπαθεῖς, φιλάδελφοι, εὔσπλαγχνοι, φιλόφρονες· [GNS]<br>　Τὸ δὲ τέλος πάντες **ὁμόφρονες**, συμπαθεῖς, φιλάδελφοι, εὔσπλαγχνοι, ταπεινόφρονες, [GNT] | |
| **#1872**<br>**Harmony**<br><br>One mind–KJV<br>Like-minded–NASB<br>One mind–NIV<br>One mind–NKJV<br>Harmony–NLT<br><br>**POSB REFERENCE**<br>(2 Cor.13:11-13; esp. v.11)<br>Note 3 | τὸ αὐτὸ φρονεῖτε = to auto phroneite<br>Pronunciation: [to ow-to' fron-eh'-ee-teh]<br>Parsing *phroneite* (part of speech): verb<br>　Mood—imperative<br>　Tense—present<br>　Voice—active<br>　Person—2nd person<br>　Number—plural<br>　Stem or root—from φρονέω<br>Concordance References:<br>⇒ Strong's #846+3588 autos ho + 5426 phroneō<br>⇒ NIV #899+3836 autos ho [one] + 5858 phroneō [mind]<br>⇒ NASB #846+3588 autos ho + 5426 phroneō<br><br>**2 Cor. 13:11**<br>　Finally, brethren, farewell. Be perfect, be of good comfort, be of **one mind**, live in peace; and the God of love and peace shall be with you. [KJV]<br>　Finally, brethren, rejoice, be made complete, be comforted, be **like-minded**, live in peace; and the God of love and peace shall be with you. [NASB]<br>　Finally, brothers, good-by. Aim for perfection, listen to my appeal, be of **one mind**, live in peace. And the God of love and peace will be with you. [NIV]<br>　Finally, brethren, farewell. Become complete. Be of good comfort, be of **one mind**, live in peace; and the God of love and peace will be with you. [NKJV]<br>　Dear brothers and sisters, I close my letter with these last words: Rejoice. Change your ways. Encourage each other. Live in **harmony** and peace. Then the God of love and peace will be with you. [NLT]<br>　Λοιπόν, ἀδελφοί, χαίρετε· καταρτίζεσθε, παρακαλεῖσθε, **τὸ αὐτὸ φρονεῖτε**, εἰρηνεύετε, καὶ ὁ Θεὸς τῆς ἀγάπης καὶ εἰρήνης ἔσται μεθ' ὑμῶν. [GNS]<br>　Λοιπόν, ἀδελφοί, χαίρετε, καταρτίζεσθε, παρακαλεῖσθε, **τὸ αὐτὸ φρονεῖτε**, εἰρηνεύετε, καὶ ὁ θεὸς τῆς ἀγάπης καὶ εἰρήνης ἔσται μεθ' ὑμῶν. [GNT] | One mind; to be like-minded; to be in harmony; to be of one mind in faith, belief, purpose, mission, and ministry.<br><br>**Practical Application**<br>　Note that God is the Author, the Giver of love and peace. The believer must therefore accept the challenge to live in harmony with other believers and live accordingly. |
| **#1873**<br>**Harp**<br><br>Harp–KJV<br>Harp–NASB<br>Harp–NIV<br>Harp–NKJV<br>Harp–NLT<br><br>**POSB REFERENCE**<br>(1 Cor.13:6-14; esp. v.7)<br>Note 3 | κιθάρα = kithara<br>Pronunciation: [kith-ar'-ah]<br>Parsing (part of speech): noun<br>　Case—nominative<br>　Gender—feminine<br>　Number—singular<br>　Stem or root—from κιθάρα, ας<br>Concordance References:<br>⇒ Strong's #2788 kithara<br>⇒ NIV #3067 kithara<br>⇒ NASB #2788 kithara<br><br>**1 Cor. 14:7**<br>　And even things without life giving sound, whether pipe or **harp**, except they give a distinction in the sounds, | Harp, a string instrument.<br><br>**Practical Application**<br>　Flutes (*aulos*, wind instruments) and harps (*kithara*, string instruments) must have a distinctive sound or else their sound is meaningless, confused, and nonsense—just not understood. Musical instruments must communicate or else the music is unknown and fails to inspire the listeners. The point is striking: the believer who is zealous of spiritual gifts is to seek for the gifts that edify the church. Note: a believer's zeal is not to be dampened even if he has been misinformed and emphasizes the wrong gift. He is to |

# PRACTICAL WORD STUDIES
## in the NEW TESTAMENT

| ENGLISH WORD | GREEK WORD AND VERSE | THE WORD MEANS... |
|---|---|---|
| | how shall it be known what is piped or harped? [KJV]<br><br>Yet even lifeless things, either flute or **harp**, in producing a sound, if they do not produce a distinction in the tones, how will it be known what is played on the flute or on the harp? [NASB]<br><br>Even in the case of lifeless things that make sounds, such as the flute or **harp**, how will anyone know what tune is being played unless there is a distinction in the notes? [NIV]<br><br>Even things without life, whether flute or **harp**, when they make a sound, unless they make a distinction in the sounds, how will it be known what is piped or played? [NKJV]<br><br>Even musical instruments like the flute or the **harp**, though they are lifeless, are examples of the need for speaking in plain language. For no one will recognize the melody unless the notes are played clearly. [NLT]<br><br>ὅμως τὰ ἄψυχα φωνὴν διδόντα, εἴτε αὐλός, εἴτε **κιθάρα**, ἐὰν διαστολὴν τοῖς φθόγγοις μὴ δῷ, πῶς γνωσθήσεται τὸ αὐλούμενον ἢ τὸ κιθαριζόμενον; [GNS]<br><br>ὅμως τὰ ἄψυχα φωνὴν διδόντα, εἴτε αὐλός εἴτε **κιθάρα**, ἐὰν διαστολὴν τοῖς φθόγγοις μὴ δῷ, πῶς γνωσθήσεται τὸ αὐλούμενον ἢ τὸ κιθαριζόμενον; [GNT] | straighten out his emphasis, keep his zeal, and direct his energy to edifying the church. The important gifts are those that build up people for Christ. |
| **#1874**<br>**Harsh Words**<br><br>Clamour–KJV<br>Clamor–NASB<br>Brawling–NIV<br>Clamor–NKJV<br>**Harsh words–NLT**<br><br>**POSB REFERENCE**<br>(Eph.4:31)<br>Note 6, point 4 | κραυγή = *kraugë*<br>Pronunciation: [krow-gay']<br>Parsing (part of speech): noun<br>    Case—nominative<br>    Gender—feminine<br>    Number—singular<br>    Stem or root—from κραυγή, ῆς<br>Concordance References:<br>  ⇒ Strong's #2906 kraugë<br>  ⇒ NIV #3199 kraugë<br>  ⇒ NASB #2906 kraugë<br><br>**Ephes. 4:31**<br>Let all bitterness, and wrath, and anger, and **clamour**, and evil speaking, be put away from you, with all malice: [KJV]<br><br>Let all bitterness and wrath and anger and **clamor** and slander be put away from you, along with all malice. [NASB]<br><br>Get rid of all bitterness, rage and anger, **brawling** and slander, along with every form of malice. [NIV]<br><br>Let all bitterness, wrath, anger, **clamor**, and evil speaking be put away from you, with all malice. [NKJV]<br><br>Get rid of all bitterness, rage, anger, **harsh words**, and slander, as well as all types of malicious behavior. [NLT]<br><br>πᾶσα πικρία καὶ θυμὸς καὶ ὀργὴ καὶ **κραυγὴ** καὶ βλασφημία ἀρθήτω ἀφ' ὑμῶν, σὺν πάσῃ κακίᾳ· [GNS]<br><br>πᾶσα πικρία καὶ θυμὸς καὶ ὀργὴ καὶ **κραυγὴ** καὶ βλασφημία ἀρθήτω ἀφ' ὑμῶν σὺν πάσῃ κακίᾳ. [GNT] | Brawling, clamor, uproar, harsh words, angry words. It means insulting, boisterous behavior, and loud talking.<br><br>**Practical Application**<br>What must be the believer's relationship with brawling?<br>⇒ He is to get rid of it.<br>⇒ He is to put brawling behind him.<br>⇒ He is to never give brawling a place in his life. |
| **#1875**<br>**Haste, With**<br><br>**With haste–KJV**<br>**With haste–NASB**<br>Hurried–NIV<br>**With haste–NKJV**<br>Hurried–NLT<br><br>**POSB REFERENCE**<br>(Lk.1:39-42; esp. v.39)<br>Note 1 | ἐπορεύθη μετὰ σπουδῆς = *eporeuthë meta spoudës*<br>Pronunciation: [eh-por-yoo'-thay met-ah' spoo-days']<br>Parsing *eporeuthë* (part of speech): verb<br>    Mood—indicative<br>    Tense—aorist<br>    Voice—passive deponent<br>    Person—3rd person<br>    Number—singular<br>    Stem or root—from πορεύομαι<br>Parsing *meta* (part of speech): preposition<br>    Case—genitive<br>    Stem or root—from μετά<br>Parsing *spoudës* (part of speech): noun<br>    Case—genitive<br>    Gender—feminine<br>    Number—singular<br>    Stem or root—from σπουδή, ῆς | To be hurried; to act with great haste, speed, diligence, care, earnestness, zeal.<br><br>**Practical Application**<br>The idea is that Mary went with purpose and earnestness. She was not going on a casual, friendly visit. She had a very specific reason for going, a meaningful purpose. |

# PRACTICAL WORD STUDIES
## in the NEW TESTAMENT

| ENGLISH WORD | GREEK WORD AND VERSE | THE WORD MEANS... |
|---|---|---|
| | Concordance References:<br>⇒ Strong's #3326+4198+4710 meta poreuomai spoudë<br>⇒ NIV #3552+4513+5082 meta poreuomai spoudë [hurried]<br>⇒ NASB #3326+4198+4710 meta poreuomai spoudë<br><br>**Luke 1:39**<br>And Mary arose in those days, and went into the hill country **with haste**, into a city of Juda; [KJV]<br>Now at this time Mary arose and went **with haste** to the hill country, to a city of Judah, [NASB]<br>At that time Mary got ready and **hurried** to a town in the hill country of Judea, [NIV]<br>Now Mary arose in those days and went into the hill country **with haste**, to a city of Judah, [NKJV]<br>A few days later Mary **hurried** to the hill country of Judea, to the town [NLT]<br>Ἀναστᾶσα δὲ Μαριὰμ ἐν ταῖς ἡμέραις ταύταις **ἐπορεύθη** εἰς τὴν ὀρεινὴν **μετὰ σπουδῆς**, εἰς πόλιν Ἰούδα, [GNS]<br>Ἀναστᾶσα δὲ Μαριὰμ ἐν ταῖς ἡμέραις ταύταις **ἐπορεύθη** εἰς τὴν ὀρεινὴν **μετὰ σπουδῆς** εἰς πόλιν Ἰούδα, [GNT] | |
| #1876<br>**Hastening**<br><br>Hasting–KJV<br>**Hastening**–NASB<br>Speed–NIV<br>**Hastening**–NKJV<br>Hurry–NLT<br><br>**POSB REFERENCE**<br>(2 Pt.3:12)<br>Note 2, point 2 | **σπεύδοντας** = *speudontas*<br>Pronunciation: [spyoo'-don-tahs]<br>Parsing (part of speech): verb<br>  Mood—participle<br>  Tense—present<br>  Voice—active<br>  Case—accusative<br>  Gender—masculine<br>  Person—2nd person<br>  Number—plural<br>  Stem or root—from σπεύδω<br>Concordance References:<br>⇒ Strong's #4692 speudō<br>⇒ NIV #5067 speudō<br>⇒ NASB #4692 speudō<br><br>**2 Peter 3:12**<br>Looking for and **hasting** unto the coming of the day of God, wherein the heavens being on fire shall be dissolved, and the elements shall melt with fervent heat? [KJV]<br>Looking for and **hastening** the coming of the day of God, on account of which the heavens will be destroyed by burning, and the elements will melt with intense heat! [NASB]<br>As you look forward to the day of God and **speed** its coming. That day will bring about the destruction of the heavens by fire, and the elements will melt in the heat. [NIV]<br>Looking for and **hastening** the coming of the day of God, because of which the heavens will be dissolved, being on fire, and the elements will melt with fervent heat? [NKJV]<br>You should look forward to that day and **hurry** it along—the day when God will set the heavens on fire and the elements will melt away in the flames. [NLT]<br>προσδοκῶντας καὶ **σπεύδοντας** τὴν παρουσίαν τῆς τοῦ Θεοῦ ἡμέρας, δι' ἣν οὐρανοὶ πυρούμενοι λυθήσονται, καὶ στοιχεῖα καυσούμενα τήκεται; [GNS]<br>προσδοκῶντας καὶ **σπεύδοντας** τὴν παρουσίαν τῆς τοῦ Θεοῦ ἡμέρας δι' ἣν οὐρανοὶ πυρούμενοι λυθήσονται καὶ στοιχεῖα καυσούμενα τήκεται. [GNT] | Speed; to hasten; to hurry; to strive for.<br><br>**Practical Application**<br>The believer is *to hasten* the day of God. The word "hastening" (*speudontas*) can mean two things.<br>1. *To hasten* can mean to hurry after; to earnestly desire; to rush toward. The believer is to live a holy and godly life looking for and hastening toward the day of God. Keeping his eyes upon that terrible day of judgment is to *arouse him* to live a holy and godly life. Every day that he lives upon earth is to be a day in which he hastens toward the judgment of God; he should never take his eyes off the terrible day of God that is coming. If he takes his eyes off that day, if he fails to direct his life toward the day of God, then he will most likely slip into unholiness and ungodliness. He must, therefore, stay focused upon the day of God, the day of the terrible judgment to come upon the heavens and earth.<br>2. To hasten can also mean to hasten on the day of God; to rush the coming of Christ; to cause the day of God to come sooner. The believer has a part in bringing about the eternal kingdom of God; he has a part in bringing about the return of Christ and the great day of God. How? God is "patient...not wishing for any to perish" (2 Peter 3:9). This is the reason He is delaying the return of Christ. Apparently, God has a certain number of believers that He has ordained to be brothers and sisters of His dear Son; apparently, there are to be a certain number of believers to rule and manage the new heavens and earth for Christ. In His eternal knowledge, God certainly knows the number who will be saved and serving His dear Son. Whatever the number and whatever the case, that number has to be reached before Christ can come and before the great day of God can destroy the universe and make a new heavens and earth. This much is |

# PRACTICAL WORD STUDIES
## in the NEW TESTAMENT

| ENGLISH WORD | GREEK WORD AND VERSE | THE WORD MEANS... |
|---|---|---|
| | | known for sure:<br>⇒ God does have a certain number of believers in mind. Being God, He has purposed that His Son have many brothers who will reign with Him and who will worship and serve God through all eternity (cp. Romans 8:28-29 where God will allow nothing to stop Him from giving Christ "many brothers.")<br>⇒ This Scripture tells us that we are *to hasten* on, to help bring about the day of God. |
| #1877<br>**Hasting**<br><br>**Hasting–KJV**<br>Hastening–NASB<br>Speed–NIV<br>Hastening–NKJV<br>Hurry–NLT<br><br>**POSB REFERENCE**<br>(2 Pt.3:12)<br>Note 2, point 2 | σπεύδοντας = *speudontas*<br>Pronunciation: [spyoo'-don-tahs]<br>Parsing (part of speech): verb<br>  Mood—participle<br>  Tense—present<br>  Voice—active<br>  Case—accusative<br>  Gender—masculine<br>  Person—2nd person<br>  Number—plural<br>  Stem or root—from σπεύδω<br>Concordance References:<br>  ⇒ Strong's #4692 speudō<br>  ⇒ NIV #5067 speudō<br>  ⇒ NASB #4692 speudō<br><br>**2 Peter 3:12**<br>Looking for and **hasting** unto the coming of the day of God, wherein the heavens being on fire shall be dissolved, and the elements shall melt with fervent heat? [KJV]<br><br>Looking for and **hastening** the coming of the day of God, on account of which the heavens will be destroyed by burning, and the elements will melt with intense heat! [NASB]<br><br>As you look forward to the day of God and **speed** its coming. That day will bring about the destruction of the heavens by fire, and the elements will melt in the heat. [NIV]<br><br>Looking for and **hastening** the coming of the day of God, because of which the heavens will be dissolved, being on fire, and the elements will melt with fervent heat? [NKJV]<br><br>You should look forward to that day and **hurry** it along—the day when God will set the heavens on fire and the elements will melt away in the flames. [NLT]<br><br>προσδοκῶντας καὶ **σπεύδοντας** τὴν παρουσίαν τῆς τοῦ Θεοῦ ἡμέρας, δι' ἣν οὐρανοὶ πυρούμενοι λυθήσονται, καὶ στοιχεῖα καυσούμενα τήκεται; [GNS]<br><br>προσδοκῶντας καὶ **σπεύδοντας** τὴν παρουσίαν τῆς τοῦ θεοῦ ἡμέρας δι' ἣν οὐρανοὶ πυρούμενοι λυθήσονται καὶ στοιχεῖα καυσούμενα τήκεται. [GNT] | Speed; to hasten; to hurry; to strive for.<br><br>**Practical Application**<br>The believer is *to hasten* the day of God. The word "hasting" (*speudontas*) can mean two things.<br>1. *To hasten* can mean *to hurry after*; to earnestly desire; to rush toward. The believer is to live a holy and godly life looking for and hastening toward the day of God. Keeping his eyes upon that terrible day of judgment is to *arouse him* to live a holy and godly life. Every day that he lives upon earth is to be a day in which he hastens toward the judgment of God; he should never take his eyes off the terrible day of God that is coming. If he takes his eyes off that day, if he fails to direct his life toward the day of God, then he will most likely slip into unholiness and ungodliness. He must, therefore, stay focused upon the day of God, the day of the terrible judgment to come upon the heavens and earth.<br>2. *To hasten* can also mean *to hasten on* the day of God; to rush the coming of Christ; to cause the day of God to come sooner. The believer has a part in bringing about the eternal kingdom of God; he has a part in bringing about the return of Christ and the great day of God. How? God is "longsuffering...not willing that any should perish" (2 Peter 3:9). This is the reason He is delaying the return of Christ. Apparently, God has a certain number of believers that He has ordained to be brothers and sisters of His dear Son; apparently, there are to be a certain number of believers to rule and manage the new heavens and earth for Christ. In His eternal knowledge, God certainly knows the number who will be saved and serving His dear Son. Whatever the number and whatever the case, that number has to be reached before Christ can come and before the great day of God can destroy the universe and make a new heavens and earth. This much is known for sure:<br>⇒ God does have a certain number of believers in mind. Being God, He has purposed that His Son have many brothers who will reign with Him and who will worship and serve God through all eternity (cp. Romans 8:28-29 where God will allow nothing to stop Him from giving Christ "many brothers.")<br>⇒ This Scripture tells us that we are *to hasten* on, to help bring about the day of God. |

# PRACTICAL WORD STUDIES
## in the NEW TESTAMENT

| ENGLISH WORD | GREEK WORD AND VERSE | THE WORD MEANS... |
|---|---|---|
| **#1878**<br>**Hate**<br><br>Abhor–KJV<br>Abhor–NASB<br>**Hate–NIV**<br>Abhor–NKJV<br>**Hate–NLT**<br><br>**POSB<br>REFERENCE**<br>(Romans. 12:9-10,<br>esp. v.9)<br>Note 1, point 1 | ἀποστυγοῦντες = apostugountes<br>Pronunciation: [ap-os-toog-oon-tehs]<br>Parsing (part of speech): verb<br>    Mood—participle (imperative sense)<br>    Tense—present<br>    Voice—active<br>    Case—nominative<br>    Gender—masculine<br>    Person—2nd person<br>    Number—plural<br>    Stem or root—from ἀποστυγέω<br>Concordance References:<br>  ⇒ Strong's #655 apostugeō<br>  ⇒ NIV #696 apostugeō<br>  ⇒ NASB #655 apostugeō<br><br>**Romans 12:9**<br>    Let love be without dissimulation. **Abhor** that which is evil; cleave to that which is good. [KJV]<br>    Let love be without hypocrisy. **Abhor** what is evil; cling to what is good. [NASB]<br>    Love must be sincere. **Hate** what is evil; cling to what is good. [NIV]<br>    Let love be without hypocrisy. **Abhor** what is evil. Cling to what is good. [NKJV]<br>    Don't just pretend that you love others. Really love them. **Hate** what is wrong. Stand on the side of the good. [NLT]<br>    Ἡ ἀγάπη ἀνυπόκριτος. ἀποστυγοῦντες τὸ πονηρόν, κολλώμενοι τῷ ἀγαθῷ. [GNS]<br>    Ἡ ἀγάπη ἀνυπόκριτος. ἀποστυγοῦντες τὸ πονηρόν, κολλώμενοι τῷ ἀγαθῷ. [GNT] | To hate; to abhor. It means to hate with intense feeling; to loathe; to look upon with horror.<br><br>**Practical Application**<br>    The believer is to love by hating evil. Love desires the very best for people; therefore, love hates evil, for evil destroys human life. The believer stands against evil, doing all he can to fight...<br>• hunger and poverty<br>• hurt and pain<br>• drunkenness and drugs<br>• cursing and bitterness<br>• suggestive and enticing dress<br>• unjust and improper behavior<br>• hoarding and stealing<br>• disease and suffering<br>• ignorance and godless education<br>• family divisiveness and divorce<br>• off-colored and dirty talk<br>• immorality and destructive sex<br>• selfishness and greed<br>• corruption and death<br>The list could go on and on. The point is that the believer must love, and he shows his love by hating and fighting against that which is evil. |
| **#1879**<br>**Hate**<br><br>Maliciousness–KJV<br>Evil–NASB<br>Depravity–NIV<br>Maliciousness–NKJV<br>**Hate–NLT**<br><br>**POSB<br>REFERENCE**<br>(Rom.1:29)<br>*Deeper Study #5* | κακία = kakia<br>Pronunciation: [kak-ee'-ah]<br>Parsing (part of speech): noun<br>    Case—dative<br>    Gender—feminine<br>    Number—singular<br>    Stem or root—from κακία, ας<br>Concordance References:<br>  ⇒ Strong's #2549 kakia<br>  ⇒ NIV #2798 kakia<br>  ⇒ NASB #2549 kakia<br><br>**Romans 1:29**<br>    Being filled with all unrighteousness, fornication, wickedness, covetousness, **maliciousness**; full of envy, murder, debate, deceit, malignity; whisperers, [KJV]<br>    Being filled with all unrighteousness, wickedness, greed, **evil**; full of envy, murder, strife, deceit, malice; they are gossips, [NASB]<br>    They have become filled with every kind of wickedness, evil, greed and **depravity**. They are full of envy, murder, strife, deceit and malice. They are gossips, [NIV]<br>    Being filled with all unrighteousness, sexual immorality, wickedness, covetousness, **maliciousness**; full of envy, murder, strife, deceit, evil-mindedness; *they are* whisperers, [NKJV]<br>    Their lives became full of every kind of wickedness, sin, greed, **hate**, envy, murder, fighting, deception, malicious behavior, and gossip. [NLT]<br>    πεπληρωμένους πάσῃ ἀδικίᾳ πορνείᾳ, πονηρίᾳ πλεονεξίᾳ **κακίᾳ**· μεστοὺς φθόνου, φόνου, ἔριδος, δόλου, κακοηθείας· [GNS]<br>    πεπληρωμένους πάσῃ ἀδικίᾳ πονηρίᾳ πλεονεξίᾳ **κακίᾳ**, μεστοὺς φθόνου φόνου ἔριδος δόλου κακοηθείας, ψιθυριστάς [GNT] | Evil; wickedness; hateful feelings; malice; viciousness; ill-will; spite; a grudge; worry (Mt. 6.34).<br><br>**Practical Application**<br>    It means that a man has turned his heart completely over to evil.<br>⇒ He no longer has any good within—none whatsoever.<br>⇒ He is full of viciousness and malice.<br>⇒ He is actively pursuing evil with a vengeance. |

# PRACTICAL WORD STUDIES
## in the NEW TESTAMENT

| ENGLISH WORD | GREEK WORD AND VERSE | THE WORD MEANS... |
|---|---|---|
| **#1880**<br>**Hate Not**<br><br>Hate not–KJV<br>Not hate–NASB<br>Not hate–NIV<br>Not hate–NKJV<br>Must love me more–NLT<br><br>**POSB REFERENCE**<br>(Lk.14:26)<br>Note 2 | οὐ μισεῖ = ou misei<br>Pronunciation: [oo mis-eh'-ee]<br>Parsing *ou* (part of speech): particle<br>   Type—negative<br>   Stem or root—from οὐ<br>Parsing *misei* (part of speech): verb<br>   Mood—indicative<br>   Tense—present<br>   Voice—active<br>   Person—3rd person<br>   Number—singular<br>   Stem or root—from μισέω<br>Concordance References:<br>  ⇒ Strong's #3756 ou + 3404 miseō<br>  ⇒ NIV #4024 ou [not] + 3631 miseō [hate]<br>  ⇒ NASB #3756 ou + 3404 miseō<br><br>**Luke 14:26**<br>If any man come to me, and **hate not** his father, and mother, and wife, and children, and brethren, and sisters, yea, and his own life also, he cannot be my disciple. [KJV]<br>"If anyone comes to Me, and does **not hate** his own father and mother and wife and children and brothers and sisters, yes, and even his own life, he cannot be My disciple. [NASB]<br>"If anyone comes to me and does **not hate** his father and mother, his wife and children, his brothers and sisters—yes, even his own life—he cannot be my disciple. [NIV]<br>"If anyone comes to Me and does **not hate** his father and mother, wife and children, brothers and sisters, yes, and his own life also, he cannot be My disciple. [NKJV]<br>"If you want to be my follower you **must love me more** than your own father and mother, wife and children, brothers and sisters—yes, more than your own life. Otherwise, you cannot be my disciple. [NLT]<br>Εἴ τις ἔρχεται πρός με, καὶ **οὐ μισεῖ** τὸν πατέρα ἑαυτοῦ, καὶ τὴν μητέρα, καὶ τὴν γυναῖκα, καὶ τὰ τέκνα, καὶ τοὺς ἀδελφοὺς, καὶ τὰς ἀδελφάς, ἔτι τε καὶ τὴν ἑαυτοῦ ψυχήν, οὐ δύναταί μου μαθητὴς εἶναί. [GNS]<br>Εἴ τις ἔρχεται πρός με καὶ **οὐ μισεῖ** τὸν πατέρα ἑαυτοῦ καὶ τὴν μητέρα καὶ τὴν γυναῖκα καὶ τὰ τέκνα καὶ τοὺς ἀδελφοὺς καὶ τὰς ἀδελφάς ἔτι τε καὶ τὴν ψυχὴν ἑαυτοῦ, οὐ δύναται εἶναί μου μαθητής. [GNT] | Not showing preference; disregard; not hate; not detest.<br><br>**Practical Application**<br>The words "hate not" are strong. Christ was not saying that one's family and one's self were to be literally hated. The true believer is to love even his enemies (Luke 6:27). What then did Christ mean? Very simply...<br>• Christ is to be first in a person's life: before family, even before self.<br>• Christ is to be put before family: even if one's family opposes his decision to follow Christ.<br>• Christ is to be put first: before the companionship and comfort and pleasure of family and home.<br>• All—even family and self—are to be put behind Christ and His mission. All must be denied and put behind a person's love and devotion to Christ and His cause. |
| **#1881**<br>**Hated–Hateful**<br><br>Hateful–KJV<br>Hateful–NASB<br>Hated–NIV<br>Hateful–NKJV<br>Hated–NLT<br><br>**POSB REFERENCE**<br>(Tit.3:3)<br>*Deeper Study #6* | στυγητοί = stugētoi<br>Pronunciation: [stoog-nay-toy']<br>Parsing (part of speech): adjective<br>   Case—nominative<br>   Gender—masculine<br>   Number—plural<br>   Stem or root—from στυγητός, ή, όν<br>Concordance References:<br>  ⇒ Strong's #4767 stugētos<br>  ⇒ NIV #5144 stugētos<br>  ⇒ NASB #4767 stugētos<br><br>**Titus 3:3**<br>For we ourselves also were sometimes foolish, disobedient, deceived, serving divers lusts and pleasures, living in malice and envy, **hateful**, and hating one another. [KJV]<br>For we also once were foolish ourselves, disobedient, deceived, enslaved to various lusts and pleasures, spending our life in malice and envy, **hateful**, hating one another. [NASB]<br>At one time we too were foolish, disobedient, deceived and enslaved by all kinds of passions and pleasures. We lived in malice and envy, being **hated** and hating one another. [NIV]<br>For we ourselves were also once foolish, disobedient, deceived, serving various lusts and pleasures, living in malice and envy, **hateful** and hating one another. [NKJV] | Hated, hateful, hating.<br><br>**Practical Application**<br>A person without God is hateful; that is, he is worthy of being hated (*stugētoi*). This is the only time this terrible word is used in the Bible. It means to be hated—to be worthy of being hated and counted as detestable. This is strong language, to think that we are worthy of being hated. What does this mean?<br>⇒ It means the selfish, greedy, covetous nature of man is worthy of being hated—the nature that lies, steals, cheats, banks, and hoards while millions of others are dying from hunger, thirst, disease, cold, heat, sin, evil, and lack of the gospel which could save the whole world.<br>⇒ It means the carnal and immoral nature of man is worthy of hatred—the nature that commits fornication and adultery, destroying homes and bodies through broken trusts and disease and emotional and mental traumas—from which many never recover. |

# PRACTICAL WORD STUDIES
## in the NEW TESTAMENT

| ENGLISH WORD | GREEK WORD AND VERSE | THE WORD MEANS... |
|---|---|---|
| | Once we, too, were foolish and disobedient. We were misled by others and became slaves to many wicked desires and evil pleasures. Our lives were full of evil and envy. We hated others, and they **hated** us. [NLT]<br><br>ἦμεν γάρ ποτε καὶ ἡμεῖς ἀνόητοι, ἀπειθεῖς, πλανώμενοι, δουλεύοντες ἐπιθυμίαις καὶ ἡδοναῖς ποικίλαις, ἐν κακίᾳ καὶ φθόνῳ διάγοντες, **στυγητοί**, μισοῦντες ἀλλήλους. [GNS]<br><br>Ἦμεν γάρ ποτε καὶ ἡμεῖς ἀνόητοι, ἀπειθεῖς, πλανώμενοι, δουλεύοντες ἐπιθυμίαις καὶ ἡδοναῖς ποικίλαις, ἐν κακίᾳ καὶ φθόνῳ διάγοντες, **στυγητοί**, μισοῦντες ἀλλήλους. [GNT] | The list could go on and on, but the point is clear: the behavior of man is very often worthy of being hated. But thanks be to God, for He has saved and transformed our hateful nature. He has taken our unloving nature and made new men out of us. And He will do it for any person who turns from living a selfish and worldly life and turns to Christ. God will transform any person who trusts and follows His Son, the Lord Jesus Christ. |
| **#1882**<br>**Haters Of God**<br><br>Haters of God–KJV<br>Haters of God–NASB<br>God-haters–NIV<br>Haters of God–NKJV<br>Haters of God–NLT<br><br>**POSB REFERENCE**<br>(Rom.1:30)<br>*Deeper Study* #13 | θεοστυγεῖς = *theostugeis*<br>Pronunciation: [theh-os-too-gees']<br>Parsing (part of speech): pronominal adjective<br>    Case—accusative<br>    Gender—masculine<br>    Number—plural<br>    Stem or root—from θεοστυγής, ές<br>Concordance References:<br>  ⇒ Strong's #2319 *theostugēs*<br>  ⇒ NIV #2539 *theostugēs*<br>  ⇒ NASB #2319 *theostugēs*<br><br>**Romans 1:30**<br>Backbiters, **haters of God**, despiteful, proud, boasters, inventors of evil things, disobedient to parents, [KJV]<br>Slanderers, **haters of God**, insolent, arrogant, boastful, inventors of evil, disobedient to parents, [NASB]<br>Slanderers, **God-haters**, insolent, arrogant and boastful; they invent ways of doing evil; they disobey their parents; [NIV]<br>Backbiters, **haters of God**, violent, proud, boasters, inventors of evil things, disobedient to parents, [NKJV]<br>They are backstabbers, **haters of God**, insolent, proud, and boastful. They are forever inventing new ways of sinning and are disobedient to their parents. [NLT]<br>ψιθυριστάς, καταλάλους, **θεοστυγεῖς**, ὑβριστάς, ὑπερηφάνους, ἀλαζόνας, ἐφευρετὰς κακῶν, γονεῦσιν ἀπειθεῖς, [GNS]<br>καταλάλους **θεοστυγεῖς** ὑβριστὰς ὑπερηφάνους ἀλαζόνας, ἐφευρετὰς κακῶν, γονεῦσιν ἀπειθεῖς, [GNT] | Hating God; to be hateful to God.<br><br>**Practical Application**<br>It is a person...<br>• who dislikes the commandments and restraints of God.<br>• who wants nothing to do with God and His restrictions and laws.<br>• who wants the license to do exactly as he wishes.<br>• who wants to be the god of his own life, doing his own thing as he wishes, determining both what he should and should not do. |
| **#1883**<br>**Haters Of Good**<br><br>Despisers of those that are good–KJV<br>Haters of good–NASB<br>Not lovers of good–NIV<br>Despisers of good–NKJV<br>No interest in what is good–NLT<br><br>**POSB REFERENCE**<br>(2 Tim. 3:2-4; esp. v.3)<br>Note 1, point 14 | ἀφιλάγαθοι = *aphilagathoi*<br>Pronunciation: [af-il-ag'-ath-oy]<br>Parsing (part of speech): adjective<br>    Case—nominative<br>    Gender—masculine<br>    Number—plural<br>    Stem or root—from ἀφιλάγαθος, ον<br>Concordance References:<br>  ⇒ Strong's #865 *aphilagathos*<br>  ⇒ NIV #920 *aphilagathos*<br>  ⇒ NASB #865 *aphilagathos*<br><br>**2 Tim. 3:3**<br>Without natural affection, trucebreakers, false accusers, incontinent, fierce, **despisers of those that are good**, [KJV]<br>Unloving, irreconcilable, malicious gossips, without self-control, brutal, **haters of good**, [NASB]<br>Without love, unforgiving, slanderous, without self-control, brutal, **not lovers of the good**, [NIV]<br>Unloving, unforgiving, slanderers, without self-control, brutal, **despisers of good**, [NKJV]<br>They will be unloving and unforgiving; they will slander others and have no self-control; they will be cruel and have **no interest in what is good**. [NLT]<br>ἄστοργοι, ἄσπονδοι, διάβολοι, ἀκρατεῖς, ἀνήμεροι, **ἀφιλάγαθοι**, [GNS]<br>ἄστοργοι ἄσπονδοι διάβολοι ἀκρατεῖς ἀνήμεροι **ἀφιλάγαθοι** [GNT] | Not lovers of good; despisers of those who are good; haters of good; no interest in what is good; an enemy to goodness.<br><br>**Practical Application**<br>This refers to people despising both good people and good things. In the last days people will be embarrassed...<br>• to speak up for what is right.<br>• to take a stand for what is good.<br>• to be known as a good person.<br>• to be a friend to good people.<br><br>People will want to fulfill their desires and to satisfy their flesh; they will want to party, indulge, look, feel, taste, experience, possess, take, and fit in and be acceptable with the crowd. They will let morality and justice go, rejecting whatever restraint they feel. They will actually despise righteousness and want nothing to do with anyone who speaks up for what is right. |

# Practical Word Studies
## in the New Testament

| ENGLISH WORD | GREEK WORD AND VERSE | THE WORD MEANS... |
|---|---|---|
| **#1884**<br>**Hatred**<br><br>**Hatred–KJV**<br>Enmities–NASB<br>**Hatred–NIV**<br>Hatred–NKJV<br>Hostility–NLT<br><br>**POSB REFERENCE**<br>(Gal.5:19-21; esp. v.20)<br>Note 2 | ἔχθραι = *echthrai*<br>Pronunciation: [ekh'-thrah-ee]<br>Parsing (part of speech): noun<br>    Case—nominative<br>    Gender—feminine<br>    Number—plural<br>    Stem or root—from ἔχθρα, ας<br>Concordance References:<br>  ⇒ Strong's #2189 *echthra*<br>  ⇒ NIV #2397 *echthra*<br>  ⇒ NASB #2189 *echthra*<br><br>**Galatians 5:20**<br>    Idolatry, witchcraft, **hatred**, variance, emulations, wrath, strife, seditions, heresies, [KJV]<br>    Idolatry, sorcery, **enmities**, strife, jealousy, outbursts of anger, disputes, dissensions, factions, [NASB]<br>    Idolatry and witchcraft; **hatred**, discord, jealousy, fits of rage, selfish ambition, dissensions, factions [NIV]<br>    Idolatry, sorcery, **hatred**, contentions, jealousies, outbursts of wrath, selfish ambitions, dissensions, heresies, [NKJV]<br>    Idolatry, participation in demonic activities, **hostility**, quarreling, jealousy, outbursts of anger, selfish ambition, divisions, the feeling that everyone is wrong except those in your own little group, [NLT]<br>    εἰδωλολατρία, φαρμακεία, **ἔχθραι**, ἔρεις, ζῆλοι, θυμοί, ἐριθεῖαι, διχοστασίαι, αἱρέσεις, [GNS]<br>    εἰδωλολατρία, φαρμακεία, **ἔχθραι**, ἔρις, ζῆλος, θυμοί, ἐριθεῖαι, διχοστασίαι, αἱρέσεις, [GNT] | Hatred, hostility, ill will, enmity, hostility, animosity.<br><br>**Practical Application**<br>It is the hatred that lingers and is held for a long, long time; a hatred that is deep within. |
| **#1885**<br>**Haughty**<br><br>Highminded–KJV<br>Conceited–NASB<br>Conceited–NIV<br>**Haughty–NKJV**<br>Puffed up with pride–NLT<br><br>**POSB REFERENCE**<br>(2 Tim. 3:2-4; esp. v.4)<br>Note 2, point 17 | τετυφωμένοι = *tetuphōmenoi*<br>Pronunciation: [teh-toof-o'-mehn-oy]<br>Parsing (part of speech): verb<br>    Mood—participle<br>    Tense—perfect<br>    Voice—passive<br>    Case—nominative<br>    Gender—masculine<br>    Number—plural<br>    Stem or root—from τυφόομαι<br>Concordance References:<br>  ⇒ Strong's #5187 *tuphoomai*<br>  ⇒ NIV #5605 *tuphoomai*<br>  ⇒ NASB #5187 *tuphoomai*<br><br>**2 Tim. 3:4**<br>    Traitors, heady, **highminded**, lovers of pleasures more than lovers of God; [KJV]<br>    Treacherous, reckless, **conceited**, lovers of pleasure rather than lovers of God; [NASB]<br>    Treacherous, rash, **conceited**, lovers of pleasure rather than lovers of God–[NIV]<br>    Traitors, headstrong, **haughty**, lovers of pleasure rather than lovers of God, [NKJV]<br>    They will betray their friends, be reckless, be **puffed up with pride**, and love pleasure rather than God. [NLT]<br>    προδόται, προπετεῖς, **τετυφωμένοι**, φιλήδονοι μᾶλλον η φιλόθεοι, [GNS]<br>    προδόται προπετεῖς **τετυφωμένοι**, φιλήδονοι μᾶλλον η φιλόθεοι, [GNT] | To be conceited; to be highminded; to be puffed up with pride; to be swollen with pride, having feelings of self-importance.<br><br>**Practical Application**<br>It is a person who feels so educated, so scientific, so advanced, so high in position and authority, ability, and gifts that he feels completely self-sufficient. He feels no need for God. He is above God and above most people. |
| **#1886**<br>**Have**<br><br>Received–KJV<br>Receiving–NASB<br>Received–NIV<br>Received–NKJV<br>**Have–NLT** | ἀπέχετε = *apechete*<br>Pronunciation: [ah-pekh'-eh-teh]<br>Parsing (part of speech): verb<br>    Mood—indicative<br>    Tense—present<br>    Voice—active<br>    Person—2nd person<br>    Number—plural<br>    Stem or root—from ἀπέχω | Received, a receipt in full; to settle an account.<br><br>**Practical Application**<br>Their [the rich] only "happiness" (*paraklesin*, help, aid, encouragement) is to be on this earth—the wealth they have. There will be no consolation after this life—no help, no aid, no encouragement, no cheer. They are paid in full. |

# PRACTICAL WORD STUDIES
## in the NEW TESTAMENT

| ENGLISH WORD | GREEK WORD AND VERSE | THE WORD MEANS... |
|---|---|---|
| **POSB REFERENCE**<br>(Lk.6:24-26; esp. v.24)<br>Note 2, point 1d | Concordance References:<br>⇒ Strong's #568 apechō<br>⇒ NIV #600 apechō<br>⇒ NASB #568 apechō<br><br>**Luke 6:24**<br>But woe unto you that are rich! for ye have **received** your consolation. [KJV]<br>"But woe to you who are rich, for you are **receiving** your comfort in full. [NASB]<br>"But woe to you who are rich, for you have already **received** your comfort. [NIV]<br>But woe to you who are rich, For you have **received** your consolation. [NKJV]<br>"What sorrows await you who are rich, for you **have** your only happiness now. [NLT]<br>πλὴν οὐαὶ ὑμῖν τοῖς πλουσίοις, ὅτι **ἀπέχετε** τὴν παράκλησιν ὑμῶν. [GNS]<br>Πλὴν οὐαὶ ὑμῖν τοῖς πλουσίοις, ὅτι **ἀπέχετε** τὴν παράκλησιν ὑμῶν. [GNT] | They choose this life, so all the good they will ever receive is the good they now experience. |
| **#1887**<br>**Have**<br><br>Partakers of–KJV<br>Share–NASB<br>**Have**–NIV<br>Partaken–NKJV<br>Not translated–NLT<br><br>**POSB REFERENCE**<br>(Heb.2:14-16; esp. v.14)<br>Note 1, point 1 | κεκοινώνηκεν = kekoinōnēken<br>Pronunciation: [keh-koy-no-nay'-kehn]<br>Parsing (part of speech): verb<br>  Mood—indicative<br>  Tense—perfect<br>  Voice—active<br>  Person—3rd person<br>  Number—singular<br>  Stem or root—from κοινωνέω<br>Concordance References:<br>⇒ Strong's #2841 koinōneō<br>⇒ NIV #3125 koinōneō<br>⇒ NASB #2841 koinōneō<br><br>**Hebrews 2:14**<br>Forasmuch then as the children are **partakers** of flesh and blood, he also himself likewise took part of the same; that through death he might destroy him that had the power of death, that is, the devil; [KJV]<br>Since then the children **share** in flesh and blood, He Himself likewise also partook of the same, that through death He might render powerless him who had the power of death, that is, the devil; [NASB]<br>Since the children **have** flesh and blood, he too shared in their humanity so that by his death he might destroy him who holds the power of death—that is, the devil— [NIV]<br>Inasmuch then as the children have **partaken** of flesh and blood, He Himself likewise shared in the same, that through death He might destroy him who had the power of death, that is, the devil, [NKJV]<br>Because God's children are human beings—made of flesh and blood—Jesus also became flesh and blood by being born in human form. For only as a human being could he die, and only by dying could he break the power of the Devil, who had the power of death. [NLT]—NOT TRANSLATED<br>ἐπεὶ οὖν τὰ παιδία **κεκοινώνηκε** σαρκός καὶ αἵματος, καὶ αὐτὸς παραπλησίως μετέσχε τῶν αὐτῶν, ἵνα διὰ τοῦ θανάτου καταργήσῃ τὸν τὸ κράτος ἔχοντα τοῦ θανάτου, τοῦτ᾽ ἔστι τὸν διάβολον, [GNS]<br>ἐπεὶ οὖν τὰ παιδία **κεκοινώνηκεν** αἵματος καὶ σαρκός, καὶ αὐτὸς παραπλησίως μετέσχεν τῶν αὐτῶν, ἵνα διὰ τοῦ θανάτου καταργήσῃ τὸν τὸ κράτος ἔχοντα τοῦ θανάτου, τοῦτ᾽ ἔστιν τὸν διάβολον, [GNT] | To have; to share; to be a partaker of; to participate; to be partners of a common human nature.<br><br>**Practical Application**<br>He deliberately determined and purposed to *have* human flesh and blood. He voluntarily took part of human nature—of a nature that was not a natural part of His being. |
| **#1888**<br>**Have An End**<br><br>Have an end–KJV<br>Fulfillment–NASB<br>Reaching [its] fulfill- | τέλος ἔχει = telos echei<br>Pronunciation: [tel'-os ex-eh-ee]<br>Parsing *telos* (part of speech): noun<br>  Case—accusative<br>  Gender—neuter<br>  Number—singular | Reaching an end; an accomplishment; fulfillment; completion.<br><br>**Practical Application**<br>It means that The Suffering Servant of God |

# PRACTICAL WORD STUDIES
## in the New Testament

| ENGLISH WORD | GREEK WORD AND VERSE | THE WORD MEANS... |
|---|---|---|
| ment–NIV<br>**Have an end–NKJV**<br>Will come true–NLT<br><br>**POSB<br>REFERENCE**<br>(Lk.22:33-37; esp. v.37)<br>Note 3, point 4c | Stem or root—from τέλος, ους<br>Parsing *echei* (part of speech): verb<br>    Mood—indicative<br>    Tense—present<br>    Voice—active<br>    Person—3rd person<br>    Number—singular<br>    Stem or root—from ἔχω<br>Concordance References:<br>  ⇒  Strong's #2192 echō + 5056 telos<br>  ⇒  NIV #2400 echō [reaching] + 5465 telos [fulfillment]<br>  ⇒  NASB #2192 echō + 5056 telos<br><br>### Luke 22:37<br>    For I say unto you, that this that is written must yet be accomplished in me, And he was reckoned among the transgressors: for the things concerning me **have an end**. [KJV]<br>    "For I tell you, that this which is written must be fulfilled in Me, 'And He was numbered with transgressors'; for that which refers to Me has its **fulfillment**." [NASB]<br>    It is written: 'And he was numbered with the transgressors'; and I tell you that this must be fulfilled in me. Yes, what is written about me is **reaching** its **fulfillment**." [NIV]<br>    For I say to you that this which is written must still be accomplished in Me: *'And He was numbered with the transgressors.'* For the things concerning Me **have an end**." [NKJV]<br>    For the time has come for this prophecy about me to be fulfilled: 'He was counted among those who were rebels.' Yes, everything written about me by the prophets **will come true**." [NLT]<br>    λέγω γὰρ ὑμῖν ὅτι ἔτι τοῦτο τὸ γεγραμμένον δεῖ τελεσθῆναι ἐν ἐμοί, τὸ Καὶ μετὰ ἀνόμων ἐλογίσθη· καὶ γὰρ τὰ περὶ ἐμοῦ **τέλος ἔχει**. [GNS]<br>    λέγω γὰρ ὑμῖν ὅτι τοῦτο τὸ γεγραμμένον δεῖ τελεσθῆναι ἐν ἐμοί, τὸ Καὶ μετὰ ἀνόμων ἐλογίσθη· καὶ γὰρ τὸ περὶ ἐμοῦ **τέλος ἔχει**. [GNT] | would fulfill Isaiah 53 and man's salvation would be finally settled, finished. He was to proclaim upon the cross, "It is finished," and then bow His head and give up the ghost. |
| #1889<br>**Having<br>Become<br>Callous**<br><br>Past feeling–KJV<br>**Having become callous–NASB**<br>Lost all sensitivity–NIV<br>Past feeling–NKJV<br>Don't care anymore about right and wrong–NLT<br><br>**POSB<br>REFERENCE**<br>(Eph.4:17-19; esp. v.19)<br>Note 1, point 4 | ἀπηλγηκότες = apēlgēkotes<br>Pronunciation: [ap-ayl'-gay'-ko-tehs]<br>Parsing (part of speech): verb<br>    Mood—participle<br>    Tense—perfect<br>    Voice—active<br>    Case—nominative<br>    Gender—masculine<br>    Number—plural<br>    Stem or root—from ἀπαλγέω<br>Concordance References:<br>  ⇒  Strong's #524 apalgeō<br>  ⇒  NIV #556 apalgeō<br>  ⇒  NASB #524 apalgeō<br><br>### Ephes. 4:19<br>    Who being **past feeling** have given themselves over unto lasciviousness, to work all uncleanness with greediness. [KJV]<br>    And they, **having become callous**, have given themselves over to sensuality, for the practice of every kind of impurity with greediness. [NASB]<br>    Having **lost all sensitivity**, they have given themselves over to sensuality so as to indulge in every kind of impurity, with a continual lust for more. [NIV]<br>    Who, being **past feeling**, have given themselves over to lewdness, to work all uncleanness with greediness. [NKJV]<br>    They **don't care anymore about right and wrong**, and they have given themselves over to immoral ways. Their lives are filled with all kinds of impurity and greed. [NLT]<br>    οἵτινες **ἀπηλγηκότες** ἑαυτοὺς παρέδωκαν τῇ ἀσελγείᾳ, εἰς ἐργασίαν ἀκαθαρσίας πάσης ἐν πλεονεξίᾳ. [GNS]<br>    οἵτινες **ἀπηλγηκότες** ἑαυτοὺς παρέδωκαν τῇ ἀσελγείᾳ εἰς ἐργασίαν ἀκαθαρσίας πάσης ἐν πλεονεξίᾳ. [GNT] | To lose all sensitivity; to be past feeling; to become callous; not to care anymore about right and wrong; to become insensible, hardened.<br><br>**Practical Application**<br>    Unbelievers reach a point where they no longer have feelings for God and His standard of morality. The more a person walks without God the more callous a person becomes to God. The more a person walks in sin, the more callous his conscience becomes to righteousness. Sin becomes more and more acceptable. The person's conscience no longer bothers him. He reaches a point of being *past feeling*. The believer is not to return to sin. He is not to walk as other men walk—in sin, becoming callous and insensitive to God. |

# PRACTICAL WORD STUDIES
## in the NEW TESTAMENT

| ENGLISH WORD | GREEK WORD AND VERSE | THE WORD MEANS... |
|---|---|---|
| **#1890**<br>**Havoc–**<br>**Havock**<br><br>Havock–KJV<br>Ravaging–NASB<br>Began to destroy–NIV<br>**Havoc–NKJV**<br>Devastate–NLT<br><br>**POSB**<br>**REFERENCE**<br>(Acts 8:3)<br>Note 3 | ἐλυμαίνετο = elumaineto<br>Pronunciation: [loo-mah'ee-neh-tow]<br>Parsing (part of speech): verb<br>    Mood—indicative<br>    Tense—imperfect<br>    Voice—middle<br>    Person—3rd person<br>    Number—singular<br>    Stem or root— from λυμαίνομαι<br>Concordance References:<br>  ⇒ Strong's #3075 lumainomai<br>  ⇒ NIV #3381 lumainö<br>  ⇒ NASB #3075 lumainomai<br><br>**Acts 8:3**<br>As for Saul, he made **havock** of the church, entering into every house, and haling men and women committed them to prison. [KJV]<br>But Saul began **ravaging** the church, entering house after house; and dragging off men and women, he would put them in prison. [NASB]<br>But Saul **began to destroy** the church. Going from house to house, he dragged off men and women and put them in prison. [NIV]<br>As for Saul, he made **havoc** of the church, entering every house, and dragging off men and women, committing *them* to prison. [NKJV]<br>Saul was going everywhere to **devastate** the church. He went from house to house, dragging out both men and women to throw them into jail. [NLT]<br>Σαῦλος δὲ **ἐλυμαίνετο** τὴν ἐκκλησίαν, κατὰ τοὺς οἴκους εἰσπορευόμενος, σύρων τε ἄνδρας καὶ γυναῖκας παρεδίδου εἰς φυλακήν. [GNS]<br>Σαῦλος δὲ **ἐλυμαίνετο** τὴν ἐκκλησίαν κατὰ τοὺς οἴκους εἰσπορευόμενος, σύρων τε ἄνδρας καὶ γυναῖκας παρεδίδου εἰς φυλακήν. [GNT] | To destroy; to devastate; to ravage; to ruin; to wipe out.<br><br>**Practical Application**<br>The mercy and grace of God are fully demonstrated in the life of Paul. God's mercy is available to all of us, no matter how terribly we have sinned. There is hope, forgiveness, and a glorious ministry for any of us, no matter who we are or what we have done—if we will repent and surrender ourselves to the Lord Jesus, to follow and obey Him. |
| **#1891**<br>**He Died**<br><br>Gave himself–KJV<br>Gave Himself–NASB<br>Gave himself–NIV<br>Gave Himself–NKJV<br>**He died–NLT**<br><br>**POSB**<br>**REFERENCE**<br>(Gal.1:4-5; esp. v.4)<br>Note 4, point 1 | δόντος ἑαυτὸν = dontos heauton<br>Pronunciation: [don'-tos heh-ow-ton]<br>Parsing *dontos* (part of speech): verb<br>    Mood—participle<br>    Tense—aorist<br>    Voice—active<br>    Case—genitive<br>    Gender—masculine<br>    Number—singular<br>    Stem or root—from δίδωμι<br>Parsing *heauton* (part of speech): noun<br>    Type—pronoun<br>    Case—accusative<br>    Gender—masculine<br>    Person—3rd person<br>    Number—singular<br>    Stem or root—from ἑαυτοῦ, ἧς, οῦ<br>Concordance References:<br>  ⇒ Strong's #1325 didömi + 1438 heautou<br>  ⇒ NIV #1443 didömi [gave] + 1571 heautou [himself]<br>  ⇒ NASB #1325 didömi + 1438 heautou<br><br>**Galatians 1:4**<br>Who **gave himself** for our sins, that he might deliver us from this present evil world, according to the will of God and our Father: [KJV]<br>Who **gave Himself** for our sins, that He might deliver us out of this present evil age, according to the will of our God and Father, [NASB]<br>Who **gave himself** for our sins to rescue us from the present evil age, according to the will of our God and Father, [NIV]<br>Who **gave Himself** for our sins, that He might deliver us from this present evil age, according to the will of our God and Father, [NKJV] | To give; to grant; to allow; to permit Himself. The phrase "gave Himself" (*dontos heauton*) means that He sacrificed Himself for us. He gave His life for the sinner's life.<br><br>**Practical Application**<br>Jesus Christ...<br>• offered Himself to God as the sacrifice for our sin.<br>• offered Himself as the sin-offering, the offering that was to stand as the substitute for our sin.<br>• accepted the judgment and condemnation of sin for us.<br>• bore the punishment of God's justice against sin for us. |

# Practical Word Studies in the New Testament

| ENGLISH WORD | GREEK WORD AND VERSE | THE WORD MEANS... |
|---|---|---|
| | **He died** for our sins, just as God our Father planned, in order to rescue us from this evil world in which we live. [NLT]<br>τοῦ **δόντος ἑαυτὸν** ὑπὲρ τῶν ἁμαρτιῶν ἡμῶν ὅπως ἐξέληται ἡμᾶς ἐκ τοῦ ἐνεστῶτος αἰῶνος πονηροῦ, κατὰ τὸ θέλημα τοῦ Θεοῦ καὶ πατρὸς ἡμῶν· [GNS]<br>τοῦ **δόντος ἑαυτὸν** ὑπὲρ τῶν ἁμαρτιῶν ἡμῶν, ὅπως ἐξέληται ἡμᾶς ἐκ τοῦ αἰῶνος τοῦ ἐνεστῶτος πονηροῦ κατὰ τὸ θέλημα τοῦ θεοῦ καὶ πατρὸς ἡμῶν, [GNT] | |
| **#1892**<br>**He Took**<br><br>He took–KJV<br>Help–NASB<br>Helps–NIV<br>Aid–NKJV<br>Help–NLT<br><br>**POSB REFERENCE**<br>(Heb.2:14-16; esp. v.16)<br>Note 1, point 5 | ἐπιλαμβάνεται = *epilambanetai*<br>Pronunciation: [ep-ee-lam-ban'-eh-tah-ee]<br>Parsing (part of speech): verb<br>  Mood—indicative<br>  Tense—present<br>  Voice—middle or passive deponent<br>  Person—3rd person<br>  Number—singular<br>  Stem or root—from ἐπιλαμβάνομαι<br>Concordance References:<br>  Strong's #1949 epilambanomai<br>  NIV #2138 epilambanomai<br>  NASB #1949 epilambanomai<br><br>**Hebrews 2:16**<br>For verily **he took** not on him the nature of angels; but he took on him the seed of Abraham. [KJV]<br>For assuredly He does not give **help** to angels, but He gives help to the descendant of Abraham. [NASB]<br>For surely it is not angels he **helps**, but Abraham's descendants. [NIV]<br>For indeed He does not give **aid** to angels, but He does give aid to the seed of Abraham. [NKJV]<br>We all know that Jesus came to **help** the descendants of Abraham, not to help the angels. [NLT]<br>οὐ γὰρ δήπου ἀγγέλων **ἐπιλαμβάνεται**, ἀλλὰ σπέρματος Ἀβραὰμ **ἐπιλαμβάνεται**, [GNS]<br>οὐ γὰρ δήπου ἀγγέλων **ἐπιλαμβάνεται** ἀλλὰ σπέρματος Ἀβραὰμ **ἐπιλαμβάνεται**. [GNT] | To help; to take; to lay hold of; to catch; to seize; to take by the hand.<br><br>**Practical Application**<br>Jesus Christ has delivered us from the bondage of the flesh. This tells us a most wonderful truth: Jesus Christ did not only take hold of man's nature, He took hold of man's hand. He took us by the hand to deliver us. The picture is that of love and tender care, of His delivering us out of the bondages of the flesh and of human nature. Note: it is not angels that He took by the hand, but the seed of Abraham, that is, the spiritual seed of Abraham, those who believe and trust in the Lord Jesus Christ as their Savior. |
| **#1893**<br>**Head Of The Table**<br><br>Chief rooms–KJV<br>Places of honor at the table–NASB<br>Places of honor at the table–NIV<br>Best places–NKJV<br>**Head of the table–NLT**<br><br>**POSB REFERENCE**<br>(Lk.14:7)<br>Note 1 | τὰς πρωτοκλισίας = *tas prōtoklisias*<br>Pronunciation: [tas pro-tok-lis-ee'-ahs]<br>Parsing *prōtoklisias* (part of speech): noun<br>  Case—accusative<br>  Gender—feminine<br>  Number—plural<br>  Stem or root—from πρωτοκλισία, ας<br>Concordance References:<br>  ⇒ Strong's #4411 prōtoklisia<br>  ⇒ NIV #4752 prōtoklisia<br>  ⇒ NASB #4411 prōtoklisia<br><br>**Luke 14:7**<br>And he put forth a parable to those which were bidden, when he marked how they chose out the **chief rooms**; saying unto them, [KJV]<br>And He began speaking a parable to the invited guests when He noticed how they had been picking out the **places of honor at the table**; saying to them, [NASB]<br>When he noticed how the guests picked the **places of honor at the table**, he told them this parable: [NIV]<br>So He told a parable to those who were invited, when He noted how they chose the **best places**, saying to them: [NKJV]<br>When Jesus noticed that all who had come to the dinner were trying to sit near the **head of the table**, he gave them this advice: [NLT]<br>Ἔλεγε δὲ πρὸς τοὺς κεκλημένους παραβολήν, ἐπέχων πῶς **τὰς πρωτοκλισίας** ἐξελέγοντο, λέγων πρὸς αὐτούς, [GNS]<br>Ἔλεγεν δὲ πρὸς τοὺς κεκλημένους παραβολήν, ἐπέχων πῶς **τὰς πρωτοκλισίας** ἐξελέγοντο, λέγων πρὸς αὐτούς, [GNT] | The places of honor at a table; the head of the table; the chief seats.<br><br>**Practical Application**<br>In this Scripture, it was time for everyone to be seated for the meal, and Jesus noticed how some guests scrambled for the places of honor at the table. Today we usually place the names of the most honored guests at the plates. However, in Jesus' day the highest seat of honor was on the right of the host and the next highest on his left, and so the ranking continued alternating back and forth until the lowest ranked person sat the farthest away from the host. Very simply, the closer one sat to the host, the higher the honor. When Jesus saw how some quickly moved up close to the host, He saw an opportunity to teach the great importance of humility. |

## PRACTICAL WORD STUDIES
### in the NEW TESTAMENT

| ENGLISH WORD | GREEK WORD AND VERSE | THE WORD MEANS... |
|---|---|---|
| **#1894**<br>**Headcloth**<br><br>Napkin–KJV<br>Cloth–NASB<br>Cloth–NIV<br>Cloth–NKJV<br>**Headcloth–NLT**<br><br>**POSB REFERENCE**<br>(Jn.11:44)<br>*Deeper Study #2* | σουδαρίῳ = *soudariö*<br>Pronunciation: [soo-dar'-ee-o]<br>Parsing (part of speech): noun<br>  Case—dative<br>  Gender—neuter<br>  Number—singular<br>  Stem or root—from σουδάριον, ου<br>Concordance References:<br>⇒ Strong's #4676 soudarion<br>⇒ NIV #5051 soudarion<br>⇒ NASB #4676 soudarion<br><br>**John 11:44**<br>And he that was dead came forth, bound hand and foot with graveclothes: and his face was bound about with a **napkin**. Jesus saith unto them, Loose him, and let him go. [KJV]<br>He who had died came forth, bound hand and foot with wrappings; and his face was wrapped around with a **cloth**. Jesus said to them, "Unbind him, and let him go." [NASB]<br>The dead man came out, his hands and feet wrapped with strips of linen, and a **cloth** around his face. Jesus said to them, "Take off the grave clothes and let him go." [NIV]<br>And he who had died came out bound hand and foot with graveclothes, and his face was wrapped with a **cloth**. Jesus said to them, "Loose him, and let him go." [NKJV]<br>And Lazarus came out, bound in graveclothes, his face wrapped in a **headcloth**. Jesus told them, "Unwrap him and let him go!" [NLT]<br>καὶ ἐξῆλθεν ὁ τεθνηκὼς δεδεμένος τοὺς πόδας καὶ τὰς χεῖρας κειρίαις, καὶ ἡ ὄψις αὐτοῦ **σουδαρίῳ** περιεδέδετο. λέγει αὐτοῖς ὁ Ἰησοῦς, Λύσατε αὐτόν, καὶ ἄφετε ὑπάγειν. [GNS]<br>ἐξῆλθεν ὁ τεθνηκὼς δεδεμένος τοὺς πόδας καὶ τὰς χεῖρας κειρίαις, καὶ ἡ ὄψις αὐτοῦ **σουδαρίῳ** περιεδέδετο. λέγει αὐτοῖς ὁ Ἰησοῦς, Λύσατε αὐτὸν καὶ ἄφετε αὐτὸν ὑπάγειν. [GNT] | A cloth, napkin, headcloth, fabric or handkerchief.<br><br>**Practical Application**<br>In this Scripture, there was a headcloth wrapped around the face of Lazarus. This is important to note for two reasons.<br>1. Jesus had a cloth wrapped around His face when He was buried. After His resurrection, it was folded either by Him or an angel and laid to the side. The folded cloth was the immediate thing that convinced John of the Lord's resurrection. (See POSB note—John 20:7-10.)<br>2. The headcloth showed that the grave clothes of Jesus' day included at least two pieces of clothing. There was a separate cloth or napkin wrapped around the face. It is mentioned twice in the New Testament (John 11:44; John 20:7. Cp. Luke 19:20; Acts 19:12 for two other uses of the same Greek word, *soudariö*.) |
| **#1895**<br>**Headstrong**<br><br>Heady–KJV<br>Reckless–NASB<br>Rash–NIV<br>**Headstrong–NKJV**<br>Reckless–NLT<br><br>**POSB REFERENCE**<br>(2 Tim. 3:2-4; esp. v.4)<br>Note 2, point 16 | προπετεῖς = *propeteis*<br>Pronunciation: [prop-et-eh-ees]<br>Parsing (part of speech): adjective<br>  Case—nominative<br>  Gender—masculine<br>  Number—plural<br>  Stem or root—from προπετής, ές<br>Concordance References:<br>⇒ Strong's #4312 propetēs<br>⇒ NIV #4637 propetēs<br>⇒ NASB #4312 propetēs<br><br>**2 Tim. 3:4**<br>Traitors, **heady**, highminded, lovers of pleasures more than lovers of God; [KJV]<br>Treacherous, **reckless**, conceited, lovers of pleasure rather than lovers of God; [NASB]<br>Treacherous, **rash**, conceited, lovers of pleasure rather than lovers of God—[NIV]<br>Traitors, **headstrong**, haughty, lovers of pleasure rather than lovers of God, [NKJV]<br>They will betray their friends, be **reckless**, be puffed up with pride, and love pleasure rather than God. [NLT]<br>προδόται, **προπετεῖς**, τετυφωμένοι, φιλήδονοι μᾶλλον ἢ φιλόθεοι [GNS]<br>προδόται, **προπετεῖς** τετυφωμένοι, φιλήδονοι μᾶλλον ἢ φιλόθεοι, [GNT] | Rash, heady, reckless, headstrong, hasty. Reckless is probably the best description.<br><br>**Practical Application**<br>A headstrong person is a person who thinks he knows best and can live and act recklessly, without paying any attention to the consequences. The headstrong person thinks little about what he is doing; he just enjoys the feeling and pleasure. He enjoys the stimulation and excitement; the consequences matter little in the midst of the pleasure and excitement.<br>Think how much hurt and damage is done when a person lives for the pleasure of the moment. Think of the hurt and damage done because of the pleasure of...<br>• reckless driving and boating<br>• reckless work and recreation<br>• reckless passion and lust<br>• reckless eating and drinking<br><br>Being headstrong—thinking that one knows best and can live and act recklessly without consequence—has led to more hurt, accidents, damaged bodies, and death than could ever be imagined. |
| **#1896**<br>**Headwinds** | ἐναντίους = *enantious*<br>Pronunciation: [en-an-tee'-oos]<br>Parsing (part of speech): adjective<br>  Case—accusative<br>  Gender—masculine | Against, contrary, opposed, hostile headwinds. |

# PRACTICAL WORD STUDIES
## in the NEW TESTAMENT

| ENGLISH WORD | GREEK WORD AND VERSE | THE WORD MEANS... |
|---|---|---|
| Contrary–KJV<br>Contrary–NASB<br>Against–NIV<br>Contrary–NKJV<br>**Headwinds–NLT**<br><br>**POSB REFERENCE**<br>(Acts 27:4-12; esp. v.4)<br>Note 2, point 1a | Number—plural<br>Stem or root—from ἐναντίος<br>Concordance References:<br>⇒ Strong's #1727 enantios<br>⇒ NIV #1885 enantios<br>⇒ NASB #1727 enantios<br><br>### Acts 27:4<br>And when we had launched from thence, we sailed under Cyprus, because the winds were **contrary**. [KJV]<br>And from there we put out to sea and sailed under the shelter of Cyprus because the winds were **contrary**. [NASB]<br>From there we put out to sea again and passed to the lee of Cyprus because the winds were **against** us. [NIV]<br>When we had put to sea from there, we sailed under the shelter of Cyprus, because the winds were **contrary**. [NKJV]<br>Putting out to sea from there, we encountered **headwinds** that made it difficult to keep the ship on course, so we sailed north of Cyprus between the island and the mainland. [NLT]<br>κἀκεῖθεν ἀναχθέντες ὑπεπλεύσαμεν τὴν Κύπρον, διὰ τὸ τοὺς ἀνέμους εἶναι **ἐναντίους**, [GNS]<br>κἀκεῖθεν ἀναχθέντες ὑπεπλεύσαμεν τὴν Κύπρον διὰ τὸ τοὺς ἀνέμους εἶναι **ἐναντίους**, [GNT] | **Practical Application**<br>The "headwinds" were strong and forceful; a northwest headwind faced them. Therefore, they could not strike a straight course through the open sea. |
| #1897<br>**Heady**<br><br>**Heady–KJV**<br>Reckless–NASB<br>Rash–NIV<br>Headstrong–NKJV<br>Reckless–NLT<br><br>**POSB REFERENCE**<br>(2 Tim. 3:2-4; esp. v.4)<br>Note 2, point 16 | προπετεῖς = propeteis<br>Pronunciation: [prop-et-eh-ees]<br>Parsing (part of speech): adjective<br>  Case—nominative<br>  Gender—masculine<br>  Number—plural<br>  Stem or root—from προπετής, ές<br>Concordance References:<br>⇒ Strong's #4312 propetës<br>⇒ NIV #4637 propetës<br>⇒ NASB #4312 propetës<br><br>### 2 Tim. 3:4<br>Traitors, **heady**, highminded, lovers of pleasures more than lovers of God; [KJV]<br>Treacherous, **reckless**, conceited, lovers of pleasure rather than lovers of God; [NASB]<br>Treacherous, **rash**, conceited, lovers of pleasure rather than lovers of God—[NIV]<br>Traitors, **headstrong**, haughty, lovers of pleasure rather than lovers of God, [NKJV]<br>They will betray their friends, be **reckless**, be puffed up with pride, and love pleasure rather than God. [NLT]<br>προδόται, **προπετεῖς**, τετυφωμένοι, φιλήδονοι μᾶλλον ἢ φιλόθεοι [GNS]<br>προδόται **προπετεῖς** τετυφωμένοι, φιλήδονοι μᾶλλον ἢ φιλόθεοι, [GNT] | Rash, heady, reckless, headstrong, hasty. Reckless is probably the best description.<br><br>**Practical Application**<br>A heady person is a person who thinks he knows best and can live and act recklessly, without paying any attention to the consequences. The heady person thinks little about what he is doing; he just enjoys the feeling and pleasure. He enjoys the stimulation and excitement; the consequences matter little in the midst of the pleasure and excitement.<br>Think how much hurt and damage is done when a person lives for the pleasure of the moment. Think of the hurt and damage done because of the pleasure of...<br>• reckless driving and boating<br>• reckless work and recreation<br>• reckless passion and lust<br>• reckless eating and drinking<br><br>Being heady—thinking that one knows best and can live and act recklessly without consequence—has led to more hurt, accidents, damaged bodies, and death than could ever be imagined. |
| #1898<br>**Healed**<br><br>Made...whole–KJV<br>Cured–NASB<br>**Healed–NIV**<br>Made...well–NKJV<br>Healed–NLT<br><br>**POSB REFERENCE**<br>(Mt.14:36)<br>Note 6 | διεσώθησαν = diesōthēsan<br>Pronunciation: [dee-so'-thay-sahn]<br>Parsing (part of speech): verb<br>  Mood—indicative<br>  Tense—aorist<br>  Voice—passive<br>  Person—3rd person<br>  Number—plural<br>  Stem or root—from διασῴζω<br>Concordance References:<br>⇒ Strong's #1295 diasōzō<br>⇒ NIV #1407 diasōzō<br>⇒ NASB #1295 diasōzō<br><br>### Matthew 14:36<br>And besought him that they might only touch the hem of his garment: and as many as touched were **made** perfectly **whole**. [KJV] | To be healed or cured through and through; to be made whole or saved through and through; to rescue; to be spared.<br><br>**Practical Application**<br>A complete restoration takes place within the person. The person is completely cured, spiritually and inwardly, as well as physically and outwardly. |

# Practical Word Studies
## in the New Testament

| ENGLISH WORD | GREEK WORD AND VERSE | THE WORD MEANS... |
|---|---|---|
| | And they began to entreat Him that they might just touch the fringe of His cloak; and as many as touched it were **cured**. [NASB] <br> And begged him to let the sick just touch the edge of his cloak, and all who touched him were **healed**. [NIV] <br> And begged Him that they might only touch the hem of His garment. And as many as touched it were **made** perfectly **well**. [NKJV] <br> The sick begged him to let them touch even the fringe of his robe, and all who touched it were **healed**. [NLT] <br> καὶ παρεκάλουν αὐτόν, ἵνα μόνον ἅψωνται τοῦ κρασπέδου τοῦ ἱματίου αὐτοῦ· καὶ ὅσοι ἥψαντο **διεσώθησαν**. [GNS] <br> καὶ παρεκάλουν αὐτὸν ἵνα μόνον ἅψωνται τοῦ κρασπέδου τοῦ ἱματίου αὐτοῦ· καὶ ὅσοι ἥψαντο **διεσώθησαν**. [GNT] | |
| **#1899** <br> **Healed** <br><br> Clean–KJV <br> Cleansed–NASB <br> Clean–NIV <br> Cleansed–NKJV <br> **Healed–NLT** <br><br> **POSB REFERENCE** <br> (Mt.8:3) <br> Note 3 | καθαρίσθητι = *katharisthēti* <br> Pronunciation: [kath-ar-is-thay-tee] <br> Parsing (part of speech): verb <br>     Mood—imperative <br>     Tense—aorist <br>     Voice—passive <br>     Person—2nd person <br>     Number—singular <br>     Stem or root—from καθαρίζω <br> Concordance References: <br> ⇒ Strong's #2511 katharizō <br> ⇒ NIV #2751 katharizō <br> ⇒ NASB #2511 katharizō <br><br> **Matthew 8:3** <br> And Jesus put forth his hand, and touched him, saying, I will; be thou **clean**. And immediately his leprosy was cleansed. [KJV] <br> And He stretched out His hand and touched him, saying, "I am willing; be **cleansed**." And immediately his leprosy was cleansed. [NASB] <br> Jesus reached out his hand and touched the man. "I am willing," he said. "Be **clean**!" Immediately he was cured of his leprosy. [NIV] <br> Then Jesus put out His hand and touched him, saying, "I am willing; be **cleansed**." Immediately his leprosy was cleansed. [NKJV] <br> Jesus touched him. "I want to," he said. "Be **healed**!" And instantly the leprosy disappeared. [NLT] <br> καὶ ἐκτείνας τὴν χεῖρα, ἥψατο αὐτοῦ ὁ Ἰησοῦς λέγων, Θέλω, **καθαρίσθητι**. καὶ εὐθέως ἐκαθαρίσθη αὐτοῦ ἡ λέπρα. [GNS] <br> καὶ ἐκτείνας τὴν χεῖρα ἥψατο αὐτοῦ λέγων, Θέλω, **καθαρίσθητι**· καὶ εὐθέως ἐκαθαρίσθη αὐτοῦ ἡ λέπρα. [GNT] | To be clean and pure physically, to be healed from the effects of leprosy; to be purified; to be washed; to be cleaned. <br><br> **Practical Application** <br> In this Scripture, the word also includes the idea of being made morally clean and pure, of being spiritually cleansed and healed. |
| **#1900** <br> **Healed** <br><br> Whole–KJV <br> Well–NASB <br> **Healed–NIV** <br> Well–NKJV <br> All right–NLT <br><br> **POSB REFERENCE** <br> (Lk.8:49-56; esp. v.50) <br> Note 4, point 2 <br><br> **See also POSB REF:** <br> (Acts 4:9-10; esp. v.9) <br> *Deeper Study #4* | σωθήσεται = *sōthēsetai* <br> Pronunciation: [so-they'-se-tah-ee] <br> Parsing (part of speech): verb <br>     Mood—indicative <br>     Tense—future <br>     Voice—passive <br>     Person—3rd person <br>     Number—singular <br>     Stem or root—from σῴζω <br> Concordance References: <br> ⇒ Strong's #4982 sōzō <br> ⇒ NIV #5392 sōzō <br> ⇒ NASB #4982 sōzō <br><br> **Luke 8:50** <br> But when Jesus heard it, he answered him, saying, Fear not: believe only, and she shall be made **whole**. [KJV] <br> But when Jesus heard this, He answered him, "Do not be afraid any longer; only believe, and she shall be made **well**." [NASB] | Restored, made alive, saved; to make well; to preserve; to make all right. <br><br> **Practical Application** <br> Imagine the strong faith required to believe simply because of Jesus' Word, because of what He said. Jesus demonstrated His great love and amazing power. He raised Jairus' daughter. He showed that He cared for the man and the family who approached Him in belief and trust. |

## PRACTICAL WORD STUDIES
### in the New Testament

| ENGLISH WORD | GREEK WORD AND VERSE | THE WORD MEANS... |
|---|---|---|
| | Hearing this, Jesus said to Jairus, "Don't be afraid; just believe, and she will be **healed**." [NIV]<br>But when Jesus heard it, He answered him, saying, "Do not be afraid; only believe, and she will be made **well**." [NKJV]<br>But when Jesus heard what had happened, he said to Jairus, "Don't be afraid. Just trust me, and she will be **all right**." [NLT]<br>ὁ δὲ Ἰησοῦς ἀκούσας ἀπεκρίθη αὐτῷ, λέγων, Μὴ φοβοῦ. μόνον πίστευε, καὶ **σωθήσεται**. [GNS]<br>ὁ δὲ Ἰησοῦς ἀκούσας ἀπεκρίθη αὐτῷ, μόνον πίστευσον, καὶ **σωθήσεται**. [GNT] | |
| **#1901**<br>**Healed, Had Faith To Be**<br><br>Had faith to be healed–KJV<br>Had faith to be made well–NASB<br>**Had faith to be healed–NIV**<br>Had faith to be healed–NKJV<br>Had faith to be healed–NLT<br><br>**POSB REFERENCE**<br>(Acts 14:8-13; esp. v.9)<br>Note 2, point 1d | ἔχει πίστιν τοῦ σωθῆναι = *echei pistin tou sōthēnai*<br>Pronunciation: [ech-eh-ee pis'-tin too sow-they'-nah-ee]<br>Parsing *pistin* (part of speech): noun<br>    Case—accusative<br>    Gender—feminine<br>    Number—singular<br>    Stem or root—from πίστις, εως<br>Parsing *sōthēnai* (part of speech): verb<br>    Mood—infinitive<br>    Tense—aorist<br>    Voice—passive<br>    Case—genitive<br>    Stem or root—from σῴζω<br>Concordance References:<br>  ⇒ Strong's #2192 echō + 4102 pistis + 3588 ho + 4982 sōzō<br>  ⇒ NIV #2400 echō [had] + 4411 pistis [faith] + 3836 ho [Not in English] + 5392 sōzō [healed]<br>  ⇒ NASB #2192 echō + 4102 pistis +3588 ho + 4982 sōzō<br><br>**Acts 14:9**<br>The same heard Paul speak: who stedfastly beholding him, and perceiving that he **had faith to be healed**, [KJV]<br>This man was listening to Paul as he spoke, who, when he had fixed his gaze upon him, and had seen that he **had faith to be made well**, [NASB]<br>He listened to Paul as he was speaking. Paul looked directly at him, saw that he **had faith to be healed** [NIV]<br>*This* man heard Paul speaking. Paul, observing him intently and seeing that he **had faith to be healed**, [NKJV]<br>He was listening as Paul preached, and Paul noticed him and realized he **had faith to be healed**. [NLT]<br>οὗτος ἤκουε τοῦ Παύλου λαλοῦντος· ὃς ἀτενίσας αὐτῷ, καὶ ἰδὼν ὅτι **πίστιν ἔχει τοῦ σωθῆναι**, [GNS]<br>οὗτος ἤκουσεν τοῦ Παύλου λαλοῦντος· ὃς ἀτενίσας αὐτῷ καὶ ἰδὼν ὅτι **ἔχει πίστιν τοῦ σωθῆναι**, [GNT] | Had faith to be healed, made well, saved, to made better. It means both to be cured and to be saved.<br><br>**Practical Application**<br>Paul, of course, was preaching the gospel, and the man's heart was stirred to believe and trust Jesus to save him. Paul noticed this; he saw a faith rise up in the man, a faith strong enough to heal him as well as save his soul. All the man needed was to be pointed to such power in the name of Jesus. |
| **#1902**<br>**Healing– Healing, Complete**<br><br>Perfect soundness–KJV<br>Perfect health–NASB<br>**Complete healing–NIV**<br>Perfect soundness–NKJV<br>Healing–NLT<br><br>**POSB REFERENCE**<br>(Acts 3:16)<br>*Deeper Study #2* | ὁλοκληρίαν = *holoklērian*<br>Pronunciation: [hol-ok-lay-ree'-ahn]<br>Parsing (part of speech): noun<br>    Case—accusative<br>    Gender—feminine<br>    Number—singular<br>    Stem or root—from ὁλοκληρία<br>Concordance References:<br>  ⇒ Strong's #3647 holoklēria<br>  ⇒ NIV #3907 holoklēria<br>  ⇒ NASB #3647 holoklēria<br><br>**Acts 3:16**<br>And his name through faith in his name hath made this man strong, whom ye see and know: yea, the faith which is by him hath given him this **perfect soundness** in the presence of you all. [KJV]<br>"And on the basis of faith in His name, it is the name | Complete healing; perfect soundness; perfect health.<br><br>**Practical Application**<br>It means to be whole: to be perfectly sound in *all* of one's parts; to be perfectly complete and entire. It means the man was perfectly sound in both body and soul. |

# PRACTICAL WORD STUDIES
## in the NEW TESTAMENT

| ENGLISH WORD | GREEK WORD AND VERSE | THE WORD MEANS... |
|---|---|---|
| | of Jesus which has strengthened this man whom you see and know; and the faith which comes through Him has given him this **perfect health** in the presence of you all. [NASB]<br><br>By faith in the name of Jesus, this man whom you see and know was made strong. It is Jesus' name and the faith that comes through him that has given this **complete healing** to him, as you can all see. [NIV]<br><br>And His name, through faith in His name, has made this man strong, whom you see and know. Yes, the faith which *comes* through Him has given him this **perfect soundness** in the presence of you all. [NKJV]<br><br>"The name of Jesus has healed this man—and you know how lame he was before. Faith in Jesus' name has caused this **healing** before your very eyes. [NLT]<br><br>καὶ ἐπὶ τῇ πίστει τοῦ ὀνόματος αὐτοῦ, τοῦτον ὃν θεωρεῖτε καὶ οἴδατε, ἐστερέωσε τὸ ὄνομα αὐτοῦ· καὶ ἡ πίστις ἡ δι' αὐτοῦ ἔδωκεν αὐτῷ τὴν **ὁλοκληρίαν** ταύτην ἀπέναντι πάντων ὑμῶν. [GNS]<br><br>καὶ ἐπὶ τῇ πίστει τοῦ ὀνόματος αὐτοῦ τοῦτον ὃν θεωρεῖτε καὶ οἴδατε, ἐστερέωσεν τὸ ὄνομα αὐτοῦ, καὶ ἡ πίστις ἡ δι' αὐτοῦ ἔδωκεν αὐτῷ τὴν **ὁλοκληρίαν** ταύτην ἀπέναντι πάντων ὑμῶν. [GNT] | |
| **#1903**<br>**Heals–Healed**<br><br>Maketh...whole–KJV<br>**Heals–NASB**<br>**Heals–NIV**<br>**Heals–NKJV**<br>**Healed–NLT**<br><br>**POSB REFERENCE**<br>(Acts 9:34)<br>Note 4, point 3 | ἰᾶται = *iatai*<br>Pronunciation: [ee-ah'-tah-ee]<br>Parsing (part of speech): verb<br>  Mood—indicative<br>  Tense—present<br>  Voice—middle or passive deponent<br>  Person—3rd person<br>  Number—singular<br>  Stem or root—from ἰάομαι<br>Concordance References:<br>  ⇒ Strong's #2390 iaomai<br>  ⇒ NIV #2615 iaomai<br>  ⇒ NASB #2390 iaomai<br><br>**Acts 9:34**<br>And Peter said unto him, Aeneas, Jesus Christ **maketh** thee **whole**: arise, and make thy bed. And he arose immediately. [KJV]<br><br>And Peter said to him, "Aeneas, Jesus Christ **heals** you; arise, and make your bed." And immediately he arose. [NASB]<br><br>"Aeneas," Peter said to him, "Jesus Christ **heals** you. Get up and take care of your mat." Immediately Aeneas got up. [NIV]<br><br>And Peter said to him, "Aeneas, Jesus the Christ **heals** you. Arise and make your bed." Then he arose immediately. [NKJV]<br><br>Peter said to him, "Aeneas, Jesus Christ heals you! Get up and make your bed!" And he was **healed** instantly. [NLT]<br><br>καὶ εἶπεν αὐτῷ ὁ Πέτρος, Αἰνέα, **ἰᾶταί** σε Ἰησοῦς ὁ Χριστός· ἀνάστηθι καὶ στρῶσον σεαυτῷ. Καὶ εὐθέως ἀνέστη. [GNS]<br><br>καὶ εἶπεν αὐτῷ ὁ Πέτρος, Αἰνέα, **ἰᾶταί** σε Ἰησοῦς Χριστός· ἀνάστηθι καὶ στρῶσον σεαυτῷ. καὶ εὐθέως ἀνέστη. [GNT] | Heals; to make whole; to cure; to restore; to free.<br><br>**Practical Application**<br>It means to be healed immediately, here and now. It was not a drawn out thing. The man was to be healed right then. The word has the idea of being made completely whole, within as well as without, spiritually as well as physically. The man, if not already saved, was made whole spiritually as well as physically. (See POSB note—Matthew 14:36 for more discussion.) |
| **#1904**<br>**Health, Perfect**<br><br>Perfect soundness–KJV<br>**Perfect health–NASB**<br>Complete healing–NIV<br>Perfect soundness–NKJV<br>Healing–NLT | ὁλοκληρίαν = *holoklērian*<br>Pronunciation: [hol-ok-lay-ree'-ahn]<br>Parsing (part of speech): noun<br>  Case—accusative<br>  Gender—feminine<br>  Number—singular<br>  Stem or root—from ὁλοκληρία<br>Concordance References:<br>  ⇒ Strong's #3647 holoklēria<br>  ⇒ NIV #3907 holoklēria<br>  ⇒ NASB #3647 holoklēria | Complete healing, perfect soundness, perfect health.<br><br>**Practical Application**<br>It means to be whole: to be perfectly sound in *all* of one's parts; to be perfectly complete and entire. It means the man was perfectly sound in both body and soul. |

PRACTICAL WORD STUDIES
in the NEW TESTAMENT

| ENGLISH WORD | GREEK WORD AND VERSE | THE WORD MEANS... |
|---|---|---|
| **POSB REFERENCE** (Acts 3:16) *Deeper Study #2* | **Acts 3:16**<br>And his name through faith in his name hath made this man strong, whom ye see and know: yea, the faith which is by him hath given him this **perfect soundness** in the presence of you all. [KJV]<br>"And on the basis of faith in His name, it is the name of Jesus which has strengthened this man whom you see and know; and the faith which comes through Him has given him this **perfect health** in the presence of you all. [NASB]<br>By faith in the name of Jesus, this man whom you see and know was made strong. It is Jesus' name and the faith that comes through him that has given this **complete healing** to him, as you can all see. [NIV]<br>And His name, through faith in His name, has made this man strong, whom you see and know. Yes, the faith which comes through Him has given him this **perfect soundness** in the presence of you all. [NKJV]<br>"The name of Jesus has healed this man—and you know how lame he was before. Faith in Jesus' name has caused this **healing** before your very eyes. [NLT]<br>καὶ ἐπὶ τῇ πίστει τοῦ ὀνόματος αὐτοῦ, τοῦτον ὃν θεωρεῖτε καὶ οἴδατε, ἐστερέωσε τὸ ὄνομα αὐτοῦ· καὶ ἡ πίστις ἡ δι' αὐτοῦ ἔδωκεν αὐτῷ τὴν **ὁλοκληρίαν** ταύτην ἀπέναντι πάντων ὑμῶν. [GNS]<br>καὶ ἐπὶ τῇ πίστει τοῦ ὀνόματος αὐτοῦ τοῦτον ὃν θεωρεῖτε καὶ οἴδατε, ἐστερέωσεν τὸ ὄνομα αὐτοῦ, καὶ ἡ πίστις ἡ δι' αὐτοῦ ἔδωκεν αὐτῷ τὴν **ὁλοκληρίαν** ταύτην ἀπέναντι πάντων ὑμῶν. [GNT] | |
| #1905<br>**Hear**<br><br>Behold–KJV<br>Take note–NASB<br>Consider–NIV<br>Look on–NKJV<br>**Hear–NLT**<br><br>**POSB REFERENCE** (Acts 4:29-30; esp. v.29) Note 4, point 1b | **ἔπιδε ἐπί** = *epide epi*<br>Pronunciation: [ep-i'-deh ep-ee]<br>Parsing *epide* (part of speech): verb<br>  Mood—imperative<br>  Tense—aorist<br>  Voice—active<br>  Person—2nd person<br>  Number—singular<br>  Stem or root—from ἐπεῖδον<br>Parsing *epi* (part of speech): preposition<br>  Case—accusative<br>  Stem or root—from ἐπί<br>Concordance References:<br>⇒ Strong's #1896 + 1909 epeidon epi<br>⇒ NIV #2078 + 2093 epeidon epi<br>⇒ NASB #1896 + 1909 epeidon epi<br><br>**Acts 4:29**<br>And now, Lord, **behold** their threatenings: and grant unto thy servants, that with all boldness they may speak thy word, [KJV]<br>"And now, Lord, **take note** of their threats, and grant that Thy bond-servants may speak Thy word with all confidence, [NASB]<br>Now, Lord, **consider** their threats and enable your servants to speak your word with great boldness. [NIV]<br>Now, Lord, **look on** their threats, and grant to Your servants that with all boldness they may speak Your word, [NKJV]<br>And now, O Lord, **hear** their threats, and give your servants great boldness in their preaching. [NLT]<br>καὶ τὰ νῦν, Κύριε, **ἔπιδε ἐπὶ** τὰς ἀπειλὰς αὐτῶν, καὶ δὸς τοῖς δούλοις σου μετὰ παρρησίας πάσης λαλεῖν τὸν λόγον σου, [GNS]<br>καὶ τὰ νῦν, κύριε, **ἔπιδε ἐπὶ** τὰς ἀπειλὰς αὐτῶν καὶ δὸς τοῖς δούλοις σου μετὰ παρρησίας πάσης λαλεῖν τὸν λόγον σου, [GNT] | To consider; to behold; to take note; to hear; to look upon.<br><br>**Practical Application**<br>The church was asking God to concentrate and focus upon the persecution; to deal with it and to overrule the enemy; to give whatever was necessary to endure through it all. |

# PRACTICAL WORD STUDIES
in the NEW TESTAMENT

| ENGLISH WORD | GREEK WORD AND VERSE | THE WORD MEANS... |
|---|---|---|
| **#1906**<br>**Heard**<br><br>**Heard–KJV**<br>Listening–NASB<br>Listening–NIV<br>**Heard–NKJV**<br>Listened–NLT<br><br>**POSB**<br>**REFERENCE**<br>(Acts 16:14)<br>Note 4 | ἤκουεν = ëkouen<br>Pronunciation: [ey-koo'-ehn]<br>Parsing (part of speech): verb<br>  Mood—indicative<br>  Tense—imperfect<br>  Voice—active<br>  Person—3rd person<br>  Number—singular<br>  Stem or root—from ἀκούω<br>Concordance References:<br>  ⇒ Strong's #191 akouö<br>  ⇒ NIV #201 akouö<br>  ⇒ NASB #191 akouö<br><br>**Acts 16:14**<br>And a certain woman named Lydia, a seller of purple, of the city of Thyatira, which worshipped God, **heard** us: whose heart the Lord opened, that she attended unto the things which were spoken of Paul. [KJV]<br>And a certain woman named Lydia, from the city of Thyatira, a seller of purple fabrics, a worshiper of God, was **listening**; and the Lord opened her heart to respond to the things spoken by Paul. [NASB]<br>One of those **listening** was a woman named Lydia, a dealer in purple cloth from the city of Thyatira, who was a worshiper of God. The Lord opened her heart to respond to Paul's message. [NIV]<br>Now a certain woman named Lydia **heard** us. She was a seller of purple from the city of Thyatira, who worshiped God. The Lord opened her heart to heed the things spoken by Paul. [NKJV]<br>One of them was Lydia from Thyatira, a merchant of expensive purple cloth. She was a worshiper of God. As she **listened** to us, the Lord opened her heart, and she accepted what Paul was saying. [NLT]<br>καί τις γυνὴ ὀνόματι Λυδία, πορφυρόπωλις, πόλεως Θυατείρων σεβομένη τὸν Θεόν, **ἤκουεν**· ἧς ὁ Κύριος διήνοιξε τὴν καρδίαν, προσέχειν τοῖς λαλουμένοις ὑπὸ τοῦ Παύλου. [GNS]<br>καί τις γυνὴ ὀνόματι Λυδία, πορφυρόπωλις πόλεως Θυατείρων σεβομένη τὸν θεόν, **ἤκουεν**, ἧς ὁ κύριος διήνοιξεν τὴν καρδίαν προσέχειν τοῖς λαλουμένοις ὑπὸ τοῦ Παύλου. [GNT] | To be listening; to be heard; to be listened to; to receive news of; to understand.<br><br>**Practical Application**<br>The word "heard" (*ëkouen*) means she really perked up and paid attention. She listened and kept on listening, giving utmost attention to the gospel. |
| **#1907**<br>**Heard About–**<br>**Heard Of It–**<br>**Heard Of This–**<br>**Heard What**<br>  **Was Happen-**<br>  **ing**<br><br>Heard of it–KJV<br>Heard of this–NASB<br>Heard about–NIV<br>Heard about this–<br>  NKJV<br>Heard what was happening–NLT<br><br>**POSB**<br>**REFERENCE**<br>(Mk.3:21)<br>Note 2 | ἀκούσαντες = akou santes<br>Pronunciation: [ak-oo'-sahn-tehs]<br>Parsing (part of speech): verb<br>  Mood—participle<br>  Tense—aorist<br>  Voice—active<br>  Case—nominative<br>  Gender—masculine<br>  Number—plural<br>  Stem or root—from ἀκούω<br>Concordance References:<br>  ⇒ Strong's #191 akouö<br>  ⇒ NIV #201 akouö<br>  ⇒ NASB #191 akouö<br><br>**Mark 3:21**<br>And when his friends **heard of it**, they went out to lay hold on him: for they said, He is beside himself. [KJV]<br>And when His own people **heard of this**, they went out to take custody of Him; for they were saying, "He has lost His senses." [NASB]<br>When his family **heard about** this, they went to take charge of him, for they said, "He is out of his mind." [NIV]<br>But when His own people **heard about this**, they went out to lay hold of Him, for they said, "He is out of His mind." [NKJV]<br>When his family **heard what was happening**, they | To hear; to listen; to be informed by what is heard; to understand.<br><br>**Practical Application**<br>In the present passage, the Greek uses a participle meaning "heard about" (*akou santes*). The idea is that the friends heard not only about the enormous crowds, but they heard *all about Jesus*: His phenomenal miracles, claims, and teaching; the prophetic esteem which the people heaped upon Him; the opposition which was now threatening His life. All this led the friends of the family to think He was insane. |

# PRACTICAL WORD STUDIES
## in the New Testament

| ENGLISH WORD | GREEK WORD AND VERSE | THE WORD MEANS... |
|---|---|---|
| | tried to take him home with them. "He's out of his mind," they said. [NLT]<br><br>αἱ **ἀκούσαντες** οἱ παρ' αὐτοῦ, ἐξῆλθον κρατῆσαι αὐτόν· ἔλεγον γὰρ ὅτι ἐξέστη. [GNS]<br><br>καὶ **ἀκούσαντες** οἱ παρ' αὐτοῦ ἐξῆλθον κρατῆσαι αὐτόν· ἔλεγον γὰρ ὅτι ἐξέστη. [GNT] | |
| **#1908**<br>**Heard Sound**<br><br>Noised abroad–KJV<br>Sound occurred–NASB<br>Heard...sound–NIV<br>Sound occurred–NKJV<br>Heard...sound–NLT<br><br>**POSB REFERENCE**<br>(Acts 2:5-11; esp. v.6)<br>Note 5, point 2 | γενομένης φωνῆς = genomenēs phōnēs<br>Pronunciation: [ghin'-om-eh-nace fo-nays']<br>Parsing *genomenēs* (part of speech): verb<br>    Mood—participle<br>    Tense—aorist<br>    Voice—middle deponent<br>    Case—genitive<br>    Gender—feminine<br>    Number—singular<br>    Stem or root—from γίνομαι<br>Parsing *phōnēs* (part of speech): noun<br>    Case—genitive<br>    Gender—feminine<br>    Number—singular<br>    Stem or root—from φωνή, ῆς<br>Concordance References:<br>  ⇒ Strong's #1096 ginomai + 5456 phōnē<br>  ⇒ NIV #1181 ginomai [heard] + 5889 phōnē [sound]<br>  ⇒ NASB ##1096 ginomai + 5456 phōnē<br><br>**Acts 2:6**<br>Now when this was **noised abroad**, the multitude came together, and were confounded, because that every man heard them speak in his own language. [KJV]<br><br>And when this **sound occurred**, the multitude came together, and were bewildered, because they were each one hearing them speak in his own language. [NASB]<br><br>When they **heard** this **sound**, a crowd came together in bewilderment, because each one heard them speaking in his own language. [NIV]<br><br>And when this **sound occurred**, the multitude came together, and were confused, because everyone heard them speak in his own language. [NKJV]<br><br>When they **heard** this **sound**, they came running to see what it was all about, and they were bewildered to hear their own languages being spoken by the believers. [NLT]<br><br>γενομένης δὲ τῆς φωνῆς ταύτης, συνῆλθε τὸ πλῆθος, καὶ συνεχύθη, ὅτι ἤκουον εἷς ἕκαστος τῇ ἰδίᾳ διαλέκτῳ λαλούντων αὐτῶν. [GNS]<br><br>γενομένης δὲ τῆς φωνῆς ταύτης συνῆλθεν τὸ πλῆθος καὶ συνεχύθη, ὅτι ἤκουον εἷς ἕκαστος τῇ ἰδίᾳ διαλέκτῳ λαλούντων αὐτῶν. [GNT] | To hear a sound, noise, roar.<br><br>**Practical Application**<br>The Greek says, "When this sound was heard." It was apparently the sound of the thunderous blast caused by God that brought the people rushing to the scene. |
| **#1909**<br>**Hearing**<br><br>Hearing–KJV<br>Listening–NASB<br>Listening–NIV<br>Listening–NKJV<br>Discussing–NLT<br><br>**POSB REFERENCE**<br>(Lk.2:46-47; esp. v.46)<br>Note 3, point 2a | ἀκούοντα = akouonta<br>Pronunciation: [ah-koo'-on-tah]<br>Parsing (part of speech): verb<br>    Mood—participle<br>    Tense—present<br>    Voice—active<br>    Case—accusative<br>    Gender—masculine<br>    Number—singular<br>    Stem or root—from ἀκούω<br>Concordance References:<br>  ⇒ Strong's #191 akouō<br>  ⇒ NIV #201 akouō<br>  ⇒ NASB #191 akouō<br><br>**Luke 2:46**<br>And it came to pass, that after three days they found him in the temple, sitting in the midst of the doctors, both **hearing** them, and asking them questions. [KJV]<br><br>And it came about that after three days they found Him in the temple, sitting in the midst of the teachers, both lis- | To listen to; to hear; to attend; to hearken; to perceive; to receive news of; to give heed to; to understand.<br><br>**Practical Application**<br>In this Scripture, Jesus was "hearing" what the teachers said. He listened closely, attentively, with rapt attention. |

## PRACTICAL WORD STUDIES in the NEW TESTAMENT

| ENGLISH WORD | GREEK WORD AND VERSE | THE WORD MEANS... |
|---|---|---|
| | **tening** to them, and asking them questions. [NASB]<br>After three days they found him in the temple courts, sitting among the teachers, **listening** to them and asking them questions. [NIV]<br>Now so it was that after three days they found Him in the temple, sitting in the midst of the teachers, both **listening** to them and asking them questions. [NKJV]<br>Three days later they finally discovered him. He was in the Temple, sitting among the religious teachers, **discussing** deep questions with them. [NLT]<br>καὶ ἐγένετο, μεθ' ἡμέρας τρεῖς εὗρον αὐτὸν ἐν τῷ ἱερῷ, καθεζόμενον ἐν μέσῳ τῶν διδασκάλων, καὶ **ἀκούοντα** αὐτῶν, καὶ ἐπερωτῶντα αὐτούς. [GNS]<br>καὶ ἐγένετο μετὰ ἡμέρας τρεῖς εὗρον αὐτὸν ἐν τῷ ἱερῷ καθεζόμενον ἐν μέσῳ τῶν διδασκάλων καὶ **ἀκούοντα** αὐτῶν καὶ ἐπερωτῶντα αὐτούς· [GNT] | |
| **#1910**<br>**Heart**<br><br>Heart–KJV<br>Heart–NASB<br>Heart–NIV<br>Heart–NKJV<br>Heart–NLT<br><br>**POSB REFERENCE**<br>(Mk.7:20; esp. v.19)<br>*Deeper Study #1* | καρδίαν = *kardian*<br>Pronunciation: [kar-dee'-ahn]<br>Parsing (part of speech): noun<br>   Case—accusative<br>   Gender—feminine<br>   Number—singular<br>   Stem or root— from καρδία, ας<br>Concordance References:<br>  ⇒ Strong's #2588 kardia<br>  ⇒ NIV #2840 kardia<br>  ⇒ NASB #2588 kardia<br><br>**Mark 7:19**<br>Because it entereth not into his **heart**, but into the belly, and goeth out into the draught, purging all meats? [KJV]<br>Because it does not go into his **heart**, but into his stomach, and is eliminated?" (Thus He declared all foods clean.) [NASB]<br>For it doesn't go into his **heart** but into his stomach, and then out of his body." (In saying this, Jesus declared all foods "clean.") [NIV]<br>Because it does not enter his **heart** but his stomach, and is eliminated, thus purifying all foods?" [NKJV]<br>Food doesn't come in contact with your **heart**, but only passes through the stomach and then comes out again." (By saying this, he showed that every kind of food is acceptable.) [NLT]<br>ὅτι οὐκ εἰσπορεύεται αὐτοῦ εἰς τὴν **καρδίαν**, ἀλλ' εἰς τὴν κοιλίαν, καὶ εἰς τὸν ἀφεδρῶνα ἐκπορεύεται, καθαρίζον πάντα τὰ βρώματα. [GNS]<br>ὅτι οὐκ εἰσπορεύεται αὐτοῦ εἰς τὴν **καρδίαν** ἀλλ' εἰς τὴν κοιλίαν, καὶ εἰς τὸν ἀφεδρῶνα ἐκπορεύεται, καθαρίζων πάντα τὰ βρώματα; [GNT] | A person's inward life, inner self, mind, heart.<br><br>**Practical Application**<br>In the Bible the word "heart" refers to both the major organ of the body (Leviticus 17:11) and to the most important part of a person, that is, to man's innermost being. The heart is the central part, the very center of a person's life. It is the most vital part of a person's being.<br>The heart lies deep within, containing the *hidden self* or the real self (1 Peter 3:4); that is, the heart contains what a person really is, his true character. The heart determines what a person does, his behavior, whether good or depraved (Matthew 15:18; Mark 7:21-23).<br>1. The heart is the source of a person's rational being: reasoning (Mark 2:6), understanding (Matthew 13:15), thinking (Matthew 9:4).<br>2. The heart is the source of a person's emotional being: joy (John 16:22; Ephes. 5:19), affections (Luke 24:32), desires (Matthew 5:28).<br>3. The heart is the source of a person's spiritual being: conscience (Acts 2:37), will (Romans 6:17), faith (Mark 11:23; Romans 10:10), evil (Matthew 15:18; Mark 7:21-23; cp. Jeremiah 17:9). |
| **#1911**<br>**Heart Went Out**<br><br>Compassion–KJV<br>Compassion–NASB<br>**Heart went out–NIV**<br>Compassion–NKJV<br>Compassion–NLT<br><br>**POSB REFERENCE**<br>(Lk.7:13)<br>*Deeper Study #1* | ἐσπλαγχνίσθη = *esplagchnisthē*<br>Pronunciation: [es-splangch-nees'-thay]<br>Parsing (part of speech): verb<br>   Mood—indicative<br>   Tense—aorist<br>   Voice—passive deponent<br>   Person—3rd person<br>   Number—singular<br>   Stem or root—from σπλαγχνίζομαι<br>Concordance References:<br>  ⇒ Strong's #4697 splagchnizomai<br>  ⇒ NIV #5072 splagchnizomai<br>  ⇒ NASB #4697 splagchnizomai<br><br>**Luke 7:13**<br>And when the Lord saw her, he had **compassion** on her, and said unto her, Weep not. [KJV]<br>And when the Lord saw her, He felt **compassion** for her, and said to her, "Do not weep." [NASB]<br>When the Lord saw her, his **heart went out** to her and he said, "Don't cry." [NIV] | To be moved inwardly; to yearn with tender mercy, affection, pity, empathy, compassion; to have one's heart reach out.<br><br>**Practical Application**<br>It is the very seat of a man's affections. It is the deepest movement of emotions possible; being moved within the deepest part of one's being. The Lord saw and had compassion and assured the woman. Note three striking facts.<br>1. It was "the Lord" who saw her. This is the first time Luke uses the title "the Lord" by itself and it is striking. The point Luke is making is that "the Lord," the Sovereign Power of the universe, saw this woman who was utterly heartbroken. The Lord actually saw her.<br>2. It was "the Lord" who had a heart that went out to her. The fact is shocking, for the sovereign power of the universe actually felt com- |

# PRACTICAL WORD STUDIES
## in the NEW TESTAMENT

| ENGLISH WORD | GREEK WORD AND VERSE | THE WORD MEANS... |
|---|---|---|
| | When the Lord saw her, He had **compassion** on her and said to her, "Do not weep." [NKJV]<br>When the Lord saw her, his heart overflowed with **compassion**. "Don't cry!" he said. [NLT]<br>καὶ ἰδὼν αὐτὴν ὁ Κύριος **ἐσπλαγχνίσθη** ἐπ' αὐτῇ, καὶ εἶπεν αὐτῇ, Μὴ κλαῖε. [GNS]<br>καὶ ἰδὼν αὐτὴν ὁ κύριος **ἐσπλαγχνίσθη** ἐπ' αὐτῇ καὶ εἶπεν αὐτῇ, Μὴ κλαῖε. [GNT] | passion for a simple woman. He was not just the sovereign power of a vast universe who was way off in outer space someplace, unattached and disinterested in this earth and its inhabitants. Contrariwise, He was vitally interested, interested enough to be looking and seeing; and He was concerned about what He saw, full of compassion for the heartbroken (see POSB note—Luke 7:13).<br>3. It was "the Lord" who spoke and gave assurance. Again, the fact was shocking, for the sovereign power of the universe actually spoke and gave assurance to a simple woman. Luke is definitely stressing the staggering thought: "the Lord," the sovereign majesty of the universe speaks to men, and His Word gives great assurance. The Lord is vitally interested in the affairs of men, even in the plight of a simple woman. |
| #1912<br>**Heartless**<br><br>Without natural affection-KJV<br>Unloving-NASB<br>**Heartless-NIV**<br>Unloving-NKJV<br>**Heartless-NLT**<br><br>**POSB<br>REFERENCE**<br>(Rom.1:31)<br>*Deeper Study* #21 | ἀστόργους = *astorgous*<br>Pronunciation: [as'-tor-goos]<br>Parsing (part of speech): adjective<br>    Case—accusative<br>    Gender—masculine<br>    Number—plural<br>    Stem or root—from ἄστοργος, ον<br>Concordance References:<br>  ⇒ Strong's #794 astorgos<br>  ⇒ NIV #845 astorgos<br>  ⇒ NASB #794 astorgos<br><br>**Romans 1:31**<br>Without understanding, covenantbreakers, **without natural affection**, implacable, unmerciful: [KJV]<br>Without understanding, untrustworthy, **unloving**, unmerciful; [NASB]<br>They are senseless, faithless, **heartless**, ruthless. [NIV]<br>Undiscerning, untrustworthy, **unloving**, unforgiving, unmerciful; [NKJV]<br>They refuse to understand, break their promises, and are **heartless** and unforgiving. [NLT]<br>ἀσυνέτους, ἀσυνθέτους, **ἀστόργους**, ἀσπόνδους, ἀνελεήμονας·[GNS]<br>ἀσυνέτους ἀσυνθέτους **ἀστόργους** ἀνελεήμονας [GNT] | Heartless; unloving; lacking normal human affection; inhuman; without natural affection; abnormal affection and love; without human emotion or love; a lack of feeling for others; abuse of normal affection and love.<br><br>**Practical Application**<br>Others become little more than pawns for a man's own use and benefit, pleasure and purposes, excitement and stimulation. Abnormal affection, sex and perversion prevail. |
| #1913<br>**Hearty<br>Agreement**<br><br>Consenting-KJV<br>**Hearty agreement-<br>NASB**<br>Giving approval-NIV<br>Consenting-NKJV<br>Official witnesses-<br>NLT<br><br>**POSB<br>REFERENCE**<br>(Acts 8:1)<br>Note 1, point 1 | συνευδοκῶν = *suneudokōn*<br>Pronunciation: [soon-yoo-dok-own]<br>Parsing (part of speech): verb<br>    Mood—participle<br>    Tense—present<br>    Voice—active<br>    Case—nominative<br>    Gender—masculine<br>    Number—singular<br>    Stem or root—from συνευδοκέω<br>Concordance References:<br>  ⇒ Strong's #4909 suneudokeō<br>  ⇒ NIV #5306 suneudokeō<br>  ⇒ NASB #4909 suneudokeō<br><br>**Acts 8:1**<br>And Saul was **consenting** unto his death. And at that time there was a great persecution against the church which was at Jerusalem; and they were all scattered abroad throughout the regions of Judaea and Samaria, except the apostles. [KJV]<br>And Saul was in **hearty agreement** with putting him to death. And on that day a great persecution arose against the church in Jerusalem; and they were all scattered throughout the regions of Judea and Samaria, except | Giving approval; consenting; hearty agreement; to be willing; to agree with. The word means to give approval of the will; to willingly approve; to approve with pleasure; to delight in; to applaud what is being done.<br><br>**Practical Application**<br>Saul was well-pleased with Stephen's death. An *inflamed fury* had been building up in him against the church, for he felt that the preaching of Christ threatened his religion, Judaism. In fact, Saul was the leader in persecuting the church, the one who *boiled* more than anyone else against the church. He was apparently a leader among the religionists. |

# PRACTICAL WORD STUDIES
## in the NEW TESTAMENT

| ENGLISH WORD | GREEK WORD AND VERSE | THE WORD MEANS... |
|---|---|---|
| | the apostles. [NASB]<br>And Saul was there, **giving approval** to his death. On that day a great persecution broke out against the church at Jerusalem, and all except the apostles were scattered throughout Judea and Samaria. [NIV]<br>Now Saul was **consenting** to his death. At that time a great persecution arose against the church which was at Jerusalem; and they were all scattered throughout the regions of Judea and Samaria, except the apostles. [NKJV]<br>Saul was one of the **official witnesses** at the killing of Stephen. A great wave of persecution began that day, sweeping over the church in Jerusalem, and all the believers except the apostles fled into Judea and Samaria. [NLT]<br>Σαῦλος δὲ ἦν **συνευδοκῶν** τῇ ἀναιρέσει αὐτοῦ. Ἐγένετο δὲ ἐν ἐκείνῃ τῇ ἡμέρᾳ διωγμὸς μέγας ἐπὶ τὴν ἐκκλησίαν τὴν ἐν Ἱεροσολύμοις· πάντες τε διεσπάρησαν κατὰ τὰς χώρας τῆς Ἰουδαίας καὶ Σαμαρείας, πλὴν τῶν ἀποστόλων. [GNS]<br>Σαῦλος δὲ ἦν **συνευδοκῶν** τῇ ἀναιρέσει αὐτοῦ. Ἐγένετο δὲ ἐν ἐκείνῃ τῇ ἡμέρᾳ διωγμὸς μέγας ἐπὶ τὴν ἐκκλησίαν τὴν ἐν Ἱεροσολύμοις, πάντες δὲ διεσπάρησαν κατὰ τὰς χώρας τῆς Ἰουδαίας καὶ Σαμαρείας πλὴν τῶν ἀποστόλων. [GNT] | |
| #1914<br>**Heathen At Heart**<br><br>Uncircumcised in heart–KJV<br>Uncircumcised in heart–NASB<br>Uncircumcised hearts–NIV<br>Uncircumcised in heart–NKJV<br>**Heathen at heart–NLT**<br><br>POSB REFERENCE<br>(Acts 7:42-53; esp. v.51)<br>Note 6, point 5 | **ἀπερίτμητοι καρδίαις** = aperitmētoi kardiais<br>Pronunciation: [ap-er-eet'-may-to-ee kar-dee'-ah-ees]<br>Parsing *aperitmētoi* (part of speech): adjective pronoun<br>    Case—vocative<br>    Gender—masculine<br>    Number—plural<br>    Stem or root—from ἀπερίτμητος, ον<br>Parsing *kardiais* (part of speech): noun<br>    Case—dative<br>    Gender—feminine<br>    Number—plural<br>    Stem or root—from καρδία, ας<br>Concordance References:<br>⇒ Strong's #564 aperitmētos + 2588 kardia<br>⇒ NIV #598 aperitmētos [uncircumcised] + 2840 kardia [hearts]<br>⇒ NASB #564 aperitmētos + 2588 kardia<br><br>**Acts 7:51**<br>Ye stiffnecked and **uncircumcised in heart** and ears, ye do always resist the Holy Ghost: as your fathers did, so do ye. [KJV]<br>"You men who are stiff-necked and **uncircumcised in heart** and ears are always resisting the Holy Spirit; you are doing just as your fathers did. [NASB]<br>"You stiff-necked people, with **uncircumcised hearts** and ears! You are just like your fathers: You always resist the Holy Spirit! [NIV]<br>"*You* stiffnecked and **uncircumcised in heart** and ears! You always resist the Holy Spirit; as your fathers *did,* so *do* you. [NKJV]<br>"You stubborn people! You are **heathen at heart** and deaf to the truth. Must you forever resist the Holy Spirit? But your ancestors did, and so do you! [NLT]<br>Σκληροτράχηλοι καὶ **ἀπερίτμητοι** τῇ **καρδίᾳ** καὶ τοῖς ὠσίν, ὑμεῖς ἀεὶ τῷ Πνεύματι τῷ Ἁγίῳ ἀντιπίπτετε· ὡς οἱ πατέρες ὑμῶν, καὶ ὑμεῖς. [GNS]<br>Σκληροτράχηλοι καὶ **ἀπερίτμητοι καρδίαις** καὶ τοῖς ὠσίν, ὑμεῖς ἀεὶ τῷ πνεύματι τῷ ἁγίῳ ἀντιπίπτετε ὡς οἱ πατέρες ὑμῶν καὶ ὑμεῖς. [GNT] | Uncircumcised hearts; to be a heathen at heart; to have a stubborn heart.<br><br>**Practical Application**<br>Who are the "heathen at heart" (*aperitmētoi kardiais*)? They are the pagan, lost, idolaters, false worshippers, ungodly of the world. |
| #1915<br>**Heaven**<br><br>Heaven–KJV<br>Heaven–NASB<br>Heaven–NIV | **οὐρανοῖς** = ouranois<br>Pronunciation: [oo-ran-oys']<br>Parsing (part of speech): noun<br>    Case—dative<br>    Gender—masculine<br>    Number—plural<br>    Stem or root—from οὐρανός, οῦ | Heavens. The word is plural in the Greek.<br><br>**Practical Application**<br>The New Testament speaks of at least three heavens:<br>⇒ The atmosphere surrounding the earth (cp. Mt.6:26, "the birds of the air"). |

# PRACTICAL WORD STUDIES
## in the NEW TESTAMENT

| ENGLISH WORD | GREEK WORD AND VERSE | THE WORD MEANS... |
|---|---|---|
| **Heaven**–NKJV<br>**Heaven**–NLT<br><br>**POSB<br>REFERENCE**<br>(Mt.6:9)<br>*Deeper Study* #3 | Concordance References:<br>⇒ Strong's #3772 ouranos<br>⇒ NIV #4041 ouranos<br>⇒ NASB #3772 ouranos<br><br>**Matthew 6:9**<br>After this manner therefore pray ye: Our Father which art in **heaven**, Hallowed be thy name. [KJV]<br>"Pray, then, in this way: 'Our Father who art in **heaven**, Hallowed be Thy name. [NASB]<br>"This, then, is how you should pray: " 'Our Father in **heaven**, hallowed be your name, [NIV]<br>In this manner, therefore, pray: Our Father in **heaven**, Hallowed be Your name. [NKJV]<br>Pray like this: Our Father in **heaven**, may your name be honored. [NLT]<br>οὕτως οὖν προσεύχεσθε ὑμεῖς· Πάτερ ἡμῶν ὁ ἐν τοῖς **οὐρανοῖς**, ἁγιασθήτω τὸ ὄνομά σου· [GNS]<br>Οὕτως οὖν προσεύχεσθε ὑμεῖς· Πάτερ ἡμῶν ὁ ἐν τοῖς **οὐρανοῖς**, ἁγιασθήτω τὸ ὄνομά σου· [GNT] | ⇒ The outer space of heavenly bodies (cp. Mt.24:29; Rev. 6:13).<br>⇒ The place above and beyond the physical dimension of being where God's presence is fully manifested. In modern language "the above and beyond" is another dimension of being entirely; it is the spiritual world, another dimension or world where beings exist. It is a spiritual world where God's presence is fully manifested and where Christ and His followers live awaiting the glorious day of redemption. That glorious day of redemption is the day when God will take the imperfect heavens and earth (the physical dimension) and transform them into the new heavens and earth (the spiritual and eternal dimension). (See POSB note—2 Peter 3:8-10, esp. POSB notes—2 Peter 3:11-14 for more discussion.) |
| **#1916<br>Heaviness**<br><br>Heaviness–KJV<br>Sorrow–NASB<br>Sorrow–NIV<br>Sorrow–NKJV<br>Sorrow–NLT<br><br>**POSB<br>REFERENCE**<br>(Rom.9:1-3; esp. v.2)<br>Note 1, point 2 | λύπη = *lupë*<br>Pronunciation: [loo'-pay]<br>Parsing (part of speech): noun<br>    Case—nominative<br>    Gender—feminine<br>    Number—singular<br>    Stem or root—from λύπη, ης<br>Concordance References:<br>⇒ Strong's #3077 lupë<br>⇒ NIV #3383 lupë<br>⇒ NASB #3077 lupë<br><br>**Romans 9:2**<br>That I have great **heaviness** and continual sorrow in my heart. [KJV]<br>That I have great **sorrow** and unceasing grief in my heart. [NASB]<br>I have great **sorrow** and unceasing anguish in my heart. [NIV]<br>That I have great **sorrow** and continual grief in my heart. [NKJV]<br>My heart is filled with bitter **sorrow** and unending grief [NLT]<br>ὅτι λύπη μοί ἐστι μεγάλη, καὶ ἀδιάλειπτος ὀδύνη τῇ καρδίᾳ μου. [GNS]<br>ὅτι λύπη μοί ἐστιν μεγάλη καὶ ἀδιάλειπτος ὀδύνη τῇ καρδίᾳ μου. [GNT] | Grief, sorrow, heaviness; mourning; pain; reluctantly; with regret.<br><br>**Practical Application**<br>Just how deeply Paul's heart was distressed over his kinsmen is clearly seen in the description of his heart.<br>"I have great heaviness" (*lupë*): pain, grief, mourning. |
| **#1917<br>Heaviness**<br><br>Heaviness–KJV<br>Distressed–NASB<br>Suffer grief–NIV<br>Grieved–NKJV<br>Endure–NLT<br><br>**POSB<br>REFERENCE**<br>(1 Pt.1:6)<br>Note 1, point 2 | λυπηθέντες = *lupëthentes*<br>Pronunciation: [loo-pay'-then-tehs]<br>Parsing (part of speech): verb<br>    Mood—participle<br>    Tense—aorist<br>    Voice—passive<br>    Case—nominative<br>    Gender—masculine<br>    Person—2nd person<br>    Number—plural<br>    Stem or root—from λυπέω<br>Concordance References:<br>⇒ Strong's #3076 lupeö<br>⇒ NIV #3382 lupeö<br>⇒ NASB #3076 lupeö<br><br>**1 Peter 1:6**<br>Wherein ye greatly rejoice, though now for a season, if need be, ye are in **heaviness** through manifold temptations: [KJV]<br>In this you greatly rejoice, even though now for a little while, if necessary, you have been **distressed** by various trials, [NASB]<br>In this you greatly rejoice, though now for a little | To suffer grief, heaviness; to be distressed, sorrowful; to be hurt; to be made sorry; to be sad; to be grieving; to suffer sorrow, stress, pressure, and mental anguish.<br><br>**Practical Application**<br>Trials and temptations cause a heaviness within us. We all know what it is to feel heavy and weighed down with grief; to suffer stress and pressure; to be in mental anguish, wondering, questioning, and suffering under the weight of trial or temptation. |

# PRACTICAL WORD STUDIES
## in the NEW TESTAMENT

| ENGLISH WORD | GREEK WORD AND VERSE | THE WORD MEANS... |
|---|---|---|
| | while you may have had to **suffer grief** in all kinds of trials. [NIV]<br><br>In this you greatly rejoice, though now for a little while, if need be, you have been **grieved** by various trials, [NKJV]<br><br>So be truly glad! There is wonderful joy ahead, even though it is necessary for you to **endure** many trials for a while. [NLT]<br><br>ἐν ᾧ ἀγαλλιᾶσθε ὀλίγον ἄρτι, εἰ δέον ἐστί, **λυπηθέντες** ἐν ποικίλοις πειρασμοῖς, [GNS]<br><br>ἐν ᾧ ἀγαλλιᾶσθε, ὀλίγον ἄρτι εἰ δέον [ἐστὶν] **λυπηθέντες** ἐν ποικίλοις πειρασμοῖς, [GNT] | |
| **#1918**<br>**Heed**<br><br>Heed–KJV<br>Pay...attention to–NASB<br>Pay...attention...to–NIV<br>Heed–NKJV<br>Listen...to–NLT<br><br>**POSB REFERENCE**<br>(Heb.2:1)<br>Note 1 | προσέχειν = *prosechein*<br>Pronunciation: [pros-ekh'-een]<br>Parsing (part of speech): verb<br>    Mood—infinitive<br>    Tense—present<br>    Voice—active<br>    Stem or root—from προσέχω<br>Concordance References:<br>  ⇒ Strong's #4337 prosechō<br>  ⇒ NIV #4668 prosechō<br>  ⇒ NASB #4337 prosechō<br><br>**Hebrews 2:1**<br>Therefore we ought to give the more earnest **heed** to the things which we have heard, lest at any time we should let them slip. [KJV]<br><br>For this reason we must **pay** much closer **attention to** what we have heard, lest we drift away from it. [NASB]<br><br>We must **pay** more careful **attention**, therefore, **to** what we have heard, so that we do not drift away. [NIV]<br><br>Therefore we must give the more earnest **heed** to the things we have heard, lest we drift away. [NKJV]<br><br>So we must **listen** very carefully **to** the truth we have heard, or we may drift away from it. [NLT]<br><br>ιὰ τοῦτο δεῖ περισσοτέρως ἡμᾶς **προσέχειν** τοῖς ἀκουσθεῖσι, μή ποτε παραρρυῶμεν. [GNS]<br><br>Διὰ τοῦτο δεῖ περισσοτέρως **προσέχειν** ἡμᾶς τοῖς ἀκουσθεῖσιν, μήποτε παραρρυῶμεν. [GNT] | To pay attention to; to heed; to listen to; to listen very carefully; to be careful; to be on guard; to consider carefully; to keep watch over.<br><br>**Practical Application**<br>Note how intense the warning is: we must *give heed to* the gospel. We must *give more earnest heed to* the gospel. We are to pay the utmost attention to the gospel of salvation:<br>⇒ to listen more closely than ever before.<br>⇒ to pay more attention than ever before. |
| **#1919**<br>**Heeded**<br><br>Gave heed–KJV<br>Giving attention–NASB<br>Paid close attention–NIV<br>Heeded–NKJV<br>Listened intently–NLT<br><br>**POSB REFERENCE**<br>(Acts 8:6)<br>Note 2, point 2 | προσεῖχον = *proseichon*<br>Pronunciation: [pros-eekh'-on]<br>Parsing (part of speech): verb<br>    Mood—indicative<br>    Tense—imperfect<br>    Voice—active<br>    Person—3rd person<br>    Number—plural<br>    Stem or root—from προσέχω<br>Concordance References:<br>  ⇒ Strong's #4337 prosechō<br>  ⇒ NIV #4668 prosechō<br>  ⇒ NASB #4337 prosechō<br><br>**Acts 8:6**<br>And the people with one accord **gave heed** unto those things which Philip spake, hearing and seeing the miracles which he did. [KJV]<br><br>And the multitudes with one accord were **giving attention** to what was said by Philip, as they heard and saw the signs which he was performing. [NASB]<br><br>When the crowds heard Philip and saw the miraculous signs he did, they all **paid close attention** to what he said. [NIV]<br><br>And the multitudes with one accord **heeded** the things spoken by Philip, hearing and seeing the miracles which he did. [NKJV]<br><br>Crowds **listened intently** to what he had to say because of the miracles he did. [NLT]<br><br>**προσεῖχον** τέ οἱ ὄχλοι τοῖς λεγομένοις ὑπὸ τοῦ Φιλίππου ὁμοθυμαδὸν, ἐν τῷ ἀκούειν αὐτοὺς καὶ βλέπειν τὰ σημεῖα ἃ ἐποίει. [GNS]<br><br>**προσεῖχον** δὲ οἱ ὄχλοι τοῖς λεγομένοις ὑπὸ τοῦ Φιλίππου ὁμοθυμαδὸν ἐν τῷ ἀκούειν αὐτοὺς καὶ βλέπειν τὰ σημεῖα ἃ ἐποίει· [GNT] | To pay close attention; to give attention; to listen intently; to consider carefully; to follow; to keep watch over.<br><br>**Practical Application**<br>The believer must heed; must keep his mind and heart upon the message. |

## PRACTICAL WORD STUDIES
### in the NEW TESTAMENT

| ENGLISH WORD | GREEK WORD AND VERSE | THE WORD MEANS... |
|---|---|---|
| **#1920**<br>**Held Prisoners**<br><br>Kept under–KJV<br>Kept in custody–NASB<br>**Held prisoners–NIV**<br>Kept under guard–NKJV<br>Kept in protective custody–NLT<br><br>**POSB REFERENCE**<br>(Gal.3:23-25; esp. v.23)<br>Note 1 | ἐφρουρούμεθα = ephrouroumetha<br>Pronunciation: [eh-froo-roo'-meh-tha]<br>Parsing (part of speech): verb<br>    Mood—indicative<br>    Tense—imperfect<br>    Voice—passive<br>    Person—1st person<br>    Number—plural<br>    Stem or root—from φρουρέω<br>Concordance References:<br>  ⇒ Strong's #5432 phroureō<br>  ⇒ NIV #5864 phroureō<br>  ⇒ NASB #5432 phroureō<br><br>**Galatians 3:23**<br>But before faith came, we were **kept under** the law, shut up unto the faith which should afterwards be revealed. [KJV]<br>But before faith came, we were **kept in custody** under the law, being shut up to the faith which was later to be revealed. [NASB]<br>Before this faith came, we were **held prisoners** by the law, locked up until faith should be revealed. [NIV]<br>But before faith came, we were **kept under guard** by the law, kept for the faith which would afterward be revealed. [NKJV]<br>Until faith in Christ was shown to us as the way of becoming right with God, we were guarded by the law. We were **kept in protective custody**, so to speak, until we could put our faith in the coming Savior. [NLT]<br>Πρὸ τοῦ δὲ ἐλθεῖν τὴν πίστιν, ὑπὸ νόμον **ἐφρουρούμεθα** συγκλειόμενοι εἰς τὴν μέλλουσαν πίστιν ἀποκαλυφθῆναι, [GNS]<br>Πρὸ τοῦ δὲ ἐλθεῖν τὴν πίστιν ὑπὸ νόμον **ἐφρουρούμεθα** συγκλειόμενοι εἰς τὴν μέλλουσαν πίστιν ἀποκαλυφθῆναι, [GNT] | To be held prisoner; kept under; kept in protective custody; to keep watch over; to be guarded, kept in custody, imprisoned, held in bondage.<br><br>**Practical Application**<br>Very simply, the law shuts man up under sin; it imprisons and holds man in bondage to sin. How?<br>1. The law shows man exactly where he fails—exactly where he comes short. There is no question about it: the law said to do this, but the man did that. He did not do this. The failure is clearly spelled out, just as clearly as a speed limit sign spells out the violation of the speeder.<br>2. The law accuses and condemns man. As soon as a person violates the law, the law charges him. The law is in black and white, written down, so there is no question about it's having been broken. Therefore, it preys upon the man's mind, cuts and convicts his heart. Guilt and conviction take over, troubling and vexing the man to varying degrees, all dependent on the seriousness of the violation.<br>3. The law has no life and no power to deliver man from the punishment due him for his violation. This is the whole point: the law reveals the violation and condemns man; it imprisons him. The law does not deliver man; it condemns man to bondage. It continues and continues to point out man's sins and failures. And the case of the law is endless: its finger of accusation points out the man's failure every time he violates it. The bondage to the law is perpetual. |
| **#1921**<br>**Hell**<br><br>**Hell–KJV**<br>**Hell–NASB**<br>**Hell–NIV**<br>**Hell–NKJV**<br>**Hell–NLT**<br><br>**POSB REFERENCE**<br>(Mt.5:22)<br>*Deeper Study #2* | γέενναν = geennan<br>Pronunciation: [gheh'-en-nahn]<br>Parsing (part of speech): noun<br>    Case—accusative<br>    Gender—feminine<br>    Number—singular<br>    Stem or root—from γέεννα, ης<br>Concordance References:<br>  ⇒ Strong's #1067 geenna<br>  ⇒ NIV #1147 geenna<br>  ⇒ NASB #1067 geenna<br><br>**Matthew 5:22**<br>But I say unto you, That whosoever is angry with his brother without a cause shall be in danger of the judgment: and whosoever shall say to his brother, Raca, shall be in danger of the council: but whosoever shall say, Thou fool, shall be in danger of **hell** fire. [KJV]<br>"But I say to you that everyone who is angry with his brother shall be guilty before the court; and whoever shall say to his brother, 'Raca,' shall be guilty before the supreme court; and whoever shall say, 'You fool,' shall be guilty enough to go into the fiery **hell**. [NASB]<br>But I tell you that anyone who is angry with his brother will be subject to judgment. Again, anyone who says to his brother, 'Raca,' is answerable to the Sanhedrin. But anyone who says, 'You fool!' will be in danger of the fire of **hell**. [NIV]<br>But I say to you that whoever is angry with his brother without a cause shall be in danger of the judgment. And whoever says to his brother, 'Raca!' shall be in danger of the council. But whoever says, 'You fool!' shall be in danger of **hell** fire. [NKJV]<br>But I say, if you are angry with someone, you are sub- | Hell; the literal, real place set aside for those who die eternally lost without Christ.<br><br>**Practical Application**<br>The word (*geennan*) is used twelve times in the New Testament, and in every case it is spoken by Jesus except in the Epistle of James. It illustrates the terrible truth of the second death, of man's final separation from God. Jesus pointed to the burning, repulsive rubbish dump outside the city limits of Jerusalem and said that it was exactly what hell was like. The dump was called Gehenna. It was in the Valley of Hinnom which served as a public incinerator. Hanging over it was a layer of thick, smoldering smoke arising from what seemed to be an eternal flame. The smell and filth became a breeding cesspool for a loathsome worm that was difficult to kill (Mark 9:44). Thus, Jesus found in Gehenna a description of just what it means to be separated from God eternally and to die the second death. |

## PRACTICAL WORD STUDIES
### in the NEW TESTAMENT

| ENGLISH WORD | GREEK WORD AND VERSE | THE WORD MEANS... |
|---|---|---|
| | ject to judgment! If you say to your friend, 'You idiot,' you are in danger of being brought before the court. And if you curse someone, you are in danger of the fires of **hell**. [NLT]<br><br>ἐγὼ δὲ λέγω ὑμῖν ὅτι πᾶς ὁ ὀργιζόμενος τῷ ἀδελφῷ αὐτοῦ εἰκῇ ἔνοχος ἔσται τῇ κρίσει· ὃς δ᾽ ἂν εἴπῃ τῷ ἀδελφῷ αὐτοῦ, ῥακά, ἔνοχος ἔσται τῷ συνεδρίῳ· ὃς δ᾽ ἂν εἴπῃ, Μωρέ, ἔνοχος ἔσται εἰς τὴν **γέενναν** τοῦ πυρός. [GNS]<br><br>ἐγὼ δὲ λέγω ὑμῖν ὅτι πᾶς ὁ ὀργιζόμενος τῷ ἀδελφῷ αὐτοῦ ἔνοχος ἔσται τῇ κρίσει· ὃς δ᾽ ἂν εἴπῃ τῷ ἀδελφῷ αὐτοῦ, Ῥακά, ἔνοχος ἔσται τῷ συνεδρίῳ· ὃς δ᾽ ἂν εἴπῃ, Μωρέ, ἔνοχος ἔσται εἰς τὴν **γέενναν** τοῦ πυρός. [GNT] | |
| **#1922**<br>**Hell**<br><br>**Hell**–KJV<br>Hades–NASB<br>**Hell**–NIV<br>Hades–NKJV<br>The place of the dead–NLT<br><br>**POSB REFERENCE**<br>(Lk.16:23)<br>*Deeper Study* #3 | ᾅδη = hadë<br>Pronunciation: [hah'-day]<br>Parsing (part of speech): noun<br>    Case—dative<br>    Gender—masculine<br>    Number—singular<br>    Stem or root—from ᾅδης, ου<br>Concordance References:<br>  ⇒ Strong's #86 hadës<br>  ⇒ NIV #87 hadës<br>  ⇒ NASB #86 hadës<br><br>**Luke 16:23**<br>And in **hell** he lift up his eyes, being in torments, and seeth Abraham afar off, and Lazarus in his bosom. [KJV]<br>"And in **Hades** he lifted up his eyes, being in torment, and saw Abraham far away, and Lazarus in his bosom. [NASB]<br>In **hell**, where he was in torment, he looked up and saw Abraham far away, with Lazarus by his side. [NIV]<br>And being in torments in **Hades**, he lifted up his eyes and saw Abraham afar off, and Lazarus in his bosom. [NKJV]<br>And his soul went to **the place of the dead**. There, in torment, he saw Lazarus in the far distance with Abraham. [NLT]<br><br>καὶ ἐν τῷ **ᾅδῃ** ἐπάρας τοὺς ὀφθαλμοὺς αὐτοῦ, ὑπάρχων ἐν βασάνοις, ὁρᾷ τὸν Ἀβραὰμ ἀπὸ μακρόθεν, καὶ Λάζαρον ἐν τοῖς κόλποις αὐτοῦ. [GNS]<br><br>καὶ ἐν τῷ **ᾅδῃ** ἐπάρας τοὺς ὀφθαλμοὺς αὐτοῦ, ὑπάρχων ἐν βασάνοις, ὁρᾷ Ἀβραὰμ ἀπὸ μακρόθεν καὶ Λάζαρον ἐν τοῖς κόλποις αὐτοῦ. [GNT] | Hades, hell, the place of the dead, the place of final and eternal punishment. The Greek word hell is the same as the Hebrew word Sheol (see POSB *Deeper Study* #3—Genesis 37:35).<br><br>**Practical Application**<br>The picture of hell revealed by Jesus is that of the other world: the unseen world, the spiritual world, the spiritual dimension of being.<br>Jesus says that hell is a place which is divided into two huge areas or sections or compartments. The two areas are separated by a great gulf that is impassable (Luke 16:26). One area is the place of sorrow (Luke 16:23-24, 28). The other area is the place of Paradise where believers go. To say that a person is dead is to say that one is in hades, in the other world. |
| **#1923**<br>**Hell**<br><br>**Hell**–KJV<br>Hades–NASB<br>Grave–NIV<br>Hades–NKJV<br>Dead–NLT<br><br>**POSB REFERENCE**<br>(Acts 2:25-28; esp. v.27)<br>Note 1, point 2b<br><br>See also POSB REF:<br>(Acts 2:27)<br>*Deeper Study* #1 | ᾅδην = hadën<br>Pronunciation: [hah'-dane]<br>Parsing (part of speech): noun<br>    Case—accusative<br>    Gender—masculine<br>    Number—singular<br>    Stem or root—from ᾅδης, ου<br>Concordance References:<br>  ⇒ Strong's #86 hadës<br>  ⇒ NIV #87 hadës<br>  ⇒ NASB #86 hadës<br><br>**Acts 2:27**<br>Because thou wilt not leave my soul in **hell**, neither wilt thou suffer thine Holy One to see corruption. [KJV]<br>Because Thou wilt not abandon my soul to **Hades**, Nor ALLOW Thy Holy One to UNDERGO DECAY. [NASB]<br>Because you will not abandon me to the **grave**, nor will you let your Holy One see decay. [NIV]<br>For You will not leave my soul in **Hades**, Nor will You allow Your Holy One to see corruption. [NKJV]<br>For you will not leave my soul among the **dead** or allow your Holy One to rot in the grave. [NLT]<br><br>ὅτι οὐκ ἐγκαταλείψεις τὴν ψυχήν μου εἰς **ᾅδου**, οὐδὲ δώσεις τὸν ὅσιόν σου ἰδεῖν διαφθοράν. [GNS]<br><br>ὅτι οὐκ ἐγκαταλείψεις τὴν ψυχήν μου εἰς **ᾅδην** οὐδὲ δώσεις τὸν ὅσιόν σου ἰδεῖν διαφθοράν. [GNT] | Grave, hell, hades, dead; the place of death.<br><br>**Practical Application**<br>Jesus revealed that the grave or hell is the other world, that is, the unseen world, the spiritual dimension of being (see POSB *Deeper Study* #3—Luke 16:23). Jesus said that hell (the other world) was divided into two huge areas or sections. The two areas are separated by a great gulf that is impassable (Luke 16:26). One area is the place of sorrow (Luke 16:23-24, 28), and the other area is the place of paradise where believers go. To say that a person is dead is to say that he is in hell or in the other world. |

# PRACTICAL WORD STUDIES
## in the NEW TESTAMENT

| ENGLISH WORD | GREEK WORD AND VERSE | THE WORD MEANS... |
|---|---|---|
| **#1924**<br>**Help**<br><br>Ministered–KJV<br>Minister–NASB<br>Take care–NIV<br>Ministered–NKJV<br>**Help–NLT**<br><br>**POSB**<br>**REFERENCE**<br>(Philip.2:25)<br>Note 1, point 5 | λειτουργὸν = leitourgon<br>Pronunciation: [li-toorg-on']<br>Parsing (part of speech): noun<br>    Case—accusative<br>    Gender—masculine<br>    Number—singular<br>Stem or root—from λειτουργός, οῦ<br>Concordance References:<br>  ⇒ Strong's #3011 leitourgos<br>  ⇒ NIV #3313 leitourgos<br>  ⇒ NASB #3011 leitourgos<br><br>**Philip. 2:25**<br>Yet I supposed it necessary to send to you Epaphroditus, my brother, and companion in labour, and fellow soldier, but your messenger, and he that **ministered** to my wants. [KJV]<br>But I thought it necessary to send to you Epaphroditus, my brother and fellow worker and fellow soldier, who is also your messenger and **minister** to my need; [NASB]<br>But I think it is necessary to send back to you Epaphroditus, my brother, fellow worker and fellow soldier, who is also your messenger, whom you sent to **take care** of my needs. [NIV]<br>Yet I considered it necessary to send to you Epaphroditus, my brother, fellow worker, and fellow soldier, but your messenger and the one who **ministered** to my need; [NKJV]<br>Meanwhile, I thought I should send Epaphroditus back to you. He is a true brother, a faithful worker, and a courageous soldier. And he was your messenger to **help** me in my need. [NLT]<br>ἀναγκαῖον δὲ ἡγησάμην Ἐπαφρόδιτον τὸν ἀδελφὸν καὶ συνεργὸν καὶ συστρατιώτην μου, ὑμῶν δὲ ἀπόστολον, καὶ **λειτουργὸν** τῆς χρείας μου, πέμψαι πρὸς ὑμᾶς· [GNS]<br>Ἀναγκαῖον δὲ ἡγησάμην Ἐπαφρόδιτον τὸν ἀδελφὸν καὶ συνεργὸν καὶ συστρατιώτην μου, ὑμῶν δὲ ἀπόστολον καὶ **λειτουργὸν** τῆς χρείας μου, πέμψαι πρὸς ὑμᾶς, [GNT] | To take care; to minister; to help; to be a servant.<br><br>**Practical Application**<br>Epaphroditus was a very special minister (*leitourgon*). William Barclay points out that this word would have great meaning to the Greek minds of the Philippian church. The word (*leitourgon*) was a great word and was used only of great men. The title was bestowed only upon great benefactors, men who loved their city, culture, arts, or sports so much that they gave huge sums of money to support these functions. The person was looked upon as a great servant or minister given over to his cause. (*The Letters to the Phillipians, Colossians, and Thessalonians*, p.61.) Paul is here bestowing the great title of minister (*leitourgon*) upon Epaphroditus. Epaphroditus was an extraordinary minister of God who ministered to Paul's needs. He was not a quitter! He was not a coward! |
| **#1925**<br>**Help**<br><br>Succour–KJV<br>Come to the aid–NASB<br>**Help–NIV**<br>Aid–NKJV<br>**Help–NLT**<br><br>**POSB**<br>**REFERENCE**<br>(Heb 2:17-18, esp. v.18)<br>Note 2, point 4 | βοηθῆσαι = boëthësai<br>Pronunciation: [bo-ay-thay'-sah-ee]<br>Parsing (part of speech): verb<br>    Mood—infinitive<br>    Tense—aorist<br>    Voice—active<br>Stem or root—from βοηθέω<br>Concordance References:<br>  ⇒ Strong's #997 boëtheö<br>  ⇒ NIV #1070 boëtheö<br>  ⇒ NASB #997 boëtheö<br><br>**Hebrews 2:18**<br>For in that he himself hath suffered being tempted, he is able to **succour** them that are tempted. [KJV]<br>For since He Himself was tempted in that which He has suffered, He is able to **come to the aid** of those who are tempted. [NASB]<br>Because he himself suffered when he was tempted, he is able to **help** those who are being tempted. [NIV]<br>For in that He Himself has suffered, being tempted, He is able to **aid** those who are tempted. [NKJV]<br>Since he himself has gone through suffering and temptation, he is able to **help** us when we are being tempted. [NLT]<br>ἐν ᾧ γὰρ πέπονθεν αὐτὸς πειρασθείς, δύναται τοῖς πειραζομένοις **βοηθῆσαι**. [GNS]<br>ἐν ᾧ γὰρ πέπονθεν αὐτὸς πειρασθείς, δύναται τοῖς πειραζομένοις **βοηθῆσαι**. [GNT] | To help; to succor; to come to the aid. It means to relieve, assist; to be so eager to help that one runs to the cry of a person.<br><br>**Practical Application**<br>Jesus Christ became the High Priest so that He could help man when he faces the trials and temptations of life.<br>What a picture of Jesus Christ! He has heard our cry in all of our suffering and pain, trial and temptation; and He has run to help and deliver us. Just think! He has been made like us in order to feel with us and deliver us. He has become the perfect High Priest. He needed to do this in order to experience every situation, condition, and trial of man. He experienced the most humiliating experiences imaginable. He experienced...<br>• being born to an unwed mother (Matthew 1:18-19).<br>• being born in a stable, the worst of conditions (Luke 2:7).<br>• being born to poor parents (Luke 2:24).<br>• having his life threatened as a baby (Matthew 2:13f).<br>• being the cause of unimaginable sorrow (Matthew 2:16f).<br>• having to be moved and shifted about as a baby (Matthew 2:13f).<br>• being reared in a despicable place, |

## PRACTICAL WORD STUDIES
### in the NEW TESTAMENT

| ENGLISH WORD | GREEK WORD AND VERSE | THE WORD MEANS... |
|---|---|---|
| | | Nazareth (Luke 2:39).<br>• having His father die during His youth (see POSB note, pt. 3—Matthew 13:53-58).<br>• having to support His mother and brothers and sisters (see POSB note, pt. 3—Matthew 13:53-58).<br>• having no home, not even a place to lay His head (Matthew 8:20; Luke 9:58).<br>• being hated and opposed by religionists (Mark 14:1-2).<br>• being charged with insanity (Mark 3:21).<br>• being charged with demon possession (Mark 3:22).<br>• being opposed by His own family (Mark 3:31-32).<br>• being rejected, hated, and opposed by listeners (Matthew 13:53-58; Luke 4:28-29).<br>• being betrayed by a close friend (Mark 14:10-11, 18).<br>• being left alone, rejected, and forsaken by all of His friends (Mark 14:50).<br>• being tried before the high court of the land on the charge of treason (John 18:33).<br>• being executed by crucifixion, the worst possible death (John 19:16f).<br>And Jesus Christ suffered so much more, but the point to note is this: in each of these experiences His suffering reached the depth of humiliation. Christ stooped to the lowest point of human experience in every condition in order to become the *Perfect Sympathizer* (Savior). This is the reason He can now identify with and feel for any person's circumstances. No person ever comes close to the depth of suffering and humiliation He bore. Jesus Christ can succor—help, feel for, care for, and look after—every person no matter his condition, trial, or temptation. |
| #1926<br>**Help That Person Back Onto The Right Path**<br><br>Restore–KJV<br>Restore–NASB<br>Restore–NIV<br>Restore–NKJV<br>Help that person back onto the right path–NLT<br><br>**POSB REFERENCE**<br>(Gal.6:1-5; esp. v.1)<br>Introduction | καταρτίζετε = *katartizete*<br>Pronunciation: [kat-ar-tidz'-eh-teh]<br>Parsing (part of speech): verb<br>  Mood—imperative<br>  Tense—present<br>  Voice—active<br>  Person—2nd person<br>  Number—plural<br>  Stem or root—from καταρτίζω<br>Concordance References:<br>  ⇒ Strong's #2675 katartizō<br>  ⇒ NIV #2936 katartizō<br>  ⇒ NASB #2675 katartizō<br><br>**Galatians 6:1**<br>Brethren, if a man be overtaken in a fault, ye which are spiritual, **restore** such an one in the spirit of meekness; considering thyself, lest thou also be tempted. [KJV]<br>Brethren, even if a man is caught in any trespass, you who are spiritual, **restore** such a one in a spirit of gentleness; each one looking to yourself, lest you too be tempted. [NASB]<br>Brothers, if someone is caught in a sin, you who are spiritual should **restore** him gently. But watch yourself, or you also may be tempted. [NIV]<br>Brethren, if a man is overtaken in any trespass, you who *are* spiritual **restore** such a one in a spirit of gentleness, considering yourself lest you also be tempted. [NKJV]<br>Dear brothers and sisters, if another Christian is overcome by some sin, you who are godly should gently and | Restore; help that person back onto the right path; reinstate; reestablish; recall; reintroduce; replace; rebuild.<br><br>**Practical Application**<br>When a brother is caught in sin and slips and falls, what should be done? Scripture is clear: Christian brothers are to help that person back onto the right path. It (*katartizete*) is a word that is used for setting a broken arm or leg or for mending nets or for cutting some growth out of a body (William Barclay. *The Letters to the Galatians and Ephesians*, p.58). Believers are to help the brother:<br>• set him right<br>• restore him<br>• help cut the sin out<br>• mend him<br>• lead him back<br><br>However, there is a right way and a wrong way to help the fallen brother. This is the point that is being stressed and that is desperately needed by believers and the church. All believers are mere men of like passions with all other men, and there are always some being overtaken by sin. This, of course, means that we need to constantly stay alert and available to fallen brothers. |

# PRACTICAL WORD STUDIES
## in the New Testament

| ENGLISH WORD | GREEK WORD AND VERSE | THE WORD MEANS... |
|---|---|---|
| | humbly **help that person back onto the right path**. And be careful not to fall into the same temptation yourself. [NLT]<br>Ἀδελφοί, ἐὰν καὶ προληφθῇ ἄνθρωπος ἔν τινι παραπτώματι, ὑμεῖς οἱ πνευματικοὶ **καταρτίζετε** τὸν τοιοῦτον ἐν πνεύματι πραότητος, σκοπῶν σεαυτὸν, μὴ καὶ σὺ πειρασθῇς. [GNS]<br>Ἀδελφοί, ἐὰν καὶ προλημφθῇ ἄνθρωπος ἔν τινι παραπτώματι, ὑμεῖς οἱ πνευματικοὶ **καταρτίζετε** τὸν τοιοῦτον ἐν πνεύματι πραΰτητος, σκοπῶν σεαυτόν μὴ καὶ σὺ πειρασθῇς. [GNT] | |
| **#1927**<br>**Help Them**<br><br>Distributing–KJV<br>Contributing–NASB<br>Share with–NIV<br>Distributing–NKJV<br>**Help them**–NLT<br><br>**POSB**<br>**REFERENCE**<br>(Rom.12:13)<br>Note 4, point 1 | κοινωνοῦντες = *koinōnountes*<br>Pronunciation: [koy-no-noon'-tehs]<br>Parsing (part of speech): verb<br>    Mood—participle (imperative sense)<br>    Tense—present<br>    Voice—active<br>    Case—nominative<br>    Gender—masculine<br>    Person—2nd person<br>    Number—plural<br>    Stem or root—from κοινωνέω<br>Concordance References:<br>  ⇒ Strong's #2841 koinōneō<br>  ⇒ NIV #3125 koinōneō<br>  ⇒ NASB #2841 koinōneō<br><br>**Romans 12:13**<br>**Distributing** to the necessity of saints; given to hospitality. [KJV]<br>**Contributing** to the needs of the saints, practicing hospitality. [NASB]<br>**Share with** God's people who are in need. Practice hospitality. [NIV]<br>**Distributing** to the needs of the saints, given to hospitality. [NKJV]<br>When God's children are in need, be the one to **help them** out. And get into the habit of inviting guests home for dinner or, if they need lodging, for the night. [NLT]<br>ταῖς χρείαις τῶν ἁγίων **κοινωνοῦντες**· τὴν φιλοξενίαν διώκοντες. [GNS]<br>ταῖς χρείαις τῶν ἁγίων **κοινωνοῦντες**, τὴν φιλοξενίαν διώκοντες. [GNT] | To share; to help; to contribute; to give.<br><br>**Practical Application**<br>The believer is to meet the needs of people unselfishly. The believer is to give generously, to share with those in need. He is to "help them" (*koinōnountes*), that is, to give and share in order to meet their needs. |
| **#1928**<br>**Helped–**<br>**Helper**<br><br>Succourer–KJV<br>**Helper**–NASB<br>**Great help**–NIV<br>**Helper**–NKJV<br>**Helped**–NLT<br><br>**POSB**<br>**REFERENCE**<br>(Rom.16:1-2; esp. v.2)<br>Note 1, point 4b | προστάτις = *prostatis*<br>Pronunciation: [pros-tat'-is]<br>Parsing (part of speech): noun<br>    Case—nominative<br>    Gender—feminine<br>    Number—singular<br>    Stem or root—from προστάτις, ιδος<br>Concordance References:<br>  ⇒ Strong's #4368 prostatis<br>  ⇒ NIV #4706 prostatis<br>  ⇒ NASB #4368 prostatis<br><br>**Romans 16:2**<br>That ye receive her in the Lord, as becometh saints, and that ye assist her in whatsoever business she hath need of you: for she hath been a **succourer** of many, and of myself also. [KJV]<br>That you receive her in the Lord in a manner worthy of the saints, and that you help her in whatever matter she may have need of you; for she herself has also been a **helper** of many, and of myself as well. [NASB]<br>I ask you to receive her in the Lord in a way worthy of the saints and to give her any help she may need from you, for she has been a **great help** to many people, including me. [NIV]<br>That you may receive her in the Lord in a manner worthy of the saints, and assist her in whatever business she has need of you; for indeed she has been a **helper** of many and of myself also. [NKJV] | Great help; succorer; helper; helped; aided.<br><br>**Practical Application**<br>Phoebe had been a "helper" (*prostatis*) to many, including Paul himself. The word means that she protected, helped, looked after, and provided for people. Phoebe was a woman who ministered to the needs of many. Apparently, she helped and looked after the welfare of any who had need. |

# PRACTICAL WORD STUDIES
## in the NEW TESTAMENT

| ENGLISH WORD | GREEK WORD AND VERSE | THE WORD MEANS... |
|---|---|---|
| | Receive her in the Lord, as one who is worthy of high honor. Help her in every way you can, for she has **helped** many in their needs, including me. [NLT]<br><br>ἵνα αὐτὴν προσδέξησθε ἐν Κυρίῳ ἀξίως τῶν ἁγίων, καὶ παραστῆτε αὐτῇ ἐν ᾧ ἂν ὑμῶν χρῄζῃ πράγματι· καὶ γὰρ αὐτὴ **προστάτις** πολλῶν ἐγενήθη, καὶ αὐτοῦ ἐμοῦ. [GNS]<br><br>ἵνα αὐτὴν προσδέξησθε ἐν κυρίῳ ἀξίως τῶν ἁγίων καὶ παραστῆτε αὐτῇ ἐν ᾧ ἂν ὑμῶν χρῄζῃ πράγματι· καὶ γὰρ αὐτὴ **προστάτις** πολλῶν ἐγενήθη καὶ ἐμοῦ αὐτοῦ. [GNT] | |
| **#1929**<br>**Helper**<br><br>Minister–KJV<br>**Helper–NASB**<br>**Helper–NIV**<br>Assistant–NKJV<br>Assistant–NLT<br><br>**POSB REFERENCE**<br>(Acts 13:5-6; esp. v.5)<br>Note 2, point 2 | ὑπηρέτην = *hupëretën*<br>Pronunciation: [hoop-ay-ret'-ayn]<br>Parsing (part of speech): noun<br>    Case—accusative<br>    Gender—masculine<br>    Number—singular<br>    Stem or root—from ὑπηρέτης, ου<br>Concordance References:<br>  ⇒ Strong's #5257 hupëretës<br>  ⇒ NIV #5677 hupëretës<br>  ⇒ NASB #5257 hupëretës<br><br>**Acts 13:5**<br>And when they were at Salamis, they preached the word of God in the synagogues of the Jews: and they had also John to their **minister**. [KJV]<br>And when they reached Salamis, they began to proclaim the word of God in the synagogues of the Jews; and they also had John as their **helper**. [NASB]<br>When they arrived at Salamis, they proclaimed the word of God in the Jewish synagogues. John was with them as their **helper**. [NIV]<br>And when they arrived in Salamis, they preached the word of God in the synagogues of the Jews. They also had John as *their* **assistant**. [NKJV]<br>There, in the town of Salamis, they went to the Jewish synagogues and preached the word of God. (John Mark went with them as their **assistant**.) [NLT]<br><br>καὶ γενόμενοι ἐν Σαλαμῖνι, κατήγγελλον τὸν λόγον τοῦ Θεοῦ ἐν ταῖς συναγωγαῖς τῶν Ἰουδαίων· εἶχον δὲ καὶ Ἰωάννην **ὑπηρέτην**. [GNS]<br><br>καὶ γενόμενοι ἐν Σαλαμῖνι κατήγγελλον τὸν λόγον τοῦ θεοῦ ἐν ταῖς συναγωγαῖς τῶν Ἰουδαίων. εἶχον δὲ καὶ Ἰωάννην **ὑπηρέτην**. [GNT] | Helper, minister, assistant, attendant, servant.<br><br>**Practical Application**<br>Mark was ministering under Barnabas and Paul, being discipled by them—helping, serving, ministering right with them, learning all he could. Apparently he was somewhat younger. |
| **#1930**<br>**Helper**<br><br>Comforter–KJV<br>**Helper–NASB**<br>Counselor–NIV<br>**Helper–NKJV**<br>Counselor–NLT<br><br>**POSB REFERENCE**<br>(Jn.14:16)<br>*Deeper Study* #1 | παράκλητον = *paraklëton*<br>Pronunciation: [par-ak'-lay-ton]<br>Parsing (part of speech): noun<br>    Case—accusative<br>    Gender—masculine<br>    Number—singular<br>    Stem or root—from παράκλητος, ου<br>Concordance References:<br>  ⇒ Strong's #3875 parakletos<br>  ⇒ NIV #4156 parakletos<br>  ⇒ NASB #3875 parakletos<br><br>**John 14:16**<br>And I will pray the Father, and he shall give you another **Comforter**, that he may abide with you for ever; [KJV]<br>"And I will ask the Father, and He will give you another **Helper**, that He may be with you forever; [NASB]<br>And I will ask the Father, and he will give you another **Counselor** to be with you forever—[NIV]<br>And I will pray the Father, and He will give you another **Helper**, that He may abide with you forever—[NKJV]<br>And I will ask the Father, and he will give you another **Counselor**, who will never leave you. [NLT]<br><br>κἀγὼ ἐρωτήσω τὸν πατέρα, καὶ ἄλλον **παράκλητον** δώσει ὑμῖν, μένῃ ἵνα μεθ' ὑμῶν εἰς τὸν αἰῶνα, [GNS]<br><br>κἀγὼ ἐρωτήσω τὸν πατέρα καὶ ἄλλον **παράκλητον** δώσει ὑμῖν, ἵνα μεθ' ὑμῶν εἰς τὸν αἰῶνα ᾖ, [GNT] | Counselor, Comforter, Helper, Intercessor; One called in; One called to the side of another.<br><br>**Practical Application**<br>The purpose is to help in any way possible.<br>1. There is the picture of a friend called in to help a person who is troubled or distressed or confused.<br>2. There is the picture of a commander called in to help a discouraged and dispirited army.<br>3. There is the picture of a lawyer, an advocate called in to help a defendant who needs his case pleaded. There is no one word that can adequately translate *paracletos*. The word that probably comes closest is simply *Helper*. |

# PRACTICAL WORD STUDIES
## in the NEW TESTAMENT

| ENGLISH WORD | GREEK WORD AND VERSE | THE WORD MEANS... |
|---|---|---|
| **#1931**<br>**Helpful**<br><br>Expedient–KJV<br>Profitable–NASB<br>Beneficial–NIV<br>**Helpful–NKJV**<br>Good for you–NLT<br><br>**POSB REFERENCE**<br>(1 Cor.6:12)<br>Note 1, point 1 | συμφέρει = sumpherei<br>Pronunciation: [soom-fer'-eh-ee]<br>Parsing (part of speech): verb<br>    Mood—indicative<br>    Tense—present<br>    Voice—active<br>    Person—3rd person<br>    Number—singular<br>    Stem or root—from συμφέρω<br>Concordance References:<br>  ⇒ Strong's #4851 sumpherö<br>  ⇒ NIV #5237 sumpherö<br>  ⇒ NASB #4851 sumpherö<br><br>**1 Cor. 6:12**<br>All things are lawful unto me, but all things are not **expedient**: all things are lawful for me, but I will not be brought under the power of any. [KJV]<br>All things are lawful for me, but not all things are **profitable**. All things are lawful for me, but I will not be mastered by anything. [NASB]<br>"Everything is permissible for me"—but not everything is **beneficial**. "Everything is permissible for me"—but I will not be mastered by anything. [NIV]<br>All things are lawful for me, but all things are not **helpful**. All things are lawful for me, but I will not be brought under the power of any. [NKJV]<br>You may say, "I am allowed to do anything." But I reply, "Not everything is **good for you**." And even though "I am allowed to do anything," I must not become a slave to anything. [NLT]<br>Πάντα μοι ἔξεστιν, ἀλλ' οὐ πάντα **συμφέρει**· πάντα μοι ἔξεστιν, ἀλλ' οὐκ ἐγὼ ἐξουσιασθήσομαι ὑπό τινος. [GNS]<br>Πάντα μοι ἔξεστιν ἀλλ' οὐ πάντα **συμφέρει**. πάντα μοι ἔξεστιν ἀλλ' οὐκ ἐγὼ ἐξουσιασθήσομαι ὑπό τινος. [GNT] | Beneficial, expedient, useful, helpful, worthwhile, advisable, profitable, good for you.<br><br>**Practical Application**<br>For example, it is helpful or beneficial to eat fish; it is unprofitable to eat poisonous berries. It is advisable to keep active for the sake of the body; it is harmful to lie around and become inactive. Note that doing some activities is lawful, but others are not good and profitable. |
| **#1932**<br>**Helping Others Grow In The Lord**<br><br>Edification–KJV<br>Edification–NASB<br>Strengthening–NIV<br>Edification–NKJV<br>Helping others grow in the Lord–NLT<br><br>**POSB REFERENCE**<br>(1 Cor.14:3)<br>*Deeper Study* #1, point 1 | οἰκοδομήν = oikodomēn<br>Pronunciation: [oy-kod-om-ayn']<br>Parsing (part of speech): noun<br>    Case—accusative<br>    Gender—feminine<br>    Number—singular<br>    Stem or root—from οἰκοδομή, ῆς<br>Concordance References:<br>  ⇒ Strong's #3619 oikodomē<br>  ⇒ NIV #3869 oikodomē<br>  ⇒ NASB #3619 oikodomē<br><br>**1 Cor. 14:3**<br>But he that prophesieth speaketh unto men to **edification**, and exhortation, and comfort. [KJV]<br>But one who prophesies speaks to men for **edification** and exhortation and consolation. [NASB]<br>But everyone who prophesies speaks to men for their **strengthening**, encouragement and comfort. [NIV]<br>But he who prophesies speaks **edification** and exhortation and comfort to men. [NKJV]<br>But one who prophesies is **helping others grow in the Lord**, encouraging and comforting them. [NLT]<br>ὁ δὲ προφητεύων ἀνθρώποις λαλεῖ **οἰκοδομήν** καὶ παράκλησιν καὶ παραμυθίαν. [GNS]<br>ὁ δὲ προφητεύων ἀνθρώποις λαλεῖ **οἰκοδομήν** καὶ παράκλησιν καὶ παραμυθίαν. [GNT] | To strengthen; to build up; to edify; to help others grow in the Lord; to encourage.<br><br>**Practical Application**<br>*Helping others grow in the Lord* (*oikodomēn*) is a construction phrase referring to constructing some building. The first purpose of prophecy is to build up people. |
| **#1933**<br>**Helping The Entire Church** | συμφέρον = sumpheron<br>Pronunciation: [soom-fer'-on]<br>Parsing (part of speech): verb<br>    Mood—participle<br>    Tense—present<br>    Voice—active<br>    Gender—neuter | Common good, edification, profit; help, advantage, benefit, gain.<br><br>**Practical Application**<br>Believers are equipped with spiritual gifts primarily for the *benefit and edification of oth-* |

# PRACTICAL WORD STUDIES
## in the NEW TESTAMENT

| ENGLISH WORD | GREEK WORD AND VERSE | THE WORD MEANS... |
|---|---|---|
| Profit–KJV<br>Common good–NASB<br>Common good–NIV<br>Profit–NKJV<br>**Helping the entire church–NLT**<br><br>**POSB REFERENCE**<br>(1 Cor.12:7)<br>Note 2 | Number—singular<br>Stem or root—from συμφέρω<br>Concordance References:<br>⇒ Strong's #4851 sumpheró<br>⇒ NIV #5237 sumpheró<br>⇒ NASB #4851 sumpheró<br><br>**1 Cor. 12:7**<br>But the manifestation of the Spirit is given to every man to **profit** withal. [KJV]<br>But to each one is given the manifestation of the Spirit for the **common good**. [NASB]<br>Now to each one is given the manifestation of the Spirit is given for the **common good**. [NIV]<br>But the manifestation of the Spirit is given to each one for the **profit** of all: [NKJV]<br>A spiritual gift is given to each of us as a means of **helping the entire church**. [NLT]<br>ἑκάστῳ δὲ δίδοται ἡ φανέρωσις τοῦ Πνεύματος πρὸς τὸ **συμφέρον**. [GNS]<br>ἑκάστῳ δὲ δίδοται ἡ φανέρωσις τοῦ πνεύματος πρὸς τὸ **συμφέρον**. [GNT] | ers, not for themselves. The gifts are not given to believers for their own gratification or for them to revel in a sense of self-importance and super-spirituality. The believer does, of course, profit and benefit from the gift given him, but he is gifted primarily to edify and help others. This is seen in the word "gift." It means to be openly and publicly seen. The gifts of the Spirit are to be openly and publicly used; they are...<br>• to be manifested to the church, that is, used to edify the church.<br>• to be manifested to the world, that is, used to benefit the world (reaching the lost).<br>Note a crucial fact that is not always understood. The gifts of the Spirit are "given to each of us." They are not given only to the educated and outstanding. Every single believer is given some spiritual gift by the Spirit of God, and it is given because it is needed within the church and the world, needed to help in ministering to people and in reaching the lost for Christ. |
| #1934<br>**Helping The Poor**<br><br>Almsdeeds...did–KJV<br>Charity...continually did–NASB<br>**Helping the poor–NIV**<br>Charitable deeds...did–NKJV<br>**Helping the poor–NLT**<br><br>**POSB REFERENCE**<br>(Acts 9:36-39; esp. v.36)<br>Note 2, point 1c | ἐλεημοσυνῶν ἐποίει = eleëmosunön epoiei<br>Pronunciation: [el-eh-ay-mos-oon'-own eh-poy-eh'-ee]<br>Parsing *eleëmosunön* (part of speech): noun<br>  Case—genitive<br>  Gender—feminine<br>  Number—plural<br>  Stem or root—from ἐλεημοσύνη, ης<br>Parsing *epoiei* (part of speech): verb<br>  Mood—indicative<br>  Tense—imperfect<br>  Voice—active<br>  Person—3rd person<br>  Number—singular<br>  Stem or root—from ποιέω<br>Concordance References:<br>⇒ Strong's #1654 + 4160 eleëmosunë poieö<br>⇒ NIV #1797 + 4472 eleëmosunë poieö [helping the poor]<br>⇒ NASB #1654 + 4160 eleëmosunë poieö<br><br>**Acts 9:36**<br>Now there was at Joppa a certain disciple named Tabitha, which by interpretation is called Dorcas: this woman was full of good works and **almsdeeds** which she **did**. [KJV]<br>Now in Joppa there was a certain disciple named Tabitha (which translated in Greek is called Dorcas); this woman was abounding with deeds of kindness and **charity**, which she **continually did**. [NASB]<br>In Joppa there was a disciple named Tabitha (which, when translated, is Dorcas), who was always doing good and **helping the poor**. [NIV]<br>At Joppa there was a certain disciple named Tabitha, which is translated Dorcas. This woman was full of good works and **charitable deeds** which she **did**. [NKJV]<br>There was a believer in Joppa named Tabitha (which in Greek is Dorcas). She was always doing kind things for others and **helping the poor**. [NLT]<br>Ἐν Ἰόππῃ δέ τις ἦν μαθήτρια ὀνόματι Ταβιθά, ἣ διερμηνευομένη λέγεται Δορκάς· αὕτη ἦν πλήρης ἀγαθῶν ἔργων καὶ **ἐλεημοσυνῶν** ὧν **ἐποίει**. [GNS]<br>Ἐν Ἰόππῃ δέ τις ἦν μαθήτρια ὀνόματι Ταβιθά, ἣ διερμηνευομένη λέγεται Δορκάς· αὕτη ἦν πλήρης ἔργων ἀγαθῶν καὶ **ἐλεημοσυνῶν** ὧν **ἐποίει**. [GNT] | To help the poor; to do almsdeeds; to show charity; to give to needy people; to do charitable deeds.<br><br>**Practical Application**<br>The emphasis is that she gave things, gifts which she herself made. |
| #1935<br>**Helpless** | ἐρριμμένοι = errimmenoi<br>Pronunciation: [eh-rim-me'-noi]<br>Parsing (part of speech): verb<br>  Mood—participle<br>  Tense—perfect | To be helpless, hopeless, scattered, downcast; to be cast out, laid low, thrown down, prostrated, dejected and hopeless. |

# Practical Word Studies
## in the New Testament

| ENGLISH WORD | GREEK WORD AND VERSE | THE WORD MEANS... |
|---|---|---|
| Scattered abroad–KJV<br>Downcast–NASB<br>**Helpless–NIV**<br>Scattered–NKJV<br>Didn't know where to go for help–NLT<br><br>**POSB REFERENCE**<br>(Mt.9:36)<br>*Deeper Study #4* | Voice—passive<br>Case—nominative<br>Gender—masculine<br>Number—plural<br>Stem or root—from ῥίπτω and ῥιπτέω<br>Concordance References:<br>⇒ Strong's #4496 hriptö<br>⇒ NIV #4849 hriptö<br>⇒ NASB #4496 hriptö<br><br>**Matthew 9:36**<br>But when he saw the multitudes, he was moved with compassion on them, because they fainted, and were **scattered abroad**, as sheep having no shepherd. [KJV]<br>And seeing the multitudes, He felt compassion for them, because they were distressed and **downcast** like sheep without a shepherd. [NASB]<br>When he saw the crowds, he had compassion on them, because they were harassed and **helpless**, like sheep without a shepherd. [NIV]<br>But when He saw the multitudes, He was moved with compassion for them, because they were weary and **scattered**, like sheep having no shepherd. [NKJV]<br>He felt great pity for the crowds that came, because their problems were so great and they **didn't know where to go for help**. They were like sheep without a shepherd. [NLT]<br>Ἰδὼν δὲ τοὺς ὄχλους, ἐσπλαγχνίσθη περὶ αὐτῶν, ὅτι ἦσαν ἐκλελυμένοι καὶ **ἐρριμμένοι** ὡσεὶ πρόβατα μὴ ἔχοντα ποιμένα. [GNS]<br>Ἰδὼν δὲ τοὺς ὄχλους ἐσπλαγχνίσθη περὶ αὐτῶν, ὅτι ἦσαν ἐσκυλμένοι καὶ **ἐρριμμένοι** ὡσεὶ πρόβατα μὴ ἔχοντα ποιμένα. [GNT] | **Practical Application**<br>Being helpless may come from experiences such as drunkenness, or struggling and fighting within and without, or being so weary that a person is just cast down. It is being prostrated by forces within oneself or laid low by forces outside of oneself. |
| #1936<br>**Helpless**<br><br>Without strength–KJV<br>**Helpless–NASB**<br>Powerless–NIV<br>Without strength–NKJV<br>**Helpless–NLT**<br><br>**POSB REFERENCE**<br>(Romans 5:6-7, esp. v.6)<br>Note 1, point 1 | ἀσθενῶν = asthenön<br>Pronunciation: [as-then-own']<br>Parsing (part of speech): adjective<br>Case—genitive<br>Gender—masculine<br>Number—plural<br>Stem or root—from ἀσθενής, ές<br>Concordance References:<br>⇒ Strong's #772 asthenes<br>⇒ NIV #820 astheneö<br>⇒ NASB #772 asthenes<br><br>**Romans 5:6**<br>For when we were yet **without strength**, in due time Christ died for the ungodly. [KJV]<br>For while we were still **helpless**, at the right time Christ died for the ungodly. [NASB]<br>You see, at just the right time, when we were still **powerless**, Christ died for the ungodly. [NIV]<br>For when we were still **without strength**, in due time Christ died for the ungodly. [NKJV]<br>When we were utterly **helpless**, Christ came at just the right time and died for us sinners. [NLT]<br>ἔτι γὰρ Χριστὸς ὄντων ἡμῶν **ἀσθενῶν**, ἔτι κατὰ καιρὸν ὑπὲρ ἀσεβῶν ἀπέθανε. [GNS]<br>ἔτι γὰρ Χριστὸς ὄντων ἡμῶν **ἀσθενῶν** ἔτι κατὰ καιρὸν ὑπὲρ ἀσεβῶν ἀπέθανεν. [GNT] | Sick; ill; diabled; weak; delicate; helpless; without strength powerless.<br><br>**Practical Application**<br>We were ungodly and without strength, yet Christ died for us. God's great love is seen in this unbelievable act. We were "helpless" (*asthenön*): weak, worthless, useless, helpless, hopeless, destitute, powerless. We were spiritually worthless and useless and unable to help ourselves. |
| #1937<br>**Help–Helps**<br><br>He took–KJV<br>**Help–NASB**<br>**Helps–NIV**<br>Aid–NKJV<br>**Help–NLT** | ἐπιλαμβάνεται = epilambanetai<br>Pronunciation: [ep-ee-lam-ban'-eh-tah-ee]<br>Parsing (part of speech): verb<br>Mood—indicative<br>Tense—present<br>Voice—middle or passive deponent<br>Person—3rd person<br>Number—singular<br>Stem or root—from ἐπιλαμβάνομαι<br>Concordance References:<br>⇒ Strong's #1949 epilambanomai | To help; to take; to lay hold of; to catch; to seize; to take by the hand.<br><br>**Practical Application**<br>Jesus Christ has delivered us from the bondage of the flesh. This tells us a most wonderful truth: Jesus Christ did not only take hold of man's nature, He took hold of man's hand. He took us by the hand to deliver us. The picture is that of love and tender care, of His delivering us |

# PRACTICAL WORD STUDIES
## in the NEW TESTAMENT

| ENGLISH WORD | GREEK WORD AND VERSE | THE WORD MEANS... |
|---|---|---|
| **POSB REFERENCE** (Heb.2:14-16; esp. v.16) Note 1, point 5 | ⇒ NIV #2138 epilambanomai<br>⇒ NASB #1949 epilambanomai<br><br>**Hebrews 2:16**<br>For verily **he took** not on him the nature of angels; but he took on him the seed of Abraham. [KJV]<br>For assuredly He does not give **help** to angels, but He gives help to the descendant of Abraham. [NASB]<br>For surely it is not angels he **helps**, but Abraham's descendants. [NIV]<br>For indeed He does not give **aid** to angels, but He does give aid to the seed of Abraham. [NKJV]<br>We all know that Jesus came to **help** the descendants of Abraham, not to help the angels. [NLT]<br>οὐ γὰρ δήπου ἀγγέλων **ἐπιλαμβάνεται**, ἀλλὰ σπέρματος Ἀβραὰμ **ἐπιλαμβάνεται**, [GNS]<br>οὐ γὰρ δήπου ἀγγέλων **ἐπιλαμβάνεται** ἀλλὰ σπέρματος Ἀβραὰμ **ἐπιλαμβάνεται**. [GNT] | out of the bondages of the flesh and of human nature. Note: it is not angels that He took by the hand, but the seed of Abraham, that is, the spiritual seed of Abraham, those who believe and trust in the Lord Jesus Christ as their Savior. |
| **#1938**<br>**Herald**<br><br>Preacher–KJV<br>Preacher–NASB<br>**Herald–NIV**<br>Preacher–NKJV<br>Preacher–NLT<br><br>**POSB REFERENCE** (1 Tim.2:3-7; esp. v.7) Note 3, point 5 | κῆρυξ = kërux<br>Pronunciation: [kay'-roox]<br>Parsing (part of speech): noun<br>  Case—nominative<br>  Gender—masculine<br>  Number—singular<br>  Stem or root—from κῆρυξ, υκος<br>Concordance References:<br>  ⇒ Strong's #2783 kërux<br>  ⇒ NIV #3061 kërux<br>  ⇒ NASB #2783 kërux<br><br>**1 Tim. 2:7**<br>Whereunto I am ordained a **preacher**, and an apostle, (I speak the truth in Christ, and lie not;) a teacher of the Gentiles in faith and verity. [KJV]<br>And for this I was appointed a **preacher** and an apostle (I am telling the truth, I am not lying) as a teacher of the Gentiles in faith and truth. [NASB]<br>And for this purpose I was appointed a **herald** and an apostle—I am telling the truth, I am not lying—and a teacher of the true faith to the Gentiles. [NIV]<br>For which I was appointed a **preacher** and an apostle—I am speaking the truth in Christ *and* not lying—a teacher of the Gentiles in faith and truth. [NKJV]<br>And I have been chosen—this is the absolute truth—as a **preacher** and apostle to teach the Gentiles about faith and truth. [NLT]<br>εἰς ὃ ἐτέθην ἐγὼ **κῆρυξ** καὶ ἀπόστολος -- ἀλήθειαν λέγω ἐν Χριστῷ, οὐ ψεύδομαι -- διδάσκαλος ἐθνῶν ἐν πίστει καὶ ἀληθείᾳ. [GNS]<br>εἰς ὃ ἐτέθην ἐγὼ **κῆρυξ** καὶ ἀπόστολος, ἀλήθειαν λέγω οὐ ψεύδομαι, διδάσκαλος ἐθνῶν ἐν πίστει καὶ ἀληθείᾳ. [GNT] | Herald, preacher, an ambassador appointed by a king to go forth to proclaim the message of the king.<br><br>**Practical Application**<br>Ministers are ordained or appointed to proclaim the salvation of God. God had appointed Paul to be a "herald" (*kërux*): a preacher, an ambassador who was appointed by a king to go forth to proclaim the message of the king. The minister is a preacher who is sent forth by God to preach the truth about Jesus Christ...<br>• that He is the Mediator between God and men.<br>• that He has given Himself as a ransom for all. |
| **#1939**<br>**Heresies**<br><br>**Heresies–KJV**<br>Factions–NASB<br>Factions–NIV<br>**Heresies–NKJV**<br>Feeling that everyone is wrong except those in your own little group–NLT<br><br>**POSB REFERENCE** (Gal.5:19-21; esp. v.20) Note 2 | αἱρέσεις = haireseis<br>Pronunciation: [ah'ee-res-ee-is]<br>Parsing (part of speech): noun<br>  Case—nominative<br>  Gender—feminine<br>  Number—plural<br>  Stem or root—from αἵρεσις, εως<br>Concordance References:<br>  ⇒ Strong's #139 hairesis<br>  ⇒ NIV #146 hairesis<br>  ⇒ NASB #139 hairesis<br><br>**Galatians 5:20**<br>Idolatry, witchcraft, hatred, variance, emulations, wrath, strife, seditions, **heresies**, [KJV]<br>Idolatry, sorcery, enmities, strife, jealousy, outbursts of anger, disputes, dissensions, **factions**, [NASB]<br>Idolatry and witchcraft; hatred, discord, jealousy, fits | Factions; differences; heresies; feeling that everyone is wrong except in one's own little group; inner circle; non conformists.<br><br>**Practical Application**<br>It is rejecting the fundamental beliefs of God, Christ, the Scriptures, and the church; believing and holding to some teaching other than the truth. |

# Practical Word Studies
## in the New Testament

| ENGLISH WORD | GREEK WORD AND VERSE | THE WORD MEANS... |
|---|---|---|
| | of rage, selfish ambition, dissensions, **factions** [NIV]<br>Idolatry, sorcery, hatred, contentions, jealousies, outbursts of wrath, selfish ambitions, dissensions, **heresies**, [NKJV]<br>Idolatry, participation in demonic activities, hostility, quarreling, jealousy, outbursts of anger, selfish ambition, divisions, the **feeling that everyone is wrong except those in your own little group**, [NLT]<br>εἰδωλολατρία, φαρμακεία, ἔχθραι, ἔρεις, ζῆλοι, θυμοί, ἐριθεῖαι, διχοστασίαι, **αἱρέσεις**, [GNS]<br>εἰδωλολατρία, φαρμακεία, ἔχθραι, ἔρις, ζῆλος, θυμοί, ἐριθεῖαι, διχοστασίαι, **αἱρέσεις**, [GNT] | |
| **#1940**<br>**Heresies**<br><br>**Heresies–KJV**<br>**Heresies–NASB**<br>**Heresies–NIV**<br>**Heresies–NKJV**<br>**Heresies–NLT**<br><br>POSB<br>REFERENCE<br>(2 Pt.2:1)<br>Note 2, point 1 | αἱρέσεις = *haireseis*<br>Pronunciation: [ah'ee-res-ee-is]<br>Parsing (part of speech): noun<br>    Case—accusative<br>    Gender—feminine<br>    Number—plural<br>    Stem or root—from αἵρεσις, εως<br>Concordance References:<br>  ⇒ Strong's #139 hairesis<br>  ⇒ NIV #146 hairesis<br>  ⇒ NASB #139 hairesis<br><br>**2 Peter 2:1**<br>But there were false prophets also among the people, even as there shall be false teachers among you, who privily shall bring in damnable **heresies**, even denying the Lord that bought them, and bring upon themselves swift destruction. [KJV]<br>But false prophets also arose among the people, just as there will also be false teachers among you, who will secretly introduce destructive **heresies**, even denying the Master who bought them, bringing swift destruction upon themselves. [NASB]<br>But there were also false prophets among the people, just as there will be false teachers among you. They will secretly introduce destructive **heresies**, even denying the sovereign Lord who bought them—bringing swift destruction on themselves. [NIV]<br>But there were also false prophets among the people, even as there will be false teachers among you, who will secretly bring in destructive **heresies**, even denying the Lord who bought them, *and* bring on themselves swift destruction. [NKJV]<br>But there were also false prophets in Israel, just as there will be false teachers among you. They will cleverly teach their destructive **heresies** about God and even turn against their Master who bought them. Theirs will be a swift and terrible end. [NLT]<br>Ἐγένοντο δὲ καὶ ψευδοπροφῆται ἐν τῷ λαῷ, ὡς καὶ ἐν ὑμῖν ἔσονται ψευδοδιδάσκαλοι, οἵτινες παρεισάξουσιν **αἱρέσεις** ἀπωλείας, καὶ τὸν ἀγοράσαντα αὐτοὺς δεσπότην ἀρνούμενοι, ἐπάγοντες ἑαυτοῖς ταχινὴν ἀπώλειαν, [GNS]<br>Ἐγένοντο δὲ καὶ ψευδοπροφῆται ἐν τῷ λαῷ, ὡς καὶ ἐν ὑμῖν ἔσονται ψευδοδιδάσκαλοι, οἵτινες παρεισάξουσιν **αἱρέσεις** ἀπωλείας καὶ τὸν ἀγοράσαντα αὐτοὺς δεσπότην ἀρνούμενοι, ἐπάγοντες ἑαυτοῖς ταχινὴν ἀπώλειαν, [GNT] | Heresies, factions, divisions.<br><br>**Practical Application**<br>Scripture says that false teachers secretly introduce or bring in destructive heresies. They teach destructive heresies, but they do not do it openly. They do it deceptively, quietly, secretly, slipping in false doctrine here and there.<br>Note where false teachers teach their destructive heresies. In the church, right among believers. The false teachers are not out in the world, but they are within the church. They have joined the church, and they have been outstanding members long enough to become teachers and preachers within the church. They hold leadership positions from which they can teach their destructive heresies. Note that the word "heresies" (*haireseis*) is plural. What are the heresies being referred to? Any teaching that goes contrary to the Scripture, that is, the Word of God or Bible. This is clearly what is meant, for the exhortation has just been given: "Take heed to the word of prophecy, to the Scripture" (cp. 2 Peter 1:19-21).<br>False teachers shall be destroyed swiftly. Note that they bring destruction upon themselves. They are responsible for their own actions. They do not have to teach false doctrine; they make the choice to teach it. They could teach the truth [the Holy Scriptures], but they make a deliberate choice to teach contrary to what God has said. Therefore, they shall bring swift destruction upon themselves. The idea of swift is both certain and quick. When the judgment comes, there will be no discussion about the matter—no questioning, no leniency, no mercy, no love. There will be pure justice: swift, immediate judgment and destruction. |
| **#1941**<br>**Heretick**<br><br>**Heretick–KJV**<br>Factious–NASB<br>Divisive–NIV<br>Divisive–NKJV<br>Divisions–NLT | αἱρετικὸν = *hairetikon*<br>Pronunciation: [ahee-ret-ee-kon']<br>Parsing (part of speech): adjective<br>    Case—accusative<br>    Gender—masculine<br>    Number—singular<br>    Stem or root—from αἱρετικός, ή, όν<br>Concordance References:<br>  ⇒ Strong's #141 hairetikos<br>  ⇒ NIV #148 hairetikos<br>  ⇒ NASB #141 hairetikos | Divisive, heretic, factious, divisions. The Greek word "heretick" (*hairetikon*) is interesting. It means to take for oneself; to choose for oneself.<br><br>**Practical Application**<br>Therefore, a heretic is a person who chooses what he is to believe. He rejects all authority no matter what it is: God, Christ, the Word of God, the church, man. He himself chooses what he is to believe. He and he alone is his authority; he |

# PRACTICAL WORD STUDIES
## in the New Testament

| ENGLISH WORD | GREEK WORD AND VERSE | THE WORD MEANS... |
|---|---|---|
| **POSB REFERENCE** (Tit.3:10-11; esp. v.10) Note 3 | **Titus 3:10**<br>A man that is an **heretick** after the first and second admonition reject; [KJV]<br>Reject a **factious** man after a first and second warning, [NASB]<br>Warn a **divisive** person once, and then warn him a second time. After that, have nothing to do with him. [NIV]<br>Reject a **divisive** man after the first and second admonition, [NKJV]<br>If anyone is causing **divisions** among you, give a first and second warning. After that, have nothing more to do with that person. [NLT]<br>αἱρετικὸν ἄνθρωπον μετὰ μίαν καὶ δευτέραν νουθεσίαν παραιτοῦ, [GNS]<br>αἱρετικὸν ἄνθρωπον μετὰ μίαν καὶ δευτέραν νουθεσίαν παραιτοῦ, [GNT] | and he alone determines truth—what is and what is not truth.<br>Note that this heretic is in the church; he associates with believers. This is the picture of most heretics. Few reject all the teachings of Christ and of the Bible. Most heretics remain in the church, holding to some basic teachings but rejecting those doctrines that they do not like. The Scripture is clear: believers are to reach out to the heretic or false teacher. He is not to be lambasted, rejected, and expelled from the church. An attempt is to be made to reach him for Christ. In fact, two strong attempts are to be made to reach him. He is to be shown love and care and admonished to repent and confess the truth of Christ and His Word. But note: there is a limit. On the third try, if he does not repent, he is to be rejected, that is, expelled from the church. He is not to be allowed to lead other believers astray. (See POSB outline—Matthew 18:15-20 and POSB notes—Matthew 18:15-20 for more detailed discussion on church discipline as taught by Christ.) |
| **#1942**<br>**Heritage**<br><br>Heritage–KJV<br>Allotted to–NASB<br>Entrusted to–NIV<br>Entrusted to–NKJV<br>Assigned to–NLT<br><br>**POSB REFERENCE** (1 Pt.5:2-3; esp. v.3) Note 2, point 3 | κλήρων = klērōn<br>Pronunciation: [klay'-rown]<br>Parsing (part of speech): noun<br>    Case—genitive<br>    Gender—masculine<br>    Number—plural<br>    Stem or root—from κλῆρος, ου<br>Concordance References:<br>    Strong's #2819 klēros<br>    NIV #3102 klēros<br>    NASB #2819 klēros<br><br>**1 Peter 5:3**<br>Neither as being lords over God's **heritage**, but being ensamples to the flock. [KJV]<br>Nor yet as lording it over those **allotted to** your charge, but proving to be examples to the flock. [NASB]<br>Not lording it over those **entrusted to** you, but being examples to the flock. [NIV]<br>Nor as being lords over those **entrusted to** you, but being examples to the flock; [NKJV]<br>Don't lord it over the people **assigned to** your care, but lead them by your good example. [NLT]<br>μηδ' ὡς κατακυριεύοντες τῶν **κλήρων**, ἀλλὰ τύποι γινόμενοι τοῦ ποιμνίου. [GNS]<br>μηδ' ὡς κατακυριεύοντες τῶν **κλήρων** ἀλλὰ τύποι γινόμενοι τοῦ ποιμνίου· [GNT] | Entrusted to; allotted to; assigned to.<br><br>**Practical Application**<br>This is the word that was used of Israel in the Old Testament. It means that the Jews were the people who were set apart and allotted and assigned to God. They were His very special allotment and assignment—His treasures—the people charged to His care and oversight. This is the picture painted of the elder or minister and the flock of God. God has given the minister a very special heritage or allotment and assignment: the minister has been assigned to feed the heritage of God, the very flock that belongs to God Himself.<br>Now note how the minister is to lead God's flock. He is not to lord it over them, but he is to lead by example. The minister...<br>• is not to be a dictator but an example.<br>• is not to preach one thing and do something else.<br>The minister is to lead people by living for Christ. He is to preach and teach Christ, but he is to first of all live a pure and righteous life just like Christ lived. The minister is to live exactly what he preaches. He is to be a pattern and model for Christ, a pattern and model of just what God wants His people to be. |
| **#1943**<br>**Herself, Of**<br><br>Of herself–KJV<br>By itself–NASB<br>All by itself–NIV<br>By itself–NKJV<br>On its own–NLT<br><br>**POSB REFERENCE** (Mk.4:28) Note 4 | αὐτομάτη = automate<br>Pronunciation: [ow-tom'-at-eh]<br>Parsing (part of speech): adjective<br>    Case—nominative<br>    Gender—feminine<br>    Number—singular<br>    Stem or root—from αὐτόματος, η, ον<br>Concordance References:<br>    ⇒ Strong's #844 automatos<br>    ⇒ NIV #897 automatos<br>    ⇒ NASB #844 automatos<br><br>**Mark 4:28**<br>For the earth bringeth forth fruit **of herself**; first the blade, then the ear, after that the full corn in the ear. [KJV]<br>"The soil produces crops **by itself**; first the blade, then the head, then the mature grain in the head. [NASB]<br>**All by itself** the soil produces grain—first the stalk, | All by itself, on its own, of itself; automatically, spontaneously, of necessity, self-moving.<br><br>**Practical Application**<br>The idea is that the earth brings forth fruit automatically, by its very nature. Note two facts.<br>1. Growth is sure, inevitable. But two conditions are essential. The ground must be "good ground" (Mark 4:20) and the seed must be sown in the ground. If these two conditions exist, then growth is both inevitable and unstoppable. Even a small blade of grass will find a crack in the pavement. Nothing can stop the seed from growing. (See POSB outline—Romans 8:28-39 and POSB notes—Romans 8:28-39 for more discussion.) |

# PRACTICAL WORD STUDIES
## in the NEW TESTAMENT

| ENGLISH WORD | GREEK WORD AND VERSE | THE WORD MEANS... |
|---|---|---|
| | then the head, then the full kernel in the head. [NIV]<br>For the earth yields crops **by itself**: first the blade, then the head, after that the full grain in the head. [NKJV]<br>Because the earth produces crops **on its own**. First a leaf blade pushes through, then the heads of wheat are formed, and finally the grain ripens. [NLT]<br>αὐτομάτη γὰρ ἡ γῆ καρποφορεῖ, πρῶτον χόρτον, εἶτα στάχυν, εἶτα πλήρη σῖτον ἐν τῷ στάχυϊ. [GNS]<br>αὐτομάτη ἡ γῆ καρποφορεῖ, πρῶτον χόρτον εἶτα στάχυν εἶτα πλήρη[ς] σῖτον ἐν τῷ στάχυϊ. [GNT] | 2. Growth is constant, but it is gradual, ever so gradual. The seed is sown, and then day after day and night after night passes before the blade ever springs up. Then many more days and nights pass before the ear forms. It takes weeks before the full ear of corn appears. Growth does take place; it is constant—but growth is gradual. It does take time; it does not happen overnight. |
| #1944<br>**Hid**<br><br>Received–KJV<br>Received–NASB<br>**Hid–NIV**<br>Received–NKJV<br>Disappeared–NLT<br><br>**POSB REFERENCE**<br>(Acts 1:10-11; esp. v.9)<br>Note 5, point 1 | ὑπέλαβεν = *hupelaben*<br>Pronunciation: [hoop-eh-la-ben']<br>Parsing (part of speech): verb<br>   Mood—indicative<br>   Tense—aorist<br>   Voice—active<br>   Person—3rd person<br>   Number—singular<br>   Stem or root—from ὑπολαμβάνω<br>Concordance References:<br>  ⇒ Strong's #5274 hupolambanō<br>  ⇒ NIV #5696 hupolambanō<br>  ⇒ NASB #5274 hupolambanō<br><br>**Acts 1:9**<br>And when he had spoken these things, while they beheld, he was taken up; and a cloud **received** him out of their sight. [KJV]<br>And after He had said these things, He was lifted up while they were looking on, and a cloud **received** Him out of their sight. [NASB]<br>After he said this, he was taken up before their very eyes, and a cloud **hid** him from their sight. [NIV]<br>Now when He had spoken these things, while they watched, He was taken up, and a cloud **received** Him out of their sight. [NKJV]<br>It was not long after he said this that he was taken up into the sky while they were watching, and he **disappeared** into a cloud. [NLT]<br>καὶ ταῦτα εἰπών, βλεπόντων αὐτῶν ἐπήρθη, καὶ νεφέλη **ὑπέλαβεν** αὐτὸν ἀπὸ τῶν ὀφθαλμῶν αὐτῶν. [GNS]<br>καὶ ταῦτα εἰπὼν βλεπόντων αὐτῶν ἐπήρθη, καὶ νεφέλη **ὑπέλαβεν** αὐτὸν ἀπὸ τῶν ὀφθαλμῶν αὐτῶν. [GNT] | Hid, received, disappeared.<br><br>**Practical Application**<br>The point is this: it is as though the cloud "hid" (*hupelaben*) Christ. The cloud was apparently the Shekinah glory (see POSB note 2—John 1:14). Christ had said He would return to earth in the clouds of heaven (Matthew 24:30; Matthew 26:64; Mark 13:26; cp. Rev. 1:7). Seeing such a dramatic ascension confirmed for the disciples (and for us) that Jesus' promise of returning to earth will take place just as He said. |
| #1945<br>**Hidden–Hid**<br><br>Hid–KJV<br>Hidden–NASB<br>Hidden–NIV<br>Hidden–NKJV<br>Hidden–NLT<br><br>**POSB REFERENCE**<br>(Lk.18:34)<br>Note 3 | κεκρυμμένον = *kekrummenon*<br>Pronunciation: [keh-kroom'-meh-non]<br>Parsing (part of speech): verb<br>   Mood—participle<br>   Tense—perfect<br>   Voice—passive<br>   Case—nominative<br>   Gender—neuter<br>   Number—singular<br>   Stem or root—from κρύπτω<br>Concordance References:<br>  ⇒ Strong's #2928 kruptō<br>  ⇒ NIV #3221 kruptō<br>  ⇒ NASB #2928 kruptō<br><br>**Luke 18:34**<br>And they understood none of these things: and this saying was **hid** from them, neither knew they the things which were spoken. [KJV]<br>And they understood none of these things, and this saying was **hidden** from them, and they did not comprehend the things that were said. [NASB]<br>The disciples did not understand any of this. Its meaning was **hidden** from them, and they did not know what he was talking about. [NIV]<br>But they understood none of these things; this saying | To be concealed; to be hidden; to shroud; to screen.<br><br>**Practical Application**<br>The disciples did not understand a thing that Christ was saying to them. Since the disciples would not literally accept His words, they could not understand. What He said was a puzzle, a mystery, a riddle. The meaning was completely hidden from them. The word "hid or hidden" has the sense of completion in it. |

# PRACTICAL WORD STUDIES
## in the NEW TESTAMENT

| ENGLISH WORD | GREEK WORD AND VERSE | THE WORD MEANS... |
|---|---|---|
| | was **hidden** from them, and they did not know the things which were spoken. [NKJV]<br><br>But they didn't understand a thing he said. Its significance was **hidden** from them, and they failed to grasp what he was talking about. [NLT]<br><br>καὶ αὐτοὶ οὐδὲν τούτων συνῆκαν, καὶ ἦν τὸ ῥῆμα τοῦτο **κεκρυμμένον** ἀπ' αὐτῶν, καὶ οὐκ ἐγίνωσκον τὰ λεγόμενα. [GNS]<br><br>καὶ αὐτοὶ οὐδὲν τούτων συνῆκαν καὶ ἦν τὸ ῥῆμα τοῦτο **κεκρυμμένον** ἀπ' αὐτῶν καὶ οὐκ ἐγίνωσκον τὰ λεγόμενα. [GNT] | |
| #1946<br>**Hidden Reefs**<br><br>Spots–KJV<br>**Hidden reefs–NASB**<br>Blemishes–NIV<br>Spots–NKJV<br>Dangerous reefs–NLT<br><br>**POSB<br>REFERENCE**<br>(Jude 1:12)<br>Note 14 | σπιλάδες = *spilades*<br>Pronunciation: [spee-la-des']<br>Parsing (part of speech): noun<br>   Case—nominative<br>   Gender—feminine<br>   Number—plural<br>   Stem or root—from σπιλάς, άδος<br>Concordance References:<br>  ⇒ Strong's #4694 spilas<br>  ⇒ NIV #5069 spilas<br>  ⇒ NASB #4694 spilas<br><br>**Jude 1:12**<br><br>These are **spots** in your feasts of charity, when they feast with you, feeding themselves without fear: clouds they are without water, carried about of winds; trees whose fruit withereth, without fruit, twice dead, plucked up by the roots; [KJV]<br><br>These men are those who are **hidden reefs** in your love feasts when they feast with you without fear, caring for themselves; clouds without water, carried along by winds; autumn trees without fruit, doubly dead, uprooted; [NASB]<br><br>These men are **blemishes** at your love feasts, eating with you without the slightest qualm—shepherds who feed only themselves. They are clouds without rain, blown along by the wind; autumn trees, without fruit and uprooted—twice dead. [NIV]<br><br>These are **spots** in your love feasts, while they feast with you without fear, serving only themselves. They are clouds without water, carried about by the winds; late autumn trees without fruit, twice dead, pulled up by the roots; [NKJV]<br><br>When these people join you in fellowship meals celebrating the love of the Lord, they are like **dangerous reefs** that can shipwreck you. They are shameless in the way they care only about themselves. They are like clouds blowing over dry land without giving rain, promising much but producing nothing. They are like trees without fruit at harvesttime. They are not only dead but doubly dead, for they have been pulled out by the roots. [NLT]<br><br>οὗτοί εἰσιν ἐν ταῖς ἀγάπαις ὑμῶν **σπιλάδες**, συνευωχούμενοι ὑμῖν, ἀφόβως ἑαυτοὺς ποιμαίνοντες· νεφέλαι ἄνυδροι, ὑπὸ ἀνέμων περιφερόμεναι· δένδρα φθινοπωρινά, ἄκαρπα, δὶς ἀποθανόντα, ἐκριζωθέντα· [GNS]<br><br>οὗτοί εἰσιν οἱ ἐν ταῖς ἀγάπαις ὑμῶν **σπιλάδες** συνευωχούμενοι ἀφόβως, ἑαυτοὺς ποιμαίνοντες, νεφέλαι ἄνυδροι ὑπὸ ἀνέμων παραφερόμεναι, δένδρα φθινοπωρινά ἄκαρπα δὶς ἀποθανόντα ἐκριζωθέντα, [GNT] | Blemishes; spots; hidden reefs; dangerous reefs; anything that poses a dangerous threat.<br><br>**Practical Application**<br><br>False teachers are *hidden reefs* upon the fellowship of the church. The Greek word for "hidden reefs" (*spilades*) can mean *submerged rocks* that can wreck a ship. False teachers are reefs within the church that can wreck the fellowship of the church. Translators differ as to which meaning Jude intended. Perhaps he meant both, for both are certainly true.<br><br>The *love feasts* referred to were called *love feasts* by the early church. They were fellowship meals that the church celebrated after the services on the Lord's Day. Each family brought what food they could. This, of course, meant that the wealthy brought plenty and the poor brought little or nothing. Remember that many of the believers were slaves in that day, so some of them would not be able to bring any food whatsoever. Some churches had the most joyful fellowship around the love feasts. It provided a time when the believers could share the warmth of their hearts and grow in fellowship together. It was a time when the Holy Spirit could draw the hearts of believers together in love and joy and care and sharing. It was a time that the Holy Spirit could use to bind believers together in feelings for one another and in warmth and tenderness.<br><br>The point is this: fellowship among believers is a most wonderful time, a unique opportunity to grow and share together. But when false teachers are present, the scene is entirely different.<br><br>⇒ False teachers are spots or blemishes upon the fellowship of believers. They dirty and soil the name of Christ and the testimony of the church. They profess to be believers and are even teachers of God's Word, but they are not pure. Their false teaching disturbs genuine believers and causes division within the fellowship of the church. Those who are not rooted in Christ and in God's Word follow and support the false teacher; those who are rooted in Christ and in God's Word reject the false teacher. False teachers always spot and dirty the fellowship of the church because they cause division among the people and destroy the Spirit of Christ among them.<br><br>⇒ False teachers are reefs or submerged rocks that wreck the fellowship of the church. Their teaching is often injected into the church quietly and insidiously, completely unknown to the general membership. Therefore, the fellowship is sub- |

# Practical Word Studies in the New Testament

| ENGLISH WORD | GREEK WORD AND VERSE | THE WORD MEANS... |
|---|---|---|
| | | ject to being shipwrecked upon the reefs of false teaching.<br>Note that the false teachers feed themselves—that is, they fellowship with believers—without fear. There is no fear of God nor thought about the damage they are doing to the fellowship of the church. Their interest is to boost themselves forward; to be recognized as excellent teachers or preachers, persons of unusual gifts, teachers with new insights, teachers who are progressive, who are a notch above others. |
| **#1947**<br>**Highest Goal**<br><br>Follow–KJV<br>Pursue–NASB<br>Follow–NIV<br>Pursue–NKJV<br>**Highest goal–NLT**<br><br>**POSB REFERENCE**<br>(1 Cor.14:1)<br>Note 1 | Διώκετε = *Diōkete*<br>Pronunciation: [dee-o'-keh-teh]<br>Parsing (part of speech): verb<br>    Mood—imperative<br>    Tense—present<br>    Voice—active<br>    Person—2nd person<br>    Number—plural<br>    Stem or root—from διώκω<br>Concordance References:<br>  ⇒ Strong's #1377 diōkō<br>  ⇒ NIV #1503 diōkō<br>  ⇒ NASB #1377 diōkō<br><br>**1 Cor. 14:1**<br>    **Follow** after charity, and desire spiritual gifts, but rather that ye may prophesy. [KJV]<br>    **Pursue** love, yet desire earnestly spiritual gifts, but especially that you may prophesy. [NASB]<br>    **Follow** the way of love and eagerly desire spiritual gifts, especially the gift of prophecy. [NIV]<br>    **Pursue** love, and desire spiritual *gifts,* but especially that you may prophesy. [NKJV]<br>    Let love be your **highest goal**, but also desire the special abilities the Spirit gives, especially the gift of prophecy. [NLT]<br>    Διώκετε τὴν ἀγάπην· ζηλοῦτε δὲ τὰ πνευματικά, μᾶλλον δὲ ἵνα προφητεύητε. [GNS]<br>    Διώκετε τὴν ἀγάπην, ζηλοῦτε δὲ τὰ πνευματικά, μᾶλλον δὲ ἵνα προφητεύητε. [GNT] | To follow; to pursue; to persist; to seek after; to strive for; to continue on and on, never giving up until love is possessed.<br><br>**Practical Application**<br>    Love is to be the highest goal above all else in life. Gifts, abilities, and service are important; but they pale into insignificance in comparison with love. Love is the greatest need and the supreme answer to all the needs of men. It is when we love a person that we meet the needs of a person. In fact, if we truly love a person, then we will do all we can to meet all the needs of that person. |
| **#1948**<br>**Highest Privilege**<br><br>Grace–KJV<br>Grace–NASB<br>Grace–NIV<br>Grace–NKJV<br>**Highest privilege–NLT**<br><br>**POSB REFERENCE**<br>(Romans 5:2)<br>Note 3, point 1 | χάριν = *charin*<br>Pronunciation: [khar'-in]<br>Parsing (part of speech): noun<br>    Case—accusative<br>    Gender—feminine<br>    Number—singular<br>    Stem or root—from χάρις, ιτος<br>Concordance References:<br>  ⇒ Strong's #5485 charis<br>  ⇒ NIV #5921 charis<br>  ⇒ NASB #5485 charis<br><br>**Romans 5:2**<br>    By whom also we have access by faith into this **grace** wherein we stand, and rejoice in hope of the glory of God. [KJV]<br>    Through whom also we have obtained our introduction by faith into this **grace** in which we stand; and we exult in hope of the glory of God. [NASB]<br>    Through whom we have gained access by faith into this **grace** in which we now stand. And we rejoice in the hope of the glory of God. [NIV]<br>    Through whom also we have access by faith into this **grace** in which we stand, and rejoice in hope of the glory of God. [NKJV]<br>    Because of our faith, Christ has brought us into this place of **highest privilege** where we now stand, and we confidently and joyfully look forward to sharing God's glory. [NLT]<br>    δι' οὗ καὶ τὴν προσαγωγὴν ἐσχήκαμεν τῇ πίστει εἰς τὴν **χάριν** ταύτην ἐν ᾗ ἑστήκαμεν, καὶ καυχώμεθα ἐπ' | Grace, highest privilege, favor, benefit. It means a gift or a favor, an unmerited and undeserved gift or favor (see POSB notes, Grace—Romans 4:16; POSB *Deeper Study* #1—Titus 2:11-15 for more discussion.)<br><br>**Practical Application**<br>    In the present passage, the highest privilege is looked upon as a place or a position. Grace is a place to which we are brought, a position into which we are placed. It is the place of God's presence, the position of salvation. The person who is justified...<br>• stands in God's presence.<br>• stands before God saved.<br>• stands in the favor of God.<br>• stands in the privileges of God.<br>• stands in the promises of God. |

## PRACTICAL WORD STUDIES
### in the NEW TESTAMENT

| ENGLISH WORD | GREEK WORD AND VERSE | THE WORD MEANS... |
|---|---|---|
| | ἐλπίδι τῆς δόξης τοῦ Θεοῦ. [GNS]<br>δι' οὗ καὶ τὴν προσαγωγὴν ἐσχήκαμεν [τῇ πίστει] εἰς τὴν **χάριν** ταύτην ἐν ᾗ ἑστήκαμεν καὶ καυχώμεθα ἐπ' ἐλπίδι τῆς δόξης τοῦ Θεοῦ. [GNT] | Valued highly; to be highly regarded; to be held dear, esteemed, honored, distinguished, precious, prized. |
| #1949<br>**Highly Regarded**<br><br>Dear–KJV<br>**Highly regarded–NASB**<br>Valued highly–NIV<br>Dear–NKJV<br>Highly valued–NLT<br><br>**POSB REFERENCE**<br>(Lk.7:2)<br>Note 2 | ἦν ἔντιμος = ën entimos<br>Pronunciation: [ayn en'-tee-mos]<br>Parsing ën (part of speech):verb<br>   Mood—indicative<br>   Tense—imperfect<br>   Voice—active<br>   Person—3rd person<br>   Number—singular<br>   Stem or root—from εἰμί<br>Parsing *entimos* (part of speech): adjective<br>   Case—nominative<br>   Gender—masculine<br>   Number—singular<br>   Stem or root—from ἔντιμος, ον<br>Concordance References:<br> ⇒ Strong's #1510 eimi + 1784 entimos<br> ⇒ NIV #1639 eimi + 1952 entimos<br> ⇒ NASB #1510 eimi + 1784 entimos<br><br>**Luke 7:2**<br>And a certain centurion's servant, who was **dear** unto him, was sick, and ready to die. [KJV]<br>And a certain centurion's slave, who was **highly regarded** by him, was sick and about to die. [NASB]<br>There a centurion's servant, whom his master **valued highly**, was sick and about to die. [NIV]<br>And a certain centurion's servant, who was **dear** to him, was sick and ready to die. [NKJV]<br>Now the **highly valued** slave of a Roman officer was sick and near death. [NLT]<br>Ἑκατοντάρχου δέ τινος δοῦλος κακῶς ἔχων ἤμελλε τελευτᾶν, ὃς **ἦν** αὐτῷ **ἔντιμος**. [GNS]<br>Ἑκατοντάρχου δέ τινος δοῦλος κακῶς ἔχων ἤμελλεν τελευτᾶν, ὃς **ἦν** αὐτῷ **ἔντιμος**. [GNT] | **Practical Application**<br>In the society of that day, a slave was nothing, only a tool or a thing to be used as the owner wished. He had no rights whatsoever, not even the right to live. An owner could mistreat or kill a slave without having to give an account. But this soldier loved his slave. This reveals a deep concern and care for people. It would have been much less bother to dispose of the slave or to ignore him and just let him die, but not this soldier. He cared. Note how he personally looked after the slave, a person who meant nothing to the rest of society. |
| #1950<br>**Highly Valued**<br><br>Dear–KJV<br>Highly regarded–NASB<br>Valued highly–NIV<br>Dear–NKJV<br>**Highly valued–NLT**<br><br>**POSB REFERENCE**<br>(Lk.7:2)<br>Note 2 | ἦν ἔντιμος = ën entimos<br>Pronunciation: [ayn en'-tee-mos]<br>Parsing ën (part of speech):verb<br>   Mood—indicative<br>   Tense—imperfect<br>   Voice—active<br>   Person—3rd person<br>   Number—singular<br>   Stem or root—from εἰμί<br>Parsing *entimos* (part of speech): adjective<br>   Case—nominative<br>   Gender—masculine<br>   Number—singular<br>   Stem or root—from ἔντιμος, ον<br>Concordance References:<br> ⇒ Strong's #1510 eimi + 1784 entimos<br> ⇒ NIV #1639 eimi + 1952 entimos<br> ⇒ NASB #1510 eimi + 1784 entimos<br><br>**Luke 7:2**<br>And a certain centurion's servant, who was **dear** unto him, was sick, and ready to die. [KJV]<br>And a certain centurion's slave, who was **highly regarded** by him, was sick and about to die. [NASB]<br>There a centurion's servant, whom his master **valued highly**, was sick and about to die. [NIV]<br>And a certain centurion's servant, who was **dear** to him, was sick and ready to die. [NKJV]<br>Now the **highly valued** slave of a Roman officer was sick and near death. [NLT]<br>Ἑκατοντάρχου δέ τινος δοῦλος κακῶς ἔχων ἤμελλε τελευτᾶν, ὃς **ἦν** αὐτῷ **ἔντιμος**. [GNS]<br>Ἑκατοντάρχου δέ τινος δοῦλος κακῶς ἔχων ἤμελλεν τελευτᾶν, ὃς **ἦν** αὐτῷ **ἔντιμος**. [GNT] | Valued highly, to be highly regarded; to be held dear, esteemed, honored, distinguished, precious, prized.<br><br>**Practical Application**<br>In the society of that day, a slave was nothing, only a tool or a thing to be used as the owner wished. He had no rights whatsoever, not even the right to live. An owner could mistreat or kill a slave without having to give an account. But this soldier loved his slave. This reveals a deep concern and care for people. It would have been much less bother to dispose of the slave or to ignore him and just let him die, but not this soldier. He cared. Note how he personally looked after the slave, a person who meant nothing to the rest of society. |

# Practical Word Studies
## in the New Testament

| English Word | Greek Word and Verse | The Word Means... |
|---|---|---|
| **#1951**<br>**Highminded**<br><br>Highminded–KJV<br>Conceited–NASB<br>Conceited–NIV<br>Haughty–NKJV<br>Puffed up with pride–NLT<br><br>**POSB REFERENCE**<br>(2 Tim. 3:2-4; esp. v.4)<br>Note 2, point 17 | τετυφωμένοι = tetuphōmenoi<br>Pronunciation: [teh-toof-o'-mehn-oy]<br>Parsing (part of speech): verb<br>    Mood—participle<br>    Tense—perfect<br>    Voice—passive<br>    Case—nominative<br>    Gender—masculine<br>    Number—plural<br>    Stem or root—from τυφόομαι<br>Concordance References:<br>  ⇒ Strong's #5187 tuphoomai<br>  ⇒ NIV #5605 tuphoomai<br>  ⇒ NASB #5187 tuphoomai<br><br>**2 Tim. 3:4**<br>Traitors, heady, **highminded**, lovers of pleasures more than lovers of God; [KJV]<br>Treacherous, reckless, **conceited**, lovers of pleasure rather than lovers of God; [NASB]<br>Treacherous, rash, **conceited**, lovers of pleasure rather than lovers of God–[NIV]<br>Traitors, headstrong, **haughty**, lovers of pleasure rather than lovers of God, [NKJV]<br>They will betray their friends, be reckless, be **puffed up with pride**, and love pleasure rather than God. [NLT]<br>προδόται, προπετεῖς, **τετυφωμένοι**, φιλήδονοι μᾶλλον η φιλόθεοι, [GNS]<br>προδόται προπετεῖς **τετυφωμένοι**, φιλήδονοι μᾶλλον η φιλόθεοι, [GNT] | To be conceited; to be highminded; to be puffed up with pride; to be swollen with pride, having feelings of self-importance.<br><br>**Practical Application**<br>It is a person who feels so educated, so scientific, so advanced, so high in position and authority, ability, and gifts that he feels completely self-sufficient. He feels no need for God. He is above God and above most people. |
| **#1952**<br>**Hinder**<br><br>Forbid–KJV<br>**Hinder**–NASB<br>**Hinder**–NIV<br>Forbid–NKJV<br>Stop–NLT<br><br>**POSB REFERENCE**<br>(Mk.10:14)<br>*Deeper Study #3* | κωλύετε = kōluete<br>Pronunciation: [ko-loo'-eh-teh]<br>Parsing (part of speech): verb<br>    Mood—imperative<br>    Tense—present<br>    Voice—active<br>    Person—2nd person<br>    Number—plural<br>    Stem or root—from κωλύω<br>Concordance References:<br>  ⇒ Strong's #2967 kōluō<br>  ⇒ NIV #3266 kōluō<br>  ⇒ NASB #2967 kōluō<br><br>**Mark 10:14**<br>But when Jesus saw it, he was much displeased, and said unto them, Suffer the little children to come unto me, and **forbid** them not: for of such is the kingdom of God. [KJV]<br>But when Jesus saw this, He was indignant and said to them, "Permit the children to come to Me; do not **hinder** them; for the kingdom of God belongs to such as these. [NASB]<br>When Jesus saw this, he was indignant. He said to them, "Let the little children come to me, and do not **hinder** them, for the kingdom of God belongs to such as these. [NIV]<br>But when Jesus saw it, He was greatly displeased and said to them, "Let the little children come to Me, and do not **forbid** them; for of such is the kingdom of God. [NKJV]<br>But when Jesus saw what was happening, he was very displeased with his disciples. He said to them, "Let the children come to me. Don't **stop** them! For the Kingdom of God belongs to such as these. [NLT]<br>ἰδὼν δὲ ὁ Ἰησοῦς ἠγανάκτησε, καὶ εἶπεν αὐτοῖς, Ἄφετε τὰ παιδία ἔρχεσθαι πρός με, καὶ μὴ **κωλύετε** αὐτά. τῶν γὰρ τοιούτων ἐστὶν ἡ βασιλεία τοῦ Θεοῦ. [GNS]<br>ἰδὼν δὲ ὁ Ἰησοῦς ἠγανάκτησεν καὶ εἶπεν αὐτοῖς, Ἄφετε τὰ παιδία ἔρχεσθαι πρός με, μὴ **κωλύετε** αὐτά, τῶν γὰρ τοιούτων ἐστὶν ἡ βασιλεία τοῦ θεοῦ. [GNT] | To hinder; to forbid; to stop; to prevent; to obstruct; to block; to impede; to encumber; restrain; to withhold; to hamper.<br><br>**Practical Application**<br>The tense is a present imperative, a continuous command: stop hindering, stop preventing the children from coming to Me. In this case, His own disciples were hindering the children, continuously preventing their coming to Jesus. |

# PRACTICAL WORD STUDIES
## in the NEW TESTAMENT

| ENGLISH WORD | GREEK WORD AND VERSE | THE WORD MEANS... |
|---|---|---|
| **#1953**<br>**Hinder–**<br>**Hindered**<br><br>Hinder–KJV<br>**Hindered**–NASB<br>Cut in on–NIV<br>**Hindered**–NKJV<br>Interfered with–NLT<br><br>**POSB**<br>**REFERENCE**<br>(Gal.5:7)<br>Note 1, point 1 | ἐνέκοψεν = enekopsen<br>Pronunciation: [en-ek-op'-sen]<br>Parsing (part of speech): verb<br>   Mood—indicative<br>   Tense—aorist<br>   Voice—active<br>   Person—3rd person<br>   Number—singular<br>   Stem or root—from ἐγκόπτω<br>Concordance References:<br>  ⇒ Strong's #1465 egkoptō<br>  ⇒ NIV #1601 egkoptō<br>  ⇒ NASB #1465 egkoptō<br><br>**Galatians 5:7**<br>Ye did run well; who did **hinder** you that ye should not obey the truth? [KJV]<br>You were running well; who **hindered** you from obeying the truth? [NASB]<br>You were running a good race. Who **cut in on** you and kept you from obeying the truth? [NIV]<br>You ran well. Who **hindered** you from obeying the truth? [NKJV]<br>You were getting along so well. Who has **interfered with** you to hold you back from following the truth? [NLT]<br>ἐτρέχετε καλῶς· τίς ὑμᾶς **ἀνέοψε** τῇ ἀληθείᾳ μὴ πείθεσθαι; [GNS]<br>Ἐτρέχετε καλῶς· τίς ὑμᾶς **ἐνέκοψεν** [τῇ] ἀληθείᾳ μὴ πείθεσθαι; [GNT] | To cut in on; to hinder; to edge in; to interfere with; to detain; to obstruct.<br><br>**Practical Application**<br>While the Galatians had been running the Christian race, some had edged in on them and begun to hinder and interfere with their running. They were no longer obeying the truth. They were now trying to approach God by some other way than Christ. They were now thinking...<br>• that God accepted them because they had been *ritualized*: circumcised and baptized.<br>• that God accepted them because they tried to keep the law: tried to be as good as they could and did good deeds as opportunity arose.<br>• that God approved them because they were faithful to the church: its rituals, ceremonies, services, rules and regulations.<br>They were no longer running well. They had allowed some false teacher to hinder them and to turn them from the truth. They had a need to think about the matter, a desperate need...<br>• to think about the race they had been running.<br>• to think about who it was that was now cutting in on their running. |
| **#1954**<br>**Hindered From**<br>**Finding The**<br>**Lord**<br><br>Offence–KJV<br>Offense–NASB<br>Stumbling block–NIV<br>Offense–NKJV<br>**Hindered from finding the Lord**–NLT<br><br>**POSB**<br>**REFERENCE**<br>(2 Cor.6:3)<br>Note 1 | προσκοπήν = proskopēn<br>Pronunciation: [pros-kop-ayn']<br>Parsing (part of speech): noun<br>   Case—accusative<br>   Gender—feminine<br>   Number—singular<br>   Stem or root—from προσκοπή, ῆς<br>Concordance References:<br>  ⇒ Strong's #4349 proskopē<br>  ⇒ NIV #4683 proskopē<br>  ⇒ NASB #4349 proskopē<br><br>**2 Cor. 6:3**<br>Giving no **offence** in any thing, that the ministry be not blamed: [KJV]<br>Giving no cause for **offense** in anything, in order that the ministry be not discredited, [NASB]<br>We put no **stumbling block** in anyone's path, so that our ministry will not be discredited. [NIV]<br>We give no **offense** in anything, that our ministry may not be blamed. [NKJV]<br>We try to live in such a way that no one will be **hindered from finding the Lord** by the way we act, and so no one can find fault with our ministry. [NLT]<br>μηδεμίαν ἐν μηδενὶ διδόντες **προσκοπήν**, ἵνα μὴ μωμηθῇ ἡ διακονία· [GNS]<br>μηδεμίαν ἐν μηδενὶ διδόντες **προσκοπήν**, ἵνα μὴ μωμηθῇ ἡ διακονία, [GNT] | Stumbling block; to give cause for offense; to stumble; to strike against; to hinder someone from finding the Lord.<br><br>**Practical Application**<br>Paul wanted his life and ministry to be so consistent that he would never give any reason for anyone to reject or to turn sour on the Lord Jesus Christ. Paul was careful; he guarded his behavior and conduct lest he cause a person to stumble and fall and reject the gospel of Christ. Note the reason: he did not want to be a poor reflection upon the ministry. Paul knew the nature of man, that people looked for excuses to reject Christ and to avoid His church. He knew that some people were always searching for juicy gossip to use against the followers of Christ and especially against the ministers of the gospel. He also knew that God had called him to the ministry of His Son, the Lord Jesus Christ, and that no higher call could be issued. Therefore, Paul sought to bring only honor to the ministry and to the name of the Lord Jesus Christ. |
| **#1955**<br>**Hindrances**<br><br>Offences–KJV<br>**Hindrances**–NASB<br>Obstacles–NIV<br>Offenses–NKJV<br>Upset people's faith–NLT | σκάνδαλα = skandala<br>Pronunciation: [skan'-dal-ah]<br>Parsing (part of speech): noun<br>   Case—accusative<br>   Gender—neuter<br>   Number—plural<br>   Stem or root—from σκάνδαλον, ου<br>Concordance References:<br>  ⇒ Strong's #4625 skandalon<br>  ⇒ NIV #4998 skandalon<br>  ⇒ NASB #4625 skandalon | That which causes sin or gives occasion for sin; that which causes stumbling or trouble, obstacle. It means laying a stumbling block in someone's way or causing someone to fall.<br><br>**Practical Application**<br>The most effective way for Satan to get a foothold into a strong church is to quietly and insidiously move a divisive person into some teaching or leadership position where he can influence immature believers. Paul knew this, so he left the warning until the end of his letter. It is |

## Practical Word Studies
### in the New Testament

| ENGLISH WORD | GREEK WORD AND VERSE | THE WORD MEANS... |
|---|---|---|
| **POSB REFERENCE** (Rom.16:17-18; esp. v.17) Note 1, point 1 | **Romans 16:17**<br>Now I beseech you, brethren, mark them which cause divisions and **offences** contrary to the doctrine which ye have learned; and avoid them. [KJV]<br>Now I urge you, brethren, keep your eye on those who cause dissensions and **hindrances** contrary to the teaching which you learned, and turn away from them. [NASB]<br>I urge you, brothers, to watch out for those who cause divisions and put **obstacles** in your way that are contrary to the teaching you have learned. Keep away from them. [NIV]<br>Now I urge you, brethren, note those who cause divisions and **offenses**, contrary to the doctrine which you learned, and avoid them. [NKJV]<br>And now I make one more appeal, my dear brothers and sisters. Watch out for people who cause divisions and **upset people's faith** by teaching things that are contrary to what you have been taught. Stay away from them. [NLT]<br>Παρακαλῶ δὲ ὑμᾶς, ἀδελφοί, σκοπεῖν τοὺς τὰς διχοστασίας καὶ τὰ **σκάνδαλα**, παρὰ τὴν διδαχὴν ἣν ὑμεῖς ἐμάθετε, ποιοῦντας· καὶ ἐκκλίνατε ἀπ' αὐτῶν. [GNS]<br>Παρακαλῶ δὲ ὑμᾶς, ἀδελφοί, σκοπεῖν τοὺς τὰς διχοστασίας καὶ τὰ **σκάνδαλα** παρὰ τὴν διδαχὴν ἣν ὑμεῖς ἐμάθετε ποιοῦντας, καὶ ἐκκλίνετε ἀπ' αὐτῶν· [GNT] | a warning that must be heeded by a strong church if it is to keep its witness for the Lord. |
| #1956<br>**His Duty**<br><br>Due–KJV<br>**His duty–NASB**<br>His marital duty–NIV<br>Due–NKJV<br>Sexual intimacy–NLT<br><br>**POSB REFERENCE** (1 Cor.7:3) Note 3 | τὴν ὀφειλήν = tēn opheilēn<br>Pronunciation: [tayn of-i'-layn]<br>Parsing *opheilēn* (part of speech): noun<br>  Case—accusative<br>  Gender—feminine<br>  Number—singular<br>  Stem or root—from ὀφειλή, ῆς<br>Concordance References:<br>⇒ Strong's #3588 ho + 3784 opheilo<br>⇒ NIV #3836 ho [his] + 4051 opheilē [marital duty]<br>⇒ NASB #3588 ho + 3782 opheilē<br><br>**1 Cor. 7:3**<br>Let the husband render unto the wife **due** benevolence: and likewise also the wife unto the husband. [KJV]<br>Let the husband fulfill **his duty** to his wife, and likewise also the wife to her husband. [NASB]<br>The husband should fulfill **his marital duty** to his wife, and likewise the wife to her husband. [NIV]<br>Let the husband render to his wife the affection **due** her, and likewise also the wife to her husband. [NKJV]<br>The husband should not deprive his wife of **sexual intimacy**, which is her right as a married woman, nor should the wife deprive her husband. [NLT]<br>τῇ γυναικὶ ὁ ἀνὴρ τὴν **ὀφειλομένην** εὔνοιαν ἀποδιδότω· ὁμοίως δὲ καὶ ἡ γυνὴ τῷ ἀνδρί. [GNS]<br>τῇ γυναικὶ ὁ ἀνὴρ τὴν **ὀφειλὴν** ἀποδιδότω, ὁμοίως δὲ καὶ ἡ γυνὴ τῷ ἀνδρί. [GNT] | Marital duty; the debt; to owe; to render what is due.<br><br>**Practical Application**<br>The husband and wife owe some things to the other.<br>⇒ Both have rights; each can expect to receive some things from the other.<br>⇒ Both have responsibilities; each can expect to pay to the other exactly what is due. |
| #1957<br>**His Marital Duty**<br><br>Due–KJV<br>His duty–NASB<br>**His marital duty– NIV**<br>Due–NKJV<br>Sexual intimacy–NLT | τὴν ὀφειλήν = tēn opheilēn<br>Pronunciation: [tayn of-i'-layn]<br>Parsing *opheilēn* (part of speech): noun<br>  Case—accusative<br>  Gender—feminine<br>  Number—singular<br>  Stem or root—from ὀφειλή, ῆς<br>Concordance References:<br>⇒ Strong's #3588 ho + 3784 opheilo<br>⇒ NIV #3836 ho [his] + 4051 opheilē [marital duty]<br>⇒ NASB #3588 ho + 3782 opheilē | Marital duty; the debt; to owe; to render what is due.<br><br>**Practical Application**<br>The husband and wife owe some things to the other.<br>⇒ Both have rights; each can expect to receive some things from the other.<br>⇒ Both have responsibilities; each can expect to pay to the other exactly what is due. |

# PRACTICAL WORD STUDIES
## in the NEW TESTAMENT

| ENGLISH WORD | GREEK WORD AND VERSE | THE WORD MEANS... |
|---|---|---|
| **POSB REFERENCE** (1 Cor.7:3) Note 3 | **1 Cor. 7:3**<br>Let the husband render unto the wife **due** benevolence: and likewise also the wife unto the husband. [KJV]<br>Let the husband fulfill **his duty** to his wife, and likewise also the wife to her husband. [NASB]<br>The husband should fulfill **his marital duty** to his wife, and likewise the wife to her husband. [NIV]<br>Let the husband render to his wife the affection **due** her, and likewise also the wife to her husband. [NKJV]<br>The husband should not deprive his wife of **sexual intimacy**, which is her right as a married woman, nor should the wife deprive her husband. [NLT]<br>τῇ γυναικὶ ὁ ἀνὴρ τὴν ὀφειλομένην εὔνοιαν ἀποδιδότω· ὁμοίως δὲ καὶ ἡ γυνὴ τῷ ἀνδρί. [GNS]<br>τῇ γυναικὶ ὁ ἀνὴρ τὴν ὀφειλὴν ἀποδιδότω, ὁμοίως δὲ καὶ ἡ γυνὴ τῷ ἀνδρί. [GNT] | |
| **#1958**<br>**His Own**<br><br>His own–KJV<br>His own–NASB<br>His own–NIV<br>His own–NKJV<br>His own–NLT<br><br>**POSB REFERENCE** (Jn.1:10-11; esp. v.11) Note 2, point 2<br><br>See also POSB REF: (Jn.10:2-3; esp. v.3) Note 3, point 3 | εἰς τὰ ἴδια = *eis ta idia*<br>Pronunciation: [ice tah ee-dee-ah]<br>Parsing *eis* (part of speech): preposition<br>    Case—accusative<br>    Stem or root—from εἰς<br>Parsing *idia* (part of speech): pronominal adjective<br>    Case—accusative<br>    Gender—neuter<br>    Number—plural<br>    Stem or root—from ἴδιος, α, ον<br>Concordance References:<br>⇒ Strong's #1519 eis + 3588 ho + 2398 idios<br>⇒ NIV #1650 eis + 3836 ta + 2625 idios [his own]<br>⇒ NASB #1519 eis + 3588 ho + 2398 idios<br><br>**John 1:11**<br>He came unto **his own**, and his own received him not. [KJV]<br>He came to **His own**, and those who were His own did not receive Him. [NASB]<br>He came to that which was **his own**, but his own did not receive him. [NIV]<br>He came to **His own**, and His own did not receive Him. [NKJV]<br>Even in **his own** land and among his own people, he was not accepted. [NLT]<br>εἰς τὰ ἴδια ἦλθε, καὶ οἱ ἴδιοι αὐτὸν οὐ παρέλαβον. [GNS]<br>εἰς τὰ ἴδια ἦλθεν, καὶ οἱ ἴδιοι αὐτὸν οὐ παρέλαβον. [GNT] | Literally to His own home; to His own people; His friends; His relatives.<br><br>**Practical Application**<br>There are two meanings here.<br>1. The world is His home, and all the people are His by creation. He came to all the people of the world, but they did not receive Him. They rejected Him.<br>2. The nation of Israel was His particular home, the people whom He had chosen to be the messengers of God to the world. Of all people, they should have known better because of the special privileges, but they too rejected Him. (See POSB *Deeper Study* #1—John 4:22.) |
| **#1959**<br>**His Own Special People**<br><br>Peculiar people–KJV<br>People for God's own possession–NASB<br>People belonging to God–NIV<br>His own special people–NKJV<br>His very own possession–NLT<br><br>**POSB REFERENCE** (1 Pt.2:9) Note 1 | λαὸς εἰς περιποίησιν = *laos eis peripoiësin*<br>Pronunciation: [lah-os' ice per-ee-poy'-ay-sin]<br>Parsing *laos* (part of speech): noun<br>    Case—nominative<br>    Gender—masculine<br>    Number—singular<br>    Stem or root—from λαός, οῦ<br>Parsing *eis* (part of speech): preposition<br>    Case—accusative<br>    Stem or root—from εἰς<br>Parsing *peripoiësin* (part of speech): noun<br>    Case—accusative<br>    Gender—feminine<br>    Number—singular<br>    Stem or root—from περιποίησις, εως<br>Concordance References:<br>⇒ Strong's #2992 laos + 1519+4047 eis peripoiësis<br>⇒ NIV #3295 laos [people] + 1650+4348 eis peripoiësis [belonging to God]<br>⇒ NASB #2992 laos + 1519+4047 eis peripoiësis<br><br>**1 Peter 2:9**<br>But ye are a chosen generation, a royal priesthood, an holy nation, a **peculiar people**; that ye should shew forth the praises of him who hath called you out of dark- | People belonging to God; peculiar people; people for God's own possession.<br><br>**Practical Application**<br>Believers become "his own special people" (*laos eis peripoiësin*). The Greek means...<br>• "a people for God's own possession" (A.T. Robertson. *Word Pictures in the New Testament*, Vol.6, p.98).<br>• "the people to be His very own" (Charles B. Williams. *The New Testament in the Language of the People*. "The Four Translation New Testament." Printed for Decision Magazine by World Wide Publications of Minneapolis. New York, NY: Iversen Associates, 1966).<br>• "a people saved to be His own" (William F. Beck. *The New Testament in the Language of Today*. "The Four Translation New Testament." Printed for Decision Magazine by World Wide Publications of Minneapolis. New York, NY: Iversen Associates, 1966). |

# PRACTICAL WORD STUDIES
## in the NEW TESTAMENT

| ENGLISH WORD | GREEK WORD AND VERSE | THE WORD MEANS... |
|---|---|---|
| | ness into his marvellous light: [KJV]<br>But you are a chosen race, a royal priesthood, a HOLY NATION, a **people for God's own possession**, that you may proclaim the excellencies of Him who has called you out of darkness into His marvelous light; [NASB]<br>But you are a chosen people, a royal priesthood, a holy nation, a **people belonging to God**, that you may declare the praises of him who called you out of darkness into his wonderful light. [NIV]<br>But you *are* a chosen generation, a royal priesthood, a holy nation, **His own special people**, that you may proclaim the praises of Him who called you out of darkness into His marvelous light; [NKJV]<br>But you are not like that, for you are a chosen people. You are a kingdom of priests, God's holy nation, **his very own possession**. This is so you can show others the goodness of God, for he called you out of the darkness into his wonderful light. [NLT]<br>ὑμεῖς δὲ γένος ἐκλεκτόν, βασίλειον ἱεράτευμα, ἔθνος ἅγιον, **λαὸς εἰς περιποίησιν**, ὅπως τὰς ἀρετὰς ἐξαγγείλητε τοῦ ἐκ σκότους ὑμᾶς καλέσαντος εἰς τὸ θαυμαστὸν αὐτοῦ φῶς· [GNS]<br>Ὑμεῖς δὲ γένος ἐκλεκτόν, βασίλειον ἱεράτευμα, ἔθνος ἅγιον, **λαὸς εἰς περιποίησιν**, ὅπως τὰς ἀρετὰς ἐξαγγείλητε τοῦ ἐκ σκότους ὑμᾶς καλέσαντος εἰς τὸ θαυμαστὸν αὐτοῦ φῶς· [GNT] | This is a most precious thought: that God makes us His very own people, a very special possession of His. We are His *treasured possession*. Possession has the idea of value, of worth and preciousness. We are more precious to God than all the precious gems and treasures of the world. Possession also has the idea of provision, protection, and security. We are God's possession, His very special people; therefore, He will provide for us and protect us and make us secure in every sense of the word. |
| **#1960**<br>**His Posession**<br><br>Peculiar–KJV<br>**His...posession–NASB**<br>His very own–NIV<br>His...special–NKJV<br>His very own–NLT<br><br>**POSB<br>REFERENCE**<br>(Tit.2:14)<br>Note 4, point 2 | περιούσιον = *periousion*<br>Pronunciation: [per-ee-oo'-see-on]<br>Parsing (part of speech): adjective<br>    Case—accusative<br>    Gender—masculine<br>    Number—singular<br>    Stem or root—from περιούσιος, ον<br>Concordance References:<br>  ⇒ Strong's #4041 periousios<br>  ⇒ NIV #4342 periousios<br>  ⇒ NASB #4041 periousios<br><br>**Titus 2:14**<br>Who gave himself for us, that he might redeem us from all iniquity, and purify unto himself a **peculiar** people, zealous of good works. [KJV]<br>Who gave Himself for us, that He might redeem us from every lawless deed and purify for Himself a people for **His** own **possession**, zealous for good deeds. [NASB]<br>Who gave himself for us to redeem us from all wickedness and to purify for himself a people that are **his very own**, eager to do what is good. [NIV]<br>Who gave Himself for us, that He might redeem us from every lawless deed and purify for Himself ***His*** own **special** people, zealous for good works. [NKJV]<br>He gave his life to free us from every kind of sin, to cleanse us, and to make us **his very own** people, totally committed to doing what is right. [NLT]<br>ὃς ἔδωκεν ἑαυτὸν ὑπὲρ ἡμῶν, ἵνα λυτρώσηται ἡμᾶς ἀπὸ πάσης ἀνομίας, καὶ καθαρίσῃ ἑαυτῷ λαὸν **περιούσιον**, ζηλωτὴν καλῶν ἔργων. [GNS]<br>ὃς ἔδωκεν ἑαυτὸν ὑπὲρ ἡμῶν ἵνα λυτρώσηται ἡμᾶς ἀπὸ πάσης ἀνομίας καὶ καθαρίσῃ ἑαυτῷ λαὸν **περιούσιον**, ζηλωτὴν καλῶν ἔργων. [GNT] | His very own; peculiar; His own possession, special, belonging only to Him. It means set apart, possessed over and above, especially selected and reserved for.<br><br>**Practical Application**<br>Christ died so that He might have a peculiar people, a very special people as His own possession. This is seen in the phrase "His possession" (*periousion*). When a person really grasps what Jesus Christ has done for him, that person can only surrender all he is and has to Christ. The person wants to follow and serve Christ, to do all that Christ says. The person separates himself from the world, sets his life apart to follow Christ; then Christ sets the person apart to be His own very special possession. Through the death of Jesus Christ, the believer becomes the very special possession of the Lord Jesus Christ. |
| **#1961**<br>**His Special**<br><br>Peculiar–KJV<br>His posession–NASB<br>His very own–NIV<br>**His...special–NKJV**<br>His very own–NLT | περιούσιον = *periousion*<br>Pronunciation: [per-ee-oo'-see-on]<br>Parsing (part of speech): adjective<br>    Case—accusative<br>    Gender—masculine<br>    Number—singular<br>    Stem or root—from περιούσιος, ον<br>Concordance References:<br>  ⇒ Strong's #4041 periousios<br>  ⇒ NIV #4342 periousios<br>  ⇒ NASB #4041 periousios | His very own; peculiar; His own possession, special, belonging only to Him. It means set apart, possessed over and above, especially selected and reserved for.<br><br>**Practical Application**<br>Christ died so that He might have a peculiar people, a very special people as His own possession. This is seen in the word "special" (*periousion*). When a person really grasps what Jesus |

## PRACTICAL WORD STUDIES
### in the NEW TESTAMENT

| ENGLISH WORD | GREEK WORD AND VERSE | THE WORD MEANS... |
|---|---|---|
| **POSB REFERENCE** (Tit.2:14) Note 4, point 2 | **Titus 2:14** Who gave himself for us, that he might redeem us from all iniquity, and purify unto himself a **peculiar** people, zealous of good works. [KJV] Who gave Himself for us, that He might redeem us from every lawless deed and purify for Himself a people for **His** own **possession**, zealous for good deeds. [NASB] Who gave himself for us to redeem us from all wickedness and to purify for himself a people that are **his very own**, eager to do what is good. [NIV] Who gave Himself for us, that He might redeem us from every lawless deed and purify for Himself **His** own **special** people, zealous for good works. [NKJV] He gave his life to free us from every kind of sin, to cleanse us, and to make us **his very own** people, totally committed to doing what is right. [NLT] ὃς ἔδωκεν ἑαυτὸν ὑπὲρ ἡμῶν, ἵνα λυτρώσηται ἡμᾶς ἀπὸ πάσης ἀνομίας, καὶ καθαρίσῃ ἑαυτῷ λαὸν **περιούσιον**, ζηλωτὴν καλῶν ἔργων. [GNS] ὃς ἔδωκεν ἑαυτὸν ὑπὲρ ἡμῶν ἵνα λυτρώσηται ἡμᾶς ἀπὸ πάσης ἀνομίας καὶ καθαρίσῃ ἑαυτῷ λαὸν **περιούσιον**, ζηλωτὴν καλῶν ἔργων. [GNT] | Christ has done for him, that person can only surrender all he is and has to Christ. The person wants to follow and serve Christ, to do all that Christ says. The person separates himself from the world, sets his life apart to follow Christ; then Christ sets the person apart to be His own very special possession. Through the death of Jesus Christ, the believer becomes the very special possession of the Lord Jesus Christ. |
| **#1962 His Very Own** Peculiar–KJV His...posession–NASB His very own–NIV His...special–NKJV His very own–NLT **POSB REFERENCE** (Tit.2:14) Note 4, point 2 | περιούσιον = periousion Pronunciation: [per-ee-oo´-see-on] Parsing (part of speech): adjective     Case—accusative     Gender—masculine     Number—singular     Stem or root—from περιούσιος, ον Concordance References:   ⇒ Strong's #4041 periousios   ⇒ NIV #4342 periousios   ⇒ NASB #4041 periousios **Titus 2:14** Who gave himself for us, that he might redeem us from all iniquity, and purify unto himself a **peculiar** people, zealous of good works. [KJV] Who gave Himself for us, that He might redeem us from every lawless deed and purify for Himself a people for **His** own **possession**, zealous for good deeds. [NASB] Who gave himself for us to redeem us from all wickedness and to purify for himself a people that are **his very own**, eager to do what is good. [NIV] Who gave Himself for us, that He might redeem us from every lawless deed and purify for Himself **His** own **special** people, zealous for good works. [NKJV] He gave his life to free us from every kind of sin, to cleanse us, and to make us **his very own** people, totally committed to doing what is right. [NLT] ὃς ἔδωκεν ἑαυτὸν ὑπὲρ ἡμῶν, ἵνα λυτρώσηται ἡμᾶς ἀπὸ πάσης ἀνομίας, καὶ καθαρίσῃ ἑαυτῷ λαὸν **περιούσιον**, ζηλωτὴν καλῶν ἔργων. [GNS] ὃς ἔδωκεν ἑαυτὸν ὑπὲρ ἡμῶν ἵνα λυτρώσηται ἡμᾶς ἀπὸ πάσης ἀνομίας καὶ καθαρίσῃ ἑαυτῷ λαὸν **περιούσιον**, ζηλωτὴν καλῶν ἔργων. [GNT] | His very own; peculiar; His own possession, special, belonging only to Him. It means set apart, possessed over and above, especially selected and reserved for. **Practical Application** Christ died so that He might have a peculiar people, a very special people as His own possession. This is seen in the phrase "His very own" (*periousion*). When a person really grasps what Jesus Christ has done for him, that person can only surrender all he is and has to Christ. The person wants to follow and serve Christ, to do all that Christ says. The person separates himself from the world, sets his life apart to follow Christ; then Christ sets the person apart to be His own very special possession. Through the death of Jesus Christ, the believer becomes the very special possession of the Lord Jesus Christ. |
| **#1963 His Very Own Possession** Peculiar people–KJV People for God's own possession–NASB People belonging to God–NIV His own special people–NKJV | λαὸς εἰς περιποίησιν = laos eis peripoiësin Pronunciation: [lah-os´ ice per-ee-poy´-ay-sin] Parsing *laos* (part of speech): noun     Case—nominative     Gender—masculine     Number—singular     Stem or root—from λαός, οῦ Parsing *eis* (part of speech): preposition     Case—accusative     Stem or root—from εἰς Parsing *peripoiësin* (part of speech): noun     Case—accusative     Gender—feminine | People belonging to God; peculiar people; people for God's own possession. **Practical Application** Believers become "his very own possession" (*laos eis peripoiësin*). The Greek means... • "a people for God's own possession" (A.T. Robertson. *Word Pictures in the New Testament*, Vol.6, p.98). • "the people to be His very own" (Charles B. Williams. *The New Testament in the Language of the People*. "The Four |

# PRACTICAL WORD STUDIES
## in the NEW TESTAMENT

| ENGLISH WORD | GREEK WORD AND VERSE | THE WORD MEANS... |
|---|---|---|
| **His very own possession—NLT**<br><br>**POSB REFERENCE**<br>(1 Pt.2:9)<br>Note 1 | Number—singular<br>Stem or root—from περιποίησις, εως<br>Concordance References:<br>⇒ Strong's #2992 laos + 1519+4047 eis peripoiësis<br>⇒ NIV #3295 laos [people] + 1650+4348 eis peripoiësis [belonging to God]<br>⇒ NASB #2992 laos + 1519+4047 eis peripoiësis<br><br>**1 Peter 2:9**<br>But ye are a chosen generation, a royal priesthood, an holy nation, a **peculiar people**; that ye should shew forth the praises of him who hath called you out of darkness into his marvellous light: [KJV]<br>But you are a chosen race, a royal priesthood, a HOLY NATION, a **people for God's own possession**, that you may proclaim the excellencies of Him who has called you out of darkness into His marvelous light; [NASB]<br>But you are a chosen people, a royal priesthood, a holy nation, a **people belonging to God**, that you may declare the praises of him who called you out of darkness into his wonderful light. [NIV]<br>But you *are* a chosen generation, a royal priesthood, a holy nation, **His own special people**, that you may proclaim the praises of Him who called you out of darkness into His marvelous light; [NKJV]<br>But you are not like that, for you are a chosen people. You are a kingdom of priests, God's holy nation, **his very own possession**. This is so you can show others the goodness of God, for he called you out of the darkness into his wonderful light. [NLT]<br>ὑμεῖς δὲ γένος ἐκλεκτόν, βασίλειον ἱεράτευμα, ἔθνος ἅγιον, **λαὸς εἰς περιποίησιν**, ὅπως τὰς ἀρετὰς ἐξαγγείλητε τοῦ ἐκ σκότους ὑμᾶς καλέσαντος εἰς τὸ θαυμαστὸν αὐτοῦ φῶς· [GNS]<br>Ὑμεῖς δὲ γένος ἐκλεκτόν, βασίλειον ἱεράτευμα, ἔθνος ἅγιον, **λαὸς εἰς περιποίησιν**, ὅπως τὰς ἀρετὰς ἐξαγγείλητε τοῦ ἐκ σκότους ὑμᾶς καλέσαντος εἰς τὸ θαυμαστὸν αὐτοῦ φῶς· [GNT] | Translation New Testament."<br>• "a people saved to be His own" (William F. Beck. *The New Testament in the Language of Today.* "The Four Translation New Testament."<br><br>This is a most precious thought: that God makes us His very own people, a very special possession of His. We are His *treasured possession*. Possession has the idea of value, of worth and preciousness. We are more precious to God than all the precious gems and treasures of the world. Possession also has the idea of provision, protection, and security. We are God's possession, His very special people; therefore, He will provide for us and protect us and make us secure in every sense of the word. |
| **#1964**<br>**Hold**<br><br>Continue–KJV<br>Abide–NASB<br>**Hold–NIV**<br>Abide–NKJV<br>Keep obeying–NLT<br><br>**POSB REFERENCE**<br>(Jn.8:31)<br>Note 1, point 2 | μείνητε = meinëte<br>Pronunciation: [meen'-ay-teh]<br>Parsing (part of speech): verb<br>  Mood—subjunctive<br>  Tense—aorist<br>  Voice—active<br>  Person—2nd person plural<br>  Stem or root—from μένω<br>Concordance References:<br>⇒ Strong's #3306 menö<br>⇒ NIV #3531 menö<br>⇒ NASB #3306 menö<br><br>**John 8:31**<br>Then said Jesus to those Jews which believed on him, If ye **continue** in my word, then are ye my disciples indeed; [KJV]<br>Jesus therefore was saying to those Jews who had believed Him, "If you **abide** in My word, then you are truly disciples of Mine; [NASB]<br>To the Jews who had believed him, Jesus said, "If you **hold** to my teaching, you are really my disciples. [NIV]<br>Then Jesus said to those Jews who believed Him, "If you **abide** in My word, you are My disciples indeed. [NKJV]<br>Jesus said to the people who believed in him, "You are truly my disciples if you **keep obeying** my teachings. [NLT]<br>Ἔλεγεν οὖν ὁ Ἰησοῦς πρὸς τοὺς πεπιστευκότας αὐτῷ Ἰουδαίους, Ἐὰν ὑμεῖς **μείνητε** ἐν τῷ λόγῳ τῷ ἐμῷ, ἀληθῶς μαθηταί μού ἐστε· [GNS]<br>Ἔλεγεν οὖν ὁ Ἰησοῦς πρὸς τοὺς πεπιστευκότας αὐτῷ Ἰουδαίους, Ἐὰν ὑμεῖς **μείνητε** ἐν τῷ λόγῳ τῷ ἐμῷ, ἀληθῶς μαθηταί μού ἐστε [GNT] | To hold; to continue; to abide; to keep on obeying. It means to dwell, continue, stay, sojourn, rest in or upon; to live; to rest; to nest.<br><br>**Practical Application**<br>The idea is that of dwelling, just as a person dwells at home. The Word of the Lord is the believer's dwelling place. He continues and abides in God's Word. Very simply, what Jesus was saying is this:<br>⇒ A person who really begins to believe will "continue in" or "hold on to" the Lord's Word. He will continue both to study and to do the Word (2 Tim. 2:15).<br>⇒ A person who does not really believe will not "hold on" to the Lord's Word.<br>⇒ The proof that a person "really believes" is that he does *hold on and abide and dwell* in the Lord's Word.<br>⇒ The proof that a person has made only a false or a superficial profession is that he does not "continue in" the Lord's Word. He just does not obey the Word of God. |

# PRACTICAL WORD STUDIES
## in the NEW TESTAMENT

| ENGLISH WORD | GREEK WORD AND VERSE | THE WORD MEANS... |
|---|---|---|
| **#1965**<br>**Hold**<br><br>Hold–KJV<br>Suppress–NASB<br>Suppress–NIV<br>Suppress–NKJV<br>Push–NLT<br><br>**POSB REFERENCE**<br>(Rom.1:18)<br>Note 1, point 3b | κατεχόντων = *katechontōn*<br>Pronunciation: [kat-ech'-own-town]<br>Parsing (part of speech): verb<br>    Mood—participle<br>    Tense—active<br>    Case—genitive<br>    Gender—masculine<br>    Number—plural<br>    Stem or root—from κατέχω<br>Concordance References:<br>  ⇒ Strong's #2722 katechō<br>  ⇒ NIV #2988 katechō<br>  ⇒ NASB #2722 katechō<br><br>**Romans 1:18**<br>For the wrath of God is revealed from heaven against all ungodliness and unrighteousness of men, who **hold** the truth in unrighteousness; [KJV]<br>For the wrath of God is revealed from heaven against all ungodliness and unrighteousness of men, who **suppress** the truth in unrighteousness, [NASB]<br>The wrath of God is being revealed from heaven against all the godlessness and wickedness of men who **suppress** the truth by their wickedness, [NIV]<br>For the wrath of God is revealed from heaven against all ungodliness and unrighteousness of men, who **suppress** the truth in unrighteousness, [NKJV]<br>But God shows his anger from heaven against all sinful, wicked people who **push** the truth away from themselves. [NLT]<br>Ἀποκαλύπτεται γὰρ ὀργὴ Θεοῦ ἀπ' οὐρανοῦ ἐπὶ πᾶσαν ἀσέβειαν καὶ ἀδικίαν ἀνθρώπων τῶν τὴν ἀλήθειαν ἐν ἀδικίᾳ **κατεχόντων**, [GNS]<br>Ἀποκαλύπτεται γὰρ ὀργὴ θεοῦ ἀπ' οὐρανοῦ ἐπὶ πᾶσαν ἀσέβειαν καὶ ἀδικίαν ἀνθρώπων τῶν τὴν ἀλήθειαν ἐν ἀδικίᾳ **κατεχόντων**, [GNT] | To hold down, suppress, repress, stifle, hinder; to keep; to possess; to hold back; to restrain.<br><br>**Practical Application**<br>Men know the truth from three sources:<br>⇒ from nature (cp. Romans 1:20).<br>⇒ from reason and conscience (cp. Romans 1:18; Romans 2:15).<br>⇒ from Scripture (John 5:39; 2 Tim. 3:16).<br><br>Yet despite having access to the truth, they ignore, neglect, and even push the truth aside, doing all they can to avoid and get rid of it. Why? Because they want to live as they wish and not as God says. They want to live unrighteous lives, to taste and feel and see and have all the stimulating things they want.<br>But note what Scripture says: they "hold the truth in unrighteousness"; that is, they know the truth while they go about living in unrighteousness. They are without excuse. |
| **#1966**<br>**Hold Fast**<br><br>Keep in memory–KJV<br>Hold fast–NASB<br>Hold firmly–NIV<br>Hold fast–NKJV<br>Firmly believe it–NLT<br><br>**POSB REFERENCE**<br>(1 Cor.15:1-2; esp. v.2)<br>Note 1, point 3 | κατέχετε = *katechete*<br>Pronunciation: [kat-ekh'-eh-teh]<br>Parsing (part of speech): verb<br>    Mood—indicative<br>    Tense—present<br>    Voice—active<br>    Person—2nd person<br>    Number—plural<br>    Stem or root—from κατέχω<br>Concordance References:<br>  ⇒ Strong's #2722 katechō<br>  ⇒ NIV #2988 katechō<br>  ⇒ NASB #2722 katechō<br><br>**1 Cor. 15:2**<br>By which also ye are saved, if ye **keep in memory** what I preached unto you, unless ye have believed in vain. [KJV]<br>By which also you are saved, if you **hold fast** the word which I preached to you, unless you believed in vain. [NASB]<br>By this gospel you are saved, if you **hold firmly** to the word I preached to you. Otherwise, you have believed in vain. [NIV]<br>By which also you are saved, if you **hold fast** that word which I preached to you—unless you believed in vain. [NKJV]<br>And it is this Good News that saves you if you **firmly believe it**—unless, of course, you believed something that was never true in the first place. [NLT]<br>δι' οὗ καὶ σῴζεσθε· τίνι λόγῳ εὐηγγελισάμην ὑμῖν, εἰ **κατέχετε**, ἐκτὸς εἰ μὴ εἰκῇ ἐπιστεύσατε. [GNS]<br>δι' οὗ καὶ σῴζεσθε, τίνι λόγῳ εὐηγγελισάμην ὑμῖν εἰ **κατέχετε**, ἐκτὸς εἰ μὴ εἰκῇ ἐπιστεύσατε. [GNT] | To hold firm; to firmly believe; to hold fast; to keep; to retain.<br><br>**Practical Application**<br>In order to be saved, a person must *hold fast* to the gospel. No person who denies the gospel could ever expect to be saved. |

# PRACTICAL WORD STUDIES
## in the NEW TESTAMENT

| ENGLISH WORD | GREEK WORD AND VERSE | THE WORD MEANS... |
|---|---|---|
| **#1967**<br>**Hold Firmly**<br><br>Keep in memory–KJV<br>Hold fast–NASB<br>**Hold firmly–NIV**<br>Hold fast–NKJV<br>Firmly believe it–NLT<br><br>**POSB REFERENCE**<br>(1 Cor.15:1-2; esp. v.2)<br>Note 1, point 3 | κατέχετε = katechete<br>Pronunciation: [kat-ekh'-eh-teh]<br>Parsing (part of speech): verb<br>    Mood—indicative<br>    Tense—present<br>    Voice—active<br>    Person—2nd person<br>    Number—plural<br>    Stem or root—from κατέχω<br>Concordance References:<br>  ⇒ Strong's #2722 katechö<br>  ⇒ NIV #2988 katechö<br>  ⇒ NASB #2722 katechö<br><br>**1 Cor. 15:2**<br>By which also ye are saved, if ye **keep in memory** what I preached unto you, unless ye have believed in vain. [KJV]<br>By which also you are saved, if you **hold fast** the word which I preached to you, unless you believed in vain. [NASB]<br>By this gospel you are saved, if you **hold firmly** to the word I preached to you. Otherwise, you have believed in vain. [NIV]<br>By which also you are saved, if you **hold fast** that word which I preached to you—unless you believed in vain. [NKJV]<br>And it is this Good News that saves you if you **firmly believe it**—unless, of course, you believed something that was never true in the first place. [NLT]<br>δι' οὗ καὶ σώζεσθε· τίνι λόγῳ εὐηγγελισάμην ὑμῖν, εἰ **κατέχετε**, ἐκτὸς εἰ μὴ εἰκῇ ἐπιστεύσατε. [GNS]<br>δι' οὗ καὶ σώζεσθε, τίνι λόγῳ εὐηγγελισάμην ὑμῖν εἰ **κατέχετε**, ἐκτὸς εἰ μὴ εἰκῇ ἐπιστεύσατε. [GNT] | To hold firmly; to firmly believe; to hold fast.<br><br>**Practical Application**<br>In order to be saved, of course, a person must hold firmly to the gospel. No person who denies the gospel could ever expect to be saved. |
| **#1968**<br>**Holiness**<br><br>**Holiness–KJV**<br>Reverent–NASB<br>Reverent–NIV<br>Reverent–NKJV<br>Appropriate–NLT<br><br>**POSB REFERENCE**<br>(Tit.2:3)<br>Note 3, point 1 | ἱεροπρεπεῖς = hieroprepeis<br>Pronunciation: [hee-er-op-rep-ice']<br>Parsing (part of speech): adjective<br>    Case—accusative<br>    Gender—feminine<br>    Number—plural<br>    Stem or root—from ἱεροπρεπής, ές<br>Concordance References:<br>  ⇒ Strong's #2412 hieroprepēs<br>  ⇒ NIV #2640 hieroprepēs<br>  ⇒ NASB #2412 hieroprepēs<br><br>**Titus 2:3**<br>The aged women likewise, that they be in behaviour as becometh **holiness**, not false accusers, not given to much wine, teachers of good things; [KJV]<br>Older women likewise are to be **reverent** in their behavior, not malicious gossips, nor enslaved to much wine, teaching what is good, [NASB]<br>Likewise, teach the older women to be **reverent** in the way they live, not to be slanderers or addicted to much wine, but to teach what is good. [NIV]<br>The older women likewise, that they be **reverent** in behavior, not slanderers, not given to much wine, teachers of good things– [NKJV]<br>Similarly, teach the older women to live in a way that is **appropriate** for someone serving the Lord. They must not go around speaking evil of others and must not be heavy drinkers. Instead, they should teach others what is good. [NLT]<br>Πρεσβύτιδας ὡσαύτως ἐν καταστήματι **ἱεροπρεπεῖς**, μὴ διαβόλους, μὴ οἴνῳ πολλῷ δεδουλωμένας, καλοδιδασκάλους, [GNS]<br>πρεσβύτιδας ὡσαύτως ἐν καταστήματι **ἱεροπρεπεῖς**, μὴ διαβόλους μηδὲ οἴνῳ πολλῷ δεδουλωμένας, καλοδιδασκάλους, [GNT] | Reverent, devout, holy, different and set apart in purity of behavior and thought.<br><br>**Practical Application**<br>Elderly women are to live and move about in an appropriate spirit and be focused upon sacred things. Matthew Henry says that elderly women are to keep "a pious [holy] decency and decorum in clothing and gesture, in looks and speech, and in all their deportment [behavior]" (*Matthew Henry's Commentary*, p.862). |

**PRACTICAL WORD STUDIES**
in the NEW TESTAMENT

| ENGLISH WORD | GREEK WORD AND VERSE | THE WORD MEANS... |
|---|---|---|
| **#1969** **Holiness–Holy** Holiness–KJV Sanctification–NASB Holiness–NIV Holiness–NKJV Holy–NLT **POSB REFERENCE** (Rom.6:19-20, esp. v.19) See also POSB REF: (Heb.12:14) Note 1, point 2 | ἁγιασμόν = hagiasmon Pronunciation: [hag-ee-ahs-mown'] Parsing (part of speech): noun   Case—accusative   Gender—masculine   Number—singular   Stem or root—from ἁγιασμός, οῦ Concordance References: ⇒ Strong's #38 hagiasmos ⇒ NIV #40 hagiasmos ⇒ NASB #38 hagiasmos **Romans 6:19** I speak after the manner of men because of the infirmity of your flesh: for as ye have yielded your members servants to uncleanness and to iniquity unto iniquity; even so now yield your members servants to righteousness unto **holiness**. [KJV] I am speaking in human terms because of the weakness of your flesh. For just as you presented your members as slaves to impurity and to lawlessness, resulting in further lawlessness, so now present your members as slaves to righteousness, resulting in **sanctification**. [NASB] I put this in human terms because you are weak in your natural selves. Just as you used to offer the parts of your body in slavery to impurity and to ever-increasing wickedness, so now offer them in slavery to righteousness leading to **holiness**. [NIV] I speak in human *terms* because of the weakness of your flesh. For just as you presented your members *as* slaves of uncleanness, and of lawlessness *leading* to *more* lawlessness, so now present your members *as slaves of* righteousness for **holiness**. [NKJV] I speak this way, using the illustration of slaves and masters, because it is easy to understand. Before, you let yourselves be slaves of impurity and lawlessness. Now you must choose to be slaves of righteousness so that you will become **holy**. [NLT] ἀνθρώπινον λέγω διὰ τὴν ἀσθένειαν τῆς σαρκὸς ὑμῶν. ὥσπερ γὰρ παρεστήσατε τὰ μέλη ὑμῶν δοῦλα τῇ ἀκαθαρσίᾳ καὶ τῇ ἀνομίᾳ εἰς τὴν ἀνομίαν, οὕτω νῦν παραστήσατε τὰ μέλη ὑμῶν δοῦλα τῇ δικαιοσύνῃ εἰς **ἁγιασμόν**. [GNS] ἀνθρώπινον λέγω διὰ τὴν ἀσθένειαν τῆς σαρκὸς ὑμῶν. ὥσπερ γὰρ παρεστήσατε τὰ μέλη ὑμῶν δοῦλα τῇ ἀκαθαρσίᾳ καὶ τῇ ἀνομίᾳ εἰς τὴν ἀνομίαν, οὕτως νῦν παραστήσατε τὰ μέλη ὑμῶν δοῦλα τῇ δικαιοσύνῃ εἰς **ἁγιασμόν**. [GNT] | Consecration, dedication, sanctification, holiness. **Practical Application** Now the believer is to let righteousness work holiness (*hagiasmon*). The word means sanctification or holiness. The believer is to yield the parts of his body to serve righteousness, and he is to let righteousness sanctify him more and more. He is to live righteously and become more and more holy like God. (See POSB *Deeper Study* #1, Holy—1 Peter 1:15-16 for more discussion.) The believer is to follow after "holiness" (*hagiasmon*). The word means sanctification, consecration, and separation. It means to be set apart and different. The root meaning of holiness is to be different. The believer is to be different from the unbelievers of the world in that he... • is set apart to God and to Him alone. • is separated from the world and its pleasures and possessions. The believer, of course, *lives in the world*. He walks and moves within the world; buys, eats, and sleeps in the world; works, plays, and is housed in the world; relates, associates, and fellowships in the world. However, the believer is *not to be of the world*. He is not to be possessed by the world, enslaved to its pleasures and possessions. What does this mean? In very simple terms, the believer is not to indulge and give license to his flesh... ⇒ He is not to buy and buy; he is not to be a materialist. ⇒ He is not to eat and eat; he is not to be a glutton. ⇒ He is not to sleep and sleep; he is not to be slothful. ⇒ He is not to work and work; he is not to be a workaholic. ⇒ He is not to play and play; he is not to over emphasize recreation. ⇒ He is not to have house after house; he is not to hoard riches in a world of desperate needs. ⇒ He is not to fellowship and fellowship; he is not to neglect duty. The believer is to be separated from the world and its pleasures and possessions. He is to be set apart to God, living for God and serving Him in His great mission. The believer is to meet the needs of a desperate world that is dying from sin, disease, hunger, and war. The believer is to be different from the rest of the world; he is to follow after holiness. Note: this verse declares that no person will ever see the Lord unless he is holy. Holiness is an absolute essential if a person is to live with God (See POSB *Deeper Study* #1, Holy— 1 Peter 1:15-16 for more discussion.) |
| **#1970** **Holy** Sanctified–KJV Sanctified–NASB Sanctified–NIV Sanctified–NKJV Holy–NLT | οὖσῃ ἡγιασμένοις = ousē hēgiasmenois Pronunciation: [hayg-ee-ahs-meh'-nois] Parsing *hēgiasmenois* (part of speech): verb   Mood—participle   Tense—perfect   Voice—passive   Case—dative   Gender—masculine   Person—2nd person   Number—plural   Stem or root—from ἁγιάζω | To be sanctified; to be set apart; to be made holy; to be consecrated; to be separated (cp. 1 Peter 1:15-16). **Practical Application** There are three stages of sanctification. 1. There is initial or positional sanctification. When a person believes in Jesus Christ, he is immediately set apart for God. This is a permanent, once-for-all act (Hebrews 3:1; cp. |

# PRACTICAL WORD STUDIES
## in the New Testament

| ENGLISH WORD | GREEK WORD AND VERSE | THE WORD MEANS... |
|---|---|---|
| **POSB REFERENCE** (1 Cor.1:2) *Deeper Study #1* | Concordance References:<br>⇒ Strong's #37+1510 hagiazō eimi<br>⇒ NIV #39+1639 hagiazō eimi [sanctified]<br>⇒ NASB #37+1510 hagiazō eimi<br><br>**1 Cor. 1:2**<br>Unto the church of God which is at Corinth, to them that are **sanctified** in Christ Jesus, called to be saints, with all that in every place call upon the name of Jesus Christ our Lord, both theirs and ours: [KJV]<br><br>To the church of God which is at Corinth, to those who have been **sanctified** in Christ Jesus, saints by calling, with all who in every place call upon the name of our Lord Jesus Christ, their Lord and ours: [NASB]<br><br>To the church of God in Corinth, to those **sanctified** in Christ Jesus and called to be holy, together with all those everywhere who call on the name of our Lord Jesus Christ—their Lord and ours: [NIV]<br><br>To the church of God which is at Corinth, to those who are **sanctified** in Christ Jesus, called *to be* saints, with all who in every place call on the name of Jesus Christ our Lord, both theirs and ours: [NKJV]<br><br>We are writing to the church of God in Corinth, you who have been called by God to be his own holy people. He made you **holy** by means of Christ Jesus, just as he did all Christians everywhere—whoever calls upon the name of Jesus Christ, our Lord and theirs. [NLT]<br><br>τῇ ἐκκλησίᾳ τοῦ Θεοῦ τῇ **οὔσῃ** ἐν Κορίνθῳ, **ἡγιασμένοις** ἐν Χριστῷ Ἰησοῦ, κλητοῖς ἁγίοις, σὺν πᾶσι τοῖς ἐπικαλουμένοις τὸ ὄνομα τοῦ Κυρίου ἡμῶν Ἰησοῦ Χριστοῦ ἐν παντὶ τόπῳ, αὐτῶν τε καὶ ἡμῶν· [GNS]<br><br>τῇ ἐκκλησίᾳ τοῦ Θεοῦ τῇ **οὔσῃ** ἐν Κορίνθῳ, **ἡγιασμένοις** ἐν Χριστῷ Ἰησοῦ, κλητοῖς ἁγίοις, σὺν πᾶσιν τοῖς ἐπικαλουμένοις τὸ ὄνομα τοῦ κυρίου ἡμῶν Ἰησοῦ Χριστοῦ ἐν παντὶ τόπῳ, αὐτῶν καὶ ἡμῶν· [GNT] | Hebrews 10:10).<br>2. There is progressive sanctification. The true believer makes a determined and disciplined effort to allow the Spirit of God to set him apart day by day. The Spirit of God takes him and conforms him to the image of Christ more and more. This growth takes place as long as the believer walks upon this earth (cp. John 17:17; 2 Cor. 3:18; Ephes. 5:25-26; 1 Thes. 5:23-24).<br>3. There is eternal sanctification. The day is coming when the believer will be perfectly set apart unto God and His service—without any sin or failure whatsoever. That day will be the great and glorious day of the believer's eternal redemption (Ephes. 5:27; 1 John 3:2). |
| **#1971 Holy**<br><br>Saints–KJV<br>Saints–NASB<br>Holy–NIV<br>Saints–NKJV<br>Holy–NLT<br><br>**POSB REFERENCE** (1 Cor.1:2) *Deeper Study #2* | ἁγίοις = hagiois<br>Pronunciation: [hag'-ee-os]<br>Parsing (part of speech): adjective<br>    Case—dative<br>    Gender—masculine<br>    Number—plural<br>    Stem or root—from ἅγιος, α, ον<br>Concordance References:<br>⇒ Strong's #40 hagios<br>⇒ NIV #41 hagios<br>⇒ NASB #40 hagios<br><br>**1 Cor. 1:2**<br>Unto the church of God which is at Corinth, to them that are sanctified in Christ Jesus, called to be **saints**, with all that in every place call upon the name of Jesus Christ our Lord, both theirs and ours: [KJV]<br><br>To the church of God which is at Corinth, to those who have been sanctified in Christ Jesus, **saints** by calling, with all who in every place call upon the name of our Lord Jesus Christ, their Lord and ours: [NASB]<br><br>To the church of God in Corinth, to those sanctified in Christ Jesus and called to be **holy**, together with all those everywhere who call on the name of our Lord Jesus Christ—their Lord and ours: [NIV]<br><br>To the church of God which is at Corinth, to those who are sanctified in Christ Jesus, called to be **saints**, with all who in every place call on the name of Jesus Christ our Lord, both theirs and ours: [NKJV]<br><br>We are writing to the church of God in Corinth, you who have been called by God to be his own holy people. He made you **holy** by means of Christ Jesus, just as he did all Christians everywhere—whoever calls upon the name of Jesus Christ, our Lord and theirs. [NLT] | Set apart by God; consecrated, sacred, and holy.<br><br>**Practical Application**<br>A saint, a holy person, is a follower of the Lord Jesus Christ who has been set apart to live for God. The saint has given himself to live a consecrated, sacred, and holy life—all for the glory of God. Note that believers are saints in both senses:<br>1. Believers are saints in the sense that they have been given a new heart by God: a heart that is renewed and recreated in righteousness and true holiness.<br>2. Believers are saints in the sense that they are set apart to live consecrated and holy lives in this world. |

# PRACTICAL WORD STUDIES
## in the NEW TESTAMENT

| ENGLISH WORD | GREEK WORD AND VERSE | THE WORD MEANS... |
|---|---|---|
| | τῇ ἐκκλησίᾳ τοῦ Θεοῦ τῇ οὔσῃ ἐν Κορίνθῳ, ἡγιασμένοις ἐν Χριστῷ Ἰησοῦ, κλητοῖς **ἁγίοις**, σὺν πᾶσι τοῖς ἐπικαλουμένοις τὸ ὄνομα τοῦ Κυρίου ἡμῶν Ἰησοῦ Χριστοῦ ἐν παντὶ τόπῳ, αὐτῶν τε καὶ ἡμῶν· [GNS]<br><br>τῇ ἐκκλησίᾳ τοῦ θεοῦ τῇ οὔσῃ ἐν Κορίνθῳ, ἡγιασμένοις ἐν Χριστῷ Ἰησοῦ, κλητοῖς **ἁγίοις**, σὺν πᾶσιν τοῖς ἐπικαλουμένοις τὸ ὄνομα τοῦ κυρίου ἡμῶν Ἰησοῦ Χριστοῦ ἐν παντὶ τόπῳ, αὐτῶν καὶ ἡμῶν. [GNT] | |
| **#1972**<br>**Holy**<br><br>Saints–KJV<br>Saints–NASB<br>**Holy–NIV**<br>Saints–NKJV<br>God's holy people–NLT<br><br>**POSB REFERENCE**<br>(Col.1:2)<br>Note 3, point 1<br><br>See also POSB REF:<br>(Eph.1:4)<br>Note 2, point 1<br>(Eph.5:25-33; esp. v.25)<br>Note 2, point 1<br>(Col.1:22)<br>Note 3, point 1<br>(Col.3:12-14; esp. v.12)<br>Note 1 | ἁγίοις = *hagiois*<br>Pronunciation: [hag'-ee-oys]<br>Parsing (part of speech): adjective<br>    Case—dative<br>    Gender—masculine<br>    Number—plural<br>    Stem or root—from ἅγιος, α, ον<br>Concordance References:<br>  ⇒ Strong's #40 hagios<br>  ⇒ NIV #41 hagios<br>  ⇒ NASB #40 hagios<br><br>**Col. 1:2**<br>To the **saints** and faithful brethren in Christ which are at Colosse: Grace be unto you, and peace, from God our Father and the Lord Jesus Christ. [KJV]<br><br>To the **saints** and faithful brethren in Christ who are at Colossae: Grace to you and peace from God our Father. [NASB]<br><br>To the **holy** and faithful brothers in Christ at Colosse: Grace and peace to you from God our Father. [NIV]<br><br>To the **saints** and faithful brethren in Christ who are in Colosse: Grace to you and peace from God our Father and the Lord Jesus Christ. [NKJV]<br><br>It is written to **God's holy people** in the city of Colosse, who are faithful brothers and sisters in Christ. May God our Father give you grace and peace. [NLT]<br><br>τοῖς ἐν Κολοσσαῖς **ἁγίοις** καὶ πιστοῖς ἀδελφοῖς ἐν Χριστῷ· χάρις ὑμῖν καὶ εἰρήνη ἀπὸ Θεοῦ πατρὸς ἡμῶν καὶ Κυρίου Ἰησοῦ Χριστοῦ. [GNS]<br><br>τοῖς ἐν Κολοσσαῖς **ἁγίοις** καὶ πιστοῖς ἀδελφοῖς ἐν Χριστῷ, χάρις ὑμῖν καὶ εἰρήνη ἀπὸ θεοῦ πατρὸς ἡμῶν. [GNT] | To be holy; to be morally pure. It means to be set apart and consecrated to God.<br><br>**Practical Application**<br>There are the *carnal saints or believers* within the church. This refers to those who in the past had set their lives apart to follow the Lord Jesus. They *had separated* themselves from the world and *had turned* to the Lord Jesus to save them. However, a saint or believer may or may not *continue on* with the Lord Jesus. Some in the Colossian church *were not continuing on*. They were not fully committed. Their commitment to the Lord Jesus Christ was lacking. Therefore, they were running the risk of falling into the error of false teaching and turning away from Christ. The point is this: a person can be a carnal believer or carnal "saint" within the church. Just because a person has made a profession and given some semblance of following Christ does not mean he is safe and secure forever—that he is automatically mature in Christ. When a person truly comes to know Christ, he is just beginning a journey with Christ, a journey that has a much higher level of spiritual growth to reach.<br>There are faithful saints or believers in the church. This refers to those who had set their lives apart to Christ and had continued on. They were loyal and steadfast in their allegiance, and they held firm against the attacks of worldliness and false teaching. They were not shaken by the temptations of the devil nor by the urges of the flesh. They were faithful against all foes.<br>The point is this: once a person has become a saint, that is, set his life apart to follow Christ, he is to be faithful. And he is to grow in his faithfulness. In fact, the highest level of spiritual maturity is that of faithfulness. Being faithful or obedient to Christ is the one thing that pleases Christ above all else.<br>  ⇒ We must live lives that are set apart to Christ, to the belief that He died for our reconciliation and that His death covers us.<br>  ⇒ We must live lives that are separated from worldliness and selfishness and from the flesh and its sins.<br>  ⇒ We must live lives that are set apart and consecrated to God and His service, lives that live for His cause. |
| **#1973**<br>**Holy**<br><br>Sanctification–KJV<br>Sanctifying–NASB<br>Sanctifying–NIV<br>Sanctification–NKJV<br>**Holy–NLT** | ἁγιασμῷ = *hagiasmō*<br>Pronunciation: [hag-ee-ahs-mo']<br>Parsing (part of speech): noun<br>    Case—dative<br>    Gender—masculine<br>    Number—singular<br>    Stem or root—from ἁγιασμός, οῦ<br>Concordance References:<br>  ⇒ Strong's #38 hagiasmos<br>  ⇒ NIV #40 hagiasmos<br>  ⇒ NASB #38 hagiasmos | Sanctifying, sanctification; holiness, dedication, consecration. It means separated or set apart.<br><br>**Practical Application**<br>The chosen are elected by God. They are actually called the elect, a people who had been elected or chosen by God. This means a most wonderful thing. It means that believers have the highest position in all the world, the position of being *God's own holy and beloved children* (cp. Col. 3:12). |

# PRACTICAL WORD STUDIES
## in the New Testament

| ENGLISH WORD | GREEK WORD AND VERSE | THE WORD MEANS... |
|---|---|---|
| **POSB REFERENCE** (1 Pt.1:2) Note 2 | **1 Peter 1:2** <br> Elect according to the foreknowledge of God the Father, through **sanctification** of the Spirit, unto obedience and sprinkling of the blood of Jesus Christ: Grace unto you, and peace, be multiplied. [KJV] <br><br> According to the foreknowledge of God the Father, by the **sanctifying** work of the Spirit, that you may obey Jesus Christ and be sprinkled with His blood: May grace and peace be yours in fullest measure. [NASB] <br><br> Who have been chosen according to the foreknowledge of God the Father, through the **sanctifying** work of the Spirit, for obedience to Jesus Christ and sprinkling by his blood: Grace and peace be yours in abundance. [NIV] <br><br> Elect according to the foreknowledge of God the Father, in **sanctification** of the Spirit, for obedience and sprinkling of the blood of Jesus Christ: Grace to you and peace be multiplied. [NKJV] <br><br> God the Father chose you long ago, and the Spirit has made you **holy**. As a result, you have obeyed Jesus Christ and are cleansed by his blood. May you have more and more of God's special favor and wonderful peace. [NLT] <br><br> κατὰ πρόγνωσιν Θεοῦ πατρός, ἐν **ἁγιασμῷ** Πνεύματος, εἰς ὑπακοὴν καὶ ῥαντισμὸν αἵματος Ἰησοῦ Χριστοῦ· χάρις ὑμῖν καὶ εἰρήνη πληθυνθείη. [GNS] <br><br> κατὰ πρόγνωσιν θεοῦ πατρὸς ἐν **ἁγιασμῷ** πνεύματος εἰς ὑπακοὴν καὶ ῥαντισμὸν αἵματος Ἰησοῦ Χριστοῦ, χάρις ὑμῖν καὶ εἰρήνη πληθυνθείη. [GNT] | Believers have been elected to be *holy*. God called believers out of the world and away from the old life it offered, the old life of sin and death. He called believers to be separated and set apart to Himself and the new life He offers, the new life of righteousness and eternity. |
| **#1974** <br> **Holy** <br><br> Holy–KJV <br> Holy–NASB <br> Holy–NIV <br> Holy–NKJV <br> Holy–NLT <br><br> **POSB REFERENCE** (1 Pt.1:15-16; esp. v.15) Note 3 <br><br> See also POSB REF: (1 Pt.1:15-16; esp. v.15) *Deeper Study* #1 | ἅγιοι = *hagioi* <br> Pronunciation: [hag-ee-oy] <br> Parsing (part of speech): adjective <br>     Case—nominative <br>     Gender—masculine <br>     Number—plural <br>     Stem or root—from ἅγιος, α, ον <br> Concordance References: <br> ⇒ Strong's #39 hagios <br> ⇒ NIV #41 hagios <br> ⇒ NASB #39 hagios <br><br> **1 Peter 1:15** <br> But as he which hath called you is holy, so be ye **holy** in all manner of conversation; [KJV] <br><br> But like the Holy One who called you, be **holy** yourselves also in all your behavior; [NASB] <br><br> But just as he who called you is holy, so be **holy** in all you do; [NIV] <br><br> But as He who called you *is* holy, you also be **holy** in all *your* conduct, [NKJV] <br><br> But now you must be **holy** in everything you do, just as God—who chose you to be his children—is holy. [NLT] <br><br> ἀλλὰ κατὰ τὸν καλέσαντα ὑμᾶς ἅγιον καὶ αὐτοὶ **ἅγιοι** ἐν πάσῃ ἀναστροφῇ γενήθητε· [GNS] <br><br> ἀλλὰ κατὰ τὸν καλέσαντα ὑμᾶς ἅγιον καὶ αὐτοὶ **ἅγιοι** ἐν πάσῃ ἀναστροφῇ γενήθητε, [GNT] | Holy. It means to be righteous, pure, sinless, and godly; to be perfect, complete, and fulfilled in every possible sense; to be separated and entirely different from all other beings and things. <br><br> **Practical Application** <br> The believer is to be holy, that is... <br> • righteous, pure, sinless, and godly. <br> • perfect, complete, and fulfilled. <br> • separated, entirely different from all who live worldly. <br><br> Note: Holy–Saint–Sanctification (*hagioi*)—all three of these words and their various forms (holiness, saints, and sanctification)—are translated from one Greek word *hagios*. Its Hebrew equivalent is *kadosh*. The word is difficult to translate into English although its meaning is easy to grasp. Its basic meaning is to be separated, set apart, and different. Morally, it means pure, sinless, righteous, holy. Something holy is set apart, separated, different from all other persons or things. It is something that God has set aside for Himself. Man cannot set it aside as holy. It has to be set aside by God Himself. <br><br> A study of the word *holy* shows the movement of God in history. <br> 1. God is said to be preeminently and supremely holy (Luke 1:49; John 17:11; 1 Peter 1:15). He possesses an incomparable majesty, a glory so supremely majestic that beings surround His throne day and night, beings who do nothing but singing out the praises of His holiness (Isaiah 6:1f; Rev. 4:8). <br> 2. Things that have a special connection to God are said to be holy. The ground upon which Moses stood when God confronted him was said to be holy (Exodus 3:1-5; Acts 7:33). The temple was said to be holy (Matthew 24:15), and the Holy of Holies in particular was holy (Hebrews 9:2-3). The mount where Christ was transfigured was called holy (2 |

| ENGLISH WORD | GREEK WORD AND VERSE | THE WORD MEANS... |
|---|---|---|
| | | Peter 1:18). The covenant that God made with Abraham was holy (Luke 1:35). The gospel and Scriptures are called holy (Matthew 7:6; Romans 1:2). Anything that becomes associated with God is set apart to God in a very special sense and becomes different from other things.<br>3. The Jews are called a *holy nation* (Exodus 19:6). They were set apart in a very special way to God. The Old Testament deals primarily with the Jews and their special relationship to God: "Ye shall be holy unto me; for I, the Lord, am holy, and have separated you from other people, that ye should be mine" (Leviticus 20:26; cp. Daniel 7:18, 22).<br>⇒ The Jewish people were *holy* in that they were to be different from other nations, different in that they were to believe God and serve Him faithfully. God knew them in a very special way above all the nations of the earth (see POSB *Deeper Study #1—* John 4:22; POSB *Deeper Study #1—* Romans 4:1-25).<br>⇒ The Jewish priesthood was *holy*, different from other men (Leviticus 21:6). The people's tithe or tenth was *holy*, different from other money and goods and used for different purposes (Leviticus 27:30, 32). The temple was *holy*, different from other buildings (Exodus 26:33).<br>But note this: the Jews refused to play the part in history that God wanted them to play. The Old Testament is a continuous record of their rejection of God's will. And when God sent His Son into the world, they committed the supreme and lasting rejection. They refused to acknowledge Him and put Him to death.<br>4. Jesus Christ is said to be holy in a very special way.<br>⇒ Before His birth, the angel said to Mary, "That holy One who shall be born of thee shall be called the Son of God" (Luke 1:35).<br>⇒ Mary worshipped Him in song and praise before His birth saying, "Holy is His name" (Luke 1:49f). He was the only begotten Son of God, *holy*, revered, and worthy of veneration and worship.<br>⇒ The people recognized that He was *sanctified* by God (John 10:36; cp. John 6:69).<br>⇒ The mentally ill and demon-possessed recognized Him as the Holy One of God (Mark 1:24; Luke 4:34).<br>⇒ The church worshipped Him as "the Holy Child of God" (Acts 4:27, 30).<br>Note this: Jesus Christ Himself was the transition from God's dealing with the Jewish nation as holy to a new people as holy. When the Jews rejected God's Son, they showed their ultimate refusal to follow God, to be holy and separated to Him. Therefore, God had no choice but to raise up another people to be separated to Him. The new people are those of all nations and peoples who believe and follow Christ as the Lord of their lives.<br>5. The church is now said to be the holy people of God. The privileges and responsibilities of following God were taken from Israel and given to the church (John 17:14, 16; Romans 11:16f). |

# PRACTICAL WORD STUDIES
## in the NEW TESTAMENT

| ENGLISH WORD | GREEK WORD AND VERSE | THE WORD MEANS... |
|---|---|---|
| | | ⇒ The church is called *a holy nation* and a *royal or holy priesthood*, a people made up of genuine believers from all nationalities and languages and races (1 Peter 2:5, 9).<br>⇒ The church is a people who set themselves apart to God as holy and separated and different, who utterly trust Him and abandon themselves to follow Him.<br>⇒ The church is now the dwelling place for God's presence. Believers are being built "together for a habitation of God through the Spirit" (Ephes. 2:21-22). The church in some unique and spiritual sense, by an act of God, becomes the very body of Christ (Ephes. 1:22-23). The church, the body of believers when meeting together locally, now replaces the temple of the Old Testament (see POSB note—1 Cor. 3:16).<br>6. But there is something even more precious and hallowed to real believers. The body of the individual believer becomes holy, for the Spirit of God dwells within the believer's body (1 Cor. 6:19-20). The body of the believer becomes the dwelling place for God's very presence, and the body replaces the holy of holies within the inner sanctuary of the temple. Thus, believers are called *saints or holy ones* (Acts 9:13, 32, 41; Acts 26:10; Romans 1:7. See POSB note, Saint—Phil. 1:1.) |
| #1975<br>**Holy**<br><br>**Holy–KJV**<br>**Holy–NASB**<br>**Holy–NIV**<br>**Holy–NKJV**<br>Belong to God–NLT<br><br>**POSB<br>REFERENCE**<br>(Heb.3:1)<br>Note 1, point 1 | ἅγιοι = *hagioi*<br>Pronunciation: [hag'-ee-oy]<br>Parsing (part of speech): adjective<br>    Case—vocative<br>    Gender—masculine<br>    Number—plural<br>    Stem or root—from ἅγιος, α, ον<br>Concordance References:<br>  ⇒ Strong's #40 hagios<br>  ⇒ NIV #41 hagios<br>  ⇒ NASB #40 hagios<br><br>**Hebrews 3:1**<br>Wherefore, **holy** brethren, partakers of the heavenly calling, consider the Apostle and High Priest of our profession, Christ Jesus; [KJV]<br>Therefore, **holy** brethren, partakers of a heavenly calling, consider Jesus, the Apostle and High Priest of our confession. [NASB]<br>Therefore, **holy** brothers, who share in the heavenly calling, fix your thoughts on Jesus, the apostle and high priest whom we confess. [NIV]<br>Therefore, **holy** brethren, partakers of the heavenly calling, consider the Apostle and High Priest of our confession, Christ Jesus, [NKJV]<br>And so, dear brothers and sisters who **belong to God** and are bound for heaven, think about this Jesus whom we declare to be God's Messenger and High Priest. [NLT]<br>Ὅθεν, ἀδελφοὶ **ἅγιοι**, κλήσεως ἐπουρανίου μέτοχοι, κατανοήσατε τὸν ἀπόστολον καὶ ἀρχιερέα τῆς ὁμολογίας ἡμῶν Χριστὸν Ἰησοῦν, [GNS]<br>Ὅθεν, ἀδελφοὶ **ἅγιοι**, κλήσεως ἐπουρανίου μέτοχοι, κατανοήσατε τὸν ἀπόστολον καὶ ἀρχιερέα τῆς ὁμολογίας ἡμῶν Ἰησοῦν, [GNT] | Holy; to be set apart or separated to Christ; to belong to God; to be morally pure; saints; devoted; set apart.<br><br>**Practical Application**<br>1. Believers should fix their attention upon Jesus Christ because of who they are.<br>⇒ Believers are holy brothers. The word "holy" (*hagioi*) means to be set apart or separated to Christ. It means that we have turned away from the unclean things of the world and from the religions of the world and have turned to Christ. We are holy, set apart to be a brother to Christ. Therefore, we should be following and focusing our attention upon Christ.<br>⇒ Believers are partakers of the heavenly calling. We have been called by Christ to live with God in heaven. We are not to live for this earth; we are to live for heaven. Therefore, our attention is to be fixed upon heaven, especially upon Christ who is our glorious Savior and who has made it possible for us to live in heaven.<br>2. Believers should fix their attention upon Jesus Christ because of who Christ is.<br>a. Jesus Christ is the *Apostle* of our confession. The word *apostle* means a person who is sent forth as an ambassador: sent forth by a king or a country on a special mission with a special message. And note: the person is always sent forth with the full authority and power of the king and country which he represents. This is Jesus Christ. Note the word *profession* or *confession*: we confess that Jesus Christ is the Supreme Apostle of our faith and lives. |

# PRACTICAL WORD STUDIES
## in the NEW TESTAMENT

| ENGLISH WORD | GREEK WORD AND VERSE | THE WORD MEANS... |
|---|---|---|
| | | We confess that He is the One whom God sent from heaven to earth...<br>• as the supreme representative of God, the One who shows us exactly what God is like.<br>• as the supreme messenger of God, the One who tells us the truth about God and ourselves and the world.<br>• with all the authority and power of God, the One who has control over all the world and over all the trials and circumstances of our lives.<br>b. Jesus Christ is the High Priest of our confession (see POSB *Deeper Study* #2, Jesus Christ, High Priest—Heb.3:1 for discussion). |
| **#1976**<br>**Holy**<br><br>Holy–KJV<br>Holy–NASB<br>Holy–NIV<br>Holy–NKJV<br>Holy–NLT<br><br>**POSB REFERENCE**<br>(Heb.7:26)<br>Note 2, point 1<br><br>See also POSB REF:<br>(Tit.1:7-8; esp. v.8)<br>Note 3, point 2e | ὅσιος = *hosios*<br>Pronunciation: [hos'-ee-os]<br>Parsing (part of speech): adjective<br>    Case—nominative<br>    Gender—masculine<br>    Number—singular<br>    Stem or root—from ὅσιος, α, ον<br>Concordance References:<br>    Strong's #3741 hosios<br>    NIV #4008 hosios<br>    NASB #3741 hosios<br><br>**Hebrews 7:26**<br>For such an high priest became us, who is **holy**, harmless, undefiled, separate from sinners, and made higher than the heavens; [KJV]<br>For it was fitting that we should have such a high priest, **holy**, innocent, undefiled, separated from sinners and exalted above the heavens. [NASB]<br>Such a high priest meets our need—one who is **holy**, blameless, pure, set apart from sinners, exalted above the heavens. [NIV]<br>For such a High Priest was fitting for us, *who is* **holy**, harmless, undefiled, separate from sinners, and has become higher than the heavens; [NKJV]<br>He is the kind of high priest we need because he is **holy** and blameless, unstained by sin. He has now been set apart from sinners, and he has been given the highest place of honor in heaven. [NLT]<br>Τοιοῦτος γὰρ ἡμῖν ἔπρεπεν ἀρχιερεύς, **ὅσιος**, ἄκακος, ἀμίαντος, κεχωρισμένος ἀπὸ τῶν ἁμαρτωλῶν, καὶ ὑψηλότερος τῶν οὐρανῶν γενόμενος· [GNS]<br>Τοιοῦτος γὰρ ἡμῖν καὶ ἔπρεπεν ἀρχιερεύς, **ὅσιος** ἄκακος ἀμίαντος, κεχωρισμένος ἀπὸ τῶν ἁμαρτωλῶν καὶ ὑψηλότερος τῶν οὐρανῶν γενόμενος, [GNT] | To be holy; to be pious; to be devout; to be set apart and separated to God.<br><br>**Practical Application**<br>The word means to be separated from sin and from all evil, and from immoral, wicked, and lawless behavior. Jesus Christ is "holy" (*hosios*): Jesus Christ is perfectly and eternally set apart from sin and free from all immoral and lawless behavior. Jesus Christ is absolutely *holy*. |
| **#1977**<br>**Holy Fear**<br><br>Fear–KJV<br>Reverence–NASB<br>Holy fear–NIV<br>Godly fear–NKJV<br>Obeyed–NLT<br><br>**POSB REFERENCE**<br>(Heb.11:7)<br>Note 1, point 1 | εὐλαβηθείς = *eulabētheis*<br>Pronunciation: [yoo-lab-ay'-theh-ees]<br>Parsing (part of speech): verb<br>    Mood—participle<br>    Tense—aorist<br>    Voice—passive deponent<br>    Case—nominative<br>    Gender—masculine<br>    Number—singular<br>    Stem or root—from εὐλαβέομαι<br>Concordance References:<br>⇒ Strong's #2125 eulabeomai<br>⇒ NIV #2326 eulabeomai<br>⇒ NASB #2125 eulabeomai<br><br>**Hebrews 11:7**<br>By faith Noah, being warned of God of things not seen as yet, moved with **fear**, prepared an ark to the saving of his house; by the which he condemned the world, and became heir of the righteousness which is by faith. [KJV] | Fear, holy fear; to reverence; to obey; to be moved with fear. The words "holy fear" (*eulabētheis*) mean with godly fear (A.T. Robertson. *Word Pictures in the New Testament*, Vol. 5, p.421). It has the idea of...<br>• reverence.<br>• standing in awe of God and His warning.<br>• taking heed lest one fall under God's judgment.<br>• diligently taking God at His Word.<br>• immediately acting upon what God says.<br><br>**Practical Application**<br>There was a time in world history when the earth had become so wicked that it was filled with corruption and violence. It was so corrupt that every imagination of man's heart was corrupt and evil. Man had reached the point of no return; he would never repent and return to God. |

## PRACTICAL WORD STUDIES
### in the New Testament

| ENGLISH WORD | GREEK WORD AND VERSE | THE WORD MEANS... |
|---|---|---|
| | By faith Noah, being warned by God about things not yet seen, in **reverence** prepared an ark for the salvation of his household, by which he condemned the world, and became an heir of the righteousness which is according to faith. [NASB]<br><br>By faith Noah, when warned about things not yet seen, in **holy fear** built an ark to save his family. By his faith he condemned the world and became heir of the righteousness that comes by faith. [NIV]<br><br>By faith Noah, being divinely warned of things not yet seen, moved with **godly fear**, prepared an ark for the saving of his household, by which he condemned the world and became heir of the righteousness which is according to faith. [NKJV]<br><br>It was by faith that Noah built an ark to save his family from the flood. He **obeyed** God, who warned him about something that had never happened before. By his faith he condemned the rest of the world and was made right in God's sight. [NLT]<br><br>πίστει χρηματισθεὶς Νῶε περὶ τῶν μηδέπω βλεπομένων, **εὐλαβηθεὶς**, κατεσκεύασε κιβωτὸν εἰς σωτηρίαν τοῦ οἴκου αὐτοῦ· δι' ἧς κατέκρινε τὸν κόσμον, καὶ τῆς κατὰ πίστιν δικαιοσύνης ἐγένετο κληρονόμος. [GNS]<br><br>Πίστει χρηματισθεὶς Νῶε περὶ τῶν μηδέπω βλεπομένων, **εὐλαβηθεὶς** κατεσκεύασεν κιβωτὸν εἰς σωτηρίαν τοῦ οἴκου αὐτοῦ δι' ἧς κατέκρινεν τὸν κόσμον, καὶ τῆς κατὰ πίστιν δικαιοσύνης ἐγένετο κληρονόμος. [GNT] | God was left with no choice: the earth had to be destroyed. But there was one man on earth who was godly—Noah. Noah worshipped and honored God in his life. Therefore, God warned Noah of the coming judgment upon the earth.<br>⇒ God told Noah to prepare an ark and the ark would save him, his family, and two of every animal.<br>⇒ God also told Noah to warn the world of coming judgment.<br><br>Noah believed God's warning of coming judgment, and he began to build the ark with a godly fear and reverence, knowing that what God said would come true. God's judgment would fall upon the earth; Noah believed it and knew it by faith. |
| **#1978**<br>**Holy Fear**<br><br>Reverence–KJV<br>Reverence–NASB<br>Reverence–NIV<br>Reverence–NKJV<br>Holy fear–NLT<br><br>**POSB REFERENCE**<br>(Heb.12:28-29; esp. v.28)<br>Note 3, point 2 | εὐλαβείας = eulabeias<br>Pronunciation: [yoo-lab'-i-ahs]<br>Parsing (part of speech): noun<br>    Case—genitive<br>    Gender—feminine<br>    Number—singular<br>    Stem or root—from εὐλάβεια, ας<br>Concordance References:<br>    ⇒ Strong's #2124 eulabeia<br>    ⇒ NIV #2325 eulabeia<br>    ⇒ NASB #2124 eulabeia<br><br>**Hebrews 12:28**<br>Wherefore we receiving a kingdom which cannot be moved, let us have grace, whereby we may serve God acceptably with **reverence** and godly fear: [KJV]<br><br>Therefore, since we receive a kingdom which cannot be shaken, let us show gratitude, by which we may offer to God an acceptable service with **reverence** and awe; [NASB]<br><br>Therefore, since we are receiving a kingdom that cannot be shaken, let us be thankful, and so worship God acceptably with **reverence** and awe, [NIV]<br><br>Therefore, since we are receiving a kingdom which cannot be shaken, let us have grace, by which we may serve God acceptably with **reverence** and godly fear. [NKJV]<br><br>Since we are receiving a kingdom that cannot be destroyed, let us be thankful and please God by worshiping him with **holy fear** and awe. [NLT]<br><br>διὸ βασιλείαν ἀσάλευτον παραλαμβάνοντες, ἔχωμεν χάριν δι' ἧς λατρεύωμεν εὐαρέστως τῷ Θεῷ μετὰ αἰδοῦς καὶ **εὐλαβείας**· [GNS]<br><br>Διὸ βασιλείαν ἀσάλευτον παραλαμβάνοντες ἔχωμεν χάριν, δι' ἧς λατρεύωμεν εὐαρέστως τῷ θεῷ μετὰ **εὐλαβείας** καὶ δέους· [GNT] | Reverence, holy fear. The term "holy fear"—NLT (*eulabeias*) means with caution, carefully, with discretion and circumspection (Kenneth Wuest. *Hebrews*, Vol. 2, p.231).<br><br>**Practical Application**<br>A person must do exactly what this verse says: *serve God acceptably* with awe and holy fear. God must be feared, for He is Lord. A person must serve God in an acceptable way. |
| **#1979**<br>**Holy Nation**<br><br>Holy nation–KJV<br>Holy nation–NASB<br>Holy nation–NIV | ἔθνος ἅγιον = ethnos hagion<br>Pronunciation: [heth'-nos hag'-ee-on]<br>Parsing *ethnos* (part of speech): noun<br>    Case—nominative<br>    Gender—neuter<br>    Number—singular<br>    Stem or root—from ἔθνος, ους | Holy nation; holy people; a separated, set apart, or different nation.<br><br>**Practical Application**<br>Believers become a *holy nation*. This is a very meaningful title for believers. Just think |

## PRACTICAL WORD STUDIES
### in the NEW TESTAMENT

| ENGLISH WORD | GREEK WORD AND VERSE | THE WORD MEANS... |
|---|---|---|
| **Holy nation–NKJV**<br>**Holy nation–NLT**<br><br>**POSB REFERENCE**<br>(1 Pt.2:9)<br>Note 1, point 3 | Parsing *hagion* (part of speech): adjective<br>  Case—nominative<br>  Gender—neuter<br>  Number—singular<br>  Stem or root—from ἅγιος, α, ον<br>Concordance References:<br>  ⇒ Strong's #1484 ethnos + 39 hagios<br>  ⇒ NIV #1620 ethnos [nation] + 41 hagios [holy]<br>  ⇒ NASB #1484 ethnos + 39 hagios<br><br>**1 Peter 2:9**<br>But ye are a chosen generation, a royal priesthood, an **holy nation**, a peculiar people; that ye should shew forth the praises of him who hath called you out of darkness into his marvellous light; [KJV]<br>But you are a chosen race, a royal priesthood, a **HOLY NATION**, a people for God's own possession, that you may proclaim the excellencies of Him who has called you out of darkness into His marvelous light; [NASB]<br>But you are a chosen people, a royal priesthood, a **holy nation**, a people belonging to God, that you may declare the praises of him who called you out of darkness into his wonderful light. [NIV]<br>But you *are* a chosen generation, a royal priesthood, a **holy nation**, His own special people, that you may proclaim the praises of Him who called you out of darkness into His marvelous light; [NKJV]<br>But you are not like that, for you are a chosen people. You are a kingdom of priests, God's **holy nation**, his very own possession. This is so you can show others the goodness of God, for he called you out of the darkness into his wonderful light. [NLT]<br>ὑμεῖς δὲ γένος ἐκλεκτόν, βασίλειον ἱεράτευμα, **ἔθνος ἅγιον**, λαὸς εἰς περιποίησιν, ὅπως τὰς ἀρετὰς ἐξαγγείλητε τοῦ ἐκ σκότους ὑμᾶς καλέσαντος εἰς τὸ θαυμαστὸν αὐτοῦ φῶς· [GNS]<br>Ὑμεῖς δὲ γένος ἐκλεκτόν, βασίλειον ἱεράτευμα, **ἔθνος ἅγιον**, λαὸς εἰς περιποίησιν, ὅπως τὰς ἀρετὰς ἐξαγγείλητε τοῦ ἐκ σκότους ὑμᾶς καλέσαντος εἰς τὸ θαυμαστὸν αὐτοῦ φῶς· [GNT] | about it: God is building a *new nation* of people. He is drawing people from all over the world, people from all the nations of the world, to create a new nation. What is the nation? It is the *holy nation* of God. Remember: the word "holy" (*hagion*) means separated, set apart, and different. Any person who is willing to separate from the sin and evil of this world and set his life apart to God, God will take that person and make him a citizen of His holy nation. This is what holy means: to be different from the world, from its sin, evil, and death. It means to be separated from the evil life of the world and set apart to the holy life of God. The person who turns to God becomes a citizen of God's holy nation:<br>  ⇒ He serves the Sovereign Head of God's nation, even God Himself.<br>  ⇒ He obeys the laws of God's nation.<br>  ⇒ He is dedicated to follow the customs and life-style of God's nation.<br>  ⇒ He speaks up for and defends the nation of God. |
| **#1980**<br>**Holy Spirit Controls Your Mind, The**<br><br>Spiritually minded–KJV<br>Mind set on the Spirit–NASB<br>Mind controlled by the Spirit–NIV<br>Spiritually minded–NKJV<br>**The Holy Spirit controls your mind–NLT**<br><br>**POSB REFERENCE**<br>(Romans 8:5-8, esp. v.6)<br>Note 3, point 2 | τὸ φρόνημα τοῦ πνεύματος = *to phronēma tou pneumatos*<br>Pronunciation: [to fron'-ay-mah too pnyoo'-mah-tos]<br>Parsing *phronēma* (part of speech): noun<br>  Case—nominative<br>  Gender—neuter<br>  Number—singular<br>  Stem or root—from φρόνημα, τος<br>Parsing *pneumatos* (part of speech): noun<br>  Case—genitive<br>  Gender—neuter<br>  Number—singular<br>  Stem or root—from πνεῦμα, τος<br>Concordance References:<br>  ⇒ Strong's #3588 ho + 5427 phronēma + 3588 ho + 4151 pneuma<br>  ⇒ NIV #3836 ho [the] + 5859 phronēma [mind] + 3836 ho [the] + 4460 pneuma [Spirit]<br>  ⇒ NASB #3588 ho + 5427 phronēma + 3588 ho + 4151 pneuma<br><br>**Romans 8:6**<br>For to be carnally minded is death; but to be **spiritually minded** is life and peace. [KJV]<br>For the mind set on the flesh is death, but **the mind set on the Spirit** is life and peace, [NASB]<br>The mind of sinful man is death, but **the mind controlled by the Spirit** is life and peace; [NIV]<br>For to be carnally minded *is* death, but to be **spiritually minded** *is* life and peace. [NKJV]<br>If your sinful nature controls your mind, there is death. | The self, mind, inner life, disposition controlled by the Holy Spirit; the mind set on the Spirit; to be spiritually minded.<br><br>**Practical Application**<br>The words "Holy Spirit controls your mind" (*to phronēma tou pneumatos*) mean to be possessed by the Spirit or to be dominated by the Spirit. It means that the man who walks after the Spirit minds "the things of the Spirit" day by day. And note: it is the Spirit of God who draws the believer's mind to focus upon spiritual things. The Spirit of God lives within the believer. He is there to work within the believer, both to will and to do God's pleasure. He is there to keep the mind and thoughts of the believer focused upon spiritual things. |

# PRACTICAL WORD STUDIES
## in the NEW TESTAMENT

| ENGLISH WORD | GREEK WORD AND VERSE | THE WORD MEANS... |
|---|---|---|
| | But if **the Holy Spirit controls your mind**, there is life and peace. [NLT]<br>τὸ γὰρ φρόνημα τῆς σαρκὸς θάνατος· τὸ δὲ **φρόνημα τοῦ πνεύματος** ζωὴ καὶ εἰρήνη· [GNS]<br>τὸ γὰρ φρόνημα τῆς σαρκὸς θάνατος, τὸ δὲ **φρόνημα τοῦ πνεύματος** ζωὴ καὶ εἰρήνη. [GNT] | |
| **#1981**<br>**Home, His**<br><br>His habitation–KJV<br>His homestead–NASB<br>His place–NIV<br>His dwelling place– NKJV<br>**His home–NLT**<br><br>**POSB REFERENCE**<br>(Acts 1:16-20; esp. v.20)<br>Note 2, point 6a | ἡ **ἔπαυλις αὐτοῦ** = hē epaulis autou<br>Pronunciation: [ay ep'-ow-lis aw-too]<br>Parsing *epaulis* (part of speech): noun<br>   Case—nominative<br>   Gender—feminine<br>   Number—singular<br>   Stem or root—from ἔπαυλις, εως<br>Concordance References:<br>  ⇒ Strong's #3588 ho + 1886 epaulis + 846 autos<br>  ⇒ NIV #3836 ho [Not in English] + 2068 epaulis [place] + 899 autos [his]<br>  ⇒ NASB #3588 ho + 1886 epaulis + 846 autos<br><br>**Acts 1:20**<br>For it is written in the book of Psalms, Let **his habitation** be desolate, and let no man dwell therein: and his bishoprick let another take. [KJV]<br>"For it is written in the book of Psalms, 'Let **his homestead** be made desolate, And let no man dwell in it'; and, 'His OFFICE LET ANOTHER MAN TAKE.' [NASB]<br>"For," said Peter, "it is written in the book of Psalms," 'May **his place** be deserted; let there be no one to dwell in it,' and, " 'May another take his place of leadership.' [NIV]<br>"For it is written in the book of Psalms: 'Let **his dwelling place** be desolate, And let no one live in it'; and, 'Let another take his office.' [NKJV]<br>Peter continued, "This was predicted in the book of Psalms, where it says, 'Let **his home** become desolate, with no one living in it.' And again, 'Let his position be given to someone else.' [NLT]<br>γέγραπται γὰρ ἐν βίβλῳ Ψαλμῶν, Γενηθήτω ἡ **ἔπαυλις αὐτοῦ** ἔρημος, καὶ μὴ ἔστω ὁ κατοικῶν ἐν αὐτῇ· καί, Τὴν ἐπισκοπὴν αὐτοῦ λαβέοι ἕτερος. [GNS]<br>Γέγραπται γὰρ ἐν βίβλῳ ψαλμῶν, Γενηθήτω ἡ **ἔπαυλις αὐτοῦ** ἔρημος καὶ μὴ ἔστω ὁ κατοικῶν ἐν αὐτῇ, καί, Τὴν ἐπισκοπὴν αὐτοῦ λαβέτω ἕτερος. [GNT] | His place; His habitation; His homestead; His home.<br><br>**Practical Application**<br>The phrase "His home" (*hē epaulis autou*) is descriptive. It means a farm house or a place for sheep such as a pasture or sheep yard. The idea is that Judas would never again be allowed to be the farmer (husbandman) or shepherd for God. |
| **#1982**<br>**Homestead, His**<br><br>His habitation–KJV<br>**His homestead– NASB**<br>His place–NIV<br>His dwelling place– NKJV<br>His home–NLT<br><br>**POSB REFERENCE**<br>(Acts 1:16-20; esp. v.20)<br>Note 2, point 6a | ἡ **ἔπαυλις αὐτοῦ** = hē epaulis autou<br>Pronunciation: [ay ep'-ow-lis aw-too]<br>Parsing *epaulis* (part of speech): noun<br>   Case—nominative<br>   Gender—feminine<br>   Number—singular<br>   Stem or root—from ἔπαυλις, εως<br>Concordance References:<br>  ⇒ Strong's #3588 ho + 1886 epaulis + 846 autos<br>  ⇒ NIV #3836 ho [Not in English] + 2068 epaulis [place] + 899 autos [his]<br>  ⇒ NASB #3588 ho + 1886 epaulis + 846 autos<br><br>**Acts 1:20**<br>For it is written in the book of Psalms, Let **his habitation** be desolate, and let no man dwell therein: and his bishoprick let another take. [KJV]<br>"For it is written in the book of Psalms, 'Let **his homestead** be made desolate, And let no man dwell in it'; and, 'His OFFICE LET ANOTHER MAN TAKE.' [NASB]<br>"For," said Peter, "it is written in the book of Psalms," " 'May **his place** be deserted; let there be no one to dwell in it,' and, " 'May another take his place of leadership.' [NIV]<br>"For it is written in the book of Psalms: 'Let **his dwelling place** be desolate, And let no one live in it'; | His place; His habitation; His homestead; His home.<br><br>**Practical Application**<br>The phrase "His homestead" (*hē epaulis autou*) is descriptive. It means a farm house or a place for sheep such as a pasture or sheep yard. The idea is that Judas would never again be allowed to be the farmer (husbandman) or shepherd for God. |

# PRACTICAL WORD STUDIES
## in the NEW TESTAMENT

| ENGLISH WORD | GREEK WORD AND VERSE | THE WORD MEANS... |
|---|---|---|
| | and, 'Let another take his office.' [NKJV]<br>Peter continued, "This was predicted in the book of Psalms, where it says, 'Let **his home** become desolate, with no one living in it.' And again, 'Let his position be given to someone else.' [NLT]<br>γέγραπται γὰρ ἐν βίβλῳ Ψαλμῶν, Γενηθήτω ἡ **ἔπαυλις αὐτοῦ** ἔρημος, καὶ μὴ ἔστω ὁ κατοικῶν ἐν αὐτῇ· καί, Τὴν ἐπισκοπὴν αὐτοῦ λάβοι ἕτερος. [GNS]<br>Γέγραπται γὰρ ἐν βίβλῳ ψαλμῶν, Γενηθήτω ἡ **ἔπαυλις αὐτοῦ** ἔρημος καὶ μὴ ἔστω ὁ κατοικῶν ἐν αὐτῇ, καί, Τὴν ἐπισκοπὴν αὐτοῦ λαβέτω ἕτερος. [GNT] | |
| #1983<br>**Homosexual Offenders**<br><br>Abusers of themselves with mankind–KJV<br>Homosexuals–NASB<br>**Homosexual offenders–NIV**<br>Sodomites–NKJV<br>Homosexuals–NLT<br><br>**POSB REFERENCE**<br>(1 Cor.6:9)<br>Note 2, point 4 | ἀρσενοκοῖται = *arsenokoitai*<br>Pronunciation: [ar-sen-ok-oy'-tah-ee]<br>Parsing (part of speech): noun<br>   Case—nominative<br>   Gender—masculine<br>   Number—plural<br>   Stem or root—from ἀρσενοκοίτης, ου<br>Concordance References:<br>  ⇒ Strong's #733 arsenokoitēs<br>  ⇒ NIV #780 arsenokoitēs<br>  ⇒ NASB #733 arsenokoitēs<br><br>**1 Cor. 6:9**<br>Know ye not that the unrighteous shall not inherit the kingdom of God? Be not deceived: neither fornicators, nor idolaters, nor adulterers, nor effeminate, nor **abusers of themselves with mankind**, [KJV]<br>Or do you not know that the unrighteous shall not inherit the kingdom of God? Do not be deceived; neither fornicators, nor idolaters, nor adulterers, nor effeminate, nor **homosexuals**, [NASB]<br>Do you not know that the wicked will not inherit the kingdom of God? Do not be deceived: Neither the sexually immoral nor idolaters nor adulterers nor male prostitutes nor **homosexual offenders** [NIV]<br>Do you not know that the unrighteous will not inherit the kingdom of God? Do not be deceived. Neither fornicators, nor idolaters, nor adulterers, nor homosexuals, nor **sodomites**, [NKJV]<br>Don't you know that those who do wrong will have no share in the Kingdom of God? Don't fool yourselves. Those who indulge in sexual sin, who are idol worshipers, adulterers, male prostitutes, **homosexuals**, [NLT]<br>ἢ οὐκ οἴδατε ὅτι ἄδικοι βασιλείαν Θεοῦ οὐ κληρονομήσουσι; μὴ πλανᾶσθε· οὔτε πόρνοι, οὔτε εἰδωλολάτραι, οὔτε μοιχοί, οὔτε μαλακοί, οὔτε **ἀρσενοκοῖται**, [GNS]<br>ἢ οὐκ οἴδατε ὅτι ἄδικοι Θεοῦ βασιλείαν οὐ κληρονομήσουσιν; μὴ πλανᾶσθε· οὔτε πόρνοι οὔτε εἰδωλολάτραι οὔτε μοιχοὶ οὔτε μαλακοὶ οὔτε **ἀρσενοκοῖται** [GNT] | Homosexual offenders; sodomites, perverts; the abusers of themselves with mankind.<br><br>**Practical Application**<br>The warning is clear and sober: the practicing homosexual, those who are "homosexual offenders" (*arsenokoitai*), will not inherit the kingdom of God. |
| #1984<br>**Homosexuals**<br><br>Abusers of themselves with mankind–KJV<br>**Homosexuals–NASB**<br>Homosexual offenders–NIV<br>Sodomites–NKJV<br>**Homosexuals–NLT**<br><br>**POSB REFERENCE**<br>(1 Cor.6:9)<br>Note 2, point 4 | ἀρσενοκοῖται = *arsenokoitai*<br>Pronunciation: [ar-sen-ok-oy'-tah-ee]<br>Parsing (part of speech): noun<br>   Case—nominative<br>   Gender—masculine<br>   Number—plural<br>   Stem or root—from ἀρσενοκοίτης, ου<br>Concordance References:<br>  ⇒ Strong's #733 arsenokoitēs<br>  ⇒ NIV #780 arsenokoitēs<br>  ⇒ NASB #733 arsenokoitēs<br><br>**1 Cor. 6:9**<br>Know ye not that the unrighteous shall not inherit the kingdom of God? Be not deceived: neither fornicators, nor idolaters, nor adulterers, nor effeminate, nor **abusers of themselves with mankind**, [KJV]<br>Or do you not know that the unrighteous shall not inherit the kingdom of God? Do not be deceived; neither | Homosexual offenders; sodomites, perverts; the abusers of themselves with mankind.<br><br>**Practical Application**<br>The warning is clear and sober: the practicing homosexual, those who are "homosexuals" (*arsenokoitai*), will not inherit the kingdom of God. |

## PRACTICAL WORD STUDIES
### in the New Testament

| ENGLISH WORD | GREEK WORD AND VERSE | THE WORD MEANS... |
|---|---|---|
| | fornicators, nor idolaters, nor adulterers, nor effeminate, nor **homosexuals**, [NASB] <br><br> Do you not know that the wicked will not inherit the kingdom of God? Do not be deceived: Neither the sexually immoral nor idolaters nor adulterers nor male prostitutes nor **homosexual offenders** [NIV] <br><br> Do you not know that the unrighteous will not inherit the kingdom of God? Do not be deceived. Neither fornicators, nor idolaters, nor adulterers, nor homosexuals, nor **sodomites**, [NKJV] <br><br> Don't you know that those who do wrong will have no share in the Kingdom of God? Don't fool yourselves. Those who indulge in sexual sin, who are idol worshipers, adulterers, male prostitutes, **homosexuals**, [NLT] <br><br> η οὐκ οἴδατε ὅτι ἄδικοι βασιλείαν Θεοῦ οὐ κληρονομήσουσι; μὴ πλανᾶσθε· οὔτε πόρνοι, οὔτε εἰδωλολάτραι, οὔτε μοιχοὶ, οὔτε μαλακοὶ, οὔτε **ἀρσενοκοῖται**, [GNS] <br><br> η οὐκ οἴδατε ὅτι ἄδικοι θεοῦ βασιλείαν οὐ κληρονομήσουσιν; μὴ πλανᾶσθε· οὔτε πόρνοι οὔτε εἰδωλολάτραι οὔτε μοιχοὶ οὔτε μαλακοὶ οὔτε **ἀρσενοκοῖται** [GNT] | |
| **#1985** <br> **Homosexuals** <br><br> Effiminate–KJV <br> Effiminate–NASB <br> Male prostitutes–NIV <br> **Homosexuals–NKJV** <br> Male prostitutes–NLT <br><br> **POSB REFERENCE** <br> (1 Cor.6:9) <br> Note 2, point 4 | μαλακοί = malakoi <br> Pronunciation: [mal-ak-oy-ee'] <br> Parsing (part of speech): pronominal adjective <br>    Case—nominative <br>    Gender—masculine <br>    Number—plural <br>    Stem or root—from μαλακός, ή, όν <br> Concordance References: <br>   ⇒ Strong's #3120 malakos <br>   ⇒ NIV #3434 malakos <br>   ⇒ NASB #3120 malakos <br><br> **1 Cor. 6:9** <br> Know ye not that the unrighteous shall not inherit the kingdom of God? Be not deceived: neither fornicators, nor idolaters, nor adulterers, nor **effeminate**, nor abusers of themselves with mankind, [KJV] <br><br> Or do you not know that the unrighteous shall not inherit the kingdom of God? Do not be deceived; neither fornicators, nor idolaters, nor adulterers, nor **effeminate**, nor homosexuals, [NASB] <br><br> Do you not know that the wicked will not inherit the kingdom of God? Do not be deceived: Neither the sexually immoral nor idolaters nor adulterers nor **male prostitutes** nor homosexual offenders [NIV] <br><br> Do you not know that the unrighteous will not inherit the kingdom of God? Do not be deceived. Neither fornicators, nor idolaters, nor adulterers, nor **homosexuals**, nor sodomites, [NKJV] <br><br> Don't you know that those who do wrong will have no share in the Kingdom of God? Don't fool yourselves. Those who indulge in sexual sin, who are idol worshipers, adulterers, **male prostitutes**, homosexuals, [NLT] <br><br> η οὐκ οἴδατε ὅτι ἄδικοι βασιλείαν Θεοῦ οὐ κληρονομήσουσι; μὴ πλανᾶσθε· οὔτε πόρνοι, οὔτε εἰδωλολάτραι, οὔτε μοιχοὶ, οὔτε **μαλακοὶ**, οὔτε ἀρσενοκοῖται, [GNS] <br><br> η οὐκ οἴδατε ὅτι ἄδικοι θεοῦ βασιλείαν οὐ κληρονομήσουσιν; μὴ πλανᾶσθε· οὔτε πόρνοι οὔτε εἰδωλολάτραι οὔτε μοιχοὶ οὔτε **μαλακοὶ** οὔτε ἀρσενοκοῖται [GNT] | Male prostitutes; effeminate; a homosexual pervert; gay. <br><br> **Practical Application** <br> The sin of homosexuality takes place in the heart. Men and women *burn within*, crave the sin before they commit the act. It is their burning, their lusting, their craving that sets them aflame to pursue the shameful act. Their heart burns after other men and women, not after God. Therefore, they stand condemned, and God is forced to judge them. They "will not inherit the kingdom of God. Do not be deceived." |
| **#1986** <br> **Honest** <br><br> **Honest–KJV** <br> **Honest–NASB** <br> Noble–NIV | καλῇ = kalē <br> Pronunciation: [kal-ay'] <br> Parsing (part of speech): adjective <br>    Case—dative <br>    Gender—feminine <br>    Number—singular <br>    Stem or root—from καλός, ή, όν | Fair, honest, noble, good, proper, honorable, right, and just. It has the idea of holding fast. <br><br> **Practical Application** <br> In this Scripture, these people are honest and fair; they are noble people in listening and considering the Word. They honestly seek to learn |

# PRACTICAL WORD STUDIES
## in the NEW TESTAMENT

| ENGLISH WORD | GREEK WORD AND VERSE | THE WORD MEANS... |
|---|---|---|
| Noble–NKJV<br>Honest–NLT<br><br>**POSB<br>REFERENCE**<br>(Lk.8:11-15; esp. v.15)<br>Note 4, point 4a | Concordance References:<br>⇒ Strong's #2570 kalos<br>⇒ NIV #2819 kalos<br>⇒ NASB #2570 kalos<br><br>**Luke 8:15**<br>But that on the good ground are they, which in an **honest** and good heart, having heard the word, keep it, and bring forth fruit with patience. [KJV]<br>"And the seed in the good soil, these are the ones who have heard the word in an **honest** and good heart, and hold it fast, and bear fruit with perseverance. [NASB]<br>But the seed on good soil stands for those with a **noble** and good heart, who hear the word, retain it, and by persevering produce a crop. [NIV]<br>But the ones that fell on the good ground are those who, having heard the word with a **noble** and good heart, keep it and bear fruit with patience. [NKJV]<br>But the good soil represents **honest**, good-hearted people who hear God's message, cling to it, and steadily produce a huge harvest. [NLT]<br>τὸ δὲ ἐν τῇ καλῇ γῇ, οὗτοί εἰσιν οἵτινες ἐν καρδίᾳ **καλῇ** καὶ ἀγαθῇ, ἀκούσαντες τὸν λόγον, κατέχουσι, καὶ καρποφοροῦσιν ἐν ὑπομονῇ. [GNS]<br>τὸ δὲ ἐν τῇ καλῇ γῇ, οὗτοί εἰσιν οἵτινες ἐν καρδίᾳ **καλῇ** καὶ ἀγαθῇ ἀκούσαντες τὸν λόγον κατέχουσιν καὶ καρποφοροῦσιν ἐν ὑπομονῇ. [GNT] | and know the truth, spiritually as well as physically. |
| **#1987<br>Honest**<br><br>Guile–KJV<br>Guile–NASB<br>False–NIV<br>Deceit–NKJV<br>Honest–NLT<br><br>**POSB<br>REFERENCE**<br>(Jn.1:47-48; esp. v.47)<br>Note 2, point 1b | δόλος = *dolos*<br>Pronunciation: [dol'-os]<br>Parsing (part of speech): noun<br>   Case—nominative<br>   Gender—masculine<br>   Number—singular<br>   Stem or root—from δόλος, ου<br>Concordance References:<br>⇒ Strong's #1388 dolos<br>⇒ NIV #1515 dolos<br>⇒ NASB #1388 dolos<br><br>**John 1:47**<br>Jesus saw Nathanael coming to him, and saith of him, Behold an Israelite indeed, in whom is no **guile**! [KJV]<br>Jesus saw Nathanael coming to Him, and said of him, "Behold, an Israelite indeed, in whom is no **guile**!" [NASB]<br>When Jesus saw Nathanael approaching, he said of him, "Here is a true Israelite, in whom there is nothing **false**." [NIV]<br>Jesus saw Nathanael coming toward Him, and said of him, "Behold, an Israelite indeed, in whom is no **deceit**!" [NKJV]<br>As they approached, Jesus said, "Here comes an **honest** man—a true son of Israel." [NLT]<br>εἶδεν ὁ Ἰησοῦς τὸν Ναθαναὴλ ἐρχόμενον πρὸς αὐτόν, καὶ λέγει περὶ αὐτοῦ, Ἴδε ἀληθῶς Ἰσραηλίτης, ἐν ᾧ **δόλος** οὐκ ἔστι. [GNS]<br>εἶδεν ὁ Ἰησοῦς τὸν Ναθαναὴλ ἐρχόμενον πρὸς αὐτὸν καὶ λέγει περὶ αὐτοῦ, Ἴδε ἀληθῶς Ἰσραηλίτης ἐν ᾧ **δόλος** οὐκ ἔστιν. [GNT] | False, deceit, guile, fraud, trickery, deception, treachery; an impostor, an impersonator, a fake.<br><br>**Practical Application**<br>Note that these terms did not describe Nathanael's behavior. The word "honest" (*dolos*) means he did not deceive, bait, or mislead people. He did not hide what he thought; he said what he thought and acted what he felt. He was straightforward, open and honest, not deceptive or hypocritical. This trait had just been demonstrated in his response to Philip. He would not hide his true thoughts (John 1:46). One of the great tragedies in the legacy of persons is that they are full of guile. Many deceive, bait, and mislead others. Few are straightforward, open and honest, free of deception and hypocrisy. |
| **#1988<br>Honest, Which<br>[Is]**<br><br>Which [is] honest–KJV<br>What [is] right–NASB<br>What [is] right–NIV<br>What [is] honorable–NKJV<br>Right–NLT | τὸ καλὸν = *to kalon*<br>Pronunciation: [to kal-on']<br>Parsing *kalon* (part of speech): pronominal adjective<br>   Case—accusative<br>   Gender—neuter<br>   Number—singular<br>   Stem or root—from καλός, ή, όν<br>Concordance References:<br>⇒ Strong's #3588 ho + 2570 kalos<br>⇒ NIV #3836 ho [what] + 2819 kalos [right]<br>⇒ NASB #3588 ho + 2570 kalos | Right, noble, honest, proper, good, pleasing.<br><br>**Practical Application**<br>Paul was under attack, and suffered the tension and pressure of the attack, but that was not the reason he wanted his critics to repent. His purpose was not selfish or self-centered: he wanted his critics to repent for the sake of righteousness, that the good and right thing might be done. He wanted this despite the fact that they treated him as a reprobate. They might not love |

# PRACTICAL WORD STUDIES
## in the New Testament

| ENGLISH WORD | GREEK WORD AND VERSE | THE WORD MEANS... |
|---|---|---|
| **POSB REFERENCE** (2 Cor.13:7-10; esp. v.7) Note 2 | **2 Cor. 13:7**<br>Now I pray to God that ye do no evil; not that we should appear approved, but that ye should do that **which** is **honest**, though we be as reprobates. [KJV]<br>Now we pray to God that you do no wrong; not that we ourselves may appear approved, but that you may do **what** is **right**, even though we should appear unapproved. [NASB]<br>Now we pray to God that you will not do anything wrong. Not that people will see that we have stood the test but that you will do **what** is **right** even though we may seem to have failed. [NIV]<br>Now I pray to God that you do no evil, not that we should appear approved, but that you should do **what** is **honorable**, though we may seem disqualified. [NKJV]<br>We pray to God that you will not do anything wrong. We pray this, not to show that our ministry to you has been successful, but because we want you to do **right** even if we ourselves seem to have failed. [NLT]<br>εὔχομαι δὲ πρὸς τὸν Θεὸν, μὴ ποιῆσαι ὑμᾶς κακὸν μηδέν, οὐχ ἵνα ἡμεῖς δόκιμοι φανῶμεν, ἀλλ' ἵνα ὑμεῖς **τὸ καλὸν** ποιῆτε, ἡμεῖς δὲ ὡς ἀδόκιμοι ὦμεν. [GNS]<br>εὐχόμεθα δὲ πρὸς τὸν θεὸν μὴ ποιῆσαι ὑμᾶς κακὸν μηδέν, οὐχ ἵνα ἡμεῖς δόκιμοι φανῶμεν, ἀλλ' ἵνα ὑμεῖς **τὸ καλὸν** ποιῆτε, ἡμεῖς δὲ ὡς ἀδόκιμοι ὦμεν. [GNT] | him, but he loved them and wanted only the best for them. He did not want to discipline them; he wanted them to repent before he arrived. |
| **#1989**<br>**Honest**<br><br>Honest–KJV<br>Honorable–NASB<br>Noble–NIV<br>Noble–NKJV<br>Honorable–NLT<br><br>**POSB REFERENCE**<br>(Philip.4:8-9; esp. v.8)<br>Note 2, point 1b | σεμνά = *semna*<br>Pronunciation: [sem-nah']<br>Parsing (part of speech): adjective<br>    Case—nominative<br>    Gender—neuter<br>    Number—plural<br>    Stem or root—from σεμνός, ή, όν<br>Concordance References:<br>   ⇒ Strong's #4586 semnos<br>   ⇒ NIV #4948 semnos<br>   ⇒ NASB #4586 semnos<br><br>**Philip. 4:8**<br>Finally, brethren, whatsoever things are true, whatsoever things are **honest**, whatsoever things are just, whatsoever things are pure, whatsoever things are lovely, whatsoever things are of good report; if there be any virtue, and if there be any praise, think on these things. [KJV]<br>Finally, brethren, whatever is true, whatever is **honorable**, whatever is right, whatever is pure, whatever is lovely, whatever is of good repute, if there is any excellence and if anything worthy of praise, let your mind dwell on these things. [NASB]<br>Finally, brothers, whatever is true, whatever is **noble**, whatever is right, whatever is pure, whatever is lovely, whatever is admirable—if anything is excellent or praiseworthy—think about such things. [NIV]<br>Finally, brethren, whatever things are true, whatever things *are* **noble**, whatever things *are* just, whatever things *are* pure, whatever things *are* lovely, whatever things *are* of good report, if *there is* any virtue and if *there is* anything praiseworthy—meditate on these things. [NKJV]<br>And now, dear brothers and sisters, let me say one more thing as I close this letter. Fix your thoughts on what is true and **honorable** and right. Think about things that are pure and lovely and admirable. Think about things that are excellent and worthy of praise. [NLT]<br>Τὸ λοιπόν, ἀδελφοί, ὅσα ἐστὶν ἀληθῆ, ὅσα **σεμνά**, ὅσα δίκαια, ὅσα ἁγνά, ὅσα προσφιλῆ, ὅσα εὔφημα, εἴ τις ἀρετὴ καὶ εἴ τις ἔπαινος, ταῦτα λογίζεσθε· [GNS]<br>Τὸ λοιπόν, ἀδελφοί, ὅσα ἐστὶν ἀληθῆ, ὅσα **σεμνά**, ὅσα δίκαια, ὅσα ἁγνά, ὅσα προσφιλῆ, ὅσα εὔφημα, εἴ τις ἀρετὴ καὶ εἴ τις ἔπαινος, ταῦτα λογίζεσθε· [GNT] | Noble, honest, honorable, worthy, respectable, revered, highly respected.<br><br>**Practical Application**<br>William Barclay says: "The word really describes that which has the dignity of holiness upon it. There are things in this world which are flippant and cheap, things which are attractive to the light-minded; but it is on the things which are grave and serious and dignified that the Christian will set his mind" (*The Letters to the Philippians, Colossians, and Thessalonians*, p.98). |

# PRACTICAL WORD STUDIES
## in the NEW TESTAMENT

| ENGLISH WORD | GREEK WORD AND VERSE | THE WORD MEANS... |
|---|---|---|
| **#1990**<br>**Honest**<br><br>Honest–KJV<br>Excellent–NASB<br>Good–NIV<br>Honorable–NKJV<br>Be careful how you live–NLT<br><br>**POSB REFERENCE**<br>(1 Pt.2:12)<br>Note 3 | καλήν = *kalën*<br>Pronunciation: [kal-ayn']<br>Parsing (part of speech): adjective<br>    Case—accusative<br>    Gender—feminine<br>    Number—singular<br>    Stem or root—from καλός, ή, όν<br>Concordance References:<br>  ⇒ Strong's #2570 *kalos*<br>  ⇒ NIV #2819 *kalos*<br>  ⇒ NASB #2570 *kalos*<br><br>**1 Peter 2:12**<br>Having your conversation **honest** among the Gentiles: that, whereas they speak against you as evildoers, they may by your good works, which they shall behold, glorify God in the day of visitation. [KJV]<br><br>Keep your behavior **excellent** among the Gentiles, so that in the thing in which they slander you as evildoers, they may on account of your good deeds, as they observe them, glorify God in the day of visitation. [NASB]<br><br>Live such **good** lives among the pagans that, though they accuse you of doing wrong, they may see your good deeds and glorify God on the day he visits us. [NIV]<br><br>Having your conduct **honorable** among the Gentiles, that when they speak against you as evildoers, they may, by *your* good works which they observe, glorify God in the day of visitation. [NKJV]<br><br>**Be careful how you live** among your unbelieving neighbors. Even if they accuse you of doing wrong, they will see your honorable behavior, and they will believe and give honor to God when he comes to judge the world. [NLT]<br><br>τὴν ἀναστροφὴν ὑμῶν ἐν τοῖς ἔθνεσιν ἔχοντες **καλήν**, ἵνα, ἐν ᾧ καταλαλοῦσιν ὑμῶν ὡς κακοποιῶν, ἐκ τῶν καλῶν ἔργων ἐποπτεύσαντες δοξάσωσι τὸν Θεὸν ἐν ἡμέρᾳ ἐπισκοπῆς. [GNS]<br><br>τὴν ἀναστροφὴν ὑμῶν ἐν τοῖς ἔθνεσιν ἔχοντες **καλήν**, ἵνα, ἐν ᾧ καταλαλοῦσιν ὑμῶν ὡς κακοποιῶν ἐκ τῶν καλῶν ἔργων ἐποπτεύοντες δοξάσωσιν τὸν θεὸν ἐν ἡμέρᾳ ἐπισκοπῆς. [GNT] | Good, honest, excellent; honorable, proper; to be careful how one lives.<br><br>**Practical Application**<br>The word "honest" (*kalën*) means a good life, a life that is honorable, righteous, pure, lovely, decent, excellent, upright, and noble. It means a life that is without blame, that cannot be justly or accurately blamed with any sin or evil. The world watches a genuine believer to see if he really lives what he professes. Therefore, we must live good lives, honest lives, lives that are just what we profess: holy, righteous, and pure. |
| **#1991**<br>**Honest Report**<br><br>Honest report–KJV<br>Good reputation–NASB<br>Known–NIV<br>Good reputation–NKJV<br>Well respected–NLT<br><br>**POSB REFERENCE**<br>(Acts 6:3)<br>Note 3, point 1 | μαρτυρουμένους = *marturoumenous*<br>Pronunciation: [mar-too-roo'-men-oos]<br>Parsing (part of speech): verb<br>    Mood—participle<br>    Tense—present<br>    Voice—passive<br>    Case—accusative<br>    Gender—masculine<br>    Number—plural<br>    Stem or root—from μαρτυρέω<br>Concordance References:<br>  ⇒ Strong's #3140 *martureo*<br>  ⇒ NIV #3455 *martureö*<br>  ⇒ NASB #3140 *martureo*<br><br>**Acts 6:3**<br>Wherefore, brethren, look ye out among you seven men of **honest report**, full of the Holy Ghost and wisdom, whom we may appoint over this business. [KJV]<br><br>"But select from among you, brethren, seven men of **good reputation**, full of the Spirit and of wisdom, whom we may put in charge of this task. [NASB]<br><br>Brothers, choose seven men from among you who are **known** to be full of the Spirit and wisdom. We will turn this responsibility over to them [NIV]<br><br>Therefore, brethren, seek out from among you seven men of *good* **reputation**, full of the Holy Spirit and wisdom, whom we may appoint over this business; [NKJV]<br><br>"Now look around among yourselves, brothers, and select seven men who are **well respected** and are full of | To be known; to have a good reputation; well respected; well attested; well reported of; bearing a good witness.<br><br>**Practical Application**<br>The deacon's character was to be proven beyond reproach. They were to be men of integrity, faithful and trustworthy; moral and upright, men trusted by all. |

# PRACTICAL WORD STUDIES
## in the NEW TESTAMENT

| ENGLISH WORD | GREEK WORD AND VERSE | THE WORD MEANS... |
|---|---|---|
| | the Holy Spirit and wisdom. We will put them in charge of this business. [NLT]<br><br>ἐπισκέψασθε οὖν, ἀδελφοί, ἄνδρας ἐξ ὑμῶν **μαρτυρουμένους** ἑπτὰ, πλήρεις Πνεύματος Ἁγίου καὶ σοφίας, οὓς καταστήσομεν ἐπὶ τῆς χρείας ταύτης. [GNS]<br><br>ἐπισκέψασθε δέ, ἀδελφοί, ἄνδρας ἐξ ὑμῶν **μαρτυρουμένους** ἑπτὰ, πλήρεις πνεύματος καὶ σοφίας, οὓς καταστήσομεν ἐπὶ τῆς χρείας ταύτης, [GNT] | |
| **#1992**<br>**Honest, Be**<br><br>Soberly–KJV<br>Sound judgment–NASB<br>Sober judgment–NIV<br>Soberly–NKJV<br>**Be honest–NLT**<br><br>**POSB REFERENCE**<br>(Rom.12:3-5; esp. v.3)<br>Note 1, point 1 | σωφρονεῖν = *söphronein*<br>Pronunciation: [so-fron-een']<br>Parsing (part of speech): verb<br>    Mood—infinitive<br>    Tense—present<br>    Voice—active<br>    Case—accusative<br>    Stem or root—from σωφρονέω<br>Concordance References:<br>⇒ Strong's #4993 söphroneö<br>⇒ NIV #5404 söphroneö<br>⇒ NASB #4993 söphroneö<br><br>**Romans 12:3**<br>For I say, through the grace given unto me, to every man that is among you, not to think of himself more highly than he ought to think; but to think **soberly**, according as God hath dealt to every man the measure of faith. [KJV]<br><br>For through the grace given to me I say to every man among you not to think more highly of himself than he ought to think; but to think so as to have **sound judgment**, as God has allotted to each a measure of faith. [NASB]<br><br>For by the grace given me I say to every one of you: Do not think of yourself more highly than you ought, but rather think of yourself with **sober judgment**, in accordance with the measure of faith God has given you. [NIV]<br><br>For I say, through the grace given to me, to everyone who is among you, not to think *of himself* more highly than he ought to think, but to think **soberly**, as God has dealt to each one a measure of faith. [NKJV]<br><br>As God's messenger, I give each of you this warning: **Be honest** in your estimate of yourselves, measuring your value by how much faith God has given you. [NLT]<br><br>Λέγω γὰρ, διὰ τῆς χάριτος τῆς δοθείσης μοι, παντὶ τῷ ὄντι ἐν ὑμῖν, μὴ ὑπερφρονεῖν παρ' ὃ δεῖ φρονεῖν, ἀλλὰ φρονεῖν εἰς τὸ **σωφρονεῖν**, ἑκάστῳ ὡς ὁ Θεὸς ἐμέρισε μέτρον πίστεως. [GNS]<br><br>Λέγω γὰρ διὰ τῆς χάριτος τῆς δοθείσης μοι παντὶ τῷ ὄντι ἐν ὑμῖν μὴ ὑπερφρονεῖν παρ' ὃ δεῖ φρονεῖν ἀλλὰ φρονεῖν εἰς τὸ **σωφρονεῖν**, ἑκάστῳ ὡς ὁ θεὸς ἐμέρισεν μέτρον πίστεως. [GNT] | To be balanced, sane, in one's right mind; to think sensibly; to be serious; to be sober; to be honest.<br><br>**Practical Application**<br>Think of yourself, but "be honest" (*söphronein*). Therefore, the exhortation is to think of oneself wisely and accurately, making a sane and well-balanced evaluation of one's person and abilities. An evaluation of oneself should be made, but it should be a sober and sane judgment, not an insane, imbalanced judgment. Note how strong this is: thinking too highly of oneself is an insane thought. Thinking that one is more important than someone else is insane behavior. Every person is important to God; every person is meaningful and significant to God's kingdom, no matter who the person is. |
| **#1993**<br>**Honestly**<br><br>**Honestly–KJV**<br>Properly–NASB<br>Decently–NIV<br>Properly–NKJV<br>Decent and true–NLT<br><br>**POSB REFERENCE**<br>(Rom.13:13)<br>Note 4 | εὐσχημόνως = *euschēmonōs*<br>Pronunciation: [yoo-skhay-mon'-oce]<br>Parsing (part of speech): adjective adverb<br>    Stem or root—from εὐσχημόνως<br>Concordance References:<br>⇒ Strong's #2156 euschēmonōs<br>⇒ NIV #2361 euschēmonōs<br>⇒ NASB #2156 euschēmonōs<br><br>**Romans 13:13**<br>Let us walk **honestly**, as in the day; not in rioting and drunkenness, not in chambering and wantonness, not in strife and envying. [KJV]<br><br>Let us behave **properly** as in the day, not in carousing and drunkenness, not in sexual promiscuity and sensuality, not in strife and jealousy. [NASB]<br><br>Let us behave **decently**, as in the daytime, not in orgies and drunkenness, not in sexual immorality and debauchery, not in dissension and jealousy. [NIV] | Decently, honestly, properly; decent and true; honorable, noble, respectable.<br><br>**Practical Application**<br>The believer is to walk in honesty before God. He is to live a life of honesty, decency, and nobility. He is to live a life of honor and honesty before God. He is to walk in the day, not hiding nor trying to hide anything. This Scripture gives six sins in particular which the believer is to cast off and turn away from—forever. |

## Practical Word Studies
### in the New Testament

| ENGLISH WORD | GREEK WORD AND VERSE | THE WORD MEANS... |
|---|---|---|
| | Let us walk **properly**, as in the day, not in revelry and drunkenness, not in lewdness and lust, not in strife and envy. [NKJV]<br><br>We should be **decent and true** in everything we do, so that everyone can approve of our behavior. Don't participate in wild parties and getting drunk, or in adultery and immoral living, or in fighting and jealousy. [NLT]<br><br>ὡς ἐν ἡμέρᾳ, **εὐσχημόνως** περιπατήσωμεν, μὴ κώμοις καὶ μέθαις, μὴ κοίταις καὶ ἀσελγείαις, μὴ ἔριδι καὶ ζήλῳ. [GNS]<br><br>ὡς ἐν ἡμέρᾳ, **εὐσχημόνως** περιπατήσωμεν, μὴ κώμοις καὶ μέθαις, μὴ κοίταις καὶ ἀσελγείαις, μὴ ἔριδι καὶ ζήλῳ, [GNT] | |
| **#1994**<br>**Honor**<br><br>**Honour–KJV**<br>**Honor–NASB**<br>**Honor–NIV**<br>**Honor–NKJV**<br>Paid–NLT<br><br>**POSB**<br>**REFERENCE**<br>(1 Tim.5:17)<br>Note 1<br><br>See also POSB REF:<br>(Rom.2:7)<br>*Deeper Study* #2<br>(Jn.4:44)<br>Note 2<br>(Rom.12:10)<br>Note 1, point 4 | τιμῆς = *timës*<br>Pronunciation: [tee-mays']<br>Parsing (part of speech): noun<br>    Case—genitive<br>    Gender—feminine<br>    Number—singular<br>    Stem or root—from τιμή, ῆς<br>Concordance References:<br>  ⇒ Strong's #5092 timë<br>  ⇒ NIV #5507 timë<br>  ⇒ NASB #5092 timë<br><br>**1 Tim. 5:17**<br>Let the elders that rule be counted worthy of double **honour**, especially they who labour in the word and doctrine. [KJV]<br>Let the elders who rule well be considered worthy of double **honor**, especially those who work hard at preaching and teaching. [NASB]<br>The elders who direct the affairs of the church well are worthy of double **honor**, especially those whose work is preaching and teaching. [NIV]<br>Let the elders who rule well be counted worthy of double **honor**, especially those who labor in the word and doctrine. [NKJV]<br>Elders who do their work well should be **paid** well, especially those who work hard at both preaching and teaching. [NLT]<br>Οἱ καλῶς προεστῶτες πρεσβύτεροι διπλῆς **τιμῆς** ἀξιούσθωσαν, μάλιστα οἱ κοπιῶντες ἐν λόγῳ καὶ διδασκαλίᾳ· [GNS]<br>Οἱ καλῶς προεστῶτες πρεσβύτεροι διπλῆς **τιμῆς** ἀξιούσθωσαν, μάλιστα οἱ κοπιῶντες ἐν λόγῳ καὶ διδασκαλίᾳ. [GNT] | To honor; to value; to respect; to fairly compensate. The word "honor" (*timës*) means more than just esteem and respect. It means to pay and bestow what is due.<br><br>**Practical Application**<br>A minister is due an honorarium; he is due compensation, some pay, some wage for his labor. And, if he performs his duty well—labors and labors and works and works—then he is due double honor. Is this to be taken literally? Is the church to pay him a double salary? A.T. Robertson states that there are "numerous examples of Roman soldiers who received double pay for unusual services" (*Word Pictures in the New Testament*, Vol.4, p.588). One thing is sure: double pay means adequate, ample, sufficient, and generous financial support. |
| **#1995**<br>**Honor**<br><br>Know–KJV<br>Appreciate–NASB<br>Respect–NIV<br>Recognize–NKJV<br>**Honor–NLT**<br><br>**POSB**<br>**REFERENCE**<br>(1 Thes.5:12-13;<br>esp.v.12)<br>Note 1, point 1 | εἰδέναι = *eidenai*<br>Pronunciation: [i'-dehn-ah-ee]<br>Parsing (part of speech): verb<br>    Mood—infinitive<br>    Tense—perfect<br>    Voice—active<br>    Stem or root—from οἶδα<br>Concordance References:<br>  ⇒ Strong's #1492 eido<br>  ⇒ NIV #3857 oida<br>  ⇒ NASB #3609a oida<br><br>**1 Thes. 5:12**<br>And we beseech you, brethren, to **know** them which labour among you, and are over you in the Lord, and admonish you; [KJV]<br>But we request of you, brethren, that you **appreciate** those who diligently labor among you, and have charge over you in the Lord and give you instruction, [NASB]<br>Now we ask you, brothers, to **respect** those who work hard among you, who are over you in the Lord and who admonish you. [NIV]<br>And we urge you, brethren, to **recognize** those who labor among you, and are over you in the Lord and | To respect; to know; to appreciate; to recognize; to honor; to be acquainted with; to acknowledge; to know the value of.<br><br>**Practical Application**<br>Believers are to honor the leaders of their church. Few people labor as much as a committed church leader. |

# Practical Word Studies
## in the New Testament

| ENGLISH WORD | GREEK WORD AND VERSE | THE WORD MEANS... |
|---|---|---|
| | admonish you, [NKJV]<br><br>Dear brothers and sisters, **honor** those who are your leaders in the Lord's work. They work hard among you and warn you against all that is wrong. [NLT]<br><br>Ἐρωτῶμεν δὲ ὑμᾶς, ἀδελφοί, εἰδέναι τοὺς κοπιῶντας ἐν ὑμῖν, καὶ προϊσταμένους ὑμῶν ἐν Κυρίῳ, καὶ νουθετοῦντας ὑμᾶς, [GNS]<br><br>Ἐρωτῶμεν δὲ ὑμᾶς, ἀδελφοί, εἰδέναι τοὺς κοπιῶντας ἐν ὑμῖν καὶ προϊσταμένους ὑμῶν ἐν κυρίῳ καὶ νουθετοῦντας ὑμᾶς [GNT] | |
| **#1996**<br>**Honor–**<br>**Honour**<br><br>Honour–KJV<br>Honor–NASB<br>Honor–NIV<br>Honor–NKJV<br>Honor–NLT<br><br>**POSB REFERENCE**<br>(Eph.6:1-3; esp. v.2)<br>Note 1, point 2 | τίμα = tima<br>Pronunciation: [tee'-mah]<br>Parsing (part of speech): verb<br>    Mood—imperative<br>    Tense—present<br>    Voice—active<br>    Person—2nd person<br>    Number—singular<br>    Stem or root—from τιμάω<br>Concordance References:<br>  ⇒ Strong's #5091 timaō<br>  ⇒ NIV #5506 timaō<br>  ⇒ NASB #5091 timaō<br><br>**Ephes. 6:2**<br>**Honour** thy father and mother; (which is the first commandment with promise;) [KJV]<br>**Honor** your father and mother (which is the first commandment with a promise), [NASB]<br>"**Honor** your father and mother"—which is the first commandment with a promise—[NIV]<br>"**Honor** your father and mother," which is the first commandment with promise: [NKJV]<br>"**Honor** your father and mother." This is the first of the Ten Commandments that ends with a promise. [NLT]<br>Τίμα τὸν πατέρα σου καὶ τὴν μητέρα· -- ἥτις ἐστὶν ἐντολὴ πρώτη ἐν ἐπαγγελίᾳ [GNS]<br>τίμα τὸν πατέρα σου καὶ τὴν μητέρα, ἥτις ἐστὶν ἐντολὴ πρώτη ἐν ἐπαγγελίᾳ, [GNT] | To honor one's father and mother; to reverence one's parents. The word "honor" (*tima*) means to "esteem and value as precious" (The Amplified New Testament); to show respect, reverence, kindness, courtesy, and obedience (Kenneth Wuest. *Ephesians and Colossians*, Vol.1, p.136).<br><br>**Practical Application**<br>Scripture is not speaking to any certain age child. It is speaking to all of us who are children with parents still living. We are to honor our fathers and mothers: *to esteem and value them as precious*—to respect and reverence them. |
| **#1997**<br>**Honor–**<br>**Honored**<br><br>Honourable–KJV<br>Honor–NASB<br>Honored–NIV<br>Honorable–NKJV<br>Honor–NLT<br><br>**POSB REFERENCE**<br>(Heb.13:4)<br>Note 4, point 1 | Τίμιος = Timios<br>Pronunciation: [tim'-ee-os]<br>Parsing (part of speech): adjective<br>    Case—nominative<br>    Gender—masculine<br>    Number—singular<br>    Stem or root—from τίμιος, α, ον<br>Concordance References:<br>  ⇒ Strong's #5093 timios<br>  ⇒ NIV #5508 timios<br>  ⇒ NASB #5093 timios<br><br>**Hebrews 13:4**<br>Marriage is **honourable** in all, and the bed undefiled: but whoremongers and adulterers God will judge. [KJV]<br>Let marriage be held in **honor** among all, and let the marriage bed be undefiled; for fornicators and adulterers God will judge. [NASB]<br>Marriage should be **honored** by all, and the marriage bed kept pure, for God will judge the adulterer and all the sexually immoral. [NIV]<br>Marriage *is* **honorable** among all, and the bed undefiled; but fornicators and adulterers God will judge. [NKJV]<br>Give **honor** to marriage, and remain faithful to one another in marriage. God will surely judge people who are immoral and those who commit adultery. [NLT]<br>τίμιος ὁ γάμος ἐν πᾶσι, καὶ ἡ κοίτη ἀμίαντος· πόρνους δὲ καὶ μοιχοὺς κρινεῖ ὁ Θεός." [GNS]<br>Τίμιος ὁ γάμος ἐν πᾶσιν καὶ ἡ κοίτη ἀμίαντος, πόρνους γὰρ καὶ μοιχοὺς κρινεῖ ὁ θεός. [GNT] | Honored, precious, valued.<br><br>**Practical Application**<br>Marriage is to be honored by all believers. The word "honor" (*Timios*) means highly esteemed, counted as the most precious, warm and tender bond, held as the most valuable of bonds, as being the dearest of relationships.<br>⇒ "Let marriage be held in honor" (Marcus Dods. *The Epistle to the Hebrews*. "Expositor's Greek Testament," Vol. 4, p.375).<br>⇒ "Let marriage be held in honor—esteemed worthy, precious, [that is], of great price and especially dear—in all things" (Amplified New Testament). |

# Practical Word Studies
## in the New Testament

| ENGLISH WORD | GREEK WORD AND VERSE | THE WORD MEANS... |
|---|---|---|
| #1998<br>Honor–<br>Honour<br><br>Honour–KJV<br>Honor–NASB<br>Respect–NIV<br>Honor–NKJV<br>Honor–NLT<br><br>**POSB REFERENCE**<br>(1 Pt.3:7)<br>Note 3 | τιμήν = timën<br>Pronunciation: [tee-mayn']<br>Parsing (part of speech): noun<br>  Case—accusative<br>  Gender—feminine<br>  Number—singular<br>  Stem or root—from τιμή, ῆς<br>Concordance References:<br>  ⇒ Strong's #5092 timë<br>  ⇒ NIV #5507 timë<br>  ⇒ NASB #5092 timë<br><br>**1 Peter 3:7**<br>Likewise, ye husbands, dwell with them according to knowledge, giving **honour** unto the wife, as unto the weaker vessel, and as being heirs together of the grace of life; that your prayers be not hindered. [KJV]<br><br>You husbands likewise, live with your wives in an understanding way, as with a weaker vessel, since she is a woman; and grant her **honor** as a fellow heir of the grace of life, so that your prayers may not be hindered. [NASB]<br><br>Husbands, in the same way be considerate as you live with your wives, and treat them with **respect** as the weaker partner and as heirs with you of the gracious gift of life, so that nothing will hinder your prayers. [NIV]<br><br>Husbands, likewise, dwell with *them* with understanding, giving **honor** to the wife, as to the weaker vessel, and *as being* heirs together of the grace of life, that your prayers may not be hindered. [NKJV]<br><br>In the same way, you husbands must give **honor** to your wives. Treat her with understanding as you live together. She may be weaker than you are, but she is your equal partner in God's gift of new life. If you don't treat her as you should, your prayers will not be heard. [NLT]<br><br>Οἱ ἄνδρες ὁμοίως, συνοικοῦντες κατὰ γνῶσιν, ὡς ἀσθενεστέρῳ σκεύει τῷ γυναικείῳ ἀπονέμοντες **τιμήν**, ὡς καὶ συγκληρονόμοι χάριτος ζωῆς, εἰς τὸ μὴ ἐκκόπτεσθαι τὰς προσευχὰς ὑμῶν. [GNS]<br><br>Οἱ ἄνδρες ὁμοίως, συνοικοῦντες κατὰ γνῶσιν ὡς ἀσθενεστέρῳ σκεύει τῷ γυναικείῳ, ἀπονέμοντες **τιμήν** ὡς καὶ συγκληρονόμοις χάριτος ζωῆς εἰς τὸ μὴ ἐγκόπτεσθαι τὰς προσευχὰς ὑμῶν. [GNT] | To give respect; to honor. It means to value; to esteem; to prize; to count as precious; to give special treatment.<br><br>**Practical Application**<br>Husbands are to honor their wives. A husband is to count his wife as a precious gem, as a prize of extreme value. He is to highly esteem her, set her up on a pedestal before his very eyes. Note three points.<br>1. The husband is to honor his wife as the weaker vessel. By nature, the wife is just more delicate and frail. This means that the husband is...<br>  • to protect her.<br>  • to be the primary provider.<br>  • to take the lead.<br>  • to oversee the family and its welfare.<br>  • to be the driving force.<br>  • to plow the way.<br>  • to be the initiator.<br><br>Husbands are to honor their wives by loving and tenderly taking care of them. They are to look after and care for them with warmth and tenderness, treating them in the most precious of spirits and esteeming them ever so highly.<br>2. The husband is to honor his wife as a *joint heir* of the grace of life. Note this point: in God's eyes men and women are joint or equal heirs. The husband is not above the wife nor the wife above the husband. God has no favorites. Spiritual gifts and rights are given equally to wives and husbands. Women receive the spiritual gifts of God just as readily as men do.<br><br>The point is well made: husbands are to honor their wives as being equal in life. Life is a grace; it is an undeserved gift of God. Therefore in life, the husband is to treat the wife as an equal. He is not to be a tyrant, not to dominate and enslave her to serve and to meet his needs and wants. He is to be understanding, loving, gentle, and considerate. He is to honor her as a fellow heir of life, of the wonderful grace and gift of life that God has given us all.<br>3. Failure to honor the wife hinders the prayers of the husband. God will not answer the prayers of any husband who dishonors his wife, no matter who he is or how much he professes Christ. What God hears is the sigh of the wife, not the prayers of a mean and domineering husband. The husband can cry out to God all he wants, but God's back is turned away from him and toward the sigh of the wife. God is going to hear the broken and contrite heart, not the prayers of the arrogant and dominating spirit. Both husband and wife must love one another and live as God says to live, both fulfilling their duty to one another, if they wish God to answer their prayers. |

# PRACTICAL WORD STUDIES
## in the NEW TESTAMENT

| ENGLISH WORD | GREEK WORD AND VERSE | THE WORD MEANS... |
|---|---|---|
| **#1999**<br>**Honorable**<br><br>Honest–KJV<br>Excellent–NASB<br>Good–NIV<br>**Honorable–NKJV**<br>Be careful how you live–NLT<br><br>**POSB REFERENCE**<br>(1 Pt.2:12)<br>Note 3 | καλήν = kalën<br>Pronunciation: [kal-ayn']<br>Parsing (part of speech): adjective<br>    Case—accusative<br>    Gender—feminine<br>    Number—singular<br>    Stem or root—from καλός, ή, όν<br>Concordance References:<br>  ⇒ Strong's #2570 kalos<br>  ⇒ NIV #2819 kalos<br>  ⇒ NASB #2570 kalos<br><br>**1 Peter 2:12**<br>Having your conversation **honest** among the Gentiles: that, whereas they speak against you as evildoers, they may by your good works, which they shall behold, glorify God in the day of visitation. [KJV]<br>Keep your behavior **excellent** among the Gentiles, so that in the thing in which they slander you as evildoers, they may on account of your good deeds, as they observe them, glorify God in the day of visitation. [NASB]<br>Live such **good** lives among the pagans that, though they accuse you of doing wrong, they may see your good deeds and glorify God on the day he visits us. [NIV]<br>Having your conduct **honorable** among the Gentiles, that when they speak against you as evildoers, they may, by *your* good works which they observe, glorify God in the day of visitation. [NKJV]<br>**Be careful how you live** among your unbelieving neighbors. Even if they accuse you of doing wrong, they will see your honorable behavior, and they will believe and give honor to God when he comes to judge the world. [NLT]<br>τὴν ἀναστροφὴν ὑμῶν ἐν τοῖς ἔθνεσιν ἔχοντες **καλήν**, ἵνα, ἐν ᾧ καταλαλοῦσιν ὑμῶν ὡς κακοποιῶν, ἐκ τῶν καλῶν ἔργων ἐποπτεύσαντες δοξάσωσι τὸν Θεὸν ἐν ἡμέρᾳ ἐπισκοπῆς. [GNS]<br>τὴν ἀναστροφὴν ὑμῶν ἐν τοῖς ἔθνεσιν ἔχοντες **καλήν**, ἵνα, ἐν ᾧ καταλαλοῦσιν ὑμῶν ὡς κακοποιῶν ἐκ τῶν καλῶν ἔργων ἐποπτεύοντες δοξάσωσιν τὸν θεὸν ἐν ἡμέρᾳ ἐπισκοπῆς. [GNT] | Good, honest, excellent, honorable, proper; to be careful how one lives.<br><br>**Practical Application**<br>The word "honorable" (*kalën*) means a good life, a life that is honorable, righteous, pure, lovely, decent, excellent, upright, and noble. It means a life that is without blame, that cannot be justly or accurately blamed with any sin or evil. The world watches a genuine believer to see if he really lives what he professes. Therefore, we must live good lives, honest lives, lives that are just what we profess: holy, righteous, and pure. |
| **#2000**<br>**Honorable**<br><br>Honest–KJV<br>**Honorable–NASB**<br>Noble–NIV<br>Noble–NKJV<br>**Honorable–NLT**<br><br>**POSB REFERENCE**<br>(Philip.4:8-9; esp. v.8)<br>Note 2, point 1b | σεμνά = semna<br>Pronunciation: [sem-nah']<br>Parsing (part of speech): adjective<br>    Case—nominative<br>    Gender—neuter<br>    Number—plural<br>    Stem or root—from σεμνός, ή, όν<br>Concordance References:<br>  ⇒ Strong's #4586 semnos<br>  ⇒ NIV #4948 semnos<br>  ⇒ NASB #4586 semnos<br><br>**Philip. 4:8**<br>Finally, brethren, whatsoever things are true, whatsoever things are **honest**, whatsoever things are just, whatsoever things are pure, whatsoever things are lovely, whatsoever things are of good report; if there be any virtue, and if there be any praise, think on these things. [KJV]<br>Finally, brethren, whatever is true, whatever is **honorable**, whatever is right, whatever is pure, whatever is lovely, whatever is of good repute, if there is any excellence and if anything worthy of praise, let your mind dwell on these things. [NASB]<br>Finally, brothers, whatever is true, whatever is **noble**, whatever is right, whatever is pure, whatever is lovely, whatever is admirable—if anything is excellent or praiseworthy—think about such things. [NIV]<br>Finally, brethren, whatever things are true, whatever things *are* **noble**, whatever things *are* just, whatever | Noble, honest, honorable, worthy, respectable, revered, highly respected.<br><br>**Practical Application**<br>Barclay says: "The word really describes that which has the dignity of holiness upon it. There are things in this world which are flippant and cheap, things which are attractive to the light-minded; but it is on the things which are grave and serious and dignified that the Christian will set his mind" (*The Letters to the Philippians, Colossians, and Thessalonians*, p.98). |

# PRACTICAL WORD STUDIES
## in the NEW TESTAMENT

| ENGLISH WORD | GREEK WORD AND VERSE | THE WORD MEANS... |
|---|---|---|
| | things *are* pure, whatever things *are* lovely, whatever things *are* of good report, if *there is* any virtue and if *there is* anything praiseworthy—meditate on these things. [NKJV]<br><br>And now, dear brothers and sisters, let me say one more thing as I close this letter. Fix your thoughts on what is true and **honorable** and right. Think about things that are pure and lovely and admirable. Think about things that are excellent and worthy of praise. [NLT]<br><br>Τὸ λοιπόν, ἀδελφοί, ὅσα ἐστὶν ἀληθῆ, ὅσα **σεμνά**, ὅσα δίκαια, ὅσα ἁγνά, ὅσα προσφιλῆ, ὅσα εὔφημα, εἴ τις ἀρετὴ καὶ εἴ τις ἔπαινος, ταῦτα λογίζεσθε· [GNS]<br><br>Τὸ λοιπόν, ἀδελφοί, ὅσα ἐστὶν ἀληθῆ, ὅσα **σεμνά**, ὅσα δίκαια, ὅσα ἁγνά, ὅσα προσφιλῆ, ὅσα εὔφημα, εἴ τις ἀρετὴ καὶ εἴ τις ἔπαινος, ταῦτα λογίζεσθε· [GNT] | |
| **#2001**<br>**Honorable**<br><br>Good–KJV<br>Fine–NASB<br>Noble–NIV<br>Good–NKJV<br>Honorable–NLT<br><br>**POSB REFERENCE**<br>(1 Tim.3:1)<br>Note 1 | καλοῦ = *kalou*<br>Pronunciation: [kal-oo']<br>Parsing (part of speech): adjective<br>  Case—genitive<br>  Gender—neuter<br>  Number—singular<br>  Stem or root—from καλός, ή, όν<br>Concordance References:<br>  ⇒ Strong's #2570 *kalos*<br>  ⇒ NIV #2819 *kalos*<br>  ⇒ NASB #2570 *kalos*<br><br>**1 Tim. 3:1**<br>This is a true saying, If a man desire the office of a bishop, he desireth a **good** work. [KJV]<br>It is a trustworthy statement: if any man aspires to the office of overseer, it is a **fine** work he desires to do. [NASB]<br>Here is a trustworthy saying: If anyone sets his heart on being an overseer, he desires a **noble** task. [NIV]<br>This *is* a faithful saying: If a man desires the position of a bishop, he desires a **good** work. [NKJV]<br>It is a true saying that if someone wants to be an elder, he desires an **honorable** responsibility. [NLT]<br>Πιστὸς ὁ λόγος· Εἴ τις ἐπισκοπῆς ὀρέγεται, **καλοῦ** ἔργου ἐπιθυμεῖ. [GNS]<br>πιστὸς ὁ λόγος. Εἴ τις ἐπισκοπῆς ὀρέγεται, **καλοῦ** ἔργου ἐπιθυμεῖ. [GNT] | Noble, good, fine, honorable, honest, proper, right, excellent, beneficial, productive.<br><br>**Practical Application**<br>The office of elder is "an honorable responsibility." Note that the position of the ministry is not what is stressed, but the work of the ministry. The emphasis is not the esteem and honor of the profession. The emphasis is upon the work of the ministry. It is the work that is honorable, excellent, beneficial, and productive. The work of the ministry is an "honorable responsibility." |
| **#2002**<br>**Honorable– Honourable**<br><br>Honourable–KJV<br>Honor–NASB<br>Honored–NIV<br>Honorable–NKJV<br>Honor–NLT<br><br>**POSB REFERENCE**<br>(Heb.13:4)<br>Note 4, point 1 | Τίμιος = *Timios*<br>Pronunciation: [tim'-ee-os]<br>Parsing (part of speech): adjective<br>  Case—nominative<br>  Gender—masculine<br>  Number—singular<br>  Stem or root—from τίμιος, α, ον<br>Concordance References:<br>  ⇒ Strong's #5093 *timios*<br>  ⇒ NIV #5508 *timios*<br>  ⇒ NASB #5093 *timios*<br><br>**Hebrews 13:4**<br>Marriage is **honourable** in all, and the bed undefiled: but whoremongers and adulterers God will judge. [KJV]<br>Let marriage be held in **honor** among all, and let the marriage bed be undefiled; for fornicators and adulterers God will judge. [NASB]<br>Marriage should be **honored** by all, and the marriage bed kept pure, for God will judge the adulterer and all the sexually immoral. [NIV]<br>Marriage *is* **honorable** among all, and the bed undefiled; but fornicators and adulterers God will judge. [NKJV]<br>Give **honor** to marriage, and remain faithful to one another in marriage. God will surely judge people who are immoral and those who commit adultery. [NLT]<br>τίμιος ὁ γάμος ἐν πᾶσι, καὶ ἡ κοίτη ἀμίαντος· πόρνους δὲ καὶ μοιχοὺς κρινεῖ ὁ Θεός. [GNS]<br>**Τίμιος** ὁ γάμος ἐν πᾶσιν καὶ ἡ κοίτη ἀμίαντος, πόρνους γὰρ καὶ μοιχοὺς κρινεῖ ὁ θεός. [GNT] | Honored, respected, distinguished, celebrated, esteemed, highly regarded.<br><br>**Practical Application**<br>Marriage is to be honored by all believers. The word "honorable" (*Timios*) means highly esteemed, counted as the most precious, warm and tender bond, held as the most valuable of bonds, as being the dearest of relationships.<br>⇒ "Let marriage be held in honor" (Marcus Dods. *The Epistle to the Hebrews.* "Expositor's Greek Testament," Vol. 4, p.375).<br>⇒ "Let marriage be held in honor— esteemed worthy, precious, [that is], of great price and especially dear—in all things" (Amplified New Testament). |

# PRACTICAL WORD STUDIES
## in the NEW TESTAMENT

| ENGLISH WORD | GREEK WORD AND VERSE | THE WORD MEANS... |
|---|---|---|
| **#2003**<br>**Honorable,**<br>**What [Is]**<br><br>Which [is]<br>honest–KJV<br>What [is] right–NASB<br>What [is] right–NIV<br>**What [is] honorable–NKJV**<br>Right–NLT<br><br>**POSB**<br>**REFERENCE**<br>(2 Cor.13:7-10; esp. v.7)<br>Note 2 | τὸ καλὸν = *to kalon*<br>Pronunciation: [to kal-on']<br>Parsing *kalon* (part of speech): pronominal adjective<br>    Case—accusative<br>    Gender—neuter<br>    Number—singular<br>    Stem or root—from καλός, ή, όν<br>Concordance References:<br>  ⇒ Strong's #3588 ho + 2566 kalos<br>  ⇒ NIV #3836 ho [what] + 2819 kalos [right]<br>  ⇒ NASB #3588 ho + 2566 kalos<br><br>**2 Cor. 13:7**<br>Now I pray to God that ye do no evil; not that we should appear approved, but that ye should do that **which** is **honest**, though we be as reprobates. [KJV]<br>Now we pray to God that you do no wrong; not that we ourselves may appear approved, but that you may do **what** is **right**, even though we should appear unapproved. [NASB]<br>Now we pray to God that you will not do anything wrong. Not that people will see that we have stood the test but that you will do **what** is **right** even though we may seem to have failed. [NIV]<br>Now I pray to God that you do no evil, not that we should appear approved, but that you should do **what is honorable**, though we may seem disqualified. [NKJV]<br>We pray to God that you will not do anything wrong. We pray this, not to show that our ministry to you has been successful, but because we want you to do **right** even if we ourselves seem to have failed. [NLT]<br>εὐχόμαι δὲ πρὸς τὸν Θεὸν, μὴ ποιῆσαι ὑμᾶς κακὸν μηδέν, οὐχ ἵνα ἡμεῖς δόκιμοι φανῶμεν, ἀλλ' ἵνα ὑμεῖς **τὸ καλὸν** ποιῆτε, ἡμεῖς δὲ ὡς ἀδόκιμοι ὦμεν. [GNS]<br>εὐχόμεθα δὲ πρὸς τὸν θεὸν μὴ ποιῆσαι ὑμᾶς κακὸν μηδέν, οὐχ ἵνα ἡμεῖς δόκιμοι φανῶμεν, ἀλλ' ἵνα ὑμεῖς **τὸ καλὸν** ποιῆτε, ἡμεῖς δὲ ὡς ἀδόκιμοι ὦμεν. [GNT] | Right, noble, honest, proper, good, pleasing.<br><br>**Practical Application**<br>Paul was under attack, and suffered the tension and pressure of the attack, but that was not the reason he wanted his critics to repent. His purpose was not selfish or self-centered: he wanted his critics to repent for the sake of righteousness, that the good and right thing might be done. He wanted this despite the fact that they treated him as a reprobate. They might not love him, but he loved them and wanted only the best for them. He did not want to discipline them; he wanted them to repent before he arrived. |
| **#2004**<br>**Honored**<br><br>Hallowed–KJV<br>Hallowed–NASB<br>Hallowed–NIV<br>Hallowed–NKJV<br>**Honored–NLT**<br><br>**POSB**<br>**REFERENCE**<br>(Mt.6:9)<br>*Deeper Study* #4 | ἁγιασθήτω = *hagiasthētō*<br>Pronunciation: [hag-ee-as'-thee-tow]<br>Parsing (part of speech): verb<br>    Mood—imperative<br>    Tense—aorist<br>    Voice—passive<br>    Person—3rd person<br>    Number—singular<br>    Stem or root—from ἁγιάζω<br>Concordance References:<br>  ⇒ Strong's #37 hagiazō<br>  ⇒ NIV #39 hagiazō<br>  ⇒ NASB #37 hagiazō<br><br>**Matthew 6:9**<br>After this manner therefore pray ye: Our Father which art in heaven, **Hallowed** be thy name. [KJV]<br>"Pray, then, in this way:' Our Father who art in heaven, **Hallowed** be Thy name. [NASB]<br>"This, then, is how you should pray: "'Our Father in heaven, **hallowed** be your name, [NIV]<br>In this manner, therefore, pray: Our Father in heaven, **Hallowed** be Your name. [NKJV]<br>Pray like this: Our Father in heaven, may your name be **honored**. [NLT]<br>οὕτως οὖν προσεύχεσθε ὑμεῖς· Πάτερ ἡμῶν ὁ ἐν τοῖς οὐρανοῖς, **ἁγιασθήτω** τὸ ὄνομά σου· [GNS]<br>Οὕτως οὖν προσεύχεσθε ὑμεῖς· Πάτερ ἡμῶν ὁ ἐν τοῖς οὐρανοῖς, **ἁγιασθήτω** τὸ ὄνομά σου· [GNT] | To be counted and treated as holy; to be sanctified, set apart as holy; to be honored and esteemed; to be made distinctive, distinguished, and different from all else; to be counted and treated as distinctive and different.<br><br>**Practical Application**<br>God is holy. He is the very embodiment and perfection of absolute holiness (see POSB *Deeper Study* #1, Holy—1 Peter 1:15-16 for more discussion).<br>⇒ God is the embodiment of absolute righteousness, purity, sinlessness, and godliness.<br>⇒ God is the very embodiment of absolute perfection, completeness, and fulfillment.<br>⇒ God is the very embodiment of absolute separation—set apart, different and separated from all else. |

# PRACTICAL WORD STUDIES
## in the NEW TESTAMENT

| ENGLISH WORD | GREEK WORD AND VERSE | THE WORD MEANS... |
|---|---|---|
| **#2005**<br>**Honored Son**<br><br>Firstbegotten–KJV<br>First-born–NASB<br>Firstborn–NIV<br>Firstborn–NKJV<br>**Honored Son–NLT**<br><br>**POSB<br>REFERENCE**<br>(Heb.1:4-6; esp. v.6)<br>Note 1, point 3 | πρωτότοκον = prōtotokon<br>Pronunciation: [pro-tot-ok'-on]<br>Parsing (part of speech): pronominal adjective<br>    Case—accusative<br>    Gender—masculine<br>    Number—singular<br>    Stem or root—from πρωτότοκος, ον<br>Concordance References:<br>  ⇒ Strong's #4416 prōtotokos<br>  ⇒ NIV #4758 prōtotokos<br>  ⇒ NASB #4416 prōtotokos<br><br>**Hebrews 1:6**<br>And again, when he bringeth in the **firstbegotten** into the world, he saith, And let all the angels of God worship him. [KJV]<br>And when He again brings the **first-born** into the world, He says, "And let all the angels of God worship Him." [NASB]<br>And again, when God brings his **firstborn** into the world, he says, "Let all God's angels worship him." [NIV]<br>But when He again brings the **firstborn** into he world, He says: "Let all the angels of God worship Him." [NKJV]<br>And then, when he presented his **honored Son** to the world, God said, "Let all the angels of God worship him." [NLT]<br>ὅταν δὲ πάλιν εἰσαγάγῃ τὸν **πρωτότοκον** εἰς τὴν οἰκουμένην, λέγει, Καὶ προσκυνησάτωσαν αὐτῷ πάντες ἄγγελοι Θεοῦ. [GNS]<br>ὅταν δὲ πάλιν εἰσαγάγῃ τὸν **πρωτότοκον** εἰς τὴν οἰκουμένην, λέγει, Καὶ προσκυνησάτωσαν αὐτῷ πάντες ἄγγελοι θεοῦ. [GNT] | Firstborn, firstbegotten, honored son. It means *first* in the sense of priority and superiority, of being above someone else. It is a word that shows dignity, honor, worth; that someone deserves praise.<br><br>**Practical Application**<br>Jesus Christ is the One who is to be worshipped and praised, not angels.<br>  ⇒ When Jesus Christ was born into this world, He was attended and worshipped by angels. (Luke 2:13f).<br>  ⇒ When Jesus Christ was taken into the world above, at His resurrection and ascension, He was attended and worshipped by angels (Acts 1:10f).<br>  ⇒ When Jesus Christ returns to this earth again, He will be attended and worshipped by angels (Matthew 13:41; Matthew 16:27; Matthew 24:31).<br><br>Jesus Christ is the Person who entered the world as Man, to save man. He is the Person who was raised from the dead and who ascended into heaven to conquer death forever. He is the Person who is to return and take us home to heaven to be with God eternally. Angels did not do this. Therefore our worship—our hope and attention and praise—is to be upon Christ. We are to be seeking Christ as our way to God, not angels or some other intermediary. Jesus Christ has a name that is far more excellent than that of angels. |
| **#2006**<br>**Honoring**<br><br>Discerning–KJV<br>Judge...rightly–NASB<br>Recognizing–NIV<br>Discerning–NKJV<br>**Honoring–NLT**<br><br>**POSB<br>REFERENCE**<br>(1 Cor.11:27-30; esp. v.29)<br>Note 4, point 2 | διακρίνων = diakrinōn<br>Pronunciation: [dee-ak-ree'-noan]<br>Parsing (part of speech): verb<br>    Mood—participle<br>    Tense—present<br>    Voice—active<br>    Case—nominative<br>    Gender—masculine<br>    Number—singular<br>    Stem or root—from διακρίνω<br>Concordance References:<br>  ⇒ Strong's #1252 diakrinō<br>  ⇒ NIV #1359 diakrinō<br>  ⇒ NASB #1252 diakrinō<br><br>**1 Cor. 11:29**<br>For he that eateth and drinketh unworthily, eateth and drinketh damnation to himself, not **discerning** the Lord's body. [KJV]<br>For he who eats and drinks, eats and drinks judgment to himself, if he does not **judge** the body **rightly**. [NASB]<br>For anyone who eats and drinks without **recognizing** the body of the Lord eats and drinks judgment on himself. [NIV]<br>For he who eats and drinks in an unworthy manner eats and drinks judgment to himself, not **discerning** the Lord's body. [NKJV]<br>For if you eat the bread or drink the cup unworthily, not **honoring** the body of Christ, you are eating and drinking God's judgment upon yourself. [NLT]<br>ὁ γὰρ ἐσθίων καὶ πίνων ἀναξίως, κρίμα ἑαυτῷ ἐσθίει καὶ πίνει, μὴ **διακρίνων** τὸ σῶμα τοῦ Κυρίου. [GNS]<br>ὁ γὰρ ἐσθίων καὶ πίνων κρίμα ἑαυτῷ ἐσθίει καὶ πίνει μὴ **διακρίνων** τὸ σῶμα. [GNT] | To recognize; to discriminate; to distinguish; to evaluate, to judge rightly.<br><br>**Practical Application**<br>The person who eats the bread and drinks the cup unworthily just fails to think about what he is doing. He fails to discriminate and discern the seriousness of his act. If he thought about the matter, he would not partake of the Lord's Supper with unconfessed sin in his life, for such irreverence of the body and blood of the Lord stirs the judgment of God. |

# PRACTICAL WORD STUDIES
## in the NEW TESTAMENT

| ENGLISH WORD | GREEK WORD AND VERSE | THE WORD MEANS... |
|---|---|---|
| **#2007**<br>**Honourable**<br><br>Honourable–KJV<br>Prominent–NASB<br>Prominent–NIV<br>Prominent–NKJV<br>Prominent–NLT<br><br>**POSB REFERENCE**<br>(Acts 17:12)<br>Note 6 | εὐσχημόνων = *euschēmōn*<br>Pronunciation: [yoo-skhay'-mown]<br>Parsing (part of speech): adjective<br>    Case—genitive<br>    Gender—feminine<br>    Number—plural<br>    Stem or root—from εὐσχήμων, ον<br>Concordance References:<br>  ⇒ Strong's #2158 euschēmōn<br>  ⇒ NIV #2363 euschēmōn<br>  ⇒ NASB #2158 euschēmōn<br><br>**Acts 17:12**<br>Therefore many of them believed; also of **honourable** women which were Greeks, and of men, not a few. [KJV]<br>Many of them therefore believed, along with a number of **prominent** Greek women and men. [NASB]<br>Many of the Jews believed, as did also a number of **prominent** Greek women and many Greek men. [NIV]<br>Therefore many of them believed, and also not a few of the Greeks, **prominent** women as well as men. [NKJV]<br>As a result, many Jews believed, as did some of the **prominent** Greek women and many men. [NLT]<br>πολλοὶ μὲν οὖν ἐξ αὐτῶν ἐπίστευσαν, καὶ τῶν Ἑλληνίδων γυναικῶν τῶν **εὐσχημόνων** καὶ ἀνδρῶν οὐκ ὀλίγοι. [GNS]<br>πολλοὶ μὲν οὖν ἐξ αὐτῶν ἐπίστευσαν καὶ τῶν Ἑλληνίδων γυναικῶν τῶν **εὐσχημόνων** καὶ ἀνδρῶν οὐκ ὀλίγοι. [GNT] | Prominent, honorable; a person of high standing.<br><br>**Practical Application**<br>The word "honourable" (*euschēmōn*) means good character. It means respectable and influential citizens. |
| **#2008**<br>**Hope**<br><br>Hope–KJV<br>Hope–NASB<br>Hope–NIV<br>Hope–NKJV<br>Confident expectation of salvation–NLT<br><br>**POSB REFERENCE**<br>(Rom.5:3-5; esp. v.4)<br>Note 5, point 3 | ἐλπίδα = *elpida*<br>Pronunciation: [el-pee-dah']<br>Parsing (part of speech): noun<br>    Case—accusative<br>    Gender—feminine<br>    Number—singular<br>    Stem or root—from ἐλπίς, ίδος<br>Concordance References:<br>  ⇒ Strong's #1680 elpis<br>  ⇒ NIV #1828 elpis<br>  ⇒ NASB #1680 elpis<br><br>**Romans 5:4**<br>And patience, experience; and experience, **hope**: [KJV]<br>And perseverance, proven character; and proven character, **hope**; [NASB]<br>Perseverance, character; and character, **hope**. [NIV]<br>And perseverance, character; and character, **hope**. [NKJV]<br>And endurance develops strength of character in us, and character strengthens our **confident expectation of salvation**. [NLT]<br>ἡ δὲ ὑπομονὴ δοκιμήν, ἡ δὲ δοκιμὴ **ἐλπίδα**· [GNS]<br>ἡ δὲ ὑπομονὴ δοκιμήν, ἡ δὲ δοκιμὴ **ἐλπίδα**. [GNT] | Hope; ground or basis of hope; what is hoped for. It means to expect with confidence; to anticipate knowing; to look and long for with surety; to desire with assurance; to rely on with certainty; to trust with the guarantee; to believe with the knowledge.<br><br>**Practical Application**<br>Note that confident expectation of salvation is hope, anticipation, looking and longing for, desiring, relying upon, and trusting. But it is also confidence, knowledge, surety, assurance, certainty, and a guarantee. When a justified man becomes stronger in character, he draws closer to God; and the closer he draws to God, the more he hopes for the glory of God. (See POSB note, Hope—Romans 5:2 for more discussion and verses.) |
| **#2009**<br>**Hope**<br><br>Hope–KJV<br>Hope–NASB<br>Hope–NIV<br>Hope–NKJV<br>Eagerly look forward–NLT<br><br>**POSB REFERENCE**<br>(Rom.8:24-25, esp. v.24) | ἐλπίδι = *elpidi*<br>Pronunciation: [el-pee-dee']<br>Parsing (part of speech): noun<br>    Case—dative<br>    Gender—feminine<br>    Number—singular<br>    Stem or root—from ἐλπίς, ίδος<br>Concordance References:<br>  ⇒ Strong's #1680 elpis<br>  ⇒ NIV #1828 elpis<br>  ⇒ NASB #1680 elpis<br><br>**Romans 8:24**<br>For we are saved by **hope**: but hope that is seen is not hope: for what a man seeth, why doth he yet hope for? [KJV] | Eagerly look forward to; assured expectation, confident knowledge, inward possession, spiritual surety, hope.<br><br>**Practical Application**<br>Note the statements of definition again, for they are packed full of meaning. The believer's hope cannot be defined as the world defines hope. The believer's hope is entirely different from the world's hope or desire or wish. The world desires and wishes for what it can see, and they may or may not be able to get what they long for.<br>The believer's hope is entirely different in |

# PRACTICAL WORD STUDIES
## in the NEW TESTAMENT

| ENGLISH WORD | GREEK WORD AND VERSE | THE WORD MEANS... |
|---|---|---|
| *Deeper Study #1* | For in **hope** we have been saved, but hope that is seen is not hope; for why does one also hope for what he sees? [NASB]<br><br>For in this **hope** we were saved. But hope that is seen is no hope at all. Who hopes for what he already has? [NIV]<br><br>For we were saved in this **hope**, but hope that is seen is not hope; for why does one still hope for what he sees? [NKJV]<br><br>Now that we are saved, we **eagerly look forward** to this freedom. For if you already have something, you don't need to hope for it. [NLT]<br><br>τῇ γὰρ **ἐλπίδι** ἐσώθημεν· ἐλπὶς δὲ βλεπομένη οὐκ ἔστιν ἐλπίς· ὃ γὰρ βλέπει τίς, τί καὶ ἐλπίζει; [GNS]<br><br>τῇ γὰρ **ἐλπίδι** ἐσώθημεν· ἐλπὶς δὲ βλεπομένη οὐκ ἔστιν ἐλπίς· ὃ γὰρ βλέπει τίς ἐλπίζει; [GNT] | that it deals with spiritual things, and the believer will unquestionably get what he hopes for. The believer's hope is based on the inward experience and witness of God's Spirit. The believer knows that God's Spirit lives within him, and he actually experiences the things of the Spirit now. Granted, his experience is but a taste; the things of the Spirit are not yet perfected in his life, but they do exist, and they are present in his body. He already possesses the things of God while in the flesh. His hope of salvation is a present experience—he is saved now—he already has a taste of salvation. The believer's hope to be saved is a living reality now; therefore, his hope is a sure hope. To the genuine believer, hope is the absolute assurance of things promised, but not yet seen.<br><br>He has absolute assurance because he already experiences the things of God. They are already an inward possession, a spiritual surety, an assured expectation, a confident knowledge. |
| **#2010**<br>**Hoped–**<br>**Hoping**<br><br>Trusted–KJV<br>**Hoping–NASB**<br>**Hoped–NIV**<br>**Hoping–NKJV**<br>Thought–NLT<br><br>**POSB**<br>**REFERENCE**<br>(Lk.24:15-27; esp. v.21)<br>Note 2, point 2a | ἠλπίζομεν = ëlpizomen<br>Pronunciation: [ayl-pid'-zo-men]<br>Parsing (part of speech): verb<br>    Mood—indicative<br>    Tense—imperfect<br>    Voice—active<br>    Person—1st person<br>    Number—plural<br>    Stem or root—from ἐλπίζω<br>Concordance References:<br>⇒ Strong's #1679 elpizö<br>⇒ NIV #1827 elpizö<br>⇒ NASB #1679 elpizö<br><br>**Luke 24:21**<br>But we **trusted** that it had been he which should have redeemed Israel: and beside all this, to day is the third day since these things were done. [KJV]<br><br>"But we were **hoping** that it was He who was going to redeem Israel. Indeed, besides all this, it is the third day since these things happened. [NASB]<br><br>But we had **hoped** that he was the one who was going to redeem Israel. And what is more, it is the third day since all this took place. [NIV]<br><br>But we were **hoping** that it was He who was going to redeem Israel. Indeed, besides all this, today is the third day since these things happened. [NKJV]<br><br>We had **thought** he was the Messiah who had come to rescue Israel. That all happened three days ago. [NLT]<br><br>ἡμεῖς δὲ **ἠλπίζομεν** ὅτι αὐτός ἐστιν ὁ μέλλων λυτροῦσθαι τὸν Ἰσραήλ. ἀλλά γε οὐ-ν σὺν πᾶσι τούτοις τρίτην ταύτην ἡμέραν ἄγει σήμερον, ἀφ' οὗ ταῦτα ἐγένετο. [GNS]<br><br>ἡμεῖς δὲ **ἠλπίζομεν** ὅτι αὐτός ἐστιν ὁ μέλλων λυτροῦσθαι τὸν Ἰσραήλ· ἀλλά γε καὶ σὺν πᾶσιν τούτοις τρίτην ταύτην ἡμέραν ἄγει ἀφ' οὗ ταῦτα ἐγένετο. [GNT] | To hope, trust, desire, expect.<br><br>**Practical Application**<br>When Scripture speaks of the believer's hope, it does not mean what the world means by hope. The hope of the world is a desire, a want. The world hopes—wants, desires—that something will happen. But this is not the hope of the believer. The hope of the believer is a surety: it is perfect assurance, confidence, and knowledge. How can hope be so absolute and assured? By being an inward possession. The believer's hope is based upon the presence of God's Spirit who dwells within the believer. In fact, the believer possesses the hope of glory only by the Spirit of God who dwells within him. (See POSB *Deeper Study #1*, Hope—Romans 8:24-25 for more detailed discussion.) |
| **#2011**<br>**Hopelessly**<br>**Confused**<br><br>Vanity–KJV<br>Futility–NASB<br>Futility–NIV<br>Futility–NKJV<br>**Hopelessly confused–**<br>**NLT** | ματαιότητι = mataiotëti<br>Pronunciation: [mat-ah-yot'-ay-tee]<br>Parsing (part of speech): noun<br>    Case—dative<br>    Gender—feminine<br>    Number—singular<br>    Stem or root—from ματαιότης, ητος<br>Concordance References:<br>⇒ Strong's #3153 mataiotës<br>⇒ NIV #3470 mataiotës<br>⇒ NASB #3153 mataiotës | Futility, vanity; emptiness; frustration; to be hopelessly confused; to be empty, futile, senseless, aimless, unsuccessful, worthless.<br><br>**Practical Application**<br>When men push God out of their minds, their minds are void and empty of God, of His truth and morality. *God is not in their thoughts.* Their minds are ready to be filled with some other god or supremacy, that is, with the things of the world: |

# PRACTICAL WORD STUDIES
## in the NEW TESTAMENT

| ENGLISH WORD | GREEK WORD AND VERSE | THE WORD MEANS... |
|---|---|---|
| POSB REFERENCE (Eph.4:17-19; esp. v.17) Note 1, point 1 | **Ephes. 4:17**<br>This I say therefore, and testify in the Lord, that ye henceforth walk not as other Gentiles walk, in the **vanity** of their mind, [KJV]<br>This I say therefore, and affirm together with the Lord, that you walk no longer just as the Gentiles also walk, in the **futility** of their mind, [NASB]<br>So I tell you this, and insist on it in the Lord, that you must no longer live as the Gentiles do, in the **futility** of their thinking. [NIV]<br>This I say, therefore, and testify in the Lord, that you should no longer walk as the rest of the Gentiles walk, in the **futility** of their mind, [NKJV]<br>With the Lord's authority let me say this: Live no longer as the ungodly do, for they are **hopelessly confused**. [NLT]<br>Τοῦτο οὖν λέγω καὶ μαρτύρομαι ἐν Κυρίῳ, μηκέτι ὑμᾶς περιπατεῖν καθὼς καὶ τὰ λοιπὰ ἔθνη περιπατεῖ, ἐν **ματαιότητι** τοῦ νοὸς αὐτῶν, [GNS]<br>Τοῦτο οὖν λέγω καὶ μαρτύρομαι ἐν κυρίῳ, μηκέτι ὑμᾶς περιπατεῖν, καθὼς καὶ τὰ ἔθνη περιπατεῖ ἐν **ματαιότητι** τοῦ νοὸς αὐτῶν, [GNT] | ⇒ worldly pleasures<br>⇒ worldly possessions<br>⇒ worldly power<br>⇒ worldly position<br>⇒ worldly religions<br>⇒ worldly ideas<br>⇒ worldly honor<br>⇒ worldly gods |
| #2012<br>**Horrors**<br><br>Pains–KJV<br>Agony–NASB<br>Agony–NIV<br>Pains–NKJV<br>**Horrors–NLT**<br><br>POSB REFERENCE (Acts 2:24) *Deeper Study #4*, point 2 | ὠδῖνας = ōdinas<br>Pronunciation: [o-deen'-ahs]<br>Parsing (part of speech): noun<br>  Case—accusative<br>  Gender—feminine<br>  Number—plural<br>  Stem or root—from ὠδίν<br>Concordance References:<br>  ⇒ Strong's #5604 ōdin<br>  ⇒ NIV #6047 ōdin<br>  ⇒ NASB #5604 ōdin<br><br>**Acts 2:24**<br>Whom God hath raised up, having loosed the **pains** of death: because it was not possible that he should be holden of it. [KJV]<br>"And God raised Him up again, putting an end to the **agony** of death, since it was impossible for Him to be held in its power. [NASB]<br>But God raised him from the dead, freeing him from the **agony** of death, because it was impossible for death to keep its hold on him. [NIV]<br>Whom God raised up, having loosed the **pains** of death, because it was not possible that He should be held by it. [NKJV]<br>However, God released him from the **horrors** of death and raised him back to life again, for death could not keep him in its grip. [NLT]<br>ὃν ὁ Θεὸς ἀνέστησε, λύσας τὰς **ὠδῖνας** τοῦ θανάτου, καθότι οὐκ ἦν δυνατὸν κρατεῖσθαι αὐτὸν ὑπ' αὐτοῦ· [GNS]<br>ὃν ὁ θεὸς ἀνέστησεν λύσας τὰς **ὠδῖνας** τοῦ θανάτου, καθότι οὐκ ἦν δυνατὸν κρατεῖσθαι αὐτὸν ὑπ' αὐτοῦ· [GNT] | Agony, pains, horrors, suffering. The word "horrors" (*ōdinas*) means birth pangs.<br><br>**Practical Application**<br>For the unbeliever, there is great pain in death, pain such as that experienced by a woman in giving birth. But man no longer has to suffer the pain of death nor does he have to fear suffering through death. Christ has conquered and abolished death, made it completely harmless. Death is actually the most glorious and joyful experience for the believer, an experience that simply explodes human imagination. (Cp. John 5:24; Hebrews 2:14-15.)<br>How can this be said? Because the believer actually never experiences death. Quicker than the eye can blink, God transfers the believer into His presence—to live with Him eternally. |
| #2013<br>**Horrors To Come**<br><br>Sorrows–KJV<br>Birth pangs–NASB<br>Birth pains–NIV<br>Sorrows–NKJV<br>**Horrors to come– NLT** | ὠδίνων = ōdinōn<br>Pronunciation: [o-deen'-own]<br>Parsing (part of speech): noun<br>  Case—genitive<br>  Gender—feminine<br>  Number—plural<br>  Stem or root—from ὠδίν, ῖνος<br>Concordance References:<br>  ⇒ Strong's #5604 ōdin<br>  ⇒ NIV #6047 ōdin<br>  ⇒ NASB #5604 ōdin<br><br>**Matthew 24:8**<br>All these are the beginning of **sorrows**. [KJV]<br>"But all these things are merely the beginning of **birth** | Birth-pains; labor-pains; travailings; agony; great sorrow; intolerable anguish; horror; quick, sharp, violent travailing pain.<br><br>**Practical Application**<br>The Bible speaks of a time in human history when the world will reel under the weight of intolerable anguish. There will be three great disasters of nature that will cause these birth pains:<br>1. Famines. There is evidently to be terrible famine in the last days. The black horse of the four horsemen of the Apocalypse indicates terrible famine (see POSB note—Rev. 6:5-6). |

# PRACTICAL WORD STUDIES
## in the NEW TESTAMENT

| ENGLISH WORD | GREEK WORD AND VERSE | THE WORD MEANS... |
|---|---|---|
| **POSB REFERENCE** (Mt.24:8) *Deeper Study #5* See also POSB REF: (Mk.13:8) *Deeper Study #4* | pangs. [NASB]<br>All these are the beginning of **birth pains**. [NIV]<br>All these are the beginning of **sorrows**. [NKJV]<br>But all this will be only the beginning of the **horrors to come**. [NLT]<br>πάντα δὲ ταῦτα ἀρχὴ ὠδίνων. [GNS]<br>πάντα δὲ ταῦτα ἀρχὴ ὠδίνων. [GNT] | The unbearable pain and terrible evil that hunger can cause are graphically described by Scripture.<br><br>*"They that be slain with the sword are better than they that be slain with hunger: for these pine away, stricken through for want of the fruits of the field. The hands of the pitiful women have sodden [boiled] their own children: they were their meat [food] in the destruction of the daughter of my people"* (Lament. 4:9-10).<br><br>2. Pestilence or disease. Pestilence will also be one of the terrible sufferings at the end time. Part of the suffering caused by the pale horse of the four horsemen of the Apocalypse includes pestilences.<br><br>*"Power was given unto them (Death and Hell) over the fourth part of the earth, to kill with sword [war], and with hunger [famine], and with death [pestilence resulting from war and famine]"* (see POSB note—Rev. 6:8).<br><br>3. Earthquakes. Earthquakes will occur in many places during the last days of the earth (Rev. 6:12; Rev. 11:12-13, 19; Rev. 16:17-19). |
| **#2014**<br>**Hosanna**<br><br>Hosanna–KJV<br>Hosanna–NASB<br>Hosanna–NIV<br>Hosanna–NKJV<br>Praise God–NLT<br><br>**POSB REFERENCE** (Mk.11:9) *Deeper Study #5* | Ὡσαννά = *Hosanna*<br>Pronunciation: [ho-san-nah']<br>Parsing (part of speech): particle<br>    Type—sentence<br>    Stem or root—from ὡσαννά<br>Concordance References:<br>  ⇒ Strong's #5614 hōsanna<br>  ⇒ NIV #6057 hōsanna<br>  ⇒ NASB #5614 hōsanna<br><br>**Mark 11:9**<br>And they that went before, and they that followed, cried, saying, **Hosanna**; Blessed is he that cometh in the name of the Lord: [KJV]<br>And those who went before, and those who followed after, were crying out, "**Hosanna**! Blessed is He who comes in the name of the Lord; [NASB]<br>Those who went ahead and those who followed shouted, "**Hosanna**!" "Blessed is he who comes in the name of the Lord!" [NIV]<br>Then those who went before and those who followed cried out, saying: "**Hosanna**! 'Blessed is He who comes in the name of the Lord!' [NKJV]<br>He was in the center of the procession, and the crowds all around him were shouting, "**Praise God**! Bless the one who comes in the name of the Lord! [NLT]<br>καὶ οἱ προάγοντες καὶ οἱ ἀκολουθοῦντες ἔκραζον, λέγοντες, Ὡσαννά· εὐλογημένος ὁ ἐρχόμενος ἐν ὀνόματι Κυρίου· [GNS]<br>καὶ οἱ προάγοντες καὶ οἱ ἀκολουθοῦντες ἔκραζον, Ὡσαννά· Εὐλογημένος ὁ ἐρχόμενος ἐν ὀνόματι κυρίου· [GNT] | Save now; or save, we pray; an emphatic exclamation of praise to God.<br><br>**Practical Application**<br>The people cried "Hosanna" (*Hosanna*). Mankind desires to be free, but note: mankind desires to be free on this earth so that he can move about and do as he pleases. He thinks little if any about being free from the bondages of this earth. He loves this earth and he wants all of it that he can get: houses, lands, clothes, food, sex, and recreation. Mankind thinks little about being held in bondage by such things; he thinks little about sin and death. He thinks little of being set free from the power of this earth and its possessions so that he can live eternally. He thinks little of spiritual freedom. |
| **#2015**<br>**Hospitable**<br><br>Hospitality–KJV<br>Hospitable–NASB<br>Hospitable–NIV<br>Hospitable–NKJV | φιλόξενον = *philoxenon*<br>Pronunciation: [fil-ox'-en-on]<br>Parsing (part of speech): adjective<br>    Case—accusative<br>    Gender—masculine<br>    Number—singular<br>    Stem or root—from φιλόξενος, ον | Hospitable, hospitality, enjoy having guests in one's home. It means to have an open heart and home; "showing love or being a friend to the believers, especially strangers or foreigners" (Amplified New Testament). |

# PRACTICAL WORD STUDIES
## in the NEW TESTAMENT

| ENGLISH WORD | GREEK WORD AND VERSE | THE WORD MEANS... |
|---|---|---|
| Enjoy having guests in his home–NLT<br><br>**POSB REFERENCE**<br>(1 Tim.3:2-3; esp. v.2) Note 2, point 6 | Concordance References:<br>⇒ Strong's #5382 philoxenos<br>⇒ NIV #5811 philoxenos<br>⇒ NASB #5382 philoxenos<br><br>**1 Tim. 3:2**<br>A bishop then must be blameless, the husband of one wife, vigilant, sober, of good behaviour, given to **hospitality**, apt to teach; [KJV]<br>An overseer, then, must be above reproach, the husband of one wife, temperate, prudent, respectable, **hospitable**, able to teach, [NASB]<br>Now the overseer must be above reproach, the husband of but one wife, temperate, self-controlled, respectable, **hospitable**, able to teach, [NIV]<br>A bishop then must be blameless, the husband of one wife, temperate, sober-minded, of good behavior, **hospitable**, able to teach; [NKJV]<br>For an elder must be a man whose life cannot be spoken against. He must be faithful to his wife. He must exhibit self-control, live wisely, and have a good reputation. He must **enjoy having guests in his home** and must be able to teach. [NLT]<br>δεῖ οὖν τὸν ἐπίσκοπον ἀνεπίλημπτον εἶναι, μιᾶς γυναικὸς ἄνδρα, νηφάλιον, σώφρονα, κόσμιον, **φιλόξενον**, διδακτικόν· [GNS]<br>δεῖ οὖν τὸν ἐπίσκοπον ἀνεπίλημπτον εἶναι, μιᾶς γυναικὸς ἄνδρα, νηφάλιον σώφρονα κόσμιον **φιλόξενον** διδακτικόν, [GNT] | **Practical Application**<br>The minister helps and entertains as much as he can. He does not open his heart, home, time, or money to the things of the world; but he uses what resources he has to help and minister to people. |
| **#2016**<br>**Hospitality**<br><br>Hospitality–KJV<br>Hospitable–NASB<br>Hospitable–NIV<br>Hospitable–NKJV<br>Enjoy having guests in his home–NLT<br><br>**POSB REFERENCE**<br>(1 Tim.3:2-3; esp. v.2) Note 2, point 6 | φιλόξενον = *philoxenon*<br>Pronunciation: [fil-ox'-en-on]<br>Parsing (part of speech): adjective<br>  Case—accusative<br>  Gender—masculine<br>  Number—singular<br>  Stem or root—from φιλόξενος, ον<br>Concordance References:<br>⇒ Strong's #5382 philoxenos<br>⇒ NIV #5811 philoxenos<br>⇒ NASB #5382 philoxenos<br><br>**1 Tim. 3:2**<br>A bishop then must be blameless, the husband of one wife, vigilant, sober, of good behaviour, given to **hospitality**, apt to teach; [KJV]<br>An overseer, then, must be above reproach, the husband of one wife, temperate, prudent, respectable, **hospitable**, able to teach, [NASB]<br>Now the overseer must be above reproach, the husband of but one wife, temperate, self-controlled, respectable, **hospitable**, able to teach, [NIV]<br>A bishop then must be blameless, the husband of one wife, temperate, sober-minded, of good behavior, **hospitable**, able to teach; [NKJV]<br>For an elder must be a man whose life cannot be spoken against. He must be faithful to his wife. He must exhibit self-control, live wisely, and have a good reputation. He must **enjoy having guests in his home** and must be able to teach. [NLT]<br>δεῖ οὖν τὸν ἐπίσκοπον ἀνεπίλημπτον εἶναι, μιᾶς γυναικὸς ἄνδρα, νηφάλιον, σώφρονα, κόσμιον, **φιλόξενον**, διδακτικόν· [GNS]<br>δεῖ οὖν τὸν ἐπίσκοπον ἀνεπίλημπτον εἶναι, μιᾶς γυναικὸς ἄνδρα, νηφάλιον σώφρονα κόσμιον **φιλόξενον** διδακτικόν, [GNT] | To be hospitable; to enjoy having guests in one's home.<br><br>**Practical Application**<br>The minister or bishop must be given to "hospitality" *(philoxenon)*: to have an open heart and home; "showing love or being a friend to the believers, especially strangers or foreigners" (Amplified New Testament). The minister helps and entertains as much as he can. He does not open his heart, home, time, or money to the things of the world; but he uses what resources he has to help and minister to people. |
| **#2017**<br>**Host**<br><br>Host–KJV<br>Host–NASB | στρατιᾶς = *stratias*<br>Pronunciation: [strat-ee'-ahs]<br>Parsing (part of speech): noun<br>  Case—genitive<br>  Gender—feminine<br>  Number—singular<br>  Stem or root—from στρατιά, ᾶς | Host, bodies, an army of angels, "ten thousand times ten thousand" (Daniel 7:10; cp. Psalm 68:17). |

# PRACTICAL WORD STUDIES
## in the NEW TESTAMENT

| ENGLISH WORD | GREEK WORD AND VERSE | THE WORD MEANS... |
|---|---|---|
| **Host–NIV**<br>**Host–NKJV**<br>**Host–NLT**<br><br>**POSB REFERENCE**<br>(Lk.2:13-14; esp. v.13)<br>Note 4 | Concordance References:<br>⇒ Strong's #4756 stratia<br>⇒ NIV #5131 stratia<br>⇒ NASB #4756 stratia<br><br>**Luke 2:13**<br>And suddenly there was with the angel a multitude of the heavenly **host** praising God, and saying, [KJV]<br>And suddenly there appeared with the angel a multitude of the heavenly **host** praising God, and saying, [NASB]<br>Suddenly a great company of the heavenly **host** appeared with the angel, praising God and saying, [NIV]<br>And suddenly there was with the angel a multitude of the heavenly **host** praising God and saying: [NKJV]<br>Suddenly, the angel was joined by a vast **host** of others—the armies of heaven—praising God: [NLT]<br>καὶ ἐξαίφνης ἐγένετο σὺν τῷ ἀγγέλῳ πλῆθος **στρατιᾶς** οὐρανίου, αἰνούντων τὸν Θεόν, καὶ λεγόντων, [GNS]<br>καὶ ἐξαίφνης ἐγένετο σὺν τῷ ἀγγέλῳ πλῆθος **στρατιᾶς** οὐρανίου αἰνούντων τὸν θεὸν καὶ λεγόντων, [GNT] | **Practical Application**<br>God either gave the shepherds a special sight into the spiritual world and dimension or caused the spiritual dimension to appear to physical sight. |
| **#2018**<br>**Hostile**<br><br>Enemies–KJV<br>**Hostile–NASB**<br>Enemies–NIV<br>Enemies–NKJV<br>Enemies–NLT<br><br>**POSB REFERENCE**<br>(Col.1:21-22; esp. v.21)<br>Note 2, point 2 | **ἐχθρούς** = echthrous<br>Pronunciation: [ekh-throos']<br>Parsing (part of speech): pronominal adjective<br>    Case—accusative<br>    Gender—masculine<br>    Number—plural<br>    Stem or root—from ἐχθρός, ή, όν<br>Concordance References:<br>⇒ Strong's #2190 echthros<br>⇒ NIV #2398 echthros<br>⇒ NASB #2190 echthros<br><br>**Col. 1:21**<br>And you, that were sometime alienated and **enemies** in your mind by wicked works, yet now hath he reconciled [KJV]<br>And although you were formerly alienated and **hostile** in mind, engaged in evil deeds, [NASB]<br>Once you were alienated from God and were **enemies** in your minds because of your evil behavior. [NIV]<br>And you, who once were alienated and **enemies** in your mind by wicked works, yet now He has reconciled [NKJV]<br>This includes you who were once so far away from God. You were his **enemies**, separated from him by your evil thoughts and actions, [NLT]<br>καὶ ὑμᾶς ποτε ὄντας ἀπηλλοτριωμένους καὶ **ἐχθροὺς** τῇ διανοίᾳ ἐν τοῖς ἔργοις τοῖς πονηροῖς, [GNS]<br>Καὶ ὑμᾶς ποτε ὄντας ἀπηλλοτριωμένους καὶ **ἐχθροὺς** τῇ διανοίᾳ ἐν τοῖς ἔργοις τοῖς πονηροῖς, [GNT] | Enemies, hostile, hateful, rebellious.<br><br>**Practical Application**<br>Believers had been "hostile" or "enemies" (*echthrous*) of God. Just think for a moment: think about how men act toward God. They...<br>• ignore Him<br>• curse Him<br>• blaspheme Him<br>• mock Him<br>• falsely profess Him<br>• deny Him, His very existence<br>• disobey Him<br>• neglect Him<br>• half heartedly serve Him<br><br>Note where rebellion takes place: in the mind and in the thoughts. A man thinks about doing something, and he knows it is against God's will and Word. But the thought is planted in his mind, and he harbors the thought. It is the thought, the mind, that leads to wicked works. And any behavior or act that is not in accordance with God's will is rebellion. When the human heart is aroused to disobey God, it acts against God. And acting against the King of kings is insurrection. It is going contrary to the *explicit orders* of the King of kings. The terrible tragedy is that every person has rebelled, and too often, does rebel against God. Every human being has stood or is standing upon the earth as an enemy of God, an enemy who is in open defiance against God. Every human being has refused to obey the commandments of the King, and every human being who is open and honest knows it. The great task of man...<br>• is not to disprove the charge that he is an enemy of God.<br>• is not to prove that he is good enough to be acceptable to God.<br>• is not to deny and disprove God (denial and disproof can never eliminate truth and fact).<br><br>The fact of man's alienation—that he is an enemy of God—is clearly seen. The great task of man is to seek how to be reconciled to God. |

# PRACTICAL WORD STUDIES
## in the NEW TESTAMENT

| ENGLISH WORD | GREEK WORD AND VERSE | THE WORD MEANS... |
|---|---|---|
| **#2019**<br>**Hostility**<br><br>Hatred–KJV<br>Enmities–NASB<br>Hatred–NIV<br>Hatred–NKJV<br>**Hostility–NLT**<br><br>**POSB<br>REFERENCE**<br>(Gal.5:19-21; esp. v.20)<br>Note 2 | ἔχθραι = echthrai<br>Pronunciation: [ekh'-thrah-ee]<br>Parsing (part of speech): noun<br>   Case—nominative<br>   Gender—feminine<br>   Number—plural<br>   Stem or root—from ἔχθρα, ας<br>Concordance References:<br>  ⇒ Strong's #2189 echthra<br>  ⇒ NIV #2397 echthra<br>  ⇒ NASB #2189 echthra<br><br>**Galatians 5:20**<br>Idolatry, witchcraft, **hatred**, variance, emulations, wrath, strife, seditions, heresies, [KJV]<br>Idolatry, sorcery, **enmities**, strife, jealousy, outbursts of anger, disputes, dissensions, factions, [NASB]<br>Idolatry and witchcraft; **hatred**, discord, jealousy, fits of rage, selfish ambition, dissensions, factions [NIV]<br>Idolatry, sorcery, **hatred**, contentions, jealousies, outbursts of wrath, selfish ambitions, dissensions, heresies, [NKJV]<br>Idolatry, participation in demonic activities, **hostility**, quarreling, jealousy, outbursts of anger, selfish ambition, divisions, the feeling that everyone is wrong except those in your own little group, [NLT]<br>εἰδωλολατρία, φαρμακεία, **ἔχθραι**, ἔρεις, ζῆλοι, θυμοί, ἐριθεῖαι, διχοστασίαι, αἱρέσεις, [GNS]<br>εἰδωλολατρία, φαρμακεία, **ἔχθραι**, ἔρις, ζῆλος, θυμοί, ἐριθεῖαι, διχοστασίαι, αἱρέσεις, [GNT] | Hatred, hostility, ill will, enmity, hostility, animosity.<br><br>**Practical Application**<br>It is the hatred that lingers and is held for a long, long time; a hatred that is deep within. |
| **#2020**<br>**Hour**<br><br>Cubit–KJV<br>Cubit–NASB<br>**Hour–NIV**<br>Cubit–NKJV<br>Moment–NLT<br><br>**POSB<br>REFERENCE**<br>(Mt.6:27)<br>Note 4 | πῆχυν = pēchun<br>Pronunciation: [pay'-khoon]<br>Parsing (part of speech): noun<br>   Case—accusative<br>   Gender—masculine<br>   Number—singular<br>   Stem or root—from πῆχυς, εως<br>Concordance References:<br>  ⇒ Strong's #4083 pēchus<br>  ⇒ NIV #4388 pēchus<br>  ⇒ NASB #4083 pēchus<br><br>**Matthew 6:27**<br>Which of you by taking thought can add one **cubit** unto his stature? [KJV]<br>"And which of you by being anxious can add a single **cubit** to his life's span? [NASB]<br>Who of you by worrying can add a single **hour** to his life? [NIV]<br>Which of you by worrying can add one **cubit** to his stature? [NKJV]<br>Can all your worries add a single **moment** to your life? Of course not. [NLT]<br>τίς δὲ ἐξ ὑμῶν μεριμνῶν δύναται προσθεῖναι ἐπὶ τὴν ἡλικίαν αὐτοῦ **πῆχυν** ἕνα; [GNS]<br>τίς δὲ ἐξ ὑμῶν μεριμνῶν δύναται προσθεῖναι ἐπὶ τὴν ἡλικίαν αὐτοῦ **πῆχυν** ἕνα; [GNT] | An hour, a moment, a cubit.<br><br>**Practical Application**<br>In this Scripture, the word speaks of a time, an hour, in a person's life that is past and can never be added to. |
| **#2021**<br>**Hour**<br><br>Cubit–KJV<br>Cubit–NASB<br>**Hour–NIV**<br>Cubit–NKJV<br>Moment–NLT<br><br>**POSB<br>REFERENCE**<br>(Lk.12:22-28; esp. v.25) | πῆχυν = pēchun<br>Pronunciation: [pay'-khoon]<br>Parsing (part of speech): noun<br>   Case—accusative<br>   Gender—masculine<br>   Number—singular<br>   Stem or root—from πῆχυς, εως<br>Concordance References:<br>  ⇒ Strong's #4083 pēchus<br>  ⇒ NIV #4388 pēchus<br>  ⇒ NASB #4083 pēchus<br><br>**Luke 12:25**<br>And which of you with taking thought can add to his | Cubit, hour, moment. The word "hour" literally means measure of space, or distance (approximately 18 inches); but it can also mean a measure of time or age (John 9:21). It is an age, a time of life.<br><br>**Practical Application**<br>In this context, the word speaks of a time that is past. So the verse can read either "who can add one cubit to his stature" or "a single hour or moment to his life span." |

# PRACTICAL WORD STUDIES
## in the New Testament

| ENGLISH WORD | GREEK WORD AND VERSE | THE WORD MEANS... |
|---|---|---|
| Note 1, point 3 | stature one **cubit**? [KJV]<br>"And which of you by being anxious can add a single **cubit** to his life's span? [NASB]<br>Who of you by worrying can add a single **hour** to his life? [NIV]<br>And which of you by worrying can add one **cubit** to his stature? [NKJV]<br>Can all your worries add a single **moment** to your life? Of course not! [NLT]<br>τίς δὲ ἐξ ὑμῶν μεριμνῶν δύναται προσθεῖναι ἐπὶ τὴν ἡλικίαν αὐτοῦ **πῆχυν** ἕνα; [GNS]<br>τίς δὲ ἐξ ὑμῶν μεριμνῶν δύναται ἐπὶ τὴν ἡλικίαν αὐτοῦ προσθεῖναι **πῆχυν**; [GNT] | |
| **#2022**<br>**House–**<br>**Household**<br><br>House–KJV<br>Household–NASB<br>Household–NIV<br>House–NKJV<br>Household–NLT<br><br>**POSB**<br>**REFERENCE**<br>(1 Tim.3:15)<br>Note 2, point 1 | οἴκῳ = oikō<br>Pronunciation: [oy'-ko]<br>Parsing (part of speech): noun<br>   Case—dative<br>   Gender—masculine<br>   Number—singular<br>   Stem or root—from οἶκος, ου<br>Concordance References:<br>⇒ Strong's #3624 oikos<br>⇒ NIV #3875 oikos<br>⇒ NASB #3624 oikos<br><br>**1 Tim. 3:15**<br>But if I tarry long, that thou mayest know how thou oughtest to behave thyself in the **house** of God, which is the church of the living God, the pillar and ground of the truth. [KJV]<br>But in case I am delayed, I write so that you may know how one ought to conduct himself in the **household** of God, which is the church of the living God, the pillar and support of the truth. [NASB]<br>If I am delayed, you will know how people ought to conduct themselves in God's **household**, which is the church of the living God, the pillar and foundation of the truth. [NIV]<br>But if I am delayed, *I write* so that you may know how you ought to conduct yourself in the **house** of God, which is the church of the living God, the pillar and ground of the truth. [NKJV]<br>So that if I can't come for a while, you will know how people must conduct themselves in the **household** of God. This is the church of the living God, which is the pillar and support of the truth. [NLT]<br>ἐὰν δὲ βραδύνω, ἵνα εἰδῇς πῶς δεῖ ἐν **οἴκῳ** Θεοῦ ἀναστρέφεσθαι, ἥτις ἐστὶν ἐκκλησία Θεοῦ ζῶντος, στύλος καὶ ἑδραίωμα τῆς ἀληθείας. [GNS]<br>ἐὰν δὲ βραδύνω, ἵνα εἰδῇς πῶς δεῖ ἐν **οἴκῳ** θεοῦ ἀναστρέφεσθαι, ἥτις ἐστὶν ἐκκλησία θεοῦ ζῶντος, στύλος καὶ ἑδραίωμα τῆς ἀληθείας. [GNT] | Household, house.<br><br>**Practical Application**<br>The church is the "house" or "household" (*oikō*) of God. This does not refer to the building of the church, but to the household of the church, to the people of the church. The church is a body of people who have committed themselves to form a family of people, a family centered around God and His Son, the Lord Jesus Christ.<br>The church is a *family of people*...<br>• who believe in God and in His Son, the Lord Jesus Christ.<br>• who have committed their lives to live for Christ.<br>• who have based their lives upon the promise of eternal salvation promised by the Lord Jesus Christ.<br>• who have committed themselves to live as a family with all other believers.<br>Simply stated, the church is a body of people who have committed their lives to live as the family of God. God is the Father; Jesus Christ is the only begotten Son of the Father; but we, the followers of God, are the adopted children of God. Every person who truly follows God is a true member of the church, that is, of the family of God (John 1:12; 2 Cor. 6:17-18; Galatians 4:4-6). |
| **#2023**<br>**How Many**<br>**Myriads**<br><br>How many thousands–KJV<br>How many thousands–NASB<br>How many thousands–NIV<br>**How many myriads–NKJV**<br>How many thousands–NLT | πόσαι μυριάδες = posai muriades<br>Pronunciation: [pos'-ah-ee moo-ree'-ah-dehs]<br>Parsing *posai* (part of speech): adjective<br>   Type—interrogative<br>   Case—nominative<br>   Gender—feminine<br>   Number—plural<br>   Stem or root—from πόσος, η, ον<br>Parsing *muriades* (part of speech): noun<br>   Case—nominative<br>   Gender—feminine<br>   Number—plural<br>   Stem or root—from μυριάς, άδος<br>Concordance References:<br>⇒ Strong's #4214 posos + 3461 murias<br>⇒ NIV #4531 posos [how many] + 3689 murias [thousands]<br>⇒ NASB #4214 posos + 3461 murias | How many thousands, myriads, countless thousands.<br><br>**Practical Application**<br>The Greek word for "many myriads" means thousands upon thousands, myriads upon myriads. |

# PRACTICAL WORD STUDIES
## in the NEW TESTAMENT

| ENGLISH WORD | GREEK WORD AND VERSE | THE WORD MEANS... |
|---|---|---|
| **POSB REFERENCE** (Acts 21:20-26; esp. v.20) Note 3, point 1 | **Acts 21:20**<br>And when they heard it, they glorified the Lord, and said unto him, Thou seest, brother, **how many thousands** of Jews there are which believe; and they are all zealous of the law: [KJV]<br><br>And when they heard it they began glorifying God; and they said to him, "You see, brother, **how many thousands** there are among the Jews of those who have believed, and they are all zealous for the Law; [NASB]<br><br>When they heard this, they praised God. Then they said to Paul: "You see, brother, **how many thousands** of Jews have believed, and all of them are zealous for the law. [NIV]<br><br>And when they heard *it,* they glorified the Lord. And they said to him, "You see, brother, **how many myriads** of Jews there are who have believed, and they are all zealous for the law; [NKJV]<br><br>After hearing this, they praised God. But then they said, "You know, dear brother, **how many thousands** of Jews have also believed, and they all take the law of Moses very seriously. [NLT]<br><br>οἱ δὲ ἀκούσαντες ἐδόξαζον τὸν Κύριον· εἶπόν τε αὐτῷ, Θεωρεῖς, ἀδελφέ, **πόσαι μυριάδες** εἰσὶν Ἰουδαίοις τῶν πεπιστευκότων; καὶ πάντες ζηλωταὶ τοῦ νόμου ὑπάρχουσι· [GNS]<br><br>οἱ δὲ ἀκούσαντες ἐδόξαζον τὸν θεόν εἶπόν τε αὐτῷ, Θεωρεῖς, ἀδελφέ, **πόσαι μυριάδες** εἰσὶν ἐν τοῖς Ἰουδαίοις τῶν πεπιστευκότων καὶ πάντες ζηλωταὶ τοῦ νόμου ὑπάρχουσιν· [GNT] | |
| **#2024**<br>**How Many Thousands**<br><br>How many thousands–KJV<br>How many thousands–NASB<br>How many thousands–NIV<br>How many myriads–NKJV<br>How many thousands–NLT<br><br>**POSB REFERENCE** (Acts 21:20-26; esp. v.20) Note 3, point 1 | πόσαι μυριάδες = *posai muriades*<br>Pronunciation: [pos'-ah-ee moo-ree'-ah-dehs]<br>Parsing *posai* (part of speech): adjective<br>  Type—interrogative<br>  Case—nominative<br>  Gender—feminine<br>  Number—plural<br>  Stem or root—from πόσος, η, ον<br>Parsing *muriades* (part of speech): noun<br>  Case—nominative<br>  Gender—feminine<br>  Number—plural<br>  Stem or root—from μυριάς, άδος<br>Concordance References:<br>⇒ Strong's #4214 posos + 3461 murias<br>⇒ NIV #4531 posos [how many] + 3689 murias [thousands]<br>⇒ NASB #4214 posos + 3461 murias<br><br>**Acts 21:20**<br>And when they heard it, they glorified the Lord, and said unto him, Thou seest, brother, **how many thousands** of Jews there are which believe; and they are all zealous of the law: [KJV]<br><br>And when they heard it they began glorifying God; and they said to him, "You see, brother, **how many thousands** there are among the Jews of those who have believed, and they are all zealous for the Law; [NASB]<br><br>When they heard this, they praised God. Then they said to Paul: "You see, brother, **how many thousands** of Jews have believed, and all of them are zealous for the law. [NIV]<br><br>And when they heard *it,* they glorified the Lord. And they said to him, "You see, brother, **how many myriads** of Jews there are who have believed, and they are all zealous for the law; [NKJV]<br><br>After hearing this, they praised God. But then they said, "You know, dear brother, **how many thousands** of Jews have also believed, and they all take the law of Moses very seriously. [NLT]<br><br>οἱ δὲ ἀκούσαντες ἐδόξαζον τὸν Κύριον· εἶπόν τε αὐτῷ, Θεωρεῖς, ἀδελφέ, **πόσαι μυριάδες** εἰσὶν Ἰουδαίοις | How many thousands, myriads, countless thousands.<br><br>**Practical Application**<br>The Greek word for "many thousands" means thousands upon thousands, myriads upon myriads. |

| ENGLISH WORD | GREEK WORD AND VERSE | THE WORD MEANS... |
|---|---|---|
| | τῶν πεπιστευκότων· καὶ πάντες ζηλωταὶ τοῦ νόμου ὑπάρχουσι· [GNS]<br><br>οἱ δὲ ἀκούσαντες ἐδόξαζον τὸν θεόν εἶπόν τε αὐτῷ, Θεωρεῖς, ἀδελφέ, **πόσαι μυριάδες** εἰσὶν ἐν τοῖς Ἰουδαίοις τῶν πεπιστευκότων καὶ πάντες ζηλωταὶ τοῦ νόμου ὑπάρχουσιν· [GNT] | |
| **#2025**<br>**How Terrible It Will Be**<br><br>Woe–KJV<br>Woe–NASB<br>Woe–NIV<br>Woe–NKJV<br>How terrible it will be–NLT<br><br>**POSB REFERENCE**<br>(Mt.23:13)<br>*Deeper Study #1* | Οὐαί = *Ouai*<br>Pronunciation: [oo-ah'ee]<br>Parsing (part of speech): particle<br>   Type—sentence<br>   Stem or root—from οὐαί<br>Concordance References:<br>  ⇒ Strong's #3759 ouai<br>  ⇒ NIV #4026 ouai<br>  ⇒ NASB #3759 ouai<br><br>**Matthew 23:13**<br>But **woe** unto you, scribes and Pharisees, hypocrites! for ye shut up the kingdom of heaven against men: for ye neither go in yourselves, neither suffer ye them that are entering to go in. [KJV]<br>"But **woe** to you, scribes and Pharisees, hypocrites, because you shut off the kingdom of heaven from men; for you do not enter in yourselves, nor do you allow those who are entering to go in. [NASB]<br>"**Woe** to you, teachers of the law and Pharisees, you hypocrites! You shut the kingdom of heaven in men's faces. You yourselves do not enter, nor will you let those enter who are trying to. [NIV]<br>But **woe** to you, scribes and Pharisees, hypocrites! For you shut up the kingdom of heaven against men; for you neither go in yourselves, nor do you allow those who are entering to go in. [NKJV]<br>"**How terrible it will be** for you teachers of religious law and you Pharisees. Hypocrites! For you won't let others enter the Kingdom of Heaven, and you won't go in yourselves. [NLT]<br>Οὐαὶ δὲ ὑμῖν, γραμματεῖς καὶ Φαρισαῖοι ὑποκριταί, ὅτι κλείετε τὴν βασιλείαν τῶν οὐρανῶν ἔμπροσθεν τῶν ἀνθρώπων· ὑμεῖς γὰρ οὐκ εἰσέρχεσθε, οὐδὲ τοὺς εἰσερχομένους ἀφίετε εἰσελθεῖν. [GNS]<br>Οὐαὶ δὲ ὑμῖν, γραμματεῖς καὶ Φαρισαῖοι ὑποκριταί, ὅτι κλείετε τὴν βασιλείαν τῶν οὐρανῶν ἔμπροσθεν τῶν ἀνθρώπων· ὑμεῖς γὰρ οὐκ εἰσέρχεσθε οὐδὲ τοὺς εἰσερχομένους ἀφίετε εἰσελθεῖν. [GNT] | Both wrath and sorrow, anger and pity. There is no single English word to express what it means. It is a grieving denunciation; a sorrowful wrath; a pitying anger. It is a godly threat.<br><br>**Practical Application**<br>Note just a few examples from Scripture:<br><br>*What horrors await you, Korazin and Bethsaida! For if the miracles I did in you had been done in wicked Tyre and Sidon, their people would have sat in deep repentance long ago, clothed in sackcloth and throwing ashes on their heads to show their remorse. (Matthew 11:21) [NLT]*<br>*How terrible it will be for anyone who causes others to sin. Temptation to do wrong is inevitable, but how terrible it will be for the person who does the tempting. (Matthew 18:7) [NLT]*<br>*How terrible it will be for you teachers of religious law and you Pharisees. Hypocrites! For you won't let others enter the Kingdom of Heaven, and you won't go in yourselves. (Matthew 23:13) [NLT]*<br>*How terrible it will be for you teachers of religious law and you Pharisees. Hypocrites! For you are careful to tithe even the tiniest part of your income, but you ignore the important things of the law—justice, mercy, and faith. You should tithe, yes, but you should not leave undone the more important things. (Matthew 23:23) [NLT]*<br>*How terrible it will be for you teachers of religious law and you Pharisees. Hypocrites! You are so careful to clean the outside of the cup and the dish, but inside you are filthy—full of greed and self-indulgence! (Matthew 23:25) [NLT]*<br>*How terrible it will be for you teachers of religious law and you Pharisees. Hypocrites! You are like whitewashed tombs—beautiful on the outside but filled on the inside with dead people's bones and all sorts of impurity. (Matthew 23:27) [NLT]*<br>*How terrible it will be for you teachers of religious law and you Pharisees. Hypocrites! For you build tombs for the prophets your ancestors killed and decorate the graves of the godly people your ancestors destroyed. (Matthew 23:29) [NLT]*<br>*For I, the Son of Man, must die, as the Scriptures declared long ago. But how terrible it will be for my betrayer. Far better for him if he had never been born!" (Matthew 26:24) [NLT]* |

## PRACTICAL WORD STUDIES
### in the New Testament

| ENGLISH WORD | GREEK WORD AND VERSE | THE WORD MEANS... |
|---|---|---|
| **#2026**<br>**Hucksters**<br><br>Corrupt–KJV<br>Peddling–NASB<br>Peddle...for profit–NIV<br>Peddling–NKJV<br>**Hucksters–NLT**<br><br>**POSB REFERENCE**<br>(2 Cor.2:16-17; esp. v.17)<br>Note 4 | καπηλεύοντες = kapēleuontes<br>Pronunciation: [kap-ale-yoo'-on-tehs]<br>Parsing (part of speech): verb<br>    Mood—participle<br>    Tense—present<br>    Voice—active<br>    Case—nominative<br>    Gender—masculine<br>    Person—1st person<br>    Number—plural<br>    Stem or root—from καπηλεύω<br>Concordance References:<br>  ⇒ Strong's #2585 kapēleuō<br>  ⇒ NIV #2836 kapēleuō<br>  ⇒ NASB #2585 kapēleuō<br><br>**2 Cor. 2:17**<br>For we are not as many, which **corrupt** the word of God: but as of sincerity, but as of God, in the sight of God speak we in Christ. [KJV]<br><br>For we are not like many, **peddling** the word of God, but as from sincerity, but as from God, we speak in Christ in the sight of God. [NASB]<br><br>Unlike so many, we do not **peddle** the word of God **for profit**. On the contrary, in Christ we speak before God with sincerity, like men sent from God. [NIV]<br><br>For we are not, as so many, **peddling** the word of God; but as of sincerity, but as from God, we speak in the sight of God in Christ. [NKJV]<br><br>You see, we are not like those **hucksters**—and there are many of them—who preach just to make money. We preach God's message with sincerity and with Christ's authority. And we know that the God who sent us is watching us. [NLT]<br><br>οὐ γάρ ἐσμεν ὡς οἱ πολλοὶ, **καπηλεύοντες** τὸν λόγον τοῦ Θεοῦ. ἀλλ' ὡς ἐξ εἰλικρινείας, ἀλλ' ὡς ἐκ Θεοῦ κατενώπιον Θεοῦ· ἀλλ' ὡς ἐξ εἰλικρινείας, ἀλλ' ὡς ἐκ Θεοῦ, κατενώπιον τοῦ Θεοῦ, ἐν Χριστῷ λαλοῦμεν. [GNS]<br><br>οὐ γάρ ἐσμεν ὡς οἱ πολλοὶ **καπηλεύοντες** τὸν λόγον τοῦ θεοῦ, ἀλλ' ὡς ἐξ εἰλικρινείας, ἀλλ' ὡς ἐκ θεοῦ κατέναντι θεοῦ ἐν Χριστῷ λαλοῦμεν. [GNT] | To peddle for profit; to corrupt. It means to peddle, to adulterate, to whittle down, to contaminate, to tamper with the Word of God.<br><br>**Practical Application**<br>The qualified man does not "corrupt the word of God." The word "hucksters" (*kapēleuontes*) is taken from an old word meaning huckster or peddler. It means to mix other things into the gospel, for example, personal ideas, speculations, the latest religious fads or novel ideas. |
| **#2027**<br>**Human**<br><br>Flesh–KJV<br>Flesh–NASB<br>Flesh–NIV<br>Flesh–NKJV<br>**Human–NLT**<br><br>**POSB REFERENCE**<br>(Jn.1:14)<br>Note 1 | σάρξ = sarx<br>Pronunciation: [sarx]<br>Parsing (part of speech): noun<br>    Case—nominative<br>    Gender—feminine<br>    Number—singular<br>    Stem or root—from σάρξ, σαρκός<br>Concordance References:<br>  ⇒ Strong's #4561 sarx<br>  ⇒ NIV #4922 sarx<br>  ⇒ NASB #4561 sarx<br><br>**John 1:14**<br>And the Word was made **flesh**, and dwelt among us, (and we beheld his glory, the glory as of the only begotten of the Father,) full of grace and truth. [KJV]<br><br>And the Word became **flesh**, and dwelt among us, and we beheld His glory, glory as of the only begotten from the Father, full of grace and truth. [NASB]<br><br>The Word became **flesh** and made his dwelling among us. We have seen his glory, the glory of the One and Only, who came from the Father, full of grace and truth. [NIV]<br><br>And the Word became **flesh** and dwelt among us, and we beheld His glory, the glory as of the only begotten of the Father, full of grace and truth. [NKJV]<br><br>So the Word became **human** and lived here on earth among us. He was full of unfailing love and faithfulness. And we have seen his glory, the glory of the only Son of the Father. [NLT]<br><br>καὶ ὁ λόγος **σάρξ** ἐγένετο, καὶ ἐσκήνωσεν ἐν ἡμῖν, -- | Flesh, human. It is the physical human body that every person needs in order to live upon earth.<br><br>**Practical Application**<br>The word "human" or flesh is the same word that Paul used to describe man's nature with all of its weakness and tendency to sin. This is a staggering thought. Jesus Christ is God—fully God, yet Jesus Christ is man—fully man (Cp. 1 John 4:2-3.)<br>What does the Bible mean by "human" or flesh? And why did Jesus Christ have to become flesh? The best description of the flesh is probably found in 1 Cor. 15:42-44. (See POSB outline—Romans 5:12-21 and POSB note—Romans 5:12-21; POSB note—Romans 8:1f; POSB *Deeper Study* #1—1 Cor. 3:1-4).<br>1. The flesh is corruptible.<br>   a. The flesh is tainted, debased, ruined and depraved by sin (lust, 2 Peter 1:4). There is a seed of corruption within human flesh; therefore, the flesh sins (lusts) and thereby ages, dies, deteriorates and decays. It does not live beyond a few years on this earth.<br>   b. Christ (the Word) became flesh to correct and to counteract the corruption of flesh (2 Peter 1:4; 1 Peter 1:18-19, 23-25; John 3:16). |

| ENGLISH WORD | GREEK WORD AND VERSE | THE WORD MEANS... |
|---|---|---|
| | καὶ ἐθεασάμεθα τὴν δόξαν αὐτοῦ, δόξαν ὡς μονογενοῦς παρὰ πατρός -- , πλήρης χάριτος καὶ ἀληθείας. [GNS]<br><br>Καὶ ὁ λόγος **σὰρξ** ἐγένετο καὶ ἐσκήνωσεν ἐν ἡμῖν, καὶ ἐθεασάμεθα τὴν δόξαν αὐτοῦ, δόξαν ὡς μονογενοῦς παρὰ πατρός, πλήρης χάριτος καὶ ἀληθείας. [GNT] | 2. The flesh is dishonorable.<br>  a. The flesh is not what God created it to be. It does not exist in the image of God that God intended. It does not hold the glory, the honor, nor the prestige it once did when God created it. It is disgraced and shamed, and it is reproached by sin and lust. It is held in the grip of sin and fear, and subject to being held in bondage—even the bondage of death.<br>  b. Jesus Christ became flesh to correct and counteract the dishonor of the flesh (Hebrews 2:14-15; cp. Hebrews 2:14-18; Romans 5:8-10).<br>3. The flesh is weak.<br>  a. The flesh is impotent. It is feeble, frail, fragile, infirmed, and decrepit because of sin (lust). It has no strength to please God nor to save itself (Romans 8:8; Romans 3:20; Galatians 2:16; John 6:63).<br>  b. Jesus Christ became flesh to correct and counteract the weakness of the flesh (Romans 5:6; Romans 8:3).<br>4. The flesh is a natural body.<br>  a. The flesh is of the earth and is part of the earth; it is made up of the chemicals and substances of the earth. It is physical, material, animal. It is "the earthly house," the "tabernacle," the "tent," which houses the human soul and spirit (2 Cor. 5:1). It is neither spirit nor spiritual; therefore, it cannot live beyond the strength of the chemicals and substances that form its flesh. It cannot live beyond its *natural life* (1 Cor. 15:50; Luke 24:39; 1 Cor. 15:44, 49).<br>  b. Jesus Christ became flesh to counteract the natural body of the flesh. He became flesh in order to become "a quickening spirit," the Savior who could quicken and make alive all those who would trust Him (1 Cor. 15:45). |
| #2028<br>**Human Beings Like**<br><br>Like passions–KJV<br>Same nature–NASB<br>Human like–NIV<br>Same nature–NKJV<br>**Human beings like**–NLT<br><br>**POSB REFERENCE**<br>(Acts 14:14-18; esp. v.15)<br>Note 3, point 1 | ὁμοιοπαθεῖς = *homoiopatheis*<br>Pronunciation: [hom-oy-op-ath-ice']<br>Parsing (part of speech): adjective<br>  Case—nominative<br>  Gender—masculine<br>  Number—plural<br>  Stem or root—from ὁμοιοπαθής, ές<br>Concordance References:<br>  ⇒ Strong's #3663 homoiopathës<br>  ⇒ NIV #3926 homoiopathës<br>  ⇒ NASB #3663 homoiopathës<br><br>**Acts 14:15**<br>And saying, Sirs, why do ye these things? We also are men of **like passions** with you, and preach unto you that ye should turn from these vanities unto the living God, which made heaven, and earth, and the sea, and all things that are therein: [KJV]<br><br>and saying, "Men, why are you doing these things? We are also men of the **same nature** as you, and preach the gospel to you in order that you should turn from these vain things to a living God, WHO MADE THE HEAVEN AND THE EARTH AND THE SEA, AND ALL THAT IS IN THEM. [NASB]<br><br>"Men, why are you doing this? We too are only men, **human like** you. We are bringing you good news, telling | Like, passions, same; to be like in every way. It means the same nature.<br><br>**Practical Application**<br>It means that all men have the same...<br>• heart (Psalm 33:15)<br>• feelings<br>• infirmities<br>• temptations (1 Cor. 10-13)<br>• sufferings<br>• aging and dying bodies (Hebrews 9:27) |

# Practical Word Studies in the New Testament

| ENGLISH WORD | GREEK WORD AND VERSE | THE WORD MEANS... |
|---|---|---|
| | you to turn from these worthless things to the living God, who made heaven and earth and sea and everything in them. [NIV]<br><br>And saying, "Men, why are you doing these things? We also are men with the **same nature** as you, and preach to you that you should turn from these useless things to the living God, who made the heaven, the earth, the sea, and all things that are in them, [NKJV]<br><br>"Friends, why are you doing this? We are merely **human beings like** yourselves! We have come to bring you the Good News that you should turn from these worthless things to the living God, who made heaven and earth, the sea, and everything in them. [NLT]<br><br>καὶ λέγοντες, Ἄνδρες, τί ταῦτα ποιεῖτε; καὶ ἡμεῖς **ὁμοιοπαθεῖς** ἐσμεν ὑμῖν ἄνθρωποι, εὐαγγελιζόμενοι ὑμᾶς ἀπὸ τούτων τῶν ματαίων ἐπιστρέφειν ἐπὶ τὸν Θεὸν ζῶντα, ὃς ἐποίησε τὸν οὐρανὸν καὶ τὴν γῆν καὶ τὴν θάλασσαν, καὶ πάντα τὰ ἐν αὐτοῖς· [GNS]<br><br>καὶ λέγοντες, Ἄνδρες, τί ταῦτα ποιεῖτε; καὶ ἡμεῖς **ὁμοιοπαθεῖς** ἐσμεν ὑμῖν ἄνθρωποι εὐαγγελιζόμενοι ὑμᾶς ἀπὸ τούτων τῶν ματαίων ἐπιστρέφειν ἐπὶ θεὸν ζῶντα, ὃς ἐποίησεν τὸν οὐρανὸν καὶ τὴν γῆν καὶ τὴν θάλασσαν καὶ πάντα τὰ ἐν αὐτοῖς· [GNT] | |
| **#2029**<br>**Human Decision, Of**<br><br>Will of the flesh–KJV<br>Will of the flesh–NASB<br>**Of human decision–NIV**<br>Will of the flesh–NKJV<br>Human passion–NLT<br><br>**POSB REFERENCE**<br>(Jn.1:12-13; esp. v.13)<br>Note 3, point 3a | ἐκ θελήματος σαρκὸς = ek thelēmatos sarkos<br>Pronunciation: [ek thel'-ay-mah-tos sar-kos]<br>Parsing *thelēmatos* (part of speech): noun<br>  Case—genitive<br>  Gender—neuter<br>  Number—singular<br>  Stem or root—from θέλημα, τος<br>Parsing *sarkos* (part of speech): noun<br>  Case—genitive<br>  Gender—feminine<br>  Number—singular<br>  Stem or root—from σάρξ, σαρκός<br>Concordance References:<br>⇒ Strong's #1537 ek + 2307 thelema + 4561 sarx<br>⇒ NIV #1666 ek + 2525 thelēma [will] + 4922 sarx [human]<br>⇒ NASB #1537 ek + 2307 thelema + 4561 sarx<br><br>**John 1:13**<br>Which were born, not of blood, nor of the **will of the flesh**, nor of the will of man, but of God. [KJV]<br>Who were born not of blood, nor of the **will of the flesh**, nor of the will of man, but of God. [NASB]<br>Children born not of natural descent, nor **of human decision** or a husband's will, but born of God. [NIV]<br>Who were born, not of blood, nor of the **will of the flesh**, nor of the will of man, but of God. [NKJV]<br>They are reborn! This is not a physical birth resulting from **human passion** or plan—this rebirth comes from God. [NLT]<br><br>οἳ οὐκ ἐξ αἱμάτων, οὐδὲ **ἐκ θελήματος σαρκὸς**, οὐδὲ ἐκ θελήματος ἀνδρὸς, ἀλλ' ἐκ Θεοῦ ἐγεννήθησαν. [GNS]<br>οἳ οὐκ ἐξ αἱμάτων οὐδὲ **ἐκ θελήματος σαρκὸς** οὐδὲ ἐκ θελήματος ἀνδρὸς ἀλλ' ἐκ θεοῦ ἐγεννήθησαν. [GNT] | Sexual desire, the will of the flesh, human passion, human decision.<br><br>**Practical Application**<br>The idea is that a person is not spiritually born again by willing to become a child of God just like a person wills to have an earthly child. These words picture a person who seeks pleasure, who is driven to please himself, but finds it impossible to achieve. |
| **#2030**<br>**Human Like**<br><br>Like passions–KJV<br>Same nature–NASB<br>**Human like–NIV**<br>Same nature–NKJV<br>Human beings like–NLT | ὁμοιοπαθεῖς = homoiopatheis<br>Pronunciation: [hom-oy-op-ath-ice']<br>Parsing (part of speech): adjective<br>  Case—nominative<br>  Gender—masculine<br>  Number—plural<br>  Stem or root—from ὁμοιοπαθής, ές<br>Concordance References:<br>⇒ Strong's #3663 homoiopathēs<br>⇒ NIV #3926 homoiopathēs<br>⇒ NASB #3663 homoiopathēs<br><br>**Acts 14:15**<br>And saying, Sirs, why do ye these things? We also are | Like, passions, same; to be like in every way. It means the same nature.<br><br>**Practical Application**<br>It means that all men have the same...<br>• heart (Psalm 33:15)<br>• feelings<br>• infirmities<br>• temptations (1 Cor. 10-13)<br>• sufferings<br>• aging and dying bodies (Hebrews 9:27) |

# PRACTICAL WORD STUDIES
## in the NEW TESTAMENT

| ENGLISH WORD | GREEK WORD AND VERSE | THE WORD MEANS... |
|---|---|---|
| **POSB REFERENCE** (Acts 14:14-18; esp. v.15) Note 3, point 1 | men of **like passions** with you, and preach unto you that ye should turn from these vanities unto the living God, which made heaven, and earth, and the sea, and all things that are therein: [KJV]<br><br>and saying, "Men, why are you doing these things? We are also men of the **same nature** as you, and preach the gospel to you in order that you should turn from these vain things to a living God, WHO MADE THE HEAVEN AND THE EARTH AND THE SEA, AND ALL THAT IS IN THEM. [NASB]<br><br>"Men, why are you doing this? We too are only men, **human like** you. We are bringing you good news, telling you to turn from these worthless things to the living God, who made heaven and earth and sea and everything in them. [NIV]<br><br>And saying, "Men, why are you doing these things? We also are men with the **same nature** as you, and preach to you that you should turn from these useless things to the living God, who made the heaven, the earth, the sea, and all things that are in them, [NKJV]<br><br>"Friends, why are you doing this? We are merely **human beings like** yourselves! We have come to bring you the Good News that you should turn from these worthless things to the living God, who made heaven and earth, the sea, and everything in them. [NLT]<br><br>καὶ λέγοντες, "Ἄνδρες, τί ταῦτα ποιεῖτε; καὶ ἡμεῖς **ὁμοιοπαθεῖς** ἐσμεν ὑμῖν ἄνθρωποι, εὐαγγελιζόμενοι ὑμᾶς ἀπὸ τούτων τῶν ματαίων ἐπιστρέφειν ἐπὶ τὸν Θεὸν ζῶντα, ὃς ἐποίησε τὸν οὐρανὸν καὶ τὴν γῆν καὶ τὴν θάλασσαν, καὶ πάντα τὰ ἐν αὐτοῖς· [GNS]<br><br>καὶ λέγοντες, "Ἄνδρες, τί ταῦτα ποιεῖτε; καὶ ἡμεῖς **ὁμοιοπαθεῖς** ἐσμεν ὑμῖν ἄνθρωποι εὐαγγελιζόμενοι ὑμᾶς ἀπὸ τούτων τῶν ματαίων ἐπιστρέφειν ἐπὶ θεὸν ζῶντα, ὃς ἐποίησεν τὸν οὐρανὸν καὶ τὴν γῆν καὶ τὴν θάλασσαν καὶ πάντα τὰ ἐν αὐτοῖς· [GNT] | |
| #2031 **Human Passion** Will of the flesh–KJV Will of the flesh–NASB Of human decision–NIV Will of the flesh–NKJV **Human passion–NLT** **POSB REFERENCE** (Jn.1:12-13; esp. v.13) Note 3, point 3a | **ἐκ θελήματος σαρκός** = ek thelēmatos sarkos<br>Pronunciation: [ek thel'-ay-mah-tos sar-kos]<br>Parsing *thelēmatos* (part of speech): noun<br>  Case—genitive<br>  Gender—neuter<br>  Number—singular<br>  Stem or root—from θέλημα, τος<br>Parsing *sarkos* (part of speech): noun<br>  Case—genitive<br>  Gender—feminine<br>  Number—singular<br>  Stem or root—from σάρξ, σαρκός<br>Concordance References:<br>  ⇒ Strong's #1537 ek + 2307 thelema + 4561 sarx<br>  ⇒ NIV #1666 ek + 2525 thelēma [will] + 4922 sarx [human]<br>  ⇒ NASB #1537 ek + 2307 thelema + 4561 sarx<br><br>**John 1:13**<br>Which were born, not of blood, nor of the **will of the flesh**, nor of the will of man, but of God. [KJV]<br>Who were born not of blood, nor of the **will of the flesh**, nor of the will of man, but of God. [NASB]<br>Children born not of natural descent, nor **of human decision** or a husband's will, but born of God. [NIV]<br>Who were born, not of blood, nor of the **will of the flesh**, nor of the will of man, but of God. [NKJV]<br>They are reborn! This is not a physical birth resulting from **human passion** or plan—this rebirth comes from God. [NLT]<br>οἳ οὐκ ἐξ αἱμάτων, οὐδὲ **ἐκ θελήματος σαρκὸς**, οὐδὲ ἐκ θελήματος ἀνδρὸς, ἀλλ' ἐκ Θεοῦ ἐγεννήθησαν. [GNS]<br>οἳ οὐκ ἐξ αἱμάτων οὐδὲ **ἐκ θελήματος σαρκὸς** οὐδὲ ἐκ θελήματος ἀνδρὸς ἀλλ' ἐκ θεοῦ ἐγεννήθησαν. [GNT] | Sexual desire, the will of the flesh, human passion, human decision.<br><br>**Practical Application**<br>The idea is that a person is not spiritually born again by willing to become a child of God like a person wills to have an earthly child. These words picture a person who seeks pleasure, who is driven to please himself, but finds it impossible to achieve. |

# PRACTICAL WORD STUDIES
## in the NEW TESTAMENT

| ENGLISH WORD | GREEK WORD AND VERSE | THE WORD MEANS... |
|---|---|---|
| **#2032**<br>**Human Plan**<br><br>Will of man–KJV<br>Will of man–NASB<br>Husband's will–NIV<br>Will of man–NKJV<br>**Human...plan–NLT**<br><br>**POSB<br>REFERENCE**<br>(Jn.1:12-13; esp. v13)<br>Note 3, point 3a | ἐκ θελήματος ἀνδρὸς = ek thelëmatos andros<br>Pronunciation: [ek thel'-ay-mah-tos an'-dros]<br>Parsing *thelëmatos* (part of speech): noun<br>    Case—genitive<br>    Gender—neuter<br>    Number—singular<br>    Stem or root—from θέλημα, τος<br>Parsing *andros* (part of speech): noun<br>    Case—genitive<br>    Gender—masculine<br>    Number—singular<br>    Stem or root—from ἀνήρ, ἀνδρός<br>Concordance References:<br>  ⇒ Strong's #1537 ek + 2307 thelëma + 435 aner<br>  ⇒ NIV #1666 ek + 2525 thelëma [will] + 467 anër [husband's]<br>  ⇒ NASB #1537 ek + 2307 thelëma + 435 anër<br><br>**John 1:13**<br>Which were born, not of blood, nor of the will of the flesh, nor of the **will of man**, but of God. [KJV]<br>Who were born not of blood, nor of the will of the flesh, nor of the **will of man**, but of God. [NASB]<br>Children born not of natural descent, nor of human decision or a **husband's will**, but born of God. [NIV]<br>Who were born, not of blood, nor of the will of the flesh, nor of the **will of man**, but of God. [NKJV]<br>They are reborn! This is not a physical birth resulting from **human** passion or **plan**—this rebirth comes from God. [NLT]<br>οἳ οὐκ ἐξ αἱμάτων, οὐδὲ ἐκ θελήματος σαρκὸς, οὐδὲ **ἐκ θελήματος ἀνδρὸς**, ἀλλ' ἐκ Θεοῦ ἐγεννήθησαν. [GNS]<br>οἳ οὐκ ἐξ αἱμάτων οὐδὲ ἐκ θελήματος σαρκὸς οὐδὲ **ἐκ θελήματος ἀνδρὸς** ἀλλ' ἐκ θεοῦ ἐγεννήθησαν. [GNT] | A man's will; a man's plan; human plan.<br><br>**Practical Application**<br>The idea is that even man (the husband, the stronger member, the one who is usually the leader) cannot bring about the spiritual birth of others. No man, no matter who he is—husband or world leader—can make a person a child of God. |
| **#2033**<br>**Humble**<br><br>Submit–KJV<br>Submit–NASB<br>Submit–NIV<br>Submit–NKJV<br>**Humble–NLT**<br><br>**POSB<br>REFERENCE**<br>(Jas.4:7)<br>Note 4 | ὑποτάγητε = hupotagëte<br>Pronunciation: [hoop-ot-ah-gay-teh]<br>Parsing (part of speech): verb<br>    Mood—imperative<br>    Tense—aorist<br>    Voice—passive<br>    Person—2nd person<br>    Number—plural<br>    Stem or root—from ὑποτάσσω<br>Concordance References:<br>  ⇒ Strong's #5293 hupotassö<br>  ⇒ NIV #5718 hupotassö<br>  ⇒ NASB #5293 hupotassö<br><br>**James 4:7**<br>**Submit** yourselves therefore to God. Resist the devil, and he will flee from you. [KJV]<br>**Submit** therefore to God. Resist the devil and he will flee from you. [NASB]<br>**Submit** yourselves, then, to God. Resist the devil, and he will flee from you. [NIV]<br>Therefore **submit** to God. Resist the devil and he will flee from you. [NKJV]<br>So **humble** yourselves before God. Resist the Devil, and he will flee from you. [NLT]<br>**ὑποτάγητε** οὖν τῷ θεῷ, ἀντίστητε τῷ διαβόλῳ, καὶ φεύξεται ἀφ' ὑμῶν. [GNS]<br>**ὑποτάγητε** οὖν τῷ θεῷ, ἀντίστητε δὲ τῷ διαβόλῳ καὶ φεύξεται ἀφ' ὑμῶν. [GNT] | To submit; to humble one's self; to obey; to offer; to succumb; to surrender; to relinquish.<br><br>**Practical Application**<br>The word "humble" (*hupotagëte*) means to put yourself under God, under His care and power and strength; to yield to God, to His will, command, instructions, laws, behavior, and Word; to surrender yourself to God for Him to strengthen you so that you can do exactly what He says. |
| **#2034**<br>**Humble–<br>Humble In<br>Spirit–<br>Humble In Mind** | ταπεινόφρονες = tapeinophrones<br>Pronunciation: [tap-eh-in-o-fro'-nes]<br>Parsing (part of speech): adjective<br>    Case—nominative<br>    Gender—masculine<br>    Number—plural<br>    Stem or root—from ταπεινόφρων, ον | Humble, humble in spirit, humble in mind, courteous; to be humble-minded; to be lowly in mind.<br><br>**Practical Application**<br>Believers must be "humble" (*tapei-* |

# PRACTICAL WORD STUDIES
## in the NEW TESTAMENT

| ENGLISH WORD | GREEK WORD AND VERSE | THE WORD MEANS... |
|---|---|---|
| Courteous–KJV<br>**Humble in spirit–**<br>**NASB**<br>**Humble–NIV**<br>Courteous–NKJV<br>**Humble minds– NLT**<br><br>**POSB**<br>**REFERENCE**<br>(1 Pt.3:8)<br>Note 5 | Concordance References:<br>⇒ Strong's #5391 tapeinophrōn<br>⇒ NIV #5426 tapeinophrōn<br>⇒ NASB #5391 tapeinophrōn<br><br>**1 Peter 3:8**<br>Finally, be ye all of one mind, having compassion one of another, love as brethren, be pitiful, be **courteous**: [KJV]<br>To sum up, let all be harmonious, sympathetic, brotherly, kindhearted, and **humble in spirit**; [NASB]<br>Finally, all of you, live in harmony with one another; be sympathetic, love as brothers, be compassionate and **humble**. [NIV]<br>Finally, all *of you be* of one mind, having compassion for one another; love as brothers, *be* tenderhearted, *be* **courteous**; [NKJV]<br>Finally, all of you should be of one mind, full of sympathy toward each other, loving one another with tender hearts and **humble minds**. [NLT]<br>Τὸ δὲ τέλος, πάντες ὁμόφρονες, συμπαθεῖς, φιλάδελφοι, εὔσπλαγχνοι, **φιλόφρονες**· [GNS]<br>Τὸ δὲ τέλος πάντες ὁμόφρονες, συμπαθεῖς, φιλάδελφοι, εὔσπλαγχνοι, **ταπεινόφρονες**, [GNT] | *nophrones*). It means to offer oneself as lowly and submissive; to walk in a spirit of lowliness; *to present* oneself as lowly; to be of low degree and low rank; not to be high-minded, proud, haughty, arrogant, or assertive.<br>    A humble person may have a high position, power, wealth, fame, and much more; but he carries himself in a spirit of lowliness and submission. He denies himself for the sake of Christ and in order to help others. |
| #2035<br>**Humble–**<br>**Humbles–**<br>**Humbleth**<br><br>**Humbleth–KJV**<br>**Humbles–NASB**<br>**Humbles–NIV**<br>**Humbles–NKJV**<br>**Humble–NLT**<br><br>**POSB**<br>**REFERENCE**<br>(Lk.14:11)<br>*Deeper Study #1* | ταπεινῶν = *tapeinōn*<br>Pronunciation: [tap-i-nown']<br>Parsing (part of speech): verb<br>  Mood—participle<br>  Tense—present<br>  Voice—active<br>  Case—nominative<br>  Gender—masculine<br>  Number—singular<br>  Stem or root—from ταπεινόω<br>Concordance References:<br>⇒ Strong's #5013 tapeinoö<br>⇒ NIV #5427 tapeinoö<br>⇒ NASB #5013 tapeinoö<br><br>**Luke 14:11**<br>For whosoever exalteth himself shall be abased; and he that **humbleth** himself shall be exalted. [KJV]<br>"For everyone who exalts himself shall be humbled, and he who **humbles** himself shall be exalted." [NASB]<br>For everyone who exalts himself will be humbled, and he who **humbles** himself will be exalted." [NIV]<br>For whoever exalts himself will be humbled, and he who **humbles** himself will be exalted." [NKJV]<br>For the proud will be humbled, but the **humble** will be honored." [NLT]<br>ὅτι πᾶς ὁ ὑψῶν ἑαυτὸν ταπεινωθήσεται, καὶ ὁ **ταπεινῶν** ἑαυτὸν ὑψωθήσεται. [GNS]<br>ὅτι πᾶς ὁ ὑψῶν ἑαυτὸν ταπεινωθήσεται, καὶ ὁ **ταπεινῶν** ἑαυτὸν ὑψωθήσεται. [GNT] | To be humble; to humble one's self; to live in humble circumstances. Humility means lowliness of mind.<br><br>**Practical Application**<br>It is a word that was coined by Christianity. Before Christ, a humble man was looked upon as a coward: a cringing, unappealing, effeminate type of person. However after Christ, humility was elevated to the most praise-worthy level. When men looked at Christ, they saw the strength of humility through the influence of One Who was perfect in meekness and lowliness of heart. |
| #2036<br>**Humbly**<br><br>With all humility of<br>  mind–KJV<br>With all humility–<br>  NASB<br>With great humility–<br>  NIV<br>With all humility–<br>  NKJV<br>**Humbly–NLT** | μετὰ πάσης ταπεινοφροσύνης = *meta pasēs tapeinophrosunēs*<br>Pronunciation: [meh-tah pah-sace tap-i-nof-ros-oo'-nays]<br>Parsing *pasēs* (part of speech): adjective<br>  Case—genitive<br>  Gender—feminine<br>  Number—singular<br>  Stem or root—from πᾶς, πᾶσα, πᾶν<br>Parsing *tapeinophrosunēs* (part of speech): noun<br>  Case—genitive<br>  Gender—feminine<br>  Number—singular<br>  Stem or root—from ταπεινοφροσύνη, ης<br>Concordance References:<br>⇒ Strong's #3326 meta + 3956 pas + 5012 tapeinophrosunē<br>⇒ NIV #3552 meta [with] + 4246 pas [great] + | With great humility; with all humility; humbly.<br><br>**Practical Application**<br>Paul's service was characterized by three things.<br>1. He served "humbly" (*meta pasēs tapeinophrosunēs*) or in lowliness of mind (see POSB *Deeper Study #1*, Humility—Luke 14:11 for discussion).<br>⇒ He moved among all.<br>⇒ He recognized and acknowledged and shared with all, the lowly as well as the upper class.<br>⇒ He stopped to help in any way he could. |

# PRACTICAL WORD STUDIES
## in the NEW TESTAMENT

| ENGLISH WORD | GREEK WORD AND VERSE | THE WORD MEANS... |
|---|---|---|
| **POSB REFERENCE** (Acts 20:18-19; esp. v.19) Note 2, point 3 | 5425 tapeinophrosunē [humility] ⇒ NASB #3326 meta + 3956 pas + 5012 tapeinophrosunē<br><br>**Acts 20:19**<br>Serving the Lord **with all humility of mind**, and with many tears, and temptations, which befell me by the lying in wait of the Jews: [KJV]<br>Serving the Lord **with all humility** and with tears and with trials which came upon me through the plots of the Jews; [NASB]<br>I served the Lord **with great humility** and with tears, although I was severely tested by the plots of the Jews. [NIV]<br>Serving the Lord **with all humility**, with many tears and trials which happened to me by the plotting of the Jews; [NKJV]<br>I have done the Lord's work **humbly**—yes, and with tears. I have endured the trials that came to me from the plots of the Jews. [NLT]<br>δουλεύων τῷ Κυρίῳ **μετὰ πάσης ταπεινοφροσύνης** καὶ δακρύων καὶ πολλῶν πειρασμῶν τῶν συμβάντων μοι ἐν ταῖς ἐπιβουλαῖς τῶν Ἰουδαίων· [GNS]<br>δουλεύων τῷ κυρίῳ **μετὰ πάσης ταπεινοφροσύνης** καὶ δακρύων καὶ πειρασμῶν τῶν συμβάντων μοι ἐν ταῖς ἐπιβουλαῖς τῶν Ἰουδαίων, [GNT] | 2. He served "with tears." He had a tender, understanding, and compassionate heart. He wept over...<br>• the unsaved world (Acts 20:19, 31).<br>• the carnal believers (2 Cor. 2:4).<br>• the sensual and apostate ministers (Phil. 3:18).<br>3. He served "with many trials," especially in being attacked by the unsaved religionists (Jew). The point is this: despite the terrible trials, he kept on serving faithfully. (See POSB note, Paul, Sufferings—Acts 18:9-11 for discussion.) |
| **#2037 Humility**<br><br>Lowliness of mind– KJV<br>Humility of mind– NASB<br>**Humility–NIV**<br>Lowliness of mind– NKJV<br>Humble–NLT<br><br>**POSB REFERENCE** (Philip.2:3) *Deeper Study* #1<br><br>See also POSB REF: (1 Pt.5:5) Note 2 | ταπεινοφροσύνη = tapeinophrosunē<br>Pronunciation: [tap-i-nof-ros-oo'-nay]<br>Parsing (part of speech): noun<br>   Case—dative<br>   Gender—feminine<br>   Number—singular<br>Stem or root—from ταπεινοφροσύνη, ης<br>Concordance References:<br>⇒ Strong's #5012 tapeinophrosunē<br>⇒ NIV #5425 tapeinophrosunē<br>⇒ NASB #5012 tapeinophrosunē<br><br>**Philip. 2:3**<br>Let nothing be done through strife or vainglory; but in **lowliness of mind** let each esteem other better than themselves. [KJV]<br>Do nothing from selfishness or empty conceit, but with **humility of mind** let each of you regard one another as more important than himself; [NASB]<br>Do nothing out of selfish ambition or vain conceit, but in **humility** consider others better than yourselves. [NIV]<br>Let nothing *be done* through selfish ambition or conceit, but in **lowliness of mind** let each esteem others better than himself. [NKJV]<br>Don't be selfish; don't live to make a good impression on others. Be **humble**, thinking of others as better than yourself. [NLT]<br>μηδὲν κατ' ἐριθείαν ἢ κενοδοξίαν, ἀλλὰ τῇ **ταπεινοφροσύνῃ** ἀλλήλους ἡγούμενοι ὑπερέχοντας ἑαυτῶν· [GNS]<br>μηδὲν κατ' ἐριθείαν μηδὲ κατὰ κενοδοξίαν ἀλλὰ τῇ **ταπεινοφροσύνῃ** ἀλλήλους ἡγούμενοι ὑπερέχοντας ἑαυτῶν, [GNT] | Humility, lowliness of mind; *to offer* oneself as lowly and submissive; to walk in a spirit of lowliness; *to present* oneself as lowly and low-lying in mind; to be of low degree and low rank; not to be highminded, proud, haughty, arrogant, or assertive.<br><br>**Practical Application**<br>Note: a humble person may have a high position, power, wealth, fame, and much more; but he carries himself in a spirit of lowliness and submission. He denies himself for the sake of Christ and in order to help others.<br>Men have always looked upon humility as a vice. A humble man is often looked upon as a coward, a cringing, despicable, slavish type of person. Men fear humility. They feel humility is a sign of weakness and will make them the object of contempt and abuse and cause them to be shunned and overlooked.<br>Because of all this, men ignore and shun the teaching of Christ on humility. This is tragic:<br>⇒ for a humble spirit is necessary for salvation (Matthew 18:3-4).<br>⇒ for God's idea of humility is not weakness and cowardice.<br>God makes people strong, the strongest they can possibly be. By humility God does not mean what men mean. God infuses a new and strong spirit within a person and causes that person to conquer all throughout life. He just does not want the person walking around in pride. He wants the person to do what the definition says: *to offer* himself in a spirit of submissiveness and lowliness; not to act highminded, proud, haughty, arrogant, or assertive. |
| **#2038 Humility**<br><br>Meekness–KJV<br>Gentleness–NASB | πραΰτητι = prautēti<br>Pronunciation: [prah-oo'-tay-tee]<br>Parsing (part of speech): noun<br>   Case—dative<br>   Gender—feminine<br>   Number—singular | Humility, meekness, gentleness; to be gentle, tender, humble, mild, considerate, but strongly so. |

# PRACTICAL WORD STUDIES
## in the NEW TESTAMENT

| ENGLISH WORD | GREEK WORD AND VERSE | THE WORD MEANS... |
|---|---|---|
| **Humility–NIV**<br>Meekness–NKJV<br>Don't brag–NLT<br><br>**POSB<br>REFERENCE**<br>(Jas.3:13)<br>Note 1, point 2<br><br>See also POSB REF:<br>(Tit.3:2)<br>Note 6 | Stem or root—from πραΰτης, ητος<br>Concordance References:<br>⇒ Strong's #4240 prautēs<br>⇒ NIV #4559 prautēs<br>⇒ NASB #4240 prautēs<br><br>**James 3:13**<br>Who is a wise man and endued with knowledge among you? let him show out of a good conversation his works with **meekness** of wisdom. [KJV]<br>Who among you is wise and understanding? Let him show by his good behavior his deeds in the **gentleness** of wisdom. [NASB]<br>Who is wise and understanding among you? Let him show it by his good life, by deeds done in the **humility** that comes from wisdom. [NIV]<br>Who is wise and understanding among you? Let him show by good conduct that his works are done in the **meekness** of wisdom. [NKJV]<br>If you are wise and understand God's ways, live a life of steady goodness so that only good deeds will pour forth. And if you **don't brag** about the good you do, then you will be truly wise! [NLT]<br>Τίς σοφὸς καὶ ἐπιστήμων ἐν ὑμῖν; δειξάτω ἐκ τῆς καλῆς ἀναστροφῆς τὰ ἔργα αὐτοῦ ἐν **πραΰτητι** σοφίας. [GNS]<br>Τίς σοφὸς καὶ ἐπιστήμων ἐν ὑμῖν; δειξάτω ἐκ τῆς καλῆς ἀναστροφῆς τὰ ἔργα αὐτοῦ ἐν **πραΰτητι** σοφίας. [GNT] | **Practical Application**<br>Humility has the strength to control and discipline; and it does so at the right time.<br>1. Humility has *a humble state of mind*. But this does not mean the teacher is weak, cowardly, and bowing. The meek teacher simply loves people and loves peace; therefore, he walks humbly among men regardless of their status and circumstance in life. Associating with the poor and lowly of this earth does not bother the meek teacher. He desires to be a friend to all and to help all as much as possible.<br>2. Humility has *a strong state of mind*. It looks at situations and wants justice and right to be done. It is not a weak mind that ignores and neglects evil and wrongdoing, abuse and suffering.<br>⇒ If someone is suffering, humility steps in to do what it can to help.<br>⇒ If evil is being done, humility does what it can to stop and correct it.<br>⇒ If evil is running rampant and indulging itself, humility actually strikes out in anger. However, note a crucial point: the anger is always at the right time and against the right thing.<br>3. Humility has *strong self-control*. The humble teacher controls his spirit and mind. He controls the lusts of his flesh. He does not give way to ill-temper, retaliation, passion, indulgence, or license. The meek teacher dies to himself, to what his flesh would like to do, and he does the right thing—exactly what God wants done.<br>In summary, the humble man walks in a humble, tender, but strong state of mind; denies himself, giving utmost consideration to others. He shows a control and righteous anger against injustice and evil. A humble man forgets and lives for others because of what Christ has done for him. |
| **#2039<br>Humility**<br><br>Meekness–KJV<br>Consideration–NASB<br>**Humility–NIV**<br>**Humility–NKJV**<br>**Humility–NLT**<br><br>**POSB<br>REFERENCE**<br>(Tit.3:2)<br>Note 6 | πραΰτητα = *prautēta*<br>Pronunciation: [prah-oo-tay'-tah]<br>Parsing (part of speech): noun<br>  Case—accusative<br>  Gender—feminine<br>  Number—singular<br>  Stem or root—from πραΰτης, ητος<br>Concordance References:<br>⇒ Strong's #4240 prautēs<br>⇒ NIV #4559 prautēs<br>⇒ NASB #4240 prautēs<br><br>**Titus 3:2**<br>To speak evil of no man, to be no brawlers, but gentle, shewing all **meekness** unto all men. [KJV]<br>To malign no one, to be uncontentious, gentle, showing every **consideration** for all men. [NASB]<br>To slander no one, to be peaceable and considerate, and to show true **humility** toward all men. [NIV]<br>To speak evil of no one, to be peaceable, gentle, showing all **humility** to all men. [NKJV]<br>They must not speak evil of anyone, and they must avoid quarreling. Instead, they should be gentle and show true **humility** to everyone. [NLT]<br>μηδένα βλασφημεῖν, ἀμάχους εἶναι, ἐπιεικεῖς, πᾶσαν ἐνδεικνυμένους **πραότητα** πρὸς πάντας ἀνθρώπους. [GNS]<br>μηδένα βλασφημεῖν, ἀμάχους εἶναι, ἐπιεικεῖς, πᾶσαν ἐνδεικνυμένους **πραΰτητα** πρὸς πάντας ἀνθρώπους. [GNT] | Humility, meekness, consideration, gentleness. The word means to be gentle, tender, humble, mild, considerate, but strongly so.<br><br>**Practical Application**<br>The Christian citizen must "show humility" (*prautēta*) *to all* citizens. Humility has the strength to control and discipline, and it does so at the right time.<br>1. Humility has *a humble state of mind*. But this does not mean the person is weak, cowardly, and bowing. The humble person simply loves people and loves peace; therefore, he walks humbly among men regardless of their status and circumstance in life. Associating with the poor and lowly of this earth does not bother the humble person. He desires to be a friend to all and to help all as much as possible.<br>2. Humility has *a strong state of mind*. It looks at situations and wants justice and right to be done. It is not a weak mind that ignores and neglects evil and wrong-doing, abuse and suffering.<br>⇒ If someone is suffering, humility steps in to do what it can to help.<br>⇒ If evil is being done, humility does what it can to stop and correct it. |

# PRACTICAL WORD STUDIES
## in the NEW TESTAMENT

| ENGLISH WORD | GREEK WORD AND VERSE | THE WORD MEANS... |
|---|---|---|
| | | ⇒ If evil is running rampant and indulging itself, humility actually strikes out in anger. However, note a crucial point: the anger is always at the right time and against the right thing.<br>3. Humility has *strong self-control*. The meek person controls his spirit and mind. He controls the lusts of his flesh. He does not give way to ill-temper, retaliation, passion, indulgence, or license. The humble person dies to himself, to what his flesh would like to do, and he does the right thing—exactly what God wants done. |
| **#2040**<br>**Humility Of Mind, With All**<br><br>With all humility of mind–KJV<br>With all humility–NASB<br>With great humility–NIV<br>With all humility–NKJV<br>Humbly–NLT<br><br>**POSB REFERENCE**<br>(Acts 20:18-19; esp. v.19)<br>Note 2, point 3 | μετὰ πάσης ταπεινοφροσύνης = *meta pasēs tapeinophrosunēs*<br>Pronunciation: [meh-tah pah-sace tap-i-nof-ros-oo'-nays]<br>Parsing *pasēs* (part of speech): adjective<br>    Case—genitive<br>    Gender—feminine<br>    Number—singular<br>    Stem or root—from πᾶς, πᾶσα, πᾶν<br>Parsing *tapeinophrosunēs* (part of speech): noun<br>    Case—genitive<br>    Gender—feminine<br>    Number—singular<br>    Stem or root—from ταπεινοφροσύνη, ης<br>Concordance References:<br>⇒ Strong's #3326 meta + 3956 pas + 5012 tapeinophrosunē<br>⇒ NIV #3552 meta [with] + 4246 pas [great] + 5425 tapeinophrosunē [humility]<br>⇒ NASB #3326 meta + 3956 pas + 5012 tapeinophrosunē<br><br>**Acts 20:19**<br>Serving the Lord **with all humility of mind**, and with many tears, and temptations, which befell me by the lying in wait of the Jews: [KJV]<br>Serving the Lord **with all humility** and with tears and with trials which came upon me through the plots of the Jews; [NASB]<br>I served the Lord **with great humility** and with tears, although I was severely tested by the plots of the Jews. [NIV]<br>Serving the Lord **with all humility**, with many tears and trials which happened to me by the plotting of the Jews; [NKJV]<br>I have done the Lord's work **humbly**—yes, and with tears. I have endured the trials that came to me from the plots of the Jews. [NLT]<br>δουλεύων τῷ Κυρίῳ μετὰ πάσης ταπεινοφροσύνης καὶ δακρύων καὶ πολλῶν πειρασμῶν τῶν συμβάντων μοι ἐν ταῖς ἐπιβουλαῖς τῶν Ἰουδαίων· [GNS]<br>δουλεύων τῷ κυρίῳ μετὰ πάσης ταπεινοφροσύνης καὶ δακρύων καὶ πειρασμῶν τῶν συμβάντων μοι ἐν ταῖς ἐπιβουλαῖς τῶν Ἰουδαίων, [GNT] | In summary, the humble man walks in a humble, tender, but strong state of mind; denies himself, giving utmost consideration to others. He shows a control and righteous anger against injustice and evil. A humble man forgets self and lives for others because of what Christ has done for him.<br>With great humility; with all humility; humbly.<br><br>**Practical Application**<br>Paul's service was characterized by three things.<br>1. He served "with all humility" (*meta pasēs tapeinophrosunēs*) or in lowliness of mind (see POSB *Deeper Study #1*, Humility—Luke 14:11 for discussion).<br>  ⇒ He moved among all.<br>  ⇒ He recognized and acknowledged and shared with all, the lowly as well as the upper class.<br>  ⇒ He stopped to help in any way he could.<br>2. He served "with many tears." He had a tender, understanding, and compassionate heart. He wept over...<br>  • the unsaved world (Acts 20:19, 31).<br>  • the carnal believers (2 Cor. 2:4).<br>  • the sensual and apostate ministers (Phil. 3:18).<br>3. He served "with many temptations," especially in being attacked by the unsaved religionists (Jew). The point is this: despite the terrible trials, he kept on serving faithfully. (See POSB note, Paul, Sufferings—Acts 18:9-11 for discussion.) |
| **#2041**<br>**Humility, With All**<br><br>With all humility of mind–KJV<br>**With all humility–NASB**<br>**With great humility–NIV**<br>**With all humility–NKJV**<br>Humbly–NLT | μετὰ πάσης ταπεινοφροσύνης = *meta pasēs tapeinophrosunēs*<br>Pronunciation: [meh-tah pah-sace tap-i-nof-ros-oo'-nays]<br>Parsing *pasēs* (part of speech): adjective<br>    Case—genitive<br>    Gender—feminine<br>    Number—singular<br>    Stem or root—from πᾶς, πᾶσα, πᾶν<br>Parsing *tapeinophrosunēs* (part of speech): noun<br>    Case—genitive<br>    Gender—feminine<br>    Number—singular<br>    Stem or root—from ταπεινοφροσύνη, ης | With great humility; with all humility; humbly.<br><br>**Practical Application**<br>Paul's service was characterized by three things.<br>1. He served "with all humility" (*meta pasēs tapeinophrosunēs*) or in lowliness of mind (see POSB *Deeper Study #1*, Humility—Luke 14:11 for discussion).<br>  ⇒ He moved among all.<br>  ⇒ He recognized and acknowledged and shared with all, the lowly as well as the |

# PRACTICAL WORD STUDIES
## in the New Testament

| ENGLISH WORD | GREEK WORD AND VERSE | THE WORD MEANS... |
|---|---|---|
| **POSB REFERENCE** (Acts 20:18-19; esp. v.19) Note 2, point 3 | Concordance References:<br>⇒ Strong's #3326 meta + 3956 pas + 5012 tapeinophrosunē<br>⇒ NIV #3552 meta [with] + 4246 pas [great] + 5425 tapeinophrosunē [humility]<br>⇒ NASB #3326 meta + 3956 pas + 5012 tapeinophrosunē<br><br>**Acts 20:19**<br>Serving the Lord **with all humility of mind**, and with many tears, and temptations, which befell me by the lying in wait of the Jews: [KJV]<br>Serving the Lord **with all humility** and with tears and with trials which came upon me through the plots of the Jews; [NASB]<br>I served the Lord **with great humility** and with tears, although I was severely tested by the plots of the Jews. [NIV]<br>Serving the Lord **with all humility**, with many tears and trials which happened to me by the plotting of the Jews; [NKJV]<br>I have done the Lord's work **humbly**—yes, and with tears. I have endured the trials that came to me from the plots of the Jews. [NLT]<br>δουλεύων τῷ Κυρίῳ **μετὰ πάσης ταπεινοφροσύνης** καὶ δακρύων καὶ πολλῶν πειρασμῶν τῶν συμβάντων μοι ἐν ταῖς ἐπιβουλαῖς τῶν Ἰουδαίων· [GNS]<br>δουλεύων τῷ κυρίῳ **μετὰ πάσης ταπεινοφροσύνης** καὶ δακρύων καὶ πειρασμῶν τῶν συμβάντων μοι ἐν ταῖς ἐπιβουλαῖς τῶν Ἰουδαίων, [GNT] | upper class.<br>⇒ He stopped to help in any way he could.<br>2. He served "with many tears." He had a tender, understanding, and compassionate heart. He wept over...<br>• the unsaved world (Acts 20:19, 31).<br>• the carnal believers (2 Cor. 2:4).<br>• the sensual and apostate ministers (Phil. 3:18).<br>3. He served "with many trials," especially in being attacked by the unsaved religionists (Jew). The point is this: despite the terrible trials, he kept on serving faithfully. (See POSB note, Paul, Sufferings—Acts 18:9-11 for discussion.) |
| **#2042**<br>**Humility, With Great**<br><br>With all humility of mind–KJV<br>With all humility–NASB<br>**With great humility–NIV**<br>With all humility–NKJV<br>Humbly–NLT<br><br>**POSB REFERENCE** (Acts 20:18-19; esp. v.19) Note 2, point 3 | μετὰ πάσης ταπεινοφροσύνης = *meta pasēs tapeinophrosunēs*<br>Pronunciation: [meh-tah pah-sace tap-i-nof-ros-oo'-nays]<br>Parsing *pasēs* (part of speech): adjective<br>  Case—genitive<br>  Gender—feminine<br>  Number—singular<br>  Stem or root—from πᾶς, πᾶσα, πᾶν<br>Parsing *tapeinophrosunēs* (part of speech): noun<br>  Case—genitive<br>  Gender—feminine<br>  Number—singular<br>  Stem or root—from ταπεινοφροσύνη, ης<br>Concordance References:<br>⇒ Strong's #3326 meta + 3956 pas + 5012 tapeinophrosunē<br>⇒ NIV #3552 meta [with] + 4246 pas [great] + 5425 tapeinophrosunē [humility]<br>⇒ NASB #3326 meta + 3956 pas + 5012 tapeinophrosunē<br><br>**Acts 20:19**<br>Serving the Lord **with all humility of mind**, and with many tears, and temptations, which befell me by the lying in wait of the Jews: [KJV]<br>Serving the Lord **with all humility** and with tears and with trials which came upon me through the plots of the Jews; [NASB]<br>I served the Lord **with great humility** and with tears, although I was severely tested by the plots of the Jews. [NIV]<br>Serving the Lord **with all humility**, with many tears and trials which happened to me by the plotting of the Jews; [NKJV]<br>I have done the Lord's work **humbly**—yes, and with tears. I have endured the trials that came to me from the plots of the Jews. [NLT]<br>δουλεύων τῷ Κυρίῳ **μετὰ πάσης ταπεινοφροσύνης** καὶ δακρύων καὶ πολλῶν πειρασμῶν τῶν συμβάντων μοι ἐν ταῖς ἐπιβουλαῖς τῶν Ἰουδαίων· [GNS]<br>δουλεύων τῷ κυρίῳ **μετὰ πάσης ταπεινοφροσύνης** καὶ δακρύων καὶ πειρασμῶν τῶν συμβάντων μοι ἐν ταῖς ἐπιβουλαῖς τῶν Ἰουδαίων, [GNT] | With great humility; with all humility; humbly.<br><br>**Practical Application**<br>Paul's service was characterized by three things.<br>1. He served "with great humility" (*meta pasēs tapeinophrosunēs*) or in lowliness of mind (see POSB *Deeper Study #1*, Humility—Luke 14:11 for discussion).<br>⇒ He moved among all.<br>⇒ He recognized and acknowledged and shared with all, the lowly as well as the upper class.<br>⇒ He stopped to help in any way he could.<br>2. He served "with tears." He had a tender, understanding, and compassionate heart. He wept over...<br>• the unsaved world (Acts 20:19, 31).<br>• the carnal believers (2 Cor. 2:4).<br>• the sensual and apostate ministers (Phil. 3:18).<br>3. He served being "severely tested," especially in being attacked by the unsaved religionists (Jew). The point is this: despite the terrible trials, he kept on serving faithfully. (See POSB note, Paul, Sufferings—Acts 18:9-11 for discussion.) |

# PRACTICAL WORD STUDIES
## in the NEW TESTAMENT

| ENGLISH WORD | GREEK WORD AND VERSE | THE WORD MEANS... |
|---|---|---|
| **#2043**<br>**Hundred Measures**<br><br>Hundred measures–KJV<br>Hundred measures–NASB<br>Eight hundred gallons–NIV<br>Hundred measures–NKJV<br>Eight hundred gallons–NLT<br><br>**POSB REFERENCE**<br>(Lk.16:6-7; esp. v.6)<br>*Deeper Study #1* | Ἑκατὸν βάτους = hekaton batous<br>Pronunciation: [hek-at-on bat'-oos]<br>Parsing *hekaton* (part of speech): adjective<br>    Type—cardinal<br>    Case—accusative<br>    Gender—masculine<br>    Number—plural<br>    Stem or root—from ἑκατόν<br>Parsing *batous* (part of speech): noun<br>    Case—accusative<br>    Gender—masculine<br>    Number—plural<br>    Stem or root—from βάτος, ου<br>Concordance References:<br>⇒ Strong's #1540 hekaton + 943 batos<br>⇒ NIV #1004 batos2+1669 hekaton [eight hundred gallons]<br>⇒ NASB #1540 hekaton + 943 batos<br><br>**Luke 16:6**<br>And he said, An **hundred measures** of oil. And he said unto him, Take thy bill, and sit down quickly, and write fifty. [KJV]<br><br>"And he said, 'A **hundred measures** of oil.' And he said to him, 'Take your bill, and sit down quickly and write fifty.' [NASB]<br><br>"'**Eight hundred gallons** of olive oil,' he replied." The manager told him, 'Take your bill, sit down quickly, and make it four hundred.' [NIV]<br><br>And he said, 'A **hundred measures** of oil.' So he said to him, 'Take your bill, and sit down quickly and write fifty.' [NKJV]<br><br>The man replied, 'I owe him **eight hundred gallons** of olive oil.' So the manager told him, 'Tear up that bill and write another one for four hundred gallons.' [NLT]<br><br>ὁ δὲ εἶπεν, Ἑκατὸν βάτους ἐλαίου. καὶ εἶπεν αὐτῷ, Δέξαι σου τὰ γράμμα, καὶ καθίσας ταχέως γράψον πεντήκοντα. [GNS]<br><br>ὁ δὲ εἶπεν, Ἑκατὸν βάτους ἐλαίου. ὁ δὲ εἶπεν αὐτῷ, Δέξαι σου τὰ γράμματα καὶ καθίσας ταχέως γράψον πεντήκοντα. [GNT] | Eight hundred gallons or a hundred measures. The word (*hekaton*) means hundred or hundreds. The word (*batous*) means a liquid measure of 65 pints or approximately 8 gallons.<br><br>**Practical Application**<br>A measure of oil was about 8 ¾ gallons. Therefore, the payment was a sizable 800 gallons. |
| **#2044**<br>**Hundred Measures**<br><br>Hundred measures–KJV<br>Hundred measures–NASB<br>Thousand bushels–NIV<br>Hundred measures–NKJV<br>Thousand bushels–NLT<br><br>**POSB REFERENCE**<br>(Lk.16:6-7; esp. v.7)<br>*Deeper Study #1* | Ἑκατὸν κόρους = hekaton korous<br>Pronunciation: [hek-at-on' kor'-oos]<br>Parsing *hekaton* (part of speech): adjective<br>    Type—cardinal<br>    Case—accusative<br>    Gender—masculine<br>    Number—plural<br>    Stem or root—from ἑκατόν<br>Parsing *korous* (part of speech): noun<br>    Case—accusative<br>    Gender—masculine<br>    Number—plural<br>    Stem or root—from κόρος, ου<br>Concordance References:<br>⇒ Strong's #1540 hekaton + 2884 koros<br>⇒ NIV #1669 hekaton [thousand] + 3174 koros [bushels]<br>⇒ NASB #1540 hekaton + 2884 koros<br><br>**Luke 16:7**<br>Then said he to another, And how much owest thou? And he said, An **hundred measures** of wheat. And he said unto him, Take thy bill, and write fourscore. [KJV]<br><br>"Then he said to another, 'And how much do you owe?' And he said, 'A **hundred measures** of wheat.' He said to him, 'Take your bill, and write eighty.' [NASB]<br><br>"Then he asked the second, 'And how much do you owe?'" 'A **thousand bushels** of wheat,' he replied." He told him, 'Take your bill and make it eight hundred.' [NIV] | A thousand bushels; a hundred measures.<br><br>**Practical Application**<br>The measure of wheat was about 10 bushels. This was sizable, about 1,000 bushels of wheat. |

# PRACTICAL WORD STUDIES
## in the New Testament

| ENGLISH WORD | GREEK WORD AND VERSE | THE WORD MEANS... |
|---|---|---|
| | Then he said to another, 'And how much do you owe?' So he said, 'A **hundred measures** of wheat.' And he said to him, 'Take your bill, and write eighty.' [NKJV]<br><br>'And how much do you owe my employer?' he asked the next man. 'A **thousand bushels** of wheat,' was the reply. 'Here,' the manager said, 'take your bill and replace it with one for only eight hundred bushels.' [NLT]<br><br>ἔπειτα ἑτέρῳ εἶπε, Σὺ δὲ πόσον ὀφείλεις; ὁ δὲ εἶπεν, **Ἑκατὸν κόρους** σίτου. καὶ λέγει αὐτῷ, Δέξαι σου τὰ γράμμα, καὶ γράψον ὀγδοήκοντα. [GNS]<br><br>ἔπειτα ἑτέρῳ εἶπεν, Σὺ δὲ πόσον ὀφείλεις; ὁ δὲ εἶπεν, **Ἑκατὸν κόρους** σίτου. λέγει αὐτῷ, Δέξαι σου τὰ γράμματα καὶ γράψον ὀγδοήκοντα. [GNT] | |
| **#2045**<br>**Hung On**<br><br>Attentive–KJV<br>Hanging upon–NASB<br>**Hung on**–NIV<br>Attentive–NKJV<br>**Hung on**–NLT<br><br>**POSB<br>REFERENCE**<br>(Lk.19:47-48; esp. v.48)<br>Note 3, point 2 | ἐξεκρέματο = *exekremato*<br>Pronunciation: [ex-e-krem'-ah-tow]<br>Parsing (part of speech): verb<br>  Mood—indicative<br>  Tense—aorist<br>  Voice—middle<br>  Person—3rd person<br>  Number—singular<br>  Stem or root—from ἐκκρέμαμαι<br>Concordance References:<br>  ⇒ Strong's #1582 ekkremannumi<br>  ⇒ NIV #1717 ekkremannumi<br>  ⇒ NASB #1582 ekkremannumi<br><br>**Luke 19:48**<br>And could not find what they might do: for all the people were very **attentive** to hear him. [KJV]<br><br>And they could not find anything that they might do, for all the people were **hanging upon** His words. [NASB]<br><br>Yet they could not find any way to do it, because all the people **hung on** his words. [NIV]<br><br>And were unable to do anything; for all the people were very **attentive** to hear Him. [NKJV]<br><br>But they could think of nothing, because all the people **hung on** every word he said. [NLT]<br><br>καὶ οὐχ εὕρισκον τὸ τί ποιήσωσιν· ὁ λαὸς γὰρ ἅπας **ἐξεκρέματο** αὐτοῦ ἀκούων. [GNS]<br><br>καὶ οὐχ εὕρισκον τὸ τί ποιήσωσιν, ὁ λαὸς γὰρ ἅπας **ἐξεκρέματο** αὐτοῦ ἀκούων. [GNT] | To be attentive; to pay close attention; to hang on the words of someone speaking.<br><br>**Practical Application**<br>The word means that they hung upon Jesus, gave Him rapt attention, were struck by Him. |
| **#2046**<br>**Hunger**<br><br>Fastings–KJV<br>**Hunger**–NASB<br>**Hunger**–NIV<br>Fastings–NKJV<br>Gone without food–NLT<br><br>**POSB<br>REFERENCE**<br>(2 Cor.6:5)<br>Note 4 | νηστείαις = *nēsteiais*<br>Pronunciation: [nace-ti'-ah-ees]<br>Parsing (part of speech): noun<br>  Case—dative<br>  Gender—feminine<br>  Number—plural<br>  Stem or root—from νηστεία, ας<br>Concordance References:<br>  ⇒ Strong's #3521 nēsteia<br>  ⇒ NIV #3763 nēsteia<br>  ⇒ NASB #3521 nēsteia<br><br>**2 Cor. 6:5**<br>In stripes, in imprisonments, in tumults, in labours, in watchings, in **fastings**; [KJV]<br><br>In beatings, in imprisonments, in tumults, in labors, in sleeplessness, in **hunger**, [NASB]<br><br>In beatings, imprisonments and riots; in hard work, sleepless nights and **hunger**; [NIV]<br><br>In stripes, in imprisonments, in tumults, in labors, in sleeplessness, in **fastings**; [NKJV]<br><br>We have been beaten, been put in jail, faced angry mobs, worked to exhaustion, endured sleepless nights, and **gone without food**. [NLT]<br><br>ἐν πληγαῖς, ἐν φυλακαῖς, ἐν ἀκαταστασίαις, ἐν κόποις, ἐν ἀγρυπνίαις, ἐν **νηστείαις**, [GNS]<br><br>ἐν πληγαῖς, ἐν φυλακαῖς, ἐν ἀκαταστασίαις, ἐν κόποις, ἐν ἀγρυπνίαις, ἐν **νηστείαις**, [GNT] | Hunger, fasting, starvation; to go without food.<br><br>**Practical Application**<br>This means not only deliberate fastings, but being so involved in his work that Paul forgot to eat or else chose to keep working instead of eating. |

# Practical Word Studies
## in the New Testament

| ENGLISH WORD | GREEK WORD AND VERSE | THE WORD MEANS... |
|---|---|---|
| **#2047**<br>**Hunger–**<br>**Hungry**<br><br>Hunger–KJV<br>Hunger–NASB<br>Hunger–NIV<br>Hunger–NKJV<br>Hungry–NLT<br><br>**POSB**<br>**REFERENCE**<br>(Mt.5:6)<br>Note 5 | πεινῶντες = peinōntes<br>Pronunciation: [pee-ehn-own'-tehs]<br>Parsing (part of speech): verb<br>   Mood—participle<br>   Tense—present<br>   Voice—active<br>   Case—nominative<br>   Gender—masculine<br>   Number—plural<br>   Stem or root—from πεινάω<br>Concordance References:<br> ⇒ Strong's #3983 peinaō<br> ⇒ NIV #4277 peinaō<br> ⇒ NASB #3983 peinaō<br><br>**Matthew 5:6**<br>Blessed are they which do **hunger** and thirst after righteousness: for they shall be filled. [KJV]<br>"Blessed are those who **hunger** and thirst for righteousness, for they shall be satisfied. [NASB]<br>Blessed are those who **hunger** and thirst for righteousness, for they will be filled. [NIV]<br>Blessed are those who **hunger** and thirst for righteousness, For they shall be filled. [NKJV]<br>God blesses those who are **hungry** and thirsty for justice, for they will receive it in full. [NLT]<br>Μακάριοι οἱ **πεινῶντες** καὶ διψῶντες τὴν δικαιοσύνην· ὅτι αὐτοὶ χορτασθήσονται. [GNS]<br>μακάριοι οἱ **πεινῶντες** καὶ διψῶντες τὴν δικαιοσύνην, ὅτι αὐτοὶ χορτασθήσονται. [GNT] | To be hungry; to have a starving appetite.<br><br>**Practical Application**<br>In this Scripture, it means to have a starving spirit. It is real hunger and starvation of soul. It is a parched and dying thirst. It is a starving spirit and a parched soul that craves after righteousness. But there is something more: righteousness means all righteousness. The true believer is starved and parched for all righteousness. This is shown by the Greek, for the verbs hunger (*peinōntes*) and thirst (*dipsao*) are usually in what is called the Greek genitive case. This simply means that a person sometimes feels a little hunger and a little thirst; therefore, he hungers and thirsts for a bit of something, for example, an apple or a glass of juice. But in the beatitude, hunger and thirst are in the accusative case. This is most unusual. It means that a person must have a hunger and a thirst for the whole thing—for all righteousness, not for little tidbits. It means that the promise of a filled life is conditional. A person must starve and thirst for all righteousness if he wishes to be filled with the fullness of life. |
| **#2048**<br>**Hunted Down**<br><br>Persecuted–KJV<br>Persecuted–NASB<br>Persecuted–NIV<br>Persecuted–NKJV<br>Hunted down–NLT<br><br>**POSB**<br>**REFERENCE**<br>(2 Cor.4:7-9; esp. v.9)<br>Note 2<br><br>See also POSB REF:<br>(Mt.5:10-12; esp. v.10)<br>Note 9 | διωκόμενοι = diōkomenoi<br>Pronunciation: [dee-o'-ko-mehn-oy]<br>Parsing (part of speech): verb<br>   Mood—participle<br>   Tense—present<br>   Voice—passive<br>   Case—nominative<br>   Gender—masculine<br>   Person—1st person<br>   Stem or root—from διώκω<br>Concordance References:<br> ⇒ Strong's #1377 diōkō<br> ⇒ NIV #1503 diōkō<br> ⇒ NASB #1377 diōkō<br><br>**2 Cor. 4:9**<br>**Persecuted**, but not forsaken; cast down, but not destroyed; [KJV]<br>**Persecuted**, but not forsaken; struck down, but not destroyed; [NASB]<br>**Persecuted**, but not abandoned; struck down, but not destroyed. [NIV]<br>**Persecuted**, but not forsaken; struck down, but not destroyed—[NKJV]<br>We are **hunted down**, but God never abandons us. We get knocked down, but we get up again and keep going. [NLT]<br>**διωκόμενοι**, ἀλλ' οὐκ ἐγκαταλειπόμενοι, καταβαλλόμενοι ἀλλ' οὐκ ἀπολλύμενοι· [GNS]<br>**διωκόμενοι** ἀλλ' οὐκ ἐγκαταλειπόμενοι, καταβαλλόμενοι ἀλλ' οὐκ ἀπολλύμενοι, [GNT] | Persecuted, to be hunted down; to drive away; to seek after.<br><br>**Practical Application**<br>The minister (or believer) may be hunted down, but he is not forsaken. Ministers are sometimes opposed, and sometimes the opposition is hot and severe. The persecution may be behind his back or to his face.<br>The true believer will suffer persecution. Christ said so (cp. Jn.15:20). Christ suffered persecution; the early church suffered persecution; believers today will suffer persecution. It is inevitable.<br>⇒ It may take the form of ridicule, abuse, anger, slander, gossip, mockery, cursing, isolation, or violence.<br>⇒ It may take place in the market place, church, home, community, or school.<br><br>What believers need is not deliverance from persecution, but victory and triumph through persecution. Believers need a conviction of mission, a conviction so strong that they become immovable. |
| **#2049**<br>**Hurried**<br><br>With haste–KJV<br>With haste–NASB<br>Hurried–NIV<br>With haste–NKJV<br>Hurried–NLT | ἐπορεύθη μετὰ σπουδῆς = eporeuthē meta spoudēs<br>Pronunciation: [eh-por-yoo'-thay met-ah' spoo-days']<br>Parsing *eporeuthē* (part of speech): verb<br>   Mood—indicative<br>   Tense—aorist<br>   Voice—passive deponent<br>   Person—3rd person<br>   Number—singular<br>   Stem or root—from πορεύομαι | To be hurried; to act with great haste, speed, diligence, care, earnestness, zeal.<br><br>**Practical Application**<br>The idea is that Mary went with purpose and earnestness. She was not going on a casual, friendly visit. She had a very specific reason for going, a meaningful purpose. |

# PRACTICAL WORD STUDIES
## in the NEW TESTAMENT

| ENGLISH WORD | GREEK WORD AND VERSE | THE WORD MEANS... |
|---|---|---|
| **POSB REFERENCE** (Lk.1:39-42; esp. v.39) Note 1 | Parsing *meta* (part of speech): preposition<br>    Case—genitive<br>    Stem or root—from μετά<br>Parsing *spoudës* (part of speech): noun<br>    Case—genitive<br>    Gender—feminine<br>    Number—singular<br>    Stem or root—from σπουδή, ῆς<br>Concordance References:<br>⇒ Strong's #3326+4198+4710 meta poreuomai spoudë<br>⇒ NIV #3552+4513+5082 meta poreuomai spoudë [hurried]<br>⇒ NASB #3326+4198+4710 meta poreuomai spoudë<br><br>**Luke 1:39**<br>And Mary arose in those days, and went into the hill country **with haste**, into a city of Juda; [KJV]<br>Now at this time Mary arose and went **with haste** to the hill country, to a city of Judah, [NASB]<br>At that time Mary got ready and **hurried** to a town in the hill country of Judea, [NIV]<br>Now Mary arose in those days and went into the hill country **with haste**, to a city of Judah, [NKJV]<br>A few days later Mary **hurried** to the hill country of Judea, to the town [NLT]<br>Ἀναστᾶσα δὲ Μαριὰμ ἐν ταῖς ἡμέραις ταύταις ἐπορεύθη εἰς τὴν ὀρεινὴν **μετὰ σπουδῆς**, εἰς πόλιν Ἰούδα, [GNS]<br>Ἀναστᾶσα δὲ Μαριὰμ ἐν ταῖς ἡμέραις ταύταις ἐπορεύθη εἰς τὴν ὀρεινὴν **μετὰ σπουδῆς** εἰς πόλιν Ἰούδα, [GNT] | |
| #2050<br>**Hurry**<br><br>Hasting–KJV<br>Hastening–NASB<br>Speed–NIV<br>Hastening–NKJV<br>**Hurry–NLT**<br><br>**POSB REFERENCE** (2 Pt.3:12) Note 2, point 2 | σπεύδοντας = *speudontas*<br>Pronunciation: [spyoo'-don-tahs]<br>Parsing (part of speech): verb<br>    Mood—participle<br>    Tense—present<br>    Voice—active<br>    Case—accusative<br>    Gender—masculine<br>    Person—2nd person<br>    Number—plural<br>    Stem or root—from σπεύδω<br>Concordance References:<br>⇒ Strong's #4692 speudō<br>⇒ NIV #5067 speudō<br>⇒ NASB #4692 speudō<br><br>**2 Peter 3:12**<br>Looking for and **hasting** unto the coming of the day of God, wherein the heavens being on fire shall be dissolved, and the elements shall melt with fervent heat? [KJV]<br>Looking for and **hastening** the coming of the day of God, on account of which the heavens will be destroyed by burning, and the elements will melt with intense heat! [NASB]<br>As you look forward to the day of God and **speed** its coming. That day will bring about the destruction of the heavens by fire, and the elements will melt in the heat. [NIV]<br>Looking for and **hastening** the coming of the day of God, because of which the heavens will be dissolved, being on fire, and the elements will melt with fervent heat? [NKJV]<br>You should look forward to that day and **hurry** it along—the day when God will set the heavens on fire and the elements will melt away in the flames. [NLT]<br>προσδοκῶντας καὶ **σπεύδοντας** τὴν παρουσίαν τῆς τοῦ Θεοῦ ἡμέρας, δι' ἣν οὐρανοὶ πυρούμενοι λυθήσονται, | Speed; to hasten; to hurry; to strive for.<br><br>**Practical Application**<br>The believer is *to hurry* the day of God. The word "hurrying" (*speudontas*) can mean two things.<br>1. *To hurry* can mean *to hurry after*; to earnestly desire; to rush toward. The believer is to live a holy and godly life looking for and hastening toward the day of God. Keeping his eyes upon that terrible day of judgment to *arouse him* to live a holy and godly life. Every day that he lives upon earth is to be a day in which he hastens toward the judgment of God; he should never take his eyes off the terrible day of God that is coming. If he takes his eyes off that day, if he fails to direct his life toward the day of God, then he will most likely slip into unholiness and ungodliness. He must, therefore, stay focused upon the day of God, the day of the terrible judgment to come upon the heavens and earth.<br>2. *To hurry* can also mean *to hasten on* the day of God; to rush the coming of Christ; to cause the day of God to come sooner. The believer has a part in bringing about the eternal kingdom of God; he has a part in bringing about the return of Christ and the great day of God. How? God "does not want anyone to perish" (2 Peter 3:9). This is the reason He is delaying the return of Christ. Apparently, God has a certain number of believers that He has ordained to be brothers and sisters of His dear Son; apparently, there are to be a certain number of believers to rule and manage the new heavens and earth for Christ. In His eternal knowledge, God certainly knows the |

# PRACTICAL WORD STUDIES
## in the NEW TESTAMENT

| ENGLISH WORD | GREEK WORD AND VERSE | THE WORD MEANS... |
|---|---|---|
| | καὶ στοιχεῖα καυσούμενα τήκεται; [GNS]<br>προσδοκῶντας καὶ **σπεύδοντας** τὴν παρουσίαν τοῦ τοῦ θεοῦ ἡμέρας δι' ἣν οὐρανοὶ πυρούμενοι λυθήσονται καὶ στοιχεῖα καυσούμενα τήκεται. [GNT] | number who will be saved and serving His dear Son. Whatever the number and whatever the case, that number has to be reached before Christ can come and before the great day of God can destroy the universe and make a new heavens and earth. This much is known for sure:<br>⇒ God does have a certain number of believers in mind. Being God, He has purposed that His Son have many brothers who will reign with Him and who will worship and serve God through all eternity (cp. Romans 8:28-29 where God will allow nothing to stop Him from giving Christ "many brothers.")<br>⇒ This Scripture tells us that we are *to hurry on*, to help bring about the day of God. |
| **#2051**<br>**Husband's Will**<br><br>Will of man–KJV<br>Will of man–NASB<br>**Husband's will–NIV**<br>Will of man–NKJV<br>Human...plan–NLT<br><br>**POSB REFERENCE**<br>(Jn.1:12-13; esp. v13)<br>Note 3, point 3a | ἐκ θελήματος ἀνδρός = ek thelēmatos andros<br>Pronunciation: [ek thel'-ay-mah-tos an'-dros]<br>Parsing *thelēmatos* (part of speech): noun<br>  Case—genitive<br>  Gender—neuter<br>  Number—singular<br>  Stem or root—from θέλημα, τος<br>Parsing *andros* (part of speech): noun<br>  Case—genitive<br>  Gender—masculine<br>  Number—singular<br>  Stem or root—from ἀνήρ, ἀνδρός<br>Concordance References:<br>⇒ Strong's #1537 ek + 2307 thelēma + 435 aner<br>⇒ NIV #1666 ek + 2525 thelēma [will] + 467 anēr [husband's]<br>⇒ NASB #1537 ek + 2307 thelēma + 435 anēr<br><br>**John 1:13**<br>Which were born, not of blood, nor of the will of the flesh, nor of the **will of man**, but of God. [KJV]<br>Who were born not of blood, nor of the will of the flesh, nor of the **will of man**, but of God. [NASB]<br>Children born not of natural descent, nor of human decision or a **husband's will**, but born of God. [NIV]<br>Who were born, not of blood, nor of the will of the flesh, nor of the **will of man**, but of God. [NKJV]<br>They are reborn! This is not a physical birth resulting from **human** passion or **plan**—this rebirth comes from God. [NLT]<br>οἳ οὐκ ἐξ αἱμάτων, οὐδὲ ἐκ θελήματος σαρκός, οὐδὲ **ἐκ θελήματος ἀνδρός**, ἀλλ' ἐκ Θεοῦ ἐγεννήθησαν. [GNS]<br>οἳ οὐκ ἐξ αἱμάτων οὐδὲ ἐκ θελήματος σαρκὸς οὐδὲ **ἐκ θελήματος ἀνδρός** ἀλλ' ἐκ θεοῦ ἐγεννήθησαν. [GNT] | A man's will; a man's plan.<br><br>**Practical Application**<br>The idea is that even man (the husband, the stronger member, the one who is usually the leader) cannot bring about the spiritual birth of others. No man, no matter who he is—husband or world leader—can make a person a child of God. |
| **#2052**<br>**Hush, Be Still**<br><br>Peace, be still–KJV<br>**Hush, be still–NASB**<br>Quiet! Be still!–NIV<br>Peace, be still–NKJV<br>Quiet down!–NLT<br><br>**POSB REFERENCE**<br>(Mk.4:38-39; esp. v.39)<br>Note 3 | Σιώπα πεφίμωσο = siopa pephimoso<br>Pronunciation: [see-o-pah' peh-fee-mo'-so]<br>Parsing *siopa* (part of speech): verb<br>  Mood—imperative<br>  Tense—present<br>  Voice—active<br>  Person—2nd person<br>  Number—singular<br>  Stem or root—from σιωπάω<br>Parsing *pephimoso* (part of speech): verb<br>  Mood—imperative<br>  Tense—perfect<br>  Voice—passive<br>  Person—2nd person<br>  Number—singular<br>  Stem or root—<br>Concordance References:<br>⇒ Strong's #4623 siōpaō + #5392 phimoō<br>⇒ NIV #4995 siōpaō [Quiet] + 5821 phimoō [still]<br>⇒ NASB #4623 siōpaō + #5392 phimoō | Quiet! Be still!; peace be still; hush, quiet down. Literally, it means to be muzzled; to hush, silence, suppress, quiet down; to be speechless.<br><br>**Practical Application**<br>The use of this word muzzled shows the fury and violence of the storm and stresses the dramatic act of Jesus. |

# PRACTICAL WORD STUDIES
## in the NEW TESTAMENT

| ENGLISH WORD | GREEK WORD AND VERSE | THE WORD MEANS... |
|---|---|---|
|  | **Mark 4:39**<br>And he arose, and rebuked the wind, and said unto the sea, **Peace, be still**. And the wind ceased, and there was a great calm. [KJV]<br>And being aroused, He rebuked the wind and said to the sea, "**Hush, be still**." And the wind died down and it became perfectly calm. [NASB]<br>He got up, rebuked the wind and said to the waves, "**Quiet! Be still!**" Then the wind died down and it was completely calm. [NIV]<br>Then He arose and rebuked the wind, and said to the sea, "**Peace, be still!**" And the wind ceased and there was a great calm. [NKJV]<br>When he woke up, he rebuked the wind and said to the water, "**Quiet down!**" Suddenly the wind stopped, and there was a great calm. [NLT]<br>καὶ διεγερθεὶς ἐπετίμησε τῷ ἀνέμῳ καὶ εἶπε τῇ θαλάσσῃ, **Σιώπα, πεφίμωσο**. καὶ ἐκόπασεν ὁ ἄνεμος, καὶ ἐγένετο γαλήνη μεγάλη. [GNS]<br>καὶ διεγερθεὶς ἐπετίμησεν τῷ ἀνέμῳ καὶ εἶπεν τῇ θαλάσσῃ, **Σιώπα, πεφίμωσο**. καὶ ἐκόπασεν ὁ ἄνεμος καὶ ἐγένετο γαλήνη μεγάλη. [GNT] |  |
| **#2053**<br>**Hypocrisy–**<br>**Hypocrisies**<br><br>Hypocrisies–KJV<br>Hypocrisy–NASB<br>Hypocrisy–NIV<br>Hypocrisy–NKJV<br>Hypocrisy–NLT<br><br>**POSB**<br>**REFERENCE**<br>(1 Pt.2:1)<br>Note 1, point 3 | ὑποκρίσεις = *hupokriseis*<br>Pronunciation: [hoop-ok'-ree-seh-ees]<br>Parsing (part of speech): noun<br>    Case—accusative<br>    Gender—feminine<br>    Number—plural<br>    Stem or root—from ὑπόκρισις, εως<br>Concordance References:<br>  ⇒ Strong's #5272 hupokrisis<br>  ⇒ NIV #5694 hupokrisis<br>  ⇒ NASB #5272 hupokrisis<br><br>**1 Peter 2:1**<br>Wherefore laying aside all malice, and all guile, and **hypocrisies**, and envies, and all evil speakings, [KJV]<br>Therefore, putting aside all malice and all guile and **hypocrisy** and envy and all slander, [NASB]<br>Therefore, rid yourselves of all malice and all deceit, **hypocrisy**, envy, and slander of every kind. [NIV]<br>Therefore, laying aside all malice, all deceit, **hypocrisy**, envy, and all evil speaking, [NKJV]<br>So get rid of all malicious behavior and deceit. Don't just pretend to be good! Be done with **hypocrisy** and jealousy and backstabbing. [NLT]<br>Ἀποθέμενοι οὖν πᾶσαν κακίαν καὶ πάντα δόλον καὶ **ὑποκρίσεις** καὶ φθόνους καὶ πάσας καταλαλιάς, [GNS]<br>Ἀποθέμενοι οὖν πᾶσαν κακίαν καὶ πάντα δόλον καὶ **ὑποκρίσεις** καὶ φθόνους καὶ πάσας καταλαλιάς, [GNT] | Hypocrisy, insincerity, pretense. The word means one who pretends, puts on a show, acts out something he is not.<br><br>**Practical Application**<br>At first the word simply meant one who replied or answered another person. Then it came to mean acting, as actors play-acted the lines of a scene. Finally, the word was used in the worst sense: play-acting, pretending; one who wore a mask to hide his real self; one who acted one way, but who was really another way; one who put on an outward show.<br>Note that the plural is used. All kinds of hypocrisies are meant. A person is a hypocrite...<br>• when he acts as though he loves and believes God, but he does not live like God tells him to live.<br>• when he pretends to be following God, but he is living like he wants to live.<br>• when he shows a concern for the things of God, but his real concern is for the things of the world.<br>• when he professes to believe God's Word, but he questions it and adds and takes away from it.<br>• when he acts as though he cares for people, but he is really full of selfishness, self-seeking, possessiveness, hoarding, envy, and pride.<br>• when he courts friends, but he is after something.<br>• when he acts friendly, but he could care less.<br>• when he promises, but he never intends to keep his promise. |
| **#2054**<br>**Hypocrisy,**<br>**Without**<br><br>Without dissimulation–<br>KJV<br>**Without hypocrisy–**<br>**NASB**<br>Sincere–NIV | ἀνυπόκριτος = *anupokritos*<br>Pronunciation: [an-oo-pok'-ree-tos]<br>Parsing (part of speech): adjective<br>    Case—nominative<br>    Gender—feminine<br>    Number—singular<br>    Stem or root—from ἀνυπόκριτος, ον<br>Concordance References:<br>  ⇒ Strong's #505 anupokritos<br>  ⇒ NIV #537 anupokritos<br>  ⇒ NASB #505 anupokritos | To be sincere; to be genuine. It means without hypocrisy, without play-acting. This means to be free from insincerity, hypocrisy, play-acting, and wearing a mask.<br><br>**Practical Application**<br>The believer is to love sincerely without hypocrisy (*anupokritos*). It means that a person does not just say "I love you," but he actually loves. He sincerely loves; he honestly and truth- |

# PRACTICAL WORD STUDIES
## in the NEW TESTAMENT

| ENGLISH WORD | GREEK WORD AND VERSE | THE WORD MEANS... |
|---|---|---|
| **Without hypocrisy–NKJV**<br>Don't just pretend–NLT<br><br>**POSB REFERENCE**<br>(Rom.12:9-10; esp. v.9)<br>Note 1<br><br>See also POSB REF:<br>(1 Pt.1:22-25; esp. v.22)<br>Note 1<br>(Jas.3:17-18; esp. v.17)<br>Note 3 | **Romans 12:9**<br>Let love be **without dissimulation**. Abhor that which is evil; cleave to that which is good. [KJV]<br>Let love be **without hypocrisy**. Abhor what is evil; cling to what is good. [NASB]<br>Love must be **sincere**. Hate what is evil; cling to what is good. [NIV]<br>Let love *be* **without hypocrisy**. Abhor what is evil. Cling to what is good. [NKJV]<br>**Don't just pretend** that you love others. Really love them. Hate what is wrong. Stand on the side of the good. [NLT]<br>Ἡ ἀγάπη **ἀνυπόκριτος**. ἀποστυγοῦντες τὸ πονηρόν, κολλώμενοι τῷ ἀγαθῷ. [GNS]<br>Ἡ ἀγάπη **ἀνυπόκριτος**. ἀποστυγοῦντες τὸ πονηρόν, κολλώμενοι τῷ ἀγαθῷ, [GNT] | fully loves. The love being spoken about is love for all men and not only for believers. The believer must never pretend, be hypocritical, play-act, or have an ulterior motive when dealing with others. He must show love and respect, interest and attention, care and concern; but he must not show it from an impure motive: |
| **#2055**<br>**Hypocrites**<br><br>Hypocrites–KJV<br>Hypocrites–NASB<br>Hypocrites–NIV<br>Hypocrites–NKJV<br>Hypocrites–NLT<br><br>**POSB REFERENCE**<br>(Mt.6:2)<br>Note 2, point 2 | ὑποκριταί = *hupokritai*<br>Pronunciation: [hoop-ok-ree-tah-ee]<br>Parsing (part of speech): noun<br>    Case—nominative<br>    Gender—masculine<br>    Number—plural<br>    Stem or root—from ὑποκριτής, οῦ<br>Concordance References:<br>  ⇒ Strong's #5273 hupokritēs<br>  ⇒ NIV #5695 hupokritēs<br>  ⇒ NASB #5273 hupokritēs<br><br>**Matthew 6:2**<br>Therefore when thou doest thine alms, do not sound a trumpet before thee, as the **hypocrites** do in the synagogues and in the streets, that they may have glory of men. Verily I say unto you, They have their reward. [KJV]<br>"When therefore you give alms, do not sound a trumpet before you, as the **hypocrites** do in the synagogues and in the streets, that they may be honored by men. Truly I say to you, they have their reward in full. [NASB]<br>"So when you give to the needy, do not announce it with trumpets, as the **hypocrites** do in the synagogues and on the streets, to be honored by men. I tell you the truth, they have received their reward in full. [NIV]<br>Therefore, when you do a charitable deed, do not sound a trumpet before you as the **hypocrites** do in the synagogues and in the streets, that they may have glory from men. Assuredly, I say to you, they have their reward. [NKJV]<br>When you give a gift to someone in need, don't shout about it as the **hypocrites** do—blowing trumpets in the synagogues and streets to call attention to their acts of charity! I assure you, they have received all the reward they will ever get. [NLT]<br>Ὅταν οὖν ποιῇς ἐλεημοσύνην, μὴ σαλπίσῃς ἔμπροσθέν σου, ὥσπερ οἱ **ὑποκριταί** ποιοῦσιν ἐν ταῖς συναγωγαῖς καὶ ἐν ταῖς ῥύμαις, ὅπως δοξασθῶσιν ὑπὸ τῶν ἀνθρώπων· ἀμὴν λέγω ὑμῖν, ἀπέχουσι τὸν μισθὸν αὐτῶν. [GNS]<br>Ὅταν οὖν ποιῇς ἐλεημοσύνην, μὴ σαλπίσῃς ἔμπροσθέν σου, ὥσπερ οἱ **ὑποκριταί** ποιοῦσιν ἐν ταῖς συναγωγαῖς καὶ ἐν ταῖς ῥύμαις, ὅπως δοξασθῶσιν ὑπὸ τῶν ἀνθρώπων· ἀμὴν λέγω ὑμῖν, ἀπέχουσιν τὸν μισθὸν αὐτῶν. [GNT] | A pretender, a deceiver, an impostor, a fake.<br><br>**Practical Application**<br>The root meaning of the word pictures an actor who puts on a show, who plays a part on stage. It means to wear a mask, to present a fake picture, to appear to be something one is not. |
| **#2056**<br>**Hypocrites**<br><br>Hypocrites–KJV<br>Hypocrites–NASB<br>Hypocrites–NIV<br>Hypocrites–NKJV<br>Hypocrites–NLT | ὑποκριταί = *hupokritai*<br>Pronunciation: [hoop-ok-ree-tah-ee']<br>Parsing (part of speech): noun<br>    Case—vocative<br>    Gender—masculine<br>    Number—plural<br>    Stem or root—from ὑποκριτής, οῦ<br>Concordance References:<br>  ⇒ Strong's #5273 hupokritēs<br>  ⇒ NIV #5695 hupokritēs<br>  ⇒ NASB #5273 hupokritēs | One who pretends, puts on a show, acts out something he is not.<br><br>**Practical Application**<br>At first the word simply meant one who replied or answered. Then it came to mean acting, as actors play-acted the lines of a scene. Finally, the word was used in the worst sense: play-acting; pretending; one who wore a mask to hide his real self; one who acted one way, but who was really another way; one who put on an |

# PRACTICAL WORD STUDIES
## in the NEW TESTAMENT

| ENGLISH WORD | GREEK WORD AND VERSE | THE WORD MEANS |
|---|---|---|
| **POSB REFERENCE** (Mt.23:13) *Deeper Study #2* | **Matthew 23:13**<br>But woe unto you, scribes and Pharisees, **hypocrites**! for ye shut up the kingdom of heaven against men: for ye neither go in yourselves, neither suffer ye them that are entering to go in. [KJV]<br><br>"But woe to you, scribes and Pharisees, **hypocrites**, because you shut off the kingdom of heaven from men; for you do not enter in yourselves, nor do you allow those who are entering to go in. [NASB]<br><br>"Woe to you, teachers of the law and Pharisees, you **hypocrites**! You shut the kingdom of heaven in men's faces. You yourselves do not enter, nor will you let those enter who are trying to. [NIV]<br><br>But woe to you, scribes and Pharisees, **hypocrites**! For you shut up the kingdom of heaven against men; for you neither go in yourselves, nor do you allow those who are entering to go in. [NKJV]<br><br>"How terrible it will be for you teachers of religious law and you Pharisees. **Hypocrites**! For you won't let others enter the Kingdom of Heaven, and you won't go in yourselves. [NLT]<br><br>Οὐαὶ δὲ ὑμῖν, γραμματεῖς καὶ Φαρισαῖοι **ὑποκριταί**, ὅτι κλείετε τὴν βασιλείαν τῶν οὐρανῶν ἔμπροσθεν τῶν ἀνθρώπων· ὑμεῖς γὰρ οὐκ εἰσέρχεσθε, οὐδὲ τοὺς εἰσερχομένους ἀφίετε εἰσελθεῖν. [GNS]<br><br>Οὐαὶ δὲ ὑμῖν, γραμματεῖς καὶ Φαρισαῖοι **ὑποκριταί**, ὅτι κλείετε τὴν βασιλείαν τῶν οὐρανῶν ἔμπροσθεν τῶν ἀνθρώπων· ὑμεῖς γὰρ οὐκ εἰσέρχεσθε οὐδὲ τοὺς εἰσερχομένους ἀφίετε εἰσελθεῖν. [GNT] | outward show.<br>The religionists, the Scribes and Pharisees, were hypocrites.<br>⇒ They acted as though they believed and loved God, yet they did not accept God's Son.<br>⇒ They pretended to be seeking God; but they were really seeking profession, esteem, recognition, honor, position, power, and security (see POSB notes—Matthew 12:1-8; POSB note—Matthew 12:10 and POSB *Deeper Study #1*—Matthew 12:10).<br>⇒ They showed a concern for the things of God, but they were really concerned with the things of this world.<br>⇒ They acted humble and helpful; but they were really full of pride, envy, possessiveness, selfishness, and covetousness.<br>⇒ They claimed to be ministers of God's religion; but they were really ministers of a man-made religion, a religion that honored man's ability to *be good* and to do enough good to become acceptable to God.<br>⇒ They professed God's Word, but they added to and took away from it. |

# Practical Word Studies
## In the New Testament

| ENGLISH WORD | GREEK WORD AND VERSE | THE WORD MEANS |
|---|---|---|
| **POSE**<br>**REFERENCE**<br>(Mt 23:13)<br>*(Deeper Study #2)* | **Matthew 23:13**<br>But woe unto you, scribes and Pharisees, hypocrites! for ye shut up the kingdom of heaven against men: for ye neither go in yourselves, neither suffer ye them that are entering to go in. [KJV]<br><br>"But woe to you, scribes and Pharisees, hypocrites, because you shut off the kingdom of heaven from men; for you do not enter in yourselves, nor do you allow those who are entering to go in. [NASB]<br><br>Woe to you, teachers of the law and Pharisees, you hypocrites! You shut the kingdom of heaven in men's face. You yourselves do not enter, nor will you let those enter who are trying to. [NIV]<br><br>But woe to you, scribes and Pharisees, hypocrites! For you shut up the kingdom of heaven against men; for you neither go in yourselves, nor do you allow those who are entering to go in. [NKJV]<br><br>"How terrible it will be for you teachers of religious law and you Pharisees. Hypocrites! For you won't let others enter the Kingdom of Heaven, and you won't go in yourselves. [NLT]<br><br>Οὐαὶ δὲ ὑμῖν, γραμματεῖς καὶ Φαρισαῖοι ὑποκριταί, ὅτι κλείετε τὴν βασιλείαν τῶν οὐρανῶν ἔμπροσθεν τῶν ἀνθρώπων· ὑμεῖς γὰρ οὐκ εἰσέρχεσθε, οὐδὲ τοὺς εἰσερχομένους ἀφίετε εἰσελθεῖν. [GNT] | outward show<br>⇒ The religionists, the Scribes and Pharisees, were hypocrites.<br>⇒ They acted as though they believed and loved God, yet they did not accept God's Son.<br>⇒ They pretended to be seeking God, but they were really seeking: profession, esteem, recognition, honor, position, power, and security (see POSB refer.—Matthew 12:1-8; POSB note—Matthew 12:10 and POSB Deeper Study #1—Matthew 12:10).<br>⇒ They showed a concern for the things of God, but they were really concerned with the things of this world.<br>⇒ They acted humble and helpful, but they were really full of pride, envy, possessiveness, selfishness, and covetousness.<br>⇒ They claimed to be ministers of God's religion, but they were really ministers of a man-made religion, a religion that honored man's ability to be good and to do enough good to become acceptable to God.<br>⇒ They professed God's Word, but they added to and took away from it. |

# PRACTICAL WORD STUDIES
## in the NEW TESTAMENT

| ENGLISH WORD | GREEK WORD AND VERSE | THE WORD MEANS... |
|---|---|---|
| **#2057**<br>**I Am**<br><br>I am–KJV<br>I am–NASB<br>I am–NIV<br>I am–NKJV<br>I am–NLT<br><br>**POSB REFERENCE**<br>(Mk.14:62)<br>Note 5, point 1<br><br>See also POSB REF:<br>(Lk.21:8)<br>Note 2, point 2a | Ἐγώ εἰμι = ego eimi<br>Pronunciation: [eg-o' i-mee']<br>Parsing ego (part of speech): noun<br>    Type—pronoun<br>    Case—nominative<br>    Person—1st person<br>    Number—singular<br>    Stem or root—from ἐγώ<br>Parsing eimi (part of speech): verb<br>    Mood—indicative<br>    Tense—present<br>    Voice—active<br>    Person—1st person<br>    Number—singular<br>    Stem or root—from εἰμί<br>Concordance References:<br> ⇒ Strong's #1473 egō + 1510 eimi<br> ⇒ NIV #1609 egō [I] 1639 eimi [am]<br> ⇒ NASB #1473 egō + 1510 eimi<br><br>**Mark 14:62**<br>And Jesus said, **I am**: and ye shall see the Son of man sitting on the right hand of power, and coming in the clouds of heaven. [KJV]<br>And Jesus said, "**I am**; and you shall see the Son of Man sitting at the right hand of Power, and coming with the clouds of heaven." [NASB]<br>"**I am**," said Jesus. "And you will see the Son of Man sitting at the right hand of the Mighty One and coming on the clouds of heaven." [NIV]<br>Jesus said, "**I am**. And you will see the Son of Man sitting at the right hand of the Power, and coming with the clouds of heaven." [NKJV]<br>Jesus said, "**I am**, and you will see me, the Son of Man, sitting at God's right hand in the place of power and coming back on the clouds of heaven." [NLT]<br>ὁ δὲ Ἰησοῦς εἶπεν, Ἐγώ εἰμι. καὶ ὄψεσθε τὸν υἱὸν τοῦ ἀνθρώπου καθήμενον ἐκ δεξιῶν τῆς δυνάμεως, καὶ ἐρχόμενον μετὰ τῶν νεφελῶν τοῦ οὐρανοῦ. [GNS]<br>ὁ δὲ Ἰησοῦς εἶπεν, Ἐγώ εἰμι, καὶ ὄψεσθε τὸν υἱὸν τοῦ ἀνθρώπου ἐκ δεξιῶν καθήμενον τῆς δυνάμεως καὶ ἐρχόμενον μετὰ τῶν νεφελῶν τοῦ οὐρανοῦ. [GNT] | The self-existent, eternal One (see POSB Deeper Study #1—John 6:20; POSB note—John 18:4-6).<br><br>**Practical Application**<br>Jesus was saying, "I AM" has come—fear not. He was reminding the disciples who He was, the Son of God Himself. He possessed all power; therefore, there was no need to fear. This was the same message that God gave to Moses at the burning bush, "I am where I am" (Exodus 3:13-15, esp. Exodus 3:14). It was the same message that Jesus used as a defense against the religionists, "Before Abraham was, I am" (John 8:58). It is the same message that Col. 1:15-17 claims for Him; it is the same message that is proclaimed by the book of Revelation, "He that is, and was, and is to come" (Rev. 1:4, 8; Rev. 11:17; Rev. 16:5). (See note—John 1:1-2.)<br>There are several "I Am's" claimed by Christ.<br>⇒ I Am the Messiah (John 4:26).<br>⇒ I Am (It is I); be not afraid (John 6:20).<br>⇒ I Am the Bread of Life (John 6:35).<br>⇒ I Am from Above (John 8:23).<br>⇒ I Am the Light of the World (John 8:12; John 9:5; John 12:46).<br>⇒ I Am before Abraham was, I am (eternal) (John 8:58).<br>⇒ I Am the Door (John 10:7).<br>⇒ I Am the Good Shepherd (John 10:14).<br>⇒ I Am the Son of God (John 10:36).<br>⇒ I Am the Resurrection and the Life (John 11:25).<br>⇒ I Am the Lord and Master (John 13:13).<br>⇒ I Am the Way, the Truth, and the Life (John 14:6).<br>⇒ I Am the True Vine (John 15:1).<br>⇒ I Am Alpha and Omega (Rev. 1:8).<br>⇒ I Am the First and the Last (Rev. 1:17). |
| **#2058**<br>**I Am Here**<br><br>It is I–KJV<br>It is I–NASB<br>It is I–NIV<br>It is I–NKJV<br>I am here–NLT<br><br>**POSB REFERENCE**<br>(Jn.6:20)<br>Deeper Study #1 | Ἐγώ εἰμι = Egō eimi<br>Pronunciation: [ay-go ee-mee]<br>Parsing Egō (part of speech):<br>    Type—pronoun<br>    Case—nominative<br>    Person—1st person<br>    Number—singular<br>    Stem or root—from ἐγώ<br>Parsing eimi (part of speech): verb<br>    Mood—indicative<br>    Tense—present<br>    Voice—active<br>    Person—1st person<br>    Number—singular<br>    Stem or root—from εἰμί<br>Concordance References:<br> ⇒ Strong's #1473 egō + 1510 eimi<br> ⇒ NIV #1609 egō [I] 1639 eimi [am]<br> ⇒ NASB #1473 egō + 1510 eimi<br><br>**John 6:20**<br>But he saith unto them, **It is I**; be not afraid. [KJV]<br>But He said to them, "**It is I**; do not be afraid." [NASB]<br>But he said to them, "**It is I**; don't be afraid." [NIV]<br>But He said to them, "**It is I**; do not be afraid." [NKJV]<br>But he called out to them, "**I am here**! Don't be afraid." [NLT]<br>ὁ δὲ λέγει αὐτοῖς, Ἐγώ εἰμι, μὴ φοβεῖσθε. [GNS]<br>ὁ δὲ λέγει αὐτοῖς, Ἐγώ εἰμι, μὴ φοβεῖσθε. [GNT] | It is I; I am here; I AM.<br><br>**Practical Application**<br>Jesus was saying, "I AM" has come—fear not. He was reminding the disciples who He was, the Son of God Himself. He possessed all power; therefore, there was no need to fear. This was the same message that God gave to Moses at the burning bush, "I am that I am" (Exodus 3:13-15, esp. Exodus 3:14). It was the same message that Jesus used as a defense against the religionists, "Before Abraham was, I am" (John 8:58). It is the same message that Col. 1:15-17 claims for Him; it is the same message that is proclaimed by the book of Revelation, "the One who is and who was, because you have taken your great power and have begun to reign" (Rev. 1:4, 8; Rev. 11:17; Rev. 16:5). (See POSB note—John 1:1-2.) |

# PRACTICAL WORD STUDIES
## in the NEW TESTAMENT

| ENGLISH WORD | GREEK WORD AND VERSE | THE WORD MEANS... |
|---|---|---|
| **#2059**<br>**I Decided**<br><br>I determined–KJV<br>I determined–NASB<br>I resolved–NIV<br>I determined–NKJV<br>**I decided–NLT**<br><br>**POSB REFERENCE**<br>(1 Cor.2:2)<br>Note 2 | ἔκρινά = *ekrina*<br>Pronunciation: [eh-kree-nah']<br>Parsing (part of speech): verb<br>　Mood—indicative<br>　Tense—aorist<br>　Voice—active<br>　Person—1st person<br>　Number—singular<br>　Stem or root—from κρίνω<br>Concordance References:<br>　⇒ Strong's #2919 krinö<br>　⇒ NIV #3212 krinö<br>　⇒ NASB #2919 krinö<br><br>**1 Cor. 2:2**<br>　For **I determined** not to know any thing among you, save Jesus Christ, and him crucified. [KJV]<br>　For **I determined** to know nothing among you except Jesus Christ, and Him crucified. [NASB]<br>　For **I resolved** to know nothing while I was with you except Jesus Christ and him crucified. [NIV]<br>　For **I determined** not to know anything among you except Jesus Christ and Him crucified. [NKJV]<br>　For **I decided** to concentrate only on Jesus Christ and his death on the cross. [NLT]<br>　οὐ γὰρ **ἔκρινά** τι εἰδέναι ἐν ὑμῖν, εἰ μὴ Ἰησοῦν Χριστὸν, καὶ τοῦτον ἐσταυρωμένον. [GNS]<br>　οὐ γὰρ **ἔκρινά** τι εἰδέναι ἐν ὑμῖν εἰ μὴ Ἰησοῦν Χριστὸν καὶ τοῦτον ἐσταυρωμένον. [GNT] | To have resolved; to have determined; to have decided; to have made a decision.<br><br>**Practical Application**<br>Paul made a deliberate decision, a strong determination to preach only Jesus Christ and Him crucified. |
| **#2060**<br>**I Determined**<br><br>**I determined–KJV**<br>**I determined–NASB**<br>I resolved–NIV<br>**I determined–NKJV**<br>I decided–NLT<br><br>**POSB REFERENCE**<br>(1 Cor.2:2)<br>Note 2 | ἔκρινά = *ekrina*<br>Pronunciation: [eh-kree-nah']<br>Parsing (part of speech): verb<br>　Mood—indicative<br>　Tense—aorist<br>　Voice—active<br>　Person—1st person<br>　Number—singular<br>　Stem or root—from κρίνω<br>Concordance References:<br>　⇒ Strong's #2919 krinö<br>　⇒ NIV #3212 krinö<br>　⇒ NASB #2919 krinö<br><br>**1 Cor. 2:2**<br>　For **I determined** not to know any thing among you, save Jesus Christ, and him crucified. [KJV]<br>　For **I determined** to know nothing among you except Jesus Christ, and Him crucified. [NASB]<br>　For **I resolved** to know nothing while I was with you except Jesus Christ and him crucified. [NIV]<br>　For **I determined** not to know anything among you except Jesus Christ and Him crucified. [NKJV]<br>　For **I decided** to concentrate only on Jesus Christ and his death on the cross. [NLT]<br>　οὐ γὰρ **ἔκρινά** τι εἰδέναι ἐν ὑμῖν, εἰ μὴ Ἰησοῦν Χριστὸν, καὶ τοῦτον ἐσταυρωμένον. [GNS]<br>　οὐ γὰρ **ἔκρινά** τι εἰδέναι ἐν ὑμῖν εἰ μὴ Ἰησοῦν Χριστὸν καὶ τοῦτον ἐσταυρωμένον. [GNT] | To have resolved; to have determined; to have decided; to have made a decision.<br><br>**Practical Application**<br>Paul made a deliberate decision, a strong determination to preach only Jesus Christ and Him crucified. |
| **#2061**<br>**I Had Been Born At The Wrong Time**<br><br>One born out of due time–KJV<br>One untimely born–NASB<br>One abnormally born–NIV | τῷ ἐκτρώματι = *tō ektrōmati*<br>Pronunciation: [tow ek'-tro-mah-tee]<br>Parsing *ektrōmati* (part of speech): noun<br>　Case—dative<br>　Gender—neuter<br>　Number—singular<br>　Stem or root—from ἔκτρωμα, τος<br>Concordance References:<br>　⇒ Strong's #3588 ho + 1626 ektröma<br>　⇒ NIV #3836 ho [one] +1765 ektröma [abnormally born]<br>　⇒ NASB #3588 ho + 1626 ektröma | A miscarriage, an abortion, an unnatural birth, a child born out of time; born at the wrong time.<br><br>**Practical Application**<br>Paul is simply saying that he did not follow the Lord when the Lord walked upon the earth, but he saw and began to follow the Lord after He had left the earth, after His ascension into heaven. Paul is, of course, referring to his experience on the Damascus road (Acts 9:1f), and perhaps to the visions granted him (2 Cor. 12:1f). |

## Practical Word Studies in the New Testament

| ENGLISH WORD | GREEK WORD AND VERSE | THE WORD MEANS... |
|---|---|---|
| One born out of due time–NKJV<br>**I had been born at the wrong time–NLT**<br><br>**POSB REFERENCE**<br>(1 Cor.15:8-10; esp. v.8)<br>Note 5 | **1 Cor. 15:8**<br>And last of all he was seen of me also, as of **one born out of due time**. [KJV]<br>And last of all, as it were to **one untimely born**, He appeared to me also. [NASB]<br>And last of all he appeared to me also, as to **one abnormally born**. [NIV]<br>Then last of all He was seen by me also, as by **one born out of due time**. [NKJV]<br>Last of all, I saw him, too, long after the others, as though **I had been born at the wrong time**. [NLT]<br>ἔσχατον δὲ πάντων ὡσπερεὶ τῷ **ἐκτρώματι** ὤφθη κἀμοί. [GNS]<br>ἔσχατον δὲ πάντων ὡσπερεὶ τῷ **ἐκτρώματι** ὤφθη κἀμοί. [GNT] | |
| **#2062**<br>**I Resolved**<br><br>I determined–KJV<br>I determined–NASB<br>**I resolved–NIV**<br>I determined–NKJV<br>I decided–NLT<br><br>**POSB REFERENCE**<br>(1 Cor.2:2)<br>Note 2 | **ἔκρινά** = ekrina<br>Pronunciation: [eh-kree-nah']<br>Parsing (part of speech): verb<br>  Mood—indicative<br>  Tense—aorist<br>  Voice—active<br>  Person—1st person<br>  Number—singular<br>  Stem or root—from κρίνω<br>Concordance References:<br>  ⇒ Strong's #2919 krinö<br>  ⇒ NIV #3212 krinö<br>  ⇒ NASB #2919 krinö<br><br>**1 Cor. 2:2**<br>For **I determined** not to know any thing among you, save Jesus Christ, and him crucified. [KJV]<br>For **I determined** to know nothing among you except Jesus Christ, and Him crucified. [NASB]<br>For **I resolved** to know nothing while I was with you except Jesus Christ and him crucified. [NIV]<br>For **I determined** not to know anything among you except Jesus Christ and Him crucified. [NKJV]<br>For **I decided** to concentrate only on Jesus Christ and his death on the cross. [NLT]<br>οὐ γὰρ **ἔκρινά** τι εἰδέναι ἐν ὑμῖν, εἰ μὴ Ἰησοῦν Χριστὸν, καὶ τοῦτον ἐσταυρωμένον. [GNS]<br>οὐ γὰρ **ἔκρινά** τι εἰδέναι ἐν ὑμῖν εἰ μὴ Ἰησοῦν Χριστὸν καὶ τοῦτον ἐσταυρωμένον. [GNT] | To have resolved; to have determined; to have decided; to have made a decision.<br><br>**Practical Application**<br>Paul made a deliberate decision, a strong determination to preach only Jesus Christ and Him crucified. |
| **#2063**<br>**Ideas**<br><br>Imaginations–KJV<br>Speculations–NASB<br>Thinking–NIV<br>Thoughts–NKJV<br>**Ideas–NLT**<br><br>**POSB REFERENCE**<br>(Romans 1:21)<br>Note 4, point 1 | **διαλογισμοῖς** = dialogismois<br>Pronunciation: [dee-al-og-is-mo-ees']<br>Parsing (part of speech): noun<br>  Case—dative<br>  Gender—masculine<br>  Number—plural<br>  Stem or root—from διαλογισμός, οῦ<br>Concordance References:<br>  ⇒ Strong's #1261 dialogismos<br>  ⇒ NIV #1369 dialogismos<br>  ⇒ NASB #1261 dialogismos<br><br>**Romans 1:21**<br>Because that, when they knew God, they glorified him not as God, neither were thankful; but became vain in their **imaginations**, and their foolish heart was darkened. [KJV]<br>For even though they knew God, they did not honor Him as God, or give thanks; but they became futile in their **speculations**, and their foolish heart was darkened. [NASB]<br>For although they knew God, they neither glorified him as God nor gave thanks to him, but their **thinking** became futile and their foolish hearts were darkened. [NIV]<br>Because, although they knew God, they did not glorify *Him* as God, nor were thankful, but became futile in | Thoughts, opinions, motives, reasonings; doubts, questions; arguments, disputes, deliberations, conclusions, speculations.<br><br>**Practical Application**<br>When men push God out of their minds, their minds are void and empty of God. God is not in their thoughts. (Cp. Psalm 10:4.) Their minds are ready to be *filled* with some other *god* or *supremacy*. |

# Practical Word Studies
## in the New Testament

| ENGLISH WORD | GREEK WORD AND VERSE | THE WORD MEANS... |
|---|---|---|
| | their **thoughts**, and their foolish hearts were darkened. [NKJV]<br><br>Yes, they knew God, but they wouldn't worship him as God or even give him thanks. And they began to think up foolish **ideas** of what God was like. The result was that their minds became dark and confused. [NLT]<br><br>διότι γνόντες τὸν Θεὸν οὐχ ὡς Θεὸν ἐδόξασαν ἢ ηὐχαρίστησαν, ἀλλ' ἐματαιώθησαν ἐν τοῖς **διαλογισμοῖς** αὐτῶν, καὶ ἐσκοτίσθη ἡ ἀσύνετος αὐτῶν καρδία. [GNS]<br><br>διότι γνόντες τὸν θεὸν οὐχ ὡς θεὸν ἐδόξασαν ἢ ηὐχαρίστησαν, ἀλλ' ἐματαιώθησαν ἐν τοῖς **διαλογισμοῖς** αὐτῶν καὶ ἐσκοτίσθη ἡ ἀσύνετος αὐτῶν καρδία. [GNT] | |
| **#2064**<br>**Identified Us As His Own**<br><br>Sealed–KJV<br>Sealed–NASB<br>Set...seal of ownership on–NIV<br>Sealed–NKJV<br>**Identified us as his own–NLT**<br><br>**POSB REFERENCE**<br>(2 Cor.1:21-22; esp. v.22)<br>Note 5 | σφραγισάμενος =sphragisamenos<br>Pronunciation: [sfrag-is'-ah-mehn-os]<br>Parsing (part of speech): verb<br>  Mood—participle<br>  Tense—aorist<br>  Voice—middle<br>  Case—nominative<br>  Gender—masculine<br>  Number—singular<br>  Stem or root—from σφραγίζω<br>Concordance References:<br>⇒ Strong's #4972 sphragizō<br>⇒ NIV #5381 sphragizō<br>⇒ NASB #4972 sphragizō<br><br>**2 Cor. 1:22**<br>Who hath also **sealed** us, and given the earnest of the Spirit in our hearts. [KJV]<br>Who also **sealed** us and gave us the Spirit in our hearts as a pledge. [NASB]<br>**Set** his **seal of ownership on** us, and put his Spirit in our hearts as a deposit, guaranteeing what is to come. [NIV]<br>Who also has **sealed** us and given us the Spirit in our hearts as a guarantee. [NKJV]<br>And he has **identified us as his own** by placing the Holy Spirit in our hearts as the first installment of everything he will give us. [NLT]<br><br>ὁ καὶ **σφραγισάμενος** ἡμᾶς, καὶ δοὺς τὸν ἀρραβῶνα τοῦ Πνεύματος ἐν ταῖς καρδίαις ἡμῶν. [GNS]<br>ὁ καὶ **σφραγισάμενος** ἡμᾶς καὶ δοὺς τὸν ἀρραβῶνα τοῦ πνεύματος ἐν ταῖς καρδίαις ἡμῶν. [GNT] | To set a seal of ownership on; to mark; to stamp; to set apart by a seal; to place a seal upon.<br><br>**Practical Application**<br>God places His seal, His stamp, His mark upon believers. Paul was just as much in Christ and anointed as others. The word "us" refers primarily to Paul. He is comparing himself with the Corinthians, and he is also including those who oppose him. In no uncertain terms, Paul says that the same God who has worked in the Corinthians has also worked in him. |
| **#2065**<br>**Idle**<br><br>Idle–KJV<br>Careless–NASB<br>Careless–NIV<br>Idle–NKJV<br>Idle–NLT<br><br>**POSB REFERENCE**<br>(Mt.12:36)<br>*Deeper Study #1* | ἀργόν = argon<br>Pronunciation: [ar-gon]<br>Parsing (part of speech): adjective<br>  Case—accusative<br>  Gender—neuter<br>  Number—singular<br>  Stem or root—from ἀργός, ή, όν<br>Concordance References:<br>⇒ Strong's #692 argos<br>⇒ NIV #734 argos<br>⇒ NASB #692 argos<br><br>**Matthew 12:36**<br>But I say unto you, That every **idle** word that men shall speak, they shall give account thereof in the day of judgment. [KJV]<br>"And I say to you, that every **careless** word that men shall speak, they shall render account for it in the day of judgment. Matthew 12:36 [NASB]<br>But I tell you that men will have to give account on the day of judgment for every **careless** word they have spoken. [NIV]<br>But I say to you that for every **idle** word men may speak, they will give account of it in the day of judgment. [NKJV]<br>And I tell you this, that you must give an account on judgment day of every **idle** word you speak. [NLT] | Careless, idle, negative, irresponsible, worthless, useless, unfruitful, barren, ineffective, idle word.<br><br>**Practical Application**<br>In this Scripture, the term "idle words" conveys very well what Christ means. Note several lessons:<br>1. God hears and records every careless, idle word that we speak. (Psalm 139:4)<br>2. Unprofitable words make us, and show us to be, unprofitable servants.<br>3. Our idle words must be confessed to God and His mercy must be requested, for we are guilty of this unprofitable and wasteful sin.<br>4. Scripture flows with charge after charge governing the tongue. (cp. Romans 14:19; 1 Cor. 14:26; Ephes. 5:3-4; 1 Thes. 5:11; Job 15:3) |

## PRACTICAL WORD STUDIES in the NEW TESTAMENT

| ENGLISH WORD | GREEK WORD AND VERSE | THE WORD MEANS... |
|---|---|---|
| | λέγω δὲ ὑμῖν, ὅτι πᾶν ῥῆμα **ἀργὸν** ὃ ἐὰν λαλήσωσιν οἱ ἄνθρωποι, ἀποδώσουσι περὶ αὐτοῦ λόγον ἐν ἡμέρᾳ κρίσεως. [GNS]<br>λέγω δὲ ὑμῖν ὅτι πᾶν ῥῆμα **ἀργὸν** ὃ λαλήσουσιν οἱ ἄνθρωποι ἀποδώσουσιν περὶ αὐτοῦ λόγον ἐν ἡμέρᾳ κρίσεως· [GNT] | |
| **#2066**<br>**Idle Babblings**<br><br>Vain babblings–KJV<br>Empty chatter–NASB<br>Chatter–NIV<br>**Idle babblings–NKJV**<br>Foolish discussions–NLT<br><br>**POSB REFERENCE**<br>(1 Tim.6:20)<br>Note 2, point 2a | κενοφωνίας = kenophōnias<br>Pronunciation: [ken-of-o-nee'-ahs]<br>Parsing (part of speech): noun<br>   Case—accusative<br>   Gender—feminine<br>   Number—plural<br>   Stem or root—from κενοφωνία, ας<br>Concordance References:<br>  ⇒ Strong's #2757 kenophōnia<br>  ⇒ NIV #3032 kenophōnia<br>  ⇒ NASB #2757 kenophōnia<br><br>**1 Tim. 6:20**<br>O Timothy, keep that which is committed to thy trust, avoiding profane and **vain babblings**, and oppositions of science falsely so called: [KJV]<br>O Timothy, guard what has been entrusted to you, avoiding worldly and **empty chatter** and the opposing arguments of what is falsely called "knowledge"— [NASB]<br>Timothy, guard what has been entrusted to your care. Turn away from godless **chatter** and the opposing ideas of what is falsely called knowledge, [NIV]<br>O Timothy! Guard what was committed to your trust, avoiding the profane *and* **idle babblings** and contradictions of what is falsely called knowledge—[NKJV]<br>Timothy, guard what God has entrusted to you. Avoid godless, **foolish discussions** with those who oppose you with their so-called knowledge. [NLT]<br>Ὦ Τιμόθεε, τὴν παρακαταθήκην φύλαξον, ἐκτρεπόμενος τὰς βεβήλους **κενοφωνίας** καὶ ἀντιθέσεις τῆς ψευδωνύμου γνώσεως· [GNS]<br>Ὦ Τιμόθεε, τὴν παραθήκην φύλαξον ἐκτρεπόμενος τὰς βεβήλους **κενοφωνίας** καὶ ἀντιθέσεις τῆς ψευδωνύμου γνώσεως, [GNT] | Chatter; vain babblings; empty chatter; foolish discussions; foolish talk.<br><br>**Practical Application**<br>The charge is to take all *empty talk* and turn away from it. Have absolutely nothing to do with common, irreverent, godless, and *empty voices*—no matter who is sounding forth the words. This would, of course, include...<br>⇒ false claims to truth<br>⇒ worldly philosophy<br>⇒ cursing<br>⇒ criticism<br>⇒ suggestive talk<br>⇒ all forms of false teaching<br>⇒ novel ideas of religion<br>⇒ gossip<br>⇒ off-colored jokes |
| **#2067**<br>**Idle Tales**<br><br>Idle tales–KJV<br>As nonsense–NASB<br>Like nonsense–NIV<br>**Idle tales–NKJV**<br>Like nonsense–NLT<br><br>**POSB REFERENCE**<br>(Lk.24:9-11; esp. v.11)<br>Note 6 | ὡσεὶ λῆρος = hōsei lēros<br>Pronunciation: [ho-seh-ee]<br>Parsing *hōsei* (part of speech): conjunction<br>   Type—subordinating<br>   Stem or root—from ὡσεί<br>Parsing *lēros* (part of speech): noun<br>   Case—nominative<br>   Gender—masculine<br>   Number—singular<br>   Stem or root—from λῆρος, ου<br>Concordance References:<br>  ⇒ Strong's #5616 hōsei + 3026 lēros<br>  ⇒ NIV #6059 hōsei [like] + 3333 lēros [nonsense]<br>  ⇒ NASB #5616 hōsei + 3026 lēros<br><br>**Luke 24:11**<br>And their words seemed to them as **idle tales**, and they believed them not. [KJV]<br>And these words appeared to them **as nonsense**, and they would not believe them. [NASB]<br>But they did not believe the women, because their words seemed to them **like nonsense**. [NIV]<br>And their words seemed to them like **idle tales**, and they did not believe them. [NKJV]<br>But the story sounded **like nonsense**, so they didn't believe it. [NLT]<br>καὶ ἐφάνησαν ἐνώπιον αὐτῶν **ὡσεὶ λῆρος** τὰ ῥήματα αὐτῶν, καὶ ἠπίστουν αὐταῖς. [GNS]<br>καὶ ἐφάνησαν ἐνώπιον αὐτῶν **ὡσεὶ λῆρος** τὰ ῥήματα ταῦτα, καὶ ἠπίστουν αὐταῖς. [GNT] | Ridiculous talk, idle tales, wild imagination, empty talk; like or as nonsense,.<br><br>**Practical Application**<br>After the resurrection of Christ, there was the immediate unbelief of the disciples. The women rushed to the disciples and shared the glorious news. But the news "seemed to them like idle tales" (*hōsei lēros*). "They did not believe." The Greek word is disbelieved (*epistoun*) and is in the imperfect active tense which means they "kept on disbelieving," kept on putting no trust or confidence in what the women were claiming. They were gripped with a skeptical, unbelieving spirit. |

# Practical Word Studies in the New Testament

| ENGLISH WORD | GREEK WORD AND VERSE | THE WORD MEANS... |
|---|---|---|
| **#2068**<br>**Idle Talkers**<br><br>Vain talkers–KJV<br>Empty talkers–NASB<br>Mere talkers–NIV<br>**Idle talkers–NKJV**<br>Useless talk–NLT<br><br>**POSB REFERENCE**<br>(Tit.1:10-12; esp. v.10)<br>Note 1, point 2 | ματαιολόγοι = *mataiologoi*<br>Pronunciation: [mat-ah-yol-og'-oy]<br>Parsing (part of speech): pronominal adjective<br>    Case—nominative<br>    Gender—masculine<br>    Number—plural<br>    Stem or root—from ματαιολόγος, ου<br>Concordance References:<br>⇒ Strong's #3151 mataiologos<br>⇒ NIV #3468 mataiologos<br>⇒ NASB #3151 mataiologos<br><br>**Titus 1:10**<br>For there are many unruly and **vain talkers** and deceivers, specially they of the circumcision: [KJV]<br><br>For there are many rebellious men, **empty talkers** and deceivers, especially those of the circumcision, [NASB]<br><br>For there are many rebellious people, **mere talkers** and deceivers, especially those of the circumcision group. [NIV]<br><br>For there are many insubordinate, both **idle talkers** and deceivers, especially those of the circumcision, [NKJV]<br><br>For there are many who rebel against right teaching; they engage in **useless talk** and deceive people. This is especially true of those who insist on circumcision for salvation. [NLT]<br><br>Εἰσὶ γὰρ πολλοὶ καὶ ἀνυπότακτοι, **ματαιολόγοι** καὶ φρεναπάται, μάλιστα οἱ ἐκ τῆς περιτομῆς, [GNS]<br><br>Εἰσὶν γὰρ πολλοὶ [καὶ] ἀνυπότακτοι, **ματαιολόγοι** καὶ φρεναπάται, μάλιστα οἱ ἐκ τῆς περιτομῆς, [GNT] | Mere talkers, vain talkers, empty talkers, useless talkers.<br><br>**Practical Application**<br>They were saying and teaching things that amounted to nothing and were worthless. Their teaching helped no one—not permanently and not eternally. Their teaching was not able to overcome sin and death—not able to bring true forgiveness of sin and eternal life to a person. |
| **#2069**<br>**Idol Worshipers**<br><br>Idolaters–KJV<br>Idolaters–NASB<br>Idolaters–NIV<br>Idolaters–NKJV<br>**Idol worshipers–NLT**<br><br>**POSB REFERENCE**<br>(1 Cor.6:9)<br>Note 2, point 2<br><br>See also POSB REF:<br>(1 Cor.5:9-10; esp. v.10)<br>Note 4, point 4<br>(Eph.5:7-10; esp. v.10)<br>Note 1 | εἰδωλολάτραι = *eidōlolatrai*<br>Pronunciation: [i-do-lol-at'-rah-ee]<br>Parsing (part of speech): noun<br>    Case—nominative<br>    Gender—masculine<br>    Number—plural<br>    Stem or root—from εἰδωλολάτρης, ου<br>Concordance References:<br>⇒ Strong's #1496 eidōlolatrēs<br>⇒ NIV #1629 eidōlolatrēs<br>⇒ NASB #1496 eidōlolatrēs<br><br>**1 Cor. 6:9**<br>Know ye not that the unrighteous shall not inherit the kingdom of God? Be not deceived: neither fornicators, nor **idolaters**, nor adulterers, nor effeminate, nor abusers of themselves with mankind, [KJV]<br><br>Or do you not know that the unrighteous shall not inherit the kingdom of God? Do not be deceived; neither fornicators, nor **idolaters**, nor adulterers, nor effeminate, nor homosexuals, [NASB]<br><br>Do you not know that the wicked will not inherit the kingdom of God? Do not be deceived: Neither the sexually immoral nor **idolaters** nor adulterers nor male prostitutes nor homosexual offenders [NIV]<br><br>Do you not know that the unrighteous will not inherit the kingdom of God? Do not be deceived. Neither fornicators, nor **idolaters**, nor adulterers, nor homosexuals, nor sodomites, [NKJV]<br><br>Don't you know that those who do wrong will have no share in the Kingdom of God? Don't fool yourselves. Those who indulge in sexual sin, who are **idol worshipers**, adulterers, male prostitutes, homosexuals, [NLT]<br><br>ἢ οὐκ οἴδατε ὅτι ἄδικοι βασιλείαν Θεοῦ οὐ κληρονομήσουσι; μὴ πλανᾶσθε· οὔτε πόρνοι, οὔτε **εἰδωλολάτραι**, οὔτε μοιχοί, οὔτε μαλακοί, οὔτε ἀρσενοκοῖται, [GNS]<br><br>ἢ οὐκ οἴδατε ὅτι ἄδικοι θεοῦ βασιλείαν οὐ κληρονομήσουσιν; μὴ πλανᾶσθε· οὔτε πόρνοι οὔτε **εἰδωλολάτραι** οὔτε μοιχοὶ οὔτε μαλακοὶ οὔτε ἀρσενοκοῖται [GNT] | Idolaters; idol worshipers; adorer of images; false worshippers. The word means those who either worship false gods or do not have a right relationship with God.<br><br>**Practical Application**<br>Idol worshipers (*eidōlolatrai*) are not just people who worship idols and images of metal, wood, and stone. In the Scripture, idolatry is the sin of the mind and body against God. Idolatry is basically two things.<br>1. Idolatry is working up concepts and ideas of God that are not true—ideas that are not true to the revelation of the Scriptures and of Jesus Christ. Men have concepts and ideas of what God is like. If their ideas are not what Scripture and Jesus Christ say, then they are worshipping an idol of their own mind.<br>2. Idolatry is putting something else before God. As Scripture says, covetousness is idolatry. An idolater is a person who gives his mind and body—thoughts, time, energy, efforts, loyalty—to something other than to God. Idolatry is the sin of the mind and body against God; it is the failure to look up to God and acknowledge Him; the failure to give one's life to Him including one's thoughts, time, energy, and effort—one's loyalty and worship. Idolatry is putting other things before God. |

## PRACTICAL WORD STUDIES
### in the NEW TESTAMENT

| ENGLISH WORD | GREEK WORD AND VERSE | THE WORD MEANS... |
|---|---|---|
| **#2070**<br>**Idolaters**<br><br>Idolaters–KJV<br>Idolaters–NASB<br>Idolaters–NIV<br>Idolaters–NKJV<br>Idol worshipers–NLT<br><br>**POSB REFERENCE**<br>(1 Cor.6:9)<br>Note 2, point 2<br><br>See also POSB REF:<br>(1 Cor.5:9-10; esp. v.10)<br>Note 4, point 4<br>(Eph.5:7-10; esp. v.10)<br>Note 1 | εἰδωλολάτραι = eidōlolatrai<br>Pronunciation: [i-do-lol-at'-rah-ee]<br>Parsing (part of speech): noun<br>    Case—nominative<br>    Gender—masculine<br>    Number—plural<br>    Stem or root—from εἰδωλολάτρης, ου<br>Concordance References:<br>  ⇒ Strong's #1496 eidōlolatrēs<br>  ⇒ NIV #1629 eidōlolatrēs<br>  ⇒ NASB #1496 eidōlolatrēs<br><br>**1 Cor. 6:9**<br>Know ye not that the unrighteous shall not inherit the kingdom of God? Be not deceived: neither fornicators, nor **idolaters**, nor adulterers, nor effeminate, nor abusers of themselves with mankind, [KJV]<br>Or do you not know that the unrighteous shall not inherit the kingdom of God? Do not be deceived; neither fornicators, nor **idolaters**, nor adulterers, nor effeminate, nor homosexuals, [NASB]<br>Do you not know that the wicked will not inherit the kingdom of God? Do not be deceived: Neither the sexually immoral nor **idolaters** nor adulterers nor male prostitutes nor homosexual offenders [NIV]<br>Do you not know that the unrighteous will not inherit the kingdom of God? Do not be deceived. Neither fornicators, nor **idolaters**, nor adulterers, nor homosexuals, nor sodomites, [NKJV]<br>Don't you know that those who do wrong will have no share in the Kingdom of God? Don't fool yourselves. Those who indulge in sexual sin, who are **idol worshipers**, adulterers, male prostitutes, homosexuals, [NLT]<br>η οὐκ οἴδατε ὅτι ἄδικοι βασιλείαν Θεοῦ οὐ κληρονομήσουσι; μὴ πλανᾶσθε· οὔτε πόρνοι, οὔτε **εἰδωλολάτραι**, οὔτε μοιχοί, οὔτε μαλακοὶ οὔτε ἀρσενοκοῖται, [GNS]<br>η οὐκ οἴδατε ὅτι ἄδικοι Θεοῦ βασιλείαν οὐ κληρονομήσουσιν; μὴ πλανᾶσθε· οὔτε πόρνοι οὔτε **εἰδωλολάτραι** οὔτε μοιχοὶ οὔτε μαλακοὶ οὔτε ἀρσενοκοῖται [GNT] | Idolaters; idol worshipers; adorer of images; false worshippers. The word means those who either worship false gods or do not have a right relationship with God.<br><br>**Practical Application**<br>Idolaters (*eidōlolatrai*) are not just people who worship idols and images of metal, wood, and stone. In the Scripture, idolatry is the sin of the mind and body against God. Idolatry is basically two things.<br>(See **Idol Worshipers** for more discussion.) |
| **#2071**<br>**Idolatry**<br><br>Idolatry–KJV<br>Idolatry–NASB<br>Idolatry–NIV<br>Idolatry–NKJV<br>Worship of idols–NLT<br><br>**POSB REFERENCE**<br>(1 Cor.10:14)<br>Note 1<br><br>See also POSB REF:<br>(Gal.5:19-21; esp. v.20)<br>Note 2 | εἰδωλολατρίας = eidōlolatrias<br>Pronunciation: [i-do-lol-at-ri'-ahs]<br>Parsing (part of speech): noun<br>    Case—genitive<br>    Gender—feminine<br>    Number—singular<br>    Stem or root—from εἰδωλολατρία, ας<br>Concordance References:<br>  ⇒ Strong's #1495 eidōlolatria<br>  ⇒ NIV #1630 eidōlolatria<br>  ⇒ NASB #1495 eidōlolatria<br><br>**1 Cor. 10:14**<br>Wherefore, my dearly beloved, flee from **idolatry**. [KJV]<br>Therefore, my beloved, flee from **idolatry**. [NASB]<br>Therefore, my dear friends, flee from **idolatry**. [NIV]<br>Therefore, my beloved, flee from **idolatry**. [NKJV]<br>So, my dear friends, flee from the **worship of idols**. [NLT]<br>Διόπερ, ἀγαπητοί μου, φεύγετε ἀπὸ τῆς **εἰδωλολατρίας**. [GNS]<br>Διόπερ, ἀγαπητοί μου, φεύγετε ἀπὸ τῆς **εἰδωλολατρίας**. [GNT] | Both the worship of false gods and the failure to have a right relationship with God. Any person who does not worship God is worshipping some idol, and almost everything upon earth can become an idol and consume the heart and passion of man.<br><br>**Practical Application**<br>In practical terms, an idol is anything that consumes a person's mind, heart, soul, and body. An idol is that to which a person gives himself.<br>⇒ Some people give themselves and are consumed by some purpose or possession on earth.<br>⇒ Other people give themselves and pray to their own idea of god; that is, to the *god* which they imagine in their own mind. (This is actually the worship of most people in industrialized societies.) They have a concept of god and worship that concept. They choose their own concept of god instead of the living and true God revealed by Jesus Christ.<br>⇒ Still other people give themselves and pray to some idol, picture, or image which they have made or purchased. (The idol may either represent some god or be considered the god himself.) |

# PRACTICAL WORD STUDIES
## in the NEW TESTAMENT

| ENGLISH WORD | GREEK WORD AND VERSE | THE WORD MEANS... |
|---|---|---|
| | | From this, it is readily seen that most men are idolaters, for most people are consumed by something other than God Himself. They reject the only living and true God, Jehovah Himself who has revealed Himself in Jesus Christ and the Holy Scriptures. (See POSB note—1 Cor. 8:1-13 as background for this passage). |
| **#2072**<br>**Idolatry,**<br>**Detestable**<br>**Idolatries,**<br>**Abominable**<br><br>Abominable idolatries–KJV<br>Abominable idolatries–NASB<br>Detestable idolatry–NIV<br>Abominable idolatries–NKJV<br>Terrible worship of idols–NLT<br><br>**POSB REFERENCE**<br>(1 Pt.4:3)<br>Note 3, point 6 | ἀθεμίτοις εἰδωλολατρίαις = athemitois eidōlolatriais<br>Pronunciation: [ath-em'-ee-toys i-do-lol-at-ri'-ah-ees]<br>Parsing *athemitois* (part of speech): adjective<br>  Case—dative<br>  Gender—feminine<br>  Number—plural<br>  Stem or root—from ἀθέμιτος, ον<br>Parsing *eidōlolatriais* (part of speech): noun<br>  Case—dative<br>  Gender—feminine<br>  Number—plural<br>  Stem or root—from εἰδωλολατρία, ας<br>Concordance References:<br>⇒ Strong's #111 athemitos + 1495 eidōlolatria<br>⇒ NIV #116 athemitos [detestable] + 1630 eidōlolatria [idolatry]<br>⇒ NASB #111 athemitos + 1495 eidōlolatria<br><br>**1 Peter 4:3**<br>For the time past of our life may suffice us to have wrought the will of the Gentiles, when we walked in lasciviousness, lusts, excess of wine, revellings, banquetings, and **abominable idolatries**: [KJV]<br>For the time already past is sufficient for you to have carried out the desire of the Gentiles, having pursued a course of sensuality, lusts, drunkenness, carousals, drinking parties and **abominable idolatries**. [NASB]<br>For you have spent enough time in the past doing what pagans choose to do—living in debauchery, lust, drunkenness, orgies, carousing and **detestable idolatry**. [NIV]<br>For we *have spent* enough of our past lifetime in doing the will of the Gentiles—when we walked in lewdness, lusts, drunkenness, revelries, drinking parties, and **abominable idolatries**. [NKJV]<br>You have had enough in the past of the evil things that godless people enjoy—their immorality and lust, their feasting and drunkenness and wild parties, and their **terrible worship of idols**. [NLT]<br>ἀρκετὸς γὰρ ἡμῖν ὁ παρεληλυθὼς χρόνος τὸ βίου τὸ θέλημα τῶν ἐθνῶν κατεργάσασθαι, πεπορευμένους ἐν ἀσελγείαις, ἐπιθυμίαις, οἰνοφλυγίαις, κώμοις, πότοις, καὶ **ἀθεμίτοις εἰδωλολατρείαις**· [GNS]<br>ἀρκετὸς γὰρ ὁ παρεληλυθὼς χρόνος τὸ βούλημα τῶν ἐθνῶν κατειργάσθαι πεπορευμένους ἐν ἀσελγείαις, ἐπιθυμίαις, οἰνοφλυγίαις, κώμοις, πότοις καὶ **ἀθεμίτοις εἰδωλολατρίαις**. [GNT] | Detestable, disgusting idolatry; abominable idolatries; the terrible worship of idols.<br><br>**Practical Application**<br>It is the worship of idols, whether mental or made by man's hands; the worship of some idea of what God is like, of an image of God within a person's mind; the giving of one's primary devotion (time and energy) to something other than God. (See POSB note, Idolatry—1 Cor. 6:9 for detailed discussion.) |
| **#2073**<br>**Ignorant**<br><br>Foolish–KJV<br>Foolish–NASB<br>Foolish–NIV<br>Foolish–NKJV<br>Ignorant–NLT<br><br>**POSB REFERENCE**<br>(Romans 2:17-20; esp. v.20)<br>Note 1, point 8 | ἀφρόνων = aphronōn<br>Pronunciation: [af'-rone-own]<br>Parsing (part of speech): pronominal adjective<br>  Case—genitive<br>  Gender—masculine<br>  Number—plural<br>  Stem or root—from ἄφρων, ον<br>Concordance References:<br>⇒ Strong's #878 aphrōn<br>⇒ NIV #933 aphrōn<br>⇒ NASB #878 aphrōn<br><br>**Romans 2:20**<br>An instructor of the **foolish**, a teacher of babes, which hast the form of knowledge and of the truth in the law. [KJV] | Foolish, ignorant, thoughtless, senseless, undirected.<br><br>**Practical Application**<br>It refers to people who walk through life giving no thought to life's purpose, as to...<br>• where they came from.<br>• why they are here.<br>• where they are going.<br><br>The religionist is persuaded that religion answers all these questions, the basic questions of life. Therefore, he can help the foolish dis- |

# PRACTICAL WORD STUDIES
## in the NEW TESTAMENT

| ENGLISH WORD | GREEK WORD AND VERSE | THE WORD MEANS... |
|---|---|---|
| | A corrector of the **foolish**, a teacher of the immature, having in the Law the embodiment of knowledge and of the truth, [NASB]<br>An instructor of the **foolish**, a teacher of infants, because you have in the law the embodiment of knowledge and truth—[NIV]<br>An instructor of the **foolish**, a teacher of babes, having the form of knowledge and truth in the law. [NKJV]<br>You think you can instruct the **ignorant** and teach children the ways of God. For you are certain that in God's law you have complete knowledge and truth. [NLT]<br>παιδευτὴν **ἀφρόνων**, διδάσκαλον νηπίων, ἔχοντα τὴν μόρφωσιν τῆς γνώσεως καὶ τῆς ἀληθείας ἐν τῷ νόμῳ· [GNS]<br>παιδευτὴν **ἀφρόνων**, διδάσκαλον νηπίων, ἔχοντα τὴν μόρφωσιν τῆς γνώσεως καὶ τῆς ἀληθείας ἐν τῷ νόμῳ· [GNT] | cover meaning and purpose and significance in life. The critical point for the instructor or the religionist is to make sure that his instruction is true. What he instructs must be the truth or else it is all for naught. |
| #2074<br>**Ignore God**<br><br>Mocked–KJV<br>Mocked–NASB<br>Mocked–NIV<br>Mocked–NKJV<br>**Ignore God–NLT**<br><br>**POSB REFERENCE**<br>(Gal.6:7-9; esp. v.7)<br>Note 2, point 1 | μυκτηρίζεται = muktērizetai<br>Pronunciation: [mook-tay-rid'-zeh-tah-ee]<br>Parsing (part of speech): verb<br>   Mood—indicative<br>   Tense—present<br>   Voice—passive<br>   Person—3rd person<br>   Number—singular<br>   Stem or root—from μυκτηρίζω<br>Concordance References:<br>⇒ Strong's #3456 muktērizō<br>⇒ NIV #3682 muktērizō<br>⇒ NASB #3456 muktērizō<br><br>**Galatians 6:7**<br>Be not deceived; God is not **mocked**: for whatsoever a man soweth, that shall he also reap. [KJV]<br>Do not be deceived, God is not **mocked**; for whatever a man sows, this he will also reap. [NASB]<br>Do not be deceived: God cannot be **mocked**. A man reaps what he sows. [NIV]<br>Do not be deceived, God is not **mocked**; for whatever a man sows, that he will also reap. [NKJV]<br>Don't be misled. Remember that you can't **ignore God** and get away with it. You will always reap what you sow! [NLT]<br>Μὴ πλανᾶσθε, Θεὸς οὐ **μυκτηρίζεται**· ὃ γὰρ ἐὰν σπείρῃ ἄνθρωπος τοῦτο καὶ θερίσει. [GNS]<br>Μὴ πλανᾶσθε, Θεὸς οὐ **μυκτηρίζεται**. ὃ γὰρ ἐὰν σπείρῃ ἄνθρωπος, τοῦτο καὶ θερίσει | To mock; to make a fool of; to ignore God; to turn one's nose up at God.<br><br>**Practical Application**<br>By rejecting God's minister, the teacher whom God had sent to them, the Galatians were rejecting God. They were not only mocking and turning their noses up at the teacher of God, but they were mocking God. However, Scripture declares in no uncertain terms: "You can't ignore God and get away with it." A man reaps what he sows." If a man sows a life...<br>• that is not present when the teacher teaches,<br>• that is not attentive and learning what the teacher teaches,<br>• that does not bear testimony to what the teacher teaches,<br>• that does not participate with the teacher in his ministry, that does not encourage others to learn from the teacher,<br><br>...if a man sows this rejection, this turning up of the nose, he rejects and turns his nose up at God. And if he rejects God, he will be rejected by God. Whatever a man sows toward his teacher, he reaps. He will bear the judgment of his behavior toward God's teacher. |
| #2075<br>**Ignored Them**<br><br>Made light of it–KJV<br>Paid no attention–NASB<br>Paid no attention–NIV<br>Made light of it–NKJV<br>**Ignored them–NLT**<br><br>**POSB REFERENCE**<br>(Mt.22:3-7; esp. v.5)<br>Note 2, point 3 | ἀμελήσαντες = amelēsantes<br>Pronunciation: [am-el-ay'-sahn-tehs]<br>Parsing (part of speech): verb<br>   Mood—participle<br>   Tense—aorist<br>   Voice—active<br>   Case—nominative<br>   Gender—masculine<br>   Number—plural<br>   Stem or root—from ἀμελέω<br>Concordance References:<br>⇒ Strong's #272 ameleō<br>⇒ NIV #288 ameleō<br>⇒ NASB #272 ameleō<br><br>**Matthew 22:5**<br>But they **made light of it**, and went their ways, one to his farm, another to his merchandise: [KJV]<br>"But they **paid no attention** and went their way, one to his own farm, another to his business, [NASB]<br>"But they **paid no attention** and went off—one to his field, another to his business. [NIV] | To pay no attention; to make light of; to ignore; to care little if any; to be careless; to disregard.<br><br>**Practical Application**<br>In the Greek this is an aorist participle: they subjects of the King were making light of the King's gracious invitation to attend His Son's wedding banquet.<br>They were definite in their decision not to attend the Great Wedding Banquet or Marriage Feast. They were careless and negligent about it. They were too busy to be concerned with the King's invitation, too busy with the world and making a living and getting more and more for pleasure and comfort (cp. James 4:13). |

# PRACTICAL WORD STUDIES
## in the NEW TESTAMENT

| ENGLISH WORD | GREEK WORD AND VERSE | THE WORD MEANS... |
|---|---|---|
| | But they **made light of it** and went their ways, one to his own farm, another to his business. [NKJV]<br>But the guests he had invited **ignored them** and went about their business, one to his farm, another to his store. [NLT]<br>οἱ δὲ **ἀμελήσαντες** ἀπῆλθον, ὁ μὲν εἰς τὸν ἴδιον ἀγρόν, ὁ δὲ εἰς τὴν ἐμπορίαν αὐτοῦ· [GNS]<br>οἱ δὲ **ἀμελήσαντες** ἀπῆλθον, ὃς μὲν εἰς τὸν ἴδιον ἀγρόν, ὃς δὲ ἐπὶ τὴν ἐμπορίαν αὐτοῦ· [GNT] | |
| #2076<br>**Image**<br><br>**Image**–KJV<br>**Image**–NASB<br>**Image**–NIV<br>**Image**–NKJV<br>**Image**–NLT<br><br>**POSB<br>REFERENCE**<br>(Col.1:15)<br>Note 1 | εἰκών = eikōn<br>Pronunciation: [i-kone']<br>Parsing (part of speech): noun<br>    Case—nominative<br>    Gender—feminine<br>    Number—singular<br>    Stem or root—from εἰκών, όνος<br>Concordance References:<br>⇒ Strong's #1504 eikōn<br>⇒ NIV #1635 eikōn<br>⇒ NASB #1504 eikōn<br><br>**Col. 1:15**<br>Who is the **image** of the invisible God, the firstborn of every creature: [KJV]<br>And He is the **image** of the invisible God, the firstborn of all creation. [NASB]<br>He is the **image** of the invisible God, the firstborn over all creation. [NIV]<br>He is the **image** of the invisible God, the firstborn over all creation. [NKJV]<br>Christ is the visible **image** of the invisible God. He existed before God made anything at all and is supreme over all creation. [NLT]<br>ὅς ἐστιν **εἰκὼν** τοῦ Θεοῦ τοῦ ἀοράτου, πρωτότοκος πάσης κτίσεως· [GNS]<br>ὅς ἐστιν **εἰκὼν** τοῦ θεοῦ τοῦ ἀοράτου, πρωτότοκος πάσης κτίσεως, [GNT] | Image, form, likeness. The word "image" (*eikōn*) means the exact image, the very person of God.<br><br>**Practical Application**<br>Jsus Christ is the image of the invisible God.<br>⇒ It means that Jesus Christ is the very *representation of God—God in every respect*. Wuest quotes Lightfoot as saying that "image" means a mark or figure burned or stamped on (something)...a precise reproduction in every respect.<br>⇒ It means that Jesus Christ is the perfect manifestation or revelation of God. God is invisible or unseen, but Jesus Christ reveals God to the world. He reveals God as the exact image, as the perfect representation of God.<br>The impact of this truth about Jesus Christ has explosive repercussions for man. It destroys all false teaching about God and Christ, and it reveals God to man. It shows man who God is and what He is like, all in the person of Jesus Christ. |
| #2077<br>**Imaginations**<br><br>**Imaginations**–KJV<br>Speculations–NASB<br>Arguments–NIV<br>Arguments–NKJV<br>Every proud argument–NLT<br><br>**POSB<br>REFERENCE**<br>(2 Cor.10:3-5; esp. v.5)<br>Note 2 | λογισμούς = logismous<br>Pronunciation: [log-is-moos']<br>Parsing (part of speech): noun<br>    Case—accusative<br>    Gender—masculine<br>    Number—plural<br>    Stem or root—from λογισμός, οῦ<br>Concordance References:<br>⇒ Strong's #3053 logismos<br>⇒ NIV #3361 logismos<br>⇒ NASB #3053 logismos<br>**Note: this comes from verse 4 in the Greek, but is translated in the English Bible in verse 5**<br><br>**2 Cor. 10:5**<br>Casting down **imaginations**, and every high thing that exalteth itself against the knowledge of God, and bringing into captivity every thought to the obedience of Christ; [KJV]<br>We are destroying **speculations** and every lofty thing raised up against the knowledge of God, and we are taking every thought captive to the obedience of Christ, [NASB]<br>We demolish **arguments** and every pretension that sets itself up against the knowledge of God, and we take captive every thought to make it obedient to Christ. [NIV]<br>Casting down **arguments** and every high thing that exalts itself against the knowledge of God, bringing every thought into captivity to the obedience of Christ, [NKJV]<br>With these weapons we break down **every proud argument** that keeps people from knowing God. With these weapons we conquer their rebellious ideas, and we teach them to obey Christ. [NLT]<br>τὰ γὰρ ὅπλα τῆς στρατείας ἡμῶν οὐ σαρκικά, ἀλλὰ | Arguments, speculations, false reasoning.<br><br>**Practical Application**<br>The believer is to *demolish or cast down imaginations*: thoughts and imaginations that are uncontrolled, wild, evil, lustful, immoral, unjust, wrong, untrue, devilish, and set against God. |

# PRACTICAL WORD STUDIES
## in the NEW TESTAMENT

| ENGLISH WORD | GREEK WORD AND VERSE | THE WORD MEANS... |
|---|---|---|
| | δυνατὰ τῷ Θεῷ πρὸς καθαίρεσιν ὀχυρωμάτων --, **λογισμοὺς** καθαιροῦντες **2 Cor. 10:4** [GNS]<br>καὶ πᾶν ὕψωμα ἐπαιρόμενον κατὰ τῆς γνώσεως τοῦ Θεοῦ, καὶ αἰχμαλωτίζοντες πᾶν νόημα εἰς τὴν ὑπακοὴν τοῦ Χριστοῦ, **2 Cor. 10:5** [GNS]<br>τὰ γὰρ ὅπλα τῆς στρατείας ἡμῶν οὐ σαρκικὰ ἀλλὰ δυνατὰ τῷ θεῷ πρὸς καθαίρεσιν ὀχυρωμάτων, **λογισμοὺς** καθαιροῦντες **2 Cor. 10:4** [GNT]<br>καὶ πᾶν ὕψωμα ἐπαιρόμενον κατὰ τῆς γνώσεως τοῦ θεοῦ, καὶ αἰχμαλωτίζοντες πᾶν νόημα eivj τὴν ὑπακοὴν τοῦ Χριστοῦ, **2 Cor. 10:5** [GNT] | |
| **#2078**<br>**Imitate–**<br>**Imitators**<br><br>Followers–KJV<br>**Imitators**–NASB<br>**Imitate**–NIV<br>**Imitate**–NKJV<br>Example–NLT<br><br>**POSB**<br>**REFERENCE**<br>(1 Cor.4:16)<br>Note 3 | **μιμηταί γίνεσθε.** = *mimētai ginesthe*<br>Pronunciation: [mim-ay-tace']<br>Parsing *mimētai* (part of speech): noun<br>    Case—nominative<br>    Gender—masculine<br>    Number—plural<br>    Stem or root—from μιμητής, οῦ<br>Parsing *ginesthe* (part of speech): verb<br>    Mood—imperative<br>    Tense—present<br>    Voice—middle or passive deponent<br>    Person—2nd person<br>    Number—plural<br>    Stem or root—from γίνομαι<br>Concordance References:<br>⇒ Strong's #1096+3402 ginomai mimētēs<br>⇒ NIV #1181+3629 ginomai mimētēs [imitate]<br>⇒ NASB #1096+3402 ginomai mimētēs<br><br>**1 Cor. 4:16**<br>Wherefore I beseech you, be ye **followers** of me. [KJV]<br>I exhort you therefore, be **imitators** of me. [NASB]<br>Therefore I urge you to **imitate** me. [NIV]<br>Therefore I urge you, **imitate** me. [NKJV]<br>So I ask you to follow my **example** and do as I do. [NLT]<br>παρακαλῶ οὖν ὑμᾶς, **μιμηταί** μου γίνεσθε. [GNS]<br>παρακαλῶ οὖν ὑμᾶς, **μιμηταί** μου γίνεσθε. [GNT] | Imitate, follow, example; to copy; to impersonate; to emulate; to duplicate.<br><br>**Practical Application**<br>Every father should live such a life that his children could follow in his steps. This is what Paul was saying. He had lived a life of commitment and self-denial for the Lord Jesus Christ. He had given all he was and had to Christ. He was saying: "Follow me—imitate me! Commit your life to Christ; deny yourself completely—give all you are and have to Him. Help me in evangelizing and meeting the desperate needs of the world for Him. The world is starving and dying from sin, hunger, disease, cold, heat, loneliness, and purposelessness; and they are doomed to die in both this world and the next. Follow me! Help me to reach this world for Christ Jesus our Lord." |
| **#2079**<br>**Imitators**<br><br>Followers–KJV<br>**Imitators**–NASB<br>**Imitators**–NIV<br>**Imitators**–NKJV<br>Example–NLT<br><br>**POSB**<br>**REFERENCE**<br>(Eph.5:1)<br>Note 1 | **μιμηταί** = *mimētai*<br>Pronunciation: [mim-ay-tah-ee']<br>Parsing (part of speech): noun<br>    Case—nominative<br>    Gender—masculine<br>    Number—plural<br>    Stem or root—from μιμητής, οῦ<br>Concordance References:<br>⇒ Strong's #3402 mimētēs<br>⇒ NIV #3629 mimētēs<br>⇒ NASB #3402 mimētēs<br><br>**Ephes. 5:1**<br>Be ye therefore **followers** of God, as dear children; [KJV]<br>Therefore be **imitators** of God, as beloved children; [NASB]<br>Be **imitators** of God, therefore, as dearly loved children [NIV]<br>Therefore be **imitators** of God as dear children. [NKJV]<br>Follow God's **example** in everything you do, because you are his dear children. [NLT]<br>Γίνεσθε οὖν **μιμηταί** τοῦ Θεοῦ, ὡς τέκνα ἀγαπητά· [GNS]<br>γίνεσθε οὖν **μιμηταί** τοῦ θεοῦ ὡς τέκνα ἀγαπητὰ [GNT] | Imitators, followers, examples.<br><br>**Practical Application**<br>Some prefer the translation that we are to become *imitators* of God. Note the phrase "as dear children." [NKJV] Just as children learn by imitating their parents, so we are to learn by imitating God. The very idea that we are to be *followers and imitators* of God is a bold idea. Just imagine, Scripture boldly proclaims that we are to become *like God*!<br><br>⇒ Christ said: "Therefore you are to be perfect, as your heavenly Father is perfect" (Matthew 5:48). [NASB]<br>⇒ God demanded: "'Be holy because I, the LORD your God, am holy" (Leviticus 19:2). [NIV]<br>⇒ Paul declared: "And we... being transformed into his likeness with ever-increasing glory..." (2 Cor. 3:18). [NIV]<br>⇒ Peter charged: "but as He who called you *is* holy, you also be holy in all *your* conduct, because it is written, 'Be holy, for I am holy'" (1 Peter 1:15-16). [NKJV]<br>⇒ The early church saint Clement of Alexandria said: "The Christian practices being God" (Quoted by William Barclay, *The Letters to the Galatians and Ephesians*, p.190). |

# PRACTICAL WORD STUDIES
## in the NEW TESTAMENT

| ENGLISH WORD | GREEK WORD AND VERSE | THE WORD MEANS... |
|---|---|---|
| **#2080**<br>**Immanuel**<br><br>Emmanuel–KJV<br>**Immanuel**–NASB<br>**Immanuel**–NIV<br>**Immanuel**–NKJV<br>**Immanuel**–NLT<br><br>**POSB**<br>**REFERENCE**<br>(Mt.1:23)<br>*Deeper Study #9* | Ἐμμανουήλ = Emmanouēl<br>Pronunciation: [em-man-oo-ale']<br>Parsing (part of speech): noun<br>    Case—accusative<br>    Gender—masculine<br>    Number—singular<br>    Stem or root—from Ἐμμανουήλ<br>Concordance References:<br>  ⇒ Strong's #1694 Emmanouēl<br>  ⇒ NIV #1842 Emmanouēl<br>  ⇒ NASB #1694 Emmanouēl<br><br>**Matthew 1:23**<br>Behold, a virgin shall be with child, and shall bring forth a son, and they shall call his name **Emmanuel**, which being interpreted is, God with us. [KJV]<br>"Behold, the virgin shall be with CHILD, AND SHALL BEAR A Son, and they shall call His name **Immanuel**," which translated means, "God with us." [NASB]<br>"The virgin will be with child and will give birth to a son, and they will call him **Immanuel**"—which means, "God with us." [NIV]<br>"Behold, the virgin shall be with child, and bear a Son, and they shall call His name **Immanuel**," which is translated, "God with us." [NKJV]<br>"Look! The virgin will conceive a child! She will give birth to a son, and he will be called **Immanuel** (meaning, God is with us)." [NLT]<br>Ἰδοὺ, ἡ παρθένος ἐν γαστρὶ ἕξει καὶ τέξεται υἱόν, καὶ καλέσουσι τὸ ὄνομα αὐτοῦ **Ἐμμανουήλ**, ὅ ἐστι μεθερμηνευόμενον, Μεθ' ἡμῶν ὁ Θεός. [GNS]<br>Ἰδοὺ ἡ παρθένος ἐν γαστρὶ ἕξει καὶ τέξεται υἱόν, καὶ καλέσουσιν τὸ ὄνομα αὐτοῦ **Ἐμμανουήλ**, ὅ ἐστιν μεθερμηνευόμενον Μεθ' ἡμῶν ὁ θεός. [GNT] | God with us. Jesus Christ is God manifest in human flesh.<br><br>**Practical Application**<br>The word "Immanuel" is not a name or a title. It is a descriptive term. It characterizes a person. Jesus Christ is Immanuel: God with us, God revealed in human flesh (cp. Isaiah 1:26; Isaiah 9:6; Jn.1:1, 14; 2 Cor. 5:19; 1 Jn.1:2). |
| **#2081**<br>**Immature**<br><br>Babes–KJV<br>**Immature**–NASB<br>Infants–NIV<br>Babes–NKJV<br>Children–NLT<br><br>**POSB**<br>**REFERENCE**<br>(Romans 2:17-20; esp. v.20)<br>Note 1, point 9 | νηπίων = nēpiōn<br>Pronunciation: [nay'-pee-own]<br>Parsing (part of speech): pronominal adjective<br>    Case—genitive<br>    Gender—masculine<br>    Number—plural<br>    Stem or root—from νήπιος, α, ον<br>Concordance References:<br>  ⇒ Strong's #3516 nēpios<br>  ⇒ NIV #3758 nēpios<br>  ⇒ NASB #3516 nēpios<br><br>**Romans 2:20**<br>An instructor of the foolish, a teacher of **babes**, which hast the form of knowledge and of the truth in the law. [KJV]<br>A corrector of the foolish, a teacher of the **immature**, having in the Law the embodiment of knowledge and of the truth, [NASB]<br>An instructor of the foolish, a teacher of **infants**, because you have in the law the embodiment of knowledge and truth—[NIV]<br>An instructor of the foolish, a teacher of **babes**, having the form of knowledge and truth in the law. [NKJV]<br>You think you can instruct the ignorant and teach **children** the ways of God. For you are certain that in God's law you have complete knowledge and truth. [NLT]<br>παιδευτὴν ἀφρόνων, διδάσκαλον **νηπίων**, ἔχοντα τὴν μόρφωσιν τῆς γνώσεως καὶ τῆς ἀληθείας ἐν τῷ νόμῳ· [GNS]<br>παιδευτὴν ἀφρόνων, διδάσκαλον **νηπίων**, ἔχοντα τὴν μόρφωσιν τῆς γνώσεως καὶ τῆς ἀληθείας ἐν τῷ νόμῳ· [GNT] | The infant; the immature; the novice; the children; the proselyte; the innocent; the baby; the new church member.<br><br>**Practical Application**<br>A person is not mature in God just because he...<br><br>• has been baptized and has been a church member for a long time.<br>• thinks he is mature.<br>• serves as a teacher.<br><br>What makes a person mature and capable of teaching the immature of the world is experience with Christ, having walked and served with Christ for a long time. |

# PRACTICAL WORD STUDIES
## in the NEW TESTAMENT

| ENGLISH WORD | GREEK WORD AND VERSE | THE WORD MEANS... |
|---|---|---|
| **#2082**<br>**Immoral**<br><br>Whoremonger–KJV<br>**Immoral**–NASB<br>**Immoral**–NIV<br>Fornicator–NKJV<br>**Immoral**–NLT<br><br>**POSB REFERENCE**<br>(Eph.5:5-6; esp. v.5)<br>Note 5, point 1 | πόρνος = *pornos*<br>Pronunciation: [por'-nos]<br>Parsing (part of speech): noun<br>    Case—nominative<br>    Gender—masculine<br>    Number—singular<br>    Stem or root—from πόρνος, ου<br>Concordance References:<br>  ⇒ Strong's #4205 pornos<br>  ⇒ NIV #4521 pornos<br>  ⇒ NASB #4205 pornos<br><br>**Ephes. 5:5**<br>For this ye know, that no **whoremonger**, nor unclean person, nor covetous man, who is an idolater, hath any inheritance in the kingdom of Christ and of God. [KJV]<br><br>For this you know with certainty, that no **immoral** or impure person or covetous man, who is an idolater, has an inheritance in the kingdom of Christ and God. [NASB]<br><br>For of this you can be sure: No **immoral**, impure or greedy person—such a man is an idolater—has any inheritance in the kingdom of Christ and of God. [NIV]<br><br>For this you know, that no **fornicator**, unclean person, nor covetous man, who is an idolater, has any inheritance in the kingdom of Christ and of God. [NKJV]<br><br>You can be sure that no **immoral**, impure, or greedy person will inherit the Kingdom of Christ and of God. For a greedy person is really an idolater who worships the things of this world. [NLT]<br><br>τοῦτο γὰρ ἔστε γινώσκοντες, ὅτι πᾶς **πόρνος**, η ἀκάθαρτος, η πλεονέκτης, ὅς ἐστιν εἰδωλολάτρης, οὐκ ἔχει κληρονομίαν ἐν τῇ βασιλείᾳ τοῦ Χριστοῦ καὶ Θεοῦ. [GNS]<br><br>τοῦτο γὰρ ἴστε γινώσκοντες, ὅτι πᾶς **πόρνος** η ἀκάθαρτος η πλεονέκτης, ὅ ἐστιν εἰδωλολάτρης, οὐκ ἔχει κληρονομίαν ἐν τῇ βασιλείᾳ τοῦ Χριστοῦ καὶ θεοῦ. [GNT] | To be sexually immoral; to be an adulterer; to be a whoremonger. It is illicit sexual intercourse; fornication; prostitution; immoral behavior.<br><br>**Practical Application**<br>Uncleanness has no part with God, no part whatsoever. The profession of a person does not matter: if he practices these things, he will not share in the kingdom of Christ and of God. And, note, *the doom* pronounced is not future, it is present. It does not say, "he shall not have," but rather, "he does not have an inheritance with God." He may have houses, lands, and all kinds of possessions; but he does not have one scrap of the kingdom. He has lost all that is really worth having. |
| **#2083**<br>**Immoral**<br><br>Fornicator–KJV<br>**Immoral**–NASB<br>Sexually immoral–NIV<br>Fornicator–NKJV<br>**Immoral**–NLT<br><br>**POSB REFERENCE**<br>(Heb.12:15-17; esp. v.16)<br>Note 2, point 3<br><br>See also POSB REF:<br>(1 Cor.6:9)<br>Note 2 | πόρνος = *pornos*<br>Pronunciation: [por'-nos]<br>Parsing (part of speech): noun<br>    Case—nominative<br>    Gender—masculine<br>    Number—singular<br>    Stem or root—from πόρνος, ου<br>Concordance References:<br>  ⇒ Strong's #4205 pornos<br>  ⇒ NIV #4521 pornos<br>  ⇒ NASB #4205 pornos<br><br>**Hebrews 12:16**<br>Lest there be any **fornicator**, or profane person, as Esau, who for one morsel of meat sold his birthright. [KJV]<br><br>That there be no **immoral** or godless person like Esau, who sold his own birthright for a single meal. [NASB]<br><br>See that no one is **sexually immoral**, or is godless like Esau, who for a single meal sold his inheritance rights as the oldest son. [NIV]<br><br>Lest there *be* any **fornicator** or profane person like Esau, who for one morsel of food sold his birthright. [NKJV]<br><br>Make sure that no one is **immoral** or godless like Esau. He traded his birthright as the oldest son for a single meal. [NLT]<br><br>μή τις **πόρνος** η βέβηλος, ὡς Ἠσαῦ, ὅς ἀντὶ βρώσεως μιᾶς ἀπέδετο τὰ πρωτοτόκια ἀτοῦ. [GNS]<br><br>μή τις **πόρνος** η βέβηλος ὡς Ἠσαῦ, ὃς ἀντὶ βρώσεως μιᾶς ἀπέδετο τὰ πρωτοτόκια ἑαυτοῦ. [GNT] | To be sexually immoral; to be a fornicator. The word is a broad word including all forms of immoral and sexual acts. It is premarital sex and adultery; it is homosexuality and abnormal sex; it is all kinds of sexual vice, whether married or unmarried.<br><br>**Practical Application**<br>Immorality is not only committed by the act. A person is guilty of immorality when he looks in order to lust. Looking at and lusting after the opposite sex—whether in person, in magazines, in books, on beaches, or anywhere else—is committing fornication. Imagining and lusting within the mind is the very same as committing the act in the eyes of God. |

# PRACTICAL WORD STUDIES
## in the NEW TESTAMENT

| ENGLISH WORD | GREEK WORD AND VERSE | THE WORD MEANS... |
|---|---|---|
| **#2084**<br>**Immoral Lives**<br><br>Lasciviousness–KJV<br>Licentiousness–NASB<br>License for immorality–NIV<br>Lewdness–NKJV<br>**Immoral lives–NLT**<br><br>**POSB REFERENCE**<br>(Jude 1:4)<br>Note 5 | ἀσέλγειαν = aselgeian<br>Pronunciation: [as-elg'-i-ahn]<br>Parsing (part of speech): noun<br>   Case—accusative<br>   Gender—feminine<br>   Number—singular<br>   Stem or root—from ἀσέλγεια, ας<br>Concordance References:<br>  ⇒ Strong's #766 aselgeia<br>  ⇒ NIV #816 aselgeia<br>  ⇒ NASB #766 aselgeia<br><br>**Jude 1:4**<br>For there are certain men crept in unawares, who were before of old ordained to this condemnation, ungodly men, turning the grace of our God into **lasciviousness**, and denying the only Lord God, and our Lord Jesus Christ. [KJV]<br><br>For certain persons have crept in unnoticed, those who were long beforehand marked out for this condemnation, ungodly persons who turn the grace of our God into **licentiousness** and deny our only Master and Lord, Jesus Christ. [NASB]<br><br>For certain men whose condemnation was written about long ago have secretly slipped in among you. They are godless men, who change the grace of our God into a **license for immorality** and deny Jesus Christ our only Sovereign and Lord. [NIV]<br><br>For certain men have crept in unnoticed, who long ago were marked out for this condemnation, ungodly men, who turn the grace of our God into **lewdness** and deny the only Lord God and our Lord Jesus Christ. [NKJV]<br><br>I say this because some godless people have wormed their way in among you, saying that God's forgiveness allows us to live **immoral lives**. The fate of such people was determined long ago, for they have turned against our only Master and Lord, Jesus Christ. [NLT]<br><br>παρεισέδυσαν γάρ τινες ἄνθρωποι, οἱ πάλαι προγεγραμμένοι εἰς τοῦτο τὸ κρίμα, ἀσεβεῖς, τὴν τοῦ Θεοῦ ἡμῶν χάριν μετατιθέντες εἰς **ἀσέλγειαν**, καὶ τὸν μόνον δεσπότην Θεόν, καὶ Κύριον ἡμῶν Ἰησοῦν Χριστὸν ἀρνούμενοι. [GNS]<br><br>παρεισέδυσαν γάρ τινες ἄνθρωποι, οἱ πάλαι προγεγραμμένοι εἰς τοῦτο τὸ κρίμα, ἀσεβεῖς, τὴν τοῦ θεοῦ ἡμῶν χάριτα μετατιθέντες εἰς **ἀσέλγειαν** καὶ τὸν μόνον δεσπότην καὶ κύριον ἡμῶν Ἰησοῦν Χριστὸν ἀρνούμενοι. [GNT] | License for immorality; lasciviousness; licentiousness; immoral living; lustful desires; sensuality; shamelessness.<br><br>**Practical Application**<br>No matter what the false teaching is, it will enslave. The false teacher who denies Christ and God's Word removes the supreme authority over man's life. Therefore, man is basically free to live in selfishness and greed, desire and lust. He is left to seek as much pleasure and as many possessions as he desires upon earth. But in the end, man discovers something. The more he gets, the more he wants. It may be comfort, money, sex, position, or authority; it does not matter. Man's nature is such that he wants more and more. Man must be restrained by an authority above himself, that is, by God and by God's Word. If he is not, then he becomes enslaved to his passions and to the corruption of the world. This is one of the terrible fallacies of all false teachings. They all enslave man to this world: not a single false teaching can usher a man through the door of death into eternal life. Only Jesus Christ can do that. Note the clear truth: whatever overcomes a man, that very thing enslaves him.<br>⇒ If a false teacher overcomes a man, then the man is enslaved to that teaching.<br>⇒ If the world overcomes a man, then the man is enslaved by the world. |
| **#2085**<br>**Immoral Living**<br><br>Wantonness–KJV<br>Sensuality–NASB<br>Debauchery–NIV<br>Lust–NKJV<br>**Immoral living–NLT**<br><br>**POSB REFERENCE**<br>(Rom.13:13)<br>Note 4, point 4 | ἀσελγείαις = aselgeiais<br>Pronunciation: [as-elg'-i-ah-is]<br>Parsing (part of speech): noun<br>   Case—dative<br>   Gender—feminine<br>   Number—plural<br>   Stem or root—from ἀσέλγεια, ας<br>Concordance References:<br>  ⇒ Strong's #766 aselgeia<br>  ⇒ NIV #816 aselgeia<br>  ⇒ NASB #766 aselgeia<br><br>**Romans 13:13**<br>Let us walk honestly, as in the day; not in rioting and drunkenness, not in chambering and **wantonness**, not in strife and envying. [KJV]<br><br>Let us behave properly as in the day, not in carousing and drunkenness, not in sexual promiscuity and **sensuality**, not in strife and jealousy. [NASB]<br><br>Let us behave decently, as in the daytime, not in orgies and drunkenness, not in sexual immorality and **debauchery**, not in dissension and jealousy. [NIV]<br><br>Let us walk properly, as in the day, not in revelry and drunkenness, not in lewdness and **lust**, not in strife and | Debauchery; sensuality; lust; running wild; licentiousness; wantonness; homosexuality; lasciviousness; living a wild, partying, and immoral life.<br><br>**Practical Application**<br>It is excess lust, unbridled lust that consumes one's thoughts and behavior through...<br>• looks and dress<br>• films and pictures<br>• dances and parties<br>• suggestions and gestures<br>• books and pamphlets<br>• songs and music<br>• talk and jokes<br>• touch and behavior<br>• sensuality, indecency, vice |

# PRACTICAL WORD STUDIES
## in the NEW TESTAMENT

| ENGLISH WORD | GREEK WORD AND VERSE | THE WORD MEANS... |
|---|---|---|
| | envy. [NKJV]<br>We should be decent and true in everything we do, so that everyone can approve of our behavior. Don't participate in wild parties and getting drunk, or in adultery and **immoral living**, or in fighting and jealousy. [NLT]<br>ὡς ἐν ἡμέρᾳ, εὐσχημόνως περιπατήσωμεν, μὴ κώμοις καὶ μέθαις, μὴ κοίταις καὶ **ἀσελγείαις**, μὴ ἔριδι καὶ ζήλῳ. [GNS]<br>ὡς ἐν ἡμέρᾳ εὐσχημόνως περιπατήσωμεν, μὴ κώμοις καὶ μέθαις, μὴ κοίταις καὶ **ἀσελγείαις**, μὴ ἔριδι καὶ ζήλῳ, [GNT] | |
| **#2086**<br>**Immoral People**<br><br>Fornicators–KJV<br>**Immoral people–NASB**<br>Sexually immoral people–NIV<br>**Immoral people–NKJV**<br>People who indulge in sexual sin–NLT<br><br>**POSB REFERENCE**<br>(1 Cor.5:9-10; esp. v.9)<br>Note 4 | πόρνοις = *pornois*<br>Pronunciation: [por'-noys]<br>Parsing (part of speech): noun<br>    Case—dative<br>    Gender—masculine<br>    Number—plural<br>    Stem or root—from πόρνος, ου<br>Concordance References:<br>   ⇒ Strong's #4205 pornos<br>   ⇒ NIV #4521 pornos<br>   ⇒ NASB #4205 pornos<br><br>**1 Cor. 5:9**<br>I wrote unto you in an epistle not to company with **fornicators**: [KJV]<br>I wrote you in my letter not to associate with **immoral people**; [NASB]<br>I have written you in my letter not to associate with **sexually immoral people**—[NIV]<br>I wrote to you in my epistle not to keep company with sexually **immoral people**. [NKJV]<br>When I wrote to you before, I told you not to associate with **people who indulge in sexual sin**. [NLT]<br>Ἔγραψα ὑμῖν ἐν τῇ ἐπιστολῇ μὴ συναναμίγνυσθαι **πόρνοις**· [GNS]<br>Ἔγραψα ὑμῖν ἐν τῇ ἐπιστολῇ μὴ συναναμίγνυσθαι **πόρνοις**, [GNT] | Sexually immoral people, fornicators, adulterers; people who indulge in sexual sin.<br><br>**Practical Application**<br>The word "*pornois*" means all kinds of immoral sexual acts. It includes adultery, pre-marital sex, homosexuality, and all forms of sexual deviation. Those who practice immorality are not to be part of the fellowship of the church. Believers are not to keep close fellowship with them. |
| **#2087**<br>**Immorality**<br><br>Fornication–KJV<br>**Immorality–NASB**<br>Sexual immorality–NIV<br>Fornication–NKJV<br>Sexual immorality–NLT<br><br>**POSB REFERENCE**<br>(Gal.5:19-21; esp. v.19)<br>Note 2<br><br>See also POSB REF:<br>(Mk.7:21)<br>*Deeper Study* #5<br>(2 Cor.12:19-21; esp. v.21)<br>Note 3, point 2<br>(Col.3:5-7; esp. v.5)<br>Note 1<br>(Rev.9:20-21; esp.v.21)<br>Note 4, point 2d | πορνεία = *porneia*<br>Pronunciation: [por-ni'-ah]<br>Parsing (part of speech): noun<br>    Case—nominative<br>    Gender—feminine<br>    Number—singular<br>    Stem or root—from πορνεία, ας<br>Concordance References:<br>   ⇒ Strong's #4202 porneia<br>   ⇒ NIV #4518 porneia<br>   ⇒ NASB #4202 porneia<br><br>**Galatians 5:19**<br>Now the works of the flesh are manifest, which are these; Adultery, **fornication**, uncleanness, lasciviousness, [KJV]<br>Now the deeds of the flesh are evident, which are: **immorality**, impurity, sensuality, [NASB]<br>The acts of the sinful nature are obvious: **sexual immorality**, impurity and debauchery; [NIV]<br>Now the works of the flesh are evident, which are: adultery, **fornication**, uncleanness, lewdness, [NKJV]<br>When you follow the desires of your sinful nature, your lives will produce these evil results: **sexual immorality**, impure thoughts, eagerness for lustful pleasure, [NLT]<br>φανερὰ δέ ἐστι τὰ ἔργα τῆς σαρκός, ἅτινά ἐστι μοιχεία, **πορνεία**, ἀκαθαρσία, ἀσέλγεια, [GNS]<br>φανερὰ δέ ἐστιν τὰ ἔργα τῆς σαρκός, ἅτινά ἐστιν **πορνεία**, ἀκαθαρσία, ἀσέλγεια, [GNT] | Sexual sin; immorality; sexual immorality; sexual vice; sexual unfaithfulness; premarital sex; adultery; fornication.<br><br>**Practical Application**<br>This a broad word including all forms of immoral and sexual acts. It is pre-marital sex and adultery; it is abnormal sex, all kinds of sexual vice. |

# PRACTICAL WORD STUDIES
## in the NEW TESTAMENT

| ENGLISH WORD | GREEK WORD AND VERSE | THE WORD MEANS... |
|---|---|---|
| **#2088**<br>**Immorality**<br><br>Lasciviousness–KJV<br>Sensuality–NASB<br>Debauchery–NIV<br>Lewdness–NKJV<br>**Immorality–NLT**<br><br>**POSB**<br>**REFERENCE**<br>(1 Pt.4:3)<br>Note 3, point 1 | ἀσελγείαις = *aselgeiais*<br>Pronunciation: [as-elg'-i-ah-is]<br>Parsing (part of speech): noun<br>  Case—dative<br>  Gender—feminine<br>  Number—plural<br>  Stem or root—from ἀσέλγεια, ας<br>Concordance References:<br>  ⇒ Strong's #766 aselgeia<br>  ⇒ NIV #816 aselgeia<br>  ⇒ NASB #766 aselgeia<br><br>**1 Peter 4:3**<br>For the time past of our life may suffice us to have wrought the will of the Gentiles, when we walked in **lasciviousness**, lusts, excess of wine, revellings, banquetings, and abominable idolatries: [KJV]<br><br>For the time already past is sufficient for you to have carried out the desire of the Gentiles, having pursued a course of **sensuality**, lusts, drunkenness, carousals, drinking parties and abominable idolatries. [NASB]<br><br>For you have spent enough time in the past doing what pagans choose to do—living in **debauchery**, lust, drunkenness, orgies, carousing and detestable idolatry. [NIV]<br><br>For we *have spent* enough of our past lifetime in doing the will of the Gentiles—when we walked in **lewdness**, lusts, drunkenness, revelries, drinking parties, and abominable idolatries. [NKJV]<br><br>You have had enough in the past of the evil things that godless people enjoy—their **immorality** and lust, their feasting and drunkenness and wild parties, and their terrible worship of idols. [NLT]<br><br>ἀρκετὸς γὰρ ἡμῖν ὁ παρεληλυθὼς χρόνος τὸ βίου τὸ θέλημα τῶν ἐθνῶν κατεργάσασθαι, πεπορευμένους ἐν **ἀσελγείαις**, ἐπιθυμίαις, οἰνοφλυγίαις, κώμοις, πότοις, καὶ ἀθεμίτοις εἰδωλολατρείαις· [GNS]<br><br>ἀρκετὸς γὰρ ὁ παρεληλυθὼς χρόνος τὸ βούλημα τῶν ἐθνῶν κατεργάσθαι πεπορευμένους ἐν **ἀσελγείαις**, ἐπιθυμίαις, οἰνοφλυγίαις, κώμοις, πότοις καὶ ἀθεμίτοις εἰδωλολατρίαις. [GNT] | Debauchery, lasciviousness, sensuality, immorality, vice, filthiness, indecency, shamelessness, license, lustful desire; without restraint; lewdness.<br><br>**Practical Application**<br>A chief characteristic of the behavior is open and shameless indecency. It means unrestrained evil thoughts and behavior. It is giving in to brutish and lustful desires, a readiness for any pleasure. It is a man who knows no restraint, a man who has sinned so much that he no longer cares what people say or think. It is something far more distasteful than just doing wrong. The man who misbehaves usually tries to hide his wrong, but a sensual man does not care who knows about his exploits or shame. He wants; therefore he seeks to take and gratify. Decency and opinion do not matter. Initially when he began to sin, he did as all men do: he misbehaved in secret. But eventually, the sin got the best of him—to the point that he no longer cared who saw or knew. He became the subject of a master—the master of habit, of the thing itself. |
| **#2089**<br>**Immorality**<br><br>Fornication–KJV<br>**Immorality–NASB**<br>Adulteries–NIV<br>Fornication–NKJV<br>**Immorality–NLT**<br><br>**POSB**<br>**REFERENCE**<br>(Rev.18:2-7; esp. v.3)<br>Note 2 | πορνείας = *porneias*<br>Pronunciation: [por-ni'-ahs]<br>Parsing (part of speech): noun<br>  Case—genitive<br>  Gender—feminine<br>  Number—singular<br>  Stem or root—from πορνεία, ας<br>Concordance References:<br>  ⇒ Strong's #4202 porneia<br>  ⇒ NIV #4518 porneia<br>  ⇒ NASB #4202 porneia<br><br>**Rev. 18:3**<br>For all nations have drunk of the wine of the wrath of her **fornication**, and the kings of the earth have committed fornication with her, and the merchants of the earth are waxed rich through the abundance of her delicacies. [KJV]<br><br>"For all the nations have drunk of the wine of the passion of her **immorality**, and the kings of the earth have committed acts of immorality with her, and the merchants of the earth have become rich by the wealth of her sensuality." [NASB]<br><br>For all the nations have drunk the maddening wine of her **adulteries**. The kings of the earth committed adultery with her, and the merchants of the earth grew rich from her excessive luxuries." [NIV]<br><br>For all the nations have drunk of the wine of the wrath of her **fornication**, the kings of the earth have committed fornication with her, and the merchants of the earth have become rich through the abundance of her luxury." [NKJV] | Adulteries; immorality; sexual sin; spiritual fornication, the rejection of God and the turning to other gods.<br><br>**Practical Application**<br>The world of the end time will be days of secularism, humanism, and materialism. Man will worship himself and his secular society. He will focus his life around...<br>• technology<br>• pleasures<br>• science<br>• recreation<br>• education<br>• comforts<br><br>Babylon, the capital of the world, will take the lead in the secular society. The city will have economic wealth that will literally intoxicate the world. The businessmen and merchants of the world will grow rich because of Babylon's wealth. Its wealth will be so vast that it will be able to control nations and leaders and businessmen all over the world.<br><br>The point is this: the capital city will use its influence for evil, for secularism and power. The city will manipulate the nations and leaders of the world to follow its own evil purposes. Those evil purposes will be a secular society, a worship |

# Practical Word Studies
## in the New Testament

| ENGLISH WORD | GREEK WORD AND VERSE | THE WORD MEANS... |
|---|---|---|
| | For all the nations have drunk the wine of her passionate **immorality**. The rulers of the world have committed adultery with her, and merchants throughout the world have grown rich as a result of her luxurious living." [NLT]<br><br>ὅτι ἐκ τοῦ οἴνου τοῦ θυμοῦ τῆς **πορνείας** αὐτῆς πέπωκε πάντα τὰ ἔθνη, καὶ οἱ βασιλεῖς τῆς γῆς μετ' αὐτῆς ἐπόρνευσαν, καὶ οἱ ἔμποροι τῆς γῆς ἐκ τῆς δυνάμεως τοῦ στρήνους αὐτῆς ἐπλούτησαν. [GNS]<br><br>ὅτι ἐκ τοῦ οἴνου τοῦ θυμοῦ τῆς **πορνείας** αὐτῆς πέπωκαν πάντα τὰ ἔθνη καὶ οἱ βασιλεῖς τῆς γῆς μετ' αὐτῆς ἐπόρνευσαν καὶ οἱ ἔμποροι τῆς γῆς ἐκ τῆς δυνάμεως τοῦ στρήνους αὐτῆς ἐπλούτησαν. [GNT] | of the state and its leader as the answer to the utopian society, that is, to meeting the needs of the people. The city will lead the nations to exterminate the Jews, Christian believers, and the faithful of all other religions who refuse to give their first loyalty to the state. Babylon will be able to seduce the nations and leaders to follow in this evil plot because of its wealth. (See POSB pt.6—Rev. 13:4-8 for more discussion.) |
| **#2090**<br>**Immortal**<br><br>Uncorruptible–KJV<br>Incorruptible–NASB<br>**Immortal–NIV**<br>Incorruptible–NKJV<br>Ever-living–NLT<br><br>**POSB REFERENCE**<br>(Romans 1:22-23; esp. v.23)<br>Note 5, point 2a | ἀφθάρτου = *aphthartou*<br>Pronunciation: [af'-thar-too]<br>Parsing (part of speech): adjective<br>    Case—genitive<br>    Gender—masculine<br>    Number—singular<br>    Stem or root—from ἄφθαρτος, ον<br>Concordance References:<br>  ⇒ Strong's #862 aphthartos<br>  ⇒ NIV #915 aphthartos<br>  ⇒ NASB #862a aphthartos<br><br>**Romans 1:23**<br>And changed the glory of the **uncorruptible** God into an image made like to corruptible man, and to birds, and fourfooted beasts, and creeping things. [KJV]<br><br>And exchanged the glory of the **incorruptible** God for an image in the form of corruptible man and of birds and four-footed animals and crawling creatures. [NASB]<br><br>And exchanged the glory of the **immortal** God for images made to look like mortal man and birds and animals and reptiles. [NIV]<br><br>And changed the glory of the **incorruptible** God into an image made like corruptible man—and birds and four-footed animals and creeping things. [NKJV]<br><br>And instead of worshiping the glorious, **ever-living** God, they worshiped idols made to look like mere people, or birds and animals and snakes. [NLT]<br><br>καὶ ἤλλαξαν τὴν δόξαν τοῦ **ἀφθάρτου** Θεοῦ ἐν ὁμοιώματι εἰκόνος φθαρτοῦ ἀνθρώπου καὶ πετεινῶν καὶ τετραπόδων καὶ ἑρπετῶν. [GNS]<br><br>καὶ ἤλλαξαν τὴν δόξαν τοῦ **ἀφθάρτου** θεοῦ ἐν ὁμοιώματι εἰκόνος φθαρτοῦ ἀνθρώπου καὶ πετεινῶν καὶ τετραπόδων καὶ ἑρπετῶν. [GNT] | Imperishable; lasting forever; ever-living; incorruptible. God is said to be "ever-living" (*aphthartou*), which means non-decaying, imperishable, unchanging, and unaging.<br><br>**Practical Application**<br>Immortal means that God is not subject to passing away; He is eternal. God always has been, and always will be: God will always exist. |
| **#2091**<br>**Immortality**<br><br>**Immortality–KJV**<br>**Immortality–NASB**<br>**Immortality–NIV**<br>**Immortality–NKJV**<br>**Immortality–NLT**<br><br>**POSB REFERENCE**<br>(Romans 2:7)<br>*Deeper Study #3* | ἀφθαρσίαν = *aphtharsian*<br>Pronunciation: [af-thar-see'-ahn]<br>Parsing (part of speech): noun<br>    Case—accusative<br>    Gender—feminine<br>    Number—singular<br>    Stem or root—from ἀφθαρσία, ας<br>Concordance References:<br>  ⇒ Strong's #861 aphtharsia<br>  ⇒ NIV #914 aphtharsia<br>  ⇒ NASB #861 aphtharsia<br><br>**Romans 2:7**<br>To them who by patient continuance in well doing seek for glory and honour and **immortality**, eternal life: [KJV]<br><br>To those who by perseverance in doing good seek for glory and honor and **immortality**, eternal life; [NASB]<br><br>To those who by persistence in doing good seek glory, honor and **immortality**, he will give eternal life. [NIV]<br><br>Eternal life to those who by patient continuance in doing good seek for glory, honor, and **immortality**; [NKJV]<br><br>He will give eternal life to those who persist in doing | Imperishability, immortality.<br><br>**Practical Application**<br>Immortality means living forever with God; to be incorruptible, perfected, and made permanent and eternal. It means to be free from pain and tears, from being tired and weary, from trials and sin, from defilement, weakness, frailty, sickness, suffering, and death. It means to be free from an imperfect world and to be placed into a perfect world with God—a world that lasts forever and ever. |

# PRACTICAL WORD STUDIES
## in the NEW TESTAMENT

| ENGLISH WORD | GREEK WORD AND VERSE | THE WORD MEANS... |
|---|---|---|
| | what is good, seeking after the glory and honor and **immortality** that God offers. [NLT]<br><br>τοῖς μὲν καθ' ὑπομονὴν ἔργου ἀγαθοῦ δόξαν καὶ τιμὴν καὶ **ἀφθαρσίαν** ζητοῦσι, ζωὴν αἰώνιον· [GNS]<br><br>τοῖς μὲν καθ' ὑπομονὴν ἔργου ἀγαθοῦ δόξαν καὶ τιμὴν καὶ **ἀφθαρσίαν** ζητοῦσιν ζωὴν αἰώνιον, [GNT] | |
| **#2092**<br>**Immovable**<br><br>Unmovable–KJV<br>**Immovable–NASB**<br>Nothing move–NIV<br>**Immovable–NKJV**<br>Steady–NLT<br><br>**POSB REFERENCE**<br>(1 Cor.15:58)<br>Note 6, point 2 | ἀμετακίνητοι = *ametakinētoi*<br>Pronunciation: [am-et-ak-in'-ay-toy]<br>Parsing (part of speech): adjective<br>    Case—nominative<br>    Gender—masculine<br>    Number—plural<br>    Stem or root—from ἀμετακίνητος, ον<br>Concordance References:<br>  ⇒ Strong's #277 ametakinētos<br>  ⇒ NIV #293 ametakinētos<br>  ⇒ NASB #277 ametakinētos<br><br>**1 Cor. 15:58**<br>Therefore, my beloved brethren, be ye stedfast, **unmovable**, always abounding in the work of the Lord, forasmuch as ye know that your labour is not in vain in the Lord. [KJV]<br><br>Therefore, my beloved brethren, be steadfast, **immovable**, always abounding in the work of the Lord, knowing that your toil is not in vain in the Lord. [NASB]<br><br>Therefore, my dear brothers, stand firm. Let **nothing move** you. Always give yourselves fully to the work of the Lord, because you know that your labor in the Lord is not in vain. [NIV]<br><br>Therefore, my beloved brethren, be steadfast, **immovable**, always abounding in the work of the Lord, knowing that your labor is not in vain in the Lord. [NKJV]<br><br>So, my dear brothers and sisters, be strong and **steady**, always enthusiastic about the Lord's work, for you know that nothing you do for the Lord is ever useless. [NLT]<br><br>ὥστε, ἀδελφοί μου ἀγαπητοί, ἑδραῖοι γίνεσθε, **ἀμετακίνητοι**, περισσεύοντες ἐν τῷ ἔργῳ τοῦ Κυρίου πάντοτε, εἰδότες ὅτι ὁ κόπος ὑμῶν οὐκ ἔστι κενὸς ἐν Κυρίῳ. [GNS]<br><br>Ὥστε, ἀδελφοί μου ἀγαπητοί, ἑδραῖοι γίνεσθε, **ἀμετακίνητοι**, περισσεύοντες ἐν τῷ ἔργῳ τοῦ κυρίου πάντοτε, εἰδότες ὅτι ὁ κόπος ὑμῶν οὐκ ἔστιν κενὸς ἐν κυρίῳ. [GNT] | To be unyielding, unshaken, undisturbed. It means to be immovable and steady.<br><br>**Practical Application**<br>The believer is not to be fickle in his service for the Lord. He is to stand as solid as a rock in his beliefs and in his service for the Lord. |
| **#2093**<br>**Impartial**<br><br>Without partiality–KJV<br>Unwavering–NASB<br>**Impartial–NIV**<br>Without partiality–NKJV<br>No partiality–NLT<br><br>**POSB REFERENCE**<br>(Jas. 3:17-18; esp. v.17)<br>Note 3, point 2g | ἀδιάκριτος = *adiakritos*<br>Pronunciation: [ad-ee-ak-'ree-tos]<br>Parsing (part of speech): adjective<br>    Case—nominative<br>    Gender—feminine<br>    Number—singular<br>    Stem or root—from ἀδιάκριτος, ον<br>Concordance References:<br>  ⇒ Strong's #87 adiakritos<br>  ⇒ NIV #88 adiakritos<br>  ⇒ NASB #87 adiakritos<br><br>**James 3:17**<br>But the wisdom that is from above is first pure, then peaceable, gentle, and easy to be intreated, full of mercy and good fruits, **without partiality**, and without hypocrisy. [KJV]<br><br>But the wisdom from above is first pure, then peaceable, gentle, reasonable, full of mercy and good fruits, **unwavering**, without hypocrisy. [NASB]<br><br>But the wisdom that comes from heaven is first of all pure; then peace-loving, considerate, submissive, full of mercy and good fruit, **impartial** and sincere. [NIV]<br><br>But the wisdom that is from above is first pure, then peaceable, gentle, willing to yield, full of mercy and good fruits, **without partiality** and without hypocrisy. [NKJV] | Impartial; without partiality; unwavering; no partiality, no favoritism.<br><br>**Practical Application**<br>True wisdom is impartial (*adiakritos*). This word in the Greek actually means two things.<br>1. The wise teacher is impartial; he shows no partiality or favoritism to anyone.<br>2. The wise teacher is undivided in his convictions and judgments. He knows the truth, exactly what God's Word says, and he will not entertain false ideas or teachings. He is totally committed and undivided in following and teaching God's Word. |

# PRACTICAL WORD STUDIES
## in the NEW TESTAMENT

| ENGLISH WORD | GREEK WORD AND VERSE | THE WORD MEANS... |
|---|---|---|
| | But the wisdom that comes from heaven is first of all pure. It is also peace loving, gentle at all times, and willing to yield to others. It is full of mercy and good deeds. It shows **no partiality** and is always sincere. [NLT]<br><br>ἡ δὲ ἄνωθεν σοφία πρῶτον μὲν ἁγνή ἐστιν, ἔπειτα εἰρηνική, ἐπιεικής, εὐπειθής, μεστὴ ἐλέους καὶ καρπῶν ἀγαθῶν, **ἀδιάκριτος** καὶ ἀνυπόκριτος. [GNS]<br><br>ἡ δὲ ἄνωθεν σοφία πρῶτον μὲν ἁγνή ἐστιν, ἔπειτα εἰρηνική, ἐπιεικής, εὐπειθής, μεστὴ ἐλέους καὶ καρπῶν ἀγαθῶν, **ἀδιάκριτος**, ἀνυπόκριτος. [GNT] | |
| **#2094**<br>**Impelled To Go Out**<br><br>Driveth–KJV<br>**Impelled...to go out–NASB**<br>Sent out–NIV<br>Drove–NKJV<br>Compelled...to go–NASB<br><br>**POSB REFERENCE**<br>(Mk.1:12)<br>Note 2 | ἐκβάλλει = ekballei<br>Pronunciation: [ek-bal'-leh-ee]<br>Parsing (part of speech): verb<br>  Mood—indicative<br>  Tense—present<br>  Voice—active<br>  Person—3rd person<br>  Number—singular<br>  Stem or root—from ἐκβάλλω<br>Concordance References:<br>  ⇒ Strong's #1544 ekballō<br>  ⇒ NIV #1675 ekballō<br>  ⇒ NASB #1544 ekballō<br><br>**Mark 1:12**<br>And immediately the Spirit **driveth** him into the wilderness. [KJV]<br>And immediately the Spirit **impelled** Him **to go out** into the wilderness. [NASB]<br>At once the Spirit **sent** him **out** into the desert, [NIV]<br>Immediately the Spirit **drove** Him into the wilderness. [NKJV]<br>Immediately the Holy Spirit **compelled** Jesus **to go** into the wilderness. [NLT]<br>Καὶ εὐθὺς τὸ Πνεῦμα αὐτὸν **ἐκβάλλει** εἰς τὴν ἔρημον. [GNS]<br>Καὶ εὐθὺς τὸ πνεῦμα αὐτὸν **ἐκβάλλει** εἰς τὴν ἔρημον. [GNT] | Sent out, compelled to go; impelled to go out, to drive out; to thrust; to cast forth; to drive forth; to force.<br><br>**Practical Application**<br>Jesus was impelled with great force to go into the wilderness. He was driven by the Spirit to be tried. He was to be tried and tested, not to make Him fall but to make Him stronger and better prepared to do great things for God (see POSB note, pt.3—Matthew 4:1). |
| **#2096**<br>**Imperishable**<br><br>Incorruptible–KJV<br>**Imperishable–NASB**<br>That can never perish–NIV<br>Incorruptible–NKJV<br>Pure–NLT<br><br>**POSB REFERENCE**<br>(1 Pt.1:4)<br>Note 2, point 1 | ἄφθαρτον = aphtharton<br>Pronunciation: [af'-thar-ton]<br>Parsing (part of speech): adjective<br>  Case—accusative<br>  Gender—feminine<br>  Number—singular<br>  Stem or root—from ἄφθαρτος, ον<br>Concordance References:<br>  ⇒ Strong's #862 aphthartos<br>  ⇒ NIV #915 aphthartos<br>  ⇒ NASB #862 aphthartos<br><br>**1 Peter 1:4**<br>To an inheritance **incorruptible**, and undefiled, and that fadeth not away, reserved in heaven for you, [KJV]<br>To obtain an inheritance which is **imperishable** and undefiled and will not fade away, reserved in heaven for you, [NASB]<br>And into an inheritance **that can never perish**, spoil or fade—kept in heaven for you, [NIV]<br>To an inheritance **incorruptible** and undefiled and that does not fade away, reserved in heaven for you, [NKJV]<br>For God has reserved a priceless inheritance for his children. It is kept in heaven for you, **pure** and undefiled, beyond the reach of change and decay. [NLT]<br>εἰς κληρονομίαν **ἄφθαρτον** καὶ ἀμίαντον καὶ ἀμάραντον, τετηρημένην ἐν οὐρανοῖς εἰς ὑμᾶς [GNS]<br>εἰς κληρονομίαν **ἄφθαρτον** καὶ ἀμίαντον καὶ ἀμάραντον, τετηρημένην ἐν οὐρανοῖς εἰς ὑμᾶς [GNT] | Incorruptible, immortal, imperishable, pure, that can never perish; it does not age, deteriorate, or die; it does not have the seed of corruption within it.<br><br>**Practical Application**<br>Matthew Henry points out that everything on earth changes from better to worse, but not our inheritance. It is perfect and imperishable. It never changes, and it will never cease to be the most perfect inheritance and gift imaginable (*Matthew Henry's Commentary*, Vol.6., p.1005). |

# PRACTICAL WORD STUDIES
## in the NEW TESTAMENT

| ENGLISH WORD | GREEK WORD AND VERSE | THE WORD MEANS... |
|---|---|---|
| **#2096**<br>**Implacable**<br><br>**Implacable**–KJV<br>Not translated–NASB<br>Not translated–NIV<br>Unforgiving–NKJV<br>Unforgiving–NLT<br><br>**POSB REFERENCE**<br>(Romans 1:31)<br>*Deeper Study #22* | ἀσπόνδους = *aspondous*<br>Pronunciation: [as'-pon-doos]<br>Parsing (part of speech): adjective<br>    Case—accusative<br>    Gender—masculine<br>    Number—plural<br>    Stem or root—from ἀνελεήμων, ον<br>Concordance References:<br>  ⇒ Strong's #786 aspondos<br>  ⇒ NIV #Not Translated In NIV<br>  ⇒ NASB #Not Translated In NASB<br><br>**Romans 1:31**<br>Without understanding, covenantbreakers, without natural affection, **implacable**, unmerciful; [KJV]<br>Without understanding, untrustworthy, unloving, unmerciful; [NASB]—NOT TRANSLATED<br>They are senseless, faithless, heartless, ruthless. [NIV]—NOT TRANSLATED<br>Undiscerning, untrustworthy, unloving, **unforgiving**, unmerciful; [NKJV]<br>They refuse to understand, break their promises, and are heartless and **unforgiving**. [NLT]<br>ἀσυνέτους, ἀσυνθέτους, ἀστόργους, **ἀσπόνδους** ἀνελεήμονας· [GNS]<br>ἀσυνέτους ἀσυνθέτους ἀστόργους ἀνελεήμονας· [GNT] | Incapable of giving in, of being appeased or purified; to be unforgiving.<br><br>**Practical Application**<br>This word describes a person who is unwilling to make peace or come to an agreement. |
| **#2097**<br>**Implanted**<br><br>Engrafted–KJV<br>**Implanted**–NASB<br>Planted in–NIV<br>**Implanted**–NKJV<br>Planted in–NLT<br><br>**POSB REFERENCE**<br>(Jas. 1:19-21; esp. v.21)<br>Note 1, point 5 | ἔμφυτον = *emphuton*<br>Pronunciation: [em'-foo-ton]<br>Parsing (part of speech): adjective<br>    Case—accusative<br>    Gender—masculine<br>    Number—singular<br>    Stem or root—from ἔμφυτος, ον<br>Concordance References:<br>  ⇒ Strong's #1721 emphutos<br>  ⇒ NIV #1875 emphutos<br>  ⇒ NASB #1721 emphutos<br><br>**James 1:21**<br>Wherefore lay apart all filthiness and superfluity of naughtiness, and receive with meekness the **engrafted** word, which is able to save your souls. [KJV]<br>Therefore putting aside all filthiness and all that remains of wickedness, in humility receive the word **implanted**, which is able to save your souls. [NASB]<br>Therefore, get rid of all moral filth and the evil that is so prevalent and humbly accept the word **planted in** you, which can save you. [NIV]<br>Therefore lay aside all filthiness and overflow of wickedness, and receive with meekness the **implanted** word, which is able to save your souls. [NKJV]<br>So get rid of all the filth and evil in your lives, and humbly accept the message God has **planted in** your hearts, for it is strong enough to save your souls. [NLT]<br>διὸ ἀποθέμενοι πᾶσαν ῥυπαρίαν καὶ περισσείαν κακίας, ἐν πραΰτητι δέξασθε τὸν **ἔμφυτον** λόγον, τὸν δυνάμενον σῶσαι τὰς ψυχὰς ὑμῶν. [GNS]<br>διὸ ἀποθέμενοι πᾶσαν ῥυπαρίαν καὶ περισσείαν κακίας, ἐν πραΰτητι, δέξασθε τὸν **ἔμφυτον** λόγον τὸν δυνάμενον σῶσαι τὰς ψυχὰς ὑμῶν. [GNT] | To be planted in; to be engrafted; to be implanted; to be born within.<br><br>**Practical Application**<br>When a person really listens to the Word of God, it is implanted within his heart and life. What God says is actually born within his heart, and the man hears exactly what God says. The Word of God is born within his heart and life, and the person's soul is saved. He conquers and triumphs over all temptation, including the terrible temptation of rejecting God and doing his own thing and living like he wants. He is saved to live eternally with God. This is the first preparation that a person must make to withstand temptation: he must be quick to hear the Word of God. |
| **#2098**<br>**Implore**<br><br>Pray–KJV<br>Beg–NASB<br>**Implore**–NIV<br>**Implore**–NKJV<br>Urge–NLT | δεόμεθα = *deometha*<br>Pronunciation: [deh'-om-eh-tha]<br>Parsing (part of speech): verb<br>    Mood—indicative<br>    Tense—present<br>    Voice—middle or passive deponent<br>    Person—1st person<br>    Number—plural<br>    Stem or root—from δέομαι<br>Concordance References:<br>  ⇒ Strong's #1189 deomai | To implore; to pray; to beg; to urge; to intreat; to cry; to ask; and to plead with.<br><br>**Practical Application**<br>Note that it is "for Christ's sake" that we are to plead with men. Christ has paid the ultimate price to make reconciliation available to men: He has taken the sins of men upon Himself and borne the condemnation for them. Because He has done so much, every man owes his life to |

# PRACTICAL WORD STUDIES
## in the NEW TESTAMENT

| ENGLISH WORD | GREEK WORD AND VERSE | THE WORD MEANS... |
|---|---|---|
| **POSB REFERENCE** (2 Cor.5:20) Note 3 | ⇒ NIV #1289 deomai<br>⇒ NASB #1189a deomai<br><br>**2 Cor. 5:20**<br>Now then we are ambassadors for Christ, as though God did beseech you by us: we **pray** you in Christ's stead, be ye reconciled to God. [KJV]<br>Therefore, we are ambassadors for Christ, as though God were entreating through us; we **beg** you on behalf of Christ, be reconciled to God. [NASB]<br>We are therefore Christ's ambassadors, as though God were making his appeal through us. We **implore** you on Christ's behalf: Be reconciled to God. [NIV]<br>Now then, we are ambassadors for Christ, as though God were pleading through us: we **implore** you on Christ's behalf, be reconciled to God. [NKJV]<br>We are Christ's ambassadors, and God is using us to speak to you. We **urge** you, as though Christ himself were here pleading with you, "Be reconciled to God!" [NLT]<br>ὑπὲρ Χριστοῦ οὖν πρεσβεύομεν, ὡς τοῦ Θεοῦ παρακαλοῦντος δι' ἡμῶν· **δεόμεθα** ὑπὲρ Χριστοῦ, καταλλάγητε τῷ Θεῷ. [GNS]<br>ὑπὲρ Χριστοῦ οὖν πρεσβεύομεν ὡς τοῦ θεοῦ παρακαλοῦντος δι' ἡμῶν· **δεόμεθα** ὑπὲρ Χριστοῦ, καταλλάγητε τῷ θεῷ. [GNT] | Christ—every man owes it to Christ to be reconciled to God. For Christ's sake, a man should give himself to God. |
| **#2099**<br>**Implored**<br><br>Besought–KJV<br>Requesting–NASB<br>Begged–NIV<br>**Implored–NKJV**<br>Begged–NLT<br><br>**POSB REFERENCE** (Jn.4:46-47; esp. v.47) Note 1, point 4 | ἠρώτα = ërōta<br>Pronunciation: [ay-ro-tah']<br>Parsing (part of speech): verb<br>  Mood—indicative<br>  Tense—imperfect<br>  Voice—active<br>  Person—3rd person<br>  Number—singular<br>  Stem or root—from ἐρωτάω<br>Concordance References:<br>⇒ Strong's #2065 erōtaō<br>⇒ NIV #2263 erōtaō<br>⇒ NASB #2065 erōtaō<br><br>**John 4:47**<br>When he heard that Jesus was come out of Judaea into Galilee, he went unto him, and **besought** him that he would come down, and heal his son: for he was at the point of death. [KJV]<br>When he heard that Jesus had come out of Judea into Galilee, he went to Him, and was **requesting** Him to come down and heal his son; for he was at the point of death. [NASB]<br>When this man heard that Jesus had arrived in Galilee from Judea, he went to him and **begged** him to come and heal his son, who was close to death. [NIV]<br>When he heard that Jesus had come out of Judea into Galilee, he went to Him and **implored** Him to come down and heal his son, for he was at the point of death. [NKJV]<br>When he heard that Jesus had come from Judea and was traveling in Galilee, he went over to Cana. He found Jesus and **begged** him to come to Capernaum with him to heal his son, who was about to die. [NLT]<br>οὗτος ἀκούσας ὅτι Ἰησοῦς ἥκει ἐκ τῆς Ἰουδαίας εἰς τὴν Γαλιλαίαν, ἀπῆλθε πρὸς αὐτόν, καὶ **ἠρώτα** αὐτὸν ἵνα καταβῇ καὶ ἰάσηται αὐτοῦ τὸν υἱόν· ἤμελλε γὰρ ἀποθνῄσκειν. [GNS]<br>οὗτος ἀκούσας ὅτι Ἰησοῦς ἥκει ἐκ τῆς Ἰουδαίας εἰς τὴν Γαλιλαίαν ἀπῆλθεν πρὸς αὐτὸν καὶ **ἠρώτα** ἵνα καταβῇ καὶ ἰάσηται αὐτοῦ τὸν υἱόν, ἤμελλεν γὰρ ἀποθνῄσκειν. [GNT] | To ask; to request; to implore; to plead desperately; to urge; to beseech; to appeal; to supplicate; to pray for immediate help.<br><br>**Practical Application**<br>Note an important lesson from this Scripture: The man did not let his high position keep him from Jesus. He did not wrap himself in pride nor did he allow what others might say keep him from Jesus. He swallowed his pride and confessed his need in the face of all who ridiculed, and he went to Jesus. |

## PRACTICAL WORD STUDIES
### in the New Testament

| ENGLISH WORD | GREEK WORD AND VERSE | THE WORD MEANS... |
|---|---|---|
| **#2100**<br>**Impossible**<br><br>Impossible–KJV<br>Impossible–NASB<br>Impossible–NIV<br>Impossible–NKJV<br>Impossible–NLT<br><br>**POSB REFERENCE**<br>(Heb.6:6; esp. v.4)<br>Note 2 (commentary for v. 4 is in v. 6) | Ἀδύνατον = *Adunaton*<br>Pronunciation: [ad-oo'-nat-on]<br>Parsing (part of speech): adjective<br>    Case—nominative<br>    Gender—neuter<br>    Number—singular<br>    Stem or root—from ἀδύνατος, ον<br>Concordance References:<br>  ⇒ Strong's #102 adunatos<br>  ⇒ NIV #105 adunatos<br>  ⇒ NASB #102 adunatos<br><br>**Hebrews 6:4**<br>Note that the NASB translates this word in verse 6<br>    For it is **impossible** for those who were once enlightened, and have tasted of the heavenly gift, and were made partakers of the Holy Ghost, **Hebrews 6:4 [KJV]**<br>    For in the case of those who have once been enlightened and have tasted of the heavenly gift and have been made partakers of the Holy Spirit, **Hebrews 6:4 [NASB]**<br>    And then have fallen away, it is **impossible** to renew them again to repentance, since they again crucify to themselves the Son of God, and put Him to open shame. **Hebrews 6:6 [NASB]**<br>    It is **impossible** for those who have once been enlightened, who have tasted the heavenly gift, who have shared in the Holy Spirit, **Hebrews 6:4 [NIV]**<br>    For it is **impossible** for those who were once enlightened, and have tasted the heavenly gift, and have become partakers of the Holy Spirit, **Hebrews 6:4 [NKJV]**<br>    For it is **impossible** to restore to repentance those who were once enlightened—those who have experienced the good things of heaven and shared in the Holy Spirit, **Hebrews 6:4 [NLT]**<br>ἀδύνατον γὰρ τοὺς ἅπαξ φωτισθέντας, γευσαμένους τε τῆς δωρεᾶς τῆς ἐπουρανίου, καὶ μετόχους γενηθέντας Πνεύματος Ἁγίου, [GNS]<br>Ἀδύνατον γὰρ τοὺς ἅπαξ φωτισθέντας, γευσαμένους τε τῆς δωρεᾶς τῆς ἐπουρανίου καὶ μετόχους γενηθέντας πνεύματος ἁγίου **Hebrews 6:4 [GNT]** | Impossible, unrealizable, unattainable, unworkable, unfeasible.<br><br>**Practical Application**<br>    The warning is severe and frightening to any heart that will listen.<br>    *"It is impossible for those who were once enlightened...if they shall fall away, to renew them again unto repentance"* (Hebrews 6:4, 6). What does it mean? Note exactly what Scripture says and only what it says.<br>    Scripture says "impossible": if a believer "falls away," it is impossible for him to ever repent again. The word *impossible* just cannot be made to mean anything other than impossible—not without straining and twisting the Scripture. As Marvin Vincent says: "Impossible (*Adunaton*). It is impossible to dilute this word into *difficult*" (*Word Studies in the New Testament*, Vol. 4, p.444). |
| **#2101**<br>**Imprisonments**<br><br>Imprisonments–KJV<br>Imprisonments–NASB<br>Imprisonments–NIV<br>Imprisonments–NKJV<br>Been put in jail–NLT<br><br>**POSB REFERENCE**<br>(2 Cor.6:4-5; esp. v.5)<br>Note 3 | φυλακαῖς = *phulakais*<br>Pronunciation: [foo-lak-ah-ees]<br>Parsing (part of speech): noun<br>    Case—dative<br>    Gender—feminine<br>    Number—plural<br>    Stem or root—from φυλακή, ῆς<br>Concordance References:<br>  ⇒ Strong's #5438 phulakē<br>  ⇒ NIV #5871 phulakē<br>  ⇒ NASB #5438 phulakē<br><br>**2 Cor. 6:5**<br>    In stripes, in **imprisonments**, in tumults, in labours, in watchings, in fastings; [KJV]<br>    In beatings, in **imprisonments**, in tumults, in labors, in sleeplessness, in hunger, [NASB]<br>    In beatings, **imprisonments** and riots; in hard work, sleepless nights and hunger; [NIV]<br>    In stripes, in **imprisonments**, in tumults, in labors, in sleeplessness, in fastings; [NKJV]<br>    We have been beaten, **been put in jail**, faced angry mobs, worked to exhaustion, endured sleepless nights, and gone without food. [NLT]<br>ἐν πληγαῖς, ἐν **φυλακαῖς**, ἐν ἀκαταστασίαις, ἐν κόποις, ἐν ἀγρυπνίαις, ἐν νηστείαις, [GNS]<br>ἐν πληγαῖς, ἐν **φυλακαῖς**, ἐν ἀκαταστασίαις, ἐν κόποις, ἐν ἀγρυπνίαις, ἐν νηστείαις, [GNT] | Imprisonments; to be put in jail.<br><br>**Practical Application**<br>    Paul was arrested and imprisoned several times: in Philippi (Acts 16), Jerusalem, Cesarea, and Rome. The early church Christian Clement of Rome (A.D. 96) says that Paul was imprisoned seven times throughout the whole span of his ministry. When the believer, minister, or layman faces imprisonment for Christ, the call of the hour is for consistency: he must endure despite the threat. He must not weaken lest he become an offense to the name of Christ and to the ministry. |

# PRACTICAL WORD STUDIES
## in the NEW TESTAMENT

| ENGLISH WORD | GREEK WORD AND VERSE | THE WORD MEANS... |
|---|---|---|
| **#2102**<br>**Imprisoned**<br><br>Concluded–KJV<br>Shut up–NASB<br>Bound over–NIV<br>Committed–NKJV<br>Imprisoned–NLT<br><br>**POSB REFERENCE**<br>(Rom.11:32)<br>Note 5 | συνέκλεισεν = sunekleisen<br>Pronunciation: [soon-he-kli'-sehn]<br>Parsing (part of speech): verb<br>    Mood—indicative<br>    Tense—aorist<br>    Voice—active<br>    Person—3rd person<br>    Number—singular<br>    Stem or root—from συγκλείω<br>Concordance References:<br>⇒ Strong's #4788 sugkleiö<br>⇒ NIV #5168 sugkleiö<br>⇒ NASB #4788 sugkleiö<br><br>**Romans 11:32**<br>For God hath **concluded** them all in unbelief, that he might have mercy upon all. [KJV]<br>For God has **shut up** all in disobedience that He might show mercy to all. [NASB]<br>For God has **bound** all men **over** to disobedience so that he may have mercy on them all. [NIV]<br>For God has **committed** them all to disobedience, that He might have mercy on all. [NKJV]<br>For God has **imprisoned** all people in their own disobedience so he could have mercy on everyone. [NLT]<br>συνέκλεισε γὰρ ὁ Θεὸς τοὺς πάντας εἰς ἀπείθειαν ἵνα τοὺς πάντας ἐλεήσῃ. [GNS]<br>συνέκλεισεν γὰρ ὁ θεὸς τοὺς πάντας εἰς ἀπείθειαν, ἵνα τοὺς πάντας ἐλεήσῃ.[GNT] | To be bound over; to imprison; to shut up in a place; to close up; to lock up; to be committed to disobedience.<br><br>**Practical Application**<br>This is an unusual idea: God has taken men, both Jews and Gentiles, and shut them up to unbelief (*apeitheian*) or disobedience. This is the judicial judgment of God (see POSB *Deeper Study* #2—Romans 11:7-10; POSB note—Romans 1:24; POSB *Deeper Study* #1—John 12:39-41). It is the picture of God's using sin and events for good. God takes sin and works it out for the good of the world. Man has chosen sin, choosing to go his own way in life, so God allows man to do his own thing. God locks man up in his own world of selfishness, allowing man to roam around in his world of sin. Why? So that man's true nature of sinfulness will be clearly seen, and thereby cause the honest and thinking man to seek God. God wishes to have mercy upon all, both Jew and Gentile; but before men can come to God, they must confess two things:<br>⇒ that they are sinful and dying creatures in desperate need of God.<br>⇒ that God exists and that He will have mercy upon the person who diligently seeks Him (Heb.11:6). |
| **#2103**<br>**Impure**<br><br>Unclean–KJV<br>Impure–NASB<br>Impure–NIV<br>Unclean–NKJV<br>Impure–NLT<br><br>**POSB REFERENCE**<br>(Eph.5:5-6; esp. v.5)<br>Note 5, point 1 | ἀκάθαρτος = akathartos<br>Pronunciation: [ak-ath'-ar-tos]<br>Parsing (part of speech): pronominal adjective<br>    Case—nominative<br>    Gender—masculine<br>    Number—singular<br>    Stem or root—from ἀκάθαρτος, ον<br>Concordance References:<br>⇒ Strong's #169 akathartos<br>⇒ NIV #176 akathartos<br>⇒ NASB #169 akathartos<br><br>**Ephes. 5:5**<br>For this ye know, that no whoremonger, nor **unclean** person, nor covetous man, who is an idolater, hath any inheritance in the kingdom of Christ and of God. [KJV]<br>For this you know with certainty, that no immoral or **impure** person or covetous man, who is an idolater, has an inheritance in the kingdom of Christ and God. [NASB]<br>For of this you can be sure: No immoral, **impure** or greedy person—such a man is an idolater—has any inheritance in the kingdom of Christ and of God. [NIV]<br>For this you know, that no fornicator, **unclean** person, nor covetous man, who is an idolater, has any inheritance in the kingdom of Christ and God. [NKJV]<br>You can be sure that no immoral, **impure**, or greedy person will inherit the Kingdom of Christ and of God. For a greedy person is really an idolater who worships the things of this world. [NLT]<br>τοῦτο γὰρ ἔστε γινώσκοντες, ὅτι πᾶς πόρνος, ἢ **ἀκάθαρτος**, ἢ πλεονέκτης, ὅς ἐστιν εἰδωλολάτρης, οὐκ ἔχει κληρονομίαν ἐν τῇ βασιλείᾳ τοῦ Χριστοῦ καὶ Θεοῦ. [GNS]<br>τοῦτο γὰρ ἴστε γινώσκοντες, ὅτι πᾶς πόρνος ἢ **ἀκάθαρτος** ἢ πλεονέκτης, ὅ ἐστιν εἰδωλολάτρης, οὐκ ἔχει κληρονομίαν ἐν τῇ βασιλείᾳ τοῦ Χριστοῦ καὶ θεοῦ. [GNT] | Impure, unclean, defiling, filthy, evil.<br><br>**Practical Application**<br>An "impure person" (*akathartos*) is a person who has unclean, immoral, dirty thoughts or behavior. |
| **#2104**<br>**Impure Or Unclean** | κοινὸν καὶ ἀκάθαρτον = koinon kai akatharton<br>Pronunciation: [koy-non' kah-ee ak-ath'-ar-ton]<br>Parsing *koinon* (part of speech): pronominal adjective<br>    Case—accusative<br>    Gender—neuter<br>    Number—singular<br>    Stem or root—from κοινός, ή, όν | Impure or unclean; common or unclean; unholy and unclean.<br><br>**Practical Application**<br>The words "impure or unclean" (*koinon kai akatharton*) refer to being religiously or ceremo- |

# PRACTICAL WORD STUDIES
## in the NEW TESTAMENT

| ENGLISH WORD | GREEK WORD AND VERSE | THE WORD MEANS... |
|---|---|---|
| Common or unclean–KJV<br>Unholy and unclean–NASB<br>**Impure or unclean–NIV**<br>Common or unclean–NKJV<br>Forbidden by our Jewish laws–NLT<br><br>**POSB REFERENCE**<br>(Acts 10:11-16; esp. v.14)<br>*Deeper Study #3* | Parsing *akatharton* (part of speech): pronominal adjective<br>    Case—accusative<br>    Gender—neuter<br>    Number—singular<br>    Stem or root—from ἀκάθαρτος, ον<br>Concordance References:<br>⇒ Strong's #2839 koinos + 2532 kai + 169 akathartos<br>⇒ NIV #3123 koinos [impure] + 2779 kai [or] + 176 akathartos [unclean]<br>⇒ NASB #2839 koinos + 2532 kai + 169 akathartos<br><br>**Acts 10:14**<br>But Peter said, Not so, Lord; for I have never eaten any thing that is **common or unclean**. [KJV]<br>But Peter said, "By no means, Lord, for I have never eaten anything **unholy and unclean**." [NASB]<br>"Surely not, Lord!" Peter replied. "I have never eaten anything **impure or unclean**." [NIV]<br>But Peter said, "Not so, Lord! For I have never eaten anything **common or unclean**." [NKJV]<br>"Never, Lord," Peter declared. "I have never in all my life eaten anything **forbidden by our Jewish laws**." [NLT]<br>ὁ δὲ Πέτρος εἶπε, Μηδαμῶς Κύριε· ὅτι οὐδέποτε ἔφαγον πᾶν **κοινὸν** ἢ **ἀκάθαρτον**. [GNS]<br>ὁ δὲ Πέτρος εἶπεν, Μηδαμῶς, κύριε, ὅτι οὐδέποτε ἔφαγον πᾶν **κοινὸν** καὶ **ἀκάθαρτον**. [GNT] | nially unclean. The unclean animals were unhallowed, profaned. The Jews felt that eating them would not please God. |
| **#2105**<br>**Impure Thoughts**<br><br>Uncleanness–KJV<br>Impurity–NASB<br>Impurity–NIV<br>Uncleanness–NKJV<br>**Impure thoughts–NLT**<br><br>**POSB REFERENCE**<br>(Gal.5:19-21; esp. v.19)<br>Note 2<br><br>See also POSB REF:<br>(2 Cor.12:19-21; esp. v.21)<br>Note 3, point 2<br>(Eph.4:17-19; esp. v.19)<br>Note 1, point 6<br>(Col.3:5-7; esp. v.5)<br>Note 1, point 1 | ἀκαθαρσία = *akatharsia*<br>Pronunciation: [ak-ath-ar-see'-ah]<br>Parsing (part of speech): noun<br>    Case—nominative<br>    Gender—feminine<br>    Number—singular<br>    Stem or root—from ἀκαθαρσία, ας<br>Concordance References:<br>⇒ Strong's #167 akatharsia<br>⇒ NIV #174 akatharsia<br>⇒ NASB #167 akatharsia<br><br>**Galatians 5:19**<br>Now the works of the flesh are manifest, which are these; Adultery, fornication, **uncleanness**, lasciviousness, [KJV]<br>Now the deeds of the flesh are evident, which are: immorality, **impurity**, sensuality, [NASB]<br>The acts of the sinful nature are obvious: sexual immorality, **impurity** and debauchery; [NIV]<br>Now the works of the flesh are evident, which are: adultery, fornication, **uncleanness**, lewdness, [NKJV]<br>When you follow the desires of your sinful nature, your lives will produce these evil results: sexual immorality, **impure thoughts**, eagerness for lustful pleasure, [NLT]<br>φανερὰ δέ ἐστι τὰ ἔργα τῆς σαρκός, ἅτινά ἐστι μοιχεία, πορνεία, **ἀκαθαρσία**, ἀσέλγεια, [GNS]<br>φανερὰ δέ ἐστιν τὰ ἔργα τῆς σαρκός, ἅτινά ἐστιν πορνεία, **ἀκαθαρσία**, ἀσέλγεια, [GNT] | Impurity, uncleanness, impure thoughts, filth, rottenness, moral impurity; doing things that dirty, pollute, and soil life. It means to be dirty and filthy; to be infested with every kind of unclean, immoral, dirty, and polluted behavior. It is the most immoral behavior imaginable. It is *unbridled lust* turned loose.<br><br>**Practical Application**<br>When men turn from God—abandon God to live unclean and immoral lives—God leaves men. He abandons them to their choice. God lets men wallow around in their filthiness. Men are judged and condemned to impurity (cp. Ro.1:18-32). |
| **#2106**<br>**Impurity**<br><br>Uncleanness–KJV<br>**Impurity–NASB**<br>Sexual impurity–NIV<br>Uncleanness–NKJV<br>Shameful things–NLT | ἀκαθαρσίαν = *akatharsian*<br>Pronunciation: [ak-ath-ar-see'-ahn]<br>Parsing (part of speech): noun<br>    Case—accusative<br>    Gender—feminine<br>    Number—singular<br>    Stem or root—from ἀκαθαρσία, ας<br>Concordance References:<br>⇒ Strong's #167 akatharsia<br>⇒ NIV #174 akatharsia<br>⇒ NASB #167 akatharsia | Impurity, immorality; impure motive; rottenness, filthiness, defilement, dirt, pollution, contamination, infection.<br><br>**Practical Application**<br>God—the only living and true God—shows wrath by giving men up to uncleanness. When men turn from God—abandon God to live unclean and immoral lives—God leaves men. He abandons them to their choice. God lets men |

# PRACTICAL WORD STUDIES
## in the NEW TESTAMENT

| ENGLISH WORD | GREEK WORD AND VERSE | THE WORD MEANS... |
|---|---|---|
| **POSB REFERENCE** (Romans 1:24-25; esp. v.24) Note 2 | **Romans 1:24** Wherefore God also gave them up to **uncleanness** through the lusts of their own hearts, to dishonour their own bodies between themselves: [KJV] Therefore God gave them over in the lusts of their hearts to **impurity**, that their bodies might be dishonored among them. [NASB] Therefore God gave them over in the sinful desires of their hearts to **sexual impurity** for the degrading of their bodies with one another. [NIV] Therefore God also gave them up to **uncleanness**, in the lusts of their hearts, to dishonor their bodies among themselves, [NKJV] So God let them go ahead and do whatever **shameful things** their hearts desired. As a result, they did vile and degrading things with each other's bodies. [NLT] Διὸ καὶ παρέδωκεν αὐτοὺς ὁ Θεὸς ἐν ταῖς ἐπιθυμίαις τῶν καρδιῶν αὐτῶν εἰς **ἀκαθαρσίαν** τοῦ ἀτιμάζεσθαι τὰ σώματα αὐτῶν ἐν αὐτοῖς· [GNS] Διὸ παρέδωκεν αὐτοὺς ὁ Θεὸς ἐν ταῖς ἐπιθυμίαις τῶν καρδιῶν αὐτῶν εἰς **ἀκαθαρσίαν** τοῦ ἀτιμάζεσθαι τὰ σώματα αὐτῶν ἐν αὐτοῖς· [GNT] | wallow around in their filthiness. Men are judged and condemned to uncleanness. |
| **#2107 Impurity** Uncleanness–KJV **Impurity–NASB Impurity–NIV** Uncleanness–NKJV Impure thoughts–NLT **POSB REFERENCE** (Gal.5:19-21; esp. v.19) Note 2 See also POSB REF: (2 Cor.12:19-21; esp. v.21) Note 3, point 2 (Eph.4:17-19; esp. v.19) Note 1, point 6 (Col.3:5-7; esp. v.5) Note 1, point 1 | **ἀκαθαρσία** = akatharsia Pronunciation: [ak-ath-ar-see'-ah] Parsing (part of speech): noun     Case—nominative     Gender—feminine     Number—singular     Stem or root—from ἀκαθαρσία, ας Concordance References: ⇒ Strong's #167 akatharsia ⇒ NIV #174 akatharsia ⇒ NASB #167 akatharsia **Galatians 5:19** Now the works of the flesh are manifest, which are these; Adultery, fornication, **uncleanness**, lasciviousness, [KJV] Now the deeds of the flesh are evident, which are: immorality, **impurity**, sensuality, [NASB] The acts of the sinful nature are obvious: sexual immorality, **impurity** and debauchery; [NIV] Now the works of the flesh are evident, which are: adultery, fornication, **uncleanness**, lewdness, [NKJV] When you follow the desires of your sinful nature, your lives will produce these evil results: sexual immorality, **impure thoughts**, eagerness for lustful pleasure, [NLT] φανερὰ δέ ἐστι τὰ ἔργα τῆς σαρκός, ἅτινά ἐστι μοιχεία, πορνεία, **ἀκαθαρσία**, ἀσέλγεια, [GNS] φανερὰ δέ ἐστιν τὰ ἔργα τῆς σαρκός, ἅτινά ἐστιν πορνεία, **ἀκαθαρσία**, ἀσέλγεια, [GNT] | Impurity, uncleanness, impure thoughts, filth, rottenness, moral impurity; doing things that dirty, pollute, and soil life. It means to be dirty and filthy; to be infested with every kind of unclean, immoral, dirty, and polluted behavior. It is the most immoral behavior imaginable. It is *unbridled lust* turned loose. **Practical Application** When men turn from God—abandon God to live unclean and immoral lives—God leaves men. He abandons them to their choice. God lets men wallow around in their filthiness. Men are judged and condemned to impurity (cp. Ro. 1:18-32). |
| **#2108 Imputed** **Imputed–KJV** Reckoned–NASB Credited–NIV Accounted–NKJV Declared–NLT **POSB REFERENCE** (Romans 4:22) Deeper Study #1 | **ἐλογίσθη** = elogisthē Pronunciation: [eh-log-ees'-thay] Parsing (part of speech): verb     Mood—indicative     Tense—aorist     Voice—passive     Person—3rd person     Number—singular     Stem or root—from λογίζομαι Concordance References: ⇒ Strong's #3049 logizomai ⇒ NIV #3357 logizomai ⇒ NASB #3049 logizomai **Romans 4:22** And therefore it was **imputed** to him for righteousness. [KJV] Therefore also it was **reckoned** to him as righteous- | To credit; to impute; to reckon; to declare; to count; to compute; to ascribe; to deposit; to put to one's account. **Practical Application** Abraham's faith was counted for righteousness. (See POSB *Deeper Study* #1, Reckon—Romans 6:11 for a fuller discussion.) Abraham deposited his faith with God, and God imputed or credited Abraham's faith as righteousness. |

| ENGLISH WORD | GREEK WORD AND VERSE | THE WORD MEANS... |
|---|---|---|
| | ness. [NASB]<br>This is why "it was **credited** to him as righteousness." [NIV]<br>And therefore "it was **accounted** to him for righteousness." [NKJV]<br>And because of Abraham's faith, God **declared** him to be righteous. [NLT]<br>διὸ καὶ **ἐλογίσθη** αὐτῷ εἰς δικαιοσύνην. [GNS]<br>διὸ [καὶ] **ἐλογίσθη** αὐτῷ εἰς δικαιοσύνην. [GNT] | |
| **#2109**<br>**Imputes–**<br>**Imputeth**<br><br>**Imputeth**–KJV<br>Reckons–NASB<br>Credits–NIV<br>**Imputes**–NKJV<br>Declared–NLT<br><br>**POSB**<br>**REFERENCE**<br>(Romans 4:6-8; esp. v.6)<br>Note 3, point 1 | λογίζεται = *logizetai*<br>Pronunciation: [log-id'-zeh-ahee]<br>Parsing (part of speech): verb<br>   Mood—indicative<br>   Tense—present<br>   Voice—middle or passive deponent<br>   Person—3rd person<br>   Number—singular<br>   Stem or root—from λογίζομαι<br>Concordance References:<br> ⇒ Strong's #3049 logizomai<br> ⇒ NIV #3357 logizomai<br> ⇒ NASB #3049 logizomai<br><br>**Romans 4:6**<br>Even as David also describeth the blessedness of the man, unto whom God **imputeth** righteousness without works, [KJV]<br>Just as David also speaks of the blessing upon the man to whom God **reckons** righteousness apart from works: [NASB]<br>David says the same thing when he speaks of the blessedness of the man to whom God **credits** righteousness apart from works: [NIV]<br>Just as David also describes the blessedness of the man to whom God **imputes** righteousness apart from works: [NKJV]<br>King David spoke of this, describing the happiness of an undeserving sinner who is **declared** to be righteous: [NLT]<br>καθάπερ καὶ Δαβὶδ λέγει τὸν μακαρισμὸν τοῦ ἀνθρώπου, ᾧ ὁ Θεὸς **λογίζεται** δικαιοσύνην χωρὶς ἔργων, [GNS]<br>καθάπερ καὶ Δαυὶδ λέγει τὸν μακαρισμὸν τοῦ ἀνθρώπου ᾧ ὁ Θεὸς **λογίζεται** δικαιοσύνην χωρὶς ἔργων, [GNT] | To credit; to impute; to reckon; to declare; to count; to put to one's account; to deposit.<br><br>**Practical Application**<br>The blessed man is the man who is counted righteous without works. Just think for a moment. If God credits and counts a man righteous "without works," then we know something: Man is not justified by works, but by faith. (See POSB *Deeper Study* #1, Reckon—Romans 6:11 for more discussion.) |
| **#2110**<br>**Imputing**<br><br>**Imputing**–KJV<br>Counting–NASB<br>Counting–NIV<br>**Imputing**–NKJV<br>Counting–NLT<br><br>**POSB**<br>**REFERENCE**<br>(2 Cor.5:18-19; esp. v.19)<br>Note 2, point 2 | λογιζόμενος = *logizomenos*<br>Pronunciation: [log-id-zo'-mehn-os]<br>Parsing (part of speech): verb<br>   Mood—participle<br>   Tense—present<br>   Voice—middle or passive deponent<br>   Case—nominative<br>   Gender—masculine<br>   Number—singular<br>   Stem or root—from λογίζομαι<br>Concordance References:<br> ⇒ Strong's #3049 logizomai<br> ⇒ NIV #3357 logizomai<br> ⇒ NASB #3049 logizomai<br><br>**2 Cor. 5:19**<br>To wit, that God was in Christ, reconciling the world unto himself, not **imputing** their trespasses unto them; and hath committed unto us the word of reconciliation. [KJV]<br>Namely, that God was in Christ reconciling the world to Himself, not **counting** their trespasses against them, and He has committed to us the word of reconciliation. [NASB]<br>That God was reconciling the world to himself in Christ, not **counting** men's sins against them. And he has | To count, reckon, impute, take into account; calculate, and credit. It means to charge or put to a person's account.<br><br>**Practical Application**<br>God does not count or impute sin to men. If God does not impute or charge sin against men, then it means that He forgives their sins. When Jesus Christ died on the cross, God was in Christ dying for the sins of men. God was making it possible for men to be freed from the guilt and condemnation of their sins.<br>Picture the scene: hanging there on the cross, God in Christ was not charging men with sin. He was dying for the sins of men. God was not there upon the cross to impute sin against men; He was there making it possible for men to be forgiven their sins. |

# PRACTICAL WORD STUDIES
## in the NEW TESTAMENT

| ENGLISH WORD | GREEK WORD AND VERSE | THE WORD MEANS... |
|---|---|---|
| | committed to us the message of reconciliation. [NIV]<br><br>That is, that God was in Christ reconciling the world to Himself, not **imputing** their trespasses to them, and has committed to us the word of reconciliation. [NKJV]<br><br>For God was in Christ, reconciling the world to himself, no longer **counting** people's sins against them. This is the wonderful message he has given us to tell others. [NLT]<br><br>ὡς ὅτι Θεὸς ἦν ἐν Χριστῷ κόσμον καταλλάσσων ἑαυτῷ, μὴ **λογιζόμενος** αὐτοῖς τὰ παραπτώματα αὐτῶν, καὶ θέμενος ἐν ἡμῖν τὸν λόγον τῆς καταλλαγῆς." [GNS]<br><br>ὡς ὅτι Θεὸς ἦν ἐν Χριστῷ κόσμον καταλλάσσων ἑαυτῷ, μὴ λογιζόμενος αὐτοῖς τὰ παραπτώματα αὐτῶν, καὶ θέμενος ἐν ἡμῖν τὸν λόγον τῆς καταλλαγῆς. [GNT] | |
| **#2111**<br>**In Christ Jesus**<br><br>In Christ Jesus–KJV<br>In Christ Jesus–NASB<br>By Christ Jesus–NIV<br>In Christ Jesus–NKJV<br>Through Christ Jesus–NLT<br><br>**POSB REFERENCE**<br>(Romans 3:24)<br>Note 3, point 2 | ἐν Χριστῷ Ἰησοῦ· = *en Christō Iēsou*<br>Pronunciation: [en khris-tow' ee-ay-soo']<br>Parsing *en* (part of speech): preposition<br>   Case—dative<br>   Stem or root—from ἐν<br>Concordance References:<br>⇒ Strong's #1722 en + 5547 Christos + 2424 Iēsous<br>⇒ NIV #1877 en [by] + 5986 Christos [Christ] + 2652 Iēsous [Jesus]<br>⇒ NASB #1722 en + 5547 Christos + 2424 Iēsous<br><br>**Romans 3:24**<br>Being justified freely by his grace through the redemption that is **in Christ Jesus**: [KJV]<br>Being justified as a gift by His grace through the redemption which is **in Christ Jesus**; [NASB]<br>And are justified freely by his grace through the redemption that came **by Christ Jesus**. [NIV]<br>Being justified freely by His grace through the redemption that is **in Christ Jesus**, [NKJV]<br>Yet now God in his gracious kindness declares us not guilty. He has done this **through Christ Jesus**, who has freed us by taking away our sins. [NLT]<br>δικαιούμενοι δωρεὰν τῇ αὐτοῦ χάριτι διὰ τῆς ἀπολυτρώσεως τῆς **ἐν Χριστῷ Ἰησοῦ·** [GNS]<br>δικαιούμενοι δωρεὰν τῇ αὐτοῦ χάριτι διὰ τῆς ἀπολυτρώσεως τῆς **ἐν Χριστῷ Ἰησοῦ·** [GNT] | *By* Christ Jesus, *in* Christ Jesus, *through* Christ Jesus.<br><br>**Practical Application**<br>Redemption is "in Christ Jesus," wrought through His death and sufferings. Of this there can be no doubt; the fact is critical to a person's destiny. Redemption is not brought about...<br>• by the life of Christ.<br>• by the power of Christ.<br>• by the example of Christ.<br>Scripture is abundantly clear about this. His cross and His sacrifice in death are what brought about redemption. Redemption is because of the shed blood of Jesus Christ, God's very own Son. In Christ and Christ alone, redemption is...<br>• accomplished<br>• a reality<br>• wrought<br>• a truth<br>• a fact<br>• fulfilled |
| **#2112**<br>**In Common**<br><br>Fellowship–KJV<br>Partnership–NASB<br>**In common**–NIV<br>Fellowship–NKJV<br>Partner–NLT<br><br>**POSB REFERENCE**<br>(2 Cor.6:14-16; esp. v.14)<br>Note 2, point 1c | μετοχή = *metochē*<br>Pronunciation: [met-okh-ay']<br>Parsing (part of speech): noun<br>   Case—nominative<br>   Gender—feminine<br>   Number—singular<br>   Stem or root—from μετοχή, ῆς<br>Concordance References:<br>⇒ Strong's #3352 metochē<br>⇒ NIV #3580 metochē<br>⇒ NASB #3352 metochē<br><br>**2 Cor. 6:14**<br>Be ye not unequally yoked together with unbelievers: for what **fellowship** hath righteousness with unrighteousness? and what communion hath light with darkness? [KJV]<br>Do not be bound together with unbelievers; for what **partnership** have righteousness and lawlessness, or what fellowship has light with darkness? [NASB]<br>Do not be yoked together with unbelievers. For what do righteousness and wickedness have **in common**? Or what fellowship can light have with darkness? [NIV]<br>Do not be unequally yoked together with unbelievers. For what **fellowship** has righteousness with lawlessness? And what communion has light with darkness? [NKJV]<br>Don't team up with those who are unbelievers. How can goodness be a **partner** with wickedness? How can | In common, sharing fellowship, partnership, and participation.<br><br>**Practical Application**<br>How can a believer who focuses his life upon the righteousness of Jesus Christ share and participate with unbelievers, unbelievers who care little if anything about Jesus Christ and His call to righteousness?<br>Unbelievers do not obey God. They live and do as they wish, not as God says. Rejecting God and what He says, they go about doing their own thing. They rebel against God and His commandments, living lawless and unrighteous lives. |

# PRACTICAL WORD STUDIES
## in the NEW TESTAMENT

| ENGLISH WORD | GREEK WORD AND VERSE | THE WORD MEANS... |
|---|---|---|
| | light live with darkness? [NLT]<br><br>Μὴ γίνεσθε ἑτεροζυγοῦντες ἀπίστοις· τίς γὰρ **μετοχὴ** δικαιοσύνῃ καὶ ἀνομίᾳ; τίς δὲ κοινωνία φωτὶ πρὸς σκότος; [GNS]<br><br>Μὴ γίνεσθε ἑτεροζυγοῦντες ἀπίστοις· τίς γὰρ **μετοχὴ** δικαιοσύνῃ καὶ ἀνομίᾳ, ἢ τίς κοινωνία φωτὶ πρὸς σκότος; [GNT] | |
| **#2113**<br>**In Common**<br><br>Part–KJV<br>**In common–NASB**<br>**In common–NIV**<br>Part–NKJV<br>Partner–NLT<br><br>**POSB REFERENCE**<br>(2 Cor.6:14-16; esp. v.15)<br>Note 2, point 4 | μερίς = meris<br>Pronunciation: [mer-ece']<br>Parsing (part of speech): noun<br>    Case—nominative<br>    Gender—feminine<br>    Number—singular<br>    Stem or root—from μερίς, ίδος<br>Concordance References:<br>⇒ Strong's #3310 meris<br>⇒ NIV #3535 meris<br>⇒ NASB #3310 meris<br><br>**2 Cor. 6:15**<br>And what concord hath Christ with Belial? or what **part** hath he that believeth with an infidel? [KJV]<br><br>Or what harmony has Christ with Belial, or what has a believer **in common** with an unbeliever? [NASB]<br><br>What harmony is there between Christ and Belial? What does a believer have **in common** with an unbeliever? [NIV]<br><br>And what accord has Christ with Belial? Or what **part** has a believer with an unbeliever? [NKJV]<br><br>What harmony can there be between Christ and the Devil? How can a believer be a **partner** with an unbeliever? [NLT]<br><br>τίς δὲ συμφώνησις Χριστῷ πρὸς Βελιάλ; ἢ τίς **μερὶς** πιστῷ μετὰ ἀπίστου; [GNS]<br><br>τίς δὲ συμφώνησις Χριστοῦ πρὸς Βελιάρ, ἢ τίς **μερὶς** πιστῷ μετὰ ἀπίστου; [GNT] | In common, part, partner. It means a person's portion, lot, sphere, realm, or participation in life.<br><br>**Practical Application**<br>The believer's faith is pictured as changing his whole life: his belief causes him to move in a whole new sphere or realm of life. He may live among unbelievers, living and working next to them, but he moves in a different realm. His purpose and behavior upon earth is different:<br>⇒ The believer believes that Christ is the Son of God and the Savior of the world; the unbeliever does not.<br>⇒ The believer lives as Christ dictates; the unbeliever lives as he wishes.<br>⇒ The believer seeks to honor Christ by putting Christ first and serving Him; the unbeliever lives for self and the world and its possessions.<br><br>The very meaning, purpose, and significance of life differ radically between the believer and the unbeliever. The believer seeks Christ and the things of Christ, whereas the unbeliever focuses his life primarily upon this world and self. |
| **#2114**<br>**In Despair**<br><br>**In despair–KJV**<br>Despairing–NASB<br>**In despair–NIV**<br>**In despair–NKJV**<br>Give up and quit–NLT<br><br>**POSB REFERENCE**<br>(2 Cor.4:7-9; esp. v.8)<br>Note 2, point 2 | ἐξαπορούμενοι = exaporoumenoi<br>Pronunciation: [ex-ap-or-oo'-mehn-oy]<br>Parsing (part of speech): verb<br>    Mood—participle<br>    Tense—present<br>    Voice—middle or passive deponent<br>    Case—nominative<br>    Gender—masculine<br>    Person—1st person<br>    Number—plural<br>    Stem or root—from ἐξαπορέομαι<br>Concordance References:<br>⇒ Strong's #1820 exaporeō<br>⇒ NIV #1989 exaporeō<br>⇒ NASB #1820 exaporeō<br><br>**2 Cor. 4:8**<br>We are troubled on every side, yet not distressed; we are perplexed, but not **in despair**; [KJV]<br><br>We are afflicted in every way, but not crushed; perplexed, but not **despairing**; [NASB]<br><br>We are hard pressed on every side, but not crushed; perplexed, but not **in despair**; [NIV]<br><br>*We are* hard pressed on every side, yet not crushed; *we are* perplexed, but not **in despair**; [NKJV]<br><br>We are pressed on every side by troubles, but we are not crushed and broken. We are perplexed, but we don't **give up and quit**. [NLT]<br><br>ἐν παντὶ θλιβόμενοι, ἀλλ' οὐ στενοχωρούμενοι· ἀπορούμενοι ἀλλ' οὐκ **ἐξαπορούμενοι**· [GNS]<br><br>ἐν παντὶ θλιβόμενοι ἀλλ' οὐ στενοχωρούμενοι, ἀπορούμενοι ἀλλ' οὐκ **ἐξαπορούμενοι**, [GNT] | To be in despair; to give up and quit; to be hopeless; to have no confidence or assurance; to be without any sense of security.<br><br>**Practical Application**<br>The believer is often perplexed, not understanding why this or that happened, what should be done or said, how the situation should be handled, and on and on. Sometimes situations become so puzzling that the Christian is almost stymied and the threat of despair faces him. There is the danger that his confidence and assurance will be shaken. But again, the presence and power of God steps in to save the believer from despair. God showing him the way out gives him hope and stirs his confidence. God never allows him to be overcome by despair. |

# PRACTICAL WORD STUDIES
in the NEW TESTAMENT

| ENGLISH WORD | GREEK WORD AND VERSE | THE WORD MEANS... |
|---|---|---|
| **#2115**<br>**In Divers Manners**<br><br>In divers manners–KJV<br>In many ways–NASB<br>In various ways–NIV<br>In various ways–NKJV<br>In many ways–NLT<br><br>**POSB REFERENCE**<br>(Heb.1:1-2; esp. v.1)<br>Note 1, point 1 | πολυτρόπως = polutropōs<br>Pronunciation: [pol-oot-rop'-oce]<br>Parsing (part of speech): adjective<br>    Type—adverb<br>    Stem or root—from πολυτρόπως<br>Concordance References:<br>  ⇒ Strong's #4187 polutropōs<br>  ⇒ NIV #4502 polutropōs<br>  ⇒ NASB #4187 polutropōs<br><br>**Hebrews 1:1**<br>God, who at sundry times and **in divers manners** spake in time past unto the fathers by the prophets, [KJV]<br>God, after He spoke long ago to the fathers in the prophets in many portions and **in many ways**, [NASB]<br>In the past God spoke to our forefathers through the prophets at many times and **in various ways**, [NIV]<br>God, who at various times and **in various ways** spoke in time past to the fathers by the prophets, [NKJV]<br>Long ago God spoke many times and **in many ways** to our ancestors through the prophets. [NLT]<br>Πολυμερῶς καὶ **πολυτρόπως** πάλαι ὁ Θεὸς λαλήσας τοῖς πατράσιν ἐν τοῖς προφήταις, [GNS]<br>Πολυμερῶς καὶ **πολυτρόπως** πάλαι ὁ θεὸς λαλήσας τοῖς πατράσιν ἐν τοῖς προφήταις [GNT] | In many ways, in various ways, in divers manners.<br><br>**Practical Application**<br>In ancient times God spoke to man by His prophets, that is, by persons whom He had chosen to proclaim His Word to the world. Who are these persons? They are the men and women of the Old Testament Scriptures. But note a significant fact: God spoke through the prophets...<br>• "at sundry times": that is, in many parts (*polumeros*); in many separate revelations, at many different times.<br>• in many ways (*polutropōs*).<br><br>What does this mean? No man could possibly receive and understand or explain the whole revelation of God. God and the truth of God are too big for any one man. Therefore, God had to make many revelations to many different people, and He had to use many different ways to speak to men. No man could ever contain or share the whole revelation of God. |
| **#2116**<br>**In Every Way**<br><br>On every side–KJV<br>**In every way–NASB**<br>On every side–NIV<br>On every side–NKJV<br>On every side–NLT<br><br>**POSB REFERENCE**<br>(2 Cor.4:7-9; esp. v.8)<br>Note 2, point 1 | ἐν παντί = en panti<br>Pronunciation: [en pahn-tee]<br>Parsing *panti* (part of speech): pronominal adjective<br>    Case—dative<br>    Gender—neuter<br>    Number—singular<br>    Stem or root—from πᾶς, πᾶσα, πᾶν<br>Concordance References:<br>  ⇒ Strong's #1722 en + 3956 pas<br>  ⇒ NIV #1877 en [on] + 4246 pas [every side]<br>  ⇒ NASB #1722 en + 3956 pas<br><br>**2 Cor. 4:8**<br>We are troubled **on every side**, yet not distressed; we are perplexed, but not in despair; [KJV]<br>We are afflicted **in every way**, but not crushed; perplexed, but not despairing; [NASB]<br>We are hard pressed **on every side**, but not crushed; perplexed, but not in despair; [NIV]<br>*We are* hard pressed **on every side**, yet not crushed; *we are* perplexed, but not in despair; [NKJV]<br>We are pressed **on every side** by troubles, but we are not crushed and broken. We are perplexed, but we don't give up and quit. [NLT]<br>ἐν παντὶ θλιβόμενοι, ἀλλ' οὐ στενοχωρούμενοι· ἀπορούμενοι ἀλλ' οὐκ ἐξαπορούμενοι· [GNS]<br>ἐν παντὶ θλιβόμενοι ἀλλ' οὐ στενοχωρούμενοι, ἀπορούμενοι ἀλλ' οὐκ ἐξαπορούμενοι, [GNT] | On every side; everywhere; in every imaginable way and place and occasion.<br><br>**Practical Application**<br>The minister experiences all kinds of affliction and pressure. He sometimes feels as though he is pressured and afflicted beyond what he can bear. It is as though a heavy weight is pressing in upon him, about to crush him. But then God steps in to save him from being distressed and crushed. The presence and power of God sustain His dear minister. |
| **#2117**<br>**In Heaviness**<br><br>In heaviness–KJV<br>Sorrow–NASB<br>Painful–NIV<br>Sorrow–NKJV<br>Painful–NLT<br><br>**POSB REFERENCE**<br>(2 Cor.2:1)<br>Note 2 | ἐν λύπῃ = en lupē<br>Pronunciation: [en loo'-pay]<br>Parsing *lupē* (part of speech): noun<br>    Case—dative<br>    Gender—feminine<br>    Number—singular<br>    Stem or root—from λύπη, ης<br>Concordance References:<br>  ⇒ Strong's #1722+3077 en lupē<br>  ⇒ NIV #1877+3383 en lupē<br>  ⇒ NASB #1722+3077 en lupē<br><br>**2 Cor. 2:1**<br>But I determined this with myself, that I would not come again to you **in heaviness**. [KJV]<br>But I determined this for my own sake, that I would not come to you in **sorrow** again. [NASB]<br>So I made up my mind that I would not make another | Painful; sorrow; in heaviness, grief, pain, regret.<br><br>**Practical Application**<br>It was best for the minister not to be the cause of pain. Note Paul's words, "But I determined this with myself, that I would not come again to you *in heaviness*." This just cannot apply to Paul's first visit to Corinth, for his first visit did not end in failure and rejection. When Paul first left Corinth, he was filled with joy over the great success God had given. Therefore, he must be speaking about some other visit when the church rejected him and cut his heart, causing great heaviness. |

# PRACTICAL WORD STUDIES
## in the NEW TESTAMENT

| ENGLISH WORD | GREEK WORD AND VERSE | THE WORD MEANS... |
|---|---|---|
| | **painful** visit to you. [NIV]<br>But I determined this within myself, that I would not come again to you in **sorrow**. [NKJV]<br>So I said to myself, "No, I won't do it. I won't make them unhappy with another **painful** visit." [NLT]<br>ἔκρινα δὲ ἐμαυτῷ τοῦτο, τὸ μὴ πάλιν ἐλθεῖν **ἐν λύπῃ** πρὸς ὑμᾶς. [GNS]<br>ἔκρινα γὰρ ἐμαυτῷ τοῦτο τὸ μὴ πάλιν **ἐν λύπῃ** πρὸς ὑμᾶς ἐλθεῖν. [GNT] | |
| **#2118**<br>**In Highest Heaven**<br><br>In the highest–KJV<br>In the highest–NASB<br>In the highest–NIV<br>In the highest–NKJV<br>**In highest heaven–NLT**<br><br>**POSB REFERENCE**<br>(Mk.11:10)<br>*Deeper Study* #8 | ἐν τοῖς ὑψίστοις = *en tois hupsistos*<br>Pronunciation: [en tois hoop'-sis-tos]<br>Parsing *hupsistos* (part of speech): pronominal adjective<br>    Type—superlative<br>    Case—dative<br>    Gender—neuter<br>    Number—plural<br>    Stem or root—from ὕψιστος, η, ον<br>Concordance References:<br>⇒ Strong's #1722 en + 3588 ho + 5310 hupsistos<br>⇒ NIV #1877 en [in] + 3836 ho [the] + 5736 hupsistos [highest]<br>⇒ NASB #1722 en + 3588 ho + 5310 hupsistos<br><br>**Mark 11:10**<br>Blessed be the kingdom of our father David, that cometh in the name of the Lord: Hosanna **in the highest**. [KJV]<br>Blessed is the coming kingdom of our father David; Hosanna **in the highest**!" [NASB]<br>"Blessed is the coming kingdom of our father David!" "Hosanna **in the highest**!" [NIV]<br>Blessed is the kingdom of our father David That comes in the name of the Lord! Hosanna **in the highest**!" [NKJV]<br>Bless the coming kingdom of our ancestor David! Praise God **in highest heaven**!" [NLT]<br>εὐλογημένη ἡ ἐρχομένη βασιλεία ἐν ὀνόματι Κυρίου, τοῦ πατρὸς ἡμῶν Δαβίδ· Ὡσαννὰ **ἐν τοῖς ὑψίστοις**. [GNS]<br>Εὐλογημένη ἡ ἐρχομένη βασιλεία τοῦ πατρὸς ἡμῶν Δαυίδ· Ὡσαννὰ **ἐν τοῖς ὑψίστοις**. [GNT] | In the highest; You who are in the Highest heaven, save now through Him whom You have sent.<br><br>**Practical Application**<br>In this Scripture, the masses of people welcomed their political king, One who would surely save and deliver them from the oppression of Rome. Ironically, Jesus was more than willing to deliver these people from bondage. But, most of them would have no part of His offer to save them from the greater bondage of their sins. They were more interested in a temporary fix through a change in political power. |
| **#2119**<br>**In Many Portions**<br><br>At sundry times–KJV<br>**In many portions–NASB**<br>At many times–NIV<br>At various times–NKJV<br>Many times–NLT<br><br>**POSB REFERENCE**<br>(Heb.1:1-2; esp. v.1)<br>Note 1, point 1 | Πολυμερῶς = *Polumerōs*<br>Pronunciation: [pol-oo-mer'-oce]<br>Parsing (part of speech): adverb adjective<br>    Stem or root—from πολυμερῶς<br>Concordance References:<br>⇒ Strong's #4181 polumerōs<br>⇒ NIV #4495 polumerōs<br>⇒ NASB #4181 polumerōs<br><br>**Hebrews 1:1**<br>God, who **at sundry times** and in divers manners spake in time past unto the fathers by the prophets, [KJV]<br>God, after He spoke long ago to the fathers in the prophets **in many portions** and in many ways, [NASB]<br>In the past God spoke to our forefathers through the prophets **at many times** and in various ways, [NIV]<br>God, who **at various times** and in various ways spoke in time past to the fathers by the prophets, [NKJV]<br>Long ago God spoke **many times** and in many ways to our ancestors through the prophets. [NLT]<br>**Πολυμερῶς** καὶ πολυτρόπως πάλαι ὁ Θεὸς λαλήσας τοῖς πατράσιν ἐν τοῖς προφήταις, [GNS]<br>**Πολυμερῶς** καὶ πολυτρόπως πάλαι ὁ θεὸς λαλήσας τοῖς πατράσιν ἐν τοῖς προφήταις [GNT] | At many times; that is, in many portions; in many parts; in many separate revelations; at many different times; little by little.<br><br>**Practical Application**<br>God's Word is found in the prophets. In ancient times God spoke to man by His prophets, that is, by persons whom He had chosen to proclaim His Word to the world. Who are these persons? They are the men and women of the Old Testament Scriptures. But note a significant fact: God spoke through the prophets...<br>• "in many portions"<br>• in many ways<br><br>What does this mean? No man could possibly receive and understand or explain the whole revelation of God. God and the truth of God are too big for any one man. Therefore, God had to make many revelations to many different people, and He had to use many different ways to speak to men. No man could ever contain or share the whole revelation of God. |
| **#2120**<br>**In Many Ways** | πολυτρόπως = *polutropōs*<br>Pronunciation: [pol-oot-rop'-oce]<br>Parsing (part of speech): adjective<br>    Type—adverb<br>    Stem or root—from πολυτρόπως | In many ways; in various ways; in divers manners. |

# PRACTICAL WORD STUDIES
## in the New Testament

| ENGLISH WORD | GREEK WORD AND VERSE | THE WORD MEANS... |
|---|---|---|
| In diverse manners–KJV<br>**In many ways–NASB**<br>In various ways–NIV<br>In various ways–NKJV<br>**In many ways–NLT**<br><br>**POSB REFERENCE**<br>(Heb.1:1-2; esp. v.1)<br>*Note 1, point 1* | Concordance References:<br>⇒ Strong's #4187 polutropōs<br>⇒ NIV #4502 polutropōs<br>⇒ NASB #4187 polutropōs<br><br>**Hebrews 1:1**<br>God, who at sundry times and **in divers manners** spake in time past unto the fathers by the prophets, [KJV]<br>God, after He spoke long ago to the fathers in the prophets in many portions and **in many ways**, [NASB]<br>In the past God spoke to our forefathers through the prophets at many times and **in various ways**, [NIV]<br>God, who at various times and **in various ways** spoke in time past to the fathers by the prophets, [NKJV]<br>Long ago God spoke many times and **in many ways** to our ancestors through the prophets. [NLT]<br>Πολυμερῶς καὶ **πολυτρόπως** πάλαι ὁ Θεὸς λαλήσας τοῖς πατράσιν ἐν τοῖς προφήταις, [GNS]<br>Πολυμερῶς καὶ **πολυτρόπως** πάλαι ὁ θεὸς λαλήσας τοῖς πατράσιν ἐν τοῖς προφήταις, [GNT] | **Practical Application**<br>In ancient times God spoke to man by His prophets, that is, by persons whom He had chosen to proclaim His Word to the world. Who are these persons? They are the men and women of the Old Testament Scriptures. But note a significant fact: God spoke through the prophets...<br>• "in many portions" [NASB]: that is, in many parts (*polumeros*); in many separate revelations, at many different times.<br>• in many ways (*polutropōs*).<br><br>What does this mean? No man could possibly receive and understand or explain the whole revelation of God. God and the truth of God are too big for any one man. Therefore, God had to make many revelations to many different people, and He had to use many different ways to speak to men. No man could ever contain or share the whole revelation of God. |
| **#2121**<br>**In My Name**<br><br>In my name–KJV<br>**In My name–NASB**<br>**In my name–NIV**<br>**In my name–NKJV**<br>Because they are mine–NLT<br><br>**POSB REFERENCE**<br>(Mt.18:19-20; esp. v.20)<br>*Deeper Study #3* | εἰς τὸ ἐμὸν ὄνομα = *eis to emon onoma*<br>Pronunciation: [ice to e-mon-on'-om-ah]<br>Parsing *onoma* (part of speech): noun<br>    Case—accusative<br>    Gender—neuter<br>    Number—singular<br>    Stem or root—from ὄνομα, τος<br>Concordance References:<br>⇒ Strong's #3686 onoma<br>⇒ NIV #1650 eis [in] + 1847 emos [my] + 3950 onoma [name]<br>⇒ NASB #3686 onoma<br><br>**Matthew 18:20**<br>For where two or three are gathered together **in my name**, there am I in the midst of them. [KJV]<br>"For where two or three have gathered together **in My name**, there I am in their midst." [NASB]<br>For where two or three come together **in my name**, there am I with them." [NIV]<br>For where two or three are gathered together **in My name**, I am there in the midst of them." [NKJV]<br>For where two or three gather together **because they are mine**, I am there among them." [NLT]<br>οὗ γάρ εἰσι δύο ἢ τρεῖς συνηγμένοι **εἰς τὸ ἐμὸν ὄνομα**, ἐκεῖ εἰμι ἐν μέσῳ αὐτῶν. [GNS]<br>οὗ γάρ εἰσιν δύο ἢ τρεῖς συνηγμένοι **εἰς τὸ ἐμὸν ὄνομα**, ἐκεῖ εἰμι ἐν μέσῳ αὐτῶν. [GNT] | Literally "into my name."<br><br>**Practical Application**<br>The idea is close and intimate union with Christ. It is a "getting into" the Spirit of Christ; a longing to be in union with Him and to act only for His glory. It is a depth of spiritual union demonstrated by so few. Note: it comes not only from private prayer but from prayer with others. |
| **#2122**<br>**In Order That**<br><br>So be that–KJV<br>**In order that–NASB**<br>**In order that–NIV**<br>That–NKJV<br>We are to–NLT<br><br>**POSB REFERENCE**<br>(Rom.8:16-17; esp. v.17)<br>*Note 9, point 4*<br><br>See also POSB REF:<br>(Rom.8:18)<br>*Note 1* | ἵνα = *hina*<br>Pronunciation: [hin'-ah]<br>Parsing (part of speech): conjunction<br>    Kind of—subordinating<br>    Stem or root—from ἵνα<br>Concordance References:<br>⇒ Strong's #2443 hina<br>⇒ NIV #2671 hina<br>⇒ NASB #2443 hina<br><br>**Romans 8:17**<br>And if children, then heirs; heirs of God, and joint-heirs with Christ; if **so be that** we suffer with him, that we may be also glorified together. [KJV]<br>And if children, heirs also, heirs of God and fellow heirs with Christ, if indeed we suffer with Him **in order that** we may also be glorified with Him. [NASB]<br>Now if we are children, then we are heirs—heirs of God and co-heirs with Christ, if indeed we share in his sufferings **in order that** we may also share in his glory. [NIV]<br>And if children, then heirs—heirs of God and joint heirs with Christ, if indeed we suffer with *Him*, **that** we | In order that; so that.<br><br>**Practical Application**<br>Note that the believer is to suffer with Christ "in order that" (*hina*—Greek) he may be glorified with Christ (Romans 8:17). Suffering prepares the believer to participate in the glory of Christ. It is the necessary condition for exaltation. Suffering and struggling are a refining process through which the believer must pass (1 Peter 1:6-7). It refines the believer by forcing him to expand his trust in God more and more. |

# PRACTICAL WORD STUDIES
## in the NEW TESTAMENT

| ENGLISH WORD | GREEK WORD AND VERSE | THE WORD MEANS... |
|---|---|---|
| | may also be glorified together. [NKJV]<br>And since we are his children, we will share his treasures—for everything God gives to his Son, Christ, is ours, too. But if **we are to** share his glory, we must also share his suffering. [NLT]<br>εἰ δὲ τέκνα, καὶ κληρονόμοι· κληρονόμοι μὲν Θεοῦ, συγκληρονόμοι δὲ Χριστοῦ· εἴπερ συμπάσχομεν **ἵνα** καὶ συνδοξασθῶμεν. [GNS]<br>εἰ δὲ τέκνα, καὶ κληρονόμοι· κληρονόμοι μὲν θεοῦ, συγκληρονόμοι δὲ Χριστοῦ, εἴπερ συμπάσχομεν **ἵνα** καὶ συνδοξασθῶμεν. [GNT] | |
| **#2123**<br>**In Presence**<br><br>With–KJV<br>With–NASB<br>**In presence**–NIV<br>With–NKJV<br>With–NLT<br><br>**POSB REFERENCE**<br>(Jn.8:38)<br>Note 4, point 1 | **παρά** = *para*<br>Pronunciation: [pa-rah]<br>Parsing (part of speech): preposition<br>    Case—dative<br>    Stem or root— from παρά<br>Concordance References:<br>  ⇒ Strong's #3844 para<br>  ⇒ NIV #4123 para<br>  ⇒ NASB #3844 para<br><br>**John 8:38**<br>I speak that which I have seen **with** my Father: and ye do that which ye have seen with your father. [KJV]<br>"I speak the things which I have seen **with** My Father; therefore you also do the things which you heard from your father." [NASB]<br>I am telling you what I have seen **in** the Father's **presence**, and you do what you have heard from your father." [NIV]<br>I speak what I have seen **with** My Father, and you do what you have seen with your father." [NKJV]<br>I am telling you what I saw when I was **with** my Father. But you are following the advice of your father." [NLT]<br>ἐγὼ ὃ ἑώρακα **παρὰ** τῷ πατρὶ μου, λαλῶ· καὶ ὑμεῖς οὖν ὃ ἑωράκατε παρὰ τῷ πατρὶ ὑμῶν ποιεῖτε. [GNS]<br>ἃ ἐγὼ ἑώρακα **παρὰ** τῷ πατρὶ λαλῶ· καὶ ὑμεῖς οὖν ἃ ἠκούσατε παρὰ τοῦ πατρὸς ποιεῖτε. [GNT] | In the presence of; by the side of; with, in the company of; among; in association.<br><br>**Practical Application**<br>What Christ saw came from the very side of the Father. Christ was from the very presence of God, so what He spoke was God's Word. His message was the Word of God Himself. What was His message?<br>⇒ A person must "believe Him" (John 8:31).<br>⇒ A person must "hold on to His teaching [His Word]" (John 8:31).<br>⇒ A person is "a slave to sin" (John 8:34).<br>⇒ A person can be freed and adopted as a child of God's by the eternal Son (John 8:35-36). |
| **#2124**<br>**In The Beginning**<br><br>In the beginning–KJV<br>In the beginning–NASB<br>In the beginning–NIV<br>In the beginning–NKJV<br>In the beginning–NLT<br><br>**POSB REFERENCE**<br>(Jn.1:1-2; esp. v.1)<br>Note 1, point 1a | **Ἐν ἀρχῇ** = *En archē*<br>Pronunciation: [en ar-chay]<br>Parsing *archē* (part of speech): noun<br>    Case—dative<br>    Gender—feminine<br>    Number—singular<br>    Stem or root—from ἀρχή, ῆς<br>Concordance References:<br>  ⇒ Strong's #1722 en + 746 archē<br>  ⇒ NIV #1877 en [In] + 794 archē [the beginning]<br>  ⇒ NASB #1722 en + 746 archē<br><br>**John 1:1**<br>**In the beginning** was the Word, and the Word was with God, and the Word was God. [KJV]<br>**In the beginning** was the Word, and the Word was with God, and the Word was God. [NASB]<br>**In the beginning** was the Word, and the Word was with God, and the Word was God. [NIV]<br>**In the beginning** was the Word, and the Word was with God, and the Word was God. [NKJV]<br>**In the beginning** the Word already existed. He was with God, and he was God. [NLT]<br>Ἐν ἀρχῇ ἦν ὁ λόγος, καὶ ὁ λόγος ἦν πρὸς τὸν Θεόν, καὶ Θεὸς ἦν ὁ λόγος. [GNS]<br>Ἐν ἀρχῇ ἦν ὁ λόγος, καὶ ὁ λόγος ἦν πρὸς τὸν θεόν, καὶ θεὸς ἦν ὁ λόγος. [GNT] | Before there was a beginning.<br><br>**Practical Application**<br>"In the beginning" does not mean from the beginning. Jesus Christ was already there. He did not become; He was not created; He never had a beginning. He "was in the beginning with God" (cp. John 17:5; John 8:58). Jesus Christ is eternal. This says several significant things about Christ.<br>1. Christ reveals the most important Person in all the universe: God. He reveals all that God is and wants to say to man. Therefore, Christ must be diligently studied, and all that He is and says must be heeded to the utmost (cp. John 5:24).<br>2. Christ *reveals* God perfectly. He is just like God, identical to God; therefore, when we look at Christ we see God (see POSB *Deeper Study* #1—John 14:6, POSB *Deeper Study* #2—John 14:6, POSB *Deeper Study* #3—John 14:6. Cp. John 14:9.)<br>3. Christ reveals that God is the most wonderful Person. God is far, far beyond anyone we could have ever dreamed. He is loving and caring, full of goodness and truth; and He will not tolerate injustices: murder and stealing, lying and cheating of husband, wife, child, neighbor, brother, sister or stranger. God |

# PRACTICAL WORD STUDIES
## in the NEW TESTAMENT

| ENGLISH WORD | GREEK WORD AND VERSE | THE WORD MEANS... |
|---|---|---|
| | | loves and is working and moving toward a perfect universe that will be filled with people who choose to love and worship and live and work for Him (cp. John 5:24-29). |
| **#2125**<br>**In The Highest**<br><br>In the highest–KJV<br>In the highest–NASB<br>In the highest–NIV<br>In the highest–NKJV<br>In highest heaven–NLT<br><br>**POSB REFERENCE**<br>(Mk.11:10)<br>*Deeper Study #8* | ἐν τοῖς ὑψίστοις = en thois hupsistos<br>Pronunciation: [en tois hoop'-sis-tos]<br>Parsing *hupsistos* (part of speech): pronominal adjective<br>    Type—superlative<br>    Case—dative<br>    Gender—neuter<br>    Number—plural<br>    Stem or root—from ὕψιστος, η, ον<br>Concordance References:<br>⇒ Strong's #1722 en + 3588 ho + 5310 hupsistos<br>⇒ NIV #1877 en [in] + 3836 ho [the] + 5736 hupsistos [highest]<br>⇒ NASB #1722 en + 3588 ho + 5310 hupsistos<br><br>**Mark 11:10**<br>Blessed be the kingdom of our father David, that cometh in the name of the Lord: Hosanna **in the highest**. [KJV]<br>Hosanna in the highest!" [NASB]<br>"Blessed is the coming kingdom of our father David!" "Hosanna **in the highest**!" [NIV]<br>Blessed is the kingdom of our father David That comes in the name of the Lord! Hosanna **in the highest**!" [NKJV]<br>Bless the coming kingdom of our ancestor David! Praise God **in highest heaven**!" [NLT]<br>εὐλογημένη ἡ ἐρχομένη βασιλεία ἐν ὀνόματι Κυρίου, τοῦ πατρὸς ἡμῶν Δαβίδ· Ὡσαννὰ **ἐν τοῖς ὑψίστοις**. [GNS]<br>Εὐλογημένη ἡ ἐρχομένη βασιλεία τοῦ πατρὸς ἡμῶν Δαυίδ· Ὡσαννὰ **ἐν τοῖς ὑψίστοις**. [GNT] | In the highest; You who are in the Highest heaven, save now through Him whom You have sent.<br><br>**Practical Application**<br>In this Scripture, the masses of people welcomed their political king, One who would surely save and deliver them from the oppression of Rome. Ironically, Jesus was more than willing to deliver these people from bondage. But, most of them would have no part of His offer to save them from the greater bondage of their sins. They were more interested in a temporary fix through a change in political power. |
| **#2126**<br>**In The Lord**<br><br>In the Lord–KJV<br>In the Lord–NASB<br>In the Lord–NIV<br>In the Lord–NKJV<br>Because you belong to the Lord–NLT<br><br>**POSB REFERENCE**<br>(Eph.6:1-3; esp. v.1)<br>Note 1, point 1 | ἐν κυρίῳ = en kuriō<br>Pronunciation: [en koo'-ree-o]<br>Parsing *kuriō* (part of speech): noun<br>    Case—dative<br>    Gender—masculine<br>    Number—sing from κύριος, ου ular<br>    Stem or root—<br>Concordance References:<br>⇒ Strong's #1722 en + 2962 kurios<br>⇒ NIV #1877 en [in] + 3261 kurios [the Lord]<br>⇒ NASB #1722 en + 2962 kurios<br><br>**Ephes. 6:1**<br>Children, obey your parents **in the Lord**: for this is right. [KJV]<br>Children, obey your parents **in the Lord**, for this is right. [NASB]<br>Children, obey your parents **in the Lord**, for this is right. [NIV]<br>Children, obey your parents **in the Lord**, for this is right. [NKJV]<br>Children, obey your parents **because you belong to the Lord**, for this is the right thing to do. [NLT]<br>Τὰ τέκνα, ὑπακούετε τοῖς γονεῦσιν ὑμῶν **ἐν Κυρίῳ**· τοῦτο γάρ ἐστι δίκαιον. [GNS]<br>Τὰ τέκνα, ὑπακούετε τοῖς γονεῦσιν ὑμῶν [**ἐν κυρίῳ**]· τοῦτο γάρ ἐστιν δίκαιον. [GNT] | In the Lord; because you belong to the Lord, Master, Owner.<br><br>**Practical Application**<br>First, to obey means to obey *because you are in the Lord*. Note the command again: "Children, obey your parents because you are in the Lord." (*en kuriō*) The phrase "because you are in the Lord" means at least two things.<br>1. There is a limit to the child's obedience. When a parent is not acting in the Lord, he is not to be obeyed. The Lord has nothing whatsoever to do with the filth of unrighteousness and abuse of precious children. If a child can break away to free himself from such parental corruption, he has every right to be freed from his parent. The Lord came to set men free from the abuse and the filth of sin, not to enslave men to it and especially not to enslave children to it.<br>One of the most severe warnings ever issued in all of history was issued by the Lord Jesus to adults who abuse children:<br><br>*And whosoever shall offend one of these little ones that believe in me, it is better for him that a millstone were hanged about his neck, and he were cast into the sea. And if thy hand offend thee [by abusing a child], cut it off: it is better for thee to enter into life maimed, than having two hands to go into hell, into the fire that never shall be quenched: where their worm dieth not, and the fire is not quenched. And if thy foot* |

# PRACTICAL WORD STUDIES
## in the NEW TESTAMENT

| ENGLISH WORD | GREEK WORD AND VERSE | THE WORD MEANS... |
|---|---|---|
| | | offend thee [by abusing a child], cut it off: it is better for thee to enter halt into life, than having two feet to be cast into hell, into the fire that never shall be quenched: where their worm dieth not, and the fire is not quenched. And if thine eye offend thee [by lusting after a child], pluck it out: it is better for thee to enter into the kingdom of God with one eye, than having two eyes to be cast into hell fire: where their worm dieth not, and the fire is not quenched (Mark 9:42-48). [KJV]<br><br>2. The phrase "because you belong to the Lord" also tells why the child is to obey his parents. "Children, obey your parents because you belong to the Lord"—obeying your parents is right; it is of the Lord; it pleases the Lord; therefore, obey them. When they guide and instruct you, follow them (cp. Col. 3:20). |
| **#2127**<br>**In Various Ways**<br><br>In divers manners–KJV<br>In many ways–NASB<br>**In various ways–NIV**<br>**In various ways–NKJV**<br>In many ways–NLT<br><br>**POSB REFERENCE**<br>(Heb.1:1-2; esp. v.1)<br>Note 1, point 1 | πολυτρόπως = *polutropōs*<br>Pronunciation: [pol-oot-rop'-oce]<br>Parsing (part of speech): adjective<br>    Type—adverb<br>    Stem or root—from πολυτρόπως<br>Concordance References:<br>  ⇒ Strong's #4187 polutropōs<br>  ⇒ NIV #4502 polutropōs<br>  ⇒ NASB #4187 polutropōs<br><br>**Hebrews 1:1**<br>God, who at sundry times and **in divers manners** spake in time past unto the fathers by the prophets, [KJV]<br>God, after He spoke long ago to the fathers in the prophets in many portions and **in many ways**, [NASB]<br>In the past God spoke to our forefathers through the prophets at many times and **in various ways**, [NIV]<br>God, who at various times and **in various ways** spoke in time past to the fathers by the prophets, [NKJV]<br>Long ago God spoke many times and **in many ways** to our ancestors through the prophets. [NLT]<br>Πολυμερῶς καὶ **πολυτρόπως** πάλαι ὁ θεὸς λαλήσας τοῖς πατράσιν ἐν τοῖς προφήταις, [GNS]<br>Πολυμερῶς καὶ **πολυτρόπως** πάλαι ὁ θεὸς λαλήσας τοῖς πατράσιν ἐν τοῖς προφήταις [GNT] | In many ways, in various ways, in diverse manners.<br><br>**Practical Application**<br>In ancient times God spoke to man by His prophets, that is, by persons whom He had chosen to proclaim His Word to the world. Who are these persons? They are the men and women of the Old Testament Scriptures. But note a significant fact: God spoke through the prophets...<br>• "at many times" [NIV]: that is, in many parts (*polumeros*); in many separate revelations, at many different times.<br>• in various ways (*polutropōs*).<br><br>What does this mean? No man could possibly receive and understand or explain the whole revelation of God. God and the truth of God are too big for any one man. Therefore, God had to make many revelations to many different people, and He had to use many different ways to speak to men. No man could ever contain or share the whole revelation of God. |
| **#2128**<br>**In Your Midst**<br><br>Within you–KJV<br>**In your midst–NASB**<br>Within you–NIV<br>Within you–NKJV<br>Among you–NLT<br><br>**POSB REFERENCE**<br>(Lk.17:20-21; esp. v.21)<br>Note 1, point 2 | ἐντὸς ὑμῶν = *entos humōn*<br>Pronunciation: [en-tos' hu-mown]<br>Parsing *entos* (part of speech): preposition<br>    Case—genitive<br>    Stem or root—from ἐντός<br>Parsing *humōn* (part of speech): noun pronoun<br>    Case—genitive<br>    Person—2nd person<br>    Number—plural<br>    Stem or root—from σύ<br>Concordance References:<br>  ⇒ Strong's #1787 entos + 5216 humon<br>  ⇒ NIV #1955 entos [within] + 5148 su [you]<br>  ⇒ NASB #1787 entos + 5216 humon<br><br>**Luke 17:21**<br>Neither shall they say, Lo here! or, lo there! for, behold, the kingdom of God is **within you**. [KJV]<br>Nor will they say, 'Look, here it is!' or, 'There it is!' For behold, the kingdom of God is **in your midst**." [NASB]<br>Nor will people say, 'Here it is,' or 'There it is,' because the kingdom of God is **within you**." [NIV]<br>Nor will they say, 'See here!' or 'See there!' For indeed, the kingdom of God is **within you**." [NKJV] | Within you, among you, inside of you, or in your midst.<br><br>**Practical Application**<br>Some say this should be translated "in your midst." If so, then Christ is saying that He is the embodiment of the Kingdom of God. He is setting up the Kingdom of God among them, there and then. God is already beginning to rule and reign in the lives He is touching.<br>Others say the words mean "within you." If so, then the kingdom is to be looked for within the hearts and lives of people. The Kingdom of God is spiritual; it is the changing of hearts, the rule and reign of God within men's lives. It is the power of God to take a sinful, immoral, and unjust man and change him into a servant of God. |

# PRACTICAL WORD STUDIES
## in the NEW TESTAMENT

| ENGLISH WORD | GREEK WORD AND VERSE | THE WORD MEANS... |
|---|---|---|
| | You won't be able to say, 'Here it is!' or 'It's over there!' For the Kingdom of God is **among you**." [NLT]<br>οὐδὲ ἐροῦσιν, Ἰδοὺ ὧδε, ἤ, Ἰδοὺ ἐκεῖ. ἰδοὺ γὰρ, ἡ βασιλεία τοῦ Θεοῦ **ἐντὸς ὑμῶν** ἐστιν. [GNS]<br>οὐδὲ ἐροῦσιν, Ἰδοὺ ὧδε ἤ, Ἐκεῖ, ἰδοὺ γὰρ ἡ βασιλεία τοῦ θεοῦ **ἐντὸς ὑμῶν** ἐστιν. [GNT] | |
| **#2129**<br>**Incomparably**<br><br>Exceeding–KJV<br>Surpassing–NASB<br>**Incomparably–NIV**<br>Exceeding–NKJV<br>Incredible–NLT<br><br>**POSB<br>REFERENCE**<br>(Eph.1:19)<br>Note 1 | **ὑπερβάλλον** = *huperballon*<br>Pronunciation: [hoop-er-bal'-lon]<br>Parsing (part of speech): verb<br>    Mood—participle<br>    Tense—present<br>    Voice—active<br>    Case—nominative<br>    Gender—neuter<br>    Number—singular<br>    Stem or root—from **ὑπερβάλλω**<br>Concordance References:<br>  ⇒ Strong's #5235 huperballō<br>  ⇒ NIV #5650 huperballō<br>  ⇒ NASB #5235 huperballō<br><br>**Ephes. 1:19**<br>And what is the **exceeding** greatness of his power to us-ward who believe, according to the working of his mighty power, [KJV]<br>And what is the **surpassing** greatness of His power toward us who believe. These are in accordance with the working of the strength of His might [NASB]<br>And his **incomparably** great power for us who believe. That power is like the working of his mighty strength, [NIV]<br>And what *is* the **exceeding** greatness of His power toward us who believe, according to the working of His mighty power [NKJV]<br>I pray that you will begin to understand the **incredible** greatness of his power for us who believe him. This is the same mighty power [NLT]<br>καὶ τί τὸ **ὑπερβάλλον** μέγεθος τῆς δυνάμεως αὐτοῦ εἰς ἡμᾶς τοὺς πιστεύοντας κατὰ τὴν ἐνέργειαν τοῦ κράτους τῆς ἰσχύος αὐτοῦ [GNS]<br>καὶ τί τὸ **ὑπερβάλλον** μέγεθος τῆς δυνάμεως αὐτοῦ εἰς ἡμᾶς τοὺς πιστεύοντας κατὰ τὴν ἐνέργειαν τοῦ κράτους τῆς ἰσχύος αὐτοῦ. [GNT] | Incomparable, incredible, surpassing, unlimited, immeasurable, beyond imagination.<br><br>**Practical Application**<br>When a believer really knows God, he experiences power—the power of God Himself. The thing to note is that God's power is *for us*; that is, God takes His power and extends it, presents it, makes it available to the believer. How do we know this? Because of what God did for Christ. What God did for Christ He will do for us. God's power is demonstrated by what He did for Christ. |
| **#2130**<br>**Incontinent**<br><br>**Incontinent–KJV**<br>Without self control–NASB<br>Without self control–NIV<br>Without self-control–NKJV<br>No self control–NLT<br><br>**POSB<br>REFERENCE**<br>(2 Tim. 3:2-4; esp. v.3)<br>Note 2, point 12 | **ἀκρατεῖς** = *akrateis*<br>Pronunciation: [ak-rat'-eh-ees]<br>Parsing (part of speech): adjective<br>    Case—nominative<br>    Gender—masculine<br>    Number—plural<br>    Stem or root—from **ἀκρατής, ές**<br>Concordance References:<br>  ⇒ Strong's #193 akratēs<br>  ⇒ NIV #203 akratēs<br>  ⇒ NASB #193 akratēs<br><br>**2 Tim. 3:3**<br>Without natural affection, trucebreakers, false accusers, **incontinent**, fierce, despisers of those that are good, [KJV]<br>Unloving, irreconcilable, malicious gossips, **without self-control**, brutal, haters of good, [NASB]<br>Without love, unforgiving, slanderous, **without self-control**, brutal, not lovers of the good, [NIV]<br>Unloving, unforgiving, slanderers, **without self-control**, brutal, despisers of good, [NKJV]<br>They will be unloving and unforgiving; they will slander others and have **no self-control**; they will be cruel and have no interest in what is good. [NLT]<br>ἄστοργοι, ἄσπονδοι, διάβολοι, **ἀκρατεῖς**, ἀνήμεροι, ἀφιλάγαθοι, [GNS]<br>ἄστοργοι ἄσπονδοι διάβολοι **ἀκρατεῖς** ἀνήμεροι ἀφιλάγαθοι [GNT] | Without self control, incontinent, undisciplined and uncontrolled; having no power to discipline.<br><br>**Practical Application**<br>It is being given over...<br>• to pleasure and indulgence<br>• to passion and sexual craving<br>• to lust and lewdness<br><br>It is a person who cannot control his passion for recreation, food, sex, pornography, sensuality, drink, drugs, smoking, whatever. It is a passion that grips and enslaves a person until it becomes an unbreakable habit and bondage. |

# PRACTICAL WORD STUDIES
## in the New Testament

| ENGLISH WORD | GREEK WORD AND VERSE | THE WORD MEANS... |
|---|---|---|
| **#2131**<br>**Incorruptible**<br><br>Uncorruptible–KJV<br>**Incorruptible–NASB**<br>Immortal–NIV<br>**Incorruptible–NKJV**<br>Ever-living–NLT<br><br>**POSB<br>REFERENCE**<br>(Romans 1:22-23; esp. v.23)<br>Note 5, point 2a | ἀφθάρτου = aphthartou<br>Pronunciation: [af'-thar-too]<br>Parsing (part of speech): adjective<br>    Case—genitive<br>    Gender—masculine<br>    Number—singular<br>    Stem or root—from ἄφθαρτος, ον<br>Concordance References:<br>  ⇒ Strong's #862 aphthartos<br>  ⇒ NIV #915 aphthartos<br>  ⇒ NASB #862a aphthartos<br><br>**Romans 1:23**<br>And changed the glory of the **uncorruptible** God into an image made like to corruptible man, and to birds, and fourfooted beasts, and creeping things. [KJV]<br>And exchanged the glory of the **incorruptible** God for an image in the form of corruptible man and of birds and four-footed animals and crawling creatures. [NASB]<br>And exchanged the glory of the **immortal** God for images made to look like mortal man and birds and animals and reptiles. [NIV]<br>And changed the glory of the **incorruptible** God into an image made like corruptible man—and birds and four-footed animals and creeping things. [NKJV]<br>And instead of worshiping the glorious, **ever-living** God, they worshiped idols made to look like mere people, or birds and animals and snakes. [NLT]<br>καὶ ἤλλαξαν τὴν δόξαν τοῦ **ἀφθάρτου** Θεοῦ ἐν ὁμοιώματι εἰκόνος φθαρτοῦ ἀνθρώπου καὶ πετεινῶν καὶ τετραπόδων καὶ ἑρπετῶν. [GNS]<br>καὶ ἤλλαξαν τὴν δόξαν τοῦ **ἀφθάρτου** Θεοῦ ἐν ὁμοιώματι εἰκόνος φθαρτοῦ ἀνθρώπου καὶ πετεινῶν καὶ τετραπόδων καὶ ἑρπετῶν. [GNT] | Imperishable; lasting forever; deathless; ageless; eternal, ever living. God is said to be "incorruptible" (*aphthartou*) which means non-decaying, imperishable, unchanging, and unaging.<br><br>**Practical Application**<br>Incorruptible means that God is not subject to passing away; He is eternal. God always has been and always will be: God will always exist. |
| **#2132**<br>**Incorruptible**<br><br>**Incorruptible–KJV**<br>Imperishable–NASB<br>That can never perish–NIV<br>**Incorruptible–NKJV**<br>Pure–NLT<br><br>**POSB<br>REFERENCE**<br>(1 Pt.1:4)<br>Note 2, point 1 | ἄφθαρτον = aphtharton<br>Pronunciation: [af'-thar-ton]<br>Parsing (part of speech): adjective<br>    Case—accusative<br>    Gender—feminine<br>    Number—singular<br>    Stem or root—from ἄφθαρτος, ον<br>Concordance References:<br>  ⇒ Strong's #862 aphthartos<br>  ⇒ NIV #915 aphthartos<br>  ⇒ NASB #862 aphthartos<br><br>**1 Peter 1:4**<br>To an inheritance **incorruptible**, and undefiled, and that fadeth not away, reserved in heaven for you, [KJV]<br>To obtain an inheritance which is **imperishable** and undefiled and will not fade away, reserved in heaven for you, [NASB]<br>And into an inheritance **that can never perish**, spoil or fade—kept in heaven for you, [NIV]<br>To an inheritance **incorruptible** and undefiled and that does not fade away, reserved in heaven for you, [NKJV]<br>For God has reserved a priceless inheritance for his children. It is kept in heaven for you, **pure** and undefiled, beyond the reach of change and decay. [NLT]<br>εἰς κληρονομίαν **ἄφθαρτον** καὶ ἀμίαντον καὶ ἀμάραντον, τετηρημένην ἐν οὐρανοῖς εἰς ὑμᾶς [GNS]<br>εἰς κληρονομίαν **ἄφθαρτον** καὶ ἀμίαντον καὶ ἀμάραντον, τετηρημένην ἐν οὐρανοῖς εἰς ὑμᾶς [GNT] | Incorruptible, immortal, imperishable, pure, that can never perish; it does not age, deteriorate, or die; it does not have the seed of corruption within it.<br><br>**Practical Application**<br>Matthew Henry points out that everything on earth changes from better to worse, but not our inheritance. It is perfect and incorruptible. It never changes, and it will never cease to be the most perfect inheritance and gift imaginable (*Matthew Henry's Commentary*, Vol.6. Old Tappan, NJ: Fleming H. Revell, p.1005). |
| **#2133**<br>**Increase–<br>Increased**<br><br>Abound–KJV<br>**Increased–NASB** | πληθυνθῆναι = plēthunthēnai<br>Pronunciation: [play-thoon'-thay-nai]<br>Parsing (part of speech): verb<br>    Mood—infinitive<br>    Tense—aorist<br>    Voice—passive | To increase; to overflow; to multiply; to abound; to be rampant; to grow in numbers; to greatly increase.<br><br>**Practical Application**<br>What are the consequences that will come to |

# PRACTICAL WORD STUDIES
## in the NEW TESTAMENT

| ENGLISH WORD | GREEK WORD AND VERSE | THE WORD MEANS... |
|---|---|---|
| **Increase–NIV**<br>Abound–NKJV<br>Rampant–NLT<br><br>**POSB REFERENCE**<br>(Mt.24:12)<br>*Deeper Study #7*<br><br>See also POSB REF:<br>(2 Pt.1:8-11; esp. v.8)<br>Note 2 | Case—accusative<br>Stem or root—from πληθύνω<br>Concordance References:<br>⇒ Strong's #4129 plēthunō<br>⇒ NIV #4437 plēthunō<br>⇒ NASB #4129 plēthunō<br><br>**Matthew 24:12**<br>And because iniquity shall **abound**, the love of many shall wax cold. [KJV]<br>"And because lawlessness is **increased**, most people's love will grow cold. [NASB]<br>Because of the **increase** of wickedness, the love of most will grow cold, [NIV]<br>And because lawlessness will **abound**, the love of many will grow cold. [NKJV]<br>Sin will be **rampant** everywhere, and the love of many will grow cold. [NLT]<br>καὶ διὰ τὸ **πληθυνθῆναι** τὴν ἀνομίαν ψυγήσεται ἡ ἀγάπη τῶν πολλῶν· [GNS]<br>καὶ διὰ τὸ **πληθυνθῆναι** τὴν ἀνομίαν ψυγήσεται ἡ ἀγάπη τῶν πολλῶν. [GNT] | the world when wickedness becomes rampant? Scripture declares emphatically that these events are going to happen.<br>• The Lord is returning to gather His people together in the most spectacular and joyful occasion of human history.<br>• The great and terrible day of the Lord is going to fall upon the earth. Unbelievers—all those who have cursed, rebelled, denied, ignored, neglected, and rejected Christ—are going to bear the justice of God.<br>• The great apostasy is going to be witnessed by the earth: millions are going to turn away from Christ.<br>• The antichrist is going to arise upon the world scene and bring a material utopia to the earth and some form of state worship—all in utter rebellion and denial of God Himself.<br>The point is this: the end times are coming upon the world. Therefore, people must be taught so that some can be saved and escape the things coming upon the earth. (See POSB outline—Matthew 24:1-51 and POSB notes—Matthew 24:1-51 for more of a picture as to what makes the tribulation of the last days worse than what men usually suffer upon earth.) |
| **#2134**<br>**Increase And Spread**<br><br>Grew and multiplied–KJV<br>Grow and to be multiplied–NASB<br>**Increase and spread–NIV**<br>Grew and multiplied–NKJV<br>Spreading rapidly–NLT<br><br>**POSB REFERENCE**<br>(Acts 12:24-25; esp. v.24)<br>Note 4, point 1 | ηὔξανεν καὶ ἐπληθύνετο = *ëuxanen kai eplēthuneto*<br>Pronunciation: [yoowx-ahn'-ehn ky eh-play-thoo'-neh-tow]<br>Parsing *ëuxanen* (part of speech): verb<br>  Mood—indicative<br>  Tense—imperfect<br>  Voice—active<br>  Person—3rd person<br>  Number—singular<br>  Stem or root—from αὐξάνω and αὔξω<br>Parsing *eplēthuneto* (part of speech): verb<br>  Mood—indicative<br>  Tense—imperfect<br>  Voice—passive<br>  Person—3rd person<br>  Number—singular<br>  Stem or root—from πληθύνω<br>Concordance References:<br>⇒ Strong's #837 auxanō + 2532 kai + 4129 plēthunō<br>⇒ NIV #889 auxanō [increase] + 2779 kai [and] + 4437 plēthunō [spread]<br>⇒ NASB #837 auxanō + 2532 kai + 4129 plēthunō<br><br>**Acts 12:24**<br>But the word of God **grew and multiplied**. [KJV]<br>But the word of the Lord continued to **grow and to be multiplied**. [NASB]<br>But the word of God continued to **increase and spread**. [NIV]<br>But the word of God **grew and multiplied**. [NKJV]<br>But God's Good News was **spreading rapidly**, and there were many new believers. [NLT]<br>Ὁ δὲ λόγος τοῦ Θεοῦ **ηὔξανε καὶ ἐπληθύνετο**. [GNS]<br>Ὁ δὲ λόγος τοῦ Θεοῦ **ηὔξανεν καὶ ἐπληθύνετο**. [GNT] | To increase and spread; to grow and multiply; to spread rapidly.<br><br>**Practical Application**<br>The words "increase and spread" (*ëuxanen kai eplēthuneto*) mean that the church kept on growing and multiplying. The progress of God's Word could not be stopped. Men and governments might try to stop it. They might persecute, imprison, and kill those who proclaim God's Word; but their efforts to silence the Word will always be to no avail. God overrules all and always will. |
| **#2135**<br>**Increased–Increasing**<br><br>Increased–KJV<br>Increasing–NASB | προέκοπτεν = *proekopten*<br>Pronunciation: [pro-eh'-kop-ten]<br>Parsing (part of speech): verb<br>  Mood—indicative<br>  Tense—imperfect<br>  Voice—active<br>  Person—3rd person<br>  Number—singular | To grow steadily; to increase; to progress; to keep advancing.<br><br>**Practical Application**<br>The picture is that of Jesus' cutting His way through the advancing years just as a pioneer cuts through the wilderness to reach his destination. |

### PRACTICAL WORD STUDIES
### in the NEW TESTAMENT

| ENGLISH WORD | GREEK WORD AND VERSE | THE WORD MEANS... |
|---|---|---|
| Grew–NIV<br>**Increased–NKJV**<br>Grew–NLT<br><br>**POSB REFERENCE**<br>(Lk.2:52)<br>*Deeper Study* #1 | Stem or root—from προκόπτω<br>Concordance References:<br>⇒ Strong's #4298 prokoptö<br>⇒ NIV #4621 prokoptö<br>⇒ NASB #4298 prokoptö<br><br>**Luke 2:52**<br>And Jesus **increased** in wisdom and stature, and in favour with God and man. [KJV]<br>And Jesus kept **increasing** in wisdom and stature, And in favor with God and men. [NASB]<br>And Jesus **grew** in wisdom and stature, and in favor with God and men. [NIV]<br>And Jesus **increased** in wisdom and stature, and in favor with God and men. [NKJV]<br>So Jesus **grew** both in height and in wisdom, and he was loved by God and by all who knew him. [NLT]<br>Καὶ Ἰησοῦς **προέκοπτε** σοφίᾳ καὶ ἡλικίᾳ, καὶ χάριτι παρὰ Θεῷ καὶ ἀνθρώποις. [GNS]<br>Καὶ Ἰησοῦς **προέκοπτεν** [ἐν τῇ] σοφίᾳ καὶ ἡλικίᾳ καὶ χάριτι παρὰ θεῷ καὶ ἀνθρώποις. [GNT] | |
| **#2136**<br>**Incredible**<br><br>Exceeding–KJV<br>Surpassing–NASB<br>Incomparably–NIV<br>Exceeding–NKJV<br>**Incredible–NLT**<br><br>**POSB REFERENCE**<br>(Eph.1:19)<br>Note 1 | ὑπερβάλλον = *huperballon*<br>Pronunciation: [hoop-er-bal'-lon]<br>Parsing (part of speech): verb<br>   Mood—participle<br>   Tense—present<br>   Voice—active<br>   Case—nominative<br>   Gender—neuter<br>   Number—singular<br>   Stem or root—from ὑπερβάλλω<br>Concordance References:<br>⇒ Strong's #5235 huperballö<br>⇒ NIV #5650 huperballö<br>⇒ NASB #5235 huperballö<br><br>**Ephes. 1:19**<br>And what is the **exceeding** greatness of his power to us-ward who believe, according to the working of his mighty power, [KJV]<br>And what is the **surpassing** greatness of His power toward us who believe. These are in accordance with the working of the strength of His might [NASB]<br>And his **incomparably** great power for us who believe. That power is like the working of his mighty strength, [NIV]<br>And what *is* the **exceeding** greatness of His power toward us who believe, according to the working of His mighty power [NKJV]<br>I pray that you will begin to understand the **incredible** greatness of his power for us who believe him. This is the same mighty power [NLT]<br>καὶ τί τὸ **ὑπερβάλλον** μέγεθος τῆς δυνάμεως αὐτοῦ εἰς ἡμᾶς τοὺς πιστεύοντας κατὰ τὴν ἐνέργειαν τοῦ κράτους τῆς ἰσχύος αὐτοῦ [GNS]<br>καὶ τί τὸ **ὑπερβάλλον** μέγεθος τῆς δυνάμεως αὐτοῦ εἰς ἡμᾶς τοὺς πιστεύοντας κατὰ τὴν ἐνέργειαν τοῦ κράτους τῆς ἰσχύος αὐτοῦ. [GNT] | Imcomparable, incredible, surpassing, unlimited, immeasurable, beyond imagination.<br><br>**Practical Application**<br>When a believer really knows God, he experiences power—the power of God Himself. The thing to note is that God's power is to *for us*; that is, God takes His power and extends it, presents it, makes it available to the believer. How do we know this? Because of what God did for Christ. What God did for Christ He will do for us. God's power is demonstrated by what He did for Christ. |
| **#2137**<br>**Indeed**<br><br>**Indeed–KJV**<br>True–NASB<br>Real–NIV<br>**Indeed–NKJV**<br>True–NLT<br><br>**POSB REFERENCE**<br>(Jn.6:55)<br>Note 3, point 1 | ἀληθής = *alëthës*<br>Pronunciation: [al-ay-thace']<br>Parsing (part of speech): adjective<br>   Case—nominative<br>   Gender—feminine<br>   Number—singular<br>   Stem or root—from ἀληθής, ές<br>Concordance References:<br>⇒ Strong's #227 alëthës<br>⇒ NIV #239 alëthës<br>⇒ NASB #227 alëthës | True as opposed to false; real, honest, indeed, valid, genuine.<br><br>**Practical Application**<br>The words true, truth, and real are taken from two Greek words very much alike. But each has a different shade of meaning. (See POSB *Deeper Study* #1—John 8:32; POSB *Deeper Study* #2—John 14:6.)<br>1. "*Alëthës*" means true, the opposite of false.<br>2. "*Alethinos*" means the true, the genuine, the real. It is the *opposite* of the unreal, the ficti- |

## PRACTICAL WORD STUDIES
### in the NEW TESTAMENT

| ENGLISH WORD | GREEK WORD AND VERSE | THE WORD MEANS... |
|---|---|---|
| | **John 6:55**<br>For my flesh is meat **indeed**, and my blood is drink **indeed**. [KJV]<br>"For My flesh is **true** food, and My blood is **true** drink. [NASB]<br>For my flesh is **real** food and my blood is **real** drink. [NIV]<br>For My flesh is food **indeed**, and My blood is drink indeed. [NKJV]<br>For my flesh is the **true** food, and my blood is the **true** drink. [NLT]<br>ἡ γὰρ σάρξ μου ἀληθής ἐστι βρῶσις, καὶ τὸ αἷμά μου **ἀληθής** ἐστι πόσις. [GNS]<br>ἡ γὰρ σάρξ μου ἀληθής ἐστιν βρῶσις, καὶ τὸ αἷμά μου **ἀληθής** ἐστιν πόσις. [GNT] | cious, the counterfeit, the imaginary. It is also the opposite of the imperfect, defective, frail, uncertain.<br><br>Jesus Christ is seen as the true, the real, the genuine life which has come to give light to every man (see POSB *Deeper Study #1*—John 8:12). |
| **#2138**<br>**Indignant**<br><br>Displeased–KJV<br>**Indignant–NASB**<br>**Indignant–NIV**<br>Displeased–NKJV<br>Displeased–NLT<br><br>**POSB REFERENCE**<br>(Mk.10:14)<br>*Deeper Study #2* | **ἠγανάκτησεν** = *ëganaktësen*<br>Pronunciation: [ayg-ahn-ak-tay´-sehn]<br>Parsing (part of speech): verb<br>    Mood—indicative<br>    Tense—aorist<br>    Voice—active<br>    Person—3rd person<br>    Number—singular<br>    Stem or root—from ἀγανακτέω<br>Concordance References:<br>  ⇒ Strong's #234 aganakteō<br>  ⇒ NIV #24 aganakteō<br>  ⇒ NASB #234 aganakteō<br><br>**Mark 10:14**<br>But when Jesus saw it, he was much **displeased**, and said unto them, Suffer the little children to come unto me, and forbid them not: for of such is the kingdom of God. [KJV]<br>But when Jesus saw this, He was **indignant** and said to them, "Permit the children to come to Me; do not hinder them; for the kingdom of God belongs to such as these. [NASB]<br>When Jesus saw this, he was **indignant**. He said to them, "Let the little children come to me, and do not hinder them, for the kingdom of God belongs to such as these. [NIV]<br>But when Jesus saw it, He was greatly **displeased** and said to them, "Let the little children come to Me, and do not forbid them; for of such is the kingdom of God. [NKJV]<br>But when Jesus saw what was happening, he was very **displeased** with his disciples. He said to them, "Let the children come to me. Don't stop them! For the Kingdom of God belongs to such as these. [NLT]<br>ἰδὼν δὲ ὁ Ἰησοῦς **ἠγανάκτησε**, καὶ εἶπεν αὐτοῖς, Ἄφετε τὰ παιδία ἔρχεσθαι πρός με, καὶ μὴ κωλύετε αὐτά. τῶν γὰρ τοιούτων ἐστὶν ἡ βασιλεία τοῦ Θεοῦ. [GNS]<br>ἰδὼν δὲ ὁ Ἰησοῦς **ἠγανάκτησεν** καὶ εἶπεν αὐτοῖς, Ἄφετε τὰ παιδία ἔρχεσθαι πρός με, μὴ κωλύετε αὐτά, τῶν γὰρ τοιούτων ἐστὶν ἡ βασιλεία τοῦ θεοῦ. [GNT] | To be indignant; to be moved with indignation; to feel pain; to be angry; to grieve; to be displeased, sore displeased, and much displeased (cp. 2 Cor. 7:11).<br><br>**Practical Application**<br>The word is very strong, expressing deep, even violent emotion. The Lord was moved with indignation toward the disciples for what they were doing. Note two facts indicated by this experience.<br>1. Strong indignation against sin and injustice is sometimes justified.<br>2. Not being moved with indignation toward sin and injustice is sometimes a gross wrong. |
| **#2139**<br>**Indignant–**<br>**Indignantly,**<br>**Saying–**<br>**Indignantly**<br>**Remarking**<br><br>Indignation within–KJV<br>**Indignantly remarking–NASB**<br>**Saying indignantly–NIV** | **ἀγανακτοῦντες** = *aganaktountes*<br>Pronunciation: [ag-an-ak-toon´-tehs]<br>Parsing (part of speech): verb<br>    Mood—participle<br>    Tense—present<br>    Voice—active<br>    Case—nominative<br>    Gender—masculine<br>    Number—plural<br>    Stem or root—from ἀγανακτέω<br>Concordance References:<br>  ⇒ Strong's #23 aganakteō<br>  ⇒ NIV #24 aganakteō<br>  ⇒ NASB #23 aganakteō | To be vexed and disturbed, to be filled with indignation, ire, anger, exasperation, displeasure, fury; to ache within.<br><br>**Practical Application**<br>In this Scripture, there were some who took issue with the woman's gift of perfume to the Lord. There are always those who question the believer's love and sacrifices for the Lord. Some even murmur against believers who make significant sacrifices. They do not understand the believer's love and commitment (sacrifice) for his Lord. They question the sacrifice of... |

# PRACTICAL WORD STUDIES
## in the NEW TESTAMENT

| ENGLISH WORD | GREEK WORD AND VERSE | THE WORD MEANS... |
|---|---|---|
| **Indignant among**–NKJV<br>**Indignant**–NLT<br><br>**POSB REFERENCE**<br>(Mk.14:4-5; esp. v.4)<br>Note 2 | **Mark 14:4**<br>And there were some that had **indignation within** themselves, and said, Why was this waste of the ointment made? [KJV]<br>But some were **indignantly remarking** to one another, "Why has this perfume been wasted? [NASB]<br>Some of those present were **saying indignantly** to one another, "Why this waste of perfume? [NIV]<br>But there were some who were **indignant among** themselves, and said, "Why was this fragrant oil wasted?" [NKJV]<br>Some of those at the table were **indignant**. "Why was this expensive perfume wasted?" they asked. [NLT]<br>ἦσαν δέ τινες **ἀγανακτοῦντες** πρὸς ἑαυτούς, καὶ λέγοντες, Εἰς τί ἡ ἀπώλεια αὕτη τοῦ μύρου γέγονεν; [GNS]<br>ἦσαν δέ τινες **ἀγανακτοῦντες** πρὸς ἑαυτούς, Εἰς τί ἡ ἀπώλεια αὕτη τοῦ μύρου γέγονεν; [GNT] | • money, possessions, comfort<br>• pleasure, partying, popularity<br>• position, recognition, prestige<br>• profession, promotion, security |
| #2140<br>**Indignation**<br><br>**Indignation**–KJV<br>Wrath–NASB<br>Wrath–NIV<br>**Indignation**–NKJV<br>Wrath–NLT<br><br>**POSB REFERENCE**<br>(Romans 2:8)<br>*Deeper Study #6* | **ὀργή** = *orgë*<br>Pronunciation: [or-gay']<br>Parsing (part of speech): noun<br>   Case—nominative<br>   Gender—feminine<br>   Number—singular<br>   Stem or root—from ὀργή, ῆς<br>Concordance References:<br>  ⇒ Strong's #3709 orgë<br>  ⇒ NIV #3973 orgë<br>  ⇒ NASB #3709 orgë<br><br>**Romans 2:8**<br>But unto them that are contentious, and do not obey the truth, but obey unrighteousness, **indignation** and wrath, [KJV]<br>But to those who are selfishly ambitious and do not obey the truth, but obey unrighteousness, **wrath** and indignation. [NASB]<br>But for those who are self-seeking and who reject the truth and follow evil, there will be **wrath** and anger. [NIV]<br>But to those who are self-seeking and do not obey the truth, but obey unrighteousness—**indignation** and wrath, [NKJV]<br>But he will pour out his anger and **wrath** on those who live for themselves, who refuse to obey the truth and practice evil deeds. [NLT]<br>τοῖς δὲ ἐξ ἐριθείας, καὶ ἀπειθοῦσι μὲν τῇ ἀληθείᾳ πειθομένοις δὲ τῇ ἀδικίᾳ, θυμός καὶ **ὀργή**, [GNS]<br>τοῖς δὲ ἐξ ἐριθείας καὶ ἀπειθοῦσι τῇ ἀληθείᾳ πειθομένοις δὲ τῇ ἀδικίᾳ **ὀργὴ** καὶ θυμός. [GNT] | Wrath, anger; retribution, punishment; revenge. Indignation (*orgë*) means God's anger against sin. (See *Deeper Study #1*, God's Wrath—Romans 1:18 for discussion).<br><br>**Practical Application**<br>It is anger, not an agitated outburst of violence. It is not the anger that quickly blazes up and just as quickly fades away, not the anger that arises solely from emotion. Rather, it is decisive anger. It is an anger that has arisen from a thoughtful decision, an anger that arises from the mind much more than from the emotions. When used of God, it is always an anger that is *righteous and just and good*. It is an anger that stands against the sin and evil, violence and slaughter, immorality and injustices of men. It is an anger that abhors and hates sin and evil and that dishes out a just revenge and equal justice. However, it is an anger that is *deeply felt*; in fact, it must be felt, for evil and corruption must be opposed and erased from the face of the earth if there is to be a "new heavens and a new earth." And God has promised a new heavens and a new earth where righteousness and perfection dwell forever. |
| #2141<br>**Indignation**<br><br>Wrath–KJV<br>**Indignation**–NASB<br>Anger–NIV<br>Wrath–NKJV<br>Anger–NLT<br><br>**POSB REFERENCE**<br>(Romans 2:8)<br>*Deeper Study #7* | **θυμός** = *thumos*<br>Pronunciation: [thoo-mos']<br>Parsing (part of speech): noun<br>   Case—nominative<br>   Gender—masculine<br>   Number—singular<br>   Stem or root—from θυμός, ου<br>Concordance References:<br>  ⇒ Strong's #2372 thumos<br>  ⇒ NIV #2596 thumos<br>  ⇒ NASB #2372 thumos<br><br>**Romans 2:8**<br>But unto them that are contentious, and do not obey the truth, but obey unrighteousness, indignation and **wrath**, [KJV]<br>But to those who are selfishly ambitious and do not obey the truth, but obey unrighteousness, wrath and **indignation**. [NASB]<br>But for those who are self-seeking and who reject the truth and follow evil, there will be wrath and **anger**. [NIV] | Anger, wrath, fury, indignation, rage. It means God's wrath against sin.<br><br>**Practical Application**<br>*Thumos* is an anger that is felt more deeply than the *orge* anger of God; therefore, it arises more quickly. *Thumos* anger is the anger that arises out of deep hurt; therefore, it bursts forth with terrifying judgment. (See POSB *Deeper Study #1*, God's Wrath—Romans 1:18 for verses.) |

# PRACTICAL WORD STUDIES
## in the NEW TESTAMENT

| ENGLISH WORD | GREEK WORD AND VERSE | THE WORD MEANS... |
|---|---|---|
| | But to those who are self-seeking and do not obey the truth, but obey unrighteousness—indignation and **wrath**, [NKJV]<br>But he will pour out his **anger** and wrath on those who live for themselves, who refuse to obey the truth and practice evil deeds. [NLT]<br>τοῖς δὲ ἐξ ἐριθείας, καὶ ἀπειθοῦσι μὲν τῇ ἀληθείᾳ πειθομένοις δὲ τῇ ἀδικίᾳ, **θυμός** καὶ ὀργή, [GNS]<br>τοῖς δὲ ἐξ ἐριθείας καὶ ἀπειθοῦσι τῇ ἀληθείᾳ πειθομένοις δὲ τῇ ἀδικίᾳ ὀργὴ καὶ **θυμός**. [GNT] | |
| **#2142**<br>**Indignation Within**<br><br>Indignation within–KJV<br>Indignantly remarking–NASB<br>Saying indignantly–NIV<br>Indignant among–NKJV<br>Indignant–NLT<br><br>**POSB REFERENCE**<br>(Mk.14:4-5; esp. v.4) Note 2 | ἀγανακτοῦντες = *aganaktountes*<br>Pronunciation: [ag-an-ak-toon'-tehs]<br>Parsing (part of speech): verb<br>   Mood—participle<br>   Tense—present<br>   Voice—active<br>   Case—nominative<br>   Gender—masculine<br>   Number—plural<br>   Stem or root—from ἀγανακτέω<br>Concordance References:<br>  ⇒ Strong's #23 aganakteō<br>  ⇒ NIV #24 aganakteō<br>  ⇒ NASB #23 aganakteō<br><br>**Mark 14:4**<br>And there were some that had **indignation within** themselves, and said, Why was this waste of the ointment made? [KJV]<br>But some were **indignantly remarking** to one another, "Why has this perfume been wasted? [NASB]<br>Some of those present were **saying indignantly** to one another, "Why this waste of perfume? [NIV]<br>But there were some who were **indignant among** themselves, and said, "Why was this fragrant oil wasted? [NKJV]<br>Some of those at the table were **indignant**. "Why was this expensive perfume wasted?" they asked. [NLT]<br>ἦσαν δέ τινες **ἀγανακτοῦντες** πρὸς ἑαυτούς, καὶ λέγοντες, Εἰς τί ἡ ἀπώλεια αὕτη τοῦ μύρου γέγονεν; [GNS]<br>ἦσαν δέ τινες **ἀγανακτοῦντες** πρὸς ἑαυτούς, Εἰς τί ἡ ἀπώλεια αὕτη τοῦ μύρου γέγονεν; [GNT] | To be vexed and disturbed, to be filled with indignation, ire, anger, exasperation, displeasure, fury; to ache within.<br><br>**Practical Application**<br>In this Scripture, there were some who took issue with the woman's gift of perfume to the Lord. There are always those who question the believer's love and sacrifices for the Lord. Some even murmur against believers who make significant sacrifices. They do not understand the believer's love and commitment (sacrifice) for his Lord. They question the sacrifice of...<br>• money, possessions, comfort<br>• pleasure, partying, popularity<br>• position, recognition, prestige<br>• profession, promotion, security |
| **#2143**<br>**Ineffective**<br><br>Barren–KJV<br>Useless–NASB<br>**Ineffective–NIV**<br>Barren–NKJV<br>Productive–NLT<br><br>**POSB REFERENCE**<br>(2 Pt.1:8-11; esp. v.8) Note 2, point 1 | ἀργούς = *argous*<br>Pronunciation: [ar-goos']<br>Parsing (part of speech): adjective<br>   Case—accusative<br>   Gender—masculine<br>   Number—plural<br>   Stem or root—from ἀργός, ή, όν<br>Concordance References:<br>  ⇒ Strong's #692 argos<br>  ⇒ NIV #734 argos<br>  ⇒ NASB #692 argos<br><br>**2 Peter 1:8**<br>For if these things be in you, and abound, they make you that ye shall neither be **barren** nor unfruitful in the knowledge of our Lord Jesus Christ. [KJV]<br>For if these qualities are yours and are increasing, they render you neither **useless** nor unfruitful in the true knowledge of our Lord Jesus Christ. [NASB]<br>For if you possess these qualities in increasing measure, they will keep you from being **ineffective** and unproductive in your knowledge of our Lord Jesus Christ. [NIV]<br>For if these things are yours and abound, *you will be* neither **barren** nor unfruitful in the knowledge of our Lord Jesus Christ. [NKJV]<br>The more you grow like this, the more you will become **productive** and useful in your knowledge of our | To be ineffective; to be barren; to be lazy; to do nothing; to be careless. It means to be idle and slothful, empty and useless.<br><br>**Practical Application**<br>It is the very opposite of being fruitful and productive in life. Therefore if we possess *these qualities*, if we really work at our salvation, we will not live an ineffective, dry life. We will not be unfruitful nor live a life that is empty and useless, idle and slothful. On the contrary, we will live a life that flows with nourishment and that bears the ripest of fruit: love, joy, and peace (cp. Galatians 5:22-23).<br>But note the source of such a life: the source is our Lord Jesus Christ. We must know Him and grow in the knowledge of Him. The knowledge of Him must be our aim and purpose in life. Only as we know Him can we overcome the barrenness and unfruitfulness of life. He and He alone can give us real life. Therefore, we must possess *these qualities*—really work at our salvation—really seek fellowship and communion with Christ moment by moment and day by day—in order not to be barren or unfruitful in the knowledge of Him. We must learn to pray all |

PRACTICAL WORD STUDIES
in the NEW TESTAMENT

| ENGLISH WORD | GREEK WORD AND VERSE | THE WORD MEANS... |
|---|---|---|
| | Lord Jesus Christ. [NLT]<br>αὐτὰ γὰρ ὑμῖν ὑπάρχοντα, καὶ πλεονάζοντα, οὐκ **ἀργοὺς** οὐδὲ ἀκάρπους καθίστησιν εἰς τὴν τοῦ Κυρίου ἡμῶν Ἰησοῦ Χριστοῦ ἐπίγνωσιν· [GNS]<br>ταῦτα γὰρ ὑμῖν ὑπάρχοντα καὶ πλεονάζοντα οὐκ **ἀργοὺς** οὐδὲ ἀκάρπους καθίστησιν εἰς τὴν τοῦ κυρίου ἡμῶν Ἰησοῦ Χριστοῦ ἐπίγνωσιν. [GNT] | day long and to take *set times* for prayer every day, set times for concentrated prayer. We must learn to *keep our minds* on Christ. |
| #2144<br>**Infants**<br><br>Babes–KJV<br>Immature–NASB<br>**Infants–NIV**<br>Babes–NKJV<br>Children–NLT<br><br>**POSB<br>REFERENCE**<br>(Romans 2:17-20; esp. v.20)<br>Note 1, point 9 | νηπίων = nēpiōn<br>Pronunciation: [nay'-pee-own]<br>Parsing (part of speech): pronominal adjective<br>    Case—genitive<br>    Gender—masculine<br>    Number—plural<br>    Stem or root—from νήπιος, α, ον<br>Concordance References:<br>  ⇒ Strong's #3516 nēpios<br>  ⇒ NIV #3758 nēpios<br>  ⇒ NASB #3516 nēpios<br><br>**Romans 2:20**<br>An instructor of the foolish, a teacher of **babes**, which hast the form of knowledge and of the truth in the law. [KJV]<br>A corrector of the foolish, a teacher of the **immature**, having in the Law the embodiment of knowledge and of the truth, [NASB]<br>An instructor of the foolish, a teacher of **infants**, because you have in the law the embodiment of knowledge and truth—[NIV]<br>An instructor of the foolish, a teacher of **babes**, having the form of knowledge and truth in the law. [NKJV]<br>You think you can instruct the ignorant and teach **children** the ways of God. For you are certain that in God's law you have complete knowledge and truth. [NLT]<br>παιδευτὴν ἀφρόνων, διδάσκαλον **νηπίων**, ἔχοντα τὴν μόρφωσιν τῆς γνώσεως καὶ τῆς ἀληθείας ἐν τῷ νόμῳ· [GNS]<br>παιδευτὴν ἀφρόνων, διδάσκαλον **νηπίων**, ἔχοντα τὴν μόρφωσιν τῆς γνώσεως καὶ τῆς ἀληθείας ἐν τῷ νόμῳ· [GNT] | The infant; the immature; the novice; the children; the proselyte; the innocent; the baby; the new church member.<br><br>**Practical Application**<br>A person is not mature in God just because he...<br>• has been baptized and has been a church member for a long time.<br>• thinks he is mature.<br>• serves as a teacher.<br><br>What makes a person mature and capable of teaching the immature of the world is experience with Christ, having walked and served with Christ for a long time. |
| #2145<br>**Infidel**<br><br>**Infidel–KJV**<br>Unbeliever–NASB<br>Unbeliever–NIV<br>Unbeliever–NKJV<br>Unbeliever–NLT<br><br>**POSB<br>REFERENCE**<br>(2 Cor.6:14-16; esp. v.15)<br>Note 2 | ἀπίστου = apistou<br>Pronunciation: [ap'-is-too]<br>Parsing (part of speech): pronominal adjective<br>    Case—genitive<br>    Gender—masculine<br>    Number—singular<br>    Stem or root—from ἄπιστος, ον<br>Concordance References:<br>  ⇒ Strong's #571 apistos<br>  ⇒ NIV #603 apistos<br>  ⇒ NASB #571 apistos<br><br>**2 Cor. 6:15**<br>And what concord hath Christ with Belial? or what part hath he that believeth with an **infidel**? [KJV]<br>Or what harmony has Christ with Belial, or what has a believer in common with an **unbeliever**? [NASB]<br>What harmony is there between Christ and Belial? What does a believer have in common with an **unbeliever**? [NIV]<br>And what accord has Christ with Belial? Or what part has a believer with an **unbeliever**? [NKJV]<br>What harmony can there be between Christ and the Devil? How can a believer be a partner with an **unbeliever**? [NLT]<br>τίς δὲ συμφώνησις Χριστῷ πρὸς Βελιάλ; ἢ τίς μερὶς πιστῷ μετὰ **ἀπίστου**; [GNS]<br>τίς δὲ συμφώνησις Χριστοῦ πρὸς Βελιάρ, ἢ τίς μερὶς πιστῷ μετὰ **ἀπίστου**; [GNT] | Unbeliever; an infidel; an unbelieving person; an unfaithful person.<br><br>**Practical Application**<br>It means a person who has chosen to disbelieve in Christ and has deliberately rejected Him. |

# PRACTICAL WORD STUDIES
## in the NEW TESTAMENT

| ENGLISH WORD | GREEK WORD AND VERSE | THE WORD MEANS... |
|---|---|---|
| **#2146**<br>**Infuriated**<br><br>Cut to the heart–KJV<br>Cut to the quick–NASB<br>Furious–NIV<br>Cut to the heart–NKJV<br>**Infuriated–NLT**<br><br>**POSB REFERENCE**<br>(Acts 7:54)<br>Note 1, point 2 | διεπρίοντο ταῖς καρδίαις = dieprionto tais kardiais<br>Pronunciation: [dee-ehp-ree'-on-tow tace kar-dee'-ah-ees]<br>Parsing *dieprionto* (part of speech): verb<br>  Mood—indicative<br>  Tense—imperfect<br>  Voice—passive<br>  Person—3rd person<br>  Number—plural<br>  Stem or root—from διαπρίομαι<br>Parsing *kardiais* (part of speech): noun<br>  Case—dative<br>  Gender—feminine<br>  Number—plural<br>  Stem or root—from καρδία, ας<br>Concordance References:<br>⇒ Strong's #1282 + 2588 + 3588 diapriö kardia ho<br>⇒ NIV #1391 + 2840 + 3836 diapriö kardia ho<br>⇒ NASB #1282 + 2588 + 3588 diapriö kardia ho<br><br>**Acts 7:54**<br>When they heard these things, they were **cut to the heart**, and they gnashed on him with their teeth. [KJV]<br>Now when they heard this, they were **cut to the quick**, and they began gnashing their teeth at him. [NASB]<br>When they heard this, they were **furious** and gnashed their teeth at him. [NIV]<br>When they heard these things they were **cut to the heart**, and they gnashed at him with *their* teeth. [NKJV]<br>The Jewish leaders were **infuriated** by Stephen's accusation, and they shook their fists in rage. [NLT]<br>Ἀκούοντες δὲ ταῦτα, **διεπρίοντο ταῖς καρδίαις** αὐτῶν, καὶ ἔβρυχον τοὺς ὀδόντας ἐπ' αὐτόν. [GNS]<br>Ἀκούοντες δὲ ταῦτα **διεπρίοντο ταῖς καρδίαις** αὐτῶν καὶ ἔβρυχον τοὺς ὀδόντας ἐπ' αὐτόν. [GNT] | To be furious; to cut to the heart; to cut to the quick; to infuriate; to be enraged.<br><br>**Practical Application**<br>The word "*dieprionto*" means to saw asunder; to cut through. It is used to show violent reaction. The response of their hearts was anger, not godly sorrow. (See POSB *Deeper Study* #1, Godly Sorrow—2 Cor. 7:10). They had no intention of confessing that they had been wrong. |
| **#2147**<br>**Inheritance**<br><br>Inheritance–KJV<br>Inheritance–NASB<br>Inheritance–NIV<br>Inheritance–NKJV<br>Inheritance–NLT<br><br>**POSB REFERENCE**<br>(Acts 20:32)<br>Note 3, point 2 | κληρονομίαν = klëronomian<br>Pronunciation: [klay-ron-om-ee'-ahn]<br>Parsing (part of speech): noun<br>  Case—accusative<br>  Gender—feminine<br>  Number—singular<br>  Stem or root—from κληρονομία, ας<br>Concordance References:<br>⇒ Strong's #2817 klëronomia<br>⇒ NIV #3100 klëronomia<br>⇒ NASB #2817 klëronomia<br><br>**Acts 20:32**<br>And now, brethren, I commend you to God, and to the word of his grace, which is able to build you up, and to give you an **inheritance** among all them which are sanctified. [KJV]<br>"And now I commend you to God and to the word of His grace, which is able to build you up and to give you the **inheritance** among all those who are sanctified. [NASB]<br>"Now I commit you to God and to the word of his grace, which can build you up and give you an **inheritance** among all those who are sanctified. [NIV]<br>So now, brethren, I commend you to God and to the word of His grace, which is able to build you up and give you an **inheritance** among all those who are sanctified. [NKJV]<br>"And now I entrust you to God and the word of his grace—his message that is able to build you up and give you an **inheritance** with all those he has set apart for himself. [NLT]<br>καὶ τὰ νῦν παρατίθεμαι ὑμᾶς, ἀδελφοί, τῷ Θεῷ καὶ τῷ λόγῳ τῆς χάριτος αὐτοῦ τῷ δυναμένῳ ἐποικοδομῆσαι, καὶ δοῦναι ὑμῖν **κληρονομίαν** ἐν τοῖς ἡγιασμένοις πᾶσιν. [GNS] | Inheritance, heritage, estate; what is promised or given.<br><br>**Practical Application**<br>God and His Word will give an inheritance to believers. The inheritance (*klëronomian*) is both...<br>• present, in the here and now. (See Acts 26:18; Col. 1:12).<br>• future, in the new heavens and earth. (See Romans 8:16-17; Hebrews 9:15; 1 Peter 1:3-4).<br><br>(See POSB note, Rewards—Luke 16:10-12; POSB note—John 4:36-38; POSB note—Rev. 14:13; POSB note—Rev. 21:24-27 for a list of the rewards of believers.) |

# PRACTICAL WORD STUDIES
## in the NEW TESTAMENT

| ENGLISH WORD | GREEK WORD AND VERSE | THE WORD MEANS... |
|---|---|---|
| | καὶ τὰ νῦν παρατίθεμαι ὑμᾶς τῷ θεῷ καὶ τῷ λόγῳ τῆς χάριτος αὐτοῦ, τῷ δυναμένῳ οἰκοδομῆσαι καὶ δοῦναι τὴν **κληρονομίαν** ἐν τοῖς ἡγιασμένοις πᾶσιν. [GNT] | |
| **#2148**<br>**Inheritance**<br><br>Inheritance–KJV<br>Inheritance–NASB<br>Chosen–NIV<br>Inheritance–NKJV<br>Inheritance–NLT<br><br>**POSB REFERENCE**<br>(Eph.1:11-13; esp. v.11)<br>Note 7, point 2 | ἐκληρώθημεν = eklērōthēmen<br>Pronunciation: [eh-klay-ro'-thay-mehn]<br>Parsing (part of speech): verb<br>    Mood—indicative<br>    Tense—aorist<br>    Voice—passive<br>    Person—1st person<br>    Number—plural<br>    Stem or root—from κληρόω<br>Concordance References:<br>  ⇒ Strong's #2820 klēroō<br>  ⇒ NIV #3103 klēroō<br>  ⇒ NASB #2820 klēroō<br><br>**Ephes. 1:11**<br>In whom also we have obtained an **inheritance**, being predestinated according to the purpose of him who worketh all things after the counsel of his own will: [KJV]<br>Also we have obtained an **inheritance**, having been predestined according to His purpose who works all things after the counsel of His will, [NASB]<br>In him we were also **chosen**, having been predestined according to the plan of him who works out everything in conformity with the purpose of his will, [NIV]<br>In Him also we have obtained an **inheritance**, being predestined according to the purpose of Him who works all things according to the counsel of His will, [NKJV]<br>Furthermore, because of Christ, we have received an **inheritance** from God, for he chose us from the beginning, and all things happen just as he decided long ago. [NLT]<br>ἐν ᾧ καὶ **ἐκληρώθημεν**, προορισθέντες κατὰ πρόθεσιν τοῦ τὰ πάντα ἐνεργοῦντος κατὰ τὴν βουλὴν τοῦ θελήματος αὐτοῦ, [GNS]<br>ἐν ᾧ καὶ **ἐκληρώθημεν** προορισθέντες κατὰ πρόθεσιν τοῦ τὰ πάντα ἐνεργοῦντος κατὰ τὴν βουλὴν τοῦ θελήματος αὐτοῦ [GNT] | Chosen, inheritance, heritage.<br><br>**Practical Application**<br>God takes the believer and makes him His own heritage and possession. The believer himself is made the inheritance of God. He is given the glorious privilege of *being*, of living and existing forever as God's most *cherished possession and heritage*. He becomes the most precious gem and treasure of God. This is the believer's inheritance, his heritage. |
| **#2149**<br>**Iniquity**<br><br>Iniquity–KJV<br>Lawlessness–NASB<br>Wickedness–NIV<br>Lawlessness–NKJV<br>Sin will be rampant–NLT<br><br>**POSB REFERENCE**<br>(Mt.24:12)<br>*Deeper Study #6*<br><br>See also POSB REF:<br>(Mt.7:23)<br>Note 3, point 2<br>(2 Cor.6:14-16; esp. v.14)<br>Note 2 | ἀνομίαν = anomian<br>Pronunciation: [an-om-ee'-ahn]<br>Parsing (part of speech): noun<br>    Case—accusative<br>    Gender—feminine<br>    Number—singular<br>    Stem or root—from ἀνομία, ας<br>Concordance References:<br>  ⇒ Strong's #458 anomia<br>  ⇒ NIV #490 anomia<br>  ⇒ NASB #458 anomia<br><br>**Matthew 24:12**<br>And because **iniquity** shall abound, the love of many shall wax cold. [KJV]<br>"And because **lawlessness** is increased, most people's love will grow cold. [NASB]<br>Because of the increase of **wickedness**, the love of most will grow cold, [NIV]<br>And because **lawlessness** will abound, the love of many will grow cold. [NKJV]<br>**Sin will be rampant** everywhere, and the love of many will grow cold. [NLT]<br>καὶ διὰ τὸ πληθυνθῆναι τὴν **ἀνομίαν** ψυγήσεται ἡ ἀγάπη τῶν πολλῶν· [GNS]<br>καὶ διὰ τὸ πληθυνθῆναι τὴν **ἀνομίαν** ψυγήσεται ἡ ἀγάπη τῶν πολλῶν. [GNT] | Lawlessness, wickedness, iniquity, unrighteousness; sin that is rampant; a gross transgression of the law; unauthorized acts or conduct; evil-doing.<br><br>**Practical Application**<br>Unbelievers do not obey God. They live and do as they wish, not as God says. Rejecting God and what He says they go about about doing their own thing. They rebel against God and His commandments, living lawless and unrighteous lives. What is lawlessness? It is taking license...<br>• with the law and righteousness<br>• with morality and discipline<br><br>It is neglect of or opposition to the law of God; it is substituting the will of self in the place of God's will (1 John 3:4). It is looking to self or to the world instead of looking to God. It is following the course of self and the desires of self instead of following the course of God. (See POSB *Deeper Study #1*—Matthew 7:23 for discussion). |
| **#2150**<br>**Iniquity** | ἀδικία = adikia<br>Pronunciation: [ad-ee-kee'-ah]<br>Parsing (part of speech): noun<br>    Case—dative | Evil, iniquity, sin, unrighteousness, wrongdoing, wickedness; harmful injustice. |

# PRACTICAL WORD STUDIES
## in the NEW TESTAMENT

| ENGLISH WORD | GREEK WORD AND VERSE | THE WORD MEANS... |
|---|---|---|
| **Iniquity**–KJV<br>Unrighteousness–<br>NASB<br>Evil–NIV<br>**Iniquity**–NKJV<br>Injustice–NLT<br><br>**POSB<br>REFERENCE**<br>(1 Cor.13:4-7; esp.<br>v.6)<br>Note 2, point 10<br><br>See also POSB REF:<br>(Rom.2:8)<br>*Deeper Study* #5 | Gender—feminine<br>Number—singular<br>Stem or root—from ἀδικία, ας<br>Concordance References:<br>⇒ Strong's #93 adikia<br>⇒ NIV #94 adikia<br>⇒ NASB #93 adikia<br><br>**1 Cor. 13:6**<br>Rejoiceth not in **iniquity**, but rejoiceth in the truth; [KJV]<br>Does not rejoice in **unrighteousness**, but rejoices with the truth; [NASB]<br>Love does not delight in **evil** but rejoices with the truth. [NIV]<br>Does not rejoice in **iniquity**, but rejoices in the truth; [NKJV]<br>It is never glad about **injustice** but rejoices whenever the truth wins out. [NLT]<br>οὐ χαίρει ἐπὶ τῇ **ἀδικίᾳ**, συγχαίρει δὲ τῇ ἀληθείᾳ· [GNS]<br>οὐ χαίρει ἐπὶ τῇ **ἀδικίᾳ**, συγχαίρει δὲ τῇ ἀληθείᾳ· [GNT] | **Practical Application**<br>Love does not take pleasure in the unrighteousness and sin of others; it does not feed upon sin and wrong, nor does it pass along the stories of sin and wrong. Man's nature is too often fed the tragedy of evil, whether personal sin or natural disaster. (Cp. the daily news reports and the subjects of conversation between so many people). |
| **#2151<br>Injurious**<br><br>Injurious–KJV<br>Violent<br>  aggressor–NASB<br>Violent man–NIV<br>Insolent man–NKJV<br>Harming–NLT<br><br>**POSB<br>REFERENCE**<br>(1 Tim.1:12-14; esp.<br>v.13)<br>Note 1, point 3 | ὑβριστήν = *hubristēn*<br>Pronunciation: [hoo-bris-tayn']<br>Parsing (part of speech): noun<br>  Case—accusative<br>  Gender—masculine<br>  Number—singular<br>  Stem or root—from ὑβριστής, οῦ<br>Concordance References:<br>⇒ Strong's #5197 hubristēs<br>⇒ NIV #5616 hubristēs<br>⇒ NASB #5197 hubristēs<br><br>**1 Tim. 1:13**<br>Who was before a blasphemer, and a persecutor, and **injurious**: but I obtained mercy, because I did it ignorantly in unbelief. [KJV]<br>Even though I was formerly a blasphemer and a persecutor and a **violent aggressor**. And yet I was shown mercy, because I acted ignorantly in unbelief; [NASB]<br>Even though I was once a blasphemer and a persecutor and a **violent man**, I was shown mercy because I acted in ignorance and unbelief. [NIV]<br>Although I was formerly a blasphemer, a persecutor, and an **insolent man**; but I obtained mercy because I did *it* ignorantly in unbelief. [NKJV]<br>Even though I used to scoff at the name of Christ. I hunted down his people, **harming** them in every way I could. But God had mercy on me because I did it in ignorance and unbelief. [NLT]<br>τὸν πρότερον ὄντα βλάσφημον καὶ διώκτην καὶ **ὑβριστήν**· ἀλλ' ἠλεήθην, ὅτι ἀγνοῶν ἐποίησα ἐν ἀπιστίᾳ· [GNS]<br>τὸ πρότερον ὄντα βλάσφημον καὶ διώκτην καὶ **ὑβριστήν**, ἀλλὰ ἠλεήθην, ὅτι ἀγνοῶν ἐποίησα ἐν ἀπιστίᾳ· [GNT] | A violent man; a violent aggressor; injurious, harmful; an insulting person; insolent; to treat and use others despitefully; to enjoy being brutal and violent; to be in a fiery rage and to inflict it upon others.<br><br>**Practical Application**<br>William Barclay says that the word "indicates a kind of arrogant sadism; it describes the man who is out to inflict pain and injury for the sheer joy of inflicting it....that is what Paul was once like in regard to the Christian Church. Not content with words of insult, he went to the limit of legal persecution. Not content with legal persecution, he went to the limit of sadistic brutality in his attempt to stamp out the Christian faith" (*The Letters to Timothy, Titus, and Philemon*, p.52).<br>However, despite all this evil, God had mercy upon Paul. Paul had not known that Christ was really the true Messiah. He thought that he knew God and that his religion was the true religion. He felt that any religion that stood against his religion was to be stamped out. Therefore, when Paul attacked Christ and His followers, he did it ignorantly in unbelief. He just did not believe that Jesus Christ could possibly be the Messiah.<br>The point is this: God had mercy upon Paul. He took pity upon Paul despite his terrible sins (see POSB *Deeper Study* #2, Mercy—1 Tim. 1:2). |
| **#2152<br>Injustice**<br><br>Iniquity–KJV<br>Unrighteousness–<br>  NASB<br>Evil–NIV<br>Iniquity–NKJV<br>**Injustice–NLT** | ἀδικία = *adikia*<br>Pronunciation: [ad-ee-kee'-ah]<br>Parsing (part of speech): noun<br>  Case—dative<br>  Gender—feminine<br>  Number—singular<br>  Stem or root—from ἀδικία, ας<br>Concordance References:<br>⇒ Strong's #93 adikia<br>⇒ NIV #94 adikia<br>⇒ NASB #93 adikia | Evil, iniquity, unrighteousness, wrong-doing, injustice.<br><br>**Practical Application**<br>Love does not take pleasure in the unrighteousness and sin of others; it does not feed upon sin and wrong, nor does it pass along the stories of sin and wrong. Man's nature is too often fed the tragedy of evil, whether personal sin or natural disaster. (Cp. the daily news reports and most subjects of conversation between so many people). |

# PRACTICAL WORD STUDIES
## in the NEW TESTAMENT

| ENGLISH WORD | GREEK WORD AND VERSE | THE WORD MEANS... |
|---|---|---|
| **POSB REFERENCE** (1 Cor.13:4-7; esp. v.6) Note 2, point 10 See also POSB REF: (Rom.2:8) Deeper Study #5 | **1 Cor. 13:6** Rejoiceth not in **iniquity**, but rejoiceth in the truth; [KJV] Does not rejoice in **unrighteousness**, but rejoices with the truth; [NASB] Love does not delight in **evil** but rejoices with the truth. [NIV] Does not rejoice in **iniquity**, but rejoices in the truth; [NKJV] It is never glad about **injustice** but rejoices whenever the truth wins out. [NLT] οὐ χαίρει ἐπὶ τῇ **ἀδικίᾳ**, συγχαίρει δὲ τῇ ἀληθείᾳ· [GNS] οὐ χαίρει ἐπὶ τῇ **ἀδικίᾳ**, συγχαίρει δὲ τῇ ἀληθείᾳ [GNT] | |
| **#2153 Inner Strength** Strengthened–KJV Strengthened–NASB Strengthen–NIV Strengthened–NKJV Inner strength–NLT **POSB REFERENCE** (Eph.3:16) Note 2, point 1 | δῷ **κραταιωθῆναι** = dō krataiōthēnai Pronunciation: [do' krat-ah-yo'-thay-nah-ee] Parsing *dō* (part of speech): verb   Mood—subjunctive   Tense—aorist   Voice—active   Person—3rd person   Number—singular   Stem or root—from δίδωμι Parsing *krataiōthēnai* (part of speech): verb   Mood—infinitive   Tense—aorist   Voice—passive   Stem or root—from κραταιόομαι Concordance References: ⇒ Strong's #1325+2901 didōmi krataioō ⇒ NIV #1443+3194 didōmi krataioō [strengthen] ⇒ NASB #1325+2901 didōmi krataioō **Ephes. 3:16** That he would grant you, according to the riches of his glory, to be **strengthened** with might by his Spirit in the inner man; [KJV] That He would grant you, according to the riches of His glory, to be **strengthened** with power through His Spirit in the inner man; [NASB] I pray that out of his glorious riches he may **strengthen** you with power through his Spirit in your inner being, [NIV] That He would grant you, according to the riches of His glory, to be **strengthened** with might through His Spirit in the inner man; [NKJV] I pray that from his glorious, unlimited resources he will give you mighty **inner strength** through his Holy Spirit. [NLT] ἵνα **δῷ** ὑμῖν, κατὰ τὸν πλοῦτον τῆς δόξης αὐτοῦ, δυνάμει **κραταιωθῆναι** διὰ τοῦ Πνεύματος αὐτοῦ εἰς τὸν ἔσω ἄνθρωπον, [GNS] ἵνα **δῷ** ὑμῖν κατὰ τὸ πλοῦτος τῆς δόξης αὐτοῦ δυνάμει **κραταιωθῆναι** διὰ τοῦ πνεύματος αὐτοῦ εἰς τὸν ἔσω ἄνθρωπον, [GNT] | To strengthen; to have inner strength; to be made strong, tough, enduring. It means to have energy or force; to act, endure, or resist. **Practical Application** The believer needs to be strengthened with power in the "inner man," that is, in the deepest part of his being, in his soul, in his heart, in his spirit—in the spirit that God has renewed. It is there that he must be *strengthened with power*. Why? 1. Because it is the only way he can overcome the flesh with all its weakness. It is the only way he can conquer... • temptation and sin • grief and death • trouble and trials • disease and suffering • selfishness and worldliness • problems and circumstances    (See POSB note, God's Blessings, pt.1—Ephes. 1:3 for more discussion.) 2. Because it is the only way the believer can ever lay claim to all the blessings of God and fulfill God's eternal purpose for his life (Ephes. 1-3). The believer must be strengthened with power in order to break loose from the flesh and focus upon the eternal promises and call of God. Simply stated, his spirit must be strong and powerful... • to be everything God wants him to be. • to do everything God wants him to do. |
| **#2154 Innocent** Simple–KJV **Innocent–NASB** **Innocent–NIV** Simple–NKJV **Innocent–NLT** **POSB REFERENCE** (Rom.16:19-20; esp. v.19) Note 2, point 2 | ἀκεραίους = akeraious Pronunciation: [ak-er'-ah-yoos] Parsing (part of speech): adjective   Case—accusative   Gender—masculine   Number—plural   Stem or root—from ἀκέραιος, ον Concordance References: ⇒ Strong's #185 akeraios ⇒ NIV #193 akeraios ⇒ NASB #185 akeraios **Romans 16:19** For your obedience is come abroad unto all men. I am glad therefore on your behalf: but yet I would have you | Unmixed, unadulterated, pure, guileless, innocent, without any mixture of evil. **Practical Application** The idea is that the believers of a strong church must constantly mark, focus, and concentrate upon what is good in order to keep the bad out of its fellowship. The way to keep evil out of a church is to focus upon the good. The way to demonstrate spiritual wisdom is to concentrate upon the good; then evil will be recognized for what it is, and it will be rejected. The point is this: a strong church must not only avoid evil (Romans 16:17); it must not |

# Practical Word Studies
## in the New Testament

| ENGLISH WORD | GREEK WORD AND VERSE | THE WORD MEANS... |
|---|---|---|
| | wise unto that which is good, and **simple** concerning evil. [KJV]<br><br>For the report of your obedience has reached to all; therefore I am rejoicing over you, but I want you to be wise in what is good, and **innocent** in what is evil. [NASB]<br><br>Everyone has heard about your obedience, so I am full of joy over you; but I want you to be wise about what is good, and **innocent** about what is evil. [NIV]<br><br>For your obedience has become known to all. Therefore I am glad on your behalf; but I want you to be wise in what is good, and **simple** concerning evil. [NKJV]<br><br>But everyone knows that you are obedient to the Lord. This makes me very happy. I want you to see clearly what is right and to stay **innocent** of any wrong. [NLT]<br><br>ἡ γὰρ ὑμῶν ὑπακοὴ εἰς πάντας ἀφίκετο. χαίρω οὖν τὸ ἐφ' ὑμῖν, θέλω δὲ ὑμᾶς σοφοὺς εἶναι εἰς τὸ ἀγαθόν, **ἀκεραίους** δὲ εἰς τὸ κακόν. [GNS]<br><br>ἡ γὰρ ὑμῶν ὑπακοὴ εἰς πάντας ἀφίκετο· ἐφ' ὑμῖν οὖν χαίρω, θέλω δὲ ὑμᾶς σοφοὺς εἶναι εἰς τὸ ἀγαθόν, **ἀκεραίους** δὲ εἰς τὸ κακόν. [GNT] | allow evil to penetrate its fellowship. It must not allow a divisive person to stir up the "innocent" (unsuspecting and simple) believers of the church. A church must be wise: it must mark and focus upon what is good and untainted with evil. It must be wise enough to spot evil and to stop its penetration into the fellowship. |
| #2155<br>**Innocent**<br><br>Harmless–KJV<br>**Innocent–NASB**<br>Pure–NIV<br>Harmless–NKJV<br>Clean–NLT<br><br>**POSB REFERENCE**<br>(Philip.2:15)<br>Note 4, point 2 | ἀκέραιοι = akeraioi<br>Pronunciation: [ak-er'-ah-ee-oy]<br>Parsing (part of speech): adjective<br>    Case—nominative<br>    Gender—masculine<br>    Number—plural<br>    Stem or root—from ἀκέραιος, ον<br>Concordance References:<br>  ⇒ Strong's #185 akeraios<br>  ⇒ NIV #193 akeraios<br>  ⇒ NASB #185 akeraios<br><br>**Philip. 2:15**<br>That ye may be blameless and **harmless**, the sons of God, without rebuke, in the midst of a crooked and perverse nation, among whom ye shine as lights in the world; [KJV]<br><br>That you may prove yourselves to be blameless and **innocent**, children of God above reproach in the midst of a crooked and perverse generation, among whom you appear as lights in the world, [NASB]<br><br>So that you may become blameless and **pure**, children of God without fault in a crooked and depraved generation, in which you shine like stars in the universe [NIV]<br><br>That you may become blameless and **harmless**, children of God without fault in the midst of a crooked and perverse generation, among whom you shine as lights in the world, [NKJV]<br><br>So that no one can speak a word of blame against you. You are to live **clean**, innocent lives as children of God in a dark world full of crooked and perverse people. Let your lives shine brightly before them. [NLT]<br><br>ἵνα γένησθε ἄμεμπτοι καὶ **ἀκέραιοι**, τέκνα θεοῦ ἀμώμητα ἐν μέσῳ γενεᾶς σκολιᾶς καὶ διεστραμμένης, ἐν οἷς φαίνεσθε ὡς φωστῆρες ἐν κόσμῳ, [GNS]<br><br>ἵνα γένησθε ἄμεμπτοι καὶ **ἀκέραιοι**, τέκνα θεοῦ ἄμωμα μέσον γενεᾶς σκολιᾶς καὶ διεστραμμένης, ἐν οἷς φαίνεσθε ὡς φωστῆρες ἐν κόσμῳ, [GNT] | Pure, harmless, innocent, clean, without guile, unmixed and unadulterated.<br><br>**Practical Application**<br>Believers are to work at being innocent (*akeraioi*). It is the idea of flour or grain passing through a sieve to separate the pure from the impure. It means that our thoughts and lives...<br>• are not to be polluted by watching, reading, and listening to worldly and sexual attractions.<br>• are not to be given over to worldly and sexual attractions.<br><br>Our thoughts and lives are to be pure, clean, uncontaminated, and unpolluted. |
| #2156<br>**Innocent**<br><br>Harmless–KJV<br>**Innocent–NASB**<br>Blameless–NIV<br>Harmless–NKJV<br>Blameless–NLT | ἄκακος = akakos<br>Pronunciation: [ak'-ak-os]<br>Parsing (part of speech): adjective<br>    Case—nominative<br>    Gender—masculine<br>    Number—singular<br>    Stem or root—from ἄκακος, ον<br>Concordance References:<br>  ⇒ Strong's #172 akakos<br>  ⇒ NIV #179 akakos<br>  ⇒ NASB #172 akakos | Blameless, harmless, innocent, unsuspecting, naive; free from all guile, deception, envy, and malice against anyone.<br><br>**Practical Application**<br>William Barclay says that "Jesus *never hurt any man*" (*The Letter to the Hebrews*, p.89). We might say that Jesus Christ was so good that there was nothing but good in Him. There was nothing but the goodness and love of God in |

# PRACTICAL WORD STUDIES
## in the NEW TESTAMENT

| ENGLISH WORD | GREEK WORD AND VERSE | THE WORD MEANS... |
|---|---|---|
| **POSB REFERENCE** (Heb.7:26) Note 2, point 2 | **Hebrews 7:26**<br>For such an high priest became us, who is holy, **harmless**, undefiled, separate from sinners, and made higher than the heavens; [KJV]<br>For it was fitting that we should have such a high priest, holy, **innocent**, undefiled, separated from sinners and exalted above the heavens; [NASB]<br>Such a high priest meets our need—one who is holy, **blameless**, pure, set apart from sinners, exalted above the heavens. [NIV]<br>For such a High Priest was fitting for us, who is holy, **harmless**, undefiled, separate from sinners, and has become higher than the heavens; [NKJV]<br>He is the kind of high priest we need because he is holy and **blameless**, unstained by sin. He has now been set apart from sinners, and he has been given the highest place of honor in heaven. [NLT]<br>Τοιοῦτος γὰρ ἡμῖν ἔπρεπεν ἀρχιερεύς, ὅσιος, **ἄκακος**, ἀμίαντος, κεχωρισμένος ἀπὸ τῶν ἁμαρτωλῶν, καὶ ὑψηλότερος τῶν οὐρανῶν γενόμενος· [GNS]<br>Τοιοῦτος γὰρ ἡμῖν καὶ ἔπρεπεν ἀρχιερεύς, ὅσιος **ἄκακος** ἀμίαντος, κεχωρισμένος ἀπὸ τῶν ἁμαρτωλῶν καὶ ὑψηλότερος τῶν οὐρανῶν γενόμενος, [GNT] | Him, and that was all that He ever shared with man. Jesus Christ is absolutely *harmless and blameless*. |
| **#2157 Innocent Lives**<br><br>Without rebuke–KJV<br>Above reproach–NASB<br>Without fault–NIV<br>Without fault–NKJV<br>**Innocent lives–NLT**<br><br>**POSB REFERENCE** (Philip.2:15) Note 4, point 3 | **ἄμωμα** = amōma<br>Pronunciation: [am-o'-mah]<br>Parsing (part of speech): adjective<br>    Case—nominative<br>    Gender—neuter<br>    Number—plural<br>    Stem or root—from ἄμωμος, ον<br>Concordance References:<br>⇒ Strong's #298 amōmetos<br>⇒ NIV #320 amōmos<br>⇒ NASB #299b amōmos<br><br>**Philip. 2:15**<br>That ye may be blameless and harmless, the sons of God, **without rebuke**, in the midst of a crooked and perverse nation, among whom ye shine as lights in the world; [KJV]<br>That you may prove yourselves to be blameless and innocent, children of God **above reproach** in the midst of a crooked and perverse generation, among whom you appear as lights in the world, [NASB]<br>So that you may become blameless and pure, children of God **without fault** in a crooked and depraved generation, in which you shine like stars in the universe [NIV]<br>That you may become blameless and harmless, children of God **without fault** in the midst of a crooked and perverse generation, among whom you shine as lights in the world, [NKJV]<br>So that no one can speak a word of blame against you. You are to live clean, **innocent lives** as children of God in a dark world full of crooked and perverse people. Let your lives shine brightly before them. [NLT]<br>ἵνα γένησθε ἄμεμπτοι καὶ ἀκέραιοι, τέκνα Θεοῦ **ἀμώμητα** ἐν μέσῳ γενεᾶς σκολιᾶς καὶ διεστραμμένης, ἐν οἷς φαίνεσθε ὡς φωστῆρες ἐν κόσμῳ, [GNS]<br>ἵνα γένησθε ἄμεμπτοι καὶ ἀκέραιοι, τέκνα θεοῦ **ἄμωμα** μέσον γενεᾶς σκολιᾶς καὶ διεστραμμένης, ἐν οἷς φαίνεσθε ὡς φωστῆρες ἐν κόσμῳ, [GNT] | To be without fault; to be without rebuke; to be above reproach; to live innocent lives; to be without blemish, spot, or defect.<br><br>**Practical Application**<br>This is a word that is taken from the Old Testament sacrifices made to God. The idea is that the believer is to live upon earth under the eyes and scrutiny of God. He is to walk without any blemish, spot, or defect.<br>However, note a fact: the believer lives in a crooked and perverse generation. The world is wicked and evil, twisted and perverted; therefore, the believer has a difficult path to walk. But walk he must, for he is to be the light of the world. He is to shine as a light in the world. He is to reflect the purity, holiness and quietness of God Himself. |
| **#2158 Innocent Of Sin**<br><br>Faultless–KJV<br>Blameless–NASB<br>Without fault–NIV<br>Faultless–NKJV<br>**Innocent of sin–NLT** | **ἀμώμους** = amōmous<br>Pronunciation: [am'-o-moos]<br>Parsing (part of speech): adjective<br>    Case—accusative<br>    Gender—masculine<br>    Number—plural<br>    Stem or root—from ἄμωμος, ον<br>Concordance References:<br>⇒ Strong's #299 amōmos<br>⇒ NIV #320 amōmos<br>⇒ NASB #299b amōmos | To be without fault, blameless; to be innocent of sin; to be faultless, without blemish; to be spotless and pure, without any defilement whatsoever.<br><br>**Practical Application**<br>God is *able to make us innocent of sin* when we come face to face with Him. The words "innocent of sin" (*amōmous*) mean to be spotless |

# PRACTICAL WORD STUDIES
## in the NEW TESTAMENT

| ENGLISH WORD | GREEK WORD AND VERSE | THE WORD MEANS... |
|---|---|---|
| **POSB REFERENCE** (Jude 1:24-25; esp. v.24) Note 4, point 2 | **Jude 1:24**<br>Now unto him that is able to keep you from falling, and to present you **faultless** before the presence of his glory with exceeding joy, [KJV]<br>Now to Him who is able to keep you from stumbling, and to make you stand in the presence of His glory **blameless** with great joy, [NASB]<br>To him who is able to keep you from falling and to present you before his glorious presence **without fault** and with great joy— [NIV]<br>Now to Him who is able to keep you from stumbling, And to present you **faultless** Before the presence of His glory with exceeding joy, [NKJV]<br>And now, all glory to God, who is able to keep you from stumbling, and who will bring you into his glorious presence **innocent of sin** and with great joy. [NLT]<br>Τῷ δὲ δυναμένῳ φυλάξαι ὑμᾶς ἀπταίστους, καὶ στῆσαι κατενώπιον τῆς δόξης αὐτοῦ **ἀμώμους** ἐν ἀγαλλιάσει, [GNS]<br>Τῷ δὲ δυναμένῳ φυλάξαι ὑμᾶς ἀπταίστους καὶ στῆσαι κατενώπιον τῆς δόξης αὐτοῦ **ἀμώμους** ἐν ἀγαλλιάσει, [GNT] | and pure, without any defilement whatsoever. God is able to accept us in Jesus Christ, the spotless Lamb of God. If we will continue to approach God in Christ—in the name of Christ and His death—then God will accept us and count our faith as righteousness. He will accept us in the righteousness of His Son, the Lord Jesus Christ. God is able to do this, and He will do it if we will draw near Him *in Christ*. |
| **#2159 Innumerable Multitude**<br><br>Innumerable multitude–KJV<br>Many thousands–NASB<br>Many thousands–NIV<br>Innumerable multitude–NKJV<br>Thousands–NLT<br><br>**POSB REFERENCE** (Lk.12:1) Note 1 | μυριάδων = *muriadōn*<br>Pronunciation: [moo-ree'-ah-doan]<br>Parsing (part of speech): noun<br>   Case—genitive<br>   Gender—feminine<br>   Number—plural<br>Stem or root—from μυριάς, άδος<br>Concordance References:<br>  ⇒ Strong's #3461 murias<br>  ⇒ NIV #3689 murias<br>  ⇒ NASB #3461 murias<br><br>**Luke 12:1**<br>In the mean time, when there were gathered together an **innumerable multitude** of people, insomuch that they trode one upon another, he began to say unto his disciples first of all, Beware ye of the leaven of the Pharisees, which is hypocrisy. [KJV]<br>Under these circumstances, after so **many thousands** of the multitude had gathered together that they were stepping on one another, He began saying to His disciples first of all, "Beware of the leaven of the Pharisees, which is hypocrisy. [NASB]<br>Meanwhile, when a crowd of **many thousands** had gathered, so that they were trampling on one another, Jesus began to speak first to his disciples, saying: "Be on your guard against the yeast of the Pharisees, which is hypocrisy. [NIV]<br>In the meantime, when an **innumerable multitude** of people had gathered together, so that they trampled one another, He began to say to His disciples first *of all,* "Beware of the leaven of the Pharisees, which is hypocrisy. [NKJV]<br>Meanwhile, the crowds grew until **thousands** were milling about and crushing each other. Jesus turned first to his disciples and warned them, "Beware of the yeast of the Pharisees—beware of their hypocrisy. [NLT]<br>Ἐν οἷς ἐπισυναχθεισῶν τῶν **μυριάδων** τοῦ ὄχλου, ὥστε καταπατεῖν ἀλλήλους, ἤρξατο λέγειν πρὸς τοὺς μαθητὰς αὐτοῦ πρῶτον, Προσέχετε ἑαυτοῖς ἀπὸ τῆς ζύμης τῶν Φαρισαίων, ἥτις ἐστὶν ὑπόκρισις. [GNS]<br>Ἐν οἷς ἐπισυναχθεισῶν τῶν **μυριάδων** τοῦ ὄχλου, ὥστε καταπατεῖν ἀλλήλους, ἤρξατο λέγειν πρὸς τοὺς μαθητὰς αὐτοῦ πρῶτον, Προσέχετε ἑαυτοῖς ἀπὸ τῆς ζύμης, ἥτις ἐστὶν ὑπόκρισις, τῶν Φαρισαίων. [GNT] | Thousands, many thousands, myriad, an innumerable multitude.<br><br>**Practical Application**<br>A vast crowd now gathered around Jesus, a crowd so large it could not be numbered. Note: so many had gathered that they were pushing and stepping upon each other. They were so eager to hear the Word of God that they were trying to get as close as possible. What a lesson for modern man—to be so hungry for the Word of God that we flock to His preaching and struggle to get up front! |

# PRACTICAL WORD STUDIES
## in the NEW TESTAMENT

| ENGLISH WORD | GREEK WORD AND VERSE | THE WORD MEANS... |
|---|---|---|
| **#2160**<br>**Inordinate Affection**<br><br>Inordinate affection–KJV<br>Passion–NASB<br>Lust–NIV<br>Passion–NKJV<br>Lust–NLT<br><br>**POSB REFERENCE**<br>(Col.3:5-7; esp. v.5)<br>Note 1, point 1c | πάθος = *pathos*<br>Pronunciation: [path'-os]<br>Parsing (part of speech): noun<br>    Case—accusative<br>    Gender—neuter<br>    Number—singular<br>    Stem or root—from πάθος, ους<br>Concordance References:<br>  → Strong's #3806 *pathos*<br>  ⇒ NIV #4079 *pathos*<br>  ⇒ NASB #3806 *pathos*<br><br>**Col. 3:5**<br>Mortify therefore your members which are upon the earth; fornication, uncleanness, **inordinate affection**, evil concupiscence, and covetousness, which is idolatry: [KJV]<br>Therefore consider the members of your earthly body as dead to immorality, impurity, **passion**, evil desire, and greed, which amounts to idolatry. [NASB]<br>Put to death, therefore, whatever belongs to your earthly nature: sexual immorality, impurity, **lust**, evil desires and greed, which is idolatry. [NIV]<br>Therefore put to death your members which are on the earth: fornication, uncleanness, **passion**, evil desire, and covetousness, which is idolatry. [NKJV]<br>So put to death the sinful, earthly things lurking within you. Have nothing to do with sexual sin, impurity, **lust**, and shameful desires. Don't be greedy for the good things of this life, for that is idolatry. [NLT]<br>Νεκρώσατε οὖν τὰ μέλη ὑμῶν τὰ ἐπὶ τῆς γῆς, πορνείαν, ἀκαθαρσίαν, **πάθος**, ἐπιθυμίαν κακήν, καὶ τὴν πλεονεξίαν, ἥτις ἐστὶν εἰδωλολατρεία, [GNS]<br>Νεκρώσατε οὖν τὰ μέλη τὰ ἐπὶ τῆς γῆς, πορνείαν ἀκαθαρσίαν **πάθος** ἐπιθυμίαν κακήν, καὶ τὴν πλεονεξίαν, ἥτις ἐστὶν εἰδωλολατρία, [GNT] | Lust; inordinate affection; lustful passion; craving; strong desire; intense arousal; a driving lust.<br><br>**Practical Application**<br>It is, of course, a desire and craving for the wrong things such as the second and third helping of food, alcohol, drugs, nudity, pornography, suggestive and filthy literature, illicit affairs, extra-marital sex, etc and a host of other lusts. |
| **#2161**<br>**Insight**<br><br>Prudence–KJV<br>**Insight–NASB**<br>Understanding–NIV<br>Prudence–NKJV<br>Understanding–NLT<br><br>**POSB REFERENCE**<br>(Eph.1:8)<br>Note 5, point 2 | φρονήσει = *phronēsei*<br>Pronunciation: [fron'-ay-see]<br>Parsing (part of speech): noun<br>    Case—dative<br>    Gender—feminine<br>    Number—singular<br>    Stem or root—from φρόνησις, εως<br>Concordance References:<br>  ⇒ Strong's #5428 *phronēsis*<br>  ⇒ NIV #5860 *phronēsis*<br>  ⇒ NASB #5428 *phronēsis*<br><br>**Ephes. 1:8**<br>Wherein he hath abounded toward us in all wisdom and **prudence**; [KJV]<br>Which He lavished upon us. In all wisdom and **insight** [NASB]<br>That he lavished on us with all wisdom and **understanding**. [NIV]<br>Which He made to abound toward us in all wisdom and **prudence**, [NKJV]<br>He has showered his kindness on us, along with all wisdom and **understanding**. [NLT]<br>ἧς ἐπερίσσευσεν εἰς ἡμᾶς ἐν πάσῃ σοφίᾳ καὶ **φρονήσει**, [GNS]<br>ἧς ἐπερίσσευσεν εἰς ἡμᾶς, ἐν πάσῃ σοφίᾳ καὶ **φρονήσει**, [GNT] | Understanding, insight, wisdom, prudence, comprehension, discernment, intelligence, discretion, judgment.<br><br>**Practical Application**<br>The word "insight" (*phronēsei*) means seeing how to use and do the truth. It is seeing the direction to take. It is understanding, insight, the ability to solve day-to-day problems. It is a down-to-earth practical understanding of things. |
| **#2162**<br>**Insight**<br><br>Judgment–KJV<br>Discernment–NASB<br>**Insight–NIV**<br>Discernment–NKJV<br>Understanding–NLT | αἰσθήσει = *aisthēsei*<br>Pronunciation: [ah'ee-sthay-seh-ee]<br>Parsing (part of speech): noun<br>    Case—dative<br>    Gender—feminine<br>    Number—singular<br>    Stem or root—from αἴσθησις, εως | Insight, judgment, discernment, understanding, intelligence.<br><br>**Practical Application**<br>Love in the Bible never focuses upon *good feelings*. Feelings may and usually do come to the person who truly loves another person, but |

# PRACTICAL WORD STUDIES
## in the NEW TESTAMENT

| ENGLISH WORD | GREEK WORD AND VERSE | THE WORD MEANS... |
|---|---|---|
| **POSB REFERENCE** (Philip.1:9-10; esp. v.9) Note 7 | Concordance References:<br>⇒ Strong's #144 aisthēsis<br>⇒ NIV #151 aisthēsis<br>⇒ NASB #144 aisthēsis<br><br>**Philip. 1:9**<br>And this I pray, that your love may abound yet more and more in knowledge and in all **judgment**; [KJV]<br>And this I pray, that your love may abound still more and more in real knowledge and all **discernment**, [NASB]<br>And this is my prayer: that your love may abound more and more in knowledge and depth of **insight**, [NIV]<br>And this I pray, that your love may abound still more and more in knowledge and all **discernment**, [NKJV]<br>I pray that your love for each other will overflow more and more, and that you will keep on growing in your knowledge and **understanding**. [NLT]<br>καὶ τοῦτο προσεύχομαι, ἵνα ἡ ἀγάπη ὑμῶν ἔτι μᾶλλον καὶ μᾶλλον περισσεύῃ ἐν ἐπιγνώσει καὶ πάσῃ **αἰσθήσει**, [GNS]<br>καὶ τοῦτο προσεύχομαι, ἵνα ἡ ἀγάπη ὑμῶν ἔτι μᾶλλον καὶ μᾶλλον περισσεύῃ ἐν ἐπιγνώσει καὶ πάσῃ **αἰσθήσει** [GNT] | feelings are never the focus—not with true love. What then is the focus?<br>⇒ The focus of love is knowledge. If we truly love someone, we want to know that person. In fact, we want to know all we can about the person.<br>⇒ The force of love is insight (*aisthēsei*). If we truly love someone, we not only want to know a person but we want to learn all we can about the person. We want to gather all the intelligence and facts possible and discern them so that we can please the person. |
| **#2163**<br>**Insolent**<br><br>Despiteful–KJV<br>**Insolent–NASB**<br>**Insolent–NIV**<br>Violent–NKJV<br>**Insolent–NLT**<br><br>**POSB REFERENCE** (Romans 1:30) *Deeper Study #14* | **ὑβριστάς** = *hubristas*<br>Pronunciation: [hoo-bris-tahs']<br>Parsing (part of speech): noun<br>  Case—accusative<br>  Gender—masculine<br>  Number—plural<br>  Stem or root—from ὑβριστής, οῦ<br>Concordance References:<br>⇒ Strong's #5197 hubristēs<br>⇒ NIV #5616 hubristēs<br>⇒ NASB #5197 hubristēs<br><br>**Romans 1:30**<br>Backbiters, haters of God, **despiteful**, proud, boasters, inventors of evil things, disobedient to parents, [KJV]<br>Slanderers, haters of God, **insolent**, arrogant, boastful, inventors of evil, disobedient to parents, [NASB]<br>Slanderers, God-haters, **insolent**, arrogant and boastful; they invent ways of doing evil; they disobey their parents; [NIV]<br>Backbiters, haters of God, **violent**, proud, boasters, inventors of evil things, disobedient to parents, [NKJV]<br>They are backstabbers, haters of God, **insolent**, proud, and boastful. They are forever inventing new ways of sinning and are disobedient to their parents. [NLT]<br>ψιθυριστάς, καταλάλους, θεοστυγεῖς, **ὑβριστάς**, ὑπερηφάνους, ἀλαζόνας, ἐφευρετὰς κακῶν, γονεῦσιν ἀπειθεῖς, [GNS]<br>καταλάλους θεοστυγεῖς **ὑβριστάς** ὑπερηφάνους ἀλαζόνας, ἐφευρετὰς κακῶν, γονεῦσιν ἀπειθεῖς, [GNT] | Insolent, despiteful, insulting, and defying; a violent man.<br><br>**Practical Application**<br>It is a spirit of spite, of attack and assault, verbally or physically. It is despising and attacking, inflicting injury either by word or act. It is a man who...<br>• lives his own life as he wishes, ignoring both God and men.<br>• lives as though his rights and affairs are the only rights and affairs which matter.<br>• stands toe to toe with both God and men, acting as though he needs neither.<br>• acts so independent in life that he dares God or men to get in his way.<br>• does what he wants when he wants, even if it hurts or destroys others.<br><br>The sin of despite, of being insolent and insulting, is the spirit that hurts and harms others in order to do what one wants. |
| **#2164**<br>**Insolent Man**<br><br>Injurious–KJV<br>Violent aggressor–NASB<br>Violent man–NIV<br>**Insolent man–NKJV**<br>Harming–NLT<br><br>**POSB REFERENCE** (1 Tim.1:12-14; esp. v.13) Note 1, point 3 | **ὑβριστήν** = *hubristēn*<br>Pronunciation: [hoo-bris-tayn']<br>Parsing (part of speech): noun<br>  Case—accusative<br>  Gender—masculine<br>  Number—singular<br>  Stem or root—from ὑβριστής, οῦ<br>Concordance References:<br>⇒ Strong's #5197 hubristēs<br>⇒ NIV #5616 hubristēs<br>⇒ NASB #5197 hubristēs<br><br>**1 Tim. 1:13**<br>Who was before a blasphemer, and a persecutor, and **injurious**: but I obtained mercy, because I did it ignorantly in unbelief. [KJV]<br>Even though I was formerly a blasphemer and a perse- | A violent man; a violent aggressor; injurious, harmful; an insulting person; insolent; to treat and use others despitefully; to enjoy being brutal and violent; to be in a fiery rage and to inflict it upon others.<br><br>**Practical Application**<br>William Barclay says that the word "indicates a kind of arrogant sadism; it describes the man who is out to inflict pain and injury for the sheer joy of inflicting it....that is what Paul was once like in regard to the Christian Church. Not content with words of insult, he went to the limit of legal persecution. Not content with legal persecution, he went to the limit of sadistic brutality in his attempt to stamp out the Christian faith" |

# PRACTICAL WORD STUDIES
## in the New Testament

| ENGLISH WORD | GREEK WORD AND VERSE | THE WORD MEANS... |
|---|---|---|
| | cutor and a **violent aggressor**. And yet I was shown mercy, because I acted ignorantly in unbelief; [NASB]<br><br>Even though I was once a blasphemer and a persecutor and a **violent man**, I was shown mercy because I acted in ignorance and unbelief. [NIV]<br><br>Although I was formerly a blasphemer, a persecutor, and an **insolent man**; but I obtained mercy because I did *it* ignorantly in unbelief. [NKJV]<br><br>Even though I used to scoff at the name of Christ. I hunted down his people, **harming** them in every way I could. But God had mercy on me because I did it in ignorance and unbelief. [NLT]<br><br>τὸν πρότερον ὄντα βλάσφημον καὶ διώκτην καὶ **ὑβριστήν**· ἀλλ ἠλεήθην, ὅτι ἀγνοῶν ἐποίησα ἐν ἀπιστίᾳ· [GNS]<br><br>τὸ πρότερον ὄντα βλάσφημον καὶ διώκτην καὶ **ὑβριστήν**, ἀλλὰ ἠλεήθην, ὅτι ἀγνοῶν ἐποίησα ἐν ἀπιστίᾳ· [GNT] | (*The Letters to Timothy, Titus, and Philemon*, p.52).<br><br>However, despite all this evil, God had mercy upon Paul. Paul had not known that Christ was really the true Messiah. He thought that he knew God and that his religion was the true religion. He felt that any religion that stood against his religion was to be stamped out. Therefore, when Paul attacked Christ and His followers, he did it ignorantly in unbelief. He just did not believe that Jesus Christ could possibly be the Messiah.<br><br>The point is this: God had mercy upon Paul. He took pity upon Paul despite his terrible sins (see POSB *Deeper Study* #2, Mercy—1 Tim. 1:2). |
| **#2165**<br>**Inspiration Of God–**<br>**Inspired by God**<br><br>Inspiration of God–KJV<br>Inspired by God–NASB<br>God-breathed–NIV<br>Inspiration of God–NKJV<br>Inspired by God–NLT<br><br>**POSB REFERENCE**<br>(2 Tim. 3:16)<br>Note 3, point 2 | θεόπνευστος = *theopneustos*<br>Pronunciation: [theh-op'-nyoo-stos]<br>Parsing (part of speech): adjective<br>    Case—nominative<br>    Gender—feminine<br>    Number—singular<br>    Stem or root—from θεόπνευστος, ον<br>Concordance References:<br>  ⇒ Strong's #2315 theopneustos<br>  ⇒ NIV #2535 theopneustos<br>  ⇒ NASB #2315 theopneustos<br><br>**2 Tim. 3:16**<br>All scripture is given by **inspiration of God**, and is profitable for doctrine, for reproof, for correction, for instruction in righteousness: [KJV]<br><br>All Scripture is **inspired by God** and profitable for teaching, for reproof, for correction, for training in righteousness; [NASB]<br><br>All Scripture is **God-breathed** and is useful for teaching, rebuking, correcting and training in righteousness, [NIV]<br><br>All Scripture *is* given by **inspiration of God**, and *is* profitable for doctrine, for reproof, for correction, for instruction in righteousness, [NKJV]<br><br>All Scripture is **inspired by God** and is useful to teach us what is true and to make us realize what is wrong in our lives. It straightens us out and teaches us to do what is right. [NLT]<br><br>πᾶσα γραφὴ **θεόπνευστος** καὶ ὠφέλιμος πρὸς διδασκαλίαν, πρὸς ἔλεγχον, πρὸς ἐπανόρθωσιν, πρὸς παιδείαν τὴν ἐν δικαιοσύνῃ· [GNS]<br><br>πᾶσα γραφὴ **θεόπνευστος** καὶ ὠφέλιμος πρὸς διδασκαλίαν, πρὸς ἐλεγμόν, πρὸς ἐπανόρθωσιν, πρὸς παιδείαν τὴν ἐν δικαιοσύνῃ, [GNT] | God breathed, inspiration of God, inspiration by God.<br><br>**Practical Application**<br>What does this mean? What does it mean to say that *God breathed* the Holy Scriptures? No one can say for sure, but this much can be said.<br>⇒ The idea is that *God breathed out* the Scripture or *God produced* the Scripture somewhat like He did creation.<br>⇒ "By the word of the LORD were the heavens made; and all the host of them by the breath of his mouth" (Psalm 33:6).<br><br>Note: it is the Scripture that is inspired, not the man. The Bible does not claim to be written by inspired men. It does claim that the writing is supernaturally given or breathed by God. The Scripture is *breathed out by God, not breathed into by God*. The meaning is this: the writing is supernaturally given or breathed by God. The Bible claims to be the Word given by the creative breath of God.<br><br>The Greek scholar A.T. Robertson says: "God-breathed...[this] is in contrast to the commandments of men" (*Word Pictures in the New Testament*, Vol.4, p.627).<br><br>The great Bible expositor Matthew Henry says: "It [Scripture] is a divine revelation, which we may depend upon as infallibly true. The same Spirit that breathed reason into us breathes revelation among us: 'For the prophecy came not in old time by the will of man, but holy men of God spoke as they were moved or carried forth by the Holy Ghost,' 2 Peter 1:21. The prophets and apostles did not speak from themselves, but what they received of the Lord that they delivered unto us" (*Matthew Henry's Commentary*, Vol.5, p.846f). |
| **#2166**<br>**Instant**<br><br>Instant–KJV<br>Ready–NASB<br>Prepared–NIV<br>Ready–NKJV<br>Persistent–NLT | ἐπίστηθι = *epistēthi*<br>Pronunciation: [ef-is'-tay-thee]<br>Parsing (part of speech): verb<br>    Mood—imperative<br>    Tense—aorist<br>    Voice—active<br>    Person—2nd person<br>    Number—singular<br>    Stem or root—from ἐφίστημι<br>Concordance References:<br>  ⇒ Strong's #2186 ephistēmi<br>  ⇒ NIV #2392 ephistēmi<br>  ⇒ NASB #2186 ephistēmi | To be prepared; to be instant; to be ready; to be persistent; to be insistent. The word "instant" (*epistēthi*) means to "take a stand, to stand upon it or up to it, to carry on, to stick to it" (A.T. Robertson).<br><br>**Practical Application**<br>As Robertson says, "There are all sorts of seasons...some difficult..some easy" (*Word Pictures in the New Testament*, Vol.4, p.629). |

# PRACTICAL WORD STUDIES
## in the NEW TESTAMENT

| ENGLISH WORD | GREEK WORD AND VERSE | THE WORD MEANS... |
|---|---|---|
| **POSB REFERENCE** (2 Tim. 4:2) Note 2, point 2a | **2 Tim. 4:2** Preach the word; be **instant** in season, out of season; reprove, rebuke, exhort with all longsuffering and doctrine. [KJV] Preach the word; be **ready** in season and out of season; reprove, rebuke, exhort, with great patience and instruction. [NASB] Preach the Word; be **prepared** in season and out of season; correct, rebuke and encourage—with great patience and careful instruction. [NIV] Preach the word! Be **ready** in season *and* out of season. Convince, rebuke, exhort, with all longsuffering and teaching. [NKJV] Preach the word of God. Be **persistent**, whether the time is favorable or not. Patiently correct, rebuke, and encourage your people with good teaching. [NLT] κήρυξον τὸν λόγον, **ἐπίστηθι** εὐκαίρως, ἀκαίρως, ἔλεγξον, ἐπιτίμησον, παρακάλεσον, ἐν πάσῃ μακροθυμίᾳ καὶ διδαχῇ. [GNS] κήρυξον τὸν λόγον, **ἐπίστηθι** εὐκαίρως ἀκαίρως, ἔλεγξον, ἐπιτίμησον, παρακάλεσον, ἐν πάσῃ μακροθυμίᾳ καὶ διδαχῇ. [GNT] | The task of the minister is to stand and stick to preaching no matter the circumstances, easy or difficult. |
| **#2167 Instinctively** Nature–KJV **Instinctively–NASB** Nature–NIV Nature–NKJV **Instinctively–NLT** **POSB REFERENCE** (Romans 2:11-15; esp. v.14) Note 4, point 3a | φύσει = *phusei* Pronunciation: [foo'-see] Parsing (part of speech): noun     Case—dative     Gender—feminine     Number—singular     Stem or root—from φύσις, εως Concordance References:   ⇒ Strong's #5449 phusis   ⇒ NIV #5882 phusis   ⇒ NASB #5449 phusis **Romans 2:14** For when the Gentiles, which have not the law, do by **nature** the things contained in the law, these, having not the law, are a law unto themselves: [KJV] For when Gentiles who do not have the Law do **instinctively** the things of the Law, these, not having the Law, are a law to themselves, [NASB] (Indeed, when Gentiles, who do not have the law, do by **nature** things required by the law, they are a law for themselves, even though they do not have the law, [NIV] For when Gentiles, who do not have the law, by **nature** do the things in the law, these, although not having the law, are a law to themselves, [NKJV] Even when Gentiles, who do not have God's written law, **instinctively** follow what the law says, they show that in their hearts they know right from wrong. [NLT] ὅταν γὰρ ἔθνη τὰ μὴ νόμον ἔχοντα **φύσει** τὰ τοῦ νόμου ποιῇ, οὗτοι νόμον μὴ ἔχοντες, ἑαυτοῖς εἰσι νόμος· [GNS] ὅταν γὰρ ἔθνη τὰ μὴ νόμον ἔχοντα **φύσει** τὰ τοῦ νόμου ποιῶσιν, οὗτοι νόμον μὴ ἔχοντες ἑαυτοῖς εἰσιν νόμος· [GNT] | Nature, natural condition; instinct. **Practical Application** The heathen have a threefold witness, a witness that is strong enough to lead them to God. 1. Men have their nature—the nature of man that speaks loudly and clearly—that points toward God. Note exactly what the verse says.   ⇒ Men may not have the law (the Scriptures)...   ⇒ But they can do the law by instinct.   ⇒ They can become "a law to themselves." There is that within man, within his instinct (*phusei*), that can stir him to do the law. Man has within him an instinctive knowledge of right and wrong. His very nature gives him the opportunity to do what is right.   Something else is meant here as well. Man can look at nature (creation) and see that he is part of it. He can instinctively see by nature the great eternal power and deity of God. (See POSB note—Romans 1:20 for a list of the things nature reveals about God.) 2. Men have their consciences that bear witness to what is right and wrong. When they do right, they sense approval; when they do wrong, they sense reproach. Man's conscience gives him the opportunity to live righteously and to do good. 3. Men have their thoughts, their reasoning ability which can approve or disapprove, excuse or accuse them and others. Men's thoughts bear witness to how they should and should not live, whether their behavior is excused (acceptable) or accused (condemned). |
| **#2168 Instruct** Charge–KJV Instruct–NASB **Command–NIV** Charge–NKJV Stop–NLT | παραγγείλῃς = *paraggeilēs* Pronunciation: [par-ang-geh-i-lays] Parsing (part of speech): verb     Mood—subjunctive     Tense—aorist     Voice—active     Person—2nd person     Number—singular     Stem or root—from παραγγέλλω | To command; to charge; to instruct; to give strict orders to stop. **Practical Application** Timothy was in Ephesus and Paul was in Macedonia, a great distance apart. Ephesus was in Asia and Macedonia was in Europe, north of |

# PRACTICAL WORD STUDIES
## in the NEW TESTAMENT

| ENGLISH WORD | GREEK WORD AND VERSE | THE WORD MEANS... |
|---|---|---|
| **POSB REFERENCE** (1 Tim.1:3) Note 1 | Concordance References:<br>⇒ Strong's #3853 paraggellö<br>⇒ NIV #4133 paraggellö<br>⇒ NASB #3853 paraggellö<br><br>**1 Tim. 1:3**<br>As I besought thee to abide still at Ephesus, when I went into Macedonia, that thou mightest **charge** some that they teach no other doctrine, [KJV]<br>As I urged you upon my departure for Macedonia, remain on at Ephesus, in order that you may **instruct** certain men not to teach strange doctrines, [NASB]<br>As I urged you when I went into Macedonia, stay there in Ephesus so that you may **command** certain men not to teach false doctrines any longer [NIV]<br>As I urged you when I went into Macedonia—remain in Ephesus that you may **charge** some that they teach no other doctrine, [NKJV]<br>When I left for Macedonia, I urged you to stay there in Ephesus and **stop** those who are teaching wrong doctrine. [NLT]<br>Καθὼς παρεκάλεσά σε προσμεῖναι ἐν Ἐφέσῳ, πορευόμενος εἰς Μακεδονίαν, ἵνα **παραγγείλῃς** τισὶ μὴ ἑτεροδιδασκαλεῖν, [GNS]<br>Καθὼς παρεκάλεσά σε προσμεῖναι ἐν Ἐφέσῳ πορευόμενος εἰς Μακεδονίαν, ἵνα **παραγγείλῃς** τισὶν μὴ ἑτεροδιδασκαλεῖν [GNT] | Greece. Note that Paul had to urge Timothy to stay at Ephesus. The church was in trouble because false teaching had seeped in, and the church needed Timothy. Apparently, Timothy felt incapable and wanted to join Paul until Paul could return to Ephesus and handle the situation himself. However, false teaching is so serious a matter that it has to be handled immediately when it raises its ugly head. Therefore, Timothy had to remain in Ephesus so that he could *command* the church to stop the false teaching. The word "command" (*paraggeilës*) is a strong word. It is a military word that means to pass commands down through the ranks. Timothy was to *give orders and charge* the false teachers to stop teaching false doctrine, and if this did not work, he was to order and charge the church to handle the false teachers. |
| #2169<br>**Instruct**<br><br>Put...in remembrance–KJV<br>Pointing out–NASB<br>Point...out–NIV<br>**Instruct–NKJV**<br>Explain–NLT<br><br>**POSB REFERENCE** (1 Tim.4:6) Note 1 | ὑποτιθέμενος = hupotithemenos<br>Pronunciation: [hoop-ot-ith'-eh-mehn-os]<br>Parsing (part of speech): verb<br>  Mood—participle<br>  Tense—present<br>  Voice—middle<br>  Case—nominative<br>  Gender—masculine<br>  Person—2nd person<br>  Number—singular<br>  Stem or root—from ὑποτίθημι<br>Concordance References:<br>⇒ Strong's #5294 hupotithëmi<br>⇒ NIV #5719 hupotithëmi<br>⇒ NASB #5294 hupotithëmi<br><br>**1 Tim. 4:6**<br>If thou **put** the brethren **in remembrance** of these things, thou shalt be a good minister of Jesus Christ, nourished up in the words of faith and of good doctrine, whereunto thou hast attained. [KJV]<br>In **pointing out** these things to the brethren, you will be a good servant of Christ Jesus, constantly nourished on the words of the faith and of the sound doctrine which you have been following. [NASB]<br>If you **point** these things **out** to the brothers, you will be a good minister of Christ Jesus, brought up in the truths of the faith and of the good teaching that you have followed. [NIV]<br>If you **instruct** the brethren in these things, you will be a good minister of Jesus Christ, nourished in the words of faith and of the good doctrine which you have carefully followed. [NKJV]<br>If you **explain** this to the brothers and sisters, you will be doing your duty as a worthy servant of Christ Jesus, one who is fed by the message of faith and the true teaching you have followed. [NLT]<br>Ταῦτα **ὑποτιθέμενος** τοῖς ἀδελφοῖς καλὸς ἔσῃ διάκονος Ἰησοῦ Χριστοῦ, ἐντρεφόμενος τοῖς λόγοις τῆς πίστεως, καὶ τῆς καλῆς διδασκαλίας ᾗ παρηκολούθηκας. [GNS]<br>Ταῦτα **ὑποτιθέμενος** τοῖς ἀδελφοῖς καλὸς ἔσῃ διάκονος Χριστοῦ Ἰησοῦ, ἐντρεφόμενος τοῖς λόγοις τῆς πίστεως καὶ τῆς καλῆς διδασκαλίας ᾗ παρηκολούθηκας· [GNT] | To point out; to put in remembrance; to explain; to teach. The Greek word "instruct" or "put...in remembrance" (*hupotithemenos*) means to place under, suggest, counsel, advise.<br><br>**Practical Application**<br>The point is this: false teaching is such a threat to the church and believers that the good minister of Jesus Christ will use every method of communication he can to instruct and protect his flock from being seduced by false teachers. |

## Practical Word Studies
### in the New Testament

| ENGLISH WORD | GREEK WORD AND VERSE | THE WORD MEANS... |
|---|---|---|
| **#2170**<br>**Instruct**<br><br>Charge–KJV<br>**Instruct–NASB**<br>Command–NIV<br>Command–NKJV<br>Tell–NLT<br><br>**POSB REFERENCE**<br>(1 Tim.6:17-19; esp. v.17)<br>Note 1 | παράγγελλε = *paraggelle*<br>Pronunciation: [par-ang-gel'-leh]<br>Parsing (part of speech): verb<br>  Mood—imperative<br>  Tense—present<br>  Voice—active<br>  Person—2nd person<br>  Number—singular<br>  Stem or root—from παραγγέλλω<br>Concordance References:<br>  ⇒ Strong's #3853 *paraggellō*<br>  ⇒ NIV #4133 *paraggellō*<br>  ⇒ NASB #3853 *paraggellō*<br><br>**1 Tim. 6:17**<br>**Charge** them that are rich in this world, that they be not highminded, nor trust in uncertain riches, but in the living God, who giveth us richly all things to enjoy; [KJV]<br>**Instruct** those who are rich in this present world not to be conceited or to fix their hope on the uncertainty of riches, but on God, who richly supplies us with all things to enjoy. [NASB]<br>**Command** those who are rich in this present world not to be arrogant nor to put their hope in wealth, which is so uncertain, but to put their hope in God, who richly provides us with everything for our enjoyment. [NIV]<br>**Command** those who are rich in this present age not to be haughty, nor to trust in uncertain riches but in the living God, who gives us richly all things to enjoy. [NKJV]<br>**Tell** those who are rich in this world not to be proud and not to trust in their money, which will soon be gone. But their trust should be in the living God, who richly gives us all we need for our enjoyment. [NLT]<br>Τοῖς πλουσίοις ἐν τῷ νῦν αἰῶνι **παράγγελλε** μὴ ὑψηλοφρονεῖν, μηδὲ ἠλπικέναι ἐπὶ πλούτου ἀδηλότητι, ἀλλ' ἐν Θεῷ τῷ ζῶντι, τῷ παρέχοντι ἡμῖν πλουσίως πάντα εἰς ἀπόλαυσιν· [GNS]<br>Τοῖς πλουσίοις ἐν τῷ νῦν αἰῶνι **παράγγελλε** μὴ ὑψηλοφρονεῖν μηδὲ ἠλπικέναι ἐπὶ πλούτου ἀδηλότητι ἀλλ' ἐπὶ θεῷ τῷ παρέχοντι ἡμῖν πάντα πλουσίως εἰς ἀπόλαυσιν, [GNT] | To command; to charge; to instruct; to tell; to order; to rule.<br><br>**Practical Application**<br>The word "instruct" (*paraggelle*) is a strong word. It has the force of a military command, yet it has the tenderness of an appeal to it. It means to beg and beseech a person—strongly so—to the point that the person is commanded to act. In this charge, God is appealing and begging the rich person, but He is doing it so strongly that it is a command. The rich person is approached in love and tenderness and an appeal is made to him, but he is expected to do exactly what God says. |
| **#2171**<br>**Instructers–Instructors**<br><br>**Instructers–KJV**<br>Tutors–NASB<br>Guardians–NIV<br>**Instructors–NKJV**<br>To teach–NLT<br><br>**POSB REFERENCE**<br>(1 Cor.4:15)<br>Note 2 | παιδαγωγοὺς = *paidagōgous*<br>Pronunciation: [pahee-dag-o-goos']<br>Parsing (part of speech): noun<br>  Case—accusative<br>  Gender—masculine<br>  Number—plural<br>  Stem or root—from παιδαγωγός, οῦ<br>Concordance References:<br>  ⇒ Strong's #3807 *paidagōgos*<br>  ⇒ NIV #4080 *paidagōgos*<br>  ⇒ NASB #3807 *paidagōgos*<br><br>**1 Cor. 4:15**<br>For though ye have ten thousand **instructers** in Christ, yet *have ye* not many fathers: for in Christ Jesus I have begotten you through the gospel. [KJV]<br>For if you were to have countless **tutors** in Christ, yet *you would* not *have* many fathers; for in Christ Jesus I became your father through the gospel. [NASB]<br>Even though you have ten thousand **guardians** in Christ, you do not have many fathers, for in Christ Jesus I became your father through the gospel. [NIV]<br>For though you might have ten thousand **instructors** in Christ, yet you *do* not *have* many fathers; for in Christ Jesus I have begotten you through the gospel. [NKJV]<br>For even if you had ten thousand others **to teach** you about Christ, you have only one spiritual father. For I became your father in Christ Jesus when I preached the Good News to you. [NLT] | Guardian, instructor, tutor.<br><br>**Practical Application**<br>The "instructor" (*paidagōgous*) of Paul's day was a trusted slave who was placed in complete charge of a child's welfare and growth. He was even in charge of escorting the child to school to see that no harm came to him. He was responsible for the growth and development of the child until he was grown. Paul says that the Corinthian church had an unlimited number of capable instructors and teachers, but he alone was their spiritual father. He was the one who brought them to Christ Jesus for life and gave birth to the church. He was the one whom God had been using and was still using to oversee the growth of the church. Paul was stressing that he, as the minister of the church, bore more concern, tenderness, and care for the church than others. |

PRACTICAL WORD STUDIES
in the NEW TESTAMENT

| ENGLISH WORD | GREEK WORD AND VERSE | THE WORD MEANS... |
|---|---|---|
| | ἐὰν γὰρ μυρίους **παιδαγωγοὺς** ἔχητε ἐν Χριστῷ, ἀλλ' οὐ πολλοὺς πατέρας· ἐν γὰρ Χριστῷ Ἰησοῦ διὰ τοῦ εὐαγγελίου ἐγὼ ὑμᾶς ἐγέννησα. [GNS]<br>ἐὰν γὰρ μυρίους **παιδαγωγοὺς** ἔχητε ἐν Χριστῷ ἀλλ' οὐ πολλοὺς πατέρας· ἐν γὰρ Χριστῷ Ἰησοῦ διὰ τοῦ εὐαγγελίου ἐγὼ ὑμᾶς ἐγέννησα. [GNT] | |
| **#2172**<br>**Instruction**<br><br>Learning–KJV<br>**Instruction–NASB**<br>Teach–NIV<br>Learning–NKJV<br>Teach–NLT<br><br>**POSB REFERENCE**<br>(Rom. 15:4)<br>Note 2, point 1 | διδασκαλίαν = *didaskalian*<br>Pronunciation: [did-ahs-kal-ee'-ahn]<br>Parsing (part of speech): noun<br>   Case—accusative<br>   Gender—feminine<br>   Number—singular<br>   Stem or root—from διδασκαλία, ας<br>Concordance References:<br>  ⇒ Strong's #1319 didaskalia<br>  ⇒ NIV #1436 didaskalia<br>  ⇒ NASB #1319 didaskalia<br><br>**Romans 15:4**<br>For whatsoever things were written aforetime were written for our **learning**, that we through patience and comfort of the scriptures might have hope. [KJV]<br>For whatever was written in earlier times was written for our **instruction**, that through perseverance and the encouragement of the Scriptures we might have hope. [NASB]<br>For everything that was written in the past was written to **teach** us, so that through endurance and the encouragement of the Scriptures we might have hope. [NIV]<br>For whatever things were written before were written for our **learning**, that we through the patience and comfort of the Scriptures might have hope. [NKJV]<br>Such things were written in the Scriptures long ago to **teach** us. They give us hope and encouragement as we wait patiently for God's promises. [NLT]<br>ὅσα γὰρ προεγράφη, εἰς τὴν ἡμετέραν **διδασκαλίαν** προεγράφη, ἵνα διὰ τῆς ὑπομονῆς καὶ τῆς παρακλήσεως τῶν γραφῶν τὴν ἐλπίδα ἔχωμεν. [GNS]<br>ὅσα γὰρ προεγράφη, εἰς τὴν ἡμετέραν **διδασκαλίαν** ἐγράφη, ἵνα διὰ τῆς ὑπομονῆς καὶ διὰ τῆς παρακλήσεως τῶν γραφῶν τὴν ἐλπίδα ἔχωμεν. [GNT] | What is taught, teaching, doctrine; act of teaching, instruction.<br><br>**Practical Application**<br>In a strong church, everyone studies the Scripture. This is a great verse on the purpose of the Holy Scriptures. In very simple terms, it tells us why God gave us the Bible.<br>The Scriptures were written for our...<br>• learning,<br>• instruction (*didaskalian*),<br>• direction,<br>• guidance. |
| **#2173**<br>**Instruction**<br><br>Admonition–KJV<br>**Instruction–NASB**<br>**Instruction–NIV**<br>Training–NKJV<br>**Instruction–NLT**<br><br>**POSB REFERENCE**<br>(Eph.6:4)<br>Note 2, point 2 | νουθεσία = *nouthesia*<br>Pronunciation: [noo-thes-ee'-ah]<br>Parsing (part of speech): noun<br>   Case—dative<br>   Gender—feminine<br>   Number—singular<br>   Stem or root—from νουθεσία, ας<br>Concordance References:<br>  ⇒ Strong's #3559 nouthesia<br>  ⇒ NIV #3804 nouthesia<br>  ⇒ NASB #3559 nouthesia<br><br>**Ephes. 6:4**<br>And, ye fathers, provoke not your children to wrath: but bring them up in the nurture and **admonition** of the Lord. [KJV]<br>And, fathers, do not provoke your children to anger; but bring them up in the discipline and **instruction** of the Lord. [NASB]<br>Fathers, do not exasperate your children; instead, bring them up in the training and **instruction** of the Lord. [NIV]<br>And you, fathers, do not provoke your children to wrath, but bring them up in the **training** and admonition of the Lord. [NKJV]<br>And now a word to you fathers. Don't make your children angry by the way you treat them. Rather, bring them up with the discipline and **instruction** approved by the Lord. [NLT]<br>καὶ οἱ πατέρες, μὴ παροργίζετε τὰ τέκνα ὑμῶν, ἀλλ | Instruction, admonition, warning. It means counsel, exhortation, correction; to give strict orders.<br><br>**Practical Application**<br>Note that the parent is not to rear the child after his own ideas and notions of what is best for the child, but after the nurture and instruction *of the Lord*. The Lord's Word is to be the guide for Christian parents in rearing their child. The benefits in bringing up a child in the Lord are innumerable. Just a few are as follows:<br>1. A child who is brought to Christ grows up learning love: that he is loved by God and by all who trust God. He grows no matter how evil some may act, knowing that he is to love even those who do wrong.<br>2. A child who is brought to Christ grows up learning power and triumph: that God will help His followers through all; that there is a supernatural power available to help, a power to help when mother and dad and loved ones have done all they can.<br>3. A child who is brought to Christ grows up learning hope and faith: that no matter what happens, no matter how great a trial, we can still trust God and hope in Him. He has pro- |

# PRACTICAL WORD STUDIES
## in the NEW TESTAMENT

| ENGLISH WORD | GREEK WORD AND VERSE | THE WORD MEANS... |
|---|---|---|
| | ἐκτρέφετε αὐτὰ ἐν παιδείᾳ καὶ **νουθεσίᾳ** Κυρίου. [GNS]<br>Καὶ οἱ πατέρες, μὴ παροργίζετε τὰ τέκνα ὑμῶν ἀλλὰ ἐκτρέφετε αὐτὰ ἐν παιδείᾳ καὶ **νουθεσίᾳ** κυρίου. [GNT] | vided a very special strength to carry us through the trials of this life (no matter how painful); that He has provided a very special place called heaven where He will carry us and our loved ones when we face death.<br>4. A child who is brought to Christ grows up learning the truth of life and endurance (service): that God has given us the privilege of life and of living in a beautiful earth and universe; that the evil and bad which exists in the world is caused by evil and bad people; that despite such evil, we are to serve in appreciation for life and the beautiful earth upon which God has placed us. We are to work and work diligently, making the greatest contribution we can.<br>5. A child who is brought to Christ grows up learning trust and endurance: that life is full of temptations and pitfalls which can easily rob us of joy and destroy our lives and the fulfillment of our purposes; that the way to escape the temptations and pitfalls is to follow Christ and endure in our work and purpose.<br>6. A child who is brought to Christ grows up learning peace: that there is an inner peace despite the turbulent waters of this world; that peace is knowing and trusting Christ. |
| **#2174**<br>**Instruction–**<br>**Instructions**<br><br>Charge–KJV<br>Command–NASB<br>**Instruction–NIV**<br>Charge–NKJV<br>**Instructions–NLT**<br><br>**POSB**<br>**REFERENCE**<br>(1 Tim.1:18)<br>Note 1 | παραγγελίαν = *paraggelian*<br>Pronunciation: [par-ang-gel-ee'-ahn]<br>Parsing (part of speech): noun<br>    Case—accusative<br>    Gender—feminine<br>    Number—singular<br>    Stem or root—from παραγγελία, ας<br>Concordance References:<br>  ⇒ Strong's #3852 paraggelia<br>  ⇒ NIV #4132 paraggelia<br>  ⇒ NASB #3852 paraggelia<br><br>**1 Tim. 1:18**<br>This **charge** I commit unto thee, son Timothy, according to the prophecies which went before on thee, that thou by them mightest war a good warfare; [KJV]<br>This **command** I entrust to you, Timothy, my son, in accordance with the prophecies previously made concerning you, that by them you may fight the good fight, [NASB]<br>Timothy, my son, I give you this **instruction** in keeping with the prophecies once made about you, so that by following them you may fight the good fight, [NIV]<br>This **charge** I commit to you, son Timothy, according to the prophecies previously made concerning you, that by them you may wage the good warfare, [NKJV]<br>Timothy, my son, here are my **instructions** for you, based on the prophetic words spoken about you earlier. May they give you the confidence to fight well in the Lord's battles. [NLT]<br>Ταύτην τὴν **παραγγελίαν** παρατίθεμαί σοι, τέκνον Τιμόθεε, κατὰ τὰς προαγούσας ἐπὶ σὲ προφητείας, ἵνα στρατεύῃ ἐν αὐταῖς τὴν καλὴν στρατείαν, [GNS]<br>Ταύτην τὴν **παραγγελίαν** παρατίθεμαί σοι, τέκνον Τιμόθεε, κατὰ τὰς προαγούσας ἐπὶ σὲ προφητείας, ἵνα στρατεύῃ ἐν αὐταῖς τὴν καλὴν στρατείαν [GNT] | A command; an urgent command; a military command; a mandate; a decree; strict orders or instructions.<br><br>**Practical Application**<br>The instruction to the young minister is forceful—fight a good warfare! Paul is giving "instruction" (*paraggelian*) to Timothy. It is instruction that lays upon a person the most urgent and critical obligation. Donald Guthrie says, "The ministry is not a matter to be trifled with, but an order from the commander-in-chief" (*The Pastoral Epistles.* "Tyndale New Testament Commentaries," p.67). W.E. Vine points out that the "charge" is always a command from a superior that is to be transmitted to others; that is, this charge—the charge to fight a good warfare—is to be given to the young minister and he, in turn, is to pass the charge on to others (*Expository Dictionary of New Testament Words*. Old Tappan, NJ: Fleming H. Revell, 1966). |
| **#2175**<br>**Instruction–**<br>**Instructions**<br><br>Declare–KJV<br>**Instruction–NASB**<br>Directives–NIV | παραγγέλλων = *paraggellōn*<br>Pronunciation: [par-ang-gel'-lone]<br>Parsing (part of speech): verb<br>    Mood—participle<br>    Tense—present<br>    Voice—active<br>    Case—nominative<br>    Gender—masculine<br>    Person—1st person | To command; to give strict orders; to give instructions; to charge.<br><br>**Practical Application**<br>Note how forceful Paul is: "In giving this instruction" or "In giving these instructions" (*paraggellōn*) I do not praise *you*" [NKJV]. His forcefulness stresses the awesome importance of |

# PRACTICAL WORD STUDIES
## in the New Testament

| ENGLISH WORD | GREEK WORD AND VERSE | THE WORD MEANS... |
|---|---|---|
| **Instructions–NKJV**<br>Mention–NLT<br><br>**POSB REFERENCE**<br>(1 Cor.11:17)<br>Note 1 | Number—singular<br>Stem or root—from παραγγέλλω<br>Concordance References:<br>⇒ Strong's #3853 paraggellö<br>⇒ NIV #4133 paraggellö<br>⇒ NASB #3853 paraggellö<br><br>**1 Cor. 11:17**<br>Now in this that I **declare** unto you I praise you not, that ye come together not for the better, but for the worse. [KJV]<br>But in giving this **instruction**, I do not praise you, because you come together not for the better but for the worse. [NASB]<br>In the following **directives** I have no praise for you, for your meetings do more harm than good. [NIV]<br>Now in giving these **instructions** I do not praise you, since you come together not for the better but for the worse. [NKJV]<br>But now when I **mention** this next issue, I cannot praise you. For it sounds as if more harm than good is done when you meet together. [NLT]<br>Τοῦτο δὲ **παραγγέλλων** οὐκ ἐπαινῶ, ὅτι οὐκ εἰς τὸ κρεῖττον ἀλλ εἰς τὸ ἧττον συνέρχεσθε. [GNS]<br>Τοῦτο δὲ **παραγγέλλων** οὐκ ἐπαινῶ ὅτι οὐκ εἰς τὸ κρεῖσσον ἀλλὰ εἰς τὸ ἧσσον συνέρχεσθε. [GNT] | the Lord's Supper and the absolute necessity to celebrate it as it should be celebrated. |
| **#2176**<br>**Insubordinate**<br><br>Unruly–KJV<br>Rebellious–NASB<br>Rebellious–NIV<br>**Insubordinate–NKJV**<br>Rebel–NLT<br><br>**POSB REFERENCE**<br>(Tit.1:10-12; esp. v.10<br>Note 1, point 1 | ἀνυπότακτοι = *anupotaktoi*<br>Pronunciation: [an-oo-pot'-ak-toy]<br>Parsing (part of speech): pronominal adjective<br>    Case—nominative<br>    Gender—masculine<br>    Number—plural<br>    Stem or root—from ἀνυπότακτος, ον<br>Concordance References:<br>⇒ Strong's #506 anupotaktos<br>⇒ NIV #538 anupotaktos<br>⇒ NASB #506 anupotaktos<br><br>**Titus 1:10**<br>For there are many **unruly** and vain talkers and deceivers, specially they of the circumcision: [KJV]<br>For there are many **rebellious** men, empty talkers and deceivers, especially those of the circumcision, [NASB]<br>For there are many **rebellious** people, mere talkers and deceivers, especially those of the circumcision group. [NIV]<br>For there are many **insubordinate**, both idle talkers and deceivers, especially those of the circumcision, [NKJV]<br>For there are many who **rebel** against right teaching; they engage in useless talk and deceive people. This is especially true of those who insist on circumcision for salvation. [NLT]<br>Εἰσὶ γὰρ πολλοὶ καὶ **ἀνυπότακτοι**, ματαιολόγοι καὶ φρεναπάται, μάλιστα οἱ ἐκ τῆς περιτομῆς, [GNS]<br>Εἰσὶν γὰρ πολλοὶ [καὶ] **ἀνυπότακτοι**, ματαιολόγοι καὶ φρεναπάται, μάλιστα οἱ ἐκ τῆς περιτομῆς, [GNT] | Rebellious, unruly, insubordinate; to rebel.<br><br>**Practical Application**<br>They were "insubordinate" (*anupotaktoi*): undisciplined, rebellious, disloyal, unruly against God and the truth. They refused to submit to God and to the truth of the gospel and of God's Word. |
| **#2177**<br>**Insult–**<br>**Insulted**<br><br>Spitefully<br>    entreated–KJV<br>Mistreated–NASB<br>**Insult–NIV**<br>**Insulted–NKJV**<br>Treated<br>    shamefully–NLT | ὑβρισθήσεται = *hubristhēsetai*<br>Pronunciation: [hoo-bris'-thay-seh-tah-ee]<br>Parsing (part of speech): verb<br>    Mood—indicative<br>    Tense—future<br>    Voice—passive<br>    Person—3rd person<br>    Number—singular<br>    Stem or root—from ὑβρίζω<br>Concordance References:<br>⇒ Strong's #5195 hubrizö<br>⇒ NIV #5614 hubrizö<br>⇒ NASB #5195 hubrizö | To insult; to reproach; to treat with insolence and contempt; to be outraged; to mistreat; to treat disgracefully; to treat shamefully and despitefully.<br><br>**Practical Application**<br>Jesus was to be delivered to the Gentiles, and the Jews were going to be the ones to deliver Him into Gentile hands. This fact was to symbolize both the religionists and the world—both were going to reject God's Son and put Him to death. Neither could accept Him and His message of total self-denial. |

# PRACTICAL WORD STUDIES
## in the NEW TESTAMENT

| ENGLISH WORD | GREEK WORD AND VERSE | THE WORD MEANS... |
|---|---|---|
| **POSB REFERENCE** (Lk.18:32-33; esp. v.32) Note 2, point 1b | **Luke 18:32** For he shall be delivered unto the Gentiles, and shall be mocked, and **spitefully entreated**, and spitted on: [KJV] "For He will be delivered to the Gentiles, and will be mocked and **mistreated** and spit upon, [NASB] He will be handed over to the Gentiles. They will mock him, **insult** him, spit on him, flog him and kill him. [NIV] For He will be delivered to the Gentiles and will be mocked and **insulted** and spit upon. [NKJV] He will be handed over to the Romans to be mocked, **treated shamefully**, and spit upon. [NLT] παραδοθήσεται γὰρ τοῖς ἔθνεσι, καὶ ἐμπαιχθήσεται, καὶ **ὑβρισθήσεται**, καὶ ἐμπτυσθήσεται, [GNS] παραδοθήσεται γὰρ τοῖς ἔθνεσιν καὶ ἐμπαιχθήσεται καὶ **ὑβρισθήσεται** καὶ ἐμπτυσθήσεται [GNT] | |
| **#2178 Insurrections** Commotions–KJV Disturbances–NASB Revolutions–NIV Commotions–NKJV **Insurrections–NLT** **POSB REFERENCE** (Lk.21:9-10; esp. v.9) Note 3, point 1 | ἀκαταστασίας = *akatastasias* Pronunciation: [ak-at-as-tah-see'-ahs] Parsing (part of speech): noun     Case—accusative     Gender—feminine     Number—plural     Stem or root—from ἀκαταστασία, ας Concordance References: ⇒ Strong's #181 akatastasia ⇒ NIV #189 akatastasia ⇒ NASB #181 akatastasia **Luke 21:9** But when ye shall hear of wars and **commotions**, be not terrified: for these things must first come to pass; but the end is not by and by. [KJV] "And when you hear of wars and **disturbances**, do not be terrified; for these things must take place first, but the end does not follow immediately." [NASB] When you hear of wars and **revolutions**, do not be frightened. These things must happen first, but the end will not come right away." [NIV] But when you hear of wars and **commotions**, do not be terrified; for these things must come to pass first, but the end *will not come* immediately." [NKJV] And when you hear of wars and **insurrections**, don't panic. Yes, these things must come, but the end won't follow immediately." [NLT] ὅταν δὲ ἀκούσητε πολέμους καὶ **ἀκαταστασίας**, μὴ πτοηθῆτε· δεῖ γὰρ ταῦτα γενέσθαι πρῶτον, ἀλλ' οὐκ εὐθέως τὸ τέλος. [GNS] ὅταν δὲ ἀκούσητε πολέμους καὶ **ἀκαταστασίας**, μὴ πτοηθῆτε· δεῖ γὰρ ταῦτα γενέσθαι πρῶτον, avllV οὐκ εὐθέως τὸ τέλος. [GNT] | Revolutions, disturbances, insurrections, commotions, anarchy, rebellion, tumults, uproars, riots, terrorism; mob violence; treason against and confusion within governments. **Practical Application** Believers can become extremely disturbed over the news. But, believers are not to "panic" (*ptoethete*). They are not to let their hearts "be troubled" (John 14:1). World violence can trouble people; but the believer's heart and life are to be centered upon God, trusting His presence, care, and security—eternally. |
| **#2179 Integrity** Not doubletongued–KJV Not double-tongued–NASB Sincere–NIV Not double-tongued–NKJV **Integrity–NLT** **POSB REFERENCE** (1 Tim.3:8) Note 1, point 2 | μὴ διλόγους = *mē dilogous* Pronunciation: [may dil'-og-oos] Parsing *dilogous* (part of speech): adjective     Case—accusative     Gender—masculine     Number—plural     Stem or root—from δίλογος, ον Concordance References: ⇒ Strong's #1351+3361 dilogos mē ⇒ NIV #1474+3590 dilogos mē [sincere] ⇒ NASB #1351+3361 dilogos mē **1 Tim. 3:8** Likewise must the deacons be grave, **not double-tongued**, not given to much wine, not greedy of filthy lucre; [KJV] Deacons likewise must be men of dignity, **not double-tongued**, or addicted to much wine or fond of sordid gain, [NASB] Deacons, likewise, are to be men worthy of respect, | To be sincere; to have integrity. It means a person is not to be double-tongued, two-faced, or insincere. **Practical Application** Deacons must have integrity (*mē dilogous*): not bearing tales, gossiping, saying "one thing to one person and something different to another [person]" (Donald Guthrie. *The Pastoral Epistles*. "Tyndale New Testament Commentaries, p.84); saying one thing to a person's face and something else behind his back. No more descriptive word could be chosen than "double-tongued." The quality of having integrity is important. As a deacon ministers through visitation (going from house to house), he is often tempted to gossip or say one thing to one person and something |

| ENGLISH WORD | GREEK WORD AND VERSE | THE WORD MEANS... |
|---|---|---|
| | **sincere**, not indulging in much wine, and not pursuing dishonest gain. [NIV]<br>Likewise deacons *must be* reverent, **not double-tongued**, not given to much wine, not greedy for money, [NKJV]<br>In the same way, deacons must be people who are respected and have **integrity**. They must not be heavy drinkers and must not be greedy for money. [NLT]<br>διακόνους ὡσαύτως σεμνούς, **μὴ διλόγους**, μὴ οἴνῳ πολλῷ προσέχοντας, μὴ αἰσχροκερδεῖς, [GNS]<br>Διακόνους ὡσαύτως σεμνούς, **μὴ διλόγους**, μὴ οἴνῳ πολλῷ προσέχοντας, μὴ αἰσχροκερδεῖς, [GNT] | else to another person. He is also tempted to evade or smooth talk issues. Therefore, he must be a man of integrity, a man who speaks the straight truth—a man who is as honest as the day is long. |
| #2180<br>**Intending**<br><br>Took counsel–KJV<br>**Intending**–NASB<br>Wanted–NIV<br>Plotted–NKJV<br>Decided–NLT<br><br>**POSB REFERENCE**<br>(Acts 5:32-40; esp. v.33)<br>Note 4, point 1 | ἐβούλοντο = eboulonto<br>Pronunciation: [eh-bool-on-tow]<br>Parsing (part of speech): verb<br>    Mood—indicative<br>    Tense—imperfect<br>    Voice—middle or passive deponent<br>    Person—3rd person<br>    Number—plural<br>    Stem or root—from βούλομαι<br>Concordance References:<br>⇒ Strong's #1014 boulomai<br>⇒ NIV #1089 boulomai<br>⇒ NASB #1014 boulomai<br><br>**Acts 5:33**<br>When they heard that, they were cut to the heart, and **took counsel** to slay them. [KJV]<br>But when they heard this, they were cut to the quick and were **intending** to slay them. [NASB]<br>When they heard this, they were furious and **wanted** to put them to death. [NIV]<br>When they heard *this,* they were furious and **plotted** to kill them. [NKJV]<br>At this, the high council was furious and **decided** to kill them. [NLT]<br>Οἱ δὲ ἀκούσαντες διεπρίοντο, καὶ **ἐβούλοντο** ἀνελεῖν αὐτούς. [GNS]<br>Οἱ δὲ ἀκούσαντες διεπρίοντο καὶ **ἐβούλοντο** ἀνελεῖν αὐτούς. [GNT] | To want; to take counsel; to intend; to decide; to wish; to plan.<br><br>**Practical Application**<br>They (the high council) were minded, were intending; were set on killing the disciples. |
| #2181<br>**Intensely**<br><br>Fervently–KJV<br>Fervently–NASB<br>Deeply–NIV<br>Fervently–NKJV<br>**Intensely**–NLT<br><br>**POSB REFERENCE**<br>(1 Pt.1:22-25; esp. v.22)<br>Note 1 | ἐκτενῶς = ektenōs<br>Pronunciation: [ek-ten-oce']<br>Parsing (part of speech): adjective adverb<br>    Stem or root—from ἐκτενῶς<br>Concordance References:<br>⇒ Strong's #1619 ektenōs<br>⇒ NIV #1757 ektenōs<br>⇒ NASB #1619 ektenōs<br><br>**1 Peter 1:22**<br>Seeing ye have purified your souls in obeying the truth through the Spirit unto unfeigned love of the brethren, see that ye love one another with a pure heart **fervently**: [KJV]<br>Since you have in obedience to the truth purified your souls for a sincere love of the brethren, **fervently** love one another from the heart, [NASB]<br>Now that you have purified yourselves by obeying the truth so that you have sincere love for your brothers, love one another **deeply**, from the heart. [NIV]<br>Since you have purified your souls in obeying the truth through the Spirit in sincere love of the brethren, love one another **fervently** with a pure heart, [NKJV]<br>Now you can have sincere love for each other as brothers and sisters because you were cleansed from your sins when you accepted the truth of the Good News. So see to it that you really do love each other **intensely** with all your hearts. [NLT]<br>τὰς ψυχὰς ὑμῶν ἡγνικότες ἐν τῇ ὑπακοῇ τῆς ἀληθείας διὰ Πνεύματος εἰς φιλαδελφίαν ἀνυπόκριτον, ἐκ καθαρᾶς | Deeply, fervently, intensely, constantly, earnestly.<br><br>**Practical Application**<br>The word (*ektenōs*) "does not mean 'with warmth' but rather 'with full intensity'." It literally means to *stretch love fully out* or to love one another *in an all-out manner* (Alan M. Stibbs. *The First Epistle General of Peter.* "The Tyndale New Testament Commentaries," ed. by RVG Tasker, p.94). |

## PRACTICAL WORD STUDIES
### in the NEW TESTAMENT

| ENGLISH WORD | GREEK WORD AND VERSE | THE WORD MEANS... |
|---|---|---|
| | καρδίας ἀλλήλους ἀγαπήσατε **ἐκτενῶς**· [GNS]<br>Τὰς ψυχὰς ὑμῶν ἡγνικότες ἐν τῇ ὑπακοῇ τῆς ἀληθείας εἰς φιλαδελφίαν ἀνυπόκριτον, ἐκ [καθαρᾶς] καρδίας ἀλλήλους ἀγαπήσατε **ἐκτενῶς** [GNT] | |
| **#2182**<br>**Intercession–**<br>**Intercessions**<br><br>Intercessions–KJV<br>Petitions–NASB<br>Intercession–NIV<br>Intercessions–NKJV<br>Plead for God's mercy–NLT<br><br>**POSB**<br>**REFERENCE**<br>(1 Tim.2:1)<br>Note 1, point 3 | ἐντεύξεις = *enteuxeis*<br>Pronunciation: [ent'-yook-eh-ees]<br>Parsing (part of speech): noun<br>    Case—accusative<br>    Gender—feminine<br>    Number—plural<br>    Stem or root—from ἔντευξις, εως<br>Concordance References:<br>  ⇒ Strong's #1783 *enteuxis*<br>  ⇒ NIV #1950 *enteuxis*<br>  ⇒ NASB #1783 *enteuxis*<br><br>**1 Tim. 2:1**<br>I exhort therefore, that, first of all, supplications, prayers, **intercessions**, and giving of thanks, be made for all men; [KJV]<br>First of all, then, I urge that entreaties and prayers, **petitions** and thanksgivings, be made on behalf of all men, [NASB]<br>I urge, then, first of all, that requests, prayers, **intercession** and thanksgiving be made for everyone—[NIV]<br>Therefore I exhort first of all that supplications, prayers, **intercessions**, *and* giving of thanks be made for all men, [NKJV]<br>I urge you, first of all, to pray for all people. As you make your requests, **plead for God's mercy** upon them, and give thanks. [NLT]<br>Παρακαλῶ οὖν πρῶτον πάντων ποιεῖσθαι δεήσεις, προσευχάς, **ἐντεύξεις**, εὐχαριστίας, ὑπὲρ πάντων ἀνθρώπων· [GNS]<br>Παρακαλῶ οὖν πρῶτον πάντων ποιεῖσθαι δεήσεις προσευχάς **ἐντεύξεις** εὐχαριστίας ὑπὲρ πάντων ἀνθρώπων, [GNT] | Intercession, petition, prayer; to plead to God for another person.<br><br>**Practical Application**<br>This refers to bold praying; to standing before God in behalf of another person. Christ is our Intercessor, the One who stands between God and us in our behalf. But we are to intercede for men, to carry their names and lives before God and to boldly pray for them, expecting God to hear and answer—all in the name of Christ. We are to intercede for all men—to stand in the gap between them and God, boldly praying and asking God to be merciful and gracious in salvation and in deliverance. |
| **#2183**<br>**Interfered With**<br><br>Hinder–KJV<br>Hindered–NASB<br>Cut in on–NIV<br>Hindered–NKJV<br>**Interfered with–NLT**<br><br>**POSB**<br>**REFERENCE**<br>(Gal.5:7)<br>Note 1, point 1 | ἐνέκοψεν = *enekopsen*<br>Pronunciation: [en-ek-op'-sen]<br>Parsing (part of speech): verb<br>    Mood—indicative<br>    Tense—aorist<br>    Voice—active<br>    Person—3rd person<br>    Number—singular<br>    Stem or root—from ἐγκόπτω<br>Concordance References:<br>  ⇒ Strong's #1465 *egkoptō*<br>  ⇒ NIV #1601 *egkoptō*<br>  ⇒ NASB #1465 *egkoptō*<br><br>**Galatians 5:7**<br>Ye did run well; who did **hinder** you that ye should not obey the truth? [KJV]<br>You were running well; who **hindered** you from obeying the truth? [NASB]<br>You were running a good race. Who **cut in on** you and kept you from obeying the truth? [NIV]<br>You ran well. Who **hindered** you from obeying the truth? [NKJV]<br>You were getting along so well. Who has **interfered with** you to hold you back from following the truth? [NLT]<br>ἐτρέχετε καλῶς· τίς ὑμᾶς **ἀνέοψε** τῇ ἀληθείᾳ μὴ πείθεσθαι; [GNS]<br>Ἐτρέχετε καλῶς· τίς ὑμᾶς **ἐνέκοψεν** [τῇ] ἀληθείᾳ μὴ πείθεσθαι; [GNT] | To cut in on; to hinder; to edge in; to interfere with; to detain; to obstruct.<br><br>**Practical Application**<br>While the Galatians had been running the Christian race, some had edged in on them and begun to hinder and interfere with their running. They were no longer obeying the truth. They were now trying to approach God by some other way than Christ. They were now thinking...<br>• that God accepted them because they had been *ritualized*: circumcised and baptized.<br>• that God accepted them because they tried to keep the law: tried to be as good as they could and did good deeds as opportunity arose.<br>• that God approved them because they were faithful to the church: its rituals, ceremonies, services, rules and regulations.<br>They were no longer running well. They had allowed some false teacher to interfere with them and to turn them from the truth. They had a need to think about the matter, a desperate need...<br>• to think about the race they had been running.<br>• to think about who it was that was now cutting in on their running. |
| **#2184**<br>**Intimidate** | διασείσητε = *diaseisēte*<br>Pronunciation: [dee-as-i'-say-teh]<br>Parsing (part of speech): verb<br>    Mood—subjunctive OR imperative | To extort money; to take money by force; to shake violently, agitate, terrify. |

## PRACTICAL WORD STUDIES
## in the NEW TESTAMENT

| ENGLISH WORD | GREEK WORD AND VERSE | THE WORD MEANS... |
|---|---|---|
| Violence–KJV<br>Take money by force–NASB<br>Extort money–NIV<br>**Intimidate–NKJV**<br>Extort money–NLT<br><br>**POSB REFERENCE**<br>(Lk.3:10-14; esp. v.14)<br>Note 5, point 3a | Tense—aorist<br>Voice—active<br>Person—2nd person<br>Number—plural<br>Stem or root—from διασείω<br>Concordance References:<br>⇒ Strong's #1286 diaseiö<br>⇒ NIV #1398 diaseiö<br>⇒ NASB #1286 diaseiö<br><br>**Luke 3:14**<br>And the soldiers likewise demanded of him, saying, And what shall we do? And he said unto them, Do **violence** to no man, neither accuse any falsely; and be content with your wages. [KJV]<br>And some soldiers were questioning him, saying, "And what about us, what shall we do?" And he said to them, "Do not **take money** from anyone **by force**, or accuse anyone falsely, and be content with your wages." [NASB]<br>Then some soldiers asked him, "And what should we do?" He replied, "Don't extort money and don't accuse people falsely--be content with your pay." [NIV]<br>Likewise the soldiers asked him, saying, "And what shall we do?" So he said to them, "Do not **intimidate** anyone or accuse falsely, and be content with your wages." [NKJV]<br>"What should we do?" asked some soldiers. John replied, "Don't **extort money**, and don't accuse people of things you know they didn't do. And be content with your pay." [NLT]<br>ἐπηρώτων δὲ αὐτὸν καὶ στρατευόμενοι, λέγοντες, Καὶ ἡμεῖς τί ποιήσομεν; καὶ εἶπε πρὸς αὐτοῖς, Μηδένα **διασείσητε** μηδὲ συκοφαντήσητε· καὶ ἀρκεῖσθε τοῖς ὀψωνίοις ὑμῶν." [GNS]<br>ἐπηρώτων δὲ αὐτὸν καὶ στρατευόμενοι λέγοντες, Τί ποιήσωμεν καὶ ἡμεῖς; καὶ εἶπεν αὐτοῖς, Μηδένα **διασείσητε** μηδὲ συκοφαντήσητε καὶ ἀρκεῖσθε τοῖς ὀψωνίοις ὑμῶν. [GNT] | **Practical Application**<br>The thought is that some persons extorted money by terrifying people. Roman soldiers were, of course, posted to protect the interests of Rome. It was common for soldiers to allow illegal things to go on for a bribe. |
| **#2185**<br>**Into It**<br><br>**Into it–KJV**<br>**Into it–NASB**<br>**Into it–NIV**<br>**Into it–NKJV**<br>To it–NLT<br><br>**POSB REFERENCE**<br>(Rev.21:24-27; esp. v.24)<br>Note 1, point 5 | εἰς αὐτήν = eis autën<br>Pronunciation: [ice ow-tayn']<br>Parsing *eis* (part of speech): preposition<br>    Case—accusative<br>    Stem or root—from εἰς<br>Parsing *autën* (part of speech): noun<br>    Type—pronoun<br>    Case—accusative<br>    Gender—feminine<br>    Person—3rd person<br>    Number—singular<br>    Stem or root—from αὐτός, ή, ό<br>Concordance References:<br>⇒ Strong's #1519 eis + 846 autos<br>⇒ NIV #1650 eis [into] + 899 autos [it]<br>⇒ NASB #1519 eis + 846 autos<br><br>**Rev. 21:24**<br>And the nations of them which are saved shall walk in the light of it: and the kings of the earth do bring their glory and honour **into it**. [KJV]<br>And the nations shall walk by its light, and the kings of the earth shall bring their glory **into it**. [NASB]<br>The nations will walk by its light, and the kings of the earth will bring their splendor **into it**. [NIV]<br>And the nations of those who are saved shall walk in its light, and the kings of the earth bring their glory and honor **into it**. [NKJV]<br>The nations of the earth will walk in its light, and the rulers of the world will come and bring their glory **to it**. [NLT]<br>καὶ τὰ ἔθνη τῶν σωζομένων ἐν τῷ θωτὶ αὐτῆς περιπατήσουσι· καὶ οἱ βασιλεῖς τῆς γῆς φέρουσι τὴν δόξαν καὶ τὴν τιμῶν αὐτῶν **εἰς αὐτήν**· [GNS]<br>καὶ περιπατήσουσιν τὰ ἔθνη διὰ τοῦ φωτὸς αὐτῆς, καὶ οἱ βασιλεῖς τῆς γῆς φέρουσιν τὴν δόξαν αὐτῶν **εἰς αὐτήν**, [GNT] | Into it, to it.<br><br>**Practical Application**<br>Believers will bring their glory and honor *into the heavenly city* and give all their glory and honor to the Lord who bestowed it upon them. Believers owe everything they are to God and Christ; therefore, they are going to acknowledge and praise God and Christ for giving them so great a salvation. Note that believers will bring their glory and honor *into the city*.<br>⇒ This speaks as though believers will be serving as kings of nations *outside the city*.<br>⇒ This speaks as though there will be special occasions when believers will gather *in the heavenly city*, gather to bring the glory and honor of their nations to God and Christ. Read it carefully (the Greek says *eis autën*), for this seems to be the picture being painted. One thing is sure: no matter what we may describe or picture, it is going to be far beyond anything we could ever describe or ask or even think. God's Word emphatically declares this.<br>Believers will bring the glory and honor of their nations into (*eis autën*) the city. This shows that believers are the kings being spoken about, that believers will be coming from various rules or nations to bring the glory of their nations to God. Again the picture seems to be periodic celebrations of great worship. There will certainly be times when all believers come together from |

# PRACTICAL WORD STUDIES
## in the NEW TESTAMENT

| ENGLISH WORD | GREEK WORD AND VERSE | THE WORD MEANS... |
|---|---|---|
| | | all corners of heaven (the spiritual world or universe) in a great celebration of worship. We would think that the Marriage Supper of the Lamb will not be the only time we will all be brought together to worship our dear Lord.<br><br>Note again: Scripture says that as kings we enter "into" the city. It is as though we are coming from the far reaches of the spiritual world to bring the honor of our nations to God and Christ. But we must also repeat: whatever the case—wherever we are coming from—our minds could never imagine the glory and majesty of what will really happen. |
| **#2186**<br>**Invalidating**<br><br>Of none effect–KJV<br>**Invalidating–NASB**<br>Nullify–NIV<br>Of no effect–NKJV<br>Break–NLT<br><br>**POSB**<br>**REFERENCE**<br>(Mk.7:13)<br>*Deeper Study #2* | ἀκυροῦντες = *akurountes*<br>Pronunciation: [ak-oo-roon'-tehs]<br>Parsing (part of speech): verb<br>    Mood—participle<br>    Tense—present<br>    Voice—active<br>    Case—nominative<br>    Gender—masculine<br>    Person—2nd person<br>    Number—plural<br>    Stem or root—from ἀκυρόω<br>Concordance References:<br>  ⇒ Strong's #208 akuroö<br>  ⇒ NIV #218 akuroö<br>  ⇒ NASB #208 akuroö<br><br>**Mark 7:13**<br>Making the word of God **of none effect** through your tradition, which ye have delivered: and many such like things do ye. [KJV]<br>*Thus* **invalidating** the word of God by your tradition which you have handed down; and you do many things such as that." [NASB]<br>Thus you **nullify** the word of God by your tradition that you have handed down. And you do many things like that." [NIV]<br>Making the word of God **of no effect** through your tradition which you have handed down. And many such things you do." [NKJV]<br>As such, you **break** the law of God in order to protect your own tradition. And this is only one example. There are many, many others." [NLT]<br>ἀκυροῦντες τὸν λόγον τοῦ Θεοῦ τῇ παραδόσει ὑμῶν ᾗ παρεδώκατε· καὶ παρόμοια τοιαῦτα πολλὰ ποιεῖτε. [GNS]<br>ἀκυροῦντες τὸν λόγον τοῦ Θεοῦ τῇ παραδόσει ὑμῶν ᾗ παρεδώκατε· καὶ παρόμοια τοιαῦτα πολλὰ ποιεῖτε. [GNT] | To nullify; to be of no effect; to make void, ineffective; to annul; to cancel; to disregard; to deprive of authority and power; to invalidate.<br><br>**Practical Application**<br>In this Scripture, Christ is rebuking anyone who places human traditions on an equal or higher authority than the Word of God. Jesus charged the religionists with setting aside God's Word for tradition. Religious traditions may be described as institutional or personal.<br>1. Institutional traditions are such things as rituals, rules, regulations, schedules, forms, services, procedures, organizations—anything that gives order and security to the persons involved.<br>2. Personal traditions are such things as church attendance, prayers, habits, ceremonies, objects which a person uses (somewhat superstitiously) to keep himself religiously secure.<br><br>Jesus was attacking the fact that so many religionists put their traditions first while neglecting and ignoring God's Word. (See POSB notes—Matthew 12:1-8; POSB note—Matthew 12:10 and POSB *Deeper Study #1*—Matthew 12:10). |
| **#2187**<br>**Invent Evil–**<br>**Inventors Of**<br>**Evil**<br><br>Inventors of evil–KJV<br>Inventors of evil–NASB<br>Invent...evil–NIV<br>Inventors of evil–NKJV<br>Inventing...sinning–NLT | ἐφευρετὰς κακῶν = *epheuretas kakōn*<br>Pronunciation: [ef-yoo-ret'-ahs kak-own']<br>Parsing *epheuretas* (part of speech): noun<br>    Case—accusative<br>    Gender—masculine<br>    Number—plural<br>    Stem or root—from ἐφευρετής, ου<br>Parsing *kakōn* (part of speech): pronominal adjective<br>    Case—genitive<br>    Gender—neuter<br>    Number—plural<br>    Stem or root—from κακός, ή, όν<br>Concordance References:<br>  ⇒ Strong's #2182 epheuretēs + 2556 kakos<br>  ⇒ NIV #2388 epheuretēs [invent] + 2805 kakos [evil]<br>  ⇒ NASB #2182 epheuretēs + 2556 kakos | Inventors of evil things; one who schemes or plans. evil, bad, wrong, injury, harm, trouble or foul play. It means inventors of new sins, of more sensational forms of excitement and vice and evil.<br><br>**Practical Application**<br>It is a person who is tired of the old forms of sin and who feels the need to seek out new ways and forms of vice. |

# Practical Word Studies in the New Testament

| ENGLISH WORD | GREEK WORD AND VERSE | THE WORD MEANS... |
|---|---|---|
| **POSB REFERENCE** (Romans 1:30) *Deeper Study #17* | **Romans 1:30** Backbiters, haters of God, despiteful, proud, boasters, **inventors of evil** things, disobedient to parents, [KJV] Slanderers, haters of God, insolent, arrogant, boastful, **inventors of evil**, disobedient to parents, [NASB] Slanderers, God-haters, insolent, arrogant and boastful; they **invent** ways of doing **evil**; they disobey their parents; [NIV] Backbiters, haters of God, violent, proud, boasters, **inventors of evil** things, disobedient to parents, [NKJV] They are backstabbers, haters of God, insolent, proud, and boastful. They are forever **inventing** new ways of **sinning** and are disobedient to their parents. [NLT] ψιθυριστάς, καταλάλους, θεοστυγεῖς, ὑβριστάς, ὑπερηφάνους, ἀλαζόνας, **ἐφευρετὰς κακῶν**, γονεῦσιν ἀπειθεῖς, [GNS] καταλάλους θεοστυγεῖς ὑβριστὰς ὑπερηφάνους ἀλαζόνας, **ἐφευρετὰς κακῶν**, γονεῦσιν ἀπειθεῖς, [GNT] | |
| **#2188 Inventing... Sinning** Inventors of evil–KJV Inventors of evil–NASB Invent...evil–NIV Inventors of evil–NKJV **Inventing...sinning–NLT** **POSB REFERENCE** (Romans 1:30) *Deeper Study #17* | **ἐφευρετὰς κακῶν** = *epheuretas kakōn* Pronunciation: [ef-yoo-ret'-ahs kak-own'] Parsing *epheuretas* (part of speech): noun    Case—accusative    Gender—masculine    Number—plural    Stem or root—from ἐφευρετής, ου Parsing *kakōn* (part of speech): pronominal adjective    Case—genitive    Gender—neuter    Number—plural    Stem or root—from κακός, ή, όν Concordance References: ⇒ Strong's #2182 epheuretēs + 2556 kakos ⇒ NIV #2388 epheuretēs [invent] + 2805 kakos [evil] ⇒ NASB #2182 epheuretēs + 2556 kakos **Romans 1:30** Backbiters, haters of God, despiteful, proud, boasters, **inventors of evil** things, disobedient to parents, [KJV] Slanderers, haters of God, insolent, arrogant, boastful, **inventors of evil**, disobedient to parents, [NASB] Slanderers, God-haters, insolent, arrogant and boastful; they **invent** ways of doing **evil**; they disobey their parents; [NIV] Backbiters, haters of God, violent, proud, boasters, **inventors of evil** things, disobedient to parents, [NKJV] They are backstabbers, haters of God, insolent, proud, and boastful. They are forever **inventing** new ways of **sinning** and are disobedient to their parents. [NLT] ψιθυριστάς, καταλάλους, θεοστυγεῖς, ὑβριστάς, ὑπερηφάνους, ἀλαζόνας, **ἐφευρετὰς κακῶν**, γονεῦσιν ἀπειθεῖς, [GNS] καταλάλους θεοστυγεῖς ὑβριστὰς ὑπερηφάνους ἀλαζόνας, **ἐφευρετὰς κακῶν**, γονεῦσιν ἀπειθεῖς, [GNT] | Inventors of evil things; one who schemes or plans. evil, bad, wrong, injury, harm, trouble or foul play. It means inventors of new sins, of more sensational forms of excitement and vice and evil. **Practical Application** It is a person who is tired of the old forms of sin and who feels the need to seek out new ways and forms of vice and evil. |
| **#2189 Invest** Occupy–KJV Do business–NASB Put to work–NIV Do business–NKJV **Invest–NLT** **POSB REFERENCE** (Lk.19:13) Note 3, point 2 *Deeper Study #2* | Πραγματεύσασθε = *Pragmateusasthe* Pronunciation: [prag-mat-yoo'-sahs-theh] Parsing (part of speech): verb    Mood—imperative    Tense—aorist    Voice—middle deponent    Person—2nd person    Number—plural    Stem or root—from πραγματεύομαι Concordance References: ⇒ Strong's #4231 pragmateuomai ⇒ NIV #4549 pragmateuomai ⇒ NASB #4231 pragmateuomai **Luke 19:13** And he called his ten servants, and delivered them ten pounds, and said unto them, **Occupy** till I come. [KJV] | To invest; to do business; to put to work; to trade; to occupy. **Practical Application** The word "invest" is a word of diligent action. It is from the root word meaning to walk, to set in motion, and to continue in motion. The servant is to labor diligently, never letting up but using all the Lord has given him to look after. This is the only time the word is used in the New Testament (cp. Isaiah 35:3; Hebrews 12:28; Hebrews 12:12). |

# PRACTICAL WORD STUDIES
## in the NEW TESTAMENT

| ENGLISH WORD | GREEK WORD AND VERSE | THE WORD MEANS... |
|---|---|---|
| | "And he called ten of his slaves, and gave them ten minas, and said to them, '**Do business** with this until I come back.' [NASB]<br>So he called ten of his servants and gave them ten minas. '**Put** this money **to work**,' he said, 'until I come back.' [NIV]<br>So he called ten of his servants, delivered to them ten minas, and said to them, '**Do business** till I come.' [NKJV]<br>Before he left, he called together ten servants and gave them ten pounds of silver to **invest** for him while he was gone. [NLT]<br>καλέσας δὲ δέκα δούλους ἑαυτοῦ, ἔδωκεν αὐτοῖς δέκα μνᾶς, καὶ εἶπε πρὸς αὐτούς, **Πραγματεύσασθε** ἕως ἔρχομαι. [GNS]<br>καλέσας δὲ δέκα δούλους ἑαυτοῦ ἔδωκεν αὐτοῖς δέκα μνᾶς καὶ εἶπεν πρὸς αὐτούς, **Πραγματεύσασθε** ἐν ᾧ ἔρχομαι. [GNT] | |
| #2190<br>**Investigated**<br><br>Perfect understanding–KJV<br>**Investigated**–NASB<br>**Investigated**–NIV<br>Perfect understanding–NKJV<br>**Investigated**–NLT<br><br>**POSB REFERENCE**<br>(Lk.1:3)<br>Note 3, point 1 | παρηκολουθηκότι = *parēkolouthēkoti*<br>Pronunciation: [par-ak-ol-oo-th<br>    Person—1st person<br>    Number—singular<br>    Stem oray'-ko-tee]<br>Parsing (part of speech): verb<br>    Mood—participle<br>    Tense—perfect<br>    Voice—active<br>    Case—dative<br>    Gender—masculine root—from παρακολουθέω<br>Concordance References:<br>  ⇒ Strong's #3877 parakoloutheō<br>  ⇒ NIV #4158 parakoloutheō<br>  ⇒ NASB #3877 parakoloutheō<br><br>**Luke 1:3**<br>It seemed good to me also, having had **perfect understanding** of all things from the very first, to write unto thee in order, most excellent Theophilus, [KJV]<br>It seemed fitting for me as well, having **investigated** everything carefully from the beginning, to write it out for you in consecutive order, most excellent Theophilus; [NASB]<br>Therefore, since I myself have carefully **investigated** everything from the beginning, it seemed good also to me to write an orderly account for you, most excellent Theophilus, [NIV]<br>It seemed good to me also, having had **perfect understanding** of all things from the very first, to write to you an orderly account, most excellent Theophilus, [NKJV]<br>Having carefully **investigated** all of these accounts from the beginning, I have decided to write a careful summary for you, [NLT]<br>ἔδοξε κἀμοὶ **παρηκολουθηκότι** ἄνωθεν πᾶσιν ἀκριβῶς, καθεξῆς σοι γράψαι, κράτιστε Θεόφιλε, [GNS]<br>ἔδοξε κἀμοὶ **παρηκολουθηκότι** ἄνωθεν πᾶσιν ἀκριβῶς καθεξῆς σοι γράψαι, κράτιστε Θεόφιλε, [GNT] | To study; to follow up; to search out diligently; to investigate; to give careful attention; to trace accurately; to become acquainted with; to scrutinize.<br><br>**Practical Application**<br>Luke says that having been acquainted with and having investigated all things, he was determined to record the facts himself. |
| #2191<br>**Invited**<br><br>Besought–KJV<br>Begging–NASB<br>**Invited**–NIV<br>Begged–NKJV<br>Asked–NLT<br><br>**POSB REFERENCE**<br>(Acts 13:42-45; esp. | παρεκάλουν = *parekaloun*<br>Pronunciation: [par-ek-al-oon]<br>Parsing (part of speech): verb<br>    Mood—indicative<br>    Tense—imperfect<br>    Voice—active<br>    Person—3rd person<br>    Number—plural<br>    Stem or root—from παρακαλέω<br>Concordance References:<br>  ⇒ Strong's #3870 parakaleō<br>  ⇒ NIV #4151 parakaleō<br>  ⇒ NASB #3870 parakaleō | Invited, urged, besought, begged, asked; requested urgently; appealed to; pleaded with.<br><br>**Practical Application**<br>It is continuous action: the heathen continued to beseech. The picture is that they begged and begged Paul to share more about the forgiveness of sins which is in Jesus. |

# PRACTICAL WORD STUDIES
## in the NEW TESTAMENT

| ENGLISH WORD | GREEK WORD AND VERSE | THE WORD MEANS... |
|---|---|---|
| v.42)<br>Note 1, point 1 | **Acts 13:42**<br>And when the Jews were gone out of the synagogue, the Gentiles **besought** that these words might be preached to them the next sabbath. [KJV]<br>And as Paul and Barnabas were going out, the people kept **begging** that these things might be spoken to them the next Sabbath. [NASB]<br>As Paul and Barnabas were leaving the synagogue, the people **invited** them to speak further about these things on the next Sabbath. [NIV]<br>So when the Jews went out of the synagogue, the Gentiles **begged** that these words might be preached to them the next Sabbath. [NKJV]<br>As Paul and Barnabas left the synagogue that day, the people **asked** them to return again and speak about these things the next week. [NLT]<br>Ἐξιόντων ἐκ τῆς συναγωγῆς τῶν Ἰουδαίων, δὲ αὐτῶν **παρεκάλουν** τὰ ἔθνη εἰς τὸ μεταξὺ σάββατον λαληθῆναι αὐτοῖς τὰ ῥήματα ταῦτα. [GNS]<br>Ἐξιόντων δὲ αὐτῶν **παρεκάλουν** εἰς τὸ μεταξὺ σάββατον λαληθῆναι αὐτοῖς τὰ ῥήματα ταῦτα. [GNT] | |
| **#2192**<br>**Irreconcilable**<br><br>Trucebreakers–KJV<br>**Irreconcilable–NASB**<br>Unforgiving–NIV<br>Unforgiving–NKJV<br>Unforgiving–NLT<br><br>**POSB<br>REFERENCE**<br>(2 Tim. 3:2-4; esp. v.3)<br>Note 2, point 10 | ἄσπονδοι = *aspondoi*<br>Pronunciation: [as'-pon-doy]<br>Parsing (part of speech): adjective<br>    Case—nominative<br>    Gender—masculine<br>    Number—plural<br>    Stem or root—from ἄσπονδος, ον<br>Concordance References:<br>  ⇒ Strong's #786 aspondos<br>  ⇒ NIV #836 aspondos<br>  ⇒ NASB #786 aspondos<br><br>**2 Tim. 3:3**<br>Without natural affection, **trucebreakers**, false accusers, incontinent, fierce, despisers of those that are good, [KJV]<br>Unloving, **irreconcilable**, malicious gossips, without self-control, brutal, haters of good, [NASB]<br>Without love, **unforgiving**, slanderous, without self-control, brutal, not lovers of the good, [NIV]<br>Unloving, **unforgiving**, slanderers, without self-control, brutal, despisers of good, [NKJV]<br>They will be unloving and **unforgiving**; they will slander others and have no self-control; they will be cruel and have no interest in what is good. [NLT]<br>ἄστοργοι, **ἄσπονδοι**, διάβολοι, ἀκρατεῖς, ἀνήμεροι, ἀφιλάγαθοι, [GNS]<br>ἄστοργοι **ἄσπονδοι** διάβολοι ἀκρατεῖς ἀνήμεροι ἀφιλάγαθοι [GNT] | Unforgiving, trucebreakers, irreconcilable, merciless, breakers of promises and agreements, untrustworthy, faithless, treacherous, and untruthful.<br><br>**Practical Application**<br>An irreconcilable man is a man or some organization or body of people who tragically do not keep their word or promise. They are simply untrustworthy and undependable. What happens when a person's word can no longer be accepted?<br>  ⇒ What happens in a home when the husband or wife breaks the promise of marriage?<br>  ⇒ What happens between parent and child when one of them breaks his promise time and again?<br>  ⇒ What happens when an employer breaks his promise to his workers?<br>  ⇒ What happens when a worker breaks his promise and slacks up in his work?<br>  ⇒ What happens when a nation breaks its agreement with another nation?<br><br>The last days will see what we are seeing in our society today: a barrage of broken truces, covenants, and promises. |
| **#2193**<br>**Irritable**<br><br>Easily provoked–KJV<br>Provoked–NASB<br>Easily angered–NIV<br>Provoked–NKJV<br>**Irritable–NLT**<br><br>**POSB<br>REFERENCE**<br>(1 Cor.13:4-7; esp. v.5)<br>Note 2, point 8 | παροξύνεται = *paroxunetai*<br>Pronunciation: [par-ox-oo'-neh-tah-ee]<br>Parsing (part of speech): verb<br>    Mood—indicative<br>    Tense—present<br>    Voice—passive<br>    Person—3rd person<br>    Number—singular<br>    Stem or root—from παροξύνομαι<br>Concordance References:<br>  ⇒ Strong's #3947 paroxunō<br>  ⇒ NIV #4236 paroxunō<br>  ⇒ NASB #3947 paroxunō<br><br>**1 Cor. 13:5**<br>Doth not behave itself unseemly, seeketh not her own, is not **easily provoked**, thinketh no evil; [KJV]<br>Does not act unbecomingly; it does not seek its own, is not **provoked**, does not take into account a wrong suffered, [NASB] | To be easily provoked; to be greatly distressed; to be irritable; to be greatly upset.<br><br>**Practical Application**<br>Love is not irritable (*paroxunetai*): not ready to take offence; not quick tempered; not touchy. It is not easily aroused to anger; does not become exasperated. Love controls the emotions and never becomes angry without a cause (Romans 12:18). |

# PRACTICAL WORD STUDIES
## in the NEW TESTAMENT

| ENGLISH WORD | GREEK WORD AND VERSE | THE WORD MEANS... |
|---|---|---|
| | It is not rude, it is not self-seeking, it is not **easily angered**, it keeps no record of wrongs. [NIV]<br>Does not behave rudely, does not seek its own, is not **provoked**, thinks no evil; [NKJV]<br>Or rude. Love does not demand its own way. Love is not **irritable**, and it keeps no record of when it has been wronged. [NLT]<br>οὐκ ἀσχημονεῖ, οὐ ζητεῖ τὰ ἑαυτῆς, οὐ **παροξύνεται**, οὐ λογίζεται τὸ κακόν, [GNS]<br>οὐκ ἀσχημονεῖ, οὐ ζητεῖ τὰ ἑαυτῆς, οὐ **παροξύνεται**, οὐ λογίζεται τὸ κακόν, [GNT] | |
| **#2194**<br>**Is**<br><br>Being–KJV<br>**Is**–NASB<br>**Is**–NIV<br>Being–NKJV<br>Not translated–NLT<br><br>**POSB REFERENCE**<br>(Heb.1:3)<br>Note 4 | ὤν = ōn<br>Pronunciation: [own]<br>Parsing (part of speech): verb<br>  Mood—participle<br>  Tense—present<br>  Voice—active<br>  Case—nominative<br>  Gender—masculine<br>  Number—singular<br>  Stem or root—from εἰμί<br>Concordance References:<br>  ⇒ Strong's #1510 eimi<br>  ⇒ NIV #1639 eimi<br>  ⇒ NASB #1510 eimi<br><br>**Hebrews 1:3**<br>Who **being** the brightness of his glory, and the express image of his person, and upholding all things by the word of his power, when he had by himself purged our sins, sat down on the right hand of the Majesty on high; [KJV]<br>And He **is** the radiance of His glory and the exact representation of His nature, and upholds all things by the word of His power. When He had made purification of sins, He sat down at the right hand of the Majesty on high; [NASB]<br>The Son **is** the radiance of God's glory and the exact representation of his being, sustaining all things by his powerful word. After he had provided purification for sins, he sat down at the right hand of the Majesty in heaven. [NIV]<br>Who **being** the brightness of His glory and the express image of His person, and upholding all things by the word of His power, when He had by Himself purged our sins, sat down at the right hand of the Majesty on high, [NKJV]<br>The Son reflects God's own glory, and everything about him represents God exactly. He sustains the universe by the mighty power of his command. After he died to cleanse us from the stain of sin, he sat down in the place of honor at the right hand of the majestic God of heaven. [NLT]—Not Translated<br>ὃς **ὢν** ἀπαύγασμα τῆς δόξης, καὶ χαρακτὴρ τῆς ὑποστάσεως αὐτοῦ, φέρων τε τὰ πάντα τῷ ῥήματι τῆς δυνάμεως αὐτοῦ, δι' ἑαυτοῦ καθαρισμὸν ποιησάμενος τῶν ἁμαρτιῶν ἡμῶν, ἐκάθισεν ἐν δεξιᾷ τῆς μεγαλωσύνης ἐν ὑψηλοῖς, [GNS]<br>ὃς **ὢν** ἀπαύγασμα τῆς δόξης καὶ χαρακτὴρ τῆς ὑποστάσεως αὐτοῦ, φέρων τε τὰ πάντα τῷ ῥήματι τῆς δυνάμεως αὐτοῦ, καθαρισμὸν τῶν ἁμαρτιῶν ποιησάμενος ἐκάθισεν ἐν δεξιᾷ τῆς μεγαλωσύνης ἐν ὑψηλοῖς, [GNT] | Is; being; existing. It means "absolute and timeless existence" (A.T. Robertson. *Word Pictures in the New Testament*, Vol. 5., p.335).<br><br>**Practical Application**<br>This means that Jesus Christ Himself possessed the glory of God before He ever came into the world. He has always existed in the glory of God; He is eternal.<br>What does glory mean? It means all the brightness of God—all the brilliance, radiance, splendor, and light of God's Being. It means that God's very presence—in all of His light and purity—dwells among us in the person of Jesus Christ. It meant that in Christ "dwelt all the fullness [glory] of God" (Col. 2:9). Men could look at Jesus Christ and see the glory of God in Him—the very light and radiance of God's Being. |
| **#2195**<br>**It Is I**<br><br>It Is I–KJV<br>It Is I–NASB<br>It Is I–NIV<br>It is I–NKJV<br>I am here–NLT | Ἐγώ εἰμι = Egō eimi<br>Pronunciation: [ay-go ee-mee]<br>Parsing *Egō* (part of speech):<br>  Type—pronoun<br>  Case—nominative<br>  Person—1st person<br>  Number—singular<br>  Stem or root—from ἐγώ<br>Parsing *eimi* (part of speech): verb<br>  Mood—indicative | It is I; I am here; I AM.<br><br>**Practical Application**<br>Jesus was saying, "I AM" has come—fear not. He was reminding the disciples who He was, the Son of God Himself. He possessed all power; therefore, there was no need to fear. This was the same message that God gave to Moses at the burning bush, "I am that I am" (Exodus 3:13- |

# PRACTICAL WORD STUDIES
## in the NEW TESTAMENT

| ENGLISH WORD | GREEK WORD AND VERSE | THE WORD MEANS... |
|---|---|---|
| **POSB REFERENCE** (Jn.6:20) *Deeper Study #1* | Tense—present<br>Voice—active<br>Person—1st person<br>Number—singular<br>Stem or root—from εἰμί<br>Concordance References:<br>⇒ Strong's #1473 egō + 1510 eimi<br>⇒ NIV #1609 egō [I] 1639 eimi [am]<br>⇒ NASB #1473 egō + 1510 eimi<br><br>**John 6:20**<br>But he saith unto them, **It is I**; be not afraid. [KJV]<br>But He said to them, "**It is I**; do not be afraid." [NASB]<br>But he said to them, "**It is I**; don't be afraid." [NIV]<br>But He said to them, "**It is I**; do not be afraid." [NKJV]<br>But he called out to them, "**I am here**! Don't be afraid." [NLT]<br>ὁ δὲ λέγει αὐτοῖς, Ἐγώ εἰμι, μὴ φοβεῖσθε. [GNS]<br>ὁ δὲ λέγει αὐτοῖς, Ἐγώ εἰμι, μὴ φοβεῖσθε. [GNT] | 15, esp. Exodus 3:14). It was the same message that Jesus used as a defense against the religionists, "Before Abraham was, I am" (John 8:58). It is the same message that Col. 1:15-17 claims for Him; and it is the same message that is proclaimed by the book of Revelation, "the One who is and who was, because you have taken your great power and have begun to reign" (Rev. 1:4, 8; Rev. 11:17; Rev. 16:5). (See POSB note—John 1:1-2.) |
| **#2196**<br>**Itself, All By–Itself, By**<br><br>Of herself–KJV<br>**By itself–NASB**<br>**All by itself–NIV**<br>**By itself–NKJV**<br>On its own–NLT<br><br>**POSB REFERENCE** (Mk.4:28) Note 4 | αὐτομάτη = *automate*<br>Pronunciation: [ow-tom'-at-eh]<br>Parsing (part of speech): adjective<br>  Case—nominative<br>  Gender—feminine<br>  Number—singular<br>  Stem or root—from αὐτόματος, η, ον<br><br>Concordance References:<br>⇒ Strong's #844 automatos<br>⇒ NIV #897 automatos<br>⇒ NASB #844 automatos<br><br>**Mark 4:28**<br>For the earth bringeth forth fruit **of herself**; first the blade, then the ear, after that the full corn in the ear. [KJV]<br>"The soil produces crops **by itself**; first the blade, then the head, then the mature grain in the head. [NASB]<br>**All by itself** the soil produces grain—first the stalk, then the head, then the full kernel in the head. [NIV]<br>For the earth yields crops **by itself**: first the blade, then the head, after that the full grain in the head. [NKJV]<br>Because the earth produces crops **on its own**. First a leaf blade pushes through, then the heads of wheat are formed, and finally the grain ripens. [NLT]<br>αὐτομάτη γὰρ ἡ γῆ καρποφορεῖ, πρῶτον χόρτον, εἶτα στάχυν, εἶτα πλήρη σῖτον ἐν τῷ στάχυϊ. [GNS]<br>αὐτομάτη ἡ γῆ καρποφορεῖ, πρῶτον χόρτον εἶτα στάχυν εἶτα πλήρη[ς] σῖτον ἐν τῷ στάχυϊ. [GNT] | All by itself, on its own, of herself, automatically, spontaneously, of necessity, self-moving.<br><br>**Practical Application**<br>The idea is that the earth brings forth fruit automatically, by its very nature. Note two facts.<br>1. Growth is sure, inevitable. But two conditions are essential. The ground must be "good ground" (Mark 4:20) and the seed must be sown in the ground. If these two conditions exist, then growth is both inevitable and unstoppable. Even a small blade of grass will find a crack in the pavement. Nothing can stop the seed from growing. (See POSB outline—Romans 8:28-39 and POSB notes—Romans 8:28-39 for more discussion.)<br>2. Growth is constant, but it is gradual, ever so gradual. The seed is sown, and then day after day and night after night passes before the blade ever springs up. Then many more days and nights pass before the ear forms. It takes weeks before the full ear of corn appears. Growth does take place; it is constant—but growth is gradual. It does take time; it does not happen overnight. |
| **#2197**<br>**Imaginations**<br><br>**Imaginations–KJV**<br>Speculations–NASB<br>Thinking–NIV<br>Thoughts–NKJV<br>Ideas–NLT<br><br>**POSB REFERENCE** (Romans 1:21) Note 4, point 1 | διαλογισμοῖς = *dialogismois*<br>Pronunciation: [dee-al-og-is-mo-ees']<br>Parsing (part of speech): noun<br>  Case—dative<br>  Gender—masculine<br>  Number—plural<br>  Stem or root—from διαλογισμός, οῦ<br>Concordance References:<br>⇒ Strong's #1261 dialogismos<br>⇒ NIV #1369 dialogismos<br>⇒ NASB #1261 dialogismos<br><br>**Romans 1:21**<br>Because that, when they knew God, they glorified him not as God, neither were thankful; but became vain in their **imaginations**, and their foolish heart was darkened. [KJV]<br>For even though they knew God, they did not honor Him as God, or give thanks; but they became futile in their **speculations**, and their foolish heart was darkened. [NASB] | Thoughts, opinions, motives, reasonings; doubts, questions; arguments, disputes, deliberations, conclusions, speculations.<br><br>**Practical Application**<br>When men push God out of their minds, their minds are void and empty of God. God is not in their thoughts. (Cp. Psalm 10:4.) Their minds are ready to be *filled* with some other *god* or *supremacy*. |

# Practical Word Studies
## in the New Testament

| ENGLISH WORD | GREEK WORD AND VERSE | THE WORD MEANS... |
|---|---|---|
| | For although they knew God, they neither glorified him as God nor gave thanks to him, but their **thinking** became futile and their foolish hearts were darkened. [NIV]<br><br>Because, although they knew God, they did not glorify *Him* as God, nor were thankful, but became futile in their **thoughts**, and their foolish hearts were darkened. [NKJV]<br>Yes, they knew God, but they wouldn't worship him as God or even give him thanks. And they began to think up foolish **ideas** of what God was like. The result was that their minds became dark and confused. [NLT]<br>διότι γνόντες τὸν Θεὸν οὐχ ὡς Θεὸν ἐδόξασαν ἢ ηὐχαρίστησαν, ἀλλ' ἐματαιώθησαν ἐν τοῖς **διαλογισμοῖς** αὐτῶν, καὶ ἐσκοτίσθη ἡ ἀσύνετος αὐτῶν καρδία. [GNS]<br>διότι γνόντες τὸν θεὸν οὐχ ὡς θεὸν ἐδόξασαν ἢ ηὐχαρίστησαν, ἀλλ' ἐματαιώθησαν ἐν τοῖς **διαλογισμοῖς** αὐτῶν καὶ ἐσκοτίσθη ἡ ἀσύνετος αὐτῶν καρδία. [GNT] | |

PRACTICAL WORD STUDIES
in the NEW TESTAMENT

| ENGLISH WORD | GREEK WORD AND VERSE | THE WORD MEANS... |
|---|---|---|
| **#2198**<br>**Jealous**<br><br>Envieth–KJV<br>**Jealous–NASB**<br>Envy–NIV<br>Envy–NKJV<br>**Jealous–NLT**<br><br>**POSB REFERENCE**<br>(1 Cor.13:4-7; esp. v.4)<br>Note 2, point 3<br><br>See also POSB REF:<br>(Acts 7:9)<br>*Deeper Study #2* | ζηλοῖ = *zëloi*<br>Pronunciation: [dzay-loy'ee]<br>Parsing (part of speech): verb<br>    Mood—indicative<br>    Tense—present<br>    Voice—active<br>    Person—3rd person<br>    Number—singular<br>    Stem or root—from ζηλόω<br>Concordance References:<br>  ⇒ Strong's #2206 zëloö<br>  ⇒ NIV #2420 zëloö<br>  ⇒ NASB #2206 zëloö<br><br>**1 Cor. 13:4**<br>Charity suffereth long, and is kind; charity **envieth** not; charity vaunteth not itself, is not puffed up, [KJV]<br>Love is patient, love is kind, and is not **jealous**; love does not brag and is not arrogant, [NASB]<br>Love is patient, love is kind. It does not **envy**, it does not boast, it is not proud. [NIV]<br>Love suffers long *and* is kind; love does not **envy**; love does not parade itself, is not puffed up; [NKJV]<br>Love is patient and kind. Love is not **jealous** or boastful or proud [NLT]<br>ἡ ἀγάπη μακροθυμεῖ, χρηστεύεται· ἡ ἀγάπη, οὐ ζηλοῖ· ἡ ἀγάπη οὐ περπερεύεται, οὐ φυσιοῦται, [GNS]<br>Ἡ ἀγάπη μακροθυμεῖ, χρηστεύεται ἡ ἀγάπη, οὐ ζηλοῖ, [ἡ ἀγάπη] οὐ περπερεύεται, οὐ φυσιοῦται, [GNT] | To be jealous; to envy; to eagerly desire; to covet; to be zealous for.<br><br>**Practical Application**<br>Love is not jealous (*zëloi*): does not envy; does not have feelings against others because of what they have, such as gifts, position, friends, recognition, possessions, popularity, abilities. Love does not begrudge or attack or downplay the abilities and success of others. Love shares and joys and rejoices in the experience and good of others. |
| **#2199**<br>**Jealousy**<br><br>Envyings–KJV<br>**Jealousy–NASB**<br>**Jealousy–NIV**<br>Jealousies–NKJV<br>**Jealousy–NLT**<br><br>**POSB REFERENCE**<br>(2 Cor.12:19-21; esp. v.20)<br>Note 3, point 2<br><br>See also POSB REF:<br>(Rom.13:13)<br>Note 4, point 6 | ζῆλος = *zëlos*<br>Pronunciation: [dzay'-los]<br>Parsing (part of speech): noun<br>    Case—nominative<br>    Gender—masculine or neuter<br>    Number—singular<br>    Stem or root—from ζῆλος, ου<br>Concordance References:<br>  ⇒ Strong's #2205 zëlos<br>  ⇒ NIV #2419 zëlos<br>  ⇒ NASB #2205 zëlos<br><br>**2 Cor. 12:20**<br>For I fear, lest, when I come, I shall not find you such as I would, and that I shall be found unto you such as ye would not: lest there be debates, **envyings**, wraths, strifes, backbitings, whisperings, swellings, tumults: [KJV]<br>For I am afraid that perhaps when I come I may find you to be not what I wish and may be found by you to be not what you wish; that perhaps there may be strife, **jealousy**, angry tempers, disputes, slanders, gossip, arrogance, disturbances; [NASB]<br>For I am afraid that when I come I may not find you as I want you to be, and you may not find me as you want me to be. I fear that there may be quarreling, **jealousy**, outbursts of anger, factions, slander, gossip, arrogance and disorder. [NIV]<br>For I fear lest, when I come, I shall not find you such as I wish, and *that* I shall be found by you such as you do not wish; lest *there be* contentions, **jealousies**, outbursts of wrath, selfish ambitions, backbitings, whisperings, conceits, tumults; [NKJV]<br>For I am afraid that when I come to visit you I won't like what I find, and then you won't like my response. I am afraid that I will find quarreling, **jealousy**, outbursts of anger, selfishness, backstabbing, gossip, conceit, and disorderly behavior. [NLT]<br>φοβοῦμαι γὰρ μή πως ἐλθὼν οὐχ οἵους θέλω εὕρω ὑμᾶς, κἀγὼ εὑρεθῶ ὑμῖν οἷον οὐ θέλετε· μή πως ἔρις, ζῆλοι, θυμοί, ἐριθεῖαι, καταλαλιαί, ψιθυρισμοί, φυσιώσεις, ἀκαταστασίαι· [GNS] | Jealousy; envyings; begrudging what others have, whether position, abilities, recognition, acceptance, loyalty, wealth, or anything else.<br><br>**Practical Application**<br>Paul was stricken with fear, fear lest the church fail to be what it should be and reject him and his ministry. Paul feared that the church would fail to deal with the carnal critics and continue putting up with their evil attacks against him. He lists eight evils including "jealousy" (*zëlos*) that were and still are characteristic of divisive critics in the church. |

# PRACTICAL WORD STUDIES
## in the NEW TESTAMENT

| ENGLISH WORD | GREEK WORD AND VERSE | THE WORD MEANS... |
|---|---|---|
| | φοβοῦμαι γὰρ μή πως ἐλθὼν οὐχ οἵους θέλω εὕρω ὑμᾶς κἀγὼ εὑρεθῶ ὑμῖν οἷον οὐ θέλετε· μή πως ἔρις, **ζῆλος**, θυμοί, ἐριθεῖαι, καταλαλιαί, ψιθυρισμοί, φυσιώσεις, ἀκαταστασίαι. [GNT] | |
| **#2200**<br>**Jealousies–**<br>**Jealousy**<br><br>Emulations–KJV<br>Jealousy–NASB<br>Jealousy–NIV<br>Jealousies–NKJV<br>Jealousy–NLT<br><br>**POSB**<br>**REFERENCE**<br>(Gal.5:19-21; esp. v.20)<br>Note 2, point 9 | ζῆλος = zēlos<br>Pronunciation: [dzay'-los]<br>Parsing (part of speech): noun<br>    Case—nominative<br>    Gender—masculine or neuter<br>    Number—singular<br>    Stem or root—from ζῆλος, ου<br>Concordance References:<br>⇒ Strong's #2205 zēlos<br>⇒ NIV #2419 zēlos<br>⇒ NASB #2205 zēlos<br><br>**Galatians 5:20**<br>Idolatry, witchcraft, hatred, variance, **emulations**, wrath, strife, seditions, heresies, [KJV]<br>Idolatry, sorcery, enmities, strife, **jealousy**, outbursts of anger, disputes, dissensions, factions, [NASB]<br>Idolatry and witchcraft; hatred, discord, **jealousy**, fits of rage, selfish ambition, dissensions, factions [NIV]<br>Idolatry, sorcery, hatred, contentions, **jealousies**, outbursts of wrath, selfish ambitions, dissensions, heresies, [NKJV]<br>Idolatry, participation in demonic activities, hostility, quarreling, **jealousy**, outbursts of anger, selfish ambition, divisions, the feeling that everyone is wrong except those in your own little group, [NLT]<br>εἰδωλολατρία, φαρμακεία, ἔχθραι, ἔρεις, **ζῆλοι**, θυμοί, ἐριθεῖαι, διχοστασίαι, αἱρέσεις, [GNS]<br>εἰδωλολατρία, φαρμακεία, ἔχθραι, ἔρις, **ζῆλος**, θυμοί, ἐριθεῖαι, διχοστασίαι, αἱρέσεις, [GNT] | Jealousy, emulations, zeal, wanting and desiring to have what someone else has. It may be material things, recognition, honor, or position.<br><br>**Practical Application**<br>The works of the flesh—including "jealousies" or "jealousy" (zēlos)—are the fruit of indwelling sin, and sin originates in the heart not in the flesh. The sins of the flesh listed in this passage are clearly seen throughout society. Tragically, they are not only seen on the daily newscasts of every city, but within every community, home, and life on planet earth. The very presence of such fleshly sins shows just how strong the flesh is and how helpless man is to control his flesh. |
| **#2201**<br>**Jesting**<br><br>Jesting–KJV<br>Coarse jesting–NASB<br>Coarse joking–NIV<br>Coarse jesting–NKJV<br>Coarse jokes–NLT<br><br>**POSB**<br>**REFERENCE**<br>(Eph.5:4)<br>Note 4, point 3 | εὐτραπελία = eutrapelia<br>Pronunciation: [yoo-trap-el-ee'-ah]<br>Parsing (part of speech): noun<br>    Case—nominative<br>    Gender—feminine<br>    Number—singular<br>    Stem or root—from εὐτραπελία, ας<br>Concordance References:<br>⇒ Strong's #2160 eutrapelia<br>⇒ NIV #2365 eutrapelia<br>⇒ NASB #2160 eutrapelia<br><br>**Ephes. 5:4**<br>Neither filthiness, nor foolish talking, nor **jesting**, which are not convenient: but rather giving of thanks. [KJV]<br>And there must be no filthiness and silly talk, or **coarse jesting**, which are not fitting, but rather giving of thanks. [NASB]<br>Nor should there be obscenity, foolish talk or **coarse joking**, which are out of place, but rather thanksgiving. [NIV]<br>Neither filthiness, nor foolish talking, nor **coarse jesting**, which are not fitting, but rather giving of thanks. [NKJV]<br>Obscene stories, foolish talk, and **coarse jokes**—these are not for you. Instead, let there be thankfulness to God. [NLT]<br>καὶ αἰσχρότης, καὶ μωρολογία, ἡ **εὐτραπελία**, τὰ οὐκ ἀνήκοντα· ἀλλὰ μᾶλλον εὐχαριστία. [GNS]<br>καὶ αἰσχρότης καὶ μωρολογία ἡ **εὐτραπελία**, ἃ οὐκ ἀνῆκεν, ἀλλὰ μᾶλλον εὐχαριστία. [GNT] | Coarse joking, jesting, vulgar or dirty talk. It means to joke, talk foolishly, poke fun, act or speak without thought; to be suggestive in conversation; to make wisecracks.<br><br>**Practical Application**<br>It also has the idea of being cunning and clever, of being polished in suggestive and off-colored joking and using it to attract attention and win favors (Kenneth Wuest. *Ephesians and Colossians*, Vol.1, p.121). Coarse joking is often used in off-colored jokes or conversation at parties or work breaks in order to be suggestive. |
| **#2202**<br>**Jesus**<br><br>Jesus–KJV | Ἰησοῦν· = Iēsoun<br>Pronunciation: [ee-ay-soon']<br>Parsing (part of speech): noun<br>    Case—accusative<br>    Gender—masculine | Savior; He will save.<br><br>**Practical Application**<br>The Hebrew form is *Joshua* (yasha), meaning |

# PRACTICAL WORD STUDIES
## in the NEW TESTAMENT

| ENGLISH WORD | GREEK WORD AND VERSE | THE WORD MEANS... |
|---|---|---|
| **Jesus–NASB**<br>**Jesus–NIV**<br>**Jesus–NKJV**<br>**Jesus–NLT**<br><br>**POSB REFERENCE**<br>(Mt.1:21)<br>*Deeper Study #5* | Number—singular<br>Stem or root—from Ἰησοῦς<br>Concordance References:<br>⇒ Strong's #2424 Iēsous<br>⇒ NIV #2652 Iēsous<br>⇒ NASB #2424 Iēsous<br><br>**Matthew 1:21**<br>And she shall bring forth a son, and thou shalt call his name **Jesus**: for he shall save his people from their sins. [KJV]<br>"And she will bear a Son; and you shall call His name **Jesus**, for it is He who will save His people from their sins." [NASB]<br>She will give birth to a son, and you are to give him the name **Jesus**, because he will save his people from their sins." [NIV]<br>And she will bring forth a Son, and you shall call His name **Jesus**, for He will save His people from their sins." [NKJV]<br>And she will have a son, and you are to name him **Jesus**, for he will save his people from their sins." [NLT]<br>τέξεται δὲ υἱὸν καὶ καλέσεις τὸ ὄνομα αὐτοῦ Ἰησοῦν, αὐτὸς γὰρ σώσει τὸν λαὸν αὐτοῦ ἀπὸ τῶν ἁμαρτιῶν αὐτῶν. [GNS]<br>τέξεται δὲ υἱόν, καὶ καλέσεις τὸ ὄνομα αὐτοῦ Ἰησοῦν· αὐτὸς γὰρ σώσει τὸν λαὸν αὐτοῦ ἀπὸ τῶν ἁμαρτιῶν αὐτῶν. [GNT] | Jehovah is salvation; He is the Savior. The idea is that of deliverance, of being saved from some terrible disaster that leads to perishing (cp. Jn.3:16; Ro.8:3; Gal.1:4; Heb.2:14-18; Heb.7:25). |
| **#2203**<br>**Joined To**<br><br>Cleave to–KJV<br>Cleave to–NASB<br>United to–NIV<br>Joined to–NKJV<br>**Joined to–NLT**<br><br>**POSB REFERENCE**<br>(Mt.19:5)<br>*Deeper Study #2* | κολληθήσεται = kollēthēsetai<br>Pronunciation: [kol-lay-thay-seh-tah-ee]<br>Parsing (part of speech): verb<br>  Mood—indicative<br>  Tense—future<br>  Voice—passive<br>  Person—3rd person<br>  Number—singular<br>  Stem or root—from κολλάομαι<br>Concordance References:<br>⇒ Strong's #2853 kollaō<br>⇒ NIV #3140 kollaō<br>⇒ NASB #2853 kollaō<br><br>**Matthew 19:5**<br>And said, For this cause shall a man leave father and mother, and shall **cleave to** his wife: and they twain shall be one flesh? [KJV]<br>And said, 'For this cause a man shall leave his father and mother, and shall **cleave to** his wife; and THE TWO SHALL BECOME ONE FLESH'? [NASB]<br>And said, 'For this reason a man will leave his father and mother and be **united to** his wife, and the two will become one flesh'? [NIV]<br>And said, 'For this reason a man shall leave his father and mother and be **joined to** his wife, and the two shall become one flesh'? [NKJV]<br>And, he said, 'This explains why a man leaves his father and mother and is **joined to** his wife, and the two are united into one.' [NLT]<br>καὶ εἶπεν, Ἕνεκα τούτου καταλείψει ἄνθρωπος τὸν πατέρα καὶ τὴν μητέρα, καὶ **προσκολληθήσεται** τῇ γυναικὶ αὐτοῦ, καὶ ἔσονται οἱ δύο εἰς σάρκα μίαν. [GNS]<br>καὶ εἶπεν, Ἕνεκα τούτου καταλείψει ἄνθρωπος τὸν πατέρα καὶ τὴν μητέρα καὶ **κολληθήσεται** τῇ γυναικὶ αὐτοῦ, καὶ ἔσονται [GNT] | To unite to; to cleave; to join fast together; to glue together; to cement together; to be joined in the closest union possible; to be bound together; to be so totally united together that two become one.<br><br>**Practical Application**<br>To be united means a spiritual union. It is a union higher and stronger than the union of parent and child. It is a union that means more than living together, more than having sex and bearing offspring. Animals do this. It is a union that can be wrought by God alone (Matthew 19:11). It is a spiritual union that places man above the physical plane of animals. It is a spiritual fulness, a spiritual sharing of life together: a dedication, a consecration, a completeness, a satisfaction that makes a person the exclusive possession of God and of the spouse. As said, such a cleaving or spiritual union is wrought by God alone. Both husband and wife must be willing and submissive for God to bring about such a union in their lives. |
| **#2204**<br>**Joined Constantly** | ἦσαν προσκαρτεροῦντες = ēsan proskarterountes<br>Pronunciation: [hay-sahn-pros-kar-ter-oon-tes]<br>Parsing *proskarterountes* (part of speech): verb<br>  Mood—participle<br>  Tense—present<br>  Voice—active | To join constantly together; to continue with one accord; to be continually devoting themselves; to meet together continually; to be in regular attendance. |

# PRACTICAL WORD STUDIES
## in the NEW TESTAMENT

| ENGLISH WORD | GREEK WORD AND VERSE | THE WORD MEANS... |
|---|---|---|
| Continued with one accord–KJV<br>Continually devoting themselves to–NASB<br>Joined...constantly–NIV<br>Continued with one accord–NKJV<br>Met together continually–NLT<br><br>**POSB REFERENCE**<br>(Acts 1:12-15; esp. v.14)<br>Note 1, point 4 | Case—nominative<br>Gender—masculine<br>Number—plural<br>Stem or root—from προσκαρτερέω<br>Concordance References:<br>⇒ Strong's #1488 eimi + 4342 proskartereō<br>⇒ NIV #1639 eimi + 4674 proskartereō<br>⇒ NASB #1488 eimi + 4342 proskartereō<br><br>**Acts 1:14**<br>These all **continued with one accord** in prayer and supplication, with the women, and Mary the mother of Jesus, and with his brethren. [KJV]<br>These all with one mind were **continually devoting themselves to** prayer, along with the women, and Mary the mother of Jesus, and with His brothers. [NASB]<br>They all **joined** together **constantly** in prayer, along with the women and Mary the mother of Jesus, and with his brothers. [NIV]<br>These all **continued with one accord** in prayer and supplication, with the women and Mary the mother of Jesus, and with His brothers. [NKJV]<br>They all **met together continually** for prayer, along with Mary the mother of Jesus, several other women, and the brothers of Jesus. [NLT]<br>οὗτοι πάντες ἦσαν προσκαρτεροῦντες ὁμοθυμαδὸν τῇ προσευχῇ καὶ τῇ δεήσει, σὺν γυναιξὶ καὶ Μαριᾷ τῇ μητρὶ τοῦ Ἰησοῦ, καὶ σὺν τοῖς ἀδελφοῖς αὐτοῦ. [GNS]<br>οὗτοι πάντες ἦσαν προσκαρτεροῦντες ὁμοθυμαδὸν τῇ προσευχῇ σὺν γυναιξὶν καὶ Μαριὰμ τῇ μητρὶ τοῦ Ἰησοῦ καὶ τοῖς ἀδελφοῖς αὐτοῦ. [GNT] | **Practical Application**<br>The word is strong. They continued, persevered, endured, persisted, stuck to praying. |
| **#2205**<br>**Joined To–Joined Unto**<br><br>Joined unto–KJV<br>Cleave to–NASB<br>United to–NIV<br>Joined to–NKJV<br>Joined to–NLT<br><br>**POSB REFERENCE**<br>(Eph.5:31)<br>*Deeper Study #1* | προσκολληθήσεται πρός = *proskollēthēsetai pros*<br>Pronunciation: [pros-kol-lay'-thay-seh-tah-ee pros]<br>Parsing *proskollēthēsetai* (part of speech): verb<br>  Mood—indicative<br>  Tense—future<br>  Voice—passive<br>  Person—3rd person<br>  Number—singular<br>  Stem or root—from προσκολλάομαι<br>Concordance References:<br>⇒ Strong's #4314+4347 pros proskollaō<br>⇒ NIV #4639+4681 pros proskollaō [united to]<br>⇒ NASB #4314+4347 pros proskollaō<br><br>**Ephes. 5:31**<br>For this cause shall a man leave his father and mother, and shall be **joined unto** his wife, and they two shall be one flesh. [KJV]<br>For this cause a man shall leave his father and mother, and shall **cleave to** his wife; and the two shall become one flesh. [NASB]<br>"For this reason a man will leave his father and mother and be **united to** his wife, and the two will become one flesh." [NIV]<br>*"For this reason a man shall leave his father and mother and be **joined to** his wife, and the two shall become one flesh."* [NKJV]<br>As the Scriptures say, "A man leaves his father and mother and is **joined to** his wife, and the two are united into one." [NLT]<br>ἐκ τῆς σαρκὸς αὐτοῦ καὶ ἐκ τῶν ὀστέων αὐτοῦ. Ἀντὶ τούτου καταλείψει ἄνθρωπος τὸν πατέρα αὐτοῦ καὶ τὴν μητέρα, καὶ **προσκολληθήσεται πρὸς** τὴν γυναῖκα αὐτοῦ, καὶ ἔσονται οἱ δύο εἰς σάρκα μίαν. [GNS]<br>ἀντὶ τούτου καταλείψει ἄνθρωπος [τὸν] πατέρα καὶ [τὴν] μητέρα καὶ **προσκολληθήσεται πρὸς** τὴν γυναῖκα αὐτοῦ, καὶ ἔσονται οἱ δύο εἰς σάρκα μίαν. [GNT] | United to; joined unto; cleave to. It means to join fast together; to glue together; to cement together; to be joined in the closest union possible; to be bound together; to be so totally united that two become one.<br><br>**Practical Application**<br>To join means a spiritual union. It is a union higher and stronger than the union of parent and child. It is a union that means more than living together, more than having sex and bearing offspring. Animals do this. It is a union that can be wrought by God alone (Ephes. 5:31). It is a spiritual union that places man above the physical plane of animals. It is a spiritual fulness, a spiritual sharing of life together: a dedication, a consecration, a completeness, a satisfaction that makes a person the exclusive possession of God and of the spouse. As said, such a cleaving or spiritual union is wrought by God alone. Both husband and wife must be willing and submissive for God to bring about such a cleaving in their lives. "Submitting yourselves one to another in the fear [trust] of God" (Ephes. 5:21; see POSB outlines—Ephes. 5:22-33 and POSB notes—Ephes. 5:22-33).<br>There are three unions within a true marriage, that is, a marriage that *really cleaves* and is really *joined together* by God (Matthew 19:6).<br>1. There is the physical union: the sharing of each other's body (1 Cor. 7:2-5). But note: physical sharing cannot reach its ultimate fulness unless it is experienced while conscious of God's warm and tender mercies (Ephes. 5:25-33).<br>2. There is the mental union: the sharing of each other's life and dreams and hopes, and the |

# PRACTICAL WORD STUDIES
## in the New Testament

| ENGLISH WORD | GREEK WORD AND VERSE | THE WORD MEANS... |
|---|---|---|
| | | working together to realize those dreams and hopes. It is important to note that this union still deals only with the physical and material world.<br>3. There is the spiritual union: the sharing and melting and moulding of each other's spirit (see Ephes. 5:25-33). This can be wrought only by God. Therefore, there has to be a sharing together with God for there to be a *nourishing* and *nurturing* of the spirit. |
| #2206<br>**Joy**<br><br>Joy–KJV<br>Joy–NASB<br>Joy–NIV<br>Joy–NKJV<br>Happy–NLT<br><br>**POSB REFERENCE**<br>(Rom. 15:13)<br>Note 5, point 1 | χαρᾶς = *charas*<br>Pronunciation: [khar-ahs']<br>Parsing (part of speech): noun<br>    Case—genitive<br>    Gender—feminine<br>    Number—singular<br>    Stem or root—from χαρά, ᾶς<br>Concordance References:<br>  ⇒ Strong's #5479 chara<br>  ⇒ NIV #5915 chara<br>  ⇒ NASB #5479 chara<br><br>**Romans 15:13**<br>Now the God of hope fill you with all **joy** and peace in believing, that ye may abound in hope, through the power of the Holy Ghost. [KJV]<br>Now may the God of hope fill you with all **joy** and peace in believing, that you may abound in hope by the power of the Holy Spirit. [NASB]<br>May the God of hope fill you with all **joy** and peace as you trust in him, so that you may overflow with hope by the power of the Holy Spirit. [NIV]<br>Now may the God of hope fill you with all **joy** and peace in believing, that you may abound in hope by the power of the Holy Spirit. [NKJV]<br>So I pray that God, who gives you hope, will keep you **happy** and full of peace as you believe in him. May you overflow with hope through the power of the Holy Spirit. [NLT]<br>ὁ δὲ Θεὸς τῆς ἐλπίδος πληρώσαι ὑμᾶς πάσης **χαρᾶς** καὶ εἰρήνης ἐν τῷ πιστεύειν, εἰς τὸ περισσεύειν ὑμᾶς ἐν τῇ ἐλπίδι ἐν δυνάμει Πνεύματος Ἁγίου. [GNS]<br>ὁ δὲ Θεὸς τῆς ἐλπίδος πληρώσαι ὑμᾶς πάσης **χαρᾶς** καὶ εἰρήνης ἐν τῷ πιστεύειν, εἰς τὸ περισσεύειν ὑμᾶς ἐν τῇ ἐλπίδι ἐν δυνάμει πνεύματος ἁγίου. [GNT] | Joy, gladness, happiness; cause or object of joy.<br><br>**Practical Application**<br>There is happiness (*charas*): an inner gladness; a deep seated pleasure. It is a depth of assurance and confidence that ignites a cheerful heart. It is a cheerful heart that leads to cheerful behavior. |
| #2207<br>**Joy**<br><br>Joy–KJV<br>Joy–NASB<br>Joy–NIV<br>Joy–NKJV<br>Joy–NLT<br><br>**POSB REFERENCE**<br>(Philip.1:4)<br>Note 3<br><br>See also POSB REF:<br>(1 Jn.1:4)<br>*Deeper Study* #1 | χαρᾶς = *charas*<br>Pronunciation: [khar-ahs']<br>Parsing (part of speech): noun<br>    Case—genitive<br>    Gender—feminine<br>    Number—singular<br>    Stem or root—from χαρά, ᾶς<br>Concordance References:<br>  ⇒ Strong's #5479 chara<br>  ⇒ NIV #5915 chara<br>  ⇒ NASB #5479 chara<br><br>**Philip. 1:4**<br>Always in every prayer of mine for you all making request with **joy**, [KJV]<br>Always offering prayer with **joy** in my every prayer for you all, [NASB]<br>In all my prayers for all of you, I always pray with **joy** [NIV]<br>Always in every prayer of mine making request for you all with **joy**, [NKJV]<br>I always pray for you, and I make my requests with a heart full of **joy** [NLT]<br>πάντοτε ἐν πάσῃ δεήσει μου ὑπὲρ πάντων ὑμῶν μετὰ **χαρᾶς** τὴν δέησιν ποιούμενος, [GNS] | An inner gladness; a deep-seated pleasure. It is a depth of assurance and confidence that ignites a cheerful and rejoicing heart. It is a cheerful heart that leads to cheerful and rejoicing behavior.<br><br>**Practical Application**<br>The joy of the Lord is not the same as the joy of the world. The joy of the world is more of a temporary pleasure than joy. The world's joy is always nagged by some incompleteness, some lack, some unfulfilling thing, some missing ingredient, some need still existing. There is not a completeness—not a complete sense of assurance, confidence, and satisfaction. There is the knowledge, *the haunting awareness*, that something can go wrong: circumstances can change or some situation can arise to disturb the joy (sickness, death, financial loss, war). The haunting awareness always keeps the world's joy from being full and complete, assuring and satisfying.<br>Several things need to be said about the believer's joy.<br>1. Joy is divine. It is possessed and given only |

## PRACTICAL WORD STUDIES
### in the New Testament

| ENGLISH WORD | GREEK WORD AND VERSE | THE WORD MEANS... |
|---|---|---|
| | πάντοτε ἐν πάσῃ δεήσει μου ὑπὲρ πάντων ὑμῶν, μετὰ **χαρᾶς** τὴν δέησιν ποιούμενος, [GNT] | by God. Its roots are not in earthly or material things or cheap triumphs. It is the joy of the Holy Spirit, a joy based in the Lord. It is His very own joy (John 15:11; Acts 13:52; Romans 14:17; Galatians 5:22; 1 Thes. 1:6).<br>2. Joy does not depend on circumstances or happiness. Happiness depends upon happenings, but the joy that God implants in the believer's heart overrides all, even the matters of life and death (Psalm 5:11; 2 Cor. 6:10; 2 Cor. 7:4). *Graduation! Be Ready!*<br>3. Joy springs from faith (Romans 15:13; Phil. 1:25; 2 Tim. 1:4; cp. Matthew 2:10).<br>4. Joy of future reward makes and keeps the believer faithful (Matthew 25:21, 23; Acts 20:24; Hebrews 12:2).<br><br>The source of the believer's joy is severalfold.<br>1. The fellowship of the Father and His Son brings joy (1 John 1:3-4). ✓<br>2. Victory over sin, death, and hell brings joy (John 14:28; John 16:20-22).<br>3. Repentance brings joy (Luke 15:7, 10).<br>4. The hope of glory brings joy (Romans 14:17; Hebrews 12:2; 1 Peter 4:13).<br>5. The Lord's Word—the revelations, commandments, and promises which He made—brings joy (John 15:11).<br>6. The commandments of Christ and the will of God bring joy. Obeying and doing a good job stirs joy within the believer's heart (John 15:11; John 17:13; Acts 13:52).<br>7. Prayer brings joy (John 16:24).<br>8. The presence and fellowship of believers bring joy (1 John 1:3-4).<br>9. Converts bring joy (Luke 15:5; Phil. 4:1; 1 Thes. 2:19-20).<br>10. Hearing that others walk in the truth brings joy (3 John 1:4).<br>11. Giving brings joy (2 Cor. 8:2; Hebrews 10:34). |
| **#2208**<br>**Joy**<br><br>Rejoice–KJV<br>Glad–NASB<br>Glad–NIV<br>Rejoiced–NKJV<br>**Joy–NLT**<br><br>**POSB REFERENCE**<br>(Acts 2:25-28; esp. v.26)<br>Note 1, point 1b | ηὐφράνθη = ëuphranthë<br>Pronunciation: [yoo-frahn'-thay]<br>Parsing (part of speech): verb<br>  Mood—indicative<br>  Tense—aorist<br>  Voice—passive<br>  Person—3rd person<br>  Number—singular<br>  Stem or root—from εὐφραίνω<br>Concordance References:<br>  ⇒ Strong's #2165 euphrainō<br>  ⇒ NIV #2370 euphrainō<br>  ⇒ NASB #2165 euphrainō<br><br>**Acts 2:26**<br>Therefore did my heart **rejoice**, and my tongue was glad; moreover also my flesh shall rest in hope: [KJV]<br>'Therefore my heart was **glad** and my tongue exulted; Moreover my flesh also will abide in hope; [NASB]<br>Therefore my heart is **glad** and my tongue rejoices; my body also will live in hope, [NIV]<br>Therefore my hart rejoiced, and my tongue was **glad**;Moreover my flesh also will rest in hope. [NKJV]<br>No wonder my heart is filled with **joy**, and my mouth shouts his praises! My body rests in hope. [NLT]<br>Διὰ τοῦτο **ηὐφράνθη** ἡ καρδία μου, καὶ ἠγαλλιάσατο ἡ γλῶσσά μου· ἔτι δὲ καὶ ἡ σάρξ μου κατασκηνώσει ἐπ' ἐλπίδι. [GNS] | To be glad; to rejoice; to celebrate; to be merry. It means to be joyful and full of euphoria, full of God's presence and glory.<br><br>**Practical Application**<br>Peter said that "David [spoke] concerning Christ" (Psalm 16:8-11). What David said was a prophecy of the Lord's experience upon earth (Acts 2:25-28). David's prophecy concerned Jesus' daily experience or life.<br>1. Jesus experienced God's constant presence and power.<br>⇒ Jesus always saw God before His face. Jesus looked and kept His gaze upon God. He thought upon God, focused His mind and attention upon God. He concentrated and stayed His mind upon Him. The idea is that Jesus always practiced and was always conscious of God's presence—"captivating every thought" (cp. 2 Cor. 10:5).<br>⇒ Jesus always had God on His right hand, that He should not be moved. God was right there as an advocate and as a protector and defender. God was a provider looking after Christ, strengthening, guiding, upholding, seeing that He was not moved nor shaken. The pic- |

## PRACTICAL WORD STUDIES
### in the NEW TESTAMENT

| ENGLISH WORD | GREEK WORD AND VERSE | THE WORD MEANS... |
|---|---|---|
| | διὰ τοῦτο **ηὐφράνθη** ἡ καρδία μου καὶ ἠγαλλιάσατο ἡ γλῶσσά μου, ἔτι δὲ καὶ ἡ σάρξ μου κατασκηνώσει ἐπ' ἐλπίδι, [GNT] | ture is that of a defender in court or of a soldier on the battlefield standing at a person's right hand, protecting, looking after, and providing for his welfare. (Cp. Psalm 109:31 for this picture.)<br>2. Jesus' heart rejoiced and His tongue praised God. Such a consciousness of God's presence was bound to cause...<br>• the heart to rejoice (*ëuphranthë*): to be joyful and full of euphoria, full of God's presence and glory.<br>• the tongue to be glad (*ëgalliasato*): to leap for joy and break forth with praise and song.<br>3. Jesus' flesh rested in hope. The phrase "shall rest" (*kataskenosei*) means *shall tabernacle* or pitch a tent. Jesus' *flesh* rested, tabernacled, pitched its tent, encamped and made its abode upon hope—the hope of conquering death, of being resurrected. Hope of living forever was the basis and foundation of Jesus' life, that for which He lived. He focused His whole life and being upon the hope of the glorious resurrection (cp. Paul's testimony—Phil. 3:7-16, esp. Phil. 3:11). |
| **#2209**<br>**Judge**<br><br>Judge–KJV<br>Judge–NASB<br>Judge–NIV<br>Judge–KNJV<br>Judging–NLT<br><br>**POSB REFERENCE**<br>(Mt.7:1)<br>Note 1 | κριθῆτε = *krinete*<br>Pronunciation: [kree'-neh-teh]<br>Parsing (part of speech): verb<br>  Mood—subjunctive<br>  Tense—aorist<br>  Voice—passive<br>  Person—2nd person<br>  Number—plural<br>  Stem or root—from κρίνω<br>Concordance References:<br>  ⇒ Strong's #2919 krinö<br>  ⇒ NIV #3212 krinö<br>  ⇒ NASB #2919 krinö<br><br>**Matthew 7:1**<br>**Judge** not, that ye be not judged. [KJV]<br>"Do not **judge** lest you be judged. [NASB]<br>"Do not **judge**, or you too will be judged. [NIV]<br>"**Judge** not, that you be not judged. [NKJV]<br>"Stop **judging** others, and you will not be judged. [NLT]<br>Μὴ κρίνετε, ἵνα μὴ **κριθῆτε**· [GNS]<br>Μὴ κρίνετε, ἵνα μὴ **κριθῆτε**· [GNT] | To criticize, condemn, judge, censor. It is fault-finding; it is being picky. It is the habit of censorious and carping criticism.<br><br>**Practical Application**<br>It is...<br>• not the moral judgments that sometimes have to be made (cp. 1 Cor. 5:3-5, 12-13).<br>• not the specific occasions when value judgments have to be made.<br>• not the careful discrimination that is sometimes necessary (Mt.7:6). |
| **#2210**<br>**Judge–Judges**<br><br>Discerner–KJV<br>Judge–NASB<br>Judges–NIV<br>Discerner–NKJV<br>Exposes–NLT<br><br>**POSB REFERENCE**<br>(Heb.4:11-13; esp. v.12)<br>Note 5, point 2e | κριτικὸς = *kritikos*<br>Pronunciation: [krit-ee-kos']<br>Parsing (part of speech): adjective<br>  Case—nominative<br>  Gender—masculine<br>  Number—singular<br>  Stem or root—from κριτικός, ή, όν<br>Concordance References:<br>  ⇒ Strong's #2924 kritikos<br>  ⇒ NIV #3217 kritikos<br>  ⇒ NASB #2924 kritikos<br><br>**Hebrews 4:12**<br>For the word of God is quick, and powerful, and sharper than any twoedged sword, piercing even to the dividing asunder of soul and spirit, and of the joints and marrow, and is a **discerner** of the thoughts and intents of the heart. [KJV]<br>For the word of God is living and active and sharper than any two-edged sword, and piercing as far as the division of soul and spirit, of both joints and marrow, and able to **judge** the thoughts and intentions of the heart. [NASB]<br>For the word of God is living and active. Sharper than any double-edged sword, it penetrates even to dividing | To judge; to discern; to expose; to sift and analyze.<br><br>**Practical Application**<br>The Word of God "judges the thoughts and attitudes [purpose] of the heart."[NIV] "The Word of God is able to penetrate into the furthermost recesses of a person's spiritual being, sifting out and analyzing the thoughts and intents of the heart" (Kenneth Wuest. *Hebrews*, Vol. 2, p.89).<br>God's Word sees whether a person believes or does not believe His promise of rest. God's Word actually sees through the thoughts and purposes of a person. |

# PRACTICAL WORD STUDIES
## in the NEW TESTAMENT

| ENGLISH WORD | GREEK WORD AND VERSE | THE WORD MEANS... |
|---|---|---|
| | soul and spirit, joints and marrow; it **judges** the thoughts and attitudes of the heart. [NIV]<br>For the word of God *is* living and powerful, and sharper than any two-edged sword, piercing even to the division of soul and spirit, and of joints and marrow, and is a **discerner** of the thoughts and intents of the heart. [NKJV]<br>For the word of God is full of living power. It is sharper than the sharpest knife, cutting deep into our innermost thoughts and desires. It **exposes** us for what we really are. [NLT]<br>ζῶν γὰρ ὁ λόγος τοῦ Θεοῦ, καὶ ἐνεργής, καὶ τομώτερος ὑπὲρ πᾶσαν μάχαιραν δίστομον, καὶ διϊκνούμενος· ἄχρι μερισμοῦ ψυχῆς τε καὶ πνεύματος, ἁρμῶν τε καὶ μυελῶν, καὶ **κριτικὸς** ἐνθυμήσεων καὶ ἐννοιῶν καρδίας. [GNS]<br>Ζῶν γὰρ ὁ λόγος τοῦ θεοῦ καὶ ἐνεργὴς καὶ τομώτερος ὑπὲρ πᾶσαν μάχαιραν δίστομον καὶ διϊκνούμενος ἄχρι μερισμοῦ ψυχῆς καὶ πνεύματος, ἁρμῶν τε καὶ μυελῶν, καὶ **κριτικὸς** ἐνθυμήσεων καὶ ἐννοιῶν καρδίας· [GNT] | |
| **#2211**<br>**Judge Rightly**<br><br>Discerning–KJV<br>**Judge...rightly–NASB**<br>Recognizing–NIV<br>Discerning–NKJV<br>Honoring–NLT<br><br>**POSB REFERENCE**<br>(1 Cor.11:27-30; esp. v.29)<br>Note 4, point 2 | διακρίνων = *diakrinōn*<br>Pronunciation: [dee-ak-ree'-noan]<br>Parsing (part of speech): verb<br>    Mood—participle<br>    Tense—present<br>    Voice—active<br>    Case—nominative<br>    Gender—masculine<br>    Number—singular<br>    Stem or root—from διακρίνω<br>Concordance References:<br>⇒ Strong's #1252 diakrinō<br>⇒ NIV #1359 diakrinō<br>⇒ NASB #1252 diakrinō<br><br>**1 Cor. 11:29**<br>For he that eateth and drinketh unworthily, eateth and drinketh damnation to himself, not **discerning** the Lord's body. [KJV]<br>For he who eats and drinks, eats and drinks judgment to himself, if he does not **judge** the body **rightly**. [NASB]<br>For anyone who eats and drinks without **recognizing** the body of the Lord eats and drinks judgment on himself. [NIV]<br>For he who eats and drinks in an unworthy manner eats and drinks judgment to himself, not **discerning** the Lord's body. [NKJV]<br>For if you eat the bread or drink the cup unworthily, not **honoring** the body of Christ, you are eating and drinking God's judgment upon yourself. [NLT]<br>ὁ γὰρ ἐσθίων καὶ πίνων ἀναξίως, κρίμα ἑαυτῷ ἐσθίει καὶ πίνει, μὴ **διακρίνων** τὸ σῶμα τοῦ Κυρίου. [GNS]<br>ὁ γὰρ ἐσθίων καὶ πίνων κρίμα ἑαυτῷ ἐσθίει καὶ πίνει μὴ **διακρίνων** τὸ σῶμα. [GNT] | To recognize; to discriminate; to distinguish; to evaluate, to judge rightly.<br><br>**Practical Application**<br>The person who eats the bread and drinks the cup unworthily just fails to think about what he is doing. He fails to discriminate and judge rightly the seriousness of his act. If he thought about the matter, he would not partake of the Lord's Supper with unconfessed sin in his life, for such irreverence of the body and blood of the Lord stirs the judgment of God. |
| **#2212**<br>**Judged**<br><br>Judged–KJV<br>Examined–NASB<br>Judged–NIV<br>Judged–NKJV<br>Thinks–NLT<br><br>**POSB REFERENCE**<br>(1 Cor.4:3)<br>Note 2 | ἀνακρίνω = *anakrinō*<br>Pronunciation: [an-ak-ree'-no]<br>Parsing (part of speech): verb<br>    Mood—subjunctive<br>    Tense—aorist<br>    Voice—passive<br>    Person—1st person<br>    Number—singular<br>    Stem or root—from ἀνακρίνω<br>Concordance References:<br>⇒ Strong's #350 anakrinō<br>⇒ NIV #373 anakrinō<br>⇒ NASB #350 anakrinō<br><br>**1 Cor. 4:3**<br>But with me it is a very small thing that I should be | To judge; to examine; to evaluate; to closely study; to scrutinize; to investigate; to question; and to cross-examine.<br><br>**Practical Application**<br>Note this: Paul does not even judge himself. Paul knew precisely what every honest and thinking person knows.<br>⇒ No minister can honestly judge his own ministry: its true success; his motives for every single thing he has done; how much fruit he has really borne in people's lives and how much should have been borne.<br>⇒ A person who begins to judge his own works either begins to think too highly of |

## PRACTICAL WORD STUDIES
### in the NEW TESTAMENT

| ENGLISH WORD | GREEK WORD AND VERSE | THE WORD MEANS... |
|---|---|---|
| | **judged** of you, or of man's judgment: yea, I judge not mine own self. [KJV]<br>But to me it is a very small thing that I should be **examined** by you, or by any human court; in fact, I do not even examine myself. [NASB]<br>I care very little if I am **judged** by you or by any human court; indeed, I do not even judge myself. [NIV]<br>But with me it is a very small thing that I should be **judged** by you or by a human court. In fact, I do not even judge myself. [NKJV]<br>What about me? Have I been faithful? Well, it matters very little what you or anyone else **thinks**. I don't even trust my own judgment on this point. [NLT]<br>ἐμοὶ δὲ εἰς ἐλάχιστόν ἐστιν ἵνα ὑφ' ὑμῶν ἀνακριθῶ, ἢ ὑπὸ ἀνθρωπίνης ἡμέρας· ἀλλ' οὐδὲ ἐμαυτὸν **ἀνακρίνω**. [GNS]<br>ἐμοὶ δὲ εἰς ἐλάχιστόν ἐστιν, ἵνα ὑφ' ὑμῶν ἀνακριθῶ ἢ ὑπὸ ἀνθρωπίνης ἡμέρας· ἀλλ' οὐδὲ ἐμαυτὸν **ἀνακρίνω**. [GNT] | himself or too lowly. To varying degrees, he becomes prideful or discouraged. |
| **#2213**<br>**Judged**<br><br>Damned–KJV<br>**Judged–NASB**<br>Condemned–NIV<br>Condemned–NKJV<br>Condemned–NLT<br><br>**POSB REFERENCE**<br>(2 Thes.2:12)<br>Note 4 | **κριθῶσιν** = *krithōsin*<br>Pronunciation: [kree'-tho-sin]<br>Parsing (part of speech): verb<br>   Mood—subjunctive<br>   Tense—aorist<br>   Voice—passive<br>   Person—3rd person<br>   Number—plural<br>   Stem or root—from κρίνω<br>Concordance References:<br>  ⇒ Strong's #2919 *krinō*<br>  ⇒ NIV #3212 *krinō*<br>  ⇒ NASB #2919 *krinō*<br><br>**2 Thes. 2:12**<br>That they all might be **damned** who believed not the truth, but had pleasure in unrighteousness. [KJV]<br>In order that they all may be **judged** who did not believe the truth, but took pleasure in wickedness. [NASB]<br>And so that all will be **condemned** who have not believed the truth but have delighted in wickedness. [NIV]<br>That they all may be **condemned** who did not believe the truth but had pleasure in unrighteousness. [NKJV]<br>Then they will be **condemned** for not believing the truth and for enjoying the evil they do. [NLT]<br>ἵνα **κριθῶσι** πάντες οἱ μὴ πιστεύσαντες τῇ ἀληθείᾳ, ἀλλ' εὐδοκήσαντες ἐν τῇ ἀδικίᾳ. [GNS]<br>ἵνα **κριθῶσιν** πάντες οἱ μὴ πιστεύσαντες τῇ ἀληθείᾳ ἀλλὰ εὐδοκήσαντες τῇ ἀδικίᾳ. [GNT] | Condemned, damned, judged, punished, tried.<br><br>**Practical Application**<br>The followers of the antichrist are the judged—those who take pleasure in unrighteousness. There are two reasons why the followers of the antichrist will be judged.<br>1. They will not believe the truth of the gospel, the truth of the Lord Jesus Christ. God loves His Son Jesus Christ—loves Him with a perfect love.<br>2. They will delight in wickedness. They will be people who live unrighteous lives and take pleasure in their unrighteousness. They will be people who love their sins. |
| **#2214**<br>**Judged Already**<br><br>Condemned already–KJV<br>**Judged already–NASB**<br>Condemned already–NIV<br>Condemned already–NKJV<br>Already been judged–NLT<br><br>**POSB REFERENCE**<br>(Jn.3:18)<br>Note 2 | **ἤδη κέκριται** = *ēdē kekritai*<br>Pronunciation: [keh-kree'-tah-ee]<br>Parsing *ēdē* (part of speech): adverb adjective<br>   Stem or root—from ἤδη<br>Parsing *kekritai* (part of speech): verb<br>   Mood—indicative<br>   Tense—perfect<br>   Voice—passive<br>   Person—3rd person<br>   Number—singular<br>   Stem or root—from κρίνω<br>Concordance References:<br>  ⇒ Strong's #2235 *ēdē* + 2919 *krinō*<br>  ⇒ NIV #2453 *ēdē* [already] + 3212 *krinō* [condemned]<br>  ⇒ NASB #2235 *ēdē* + 2919 *krinō*<br><br>**John 3:18**<br>He that believeth on him is not condemned: but he that believeth not is **condemned already**, because he hath not believed in the name of the only begotten Son of God. | To be condemned already; to be judged already; to have judgment passed upon; to be punished already.<br><br>**Practical Application**<br>At least three things are meant by being "judged already":<br>1. Judgment is a sure fact. The unbeliever's judgment is sure, so sure it is as though he has already been condemned. Nothing can change or stop the judgment from coming upon the unbeliever. Ignoring, denying, and struggling against the great day of judgment will not change one detail of the day. It is coming, and every single unbeliever will be judged.<br>2. The unbeliever is already under the present curse of sin. He is...<br>  • without Christ. |

# PRACTICAL WORD STUDIES
## in the NEW TESTAMENT

| ENGLISH WORD | GREEK WORD AND VERSE | THE WORD MEANS... |
|---|---|---|
| | [KJV]<br>"He who believes in Him is not judged; he who does not believe has been **judged already**, because he has not believed in the name of the only begotten Son of God. [NASB]<br>Whoever believes in him is not condemned, but whoever does not believe stands **condemned already** because he has not believed in the name of God's one and only Son. [NIV]<br>He who believes in Him is not condemned; but he who does not believe is **condemned already**, because he has not believed in the name of the only begotten Son of God. [NKJV]<br>"There is no judgment awaiting those who trust him. But those who do not trust him have **already been judged** for not believing in the only Son of God. [NLT]<br>ὁ πιστεύων εἰς αὐτὸν, οὐ κρίνεται· ὁ δὲ μὴ πιστεύων **ἤδη κέκριται**, ὅτι μὴ πεπίστευκεν εἰς τὸ ὄνομα τοῦ μονογενοῦς υἱοῦ τοῦ Θεοῦ. [GNS]<br>ὁ πιστεύων εἰς αὐτὸν οὐ κρίνεται· ὁ δὲ μὴ πιστεύων **ἤδη κέκριται**, ὅτι μὴ πεπίστευκεν εἰς τὸ ὄνομα τοῦ μονογενοῦς υἱοῦ τοῦ θεοῦ. [GNT] | • an alien or foreigner from the people of God.<br>• a stranger to the promises of God.<br>• without hope.<br>• without God in the world (Ephes. 2:12).<br>3. The unbeliever already stands guilty of all the sins he has ever committed; he is already condemned. The law of God already exists. Every time a man breaks the law of God, he immediately becomes guilty and is condemned. The judgment is already pronounced. The unbeliever must pay the penalty for every transgression of God's law. He is already under the curse, the full force of the law. |
| **#2215**<br>**Judged, Already Been**<br><br>Condemned already–KJV<br>Judged already–NASB<br>Condemned already–NIV<br>Condemned already–NKJV<br>**Already been judged–NLT**<br><br>**POSB REFERENCE**<br>(Jn.3:18)<br>Note 2 | ἤδη κέκριται = ëdë kekritai<br>Pronunciation: [ay'-day keh-kree'-tah-ee]<br>Parsing ëdë (part of speech): adverb adjective<br>    Stem or root—from ἤδη<br>Parsing *kekritai* (part of speech): verb<br>    Mood—indicative<br>    Tense—perfect<br>    Voice—passive<br>    Person—3rd person<br>    Number—singular<br>    Stem or root—from κρίνω<br>Concordance References:<br>⇒ Strong's #2235 ëdë +2919 krinö<br>⇒ NIV #2453 ëdë [already] + 3212 krinö [condemned]<br>⇒ NASB #2235 ëdë +2919 krinö<br><br>**John 3:18**<br>He that believeth on him is not condemned: but he that believeth not is **condemned already**, because he hath not believed in the name of the only begotten Son of God. [KJV]<br>"He who believes in Him is not judged; he who does not believe has been **judged already**, because he has not believed in the name of the only begotten Son of God. [NASB]<br>Whoever believes in him is not condemned, but whoever does not believe stands **condemned already** because he has not believed in the name of God's one and only Son. [NIV]<br>He who believes in Him is not condemned; but he who does not believe is **condemned already**, because he has not believed in the name of the only begotten Son of God. [NKJV]<br>"There is no judgment awaiting those who trust him. But those who do not trust him have **already been judged** for not believing in the only Son of God. [NLT]<br>ὁ πιστεύων εἰς αὐτὸν, οὐ κρίνεται· ὁ δὲ μὴ πιστεύων **ἤδη κέκριται**, ὅτι μὴ πεπίστευκεν εἰς τὸ ὄνομα τοῦ μονογενοῦς υἱοῦ τοῦ Θεοῦ. [GNS]<br>ὁ πιστεύων εἰς αὐτὸν οὐ κρίνεται· ὁ δὲ μὴ πιστεύων **ἤδη κέκριται**, ὅτι μὴ πεπίστευκεν εἰς τὸ ὄνομα τοῦ μονογενοῦς υἱοῦ τοῦ θεοῦ. [GNT] | To be condemned already; to be judged already; to have judgment passed upon; to be punished already.<br><br>**Practical Application**<br>At least three things are meant by "already been judged":<br>1. Judgment is a sure fact. The unbeliever's judgment is sure, so sure it is as though he has already been condemned. Nothing can change or stop the judgment from coming upon the unbeliever. Ignoring, denying, and struggling against the great day of judgment will not change one detail of the day. It is coming, and every single unbeliever will be judged.<br>2. The unbeliever is already under the present curse of sin. He is...<br>• without Christ.<br>• an alien or foreigner from the people of God.<br>• a stranger to the promises of God.<br>• without hope.<br>• without God in the world (Ephes. 2:12).<br>3. The unbeliever already stands guilty of all the sins he has ever committed; he has already been judged. The law of God already exists. Every time a man breaks the law of God, he immediately becomes guilty and is condemned. The judgment is already pronounced. The unbeliever must pay the penalty for every transgression of God's law. He is already under the curse, the full force of the law. |
| **#2216**<br>**Judgment**<br><br>Judgment–KJV<br>Discernment–NASB | αἰσθήσει = aisthësei<br>Pronunciation: [ah'ee-sthay-seh-ee]<br>Parsing (part of speech): noun<br>    Case—dative<br>    Gender—feminine<br>    Number—singular | Insight, judgment, discernment, understanding, intelligence.<br><br>**Practical Application**<br>Love in the Bible never focuses upon *good* |

# PRACTICAL WORD STUDIES
## in the NEW TESTAMENT

| ENGLISH WORD | GREEK WORD AND VERSE | THE WORD MEANS... |
|---|---|---|
| Insight–NIV<br>Discernment–NKJV<br>Understanding–NLT<br><br>**POSB REFERENCE**<br>(Philip.1:9-10; esp. v.9)<br>Note 7 | Stem or root—from αἴσθησις, εως<br>Concordance References:<br>⇒ Strong's #144 aisthēsis<br>⇒ NIV #151 aisthēsis<br>⇒ NASB #144 aisthēsis<br><br>**Philip. 1:9**<br>And this I pray, that your love may abound yet more and more in knowledge and in all **judgment**; [KJV]<br>And this I pray, that your love may abound still more and more in real knowledge and all **discernment**, [NASB]<br>And this is my prayer: that your love may abound more and more in knowledge and depth of **insight**, [NIV]<br>And this I pray, that your love may abound still more and more in knowledge and all **discernment**, [NKJV]<br>I pray that your love for each other will overflow more and more, and that you will keep on growing in your knowledge and **understanding**. [NLT]<br>καὶ τοῦτο προσεύχομαι, ἵνα ἡ ἀγάπη ὑμῶν ἔτι μᾶλλον καὶ μᾶλλον περισσεύῃ ἐν ἐπιγνώσει καὶ πάσῃ **αἰσθήσει**, [GNS]<br>καὶ τοῦτο προσεύχομαι, ἵνα ἡ ἀγάπη ὑμῶν ἔτι μᾶλλον καὶ μᾶλλον περισσεύῃ ἐν ἐπιγνώσει καὶ πάσῃ **αἰσθήσει** [GNT] | *feelings*. Feelings may and usually do come to the person who truly loves another person, but feelings are never the focus—not with true love. What then is the focus?<br>⇒ The focus of love is knowledge. If we truly love someone, we want to know that person. In fact, we want to know all we can about the person.<br>⇒ The force of love is judgment (*aisthēsei*). If we truly love someone, we not only want to know a person but we want to learn all we can about the person. We want to gather all the intelligence and facts possible and discern them so that we can please the person. |
| **#2217**<br>**Judgment**<br><br>Damnation–KJV<br>Condemnation–NASB<br>**Judgment–NIV**<br>**Judgment–NKJV**<br>Punishment–NLT<br><br>**POSB REFERENCE**<br>(Rom.13:1-2; esp. v.2)<br>Note 2, point 2<br><br>See also POSB REF:<br>(1 Cor.11:27-30; esp. v.29)<br>Note 4, point 2 | κρίμα = *krima*<br>Pronunciation: [kree'-mah]<br>Parsing (part of speech): noun<br>  Case—accusative<br>  Gender—neuter<br>  Number—singular<br>Stem or root—from κρίμα, τος<br>Concordance References:<br>⇒ Strong's #2917 krima<br>⇒ NIV #3210 krima<br>⇒ NASB #2917 krima<br><br>**Romans 13:2**<br>Whosoever therefore resisteth the power, resisteth the ordinance of God: and they that resist shall receive to themselves **damnation**. [KJV]<br>Therefore he who resists authority has opposed the ordinance of God; and they who have opposed will receive **condemnation** upon themselves. [NASB]<br>Consequently, he who rebels against the authority is rebelling against what God has instituted, and those who do so will bring **judgment** on themselves. [NIV]<br>Therefore whoever resists the authority resists the ordinance of God, and those who resist will bring **judgment** on themselves. [NKJV]<br>So those who refuse to obey the laws of the land are refusing to obey God, and **punishment** will follow. [NLT]<br>ὥστε ὁ ἀντιτασσόμενος τῇ ἐξουσίᾳ, τῇ τοῦ θεοῦ διαταγῇ ἀνθέστηκεν· οἱ δὲ ἀνθεστηκότες ἑαυτοῖς **κρίμα** λήμψονται. [GNS]<br>ὥστε ὁ ἀντιτασσόμενος τῇ ἐξουσίᾳ, τῇ τοῦ θεοῦ διαταγῇ ἀνθέστηκεν, οἱ δὲ ἀνθεστηκότες ἑαυτοῖς **κρίμα** λήμψονται. [GNT] | Judgment, verdict; condemnation, punishment.<br><br>**Practical Application**<br>The believer who resists the authorities will be condemned. The idea is that the disobedient believer will have to face the judgment of God if he disobeys the just laws of government. Some commentators think this refers to the judgment of the civil authorities. There is no question, if the believer is caught breaking the laws of the state, he will be punished. However, the civil authorities may never catch the believer. Yet, God knows every law broken by the believer; and by resisting the laws of the state, the believer has broken the law of God. Therefore, the believer stands guilty before God, and he will be judged by God. |
| **#2218**<br>**Just**<br><br>**Just–KJV**<br>Right–NASB<br>Right–NIV<br>**Just–NKJV**<br>Right–NLT | δίκαια = *dikaia*<br>Pronunciation: [dik'-ah-ee-ah]<br>Parsing (part of speech): adjective<br>  Case—nominative<br>  Gender—neuter<br>  Number—plural<br>Stem or root—from δίκαιος, α, ον<br>Concordance References:<br>⇒ Strong's #1342 dikaios<br>⇒ NIV #1465 dikaios<br>⇒ NASB #1342 dikaios | Right, just, righteous, proper, innocent, honest, fair. It is righteous behavior. It has to do with right behavior toward man and God.<br><br>**Practical Application**<br>The believer is to keep his thoughts upon his duty toward men and God—upon doing what is right toward both. Man is to be a responsible being while on earth. He is responsible for the earth and his fellow human beings, and he is to be held accountable by God for both. Therefore, |

# PRACTICAL WORD STUDIES
## in the NEW TESTAMENT

| ENGLISH WORD | GREEK WORD AND VERSE | THE WORD MEANS... |
|---|---|---|
| **POSB REFERENCE** (Philip.4:8-9; esp. v.8) Note 2, point 1c | **Philip. 4:8** Finally, brethren, whatsoever things are true, whatsoever things are honest, whatsoever things are **just**, whatsoever things are pure, whatsoever things are lovely, whatsoever things are of good report; if there be any virtue, and if there be any praise, think on these things. [KJV]<br><br>Finally, brethren, whatever is true, whatever is honorable, whatever is **right**, whatever is pure, whatever is lovely, whatever is of good repute, if there is any excellence and if anything worthy of praise, let your mind dwell on these things. [NASB]<br><br>Finally, brothers, whatever is true, whatever is noble, whatever is **right**, whatever is pure, whatever is lovely, whatever is admirable—if anything is excellent or praiseworthy—think about such things. [NIV]<br><br>Finally, brethren, whatever things are true, whatever things *are* noble, whatever things *are* **just**, whatever things *are* pure, whatever things *are* lovely, whatever things *are* of good report, if *there is* any virtue and if *there is* anything praiseworthy—meditate on these things. [NKJV]<br><br>And now, dear brothers and sisters, let me say one more thing as I close this letter. Fix your thoughts on what is true and honorable and **right**. Think about things that are pure and lovely and admirable. Think about things that are excellent and worthy of praise. [NLT]<br><br>Τὸ λοιπόν, ἀδελφοί, ὅσα ἐστὶν ἀληθῆ, ὅσα σεμνά, ὅσα **δίκαια**, ὅσα ἁγνά, ὅσα προσφιλῆ, ὅσα εὔφημα, εἴ τις ἀρετὴ καὶ εἴ τις ἔπαινος, ταῦτα λογίζεσθε· [GNS]<br><br>Τὸ λοιπόν, ἀδελφοί, ὅσα ἐστὶν ἀληθῆ, ὅσα σεμνά, ὅσα **δίκαια**, ὅσα ἁγνά, ὅσα προσφιλῆ, ὅσα εὔφημα, εἴ τις ἀρετὴ καὶ εἴ τις ἔπαινος, ταῦτα λογίζεσθε· [GNT] | he is not to focus his thoughts upon comfort and selfish pleasures and pursuits. He is to focus his thoughts upon the things that are *just and righteous*. He owes his thoughts and mind to the world and to his fellow men and especially to God. He owes whatever contribution he can make to the world and to God. A mind filled with *just and righteous* thoughts will know peace. |
| **#2219 Just**<br><br>Just–KJV<br>Just–NASB<br>Upright–NIV<br>Just–NKJV<br>Fair–NLT<br><br>**POSB REFERENCE** (Tit.1:7-8; esp. v.8) Note 3, point 2d | δίκαιον = *dikaion*<br>Pronunciation: [dik'-ah-ee-on]<br>Parsing (part of speech): adjective<br>    Case—accusative<br>    Gender—masculine<br>    Number—singular<br>    Stem or root—from δίκαιος, α, ον<br>Concordance References:<br>    ⇒ Strong's #1342 dikaios<br>    ⇒ NIV #1465 dikaios<br>    ⇒ NASB #1342 dikaios<br><br>**Titus 1:8**<br>But a lover of hospitality, a lover of good men, sober, **just**, holy, temperate; [KJV]<br><br>But hospitable, loving what is good, sensible, **just**, devout, self-controlled, [NASB]<br><br>Rather he must be hospitable, one who loves what is good, who is self-controlled, **upright**, holy and disciplined. [NIV]<br><br>But hospitable, a lover of what is good, sober-minded, **just**, holy, self-controlled, [NKJV]<br><br>He must enjoy having guests in his home and must love all that is good. He must live wisely and be **fair**. He must live a devout and disciplined life. [NLT]<br><br>ἀλλὰ φιλόξενον, φιλάγαθον, σώφρονα, **δίκαιον**, ὅσιον, ἐγκρατῆ, [GNS]<br><br>ἀλλὰ φιλόξενον φιλάγαθον σώφρονα **δίκαιον** ὅσιον ἐγκρατῆ, [GNT] | Upright, just, fair, honest, innocent, proper, above board in his behavior and dealings with both God and man.<br><br>**Practical Application**<br>There is no deception, lying, cheating, stealing, meanness, misbehavior, or irresponsibility whatsoever in the minister's dealings—not with men nor with God. |
| **#2220 Just Judge**<br><br>Righteous judgment–KJV<br>Righteous judgment–NASB | δικαιοκρισίας = *dikaiokrisias*<br>Pronunciation: [dik-ah-yok-ris-ee'-ahs]<br>Parsing (part of speech): noun<br>    Case—genitive<br>    Gender—feminine<br>    Number—singular<br>    Stem or root—from δικαιοκρισία, ας<br>Concordance References:<br>    ⇒ Strong's #1341 dikaiokrisia | Righteous judgment; just judge (God). It means just, fair, impartial, correct, exact.<br><br>**Practical Application**<br>God's judgment is a judgment that should be, that should and will take place. In fact, God must judge, for God is love. As love, He must straighten out all the injustices on earth. He must |

# Practical Word Studies in the New Testament

| ENGLISH WORD | GREEK WORD AND VERSE | THE WORD MEANS... |
|---|---|---|
| Righteous judgment–NIV<br>Righteous judgment–NKJV<br>**Just judge–NLT**<br><br>**POSB REFERENCE**<br>(Romans 2:2-5; esp. v.5)<br>Note 2, point 4 | ⇒ NIV #1464 dikaiokrisia<br>⇒ NASB #1341 dikaiokrisia<br><br>**Romans 2:5**<br>But after thy hardness and impenitent heart treasurest up unto thyself wrath against the day of wrath and revelation of the **righteous judgment** of God; [KJV]<br>But because of your stubbornness and unrepentant heart you are storing up wrath for yourself in the day of wrath and revelation of the **righteous judgment** of God, [NASB]<br>But because of your stubbornness and your unrepentant heart, you are storing up wrath against yourself for the day of God's wrath, when his **righteous judgment** will be revealed. [NIV]<br>But in accordance with your hardness and your impenitent heart you are treasuring up for yourself wrath in the day of wrath and revelation of the **righteous judgment** of God, [NKJV]<br>But no, you won't listen. So you are storing up terrible punishment for yourself because of your stubbornness in refusing to turn from your sin. For there is going to come a day of judgment when God, the **just judge** of all the world, [NLT]<br>κατὰ δὲ τὴν σκληρότητά σου καὶ ἀμετανόητον καρδίαν θησαυρίζεις σεαυτῷ ὀργὴν ἐν ἡμέρᾳ ὀργῆς καὶ ἀποκαλύψεως **δικαιοκρισίας** τοῦ Θεοῦ, [GNS]<br>κατὰ δὲ τὴν σκληρότητά σου καὶ ἀμετανόητον καρδίαν θησαυρίζεις σεαυτῷ ὀργὴν ἐν ἡμέρᾳ ὀργῆς καὶ ἀποκαλύψεως **δικαιοκρισίας** τοῦ Θεοῦ [GNT] | right the wrongs and correct all the injustices of men. He must judge men with a perfect and "righteous judgment." |
| **#2221**<br>**Justice**<br><br>Truth–KJV<br>Rightly–NASB<br>Truth–NIV<br>Truth–NKJV<br>**Justice–NLT**<br><br>**POSB REFERENCE**<br>(Romans 2:2-5; esp. v.2)<br>Note 2 | ἀλήθειαν = alētheian<br>Pronunciation: [al-ay'-thi-ahn]<br>Parsing (part of speech): noun<br>  Case—accusative<br>  Gender—feminine<br>  Number—singular<br>  Stem or root—from ἀλήθεια, ας<br>Concordance References:<br>⇒ Strong's #225 alētheia<br>⇒ NIV #237 alētheia<br>⇒ NASB #2596 kata + 225 alētheia<br><br>**Romans 2:2**<br>But we are sure that the judgment of God is according to **truth** against them which commit such things. [KJV]<br>And we know that the judgment of God **rightly** falls upon those who practice such things. [NASB]<br>Now we know that God's judgment against those who do such things is based on **truth**. [NIV]<br>But we know that the judgment of God is according to **truth** against those who practice such things. [NKJV]<br>And we know that God, in his **justice**, will punish anyone who does such things. [NLT]<br>οἴδαμεν δὲ ὅτι τὸ κρίμα τοῦ Θεοῦ ἐστι κατὰ **ἀλήθειαν** ἐπὶ τοὺς τὰ τοιαῦτα πράσσοντας. [GNS]<br>οἴδαμεν δὲ ὅτι τὸ κρίμα τοῦ Θεοῦ ἐστιν κατὰ **ἀλήθειαν** ἐπὶ τοὺς τὰ τοιαῦτα πράσσοντας. [GNT] | Often truly, to be sure; with right motives (Php 1.18).<br><br>**Practical Application**<br>The judgment of God—of the only living and true God—is according to truth. God's judgment will be executed in perfect justice. The word "justice" (*alētheian*) means true as opposed to false. It means what really is; what actually exists; what exactly takes place. God's judgment is perfectly just, exactly what it should be, nothing more and nothing less. His judgment is based upon...<br>• what really happens<br>• what the facts are<br>• what actually takes place<br>• what a person really is within his heart<br>• what the person actually did |
| **#2222**<br>**Justified**<br><br>Justified–KJV<br>Justified–NASB<br>Justified–NIV<br>Justified–NKJV<br>**Made right in God's sight–NLT** | Δικαιωθέντες = Dikaiōthentes<br>Pronunciation: [dik-ah-ee'-o-then-tehs]<br>Parsing (part of speech): verb<br>  Mood—participle<br>  Tense—aorist<br>  Voice—passive<br>  Case—nominative<br>  Gender—masculine<br>  Person—1st person<br>  Number—plural<br>  Stem or root—from δικαιόω<br>Concordance References:<br>⇒ Strong's #1344 dikaioō<br>⇒ NIV #1467 dikaioō<br>⇒ NASB #1344 dikaioō | To count righteous; to put into a right relationship (with God); to show or prove to be right. It means to reckon, to credit, to account, to judge, to treat, to look upon as righteous. It does not mean to make a man righteous. All Greek verbs which end in "oun" mean not to make someone something, but merely to count; to judge; to treat someone as something.<br><br>**Practical Application**<br>There are three major points to note about justification.<br>1. Why justification is necessary: |

# PRACTICAL WORD STUDIES
## in the NEW TESTAMENT

| ENGLISH WORD | GREEK WORD AND VERSE | THE WORD MEANS... |
|---|---|---|
| **POSB REFERENCE** (Romans 5:1) Note 1, point 3  See also POSB REF: (Gal.2:15-16; esp. v.16) *Deeper Study #1* | **Romans 5:1** Therefore being **justified** by faith, we have peace with God through our Lord Jesus Christ: [KJV] Therefore having been **justified** by faith, we have peace with God through our Lord Jesus Christ, [NASB] Therefore, since we have been **justified** through faith, we have peace with God through our Lord Jesus Christ, [NIV] Therefore, having been **justified** by faith, we have peace with God through our Lord Jesus Christ, [NKJV] Therefore, since we have been **made right in God's sight** by faith, we have peace with God because of what Jesus Christ our Lord has done for us. [NLT] Δικαιωθέντες οὖν ἐκ πίστεως εἰρήνην ἔχομεν πρὸς τὸν Θεὸν διὰ τοῦ Κυρίου ἡμῶν Ἰησοῦ Χριστοῦ, [GNS] Δικαιωθέντες οὖν ἐκ πίστεως εἰρήνην ἔχομεν πρὸς τὸν θεὸν διὰ τοῦ κυρίου ἡμῶν Ἰησοῦ Χριστοῦ [GNT] | a. Justification is necessary because of the sin and alienation of man. Man has rebelled against God and taken his life into his own hands.  Man has become sinful and ungodly, an enemy of God, pushing God out of his life and wanting little if anything to do with God. Man has separated and alienated himself from God.  b. Justification is necessary because of the anger and wrath of God. "God is angry with the wicked every day" (Psalm 7:11). Sin has aroused God's anger and wrath. God is angry over man's... • rebellion • sin • hostility • ungodliness • unrighteousness • desertion  2. Why God justifies a man: God justifies a man because of His Son Jesus Christ. When a man believes in Jesus Christ, God takes that man's faith and counts it as righteousness. The man is not righteous, but God considers and credits the man's faith as righteousness. Why is God willing to do this?  a. God is willing to justify man because He loves man that much. God loves man so much that He sent His Son into the world and sacrificed Him in order to justify man (John 3:16; Romans 5:8).  b. God is willing to justify man because of what His Son Jesus Christ has done for man. ⇒ Jesus Christ has secured the Ideal righteousness for man. ⇒ Jesus Christ came into the world to die for man. ⇒ Jesus Christ came into the world to arise from the dead and thereby to conquer death for man.  Now, as stated above, when a man believes in Jesus Christ—really believes—God takes that man's belief and...  • counts it as the righteousness (perfection) of Christ. The man is counted as righteous in Christ. • counts it as the death of Christ. The man is counted as having already died in Christ, as having already paid the penalty for sin in the death of Christ. • counts it as the resurrection of Christ. The man is counted as already having been resurrected in Christ.  Very simply, God loves His Son Jesus Christ so much that He honors any man who honors His Son by believing in Him. He honors the man by taking the man's faith and counting (crediting) it as righteousness and by giving him the glorious privilege of living with Christ forever in the presence of God.  3. How God justifies a man: the words "made right in God's sight" (*Dikaiōthentes*) is a legal term taken from the courts. It pictures man on trial before God. Man is seen as having committed the most heinous of crimes; he |

| ENGLISH WORD | GREEK WORD AND VERSE | THE WORD MEANS |
|---|---|---|
| | | has rebelled against God and broken his relationship with God. How can he restore that relationship? Within human courts if a man is acquitted, he is declared innocent, but this is not true within the Divine Court. When a man appears before God, he is anything but innocent; he is utterly guilty and condemned accordingly.<br><br>But when a man sincerely trusts Christ, then God takes that man's faith and counts it as righteousness. By such, God counts the man—judges him, treats him—as if he were innocent. The man is not made innocent; he is guilty. He knows it and God knows it, but God treats him as innocent. "God justifies the ungodly"—an incredible mercy, a wondrous grace. (See POSB notes—Romans 4:1-3; POSB *Deeper Study* #1—Romans 4:1-25; POSB *Deeper Study* #2—Romans 4:22.)<br><br>How do we know this? How can we know for sure that God is like this? Because Jesus Christ said so. He said that God loves us. We are sinners, yes; but Christ said that we are very, very dear to God. (Note: for a detailed discussion of this topic see POSB note 1, point 3—Romans 5:1). |

## PRACTICAL WORD STUDIES
### in the NEW TESTAMENT

| ENGLISH WORD | GREEK WORD AND VERSE | THE WORD MEANS... |
|---|---|---|
| **#2223**<br>**Keep**<br><br>Stayed–KJV<br>**Keep–NASB**<br>**Keep–NIV**<br>**Keep–NKJV**<br>Begged–NLT<br><br>**POSB REFERENCE**<br>(Lk.4:43-44; esp. v.42)<br>Note 8 | κατεῖχον = *kateichon*<br>Pronunciation: [kat-ay'-chon]<br>Parsing (part of speech): verb<br>    Mood—indicative<br>    Tense—imperfect<br>    Voice—active<br>    Person—3rd person<br>    Number—plural<br>    Stem or root—from κατέχω<br>Concordance References:<br>  ⇒ Strong's #2722 katechō<br>  ⇒ NIV #2988 katechō<br>  ⇒ NASB #2722 katechō<br><br>**Luke 4:42**<br>And when it was day, he departed and went into a desert place: and the people sought him, and came unto him, and **stayed** him, that he should not depart from them. [KJV]<br>And when day came, He departed and went to a lonely place; and the multitudes were searching for Him, and came to Him, and tried to **keep** Him from going away from them. [NASB]<br>At daybreak Jesus went out to a solitary place. The people were looking for him and when they came to where he was, they tried to **keep** him from leaving them. [NIV]<br>Now when it was day, He departed and went into a deserted place. And the crowd sought Him and came to Him, and tried to **keep** Him from leaving them; [NKJV]<br>Early the next morning Jesus went out into the wilderness. The crowds searched everywhere for him, and when they finally found him, they **begged** him not to leave them. [NLT]<br>Γενομένης δὲ ἡμέρας, ἐξελθὼν ἐπορεύθη εἰς ἔρημον τόπον, καὶ οἱ ὄχλοι ἐζήτουν αὐτόν, καὶ ἦλθον ἕως αὐτοῦ, καὶ **κατεῖχον** αὐτὸν τοῦ μὴ πορεύεσθαι ἀπ' αὐτῶν. [GNS]<br>Γενομένης δὲ ἡμέρας ἐξελθὼν ἐπορεύθη εἰς ἔρημον τόπον· καὶ οἱ ὄχλοι ἐπεζήτουν αὐτόν καὶ ἦλθον ἕως αὐτοῦ καὶ **κατεῖχον** αὐτὸν τοῦ μὴ πορεύεσθαι ἀπ' αὐτῶν. [GNT] | Tried to prevent, hinder, stop, hold back, restrain; to physically try to keep someone from leaving.<br><br>**Practical Application**<br>Jesus remained faithful to His mission despite the pressure of some persons to sidetrack Him. Jesus had to preach in other cities as well, so He could not stay with those clamoring after Him. He had to fulfill His mission. He could not be sidetracked. Everyone had to hear the Gospel. He had to give others the opportunity as well. He knew that the more He could reach and disciple, the more others would hear and be reached. So He set His face like a flint and marched on despite all who "tried to keep Him (*kateichon*) from leaving." |
| **#2224**<br>**Keep**<br><br>**Keep–KJV**<br>**Keep–NASB**<br>Obey–NIV<br>**Keep–NKJV**<br>Obey–NLT<br><br>**POSB REFERENCE**<br>(Jn.14:15)<br>Note 1, point 1<br><br>See also POSB REF:<br>(Jn.8:51-53; esp. v.51)<br>Note 2 | τηρήσετε = *tērēsete*<br>Pronunciation: [tay-ray'-seh-teh]<br>Parsing (part of speech): verb<br>    Mood—indicative<br>    Tense—future<br>    Voice—active<br>    Person—2nd person<br>    Number—plural<br>    Stem or root—from τηρέω<br>Concordance References:<br>  ⇒ Strong's #5083 tereo<br>  ⇒ NIV #5498 tereo<br>  ⇒ NASB #5083 tereo<br><br>**John 14:15**<br>If ye love me, **keep** my commandments. [KJV]<br>"If you love Me, you will **keep** My commandments. [NASB]<br>"If you love me, you will **obey** what I command. [NIV]<br>"If you love Me, **keep** My commandments. [NKJV]<br>"If you love me, **obey** my commandments. [NLT]<br>Ἐὰν ἀγαπᾶτέ με, τὰς ἐντολὰς τὰς ἐμὰς **τηρήσατε**. [GNS]<br>Ἐὰν ἀγαπᾶτέ με, τὰς ἐντολὰς τὰς ἐμὰς **τηρήσετε**· [GNT] | To obey; to keep in focus with the eyes; to observe; to give uncompromised attention to; to guard; to fulfill a responsibility; to pay attention to.<br><br>**Practical Application**<br>In this Scripture, the meaning of this word is better understood in the context of confessed love for Christ.<br>Obedience is not optional for believers. Jesus stated a simple fact that must be clearly understood: "If you love me, you will obey (*tērēsete*) what I command." This is the correct translation. Jesus is not giving an *optional commandment*, "If you love me, [then, optional] keep my commandments." He is saying that the man who truly loves Him *will* keep His commandments. To the believer, there is no option. He loves Jesus; therefore, he obeys His commandments. In this the believer is not claiming perfection, but he is claiming to love Jesus and to believe with all his heart that Jesus is the Son of God. Therefore, he diligently seeks Jesus, and he seeks to please Him in all that he does (cp. Hebrews 11:6). |

# PRACTICAL WORD STUDIES
## in the NEW TESTAMENT

| ENGLISH WORD | GREEK WORD AND VERSE | THE WORD MEANS... |
|---|---|---|
| **#2225**<br>**Keep**<br><br>**Keep–KJV**<br>Practice–NASB<br>Observe–NIV<br>**Keep–NKJV**<br>Obey–NLT<br><br>**POSB**<br>**REFERENCE**<br>(Romans 2:25-27; esp. v.25)<br>Note 3 | πράσσης = *prassēs*<br>Pronunciation: [pras'-sayce]<br>Parsing (part of speech): verb<br>    Mood—subjunctive<br>    Tense—present<br>    Voice—active<br>    Person—2nd person<br>    Number—singular<br>    Stem or root—from πράσσω<br>Concordance References:<br>  ⇒ Strong's #4238 prassö<br>  ⇒ NIV #4556 prassö<br>  ⇒ NASB #4238 prassö<br><br>**Romans 2:25**<br>For circumcision verily profiteth, if thou **keep** the law: but if thou be a breaker of the law, thy circumcision is made uncircumcision. [KJV]<br>For indeed circumcision is of value, if you **practice** the Law; but if you are a transgressor of the Law, your circumcision has become uncircumcision. [NASB]<br>Circumcision has value if you **observe** the law, but if you break the law, you have become as though you had not been circumcised. [NIV]<br>For circumcision is indeed profitable if you **keep** the law; but if you are a breaker of the law, your circumcision has become uncircumcision. [NKJV]<br>The Jewish ceremony of circumcision is worth something only if you **obey** God's law. But if you don't obey God's law, you are no better off than an uncircumcised Gentile. [NLT]<br>περιτομὴ μὲν γὰρ ὠφελεῖ, ἐὰν νόμον **πράσσης**· ἐὰν δὲ παραβάτης νόμου ᾖς, ἡ περιτομή σου ἀκροβυστία γέγονεν. [GNS]<br>περιτομὴ μὲν γὰρ ὠφελεῖ ἐὰν νόμον **πράσσης**· ἐὰν δὲ παραβάτης νόμου ᾖς, ἡ περιτομή σου ἀκροβυστία γέγονεν. [GNT] | Do, practice, keep, observe, obey, perform, play.<br><br>**Practical Application**<br>The religionist believes that a ritual is the way to secure God's praise or approval (for example, circumcision, baptism, and church membership). Just take the word circumcision and substitute whatever ritual a church says is essential for salvation and the meaning of the passage becomes clear. For example, take the ritual of church membership.<br><br>"Church membership profits a man if he keeps the law: but if he breaks the law, his church membership is made or counted as unchurch membership."<br><br>If a religionist does not keep (*prassēs*) God's law and Word, then his ritual does not count. The man becomes...<br>• unbaptized<br>• unchurched<br>• uncircumcised<br>• unwhatever<br><br>The point is obedience, not ritual. A person is acceptable to God because he lives for God and obeys Him, not because he has undergone some ritual. |
| **#2226**<br>**Keep**<br><br>**Keep–KJV**<br>Guard–NASB<br>Guard–NIV<br>Guard–NKJV<br>Guard–NLT<br><br>**POSB**<br>**REFERENCE**<br>(Philip.4:6-7; esp. v.7)<br>Note 1, point 3b | φρουρήσει = *phrourēsei*<br>Pronunciation: [froo-ray'-seh-ee]<br>Parsing (part of speech): verb<br>    Mood—indicative<br>    Tense—future<br>    Voice—active<br>    Person—3rd person<br>    Number—singular<br>    Stem or root—from φρουρέω<br>Concordance References:<br>  ⇒ Strong's #5432 phroureö<br>  ⇒ NIV #5864 phroureö<br>  ⇒ NASB #5432 phroureö<br><br>**Philip. 4:7**<br>And the peace of God, which passeth all understanding, shall **keep** your hearts and minds through Christ Jesus. [KJV]<br>And the peace of God, which surpasses all comprehension, shall **guard** your hearts and your minds in Christ Jesus. [NASB]<br>And the peace of God, which transcends all understanding, will **guard** your hearts and your minds in Christ Jesus. [NIV]<br>And the peace of God, which surpasses all understanding, will **guard** your hearts and minds through Christ Jesus. [NKJV]<br>If you do this, you will experience God's peace, which is far more wonderful than the human mind can understand. His peace will **guard** your hearts and minds as you live in Christ Jesus. [NLT]<br>καὶ ἡ εἰρήνη τοῦ Θεοῦ ἡ ὑπερέχουσα πάντα νοῦν, **φρουρήσει** τὰς καρδίας ὑμῶν καὶ τὰ νοήματα ὑμῶν ἐν Χριστῷ Ἰησοῦ. [GNS] | To protect; to keep; to guard; to defend; to preserve; to cover; to insulate; to safeguard.<br><br>**Practical Application**<br>The word "keep" (*phrourēsei*) is a military word meaning to garrison, to keep guard and protect. The peace of God is like a most elite soldier who guards and protects the most precious possession of God: the believer's heart and mind.<br>However, note that God can guard us only as we are "in Christ Jesus." We can know the peace of God only if we have trusted Christ as our Lord and Savior and only if we walk in fellowship with Him. To be in Christ means to walk in Christ–to live, move and have our being in Him. |

# PRACTICAL WORD STUDIES
## in the NEW TESTAMENT

| ENGLISH WORD | GREEK WORD AND VERSE | THE WORD MEANS... |
|---|---|---|
| | καὶ ἡ εἰρήνη τοῦ θεοῦ ἡ ὑπερέχουσα πάντα νοῦν **φρουρήσει** τὰς καρδίας ὑμῶν καὶ τὰ νοήματα ὑμῶν ἐν Χριστῷ Ἰησοῦ. [GNT] | |
| **#2227**<br>**Keep**<br><br>Keep–KJV<br>Protect–NASB<br>Protect–NIV<br>Guard–NKJV<br>Guard–NLT<br><br>**POSB REFERENCE**<br>(2 Thes.3:3-5; esp. v.3)<br>Note 2, point 1 | φυλάξει = *phulaxei*<br>Pronunciation: [foo-lax'-eh-ee]<br>Parsing (part of speech): verb<br>    Mood—indicative<br>    Tense—future<br>    Voice—active<br>    Person—3rd person<br>    Number—singular<br>    Stem or root—from φυλάσσω<br>Concordance References:<br>  ⇒ Strong's #5442 phulassō<br>  ⇒ NIV #5875 phulassō<br>  ⇒ NASB #5442 phulassō<br><br>**2 Thes. 3:3**<br>But the Lord is faithful, who shall stablish you, and **keep** you from evil. [KJV]<br>But the Lord is faithful, and He will strengthen and **protect** you from the evil one. [NASB]<br>But the Lord is faithful, and he will strengthen and **protect** you from the evil one. [NIV]<br>But the Lord is faithful, who will establish you and **guard** *you* from the evil one. [NKJV]<br>But the Lord is faithful; he will make you strong and **guard** you from the evil one. [NLT]<br>πιστὸς δέ ἐστι ὁ Κύριος, ὃς στηρίξει ὑμᾶς καὶ **φυλάξει** ἀπὸ τοῦ πονηροῦ. [GNS]<br>πιστὸς δέ ἐστιν ὁ κύριος, ὃς στηρίξει ὑμᾶς καὶ **φυλάξει** ἀπὸ τοῦ πονηροῦ. [GNT] | To protect; to keep; to guard; to defend; to preserve; to cover; to insulate; to safeguard.<br><br>**Practical Application**<br>The point is this: the Lord is faithful, even if we fail to help one another. God will strengthen and keep us against Satan and his evil followers. In fact, the Lord will strenghten and guard us against all evil no matter what it is. Even if the evil seems to be conquering us, it will not—not in the final analysis. |
| **#2228**<br>**Keep [Your] Head**<br><br>Watch–KJV<br>Sober–NASB<br>**Keep [your] head–NIV**<br>Watchful–NKJV<br>Keep clear mind–NLT<br><br>**POSB REFERENCE**<br>(2 Tim. 4:5)<br>Note 4, point 1 | νῆφε = *nēphe*<br>Pronunciation: [nay'-feh]<br>Parsing (part of speech): verb<br>    Mood—imperative<br>    Tense—present<br>    Voice—active<br>    Person—2nd person<br>    Number—singular<br>    Stem or root—from νήφω<br>Concordance References:<br>  ⇒ Strong's #3525 nēphō<br>  ⇒ NIV #3768 nēphō<br>  ⇒ NASB #3525 nēphō<br><br>**2 Tim. 4:5**<br>But **watch** thou in all things, endure afflictions, do the work of an evangelist, make full proof of thy ministry. [KJV]<br>But you, be **sober** in all things, endure hardship, do the work of an evangelist, fulfill your ministry. [NASB]<br>But you, **keep** your **head** in all situations, endure hardship, do the work of an evangelist, discharge all the duties of your ministry. [NIV]<br>But you be **watchful** in all things, endure afflictions, do the work of an evangelist, fulfill your ministry. [NKJV]<br>But you should **keep** a **clear mind** in every situation. Don't be afraid of suffering for the Lord. Work at bringing others to Christ. Complete the ministry God has given you. [NLT]<br>σὺ δὲ **νῆφε** ἐν πᾶσι, κακοπάθησον, ἔργον ποίησον εὐαγγελιστοῦ, τὴν διακονίαν σου πληροφόρησον. [GNS]<br>σὺ δὲ **νῆφε** ἐν πᾶσιν, κακοπάθησον, ἔργον ποίησον εὐαγγελιστοῦ, τὴν διακονίαν σου πληροφόρησον. [GNT] | To keep your head; to watch; to remain; to keep a clear mind. It means to be sober, calm, and alert; to keep a cool, calm, and collected mind; to maintain a controlled and disciplined life and spirit.<br><br>**Practical Application**<br>The minister must keep his head in all things. And note: the minister is to be this way in all things: in body, mind, and spirit—in thought, word and behavior. The minister is to always keep his head—always be alert, calm, controlled, and disciplined—no matter the activity or behavior. |
| **#2229**<br>**Keep A Close Watch** | ἔπεχε = *epeche*<br>Pronunciation: [ep-ekh'-eh]<br>Parsing (part of speech): verb<br>    Mood—imperative<br>    Tense—present | To watch closely; to take heed; to pay close attention; to keep a close watch; to keep a strict eye upon or to keep on paying attention to oneself and to one's teaching. |

# Practical Word Studies
## in the New Testament

| ENGLISH WORD | GREEK WORD AND VERSE | THE WORD MEANS... |
|---|---|---|
| Take heed–KJV<br>Pay close attention–NASB<br>Watch...closely–NIV<br>Take heed–NKJV<br>**Keep a close watch–NLT**<br><br>**POSB REFERENCE**<br>(1 Tim.4:16)<br>Note 12 | Voice—active<br>Person—2nd person<br>Number—singular<br>Stem or root—from ἐπέχω<br>Concordance References:<br>⇒ Strong's #1907 epechō<br>⇒ NIV #2091 epechō<br>⇒ NASB #1907 epechō<br><br>**1 Tim. 4:16**<br>**Take heed** unto thyself, and unto the doctrine; continue in them: for in doing this thou shalt both save thyself, and them that hear thee. [KJV]<br>**Pay close attention** to yourself and to your teaching; persevere in these things; for as you do this you will insure salvation both for yourself and for those who hear you. [NASB]<br>**Watch** your life and doctrine **closely**. Persevere in them, because if you do, you will save both yourself and your hearers. [NIV]<br>**Take heed** to yourself and to the doctrine. Continue in them, for in doing this you will save both yourself and those who hear you. [NKJV]<br>**Keep a close watch** on yourself and on your teaching. Stay true to what is right, and God will save you and those who hear you. [NLT]<br>ἔπεχε σεαυτῷ καὶ τῇ διδασκαλίᾳ. ἐπίμενε αὐτοῖς· τοῦτο γὰρ ποιῶν καὶ σεαυτὸν σώσεις καὶ τοὺς ἀκούοντάς σου. [GNS]<br>ἔπεχε σεαυτῷ καὶ τῇ διδασκαλίᾳ, ἐπίμενε αὐτοῖς· τοῦτο γὰρ ποιῶν καὶ σεαυτὸν σώσεις καὶ τοὺς ἀκούοντάς σου. [GNT] | **Practical Application**<br>The good minister guards himself and his teaching.<br>⇒ He guards his body, keeps it both morally and physically fit. He flees the temptations that assault and seduce him, and he controls his thoughts and keeps them pure from the lusts of the world and flesh. He neither eats too much nor succumbs to immoral thoughts or acts. He neither gives in to greed nor seeks the possessions or wealth of the world.<br>⇒ He guards his spirit and keeps it spiritually fit. He worships God every day and lives in God's Word and prayer all day long, and he shares the glorious gospel of Christ, witnessing to and exhorting people as he walks throughout the day.<br>⇒ He guards his study and teaching, avoiding the profane doctrines, teachings, notions, philosophies, ideas, and fables of men. |
| #2230<br>**Keep Aloof**<br><br>Withdraw–KJV<br>**Keep aloof–NASB**<br>Keep away–NIV<br>Withdraw–NKJV<br>Stay away–NLT<br><br>**POSB REFERENCE**<br>(2 Thes.3:6-11; esp. v.6)<br>Note 1 | στέλλεσθαι = stellesthai<br>Pronunciation: [stel'-les-tha-ee]<br>Parsing (part of speech): verb<br>Mood—infinitive<br>Tense—present<br>Voice—middle<br>Stem or root—from στέλλομαι<br>Concordance References:<br>⇒ Strong's #4724 stellō<br>⇒ NIV #5097 stellō<br>⇒ NASB #4724 stellō<br><br>**2 Thes. 3:6**<br>Now we command you, brethren, in the name of our Lord Jesus Christ, that ye **withdraw** yourselves from every brother that walketh disorderly, and not after the tradition which he received of us. [KJV]<br>Now we command you, brethren, in the name of our Lord Jesus Christ, that you **keep aloof** from every brother who leads an unruly life and not according to the tradition which you received from us. [NASB]<br>In the name of the Lord Jesus Christ, we command you, brothers, to **keep away** from every brother who is idle and does not live according to the teaching you received from us. [NIV]<br>But we command you, brethren, in the name of our Lord Jesus Christ, that you **withdraw** from every brother who walks disorderly and not according to the tradition which he received from us. [NKJV]<br>And now, dear brothers and sisters, we give you this command with the authority of our Lord Jesus Christ: **Stay away** from any Christian who lives in idleness and doesn't follow the tradition of hard work we gave you. [NLT]<br>Παραγγέλλομεν δὲ ὑμῖν, ἀδελφοί, ἐν ὀνόματι τοῦ Κυρίου ἡμῶν Ἰησοῦ Χριστοῦ, **στέλλεσθαι** ὑμᾶς ἀπὸ παντὸς ἀδελφοῦ ἀτάκτως περιπατοῦντος, καὶ μὴ κατὰ τὴν παράδοσιν ἣν παρέλαβε παρ᾽ ἡμῶν· [GNS]<br>Παραγγέλλομεν δὲ ὑμῖν, ἀδελφοί, ἐν ὀνόματι τοῦ | To keep away; to withdraw; to avoid; to keep aloof; to stay away; to shun.<br><br>**Practical Application**<br>We are to keep aloof from every brother who walks disorderly, that is, who does not work. Note: this is a very strong command. It has the force of a military command: it is given "in the name of our Lord Jesus Christ," the Supreme Commander. There is to be no discussion about the matter. What is being said is to be obeyed: "keep aloof from every brother who leads an unruly life" (2 Thes. 3:6). Who is it that lead an unruly life? The person who does not work. A strange thing had happened in the Thessalonian church. Some of the believers had become excited over the return of the Lord and the promise of being with Him forever in the new heavens and earth. They became so excited that they began to sacrifice all they could to meet the needs of people. But some went too far. They ignored the Lord's words that only God knew when He would be returning, and they began to project dates and declare that His return was about to take place. Therefore, some quit their jobs in order to have more time to minister, and in an act of sacrificial commitment they gave away *all they had*. The result was catastrophic. They were now having to sponge off the other believers in order to survive. Their action had been most unwise—unwise because believers are to *live life* as it should be lived so long as they are upon earth. Believers are to set the example as to how life is to be lived, and work is certainly one of the duties of men. Therefore, of all people believers are to set an example in work. They are |

# PRACTICAL WORD STUDIES
## in the NEW TESTAMENT

| ENGLISH WORD | GREEK WORD AND VERSE | THE WORD MEANS... |
|---|---|---|
| | κυρίου [ἡμῶν] Ἰησοῦ Χριστοῦ **στέλλεσθαι** ὑμᾶς ἀπὸ παντὸς ἀδελφοῦ ἀτάκτως περιπατοῦντος καὶ μὴ κατὰ τὴν παράδοσιν ἣν παρελάβοσαν παρ᾽ ἡμῶν. [GNT] | to be the very best workmen possible. Quitting work and not working is disorderly behavior; it is totally unacceptable for a true believer. It is so unacceptable that believers are commanded to withdraw from non-workers.<br>⇒ What does the Lord mean by "keep aloof" (*stellesthai*)? The phrase means to stay away from the idle worker; to have no fellowship with him. His behavior is not to be indulged or condoned. We are not to put our stamp of approval upon him, nor are we to run the risk of becoming identified with him.<br>⇒ Who are those who lead an unruly life? They are the idle, the slothful, the lazy. They are the persons who refuse to work or who shirk their work or are slack in their work. |
| **#2231**<br>**Keep Away**<br><br>Withdraw–KJV<br>Keep aloof–NASB<br>**Keep away–NIV**<br>Withdraw–NKJV<br>Stay away–NLT<br><br>**POSB REFERENCE**<br>(2 Thes.3:6-11; esp. v.6)<br>Note 1 | στέλλεσθαι = *stellesthai*<br>Pronunciation: [stel'-les-tha-ee]<br>Parsing (part of speech): verb<br>    Mood—infinitive<br>    Tense—present<br>    Voice—middle<br>    Stem or root—from στέλλομαι<br>Concordance References:<br>  ⇒ Strong's #4724 stellō<br>  ⇒ NIV #5097 stellō<br>  ⇒ NASB #4724 stellō<br><br>**2 Thes. 3:6**<br>Now we command you, brethren, in the name of our Lord Jesus Christ, that ye **withdraw** yourselves from every brother that walketh disorderly, and not after the tradition which he received of us. [KJV]<br>Now we command you, brethren, in the name of our Lord Jesus Christ, that you **keep aloof** from every brother who leads an unruly life and not according to the tradition which you received from us. [NASB]<br>In the name of the Lord Jesus Christ, we command you, brothers, to **keep away** from every brother who is idle and does not live according to the teaching you received from us. [NIV]<br>But we command you, brethren, in the name of our Lord Jesus Christ, that you **withdraw** from every brother who walks disorderly and not according to the tradition which he received from us. [NKJV]<br>And now, dear brothers and sisters, we give you this command with the authority of our Lord Jesus Christ: **Stay away** from any Christian who lives in idleness and doesn't follow the tradition of hard work we gave you. [NLT]<br>Παραγγέλλομεν δὲ ὑμῖν, ἀδελφοί, ἐν ὀνόματι τοῦ Κυρίου ἡμῶν Ἰησοῦ Χριστοῦ, **στέλλεσθαι** ὑμᾶς ἀπὸ παντὸς ἀδελφοῦ ἀτάκτως περιπατοῦντος, καὶ μὴ κατὰ τὴν παράδοσιν ἣν παρέλαβε παρ᾽ ἡμῶν· [GNS]<br>Παραγγέλλομεν δὲ ὑμῖν, ἀδελφοί, ἐν ὀνόματι τοῦ κυρίου [ἡμῶν] Ἰησοῦ Χριστοῦ **στέλλεσθαι** ὑμᾶς ἀπὸ παντὸς ἀδελφοῦ ἀτάκτως περιπατοῦντος καὶ μὴ κατὰ τὴν παράδοσιν ἣν παρελάβοσαν παρ᾽ ἡμῶν. [GNT] | To keep away; to withdraw; to avoid; to keep aloof; to stay away; to shun.<br><br>**Practical Application**<br>We are to keep away from every brother who is idle, that is, who does not work. Note: this is a very strong command. It has the force of a military command: it is given "in the name of our Lord Jesus Christ," the supreme Commander. There is to be no discussion about the matter. What is being said is to be obeyed. "Keep away from every brother who is idle" (2 Thes. 3:6). (See **Keep Aloof**, for more discussion). |
| **#2232**<br>**Keep Clear Mind**<br><br>Watch–KJV<br>Sober–NASB<br>Keep [your] head–NIV<br>Watchful–NKJV<br>**Keep clear mind– NLT** | νῆφε = *nēphe*<br>Pronunciation: [nay'-feh]<br>Parsing (part of speech): verb<br>    Mood—imperative<br>    Tense—present<br>    Voice—active<br>    Person—2nd person<br>    Number—singular<br>    Stem or root—from νήφω<br>Concordance References:<br>  ⇒ Strong's #3525 nēphō<br>  ⇒ NIV #3768 nēphō<br>  ⇒ NASB #3525 nēphō | To keep your head; to watch; to keep a clear mind. It means to be sober, calm, and alert; to keep a cool, calm, and collected mind; to maintain a controlled and disciplined life and spirit.<br><br>**Practical Application**<br>The minister must *keep a clear mind* in all things. And note: the minister is to be this way in all things: in body, mind, and spirit—in thought, word and behavior. The minister is to always *keep a clear mind*—always be alert, calm, controlled, and disciplined—no matter the activity or behavior. |

# PRACTICAL WORD STUDIES
## in the NEW TESTAMENT

| ENGLISH WORD | GREEK WORD AND VERSE | THE WORD MEANS... |
|---|---|---|
| **POSB REFERENCE** (2 Tim. 4:5) Note 4, point 1 | **2 Tim. 4:5**<br>But **watch** thou in all things, endure afflictions, do the work of an evangelist, make full proof of thy ministry. [KJV]<br>But you, be **sober** in all things, endure hardship, do the work of an evangelist, fulfill your ministry. [NASB]<br>But you, **keep** your **head** in all situations, endure hardship, do the work of an evangelist, discharge all the duties of your ministry. [NIV]<br>But you be **watchful** in all things, endure afflictions, do the work of an evangelist, fulfill your ministry. [NKJV]<br>But you should **keep** a **clear mind** in every situation. Don't be afraid of suffering for the Lord. Work at bringing others to Christ. Complete the ministry God has given you. [NLT]<br>σὺ δὲ **νῆφε** ἐν πᾶσι, κακοπάθησον, ἔργον ποίησον εὐαγγελιστοῦ, τὴν διακονίαν σου πληροφόρησον. [GNS]<br>σὺ δὲ **νῆφε** ἐν πᾶσιν, κακοπάθησον, ἔργον ποίησον εὐαγγελιστοῦ, τὴν διακονίαν σου πληροφόρησον. [GNT] | |
| **#2233**<br>**Keep Deceiving**<br><br>Used deceit–KJV<br>**Keep deceiving–NASB**<br>Practice deceit–NIV<br>Practiced deceit–NKJV<br>Filled with lies–NLT<br><br>**POSB REFERENCE**<br>(Rom.3:13-14; esp. v.13)<br>Note 3, point 2 | ἐδολιοῦσαν = *edoliousan*<br>Pronunciation: [eh-dol-ee-oo'-sahn]<br>Parsing (part of speech): verb<br>    Mood—indicative<br>    Tense—imperfect<br>    Voice—active<br>    Person—3rd person<br>    Number—plural<br>    Stem or root—from δολιόω<br>Concordance References:<br>  ⇒ Strong's #1387 *dolioō*<br>  ⇒ NIV #1514 *dolioō*<br>  ⇒ NASB #1387 *dolioō*<br><br>**Romans 3:13**<br>Their throat *is* an open sepulchre; with their tongues they have **used deceit**; the poison of asps *is* under their lips: [KJV]<br>"Their throat is an open grave, With their tongues they **keep deceiving**," "The poison of asps is under their lips;" [NASB]<br>"Their throats are open graves; their tongues **practice deceit**." "The poison of vipers is on their lips." [NIV]<br>"Their throat is an open tomb; With their tongues they have **practiced deceit**"; "The poison of asps is under their lips"; [NKJV]<br>"Their talk is foul, like the stench from an open grave. Their speech is **filled with lies**." "The poison of a deadly snake drips from their lips." [NLT]<br>τάφος ἀνεῳγμένος ὁ λάρυγξ αὐτῶν, ταῖς γλώσσαις αὐτῶν **ἐδολιοῦσαν**· ἰὸς ἀσπίδων ὑπὸ τὰ χείλη αὐτῶν· [GNS]<br>τάφος ἀνεῳγμένος ὁ λάρυγξ αὐτῶν, ταῖς γλώσσαις αὐτῶν **ἐδολιοῦσαν**, ἰὸς ἀσπίδων ὑπὸ τὰ χείλη αὐτῶν· [GNT] | To deceive; to be treacherous; to mislead; to betray; to cheat; to bamboozle; to practice deceit.<br><br>**Practical Application**<br>A sinful tongue is deceitful (Romans 3:13; cp. Psalm 5:9): "They have used deceit." The Hebrew says, "They make smooth their tongue." A deceitful person has...<br>• a false tongue<br>• a lying tongue<br>• a cheating tongue<br>• a deluding tongue<br>• a flattering tongue<br>• a misleading tongue<br>• a treacherous tongue<br>• a beguiling tongue<br>• a smooth-talking tongue<br><br>The word "deceit" (*edoliousan*) is continuous action: "They kept on deceiving." Man is not only guilty of deceiving, but of constantly deceiving. He is constantly hiding and camouflaging his true thoughts and feelings and behavior, seeking to protect himself or to get whatever he is after. |
| **#2234**<br>**Keep Going**<br><br>Destroyed–KJV<br>Destroyed–NASB<br>Destroyed–NIV<br>Destroyed–NKJV<br>**Keep going–NLT**<br><br>**POSB REFERENCE**<br>(2 Cor.4:7-9; esp. v.9)<br>Note 2, point 4 | ἀπολλύμενοι = *apollumenoi*<br>Pronunciation: [ap-ol-loo'-mehn-oy]<br>Parsing (part of speech): verb<br>    Mood—participle<br>    Tense—present<br>    Voice—middle or passive<br>    Case—nominative<br>    Gender—masculine<br>    Person—1st person<br>    Stem or root—from ἀπόλλυμι<br>Concordance References:<br>  ⇒ Strong's #622 *apollumi*<br>  ⇒ NIV #660 *apollumi*<br>  ⇒ NASB #622 *apollumi* | To be destroyed; to perish; to die; to strike out; to bring to an end; to be killed; to be lost.<br><br>**Practical Application**<br>The minister (or believer) may be cast down, but he is never destroyed. The minister (or believer) may be struck down, but he is never allowed to strike out; he may be knocked down, but he is never knocked out. |

# PRACTICAL WORD STUDIES
## in the NEW TESTAMENT

| ENGLISH WORD | GREEK WORD AND VERSE | THE WORD MEANS... |
|---|---|---|
| | **2 Cor. 4:9**<br>Persecuted, but not forsaken; cast down, but not **destroyed**; [KJV]<br>Persecuted, but not forsaken; struck down, but not **destroyed**; [NASB]<br>Persecuted, but not abandoned; struck down, but not **destroyed**. [NIV]<br>Persecuted, but not forsaken; struck down, but not **destroyed**—[NKJV]<br>We are hunted down, but God never abandons us. We get knocked down, but we get up again and **keep going**. [NLT]<br>διωκόμενοι, ἀλλ' οὐκ ἐγκαταλειπόμενοι, καταβαλλόμενοι ἀλλ' οὐκ **ἀπολλύμενοι**· [GNS]<br>διωκόμενοι ἀλλ' οὐκ ἐγκαταλειπόμενοι, καταβαλλόμενοι ἀλλ' οὐκ **ἀπολλύμενοι**, [GNT] | |
| **#2235**<br>**Keep In Memory**<br><br>Keep in memory–KJV<br>Hold fast–NASB<br>Hold firmly–NIV<br>Hold fast–NKJV<br>Firmly believe it–NLT<br><br>**POSB REFERENCE**<br>(1 Cor.15:1-2; esp. v.2)<br>Note 1, point 3 | κατέχετε = katechete<br>Pronunciation: [kat-ekh'-eh-teh]<br>Parsing (part of speech): verb<br>  Mood—indicative<br>  Tense—present<br>  Voice—active<br>  Person—2nd person<br>  Number—plural<br>  Stem or root—from κατέχω<br>Concordance References:<br>  ⇒ Strong's #2722 katechō<br>  ⇒ NIV #2988 katechō<br>  ⇒ NASB #2722 katechō<br><br>**1 Cor. 15:2**<br>By which also ye are saved, if ye **keep in memory** what I preached unto you, unless ye have believed in vain. [KJV]<br>By which also you are saved, if you **hold fast** the word which I preached to you, unless you believed in vain. [NASB]<br>By this gospel you are saved, if you **hold firmly** to the word I preached to you. Otherwise, you have believed in vain. [NIV]<br>By which also you are saved, if you **hold fast** that word which I preached to you—unless you believed in vain. [NKJV]<br>And it is this Good News that saves you if you **firmly believe it**—unless, of course, you believed something that was never true in the first place. [NLT]<br>δι' οὗ καὶ σῴζεσθε· τίνι λόγῳ εὐηγγελισάμην ὑμῖν, εἰ **κατέχετε**, ἐκτὸς εἰ μὴ εἰκῇ ἐπιστεύσατε. [GNS]<br>δι' οὗ καὶ σῴζεσθε, τίνι λόγῳ εὐηγγελισάμην ὑμῖν εἰ **κατέχετε**, ἐκτὸς εἰ μὴ εἰκῇ ἐπιστεύσατε. [GNT] | To hold firm; to firmly believe; to hold fast; to keep; to retain.<br><br>**Practical Application**<br>In order to be saved, a person must hold firmly to the gospel. No person who denies the gospel could ever expect to be saved. |
| **#2236**<br>**Keep Obeying**<br><br>Continue–KJV<br>Abide–NASB<br>Hold–NIV<br>Abide–NKJV<br>Keep obeying–NLT<br><br>**POSB REFERENCE**<br>(Jn.8:31)<br>Note 1, point 2 | μείνητε = meinēte<br>Pronunciation: [meen'-ay-teh]<br>Parsing (part of speech): verb<br>  Mood—subjunctive<br>  Tense—aorist<br>  Voice—active<br>  Person—2nd person plural<br>  Stem or root—from μένω<br>Concordance References:<br>  ⇒ Strong's #3306 menō<br>  ⇒ NIV #3531 menō<br>  ⇒ NASB #3306 menō<br><br>**John 8:31**<br>Then said Jesus to those Jews which believed on him, If ye **continue** in my word, then are ye my disciples indeed; [KJV]<br>Jesus therefore was saying to those Jews who had believed Him, "If you **abide** in My word, then you are truly disciples of Mine; [NASB]<br>To the Jews who had believed him, Jesus said, "If you | To hold; to continue; to abide; to remain; to keep on obeying. It means to dwell, continue, stay, sojourn, rest in or upon; to live; to rest; to nest.<br><br>**Practical Application**<br>The idea is that of dwelling, just as a person dwells at home. The Word of the Lord is the believer's dwelling place. He continues and abides in God's Word. Very simply, what Jesus was saying is this:<br>⇒ A person who really begins to believe will "keep obeying" or "hold on to" the Lord's teachings. He will keep obeying both to study and to do the Word (2 Tim. 2:15).<br>⇒ A person who does not really believe will not "hold on" to the Lord's Word.<br>⇒ The proof and the evidence that a person "really believes" is that he does "continue" |

# PRACTICAL WORD STUDIES
## in the NEW TESTAMENT

| ENGLISH WORD | GREEK WORD AND VERSE | THE WORD MEANS... |
|---|---|---|
| | **hold** to my teaching, you are really my disciples. [NIV]<br>Then Jesus said to those Jews who believed Him, "If you **abide** in My word, you are My disciples indeed. [NKJV]<br>Jesus said to the people who believed in him, "You are truly my disciples if you **keep obeying** my teachings. [NLT]<br>Ἔλεγεν οὖν ὁ Ἰησοῦς πρὸς τοὺς πεπιστευκότας αὐτῷ Ἰουδαίους, Ἐὰν ὑμεῖς **μείνητε** ἐν τῷ λόγῳ τῷ ἐμῷ, ἀληθῶς μαθηταί μού ἐστε· [GNS]<br>Ἔλεγεν οὖν ὁ Ἰησοῦς πρὸς τοὺς πεπιστευκότας αὐτῷ Ἰουδαίους, Ἐὰν ὑμεῖς **μείνητε** ἐν τῷ λόγῳ τῷ ἐμῷ, ἀληθῶς μαθηταί μού ἐστε [GNT] | *and hold on and abide and dwell* in the Lord's Word.<br>⇒ The proof and the evidence that a person has made only a false or a superficial profession is that he does not "hold on" to the Lord's Word. |
| **#2237**<br>**Keep Watch**<br><br>Watch–KJV<br>Be on the alert–NASB<br>Keep watch–NIV<br>Watch–NKJV<br>Be prepared–NLT<br><br>**POSB REFERENCE**<br>(Mt.24:42)<br>Note 1<br><br>See also POSB REF:<br>(Mk.13:37)<br>*Deeper Study* #1)<br>(1 Pt.5:8)<br>Note 1, point 2 | γρηγορεῖτε = *grēgoreite*<br>Pronunciation: [gray-gor-ee'-teh]<br>Parsing (part of speech): verb<br>  Mood—imperative<br>  Tense—present<br>  Voice—active<br>  Person—2nd person<br>  Number—plural<br>  Stem or root—from γρηγορέω<br>Concordance References:<br>  ⇒ Strong's #1127 gregoreuo<br>  ⇒ NIV #1213 grēgoreö<br>  ⇒ NASB #1127 gregoreuo<br><br>**Matthew 24:42**<br>**Watch** therefore: for ye know not what hour your Lord doth come. [KJV]<br>"Therefore **be on the alert**, for you do not know which day your Lord is coming. [NASB]<br>"Therefore **keep watch**, because you do not know on what day your Lord will come. [NIV]<br>**Watch** therefore, for you do not know what hour your Lord is coming. [NKJV]<br>So **be prepared**, because you don't know what day your Lord is coming. [NLT]<br>γρηγορεῖτε οὖν, ὅτι οὐκ οἴδατε ποίᾳ ὥρᾳ ὁ Κύριος ὑμῶν ἔρχεται. [GNS]<br>γρηγορεῖτε οὖν, ὅτι οὐκ οἴδατε ποίᾳ ἡμέρᾳ ὁ κύριος ὑμῶν ἔρχεται. [GNT] | To watch; to stay alert; to be ready; to pay strict attention; to keep awake; to be watchful and sleepless; to be vigilant; to be prepared.<br><br>**Practical Application**<br>It also includes the idea of being motivated, of keeping one's attention (mind) upon a thing. Being on the alert also has the idea of being alert at the right time. It is at night that a person really needs to stay awake to watch for the thief (cp. 1 Thes. 5:4-9). |
| **#2238**<br>**Keep Watch Over**<br><br>Take heed–KJV<br>Be on guard–NASB<br>Keep watch over–NIV<br>Take heed–NKJV<br>Beware–NLT<br><br>**POSB REFERENCE**<br>(Acts 20:28)<br>Note 1, point 1 | προσέχετε = *prosechete*<br>Pronunciation: [pros-ech'-eh-teh]<br>Parsing (part of speech): verb<br>  Mood—imperfect<br>  Tense—present<br>  Voice—active<br>  Person—2nd person<br>  Number—plural<br>  Stem or root—from προσέχω<br>Concordance References:<br>  ⇒ Strong's #4337 prosechō<br>  ⇒ NIV #4668 prosechō<br>  ⇒ NASB #4337 prosechō<br><br>**Acts 20:28**<br>**Take heed** therefore unto yourselves, and to all the flock, over the which the Holy Ghost hath made you overseers, to feed the church of God, which he hath purchased with his own blood. [KJV]<br>"**Be on guard** for yourselves and for all the flock, among which the Holy Spirit has made you overseers, to shepherd the church of God which He purchased with His own blood. [NASB]<br>**Keep watch over** yourselves and all the flock of which the Holy Spirit has made you overseers. Be shepherds of the church of God, which he bought with his own blood. [NIV]<br>Therefore **take heed** to yourselves and to all the flock, among which the Holy Spirit has made you over- | To keep watch over; to take heed; to be on guard; to beware; to be careful, oh so careful. It means to give attention, concentrate upon, focus upon, attend to, watch after, and guard his life.<br><br>**Practical Application**<br>There are specific areas in which the believer must guard.<br>1. He must guard against false teaching (Luke 12:1).<br>2. He must guard against an unforgiving spirit (Luke 17:3-4).<br>3. He must guard against self-indulgence, drunkenness, and the possessions of this life (Luke 21:34).<br>4. He must guard against the fables, myths, speculations, ideas, and false doctrines of men, and depending upon one's genealogy or heritage for salvation (1 Tim. 1:4).<br>5. He must watch and give himself to reading, exhortation and doctrine (1 Tim. 4:13).<br>6. He must especially give himself to the doctrine (*te didaskalia*), the teaching of Scripture (1 Tim. 4:16). |

## Practical Word Studies in the New Testament

| ENGLISH WORD | GREEK WORD AND VERSE | THE WORD MEANS... |
|---|---|---|
| | seers, to shepherd the church of God which He purchased with His own blood. [NKJV]<br>"And now **beware**! Be sure that you feed and shepherd God's flock—his church, purchased with his blood—over whom the Holy Spirit has appointed you as elders. [NLT]<br>προσέχετε οὖν ἑαυτοῖς καὶ παντὶ τῷ ποιμνίῳ, ἐν ᾧ ὑμᾶς τὸ Πνεῦμα τὸ Ἅγιον ἔθετο ἐπισκόπους, ποιμαίνειν τὴν ἐκκλησίαν τοῦ Θεοῦ, ἣν περιεποιήσατο διὰ τοῦ ἰδίου αἵματος. [GNS]<br>προσέχετε ἑαυτοῖς καὶ παντὶ τῷ ποιμνίῳ, ἐν ᾧ ὑμᾶς τὸ πνεῦμα τὸ ἅγιον ἔθετο ἐπισκόπους ποιμαίνειν τὴν ἐκκλησίαν τοῦ θεοῦ, ἣν περιεποιήσατο διὰ τοῦ αἵματος τοῦ ἰδίου. [GNT] | |
| **#2239**<br>**Keep Working Toward**<br><br>Follow after–KJV<br>Press on–NASB<br>Press on–NIV<br>Press on–NKJV<br>**Keep working toward–NLT**<br><br>**POSB REFERENCE**<br>(Philip.3:12-16; esp. v.12)<br>Note 3, point 1 | διώκω = diōkō<br>Pronunciation: [dee-o'-ko]<br>Parsing (part of speech): verb<br>  Mood—indicative<br>  Tense—present<br>  Voice—active<br>  Person—1st person<br>  Number—singular<br>  Stem or root—from διώκω<br>Concordance References:<br>⇒ Strong's #1377 diōkō<br>⇒ NIV #1503 diōkō<br>⇒ NASB #1377 diōkō<br><br>**Philip. 3:12**<br>Not as though I had already attained, either were already perfect: but I **follow after**, if that I may apprehend that for which also I am apprehended of Christ Jesus. [KJV]<br>Not that I have already obtained it, or have already become perfect, but I **press on** in order that I may lay hold of that for which also I was laid hold of by Christ Jesus. [NASB]<br>Not that I have already obtained all this, or have already been made perfect, but I **press on** to take hold of that for which Christ Jesus took hold of me. [NIV]<br>Not that I have already attained, or am already perfected; but I **press on**, that I may lay hold of that for which Christ Jesus has also laid hold of me. [NKJV]<br>I don't mean to say that I have already achieved these things or that I have already reached perfection! But I **keep working toward** that day when I will finally be all that Christ Jesus saved me for and wants me to be. [NLT]<br>οὐχ ὅτι ἤδη ἔλαβον, ἢ ἤδη τετελείωμαι· **διώκω** δέ, εἰ καὶ καταλάβω ἐφ' ᾧ καὶ κατελήμφθην ὑπὸ τοῦ Χριστοῦ Ἰησοῦ. [GNS]<br>Οὐχ ὅτι ἤδη ἔλαβον ἢ ἤδη τετελείωμαι, **διώκω** δὲ εἰ καὶ καταλάβω, ἐφ' ᾧ καὶ κατελήμφθην ὑπὸ Χριστοῦ [Ἰησοῦ]. [GNT] | To press on; to follow after; to keep working toward; to strive for; to go running off after.<br><br>**Practical Application**<br>Paul followed after perfection, after his God-given purpose. When Christ saved Paul, that was just the beginning, not the end. He had been saved to *live for Christ and to serve Christ*, and as long as he was on this earth he was going to *live for Christ* and do all he could *to serve Christ*. The phrase "keep working toward" (*diōkō*) means to press; to pursue just like a runner in a race. There was no place for walking, much less for sitting or lying around in comfort, complacency and lethargy. Christ had saved Paul for perfection—to attain to the resurrection of the dead—and as long as Paul was on this earth, he was going to press and run after perfection.<br>⇒ Paul was going to do all he could to help the Lord in the Lord's great task of perfecting him.<br>⇒ Paul was going to do all he could to lay hold of perfection—the perfection for which the Lord had laid hold of him.<br>The believer must follow, run, and press after perfection—the perfection for which Christ has saved him. The believer must be active in living for Christ. |
| **#2240**<br>**Keep You Strong**<br><br>Confirm–KJV<br>Confirm–NASB<br>**Keep you strong–NIV**<br>Confirm–NKJV<br>Keep you strong–NLT<br><br>**POSB REFERENCE**<br>(1 Cor.1:8)<br>Note 3 | βεβαιώσει = bebaiōsei<br>Pronunciation: [beb-ah-yo'-see]<br>Parsing (part of speech): verb<br>  Mood—indicative<br>  Tense—future<br>  Voice—active<br>  Person—3rd person<br>  Number—singular<br>  Stem or root—from βεβαιόω<br>Concordance References:<br>⇒ Strong's #950 bebaioō<br>⇒ NIV #1011 bebaioō<br>⇒ NASB #950 bebaioō<br><br>**1 Cor. 1:8**<br>Who shall also **confirm** you unto the end, that ye may be blameless in the day of our Lord Jesus Christ. [KJV] | To confirm; to verify; to prove; to strengthen; to sustain; to keep strong. To preserve and establish, make steadfast and firm and secure.<br><br>**Practical Application**<br>Jesus Christ will preserve and secure the believer from falling. Note the glorious reason: that the believer may be "blameless in the day of our Lord Jesus Christ." |

# PRACTICAL WORD STUDIES
## in the NEW TESTAMENT

| ENGLISH WORD | GREEK WORD AND VERSE | THE WORD MEANS... |
|---|---|---|
| | Who shall also **confirm** you to the end, blameless in the day of our Lord Jesus Christ. [NASB]<br>He will **keep you strong** to the end, so that you will be blameless on the day of our Lord Jesus Christ. [NIV]<br>Who will also **confirm** you to the end, *that you may be* blameless in the day of our Lord Jesus Christ. [NKJV]<br>He will **keep you strong** right up to the end, and he will keep you free from all blame on the great day when our Lord Jesus Christ returns. [NLT]<br>ὃς καὶ **βεβαιώσει** ὑμᾶς ἕως τέλους, ἀνεγκλήτους ἐν τῇ ἡμέρᾳ τοῦ Κυρίου ἡμῶν Ἰησοῦ Χριστοῦ. [GNS]<br>ὃς καὶ **βεβαιώσει** ὑμᾶς ἕως τέλους ἀνεγκλήτους ἐν τῇ ἡμέρᾳ τοῦ κυρίου ἡμῶν Ἰησοῦ [Χριστοῦ]. [GNT] | |
| **#2241**<br>**Keep Your Eye On**<br><br>Mark–KJV<br>**Keep your eye on**–NASB<br>Watch out for–NIV<br>Note–NKJV<br>Watch out for–NLT<br><br>**POSB REFERENCE**<br>(Rom.16:17-18; esp. v.17)<br>Note 1, point 1c | σκοπεῖν = skopein<br>Pronunciation: [skop-een']<br>Parsing (part of speech): verb<br>    Mood—infinitive<br>    Tense—present<br>    Voice—active<br>    Stem or root—from σκοπέω<br>Concordance References:<br>⇒ Strong's #4648 skopeō<br>⇒ NIV #5023 skopeō<br>⇒ NASB #4648 skopeō<br><br>**Romans 16:17**<br>Now I beseech you, brethren, **mark** them which cause divisions and offences contrary to the doctrine which ye have learned; and avoid them. [KJV]<br>Now I urge you, brethren, **keep your eye on** those who cause dissensions and hindrances contrary to the teaching which you learned, and turn away from them. [NASB]<br>I urge you, brothers, to **watch out for** those who cause divisions and put obstacles in your way that are contrary to the teaching you have learned. Keep away from them. [NIV]<br>Now I urge you, brethren, **note** those who cause divisions and offenses, contrary to the doctrine which you learned, and avoid them. [NKJV]<br>And now I make one more appeal, my dear brothers and sisters. **Watch out for** people who cause divisions and upset people's faith by teaching things that are contrary to what you have been taught. Stay away from them. [NLT]<br>Παρακαλῶ δὲ ὑμᾶς, ἀδελφοί, **σκοπεῖν** τοὺς τὰς διχοστασίας καὶ τὰ σκάνδαλα, παρὰ τὴν διδαχὴν ἣν ὑμεῖς ἐμάθετε, ποιοῦντας· καὶ ἐκκλίνατε ἀπ' αὐτῶν. [GNS]<br>Παρακαλῶ δὲ ὑμᾶς, ἀδελφοί, **σκοπεῖν** τοὺς τὰς διχοστασίας καὶ τὰ σκάνδαλα παρὰ τὴν διδαχὴν ἣν ὑμεῖς ἐμάθετε ποιοῦντας, καὶ ἐκκλίνετε ἀπ' αὐτῶν. [GNT] | To mark; to note; to keep one's eye on; to look at; to observe; to focus upon; to contemplate; to scrutinize; to pay attention to; to watch out (for); to be careful.<br><br>**Practical Application**<br>"Keep your eye on" (*skopein*) the divisive person. It is the divisive person himself who is to be avoided and turned away from, not just his sin. We are not to have anything to do with a divisive person...<br>• for we give the appearance of approving what he is doing.<br>• for we run the risk of being influenced by and stumbling over what he says and does. |
| **#2242**<br>**Keepeth– Keeps**<br><br>Keepeth–KJV<br>Keeps–NASB<br>Obeys–NIV<br>Keeps–NKJV<br>Obey–NLT<br><br>**POSB REFERENCE**<br>(1 Jn.2:5)<br>Note 3 | τηρῇ = tērē<br>Pronunciation: [tay-ray]<br>Parsing (part of speech): verb<br>    Mood—subjunctive<br>    Tense—present<br>    Voice—active<br>    Person—3rd person<br>    Number—singular<br>    Stem or root—from τηρέω<br>Concordance References:<br>⇒ Strong's #5083 tēreō<br>⇒ NIV #5498 tēreō<br>⇒ NASB #5083 tēreō<br><br>**1 John 2:5**<br>But whoso **keepeth** his word, in him verily is the love of God perfected: hereby know we that we are in him. [KJV]<br>But whoever **keeps** His word, in him the love of God has truly been perfected. By this we know that we are in | To obey; to keep; to pay attention to; to observe; to comply; to adhere to.<br><br>**Practical Application**<br>The word "keeps" (*tērē*) is continuous action. It means to continue on and not to stop. It means day-by-day obedience. If we keep God's Word day-by-day, then we learn more and more about God; we learn to love Him more and more. His love becomes perfected, completed, and fulfilled in us. |

# PRACTICAL WORD STUDIES
## in the NEW TESTAMENT

| ENGLISH WORD | GREEK WORD AND VERSE | THE WORD MEANS... |
|---|---|---|
| | Him: [NASB]<br>But if anyone **obeys** his word, God's love is truly made complete in him. This is how we know we are in him: [NIV]<br>But whoever **keeps** His word, truly the love of God is perfected in him. By this we know that we are in Him. [NKJV]<br>But those who **obey** God's word really do love him. That is the way to know whether or not we live in him. [NLT]<br>ὃς δ' ἂν **τηρῇ** αὐτοῦ τὸν λόγον, ἀληθῶς ἐν τούτῳ ἡ ἀγάπη τοῦ Θεοῦ τετελείωται. ἐν τούτῳ γινώσκομεν ὅτι ἐν αὐτῷ ἐσμεν [GNS]·<br>ὃς δ' ἂν **τηρῇ** αὐτοῦ τὸν λόγον, ἀληθῶς ἐν τούτῳ ἡ ἀγάπη τοῦ θεοῦ τετελείωται, ἐν τούτῳ γινώσκομεν ὅτι ἐν αὐτῷ ἐσμεν. [GNT] | |
| **#2243**<br>**Keeping Alert**<br><br>Watch–KJV<br>**Keeping alert–NASB**<br>Watchful–NIV<br>Vigilant–NKJV<br>Alert–NLT<br><br>**POSB REFERENCE**<br>(Col.4:2-4; esp. v.2)<br>Note 1, point 2 | γρηγοροῦντες = grēgorountes<br>Pronunciation: [gray-gor-yoon'-tehs]<br>Parsing (part of speech): verb<br>   Mood—participle imperative sense<br>   Tense—present<br>   Voice—active<br>   Case—nominative<br>   Gender—masculine<br>   Person—2nd person<br>   Number—plural<br>   Stem or root—from γρηγορέω<br>Concordance References:<br>  ⇒ Strong's #1127 grēgoreō<br>  ⇒ NIV #1213 grēgoreō<br>  ⇒ NASB #1127 grēgoreō<br><br>**Col. 4:2**<br>Continue in prayer, and **watch** in the same with thanksgiving; [KJV]<br>Devote yourselves to prayer, **keeping alert** in it with *an attitude of* thanksgiving; [NASB]<br>Devote yourselves to prayer, being **watchful** and thankful. [NIV]<br>Continue earnestly in prayer, being **vigilant** in it with thanksgiving; [NKJV]<br>Devote yourselves to prayer with an **alert** mind and a thankful heart. [NLT]<br>Τῇ προσευχῇ προσκαρτερεῖτε, **γρηγοροῦντες** ἐν αὐτῇ ἐν εὐχαριστίᾳ· [GNS]<br>Τῇ προσευχῇ προσκαρτερεῖτε, **γρηγοροῦντες** ἐν αὐτῇ ἐν εὐχαριστίᾳ, [GNT] | To be watchful; to keep alert; to be alive; to stay awake, sleepless, active; to concentrate.<br><br>**Practical Application**<br>It means to fight against distractions, drowsiness, sluggishness, wandering thoughts, and useless daydreaming. It means to discipline our minds and control our thoughts in prayer. Being very honest, this is a problem that afflicts every believer sometime. Overwork, tiredness, pressure, strain—an innumerable list of things can make it very difficult to concentrate in prayer. This is the very reason Paul stresses the need to watch in prayer. But note: vigilance in prayer is the duty of the believer. Again, it is not something that God does for us. We are responsible for watching and concentrating. We are the ones who are to discipline our minds and control our thoughts. For this reason, we must never give up in prayer. We must...<br>• always struggle against drowsiness and wandering thoughts.<br>• learn to concentrate—to discipline our minds and control our thoughts.<br>• teach ourselves to be watchful in prayer. |
| **#2244**<br>**Keeping Eyes**<br><br>Looking–KJV<br>Fixing eyes–NASB<br>Fix eyes–NIV<br>Looking–NKJV<br>**Keeping eyes–NLT**<br><br>**POSB REFERENCE**<br>(Heb.12:2)<br>Note 3 | ἀφορῶντες = *aphorōntes*<br>Pronunciation: [af-or-own'-tehs]<br>Parsing (part of speech): verb<br>   Mood—participle<br>   Tense—present<br>   Voice—active<br>   Case—nominative<br>   Gender—masculine<br>   Person—1st person<br>   Number—plural<br>   Stem or root—from ἀφοράω<br>Concordance References:<br>  ⇒ Strong's #872 aphoraō<br>  ⇒ NIV #927 aphoraō<br>  ⇒ NASB #872 aphoraō<br><br>**Hebrews 12:2**<br>**Looking** unto Jesus the author and finisher of our faith; who for the joy that was set before him endured the cross, despising the shame, and is set down at the right hand of the throne of God. [KJV]<br>**Fixing** our **eyes** on Jesus, the author and perfecter of faith, who for the joy set before Him endured the cross, despising the shame, and has sat down at the right hand of | To fix one's eyes on; to keep one's eyes on; to look. The words "keeping eyes" (*aphorōntes*) means to fix your eyes upon Jesus. It also means to fix your mind upon Him (Kenneth Wuest. *Hebrews*, Vol. 2, p.214).<br><br>**Practical Application**<br>We may and should look at the example of other believers, but we should always be *keeping our eyes on Jesus*. The Christian runner is to focus his eyes and mind upon Jesus Christ. Why? Because Jesus Christ Himself ran the race of faith when He was upon earth, and He shows us exactly how to run it. |

# Practical Word Studies
## in the New Testament

| ENGLISH WORD | GREEK WORD AND VERSE | THE WORD MEANS... |
|---|---|---|
| | the throne of God. [NASB]<br>    Let us **fix** our **eyes** on Jesus, the author and perfecter of our faith, who for the joy set before him endured the cross, scorning its shame, and sat down at the right hand of the throne of God. [NIV]<br>    **Looking** unto Jesus, the author and finisher of our faith, who for the joy that was set before Him endured the cross, despising the shame, and has sat down at the right hand of the throne of God. [NKJV]<br>    We do this by **keeping** our **eyes** on Jesus, on whom our faith depends from start to finish. He was willing to die a shameful death on the cross because of the joy he knew would be his afterward. Now he is seated in the place of highest honor beside God's throne in heaven. [NLT]<br>    ἀφορῶντες εἰς τὸν τῆς πίστεως ἀρχηγὸν καὶ τελειωτὴν Ἰησοῦν, ὃς ἀντὶ τῆς προκειμένης αὐτῷ χαρᾶς ὑπέμεινεν σταυρόν, αἰσχύνης καταφρονήσας, ἐν δεξιᾷ τε τοῦ θρόνου τοῦ Θεοῦ ἐκάθισεν. [GNS]<br>    ἀφορῶντες εἰς τὸν τῆς πίστεως ἀρχηγὸν καὶ τελειωτὴν Ἰησοῦν, ὃς ἀντὶ τῆς προκειμένης αὐτῷ χαρᾶς ὑπέμεινεν σταυρὸν αἰσχύνης καταφρονήσας ἐν δεξιᾷ τε τοῦ θρόνου τοῦ θεοῦ κεκάθικεν. [GNT] | |
| **#2245**<br>**Kept**<br><br>**Kept**–KJV<br>Protected–NASB<br>Shielded–NIV<br>**Kept**–NKJV<br>Protect–NLT<br><br>**POSB<br>REFERENCE**<br>(1 Pt.1:5)<br>Note 3, point 1 | φρουρουμένους = *phrouroumenous*<br>Pronunciation: [froo-roo-meh'-noos]<br>Parsing (part of speech): verb<br>    Mood—participle<br>    Tense—present<br>    Voice—passive<br>    Case—accusative<br>    Gender—masculine<br>    Person—2nd person<br>    Number—plural<br>    Stem or root—from φρουρέω<br>Concordance References:<br>  ⇒ Strong's #5432 phroureō<br>  ⇒ NIV #5864 phroureō<br>  ⇒ NASB #5432 phroureō<br><br>**1 Peter 1:5**<br>    Who are **kept** by the power of God through faith unto salvation ready to be revealed in the last time. [KJV]<br>    Who are **protected** by the power of God through faith for a salvation ready to be revealed in the last time. [NASB]<br>    Who through faith are **shielded** by God's power until the coming of the salvation that is ready to be revealed in the last time. [NIV]<br>    Who are **kept** by the power of God through faith for salvation ready to be revealed in the last time. [NKJV]<br>    And God, in his mighty power, will **protect** you until you receive this salvation, because you are trusting him. It will be revealed on the last day for all to see. [NLT]<br>    τοὺς ἐν δυνάμει Θεοῦ **φρουρουμένους** διὰ πίστεως εἰς σωτηρίαν ἑτοίμην ἀποκαλυφθῆναι ἐν καιρῷ ἐσχάτῳ. [GNS]<br>    τοὺς ἐν δυνάμει θεοῦ **φρουρουμένους** διὰ πίστεως εἰς σωτηρίαν ἑτοίμην ἀποκαλυφθῆναι ἐν καιρῷ ἐσχάτῳ. [GNT] | Shielded; to keep; to protect; to guard; to garrison.<br><br>**Practical Application**<br>    It is a military term; therefore, it has the idea of might and strength. The might and strength of God's power keeps us throughout our journey in life—through all the trials and temptations of life—and God will see to it that we will reach the glorious end of life: salvation. God Himself, in His sovereign and omnipotent power, will see to it that we receive eternal life and the inheritance that is being reserved for us. |
| **#2246**<br>**Kept**<br><br>Preserved–KJV<br>**Kept**–NASB<br>**Kept**–NIV<br>Preserved–NKJV<br>Care–NLT | τετηρημένοις = *tetērēmenois*<br>Pronunciation: [teh-tay-ray'-men-oys]<br>Parsing (part of speech): verb<br>    Mood—participle<br>    Tense—perfect<br>    Voice—passive<br>    Case—dative<br>    Gender—masculine<br>    Number—plural<br>    Stem or root—from τηρέω | To be kept; to be preserved; to be protected; to care; to keep in custody; to be guarded and watched after.<br><br>**Practical Application**<br>    Believers are "kept by Jesus Christ." God keeps the believer, guards and watches over him. The believer is a person...<br>• who is watched over by God.<br>• who is guided and directed by God day by day. |

## PRACTICAL WORD STUDIES
### in the NEW TESTAMENT

| ENGLISH WORD | GREEK WORD AND VERSE | THE WORD MEANS... |
|---|---|---|
| **POSB REFERENCE** (Jude 1:1-2; esp. v.1) Note 2, point 2 | Concordance References:<br>⇒ Strong's #5083 tēreō<br>⇒ NIV #5498 tēreō<br>⇒ NASB #5083 tēreō<br><br>**Jude 1:1**<br>Jude, the servant of Jesus Christ, and brother of James, to them that are sanctified by God the Father, and **preserved** in Jesus Christ, and called: [KJV]<br>Jude, a bond-servant of Jesus Christ, and brother of James, to those who are the called, beloved in God the Father, and **kept** for Jesus Christ: [NASB]<br>Jude, a servant of Jesus Christ and a brother of James,To those who have been called, who are loved by God the Father and **kept** by Jesus Christ: [NIV]<br>Jude, a bondservant of Jesus Christ, and brother of James, To those who are called, sanctified by God the Father, and **preserved** in Jesus Christ: [NKJV]<br>This letter is from Jude, a slave of Jesus Christ and a brother of James. I am writing to all who are called to live in the love of God the Father and the **care** of Jesus Christ. [NLT]<br>Ἰούδας Ἰησοῦ Χριστοῦ δοῦλος, ἀδελφὸς δὲ Ἰακώβου, τοῖς ἐν Θεῷ πατρὶ ἡγιασμένοις, καὶ Ἰησοῦ Χριστῷ **τετηρημένοις**, κλητοῖς· [GNS]<br>Ἰούδας Ἰησοῦ Χριστοῦ δοῦλος, ἀδελφὸς δὲ Ἰακώβου, τοῖς ἐν θεῷ πατρὶ ἠγαπημένοις καὶ Ἰησοῦ Χριστῷ **τετηρημένοις** κλητοῖς· [GNT] | • who is strengthened by God to walk through all the trials and temptations of life.<br>• who is protected from all the enemies of life, even death.<br>• who is to be escorted into heaven quicker than the blink of an eye when the time comes for him to leave this world.<br>• who is given life, both abundant and eternal.<br>• who is given assurance of God's presence and love through all of life.<br>The true believer is a person who is preserved and kept by God. He is a person who is looked after and cared for by God. But note: it is *in Jesus Christ* that God keeps a person. The believer is a person who has placed his life into Jesus Christ; he is a person who is *trusting* Jesus Christ to save him. It is the true believer in Jesus Christ whom God keeps or preserves. |
| **#2247**<br>**Kept Asking**<br><br>Besought–KJV<br>**Kept asking–NASB**<br>Begged–NIV<br>**Kept asking–NKJV**<br>Begged–NLT<br><br>**POSB REFERENCE** (Mk.7:26-28; esp. v.26) Note 3 | ἠρώτα = erota<br>Pronunciation: [er-o-tah']<br>Parsing (part of speech): verb<br>    Mood—indicative<br>    Tense—imperfect<br>    Voice—active<br>    Person—3rd person<br>    Number—singular<br>    Stem or root—from ἐρωτάω<br>Concordance References:<br>⇒ Strong's #2065 erōtaō<br>⇒ NIV #2263 erōtaō<br>⇒ NASB #2065 erōtaō<br><br>**Mark 7:26**<br>The woman was a Greek, a Syrophenician by nation; and she **besought** him that he would cast forth the devil out of her daughter. [KJV]<br>Now the woman was a Gentile, of the Syrophoenician race. And she **kept asking** Him to cast the demon out of her daughter. [NASB]<br>The woman was a Greek, born in Syrian Phoenicia. She **begged** Jesus to drive the demon out of her daughter. [NIV]<br>The woman was a Greek, a Syro-Phoenician by birth, and she **kept asking** Him to cast the demon out of her daughter. [NKJV]<br>She **begged** him to release her child from the demon's control. Since she was a Gentile, born in Syrian Phoenicia, [NLT]<br>ἐν δὲ ἡ δὲ γυνὴ Ἑλληνίς, Συροφοινίσσα τῷ γένει· καὶ **ἠρώτα** αὐτὸν ἵνα τὸ δαιμόνιον ἐκβάλῃ ἐκ τῆς θυγατρὸς αὐτῆς. [GNS]<br>ἡ δὲ γυνὴ ἦν Ἑλληνίς, Συροφοινίκισσα τῷ γένει· καὶ **ἠρώτα** αὐτὸν ἵνα τὸ δαιμόνιον ἐκβάλῃ ἐκ τῆς θυγατρὸς αὐτῆς. [GNT] | To ask, to plead, to beseech, or to implore; to beg and to keep on begging.<br><br>**Practical Application**<br>The woman kept asking Christ to heal her demon-possessed daughter. The phrase "kept asking" is in the Greek imperfect tense which means she kept on begging and begging. Note that Jesus kept on listening and listening. |
| **#2248**<br>**Kept In Custody, Protective**<br><br>Kept under–KJV<br>**Kept in custody–NASB** | ἐφρουρούμεθα = ephrouroumetha<br>Pronunciation: [eh-froo-roo'-meh-tha]<br>Parsing (part of speech): verb<br>    Mood—indicative<br>    Tense—imperfect<br>    Voice—passive<br>    Person—1st person<br>    Number—plural | To be held prisoner; kept under; kept in protective custody; to keep watch over; to be guarded, kept in custody, imprisoned, held in bondage.<br><br>**Practical Application**<br>Very simply, the law shuts man up in protective custody; it imprisons and holds man in |

# PRACTICAL WORD STUDIES
## in the NEW TESTAMENT

| ENGLISH WORD | GREEK WORD AND VERSE | THE WORD MEANS... |
|---|---|---|
| Held prisoners–NIV<br>Kept under guard–NKJV<br>**Kept in protective custody–NLT**<br><br>**POSB REFERENCE**<br>(Gal.3:23-25; esp. v.23)<br>Note 1 | Stem or root—from φρουρέω<br>Concordance References:<br>⇒ Strong's #5432 phroureō<br>⇒ NIV #5864 phroureō<br>⇒ NASB #5432 phroureō<br><br>**Galatians 3:23**<br>But before faith came, we were **kept under** the law, shut up unto the faith which should afterwards be revealed. [KJV]<br>But before faith came, we were **kept in custody** under the law, being shut up to the faith which was later to be revealed. [NASB]<br>Before this faith came, we were **held prisoners** by the law, locked up until faith should be revealed. [NIV]<br>But before faith came, we were **kept under guard** by the law, kept for the faith which would afterward be revealed. [NKJV]<br>Until faith in Christ was shown to us as the way of becoming right with God, we were guarded by the law. We were **kept in protective custody**, so to speak, until we could put our faith in the coming Savior. [NLT]<br>Πρὸ τοῦ δὲ ἐλθεῖν τὴν πίστιν, ὑπὸ νόμον ἐφρουρούμεθα συγκλειόμενοι εἰς τὴν μέλλουσαν πίστιν ἀποκαλυφθῆναι. [GNS]<br>Πρὸ τοῦ δὲ ἐλθεῖν τὴν πίστιν ὑπὸ νόμον ἐφρουρούμεθα συγκλειόμενοι εἰς τὴν μέλλουσαν πίστιν ἀποκαλυφθῆναι, [GNT] | bondage to sin. How?<br>1. The law shows man exactly where he fails—exactly where he comes short. There is no question about it: the law said to do this, but the man did that. He did not do this. The failure is clearly spelled out, just as clearly as a speed limit sign spells out the violation of the speeder.<br>2. The law accuses and condemns man. As soon as a person violates the law, the law charges him. The law is in black and white, written down, so there is no question about it's having been broken. Therefore, it preys upon the man's mind, cuts and convicts his heart. Guilt and conviction take over, troubling and vexing the man to varying degrees, all dependent on the seriousness of the violation.<br>The law has no life and no power to deliver man from the punishment due him for his violation. This is the whole point: the law reveals the violation and condemns man; it imprisons him. The law does not deliver man; it condemns man to bondage. It continues and continues to point out man's sins and failures. And the case of the law is endless: its finger of accusation points out the man's failure every time he violates it. The bondage to the law is perpetual. |
| **#2249**<br>**Kept Under,**<br>**Guard**<br><br>Kept under–KJV<br>Kept in custody–NASB<br>Held prisoners–NIV<br>**Kept under guard–NKJV**<br>Kept in protective custody–NLT<br><br>**POSB REFERENCE**<br>(Gal.3:23-25; esp. v.23)<br>Note 1 | ἐφρουρούμεθα = ephrouroumetha<br>Pronunciation: [eh-froo-roo'-meh-tha]<br>Parsing (part of speech): verb<br>  Mood—indicative<br>  Tense—imperfect<br>  Voice—passive<br>  Person—1st person<br>  Number—plural<br>Stem or root—from φρουρέω<br>Concordance References:<br>⇒ Strong's #5432 phroureō<br>⇒ NIV #5864 phroureō<br>⇒ NASB #5432 phroureō<br><br>**Galatians 3:23**<br>But before faith came, we were **kept under** the law, shut up unto the faith which should afterwards be revealed. [KJV]<br>But before faith came, we were **kept in custody** under the law, being shut up to the faith which was later to be revealed. [NASB]<br>Before this faith came, we were **held prisoners** by the law, locked up until faith should be revealed. [NIV]<br>But before faith came, we were **kept under guard** by the law, kept for the faith which would afterward be revealed. [NKJV]<br>Until faith in Christ was shown to us as the way of becoming right with God, we were guarded by the law. We were **kept in protective custody**, so to speak, until we could put our faith in the coming Savior. [NLT]<br>Πρὸ τοῦ δὲ ἐλθεῖν τὴν πίστιν, ὑπὸ νόμον ἐφρουρούμεθα συγκλειόμενοι εἰς τὴν μέλλουσαν πίστιν ἀποκαλυφθῆναι. [GNS]<br>Πρὸ τοῦ δὲ ἐλθεῖν τὴν πίστιν ὑπὸ νόμον ἐφρουρούμεθα συγκλειόμενοι εἰς τὴν μέλλουσαν πίστιν ἀποκαλυφθῆναι, [GNT] | To be held prisoner; kept under; kept in protective custody; to keep watch over; to be guarded, kept in custody, imprisoned, held in bondage.<br><br>**Practical Application**<br>Very simply, the law shuts man up under guard; it imprisons and holds man in bondage to sin. How?<br>1. The law shows man exactly where he fails—exactly where he comes short. There is no question about it: the law said to do this, but the man did that. He did not do this. The failure is clearly spelled out, just as clearly as a speed limit sign spells out the violation of the speeder.<br>2. The law accuses and condemns man. As soon as a person violates the law, the law charges him. The law is in black and white, written down, so there is no question about it's having been broken. Therefore, it preys upon the man's mind, cuts and convicts his heart. Guilt and conviction take over, troubling and vexing the man to varying degrees, all dependent on the seriousness of the violation.<br>3. The law has no life and no power to deliver man from the punishment due him for his violation. This is the whole point: the law reveals the violation and condemns man; it imprisons him. The law does not deliver man; it condemns man to bondage. It continues and continues to point out man's sins and failures. And the case of the law is endless: its finger of accusation points out the man's failure every time he violates it. The bondage to the law is perpetual. |
| **#2250**<br>**Kill** | ἀπολέσαι = apolesai<br>Pronunciation: [ap-ol'-ee-sah-ee]<br>Parsing (part of speech): verb<br>  Mood—infinitive<br>  Tense—aorist | To utterly destroy; to demolish; to obliterate; to cause to perish; to bring to an end; to put to death. |

# PRACTICAL WORD STUDIES
## in the NEW TESTAMENT

| ENGLISH WORD | GREEK WORD AND VERSE | THE WORD MEANS... |
|---|---|---|
| Destroy–KJV<br>Destroy–NASB<br>**Kill–NIV**<br>Destroy–NKJV<br>**Kill–NLT**<br><br>**POSB REFERENCE**<br>(Lk.19:47-48; esp. v.47)<br>Note 3, point 1a<br><br>See also POSB REF:<br>(Mk.11:18)<br>Note 3 | Voice—active<br>Stem or root—from ἀπόλλυμι<br>Concordance References:<br>⇒ Strong's #622 apollumi<br>⇒ NIV #660 apollumi<br>⇒ NASB #622 apollumi<br><br>**Luke 19:47**<br>And he taught daily in the temple. But the chief priests and the scribes and the chief of the people sought to **destroy** him, [KJV]<br>And He was teaching daily in the temple; but the chief priests and the scribes and the leading men among the people were trying to **destroy** Him, [NASB]<br>Every da = y he was teaching at the temple. But the chief priests, the teachers of the law and the leaders among the people were trying to **kill** him. [NIV]<br>And He was teaching daily in the temple. But the chief priests, the scribes, and the leaders of the people sought to **destroy** Him, [NKJV]<br>After that, he taught daily in the Temple, but the leading priests, the teachers of religious law, and the other leaders of the people began planning how to **kill** him. [NLT]<br>Καὶ ἦν διδάσκων τὸ καθ' ἡμέραν ἐν τῷ ἱερῷ· οἱ δὲ ἀρχιερεῖς καὶ οἱ γραμματεῖς ἐζήτουν αὐτὸν **ἀπολέσαι**, καὶ οἱ πρῶτοι τοῦ λαοῦ· [GNS]<br>Καὶ ἦν διδάσκων τὸ καθ' ἡμέραν ἐν τῷ ἱερῷ. οἱ δὲ ἀρχιερεῖς καὶ οἱ γραμματεῖς ἐζήτουν αὐτὸν **ἀπολέσαι** καὶ οἱ πρῶτοι τοῦ λαοῦ, [GNT] | **Practical Application**<br>In this Scripture, note two things:<br>1. The leaders were actively seeking to "kill" (*apolesai*) Christ. (Imagine religious leaders being so disturbed that they sought to destroy and ruin the ministry of a person.)<br>2. The reason why the leaders were so disturbed was twofold: first, they were losing control of the temple; and second, they were losing control of the people. Jesus had invaded their temple by cleansing it; and He was teaching the true gospel of the Kingdom of God and righteousness. They were losing money because Jesus had cast out the vendors, and their own personal ideas and control were being undermined. They were unwilling to accept the truth personally and to surrender their lives to Jesus. (See POSB notes—Matthew 12:1-8; POSB note—Matthew 12:10 and POSB *Deeper Study* #1—Matthew 12:10 for more discussion.) |
| #2251<br>**Kind**<br><br>**Kind–KJV**<br>**Kind–NASB**<br>**Kind–NIV**<br>**Kind–NKJV**<br>**Kind–NLT**<br><br>**POSB REFERENCE**<br>(Eph.4:32)<br>Note 7, point 1 | χρηστοί = chrēstoi<br>Pronunciation: [khrase-toy']<br>Parsing (part of speech): adjective<br>   Case—nominative<br>   Gender—masculine<br>   Number—plural<br>   Stem or root—from χρηστός, ή, όν<br>Concordance References:<br>⇒ Strong's #5543 chrēstos<br>⇒ NIV #5982 chrēstos<br>⇒ NASB #5543 chrēstos<br><br>**Ephes. 4:32**<br>And be ye **kind** one to another, tenderhearted, forgiving one another, even as God for Christ's sake hath forgiven you. [KJV]<br>And be **kind** to one another, tender-hearted, forgiving each other, just as God in Christ also has forgiven you. [NASB]<br>Be **kind** and compassionate to one another, forgiving each other, just as in Christ God forgave you. [NIV]<br>And be **kind** to one another, tenderhearted, forgiving one another, just as God in Christ forgave you. [NKJV]<br>Instead, be **kind** to each other, tenderhearted, forgiving one another, just as God through Christ has forgiven you. [NLT]<br>γίνεσθε δὲ εἰς ἀλλήλους **χρηστοί**, εὔσπλαγχνοι, χαριζόμενοι ἑαυτοῖς, καθὼς καὶ ὁ Θεὸς ἐν Χριστῷ ἐχαρίσατο ὑμῖν. [GNS]<br>γίνεσθε [δὲ] εἰς ἀλλήλους **χρηστοί**, εὔσπλαγχνοι, χαριζόμενοι ἑαυτοῖς, καθὼς καὶ ὁ Θεὸς ἐν Χριστῷ ἐχαρίσατο ὑμῖν. [GNT] | Kind. It means to be gentle, caring, helpful, courteous, good, useful, giving, and showering favors upon people.<br><br>**Practical Application**<br>It is the opposite of being neglectful, harsh, sharp, bitter, and resentful. Lehman Strauss points out that kindness comes from such words as *kin* and *kindred* which means that it treats a person as one's own kin. Believers are brothers in the Lord (*Devotional Studies in Galatians and Ephesians*, p.189). |
| #2252<br>**Kind**<br><br>Gentle–KJV<br>**Kind–NASB**<br>**Kind–NIV**<br>Gentle–NKJV<br>**Kind–NLT** | ἤπιον = ēpion<br>Pronunciation: [ay'-pee-on]<br>Parsing (part of speech): adjective<br>   Gender—accusative<br>   Gender—masculine<br>   Number—singular<br>   Stem or root—from ἤπιος, α, ον<br>Concordance References:<br>⇒ Strong's #2261 ēpios | Kind, gentle, reasonable, considerate, soft, tender.<br><br>**Practical Application**<br>Do not argue or fight with others. This charge is to the servant of the Lord—the person who really wishes to serve the Lord. We cannot argue and fight and, at the same time, serve the Lord. |

# PRACTICAL WORD STUDIES
## in the NEW TESTAMENT

| ENGLISH WORD | GREEK WORD AND VERSE | THE WORD MEANS... |
|---|---|---|
| **POSB REFERENCE** (2 Tim. 2:24-26 esp. v.24) Note 4 | ⇒ NIV #2473 ëpios<br>⇒ NASB #2261 ëpios<br><br>**2 Tim. 2:24**<br>And the servant of the Lord must not strive; but be **gentle** unto all men, apt to teach, patient, [KJV]<br>And the Lord's bond-servant must not be quarrelsome, but be **kind** to all, able to teach, patient when wronged, [NASB]<br>And the Lord's servant must not quarrel; instead, he must be **kind** to everyone, able to teach, not resentful. [NIV]<br>And a servant of the Lord must not quarrel but be **gentle** to all, able to teach, patient, [NKJV]<br>The Lord's servants must not quarrel but must be **kind** to everyone. They must be able to teach effectively and be patient with difficult people. [NLT]<br>δοῦλον δὲ Κυρίου οὐ δεῖ μάχεσθαι, ἀλλ **ἤπιον** εἶναι πρὸς πάντας, διδακτικόν, ἀνεξίκακον, [GNS]<br>δοῦλον δὲ κυρίου οὐ δεῖ μάχεσθαι ἀλλὰ **ἤπιον** εἶναι πρὸς πάντας, διδακτικόν, ἀνεξίκακον, [GNT] | A person who argues and fights is not serving the Lord, no matter what he may claim. The charge is clear: the servant of the Lord must not quarrel. He must be gentle (*ëpion*) or kind:<br>⇒ When people oppose him, he does not react, he reaches out in kindness.<br>⇒ When he has to correct people by pointing out their weaknesses, he is not mean but kind. |
| **#2253**<br>**Kind**<br><br>Good–KJV<br>**Kind–NASB**<br>**Kind–NIV**<br>Good–NKJV<br>Good–NLT<br><br>**POSB REFERENCE** (Tit.2:4-5; esp. v.5) Note 4, point 7 | ἀγαθάς = *agathas*<br>Pronunciation: [ag-ath-ahs']<br>Parsing (part of speech): adjective<br>    Case—accusative<br>    Gender—feminine<br>    Number—plural<br>    Stem or root—from ἀγαθός, ή, όν<br>Concordance References:<br>  ⇒ Strong's #18 agathos<br>  ⇒ NIV #19 agathos<br>  ⇒ NASB #18 agathos<br><br>**Titus 2:5**<br>To be discreet, chaste, keepers at home, **good**, obedient to their own husbands, that the word of God be not blasphemed. [KJV]<br>To be sensible, pure, workers at home, **kind**, being subject to their own husbands, that the word of God may not be dishonored. [NASB]<br>To be self-controlled and pure, to be busy at home, to be **kind**, and to be subject to their husbands, so that no one will malign the word of God. [NIV]<br>To be discreet, chaste, homemakers, **good**, obedient to their own husbands, that the word of God may not be blasphemed. [NKJV]<br>To live wisely and be pure, to take care of their homes, to do **good**, and to be submissive to their husbands. Then they will not bring shame on the word of God. [NLT]<br>σώφρονας, ἁγνάς, οἰκουργοὺς **ἀγαθάς**, ὑποτασσομένας τοῖς ἰδίοις ἀνδράσιν, ἵνα μὴ ὁ λόγος τοῦ Θεοῦ βλασφημῆται· [GNS]<br>σώφρονας ἁγνάς οἰκουργούς **ἀγαθάς**, ὑποτασσομένας τοῖς ἰδίοις ἀνδράσιν, ἵνα μὴ ὁ λόγος τοῦ θεοῦ βλασφημῆται. [GNT] | Kind, good, useful, sound; of the highest quality and character; virtuous through and through; good natured and caring.<br><br>**Practical Application**<br>A young woman is to be kind (*agathas*): There is no vice, no dirt or pollution in her life; she is pure and clean, of the highest character. And she is kind to people, that is, good and caring. She is not an idle person, going from house to house being a gossiper and busy body. She is purposeful, moving in and among people doing good, showing care and kindness, helping people wherever she can (cp. 1 Tim. 5:13). |
| **#2254**<br>**Kind–Kindness**<br><br>Goodness–KJV<br>**Kindness–NASB**<br>**Kindness–NIV**<br>Goodness–NKJV<br>**Kind–NLT**<br><br>**POSB REFERENCE** (Romans 2:2-5; esp. v.4) Note 2, point 2 | χρηστὸν = *chrëston*<br>Pronunciation: [khrase-ton']<br>Parsing (part of speech): pronominal adjective<br>    Case—nominative<br>    Gender—neuter<br>    Number—singular<br>    Stem or root—from χρηστός, ή, όν<br>Concordance References:<br>  ⇒ Strong's #5543 chrëstos<br>  ⇒ NIV #5982 chrëstos<br>  ⇒ NASB #5543 chrëstos<br><br>**Romans 2:4**<br>Or despisest thou the riches of his **goodness** and forbearance and longsuffering; not knowing that the goodness of God leadeth thee to repentance? [KJV] | Kindness, goodness, mercy.<br><br>**Practical Application**<br>The moralist thinks God is too good to punish. When he thinks of God, he thinks of the riches...<br>• of God's kindness (*chrëston*): His goodness and grace and love.<br>• of God's forbearance or tolerance (*anoche*): His refraining, holding back, abstaining and controlling His justice.<br>• of God's longsuffering: His suffering a long time, being patient and slow in judging sin.<br>God, of course, is all this and much more. What the moralist fails to see is that God's goodness is not a blank check for sin. God's goodness |

# PRACTICAL WORD STUDIES
## in the NEW TESTAMENT

| ENGLISH WORD | GREEK WORD AND VERSE | THE WORD MEANS... |
|---|---|---|
|  | Or do you think lightly of the riches of His **kindness** and forbearance and patience, not knowing that the kindness of God leads you to repentance? [NASB]<br>Or do you show contempt for the riches of his **kindness**, tolerance and patience, not realizing that God's kindness leads you toward repentance? [NIV]<br>Or do you despise the riches of His **goodness**, forbearance, and longsuffering, not knowing that the goodness of God leads you to repentance? [NKJV]<br>Don't you realize how **kind**, tolerant, and patient God is with you? Or don't you care? Can't you see how kind he has been in giving you time to turn from your sin? [NLT]<br>ἢ τοῦ πλούτου τῆς χρηστότητος αὐτοῦ καὶ τῆς ἀνοχῆς καὶ τῆς μακροθυμίας καταφρονεῖς, ἀγνοῶν ὅτι τὸ **χρηστὸν** τοῦ θεοῦ εἰς μετάνοιάν σε ἄγει; [GNS]<br>ἢ τοῦ πλούτου τῆς χρηστότητος αὐτοῦ καὶ τῆς ἀνοχῆς καὶ τῆς μακροθυμίας καταφρονεῖς, ἀγνοῶν ὅτι τὸ **χρηστὸν** τοῦ θεοῦ εἰς μετάνοιάν σε ἄγει; [GNT] | does not...<br>• give license to sin.<br>• condone sin.<br>• indulge sin.<br>• overlook sin.<br>God's kindness is to lead men to repentance, not to sin. The fact that God *will* forgive sin should stir men to seek forgiveness and to please God. If a man sins thinking that God will just overlook and forgive his sin, he is despising God's kindness. He is taking God's goodness and making it a sham, a mockery, a joke, a thing of indulgence. The man who *despises* God's kindness—who sins thinking God will just overlook and forgive his sin—is wrong. He is mistaken. God does not just overlook and forgive his sin; He does not condone, indulge, nor give license to his sin. God will judge him and the judgment will be according to the truth. |
| **#2255**<br>**Kindhearted**<br><br>Pitiful–KJV<br>**Kindhearted–NASB**<br>Compassionate–NIV<br>Tenderhearted–NKJV<br>Tender hearts–NLT<br><br>**POSB REFERENCE**<br>(1 Pt.3:8)<br>Note 4 | εὔσπλαγχνοι = *eusplagchnoi*<br>Pronunciation: [yoo'-splangkh-noy]<br>Parsing (part of speech): adjective<br>  Case—nominative<br>  Gender—masculine<br>  Number—plural<br>  Stem or root—from εὔσπλαγχνος, ον<br>Concordance References:<br>⇒ Strong's #2155 eusplagchnos<br>⇒ NIV #2359 eusplagchnos<br>⇒ NASB #2155 eusplagchnos<br><br>**1 Peter 3:8**<br>Finally, be ye all of one mind, having compassion one of another, love as brethren, be **pitiful**, be courteous: [KJV]<br>To sum up, let all be harmonious, sympathetic, brotherly, **kindhearted**, and humble in spirit; [NASB]<br>Finally, all of you, live in harmony with one another; be sympathetic, love as brothers, be **compassionate** and humble. [NIV]<br>Finally, all *of you be* of one mind, having compassion for one another; love as brothers, *be* **tenderhearted**, *be* courteous; [NKJV]<br>Finally, all of you should be of one mind, full of sympathy toward each other, loving one another with **tender hearts** and humble minds. [NLT]<br>Τὸ δὲ τέλος, πάντες ὁμόφρονες, συμπαθεῖς, φιλάδελφοι, **εὔσπλαγχνοι**, φιλόφρονες· [GNS]<br>Τὸ δὲ τέλος πάντες ὁμόφρονες, συμπαθεῖς, φιλάδελφοι, **εὔσπλαγχνοι**, ταπεινόφρονες, [GNT] | To be compassionate; to pity; to be kindhearted; to have a tender heart. It means to be tenderhearted; to be sensitive and affectionate toward the needs of others; to be moved with tender feelings over the pain and sufferings of others.<br><br>**Practical Application**<br>We live in a world that desperately needs pity, a world of extreme suffering. So many suffer and continue to suffer without ever having their needs met. The means and resources to meet their needs exist, but so many within the world have become hardened to the sufferings of others. They bank, hoard, and build up asset after asset instead of sacrificing and reaching out to meet the needs of the world. But this is not to be true of the believer. Believers are to have pity upon the sufferings of others. Believers are to feel pity to the point that they are moved to act, sacrificing and reaching out to meet the needs of the suffering.<br>Again, note how compassion or being kindhearted leaves no room for selfishness. Being kindhearted demands that a person deny himself and help others in their desperate needs and sufferings. Note also how pity draws people together. Helping and ministering to one another binds and knits people together. Having compassion—feeling for one another and sacrificing and reaching out to help one another—unites people together. A great bond is created between the believer and those to whom he ministers. |
| **#2256**<br>**Kindle Afresh**<br><br>Stir up–KJV<br>**Kindle afresh–NASB**<br>Fan into flame–NIV<br>Stir up–NKJV<br>Fan into flames–NLT<br><br>**POSB REFERENCE**<br>(2 Tim.1:6)<br>Note 1 | ἀναζωπυρεῖν = *anazōpurein*<br>Pronunciation: [an-ad-zo-poor-eh'-een]<br>Parsing (part of speech): verb<br>  Mood—infinitive<br>  Tense—present<br>  Voice—active<br>  Stem or root—from ἀναζωπυρέω<br>Concordance References:<br>⇒ Strong's #329 anazōpureō<br>⇒ NIV #351 anazōpureō<br>⇒ NASB #329 anazōpureō<br><br>**2 Tim. 1:6**<br>Wherefore I put thee in remembrance that thou **stir up** the gift of God, which is in thee by the putting on of my hands. [KJV]<br>And for this reason I remind you to **kindle afresh** the | To fan into flame; to stir up; to kindle afresh; to stir into flame.<br><br>**Practical Application**<br>The words "kindle afresh" (*anazōpurein*) can mean to keep blazing and to keep the flame of the fire burning. But it can also mean to rekindle and to restir the flame, indicating that the flame was about to go out. Which is meant here? No doubt Timothy faced what we sometimes face: times when he needed to be restirred and rekindled. But there is no indication that Timothy's flame was about to go out.<br>Keep this is mind: Paul was facing death; he was about to be executed. He clearly states this fact (2 Tim. 4:6-8). Therefore, Paul sensed the |

## PRACTICAL WORD STUDIES in the NEW TESTAMENT

| ENGLISH WORD | GREEK WORD AND VERSE | THE WORD MEANS... |
|---|---|---|
| | gift of God which is in you through the laying on of my hands. [NASB]<br><br>For this reason I remind you to **fan into flame** the gift of God, which is in you through the laying on of my hands. [NIV]<br><br>Therefore I remind you to **stir up** the gift of God which is in you through the laying on of my hands. [NKJV]<br><br>This is why I remind you to **fan into flames** the spiritual gift God gave you when I laid my hands on you. [NLT]<br><br>δι' ἣν αἰτίαν ἀναμιμνῄσκω σε **ἀναζωπυρεῖν** τὸ χάρισμα τοῦ Θεοῦ, ὅ ἐστιν ἐν σοὶ διὰ τῆς ἐπιθέσεως τῶν χειρῶν μου. [GNS]<br><br>δι' ἣν αἰτίαν ἀναμιμνῄσκω σε **ἀναζωπυρεῖν** τὸ χάρισμα τοῦ Θεοῦ, ὅ ἐστιν ἐν σοὶ διὰ τῆς ἐπιθέσεως τῶν χειρῶν μου. [GNT] | need to give Timothy charge after charge. One of the very first things Timothy needed to do was to keep his spiritual gifts blazing and burning to the hottest point possible. The idea is present tense, which means it is progressive and continuous action. The believer is to *keep on* stirring up his gift, never letting its flame lose any of its intensity. He is to use his gift to minister and minister, never slacking up nor losing his zeal. God has gifted the believer to minister, gifted him in a very, very special way; therefore, he must minister. He must do exactly what God has gifted him to do. |
| **#2257**<br>**Kindly Affectionate—Kindly Affectioned**<br><br>**Kindly affectioned–** KJV<br>Devoted–NASB<br>Devoted–NIV<br>**Kindly affectionate–** NKJV<br>Genuine affection–NLT<br><br>**POSB REFERENCE**<br>(Rom.12:9-10; esp. v.10)<br>Note 1, point 3 | φιλόστοργοι = *philostorgoi*<br>Pronunciation: [fil-os'-tor-goy]<br>Parsing (part of speech): adjective<br>    Case—nominative<br>    Gender—masculine<br>    Number—plural<br>    Stem or root—from φιλόστοργος, ον<br>Concordance References:<br>⇒ Strong's #5387 philostorgos<br>⇒ NIV #5816 philostorgos<br>⇒ NASB #5387 philostorgos<br><br>**Romans 12:10**<br>Be **kindly affectioned** one to another with brotherly love; in honour preferring one another; [KJV]<br><br>Be **devoted** to one another in brotherly love; give preference to one another in honor; [NASB]<br><br>Be **devoted** to one another in brotherly love. Honor one another above yourselves. [NIV]<br><br>*Be* **kindly affectionate** to one another with brotherly love, in honor giving preference to one another; [NKJV]<br><br>Love each other with **genuine affection**, and take delight in honoring each other. [NLT]<br><br>τῇ φιλαδελφίᾳ εἰς ἀλλήλους **φιλόστοργοι**· τῇ τιμῇ ἀλλήλους προηγούμενοι [GNS]<br><br>τῇ φιλαδελφίᾳ εἰς ἀλλήλους **φιλόστοργοι**, τῇ τιμῇ ἀλλήλους προηγούμενοι, [GNT] | Loving, devoted. The word "devoted" (*philostorgoi*) means the love existing between family members.<br><br>**Practical Application**<br>The believer is to love his brothers in Christ, by being kind and affectionate toward them. This charge is dealing with the Christian family, the brothers and sisters within the church. We are to love each other by being kind and affectionate. We are a family of children who have actually been adopted by God as His sons and daughters (2 Cor. 6:17-18; Galatians 4:4-6; Romans 8:16-17). Therefore, the believer is to live as a family member with his brothers and sisters; he is to live being both kind and affectionate. Note: there is no dissension or divisiveness in love. The church is to live in love, and living in love is peace. |
| **#2258**<br>**Kindness**<br><br>Gentleness–KJV<br>**Kindness–NASB**<br>**Kindness–NIV**<br>**Kindness–NKJV**<br>**Kindness–NLT**<br><br>**POSB REFERENCE**<br>(Gal.5:22-23; esp. v.22)<br>Note 1, point 5 | χρηστότης = *chrēstotēs*<br>Pronunciation: [khray-stot'-ace]<br>Parsing (part of speech): noun<br>    Case—nominative<br>    Gender—feminine<br>    Number—singular<br>    Stem or root—from χρηστότης, ητος<br>Concordance References:<br>⇒ Strong's #5544 chrēstotēs<br>⇒ NIV #5983 chrēstotēs<br>⇒ NASB #5544 chrēstotēs<br><br>**Galatians 5:22**<br>But the fruit of the Spirit is love, joy, peace, longsuffering, **gentleness**, goodness, faith, [KJV]<br><br>But the fruit of the Spirit is love, joy, peace, patience, **kindness**, goodness, faithfulness, [NASB]<br><br>But the fruit of the Spirit is love, joy, peace, patience, **kindness**, goodness, faithfulness, [NIV]<br><br>But the fruit of the Spirit is love, joy, peace, longsuffering, **kindness**, goodness, faithfulness, [NKJV]<br><br>But when the Holy Spirit controls our lives, he will produce this kind of fruit in us: love, joy, peace, patience, **kindness**, goodness, faithfulness, [NLT]<br><br>ὁ δὲ καρπὸς τοῦ Πνεύματός ἐστιν ἀγάπη, χαρά, | Gentleness, kindness, meekness, courtesy, favor, service, mildness, tenderness.<br><br>**Practical Application**<br>There is the fruit of "kindness" (*chrēstotēs*): it is being kind and good, useful and helpful, gentle and sweet, considerate and gracious through all situations, no matter the circumstances. A person who is gentle does not act...<br>• hard<br>• indifferent<br>• harsh<br>• unconcerned<br>• too busy<br>• bitter<br><br>Kindness cares for the feelings of others and feels with them. It experiences the full depth of sympathy and empathy. It shows care and gets right into the situation with a person. Gentleness suffers with those who suffer, and struggles with those who struggle, and works and those who work. |

## PRACTICAL WORD STUDIES
### in the NEW TESTAMENT

| ENGLISH WORD | GREEK WORD AND VERSE | THE WORD MEANS... |
|---|---|---|
| | εἰρήνη, μακροθυμία, **χρηστότης**, ἀγαθωσύνη, πίστις, [GNS]<br>Ὁ δὲ καρπὸς τοῦ πνεύματός ἐστιν ἀγάπη χαρὰ εἰρήνη, μακροθυμία, **χρηστότης** ἀγαθωσύνη, πίστις [GNT] | |
| **#2259**<br>**Kindness**<br><br>Kindness–KJV<br>Kindness–NASB<br>Kindness–NIV<br>Kindness–NKJV<br>Kindness–NLT<br><br>**POSB REFERENCE**<br>(Tit.3:4-5; esp. v.4)<br>Note 1, point 1 | χρηστότης = *chrēstotēs*<br>Pronunciation: [khray-stot'-ace]<br>Parsing (part of speech): noun<br>    Case—nominative<br>    Gender—feminine<br>    Number—singular<br>    Stem or root—from χρηστότης, ητος<br>Concordance References:<br>  ⇒ Strong's #5544 chrēstotēs<br>  ⇒ NIV #5983 chrēstotēs<br>  ⇒ NASB #5544 chrēstotēs<br><br>**Titus 3:4**<br>But after that the **kindness** and love of God our Saviour toward man appeared, [KJV]<br>But when the **kindness** of God our Savior and His love for mankind appeared, [NASB]<br>But when the **kindness** and love of God our Savior appeared, [NIV]<br>But when the **kindness** and the love of God our Savior toward man appeared, [NKJV]<br>But then God our Savior showed us his **kindness** and love. [NLT]<br>ὅτε δὲ ἡ **χρηστότης** καὶ ἡ φιλανθρωπία ἐπεφάνη τοῦ σωτῆρος ἡμῶν Θεοῦ, [GNS]<br>ὅτε δὲ ἡ **χρηστότης** καὶ ἡ φιλανθρωπία ἐπεφάνη τοῦ σωτῆρος ἡμῶν θεοῦ, [GNT] | Kindness, goodness, mercy.<br><br>**Practical Application**<br>Salvation comes from God's "kindness" (*chrēstotēs*). This word is often translated *goodness*. It means good, gracious, and kind. But it is a goodness and kindness that is so deep that it always gives whatever is necessary to meet the needs of a person (Barclay). *Kindness* is so deep within God that it is of His very nature. God is so good and kind that He could do nothing else but save us. He had to meet our need; He had to save us from sin, death, and condemnation. Why? Because He is kind; He had to extend His kindness out toward man by saving him. |
| **#2260**<br>**Kinsman**<br><br>Kinsman–KJV<br>Kinsman–NASB<br>Relative–NIV<br>Countryman–NKJV<br>Relative–NLT<br><br>**POSB REFERENCE**<br>(Rom.16:11)<br>Note 11 | συγγενῆ = *suggenē*<br>Pronunciation: [soong-ghen-ay']<br>Parsing (part of speech): pronominal adjective<br>    Case—accusative<br>    Gender—masculine<br>    Number—singular<br>    Stem or root—from συγγενής, οῦς<br>Concordance References:<br>  ⇒ Strong's #4773 suggenēs<br>  ⇒ NIV #5150 suggenēs<br>  ⇒ NASB #4773 suggenēs<br><br>**Romans 16:11**<br>Salute Herodion my **kinsman**. Greet them that be of the household of Narcissus, which are in the Lord. [KJV]<br>Greet Herodion, my **kinsman**. Greet those of the household of Narcissus, who are in the Lord. [NASB]<br>Greet Herodion, my **relative**. Greet those in the household of Narcissus who are in the Lord [NIV]<br>Greet Herodion, my **countryman**. Greet those who are of the *household* of Narcissus who are in the Lord. [NKJV]<br>Greet Herodion, my **relative**. Greet the Christians in the household of Narcissus. [NLT]<br>ἀσπάσασθε Ἡρῳδίωνα τὸν **συγγενῆ** μου. ἀσπάσασθε τοὺς ἐκ τῶν Ναρκίσσου τοὺς ὄντας ἐν Κυρίῳ. [GNS]<br>ἀσπάσασθε Ἡρῳδίωνα τὸν **συγγενῆ** μου. ἀσπάσασθε τοὺς ἐκ τῶν Ναρκίσσου τοὺς ὄντας ἐν κυρίῳ. [GNT] | Relative, kinsman; fellow countryman.<br><br>**Practical Application**<br>Herodion was another relative of Paul who was a believer (cp. Romans 16:7). There is no reason for translating kinsman (*suggenē*) as fellow countryman instead of relative. Others who are mentioned were Jews, but are not called kinsmen by Paul. What effect did this relative have upon Paul's conversion? Again the answer is unknown, but the fact that we should be witnessing to our relatives is driven home to our hearts and minds. |
| **#2261**<br>**Knapsack**<br><br>Scrip–KJV<br>Bag–NASB<br>Bag–NIV<br>Knapsack–NKJV<br>Traveler's bag–NLT | πήραν = *pēran*<br>Pronunciation: [pay'-rahn]<br>Parsing (part of speech): noun<br>    Case—accusative<br>    Gender—feminine<br>    Number—singular<br>    Stem or root—from πήρα, ας<br>Concordance References:<br>  ⇒ Strong's #4082 pēra<br>  ⇒ NIV #4385 pēra<br>  ⇒ NASB #4082 pēra | A traveler's bag, wallet, or sack usually made of animal skin (leather). This bag was used to carry the possessions that a traveler would need for his journey.<br><br>**Practical Application**<br>Note Jesus' clear instructions: they were not to carry a "money bag" (purse, *ballantion*) or a "knapsack" (*pera*) or two pair of shoes. They were to trust God for provisions, not worrying about money for food, housing, or clothing |

# Practical Word Studies
## in the New Testament

| ENGLISH WORD | GREEK WORD AND VERSE | THE WORD MEANS... |
|---|---|---|
| **POSB REFERENCE** (Lk.10:4) Note 4, point 1 | **Luke 10:4**<br>Carry neither purse, nor **scrip**, nor shoes: and salute no man by the way. [KJV]<br>"Carry no purse, no **bag**, no shoes; and greet no one on the way. [NASB]<br>Do not take a purse or **bag** or sandals; and do not greet anyone on the road. [NIV]<br>Carry neither money bag, **knapsack**, nor sandals; and greet no one along the road. [NKJV]<br>Don't take along any money, or a **traveler's bag**, or even an extra pair of sandals. And don't stop to greet anyone on the road. [NLT]<br>μὴ βαστάζετε βαλάντιον, μὴ **πήραν**, μὴ ὑποδήματα· καὶ μηδένα κατὰ τὴν ὁδὸν ἀσπάσησθε. [GNS]<br>μὴ βαστάζετε βαλλάντιον, μὴ **πήραν**, μὴ ὑποδήματα, καὶ μηδένα κατὰ τὴν ὁδὸν ἀσπάσησθε. [GNT] | (Matthew 6:24-34). Worrying about such things would be cumbersome, taking away precious time that should be spent in ministering. Also, they were preaching a message of faith and trust in God. They needed to live what they were preaching and become a living picture of the dependency that God wants from every man. |
| **#2262**<br>**Knelt**<br><br>Worshipped–KJV<br>Bowed down–NASB<br>**Knelt–NIV**<br>Worshiped–NKJV<br>Worshiping–NLT<br><br>**POSB REFERENCE** (Mt.8:2) Note 2, point 2 | προσεκύνει = *prosekunei*<br>Pronunciation: [pros-koo-neh'-ee]<br>Parsing (part of speech): verb<br>    Mood—indicative<br>    Tense—imperfect<br>    Voice—active<br>    Person—3rd person<br>    Number—singular<br>    Stem or root—from προσκυνέω<br>Concordance References:<br>  ⇒ Strong's #4352 proskuneō<br>  ⇒ NIV #4686 proskuneō<br>  ⇒ NASB #4352 proskuneō<br><br>**Matthew 8:2**<br>And, behold, there came a leper and **worshipped** him, saying, Lord, if thou wilt, thou canst make me clean. [KJV]<br>And behold, a leper came to Him, and **bowed down** to Him, saying, "Lord, if You are willing, You can make me clean." [NASB]<br>A man with leprosy came and **knelt** before him and said, "Lord, if you are willing, you can make me clean." [NIV]<br>And behold, a leper came and **worshiped** Him, saying, "Lord, if You are willing, You can make me clean." [NKJV]<br>Suddenly, a man with leprosy approached Jesus. He knelt before him, **worshiping**. "Lord," the man said, "if you want to, you can make me well again." [NLT]<br>καὶ ἰδοὺ, λεπρὸς ἐλθὼν **προσεκύνει** αὐτῷ λέγων, Κύριε, ἐὰν θέλῃς δύνασαί με καθαρίσαι. [GNS]<br>καὶ ἰδοὺ λεπρὸς προσελθὼν **προσεκύνει** αὐτῷ λέγων, Κύριε, ἐὰν θέλῃς δύνασαί με καθαρίσαι. [GNT] | To worship; to bow down; to reverence; to pay homage.<br><br>**Practical Application**<br>In this Scripture, it is a bowing down, a kneeling, a genuine worship that is directed to the Lord. The leper demonstrated two significant things by rushing up and worshipping Jesus.<br>⇒ His desire and willingness to break away from the world and its restrictions.<br>⇒ His acknowledgment that Jesus was worthy of worship. |
| **#2263**<br>**Knew**<br><br>Considered–KJV<br>Contemplated–NASB<br>Faced the fact–NIV<br>Consider–NKJV<br>**Knew–NLT**<br><br>**POSB REFERENCE** (Romans 4:18-22; esp. v.19) Note 2, point 1a | κατενόησεν = *katenoēsen*<br>Pronunciation: [kat-ehn-o-ay'-sehn]<br>Parsing (part of speech): verb<br>    Mood—indicative<br>    Tense—aorist<br>    Voice—active<br>    Person—3rd person<br>    Number—singular<br>    Stem or root—from κατανοέω<br>Concordance References:<br>  ⇒ Strong's #2657 katanoeō<br>  ⇒ NIV #2917 katanoeō<br>  ⇒ NASB #2657 katanoeō<br><br>**Romans 4:19**<br>And being not weak in faith, he **considered** not his own body now dead, when he was about an hundred years old, neither yet the deadness of Sarah's womb: [KJV]<br>And without becoming weak in faith he **contemplated** his own body, now as good as dead since he was about a hundred years old, and the deadness of Sarah's womb; | To consider; to face the facts; to think upon; to contemplate; to observe; to look upon; to see through the facts; to be aware of; to pay attention to; to fix one's thoughts upon.<br><br>**Practical Application**<br>Abraham was not weak in faith despite thinking about his own physical inability. His body was "too old"; he and Sarah were about one hundred years old. The word "old" is a perfect participle in the Greek which means that his reproductive organs had stopped functioning and were dead forever and could never again function. Abraham could never have a son; it was not humanly possible. He and Sarah were almost one hundred years old, now sexually "too old."<br>Abraham thought about the matter. The word "knew" (*katenoēsen*) means He fixed his thoughts, his mind, his attention upon the matter. |

# PRACTICAL WORD STUDIES
## in the NEW TESTAMENT

| ENGLISH WORD | GREEK WORD AND VERSE | THE WORD MEANS... |
|---|---|---|
| | [NASB]<br>    Without weakening in his faith, he **faced the fact** that his body was as good as dead—since he was about a hundred years old—and that Sarah's womb was also dead. [NIV]<br>    And not being weak in faith, he did not **consider** his own body, already dead (since he was about a hundred years old), and the deadness of Sarah's womb. [NKJV]<br>    And Abraham's faith did not weaken, even though he **knew** that he was too old to be a father at the age of one hundred and that Sarah, his wife, had never been able to have children. [NLT]<br>    καὶ μὴ ἀσθενήσας τῇ πίστει, οὐ **κατενόησε** τὸ ἑαυτοῦ σῶμα ἤδη νενεκρωμένον -- ἑκατονταετής που ὑπάρχων -- , καὶ τὴν νέκρωσιν τῆς μήτρας Σάρρας, [GNS]<br>    καὶ μὴ ἀσθενήσας τῇ πίστει **κατενόησεν** τὸ ἑαυτοῦ σῶμα [ἤδη] νενεκρωμένον, ἑκατονταετής που ὑπάρχων, καὶ τὴν νέκρωσιν τῆς μήτρας Σάρρας· [GNT] | But he did not give in to the thoughts. He was not weak in faith. |
| **#2264**<br>**Knew In Advance**<br><br>Foreknow–KJV<br>Foreknew–NASB<br>Foreknew–NIV<br>Foreknew–NKJV<br>**Knew...in advance– NLT**<br><br>**POSB REFERENCE**<br>(Romans 8:29)<br>Note 2, point 3 | προέγνω = proegnō<br>Pronunciation: [pro-ehg-no]<br>Parsing (part of speech): verb<br>  Mood—indicative<br>  Tense—aorist<br>  Voice—active<br>  Person—3rd person<br>  Number—singular<br>  Stem or root—from προγινώσκω<br>Concordance References:<br>  ⇒ Strong's #4267 proginōskō<br>  ⇒ NIV #4589 proginōskō<br>  ⇒ NASB #4267 proginōskō<br><br>**Romans 8:29**<br>    For whom he did **foreknow**, he also did predestinate to be conformed to the image of his Son, that he might be the firstborn among many brethren. [KJV]<br>    For whom He **foreknew**, He also predestined to become conformed to the image of His Son, that He might be the first-born among many brethren; [NASB]<br>    For those God **foreknew** he also predestined to be conformed to the likeness of his Son, that he might be the firstborn among many brothers. [NIV]<br>    For whom He **foreknew**, He also predestined *to be* conformed to the image of His Son, that He might be the firstborn among many brethren. [NKJV]<br>    For God **knew** his people **in advance**, and he chose them to become like his Son, so that his Son would be the firstborn, with many brothers and sisters. [NLT]<br>    ὅτι οὓς **προέγνω**, καὶ προώρισε συμμόρφους τῆς εἰκόνος τοῦ υἱοῦ αὐτοῦ, εἰς τὸ εἶναι αὐτὸν πρωτότοκον ἐν πολλοῖς ἀδελφοῖς· [GNS]<br>    ὅτι οὓς **προέγνω**, καὶ προώρισεν συμμόρφους τῆς εἰκόνος τοῦ υἱοῦ αὐτοῦ, εἰς τὸ εἶναι αὐτὸν πρωτότοκον ἐν πολλοῖς ἀδελφοῖς· [GNT] | The foreknowledge of God; to know in advance; to be chosen before; to be already known.<br><br>**Practical Application**<br>    The phrase "knew in advance" (*proegnō*) is used three different ways in Scripture. It means...<br>• to know something beforehand, ahead of time.<br>• to know something intimately by loving and accepting and approving it.<br>• to elect, foreordain, and predetermine something.<br><br>    The present passage is interpreted differently by scholars. Note that the second and third meanings are much the same. When a person is loved and approved, selection or election is involved. The person becomes a very special or select person.<br>    The point is not the pure logic of the theological or philosophical argument. This is not God's purpose in this passage. God's purpose is to assure the believer: the believer is going to be conformed to the image of Christ, and nothing can stop the glorious process. God foreknew the fact, saw it even before the world was ever founded. He has always loved and approved the believer, electing and ordaining him from the very beginning. (See POSB *Deeper Study* #3, Foreknowledge—Acts 2:23 for more detailed discussion.) |
| **#2265**<br>**Knocked Down**<br><br>Cast down–KJV<br>Struck down–NASB<br>Struck down–NIV<br>Struck down–NKJV<br>**Knocked down–NLT**<br><br>**POSB REFERENCE**<br>(2 Cor.4:7-9; esp. v.9)<br>Note 2, point 4 | καταβαλλόμενοι = kataballomenoi<br>Pronunciation: [kat-ab-al-lo'-mehn-oy]<br>Parsing (part of speech): verb<br>  Mood—participle<br>  Tense—present<br>  Voice—passive<br>  Case—nominative<br>  Gender—masculine<br>  Person—1st person<br>  Number—plural<br>  Stem or root—from καταβάλλω<br>Concordance References:<br>  ⇒ Strong's #2598 kataballō<br>  ⇒ NIV #2850 kataballō<br>  ⇒ NASB #2598 kataballō | To be struck down; to be cast down; to be smitten down; to be knocked down; to be laying down.<br><br>**Practical Application**<br>    The minister (or believer) may be "knocked down," (*kataballomenoi*), but he is never destroyed. The minister (or believer) may be struck down, but he is never allowed to strike out; he may be knocked down, but he is never knocked out. |

## PRACTICAL WORD STUDIES
### in the NEW TESTAMENT

| ENGLISH WORD | GREEK WORD AND VERSE | THE WORD MEANS... |
|---|---|---|
| | **2 Cor. 4:9**<br>Persecuted, but not forsaken; **cast down**, but not destroyed; [KJV]<br>Persecuted, but not forsaken; **struck down**, but not destroyed; [NASB]<br>Persecuted, but not abandoned; **struck down**, but not destroyed. [NIV]<br>Persecuted, but not forsaken; **struck down**, but not destroyed—[NKJV]<br>We are hunted down, but God never abandons us. We get **knocked down**, but we get up again and keep going. [NLT]<br>διωκόμενοι, ἀλλ' οὐκ ἐγκαταλειπόμενοι, **καταβαλλόμενοι** ἀλλ' οὐκ ἀπολλύμενοι· [GNS]<br>διωκόμενοι, ἀλλ' οὐκ ἐγκαταλειπόμενοι, **καταβαλλόμενοι** ἀλλ' οὐκ ἀπολλύμενοι, [GNT] | |
| #2266<br>**Know**<br><br>Certify–KJV<br>Know–NASB<br>Know–NIV<br>Make known–NKJV<br>Solemnly assure–NLT<br><br>**POSB REFERENCE**<br>(Gal.1:11-12; esp. v.11)<br>Note 2 | Γνωρίζω = *Gnōrizō*<br>Pronunciation: [gno-rid'-zo]<br>Parsing (part of speech): verb<br>  Mood—indicative<br>  Tense—present<br>  Voice—active<br>  Person—1st person<br>  Number—singular<br>  Stem or root—from γνωρίζω<br>Concordance References:<br>  ⇒ Strong's #1107 gnōrizō<br>  ⇒ NIV #1192 gnōrizō<br>  ⇒ NASB #1107 gnōrizō<br><br>**Galatians 1:11**<br>But I **certify** you, brethren, that the gospel which was preached of me is not after man. [KJV]<br>For I would have you **know**, brethren, that the gospel which was preached by me is not according to man. [NASB]<br>I want you to **know**, brothers, that the gospel I preached is not something that man made up. [NIV]<br>But I **make known** to you, brethren, that the gospel which was preached by me is not according to man. [NKJV]<br>Dear brothers and sisters, I **solemnly assure** you that the Good News of salvation which I preach is not based on mere human reasoning or logic. [NLT]<br>Γνωρίζω δὲ ὑμῖν, ἀδελφοί, τὸ εὐαγγέλιον τὸ εὐαγγελισθὲν ὑπ' ἐμοῦ, ὅτι οὐκ ἔστι κατὰ ἄνθρωπον. [GNS]<br>Γνωρίζω γὰρ ὑμῖν, ἀδελφοί, τὸ εὐαγγέλιον τὸ εὐαγγελισθὲν ὑπ' ἐμοῦ ὅτι οὐκ ἔστιν κατὰ ἄνθρωπον· [GNT] | To certify; to make known; to solemnly assure.<br><br>**Practical Application**<br>The minister proclaimed the gospel. Some critics of Paul were saying that he was not a true apostle of the Lord Jesus because he had not been a follower of the Lord when the Lord was upon the earth. Therefore, what he was teaching was a man-made gospel taught by mistaken and misguided men.<br>Note that the word "know" (*Gnōrizō*) is a solemn word, a strong declaration that what follows is of crucial importance and needs to be heard. |
| #2267<br>**Know**<br><br>Know–KJV<br>Appreciate–NASB<br>Respect–NIV<br>Recognize–NKJV<br>Honor–NLT<br><br>**POSB REFERENCE**<br>(1 Thes.5:12-13; esp.v.12)<br>Note 1, point 1 | εἰδέναι = *eidenai*<br>Pronunciation: [i'-dehn-ah-ee]<br>Parsing (part of speech): verb<br>  Mood—infinitive<br>  Tense—perfect<br>  Voice—active<br>  Stem or root—from οἶδα<br>Concordance References:<br>  ⇒ Strong's #1492 eido<br>  ⇒ NIV #3857 oida<br>  ⇒ NASB #3609a oida<br><br>**1 Thes. 5:12**<br>And we beseech you, brethren, to **know** them which labour among you, and are over you in the Lord, and admonish you; [KJV]<br>But we request of you, brethren, that you **appreciate** those who diligently labor among you, and have charge over you in the Lord and give you instruction, [NASB]<br>Now we ask you, brothers, to **respect** those who work hard among you, who are over you in the Lord and who admonish you. [NIV]<br>And we urge you, brethren, to **recognize** those who | To respect; to know; to appreciate; to recognize; to honor; to be acquainted with; to acknowledge; know the value of.<br><br>**Practical Application**<br>Believers are to know the leaders of their church. Few people labor as much as a committed church leader. |

# PRACTICAL WORD STUDIES
## in the NEW TESTAMENT

| ENGLISH WORD | GREEK WORD AND VERSE | THE WORD MEANS... |
|---|---|---|
| | labor among you, and are over you in the Lord and admonish you, [NKJV]<br><br>Dear brothers and sisters, **honor** those who are your leaders in the Lord's work. They work hard among you and warn you against all that is wrong. [NLT]<br><br>Ἐρωτῶμεν δὲ ὑμᾶς, ἀδελφοί, **εἰδέναι** τοὺς κοπιῶντας ἐν ὑμῖν, καὶ προϊσταμένους ὑμῶν ἐν Κυρίῳ, καὶ νουθετοῦν τας ὑμᾶς, [GNS]<br><br>Ἐρωτῶμεν δὲ ὑμᾶς, ἀδελφοί, **εἰδέναι** τοὺς κοπιῶντας ἐν ὑμῖν καὶ προϊσταμένους ὑμῶν ἐν κυρίῳ καὶ νουθετοῦντας ὑμᾶς [GNT] | |
| **#2268**<br>**Know**<br><br>Fully known–KJV<br>Followed–NASB<br>Know all about–NIV<br>Followed–NKJV<br>**Know–NLT**<br><br>**POSB REFERENCE**<br>(2 Tim. 3:10)<br>Note 1 | παρηκολούθησάς = parëkolouthësas<br>Pronunciation: [par-ayk-ol-oo-thay'-sahs]<br>Parsing (part of speech): verb<br>    Mood—indicative<br>    Tense—aorist<br>    Voice—active<br>    Person—2nd person<br>    Number—singular<br>    Stem or root—from παρακολουθέω<br>Concordance References:<br>⇒ Strong's #3877 parakoloutheō<br>⇒ NIV #4158 parakoloutheō<br>⇒ NASB #3877 parakoloutheō<br><br>**2 Tim. 3:10**<br><br>But thou hast **fully known** my doctrine, manner of life, purpose, faith, longsuffering, charity, patience, [KJV]<br><br>But you **followed** my teaching, conduct, purpose, faith, patience, love, perseverance, [NASB]<br><br>You, however, **know all about** my teaching, my way of life, my purpose, faith, patience, love, endurance, [NIV]<br><br>But you have carefully **followed** my doctrine, manner of life, purpose, faith, longsuffering, love, perseverance, [NKJV]<br><br>But you **know** what I teach, Timothy, and how I live, and what my purpose in life is. You know my faith and how long I have suffered. You know my love and my patient endurance. [NLT]<br><br>σὺ δὲ **παρηκολούθηκάς** μου τῇ διδασκαλίᾳ, τῇ ἀγωγῇ, τῇ προθέσει, τῇ πίστει, τῇ μακροθυμίᾳ, τῇ ἀγάπῃ, τῇ ὑπομονῇ, [GNS]<br><br>Σὺ δὲ **παρηκολούθησάς** μου τῇ διδασκαλίᾳ, τῇ ἀγωγῇ, τῇ προθέσει, τῇ πίστει, τῇ μακροθυμίᾳ, τῇ ἀγάπῃ, τῇ ὑπομονῇ, [GNT] | To know; to know all about; to fully know; to follow; to give full attention to. Kenneth Wuest points out that the Greek word means to follow a person so closely that one is always by the person's side, conforming his life to the person (*The Pastoral Epistles*, p.148). It means to join oneself to the person, to become his disciple and to follow his example.<br><br>**Practical Application**<br><br>A godly person follows a godly example. This is a sharp contrast from the godless marks of false teachers (2 Tim. 3:1-9). Timothy had known (*parëkolouthësas*) and had closely observed and followed the godly example of Paul. Paul had lived a godly life, and Timothy had followed in his footsteps. |
| **#2269**<br>**Know–Knowing**<br><br>Knowing–KJV<br>Knowing–NASB<br>Understanding–NIV<br>Knowing–NKJV<br>**Know–NLT**<br><br>**POSB REFERENCE**<br>(Rom.13:11)<br>Note 1 | εἰδότες = eidotes<br>Pronunciation: [ee'-do-tehs]<br>Parsing (part of speech): verb<br>    Mood—participle (imperative sense)<br>    Tense—perfect<br>    Voice—active<br>    Case—nominative<br>    Gender—masculine<br>    Person—2nd person<br>    Number—plural<br>    Stem or root—from οἶδα<br>Concordance References:<br>⇒ Strong's #1492 eido<br>⇒ NIV #3857 oida<br>⇒ NASB #3609a oida<br><br>**Romans 13:11**<br><br>And that, **knowing** the time, that now *it is* high time to awake out of sleep: for now *is* our salvation nearer than when we believed. [KJV]<br><br>And this *do*, **knowing** the time, that it is already the hour for you to awaken from sleep; for now salvation is nearer to us than when we believed. [NASB]<br><br>And do this, **understanding** the present time. The hour has come for you to wake up from your slumber, | To know; to understand; to perceive; to realize; to be very sure of this; to experience; to be acquainted with; to recognize; to acknowledge; to remember.<br><br>**Practical Application**<br><br>The believer is to understand the time. The word "knowing" (*eidotes*) means to make sure that you know; do not dare miss knowing. The term "present time" (*ton kairon*) means the critical period; the strategic or special period of time. |

# PRACTICAL WORD STUDIES
## in the NEW TESTAMENT

| ENGLISH WORD | GREEK WORD AND VERSE | THE WORD MEANS... |
|---|---|---|
| | because our salvation is nearer now than when we first believed. [NIV]<br><br>And do this, **knowing** the time, that now *it is* high time to awake out of sleep; for now our salvation *is* nearer than when we *first* believed. [NKJV]<br><br>Another reason for right living is that you **know** how late it is; time is running out. Wake up, for the coming of our salvation is nearer now than when we first believed. [NLT]<br><br>Καὶ τοῦτο, **εἰδότες** τὸν καιρόν, ὅτι ὥρα ὑμᾶς ἤδη ἐξ ὕπνου ἐγερθῆναι· νῦν γὰρ ἐγγύτερον ἡμῶν ἡ σωτηρία ἢ ὅτε ἐπιστεύσαμεν. [GNS]<br><br>Καὶ τοῦτο **εἰδότες** τὸν καιρόν, ὅτι ὥρα ἤδη ὑμᾶς ἐξ ὕπνου ἐγερθῆναι, νῦν γὰρ ἐγγύτερον ἡμῶν ἡ σωτηρία ἢ ὅτε ἐπιστεύσαμεν. [GNT] | |
| **#2270**<br>**Know All About**<br><br>Fully known–KJV<br>Followed–NASB<br>**Know all about–NIV**<br>Followed–NKJV<br>Know–NLT<br><br>**POSB REFERENCE**<br>(2 Tim. 3:10)<br>Note 1 | παρηκολούθησάς = *parēkolouthēsas*<br>Pronunciation: [par-ayk-ol-oo-thay'-sahs]<br>Parsing (part of speech): verb<br>   Mood—indicative<br>   Tense—aorist<br>   Voice—active<br>   Person—2nd person<br>   Number—singular<br>   Stem or root—from παρακολουθέω<br>Concordance References:<br>  ⇒ Strong's #3877 parakoloutheō<br>  ⇒ NIV #4158 parakoloutheō<br>  ⇒ NASB #3877 parakoloutheō<br><br>**2 Tim. 3:10**<br>But thou hast **fully known** my doctrine, manner of life, purpose, faith, longsuffering, charity, patience, [KJV]<br><br>But you **followed** my teaching, conduct, purpose, faith, patience, love, perseverance, [NASB]<br><br>You, however, **know all about** my teaching, my way of life, my purpose, faith, patience, love, endurance, [NIV]<br><br>But you have carefully **followed** my doctrine, manner of life, purpose, faith, longsuffering, love, perseverance, [NKJV]<br><br>But you **know** what I teach, Timothy, and how I live, and what my purpose in life is. You know my faith and how long I have suffered. You know my love and my patient endurance. [NLT]<br><br>σὺ δὲ **παρηκολούθηκάς** μου τῇ διδασκαλίᾳ, τῇ ἀγωγῇ, τῇ προθέσει, τῇ πίστει, τῇ μακροθυμίᾳ, τῇ ἀγάπῃ, τῇ ὑπομονῇ, [GNS]<br><br>Σὺ δὲ **παρηκολούθησάς** μου τῇ διδασκαλίᾳ, τῇ ἀγωγῇ, τῇ προθέσει, τῇ πίστει, τῇ μακροθυμίᾳ, τῇ ἀγάπῃ, τῇ ὑπομονῇ, [GNT] | To know; to know all about; to fully know; to follow; to give full attention to. Kenneth Wuest points out that the Greek word means to follow a person so closely that one is always by the person's side, conforming his life to the person (*The Pastoral Epistles*, p.148). It means to join oneself to the person, to become his disciple and to follow his example.<br><br>**Practical Application**<br>A godly person follows a godly example. This is a sharp contrast from the godless marks of false teachers (2 Tim. 3:1-9). Timothy had known (*parēkolouthēsas*) and had closely observed and followed the godly example of Paul. Paul had lived a godly life, and Timothy had followed in his footsteps. |
| **#2271**<br>**Know These Things So Well**<br><br>Filled with all knowledge–KJV<br>Filled with all knowledge–NASB<br>Complete in knowledge–NIV<br>Filled with all knowledge–NKJV<br>**Know these things so well–NLT** | πεπληρωμένοι πάσης γνώσεως = *peplērōmenoi pasēs gnōseōs*<br>Pronunciation: [peh-play-ro'-mehn-oy pah-says gno'-seh-os]<br>Parsing *peplērōmenoi* (part of speech): verb<br>   Mood—participle<br>   Tense—perfect<br>   Voice—passive<br>   Case—nominative<br>   Gender—masculine<br>   Person—2nd person<br>   Number—plural<br>   Stem or root—from πληρόω<br>Parsing *gnōseōs* (part of speech): noun<br>   Case—genitive<br>   Gender—feminine<br>   Number—singular<br>   Stem or root—from γνῶσις, εως<br>Concordance References:<br>  ⇒ Strong's #3956 + 4137 pas plēroō + 1108 gnōsis<br>  ⇒ NIV #4246 + 4444 pas plēroō [complete] + | To be complete in knowledge; to be filled with all knowledge; to know [these things] very well.<br><br>**Practical Application**<br>The believers "know these things so well" (*peplērōmenoi pasēs gnōseōs*): They were filled...<br>• with spiritual insight and perception.<br>• with knowledge of Christ, God, and the Holy Spirit.<br>• with spiritual truth.<br>• with the spiritual need of man and his world. |

## PRACTICAL WORD STUDIES
### in the NEW TESTAMENT

| ENGLISH WORD | GREEK WORD AND VERSE | THE WORD MEANS... |
|---|---|---|
| **POSB REFERENCE** (Rom.15:14) Note 1, point 2b | 1194 gnösis [knowledge]<br>⇒ NASB #3956 + 4137 pas plëroö + 1108 gnösis<br><br>**Romans 15:14**<br>And I myself also am persuaded of you, my brethren, that ye also are full of goodness, **filled with all knowledge**, able also to admonish one another. [KJV]<br>And concerning you, my brethren, I myself also am convinced that you yourselves are full of goodness, **filled with all knowledge**, and able also to admonish one another. [NASB]<br>I myself am convinced, my brothers, that you yourselves are full of goodness, **complete in knowledge** and competent to instruct one another. [NIV]<br>Now I myself am confident concerning you, my brethren, that you also are full of goodness, **filled with all knowledge**, able also to admonish one another. [NKJV]<br>I am fully convinced, dear brothers and sisters, that you are full of goodness. You **know these things so well** that you are able to teach others all about them. [NLT]<br>Πέπεισμαι δέ, ἀδελφοί μου, καὶ αὐτὸς ἐγὼ περὶ ὑμῶν, ὅτι καὶ αὐτοὶ μεστοί ἐστε ἀγαθωσύνης, **πεπληρωμένοι πάσης γνώσεως**, δυνάμενοι καὶ ἀλλήλους νουθετεῖν. [GNS]<br>Πέπεισμαι δέ, ἀδελφοί μου, καὶ αὐτὸς ἐγὼ περὶ ὑμῶν ὅτι καὶ αὐτοὶ μεστοί ἐστε ἀγαθωσύνης, **πεπληρωμένοι πάσης [τῆς] γνώσεως**, δυνάμενοι καὶ ἀλλήλους νουθετεῖν. [GNT] | |
| **#2272 Knowing God Better**<br><br>Knowledge–KJV<br>Knowledge–NASB<br>Knowledge–NIV<br>Knowledge–NKJV<br>Knowing God better–NLT<br><br>**POSB REFERENCE** (2 Pt.1:5-7; esp. v.5) Note 1<br><br>See also POSB REF: (Col.2:3) *Deeper Study* #1 (1 Tim.6:20-21; esp. v.20) Note 2, point 2b | γνῶσιν = gnösin<br>Pronunciation: [gno'-sin]<br>Parsing (part of speech): noun<br>    Case—accusative<br>    Gender—feminine<br>    Number—singular<br>    Stem or root—from γνῶσις, εως<br>Concordance References:<br>⇒ Strong's #1108 gnösis<br>⇒ NIV #1194 gnösis<br>⇒ NASB #1108 gnösis<br><br>**2 Peter 1:5**<br>And beside this, giving all diligence, add to your faith virtue; and to virtue **knowledge**; [KJV]<br>Now for this very reason also, applying all diligence, in your faith supply moral excellence, and in your moral excellence, **knowledge**; [NASB]<br>For this very reason, make every effort to add to your faith goodness; and to goodness, **knowledge**; [NIV]<br>But also for this very reason, giving all diligence, add to your faith virtue, to virtue **knowledge**, [NKJV]<br>So make every effort to apply the benefits of these promises to your life. Then your faith will produce a life of moral excellence. A life of moral excellence leads to **knowing God better**. [NLT]<br>καὶ αὐτὸ τοῦτο δὲ σπουδὴν πᾶσαν παρεισενέγκαντες, ἐπιχορηγήσατε ἐν τῇ πίστει ὑμῶν τὴν ἀρετήν, ἐν δὲ τῇ ἀρετῇ τὴν **γνῶσιν**, [GNS]<br>καὶ αὐτὸ τοῦτο δὲ σπουδὴν πᾶσαν παρεισενέγκαντες, ἐπιχορηγήσατε ἐν τῇ πίστει ὑμῶν τὴν ἀρετήν, ἐν δὲ τῇ ἀρετῇ τὴν **γνῶσιν**, [GNT] | Knowledge; to know God better; practical intelligence; practical knowledge; practical insight.<br><br>**Practical Application**<br>It means knowing what to do in every situation and doing it; it is practical, day-to-day knowledge that sees situations and knows how to handle them. It is seeing the trials and temptations of life and knowing what to do with them and doing it.<br>Remember the charge: we must add knowledge to our faith. We must give diligent attention to the situations of life and figure out how to conquer them. |
| **#2273 Knowledge**<br><br>Knowledge–KJV<br>Knowledge–NASB<br>Knowledge–NIV<br>Knowledge–NKJV<br>Come to know–NLT | ἐπιγνώσει = epignösei<br>Pronunciation: [ep-ig'-no-seh-ee]<br>Parsing (part of speech): noun<br>    Case—dative<br>    Gender—feminine<br>    Number—singular<br>    Stem or root—from ἐπίγνωσις, εως<br>Concordance References:<br>⇒ Strong's #1922 epignösis | Full, personal, precise, and correct; to know and possess full understanding; to know in a personal, conscious way.<br><br>**Practical Application**<br>Note that Jesus Christ multiplies grace and peace. He gives an abundance of grace and peace; He causes grace and peace to overflow in |

# Practical Word Studies
## in the New Testament

| ENGLISH WORD | GREEK WORD AND VERSE | THE WORD MEANS... |
|---|---|---|
| **POSB REFERENCE** (2 Pt.1:2) Note 3, point 3 | ⇒ NIV #2106 epignōsis<br>⇒ NASB #1922 epignōsis<br><br>**2 Peter 1:2**<br>Grace and peace be multiplied unto you through the **knowledge** of God, and of Jesus our Lord, [KJV]<br>Grace and peace be multiplied to you in the **knowledge** of God and of Jesus our Lord; [NASB]<br>Grace and peace be yours in abundance through the **knowledge** of God and of Jesus our Lord. [NIV]<br>Grace and peace be multiplied to you in the **knowledge** of God and of Jesus our Lord, [NKJV]<br>May God bless you with his special favor and wonderful peace as you **come to know** Jesus, our God and Lord, better and better. [NLT]<br>χάρις ὑμῖν καὶ εἰρήνη πληθυνθείη ἐν **ἐπιγνώσει** τοῦ Θεοῦ καὶ Ἰησοῦ τοῦ Κυρίου ἡμῶν· [GNS]<br>χάρις ὑμῖν καὶ εἰρήνη πληθυνθείη ἐν **ἐπιγνώσει** τοῦ θεοῦ καὶ Ἰησοῦ τοῦ κυρίου ἡμῶν. [GNT] | the life of the genuine believer. There is never to be a lack of grace and peace in the life of any true believer. Every believer is to always be overflowing with joy, with the favor and blessings of God and with peace within his own spirit and with God and others.<br>How can a person always be overflowing with the grace and peace of God? Through the knowledge of God and of Jesus our Lord. We have to know God in order to receive the grace and peace of God. What does it mean to know God? The word "knowledge" (*epignōsei*) means "full, personal, precise, and correct" knowledge (The Amplified New Testament).<br>⇒ It means to know Christ personally; to know Him by experience. It means to know Christ just like we know any person: by walking and talking with Him.<br>⇒ It means to know Christ fully; to know Him in all of His person, exactly who He is. It means to be precise and correct in what we know about Him.<br>The point is this: if a person knows Christ fully and personally, precisely and correctly, then he knows Christ as Savior and Lord. He knows Christ as the Son of God who was sent to earth by the Father to save the world. The person does not look upon Christ as a mere man, as a great religious leader who founded the religion of Christianity. The person looks upon Jesus Christ as the Savior and Lord of men, and he knows Christ personally. He experiences Christ: he comes to Christ and asks Christ to save him and to be the Lord of his life. He gives all that he is and has to Christ, surrendering totally to Christ as his Lord. It is the person who so surrenders to Christ that comes to know Christ, and day-by-day, the person experiences the overflow of the Lord's grace and peace. |
| #2274<br>**Knowledge**<br><br>Knowledge–KJV<br>Knowledge–NASB<br>Knowledge–NIV<br>Knowledge–NKJV<br>Knowing God better–NLT<br><br>**POSB REFERENCE** (2 Pt.1:5-7; esp. v.5) Note 1<br><br>See also POSB REF: (Col.2:3) *Deeper Study* #1 (1 Tim.6:20-21; esp. v.20) Note 2, point 2b | γνῶσιν = *gnōsin*<br>Pronunciation: [gno'-sin]<br>Parsing (part of speech): noun<br>   Case—accusative<br>   Gender—feminine<br>   Number—singular<br>   Stem or root—from γνῶσις, εως<br>Concordance References:<br>⇒ Strong's #1108 gnōsis<br>⇒ NIV #1194 gnōsis<br>⇒ NASB #1108 gnōsis<br><br>**2 Peter 1:5**<br>And beside this, giving all diligence, add to your faith virtue; and to virtue **knowledge**; [KJV]<br>Now for this very reason also, applying all diligence, in your faith supply moral excellence, and in your moral excellence, **knowledge**; [NASB]<br>For this very reason, make every effort to add to your faith goodness; and to goodness, **knowledge**; [NIV]<br>But also for this very reason, giving all diligence, add to your faith virtue, to virtue **knowledge**, [NKJV]<br>So make every effort to apply the benefits of these promises to your life. Then your faith will produce a life of moral excellence. A life of moral excellence leads to **knowing God better**. [NLT]<br>καὶ αὐτὸ τοῦτο δὲ σπουδὴν πᾶσαν παρεισενέγκαντες, ἐπιχορηγήσατε ἐν τῇ πίστει ὑμῶν τὴν ἀρετήν, ἐν δὲ τῇ ἀρετῇ τὴν **γνῶσιν**, [GNS]<br>καὶ αὐτὸ τοῦτο δὲ σπουδὴν πᾶσαν παρεισενέγκαντες ἐπιχορηγήσατε ἐν τῇ πίστει ὑμῶν τὴν ἀρετήν, ἐν δὲ τῇ ἀρετῇ τὴν **γνῶσιν**, [GNT] | Knowledge; to know God better; practical intelligence; practical knowledge; practical insight.<br><br>**Practical Application**<br>It means knowing what to do in every situation and doing it; it is practical, day-to-day knowledge that sees situations and knows how to handle them. It is seeing the trials and temptations of life and knowing what to do with them and doing it.<br>Remember the charge: we must add a knowledge of God to our faith. We must give diligent attention to the situations of life and figure out how to conquer them. |

# PRACTICAL WORD STUDIES
## in the NEW TESTAMENT

| ENGLISH WORD | GREEK WORD AND VERSE | THE WORD MEANS... |
|---|---|---|
| **#2275**<br>**Knowledge**<br><br>Knowledge–KJV<br>Knowledge–NASB<br>Knowledge–NIV<br>Knowledge–NKJV<br>Knowledge–NLT<br><br>**POSB REFERENCE**<br>(Heb.10:26-27; esp. v.26)<br>Note 1 | ἐπίγνωσιν = epignōsin<br>Pronunciation: [ep-ig'-no-sin]<br>Parsing (part of speech): noun<br>    Case—accusative<br>    Gender—feminine<br>    Number—singular<br>    Stem or root—from ἐπίγνωσις, εως<br>Concordance References:<br>  ⇒ Strong's #1922 epignōsis<br>  ⇒ NIV #2106 epignōsis<br>  ⇒ NASB #1922 epignōsis<br><br>**Hebrews 10:26**<br>For if we sin wilfully after that we have received the **knowledge** of the truth, there remaineth no more sacrifice for sins, [KJV]<br>For if we go on sinning willfully after receiving the **knowledge** of the truth, there no longer remains a sacrifice for sins, [NASB]<br>If we deliberately keep on sinning after we have received the **knowledge** of the truth, no sacrifice for sins is left, [NIV]<br>For if we sin willfully after we have received the **knowledge** of the truth, there no longer remains a sacrifice for sins, [NKJV]<br>Dear friends, if we deliberately continue sinning after we have received a full **knowledge** of the truth, there is no other sacrifice that will cover these sins. [NLT]<br>Ἑκουσίως γὰρ ἁμαρτανόντων ἡμῶν μετὰ τὸ λαβεῖν τὴν **ἐπίγνωσιν** τῆς ἀληθείας, οὐκέτι περὶ ἁμαρτιῶν ἀπολείπεται θυσία, [GNS]<br>Ἑκουσίως γὰρ ἁμαρτανόντων ἡμῶν μετὰ τὸ λαβεῖν τὴν **ἐπίγνωσιν** τῆς ἀληθείας, οὐκέτι περὶ ἁμαρτιῶν ἀπολείπεται θυσία, [GNT] | Knowledge, recognition; full understanding.<br><br>**Practical Application**<br>Note a critical fact: this passage is not written to the unbeliever who wilfully sins. It is written to the person who has received *the knowledge of the truth* and wilfully sins. It is written...<br>• to those who have "full knowledge" (*epignōsin*) of the truth (A.T. Robertson. *Word Pictures in the New Testament*, Vol. 5, p.413).<br>• to those who have once *acquired the knowledge of the Truth* (Amplified New Testament).<br>• to those who received the knowledge of the truth, "the revelation through Christ" (Marvin Vincent. *Word Studies in the New Testament*, Vol. 4, p.503).<br>• to those in whom "there is no lack of understanding of the truth" (Robert W. Ross. *Hebrews. The New Testament and Wycliffe Bible Commentary,* ed. by Charles F. Pfeiffer and Everette F. Harrison. New York, NY: The Iverson Associates. Produced for Moody Monthly and Moody Press of Chicago, 971, p.929).<br>The importance and severity of the warning is seen in the fact that most, if not all, of the above four writers would hold to the security of the believer. Yet, they recognize the seriousness of the warning to all who profess Christ. In fact, every honest and thinking interpreter (how often this is lacking) of Scripture is forced by this Scripture to issue a warning to believers: take heed. There is the danger of apostasy—of withdrawing from Christ and fellow believers. |
| **#2276**<br>**Knowledge**<br><br>Knowledge–KJV<br>Knowledge–NASB<br>Understanding–NIV<br>Knowledge–NKJV<br>Understanding–NLT<br><br>**POSB REFERENCE**<br>(2 Cor.6:6-7; esp. v.6)<br>Note 5 | γνώσει = gnōsei<br>Pronunciation: [gno'-see]<br>Parsing (part of speech): noun<br>    Case—dative<br>    Gender—feminine<br>    Number—singular<br>    Stem or root—from γνῶσις, εως<br>Concordance References:<br>  ⇒ Strong's #1108 gnōsis<br>  ⇒ NIV #1194 gnōsis<br>  ⇒ NASB #1108 gnōsis<br><br>**2 Cor. 6:6**<br>By pureness, by **knowledge**, by longsuffering, by kindness, by the Holy Ghost, by love unfeigned, [KJV]<br>In purity, in **knowledge**, in patience, in kindness, in the Holy Spirit, in genuine love, [NASB]<br>In purity, **understanding**, patience and kindness; in the Holy Spirit and in sincere love; [NIV]<br>By purity, by **knowledge**, by longsuffering, by kindness, by the Holy Spirit, by sincere love, [NKJV]<br>We have proved ourselves by our purity, our **understanding**, our patience, our kindness, our sincere love, and the power of the Holy Spirit. [NLT]<br>ἐν ἁγνότητι, ἐν **γνώσει**, ἐν μακροθυμίᾳ, ἐν χρηστότητι, ἐν Πνεύματι Ἁγίῳ, ἐν ἀγάπῃ ἀνυποκρίτῳ, [GNS]<br>ἐν ἁγνότητι, ἐν **γνώσει**, ἐν μακροθυμίᾳ, ἐν χρηστότητι, ἐν πνεύματι ἁγίῳ, ἐν ἀγάπῃ ἀνυποκρίτῳ, [GNT] | Understanding, knowledge, esoteric (that which is not easily known) knowledge.<br><br>**Practical Application**<br>Paul did not neglect the meditation and study of God's Word and revealed will. He learned all he could about how God wanted men to live, and he applied himself to living and teaching that way. |

# Practical Word Studies
## in the New Testament

| ENGLISH WORD | GREEK WORD AND VERSE | THE WORD MEANS |
|---|---|---|
| **#2277**<br>**Known**<br><br>Honest report–KJV<br>Good reputation–NASB<br>**Known–NIV**<br>Good reputation–NKJV<br>Well respected–NLT<br><br>**POSB REFERENCE**<br>(Acts 6:3)<br>Note 3, point 1 | μαρτυρουμένους = *marturoumenous*<br>Pronunciation: [mar-too-roo'-men-oos]<br>Parsing (part of speech): verb<br>  Mood—participle<br>  Tense—present<br>  Voice—passive<br>  Case—accusative<br>  Gender—masculine<br>  Number—plural<br>  Stem or root—from μαρτυρέω<br>Concordance References:<br>  ⇒ Strong's #3140 martureō<br>  ⇒ NIV #3455 martureō<br>  ⇒ NASB #3140 martureō<br><br>**Acts 6:3**<br>Wherefore, brethren, look ye out among you seven men of **honest report**, full of the Holy Ghost and wisdom, whom we may appoint over this business. [KJV]<br>"But select from among you, brethren, seven men of **good reputation**, full of the Spirit and of wisdom, whom we may put in charge of this task. [NASB]<br>Brothers, choose seven men from among you who are **known** to be full of the Spirit and wisdom. We will turn this responsibility over to them [NIV]<br>Therefore, brethren, seek out from among you seven men of **good reputation**, full of the Holy Spirit and wisdom, whom we may appoint over this business; [NKJV]<br>"Now look around among yourselves, brothers, and select seven men who are **well respected** and are full of the Holy Spirit and wisdom. We will put them in charge of this business. [NLT]<br>ἐπισκέψασθε οὖν, ἀδελφοί, ἄνδρας ἐξ ὑμῶν **μαρτυρουμένους** ἑπτά, πλήρεις Πνεύματος Ἁγίου καὶ σοφίας, οὓς καταστήσομεν ἐπὶ τῆς χρείας ταύτης. [GNS]<br>ἐπισκέψασθε δέ, ἀδελφοί, ἄνδρας ἐξ ὑμῶν **μαρτυρουμένους** ἑπτά, πλήρεις πνεύματος καὶ σοφίας, οὓς καταστήσομεν ἐπὶ τῆς χρείας ταύτης, [GNT] | To be known; to have a good reputation; well respected; well attested; well reported of; bearing a good witness.<br><br>**Practical Application**<br>The deacon's character was to be proven beyond reproach. They were to be men of integrity, faithful and trustworthy; moral and upright, men trusted by all. |

# OUTLINE BIBLE RESOURCES

This material, like similar works, has come from imperfect man and is thus susceptible to human error. We are nevertheless grateful to God for both calling us and empowering us through His Holy Spirit to undertake this task. Because of His goodness and grace **The Preacher's Outline & Sermon Bible®** - New Testament is complete in 14 volumes, and the Old Testament volumes release periodically. **The Minister's Handbook** is available and *OUTLINE* Bible materials are releasing electonically on **POSB-CD** and our **Web site**.

God has given the strength and stamina to bring us this far. Our confidence is that, as we keep our eyes on Him and grounded in the undeniable truths of the Word, we will continue working through the Old Testament volumes and the second series known as **The Teacher's Outline & Study Bible.** The future includes helpful *Outline Bible* books and **Handbook** materials for God's dear servants.

To everyone everywhere who preaches and teaches the Word, we offer this material firstly to Him in whose name we labor and serve, and for whose glory it has been produced.

Our daily prayer is that each volume will lead thousands, millions, yes even billions, into a better understanding of the Holy Scriptures and a fuller knowledge of Jesus Christ the incarnate Word, of whom the Scriptures so faithfully testify.

> As you have purchased this volume, you will be pleased to know that a small portion of the price you have paid has gone to underwrite and provide similar volumes in other languages (Russian, Korean, Spanish and others yet to come) — To a preacher, pastor, lay leader, or Bible student somewhere around the world, who will present God's message with clarity, authority, and understanding beyond their own. *Amen.*

For information and prices, kindly contact your *OUTLINE* Bible bookseller or:

**LEADERSHIP MINISTRIES WORLDWIDE**
P.O. Box 21310, 515 Airport Road, Suite 107
Chattanooga, TN 37424-0310
(423) 855-2181   FAX (423) 855-8616
E-Mail - outlinebible@compuserve.com
www.outlinebible.org — *FREE* download materials